NEW
ROCK
RECORD

NEW ROCK RECORD

TERRY HOUNSOME

Facts On File Publications
460 Park Avenue South
New York, N.Y. 10016

NEW ROCK RECORD

Original limited edition (*Rockmaster,* 1978) and revised, expanded edition (*Rock Record,* 1979) published and produced in the United Kingdom by Terry Hounsome; published in the United States of America by Facts On File, Inc.

This edition published in the United Kingdom in 1981 by Blandford Books Ltd., as *New Rock Record.*

This edition published in the United States of America in 1981 by Facts On File, Inc.

Library of Congress Cataloging in Publication Data
Hounsome, Terry.
  New rock record.

  Includes index.
  1. Rock music—Discography.
I. Title.
ML156.4.R6H68   016.7899'12454   81-12489
ISBN 0-87196-774-X   AACR2
ISBN 0-87196-770-7 (pbk.)

Printed in the United States of America

10 9 8 7 6 5 4 3 2 1

Contents

Introduction

This second edition of NEW ROCK RECORD has taken 7 years to produce in its present form. It lists groups and artistes together with their LP records and the musicians who have played with them. It includes an index to all the groups and musicians.

This edition now contains some 6,000 entries; 40,000 LP records and 35,000 different musicians. It takes in all forms of "Rock" music from its roots to the present day; as well as mainstream Rock it also contains much information on Pop, Soul, Reggae, Jazzrock, Blues, Country and Folk.

Imports (to Britain) and reissues (with different catalogue numbers) are listed together with some EPs, but singles and bootlegs are beyond the scope of this edition. Catalogue numbers are listed from many countries but only if this number is different from the British release. It is not intended to list every countries release of a particular record. The current availibility of any record is not listed as albums are continually being reissued from many countries. The dates stated in the entries are generally the date on the album or cover. Material has been added to early 1983.

The aim of NEW ROCK RECORD is to provide a useful and as accurate as possible guide to rock music albums and the people who have made them. As a discography its main purpose is to aid identification: It does not set out to review the records or musicians, for this reason, apart from a few factual notes, no text has been included.

The size of each entry is governed by the amount of information available not the relative importance of each group or artiste. Each entry carries a code symbol consisting of its initial letter and running order number. Check in the index for the symbol of any particular group or artistes precise location.

In many entries musicians have been linked by symbols to the albums or dates on which they played; musicians are listed even if they have played only on one track of a particular LP. Many musicians play more than one instrument and where space permits these have been listed but not the make or specific type of instrument, this abbreviation should be taken as a general indication. Instruments are listed in groups, e.g. Guitar covers all types of guitar. String sections and orchestras are described as such and not by individual musicians.

Wherever possible the appearance of a musician on an album has been indicated by coding the album alphabetically or numerically and placing the code after the musicians name and instrument. Where musicians have been known to belong to a group at a particular date, the date has been stated and coded. In some cases where both albums and dates are listed, a mixture of alphabetical and numerical symbols have been used.

The entries run in alphabetical order , though some entries are not in totally strict order. Also, some entries were allocated numbers but have been subsequently withdrawn as unsuitable for inclusion in this edition. Some entries have been continued over to the next page, these have been indicated at the top and bottom of the relevant pages.

The editor is aware that some entries are incomplete and that there are some omissions. Anyone-musicians or collectors- who is able to supply further information or any other suggestions is invited to contact him by letter or telephone at the address given below. Correspondents requiring a reply are requested to enclose a stamped addressed envelope or an international reply coupon.

Terry Hounsome,
13, Stanton Road,
Regents Park,
Southampton,
Hampshire,
England.
SOI 4HF
Tele. 0703 771639.

How to use this book

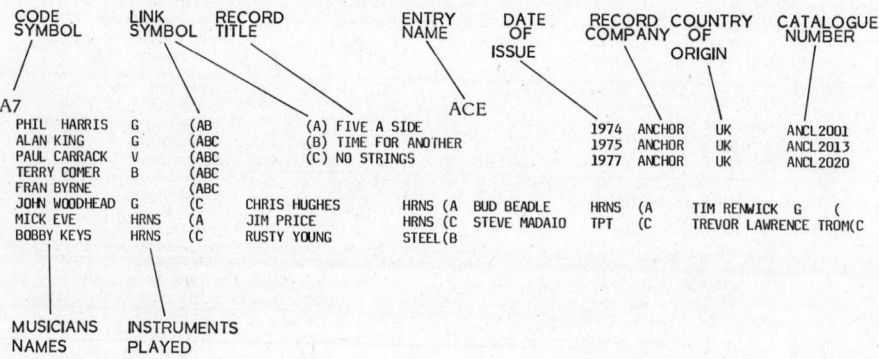

CODE
SYMBOL

LINK RECORD
SYMBOL TITLE

ENTRY
NAME

DATE
OF
ISSUE

RECORD COUNTRY
COMPANY OF
ORIGIN

CATALOGUE
NUMBER

A7

ACE

PHIL HARRIS	G	(AB		(A) FIVE A SIDE	1974	ANCHOR	UK	ANCL 2001
ALAN KING	G	(ABC		(B) TIME FOR ANOTHER	1975	ANCHOR	UK	ANCL 2013
PAUL CARRACK	V	(ABC		(C) NO STRINGS	1977	ANCHOR	UK	ANCL 2020
TERRY COMER	B	(ABC	
FRAN BYRNE		(ABC	
JOHN WOODHEAD	G	(C	CHRIS HUGHES	HRNS (A	BUD BEADLE	HRNS (A	TIM RENWICK G (
MICK EVE	HRNS	(A	JIM PRICE	HRNS (C	STEVE MADAIO	TPT (C	TREVOR LAWRENCE TROM(C
BOBBY KEYS	HRNS	(C	RUSTY YOUNG	STEEL (B

MUSICIANS
NAMES

INSTRUMENTS
PLAYED

Acknowledgements

I would like to thank the following people, [friends, musicians and readers] from all over the world for the help, sympathy, encouragement, inspiration, the many letters and the odd record or tape.

Clive Ablett,
Ross John Angel,
Bjerkem Brynjar,
Louis Behials,
Paul Barber,
B.N.Broomfield,
M Brusselman,
Paul Cole,
Cob Records,
Gerald Chute,
Chris Curry,
Pete Drewson,
George Davenport,
Geoff Eldridge,
D.A. Eames,
Neal Farnsworth,
Peter Fippl,
M. Fitzgerald,
D.Goodyear,
Paul Gilbert,
Josh Greer,
Ron Hockings,
John Huggins,
Peter Hiley,
Michael Harris,
John Harrelson,
Arlo Hegler,
Tom Jasivkowiez,
Bernard Koob,
Dieter Kiefer,
Alan Lord,
Logo Records,
Allan Levine,
G lewis,
Bernd Matheja,
Paul Mann,
Alasdair Macdonald,
Barry Margolis,
Andy Neal,
Jack Nadelle,
Terry Osborn,
Ted Pinch,
Pye
  David Powell,
Jeff Parr,
G.R.Ritchie,
Red Lightnin',
Wilhelm Reber,
Dave Smith,
Shades,
R Slaymaker,
R Sturgen,
Wolfgang Siebert,
Gary Stokes,
John Tobler,
Uwe Tessnow,
Crofton Thorpe,
Mark Volman,
C Wood,
Francis M Ward,
Jeff Wells,
Kirmo Wilen,
Clifton Yorks,

Brett 'Buddy' Ascott,
Armadillo Records,
Jeff Brown,
Michael Bates,
Phil Broughton,
Walter Becker,
Tim Chambre,
Geoff Cox,
Cruisin' Records,
Paul Cross,
Fred Dellar,
Tim Deal,
K.Disney,
E.ML Records,
John Eagle,
Scott Friedberg,
John Farrah,
Kurt Glaso,
G.I Records,
Natalie Gomillian,
Bill Gurney,
Phil Harwood
Derek Henderson,
Stephen Hammonds,
Jurgen Heeger,
Christian Hanell,
Wolfgang Jensen,
Neil Jeffries,
Detlef Krug,
Phil King,
Bernard leonard,
Neil Littman,
Chris Lorimer,
Andy Lynch,
Hugh Maclain,
J Matlathronas,
Ed Mechem,
Rob Morrish,
Zbignew Nowara,
Lars Nilsson,
Norbert Obermanns,
Bob Pearce,
John Philpin,
Maurizio Petitti,
Les Raphael,
Peter Redman,
Peter Ried,
Tony Reynolds,
Eiji Sashida,
Carol Shipp
Jim Seymour,
Rainer Steinike,
John B Sacksteder,
Henning Sander,
Gerhard Taufer,
Dick Tomli,
Tumbleweed Connection,
Virgin Records,
Ludwig Webel,
Paul Williams,
Muddy Waters,
Deena Weinstein,
Steve York,

Roy Arblaster,
Ash & Gloria,
Marc Barthemy,
Hugh Byron,
Adrian Booth,
Olaf Benzinger,
John Clare
Roger Chapman,
Chilli Charles,
Andrew Craven,
Decca Records,
Andy Dobbs,
Pete Drewery,
Everly Brothers,
John W. Edwards
George Forrester,
Klaus Freestad,
Kurt Gaile,
Dave Greenhaulgh,
Stephen Green,
Andrew Gibbons,
Guy Hamilton,
Steve Hammond,
E.P.Hopper,
Phill Hall,
Jim Hill,
Ian Jones,
Derek King,
Nigel Keatley,
Ferninand Kother,
Spencer Liegh,
Jeff Lambert,
Ian Lumsden,
Bob Lyons,
Steve Morgan,
Andy Maunder,
Rod Mortimer,
Gordon Mackay,
Richard Norris,
Knut Olsson,
Oasis,
Frank Plouright,
Deb Pal,
Anthony Parr,
Andy Read,
Paul Renk,
Jermy Robinson,
Peter Richmond,
Richard Sadler,
Paul Soper,
George Sepetjian,
Harvey Shields,
Willie Sugg,
Malc Tipping,
David Thompson,
Julian Thomas,
United Artist,
Vinyl Solution,
Paul Williams,
Arthur Wood,
Stephen Weeks,
Stephen Young,
Pete York,

Erroll Antzis,
R.G.Allen,
David Bragg,
Vytenis Babrauskas,
Beano's
Steve Blamire
Henry's Records
Randy California,
Bill Cullen,
Max Cripps,
Alan Dawson,
C.D.Davies,
Klaus Damrau,
Ezy Ryder Records
T Evans,
Donald Fagen,
Steven Feigenbaum,
John Grave,
David Ginsburg,
John Guest,
Wolfgang Giese,
Bruno Haas,
Stuart Heather,
David Hayhoe,
Richard Hughes,
Bernie Hein,
Robert Jackson,
Freddie King,
William.F.Krober,
Howard Kaylan,
Line Records (Germany)
Bri Lockyear,
Graham liddell,
Barry Lazell,
Gary Moberley,
Bert Muirhead,
Bob Metcalfe,
Torben Nielsen,
Chris Newby,
Ingrid Olsson,
Olaf Owre,
Polydor,
Chris Pouncy
Charlie Pritchard,
Norman Read,
Replay's,
L Rogoff,
Wilf Roach,
Summit Records,
Harry Shapiro,
Roger Seaman,
John Stewart,
Martin Storkman,
Mike Tesise,
David Teeitlel,
Mark Tyrell,
Jan Van Neck,
Ian Walker,
W.E.A. ,
Mel Wright,
George Walker,
Paul Yaersley,
J Young.

And all the others i have forgotten or missed.

And a special thanks to my family, Chris, my wife, for the typing, indexing, sorting and a LOT of patience. My children : Claire, Steven and Jonathan for the coffee they have made and the help they have given.

Abbreviations

ACC	ACCORDIAN
A'HARP	AUTOHARP
B	BASS
BAN	BANJO
BAZ	BAZOUKI
BOD	BODHRAN
BOMBA	BOMBARDE
CLAR	CLARINET
COMP	COMPILATION ALBUM
CONC	CONCERTINA
D	DRUMS
DBL	DOUBLE ALBUM SET
DOB	DOBRO GUITAR
DULC	DULCIMER
EURO	EUROPEAN
FDL	FIDDLE
FLT	FLUTE
FR	FRANCE
G	GUITAR
GERM	GERMANY
HCA	HARMONICA
HRNS	HORNS(TRUMPETS,TROMBONES, TUBA ETC)
IT	ITALY
JAP	JAPAN
K	KEYBOARDS(ALL TYPES)
MAND	MANDOLIN
MEL	MELODEON
NOR	NORWAY
ORG	ORGAN
PERC	PERCUSSION
PNO	PIANO
R I	RE ISSUE
SAX	SAXOPHONE
SIT	SITAR
STEEL	STEEL GUITAR /PEDAL STEEL GUITAR
STR	STRINGS(VIOLIN, CELLO, BASS VIOLA)
SYN	SYNTHESIZER
SWED	SWEDEN
TPT	TRUMPET
TROM	TROMBONE
UK	GREAT BRITAIN
US	UNITED STATES OF AMERICA
V	VOCALS/ BACKING VOCALS
VLA	VIOLA
VLN	VIOLIN
WIND	SAXOPHONE,FLUTE, CLARINET ETC

THIS BOOK IS DEDICATED TO:

Freddie King – Roger Chapman
Randy California – Steely Dan
Muddy Waters – Kraan
Fabulous Thunderbirds – Z Z Top

Musicians & Record Collectors
Everywhere

Chris, Claire, Steven & Jon

And
All my friends & family

DIRECTORY

Directory

A B SKHY

A1

JIM MARCOTTE	B	(AB	
DENNIS GEYER	G/V	(AB	
TERRY ANDERSEN	D/V	(A	
HOWARD WALES	K	(A	
OTIS HALE	FLT	(A	
BUD BRISBOIS	TPT	(A	
DAVE ROBERTS	TROM	(A	
WALLY ROSE	PNO	(B	

(A) A B SKHY
(B) RAMBLING ON

RICK JAEGER	D	(B	CURLEY COOKE
RUSSELL DASHIELL	G	(A	LAROON HOLT
PHILLIP PRUDEN	SAX	(A	JIM HORN
SAM McCUE	G V	(A	BEN SIDRAN

| 1969 MGM | | SE4628 |
| 1970 MGM | | SE4676 |

G	(B	JIM LIBAN	HCA(A
TPT	(A	MARVIN BROWN	TPT(A
SAX	(A	DONALD WALDROP	TROM(A
K	(B	ELVIN BISHOP	G (B

A2

AC,DC

ANGUS YOUNG	G	(ABCDEFGH
MALCOLM YOUNG	G	(ABCDEFGH
PHIL RUDD	D	(ABCDEFGH
BRIAN JOHNSON	V	(GH
BON SCOTT	V	(ABCDEF
CLIFF WILLIAMS	B	(DEFGH
MARK EVANS		(ABC
ROBERT JOHN LANGE	PROD	(GH

(A) HIGH VOLTAGE
(B) DIRTY DEEDS DONE CHEAP
(C) LET THERE BE ROCK
(D) POWERAGE
(E) IF YOU WANT BLOOD
(F) HIGHWAY TO HELL
(G) BACK IN BLACK
(H) FOR THOSE ABOUT TO ROCK

1976 ATLANTIC	UK K50257 US SD36142
1976 ATLANTIC	UK K50323 US 16033
1977 ATLANTIC	UK K50366 US SD36151
1978 ATLANTIC	UK K50483 US SD19180
1978 ATLANTIC	UK K50532 US 19212
1979 ATLANTIC	UK K50628 US 19244
1980 ATLANTIC	UK K50735 US 16018
1981 ATLANTIC	UK K50851 US 11111

A2A

AALON

AALON BUTLER

(A) CREAM CITY

19 ARISTA US 4127

A2B

ADC BAND

(A) RENAISSANCE
(B) BROTHER LUCK

| 1980 COTILLION | US 5221 |
| 1981 ATLANTIC UK | K50795 US 16041 |

A2C

AK BAND

(A) MANHOLE KIDS

1981 RCA LP 5024

A2D

THE A's

RICHARD BUSH	V	(AB
RICK DiFONZO	G	(AB
TERRY BORTMAN	B	(AB
MIKE SNYDER	D	(AB

(A) THE A's
(B) A WOMANS GOT THE POWER

| 1981 ARISTA | US 4238 |
| 1981 ARISTA | US 9554 |

| ROCCO NOTTE | K | (AB |

A2E

CHRIS SLACK	G	(
CHRIS HOWARD	B	(
JOHN THORNE	D	(

A TO Z

(A) WITCH OF BERKELEY

1980 POLYDOR UK 2383 587

| MARV ? | G | (| JULA HARRINGTON | V (|

A3

FRANK CLARK	D	(AB
DAVE SKILLIN	V	(AB
STAN ALDOUS	B	(AB
PADDY COULTER	K	(A

AARDVARK

(A) PRE LP LINE UP
(B) AARDVARK

1970 NOVA GER 12024 UK SDN .17

| STEVE MILLINER | K | (B |

A3A

CHRIS WILLIAMS	V	(
CHARLY SCHADE	G	(
CHRIS BARUTZKY	K SYN(	
KLAUS KOHHASE	B	(
ALLAN WARREN	D	(

ABACUS

(A) ABACUS
(B) EVERYTHING YOU NEED
(C) JUST A DAYS JOURNEY AWAY
(D) MIDWAY

1971		
1972 ZEBRA	GER 2949 002
1972 POLYDOR	2371 270
1974 ZEBRA	GER 2949 013

A4

ANNA ULVAEUS	V	(123A>Z
BENNY ANDERSSON	K V	(4 A>Z
ANNIFRID LYNGSTAD-FREDRIKSSON	V(A>Z	
BJORN ULVAEUS	G V	(4 A>Z

ANDERS DAHL	STR	(E
MALANDO GASSAMA	PERC	(BEGJ
AKE SUNKVIST	PERC	(KZ
JANNE SCHAFFER	G	(BCDEGJK
ANDREW EIJAS	HRNS	(JZ
PER LINDVALL	D	(K
KAJTEK WOJCIECHOWSKI	SAX(	JK
JANNE KLING	WIND	(J
PAUL HARRIS	PNO	(J
LASSE WELLANDER	G	(CEGJK
LARS CARLSSON	HRNS	(EGJK
ULF ANDERSSON	SAX	(C
PER SAHLBERG	B	(B
CHRISTER EKLUND	SAX	(B
RUTGER GUNNARSON	B	(BCEGJK
MIKE WATSON	B	(CJK
ANDERS GLENMARK	G	(E
OLA BRUNKERT	D	(BCEGJK
FINN SJOBERG	G	(B
ROGER PALM	D	(CEF
BRUNO GLENMARK	TPT	(C
JOE GALDO	D	(J
ARNOLD PASEIRO	B	(J
ISH LEDESMA	G	(J
GEORGE TERRY	G	(J
HALLDOR PALSSON	SAX	(J
JOHAN STENGARD	SAX	(J
NILS LANDGREN	TROM	(J
ROLF ALEX	D	(J
JAN RISBERG	OBOE	(J
MATS RONANDER	G	(Z

ABBA

(A) RING RING
(B) WATERLOO
(B) WATERLOO
(B) WATERLOO
(B) WATERLOO
(C) ABBA
(C) ABBA
(C) ABBA
(D) GREATEST HITS
(D) GREATEST HITS
(D) GREATEST HITS
(E) ARRIVAL
(E) ARRIVAL
(E) ARRIVAL
(F) GOLDEN DOUBLE
(G) THE ALBUM
(G) THE ALBUM
(H) LES PLUS GRANDS SUCCES
(J) VOULEZ VOUS
(J) VOULEZ VOUS
(K) SUPER TROUPER
(K) SUPER TROUPER
(L) GREATEST HITS VOL 2
(L) GREATEST HITS VOL 2
(M) VISITORS
(M) VISITORS
(Z) LIVE LINE-UP NOV 1979
( ) CIRACIAS POR LAS MUSICA

SOLO ALBUMS
(1) AGNETHA(ANNA)
(2) AGNETHA 2(ANNA)
(3) AGNETHA
(4) LYCKA(BENNY & BJORN)
( ) SORN JAG AR
( ) 11 WOMEN IN A HOUSE
( ) BASTA   (AGNETHA)
( ) TEN YEARS WITH (AGNETHA)

1973 POLAR	SWED 242	RCA AUST 102323
1974 EPIC	UK 80179	ATLANTIC US 18101
1974 POLAR	SWED 252	RCA AUST 14003
1974 VOGUE	FR 28047	POLYDOR GER 2374111
19 EPIC	UK 32009	
1975 EPIC	UK 80835	ATLANTIC US 18146
1975 POLAR	SWED 262	RCA AUST 14013
1975 VOGUE	FR 28039	
1976 EPIC	UK 69218	ATLANTIC US 18189
1976 POLAR	SWED 266	RCA AUST 14020
1976 VOGUE	FR 28047	ATLANTIC CAN 19114
1976 EPIC	UK 86018	ATLANTIC US 18207
1976 VOGUE	FR 20238	RCA AUST 14034
1976 POLAR	SWED 272	
1977 VOGUE	FR 685	
1977 EPIC	UK 86052	ATLANTIC US 19164
1977 POLAR	SWED 282	RCA AUST 14060
197 RCA	FR 13036	
1979 EPIC	UK 86086	ATLANTIC US 16000
1979 POLAR	SWED 292	RCA AUST 14135
1980 EPIC	UK 10022	ATLANTIC US 16023
1980 POLAR	SWED 322	
1980 EPIC	UK 10017	ATLANTIC US 16009
1980 POLAR	SWED 312	
1981 EPIC	UK 10032	ATLANTIC US 19332
1981 POLAR	SWED 342	
1981 EPIC	UK 86123	

1968 CUPOL	SWED 1002
1969 CUPOL	SWED 1003
1974 EMBASSY UK	31094
1970 POLAR	SWED 113
1970	
1972	
1973	
1979	

A2

A2A

A2B

A2C

A2D

A2E

A3

A3A

A4

JOHN ABERCROMBIE

```
   JOHN ABERCROMBIE  G   (ALL     (A) FRIENDS                          1971 OBLIVION        US        003
   DAVE HOLLAND      D   (CDI     (A) FRIENDS                          1975 CAROLINE        UK        1511
   JACK DEJOHNETTE   D   (BCDGI   (B) TIMELESS                         1975 ECM                       1047
   RALPH TOWNER      (H            (C) GATEWAY                          1975 ECM                       1061
   JAN HAMMER        K   (B        (D) CLOUD DANCE                      1976 ECM                       1062
   JEFF WILLLIAMS    G   (A        (E) PILGRIM & THE STARS             1976 ECM                       1063
   CLINT HOUSTON     B   (A        (F) UNTITLED                        197  ECM                       1074
   MARC COHEN        SAX  (A       (G) PICTURES                        1977 ECM                       1079
   RICHIE BEIRACH    PNO  (KL      (H) SARGASSA SEA                    1976 ECM                       1080
   GEORGE MRAZ       B   (KL       (I) GATEWAY 2                       1978 ECM                       1105
   PETER DONALDSON   D   (JK       (J) CHARACTERS                      1978 ECM                       1117
   COLIN WALCOTT     TABLA(D       (K) ARCADE                          1979 ECM                       1133
                                   (L) M                               1980 ECM                       1191
                                   (M) STRAIGHT FLIGHT                 1982 JAM               ·       5001
```
MICK ABRAHAMS
```
   MICK ABRAHAMS     G V  (ALL     (A) MICK ABRAHAMS                   1971 CHRYSALIS UK 9147 US A&M  4312
   BOB SARGEANT      G V K(AB      (B) AT LAST                         1972 CHRYSALIS US 1005
   RITCHIE DHARMA    D   (AB       (C) LEARNING TO PLAY GUITAR WITH..  1975 SRT          SRTM          73313
   WALT MONAGHAN     B   (AB       (1) AUG> SEPT 1978
   JACK LANCASTER    WIND (B
   TOM DOWNING       FDL G(1   DAVE BRISTOW     PNO  (1   PETE CLEMMINS              (B
```
ABSOLUTELY ELSEWHERE
```
   PAUL FISHMAN      K   (A        (A) IN SEARCH OF ANCIENT GODS       1976 WB           UK           K56192
   BILL BRUFORD      D   (A
   PHILIP SAATCHI    G   (A   JON ASTROP       B   (A
```
NATHAN ABSHIRE & THE PINEGROVE BOYS
```
   NATHAN ABSHIRE    ACC  (        (A) THE LEGENDARY JAY MILLER SESSION VOL 13  1978 FLYRIGHT    LP 535
```
MIKE ABSALOM
```
   MIKE ABSALOM      (ALL          (A) SAVE THE LAST GHERKIN FOR ME    1969 SAYDISC                   SDL162
                                   (B) MIKE ABSALOM                    1971 VERTIGO                   6360 053
                                   (C) HECTOR AND OTHER PECCADILLOS    1973 PHILIPS
```
ABYSSINIANS
```
   BERNARD COLLINS   (              (A) FORWARD TO ZION                19   KLIK                     KLP9023
   DONALD MANNING    (              (B) ARISE                          1978 FRONT LINE               FL1019
   UNFORD MANNING
   JAH JERRY   G   (AB  FRANKLYN WAUL   K   (AB  EARL SMITH    G   (AB  CARLTON MANNING   G   (A
   ROBBIE SHAKESPEARE B (AB  PABLO BLACK    K   (AB  SLY DUNBAR   D   (AB  MICHAEL COOPER   K   (AB
   DEVON RICHARDSON  D  (AB  RAS JAWBONE    D   (AB  LLOYD PARKS   B   (AB  BONGO HERMAN    PERC (AB
   WINSTON BOWEN  G   (AB  GLEN DE COSTA  SAX  (A   CEDRIC BROOKS SAX  (AB  BOBBY ELLIS     TPT  (AB
   HERMAN MARQUIS  SAX  (AB  GEORGE FULLWOOD B  (AB  SANTA         D   (AB  TONY ALLEN      G    (AB
   TOMMY McCOOK   WIND (AB  VIVIAN HALL    TPT  (AB
```
ACCOLADE
```
   GORDON GILTRAP    G   (1        (A) ACCOLADE                        1970 COLUMBIA        UK   SCX 6405
   DON PARTRIDGE     G   (1        (B) ACCOLADE 2                      1971 REGAL ZONOPHONE UK SLRZ 1024
   BRIAN CRESSWELL   (1            (1) 1969
   MALCOLM POOLE     B   (1   IAN HOLT         (1
```
ACADEMY
```
   POLLY PERKINS     V   (A        (A) POP LORE ACCORDING TO ..        1969 MORGAN BLUE TOWN UK       5001
   DAMON J HARDY     V   (A
   RICHARD COBBY     G   (A   DICK WALTER FLT  (A
```
ACCELERATES
```
   CHRIS MARTIN      V   (A        (A) THE ACCELERATES(EP)             1979   SPIV RECORDS   UK
   TONY DOYLE        B V  (A
   MARTIN SMITH      G   (A   BRIAN DAMAGE D  (A   KATHY FREEMAN     G   (A
```
ACCEPT
```
   UDO DIRKSCHNEIDER V  (A         (A) ACCEPT                          1979 BRAIN       UK       0060 188
   PETER BALTES      B V (A        (B) I'M A REBEL                     1980 LOGO UK 1025 PASSPORT US 9849
   WOLF HOFFMAN      G   (A
   JORG FISCHER      G   (A   STEFAN KAUFMAN   D   (A   FRANK FRIEDRICH   D   (A
```
ACCIDENTS
```
                                   (A) KISS ME ON THE APOCALYPSE       19   HOOK LINE & SINKER
```
ACE
```
   PHIL HARRIS       G   (AB       (A) FIVE A SIDE                     1974 ANCHOR        UK   ANCL 2001
   ALAN BAM KING     G   (ABC      (B) TIME FOR ANOTHER                1975 ANCHOR        UK   ANCL 2013
   PAUL CARRACK      V   (ABC      (C) NO STRINGS                      1977 ANCHOR        UK   ANCL 2020
   TERRY COMER       B   (ABC      (C) NO STRINGS                      1977 CARRERE       FR        68037
   FRAN BYRNE        D   (ABC
   JOHN WOODHEAD  G   (C  CHRIS HUGHES     HRNS (A   BUD BEADLE    HRNS (A  TIM RENWICK    G   (
   MICK EVE    HRNS (A  JIM PRICE       HRNS (C   STEVE MADAIO  TPT  (C  TREVOR LAWRENCE TROM(C
   BOBBY KEYS  HRNS (C  RUSTY YOUNG    STEEL(B   STEVE WITHERINGTON D  (
```
JOHNNY ACE
```
   JOHNNY ACE             (A        (A) JOHNNY ACE MEMORIAL ALBUM       1971 DUKE  ?  RI 1981  ACE UK CH40
```
ACE SPECTRUM
```
                                   (A) JUST LIKE THE MOVIES            19   ATLANTIC      US        18185
```
ACES
```
   LOUIS MYERS       V G HCA(ABC   (A) CHICAGO BEAT                    1976 BLACK & BLUE            33508
   DAVE MYERS        B   (ABC      (B) ACES & GUESTS                   1977 MCM          FR        900293
   FRED BELOW        D   (C        (C) KINGS OF CHICAGO BLUES          19   VOGUE        FR         30174
   SAM LAWHORN       G   (C
   EDDIE TAYLOR      G   (C
```
ACHE
```
   STEEN TOFT ANDERSEN B HCA(B     (A) DE HOMINE URBANO               1970 PHILIPS?                 841906
   GLENN FISCHER     D PERC(A       (B) BLA SOM ALTID                  1977 KHF          DK        ROLP 6570
   JOHNNIE GELLETT   V K G (B
   PETER MELLIN      K G  (A   FINN OLAFSSON    G K (AB  TORSTEN OLAFSSON  B V (A   GERT SMEDEGARD  D  (B
   PER WIUM          K   (B
```

DAVID ACKLES

```
A9
    DAVID ACKLES       V    (ALL      (A) DAVID ACKLES              1968 ELEKTRA US EKS 74022 UK 71 K42020
    MICHAEL FONFARA    ORG  (A        (B) SUBWAY TO THE COUNTRY     1970 ELEKTRA US EKS 74060 UK 71 K42092
    DOUG HASTINGS      G    (A        (C) AMERICAN GOTHIC           1972 ELEKTRA US EKS 75032 UK    K42112
    JOHN KELIEHOR      PERC (A        (D) FIVE & DIME               1973 CBS      US      32466
    DAWN WEIS          PICC (D
    GEORGINA MOHAMMED  FLT  (D  LOREN PICKFORD   WIND (D  EARL DUMLER      WIND (D  JAMES KANTER    CLAR  (D
    EUGENE CIPRIANO    SAX  (D  TODD MILLAR      HRNS (D  ROBERT HENDERSON HRNS (D  RUSSELL KIDD    TPT   (D
    ZIGMANT KANSTUL    TPT  (D  JOHN DALEY       TROM (D  EDMOND WELTER    TUBA (D  COLIN BAILEY    PERC  (D
    LOU ANNE NEILL     HARP (D  BRUCE LANGHORNE  G    (D  JAMIE GRAHAM     G    (D  RED RHODES      STEEL (D
    DEAN TORRANCE      V    (D  DOUGLAS GRAHAM   V    (A  DANNY WEIS       G    (A  JERRY PENROD    B     (A
```

BARBARA ACKLIN

```
A9A
    BARBARA ACKLIN     V    (AB       (A) LOVE MAKES A WOMAN        19   BRUNSWICK US     754137
                                      (B) SEVEN DAYS OF NIGHT       19   BRUNSWICK US     754148
```

ACQUA FRAGILE

```
A9B
    PIERO CANAVERA     D G V(AB        (A) ACQUA FRAGILE            1973 NUMERO UNO      IT      55656
    GINO CAMPANINI     G V  (AB        (B) MASS MEDIA STARS         1974 DISCHI IT 6150 IMPORT 1005
    FRANZ DOND         B    (AB
    BERNARDO LANZETTI  V G  (AB  MAURIZIO MORI    K V  (AB  CLAUDIO FABI   PNO (B
```

ACTION

```
A9C
    ALAN BAM KING      G    (A        (A) THE ULTIMATE ACTION       1980 EDSEL       UK      ED  101
    REG KING           V    (A
    PETE WATSON        G    (A  MIKE EVANS     B   (A  ROGER POWELL   D  (A  GEORGE MARTIN  PROD(A
```

ACROBAT

```
A9D
    BILLY JONES        G    (A        (A) ACROBAT                   1972 TMI         US      1004
```

ADAM & THE ANTS

```
A10
    ADAM ANT           V    (ALL      (1) NOVEMBER 1977
    JOHNNY BIVOUAC     G    (1        (A) DIRK WEARS WHITE SOX      1979 DO IT           RIDE   3
    ANDY WATSON        B    (1        (B) KINGS OF THE WILD FRONTIER 1980 CBS UK 84549   US  37033
    DAVE BARB          D    (1        (C) STAND AND DELIVER         1981
    MATTHEW ASHMAN     G K  (A        (D) PRINCE CHARMING           1981
    ANDREW WARREN      B    (A
    KEVIN MOONEY       B    (BCD  MARCO PIRRONI  G   (BCD  TERRY LEE MIALL  D(BCD  CHRIS 'MERRICK'HUGHES D(BCD
```

ARTHUR ADAMS

```
A11
    ARTHUR ADAMS       G V  (ABC      (A) ITS PRIVATE TONIGHT       1972      BLUE THUMB   BT 543
    PHIL UPCHURCH      G    (A        (B) HOME BREW                 197       FANTASY  US  9479
    WILTON FELDER      B    (A        (C) MIDNIGHT SERENADE         19        FANTASY      9523
    JOE SAMPLE         K    (A        (D) I LOVE LOVE LOVE MY LADY  1979      A&M      US  4752
    SHIRLEY MATTHEWS   V    (A
    GENE ESTES         VIBES(A  ERNIE WATTS    HRS (A  PAUL HUMPHREY  D  (A  MIKE ALTSCHUL  HRS (A
    JACK KELSO         HRS (A   PAUL HUBINON   HRS (A  BILL GREEN     HRS (A  CHUCK FINDLEY  HRS (A
    BOBBYE HALL        PERC(A   GEORGE BOHANON HRS (A  JAMES JAMESON  B  (B  DENNIS COFFEY  G   (B
    EARL PALMER        D   (B   VANETTA FIELDS V   (A  CLYDIE KING    V  (A
```

DOUGLAS ADAMS

```
A11A
    DOUGLAS ADAMS      V    (A        (A) THE HITCHIKERS GUIDE TO THE GALAXY 1979 ORIGINAL   UK    ORA42
    BERNIE LEADON      (A
    TIM SOUSTER        (A   PADDY KINGSLAND (A
```

JAY BOY ADAMS

```
A11B
    JAY BOY ADAMS      (AB       (A) JAY BOY ADAMS             1978 ATLANTIC     US      18221
                                 (B) FORK                     1980 ATLANTIC     US      19195
```

JOHNNY ADAMS

```
A12
    JOHNNY ADAMS       (ABC      (A) HEART & SOUL              19   SSS INT    US      SSS5
                                 (A) HEART & SOUL              19   CHARLY     UK  CR 30154
                                 (B) AFTER ALL THE GOOD IS GONE 19  ARIOLA     US  SW 50036
                                 (C) STAND BY ME               19  CHELSEA    US      S 25
                                 (D) RECONSIDER ME             1976 CHARLY EP          CEP 102
```

DANNY ADLER

```
A12A
    DANNY ADLER        G K V(A        (A) THE DANNY ADLER STORY     1979 DO IT           RIDE 2
    NICK PLYTAS        K    (A
    JULIAN SCOTT       B    (A  JUSTIN HILDRITH  D (A  NICK MONNAS    D     (A
```

ADVENTURERS

```
A12B
                                 (A) CANT STOP TWISTING        19   COLUMBIA           174/
```

ADVERTISING

```
A13
    TOT TAYLOR         G K  (A        (A) JINGLES                   1978 EMI UK          EMC 3253
    PAUL BULTITUDE     D    (A
    DENNIS SMITH       B    (A  SIMON BOSWELL G (A
```

ADVERTS

```
A14
    GAYE ADVERT        B    (A1B      (1) MARCH 1978 GIG
    T V SMITH          V    (A1B      (A) CROSSING THE RED SEA      1978   BRIGHT   UK  BRL 201
    TOM NEWMAN         SYN  (B        (A) CROSSING THE RED SEA      1981   BUTT     RI  ALS0002
    LAURIE DRIVER      D    (A        (B) CAST OF THOUSANDS         1979 RCA UK     PL25246
    HOWARD PICKUP      G    (A1B
    JOHN TOWE          D    (1   TIM GROSS    K  (C    ROD LATTER   D  (B   RICHARD STRANGE  SYN (B
```

AERIAL

```
A15
    LAURIE CURRIE      D V   (A       (A) IN THE MIDDLE OF THE NIGHT 1978 CAPITOL GER 8590 UK/US 11828
    MALCOLM BUCHANAN   K    (A
    BRIAN MIESSNER     B V G (A   GARY O'CONNOR     G B V (
```

AEROSMITH

```
A16
    STEVE TYLER        HCA PERC K B V(ABCDEF (A) AEROSMITH          1973 CBS UK 65486   US 32005
    BRAD WHITFORD      G       ( BCD EF      (B) GET YOUR WINGS     1974 CBS UK 80015   US 32847
    JOEY KRAMER        D V     ( BCDEF       (C) TOYS IN THE ATTIC  1975 CBS UK 80773   US 33479
    SCOTT CUSHNIE      PNO     ( C           (D) ROCKS              1976 CBS UK 81379   US 34165
    JOE PERRY          V B G PERC (ABCDEF    (E) DRAW THE LINE      1977 CBS UK 82147   US 34865
    TOM HAMILTON       B G     (BCDEF        (F) LIVE BOOTLEG       1978 CBS UK 88325   US 35564
    JAY MESSINA        PERC    (C            (G) NIGHT IN THE RUTS  1979 CBS UK 83680   US 36050
    PAUL PRESTOPINO    BANJ    (D            (H) GREATEST HITS      1980 CBS UK 84704   US 36865
```

AFFINITY

```
   LINDA HOYLE       V    (A        (A) AFFINITY              1970 VERTIGO         UK  6360004
   MIKE JOPP         G    (A        (A) AFFINITY              1970 PARAMOUNT       US  PAS5027
   MO FOSTER         B    (A
   GRANT SERPELL     D    (A        LYNTON NAIFF          K    (A
A18                                                                                           A18
                                    (A) AFTER TEA            19   ACE OF CLUBS UK    SCLR 1251
A19                                 AFTER TEA                                                 A19
                                    AFTER THE FIRE
   PETER BANKS       K    (BCD      (A) SIGNS OF CHANGE      1978 RAPID        UK   RR 001
   IVOR TWIDELL      D    (B        (B) LASER LOVE           1979 CBS          UK   83795
   ANDY PIERCY       V G B (BCD     (C) 80F                  1980 EPIC         UK   84545
   TIM HAYWELL       B    (         (D) BATTERIES NOT INCLUDED 1982 CBS        UK   85566
   NICK BATTLE       B    (
   JOHN RUSSELL      G    (BCD      PETE KING             D    (CD
A19A                                AGITATION FREE                                            A19A
   LUTZ ULBRICH      G K  (ABC      (A) MALESCH             1972 VERTIGO    UK    6360 607
   ULI POP           BONGO (A       (A) MALESCH             1978 ATMOSPHERE       IRI 5001
   JORG SCHWENKE     G    (AC       (B) 2ND ALBUM           1973 VERTIGO    UK    6360 615
   ERHARD GROSSKOPF        (C       (B) 2ND ALBUM           1979 ATMOSPHERE       IRI 5002
   MICHEL GUNTER     B    (ABC      (C) LAST                1976 BARCLAY    FR      80615
   MICHAEL HOENIG    K SYN (ABC
   BURGHARD RAUSCH   K D V (ABC  GUSTAV LUTHJENS  G  (    PETER MICHAEL HAMEL  K (A  STEFAN DIEZ  G   (B
   DIETMAR BURMEISTER D    (C
A19C                                AGAIN AGAIN                                               A19C
                                    (A) THE WAY WE WERE(EP)  1979    DO IT     UK   DUN IT 7
A19D                                AGGREGATION                                               A19D
                                    (A) MIND ODYSSEY         19      LHI       US     12008
A20                                 AGNES STRANGE                                            A20
   JOHN WESTWOOD     G    (A        (A) STRANGE FLAVOUR      1975  BIRDSNEST   UK   BRL 9000
   ALAN GREEN        B    (A
   DAVE RODWELL      D    (A
A20A                                AGORA                                                     A20A
   ROBERTO BACCHIOCCHI K V (A       (A) AGORA                1975 ATLANTIC       EURO 50171
   RENATO GASPARINI  G    (A
   OVIDIO URBANI     SAX V(A   PAOLO COLA FRANCESCO B V   (A MAURA MENCARONI   D V  (A
A21                                 DON AGRATI                                                A21
   DON AGRATI       V K B D (A      (A) HOME GROWN           1973 ELEKTRA UK K42141 US EKS 75057
   JAMES GANDUGLIA   PERC (A
   GIL ROGERS        G    (A   RIC RICCIO       FLT (A  KARLA PAYNE    B   (A  SKIP SHORTLEDGE     HRS
   PHIL AYLING       HRS  (A   BOB CASSENS      B   (A  MIKE FRANCIS   HRS (A  FRED LAWRENCE    HRS (A
   LIZA REY          HARP (A   DAVE KAUFMAN     HRS (A  JIM STOUDER    CLAR (A
A21A                                AIM                                                       A21A
   MICHAEL OVERLY    V FLT(A        (A) AIM FOR THE HIGHEST  1973 BLUE THUMB      US  BTS 64
   WARREN PEMBERTON  D    (A
   DAVID M SHERR     OBOE (A   ALAN ESTES       CONGA(A  LOREN NEWKIRK  K   (A  PATRICK O'CONNOR    (A
A22                                 CHARLIE AINLEY                                            A22
   CHARLIE AINLEY    V G  (AB       (A) TOO MUCH IS NOT ENOUGH 1978 NEMPEROR US35080
   HENRY SPINETTI    D    (A        (B) BANG YOUR DOOR      1978 NEMPEROR US 35648 EMI UK 3285
   ROB HENDRY        G    (1        (1) LIVE DATE NOV 1979
   CHARLIE HARRISON  B    (A
   RICHARD WORTHY    G    (AB  JOHN PORTER      G B (A  PRESTON HEYMAN  PERC (A  TOM WILDY   HCA    (A
   MEL COLLINS       HRS  (A   KOKOMO           V   (A  JO PARTRIDGE    G MAND(A  MICK WEAVER   K   (A
   PETE WINGFIELD    K    (A   MIKE STOREY      K   (A  DAVID HENTSCHEL SYN (A  STUART ELLIOTT D PERC(B
   CHAS HODGES       B    (B   HOWIE CASEY      HRS (B  TONY ASHTON     ORG (B  MARTIN FRITH    HRNS(B
   ROBIN BIBI        G    (1   SAM HARLEY       B   (1  RON TELEMACQUE  D   (1
A22A                                AIR                                                       A22A
   TOM COPPOLA       K    (A        (A) AIR                  1971 EMBRYO      US      SD733
   JOHN SIEGLER      B    (A
   COOGIE            K V  (A   MARK ROSENHAGEN     D    (A
A22B                                AIR RAID                                                  A22B
   RICK BROWN        D    (A        (A)AIR RAID              1981 20th CENTURY
   ARTHUR OFFEN      V K  (A
   RICK HINKLE       G    (A   TOMMY WALKER     B   (A
A22C                                AIR SUPPLY                                                A22C
   RUSSELL HITCHCOCK V    (AB       (A) LOST IN LOVE         1980 ARISTA US 4268 UK SPART 1138
   GRAHAM RUSSELL    G V  (AB       (B) THE ONE THAT YOU LOVE 1981 ARISTA US 9551 UK SPART 1169
   TOMMY EMMANUEL    G    (A
   RALPH COOPER      D    (AB  FRANK ESTER SMITH K  (AB DAVID MOYSE    G V (AB REX GOH    B V (B
   CRISTON BARKER    B V  (A   DAVID GREEN      K   (B  SAM McNALLY    K   (A
A22D                                AIRBORNE                                                  A22D
   LARRY STEWART     V G K(A        (A) AIRBORNE             1979 CBS          US  36076
   BEAU HILL         V G K(A
   JOHN PEARCE       B V  (A   MIKE BAIRD       D   (A  DAVID ZYCHEK   G V (A
A23                                 JANE AIRE & BELVEDERES                                    A23
   JANE AIRE         V    (A        (A) JANE AIRE & THE BELVEDERES 1979 VIRGIN UK  V2134
   CHRIS PYNE        TROM (A        (B) JANE AIRE           19  STIFF     UK   SEEZ 11
   PIETRO NARDINI    G K  (A
   GALEN STUDEBAKER  D    (   EMILY RUTH      VLN       FRANCOIS DE CHANCY GK     CHRIS BUTLER    B
   ROBERT LU EDMUNDS G    (A  GAVIN POVEY     K   (A  GLYN HAVARD     B   (A  JOHN MOSS     D      (A
   CHRIS JENKINS     G    (A  MARTIN DROVER   TPT (A  MIKE DAVIS      TPT (A  MALCOLM GRIFFITHS TROM (A
   GEOFF DALEY       SAX  (A  RAY WARLEIGH    SAX (A  JOAN ASHLEY     V   (A  KIRSTY MACCOLL    V  (A
   RACHEL SWEET      V    (A  DAVID ARNOLD    PERC(A
A24                                 AIRTO                                                     A24
   AIRTO MOREIRA     PERC V D(ALL    (A) SEEDS ON THE GROUND 19  POLYDOR 2310 040  BUDDAH 5085
   FLORA PURIM       V PERC(BJH      (B) FINGERS            1973 CTI CTI18            6028
   HUGO FATTORUSO    K V  (B         (C) VIRGIN LAND        1974 CTI CTI23  SALVATION 701
   RINGO THIELMANN   B V  (B         (D) IN CONCERT         1974 CTI CTI21
   SIVUCA            G    (J         (E) FREE               19   CTI                 6020
   HERMETO           K FLT(J         (G) IDENTITY           1976 ARISTA UK ARTY119 PATHE FR 4068
       (CONTINUED)
```

[4]

AIRTO

```
DEODATO             (D      (H) PROMISES OF THE SUN    1976 ARISTA US AL4116 PATHE FR 98770
STANLEY CLARKE    B (F      (I) I'M FINE               19   WEA                    K59420
JOE FARRELL         (F      (J) THE ESSENTUAL AIRTO    19   BUDDAH  25668          870C3/2
CHICK COREA       K (F      (K) NATURAL FEELINGS       197  SKYE              US    21
DAVID AMARO       G (BG
JORGE FATTORUSO   D V (B  RON CARTER  B  (J  KEITH JARRETT  K  (F
```

(GINGER BAKERS) AIRFORCE

```
GINGER BAKER      D (ABCD   (A) AIRFORCE          1970 POLYDOR UK 2662 001 US ATCO 703
STEVE WINWOOD     K V G(A   (B) AIRFORCE 2        1970 POLYDOR UK 2383 029 US ATCO 33343
RICK GRECH        B (AB     (C) FREE KINGS        19   KARUSSELL      GERM 2499 018
CHRIS WOOD        SAX (A    (D) POP GIANTS VOL 10 19   BRUNSWICK           2011 521
HAROLD McNAIR     SAX (AB
PHIL SEAMAN       D (A    DENNY LAINE   G V (AB  GRAHAM BOND   K SAX(AB  BUD BEADLE  WIND (A
DIANE STEWART     V (B    REMI KABAKA  PERC (A   KEN CRADDOCK  K  (B  ALIKI ASHMAN     V(B
STEVE GREGORY     HRNS (B  COLIN GIBSON  B  (B   NEEMOI ACQUAYE PERC (B CATHERINE JAMES B(B
ROCKY DZIDZORNU   PERC (B
```

AIRPLAY

```
DAVID FOSTER      K V  (A   (A) AIRPLAY          1980 RCA        US      1 3099
JAY GRAYDON       G V  (A
TOMMY FUNDERBURK  V    (A  JEFF PORCARO D  (A  MIKE BAIRD     D  (A
```

AIRWAVES

```
RAY MARTINEZ      G V K(AB   (A) NEW DAY        1978 MERCURY UK 9109 613 A&M US 4689
DAVE CHARLES      D   (AB    (B) NEXT STOP      1979 MERCURY UK 9109 625 A&M US 4763
JOHN DAVID        V K G(AB
PAUL COBBOLD      CELLO(AB  TED BUNTIN   (B  PAT MORAN    PROD (A
```

AIZZ

```
                            (A) THE WITCH OF BERKELY  1980 POLYDOR   UK    2383 587
```

AKA & THE CHARLATANS

```
                            (A) HEROES ARE LOSERS    1978 VANITY   (EP)      VEIN 1
```

AKIDO

```
NEEMOI SPEEDY ACQUAYE PERC(A  (A) AKIDO          1972 MERCURY   US     SRM1 644
```

JAN AKKERMAN

```
JAN AKKERMAN      G   (ALL   (A) PROFILE         1972 HARVEST UK SHSP4026 US SIRE 7407
KAZ LUX           V   (D     (B) GUITAR FOR SALE 1973 BOVEMA EURO  51105
JOACHIM KUHN      B   (E     (C) TABERNAKEL      1974 ATLANTIC UK K 40522  US ATCO 7032
BRUNO CASTELUCCI  D   (EG    (D) ELI            1977 ATLANTIC UK K 50320 US ATCO 18210
RAY LUCAS         D   (C     (E) JAN AKKERMAN   1978 ATLANTIC UK K 50420 US ATCO 19159
CARMINE APPICE    D   (C     (F) ARANJUEZ       1978 CBS       UK   81843
GEORGE FLYNN      K   (C     (G) LIVE           1979 ATLANTIC UK K 50560
BERT RUITER       B   (A     (H) TALENT FOR SALE 19  M F P    NL    5036
PIERRE VAN DER LINDEN D(ADE  (J) 3             1979 ATLANTIC UK K50664
HENRY RONDE       STEEL(J    (K) TRANSPARENT   1980 ARIOLA NL   203 043
DANIEL WAITZMAN   FLT  (C    (L) BEST OF       1980 ATLANTIC NL  50740
FRANS SMIT        D   (A     (M) ALL IN THE FAMILY 1981 ARIOLA   655 137
FERRY MAAT        PNO  (A    (N) MEDITATION    19   POLYDOR EURO 2441 089
JIM CHAMPAGNOLA   SAX  (M    ( ) A PHENOMENON  1979 EMI     EURO 26189
AF TOMBOEL        PERC (M
EDDIE CONRAD      PERC (M  JAAP VAN EYCK   B  (A  JASPER VAN'T HOF K (DG  TOM BARLAGE  SAX K (G
WILLEM ENNES      K  (G  RICK VAN DER LINDEN K (D  WARWICK READING B (D  RICHARD DE BOIS  D  (D
MARGARET ESHUIS   V  (D  MAGGIE McNEAL   V  (D  PATRICIA PAAY   V  (D  CEES VAN DER LAARSE B(EG
NEPPIE NOYA      PERC (DEGJ TIM BOGERT   B  (C  PETER SCHON     K  (J  DUANE HITCHINS  K  (J
BUNNY BRUNEL      B  (J  DAVID KELFIELD  D  (J  YVETTE CASON    V  (J  WILLY DEE        V  (J
JODY PYPER        V  (J  KIMM HEKKER     V  (J  MARGO THUNDER   V  (J  RON BIJTELELAAR  B(B
SINEY WACHTEL     D  (B  COCKY AKKERMAN  D  (B  GENE SANTION    B  (J  JON FADDIS     TPT(J
ALAN RUBIN        HRNS (J  TOM MALONE   TROM (J  DAVID TAYLOR   TROM (J  JIM ODGREN    SAX (J
TONY SCOTT        WLAR V(N CEES SCHNOMA  K  (N  WIM ESSED       B  (N  BRUNO CASTELUCCI D (JN
JON CLARK         HRNS (J  HOWARD JHOA  SAX (J  PETE GORDON    HRNS (J  MIKE BRECKER  SAX (J
```

ALABAMA

```
RANDY OWEN        G V  (AB   (A) MY HOME'S IN ALABAMA  1980 RCA           1 3644
TEDDY GENRTY      B V  (AB   (B) FEELS SO RIGHT        1981 RCA           5025
MARK HERNDON      D V  (AB
JEFF COOK         G K V (AB
```

ALABAMA STATE TROUPERS

```
DON NIX           G V  (A   (A) ALABAMA STATE TROUPERS  1972 ELEKTRA  US  EKS75022
FURRY LEWIS       V G  (A
CLAYTON IVEY      PNO  (A  TIPPY ARMSTRONG G (A  FRED PROOTY   D  (A  BOB WRAY       B (A
KEN WOODLEY       K    (A  CAROLYN WATKINS V (A  JEANNIE GREENE V  (A  BRENDA PATTERSON V(A
WAYNE PERKINS     G    (A  MARIANNE WATKINS V (A  MARLINE GREENE V  (A  MARY ANDERSON  V (A
TARP TARRANT      D    (A
```

ALAMO

```
KEN WOODLEY       K V  (A   (A) ALAMO          1971 ATLANTIC  US       8279
LARRY RASPBERRY   G    (A
RICHARD ROSEBROUGH G   (A  LARRY DAVIS  B  (A
```

ALBATROSS

```
PETER BARRON      B    (B   (A) ALBATROSS           19?  ?
KIM BRYANT        D    (B   (B) A BREATH OF FRESH AIR  19? REPRISE  US    4002
LINDSAY BJERRE    G V  (B   (C) GOING EASY          19   HARVEST  US  SMAS 671
```

ALBERT

```
OTIS SMITH        V    (AB   (A) ALBERT         1970 PERCEPTION  US
PAUL DICKLER      G    (B    (B) THE ALBERT     1971 PERCEPTION  US       9
MICHAEL GIBSON    TROM (AB
BARRY LAZAROWITZ  D    (AB HOWARD WYETH K  (AB RICHARD MEISTERMAN TPT(B  FRANK VICARI  SAX (B
JAY SILVA         TPT  (B  PETER PETRUCCELLI B(B JON HUSTON     HRNS (AB  MIKE MATTIO  TPT (A
JAY THOMAS        TPT  (A  JOE BRAZIL  SAX (A  STEVE McCORD   G B (A  BILLY ELMIGER B (A
```

ALBERTO Y LOS TRIOS PARANOIAS

```
CHRIS LEE         V G  (ABCD  (A) ALBERTO Y LOS TRIOS PARANOIAS 1976 TRANSATLANTIC TRA 316
BOB HARDING       V G B (ABCD  (B) ITALIANS FROM OUTER SPACE    1977 TRANSATLANTIC TRA 349
BRUCE MITCHELL    PERC (ABCD  (C) SNUFF ROCK (EP)              1977 STIFF         LAST 2
```

(CONTINUED)

ALBERTO Y LOS TRIOS PARANOIAS

```
TONY BOWERS        G B   (ABCD      (D) SKITE                          1978 LOGO           1009
SIMON WHITE        STEEL (ABCD      (E) WORST OF THE BERTS             1980 LOGO           4008
JIMMY HIBBERT      V B   (ABCD
LES PRYOR          V     (ABCD  CHAS JANKEL      K       (D ROGER RUSKIN SPEAR SAX(D  ALBIE DONNELLY HRS(A
GRAHAM ROBERTSON   HRS   (A DAVE TOMLINSON CLAR SYN    (A ANTHONY MOORE     ORG (A    PETER TENNER   PROD(A
```

THE ALBION BAND

```
ASHLEY HUTCHINGS   B V   (ALL      THE ALBION COUNTRY BAND
MARTIN CARTHY      V G   (EFMO     (A) JAN 1972  (B) JAN OCT 1972 (C) OCT 1972 (D) DEC 1972 (E) 1973
SUE HARRIS   V OBOE DULC(EF        (F) BATTLE OF THE FIELD            1976 ISLAND    UK      HELP 25
JOHN KIRKPATRICK V CONC(AEFO       ETCHINGHAM STEAM BAND
MARTIN NICHOLLS    SACKBUTS(F       (G) JAN 1974 JULY 1974  (H) SUMMER 1974 (J) APRIL 1975
SIMON NICOL V G K DULC (ABCDEFKLMN  ALBION DANCE BAND
ROGER SWALLOW      D     (EF       (K) FORMED 1975
DAVE MATTACKS      D     (BCEFJKLM  (L) THE PROSPECT BEFORE US         1977 HARVEST UK SHSP4059
JOHN IVESON        SACKBUTS(F       ALBION BAND
COLIN SHEEN        SACKBUTS (F      (M) RISE UP LIKE THE SUN           1978 HARVEST UK SHSP4092 FR 06612
PAUL BEER          SACKBUTS(F       (N) ALBION RIVER HYMN MARCH  1979
STEVE ASHLEY       V G HCA  (B      (O) LARK RISE TO CANDLEFORD        1980 CHARISMA   UK        CD 54020
ROYSTON WOOD       V CONC  (AB
SUE DRAHEIM    FDL BANJO(ABC  ANDY FAIRWEATHER LOW V(M  RICHARD THOMPSON G V(ACDM  LINDA THOMPSON V (CDM
BILL CADDICK       V PERC(O  SHIRLEY COLLINS  V  (DGHJKL JOHN WATCHAM       (D   TERRY POTTER   HCA(GJ
PETER KNIGHT       FDL  (J   JOHN RODD    V CONC(KL  WILL DUKE    CONC MEL(K   MADDY PRIOR    V (N
JOHN SOTHCOTT      VIELLE(KLN  PHIL PICKETT WIND K (LMN  MICHAEL GREGORY  D (KLMO  PETE BULLOCK K WIND(MNO
JOHN TAMS          V MEL(LMO  RIC SANDERS     VLN (M   GRAEME TAYLOR  G K (LMO  DAVE BRISTOW    K (M
KATE McGARRIGLE    V     (M   JULIE COVINGTON V  (M   PAT DONALDSON    V (M   HOWARD EVANS   HRNS(O
DOUG MORTER        G     (O   BRIAN PROTHEROE K V O   STEVE SAUNDERS  TROM (O   MARTIN SIMPSON BAN(O
IAN HOLDER         ACC   (GHJ  VIC GAMMON      (HJ   EDDIE UPTON      V HCA(JKL
```

ALCO

```
TIM CAESAR         V     (A      (A) THREADS OF LIFE                  1972 ALCO      ALC 530
JULIAN CAESAR      D V K(A
PAUL FIDLIN        B G V (A  BEN BROOKE   G B V   (A  MARTIN KENNARD    V  (A  RICHARD WILLIAMS V (A
JONATHAN PALMER    V     (A  STEPHEN HARBACH   V  (A  NORMAN FRASER     V  (A  RAY DAVISON V      (A
ITCHEN ORCHESTRA   (A
```

ALDA RESERVE

```
BRAD ELLIS         K V   (A      (A) LOVE GOES ON                     1979 SIRE GERM 201 042  UK SRK 6079
MARK SUALL         G V   (A
MATTHEW PATUTO     D V   (A  TONY SHANAHAN     B V (A
```

ALESSI BROTHERS

```
BOBBY ALESSI       V G   (ABC     (A) ALESSI                          1977 A&M UK AMLH64608 US 4608
BILLY ALESSI       K V   (ABC     (B) ALL FOR A REASON                1978 A&M UK AMLH68446 US 4657
JAMES DIVISEK      D     (C       (C) DRIFTIN'                        1978 A&M UK AMLH64713 US 4713
DENNIS BELFIELD    B     (C       (D) WORDS & MUSIC                   1979 A&M UK AMLH64776 US 4776
JIM SEALS          SAX   (C
LOUIE SHELTON      G     (C  BRIAN WHITCOMB    K  (C  STEVE PORCARO    SYN (C  ALAN ESTES PERC (C
VINCE CHARLES      PERC  (C  ED GREENE         D  (C  DAVID HUNGATE    B   (C  LEE RITENOUR G  (C
MELVIN WATSON      G     (C  GREG PHILLINGANES K  (C  ABE LABORIEL     B   (C  RICHIE HAVENS V  (C
MICHAEL BAIRD      D     (C  DASH CROFTS       V  (C  GREG MATHIESON   K   (C  DON MENZA   SAX (C
MIKE MELVION       G     (A  DENNID BUDIMIR    G  (A  RAY PARKER       G   (A  JIM HUGHART       (A
SCOTTY EDWARDS     G     (A  JEFF PORCARO      D  (A  HAL BLAINE       D   (A  JOHN GUERIN    D (A
TOM SCOTT          WIND  (A  VIC FELDMAN       VIBES(A  EMIL RICHARDS  VIBES(A  BONAS HOWE     PERC(A
FRANK RIVIOLI      D     (A  STEVE GADD        D  (B  ANDY NEWMARK     D   (B  WILL LEE       B  (B
RICHARD TEE        K     (B  JOHN TROPEA       G  (B  CHARLIE BROWN    SAX (B  DAVID SPINOZZA G  (B
MICHAEL CHIMES     (B   BOB RILEY            (B  RAPHAEL GOLDFIELD B  (B  JIMMY RIPPETOE G  (B
DAWN KAROL         (B   DAVID SANBORN   HRNS (B  RANDY BRECKER    HRNS (B  MICHAEL BRECKER HRN(B
ALAN RUBIN         HRNS (B   GEORGE YOUNG    HRNS (B  RONNIE CUBER     HRNS (B  WAYNE ANDREA    HRN(B
JOE DEANGELES      HRNS (B
```

ARTHUR ALEXANDER

```
ARTHUR ALEXANDER   V     (ALL     (A) ALEXANDER THE GREAT         19   LONDON          RED  1364
                                  (B) ARTHUR ALEXANDER            19   LONDON          RED  1401
                                  (C) YOU BETTER MOVE ON          1962 LONDON   UK     HAD  2457
                                  (C) YOU BETTER MOVE ON          1962 DOT      US          25434
                                  (D) ARTHUR ALEXANDER            197  WB       US          2567
```

WILLY ALEXANDER & THE BOOM BOOM BAND

```
WILLY ALEXANDER    V K   (AB      (A) WILLY ALEXANDER & BOOM BOOM BAND 1978 MCA UK MCF 2835  US 2323
BILLY LOOSIGIAN    G     (AB      (B) MEAN WHILE BACK IN THE STATES    1979 MCA UK MCF 2876  US 3052
SEVERIN GROSSMAN   B     (AB
DAVID McLEAN       D PERC(AB
```

ALEXANDER RABBIT

```
C HOLMER           (A       (A) THE HUNCHBACK OF NOTRE DAME    1970 MERCURY   US        61291
B BRADBURY         (A
L DEMSKI           (A   S SCHEIER       (A  C J BRODOWICZ    (A
```

ALEXIS

```
RANDY REEDER       D     (A      (A) ALEXIS                       1977 MCA       US         2260
LARRY BRADEN       B V   (A
DAVE PETERS        SAX K(A  ROBBIE FALLBERO   G  (A  EDDIE ULIBARRI   K V (A  DICK WALKER    K V(A
```

ALFALPHA

```
NICK LAIRD CLOWES V HCA G  (A    (A) ALFALPHA                     1977 EMI   UK   EMC 3213
ANDY HARLEY        V G   (A
SAM HARLEY         B G   (A  STEVE CHAPMAN     D  (A  ADRIAN REA       D  (A  RAY COOPER     PERC(A
JIM CUOMO          SAX K(A  B J COLE          STEEL(A  JOHN MEALING    PNO (A  DEL NEWMAN K   (A
FRED SHUSTER       G     (A  ISAAC GUILLORY    G  (A
```

ALICE

```
DOUDON WEISS       D     (AB      (A) ALICE                      1970 METRONOME    FR   MLP15391
ALAN SUZAN         V B   (AB      (A) ALICE                      19   BYG          FR     529016
PAUL SEMANA        G     (B       (B) ARRETEZ LA MONDE           1973 POLYDOR      FR   2393 043
LUC BERTIN         K     (B
IAN GELFS          G V   (B  BRUNO BESSE       G  (A  SYLVAIN DUPLANT  B V (A
```

```
A33B                              ALIAS                                              A33B
   JOJO BILLINGSLEY    V  (A     (A) CONTRABAND              1979 MERCURY        US   SRM1 3800
   DORMAN COGBURN      G  (A
   JIMMY DAUGHERTY     V  (A   BARRY HARWOOD    G   (A   ARTIMUS PYLE    D  (A   RICKY POWELL   B  (A
   BILLY POWELL        K  (A   LEON WILKESON    B   (A
A33C                              ALIBI                                              A33C
                                (A) FRIENDS                1980 MAGNET UK 5034 POLYDOR US 6292
A33D                              ALIEN                                              A33D
                                (A) SONS OF THE UNIVERSE    1980 ELEKTRA        US   221
A33E                          ALIOTTA HAYNES                                         A33E
   MITCH ALIOTTA      G B V(ABCD    (A) ALIOTTA HAYNES MUSIC       1970 AMPEX     US   1010B
   SKIP HAYNES        B G V(ABCD    (B) ALIOTTA HAYNES JEREMIAH    1970 AMPEX     US   10119
   TED ALIOTTA        B V  (A       (C) LAKE SHORE DRIVE           19   BIG FOOT  US   714
   JOHN JEREMIAH      K V  (BCD      (D) SLIPPIN AWAY              1977 LITTLE FOOT US  711
   RON ZETA           D    (B
   ROB PARISIO        D V  (D
A33F                          ALIVE & KICKIN'                                        A33F
                                (A) ALIVE & KICKIN'         197  ROULETTE        US   47052
A34                             ALKATRAZ                                             A34
   WILL YOUATT         G  (A    (A) DOING A MOONLIGHT        1976 UA/ROCKFIELD UAS 30001
   JAMES DAVIES        G  (A
   JEFF SINGER         B  (A  STUART HALLIDAY  G   (A   JIMMY JEWEL   SAX (A   CLIVE JOHN    K  (A
   RAY MARTINEZ        G  (A
A34A                            ALKATRAZZ                                            A34A
   CRAIG STEVENS       V  (A    (A) YOUNGBLOOD              1981 RCA           UK    5023
   BOB JENNER          G  (A
   GARY BEVEN          B  (A  NICK PARSONS    D   (A
A34B                           BARRY ALLEN                                           A34B
   BARRY ALLEN            (      (A) BARRY ALLEN            19   UNI           US    73104
A35                           DAEVID ALLEN                                           A35
   DAEVID ALLEN       V G  (ALL   (A) OBSOLETE(DASHIELL HEDAYAT)  1971 SHANDAR FR 10009 CBS UK 83512
   DASHIELL HEDAYAT        (A     (B) BANANA MOON               1975 CAROLINE         UK C1512
   ROBERT WYATT       G D V(B      (B) BANANA MOON               1971 BYG  FR        529 345
   ARCHIE LEGGET      B    (B      (B) BANANA MOON               197  CHARLY       CR   30165
   GARY WRIGHT        VLN  (B      (C) GOOD MORNING              1976 VIRGIN     UK    V2054
   GERRY FIELDS       VLN  (B      (D) NOW IS THE HAPPIEST TIME.........1977 AFFINITY      AFF3
   BARRY ST JOHN      V    (B      (E) N'EXISTE PAS             1979 CHARLY        UK   CRL5015
   PIP PYLE           D    (AB
   CHRISTIAN TRITSCH  G    (AB  NICK EVANS     TROM (B  GILLIE'SHAKTI YONI'SMYTH V(ABC  DIDIER MALHERBE FLT (A
   MAGGIE BELL        V    (B   WILLIAM BURROUGHS V   (A  SAM WYATT    V   (A  PEPE MILAN     G  (CDE
   ANN CAMPS          V    (C   TONY PASCUAL   K G (C  TONY ARES    B   (C  JUAN BIBLIONI  G  (D
   TONI TREE FERNANDEZ G   (C   SAM GOPAL      PERC (D  VICTOR PERAINO  K  (D  VERA VIOLIN    VLN(D
   XAVER RIBA         VLN  (D   CHRIS CUTLER   D   (C  ANGEL ADUANA  BANJO (E  RONALD WALTHEN   (E
   BRIAN DAMAGE       D    (E   GEORGE BISHOP  SAX  (E
A35A                          LUTHER ALLISON                                         A35A
   LUTHER ALLISON     G V  (AB   (A) LOVE ME MAMA(BLUES NEBULAE)  1969 DELMARK    us         DS625
   WITH                          (B) NIGHT LIFE              1976 GORDY     US    US  G 974V1
   RICHARD TEE        K    (B    (C) LUTHERS BLUES           1973 GORDY     US    US   967
   ROBIN KENYATTA     SAX  (B    (D) BA NEWS IS COMING       1973 GORDY US 964  VOGUE  523023
   GERRY BROWN        D    (B
   K J KNIGHT         D    (C  STEVE KHAN     G    (B  JOHN LEE     B   (B  JEFFREY ALDRICH  B  (B
   MICHAEL CARVIN     D    (B  LARRY BYRNE    K    (B  DR JOHN      K   (B  RAY ANDERSON    TROM(B
   JIM SOLBERG        G    (B  RALPH McDONALD PERC (B  RANDY BRECKER  TPT (B  MICHAEL BRECKER  SAX(B
   LEW DEL GATTO      SAX  (B  RICHARD DRAKE  SAX  (B  BRUCE JOHNSTONE SAX (B  TASHA THOMAS    V  (B
   MAERETHA STEWART   V    (B  HILDA HARRIS   V    (B  GAIL KANTOR  V   (B  DAVID NEWMAN    SAX(B
   ANDREW SMITH       D    (CD  BOB BABBITT    B    (C  GARY BEAM    B   (C  PAUL WHITE      K  (CD
   TOM CURRY          K    (C  RAY GOODMAN    G    (CD  GENE BLOCK   G   (C
   GARFILED ANYOVE    HCA  (D
A35B                          MICHAEL ALLEN                                          A35B
   MICHAEL ALLEN          (ALL   (A) ACT ONE               19?  LONDON        US    544
                                 (B) LOVE OF MIKE           19?  LONDON        US
                                 (C) SOMETHING SPECIAL      19   MGM           US    4762
A35C                           PETER ALLEN                                           A35C
   PETER ALLEN        K V  (ALL   (A) CONTINENTAL AMERICA   1975 A&M           UK    AMLS 63643
   FRED THALER        D    (C     (B) TAUGHT BY EXPERTS     1976 A&M           UK    AMLH 64584
   DAVE PARLATO       B    (C     (C) IT IS TIME FOR PETER ALLEN 1977 A&M       UK    AMLH 63706
   RUBIN RIVERA       CELLO(C     (D) I COULD HAVE BEEN A SAILOR 1979 A&M       UK    AMLH 64739
   MIKE WARREN        G    (C     (E) BI-COASTAL            1980 A&M           UK    AMLH 64825
   JOHN GUTH          G    (C
   TIM MAY            G    (C  MARSHALL ROSENBERG PERC (C  DAVID FOSTER  K   (C  ED GREENE  D    (E
   MIKE PORCARO       B    (E  DAVID WILLIAMS G    (E  PAULINHO DACOSTA PERC (E  EUGENE MEROS   SAX(E
   RICHARD PAGE       V    (E  STEVE GEORGE   V    (E  TOM KEANE    K   (E  STEVE LUKATHER  G  (E
   GARY HERBIG        SAX  (E  RALPH HUMPHRIES D   (E  DAVE McDANIEL  B   (E  LON PRICE  SAX  (E
   CARLOS VEGA        D    (E  RICHIE ZITO    G    (E  LARRY WILLIAMS  K  (E  JAY GRAYDON G   (E
   ERICH BULLING      STR  (E  JOSE ROSSY     PERC (E  JERRY HEY    HRNS (E
A35D                           TERRY ALLEN                                           A35D
   TERRY ALLEN        K V  (ALL   (A) JUAREZ               1975 LANDFALL            1394
   LLOYD MAINES       G V  (BC    (B) LUBBOCK              1978 FATE                33997
   KENNY MAINES       B V  (BC    (C) SMOKIN' THE DUMMY    1980 FATE                38121
   DONNIE MAINES      D V  (C
   RICHARD BOWDEN     FDL V(ABC  JESSE TAYLOR   G V  (C  JOE ELY      HCA (BC  PONT BOONE ACC   (BC
   ALAN SHINN         PERC (BC  MIKE MEYERS    PERC (C  MONTE WILLIAMS K SYN (C  TOMMIE ANDERSON HRNS(BC
   MARK ANTHONY       HRNS (BC  JACK DELAHUNTY CLAR (C  DON CALDWELL  SAX (C  JO HARVEY ALLEN V  (BC
   GREG DOUGLAS       G    (A   PETER KAUKONEN G    (A  DIANE HARRIS  V   (A  JIMMY HOWELL    PROD(A
   CURTIS McBRIDE     D    (B   LUIS MARTINEZ  G    (B  JESSE TAYLOR  G   (B  RUSS STANDEFER  HRN (B
   SYLVESTER RICE     V    (B   GIVEN HEWITT   V    (B  SUZANNE PAULK  V   (B  FREDDY PRIDE    V  (B
   MIKE AUSTIN        V    (B   VINCENT THOMAS V    (B  JIMMY SAMPSON  V   (B  STRINGS & BAND     (B
```

[7]

DUANE ALLMAN

DUANE ALLMAN	G	(ALL	(A) ANTHOLOGY	1972	CAPRICORN	UK K 67502	US 0108
			(A) ANTHOLOGY	1974	CAPRICORN	2659 035	
			(B) ANTHOLOGY VOL 2	1974	CAPRICORN	UK 2659037	US 0139
			(C) BEST OF DUANE ALLMAN	1979	CAPRICORN	2429 187	

GREGG ALLMAN

GREGG ALLMAN	K V	(ALL	(A) LAID BACK	1973	CAPRICORN	UK 2429 103	K4750B
CHER	V	(D	(A) LAID BACK	1973	CAPRICORN US		CP 0116
NEIL LARSEN	K	(CD	(B) GREGG ALLMAN TOUR (DBL)	1974	CAPRICORN	UK 2659 038	US 0141
MAC REBENNACK	K	(C	(C) PLAYIN' UP A STORM	1977	CAPRICORN	UK 2473 131	US 0181
DAVID LUELL	SAX	(C	(D) TWO THE HARD WAY	1977	W B	UK K 56436	US 3120
BILL STEWART	D	(ABCD					

JOHN HUG	G	(CD	RICKY HIRSCH	G	(CD	FRED BECKMAIER	B	(C	WILLIE WEEKS	B	(CD
RED CALLENDER	B	(C	STEVE MADAIO	HRNS	(C	MILT HOLLAND	PERC	(C	PAT RIZZO	HRNS(C
CLYDIE KING	V	(CD	SHIRLEY MATTHEWS	V	(CD	VANETTA FIELDS	V	(CD	JIM HORN	HRNS(D
RON EADES	SAX	(D	HARRISON CALLOWAY	HRS	(D	PAT HENDERSON	V	(D	DOUG HAYWOOD	V (D
DENNIS GOODE	TROM	(D	HARVEY THOMPSON	SAX	(D	TIM SCHMIT	V	(D	SID SHARP	STRINGS(D
BOBBYE HALL	PERC	(D	SCOTT BOYER	G	(ABD	FRED TACKETT	V	(D	MICKEY RAPHAEL	HCA (D
RANDALL BRAMBLETT	SAX	(D	BEN CAULEY	TPT	(D	RUSSELL MORRIS	V	(D	STEVE BECKMAIER	G (C
BILL PAYNE	K	(C	VICTOR FELDMAN	PERC	(C	TOMMY TALTON	G	(AB	JOHNNY LEE JOHNSON	D(B
KENNY TIBBETTS	B	(B	CHUCK LEAVELL	PNO	(B	DAVID BROWN	SAX	(B	ED FREEMAN	STR(A
HAROLD WILLIAMS	SAX	(B	TODD LOGAN	TPT	(B	PETER EKLUND	TPT	(B	ANNIE SUTTON	V (B
ERIN DICKINS	V	(B	LYNN RUBIN	V	(B	JOHNNY SANDLIN	PROD	(AB	RUSS TITELMAN	PROD(C
LENNY WARONKER	PROD	(C	BUZZ FEITEN	G	(A	CHARLIE HAYWARD	B	(A	DAVID NEWMAN	SAX (A
JAIMOE JAI JOHANSON	PERC	(A	PAUL HORNSBY	K	(A	JIMMY NAILS	G	(A	BUTCH TRUCKS	PERC (A
MAERETHA STEWART	V	(A	HELENE MILES	V	(A	HILDA HARRIS	V	(A	ALBERT ROBINSON	V (A
CARL HALL	V	(A	JUNE McGRUDER	V	(A	LYNDA NOVEMBER	V	(A	EILEEN GILBERT	V (A
EMILY HOUSTON	V	(A								

ALLMAN BROTHERS BAND

GREGG ALLMAN	K V	(ALL	(A) THE ALLMAN BROTHERS BAND		1969	ATCO	US	SD33308
DUANE ALLMAN	G	(ABCDI	(A) THE ALLMAN BROTHERS BAND		1969	CAPRICORN	UK	228 033
BERRY OAKLEY	B	(ABCDE	(A) THE ALLMAN BROTHERS BAND		1969	CAPRICORN	UK	0196
RICHARD BETTS	G V	(ABCDEFGHJKL	(B) IDLEWILD SOUTH		1970	ATCO	US	SD 33342
JAI JOHANSON	PERC	(ABCDEFHJL	(B) IDLEWILD SOUTH		1970	CAPRICORN	UK	2400 032
BUTCH TRUCKS	PERC	(ABCDEFHJKL	(B) IDLEWILD SOUTH		1970	CAPRICORN	UK	0197
THOM DOUCETTE	HCA	(B	(C) LIVE AT FILLMORE EAST	(DBL)	1971	CAPRICORN	UK	K 60011
CHUCK LEAVELL SYN	PNO V	(EFH	(C) LIVE AT FILLMORE EAST	(DBL)	1971	CAPRICORN	UK	2659 039
LAMAR WILLIAMS	B	(EFH	(C) LIVE AT FILLMORE EAST	(DBL)	1971	CAPRICORN US 2/802		0131
LES DUDEK	G	(E	(C) LIVE AT FILLMORE EAST	(DBL)	1971	POLYDOR		2639 102
TOMMY TALTON	G	(G	(D) EAT A PEACH	(DBL)	1972	CAPRICORN	UK	K 67501
JOHNNY SANDLIN	G PERC	(F	(D) EAT A PEACH	(DBL)	1972	CAPRICORN	UK	2659 034
BILL STEWART	PERC	(F	(D) EAT A PEACH	(DBL)	1972	CAPRICORN	US	2C4 0102
DAN TOLER	G	(JKL	(D) EAT A PEACH	(DBL)	1972	POLYDOR		2639 101
DAVID GOLDFLIES	B	(JKL	(E) BROTHERS & SISTERS		1973	CAPRICORN	US	CP 0111
DAVID TOLER	D	(KL	(E) BROTHERS & SISTERS		1971	CAPRICORN	UK	2429 102
CHARLIE DANIELS	FDL	(KL	(E) BROTHERS & SISTERS		1974	CAPRICORN	UK	K 47507
CHIP YOUNG	V	(L	(F) WIN LOOSE OR DRAW		1975	CAPRICORN	UK	2476 116
MARK MORRIS	PERC	(KL	(F) WIN LOOSE OR DRAW		1975	CAPRICORN	US	CP 0156
JOHNNY COBB	V PNO	(L	(G) THE ROAD GOES ON FOREVER (DBL)		1975	CAPRICORN	UK	2637 101
TOM COBB	V	(L	(G) THE ROAD GOES ON FOREVER (DBL)		1975	CAPRICORN	US	2CP 0164
THOMAS CAINE	V	(L	(H) WIPE THE WINDOWS,....... (DBL)		1976	CAPRICORN	UK	2637 103
MIKE LAWLER	K	(KL	(H) WIPE THE WINDOWS,....... (DBL)		1976	CAPRICORN	US	CP 0177
JIMMY HALL	SAX V	(KL	(J) ENLIGHTENED ROGUES		1979	CAPRICORN	UK	POLD5016
JIM ESSERY	HCA	(JK	(K) REACH FOR THE SKY		1980	ARISTA US 9535	UK	SPART 1146
SHERRY CAINE	V	(L	(K) REACH FOR THE SKY		1980	ARISTA	NL	202 843
BONNIE BRAMLETT	V	(J	(L) BROTHERS OF THE ROAD		1981	ARISTA	UK	SPART 1176
MIMI HART	V	(J						
JOE LALA	PERC	(J	(AB) BEGINNINGS	(DBL)	1973	ATCO	US	SD 2 805
GREG GUIDRY	V	(L	(AB) BEGINNINGS	(DBL)	1974	CAPRICORN	UK	2569 040
JOY LANNON	V	(L	(AB) BEGINNINGS	(DBL)	1974	CAPRICORN	UK	K 60046
DONNA McELROY	V	(L	(AB) BEGINNINGS	(DBL)	1974	CAPRICORN	US	2CX 0123
KEITH ENGLAND	V	(L	( ) THE ALLMAN BROTHERS	(DBL)	19	ATLANTIC		K 60070
JEFF SILVERMAN	V	(L	( ) ALL MENS BROTHERS	(DBL)	19	ATCO	US	40424
RANDALL HART	V	(L	( ) THE BEST OF		1980	CAPRICORN	UK	2429 198
PETER KINGSBERRY	V	(L	( ) DUANE & GREGG		1973	POLYDOR	UK	2310 235
JOE PIZZULO	V	(L	( ) DUANE & GREGG		197	SPRINGBOARD	US	4046
JOHN RYAN	PROD	(L	( ) DUANE & GREGG		1972	POLYDOR	GER	2310 235
			( ) DUANE & GREGG		19	BOLD		33301

ALLMAN JOYS

GREGG ALLMAN	K V	(A	(A) ALLMANJOYS	1973	DIAL US		DL6005
DUANE ALLMAN	G V	(A	(A) ALLMANJOYS	197	MERCURY	UK	6398 005
RALPH BALINGER	D	(A					
RONNIE WILKIN	PNO	(A	TOMMY AMATO	D	(A	BOBBY DENNIS	G (A	JACK JACKSON	G (A

ALMA ATA

PHIL DRESHER	V	(A	(A) DREAMS	19	CAIN	GERM	CL 4793
LESLIE FORSTER	B	(A					
DAGMAR HORN	G V	(A	JOE SCHAFER	G V	(A	TOMMY VIEWEG	D (A	RANDY KWIZOROWSKI	K V(A
LUDWIG GOTZ	TROM	(A	JORG SEEMAN	TPT	(A	MARTI URIGSHARDT	SAX (A

JOHNNY ALMOND

JOHNNY ALMOND	SAX K(ALL	(A) MUSIC MACHINE PATENT PENDING	1969	DERAM	UK SML 1043	US 18030
WITH		(B) MUSIC MACHINE HOLLYWOOD BLUES	1970	DERAM	UK SML 1057	US 18037
JEFF CONDON	HRNS (A					

JIMMY CRAWFORD	G	(A	ROGER SUTTON	B	(A	JOHNNY WIGGINS	K	(A	STEVE HAMMOND	G (A
ALAN WHITE	D	(A	CHARLES KYNARD	ORG	(B	JOE PASS	G	(B	RAY NEOPOLITAN	B (B
EARL PALMER	B	(B	JOE HARRIS	HRS	(B	HADLEY CALIMAN	HRS	(B	CURTIS AMY	SAX(B
PAUL WILLIAMS		(A	ZOOT MONEY		(A					

ALPHA BAND

```
    STEVE SOLES        V G  (ABC        (A) ALPHA BAND                    1977 ARISTA UK ARTY 143 US AB 4102
    T BONE BURNETT     V G  (ABC        (B) SPARK IN THE DARK            1977 ARISTA UK           US AB 4145
    DAVID JACKSON      B    (A          (B) SPARK IN THE DARK            1977 PATHE               FR 06860066
    MATT BETTON        D    (AB         (C) STATUE MAKERS OF HOLLYWOOD   1978 ARISTA UK SPART1039US AB 4279
    DAVID MINER        B    (BC         (C) STATUE MAKERS OF HOLLYWOOD   1978 PATHE               FR 06860885
    CINDY BULLENS      V    (BC
    EVERETT BRYSON     PERC (C   LEE PASTORA       (C   K O THOMAS    K  (AB  DAVID MANSFIELD  G (ABC
    ROSCOE WEST        V    (A   ROSANNA TAPLIN V  (A   JOE CORRERO   D  (B   BILLY MAXWELL      (BC
    RINGO STARR        D    (B   MIKE UTLEY        K  (B  OSAU KITAJIMA KOTO(B   GEOFFREY HALES   D (B
```

ALPHA RALPHA

```
    MICHAEL MARESKA      G   (A          (A) ALPHA RALPHA               19   WEA        K 56330
    CHARLIE CHARRIROW B      (A
    EMMANUEL LACORDAIRE PERC(A CLAUDE ALVAREZ  PERC G(A  JEAN GARDET   K  (A
```

ALPHATAURAS

```
    PIETRO PELLEGRINI  K   (A           (A) ALPHATAURAS                 1973 MAGMA         ITALY  18001
    GUIDO WASSERMAN    G   (A
    GIORGIO SANTANDERE D  (A   ALFONSO OLIVE   B  (A  MICHELE BAVARO   V  (A
```

ALQUIN

```
    FERDINAND BAKKER   G K V(ABCDEF      (A) MARKS                      1972 POLYDOR 2646 101  UK  2480 152
    THUNDERTHIGHS      V   (             (A) MARKS                      1972 POLYDOR              2419 060
    RONALD OTTENHOFF   HRS (ABCDEF       (B) MOUNTAIN QUEEN             1973 POLYDOR          UK  2480 179
    DICK FRANSSEN      K   (ABCDEF       (C) NOBODY CAN WAIT FOREVER    19   POLYDOR 2925 045 UK  2480 262
    MICHAEL VAN DIJK   V   (CDEF         (C) NOBODY CAN WAIT FOREVER    1975 RCA              US  APLI 1061
    HEIN MARS          D   (ABC          (D) CRASH                      19   POLYDOR              2646 101
    PAUL WESTSTRATE    D   (ABC          (E) BEST KEPT SECRET           1976 POLYDOR              2925 045
    JOB TARENSKEEN     WIND (ABCDEF       (F) ON TOUR                    1976 POLYDOR              2441 067
    JAN VISSEN         B   (F
```

SHIRLEY ALSTON

```
    SHIRLEY ALSTON     V   (ALL          (A) WITH ALITTLE HELP          1975 LONDON         SHA   8491
    FLAMINGO'S         V   (A            (B) LADY ROSE                  1977 STRAWBERRY      US STW 6004
    THE DRIFTERS       V   (A            (C) SINGS SHIRELLES GREATEST HITS 1977 STRAWBERRY   US STW 6006
    BELMONTS           V   (A
    HERMANS HERMITS    V   (A   THE 5 SATINS     V  (A   DANNY & THE JUNIORS   V  (A
    SHEP & THE LIMLITES V  (A
```

ALTERED IMAGES

```
    CLARE GROGAN       V   (A            (A) HAPPY BIRTHDAY             1981 EPIC           UK    84893
```

ALTERNATIVE T V

```
    MICKY SMITH        B   (1            (A) THE IMAGE HAS CRACKED      1978 DEPTFORD FUN CITY  DPL 01
    ALEX FERGUSSON     G   (123D         (B) WHAT YOU SEE IS WHAT YOU ARE 1978 DEPTFORD FUN CITY DLP 02
    MARK PERRY         V G (ABCD12345    (C) VIBING UP THE SENILE MAN   1979 DEPTFORD FUN CITY  DLP 03
    JOHN TOWE          D   (12           (D) LIVE AT THE RAT CLUB 77    1979 CRYSTAL           CLP 001
    DAVE GEORGE        D   (C5           (E) ACTION TIME VISION (COMP)  1979 DEPTFORD FUN CITY  LPS005
    MARK LINEHAM       G   (             (F) STRANGE KICKS              1981 IRS          UK    70023
    TYRONE THOMAS      B   (A234D        (1) APRIL 1977      (2)MAY JULY 1977    (3) AUG OCT  1977
    CHRIS BENNETT      D   (AD34         (4) OCT 1977 1978    (5) 1979           (B) WITH HERE & NOW
    DENNIS BURNS       B   (ABC45
```

ALTERNATIVES

```
                                        (A) ALTERNATIVES               197  WB           US    31873
```

ALTHEA & DONNA

```
    ALTHEA             V   (A            (A) UPTOWN TOP RANKING         1978 FRONT LINE          FL 1012
    DONNA              V   (A
```

AMAZING RHYTHM ACES

```
    BARRY BYRD BURTON  V G (ABCD         (A) STACKED DECK              1975  ABC UK ABCL5152  US ABCD 913
    BILLY EARHEART     K   (ABCDEF        (B) TOO STUFFED TOO JUMP      1976  ABC UK ABCL5160  US ABCD 940
    JIM KERSHAW        G   (A            (B) TOO STUFFED TO JUMP       1976  CARRERE       FR     68024
    BUTCH McDADE       V D (ABCDEF        (C) TOUCAN DO IT TOO          1976  ABC UK ABCL5219  US AB 1005
    JAMES HOOKER       K V (ABCDEF        (C) TOUCAN DO IT TOO          1976  CARRERE       FR     1005
    JEFF DAVIS         B   (ABCDEF        (D) BURNING THE BALLROOM DOWN 1978  ABC UK ABCL5244  US AA 1063
    RUSSELL SMITH      V G (ABCDEF        (D) BURNING THE BALLROOM DOWN 1978  CARRERE       FR     68057
    DUNCAN CAMERON     G V (EF           (E) AMAZING RHYTHM ACES       1979  ABC UK ABCL5267 CBS US 36083
    JIMMY JOHNSON      G   (E            (F) HOW THE HELL DO YOU SPELL RHYTHUM 1980 WB UK K 56859 US 3476
    ROGER HAWKINS      D   (E
    HARRISON CALLOWAY  TPT (E   RONNIE EADES      SAX  (E   HARVEY THOMPSON   SAX  (E
    CHARLES ROSE       TROM(E   LLOYD BARRY       TPT  (E   BEN CAULEY        TPT  (E
    JOAN BAEZ          V   (E   LIZA GILKYSON     V    (E
```

AMBERGRIS

```
    LARRY HARLOW       K PERC(A          (A) AMBERGRIS                  1970 PARAMOUNT           PAS 5014
    JERRY WEISS        B K  (A
    CHARLIE CAMILLARI  TPT (A   HARRY MAX         B VLN TPT(A  GIL FIELDS        D   (A
    GLEN JOHN MILLER   TROM(A   JIMMY MAELEN      V PERC  (A  LEWIS KAHN        TROM VLA(A
    BILLY SHAY         G HCA(A
```

AMBROSE SLADE

```
    JIM LEE            B VLN(A           (A) AMBROSE SLADE              1969 FONTANA             SRF67598
    DON POWELL         D   (             (A) BEGINNINGS                 1969 FONTANA             STL 5492
    NODDY HOLDER       G V (A
    DAVE HILL          G   (A
```

AMBROSIA

```
    CHRISTOPHER NORTH  K V (ABCDE        (A) AMBROSIA                  1975  20th CENTURY        BT 434
    DAVID PACK         G K V(ABCDE        (A) AMBROSIA                  1975  DISCODIS      FR     199
    JOE PUERTA         B G V(ABCDE        (B) SOMEWHERE I'VE NEVER TRAVELLED 1976 20th CENTURY    BTH 510
    BURLEIGH DRUMMOND  D PERC V(ABCDE     (B) SOMEWHERE I'VE NEVER TRAVELLED 1976 DISCODIS   FR     224
    IAN UNDERWOOD      SAX (AB           (C) LIFE BEYOND L A           1978  W B US 3135   UK  K 56525
    RUTH UNDERWOOD     MARIMBA(AB         (D) ONE EIGHTY                1980  W B US 3368   UK  K 56811
    JIM HORN           SAX (E            (E) ROAD ISLAND               1982  W B US 3638   UK  K 56968
    DAVID LEWIS        K   (DE
    ROYCE JONES        V   (DE   ERNIE WATTS      SAX  (D   JOE SAMPLE        PNO  (C
    CLIFF WOOLLEY      HCA (C    DANIEL KOBIALKA  VLN  (CD  MARTY KRYSTALL    SAX  (C
    JAMES WEST         V   (C    JAMES GUTHRIE    SAX  (E
```

AME SON

MARK BLANC	D	(	(A) AME SON	19	BYG	FR	529 325
BERNARD LAVIALLE	G	(	(A) CATALYSE	19	METRONOME	GER MLP 15 373	
PATRICK FONTAINE	B	(					
FRANCOIS GARRELL	FLT	(					

A49   AMEN CORNER   A49

ANDY FAIRWEATHER LOW	V G	(ALL	(A) ROUND AMEN CORNER	1968	DERAM	UK	DML 1021
NEIL JONES	G	(	(B) NATIONAL WELSH COAST LIVE	1979	IMMEDIATE	UK	IMSP 023
BLUE WEAVER	K	(	(C) FAREWELL MAGNIFICENT SEVEN	1969	IMMEDIATE	UK	IMSP 028
ALAN JONES	SAX	(	(D) WORLD OF AMEN CORNER	1969	DECCA	UK	SPA 33
MIKE SMITH	SAX	(	(E) AMEN CORNER & SMALL FACES	1975	NEW WORLD		NW 6001
CLIVE TAYLOR	B	(	(F) RETURN OF THE MAGNIFICENT SEVEN	1976	IMMEDIATE	UK	IML 1004
DENNIS BRYON	D	(	(G) GREATEST HITS	1978	IMMEDIATE	UK	IML 2004

A50   AMERICA   A50

GERRY BECKLEY	G V	(ALL	(A) AMERICA	1971	WB UK	K 46093	US	2576	
DEWEY BUNNELL	D G V	(ALL	(B) HORSE WITH NO NAME	19	WB UK	K 46157			
DAN PEEK	G V	(ABCDEFGHIJ	(C) HOMECOMING	1972	WB UK	K 46180	US	2655	
DAVE ATTWOOD	D	(AG	(D) HAT TRICK	1973	WB UK	K 56016	US	2728	
RAY COOPER	PERC	(AG	(E) HOLIDAY	1974	WB UK	K 56046	US	2808	
JOE OSBORN	B	(CG	(F) HEARTS	1975	WB UK	K 56115	US	2852	
DAVID DICKEY	B	(FGHIJK	(G) HISTORY (GREATEST HITS)	1975	WB UK	K 56169	US	3110	
GEORGE MARTIN	PNO	(H	(H) HIDEAWAY	1976	WB UK	K 56236	US	2932	
JIMMY CALIRE	K SAX	(IJK	(I) HARBOR	1976	WB UK	K 56351	US	3017	
CLYDIE KING	V	(FG	(J) LIVE	1977	WB UK	K 56434	US	3136	
JESSICA SMITH	V	(FG	(K) SILENT LETTER	1979	CAPITOL		UK US	11950	
HAL BLAINE	D	(CG	(L) ALIBI	1980	CAPITOL		UK US	12098	
DAVID LINDLEY	STEEL	(A	(M) VIEW FROM THE GROUND	1982	CAPITOL			12209	
RUSS BALLARD	V	(M							
GARY MALLABER	D	(C	HENRY DILTZ	BAN	(CG	TOM WALSH	PERC	(IJKM	
WILLIE LEACOX	D	(HIJGKM	VANETTA FIELDS	V	(FG	MIKE WOODS	G	(K	
LARRY CARLTON	SITAR	(J	CHESTER McCRACKEN	PERC	(G	KIM HAWORTH	D	(G	
DEAN PARKS	G	(M	STEVE LUKATHER	G	(M	MARK ISHAM	SYN	(M	
CARL WILSON	V	(M	CHRISTOPHER CROSS	V	(M	TOM KELLY	V	(M	
TIM SCHMIDT	V	(M	BRAD PALMER	B	(M	CHRIS SOTE	K SYN	(M	
ALVIN TAYLOR	D	(M	RICK NEIGHER	G	(M	MIKE PORCARO	B	(M	
SARA TAYLOR	V	(M	CHUCK KIRKPATRICK	V	(M	BOBBY COLLOMBY	PROD	(M	
HADLEY HECKENSMITH	G	(M	BILL MUMY	G	(M	JEFF PORCARO	D	(M	
JAI WINDING	K SYN	(M							

A50A   AMERICAN BLUES LEGENDS   A50A

JOHNNY BARNES	CLAR	(A	(A) AMERICAN BLUES LEGENDS	1972	POLYDOR		2460 186		
EDDIE TAYLOR	G	(A	(A) AMERICAN BLUES LEGENDS	1974	BIG BEAR	USBM150202	UK	BEAR 1	
BIG JOHN WRENCHER	V HCA	(A	( ) AMERICAN BLUES LEGENDS	1975	BIG BEAR			BEAR 8	
DR ROSS	V G HCA	(A							
COUSIN JOE PLEASANT	V PNO	(A	G P JACKSON	V G	(A	BOB HALL	PNO	(A	
BOB BRUNNING	B	(A	PETE YORK	D	(A	ROGER HILL	G	(A	
GRAHAM GALLERY	B	(A	GEORGE CHISHOLM	TROM	(A	COLIN SMITH	TPT	(A	

A51   AMERICAN BREED   A51

GARY LOIZZO	V G	(ABC	(A) AMERICAN BREED	1967	DOT DOLPO255	ATLANTIC	38002	
CHUCK COLBERT	B	(ABC	(B) BEND ME SHAPE ME	1968	DOT SLPD 502	ATLANTIC	38003	
AL CINER	G	(ABC	(C) PUMPKIN,POWDER,SCARLET & GREEN	1968	ATLANTIC		38006	
LEE GRAZIANO	D	(ABC	(D) LONELY SIDE OF THE CITY	1968	ATLANTIC		38008	
SKEET BRUSHOR		(C						
RALPH CRAIG		(C	BOBBY LEWIS		(C	LEN DRUSS		(C
ART HOYLE		(C	JOEL VANCE		(C	JOHN HOWELL		(C
BOB KEENE		(C	CLARK WEBER		(C			

A51A   AMERICAN DREAM   A51A

NICK JACKSON	G K V	(A	(A) AMERICAN DREAM	197	AMPEX	US	81001
DON LEE VAN WINKLE	G V	(A					
NICKY INDELICATO	G V	(A	DON FERRIS	B V	(A	MICKY BROOKS	D	(A

A51B   AMERICAN EAGLE   A51B

GREG BECK	G V	(A	(A) AMERICAN EAGLE	1970	DECCA	US	75258
GENE HUBBARD	K V B	(A					
ROBERT LOWERY	V	(A	FRED ZEUFELDT	D V	(A		

A51C   AMERICAN ECHOES   A51C

		(A) LAST TRAIN TO CLARKESVILLE	19	BLUEPORT	BLU 7

A52   AMERICAN FLYER   A52

STEVE KATZ		(AB	(A) AMERICAN FLYER	1976	UA	US	UALA 650	
ERIC KAZ		(AB	(A) AMERICAN FLYER	1976	UA	UK	UAS29991	
DOUG YULE		(AB	(B) SPIRIT OF A WOMAN	1977	UAS	UK	UAS30078	
CRAIG FULLER		(AB	(B) SPIRIT OF A WOMAN	1977	UA	US	UALA 720	
J D SOUTHER		(B						
LINDA RONSTADT	V	(B	SYLVIA TYSON	V	(B	TRACY NELSON	V	(B
BEN MINK		(B	WHITEY GLAN	D	(B	PRAKASH JOHN	B	(B
BOBBY KEYS	HRS	(B	JERRY SCHEFF		(B	JOHN KAPEC		(B
ALVIN TAYLOR	D	(B	FRED BECKMAIER	B	(A	LARRY CARLTON	G	(A
SCOTT EDWARDS	B	(A	GARY COLEMAN	PERC	(A	RUSTY YOUNG	STEEL	(A
JOE SAMPLE	K	(A	LELAND SKLAR	B	(A	ERNIE WATTS	SAX	(A
BYRON BERLINE	FDL	(A	EARL DUMLER	HRN	(A	VINCE DEROSA	HRNS	(A
HARRY BLUESTONE STRINGS		(A						

A53   AMERICAN GYPSY (1)   A53

JOE SKEEFE	B V K	(A	(A) AMERICAN GYPSY	1975	CHESS/CADET	CH 60034	
STEVE CLISBY	K HCA V	(A	( ) AMERICAN GYPSY	1975	BTM	BTM 1001	
MICHAEL HAMANE	G V	(A	( ) AMERICAN GYPSY	1975	CHESS	BTM 5003	
DALE HARREL Jr	G V	(A	( ) ANGEL EYES	19	PHILIPS	6410 066	
RICHARD JAMES	PERC D	(A					
LORENZO MILLS	PERC V	(A					

AMERICAN GYPSY (2)

```
JOE LALA          PERC (B
WILLIE WEEKS      B    (B
BILL LORDAN       D    (A
JAMES WALSH       V K D (ABD
ENRICO ROSENBAUM  PERC V G(ABD
JAY EPSTEIN       D    (A
```

(A) GYPSY	1971 CBS UK 66270 METROMEDIA US 1031	
(B) IN THE GARDEN	1972	METROMEDIA US 1044
(C) UNLOCK THE DEAD GATES	1973 RCA	US APLI0093
(D) ANTITHESIS	1972 RCA	US LSP 4775

JAMES JOHNSON   V G   (ABD   DONI LARSON   B   (A

AMERICAN NOISE

```
TOMMY RICH        D    (A
CRAIG BLAZER      G    (A
GEORGE SIPL       K    (A
```

(A) AMERICAN NOISE   1980   PLANET NL 52236   US P8

JERRY MORAN   K   (A   BRUCE BLAZER   G   (A

AMERICAN STANDARD BAND

(A) AMERICAN STANDARD BAND   1979   ISLAND   ILPS9450

AMERICAN TEARS

```
MARK MANGOLD        K V  (ABC
GLENN KITHCART      D    (C
KIRK POWERS         B V  (C
CRAIG EVAN BROOKS   G V  (C
GARY SONNY          B    (A
```

(A) BRANDED BAD	1974	CBS	US KC 33038
(B) TEARGAS	1975	CBS	US PC 33847
(C) POWERHOUSE	1977	CBS	US PC 34676

TOMMY GUNN   D   (AB   GREG BAZE   B   (B

AMERICAN TRAIN

```
TOM HOWE          G    (
CHRIS SCHINDLER   B
```

MIKE SKINNER   D   JOHN SULLIVAN   V

AMM II

```
KEITH ROWE        G    (A
EDDIE PROVOST     D    (A
LOU GARE          SAX  (A
```

(A) IT HAS BEEN AN ORDINARY DAY   1980   JAPO   60031

AMON DUUL

```
RAINER BAUER        G V    (ABCDEF
ULLRICH LEOPOLD     B      (ABCDEF
PETER LEOPOLD       D      (ABDE
HELGE FILANDA       V PERC(ABCDEF
WOLFGANG KRISCHKE   K PERC(ABDEF
ELLA BAUER          V PERC(ABCDEF
ANGELIKA FILANDA    V PERC(ABDEf
USCHI OBERMEIER     PERC (ABDE
KLAUS ESSER         G    (C
```

(A) AMON DUUL	1969 PROPHESY	1003
(B) COLLAPSING	1969 METRONOME	SMLP 012
(C) PARA DIESWARTS DUUL	1969 OHR	GER 56068
(D) DISTASTER	1971 BASF	GER 29 290 79/4
(E) THIS IS AMON DUUL	1973 BRAIN	GER 200 146
(F) MINNELIED	1975 BRAIN	GER 0040 149

AMON DUUL II

```
CHRIS KARRER    SAX G V  (ABCDEFGHJKLP
JOHN WEINZIERL          G (ABCDEFGHJLO
FALK ROGNER            B (ABCDEFGHJK
RENATE KNAUP           V (ABCDEFGHJK
CHRISTIAN 'STRAT'THIELE VLN V(AB
DIETER SERFAS          D (A
PETER LEOPOLD          D (ABCDEFGHJKOP
DAVE ANDERSON          B (AB
RAINER BAUER           G V (B
ULLRICH LEOPOLD        B (B
THOMAS KEYSERLING      FLT (B
LOTHAR MEID            B V (CDEGHJ
KARL HEINZ HAUSMANN    K (CD
JIMMY JACKSON          K (CE
AL GROMER              SITAR (CE
ROLF ZACHER            V (CE
OLAF KUBLER   PROD SAX (ABCDEFH
PAUL HEYDA             VLN (E
PANDIT SHANKAR         TABLA (E
LIZ VAN NEIENHOFF      TABLA (E
ROBBY HEIBL B G VLN V  (FK
LEE HARPER             TPT (HK
BOBBY JONES            SAX (HK
HERMANN JALOWITZKI     PERC (H
PETER KRAMPER          SYN (EF
HELMUT SONNLEIFNER     VLN (K
ERIK EBERT             (P
DANNY FICHELSCHER      D PERC(DEG
```

(A) PHALLUS DEI	1969 LIBERTY		LBS 83279
(A) PHALLUS DEI	1972 SUNSET	RI	50257
(B) YETI	1970 LIBERTY LSP 101/2		83359/60
(C) DANCE OFTHE LEMMINGS (DBL)	1971 UA US 9954	UK	60003/4
(C) TANZ DER LEMMINGE (DBL)	1971 LIBERTY	GER	83473 /74
(D) CARNIVAL IN BABYLON	1972 UA US 5586	UK	UAG 29327
(E) WOLF CITY	1972 UA US LA 017	UK	UAG 29406
(F) VIVA LA TRANCE	1973 UA US LA 198	UK	UAS 29504
(G) LIVE IN LONDON	1974 UA USP 102	UK	UAS 29466
(H) HI JACK	1974 NOVA	GER	6/22056
(H) HI JACK	1974 ATCO US 36108	UK ATLANTIC K50136
(J) LEMMINGMANIA	1975 UA		UAS 29723
(K) MADE IN GERMANY	1975 NOVA		628350
(K) MADE IN GERMANY	1975 ATCO US 36119	UK ATLANTIC K50182
(L) PYRAGONY	1976 NOVA		622890
(M) CLASSIC GERMAN ROCK SCENE	197 SONOPRESSE	FR	29770/71
(O) ALMOST LIVE	1977 NOVA	GER	623305
(P) ONLY HUMAN	1978 STRAUD	GER	623561
(P) ONLY HUMAN	1978 VINYL	UK LV 1004

```
KEITH FORSEY    PERC  (F    CHRIS BALDER         STR (H
LUDWIG POPP     HRN   (H    BOB CHATWIN          TPT (H
RUDY NAGORA     SAX   (H    THOR BALDURSSON      K   (HK
WILD WILLY      ACC V (H    HEINZ BECKER         PERC (K
NANDO TISCHER   G V   (K    JURGEN KORULETSCH    V   (K
KLAUS EBERT     B     (LO   STEFAN ZAUNER        K   (LOP
JOY ALASKA      V     (D    DESMOND BONNER       V   (F
```

ANARCHIC SYSTEM

(A) CHERIE SHA LA LA	19	DISCODIS	FR 85064/65
(B) GENERATION	19	DISCODIS	FR 7 00005
(C) SPECIAL CLUBS	19	DISCO DIS	FR 70008/9

ANCIENT GREASE

```
JOHN WEATHERS         D    (A
GARY PICKFORD HOPKINS V    (A
PHIL RYAN             K    (A
```

(A) WOMEN & CHILDREN FIRST   1970 MERCURY UK 6338 033   US 61305

ERIC ANDERSEN

```
ERIC ANDERSEN  HCA V G (ALL
 WITH
DEBBIE GREENE       G PNO(ABCDEJ
DEBORAH ANDERSEN    V    (K
JOHN GUERIN         D    (K
RUSS KUNKEL         D    (K
SCOTT EDWARDS       B    (K
DEAN PARKS          G    (K
TOM HENSLEY         PNO  (K
HOWARD EMERSON      G    (K
GARY COLEMAN        PERC (K
TOM SCOTT           SAX  (KL
TOM SELLERS         K    (K
EMANUEL MOSS        VLN  (K
CHRIS BOND          G    (K
```

(A) TODAY IS THE HIGHWAY	1965 FONTANA	UK	TFL6061
(A) TODAY IS THE HIGHWAY	1965 VANGUARD		VSD 79157
(B) 'BOUT CHANGES & THINGS	1966 VANGUARD		VSD 79206
(C) 'BOUT CHANGES & THINGS TAKE 2	1968 FONTANA	UK	STFL 6068
(C) 'BOUT CHANGES & THINGS TAKE 2	1967 VANGUARD		VSD 79236
(D) MORE HITS FROM TIN CAN ALLEY	1968 VANGUARD		SVRL19003
(D) MORE HITS FROM TIN CAN ALLEY	1968 VANGUARD		VSD 79271
(E) A COUNTRY DREAM	1969 VANGUARD		VSD 6540
(F) AVALANCHE	1970 W B	US	WS 1748
(G) ERIC ANDERSEN	1970 W B	US	WS 1806
(H) THE BEST OF ERIC ANDERSEN (DBL)	1971 VANGUARD		VSD 7/8
(J) BLUE RIVER	1973 CBS	UK	65145
(J) BLUE RIVER	1973 CBS	US	31062
(K) BE TRUE TO YOU	1975 ARISTA	UK	ARTY 114
(K) BE TRUE TO YOU	1975 ARISTA	US	4033

(CONTINUED)

```
RICHARD BENNETT      G    (K        (L) SWEET SUPRISE              1976 ARISTA        US    4075
ERNIE WATTS          SAX  (K        (M) THE BEST SONGS            1977 ARISTA        US    4128
ANDY ROBINSON        V    (K        (M) THE BEST SONGS            1977 PATHE         FR    4148
ALAN LINDGREN        K    (K        (N) STAGE                     19   CBS           US    65571
DENNIS ST JOHN       D    (K
EMORY GORDY          B    (K    JENNIFER WARREN    V    (K    MAXINE WILLARD     V    (K    GINGER BLAKE       V  (K
JULIA TILLMAN        V    (K    DOUG HAYWOOD            (K    JACKSON BROWNE     V    (K    HERB PEDERSEN      V  (K
MIKE CONDELLO        V    (K    JONI MITCHELL      V    (KJ   RAY BUCKWICH       V    (K    ORWIN MIDDLETON    V  (K
MARIA MULDAUR        V    (K    PAUL HARRIS        K    (CDG  HARVEY BROOKS      B    (BC   HERBIE LOVELL      D  (CDE
MARK SPORER          B    (KJ   JESSE EHRLICH      CELLO (K   ANDY JOHNSON       G VIBES (EFJ GARRY CARRIGAN   PERC(J
NORBERT PUTNAM       B    (DJ   WELDON MYRICK      STEEL(EJ   TEMPLE RISES       V    (J    KENNY BUTTREY      D  (DJ
GLEN SPREEN          K    (J    EDDIE HINTON       G    (J    DAVID BRIGGS       K    (DJ   FARRELL MORRIS     VIBES(J
HUGH McCRACKEN       G    (J    GRADY MARTIN       G    (J    JIM McKEVITT       D    (J    BOB RAFKIN         G  (D
DAVID BROMBERG       G    (J    DON THOMAS         G    (D    KEVIN KELLY        ACC  (J    RICHARD SCHLOSSER  D  (J
AL COOPER            G    (D    LAVERNA MOORE      V    (J    MILLE KIRKHAM      V    (J    AMOS GARRETT       G  (D
SONJA MONTGOMERY     V    (D    JORDANAIRES   V         (J    BOB BUSHELL        B    (D    FLORENCE WARNER    V  (J
JOE MACK             B    (D    STEVE ANANDER      B    (DF   PAUL GRIFFIN       PNO  (D    AL ROGERS          D  (D
BOBBY GREGG               (D    DOC BUTLER         HRN  (J    GREGG DEVINS       PERC (D    BILL PURSELL       PNO(E
JACK JENNINGS        PERC (D    LEE CRABTREE       PNO  (F    CHARLIE McCOY      HCA  (E    CHUCK RAUNEY       B  (F
BRUCE LANGHORN       G B  (F    JAYDEE MANNESS     G    (F    ERIC GALE          G    (F    CHRIS PARKER       D  (L
RICHARD BELL         K    (L    TONY BROWN         B    (L    ARLEN ROTH         G    (L    DAVID MANSFIELD    VLN STEEL(L
ANTONIO RAMOS        PERC (L    TOM SELLERS        K    (L    SISTER JOON        G    (L    TIM SCHMIT         V  (L
BEN KEITH            STEEL(L    JOHN BATDORF       V    (L    BRENT MYDLAND      V    (L    TOM P SALISBURY    K  (O
RANDY CIARLANTE      D    (O    BRAD STAHL         B V  (O    ROBERT LUSTGARTTEN G    (O
```

A59A   AL ANDERSON   A59A

```
AL ANDERSON          K G V (A        (A) AL ANDERSON            1972     VANGUARD US 79324    VSQ 40018
TOM STALEY           D    (A
TERRY ADAMS          PNO  (A    DON ADAMS          TROM (A    AL LEPAK           B    (A
```

A59B   CASEY ANDERSON   A59B

```
CASEY ANDERSON       G V  (ALL       (A) GOIN' PLACES           196      ELEKTRA    US    7192
CARL LYNCH           G    (E         (B) BAG I'M IN             196      ATCO       US    33149
BOBBY BUSHNELL       B    (E         (C) MORE PRETTY GIRLS THAN ONE 196  ATCO       US    33166
PANAMA FRANCIS       D    (E         (D) LIVE AT THE ICEHOUSE   1964     ATCO       US    33172
                                     (E) BLUES IS A WOMAN GONE  1965     ATCO       US    33176
```

A59B   DON ANDERSON   A59B

```
DON ANDERSON         V PNO (AB       (A) FEELIN' ALRIGHT        1972     INTERCORD           26007/5
KEITH FORSEY         D    (A         (B) EAGLE FLIES            1973     INTERCORD           26012/5
LOTHAR MEID          B    (A
ANDY MANX            G    (A    VILKO ZANKI        G B  (AB   PAUL VINCENT       G    (A
JOY FLEMING          V    (A    MAX GREGER JR      K    (A    RAINER PIETSCH     HCA K V(A
RALF MOWY            WIND (A    THOR BALDERURSSON  K V  (B    GERHARD SPIRKA     B    (B
ERNST VOSTER         G V  (B    ROLF BAUM          D    (B    FREDERIC RABOLD    HRNS (B
```

A60   IAN A ANDERSON   A60

```
IAN A ANDERSON       V G  (ALL       (A) STEREO DEATH BREAKDOWN        1969 LIBERTY               LBS83242
AL JONES             G    (B         (B) BOOK OF CHANGES               1970 FONTANA               STL 5542
DAVE JEFF            HCA  (B         (C) ROYAL YORK CRESENT            1970 VILLAGE THING UK  VTS   3
PICK WITHERS         D    (D         (D) A VULTURE IS NOT A BIRD YOU CAN...1971 VILLAGE THING UK VTS 9
KIPPS BROWN          ORG  (D         (E) SINGER SLEEPS ON             197  VILLAGE THING UK  VTS  18
JOHN TURNER          B    (BD        (1) COUNTRY BLUES BAND 1968
KEITH WARMINGTON     HCA  (D         (2) COUNTRY BLUES BAND 1968
PAUL ROWAN           HCA  (1
BOB ROWE             B    (12AB  CHRIS TURNER            (2A   PETE MORAN         V    (E
PETE SIDDONS         BOUZ (E    MIKE COOPER        G    (E    LES CALVERT        K B  (E
IAN FOSTER           D    (E    BILL BOAZMAN       G V  (E    MAGGIE HOLLAND     G    (E
BOB HALL             PNO  (B    KEITH CHRISTMAS    D    (B    RON NEEDS          MAND (A
PETE HOSSELL         JUG  (A    MEL RIGHT          D    (B    BRIAN CLAXTON           (A
```

A60A   JON ANDERSON   A60A

```
JON ANDERSON         ALL  (AB       (A) OLIAS OF SUNHILLOW     1976 ATLANTIC UK K50261 US SD18180
BRIAN GAYLOR         SYN  (A        (B) SONG OF SEVEN          1980 ATLANTIC UK K50756 US  16021
DAVE LAWSON               (C        (C) ANIMATION              1982 ATLANTIC            US  19355
KEN FREEMAN          STR  (A
IAN BARINSON         G B V (B    JOHN GIBLIN        B    (BC   RONNIE LEAHY       K    (BC
MORRIS PERT          D    (BC   DICK MORRISSEY     SAX  (BC   CHRISTOPHER RAINBOW V   (BC
JOHNNY DANKWORTH     SAX  (B    SIMON PHILIPS      D    (BC   JACK BRUCE         B    (BC
CLEM CLEMPSON        G    (BC   MEL                B    (B    DAVE SANCIOUS           (C
STEFANO CERRI        D    (C    BROTHER JAMES           (C    BILLY KRISTIAN          (C
BRETT MORGAN         D    (C    BLUE WEAVER        K    (C    IAN WALLACE        D    (C
TONY STANTON              (C    CHRIS PYNE              (C    HENRY LOWTHER      HRNS (C
DELMAY STRING QUARTET     (C
```

A61   MILLER ANDERSON   A61

```
MILLER ANDERSON      G V  (A        (A) BRIGHT CITY           1971 DERAM   UK SDL 3  US 18062
WITH
MICK WEAVER          K    (A    PETER DINES        K    (A    GARY THAIN         B    (A
ERIC DILLON          D    (A    NEIL HUBBARD       G    (A    LYN DOBSON         FLT  (A
HAROLD BECKETT       HRNS (A    MADELINE BELL      V    (A    LIZA STRIKE        V    (A
TRACY MILLER         V    (A
```

A62   HARVEY ANDREWS   A62

```
HARVEY ANDREWS       V G  (ALL       (A) PLACES & FACES        1970 DECCA                SDN 9
WITH                                 (B) WRITER OF SONGS       1972 CUBE                 HIFLY 10
TED TAYLOR           K    (B         (B) WRITER OF SONGS       1981 BEESWING    UK RI LBEE 002
MIKE MORAN           PNO  (C         (C) FRIENDS OF MINE       1977 ELECTRICAL           GNAT  2
GRAHAM COOPER        G    (CD        (C) FRIENDS OF MINE       1973 FLY                  HIFLY 15
TERRY COX            D    (C         (D) FANTASIES FROM A CORNER SEAT 1975 TRANSATLANTIC TRA 298
ROY BABBINGTON       B    (BC        (E) SOMEDAY               1976 TRANSATLANTIC        TRA 329
CHRIS KARAN          D    (C         (F) BRAND NEW DAY         1980 POLYDOR              2383 595
GEOFF BODENHAM       G V  (F
PHIL KENZIE          SAX  (C    DAVE COXHILL       SAX  (C    JIMMY HELMS        TPT  (C
     (CONTINUED)
```

HARVEY ANDREWS

MIKE BAILEY	TPT	(C	BERNIE HOLLAND	G	(E	MARK WARNER	G	(E
BOB JONES	G	(E	PETE WILLSHER	STEEL	(E	PETE WINGFIELD	K	(DE
JIM TOOMEY	D	(E	MO FOSTER	B	(E	CHRIS MERCER	SAX	(E
RON CARTHY	TPT	(E	GRAHAM PRESKETT	MAN VLN(C		PAUL KEOGH	G	(BC
DAVE MATTACKS	D	(BC	DAVE CARTWRIGHT	G HCA	(C	FRANCIS MONKMAN	K	(C
MIKE PAGE	SAX	(C	PAT DONALDSON	B	(D	RICHARD THOMPSON	G	(D
LINDA THOMPSON	V	(D	BOB FALLOON	G	(B	STAN GORMAN	D	(B
RALPH McTELL	G	(B	DAVE PEGG	B	(B	COZY POWELL	D	(B
IAN THOMPSON	B	(B	RICK WAKEMAN	K	(B	LES THATCHER	G	(B

MARK ANDREWS & THE GENTS

MARK ANDREWS	K V	(A	(A) BIG BOY			1979	A&M US 4812	UK	AMLH68513
MARTIN SAWTELL	B V	(A						
LARRY TOLFREE	D	(A	BRIAN KEMP	K V	(A	BARRY LINES	G V	(A

ANDROMEDA

JOHN CANN	G V	(A	(A) ANDROMEDA	1969 RCA	SF 8031
MICK HAWKSWORTH	B V	(A			
IAN McCLANE	D V	(A			

ANDWELLA'S DREAM

DAVE LEWIS	G K V	(ABC	(A) LOVE & POETRY	1969	CBS	63673
NIGEL SMITH	B	(ABC	(B) WORLD'S END	1970	REFLECTION UK	REF 1010
GORDON BARTON	D	(ABC	(B) WORLD'S END	1970	DUNHILL US	50095
DAVE McDOUGALL	K	(BC	(C) PEOPLE'S PEOPLE	1971	REFLECTION UK	REFL 10
DAVE STRUTHERS	B V	(C	(C) PEOPLE'S PEOPLE	1971	DUNHILL US	50105
JACK McCULLOCH	D	(B				
BOB DOWNES	FLT PERC(A		DORIS TROY	V	(C	LIZA STRIKE	V	(C
PHIL GILLIN	PROD C					

ANGE

DANIEL HAAS	B G	(BCDE	(A) IN CONCERT	1971	RCA	PL 37153
FRANCIS DECAMPS	K V	(BCDEFGH	(B) CARICATURES	1972	PHILIPS 6325 181	6332 066
JEAN MICHEL BREZOVAR	G V	(BCDE	(C) LA CIMETIERE DES ARLEQUINS	1974	PHILIPS 6325 037	9101 022
JEAN PIERRE GUICHARD	D	(H	(D) AU DELA DU DELIRE	1975	PHILIPS	9101 004
GERALD JELSCH	D	(BCD	(E) EMILE JACOTEY	1975	PHILIPS	9101 012
GUENOLE BIGER	G D	(E	(F) PAR LE FILS DU MANDARIN	1976	PHILIPS	9101 090
CHRISTIAN DECAMPS	K V	(BCDEFGH	(G) ANGE TOME	(DBL)	1977	PHILIPS	6641 715
ERIC BIBONNE	V	(D	(H) GUET APENS	1978	PHILIPS	9101 184
HENRY LOUSTAU	VLN	(D				
MICHEL LEFLOCH	V	(D	CLAUDE LEMET	G B FLT	(H	GERALD RENARD	B	(H

ANGEL

BARRY BRANT	D V	(ABCDEF	(A) ANGEL	1976	CASABLANCA UK CBC 4007 US	7021
'PUNKY' EDWIN MEADOWS	G	(ABCDEF	(B) HELLUVA BAND	1976	CASABLANCA UK CBC 4010 US	7028
FRANK DIMINO	V	(ABCDEF	(C) ON EARTH AS IT IS IN HEAVEN	1977	CASABLANCA UK CAL 2002 US	7043
FELIX ROBINSON	B	(DEF	(C) ON EARTH AS IT IS IN HEAVEN	1977	CASABLANCA FR	CBLA71007
GREGG GIUFFRIA	K	(ABCDEF	(D) WHITE HOT	1978	CASABLANCA UK CSL 2023 US	7085
MICKEY JONES	B	(ABC	(E) SINFUL	1979	CASABLANCA US	7127
			(F) LIVE WITHOUT A NET	1980	CASABLANCA UK 2703 US	7203

ANGEL CITY

DOC NEESON	V	(C	(A) FACE TO FACE	1978	EPIC US 36344	UK 84253
JOHN BREWSTER	G V	(C	(B) DARKROOM	1980	EPIC US 36543	UK 84502
RICK BREWSTER	G K	(C	(C) NIGHT ATTACK	1981	EPIC	UK 85480
GRAHAM BIDSTRUP	D	(				
CHRIS BAILEY	B V	(C	MURRAY BURNS	K	(A	BRENT ECCLES	D	(C

ANGELIC UPSTARTS

MENSI	V	(	(A) WE GOTTA GET OUT OF THIS PLACE	1980	WB	UK	K56806
STEVE	B	(	(B) LIVE	1981	EMI	UK	ZEM 102
MOND	G	(	(C) 2,000,000 VOICES	1981	ZONOPHONE	UK	ZONC104
STICKS	D	(				

ANGELO

ANGELO	V K	(A	(A) ANGELO		1977	FANTASY	F9507
LEE RITENOUR	G	(A					
DAVID AMARO	G	(A	BILL DICKENSON	B	(A	JIM GORDON	D	(A
LAUDIR DE OLIVEIRA	PERC	(A	DAVID SERAPHINE	D	(A	TOM SCOTT	WIND	(A
LEE LOUGHNAME	TPT	(A	MIKE BARONE	TROM	(A	DONALD BYRD	HRN	(A
PETER CETERA	V	(A	CARL WILSON	V	(A			

ANGELWITCH

KEVIN HEYBOURNE	G	(	(A) ANGELWITCH	1980	BRONZE	UK	BRON 532
KEVIN RIDDLES	B					
DAVE HOGG	D	(				

ANGLETRAX

JERRY MINGE	K	(A	(A) ANGLETRAX	1979	ARIOLA	AHAL8009
MARTIN HEATH	B	(A				
RENE RENNO	G	(A	WENDY HERMAN	V	(A	DAN WHO	D	(A
LIN JAMMET	G	(A				

ANIMALS

ALAN PRICE	K	(ABCDEI	(A) IN THE BEGINNING	(EP)	1965	DECCA DFE8643	WAND 690
JOHN STEEL	D	(ABCDEI	(B) THE ANIMALS	1964	COLUMBIA	UK	33SX1669
HILTON VALENTINE	G	(ABCDEFGI	(B) THE ANIMALS	1969	STARLINE	UK	SRS 5006
CHAS CHANDLER	B	(ABCDEFGI	(C) THE ANIMALS	1964	M G M	US	SE 4264
ERIC BURDON	V	(ABCDEFGHIM	(C) GET YOURSELF A COLLEGE GIRL	1965	M G M	US	SE 4273
DAVE ROWEBERRY	K	(G	(D) ANIMALS ON TOUR	1965	M G M	US	SE 4281
JOHN WEIDER	B G	(LMN	(E) ANIMAL TRACKS	1965	COLUMBIA	UK	33SX1708
VIC BRIGGS	G B	(LM	(E) ANIMAL TRACKS	1965	M G M	US	SE 4305
DANNY McCULLOCH	B G V	(LM	(F) BRITISH GO GO	1965	M G M	US	SE 4306
BARRY JENKINS	D	(GLMN	(G) ANIMALISM	1966	DECCA	UK	LK 4797
ANDY SOMERS(SUMMERS)	G	(N	(G) ANIMALISM	1966	M G M	US	SE 4414
ZOOT MONEY	K	(N	(H) AMINALIZATION	1966	M G M	US	SE 4384
GEORGE BRUNO	K V	(L	(I) MOST OF THE ANIMALS	1966	COLUMBIA	UK	SX 6035
			(I) MOST OF THE ANIMALS	1973	M F P	UK	MFP 5218

(CONTINUED)

ANIMALS

(J) WIND OF CHANGE		1967	M G M	US	CS 8052
(J) WIND OF CHANGE		1971	M G M	UK	2354 001
(J) WIND OF CHANGE		1967	M G M	US	SE 4484
(K) ERIC IS HERE		1967	M G M	US	SE 4433
(L) EVERYONE OF US		1968	M G M	US	SE 4553
(M) TWAIN SHALL MEET		1968	M G M		CS 8074
(M) TWAIN SHALL MEET		1968	M G M	US	SE 4537
(N) LOVE IS	(DBL)	1969	VERVE		6651 09/10
(N) LOVE IS		1969	M G M		CS 8104
(N) LOVE IS		1968	M G M	US	SE 4591
(N) LOVE IS		1971	M G M	UK	2619 002
(N) LOVE IS		1972	M G M	US	690
(JM)WIND OF CHANGE/TWAIN SHALL MEET	19		M G M		2642 004
( ) ANIMALS ANTHOLOGY 64 65	19		RAK	EURO	184 97238/9
( ) BEST OF THE ANIMALS		1966	M G M	US	SE 4324
( ) BEST OF THE ANIMALS		1967	M G M	US	4454
( ) BEST OF THE ANIMALS	(DBL)	1973	ABCKO		AB 4226
( ) BEST OF THE ANIMALS		19	SPRINGBOARD	US	4025
( ) BEST OF THE ANIMALS		19	PATHE	FR	CO62 91190
( ) BEST OF VOL2		1967	M G M	US	SE 4454
( ) GREATEST HITS		1969	M G M	US	SE 4602
( ) IN THE BEGINNING		1973	WAND		V6 5083
( ) ERIC BURDON & THE ANIMALS		1975	POLYDOR		2356 142
( ) NEWCASTLE 63		1976	D J M		DJSL 069
( ) NEWCASTLE 63		1977	CHARLY	UK	CR 30016
( ) LIVE IN NEWCASTLE		1976	D J M		DJB26069
( ) WITH SONNY BOY WILLIAMSON 63		1977	CHARLY	UK	CR 30018
( ) WILD ANIMALS		1966	DECCA	IMP	XLB 646028
( ) HITS OF THE ANIMALS		1969	COLUMBIA	IMP	SGHX 10048
( ) HOUSE OF THE RISING SUN		1970	EMI	IMP	048 50731
( ) STAR PORTRAIT		1971	M G M	IMP	665 102
( ) POP HISTORY		1971	M G M	IMP	2625 011
( ) MADMAN		1971	M G M	IMP	2674 044
( ) EARLY ANIMALS WITH ERIC BURDON		1973	PICKWICK	IMP	SPS 3330
( ) BEFORE WE WERE SO RUDELY INTERUPTED 77			BARN		2314 104
( ) BEFORE WE WERE SO RUDELY INTERUPTED 77			JET	US	JTLA790H
( ) NIGHTTIME IS THE RIGHT TIME		19	SPRINGBOARD	US	4065
( ) LET IT ROCK		1980	INTERCORD	NL	128611
( ) ERIC BURDON & THE ANIMALS		19	CHARLY		30197

(EP's)

ANIMALS IS HERE	1964	COLUMBIA	UK	SEG 8374
ANIMALS(BOOM BOOM)	1965	COLUMBIA	UK	SEG 8400
ANIMALS No2(I'M IN LOVE AGAIN)	1965	COLUMBIA	UK	SEG 8439
ARE BACK	1966	COLUMBIA	UK	SEG 8452
ANIMAL TRACKS	1966	COLUMBIA	UK	SEG 8499

A67A

UWE BICK	D V	(A
JURGENS JONUSCHIES	B V	(A
WERNER HOSTERMANN	K V	(A
HANS KAMPER	G V	(AB
MARTIN HABENICHT	B	(B

ANNEXUS QUAM

(A) ANNEXUS QUAM(OSMOSE)		1970	OHR	GER	56007
(B) BEZIEHUNGEN		1972	OHR	GER	556028

HARALD KLEMM	G FLT V(AB	OVE VOLQUARTZ	SAX (AB

A67C

CLIVE GREGSON	G V	(A
NICK SIMPSON		(
MEL HARLEY	D	(A
PHIL BARNES		

ANY TROUBLE

(A) WHERE ARE ALL THE NICE GIRLS	1980	STIFF UK SEEZ 25 US USE 6
(B) WHEELS IN MOTION	1981	STIFF UK SEEZ 37

CHRIS PARKS   G V   (A

A67D

BILLY JONES	
JIM DONLINGER	
JIM NYEHOLT	
BILLY HERMAN	

AORTA

(A) AORTA	1969	CBS		CS 9785
(B) AORTA 2	1970	HAPPY TIGER	US	1010

A67E

APHRODOITES CHILD

VANGELIS PAPATHANASSIOU K B (ALL		(A) END OF THE WORLD	1969	MERCURY	UK	SMCL20140
DEMIS ROUSSOS V B G (ALL		(AF)END OF THE WORLD RAIN & TEARS	19	VERTIGO		6333 008
LUCAS SIDERAS D V (ALL		(B) ITS FIVE O'CLOCK	19	VERTIGO		6333 009
WITH		(C) 666,APOCALYPSE OF JOHN	1972	VERTIGO		6673 001
		(C) 666,APOCALYPSE OF JOHN	1972	VERTIGO		6641 581
SILVER KOULOURIS G PERC AC		(C) 666,APOCALYPSE OF JOHN	197	VERTIGO	US	500
VANNIS TSAROUCHIS V (C		(D) APHRODITES CHILD	1978	MERCURY		6886 650
IRENE PAPAS V (C		(D) APHRODITES CHILD	19	MERCURY	US	VEL 2 500
JOHN FROST V (C		(D) APHRODITES CHILD	1975	MERCURY		138 351
ARRIS HALKITIS B SAX V PERC (C		(E) BEST OF	1975	MERCURY		6333 002
MICHEL RIPOCHE TROM SAX (C		(E) BEST OF	19	VERTIGO		6583 025
		(F) RAIN & TEARS	1975	VERTIGO/PHILIPS		6483 035
		(H) GREATEST HITS	1981	FONTANA		6420 006

A67F

ANIMATED EGG

(A) ANIMATED EGG	196	ALSHIRE	US	5104

A67G

ANNO DOMINI

DAVE MERCER	G B V	(A	
'TIGER' TAYLOR	G V	(A	
KERRY SCOTT	V PER	(A	

(A) ON THE NEW DAY	1971	DERAM		SLM 1085

JOHN JONES   G   (A

A67H

BARTHOLOMEW	G V	(A
BOBBY HOWE	D V	(A
GREGG HOLLISTER	B V	(A

ANTHEM

(A) ANTHEM	1970	BUDDAH	US	5071

A67J

ANTI PASTI

(A) THE LAST CALL	1981	RONDELET	UK	ABOUT 5

A67K   ANYONES DAUGHTER   A67K

HARALD BARETH	B V	(A	(A) ADONIS		1979	BRAIN		0060 186
UWE KARPA	G	(A						
KONO KONOPIK	D	(A	MATTHIAS ULMER	K	(A			

A67L   APPALOOSA   A67L

AL KOOPER	K	(A	(A) APPALOOSA		1971	CBS	US	9819
JOHN CROMPTON	V	(A						
ROBIN BATTEAU	VLN	(A	GENO ROSOU	STR	(A	DAVID REISER	B	(A

A67M   APPLEJACKS   A67M

AL JACKSON	V	(A	(A) APPLEJACKS		1964	DECCA	UK	LK 4635
MARTIN BAGGOTT	G	(A						
PHIL CASH	G	(A	MEGAN DAVIES	B	(A	DON GOULD	K	(A
GERRY FREEMAN	D	(A						

A67N   CARMINE APPICE   A67N

CARMINE APPICE	D V	(A	(A) CARMINE APPICE		1981	WEA	UK K99196	
DANNY JOHNSON	G	(A						
JAY DAVIS	B	(A	DUANE HITCHINGS	K	(A			

A67P   APACHE   A67P

JOE MESSINA	V	(A	(A) APACHE		1981	ATCO	UK	K50826
GARY T AMOS	D	(A						
TOM CLIFFORD	B	(A	DENNIS SHEAHAN	G	(A	PETER ARENDT	G K	(A

A68   APPLETREE THEATRE   A68

TERENCE BOYLAN	(	(A) PLAYBACK		19	POLYDOR UK 2353 051 US VERVE3042		
JOHN BOYLAN	(A						
LARRY CORYELL	G	(A	CHUCK RAINEY	B	(A	CHUCK ISRAELS	(A
HERB LOVELLE	(A	ERIC GALE	G	(A			

A68A   APPLE PIE MOTHERHOOD   A68A

JEFF LABES	K	(AB	(A) APPLE PIE MOTHERHOOD BAND		1968	ATLANTIC	US	SD 8189
TED DEMOS	G V	(AB	(B) APPLE PIE		1969	ATLANTIC	US	SD 8233
JOE CASTAGNO	G	(A						
JACK BRUNO	G V	(AB	DICK BARNABY	B	(AB	BRUCE PAINE	V	(B
ADAM MEYERS	HCA V	(A	MICHAEL SORAFINE	G V	(A			

A68B   APPLE & APPLEBERRY   A68B

	(A) APPLE & APPLEBERRY	1974	ABC	US	802

A69   APRIL WINE   A69

RICK MORRISON	SAX	(A	(A) ON RECORD		1972	AQUARIUS	US	503
BRIAN GREENWAY	G V	(HJKL	(A) APRIL WINE		1972	BIG TREE	US	2012
JERRY MERCER	D V	(BCDEFGHJK	(B) ELECTRIC JEWELS		1973	AQUARIUS	US	AQR 504
STEVE LANG	B V	(EFGHJKL	(C) LIVE		1974	AQUARIUS	US	AQR 505
JIM CLENCH	B V	(ABCD	(D) STAND BACK		1975	BIG TREE	US89506 AQUARIUS506	
MYLES GOODWYN	V G K	(ALL	(E) WHOLE WORLDS GONE CRAZY		1976	LONDON	UK	SHU 8503
GARY MOFFET	G V	(BCDEFGHJK	(E) WHOLE WORLDS GONE CRAZY		1976	LONDON	US	PS 675
DAVID HENMAN	G	(AB	(F) FOREVER FOR NOW		1976	AQUARIUS		AQR 511
RITCHIE HENMAN	D	(AB	(G) LIVE AT THE EL MOCAMBO		1977	LONDON	UK	SHU 8510
KEITH JOLLIMORE	FLT	(G	(G) LIVE AT THE EL MOCAMBO		1977	LONDON	US	PS 699
RICHARD NEWELL	HCA	(B	(H) FIRST GLANCE		1978	CAPITOL		11852
PIERRE SENECAL	K	(B	(J) HARDER ...FASTER		19	CAPITOL	US	12013
AL NICHOLS	V	(B	(K) GREATEST HITS		1979	AQUARIUS	US	AQR 525
PAM MARSH	V	(BF	(L) NATURE OF THE BEAST		1981	CAPITOL		12125
MARY LOU GAUTHIER	V	(A	(EP) UNRELEASED LIVE		1979	CAPITOL 12CL18		
DWAYNE FORD	K	(E						
FRANK LUDWIG	K	(E	FRANK MARINI	G	(E	SERGE LUCAS	K	(E
BILLY SZAWLOWSKI	V	(E	BARRY KEAN	PERC	(F	JUDY RICHARDS	V	(F
GAIL MEZO	V	(F	TONY GRANT	V	(F	BRIAN GREENWAY	G V	(HJ

A70   AQUARIAN DREAM   A70

(A) FANTASY		1978	ELEKTRA	K	52109
(B) NORMAN CONNORS PRESENTS A' DREAM		19	BUDDAH	US	5672
(C) AQUARIAN DREAM		1980	BUDDAH	UK	08
(D) CHANCE TO DANCE		1980	ELEKTRA	US	205

A71   AQUILA   A71

RALPH DENYER	V G	(A	(A) AQUILA		1970	RCA		SF 8126
PHIL CHILDS	B K	(A						
GEORGE LEE	WIND	(A	MARTIN WOODWARD	K	(A	JAMES SMITH	D	(A

A71A   AQSAK MABOUL   A71A

MARC HOLLANDER	K WIND	(A	(A) UN PEU DE L'AME DES BANDITS		1979	ATEM	BELG	002
CATHERINE JAUNIAUX	V	(A						
FRED FRITH	G VLN B	(A	MICHEL BERCKMANS	WIND	(A	FRANK WUYTS	D	(A
CHRIS CUTLER	D	(A	DENIS VAN HECKE	STR G	(A			

A71B   AQUATONES   A71B

(A) THE AQUATONES SING	19	FARGO		5001

A72   ARBRE   A72

PAUL CAFFREY	V G	(AB	(A) TIME & AGAIN		1976	DJM	DJF20480
TONY DAVISON	B	(AB	(B) ARBRE		1978	DJM	DJF20527
ROGER ASKEW	G PNO	(AB					
BILL BISSET	D	(AB	PHIL CAFFREY	V G	(AB	PETER CAFFREY	G V	(AB

A72A   DAN ARBRAS   A72A

DAN ARBRAS	G V	(ALL	(A) DOUAR NEVEZ		1977	HEXAGONE	FR	883 009
PATRIG MOLARD	WIND	(ABC	(B) ALLEZ DIRE A LA VILLE		1978	HEXAGONE	FR	883 021
BENOIT WIDEMANN	K SYN	AABC	(C) THE EARTH LAMENT		1979	HEXAGONE	FR	883 034
DAVE PEGG	B	(A						
MICHEL SANTANGELI	D	(ABC	MARC CHANTEREAU	PERC	(A	EMMANUELLE PARRENIN	VIELLE	(A
GUY DELACROIX	B	(B	FRANCIS MOZE	B	(BC	PATRICK AUDOIN	K	(BC
DONINIQUE WIDIEZ		(B						

A72B   ARC (US)   A72B

BOBBY SAVENE	B V	(A	(A) ARC		1978	LIFESONG	US	35413
WAYNE GEORGE	K V	(A						
EDDIE KOSOWSKI	G V	(A	STEVE SZCZESNIAK	D V	(A			

A73   ARC   A73

MICK GALLAGHER	K G V	(A	(A) ARC AT THIS		1971	DECCA	SKLR5077
JOHN TURNBULL	G	(A					
TOM DUFFY	B V	(A	DAVID MONTGOMERY	D	(A		

A73A   ARCADIUM   A73A

GRAHAM BEST	B V	(A	(A) ARCADIUM(BREATHE AWHILE)		1969	MIDDLE EARTH	MDLS 302
ALAN ELLWOOD	K V	(A					
JOHN PARKER	D	(A	ROBERT ELLWOOD	(A	MIGUEL SEGIDES	(A	

A74   NEIL ARDLEY   A74

NEIL ARDLEY	K SYN	(ALL	(A) WESTERN UNION	1965	DECCA	UK	SKL 4690
TONY REEVES	B	(A	(B) DEJEUNER SUR L'HERBE	1969	VERVE	UK	SVLP 9236
JON HISEMAN	D	(AD	(C) GREEK VARIATIONS(1 SIDE)	1970	COLUMBIA	UK	SCX 6414
JACK BRUCE	B	(BC	(D) SYMPHONY OF AMARANTHS	1972	REGAL ZONOPHONE		SLRZ 1028
JEFF CLYNE	B	(CD	(E) KALEIDOSCOPE OF RAINBOWS	1976	GULL	UK	GULP 1018
BOB BERTLES	WIND	(E	(F) HARMONY OF SPHERES	1979	DECCA	UK	TXSR 133
PAUL BUCKMASTER	CELLO	(E					

IAN CARR	HRNS	(EABCDEF	GEOFF CASTLE	K	(EF	TONY COE	WIND	(EF	DAVE McCRAE	K (E
ROGER SELLERS	D	(E	KEN SHAW	G	(E	BRIAN SMITH	WIND	(E	ROGER SUTTON	B (E
BARBARA THOMPSON	WIND	(EF	TREVOR TOMKINS	PERC	(EF	STAN SULZMANN	WIND	(E	JOHN TAYLOR	K (E
JOHN MARTYN	G	(F	BILLY KRISTIAN	B	(F	RICHARD BURGESS	D	(F	PEPI LEMER	V (F
NORMA WINSTONE	V	(F	MICK PALMER	HRNS	(A	TONY DUDLEY	HRNS	(A	BOB LEAPER	HRNS(A
MIKE PHILLIPSON	HRNS	(A	JOHN MUMFORD	HRNS	(A	PAUL RUTTERFORD	HRNS	(A	PETER HARVEY	HRNS(A
DICK HART	HRNS	(AD	LES CARTER	WIND	(A	TREVOR WATTS	WIND	(A	DAVE GELLY	WIND K(ABD
TOM HARRIS	WIND	(A	SEBASTIAN FREUDENBERG	WIND	(A	MIKE BARRETT	K	(A	DEREK WATKINS	HRNS(BD
HARRY BECKETT	HRNS	(BD	HENRY LOWTHER	HRNS	(BD	MIKE GIBBS	HRNS	(BC	DEREK WADSWORTH	HRNS(BD
TONY RUSSELL	HRNS	(B	GEORGE SMITH	HRNS	(B	JIM PHILLIPS	WIND	(B	JOHN MARSHALL	D (C
DICK HECKSTAL SMITH	WIND	(BD	FRANK RICOTTI	PERC	(BCD	DON RENDELL	HRNS	(CD	KARL JENKINS	WIND K (CD
NIGEL CARTER	HRNS	(D	JOHN CLEMENSON	WIND	(D	RAY PREMRU	HRNS	(D	BUNNY GOULD	WIND(D
STAN TRACEY	K	(D	ALAN BRANSCOMBE	K	(D	CHRIS LAURENCE	B	(D	NORMA WINSTON	V (D
IVOR CUTLER	V	(D								

A74A   AREA   A74A

DEMETRIO STATOS	V K	(AB	(A) CRAC		19	BARCLAY	IT	940 512
ARES TAVOLAZZI	B	(A	(B) ARBEIT MACHT FREI		1973	CRAMPS		5101
PATRIZIO FARISELLI	K	(AB						
GIAMPAOLO TOFANI	G	(AB	PATRICK ERARD OJIVAS	B	(B			

A74B   ARDO DOMBEC   A74B

HELMUT HECHMAN	WIND	(A	(A) ARDO DOMBEC		1971	BASF/PILZ	GER 2021095/2
WOLFGANG SPILLNER	D V	(A					
HARALD GLEN	G V	(A	MICHAEL UFER	B	(A		

A75   AREA CODE 615   A75

WELDON MYRICK STEEL	G	(AB	(A) AREA CODE 615	1969	POLYDOR	UK	583572
BOBBY THOMPSON BAN	K	(AB	(A) AREA CODE 615	1969	POLYDOR	US	24 4002
BUDDY SPICHER	FDL	(AB	(B) A TRIP IN THE COUNTRY	1970	POLYDOR		2425 023
CHARLIE McCOY	HCA	(AB	(B) A TRIP IN THE COUNTRY	1970	POLYDOR	US	24 4025
MAC GAYDEN	G	(AB	(AB)AREA CODE/A TRIP	(DBL)	1974	POLYDOR	2683 040
WAYNE MOSS	B G	(AB					
KENNY BUTTREY	D	(AB	NORBERT PUTNAM	B	(AB	KEN LAUBER	PNO	(A
DAVID BRIGGS	PNO	(B					

A76   JOSE 'CHEPITO' AREAS   A76

JOSE CHEPITO AREAS	PERC	(A	(A) JOSE CHEPITO AREAS		1974	CBS US 33062	UK 80296

A77   ARGENT   A77

ROD ARGENT	K V	(ABCDEFGH	(A) ARGENT	1970	CBS	UK	63781
ROBERT HENRIT	D	(ABCDEFGH	(A) ARGENT	1970	EPIC	US	26525
JIM RODFORD	B	(ABCDEFGH	(B) RING OF HANDS	1971	EPIC	UK	64190
RUSS BALLARD	G V	(ABCDEF	(B) RING OF HAND	1971	EPIC	US	30128
JOHN VERITY	V	(GH	(C) ALL TOGETHER NOW	1972	CBS	UK	64962
JOHN GRIMALDI	G	(GH	(C) ALL TOGETHER NOW	1972	EPIC	US	31556
PHIL COLLINS	PERC	(H	(D) IN DEEP	1973	EPIC	UK	65475
DEREK GRIFFITHS	G	(D	(D) IN DEEP	1973	EPIC	US	32195
			(E) NEXUS	1974	EPIC	UK	65924
			(E) NEXUS	1974	EPIC	US	32573
			(F) ENCORE	(DBL) 1974	EPIC	UK	88063
			(F) ENCORE	(DBL) 1974	EPIC	US	33079
			(G) CIRCUS	1975	EPIC	UK	80691
			(G) CIRCUS	1975	EPIC	US	33422
			(H) COUNTERPOINT	1975	RCA	UK	RS 1020
			(H) COUNTERPOINT	1975	U A	US	LA 560G
			( ) BEST OF ARGENT	1976	EPIC	UK	81321
			( ) HOLD YOUR HEAD UP	1978	EMBASSY	UK	31640
			( ) ANTHOLOGY	197	EPIC	US	33955
			( ) SILVER PLATED	197	EPIC	US	26285

A78   ROD ARGENT   A78

ROD ARGENT	K V	(A	(A) MOVING HOME		1978	MCA	MCF 2854
WITH							
PHIL COLLINS	PERC	(A	MORRIS PERT	PERC	(A	ALPHONSO JOHNSON	B (A
CLIVE CHAMAN	B	(A	GARY MOORE	G	(A	JACK LANCASTER	WIND (A

A79   ARIEL   A79

MICHAEL RUDD	V G	(AB	(A) STRANGE FANTASTIC DREAM		1973	HARVEST	SHSP4028
WILLIAM PUTT	B	(AB	(B) ROCK N ROLL SCARS		1974	HARVEST	SHSP4039
HARVEY JAMES	G	(B					
JOHN LEE	D	(B	JOHN MILLS	K	(A	TIM GAZE	G V	(A
NIGEL MACARA	D V	(A					

A80   ARIZONA   A80

PETER KUCH		(B	(A) ARIZONA		1976	RCA	SF 8465
DOUG HOLZWARTH		(B	(A) ARIZONA		1976	RCA	US LPL1 5123
MARY DOBBINS		(B	(B) LOWDOWN		1977	RCA	PL 25103
WILLIE KNOWLES		(B					
PAT MURPHY		(B	KEN ASHBY		(B		

```
    KEITH RELF           V HCA (A     (A) ARMAGEDDON                      1975   A&M US SP4513   UK AMLH 64513
    LOUIS CENNAMO        B     (A
    BOBBY CALDWELL       D V   (A     MARTIN PUGH          G      (A
```

```
    JOAN ARMATRADING     V G (ALL     (A) WHATEVERS FOR US              1974  CUBE  2338 023   UK      HIFLY 12
    RAY COOPER           PERC(AJ      (A) WHATEVERS FOR US              1972  A&M               US         4382
    HENRY SPINETTI       D   (ADE     (B) BACK TO THE NIGHT            1975  A&M   US 4525  UK      AMLH 68305
    ROBBIE SHAKESPEARE   B   (J       (B) BACK TO THE NIGHT            1982  A&M   UK RI AMID 112
    DAVEY JOHNSTONE      G   (A       (C) JOAN ARMATRADING             1976  A&M   US 4588  UK      AMLH64588
    KENNEY JONES         D   (CD      (D) SHOW SOME EMOTION            1977  A&M   US 4663  UK      AMLH 68433
    TONY CARR            D   (BC      (E) TO THE LIMIT                 1978  A&M                       AMLH 64732
    CHRIS KARAN          PERC(B       (F) STEPPING OUT                 1979  A&M                       AMLH 64789
    LON PRICE            WIND(F        (G) ME MYSELF I                  1980  A&M                       AMLH 64809
    RON MATTHEWSON       B   (B       (H) HOW CRUEL ½ LP               1980  A&M US 3302      NL         63302
    DAVE MARKEE          B   (CDE      (J) WALK UNDER LADDERS           1981  A&M               UK AMLH 64876
    DAVE BROOKS          SAX (B       (1) 1975 TOUR    (2) 1975 TOUR    (3) 1977 IN CONCERT TV SHOW
    COLIN PINCOTT        G   (B
    JEAN ROUSSEL         K   (B    JOHN HALSEY      D    (B   ANDY SOMERS     G    (B   PETE GAGE        K G (B
    BERNIE HOLLAND       G   (B    SHAMSI SARUMI   PERC (B   PHIL CHEN       B    (B   TONY NEWMAN      D   (B
    GASPAR LAWAL         PERC(B    JERRY DONAHUE  G (CD23   DAVE MATTACKS    D    (C2  JIMMY JEWELL     SAX (C
    B J COLE             STEEL(C   PAT DONALDSON   B    (2   GERRY CONWAY    D    (AB  BRYAN GAROFALO   B   (D3
    DAVID KEMPER         D   (D3   JOHN BUNDRICK   K    (D   GEORGIE FAME    K    (D   PETE CLARKE      V   (D
    JOE SCOTT            V   (D    MEL COLLINS     SAX (DJ   TIM HINKLEY     K    (D   GRAHAM LYLE      G   (C
    PETE WOOD            K   (C    BRYN HAWORTH   G MAND(2C   ALBERT LEE      G    (2   QUITMAN DENNIS   SAX (E3
    RED YOUNG            K   (3EF  PHILIP PALMER   K    (E   THE MOVIES           (1   DICK SIMS        K   (E
    MARCUS MILLER        B   (G    STEVE YORK    B HCA (B   WILL LEE        B    (G   ANTON FIG        D   (G
    CHRIS SPEDDING       G   (G    HIRAM BULLOCK   G    (G   RICKY HIRSCH    G    (FG  DANNY FEDERICI   K   (G
    PAUL SCHAEFFER       PNO (G    CLIFFORD CARTER PNO  (G   PHILLIP ST JOHN PNO  (G   CLARENCE CLEMONS SAX (G
    GEORGE KERR          V   (G    SAMMY TURNER    K    (F   RITCHIE HAYWARD D    (F   BILL BODINE      B   (F
    LARRY STEELE         B   (A    PAM NESTER      V    (A   JERRY MAROTTA   D V  (J   TONY LEVIN       B   (J
    HUGH BURNS           G   (J    THOMAS DOLBY    SYN  (J   GARY SANFORD    G    (J   NICK PLYTAS      K   (J
    DICK CUTHELL         HRNS(J    RICO RODRIGUEZ  HRNS (J   ANDY PARTRIDGE  G    (J   JULIAN DIGGLE    PERC(J
    SLY DUNBAR           D   (J
```

```
    FRANKIE ARMSTRONG   V     (AB     (A) LOVELY ON THE WATER          1972  TOPIC       UK        12TS 216
    JEFF LOWE      DULC/WIND (A        (B) SONGS & BALLADS              1975  TOPIC       UK        12TS 273
    JACK WARSHAW       G BAN(A         (C) AND THE MUSIC PLAYS          1981  BRIAR       US            4211
    ANDREW BROWN       FDL   (B
    GRAHAM GOFFEE      G     (B    SUSIE ROTHFIELD  DULC V(B  HEATHER WOOD   V   (B   BRIAN PEARSON    V (B
```

```
    KEVIN ARMSTRONG          (A      (A) HOW THE WEST WAS WON         1981  NEW OPIUM         UK OVAL302
```

```
    ROB JONES           V    (A      (A) WHEN                         1980  ACE  (EP)        ACE   20
    ROB HILL            G    (A
    JAIME CORTINAS      B    (A   GARY FOSTER     D    (A  ANDY BRISCOE    SYN (A   PHIL MARTIN G    (A
```

```
    BILLY BOY ARNOLD  V HCA(ALL      (A) KING OF CHICAGO BLUES VOL 3  1975  VOGUE                   30285
    WITH                             (B) BLOW THE BACK OFF IT         1975  RED LIGHTNIN    RL   0012
    JOHNNY WALKER       PNO  (C      (C) SINNERS PRAYER               1976  RED LIGHTNIN    RL   0014
    CHRIS MOSS          D    (C      (D) MORE BLUES ON THE SOUTH SIDE  197  BELLAPHON 40108 PRESTIGE 7389
    ODELL CAMPBELL      B    (BC      (E) CHECKIN' IT OUT              1979  RED LIGHTNIN    RL   0024
    LOUIS MYERS         G    (C      (F) CRYING & PLEADING            1980  CHARLY          CRB 1016
    SAMMY LAWHORN       G    (C      (G) I WISH YOU WOULD   (EP)      1980  CHARLY          UK CTD 117
    PETER SHERTSER      PROD (E
    BO DIDDLEY          G    (B   OTIS SPAN      PNO  (B  JEROME GREEN    PERC(B   FRED BELOW     D  (B
    REYNOLDS HOWARD     D    (B   JAMES BRADFORD  B    (B  CLIFTON JAMES   D   (B   HENRY GRAY     PNO (B
    JODY WILLIAMS       G    (B   SUNNYLAND SLIM PNO  (B  MILTON RECTOR   B   (B   EARL PHILLIPS  D  (B
    QUINN WILSON        B    (B   SYLVESTER THOMPSON G (B  MACK THOMPSON   G   (B   MIGHTY JOE YOUNG G (E
    LAFAYETTE LEAKE     PNO  (D   JEROME ARNOLD   B    (D  JUNIOR BLACKMAN D   (D   TONY McPHEE    G  (E
    WILGER CAMPBELL     D    (E   ALAN FISH       B    (E
```

```
    P P ARNOLD          V    (ALL     (A) FIRST LADY                  1967  IMMEDIATE          IMSP 011
    LEE JACKSON         B    (         (B) KAFUNTA                     1968  IMMEDIATE          IMSP017
    KEITH EMERSON       K    (         (C) GREATEST HITS               1977  IMMEDIATE          IML2006
    DAVY O'LIST         G    (
    BRIAN DAVISON       D    (
```

```
    DYAN BIRCH          V    (ABC     (A) ARRIVAL                     1970  LONDON       US         576
    FRANK COLLINS       V    (ABC     (A) ARRIVAL                     1970  DECCA              SKL5055
    PADDY McHUGH        V    (ABC     (B) HEARTBREAK KID              1973  CBS                  70125
    TONY O'MALLEY       V K  (ABC     (C) ARRIVAL                     1972  CBS                  64733
    CARROLL CARTER      V    (ABC
    RALPH PEREIRA       G    (C    LEE SUTHERLAND   B   (C  GLEN LEFLEUR    D   (C   DON HUME       B  (A
    LLOYD COURTENAY     D    (A    RON CARTHY      TPT  (D  ED RAY-SMITH   TROM (B   ROY CARTER    OBOE (D
    PETE ZORN          HRNS (D    PHIL CHEN       B    (D  GEORGE LEE      SAX (C
```

```
    DON NIXON         B V PERC(AB     (A) RUMOURS                     1976  VANGUARD       US VSD 79369
    ROBERT KIRKLAND   G V PERC(AB     (B) SUDDENLY                    1980  WB             US       3429
    SCOTT DAVISON     D PERC(AB
    MARTY STOOT         K    (AB  DON BROOKS    HCA   (A  LARRY PACKER    FDL (A   ERIC WEISSBERG  BANJ(A
    SANFORD ALLEN            (A   STRING SECTION
```

```
    DAVIE ALLAN         G V  (A      (A) APACHE'65                    1965  TOWER         US        5002
    STEVE PUGH          B    (A      (B) BLUES THEME                  1967  TOWER         US        5078
    LARRY BROWN         D    (A      (C) CYCLE DELIC SOUNDS           1968  TOWER         US        5094
    PAUL JOHNSON        G    (A      (D) WILD IN THE STREETS           196  TOWER         US        5139
```

ARS NOVA

JOHN PIERSON	TROM V(AB		(A) ARS NOVA		1968 ELEKTRA	US	EKS74020
WYATT DAY	G K V (AB		(B) SUNSHINE & SHADOWS		1969 ATLANTIC		SD 8221
WARREN BERNHARDT	K (B		(B) SUNSHINE & SHADOWS		1969 ATLANTIC		588 196
MAURY BAKER	PERC K (A						
GIOVANNI PAPALIA	G (A	SAM BROWN	G (B	JIMMY OWENS	TPT (B	BILL FOLWELL	TPT B(A
ART KOENIG	B (B	JOE HUNT	D (B	JONATHAN RASKIN	B G V(A		

ART

LUTHER GROSVENOR	G (A	(A) SUPERNATURAL FAIRYTALES	1967 ISLAND	ILP 967
MIKE KELLIE	D (A			
MIKE HARRISON	V K (A	GREG RIDLEY B (A		

ART & LANGUAGE

MAYO THOMPSON	(A	(A) CORRECTED SLOGANS	197 MUSIC LANGUAGE US	1848
JESSE CHAMBERLAIN	(			

ART BEARS

FRED FRITH	G VLN K(ABC	(A) HOPES & FEARS	1978 RE	2188
CHRIS CUTLER	D PERC(ABC	(A) HOPES & FEARS	1978 RANDOM RADAR	RRR 004
DAGMAR KRAUSE	V (ABC	(B) WINTER SONGS	1979 RE	RE0618
GEORGE BORN	V (A	(C) THE WORLD AS IT IS TODAY	1981 RE	6622
LINDSAY COOPER	WIND (A			
TIM HODGKINSON	K WIND(A			

ART ENSEMBLE OF CHICAGO

ROSCOE MITCHELL	SAX (ALL	(A) PHASE ONE	19 AMERICA		AM 6116
LESTER BOWIE	TPT (ALL	(A) PHASE ONE	19 PRESTIGE	US	10064
MALACHI FAVORS	B (ALL	(B) WITH FONTELLA BASS	19 AMERICA		AM 6117
JOESEPH JARMAN	WIND (ALL	(B) WITH FONTELLA BASS	19 PRESTIGE		PR 10049
DON MOYE	D (ALL	(C) SPIRITUAL	1974 POLYDOR		2383 098
FONTELLA BASS	V (BJP	(C) SPIRITUAL	1974 FREEDOM		28 428
		(D) FANFARE FOR WARRIORS	1974 ATLANTIC	US	SD 1651
		(D) FANFARE FOR WARRIORS	1977 ATLANTIC	UK	K 50304
		(E) TUTAMKHAMUN	1975 FREEDOM		28 473
		(F) PEOPLE IN SORROW	19 PATHE		2C062 10523
		(F) PEOPLE IN SORROW	19 NESSA	US	N3
		(G JACKS ONLY YOUR HOUSE	1978 AFFINITY		AFF 9
		(I) CHI CONGA	19 PAULA	US	LPS 4001
		(J) LES STANCES A SOPHIE	19 NESSA	US	N4
		(K) THE PARIS SESSION (1969)	1975 FREEDOM	US	AL 1903
		(K) THE PARIS SESSION (DBL)	197 FREEDOM		41106 /7
		(L) CERTAIN BLACKS	19 INNERCITY	US	IC 1004
		(M) NICE GUYS	1979 ECM		ECM 1126
		(N) REESE & THE SMOOTH ONES	197 FREEDOM		AFF 22
		(O) LIVE PART ONE	197		
		(P) LIVE PART TWO	197 BYG	FR	2401
		(Q) FULL FORCE	1980 ECM		1167

ART OBJECTS

(A) BAGPIPE MUSIC	1981 HEARTBEAT	HB5

ART ZOYD

ROCCO FERNANDEZ	G V (ABC	(A) SYMPHONIE POUR LE JOUR...	1976 ART ZOYD		001
THIERRY ZABOITZEFF	B V (ABC	(B) MUSIQUE POUR L'ODYSSEE	1979 ATEM GER 7002	UK RE	RR3
JEAN PIERRE SOAREZ	TPT (ABC	(C) GENERATION SANS FUTUR	1980 ATEM	GER	7007
FRANK CARDON	VLN (B				
ALAIN ECKERT	G PERC(AC	GERERD HOURBETTE	VLN SAX(ABC	MICHEL THOMAS SAX (B	
MICHEL BERCKMANS	WIND (B	DANIEL DENIS	PERC (BC	PATRICIA DALLIO PNO (C	
GILLES RENARD	SAX (C				

ARTFUL DODGER

STEVE BRIGADA	B PERC(ABCD	(A) ARTFUL DODGER	1975 CBS	US	PC 33811
STEVE COOPER	B (ABCD	(B) HONOUR AMONG THIEVES	1976 CBS	US	PC 34273
GARY COX	G V (ABC	(C) BABES ON BROADWAY	1977 CBS	US	PC 34846
GARY HERREWIG	G V (ABCD	(D) RAVE ON	1980 ARIOLA US 1503	NL	202 804
BILL PALISELLI	V (ABCD				
PETE BONTA	K G (D				

ARTI & MESTIERI

FURIO CHIRICO	D PERC(A	(A) TILT	1974 CRAMPS	IT	CRSLP5501
BEPPE CROVELLA	K SYN (A	(B) GIRO DI VALZEPER	19 BARCLAY		940 518
MARCO GALLESI	B (A				
ARTURO VITALE	WIND (A	GIGI VENEGONI G SYN (A			

ARTISTICS

(A) I'M GONNA MISS YOU	19 BRUNSWICK	754123
(B) ARTICULATE	19 BRUNSWICK	754139
(C) WHAT HAPPENED	19 BRUNSWICK	754153
(D) GET MY HANDS ON SOME LOVIN'	19 OKEH	14119

ARTWOODS

ART WOOD	V (A	(A) ART GALLERY	1964 DECCA	LK 4830
JON LORD	K (A	(A) ARTWOODS	1973 SPARK	SRLM2006
KEEF HARTLEY	D (A	(B) ART GALLERY	1974 ECLIPSE	ECS 2025
DEREK GRIFFITHS	G (A	(C) JAZZ IN JEANS (EP)	1966 DECCA	DFE 8654
MALCOLM POOLE	B (A			

ARZACHEL

STEVE HILLAGE	G V (A	(A) ARZACHEL	1969 EGG EURO	ROULETTE US 42036
MONT CAMPBELL	B (A			
CLIVE BROOKS	D (A	DAVE STEWART K (A		

ASCEND

AMIN MOHAMMED	SITAR B (A	(A) CREATURES OF LIGHT & DARKNESS	1978	
CHRIS BISCOE	SAX (A			
NICK JONES	G (A	EDDY SAYER D (A	PETER LEMER K (A	
GRAHAME SMITH	VLN (A			

ASGARD

JAMES SMITH	V (A	(A) IN THE REALM OF
TED BARTLETT	V (A	
RODNEY HARRISON	G V (A	PETER ORGIL VLN (A
IAN SNOW	D (A	

(A) IN THE REALM OF   1972   THRESHOLD   THS 6

PETER ORGIL   VLN (A   DAVE COOK   B (A

DOUG ASHDOWN

DOUG ASHDOWN	G V (A	(A) A WINTER IN AMERICA 1977 DECCA TXSR 125
MARK PONCH	G (A	
TIM PARTRIDGE	B (A	PEE WEE CLARK STEEL (A JOE ALLAN B (A
STU BASEORE	STEEL (A	RUSSELL DUNLOP D (A TONY BUCHANAN WIND (A
LAURIE LONDON	D (A	DAVID BRIGGS PNO (A WAYNE FINDLAY K (A
KIM RYRIE	SYN (A	ROY RITCHIE K (A TROY SEALS G (A
DECLAN AFFLEY	WIND (A	JOHN JACKSON G (A IAN BLOXSOM PERC (A
NORMA STONEMAN	V (A	DAVID COOPER V (A

ASHFORD & SIMPSON

NICKOLAS ASHFORD	V PROD(ALL	(A) GIMME SOMETHING REAL	1974	WB UK K 46283 US BS 2739
VALERIE SIMPSON	V K PROD(ALL	(B) I WANNA BE SELFISH	1974	WB UK K 56050 US BS 2789
ELLIOTT RANDALL	G (C	(C) COME AS YOU ARE	1976	WB UK K 56159 US BS 2858
RICHARD TEE	K (CK	(D) SEND IT	1977	WB UK /K US BS 3088
FRANCISCO CENTENO	B (CFBDJK	(E) SO SO SATISFIED	1977	WB US BS 2992
RALPH McDONALD	PERC (ABCFJ	(F) IS IT STILL GOOD TO YOU	1978	WB UK K 56547 US BS 3219
RICK MAROTTA	D (C	(G) KEEP IT COMING	197	TAMLA US T 7351
STEVE JORDAN	D (F	(H) STAY FREE	1979	WB UK K 56703 US 3357
JOHN DAVID	HRNS (F	(J) A MUSICAL AFFAIR	1980	WB UK K 56840 US 3458
STEVE GADD	D (C	(K) SECRET OPERA	1982	EMI UK 12207
JOHN SUSSEWELL	D (F			
LEROY PENDARVIS	HRNS (ABJ	JOSHIE ARMSTEAD V (ABC	JEFF MIRANOV	G (C
RAY SIMPSON	V (CBDF	DON GROLNICK K (C	GEORGE YOUNG	HRNS (CJ
RAY CHEW	K (FDJK	PAUL RISER STRINGS(FABDJ	ULLANDA McCULLOUGH	V (FDJK
ERIC GALE	G (CFDJK	HUGH McCRACKEN G (C	JERRY FRIEDMANN	G (AB
ROBERT KREINER BABBIT	B (AB	PHILLIP WOO SYN (D	EDDIE DANIELS	FLT (J
ANDREW SMITH	D (AB	YOGI HORTON D (K	CORNELL DUPREE	G (B
DAVID TOFANI	SAX (K	STEVE KHAN G (D	JOHN TROPEA	G (A
CHARLES COLLINS	D (AB	FRANK OWENS K (B	KEITH LOVING ILLEDGE	G (B
DAVID CAREY	PERC (ABD	CHRIS PARKER D (DJK	ROBERT SOBINO	K (B
ROB MOUNSEY	SYN HRNS(JK	JOHN SUSSWELL D (D	CRUSHER BENNETT	PERC (K

ASHKAN

STEVE BAILEY	V (A	(A) IN FROM THE COLD 1970 NOVA UK SRNR 1 US SIRE 97017
RON BENDING	B V (A	
TERRY SIMS	PERC (A	BOB WESTON G V (A

STEVE ASHLEY

STEVE ASHLEY	HCA V G (AB	(A) STROLL ON 1974 GULL US 6-401 UK GULP1003
RICHARD BYERS	G (B	(B) SPEEDY RETURN 1975 GULL UK GULP1012
ROYSTON MITCHELL	K (B	
MADDY PRIOR	SPOONS(B	DENNIS LOPEZ PERC (B DAVE PEGG B (B
DAVE MATTACKS	D (B	LYLE HARPER B (B SIMON PHILLIPS D (B
BARRY DRANSFIELD	(A	ASHLEY HUTCHINGS B (A LEA NICHOLSON (B
SIMON NICOL	G (A	B J COLE STEEL (A CLAIRE DAWSON (A
RAINER SCHUELEIN	(A	DANNY THOMPSON B (A BRIAN DIPROVE (A
SUE DRAHEIM	(A	REDD McREADY (A CHRISTOPHER TAYLOR (A
ROYSTON WOOD	(A	THOM FRIEDLEIN (A CHRIS KARAN PERC (A
DARRYL RUNSWICK	B (A	RICHARD TAYLOR (A

ASHMAN REYNOLDS

ALIKI ASHMAN	V (A	(A) STOP OFF 1972 POLYDOR US 5507 UK 2383 114
HARRY REYNOLDS	B G V (A	
BOB WESTON	G (A	MICKEY KEEN G (A ROD EDWARDS K V G (A
KEITH BOYCE	D (A	TONY CLARKE PERC (A MADELINE BELL V (A
LIZA STRIKE	V (A	LADBROKE HORNS HRNS (A

ASH RA (TEMPLE)

MANUEL GOETTSCHING	G SYN (ALL	(A) ASH RA TEMPLE	1971	OHR OMM 556013
UDI ARNDT	G (H	(B) SCHWINGUNGEN	1972	OHR OMM 556020
LUTZ ULBRICH	G (I	(C) SEVEN UP	1973	KOMISCHE KM 58001
KLAUS SCHULZE	K (ADF	(D) JOIN IN	1973	OHR OMM 556032
HARMUT ENKE	B G (ABCD	(E) STARRING ROSI	1973	KOMISCHE KM 58007
WOLFGANG MULLER	B (B	(F) INVENTIONS FOR ELECTRIC GUITAR	19	KOMISCHE KM 58015
HARALD GROSSKOPF	D SYN (EI	(F) INVENTIONS FOR ELECTRIC GUITAR	19	BARCLAY 840066
MATHIAS WEHLER	SAX (B	(G) NEW AGE OF EARTH	1977	VIRGIN V 2080
ROSI MULLER	V PERC(ED	(G) NEW AGE OF EARTH	1977	ISADORA ISA 9003
ULI POP	PERC (B	(H) BLACKOUTS	1977	VIRGIN V 2091
DIETER DIERKS	B PERC(CE	(H) BLACKOUTS	1977	POLYDOR 2373 740
MIKKY DOWE	V FLT(C	(I) CORRELATIONS	1979	VIRGIN NL V 2117
STEVE SCHROYDER	K (C	(J) BELLE ALLIANCE	1980	VIRGIN NL 202 284
DIETMAR BURMEISTER	D (C			
HARALD GROSSKOPF	D (E			
TOMMIE ENGEL	D (C	ROLF ULRICH KAISER PROD (D		

MARK ASHTON

MARK ASHTON	G V (AB	(A)MARK ASHTON	1978 20TH CENTURY US 520
STEVE GOULD	G (B	(B) SOLO	1979 ARISTA ARL 5023
MICK FEAT	B (B		
PETER VAN HOOKE	D (B	PHIL WAINMAN D (B WINSTON DELANDRO G (B DEREK AUSTIN K (B
TONY BRAUNAGEL	D (B	TERRY WILSON B (B BOB WESTON G (B PETE WILLSHER STEEL(B
CHRIS FLETCHER	PERC (B	MIGUEL BARRADOS D (B	

ASIA

JOHN WETTON	B V K (A	(A) ASIA 1982 GEFFEN UK 85577 GHS 2008
STEVE HOWE	G V (A	
GEOFFREY DOWNES	K (A	CARL PALMER D (A

ASHTON & LORD

TONY ASHTON	K V (A	(A) FIRST OF THE BIG BANDS 1974 PURPLE UK 3507 US WB 2778
JON LORD	(A	(A) FIRST OF THE BIG BANDS 1974 PATHE FR 2C064 95592

ASHTON GARDNER & DYKE

```
TONY ASHTON        K V   (ABCD     (A) ASHTON GARDNER & DYKE              1969  POLYDOR          583  081
KIM GARDNER        B     (ABCD     (B) WHAT A BLOODY LONG DAY ITS BEEN    1972  CAPITOL     EAST 862
ROY DYKE           D     (ABCD     (C) THE WORST OF                       1971  CAPITOL     EST  563
JOHN MUMFORD       TPT   (B        (D) THE LAST REBEL    (SOUNDTRACK)     1971  CAPITOL
DAVE CASWELL       TPT   (B
LYLE JENKINS       WIND  (B.       MICK LIBER       G      (BC    JIM PRICE              TPT (C
STAN WEBB          G     (C        GEORGE OHARA SMITH G    (C     PAUL PILNIK            G   (C
ROSETTA HIGHTOWER  V     (C        CHRIS BARBER     TROM   (C     P P ARNOLD             V   (C
MADELINE POULET(BELL?) V (C        B J COLE         STEEL  (C     CEDRIC CLAYTON         G   (C
ROMULUS WOODWORTH  G     (C        MOXY             HCA    (C     PHIL & BOOGIE BAND         (C
```

RICHARD ASHWORTH & WHITE DUB

```
RICHARD ASHWORTH         (AB       (A) M 3 REVISITED     (EP)     19   OVERDRIVE     ORDER 1
                                   (B) SURREY SKYLINE    (EP)     19   OVERDRIVE     ORDER 2
```

ASLEEP AT THE WHEEL

```
RAY BENSON       G V   (ABCDEFGHI  (A) COMIN' RIGHT AT YA             1973 UA US LA 038  UK  UAS29454
LEROY PRESTON    G D V (ABCDEFGHI  (B) COMIN' RIGHT AT YA             1978 SUNSET        UK  SNS50415
CHRIS O'CONNELL  V G   (ABCDEFGHI  (B) ASLEEP AT THE WHEEL           1974 EPIC US           33097
FLOYD DOMINO     PNO   (ABCDEFGHI  (C) TEXAS GOLD                    1975 CAPITOL       UK  EST11441
TONY GARNIER     B     (DFG        (D) WHEELIN 'N' DEALIN            1976 CAPITOL           EST11546
DANNY LEVIN      MAN FDL(CDFG(      (E) TEXAS COUNTRY  (ONE SIDE)    1976 UA            US  UALA 574
ED VIZARD        SAX   (C          (F) THE WHEEL                     1977 CAPITOL           EST11620
SCOTT HENNIGE    D     (CD         (G) COLLISION COURSE              1978 CAPITOL           EST11726
LINK DAVIS       FDL SAX(DFG       (H) SERVED LIVE                   1979 CAPITOL       ST    11945
JOHNNY GIMBLE    FDL   (ABCD       (I) FATHERS & SONS (DBL)1WHEEL 1 WILLS197 EPIC       US    33782
LUCKY OCEANS     D STEEL(ABCDEFGHI (J) FRAMED                        1980 MCA           US    5131
BILLY JOOR       TPT   (C
BILLY BRIGGS     SAX   (C    DAVID POE       SAX   (C   TOMMY ALLSUP      B   (C   BOBBY WOMMACK   TPT(C
MIKE O'DOWD      WIND  (C    HURSHAL W WIGGINGTON V (C  BILL MABRY       FDL  (DFG DENNIS SOLEE   SAX(D
JOEL SONNIER     ACC   (D    LINDA HARGROVE  G     (D   BUCKY MEADOWS     G   (D   TINY MOORE      MAND(D
ELDON SHAMLIN    G     (D    JACO       WIND       (F   ED FREEMAN       PNO  (    GENE DOBKIN     B  (A
BUDDY SPICHER    FDL   (A    RICHARD CASONA  FDL   (A   ANDREW STEIN     FDL  (AG  LEON RAUSCH     V  (F
PAT RYAN         WIND  (FG   CHRIS YORK      D     (FG  DOLORES HALL     V    (G   BENNY DIGGS     V  (G
PHILLIP BALLOU   V     (G    BOB WILLS       FDL HRN (I ARNETT COBB      SAX  (D
```

VERA & GARY ASPEY

```
VERA ASPEY       V G   (AB        (A) FROM THE NORTH       1975  TOPIC    12TS 255
GARY ASPEY       V G   (AB        (B) A TASTE OF HOTPOT    1976  TOPIC    12TS 299
BERNARD WRIGLEY  V CONC(A
WILF DARLINGTON  V MAND(A
```

VERA ASPEY

```
VERA ASPEY       V G   (A        (A) THE BLACKBIRD        1977  TOPIC    12TS 356
DAVE GOTLIFFE    PNO   (A
JOHN LUCE        G     (A
```

ASSASSIN OF SILENCE

```
JIM CURNUTTE     V SYN G B(A      (A) BENEATH ALL THE MADNESS    1979  NEUROLOGICAL     5001
JANE CHAFIN      K V   (A
ELLIOT THORNE    D V   (A   ROBIN JAMESON    B   (A   WILLIE MAC   B    (A
MARK SEGAL       D     (A   PHIL CULP        B   (A   KEVIN LAMB   PNO FLT(A
```

ASSAGAI

```
LOUIS MOHOLO     D     (AB        (A) ASSAGAI       1971  VERTIGO          6360 030
DUDU PUKWANA     SAX   (AB        (B) ZIMBABWE      1972  PHILIPS          6308 079
MONGEZI FEZA     TPT   (AB        ( ) ASSAGAI       1975  CONTOUR         2879 394
BIZO MNGQIKANA   SAX   (AB        ( ) AFROROCK      1971  SOUNDS SUPERB UK SPR 90054
FRED COKER       G     (A
CHARLES ONONOGBO B     (A    TERRI QUAYE     CONGA (B  FRED FREDERICKS  SAX (B
MARTHA MDENGE    V     (B    TONY DUHIG            (B  JON FIELD            (B
GLYN HAVARD            (B    SMILEY DE JONNES PERC (B
```

ASSOCIATES

```
BILLY McKENZIE   V     (A        (A) AFFECTIONATE PUNCH    1980  FICTION UK FIX 1 2383 585
ALAN RANKINE     G B K (A
NIGEL GLOCKLER   D     (A   ROBERT SMITH    V    (A   JOHN MURPHY    D    (
MICHAEL DEMPSEY  B     (
```

ASSEMBLED MULTITUDE

```
                                 (A) ASSEMBLED MULTITUDE   197  ATLANTIC   US  8262
```

ASSOCIATION

```
RUSS GIGUERE      G V      (ABCDEFGH  (A) AND THEN...ALONG CAME ASSOCIATION 1966 VALIENT  US   VLS 25002
JIM YESTER    SAX V G K    (ABCDEFGHIJ(A) AND THEN...ALONG CAME ASSOCIATION 1966 LONDON   UK   HAT 8305
TED BLUECHEL      D V      (ABCDEFGHIJ(A) AND THEN...ALONG CAME ASSOCIATION 1966 W B      US       1702
BRIAN COLE    CLAR B V     (ABCDEFGHIJ(B) RENAISSANCE                       1967 VALIENT  US   VLS 25004
TERRY KIRKMAN   D V WIND   (ABCDEFGHIJ(B) RENAISSANCE                       1967 LONDON   UK   HAT 8313
GARY ALEXANDER    G V      (ABEGHIJ   (B) RENAISSANCE                       1967 W B      US   WS  1704
LARRY RAMOS SAX HCA G V    (CDEFGHIJ  (C) INSIGHT OUT                       1967 LONDON   UK   MHAT 8342
RICHARD THOMPSON  G V      (IJ        (C) INSIGHT OUT                       1967 WB       US   WS  1696
                                      (D) BIRTHDAY                          1968 WB       US   WS  1733
                                      (E) GREATEST HITS                     1969 WB       US   WS  1767
                                      (F) GOODBYE COLUMBUS  (SOUNDTRACK)    1969 WB       US   WS  1786
                                      (G) ASSOCIATION                       1969 WB       US   WS  1800
                                      (H) LIVE               (DBL)          1970 WB       US   2WS 1868
                                      (I) STOP YOUR MOTOR                   1971 WB       US   WS  1927
                                      (J) WATERBEDS IN TRINIDAD             1972 CBS      UK   S   65009
                                      (J) WATERBEDS IN TRINIDAD             1972 CBS      US   KC  31348
                                      (K) THE ASSOCIATION                   1981 WB       UK       K26012
```

ASTRONAUTS

```
BOB DEMMON       G TPT K(AB       (A) SURFIN' WITH THE ASTRONAUTS   1963  RCA   US  2760
RICH FIFIELD     G V    (A        (B) TRAVELIN' MAN                 1967  RCA   US  3733
DENNIS LINDSEY   G      (A
JIM GALLAGHER    D      (A   STORMY PATTERSON    B V   (A
```

```
A107
   BRINSLEY FORDE   PERC G V   (AB
   DON GRIFFITHS   PERC G V   (ABC
   BUNNY McKENZIE      HCA   (A
   COURTNEY HEMMINGS PERC V K(AC
   GEORGE OBAN        PERC B(ABC
   TREVOR BOW         PERC  (A
   TONY GADD          K V   (B
   VIN GORDON         TPT   (C
A108
```

ASWAD

(A) ASWAD	1976	ISLAND	UK	ILPS9399
(B) HULET	1980	ISLAND UK 9611 GROVE GMLP 6
(C) SHOWCASE	1981	GROVE		ASWAD 1

```
ANGUS GAYE        D K   (AB   CANDY McKENZIE V    (A
DELROY WASHINGTON  V     (A   ADETOKUMBA ILLORIN G  (A
KARL PITTERSON           (C   BONGO LEVI     V      (C
MIKE ROSE         TPT     (C
```

ATACAMA   A108

(A) ATACAMA	1971	CHARISMA	UK	CAS 1039
(B) SUN BURNS UP ABOVE	1972	CHARISMA	UK	CAS 1060

A108A   ATHLETICO SPIZZ 80   A108A

(A) DO A RUNNER	1980	A&M	UK	AMLE 68514

A109   PETE ATKIN   A109

```
PETE ATKIN   G V PNO   (ALL
STEVE COOK      B      (A
BRIAN ODGERS    B      (A
TONY MARSH      D      (A
HENRY MACKENZIE CLAR   (A
RUSSELL DAVIES  HRNS   (A
ALBERT HALL     HRNS   (A
FRANK RICOTTI   PERC   (D
CHRIS SPEDDING  G      (BC
HERBIE FLOWERS  B      (BC
KENNY CLARE     D      (B
DENNIS CLIFT    TPT
LEON CALVERT    HRNS   (B
DAI DAVIS       TROM   (B
ALAN PARKER     G      (B
TONY COE        WIND   (D
ALAN WAKEMAN    WIND   (BC
MIKE MORAN      K      (CD
RALPH IZEN      TPT    (C
DICK HART       TUBA   (C
RONNIE ROSS     SAX    (E
NEIL CAMPBELL   G      (F
GAYE BROWN      V      (F
```

(A) BEWARE OF THE BEAUTIFUL STRANGER	1970	FONTANA	UK	6309 011
(A) BEWARE OF THE BEAUTIFUL STRANGER	1974	RCA		SF 8387
(B) DRIVING THROUGH MYTHICAL AMERICA	1971	PHILIPS		6308 070
(B) DRIVING THROUGH MYTHICAL AMERICA	1974	RCA		SF 8386
(C) A KING AT NIGHTFALL	1973	RCA		SF 8336
(D) THE ROAD OF SILK	1974	RCA		LPLI 5014
(E) SECRET DRINKER	1974	RCA		LPLI 5062
(F) LIVE LIBEL	1975	RCA		RS 1013
( ) MASTER OF REVELS (BEST OF)	1977	RCA		PL 25041
(G) RIDERS TO THE WORLDS END (CASS)	19	RCA		PK 11677

(NOTE (A) RECORDS HAVE ONE DIFFERENT TRACK)

```
JIM WORTLEY    TROM   (B    RICHARD IHNATON WIEZ WIND (B
BARRY MORGAN   D      (BC   DAVE BELL       B      (B
CLIVE BAKER    TPT    (BC   DARRYL RUNSWICK  B     (DEF
DON FAY        SAX    (B    BARRY DE SOUZA   D     (E
RAY COOPER     PERC   (C    TERRY COX        D     (D
NAT PECK       TROM   (C    BILL GELDARD    TROM   (C
BOB SYDOR      WIND   (C    MIKE PAGE       WIND   (C
HOWARD BALL    STRINGS(C    CLIVE JAMES     LYRICS (
DICK LEVENS    B      (F    JEFF SEOPARDIE   D     (F
DIANE LANGTON  V      (F    ANNABEL LEVENTON V     (F
```

A110   CHET ATKINS   A110

CHET ATKINS AT HOME	RCA	1958	LPM	1544	FROM NASHVILLE WITH LOVE	RCA	1966		
SESSION WITH	RCA	1959	LPM	1090	GUITAR WORLD	RCA	1967	LSP	3728
STRINGING ALONG WITH	RCA	1959	LPM	1236	PICKS THE BEST	RCA	1967	LSP	3818
IN THREE DIMENSIONS	RCA	1959	LPM	1197	PICKS THE BEST	RCA	1967	ANLI	0981
FINGER STYLE GUITAR	RCA	1959	LPM	1383	MR ATKINS GUITAR PICKER	CAMDEN	196	CDS	1090
HI FI FOCUS	RCA	1959	LPM	1577	MR ATKINS GUITAR PICKER	CAMDEN	196	CASX2464E
IN HOLLYWOOD	RCA	195	LPM	1993	CLASS GUITAR	RCA	1967	LSP	3885
HUM & STRUM ALONG	RCA	1959	LPM	2025	CHET	CAMDEN	1967	CDS	1014
MISTER GUITAR	RCA	1960	LPM	2103	CHET	CAMDEN	196		2182
TEENSVILLE	RCA	1960	LPM	2161	SOLO FLIGHTS	RCA	1968	LSP	3922
TEENSVILLE	RCA UK	1960	RD	27168	SOLO FLIGHTS	RCA	1968	RD	7934
THE OTHER CHET ATKINS	RCA	1960	LPM	2175	COUNTRY PICKIN'	19			X9006
WORKSHOP	RCA	1961	RD	27214	REMINISCING (HANK SNOW)	RCA	1964	RD	7691
WORKSHOP	RCA	1961	LPM	2232	REMINISCING (HANK SNOW)	RCA	1964	LSP	2952
MOST POPULAR GUITAR	RCA	1961	LPM	2346	SOLID GOLD 68	RCA	1968	LSP	4061
& HIS GUITAR	CAMDEN	1961	CDN	160	HOMETOWN GUITAR	RCA	1968	LSP	4017
BACK HOME HYMNS	RCA	1962	CDN	165	LOVERS GUITAR	RCA	1969	LSP	4035
DOWN HOME	CAMDEN	1962	CDN	165	SOLID GOLD 69	RCA	1969	LSP	4244
DOWN HOME	RCA	1962	LSP	2450	C B ATKINS & C E SNOW	RCA	1969	LSP	4254
DOWN HOME	CAMDEN	1962	SND	5016	THIS IS CHET ATKINS	RCA	19	VPS	4254
CARRIBBEAN GUITAR	RCA	1962	LSP	2549	BY SPECIAL REQUEST	RCA	1970	LSP	5254
CHRISTMAS WITH CHET	RCA	1962	LSP	2423	SOLID GOLD 70	RCA	1970	LSP	4244
THE POPS GOES COUNTRY	RCA	196	LSC	2870	SOLID GOLD 70	RCA	1970	SF	8092
CHET PICKS ON THE POPS	RCA	196	LSC	3104	ME & JERRY	RCA	19	LSA	3033
RELAXIN' WITH CHET	RCA	1969	INTS	1004	ME & JERRY	RCA	1971	LSP	4396
RELAXING WITH CHET	RCA	1969	CAM	2292	GUITAR PICKER	CAMDEN	1971		2464
TRAVELLIN' GUITAR	RCA	19	INTS	1141	YESTERGROOVIN'	RCA	1970	LSP	4331
TRAVELLIN'	RCA	19	LSP	2678	YESTERGROOVIN'	RCA	1970	SF	8130
THE EARLY YEARS	CAMDEN	19	CAS	659	ME & CHET	RCA	19	LSA	3091
OUR MAN IN NASHVILLE	RCA	1963	LSP	2616	ME & CHET	RCA	1972	ANLI	2167
OUR MAN IN NASHVILLE	RCA	19	SE	7529	FOR THE GOOD TIMES	RCA	1971	LSP	4464
GUITAR COUNTRY	RCA	1964	LSP	2783	NOW & THEN	RCA	1972		6079
PROGRESSIVE PICKIN'	RCA	1964	LSP	2908	NASHVILLE GOLD	RCA	1972	CAS	2551
BEST OF	RCA	1964	LSP	2887	FINGER PICKIN' GOOD	RCA	19	CAS	2600
BEST OF	RCA	196	RD	7664	PICKS THE HITS	RCA	1973	LSA	3121
& HIS OTHER GUITAR	RCA	19			STRUM ALONG GUITAR METHOD	RCA	1973	PRP	36932
PICKS ON THE POPS	RCA	19	LSC	3104	PICKS THE HITS	RCA	19	LSP	4754
IN CONCERT	CAMDEN	19	CPL2	1014	PICKS ON JERRY REED	RCA	1974	APLI	0545
PICKIN' MY WAY	RCA	19	LSA	3051	SUPERPICKERS	RCA	1974	APLI	0329
PICKIN' MY WAY	RCA	1970	LSP	4585	ALONE	RCA	19	APLI	0159
MY FAVOURITE GUITARS	RCA	1965	LSP	3316	GOES TO THE MOVIES	RCA	19	APLI	0845
MY FAVOURITE GUITARS	RCA	1965	RD	7710	THE NIGHT ATLANTA BURNED	RCA	1975	APLI	1233
MORE OF THAT GUITAR COUNTRY	RCA	1965	LSP	3429	FAMOUS COUNTRY MUSIC MAKERS	RCA	1975	DPS	2063
TEENSCENE	RCA	19	ACLI	7005	LOVE LETTERS	CAMDEN	19	ACLI	7042
TEENSCENE	RCA	19	SF	7602	CHET & BOOTS	CAMDEN	19	CAS	2523
AMERICAN SALUTE	RCA	19	LSC	3277	THE BEST OF CHET & FRIENDS	RCA	1976	APLI	1985
GUITAR COUNTRY	RCA	1965			CHESTER & LESTER	RCA	1976	APLI	1167
PICKS ON THE BEATLES	RCA	1966	LSP	3531	CHESTER & LESTER	RCA	1977	LPS	3290
PICKS ON THE BEATLES	RCA	1966	SF	7813	ME & MY GUITAR	RCA	1977	PL	12405
BEST OF VOL 2	RCA	1965	LSP	3558	CHET FLOYD & DANNY	RCA	1977	APLI	2311
BEST OF VOL 2	CAMDEN	19	CAS	10261	GUITAR MONSTERS (LES PAUL)	RCA	1978	PL	1286
PICKS ON THE BEATLES(REISSUE)RCA		1977	ANLA	2002	GUITAR MONSTERS (LES PAUL)	RCA	1978	APLI	2786
BEST OF CHET ATKINS	RCA	1966			LEGENDARY PERFORMER	RCA	1978	PL	12503
MUSIC FROM NASHVILLE	CAMDEN	1966	CAM	981	FIRST NASHVILLE GUIT QUARTET	RCA	1979	AHLI	3302
THE GUITAR GENIUS	CAMDEN	1963	CDS	1067					
THE GUITAR GENIUS	CAMDEN	1963	CAS	753					
```
```

A111　　　　　　　　　　　　　ATLANTA RHYTHM SECTION　　　　　　　　　　　　　A111

PAUL GODDARD	B G	(ALL	(A) ATLANTA RHYTHM SECTION	1972	MCA	UK	MAPS	5594
BARRY BAILEY	G B	(ALL	(A) ATLANTA RHYTHM SECTION	1972	DECCA	US		5265
J R COBB	G B V	(ALL	(B) BACK UP AGAINST THE WALL	1974	MCA	UK MCF 2670		6465
RONNIE HAMMOND	V	(ALL	(B) BACK UP AGAINST THE WALL	1974	DECCA	US		5390
DEAN DAUGHTRY	K	(ALL	(C) THIRD ANNUAL PIPE DREAM	1975	POLYDOR	UK 2391 136 US		6027
ROBERT NIX	D V	(ABCDEFGHI	(D) DOG DAYS	1976	POLYDOR	UK 2391 179 US		6041
MYLON LEFEVRE	V	(C	(E) RED TAPE	1976	POLYDOR	UK 2391 223 US		6060
MIKE HUEY	CONGA	(C	(F) ROCK'N'ROLL ALTERNATIVE	1977	POLYDOR	UK 2391 255 US		6080
PAUL DAVIS	V	(G	(G) CHAMPAGNE JAM	1978	POLYDOR	UK 2391 319 US		6134
ROY YEAGER	D	(IJK	(H) ARE YOU READY (DBL)	1980	POLYDOR	UK 2672 050 US		6236
BUDDY BUIE	V	(K	(I) UNDERDOG	1979	POLYDOR	UK 2391 398 US		6200
STEVE McRAY	K V	(K	(J) BOYS FROM DORAVILLE(DIFF US/UK)1980	POLYDOR	UK 2391 467 US		6285
BILLY LEE RILEY	HCA	(B	(AB) ATLANTA RHYTHM SECTION(DBL)	19	MCA	US		4114
HUGH BABY JARRET	V	(C	(K) QUINELLA	1981	CBS	UK 85320		
JO JO BILLINGSLEY	V	(G						
ARTIMUS PYLE	PERC	(G						
MARK DENNY	SYN	(K	STEVE HAMMOND	V	(J RICK MAXWELL	STEEL(J	
STRAY STRATON		(J	RODNEY JUSTO	V	(A		

A112　　　　　　　　　　　　　ATLANTIC BRIDGE　　　　　　　　　　　　　A112

MIKE TRAVIS	D	(A	(A) ATLANTIC BRIDGE	1970	DAWN	DNLS 3014
MIKE McNAUGHT	K	(A	(B) I CANT LIE TO YOU (EP)	1971	DAWN	DNX 2507
JIM PHILLIPS	SAX	(A				
DARYL RUNSWICK	B	(A				

A112A　　　　　　　　　　　　　ATLANTICS　　　　　　　　　　　　　A112A

RAY BOY FERNANDES	D PERC(A	(A) BIG CITY ROCK	1979	ABC	US	AA	1134
FRED PINEAU	G	(A						
B WILKINSON	B V K(A	TOM HAUCK	G V	(A	BOBBY MARRON	V	(A

A113　　　　　　　　　　　　　ATLANTIS　　　　　　　　　　　　　A113

GASPAR LAWAL	PERC	(B	(A) ATLANTIS	1973	VERTIGO	UK 6360 609	US VEL1016
INGA RUMPF	V PERC(ALL	(B) ITS GETTING BETTER	1974	VERTIGO	UK 6360 614	US VEL1018
JEAN JACQUES KRAVETZ K	(ABCD	(C) ATLANTIS	1974	POLYDOR	UK 2391 176	US PD 6513
RINGO FUNK	D	(BCDFGH	(D) OH BABY	1974	VERTIGO	UK 6360 621	
CURT CRESS	D	(A	(D) OH BABY	1974	VENUS	US 1009	
KARL HEINZ SCHOTT	B	(ALL	(E) ALLEY CAT	19	VERTIGO	UK 6360 127	
DIETER BORNSCHLEGEL	G	(B	(F) LIVE	(DBL)	1974	VERTIGO	6623 900
RAINER MARZ	G V	(GH	(F) LIVE	(DBL)	19	VENUS	US 1010
REEBOP BAAH	PERC	(A	(G) TOP OF THE BILL	1976	VENUS	F1002
JEAN ROUSSEL	K	(a	(H) GET ON BOARD	1975	VENUS	1011
INGO BISCHOFF	K	(G				
LINDA FIELD	V	(C	JACKIE DIEZ	V	(A	FRANK DIEZ	(Agh
ADRIAN ASKEW	K G V	(CDEGH	ALEX CONTI	G V	(CDF	JASPER VAN'T' HOF	PNO (C
GERALD HARTWIG	B	(G					

A113A　　　　　　　　　　　　　ATLAS　　　　　　　　　　　　　A113A

DARREL WILKES	G V	(A	(A) AGAINST ALL THE ODDS	1978	ATLAS	WIL 001
PAUL GREENWOOD	K B	(A				
N H K PLEASANT	D PERC(A				

A114　　　　　　　　　　　　　ATOLL　　　　　　　　　　　　　A114

MICHEL TAILLET	K	(AB	(A) L'ARAIGNEE MAL	1975	EURODISC	FR 913	002
RICHARD AUBERT	VLN	(A	(B) TERTIO	1978	ARIOLA	ARL	5008
CHRISTIAN BEYA	G	(AB	(B) TERTIOS	1978	EURODISC	FR 913 132	
ANDRE BALZER	PERC	(AB					
ALAIN GOZZO	D	(AB	JEAN LUC THILLOT	B	(AB		

A115　　　　　　　　　　　　　ATOMIC ROOSTER　　　　　　　　　　　　　A115

VINCENT CRANE	K	(ALL	(A) ATOMIC ROOSTER	1970	B &C	UK	CAS	1010
CARL PALMER	D	(A	(B) DEATH WALKS BEHIND YOU	1970	B & C	UK	CAS	2026
NICK GRAHAM	B	(A	(B) DEATH WALKS BEHIND YOU	1971	ELEKTRA	US	EKS	74094
RICK PARNELL	D	(DEF	(C) IN HEARING OF	1971	PEGASUS	UK	PEG	1
STEVE BOLTON	G	(D	(C) IN HEARING OF	1971	ELEKTRA	US		74109
JOHN MANDELLA	G	(EF	(D) MADE IN ENGLAND	1972	DAWN	UK	DNLS	3038
PRESTON HEYMAN	D	(H	(D) MADE IN ENGLAND	1972	ELEKTRA	US		75039
CHRIS FARLOWE	V	(DEF	(E) ATOMIC ROOSTER IV	1973	ELEKTRA	US	EKS	75074
JOHN CANN	G	(BC	(F) NICE & GREASY	1973	DAWN UK DNLS3049	GER BRAIN 1033
PAUL HAMMOND	D	(BC	(G) ASSORTMENT	1974	B & C	UK	CS	9
DORIS TROY	V	(D	(H) HOME TO ROOST	1977	MOONCREST	UK	CDR	2
BILL SMITH	B	(D	(I) THIS IS ATOMIC ROOSTER	1977	BRAIN	GER 200		151
LIZA STRIKE	V	(D	(J) ATOMIC ROOSTER	1980	EMI	UK	EMC	3341
PETER FRENCH	V	(C						

A115A　　　　　　　　　　　　　ATTILA　　　　　　　　　　　　　A115A

| BILLY JOEL | K V | (A | (A) ATTILA | 1970 | EPIC | 30030 | 26282 |
| JON SMALL | D | (A | | | | | |

A116　　　　　　　　　　　　　ATTITUDES　　　　　　　　　　　　　A116

DANNY KOOTCH	G	(AB	(A) ATTITUDES	1975	DARK HORSE		AMLH22008
JIM KELTNER	D	(AB	(B) GOOD NEWS	1977	DARK HORSE	K	56385
PAUL STALLWORTH	B V	(AB	(B) GOOD NEWS	1977	DARK HORSE	US	3021
DAVID FOSTER	K	(AB					

WITH

VENETTE GLOUD	V	(A	CARMEN TWILLIE	V	(A	KATHRYN COLLIER	V	(A
COSMO DE AGUERO	CONGA	(A	CHUCK HIGGINS	V	(AB	PAT MURPHY	CONGA(AB
WADDY WACHTEL	G	(B	JESSE ED DAVIS	G	(A	VINCE CHARLES	PERC (Ab
MARVIN BRAXTON	HCA	(B	TOWER OF POWER	HRNS	(B	DONNY GERRARD	V	(B
JAY GRAYDON	G	(B	JAY LEWIS	G	(B	GEORGE BELL	FLT	(B
RINGO STARR	D	(B	EMIL RICHARDS	PERC	(B	JORGE CALDERON	V	(B
			BOOKER T JONES	K	(B	YVONNE RANKIN	V	(B

A116A　　　　　　　　　　　　　ATTRACTIONS　　　　　　　　　　　　　A116A

(A) MAD ABOUT THE WRONG BOY　　　　1980 F BEAT UK 8UK WEA NL 58158

A116B　　　　　　　　　　　　　AU PAIRS　　　　　　　　　　　　　A116B

LESLEY	G V	(A	(A) PLAYING WITH A DIFFERENCE SEX	1981	HUMAN	UK	HUMAN 1
PAUL	G V	(A					
JANE	B	(A	PETE	D	(A		

```
    PETER PINCKNEY      G V    (A      (A) AUBREY SMALL              1971   POLYDOR        UK   2383 048
    ROD TAYLOR          K V    (A
    ALAN CHRISTMAS      G      (A      DAVID YEARLEY      B      (A    GRAHAM HUNT      D G V(A
```

```
    TONY CONNOR         D      (ABCDE  (A) AUDIENCE                  1969   POLYDOR         583  065
    GUS DUDGEON    PROD PERC   (CD     (B) FRIENDS FRIENDS FRIENDS   1970   CHARISMA        CAS  1012
    TREVOR WILLIAMS     B K V  (ABCDE  (C) HOUSE ON THE HILL         1971   CHARISMA        CAS  1032
    KEITH GEMMELL       WIND   (ABCDE  (C) HOUSE ON THE HILL         1971   ELEKTRA      US EKS 74100
    JIM PRICE           HRNS   (D      (D) LUNCH                     1972   CHARISMA     UK CAS  1054
    BOBBY KEYS          SAX    (D      (D) LUNCH                     1972   ELEKTRA      US EKS 75026
    NICK JUDD           K      (D      (E) YOU CANT BEAT THEM        1973   CHARISMA     UK   CS 7
    HOWARD WERTH        G V    (ABCDE
    CHRIS BROUGH        PROD   (A
```

```
    MICK AUDSLEY                       (A) DARK & DEVIL WATERS       1973   SONET          SNTF 641
                                      (B) STORYBOARD                1974   SONET          SNTF 659
```

```
    BRIAN AUGER         K V    (ALL    (A) OPEN                    1967 ATCO   US 33256 MARMALADE  607 002
    ROY SWINFIELD       FLT    (B      (A) OPEN                    19   POLYDOR RI                 2438 304
    JIMMY PAGE          G      (M      (B) DEFINITELY WHAT         1968 ATCO   US 33273 MARMALADE  607 003
    I BEERS             WIND   (B      (B) DEFINITELY WHAT         19   POLYDOR RI GER             184 182
    JULIE DRISCOLL(TIPPETTS) V(ACORS   (C) STREETNOISE      (DBL)  1968 ATCO   US 2701  MARMALADE 608005/6
    RICK LAIRD          B      (        (C) STREETNOISE      (DBL)  1968 KARUSSELL RI      GER    2674 014
    PHIL KINORRA        D      (        (D) BEFOUR                 1970 RCA US 4372    UK          SF 8101
    GLEN HUGHES         SAX    (        (E) OBLIVION EXPRESS       1971 RCA US 4462    UK          SF 8170
    MICK WALLER         D      (MS      (F) A BETTER LAND          1971 RCA US 4540    UK POLYDOR 2383 062
    ROD STEWART         V      (        (G) SECOND WIND            1972 RCA US 4703    UK POLYDOR 2383 104
    DAVE AMBROSE        B      (ABCDR   (H) CLOSER TO IT           1973 RCA US 0140    UK CBS       65625
    CLIVE THACKER       D      (ABCDRS  (J) STRAIGHT AHEAD         1974 RCA US 0454       UK CBS    80058
    COLIN ALLEN         D      (D       (K) LIVE OBLIVION   VOL 1  1974 RCA US 2481 US            0645
    JACK MILLS          G      (HJKLNX  (L) LIVE OBLIVION   VOL 2 (DBL) 1974 RCAUS 1230
    JOHN McLAUGHLIN     G      (        (X) REINFORCEMENTS         1974 RCA US 1210
    DAVID DOYLE         D      (X       (M) DONT SEND ME NO FLOWERS 1969            MARMALADE 608 004
    STEVE FERRONE       D      (JKL     (M) JAM SESSION            1975 CHARLY     UK           30011
    ROGER SUTTON        B      (DS      (N) HAPPINESS HEARTACHES   1977 WB US BS2981 UK           56326
    JIM MULLEN          G      (EFG     (O) ENCORE                 1978 WB US BSK3153 UK         K56458
    GODFREY MACLEAN     D      (H       (P) BEST OF BRIAN AUGER & TRINITY 1970 POLYDOR         2334 004
    MIRZA AL SHARIF     PERC   (J       (Q) BRIAN AUGER & THE TRINITY 19 POLYDOR             2384 062
    DAVE CRIGGER        D      (O       (R) GENESIS(TRINITY)       1975 POLYDOR US 6505    UK  2383 277
    CLEM CATTINI        D      (S       (S) LONDON 1964 67         1977 CHARLY        UK       CR300019
    ALEX LIGERTWOOD     V      (GKLNX   (T) THIS IS                1975 METRONOME     GER       200149
    LENNOX LAINGTON     D      (HJNX    ( ) STAR PORTRAIT(DBL COMP) 19 POLYDOR                2625 008
    DAVID McDANIELS     B      (O       ( ) BRIAN AUGER            19   SPRINGBOARD   US     SPB 4044
    GEORGE DOERING      G      (O       ( ) THE BEST OF BRIAN AUGER 19 RCA   US 2249
    MAXINE WILLARD      V      (O       ( ) JULIE DRISCOLL & BRIAN AUGER 1968 MFP             1265
    LENNY WHITE         D      (N       ( ) ATTENTION             19 FONTANA               9294 901
    A McGAVIN           WIND   (B       ( ) POP HISTORY VOL 26    1972 POLYDOR                26680
    J BUCK              FLT    (B       ( ) IN & OUT              1969 KARUSSELL            2345 004
    RICK BROWN          B      (MS
    LONG JOHN BALDRY V  (
    CLIVE CHAMAN        B      (NX      SONNY BOY WILLIAMSON (RICE MILLER) HCA (M    JOE HARRIOT   SAX (M
    ALAN SKIDMORE       SAX    (M       VIC BRIGGS        G      (S    GARY BOYLE     G      (ADR
    BARRY REEVES        D      (D       BARRY DEAN        G      (EFGHJKL ROBBIE McINTOSH D   (EFG
    JESSICA SMITH       V      (O       STRING SECTION            (B    ALBERT HALL    TPT  (B
    GREG BOWEN          TPT    (B       DEREK WATKINS     TPT    (B    LENNIE CALVERT TPT(B
    DEREK HEALEY        TPT    (B       S REYNOLDS        TPT    (B    D CAMPBELL     TPT  (B
    CLIFF HARDIE        TROM   (B       ALF REECE         TROM   (B    J SIMCOCK      TROM (B
    P POUCHER           TROM   (B       B ALTRAM          TROM   (B    T RANDALL      WIND (B
```

```
    MIKE AULDRIDGE  DOBRO V G(ALL   (A) DOBRO           1972 SONET UK SNTF657 US TAKOMA 1033
    DAVID BROMBERG      G      (AB  (B) BLUES & BLUEGRASS 1977 SONET UK SNTF673 US TAKOMA 1041
    VASSAR CLEMENTS     FDL    (AB  (C) MIKE AULDRIDGE  1976 FLYING FISH US FLY 0003
    CHARLIE WALLER      G      (A   (D) OLD DOG         19   FLYING FISH US FF054+FLY 0004
    BUCK GRAVES         DOB    (A   (E) SLIDIN' SMOKE   1979 FLYING FISH US FF080
    BILL EMERSON        BANJO(A
    JOHN DUFFY          G MAND(AB DOYLE LAWSON MAND G   (AB TOM GREY      B   (AB BEN ELDRIDGE  BAN G(AB
    ED FERRIS           B      (A  STEVE BURGH        B   (A  BILL YATES    B   (A  JEFF NEWMAN       (E
    JOHN STARLING       G      (B  RICK SCAGGS        G   (B  BOB LAWRENCE  D   (B  GERRY MULE    G   (B
    LOWELL GEORGE       G      (B  TOM GUIDERA        G   (B  FAYSSOUX STARLING V (B  LINDA RONSTADT V (B
    PAUL CRAFT          G      (B
```

```
    LARRY MARTIN        D V    (AB     (A) BLUESVIBES        1969   SIRE LONDON   US       97007
    WAYNE CEBALLOS  HCA V G K(AB       (B) RESURRECTION      1969   FILLMORE/CBS  US       30002
    KEN NEWELL          B V    (AB
```

```
    AL LATHAN           V PERC(A       (A) AURA              1971   MERCURY      US   SRM1 620
    BILL WALDNER        G      (A       (B) AURA II?          1972   GUINNESS     US
    FRED ENTESARI       SAX    (A
    ANDY FOERTSCH       TROM   (A  DENNIS HORAN     D   (A  JERRY SMITH   B V  (A  GEORGE BARR   TPT V (A
    SAM ALESSI          K      (A  CHUCK GREENBERG  WIND(A  TERRY QUAYE   PERC (A
```

```
    BILL STAEBELL       B      (AB     (A) GLIDER            1978   CHRYSALIS US/UK   CHR 1172
    RON WAGNER          D      (AB     (B) CITY SLICKER      1979   CHRYSALIS US/UK   CHR 1210
    RICHARD C BRAUN     TPT    (AB
    STEPHEN KUJALA      WIND   (AB STEVEN REHBEIN   PERC (AB JOHN SERRY JNR K  (A  BIFF HANNON   PNO (B
    STACEY O'BRIEN      V      (B  GLORIA O'BRIEN   V   (B  DONNA DELORY  V   (B  LEE RITENOUR  G   (B
    JEFF TKAZYAK        HRNS   (B  STEVE JOHNSON    HRNS(B  ROBERT PAYNE  HRNS(B  STACY CLINGER V   (B
    TIM MAY             G      (B  AFREEA TREES     V   (B  GLORIA GOLDSMITH V (B
```

PATTI AUSTIN

PATTI AUSTIN	V (ALL	(A) END OF A RAINBOW	1976 CTI			CTI 5001
WITH		(B) HAVANA CANDY	1977 CTI			CTI 5006
DAVE GRUSIN	PNO (B	(C) LIVE AT THE BOTTOM LINE	1979 CTI			7086
ERIC GALE	G (ABE	(D) BODY LANGUAGE	1980 CTI	UK 2406 013	US	36503
STEVE KHAN	G (AB	(E) EVERY HOME SHOULD HAVE ONE	1980 QWEST		UK	K56931
HUGH McCRACKEN	G (B					
WILL LEE	B (BCD	STEVE JORDAN D (B	RALPH McDONALD	PERC(BE	ERNIE WATTS	SAX (E
CHRIS PARKER	D (E	MICHAEL BRECKER SAX(ABCD	RICHARD TEE	K (ABE	FRANCISCO CENTENO	B(B
ANTHONY JACKSON	B (BE	BOB JAMES K (E	EDDIE WATKINS	B (E	SYN	(E
DAVE VALENTIN	PERC (B	FRANK GRAVIS B (B	ALAN RUBIN	TPT (B	MARVIN STAMM	TPT(B
WAYNE ANDRE	TROM (B	GERRY NIEWOOD SAX (B	LOU MARINI	SAX (B	RONNIE CUBER	SAX(B
LANI GROVES	V (B	GWEN GUTHRIE V (B	YOLANDA McCULLOUGH	V (B	KEN WILLIAMS	V (B
JEFF BERLIN	B (A	STEVE GADD D (A	RANDY BRECKER	HRNS (AD	STRINGS	(B
GLORIA AGOSTINI	HARP (A	RANDY McCORMACK K (D	JEREMY WALL	K (D	DUNCAN CAMERON	G (D
DAVID HOOD	B (D	ROGER HAWKINS D (D	MICKEY BUCKINS	PERC (D	JOHN TROPEA	G (D
JERRY DODGION	SAX (D	JIM PUGH TROM (D	AVA ALDRIDGE	V (D	MARIE TOMLINSON CLARKE	V(D
CINDI RICHARDSON	V (D	JAMES INGRAM V (E	LOUIS JOHNSON	B (E	JOHN ROBINSON	D (E
GREG PHILLINGANES	K SYN(E	DAVID FOSTER SYN (E	MICHAEL BODDICKER	SYN (E	PAULINHO DA COSTA	PERC(E
STEVE LUKATHER	G (E	LEON PENDARVIS K (C	CRUSHER BENNETT	PERC (C	BABI FLOYD	V (C
DAVID SPINOZZA	G (C	PAT REBILLOT K (C	FRANK FLOYD	V (C	WILLIAM McCULLOUGH	V (C
CHARLES COLLINS	D (C					

SIL AUSTIN

SIL AUSTIN	SAX (	( ) HONEY SAX	19	POLYDOR 583 758	US SSS	SSST 4
		( ) SLOW ROCK ROCK	19	WING	US	MGW 12168
		( ) EVERYTHINGS SHAKIN'	19	MERCURY	US	MG 20320
		( ) GO SIL GO	19	MERCURY	US	3348
		( ) SILVER SCREEN	19	SSS	US	SSS 14
		( ) PLAYS PRETTY	19	MERCURY	US	60096
		( ) SOFT SOUL	19	SSS	US	SSS 8

TOM AUSTIN

TOM AUSTIN	K V (A	(A) EMPTY NIGHTS	1977	FIRST AMERICAN US		7707
CHRIS LEIGHTON	D (A					
DAVE RAYNOR	G V (A	TERRY LAUBER STEEL (A	DON McKINNEY	V (A		
JOE CHEMAY	B (A	DALE BOBBIT B (A	RICH OLSON	G (A		
MARDI SHERIDAN	G (A	ROGER PEASE CONGA (A	KELLEY HARLAND	V (A		
JIM BREDOUW	V (A					

AUTOMATIC FINE TUNING

PAT McDONNELL	G (A	(A) AUTOMATIC FINE TUNING	1976	CHARISMA	CAS 1122
ROBERT CROSS	G (A				
DAVID BALL	D (A	TREVOR DARKS B (A			

AUTOMATIC MAN

MICHAEL SHRIEVE	D (A	(A) AUTOMATIC MAN	1976 ISLAND UK ILPS9397
PAT THRALL	G V (AB	(B) VISITORS	1977 ISLAND UK ILPS9429 ANTILLES US 7062
BAYETE	K V (AB		
DON HARVEY	B (AB	JEROME RIMSON B (B	GLENN SYMMONDS D (B
TODD COCHRAN	K V (AB		

AUTOSALVAGE

THOMAS DANAHER	V G (A	(A) AUTOSALVAGE	1968 RCA US LSP3940
DARIUS DAVENPORT	V G K B (A		
RICK TURNER	DULC BANJO G(A	SKIP BOONE B PNO (A	

AUTUMN PEOPLE

LARRY CLARK	G V (A	(A) AUTUMN PEOPLE	1976	SOUNDTECH	US 3020
DANNY POFF	K V (A				
CLIFF SPIEGEL	B V (A	STEVE BARRAZA D V (A			

AVALANCHE

ADRIAN CAMPBELL	V (A	(A) AVALANCHE	1976	BOOTLEG	AUSTRALIA 059
TONY NAYLOR	G V (A	(A) AVALANCHE	1977	ABC	US 1000
CLIVE HARRISON	B V (A				
GEOFF COX	D (A				

JOHNNY AVERAGE BAND

JOHNNY AVERAGE	(A	(A) SOME PEOPLE	1981 WB US 3514

AVERAGE WHITE BAND

ALAN GORRIE	V G B (ALL	(A) SHOW YOUR HAND	1973 MCA UK MUPS 486 74 MCF2514
ROBBIE McINTOSH	D (ABCD	(A) SHOW YOUR HAND	1973 MCA US 345
ROGER BALL	K SAX(ALL	(B) AVERAGE WHITE BAND	1974 ATLANTIC UK K50058 US 7308
ONNIE McINTYRE	V G (ALL	(B) AVERAGE WHITE BAND	197 ATLANTIC US RI 19116
HAMISH STUART	G B V (ALL	(B) AVERAGE WHITE BAND	1980 RCA INT UK 5049
MALCOLM DUNCAN	SAX (ALL	(C) CUT THE CAKE	1975 ATLANTIC UK K50146 US18140
STEVE FERRONE	D (CEFGHJKLMN	(D) PUT IT WHERE YOU WANT IT	1975 MCA UK MCF 270 US 475
CORNELL DUPREE	G (H	(E) SOUL SEARCHIN'	1976 ATLANTIC UK K50272 US 18179
RANDY BRECKER	HRNS (BEHJN	(E) SOUL SEARCHIN'	1980 RCA INT UK 5058
MICHAEL BRECKER	HRNS (BEHJ	(F) PERSON TO PERSON	1976 ATLANTIC UK K60127 US 1002
MARVIN STAMM	TPT (BE	(G) BENNY & US	1977 ATLANTIC UK K50384 US 19105
AIRTO MOREIRA	PERC (J	(H) WARMER COMMUNICATIONS	1978 RCA UK XL 13053
LEW DELGATTO	SAX (HJ	(H) WARMER COMMUNICATIONS	1978 ATLANTIC US SD 19162
MEL DAVIS	TPT (B	(J) FEEL NO FRET	1979 RCA UK 3063 RI 81 INT5140
BEN E KING	V (G	(K) VOL7	1980 ATLANTIC RI US 19266
KEN BISCEL	K (B	(L) THE BEST OF	1979 RCA UK 3101 RI INTS 5139
ROBIM CLARK	V (H	(M) SHINE	1980 ARISTA US 9523
ZECA DA CUICA	(J	(M) SHINE	1980 RCA UK 3123
DAVID FOSTER	PROD K(KM	(N) CUPIDS IN FASHION	1982 RCA RCALP6052
DEBRA GRAY	V (G	(NB) (D) IS A SLIGHTLY DIFFERENT REISSUE OF (A)	
RALPH McDONALD	PERC (B		
LUIS DOS SANTOS	(J	RAY BARRETTO CONGA(CH	GLENN FERRIS TROM (B	LUTHER VANDROSS V (J
TOM MALONE	TROM (H	RONNIE CUBER SAX (E	BARRY ROGERS TROM (EH	JIM MULLEN G (E
CARLOS MARTIN	PERC (E	DAVE BRIGATI V (E	EDDIE BRIGATI V (E	RUBENS BASSINI PERC(H
NICHOLAS MARRERO	PERC (G	PAIL LANI PERC (M	BRENDA RUSSELL V (M	LENNY CASTRO PERC(M
PAULINHO DACOSTA	PERC (M	GARY GRANT TPT (KM	LEW McCREARY TROM (M	ERNIE WATTS SAX (KM
DAN HARTMAN	K V PROD(N	RICHIE STOOTS G (N	JERRY HEY HRNS (KM	LARRY HALL TPT (M
BILL REICHENBACH	TROM(KM	KIM HUTCHCROFT SAX (M	ARIF MARDIN PROD (K	JEFF BOVA SYN (N
SAMMY FIGUERA	PERC (N	JOE MELOTTI V (N		

[24]

```
A131A                          AVIARY                                        A131A
  BRAD LOVE        K V  (A           (A) AVIARY          1979 EPIC US 35716  UK    EPC 83572
  PAUL MADDEN      K    (A
  KEN STEINMONTS   B V  (A  TOBY BOWEN  G  (A   RICHARD BRYANS D V    (A
A131B                          AVIATOR                                       A131B
  MICK ROGERS      G V  (AB          (A) AVIATOR        1979 HARVEST UK SHSP4096 US EMI17012
  CLIVE BUNKER     D    (AB          (B) TURBULENCE     1980 HARVEST UK SHSP4107
  JOHN G PERRY     B V  (AB
  JACK LANCASTER   WIND (A
A131C                          AXE                                          A131C
  MICHAEL TURPIN   B V  (AB          (A) AXE            1979 MCA US 3171
  TEDDY MUELLER    D    (AB          (B) LIVING ON THE EDGE  1980 MCA US 3224  UK  3033
  BOBBY BARTH      G V  (AB
  EDGAR RILEY JR.  K V  (AB MICHAEL OSBORNE  G V (AB
A131D                      DAVID AXELROD                                    A131D
  DAVID AXELROD    V    (ALL         (A) SONGS OF INNOCENCE  1968 CAPITOL UK ST2982  US 11362
  WITH                               (B) ROCK MESSIAH       1972 RCA              US  4636
  NDUGU LEON CHANCLER D (D           (C) THE AUCTION        1974 MCA UK MCF2664 US DECCA 75355
  MAILTO CORREA    PERC (D           (D) SERIOUSLY DEEP     1975 POLYDOR UK 2391 193 US  6050
  JIM HUGHART      B    (DF          (E) HEAVY AXE         1975 FANTASY    US        9456
  GARY COLEMAN     VIBES (AD         (F) STRANGE LADIES    1978 MCA          US     2283
  BILLY FENDER     G    (DF          (G) MARCHIN'         1980 MCA          US     3199
  JOHN MORELL      G    (D
  STRINGS          (A  EUGENE SNOOKYYOUNG TPT (D   JIMMY CLEVELAND   TROM (DF  DICK HYDE   TROM (D
  JEROME RICHARDSON SAX  (D  ERNIE WATTS     WIND (DF JAY MIGLIORI    WIND (D   GENE CIPRIANO WIND(D
  JOE SAMPLE       K   (D  BENJAMIN BARRETT    (A  ARNOLD BELNICK        (A   AL CASEY     G   (C
  VINCENT DE ROSA  HRNS (A  ALVIN DINKIN       (C  ALLEN DI RIENZO       (A   GENE ESTES  PERC (A
  FREDDIE HILL     TPT (A  BILL HINSHAW        (A  HARRY HYAMS           (A   TONY TERRAN      (A
  PETE WYANT       (A  CAROLE KAYE      B     (A  RICHARD LEITH    TROM (A   ARTHUR MANEBE  HRNS (A
  LEW McCREARY     HRNS (A  OLLIE MITCHELL  TPT (A  EARL PALMER      D   (A   HOWARD ROBERTS  G  (A
  NATHAN ROSS      (A  MYRON SANDLER       (A  HAROLD SCHNEIER       (A   HENRY SIGISMONTI WIND(A
  MARSHALL SOSSON  (A  DON RANDI        K   (E  BOBBY BRYANT     TPT (E
A131E                         AXISPOINT                                     A131E
  EDDIE HARDIN     K V  (AB          (A) AXIS POINT       1979 RCA              PL 30039
  CHARLIE WITNEY   G    (AB          (B) BOAST OF THE TOWN 1980 RCA             PL 25277
  CHARLIE McCRACKEN B V (AB
  ROB TOWNSEND     (AB JOHN GUSTAFSON   B   (A  LOUIE AUSTIN    V   (A  LES BINKS   D   (A
  COLIN JENNINGS   PERC (A
A131F                        AXIS(ITALY)                                    A131F
  DEMIS VISVIKIS   K V  (ALL         (A) ELA ELA /OSANNA   1971 RIVIERA    IT       521 192
  GEORGE CHATZIATHANASSIOU D V(AB    (B) AXIS             1971 RIVIERA    IT        95010
  ALECOS CARACANDAS G V  (AB         (C) AXIS             1973 RIVIERA    IT        95014
  ALEXANDROS FANTIS B    (C
  CHRIS STASSINOPOULOS    D   (C   GEORGE HADJIATHNASSIOU    D (C
A131G                         AXIS(US)                                      A131G
  VINNY APPICE     D V  (A           (A) ITS A CIRCUS WORLD 1978 RCA US  AFLI 2950
  DANNY JOHNSON    G    (A
  KEN AARONSON     B    (A  JAY DAVIS       B V (A
A132                        HOYT AXTON                                       A132
  HOYT AXTON       G V  (ALL         (A) GREENBACK DOLLAR    1964 STATESIDE UK SL10082 US HORIZON  1601
  MIKE BOTTS       D    (LN          (B) THUNDER & LIGHTNIN' 1964 STATESIDE UK SL10096 US HORIZON  1613
  DAVID JACKSON    PNO B(JLN         (C) EXPLODES           196  JOY          JOYS119 US VEEJAY   1098
  FRANCISCO ARELLANO TPT (N          (D) SINGS BETTY SMITH  196  EXODUS              US           301
  SAMMY CREASON    D    (JN          (E) JOY TO THE WORLD   196  CAPITOL             US      EST 788
  MIKE UTLEY       K    (JN          (F) SATURDAYS CHILD    196  VEEJAY              US          1127
  JAMES BURTON     G    (JLNQ        (G) COUNTRY ANTHEM     19   CAPITOL             US       SMAS850
  RED RHODES       STEEL(JN          (H) LESS THAN A SONG   1973 A&M   UK AMLH 64376 US A&M      4376
  RALPH MOONEY     STEEL(JN          (J) LIFE MACHINE       1974 A&M   UK AMLH 63604 US A&M      3604
  JEFF BAXTER      G    (LNOQ        (K) MY GRIFFIN IS GONE 1974 CBS                 US        33103
  HANK DEVITO      STEEL(N           (L) SOUTHBOUND         1975 A&M   UK AMLH 64510 US A&M      4510
  BOB WILSON       K    (N           (M) FEARLESS           1976 A&M   UK AMLH 64571 US A&M      4571
  WILLIAM GRIFFIN  V(N               (N) ROADSONGS          1977 A&M   UK AMLH 64669 US A&M      4669
  RONEE BLAKLEY    V    (JN          (O) SNOW BLIND FRIEND  1977 MCA   UK MCF 2803   US MCA      2263
  BOB LIND         G    (J           (P) FREE SAILIN'       1978 MCA   UK MCF 2831   US MCA      2319
  ROGER JOHNSON    AUTOHARP(LN       (Q) RUSTY OLD HALO     1979 YOUNGBLOOD UK  800  US JEREMIAH 5000
  MAX BENNETT      B    (LN          (Q) RUSTY OLD HALO     1980 MFP       UK     50520
  JIM KELTNER      D    (JN          (R) WHERE DID THE MONEY GO 1980              US JEREMIAH 5001
  LOREN NEWKIRK    PNO  (JN          (R) EVERYBODY'S GOIN ON ROAD 1980 YOUNGBLOOD UK 4BP120
  MARK VOLMAN      V    (JN          (S) LIVE (DBL)         1981               US JEREMIAH 5002
  HOWARD KAYLAN    V    (JN
  LARRY CARLTON    G    (N  BEN BENAY       G   (N  MIKE OMARTIAN   K  (N  JOE SAMPLE    K  (N
  GARY COLEMAN     PERC (N  MARC EDELSTEIN  V   (N  CLAUDIA LENNEAR V  (N  DONNA WEISS   V  (N
  ROBERT ROGERS    V    (N  RONALD WHITE    V   (N  KATHY SMITH     V  (N  LARRY MUHOBERAC PNO (N
  NICOLETTE LARSON V    (N  LINDA RONSTADT  V  (JN  JERRY SCHEFF    B  (LN DICK HYDE    TROM(N
  GAIL DAVIES      TAMB (JN LEE SKLAR       B  (JN  TEDA BRACCI     V  (N  RON CORNELIUS G  (N
  MAC GAYDEN       G    (N  KARL HIMMEL     D   (J  TIM DRUMMOND    B  (N  TOM SCOTT     WIND(N
  TERRY REID       G    (J  DR ERIC HORD    V   (J  DOUG DILLARD    BANJ (JL MILT HOLLAND PERC(J
  LEE MONTGOMERY   G    (JL CLYDIE KING     V   (J  MERRY CLAYTON   V  (J  SHIRLEY MATTHEWS V (J
  SKITCHY WASHBURN V    (J  DENNY BROOKS    V   (J  MIMI FARINA     V  (J  KATHY WARD    V  (O
  DONNA ROBERTS    K    (O  JACK SKINNER    B   (O  ALAN THORNHILL  V  (O  PETE GRANT AUTOHARP (O
  GARY WATTMAN     D    (O  PIERRE LA PORTE HCA (O  JIM MESSINA     G  (O  BYRON BERLINE  FDL MAN(O
  JOE LAMANO       B    (L  GEORGE CLINTON  PNO (L  MARTY HOWARD    G  (LN DICK ROSMINI  G  (LN
  VICTOR FELDMAN   PERC (L  PAUL LEWINSON   K   (L  JOHNNY ROTELLA  WIND (L JOHN GUERIN   D  (L
  JOHN HARTFORD    FDL  (L  FRANK REKARD    G   (L  JUDY ELLIOTT    V  (L  ERNIE CARLSON TROM(N
  EMORY GORDY      B    (JNQ GUSTAVO RAMOS  TPT (N  RENEE ARMAND    V  (JLN JEFF PORCARO  D  (N
  ED KOLLIS        HCA  (N  DANA BRADY      V  (JN  WARREN MOORE    V  (N  MARK DAWSON   G V (JLNO
  GARTH HUDSON     K    (Q  STEPHEN STILLS  G V (Q  JOHN McUEN         (Q  PAUL BUTTERFIELD HCA (Q
  Dr JOHN          K    (Q  MARLENE PRINS   V   (Q  DAVID WOODFORD     (Q  DICK STEWART  (Q
  GLEN HARDIN      K    (Q  BOB FRAZIER     (Q  BAMBI ROBERTS   V  (Q  DONNA WASHBURN V  (N
```

KEVIN AYERS

KEVIN AYERS PROD V G (ALL				(A) JOY OF A TOY	1970	HARVEST	UK		SHVL 763
WITH				(B) SHOOTING AT THE MOON	1971	HARVEST	UK		SHSP 4005
TONY CARR	D	(CH		(AB)JOY OF A TOY/SHOOTING AT THE MOON	1975	HARVEST	DBL UK		SHDW 407
JOHN VAN DERRICK	VLN	(C		(AB)JOY OF A TOY/SHOOTING AT THE MOON	19	PATHE	DBL FR	C18452277/8	
ROBERT WYATT	D V	(ABCDF		(C) WHATEVERSHEBRINGSWESING	1972	HARVEST	UK		SHVL 800
ROB TAIT	D	(C		(D) BANANAMOUR	1973	HARVEST	UK		SHVL 807
DIDIER MALHERBE	WIND	(C		(CD)WHATEVERSHEBRINGSWESING/BANANAMOUR		PATHE	DBL FR	C15052507/8	
MIKE RATLEDGE	K	(ABDE		(E) CONFESSIONS OF DR DREAM	1974	ISLAND	UK		ILPS 9263
HUGH HOPPER	B	(A		(F) JUNE 1st 1974	1974	ISLAND	UK		ILPS 9291
DAVID BEDFORD	K	(ABCDH		(G) SWEET DECEIVER	1975	ISLAND	UK		ILPS 9322
LOL COXHILL	SAX	(BEH		(H) ODD DITTIES	1976	HARVEST	UK		SHSM 2005
MIKE OLDFIELD	G B V	(BCEHF		(J) YES WE HAVE NO MANANAS	1976	HARVEST	UK		SHSP 4057
WILLIAM MURRAY	D	(C		(J) YES WE HAVE NO MANANAS	1976	ABC	US		ABC 1021
RICHARD SINCLAIR	B	(BH		(K) RAINBOW TAKEAWAY	1978	HARVEST	UK		SHSP 4085
DAVE DUFORT	D	(CH		(L) THATS WHAT YOU GET BABE	1980	HARVEST	UK		SHSP 4016
GERRY FIELD	VLN	(C		(L) THATS WHAT YOU GET BABE	1980	HARVEST	NL		062 63637
HOWIE CASEY	G	(D							

ROY SMITH-FIELD	PICC	(H	ARCHIE LEGGET	B	(DFH	DAVE CASWELL	TPT	(D	MICK FINCHER	D	(HB
KEITH BATCHELOR	FLT	(H	LYLE JENKINS	SAX	(D	RICHARD COUGHLAN	D	(H	ROB TOWNSEND	D	(JK
TRISTAM FRY	PERC	(D	DAVE SINCLAIR	K	(H	BILLY LIVSEY	K	(JK	OLLIE HALSALL	B G(EFGJK	
B J COLE	STEEL(J		RICK WILLS	B	(J	MARK WARNER	G	(E	TONY NEWMAN	D	(J
EDDIE SPARROW	PERC	(DHF	SAMMY MITCHELL	G	(E	ROGER POPE	D	(J	RON PRICE	PNO(DH	
RUPERT HINE	K	(E	RAY COOPER	PERC	(E	LIZA STRIKE	V	(DH	JOHN PERRY	B	(E
SEAN MILLIGAN	V	(E	BARRY ST JOHN	V	(DH	MIKE GILES	D	(E	LADYBIRDS	V	(H
DORIS TROY	V	(DEH	ROSETTA HIGHTOWER V		(E	JOHN ALTMAN	CLAR	(G	GEORGE ZOOT MONEY K	(J	
CHARLIE McCRACKEN	B G	(JK	DUNCAN BROWN	TPT	(H	JACOB MAGNUSSON	V K	(G	CAL BATCHELOR	G	(E
CHARLIE ROSE	HRNS	(G	BRIDGET ST JOHN	V	(BH	RONNIE EADES	HRNS	(G	HENRY CRALLAN	PNO	(E
HARRISON CALLOWAY	HRNS	(G	JOANNE WILLIAMS	V	(E	STEVE NYE	ORG	(E	STEVE HILLAGE	G	(D
HARRY SMITH		(H	MIKE MORAN	PNO	(E	FRED SMITH	D	(G	ELTON JOHN	PNO	(G
NICO	V	(EF	BIAS BOSHELL	PNO	(E	CHILI CHARLES	D	(G	MICK FEAT	B	(J
ANDY ROBERTS	G	(J	NICK ROWLEY	K	(J	FUZZY SAMUELS	B	(G	TREVOR JONES	B	(E
JOHN GUSTAFSON	B	(E	HARVEY THOMPSON	HRNS	(G	GRAHAM PRESKETT	VLN	(K	BARRY DE SOUZA	D	(K
ROGER SAUNDERS	G	(J	ANTHONY MOORE		(K	DAEVID ALLEN		(B	HULLOO CHOIR	V	(E
BRIAN ENO	V SYN	(F	JOHN CALE VIOLA		(F	RABBIT BUNDRICK	K	(F	PETER JENNER	PROD (ABH	
ANDREW KING	PROD	(CDH	MALCOLM JONES	PROD	(H						

ROY AYERS

ROY AYERS		( ) VIRGO VIBES	19	ATLANTIC	US	SD	1488
WAYNE HENDERSON	(*	( ) DADDY BUG & FRIEND	19	ATCO	US	SD	1692
		( ) UBIQUITY	1975	POLYDOR	US	PD	6046
		( ) TEARS TO A SMILE	19	POLYDOR	US		
		( ) MYSTIC VOYAGE	1975	POLYDOR	US	PD	6057
		( ) RED BLACK & GREEN	197	POLYDOR	US	PD 1-6078	
		( ) VIBRATIONS	1976	POLYDOR	UK	2391 256	
		( ) EVERYBODY LOVES THE SUNSHINE	1976	POLYDOR	US	PD 16070	
		( ) LIFELINE	1977	POLYDOR	US	2391 292	
		( ) YOU SEND ME	1978	POLYDOR	UK	2391 365	
		( ) LETS DO IT	1978	POLYDOR	UK	2490 145	
		(*) STEP INTO OUR LIFE	1978	POLYDOR	US	PD 16179	
		(*) STEP INTO OUR LIFE	1978	POLYDOR	UK	2391 380	
		(*) STEP INTO OUR LIFE	1978	POLYDOR	UK	POLS 1004	
		( ) FEVER	1979	POLYDOR	UK	2391 396	
		( ) THE BEST OF (LOVE FANTASY)	1979	POLYDOR	UK	2391 429	
		( ) AFRICA CENTRE OF THE WORLD	1981	POLYDOR	UK	2391 157	

AYERS ROCK

CHRIS BROWN	G V	(AB	(A) BIG RED ROCK	1975	A&M US 4523	UK	AMLH64523	
COL COUGHAN	WIND V(AB		(B) BEYOND	1976	A&M US 4565			
JAMES DOYLE	G	(AB						
DUNCAN McGUIRE	B	(AB	MARK KENNEDY	D	(AB			

AZTEC TWO STEP

NEAL SHULMAN	V G	(ALL	(A) AZTEC TWO STEP	1972 ELEKTRA	UK K42118	US EKS 75031				
DAVID VAUGHT	B	(A	(B) SECOND STEP	1975 RCA		UK RS1034	US AFLI 1161			
SPANKY McFARLANE	V	(A	(C) TWOS COMPANY	197 RCA			US AFLI 1497			
PETER KLIEMES	BANJO(A		(D) ADJOINING SUITES	197 RCA			US AFLI 2453			
BOBBY TORRES	CONGA(A									
REX FOWLER	G V	(ALL	JOHN SEITER	D	(A	JERRY YESTER BANJO V PNO(A		RANDY BENSON	V	(A
DOUG DILLARD	BANJO(A		JOHN SEBASTIAN	HCA	(A	DENNIS WITCHER	V	(A	JOHN TROPEA	G	(B
KEN ASCHER	K	(B	DON PAYNE	B	(B	ALLEN SCHWARZBERG	D	(B	EMILE LATIMER	PERC	(B
DON ELLIOTT	VIBES(B		FRANK SIMS	V	(B	GEORGE SIMS	V	(B	DAVID KONDZIELA	V	(B

AZTECA

BOB FERREIRA	WIND	(B	(A) AZTECA	197	CBS			65011		
PAT O'HARA	TROM	(B	(B) PYRAMID OF THE SUN	1973	CBS	US	KC 32451		
TOM HARREL	HRNS	(B							
MEL MARTIN	WIND	(B	WENDY HAAS	V	(B	ERROL KNOWLES	V	(B	PETE ESCOVEDO	PER V(B
PAUL JACKSON	B	(B	BILL COURTIAL	G	(B	GEORGE MURIBUS	K	(B	FLIP NUNEZ	ORG	(B
GEORGE DI QUATRO	K	(B	COKE ESCOVEDO	PERC	(B	VICTOR PANTOJA	CONGA(B		JOHN BRINCK	D	(B
LENNY WHITE	D	(B	RICO REYES	V	(B	TOM RUTLEY	B	(B	TONY JUNCALE	B	(B
MIKE NOCK	K	(B	NEAL SCHON	G	(B						

AZTECS

BILLY THORPE	G V	(B	(A) LIVE AT SUNBURY (DBL)	19	HAVOC	NZ	HST4003/4	
PAUL WHEELER	B	(B	(B) THE HOAX IS OVER	1970	INFINITY	AUS	934 092	
KEVIN MURPHY	PERC	(B						
WARREN MORGAN	K	(B	LOBBY LOYDE	G	(A			

B BUMBLE & THE STINGERS

WILLIAM 'B' BUMBLE	G	(A	(A) PIANO STYLINGS OF B BUMBLE (EP)	19	STATESIDE	UK SE	1001	
RON BRADY	D	(A						
FRED RICHARD	PNO	(A						

B2   B B BLUNDER   B2

```
BRIAN GODDING V PNO G K  (A     (A) WORKERS PLAYTIME            1971    U A           UK   UAG 29156
KEVIN WESTLAKE      D G  (A
BRIAN BELSHAW       B V  (A     JULIE DRISCOLL       V    (A    BARRY JENKINS     D    (A
BRIAN AUGER         K    (A     MARK CHARIG          TPT  (A    MICK TAYLOR       G    (A
CHRIS KIMSEY        PNO  (A     NICK EVANS           TROM (A    GRAHAM SMITH      PERC (A
```

B2A   B52s   B2A

```
KEITH STRICKLAND    D    (ABC    (A) B52'S           1979   ISLAND UK ILPS9580 US WB 3255
CINDY WILSON        V G  (ABC    (B) WILD PLANET     1980   ISLAND UK ILPS59622 US WB 3471
RICKY WILSON        G    (ABC    (C) PARTY MIX       1981   ISLAND UK IPM 1001
FRED SCHNEIDER      K V  (ABC
KATE PIERSON        V G K (ABC   CHRIS BLACKWELL    PROD(AB
```

B2B   B MOVIES   B2B

```
                                 (A) TAKE THREE      (EP)    1980   DEAD GOOD     UK   DEAD9
B3                                     B T EXPRESS                                          B3
JAMAL RASOOL        B V  (E      (A) DO IT TILL YOURE SATISFIED  1975  PYE      UK   NSPL28207
LESLIE MING         D    (E      (A) DO IT TILL YOURE SATISFIED  1975  ROADSHOW US   SDS  5117
RICHARD THOMPSON    G V  (E      (B) NON STOP                    1976  EMI      UK   INA 1501
KASHIF SALEEM       K V  (E      (B) NON STOP                    1976  ROADSHOW US   RS 41001
DENNIS ROWE         PERC V(E     (C) ENERGY TO BURN              1977  EMI      UK   INA 1502
CARLOS WARD    WIND K V  (E      (C) ENERGY TO BURN              1977  CBS      US   PC 34178
                                 (D) FUNCTION AT THE JUNCTION    19    CBS           34702
                                 (D) FUNCTION AT THE JUNCTION    1977  EMI      UK   INS 3009
                                 (E) SHOUT                       19    CBS      US   JC 35078
                                 (E) SHOUT                       1978  EMI      UK   INS 3016
                                 (F) 1980                        1980  EXCALIBRE UK 5002 US  36333
                                 (G) GREATEST HITS               1980  CBS           US       36923
                                 (H) OLD GOLD , FUTURE GOLD      1980  EXCALIBRE UK 5001
B3A                                    B Z N                                                B3A
                                 (A) MAKING A NAME               19    NEGRAM             NN2
                                 ( ) GREATEST HITS               1980  MERCURY   NL   9198 681
                                 ( ) IN THE BEGINNING            1980  POLYDOR   NL   2426 024
                                 ( ) GREEN VALLEYS               1980  MERCURY   NL   6423 371
                                 ( ) BEST OF                     1980  M F P     NL     58018
B4                               REBOP KWAKU BAAH                                          B4
REBOP KWAKU BAAH    PERC (ABC    (A) REBOP              1972   ISLAND    US    SW 9304
STEVE WINWOOD       K G V(A      (B) ANTHONY REBOP KWAKU BAAH 1973 PHILIPS SWED 6316 008
CHRIS WOOD          FLT  (A      (C) TRANCE             1977   ISLAND    UK    ILPS 9491
ROSCO GEE           B    (A
DELISLE HARPER      B    (A      CONRAD ISADORE   D    (A     JUNIOR KERR      G    (A
JEAN ROUSSEL        K    (A      GORDON HUNTE     G    (A     RABBIT           K    (A
PETER VANDERPUIJE   WIND (A      CHRIS MERCER     WIND (A     ROGER CAWKWELL   WIND (A
GEORGE LEE          WIND (A      KENNY WHEELER    TPT  (A     EDDIE QUANSAH    TPT  (A
THE VOICE OF AFRICA V    (A      MAFFY FALAY      TPT  (B     ULF ANDERSSON    SAX  (B
GUNNAR BERGSTEN     SAX  (B      BOBO STENSON     K    (B     JANNE SCHAFFER   G    (B
BENGT DAHLEN        B    (B      LUKAS LINDHOLM   B    (B     ERIK DAHLBACK    D    (B
RUNE CARLSSON       D    (B      ABDELLCADA ZEF ZEF V (C      MOHAMED BEN HAMOU SAIDI (C
ABDELLA EL HILALLI  PERC (C      BEN MOHAMED ZAIN FLT (C
SIDI JILLALA        (C           GANOUS ENSEMBLE  V   (C
B5                               BABE RUTH                                                  B5
DAVE PUNSHON        K    (A1     (A) FIRST BASE        1972 HARVEST UK SHSP4022  US11151
ALAN SHACKLOCK      G    (123ABC (B) AMAR CABALLERO    1973 HARVEST UK SHVL812  US   11275
DAVE HEWITT         B    (A12345BC (C) BABE RUTH       1975 HARVEST UK SHSP4038 US   11367
JENNY HAAN          V    (ABC1234 (D) STEALIN HOME     1975 CAPITOL    US/UK    11451
ED SPEVOCK          D    (23456CDE (E) KIDS STUFF      1976 CAPITOL UK 23739    US   11515
BERNIE MARSDEN      G    (456E   (F) BEST OF           1977 HARVEST UK SHSM2019
ELLIE HOPE          V    (56E
GASPAR LAWAL        PERC (AB     (1) 1971  (2) 1973  (3) 1975  (4) 1975  (5) 1976  (6) 1976
RAY KNOTT           B    (6
CHRIS HOLMES        K    (2      DICK POWELL      D    (AB1   BRENT CARTER     SAX  (A
JEFF ALLEN          D    (A      RAY HARRIS       HRNS (B     DUNCAN LAMONT    FLT  (B
STEVE GREGORY       SAX  (B      DAVE WHITE       FLT  (B     KEITH CHRISTIE   TROM (B
RAY PREMRU          TROM (B      JACK ELLORY      FLT  (B     BRIAN WARREN     FLT  (B
RON CARTHY          TPT  (B      BUD BEADLE       SAX  (B     NICK MOBBS       PERC (B
ANGELITO PEREZ      V PERC(B     NEIL MURRAY      B    (E     DON AIREY        K SYN(E
FRANK RICOTTI       VIBES (E     TONY CARR        PERC (E     CHRIS KARAN      PERC (E
HARRY MIER          OBOE (A
B6                               BABY                                                       B6
JOHNNY LEE SCHELL   V K G (AB    (A) BABY              1976 MERCURY US 1 1062 LONESTARR 6264
TOM SCOTT           WIND (B      (B) WHERE DID ALL THE MONEY GO 1977 CHELSEA      CHL  517
STEVE CRANE         B V  (AB
WOODIE PUTMAN       D    (B      JOHN MARK CAMP   G V  (B
B7                               BABY GRAND                                                 B7
DAVID KAGAN         V    (AB     (A) BABY GRAND        1978 ARISTA UK SPART1061 US AB4148
ERIC BAZILIAN       G V  (AB     (B) ANCIENT MEDICINE  1979 ARISTA            US   4200
ROB HYMAN           K V  (AB
RALPH SCHUCKETT     K    (A      JOHN SIEGLER     B    (A     RICK CHERTHOFF   PERC (A
MICHAEL BRECKER     HRNS (A      DAVID DARTH PRATER D  (A     RICK MAROTTA     D    (A
B7A                              BABY RAY                                                   B7A
BABY RAY                 (A      (A) WHERE THE SOUL IS    19  IMPERIAL   US   12335
B7B                              BABYFACE                                                   B7B
EDGAR RILEY         K V  (A      (A) BABYFACE          1977 ASI        US     213
BOB MILES           D    (A
MICHAEL TURPIN      B V  (A      BOBBY BARTH      G V  (A
B8                               BABYS                                                      B8
JOHN WAITE          B V  (ABCDE  (A) BABYS             1976 CHRYSALIS       1129
MIKE CORBY          K G  (ABC    (B) BROKEN HEART      1977 CHRYSALIS       1150
WALT STOCKER        G    (ABCDE  (C) HEAD FIRST        1979 CHRYSALIS       1195
TONY BROCK          D V  (ABCDE  (D) UNION JACKS       1980 CHRYSALIS       1267
MARTI McCALL        V    (C      (E) ON THE EDGE       1980 CHRYSALIS       1305
JONATHAN CAIN       G K V (DE    (F) ANTHOLOGY         1981 CHRYSALIS       1351
DIANA LEE           V    (C
       (CONTINUED)
```

BABYS

ROBB LAWRENCE	MAND	(C	PAT HENDERSON	V	(BC	(CONTINUED)	
MIKE JAPP	V	(C	BOBBYE HALL	PERC	(C	KEVIN KELLY	PNO (C
JOHN SINCLAIR	SYN	(C	RICKY PHILLIPS	B	(CDE	MYRNA MATTHEWS	V (BC
JACK CONRAD	B	(C	ANNE MARIE LECLERC	V	(DE	LISA ROBERTS	V (BC

BACHDENKEL

PETER KIMBERLEY	B K V	(AB	(A) STALINGRAD		1977	INITIAL	IRL 002
COLIN SWINBURNE	G V	(AB	(B) LEMMINGS		1978	INITIAL	IRL 001
BRIAN SMITH	D	(AB					
KAREL BEER	K G	(AB	IRVIN MOWREY	V	(A	ANDY SCOTT	K (A

RANDY BACHMAN

RANDY BACHMAN	G V B	(AB	(A) SURVIVOR		1978	POLYDOR	UK 2490 146
WITH			(A) SURVIVOR		1978	POLYDOR	US PD1 6141
BURTON CUMMINGS	K	(A	(B) AXE		19	RCA	US LSP 4349
JEFF PORCARO	D	(A					
IAN GARDINER	D	(A	TOM SCOTT	SAX	(A	BECKY LOPEZ	(A
PATTY BROOKS	V	(A	PETSYE POWELL	V	(A		

BACHMAN TURNER OVERDRIVE

RANDY BACHMAN	G V	(ALL	(A) BACHMAN TURNER OVERDRIVE		1973	MERCURY UK 6499 509	US SRM1 673
TIM BACHMAN	V	(AB	(B) BACHMAN TURNER OVERDRIVE 2		1974	MERCURY UK 6338 482	US SRM1 693
BLAIR THORNTON	G V B	(CDEFGHJ	(C) NOT FRAGILE		1974	MERCURY UK 9100 007	US SRM11004
ROBBIE BACHMAN	PERC D V	(ABCDGJ	(D) FOUR WHEEL DRIVE		1975	MERCURY UK 9100 012	US SRM11027
FRED TURNER	B V	(ALL	(D) FOUR WHEEL DRIVE		1975	MERCURY	GERM 6338 566
JIM CLENCH	D	(JH	(E) AS BRAVE BELT		1975	WB UK K 54036	US MS 2210
FRANK TROWBRIDGE	G	(C	(F) HEAD ON		1976	MERCURY UK 9100 020	US SRM11067
BARRY KEANE	PERC	(A	( ) THE BEST OF		1976	MERCURY UK 9100 026	US SRM11101
			(G) FREEWAYS		1977	MERCURY UK 9100 035	US SRM13700
			(H) STREET ACTION		1978	MERCURY UK 9100 051	US SRM13713
			(J) ROCK'N'ROLL NIGHTS		1979	MERCURY	US SRM13748
			(K) GREATEST		1980	MERCURY NL 9279 123	

BACK DOOR

COLIN HODGKINSON	B	(ALL	(A) BACK DOOR		1972	BLAKEY	BLP 5989
FELIX PAPPALARDI	K	(C	(A) BACK DOOR		1973	WB	K 46231
ADRIAN TILBROOK	D	(	(A) BACK DOOR		1973	WB	US BS 2753
RON ASPERY K FLT SAX		(ALL	(B) EIGHTH STREET NITES		1973	WB	K 46265
TONY HICKS	D	(ABC	(C) ANOTHER FINE MESS		1975	WB	K 56098
BERNIE HOLLAND	G	(C	(D) ACTIVATE		1976	WB	K 56243
PETER THORUP	V	(C					
DAVE McRAE	K	(C					

BACKSTAGE

(A) BACKSTAGE	1979 SONET UK SNTF 852

BACK STREET CRAWLER

PAUL KOSSOFF	G	(AB	(A) THE BAND PLAYS ON		1975	ATLANTIC	K 50173
TERRY WILSON-SLESSER	V	(AB	(A) THE BAND PLAYS ON		1975	ATCO	36125
MIKE MONTGOMERY	K	(AB	(B) SECOND STREET		1976	ATLANTIC	K 50267
TONY BRAUNAGEL	D V(	(AB					
TERRY WILSON	B V	(AB	GEOFF WHITEHORN	G	(B	PETE VANDER PUIJE	SAX (A
GEORGE LARNYOH	WIND	(A	EDDIE QUANSAH	HRNS	(A	JOHN RABBIT BUNDRICK	V (B

BACKHAUSEN

PETER BACKHAUSEN	V K G D	(A	(A) PLANET SHOW		1979	SKY	SKY 037
KARL GILLAUT	G	(A					
STEFFI STEPHAN	B	(A	BERTRAM ENGEL	D	(A	SIDDARTHA GAUTAMA	D (A
KARL SCHOTT	B	(A	GEOFF PEACEY	K	(A	GEORG FUNKE	B (A
WILLY TJON AJONG	K	(A					

BACONFAT

GEORGE SMITH	V HCA	(B	(A) GREASE ONE FOR ME		1970	BLUE HORIZON	7 63858
BUDDY REED	G V	(AB	(B) TOUGH DUDE		1971	BLUE HORIZON	2431 001
DICK INNES Jr	D	(AB					
GREGG SCHAEFER	G HCA	(AB	JERRY SMITH	B	(AB	ROD GINGERMAN PIAZZA	V HCA (AB
J D NICHOLSON	V PNO	(AB					

BAD BOY

STEVE GRIMM	G V	(ABC	(A) THE BAND THAT MADE MILWAUKEE FAMOUS	1977	UA	US LA 781	
JOE LAVIE	K G V	(AB	(B) BACK TO BACK		1978	UA	US LA 869
JOHN MARCELLI	B	(ABC	(C) PRIVATE PARTY		1980	STREETWISE	US 4321
LARS HANSON	D	(AB					
EARL SLICK	G	(B	HECTOR'JACKIE'RAMES	D V	(C	STEVE HUNTER	G (A
SCOTT STEPHAN	G V	(C	BARRY GOLDBERG	K	(B	CLAUDE PEPPER	D (B

BAD COMPANY

PAUL RODGERS	PNO V G	(ALL	(A) BAD COMPANY		1974	ISLAND UK	ILPS 9279
SIMON KIRKE	D	(ALL	(A) BAD COMPANY		1974	SWANSONG US 8410 RI 77	8510
BOZ BURRELL	B	(ALL	(B) STRAIGHT SHOOTER		1975	ISLAND UK	ILPS 9304
MICK RALPHS	G K	(ALL	(B) STRAIGHT SHOOTER		1975	SWANSONG US 8413 RI	8502
MEL COLLINS	SAX	(AD	(C) RUN WITH THE PACK		1976	ISLAND UK	ILPS 9346
SUE & SUNNY	V	(A	(C) RUN WITH THE PACK		1976	SWANSONG US 8415 RI 77	8503
			(D) BURNING SKY		1977	ISLAND UK	ILPS 9441
			(D) BURNING SKY		1977	SWANSONG US	8500
			(E) DESOLATION ANGELS		1979	SWANSONG UK	SSK59408
			(E) DESOLATION ANGELS		1979	SWANSONG US	8506
			(F) ROUGH DIAMONDS		1982	SWANSONG US	SSK 59419

BAD MANNERS

BUSTER BLOODVESSEL	V	(	(A) SKA'N'B	1980 MAGNET UK 5033
			(B) LOONIE TUNES	1980 MAGNET UK 5038
			(C) GOSH IT'S..	1980 MAGNET UK 5043

BADFINGER

```
PETE HAM           V G   (ABCDEF   (A) MAGIC CHRISTIAN MUSIC        1970 APPLE    UK SAPCOR12 US      3364
TOM EVANS          V B   (ABCDEFGH (B) NO DICE                      1970 APPLE    UK SAPCOR 16 US     3367
JOEY MOLLAND       G V   (ABCDEFGH (C) STRAIGHT UP                  1972 APPLE    UK SAPCOR 19 US     3387
PETER CLARK              (G        (D) BADFINGER                    1974 WB       UK K56023 US        2762
DAVID MALLONY      V     (G        (E) ASS                          1974 APPLE    UK SAPCOR 27 US     3411
DUANE HITCHINGS    SYN   (G        (F) WISH YOU WERE HERE           1975 WB                US        2827
ANDY NEWMARK       D     (G        (G) AIRWAVES                     1979 ELEKTRA UK K52129   US      6E 129
STEVE FORMAN       PERC  (G        (H) SAY NO MORE                  1981 RADIO RECORD         16030
KEN HARCK          D     (G
MIKE GIBBINS       D     (ABCDEF   JOE TANSIN        G    (G        NICKY HOPKINS K       (G
TONY KAYE          K     (GH       RICHARD BRYANS    D    (H        GLENN SHERBA  G       (H
```

BADGER

```
TONY KAYE          K     (AB       (A) ONE LIVE BADGER              1973 ATLANTIC UK K40473  US      7022
ROY DYKE           D     (AB       (B) WHITE LADY                   1974 EPIC     UK 80009   US      32831
DAVID FOSTER       B V   (A
BRIAN PARRISH      G V   (A        JACKIE LOMAX      G V  (B        JOAN HARMON V (B
BRY HAWORTH        G     (B        PAUL PILNICK      G    (B        BARRY BAILEY  G       (B
JOHN LANGO         TROM  (B        KIM GARDNER       B    (B        LESTER CALISTE TPT    (B
BOBBY MONTGOMERY   V     (B        TERESIPA HENRY    V    (B        CARL BLOUIN   WIND    (B
JESSIE SMITH       V     (B        JEFF BECK         G    (B        ALVIN THOMAS  SAX     (B
MERCEDES DAVIS     V     (B        ALLEN TOUSSAINT   K PERC(B
```

JOAN BAEZ

```
JOAN BAEZ          G V   (ALL      (A) JOAN BAEZ                    1960 VANGUARD     VSD79073   VSD  2077
WITH                              (A) JOAN BAEZ                    1960 FONTANA                 STFL 6002
HAL RUGG           G     (LM       (B) JOAN BAEZ  2                 1961 VANGUARD     VSD 79094  VSD  2097
JERRY REED         G     (LM       (B) JOAN BAEZ  2                 1961 FONTANA                 STFL 6025
JERRY KENNEDY      G     (LM       (C) IN CONCERT                  1962 VANGUARD     VSD79112   VSD  2122
HAROLD BRADLEY     G     (LM       (C) IN CONCERT                  1962 FONTANA                 STFL 6033
PETE WADE          G     (LMR      (D) IN CONCERT 2                1963 VANGUARD     VSD79113   VSD  2133
TOMMY JACKSON      FDL   (LM       (D) IN CONCERT 2                1963 FONTANA                 STFL 6035
BUDDY SPICHER      FDL   (LM       (E) JOAN BAEZ 5                 1964 VANGUARD                VSD79160
JUNIOR HUSKY       B     (LM       (E) JOAN BAEZ 5                 1964 FONTANA                 STFL 6043
NORBERT PUTNAM     B     (LMQR     (F) FAREWELL ANGELINA           1965 VANGUARD     VSD 23006
HARGUS PIG ROBBINS K     (LM       (F) FAREWELL ANGELINA           1965 FONTANA                 STFL 6058
KENNY BUTTREY      D     (LMQR     (G) NOEL                        1966 VANGUARD     VSD79230   VSD 23018
FRED CARTER        MAND  (LM       (G) NOEL                        1966 FONTANA                 STFL 6078
BILL PURCELL       K     (LM       (H) PORTRAIT                    1966 VANGUARD                SVRL19025
GRADY MARTIN       G     (LMQ      (J) JOAN                        1967 VANGUARD     VSD79240   VSD 23011
JIM GORDON         D     (         (J) JOAN                        1967 FONTANA                 STFL 6082
LARRY CARLTON      G     (X        (K) BAPTISM                     1968 VANGUARD     SVRL19000  VSD 79275
DEAN PARKS         G     (1X       (L) ANY DAY NOW                 1968 VANGUARD     VSD79306/7  55/66
JOE SAMPLE         K     (X        (M) DAVIDS ALBUM                1969 VANGUARD     VSD79308   SVRL19050
DAVID PAICH        K     (X        (N) ONE DAY AT A TIME           1970 VANGUARD     VSD79310   VSD 23010
LARRY KNECHTEL     K     (X        (O) FIRST TEN YEARS             1970 VANGUARD                VSD  6560
REINHOLD PRESS     B     (1X       (P) BLESSED ARE                 1971 VANGUARD                VSD6570/1
RED RHODES         STEEL (X        (Q) CARRY IT ON                 1972 VANGUARD     VSD79313    519042
JIM HORN           SAX   (X        (R) COME FROM THE SHADOWS       1972 A&M   US 4339   UK   AMLH64339
MALCOLM CECIL      SYN   (X1       (S) THE BALLAD BOOK             1972 VANGUARD                VSD 41/42
HAMPTON HAWES      K     (X        (T) WHERE ARE YOU NOW MY SON    1973 A&M   US 4390   UK   AMLH64390
TOM SCOTT          WIND  (UX       (U) GRACIAS A LA VIDA (HERES TO LIFE)1974 A&M               AMLH63614
MAX BENNETT        B     (X        (V) CONTEMPORARY BALLAD BOOK    1974 VANGUARD                VSD 49/50
JOHN GUERIN        D     (X        (W) PROFILES                    1974 IRL                    IC054 95128
RICK LOTEMPIO      G     (X        (X) DIAMONDS & RUST             1975 A&M          AMLH64527
OLLIE MITCHELL     TPT   (X        (Y) LIVE IN JAPAN               1975 VANGUARD                GP   315
DONALD DUNN        B     (1        (Z) LOVE SONG ALBUM             1976 VANGUARD                VSD 79/80
JONI MITCHELL      V     (UX       ( ) FROM EVERY STAGE            1976 A&M   US 3704   UK   AMLH64704
BUCK MONARI        TPT   (X        (1) GULF WINDS                  1976 A&M   US 4603   UK   AMLH64603
BILL WOOD          V     (9        ( ) BLOWING AWAY                1977 PORTRAIT US 34697 UK       82011
TED ALEVIZOS       V     (9        ( ) GOLDEN HOUR                 1972 PYE          GH 843
PETE DRAKE         STEEL (LM       ( ) HITS THE GREATEST & OTHERS  1973 VANGUARD                VSD 79332
JOHNNY GIMBLE            (L        ( ) GREATEST HITS               19   IRL          Ic062 93622
DAVID BRIGGS            (LR        ( ) BEST OF                     1977 A&M          AMLH64665
STEPHEN STILLS          (L        ( ) INTRODUCTION TO/FAREWELL ANGELINA 1976 ARL    IC18892665/6
MILT HOLLAND       PERC  (U        (9) THE BEST OF                 1968 SAGA         EROS  8075
JIM HUGHART        B     (U        ( ) GOLDEN HOUR VOL 2           19   PYE   GH 863
LALO LINDGRON      HARP  (U        ( ) HOUSE OF THE RISING SUN     1978 MUSIDISC                1367
EDGARLUSTGARTEN    CELLO (U        ( ) SUPER DISC OF JOAN BAEZ     19   A&M          GXM 9002
SALLY STEVENS      V     (U        ( ) HONEST LULABY               1979 PORTRAIT                PRT 83474
TOMMY TEDESCO      G     (U        ( ) COUNTRY MUSIC               1979 VANGUARD                VSD  105
JACKIE WARD        V     (U        ( ) SPOTLIGHT ON                1980 PORTRAIT                1008
ANDRA WILLIS       V     (U        ( ) LIVE IN CONCERT             1980 PORTRAIT UK              84790
BRUCE LANGHORN     G     (F        ( ) MAGIC OF JOAN BAEZ          1981 K TEL  UK   NE 1114
RALPH RINZLER      MAND  (F
RUSS SAVAKUS       B     (F        RICHARD ROMOFF       B          (F   DAVID HARRIS        V     (Q
RICHARD FESTINGER  G     (Q        STUART BASORE        STEEL      (R   CHARLIE McCOY       HCA   (R
FARRELL MORRIS     PERC  (R        WELDON MYRICK        STEEL      (R   GLEN SPREEN         K     (R
JOHN BUCK WILKINS  G     (R
```

HENRY BADOWSKI

```
HENRY BADOWSKI    V SAX B K(A      (A) LIFE IS GRAND               1981 A&M          UK AMLH 68527
JAMES STEPHENSON  G B    (A
ALEXSANDER KOLKOWSKI VLN (A        WALLY BRILL          PROD  (A
```

BAG

```
JIMMY CURTISS            (A        (A) REAL                        1969 DECCA         US          75057
```

EDDIE BAIRD

```
EDDIE BAIRD       G K V (A         (A) HARD GRAFT                  1976 DJM           UK          467
```

DUCK BAKER

```
DUCK BAKER        G V   (ALL       (A) THERES SOMETHING FOR EVERYONE 1977 KICKING MULE US 124 UK SNKF116
WITH                              (B) WHEN YOU WORE A TULIP       19   KICKING MULE US 135 UK SNKF123
STEFAN GROSSMAN    G    (C         (C) KING OF BONGO BONG         1977 KICKING MULE US 144 UK SNKF137
MIKE PIGGOTT      VLN   (C         (D) FINGER STYLE JAZZ GUITAR   1979 KICKING MULE        UK SNKF154
```

GINGER BAKER

```
GINGER BAKER          D    (ALL   (A)STRATAVARIOUS                          1972 POLYDOR UK 2383 133 US ATCO 7015
CHRIS SPEDDING        G    (E     (B) FELI RANSOME KUTI & THE AFRICA BAND 72 REGAL ZONOPHONE  UK    SLRZ 1023
RICK GRECH            B V  (E     (C) AT HIS BEST                          1973 POLYDOR UK 2659 023 US      3504
HENRY THOMAS          B    (1     (D) POP HISTORY                          19   POLYDOR                2668 002
MIKE DAVIS            G    (1     (E) ELEVEN SIDES OF BAKER                1977 MOUNTAIN UK 5005   US SIRE 7532
JOHN MIZAROLLI        G    (1     (E) ELEVEN SIDES OF BAKER                1977 PHONOGRAM               6370 419
FELI RANSOME KUTI          (B     (1) 1980 LIVE BAND
DELISLE HARPER        B    (E
LOUISE ARTHURWORREY   V    (E     KOFI OSAPANIN       PERC (E   OLU GEORGE        PERC (E
STAN SULZMANN         SAX  (E     JEFF DALY           SAX  (E   DEREK WADSWORTH   TROM (E
SNIPS                 V    (E     KUMA HARADA         B    (E   HERBIE FLOWERS    B    (E
EUNICE A GREEN        V    (E     MIKE DEACON         K    (E   KOJO OSAPANIN     PERC (E
IAN HAMER             TPT  (E     ALAN SKIDMORE       SAX  (E   EDDIE MORDUE      SAX  (E
WALLY SMITH           TROM (E
```

BAKER GURVITZ ARMY

```
GINGER BAKER           D PERC(ABC  (A) BAKER GURVITZ ARMY       1974 VERTIGO      UK   9103  201
ADRIAN GURVITZ         G V  (ABC   (A) BAKER GURVITZ ARMY       1974 JANUS        US         7015
PAUL GURVITZ           B V  (ABC   (B) ELYSIAN ENCOUNTER        1975 MOUNTAIN     UK   TOPS 101
SNIPS                  V    (BC    (B) ELYSIAN ENCOUNTER        1975 ATCO         US        36123
PETER LEMER            K    (B     (C) HEARTS ON FIRE           1976 MOUNTAIN     UK   TOPS 111
JOHN NORMAN MITCHELL VIBES K(A     (C) HEARTS ON FIRE           1976 PHONOGRAM    EURO 9103  206
MADELINE BELL          V    (A     (C) HEARTS ON FIRE           1976 ATCO         US        36137
ROSETTA HIGHTOWER      V    (A
BARRY ST JOHN          V    (A     LIZA STRIKE       V     (A
```

LAVERN BAKER

```
LAVERN BAKER          V    (ALL    (A) LET ME BELONG TO YOU      1974 BRUNSWICK    US      754160
                                   (B) SINGS BESSIE SMITH        1976 ATLANTIC     GER  ATL51241
                                   (C) HER GREATEST RECORDINGS   19   ATLANTIC     US
```

MICKEY BAKER

```
MICKEY BAKER          G    (ALL    (A) TAKE A LOOK INSIDE              1975 BIG BEAR          BEAR 5
WILLY MABON           K HCA (A     (B) THE BLUES IN ME                1975 BLACK & BLUE       33507
FRITZ OZMEC           D    (C      (C) UP ON THE HILL                 1975 ROOTS      US      SL 517
DAN ARMSTRONG         B    (A      (D) BLUES & JAZZ GUITAR OF M BAKER 197  KICKING MULE UK SNKF127 US 142
PETE MORGAN           B    (A      (E) JAZZ ROCK GUITAR              1978 KICKING MULE UK SNKF145 US 140
PETE YORK             B    (A
KIERAN O'CONNOR       PERC (A      KEN ELLIOTT       K     (A    DYAN BIRCH        V    (A
PADDY McHUGH          V    (A      FRANK COLLINS     V     (A    MARTIN WICHTL     SAX  (C
FRANK MANTOOTH        PNO  (C      KARL KRBAVAC      B HCA (C
```

BAKERLOO

```
DAVE CLEMPSON      G HCA K  (A     (A) BAKERLOO               1969 HARVEST      UK    SHVL  762
TERRY POOLE        B        (A
KEITH BAKER        D        (A     JERRY SALISBURY   TPT   (A
```

BALANCE

```
PEPPY CASTRO       V    (AB        (A) BALANCE                1981 PORTRAIT
BOB KULICK         G    (AB        (B) IN FOR THE COUNT       1982 PORTRAIT  UK    85787
DOUG KATSAROS      K V  (AB
JOHN SIEGLER       B    (A         ANDY NEWMARK      D     (A    CHUCK BURGI       D    (B
DENNIS FELDMAN     B    (B
```

LONG JOHN BALDRY

```
LONG JOHN BALDRY  V HCA(ALL   (A) LONG JOHNS BLUES           1964 U A ULP1081 ASCOT   US 13022
WITH                          (A) LONG JOHNS BLUES           1971 UA      US              UAS5545
RAY JACKSON       MAND (E     (B) LOOKING AT LONG JOHN       1966 U A SULP1146  SUNSET    50109
KATHI McDONALD    V    (K     (C) LET THE HEARTACHE BEGIN    1968 PYE    UK NSPL 18208
ALAN MURPHY       G    (KJ    (D) LET THERE BE LONG JOHN     1968 PYE    UK NSPL 18228
IAN ARMITT        K    (AEFJ  (E) IT AINT EASY               1971 WB  US 1921    UK      K 46008
RONNIE WOOD       G    (E     (F) EVERYTHING STOPS FOR TEA   1972 WB             K 46160
SAM MITCHELL      STEEL(EF    (G) HEARTACHES (GOLDEN HOUR)   1974 PYE            GH    572
MAGGIE BELL       V    (E     (H) GOOD TO BE ALIVE           1976 CASABLANCA  US         7012
MICKEY WALLER     PERC (F     (J) WELCOME TO THE CLUB        1977 CASABLANCA  US         7035
ALAN SKIDMORE     SAX  (E     (K) BALDRY'S OUT               1979 EMI US 17015  UK     AML3002
JIMMY HOROWITZ    K    (FHJK  (L) BLUES(HOOCHIE COOCHIE MEN) 19   UA      US              5543
JEFF BRADFORD     G HCA(A     (M) LONG JOHN BALDRY           1980 EMI US 17038  NL      86263
CLIFF BARTON      B    (A     ( ) WAIT FOR ME                1969 JANUS US       7002
RICK BROWN        B    (F
BILL LAW          D    (A    ELTON JOHN      PNO (EF  CALEB QUAYE       G   (E   DAVE GLOVER     B    (E
IAN DUCK          V HCA(E    ROGER POPE      D   (E   DAVEY JOHNSTONE   G   (F   NIGEL OLSSON    D    (F
KLAUS VOORMANN    B    (F    RAY COOPER      PERC(F   STEFAN DELFT      VLA (F   JAMES LITHERLAND G  (F
ROBERT WESTON     G    (F    BILL SMITH      B   (F   JOHN DENTITH      D   (F   LIZA STRIKE     V   (FHJ
DORIS TROY        V    (F    BARRY ST JOHN   V   (F   TERRY STANNARD    D   (F   JOHN PORTER     B   (F
ROD STEWART       BANJ (F    MADELINE BELL   V   (FJ  DAVID BALL        G   (H   DENNIS BALL     B   (H
TONY NEWMAN       D    (H    JON FIELD       FDL (H   ANDY BOWN         G   (HJ  JOHN MEALING    ORG (H
LESLEY DUNCAN     V    (HJ   SUE GLOVER      V   (H   NEIL SHEPHERD     V   (H   JESSE ED DAVIS  G   (J
JOHN JARVIS       PNO  (J    PETER GAVIN     D   (J   KLAUS VOORMANN    B   (J   GEORGE CHISHOLM TROM (J
NEIL LANCASTER    V    (J    MICK CLARKE     G   (K   ROY YOUNG         K V (K   SAM MITCHELL    G   (HJ
TERRY COX         D    (H    MIKE FRENCH     FDL (H   PETE STANLEY      BANJ(H   CHRIS HUGHES    SAX  (H
BOB COHEN         G    (H    MIKE DRISCOL    D   (H   KAY GARNER        V   (HJ  FRED TACKETT    G   (J
JIM KELTNER       D    (J    TOM BROWN       SAX (J   DAVID SNELL       HARP(J   TONY BURROWS    V   (J
CHAS MILLS        V    (J    JAMES LEE FISH  B   (K   JEFF SEITZ        D   (K   CAROL BECKER    V   (K
TRACY BALIN       V    (K    MICHAEL ICEBERG SYN (K   RAY WARLEIGH      SAX (K   TIM SADLER      V   (K
KIM KELLY         V    (K    STEPHEN BRUCE   V   (K   ORCHESTRA             (F
```

MARTY BALIN

```
MARTY BALIN       G V  (A     (A) BALIN                 1981 EMI       US    17054
JOHN JARVIS       K    (A
JOHNNY DECARO     G V  (A     MARK CUMMINGS    K V (A   BILLY LEE LEWIS   D V (A
RICHARD BASSIL    B V  (A     NEIL LARSEN      K   (A   MICHAEL BODDICKER K   (A
JOHN HUG          G    (A     KEN WATSON       PERC(A   BOBBYE HALL       PERC(A
STEVE FORMAN      PERC (A     BILL CHAMPLIN    V   (A   RICK NOWELS       V   (A
DAVID E LANDAU    V    (A
```

MARCIA BALL

```
MARCIA BALL        V   (A    (A) CIRSUIT QUEEN              1978   CAPITOL      US   ST  11752
                             (B) FREDA & THE FIREDOGS LIVE  1980   BIG WHEEL    US   NR  10876
```

HANK BALLARD

```
HANK BALLARD       V   (ALL  (A) HANK BALLARD & THE MIDNIGHTERS  19   STARDAY     US      K5003X
WITH                         ( ) HANK BALLARD & THE MIDNIGHTERS  19   POWERPAK    US   PO 276
LAWSON SMITH                 ( ) HANK BALLARD BIGGEST HITS       19
NORMAN THRASHER              ( ) THOSE LAZY LAZY DAYS            19
BILLY DAVIS                  ( ) GLAD SONGS SAD SONGS            19
HENRY BOOTH                  ( ) JUMPIN' HANK BALLARD            19   LONDON HA 8101  US KING  793
CHARLES SUTTON               ( ) GREATEST JUKE BOX HITS          19   KING        US       541
ARTHUR PORTER                ( ) HANGING WITH HANK              19   STANG       US   ST 1031
SONNY WOODS                  ( ) SPOTLIGHT ON HANK BALLARD       19   STARDAY GUSTO US  SK  740
                             ( ) CANT KEEP A GOOD MAN DOWN       19   KING        US      1052
                             ( ) FINGER POPPIN TIME             19   KING        US       700
```

LARRY BALLARD

```
LARRY BALLARD      V   (ALL  (A) YOUNG BLOOD & SWEET COUNTRY MUSIC 1974   ELEKTRA   US       7E1024
                             (B) HONKY TONK HEAVEN              1976   CAPITOL   US   ST 11520
                             (C) WAITING IN THE WINGS           1977   CAPITOL   US   ST 11662
```

RUSS BALLARD

```
RUSS BALLARD V D K B G HCA(ALL  (A) RUSS BALLARD              1974   EPIC US 33252   UK EPC 80341
NICK NEWELL        SAX  (AB   (B) WINNING                     1976   EPIC US 34093   UK EPC 69210
CHRIS MERCER       SAX  (AB   (C) AT THE THIRD STROKE         1978   EPIC US 35035   UK EPC 82629
STEVE GREGORY      SAX  (A    (D) RUSS BALLARD & THE BARNET DOGS 1980 EPIC US 36186  UK EPC 83867
MICK EVE           SAX  (A    (E) INTO THE FIRE               1981   EPIC US 36993
RABBIT BUNDRICK    K    (B
DENNIS BELFIELD    B    (A    MIKE BAIRD       D   (C    CRAIG DOERGE     K   (C
STEVE FREDIANI     HRNS (C    TOM SCOTT        SAX (C    DAVID HUNGATE    B   (C
BOBBYE HALL        PERC (C    DAVID FOSTER     K   (C    FRED TACKETT     G   (C
DAVE HENSON        V    (C    LEE SKLAR        B   (C    JEFF PORCARO     D   (C
MIKE PORCARO       B    (C    KEITH OLSEN      PERC(C    DAVID PAICH      K   (C
TOM KELLY          V    (C    DAVE MATTACKS    D   (B    DAVE MARKEE      B   (B
CHRIS KARAN        PERC (B    GEOFF SKATES         (B    PETE ZORN        B   (B
TERRY STARR        TPT  (B    PIP WILLIAMS         (B    MADELINE BELL    V   (B
SUNNY LESLIE       V    (B    JOANNE WILLIAMS  V   (B    LIZA STRIKE      V   (B
DAVE WINTOUR       B    (DE   BILL ROBERTS     G V (DE   ROB HENRIT       D   (DE
RICHARD BLANSHARD  V    (DE   LESLIE MORGAN    D   (D
```

BALLIN' JACK

```
GLENN THOMAS       G    (A    (A) BALLIN' JACK               1970   CBS US  30344 UK    64210
LUTHER RABB        B V  (A    (B) BUZZARD LUCK                1972   CBS US  31468
JIM COILE          WIND (A    (C) SPECIAL PRIDE               1973   MERCURY   US    1 672
RONNIE HAMMON      D    (A    (D) LIVE AND IN COLOR           1974   MERCURY   US    1 700
TIM McFARLAND      PNO  (A
JIM WALTERS        TPT  (A
```

BALLS

```
TREVOR BURTON      B    (ABCD  (A) 1969      (B) 1969      (C) 1970 SUMMER   (D) 1970 LATE
DENNY LAINE        G V  (ABCD
ALAN WHITE         D    (B     JACKIE LOMAX     G V (C    STEVE GIBBONS    V G (D
MIKE KELLIE        D    (CD    DAVE MORGAN      B   (A    KEITH SMART      D   (A
RICHARD TANDY      K    (CD
```

BALTIK

```
JANNE SCHAFFER     G    (A    (A) BALTIK                     1973   CBS          SWED    65581
BJORN JASON LINDH  FLT  (A
JOHN GUSTAFSON     B    (A
```

BAMA

```
                              (A) GHETTO'S OF MY MIND         1974   CHESS               50032
```

BAMBOO

```
DAVE RAY      HCA V G  (A    (A) BAMBOO                      1969   ELEKTRA   US  EKS 74048
WILL DONIGHT   V B PNO (A
DANIEL LEE HALL V K G  (A    SANFORD KONIKOFF  D   (A    RED RHODES      STEEL   (A
PETER HODGSON  B       (A    BRENDAN HARKIN    PERC (A   KEN JENKINS     B       (A
```

BAMBOO ZOO

```
                              (A) LOOK, LISTEN, CONSUME       1981   PHONEY    UK   PHOG8101
```

BANCHEE

```
PETER ALONGI       G V  (B    (A) BANCHEE                    1969   ATLANTIC   US
JOSE MIGUEL DE JESUS G V (B   (B) THINKIN'                   1971   POLYDOR US 24 4066 UK 242507?
FERNANDO ROMAN     PERC V(B
MICHAEL MARINE     B V  (B    VICTOR DIGILIE    D   (B
```

BANCO

```
PIER LUIGI CALDERONI D (D    ( ) BANCO DEL MUTUO SOCCORSO    1972   ORIZZONTE  ITAL ORL  8041
FRANCESCO DI GIACOMO V (D    ( ) DARWIN                      1972   ORIZZONTE  ITAL ORL  8094
RENATO D'ANGELO   B G  (D    ( ) LO SONO NATO LIBERO         1973   ORIZZONTE  ITAL ORL  8202
GIANNA NOCENZI  K CLAR(D     (D) BANCO                       1975   MANTICORE  UK   K  53507
VITTORIO NOCENZI  K    (D    (D) BANCO                       1975   MANTICORE  US   MA6  505
                             ( ) GAROGANO ROSSO              1976   ORIZZONTE  ITAL ORL  8334
                             ( ) AS IN A LAST SUPPER          1976   MANTICORE          28004
                             ( ) DI TEARO                    19     DISCHI     ITAL SMRL 6226
                             ( ) CANTO DI PRIMAVERA           19     DISCHI     ITAL SMRL 6247
                             ( ) CAPOLINEA                   19     DISCHI     ITAL SMRL 6260
```

THE BAND

```
ROBBIE ROBERTSON  G V K (ALL  (A) MUSIC FROM THE BIG PINK     1968   CAPITOL        ST  2955
RICK DANKO      B V VLN (ALL  (B) THE BAND                    1969   CAPITOL        EST  132
RICHARD MANUEL  D K V   (ALL  (AB)MILESTONES                  1973   EMI    IMP  5C18450195/6
LEVON HELM      V D G   (ALL  (C) STAGE FRIGHT                1970   CAPITOL        EASW 425
GARTH HUDSON    K SAX   (ALL  (D) CAHOOTS                     1971   CAPITOL        EAST 651
WITH                          (E) ROCK OF AGES                1972   CAPITOL        EASSP 11
TOM MALONE         HRNS (HJ   (E) ROCK OF AGES                1972   CAPITOL        SABB11045
JIM GORDON         HRNS (HJ   (F) MOONDOG MATINEE             1973   CAPITOL        ESW 11214
    (CONTINUED)
```

THE BAND

JOHN SIMON   K HRNS (BEHJ
LARRY PACKER   VLN   (HJ
VAN MORRISON   V   (DJ
ALLEN TOUSSAINT   K   (D
SNOOKY YOUNG   HRNS   (E
HOWARD JOHNSON   HRNS   (EJ
DOC POMUS   (E
JOE FARRELL   HRNS   (E
EARL McINTYRE   TROM   (E
J D PARRAN   WIND   (E
BOBBY CHARLES   V   (EJ
BOB DYLAN   V G   (EJ
Dr JOHN   K PERC (EJ
RICH COOPER   HRNS   (J
RONNIE HAWKINS   V   (J
NEIL DIAMOND   V G   (J
MUDDY WATERS   G V   (J
ERIC CLAPTON   G V   (J
EMMYLOU HARRIS   V G   (J

(G) NORTHERN LIGHTS SOUTHERN CROSS
(H) ISLANDS
(J) THE LAST WALTZ   TRIPLE
(J) THE LAST WALTZ   TRIPLE
( ) THE BEST OF THE BAND
( ) THE BEST OF THE BAND
( ) THE BEST OF THE BAND
( ) MASTERS OF ROCK
( ) IN CONCERT
( ) ANTHOLOGY
( ) ANTHOLOGY

BILLY MUNDI   (F
JERRY HEY   HRNS   (J
NEIL YOUNG   V G   (J
DENNIS ST JOHN   D   (J
BOB MARGOLIN   G   (J
RINGO STARR   D   (J
STAPLES SINGERS   V   (J

(CONTINUED)   B29
1975 CAPITOL   EST 11440
1977 CAPITOL   EST 11602
1978 WB   UK   K   66076
1978 WB   US   3WS 3146
1976 CAPITOL   EAST23927
1976 CAPITOL   US   ST 11553
1976 CAPITOL   UK   ST 3927
1975 EMI INT   IC 054 81735
1973 EMI   IMP   5C 054 81466
1978 CAPITOL   ESTSP 19
1978 CAPITOL   US   SKBO11856

BEN KEITH   (F
CHARLIE KEAGLE   HRNS   (J
JONI MITCHELL   V G   (J
PAUL BUTTERFIELD HCA V (J
PINETOP PERKINS   K   (J
RON WOOD   G   (J
BYRON BERLINE   FDL   (G

B30 BAND OF JOY

ROBERT PLANT   V   (
JOHN BONHAM   D   (
PAUL LOCKEY   G V (
MICHAEL CHETWOOD K   (

(A) BAND OF JOY   1978 POLYDOR US 6133 UK 2310 588

KEVIN HAMMOND   G V (JOHN PASTERNAK   B V (
FRANCESCO NIZZA   D   (

B30A BAND OF THIEVES

(A) BAND OF THIEVES   1979 OVAL   US   1727

B31 BANDIT

JAMES LITHERLAND G   (A
GRAHAM BROAD   D K (A
DANNY McINTOSH   G V (AB*
JIM DIAMOND   V   (A
CLIFF WILLIAMS   B V (A
TONY LESTER   B V (B

(A) BANDIT   1977 ARISTA US 4113 UK ARTY 148
*(B) PARTNERS IN CRIME 1978 ARIOLA US 50042 UK ARL 5010
(C) HIT & RUN   1980 ARIOLA US 50067

THEODORE THUNDER D V (B   GERRY TREW   V   (B
MICK GRABHAM   G V (B*
TWO DIFFERENT COVERS GIVING DIFFERENT GUITARIST

B31A BANDIT (US)

JOEY NEWMAN   G V (A
KEVIN BARNHILL   B V G (A
TIMOTHY EATON   V   (A

(A) BANDIT   1975 ABC   US   918

DAVID DELLA ROSSA GV   (A   DANNY GORMAN   D   (A

B31B BANDERA

(A) HYPE INTO SELLING YOUR HEAD 1980 JSP UK 1018

B32 BANDOGGS

TONY ROSE   (
NIC JONES   (
PETE COE   (

(A) BANDOGGS   1978 TRANSATLANTIC   LTRA 504

CHRIS COE

B32A BANG

TONY D'IORIO   D   (A
FRANK FERRARA   B V (ABC
FRANK GLICKEN   G V (ABC
DURIS MAXWELL   D   (B
BRUCE GARY   D   (BC
SHIRLEY MATTHEWS V   (B

(A) BANG   1972 CAPITOL   US   11015
(B) MOTHER/BOW TO THE KING 1972 CAPITOL US 11110
(C) BANG MUSIC   1973 CAPITOL   US   11190

JEFFREY CHEEN   PERC (B   CLYDIE KING   V   (B
VANETTA FIELDS   V   (B

B33 BANGOR FLYING CIRCUS

MICHAEL TEGZA   D PERC (A
DAVID WOLINSKI   PERC K V B (A
ALAN DE CARLO   PERC G V (A

(A) BANGOR FLYING CIRCUS 1969 STATESIDE UK SSL5022 US DUNHILL 50069

B33A DARRELL BANKS

DARRELL BANKS   (A

(A) DARRELL BANKS IS HERE 19 ATCO US SD 33216 VOLT US 6002

B34 PETER BANKS

PETER BANKS   G   (ABC
JAN AKKERMAN   G   (AB
STEVE HACKETT   G   (B
RAY BENNETT   B   (B
JOHN WETTON   B   (B

(A) PETER BANKS & JAN AKKERMAN 19 SOVEREIGN SVNA 7250
(B) PETER BANKS   1973 SOVEREIGN   SVNA 7256
(B) TWO SIDES OF PETER BANKS 1973 CAPITOL   SMAS11217

PHIL COLLINS   D   (B   MIKE HOUGH   D   (B

B34A ROSE BANKS

ROSE BANKS   V   (A

(A) ROSE   1976 MOTOWN US 6/845 UK STML 12024

B34B TONY BANKS

TONY BANKS   K G B (A
KIM BEACON   V   (A
CHESTER THOMPSON D   (A

(A) A CURIOUS FEELING   1979 CHARISMA US 2207 UK CAS 1148

B35 BANZAI

EVERT VERHEES   G V K B (A
PETER TORFS   K V (A
JOHN McO   G V (A

(A) HORANATA   19   DELTA   DG 10 001

LUDWIG KERMAT   VIBES PERC (A ERRY FOX   D PERC (A

B36 BAR KAYS

JIMMY KING   (*
RONNIE CALDWELL   (*
PHALIN JONES   (*
CARL CUNNINGHAM   (*
FRANK THOMPSON   (
JAMES ALEXANDER   (
BEN CAULEY   (
LLOYD SMITH   (
CHARLES ALLEN   (
MICHAEL BEARD   (
WINSTON STEWART   (
HARVEY HENDERSON   (

( ) SOUL FINGER   19   ATCO   228   030
( ) SOUL FINGER   19   ATCO   SD 33287
( ) SOUL FINGER   19   ATLANTIC   K 40184
( ) GOTTA GROOVE   1969 STAX STATS1009 RI 80 4130
( ) GOTTA GROOVE   1969 VOLT   6004
( ) BLACK ROCK   19   POLYDOR   2362 003
( ) DO YOU SEE   19   POLYDOR   2325 087
( ) COLD BLOODED   1976 STAX   STX 1033
( ) TOO HOT TO STOP   1976 MERCURY   SRM 11099
( ) FLYING HIGH ON YOUR LOVE 1978 MERCURY UK 9100 048
( ) FLYING HIGH ON YOUR LOVE 1978 MERCURY   SRM 1181
( ) MONEY TALKS   1979 STAX   STX 3023
( ) MONEY TALKS   1979 STAX   4106
( ) DO YOU SEE WHAT I SEE 19 VOLT   US   8001

(CONTINUED)

BAR KAYS

( ) IN JOY		1980	MERCURY		3781
( ) LIGHT OF LIFE		1980	MERCURY		3732
( ) AS ONE		1981	MERCURY	UK 6337	108
( ) BLACK LIGHT		19	VOLT	US	6011

(*) THE FOUR MEMBERS WHO DIED WITH OTIS REDDING(*)

BARBARELLA

B36A

GERNER BRESSEN	V FLY (A
HENNING POLD	V B (A
TERJE BARNHOLDT	D (A
KAARE BARKOU	K V (A

(A) FIRST LOVE	1975	ARTIST	DENMARK	515
(B) BARBARELLA?	1976	ARTIST	DENMARK	?

KENNETH CARTER   G V   (A

BARBARIANS

B36B

JERRY CAUSI	B (A
JEFF MORRIS	G (A
BRUCE BENSON	G (A

(A) THE BARBARIANS	1979	RHINO	US RI	008

VICTOR MOULTON   D V   (A

BILL BARCLAY

B36C

BILL BARCLAY   V   (ALL

(A) ALMOST ALIVE	1974	GM	GHL	1016
(B) THERE WAS THIS BLOKE	1975	RUBBER	RUB	010
(C) VIVA DUNBAR	1976	PYE	PKL	5555
(D) HALF ALIVE	1979	SAFARI	BOOB	1

BARCLAY JAMES HARVEST

B37

JOHN LEES	G V	(ALL
STEWART WOLSTENHOLME	K	(A>L
MEL PRITCHARD	D	(ALL
LES HOLROYD	B	(ALL
ALAN PARSONS	J HARP	(B
KEVIN McALEA	K	(M
BARRY THOMAS	V	(D
BILL NEWTON	V	(D
NORMAN BROWN	V	(D
NAT WHITWORTH	V	(D
GEORGE WALL	V	(D
DAVE BROWNING	TPT	(D
LENNIE MOAKES	TPT	(D
DON BANKS	TPT	(D
BROM HARVEY	TPT	(D
FRANK DIXON	TROM	(D
MUFF KING	TROM	(D
FRANK BRIERLEY	TROM	(D
AUSTIN GLEAVE	TROM	(D
KEVIN McALEA	K	(M
ALAN FAWKES	SAX	(M
SYMPH ORCH		(ABCD

(A) BARCLAY JAMES HARVEST	1970	HARVEST		SHVL	770
(B) ONCE AGAIN	1971	HARVEST		SHVL	788
(C) OTHER SHORT STORIES	1971	HARVEST		SHVL	794
(D) BABY JAMES HARVEST	1972	HARVEST		SHSP	4023
( ) EARLY MORNING ONWARDS	1972	STARLINE	UK SRS	5126
(E) EVERYONE IS EVERYBODY ELSE	1974	POLYDOR		2383	286
(F) LIVE	1974	POLYDOR		2683	052
(G) TIME HONOURED GHOSTS	1975	POLYDOR		2383	361
(G) TIME HONOURED GHOSTS	1975	POLYDOR	US		6517
(H) OCTOBERON	1976	POLYDOR		2442	144
(H) OCTOBERON	1976	MCA	US		2234
( ) BEST OF VOL 1	1977	HARVEST	UK	SHSM	2013
(I) GONE TO EARTH	1978	POLYDOR		2442	148
(I) GONE TO EARTH	1978	MCA	US		2302
(J) LIVE TAPES	1978	POLYDOR		PODV	2001
(K) NUMBER 12	1978	POLYDOR		2442	153
(K) NUMBER 12	1978	POLYDOR		POLD	5006
( ) BEST OF VOL 2	1979	HARVEST		SHSM	2023
(L) MOCKINGBIRD (THE EARLY YEARS)	1980	HARVEST	EURO	05607236	
(M) EYES OF THE UNIVERSE	1980	POLYDOR		POLD	5029
( ) BEST OF VOL 3	1981	HARVEST	UK	SHSM	2033
(N) TURN OF THE TIDE	1981	POLYDOR	UK	POLD	5040
(O) CONCERT FOR THE PEOPLE	1982	POLYDOR	UK	POLD	5052

NICKEY BARCLAY

B38

NICKEY BARCLAY		(
WITH		
WADDY WACHTEL	G	(A
JEFF RICH	B	(A

(A) DIAMOND IN A JUNKYARD	1976	ARIOLA		AAS 1503
(A) DIAMOND IN A JUNKYARD	1976	ARIOLA	US	ST 5006

BUGS PEMBERTON   D   (A

PETER BARDENS

B39

PETER BARDENS	K V	(ALL
WITH		
ANDY GEE	G	(ABC
BRUCE THOMAS	B	(AC
ALAN MARSHALL	V PERC	(AC
STEVE ELLIS	V	(AC
REG ISADOR	D	(ABC
ROCKY	PERC	(AC
DAVID WOOLEY	V	(AC
JOHN OWEN	B	(BC
VIC LINTON	G	(C
MAXINE OFFLA	V	(BC
GUS ISADORE	G V	(D
PETE SHADE	VIBES	(D

(A) THE ANSWER	1970	TRANSATLANTIC	UK	TRA	222
(A) THE ANSWER	1970	VERVE	US		3088
(A) THE ANSWER	1970	METRONOME	IMP MPL 15	389	
(B) PETER BARDENS	1971	TRANSATLANTIC	UK	TRA	243
(B) WRITE MY NAME IN DUST	1971	VERVE MGM	US		3091
(C) VINTAGE 69	1976	TRANSATLANTIC	UK	TRASAM36	
(D) HEART TO HEART	1979	ARISTA		SPART1108	

LINDA LEWIS	V	(ABC	PETER GREEN	G	(C
VICTOR BROX	VLN V	(B	LIZA STRIKE	V	(BC
JUDY POWELL	V	(BC	ANITA POLLINGER	V	(BC
PETER VAN HOOKE	D	(D	STAN SCRIVENER	B	(D
MEL COLLINS	SAX	(D	CHRIS KARAN	PERC	(D

BARDOT

B40

RAY McRINER	V G	(A
CHRIS BRADFORD	V	(A
LAURIE ANDREW	V	(A
GEOFF WESTBY	K	(A
BOB YOUNG	HCA	(A

(A) ROCKIN IN RHYTHM	1978	RCA		PL 25121

PIP	G	(A	FRANK RICOTTI	D	(A
MIKE GILES	D	(A	DAVE MARKEE	B	(A

BAREFOOT JERRY

B41

WAYNE MOSS G V K B PERC		(ALL
MAC GAYDEN G V K		(A
JOHN HARRIS	K	(ABC
KEN BUTTREY	D	(ABC
RUSS HICKS STEEL G V HRS		(BCDEF
KENNY MALONE	D	(BC
BUDDY SPICHER	FDL	(BC
DAN FLICKENGER	K	(B
TOM KNOX	K	(B
BUDDY BLACKMON BANJ DOBRO		(F
DAVE DORAN	B V G	(C
FRED NEWELL V B BANJO		(CD
BARRY CHANCE	K B G	(EF
COSTO DAVIS	STRING	(E
CHARLIE McCOY HCA V FLT PNO		(DEF
JIM COLVARD	G B	(DE
BOBBY THOMPSON	B V G	(BCD
BUDDY SKIPPER	HRNS V PERC	(CD
JIM ISBELL		(D
MIKE McBRIDE B G PERC		(F

(A) SOUTHERN DELIGHT	1971	CAPITOL		EST	786
(B) BAREFOOT JERRY	1972	WB	US	BS	2641
(B) BAREFOOT JERRY	1972	WB	UK	K	46268
(C) WATCHIN' TV	1974	MONUMENT KZ32926		MC	6631
(C) WATCHIN' TV	1979	CRIMINAL	UK RI TAKE 2		
(D) YOU CANT GET OFF WITH YOUR SHOES ON 75		MONUMENT		MNT	80695
(D) YOU CANT GET OFF WITH YOUR SHOES ON 75		MONUMENT		MC	6631
(D) YOU CANT GET OFF WITH YOUR SHOES ON 75		MONUMENT		KZ	33381
(E) KEYS TO THE COUNTRY	1976	CBS			34252
(E) KEYS TO THE COUNTRY	1976	MONUMENT	US	MG	7605
(F) BAREFOOTIN'	1977	MONUMENT		MG	7610
(F) BAREFOOTIN'	1977	MONUMENT		MNT	82413
(AB)GROCERY	DBLE	1976	MONUMENT		KZ 33381
(AB)GROCERY	DBL	1976	MONUMENT		33909
(AB)GROCERY	DBL	1976	MONUMENT		MP 8603

SI EDWARDS	PERC	(CDEF	STEVE DAVIS	K	(E
JOHN MOSS	HRNS	(EF	WARREN HARTMAN	K	(DE
TERRY DEARMORE	B G	(DE	BILLY SWAN	V	(D

[33]

B41A

PATRICK BARNES

B41A
PATRICK BARNES   G   (A   (A) GUITAR   1980   STIFF   SEEZ 22
B41B
JESSE BARISH   B41B
JESSE BARISH   G V FLT(ALL   (A) JESSE BARISH   1979   RCA   US   1 2555
JAY DAVID   D V   (B   (B) MERCURY SHOES   1980   RCA   US   1 3420
AUSTIN DELONO   K V G   (B
DOUG KILLMER   B V   (B   JAMES RALSTON   G V   (B   JOHNNY FONTAYNE DECARO G V (B
JOHN HUG   G   (B   MARTY BALIN   V   (AB   GREG PHILLINGANES   SYN (B
STEVE FORMAN   PERC   (B   TOMMY VIG   PERC   (B   ALTO REED   SAX (B
B41C
MAX D BARNES   MAX D BARNES   B41C
MAX D BARNES   (A   (A) ROUGH AROUND THE EDGES   1980   OVATION   US   1749
B42
BRUCE MECHAN   G V   (A   BAROOGA BANDIT   B42
DAN O'CONNELL   B V   (A   (A) COME SOFTLY   1979   CAPITOL   EST 11924
MAT DE RAAD   K V   (A   FRANZ DE RAAD   D V   (A   DREW ABBOTT   G   (A
CHARLIE MARTIN   PERC V(A   TOM NEME   G   (A   ALTO REED   WIND (A
MICHAEL STOKES   PERC (A
B42A
DEAN NIMMER   D   (A   BAROQUES   B42A
RICK BIENIEWSKI   B   (A   (A) THE BAROQUES   1967   CHESS   US   1516
JAY BERKENHAGEN   G K V   (A   JACQUES HUTCHINSON   G V   (A
B42B
WALT BARR   G   (ABC   WALTER BARR   B42B
ROY BEAVERMAN   K   (ABC   (A) FIRST VISIT   1978   MUSE   US   5172
DOUG HODGES   B   (A   (B) EAST WINDS   1979   MUSE   US   5210
JACK TURCHIN   D   (A
BRIAN ROSE   D   (C   BILL KUHNE   B   (B   MARK LEON   D   (B
JULIE LONG   V   (B   BRYAN TILFORD   B   (C   SANFORD   PERC (C
B43   JACK LECOMPTE   PERC   (B
JOAN A VIDAL   K   (ABCDE   BARRABAS   B43
JOSE LUIS TEJADA   V HCA   (ABCDE   (A) POWER   1973   RCA   US   SPLI 2000
ENRIQUE MORALES   G V   (ABCDE   (B) BARRABAS   1975   ATLANTIC   K 50152
ERNESTO DUARTE WIND PERC V(ABCDE   (B) BARRABAS   1975   ATLANTIC   US   913 092
MIGUEL MORALES   G B V   (ABCDE   (B) BARRABAS   1975   ATCO   US   36110
DANIEL LOUIS   D   (DE   (C) RELEASE   1975   ATLANTIC   913 207
JOSE MARIA MOLL   D   (AB   (D) HEART OF THE CITY   1975   ATLANTIC   ATC 9590
MAXINE WATERS   V   (B   (D) HEART OF THE CITY   1975   ATCO   US   36 118
PATTI WATERS   V   (B   (D) HEART OF THE CITY   1975   ATLANTIC   913 039
JULIA WATERS   V   (B   (E) HI JACK   19   ATLANTIC   87912
HERNANOS MORALES   V   (B   (F) WATCH OUT   19   ATCO   US   36 136
B43A   (F) WATCH OUT   1976   ATLANTIC   UK   K50285
JOHNNY LA PORTE   G   (ABCDE   BARRELHOUSE   B43A
TINEKE SCHOEMAKER V   (ABCDE   (A) BARRELHOUSE   1974   MUNICH   BM 150205
BARRELHOUSE BAILEY PNO   D   (B) WHO'S MISSING   1975   MUNICH   BM 150213
BOB DROS   D   (ABCDE   (C) HARD TO COVER   1977   MUNICH   BM 150214
JAY WALKER   B   (A   (D) BEWARE   1979   ARIOLA   NL   200 895
HAN VAN DAM   PNO   (BC   (E) GOT TO GET TOGETHER   1981   ARIOLA   NL   203 461
JAN WILLEM SLIGTING B   (BC
JEFF REYNOLDS   TPT   (E   GUS LA PORTE   G   (CDE   HANS DULFER   SAX (DE
B43B   ROB VAN DONSELAAR   K   (E
                                       BARRELHOUSE BUCK   B43B
B43C   (A) BARRELHOUSE BUCK   19   FOLKWAYS   3554
                                       ELIZABETH BARRACLOUGH   B43C
ELIZABETH BARRACLOUGH G V (ALL   (A) ELIZABETH BARRACLOUGH   1978   BEARSVILLE UK K55520 US   6978
DAVE LEWIS   D   (A   (B) HI   1979   BEARSVILLE   US   6992
KENNY BUTTREY   D   (A
CHARLIE McCOY   HCA   (A   MALCOLM MORTIMORE   D   (A   MIKE LEECH   B   (A
IAN HAMPTON   B   (A   RUSS HICKS   G   (A   MICK HODGKINSON K B G(A
BOB BOUCHER   B   (A   TODD RUNDGREN   G   (A   AARON NESBIT   K   (B
PAUL BUTTERFIELD   HCA   (AB   LEROY HODGES   B   (B   GENE CHRISMAN   D   (B
WILLIE MITCHELL   PNO   (B   JACK HOLDER   SYN   (B   ANDREW LOVE   SAX (B
ERMA SHAW   V   (B   ELIZABETH SMITH   V   (B   ROMELL GREENLEE   V   (B
B43D
JEREMY GLUCK   V   (A   BARRACUDAS   B43D
ROBIN WILLS   G   (A   (A) DROP OUT WITH   1981   REGAL ZONOPHONE UK   ZON0103
NICK TURNER   D   (A   DAVID BUCKLEY   B   (A
B43E
NORMAN BARRATT   G V   (A   BARRATT BAND   B43E
TIM HATWELL   B V   (A   (A) PLAYING IN THE CITY   1981   CHAPEL LANE   UK   8005
RUSSELL CALDWELL   D   (A   DAVE MORRIS   K V   (A   WALTER BOLLARD   K   (A
B44
SYD BARRETT   G V   (AB   SYD BARRETT   B44
JERRY SHIRLEY   D   (B   (A) MADCAP LAUGHS   1970   HARVEST   SHVL 765
DAVID GILMOUR PROD B G   (AB   (A) MADCAP LAUGHS   1970   HARVEST   US   SABB11314
RICHARD WRIGHT PROD K   (A   (B) BARRETT   1970   HARVEST   SHSP 4007
ROGER WATERS   PROD B(A   (AB) MADCAP/BARRETT (DBL)   1974   HARVEST   SHDW 404
MALCOLM JONES   PROD   (A   (AB) MADCAP/BARRETT (DBL)   197   PATHE   FR C18450350/1
MIKE RATLEDGE   K   (A
WILLIE WILSON   D   (AB   ROBERT WYATT   D   (A   HUGH HOPPER   B   (A
B44A   VIC SEYWELL   HRN   (A
RONNIE BARRON   (A   RONNIE BARRON   B44A
                                    (A) REVEREND ETHER   1971   DECCA   US   DL 75303
B44B
                                       BARRINO BROTHERS   B44B
                                    (A) I SHALL NOT BE MOVED   19   INVICTUS   US   7308

DUKE D'MOND	V	(ALL	( ) CALL UP THE GROUPS	1964	COLUMBIA	UK	33SX 1648	
BARRON ANTHONY	V	(ALL	( ) BARRON KNIGHTS	1966	COLUMBIA	UK	SX 6007	
PEANUTS LANGFORD	G V	(ALL	( ) SCRIBED	1967	COLUMBIA	UK	SCX 6176	
BUTCH BAKER	G V	(ALL	( ) KNIGHTS OF LAUGHTER	1975	PENNYFARTHING		PAGS 533	
DAVE BALLINGER	D	(ALL	( ) ONE MANS MEAT	1973	PENNYFARTHING		PELS 536	
			( ) LIVE IN TROUBLE	1977	EPIC		EPC 82451	
			( ) NIGHT GALLERY	1978	EPIC		EPC 83221	
			( ) KNIGHTS OF LAUGHTER	1979	PICKWICK		SHM 981	
			( ) TEACH THE WORLD TO LAUGH	1979	CBS		83891	
			( ) JESTA GIGGLE	1980	epic	UK	84550	

B45A   NEIL BASHAN   B45A

NEIL BASHAN		(AB	(A) YOU GOT THE POWER	1978	ARIOLA		ARL 5005	
PETE VAN HOOKE	D	(AB	(B) HIGH ON A EASY FEELING	1979	ARIOLA		ARL 5026	
ROY BABINGTON	B	(B						
PAUL WESTWOOD	B	(B	RAY RUSSELL	G	(B	LYNTON NAIFF	K	(B
VICKY BROWN	V	(B	HELEN CHAPELL	V	(B	LIZA STRIKE	V	(B
GARY OSBORNE	V	(B						

B45B   JON BARTEL   B45B

JON BARTEL	K	(AB	(A) JON BARTEL	1968	PERCEPTION	US	
LOU STELLUTE	HRNS	(B	(B) THE JON BARTEL THING	1969	CAPITOL	US	274
LARRY O'BRIAN	STR	(B					
ABE BLASINGAME	PERC	(B					

B45C   MICHAEL BARTON & THE GROOVERS   B45C

MICHAEL BARTON	V K PERC	(A	(A) ST GEORGE IS CROSS RUPERT	1981	CERBENIS BITE	UK		
MICKEY FINN	PERC	(A						
ROB LUCAS	K G	(A	ROYSTON LUCAS	B V	(A	MONKEY	K V	(A
RICHARD JOHNS	SAX	(A	ROY BACKHOUSE	K	(A	VALERIE BURROWES	V	(A

B45D   GARY BARTZ   B45D

GARY BARTZ		(A	(A) BARTZ	1980	ARISTA	US	4263

B45E   ROBBIE BASHO   B45E

ROBBIE BASHO	G V	(ALL	(A) THE FALCONERS ARM 1	1967	TAKOMA	US	1017
KREHE RITTER	HRNS	(C	(B) THE FALCONERS ARM 2	1968	TAKOMA	US	1018
MOREEN LIBET	VLA	(C	(C) VENUS IN CANCER	1969	BLUE THUMB	US	10
VICTOR CHANCELLOR	G	(C	(D) SONG OF THE STALLION	1972	TAKOMA	US	1031
			(E) VISIONS OF THE COUNTRY	1979	WINDHAM HILL	US	1005
			(F) ART OF ACOUSTIC STEEL GUITAR	1980	WINDHAN HILL	US	1010

B45F   BASEMENT FIVE   B45F

DENNIS MORRIS		(A	(A) 1965/80	1980 ISLAND UK ILPS9641 ANTILLES US7082
RICHARD DUDANSKI		(A		
J R		(A		
LEO		(A		

B46   MICHAEL BASS   B46

MICHAEL BASS PERC K V TROM	(A	(A) PARCHESI PIE	1978	RANDOM RADAR	RRR 3 14	
WITH						
DAVE NEWHOUSE WIND K V	(A	GLENN WISER B G V	(A			

B47   BASTARD   B47

CARLOS BASTARDOS	V B	(AB	(A) BACK TO NATURE	1977	NOVA		6 23288
KEITH KOSSOFF	G	(AB	(B) TEARING NIGHTS	1978	NOVA		6 23619
THEO TREMOLO	G	(AB	(C) LIVE & ALIVE	1980	LAVA	TCH	80535
TOTO PETTICOATO	D	(AB					
ULI MEIBER	G	(B	KARL ROTHERT	B	(B		

B47A   BATDORF & RODNEY   B47A

MARK RODNEY	G V K	(ALL	(A) OFF THE SHELF	1971	WEA		US	SD	8298	
JOHN BATDORF	G V K	(ALL	(B) BATDORF & RODNEY	1972	ASYLUM				5056	
RUSS KUNKEL	D	(C	(C) LIFE IS YOU	1975	ARISTA US 4041 UK	ARTY 112				
SCOTT EDWARDS	B	(C								
RICK CARLOS	B	(C	DEAN PARKS	G	(C	GARY COLEMAN	PERC	(C	
TOM HENSLEY	K	(C	GINGER BLAKE	V	(C	MAXINE WILLARD	V	(C	
JULIA TILLMAN	V	(C	MARTY GWINN	V	(C	JOE SIDORE	V	(C	
TOM SELLERS	K	(C	STRINGS		(C	RICK CARLOS	B	(B	
JOHN MAUCERI	D	(B	JIM HASKELL	K	(B	CHRIS ETHRIDGE	B	(A	
JOHN BARBATA	D	(A	BARRY BECKETT	K	(B	ROGER HAWKINS	D	(A	
DAVID HOOD	B	(A							

B47B   MIKE BATT   B47B

MIKE BATT		(	( ) SCHIZOPHONIA	1977	EPIC		EPC 82001		
FRANK RICOTTI	PERC	(C	(B) TAROT SUITE	1979	EPIC		EPC 86099		
FRANK McDONALD	B	(C	(C) WAVES	1980	EPIC		EPC 84617		
CLEM CATTINI	D	(B	(D) 6 DAYS IN BERLIN	1981	EPIC		85149		
CHRIS SPEDDING	G	(B							
RAY COOPER	PERC	(B	TERRY COX	D	(B	RICK KEMP	B	(B
ROGER CHAPMAN	V	(B	RAY RUSSELL	G	(C	EDDIE COWARD	CONG	(C
B J COLE	STEEL	(BC	MEL COLLINS	SAX	(BC	TREVOR MORAIS	D	(CB
JIM CREGAN	G	(BC	NIGEL JENKINS	G	(C	AMSTERDAM CHAMBER ORCH		(C
HAROLD FISHER	D	(B	FRANK McDONALD	B	(B	TONY CARR	PERC	(B
ROY MORGAN	PERC	(B	MARTIN KERSHAW	G	(B	RICKY HITCHCOCK	G	(B
RORY GALLAGHER	G	(B	RAY COOPER	PERC	(B	LES THATCHER	G	(B
COLIN BLUNSTONE	V	(B	TONY McPHEE	G	(B	CHRIS KARAN	PERC	(B

B47C   DAVID BATTEAU   B47C

DAVID BATTEAU	V G	(A	(A) HAPPY IN HOLLYWOOD	1976	A&M		AMLH64576		
WITH									
WILLIE WEEKS	B	(A	KENNY ALTMAN	B	(A	JEFF PORCARO	D	(A
MILT HOLLAND	PERC	(A	DAVID PAICH	K	(A	ROY DAVIES	K	(A
DAVID SPINOZZA	G	(A	ROBERT AHWAI	G	(A	STEVE GREGORY	FLT	(A
MICHAEL BAILEY	TPT	(A	MARTIN DROVER	TPT	(A	CHRIS MERCER	SAX	(A
DENIECE WILLIAMS	V	(A	JULIA TILLMAN	V	(A	MAXINE WILLARD	V	(A
JOAN SLIWIN	V	(A							

STIV BATORS

STIV BATORS	V	(A
FRANK SECICH	B V	(A
GEORGIE HAMSON	G V	(A
THOM WILSON	PROD	(A

(A) DISCONNECTED   1980 BOMP   BLP 4015

DAVID QUINTON   D   (A   GREG SHAW   PROD (A

BATTEAUX

DAVID BATTEAU	G V	(A
ROBIN BATTEAU	VLN G V	(A
PETER FREIBERGER	B	(A
ROBIN LANE	V	(A
JOHN GUERIN	D	(A
SHELBY FLINT	V	(A

(A) BATTEAUX   1974 CBS   US   32063

ANDY NEWMARK	D	(A	MILT HOLLAND	PERC (A
SALLY STEVENS	V	(A	DOUG McCLARAN	K	(A
TOM SCOTT	WIND	(A	JACKIE WARD	V	(A

BATTI MAMZELLE

PETER DUPREY	B V	(A
WINSTON DELANDRO	G K	(A
RICHARD BAILEY	D V	(A
RUSSELL VALDEZ	PERC	(A

(A) I SEE THE LIGHT   1974 CUBE HI FLY 17   2326 037

| MIGUEL BARRADAS | PERC | (A | RALPH RICHARDSON | PERC (A |
| FRANK INCE | CONGA | (A | JIMMY CHAMBERS | CONGAS(A |

BATTERED ORNAMENTS

NISAR AHMED KHAN	FLT V	(A
CHRIS SPEDING	G K V	(A
ROGER POTTER	B V	(A

(A) MANTLE PIECE   1969 HARVEST   UK SHVL 758

| PETE BAILEY | PERC V | (A | ROB TAIT | D V | (A |

SKIP BATTIN

SKIP BATTIN	B V	(AB
CLARENCE WHITE	G	(A
BILLY MUNDI	D	(A
JOHN GUERIN	D	(A
SNEAKY PETE KLEINOW	STEEL	(B
GAIL KANTOR	V	(B
NADRA THOMAS	V	(B

(A) SKIP   1973 SIGNPOST UK SG4255 US 8408
(B) NAVIGATOR   1981 APPALOOSA IT 014

ROGER McGUINN	G V	(A	SPANKY McFARLANE	V	(A
DAVID HINES	G	(B	GREGG HARRIS	G	(B
JACK BRUNO	D	(B	BRIAN ELLIOT	PNO	(B
BRYAN POLAND	PERC	(B

LUCIO BATTISTI

LUCIO BATTISTI	V	(ALL
RAY PARKER	G	(D
DENNIS BUDIMIR	G	(D
DANNY FERGUSON	G	(D
MIKE MELVOIN	K	(D
SCOTTY EDWARDS	B	(D
HAL BLAINE	D	(D

(A) IL MIO CANTO LIBERO   1973 COLUMBIA   SCX 6540
(B) IL NOSTRO CARO ANGELO   1975 VOGUE   LDM 30254
(C) ANIMA LATINA   1975 VOGUE   LDM 30282
(D) IMAGES   1978 RCA   PL 31889

| JIM HUGHART | B | (D | ED GREENE | D | (D |
| MICHAEL BODDICKER | K | (D |

BATTLEFIELD BAND

ALAN REID	G V K SYN	(ALL
BRIAN McNEILL	VLN V	(ALL
RICKY SCAGGS	WIND	(AC
JAMIE McMEMEMY	G MAN V	(BD
JOHN GAHAGAN	CONC	(B
JENNY CLARK	G V	(E
DUNCAN McGILLIVRAY	WIND G V	(EFG
ALEC DUDGEON	D	(E
PAT KILBRIDE	G V	(D
SYLVIA BARNES	G V	(F

(A) BATTLEFIELD BAND   1976 ARFOLK   FR 349
(B) THE BATTLEFIELD   1977 TOPIC   UK 12TS313
(C) BATTLEFIELD BAND 2   1977 ARFOLK   FR 358
(D) AT THE FRONT   1978 TOPIC   UK 12TS381
(E) STAND EASY   1979 TOPIC   UK 12TS404
(F) PREVIEW   (EP) 1980 TEMPLE   UK ETP 10
(G) HOME IS WHERE THE VAN IS   1980 TEMPLE   UK TP 005
(G) HOME IS WHERE THE VAN IS   1981 FLYING FISH US   250

GED FOLEY   G MAND V WIND(G

BAUHAUS

KEVIN HASKINS	D	(ABC
DAVID JAY	B	(ABC
PETER MURPHY	V	(ABC
DANIEL ASH	G	(ABc

(A) IN THE FLAT FIELD   1980 4AD   UK CAD 13
(B) MASK   1981 BEGGARS BANQUET UK BEGA 29
(C) THE SKY'S GONE OUT   1982 BEGGARS BANQUET UK BEGA 45
(C+) PRESS THE EJECT(FREE WITH C)   1982 BEGGARS BANQUET UK BEGA 38

PETER BAUMANN

PETER BAUMANN	K	(AB
W THIERFELD	D	(B
B JOBSKI	HRNS	(B
CARSTEN BOHN	K D	(C
MIKE DAWE	D	(C
LINDSAY KAY BRYNAN	V	(C

(A) ROMANCE 76   1977 VIRGIN   UK   2069
(B) TRANS HARMONIC NIGHTS   1979 VIRGIN   2124
(C) REPEAT REPEAT   1981 VIRGIN   2214

RITCHIE FLIEGLER   G   (C   JOHN TROPEA   G   (A

BAUTISTA

ROLAND BAUTISTA	G V	(A
CHIP STEEN	PERC	(A
BOBBY LYLE	K SYN	(A
DONALD BECK	B	(A

(A) BAUTISTA   1977 ABC   US   1003

STEVE GUTIERREZ   D   (A   VICTOR FELDMAN   VIBES(A

BAXTER

STEVE BELGRADE	G V	(A
DOUG ARIOLI	G V	(A
LAWRENCE DI NATALE	D	(A

(A) BAXTER   1973 PARAMOUNT   US   6050

STEVEN KIRSHENBAUM K SYN   (A   EDWIN PERRY   B V   (A

CAROL BAYER SAGER

CAROL BAYER SAGER	V	(ALL
LEE SKLAR	B	(ABC
JOHNNY VASTANO	G V	(A
ARTIE BUTLER	K	(A

(A) CAROL BAYER SAGER   1977 ELEKTRA US 7E1100   UK K52059
(B) TOO   1978 ELEKTRA US 6E 151   UK K52093
(C) SOMETIMES LATE AT NIGHT   1981 EPIC   UK 85110

PETER ALLEN	V K	(A	LANCE QUINN	G	(A	ALAN ESTES	PERC (A	BRENDA RUSSELL	V	(A
GENE PAGE	STR	(A	EMORY GORDY	B	(A	PAUL BUCKMASTER	SYN	(A	WILL LEE	B	(A
JERRY FRIEDMAN	G	(A	MADELINE KOHN	V	(A	HUGH McCRACKEN	G	(A	ANDY NEWMARK	D	(A
NINO TEMPO	SAX	(B	ED GREENE	D	(B	DAVID FOSTER	K STR(BC	STEVE FORMAN	PERC(B
BILL CHAMPLIN	V	(B	REINNE PRESS	B	(BC	ALICE COOPER	V	(B	IRA NEWBORN	G	(B
JEFF PORCARO	D	(C	BURT BACHARACH	PNO	(C	GEORGE YOUNG	SAX	(C	STEVE GEORGE	V	(C
MICHAEL JACKSON	V	(C	FRANN GOLDE	V	(C	JERRY HEY	HRNS	(C	FRED TACKETT	G	(C
DENNIS ST JOHN	D	(C	RICHARD BENNETT	G	(C	THOM HENSLEY	PNO	(C	KING ERRISSON	PERC(C
WARREN LUENING	HRNS	(C	RAY GRAYDEN	G	(BC	MELISSA MANCHESTER	K V	(ABC	LEE RITENOUR	G	(ABC
NICKY HOPKINS	K	(A	RUSS KUNKEL	D	(AB	BOB CRANSHAW	B	(A	ALAN SCHWARTZBERG	D(A
ABIGAIL HANESS	V	(A	TONY ORLANDO	V	(A	MARVIN HAMLISCH	G STR(ABC	JIM KELTNER	D	(AC
BRUCE ROBERTS	V PNO(ABC	AL GORGONI	G	(A	ROY MARKOWITZ	D	(A	THOM COTELLA	G	(AB
GARNETT BROWN	TROM	(A	BETTE MIDLER	V	(A	DON COSTA	STR	(B	DAVID HUNGATE	B	(B
									(CONTINUED)

CAROL BAYER SAGER

STEVE LUKATHER	G	(BC	MICHAEL McDONALD	V	(B	JIM GORDON	D	(B	STEVE PORCARO	SYN (B
CRAIG DOERGE	K	(B	DAVID CAMPBELL	STR	(B	MICHAEL LANG	K	(C	ED WALSH	SYN(C
RICHARD PAGE	V	(C	PAUL JACKSON	G	(C	PAULINHO DACOSTA	PERC	(C	JOANN HARRIS	V (C
TIM MAY	G	(C	IAN UNDERWOOD	SYN	(C	NEIL DIAMOND	G	(C	DOUG RHONE	G (C
ALAN LINDGREN	SYN	(C	VINCE CHARLES	PERC	(C	VENNETTE GLOUD	V	(C	JENNIFER SLOAN	V (B
CARMEN TWILLIE	V	(B	RICHIE ZITO	G	(B	DAVID LASLEY	V	(B	LUTHER VANDROSS	V (B
RICHARD DAVID	B	(B	JIM HUGHART	B	(B	SKIP REDWINE	K	(B	MICHAEL RUBINI	G (B

BAZAAR

(A) ORIENTAL WIND   1981 SONET   UK SNTF 864

BE BOP DELUXE

BILL NELSON	G V	(ALL	(A) AXE VICTIM	1974 HARVEST US SM 11689 UK SHVL 813		
ROBERT BRYAN	B	(AH	(B) FUTURAMA	1975 HARVEXT US ST 11432 UK SHSP4045		
NICHOLAS DEW	D	(AH	(C) SUNBURST FINISH	1976 HARVEST US ST 11478 UK SHSP4053		
IAN PARKIN	G	(AH	(D) MODERN MUSIC	1976 HARVEST US ST 11575 UK SHSP4058		
RICHARD BROWN	K	(	(E) HOT VALVES (EP)	1976 HARVEST	UK HAR 5117	
MILTON REAME JAMES K		(	(F) LIVE IN THE AIR AGE (DBL)	1977 HARVEST US 11666 UK SHVL 816		
PAUL JEFFREYS	B	(	(G) DRASTIC PLASTIC	1978 HARVEST FR 06598	UK SHSP4091	
SIMON FOX	D	(BCDEFGH	(H) THE BEST OF & THE REST (DBL)	1978 HARVEST	UK SHDW 410	
CHARLIE TUMAHAI	B	(BCDEFGH				
ANDREW CLARK	K	(CDEFGH	NICK CLARK	G	(	JENNY HAAN V (A

BRIAN WILSON	(	MIKE LOVE	(	AL JARDINE	G (	DENNIS WILSON	(
BRUCE JOHNSTON	(	BLONDI CHAPMAN	(	CARL WILSON	(	RICK FATAAR	D (
JAMES GUERCIO	(	DAVID MATTS	(	GLEN CAMPBELL	(		

WITH

TONI TENNILLE	V	MARILYN WILSON	V	STEVE DOUGLAS	SAX (	JACK NIMITZ	SAX(
MIKE ALTSCHUL	SAX (	DENNIS DREITH	SAX (	JOHN J KELSO	SAX (	JAY MIGLIORI	SAX(
PLAS JOHNSON	SAX (	JULES JACOBS	CLAR (	CAROL LEE MILLER A'HARP (		GENE ESTES	PERC (
JULIUS WECHTER	PERC (	HAL BLAINE	D (	DENNIS DRAGON	D (	RON ALTBACH	PNO(
ED CARTER	G (	BILLY HINSCHE	G (	BEN BENAY	G (	JERRY COLE	G (
TOMMY TEDESCO	G (	LYLE RITZ	B (	TIM DRUMMOND	B (	RAY POLMAN	B (
JAMES HUGHART	B (	BOBBY SHEW	TPT (	GARY GRIFFIN	K (	MIKE KOWALSKI	D (
CHRIS MIDDAUGH	STEEL(	MICHAEL ANDREAS	HRNS (	CHARLES LLOYD	HRNS (	LANCE BUTLER	HRNS(
JOHN FOSS	HRNS(	VICTOR FELDMAN	PERC (	STEVE FORMAN	PERC (	MIKE MAROS	K (
BOB ESTY	SYN (	WAH WAH WATSON	G (	JOE CHEANAY	B (	ED CARTER	G B (
CARLOS FIGUEORA	D (	JIM GUERICO	B (	STERLING SMITH	K (	PHIL SHENDALE	(
JOEL PERSKIN	SAX (	GARY MALLABER	D (	RITCHIE ZITO	G (	MIKE BAIRD	D (
JIMMY LYONS	G (						

SURFIN SAFARI	1962 CAPITOL	T1808	SO TOUGH	19	BROTHER	2090
SURFIN SAFARI	1962 CAPITOL	SY 4572	HOLLAND	1973 REPRISE	K 54008	
SURFIN SAFARI	1981 GREENLIGHT UK	2014	HOLLAND	1973 BROTHER	2118	
SURFIN U S A	1963 CAPITOL	ST 1890	SUNFLOWER/SURFS UP (DBL)	1973 EMI	5C184502156	
SURFER GIRL	1963 CAPITOL	ST 1981	IN CONCERT	1973 REPRISE	84001	
SURFER GIRL	19 PICKWICK	SPC3351	ENDLESS SUMMER	1974 CAPITOL	EAST11307	
GREAT CONCERT	19 PICKWICK	SPC 3309	ENDLESS SUMMER	1981 MFP	50528	
LITTLE DEUCE COUPE	1963 CAPITOL	ST 1998	FRIENDS /SMILEY SMILE DBL	1974 CAPITOL	2MS 2167	
LITTLE DEUCE COUPE	1981 GREENLIGHT UK	2025	VERY BEST OF 63-69	1974 ELECTROLA IC15281482		
SHUT DOWN VOL 2	1964 CAPITOL	ST 2027	STARS OF THE SIXTIES	1974 BOVEMA	5C05081596	
ALL SUMMER LONG	1964 CAPITOL	ST 2110	DO YOU WANNA DANCE	1975 EMI	140502545	
ALL SUMMER LONG	1973 MFP	50065	DO YOU WANNA DANCE	1971 MFP	5235	
CHRISTMAS ALBUM	1964 CAPITOL	ST 2164	WILD HONEY/20 20 (DBL)	1975 REPRISE US 2MS 2166		
CHRISTMAS ALBUM	1977 CAPITOL	CAP1014	WILD HONEY/FRIENDS	1975 CAPITOL	ESTSP 14	
BEACH BOYS CONCERT	1964 CAPITOL	ST 2198	OLDIES	1975 EMI	048 0776	
BEACH BOYS TODAY	1965 CAPITOL	ST 2269	GOOD VIBRATIONS BEST OF	19 REPRISE	K 2280	
SUMMER DAYS SUMMER NIGHTS	1965 CAPITOL	ST 2354	GOOD VIBRATIONS	1975 REPRISE	K 52223	
SUMMER DAYS SUMMER NIGHTS	1978 CAPITOL	CAPS 1023	GOOD VIBRATIONS	1975 REPRISE	6484	
BEACH BOYS PARTY	1965 CAPITOL	ST 2398	GOOD VIBRATIONS(BEST OF)	1975 BROTHER	2223	
BEACH BOYS PARTY	1965 CAPITOL	MAS 2398	GOOD VIBRATIONS	197 M F P	50234	
PET SOUNDS	1966 CAPITOL	ST 2458	GOOD VIBRATIONS	197 PICKWICK	SPC3769	
PET SOUNDS	1966 CAPITOL	MS 2197	SPIRIT OF AMERICA DBL	1975 CAPITOL	SVBB11384	
PET SOUNDS	19 BROTHER US	2083	SPIRIT OF AMERICA DBL	1975 CAPITOL	VMP1007	
PET SOUNDS	1981 GREENLIGHT UK	2002	15 BIG ONES	1976 REPRISE	2251	
BEST OF THE BEACH BOYS	1966 CAPITOL	ST 2545	15 BIG ONES	1976 REPRISE	K 54079	
BEST OF THE BEACH BOYS	1966 CAPITOL	ST20856	STACK O TRACKS	1976 CAPITOL	DKAD2893	
SMILEY SMILE	1967 CAPITOL	ST 9001	STACK O TRACKS	1977 CAPITOL	EST24009	
SMILEY SMILE (GERM)	1967 CAPITOL	SMK 74330	20 GOLDEN GREATS	1977 CAPITOL	EMTV1	
SMILEY SMILE	19 BROTHER	9001	LOVE YOU	1977 REPRISE	K 54087	
BEST OF VOL 2	1967 CAPITOL	ST 2706	LOVE YOU	1977 REPRISE	MSK 2258	
BEST OF VOL 2	1967 CAPITOL	ST20956	M I U	1978 REPRISE	MSK 2268	
WILD HONEY	1968 CAPITOL	ST 2859	M I U	1978 REPRISE	K 54102	
FRIENDS	1968 CAPITOL	ST 2895	40 GREAT HITS (DBL)	19 CAPITOL	CAPITOL 1/2	
FRIENDS (GERM)	1968 CAPITOL	SMK 74456	30 GREATEST HITS'TRIPLE)	19 CAPITOL	2813	
CALIFORNIA GIRLS (FRENCH)	19 CAPITOL	T 20740	BEACH BOYS	19 PICKWICK US SPC3221		
BEST OF VOL 3	1968 CAPITOL	ST 2945	FUN FUN FUN (DBL)	19 CAPITOL	SF702/703	
BEST OF VOL 3	1968 CAPITOL	ST21142	FUN FUN FUN (DBL)	19 CAPITOL US STB 701		
BEACH BOYS	1970 M F P	MFP 1382	GIRLS	19 CAPITOL GER 05480 627		
20/20	1969 CAPITOL	EST 133	L A LIGHT ALBUM	1979 CARIBOU	UK 86081	
CLOSE UP	1969 CAPITOL	EST 253	GIRLS ON THE BEACH	19 CAPITOL	CAPS 1037	
LONDON 69	1969 CAPITOL	ST 11584	ALL SUMMER LONG CALIFORNIS	19 CAPITOL	US 500	
SUNFLOWER	1970 REPRISE	6382	1962/65 (DBL)	1980 CAPITOL	82292	
SUNFLOWER	1970 STATESIDE	SSLA 8251	1966/69 (DBL)	1980 CAPITOL	82294	
SUNFLOWER	1980 CARIBOU UK RI 31773		KEEP THE SUMMER ALIVE	1980 CARIBOU	UK 86109	
BUG IN	1970 STARLINE	SRS 5014	KEEP THE SUMMER ALIVE	1980 CARIBOU	US 36283	
GREATEST HITS	1970 CAPITOL	ST21628	(EPs)			
SURFS UP	1971 REPRISE	6453	SURFIN USA	196 CAPITOL	20540	
SURFS UP	1971 STATESIDE	SSL10313	FUN FUN FUN	196 CAPITOL	20603	
SURFS UP	1980 EMBASSY	UK 31774	4 BY THE BEACH BOYS	196 CAPITOL	1/ 5267	
BEACH BOYS	1971 STARLINE	SRS 5074	SAIL ON SAILOR	1977 REPRISE	k14481	
LIVE IN LONDON	1972 CAPITOL	ST21715				
LIVE IN LONDON	1977 M F P	50345				
SO TOUGH	1972 REPRISE	K 44184				
SO TOUGH	1972 REPRISE	2083				

			BEACON STREET UNION					B57
PAUL TARTACHNY	G V	(AB	(A) EYES OF THE BEACON STREET UNION	1968	MGM UK 8069	US	SE	4517
WAYNE ULAKY	B V	(AB	(B) CLOWN DIED IN MARVIN GARDENS	1968	MGM	US	SE	4568
JOHN WRIGHT	V PERC	(AB						
RICHARD WEISBURG	D	(AB	ROBERT RHODES	K WIND	(AB			

RICHARD T BEAR

								B57A
RICHARD T BEAR	K	(A	(A) RED HOT & BLUE	1979	RCA		PL	12927
ALLAN SCHWARZBERG	D PERC	(A	(B) BEAR	1980	RCA			13313
LES DUDEK	G	(A						
ELLIOTT RANDALL	G	(A						
STEVE GELFAND	B	(A	MIKE FINNIGAN	K	(A	NEIL JASON	B	(A
GEORGE GOMEZ	G	(A	PAUL SCHAEFFER	K	(A	GORDON GRODY	V	(A
JOHN BARRANCO	V	(A	BOB GURLAND	TPT	(A	ANNIE SUTTON	V	(A
DIVA GRAY	V	(A	SHARON LEE WILLIAMS	V	(A	ZULEMA CUSSEAUX	V	(A
TRACY RICHARDSON	V	(A	BILLY SQUIER	G	(A	KATHY INGRAHAM	V	(A
CHRISTINE FAITH	V	(A	DAVE WOODS	TPT	(A	JACK ZAZA	ACC	(A
RANDY BRECKER	HRNS	(A	MICHAEL BRECKER	HRNS	(A	GEORGE YOUNG	HRNS	(A
RON CUBER	HRNS	(A	TONY PRICE	HRNS	(A	TOM MALONE	HRNS	(A

BEADGAME

					B57B
(A) WELCOME	19	AVCO	US	33009	

BEANS

					B57C
(A) BEANS	1972	AVALANCHE	US	9200	

BEAR

							B57D
ARTIE TRAUM	G V	(A	(A) BEAR	1968	VERVE	US	3059
ERIC KAZ	K V	(A					
DARIUS DAVENPORT	D	(A					

BEAR MOUNTAIN

							B57E
FRANK FORD	D	(A	(A) ONE MORE DAY	19	PREDATOR	US	1001
BILL KEISLER	B	(A					
CAM EMPENS	K V	(A	BILL RICHARDSON	G V	(A		

BEARFOOT

							B57F
DWAYNE FORD FLT K G V		(ABC	(A) BEARFOOT	1973	EPIC	US	32146
TERRY DANKE	B V	(AB	(B) FRIENDS	1973	EPIC	CAN	32653
JIM ATKINSON	G V	(ABC	(C) PASSING TIME	1975	EPIC	CAN	33530
HUGH BROCKIE	G BAN	(ABC					
GARY HOLT	B	(C	DANNY McBRIDE	G	(C	BRIAN HILTEN	D	(A
KENNY MALONE	D	(C	PRAKASH JOHN	B	(C	CHRIS VICKERY	B	(C
BRUCE PENNYCOOK	HRNS	(C	DAVE McMURDOW	HRNS	(C	MALCOLM TOMLINSON	PERC	(C
WHITEY GLAN	D	(C	LARRY LONDON	PERC	(C			

BEARS

							B58
GEORGE GIL	G	(	(A) BEARS	1981	OK	UK	3001
RON WEST	B						
CALLY	D		KRIS KERSHAW	SAX			

THE BEAST

							B58A
DAVID RAINES	V	(AB	(A) PRELUDE FOR TODAY	1969	COTILLION	US	9012
ROBERT YEAZEL	G V	(AB	(B) BEAST	1970	EVOLUTION	US	2017
GERRY FIKE	K	(AB					
LARRY FERRIS	D	(AB	MICHAEL KERNS	WIND	(AB	KEN PASSARELLI	B HCA	(A
DOMINICK TODERO	TPT	(A	ROBERT BRYANT	B	(B			

BEAT

							B58B
DAVE WAKELING	G	(ABC	(A) I JUST CANT STOP IT	1980	BEAT UK 001	SIRE US	6091
ANDY COX	G	(AB	(B) WHA'APPEN ??	1981	GO FEET UK BEET 3		
RANKIN ROGER	V	(AB					
SAXA	SAX	(AB	DAVID STEELE	B	(A	DAVID WRIGHT	K	(A
EVERETT MARTIN	D	(A	BOB SARGEANT	PROD	(A	BUCK CHARLERY	V	(

BEATPUMP

					B58C
FIVE MONTH PLAN	1980	SLOWLORRIES	UK	SLOW 1	

THE BEATLES

JOHN LENNON	G V K	(ALL				
PAUL McCARTNEY	B G K	V(ALL				
GEORGE HARRISON	G V	(ALL				
RINGO STARR	D V	(ALL				
WITH						
PETE BEST	D		PATTI BOYD	V		
STUART SUTCLIFFE	G		GARY LEEDS	V	RONNIE SCOTT	SAX
KLAUS VOORMANN	B		JANE ASHER	V	BILL JACKMAN	SAX
ERIC CLAPTON	G		KEITH MOON	V	BILL POVEY	SAX
GEORGE MARTIN	K		GRAHAM NASH	V	HARRY KLEIN	SAX
BILLY PRESTON	K		SOUNDS INC		DAVID JONES	TPT
TONY SHERIDAN	G V		LES CONDON	HRN	NEIL ASPINAL	V
ANDY WHITE	D		IAN HAMER	HRN	GEOFF EMERICK	V
MICK JAGGER	V		EDDIE THORNTON	HRN	FRANK CLARKE	B
KEITH RICHARD	V		ALAN BRANSCOMBE	SAX	ANIL BHAGWAT	V
YOKO ONO	V		PETER COE	SAX	PHIL JONES	TPT
MARIANNE FAITHFUL	V		BLACK DYKE MILLS BAND		NICKY HOPKINS	K
					JESSIE ROBINS	V
					BRIAN JONES	SAX

EPs			
BEATLES HITS	1963	PARLOPHONE	GEP 8880
TWIST & SHOUT	1963	PARLOPHONE	GEP 8882
BEATLES NO 1	1963	PARLOPHONE	GEP 8883
ALL MY LOVIN'	1964	PARLOPHONE	GEP 8891
LONG TALL SALLY	1964	PARLOPHONE	GEP 8913
HARD DAYS NIGHT	1964	PARLOPHONE	GEP 8920
HARD DAYS NIGHT 2	1964	PARLOPHONE	GEP 8924
BEATLES FOR SALE	1965	PARLOPHONE	GEP 8931
BEATLES FOR SALE 2	1965	PARLOPHONE	GEP 8938
MILLION SELLERS	1965	PARLOPHONE	GEP 8946
YESTERDAY	1965	PARLOPHONE	GEP 8948
NOWHERE MAN	1966	PARLOPHONE	GEP 8952
MAGICAL MYSTERY TOUR	1967	PARLOPHONE	SMMT 1
MY BONNIE	19	POLYDOR	H 21 610

LPs

THE BEATLES & TONY SHERIDAN		1962	CONTOUR		CN	2007
THE EARLY YEARS		1962	CONTOUR			2870111
THE BEATLES FIRST		19	POLYDOR			24001
IN THE BEGINNING		19	POLYDOR		2664	107
THIS IS WHERE IT STARTED		19				
PLEASE PLEASE ME	MONO	1963	PARLOPHONE	UK	PMC	1202
"	MONO	1963	PARLOPHONE	UK	PCS	3042
"		1963	EMI	EURO		04219
"		1966	ODEON	JAP		7548
"		1969	APPLE	JAP		AP8675
"		1976	APPLE	JAP		80550
WITH THE BEATLES	MONO	1963	PARLOPHONE	UK	PMC	1206
"	STEREO	1963	PARLOPHONE	UK	PCS	3045
"		196	EMI	EURO		04181
"		1966	ODEON	JAP		7549
"		1969	APPLE	JAP	AP	8678
"		1976	APPLE	JAP		80551
INTRODUCING THE BEATLES		1964	VEE JAY	US		SR1062
NUMBER 2		1964	ODEON	JAP		7058
"		1967	ODEON	JAP		8027
"		1970	APPLE	JAP		8027
"		1976	APPLE	JAP		70101
THE BEATLES		1964	MGM	US		4215
"		1964	ODEON	JAP		7041
"		1967	ODEON	JAP		8026
"		1970	APPLE	JAP		8026
"		1976	APPLE	JAP		70100
MEET THE BEATLES		1964	CAPITOL	US		2047
"		1970	APPLE	JAP	AP	80011
"		1975	APPLE	JAP		80562
NUMBER 5		1964	ODEON	JAP		7103
"		1967	ODEON	JAP		8028
"		1970	APPLE	JAP		8028
"		1976	APPLE	JAP		70102
BEATLES SECOND		1964	CAPITOL	US		2080
"		1970	APPLE	JAP		AP80012
"		1976	APPLE	JAP		80563
SOMETHING NEW		1964	CAPITOL	US		2108
"		19	EMI	EURO		04600
"		1970	APPLE	JAP		80033
"		1976	APPLE	JAP		80564
AINT SHE SWEET		1964		US		
BEATLES STORY		1964	CAPITOL	US		2222
"		1966	ODEON	JAP		7553
"		1969	APPLE	JAP		8676/7
"		1976	APPLE	JAP		77007/8
HARD DAYS NIGHT	MONO	1964	PARLOPHONE	UK	PMC	1230
"	STEREO	1964	PARLOPHONE	UK	PCS	3058
"		1964	EMI	EURO		04145
"		1964	ODEON	JAP		7123
"		1967	ODEON	JAP		8147
"		1970	APPLE	JAP		AP8147
"		1976	APPLE	JAP		80552
"		1964	U A	US	3366	64
BEATLES FOR SALE	MONO	1964	PARLOPHONE	UK	PMC	1240
"	STEREO	1964	PARLOPHONE	UK	PCS	3062
"		1964	EMI	EURO		04200
"		1965	ODEON	JAP		7179
"		1968	ODEON	JAP		8442
"		1976	APPLE	JAP		80553
BEATLES 65		1965	CAPITOL	US		2228
"		1965	EMI	EURO		04201
EARLY BEATLES		1965	CAPITOL	US		2309
"		1970	APPLE	JAP		80034
"		1976	APPLE	JAP		80565
BEATLES VI		1965	CAPITOL	US		2358
"		1970	APPLE	JAP		80035
"		1976	APPLE	JAP		80566
HELP		1965	PARLOPHONE	UK	PMC	1255
"	STEREO	1965	PARLOPHONE	UK	PCS	3071
"		1965	EMI	EURO		04257
"		1965	ODEON	JAP		7387
"		1967	ODEON	JAP		8151
"		1970	APPLE	JAP		8151
"		1970	APPLE	JAP		80060
"		1965	CAPITOL	US		2386
"		1976	APPLE	JAP		80567
RUBBER SOUL	MONO	1966	PARLOPHONE	UK	PMC	1267
"	STEREO	1966	PARLOPHOONE	UK	PCS	3075
"		1966	CAPITOL	US		2442
"		1966	EMI	EURO		04115
"		1966	ODEON	JAP		7450
"		1967	ODEON	JAP		8156
"		1970	APPLE	JAP		8156
"		1976	APPLE	JAP		80555
YESTERDAY & TODAY		1966	CAPITOL	US		2553
"		1970	APPLE	JAP		80061
"						

Title		Year	Label	Country		Number
REVOLVER		1966	PARLOPHONE	UK	PCS	7009
"		1966	CAPITOL	US		2576
"		1966	EMI	EURO		04097
"		1966	ODEON	JAP		7600
"		1968	ODEON	JAP		8443
"		1969	APPLE	JAP		8443
"		1976	APPLE	JAP		80556
COLLECTION OF OLDIES		1967	PARLOPHONE	UK	PCS	7016
"		1967	ODEON	JAP		8016
"		1970	APPLE	JAP		8016
"		1976	APPLE	JAP		80557
SGT PEPPER		1967	PARLOPHONE	UK	PCS	7027
"		1967	CAPITOL	US		2653
"		1967	EMI	EURO		04177
"		1967	ODEON	JAP		8163
"		1969	APPLE	JAP		8163
"		1976	APPLE	JAP		80668
MAGICAL MYSTERY TOUR		1968	CAPITOL	US		2835
"		1976	EMI	UK	PCTC	255
"		1969	APPLE	JAP		9728
"		1976	APPLE	JAP		80569
THE BEATLES WHITE (DBL)		1968	PARLOPHONE	UK		PCS7067/8
"		1968	APPLE	US		101
"		1969	APPLE	JAP		8570/1
"		1976	APPLE	JAP		77001/2
YELLOW SUBMARINE		1969	APPLE	UK	PCS	7070
"		1969	APPLE	IMP		74585
"		1969	EMI	EURO		04002
"		1969	APPLE	JAP		8610
"		1976	APPLE	JAP		80559
"		1969	CAPITOL	US		153
ABBEY ROAD		1969	APPLE	UK	PCS	7088
"		1969	CAPITOL	US	SO	383
"		1969	EMI	EURO		04243
"		1969	APPLE	JAP		8815
"		1976	APPLE	JAP		80560
BEATLES AGAIN		19	EMI	EURO		04348
"		19	APPLE	JAP		8940
LET IT BE		1970	APPLE	UK	PCS	7096
"		1970	APPLE	US		34001
"	BOX SET	1970	APPLE			PXS1
"		1970	EMI	EURO		04433
"		1970	APPLE	JAP		9009
"		1971	APPLE	JAP	AP	80189
"		1976	APPLE	JAP		80561
HEY JUDE		1970	CAPITOL	US	SW	385
"		1970	APPLE		CPCS	106
"		1970	APPLE	JAP		8940
"		1976	APPLE	JAP		80570
1962 66	DBL	1973	PARLOPHONE	UK	PCSP	717
"	DBL	1973	CAPITOL	US		SEBX11842
"	DBL	1973	CAPITOL	US		3403
"	DBL	1973	EMI	EURO		05307
"	DBL	1973	APPLE	JAP	AP	9032
"	DBL	1976	APPLE	JAP		77003/4
1967 70	DBL	1973	PARLOPHONE	UK	PCSP	718
"	DBL	1973	CAPITOL	US		SEBX11843
"	DBL	1973	CAPITOL	US		3404
"	DBL	1973	EMI	EURO		05309/0
"	DBL	1973	APPLE	JAP	AP	9033
"	DBL	1976	APPLE	JAP		77005/6
THE EARLY YEARS		1973	EMI	IMP	2870	111
"		1975	APPLE			2309
PORTRAIT OF		1975	POLYDOR			
RARITIES		19	PARLOPHONE	UK	PMC	1001
LIVE AT THE STAR CLUB HAMBURG		1977	BELLAPHON	GERM	BLS	5560
"		1977	ATLANTIC	US	SD2	7001
"		1977	RCA			7375
LIVE AT THE HOLLYWOOD BOWL		1977	EMI	UK		EMTV 4
"		1977	EMI	EURO		06377
"		1977	CAPITOL	US		SMAS11638
ROCK'N'ROLL		1976	PARLOPHONE	UK	PCSP	719
"		1976	CAPITOL	US		SKB011537
"		1976	EMI	EURO		06137/8
"		1976	ODEON	JAP		77009
LOVE SONGS		1977	PARLOPHONE	UK	PCS	7211
"		1977	CAPITOL	US		SKBL11711
"		1977	PATHE	FR		C15406550/1
BEATLES BEAT		19	PATHE	FR		C07204363
BEATLES GREATEST		19	PATHE	FR		C06204207
BEATLES TAPES		1977	POLYDOR		2683	068
LIVE AT THE STAR CLUB		1977	LINGASONG			LNL1
LIVE AT THE STAR CLUB		1977	BELLAPHON			15233
BEATLES BALLADS		1980	PARLOPHONE		PCS	7214
HEAR THE BEATLES TELL ALL		1981	CHARLY		CRV	202

RICHARD KERSEY	G V	(A	(A) LIVE					
ROBBY MATTHES	B V	(A	(B) TAKING MY TIME		1977	TELDEC	GER	623179
KLAUS LARISEL	G V	(A			1980	INTERCORD	NL	148504
CHRISTIAN ENGEL	D V	(A						

B60   **BEAU**   B60

```
      C J T MIDGLEY(BEAU) G V  (AB      (A) BEAU                    1969  DANDELION    UK       63751
      JIM MILNE               (B       (B) CREATION                1971  DANDELION    UK   DAN 8006
      STEVE CLAYTON           (B
B61                                 BEAU BRUMMELS                                                  B61
      SAL VALENTINO      V   (ABCDEFGHJ (A) INTRODUCING            1965  AUTUMN        SLP  103
      RON ELLIOTT        G v (ABCDEFGHJ (B) BEAU BRUMMELS          19    AUTUMN        SLP  104
      RON MEAGHER        G B V (ABDEFJ  (C) BEAU BRUMMELS          1966  PYE           NPL 28062
      DECLAN MULLIGAN    BG V (AJ       (D) BEAU BRUMMELS 66       1966  W B           WS  1644
      JON PETERSON       D   (AJBD      (E) TRIANGLE               1967  W B           WS  1692
      WITH                             (F) BEST OF                 1967  VAULT         LPS  114
      VAN DYKE PARKS     K   (E         (G) VOL 44                 196   VAULT         LPS  121
      JERRY REED         G   (H         (H) BRADLEYS BARN          1968  W B           WS  1760
      NORBERT PUTNAM     B   (H         (J) THE BEAU BRUMMELS      1975  W B           WS  2842
      DAVID BRIGGS       K   (H         (K) GREATEST HITS          19    JAS           JAS 5000
      KENNY BUTTREY      D   (H         ( ) BEAU BRUMMELS SING     19    POST      US       6000
      DAN LEVITT         G BAN (J       ( ) BEST OF 1964/68        1981  RHINO     US       101
      MARK JORDAN        PNO (J
      VICTOR FELDMAN     PERC (J
B61A                                  BEAUREGARD                                                  B61A
                                       (A) BEAUREGARD             19    SOUND PROD
B61B                                   D BEAVER                                                   B61B
      D BEAVER           K V  (A        (A) COMBINATIONS           1973  TMI           BTLI 0118
      PAUL ALLAN TAYLOR  G V  (A
      JIMMY JAMISON      V    (A        TOMMY CATHEY      B   (A   JOEL WILLIAMS  G D  (A
      CARL MARSH         WIND (A        J A SPELL         FDL (A   STEVE SPEAR    B    (A
      JIMMY TARBUTTON    G    (A        DAVID MAYO      V PNO (A   RENI CROOK     V    (A
      LEO LEBLANC        STEEL (A       RUDY GARNER      CLAR (A   JACKIE COOK    V    (A
B62                                 BEAVER BROTHERS                                               B62
      GEOFF GILL      V K G B D(A       (A) VENTRILOQUISMS         197   AURA          AUL  701
      CLIFF WADE         K V  (A
      CAPRIOL SINGERS    V    (A
B63                                 BEAVER & KRAUSE                                               B63
      PAUL BEAVER     K SYN(ALL         (A) RAGNAROK ELECTRONIC FUNK 1969 LIMELIGHT US      86069
      BERNARD KRAUSE  K SYN(ALL         (B) IN A WILD SANCTUARY    1970  W B           WS  1850
      WITH                             (C) GANDHARVA              1971  W B       US  WS  1909
      MIKE BLOOMFIELD    G    (C        (C) GANDHARVA              1971  W B       UK   K 46130
      RAY BROWN          B    (C        (D) ALL GOOD MEN           1972  W B       UK   K 46184
      RIK ELSWIT         G    (C        (D) ALL GOOD MEN           1972  W B       US   BS 2624
      LEE CHARLTON       D    (C        (E) GUIDE TO ELECTRONIC MUSIC 1975 NONSUCH UK   K 73018
      ROD ELLICOTT       B    (C
      LAMONT JOHNSON     K    (C        MIKE LANG         K   (C   GAIL LANGTON   HARP (C
      GEORGE MARCH       D    (C        RONNIE MONTROSE   G   (C   GERRY MULLIGAN SAX  (C
      HOWARD ROBERTS     G    (ABC      BUD SHANK        SAX  (AAB  PATRICE HOLLOWAY V  (C
      CLYDIE KING        V    (C        PAUL LAGOS        D   (A   DAVE GRUISIN   K    (A
      MILT HOLLAND       PERC (AB       EVENGELINE CARMICHAEL V (CD VANETTA FIELDS V   (CD
      RON LEE HICKLIN    V    (CD       BILL KING         V   (CD  LEWIS MOCFORD  C    (CD
      EDNA WRIGHT        V    (CD       ELIZABETH WILSON  V   (D   CRIS WILLIAMSON V   (D
      ADRIENNE ANDERSON  V    (D
B63A                                   BEAVERTEETH                                                B63A
                                       (A) BEAVER TEETH           1977  RCA            1 2076
                                       (B) DAM IT                 1978  RCA            1 2574

B64                                    JEFF BECK                                                  B64
      JEFF BECK       G B  (ALL         (1) PRE FIRST LP LINE UP  (2) PRE FIRST LP LINE UP
      WITH                             (A) TRUTH                  1968  COLUMBIA  UK  SCX  6293
      JET HARRIS         B    (1        (A) TRUTH                  1968  EPIC      US  PE  26413
      VIV PRINCE         D    (1        (B) BECK OLA               1969  COLUMBIA  UK  SCX  6351
      RAY COOK           D    (2        (B) BECK OLA               1973  PATHE     FE 2C062 90496
      RON WOOD           G    (AB2      (B) BECK OLA               1975  EPIC      US  BN  26478
      ROD STEWART        V    (AB2      (AB)TRUTH/ BECK OLA        19    EPIC      US  BG  33779
      NICKY HOPKINS      K    (AB       (C) ROUGH & READY          1971  EPIC UK 64619 US     30973
      TONY NEWMAN        D    (B        (D) THE JEFF BECK GROUP    1972  EPIC UK 64899 US     31331
      MAX MIDDLETON      K    (CDEF      (CD) ROUGH & READY/JEFF BECK GROUP DB 19 EPIC US  PE 30973
      COZY POWELL        D    (CDX      (E) BLOW BY BLOW           1975  EPIC UK 69117 US     33409
      BOB TENCH          G V  (CDX      (F) WIRED                  1976  EPIC UK 86012 US     33849
      PHIL CHEN          B    (E        (G) LIVE                   1977  EPIC UK 86025 US     34433
      WILBUR BASCOMB     B    (F        (H) THERE & BACK           1980  EPIC UK 83288
      FERNANDO SAUNDERS  B V G (G       ( ) MASTER OF ROCK  1974 EMI 054 92207 FR PATHE 06295122
      JOHN PAUL JONES    ORG  (A        (B) THE MOST OF JEFF BECK  1971  M F P     UK  MFP 5219
      SIMON PHILLIPS     D    (H        ( ) BEST OF JEFF BECK      19    CBS       HOLL     92207
      TONY HYMAS         K    (H        (X) GOT THE FEELING & OTHERS (EP) 1972 PLAYBACK     1026
      MO FOSTER          B    (H        (X) GOT THE FEELING        1972  CBS       US       31546
      STEVE KINDLER      VLN K (G       ( ) JEFF BECK GOLDEN DISC  1974  CBS SONY  JAP ECPN 23
      TONY SMITH         D V  (G
      JAN HAMMER         K    (FGH  RICHARD BAILEY D  (EF  NARADA MICHAEL WALDEN D(F CLIVE CHAMAN B (CDMX
      MICK WALLER        D    (A    AYNSLEY DUNBAR D  (A   KEITH MOON        D(A
B64A                                BECK BOGERT & APPICE                                          B64A
      JEFF BECK          G    (AB       (A) BECK BOGERT & APPICE   1973  EPIC      UK  EPC 65455
      CARMINE APPICE     D    (AB       (A) BECK BOGERT & APPICE   1973  EPIC      US  KE  32140
      TIM BOGERT         B    (AB       (B) LIVE IN JAPAN          1975  EPIC      JAP EPCO  58
      DANNY HUTTON       V    (A        (C) LIVE IN JAPAN (DBL)    1973  CBS/SONY  JAP ECPJ11/12
      DUANE HITCHINGS    K    (A        (D) ALIVE                  1974  EPIC              22001
      JIM GREENSPOON     PNO  (A
```

[41]

JOE BECK

JOE BECK	G V	(ALL	(A) NATURE BOY		1969	VERVE	US	FTS 3081
STEVE KHAN	G	(C	(B) WATCH THE TIME		1977	POLYDOR		2391 257
DON GROLNICK	K	(C	(B) WATCH THE TIME		1977	POLYDOR	US	PD 6092
WILL LEE	B	(C	(C) BECK		1977	KUDU		KU 21
CHRIS PARKER	D	(C	(C) BECK		1975	KUDU	US	KU 2151
DAVID SANBORN	SAX	(C	(D) ROCK ENCOUNTER		19	POLYDOR		2925 024
SABICAS	G	(D						

BECKETT

ROBERT BARTON	G V	(A	(A) BECKETT		1974	RAFT	UK	RA 48502
KENNY MOUNTAIN	G V	(A						
TERRY WILSON-SLESSER	V	(A	KEITH FISHER	D	(A	FRANKIE GIBBONS	B	(
IAN MURRAY	B	(A	TIM HINKLEY	K	(A			

HARRY BECKETT

HARRY BECKETT	HRND	(ALL	(A) FLARE UP		1971	PHILIPS		6308 026
JOHN SURMAN	SAX	(A	(B) WARM SMILES		1972	RCA		SF 8225
MIKE OSBORNE	SAX	(ABC	(C) THEME FOR FEGA		1973	RCA		SF 8264
ALAN SKIDMORE	SAX	(AC	(D) JOY UNLIMITED		1975	CADILLAC		SGC 1004
FRANK RICOTTI	VIBES PERC	(ABC	(E) MEMORIES OF BACARES		1976	OGUN		OG 800
JOHN TAYLOR	K	(ABC	(F) GOT IT MADE		1978	OGUN		OG 020
CHRIS LAURENCE	B	(ABC						
JOHN WEBB	D	(ABCE	RAY RUSSELL	G	(DEF	BRIAN MILLER	K	(DE
DARYL RUNSWICK	B	(DE	NIGEL MORRIS	D	(D	MARTIN DAVID	PERC	(DF
ROBIN JONES	PERC	(E	PETE LEMER	K	(F	ALAN JACKSON	D	(F
ROY BABBINGTON	B	(F						

BECKIES

MICHAEL BROWN	K	(A	(A) THE BECKIES		1976	SIRE	US	SASD 7159
MAYO JAMES McALLISTER		(A						
GARY HODGDEN		(A	SCOTT TRUSTY		(A			

BECKMEIER BROTHERS

FRED BECKMEIER	V B	(A	(A) BECKMEIER BROTHERS		1979	CASABLANCA	US	7147
STEVE BECKMEIER	G	(A						
DAVID KALISH	G	(A	GARY FERGUSON	D	(A	RICHIE HAYWARD	D	(A
DAVID SHAW	D	(A	NEIL LARSEN	K	(A	STEVE BERLIN	SAX	(A
R A MARTIN	K HRNS	(A						

DAVID BEDFORD

DAVID BEDFORD	K	(ALL	(A) NURSES SONG WITH ELEPHANTS	1972	DANDELION		2310 165
WITH			(B) STARS END	1974	VIRGIN	V	2020
MICHAEL OLDFIELD	G B	(ABCDEF	(C) ORCHESTRAL TUBULAR BELLS	1975	VIRGIN	V	2026
CHRIS CUTLER	PERC	(B	(D) RIME OF THE ANCIENT MARINER	1975	VIRGIN	V	2038
DIANE COULSON	V	(D	(E) ODYSSEY	1976	VIRGIN	V	2070
LUCY BLACKBURN	V	(D	(E) ODYSSEY	1976	POLYDOR		2933 735
KEVIN AYERS	V	(A	(F) INSTRUCTIONS FOR ANGELS	1977	VIRGIN	V	2090
DARYL RUNSWICK	B	(B	(F) INSTRUCTIONS FOR ANGELS	1977	POLYDOR		2437 738
MIKE RATLEDGE	SYN	(F					
GILBERT BIBERIAN	G	(A	OMEGA PLAYERS	G	(A	QUEEN'S COLLEGE CHOIR V	(ADE
JOHN PEEL	REC	(A	SEBASTIAN BELL	FLT	(A	ROBERT POWELL	V	(D
ANDY SUMMERS	G	(E	ANNE MURRAY	REC	(E	ROSALIND KANDLER	REC	(E
LAYNE HALSTEAD	OBOE	(E	NICOLETTE ALVEY	K V	(E	VICKY COOPER	V	(E
SOPHIE DICKSON	V	(E	ELLY LEMOS		(E	SERENA MACREADY-SELLARS		(E
MEGAN POWELL	V	(E	DAISY GOODWIN	V	(E	MAI DICKSON	V	(E
JUDY PLANT	V	(E					

BEDLAM

COZY POWELL	D	(A	(A) BEDLAM		1973	CHRYSALIS		CHR 1048
FRANCESCO AIELLO	V	(A						
DENNIS BALL	B	(A	FELIX PAPPALARDI	K	(A	MAX MIDDLETON	K	(A
DABE BALL	G	(A						

BEE GEES

MAURICE GIBB	V	(ALL	(A) BEE GEES FIRST	1967	POLYDOR	UK 583 012	US ATCO 33223		
ROBIN GIBB	V	(ALL	(B) HORIZONTAL	1968	POLYDOR	UK 583 020	US ATCO 33233		
COLIN PETERSEN	D	(ABCDEG	(C) RARE PRECIOUS & BEAUTIFUL	1968	POLYDOR	UK 236 221	US ATCO 33264		
DENNIS BYRON	D	(TWZabY	(D) IDEA	1968	POLYDOR	UK 583 036	US ATCO 33253		
BARRY GIBB	V G	(ALL	(E) RARE PRECIOUS & BEAUTIFUL VOL 2	1968	POLYDOR	UK 236 513	US ATCO 33321		
VINCE MELOUNEY	G	(ABCD	(F) RARE PRECIOUS & BEATIFUL VOL 3	1969	POLYDOR	UK 236 556			
ALAN KENDALL	G B	(TWYZab	(G) ODESSA	1969	POLYDOR	UK 582049/50	US ATCO 2702		
BLUE WEAVER	K	(TWZabY	(G) ODESSA	1969	POLYDOR	2674 012	US RSO 3007		
GARY BROWN	SAX	(a	(H) THE BEST OF	1969	POLYDOR	UK 583 063			
HAROLD COWART	B	(ac	(I) CUCUMBER CASTLE	1970	POLYDOR	UK 2383 010	US 33327		
JOE LALA	PERC	(aWY	(J) SOUND OF LOVE	1970	POLYDOR	UK 2447 005			
HERBIE MANN	FLT	(a	(K) TWO YEARS ON	1970	POLYDOR	UK 2310 069	US 33353		
GEORGE TERRY	G	(ac	(L) MARLEY PURT DRIVE	1970	POLYDOR	UK 2447 012			
DANIEL BEN ZEBULON	PERC	(a	(M) TRAFALGAR	1971	POLYDOR	UK 2383 052	US ATCO 7003		
BILL PURSE	HRNS	(a	(N) TO WHOM IT MAY CONCERN	1972	POLYDOR	UK 2383 139	US ATCO 7012		
STAN WEBB	HRNS	(a	(O) LIFE IN A TIN CAN	1973	RSO	UK 2394 102			
NEIL BONSANTI	HRNS	(a	(P) THE BEST OF VOL 2	1973	RSO	UK 2394 106	US SO 875		
PETER GRAVES	HRNS	(a	(Q) GOTTA GET A MESSAGE TO YOU	1973	CONTOUR	2870 404			
WHIT SIDENER	HRNS	(a	(R) MrNATURAL	1974	RSO	UK 2394 132			
KENNY FAULK	HRNS	(a	(T) MAIN COURSE	1975	RSO	UK 2394 150	US 3024		
JAMES PANKOW	HRNS	(a	(U) PORTRAIT	1975	POLYDOR	UK 2482 092			
WALTER PARAZAIDER	HRNS	(a	(V) S W A L K (SOUNDTRACK)	197	POLYDOR	UK 2383 043			
LEE LOUGHNANE	HRNS	(a	(W) CHILDREN OF THE WORLD	1976	RSO		US 1 3003		
JIM WESTLEY	K	(	(X) GOLD	197	RSO		US 1 3006		
BRIAN GLASCOCK	D	(	(Y) HERE AT LAST.....LIVE	1977	RSO	UK 2658 120	US 1 3901		
GEOFF BRIDGEFORD	D	(	(Z) SATURDAY NIGHT FEVER(SOUNDTRACK)	1977	RSO	UK 2658 123	US 2 4001		
JIM KELTNER	D	(O	(a) SPIRITS HAVING FLOWN	1979	RSO	UK RSBG 1	US 1 3041		
SNEAKY PETE	STEEL	(O	(b) BEE GEES GREATEST	1979	RSO	UK RSDX001	US 4200		
RICK GRECH	B	(O	(c) LIVING EYES	1981	RSO	UK RSBG 002			
MANHATTAN HORNS		(							
BONAROO HRNS		(WYac	EARLY DAYS VOL 1	1978	PICKWICK		SHM 971		
ARIF MARIN	PROD	(T	EARLY DAYS VOL 2	1978	PICKWICK		SHM 973		
RAY BARETTO	D	(T	EARLY DAYS VOL 3	1978	PICKWICK		SHM 982		
STEPHEN STILLS	PERC	(W	BONANZA	1978	PICKWICK		PDA 048		

(CONTINUED)

[42]

```
ALBHY GALUTEN SYN B PROD (WYac    JOEY MURCIA        G     (Y    JEFF PORCARO      D    (c
KARL RICHARDSON      PROD (WYac    CHUCK KIRKPATRICK  G     (c    DON FELDER        G    (c
GEORGE BITZER     PROD SYN(c       JOE GALDO          D     (c    JOE FARRELL       SAX  (T
BOB GLAUB            B    (c        GARY BROWN         SAX   (Wa   GEORGE PERRY      B    (W
DONNY BROOKS         HCA  (c        RICHARD TEE        K     (c    RALPH McDONALD    PERC (c
GEOFF WESTLEY        K    (Y        RUSS KUNKEL        D     (c    DAVID WOLINSKI    K    (c
STEVE GADD           D    (c
```

B72   CAPTAIN BEEFHEART   B72

```
CAPTAIN BEEFHEART              (A) SAFE AS MILK                1967   BUDDAH        US  BDS  5001
(DON VAN VLIET)   G V HCA(ALL   (A) SAFE AS MILK                1970   BUDDAH        US  BDS  5063
                               (A) SAFE AS MILK                1968   PYE INT       UK  NPL 28110
RY COODER         G    (A       (B) DROP OUT BOOGIE             1967   BUDDAH            2349 002
                               (C) STRICTLY PERSONAL           1968   LIBERTY LBR1006       83172
ANTENNAE JIM SEMENS)           (C) STRICTLY PERSONAL           19     UA UAS29540   SUNSET 50208
(JEFF COTTON)     G    (ACDEH   (C) STRICTLY PERSONAL           1968   BLUE THUMB    US  BTS    1
                               (C) STRICTLY PERSONAL(ROCKFILE)  19     LIBERTY           LBR 1006
ZOOT HORN ROLLO                (D) TROUT MASK REPLICA(DBL)      1969   STRAIGHT      US  STS 1053
(BILL HARKLEROAD) G    (DEFGJ   (D) TROUT MASK REPLICA(DBL)     1969   REPRISE           K 64026
                               (D) TROUT MASK REPLICA(DBL)      1969   REPRISE       US  RS  2027
ROCKETTE MORTON                (E) LICK MY DECALS OFF           1970   STRAIGHT      US  STS 1063
(MARK BOSTON)     B G  (DEFGJ   (E) LICK MY DECALS OFF          1970   REPRISE           K 44244
                               (E) LICK MY DECALS OFF           1970   REPRISE       US  RS  6240
ED MARIMBA(ART TRIPP) K D (FGJ  (E) LICK MY DECALS OFF          19     ELECTROLA     IC 062 92092
                               (F) SPOTLIGHT KID                1971   REPRISE       UK  K 44162
OREJON (ROY ESTRADA) B   (G     (F) SPOTLIGHT KID               1971   REPRISE       US  RS  2050
                               (G) CLEAR SPOT                   1972   REPRISE           UK K54007
SNOUFFER(ALEX ST CLAIRE)G (ACHJ (G) CLEAR SPOT                  1972   REPRISE       US  MS  2115
                               (H) MIRROR MAN                   1971   BUDDAH            2365 022
DRUMBO ( JOHN FRENCH) D (ACDEFHLM (H) MIRROR MAN                1974   BUDDAH            BDLP 4004
                               (H) MIRROR MAN                   19     BUDDAH        US  BDS 5077
WINGED EEL FINGERLING          (J) UNCONDITIONALLY GUARANTEED   1974   VIRGIN        UK  V  2015
(ELLIOT INGBER)   G    (1FK     (J) UNCONDITIONALLY GUARANTEED  1974   MERCURY       US  SRM1 709
JEFF MORRIS TEPPER G   (LM      (K) BLUEJEANS & MOONBEAMS       1974   VIRGIN        UK  V  2123
ERIC DREW FELDMAN  B K (LM      (K) SHINEY BEAST BAT CHAIN PULLER 1978  W B          US  BSK 3256
ROBERT WILLIAMS    D   (LM      (L) CAPT BEEFHEART FILE         1977   PYE           UK  FILD 008
MARC MARCELLINO    K   (CH      (M) DOC AT THE RADAR STATION    1980   VIRGIN        UK  V  2172
BRUCE FOWLER      TROM (LM      ( ) PLASTIC FACTORY             19     BUDDAH        GER 2318 014
MASCARA SNAKE     CLAR (DE      (1) LIVE TOUR BAND
JERRY HANDLEY      B   (ACDEH   ( ) BONGO FURY                  1975   DISCREET          2334
ANDY DIMARTINO     G   (J
JIMMY CARL BLACK   D   (1       HERB BETMEN               (A    RUSS TITELMAN     G    (A
TED CACTUS             (F       DEL SIMMONS         WIND  (J    RHYS CLARK        D    (F
TY GRIMES         PERC (K       GREG DAVIDSON       G     (1    DOUG MOON         G    (DE
MARK GIBBONS       K   (K       MILT HOLLAND        PERC  (G    DEAN SMITH        G    (K
GARY LEWIS         G   (LM      BOB WEST            B     (K    MICHAEL SMOTHERMAN K V (K
                               GENE PELLO          D     (K    JIMMY CARAVAN     K    (K
```

B73   BEES MAKE HONEY   B73

```
BARRY RICHARDSON  B SAX (ABCDE  (A) MUSIC EVERY NIGHT              1972   EMI           EMC 3013
RUAN O'LOCHLAINN  G K SAX (AB   (B) 1971/72    (C) 1973   (D) 1974    (E) 1974
MICK MOLLOY        G    (ABCD   ( ) BEES MAKE HONEY (SYVIE) (EP)    1977   CHARLY        CEP  117
DEKE O'BRIEN       G    (ABCD
BOB CEEMANBERG     D    (AB
FRAN BYRNE         D    (ABCD   CLIFF BILLETT       TPT   (A    GERRY HOGAN       STEEL(A
MALCOLM MORLEY     G    (C      ROD DEMICK          B     (DE   ED DEAN           G    (E
KEVIN McALEA      PNO   (E      WILLIE FINLAYSON    G     (E    JEDD KELLY        D    (A
```

B74   BEGGARS OPERA   B74

```
MARTIN GRIFFITHS  V PERC(ABC    (A) ACT ONE                     1970   VERTIGO           6360 018
ALAN PARK          K   (ABCDE   (A) ACT ONE                     197    VERVE         US      5080
RAYMOND WILSON     D   (ABC     (B) WATERS OF CHANGE            1971   VERTIGO       UK  6360 054
RICKY GARDINER    G V  (ABCDEF  (C) PATHFINDER                 1972   VERTIGO       UK  6360 073
MARSHALL ERSKINE  B FLT (AB     (D) GET YOUR DOG OFF ME         1973   VERTIGO       UK  6360 090
GORDON SELLAR    B G V (BCDEF   (E) SAGITTARY                  19     JUPITER       GER    88907
VIRGINIA SCOTT     V   (BEF     (F) BEGGARS CANT BE CHOOSERS    19     JUPITER       GER    27702
LINNIE PATERSON    V   (D       (G) LIFELINE                   197    VERTIGO       GER 6350 060
COLIN FAIRLIE      D   (DE
PETE SCOTT         V   (F       CLEM CATTINI        D     (F
```

B74A   ADRIAN BELEW   B74A

```
ADRIAN BELEW      G D V(A       (A) LONE RAUNO                  1982   ISLAND        UK  ILPS 9675
CHRISTY BLEY      K V  (A
WILLIAM JANSSEN   SAX V (A       AUDIE BELEW         K     (A    J CLIFTON MAYHUGH B V  (A
```

B75   GRAHAM BELL   B75

```
GRAHAM BELL        V G  (A       (A) GRAHAM BELL                 1972   CHARISMA      UK  CAS 1061
MEL COLLINS       SAX   (A
RON CORNELIUS      G    (A       TIM DRUMMOND        B     (A    IAN WALLACE       D    (A
TIM HINKLEY        K    (A       BOB WILSON          K     (A    GASPAR LAWAL      PERC (A
DEREK QUINN       PERC  (A
```

B75A   JIMMY BELL   B75A

```
JIMMY BELL        PNO   (A       (A) STRANGER IN YOUR TOWN       197    JSP           UK      1007
```

B76   MADELINE BELL   B76

```
MADELINE BELL      V   (ALL      BELLS A POPPIN'                          1967   PHILIPS       SBL 7818
                                DOIN' THINGS                             1969   PHILIPS       SBL 7865
                                MADELINE BELL                            1971   PHILIPS       6308 053
                                16 STAR TRACKS BY MADELINE BELL          1971   PHILIPS       6308 066
                                COMIN' ATCHA                             1974   RCA           SF  8393
                                THIS IS ONE GIRL                         1976   PYE           NSPL18483
```

MAGGIE BELL

MAGGIE BELL	V	(ABC	(A) QUEEN OF THE NIGHT	1973	POLYDOR		2383 239
WITH			(A) QUEEN OF THE NIGHT	1973	ATLANTIC	US	7293
REGGIE YOUNG	G	(A	(B) SUICIDE SAL	1975	POLYDOR		2383 313
CORNELL DUPREE	G	(A	(B) SUICIDE SAL	1975	SWANSONG	US	SS 8412
JOHN HUGHEY	STEEL	(A	(D) GREAT ROCK SENSATION	19	POLYDOR	IMP	2499 107
MICKEY KEENE	G	(B					
HUGH McCRACKEN	G	(A	RICHARD TEE	K	(A	ARTHUR JENKINS	K	(A
LEON PENDARVIS	K	(A	BARRY GOLDBERG	K	(A	CHUCK RAINEY	B	(A
BILL SALTER	B	(A	STEVE GADD	D	(A	RALPH McDONALD	PERC	(A
SWEET INSPIRATION	V	(A	PAUL FRANCIS	D	(B	DELISLE HARPER	B	(B
PETE WINGFIELD	K	(B	ROY DAVIES	K	(B	BRIAN BREEZE	G V	(B
TERRY	G	(B	HUGH BURNS	G	(B	JIMMY PAGE	G	(B
RAY GLYNN	G	(B	JIMMY JEWELL	SAX	(B	CUDDLEY JUDD	BAGPIPES	(B
BILLY LAWRIE	V	(B	MARK LONDON	V	(B			

WILLIAM BELL

WILLIAM BELL	V	(ALL	PHASES OF REALITY	19	STAX	US 3005	2362 027
SWEET INSPIRATION	V		BOUND TO HAPPEN	1974	STAX		2363 002
BOOKER T JONES			COMIN BACK FOR MORE	1977	MERCURY		9100 038
AL JACKSON	PERC	(X	COMIN BACK FOR MORE	19	MERCURY	US	SRM1 1146
CARSON WHITSETT	K	(X	ITS TIME YOU TOOK ANOTHER LISTEN	19	MERCURY	US	SRM1 1193
HORACE SHIPP JR	G	(X	(X) RELATING	19	STAX	US 5502	STX 1010
DUCK DUNN	B	(X	BOUND TO HAPPEN	19	STAX	US 2014	STX 1050
JAMES McDUFF	K	(X	WOW WILLIAM BELL	19	STAX	US 2037	
HAROLD BEANE	G	(X					
BOBBY MANUEL	G	(X					

BELL & ARC

MICK GALLAGHER	K	(A	(A) BELL & ARC	1971	CHARISMA	UK	CAS 1053
GRAHAM BELL	V G	(A	(A) BELL & ARC	1971	CBS	US	31142
TOM DUFFY	B	(A					
JOHN WOODS	PERC	(A	ALAN WHITE	PERC D	(A	JOHN TURNBULL	G	(A
STEVE GREGORY	SAX	(A	BUD BEADLE	SAX	(A	ROB TAIT	D	(A
JEFF CONDON	CORNET	(A	KEN CRADDOCK	G	(A			

BELL & JAMES

LEROY BELL	G D PERC	(A	(A) BELL & JAMES	1978	A&M US 4728	UK	AMLH 64728
THOM BELL	PROD	(A					
CASEY JAMES	G B K SYN	(A	CARLA BENSON	V	(A	HARRIET THARPE	V	(A
YVETTE BENTON	V	(A	M F S B ORCHESTRA		(A			

BELLAMY BROTHERS

DAVID BELLAMY	V G	(ALL	(A) LET YOUR LOVE FLOW	1976	W B US 2941	UK	K56242
HOWARD BELLAMY	V G	(ALL	(B) PLAIN & FANCY	1977	W B US 3034	UK	K56357
RICHARD BENNETT	G	(ABC	(C) BEAUTIFUL FRIENDS	1978	W B US 3176	UK	K56485
DOUG RHONE	G	(AC	(D) TWO & ONLY	1979	W B	337	
DENNIS ST JOHN	D	(A	(E) YOU CAN GET CRAZY	1980	W B		K56777
ALAN LINDGREN	K	(ABC	(F) SONS OF THE SUN	1980	W B	UK	K56872
KING ERRISON	PERC	(AB					
EMORY GORDY	B	(AC	MIKE HUEY	D	(B	JOHN SELK	B	(B
ALAN ESTES	PERC	(E	BOBBY BRUCE	FDL	(E	DANNY JONES	STEEL	(EF
CARL CHAMBERS	G	(E	JON LAFRANDE	K	(EF	RODNEY PRICE	D	(EF
JESSE CHAMBERS	B	(EF	CARLOS VEGA	D	(E	RICKY SKAGGS	FDL MAND	(F
BOBBIE HALL	PERC	(F	REINIE PRESS	B	(C	RICK SCHLOSSER	D	(C
RANDY FERRELL	G	(F	MICHAEL LLOYD	PROD	(F			

BELMONTS

FRED MILANE	V	(ABC	(A) CARNIVAL OF HITS	196	SABRINA	US	5001
ANGELO D'ALE.	V	(ABC	(B) SUMMER LOVE	196	DOT	US	25949
FRANK LYNDON	V	(C	(C) CIGARS ACAPPELLA CANDY	1972	BUDDAH	US	5123
CARLO MASTRANGELO	V	(A					

PAT BENATAR

PAT BENATAR	V	(ALL	(A) IN THE HEAT OF THE NIGHT	1979	CHRYSALIS		CHR1236
SCOTT ST CLAIR SHEETS	G	(ABC	(B) CRIME OF PASSION	1980	CHRYSALIS		CHR1245
ROGER CAPPS	B V	(ABCD	(C) PRECIOUS TIME	1981	CHRYSALIS		CHR1346
NEIL GERALDO	G K V	(ABCD	(D) GET NERVOUS	1982	CHRYSALIS		CHR1396
MYRON GROMBACHER	D	(ABCD					
GLEN HAMILTON	D	(B	CHARLIE GIORDANO	K	(D			

DAVID BENDETH

DAVID BENDETH	PROD G V	(AB	(A) ADRENALIN	1979	SIDEWALK		SWK 2004
JOHN CLEVELAND HUGHES	K	(AB	(B) JUST DESERT	1981	ENSIGN		ENVY 502
MARCUS MILLER	B	(A					
LENNY WHITE	D	(A	RANDY BRAMWELL	B	(AB	DAVID SPAN	D	(A
MEMO ACEVEDO	PERC	(AB	ROBERT BOYER	V	(AB	JOHN JOHNSON	SAX	(A
FRED BOYER	V	(AB	BILLY COBHAM	D	(AB	LOU POMANTI	K SYN	(B
CHUCK BURGI	D	(B	SELWYN PITT	V	(B	MICHAEL STUART	SAX	(B
MIKE MALONE	TPT	(A	DON ENGLARD	SAX	(B	TERRY LUKISKI	TROM	(B
DAVID DUNLOP	TPT	(A					

BRIAN BENNETT

BRIAN BENNETT	D	(ALL	(A) CHANGE OF DIRECTION	1968	COLUMBIA	UK	SCX 6144
ALAN PARKER	G	(C	(B) THE ILLUSTRATED LONDON PRIDE	1969	STUDIO 2	UK	TWO 268
ALAN HAWKSHAW	K	(C	(C) ROCK DREAMS	1977	DJM	UK	20499
LES HURDLE	B	(C	(D) VOYAGE	1978	DJM	UK	20532
TONY RIVERS	V	(C					
JOHN PERRY	V	(C	STUART CALVER	V	(C	CLIFF RICHARD	V	(C
PETE WILLSHER	STEEL	(C	JOE BROWN	V	(C	JIM LAWLESS	CONGA	(C
JOE FAGIN	V	(C	TERRY BRITON	G	(C	ALAN TARNEY	B	(C
GRAHAM TODD	PNO	(C					

CLIFF BENNETT

CLIFF BENNETT	V	(ALL	(A)	CLIFF BENNETT & THE REBEL ROUSERS	1964	PARLOPHONE	UK	PMC 1242
ROY YOUNG	K V	(B	(B)	DRIVING YOU WILD	1966	REGAL ZONOPHONE		REG 1035
MICK BURT	D	(B	(B)	DRIVING YOU WILD	1966	M F P	UK	MFP 1121
CHAS HODGES	G	(	(C)	GOT TO GET YOU INTO MY LIFE	1968	PARLOPHONE	UK	PCS 7017
MOSS GROVES	SAX	(B	(D)	BRANCHES OUT	1968	PARLOPHONE	UK	PCS 7054
SID PHILLIPS	SAX	(B	(E)	REBELLION	1971	CBS	US	64487
JOHN GRAY	B	(E	(F)	CLIFF BENNETT & THE REBEL ROUSERS	1978	EMI	UK	NUT 14
MAREK KLUCZYNSKI	FLT	(E						
DEREK WIER	PERC	(E	ROBERT SMITH	G	(E	BOBBY THOMPSON	B	(B
DAVE WENDELLS	B	(B						

DUSTER BENNETT

DUSTER BENNETT V G HCA PERC(ALL			(A)	SMILING LIKE IM HAPPY	1968	BLUE HORIZON		7 63208
WITH			(B)	BRIGHT LIGHTS	1969	BLUE HORIZON		7 63221
PETER GREEN	G	(A	(C)	12 DBs	1970	BLUE HORIZON		7 63868
JOHN McVIE	B	(A	(D)	FINGERTIPS	1974	TOADSTOOL AUSTRALIA		L 35436
HAM RICHMOND	K	(A	(E)	BENNETT	19	BLUE HORIZON	US	4812
STELLA SUTTON	V	(AB	(F)	JUSTA	19	BLUE HORIZON	US	4804
MICK FLEETWOOD	D	(A						
TOP TOPHAM	G	(BC						
TONY MILLS	B	(BC	NICKY HOPKINS	K	(D	JOHN SIOMOS	D	(D
RICK WILLS	B	(D	HUGH BURNS	G	(D	MORRIS PERT	PERC (D
PETER FRAMPTON	G	(D	TERRY STANNARD	D	(D	LIZA STRIKE	V	(D
ROB ROBERTSON	B	(D	PHIL WAINMAN	D	(D	PETE WINGFIELD	K	(D
PIP WILLIAMS	G	(D	BARRY ST JOHN	V	(D	LINDA KENDRICK	V	(D
ANN SIMMONDS	V	(D	BOZ BURRELL	B	(D	IAN WALLACE	D	(D
BILLY GRAHAM	HRNS	(D	HOWIE CASEY	HRNS	(D	DICK PARRY	HRNS (D
REG BROOKS	HRNS	(D	CECIL MOSS	HRNS	(D	JOHNNY HUCKRIDGE	HRNS (D
MIKE DAVIS	HRNS	(D	JOHN DONNELLY	HRNS	(D	PETER BLUE	B	(B

BENNINGHOFF'S BAD ROCK BLUES BAND

		(A)	CHURCH BACH	1972	SSS	US	17

MARC BENNO

MARC BENNO	G V K	(ALL	(A)	MARC BENNO	1970	A&M	US	SP 4273
WITH			(B)	MINNOWS	1971	A&M	UK	AMLS64303
CLARENCE WHITE	G	(B	(B)	MINNOWS	1971	A&M	US	SP 4303
JESSE ED DAVIS	G	(BC	(C)	AMBUSH	1972	A&M	UK	AMLS64634
BOBBY WOMACK	G	(B	(C)	AMBUSH	1972	A&M	US	SP 4364
JERRY McGEE	G	(AB	(D)	LOST IN AUSTIN	1979	A&M US 4769	UK	AMLH64767
CARL RADLE	B	(BCD						
JERRY SCHEFF	B	(BA	CHUCK COMANICO	B	(B	GARY ILLINGSWORTH	K	(B
JIM KELTNER	D	(BCD	NICK DE CARO	ACC	(B	RITA COOLIDGE	V	(BA
CLYDIE KING	V	(B	VENETTA FIELDS	V	(B	MIKE UTLEY	K	(C
BOBBY KEYS	SAX	(C	BOOKER T JONES	HRNS G	(C	RAY BROWN	B	(C
BONNIE BRAMLETT	V	(C	ALBERT LEE	G	(D	ERIC CLAPTON	G V	(D
DICK SIMS	K	(D	DICK MORRISSEY	SAX	(D	BOOKER T JONES	K	(A
RY COODER	G	(A	JIM HORN	WIND	(A	JIMMY KARSTEIN	D	(A
SANDY KONIKOFF	TROM	(A	PRISCILLA COOLIDGE	V	(A			

BENOIT

DAVE BENOIT	K SYN	(AB	(A)	HEAVIER THAN YESTERDAY	1977	AVI	US	6025
DAVE WILLIAMS	B	(A	(B)	CAN YOU IMAGINE	1980	AVI	US	6074
GARY FERGUSON	D	(AB						
WADE SHORT	B	(B	DAVID SHERR	WIND	(A	JOHN WHELLOCK	G	(B
LAURIN RINDER	PERC	(A	MARCELINE VALDEZ	PERC	(B	RON KINK	TPT	(A

GEORGE BENSON

GEORGE BENSON	G V(ALL		(A)	ITS UPTOWN	1966	CBS	US	CS 9325
WITH			(B)	GEORGE BENSON COOKBOOK	19	CBS	US	CS 9413
RON CUBER	SAX(ATXI		(C)	BENSON BURNER (DBL)	19	CBS	US	CH 33569
JIMMY LOVELACE	D	(A	(D)	WILLOW WEEP FOR ME	19	CBS		63533
LONNIE SMITH	K	(A	(E)	BEYOND THE BLUE HORIZON	19	CTI	US	CTI 6009
PHIL UPCHURCH	G	(LPTX	(F)	WHITE RABBIT	1972 CTI US 6015		UK	CTI 6
JORGE DALTO	K	(LPX	(G)	BODY TALK	1974 CTI US 6033		UK	CTI 20
HARVEY MASON	D	(LPX	(H)	BAD BENSON	1974 CTI		US	CTI 6045
RALPH McDONALD	PERC(LPX		(I)	GOOD KING BAD	1976 CTI		UK	CTI 6062
LEE RITENOUR	G	(WX	(J)	BENSON & FARRELL	1977 CTI		US	CTI 6069
GEORGE DUKE	K	(W	(K)	IN CONCERT	1977 CTI		US	CTI 6072
HERBIE HANCOCK	K	(WFX	(L)	BREEZIN'	1976 W B US 3111		UK	K 56199
JOE FARRELL	HRNS(JYX		(M)	SHAPE OF THINGS TO COME	1976 A&M		US	SP 3014
RONNIE FOSTER	K	(LPTX	(N)	TELL IT LIKE IT IS	197 A&M		US	SP 3020
STANLEY BANKS	B	(LPX	(O)	THE OTHER SIDE OF ABBEY ROAD	1976 A&M		US	SP 3028
JACK McDUFF	K	(RV	(P)	IN FLIGHT	1977 W B US 2983		UK	K 56327
DON GROLNICK	K	(TJ	(Q)	SUMMERTIME	1977 EMBASSY		UK	EMB 31566
CLIFF CARTER	K	(T	(R)	BENSON & McDUFF	1977 PRESTIGE		UK	PR 2407
WILBUR BASCOMB	B	(T	(S)	WEEKEND IN L.A. (LIVE) (DBL)	1978 W B		UK	K 66074
WAYNE DOCKERY	B	(TK	(T)	SPACE ALBUM	1978 CTI			7085
MARVIN CHAPELL	D	(TK	(U)	STORMY WEATHER	19 EMBASSY		UK	EMB 31689
RAY ARMANDO	PERC(TK		(V)	LIVING INSIDE YOUR LOVE	1979 WB		UK	K 66085
JOHNNY GRIGGS	PERC(TK		(W)	GIVE ME THE NIGHT	1980 WB US 3453		UK	K 56823
SUE EVANS	PERC(TX		(X)	THE GEORGE BENSON COLLECTION	1981 WB		UK	K 66107
FRED WESLEY	TROM(T		(Y)	THE BEST OF	19 CTI			66035
STEVE LUKATHER	G	(X						
JAY BERLINER	G	(XF	RON CARTER	B	(XF	BILLY COBHAM	D	(XF	AIRTO MOREIRA PERC	(XF
PHIL KRAUS	PERC(X		STEVE GADD	D	(KTX	ROBERT POWELL	B	(X	CHARLES CONVINTON K	(X
LEO MORRIS	B	(X	JOHNNY PACHECO	PERC(X		BURT COLLINS	TPT	(X	JOE SHEPLEY TPT	(X
MARVIN STAMM	WIND(X		WAYNE ANDRE	HRNS(X		ALAN RAPH	HRNS	(X	BUDDY LUCAS SAX	(X
WILL LEE	B	(KTXJ	EARL KLUGH	G	(XF	DON ASHWORTH	K	(X	GEROME RICHARDSON K	(X
BOB JAMES	K	(X	ERNIE HAYES	K	(X	GERRY JEMMOTT	B	(X	JEFF PORCARO D	(X
JAY GRAYDON	G SYN(X		DAVID PAICH	SYN (XW		CHUCK FINDLEY	TPT	(X	GARY HERBIG WIND	(X
VANETTE GLOUD	V	(X	CARMEN TWILLEY	V	(X	BILL CHAMPLIN	V	(X	BILL REICHENBACH TROM	(X
MIKE BAIRD	PERC(X		DAVID FOSTER	K SYN(XW		JAI WINDING	PNO	(X	ARETHA FRANKLIN V	(X
LOUIS JORDAN	B	(X	BUZZY FEITEN	G	(X	PAULINHO DA COSTA	PERC (XW		EDDIE DANIELS SAX	(X
(CONTINUED)								

GEORGE BENSON

MARCY LEVY	V	(X	MARK STEVENS	V	(X	ABRAHAM LABORIEL	B	(XW
RICHARD TEE	K	(XW	MICHAEL BODDICKER	SYN	(XW	PATTI AUSTIN	V	(XW
JOCELYN ALLEN	V	(XW	TOM BAHLER	V	(XW	JIM GILSTRAP	V	(XW
KIM HUTCHCROFT	WIND	(WX	LARRY WILLIAMS	WIND	(WX	ERIC GALE	G	(TXJ
GARY KING	B	(JX	ANDY NEWMARK	D	(KTXJ	DAVID FRIEDMAN	PERC	(X
GREG PHILLINGANES	PNO	(XW	MICHAEL OMARTIAN	K	(X	HERBERT LAWS	FLT	(KTX
PHIL BODNER	WIND	(X	PATTI AUSTIN	V	(X	CHAKA KHAN	V	(X
HAMISH STUART	G	(X	STEVE FERRONE	D	(X	RALPH CRUZ	PERC	(X
GEORGE MARGE	FLT	(X	KEN BISCHEL	SYN	(X	RANDY BRECKER	TPT	(TX
MICHAEL BRECKER	SAX	(X	BARRY ROGERS	TROM	(X	MICHAEL MASSER	PNO	(X
CARLOS VEGA	D	(W	CLAIRE FISCHER	K	(W	ARIF MARDIN	PROD	(X
NEIL STUBENHAUS	B	(X	TOMMY LIPUMA	PROD	(X	GEORGE RICCI	CELLO	(X
RONNIE CUBER	SAX	(X	CREED TAYLOR	PROD	(X	EMANUEL VARDI	VLA	(X
NICKY MARRERO	PERC	(J	DAVID TOFANI	FLT	(J	SONNY BRAVO	PNO	(J
JOSE MADERA	PERC	(J	MICHAEL COLLAZA	PERC	(J			

(CONTINUED)						
JOHN ROBINSON	D	(XW				
DIVA GRAY	V	(XW				
JERRY HEY	TPT	(WX				
FRANK VICARI	SAX	(X				
JEROME RICHARDSON	FLT	(X				
ARTHUR JENKINS	PNO	(X				
EDDIE DANIELS	FLT	(XJ				
GEORGE YOUNG	SAX	(X				
QUINCY JONES	PROD	(WX				
SUE EVANS	PERC	(X				
MAX POLLIKOFF	VLN	(X				
RAOWL POLIKIAN	VLN	(X				
STEVE KHAN	G	(J				

OSCAR BENTON BLUES BAND

OSCAR BENTON	G V	(ALL	(A) FEEL SO GOOD			1969 DECCA		no 418	
H J B HAWKINS	B	(A	(B) BENTON 71			1971 DECCA		SLK 16724	
BARRELHOUSE BAILEY	PNO	(ABC	(C) DRAGGIN' AROUND			197 IMPERIAL		054 24550	
LONESOME TANNY LANT	D	(AB							
JAY WALKER	B D	(BC	GUS LAPORTE	G B	(BC JOHNNY LAPORTE	G	(C RUUEL BRINK	SAX	(C

BUSTER BENTON

BUSTER BENTON	G V	(ABC	(A) BLUES BUSTER		19 RED LIGHTNIN'	UK		RL 0026
RON SCOTT	SAX	(AB	(B) SPIDER IN MY STEW		1978 RONN US 7536	JAP P VINE		3502
CAREY BELL	HCA	(AB	(C) IS THE FELLING		1980 RONN US 7535			
LAFAYETTE LEAKE	PNO	(AB	(AB) HAVE 8 TRACKS THE SAME)					
JIMMY JOHNSON	G	(AB	(EP) SWEET 94		1980 CHARLY			CTD 119
NOLAN STRUCK	B	(AB						
RAY ALLISON	D	(AB	MIGHTY JOE YOUNG	G	(B WILLIE DIXON	B	(B JAMES GREEN	B	(B
BILLY DAVENPORT	D	(B						

BERLIN BLONDES

(A) BERLIN BLONDES	1980 EMI	UK	3346

BYRON BERLINE

BYRON BERLINE	FDL	(ALL	(A) & SUNDANCE	1977 MCA	US	2217
			(B) LIVE AT McCABES	1978 TAKAMO US 1061	RI 80	7061

CHUCK BERRY

CHUCK BERRY	G V	(ALL	( ) ROCK ROCK	19	CHESS	US		1515
WITH			( ) AFTER SCHOOL SESSIONS	1958	CHESS	US	LP	1426
			( ) ONE DOZEN BERRY'S	1958	CHESS	US	LP	1432
BO DIDDLEY	G	(	( ) ONE DOZEN BERRY'S	1958	LONDON	UK		2132
JOHNNY JOHNSON	PNO	(	( ) CHUCK BERRY IS ON TOP	19	CHESS	US	LP	1435
WILLIE DIXON	B	(	( ) ROCKIN' AT THE HOPS	19	CHESS	US	LP	1448
JASPER THOMAS	D	(	( ) NEW JUKE BOX HITS	19	CHESS	US	LP	1456
JEROME GREEN	PERC	(	( ) NEW JUKE BOX HITS	1960	PYE INT	UK	NPL	28019
OTIS SPANN	PNO	(	( ) CHUCK BERRY	1960	PYE INT	UK	NPL	28024
EDDIE HARDY	D	(	( ) CHUCK BERRY	19	CHESS	US		60032
L C DAVIS	SAX	(	( ) CHUCK BERRY	1967	MARBLE ARCH	UK	MAL	611
JIMMIE ROGERS	G	(	( ) ON STAGE	1960	CHESS	US	LP	1480
FRED BELOW	D	(	( ) ON STAGE	1960	PYE INT	UK	NPL	28027
LAFAYETTE LEAKE	PNO	(	( ) MORE CHUCK BERRY	1960	CHESS	US	LP	1465
G SMITH	B	(	( ) MORE CHUCK BERRY	1960	PYE INT	UK	NPL	28028
MATT MURPHY	G	(	( ) TWIST	1960	CHESS	US	LP	1466
ODIE PAYNE	D	(	( ) LATEST & GREATEST	196	PYE INT	UK	NPL	28031
PAUL WILLIAMS	PNO	(	( ) YOU NEVER CAN TELL	1964	PYE INT	UK	NPL	28039
THE FIVE DIMENSIONS (GB)			( ) YOU NEVER CAN TELL	1967	MARBLE ARCH	UK	MAL	702
MARTHA BERRY	V	(	( ) GREATEST HITS	1964	CHESS	US	LP	321
WAYNE GABRIEL	G	(	( ) GREATEST HITS	1964	CHESS	US	LP	1485
ADAM IPPOLITO	PNO	(	( ) GREATEST HITS	1967	MARBLE ARCH	UK	MAL	660
GARY VAN SCYOC	B	(	( ) 2 GREAT GUITARS	1964	PYE INT	UK	NPL	28047
STAN BRONSTEIN	SAX	(	( ) CHUCK BERRY IN LONDON	1965	CHESS	UK		4005
RICK FRANK	D	(	( ) CHUCK BERRY IN LONDON	1965	CHESS	US	LP	1495
BILLY PEEK	G	(	( ) FRESH BERRYS	1965	CHESS	UK		4506
RON NEED	D	(	( ) FRESH BERRYS	1965	CHESS	US	LP	1498
GREY EDRICK	B	(	( ) ST LOUIS TO LIVERPOOL	196	CHESS	US	LP	1488
ELLIOTT RANDALL	G	(	( )BACK HOME	196	CHESS	US	LP	1550
WILBUR BASCOMB	B	(	( ) GOLDEN HITS	1967	MERCURY			61103
ERNIE HAYES	PNO	(	( ) FROM ST LOUIS TO FRISCO	19	MERCURY			6463 015
INGRID BERRY	V	(	( ) AT THE FILLMORE	1967	MERCURY			6463 016
EQUADORS	V	(	( ) AT THE FILLMORE	19	MERCURY			SMCL20110
STEVE MILLER BAND			( ) MEDLEY	1967	MERCURY			6851 002
KENNY BUTTREY	D	(	( ) IN MEMPHIS	1967	MERCURY			6430 022
JIM MARSALA	B	(	( ) IN MEMPHIS	19	MERCURY			SMCL20110
BOB WRAY	B	(	( ) CONCERTO IN B GOODE	1969	MERCURY			61233
PETER JOHN HOGAN	HCA	(	( )HOME AGAIN	1971	CHESS			6310 113
CHUCK BERNARD		(	( )ST LOUIS TO FRISCO TO MEMPHIS DBL	1972	PHILIPS			6619 008
DEREK GRIFFITHS	G	(	( )ST LOUIS TI FRISCO TO MEMPHIS DBL	1972	MERCURY	US		2 .6501
IAN McLAGEN	K	(	( ) THE LONDON SESSIONS	1972	CHESS	UK		6310 122
KENNY JONES	D	(	( ) THE LONDON SESSIONS	1972	CHESS	US		50001
ONNIE McINTYRE	G	(	( ) THE LONDON SESSIONS	19	CHESS	US		60020
DAVE KAFINETTI	K	(	( ) SAN FRANCISCO DUES	1972	CHESS	UK	6310	115
NIC POTTER	B	(	( ) SAN FRANCISCO DUES	1972	CHESS			50008
ROBBIE McINTOSH	D	(	( ) BACK HOME	1972	CHESS			50024
			( ) GOLDEN DECADE	1972	CHESS	US		1514
			( ) GOLDEN DECADE	1972	CHESS			6641 018
			( ) GOLDEN DECADE VOL 2	1973	CHESS			6641 058
			( ) GOLDEN DECADE VOL 2	1973	CHESS	US		60023
			( ) BIO	1973	CHESS			50043
			( ) BIO	1973	CHESS		6499	650

(CONTINUED)

CHUCK BERRY

( ) BACK IN THE USA	1973	PHILIPS		6336 216
( ) ALLTIME GREATEST R'N'R PARTY HITS	1974	CHESS		6310 130
( ) ALLTIME GREATEST R'N'R PARTY HITS	1974	CHESS	US	ACB 00208
( ) GOLDEN DECADE VOL 3	1974	CHESS		6641 177
( ) GOLDEN DECADE VOL 3	1974	CHESS		50039
( ) GOLDEN DECADE VOL 3	1974	CHESS	US	60028
( ) I'M A ROCKER	1975	CONTOUR CAN 2019 UK	6870 638
( ) CHUCK BERRY 75	1975	CHESS	UK	9109 101
( ) CHUCK BERRY 75	1975	CHESS US 60032		50047
( ) MOTORVATIN'	1976	CHESS	UK	9286 690
( ) MOTORVATIN'	1976	CHESS	NL	9283 020
( ) GREATEST HITS	1977	ARCHIVE	US	321
( ) SWEET LITTLE SIXTEEN R'N' R HITS	1976	PHILIPS	UK	SON 006
( ) ROCKIT	1979	ATLANTIC	UK	K 50648
( ) ROCKIT	1979	ATCO	US	SD38118
( ) CHUCK BERRY	19	IMPACT	FR	6499671
( ) LOUISIANA	19	CHESS	US	26 130
( ) THE SECOND COMING	19	W B	US	0598
( ) WILD BERRY'S	19	PICKWICK	US	SPC 3392
( ) AMERICA'S HOTEST WAX	19	REELIN'	US	001
( ) FLASHBACK DBL	19	PICKWICK	US	PTP 2061
( ) THE BEST OF	19	STARDAY	US	
( ) CHUCK BERRY VOL I	19	IMPACT	FR	6886 403
( ) CHUCK BERRY VOL 2	19	IMPACT	FR	6886 407
( ) CHUCK BERRY	19	IMPACT	FR	6995 402
( ) CHUCK BERRY & FRIENDS	19	ARISTOCRAT	US	BR 100
( ) 20 GOLDEN GREATS	1979	HAMMER	UK	HMR 9003
( ) SPOTLIGHT	1980	CHESS	UK	1003
( ) MODS & ROCKERS	1980	MERCURY	UK	6336 635
() GREATEST HITS	1981	WHITE DOVE	UK	957
( ) ROCKIN' WITH	1981	MERCURY	UK	9279140
(EP) CHUCK & BO	196	PYE INT	UK	NEP 44009
(EP) CHUCK BERRY	196	PYE INT	UK	NEP 44011
(EP) CHUCK & BO 2	196	PYE INT	UK	NEP 44012
(EP) THIS IS CHUCK BERRY	196	PYE INT	UK	NEP 44013
(EP) CHUCK & BO 3	196	PYE INT	UK	NEP 44017
(EP) BEST OF	1964	PYE INT	UK	NEP 44018
(EP) HITS	1964	PYE INT	UK	NEP 44028
(EP) BLUE MOOD	1965	PYE INT	UK	NEP 44033
(EP) PROMISED LAND	1964	CHESS	UK	CRE 6002
(EP) COME ON	1965	CHESS	UK	CRE 6005
(EP) R& B WITH CHUCK BERRY	196	LONDON	UK	EPU 1053
(EP) REELIN & ROCKIN	196	LONDON	UK	EPM 1188
(EP) I GOT A BOOKING	19	CHESS	UK	CRE 6012
(EP) YOU CAME A LONG WAY FROM ST LOUIS	19	CHESS	UK	CRS 6016

DAVE BERRY

DAVE BERRY	V	(ALL	(A) DAVE BERRY	1964	DECCA	UK	LK 4653
			(B) A DOZEN BERRY'S	1966	ACE OF CLUBS	UK	SCL 1218
			(C) SPECIAL SOUND OF DAVE BERRY	1968	DECCA	UK	LK 4823
			(D) DAVE BERRY 68	1968	DECCA	UK	LK 4932
			(E) REMEMBERING	1976	DECCA	UK	REM 3

MIKE BERRY

MIKE BERRY	V	(ALL	(A) DRIFT AWAY	1972	YORK	UK	FYK 409
MEL JONES	D	(B	(B) ROCKS IN MY HEAD	1976	POLYDOR	UK	2383 392
GERRY CONWAY	D	(B	(B) ROCKS IN MY HEAD	1976	SIRE	US	7524
KEN LUNDGREN	B	(B	(C) I'M A ROCKER	1980	EPIC	US	36071
BILLY KUY	G	(B					
GEOFF WHITEHORN	G	(B	CHAS HODGES	K	(B	ANDY PARKER	G	(B
TERRY BRITTON	G	(B	CLEM CATTINI	D	(B	GRAHAM TODD	K	(B
KEN FREEMAN	SYN	(B				

PETE BEST

PETE BEST	D V	(A	(A) THE PETE BEST STORY	1966 SAVAGE 71/2 BEST FAN CLUB 100
GEORGE HARRISON	G V	(A		
PAUL McCARTNEY	B V G	(A	JOHN LENNON	G V	(A	STUART SUTCLIFFE	B	(A

BETHLEHAM ASYLUM

DANNY FINLAY	G V	(AB	(A) COMMIT THYSELF	1970	AMPEX	US	10106
CHARLES DECHANT	WIND V	(AB	(B) BETHLEHEM ASYLUM	1971	AMPEX	US	10124
CHRISTIAN GANDH	K FLT	(AB					
JIMMY NEIMAN	B V,	(AB	BUDDY HELM	D	(AB		

BETHNAL

GEORGE CSAPO	V K VLN	(AB	(A) DANGEROUS TIMES	1978	VERTIGO	UK	9102 020
EVERTON WILLIAMS	B V	(AB	(B) CRASH LANDING	1978	VERTIGO	UK	9102 029
PETE DOWLING	D	(AB					
NICK MICHAELS	G	(AB					

DICKIE BETTS

RICHARD(DICKIE)BETTS	G V	(ALL	(A) HIGHWAY CALL	1975	CAPRICORN	UK	2429 117
WITH			(A) HIGHWAY CALL	1975	CAPRICORN	US	0123
DAVE TOLER	D	(1C	(B) DICKIE BETTS & GREAT SOUTHERN	1977	ARISTA	UK SPARTY 1005
DAN TOLER	G V	(BC	(B) DICKIE BETTS & GREAT SOUTHERN	1977	ARISTA	US	4123
KEN TIBBETTS	B	(B	(C) ATLANTA BURNING DOWN	1978	ARISTA	UK SPARTY 1046
TOM BROOME	K V	(B	(C) ATLANTA BURNING DOWN	1978	ARISTA	US	4168
DONNIE SHARBONO	D	(1BC	(1) 1978 UK TOURING BAND				
JERRY THOMPSON	PERC	(					
DAVID GOLDFLIES	B	(1C	CHUCK LEAVELL	PNO	(A	DAVID WALSHAW	D PERC	(A
MICHAEL WORKMAN	K V	(1	JOHN HUGHEY	STEEL	(A	JOHNNY SANDLIN	B PERC	(A
DON JOHNSON	V	(B	TOMMY TALTON	G	(A	STRAY STRATON	B V	(A
TOPPER PRICE	HCA	(BC	WALTER POINDEXTER	BAN V	(A	FRANK POINDEXTER	DOBRO V	(A
MICKEY THOMAS	V	(B	OSCAR UNDERWOOD	MAND	(A	LEON POINDEXTER	G V	(A
VASSAR CLEMENTS	FDL	(A	JEFF HANNA	G	(A	REESE WYNANS	HCA	(AC
BUCK	V	(A	DOTTIE	V	(A	REBA	V	(A
BONNIE BRAMLETT	V	(C	CLYDIE KING	V	(C	SHIRLEY MATTHEWS	V	((C

```
    ROBERTO DETREE        G      (ABCD    (A) EINSTIEG                        19    VERTIGO      GER      1001
    JIMMY J GALWAY        FLT    (A       (B) AND THE WATERS OPENED          19    VERTIGO      GER  6360 612
    ROBERT ELISCU         WIND   (ABCD    (C) DHARANA                        19    VERTIGO      GER  6360 619
    COTCH BLACK           PERC D(ABC      (D) HESSE BETWEEN MUSIC            19    ELECTROLA    GER  062 29546
    ULRICH STRANZ                (A
    PETER MICHAEL HAMEL   K      (ABCD   ANATOL ARKUS      SYN   (C    TOM VANDERGELD      VIBES     (D
    GARY TODD             B      (C      JERZY ZIEMBROWSKI  B    (D    HOLGER BRANDT       D         (D
    AL GROMER             SIT    (D      PETER MULLER            (D    DURU OMSON          D     (B
    CHARLES CAMPBELL      CONGA  (CD     APARNA CHAKRAVARTI TAMB  (C    BOBBY JONES         WIND (D
    FRANZ LEHRNDORFER     K      (D      GERT WESTPHAL      V     (D
```

```
    ALEX BEVAN            G V    (A      (A) NO TRUTH TO SELL               1971   BIG TREE     US       2006
    ROLLY BROWN           G      (A
    JIM NICE              B      (A     TOM BAKER          PNO   (A
```

```
    BHAGAVAN DAS          V PERC (A      (A) AH                (DBL)        1972   BHAGAVAN DAS US       1080
```

```
    HANSI BIEBL           G V    (A      (A) FIRST                          1979   AMIGA        GDR  855716
    MICHAEL KASZUBOWSKI   B      (A
    PETER KRAUSE          D      (A     BERND KLEINOW       HARP  (A
```

```
    ATLI GRUND            G V    (A      (A) BIG BALLS & THE GREAT WHITE IDIOT 1977  NOVA             6 23280
    ALFRED GRUND          B V    (A
    PETER GRUND           D V    (A     WOLFGANG LORENZ    G V   (A    BARON ADOLF KAISER   V        (A
```

```
    BIG BOPPER(J P RICHARDSON V          (A) CHANTILLY LACE                  1958   MERCURY            20432
    DIED 1959 IN PLANE CRASH WITH        (A) CHANTILLY LACE                  1974   CONTOUR          6870 531
    BUDDY HOLLY                          (A) CHANTILLY LACE                  19    PICKWICK     US      3565
```

```
    CHRIS SHAKESPEARE     V              (A) ROLLS ON & ROCKS OFF(4 TRACKS)   CASSETTE ONLY COMP
    NICK GUYLER           G
    ARNIE COTRELL         G V           RONNIE TAYLOR      SAX         JOSS JONES          B     (
    SIMON TILLEY          D             BOB PETTIT         SAX         MARTIN WHITE        TROM
    CHRIS BROWN           G
```

```
    JANIS JOPLIN          V      (AB     (A) BIG BROTHER & THE HOLDING COMPANY 1968  LONDON      UK   SHT  8377
    SAM ANDREWS           G B V  (ABCD   (A) BIG BROTHER & THE HOLDING COMPANY 1967  FONTANA          TL   5457
    JAMES GURLEY          B      (ABCD   (A) BIG BROTHER & THE HOLDING COMPANY 1967  MAINSTREAM  US        6099
    DAVID GETZ            D PNO  (ABCD   (A) BIG BROTHER & THE HOLDING COMPANY 1967  CBS  9700   US   KC  30631
    PETE ALBIN            B G    (ABCD   (B) CHEAP THRILLS                    1968   CBS         UK       63392
    NICK GRAVENITES       V      (CD     (B) CHEAP THRILLS                    1968   CBS         US   PC  9700
    DAVID SCHALLOCK       G V    (CD     (C) BE A BROTHER                     1971   CBS         UK       64118
    MIKE FINNIGAN         K V    (CD     (C) BE A BROTHER                     1971   CBS         US   KC  30222
    KATHY McDONALD        V      (CD     (D) HOW HARD IT IS                   1971   CBS         US   KC  30738
    IRA KAMIN             K      (C
    TOWER OF POWER        HRNS   (C     JOHN SIMON         PNO   (B
```

```
    FRANKIE BRUNSON       V      (A      (A) BIG DADDY'S BLUES               196    GEE          US       704
                                         (B) TWIST PARTY                     196    REGENT       US      6106
```

```
    ART MUNSON            G V    (A      (A) BIG FOOT                        1968   WINRE        US      1004
    VIRGIL BECKHAM        B V    (A
    SPENCER EARNSHAW      D      (A     GERARD BELISLE    HRNS V (A    DAVID GARLAND       K HRNS V(A
```

```
    JOE SHIKANY           G V    (A      (A) BIG HORN                        1978   CBS          US      35618
    MICHAEL IPSEN         B V    (A
    STEVE ADAMEK          D V    (A     BOB MARCY         WIND V(A    PETER DAVIS         K V   (A
```

```
    BIG JOHN GOODISON     V      (ALL    (A) ACT 1                          1974   DJM                DJLPS 438
    PIP WILLIAMS          G      (A      (B) ACT 2                          1975   DJM                DJLPS 463
    COLIN FLETCHER        K V    (A      (C) ON THE ROAD                    1977   DJM                DJF 30511
    MIKE GREGORY          D      (A
    PHIL WAINMAN          D V    (A
```

```
    BIG JOE               V      (A      (A) KEEP ROCKING & SWINGING        197    ?                  LAP  001
    SLY DUNBAR            D      (A      (B) AFRICAN PRINCESS               1978   TROJAN      UK TRLS 152
    JOHNNY CLARKE         PNO    (A
    CARLTON DAVIS         D      (A     ROBBIE SHAKESPEARE  B    (A    LLOYD SPARKS        B     (A
    EARL SMITH            G      (A     BOOFA              G    (A    TONY CHIN           G     (A
    ANSEL COLLINS         ORG    (A     BERNARD HARVEY     ORG  (A    AUSSIE HEBERT       PNO   (A
```

```
    MACEO MERRYWEATHER    V PNO  (A      (A) VOLUME ONE                     1976   RCA               17204
    TAMPA RED             G      (B      (B) BIG MACEO                      19    RCA          FR  730 577
    ALFRED ELKINS         B      (B
    CLIFFORD JONES        D      (B     LITTLE T(TYRELL DIXON) D   (B    CHARLIE SANDERS     D     (B
    BIG CRAWFORD          B      (B     EDDIE BOYD         PNO   (B
```

```
                                         (A) BIG MOUTH                      19    SPINDIZZY   US  31024
```

```
    JOHN WEATHERS         D      (A      (A) BLUEBELL WOOD                   1971   PEGASUS     UK   PEG     4
    PHIL RYAN             K      (A
    GARY PICKFORD HOPKINS V G            RAY TAFF WILLIAMS  G     (A    RITCHIE FRANCIS     B PNO V  (A
```

```
    ALEX CHILTON          V      (ABC    (A) RADIO CITY                     1971   ARDENT      US  ADS  2803
    CHRIS BELL            G V    (A      (B) BIG STAR                       1972   ARDENT      US  ADS  1501
    ANDY HUMMELL          B      (AB     (AB) RADIO CITY/BIG STAR           1978   STAX            SXSP  302
    JODY STEPHENS         D      (ABC    (C) THIRD ALBUM                    1978   AURA            AUL   703
    TOMMY CATHY           B      (C      (C) THIRD ALBUM                    1978   PVC         US        7903
    STEVE CROPPER         G      (C
    CARL MARSH            SYN    (C     RICHARD ROSEBROUGH  D     (BC   WILLIAM MURPHY      B     (C
    LEE BAKER             G      (C     JIM DICKINSON      K G PROD(C    DANNY JONES               (B
    TOMMY McCLURE         B      (C     TAPT TARRENT    [48]  D    (C
```

BIG THREE (UK)

```
    BRIAN GRIFFITHS      G    (AB      (A) LIVE AT THE CAVERN      (EP)   1963   DECCA           UK   DFE  8552
    JOHN GUSTAFSON       B    (AB      (B) RESURECTION                    1973   POLYDOR         UK   2383  199
    JOHN HUTCHINSON      D    (A
    PETER ROBINSON       PNO  (B       HENRY LOWTHER       HRN    (B      JOHN SMITH            TUBA (B
    LES THATCHER         BANJO (B      MICK GRABHAM        G      (B      NIGEL OLSSON          D    (B
```

BIG THREE (US)

```
    CASS ELLIOTT         V    (        (A) BIG THREE                      196    ROULETTE        US   42000
    TIM ROSE             V    (        ( ) BIG THREE                      19     FM              US     307
    DENNY DOHERTY        V    (        ( ) LIVE AT RECORDING STUDIO       19     FM              US     311
```

BIG YOUTH

```
    BIG YOUTH            PERC V(ALL     (A) SCREAMING TARGET              1973   TROJAN          TRLS   61
    TONY CHIN            G    (E        (B) NATTY CULTURAL DREAD          1976   TROJAN          TRLS  123
    KEITH STERLING       PNO  (E        (C) HIT THE ROAD JACK             1976   TROJAN          TRLS  137
    EARL SMITH           G    (E        (D) DREADLOCKS DREAD              1976   KLIK            KLP  9001
    SANTA                D    (E        (D) DREADLOCKS DREAD              1978   FRONT LINE      FL   1014
    GEORGE FULLWOOD      B    (E        (E) ISAIAH FIRST PROPHET OF OLD   1978   FRONT LINE      FL   1011
    EARL LINDO           K    (E        (F) REGGAE GI DEM DUB             1979
    VINCENT GORDON       TROM (E        (G) REGGAE PHENOMENON            1977    BIG YOUTH       BYD    1
    HERMAN MARQUIS       SAX  (E        (H) EVERYDAY SKANK(BEST OF)       19     TROJAN          TRLS  189
    BOBBY ELLIS          TPT  (E
    S MORRIS             PERC (E        STICKY              PERC   (E     RITA MARLEY           V    (E
    JUDY MOWATT          V    (E        SKINFLESH & BONES BAND     (D
```

TRAVIS BIGGS

```
    TRAVIS BIGGS         (A             (A) SOLAR FUNK                    1980   MCA             US     3154
```

BIJOU

```
    VINCENT PALMER       G V  (ABCDE    (A) DANSE AVEC MOI                1977   PHILIPS         9101  138
    PHILIPPE DAUGA       B V  (ABCDE    (B) OK CAROLE                     1978   PHILIPS         9101  178
    DYNAMITE YAN         D    (ABCDE    (C) PAS DORMIR                    1979   PHILIPS         9101  272
    JEAN WILLIAM THOURY  PROD (ABDE     (D) EN PUBLIC                     1980   PHILIPS         6313  059
    RON MAEL             PROD (C        (E) FAMOUS DIMPLES                1981   PHILIPS         6313  139
    RUSSELL MAEL         PROD (C
```

BILLION DOLLAR BABIES

```
    MICHAEL BRUCE        G V  (A        (A) BATTLE AXE                    1977   POLYDOR         UK   2391  273
    NEAL SMITH           D    (A        (A) BATTLE AXE                    1977   POLYDOR         US     1 6100
    DENNIS DUNAWAY       B    (A
    BOB DOLIN            K    (A        MIKE MARCONI        G V    (A
```

TREVOR BILLMUSS

```
    TREVOR BILLMUSS      (A             (A) FAMILY APOLOGY                1970   CHARISMA        CAS  1017
```

BINTANGS

```
    JIM CUOMO            WIND (C        (A) BLUES ON THE CEILING          1969   DECCA NL        6440 676
    LEO                  PERC (C        (B) RIDIN' ON THE                 1970   DECCA
    GUS PLEINES          V HCA (CDE     (C) GENUINE BULL                  1975   RCA             NL   YHPL10982
    JAPIE CASTRICUM      G PNO (C       (D) NIGHT FIGHTER                 1979   ARIOLA          NL    200  525
    JACK VAN SCHIE       G    (CDE      (E) MICKEY FINN                   1980   ARIOLA          NL    202  119
    FRANK KRAAIJEVELD    B V  (C
    HARRY SCHIERBEEK     D PERC(C       ALBERT SCHIERBEEK   PERC G (C     WILLEM                PERC(C
```

BILLY & THE BEATERS

```
    BILLY VERA           G V  (A        (A) BILLY & THE BEATERS           1981   ALFA
    JEFF BAXTER          G    (A
    BRYAN CUMMINGS       SAX  (A        JIM EHINGER         PNO    (A     CHUCK FIORE           B    (A
    GEORGE MARINELLI     SAX  (A        JERRY PETERSON      SAX    (A     LON PRICE             SAX  (A
    RON VIOLA            SAX  (A        BEAU SEGAL          D      (A
```

TONY BIRD

```
    TONY BIRD            V G  (AB       (A) TONY BIRD                     1976   CBS US 34324    UK   81183
    WITH                                (B) BIRD OF PARADISE              1978   CBS US 34988    UK   82498
    EMMANUEL RENTZOS     K    (A
    WINSTON DELANDRO     G    (A        RICHARD BAILEY      D      (A     ERNEST BAIDO          B    (A
    LUCKY RANKU          G    (A        JAMES MENE          D      (A     ERNEST MOTHLE         B    (A
    JOHN KIRKPATRICK     CONC/ACC (A    GRAHAM SMITH        HCA    (A     SETH SIBANDA          V    (B
    KWA ZULU SINGERS     V    (A        T L BEDEAU          SAX    (A     GEORGE LEE            SAX  (A
    STEPHEN AMAZING      B    (A        JEREMY TAYLOR       G      (A     ARLEN ROTH            G BAN(B
    JOEL REIFF           B    (B        JOHN SIEGLER        B      (B     STU WOODS             B    (B
    FRANK CENTENO        B    (B        CHRISTOPHER PARKER  D      (B     RICHARD CROOKS        D    (B
    BARRY LAZAROWITZ     PERC (B        CRUSHER BENNETT     PERC   (B     FALUMI PRINCE         PERC (B
    JOHN LISSAUER        V K PERC (B    DOMINIC CORTESE     ACC    (B     MORRIS GOLDBERG       WIND (B
    DAVID SAMUELS        PERC (B        MAERETHA STEWART    V      (B     DEBORAH MACDUFFIE     V    (B
    JOHN CROWDER         V    (B        LINDA TSHABALALA    V      (B     SELAELO DAN MAREDI    V    (B
    RON GETMAN           V    (B        GORDON GRODY        V      (B     THEMBI MISHALI        V    (B
    THEMBA NTINGA        V    (B        FANA DAVID KEKANA   V      (B
```

BIRDS

```
    RON WOOD             G              (A) HARD UP HEROES (1TRACK)       1974   DECCA           DPA 3009/ 10
    ALISTAIR McKENZIE    V
    KIM GARDNER          B              TONY MUNROE         G            PETE McDANIELS         D
```

BIRTH CONTROL

```
    BERND NOSKE          D PERC V (ABCFGHI  (A) BIRTH CONTROLL            1969   METRONOME       MLP15 336
    DIRK STEFFENS        G V  (D        (A) BIRTH CONTROL                 1971   CHARISMA CAS1036 PROPHESY US1002
    BRUNO FRENZEL        G V  (ABCDEFGHI (B) OPERATION                    1971   OHR             GER    556 015
                                        ( ) GOLD ROCK                    1973   METRONOME       0040  019
    PETER FEOLLER        B V  (DFG       (C) HOODOO MAN                   1974   CBS                  65316
    HORST STACHELHAUS    B    (HI        (D) RE BIRTH                     1974   CBS                  65963
    MANFRED VON BOHR     D    (HI        (E) LIVE                         1974   CBS                  88088
    ZEUS B HELD          V SAX K (DFGHI  (F) PLASTIC PEOPLE               1975   CBS                  80921
    REINHOLD SOBOTTA     K    (A         (G) BACKDOOR POSSIBILITIES       1976   BRAIN           0060  019
    WOLFGANG NEUSER      K    (A         (H) INCREASE                     1977   BRAIN 0060 019   0040  122
    BERND KOSCHMIDDER    B    (ABC       (I) TITANIC                      1978   BRAIN           0060  149
    JOCKEN VAN GRUMBKOW  CELLO (F        (J) LIVE 79                      1979   BRAIN           0060  240
    FRIEDEMANN LEINER    FLT  (F         (K) DEAL DONE AT NIGHT           1980   ARIOLA          203  423
    CHRIS NOPPENEY       VLA  (F
    BERND NOSKE          D V  (K         JURGEN GOLDSCHMIDT  B      (K     WOLFGANG HOM          K    (K
    BRUNO FRENZEL        G V  (K
```

BIRTHA

```
SHELE PINIZZOTTO    G V   (AB    (A) BIRTHA                      1972  PROBE           SPBA 6267
LIVER FAVELA        V PERC D (AB  (A) BIRTHA                     1972  ABC DUNHILL     DSK 50127
SHERRY HAGLER       K     (AB    (B) CANT STOP THE MADNESS       1973  PROBE           SPBA 6272
ROSEMARY BUTLER     B V   (AB
```

BIRTHDAY PARTY

```
NICK CAVE           V     (A     (A) PRAYERS ON FIRE             1981  4AD        UK   CAD 104
ROWLAND HOWARD      G     (A
MICK HARVEY         G K   (A     TRACY PEW        WIND  (A    PHIL CALVERT     D  (A
```

BISCUIT DAVIS

```
TOM BAILEN          G V   (A     (A) PLAYING ON THE MOON         1973  FLYING DUTCHMAN US  12014
TODD ZIMMERMAN      B     (A
```
```
BOB THIELE          G K V (A     DERRICK HOITSMAN  G VLN V(A  ROBERT ANTHOINE D   (A
```

ELVIN BISHOP

```
ELVIN BISHOP        G V   (ALL   (A) ELVIN BISHOP              1969  FILLMORE          30001
WITH                             (B) FEEL IT                   1970  CBS               30239
STEVEN MILLER       PNO   (ABC   (B) FEEL IT                   1970  EPIC              64180
JOHN CHAMBERS       D     (ABC   (C) ROCK MY SOUL              19    EPIC              31563
APPLEJACK           HCA   (A     (C) APPLEJACK                 19    EPIC              65295
ALBERT GIANQUINTO   PNO   (A     (D) BEST OF (CRABSHAW RISING) 1972  EPIC              33693
ART STAVRO          B     (A     (E) LET IT FLOW               1974  CAPRICORN  UK     2429116
JO BAKER            V PERC(BEFC   (E) LET IT FLOW               1974  CAPRICORN  US     CP 0134
KIP MAERCKLEIN      B     (BC     (F) JUKE JOINT JUMP           1975  CAPRICORN  UK     2429 127
PERRY WALSH         V HCA (BC     (F) JUKE JOINT JUMP           1975  CAPRICORN  US     CP  0151
MIKE CARABELLO      PERC  (B      (G) STRUTTIN' MY STUFF        1976  CAPRICORN  UK     2429 136
CHEPITO AREAS       PERC  (B      (G) STRUTTIN' MY STUFF        1976  CAPRICORN  US     CP  0165
POINTER SISTERS     V     (B      (H) HOMETOWN BOY MAKES GOOD   1976  CAPRICORN  UK     2429 147
PHIL AABERG         K     (EFGHJ  (H) HOMETOWN BOY MAKES GOOD   1976  CAPRICORN  US     CP  0176
DON BALDWIN         D V   (EFGHIJ (I) RAISIN' HELL              1977  CAPRICORN  UK     2637 104
JOHN VERNAZZA       G     (EFGHIJ (I) RAISIN' HELL              1977  CAPRICORN  US     2CP 0185
MICK THOMAS         V     (EFGHIJ (J) THE BEST OF               1979  CAPRICORN  UK     2429 189
TOY CALDWELL        STEEL (E
JOHN SANDLIN  G PERC(EF  DICKIE BETTS     G  (EF  SLY STONE     K  (E  CHARLIE DANIELS V FDLG(E
ROSS MASON    B     (F   RICK KELLOGG    HCA (F   STEPHEN STILLS G V (F  ROSS HAYASHIDA V   (FH
BILL SLAIS    K     (GHIJ MIKE KECK       K  (G   TERRY HANCK   SAX (G  RENI SLAIS      V   (H
DEBBIE CATHEY V     (EI   MELVIN SEALS    K  (IJ  CHUCK BROOKE  HRNS (IJ BOB CLAIRE     HRNS (IJ
DAVE GROVER   HRNS  (IJ   BILL LAMB       HRNS (IJ MIC GILLETTE HRNS (HI STEVE KUPKA    HRNS (HI
GREG ADAMS    HRNS  (HI   PAUL HORNSBY    K  (E   BILL MEEKER   D  (EC  JEROME JOSEPH   CONGA(E
DAVID WALSHAW PERC  (E    RANDALL BRAMBLETT SAX (E DAVID BROWN  SAX (E  HAROLD WILLIAMS SAX(E
VASSAR CLEMENTS STRINGS(E GIDEON DANIELS  V  (E   ANNIE SAMPSON V  (E  TOWER OF POWER  HRNS(H
JUNE POINTER  V     (F    MICHAEL BROOKS B(EFGHJ RON STALLINGS V SAX(C MILT HOLLAND    PERC(C
MEL ELLISON   SAX   (C    DENNIS MARCELINO SAX (C DELANEY BRAMLETT G PROD V(C JIM GORDON CLAR(C
BOBBY BLACK   FDL   (C    CLYDIE KING      V  (C  VANETTA FIELDS V  (C GLORIA JONES    V  (C
SHIRLEY MATTHEWS V  (C
```

STEPHEN BISHOP

```
STEPHEN BISHOP  TROM V G(ALL  (A) CARELESS              1976  ABC  US 954   UK  ABCL 5201
ANDREW GOLD       G    (A     (B) BISH                  1978  ABC  US 1082  UK  ABCL 5252
MAC CRIDLIN       B    (A     (C) RED CAB TO MANHATTAN  1980  WB   US 3473  UK  K 56853
TOMMY VIG         PERC (B
MICHAEL STATON V STEEL(AB VICTOR FELDMAN   PERC (A  STEVE PORCARO  SYN (B  STEVE PAIETTA   ACC (A
LARRY BROWN       D    (A    LEE RITENOUR    G  (A  CRAIG DOERGE   K  (A  REINIE PRESS    B  (A
JIM GORDON        D    (A    CHAKA KHAN      V  (AB ALAN LINDGREN  SYN (A  LARRY KNECHTEL  K  (A
ERIC CLAPTON      G    (AC   RAY PIZZI      SAX (A  MAX BENNETT    B  (A  JOHN GUERIN     D  (A
ART GARFUNKEL     V    (ABC  TOMMY TEDESCO  MAND (A JEFFREY STATON G V B (ABC LEAH KUNKEL   V  (AB
ED SHAUGHNESSY    D    (B    RAY BROWN       B  (B  RICK SCHLOSSER D  (B  DAVID FOSTER    K  (B
GREG PHILLINGANES K    (B    MIKE McDONALD   V  (B  LEE SKLAR      B  (B  ABE LABORIEL    B  (B
DAVID HUNGATE     B    (B    JOHN JARVIS     K  (AB TOM SCOTT      SAX (B  RAY POUNDS      D  (B
NATHAN WATTS      B    (B    MICHAEL SEMBELLO G (B  RAY PARKER     G  (B  PAULINHO DA COSTA  PERC(B
KEITH HOLLAR      B    (B    BILL PAYNE      K  (B  STEVE CROPPER  G  (B  NATALIE COLE    V  (B
HAL ATKINSON      D    (B    DAVID SHIELDS   B  (B  BOBBY CHADWICK K  (B  ANDY NEWMARK    D  (C
WILLIE WEEKS      B    (C    DON GROLNICK    K  (C  DAVID SPINOZZA G  (C  SID McGINNIS    G  (C
CHRIS STAINTON    PNO  (C    CLIVE ANSTEE    STR (C JOHN GIBLIN    B  (C  PHIL COLLINS    D  (C
CHRIS PARKER      D    (C    NEIL JASON      B  (C  HUGH McCRACKEN G  (C  JEFF MIRONOV    G  (C
PHOEBE SNOW       V    (C    NEIL LARSEN     K  (C  STEVE GADD     D  (C  DENNIS BELFIELD D  (C
GARY BROOKER      PNO  (C    JOHN TROPEA     G  (C  DEAN PARKS     G  (C  BUZZY FEITEN    G  (C
MIKE MAINIERI     SYN  (C    LENNY CASTRO   PERC (C DAVID LASLEY   V  (C  ARNOLD McCULLER V  (C
JAY GRAYDON       G    (A    BARLOW JARVIS   K  (C  RUSS KUNKEL    D  (C
```

BIZARROS

```
NICK NICKOLLS     V    (     (A) LADY DUBONETTE   (EP)    1976  GORILLA
GERRY PARKINS     G    (     (B) BIZARROS                 1979  MERCURY      US
TERRY WALKER      G    (     (C) RUBBER CITY REBELS       19    CLONE        UK   CL001
```

BILL BLACK COMBO

```
BILL BLACK        B    (
BOB TUCKER        G V  (*    BILL BLACK COMBO       19    ZODIAC     US        5006
RONNIE SCAIFE     G    (*    SAXY JAZZ              1960  HI  US 32002
ROBERT GLADNEY    SAX V (*   SOLID & RAUNCHY        1962  HI  US 32003  LONDON UK  2310
PHIL MUNSEY       B    (*    THAT WONDERFUL FEELING 1961  HI  US 32004
BILL COMPTON      D    (*    MOVIN'                 1962  HI  US 32004  LONDON UK  2433
GIL MICHAEL       STEEL FDL (* RECORD HOP           196   HI  US 32006
LARRY ROGERS      HCA  (*    LETS TWIST             196   HI  US 32006  LONDON UK  2427
DANNY HOGAN       V    (*    UNTOUCHABLE SOUND      1963  HI  US 32009  LONDON UK  8080
BUTCH CARTER      V    (*    GREATEST HITS          1963  HI  US 32012  LONDON UK  8113
                             PLAYS THE BLUES        196   HI  US 32015
                             PLAYS CHUCK BERRY      1964  HI  US 32017  LONDON UK  8187
                             GOES BIG BAND          1964  HI  US 32020
                             MORE SOULID & RAUNCHY  1965  HI  US 32023
                             ALL TIMERS             1966  HI  US 32032
                             BLACK LACE             1967  HI  US 32033
                             KING OF THE ROAD       1967  HI  US 32036
                             THE MEMPHIS SCENE      1967  MEGA US 1008
                             THE BEAT GOES ON       1968  HI  US 32041  LONDON UK  8367
                             TURN ON YOUR LOVE LIGHT 1969 HI  US 32044  LONDON UK  8373
(CONTINUED)                  SOULIN' THE BLUES      1969  HI  US 32047  LONDON UK  8389
```

[50]

BILL BLACK COMBO   (CONTINUED)

RAINDROPS KEEP FALLING		1970	CBS		59957
JUKE BOX FAVOURITES		19	MEGA	US 1014 NASHVILLE UK 2003	
MORE MAGIC		19	HI	US 32061	
ROCK'N'ROLL FOREVER		1973	MEGA	US 5008 NASHVILLE uk 2005	
BILL BLACK IS BACK		1974	MEGA	US 600 NASHVILLE UK 2007	
GREATEST HITS VOL 2		19	HI	US 32078	
SOLID & COUNTRY		1975	HI	US 32088	
WORLDS GREATEST HONKY TONK BAND		1975	HI	US 32093	
(*) ITS HONKY TONK TIME		1977	HI	US 32104 LONDON UK 140	
BLACK WITH SUGAR		19	CBS	UK 63672	
MR BEAT		19	HI	US 52604	
MEMPHIS TENNESSEE		1977	HI	US 5006	
AWARD WINNERS		1977	HI	US 8004	

PABLO BLACK
PAUL DIXON   (( ) MR MUSIC ORIGINALLY   1978   STUDIO ONE
BLACK ACE
                                    (A) BLACK ACE   19   ARHOOLIE   US   1003
BLACK CAT BONES
SIMON KIRKE   D   ((A) BARBED WIRE SANDWICH   1970   NOVA   SDN   15
PAUL KOSSOFF   G   (
STU BROOKS   B   (A   DEREK BROOKS   G   (A   BOB WESTON   G   (
TERRY SIMMS   (PAUL TILLER   (BRIAN SHORT   V   (A
ROD PRICE   G V (A   STEVE MILLINER   PNO (PHIL LENOIR   D   (A
ROBIN SYLVESTER   PNO (A
BLACK HEAT
                               ( ) BLACK HEAT   19   ATLANTIC   US   7237
                               ( ) NO TIME TO BURN   1973   JAM   JAL   104
                               ( ) NO TIME TO BURN   1974   ATLANTIC   US   SD   7294
                               ( ) KEEP ON RUNNING   1975   ATLANTIC   US   18128
BLACK IVORY
                               ( ) DONT TURN AROUND   1972   TODAY   1005
                               ( ) FEEL IT   1976   BUDDAH   US   5644
                               ( ) BLACK IVORY   1977   BUDDAH   US   5658
                               ( ) HEAVY HEAVY   1980   BUDDAH   US   5722
BLACK MERDA
ANTHONY HAWKINS   G   (A   (A) BLACK MERDA   197   CHESS 1511   569517
CHARLES HAWKINS   G   (A   (B) LONG BURN THE FIRE   197   JANUS   US   3042
TYRONE HITE   D   (A
BLACK OAK ARKANSAS
JIM DANDY MANGRUM V   (ALL   ( ) THE KNOWBODY ELSE   1969   STAX   US
RICKY REYNOLDS   G   (ABCDEFGHIJN (A) BLACK OAK ARKANSAS   1971 ATLANTIC UK 2400180 US ATCO 33354
JIMMY HENDERSON   G   (HIJKLMO (B) BLACK OAK ARKANSAS   19   ATLANTIC   UK   K 40215
STAN KNIGHT   G   (ABCDEFGHIJKLN(B) KEEP THE FAITH   1972   ATCO   US   SD 33381
PAT DAUGHERTY   B   (ABCDEFGHIJKLN(C) IF AN ANGEL CAME TO SEE YOU 1972 ATCO   US   SD 7008
RUBY STARR   V   (FKLN   (D) RAUNCH & ROLL   1973 ATLANTIC UK K40451 US ATCO 7019
TOMMY ALDRIDGE   D   (CDEFGHIJKLN (E) HIGH ON A HOG   1974   ATLANTIC   UK   K 40538
A K A DORK JACKSON   (E) HIGH ON A HOG   1974   ATCO   US   SD 7035
HARVEY JETT   G   (ACEN   (F) STREET PARTY   1974   ATLANTIC   UK   K 50057
GREG REDING   G V K((F) STREET PARTY   1974   ATCO   US   36101
JACK HOLDER   SAX G K(MO   (G) HOT & NASTY   1974   ATLANTIC   UK   K 20083
JOEL WILLIAMS   D   (MO   (H) AINT LIFE GRAND   1975   ATLANTIC   UK   K 50150
WAYNE EVANS   D   (ABGN   (I) X RATED   1975   MCA   UK   MCF 2734
ANDY TANAS   V B (MO   (I) X RATED   1975   MCA   US   2155
                               ( ) EARLY TIMES   1975   STAX   5504
                               (J) LIVE MUTHA   1976   ATLANTIC   UK   K50220
                               (J) LIVE MUTHA   1976   ATCO   US   36128
                               (K) BALLS OF FIRE   1976   MCA   UK 2762 US MCA   2199
                               (L) 10 YEAR OVERNIGHT SUCCESS 1976   MCA   US   2224
                               (M) RACE WITH THE DEVIL   1977   CAPRICORN   UK   2429 156
                               (M) RACE WITH THE DEVIL   1977   CAPRICORN   US   CP 0191
                               (N) BEST OF   1977   ATCO   US   SD 36150
                               (O) I'D RATHER BE SAILING   1978   CAPRICORN   US   CP 0207
BLACK PEARL
B B FIELDINGS   (A   (A) BLACK PEARL   1969   ATLANTIC   US   8220
GEOFF MORRIS   (A   (B) LIVE   19   PROPHESY   US   1001
JERRY CAUSI   (A
MOULTY   D   (A
BLACK ROSE
LES DUDEK   G V (A   (A) BLACK ROSE   1980   CASABLANCA   NBLP 7234
CHER   V   (A
MAX GRONENTHAL   V   (A   JOHN TOWNSEND   V   (A   GARY FERGUSON   D   (A
MICHAEL FINNIGAN K V (A   WARREN HAM   V   (A   RON RITCHOTTE   G V (A
TREY THOMPSON   B   (A   STEVE PORCARO   K   (A   MICHAEL BODDICKER K   (A
DAVID PAICH   V   (A   JAMES NEWTON HOWARD K   (A   PHIL BROWN   G   (A
BLACK SABBATH
TONY IOMMI   G   (ALL   (A) BLACK SABBATH   1970   VERTIGO   UK   V06
GEEZER BUTLER   B   (ALL   (A) "   1974   WWA   WWA   006
BILL WARD   D V (ABCDEFGHJ (A) "   1977   NEMS   UK   NEL 6002
OZZIE OSBOURNE   V HCA (ABCDEFGHJ (A) "   197   WB   US   1871
                               (A) "   197   WEA   913   193
                               (A) "   1980   NEMS   UK   6017
GERALD WOODRUFFE K   (G   (B) PARANOID   1970   VERTIGO   UK   6360 011
RONNIE JAMES DIO V   (JKI   (B) "   1975   WB   US   WS4 1887
RICK WAKEMAN   K   (E   (B) "   1977   NEMS   UK   NEL 6003
VINNIE APPICE   D   (K   (B) "   19   WB   US   K 3104
ROGER BAIN   PROD (AB   (B) "   1980   ARIOLA   NL   203 148
                               (B) "   19   WEA   913   194

(CONTINUED)

(C)	MASTER OF REALITY	1971	VERTIGO	UK	6360 050
(C)	"	1974	WWA		WWA 008
(C)	"	1977	NEMS	UK	NEL 6004
(C)	"	1971	WB	US	BS 2562
(C)	"	197	WEA		913 195
(D)	BLACK SABBATH 4	1972	VERTIGO	UK	6360 071
(D)	"	1974	WWA		WWA 009
(D)	"	1977	NEMS	UK	NEL 6005
(D)	"	197	WB	US	BS 2602
(D)	"	197	WEA		913 196
(E)	SABBATH BLOODY SABBATH	1973	VERTIGO	UK	6360 115
(E)	"	1974	WWA		WWA 005
(E)	2	197	WB	US	BS 2695
(F)	SABOTAGE	1975	VERTIGO	UK	9119 001
(F)	"	197	WB	US	BS 2822
(F)	"	1980	NEMS	UK	6018
(G)	TECHNICAL ECSTACY	1976	VERTIGO	UK	9102 750
(G)	"	1976	WB	US	BS 2969
(H)	NEVER SAY DIE	1978	VERTIGO	UK	9102 751
(H)	"	197	WB	US	K 3186
(I)	HEAVEN & HELL	1980	VERTIGO	UK	9102 752
(I)	"	1980	VERTIGO	NL	6302 017
(I)	"	1980	WB	US	3372
(J)	LIVE AT LAST	1980	NEMS CASSETTE	UK	BSC 001
(J)	"	1980	ARIOLA	NL	203 049
(K)	MOB RULES	1981	VERTIGO	UK	6302 119

COMPILATION ALBUMS

( )	ATTENTION (	1975	VERTIGO		6438 057
( )	ATTENTION (	19	WWA		WWA 101
( )	BLACK SABBATH VOL 2(COMP)	1975	VERTIGO	UK	9199 133
( )	WE SOLD OUR SOULS FOR ROCK'N'ROLL	1976	VERTIGO	UK	6641 335
( )	WE SOLD OUR SOULS FOR ROCK'N'ROLL	1977	NEMS	UK	NALD 101
( )	WE SOLD OUR SOUL FOR ROCK'N'ROLL	19	WB	US	BS 2923
( )	GREATEST HITS	1977	NEMS	UK	NELS 6009
( )	GREATEST HITS	1977	WEA		913 192

B115A   BLACK SHEEP   **B115A**

LOUIS GRAMMATICE	V	(AB	(A) BLACK SHEEP			1975	CAPITOL	US	11369
BRUCE TURGEN	B	(AB	(B) ENCOURAGING WORDS			1975	CAPITOL	US	11447
LARRY CROZIER	K	(AB						
DONALD MANCUSE	G	(AB	RON ROCCO	D	(A	MIKE BENAFEDE	D	(B

B116   BLACK SLATE   **B116**

DESMOND MAHONEY	D	(A	(A) AMIGO			1980	TCD TLDLP 1	ENSIGN	ENVY15
KEITH DRUMMOND	V	(A	(B) SIRENS IN THE CITY			1981	ENSIGN		ENVY505
CHRIS HANSON	G	(A						
ELROY BAILEY	B	(A	CLEDWYN ROGERS	G	(A	ANTHONY BRIGHTLY	K	(A
NICKY RIDGUARD	TROM	(A	RUDY HOLMES	SAX	(A	HERSCHEL HOLDER	TPT	(A
RAY CARNESS	SAX	(A						

B116A   BLACK SUN   **B116A**

JACK SIDNEY	PERC	(A	(A) BLACK SUN			1978	ROCKLAND		2424 181
RONNIE COBEN	D	(A						
STEVE McLOGAN	B	(A	SAM BUCCO	G	(A	JOHN SPRINGFIELD	G V	(A
ARFAN DERSON	G	(A	PHIL WALTER	K V	(A	BRUCE McGUINNS	K	(A
WALLY HAMILTON	K	(A	JEFF SHAPER	K	(A	RICHARD ELSON	SYN	(A
STEVE LASKER	SYN	(A	LENNY GARCIA	V	(A	MICHAEL LEONARDO	HRNS	(A

B117   BLACK UHURU   **B117**

MICHAEL ROSE	V	(CFFG	(A) LOVE CRISIS			1978	THIRD WORLD		TWS 925
PUMA JONES	V	(CFG	(B) SHOWCASE			197	D ROY		
DICKIE SIMPSON	V	(CFG	(C) BLACK UHURU			1979	VIRGIN	UK	1004
SLY DUNBAR	D	(CDFG	(C) BLACK UHURU			1980	BUTT	UK	ONLY2
ROBBIE SHAKESPEARE	B G	(CFG	(D) SINSEMILLA			1980	ISLAND	UK	ILPS 9593
RUDOLF DENNIS	(		(E) BLACKSOUND OF FREEDOM			1981	GREENSLEEVES	UK	GREL 23
DON CARLOS	(		(F) RED			1981	ISLAND	UK	ILPS 9625
DOUGIE BRYAN	G	(FG	(F) RED			1981	ISLAND	GER	203 775
KEITH STERLING	ORG	(CF	(G) CHILL OUT			1982	ISLAND	GER	204 698
BARRY REYNOLDS	G	(FG						
WINSTON WRIGHT	ORG	(C	RADCLIFFE BRYAN	G	(CF	RANCHIE McLEAN	ORG	(FG
STICKY THOMPSON	PERC	(FG	MIKEY CHUNG	G	(FG	ROBERT LYN	PNO	(FG
SKY JUICE	PERC	(G	ANSELL COLLINS	K	(G			

B118   BLACK VELVET   **B118**

PETE MORRIS			(A) THIS IS BLACK VELVET			1971	BEACON		BENS 16
CLINTON CREASEY			(B) PEOPLE OF THE WORLD			1972	PYE		NSPL18392
LYNTON STEEL			(C) CAN YOU FEEL IT			1973	SEVEN SUN		SUN LP1
BRIAN CLARK			(D) LOVE CITY			19	OKEH	US	14130

B119   BLACK WIDOW   **B119**

JIM GANNON V G VIBES		(AB	(A) SACRIFICE			1970	CBS US 6786	UK	63948
ZOOT TAYLOR	K	(ABC	(B) BLACK WIDOW			1970	CBS		64133
KIP TREVOR	V G	(ABC	(C) THREE			1971	CBS		64562
CLIVE JONES	WIND	(ABC						
BOB BOND	B	(A	JOHN CULLEY	G V	(C	CLIVE BOX	D	(A
ROMEO CHALLENGER	D	(BC	GEOFF GRIFFITHS	B V	(BC			

B120   BLACKBEARD   **B120**

DENNIS 'BLACKBEARD'BOVELL	B G K	(AB	(A) STRICTLY DUB WIZE			1978	TEMPUS		TEM 001
NICK BAILEY	SYN	(B	(A) STRICTLY DUB WISE			197	LIBERTY (ROCKFILE)		LBR 1013
TONY ROBINSON	K	(B	(B) I WAH DUB			1980	MORE CUT		RDC 2002
ANGUS GAYE	D	(B						
JOHN KPIAYE	G	(B	PATRICK TENYUE	K V	(	JULIO FINN	HCA	(B
JAH BUNNY	D	(B						

B121
  BLACKBLOOD

BLACKBLOOD
B121

( ) BLACKBLOOD			1976	BRADLEY	UK	BLAK 9001
( ) BLACKBLOOD			19	MAINSTREAM	US	416
( ) BLOOD BROTHER BLOOD SISTER			19	CHRYSALIS	US	1144

B122

BLACKBYRDS
B122

KEVIN TONEY	K	(E	(A) BLACKBYRDS FIRST	1975	FANTASY		FT 9444
KEITH KILLGO	D	(E	(B) FLYING START	197	FANTASY		FT 522
JOE HALL	B	(E	(B) FLYING START	197	FANTASY	US	FT 9472
ORVILLE SAUNDERS	G	(E	(C) CITY LIFE	197	FANTASY	US	FT 9490
STEPHEN JOHNSON	SAX	(E	(D) UNFINISHED BUSINESS	197	FANTASY	US	FT 9518
			(E) ACTION	1978	FANTASY	UK	FT 534
			(E) ACTION	1978	FANTASY	US	FT 9535
			(F) BETTER DAYS	1980	FANTASY	UK	9602

B123

BLACKFOOT
B123

GREG WALKER	B	(ABCDEF	(A) NO RESERVATIONS	1975	ISLAND	UK	ILPS 9326
RICK MEDLOCKE	G V	(ABCDEF	(B) FLYIN' HIGH	1976	EPIC	US	PE 34378
JACKSON SPIRES	D V	(ABCDEF	(C) STRIKES	1979	ATCO US 38112	UK	K50603
PAT McCAFFREY	K	(CDE	(D) TOMCATTIN'	1980	ATCO US 32101	UK	K 50702
CHARLIE HARGRETT	G	(ABCDEF	(E) MARAUDER	1981	ATCO US 32107	UK	K 50799
CYNTHIA DOUGLAS	V	(C	(F) HIGHWAY SONG'LIVE'	1982	ATCO		K 50910
ROGER HAWKINS		(					
BARRY BECKETT		(	SUZI STORM	V	(	LAURA STRUZICK	V	(
BARBARA WYRICK		(	SHORTY MEDLOCKE	HCA BAN(DE	DONNA DAVIS	V	(CDE
PAMELA VINCENT	V	(CDE	HENRY WEEK	PERC	(CDE	DR DAVE CAVENDER	TPT	(E
PETER RUTH	HCA	(D	DAVID CAVENDER	HRNS	(E	CUB CODA	HCA	(C
MELODY McCULLY	V	(D					

B123A

J D BLACKFOOT
B123A

J D BLACKFOOT		(ALL	(A) THE ULTIMATE PROPHECY	1970	MERCURY	US	61288
STERLING SMITH	B G	(A	(B) SONG OF CRAZY HORSE	1974	FANTASY	US	9468
JEFF WHITLOCK	G	(A	(C) SOUTHBOUND & GONE	1975	FANTASY	US	9487
CRAIG FULLER	G	(A					
PHIL STOKES	B	(A	DAN WALDRON	D	(A	GEORGE MOBLEY	G	(A
BUDD FOWLER	B K V	(A	BILLY CARROLL	D V	(A			

B124

BLACKFOOT SUE
B124

TOM FARMER		(A	(A) NOTHING TO HIDE	1973	JAM		JAL 104
DAVE FARMERS		(A	(B) GUN RUNNING	1975	DJM		DJLPS 455
EDDIE GALGA		(A	(C) STRANGERS	1974		US	1007
ALAN JONES		(A					

B124A

BLACKJACK
B124A

MICHAEL BOLOTIN	V	(AB	(A) BLACKJACK	1979 POLYDOR US PD16215 UK 2391 411
BRUCE KULICK	G	(AB	(B) WORLDS APART	1980 POLYDOR US PD16279
SANDY GENNARO	D	(AB		
JIMMY HASLIP	B	(AB	JAN MULLANEY	K (A	CHUCK KIRKPATRICK	V	(A
TONY BATTAGLIA	V	(A		

B124B

BLACKSTONE(CAN)
B124B

JOHN FINLAY	V	(A	(A) ON THE LINE	1972	GRT	CAN	9230 1025
MICHAEL FONFARA	K	(A					
PETER HODGSON	B	(A	LARRY LEISHMAN	G V HCA(A	DANNY WEIS	G	(A
ZEKE SHEPPARD	HCA V	(A	RICHARD STEINBERG	D	(A			

B124C

BLACKSTONE(US)
B124C

TOM FLYNN	V	(A	BLACKSTONE	1971	EPIC	US	30470
KEVIN COLLINS	K	(A					
TOM BUTLER	B	(A	DAVE DESROCHERS	G	(A	MAX WEINBERG	D	(A

B125

BLACKWATER JUNCTION
B125

( ) BLACKWATER JUNCTION		1973	MCA	MUPS 469
( ) BLACKWATER JUNCTION		1974	MCA	MCF 2663
( ) BLACKWATER JUNCTION		196	DJM	DJF 20465

B125A

TIM BLAKE
B125A

TIM BLAKE	SYN	(AB	(A) CRYSTAL MACHINE	1977	EGG	900 545
			(B) BLAKES NEW JERUSALEM	1978	EGG 90288 BARCLAY	7005

B125B

BLACKWELL
B125B

JOHN BUNDRICK	K	(A	(A) BLACKWELL	1970	ASTRO	us	9010
GLENN GIBSON	V	(A					
TERRY WILSON	B	(A	RANDY DEHART	D	(A	JIMMY SMITH	G	(A

B125C

OTIS BLACKWELL
B125C

OTIS BLACKWELL	D	(A	(A) THESE ARE MY SONGS	1978	INNER	US	1032

B125D

HAL BLAINE
B125D

HAL BLAINE	D	(ABC	(A) DRUMS A GO GO	1966	DUNHILL	US	50002
			(B) PSYCHEDELIC	1967	DUNHILL	US	50019
			(C) HAVE FUN, PLAY DRUMS	196	DUNHILL	US	50035

B125E

JOHN BLAIRE
B125E

JOHN BLAIRE	V SIT	(ABC	(A) MYSTICAL SOUL	1971	A&R	US	7100 002
GEORGIE COPPELA	V	(C	(B) SOUTHERN LOVE	1976	CBS	US	33950
CLIFF CARTER	K	(C	(C) WE BELONG TOGETHER	1977	CTI	US	7 5004
GARY KING	B	(C					
STEVE GADD	D	(C	HIRAM BULLOCK	G	(C	SUE EVANS	PERC	(C
RAY MANTILLA	PERC	(C	HUGH McCRACKEN	HCA	(C	IRENE CARA	V	(C
KIM CARLSON	V	(C	GORDON GRODY	V	(C	JOCELYN SHAW	V	(C

B125F

NORMAN BLAKE
B125F

NORMAN BLAKE	G V	(ALL	(A) HOME IN SULPHUR SPRINGS	19	ROUNDER	US	0012
			(B) WHISKEY BEFORE BREAKFAST	19	ROUNDER	US	0063
			(C) FIELDS OF NOVEMBER	19	FLYING FISH	US	004
			(D) LIVE AT McCABES	19			
			(E) BLACKBERRY BLOSSOM	19	FLYING FISH		005

[53]

RONNEE BLAKLEY

```
    RONNEE BLAKLEY        K G V(ALL    (A) RONNEE BLAKLEY                    1972  ELEKTRA      US    75027
    ROGER HAWKINS         D     (B     (B) WELCOME                           1975  WB US 2890 UK   K 56174
    BARRY BECKETT         K     (B
    DAVID HOOD            B     (B     PETE CARR            G     (B     JIMMY JOHNSON       G     (B
    REGGIE YOUNG          G     (B     EDDIE HINTON         G     (B     MUSCLE SHOALS       HRNS (B
    JOHNNY GIMBLE         FDL   (B     JOHN HUGHEY          STEEL (B     BUDDY EMMONS        STEEL(B
    RANDY McCORMICK       V     (B     JERRY BRIDGES        V     (B     GERRY MASTERS       B     (B
```

BOBBY BLAND

```
    BOBBY BLAND          V     (ALL    (A) BAREFOOT ROCK AND YOU GOT ME    196  DUKE US X72
    WITH                               (B) LIKE ER RED HOT                 196  DUKE US X73
    MIKE OMARTIAN        K     (LMQN    (C) TWO STEPS FROM THE BLUES        196  DUKE US X74
    LARRY CARLTON        G     (LM      (D) HERES THE MAN                   196  DUKE US X75   VOCALION  160183
    ED GREENE            D     (LMQ     (E) CALL ON ME                      196  DUKE US X77   VOCALION   8041
    PAUL HUBINON         HRNS  (LM      (F) AINT NOTHIN' YOU CAN DO         196  DUKE US X78   VOCALION   8034
    LEW McCREARY         HRNS  (M       (G) SOUL OF THE MAN                 196  DUKE US X79   VOCALION   8027
    SID SHARP            STRING(LMQ     ( ) BEST OF BOBBY BLAND             1973 DUKE US X84
    MAXINE WILLARD       V     (LMQ     ( ) BEST OF VOL 2                   19   DUKE US X86
    JOHN KELSO           HRNS  (LM      (H) TOUCH OF THE BLUES              19   DUKE US X88   VOCALION    974
    ERNIE WATTS          HRNS  (LMQ     (I) A PIECE OF GOLD                 1969 ACTION UK  ACLP6006
    PETER CHRISTLIEB     HRNS  (M       (J) SPOTLIGHTING THE MAN            19   DUKE US X89
    JULIA TILLMAN        V     (LMQ     (K) INTROSPECTIVE OF THE EARLY YEARS 19  DUKE US D92   ABC     US  92/2
    JOE SCOTT            TPT   (         (L) HIS CALIFORNIA ALBUM           1973 ABC   UK ABCL5044 DUNHILL US 50163
    PAT HARE             G     (         (M) DREAMER                        1974 ABC   UK ABCL5053 DUNHILL US 50169
    SCOTT EDWARDS        B     (Q        (N) TOGETHER FOR THE FIRST TIME    1974 ABC   UK ABCD605  DUNHILL US 50190
    JAY GRAYDON          G     (Q        (N) TOGETHER FOR THE FIRST TIME    197  IMPULSE    US
    RAY PARKER           G     (Q        (O) TOGETHER AGAIN...LIVE          1976 IMPULSE             AMPL 8027
    LEE RITENOUR         G     (Q        (P) GET ON DOWN                    1975 ABC   UK ABCL5139 ABC    US 895
    STEVE BARRY          PERC  (Q        (Q) REFLECTIONS IN BLUE            1977 ABC   UK ABCD5196 ABC    US1018
    CHUCK FINDLEY        HRNS  (LQ       (R) COME FLY WITH ME               1978 ABC   UK ABCL5249 abc    US1075
    ORRIN WATERS         V     (Q        (S) GREATEST HITS (CASSETTE)       1979 fairway    uk   BBBC 1400
    LUTHER WATERS        V     (Q        (T) I FEEL GOOD , I FEEL FINE      1979 MCA        MCA    US 3157
    MICHAEL PRICE        V     (Q        (U) SWEET VIBRATIONS               1980 MCA   UK 5145
    DAN WALSH            V     (Q        (V) WOKE UP SCREAMING              1982 ACE   UK CH41
    DICK HYDE            HRNS  (L
    MEL BROWN            G     (LM      DAVID COHEN          G     (L     MAX BENNETT         B     (L
    BEN BENAY            G     (LM      DEAN PARKS           G     (LMQ   JUNIOR PARKER             (A
    WILTON FELDER        B     (LMQ     JIM HORN             HRNS  (MQ    TONY TERRAN         HRNS (M
    GINGER BLAKE         V     (LMQ     WAYNE BENNETT        G     (      B B KING            G V  (NO
    CHUCK RAINEY         B     (Q       VICTOR FELDMAN       PERC  (Q     NINO TEMPO          HRNS (Q
    PHIL UPCHURCH        B     (U       CURTIS ROBINSON      B     (U     DAVID ERVIN         SYN  (U
    WARREN HAYGOOD       PERC  (U       MONK HIGGINS         PNO   (U     KENNETH ELLIOTT     D    (U
    BILLY McCOY          PNO   (U       GEORGE SMITH         HCA   (U     FREDDY ROBINSON     G    (U
    ROGER WALLACE        HRNS  (U       GEORGE BOHANON       TROM  (U     SWEET SPIRIT        V    (UT
    DON MYRICK           SAX   (U       FRED JACKSON         HRNS  (U     NOLAN SMITH         HRNS (U
    STEVE MADAIO         HRNS  (Q       ALSO SEE B B KING FOR LINE UP OF (N)
```

BLANKET OF SECRECY

```
                                       (A) WALLS HAVE EARS                 1982  F BEAT       UK    LP16
```

BLAST

```
                                       (A) BLAST                           1980  CBS          US    36012
```

CHARLIE BLEAK

```
    CHARLIE BLEAK              (A        (A) LET ME IN                      1977  PIP          US    6817
```

SERGE BLENNER

```
    SERGE BLENNER             (A        (A) LA VOGUE                        1980  SKY                042
```

LYNN BLESSING

```
    LYNN BLESSING        VIBES HCA (A    (A) SUNSET PAINTER                 1969  EPIC         US    26488
    MEL TELFORD          D     (A
    WOLFGANG MELZ        B     (A       JOHN BECK            G     (A     ROBERT HIRTH        G    (A
    SNEAKY PETE          STEEL (A
```

CARLA BLEY

```
    CARLA BLEY           V K   (ALL     (A) ESCALATOR OVER THE HILL        1972  JCOA              EOTH   3
    ROSEWELL RUDD        TROM V(ADEFG    (A) ESCALATOR OVER THE HILL        1974  JCOA              JT   4001
    PERRY ROBINSON       CLAR  (AB       (A) ESCALATOR OVER THE HILL        1974  BARCLAY           840050 1 2
    GATO BARBIERI        SAX   (AB       (A) ESCALATOR OVER THE HILL        1974  JCOA         US   1003 4 5
    CHARLIE HADEN        B V   (AF       (B) TROPIC APPETITES               1974  VIRGIN JCOA       WATT   1
    MIKE MANTLER         TPT PNO(ABCDEFGH (C) 13/3/4                        1975  VIRGIN            WATT   3
    PAUL MOTIAN          D PERC(AB       (D) DINNER MUSIC                   1977  VIRGIN            WATT   6
    BOB STEWART          V TUBA(ACDEF     (D) DINNER MUSIC                   1977  ECM               2313 106
    KAREN MANTLER        V GLOC(AF       (E) EUROPEAN TOUR                  1977  VIRGIN            WATT   8
    JULIE TIPPETTS       V     (B        (E) EUROPEAN TOUR                  1977  ECM               2313 108
    HOWARD JOHNSON       WIND  (B        (F) MUSIQUE MECANIQUE              1979  WATT              WATT   9
    DAVID HOLLAND        CELLO (B        (F) MUSIQUE MECANIQUE              1979  ECM               2313 109
    TONY MARCUS          VLN   (B        (G) EUROPEAN TOUR LINE UP 78
    CARLOS WARD          SAX   (DH       (H) SOCIAL STUDIES                 1981  WATT              WATT  11
    TONY DAGRADI         WIND  (H
    RICHARD TEE          K     (D        ERIC GALE            G     (D     CORNELL DUPREE      G    (D
    GORDON EDWARDS       B     (D        STEVE GADD           D     (D     ELTON DEAN          SAX  (EG
    GARY WINDO           SAX   (EF       JOHN CLARK           HRNS  (EF    TERRY ADAMS         PNO  (EF
    HUGH HOPPER          B     (EG       ANDREW CYRILLE       D     (EG    STEVE SWALLOW       B    (FH
    D. SHARPE            D     (FH       EUGENE SHADBOURNE    G     (F     SAM BROWN           G    (
    RON McCLURE          B     (         DON CHERRY           TPT PERC (A  JACK BRUCE          V B  (A
    DON PRESTON          SYN   (A        JOHN McLAUGHLIN      G     (A     LINDA RONSTADT      V    (A
    PAUL JONES           V     (A        ORCHESTRA & STRINGS        (AC    GARY VOLENTE        CLAR (H
    JOE DALEY            WIND  (H        EARL McINTYRE        HRNS  (H
```

BLIFFERT

```
    FRED BLIFFERT        G V   (A        (A) YOU'LL LIKE BLIFFERT           19    0            US     1
```

BLINKY

```
                                       (A) JUST WE TWO                     19    GORDY        US    945
```

BLIND FAITH

B134 (left) ... B134 (right)

```
B134                        BLIND FAITH                                    B134
   ERIC CLAPTON     G V       (A) BLIND FAITH      1969   POLYDOR    UK   583  059
   STEVE WINWOOD    K V       (A) BLIND FAITH      1969   RSO        US   1  3016
   RICK GRECH      B V        (A) BLIND FAITH      1969   ATCO       US      33304
   GINGER BAKER    D
B134A                        BLISS BAND                                   B134A
   PAUL BLISS      V K    (A   (A) DINNER WITH RAOUL  1978  CBS       US      35511
   ANDY BROWN      B V    (A
   NIGEL ELLIOT    D      (A   ALAN PARK        K      (A   PHIL PALMER      G V     (A
   MAUREEN McDONALD V     (A   VENETTA FIELDS   V      (A   SHIRLEY MATTHEWS V       (A
   MIKE McDONALD   V      (A   KEITH KNUDSON    V      (A   JEFF BAXTER   PROD G STEEL(A
   GREG ADAMS      HRNS   (A   MICK GILLETTE    HRNS   (A   LENNY PICKETT    HRNS  (A
   EMILLO CASTILLO HRNS   (A   STEPHEN KUPKA    HRNS   (A   VICTOR FELDMAN   PERC  (A
B135                        RORY BLOCK                                    B135
   RORY BLOCK      V G   (ALL  (A)RORY  BLOCK        1975   RCA        US      10733
WITH                        (B) RORY BLOCK (I'M IN LOVE) 1976 BLUE GOOSE  BG   2022
   BILL PAYNE      K     (C   (C) INTOXICATION/ BITTER  1977  CHRYSALIS UK  CHR 1157
   ROLAND JOHN HINES B V (C   (D) YOU'RE THE ONE     1978   CHRYSALIS  US  CHR 1233
   BRIAN LEONARD   PERC  (A   (E) HIGH HEELED BLUES  1982   ROUNDER    US      3061
   KEITH BENSON    D     (D
   BRIAN RUSSELL   G     (A   FRED LIPSIUS     K SAX  (A   PENTI GLAN       D       (A
   DICK SMITH      PERC  (A   AL BRISCOE       STEEL  (A   DANNY WEISS      G       (A
   PRAKASH JOHN    B     (A   MICHAEL FONFARA  K      (A   IAN GUENTHER     FDL     (A
   SAM CLAYTON     CONGA V(C   RICK SCHLOSSER  D      (C   FRED TACKETT     G       (C
   JACK ASHFORD    PERC  (C   WILLIAM COLLETTE FLT    (C   WILLIAM SMITH    K       (C
   JIM HORN        SAX   (C   RITCHIE HAYWARD  D V    (C   PAUL STALLWORTH  B       (C
   JOE PORCARO     CONGA (C   REV JAMES CLEVELAND CHOIR (C CINDY BULLENS    V       (C
   ARTIE TRAUM     G     (B   ROLEY SALLEY     B      (B   PAT MURRAY      CONGA(B
   ERIC VALDINA    D     (D   ALAN SEIDLER     PNO    (D   KEN KOSEK        FDL     (B
   PROF COTTON KENT K    (D   VINCE FAY        B      (D   JAMES WILLIAMS   B       (D
   LENNY PAKULA    K     (D   DENNIS HARRIS    G      (D   LARRY WASHINGTON PERC    (D
   RONNIE JAMES    G     (D   T J TINDALL      G      (D   JIMMY MAELEN     PERC    (D
   GORDON TITCOMB  STEEL (D   BOBBY ELI      PERC G   (D   GRANT MACAVOY    D       (D
   BRUCE GRAY      K     (D   DEXTER WANSEL    SYN    (D   VINCE WARSAVAGE  PERC    (D
   BARBARA INGRAM  V     (D   EVETTE BENTON    V      (D   CARLA BENSON     V       (D
B136                        BLODWYN PIG                                   B136
   JACK LANCASTER  WIND  (AB  (A) AHEAD RINGS OUT     1969   ISLAND     UK   ILPS 9101
   MICK ABRAHAMS   G     (AB  (A) AHEAD RINGS OUT     1969   A&M        US   AM   4210
   ANDY PYLE       B     (AB  (B) GETTING TO THIS     1970   CHRYSALIS  UK   ILPS 9122
   RON BERG        D     (AB  (B) GETTING TO THIS     1970   A&M        US        4243
   GRAHAM WALLER   K     (B
   PETER BANKS     G     (    CLIVE BUNKER     D      (
B137                        BLONDE ON BLONDE                              B137
   GRAHAM DAVIS  BANJ V G B (C  (A) CONTRASTS         1969   PYE        UK   NSPL 18288
   RICHARD JOHN    B     (A   (A) CONTRASTS           1969   JANUS      US        3003
   GARETH JOHNSON  G     (ABC  (B) REBIRTH            1970   EMBER      UK   NR   5049
   DAVE THOMAS  HCA B V G (BC  (C) REFLECTIONS ON A LIFE 1971 EMBER     UK   NR   5058
   LES HICKS     PERC D(ABC   (D) BLONDE ON BLONDE    1972   EMBER      UK
   KIP             MELLA (C
   RICHARD HOPKINS B K   (A   RALPH DENYER     G V    (A
B138                        (AMAZING)BLONDEL                              B138
   TERRY WINCOTT   V G K (ABCDEFGH  (A) AMAZING BLONDEL  1970  BELL      UK   SBLL 131
   EDDIE BAIRD     V G   (ABCDEFGH  (B) EVENSONG     1970   ISLAND     UK   ILPS 9136
   JIM CAPALDI     D     (C   (B) EVENSONG           1970   ISLAND     US        9303
   JOHN GLADWIN    V G B (ABCD  (C) FANTASIA LINDUM  1971  ISLAND UK ILPS 9156 US  9310
   WILLIAM MURRAY  D     (FG   (D) ENGLAND 72        1972  ISLAND UK ILPS 9205 US  9327
   MICK FEAT       G     (FGH  (E) BLONDEL           1973  ISLAND UK ILPS 9257 US  9339
   EDDIE JOBSON    K VLN (F    (F) MULGRAVE STREET   1974   DJM  DJF 20443 +   DJLPS 443
   ALAN SPENNER    B     (F    (G) INSPIRATION       1975   DJM  DJF 20446 +   DJLPS446
   PAUL KOSSOFF    G     (F    (H) BAD DREAMS        1976   DJM             DJLPS 472
   SUE GLOVER      V     (EF   (H) BAD DREAMS        1976   DJM             DJF 20472
   SUNNY LESLIE    V     (EF   (I) LIVE IN TOKYO     1977   DJM                 48089
   SIMON KIRKE     D     (EF   (I) LIVE IN TOKYO     1977   DJM             DJF 20503
   JOHN RABBIT BUNDRICK K (F  (FG) MULGRAVE/INSPIRATION 197  DJM     US    2239 701
   STEVE WINWOOD   B     (E
   ADRIAN HOPKINS  K     (CE   BOZ BURRELL      B      (F   MICK RALPHS      G     (F
   PAT DONALDSON   B     (F    PAUL RODGERS     V      (C   CHRIS KARAN     PERC  (B
   ADAM SKEAPING   VLN   (B    DAVE SKINNER     PNO    (G   MEL COLLINS     SAX   (G
   JACK LAROQUE    (C         JOHN GILSTON     D      (H
B139                        BLONDIE                                       B139
   DEBBIE HARRY    V     (ALL  (A) BLONDIE           1976   PRIVATE STOCK   PS   2023
   CHRIS STEIN     G     (ALL  (A) BLONDIE           1976   PRIVATE STOCK   PVLP 1017
   CLEM BURKE      D (ABCF456789DEG(A) BLONDIE       1977   CHRYSALIS  UK   CHR 1165
   JIMMY DESTRI    K  (ABCDEF789G(A) BLONDIE         1978   PHONOGRAM  FR   6307 616
   GARY VALENTINE  B     (A67  (B) PLASTIC LETTERS   1978   CHRYSALIS  UK   CHR 1166
   FRANK INFANTE  B G (BCDE89FG (B) PLASTIC LETTERS  1978   PHONOGRAM  FR   6307 617
   NIGEL HARRISON  B     (CDE9FG  (C) PARALLEL LINES 1978   CHRYSALIS  UK   CHR 1192
   DALE POWERS     V     (BC   (C) PARALLEL LINES    1978   CHRYSALIS PIC DISC   5001
   BILLY O'CONNOR  D     (123  (C) X OFFENDER        19     SONOPRESSE FR   PS 69673
   FRED SMITH      B     (1234 (D) EAT TO THE BEAT   1979   CHRYSALIS  UK   CDL 1225
   JULIE           V     (1    (E) AUTO AMERICANS    1980   CHRYSALIS  UK   CDL 1290
   ROBERT FRIPP    G     (C    (F) THE BEST OF BLONDIE 1981  CHRYSALIS UK   CHR 1337
   WAH WAH WATSON  G     (E    (G) THE HUNTER        1982   CHRYSALIS  UK   CHR 1384
   JACKIE          V     (1    (1) AUTUMN 74  (2) OCT 74 JAN 75  (3) JAN 75 MAY 75  (4) MAY 75
   IVAN KRAL       G     (2    (5) MAY 75 AUG 75 (6) AUT 75  (7) OCT 75 AUG 77  (8)AUG 77 (9) NOV 79
   TISH            V     (2
   SNOOKIE         V     (2    LORNA LOFT       V      (D   DONNA DESTRI     V     (D
   ELLIE GREENWICH V     (D    MIKE CHAPMAN     V      (D   RANDY HENNES    HCA   (D
   EMIL RICHARDS   PERC  (E    OLLIE BROWN      PERC   (E   TOM SCOTT       SAX   (E
   MARK VOLMAN     V     (E    HOWARD KAYLAN    V      (E   RANDY HENNES    HCA   (D
   ALEX ACUNA      PERC  (E    STEVE GOLDSTEIN  K      (E   RAY BROWN        B    (E
   SCOTT LESSER    PERC  (E    THE 'B' GIRLS    V      (E
```

BLONKER

```
KAY JESSEN          V PERC(A      (A) DIE ZEIT STEHT STILL   1979   BRAIN      0060 104
THOMAS GRUTZMACHER  B PERC(A      (B) WINDMILLS              1981   PHILIPS    GER 6435 125
NICOLAS STALLARD       (A
HELGE TILLMAN          (AB         DIETER GEIKE      G PERC (AB    FRANK HIEBER    B   (B
WOLFGANG SCHLUTER   VIBES (B       JOCHEN PETERSEN   SYN (B       PETER FRANKEN   PERC (B
FRANK FISCHIER      B  (B
```

BLOOD

```
                                  (A) BLOOD                  19    ENTERPRISE          ENTF 3002
```

BLOOD SWEAT & TEARS

```
AL KOOPER           K V  (AM      (A) CHILD IS FATHER TO THE MAN    1968  CBS      UK           63296
BOBBY COLOMBY       D  (ABCDEFGHIJKMZ (A) CHILD IS FATHER TO THE MAN 1968 CBS      US    PC     9619
STEVE KATZ          V G  (ABCDEM   (A) THE FIRST ALBUM              1973  EMBASSY  UK    EMB 31028
JIM FIELDER         B    (ABCDEFM  (A) THE FIRST ALBUM              1977  EMBASSY  UK    EMB 31492
RANDY BRECKER       TPT  (AM       (B) BLOOD SWEAT & TEARS          1969  CBS      UK           63504
JERRY WEISS         TPT  (AM       (B) BLOOD SWEAT & TEARS          1969  CBS      US    PC     9720
DICK HALLIGAN       TROM (ABCDM    (C) THREE                        1970  CBS      UK           64024
FRED LIPSIUS        PNO SAX (ABCDM (C) THREE                        1970  CBS      US    KC    30090
DAVID CLAYTON THOMAS V (BCDHIJKMZ  (D) FOUR                         1971  CBS      UK           64355
CHUCK WINFIELD      TPT  (BCDEFM   (D) FOUR                         1971  CBS      US    KC    30590
LEW SOLOFF          TPT  (BCDEFM   (E) NEW BLOOD                    1972  CBS      UK           65252
BOBBY DOYLE         V    (         (E) NEW BLOOD                    1972  CBS      US    KC    31780
JERRY FISCHER       V    (EG       (F) NO SWEAT                     1973  CBS      UK           65725
JERRY LA CROIX      V    (G        (F) NO SWEAT                     1973  CBS      US    KC    32180
TONY KLATKA         SAX  (GHIJKZ   (G) MIRROR IMAGE                 1974  CBS      UK           80153
LARRY WILLIS        K    (EFGHIJKZ (G) MIRROR IMAGE                 1974  CBS      US    KC    32929
GEORGE WADENIUS     G    (EFGHI    (H) NEW CITY                     1975  CBS      UK           80784
DAVE BARGERON       TROM (DEFGHIJKZ (H) NEW CITY                    1975  CBS      US    PC    33484
DON HECKMAN         CLAR (D        (I) IN CONCERT                   1976  CBS NL 22006 SONY JAP 139/140
RON McCLURE         B    (GHJ      (J) MORE THAN EVER               1976  CBS      UK           81465
BILL TILLMAN        SAX  (GHIJKZ   (J) MORE THAN EVER               1976  CBS      US    PC    34233
JERRY HYMAN         TROM (BM       (K) BRAND NEW DAY                1978  ABC      UK    ABCL 5234
ALAN RUBIN          TPT  (B        (K) BRAND NEW DAY                1978  ABC      US           1015
MIKE SMITH          CONGA (D       (K) BRAND NEW DAY                1978  CARRERE  FR           68055
LOU MARINI          WIND (EF       (BC) BLOOD SWEAT & TEARS/THREE (DBL)  1976  CBS  NL          22015
JOE GIORGIANNI      TPT  (I        (  ) GREATEST HITS               1972  CBS      US    PC 31170
STEVE KAHN          G    (IJ       (  ) BLOOD SWEAT & TEARS         1978  HALLMARK       SHM   963
MIKE STERN          G    (IJKZ     (M) CLASSIC B S T                1980  CBS                  31824
DON ALIAS           PERC (IJKZ     (N) NUCLEAR BLUES                1980  MCA      UK    MCF  3061
DANNY TRIPHAN       B    (JKZ      (Z) 1976 JAPAN TOUR
FOREST BATCHELL     TPT  (JKZ
RON McCURDY         PERC (K    JIMMY MEAULIN    PERC (F   TOM MALONE       HRNS (F   DAVE HENTSCHEL   SYN  (F
FRANK RICOTTI       PERC (K    PAUL BUCKMASTER  SYN  (F   VALERIE SIMPSON  V    (F   STEVE TYRELL     PERC (F
GARY KING           B    (J    RICHARD TEEE     K    (J   HUGH McCRACKEN   G    (J   ERIC WEISSBERG BAN G (J
BOB JAMES           K    (J    ERIC GALE        G    (J   JOHN FADDIS      TPT  (J   MARVIN STAMM     TPT  (J
DAVE TAYLOR         TROM (J    ARNIE LAWRENCE   SAX  (J   DAVE FRIEDMAN    PERC (J   SID WEINBERG     OBOE (J
PATTI AUSTIN        V    (J    VIVIAN CHERRY    V    (J   LANI GROVES      V    (J   GWEN GUTHRIE     V    (J
YOLANDA McCULLOGH   V    (J    FRANK FLOYD      V    (J   WILLIAM EATON    V    (J   ZACHARY SANDERS  V    (J
CHAKA KHAN          V    (J    WILLIE SMITH     K V  (K   PETE JOLLY            (K   TOMMY MORGAN     HCA  (K
PAUL STALLWORTH     B    (K    PETER GRAVES     HRNS (K   STU BLUMBERG     TPT  (K   TOM PETERSON     WIND (K
ERNIE WATTS         HRNS (K    JOHN ROSENBURG   TPT  (K   JOHN ALTSCHUL    HRNA (K   JOHN GROSS  SAX       (K
JOHN MITCHELL       HRNS (K    VANETTA FIELDS   V    (K   BRENDA BRYANT    V    (K   MIKE FINNIGAN    K    (K
CARL GRAVES         V    (K    TISH SMITH       V    (K   ROY HALEE        TPT  (K   BOB PAYNE            (K
GLEN GARRETT             (K    KING ERRISON          (K   RAY REED              (K
```

BLOODROCK

```
STEVE HILL          K V  (ABCDEFG  (A) BLOODROCK                    1969  CAPITOL  US      ST    435
ED GRUNDY           B V  (ABCDEFG  (B) BLOODROCK TWO                1970  CAPITOL  US      ST    491
WARREN HAM          V WIND(fg      (C) BLOODROCK THREE              1971  CAPITOL  US      EST   765
RICK COBB           D PERC(BCDEF   (D) LIVE                         1972  CAPITOL  US      SVBB11038
NICK TAYLOR         V D  (ABCDEFG  (E) U S A                        1971  CAPITOL  US      SM    645
JIM RUTLEDGE        V D  (ABCDE    (F) PASSAGE                      1973  CAPITOL  US      SW  11109
LEE PICKENS         G V  (ABCDE    (G) WHIRLWIND TONGUES            1973  CAPITOL  US      EST 11259
                                   (H) BLOODROCK'N' ROLL            19    CAPITOL  US      SM  11417
```

BLOODSTONE

```
HARRY WILLIAMS      V PERC(ABCD    (A) BLOODSTONE                   1972  DECCA    UK    TXS    110
CHARLES McCORMICK   B V  (ABCD     (B) NATURAL HIGH                 1973  DECCA    UK    SKL   5150
CHARLES LOVE        G V  (ABCD     (B) NATURAL HIGH                 1973  LONDON   US           620
WILLIS DRAFFEN      G    (ABCD     (C) UNREAL                       1974  DECCA    UK    SKL   5156
ROGER DURHAM        V PERC(ABC     (C) UNREAL                       1974  LONDON   US           634
EDDIE SUMMERS       D    (A        (D) I NEED TIME                  1974  DECCA    UK    SKL   5185
HARRY WILKINS       G B  (C        (D) I NEED TIME                  1974  LONDON   US           647
DARRYL CLIFTON      D.   (C        (E) RIDDLE OF THE SPHINX         1975  DECCA    UK    SKL   5202
MARVIN WEBB                        (E) RIDDLE OF THE SPHINX         1975  LONDON   US           654
                                   (F) LULLABY OF BROADWAY          1976  DECCA    UK    SKL   5238
                                   (G) TRAIN RIDE TO HOLLYWOOD      197   LONDON   US           665
                                   (H) DO YOU WANNA DO A THING      197   LONDON   US           671
                                   (J) DONT STOP                    1979  TAMLA    UK    STML12097
```

MIKE BLOOMFIELD

```
MIKE BLOOMFIELD     K G V  (ALL    (A) SUPER SESSION               1968  CBS      UK           63396
MARK NAFTALIN       K    (BCKMN    (A) SUPER SESSION               1968  CBS      US    CS    9701
IRA KAMIN           K    (BCHLM    (A) SUPER SESSION               1973  EMBASSY  UK    EMB 31029
JOHN KAHN           B    (BCD      (B) ITS NOT KILLING ME          1969  CBS      UK           63652
BOB JONES           D V  (BCJLKMN  (C) LIVE AT BILL GRAHAMS FILLMORE WEST 1969  CBS  UK         63816
DINO ANDINO         CONGA (C       (C) LIVE AT BILL GRAHAMS FILLMORE WEST 1969  CBS  US    CS  9893
NOEL JEWKIS         SAX  (C        (D) LIVE ADVENTURES             1969  CBS      UK           66216
JOHN WILMETH        TPT  (C        (E) TRY IT BEFORE YOU BUY IT    1973  CBS      UK    PC 33173
JESSE ED DAVIS      G    (C        (F) TRIUMVIRATE                 1973  CBS      UK           65659
TAJ MAHAL           V    (C        (F) TRIUMVIRATE                 1973  XBS      US    CS 32172
NICK GRAVENITES     V    (BCHJK    (G) MILL VALLEY SESSION         1976  POLYDOR
AL KOOPER           K V G  (AD     (H) IF YOU LOVE THOSE BLUES     1977  GUITAR PLAYER  US       3002
STEPHEN STILLS      V G  (A        (H) IF YOU LOVE THOSE BLUES     1977  SONET    UK    SNTF  726
```

        (CONTINUED)

MIKE BLOOMFIELD

```
CARLOS SANTANA        G     (D
DOUG KILMER           B     (HLM
DR. JOHN              PNO G (F
CHRIS ETHRIDGE        B     (D
ERIC KRISS            K     (H
DAVE SHOREY           B V   (L
JAMES GORDON          HRNS  (F
BENNIE PARKS          PERC  (F
BARRY GOLDBERG        K     (M
JESSIE SMITH          V     (F
ROY RUBY              K     (B
RON STALLINGS         SAX   (BD
MARK ADAMS            HCA   (MN
MARCUS DOUBLEDAY      TPT   (B
DIANE TRIBUNO         V     (F
GEORGE BOHANON        TROM  (F
JOHN HAMMOND        V G HCA (F
JEROME JUMONVILLE     HRNS  (F
MARK TEEL             SAX   (B
FRED STAEHLE          D     (F
GERALD OSHITA         SAX   (B
SKIP PROKOP           D  .  (D
TOM DONLINGER         D     (H
CRAIG KILBY           TROM  (L
MARGARET EDMONSON           (O
CARL SEVEREIOL        B     (N
HART McNEE            SAX   (P
CLAY COTTON           K     (KN
SOMA                  B     (K
CHUCK BENNETT         TROM  (K
JERRY MARTINI         SAX   (K
ANDREW GOLDSTEIN      TROM  (K
```

(J) ANALINE
(J) ANALINE
(J) ANALINE
(K) COUNT TALENT & THE ORIGINALS
(L) MICHAEL BLOOMFIELD
(M) BETWEEN THE HARD PLACE
(N) LIVING IN THE FAST LANE
(N) LIVING IN THE FAST LANE
(O) LIVE IN ITALY
(P) CRUISIN' FOR BRUISIN'
(R) GOSPEL DUETS
(S) RED HOT & BLUES

1977	TAKOMA	US		1059
1977	SONET	UK	SNTF	749
1977	CBS	US	TRK	82516
1978	CLOUDS	US		
1978	TAKOMA	US		1063
1979	TAKAMO US 7070 LINE GER			5110
1980	WATERHOUSE	US		11
1981	LINE	GER		5104
1980	MAMA BARLEY	IT		001
1981	TAKOMA	US		7091
1981	KICKING MULE US/SONET UK			164
1981		US		2328

```
SNOOKY FLOWERS        SAX   (C
ROBBIE MONTGOMERY     V     (F
THOMAS JEFFERSON KAYE G V   (F
LORRAINE REBENNACK    B     (F
RICHARD SANTI         ACC   (B
FRED OLSEN            G     (B
ACE OF CUPS           V     (B
ELVIN BISHOP         G      (D
HART McNEE           SAX    (H
WOODY HARRIS                (RO
DERRICK WALKER       HCA    (P
HENRY ODEN           B      (P
KING PERKOFF         SAX    (P
DWIGHT DAILY         D      (N
RAY LOECKLE          SAX    (K
TED ASHFORD          K      (K
DENNIS MARCELLINO    SAX    (K
```

```
JOHN BOUDREAUX           PERC (F
ROGER TROY               B    (HJKMN
RICHARD BLUE MITCHELL HRNS    (F
MICHAEL MELFORD  MAND G V     (B
ANNA RIZZO               V    (JKN
RED RHODES               STEEL(B
MARCIA ANN TAYLOR        V    (J
ROOSEVELT GOOK           K    (D
DAVE NEDITCH             B    (D
TREVES BLUES BAND             (O
GEORGE MARSH             D    (N
TOM RIZZO                D    (P
FRANK BINER              V    (N
MARCIA ANN TAYLOR        V    (K
CAL LEWISTON             TPT  (K
JACK BLADES              B    (K
MAX HESKETT              TPT  (K
```

STEVE BLOOMFIELD

(A) ROCKABILLY ORIGINALS

```
STEVE BLOOMFIELD      G     (
```

1978	CHARLY		CR	30159

BLOOMSBURY PARK

(A) BLOOMSBURY PEOPLE

1970	MGM	US	4678

```
DING LORENZ           D     (A
DENNIS LANTING        G V   (A
JON WYDERKA           V PERC (A
GREG JANICK           SAX K  (A
```

SIGMUND SNOPEK   K TROM(A   PAUL DUJARDIN   B VTROM(A

BLOONTZ

(A) BLOONTZ

1973	EVOLUTION	US	3020

```
TONY BRAUNAGEL        D     (A
ANDY CHAPMAN          V     (A
DAVID L KEALEY        G     (A
JIMMY DON             G     (A
LINDA LAWLEY          V     (A
```

MICHAEL JOHN MONTGOMERY K (A   TERRY WILSON   B G (A
STEVE RADNEY   G   (A   MARGARET DORN   V   (A
SHARON REDD   V   (A   ZENOBIA   V   (A

BLOSSOMS

(A) THE BLOSSOMS

1972	MGM LION		LN 1007

BLOSSOM TOES

(A) WE ARE EVER SO CLEAN
(B) IF ONLY FOR A MOMENT

1967	MARMALADE	UK	607001
1969	MARMALADE	UK	608010

```
BRIAN GODDING         G V K (AB
BRIAN BELSHAW         B V   (AB
JIM CREGAN            G V   (AB
KEVIN WESTLAKE        D     (A
SEAN PHILLIPS         SITAR G(B
```

BARRY REEVES   D PERC (B   POLI PALMER   D   (B

BLOW FLY

( ) ZODIAC PARTY
( ) BLOW FLY PARTY

1978	WEIRD WORLD		2031
1980	WEIRD WORLD		2034

BLUE

(A) BLUE
(A) BLUE
(B) LIFE IN THE NAVY
(C) ANOTHER NIGHT TIME FLIGHT
(D) FOOLS PARTY

1973	RSO	US	873
1973	RSO	UK	2394 105
1974	RSO	UK	2394 133
1977	ROCKET UK ROLL 7 US		2290
1979	ROCKET	UK	TRAIN 4

```
IAN MACMILLAN         B G V (ABCD
HUGH NICHOLSON        G V K (ABCD
SMIGGY                G V   (B
TIMI DONALD           D V   (A
BEN KEITH             STEEL (B
RAY COOPER            PERC  (C
CHARLIE SMITH         D     (CD
```

DAVID NICHOLSON   B K   (CD

DAVID BLUE

(A) SINGER SONGWRITER (3 TRACKS)
(B) DAVID BLUE
(C) 23 DAYS IN SEPTEMBER
(D) ME
(E) STORIES
(E) STORIES
(F) NICE BABY & THE ANGEL
(G) COMIN' BACK FOR MORE
(G) COMIN' BACK FOR MORE
(H) CUPIDS ARROW

1965	ELEKTRA			
1966	ELEKTRA	US	EKS	74003
1968	REPRISE	US		6293
1970	REPRISE	US	RS	6375
1972	ASYLUM		SYL	9001
1972	ASYLUM			5052
1973	ASYLUM		SYL	9009
1975	ASYLUM		SYL	9025
1975	ASYLUM			1043
1976	ASYLUM UK K53056		SYL	1077

```
DAVID BLUE(COHEN)     G     (ALL
WITH
BOB RAFKIN            B G   (EF
RUSS KUNKEL           D     (E
JAMES KARSTEIN        D     (E
DAVID LINDLEY      G VLN    (FH
JOHN BARBATA          D     (E
RY COODER             G     (E
MILT HOLLAND          PERC  (E
RALPH SCHUCKETT       K     (E
PETE JOLLY            ACC   (E
CHRIS ETHRIDGE        B     (EF
HARVEY BROOKS         B     (B
BUDDY SALZMAN         D     (B
GLENN FRAY            V     (F
GRAHAM NASH         G V K   (F
DANNY KOOTCH          G     (G
DAN PEEK              V     (G
BEN KEITH            STEEL  (G
JOHN GUERIN          D V    (G
KREAG COFFEY          HCA   (G
CAROL CARMICHAEL      V     (G
LEVON HELM            D     (H
AUBURN BARRELL JR     G     (H
BILL SCHWARTZ         V     (H
PATTIE BROOKS         V     (H
```

```
RITA COOLIDGE        V      (E
MONTE DUNN           G      (B
CHARLIE McCOY        HCA    (D
JENNIFER WARREN      V      (F
BEN BENAY            G      (G
ROBBIN FORD          G      (G
LARRY NASH           K      (G
MAX BENNETT          B      (G
DEWEY BUNNELL        V      (G
DICK HAMILTON        SYN    (G
KARIN LAMM           V      (G
MIKE BAIRD           D      (H
JESSE ED DAVIS       G      (H
JACKIE LOMAX         V      (H
```

```
PAUL HARRIS          K      (B
HERBERT LOVELLE      D      (B
TERRY ADAMS        CELLO    (F
DAVE MASON         G V      (F
LARRY CARLTON        G      (G
DON FELDER           G      (G
TOM HENSLEY          K      (G
RENIE PRESS          B      (G
BOB DYLAN            HCA    (G
JONI MITCHELL        V      (G
JERRY BECKLEY        V      (G
DUCK DUNN            B      (H
BARRY GOLDBERG       K      (H
PHYLLIS BROWN        V      (H
```

B149A   BLUE ASH   B149A

```
B149A                                    BLUE ASH                                    B149A
    BILL BARTOLIN      V G  (AB    (A) NO MORE NO LESS        19     MERCURY        SRM 1 666
    JIM KENDZOR        V    (AB    (B) FRONT PAGE NEWS        1978   PLAYBOY             34918
    FRANK SECICH       V B  (AB
    DAVID EVANS        D V  (A
B149B                                    BLUE ANGEL                                  B149B
    CYNDI LAUPEN       V    (A     (A) BLUE ANGEL             1980   POLYDOR     UK 2391 486
    JOHN TURI          K SAX (A
    LEE BROVITZ        B    (A     JOHNNY MORELLI    D    (A  ARTHUR NEILSON    G   (A
    ROY HALEE          PROD (A
B149C                                    BLUE BAND                                   B149C
    JAN DAMEN          B    (A     (A) SLITHERING            19     ARIOLA  NL  200 646 320
    HERMAN WILBRINK    G    (A
    H J VOX            V K  (A     FRANS JONGMANS    G    (A  FRED VELTMAN      D   (A
B150                                     BLUE CHEER                                  B150
    PAUL WHALEY        D    (BCE   (A) VINCEBUS ERUPTUM       1968   PHILIPS           600 264
    RANDY HOLDEN       G    (C     (A) VINCEBUS ERUPTUM       1967   PHILIPS 9001 UK SBL7839
    DICK PETERSON      B V G (ABCDE (B) OUTSIDE INSIDE        1968   PHILIPS           600 278
    GENE ESTES         PERC (C     (B) OUTSIDE INSIDE         1968   PHILIPS        SBL 7860
    BRUCE'LEIGH'STEPHENS G  (ABCDE (C) NEW IMPROVED           1969   PHILIPS           600 305
    GENE ESTES              (      (C) NEW IMPROVED           1974   PHILIPS        SBL 7896
    ERIC ALBRONDA      PROD (C     (C) NEW IMPROVED           1969   PHILIPS    GER 852 136
    BURNS KELLOGG      K    (BCDE  (D) BLUE CHEER             1969   PHILIPS           600 333
                                   (D) BLUE CHEER             19     PHILIPS    GER 6336 001
    NORMAN MAYALL      D G  (DE    (E) ORIGINAL HUMAN BEINGS  1970   PHILIPS 6336 004  600 347
    GARY YODER         G HCA V(DE  (F) OH PLEASANT HOPE       19     PHILIPS           600 350
B150A                                    BLUE GOOSE                                  B150A
    ALAN CULLAN        V G SYN(A   (A) BLUE GOOSE             1975   ANCHOR            2005
    SEAN LOCKE         D    (A
    NICK SOUTH         B    (A     MIKE TODMAN     G    (A   NICK HOGARTH    K    (A
    ALEXIS KORNER      V    (A     STEVE MARRIOTT  V    (A   JOEY MOLLAND    V    (A
    CHRIS PERRY        D    (A
B151                                     BLUE JAYS                                   B151
    JOHN LODGE         B V  (      (A) THE BLUE JAYS          1975   THRESHOLD   UK  THS  1
    JUSTIN HAYWARD     G V  (
    GRAHAM DEACON      D    (      KIRK DUNCAN     PNO   (   JIM COCKNEY     VLN  (
    TOM TOMPKINS       CELLO (
B151A                                    BLUE MAGIC                                  B151A
    WALTER SMITH       V    (E     (A) BLUE MAGIC           19  ATCO US 7038  UK  K40532
    VERNON SAWYER           (ABCD  (B) MAGIC OF THE BLUE    19  ATCO US 36103 UK  K50112
    RICHARD  PRATT     V    (ABCDE (C) 13 BLUE MAGIC LANE   19  ATCO US 36120 UK  K50181
    WENDELL SAWYER     B    (ABCD  (D) MYSTIC DRAGONS       19  ATCO          US      36140
    KEITH BEATON       V    (ABCDE (E) MESSAGE             19  ATCO          US      38104
    TED MILLS          K    (ABCDE
B151B                                    BLUE JUG BAND                               B151B
    CLINT DELONG       G V  (A     (A) BLUE JUG            1975   CAPRICORN          0158
    ED RATZELOFF       V G  (A
    BILL LITTLE        K    (A     BILL BURNETT    B    (A   MAC PAUL WALKLEY  D  (A
    RUFUS THIBODAUX    VLN  (A     RANDY SCRUGGS   G    (A
B152                                     BLUE MINK                                   B152
    MADELINE BELL      V    (ALL   (A) OUR WORLD            1970   PHILIPS  UK  6308 024
    ROGER COOK         V    (ALL   (B) MELTING POT          1970   PHILIPS  UK  SBL 1029
    BARRY MORGAN       D    (ALL   (B) MELTING POT          1970   PHILIPS  US  600  323
    HERBIE FLOWERS     B    (ALL   (C) LIVE AT THE TALK OF THE TOWN 1972 REGAL ZONOPHONE SLRZ 1029
    ALAN PARKER        G    (ALL   (D) A TIME OF CHANGE     1972   REGAL ZONOPHONE SRZA 8507
    ANN ODELL          K    (FGH   (E) REAL MINK            1971   PHILIPS  US  600  339
    ROGER COULAM       K    (ABCDEFG ( ) BEST OF BLUE MINK  1973   PHILIPS  UK  6382 077
    RAY COOPER         PERC (FGH   (F) BLUE MINK            1973   MCA      US       332
    ALLAN CLARKE       HCA  (D     (G) ONLY WHEN I LAUGH    1973   EMI      UK  EMA  756
    DEREK WATKINS      TPT  (D     (H) FRUITY               1974   EMI      UK  EMC 3021
                                   (J) THE BEST OF BLUE MINK 1974  EMI      UK  EMC 3043
                                   (K) HIT MAKING WORLD OF BLUE MINK 1975 DECCA UK  SPA  437
                                   (L) ATTENTION            1975   PHONOGRAM         6434 064
B152A                                    BLUE MOUNTAIN EAGLE                          B152A
    DAVID PRICE        G V  (A     (A) BLUE MOUNTAIN EAGLE   197    ATCO     US       33324
    RANDY FULLER       B G V (A    (B) SECOND                197    ATCO     US
    BOB JONES          G V  (A
    JOEY NEWMAN        G K V (A     DON PONCHER     D V    (A
B153                                     BLUE NOTES                                  B153
    LOUIS MOHOLO       D    (AB    (A) BLUE NOTES FOR MONGEZI (DBL) 1977 OGUN      OGD 001/2
    JOHNNY MBIZO DYAM  B    (AB    (B) BLUE NOTES IN CONCERT VOL1  1978 OGUN      OG  220
    CHRIS McGREGOR     PNO  (AB
    DUDU PUKWANA       SAX  (AB
B154                                     BLUE OYSTER CULT                            B154
    ERIC BLOOM         G V K(ABCDEFGHJKL(A) BLUE OYSTER CULT  1973 CBS UK 64904 US    31063
    ALLEN LANIER       K K V(ABCDEFGHJKL(A) BLUE OYSTER CULT  1981 CBS        UK RI   32025
    ALBERT BOUCHARD    D G V(ABCDEFGHJKL(B) TYRANNY & MUTATION 1974 CBS UK 65331 US   32107
    JOE BOUCHARD       B V G(ABCDEFGHJKL(B) TYRANNY & MUTATION 1981 CBS       UK RI   32056
    DONALD ROESER      G V K(ABCDEFGHJKL(C) SECRET TREATIES   1974 CBS UK 80103 US    32858
    PATTI SMITH        V    (E     (C) SECRET TREATIES        1981 CBS        UK RI   32055
    RANDY BRECKER      HRNS (E     (D) ON YOUR FEET OR ON YOUR KNEES 1975 CBS UK 88116 US 33317
    MARK RIVERA        SAX  (J     (E) AGENTS OF FORTUNE      1976 CBS UK 81385 US    34164
    MICHAEL BRECKER    HRNS (E     (F) SPECTRES               1977 CBS UK 86050 US    35019
    ELLEN FOLEY        V    (HJK   (G) SOME ENCHANTED EVENING 1978 CBS UK 86074 US    35563
    GENYA REVAN        V    (H     (H) MIRRORS                1979 CBS UK 86087 US    36009
    MICKEY RAPHAEL     HCA  (H     (J) CULTOSAURUS ERECTUS    1980 CBS UK 86120 US    36550
    WENDY WEBB         V    (H     (K) FIRE OF UNKNOWN ORIGIN 1981 CBS UK 85137 US    37389
    RICK DOWNEY        D    (L     (L) ETL                    1982 CBS UK 22203

        (CONTINUED)
```

B154　　　　　　　　　　　　　　BLUE OYSTER CULT　　　(CONTINUED)　　　　　　　　B154
　　KARLA DEVITO　　　　V　　(JK　　(EP) IN MY MOUTH OR ON THE GROUND　1972　REICHSTAG　US　　1106
　　SANDY JEAN　　　　　V　　(K
　　BILL CIVITELLA　　PERC　(K　　TONY CEDRONE　　　PERC　(K　　SANDY PEARLMAN　　PROD (BCDE
　　MURRAY KRUGMAN　　PROD　(BCDE　DAVID LUCAS　　　　PROD　(E
B154A　　　　　　　　　　　　　　BLUE STEEL　　　　　　　　　　　　　　　　　　B154A
　　LEONARD ARNOLD　　G V　(AB　　(A) NO MORE LONELY NIGHTS　　1979　INFINITY INF9018　+ INS2011
　　RICHARD BOWDEN　　G V　(AB　　NOTHING BUT TIME　　　　　　1981　ASYLUM　　US　　6E308
　　HOWARD BURKE　　　G V　(AB
　　MARC DURAM　　　　B　　(AB　　MICKEY McGEE　　　　D　　(A　　REX CAUGHROM　　　K　(B
　　SKIP EDWARDS　　　K　　(B　　DON HENLEY　　　　　V　　(B　　KAREN BOWDEN　　　V　(B
　　DAVID DICKEY　　　B V　(B　　JOHN HERRON　　　　K　　(B　　MARIUS PENCZNER　K　(B
　　CLARENCE CLEMONS　SAX　(B　　KRISTINE ARNOLD　　V　　(B　　JANIS GILL　　　　V　(B
　　MICHEAL HUEY　　　D　　(AB
B154B　　　　　　　　　　　　　　BLUES BAND　　　　　　　　　　　　　　　　　　B154B
　　PAUL JONES　　　　V HCA (AB　　(A) OFFICIAL BOOTLEG ALBUM　1980　ARISTA　　　BBBP 101
　　TOM McGUINNESS　　G　　(AB　　(B) READY　　　　　　　　　1980　ARISTA　　　　BB 2
　　HUGHIE FLINT　　　D　　(AB
　　DAVE KELLY　　　　G V　(AB　BOB HALL　　　PNO　(A　IAN STEWART　PNO　(B　GARY FLETCHER　B (AB
　　GERAINT WATKINS　PNO　(B　ROCKIN' DOPSIE　ACC　(B　CHESTER ZENO　PERC (B
B154C　　　　　　　　　　　BLUE RIVERS & THE MAROONS　　　　　　　　　　　　B154C
　　　　　　　　　　　　　　　　(A) BLUE BEAT IN MY SOUL　　1967　COLUMBIA　UK　SX 6192
B154D　　　　　　　　　　　　　　BLUE ROSE　　　　　　　　　　　　　　　　　　B154D
　　TERRY FURLONG　　G　　(A　　(A) BLUE ROSE　　　　　　　1972　EPIC　　　　US 31252
　　DAVE THOMSON　　　G B　(A
　　STU PERRY　　　　　D　　(A　　JOHN URIBE　　　　　B　　(A　　DON PONCHER　　　D　(A
B154E　　　　　　　　　　　　　　BLUE SHOUTERS　　　　　　　　　　　　　　　　B154E
　　GEORGE J STEINMANN G HCA V(A　(A) LIVE AT KULTUR KARUSSELL　19　BELLAPHON　　33005
　　MAX GUGGER　　　　SAX V (A
　　ADI TOSETTO　　　　B　　(A　　KLAUS FRIEDLI　　　PNO　(A　ANDRE BURI　　　D　(A
B155　　　　　　　　　　　　　　BLUES BROTHERS　　　　　　　　　　　　　　　B155
　　JOLIET JAKE BLUES　V　(ALL　　(A) BRIEFCASE FULL OF BLUES　1978　ATLANTIC　　UK　K 50556
　　(JOHN BELUSHI)　　　　　　　(B) BLUES BROTHERS (SOUNDTRACK)　1980　ATLANTIC US 16017 UK K 50715
　　ELWOOD BLUES　　　HCA V (ALL　(C) MADE IN AMERICA　　　1980　ATLANTIC US 16025 UK K 50768
　　(DAN AKROYD)　　　　　　　(D) BEST OF THE BLUES BROTHERS　1981　ATLANTIC
　　PAUL SHAFFER　　　K V　(AC
　　STEVE CROPPER　　G　　(ABC　MATT MURPHY　　　　G　　(ABC　DONALD DUCK DUNN　B　(ABC
　　STEVE JORDAN　　　D V　(ABC　LOU MARINI　　　　SAX V(ABC　ALAN RUBIN　　　TPT V(ABC
　　TOM SCOTT　　　　SAX V (AC　TOM MALONE　　　　HRS　(ABC　MURPHY DUNNE　　K　(BC
　　JEFF MIRONOV　　　G　　(C　　CAB CALLOWAY　　　V　　(B　　JAMES BROWN　　　V　(B
　　RAY CHARLES　　　V　　(B　　ARETHA FRANKLIN　V　　(B　　WILLIE HALL　　　D　(B
　　BRENDA CORBETT　　V　　(B　　MARGARET BRANCH　V　　(B　　CAROLINE FRANKLIN V (B
　　PATTI AUSTIN　　　V　　(B　　VIVIAN CHERRY　　V　　(B　　YOLLANDA McCULLOUGH V (B
　　REV JAMES CLEVELAND CHOIR (B　ELLIOTT RANDALL　G　　(B　　KEIV GINSBERG　　G　(B
　　HIRAM BULLOCK　　G　　(B　　LARRY WILLIS　　　K　　(B　　TERRY FRYER　　　K　(B
　　BILL PAYNE　　　　K　　(B　　JOHN SPRINGER　　K　　(B　　RICHARD T BEAR　K　(B
　　JOHN HASON　　　　K　　(B　　ARTHUR DICKSON　　D　　(B　　DAVID WESTON　　　B　(B
　　LEW DEL GATTO　　HRNS (B
B155A　　　　　　　　　　　　　BLUES DIMENSIONS　　　　　　　　　　　　　　B155A
　　HELMIG VAN DER VEGT K　(A　　(A) BLUES DIMENSION　　　1969　DECCA　　GERM　ND254
　　RUDY VAN DIJK　　SAX　(A
　　HERMAN DEINUM　　B　　(A　　HANS LAFAILLE　　　D　　(A　　RIPKE　　　　　(A
B155B　　　　　　　　　　　　　BLUES IMAGE　　　　　　　　　　　　　　　　　B155B
　　FRANK 'SKIP' CONTE　K　(ABC　(A) BLUES IMAGE　　　　　1969　ATCO　　　US　33300
　　MIKE PINELLA　　　G V　(AB　　(B) OPEN　　　　　　　　　1970　ATCO　　　US　33317
　　MALCOLM JONES　　B　　(ABC　(C) RED WHITE & BLUES IMAGE　1970　ATCO　　　US　33348
　　MANUEL BERTEMATTI　D V　(ABC　(C) RED WHITE & BLUES IMAGE　1971　ATLANTIC　UK　2400 120
　　JOE LALA　　　　　PERC (ABC
　　DENNIS CORRELL　　V　　(BC　KENT HENRY　　　　　G　　(C
B156　　　　　　　　　　　　　BLUES INCORPORATED　　　　　　　　　　　　　B156
　　CYRIL DAVIES　　　V HCA (　　(A) BLUES INC/ALEXIS KORNER ALL STARS 19　TRANSATLANTIC　TRASAM 7
　　ALEXIS KORNER　　G V　(
　　MICK JAGGER　　　V HCA (　　CHARLIE WATTS　　　D　　(　　IAN ARMITT　　　K　(
　　DICK HECKSTALL SMITH SAX (　JOHN PARKER　　　　　　(　　RONNIE JONES　　　　(
　　JACK BRUCE　　　　B　　(　　GRAHAM BOND　　　K SAX (　　GINGER BAKER　　　D　(
B157　　　　　　　　　　　　　BLUES MAGOOS　　　　　　　　　　　　　　　　　B157
　　PEPPY THIELHEIM　　G V　(ABCDEF　(A) BLUES MAGOOS　　　1966　FONTANA　　　STL 5402
　　RALPH SCALA　　　V K　(ABCD　(B) PSYCHEDELIC LOLLIPOP　1966　MERCURY
　　RON GILBERT　　　B　　(ABCD　(C) ELECTRIC COMIC BOOK　1967　MERCURY
　　GEOFF DAKING　　　D　　(ABCD　(D) BASIC BLUES MAGOOS　1968　MERCURY　US　ST 61167
　　MIKE ESPOSITO　　G　　(BCDA　(E) NEVER GOING BACK TO GEORGIA　1969　ABC　US　ABCS 697
　　JOHN LIELLO　　VIBES PERC (EF　(F) GULF COAST BOUND　　1970　ABC　　US　ABCS 710
　　ERIC KAZ　　　HCA V K　(EF　(F) GULF COAST BOUND　　1972　PROBE　US　SPB 1024
　　RICHIE DICKON　　PERC (EF
　　ROGER EATON　　　B V　(E　　HERB LOVELL　　　　D　　(E　　DEAN EVANSON　　FLT　(E
　　TITO　　　　　　CONGA (E　　SOTO　　　　　　　SAX　(E　　PEE WEE ELLIS　PERC (F
　　COOKER LOPRESTI　B　　(F　　JIM PAYNE　　　　　D　　(F　　DADDY YA YA　　PERC (F
B158　　　　　　　　　　　　　BLUES PROJECT　　　　　　　　　　　　　　　　B158
　　AL KOOPER　　　　K　　(ABCG　(A) LIVE AT THE CAFE AU GO GO　1966　VERVE　　FT　3000
　　STEVE KATZ　　　　G　　(AGBC　(B) PROJECTIONS　　　　1967　VERVE　　FTS 3008
　　TOMMY FLANDERS　　V　　(AEF　(B) PROJECTIONS　　　　1969　VERVE　　SVLP 6009
　　DANNY KALB　　　　G　　(ALL　(C) LIVE AT THE TOWN HALL　1967　VERVE　　FTS 3025
　　ANDY KULBERG　　B　　(ABCDG　(D) PLANNED OBSOLESCENCE　1968　VERVE　　FTS 3046
　　RAY BLUMENFIELD　D　　(ABCDEFG　(E) LAZARUS　　　　　　1971　CAPITOL　ST　872
　　RICHARD GREENE　VLN　(D　　(F) BLUES PROJECT　　　　1972　CAPITOL　EST 11017
　　DON KRETMAR　　SAX　(DEF　(F) BLUES PROJECT　　　　197　MGM　　GAS 118
　　JOHN GREGORY　　G V　(D　　(G) REUNION IN CENTRAL PARK　1973　MCA　US　8003
　　DAVID COHEN　　　G K　(EF　　( ) BEST OF　　　　　　　197　VERVE　　FTS 3069
　　BILL LUSSENDEN　　G　　(F　　( ) POP HISTORY　　　　19　POLYDOR　　2625 020

　　　　　　　　　　　　　　　　　　　　　　　　　　(CONTINUED)

[59]

B158   (CONTINUED)   **BLUES PROJECT**   B158

```
  JOHN KOERNER        (Z    (Z) BLUES PROJECT              196   ELEKTRA      US  EKS 7264
  GEOFF MULDAUR       (Z
  DAVE RAY            (Z    IAN BUCHANAN         (Z    MARK SPOELSTRA      (Z
  ERIC VON SCHMIDT    (Z    TONY GLOVER          (Z    FRITZ RICHMOND      (Z
  JOHN SEBASTIAN      (Z    DOUG POMEROY         (Z    BOB (DYLAN) LANDY   (Z
```

B159   **BLUESOLOGY**   B159

```
  ELTON JOHN        ORG     (A) RARE TRACKS(ONE TRACK)    1975  POLYDOR      UK  2482 274
  MARC CHARIG       CORNET
  ELTON DEAN        SAX     FRED GANDY           B     JOHN BALDRY         V
  PETE GAVIN        D       NEIL HUBBARD         G     MICK INKPEN         D
  PAT HIGGS         TPT     ALAN WALKER          V     JIMMY HOROWITZ      K
  REX BISHOP        B       DAVE MURPHY          SAX   CALEB QUAYE         G
  STUART BROWN      V       MARSHA HUNT          V     BERNIE HOLLAND      G
```

B159A   **BLUESPLIZ**   B159A

```
  JORG FUNKE      V HCA FLT(A   (A) EYES DON'T LIE        1979  Z                193
  SIGGI SCHWARZ   G       (A
  PIT ZAEPERNICK  B       (A   DIETER FUNKE         D     (A   ROMI SCHICKLE   K  (A
  HARRY BERGER    SAX     (A
```

B160   **COLIN BLUNSTONE**   B160

```
  COLIN BLUNSTONE   V G   (ALL   (A) ONE YEAR             1971  EPIC UK 64557   US 30974
  PETE WINGFIELD    K     (BC    (B) ENNISMORE            1973  EPIC UK 65278   US 31994
  DEREK GRIFFITHS   G     (BC    (C) JOURNEY              1974  EPIC UK 65805   US 32962
  JIM TOOMEY        D     (BC    (D) PLANES               1976  EPIC UK 81592
  ROBERT HENRIT     D     (B     (E) NEVER EVEN THOUGHT   1978  EPIC UK 82835   RCA US 12903
  BYRON LYEFOOR     D     (B     (E) NEVER EVEN THOUGHT   1978  ROCKET          SCAN  61328
  ROD ARGENT        K     (BCF   (F) LATE NIGHTS IN SOHO  1979  ROCKET          NL  9103 510
  MIKE SNOW         K G   (B
  PHIL DENNYS       K     (B     RUSS BALLARD    K G  (B    STEVE BINGHAM    B    (B
  JIM RODFORD       B     (B     MIKE COTTON     HRNS (C    NICK NEWELL      HRNS (C
  JOHN BEECHAM      HRNS  (C     DUNCAN BROWNE   G    (C    RICHARD KERR     PNO  (C
  KINGS SINGERS     V     (C     TERRY POOLE     D    (BC   JOHN GIBLIN      B    (F
  MIKE MORAN        K     (F     JOHN VERITY     V    (F    KATE KISSOON     V    (F
  CLEM CLEMPSON     G     (F     SIMON PHILLIPS  D    (F    PAUL KOEGH       G    (F
  MAURICE PERT      PERC  (F     JIMMY CHAMBERS  V    (F    STEVIE LANGE     V    (F
```

B160A   **BLURT**   B160A

```
  TED MILTON     V SAX  (AB   (A) FACTORY QUARTET (1 SIDE OF DBL)  198   FACTORY    UK  FACT24
  JAKE MILTON    D V    (AB   (B) IN BERLIN                        1981  ARMAGEDDON UK  ARM 6
  PETE CRISS     G TROM (AB
```

B160B   **BO GRUMPUS**   B160B

```
  ED MOTTAU        G     (B    (A) BO GRUMPUS           1968
  JIM COLEGROVE    B G   (B    (B) BEFORE THE WAR       1968  ATCO        US  33246
  FELIX PAPPALARDI K B G (B
  JO HUTCHINSON    G B K (B    HERB LOVELLE     D   (B    RONNIE BLAKE    D   (B
  N D SMART        D     (B
```

B161   **BO STREET RUNNERS**   B161

```
  MICK FLEETWOOD   D     (A    (A) READY STEADY WIN (1 TRACK)  1964  DECCA    UK  LK 4634
  TIM HINKLEY      K     (A    (1) 1963
  JOHN DOMINIC     V     (A1
  MIKE PATTO       V     (A    GARY THOMAS     G    (1    GLYN THOMAS     D    (1
  DAVE CAMERON     B     (1    ROYSTON FRY     K    (1
```

B161A   **BOA**   B161A

```
  BEAU MAGGI       G HCA V(A   (A) SCHIZIOD              1975  WOODEN NICKEL    0790
  THOMAS OBOMSAWIN G V    (A
  ROGER ALTHER     D      (A   RONALD STOCKERT  G V K (A   DENNIS BELFIELD  B V K  (A
  ROBERT ZINNER    G      (A   LEWIS MARK       G     (A   MICKEY McMEEL    D V    (A
  ROGER KAHN       K V    (A   MARTIN HILL      B V   (A
```

B161B   **BOATZ**   B161B

```
  THOM FLORA       K V    (A   (A) BOATZ                1979  CAPRICORN   US  CPN 0222
  GARY BAKER       B V    (A
  PETE CARR        G      (A   RICK POWELL      D   (A    ROGER CLARK     D   (A
  STEVE NATHAN     K      (A
```

B162   **BOB & EARL**   B162

```
  BOB RELF         V      (ALL  (A) BOB & EARL           19    CRESTVIEW   US       3055
  EARL NELSON      V      (ALL  (B) TOGETHER             19    JOY         U   JOYS 199
                                (C) BOB & EARL           1969  B&C         U   BCB    1
                                (D) HARLEM SHUFFLE       1971  JAYBOY           2004
```

B163   **BOB & MARCIA**   B163

```
  BOB ANDY         V      (     (A) YOUNG GIFTED & BLACK  1976  TROJAN          TBL 122
  MARCIA GRIFFITHS V      (
```

B164   **BOBBIDAZZLER**   B164

```
  GRANT GULLICKSON V      (A   (A) BOBBIDAZZLER         1978  RCA              PL 12196
  LANCE GULLICKSON V      (A   (A) BOBBIDAZZLER         1977  RCA         US  APLI 2196
  JAMES DIVISEK    D      (A
  GEORGE MARINELLI G      (A   BRIAN WHITCOMB   K   (A    DENNIS BELFIELD  B   (A
  FRED DIVISEK            (A   PETE HENDERSON       (A    JAY LEWIS        G   (A
  TONY PELUSO            (A   STEVE PINKSTON       (A
```

B164A   **ROLAND BOCQUET**   B164A

```
  ROLAND BOCQUET   K      (A   (A) PARADIA              19    COBRA       GERM    60015
  DIDIER DUFRESNE  B      (A
  MAXIME GOETZ     G      (A   GERARD GEOFFROY   FLT  (A
```

B165   **BODACIOUS**   B165

```
  MARTY BALIN      G V    (A   (A) BODACIOUS D F        1974  RCA         US  APLI02067
  GREG DEWEY DAGREAZE D   (A   (A) BODACIOUS D F        1974  RCA         UK  SF  8391
  VIC SMITH        G      (A
  MARK RYAN        B      (A   CHARLIE HICKOX   K   (A
```

B165A   **BODAST**   B165A

```
   STEVE HOWE          G    (A      (A) BODAST TAPES(60's)        1981   CHERRY RED        BRED  12
   CLIVE MULDOON       G V  (A
   BOBBY CLARKE        D    (A      DAVE CURTIS       B V  (A    CLIVE SKINNER     G V  (A
B166                        CURT BOETCHER                                                       B166
   CURT BOETCHER   . V K G  (A      (A) THERE'S AN INNOCENT FACE  1973   ELEKTRA      US   EKS 75037
   WITH
   WEBB BURREL         V G K (A     RED RHODES        STEEL (A   SKIP KONTE        K    (A
   RIC DE LONG         B    (A      WAYNE YENTIS      SYN  (A    LES THORNTON      TUBA (A
   TESSIE              PERC (A      WILLIS MASONHEIMER TUBA (A
B166A                       BOGEY BOYS                                                          B166A
   JIMMY SMYTH         G    (AB     (A) FRIDAY NIGHT             1979   CHRYSALIS    UK   CHR  1241
   PAUL MORAN          D    (AB     (B) JIMMY DID IT             1980   CHRYSALIS    UK   CHR  1298
   DONALD NAGLE        B V  (AB
   JOHN KEOGH          K    (A      LEO LYONS         PROD (A
B166B                       BOFFALONGO                                                          B166B
   BASIL MATYCHAK      K V  (A      (A) BOFFALONGO              1969   UA           US        6726
   KEITH GINSBERG      G    (A
   LARRY HOPPEN        B V  (A      RITCHIE           D    (A   WELLS KELLY       D    (
B166C                       TIM BOGERT                                                          B166C
   TIM BOGERT               (A      (A) PROGRESSIONS            1981
B168                        MARC BOLAN & T REX                                                  B168
   MARC BOLAN          G V  (ALL    (A) MY PEOPLE WERE FAIR     1968   REGAL ZONOPHONE UK  SLRZ 1003
   WITH                             (B) PROPHET SEERS & SAGES   1968   REGAL ZONOPHONE UK  SLRZ 1005
   STEVE TOOK   D B PNO PERC (ABC   (AB) MY PEOPLE/PROPHET      1972   CUBE/FLY     UK   TOOFA  3
   MICKY FINN       PERC V(69/75    (C) UNICORN                1969   REGAL ZONOPHONE UK  SLRZ 1007
   TONY VISCONTI   PROD PNO (BCDEF  (C) UNICORN                19     BLUE THUMB   US
   JOHN PEEL           V    (AC     (D) BEARD OF STARS         1970   REGAL ZONOPHONE UK  SLRZ 1013
   BILL LEGEND         D    (71/74  (CD) UNICORN/BEARD OF STARS DBL 1972  CUBE        UK   TOOFA  9
   STEVE TURNER        B    (       (E) T REX                  1970   FLY          UK   HIFLY  2
   STEVE CURRIE        B    (70/76  (F) ELECTRIC WARRIOR       1971   FLY          UK   HIFLY  6
   IAN McDONALD        SAX  (F      ( ) THE BEST OF T REX      1971   FLY          UK   TON    2
   JACK GREEN          G    (73/75  (G) BOLAN BOOGIE           1972   FLY          UK   HIFLY  8
   PAT HALL            V    (73?75  (G) BOLAN BOOGIE           197    CUBE         UK  HIFLY   8
   GLORIA JONES        V    (73/76  (J) RIDE A WHITE SWAN      1972   MFP          UK   MFP  5274
   DINO JONES          V    (75/77  (K) HARD ON LOVE           1972   TRACK        UK   2406  101
   TYRONE SCOTT        K V  (75/76  (M) THE SLIDER             1972   EMI          UK   BLN  5001
   HERBIE FLOWERS      B    (76/77  (N) TANX                   1972   EMI          UK   BLN  5002
   TONY NEWMAN         D    (76/77  ( ) GREAT HITS             1972   EMI          UK   BLN  5003
   HOWARD KAYLAN       V    (FMS    (Q) ZINC ALLOY             1974   EMI          UK   BLNA 7751
   MARK VOLMAN         V    (FMS    (R) BEGINNING OF DOVES     1974   TRACK        UK   2410  201
   DAVY LUTTON         D    (74/76  (S) LIGHT OF LOVE          1974   CASABLANCA        NBLP 7005
   MILLER ANDERSON     G    (       (T) ZIP GUN                1975   EMI          UK   BLN  7752
   RICK WAKEMAN        K    (F      (U) GET IT ON              1975   MFP          UK        90059
   BURT COLLINS        HRNS (F      (V) FUTURISTIC DRAGON      1976   EMI          UK   BLN  5004
   LONNIE JORDAN            (S      (W) DANDY IN THE UNDERWORLD 1977  EMI          UK   BLN  5005
   DANNY THOMPSON           (S      (X) WORDS & MUSIC          1978   CUBE         UK   HIFLD  1
   B J COLE            STEEL (S     ( ) GREATEST HITS VOL 1    1978   PICKWICK     UK   SHM   953
                                    ( ) T REX COLLECTION  (DBL) 1978  PICKWICK     UK   PDA  044
                                    ( ) SOLID GOLD            1979   EMI          UK   NUT    5
B168A                       BOLD                                                                B168A
   TIM GRIFFIN         D V  (A      (A) BOLD                   196    ABC          US         705
   MICHAEL CHMURA      K    (A
   ROBERT LAPALM       G V  (A      STEPHEN WALKER   . B V  (A   DICK LAFRENIERE   G    (A
B169                        TOMMY BOLIN                                                         B169
   TOMMY BOLIN         G V K (AB    (A) TEASER                 1975   ATLANTIC     UK   K   50208
   STANLEY SHELDON     K    (A      (A) TEASER                 1975   NEMPEROR US 436   RI  37534
   DAVID FOSTER        K    (A      (B) PRIVATE EYES           1976   CBS          UK        81612
   JEFF PORCARO        D    (A      (B) PRIVATE EYES           1976   CBS          US   C   34329
   PRAIRIE PRINCE      D    (A
   PHIL COLLINS        PERC (A      JAN HAMMER        K    (A   DAVID SANBORN     SAX  (A
   SAMMY ZIGUERON      PERC (A      NARADA MICHAEL WALDEN D (A   PAUL STALLWORTH   B    (A
   BOB BERGE           D    (A      RON FRANSEN       K    (A   BOBBY BERGE       D    (B
   BOBBYE HALL         PERC (B      MARK STEIN        K V  (B   NORMA JEAN BELL  SAX PERC (B
   REGGIE McBRIDE      B V  (B
B169A                       MICHAEL BOLOTIN                                                     B169A
   MICHAEL BOLOTIN     V G  (AB     (A) MICHAEL BOLOTIN        1975   RCA UK SF 8451 US APLI 0992
   WILBUR BASCOMB      B    (A      (B) EVERY DAY OF MY LIFE   1976   RCA          US   APLI 1550
   PATRICK HENDERSON   PNO  (AB
   JAN MULLANEY        ORG  (B      BILLY ELWORTHY    G    (B   GARY FERRARO      B    (B
   JAY MICHAELS        D    (B      PAPA JOHN CREACH  FDL  (B   COLINA PHILLIPS   V    (B
   SHARON LEE WILLIAMS V    (B      RHONDA SILVER     V    (B   WAYNE PERKINS          (A
   DAVE SANBORN        SAX  (A      BERNARD PURDIE    D    (A   JIM HORN          SAX  (A
   DENNY MOROUSE       SAX  (A      MARY McCREARY     V    (A   MARCY LEVY        V    (A
   LANI GROVES         V    (A      BARBARA MASSEY    V    (A   FRED BOVA         G    (A
   WALT RICHMOND       K    (A      ANDY NEWMARK      D    (A   GEORGE STURTEVANT FLT  (A
B170                        BONAROO                                                            B170
   BILL CUOMO          K V  (A      (A) BONAROO                1974   WB           UK   K   56096
   MICHAEL HOSSACK D PERC V (A
   ROBERT LICHTIG  B HRNS V (A      JERRY WEEMS       G V  (A   BOBBY WINKELMAN   G V  (A
   MILT HOLLAND        PERC (A
B171                        GRAHAM BOND                                                        B171
   GRAHAM BOND  K SAX V     (ALL    (A) THE SOUND OF 65        1965   COLUMBIA     UK   33SX 1711
   DICK HECKSTALL SMITH SAX (ABCJ   (B) THERE'S A BOND A BETWEEN US 1966 COLUMBIA   UK   33SX 1750
   GINGER BAKER        D    (ABCJ   (C) SOLID BOND      (DBL)  1970   WB UK  3001  UK RI K 66004
   JOHN McLAUGHLIN     G    (C      (C) SOLID BOND            1970   WB           US         2555
   JACK BRUCE          B    (ABCJ   (D) HOLY MAGICK            1971   VERTIGO      UK   6360 021
   DEREK FOLEY         G    (H      (D) HOLY MAGICK            1971   MERCURY      US        61327
   JON HISEMAN         D    (C      (E) WE PUT OUR MAGICK ON YOU 1971 VERTIGO      UK   6360 042
   TERRY POOLE         G B  (E      (E) WE PUT OUR MAGICK ON YOU 1974 PHILIPS           SRMI 612
```

(CONTINUED)

B171   (CONTINUED)   GRAHAM BOND   **B171**

DIANE STEWART	V	(DE1LKH	(F) BOND IN AMERICA	1971	PHILIPS		6499200/1
HENRY WILLIAMS	G	(E	(F) BOND IN AMERICA	1971	MERCURY	UK	6499200/1
GASPAR LAWAL	PERC	(E	(G) THIS IS GRAHAM BOND	1972	PHILLIPS		6382 010
STEVE GREGORY	SAX	(E	(H) 2 HEADS ARE BETTER THAN ONE	1972	CHAPTER 1	UK	CHSR 813
JOHN WEATHERS	D	(E	(H) 2 HEADS ARE BETTER THAN ONE	1972	PATHE	FR	C064 93869
VICTOR BROX	V	(D	(J) BEGINNING OF JAZZ ROCK	1977	CHARLY		CR 30017
ANNETTE BROX	V	(D	(K) MIGHTY GRAHAM BOND	1968	PULSAR		AR 10606
PETE BROWN		(H	(L) LOVE IS THE LAW	1968	PULSAR		AR 10604
ERICA BOND	V	(H	(M) FACES & PLACES VOL 4	19	BYG	FR	529 904
RIC GRECH	B	(D	(1) INITIATION 1969 NO RECORDS				
STEVE YORK	B	(D					
JOHN GROSS	SAX	(D	ALEX DMOCHOWSKI	B	(D	PETE BAILEY	PERC (D
ALIKI ASHMAN	V	(D	DAVE HOWARD	SAX	(1	DAVE USHER	WIND B V (1
KEITH BAILEY	D	(1D	KEVIN STACEY	G	(1D	GODFREY McLEAN	D (D
JOHN MOORSHEAD	G	(D	JERRY SALISBURY	HRNS	(D	HAL BLAINE	D (L
EDDIE HOH	D	(KH	HARVEY MANDEL	G	(H	HARVEY BROOKS	K (K
RAY RUSSELL	G	(	DELISLE HARPER	B V	(H	MICK HUTCHINSON	G (H
SUE WOOLLEY	V	(H	MICK WALKER	V PERC	(H	DAVE SHEEHAN	D PERC (L
MAX BENNETT	B	(K	ALAN RUSHTON	D	(	DAVE QUINCEY	SAX (
NEIL HUBBARD	G	(	BOB WESTON	G	(		

B171A   PETER BOND   **B171A**

PETER BOND		(AB	(A) ITS ALL RIGHT FOR SOME	1977	TRAILER		LER2108
			(B) A DUCK ON HIS HEAD	1980	HIGHWAY		SHY 7012

B172A   GARY 'US' BONDS   **B172A**

GARY US BONDS	V	(ALL	(A) DANCE TILL QUARTER TO THREE	19	LEGRAND	US	3001
J T BOWEN	SAX	(E	(B) TWIST THE CALYPSO	19	LEGRAND	US	3002
CLARENCE CLEMONS	SAX	(DE	(C) GREATEST HITS	19	LEGRAND	US	3003
JOE MARTIN	G V	(E	(D) DEDICATION	1981	EMI	UK	3017
GEORGE RUIZ	B V	(E	(E) ON THE LINE	1982	EMI	UK	3022
BILL DERBY	G V	(E					
DANNY FEDERICI	K	(DE	JOHN CLEMENTE	B	(D	MIKE MICARA	D (DE
STEVE VAN ZANT	B G V	(DE	ROB PARISSI	G	(D	ROY BITTAN	K (DE
JOEY STANN	SAX V	(DE	ED MANION	SAX	(D	RICK GAZDA	V (D
BEN E KING	V	(D	ELLI GREENWICH	V	(D	ULA HEDWIG	V (D
CAROL SYLVAN	V	(D	GARY TALLENT	B	(DE	MAX WEINBERG	D (DE
LOUIE CONTE	G	(D	BRUCE SPRINGSTEEN	G V	(D	RUSTY CLOUD	K (DE
LA BAMBA	TROM	(D	MICHAEL SPENGLER	TPT	(D	CHUCK JACKSON	V (DE
MIKIE HARRIIS	V	(D	BRANDA HILLIARD	V	(D	CAROL WILLIAMS	V (D

B173   BONES   **B173**

CASEY CUNNINGHAM	D	(A	(A) BONES	1972	SIGNPOST 8402		4251
JIMMY FARAGHER	SAX B V	(A					
DANNY FARAGHER HRS HCA K V		(A	GREG TORNQUIST	G V HCA	(A		

B174   BONEY M   **B174**

MARCIA BARRETT	V	(CD	(A) TAKE THE HEAT OFF ME	1976	ATLANTIC UK K 50314 ATCO US 36143
LIZ MITCHELL	V	(CD	(B) LOVE FOR SALE	1977	ATLANTIC UK K 50385 US 19145
OBBY FARRELL	V	(CD	(C) NIGHT FLIGHT TO VENUS	1978	ATLANTIC UK K 50498 SIRE US 6062
MAIZIE WILLIAMS	V	(CD	(D) OCEANS OF FANTASY	1979	ATLANTIC UK K 50610
WITH					

KEITH FORSEY	D	(CD	NICK WOODLAND	G	(CD	GEORG DELGALTE	TROM (D
MATS BJORKLUND	G	(CD	GARY UNWIN	B	(CD	CHICO DE LOS REYES	(C
FRANK FARIAN	V	(D	PRECIOUS WILSON	V	(D	R BESSER	B (D
M CRETU	K	(D	JIM POLIVKA	TPT	(D	SCOT NEWTON	TPT (D
LISA GRODANIER	SAX	(D	BOBBY STERN	SAX	(D	LANCE BURTON	SAX (D
GEOFF STRADLING	TROM	(D	ETIENNE CAP	TPT	(D	WALTER RAB	TPT D(C
KARL BARTELMES	TPT	(D	BENNY GEBAVER	SAX	(D	DINO SOLERA	WIND (D
GEORG DELAGALTE	TROM	(D					

B174A   JUKE BOY BONNER   **B174A**

JUKE BOY BONNER	HCA V G	(ALL	(A) I'M GOING BACK TO THE COUNTRY	1968	ARHOOLIE	F	1036
BRUCE LANGMAN	G V	(C	(B) THE STRUGGLE	19	ARHOOLIE	F	1045
RON SKINNER	B	(C	(C) THINGS AINT RIGHT	1969	LIBERTY		83319
MEL WRIGHT	D	(C	(D) LEGACY OF THE BLUES	19	SONET		SNTF 634
JOHN LEWIS	K	(C	(D) LEGACY OF THE BLUES	19	GNP CRESCENDO	US	GNP 10015
			(E) LOUISIANA BLUES	19	STORYVILLE		SLP 177
			(F) ONE MAN TRIO	1979	FLYRIGHT		FLY 548

B174B   GRAHAM BONNET   **B174B**

GRAHAM BONNET	V	(AB	(A) GRAHAM BONNET	1977	RING O RECORDS	UK	2320 103
MIKE GILES	D	(A	(B) LINE UP	1981	VERTIGO	UK	6302 151
COZY POWELL	D	(B					
DAVE MARKEE	B	(A	CATHERINE HOWE	V	(A	MICK MOODY	G (AB
PIP WILLIAMS	G MAND	(A	JACQUIE SULLIVAN	V	(A	JOY YATES	V (A
STEVIE LANGE	V	(A	FRANK RICOTTI	PERC	(A	PETER ZORN	SAX (A
TERRY POPPLE	D	(A	COLIN GIBSON	B	(A	KEN CRADDOCK	PNO (A
GRAHAM PRESKETT	G	(A	TONY HYMAS	K	(A	BARDOT	V (A
GARY TWIGG	B	(B	FRANCIS ROSSI	K G V	(B	JOHN COOK	K (B
KIRBY	G	(B	IAN LYNN	K	(B	CHRISSIE STEWART	B (B
RICHARD PARFITT	G	(B	NEIL MURRAY	B	(B	JON LORD	K (B
MEL COLLINS	SAX	(B	MARTIN DITCHAM	PERC	(B	ADRIAN LEE	K (B
RUSS BALLARD	G	(B	ANDY BOWN	K	(B		

B174C   BONGO TEENS   **B174C**

		(A) BONGO TEENS	19	ORIGINAL SOUND US	5009

B174D   BONGOS   **B174D**

		(A) THE BONGOS	1980	FETISH	UK	FET005

B174E   BONNEVILLES   **B174E**

BOBBIE MARKT	SAX V	(A	(A) MEET THE BONNEVILLES	196	DRUM BOY	US	1001
VINCE MAGNA	G	(A					
WENDY COLBY	V	(A					

SEAN BONNIWELL'S MUSIC MACHINE

SEAN BONNIWELL	V G	(AB
KIETH OLSEN	B V	(A
MARK LANDON	G	(A
DOUG RHODES	K V	(A

RON EAGER   G D   (A

Album	Year	Label	Country	Cat No
(A) BONNIWELL MUSIC MACHINE	1968	WB	US	1732
(B) TURN ON THE MUSIC MACHINE	1967	ORIGINAL SOUND	US	8875

KARLA BONOFF   B175

KARLA BONOFF	V K G	(ALL							
WITH									
RUSS KUNKEL	D	(ABC	MICHAEL BOTTS	D	(A	ANDREW GOLD	G K	(ABC
MARK JORDAN	K	(C	JAI WINDING	PNO	(A	WADDY WACHTEL	G V	(AC
LEE SKLAR	B	(A	KENNY EDWARDS	G MAND B V	(AC	BROCK WALSH	V	(AC
LINDA RONSTADT	V	(A	STEVE FORMAN	PERC	(ABC	GLENN FREY	V	(A
GREG LADANYI	PERC	(A	WENDY WALDMAN	V	(A	STRING SECTION		(B
J D SOUTHER	V	(AC	GARTH HUDSON		(B	DANNY KORTCHMAR		(BC
DAN DUGMORE	STEEL	(A	PHIL KENZIE	SAX	(C	TIM SCHMIT	V	(C
DON HENLEY		(BC	DAVID SANBORN	SAX	(C	DAVID WOLINSKI	SYN K	(C
DAVID LINDLEY		(B	VICTOR FELDMSN	VIBES	(C	JOE WALSH	G	(C
BILL PAYNE	K	(C						
IRA INGBER	G	(C						

Album	Year	Label	Country	Cat No	Country	Cat No
(A) KARLA BONOFF	1977	CBS	US	34672	UK	82455
(B) RESTLESS NIGHTS	1979	CBS	US	35799	UK	83587
(C) WILD HEART OF THE YOUNG	1982	CBS	US	37444		

JACK BONUS   B177

JACK BONUS	V G SAX FLT K	(A	FREDDIE ROULETTE	G	(A	TONY SMITH	D	(A
TOM COSTER	K	(A	STRING SECTION		(A	JAMIE HOWELL	G	(A
BRUCE CONTE	G	(A	JON DETHERAGE	PNO	(A	SKIP OLSON	B	(A
ED BOGAS	VLN	(A	CHRIS ROWAN	G	(A	DAVID DIADEM	MAND K	(A
ANDY LIFLAND	D	(A	GLENN CRONKHITE	D	(A	EDDIE ADAMS	B	(A
LORIN ROWAN	G	(A	IVORY SMYLIE	CONGA	(A	JACK DORSEY	D	(A
BILLY WOLF	B	(A	BENNY VELARDE	PERC	(A	KEN BALZELL	TPT	(A
STAN MONTEIRO	CLAR	(A						
JACKIE KING	G	(A						
STEVE TURRE	TROM	(A						

Album	Year	Label	Country	Cat No
(A) JACK BONUS	1972	GRUNT		FTR 1005

BONZO DOG DO DAH BAND   B178

NEIL INNES	K B G V PROD	(ALL
VIVIAN STANSHALL	V TPT PROD	(ALL
ROGER RUSKIN SPEAR	SAX	(ALL
DAVE CLAGUE	B	(BEH
BUBS WHITE	G	(FH
RODNEY SLATER	SAX	(ABCDEH
TONY KAYE	K	(F
LEGS LARRY SMITH	D	(ALL
VERNON NOWELL	B BJO	(AEH
SAM SPOONS	PERC	(AEH
DENNIS COWAN	B V	(CDFH
DICK PARRY	WIND	(FH
ANDY ROBERTS	G	(FH
DAVE RICHARD	B	(FH
HUGHIE FLINT	D	(FH
GERRY BRON	PROD	(AB
GUS DUDGEON	PROD	(FH
BOB KERR	HRNS V	(AG
DAVE RICHARDS	B	(F
LEON WILLIAMS	TPT	(
JAMES CHAMBERS	WIND	(

Album	Year	Label	Country	Cat No
(A) GORILLA	1967	LIBERTY	UK	LBS 83056
((A) GORILLA	1970	SUNSET	UK	SLS 50160
(A) GORILLA	19	IMPERIAL	US	12370
(B) DOUGHNUT IN GRANNYS GREENHOUSE	1968	LIBERTY	UK	LBS 83158
(B) DOUGHNUT IN GRANNYS GREENHOUSE	1971	SUNSET	UK	SLS 50210
(C) TADPOLES	1969	LIBERTY	UK	LBS 83257
(C) TADPOLES	1969	LIBERTY	US	12445
(D) KEYNSHAM	1969	LIBERTY	UK	LBS 83290
(D) KEYNSHAM	1975	SUNSET	UK	SLS 50375
(D) KEYNSHAM	19	IMPERIAL	US	12457
(E) THE BEAST OF THE BONZOS (COMP)	1970	LIBERTY	UK	LBS 83332
(E) THE BEAST OF THE BONZOS (COMP)	19	UA	US	5517
(F) LETS MAKE UP & BE FRIENDLY	1972	UA	UK	UAS 29288
(F) LETS MAKE UP & BE FRIENDLY	1978	SUNSET	UK	SLS 50418
(C) URBAN SPACEMAN	1973	SUNSET	UK	SLS 50350
(C) URBAN SPACEMAN	197	IMPERIAL	US	12432
(H) HISTORY OF THE BONZOS (DBL)	1974	UA	UK	UAD60071/2
(H) HISTORY OF THE BONZOS (DBL)	1974	UA	US	LA 321 H

SYD NICHOLLS   BJO   (RAYMOND LEWITT   TUBA (

JAMES BOOKER   B179

JAMES BOOKER   PNO V   (AB

Album	Year	Label	Country	Cat No
(A) JUNCO PARTNERS	1976	ISLAND	UK	HELP 26
(B) NEW ORLEANS PIANO WIZZARD LIVE	1977	ROUNDER	US	2022

BOOKER T & THE MG's   B180

BOOKER T JONES	K G B	(ALL
WITH		
STEVE CROPPER	G	(
LOUIS STENBERG	D	(
AL JACKSON	D	(
DONALD DUCK DUNN	B	(
WILLIE HALL	D	(
DAVID T WALKER	G	(
JIM KELTNER	D	(
SAMMY CREASON	D	(
BOB GLAUB	B	(
ALEXANDER SMITH	B	(
BOBBYE HALL	PERC	(

Album	Year	Label	Country	Cat No
GREEN ONIONS	1962	LONDON	UK	1640 354
GREEN ONIONS	1966	ATLANTIC	UK	587 033
GREEN ONIONS	1980	ATLANTIC	UK	K 40072
GREEN ONIONS	19	STAX	US	STAX 701
GREEN ONIONS	19	PICKWICK		SHM 3031
AND NOW	1966	STAX	UK	589 002
AND NOW	1966	STAX	US	STAX 711
AND NOW	19	ATLANTIC		7711
IN THE XMAS SPIRIT	19	STAX	US	STAX 715
HIP HUG HER	196	STAX	US	STAX 717
BACK TO BACK(WITH MARKEYS)	19	STAX	US	STAX 720
DOING OUR THING	1968	ATLANTIC	UK	2464 011
DOING OUR THING	1968	STAX	US	1040
DOING OUR THING	19	STAX	US	STAX 724
DOING OUR THING	19	ATLANTIC		7724
BEST OF	1968	ATLANTIC	UK	228 015
BEST OF	19	STAX	UK	2325 018
BEST OF	19	STAX	US	8202
BEST OF	1980	ATLANTIC	UK	K 50749
BEST OF	197	ATLANTIC	UK	K 40072
UPTIGHT	1968	STAX	UK	SXATS1005
UPTIGHT	1968	STAX	US	2006
SOUL LIMBO	1968	STAX	UK	SXATS1001
SOUL LIMBO	1968	STAX	UK	2325 001
SOUL LIMBO	19	STAX	US	2001
McLEMORE AVENUE	1970	STAX	UK	2326 016
McLEMORE AVENUE	1970	STAX	US	2027
McLEMORE AVENUE	1970	STAX		SXATS1031
BOOKER T SET	1970	STAX	UK	2326 012
BOOKER T SET	1970	STAX	UK	SXATS1015
BOOKER T SET	19	STAX	UK	2325 003
BOOKER T SET	19	STAX	US	STAX 2009
MELTING POT	1972	STAX	UK	2325 030
MELTING POT	1972	STAX	US	STAX 1054
MELTING POT	197	STAX	US	STAX 2035

(CONTINUED)

BOOKER T & THE MG's   (CONTINUED)

STAR COLLECTION	1973	WB	MID 30042
STAR COLLECTION	19	WB	UK MID 20032
GREATEST HITS	1974	STAX	UK STX 1017
GREATEST HITS	19	ATLANTIC	US 2033
GREATEST HITS	1974	STAX	UK 2362 002
MEMPHIS SOUND	1975	STAX	UK STX 1037
UNION EXTENDED	1976	STAX	UK STXS 2041
UNION EXTENDED	1976	STAX	UK STX 1045
POP HISTORY	19	POLYDOR	2625 013
POP HISTORY	19	POLYDOR	2612 016
UNIVERSAL LANGUAGE	19	ASYLUM	US 7E 1093
UNIVERSAL LANGUAGE	19	ASYLUM	UK K 53057
GET READY	19	ATLANTIC	UK228 004
TIME IS TIGHT (MARKEYS)1979	STAX		UK STAX 3007
SOUL DRESSING	19	STAX	USSTAX 705

B180A   BOOKS   **B180A**

(A) EXPERTISE   1980   LOGO   UK   VOLUME 1

B180B   BOOMERANG   **B180B**

MARK STEIN	K V (A
JAMES GALLUZI	D (A
RICHARD RAMERIZ	G (A

(A) FIRST   19   RCA   LSP 4577

B181

JO CASMIR   B V   (A

BOOMTOWN RATS   **B181**

BOB GELDOF	V SAX (ALL
JOHNNIE FINGERS	K V (ALL
GERRY COTT	G (ABC
PETE BRIQUETTE	B V (ABC
GERRY ROBERTS	G V (ABC
SIMON CROWE	D V (ABC
ANDY DUNCAN	PERC (D
ALBE DONNELLY	SAX (D
DAVE McCHALE	SAX (A
TOM WINTER	BOUZ (D

(A) THE BOOMTOWN RATS	1977	ENSIGN		ENVY1
(A) THE BOOMTOWN RATS	1977	MERCURY	US	SRM 1188
(A) THE BOOMTOWN RATS	1977	MERCURY 6310950		9102 800
(B) TONIC FOR THE TROOPS	1978	ENSIGN ENVY3	CBS	US 35750
(B) TONIC FOR THE TROOPS	1978	MERCURY	GER	6310 954
(C) FINE ART OF SURFACING	1979	ENSIGN UK ROX 11		
(C) FINE ART OF SURFACING	1979	MERCURY	GER	6310 960
(D) MONDO BONGO	1980	MERCURY	UK	6359 042
(D) MONDO BONGO	1980	MERCURY	GER	6359 042

B181A   BOONES FARM   **B181A**

KENT SPRAGUE	V PERC(A
GARY STOVALL	G V (A
BRAD PALMER	V B G (A

(A) BOONES FARM   1972   COLUMBIA   US   31408

FRED DARLING   D   (A   MILT HOLLAND   PERC (A

B181B   BOOT   **B181B**

MIKE MYCZ	G V (AB
JIM O'BRECK	D (AB
BRUCE KNOX	G V (AB
DAN ELIASSEN	V B (AB

(A) BOOT	1972	AGAPE	US 2601
(B) TURN THE OTHER CHEEK	1977	GUINNESS	US 36002

B182   KEN BOOTHE   **B182**

KEN BOOTHE   V   (ALL

(A) BLACK GOLD & GREEN	19	TROJAN	UK TRLS 58
(B) LETS GET IT ON	1974	TROJAN	UK TRLS 83
(C) EVERYTHING I OWN	1974	TROJAN	UK TRLS 95
(D) FREEDOM STREET	1975	TROJAN	UK TRLS 120
(E) LIVE GOOD	1978	U A	LA 801
(F) 20 GREATEST REGGAE HITS	1979	CHARMERS	
(G) BLOOD BROTHERS	1978	TROJAN	UK TRLS 148
(H) WHO GETS YOUR LOVE	1979	TROJAN	UK TRLS 164

B182A   BOOTS   **B182A**

WERNER KRABBE	V HCA (A
WILI GRUN	ORG (A
BOB BRESSER	B (A

(A) HERE ARE THE BOOTS   1966   TELEFUNKEN   GERM SLE 14399

HEINZ HOFF   D   (A   JOERG SCHULTE   G   (A

B183   BOOTSY'S RUBBER BAND   **B183**

WILLIAM BOOTSY COLLINS	GVB(ABC
WITH	
PHELPS COLLINS	B G (ABC
GARY SHIDER	G (AB
MIKE HAMPTON	G (AB
FRANKIE KASH WADDY	D (ABC
BOOGIE	D (AB
GARY COOPER	D V (ABC
CASPER	B D G (ABC
RANDY BRECKER	SAX (AB
BERNIE WORRELL	K (AB
LESLYN BAILEY	V (A
RICHARD GRIFFITHS	HRNS (BC

(A) STRETCHIN OUT	1976	WB	UK K56200
(A) STRETCHIN OUT	1976	WB	UK B2920
(B) AAH...THE NAME IS BOOTSY BABY	1977	WB	UK K 56302
(B) AAH...THE NAME IS BOOTSY BABY	1977	WB	US 2972
(C) PLAYER OF THE YEAR	1978	WB	UK K56424
(C) PLAYER OF THE YEAR	1978	WB	US K 3093
(D) THIS BOOT IS MADE FOR FONK'N	1979	WB	UK K 56615

FRED WESLEY	TROM	(ABC	MACEO PARKER	SAX	(ABC
RICK GARDNER	TPT	(ABC	MICHAEL BRECKER	TPT	(A
SONNY TALBERT	K	(A	FREDRICK ALLEN	K	(A
ROBERT JOHNSON	V	(ABC	JOEL JOHNSON	K	(BC
GLEN GOINS	G	(B	JEROME BRAILEY	D	(B

B183A   BOPCATS   **B183A**

(A) ROCK'N'ROLL GRAFFITI   1980   MAGNUM FORCE   MFLP 001

B183B   BORDERLINE   **B183B**

JIM ROONEY	G V (A
DAVID GARSHEN	G V (A
JOHN GARSHEN	G V (A
BILL MUNDI	D (A
CAMPO MALAGVA	K (A
KEN COSSECK	FDL (A

(A) SWEET DREAMS AND QUIET DESIRES   1972   AVALANCHE   US   LA016

BEN KEITH	STEEL	(A	JIM COLGROVE	B	(A
JOHN SIMON	K	(A	DICK HARDLE	K	(A
DAVID SANBORN	SAX	(A	VASSAR CLEMENTS	FDL	(A

B183C   KEVIN BORICH EXPRESS   **B183C**

KEVIN BORICH	G V (A
TIM PARTRIDGE	B (A
JOHN ANNAS	D (A

(A) LIVE   1979   AVENUE   US   L37139

JOHN WATSON   D   (A

B183D   BOSS BROTHERS   **B183D**

JON ASH	K SYN V(A
STEVE WHALLEY	G V (A
MIKE SMITH	D (A
LENNI	SAX (A
IAN WILSON	G V K(A

(A) STALLING FOR TIME   1980   MERCURY   UK   9109 632

JON LEVENSON	G B	(A	MELANIE HARROLD	V	(A
RITCHIE BRUNTON	G	(A	DAVID PETERS	HCA	(A

BOSTON

BARRY GOULDREAU	G PERC	(AB
TOM SCHOLZ	G K	(AB
SIB HASHAIN	D	(AB
BRADLEY DELP	V G	(AB
FRAN SHEEHAN	B PERC	(AB
JIM MASDEA	D	(A

B184

Album	Year	Label			
(A) BOSTON	1976	EPIC UK EPCB1622	RI	32038	
(A) BOSTON	1976	EPIC	US	BL	34188
(B) DONT LOOK BACK	1978	EPIC UK EPC86057	RI	32048	
(B) DONT LOOK BACK	1978	EPIC	US	FE	35050

BOSTON TEA PARTY

B184A

RICHARD DE PERNA	B	(A
ROBERT DE PERNA	K	(A
TRAVIS FIELDS	V	(A
DAVE NOVOGROSKI	D	(A
MIKE STEVENS	G	(A

Album	Year	Label		
(A) THE BOSTON TEA PARTY	19	FLICKDISC	US	45000

SIMON BOSWELL

B184B

SIMON BOSWELL (A

Album	Year	Label		
(A) THE MIND PARASITES	1975	TRANSATLANTIC	UK	TRA 307

BOTHY BAND

B185

TRIONA O'DONNELL	K V	(ABCD
PADDY KEENAN	PIPES	(ABCD
TOMMY PEOPLES	FDL	(C
MATT MOLLOY	WIND	(ABCD
DONAL LUNNY	G K	(ABCD
MICHAEL O'DONNELL	G	(ABCD
KEVIN BURKE	FDL	(D
PADDY GLACKIN	FDL	(AB
TONY McMAHON		(A

Album	Year	Label		
(A) BOTHY BAND	1976	POLYDOR	UK	2383 379
(A) BOTHY BAND	1976	MULLIGAN	IR	LUN 002
(B) OLD HAG YOU HAVE KILLED ME	1976	MULLIGAN	IR	LUN 007
(B) OLD HAG YOU HAVE KILLED ME	1976	POLYDOR	UK	2383 417
(C) OUT OF THE WIND	1977	POLYDOR	UK	2383 456
(C) OUT OF THE WIND	1977	MULLIGAN	IR	LUN
(D) AFTER HOURS	1979	POLYDOR	UK	2383 530
(D) AFTER HOURS	1979	MULLIGAN	IR	LUN 030

BOULDER

B185A

Album	Year	Label
(A) BOULDER	1979	ARISTA

CHRISTIAN BOULE

B185B

CHRISTIAN BOULE

Album	Year	Label	
( ) PHOTO MUSIC	19	POLYDOR	2473 086

DAVID BOWIE

B186

DAVID BOWIE V G SAX K (ALL

WITH

CARLOS ALOMAR	G	(1LMOPRST
DENNIS DAVIES	PERC	(1LMOPRST
GEORGE MURRAY	B	(1MOPRST
BRIAN ENO	K	(OPS
ROBERT FRIPP	G	(PT
SIMON HOUSE	VLN	(1RS
ROGER POWELL	K	(1RS
MICK RONSON	G	(CDEFG
STACEY HAYDEN	G	(
MICK WAYNE	G	(B
TIM RENWICK	G	(B
TONY VISCONTI	B WIND	(BCPT
HERBIE FLOWERS	B	(BJK
JOHN CAMBRIDGE	D	(B
PAUL BUCKMASTER	CELLO	(B
BENNY MARSHALL	HCA	(B
DIANE SUMLER	V	(L
LUTHER VANDROSS	V	(L
ROY YOUNG	PNO	(O
RICKY GARDINER	G	(O
ANDY NEWMARK	D	(L
JOHN LENNON	V G	(L
DAVID SANBORN	SAX	(LK
LARRY WASHINGTON	PERC	(L
TONY NEWMAN	D	(JK
KEN FORDHAM	WIND	(FG
JUANITA FRANKLIN	V	(F
AVA CHERRY	V	(L
ALAN PARKER	G	(J
MIKE GARSON	G	(JK
ADRIAN BELEW	G	(1 RS
ROBIN CLARK	V	(L
SEAN MAYES	K	(RS
KEITH CHRISTMAS	G	(B
TERRY COX	D	(B
RICK WAKEMAN	K	(BDE
ANTONIA MAASS	V	(P
MARY VISCONTI	V	(O
IGGY POP	V	(O
MIKE KAMEN	K	(K
RICHARD GRANDO	WIND	(K
WILLY WEEKS	B	(L
TREVOR BOLDER	B	(DEFG
LINDA LEWIS	V	(F
ROY BITTAN	K	(MT
MICJ WOODMANSEY	D	(CDEF
MICHAEL GARSON	K	(FGL
PETE TOWNSHEND	V	(T
LYNN MAITLAND	V	(T
GUI ANDRESINO	V	(K
EARL SLICK	G	(KLM
MAC CORMACK	V	(FG
JOHN MAYER	K	(1
JEAN FINEBERG	V	(L
ANTHONY HINTON	V	(L
RALPH MACE	K	(C
MICHI HIROTA	V	(T
CHRIS PORTER	V	(T
WARREN PEACE	V	(KLM
EMIR KSASAN	B	(L
RALPH McDONALD	PERC	(L
PABLO ROSARIO	PERC	(LK
CHUCK HAMMER	G	(T
JEAN MILLINGTON	V	(L
AYNSLEY DUNBAR	D	(GJ
ANDY CLARK	SYN	(T

Album	Year	Label			
(A) DAVID BOWIE(LOVE YOU TILL TUES)	1967	DERAM		SML	1007
(A) DAVID BOWIE(TWO TRACK LESS)	1967	DERAM			18003
(A) THE WORLD OF DAVID BOWIE	1970	DECCA		SPA	58
(B) MAN OF WORDS/ SPACE ODDITY	1969	PHILIPS	UK	SBL	7912
(B) MAN OF WORDS /SPACE ODDITY	1969	MERCURY	US	ST	61246
(B) MAN OF WORDS /SPACE ODDITY	1969	RCA		LPS	4813
(C) MAN WHO SOLD THE WORLD	1970	RCA		LPS	4816
(C) MAN WHO SOLD THE WORLD	1970	PHILIPS		461	006
(C) MAN WHO SOLD THE WORLD	1971	MERCURY US 61325 UK 6338			041
(D) HUNKY DORY	1971	RCA US AFLI4623 UK		SF	8244
(D) HUNKY DORY	197	RCA		443	041
(E) RISE & FALL OF ZIGGY STARDUST	1972	RCA US AFLI4702 UK		SF	8287
(E) RISE & FALL OF ZIGGY STARDUST	1972	RCA		443	051
(F) ALADDIN SANE	1973	RCA		RS	1001
(F) ALADDIN SANE	1973	RCA CPRS4543		AFLI	4852
(F) ALADDIN SANE	1973	RCA		461	004
(G) PIN UPS	1973	RCA AFLI0291		RS	1003
(H) IMAGES 66 67	1973	LONDON US 628/9 UK		DPA3017/8	
(J) DIAMOND DOGS	1974	RCA		APLI	0576
(K) LIVE	1974	RCA		APL2	0771
(L) YOUNG AMERICANS	1975	RCA US AFLI0998 UK		RS	1006
(M) STATION TO STATION	1976	RCA		APLI	1327
(N) CHANGESONEBOWIE	1976	RCA AFLI1732		RS	1055
(O) LOW	1977	RCA		PL	12030
(P) HEROES	1977	RCA		PB	1121
(P) HEROES	1977	RCA		AFLI	2522
(P) HEROES	1977	RCA		PL	42373
( ) STARTING POINT	1977	LONDON		LC	50007
(Q) PETER & THE WOLF	1978	RCA		RL	12743
(R) STAGE	1978	RCA		\PL	02913
(S) LODGER	1979	RCA AZLI 3254		BOW	LP1
( ) GOLDEN DOUBLE	1979	RCA	JAP	SRA9503/4	
( ) BEST OF	1980	K TEL		NE	1111
( )PROFILE	19	TELDEC	GERM	624009	
(T) SCARY MONSTERS	1980	RCA		BOW	K2
(T) SCARY MONSTERS	1980	RCA		PL	13647
( ) BEGINNINGS VOL 1	19	DERAM			
( ) BEGINNINGS VOL 2	19	DERAM			621680
(U) CHANGESTWOBOWIE	1981	RCA		AFLI4204	
(V) ANOTHER FACE	1981	DECCA		TAP	17
(1) 1978 TOUR BAND					

BOWLES BROTHERS BAND

B187

BRIAN BOWLES	G V	(A
RICHARD LEE	B	(A
JULIAN SMEDLEY	G V VLN	(A
CHARLES SEAWARD	FLT	(A
CHRIS KARAN	PERC	(A
SUE JONES DAVIS	V	(A
JONATHAN WADE	K	(A
ROGER RETTIG	STEEL	(A
RICHARD MARCANGELO	D	(A
COLIN FRECHTER	PNO	(A

Album	Year	Label		
(A) ROGER BUYS A FRIDGE	1978	DECCA	TXS	127

JIMMY BOWEN

B187A

JIMMY BOWEN	B V	(A
BUDDY KNOX	G	(A
DAVE ALLDRED		(A
DON LANIER		(A

Album	Year	Label		
(A) JIMMY BOWEN	19	ROULETTE	US	25004

ALAN BOWN SET

ALAN BOWN	TPT	(ALL	(A) LONDON SWINGS	(½ LP)	1966	PYE		NPL	18121
WITH			(B) OUTWARD BOWN		1967	VERVE US 3062	MGM US	CUBLM	1
JOHN GOODSALL	G	(	(B) OUTWARD BOWN		1967	MUSIC FACTORY	UK	M F	12000
JESS RODEN	V	(CD	(C) THE ALAN BOWN		1968	DECCA		SML	1049
ROBERT PALMER	V	(	(D) SECOND ALBUM		1968	DERAM			
DAVE GREEN	SAX	(	(D) SECOND ALBUM		1968	MGM	US		
STAN HALDANE	B V	(BCE	(E) LISTEN		1970	ISLAND 6339022 GER UK ILPS9131			
PETE BURGESS	G V	(	(F) STRETCHIN' OUT		1971	ISLAND		ILPS	9163
VIC SWEENEY	D	(BCEF							
DAVE LAWSON	K	(	TERRY STANNARD	D	(	JOHN ANTHONY HELLIWELL SAX (BCEF			
GORDON NEVILLE	V	(EF	ANDY BROWN	B V	(F	JEFF BANNISTER	K V	(BCEF	
TONY CATCHPOLE	G	(CEF	JOHN HEMMINGS	TROM	(C	MEL COLLINS		PERC (E	

ANDY BOWN

ANDY BOWN	G V	(ALL	(A) GONE TO MY HEAD		1972	MERCURY	UK	6310	002
WITH			(A) GONE TO MY HEAD		1972	MERCURY	IMP	SRM	1625
HAROLD FISHER	PERC	(D	(B) ANDY BOWN SWEET WILLIAM		1973	G M		GML	1001
FRANK RICOTTI	D	(D	(C) COME BACK ROMANCE		1976	EMI		EMC	3176
MO FOSTER	B	(D	(D) GOOD ADVICE		1978	EMI		EMC	3283
DAVE MARKEE	B	(D	(E) DROWNED IN TEXAS		19	SONOPRESSE	FR	06806605	
GEOFF WESTLEY	G	(D							
PHIL PALMER	G	(D	CHRIS NEILL	V	(D	DOMINIC BUGATTI	V	(D	
FRANK MUSKER	V	(D	SHARAN CAMPBELL	V	(D	NICO RAMSDEN	G	(B	
BARRY DE SOUZA	D	(B	CHRIS BELSHAW	B	(BA	B J COLE	STEEL (B		
GLEN LEFLEUR	PERC	(B	JIMMY HOROWITZ	CELESTE(BA		SKAILA KANGA	HARP (B		
CAROLINE ATTARD	V	(AB	LESLEY DUNCAN	V	(AB	SUE GLOVER	V	(B	
SUNNY LESLIE	V	(B	STRINGS		(B	MARTIN JENNER	G	(C	
CHRIS RAE	G	(C	TERRY SMITH	G	(C	TERRY STANNARD	D	(C	
MICKY WALLER	D	(A	LIZA STRIKE	V	(A	PETER FRAMPTON	V	(A	
JOHN MEALING	K SYN (C		PETE ZORN	SAX	(C	CHAS CRONK	B	(C	
PADDY McHUGH	V	(C	FRANK COLLINS	V	(C	DIANE BIRCH	V	(C	
TOM ALLOM	V	(C	RAY JACKSON	HCA	(C	GLEN LEFLEUR	D	(C	

BOX TOPS

ALEX CHILTON	G V	(ALL	(A) THE LETTER NEON RAINBOW	1968	STATESIDE	UK	SSL 10218	
GARY TALLEY	G	(123	(A) THE LETTER NEON RAINBOW	1968	BELL	US	6011	
HAROLD CLOUD	B	(3	(B) CRY LIKE A BABY	1968	STATESIDE	UK	105	
BILL CUNNINGHAM	K B	(12	(B) CRY LIKE A BABY	1968	BELL	US	6017	
JOHN EVANS	G K	(1	(C) NON STOP	1968	BELL	US	6023	
RICK ALLEN	B K	(2	( ) SUPERHITS	196	BELL	US	6025	
SWAIN SCHARFER	K	(3	(E) DIMENSIONS	1968	BELL	US	6032	
DANNY SMYTHE	D	(1	( ) THE BEST OF THE BOX TOPS	1974	SOUNDS SUPERB	UK	SPR 90051	
TOM BOGGS	D	(23						

BOXER

MIKE PATTO	V K	(ABC	(A) BELOW THE BELT	1975	VIRGIN 27030 GER UK		V2049	
OLLIE HALSALL	G K	(AB	(A) BELOW THE BELT	1975	VIRGIN	US	PZ 34115	
KEITH ELLIS	B	(BA	(B) BLOODLETTING(NOT RELEASED UNTIL 1979	1976	VIRGIN	UK	V2073	
TONY NEWMAN	D	(AB	(C) ABSOLUTELY	1977	EPIC	UK	EPC 82151	
CHRIS STAINTON	K	(CB	(C) ABSOLUTELY	1977	EPIC	US	PE 34812	
TIM BOGERT	B V	(C						
ADRIAN FISHER	G	(C	EDDIE TUDURI	D	(C	BOZ BURRELL	V	(B
BOBBY TENCH	V	(B	TIN HINKLEY	K	(B	JEFF GLIXMAN	PROD (C	

EDDIE BOYD

EDDIE BOYD	V PNO	(ALL	(A) FIVE LONG YEARS	19	FONTANA		STJL 905	
WITH			(B) & HIS BLUES BAND	1967	DECCA UK		SKL 4872	
PETER GREEN	G	(C	(C) 7936 SOUTH RHODES	1968	BLUE HORIZON	UK	7 63202	
JOHN McVIE	B	(C	(C) 7936 SOUTH RHODES	1968	EPIC	US	26409	
MICK FLEETWOOD	D	(C	(D) LIVE	1968	STORYVILLE		SLP 268	
STOCKHOLM SLIM	V	(E	(E) LEGACY OF THE BLUES VOL 10	1974	SONET	UK	SNTF 670	
ED THIGPEN	D	(E	(E) LEGACY OF THE BLUES VOL 10	1974	GNP	US	10020	
ROLF ALM	B	(E	(F) VACATION FROM THE BLUES	1976	JEFFERSON	SWED	601	
LESTER JONES	B	'F	(G) DUST MY BROOM	19	LONDON	US	554	
CHRISTER ECKLUND	SAX	(E						
PEPS PERSSON	G HCA	V(E	SAM LANGHORN	G	(F	RICO COLLINS	SAX	(F	WILLIE COBBS	B HCA(F
BONES	D	(F	EDDIE KING MILTON G	(F	CHINK EVANS	D	(F	DAYLIGHTERS	V	(F
ERNEST COTTON	SAX	(F	PERCY WALKER	D	(F	JIMMY CONLEY	SAX	(F	FRED BELOW	D	(F
ROBERT JR LOCKWOOD G	(F	RONALD WILSON	SAX	(F	BOB CARTER	B	(F	SONNY ALLEN	D	(F
WILLIE JONES	B	(F	CHRISTINE KITRELL V	(F	L C McKINLEY	G	(F	ALFRED ELKINS	B	(F
LOUIS MYERS	G	(F						

TERENCE BOYLAN

TERENCE BOYLAN	G V	(ALL	(A) ALIAS BOONA	1969	VERVE FORECAST	US	FTS 3070	
WITH			(B) TERENCE BOYLAN	1977	ELEKTRA	US	7E 1091	
WALTER BECKER	G B	(A	(C) SUZY	1980	ELEKTRA	US	6E 201	
DONALD FAGAN	K V	(AB						
HERB LOVELLE	D	(A	JIMMY JOHNSON	D	(A	DARIUS DAVENPORT	D	(A	JIM GORDON D	(BC
RUSS KUNKEL	D	(BC	JEFF PORCARO	D	(B	CHUCK RAINEY	B	(B	DAVID JACKSON	B	(B
LEE SKLAR	B	(BC	DEAN PARKS	G	(B	VICTOR FELDMAN	PERC (BC		JAI WINDING	K	(BC
TIM SCHMIT	V	(BC	JOHN KLEMMER	SAX	(B	GARY FOSTER	SAX	(BC	WILTON FELDER	B	(B
DON HENLEY	V	(BC	BEN BENAY	G	(BC	MICKEY McGEE	D	(B	AL KOOPER	ORG	(B
DON EVANS	G	(B	DAVID PAICH	K	(B	BOB GLAUB	B	(B	STEVE LUKATHER	G	(B
DODIE PETIT	V	(B	JOHN GUERIN	D	(B	MAX BENNETT	B	(B	TOM KELLY	V	(B
DENNIS WHITTED	D	(C	WILL McFARLANE	G B	(C	JOHN HOLBROOK	B	(C	ED GREENE	D	(C
MICHAEL PORCARO	B	(C	MICHAEL OMARTIAN	PERC (C		JEFF BAXTER	G	(C	LARRY CARLTON	G	(C
PAUL HARRIS	PERC	(C	JAY GRAYDON	G	(C	DON FELDER	G	(C	DAVID KEMPER	D	(C
CHEVY CHASE	PERC	(C	EMIL RICHARDS	PERC (C		MIRANDA McGRATH	V	(C	ALMA BOYLAN	V	(C

TOMMY BOYCE & BOBBY HART

TOMMY BOYCE	G V	(A	(A) TEST PATTERNS	19	A&M	US	SP 7126	
BOBBY HART	K V	(A						
LOUIE SHELTON	G	(A	WAYNE IRVIN	G	(A	LARRY TAYLOR	B	(A
GERRY McGEE	G	(A	BILLY LEWIS	D	(A			

GARY BOYLE

GARY BOYLE	G	(AB	(A) THE DANCER	1977	GULL 163305 GER UK	GULP 1020
WITH			(B) ELECTRIC GLIDE	1978	GULL 148309 GER UK	GULP 1028
ROBIN LUMLEY	K	(A	(C) STEP OUT	1980	INTERCORD	GER	145 623
ROD ARGENT	K	(A	(C) STEP OUT	1981	PICK UP	UK	80305
DONI HARVEY	B	(A				
SIMON PHILLIPS	D	(AB	ZOE KRONBERGER	K	(A	DAVE McCRAE	K	(A
STEVE SHONE	B	(A	JEFF SEOPARDI	D	(A	MAGGIE PERT	V	(A
MORRIS PERT	PERC	(A	ROBERT AHWAI	G	(B	PETE JACOBSON	K	(B
JOHN GIBLIN	B	(B	SIMON MORTON	PERC	(B	PHIL CHEN	B	(B
RICHARD BAILEY	D	(B	KENNY SHAW	G	(B	GARY MOORE	G	(B
PAUL BIRCHALL	K	(C	GARY CULSHAW	B	(C	GRAHAM DEAN	D	(C
JANNE SCHAFFER	G	(C	STEFAN NILSSON	SYN	(C	BJORN JASON LINDH	FLT	(C
JACOB ANDERSON	PERC	(C				

THE BOYS

MATT DANGERFIELD	V G	(ABCD	(A) THE BOYS	1977	NEMS	UK	NELS 6001
CASINO STEEL	PNO	(ABC	(B) ALTERNATIVE CHARTBUSTERS	1978	NEMS	UK	NELS 6015
KID REID	V B	(ABCD	(C) TO HELL WITH THE BOYS	1978	SAFARI 8002 NL UK	1 2 BOYS
JACK BLACK	D	(ABCD	(D) BOYS ONLY	1980	SAFARI 8004 NL UK	BOYS 4
JOHN PLAIN	G	(ABCD				

BOYS NEXT DOOR

NICK CAVE	V K SAX	(AB	(A) BOYS NEXT DOOR(EP)	19	MISSING LINK AUST	LEP 3
TRACY PEW	B CLAR	(AB	(B) DOOR DOOR	1979	MUSHROOM AUST	36931
PHIL CALVERT	D	(AB				
ROWLAND HOWARD	G SAX	(AB	MICK HARVEY G K SYN B		(AB

BOYZZ

MIKE TAFOYA	G	(A	(A) TOO WILD TO TAME	1978	EPIC	UK	EPC 82995
DIRTY DAN BUCK	V PERC	(A				
GIL PINI	G V	(A	ANATOLE HALINKOVICH	K	(A	KENT COOPER	PERC V	(A
DAVID ANGEL	B	(A	LOU DELGATTO	SAX	(A	LOU MARINI	SAX	(A
SAM BURTIS	TROM	(A	ALAN RUBIN	TPT	(A			

BRAINBOX

JAN AKKERMAN	G K	(A	(A) BRAINBOX	1971	CAPITOL	IMP ST 596
HERMAN MEYER	G	(B	(A) BRAINBOX	1970	PARLOPHONE	UK	PCS 7094
ANDRE REYNEN	B	(A	(A) BRAINBOX	1970	IMPERIAL	NL	054 24082
PIERRE VAN DER LINDEN		(A	(B) BEST OF	1972		
CASIMIERZ LUX	V PERC	(AB	(C) PARTS	19	HARVEST	056 24551
TOM BARIACHER	FLT	(A				
FRANS SMIT	PERC	(BC	JOHN SCHUURSMA	(B	RUDI DE QUELJOE	(B
ROBERT VERWEY	B K	(C	RON MEYJES	G HCA	(C	MICHAEL VON DIJK	V FLT	(C

BRAINS

TOM GRAY	K V	(A	(A) BRAINS	1980	MERCURY UK 6337103 US 1 3835
RICK PRICE	G V	(A	(B) ELECTRONIC EDEN	1981	MERCURY
BRYAN SMITHWICK	B	(A			
CHARLES WOLFF	D V	(A			

BRAHMAN

VICTOR STEWART	V	(A	(A) BRAHMAN	1971	MERCURY	US	61348
ROBBIE KING	K	(A				
EDDIE PATTERSON	G	(A	DURIS MAXWELL	V D	(A	D LANZ	(A

SCOTT BRADFORD

SCOTT BRADFORD	K	(A	(A) ROCK SLIDE	1969	PROBE	US	4509
NATHAN DAVIS	WIND	(A				
STU MARTIN	PERC	(A	GUNTHER LENZ	B	(A	PHILIP CATHERINE	G	(A
JANET MORALES	TPT	(A	NICK KLETCHKOVSKY	B	(A	VINAGRE	PERC	(A

BRIAN BRAIN

MARTIN'BRIAN BRAIN'ATKINS	V	(A	(A) UNEXPECTED NOISES	1980	SECRET	UK	BRAIN 1
PETE JONES	B V	(A				
GEOFF SMYTH	G V	(A	JOHN MADDEN	V	(A	BOBBY SURGEONOR	G SYN V B	(A
BILLY	K SAX	(A	JOHN CATHERALL	B	(A	GARY SMALLMAN	D	(A

BRAINCHILD

BILL EDWARDS	B V	(A	(A) HEALING OF THE LUNITIC OWL	1970	A&M	NL	979
BRIAN WILSHAW	WIND	(A				
HARVEY COLES	B V	(A	DAVE MULLER	D	(A	CHRIS JENNINGS	K	(A
LLOYD WILLIAMS	TPT	(A	IAN GOSS	TROM	(A	PAT STRACHAM	TROM	(A

BRAINSTORM

			(A) STORMIN'	1977	RCA	UK	PL 12048
			(A) STORMIN'	197	CBS	US	35327
			(b) JOURNEY TO THE NIGHT	1978	TABU	
			(b) JOURNEY TO THE NIGHT	19	CBS	US	JZ 2048
			(C) FUNKY ENTERTAINMENT	1979	TABU	UK	TBU 83736

BRAINSTORM

EDDY VON OVERHEIDT	K V	(AB	(A) SMILE A WHILE	1972	SPIEGELEI	GERM	28505
ROLAND SCHAEFFER	G K	(AB	(B) SECOND SMILE	1974	SPIEGELEI	GERM	28596
JOACHIM KEINZER	D	(AB				
RAINER BODENSOHN	B FLT V	(AB	ENNO DERNOV	G B	(B

BRAINTICKET

JOEL VANDROOGENBROECK	FLT K V	(ABC	(A) PSYCHONAUT	19	BELLAPHON	BLPS19104
ROLF HUG	V G PERC	(A	(B) COTTON WOOD HILL	1971	BELLAPHON	GERM	19019
MARTIN SACHER	B FLT	(A	(C) CELESTRIAL SEA	1974	RCA	SF 8398
BARNEY PALM	D PERC	(A				
JANE FREE	V PERC	(A	CAROLE MURIEL	V	(A	PETER GOOD	VIBES	(A
COSMO LAMPIS	D	(B	WOLFGANG PAAP	PERC	(B	DAWN MUIR	V	(B
HELLMUTH KELBE	K	(B	RON BAER	G	(B	WERNI PRAHLACH	B	(B

BRAKES

JOE FADIL	G V	(A	(A) FOR WHY YOU KICKA MY DONKEY	1979	MAGNET 624179 GER UK MAGL5029
KEITH WILSON	G V	(A			
JOHN BROWN	D	(A	BOB PENNY	B	(A

```
      RANDALL BRAMBLETT K V G SAX(AB   (A) THAT OTHER MILE            1975  POLYDOR    US    6045
      CHUCK LEAVELL     K      (A      (B) LIGHT OF THE NIGHT         1976  POLYDOR    US    6064
      SCOTT BOYER       G      (A
      WILL LEE          B V    (A      TOMMY TALTON      G    (A      ERIC WEISSBERG  STEEL     (A
      HUGH McCRACKEN    G      (A      ANDY MUSEN        B    (A      DAVID BROWN     B        (A
      CHRIS PARKER      D      (A      PAUL HORNSBY      K    (A      ELLIOTT RANDALL G        (A
      BOB MANN          G      (A      RICK MAROTTA      D    (A      AL GORGONI      G        (A
```

B200   BONNIE BRAMLETT   B200

```
      BONNIE BRAMLETT   V    (ALL     (A) SWEET BONNIE BRAMLETT       1973  CBS        UK    65001
      WITH                            (B) ITS TIME                    1975  CAPRICORN  UK  2429 125
      BARRY BECKETT     K    (C       (B) ITS TIME                    1975  CAPRICORN  US    0148
      DAVID HOOD        B    (C       (C) LADY'S CHOICE               1976  CAPRICORN  UK  2429 145
      JOHNNY SANDLIN    G    (C       (C) LADY'S CHOICE               1976  CAPRICORN  US    0169
      ROGER HAWKINS     D    (C       (D) MEMORIES                    1978  CAPRICORN  UK  2429 162
      TOMMY TALTON      G    (CB      (D) MEMORIES                    1978  CAPRICORN  US    0199
      HARVEY THOMPSON   HRNS (C
      RICHARD BETTS     G    (C       RANDALL BRAMBLETT  SAX  (CB     ANITA BALL               (C
      CHARLES ROSE      HRNS (C       RON EADES          HRNS (C      HARRISON CALLOWAY HRNS (C
      RICKY HIRSCH      G    (CB      PAUL HORNSBY       K    (CB     CHUCK LEAVELL     PNO  (CB
      GREGG ALLMAN      ORG  (CB      DIANNE DAVIDSON    V    (C      JOE ENGLISH       D    (D
      KENNY TIBBETTS    B PERC(B      JERRY THOMPSON     D    (B      SCOTT BOYER       G    (BD
      JAIMOE            CONGAS(B      EARL FORD          TROM (B      LAGATHA BECK-SMALLWOOD V (B
      SHIRLEY MATTHEWS  V    (B       DAVID BROWN        SAX  (B      ROBERT MARTIN     K SAX(D
      BIG BILL STEWART  D    (B       BUTCH TRUCKS       CONGAS(B     EDDIE HINTON      G    (BD
      JOHNNY SANDLIN    G PERC(B      TOM RIDGEWAY       SYN  (B      LEO LABRANCHE     TPT  (B
      CLYDIE KING       V    (B       HAROLD WILLIAMS    SAX  (B      JIMMY NAILS       G    (D
      JAY ARMENTROUT    D    (D
```

B201   DELANEY BRAMLETT   B201

```
      DELANEY BRAMLETT  G V  (ALL     (A) MOBIUS STRIP                19    CBS        US  KC 32420
      WITH                            (B) SOMETHINGS COMING           1972  CBS        UK    65131
      SPIDER TAYLOR     G    (D       (C) GIVING BIRTH TO A SONG      19    MGM        US  M3G 5011
      RANDY SHARP       G    (D       (D) CLASS REUNION               1977  PRODIGAL   US  P7 10017
      CHUCK RAINEY      B    (D       (D) CLASS REUNION               1977  PRODIGAL   US  PDL 2005
      CHRIS ETHRIDGE    B    (D
      RICK SUTHERLAND   K    (CD      JIM HOBSON         K    (CD     STU PERRY         D    (CD
      JIM KELTNER       D    (D       CHUCK FINDLEY      HRNS (D      OLLIE MITCHELL    HRNS (D
      JACKIE KELSO      HRNS (D       DICK HYDE          HRNS (D      QUITMAN DENNIS    HRNS (D
      CLYDIE KING       V    (BD      SHIRLEY MATTHEWS   V    (BD     MONALISA YOUNG    V    (D
      SUSIE ALLANSON    V    (D       PAT ERICKSON       V    (D      PATTI QUATRO      V    (D
      STRINGS                (D       JIM McGREW         G    (C      VICTOR PANTOJA    PERC (C
      NICK VAN MAARTH   G    (C       FRED RIVERA        B    (C      COLE KESLER       HCA  (C
      RON GRAYSON       D PERC(B      MILT HOLLAND       PERC (B      TIM HEDING        K    (B
      ROBERT WILSON     B    (B       DARRELL LEONARD    HRNS (B      LARRY SAVORE      HRNS (B
      JOE DAVIS         SAX  (B       JIM GORDON         SAX  (B      JERRY JUMONVILLE  SAX  (B
      GLORIA JONES      V    (B       BILLY PRESTON      K    (B      JERRY McGEE       G    (B
      BEN BENAY         G    (B       VANETTA FIELDS     V    (B
```

B202   DELANEY & BONNIE BRAMLETT   B202

```
      DELANEY BRAMLETT  G V  (ALL     (A) HOME(67)                    1969  STAX       US      2026
      BONNIE BRAMLETT   V    (ALL     (A) HOME                        1974  STAX       UK  2362 001
      WITH                            (B) ACCEPT NO SUBSTITUTE        1969  ELEKTRA    US  EKS 74039
      BOOKER T JONES    K    (A       (B) ACCEPT NO SUBSTITUTE        1969  APPLE      UK  SAPCOR 7
      DONALD DUNN       B    (A       (B) ACCEPT NO SUBSTITUTE        1971  ELEKTRA    UK  K 42024
      STEVE CROPPER     G    (A       (C) ON TOUR                     1970  ATLANTIC   UK  2400 013
      AL JACKSON        D    (A       (C) ON TOUR                     1970  ATCO       US     33326
      BEN BENAY         G    (DE      (C) ON TOUR                     1971  ATLANTIC   UK  K 30030
      DUANE ALLMAN      G    (D       (D) TO BONNIE FROM DELANEY      1970  ATLANTIC   US  2400 029
      JERRY JUMONVILLE  SAX  (D       (D) TO BONNIE FROM DELANEY      1970  ATCO       US     33341
      FRANK MAYES       SAX  (D       (D) TO BONNIE FROM DELANEY      1971  ATLANTIC   UK  K
      DARRYL LEONARD    HRNS (D       (E) MOTEL SHOT                  1971  ATCO       US     33358
      JIM GORDON        K    (D       (F) COUNTRY LIFE                197   ATCO       US     33383
      KENNY GRADNEY     B    (DE      (G) GENESIS                     1971  LONDON     UK  ZGL   113
      CHUCK MORGAN      D    (D       (G) GENESIS                     1971  CRECSENDO  US      2054
      KING CURTIS       SAX  (D       (H) TOGETHER                    1972  CBS        UK     64959
      CHARLIE FREEMAN   G    (D       (H) TOGETHER                    1972  CBS        US  KC 31377
      BOBBY WHITLOCK    K V  (ABCD    (I) BEST OF                     1973  ATLANTIC   UK  K 40429
      TOM McCLURE       B    (D
      JERRY SCHEFF      B    (D       RITA COOLIDGE      V    (BC     TEX JOHNSON       CONGA (C
      RON TUTT          D    (D       SAMMY CREASON      D    (D      ANDREW LOVE       SAX   (D
      ED LOGAN          SAX  (D       FLOYD NEWMAN       SAX  (D      WAYNE JACKSON     TPT   (D
      JACK HALE         TROM (D       SAM CLAYTON        CONGA (D     ALAN ESTES        PERC  (D
      LITTLE RICHARD    PNO  (D       MIKE UTLEY         PNO  (D      JIM DICKINSON     PNO   (D
      SNEAKY PETE KLEINOW STEEL (D    ERIC CLAPTON       G    (C      DAVE MASON        G     (CE
      CARL RADLE        B    (BCE     JIM GORDON         D    (C      JIM PRICE         HRNS  (BC
      BOBBY KEYS        SAX  (BCE     GEORGE HARRISON    G    (       LEON RUSSELL      G K   (BEG
      JERRY McGEE       G    (B       JIM KELTNER        D    (BE     ISAAC HAYES       V     (A
      WILLIAM BELL      V    (A       EDDIE FLOYD        V    (A      GLEN CAMPBELL     G     (G
      BILLY PRESTON     K    (H       EDDY KENDRICKS     V    (H      MERRY CLAYTON     V     (H
      VANETTA FIELDS    V    (H       JOHN HARTFORD      BANJ (E      CLARENCE WHITE    G V   (E
      JOE COCKER        V    (E       BOBBY WOMACK       G    (H      AL CASEY          G     (G
      BILLY STRANGE     G    (G       JAMES BURTON       G    (G      HAL BLAINE        D     (G
```

B203   BRAND X   B203

```
      PERCY JONES       B    (ABCDEFG  (A) UNORTHODOX BEHAVIOUR       1976  CHARISMA  UK CAS 1117 EURO 6369977
      ROBIN LUMLEY      K    (ABCFEG   (B) MOROCCAN ROLL              1977  CHARISMA  UK CAS 1126 EURO 9124010
      JOHN GOODSALL     G    (ABCDFEG  (B) MOROCCAN ROLL              1977  PASSPORT  US               98022
      PRESTON HEYMAN    D    (         (C) LIVE STOCK                 1977  CHARISMA  UK CLASS 5
      PHIL COLLINS      PERC (ABCFEG   (C) LIVE STOCK                 1977  PASSPORT  US                9824
      JOE BLOCKER       PERC (         (D) MASQUES                    1978  CHARISMA  UK CAS 1138 EURO 9124030
      MORRIS PERT       PERC (BDFCE    (D) MASQUES                    1978  PASSPORT  US                9829
```

            (CONTINUED)

BRAND X

			(CONTINUED)			
KENWOOD DENNARD	D	(C	(E) PRODUCT	1979	CHARISMA	UK CAS 1147 EURO 9124045
JACK LANCASTER	WIND	(A	(E) PRODUCT	1979	PASSPORT	US	9840
CHUCK BURGI	D	(D	(F) DO THEY HURT	1980	CHARISMA	UK CAS 1151 EURO 9124059
PETER ROBINSON	K	(FDEG	(G) IS THERE ANYTHING ABOUT	1982	CBS	UK	85967
MIKE CLARKE	D	(FE				
JOHN GIBLIN	B	(EFG	RAPHAEL RAVENSCROFT	SAX	(G	STEVEN SHORT	V D	(G

BRANDYWINE

ALBERT MILLER	K V	(A	(A) AGED	1970	BRUNSWICK	US	754171
EDWARD STASIUM	G V	(A				
CHIP MILES	D PERC	(A	MIKE CARUSE	B	(A	CLIFF DAVIS	WIND	(A
SONNY SEALS	WIND	(A	BILLY HOWELL	TROM	(A	PASQUALE SALERNE	TPT	(A

BRASS CONSTRUCTION

LARRY PAYTON	D	(	(A) BRASS CONSTRUCTION		1976 UA	UK	UAS 29913
SANDY BILLUPS	V PERC	(	(A) BRASS CONSTRUCTION		1976 UA	US	LA 545G
WAYNE PARRIS	TPT	(	(B) 2		1976 UA	UK	UAS 30016
WADE WILLIAMSON	B	(	(B) 2		1976 UA	US	LA 677G
MICHAEL GRUDGE	SAX	(	(C) 3		1978 UA	UK	UAS 30124
RANDY MILLER	V K	(	(C) 3		1978 UA	US	LA 775H
MORRIS PRICE	TPT	(	(D) 4		1978 UA	UK	UAS 30210
JESSE WARD	SAX	(	(D) 4		1978 UA	US	LA 916H
JOSEPH ARTHUR WONG	G	(	(E) 5		1980 LIBERTY		
			(F) 6		1981 LIBERTY		

CHRIS BRAUN BAND

CHRIS BRAUN	V	(AB	(A) BOTH SIDES	1972		
KLAUS MELCHERS	K	(B	(B) FOREIGN LADY	1974	PAN	87586
BERND ADAM KEWITZ	G SAX	(B				
JOCHEN BERNSTEIN	B	(B	ELMAR KROHN	D	(B	JIGGS WHIGHAM	(B
PETER HAST	PERC	(B				

RICHARD BRAUTIGAN

RICHARD BRAUTIGAN			(A) LISTENING TO	19	STRAIGHT	ST	424

BRAVE BELT

RANDY BACHMAN	G V	(AB	(A) BRAVE BELT	19	REPRISE	US	6447
FRED TURNER	B V	(AB	(B) BRAVE BELT II	19	REPRISE	US	2057
ROBIN BACHMAN	D V	(B				
CHAD ALLEN	K V	(A				

BREAD

DAVID GATES G K V VLN	(ALL	(A) BREAD	1969	ELEKTRA	UK	K	42029
LARRY KNECHTEL K G B HCA	(DEFH	(A) BREAD	1969	ELEKTRA	US	EKS 74044
RON EDGAR	D	(A	(A) BREAD	1976	ELEKTRA	FR	22014
JAMES GRIFFIN	K G V	(ABCDEFH	(B) ON THE WATER	1970	ELEKTRA	UK	K	42050
MIKE BOTTS	D	(BCDEFH	(B) ON THE WATER	1970	ELEKTRA	US	EKS 74076
DEAN PARKS	G	(H	(C) MANNA	1971	ELEKTRA	UK	K	52001
ROB ROYER	B	(ABCF	(C) MANNA	1971	ELEKTRA	US	EKS 74086
TOM SCOTT	WIND	(H	(C) MANNA	197	ELEKTRA	UK	K 42081
JIM GORDON	D	(A	(D) BABY IM A WANT YOU	1972	ELEKTRA	UK	K	42100
MIKE BODDICKER	K	(H	(D) BABY IM A WANT YOU	1972	ELEKTRA	US	EKS 75015
			(E) GUITAR MAN	1972	ELEKTRA	UK	K	52004
			(E) GUITAR MAN	1972	ELEKTRA	US	EKS 75047
			(F) BEST OF BREAD	1974	ELEKTRA	UK	K	42115
			(F) BEST OF BREAD	1974	ELEKTRA	US	EKS 75076
			(F) BEST OF BREAD	1974	ELEKTRA	EQ	5056
			(G) BEST OF VOL 2	1974	ELEKTRA	UK	K	42161
			(G) BEST OF VOL 2	1974	ELEKTRA	US	7E	1005
			(H) LOST WITHOUT YOUR LOVE	1977	ELEKTRA	UK	K	52044
			(H) LOST WITHOUT YOUR LOVE	1977	ELEKTRA	US	7E	1094
			(I) SOUND OF BREAD	1977	ELEKTRA	UK	K	52062

BREAD LOVE & DREAMS

ANGIE REW	V FLT	(ABC	(A) BREAD LOVE & DREAMS	1969	DECCA	UK	SKL	5008
DAVID McNIVEN	V K G	(ABC	(B) STRANGE TALE OF CAPTAIN SHANNON	1970	DECCA	UK	SKL	5048
CAROLYN DAVIS	G V	(ABC	(C) AMARYLLIS	1971	DECCA	UK	SKL	5081
DANNY THOMPSON	B	(C				
TERRY COX	D	(C	JOHN ROMSEY	D	(	ALAN TRAJAN	K	(C
DAVE RICHMOND	B	(C				

BREAKFAST SPECIAL

RICHARD CROOKS	D	(A	(A) BREAKFAST SPECIAL	1976	ROUNDER	US	3012
ROGER MASON	B V	(A				
ANDY STATMAN	SAX V MAN	(A	TONY TRISCHKA	BJO STEEL	(A	JOE VAL	(A
MARGUERITE CLARK	V	(A	KENNY KOSEK	FDL V	(A	STACY PHILLIPS	G TPT	(A
JIM TOLLES	G	(A	STEVE BURGH	G	(A	MOSHE SAVITSKY	G	(A

FRANCOIS BREANT

FRANCOIS BREANT	K V	(AB	(A) SONS OPTIQUES			
EMANUEL LACORDAIRE	D PERC	(B	(B) VOYEUR EXTRA-LUCIDE	1979	BARCLAY	FR	BA215
JEAN MICHEL KAJDAN	G	(B				
GUY KHALIFA	K V	(B	FELIX BLANCHARD	K	(B	MICK MARTIN	G	(B
PASCAL ARROYO	B	(B	DIDIER LOCKWOOD	VLN	(B	STELLA VANDER	V	(B
KLAUS BLASQUIZ	V	(B	LIZA DELUXE	V	(B		

BREATHLESS

MARK AVSEC	K V	(AB	(A) BREATHLESS	1979	EMI	UK	17013
BOB BENJAMIN	B	(AB	(B) NOBODY LEAVES THIS SONG ALIVE	1980	EMI	UK	17041
ALAN GREENE	G	(AB				
JONAH KOSLEN	G V	(AB	RODNEY PSYKA	PERC	(AB	KEVIN VALENTINE	D	(AB

THE BRECKER BROTHERS

RANDY BRECKER	HRNS	(ALL	(A) THE BRECKER BROTHERS	1975	ARISTA	UK	ARTY 103
MICHAEL BRECKER	HRNS	(ALL	(A) THE BRECKER BROTHERS	1975	ARISTA	US	AL 4037
DAVE SANBORN	SAX	(AB	(B) BACK TO BACK	1976	ARISTA	UK	ARTY 128
DON GROLNICK	K	(ABE	(B) BACK TO BACK	1976	ARISTA	US	AL 4061
BOB MANN	G	(AB	(C) DONT STOP THE MUSIC	1977	ARISTA	UK SPARTY 1007
WILL LEE	B V	(AB	(D) HEAVY METAL BE-BOP	1978	ARISTA	UK	SPART1070

(CONTINUED)

B208   (CONTINUED)   THE BRECKER BROTHERS   B208
   HARVEY MASON   D   (A   (D) HEAVY METAL BE-BOP   1978   ARISTA US 4085 NL   202 113
   SAMMY FIGUEROA   PERC   (BD   (E) DETENTE   1980   ARISTA US 4272 NL   202 380
   RAFAEL CRUZ   PERC   (BD   (F) STRAPHANGIN'   1981   ARISTA US 9550 NL   203 464
   TERRY BOZZIO   G   (D
   NEIL JASON   B V   (DE   PATTI AUSTIN   V   (B   DIANE SUMLER   V   (B
   BARRY FINNERTY   G   (DF   RALPH MACDONALD   PERC   (ABE   ALLEE WILLIS   V   (B
   KASH MONET   PERC   (D   JEFF SCHOEN   V   (D   ROY HERRING   V   (D
   PAUL SCHAEFFER   K   (D   VICTORIA   TAMB   (D   ALLEN SCHWARZBERG   D   (D
   STEVE KHAN   G   (B   CHRIS PARKER   D   (B   STEVE GADD   D   (BE
   LEW DELGATTO   SAX   (B   DAVE FRIEDMAN   PERC   (B   LUTHER VANDROSS   V   (B
   ROBIN CLARK   V   (B   D J ROGERS   V   (E   JEFF MIRANOV   G   (E
   AIRTO   PERC   (E   HIRAM BULLOCK   G   (E   DAVID SPINOZZA   G   (E
   PAULINHO DACOSTA   PERC   (E   MARK GRAY   K   (EF   MARCUS MILLER   B   (EF
   STEVE JORDAN   D   (E   CARL CARLWELL   V   (E   RICHIE MORALES   D   (F
B208A   RANDY BRECKER   B208A
   RANDY BRECKER   HRNS   (A   (A) SCORE   19   SOLID STATE US   18051
   MICHAEL BRECKER   SAX   (A
   JERRY DODGION   FLT   (A   LARRY CORYELL   G   (A   HAL GALPER   K   (A
   EDDIE GOMEZ   B   (A   CHUCK RAINEY   B   (A   MICKEY ROKER   D   (A
   BERNARD PURDIE   D   (A
B208B   JOE BREEN   B208B
   JOE BREEN   G V PERC(A   (A) MORE THAN MEETS THE EYE   1978   VERTIGO   NL   6370 430
   HENRY SPINETTI   D   (A
   MO FOSTER   B   (A   RICK HITCHCOCK   G   (A   ROGER GLOVER   K HCA(A
   DAVE MARKEE   B   (A   DAVE MACRAE   K   (A   LIZA STRIKE   V   (A
   JOANNE STONE   V   (A   VICKY BROWN   V   (A   JOHN PERRY   B   (A
   TONY HYMAS   K   (A   RAY GLYNN   SITAR G(A   HUGH BURNS   G   (A
   JON LORD   K SYN (A   BARRY DESOUZA   D   (A   BOB BENHAM   G   (A
B208C   BREEZE   B208C
   ED VAN TOOVENBURG G V   (A   (A) ITS ONLY A MATTER OF TIME   19   ELECTROLA   EURO 064 82423
   FRED JANSEN   G V   (A
   BART VAN SCHOONHOVEN G V (A   HANS JANSEN   K   (A   LOUIS DOBEY   D   (A
   PIET JAN BLAUW   PERC   (A   FREEK BERRIER   K   (A   JAN HOLLESTELLE   B   (A
   CLAUS VAN MECHELEN SAX   (A   ROB MEYN   PERC   (A
B208D   BRENDA & THE TABULATIONS   B208D
                                             (A) DRY YOUR EYES   19   DIONN   US   2000
                                             (B) BRENDA & THE TABULATIONS   19   TOP & BOTTOM US   100
B208E   BRETHREN   B208E
   TOM COSGROVE   G V   (AB   (A) BRETHREN   19   TIFFANY   US   0013
   STU WOODS   B V   (AB   (B) MOMENT OF TRUTH   19   TIFFANY   US   0015
   RICK MAROTTA   D   (AB
   MIKE GARSEN   K   (AB   DR JOHN   K   (A   RUSTY YOUNG   STEEL   (A
   PATRICK   PNO   (A   THE BLOSSOMS   V   (A   RALPH McDONALD   PERC (B
   BARRY ROGERS   TROM   (B   DAVE LIEBMAN   SAX   (B   MAERETHA STEWART   V   (B
   ALBERTINE ROBINSON V   (B   TASHA THOMAS   V   (B   MARILYN JACKSON   V   (B
   ADRIENNE ALBERT   V   (B   AMANDA AMBROSE   V   (B
B209   PAUL BRETT   B209
   PAUL BRETT   G V   (ALL   (A) PAUL BRETT SAGE   1970   PYE UK NSPL18347 US JANUS3026
   WITH   (B) JUBILATION FOUNDRY   1971   DAWN   UK   DNLS 3021
   NICKY HIGGINBOTTOM WIND (A   (C) SCHIZOPHRENIA   1972   DAWN   UK   DNLS 3032
   DEREK AUSTIN   K   (H   (D) PAUL BRETT   1973   BRADLEY   UK   BRADL1001
   BOB VOICE   PERC   (A   (E) CLOCKS   1974   BRADLEYS   UK   BRADL1004
   DICK DUFALL   B   (A   (F) PHOENIX FUTURE   1975   PHOENIX FUTURE UK
   MEL COLLINS   SAX   (H   (G) EARTHBIRTH   1977   RCA   UK   PL 25080
   STEVE GREGORY   SAX   (H   (H) INTERLIFE   1978   RCA I2962 US UK   PL 25149
   DAVID GRIFFITHS   B   (EH   (I) ECLIPSE   1979   RCA   UK   PL 25219
   DELISLE HARPER   B   (H   (J) GUITAR TREK   1980   RCA   UK   PL 25283
   ROD COOMBES   D   (H
   TOM NICHOL   D   (IJ   DAVE OLNEY   B   (I   GRAHAM JARVIS   D   (I
   ROB YOUNG   K   (I   CHRIS MERCER   SAX   (I   RAY WARLEIGH   SAX   (I
   JOHNNY JOYCE   G   (I   ALAN TODD   G   (IJ   TOM NEWMAN   V   (I
   DAVE WILLIAMS   B   (I   RICHARD HARVEY   K   (J   PAUL TOWNSHEND   B   (J
   MIKE PIGGOTT   VLN G (DE   NICK STERLING   CELLO (D   DELISLE HARPER   B   (DH
   ROB YOUNG   K FDL (DI
B209A   BREWER & FARNER   B209A
   DON BREWER   (A   (A) MONUMENTAL FUNK   1974   QUADICO   US   QLP 7401
   MARK FARNER   (A
B210   BREWER & SHIPLEY   B210
   MIKE BREWER   G V   (ALL   (A) DOWN IN L A   1968   A&M   US   SP   4154
   TOM SHIPLEY   B V   (ALL   (B) WEEDS   1969   KAMA SUTRA   UK   2361 005
   WITH   (B) WEEDS   1969   KAMA SUTRA   US   BS   2016
   JERRY GARCIA   G   (C   (C) TARKIO ROAD   1970   KAMA SUTRA   UK   2316 001
   NICKY HOPKINS   K   (B   (C) TARKIO ROAD   1971   KAMA SUTRA   US   BS   2024
   MARK NAFTALIN   K   (BCDE   (C) TARKIO ROAD   19   KAMA SUTRA   2319 004
   RED RHODES   STEEL (B   (D) SHAKE OFF THE DEMON   1972   KAMA SUTRA   US   BS   2039
   BILLY MUNDI   D   (E   (E) RURAL SPACE   1973   KAMA SUTRA   UK   2319 028
   PRAIRIE PRINCE   D   (E   (E) RURAL SPACE   1973   KAMA SUTRA   US   BS   2058
   FRED BURTON   G   (CE   (F) BREWER & SHIPLEY   1974   CAPITOL   US   ST 11261
   JOHN KAHN   B   (BCDE   (G) WELCOME TO RIDDLE BRIDGE 1975   CAPITOL   UK   EST 11402
   LEON OAKLEY   CORNET (E   (H) NOT FAR FROM FREE   1978   MERCURY   US   9100 044
   BILL VITT   D   (CE   ( ) BEST OF   19   KAMA SUTRA   US   2-2613
   TURK MURPHY   TROM   (E
   PHIL HOWE   WIND   (E   JAMES MAIHACK   TUBA   (E   BUDDY CAGE   K   (E
   MIKE LEECH   B   (G   NORBERT PUTNAM   B   (G   DAVID BRIGGS   K   (G
   REGGIE YOUNG   G   (G   CHRIS LEUZINGER   G   (G   PAUL FRANKLIN   STEEL(G
   WELDON MYRICK   G   (G   KEN BUTTREY   D   (G   CHARLIE McCOY   HCA (G
   FARRELL MORRIS   PERC   (G   SHANE KEISTER   SYN   (G   CHARLES ROSE   HRNS (G
   RONNIE EADES   KRNS   (G   HARVEY THOMPSON   HRNS   (G   HARRISON CALLOWAY   HRNS (G

      (CONTINUED)

BREWER & SHIPLEY

MARY HOLLADAY	V	(G	GINGER HOLLADAY	V	(G	MIKE BLOOMFIELD	G	(B
JIM MESSINA		(A	BOB JONES	D	(BC	NICK GRAVENITES	V	(BC
JOHN CIPOLINA	V	(D	SPENCER DRYDEN	D	(D	RICHARD GREENE	VLN	(B
NOEL JEWEKS	FLT	(C	DIANE TRIBUNO	V	(C	DANNY COX	V	(C
JOSE CHEPITO AREAS		(D	ROBERT HUBERMAN	B	(B	IRA KAMIN	K	(B
FRED OLSEN	G	(B	PHIL FORD	TABLA	(B	APLLE JACK	HCA	(B
REINOL ANDINO	CONGA	(B	LITTLE JOHN HARTEMAN	D	(D	GLENN WALTERS	D	(D
DAVID LAFLAMME	VLN	(D	JESSE ED DAVIS	G	(F	GARY MALLABER	D	(F
DOUG HAYWOOD	B	(F	MICHAEL OMARTIAN	PNO	(F	JOHN BOYLAN	K SYN(F
BUDDY EMMONS	STEEL	(F	BUD SHANK	WIND	(F	STEVE CASH	HCA	(F
AL KOOPER	ORG	(F	BILL PERKINS	WIND	(F	LARRY KNIGHT	G PERC(F
RUSS KUNKEL	D	(F	SNEAKY PETE KLEINOW	STEEL	(F			

BREWERS DROOP

RON WATTS	V PERC(A	(A) OPENING TIME	1972 RCA UK SF 8301
STEVE DARRINGTON	K HCA V (A		
JOHN McKAY	G V	(A	BOB WALKER D PERC (A MALCOLM BARRETT B VLN (A
PETE DUNCAN	HRNS	(A	DAVE GELLY SAX (A JOHN WILLIAMS SAX (A

BRICK

JIMMY BROWN	WIND V(AB	(A) GOOD HIGH	1976 BANG SHOT 003
RAY RANSOM	B V	(AB	(B) BRICK 1978 BANG SHOT 004
REGI HARGIS	G V	(AB	(C) STONEHEART 1979 BANG US 35969
EDDIE IRONS	K V	(AB	(D) WAITING ON YOU 1980 BANG US 36262

ALICIA BRIDGES

ALICIA BRIDGES	V	(AB	(A) ALICIA BRIDGES 1978 POLYDOR UK 2391 364
RANDY McCORMICK	K	(AB	(B) PLAY IT AS IT LAYS 1979 POLYDOR US 6219
TOM ROBB	B	(AB	
ROY YEAGER	D	(A	KEN BELL G (AB JAMES STROUD D (B
STEVE BUCKINGHAM	G	(AB	MICKEY BUCKINS G PERC (AB JOHN FRISTOE G V (AB
ALAN FEINGOLD	ORG	(AB	STEVE McRAY ORG (AB BERNADINE MITCHELL V (A
VINNI O'NEAL	V	(A	KEITH'DOC'SAMUELS V (A JAY SCOTT SAX (B
LARRY BYRAM	G	(B	

DEE DEE BRIDGEWATER

DEE DEE BRIDGEWATER	V	(AB	(A) JUST FAMILY 1978 ELEKTRA UK K 52067
WITH			(A) JUST FAMILY 1978 ELEKTRA US 6E 119
STANLEY CLARKE	B	(A	(B) DEE DEE BRIDGEWATER 19 ATLANTIC US 18188
CHICK COREA	K	(A	
GEORGE DUKE	K	(A	ALPHONSO JOHNSON B (A RAY GOMEZ G (A
HARVEY MASON	D	(A	SCARLET RIVERA VLN (A DAVID T WALKER D (A
AIRTO MOREIRA	PERC	(A	

MARC BRIERLEY

MARC BRIERLEY	(A) HELLO	19 CBS UK 63835

BRIGATI

EDDIE BRIGATI	V	(A	(A) LOST IN THE WILDENESS 19 ELEKTRA US 7E 1074
DAVID BRIGATI		(A	

ANN BRIGGS

ANN BRIGGS		(AB	(A) ANN BRIGGS 1971 TOPIC UK 12TS 207
			(B) THE TIME HAS COME 1971 CBS UK 64612

BRIAN BRIGGS

BRIAN BRIGGS	ALL INST (A	(A) BRAIN DAMAGE 1981 BEARSVILLE 6996
RANDY VANWARMER	V	(A	
SHANE FONTAYNE	G	(A	JOHNNY AVERAGE K (A RALPH CARNEY SAX (A
PATTY CAKES	V	(A	SUZY RONSON V (A LOUIS ROLAND D (A
WILLIE WILCOX	D	(A	JOHN HOLBROOK PROD (A IAN KIMMET PROD (A

BRIGHTWINTER

(A) A BAND FOR ALL SEASONS	1975 MYRR MYR 1030

BRINSLEY SCHWARZ

BRINSLEY SCHWARZ	G V	(ALL	(A) BRINSLEY SCHWARZ 1970 UA UK UAS 29111
NICK LOWE	B V	(ALL	(A) BRINSLEY SCHWARZ 1970 CAPITOL US SWBC11869
BARRY LANDER	K	(	(B) DESPITE AT ALL 1970 LIBERTY UK LBG 83427
BOB ANDREWS	K	(ABCDEG	(C) SILVER PISTOL 1972 UA US 5566 UK UAS 29217
IAN GOMM	G	(CDEFG	(D) NERVOUS ON THE ROAD 1972 UA US 5647 UK UAS 29374
PETER WHALE	D	(	(E) PLEASE DONT EVER CHANGE 1973 UA UK UAS 29489
BILLY RANKIN	D	(ABCDEFG	(F) NEW FAVOURITES 1974 UA UK UAS 29641
DAVE JACKSON	SAX	(B	(G) ORIGINAL GOLDEN GREATS 1974 UA UK USP 101
JOHN WEIDER	FDL	(B	(H) 15 THOUGHTS OF BRINSLEY SCHWARZ 1978 UA UK UAK 30177
B J COLE	STEEL	(B	
DAVE EDMUNDS	V	(F	

BRITISH DISASTERS

(A) BREAKDOWN	197 ZED (EP)

BRITISH LIONS

JOHN FIDDLER	V G	(AB	(A) THE BRITISH LIONS 1978 VERTIGO UK 9102 019
BUFFIN GRIFFIN	D V	(AB	(B) TROUBLE WITH WOMEN 1980 CHERRY RED UK ARED 7
OVEREND WATTS	B	(AB	
RAY MAJOR	G	(AB	MORGAN FISHER K (AB BRUCE IRVINE G (B

DAVID BROADSTREET

DAVID BROADSTREET	G V	(AB	(A) DAVID BROADSTREET 1977 A&M CAN 9026
CARL KEESEE	B V CLAR(AB	(B) DREAMING IN COLOUR 1978 A&M CAN 9032
LANCE QUINN	G	(AB	
JERRY MAROTTA	D	(A	BOB MANN G (AB PETER PHILLIPS K (A
JIM NEIL	D V	(B	DOUG RILEY K (B STEVE KENNEDY SAX (A
CHRIS DADRICK	ORG	(B	MATT ZIMBEL PERC (B MICHAEL LEWIS V (B
BILL HUGHES	V	(B	

BROKEN GLASS

MILLER ANDERSON	G V	(A	(A) BROKEN GLASS 1975 CAPITOL UK EST 11510
STAN WEBB	G V	(A	
ROBBIE BLUNT	G	(A MAC POOLE D (A ROB RAWLINSON B (A TONY ASHTON K (A

BROKEN HOME

DICKEN	V G (A		(A) BROKEN HOME		1980 WB	UK	K 58148	
PETE CROWTHER	B K G(A							
RONY WILLSON	G V (A	PETE BARNACLE	D V (A	RORY WILLSON	(			

DAVID BROMBERG

DAVID BROMBERG	V G (ALL		(A) DAVID BROMBERG	1971 CBS	US 31104	UK 64906	
JODY STECHER	MAND V(AB		(B) DEMON IN DISGUISE	1972 CBS	US 31753		
STEVE BURGH	B V (ABC		(C) WANTED DEAD OR ALIVE	1974 CBS	US 32717		
DAVID NICHTERN	K V (AB		(D) MIDNIGHT ON THE WATER	1975 CBS	US 33397	UK 80885	
DAVID AMRAN	HRNS (A		(E) HOW LAT'LL YA PLAY TILL (DBL)	1976 FANTASY	US 79007	UK 53	
VASSAR CLEMENTS	FDL (AJK		(F) RECKLESS ABANDON	1977 FANTASY	US 9540	UK 536	
NORMAN BLAKE	G (A		(F) RECKLESS ABANDON	1977 MUSIDISC		5960	
RANDY SCRUGGS	B (A		(G) BANDIT IN A BATHING SUIT	1978 FANTASY	US 9555	UK 548	
JERRY GARCIA	G (BC		(G) BANDIT IN A BATHING SUIT	1978 MUSIDISC		5966	
PHIL LESH	B (BC		(H) MY OWN HOUSE	1978 FANTASY	F	9572	
NEIL ROSSI	FDL (C		( ) BEST OF OUT OF THE BLUES	19 CBS	US 34467		
WILLOW SCARLET	HCA (ABC		(J) HILLBILLY JAZZ VOL 1	1977 SONET		UK SNTF721	
ANDY STATMAN	MAND SAX(BC		(K) HILLBILLY JAZZ VOL 2	1977 SONET		UK SNTF722	
WINNIE WINSTON	BANJO (C		(L) MY OWN HOUSE	1979 FANTASY	US 9572		
GARTH HUDSON	K (M		(M) YOU SHOULD SEE	1980 FANTASY	US 9590	UK WEA K58148	
BILL KRUTZMANN	D (B						
TRACY NELSON	V (BC	JOE FERGUSON SAX (C	HUNGRIA GARCIA PERC (C	KEITH GODCHAUX K (BC
JEFF GUTCHEON	K (CB	JOEY HARRISON SCARBURY V(G	TONY MARKELLIS B (C	JOHN PAYNE WIND (C
JAY UNGAR	FDL(CD	JACK LEE V (BC	ANDY McMAHON V (BC	SWEET INSPIRATION V ((C
EVAN STOVER	FDL(D	BILLY NOVICK CLAR (D	PAUL FLEISHER WIND (D	BRIAN AHERN G (D
HUGH McDONALD	B (DEF	JESSE ED DAVIS G (D	Dr JOHN PNO (DE	JOE DARENSBEOURG CLAR(D
LYNDON UNGAR	V (D	LINDA RONSTADT V (D	EMMYLOU HARRIS V (D	HAIM SHTRUM V (D
RICHARD FEGY	G FDL (DEFGHM	BUDDY CAGE G (D	ERNIE WATTS SAX (D	BERNIE LEADON G (DE
BONNIE RAITT	V (D	JOHN HERALD V (D	BRANTLEY KEARNS V (DE	DOYLE LAWSON V (D
RICKY SKAGGS	V (D	RED RHODES STEEL(D	BILL KREUTZMANN D (BC	CURT LINBERG TROM(EFG
JOHN FIRMIN	SAX(EFG	GEORGE KINDLER FDL (EFGH	HANK DE VITO STEEL(E	HERB PEDERSEN V (EG
JIM ROTHERMEL	WIND(E	JANE SHARP V (E	PHOEBE SNOW V (E	STEVE MADAIO TPT (F
LANCE DICKERSON	D (FG	STEVE FORMAN PERC (F	DANIEL MOORE V (F	MATTHEW MOORE V (F
JIM PRICE	V (F	DARRELL LEONARD TPT (F	BILL KURASCH (F	BUDDY COLLETTE (F
PEGGY SANDVIG	PNO(F	DONNA GODCHAUX V (B	DAVID SCHALLOCK B V (G	MARTHA E WASH V (G
MARGARET REDMOND	V (G	MARILYN BRYANT V (G	RUDY COPELAND PNO (G	STEVE MOSLEY D V(ACE
RICHARD GRANDO	SAX(A	TUT TAYLOR MAND (A	PETER ECKLUND HRNS (CDEFM	KEN KOSEK FDL (B
TOM SHECHAN	B (B	JO ARMSTEAD V (B	HILDA HARRIS V (B	TASHA THOMAS V (B

BRONCO

KEVIN GAMMOND	G V (AB		(A) COUNTRY HOME	1970	ISLAND US 9300	UK ILPS 9124	
JESS RODEN	V (AB		(B) ACE OF SUNLIGHT	1971	ISLAND US 9309	UK ILPS 9161	
ROBBIE BLUNT	G V (AB		(C) SMOKIN' MIXTURE	1973	POLYDOR	UK 2383 215	
JOHN PASTERNAK	B (AB						
PETE ROBINSON	D (AB	JEFF BANNISTER PNO (A	CLIFFORD WARD V (A	
IAN HUNTER	K (B	PAUL BENNETT V (B	TREVOR LUCAS V (B	
TERRY ALLEN	ORG (B	PAUL DAVENPORT PNO (B	MICK RALPHS K (B	

STANLEY BRONSTEIN

STANLEY BRONSTEIN	V SAX (AB		(A) OUR ISLAND	19	MUSE	US MR 5072	
WITH			(B) LIVING ON THE AVENUE	1976	MUSE	MR 5113	
DANNY SALZMAN	K (B						
DOROTHY TERRELL	V (B	STEVE TARSHIS G (B	VAL BURKE B (B	
ARNOLD RAMSEY	D (B	ANGEL JUSTINADO PERC (B	DENNIS BELL K (B	
LARRY ROSEN	PERC (B	TERRI BRONSTEIN V (B	SHERROIL JENNINGS V (B	
CLAUDETTE WASHINGTON	V (B						

BRONX CHEER

TONY KNIGHT	JUG PERC(AB		(A) BARREL HOUSE PLAYER (EP)	1971 DAWN	DNX 2522	
JOHN REED	G MAND (AB		(B) GREATEST HITS	1972 DAWN	DNLS 3034	
BRIAN COOKMAN	H HCA (AB					
CHAS JOHNSON	K (AB					

HERMAN BROOD

HERMAN BROOD	K V (ALL		(A) THE FLASH & DANCE BAND	1975 UNIVERSE HOT 108	ARIOLA 200231	
HANS LAFAILLE	D (A		(B) IN VITESSE	1975 REPRISE	REPN54058	
PAUL BAGMEIJER	B (B		(C) STREET (WITH WILD ROMANCE)	1977 AVES INT 146506	ARIOLA 28711	
ROB TEN BOKUM	G B V(B		(D) SHPRITSZ (WITH WILD ROMANCE)	1978 AVES INT	146 503	
HERMAN VAN BOEYEN	D V (B		(E) CHA CHA	1978 AVES INT	146 507	
MARGRIET HILDE	V (B		(F) HERMAN BROOD & WILD ROMANCE	1979 ARIOLA	ARL 5029	
ROB VAN DONSELAAR	K (B		(G) GO NUTZ	1980 AVES INT	146 527	
BIG JOHN	HCA (B		(H) SOUNDTRACK CHA CHA (5 TRACKS)	1980 CBS	70183	
FERDIE KARMELK	G HCA V(C		(I) WAIT A MINUTE	1980 AVES INT	146 532	
KIM FOWLEY	(I		(J) MODERN TIMES REVIVE	1981 ARIOLA GER 6635	NL 204206	
AD SCHAAP	SAX (J		(K) IN A BAD MOOD	1980 ARIOLA	US 50055	
DAVID HOLLESTELLE	K V (J					
GERRIT VEEN	B (C	PETER WALRECHT D (C	ELLEN PIEBES V (C	RIA RUITER V (C
JAN AKKERMAN	G (C	FREDDIE CAVALLI B (DEGH	ANI MEERMAN D (DEGHF	DANNY LADEMACHER G(DEFGHJ
BERTUS BORGERS	SAX (DEJ	ROBERT JAN STIPS K (DJ	MONIKA TJEN AKWOEI V (DE	JOSEE VAN LERSEL V (DE
LENNY MACALUSO	G (HG	ERIC NELSON B (H	ROGER GORDEN D (HG	CRAIG KRAMPH D (HG
STEPHEN HINES	K (HG	PAGE PORRAZZO PERC (HG	D'SRNEL PERSHING K (H	RYAN UIYATE PERC (H
RICK KELLIS	SAX (HG	PETER BOOTSMAN G (J	GEORGE KOOYMANS G (J	BERT HANSEN HCA (J
GINO VAIN	B (J	JAN HOLLANDER SAX (J	DEE DEE V (J	RUUD VAN DIJK SAX (J
EDNA WRIGHT	V (G	DARLENE LOVE V (G	CHUCK FRANCOUR V (G	MARTIN OSTERWIJK TROM(J
FLOOR VAN ZUTPHEN	(D	PETER WALRECHY (D	FREDDIE CAVALLI (J	

GARY BROOKER

GARY BROOKER	K V (A		(A) NO MORE FEAR OF FLYING	1979 CHRYSALIS	US UK 1224	
TIM RENWICK	G (A					
BRUCE LYNCH	B (A	B J COLE STEEL (A	DAVE MATTACKS D (A	
CHRIS SMITH	HCA (A	STEPHANIE DESYKES V (A	CLAIRE TORRY V (A	
RICHARD MYHILL	V (A	DAVE REILLY V (A	GONZALES HORNS (A	

BROOKLYN BRIDGE

```
JOHNNY MAESTRO      B V  (ALL      (A) THE BROOKLYN BRIDGE      1968  BUDDAH              US   5034
FRED FERRARA        V G TPT(ABC     (B) THE SECOND BRIDGE       1969  BUDDAH              US   5042
LES CAUCHI          V PNO (ABC     (C) DAY IS DONE             1970  BUDDAH              US   5065
MIKE GREGORIA       V PNO (AB      (D) BRIDGE IN BLUE          1972  BUDDAH              US   5107
JIMMY ROSICA        B V G (ABC
TOMMY SULLIVAN      SAX G V(ABC    CAROLYN WOOD(SULLIVAN) ORG   (ABC   RICHIE MACIOCE        G    (ABC
ARTIE CANTANZARITA  D TPT (ABC     SHELLY DAVIS         K TPT  (ABC   JOE RUVIO           SAX V(ABC
```

B225 BROOKLYN DREAMS B225

```
JOE ESPOSITO        G V  (AB      (A) BROOKLYN DREAMS         1978  RCA                 XL   13047
EDDIE HOKENSON      V PERC(AB      (B) SLEEPLESS NIGHTS        1979  RCA                 XL   13071
BRUCE SUDANO        K V G (AB
WITH
ANDRE FISCHER          (A    DENNIS BELFIELD    B   (A    VEYLER HILDERBRAND B  (A    AL CINER              (A
TONY D EISENBARGER     (A    RON STOCKERT       K   (A    SNUFFY WALDEN      G  (A    SKIP KONTE K          (A
JOE LALA         PERC (A    DONNA SUMMER       V   (A    TONY MAIDEN        G  (A    MARK OLSON        K   (A
ED GREENE        D    (B    MIKE BAIRD         D   (B    CHUCK RAINEY       B  (B    SCOTT EDWARDS     B   (B
DAVID HUNGATE    B    (B    JAY GRAYDON        G   (B    THOM ROTELLA       G  (B    BOB ESTY          PNO (B
JAI WINDING      K    (B    VICTOR FELDMAN     PERC(B    DAN WYMAN          SYN(B    LEE RITENOUR      G   (B
JERRY JUMONVILLE SAX  (B    JERRY DOUCETTE     G   (B    GAIL LEVANT        HARP(B   LEW SOLOFF        TPT (B
BARRY ROGERS     TROM (A    MICHAEL BRECKER    SAX (B    LEW DELGATTO       SAX (B   JERRY HEY         TPT (B
STEVE MADAIO     TPT  (B    CHUCK FINDLEY      TPT (B    GARY HERBIG        SAX (B   JOHN KIP          SAX (B
DAVID LUELL      SAX  (B    DICK HYDE          TROM(B    BILL REICHENBACH   TROM(B   STRINGS               (B
VOCAL BACKING         (B
```

B226 ELKIE BROOKS B226

```
ELKIE BROOKS        V    (ALL      (A) RICH MANS WOMAN        1975  A&M    US 4556  UK   AMLH64554
DAVID KEMPER        D    (A        (B) TWO DAYS AWAY          1977  A&M    US 4631  UK   AMLH68409
JEAN ROUSSEL        K    (CDB      (C) SHOOTING STAR          1978  A&M    US 4695  UK   AMLH64695
ELLIOTT RANDALL     G    (C        (D) LIVE & LEARN           1979  A&M             UK   AMLH68509
JERRY WHITMAN       V    (A        (E) PEARL                  1981
NINO TEMPLE         SAX  (A
JERRY KNIGHT        B    (C    BEN BENAY          G   (AD   MAX BENNETT        B  (A    ANDY NEWMARK      D   (C
MIKE BODDIKER       SYN  (AD   ALAN ESTES         PERC(A    PETE GAGE          G  (C    GENE ESTES        PERC(A
JOHN GUERIN         D    (A    SIMON MORTON       PERC(C    DAVID PAICH        K  (A    STAN FARBER       V   (A
JIM GILSTRAP        V    (AD   VENETTA FIELDS     V   (AD   GERRY GARRETT      V  (A    RON HICKLIN       V   (A
CLYDIE KING         V    (A    GENE MORFORD       V   (A    VERLENE ROGERS     V  (A    JOHN BARNES       K   (D
SCOTT EDWARDS       B    (D    JAMES GADSON       D   (A    HAL BLAINE         D  (D    MARLO HENDERSON   G   (D
TIM MAY             G    (D    SPENCER BEAN       D   (D    TOWER OF POWER     HRNS(D    PAULINHO DA COSTA PERC(D
DARLENE LOVE        V    (D    ORRIN WATERS       V   (D    JULIA TILLMAN      V  (D    ED WATKINS        B   (D
MAGGIE HENRY        V    (D    ED GREENE          D   (D    PAUL WARREN        G  (D    CORKY HALE        HARP(D
OLIVER LEIBER       G PERC(D    MARCIA LEVY         V   (D    FRED TACKETT       G  (D    BRYAN GAROFALO    B   (D
LENNY PICKETT       FLT  (D    EDNA WRIGHT        V   (D    STEVE BURGH        G  (A    DENNIS KOVARIK    B   (A
STEVE YORK          B    (B    ISAAC GUILLORY     G   (B    TREVOR MORAIZ         (B
```

B226A LONNIE BROOKS B226A

```
LONIE BROOKS        G V  (AB      (A) BROKE & HUNGRY         1969  US
CASEY JONES         D    (B        (B) BAYOU LIGHTNING        1979  SONET        UK         SNTF  798
BOB LEWIS           G    (B
ROB WATERS          K    (B    HARLAN TENSON      B   (B    BILLY BRANCH       HCA (B
```

B227 PAUL BROOKS B227

```
PAUL BROOKS                       ( ) STEPS FROM BEYOND      19    STATE           ETAT  21
```

B227A TERRY BROOKS & STRANGE B227A

```
TERRY BROOKS        G V  (A        (A) TO EARTH WITH LOVE     1980 STAR PEOPLE          SPR   005
JOHN KOTCH          K    (A
DONNIE CAPETTA      B    (A    JIM CHAPMAN        D   (A
```

B228 BROTHER BUNG B228

```
BOB PEARCE       V G HCA  (A        (A) BLUES CRUSADE (EP)      1968    AVENUE ARTISTS    BEV  1055
BOB GORMAN          G V   (A
KEVIN FRANCIS       B V   (A    ROGER CHANTLER     D   (A
```

B228A BROTHER FOX & THE TAR BABY B228A

```
JOE SANTANGELO      K    (A        (A) BROTHER FOX & THE TAR BABY  1969 CAPITOL US 544 ORACLE CAN   703
RICHIE BARTLETT     G    (A
TOM BALLIVEAU       B    (A    BILL GARR          D   (A    STEVE HIGH          V PERC (A
DAVE CHRISTIANSEN   G    (A
```

B228B BROTHER TO BROTHER B228B

```
                                  (A) IN THE BOTTLE          1974  TURBO               TU   7013
```

B228C BROTHERHOOD B228C

```
DRAKE LEVIN         G V  (AB      (A) BROTHERHOOD            1968  RCA                 US   4092
PHIL VOLK           B V  (AB      (B) BROTHERHOOD BROTHERHOOD 1969  RCA                US   4228
MICHAEL SMITH       D    (A
GUY WEBSTER         D    (B
```

B229 BROTHERHOOD OF BREATH B229

```
CHRIS McGREGOR      K    (ALL     (A) BROTHERHOOD OF BREATH  1971  NEON                NE   2
HARRY MILLER        B    (ALL     (B) BROTHERHOOD           1972  RCA                 SF8269
EVAN PARKER         SAX  (CD      (C) LIVE AT WILLISAU       1974  OGUN                OG   100
NICK EVANS          TROM (ABC     (D) PROCESSION            1978  OGUN                OG   524
MONGEZI FEZA        TPT  (ABC
DUDU PUKWANA        SAX  (ALL    MIKE OSBORNE       SAX (ABD   GARY WINDO         SAX (BC
JOHNNY DYANNI       B    (D      MALCOLM GRIFFITHS  TROM(AB    RADU MALFATTI      TROM(CD
MARC CHARIG         TPT  (ALL    HARRY BECKETT      TPT (ALL   RONNIE BEER        WIND (D
ALAN SKIDMORE       SAX  (AB      JOHN SURMAN        SAX (A     BRUCE GRANT        WIND (D
```

B230 EDGAR BROUGHTON BAND(THE BROUGHTONS) B230

```
EDGAR BROUGHTON G V K B HCA(ALL    (A) WASA WASA           1969  HARVEST      UK    SHVL 757
STEVE BROUGHTON D V K B G  (ALL    (A) WASA WASA           1969  EMI/HARVEST  EURO   04083
ARTHUR GRANT    G B V K   (ABCDEFGH1 (C) SING BROTHER SING  1970  HARVEST      UK    SHVL 772
JOHNNY VAN DERRICK VLN    (C        (C) EDGAR BROUGHTON BAND 1971  HARVEST UK SHVL791 EURO 04774
VICTOR UNITT V G HCA K    (CDE      (D) INSIDE OUT         1972  HARVEST      UK    SHTC 252
P HAROLD FATT       V     (C        (E) OORA              1973  HARVEST UK SHVL810 EURO 94260
DAVID BEDFORD       PNO   (CE       (F) BANDAGES          1975  NEMS         UK    NEL  6006
MIKE OLDFIELD MAND G HARP (CF       (G) PARLEZ VOUS ENGLISH 1979  BABYLON            Z  80007
JOHN THOMAS         G     (FH       (H) LIVE HITS HARDER  1979  BB               BB201009
```

(CONTINUED)

B230 (CONTINUED) EDGAR BROUGHTON BAND (The BROUGHTONS)

```
LEI ALOAH MEI        V    (F      ( ) MASTERS OF ROCK               1975  EMI                       IC054 9548
PETE KNUDSEN         K    (F      (X) BUNCH OF 45s                  1975  HARVEST           UK      SHSM 2001
DUNCAN BRIDGEMAN     K    (1      (G) PARLEZ VOUS ENGLISH           1979  INFINITY                  INS  3027
DIGGER DAVIS         G    (F      (1) BROUGHTONS 1979/80
MADELINE BELL        V    (E
DORIS TROY           V    (E      LISA STRIKE          V    (E      MAGGIE THOMAS         V   (E
RICHARD DE BASTION   K V  (G      PETE TOLSEN          G    (G      TOM NORDEN          G V  (G1
ALLAN SMITH          SAX  (G      PETER HOPE EVANS     HCA  (G      VICKI GAFFEE        CELLO(G
SUSIE O'LIST         V    (G      LOZ BROUGHTON        V    (G      SHAZZI SCOOT          V   (G
SALLY BROUGHTON      V    (G      ALI KIMBALL          V    (G      TAMARA KIMBALL        V   (G
SHELLEY WATSON       V    (G      KAY KARNERA          V    (G      TERRY COTTAM          G   (H
PETER JENNER         PROD (X      TAMARA KARNERA       V    (G
```

B231 ARTHUR BROWN

```
ARTHUR BROWN         V    (ALL    (A) THE CRAZY WORLD OF ARTHUR BROWN   1968  TRACK US 8190 UK    2407 012
VINCENT CRANE        K    (AG     (A) THE CRAZY WORLD OF ARTHUR BROWN   1968  TRACK GER 184165 UK 613  005
DRACHEN THEAKER      D    (AEF    (B) GALACTIC ZOO DOSSIER              1972  POLYDOR         UK  2310 130
CARL PALMER          D    (       (C) KINGDOM COME                     1973  POLYDOR         UK  2310 178
ANDY DALBY           G    (BCDEG  (C) KINGDOM COME                     19    TRACK           US  GUD2003/4
KEITH TIPPETT        K    (E      (D) THE JOURNEY                      1973  POLYDOR         UK  2310 254
McCULLOUGH           K    (F      (D) THE JOURNEY                      1974  PASSPORT        US       98003
CHARLIE CHARLES      D    (E      (E) DANCE                            1974  GULL US 6/405   UK  GULP 1008
LEE ROBINSON         B    (E      (F) LOST EARS    (PUDDLETOWN EXPRESS) 1976 GULL           UK  G 2003/4
PETE SOLLEY          K    (E      (G) CHISHOLM IN MY BOSOM             1978  GULL           UK  GULP 1023
MALCOLM FLYNN        PERC (E      (H) FASTER THAN THE SPEED OF SOUND   1980  WEA            NL       58088
BOBBIE McGHEE        V    (G
LLOYD PARKS          B    (E      CHARLIE DUNBAR       D    (E      THUNDERTHIGHS         V   (E
GEORGE KAHN          SAX  (E      PAT LEWIS            PERC (E      JAMES MORGAN          B   (E
STEVE YORK           B    (E      RANCHIE McCLEAN      G    (E      ERROL NELSON          K   (E
PHIL SHUTT           B    (BCD    MARTIN STEER         D    (BC     MICHAEL HARRIS        K   (BC
SEAN NICHOLAS        B    (A      DESMOND FISHER       B    (B      JULIAN BROWN          V   (B
VICTOR PERAINO       K    (D      DENNIS TAYLOR        B    (F      GEORGE KHAN         SAX   (F
JOHN MARSHALL        D    (F      ANDROID FUNNEL       G    (F      RICK KULACK           G   (G
EUGENE DILEBERO      G    (G      JOHN McBURNIE        G    (G      ROBERT KIRBY          K   (G
DELISLE HARPER       B    (G      CHAS CRONK           B    (G      NORMAN WATTROY        B   (G
PHIL CRANHAM         B    (G      STEVE HOLLY          D    (G      JOHN LINGWOOD         D   (G
MORRIS PERT          PERC (G      ROBIN JAMES          PERC (G      TONY UTER           PERC (GD
JACQUIE SULLIVAN     V    (G      R J LANGE            V    (G
```

B231A BOBBY BROWN

```
BOBBY BROWN          MULTI (A     (A) THE ENLIGHTENING BEAM OF AZONDA  1972  DESTINY        US       4002
```

B232 BUSTER BROWN

```
BUSTER BROWN                      (A) RAISE A RUCKUS TONIGHT           1976  DJM                   DJM 22037
                                  ( ) NEW KING OF THE BLUES            19    FIRE           US        102
                                  ( ) GET DOWN WITH BUSTER BROWN       19    SOUFLEC        US       2014
```

B232A CHARLES BROWN

```
CHARLES BROWN        V    (ALL    (A) BLUES & BROWN                    19    JEWEL          US       5006
                                  (B) DRIFTIN' BLUES                   19    MAINSTREAM US368 US SCORE 4011
                                  (C) CHARLES BROWN                    1975  BULLDOG               BDL 1001
                                  (D) SUNNYLAND                        1979  ROUTE 66                 KIX5
                                  ( ) BALLADS                          19    MAINSTREAM     US       6035
                                  ( ) BOSS OF THE BLUES                19    MAINSTREAM             56007
                                  ( ) WILL GRIP YOUR HEART             19    KING           US        878
                                  ( ) SINGS XMAS SONGS                 19    KING           US        775
                                  ( ) LEGEND                           19    BLUESWAY       US       6039
```

B233 CLARENCE 'GATEMOUTH' BROWN

```
CLARENCE GATEMOUTH BROWN HCA FDL(ALL(A)COLD STRANGE                   1973  BLACK & BLUE          33096
LARRY SIEBERTH       K    (L      (B) SINGS LOUIS JORDAN               1974  BLACK & BLUE          33053
WITH                              (C) GATES ON THE HEAT                1975  BARCLAY               80603
JACK McVEA           SAX  (E      (D) DOWN SOUTH IN BAYOU COUNTRY      1975  BARCLAY               90002
GEORGE ALEXANDER     TPT  (E      (E) SAN ANTONIO BALLBUSTER           1975  RED LIGHTNING         RL  0010
WILMER SHAKESLINER   SAX  (E      (E) SAN ANTONIO BALLBUSTER           1979  CHARLY         CR     30169
GERALDINE CARELL     V    (D      (F) BOGALUSA BOOGIE MAN              1976  BARCLAY               90035
LEON MEDICH          B    (D      (G) BLACKJACK                        1976  MUSIC IS MEDICINE      9002
BILL EVANS           V    (D      (H) HOUSE OF THE BLUES VOL 3         19    BLUE STAR      US     80603
CLARENCE GREEN       PNO  (D      (J) THE BLUES AINT NOTHIN'           19    BLACK & BLUE          33033
GARY BARDWELL        V    (D      (K) MAKIN' MUSIC(ROY CLARK)          1979  ABC            UK    MCF 3009
HAROLD EASTON        D    (E      (LO ALRIGHT AGAIN                    1981  ROUNDER        US     2028
DAVID FENDER         K    (L
IRVIN REASON         SAX  (E      CARL OWENS      PNO (E  DUKE BARKER     D   (E  BILL HARVEY     SAX (E
FRED FORD            SAX  (E      JOHNNY PARKER   B   (E  PLUMA DAVIS     TROM (E JIMMY McCRACKLIN K(E
HENRY BOOZIER        TPT  (E      JOE TOUSSAINT   B   (E  SAN FRISCO JEFF D   (E  JOE SCOTT       TPT (E
AL GREY              TROM (E      ALLEN CLARK     SAX (E  CARL LOTT       B   (E  JOHNNY BOARD    SAX (E
BOB LITTLE           SAX  (E      PAUL MONDAY     PNO (E  RAY JOHNSON     B   (E  ELLIS BARTES    D   (E
EMILE RUSSELL        D    (E      NAT DOUGLAS     G   (E  NATHAN WOODARD  TPT (E  DON BUZZARD   STEEL(DG
RED LANE             G    (DL     JIM EHINGER     PNO (D  JULIUS FARMER   B   (D  DOUG MORGANO    G   (D
JACK HUFFMAN         D    (E      DAVID CRAIG     V   (D  CHARLIE GRESSETT V  (D  HOYT GARRICK    V   (D
ROD RODEY            K    (G      DAVID PETERS    D   (G  JEFF FOLLARD    G   (G  BOBBY CAMPO   HRNS(G
MIET BUCKNER         ORG  (AB     MICHAEL SILVA   D   (AB ARNETT COBB     SAX (AB JAY MacSHANN    PNO (A
ROLAND LOBLIGEOIS    B    (A      PAUL GUNTHER    D   (A  LLOYD HERRMAN   SAX (L  BILL SAMUEL     SAX (L
ALVIN TYLER          SAX  (L      JOE SUNSERI     SAX (A  STANTON DAVIS   TPT (L  JIM McMILLEN    TROM(L
```

B233A DANNY JOE BROWN

```
DANNY JOE BROWN      V    (A      (A) DANNY JOE BROWN & BAND           1981  EPIC
BUZZY MEEKINS        B    (A
STEVE WHEELER        G    (A      JOHN GALVIN          K    (A      BOBBY INGRAM          G   (A
KENNY McVAY          G    (A      JIMMY GLENN          D    (A
```

DENNIS BROWN	V	(ABCD	(A) MEETS HIPPY HARRY	19	GOLDEN AGE	UK	PIOLP 2	
HIPPY HARRY	V	(A	(B) SUPER HITS	19	TROJAN	UK	TRLS 57	
SLY DUNBAR	D	(D	(C) JUST DENNIS	1975	TROJAN	UK	TRLS 107	
LLOYD PARKS	B	(D	(D) VISIONS OF	1978	LIGHTNING	UK	LIP 7	
FRANKLYN WAUL	K	(D	(E) WESTBOUND TRAIN	1978	THIRD WORLD		TWS 934	
CLIVE HUNT	TPT	(I	(F) WORDS OF WISDOM	1979	LASER	UK	LASL 1	
DANNY WALTERS	SAX	(I	(G) LIVE IN MONTREUX	1979	LASER	UK	LASL 5	
DEAN FRASER	SAX	(I	(H) WOLF & LEOPARDS	1979	EMI	UK	EMC 330	
SKULLY	PERC	(I	(I) SPELLBOUND	1980	LASER UK LASL8 NL WEA		82738	
TAMLINS	V	(I	(J) JOSEPHS COAT OF MANY COLOURS	1980	LASER UK LASL6			
KEITH STIRLING	K	(I						
VIN GORDON	TROM	(D	ERROL NELSON	K	(D	HAROLD BUTLER	K	(D
TOMMY McCOOK	SAX	(D	BOBBY ELLIS	TPT	(D	ERIC LAMONT	G	(D
STICKY	PERC	(D	ROBBIE SHAKESPEARE	G	(D	LENNOX GORDON	G	(D
HERMAN MARQUIS	SAX	(D	ROBERT XYN	K	(I	GLADSTONE ANDERSON	K	(I
STYLE SCOTT	D	(I	ANSEL COLLINS	K	(I	NOEL BAILEY	G	(I
WILLIE LINDO	G	(I	DAVID MADDEN	TPT	(I			

JAMES BROWN	V	(ALL	AMAZING JAMES BROWN	196	KING	US		743
			AT THE APOLLO	196	KING	US		826
			AT THE APOLLO	196	LONDON	UK	HA	8184
			AT THE APOLLO	196	POLYDOR	UK	583729/30	
			AT THE APOLLO	19	POLYDOR	U	2612	005
			AT THE APOLLO	19	POLYDOR	UK	657	107
			AT THE APOLLO	1975	POLYDOR		2482	184
			AT THE APOLLO	19	POLYDOR		2659	011
			PURE DYNAMITE	196	KING	US		883
			PURE DYNAMITE	196	LONDON	UK	HA	8177
			UNBEATABLE HITS	19	KING	US		919
			UNBEATABLE HITS	196	LONDON	UK	HA	8203
			PLEASE PLEASE	196	LONDON	UK	HA	8231
			PLEASE PLEASE	196	KING	US		909
			TOURS THE USA	1965	LONDON	UK	HA	8240
			PAPAS GOT A BRAND NEW BAG	196	LONDON	UK	HA	8262
			PAPAS GOT A BRAND NEW BAG	19	POLYDOR		657	001
			PAPAS GOT A BRAND NEW BAG	196	KING	US		938
			PAPAS GOT A BRAND NEW BAG	1966	PYE	UK	NPL	28099
			PAPAS GOT A BRAND NEW BAG	19	POLYDOR	UK	2334	009
			NIGHT TRAIN	196	POLYDOR	UK	657	106
			GRITS & SOUL	1965	PHILIPS	UK	BL	7664
			SHOWTIME	196	SMASH	US	MGS	27054
			PLAYS JAMES BROWN	1966	PHILIPS		BL	7697
			PLAYS RHYTHM & BLUES	19	PHILIPS	US		14575
			PLAYS JAMES BROWN	1966	SMASH	US	MGS	27072
			I GOT YOU	1966	PYE INT	UK	NPL	29074
			I GOT YOU	1966	KING	US		946
			ITS A MANS WORLD	1966	PYE INT	UK	NPL	28079
			ITS A MANS WORLD	1966	POLYDOR		657	111
			CHRISTMAS ALBUM	1966	PYE INT	UK	NPL	28097
			RAW SOUL	196	POLYDOR		657	123
			RAW SOUL	196	PYE INT	UK	NPL	28103
			RAW SOUL	196	KING	US		1016
			LIVE AT THE GARDEN	196	POLYDOR		658	041
			LIVE AT THE GARDEN	196	PYE INT	UK	NPL	28104
			COLD SWEAT	196	POLYDOR		658	043
			PRESENTS HIS SHOW OF TOMORROW	19	POLYDOR		658	073
			I CAN'T STAND MYSELF	196	POLYDOR		658	077
			HANDFUL OF SOUL	1967	PHILIPS		SBL	7761
			PLAYS THE REAL THING	1967	PHILIPS		SBL	7823
			PLAYS THE REAL THING	1967	SMASH	US		67093
			JAMES BROWN SHOW	1967				
			22 GIANT HITS		SMASH	US		67109
			PLAYS THE NEW BREED	1968	SMASH	US	MGS	27080
			NOTHING BUT SOUL	1968	POLYDOR		658	101
			I GOT A FEELING	196	POLYDOR		658	105
			I GOT A FEELING	196	KING	US		1031
			SOUL PARTY	19	POLYDOR		658	106
			OUT OF SIGHT	1968				
			SAY IT LOUD I'M BLACK & I'M PROUD	19	KING	US		1047
			SAY IT LOUD I'M BLACK & I'M PROUD	19	POLYDOR	UK	583	741
			GETTIN' DOWN TO IT	19	KING	US		1051
			GETTIN' DOWN TO IT		POLYDOR		658	151
			GETTIN' DOWN TO IT	19	POLYDOR	UK	583	742
			THINKING ABOUT LITTLE WILLIE	19	KING	US		1038
			REVOLUTION OF THE MIND	1972	POLYDOR US 25 3003 UK 2675034			
			THE POPCORN	19	KING	US		1055
			THE POPCORN	19	POLYDOR		184	319
			THE POPCORN	19	POLYDOR		658	172
			GET ON THE GOOD FOOT	1973	POLYDOR		2675	054
			GET ON THE GOOD FOOT	1973	POLYDOR		2659	018
			GET ON THE GOOD FOOT	1973	POLYDOR	US	PD	23004
			SOUL BROTHER No 1	1973	POLYDOR			
			HOT PANTS	197	POLYDOR	US	PD	4054
			ITS A MOTHER	19	POLYDOR		658	371
			ITS A MOTHER	19	KING	US		1063
			SLAUGHTERS BIG RIP OFF	1973	POLYDOR	UK	2391	084
			SLAUGHTERS BIG RIP OFF	1973	POLYDOR		2490	119
			AINT IT FUNKY	19	KING	US		1092
			THERE IT IS	19	POLYDOR		2391	033
			THERE IT IS	19	POLYDOR	US	PD	5028

(CONTINUED)

THE PAYBACK	1974	POLYDOR	UK	2659 030
THE PAYBACK	1974	POLYDOR	US	PD23007
THE PAYBACK		POLYDOR		2675 082
HELL	1974	POLYDOR	UK	2659 036
HELL	1974	POLYDOR	US	PD29001
HELL	1974	POLYDOR		2669 018
REALITY	1974	POLYDOR	UK	2391 164
REALITY	1974	POLYDOR		PD 6039
SOUL CLASSICS	1974	POLYDOR		2391 057
SOUL CLASSICS	1974	POLYDOR	US	PD 5401
BLACK CAESAR	1974	POLYDOR	UK	2490 117
MISTER DYNAMITE		POLYDOR		2357 004
THIS IS	19	PHILIPS		6336 210
SOUL ON TOP	19	POLYDOR	UK	2310 022
SOUL ON TOP	19	KING	US	KS 1100
IT'S A NEW DAY	197	POLYDOR	UK	2310 029
IT'S A NEW DAY	197	KING	US	1095
SHO IS FUNKY DOWN HERE	19	KING	US	1110
SHE IS FUNKY	197	POLYDOR	UK	2310 089
SUPER BAD	197	KING	US	KS 1127
SEX MACHINE	19	POLYDOR	UK	2625 004
SEX MACHINE	19	KING	US	71115
SEX MACHINE TODAY	1975	POLYDOR	UK	2391 175
SEX MACHINE TODAY	1975	POLYDOR	US	PD 6042
EVERYBODYS DOIN' THE HUSTLE	1975	POLYDOR	UK	2391 197
EVERYBODYS DOIN' THE HUSTLE	1975	POLYDOR	US	PD 6054
HOT	197	POLYDOR	US	PD 6059
SEX MACHINE LIVE	197	POLYDOR 9004		PD29004
SOUL CLASSICS VOL 2	1975	POLYDOR 5402	UK	2391 116
SOUL CLASSICS VOL 3	1975	POLYDOR	UK	2391 166
THE BEST OF JAMES BROWN	1975	POLYDOR	UK	2343 036
GET UP OFFA THING	1976	POLYDOR	UK	2391 228
GET UP OFFA THING	1976	POLYDOR	US	PD 6071
BODY HEAT	1976	POLYDOR US 6093 UK		2391 258
POP HISTORY	19	POLYDOR		2625 009
MUTHAS NATURE	1977	POLYDOR	UK	2391 300
MUTHAS NATURE	1977	POLYDOR	US	PD16111
SOLID GOLD	1977	POLYDOR	UK	2679 044
JAM 1980'S	1978	POLYDOR	UK	2391 343
JAM 1980'S	1978	POLYDOR	US	PD16140
TAKE A LOOK AT THOSE CAKES	197	POLYDOR	US	PD16181
TAKE A LOOK AT THOSE CAKES	1979	POLYDOR		2391 384
ORIGINAL DISCO MAN	1979	POLYCOR US 6212 UK		2391 412
SOUL SYNDROME	1980	RCA PL25334	ALP	5006
PEOPLE	1980	POLYDOR US 6258		
HOT ON THE ONE	1980	POLYDOR US 6290		

B236   JOE BROWN   B236

JOE BROWN	G V	(ALL	(A) PICTURE OF YOU	1962	GOLDEN GUINEA	UK	GGL 0146
VICKI BROWN	V	(E	(B) LIVE	1963	PICCADILLY	UK	NPL 38006
RAY GLYNN	G MAND	(E	(C) HERE COMES JOE BROWN	196	GOLDEN GUINEA	UK	GGL 0231
PETE OAKMAN	B VLN	(E	(D) PICTURE OF JOE BROWN	19	ACE OF CLUBS	UK	ACL 1127
DAVE HYNES	D	(E	(E) BROWNS HOME BREW	1972	BELL	UK	BELLS 208
JEFF PETERS	B V	(E	(F) TOGETHER	1974	VERTIGO	UK	6360 114
KIRK DUNCAN	PNO	(E	(G) JOE BROWN COLLECTION	1974	GOLDEN HOUR	UK	GH 583
			(H) JOE BROWN LIVE	1977	POWER EXCHANGE	UK	PXLS 2002
			(EP) HIT PARADE	196	PICCADILLY	UK	NEP 34025
			(EP) ALL THINGS BRIGHT	196	PICCADILLY	UK	NEP 34026
			(EP) A PICTURE OF YOU	1962	DECCA	UK	DFE 8500

B236A   KEISA BROWN   B236A

KEISA BROWN	V	(A	(A) KEISA BROWN ...LIVE	19	LITTLE STAR	US	1001

B236B   MEL BROWN   B236B

MEL BROWN	G	(AB	(A) BIG FOOT COUNTRY GIRL	19	IMPULSE		AS 9249
CLIFFORD COULTER	K	(C	(B) IMPULSIVELY	19	IMPULSE	US	9266
JOHNNY CARSWELL	K	(C	(C) I'D RATHER SUCK MY THUMB	19	BLUE THUMB	US	9186
MATTHEW KELLY	HCA	(C					
BOB WEST	B	(C	GREG FERBER	D	(C		

B237   PETE BROWN   B237

PETE BROWN V PERC LYRICS	(ALL		(A) A MEAL YOU CAN SHAKE HANDS WITH	1969	HARVEST	UK	SHVL 752
DICK HECKSTALL SMITH SAX	(AE		(B) ART SCHOOL DANCE GOES ON FOREVER	1970	HARVEST	UK	SHVL 768
JIM MULLEN	G B	(BCE	(C) THOUSANDS ON A RAFT	1970	HARVEST	UK	SHVL 782
ROGER BRUNN	B	(BE	(D) NOT FORGOTTEN ASSOCIATION	1973	DERAM	UK	SML 1103
DAVE THOMPSON	D	(BCE	(E) MY LAST BAND	1977	HARVEST	UK	SHSM 2017
ROB TAIT	D	(ABCE	(F) BACK TO FRONT LINE UP 1977				
CHRIS SPEDDING	G	(AE	(1) JAZZ POETRY GROUP 1966 (2) 1966/67 (B)&(C) PIBLIKO				

JOHN SURMAN	SAX	(1						
PETE BAILEY	PERC	(AE	ROGER BUTCH POTTER	B	(AE	CHARLIE HART	K	(AE
BIMBO ACOCK	SAX	(F	BRIAN BREEZE	G	(E	PHIL RYAN	K	(E
LYN MAKINELL	K	(F	JOHN WEATHERS	D	(E	BOB EMMINES		(
DILL KATZ	B	(F	IAN LYNN	K	(F	HELEN HARDY	V	(F
STEVE GLOVER	PERC B	(CE	ED SPEVOCK	D	(D	GEORGE KAHN		(AE
JEFF CLYNE	B	(D	MAX MIDDLETON	K	(D	NISAR AHMED]	SAX	(AE
DEREK FOLEY	G	(D	RAY 'TAFF' WILLIAMS	G	(D	TONY HUDD	G	(D
HENRY LOWTHER	TPT	(D	JACK LANCASTER	WIND	(D	VIV STANSHALL	TUBA	(D
PETER LEMUR		(1	ALAN JACKSON		(1	RON RUBIN	B	(1
VINCENT CRANE		(1	TONY ROBERTS		(2	DANNY THOMPSON		(2
PHIL SEAMAN	D	(2	HENRY LOWTHER	HRNS	(2	LAURIE ALLEN	D	(2
JEFF SEOPARDI	D	(F						

RANDY BROWN

RANDY BROWN	V	(ALL	(A) WELCOME TO MY ROOM	1978	PARACHUTE US 9005	RRL	1005	
CHUCK BROOKS	G	(ABCD	(B) INTIMATELY	1979	PARACHUTE	RRL	2007	
PAUL JACKSON	G	(B	(C) MIDNIGHT DESIRE	1980	CHOCOLATE		2010	
EDDIE WATKINS	B	(B	(D) RANDY	1981	CHOCOLATE		2017	
ELVIRA COLLINS	PERC	(B						
EDDIE BROWN	CONGA	(A	PATTI BROOKS	V	(AB	BRENDA RUSSELL	V	(B
SHARON LEE	V	(B	JAMES GADSON		(B	LARRY FARRON	K	(B
J MICHAEL DONIS	PNO	(B	KEITH BASS	PNO	(B	CARL HAMPTON	PNO	(A
BOB ZIMMITTI	PERC	(C	WAYNE STALLING	K	(A	BOBBY BRYANT	TPT	(C
GARY FERGUSON	D	(A	BILL GREEN	SAX	(C	ROGER HAWKINS	D	(C
WILLIE HALL	D PERC	(D	ROBERT RUSSELL	B	(D	HOMER BANKS	PERC	(D
SONNY SEALS	SAX	(D	BILL McFARLAND	TROM	(D			

RAY BROWN

RAY BROWN	B	(ALL	(A) SOMETHING FOR LESTER	19	CONTEMPORARY	US	7641
			(B) BROWN'S BAG	19	CONCORD JAZZ	US	19

ROY BROWN

ROY BROWN	V	(ALL	(A) HARD TIMES	1973	BLUESWAY	BLS	6056	
WITH			(B) HARD LUCK BLUES	19	STARDAY/KING	KS	1130	
FREDDIE HILL	TPT	(A	(C) BLUES ARE ALL BROWN	19	BLUESWAY	US	BLS	6019
GARY COLEMAN	PERC	(A	(D) & WYNONIE HARRIS	19	KING	US	607	
EARL PALMER	D	(A	(E) SINGS 24 HITS	19	KING	US	956	
DON RANDI	PNO	(A	(F) GOOD ROCKING TONIGHT	1978	ROUTE 66	US	KIK	6
ARTHUR WRIGHT	B	(A	(G) CHEAPEST PRICE IN TOWN	19	FAITH		91020	
DENNIS BUDIMIR	G	(A	(H) LAUGHING BUT CRYING	1978	ROUTE 66		KIX 2	
JEFF KAPLAN	G	(A						
MEL MOORE	TPT	(A	JOHN EWING	TROM	(A	JIM HORN	SAX	(A
JOHNNY WILLIAMS	SAX	(A	HERMAN RILEY	SAX	(A	JIMMY CARMICHAEL	PNO	(A
MEL BROWN	G	(A	CHARLES WRIGHT	G	(A	BOB WEST	B	(A
ABE MILES	D	(A	ALAN ESTES	PERC	(A	CLIFFORD SCOTT	SAX	(A
CAROL KAYE	B	(A	TONY TERRAN	TPT	(A	RICHARD LEITH	TROM	(A

RUTH BROWN

RUTH BROWN	V	(ALL	(A) THE BEST OF RUTH BROWN	19	ATLANTIC		8080
			(B) MISS RHYTHM	19	ATLANTIC		8026
			(C) RUTH BROWN	19	ATLANTIC		8004
			(D) SUGAR BABE	1976	PRESIDENT		1067

SHIRLEY BROWN

SHIRLEY BROWN	V	(ALL	(A) WOMAN TO WOMAN	1978	STAX UK STX3005	US TRUTH 4206	
AL JACKSON	D	(A	(A) WOMAN TO WOMAN	1980	STAX RI US 4135		
DONALD DUNN	B	(AB	(B) SHIRLEY BROWN	1977	ARISTA US 4129 UK SPARTY 1017		
BOBBY MANUEL	G	(A	(C) FOR THE REAL FEELING	1979	STAX UK STX3014	UA	4128
MARVELL THOMAS	K	(AB					
LESTER SNELL	K	(ABC	MEMPHIS HORNS		(AC	CHARLES SHALMERS SINGERS V	(A
WILLIE HALL	D	(B	DONNO RHODES	V	(B	SANDRA RHODES	V	(B
D J ROGERS	V	(B	CARL MARSH	SYN	(C	DONALD O'CONNOR	SYN	(C
JIMMY McGHEE	G	(C	MICHAEL TOLLS	G	(C	RAY GRIFFIN	B	(C
BLAIR CUNNINGHAM	D	(C	TERRY JOHNSON	PERC	(C	MICHAEL BAIRD	PERC	(C
HOT BUTTERED SOUL	V	(C	MEMPHIS SYM ORCH		(AC			

THE STANKY BROWN BAND

JAMES BROWN	K V	(ABC	(A) STANKY BROWN	1978	SIRE	US	SRIX 6053
RICHARD BUNKIEWICZ	B	(ABC	(B) OUR PLEASURE TO SERVE YOU	1976	SIRE		7516
JERRY CORDASCO	B	(ABC	(C) IF THE LIGHT DONT GET YOU	1977	SIRE	US	7529
JEFFREY LEYNOR	G	(ABC					
ALLAN ROSS	SAX	(BC	BOB MESSANO	G V	(A	JOHN ZANGRANDO	WIND	(A
JIMMY MILLER	G	(C	ELLIOTT RANDALL	G	(C	JIMMY MAELIN	PERC	(C
WERNER FRITZSCHING	G	(C	DAVID LASLEY	V	(C	LYNN PITNEY	V	(C
ARNOLD McCULLER	V	(C					

BROWN DUST

VINNIE PARELO	D	(A	(A) BROWN DUST	1972 FAMILY	US	2701	
FRANK RAMES	SAX V	(A					
PAUL CISNERES	HRNS	(A	LARRY NORAGER	G	(A	CARLES LONGORIA	B V	(A	GEORGE STANLEY	SAX	(A

DUNCAN BROWNE

DUNCAN BROWNE	G V	(ALL	(A) GIVE ME TAKE YOU	19	IMMEDIATE	IMP	Z12 52012
WITH			(A) GIVE ME TAKE YOU	1968	IMMEDIATE	UK	IMSP 018
TONY HYMAS	K	(CD	(B) DUNCAN BROWNE	1973	RAK	UK	SRKA 6754
JOHN GIBLIN	B	(CD	(C) WILD PLACES	1978	LOGO UK 1007 US SIRE		6065
SIMON PHILLIPS	D	(CD	(D) STREETS OF FIRE	1979	LOGO UK 1016 US SIRE		6080
DICK MORRISSEY	SAX	(D					
JOHN BUNDRICK	K	(B	SUZI QUATRO	V	(B	ROBERT HENRIT	D	(B
JOHN CAMERON	PNO	(B	KEITH HODGE	V	(B	JIM RODFORD	B	(B
TONY CARR	V	(B					

JACKSON BROWNE

JACKSON BROWNE	G V	(ALL	(A) FIRST ALBUM (UNRELEASED)	1967	ELEKTRA	US		
WITH			(B) JACKSON BROWNE	1972	ASYLUM UK SYL9002	RI	K 53022	
RUSS KUNKEL	D	(CEFG	(B) JACKSON BROWNE	1972	ASYLUM	US	SD 5051	
JIM GORDON	D	(E	(C) FOR EVERYMAN	1973	ASYLUM UK 4003	RI	K 43003	
CHUCK RAINEY	B	(E	(C) FOR EVERYMAN	1973	ASYLUM	US	SD 5067	
JOYCE EVERSON	V	(D	(D) LATE FOR THE SKY	1974	ASYLUM UK SYL 9018	RI	K 43007	
BILL PAYNE	K	(CEG	(D) LATE FOR THE SKY	1974	ASYLUM	US	7E 1017	
LOWELL GEORGE	G	(E	(E) THE PRETENDER	1976	ASYLUM UK K53048	US	7E 1079	
FRED TACKETT	G	(E	(F) RUNNING ON EMPTY	1978	ASYLUM UK K53070	US	6E 1131	
JOHN HALL	G	(CE	(G) HOLD OUT	1980	ASYLUM UK K52226	US	5E 511	
MIKE UTLEY	K	(CE						
JIM HORN	HRNS	(E	ALBERT LEE	G	(BE	LELAND SKLAR	B	(EF	ROY BITTAN	PNO	(E
ARTHUR GERST		(E	JON LANDAU	V PROD	(E	BOB GLAUB	B	(EG	BONNIE RAITT	V	(CE
ROSEMARY BUTLER	V	(EFG	JEFF PORCARO	D	(E	GARY COLEMAN	PERC	(E	J D SOUTHER	V	(CE
DON HENLEY	V	(CDE	CHUCK FINDLEY	HRNS	(E	DICK HYDE	HRNS	(E	QUITMAN DENNIS	HRN	(E
DAVID CROSBY	V	(BE	GRAHAM NASH	V	(E	MARK JORDAN	K	(	JOHN MAUCERN	D	(E

(CONTINUED)

[77]

(CONTINUED)   JACKSON BROWNE   B244

```
BRYAN GAROFALO      B   (E    DANNY KORTCHMAR   G   (FG  DOUG HAYWOOD      B V (CDFG SNEAKY PETE KLEINOW STEEL(BC
MICKY McGEE         D   (C    JIM KELTNER       D   (C   SPOONER OLDHAM    ORG  (C   GARY MALLABER       D  (C
BETH FICHET         V   (D    DAVID PAICH       PNO (C   ROCKADAY JOHNNIE  PNO  (C   GLENN FREY          V  (C
JONI MITCHELL       PNO (C    WILTON FELDER     B   (C   LARRY ZACK        D    (D   JAI WINDING         K  (D
CLARENCE WHITE      K   (D    DAVID JACKSON     PNO (B   JESSE ED DAVIS    G    (B   JIM GORDON          ORG(B
JIM FADDEN          HCA (B    DAVID CAMPBELL    VLA (BE  LEAH KUNKEL       V    (B   DAVID LINDLEY       G VLN(CDEFG
CRAIG DOERGE        K  (BEFG  LEWIS F DAMIAN    G V (E   JOEL BERNSTEIN    V    (F   ROBERT GUTIERREZ  G V (E
DAN FOGELBERG       V   (D    TERRY REID        V   (D   PERRY LINDLEY     V    (D   FRITZ RICHMOND      JUG (D
JOE LALA            PERC (G   RICK MAROTTA      D   (G   AL SCHMITT        PROD (D
```

B245   SEVERIN BROWNE   B245

```
SEVERIN BROWNE   V PNO G  (ALL   (A) SEVERIN BROWNE                    1973   MOWEST       US    M774L
WITH                             (B) NEW IMPROVED                      1974   MOTOWN       US     6 779
JOHN GUERIN        D    (A       (B) LOVESONGS                         1974   MOWEST       UK    MWS 7005
EMORY GORDY        B    (A
SNEAKY PETE KLEINOW STEEL (A     MERLE BREGANTE   D    (A    JEFF PORCARO      D     (B
RUSS KUNKEL        D    (B       DAVID HUNGATE    B    (B    DAVID PAICH       ACC   (B
RICHARD BENNETT    G STEEL (AB   ALAN LINDGREN    K SYN (AB  JOE PORCARO       PERC  (B
BOBBY TORRES       PERC (B       STEVE LEEDS      SAX  (B    ROBERT GRINNEDGE  STDRUM (B
DEAN WEBB          MAND (B       JENNIFER WARREN  V    (B    CAROL CARMICHAEL  V     (A
BOBBI THOMAS       V    (B       JULES SHEAR      V    (B    DENNIS CONWAY     D     (A
STEVE LE FEVER     B    (A       RAY KELLY        CELLO (A   MAURY MANSEAU     G     (A
BRUCE BUELL        B    (A       KING ERRISON     CONGAS (A
```

B246   BROWNSVILLE STATION   B246

```
HENRY WEEK       D V    (CDGH   (A) BROWNSVILLE STATION           19     PALLADIUM     US          1004
JIM BRUZZESE     PERC   (A      (A) BROWNSVILLE STATION           19     PRIVATE STOCK US          2026
CUBBY KODA       G HCA V(ABCDGH (B) A NIGHT ON THE TOWN           1972   BIG TREE      US   BTS    2010
MICHAEL LUTZ     B G V K (ABCDGH(C) YEAH!                         1973   BIG TREE      US   BT     2102
BRUCE NAZARIAN   G K V  (HG     (D) SCHOOL PUNKS                  1974   BIG TREE      US         89500
TONY DRIGGINS    B V    (AB     (E) SMOKIN' IN THE BOYS ROOM      19     PHILIPS            6369 804
T J CRONLEY      D      (A      (F) MOTOR CITY CONNECTION         1975   BIG TREE           89510
PAT McCAFREY     K      (A      (G) BROWNSVILLE STATION           1977   P STOCK US 2026 UK PVLP 1021
AL NALLI         ACC    (A      (H) AIR SPECIAL                   1978   EPIC   US 35606 UK  EPC 83161
DAVID WECK       D      (B
```

B246A   BROWNSTONE   B246A

```
BARBARA LOPEZ      V    (A       (A) BROWNSTONE                       19
MICHAEL FRASS      K V  (A
DAVID P HOFFMAN    G V  (A       SAMUEL JOHNSON   D    (A    STEVE SEIBERG     B V  (A
DOUGLAS WELBAUM    G    (A
```

B247   ANNETTE & VICTOR BROX   B247

```
VICTOR BROX        V K  (A       (A) ROLLIN' BACK                     1974   SONET        UK   SNTF 663
ANNETTE BROX       V PERC(A
JEFF WALTERS       WIND (A       GLEN CARTLIDGE   G SAX (A   HARVEY ROSE       B V  (A
CHARLENE COLLINS   V    'A       RAY WARLEIGH     SAX  (A    BRUCE MITCHELL    PERC (A
LOUIS HUTCHINSON   V    (A       GORDON REED      V    (A    TONY MOSS         B    (A
PAUL BURGESS       PERC D(A      JOHN MOORSHEAD   G    (A    ALEX DMOCHOWSKI   B    (A
RAY RUSSELL        G    (A       LARRY GANNON     G    (A    PETE WAUGH        G V  (A
JOHN PORTER        G    (A       KEITH BAILEY     D    (A    LOL CREME         D    (A
BRIAN KEITH        TROM V(A      GERALDINE CONNOR V    (A    JOYCE HOBSON      V    (A
JUNE LEWIS         V    (A       TOSH RYAN-CARTER SAX  (A    DAVE LOWARCH      G    (A
```

B248   JACK BRUCE   B248

```
JACK BRUCE         B V k (ALL    (A) SONGS FOR A TAYLOR            1969   POLYDOR      UK    583  058
DICK HECKSTALL SMITH SAX (AB     (A) SONGS FOR A TAYLOR            1969   ATCO         US         33306
CHRIS SPEDDING     G    (AC      (A) SONGS FOR A TAYLOR            1969   POLYDOR      GER   184  320
JOHN McLAUGHLIN    G    (B       (B) THINGS WE LIKE               1970   POLYDOR      UK   2343 033
JON HISEMAN        D    (AB      (B) THINGS WE LIKE               1970   ATCO         US         33349
JOHN MARSHALL      D    (AC      (B) THINGS WE LIKE               1970   POLYDOR      GER  2310 077
ART THEMEN         SAX  (A       (C) HARMONY ROW                  1971   POLYDOR      UK   2310 107
HENRY LOWTHER      HRNS (A       (C) HARMONY ROW                  1971   ATCO         US         33365
HARRY BECKETT      HRNS (A       (C) HARMONY ROW                  1971   POLYDOR           2385 065
JOHN MUMFORD       HRNS (A       (D) OUT OF THE STORM             1974   POLYDOR      UK   2394 143
MITCH MITCHELL     D    (C       (D) OUT OF THE STORM             1974   RSO               4805
LARRY CORYELL      G    (C       (D) OUT OF THE STORM             1974   RSO               2479 123
MIKE MANDEL        K    (C       (E) HOWS TRICKS                  1977   RSO          UK   2394 180
GRAHAM BOND        K    (         (E) HOWS TRICKS                 1977   RSO          US   1-3021
MICK TAYLOR        G    (1       ( ) POP GIANTS No. 14 (COMP)     19     BRUNSWICK    IMP  2911 525
JIM GORDON         D    (D       ( ) AT HIS BEST      (DBL)       1974   RSO               2659 024
SIMON PHILLIPS     D    (E       ( ) AT HIS BEST      (DBL)       1972   POLYDOR      US    PD 3505
HUGH BURNS         G    (E       (1) JACK BRUCE BAND 1977
RONNIE LEAHY       K    (1       (F) IVE ALWAYS WANTED TO DO THIS 1980   EPIC         UK        84672
CLEM CLEMSON       G    (F       (G) BRUCE LORDAN TROWER BLT      1981   CHRYSALIS          1324
JIM KELTNER        D    (D       (H) TRUCE                        1982   CHRYSALIS          1352
FELIX PAPPALARDI   V PERC(A
TONY HYMAS         K V  (E       CARLA BLEY       K V  (1    BILLY COBHAM      D    (F
DAVID SANCIOUS     K G  (F       ROBIN TROWER     G    (GH   BILL LORDAN       D    (G
REG ISIDORE        D    (H       STEVE HUNTER     G    (1    BRUCE GARY        D    (1
```

B249   BILL BRUFORD   B249

```
BILL BRUFORD       D    (ALL     (A) FEELS GOOD TO ME             1978   POLYDOR US 6149 UK  2310 579
WITH                             (A) FEELS GOOD TO ME             1978   POLYDOR              2302 075
DAVE STEWART       K    (ABCD    (B) ONE OF A KIND                1979   POLYDOR US 6205 UK  2302 091
JEFF BERLIN        B    (ABCD    (B) ONE OF A KIND                1979   POLYDOR US     POLD 5020
ALLAN HOLDSWORTH   G    (AB      (C) BRUFORD TAPES                1980   POLYDOR            BRUBOOT28
NEIL MURRAY        B    (A       (D) GRADUALLY GOING TORNADO      1980   POLYDOR US 6261 UK  EGLP 104
ANNETTE PEACOCK    V    (A
JOHN GOODSALL      G    (A
JOHN CLARK         G    (CD      KENNY WHEELER    HRNS (A    GEORGIE BORN      CELLO (D
BARBARA GASKIN     V    (D       AMANDA PARSONS   V    (D
```

BOB BRUNNING	B	(ABC	(A) BULLEN STREET BLUES	1968	SAGA	FID	2118
BIG SUNFLOWER(BOB HALL)PNO(ABC			(B) SUNFLOWER BLUES BAND	196	GEMINI	GM	2010
MICK HALLS	G	(A	(C) TRACKSIDE BLUES	1969	SAGA	EROS	8132
COLIN JORDAN	G	(AC					
PETER FRENCH	V	(A	JEFF RUSSELL	D	(A	PAT GROVER	V G	(B
LEO MANNING	D	(B	JO ANNE KELLY	V	(B	JOHN O'LEARY	HCA	(B
STEVE RYE	HCA	(B	KEITH NELSON	BANJO	(B	BARRY GUARD	D	(B
PETE BANHAM	D	(C	PETER GREEN	G V	(C			

(A) BRUSH ARBOR	1973	CAPITOL	US 11158
(B) BRUSH ARBOR II	1973	CAPITOL	US 11209
(C) PAGE ONE	1976	MONUMENT	US 6637
(D) STRAIGHT 251	1977	MONUMENT	US 7613

PEABO BRYSON	V	(ALL	(A) REACHING FOR THE SKY	1978	CAPITOL	EST 11729
WITH			(B) CROSSWINDS	1978	CAPITOL	ST 11875
PAUL LIBMAN	K	(A	(C) PARADISE	1980	CAPITOL	12-63
SONNY SEALS	SAX	(A				
TERRY FRYER	SYN	(A	BOBBY CHRISTIAN	PERC	(A	DAN LEAKE	G	(A
ROSS TRAUT	G	(A	LARRY BALL	B	(A	MORRIS JENNINGS	D	(A

ROD PRINCE	G V	(A	(A) BUBBLE PUPPY	19
TODD POTTER	G	(A		
ROY COX	B	(A	M TAYLOR	D	(A

ROY BUCHANAN	G V	(ALL	(A) ROY BUCHANAN	1972	POLYDOR	UK	2391 042
WITH			(A) ROY BUCHANAN	1972	POLYDOR	US	PD 5033
STEVE CROPPER	G	(G	(B) SECOND ALBUM	1973	POLYDOR	UK	2391 062
DIVA GRAY	V	(G	(B) SECOND ALBUM	1973	POLYDOR	US	PD 5046
RHETTA HUGHES	V	(G	(C) THATS WHAT I'M HERE FOR	1974	POLYDOR	UK	2391 114
LAURA WILLIAMS	V	(G	(C) THATS WHAT I'M HERE FOR	1974	POLYDOR	US	PD 6020
RON FOSTER	V	(G	(D) RESCUE ME	1975	POLYDOR	UK	2391 152
RAY GOMEZ	G	(GH	(E) LIVE STOCK	1975	POLYDOR	US	PD 6048
STANLEY CLARKE	G	(G	(F) A STREET CALLED STRAIGHT	1976	POLYDOR	UK	2391 233
NARADA MICHAEL WALDEN	D	(G	(F) A STREET CALLED STRAIGHT	1976	ATLANTIC	US	SD 18170
MALCOLM LUKENS	K	(GEF	(G) LOADING ZONE	1977	POLYDOR	UK	2391 295
JAN HAMMER	K	(G	(G) LOADING ZONE	1977	ATLANTIC	US	18138
SCOTT MUSMANNO	V	(G	(H) NOT ALONE	1978	ATLANTIC	US	SD 19170
DENNIS PARKER	B	(G	( ) ROY BUCHANAN	1976	POLYDOR	UK	2482 275
DAVID GARIBALDI	D	(G	( ) IN THE BEGINNING	19	POLYDOR	US	PD 6035
DONALD DUCK DUNN	B	(G	(K) MY BABA	1980	WATERHOUSE	US	12
JIM ROMEYN	SYN	(D					
WILL LEE	B	(GF	TOM FLYE	PERC	(D	ARMANDO PERAZA	CONGA(D
DICK HEINTZE	K	(BAC	TEDDY IRWIN	G	(AB	JERRY MERCER	D	(AB
DON PAYNE	B	(B	CHUCK TILLEY	V	(AB	NED DAVIS	D	(AB
BILLY PRICE	V	(CE	JOHN HARRISON	B V	(CEF	ROBBIE MAGRUDER	D	(C
BILL SHEFFIELD	V	(D	NEIL LARSEN	K	(D	KENNY TIBBETTS	B	(D
BILL STEWART	D	(D	GREG ADAMS	TPT	(D	LENNY PICKETT	SAX	(D
MIMI CASTILLO	SAX	(D	MIC GILLETTE	HRNS	(D	STEPHEN KUPKA	SAX	(D
ED FREEMAN	K	(D	VENETTA FIELDS	V	(D	CARLENE WILLIAMS	V	(D
WILLIE WEEKS	B	(H	ANDY NEWMARK	D	(FH	GARY ST CLAIR	V	(H
LUTHER VAN DROSS	V	(H	KRYSTAL DAVIS	V	(H	ALFA ANDERSON	V	(H
DAVIS LASLEY	V	(H	PETE VAN ALLEN	B	(A	PAUL JACOBS	K V	(K
GORDON JACKSON	B	(K	BYRD FOSTER	D	(EFG	RICHARD CROOK	D	(K
DON BRUBECK	D	(K					

ALAN THACKER	G FDL	(AB	(A) MORNING COMES	1976	MCA	UK	MCF 2771
DICK HALLEY	B BANJ	(AB	(A) MORNING COMES	1976	MCA	US	MCA 2218
DICK VERUCCHI	D PERC	(AB	(B) BUCKACRE	1978	MCA	US	MCA 2365
DARRELL DATA	STEEL G V	(AB					
LES LOCKRIDGE	G	(A	DAVID ANSON	PNO K V	(B			

RONN PRICE	V B G	(A	(A) BUCKEYE	1979	POLYDOR US 6213 UK 2391 16
THOM FOWLE	G V	(A			
GABRIEL KATONA	K V	(A	BEAVER PARKER	D PERC V(A	

L A	G V	(A	(A) LOOK AT ME NOW	1976	UTOPIA	US 1 1823
ROSCO	G V	(A			
JAY	B V	(A	BUZZARD	D V	(A	BOBBY	TPT K	(A
LONGDOG	K HCA HRNS	(A			

LINDSEY BUCKINGHAM	G V	(A	(A) LAW & ORDER	1981 MERCURY UK 6302 167 ASYLUM US 5E561
MICK FLEETWOOD	D	(A		
GEORGE HAWKINS	B	(A	CAROL HARRIS	V	(A	CHRISTINE McVIE	V	(A

STEVIE NICKS	V	(A1	(A) BUCKINGHAM NICKS	1973	POLYDOR US PD5058 UK 2391 093
LINDSEY BUCKINGHAM	G V	(A1	(1) PRE LP LINE UP 'FRITE' 1971	
GARY'HOPPY' HODGES	D	(A		
JIM KELTNER	D	(A	JERRY SCHEFF	B	(A	ROBERT'WADDY'WACHTEL	G	(A
MARK TULIN	B	(A	RON TUTT	D	(A	PEGGY SANDVIG	K	(A
JORGE CALDERON	PERC	(A	MONTY STARK	SYN	(A	XAVIER PACHECO	K V	(1
BRIAN KANE	G	(1	BOB GEARY	D	(1	TOM CRIEFF	B	(

DENNY TUFANO	V	(	(A) KIND OF DRAG	1966	USA	US	107
CARL GIAMMARESE	G	(	(B) TIME & CHANGES	1967	CBS	US	2669
JON JON POULOS	D	(	(C) PORTRAITS	1968	CBS	US	2798 9598
NICK FORTUNE	B	(	(D) IN ONE EAR & GONE TOMORROW	1968	CBS	US	9703
MARTY GREBB	K	(	(E) GREATEST HITS	1969	CBS	US	9812
DENNIS MICCOLI	K	(	(F) MADE IN CHICAGO	1975	CBS	US	33333

```
TIM BUCKLEY        G V  (ALL      (A) TIM BUCKLEY                   1966 ELEKTRA      US   EKS 74004
WITH                              (A) TIM BUCKLEY                   1971 ELEKTRA      UK   K  42010
LEE UNDERWOOD      G K  (ABCDEFGJ  (B) GOODBYE & HELLO              1967 ELEKTRA      US   EKS  7318
VAN DYKE PARKS     PNO  (A         (B) GOODBYE & HELLO              1971 ELEKTRA      US   EKS 74028
BILLY MUNDI        D    (A         (B) GOODBYE & HELLO              1971 ELEKTRA      UK   K  42070
JIMMY BOND         B    (B         (C) HAPPY SAD                    1968 ELEKTRA      US   EKS 74045
DON RANDI          K    (B         (C) HAPPY SAD                    1971 ELEKTRA      UK   K  42072
BRIAN HARTZLER     G    (B         (D) BLUE AFTERNOON               1969 STRAIGHT     US   STS 1060
CARTER COLLINS     CONGAS(BCDEG    (D) BLUE AFTERNOON               1970 WB           US RI WS 1842
JERRY YESTER       K    (B         (E) LORCA                        1970 ELEKTRA      US   EKS 74074
JIMMY MADISON      D    (D         (E) LORCA                        1971 ELEKTRA      US   K42053
DAVID FRIEDMAN     PERC (CD        (F) STARSAILOR                   1970 STRAIGHT     US   STS 1064
JIM FIELDER        B    (ABJ       (F) STARSAILOR                   1971 WB           US   WS 1881
JOHN MILLER        B    (CD        (F) STARSAILOR                   197  ELECTROLA    GERM IC06292094
EDDIE HOH          PERC (B         (G) GREETINGS FROM L A           1972 WB           US   BS 2631
DAVE GUARD         PERC (B         (G) GREETINGS FROM L A           1972 WB           UK   K 46176
BERNIE MYSIOR      B    (H         (H) SEFRONIA                     1973 DISCREET     UK   K 49201
BUDDY HELM         D    (H         (H) SEFRONIA                     1974 DISCREET     US   MS 2157
MARK TIERNAN       K    (HJ        (J) LOOK AT THE FOOL             1974 DISCREET     UK   K 59204
JOE FALSIA         G    (HJG       (J) LOOK AT THE FOOL             1974 DISCREET     US   DS 2201
JOHN FARSHA        G    (B
MIKE MELVOIN    PNO  (J   CHUCK RAINEY      B    (JG   EARL PALMER      D    (J   KING ERR1SON    PERC(GHJ
JESSE EHRLICH   CELLO(J   DAVID BLUEFIELD   K    (J    JIM HUGHART      B    (J   CARY COLEMAN    PERC(J
ANTHONY TERRAN  HRNS (J   WILLIAM PETERSON  HRNS (J    RICHARD NASH     HRNS (J   JOHNNY ROTELLA  HRNS (J
VENETTA FIELDS  V    (JG  CLYDIE KING       V    (JG   SHIRLEY MATTHEWS V    (J   JOHN BALKIN     B   (DEF
BUZZ GARDNER    HRNS (F   BUNK GARDNER      HRNS (F    MAURY BAKER      PERC (F   BOB RAFKIN      G    (H
KENNETH WATSON  PERC (H   ERIC DUMLER       HRNS (H    FRED SELDON      FLT  (H   MYRNA MATTHEWS  V    (H
SHARON BEARD    V    (H   LISA ROBERTS      V    (H    TOM SCOTT        SAX  (H   DENNY RANDELL   K    (H
MARCIA WALDORF  V    (H   LARRY BUNKER      PERC (H    TERRY HARRINGTON SAX  (J   ED GREENE       D    (G
PAUL NORROS     SAX  (G   EUGENE SIEGEL     SAX  (G    KEVIN KELLY      PNO  (G   LORNA M WILLARD V    (G
REINHOLD PRESS  B    (HG  JERRY GOLDSTEIN   PERC (G    STRINGS               (G   ALENA           DANCE(G
```

```
DUB CAMPBELL              G VLN(ALL   (A) BUCKWHEAT                 1971  LONDON US 595   UK SHU  8423
MICHAEL BUCKY MOTHERMAN K V(ALL       (B) MOVING ON                1972  LONDON US 609   UK SHU  8429
RANDY JAMES              G    (A      (C) CHARADE                   1973  LONDON US 621   UK SHU  8444
MARK DURHAM             B    (ALL     (D) HOT TRACKS                1975  LONDON US 635   UK SHU  8470
RICK GILBERT           D    (C
SONNY RAY              D    (D        DEAN SMITH       G V  (D  DEBBIE CAMPBELL    G V (BCD
```

```
PETER CALICHER    K    (A      (A) BUDDY ODOR IS A GAS      1979  ARIOLA       UK   5045
MEIKE TOUW        V    (A
JAN CEESTANS      SAX  (A      JOSEE IERSEL      V    (A   HUUB JANSSEN    PERC (A
RUUD BOS          HRNS (A      FRED LEEFLANG     HRNS (A   R J STIPS       K PROD(A
BARNY HAY         V    (A      GERHARD VAN DOOREN B   (A   BART TERLAAK    D    (A
MAX MOLLINGER     D    (A
```

```
BURKE SHELLEY   B V  (ALL       (A) BUDGIE                            1971 MCA         UK   MKPS 2018
TONY BOURGE     G V  (ABCDEFGHK  (A) BUDGIE                            1974 MCA         UK   MCF  2506
RAY PHILLIPS    D    (ABCHK      (B) SQUAWK                            1972 MCA         UK   MKPS 2023
JOHN THOMAS     G    (FLM        (B) SQUAWK                            1972 KAPP        US        3669
PETE BOOT       D    (DH         (B) SQUAWK                            1974 MCA         UK   MCF  2502
STEVE WILLIAMS  D    (EFGHIJLM   (C) NEVER TURN YOUR BACK ON A FRIEND  1973 MCA         UK   MDKS 8010
ROB KENDRICK    G    (          (C) NEVER TURN YOUR BACK ON A FRIEND  1974 MCA         UK   MCG  3513
MYF ISAAC       G    (          (D) IN FOR THE KILL                   1974 MCA         UK   MCF  2546
DUNCAN MACKAY   K    (M         (D) IN FOR THE KILL                   1974 BARCLAY     FR   410026
                               (D) IN FOR THE KILL                   1974 MCA         US        429
                               (E) BANDOLIER                         1975 MCA         UK   MCF  2723
                               (E) BANDOLIER                         1975 A&M         US        4618
                               (F) IF I WAS BRITANNIA I'D WAIVE...   1976 A&M         UK   AMLH68377
                               (F) IF I WAS BRITANNIA I'D WAIVE...   1976 A&M         US        4593
                               (G) IMPECKABLE                        1978 A&M         UK   AMLH64675
                               (G) IMPECKABLE                        1978 A&M         US        4675
                               (H) THE BEST OF                       1976 MCA         UK   MCF  2766
                               (I) IF SWALLOWED DO NOT INDUCE VOMIT  1980 ACTIVE   EP UK   BUDGIE  1
                               (J) POWER SUPPLY                      1980 ACTIVE      UK   ACTLP  1
                               (K) BEST OF                           1981 CUBE        UK   HIFLY 36
                               (L) NIGHTFLIGHT                       1981 RCA         UK   LP    6003
                               (M) DELIVER US FROM EVIL              1982 RCA         UK   RCALP 6054
```

```
NORTON BUFFALO  V HCA PERC(AB   (A) LOVING IN THE VALLEY OF THE MOON 1977  CAPITOL     UK US 11625
WITH                           (B) DESERT HORIZON                   1978  CAPITOL     UK US 11847
DAVE SHAPIRO    G MAND    (AB
FRED JONES      STEEL (AB   PHIL RICHARDSON    VLN  (AB   GARY CRELLER     B    (AB
KIRK HARWOOD    D    (AB    TRAMAINE HAWKINS   V    (A    JOHN McFEE G VLN STEEL (AB
BYRON ALLRED    K    (AB    DAVID LADD         FLT  (AB   JOHN CIAMBOTTI   B    (A
BOB McFEE       B    (AB    SEAN HOPPER        B    (A    LYNETTE HAWKINS  V    (A
MICKEY HART     PERC (AB    FEDDIE SMITH       V    (A    STRING SECTION        (A
JOHN HOBBS      K    (B     JOE CHEMAY         B    (B    GREG DOUGLAS     G    (B
GARY MALLABER   D    (B     WILLIAM CHAMPLIN   V    (B    BOBBY BLACK      STEEL(B
GREG ADAMS      HRNS (B     MICK GILLETTE      HRNS (B    LENNY PICKETT    HRNS (B
MIMI CASTILLO   HRNS (B     BOBBY KIMBALL      V    (B    NICOLETTE LARSON V    (B
STEVE KUPKA     HRNS (B
```

BUFFALO SPRINGFIELD

NEIL YOUNG	G V HCA(ALL	(A) BUFFALO SPRINGFIELD	1967	ATCO US 33200	UK 587 070	
		(A) THE BEGINNING (REISSUE)	1973	ATLANTIC	UK RI K30028	
STEPHEN STILLS	G V K (ALL	(B) BUFFALO SPRINGFIELD AGAIN	1967	ATCO	US SD 33226	
DEWEY MARTIN	D (ALL	(B) BUFFALO SPRINGFIELD AGAIN	1968	ATLANTIC	UK 587 091	
RICHIE FURAY	G V (ABCF.F	(B) BUFFALO SPRINGFIELD AGAIN	1971	ATLANTIC	UK K 40014	
BRUCE PALMER	B (ABEF	(C) LAST TIME AROUND	1969	ATCO	228 024	
KEN KOBLUN	B (	(C) LAST TIME AROUND	1971	ATLANTIC	UK K 40077	
BOBBY WEST	B (B	(C) LAST TIME AROUND	1969	ATCO	US SD 33256	
DOUG HASTINGS	G V (A	(D) EXPECTING TO FLY	1970	ATLANTIC	UK 2462 012	
JIM FIELDER	B (A	(E) THE BEST OF/ RETROSPECTIVE	1969	ATCO	US SD 33283	
JIM MESSINA	B V (CEF	(E) THE BEST OF/ RETROSPECTIVE	1972	ATLANTIC	UK K 40071	
CHARLIE CHIN	BANJO (B	(E) THE BEST OF/ RETROSPECTIVE	1972	ATCO	US SD 38105	
JAMES BURTON	G (B	(F) BUFFALO SPRINGFIELD (DBL)	1973	ATLANTIC	UK K 70001	
JACK NITZSCHE	K (B	(F) BUFFALO SPRINGFIELD (DBL)	1973	ATCO	US SD 2 80G	
DON RANDI	PNO (B	( ) STAR COLLECTION	19	WEA MIDI	UK K 30037	

JIMMY BUFFETT

JIMMY BUFFETT	G V (ALL	(A) DOWN TO EARTH	1972 BARNABY	US	Z 30093
WITH		(B) A WHITE SPORTS COAT & A PINK..	1973 PROBE	UK	SPB 1078
REGGIE YOUNG	G (BCD	(B) A WHITE SPORTS COAT...	1973 DUNHILL	US	X 60150
LANNY FIEL	G (ACGK	(B) A WHITE SPORTS COAT.....	1974 ABC	UK	ABCL 5036
DOYLE GRISHAM	STEEL(BCDEO	(C) LIVING & DYING IN 3/4 TIME	1974 ABC	US	ABCL 5047
TOMMY COGBILL	B (CD	(C) LIVING & DYING IN 3/4 TIME	1974 DUNHILL	US	D 50132
MIKE UTLEY	K (BCDFHIJLMO	(D) A.1.A	1975 ABC	UK	ABCL 5065
SAM CREASON	D (BCDF	(D) A.1.A	1975 DUNHILL	US	D 50183
BRENDA BRYANT	V (M	(E) RANCHO DELUXE (SOUNDTRACK)6TRACKS	1975 UA	US	LA 466G
GREG TAYLOR	HCA (BCDFHIJLMO	(F) HAVANA DAYDREAMING	1976 ABC	US	ABCD 914
FARRELL MORRIS	PERC (BCDFHIO	(F) HAVANA DAYDREAMING	1976 ABC	UK	ABCL 5148
DAVID BRYANT	V (CDF	(G) HIGH CUMBERLAND JUBILEE(1972)	1976 BARNABY		BR 6014
DON GANT	V (BCDF	(H) CHANGES IN LATITUDES	1977 ABC	UK	ABCL 5218
BUZZ CASON	V (ABCDFGK	(H) CHANGES IN LATITUDES	1977 ABC	US	ABC 990
BERGEN WHITE	V (CDFGK	(I) SON OF A SAILOR	1978 ABC	UK	ABCL 5242
BILL PUETT	HRNS (CH	(I) SON OF A SAILOR	1978 ABC	US	ABC 1046
STEVE GOODMAN	G (BDFI	(J) YOU HAD TO BE THERE (DBL)	1979 ABC		AK 1108/2
PAULETTE BROWN	V (M	(J) YOU HAD TO BE THERE (DLE)	1979 MCA		MCDW 451
JAY SPELL	K (IJL	(K) BEFORE THE SALT (A/G COMP)	1979 BARNABY	US	2BR 6019
DEBBIE McCALL	V (IJMO	(M) VOLCANO	1979 MCA	US	5102
ROGER BARTLETT	G (DFH	(M) VOLCANO	1979 MCA UK	MCG	4005
PHILLIP FAJARDO	D (E	(N) COCONUT TELEGRAPH	1981 MCA	US	5169
JOHNNY MONTEZUMA	PERC (M	(O) SOMEWHERE OVER CHINA	1982 MCA		5287

DON DOUGLAS	BANJ (M									
JERRY McGEE	G (F	JOE OSBORN	B (F	STEVE FORMAN	PERC (M	JOHNNY GIMBLE	FDL (F		
GINGER HOLLADAY	V (FI	ANITA BALL	V (F	MUSCLE SHOALS HORNS	(F	HARRY DAILEY	B(FHIJLMO		
BARRY CHANCE	G (J	MICHAEL GARDNER	D (H	KENNY BUTTREY	D (H	MIKE JEFFREY	G (H		
SHELLEY KURLAND	STRINGS(M	RUSS KUNKEL	D (M	ANDY McMAHON	K V (M	STEVE SYKES	G V (M		
BARRY CHANCE	G (JLM	NORBERT PUTNAM	B (IMO	HARVEY THOMPSON	SAX (I	JANIE FRICKE	V (I		
LEA JANE BERINATI	V (I	PENNY NICHOLS	V (I	LARRY LEE	V (I	VANETTA FIELDS	V (M		
JAMES TAYLOR	G V (M	JAMES ELMER	B (M	TIM KREKEL	B (IL	SHANE KEISTER	SYN (B		
PHIL ROYSTER	CONGAS(B	ED WILLIAMS	B (B	BOBBY THOMPSON	BANJ (GK	PAUL TABET	D (GK		
RICK FIEL	B (GK	SANDY GOODRUM	K (M	JACKIE DANGLER	PERC (M	BILL JONES	REC (M		
DAVE LOGGINS	V (MO	HUGH TAYLOR	V (M	ALEX TAYLOR	V (M	VASSAR CLEMENTS	FDL (B		
DON KLOETZE	V (GK	TRAVIS TURK	D (AK	KARL HIMMEL	D (AK	BOB COOK	B G (AK		
DAVE HANEY	B (AK	WILFRED TUILT	G (M	JUAN CADIZ	V (M	MARVIN GARDENS	PERC (B		
MATT'MATTY DREAD'BETTON	D(O	JOSH LEO	G (O	M L BENOIT	CONGA(O	HANK DEVITO	STEEL(O		
FLORENCE WARNER	V (O	CHRISTIAN BACCHELLIER	V(O	DAVID LOGGINS	V (O	FREDDY FISHSTICK	V (O		

BUGGLES

TREVOR HORN	B V (A	(A) THE AGE OF PLASTIC	1979	ATCO
GEOFFREY DOWNES	K (A			

BULL

BARRY BULL GORDON	G B V (A	(A) THIS IS BULL	1970	PARAMOUNT	US	PA 5028
ANDY MUSON	B (A					
PAUL GRIFFIN	K (A	HERB LOVELL	D (A	CARLA CALDRWELL	V (A	
HILDA HARRIS	V (A	EILEEN GILBERT	V (A	TASHA THOMAS	V (A	
STRINGS	(A					

BULLDOG BREED

	(A) MADE IN ENGLAND	1970 NOVA	UK SDN 5

BULLDOZER

	(A) BULLDOZER	197 RCA	FR PL 37161

BULLFROG

SEBASTIAN LEITNER	G (	(A) BULLFROG	1976 SKY 006 ANNUIT	US 1003
GERD HOCH	V (	(B) HIGH IN SPIRITS	1977 SKY 012	
VINCENT TROST	B (			
HARALD KALTENECKER	K (	BRUNO PEROSA PERC (		

SANDY BULL

SANDY BULL	MULTI (ALL	(A) FANTASIES	19	VANGUARD	US VSD 79119
BILLY HIGGINS	D (AB	(B) INVENTIONS FOR GUITAR & BANJO	1965	VANGUARD	US VSD 79191
DENNIS CHARLES	PERC (C	(C) E PLURIBUS UNUM	1965	VANGUARD	US VSD 6513
		(D) DEMOLITION DERBY	1972	VANGUARD	US VSD 6578

BULL ANGUS

GENO CHARLES	D (A	(A) BULL ANGUS	19	MERCURY US SRM 1619
LARRY LAFALCE	G V (A			
RON PICCOLO	K V (A	DINO PAOLILLO G V (A	FRANKIE PREVITE V REC PERC(A	
LENNY VENDITTI	B (A			

BULLDOG

BILLY HOCHER	B V (A	(A) BULLDOG	1972	MCA US 5370	UK MCF 2662
ERIC THORNGREN	G (A	(A) BULLDOG	1972	MCA 510072	US DECCA 75370
JOHN TURK	K V (A	(B) SMASHER	1974	BUDDAH	840 031
GENE CORNISH	G (A	(B) SMASHER	197	BUDDAH US 5600	UK BDLP 4007
DINO DANELLI	D (A				

CINDY BULLENS

CINDY BULLENS	V G	(ALL	(A) DESIRE WIRE		1978	UA US 933	UK UAG 30217
ROGER FREELAND	B	(A	(B) STEAL THE NIGHT		1980	CASABLANCA	7185
JEFF MIRANOV	G	(A					
MARK DOYLE	G	(AB	DAVID MANSFIELD	G	(A	LOU MARINI	SAX (A
LANCE QUINN	G	(A	DANNY GATTON	G	(A	GEORGE YOUNG	SAX (A
LEON PENDARVIS	K	(A	BILLY MERNIT	K V	(A	ROB MOUNSEY	K (A
PAUL SCHAEFFER	K	(A	NEIL JASON	B	(A	BOB BABITT	B (A
JERRY PETERSON	SAX	(A	JERRY MAROTTA	D	(A	ALLEN SCHWARZBERG	D (A
KENNY BISCHEL	SYN	(A	JIMMY MAELEN	PERC	(A	JON JOYCE	V (AB

BULLET

HARRY LANG	V G	(A	(A) BULLET		1977	pbr	us 7003
PAUL GOODING	K						
STEVE THOMAS	B V	(	JOHN SHAW	G V	(	GRAHAM SPEARS	D (

BULLSEYE

THOMAS FERRARA	G V	(A	(A) ON TARGET		1979	CBS	US 35973
ALAN CHILDS	D	(A					
KEVIN CLOUGHERTY	B V	(A	MANNY DEMAGISTRIS	G V	(A	THOMAS GRAVES	K V (A

BUMBLE BEE SLIM

AMOS EASTON[BUMBLE BEE SLIM]		(A) EVERYBODY'S FISHING	1977	MAGPIE	PY 1808

THE BUNCH

SANDY DENNY	V	(A	(A) THE BUNCH ROCK ON		1972	ISLAND UK ILPS9189 US A&M4354	
RICHARD THOMPSON	G V	(A					
TREVOR LUCAS	G V	(A	ASHLEY HUTCHINGS	V	(A	GERRY CONWAY	D (A
IAN WHITEMAN	PNO	(A	ROGER BALL	SAX	(A	LINDA PETERS	V (A
TONY COX	PNO	(A	PAT DONALDSON	B	(A	DAVE MATTACKS	D (A
MALCOLM DUNCAN	SAX	(A	MIKE ROSEN	TPT	(A		

ROMAN BUNKA

ROMAN BUNKA	G V K	(A	(A) DEIN KOPF IST EIN SCHLAFENDES AUTO 1980 PRIVATE RELEASE		F667342	
GERALD LUCIANO HARTWIG B SITAR	(A					
FREDDY SETZ	D PNO	(A	SUN A YOON	V	(A	CHILLI BABA	V (A

BUOYS

CHRIS HANLON	D	(A	(A) THE BUOYS	1971	WAND WNS 15 SCEPTRE 24001	
BILL KELLY	G FLT	(A				
CARL SIRACUSE	G K	(A	GERRY HLUDZIK	B	(A	FRAN BROZENA	G K (A

WILBURN BURCHETTE

WILBURN BURCHETTE	G	(ALL	(A) OCCULT CONCERT	1971	AMES	US 7014
			(B) OPENS THE SEVEN GATE	1972	EBOS	US 0001
			(C) GUITAR GRIMOIRE	1973	BURCHETTE	US 001
			(D) PSYCHIC MEDITATION MUSIC	1974	BURCHETTE	US 002
			(E) MUSIC OF THE GODHEAD	1975	BURCHETTE	US 003
			(F) TRANSCENDENTAL MUSIC	1976	BURCHETTE	US 004
			(G) MIND STORM	1977	BURCHETTE	US 007

ERIC BURDON

ERIC BURDON	V	(ALL	(A) GUILTY		1971	UA	UK UAG 29251
WITH			(A) GUILTY		1971	MGM	US SE 4791
JIMMY WITHERSPOON	V	(A	(B) SUN SECRETS		1974	CAPITOL	EST 11359
BOB MERCEREAU	HCA	(A	(C) STOP		1975	CAPITOL	EST 11426
LEE OSKAR	HCA	(A	(D) POP HISTORY(DBL)		197	POLYDOR	2625 011
PAPA DEE ALLEN	PERC	(A	(E) STAR PORTRAIT(DBL)		197	VERVE	2629 001
HAROLD BROWN	D	(A	(E) STAR PORTRAIT(DBL)		197	MGM	2624 024
GEORGE SURANOVICH	D	(AC	(F) SURVIVOR		1978	POLYDOR	UK 2302 078
CHARLES MILLER	SAX	(A	(F) SURVIVOR		1978	POLYDOR	2310 577
HOWARD SCOTT	G	(A	(1) 1978 MARCH TOUR				
JOHN STERLING	G	(ACJ	(G) MADMAN		1976	KARUSSELL	GERM 2674 004
LONNIE JORDAN	K	(A	(H) DARKNESS DARKNESS		1980	POLYDOR	GER 2344 147
GLENN PENNISTON	D	(1H	(I) LAST DRIVE	(FIRE DEPT)	1980	ARIOLA	EURO 202 800
TERRY RYAN	K	(AC	( ) IN THE BEGINNING		19	WAND	US 690
SNUFFY WALDEN	G	(J	(J) COMEBACK (SOUNDTRACK)		1982	LINE GER	LLP 5202
B B DICKERSON	B	(A					
GEOFF WHITEHORN	G	(F	ALVIN TAYLOR	D	(BCF	LARRY STEELE	G (1
MORRIS WHEELOCK	PERC	(C	KIM KESTERSON	B	(AC	KENNY PARRY	G (F
AALON BUTLER	G	(B	DELISLE HARPER	B	(1	ZOOT MONEY	K (F
DAVE DOVER	D	(F	RANDY RICE	B	(BC	RABBIT	K (F
COLIN PINCOTT	G	(F	JUERGEN FRITZ	K	(F	ALEXIS KORNER	G (F
FRANK DIETZ	G	(FI	STEFFI STEPHEN	B	(F	P P ARNOLD	V (F
MAGGIE BELL	V	(F	VICKI BROWN	V	(F	BRIAN ROBERTSON	G (H
BOBBY TENCH	G	(H	HENRY McCULLOGH	G	(H	CHRIS STEWART	B (H
MICK WEAVER	K	(H	MEL COLLINS	HRNS	(H	JOHN PERRY	V (H
JACKIE CARTER	V	(I	BERND GAERTIG	G V	(I	JEAN JACQUES KRAVETZ	K (I
REGINALD WORTHY	B	(I	BERTRAM ENGEL	D V K	(I	NIPPY NOYA	PERC (I
STEVE GOLDSTEIN	K	(J	LUIS CABEZA	K	(J	BILL McCUBBON	B (J
TERRY WILSON	B	(J	TONY BRAUNAGLE	D	(J	TOM VIRGIL	SAX (J
BOBBY MARTIN	SAX	(J	LYNN CAREY	V	(J	LISA SCOTT	V (J
DEBI NEAL	V	(J	KATE MARKOVITZ	V	(J	JOYCE ANGAROLA	V (J
HONEY BROWN	V	(J					

SONNY BURGESS

SONNY BURGESS		(	(A) LEGENDARY SUN PERFORMERS	19	CHARLY UK CR 30136
			(B) OLD GANG	1977	LAKE COUNTY LP 503
			(EP)SONNY BURGESS(WE WANNA BOOGIE)	19	CHARLY UK CEP 103

KEN BURIGAN

KEN BURGAN		(A	(A) THE BIG WOW WOW STRAIN	1974	BLUE THUMB	US BTS 6016
GUS CONTOS		(A				
JOHN GIRTON		(A	WILTON FELDER	(A	HARVEY MASON	(A
HILARY HAMBERG		(A	PAUL HUMPHREY	(A	MIKE SALTSBERG	(A

KEVIN BURKE

KEVIN BURKE	FDL	(	(A) IF THE CAT FITS	1978	ROCKBURGH ROC 105	
			(A) IF THE CAT FITS	1979	MULLIGAN LUN 021	
			(B) PROMENADE	1979	MULLIGAN LUN 028	

SOLOMON BURKE

SOLOMON BURKE	V	(ALL	( ) GREATEST	1963	LONDON	UK	HAK 8018
			( ) GREATEST HITS	19	ATLANTIC		8067
			( ) IF YOU NEED ME	19	ATLANTIC		8085
			( ) ROCK'N'SOUL	1964	ATLANTIC		8096
			( ) ROCK'N'SOUL	1964	ATLANTIC	UK	ATL 5009
			( ) THE BEST OF	19	ATLANTIC		8109
			( ) I WISH I KNEW	19	atlantic		88185
			( ) KING OF ROCK'N' SOUL	1966	ATLANTIC	UK	590 004
			( ) PROUD MARY	1969	BELL		SBLL 118
			( ) PROUD MARY	1969	BELL	US	6033
			( ) ELECTRONIC MAGNETISM	19	POLYDOR		2315 048
			( ) ELECTRONIC MAGNETISM	19	MGM	US	4767
			( ) HISTORY	1972	PRIDE	US	8131
			( ) I HAVE A DREAM	1974	DUNHILL	US	50161
			( ) MUSIC TO MAKE LOVE BY	1975	CHESS		9109 102
			( ) WERE ALMOST HOME	19	mgm	us	4830
			( ) MUSIC TO MAKE LOVE BY	197	CHESS	US	60042
			( ) STAR COLLECTION	1975	ATLANTIC	UK	K 20064
			( ) GET UP AND DO SOMETHING...	197	MGM		
			( ) BACK TO MY ROOTS	19	CHESS	US	19002
			( ) FROM THE HEART	1980	CHARLY	UK	CRB 1024

J J BURNEL

J J BURNEL		(A	(A) EUROMAN COMETH	1979	UA	GER	62557

B272

BURLESQUE

B272

IAN TRIMMER	SAX V	(AB	(A) ACUPUNCTURE	1977	ARISTA		ARTY 151
BILLY JENKINS	G V	(AB	(B) BURLESQUE	1977	ARISTA	UK	SPARTY 102B
STEVE PARR	K	(AB					
STEVE HUGHES	B V	(AB	PAUL WARREN	D	(A	KEVIN CURRIE	D	(B

B272A

DORSEY BURNETTE

B272A

DORSEY BURNETTE	V	(A	(A) DORSEY BURNETTE	1963 DOT US LONDON UK	HAD 8050
			(B) TALL OAK TREE	1979	ERA	US	102
			(C) GREATEST HITS	196	ERA	US	800
			(D) HERE & NOW	1972	CAPITOL	US	11094
			(E) DORSEY BURNETTE	1973	CAPITOL	US	11219
			(F) COMIN' BACK (DBL)	197	TRIP	US	8506
			(G) DORSEY BURNETTE	197	BUCKBOARD	US	1024
			(H) BERTHA LOU DEVILS QUEEN	197	ZIRKON	CAN	104
			(J) THINGS I TREASURE	1977	CALLIOPE	US	7006
			(K) THE GOLDEN HITS	1979	GUSTO	US	0050

B272B

BILLY BURNETTE

B272B

BILLY BURNETTE	G V	(ALL	(A) BILLY BURNETTE	1972	ENTRANCE	US	31228
EDDY ANDERSON	PERC	(C	(B) BILLY BURNETTE	1979	POLYDOR	US	6187
HAYWOOD BISHOP	D	(C	(C) BETWEEN FRIENDS	1979	POLYDOR	US	6242
CHRIS ETHRIDGE	B	(C	(D) BILLY BURNETTE	1980	CBS	US	36792
TOMMY COGBILL	B	(C	(E) GIMME YOU	1981	CBS	US	37460
REGGIE YOUNG	G	(C					
PHILLIP DONNELLY	G	(C	DAN PENN	V	(C	SHANE KEISTER	K	(C
CHIPS MOMAN	G V	(C	BOBBY EMMONS	K	(C	JOHNNY CHRISTOPHER	G V	(C
RICHARD MAINEGRA	V	(C	TONI WINE	V	(C	JEFF WEST	V	(C
KIMME GARDNER	B	(D	CHRIS BROSIUS	G V	(D	IAN WALLACE	D V	(D
DAVID HOOD	B	(D	ROGER HAWKINS	D	(D	BARRY BECKETT	K	(D
JIMMY JOHNSON	G	(E	WAYNE PERKINS	G	(E	DUNCAN CAMERON	G	(E
RONNIE EADES	SAX	(E	HARVEY THOMPSON	SAX	(E	PHILLIP HUMPHREY	SAX	(E
AVA ALDRIDGE	V	(E	CINDY RICHARDSON	V	(E	KIM MORRISON	V	(E

B273

HANK C BURNETTE

B273

HANK C BURNETTE	G V	(ALL	(A) SPINNIN' ROCK BOOGIE	1974	SOUTHERN SOUND UK	
			(B) DONT MESS WITH MY DUCKTAIL	1976	SONET	UK	SNTF 693
			(C) ROCKABILLY GASSEROONIE	1978	SONET	UK	SNTF 750
			(D) HOT LICKS & FANCY TRICKS	1979	SONET	UK	SNTF 792

B274

JOHNNY BURNETTE

B274

JOHNNY BURNETTE	G V	(ALL	(A) DREAMIN'	196	LONDON	UK	HAG 2306
DORSEY BURNETTE	B V	(	(A) DREAMIN'	196	LIBERTY	US	LRP 3183
PAUL BURLISON	D	(	(A) DREAMIN'	19	SUNSET	UK	SLS 50007
			(A) DREAMIN'	19	SUNSET	US	SUS 6179
			(B) ROCK'N'ROLL TRIO	1956	CORAL 10"	UK	LVC 10041
			(B) ROCK'N'ROLL TRIO	1966	ACE OF HEARTS	UK	AH 120
			(B) ROCK'N'ROLL TRIO	1971	CORAL		CP 61
			(B) ROCK'N'ROLL TRIO	1974	CORAL MCA		CRLM 1043
			(B) ROCK'N'ROLL TRIO	1978	CORAL MCA		CDLM 8054
			(C) TEAR IT UP	1969	CORAL		CP 10
			(C) TEAR IT UP	1974	CORAL		CRLM 1022
			(C) TEAR IT UP	1975	MCA		COPS 6355
			(C) TEAR IT UP	1978	SOLID SMOKE	US	3001
			( ) JOHNNY BURNETTE	196	LONDON		HAG 2349
			( ) JOHNNY BURNETTE SINGS	196	LONDON		HAG 2375
			( ) JOHNNY BURNETTE SINGS	196	LONDON		SAH 6175
			( ) JOHNNY BURNETTE SINGS	196	LIBERTY	US	LST 7190
			( ) JOHNNY BURNETTE SINGS MONO	196	LIBERTY	US	LRP 3190
			( ) VERY BEST OF	19	UA	US	LA432
			( ) BEST OF	19	SUNSET	CAN	SS 4028
			( ) HITS & OTHER FAVOURITES	19	LIBERTY	UK	LBY 1006
			( ) HITS & OTHER FAVOURITES	19	LIBERTY	US	LST 7206
			( ) 10th ANNIVERSARY ALBUM	1974	U A		UAS 29643
			( ) 10th ANNIVERSARY ALBUM	1978	SUNSET		SLS 50413
			( ) STARS OF ROCK'N'ROLL VOL 1	1979	MCA	FR	410 074
			( ) TOGETHER AGAIN	197	SOLID SMOKE	US	8005

ROCKY BURNETTE

ROCKY BURNETTE	V	(A	(A) SON OF ROCK'N'ROLL	1979	EMI US 17033	UK	EMC 3323
STEVE DEUTSH	B	(A					
RON COLEMAN	G	(A	RICK CROY	D	(A	BIFF DAWES	B	(A
DAVE EDMUNDS	G	(A	MIKE PORTER	D	(A	BILL HOUSE B PERC K	(A
JOHN HUNT	G	(A	STEVE TURNER	D	(A	CURTIS STONE	B	(A
BILLY WALKER	G	(A	CHRIS BROSIUS	G V	(A	BILLY BURNETTE	G	(A
JOHN HOBBS	K	(A	RANDY STERN	K	(A	MEL COLLINS	HRNS	(A
DENNIS DREITH	HRNS	(A	JOE RAMANO	HRNS	(A	STANLEY BEHRENS	HCA	(A
JIM SEITER	PERC	(A	BILLY GRAHAM	V	(A			

T BONE BURNETT

T BONE BURNETT	G V	(A	(A) TRUTH DECAY	1980	CHRYSALIS CHR1317	LINE GER 5109
DAVID MANSFIELD	G	(A					
DAVID MINER	B	(A	DAVID KEMPER	D	(A	K O THOMAS	PNO	(A
STEVEN SOLES	V	(A	BILLY SWAN	V	(A	JERRY McGEE	G	(A
JUDE JOHNSON		(A	STEPHEN BRUTON		(A	GARY MONTGOMERY		

BURNIN' RED' IVANHOE

KIM MENZER	WIND VLN	(ACEFJ	(A) M144	DBL	1969	SONET	DK	SLPS1512/3
OLE FICK	G V	(ACEFJ	(B) KOKSI LADY (EP)		1969	SONET	DK	6092
KARSTEN VOGEL	SAX K	(ACEFJ	(C) BURNIN' RED IVANHOE		1970	SONET	DK	SLPS 1522
JESS STAEHR	B PERC	(CEFJ	(C) BURNIN' RED IVANHOE		1970	WB	UK	K 44062
BO THRIGE ANDERSEN	D	(ACEFJ	(C) BURNIN' RED IVANHOE		1970	WB	DK	3013
STEFFEN ANDERSON	B	(A	(D) 6 ELEFANTSKOVCIKADEVISER		1971	SONET	DK	SLPS 1528
STEEN CLAESSON	G	(A	(E) WWW		1971	SONET	DK	ALSP 1530
JOHN TCHICAI	SAX	(A	(E) WWW		1971	DANDELION	UK	2310 145
HUGH STEINMETZ	TPT	(A	(E) WWW		1980	TELDEC	GERM	
MATS VINDING	B	(	(F) MILEY SMILE		1972	SONET	DK	SLPA 1540
CLAUS BOEHLING	G	(	(F) MILEY SMILE		1972	TELEFUNKEN	GERM	SLE 14687
KENNETH KNUDSON	K	(	(F) MILEY SMILE		1980	TELDEC		
TONY REEVES	PROD	(C	(G) RIGHT ON		1974	SONET	DK	SLPS 1549
EDDIE LEE BEPPEAUX	PROD	(C	(H) BURNIN' LIVE 1970-72 (CASSETTE)	1974	INSTANT		INS 2
			(J) SHORTS		198	PICKUP		80304

BURNING SPEAR

WINSTON RODNEY	V PERC	(ABCDEFGH	(A) MARCUS GARVEY	1975	ISLAND		ILPS 9377
DELROY HINES	V	(AC	(B) MAN IN THE HILLS	1976	ISLAND		ILPS 9412
RUPERT WILLINGTON	V	(AC	(C) GARVEY'S GHOST	1976	ISLAND/MANGO		ILPS 9382
PHILIP FULLWOOD	CONGA	(E	(D) DRY & HEAVY	1977	ISLAND MANGO		MLPS 9431
GEORGE LEE	SAX	(E	(E) LIVE	1977	ISLAND		ILPS 9513
ANGUS GAYE	D	(EDH	(E) LIVE	1977	PHONOGRAM	IMP	9101 680
CHINNA RANCHIE	G	(DH	(E) LIVE	1977	ISLAND	NL	200 511
EARL SMITH	G	(ACD	(F) HARDER THAN THE REST	1979	ISLAND		ILPS 9567
BRINSLEY FORDE	G	(EH	(G) HAIL H.I.M.	1980	RADIC		RDC 2003
ROBBIE SHAKESPEARE	B	(ACDH	(H) SOCIAL LIVING	1980	STOP	UK	stop 1001
BOBBY ELLIS	TPT	(ACDEGH	(J) LIVING DUB	1980	ISLAND	UK	ILPS 9556
COURTNEY HEMMINGS	K	(EH					
DONALD GRIFFITHS	G	(E	DONALD GRIFFITHS	G	(EH	DIRTY HARRY	HRNS	(H
GEORGE OBAN	B	(EH	ASTON BARRETT	PERC B	(ACDGH	TONY CHIN	G	(AC
LEROY WALLACE	D	(ACDH	TYRONE DOWNIE	K	(ACG	CARLTON SAMUELS	FLT	(AC
WIRE LINDO	K	(DGH	EGBERT EVANS	HRNS	(G	ROOTS KINSLEY	G	(DH
NELSON MILLER	D	(G	HERMAN MARQUIS	SAX	(ACDGH	RICO	HRNS	(H
JUNIOR MARVIN	G	(G	RICHARD HALL	SAX	(ACD	SKULLY	PERC	(D
BERNARD HARVEY	K	(ACDH	STICKY	PERC	(DH	VIN GORDON	TROM	(ACDH

EDDIE GUITAR BURNS

EDDIE GUITAR BURNS	G V	(AB	(A) BOTTLE UP & GO	1972	ACTION	UK	ACMP 100
WITH			(B) DETROIT BLACKBOTTOM	1975	BIG BEAR	UK	BEAR 7
PAT GROVER	G	(A					
BOB HALL	PNO	(AB	ERWIN HELFER	PNO	(A	BOB BRUNNING	B	(A
JOHN HUNT	D	(A	JIMMY JEWELL	SAX	(A	DAVE GELLY	SAX	(A
BOB WILSON	B G	(B	ROGER HILL	G	(B	PETER YORK	D	(B

RANDY BURNS

RANDY BURNS	V G	(ALL	(A) OF LOVE & WAR	1966	E.S.P.		ESP 1039
WITH			(B) EVENING OF MAGICIAN	1968	E.S.P.		ESP 1089
BRUCE SAMUELS	V B	(DEF	(C) SONG FOR UNCERTAIN LADY	1970	E.S.P.		ESP 2007
MATT KASTNER	V G K	(DEF	(D) SKYDOG BAND	1971	MERCURY		SR 61329
JOHN O'LEARY	D	(D	(E) I'M A LOVER NOT A FOOL	1972	POLYDOR	US	PD 5039
A J MULHERN	V	(DEF	(F) STILL ON OUR FEET	1973	POLYDOR	US	PD 5049
DAVID BROMBERG	G	(D					
OZ	PNO	(D	DAVID MOHN	D PERC V	(EF	DAVID TWEEDY	K V	(F
BEN KEITH	STEEL	(E					

PETER BURSCH & BROESELMASHINE

PETER BURSCH	G V	(ALL	(A) BROESELMASHINE	1971	PILZ	GER	
KLAUS DAPPER	WIND B	(BC	(B) PETER BURSCH UND DIE BROESELMASCHINE 76	XENOPHON	GER	161012
WILLI KISSMER	G V	(BC	(C) I FEEL FINE	1978	SPIEGELEI	GER	160 610
MAHENDRA KAPADIA	PERC	(B	(D) PETER BURSCH	1981	PLANE	GER	88264
JAN FRIDE	D PERC	(D					
MANI NEUMEIER	PERC	(B	ROLAND SCHAEFFER	B	(B	MIKE GOSSEN	D PERC	(C
GUNDI JOECKER	V	(C	WALDO KARPENKIEL	D PERC	(C			

JAMES BURTON

JAMES BURTON	G V	(AB	(A) GUITAR SOUNDS OF JAMES BURTON	1971	A&M	UK	AMLS64293
RALPH MOONEY		(B	(B) CORN PICKIN' & SLICK SLIDIN	196	CAPITOL	US	

BUSH

ROY KENNER	CONGAS V	(A	(A) BUSH	1970	PROBE	UK	SPB 1012
DOM TROIANO	G V	(A	(A) BUSH	1970	DUNHILL	US	50086
PRAKASH JOHN	B V	(A					
PENTTI J GLAN	D	(A					

KATE BUSH

KATE BUSH	V K	(ALL	IAN BAIRNSON	G	(ABC	DUNCAN MACKAY	K	(ABC
PRESTON HEYMAN	D	(C	PAUL KEOGH	G	(A	ALAN PARKER	G	(A
DEL PALMER	B	(BC	ALAN SKIDMORE	SAX	(A	MORRIS PERT	PERC	(AC
BARRY DE SOUZA	D	(A	CHARLIE MORGAN	D	(B	BRIAN BATH	G	(BC
DAVID PATON	B	(AB	RICHARD HARVEY	RECORDER	(B	STUART ELLIOTT	D	(ABC
BRUCE LYNCH	B	(A	MAX MIDDLETON	K	(C	ALAN MURPHY	G	(C
ANDREW POWELL	K	(AB	GARY HURST	V	(C	ANDREW BRYANT	V	(C
PADDY BUSH	V HCA MAND	(ABC	ROY HARPER	V	(C	ROLAND	PERC	(C
FRANCIS MONKMAN	K	(B	ADAM SKEAPING	VLA	(C	JO SKEAPING	LIRONI	(C
JOHN GIBLIN	B	(C						
KEVIN BURKE	VLN	(C						
MIKE MORAN	K	(C						
MARTYN FORD ORCH		(C						
LARRY FAST	K	(C						

Album	Year	Label				
(A) THE KICK INSIDE	1978	EMI US 11761	UK	EMC	3223
(B) LIONHEART	1978	EMI US 17008	UK	EMA	787
(C) NEVER FOR EVER	1980	EMI	UK	EMA	794

BUSBOYS

BRIAN O'NEAL	V K	(A			
VICTOR JOHNSON	G	(A			
KEVIN O'NEAL	B	(A			
STEVE FELIX	D	(A	GUS LOUNDERMAN	V	(A

Album	Year	Label
(A) MINIMUM WAGE ROCK'N'ROLL	1980	ARISTA

BILLY BUTLER

BILLY BUTLER	V	(A

Album	Year	Label	
(A) RIGHT TRACK	19	OKEH	14115

JERRY BUTLER

JERRY BUTLER	V	(ALL
WITH		
BETTY EVERETT	V	(*
THELMA HOUSTON	V	(+
JAMES GADSON	D	(R
JAMES JAMERSON	B	(R
H B BARNUM	K	(R
JOE SAMPLE	K	(R
DENNIS COFFEY	G	(R
DAVID T WALKER	G	(R
GENE ESTES	VIBES	(R
RICHARD EVANS	B	(S
MARVIN YANCY	K	(S
PHIL UPCHURCH	G	(S
BILLY BUTLER	G	(S
FRED WALKER	VIBES	(S
JIM SEALS	SAX	(S
KITTI HAYWARD SINGERS	V	(S
LEROY HUTSEN	V	(S
MATTIE BUTLER	V	(S
FRED CASH	V	(S
TENNISON STEPHENS	K V	(S
SOLA BOBROV	STR	(S

Album	Year	Label		
HE WILL BREAK YOUR HEART	1963	STATESIDE	UK SL	10032
HE WILL BREAK YOUR HEART	1963	VEE JAY	US	1029
FOLK SONGS	1963	STATESIDE	UK SL	10050
FOLK SONGS	1963	VEE JAY	US	1057
THEY'RE DELICIOUS TOGETHER	19	VEE JAY	US	1099
THEY'RE DELICIOUS TOGETHER	19	JOY	JOYS	123
ALL TIME HITS	19	TRIP	US	8011
16 GREATEST HITS	19	TRIP	US	TOP16-45
JUST BEAUTIFUL	19	KENT	US	536
STARRING BETTY EVERETT	(*)19	TRADITION	US	2073
FOR YOUR PRECIOUS LOVE	19	JOY	JOY	104
LOVE ME	1968	JOY	JOYS	126
LOVE ME	1968	FONTANA	TL	5264
GIFT OF LOVE	1968	SUNSET	US	5216
ICE MAN COMETH	19	MERCURY	US	61198
JERRY BUTLER	19	PICKWICK	US	3202
STARRING	1969	TRADITION	US	2068
TOGETHER	19	BUDDAH	US	7507
VERY BEST	19	BUDDAH	US	4001
VERY BEST OF	19	UA	US	UASLA498
(R) POWER OF	1973	MERCURY	US	SRM1 689
(S) SWEET 16	1974	MERCURY	US	SRM11006
SUITE FOR A SINGLE GIRL	19	TAMLA	UK	STML12052
SUITE FOR A SINGLE GIRL	19	MOTOWN	US	M7878
IT ALL COMES OUT	19	TAMLA	UK	STML12073
IT ALL COMES OUT	19	MOTOWN	US	M7892
LOVE'S ON THE MENU	1976	TAMLA	UK	STML12032
LOVE'S ON THE MENU	1976	MOTOWN	US	M7850
THELMA HOUSTON & JERRY	(+)197	MOTOWN	US	M7887
THELMA HOUSTON & JERRY	(+)197	PATHE	FRCO66	9912
SPICE OF LIFE	1972	MERCURY	6338	102
SPICE OF LIFE	1972	MERCURY	US	2/7502
BEST OF	1972	MERCURY	6430	401
BEST OF	1972	MERCURY	US	61281
LOVE WE HAVE	1972	MERCURY		1/660
MR DREAM MERCHANT	19	MERCURY	US	20118
THE SOUL GOES ON	19	MERCURY	US	SR 61171
STUFF DREAMS ARE MADE OF	19	MERCURY		855 006
THE SAGITTARIUS MOVEMENT	19	MERCURY	US	SR 61347
MAKE IT EASY ON YOURSELF	1976	DJM		DJD 28027
MAKE IT EASY ON YOURSELF	197	JOY	JOY	171
GOLDEN HITS	19	MERCURY	US	61151
NOTHING SAYS I LOVE YOU	1978	PHILADELPHIA	PIR83810	
NOTHING SAYS I LOVE YOU	1978	PHIL LA	US	35510
THEMLA HOUSTON & JERRY	1977	MOTOWN	UK	STML12063
TWO TO ONE	1978	MOTOWN	UK	STML12092
UP ON LOVE	1980	CHARLY		1005
BEST LOVE	1981	PHILLADELPHIA	US	36413

PAUL BUTTERFIELD & THE BUTTERFIELD BLUES BAND

Personnel			Album	Year	Label			
PAUL BUTTERFIELD	V HCA	(ALL	(A) OFFER YOU CANT REFUSE(1SIDE 1963)	1972	RED LIGHTNIN		R	008
SAM LAY	D V	(ABM	(B) BUTTERFIELD BLUES BAND	1965	ELEKTRA	US	EKS	7294
JEROME ARNOLD	B	(ABCM	(B) BUTTERFIELD BLUES BAND	1965	ELEKTRA	UK	K	42004
SMOKEY SMOTHERS	G	(A	(B) BUTTERFIELD BLUES BAND	1975	MIDI			22004
ELVIN BISHOP	G V	(BCDEM	(C) EAST WEST	1966	ELEKTRA	US	EKS	7315
MIKE BLOOMFIELD	G	(BCM	(C) EAST WEST	197	ELEKTRA	UK	K	42006
BILLY DAVENPORT	D	(C	(D) RESURRECTION OF PIGBOY CRABSHAW	19	ELEKTRA	UK US		74015
BUGSY MAUGH	B V	(DE	(D) RESURRECTION OF PIGBOY CRABSHAW	1971	ELEKTRA	UK	K 42017	
PHIL WILSON	D	(DEF	(E) IN MY OWN DREAM	1968	ELEKTRA	UK US	EKS74025	
DAVE SANBORN	SAX	(DEFGHJL	(E) IN MY OWN DREAM	1976	ELEKTRA	UK	K	42042
KEITH JOHNSON	TPT	(DEF	(F) KEEP ON MOVING	1969	ELEKTRA	US	EKS	74053
GENE DINWIDDIE	SAX	(DEFGHJ	(F) KEEP ON MOVING	1971	ELEKTRA	UK	K	42033
STEVE MADAIO	TPT	(FGH	(G) LIVE	1970	ELEKTRA	US	7E	2001
BUZZY FEITEN	G V K	(F	(G) LIVE	1976	ELEKTRA	UK	K	42095
ROD HICKS	V B	(FG	(H) SOMETIMES I JUST FEEL LIKE SMILIN'	1971	ELEKTRA	US	EKS	75013
BIG BLACK	V PERC	(H	(H) SOMETIMES I JUST FEEL LIKE SMILIN'	1971	ELEKTRA	UK	K	42095
RALPH WASH	V G	(GH	(J) BETTER DAYS	1973	BEARSVILLE	US	BR	2119
DENNIS WHITTED	D V	(HJ	(J) BETTER DAYS	1973	BEARSVILLE	UK	K	45515
BOBBYE HALL	PERC	(H	(K) IT ALL COMES BACK	1974	BEARSVILLE	US	BR	2170

(CONTINUED)

```
GEORGE DAVIDSON      D    (GH       (K) IT ALL COMES BACK              1974  BEARSVILLE   UK    K 45517
TREVOR LAWRENCE      SAX  (FH       (L) PUT IT IN YOUR EAR             1975  BEARSVILLE   US    BR  6960
TED HARRIS           PNO  (FGH      (L) PUT IT IN YOUR EAR             1976  BEARSVILLE   UK    K 55509
RONNIE BARRON        K V  (JK       (M) WHATS SHAKIN'                  19    ELEKTRA      US    EKS 4002
CHRISTOPHER PARKER D       (JKL     (M) WHATS SHAKIN'                  1973  MIDI               22003
BOBBY CHARLES        V    (JK       (N) GOLDEN BUTTER    (BEST OF)     1972  ELEKTRA      US    7E 2005
GEOFF MULDAUR        V G VIBES      (JK (N) GOLDEN BUTTER (BEST OF)    1972  ELEKTRA      UK    K 62011
AMOS GARRETT         G    (JK       (EP) WITH JOHN MAYALL             196    DECCA        UK    DFE 8673
MARK NAFTALIN        K    (BCDEm     (O) NORTH SOUTH                   1981  WB                 6995
MARIA MULDAUR        V    (JK  FRED BECKMEIER    B   (F   J D PARRAN   SAX  (J  BILLY RICH     B   (JK
HOWARD JOHNSON       HRNS (JK  SAM BURTIS      TROM (J   PETE ECKLUND  TPT  (J  AL KOOPER     ORG  (E
CLYDIE KING          V    (GH  VANETTA FIELDS   V  (GH   OMA DRAKE     V   (GH  MERRY CLAYTON  V   (GH
GARY BROCKS          TROM (J   JERRY RAGOVOY   PNO (F    STAN SHAFRAN  TPT  (J  CHUCK RAINEY   B   (L
TIM DRUMMOND         B    (L   JAMES JAMESON    B  (L    GORDON EDWARDS B   (L  LEVON HELM     D PERC(L
BERNARD PURDIE       D    (L   STEVEN KROON     D  (L    LLOYD MICHELS TPT  (L  IRVING MARKOWITZ TPT (L
AL DERISI            TPT  (L   SONNY RUSSO    TROM (L    HENRY GLOVER  K    (L  GARTH HUDSON   K   (L
RICHARD BELL         K    (L   FRED CARTER      G  (L    BEN KEITH     G    (L  ERIC GALE      G   (L
JOHN HOLBROOK        G    (L   NICK JAMESON     G  (L    FRANK WEST    SAX  (L  SELDON POWELL  SAX (L
BABE CLARKE          SAX  (L   MEL TAX        SAX (L    GAIL KANTOV   V    (L  ERN DICKENS    V   (L
ANN SUTTON           V    (L   EVANGELINE CARMICHAEL V(L LORNA WILLARD V    (L  JULIA TILLMAN  V   (L
ANDREA WILLIS        V    (L   JEROME RICHARDSON SAX (L  CLIFF SHANK   SAX  (L  WILBUR SCHWARTZ SAX (L
GENE CIPRIANO        SAX  (L
```

THE BUTTS BAND
B283

```
JOHN DENSMORE        D    (AB       (A) THE BUTTS BAND                1974  BLUE THUMB   UK    ILPS 9260
BOBBY KRIEGER        G    (AB       (A) THE BUTTS BAND                1975  BLUE THUMB   US          63
JESS RODEN           V G  (A        (B) HEAR & NOW                    1975  ABC          UK    ABCL 5117
PHIL CHEN            B G  (A        (B) HEAR & NOW                    1975  VOGUE        FR    10042
ROY DAVIES           K SYN(A        (B) HEAR & NOW                    1975  BLUE THUMB   US    BT  6018
ALLAN SHARP          CONGA (A
MICK WEAVER          K    (A   LARRY McDONALD      CONGA  (A   MICHAEL STULL    V G (B
MIKE BERKOWITZ       D    (B   KARL RUCKNER        B    (B     ALEX RICHMAN     V K (B
BOBBYE HALL          CONGAS(B
```

BUX
B283A

```
RALPH MORMAN         V    (A        (A) WE CAME TO PLAY              1976  CAPITOL      US    11459
PUNKY MEADOWS        G    (A
JAMES NEWLON         G V  (A   ROCKY ISAAC    D      (A   MICKEY JONES    B   (A
PAUL CHANSKY         PNO  (A
```

BUZZCOCKS
B284

```
HOWARD DEVOTO        V    (1        (1) SPIRAL SCRATCH      (EP)     1977  NEW HORMONES UK    ORG  1
PETE SHELLEY         G V  (AB1      (A) ANOTHER MUSIC IN A DIFFERENT KITCHEN 1977 UA    UK    UAG 30159
STEVE DIGGLE         B G  (AB       (B) LOVE BITES                   1978  UA           UK    UAG 30197
STEVE GARVEY         B    (AB       (B) LOVE BITES                   1978  SONGPRESSE   FR    062 61897
GARTH SMITH          B    (B        (C) DIFFERENT KINDS OF TENSION   1979  UA UK UAG30260 US A&M 009
JOHN MAHER           D    (AB1      (D) SINGLES GOING STEADY         1979  UA UK UAG30279 US A&M 001
                                    (2) ARE EVERYTHING +5 (EP)       1981  IRS                9701
```

BOBBY BYRD
B284B

```
BOBBY BYRD                (A        (A) I NEED HELP                  19    KING         US    1119
```

JOE BYRD & THE FIELD HIPPIES
B284C

```
JOE BYRD              K V SYN(A      (A) THE AMERICAN METAPHYSICAL CIRCUS 1969 CBS       US    7317
VICTORIA BOND         V    (A
SUSAN DE LANGE        V    (A   GREGG KOVER     D     (A   TOM SCOTT       WIND (A
ED SHEFTEL            TPT  (A   TED GREENE      G     (A   JOHN CLAUDER    D    (A
DANA CHALBERG         WIND (A   FRED SELDEN     WIND  (A   MEYER HIRSCH    WIND (A
DON KERIAN            TPT  (A   CHUCK BENNETT   TROM  (A   RAY CAPPOCCHI   HRNS (A
```

BYRDS
B285

```
ROGER McGUINN    V G BANJO (ALL     (A) EARLY FLIGHT  (JET SET)     19    CBS          ST    1014
GENE CLARK           G V  (ABCDOPQ  (A) EARLY FLIGHT  (JET SET)     19    TOGETHER     SST   1001
MIKE CLARKE          D    (BCDEFGOP (B) PREFLYTE                    1964  BUMBLE       US    GEXP 8001
CHRIS HILLMAN    B V MAND (BCDEFGHOPQ(B) PREFLYTE                   1972  CBS          US KC 32183
DAVID CROSBY         G V  (ABCDEOP  (B) PREFLYTE                    19    ARIOLA       HOLL  86468
KEVIN KELLEY         D    (HP       (C) MR TAMBOURINE MAN           1965  CBS          UK    62571
GRAM PARSONS         G V  (HPQ      (C) MR TAMBOURINE MAN           1965  CBS          US CS 9172
SNEAKY PETE KLEINOW STEEL (M        (C) MR TAMBOURINE MAN           19    EMBASSY            31057
DOUG DILLARD         G V  (         (C) MR TAMBOURINE MAN           19    EMBASSY            31503
CLARENCE WHITE       G V  (HJKLMNPR (D) TURN TURN TURN              1966  CBS          UK    62652
JOHN YORK            B    (JKPR     (D) TURN TURN TURN              1966  CBS          US CS 9254
SKIP BATTIN          B    (LMNRP    (D) TURN TURN TURN              19    EMBASSY            31526
GENE PARSONS         D    (JKLMNP   (D) TURN TURN TURN              1976  EMBASSY      UK    31257
JOHN GUERIN               (         (CD) MR TAMBOURINE/TURN TURN TURN 19  CBS                22018X2
EARL P BALL          PNO  (M        (E) FIFTH DIMENSION             1966  CBS          UK    62783
JIMMI SEITER         PERC (M        (E) FIFTH DIMENSION             1966  CBS                9349
PAUL POLENA     HRNS STRGS(M        (F) YOUNGER THAN YESTERDAY      1967  CBS          UK    62988
BYRON BERLINE        FDL  (M        (F) YOUNGER THAN YESTERDAY      1967  CBS          US CS 9442
LARRY KNECHTEL       K    (M        ( ) GREATEST HITS               1967  CBS          UK    63107
TERRY MELCHER        PNO  (M        ( ) GREATEST HITS               196   CBS          IMP   66298
                                    ( ) GREATEST HITS               19    CBS                9516
JON CORNEAL          D    (H        (G) NOTORIOUS BYRD BROTHERS     1968  CBS          UK    63169
LLOYD GREEN          STEEL (H       (G) NOTORIOUS BYRD BROTHERS     1968  CBS          US CS 9575
JAYDEE MANESS        STEEL (H       (H) SWEETHEART OF THE RODEO     1968  CBS          UK    63353
JOHN HARTFORD        BANJ G(H       (H) SWEETHEART OF THE RODEO     1968  CBS          US CS 9670
ROY M HUSKY          B    (H        (H) SWEETHEART OF THE RODEO     19    EMBASSY            EMB 31124
                                    (GH) SWEETHEART / NOTORIOUS BYRD BROS 1976 CBS           22040
                                    (J) DR BYRDS & MR HYDE          1969  CBS          UK    63545
                                    (J) DR BYRDS & MR HYDE          1969  CBS          US CS 9755
                                    (K) BALLAD OF EASY RIDER        1970  CBS          UK    63795
                                    (K) BALLAD OF EASY RIDER        1970  CBS          US CS 9942
                                    (L) UNTITLED          (DBL)     1970  CBS          UK    66253
                                    (L) UNTITLED          (DBL)     1970  CBS          US G  30127
```

(CONTINUED)

BYRDS

			(CONTINUED)				B285
(M)	BYRDMANIAX		1971	CBS	UK		64389
(M)	BYRDMANIAX		1971	CBS	US	KC	30640
(N)	FARTHER ALONG		1972	CBS	UK	KC	64676
(N)	FARTHER ALONG		1972	CBS LE10215	US	KC	31050
( )	GREATEST HITS VOL 2		1972	CBS	UK		64650
( )	GREATEST HITS VOL 2		1972	CBS	US	PC	31795
(O)	THE BYRDS		1973	ASYLUM	UK	SYLA	8754
(O)	THE BYRDS		1973	ASYLUM	US	SD	5058
(O)	THE BYRDS		19	WEA		K	53006
( )	HISTORY OF THE BYRDS		1973	CBS	UK		68242
( )	L A FULL CIRCLE		19	WEA	HOLL		23000
( )	L A FULL CIRCLE		19	MERCURY	US	SRM	11074
( )	GREATEST HITS VOL 3		19	CBS	UK		64966
( )	MR TAMBOURINE MAN(COMP DBL)		19	CBS	UK		66298
( )	MR TAMBOURINE MAN/TURN TURN		1975	CBS			33645
( )	SINGLES 1965 67		1980	CBS			31851
(P)	PLAY DYLAN		1980	CBS US 36293	UK		31795
(Q)	DOIN ALL RIGHT		1978	EXCITABLE	US		4506
(R)	EASY RIDERS (69/70)		1981	PENGUIN	US	EGG	FIVE

DAVID BYRON

DAVID BYRON	V	(AB	(A)	TAKE NO PRISONERS		1975 BRONZE UK ILPS9342 US MERCURY1074
LOU STONEBRIDGE	K	(A	(B)	BABY FACED KILLER		1978 ARISTA UK SPARTA 1077
DENNY BALL	B	(A	(C)	THIS DAY & AGE		1980 ARISTA US 4258
LEE KERSLAKE	D PERC	(A				
STUART ELLIOTT	D	(B	BARRY DE SOUZA	D	(B	THOMMY PRICE	D V	(C
LESTER FRY	PERC	(B	PETE THOMPSON	PERC	(A	ALAN JONES	B	(B
DANIEL BOONE	G K	(B	MICK BOX	G	(A	JOEY VASTA	B V	(C
MATT LAMBERT	G V	(C	ROBERT SARZO	G	(A	TOM MORRONGEILLO	G	(A
MICHAEL KENNY	V	(A	BERNARD KENNY	G	(A			

BYRON BAND

DAVID BYRON	V	(A	(A)	ON THE ROCKS			
ROBIN GEORGE	G	(A				1982 CREOLE UK CRX2	
MEL COLLINS	SAX	(A					
JOHN SHEARER	D	(A	BOB JACKSON	K	(A	ROGER FLAVELLE	B	(A

BYSTANDERS

VIC OAKLEY	V	(1	(1)	1968			
RAY WILLIAMS	B	(1					
JEFF JONES	D	(1	CLIVE JOHN	K V	(1	MICKEY JONES	G V	(1

BYZANTIUM

NICO RAMSDEN	G V	(A	(A)	BYZANTIUM		1972 A&M UK AMLS68104 US WB 2659
CHAS JANKEL	G V	(AB	(B)	SEASONS CHANGING		1972 A&M UK AMLH68163
ROBIN LAMBLE	B V G	(AB				
STEVE CORDUNER	D	(AB	MICK BARAKAN	G V	(B	FRANK RICOTTI	PERC	(B
DAVID HENTSCHEL	SYN	(B	JAMIE RUBINSTEIN	G V	(B	B J COLE	STEEL	(B
ROBIN SYLVESTER	SYN	(B					

ROY C

ROY C	V	(AB	(A)	SEX & SOUL		1975	MERCURY	9100 017
			(B)	MORE SAX & SOUL		19	MERCURY	6338 849

C C P P

A CECCARELLI	D	(	(A)	C.C.P.P.		19	FLAMOPHONE	2933 104
M CHANTEREAU	PNO	(						
C PADOVAN	B	(	SLIM PEZIN	G	(			

C C S

ALEXIS KORNER	G V	(ALL	(A)	C C S		1970	RAK UK SRKA 6751 US Z30559
LES CONDON	TPT	(DA	(A)	C C S		19	CBS GER 91783
PETER THORUP	V	(AD	(B)	C C S 2		1972	RAK UK SRAK503 US 31569
JOHN CAMERON	PNO	(A	(B)	C C S 2		1972	RAK GER 93232
GREG BOWEN	TPT	(AD	(C)	THE BEST BAND IN THE LAND		1973	RAK UK SRAK 504
TONY FISHER	TPT	(AD	(C)	THE BEST BAND IN THE LAND		1973	RAK GER 94611
HAROLD BECKETT	TPT	(AD	(D)	THE BEST OF C C S		1977	RAK UK SRAK 527
BILL LE SAGE	VIBES	(D	(D)	THE BEST OF C C S		1977	RAK GER 99020
HENRY LOWTHER	TPT	(AD					
KENNY WHEELER	TPT	(AD	JOHN MARSHALL	TROM	(AD	BRIAN PERRIN	TROM	(DA
DON LUSHER	TROM	(DA	BILL GELDARD	TROM	(DA	NEIL SANDERS	HRNS	(DA
HAROLD McNAIR	WIND	(AD	TONY COE	WIND	(AD	PETE KING	WIND	(AD
DANNY MOSS	WIND	(AD	BOB EFFORD	WIND	(AD	RON MOSS	WIND	(AD
ALAN PARKER	G	(DA	HERBIE FLOWERS	B	(DA	SPIKE HEATLEY	B	(DA
BARRY MORGAN	D	(DA	TONY CARR	D	(DA	JIM LAWLESS	PERC	(DA

C M U

RICHARD JOSEPH	G V	(AB	(A)	OPEN SPACES		1971	TRANSATLANTIC UK TRA 237
LARRAINE ODELL	G	(AB	(B)	SPACE CABARET		1972	TRANSATLANTIC UK TRA 259
IAN HAMLETT	G	(A					
LEARY HASSON	K	(AB	ROGER ODELL	D	(AB	ED LEE	G B	(A
JAMES GORDON	G K V	(A	STEVE COOK	B	(B			

C O B (Clives Own Band)

CLIVE PALMER	BANJO V G	(AB	(A)	THE SPIRIT OF LOVE		1971	CBS	69010
JOHN BIDWELL	BANJO K V	(AB	(B)	MOYSHE McSTIFF		1972	POLYDOR	2383 161
MICK BENNETT	PERC V K	(AB						
RALPH McTELL	G D	(A	STEVE BONNETT	B	(A	URSULA SMITH	CELLO	(A
GENEVIEVE BAKER		(B	DEMELZA VAL BAKER		(B			

CABOOSE

GARY JOHNS	V	(A	(A)	CABOOSE		19	ENTERPRISE US ENS 1015
WALTER RAMSEY	K	(A					
TOMMY CATHEY	B V	(A	JACKIE COOK	G	(A	JOEL WILLIAMS	PERC	(A
PAT KARR	V	(A					

C4B

CABARET VOLTAIRE

C4B

CHRISTOPHER R WATSON ELECT(AB	(A) MIX UP	1979	ROUGH TRADE	UK	ROUGH 4
HAYDN BOYES-WESTON D (A	(B) LIVE AT YMCA	1980	ROUGH TRADE	UK	ROUGH 7
RICHARD KIRK G WIND(AB	(C)VOICE OF AMERICA	1980	ROUGH TRADE	UK	ROUGH 11
STEPHEN MALLINDER B PERC V(AB	(D) RED MECCA	19	ROUGH TRADE	UK	ROUGH 27
MICK ALLDAY D (D	(D) RED MECCA	19	ROUGH TRADE	GER	6435 117
	( ) 3 CREPUSCULE TRACKS	1981	BRUITS	BELG	018

C5

CACTUS

C5

RUSTY DAY	V	(ABC	(A) CACTUS	1970	ATLANTIC	UK	2400 020
JIM McCARTY	G	(ABC	(A) CACTUS	1970	ATCO	US	SD 33340
TIM BOGERT	B	(ABCD	(B) ONE WAY OR ANOTHER	1971	ATLANTIC	UK	2460 114
CARMINE APPICE	D	(ABCD	(B) ONE WAY OR ANOTHER	1971	ATCO	US	33356
PETER FRENCH	V	(D	(B) ONE WAY OR ANOTHER	1972	ATLANTIC	UK	K 40216
DUANE HITCHINGS	K	(D	(C) RESTRICTIONS	1972	ATLANTIC	UK	K40307
WERNER FRITZSCHINGS	G	(D	(C) RESTRICTIONS	1971	ATCO	US	SD 33377
RON LEEJACK	G	(C	(D) 'OT & SWEATY	1972	ATLANTIC	UK	K 50013
ALBHY GALUTEN	PNO	(C	(D) 'OT & SWEATY	1972	ATCO	US	SD 7011
DUANE HITCHINGS	K	(C					

C5A

CADETS

C5A

(A) ROCKIN'N' REELIN'	19	CROWN	US	5015
(B) THE CADETS	19	CROWN	US	5370

C6

VINCE CADILLAC

C6

VINCE CADILLAC	G V	(A	(A) MODERN BOY	1978	SATRIL	UI	SATL 4010
TRIGGER LYONS	B	(A					
TIM FRANKS	D	(A					
TONY TODD	G	(A	DAVE EPPEL G (A	LARRY BARTLETT K (A
PAUL JENKINS	G	(A	MIKE SMITH V (A	JOHN PORTER V (A
PETE WINGFIELD	K V	(A	PAUL WESTWOOD B (A	RICK HITCHCOCK G (A
PETER LEMER	PNO	(A	BARRY MORGAN D (A	BARRY DE SOUZA D (A

C6A

CADILLACS

C6A

(A) FABULOUS CADILLACS	19	JUBILEE	US	1045
( ) CRAZY CADILLACS	19	JUBILEE	US	1089
( ) TWISTING WITH	196	JUBILEE	US	5009

C6B

BRIAN CADD

C6B

BRIAN CADD	K V SYN(ALL	(A) BRIAN CADD	1973 CHELSEA US 10163 AUST BOOTLEG 023
GEOFF FOX	D	(C	(B) ?	1973
GUS FENWICK	B	(C	(C) MOONSHINE	1974 CHELSEA US 502 AUST BOOTLEG 044
TONY NAYLOR	G	(C	(D) ?	1975
CHARLIE GOULD	G	(C	(E) WHITE ON WHITE	1975 CAPITOL US 11573
ALAN HAWKIN	G BAN (C	(F) YESTERDAYDREAMS	1978 CAPITOL US 11681
RUSS HAWKING	G	(C					

MIKE BURKE	STEEL (C	JIM CONWAY	HCA (C	JEFF HALES	PERC (C	MICK CONWAY	JUG (C
FRED OLBREI	FDL (C	PETER BEST	V SYN (C	STEVE COONEY	MAND (C	IVAN HUTCHISON PNO (C
PHINEAS BROWNE	STR (C	LYNN CASEY	V (C	BILLY PAYNE	K SYN (C	WILLIAM SMITH K SYN (E
NIGEL OLSSON	D (E	GARY COLEMAN	PERC(E	DEE MURRAY	B (E	BEN BENAY G BANJ (E
STEVE CROPPER	G (E	RITCHIE ZITE	G (EF	SNEAKY PETE	STEEL (E	REGGIE McBRIDE B (F
MIKE PORCARO	B (F	DAVID WINTOUR	B (F	RICHIE HAYWARD	D (F	DOUG LAVERY D (F
JEFF PORCARO	D (F	ALVIN TAYLOR	D (F	STEVE BECKMEIER	G (F	JOHN BELAND G (F
RICHARD BENNETT	G (F	DAVID KALISH	G (F	STEVE LUKATHER	G (F	MICHAEL STEWART G (F
JESSE ED DAVIS	G (F	J D MANESS	STEEL(F	DAVEY JOHNSON	MAND (F	MIKE FINNIGAN K (F
MARK T JORDAN	K (F	LARRY KNECHTEL	K (F	MIKE MORAN	K (F	JAY GRAYDON SYN (F
OLIVER C BROWN	PERC (F						

C7

CADO BELLE

C7

COLIN TULLY	SAX (BA	(A) CADO BELLE	1976	ANCHOR	UK/US	ANCL 2015
DAVY ROY	D	(AB	(B) CADO BELLE (EP)	1977	ANCHOR	UK	AN 1
STUART MACKILLOP	K	(AB					
GAVIN HODGSON	B	(AB	MAGGIE REILLY V (AB	ALAN DARBY G (AB
PADDY McHUGH	V	(AB	FRANK COLLINS V (A		

C8

CAFE JACQUES

C8

CHRISTOPHER THOMPSON G V (AB	(A) ROUND THE BACK	1977	EPIC UK 82315 US 35294
MICHAEL OGLETREE D G (AB	(B) CAFE JACQUES INTERNATIONAL	1978	EPIC UK 83042 US 35697
COLIN NELSON B (AB							
PETER VEITCH K (AB	GEOFFREY RICHARDSON G FLT(AB JOHN PERRY B (AB PHIL COLLINS PERC (AB

C9

CAFE SOCIETY

C9

RAPHAEL DOYLE	G V	(A	(A) CAFE SOCIETY	1975	KONK	KONK 102
HEREWARD KAYE	V PNO G	(A					
TOM ROBINSON	V B G PNO(A	JOHN GOSLING K (A MICK AVORY D (A JOHN BEECHAM HRNS (A
JIM FRANKS	D	(A	ROBIN WILLIAMS FDL (A NICK SOUTH B (A PHIL PALMER G (A
PAT DONALDSON	B	(A	LOUIS STEWART G (A ROY DYKE D (A

C9A

JONATHAN CAIN BAND

C9A

JONATHAN CAIN	K V	(A	(A) WINDY CITY BREAKDOWN	1977	BEARSVILLE	US	6969
JIMMY ARNOLD	G V	(A					
TOMMY CAIN	D	(A	GARY RICHWINE B V (A RALPH MACDONALD PERC (A BOBBYE HALL PERC (A

C10

CAJUN MOON

C10

ALLAN TAYLOR	G V	(A	(A) CAJUN MOON	1976	CHRYSALIS	UK	CHR 1116
JOHN GILLASPIE	K WIND(AB	(B) LATER LINE UP					
BRIAN GOLBEY	FDL G (AB						
DIK CADBURY	G V	(B					

C11

CAKE

C11

BARBARA MORILLO	V	(AB	(A) CAKE	1967	DECCA	DL 74927
JANETTE JACOBS	V	(AB	(A) CAKE	1968	MCA	MUPS 303
ELEANOR BAROOSHIAN	V	(AB	(B) A SLICE OF CAKE	1968	DECCA	DL 75039
MIKE MELVOIN	ORG	(	(B) A SLICE OF CAKE	1969	MCA	MUPS 390
DAVID COHEN	G	(					
MIKE DEASY	G	(	CAROL KAYE B (LESLIE MILTON D (

C11A

CALDARA

C11A

JOHN ATKINS	SYN K (A	(A) A MOOG MASS	1972	KAMA SUTRA	2319 020
TOBY SAKS	CELLO (A					

JORGE CALDERON

JORGE CALDERON	V G	(A	(A) CITY MUSIC			1975	WB	US BS 2904
WADDY WACHTEL	V G K	(A						
HOPPY HODGES	D	(A	WILLIE WEEKS	B	(A	MAYUTO	PERC (A	
PAT RIZZO	HRNS	(A	STEVE MADAIO	HRNS	(A	WILLIAM SMITH	V K (A	
TESSE COEN	PERC V	(A	YVONNE RANKIN	V	(A	ANDY NEWMARK	D (A	
JAMES GADSON	D	(A	VICTOR FELDMAN	PERC	(A	PAUL PAYDOS	PERC (A	
RUSS TITELMAN	PERC	(A	VALERIE CARTER	V	(A	PAUL STALLWORTH	V (A	
BOBBY LYLE	K	(A	JIM KELTNER	D	(A	NICK DE CARO	SYN (A	
BOBBYE HALL	PERC	(A						

BOBBY CALDWELL

BOBBY CALDWELL	B G K SYN V	(AB	(A) BOBBY CALDWELL			1978	CLOUDS	8804
BRUCE EMODAMENT	K	(B	(A) BOBBY CALDWELL			1978	TKR (CBS)	83362
JOHN PAULUS	B	(B	(B) CAT IN THE HAT			1980	TK UK 83386 US CLOUDS	8810
ED GREENE	D	(AB						
HAROLD SEAY	D	(AB	JOE GALDO	D	(AB	BENNY LATIMORE	K (A	
STEVE MEALY	G	(A	ALFONS KETTNER	G	(A	GEORGE PERRY	B (AB	
RICHIE VELASQUEZ	B	(A	MIKE LEWIS	SAX	(B	CHRIS COLELESSOR	WIND (B	
JEFF KIEVET	HRNS	(B	JERRY PEEL	HRN	(B	JAMES MARSHALL	TROM (B	
ANDY NEWMARK	D	(B	MARK COLBY	SAX	(B	HOLLIS BURRIDGE	HRNS (B	
GARY LINDSAY	CLAR	(B						

JOHN CALE

JOHN CALE	VLA G K B V	(ALL	(A) VINTAGE VIOLENCE			1970	CBS	64256
WITH			(A) VINTAGE VIOLENCE			1970	CBS	US CS 1037
TERRY RILEY	SAX K	(B	(B) CHURCH OF ANTHRAX			1971	CBS	UK 64259
PHIL MANZANERA	G	(EF	(B) CHURCH OF ANTHRAX			1971	CBS	US CS 30131
BRIAN ENO	K	(EFGJ	(C) ACADEMY OF PERIL			1972	REPRISE	UK K 44212
NICO	V	(J	(B) ACADEMY OF PERIL			1972	REPRISE	US MS 2079
CHRIS SPEDDING	G	(FG	(D) PARIS 1919			1973	REPRISE	UK K 44239
TIM DONALD	D	(FG	(D) PARIS 1919			1973	REPISE	US MS 2131
PAT DONALDSON	B	(FG	(E) FEAR			1974	ISLAND	UK/US ILPS9301
CHRIS THOMAS	K	(F	(F) SLOW DAZZLE			1975	ISLAND	UK/US ILPS9317
GERRY CONWAY	D	(F	(G) HELEN OF TROY			1975	ISLAND	UK/US ILPS9350
GEOFF MULDAUR	V	(F	(G) HELEN OF TROY			1975	PHONOGRAM	EUR 9123 002
PHIL COLLINS	D	(G	(H) GUTS			1977	PHONOGRAM	EUR 9101 672
OLLIE HALSALL	G	(J	(H) GUTS			1977	ISLAND	UK/US ILPS9459
JOHN RABBIT BUNDRICK	K	(J	(J) JUNE 1 1974 (NICO ENO KEVIN AYERS)			1974	ISLAND	UK/US ILPS9291
ADAM MILLER	V	(BC	(K) SABOTAGE LIVE			1979	SPY	US 004
ARCHIE LEGGET	B	(EJ	(L) HORI SOIT			1981	A&M	UK 64849
KEVIN AYERS	B	(J	(EP) ANIMAL JUSTICE			1977	ILLEGAL	UK IL003
EDDIE SPARROW	D	(J						
ROBERT WYATT	PERC	(J	LIZA STRIKE	V	(EJ	IRENE CHANTER	V (EJ	DOREEN CHANTER V (EJ
MIKE OLDFIELD	G	(J	RICHARD THOMPSON	G	(E	BRIAN TURRINGTON	B (E	BOBBY COLOMBY D (B
BRYN HAWORTH	B	(E	JUDY NYLON	V	(E	MICHAEL DESMARAIS	D (E	MARK AARON G (K
DOUG BRAWNE	D	(K	GEORGE SCOTT	B	(K	HARVEY BROOKS	B (A	SANDY KONIKOFF D (A
BOBBY GREGG	D	(B	RICHIE HAYWARD	D	(D	LOWELL GEORGE	G (D	UCLA ORCH (D
R P O		(C	FRED SMITH	D	(EH	TREVOR BURTON	B (H	RAYMOND DUFFY D (H
KEITH SMART	PERC	(J	ANDY MACKAY	SAX	(FH	JOHN WOOD	SYN (FH	TONY CARR PERC(H
BARRY STJOHN	V	(H	JOE BIDWELL	K V	(K	DEERFRANCE	PERC V(K	JOHN McCLURE PROD(B
MEREN STEIN	PROD	(H	RON WOOD	G	(C	DEL NEWMAN	D (C	STURGIS NIKICLES G V (L
JIM GORDON	K V	(L	PETER MUNY	B V	(L	ROBERT MEDICI	D V (L	
JOHN GATCHELL	TPT	(L	BOMBERETTES(MODETTES) V		(L	CHRIS THOMAS	PROD (D	

J J CALE

J J CALE	PNO B D G V	(ALL	(A) NATURALLY		1971	A&M	UK AMLS68105
WITH			(A) NATURALLY		1973	SHELTER	UK ISA 5003
KARL HIMMEL	D	(ACDEFG	(A) NATURALLY		1971	SHELTER	US 8908
CHUCK BROWNING	G D	(AD	(A) NATURALLY		1972	CARRERE	FR 67614
TIM DRUMMOND	D	(AC	(A) NATURALLY		1972	SHELTER US 2122	52009
CARL RADLE	B	(AE	(B) REALLY		1972	A&M	UK AMLS68157
NORBERT PUTNAM	B	(AB	(B) REALLY		1972	SHELTER	UK ISA 5002
BOB WILSON	PNO	(A	(B) REALLY		1972	SHELTER US 8912	52015
DAVID BRIGGS	K	(ABEFG	(B) REALLY		1972	CARRERE	FR 67613
JERRY WHITEHURST	K	(AC	(C) OKIE		1972	A&M	UK AMLS68261
WELDON MYRICK	STEEL	(AC	(C) OKIE		1974	SHELTER	UK ISA 5004
BUDDY SPICHER	FDL	(A	(C) OKIE		1974	SHELTER US 2107	
SHORTY LAVENDER	FDL	(A	(C) OKIE		197	CARRERE	FR 67608
WALTER HAYNES	DOBRO	(A	(D) TROUBADOUR		1976	SHELTER	UK ISA 5011
MAC GAYDEN	G	(ABC	(D) TROUBADOUR		1976	CARRERE	FR 67618
ED COLIS	HCA	(A	(D) TROUBADOUR		1976	SHELTER	US 52002
DIANE DAVIDSON	V	(A	(E) No 5		1979	SHELTER	UK ISA 5018
ROGER HAWKINS	D	(B	(E) No 5		1979	MCA	US 3163
DAVID HOOD	B	(B	(F) SHADES		1980	SHELTER	UK ISA 5021
BOBBY MOORE	B	(G	(F) SHADES		1980	MCA	US 5158
TONY MIGLIORI	PNO	(G	(G) GRASSHOPPER		1982	MERCURY	US SRMI 4038
BILL KENNER	MAND	(E					

PAUL DAVIS	G	(C	BARRY BECKETT	K	(B	JIMMY JOHNSON	G (B	JOAN SWEENEY	K (B
DON SHEFFIELD	TPT	(BE	BOB PHILLIPS	TPT	(B	BILL HUMBLE	TROM (B	NORMAN RAY	SAX (B
FARRELL MORRIS	D VIBES	(BCDEG	BOBBY WOODS	K	(BD	KENNY BUTTREY	D (BDEFG	GEORGE SOULE	D (B
BOB RAY	B	(B	ROBERT TARRANT	PERC	(B	JIMMY CAPPS	G (B	KOSSIE GARDNER	ORG (B
JOE ZINKAN	B	(B	JOSH GRAVES	DOBRO	(B	VASSAR CLEMENTS	FDL (B	CHARLIE McCOY	HCA (B
JIMMY KARSTEIN	D	(BDEFG	GARY GILMORE	B	(B	BILL BOATMAN	G (BDEFG	CHARLES DUNGEY	B (DG
REG YOUNG	G	(CDFG	LLOYD GREEN	STEEL	(D	TOMMY COGBILL	B (CDFG	HAROLD BRADLEY	G (CDG
JOE OSBORN	B	(D	AUDIE ASHWORTH	PERC	(D	DON TWEEDY	K (D	BUDDY HARMON	D (DGE
BUDDY EMMONS	STEEL	(D	BILL RAFFENSPEGER	B	(D	J J ALLISON	PERC (D	GORDON PAYNE	G (C
GEORGE TIDWELL	TPT	(CDE	DENNIS GOODE	TROM(CDE		BILLY PUETT	SAX (CD	KENNY MALONE	D (CD
GARY PAXTON	V	(D	BILL PURSELL	K	(C	MIKE LEECH	B (C	RED SPIVEY	K (C
BEEGIE CRUZER	K	(C	JOEL GREEN	B	(C	JERRY SMITH	K (C	GRADY MARTIN	G (C
PIG ROBBINS	K	(E	TERRY PERKINS	D	(C	BILLY COX	B (E	CHRISTINE LAKELAND	K V(EFG
SHERRY PORTER	V	(E	STRING SECTION		(E	TERRY WILLIAMS	HRNS (E	NICK RATHER	B (EFG
LARRY BELL	K	(EF	CAROL KAYE	B	(F	BOBBY EMMONS	K (FG	MICHAEL RHODES	B (F
EMORY GORDY	B	(F	JAMES BURTON	G	(F	BILL PAYNE	PNO (F	LEON RUSSELL	PNO (F
RUSS KUNKEL	D	(F	TOMMY TEDESCO	G	(F	JOHNNY CHRISTOPHER	G (F	HAYWARD BISHOP	D (F
JIM KELTNER	D	(F	GLEN D HARDIN	K	(F	HAL BLAINE	D (F	GARY ALLEN	D (FG
GORDON SHRYCOCK	G	(F	DENNIS SOLEE	SAX	(FG	STEVE GIBSON	G (G	RAY EDENTON	G (G
MIKE LAWLER	SYN	(G	TERRY McMILLIAN	HCA	(G	ROBERT GREENIDGE	PERC (G	MARILYN DAVIS	V (G

CALICO

```
    JERRY OATES          G V   (AB    (A) CALICO                          1975   UA              US   UALA  454
    KEITH IMPELLITIER    G V   (AB    (B) CALICO 2                        1976   UA              US   UALA  659
    BULL MINOR           D V   (B
    TOM MORREL           STEEL  (B     JOHN McCLURE         K      (B      MIKE REDDEN          D     (B
    DAVE KIRBY           G     (B      KENNY MALONE         D      (A      BILL ROBERTSON       D     (B
    JOE COPELAND         G     (A      JOE ALLEN            B      (A      BUDDY SPICHER        FDL   (B
    LARRY HEATH          B FDL V(A     HOWARD BARNARD       STEEL B(A      JIMMY COLVARD        G     (A
    LLOYD GREEN          STEEL G(A     REGGIE YOUNG         G      (A      BOBBY THOMPSON       G     (A
    CHUCK COCHRAN        K     (A      BOBBY WOOD           K      (A
```

C15A   RANDY   C15A

```
    RANDY CALIFORNIA     G V   (AB    (A) KAPTAIN KOPTER & THE TWIRLY BIRDS 1972   EPIC  US 31755 UK   EPC 65381
    CHARLY BUNDY         B     (A     (A) KAPTAIN KOPTER & THE TWIRLY BIRDS 1980   CBS            UK RI     31829
    TIM McGOVERN         D     (A     (B) EURO AMERICAN                    1982   LINE           GER     LLP5149
    CASS(ED CASSIDY)STRANGE  D(AB
    NOEL(CLIT McTORIUS)REDDING B(A    LARRY KNIGHT         B      (AB      MITCH(HENRY MANCHOVITZ)MITCHELL D(A
    CURLEY SMITH         D     (B      BRUCE GARY           D      (B      MARK ANDES           B     (B
    JOHN LOCKE           K     (B      GEORGE VALUCK        K V    (B      JAY FERGUSON         V     (B
    TOM HALL             G     (B      MATT ANDES           G      (B
```

C15B   CALIFORNIA EARTHQUAKE   C15B

```
    BRIAN GRIFFIN        ORG   (A     (A) CALIFORNIA EARTHQUAKE            1971   UA              US   UAS  6801
    ROY SMITH            V     (A
    JIM GORDON           D     (A      JOHN GUERIN                 (A      DENNIS POTTER              (A
    BILL CONNORS               (A      MIKE BARROWMAN       HRNS   (A      JOEL PORTER          HRNS  (A
    MAYO TIANA           HRNS  (A      JON CLARKE           HRNS   (A      DON ROBERTS          HRNS  (A
```

C16   MISSISSIPPI JOE CALLICOTT

```
    MISSISSIPPI JOE CALLICOTT  (       ( ) PRESENTING THE COUNTRY BLUES   1972   BLUE HORIZON US 4606 UK863227
```

C17   TERRY CALLIER   C17

```
    TERRY CALLIER             (ALL    (A) OCCASIONAL RAIN                 1972   CADET           US       50007
    MINNIE RIPERTON      V    (D      (B) WHAT COLOUR IS LOVE             1974   CADET           US       50019
    SIDNEY BARNES        V    (D      (C) I JUST CANT HELP MYSELF         1975   CADET           US       50041
    JYNEAN BELL          V    (D      (D) FIRE ON ICE                     1978   ELEKTRA US 6E143      UK K52096
    ELLIE WILLIS         V    (D      (D) TURN ON YOUR LOVE               1979   ELEKTRA US  189       UK K52140
    CYNTHIA WHITE        V    (D
    PHIL UPCHURCH        G    (D      W ROSS TRAUT         G      (D      DANNY LEAKE          G     (D
    CHARLES FEARING      G    (D      LARRY WADE           G      (D      EDDIE HARRIS         SAX   (D
    FRED JACKSON         SAX  (D      CHARLES OWEN         SAX    (D      CORINNE ALBRIGHT     SAX   (D
    GARNETT BROWN        TROM (D      GEORGE BOHANON       TROM   (D      STEVE MADAIO         TPT   (E
    LARRY WADE           G    (E      ROBERT WHITE         G      (E      JIMMY CLEVELAND      TROM  (D
    PAUL SERRANO         TPT  (D      KENNETH MASON        TPT    (D      EUGENE YOUNG         TPT   (D
    REGINALD BURKE       K    (DE     MICHAEL BODDICKER    SYN    (D      SCOTT EDWARDS        B     (D
    PAUL N HUMPHREY      D    (E      JAMES GADSON         D      (DE     FRED WALKER          PERC  (E
    MORRIS JENNINGS      PERC (E      SONNY BURKE          K      (E      EARL VAN DYKE        K     (E
    KINI BURKE           B    (E      JAMES JAMERSON       B      (E      WAH WAH WATSON       G     (E
    DAVID T WALKER       G    (E      OLIVER BROWN         PERC   (E      FRED WESLEY          TROM  (E
    ERNIE WATTS          SAX  (E      GAIL LEVANT          HARP   (E      STRINGS                    (E
```

C18   ROBERT CALVERT   C18

```
    ROBERT CALVERT PERC V TPT (ABC    (A) CAPTAIN LOCKHEED & THE STARFIGHTERS 74  UA  US 1011  UK   UAG 29507
    PAUL RUDOLPH         B G   (AB    (B) LUCKY LEIF & THE LONGSHIPS      1975   UA              UK   UAG 29852
    SIMON KING           D     (A     (C) HYPE(SONGS OF TOM MAHLER)       198    ASIDE           UK   IF 0311
    NIK TURNER           SAX   (AC
    LEMMY                G B   (A      ANDY ROBERTS         G      (B      DEL DETTMAR          SYN   (A
    DAVE BROCK           G     (A      TWINK                D      (A      ARTHUR BROWN         V     (A
    ADRIAN WAGNER        K     (A      VIV STANSHALL        V      (A      JIM CAPALDI          V     (A
    TOM MITTELDORF       V     (A      RICHARD EALING       V      (A      SIMON HOUSE          VLN   (BC
    MIKE NICHOLS         D PERC (      (B  MICHAEL MOORCOCK BANJO(AC       SAL MAIDA            B     (B
    BRIAN TURRINGTON     PNO   (
```

C19   CAMEL   C19

```
    PETER BARDENS        K    (ABCDEFG (A) CAMEL                          1973   MCA MUPS473 UK MAPS 6477
    ANDY LATIMER  V G FLT (ABCDEFGHJ  (A) CAMEL                          1980   MCA             NL 201 350
    DOUG FERGUSON        B    (ABCDF   (A) CAMEL                          1974   MCA MCF2665 GER  900 095
    ANDY WARD            D PERC(ABCDEFGHJ (B) MIRAGE                      1974   DERAM           UK   SML  1107
    RICHARD SINCLAIR     B V  (EFG     (B) MIRAGE                         1974   DECCA              278135
    COLIN BASS           B V  (HJ      (B) MIRAGE                         1974   JANUS US 7009
    MEL COLLINS          SAX  (FGHJ    (C) SNOW GOOSE                     1975   DERAM           UK   SKLR 5207
    DUNCAN MACKAY        K    (J       (C) SNOW GOOSE                     1975   DECCA              278136
    JAN SCHELHAAS        PNO  (JH      (C) SNOW GOOSE                     1975   JANUS US 7016 NOVA GER 6 22250
    CHRIS GREEN          CELLO (J      (D) MOONMADNESS                    1976   DERAM           UK   TXSR  115
    GASPAR LAWAL         PERC (J       (D) MOONMADNESS                    1976   DECCA 278115 NOVA GER 6 22500
    HERBIE FLOWERS       TUBA (J       (D) MOONMADNESS                    1976   JANUS US 7024 JAP UA     1035
    KIT WATKINS          K FLT (H      (E) RAINDANCE                      1977   GAMA  UK TXSR 124
    PHIL COLLINS         PERC (H       (E) RAINDANCE                      1977   DECCA              260015
    RUPERT HINE          V    (H       (F) A LIVE RECORD(DBL)             1978   DECCA UK DBCR7/8 NOVA GER28453
                                       (G) BREATHLESS                     1978   DECCA           UK   TXSR  132
    DAVID SINCLAIR       K    (F       (G) BREATHLESS                     1978   ARISTA          US        4206
                                       (G) BREATHLESS                     1978   NOVA            GER      23570
                                       (H) I CAN SEE YOUR HOUSE FROM HERE 1979   DECCA           UK   TXSR  137
                                       (H) I CAN SEE YOUR HOUSE FROM HERE 1979   ARISTA          US        4254
                                       (H) I CAN SEE YOUR HOUSE FROM HERE 1979   GAMA            GER      24132
                                       (J) NUDE                           1981   DECCA           UK   SKL  5323
```

C20   CAMEO   C20

```
    LARRY BLACKMON       D    (BCDEF   (A) CARDIAC ARREST                 1977   CASABLANCA UK CAL  2015
    TOM CAMPBELL         K    (F       (A) CARDIAC ARREST                 1977   CHOCOLATE US        2003
    GREGORY JOHNSON      K V  (BCDEF   (B) WE ALL KNOW WHO WE ARE         1978   CASABLANCA      CAL  2026
    STEPHEN MOORE        V    (F       (B) WE ALL KNOW WHO WE ARE         1978   CHOCOLATE US        2004
    TOMI JENKINS         V    (BCDEF   (C) UGLY EGO                       1978   CASABLANCA      CAL  2038
    NATHAN LEFTENANT     TPT  (BCDEF   (D) SECRET OMEN                    1979   CASABLANCA      CAL  2058
    JERYL BRIGHT         V TROM(F      (D) SECRET OMEN                    1979   CHOCOLATE US        2008
    CHARLES SAMSON       G    (B       (E) CAMEOSIS                       1979   CHOCOLATE US        2011
    ARNETT LEFTENANT     SAX  (BCDEF   (F) FEEL ME                        1980   CASABLANCA      CAL  2016
    ERIC DURHAM          G    (BC      (F) FEEL ME                        1980   CHOCOLATE US        2016
    WAYNE COOPER         V    (BC      AARON MILLS          G V    (F
    GARY DOW             B    (BC      ANTHONY COCKETT             (C      ANTHONY LOCKETT      G V   (F
    JOSE ROSSY           PERC (F       ARTHUR YOUNG         TPT    (F      RANDY STERN          K     (F
```

JOHN CAMERON

```
  JOHN CAMERON       PNO  (AB    (A) COVER LOVER                  1967  COLUMBIA      UK   SCX  6116
  DANNY THOMPSON     B    (B     (B) OFF CENTRE                   1969  DERAM         UK   SML  1044
  TONY CARR          D    (B
  HAROLD McNAIR      SAX  (B
```
JEFF CAMPBELL

```
  JEFF CAMPBELL      V G  (A    (A) LIVE ON THE WIRE              1979  ONEINE
  DAVID JAUREQUI     G    (A
  DAVID KOPPENHAUER  G    (A    BILLY LISKA        B      (A     KEVIN REDDING    D    (A
  TONY TANNER        PERC (A    DOUG FREEMAN       G      (A     CHARLIE          G    (A
  ROB LIEBERMAN      G    (A    RICK STURBINS      PNO    (A     SUE RUEDA        V    (A
```
DICK CAMPBELL

```
  DICK CAMPBELL      G V  (A    (A) SINGS WHERE ITS AT           1965  MERCURY       SR 61060
  MICHAEL BLOOMFIELD G    (A
  JIMMY VINCENT      G    (A    PETER CETERA       B      (A     MARK NAFTALIN    K    (A
  MARTY GREBB        K TAMB(A    ARTIE SULLIVAN     V TAMB (A     PAUL BUTTERFIELD HCA  (A
  BILLY HERMAN       D    (A    LARRY WRICE        D      (A     SAM LAY          D    (A
```
JUNIOR CAMPBELL

```
  JUNIOR CAMPBELL    V    (A    (A) SECOND TIME AROUND           1974  DERAM         UK   SML  1106
                                (B) COLLECTION                   19    GALE 10"            M501
```
PATRICK CAMPBELL-LYONS

```
  PATRICK CAMPBELL-LYONS   (A    (A) ME & MY FRIEND              1973  SOVEREIGN     UK   SVNA 7258
  BOBBY HARRISON           (A
  PETER DENNIS             (A    DANNY DEMON            (A       SYLVIA SCHUSTER        (A
  BOB SARGEANT             (A    JIM FRANK              (A       CHOIRS            V   (A
```
ROBERT CAMPBESS

```
  ROBERT CAMPBESS          (A    (A) LIVING IN THE SHADOW        1977  DECCA         UK   SHL  5285
```
RAY CAMPI & THE ROCKABILLY REBELS

```
  RAY CAMPI          V    (ALL   (A) ROCKABILLY LIVES            197   ROLLIN' ROCK             004
                                 (B) ROCKABILLY REBEL            197   ROLLIN' ROCK             006
                                 (C) EAGER BEAVER BOY            1976  ROLLIN' ROCK             008
                                 (D) ROCKABILLY ROCKET           1977  ROLLIN' ROCK             013
```
CAMPO DI MARTE

```
  ENRICA ROSA        G K V(A    (A) CAMPO DI MARTE               1973  UA            ITALY     29497
  MAURO SARTI        D V FLT(A
  ALFREDO BARDUCCI   FLT K V(A   C FELICE MARCOVECCHIO D    (A    PAUL RICHARD      B V  (A
```
CAN

```
  MALCOLM MOONEY     V    (ADGJ  (A) MONSTER MOVIE         1969 UA  UK UAS29094     GER       83342
  JAKI LIEBEZEIT     D (ABCDEFGHJKLMNQ(B)TAGO MAGO      DBL 1971 UA  UK UAD 60009/0
  IRMIN SCHMIDT   V K( (ABCDEFGHKLJMNQ(B) TAGO MAGO     DBL 1971 UA     EURO                   29211/2
  MICHAEL KAROLI  G VLN(ABCDEFGHJKLMNQ(C) EGE BAMYASI       1972 UA  US 063         UK UAS 29414
  HOLGER CZUKAY     B (ABCDEFHKLGJ  (D) DEEP END (SOUNDTRACKS) 1970 UA GER 83437     UK      UAS 29283
  KENJI'DAMO' SUZUKI V (BCDEKGJ  (E) FUTURE DAYS          1973 UA  US 213          UK      UAS 29505
  ROSKO GEE          B    (MNQ   (F) SOON OVER BABALUMA   1974 UA  US 343          UK      UAG 29673
  PETER GILMORE      V    (L     (G) LIMITED EDITION      1974 UA     UK           USP      103
  RENE TINNER        V    (L     (H) LANDED               1975 VIRGIN UK V2041     HORZU GER29600
  REEBOP KWAKU BAAH  PERC (MNQ   (J) UNLIMITED EDITION (DBL) 1976 CAROLINE         UK   CAD 3001
  OLAF KUBLER        SAX  (HQ    (K) OPENER               1976 SUNSET              UK   SLS 50400
                                 (L) FLOW MOTION          1976 VIRGIN UK V2071 HARVEST GER  31837
                                 (L) FLOW MOTION          1976 POLYDOR               2473 710
                                 (M) SAW DELIGHT          1977 VIRGIN UK V2079 HARVEST GER  32156
                                 (M) SAW DELIGHT          1977 POLYDOR               2473 712
                                 (N) OUT OF REACH         1978 LIGHTNING LIG4   PETERS INT  9024
                                 (N) OUT OF REACH         1978 HARVEST              GER     32715
                                 (O) CANNIBALISMS (COMP DBL) 1978 UA     UK            UDM 105/6
                                 (P) CLASSIC GERMAN ROCK SCENE 19 SONOPRESSE       FR   29772 /73
                                 (Q) CAN                  1979 LASER UK LASL2 HARVEST GER  45099
```
CANDYMEN

```
  JOHN RAINEY ADKINS G   (AB    (A) THE CANDYMEN                 1967
  RODNEY JUSTO       V   (AB    (B) BRING YOU CANDYPOWER         1968  ABC           US   ABCS 633
  DEAN DAUGHTRY      K   (AB
  BILLY GILMORE      B   (AB    BOB NIX            D      (AB
```
CANIS MAJOR

```
  JACQUELINE BODINEAD V  (A     (A) BUTTERFLY QUEEN              1980  GEM           GEM 109
  TONY BODINEAD      G V (A
  MICK GROVES        G   (A
  SIMON COOPER       B   (A     JOHN PEPE          K      (A     GARY WISE        D    (A
```
CANNED HEAT

```
  BOB HITE         V (ABCDGLMNEFJR (A) CANNED HEAT              1967  LIBERTY       US   LST  7526
  HENRY VESTINE    G (ABCDLMNJE  (A) CANNED HEAT               1967  LIBERTY       UK        83059
  AL WILSON        G V (ABCDGEFJ (A) CANNED HEAT               1972  U A UK UAG29304 SUNSET   50321
  LARRY TAYLOR     B   (ABCDGEF  (B) BOOGIE WITH CANNED HEAT   1968  LIBERTY       UK   LBS 83103
  FRANK COOK       D   (EA       (B) BOOGIE WITH CANNED HEAT   1968  LIBERTY US LST7541 RI   10105
  FITO DE LA PARRA D (BCDGLMNFJ  (B) BOOGIE WITH CANNED HEAT   197   UA            UK   UAG 29298
  JAMES SHANE      G   (MN       (C) LIVING THE BLUES      DBL 1969  LIBERTY       UK   LDS 84001
  ED BEYER         K   (MN       (C) LIVING THE BLUES      DBL 1968  LIBERTY            27200
  RICHARD HITE     B   (MNR      (C) LIVING THE BLUES      DBL 1969  UA            US        9955
  HARVERY MANDEL   G   (GLF      (C) LIVING THE BLUES      DBL 19    UA                 29258/9
  JOEL SCOTT HILL  V G (L        (D) HALLELUJAH               1969  LIBERTY       UK   LBS 83239
  ANTONIO BARRADA  B   (LJ       (D) HALLELUJAH               1969  LIBERTY       US   LST  7618
  CHRIS MORGAN     G   (         (E) VINTAGE HEAT             1970  JANUS US JSL3009 GER   19021
  GENE TAYLOR      K   (         (F) LIVE IN EUROPE           1970  LIBERTY       UK   LBS 83333
  STAN WEBB        G   (         (F) LIVE IN EUROPE           1970  LIBERTY       US        5509
  MEMPHIS SLIM         (K        (G) FUTURE BLUES             1970  LIBERTY       UK   LBS 83364
  JOHN LEE HOOKER  V   (J        (G) FUTURE BLUES             1970  LIBERTY       US   LST 11002
  SUNNYLAND SLIM   PNO (B        (H) COOKBOOK                 1970  LIBERTY       UK   LBS 83303
  MARK NAFTALIN    K   (D        (H) COOKBOOK                 1969  LIBERTY US LST11000 RI  10106
  SKIP DIAMOND     V   (D        (H) COOKBOOK                 1975  SUNSET             SLS 50377
  ELLIOT INGBER    V   (D        (J) HOOKER & HEAT        DBL 1971  LIBERTY       UK   LPS 103/4
  JAVIER BATISE    V   (D        (J) HOOKER & HEAT        DBL 1971  LIBERTY       US   35002-1/2
                                                                         (CONTINUED)
```

```
C26    (CONTINUED)                    CANNED HEAT                                    C26
    MIKE PACHECO      PERC  (D    (K) MEMPHIS HEAT                    1971  BARCLAY           80607
    ERNEST LANE       K     (DGL  ( ) LIVE AT THE TOPANGA CORRAL      1971  WAND                693
    DR JOHN           K     (G    ( ) LIVE AT THE TOPANGA CORRAL      1976  DJM          DJS 26072
    LITTLE RICHARD    PNO   (L    ( ) LIVE AT THE TOPANGA CORRAL      197   PICKWICK     SPC  3364
    CLIFFORD SOLOMON  SAX   (L    ( ) LIVE AT THE TOPANGA CORRAL      19    METROMOME        200 102
                                  (L) HISTORICAL FIGURES             1972  UA        UK UAG 29304
    CHARLES LLOYD     FLT   (L    (L) HISTORICAL FIGURES             1972  UA        US      5557
    KEVIN BURTON      ORG   (L    ( ) PORTRAIT  VOL 1 & 2            19    UA           29320 /21
    RAY BUSHBAUM      PNO   (L    (M) NEW AGE                        1973  UA        UK UAS 29455
    CLARA WARD SINGERS V    (M    (M) NEW AGE                        1973  UA        US UALA 049F
    HARRISON CALLOWAY TPT   (N    (N) ONE MORE RIVER TO CROSS        1974  ATLANTIC  UK  K 50026
    CHARLES ROSE      TROM  (N    (N) ONE MORE RIVER TO CROSS        1974  ATLANTIC  US SD  7289
                                  (N) ONE MORE RIVER TO CROSS        1978  STRAND    GER     23683
    RONNIE EADES      SAX   (N    (O) ROLLIN' & TUMBLIN'             1973  SUNSET       SLS 50321
    HARVEY THOMPSON   SAX         (R) HUMAN CONDITION                197   SONET     UK SNTF  783
                                  (R) HUMAN CONDITION                197 TAKOMA         7066
                                  ( ) COLLAGE                        19    SUNSET       SLS 50225
                                  ( ) CANNED HEAT                    19  SUNSET    NL  60024/5
                                  ( ) COLLAGE                        19    SUNSET    US     5298
                                  ( ) BEST OF                        19  SCEPTER        18017
                                  ( ) MASTERS OF ROCK                19    UA        NL     92656
                                  ( ) ORIGINAL CANNED HEAT           19    SPRINGBOARD US SPB 4026
                                  ( ) BOOGIE WITH HOOKER & HEAT      19    SPRINGBOARD US TSX 3501
                                  ( ) BOOGIE WITH HOOKER & HEAT      19    MUSIDISC     ALB  202
                                  ( ) HISTORY OF                     19    SONOPRESSE/UA   29862/63
                                  ( ) VERY BEST OF                   19    UA           UASLA431E
C26A                                  CANNED ROCK                                    C26A
    DOUGIE KENNARD  G SYN V (AB   (A) KINETIC ENERGY                 1978  CANNED ROCK UK CAN  002
    PETE BUCKBY     D PERC V (AB  (B) LIVE                           1979  CANNED ROCK UK CAN  003
    DON MAXWELL     B G V   (AB
C27                                   ACE CANNON                                     C27
    ACE CANNON        SAX   (ALL  ( ) TUFF                           186   HI        US     32007
                                  ( ) LOOKING BACK                   1962  HI        US     32008
                                  ( ) MOANING SAX                    1964  HI        US     32014
                                  ( ) ACES HIGH                      1964  HI        US     32016
                                  ( ) GREAT SHOW TUNES               1964  HI        US     32019
                                  ( ) CHRISTMAS CHEER                1964  HI        US     32022
                                  ( ) LIVE                           1965  HI        US     32025
                                  ( ) NASHVILLE HITS                 1965  HI        US     32028
                                  ( ) SWEET & TUFF                   1966  HI        US     32030
                                  ( ) MISTY SAX                      1967  HI        US     32035
                                  ( ) MEMPHIS GOLDEN HITS            1968  HI        US     32040
                                  ( ) IN THE SPOTLIGHT               1969  HI        US     32046
                                  ( ) INCOMPARABLE SAX               197   HI        US     32048
                                  ( ) ACE OF SAX                     1970  LONDON    UK SHU 8407
                                  ( ) ACE OF SAX                     1970  HI        US     32051
                                  ( ) HAPPY & MELLOW                 1970  HI        US     32057
                                  ( ) COOL & SAXY                    197   HI        US     32060
                                  ( ) BLOWING WILD                   197   HI        US     32067
                                  ( ) COUNTRY CANNON                 197   HI        US     32071
                                  ( ) BABY DONT GET HOOKED ON ME     1973  HI        US SHL 32076
                                  ( ) COUNTRY COMFORT                197   LONDON    US     32080
                                  ( ) THAT MUSIC CITY FEELING        1974  HI        US     32086
                                  ( ) THAT MUSIC CITY FEELING        1974  LONDON    UK SHU 8478
                                  ( ) SUPER SAX                      1975  LONDON    US     32090
                                  ( ) VERY BEST OF ACE CANNON        1975  LONDON    UK SHU 8486
                                  ( ) SAX MAN                        1978  LONDON    US HLP 8003
C28                                   FREDDY CANNON                                  C28
    FREDDY CANNON     V     (ALL  ( ) THE EXPLOSIVE FREDDY CANNON    1960  TOP RANK  UK  25 / 018
                                  ( ) THE EXPLOSIVE FREDDY CANNON    1960  SWAN      US     502
                                  ( ) THE EXPLOSIVE FREDDY CANNON    1976  SONIC        SON  007
                                  ( ) HAPPY SHADES OF BLUE           1962  TOP RANK  UK  35 / 106
                                  ( ) HAPPY SHADES OF BLUE           1962  SWAN      US     504
                                  ( ) FREDDY CANNON FAVOURITES       1961  TOP RANK  UK  35 / 113
                                  ( ) FREDDY CANNON FAVOURITES       1961  SWAN      US     505
                                  ( ) BANG ON                        1963  STATESIDE UK SL 10013
                                  ( ) BANG ON                        1963  SWAN      US     507
                                  ( ) STEPS OUT                      1964  STATESIDE UK SL 10062
                                  ( ) STEPS OUT                      1964  SWAN      US     511
                                  ( ) HITS                           19    WB        US WS 1544
C28A                                  CANO                                           C28A
    MARCEL AYMAR     G V   (ABC   (A) TOUS DANS L'MEME BATEAU        1976  A&M       CAN    9024
    DAVID C BURT     G HCA (ABC   (B) AU NORD DE NOTRE VIE           1977  A&M       CAN    9028
    MICHEL DASTI     D     (ABC   (C) ECLIPSE                        1978  A&M       CAN    9033
    JOHN DEERR       B K TROM(ABC
    MICHEL KENDEL    K V B (ABC  WASYL KOHUT     VLN MAN(ABC  RACHEL PAIEMENT  G V  (ABC
    ANDRE PAIEMENT   G B V (AB   MERV DEERR      TROM   (A    NICK AYOUB       CLAR (A
    KIM DESCHAMP     G     (B    MONIQUE PAIEMENT V FLT (BC   MATT ZIMBEL      PERC (C
    FAMILLE ARMIN    STR   (C    DAN ENGLERT     SAX    (C    RICK FRANCIS     G    (B
    ALISON REYNOLDS  SRT   (B    JIMMY TANAKA    PERC   (A
C29                                   CAPABILITY BROWN                               C29
    TONY FERGUSON    V G B (B    (A) FROM SCRATCH                    1972  CHARISMA  UK CAS 1056
    DAVE NEVIN       K V G B (B  (B) VOICE                           1973  CHARISMA  UK CAS 1068
    ROGER WILLIS     V D K (B    (C) LIAR                            1976  CHARISMA  UK     CS5
    GRAHAME WHITE    V K G (B
    KENNY ROWE       B V PERC(B  JOE WILLIAMS    V PERC (B
```

```
JIM CAPALDI         V D  (ALL      (A) OH HOW WE DANCED           1972  ISLAND      UK   ILPS 9187
ROGER HAWKINS       D    (ABCE     (A) OH HOW WE DANCED           1972  PHONOGRAM   EURO 6896 015
DAVID HOOD          B    (ABCE     (B) WHALE MEAT AGAIN           1974  ISLAND      UK   ILPS 9254
PETE CARR           G    (BCE      (B) WHALE MEAT AGAIN           1974  PHONOGRAM   EURO 9101 634
JIMMY JOHNSON       G    (ABCE     (C) SHORT CUT DRAW BLOOD       1975  ISLAND      UK   ILPS 9336
BARRY BECKETT       PNO  (ABCE     (C) SHORT CUT DRAW BLOOD       1975  PHONOGRAM   EURO 6396 045
STEVE WINWOOD       K B G (ABCE    (D) PLAY IT BY EAR             1977  ISLAND      UK   ILPS 9497
MUSCLE SHOALS       HRNS (ABC      (E) THE CONTENDER              1978  POLYDOR     UK   2383 490
RABBIT BUNDRICK     K    (BC       (F) DAUGHTER OF THE NIGHT      1979  RSO         US   1- 3037
JEAN ROUSSEL        B K  (BC       (G) ELECTRIC NIGHTS            1979  POLYDOR     UK   2383 534
POTATO SMITH        V    (B        (H) THE SWEET SMELL OF...SUCCESS 1980 CARRERE UK CAL116 NL 67533
JOHN BARNES         K    (D
LAURENCE PEABODY    V    (B    CHRIS STAINTON    K    (B    REMI KABAKA        PERC (BC  REBOP KWAKU BAAH PERC (ABC
RAY ALLEN           SAX  (CEGH PHILIP CHEN       B    (C    JESS RODEN         G    (C   GERRY CONWAY    D    (C
ROSKO GEE           B    (CG  CHRIS SPEDDING     G    (C    PETER YARROW       G    (C   RICK GRECH      B    (A
PAUL KOSSOFF        G    (ACE  RICO RODRIGUES    TROM (C    SUE GLOVER         V    (A   SUNNY LESLIE    V    (A
CHRIS WOOD          WIND (AC   DAVE MASON        HCA  (A    JIM GORDON         D    (A   TREVOR BURTON   B    (A
MIKE KELLIE         D    (A    BOB GRIFFIN       PNO  (A    TREVOR MORAIS      D    (EG  ALAN SPENNER    B    (EGH
PETER BONAS         G B  (EGH  PHIL CAPALDI    V PERC (EGH  RALPH RICHARDSON   D    (EJACKIE McAULEY    G    (E
CHRIS PARREN        K    (EGH  ED GREENE         D    (E    DAVID SHIELDS      B    (E   CHUCK RAINEY    K    (E
RAY PARKER          G    (E    DEAN PARKS        G    (E    MEL COLLINS        HRNS (H   ROB MASON       D    (H
BRENT FORBES        B    (H    MICK FEAT         B    (H    SIMON KIRKE        D    (G   PETER COX       V    (G
CHRIS STEWART       B    (B    BUBS WHITE        B    (B    DEREK QUINN        PERC (B   GASPAR LAWAL    PERC (B
```

```
JAMIE LYONS         V    (A        (A) CAPITOL CITY ROCKETS      1973  ELEKTRA     US        75059
ROBERT HILL         G V  (A
JERRY HERTIG        D    (A    MICHAEL WARNER    G V  (A    ERIC MOORE         B    (A
```

```
DANNY McKEN         G V  (A        (A) HEADLINE NEWS            1979  GREENSLEVES
PAULINE SPENCER     V    (A
PAULETTE HAYDEN     V-   (A    JUNIOR BROWN      B    (A    RODERICK HARVEY    D    (A
EARL LYNCH          K V  (A    GEORGE SCARLETT   G    (A    WENTY STEWART      PERC (A
```

```
                                   DANCE THE COOL JERK         19    ATCO        US   190
                                   WE GOT A THING              19    ATCO        US   201
```

```
LARRY'RHINO'RHEINHART G (ABC      (A) CAPTAIN BEYOND           1972  CAPRICORN   UK   K 47503
LEE DORMAN          B V K (ABC     (A) CAPTAIN BEYOND           1972  CAPRICORN   US   CP 0105
ROD EVANS           V    (AB       (B) SUFFICIENTLY BREATHLESS  1973  CAPRICORN   US   CP 0115
BOBBY CALDWELL      D V K (AC      (C) DAWN EXPLOSION           1977  WB          US   BS 3047
GUILLE GARCIA       PERC (B
MARTY RODRIGUEZ     D    (B    REESE WYNANS      PNO  (B    PAUL HORNSBY       K    (B
WILLY DAFFERN       V    (C
```

```
CLIVE TIMPERLEE     G    (          (NO ALBUMS)
MARTIN LAMBLE       D    (
```

```
C34
GILBERT CARANHAC                   (A) THE DOBRO               1975  CHANT DU MONDE   LDX 74508
```

```
RICHARD COUGHLAN    D    (ALL      (A) CARAVAN                  1968  VERVE            6011
PYE HASTINGS        G V  (ALL      (A) CARAVAN                  1968  MGM         UK   2353 058
DAVE SINCLAIR       K    (ABCEFG145LZM (A) CARAVAN              1972  POLYDOR     UK   2353 058
RICHARD SINCLAIR    B    (ABCD12M  (B) IF I COULD DO IT ALL OVER AGAIN...1970 DECCA UK  SKL 5052
GEOFF RICHARDSON V G VLN(EFGK34567JZL (B) IF I COULD DO IT ALL OVER AGAIN...1970 METRONOME FR MLP15 375
STEVE MILLER        K    (D2       (B) IF I COULD DO IT ALL OVER AGAIN...1970 CARRERE FR  44002
BROTHER JAMES       WIND (D        (B) IF I COULD DO IT ALL OVER AGAIN...1970 LONDON US PS 582
MIKE WEDGWOOD       B    (GK567JZ  (C) IN THE LAND OF THE GREY & PINK 1971 DERAM UK   SDL 1
JOHN G PERRY        B V  (EF4      (C) IN THE LAND OF THE GREY & PINK 1971 LONDON US 593 JAP LAX 1040
MEL COLLINS         SAX  (M        (C) IN THE LAND OF THE GREY & PINK 19  MOTORS FR  2445 203
JIM HASTINGS        WIND (CDE      (C) IN THE LAND OF THE GREY & PINK 197 CARRERE FR  44007
DEREK AUSTIN        K    (3        (D) WATERLOO LILY            1972  DERAM       UK   SDL 8
STUART EVANS        B    (3        (D) WATERLOO LILY            1972  LONDON      US   PS 615
DEK MESSECAR        B V  (K7L      (D) WATERLOO LILY            1980  VOGUE FR 6001 GER BRAIN 1010
JAN SCHELHAAS       K    (6JK      (E) FOR GIRLS WHO GROW PLUMP IN NIGHT 1973 DERAM UK  SKLR 12
DAVE GRINSTEAD      PERC (C        (E) FOR GIRLS WHO GROW PLUMP IN NIGHT 1973 LONDON US 627 JAP LAX 1041
FRANK RICOTTI       PERC (E        (E) FOR GIRLS WHO GROW PLUMP IN NIGHT 1980 VOGUE FR  6006
RUPERT HINE         SYN  (E        (F) & THE NEW SYMPHONIA      1974  DERAM       UK   SKLR 1110
TONY COE            WIND (E        (F) & THE NEW SYMPHONIA      1974  LONDON      US   PS 650
TOMMY WHITTLE       WIND (E        (F) & THE NEW SYMPHONIA      1980  VOGUE FR 6008 GER BRAIN 1054
HARRY KLEIN         WIND (E        (G) CUNNING STUNTS           1975  DERAM       UK   SKLR 5210
PETE KING           WIND (E        (G) CUNNING STUNTS           1975  BTM              BTM 5000
BARRY ROBINSON      WIND (E        (G) CUNNING STUNTS           197   RCA         GER  26 21544
HENRY LOWTHER       HRNS (E        (G) CUNNING STUNTS           197   BTM              BTM 1003
CHRIS PYNE          TROM (E        (H) CANTERBURY TALES  (DBL COMP)  1976 DECCA   UK   DKLR81/82
JOHN BEECHAM        TROM (E        (J) BLIND DOG AT ST DUNSTANS 1976  BTM UK BTM1007 US ARISTA 4088
MIKE COTTON         TPT  (E        (K) BETTER BY FAR            1977  ARISTA      UK SPARTY 1008
DAVID HITCHCOCK     PROD (EG       (K) BETTER BY FAR            1977  ARISTA      US   AB  4134
JILL PRYOR          V    (E        (K) BETTER BY FAR            1977  PATHE       FR 0C64 99089
PAUL BUCKMASTER     CELL (E        (L) THE ALBUM               1980  KINGDOM     UK   KVL 9003
VIVKI BROWN         V    (K        (L) THE ALBUM               1980  KINGDOM     NL   574015
FIONA HIBBERT       HARP (K        (M) BACK TO FRONT           1982  KINGDOM     UK   5011
TONY VISCONTI       REC  (K        ( ) THIS IS CARAVAN          19    BRAIN       GERM 200164
                                   ( ) THE BEST OF             1978  LONDON      US   50011
                                   (Z) THE BEST OF CARAVAN LIVE 1980 KINGDOM     FR   426002
                                   ( ) CARAVAN VOL1            19    POLYDOR          2445 202
                                   ( ) CARAVAN VOL2            19    POLYDOR          2445 203
```

```
GUY CARAWAN         DULC (A        (A) THE TELLING TAKES ME HOME  19  CUR NON     US        722
```

C35   GLENN CARDIER   C35
```
C35                    GLENN CARDIER                                        C35
   GLENN CARDIER            (A) GLENN CARDIER        1976  EMI          UK  EMC 3115
C35A                         CARGO                                          C35A
   MIKE PROUDFOOT    G   (A  (A) SIMPLE THINGS        1969  RINGSIDE         RS  104
   NORM FOSTER       D   (A
   RAY PARKER        ORG (A  GARTH VAGAN       B   (A
C35B                         CARGOE                                         C35B
   BILL PHILLIPS         (   (A) CARGOE              1972  ARDENT       US  ADS 2802
   TOMMY RICHARD         (
   MAX WISLEY           (   TIM BENTON            (
C35C                         CARILLO                                        C35C
   DAVID DONEN       D   (A  (A) RINGS AROUND THE MOON 1978 ATLANTIC    US SD 19176
   KEVIN KEANE       B V (A  (B) STREET OF DREAMS    1979  ATLANTIC     US   19235
   LUKE SPAGNUDO   LYRICS(A
   FRANK CARILLO     V G (A  JAN MULLANEY      K V  (A  KRISTI BARTON    V   (A
   YVONNE ELLIMAN    V   (A  RICK SILECHIO     G    (A
C35D                        DAVE CARLSEN                                    C35D
   DAVE CARLSEN          (A  (A) A PALE HORSE        1973  SPARK        UK  SRLP 110
   KEITH MOON        D   (A
   HENRY McCULLOUGH  G   (A  NOEL REDDING      B    (A  SPENCER DAVIS        (A
   ROY ALLEN            (A  STEVE GREENE           (A  MIKE DAY             (A
   ROY HARRIS           (A  DICK PALMER            (A  BOB JELFS            (A
   BERNIE O'GORMAN      (A  KEN LAWS               (A  ALAN DICKENSON       (A
   LES SAMSON           (A
C35E                      THUMBS CARLLILE                                   C35E
   THUMBS CARLLILE  G DOB (A  (A) ON HIS OWN         19    GEMINI       US   101
C36                         LARRY CARLTON                                   C36
   LARRY CARLTON     G   (ALL (A) SINGING PLAYING    1973  BLUE THUMB   US  BST 46
   GREG MATHIESON    K   (BC  (B) LARRY CARLTON      1978  WB UK K56548 US  BSK3221
   JEFF PORCARO      D   (B   (C) LIVE IN JAPAN      1979  WB GER 56721 JAP P 10643
   PAULINHO DA COSTA PERC (BC (D) STRIKES TWICE      1980  WB UK K56723 US  BSK3380
   WILLIAM'SMITTY' SMITH V (B
   ABE LABORIEL      B   (D  ROBERT POPWELL    B    (D  JOHN FERRARO         (DC
   GREG MATHIESON    K   (D  DON FREEMAN       K    (D  BRIAN MANN       K   (D
   TERRY TROTTER     K   (D  NEIL STUBENHAM    B    (C  MICHAEL OMARTIAN K   (A
   ALAN ESTES        PERC (A JIM GORDON        D    (A  MICHAEL MILLS    PERC (A
   OMA DRAKE         V   (A  RON TUTT          D    (A  JOE OSBORNE      B   (A
   JULIA TILLMAN     V   (A  MAXINE WILLARD    V    (A  WILTON FELDER    B   (A
   JOE SAMPLE        K   (A  STIX HOOPER       D    (A  MAX BENNETT      B   (A
   JOHN GUERIN       D   (A  REINIE PRESS      B    (A  CHRIS NELSON     V   (A
C37                          CARMEN                                         C37
   DAVID ALLEN       G V (ABC (A) FANDANGOS IN SPACE  1973  REGAL ZONOPHONE UK SRZA 8518
   ANGELA ALLEN      V K (ABC (A) FANDANGOS IN SPACE  1973  DUNHILL      US  DP 50192
   ROBERTO AMARAL    V PERC(ABC (B) DANCING ON A COLD WIND 1975 REGAL ZONOPHONE UK SLRZ1040
   PAUL FENTON       D   (ABC (C) THE GYPSIES         1976  MERCURY      US  SRM1 1047
   JOHN GLASCOCK     B V (ABC
   DAVID KATZ        STR (A   CHRIS KARAN       PERC  (B  TONY VISCONTI    WIND (B
   MARY VISCONTI     V   (B
C38                        ERIC CARMEN                                      C38
   ERIC CARMEN       V K D (ALL (A) ERIC CARMEN        1976 ARISTA UK ARTY 120 US  4057
   JEFF PORCARO      D   (B   (B) BOATS AGAINST THE CURRENT 1977 ARISTA UK SPARTY1015US 4124
   ANDREW GOLD       G V (B   (C) CHANGE OF HEART     1978 ARISTA UK SPART1068 US 4184
   MICHAEL BODDIKER  K   (B   (D) TONIGHT YOU'RE MINE 1980 ARISTA UK SPART1134 US 9513
   TOMMY MORGAN      HCA (C
   BRUCE JOHNSTON    V   (C  JOE CHEMAY        V    (C  JAMES NEWTON HOWARD SYN (C  BURTON CUMMINGS PNO  (C
   RICHARD REISING   G V (BCA MIKE PORCARO     B    (C  VALERIE CARTER    V    (C  BOBBY KEYS     SAX  (B
   JAI WINDING       K   (C  DONNY GERRARD     V    (C  RUSS KUNKEL       D    (C  TOM SCOTT      SAX  (B
   DANIEL KORTCHMAR  G   (C  LEE SKLAR         B    (C  RICHIE ZETO       D    (BC PAULINHO DA COSTA PERC(C
   CRAIG DOERGE      K   (C  JIM HORN          SAX  (B  LAURA ALLEN       V    (C  FRED TACKETT   G    (C
   OLLIE BROWN       PERC (B JOE PORCARO       PERC (C  DAVID PAICH       K    (C  STEVE MADAIO   TPT  (B
   BRIAN RUSSELL     V   (C  BRENDA RUSSELL    V    (C  SAMANTHA SANG     V    (C  MIKE BOTTS     D    (C
   DAVE WINTOUR      B   (B  GENE ESTES        PERC (B  NIGEL OLSSON      D    (BC CURT BOETCHER  V    (C
   GEORGE SIPL       K V (A  STEVE KNILL       B V  (A  DWIGHT KRUEGER    D    (A  DAN HUDLICKA   G V  (A
   MICHAEL McBRIDE   D V (C
C38A                        KIM CARNES                                      C38A
   KIM CARNES       V PNO(ALL (A) REST ON ME         1970 AMOS          US    7016
   GLEN D HARDIN    PNO (A    (B) KIM CARNES         1975 A&M US 4548   UK    64548
   LARRY MUHOBERAC  K   (A    (C) SAILIN'            1976 A&M US 4606   UK    64606
   LARRY CARLTON    G   (A    (D) ST VINCENT'S COURT 1979 EMI US 17004  UK    3001
   MIKE DEASY       G   (A    (E) ROMANCE DANCE      1980 EMI US 17030  UK    3012
   JAMES BURTON     G   (A    (F) MISTAKES & IDENTITY 1981 EMI US 17052 UK    3018
   GIL ROGERS       G   (A    (G) VOYEUR             1982 EMI          UK    3026
   DUANNE HITCHINGS SYN (G
   REINE PRESS      B   (AD BILL PERRY        B    (A  ED GREENE         D    (A  DENNIS ST JOHN D   (A
   MIKE SETTLE      V   (A  BROOKS HUNNICUTT  V    (A  ETHAN GOYA        V    (A  DANNY TIMMS    V   (AD
   DAVE ELLINGSON V G BJ(ABCDF JIM KELTNER    D    (B  LELAND SKLAR      B    (BD DEAN PARKES    G   (B
   DAVID FOSTER     PNO (B  STEVE FORMAN      PERC (B  MICHAEL UTLEY     K SYN(B  MAXINE WILLARD V   (BCEF
   JULIA TILLMAN    V   (BCEF MENTOR WILLIAMS V    (B  DAVID HOOD        B    (C  ROGER HAWKINS  D   (C
   BARRY BECKETT    K   (C  PETE CARR         G DOB(C  JIMMY JOHNSON     G    (C  TOM ROADY      PERC(C
   BILL CUOMO       K   (DEFG DAVID GRISMAN   MAND V(C BLACKIE SCHACKNER HCA  (C  DOMINIC GENOVA B   (D
   MATT BETTON      D   (D  STEVE GEYER       G MAN(DE JOHN BELAND       G MAN(DE LARRY HIRSCH   PERC(D
   GARY MONTGOMERY  HCA (D  DANIEL MOORE      V    (DF JERRY PETERSON    SAX  (DFG VICTOR FELDMAN PERC(D
   BOBBY COCHRAN    G   (D  BOBBIE HALL       PERC (D  ETAN McELROY      V    (D  TIM WEISBERG   FLT (D
   BRIAN CADD       V   'D  RICHIE HAYWARD    D    (D  RON BARRON        ORG  (D  JIM W GORDON   ORG(D
   DAVID JACKSON    B   (D  MATTHEW MOORE     V    (D  DARRELL LEONARD   TPT  (D  ERIC NELSON    B   (E
   CRAIG KRAMPF     D V (EFG MIKE PICCIRILLO  G V  (E  SCOTT EDWARDS     B    (E  PATRICK BOLEN  V   (E
   MIKE THOMPSON    K   (E  DAVID HUNGATE     B    (E  KIN VASSEY        V    (E  HERB PEDERSEN  V   (E
   RAPHAEL RAVENSCROFT SAX(E EDNA WRIGHT      V    (E  DARLENE LOVE      V    (E  JOEL PESKIN    SAX(E
   STEVE GOLDSTEIN  K   (FG BRIAN GAROFALO    B V  (FG CRAIG HULL        G V  (FG JOSH LEO       G V(FG
   WADDY WACHTEL    G   (FG DON FRANCISCO     PERC (F  M L BENOIT        PERC (F  DANNY KORTCHMAR G  (F
   WENDY WALDMAN    V   (F
```

CARPENTERS

RICHARD CARPENTER	K V	(ALL	(A) CLOSE TO YOU	1970	A&M			AMLS 998
KAREN CARPENTER	D V	(ALL	(A) CLOSE TO YOU	1970	A&M	US		4271
JOE OSBORN	B	(ABDEM	(B) THE CARPENTERS	1971	A&M			6 3502
BOB MESSENGER	B WIND	(ABDEL	(C) TICKET TO RIDE	1972	A&M			6 4205
RON GORDON	D	(E	(C) TICKET TO RIDE	1972	HAMLET	UK		AMLP8001
DOUG STRAWN	K WIND V	(ABEL	(D) A SONG FOR YOU	1972	A&M			6 3511
JIM HORN	WIND	(AB	(E) NOW & THEN	1973	A&M			6 3519
HAL BLAINE	D	(ABDE	(F) THE SINGLES 69 73	1974	A&M			6 3601
TIM WEISBERG	FLT	(D	(G) HORIZON	1975	A&M			6 4530
LOUIE SHELTON	G	(D	(H) A KIND OF HUSH	1976	A&M			6 4581
TONY PELUSO	G B K V	(DELM	(J) CARPENTER COLLECTION	197	A&M			CARP 1000
RED RHODES	STEEL	(D	(K) LIVE IN JAPAN	1975	A&M			GSW301/02
EARL DUMLER	WIND	(DEM	(L) LIVE AT THE PALLADIUM	1977	A&M			6 8403
NORM HERZBERG	WIND	(D	(M) PASSAGE	1977	A&M			6 4703
DANNY WOODHAMS	B	(A	(N) THE SINGLES 74 78	1978	A&M			19748
CUBBY O'BRIEN	D	(L	(M) MADE IN AMERICA	1980	A&M	US		3723
TOM SCOTT	WIND	(EM						
GARY SIMS	G	(E	BUDDY EMMONS	STEEL (E	JAYDEE MANESS	STEEL (EM	PETE JOLLY	PNO (M
DAVID LUELL	SAX	(M	KURT McGETTRICK	SAX (M	JACKIE KELSO	SAX (M	WALLY SNOW	PERC (M
RAY PARKER	G	(M	CARLENA WILLIAMS	V (M	BOBBY BRUCE	FDL (M	TOM HENSLEY	PNO (M
LEON RUSSELL	PNO	(M	LARRY MUHOBERAC	PNO (M	RON TUTT	D (M	TOMMY VIG	PERC (M
JERRY STEINHOLTZ	PERC	(M	ED GREENE	D (M	JULIA TILLMAN	V (M	MAXINE WILLARD	V (M
GAYLE LEVANT	HARP	(M	LARRY McNEALY	BANJ (M	LEE RITENOUR	G (M	VINCE CHARLES	D (M

PAUL CARRACK

PAUL CARRACK	V	(A	(A) THE NIGHTBIRD	1980	VERTIGO			6359 016
RICHAR BAILEY	D	(A						
ANDY NEWMARK	D	(A	JEFF SEOPARDIE	D (A	ALAN SPENNER	B (A		
KUMA HARADA	B	(A	TIM RENWICK	G (A	NEIL HUBBARD	G (A		
WINSTON DELANDRO	G	(A	NEVILLE MURRAY	PERC (A	DYAN BIRCH	V (A		
ALAN BAM KING	V	(A	NOEL McCALLA	V (A	MEL COLLINS	HRNS (A		
MARTIN DROVER	HRNS	(A	MALCOLM GRIFFITHS	HRNS (A	GUY BARKER	HRNS (A		

JOE 'KING' CARRASCO

JOE'KING' CARRASCO	V G	(AB	(A) & THE EL MOLINO BAND	1979	BIG BEAT	UK		WIK 11
IKE RITTER		(A	(B) JOE KING CARRASCO & THE CROWNS	1980	STIFF	UK		SEEZ 28
MIKE NAVARRO		(B						
KRIS CUMMINGS		(B	BRAD KIZER	(B	AUGIE MEYERS	(A		
ROCKY MORALES		(A	ARTURO GONZALES	(A				

CARPETTES

NEIL THOMPSON	G V	(ABC	(A) CREAM OF THE YOUTH(EP)	1978	SMALL WONDER	UK		SMALL3
TIM WILDER	D	(ABC	(B) FRUSTRATION PARADISE	1979	BEGGARS BANQUET	UK		BEGA14
GEORGE MADDISON	B	(ABC	(C) FIGHT AMONGST YOURSELVES	1980	BEGGARS BANQUET	UK		BEGA21

PETE CARR

PETE CARR	G V	(ALL	(A) NOT A WORD ON IT	1975	BIG TREE	US		BT 89518
ROGER CLARK	D	(AB	(B) MULTIPLE FLASH	1978	BIG TREE	US		BT 76009
TIM HENSON	K SYN	(AB						
CHUCK LEAVEL	K	(A	CLAYTON IVEY	K (A	TOM ROADY	PERC (A		
LENNY LEBLANC	B	(A	HARVEY THOMPSON	SAX (AB	BOB WRAY	B (B		
ROBERT BYRNE	V	(B	ROGER HAWKINS	D (A	GARY BAKER	B (B		
STEVE NATHAN	K	(B	BUTCH LEADFORD	B (B	RANDY McCORMICK	K (B		

BARBARA CARROLL

BARBARA CARROLL	PNO K	(A	(A) FROM THE BEGINNING	1977	UA	US		UALA 778H
EUGENE BIANCO	HARP	(A	(A) FROM THE BEGINNING	1978	UA	UK		UAG 30168
IRWIN MARKOWITZ	HRNS	(A						
MARVIN STAMM	HRNS	(A	JAY LEONHART	B (A	STEVE GADD	D (A		
STEVE THORNTON	PERC	(A	RUSSELL GEORGE	B (A	HUGH McCRACKEN	G (A		
BOB ROSE	G	(A	CRUSHER BENNETT	PERC (A	GEORGE DEVENS	VIBES (A		
JAY BERLINER	G	(A	RICHARD DAVIS	B (A	BILL LAVORGNA	D (A		
RON CARTER	B	(A						

JIM CARROLL

JIM CARROLL	V	(A	(A) CATHOLIC BOY	1980	ATCO	US		18132
BRIAN LINSLEY	G	(A						
STEVE LINSLEY	B	(A	TERRELL WINN	G (A	WAYNE WOODS	D (A		
ALLEN LANIER	K	(A	BOBBY KEYS	SAX (A	AMY KANTNER	V (A		
JON TIVER	G	(A	SALLY	V (A	NEON	V (A		
HILARY	V	(A	JANET	V (A	LENNY KAYE	G (A		

CARS

RIC OCASEK	G V	(ABCD	(A) THE CARS	1978	ELEKTRA	UK		K52088
ELLIOT EASTON	G V	(ABCD	(A) THE CARS	1978	ELEKTRA	US		6E 135
DAVID ROBINSON	D V	(ABCD	(B) CANDY O	1979	ELEKTRA	UK		K 52148
BEN ORR(ORZECHOWSKI)	B V	(ABCD	(C) PANORAMA	1980	ELEKTRA	UK		K 52240
GREG HAWKES	K V	(ABCD	(D) SHAKE IT UP	1981	ELEKTRA	US		5E 567
ROY THOMAS BAKER	PROD	(	(D) SHAKE IT UP	1981	ELEKTRA	US		K 52330

CARSON

BRODERICK SMITH	V HCA	(A	(A) BLOWN	19	HARVEST	UK		SHVL 608
SLEEPY GREG LAWRIE	G	(	(B) ON THE AIR(LIVE)	19	PATHE	FR	064	81774
IAN WINTER	G	(						
GARY CLARKE	B	(	TONY LUNT	D (				

CARLENE CARTER

CARLENE CARTER	V G PNO	(ALL	(A) CARLENE CARTER	1978	WB US BSK3204	UK		K 56502
MARTIN BELMONT	G	(D	(B) TWO SIDES TO EVERY WOMAN	1979	WB UK BSK3375			
DAVE EDMUNDS	G V	(C	(C) MUSICAL SHAPES	1980	F BEAT	UK		XXLP3
ANDREW BODNAR	B	(A	(D) BLUE NUN	1981	F BEAT	UK		LP12
STEVE GOULDING	D	(A						
BRINSLEY SCHWARZ	G V	(A	BOB ANDREWS	K V (AB	CHRIS GOWER	TROM (A	JOHN EARLE	SAX (A
NICK LOWE	B	(ACD	GRAHAM PARKER	G (A	TERRY WILLIAMS	D (AC	RAY BEARIS	SAX (A
DICK HANSON	HRNS	(A	KEVIN WELLS	D (C	BILLY BREMNER	G (CD	JOHN McFEE	G (C
JOHN CIAMBOTTI	B	(C	SEAN HOPPER	K (C	ROGER RETTIG	STEEL (C	BETTY BRIGHT	V (D
GINNY CLEE	V	(D	GLENN TILBROOK	V (D	BOBBY IRWIN	D (D	JAMES ELLER	V B (D
MARTIN BELMONT	G	(D	HUGH GOWER	G (D	JERRY MAROTTA	D (B	ALAN SCHWARZBURG	D (B

(CONTINUED)

BOB BABBIT	B	(B	HUGH McDONALD	B	(B	JEFF MIRONOU	G	(B	CHARLIE BROWN	G	(B
LANCE QUINN	G	(B	WERNER FRITZSCHING	G	(B	BOBBY BLAINE	K	(B	PAT REBILLOT	K	(B
PAUL SCHAFER	K	(B	ROB MOUNSEY	K	(B	CLARENCE CLEMMONS	SAX	(B	ROBERT LEE PATTON	SAX	(D
RANDY SINGER HENNES	HCA	(B	SUE EVANS		PERC (B	ANN OBRIEN	V	(B	AL DOWNING	V	(D

CLARENCE CARTER	V G K	(ALL	(A) THIS IS	1968	ATLANTIC	UK	588 152
KEN BALL	G	(J	(A) THIS IS	1968	ATLANTIC	US	SD 8192
CARL'FROG' WILLIAMS	G	(J	(B) THE DYNAMIC	1968	ATLANTIC	UK	588 172
STEVE NATHAN	K	(J	(B) THE DYNAMIC	1968	ATLANTIC	US	SD 8199
ROGER CLARK	D	(J	(C) TESTIFYIN'	1969	ATLANTIC	UK	588 191
BOB WRAY	B	(J	(C) TESTIFYIN'	1969	ATLANTIC	US	SD 8238
MICKEY BUCKIN	PERC	(J	(D) PATCHES	1970	ATLANTIC	UK	2400 027
DUNCAN CAMERON	STEEL	(J	(D) PATCHES	1970	ATLANTIC	US	SD 8267
MUSCLE SHOALS	HRNS	(J	(E) SIXTY MINUTES	1974	FAME		186
COLLETTE SIMPSON	V	(J	(F) REAL	1974	ABC	US	ABCD 833
MICHELLE MORGAN	V	(J	(F) REAL	1974	ANCHOR	UK	ABCL 5060
JERRY WALLACE	V	(J	(G) LONELINESS & TEMPTATION	1975	ABC	US	ABCD 896
CINDY RICHARDSON	V	(J	(H) HEART FULL OF SONG	1976	ABC	US	ABCD 943
PATRICIA COOLEY	V	(J	( ) THE BEST OF	1972	ATLANTIC US 8282		40245
			(J) IN PERSON	1981	VENTURE	US	1009

RON CARTER	B	(ALL	(A) BLUES FARM	1973	CTI	US	6027
WITH			( ) ALL BLUES	1974	CTI	US	6037
BILLY COBHAM	D	(AJ	( ) ALONE TOGETHER	19	MILESTONE	US	904
BOB JAMES	K	(A	( ) MAGIC	19	PRESTIGE	US	24053
GENE BERTONCINI	G	(A	( ) OUT FRONT	19	PRESTIGE	US	7397
SAM BROWN	G	(A	( ) SPANISH BLUE	1975	CTI	US	6051
STEVE GADD	D	(G	(G) ANYTHING GOES	1975	KUDU		KU 25
JIMMY MADISON	D	(G	( ) WHERE	19	PRESTIGE	US	7843
BARRY ROGERS	TROM	(G	( ) UPTOWN CONVERSATION	197	EMBRYO		SD 521
ERIC GALE	G	(G	(J) YELLOW & GREEN	1976	CTI		63004
GEORGE DEVENS	PERC	(G	(J) YELLOW & GREEN	1976	CTI	US	6064
RALPH McDONALD	PERC	(AG	(K) PASTELS	1977	MILESTONE		9073
HUBERT LAWS	FLT	(AG	( ) SONG FOR YOU	1979	MILESTONE		9086
RANDY BRECKER	HRNS	(G	( ) PARADE	1979	MILESTONE		9088
HARVEY MASON	D	(K	(O) PATRAO	1980	MILESTONE		9099
ALAN RUBIN	HRNS	(G					
DON GROLNICK	K	(GJ	RICHARD TEE	K	(AG	CHET BAKER	TPT	(O
MICHAEL BRECKER	HRNS	(G	DAVE SANBORN	SAX	(G	PHIL WOODS	SAX	(G
PATTI AUSTIN	V	(G	MARILYN JACKSON	V	(G	MAERETHA STEWART	V	(G
KENNY BARRON	PNO	(JK	HARVEY MANDEL	G	(J	HUGH McCRACKEN	G	(JK
ARTHUR JENKINS	PERC	(G	DOM UM ROMAO	PERC	(J	BEN RILEY	D	(J
KENNY BARON	PNO	(O	JACK DEJOHNETTE	D	(O	EDISON MACHADO	D	(O
ALOISIO AGUIAR	PNO	(O	AMOURY TRISTAO	G	(O	NANA VASCONCELOS	PERC	(O

VALERIE CARTER	V	(ALL	(A) JUST A STONES THROW AWAY	1977	CBS	US	PC 34155
WITH			(A) JUST A STONES THROW AWAY	1977	CBS	UK	81958
BILL PAYNE		(A	(B) WILD CHILD	1978	CBS	US	JC 35084
LOWELL GEORGE	G	(A	(B) WILD CHILD	1978	CBS	UK	82556
JEFF PORCARO	D	(AB					
BOB GLAUB	B	(A	FRED TACKETT	G	(AB	SAM CLAYTON	PERC	(A
CHARLES RAINEY	B	(AB	JOHN HALL		(A	ERNIE WATTS	SAX	(A
TOM JANS		(A	HERB PEDERSEN		(A	MIKE UTLEY	K	(AB
JOHN SEBASTIAN		(A	JACKSON BROWNE		(A	OSCAR BRASHEAR	HRNS	(A
MIKE HARRIS		(A	LOUIS SATTERFIELD		(A	DON MYRICK	SAX	(AB
DAVID CAMPBELL		(A	LARRY DUNN		(A	AL McKAY		(A
VERDINE WHITE	B	(AB	FRED WHITE		(A	ANDREW WOOLFOLK		(A
JERRY PETERS		(A	SKIP SCARBOROUGH		(A	GEORGE BOHANON		(A
PAUL BARRERE		(A	COLIN CAMERON		(A	VICTOR FELDMAN	PERC	(B
DAVID HUNGATE	B	(B	STEVE LUKATHER	G	(B	JAMES NEWTON HOWARD	K	(B
STEVE PORCARO	SYN	(B	RAY PARKER	G	(B	JAY GRAYDON	G	(B
VINI PONCIA	V	(B	WENDY HAAS	V	(B	DAVID LASLEY	V	(B
TOMMY SAVIANO	SAX	(B	DAVEY JOHNSTONE	G	(B	LENNY CASTRO	PERC	(B
CHUCK FINDLEY	HRNS	(B	STEVE MADAIO	HRNS	(B	JIM HORN	HRNS	(B

JOHN(JOHN SHAKESPEARE)CARTER	V B G		
KEN (KEN JAMES) LEWIS	V K		
JIMMY PAGE	G	VIV PRINCE	D

MARTIN CARTHY	V G	(ALL	(A) MARTIN CARTHY	1965	FONTANA	STL	5269
WITH			(A) MARTIN CARTHY	1977	TOPIC	12TS	340
DAVE SWARBRICK	VLN	(ABCDEHI	(B) SECOND ALBUM	1966	FONTANA	STL	5362
MADDY PRIOR	V	(K	(B) SECOND ALBUM	1977	TOPIC	12TS	341
LEON ROSSELSON		(F	(C) BYKER HILL	196	FONTANA	STL	5434
			(C) BYKER HILL	1977	TOPIC	12TS	342
			(D) BUT TWO CAME BY	1968	FONTANA	STL	5477
			(D) BUT TWO CAME BY	1977	TOPIC	12TS	343
			(E) PRINCE HEATHEN	1969	FONTANA	STL	5529
			(E) PRINCE HEATHEN	1977	TOPIC	12TS	344
			(F) THE WORD IS	19	TRAILER	LER	3015
			(G) LANDFALL	1971	PHILIPS	6309	049
			(G) LANDFALL	1977	TOPIC	12TS	345
			(H) SELECTIONS	1971	PEGASUS		PEG 6
			(I) THIS IS MARTIN CARTHY	1972	PHILIPS	6282	022
			(J) SWEET WIVELSFIELD	1974	DERAM	SML	1111
			(K) SHEARWATER	1975	MOONCREST	CREST	25
			(K) SHEARWATER	197	PEGASUS	PEG	12
			(L) CROWN OF HORN	1976	TOPIC	12TS	300
			(M) BECAUSE ITS THERE	1979	TOPIC 12TS289 ROUNDER US 3031		

C47A — DAVE CARTWRIGHT

DAVE CARTWRIGHT	V G K(ALL	
GARY TAYLOR	G B	(D
JIM GANNON	*G	(D
DAVE MATTACKS	D	(D
PETE SOLLEY	K	(D
PETE WILSHIRE	STEEL(D	
ROY BABBINGTON	B	(B
BARRY DESOUZA	D	(B
MO FOSTER	B	(B

(A) A LITTLE BIT OF GLORY
(B) BACK TO THE GARDEN
(C) DONT LET YOUR FAMILY DOWN
(D) MASQUERADE

MARTIN JENNER	G		(D
MIKE MORAN	K		(B
TED TAYLOR	K		(B
RAY FENWICK	G		(B

1972	TRANSATLANTIC	TRA 255
1973	TRANSATLANTIC	UK TRA 267
1975	TRANSATLANTIC	UK TRA 284
1976	DJM	UK DJF 20489

TONY JACKSON	V	(D
CHRIS KARAN	D	(B
PAUL KOEGH	G	(B
GRAHAM PRESKOTT	VLN	(B

CARTOON

C47B

DEREK CREIGAN	G V	(A
MIKE ALLISON	G	(A
CHICK E COFFILS	D	(A

(A) CARTOON

MO TROWERS	G	(A

1969	ATLANTIC	UK 588 174

JIMMY PAGE	G	(A

CASABLANCA

C48

BARRY CLARKE	V G	(A
DAVID COSTA	G V	(A
JUANITA FRANKLIN	V	(A
STEVE BINGHAM	B	(A
BRUCE ROWLAND	D	(A
GRAHAM PRESKETT	VLN	(A
LUIS JARDIM	PERC	(A
PHILIP CHEN	B	(A

(A) CASABLANCA

ALIKI ASHMAN	V	(A
TERRY STANNARD	D	(A
TREVOR VALLIS	B	(A
JOHNNY WILSON	D	(A
PAUL VIGRASS	V	(A

1974	ROCKET	PIGL 7

BILLY LIVSEY	K	(A
LOL COXHILL	WIND	(A
NICK JUDD	K	(A
BIAS BOSHELL	B	(A
GARY OSBORNE	V	(A

AL CASEY

C49

AL CASEY	G	(ALL

(A) SURFIN' HOOTENANY
(B) JUMPIN' WITH AL
(C) GUITAR ODYSSEY

1963	STACY	US STM 100
1974	BLACK & BLUE	33056
1976	JAZZ ODYSSEY	JO 012

JOHNNY CASH

C50

JOHNNY CASH
WITH
JUNE CARTER CASH
THE CARTER FAMILY

HELEN CARTER	V					
CARLENE CARTER	V	ANITA CARTER	V	ROSANNE CASH	V	CINDY CASH	V
STATLER BROTHERS		KRIS KRISTOFFERSON	V	BILLY LEE RILEY	G	LARRY BUTLER	
LARRY GATLIN		JAN HOWARD		RON TUTT		REINIE PRESS	
DAVID FOSTER		LARRY MUHOBERAC		RON ELLIOTT		RY COODER	G
JAMES BURTON	G	RUSS TITELMAN		JERRY COLE		VICTOR FELDMAN	PERC
JOE PORCARO	PERC	GENE ESTES		NICK DE CARO		GENE CIPRIANO	SAX
REGGIE YOUNG		KENNY MALONE		HENRY STRZELECKI		SHANE KEISTER	K
TEDDY IRWIN		DAVID ALAN COE	V	JACKIE WARD	V	RON HICKLIN SINGERS	V
JIMMY CAPPS	G	ROSEY NIX	V	MARSHALL GRANT	B	JORDANAIRES	V
WES HOLLAND	D	BOB WOOTTON	G	CARL PERKINS	V	LUTHER PERKINS	G
CHARLIE McCOY	HCA	CHUCK COCHRAN		JOE ALLEN		EARL SCRUGGS	BANJO
OAKRIDGE BOYS	V	LARRY McCOY		RAY EDENTON		JERRY HENSLEY	G
JACK ROUTH	G	EARL BALL	PNO	MARK MORRIS	PERC	MICHAEL BACON	CELLO
SAM MULLINS	STRINGS	KATHLEEN BRIMM	V	RED LANE		BILL PURSELL	
TOMMY ALSUP	G	JACK CLEMENT	G	JACK HALE	HRNS	BOB LEWINS	HRNS
JOEL SONNIER	HCA	DENNIS GOODE	TROM	BILLY PUETT	WIND	WAYNE JACKSON	TPT
GENE LOWERY SINGERS	V	RICH SCHULMAN	V	JIMMY WILSON	PNO	JAMES VAN EATON	D
RODNEY CROWELL	V					

WITH HIS HOT & BLUE GUITAR	1957 SUN	SLP 1220	TRUE WEST	1965 CBS	62538
SONGS THAT MADE HIM FAMOUS	1958 SUN	US SLP1235	TRUE WEST	1965 CBS	US C2S 838
SONGS THAT MADE HIM FAMOUS	1967 LONDON	HAS 2157	MEAN AS HELL	1966 CBS	US CS 9246
FABULOUS JOHNNY CASH	1959 SUN	62042	TRUE WEST 2	196 CBS	62591
GREATEST JOHNNY CASH	1959 SUN	US SLP1240	EVERYBODY LOVES A NUT	1966 CBS	62717
HYMNS BY JOHNNY CASH	1959 CBS	US CSB125	EVERYBODY LOVES A NUT	1966 CBS	US CS 9292
HYMNS BY JOHNNY CASH	1971 HALLMARK	SHM 739	HAPPINESS IS YOU	1966 CBS	62760
SINGS HANK WILLIAMS	1960 SUN	US SLP1245	GREATEST HITS	1967 CBS	63062
SINGS HANK WILLIAMS	196 LONDON	NZ HAM6195	GREATEST HITS 1	1967 CBS	US CS 9478
SINGS HANK WILLIAMS	196 SUN	US 125	CARRYIN' ON	1967 CBS US9528 UK 63105
SONGS OF OUR SOIL	1959 CBS	US CS 8148	OLD GOLDEN THROAT	1968 CBS	63318
NOW THERE WAS A SONG	1960 PHILIPS	BBL 7358	OLD GOLDEN THROAT	1975 CHARLY	CR 30005
NOW THERE WAS A SONG	1960 CBS	US CS 8254	THE HOLY LAND	1968 CBS	63428
NOW THERE WAS A SONG	1960 CBS	62028	THE HOLY LAND	196 CBS	US KCS9726
RIDE THIS TRAIN	1960 CBS	62575	LEGENDS & LOVE SONGS	1968 CBS	CAN DS 363
RIDE THIS TRAIN	1960 CBS	8255	MORE OLD GOLDEN THROAT	1969 CBS	63521
NOW HERES JOHNNY CASH	1961 SUN	US SLP1255	SINGING STORY TELLER	1969 SUN	US 115
RIDE THIS TRAIN	1960 CBS	US CS 8255	SINGING STORY TELLER	19 BUCKBOARD US BBS1021
HYMNS FROM THE HEART	1962 CBS	US CS8522	JACKSON	1969 CBS	US CS 9528
ALL ABOARD THE BLUE TRAIN	1962 SUN	US SLP1270	FROM SEA TO SHINING SEA	1968 CBS	62972
SOUND OF JOHNNY CASH	1962 CBS	US CS 8602	AT FOLSOM PRISON	1968 CBS	63308
BLOOD SWEAT & TEARS	1963 CBS	US CS 8730	AT FOLSOM PRISON	1968 CBS	US CS 9639
BLOOD SWEAT & TEARS	1963 CBS	UK 65163	AT SAN QUENTIN	1969 CBS	63629
RING OF FIRE	1963 CBS	62171	AT SAN QUENTIN	19 CBS	28090/9
RING OF FIRE	1963 CBS	US CS 8853	AT SAN QUENTIN	1969 CBS	US CS 9827
CHRISTMAS SPIRIT	1963 CBS	62284	HELLO IM JOHNNY CASH	1969 CBS US9943 uk 63796
KEEP ON THE SUNNYSIDE	1964 CBS	US CS 8952	WORLD OF JOHNNY CASH	1970 CBS	66237
I WALK THE LINE	1964 CBS	US CS8990	WORLD OF JOHNNY CASH	1970 CBS	CG 29
I WALK THE LINE	19 HILLTOP US	6097	HIS GREATEST HITS VOL 2	19 CBS	US 30887
I WALK THE LINE	19 SUN	139	JOHNNY CASH SHOW	1970 CBS	64089
I WALK THE LINE	196 CBS	UK 62371	ORIGINAL GOLDEN HITS 1	1970 SUN	6467 001
I WALK THE LINE	1974 CBS	70083	ORIGINAL GOLDEN HITS 1	19 SUN	US 100
I WALK THE LINE	1974 HALLMARK UK SHM 849	ORIGINAL GOLDEN HITS 2	1970 SUN	6467 007
BITTER TEARS	1964 CBS US 9048 UK62463	ORIGINAL GOLDEN HITS 2	19 SUN	US 101
LORENA	1964 CBS	GERM 52705	THE GREAT JOHNNY CASH	1970 HALLMARK	SHM 696
COUNTRY ROUND UP	1964 FONTANA	301	ORIGINAL JOHNNY CASH	1970 CHARLY	CR 30113
ORIGINAL SUN SOUND OF J C	1964 SUN	US SLP1275	LITTLE FAUSS & BIG HALSY	1970 CBS	70087
ORIGINAL SUN SOUND OF J C	1967 LONDON	HAS8220	THE MAN & HIS WORLD	1971 SUN	6641 008
ORANGE BLOSSOM SPECIAL	1965 CBS	62501	TRAINS & RIVERS	1971 SUN	6467012
ORANGE BLOSSOM SPECIAL	1965 CBS	US CS 9109	TRAINS & RIVERS	197 SUN	US 104

(CONTINUED)

[97]

JOHNNY CASH

Title	Year	Label	Country	No.	Title	Year	Label	Country	No.
SHOWTIME	197	SUN	US	106	FOLSOM & SAN QUENTIN	1976	CBS DBL	US	33639
GET RHYTHM	1971	SUN US105		6467 014	JOHN R CASH	1974	CBS		33370 80634
UNDERSTAND YOUR MAN	1971	HARMONY	US	30916	RIDING THE RAILS	1975	CBS		88153
A MAN IN BLACK	1971	CBS		64331	CHILDRENS ALBUM	1975	CBS	US	32898
MAN IN BLACK	1971	CBS		30550	LOOK AT THEM BEANS	1975	CBS		81012
THE LEGEND	197	SUN	US	2 118	LOOK AT THEM BEANS	1975	CBS	US	34193
ROUGH CUT KING OF COUNTRY	197	SUN	US	122	I FORGOT TO REMEMBER	1975	HALLMARK		SHM 884
THE MAN THE WORLD HIS MUSIC	197	SUN	US	126	BALLAD OF TEENAGE QUEEN	1975	HALLMARK		SHM 862
PORTRAIT	197	CBS		64516	STORY OF A BROKEN HEART	1976	HALLMARK		SHM 897
GIVE MY LOVE TO ROSE	1972	CBS	US	31256	KING OF COUNTRY	1975	MUSIDISC		174
INTERNATIONAL SUPERSTAR	1972	CBS	GERM	67284	SPOTLIGHT ON JOHNNY CASH	1975	SUN	NL	SPL01
A THING CALLED LOVE	1972	CBS 31332		64898	COLLECTION	1976	PICKWICK		PDA 005
JOHNNY CASH	197	EMBASSY		31495	DESTINATION VICTORIA STATION	1976	CBS	US	VS150
JOHNNY CASH	1974	EMBASSY		31039	MAKING A LEGEND	1976	CHARLY		18051
SHOWTIME	197	SUN		6467 016	JOHNNY CASH	19	PICKWICK	US	2052
JOHNNY CASH SONG BOOK	1972	HARMONY	US	31602	KINGS OF COUNTRY DBL	19	FESTIVAL US		174
CHRISTMAS & THE CASH FAMILY	1972	CBS	US	31764	SONGBOOK	19	CBS		EUR51357
ORIGINAL GOLDEN HITS 3	1972	SUN		6467 022	IN SWEDEN	1976	CBS		65308
ORIGINAL GOLDEN HITS 3	197	SUN	US	127	STRAWBERRY CAKE	1976	CBS 34088		81211
GOSPEL ROAD	1973	CBS	US	32253	ONE PIECE AT A TIME	1976	CBS		81416
GOSPEL ROAD	1973	CBS	UK	68243	ONE PIECE AT A TIME	1976	CBS	US	34193
SUNDAY MORNING COMING DOWN	197	CBS	US	32240	LAST GUNFIGHTER BALLAD	1977	CBS		81566
MAGNIFICENT JOHNNY CASH	1972	HALLMARK		SHM 777	LAST GUNFIGHTER BALLAD	1977	CBS	US	34314
COUNTRY & WESTERN SUPERSTAR	1973	CBS	GERM	68224	THE RAMBLER	1977	CBS	US	34833
AMERICA	1973	CBS 31645		65163	THIS IS JOHNNY CASH	197	HARMONY	US	11342
SUNDAY DOWN SOUTH	1973	SUN 119	US	6467024	I WOULD LIKE TO SEE YOU	1978	CBS UNISSUED		82676
ANY OLD WIND THAT BLOWS	1973	CBS		65431	I WOULD LIKE TO SEE YOU	1978	CBS	US	35313
ANY OLD WIND THAT BLOWS	197	CBS	US	KC32091	GONE GIRL	1978	CBS 35646		83323
J CASH & HIS WOMAN	1973	CBS		65689	ANY OLD WIND	1978	CBS	US	32091
J CASH & HIS WOMAN	1973	CBS	US	KC32443	UNISSUED JOHNNY CASH	1878	BEAR FAM GER		15016
MIGHTY JOHNNY CASH	1973	HALLMARK		SHM 804	JOHNNY & JUNE	1978	BEAR FAM GER		15030
FIVE FEET HIGH & RISING	1974	CBS	US	32951	ITCHY FEET 20 FOOT TAPPERS	1978	CBS		10009
AT OSTERAKER PRISON	1974	CBS	HOLL	65308	COLLECTION VOL 2	1978	PICKWICK	PDA	033
FOLSOM PRISON BLUES	1974	HALLMARK		SHM 822	RING OF FIRE	1979	HALLMARK		SHM 998
SOUND OF J CASH	197	EMBASSY		31081	SILVER	1979	CBS		36086
BALLADS OF AMERICAN INDIANS	1974	HARMONY	US	32388	ROCK ISLAND LINE	19	HILLTOP	US	6101
BLUE TRAIN	197	SHARE	US	5002	WITH JERRY LEE LEWIS	19	SUN	US	125
BLUE TRAIN	1979	SUN		141	THE BARON	19	CBS		37179
UNKIE & JUICEHEAD	1974	CBS		80347	ROCKABILLY BLUES	19	CBS		36779
JUNKIE & JUICEHEAD	1974	CBS	US	33086	WALLS OF PRISONS	19	HARMONY		30138
ROUGH CUT KING	1974	SUN		6870 605	GREATEST HITS VOL 3	1979	CBS	US	35637
GENTLE GIANT OF COUNTRY	1974	SUN		6641 161	JOHNNY CASH TODAY	1978	K TEL	CAN	NC424
PRECIOUS MEMORIES	1976	CBS	US	33087	HOT'N'BLUE GUITAR RI	1980	CHARLY		CRM 2013
RAGGED OLD FLAG	1974	CBS		80113	BALLAD OF A TEENAGE QUEEN(EP)	1976	CHARLY		
RAGGED OLD FLAG	1974	CBS	US	32917					

CASHMAN (PISTILL) & WEST

GENE PISTILL	G V	(AB	(A) CASHMAN PISTILL & WEST		1969	EMI		UK	EST 211
TERRY CASHMAN	V	(ALL	(B) BOUND TO HAPPEN(C P W)		19	ABC		US	629
TOMMY WEST	V K G	(ALL	(C) SONG OR TWO		1972	DUNHILL US 50126	UK PROBE 6270		
TOM MORGAN	HCA	(C	(D) MOONDOG SERENADE		1973	DUNHILL		US	DSX 50141
RAY POHLMAN	B	(CD	(D) MOONDOG SERENADE		1973	PROBE UK 6226 RI ABC 74			5058
GARY KATZ	V	(C	(E) LIFESONG		1974	ABC		UK	ABCL 5058
MIKE OMARTIAN	K	(CD							
JEFF BAXTER	STEEL	(CD	STEVE BARRI	PERC	(C	BEN BENAY	HCA G	(CD	
GARY COLEMAN	PERC	(CD	JIMMIE HASKELL	ACC	(CD	EDDIE LAMBERT	V	(D	
LOUIS SHELTON	G	(C	JIM GORDON	D	(CD	AL GORGONI	G	(B	
HUGH McCRACKEN	G	(B	SAL DETROIA	G	(B	ARTIE KAPLAN	FLT	(B	
JOE MACHO	B	(B	BOBBY GREGG	D	(B				

CASINO

(A) CASINO		1976	STATE		ETAT	5
(A) CASINO		1976	MCA	US		2191

TERRY CASHMAN

TERRY CASHMAN	G V	(A	(A) TERRY CASHMAN		1976	LIFESONG	US	6006
TOMMY WEST	K V	(A						
HENRY GROSS	G	(A	DAVID SANBORN	SAX	(A	RICK MAROTTA	D	(A

CASIOPEA

ISSEI NORO	G K	(A	(A) MINT JAMS		1982	ALFA		ALF 85869
MINORU MUKAIYA	K	(A						
TETSUO SAKURAI	G H	(A	AKIRA JIMBO	K B	(A			

JEAN PIERRE CASTELAIN

JEAN PIERRE CASTELAIN	G	(ALL	(A) DE MES YEUX VU		19	WEA		46155
			(B) ALBERIA		19	WEA		46285
			(C) LA SOURIS S'EN VA EN GUERRE		19	WEA		56188
			(D) LE MIROIR	DBL	19	WEA		86011

DAVID CASTLE

DAVID CASTLE		(AB	(A) CASTLE IN THE SKY		1977	PARACHUTE US 9002	UK RRL2001	
ANDY BELLING	PNO	(A	(B) LOVE YOU FOREVER		1979	PARACHUTE US 9015	UK RRL2009	
CLARK GASSMAN	PNO	(A						
CHUCK RAINEY	B	(AB	ABRAHAM LABORIEL	B	(A	JAMES GADSON	D	(AB
RICK SHLOSSER	D	(A	BEN BENAY	G	(A	LEE RITENOUR	G	(A
TREVOR VEITCH	G	(A	JAY GRAYDON	G	(A	DOROTHY ASHBY	HARP	(A
JIM HORN	SAX	(A	WILLIAM PERKINS	SAX	(A	BOBBYE HALL	PERC	(A
STEVE MADAIO	TPT	(A	CHARLES FINDLEY	TPT	(A	JERRY SOMMERS	D	(B
JAMES L ROLLESTON	B	(B	PATRICK McCLURE	G	(B	MIKE BODDICKER	SYN	(B
STEVE FORMAN	PERC	(B	DENNIS TREMBLY	B	(B			

CASTON & MAJORS

LEONARD CASTON	V	(A	(A) CASTON & MAJORS		1974	MOTOWN	US	6 814
KATHY WAKEFIELD	V	(A						
MATTIE LYRICKS	V	(A	TERRY McFADDIN	V	(A	ERROL SOBER	V	(A

C53

JIMMY CASTOR BUNCH

```
C53                                    JIMMY CASTOR BUNCH                                      C53
  JIMMY CASTOR        (ALL       ( ) ITS JUST BEGUN          1972  RCA            US    4640
  GERRY THOMAS     K  (F         ( ) PHASE TWO               1972  RCA            US    4783
  DOUGLAS GIBSON   B  (F         ( ) DIMENSION 3             1973  RCA            APDI  0103
  LANDON FRIDE  CONGA (F         ( ) THE EVERYTHING MAN      1974  ATLANTIC       UK  K 50052
  ELLWOOD HENDERSON D (F         ( ) THE EVERYTHING MAN      1973  RCA            UK    0313
  JEFFREY GRIMES   G  (F         (F) SUPER SOUND             1975  ATLANTIC       UK  K 50190
                                 (F) SUPER SOUND             1975  ATCO           US  SD 18150
                                 ( ) BUTT OF COURSE          1975  ATLANTIC       UK  K 50120
                                 ( ) BUTT OF COURSE          1975  ATCO           US  SD 18124
                                 ( ) E MAN GROOVIN           1976  ATLANTIC       UK  K 50295
                                 ( ) E MAN GROOVIN           1976  ATCO           US  SD 18186
                                 ( ) BEST OF                 1976  RCA            US    0877
                                 ( ) HEY LEROY               197   SMASH          US  MGS 27091
                                 ( ) MAXIMUM STIMULATION     1977  ATLANTIC       US  SD 19111
                                 ( ) 'C'                     1980  LONG DISTANCE  US    1201
                                        CASUALS
C55                              (A) HOUR WORLD              1969  DECCA          UK  SKL 5001          C55
  JOHN TEBB      V ORG(A
  HOWARD NEWCOMB   G  (A         BOB OBRIEN         D   (A   STEVE WALLACE    B   (
  ALAN TAYLOR   FL B V(A         LLOYD COURTNEY     D   (
  ROGER GREY       D  (                  CAT
C55A                             (A) CAT                     1970  RCA            US    4267          C55A
  MIKE McQUEEN     G  (A
  PHIL MULHOLLAND  D  (A         GRAHAM FIDLER      B V (A   JIM CAMPBELL     V   (A
  GARY O'CONNOR  G K  (A               CAT MOTHER                                                      C56
C56                              (A) THE STREET GIVETH       1969  POLYDOR        184   300
  ROY MICHAELS   B G V (ABCD     (A) THE STREET GIVETH       1969  POLYDOR        24  4001
  MICHAEL EQUINE D G V (ABCD     (B) ALBION DOOWAH           1970  POLYDOR        2425  021
  LARRY PACKER     G V (AB       (B) ALBION DOOWAH           1970  POLYDOR        24  4023
  BOB SMITH      K D V (ABCD     (C) LAST CHANCE DANCE       1973  UA             UAG 29481
  CHARLIE CHIN BANJO G V (A      (C) LAST CHANCE DANCE       1973  POLYDOR        5042
  JAY UNGAR         G V (BC      (D) CAT MOTHER              1974  BARCLAY        920   285
  PAUL JOHNSON     G  (B         (D) CAT MOTHER              1972  UA             UAG 29313
  LYNDON LEE HARDY V  (B         (D) CAT MOTHER              1974  POLYDOR        24  5017
  CHARLIE HARCOURT    (D
  STEVE DAVIDSON PERC (DC
  CHARLIE PRITCHARD G (          JOHN CHAMBERLAIN   MAND (C  BUZZY LINHART    VIBES (C
  VELLA CAMERON    V  (C               CATAPILLA                                                       C57
C57                              (A) CATAPILLA               1971  VERTIGO US 1006 UK  6360 029
  THIERRY RHEINHARDT WIND (A     (B) CHANGES                 1972  VERTIGO        6360 074
  ANNA MEEK        V  (AB
  HUGH EAGLESTONE SAX (AB        DAVE TAYLOR        B   (A   MALCOLM FRITH    D   (A
  ROBERT CALVERT  SAX (AB        BRYAN HANSON       D   (B   CARL WASSARD     B   (B
  GRAHAM WILSON    G  (AB              CATES GANG
  RALPH RAWLINSON  K  (B         (A) WANTED                  1970  METROMEDIA     US    1029          C57A
C57A                             (B) COME BACK HOME          1973  METROMEDIA     US    1052
  ERNIE CATE     K V  (AB
  EARL CATE      G V  (AB
  TERRY CAGLE         (A
  BILL WRIGHT      B  (A             THE CATE BROTHERS                                                 C58
C58                              (A) THE CATE BROTHERS       1975  ASYLUM         UK  SYL 9030
  ERNIE CATE     V K  (ALL       (A) THE CATE BROTHERS       1975  ASYLUM         US  7E 1050
  EARL CATE      V G  (ALL       (A) THE CATE BROTHERS       1975  ASYLUM         EURO 24 4001
  NIGEL OLSSON     D  (A         (A) THE CATE BROTHERS       1976  ASYLUM         UK  K 53019
  ED GREENE        D  (A         (B) IN ONE EYE              1976  ASYLUM         UK  K 53049
  LELAND SKLAR     B  (A         (B) IN ONE EYE              1976  ASYLUM         US  7E 1080
  SCOTT EDWARDS    B  (A         (C) THE CATE BROTHERS BAND  1977  ASYLUM         UK  K 53064
  STEVE CROPPER    G  (AB        (C) THE CATE BROTHERS BAND  1977  ASYLUM         US  7E 1116
  MICHAEL BAIRD    D  (AB        (D) FIRE ON THE TRACKS      1979  ATLANTIC       US  SD 19240
  KLAUS VOORMANN   B  (A         (D) FIRE ON THE TRACKS      1979  ATLANTIC       GERM ATL 50627
  DAVID FOSTER     K  (B
  DONALD DUNN      B  (B         GEORGE TERRY       G   (D   PAUL HARRIS      K   (D
  STEVE FORMAN   PERC (B         ALBERT SINGLETON   V   (B   JAY GRAYDON      K   (B
  TERRY CAGLE    D V  (BCD       BOBBY KEYS         HRNS (B  SID SHARP        VLN (B
  JIM HORN        SAX (B         VERNA RICHARDSON   V   (B   LISA ROBERTS     V   (B
  BROOKS HUNNICUTT V  (B         RON EOFF           B   (CD  JOE LALA         PERC (CD
  WILLIE HALL    PERC (B         STEVE MADAIO       TPT (C   MARK UNDERWOOD   TPT (C
  TIM SCHMIT       V  (C         JOHN PHILLIPS      SAX (C   LINDA SMALL      TROM (C
  JERRY JUMONVILLE SAX (C        KING ERRISON       PERC (A  CARL MARCH       SYN (A
  JOEL PESKIN     SAX (C         JULIA TILLMAN      V   (A   GARY COLEMAN     PERC (A
  MAXINE WILLARD   V  (A         WILLIAM SMITTY SMITH K (A   BOB GLAUB        B   (A
  LEVON HELM     D V  (AD              CATFISH                                                        C58A
C58A                             (A) GET DOWN                1970  EPIC           UK  EPC 64006
  BOB HODGE      V G K (AB       (B) LIVE CATFISH            1971  EPIC           UK  EPC 64408
  MARK MANKO          (A
  HARRY PHILLIPS   K  (AB        W R COOKE          (A       DALLAS HODGE     G   (A
  JIMMY OPTNER        (A         JIM DEMERS         D   (B   JOHN HILL        PNO (B
  DENNIS CRANNER   B  (B             CATFISH HODGE                                                    C59
C59                              (A) DYNASAURS & ALLEYCATS   1974  EASTBOUND      US    2008
  BOB 'CATFISH' HODGE V G K (ALL (B) SOAP OPERA'S            1975  20th CENTURY         W 202
  DALLAS HODGE     G  (A         (C) EYEWITNESS  BLUES       1979  ADELPHI        AD  4113
  LARRY ZACK       D  (B         (D) 'BOUT WITH THE BLUES    1981  ADELPHI        US
  CRISPIN CIOE   SAX  (A
  JOHN BADANJEK    D  (B         DR JOHN            K   (B   WAYNE COOK       K   (B
  DENNIS KOVARIK   B  (B         BONNIE RAITT       G   (B   JAMES MONTGOMERY HARP (B
  SNEAKY PETE KLEINOW STEEL (B   COTTON KENT        K   (C   FREEBO           V   (C
  BOB SCARF       WIND (B        JOHN LEE           D   (C   DUANE CAMPBELL   B   (C
  JIM THACKERY     G  (C         JIMMY POWERS       HCA (C   DIANA CRAWFORD   V   (C
  DAVID NAMERDY    G  (C         JAMES COTTON       HCA (C   DOUG FAGAN       SAX (C
  DIXIE D BALLIN   V  (C         SAVOY BEARD        SAX (C   GEORGE McWHIRTER TROM (C
  JAMIE MACKINNON SAX (C         WILLIAM LANDLESS   B   (A   AL WERNEKEN      G   (A
  BOB BABITCH     PNO (A         JIM McCARTY        G   (A   CARTER THRELKELD TROM (A
  DAVE CHAMBERS    D  (A
```

C60   CATHARSIS   C60

```
PATRICK MOULIA     G K V (ABCGHK    (A) CATHARSIS                    19   DISCODIS    FR   AZSH 1025
CHARLIE EDDI       D     (ABCFGHKN   (A) CATHARSIS                    19   SARAVAH               10025
YVES DE ROUBAIX    G V   (ABCGHKN    (B) CATHARSIS 2                  19   DISCODIS    FR   AZSH 1035
ROLAND BOCQUET     K V   (ABCFGJK    (B) CATHARSIS 2                  19   SARAVAH               10035
ALAIN GEOFFROY     K V   (ACGH       (C) CATHARSIS                    19   EXPLOSIVE        558  004
CHARLOTTE          V VLN (ACGK       (D) POP POEMS                    19                       528002
NILES BROWN        G VLN (AG         (E) RIMBAUD C'EST TOI            19   PATHE       FR   064 11473
CLAUDE             G SITAR(F         (F) LE BOLERO DU VEAU DES DAMES  19   SONOPRESSE  FR   ST 69612
MICHEL             B     (F          (G) VOL 1 MASQ                   19   FESTIVAL    FR       650
                                     (H) VOL 2 LES CHEVRONS          19   FESTIVAL    FR       651
                                     (J) 32 MARS                     19   MUSIDISC    FR    600507
                                     (J) 32 MARS                     19   FESTIVAL    FR       652
                                     (K) VOL 4 ILLUMINATIONS         19   FESTIVAL    FR       655
                                     (L) VOL 5 LE BOLERO             19   FESTIVAL    FR       676
                                     (M) VOL 6 ET S'AIMER            19   FESTIVAL    FR       678
                                     (N) ET S'AIMER ET MOURIR        19   MUSIDISC    FR   FLD 678
```

C61   PHILIP CATHERINE   C61

```
PHILIP CATHERINE G B K   (ALL   (A) STREAM              1972   WB        FR      46049
LARRY CORYELL      G      (DE    (B) SEPTEMBER MAN       1974   WB        GERM    46562
PALLE MIKKELBORG   TPT    (B     (C) GUITARS             1975   ATLANTIC  UK    K 50193
CHARLIE MANIANO    WIND   (BC    (D) TWIN HOUSE          1977   ATLANTIC  UK    K 50342
JOHN LEE           B      (BC    (E) SPLENDID            1978   ATLANTIC  UK    K 52086
GERRY BROWN        D      (BC    (F) BABEL               1980   ELEKTRA          52244
ROB FRANKEN        K      (C
JASPER VAN HOF     K      (BC
```

C61A   CATS (1)   C61A

```
DANNY WESTON       G      (A    (A) CATS                1980  ELEKTRA NL 52239 US 6E  275
DENNIS TILLI       B      (A
FRED ZARRA         K SYN V(A    MICHAEL CORR    V    (A    PETER KELTZ     G    (A
TOMMY STEWART      D V    (A
```

C61B   CATS (2)   C61B

```
AL CAPPS           (A    (A) LOVE IN YOUR EYES    1979 FANTASY US 9447 EMI NL   25100
GORDON MARRON      (A
REID DEILICH       (A    PIET VEERMAN         (A    ARNOLD MUHREN         (A
CEES VEERMAN       (A    BEN BENAY       G    (A    CRAIG FALL       G    (A
KING ERRISSON  PERC (A   LARRY MUHOBERAC K    (A    MICHAEL OMARTIAN K    (A
TOM HENSLEY    K   (A    EARLE DUMLER    WIND (A    BUDDY EMMONS     STEEL  (A
ROBERT HARDAWAY K  (A    PAUL HUBINON    TPT  (A    CHARLES FINDLEY  TPT  (A
DALTON SMITH   TPT (A    REINIE PRESS    B    (A    JOHN RAINES      D    (A
JOHN ROTELLA   SAX (A
```

C62   FELIX CAVALIERE   C62

```
FELIX CAVALIERE  V K (AB    (A) FELIX               1974  BEARSVILLE          US  6955
EARL FORD       TROM (B     (B) DESTINY             1975  BEARSVILLE UK K55505 US 6958
ED LOGAN        SAX  (B     (C) CASTLES IN THE AIR  1979  EPIC  35990   UK       83817
EN BISCHEL      SYN  (B
BUZZ FEITEN     G    (B     STEVE KHAN      G    (B    MERVIN BRONSON   B    (B
JACK SCARANGELLLA D  (B     GEORGE YOUNG    SAX  (B    GAIL BOGGS       V    (B
RICK MAROTTA    D    (B     ALAN RUBIN      TPT  (B    WAYNE ANDRE      SAX  (A
JOE FARRELL     SAX  (B     TONY JIMINEZ    PERC (B    DIANE SCANLON    V    (B
EDGAR MATTHEWS  TPT  (B     LAURA NYRO      V    (B    DARCY MILLER     V    (B
WILL LEE        B    (B     DINO DANELLI    D    (B    MICHAEL BRECKER  SAX  (B
DAVE SANBORN    SAX  (B     TOM MALONE      TROM (B    JEFF SOUTHWORTH  G    (B
LESLIE WEST     G    (B     VICTOR MATTSON  SAX  (B    ELLIOT RANDALL   G    (B
EDDIE RIVERA    B    (B     NANCY O'NEILL   V    (B
```

C62A   ANDRE CECCARELLI   C62A

```
ANDRE CECCARELLI D  (A    (A) ANDRE CECCARELLI    19    SONOPRESSE FR   500 002
JANNIK TOP       (         (B) CECCARELLI          1979  INNER      US      1057
HENRI GIORDANO   (A
FRANCOIS JEANNEAU (A      DIDIER LOCKWOOD       (A   CHRISTIAN ESCOUDE      (A
JEAN CLAUDE CHAVANAT      (A  ALEX LIGERTWOOD   (A
```

C62B   CELEBRATION   C62B

```
RON ALTBACH     K    (A    (A) CELEBRATION        1978  PACIFIC ARTS  US  PAC7 122
CHARLES LLOYD   SAX  (A
KIM CALKINS     D    (A    PAUL FAUERSO   K V  (A    DAVE ROBINSON    V    (A
TIM WESTON      G    (A    KEVIN BRANDON  B    (A    AL PERKINS       G    (A
MIKE LOVE       V    (A    WELLS KELLY         (A    ED CARTER             (A
GARY GRIFFIN    K    (      MIKE KOWALSKI  D    (     STEVE LEACH      V    (A
IRENE CATHAWAY  V    (A    LINDA MALLAH   V    (A    SUZANNE WALLACH  V    (A
```

C62C   CELLATRON & THE INVISIBLE   C62C

```
CELLUTRON       SYN K(A    (A) REFLECTING ON THE FIRST WATCH  1978  GREEN MOUNTAIN US   4015
INDIANA STRAIGHT G   (A
SPACEBOY        SYN  (A    D TSIORBAS     SYN  (A    A TSIERBAS     SYN V(A
```

C62D   CENTAURUS   C62D

```
JOEY BELFIORE   D    (A    (A) CENTAURUS          1978  AZRA      US       61549
NICK PAINE      G    (A
LOUIS MERLINO   V    (A    NICK COSTELLO  B    (A
```

C63   CENTIPEDE   C63

```
JOHN MARSHALL    D    (A    (A) SEPTOBER ENERGY          1971  NEON            NE9
TONY FENNELL     D    (A    (A) SEPTOBER ENERGY  REISSUE 1974  RCA        DPS 5042
ROBERT WYATT     D    (A
BRIAN GODDING    G    (A
JULIE TIPPETT    V    (A    BRIAN BELSHAW   B    (A    MAGGIE NICHOLLS  V    (A
MONGEZI FEZA     HRN  (A    MIKE PATTO      V    (A    BOZ BURRELL      V    (A
MARK CHARIG      CORNET(A   ALAN SKIDMORE   SAX  (A    ROY BABBINGTON   B    (A
MICK COLLINS     TPT  (A    LARRY STABBINS  SAX  (A    JILL LYONS       B    (A
PETER PARKES     TPT  (A    GARY WINDO      SAX  (A    HARRY MILLER     B    (A
ELTON DEAN       SAX  (A    BRIAN SMITH     SAX  (A    JEFF CLYNE       B    (A
JAN STEEL        SAX  (A    DAVE WHITE      SAX  (A    DAVE MARKEE      B    (A
IAN McDONALD     SAX  (A    KARL JENKINS    SAX  (A    KEITH TIPPETT    PNO  (A
DUDU PUKWANA     SAX  (A    JOHN WILLIAMS   SAX  (A    IAN CARR         TPT  (A
                           LARGE STRING SECTION (A
```

CERTAIN RATIO
(A) TO EACH ...
19 FACTORY UK FACT 35

C63A

C63B

ANTONIO SPANGNOLO	G B	(A
GIULIO D'AMBROSIA	WIND	(A
GIANLUIGI DI FRANCE	V FLT(	A

CERVELLO
(A) MELOS
1973 DISCHI RICORDI IT 6119

C63B

C63C

CESAR ASCARRUNZ	PNO	(A
MARK LEVINE	PNO	(A
MERL SANDERS	PNO	(A
JOE JAMMER	G	(A
MARTIN FIERRE	SAX	(A
STEVE MARCUS	SAX	(A

| CORRADO RUSTICI | G V FLT | (A |
| REMIGIO ESPOSITE | D | (A |

C63C

CESAR
(A) CESAR 830
1975 FLYING DUTCHMAN US 0830

HAROLD MARTIN	B	(A	THOMAS RUTLEY	B	(A
STEPHEN BUSFIELD	G	(A	JIM VINCENT	G	(A
HADLEY CALIMAN	WIND	(A	JOSEPH ELLI JR	TPT	(A

C63D

PETER CETERA	G V	(A
STEVE LUKATHER	G	(A
MICHAEL BODDICKER	SYN	(A
CHRIS PINNICK	G	(A
CRAIG HULL	G	(A
KENNY EDWARDS	G	(A
JOSH LEO	G	(A

PETER CETERA
(A) PETER CETERA
1981 FULL MOON FMH 3624

C63D

RICH EAMES	K	(A	BOB GLAUB	B	(A
DAVID WOLINSKI	SYN	(A	CRAIG DOERGE	K	(A
MICHAEL BOTTS	D	(A	CARL WILSON	G	(A
RICKY FATAAR	D	(A	WILLIAM SMITH	K	(A .
MARK GOLDENBERG	G	(A

C64

| CHA LAWA | | (A |

CHA LAWA
(A) EXODUS DUB
1978 SKYNOTE

C64

C64A

CHACALS DE BETHUNE
(A) LA MALEDICTION DES ROCKERS
197 BARCLAY FR 521194

C64A

C64B

| CHAD STUART | G V | (ALL |
| JEREMY CLYDE | G V | (ALL |

CHAD & JEREMY

(A) BEFORE & AFTER	1964		
(B) I DONT WANNA LOOSE YOU BABY	1965	EMBER		5031
(C) BEST OF	1967	EMBER		5036
(D) MORE	1966		
(E) DISTANT SHORES	1966	CBS	
(F) OF CABBAGES & KINGS	1967	CBS US 9471		2671
(G) THE ARK	1968	CBS	US	9699

C64B

C65

JAMES MADISON	G V	(A
PHIL MANNING	G	(A
IAN CLYNE	K	(A
GREG LAWRIE	G	(A

CHAIN
(A) TWO OF A KIND
1973 MUSHROOM AUST 35017

C65

| GEORGE BEAUFORD | HCA V | (A | BARRY SULLIVAN | B | (A |
| BARRY HARVEY | D | (A | MAL CAPEWELL | WIND | (A |

C66

CHAIN REACTION
(A) INDEBTED TO YOU
1977 GULL GULP1021

C66

C67

GENERAL NORMAN JOHNSON	V	(
EDDIE CURTIS	V	(
HARRISON KENNEDY	V	(
DANNY WOODS	V	(

CHAIRMEN OF THE BOARD

(A) CHAIRMEN OF THE BOARD	1970	INVICTUS	UK	SVT 1002
(A) CHAIRMEN OF THE BOARD	1970	INVICTUS	US	7300
(B) IN SESSION	1971	INVICTUS	UK	SVT 1003
(B) IN SESSION	1971	INVICTUS	US	7304
(C) BITTERSWEET	1972	INVICTUS	UK	SVT 1006
(D) GREATEST HITS	1973	INVICTUS	UK	SVT 1009
(E) SKIN I'M IN	1974	INVICTUS	UK	65868
(E) SKIN I'M IN	1974	INVICTUS	US	35526
(F) MEN ARE GETTING SCARCE	19	INVICTUS	US	9801

C67

C68

RICHARD DELVECCHIO(DELVY)	D(ABF
GLENN GREY	G	(AB
JIM ROBERTS	K	(AB
RANDY NAVERT	B	(ABF
DON LANDIS	G	(AB
NICK HEFNER	SAX	(B
ED FOURNIER	G	(F
ART FISHER	G	(F

CHALLENGERS

(A) SURFBEAT	1963	STATESIDE	UK	SL 10030
(A) SURFBEAT	1963	VAULT	US	100
(B) SURFING WITH THE CHALLENGERS	196	VAULT	US	101
(C) TEENAGE FAIR	196	GNP	US	2010
(D) MAN FROM UNCLE	196	GNP	US	2018
(E) CALIFORNIA KICKS	196	GNP	US	2025
(F) WIPE OUT	1967	VOCALION		SAVN 8069
(F) WIPE OUT	1966	GNP	US	2031
(G) 25 GREATEST HITS	1967	GNP	US	609
(H) LIGHT MY FIRE	1969	GNP	US	2045
(J) VANILLA FUNK	1970	GNP	US	2056
(K) WHERE WERE YOU THE SUMMER OF 62	19	FANTASY	US	9443
(L) BEST OF	1982	RHINO	US	RNLP 053

C68

C68A

CATHY CHAMBERLAIN

| (A) RAG'N ROLL REVUE | 1976 | BUDDAH | US | 5686 |
| (B) RAG'N ROLL REVUE | 1977 | wb | US | 3032 |

C68A

CATHY CHAMBERLAIN	V CONC(AB
FRED MOORE	D V	(AB
STU BROWN	B HRNS(A
KAL DAVIS	G	(A
MARIA MULDAUR	V FDL(A
JOHN MILLER	B	(A
KENNY DAVERN	WIND	(B
MILT HINTON	B	(B
ELLIOTT RANDALL	G	(B

RICHARD LOOK	K V	(AB	TONY PARENTI	CLAR(A
HARVEY BROOKS	B	(A	BILLY FAIER	BAN	(A
LOUIE MATCALF	TPT	(A	LARRY PACKER	STR	(A
WARREN VACHE JR	CORNET	(B	KASH MONET	D	(B
JACK GALE	TROM	(B	HOWARD JOHNSON	D HRNS(B
NEIL JASON	B	(B	DAVID BROMBERG	G	(B

C69

LESTER CHAMBER	V HCA	(ALL
WILLIE CHAMBERS	G V	(ALL
GEORGE CHAMBERS	B	(ALL
JOE CHAMBERS	G V	(ALL
WITH
BRIAN KEENAN	D	(
STEVE CROPPER	G	(0

CHAMBERS BROTHERS

(A) PEOPLE GET READY	1965	VAULT	US	9003
(A) PEOPLE GET READY	1966	VOCALION	UK	SAVL 8058
(B) NOW	1966	VAULT	US	115
(C) SHOUT	1968	VAULT	US	120
(D) THE TIME HAS COME TODAY	1968	CBS	US	9522
(D) THE TIME HAS COME TODAY	1968	DIRECTION	UK	63407
(E) A NEW TIME A NEW DAY	1968	CBS	US	9671
(E) A NEW TIME A NEW DAY	1968	DIRECTION	UK	63451
(E) A NEW TIME A NEW DAY	1968	CBS	US	33642
(F) LIVE AT FILLMORE EAST	1970	CBS	US	20
(G) FEELING THE BLUES	1970	LIBERTY	UK	LBS83276
(G) FEELING THE BLUES	1970	VAULT	US	128
(H) A NEW GENERATION	1971	CBS	US	30032

C69

(CONTINUED)

C69   (CONTINUED)
                                    CHAMBERS BROTHERS   C69
                          (H) A NEW GENERATION   1971   CBS   UK   64156
                          (I) OH MY GOD   1972   CBS   US   31158
                          (J) UNBONDED   1973   AVCO   US   11013
                          (K) LOVE PEACE & HAPPINESS   1974   CBS   US   KGP20
                          (K) LOVE PEACE & HAPPINESS   1974   CBS   UK   66228
                          (L) RIGHT MOVE   1975   AVCO   US   69003
                          ( ) BEST OF   19   MUSIDISC   FR   6018
                          (DE) TIME HAS COME/NEW DAY DBL 19   CBS   US   33642
                          ( ) THE BEST OF   19   FANTASY   US   24718
                          ( ) GREATEST HITS   19   CBS US 30871   VAULT   135
                          (O) LIVE IN CONCERT ON MARS   1977   CHELSEA 548 ROXBURY 106
C69A   CHAMELEON CHURCH   C69A
     TED NYERS   G V (A   (A) CHAMELEON CHURCH   1968   MGM   4574
     TONY SCHEUREN   G B V(A
     KYLE GARRAHAN   V G K B(A   CHEVY CHASE   V D K(A
C69B   CHAMPAIGN   C69B
     PAULIE CARMAN   V   (A   (A) CHAMPAIGN   1981   CBS
     RENA JONES   V   (A
     ROCKY MAFFITT   PERC (A   MICHAEL DAY   K G   (A   HOWARD REEDER   G   (A
     DANA WALDEN   K   (A   MICHAEL REED   B   (A
C70   CHAMPION   C70
     GARY BELL   V G (A   (A) CHAMPION   1978   EPIC US 35438 UK   83179
     CLEM CLEMPSON   G   (A
     DAMON BUTCHER   K   (A   WILLIE BATH   B   (A   GEOFF BRITTON   D   (A
     JEFF RICH   D   (A
C70A   BILL CHAMPLIN   C70A
     BILL CHAMPLIN   V G K(A   (A) RUNAWAY   1981   ELEKTRA   US   5E563
     KENNY LOGGINS   PROD V(A
     JOHN ROBINSON   D   (A   JAMES NEWTON HOWARD   STR (A DAVID FOSTER PROD SYN V D K(A
     JON PIERCE   B   (A   STEVE LUKATHER   G   (A TOM KELLY   V   (A
     ED GREENE   D   (A   RICHARD PAGE   V   (A PAUL LANI   PERC (A
     LARRY TOLBERT   D   (A   ABRAHAM LABORIEL   B   (A JAY GRAYDON   G   (A
     VENNETTE GLOUD   V   (A   GARY HERBIG   SAX (A JERRY HEY   HRNS (A
     HUMBERT GATICA   PERC (A   TOM SCOTT   SAX (A GARY GRANT   TPT (A
     CHUCK FINDLEY   TPT (A   KIM HUTCHCROFT   SAX (A LARRY WILLIAMS   SAX (A
     BILL REICHENBACH   TROM (A   CHARLIE LOPER   TROM (A TAMARA MATOESIAN   V   (A
     CARMEN GRILLO   V   (A   JEFF PORCARO   D   (A LEE SKLAR   B   (A
C71   CHAMPS   C71
     GLEN CAMPBELL   G   ( ) EVERYBODY'S ROCKIN'   1960   CHALLENGE US 605   2500
     CHUCK RIO   SAX   ( ) GO CHAMPS GO   196   LONDON   UK   HAH 2152
     BOBBY MORRIS   B   ( ) GO CHAMPS GO   196   CHALLENGE   US   601
     DAVE BURGESS   G   ( ) GREAT DANCE HITS   196   LONDON   UK   HAH 2451
     JIMMY SEALS   SAX   ( ) GREAT DANCE HITS   196   CHALLENGE   US   613
     DALE NORRIS   G   ( ) BEST OF THE CHAMPS   1977   LONDON   UK   ZGH 141
     DEAN BEARD   PNO   ( ) PLAY ALL AMERICAN   19   CHALLENGE   US   2514
     GENE ALDEN   D   ( ) PLAY JOSHUA LOGAN ALL AMERICAN 19 CHALLENGE   US   614
     VAN NORMAN   B
C72 DASH CROFTS   D   GENE CHANDLER   C72
     GENE CHANDLER   V   (ALL   GENE CHANDLER   1967   CHECKER   3003
     CLIFF DAVIS   SAX (L   THERE WAS A TIME   197   MCA   UK   MUPS 367
     JONI BERLMON   V   (M   THERE WAS A TIME   19   BRUNSWICK   US   754131
     THERESA DAVIS   V   (M   ALBUM   1974   JOY   JOYS 136
     RHONDA GRAISON   V   (M   DUKE OF EARL   1976   DJM   DJB 26077
                                     GET DOWN   19   20TH CENTURY   US   578
                                     LIVE ON STAGE   19   ACTION   6010
                                     WHEN YOU'RE No1   1979   20TH CENTURY   UK   598
                                     SITUATION   1970   MERCURY   US   SR 61304
                                     THE GIRL DONT CARE   19   BRUNSWICK   US   54124
                                     TWO SIDES OF   19   BRUNSWICK   US   754149
                                     (L)GET DOWN   19   20TH CENTURY   US   578
                                     (M)GENE CHANDLER   1980   20TH CENTURY   US   605
                                     JUST BE TRUE   1980   CHARLY   UK   1007
                                     NOTHING CAN STOP ME   (EP)   1980   CHARLY   UK   CTD 116
C72A   CHANGO   C72A
     GEORGE TACKTIKES   G V (A   (A) CHANGO   1975   ABC   US   872
     REINEL ANDINE   PERC V(A   (B) HONEY IS SWEETER THAN BLOOD 1976 MERCURY   US   1103
     PEPE GOMEZ   D V (AB
     MIKE CRUZ   PERC V(B   KEN WEISSMAN   D   (B   BURLIN SPEAKES   G B V   (AB
     THOMAS ALLETTO   K V (A   CHARLES ROOK   G   (B   MICHAEL BRITTON   PERC   (A
     MARTY GREBB   SAX K(B
C73   BRUCE CHANNEL   C73
     BRUCE CHANNELL   V   (ALL   HEY BABY   19   SMASH   US   27008
                                      GOIN BACK TO LOUISIANA   19   SONET   SNT 301
C74   CHANTAYS   C74
     BRIAN CARMAN   PIPELINE   1963   LONDON UK 8087 DOT US 25516
     BOB MARSHALL   PIPELINE   1974   CONTOUR   UK   2879 389
     WARREN WATERS
     BOB WELCH   BOB SPICKARD
C74A   CHANTELS   C74A
                                      WE ARE THE CHANTELS   19   END   US   301
                                      HERE'S OUR SONG AGAIN   19   END   US   312
C75   CHANTERS SISTERS   C75
     DOREEN CHANTER   K V (ALL   (A) BIRDS OF A FEATHER   1970   PAGE ONE   UK   POLS 027
     IRENE CHANTER   K V (ALL   (B) FIRST FLIGHT   1976   POLYDOR UK6075 UK   2383 382
     RAY WARLEIGH   WIND (D   (C) READY FOR LOVE   1978   SAFARI   LONG 3
     PETE WINGFIELD   K   (D   (D) SHOULDER TO SHOULDER   1978   SAFARI   LONG 4
     HENRY SPINETTI   D   (D
     DAVE MARKEE   B   (D   RAY RUSSELL   G   (D   MICK MOODY   G   (D
         (CONTINUED)

[102]

CHANTER SISTERS

SIMON PHILLIPS	D	(D	JOHN GIBLIN	B	(D	TONY HYMAS	CLAR PNO	(D
RAY COOPER	PERC	(BD	HUGH BURNS	G	(BD	CHRIS MERCER	SAX	(D
MARTIN DROVER	WIND	(D	JIMMY CHAMBERS	V	(D	TONY JACKSON	V	(D
NEIL HUBBARD	G	(B	BARRY MORGAN	D	(B	HERBIE FLOWERS	B	(B
MIKE MORAN	K	(B	JEFF DALY	SAX	(B	MADELINE BELL	V	(B
KENNY MALONE	D PERC	(C	MIKE LEECH	B	(C	REGGIE YOUNG	G	(C
JIMMY COUARD	G	(C	JOHNNY CHRISTOPHER	G	(C	BOBBY WOODS	K	(C
CHARLES COCHRAN	K	(C	HARVEY THOMPSON	HRNS	(C	HARRISON CALLAWAY	HRNS	(C
RONNIE EADES	SAX	(C	GARY BROWN	SAX	(C			

HARRY CHAPIN

HARRY CHAPIN	G V	(ALL	(A) HEADS & TALES	1971 ELEKTRA US EKS75023 UK K42107
TIM SCOTT	CELLO	(CEGH	(B) SNIPER & OTHER LOVE SONGS	1972 ELEKTRA US EKS75042 UK K42125
JOHN WALLACE	B V	(BCEGHKLFJ	(C) SHORT STORIES	1973 ELEKTRA US EKS75065 UK K42155
PAUL LEKA	K	(CEG	(D) VERITIES & BALDERDASH	1974 ELEKTRA US 7E 1012 UK K52007
JEANNE FRENCH	V	(C	(E) PORTRAIT GALLERY	1975 ELEKTRA US 7E 1041 UK K52023
BUDDY SALZMAN	D	(C	(F) ON THE ROAD TO KINGDOM COME	1976 ELEKTRA US 7E 1082 UK K52040
HOWIE FIELDS	D	(HGKLFJ	(G) GREATEST STORIES LIVE	1976 ELEKTRA US 7E 2009 UK K62017
JOHN TROPEA	G	(EG	(H) DANCE BAND ON THE TITANIC	1977 ELEKTRA US 9E 301 UK K62021
TOM CHAPIN	G BANJ	(GHLJ	(J) LIVING ROOM SUITE	1978 ELEKTRA US 6E 142 UK K52089
STEVE CHAPIN	PNO V	(EGHFKLJ	(K) LEGENDS OF THE LOST & FOUND	1979 ELEKTRA UK K62026
ALLEN SCHWARZBERG	D	(EG	(L) SEQUEL	1980 BOADWALK US 36872 CBS UK 84996
ED BEDNARSKI	CLAR	(EG		

FRANK PORTO	ACC	(E	DONNA D REILLY	V	(H	ROB WHITEWHISTLE		(E	KEN SMITH	PERC	(E
BOB SPRINGER	PERC	(EG	KRIS KRISTOFFERSON	V	(E	RITA COOLIDGE	V	(E	BILLY SWAN	V	(E
GEORGE SIMS	V	(EG	ELLIOT RANDALL	G	(H	DOUG WALKER	G B	(GH	DON PEAK	SYN	(E
DAVE KONZIELA	V	(E	FRANK SIMMS	V	(E	RON BACCHIOCCHI	PERC	(EG	SCOTT SPRAY		(EG
BOB SMITH		(EG	PAUL GABRIEL		(EG	JIMMY KEYES		(EG	GENE BIANCO	HARP	(E
SUE WHITE	V	(EG	KATHY RAMOS	V	(EG	KATHY PORTER	V	(E	CAROLYN WILLIS	V	(E
MARTY McCALL	V	(E	JACKIE WARD	V	(E	CHERYL FERRIO	V	(G	JEFF GROSS	V	(EH
JIM KELTNER	D	(J	NEIL JASON	B	(J	LOU VOLPE	G	(J	BOB COWSILL	G	(J
BILL PAYNE	K	(J	ERNIE WATTS	SAX	(J	DENNIS FRICK	WIND	(J	STEVE FORMAN	PERC	(J
DAVID BURGEN	HCA	(J	STEVE MADAIO	TPT	(J	CHUCK FINDLEY	TPT	(E	GEORGE BOHANNON	TROM	(J
TOM SMITH		(G	TIM MOORE	K	(EG	SHEILA TURNER	V	(E	J FLOOD	V	(E
GEOFF PARKER	V	(E	JOAN FISHMAN	V	(E	JUDI PARKER	V	(E	PAUL HUBINON	WIND	(E
BUD BRISBOIS	WIND	(E	JACKIE KELSO	WIND	(EJ	JAY MIGLIORI	WIND	(E	JIM HORN	SAX	(E
GEORG BOHANON	WIND	(E	CHRISTINE FAITH	V	(G	MARY MUNDY	V	(G	BETSY WAGER	V	(G
STEVE GADD	D	(H	NEIL JASON	B	(H	BUZZ BRAUNER	SAX	(H	HARRY DEVITO	TROM	(H
ARTHUR JENKINS	PERC	(H	CHRIS WAITE	PERC	(H	VICTORIA	CONGA	(H	NANCY NEWMAN	V	(H
CRAIG MITCHELL	V	(H	THEODORE MARNEL	V	(H	STEVE RANDALL	V	(H	MARSH LYNN GOLDBERG	V	(H
JOHN QUAYLE	V	(H	ART KRAHULCK	V	(H	BARBRA CARR		(H	MIKE SOLOMON	V	(H
BARBARA LINDQUIST	V	(H	BERNIE KEISING	V	(H	STEVE CHAPIN PNO V		(EGHKL	DAVE ARMSTRONG	HCA	(J
DON PAYNE	B	(J	BOBBY CARLIN	D	(C	TOMI LEE BRADLEEY	V	(J	KIM SCHOLES	CELLO	(HKJ
MICHAEL MASTERS	CELLO	(CEG	RON PALMER	G V	(CEGH	YVONNE CABLE	CELLO	(L	JOE LALA	PERC	(L
CHUCK KIRKPATRICK	V	(L	HOWARD ALBERT	SYN	(L	CHARLES CHALMERS	V	(L	SANDRA RHODES	V	(L
DONNA RHODES	V	(L	RON EVANUIK	CELLO	(F	DONNA FEIN	V	(F	MUFFY HENDRIX	V	(F
CAROLYN DENNIS	V	(F	BOBBYE HALL	PERC	(F	BUZZ BRAUNER	REC	(F	DICK HYDE	TROM	(F
THE COWSILLS	V	(J	DIXIE HUMMINGBIRDS	V	(J						

BLONDIE CHAPLIN

BLONDIE CHAPLIN	V G B PERC	(A	(A) BLONDIE CHAPLIN	1977 ASYLUM US 1095 UK K53062				
RICKY FATAAR	D PERC	(A						
DAVID MASON	PNO	(A	RICHARD TEE	K	(A	GARTH HUDSON	ACC	(A
JOHN HARTMAN	PNO	(A	STEVE LAWRENCE	SAX	(A	KENNY WALTER	TROM	(A
HOWARD TSUKAMOTO	B	(A	TOM BRAY	HRNS	(A	CARLOS MUNOZ	ORG	(A
BRYAN GAROFALO	B	(A	CLYDIE KING	V	(A	VANEETA FIELDS	V	(A
KENNY GRADNEY	B	(A	DANIEL MOORE	V	(A	CAROL HOLMES	V	(A
MATTHEW MOORE	V	(A	RITA JEAN BODINE	V	(A			

MARSHALL CHAPMAN

MARSHALL CHAPMAN	G V	(ALL	(A) ME I'M FEELIN FREE	1977 EPIC US 34422
MIKE DESPAPAS	G	(BC	(B) JADED VIRGIN	1978 EPIC US 35341
JEFF SMITH	G V	(BC	(C) MARSHALL	1979 EPIC US 36192
WILLIS BAILEY	D	(B		

TOM COMET	B	(B	STEVE SCHAFFER	B	(C	JERRY KREEN	D	(C	BOBBY EMMONS	K	(C
TERRY McMILLAN	PERC HCA	(C	REGGIE YOUNG	G	(A	TEDDY IRWIN	G	(A	TED REYNOLDS	B	(A
BUDDY EMMONS	STEEL	(A	JERRY CARRIGAN	D	(A	HARGUS PIG ROBBINS	PNO	(A	YVONNE HODGES	V	(A
BILLY PUETT	HRNS	(A	ANITA BALL	V	(A	GINGER HOLLADAY	V	(A	JANIE FRICKE	V	(A
LEA JANE BERINATI	V	(A	AL KOOPER	K G B	(B	PHIL AABERG	PNO	(B	DAVID WILCZEWSKI	SAX	(B
JAMES BURTON	G	(C	RON HICKLIN SINGERS	V	(B	BILLY SANFORD	G	(C	PETE DRAKE	STEEL	(A
FRED NEWELL	G	(C	MARY ANN KENNEDY	V	(C	PAM ROSE	V	(C	ERNIE ROWELL	V	(C

MICHAEL CHAPMAN

MICHAEL CHAPMAN	G K V	(ALL	(A) RAINMAKER	1969 HARVEST UK SHVL 755
WITH			(B) FULLY QUALIFIED SURVIVOR	1969 HARVEST US 816 UK SHVL 764
RAY LAIDLAW	D	(N	(B) FULLY QUALIFIED SURVIVOR	1979 CRIMINAL UK TAKE3
RICK KEMP	B	(ABCDEFGKM	(C) WINDOW	1971 HARVEST UK SHVL 786
BARRY MORGAN	D	(ABK	(D) WRECKED AGAIN	1971 HARVEST UK SHVL 798
ANDY LATIMER	G	(HJ	(D) WRECKED AGAIN	1971 POLYDOR GERM 2310 192
DANNY THOMPSON		(A	(E) MILLSTONE GRIT	1973 HARVEST UK SML 1105
CLEM CLEMPSON	G	(AK	(F) DEAL GONE DOWN	1974 HARVEST UK SML 1114
NORMAN HAINES		(AK	(G) PLEASURES OF THE STREET	1975 NOVA GERM 622321
ALEX DMOCHOWSKI	B	(AK	(H) SAVAGE AMUSEMENT	1976 GAMA DECCA UK SKLR 5242
AYNSLEY DUNBAR	D	(AK	(J) THE MAN WHO HATED MORNINGS	1977 DECCA UK SKLR 5290
MICK RONSON	G	(ABJK	(J) THE MAN WHO HATED MORNINGS	1978 CRIMINAL UK STEAL3
GUS DUDGEON		(B	(K) LIVED HERE	1977 CUBE UK GNAT 1
PAUL BUCKMASTER	CELLO	(B	(L) PLAYING GUITAR THE EASY WAY	1979 CRIMINAL UK STEAL2
JOHNNY VAN DERRICK	VLN	(BCG	(M) LIFE ON THE CEILING	1978 CRIMINAL US 7138 UK STEAL5
ANDRU CHAPMAN	V	(N	(N) LOOKING FOR ELEVEN	1980 CRIMINAL UK STEAL9
B J COLE	STEEL	(J	( ) LADY ON THE ROCKS	19 INTERCORD GER 126 309
HAROLD FATT	G	(CK		

PETE WINGFIELD	K	(J	JOHN McBURNIE	V	(J	RICHIE DHARMA	D	(CK	VIV McAULIFFE	V	(J
PRELUDE	V	(F	ALEX ATTERSON	PNO	(CE	PICK WITHERS	D	(DK	RAY MARTINEZ	G	(DK
JACK EMBLOW	ACC	(D	LIZA STRIKE	V	(D	CLAUDETTE HOUCHEN	V	(D	NEIL LANCASTER	V	(D

(CONTINUED)

C78 (CONTINUED)

MICHAEL CHAPMAN

```
ALBERT HAMMOND    V   (D    KEEF HARTLEY    D (EGHJ  NIGEL PEGRUM    D  (F    MADDY PRIOR      V  (F
BRIDGET ST JOHN   V   (F    PETER WOOD      K  (H    LEO LE BLANC    STEEL(H  MUTT                (GH
STEVIE            V   (GH   FUZZ            V  (GH   STEFFI STEFAN       (G    ACHIM REICHEL       (G
PAUL SUTTON       G   (G    ROD CLEMENTS    B  (JN   ANDY ROBERTS    G  (      HENRY McCULLOUGH  G (
TIM RENWICK       G   (H    PHIL PALMER     G  (M    ANDY RICHARDS   K  (M     DAVE MATTACKS    D  (M
DAVY WOOD         K   (N    LESLEY DUNCAN   V  (M    AL HODGE        V  (M
```

ROGER CHAPMAN

```
ROGER CHAPMAN     V   (ALL    (A) CHAPPO                      1979 ARISTA UK SPART1083  LINE GER 5097
WITH                          (B) LIVE IN HAMBURG             1979 ACROBAT UK ACRO 6    LINE GER 5103
DAVE MARKEE       B   (A      (C) MAIL ORDER MAGIC            1980                      LINE GER 5080
BRIAN ODGERS      B   (A      (D) HYENAS ONLY LAUGH FOR FUN   1981                      LINE GER 5125
BILLY LIVSEY      K   (A      (E) HE WAS SHE WAS....(DBL)     1982                      LINE GER 6011
JOHN HALSEY       D   (C
LES BINKS         D   (C    GEOFF WHITEHORN  G (ABCDE  MICK MOODY   G  (A    HENRY SPINETTI  D  (A
SIMON MORTON      PERC (A   RAY COOPER       PERC(A    RON ASPERY   SAX(A    POLI PALMER     SYN(ACDE
PETER HOPE EVANS  HCA  (A   JOY YATES        V  (A     VICKI BROWN  V  (A    JIMMY CHAMBERS  V  (
GEORGE CHANDLER   V   (A    MEL COLLINS      SAX (B    TIM HINKLEY  K  (BCDE JEROME RIMSON  B V (BCD
JOHN WETTON       B   (C    STRETCH          D  (BDE   HELEN HARDY  V  (B    KATHI O'DONOGHUE    V (B
MITCH MITCHELL    D   (C    STEVE SIMPSON    VLN G (DE NICK PENTELOW SAX(DE  ALAN COULTER    D  (D
BOZ BURRELL       B   (E
```

CHARGE

```
ROSETTA HIGHTOWER V  (A     (A) CHARGE                  1974  FRESH AIR      6308 900
LEE VANDERBILT    V  (A
MIKE WOODS        G  (A     NEIL HUBBARD    G    (A     ALAN SPENNER    B  (A
GODFREY MACLEAN   D  (A     SMILEY DE JONNES PERC (A    CHRIS STAINTON  ORG (A
CHRIS MERCER      SAX (A    STEVE GREGORY   SAS  (A     RON CARTHY      TPT (A
```

MARK CHARIG

```
MARK CHARIG       TPT (A    (A) PIPEDREAM           1977 OGUN        OG710
KEITH TIPPETT     K PERC V(A
ANN WINTER        V   (A
```

CHARIOT

```
MICHAEL KOPLAN    G V (A    (A) CHARIOT             1968 NATIONAL GENERAL   NG2003
LARRY GOULD       B V
PUG BAKER         D
```

CHARITY

```
JEFF OXMAN        V  (A     (A) NEW                 1969 UNI         73061
BLOSSOMS          V  (A
WALT FLANNERY        (A     KENT HENRY      G   (A   JAMES PETERS        (A
JOHN CORTINAS        (A
```

CHARLATANS

```
DAN HICKS         V D G (12  (A) THE CHARLATANS     1969 PHILIPS   US 600  309
RICHARD OLSEN     B   (A123  (B) THE CHARLATANS     1979 GROUCHO   IT  MAR X
MICHAEL FERGUSON  K   (1     (1) 64 67      (2) 67 68  (C) 68 69
MIKE WILHELM      V G (A123
PATRICK BOGERTY   PNO (2     TERRY WILSON    D   (A23  DARRYL DEVORE   K  (A3
SAM LINDE         D   (1     GEORGE HUNTER   V   (12
```

BOBBY CHARLES

```
BOBBY CHARLES(ROBERT GUIDRY)(A   (A) BOBBY CHARLES   1972 BEARSVILLE US 2104  UK K45516
AMOS GARRETT      G   (A
DR JOHN           K   (A
```

CHILI CHARLES

```
CHILLI CHARLES    D V K (AB  (A) BUSY CORNER        1974 VIRGIN     UK   V2009
DEL RICHARDSON    G   (AB    (B) QUICKSTEP          1975 VIRGIN     UK   V2028
ROBERT BAILEY     K   (AB
JOE JAMMER        G   (B     MEL COLLINS     SAX (A   GORDON SMITH   G  (A
FUZZY SAMUELS     B   (A     PAT ARNOLD      V   (A   KENNY COLE     V  (A
PHIL BECQUE       B   (A     JEAN ROUSSEL    B K (B   BROTHER JAMES  V  (B
VICKY BUSISWE MHLONGO  V (B  GEORGE LARNYOH  SAX (B   EDDIE QUANSAH  TPT (B
PETE VANDER PUIJE SAX (B     JON PIRANA      V   (B   SUZY SHUTE     V  (B
```

RAY CHARLES

```
RAY CHARLES       K V (ALL   (EPs) HIT THE ROAD JACK          19 HMV   7EG 8729
                                   I CANT STOP LOVING YOU      19 HMV   7EG 8781
                                   BALLAD STYLE OF RAY CHARLES 19 HMV   7EG 8783
                                   BALLAD STYLE OF RAY CHARLES 19 HMV   GES 5864
                                   SWINGING STYLE              19 HMV   7EG 8801
                                   SWINGING STYLE              19 HMV   GES 5871
                                   BABY ITS COLD OUTSIDE       19 HMV   7EG 8807
                                   TAKE THESE CHAINS           19 HMV   7EG 8812
                                   BUSTED                      19 HMV   7EG 8841
LPs                                RAY CHARLES SINGS           19 HMV   7EG 8861
```

```
RAY CHARLES                1957 ATLANTIC      8006    IN PERSON               1960 ATLANTIC US   8039
RAY CHARLES (HALLELUJAH)   19   ATLANTIC UK 587056    IN PERSON               1960 LONDON   UK   2284
THE GREAT R C              1958 ATLANTIC US   1259    GENIUS SINGS THE BLUES  1960 ATLANTIC      8052
THE GREAT R C              1958 LONDON   UK  15134    GENIUS SINGS THE BLUES  1960 LONDON   UK  15238
RAY CHARLES AT NEWPORT     1958 ATLANTIC      1289    DEDICATED TO YOU        1960 HMV      UK   1362
RAY CHARLES AT NEWPORT     1958 LONDON   UK   6008    DEDICATED TO YOU        1961 HMV      UK   1449
RAY CHARLES AT NEWPORT     197  ATLANTIC UK K30032    DEDICATED TO YOU        1961 ABC      UK    355
ORIGINAL RAY CHARLES       19   LONDON   UK   8022    GENIUS+SOUL=JAZZ        1960 ATLANTIC       A2
YES INDEED                 1958 ATLANTIC      8025    GENIUS+SOUL=JAZZ        1961 HMV      UK   1384
YES INDEED                 1958 LONDON   UK   2168    GENIUS+SOUL=JAZZ        1961 HMV      UK   1475
WHAT'D I SAY               1959 ATLANTIC      8029    DO THE TWIST            196  ATLANTIC      8054
WHAT'D I SAY               1959 LONDON   UK   2226    GENIUS HITS THE ROAD    196  ABC      US    335
WHAT'D I SAY               19   ATLANTIC UK 588161    GENIUS HITS THE ROAD    1960 HMV      UK   1387
WHAT'D I SAY               1971 ATLANTIC UK K40029    GENIUS HITS THE ROAD    1960 HMV      UK   1320
GENIUS OF R C              1959 ATLANTIC      1312    & BETTY CARTER          1960 HMV      UK   1520
RAY CHARLES                1959 XTRA          1103    & BETTY CARTER          1960 COLUMBIA     340742
SOUL BROTHERS              1959 LONDON   UK   6030    & BETTY CARTER          196  ABC      US    385
SOUL BROTHERS              19   ATLANTIC US   1279    & BETTY CARTER          196  HMV      UK   1414
RAY CHARLES SEXTET         1960 LONDON   UK  15178    MODERN SOUNDS IN C&W    196  HMV      UK   1580
RAY CHARLES SEXTET         1960 ATLANTIC      1304    MODERN SOUNDS IN C&W    196  ABC      US    410
```

(CONTINUED)

RAY CHARLES

Title	Year	Label	Country	Number
MODERN SOUNDS IN C&W 2	196	HMV	UK	1613
MODERN SOUNDS IN C&W 2	196	ABC	US	435
SOUL MEETING(MILT JACKSON)	1962	ATLANTIC	US	1360
SOUL MEETING(MILT JACKSON)	197	ATLANTIC		K50234
SOUL MEETING(MILT JACKSON)	1963	LONDON	UK	8046
GREATEST HITS	1962	ABC	US	415
GREATEST HITS	196	HMV	UK	1482
GREATEST HITS	196	HMV	UK	1626
STORY VOL 1	1962	ATLANTIC		8063
STORY VOL 1	1962	LONDON	UK	8023
STORY VOL 2	1962	ATLANTIC		8064
STORY VOL 2	1962	LONDON	UK	8024
STORY VOL 3	1963	ATLANTIC		8083
GREAT HITS	1963	HMV	UK	1482
GREAT HITS	1963	ATLANTIC		7101
RECIPE FOR SOUL	1963	ABC	US	465
RECIPE FOR SOUL	1963	HMV	UK	1678
SWEET & SOUR TEARS	1963	ABC	US	480
SWEET & SOUR TEARS	1963	HMV	UK	1728
SWEET & SOUR TEARS	1963	HMV	UK	1537
C&W MEETS R&B	196	HMV	UK	1630
C&W MEETS R&B	196	HMV	UK	1914
STORY VOL 4	1964	ATLANTIC		8094
HAVE A SMILE WITH ME	1964	HMV	UK	1566
HAVE A SMILE WITH ME	1964	HMV	UK	1795
LIVE	196	ATLANTIC	US	2503
IN CONCERT	1965	HMV	UK	1872
IN CONCERT	1965	HMV	UK	1606
IN CONCERT	1965	ABC	US	500
TOGETHER AGAIN	1965	ABC	US	520
TOGETHER AGAIN	1965	HMV	UK	
SENSATIONAL	1965	SOCIETY		998
CINCINNATI KID	1965	MGM	US	SE4313
CRYING TIME	1966	HMV	UK	3533
CRYING TIME	1966	HMV	US	344
RAYS MOOD	1966	HMV	UK	3574
RAYS MOOD	1966	ABC	US	550
LISTEN	1967	HMV	UK	3630
LISTEN	1967	ABC	US	595
A MAN & HIS SOUL	1967	ABC		590
LE GRAND	196	ATLANTIC	FR	332030
IN THE HEAT OF THE NIGHT	1967	U A	US	5160
GREAT HITS (5LP SET)	19	LONGINES	US	95647
14 ORIGINAL HITS	19	STARDAY	US	K 5011
GREATEST HITS VOL 2	19	STATESIDE		UK10241
LOVE COUNTRY STYLE	1969	PROBE		1015
LOVE COUNTRY STYLE	19	ABC		707
IM ALL YOURS BABY	1969	ABC		675
IM ALL YOURS BABY	1969	STATESIDE		10281
DOING HIS THING	1959	ABC	US	695
DOING HIS THING	1970	STATESIDE		10293
THE ARTISTRY OF	19	BARONET	US	111
3 OF A KIND	19	DESIGN	US	909
PORTRAIT OF RAY	1969	STATESIDE	UK	10269
PORTRAIT OF RAY	1969	ABC	US	625
MY KIND OF JAZZ	1970	TANGERINE		6495 001
FOCUS ON	1975	LONDON		F051/2
MY KIND OF JAZZ	1970	TANGERINE		TRCS1512
VOLCANIC ACTION	1971	PROBE		1039
VOLCANIC ACTION	1971	ABC	US	726
PRESENTS THE RAELETTES	1972	TANGERINE	US	1515
JAZZ NUMBER TWO	1973	TANGERINE	US	1516
MESSAGE FROM THE PEOPLE	1972	PROBE		1060
MESSAGE FROM THE PEOPLE	1972	ABC	US	755
25th ANNIVERSARY(DBL)	1972	ATLANTIC	UK	K60014
25th ANNIVERSARY(DBL)	1971	ABC	US	731
ORIGINAL RAY CHARLES	1972	BOULEVARD		4005
GENIUS IN CONCERT L A	1973	BLUESWAY		6053
ALLTIME GREAT C&W HITS	1973	PROBE	UK	108
THE FANTASTIC	19	MUSIDISC		ALB103
MEMORIES OF MOVIE FAN	19	ATLANTIC		SD 263
INCOMPARABLE	19	MUSIDISC		CV 964
STAR COLLECTION	1978	MIDI	FR	20015
BEST OF	19	POLYDOR		2472 044
THROUGH THE EYES OF LOVE	1973	PROBE	UK	1066
THROUGH THE EYES OF LOVE	1973	ABC	US	765
THE GREATEST HITS(5 LP SET)	1974	CROSSOVER		95647
COME LIVE WITH ME	1974	LONDON	UK	8467
ROCKIN WITH RAY	19	ARCH		358
COME LIVE WITH ME	1974	CROSSOVER		9000
WORLD OF RAY CHARLES VOL 2	1975	DECCA	UK	422
WORLD OF RAY CHARLES	1974	ARGO	UK	SPA361
LIVE IN JAPAN DBL	1975	CROSSOVER		535/6
RENAISSANCE	1975	LONDON	UK	8485
RENAISSANCE	1975	CROSSOVER		9005
MY KIND OF JAZZ VOL 3	1975	CROSSOVER		9007
THE GREAT R C	19	MUSIDISC		1232
HONEY HONEY	19	XTRA		1103
PORGY & BESS(CLEO LAINE)	1976	RCA	US	2 1831
PORGY & BESS(CLEO LAINE)	1976	LONDON		D 31/2
THE BEST OF	19	MCP	US	8029
RAY CHARLES	19	EVEREST	US	244
RAY CHARLES VOL2	19	EVEREST	US	292
RAY CHARLES	19	UPFRONT	US	UPF170
RAY CHARLES	19	UPFRONT	US	UPF192
TRUE TO LIFE	1977	LONDON		8509
TRUE TO LIFE	1977	ATLANTIC		19142
WHAT HAVE DONE TO THEIR SONG	1977	LONDON		ZGU 139
LOVE & PEACE	1978	LONDON		8519
BLUES	1978	EMBER	UK	CJS854
LOVE & PEACE	1978	ATCO		19199
FABULOUS RAY CHARLES	1978	MUSIDISC		CV1288
AIN'T IT SO	1979	LONDON	UK	SHL8537
SUPERDISC OF R C	1979	A&M		GXM9012
20 GOLDEN PIECES OF R C	1979	BULLDOG		BDL2012
BROTHER RAY	1980	ATLANTIC	US	19281

RONNIE CHARLES

RONNIE CHARLES		(A
LOU REIZNER	PROD	(A
KEITH TIPPETT	K	(A

(A) PRESTIDIGITION	1975	20CENTURY	BT 491

SPEEDY KEEN	V	(A	HERBIE FLOWERS	B	(A

ROBERT CHARLEBOIS

ROBERT CHARLEBOIS	V	(A
RICHARD PROVENCAL	PERC	(A
DANIEL HUBERT	B	(A
FRANK ZAPPA	G	(A

(A) SWING CHARLEBOIS SWING	1977	RCA	6436

JEAN MARIE BENOIT	K	(A	MARCEL BEACHAMP	K	(A

CHARLIE

JOHN ANDERSON	B V	(ABCD
TERRY THOMAS	G V	(ABCD
STEVE GADD	D PERC	(ABCD
JULIAN COLBECK	K	(CD
EUGENE ORGAN	G V	(CD
GRAEME QUINTON-JONES	K	(A
MARTIN SMITH	G V	(A
SHEP LONSDALE	D	(D
VICTOR PAZ	TPT	(D
ARNIE LAWRENCE	SAX	(D
PHILLIP TODD	FLT	(D

(A) FANTASY GIRLS	1976	POLYDOR	UK	2382 373
(A) FANTASY GIRLS	1976	CBS	US	34081
(B) NO SECOND CHANCE	1977	POLYDOR	UK	2383 422
(B) NO SECOND CHANCE	1977	JANUS	US	7032
(C) LINES	1978	POLYDOR	UK	2383 487
(C) LINES	1978	JANUS	US	7036
(D) FIGHT DIRTY	1979	POLYDOR UK 2443 161 +		5017
(D) FIGHT DIRTY	1979	ARISTA	US	4239

LAWRENCE FELDMAN	SAX	(D	PETE THOMS	TROM	(D
DAVID POTTS	FLT	(D	RAY COOPER	PERC	(D

CHARLIE & THE PEP BOYS

CHARLIE WOODS-PEARSON	V	(A
MICHAEL STERN	G	(A
ALAN ADKINS	G	(A
MICHAEL ZACK	D	(A
LEFTY POTOMAC	K	(A

(A) DADDY'S GIRL	1976	A&M UK AMLH64563	US 4563

BOBBY MANRIQUEZ	G	(A	ROLF HANSON	B	(A
MICHAEL S	SAX	(A	CRAIG RYAN	TPT	(A

CHARLIE & THE WIDE BOYS

CHARLIE AINLEY	V	(AB
RICHARD WORTHY	G	(AB
GREG PHILLIPS	V PERC	(AB
NIGEL CHAPPELL	B	(AB

(A) CHARLIE & THE WIDE BOYS (EP)	1974	ANCHOR	ANCE 1007
(B) GREAT COUNTRY ROCKERS	1976	MFP ANCHOR	50293

GUY EVANS	D	(AB	SIMON FRASER	G	(AB

CHARLIE BOY

CHARLIE NEWPORT	G V	(A
EDDY WILLIAMS	B V	(A
STEVE HODGES	V	(A
FRED LLOYD	K	(A

(A) INTRODUCING CHARLIE BOY	19	RELEASE	BRL 4076

BRIAN ROPER	D V	(A	BILLY ROPER	G STEEL V	(A
BRENDAN BONASS	G	(A			

C88 CHARTREUSE

PAUL JEFFREYS	B						
MILTON REAME-JAMES	K						
JEFF FAULKNER	G		MALCOLM ASHMAN	D		ROB ELLIOT	V

C89 CHAS & DAVE

CHAS HODGES	V G K	(ALL	(A) ONE FING 'N'ANUVVER	1975	RETREAT RT6004	NUT	NUT17
DAVE PEACOCK	B V FDL	(ALL	(B) CHAS & DAVE	1978	ROCKNEY		OCKNEY 1
ALBERT LEE	G	(D	(C) ROCKNEY	1978	EMI		EMC 3288
ERIC CLAPTON	G	(D	(D) DONT GIVE A MONKEYS	1979	EMI		
DAVE EDMUNDS	G	(D	(E) MUSTN'T GRUMBLE	1981	ROCKNEY		909
MICKEY BURT	D	(ALL					

C90 CHASE

BILL CHASE	TPT	(ABCD	(A) CHASE	1971	EPIC/CBS	UK	64544
ALAN WARE	TPT	(A	(A) CHASE	197	EPIC	US	30472
JERRY VAN BLAIR	TPT V	(A	(B) ENNEA	1972	EPIC/CBS	UK	64710
PHIL PORTER	K	(A	(B) ENNEA	1972	EPIC	US	31097
DENNIS JOHNSON	B V	(A	(C) PURE MUSIC	1974	EPIC	UK	80017
ANGEL SOUTH	G V	(A	(C) PURE MUSIC	1974	EPIC	US	32572
JAY SOLLENBERGER	TPT	(C	(D) GET IT ON	197	EPIC	US	26297
TED PIERCEFIELD	TPT V	(A	(AB) CHASE/ENNEA	1976	EPIC	US	33737
DARTANYAN BROWN	B V	(C					
JAY BURRID	PERC	(A	JIM OATTS	TPT	(C	JOHN EMMA	G	(C
TERRY RICHARDS	V	(A	JOE MORRISSEY	TPT	(C	JIM PETERIK	V	(C
WALLY YOHN	K	(C	TOM GORDON	D	(C		

C90A SAM CHATMON

SAM CHATMON	G V	(AB	(A) THE MISSISSIPPI SHEIK	1974	BLUE GOOSE		2006
			(B) SAM CHATMON	197	ROUNDER	US	2028

C90B CHINGA CHAVIN

CHINGA CHAVIN	V	(A	(A) COUNTRY PORN	1976	CHINGA	666
BOB HARMANN	B	(A				
FORREST BERRY	G V	(A				

C92 CHEAP TRICK

RICK NIELSEN	G	(ABCDEFG	(A) CHEAP TRICK	1977	EPIC US 34400 1980 UK		81917
TOM PETERSSON	B	(ABCDEFG	(B) IN COLOR	1977	EPIC	UK	82214
ROBIN ZANDER	V	(ABCDEFG	(B) IN COLOR	1977	EPIC	US	34884
BUN E CARLOS	D	(ABCDEFG	(C) HEAVEN TONIGHT	1978	EPIC	UK	82679
XENO	V	(	(C) HEAVEN TONIGHT	1978	EPIC	US	35312
PETE COMITA	B	(	(D) LIVE AT BUDOKAN	1978	EPIC	UK	86083
JAI WINDING	K	(E	(D) LIVE AT BUDOKAN	1978	EPIC	US	35795
TOM WERMAN	PROD	(E	(E) DREAM POLICE	1979	EPIC US 33773	UK	85322
JACK DOUGLAS	PROD	(G	(F) ALL SHOOK UP	1980	EPIC US 36498	UK	86124
			(G) FOUND ALL THE PARTS	1980	EPIC 10"	US	36453
			(EP) OVER THE EDGE	19	EPIC	JAP	084P

C93 CHUBBY CHECKER

CHUBBY CHECKER	V	(ALL	CHEQUERED	19	LONDON	UK	SHZ 8419

TWIST	1962	COLUMBIA	UK
DONT KNOCK THE TWIST	1962		
TWIST WITH	1962	PARKWAY	US	P7001
ITS PONY TIME	1962		
LETS TWIST AGAIN	1962	PARKWAY	US	P7004
YOUR TWIST PARTY	1962	PARKWAY	US	P7007
TWISTIN' AROUND THE WORLD	1962	PARKWAY	US	P7008
FOR TEEN TWISTERS ONLY	19	PARKWAY	US	P7009
TWISTIN' AROUND THE WORLD	1962	GOLDEN GUINEA	UK	GGL 0236
ALL THE HITS	1963	PARKWAY		P7014
LIMBO PARTY	1963	PARKWAY	US	P7020
BIGGEST HITS	1963		
LETS LIMBO SOME MORE	1963		
BEACH PARTY	1963		
TWIST IT UP	196		
CHUBBY CHECKER & BOBBY RYDELL	19	CAMEO		C1013
DISCOTHEQUE	19		
FOLK ALBUM	1964	PARKWAY		P7040
DOWN TO EARTH	1963	CAMEO		C1029
GOLDEN HITS	196	CAMEO	US	C1063
DANCIN' PARTY (EP)	1963	CAMEO		CPE 550
GREATEST HITS	1976	LONDON	UK	HAU 8492
GREATEST HITS	19	ABKCO		4219

C94 CHEECH & CHONG

RICHARD CHEECH MARIN		(ALL	(A) CHEECH & CHONG	1971	A&M UK AMLS67010 US WB	3250
THOMAS CHONG		(ALL	(B) BIG BAMBU	1972	A&M UK AMLH67014 US WB	3251
GEORGE HARRISON	G	(C	(C) LOS COCHINOS	1973	ODE UK ODE77019 US WB	3252
KLAUS VOORMANN	B	(C	(D) WEDDING ALBUM	1974	ODE UK ODE77025 US WB	3253
JIM KARSTEN	D	(C	(E) SLEEPING BEAUTY	1976	ODE UK ODE77040 US WB	3254
JIM KELTNER	D	(C	(F) LETS MAKE UP A NEW DOPE DEAL	19	WB UK K56809 US WB	3391
CAROLE KING	PNO	(C	(G) UP IN SMOKE	1978	WB	US WB	3249
NICKY HOPKINS	K	(C					
TOM SCOTT	SAX	(C					
DICK HYDE	HRNS	(C	BILLY PRESTON	ORG	(CG	GEORGE BOHANNON	HRNS	(C
WADDY WACHTEL	G	(G	PAUL HUBINON	HRNS	(C	DANNY KORTMAR	G	(G
STANLEY SHELDON	B	(G	RICK MAROTTA	D	(G	JAI WINDING	K	(G
			ANDY MUSON	B	(G		

C94A CHEFS

			(A) THE CHEFS	19	ATTRIX	UK	RB10

C95 CHELSEA

GENE OCTOBER	V G	(A	(A) CHELSEA	1979	STEP FORWARD	UK	SFLP 2
BRIAN JAMES	G	(A	(B) ALTERNATIVE HITS	1980	STEP FORWARD	UK	SFLP 5
BILLY IDOL	V						
JOHN TOWE	D	(	TONY JAMES	B		BOY CARIE	D	
BOB JESSIE	B	(	MARTI STACEY	G		GARY FORTUNE	D	
JAMES STEVENSON	G V	(A	GEOFF MYLES	B	(A	STEVE L JONES	D	
DAVE MARTIN	G V	(A	CHRIS BASHFORD	D V	(A	ROBIN	K	(A

CHELSEA BEIGE

```
KENNY LEHMAN        WIND (A     (A) MAMA MAMA LET YOUR SWEET BIRD SING 1971 EPIC      US      3041
BILLY SCHWARTZ      G    (A
JOHN SCORZELLO      TPT  (A     ALLAN SPRINGFIELD    V PNO(A    CHRIS EFTHIMIAM    D    (A
STAFFORD L JAMES    B    (A
```

C96   CHER   C96

```
CHER            V   (ALL    (A) ALL I REALLY WANT TO DO        1965  LIBERTY      UK    SLBY 3058
FRANK CAPP      D   (A      (A) ALL I REALLY WANT TO DO        196   IMPERIAL     US    12292
JESSE SAILES    D   (A      SONNY SIDE OF CHER                 1966  LIBERTY      UK    SLBY 3072
SHARKEY HALL    D   (A      SONNY SIDE OF CHER                 196   IMPERIAL     US    12301
HAROLD BATTISTE PNO (A      CHER                               1967  LIBERTY      UK    SLBY 3081
MIKE RUBINI     K   (A      CHER                               196   IMPERIAL     US    12320
BILL MARX       K   (A      WITH LOVE                          1968  IMPERIAL     US    12358
LYLE RITZ       B   (A      BACKSTAGE                          1968  IMPERIAL     US    12373
CLIFF HILLS     B   (A      GOLDEN GREATS                      1968
RENE HALL       B   (A      3614 JACKSON HIGHWAY               19    ATCO         US    33298
MEL POLLEN      B   (A      CHER                               1971  MCA          UK    MUPS 438
DON PEAKE       G   (A      CHER                               1974  MCA          UK    MCF  2508
BARNEY KESSEL   G   (A      CHER                               1972  KAPP         US    5549
STEVE MANN      G   (A      CHER(SUPERPAX 1)                   19    UA           US    UXS  88
MONTE DUNN      G   (A      CHER(SUPERPAX 2)                   19    UA           US    UXS  94
MIKE POST       G   (A      CHER                               19    CBS          US    3649
JEFF KAPLAN     G   (A      SINGS THE HITS                     19    SPRINGBOARD  US    4029
RANDY STEVLING  G   (A      GREATEST HITS                      19    SPRINGBOARD  US    4028
JULIUS WECHTER  PERC (A     FOXY LADY                          1972  MCA US 2019  MUPS  459
GENE ESTES      PERC (A     FOXY LADY                          197   KAPP         US    KRS  5514
BRIAN STONE     PERC (A     FOXY LADY                          197   MCA          UK    MCF  2521
FRANK DEVITO    PERC (A     HITS OF CHER                       1972  UA           US    UAS 29317
MICHEL RUBINI   K   (O      (O)BITTERSWEET WHITE LIGHT         1973  MCA US 2101  UK    MUPS 484
JOE SAMPLE      K   (O      (O)BITTERSWEET WHITE LIGHT         1974  MCA          UK    MCF  2511
DEAN PARKS      G   (O      HALF BREED                         1974  MCA          UK    MCF  2501
JEFF PORCARO    D   (O      HALF BREED                         1974  MCA          US    2104
DAVID PAICH     K   (O      DARK LADY                          1974  MCA          UK    MCF  2559
TED DALE        K   (O      DARK LADY                          1974  MCA          US    2113
                            STARS                              1975  WB           US    2850
                            STARS                              1975  WB           UK    K 56111
                            GOLDEN HITS                        1975  SUNSET       UK    SLS 50378
                            GOLDEN HITS                        19    UA           UK    UAS 29317
                            THIS IS CHER                       197   SUNSET       US    5276
                            GREATEST HITS                      1975  MCA          UK    MCF  2597
                            GREATEST HITS                      197   MCA          US    2127
                            I'D RATHER BELIEVE IN YOU          1977  WB           US    BS 2898
                            I'D RATHER BELIEVE IN YOU          1977  WB           UK    K 56292
                            CHERISHED                          1977  WB           US    S 3046
                            CHERISHED                          1977  WB           UK    K 56401
                            TAKE ME HOME                       19    CASABLANCA   US    7133
                            TAKE ME HOME                       1979  CASABLANCA   UK    CAL 2047
                            PRISONER                           1979  CASABLANCA   US    7184
```

      CHERUBIN

```
ANDY MARX          G V   (AB    (A) OUR SUNRISE                  1974  UA           GER   29688
BO BORN            K     (AB    (B) CHERUB SAFETY MATCH          1975  UA           GER   29780
PIT TREJA          PERC V(AB
EBERHARD WILLHELM  D V   (AB    THOR BALDURSON       K    (AB   BLANDINE ANTONIO MARINHO  B V(A
LUCY NEALE         V     (B     KEITH FORSEY         D    (B    RAINER PIETSCH       V   (B
GARRY HUNWYN       B     (B     MICHAEL HODJERA      G V  (A    DIETER BAUER         B   (A
FRANK BAUM         STEEL (A     WOLFGANG GRUDE       WIND (A
```

      CHEROKEE

```
CRAIG KRAMPF       D ACC(A     (A) CHEROKEE                      1971  ABC          US    719
DAVID DONALDSON    G HCA (A
GEORGE DONALDSON   G SAX (A     ROBERT DONALDSON     K V  (A    TOM LATONDRE         TPT  (A
CHRIS HILLMAN      MAND B(A     SNEAKY PET KLEINOW   STEEL (A   FLOYD 'GIB' GUILBEAU VLN  (A
```

      CHERRY PEOPLE

```
PUNKY MEADOWS      G     (A     (A) THE CHERRY PEOPLE            19    HERITAGE     US    35000
ROCKY ISAAC        D     (A
CHRIS GRIMES             (A     DOUGY GRIMES         V    (A    JAN ZUKOWSKI         B    (A
```

      CHEVY

```
                               (A) CHEVY                         1980  AVATAR       UK    AALP 5001
```

      CHEYNES

```
PETER BARDENS      K V
ROGER PEACOCK      V
PHIL SAWYER        G    MICK FLEETWOOD D        EDDIE LYNCH     G     PETER HOLLIS    B
```

      CHI LITES

```
EUGENE RECORD                  GIVE IT AWAY                      1968  MCA          UK    MUPS 397
MARSHALL THOMPSON              GIVE IT AWAY                      1968  BRUNSWICK    US    754152
                               I LIKE YOUR LOVIN                 19    BRUNSWICK    US    754152
ROBERT LESTER                  GIVE MORE POWER TO THE PEOPLE     1971  MCA          UK    MUPS 437
CREADEL JONES                  GIVE MORE POWER TO THE PEOPLE     1971  BRUNSWICK    US    754170
                               GIVE MORE POWER TO THE PEOPLE     1976  BRUNSWICK          BRLS 3011
                               A LONELY MAN                      1972  MCA          UK    MUPS 457
                               A LONELY MAN                      1972  BRUNSWICK    US    754179
                               A LONELY MAN                      1976  BRUNSWICK          BRLS 3012
                               GREATEST HITS                     1972  BRUNSWICK    UK    BRLS 3003
                               GREATEST HITS                     1972  BRUNSWICK    US    754184
                               A LETTER TO MYSELF                1973  BRUNSWICK    UK    BRLS 3007
                               A LETTER TO MYSELF                1973  BRUNSWICK    US    754118
                               THE CHI LITES                     1974  BRUNSWICK    UK    BRLS 3009
                               THE CHI LITES                     1974  BRUNSWICK    US    754197
                               TOBY                              1974  BRUNSWICK    UK    BRLS 3010
                               TOBY                              1974  BRUNSWICK    US    754200
```

(CONTINUED)

CHI LITES   (CONTINUED)

HALF A LOVE		1975	BRUNSWICK	UK	BRLS 3015
HALF A LOVE		1975	BRUNSWICK	US	754204
HALF A LOVE		1978	LONDON	UK	SHU 8521
HAPPY BEING LONELY		1976	MERCURY	UK	9100 027
HAPPY BEING LONELY		1976	MERCURY	US	SRM1 1118
VERY BEST OF THE CHI LITES		1976	BRUNSWICK	UK	BRLS 3023
CHILITETIME (COMP)		1976	LONDON	UK	SHU 8520
GREATEST HITS VOL 2		19	BRUNSWICK	US	754208
THE FANTASTIC CHI LITES		1977	MERCURY	UK	9100 041
THE FANTASTIC CHI LITES		1977	MERCURY	US	SRM1 1147
HEAVENLY BODY		1980	20TH CENTURY		619

CHIC

NORMA JEAN	V	(A	(A) CHIC		1978	ATLANTIC UK K50441 US	19153
BERNARD EDWARDS	V K	(ABC	(B) C'EST CHIC		1978	ATLANTIC UK K50565 US	19209
DIVA GRAY	V	(ABC	(C) RISQUE		1979	ATLANTIC UK K50634 US	16003
LUCI MARTIN	V	(BC	(D) GREATEST HITS		1979	ATLANTIC UK K50686 US	16011
VALERIE HAYWOOD	VLN	(	(E) REAL PEOPLE		1980	ATLANTIC UK K50711 US	16016
ALFA ANDERSON	V	(ABC	(F) CHIC CHIC		1981	ATLANTIC	
TONY THOMPSON	D	(ABC	(G) TAKE IT OFF		1981	ATLANTIC UK K50843 US	19323
DAVID LASLEY	V	(ABC					
LUTHER VANDROSS	V	(ABC					

ANDY SCHWARTZ	K	(ABC	RAYMOND JONES	K	(BC	ROBERT SABINO	K	(ABC
JON FADDIS	HRNS	(ABC	BARRY ROGERS	TROM	(ABC	SAMMY FIGUEROA	PERC	(ABC
KENNY LEHMAN	WIND	(A	DAVID FRIEDMAN	PERC	(A	ROBIN CLARK	V	(A
GEORGE YOUNG	WIND	(A	GLORIA AGOSTINI	HARP	(A	TOM COPPOLA	K	(A
MARIANNE CARROLL	VLN	(B	CHERYL HONG	VLN	(B	JOE ROSSY	PERC	(BC
ELLEN SEELING	HRNS	(BC	ALEX FOSTER	HRNS	(BC	KAREN MILNE	VLN	(B
						JEAN FINEBERG	HRNS	(BC

CHICAGO

PETER CETERA	B G V	(ALL	(A) CHICAGO TRANSIT AUTHORITY	(DBL)	1968	CBS UK 66221	US	PG8
ROBERT LAMM	K V	(ALL	(B) CHICAGO	(DBL)	1970	CBS UK 66233	US	2G24
TERRY KATHBS	G V	(A'TO'L	(C) CHICAGO 3	(DBL)	1971	CBS UK 66260	US	30110
JAMES PANKOW	TROM	(ALL	(D) CHICAGO 4	(LIVE)	1971	CBS UK 66405	US	30865
LEE LOUGHNANE V PERC TPT	(ALL		(E) CHICAGO 5		1972	CBS UK 69018	US	31002
WALTER PARAZEIDER	WIND	(ALL	(F) CHICAGO 6		1973	CBS UK 69041	US	32400
DANIEL SERAPHINE	D	(ALL	(G) CHICAGO 7	(DBL)	1974	CBS UK 88015	US	32810
LAUDIR DE OLIVEIRA	PERC	(ILMN	(H) CHICAGO 8		1975	CBS UK 69130	US	33130
DONNIE DACUS	G	(MN	(I) GREATEST HITS		1975	CBS UK 69222	US	33900
CARL WILSON	V	(L	(J) LIVE IN JAPAN 1972		1975	CBS/SONY JAP		SCPS31/32
DAVID WOLINSKI	SYN	(L	(K) CHICAGO 10		1976	CBS UK 86101	US	34260
TIM CETERA	V	(L	(L) CHICAGO XI		1977	CBS UK 86031	US	34860
CHAKA KHAN	V	(L	(M) HOT STREETS		1978	CBS UK 86069	US	35512
BLUE WEAVER	SYN	(M	(N) No13		1979	CBS UK 86093	US	36105
MAYNARD FERGUSON	TPT	(N	(O) CHICAGO XIV		1980	CBS UK 86118	US	36517
AIRTO MOREIRA	PERC	(N	(P) GREATEST HITS VOL 2		1981	CBS	US	37682
			( ) AT CARNEGIE HALL 4 LP SET		19	CBS		
			(Q) CHICAGO 16	CASSETTE 198	CBS UK 499235			

CHICKEN SHACK

STAN WEBB	G V	(ALL	(A) 40 BLUE FINGERS		1968	BLUE HORIZON	UK	7 63203
CHRISTINE PERFECT	K V	(ABK	(B) O.K. KEN		1968	BLUE HORIZON	UK	7 63209
ANDY SYLVESTER	B	(ABCDK	(C) 100 TON CHICKEN		1969	BLUE HORIZON	UK	7 63218
DAVE BIDWELL	D	(ABCDK	(D) ACCEPT		1970	BLUE HORIZON	UK	7 63861
BOB DAISLEY	B	(F	(D) ACCEPT		1970	BLUE HORIZON	US	4809
PAUL RAYMOND	V K	(CDK	(E) IMAGINATION LADY		1971	DERAM	UK	SDL5
JOHN GLASCOCK	B	(E	(E) IMAGINATION LADY		1972	DERAM	US	18063
PAUL HANCOX	D	(E	(F) UNLUCKY BOY		1973	DERAM	UK	SML1100
CHRIS MERCER	SAX	(F	(F) UNLUCKY BOY		1973	LONDON	US	632
ED SPEVOCK	D	(H1J	(G) GOODBYE	(LIVE)	1974	NOVA 6 21579	GER	SDL8008
STEVE YORK	B	(1J	(G) GOODBYE		1974	LANDON	JAP	LAX1035
ROBBIE BLUNT	G	(1HJ	(FG) STAN THE MAN	DBL	1977	NOVA	GER	6 28375
DAVE WINTHROP	SAX	(1HJ	(H) THE CREEPER		1978	EURODISC		913 203
PAUL MARTINEZ	B	(H	(H) THE CREEPER		1978	ARIOLA	GER	25891
ALAN ELLIS	TPT	(AK	(J) THATS THE WAY WE ARE		1978	SHARK	GER	148 501
DAVE WILKINSON	K	(G	(K) IN THE CAN	(COMP)	1980	CBS	UK	31811
ROB HULL	B	(G	(AB) GOLDEN ERA OF POP MUSIC	(DBL)	1977	CBS	UK	68252
ALAN POWELL	D	(G	(BC) GOLDEN ERA OF POP MUSIC	(DBL) 2	1977	CBS		68253
TONY ASHTON	K	(FH	(EF) DOUBLE		1977	DERAM		3032/1-2
DON FEY	SAX	(B	(L) CHICKEN SHACK		1979	GULL	UK	GULP 1034
BUD BEADLE	SAX	(B	(1) LIVE 78 GIG					
ALISON YOUNG	V	(D	(M) ROADIES		1981	RCA		PL 25337
DICK HECKSTALL SMITH SAX	(A							
RODERICK LEE	TPT	(B	TERRY NOONAN	TPT	(B	WALTER HORTON	HCA	(B
JOHNNY ALMOND	SAX	(AB	STEVE GREGORY	SAX	(B	ALAN SCOTT	B	(L
PAUL BUTLER	G V	(L	RIC LEE	D	(L			

CHIEFTAINS

PADDY MOLONEY	PIPES	(ALL	(A) CHIEFTAINS 1	1965	CLADDAGH IRL CC2 ISLAND 76 RI	ILPS9364
SEAN POTTS	WHISTLE	(ALL	(A) CHIEFTAINS 1	1978	CBS	RI 82986
SEAN KEANE	FDL	(BCDEFGHJK	(B) CHIEFTAINS 2	1969	CLADDAGH IRL CC7 ISLAND 76 RI	ILPS9365
MARTIN FAY	FDL	(ALL	(B) CHIEFTAINS 2	1978	CBS	RI 82988
MICK TUBRIDY	FLT	(ABCDEFGHJ	(C) CHIEFTAINS 3	1971	CLADDAGH IRL RRC10 ISLAND 76 RI	ILPS9379
PEADAR MERCIER	BODHRAN	(BCDE	(C) CHIEFTAINS 3	1978	CBS	RI 82987
DEREK BELL	HARP	(EFGHJK	(D) CHIEFTAINS 4	1973	CLADDAGH IRL RRC14 ISLAND 76 RI	ILPS9380
KEVEN CONNEFF	BODHRAN	(FHJ	(D) CHIEFTAINS 4	1978	CBS	RI 82989
RONNIE McSHANE	PERC	(EF	(E) CHIEFTAINS 5	1975	CLADDAGH IRL CC16 ISLAND 76 RI	ILPS9334
DOLORES KEANE	V	(E	(E) CHIEFTAINS 5	1978	CBS	RI 82991
MATT MOLLOY	FLT	(K	(F) BONAPARTES RETREAT	1976	ISLAND UK ILPS9432 CBS 78 RI	82990
JOLYON JACKSON	CELLO	(K	(G) LIVE	1977	ISLAND UK ILPS9501 CBS 78 RI	82985
RATHCOOLE PIPE BAND		(K	(H) CHIEFTAINS 7	1978	CLADDAGH IRL CC24	
DAVID FALLON	BOD	(A	(H) CHIEFTAINS 7	1978	CBS UK 82814	US 35612
SEAN O'RIADA		(A	(J) CHIEFTAINS 8	1979	CBS UK 83262	US
			(K) BOIL THE BREAKFAST EARLY	1980	CBS UK 84081	US 36401

```
C103                              CHIFFONS                                              C103
    JUDY CRAIG        V  (      (A) THE CHIFFONS           1963 LAURIE US 2018 UK STATESIDE 10040
    BARBARA LEE       V  (      (B) ONE FINE DAY           196  LAURIE US 2020
    PATRICIA BENNET   V  (      (C) SWEET TALKIN' GUY      1966 LAURIE US 2036 UK STATESIDE 10190
    SYLVIA PETERSON   V  (      (C) SWEET TALKIN' GUY      1972 LONDON        UK      ZGP 125
                              (D) SWEET TALKIN'            1972 PHASE 4       UK      PFS4256
                              (E) EVERYTHING YOU ALWAYS WANTED TO HEAR19 LAURIE US 4001  UK   1001
                              (F) PICK HITS                1976 SONIC        UK      SON 005
                              (EP) THEY'RE SO FINE          19  STATESIDE    UK      SE1012
C103A                            CHILDREN                                             C103A
                              (A) REBIRTH                   19  ATCO         US      33271
C103B                            CHIKKIN                                              C103B
    DAVID TONLINSON   D V (A    (A) WHICH CAME FIRST       1978 EGG          CAN     3690
    EDDY VALIQUETTE   G V (A
    GREG EVANS        B V SYN(A
C103C                   DESMOND CHILD & ROUGE                                         C103C
    DESMOND CHILD     K V (AB   (A) DESMOND CHILD & ROUGE  1979 CAPITOL              EST 11908
    DAVID LANDAU      G   (A    (B) RUNNERS IN THE NIGHT   1979 CAPITOL              EST 11909
    ALAN SCHWARTZBERG D   (A
    JERRY MAROTTA     D   (B  JOHN SUSSWELL    D   (A   NEIL JASON       B   (A   JOHN SIEGLER   B  (AB
    PAUL SHAFFER      K   (A  RALPH SHUCKETT   K   (A   JIMMY MEAULIN   PERC (A   RUBINS BASSINI PERC(A
    ELLIOTT RANDALL   G   (A  JEFF MIRANOFF    G   (A   JOE CARO         G   (A   JEFF LAYTON    G  (A
    LARRY SALTZMAN    G   (A  MARIA VIDAL      V   (AB  RANDY COURTS     K   (B   MYRIAN VALLE   V  (AB
    BETTE SUSSMANN    K   (B  DIANNE CRASSELLI V   (AB  G SMITH          G   (B
C105              CHILLI WILLI & THE RED HOT PEPPERS                                   C105
    MARTIN STONE      G MAND(AB  (A) KINGS OF THE ROBOT RHYTHM  1972 REVELATION  UK     REV 002
    SNAKEFINGERS LITHMAN  G  (AB  (B) BONGOS OVER BALHAM    1974 MOONCREST      UK     CREST 21
    PETE THOMAS       D   (B    (B) BONGOS OVER BALHAM     1974 NOVA           GER    6 23101
    BOB ANDREWS       SAX K(AB
    P C BAILEY  BAN SAX G  (B  WILL STALLIBRASS  HCA (B   RED RHODES   STEEL(B   JO ANN KELLY   V  (AB
    JACQUI McSHEE     V   (B  SOPHIE ISRAEL     V   (B   CAROL GRIMES  V  (B   NICK LOWE      B  (A
    BILLY RANKIN      D   (B  ENGLISH JOHN FOX  B   (A   BARRY EVERETT PERC (A   DAVE VORHAUS   SYN (A
    PAUL RILEY        B   (B
C106                             CHILLIWACK                                            C106
    BILL HENDERSON    G V (ALL   (A) CHILLIWACK           1971 LONDON UK SHU 8418  US 71040
    HOWARD FROESE     V G K((EF   (B) CHILLIWACK           1971 A&M                US  3509
    CLAIRE LAWRENCE WIND K B(AB  (C) ALL OVER YOU          1972 A&M                US  4375
    GKENN MILLER      B V (ADEF   (D) CHILLIWACK           1974 SIRE               US  7506
    ROSS TURNEY       D   (ABDEF  (E) ROCKERBOX            1975 SIRE UK 9103 250   US  7511
    JOAN HENDERSON    V   (C    (F) DREAMS DREAMS DREAMS   1977 MUSHROOM          US  5006
    ROBBIE KING       PNO (C    (G) LIGHTS FROM THE VALLEY 1978 MUSHROOM          US  5011
    BOB BUCKLEY       K   (C    (H) BREAKDOWN IN PARADISE  1980 MUSHROOM          US  5016
    JOHN ROLES        G V (H    (J) WANNA BE A STAR        1981 MILLENIUM         BXL 17759
    BRIAN MACLEOD     D   (H
    AB BRYANT         B   (H
C106A                           ALEX CHILTON                                         C106A
    ALEX CHILTON    PROD V (ALL  (A) ONE DAY IN NEW YORK   1977 ORK 81978  TRIO JAP    2007
    JON TIVEN     PROS G V (A    (B) LIKE FLIES ON SHERBET 1980 AURA          UK      710
    RICHARD ROSEBROUGH D (AB    (C) BACHS BOTTOM          1981 LINE          GER    LP5081
    RICH CLARK        K V (A    (1) 1980  TOUR BAND
    TOMMY HOEN        K V (A
    DAVID BEAVER      K   (A  KEN WOODLEY      B   (A   THE COSSACKS      (A  LISA ALDRIDGE   (B
    LEE BAKER            (B  JIM DICKINSON  PROD (B   ROSS JOHNSON       (B  MIKE LADD       (B
    JIM LANCASTER        (B  SID SELRIDGE        (B   MATTHEW SELIGMANN B (1  MORRIS WINDSOR D (1
    KNOX           G  (1  CHARLES BALL    PROD (A
C106B                             CHIMO                                               C106B
    TONY COLLACOTT    PNO (A    (A) CHIMO                 1971 EPIC           US     30329
    ROSS RABY         ORG V(A
    JOHN JOHNSON      B V (A  ANDY CREE    D   (A   BREEN LEBOEUF    V   (A
C107                              CHINA                                                C107
    DAVEY JOHNSTONE   G   (A    (A) CHINA                 1977 ROCKET         UK     ROLL 9
    JAMES NEWTON HOWARD K (A
    COOKER LOPRESTI   B   (A  DENNIS CONWAY    D   (A   JO PARTRIDGE     G   (   ROGER POPE     D  (A
    ELTON JOHN        V   (A  KIKI DEE         V   (A   CARMEN TWILLIE   V   (A   CATHY COLLIER  V  (A
    VENETTE GLOUD     V   (A  SID POONYA     PERC (A
C107A                      CHOCOLATE & CLAY                                           C107A
    GEORGE'CHOCOLATE' PERRY B(A  (A) CHOCOLATE & CLAY      1977 cat            us     2610
    CLAY CROPPER      G K (A
    JOE MILLER        SAX (A  HAROLD SEAY      D   (A
C107B                    CHOCOLATE WATCHBAND                                          C107B
    GARY OSBORNE      V   (A    (A) NO WAY OUT             1967 TOWER          US     5096
                              (B) THE INNER MYSTIQUE      196  TOWER          US     5106
                              (C) ONE STEP BEYOND         196  TOWER          US     5153
C107C                     CHINESE PUZZLE                                             C107C
    DAVID RODENBLOOM  G V (A    (A) INSIDE OUTSIDE         1980 REBUS          US     10 001
    DAVID HOFSTRA     B   (A
    JOHN MERNIT       D   (A
C107D                        CHOCLATE MILK                                           C107D
                              (A) CHOCOLATE MILK          19   RCA            US     APLI 1399
                              (B) COMIN'                  1977 RCA UK PL11830  US     APLI 1830
                              (D) WE'RE ALL IN THIS TOGETHER 19 RCA           US     APLI 2331
C107E                            CHOPPER                                             C107E
    GEORGE LEGION     G V (A    (A) CHOPPER               1979 A&M            US     4715
    PETER BUNCH       G V (A
    BRAD SEIP         D   (A  KIM BULLARD  K V (A  GERY LINK       B V  (A
C108                              CHOPYN                                              C108
    ANN ODELL         K V (A    (A) GRAND SLAM            1975 JET            UK     LP 08
    DENNY McCAFFREY   V   (A
    RAY RUSSELL       G V (A  KLYDE McMULLIN   G V (A   SIMON PHILLIPS  D   (A   SIMON COLCLOUGH  V PERC(A
```

CHORDS

```
    BRETT ASCOTT      D    (A       (A) SO FAR AWAY                        1980 POLYDOR UK  POLS 1019  2383 575
    CHRIS POPE        G V  (A       (A) SO FAR AWAY   (DIFF TRACKS)        1980 METRONOME       GER    60 312
    MARTIN MASON      B V  (A
    BILLY HASSETT     G V  (A   MICK TALBOT PNO (A
```
C108B   RANDLE CHOWNING BAND   C108B
```
    RANDLE CHOWNING V G HCA (A      (A) HEARTS ON FIRE                     1978 A&M             US   4715
    KEN SHEPHERD      G V  (A
    LARRY VAN FLEET   B V  (A   LLOYD HICKS  D V PERC(A RICHARD TEE    PNO V  (A BOB STEHL  LYRICON(A
    JASON LAMASTER    G    (A   PAUL LEKA    K    (A  KAT EPPLE        FLT (A   RON BACCHIOCCHI K (A
    STAN SWARTZ     SAX K(A  RAY GANTEK   STEEL(A   STEVEN GASPER      ORG (A
```
C108C   CHRISMA   C108C
```
    G DURINI          D    (A       (A) CHINESE RESTAURANT                 1977 POLYDOR      IT  2448 060
    E VEVEY           G    (A
    MAURIZIO          SYN  (A   CHRISTINA        D B K SYN(A
```
C108D   LOU CHRISTIE   C108D
```
    LOU CHRISTIE      V    (ALL      (A) LOU CHRISTIE                      1963 ROULETTE     US   25208
    MADISON MASON     G    (J        (B) STRIKES BACK                      19   CE&CO        US   1231
    DON THOMAS        G    (J        (C) STRIKES AGAIN                     19   ROULETTE     US   25332
    TONY LEVIN        B    (J        (C) STRIKES AGAIN                     19   COLPIX       US   4001
    WALTER YOST       B    (J        (D) LIGHTNIN STRIKES                  19   MGM          US   4360
    BUDDY SALTZMAN    D    (J        (E) PAINTER OF HITS                   19   MGM          US   4394
    TONY ROMERO       K    (J        (F) LOU CHRISTIE & THE CLASSICS       19   SPINERAMA    US   173
    PAUL PRESTOPINE   BAN  (J        (G) PAINT AMERICA LOVE                19   BUDDAH       US   5073
    RUSSELL GEORGE    FDL  (J        (H) LOU CHRISTIE                      19   3 BROTHERS   US   2000
    LARRY PACKER      FDL  (J        (J) LOU CHRISTIE                      1974 CTI          UK   24
    MARC HAROWITZ     STEEL(J
    ERIC WEISSBERG    STEEL (J
```
C109   KEITH CHRISTMAS   C109
```
    KEITH CHRISTMAS G V PERC(ALL     (A) STIMULUS                          1969 RCA              SF 8059
    WITH                             (B) FABLE OF THE WINGS                1970 B+C          CAS  1015
    PAT DONALDSON     B    (B        (C) PIGMY                             1971 B+C          CAS  1041
    GERRY CONWAY      D    (B        (D) BRIGHTER DAY                      1974 MANTICORE        K 53503
    BOB STEWART       K    (B        (E) STORIES FROM A HUMAN ZOO          1976 ATLANTIC         K 13515
    ROGER POWELL      D    (B        (E) STORIES FROM A HUMAN ZOO          1976 ATLANTIC   UK    K 53509
    IAN WHITEMAN      K    (B        (F) KEITH CHRISTMAS                   19   POLYDOR          244 511
    SHELAGH McDONALD  V    (D
    ALAN SPENNER      B    (D   IAN WALLACE    D  (D    NEIL HUBBARD    G  (D   EDDIE MORDUE   SAX (D
    RAY WARLEIGH    SAX    (D   MEL COLLINS  SAX  (D    MALCOLM GRIFFITHS TROM (D HENRY LOWTHER TPT (D
    MARTIN DROVER   TPT    (D   DARRYL RUNSWICK B (D    IAN McDONALD    K  (D   PETE SOLLEY    K  (D
    TOMMY REILLY    HCA    (D   SKAILA KANGA HCA  (D    WILL WATSON   HRNS (D   STEVE CROPPER  G  (E
    SNUFFY WALDEN     G    (E   DAVID NICHTERN G  (E    DONALD DUNN     B  (E   WILLIAM SMITH  K  (E
    DAVID KEMPER      D    (E   PETER BERNSTEIN V SYN(E WENDY WALDMAN   V  (E   DANIEL MOORE   V  (E
    KEITH TIPPETT   PNO    (B   MIKE EVANS     B  (B
```
C109A   CHRISTOPHER   C109A
```
    RICHARD AVITTS    G    (A       (A) CHRISTOPHER                        19   METROMEDIA       1024
    DOUG WALDEN       B    (A
    JOHN SIMPSON      D    (A   TERRANCE HAND   D  (A  DOUG TULL    PERC (A  RON CRAMER   PERC (A
```
C109B   CHRISTOPHER MILK   C109B
```
    JOHN MENDELSOHN V D K(AB         (A) CHRISTOPHER MILK                  1971 UA           US   SP066
    Mr TWISTER        V    (AB       (B) SOME PEOPLE WILL DRINK ANYTHING   1972 REPRISE      US   2111
    THE KIDDO       B V    (AB
    DONNY ALVARADO  G V    (A   G WHIZZ      D       (AB  RALPH OSWALD    G SAX(AB
```
C110   CHROME   C110
```
    JOHN L CYBORG   DATA (ACDE        (A) THE VISITATION                   1976 SIREN         DE1000
    DAMON EDGE      V G K(ABCDE       (B) ALIEN SOUNDTRACKS                1977 SIREN         DE2200
    GARRY SPAIN     B G V(ABC         (C) HALF LIP MACHINE MOVES           1979 SIREN         DE 333
    HELIOS CREED    V G B(ABCDE       (D) RED EXPOSURE                     1980 BEGGARS BANQUET UK BEGA15
    JOHN LAMBDIN      G    (B         (E) READ ONLY MEMORY(EP)             1979 SIREN US 002   RED UK 12 002
```
C110A   CHRONICLE   C110A
```
    NOBUO HOICHI      B    (C         (A) LIVE AT THE WHISKY A GO GO       1975 EXPRESS     JAP   72037
    KEII SHIKAWA    B V    (C         (B) IMA WA TOKI NO SUBETE            1975 EXPRESS     JAP   72088
    KENJI MISHIRO   K V    (C         (C) LIKE A MESSAGE FROM THE STORM    1977 ALL EARS          11477
    OSAMU TAKEDA    D V    (C
```
C111   CHRYSALIS   C111
```
    PAUL ALBUM        B    (A         (A) DEFINITION                       1968 MGM          US   4547
    J SPIDER BARBOUR  V    (A
    RALPH KOTKOV    K V    (A   NANCY NAIN      V    (A   JOHN SABIN      G  (A
    DAHAUD SHAAR      D    (A
```
C111A   CHUNKY NOVI & ERNIE   C111A
```
    CHUNKY          V K    (A         (A) CHUNKY NOVI & ERNIE              1976 REPRISE      US   2146
    NOVI        VLN SYN K V(A         (A) CHUNKY NOVI & ERNIE              1977 WB           US   3030
    ERNIE           B V    (A
    RUSS KUNKEL       D    (A   STEVE FORMAN  PERC  (A   MILT HOLLAND   PERC (A
    BOBBYE HALL     PERC   (A   JIM COWGER    WIND  (A   IAN UNDERWOOD  SYN WOOD(A
    ELLEN LAZARES     G    (A   LEE RITENOUR    G   (A   TIRAN PORTER    V  (A
    DOUG LIVINGSTON STEEL BAN (A JAY GRAYDON     G   (A
```
C111B   THE CHURCH   C111B
```
    STEVE KILBEY  V K B (ABC          (A) OF SKIN & HEART                  1981 PARLOPHONE        PCS 7583
    NICK WARD       D V    (A         (B) THE CHURCH                       1982 CARRERE          CAL 130
    PETER KOPPES      G    (ABC       (C) BLURRED CRUSADE                  1982 CARRERE          CAL 140
    MARTY WILSON-PIPER G  (ABC
    BOB CLEARMOUNTAIN PROD (C   RICHARD PLOOG   D      (BC
```
C112   CHICK CHURCHILL   C112
```
    CHICK CHURCHILL K V    (A         (A) YOU & ME         1973 CHRYSALIS UK US CHR1051 GER  6307 525
    LEO LYONS         B    (A
    RIC LEE           D    (A   MARTIN BARRE    G    (A   BERNIE MARSDEN  G   (A
    BILL JACKMAN    SAX    (A   COZY POWELL     D    (A   GARY PICKFORD HOPKINS V (A
    ROGER HODGSON   G B    (A   RICK DAVIES     D    (A
```

CHURLS
C113

BRAD FOWLES	D	(	(A) THE CHURLS	196	A&M	US	4169
HARRY SOUTHWORTH AMES	G	(	(B) SEND ME NO FLOWERS	196	A&M	US	4233
SAM HURRIE	G	(					
JOHN BARR	B	(	BOB O'NEILL	V	(		

C113A

CHUTE LIBRE
C113A

GILLES DOUIEB	B	(	(A) CHUTE LIBRE	19	PATHE		066 14359
OLIVIER HUTMAN	K	(	(B) ALI BABA	19	PATHE		068 14522
PATRICE CINILU	G						
MINO CINILU	PERC	(	DENNIS BARBIER	FLT	(	ERIC LETOURNEUX	SAX (A
PIERRE JEAN GIDEN	SAX	(					

C113B

CICHLIDS
C113B

DEBBIE MASCARO	G	(A	(A) BE TRUE TO YOUR SCHOOL	1980	BOLD	US	306
ALLAN PORTMAN	G	(A					
SUSAN ROBINS	B K	(A	BOBBY TAK	D	(A		

C113C

CIGARETTZ
C113C

			(A) CRAWL RITE OUTTA MY SKIN	1979	CANCER	UK	34794

C114

CIMARONS
C114

CARL LEVY	K G V	(BCD	(A) IN TIME	1974	TROJAN		TRLS 87
FRANKLYN DUNN	B K V	(BCD	(B) ON THE ROCK	1976	VULCAN		VULA 501
WINSTON REID	V PERC	(BCD	(C) LIVE AT THE ROUNDHOUSE	1978	POLYDOR		2383 489
LOCKSLEY GICHIE	G V	(BCD	(D) MAKA	1978	POLYDOR		2383 512
MAURICE ELLIS	D	(BCD	(E) FREEDOM STREET	1980	VIRGIN	NL	203 092

C115

CIRCUS (1)
C115

PHILIP GOODHAND TAIT	K	(	(A) CIRCUS	1969	TRANSATLANTIC		TRA 207
MEL COLLINS	SAX	(A	(A) CIRCUS	1969	METRONOME		15 360
IAN JELFS	G V	(A	(B) LISTEN TO THE BAND	19	TRANSATLANTIC		
CHRIS BURROWS	D	(A	(C) CIRCUS	1977	PHASE 4	UK	4122
ALAN BUNN		(					
KEITH BLEASBY		(A	NB PREVIOUSLY THE STORMVILLE SHAKERS				
KIRK RIDDLE	B	(A					

C115A

CIRCUS (2)
C115A

RAY CYR	D PERC	(A	(A) CIRCUS	1974	HEMISPHERE	US	6679
JIM ASH	D V PERC	(B	(B) BAND 1975				
WAYNE KESTRASKI	B V	(AB					
RANDY GLADOWSKI	G V	(AB	BRETT PETERSON DOB G BAN V (A		FRED OMERNIK	K V	(A

C116

CIRCUS MAXIMUS
C116

BOB BRUNO	G V K	(AB	(A) CIRCUS MAXIMUS	1967	VANGUARD		VSD 79260
DAVID SCHERSTROM	D	(AB	(B) NEVERLAND REVISITED	1968	VANGUARD		VSD 79274
GARY WHITE	B V	(AB					
PETER TROUTNER	G V	(AB	JERRY JEFF WALKER	V G	(A		

C116A

CITTA FRONTALE
C116A

ENZE AVITABILE	WIND	(A	(A) EL TOR	1975	FONIT	IT	45
MASSIMO GUARINE	D PERC	(A					
RINE ZURZELE	B	(A	GIANNI GUARRACINE	G SYN V	(A	PAOLO RAFFONE	K (A
LINO VAIRETTI	G V HCA K	(A					

C117

CITY
C117

CAROLE KING	K V	(A	(A) NOW THAT EVERYTHINGS BEEN SAID	1969	ODE	US	Z12 44012
DANNY KORTCHMAR	G V	(A					
JIM GORDON	D	(A	CHARLES LARKEY	B	(A		

C117A

CITY
C117A

GEORGI GOGOW	B G VLN	(AB	(A) FIRST	1978	AMIGA	GDR	855586
TONI KRAHL	V VLN	(AB	(B) DREAMLAND	1980	POOL		624391
KLAUS SELMKE	D	(AB					
FRITZ PUPPEL	G	(AB	PITTI	G	(B	RITCHIE	K (B

C118

CITY BOY
C118

LOL MASON	V	(ABCDEF	(A) CITY BOY	1976	VERTIGO UK 6360 126	US MERCURY	1098
STEVE BROUGHTON	V G	(ABCDE	(B) DINNER AT THE RITZ	1976	VERTIGO UK 6360 136	US MERCURY	1121
MAX THOMAS	V K	(ABCDEF	(C) YOUNG MEN GONE WEST	1977	VERTIGO UK 6360 151	US MERCURY	1182
FIACHRA TRENCH	PNO	(B	(C) YOUNG MEN GONE WEST	1977	PHONOGRAM		9102 018
R J LANGE	B	(BDE	(D) BOOK EARLY	1978	VERTIGO UK 9102 028	US MERCURY	13737
B J COLE	STEEL	(B	(E) DAY THE EARTH CAUGHT FIRE	1979	VERTIGO UK 9102 036		
ROGER KENT	D	(AB	(F) HEAD ARE ROLLING	1980	VERTIGO UK 6359 024	US ATLANTIC	19285
ROY WARD	D	(DEF					
DAVE JACKSON	SAX	(B	VANDERGRAAF GENERATOR V	(B	JACK HOLSTEIN	FDL	(B
MIKE SLAMER	V	(ABCDEF	CHRIS DUNN	G B	(ABCDE	TONY BRAUNAGEL	D (C
ALBIE DONNELLY	SAX	(C	GEOFF TRISTRAM	CLAR	(C	FRANK RICOTTI	PERC (C
GREG MATHIESON	K	(D	MERLE ANGER	G	(D	ROY BABBINGTON	B (D
KENDAL STUBBS	B PERC	(E	HUEY LEWIS	HCA	(E	TIM FRIESE-GREENE	SYN (E
DEREK KING	PNO	(E					

C118A

CITY LIGHTS
C118A

LELAND BOBBE	D	(A	(A) SILENT DANCING	1975	SIRE	US	7512
MARL ABEL	B V	(A					
DON WILKINS	K V	(A	JOHN BERENZY	G V	(A		

C118B

CITY WAITES
C118B

ROD SKEAPING	VLN	(AB	(A) A GORGEOUS GALLERY OF GALLANT INVENTIONS	1974	EMI		EMC 3017
JOE SKEAPING		(A	(B) CITY WAITES		1976	DECCA	SKL 5264
DOUG WOOTON		(AB					
LUCIE FINCH		(AB	KEITH THOMPSON		(B		

C119

CLANCY
C119

DAVE SKINNER	K V	(AB	(A) SERIOUSLY SPEAKING	1975	W B	UK	K 56103
GASPAR LAWAL	PERC V	(AB	(B) EVERYDAY	1975	W B	UK	K 56206
ERNIE GRAHAM	G V	(AB					
DAVE VASCO	G V	(AB	COLIN BASS	B V	(AB	SAM MITCHELL	DOBRO (B
JIM CUOMO	SAX	(AB	BARRY FORD	D V	(AB		

Personnel		Album	Year	Label		Catalogue
MAIRE BRENNAN	HARP V (ALL	(A) CLANNAD	1973	PHILIPS	IR	6392 013
PAUL BRENNAN	G V PERC FLT (ALL	(B) CLANNAD 2	1974	GAEL LINN IR 041 INTERCORD GER 160 058		
DONAL LUNNY	G PERC SYN (B	(B) CLANNAD 2	1974	SHANACHIE US 79007		
CIARAN BRENNAN	B G V K (ALL	(C) DULAMAN	1976	GAEL LINN IR 058 INTERCORD GER 160 065		
ROBBIE BRENNAN	D (B	(C) DULAMAN	1976	SHANACHIE US 79008		
PADRAIG DUGGAN	G V MAND (ALL	(D) CLANNAD IN CONCERT	1978	OGHAM US IR 5001 INTERCORD GER 160 124		
JOHN WADHAM	D (A	(E) CRANN ULL	1980	TARA IR 3007 INTERCORD GER 160 153		
GRAINNE McMONAGLE	WHISTLE(A	(E) CRANN ULL	1981	PHILIPS	UK	6373 016
MICHAEL O'DOMHNAILL	G V (B	(F) FUAIM	1982	TARA	IR	3008
PADRAIG O'DOMHNAILL	V (B					
NOEL DUGGAN	G V (ALL	EITHNE BRENNAN	K V PERC(EF	TRIONA O'DOMHNAILL	K	(B
NICKY RYAN	V (C	PAT O'FARREL	G	(F	NOEL BRIDGEMAN	D PERC(F
NEIL BUCKLEY	WIND (F					

Personnel			Album	Year	Label		Catalogue	
ERIC CLAPTON	G V (ALL		(A) ERIC CLAPTON	1970	POLYDOR US PD13008 UK 2383 021			
WITH			(A) ERIC CLAPTON	1976	RSO		UK 2394 186	
CARL RADLE	B (ABEFGJKLN		(B) HISTORY OF	1972	RSO 2659 012 RI 2671 107			
JAMIE OLDAKER	D (EFGJKLN		(B) HISTORY OF	197	ATCO	US	SD1 803	
DICK SIMS	K (EFGJKLN		(B) HISTORY OF	197	POLYDOR		2668 011	
GEORGE TERRY	G (EFGJKLN		(C) AT HIS BEST	1972	POLYDOR US 3503 UK 2659 025			
YVONNE ELLIMAN	V (EFJL		(D) RAINBOW CONCERT	1973	RSO	UK 2394 116		
SERGIO RODRIGUEZ	PERC (J		(E) 461 OCEAN BOULEVARD	1974	RSO US 1 3023	UK 2479 118		
ALBHY GALUTEN	PNO (EFJ		(E) 461 OCEAN BOULEVARD	1974	RSO		4801	
TOM BERNFELD	V (E		(F) THERE'S ONE IN EVERY CROWD	1974	RSO US 4806	UK 2479 132		
RICK GRECH	B (D		(G) E C WAS HERE	1975	RSO EURO 2479154 UK 2394 160			
JIM KARSTEIN	D (D		(H) BLUES WORLD OF E C	1975	DECCA	UK SPA 387		
RONNIE WOOD	G (DJ		(I) THE BEST OF E C	1975	POLYDOR		2482 143	
STEVE WINWOOD	K V (DB		(J) NO REASON TO CRY	1976	RSO US 1 3004	UK 2479 179		
BOBBY WHITLOCK	K V (AB		(L) SLOWHAND	1977	RSO US 1 3030	UK 2479 201		
GRAHAM LYLE	V (N		(M) CLAPTON	1978	RSO		UK 2479 702	
JIM FOX	D (E		(N) BACKLESS	1978	RSO US 1 3039	UK 2479 221		
SONNY CURTIS	V (		(N) BACKLESS	1978	RSO EURO 2394 213	RSD 5001		
ALBERT LEE	G (O1P		(O) JUST ONE NIGHT	1980	RSO 24202	UK 2479 240		
LEON RUSSELL	PNO (A		( ) POP GIANTS	19	BRUNSWICK		2911 518	
JIM GORDON	D (AB		( ) POP HISTORY	19	POLYDOR		2668 001	
BENNY GALLAGHER	V (N		( ) CLAPTON BECK & PAGE	1973	ELECTROLA		048 51780	
HENRY SPINETTI	D (O1P		( ) GREATEST HITS	1976	TELDEC	GER	622282	
CHRIS STAINTON	K (O		( ) POP MUSIC	19	POLYDOR	FR	2458 111	
DAVE MARKEE	B (O1		(P) ANOTHER TICKET	1981	RSO US 1 3095	UK 2479 285		
JERRY ALLISON	V (A		(Q) ERIC CLAPTON 4 LP SET	1981	RSO NL 2658 276			
MARCY LEVY	V (FGJKLN		(R) STEPPIN OUT	1982	DECCA	UK	TAB21	
GARY BROOKER	K (1P		(1) 1980 TOUR					
AL JACKSON	D (E							

PETE TOWNSHEND	G V (D	JIM CAPALDI	D (D	REBOP	PERC (D	DELANEY BRAMLETT	G V (AB
CHRIS DREJA	G (B	JIM McCARTY	D (B	JOHN MAYALL	V K (B	HUGHIE FLINT	D (B
GINGER BAKER	D (B	PAUL JONES	HCA (B	FELIX PAPPALARDI	K (B	BONNIE BRAMLETT	V (AB
JIM PRICE	HRNS (AB	RITA COOLIDGE	V (AB	PAUL SAMWELL SMITH	B (B	KEITH RELF	V (B
JOHN McVIE	B (B	JACK BRUCE	B V (B	STEVE ANGELO	V (B	L'ANGELO MISTERIOSO	G (B
BOBBY KEYS	SAX (AB	DAVE MASON	G (B	TEX JOHNSON	PERC (B	KING CURTIS	SAX (J
LEON RUSSELL	PNO (B	DUANNE ALLMAN	G (J	ED ANDERSON	(J	BOB DYLAN	V (J
RICK DANKO	B (J	BOB ELLIS	TPT (J	GEOFF HARRISON	(J	GARTH HUDSON	K SAX(J
RICHARD MANUEL	D (J	NAT JEFFERY	(J	DICK LA PALM	(J	BILLY PRESTON	K (J
WILTON SPEARS	(J	DOMINIC LUMETTA	(J	LARRY SAMUELS	(J	BRAINS BRADLEY	(J
JESSE ED DAVIS	G (J	TERRY DANKO	PERC(J	KONRAD KRAMER	(J	GEORGIE FAME	K (J
LEVON HELM	D (J	RALPH MOSS	PERC(J	DREAD LEVER	(J	CHRIS JAGGER	V (J
ROBBIE ROBERTSON	G K (J	SANDY CASTLE	V (J	MICK TURNER	(J	WAH WAH WATSON	G (J
JOHN SIMON	K (A	STEPHEN STILLS	G (A	MEL COLLINS	HRNS (L		

Personnel		Album	Year	Label			Catalogue
DAVE CLARK	D V (ALL	A SESSION WITH	1963	COLUMBIA UK			33SX 1598
MIKE SMITH	K V (ALL	A SESSION WITH	1968	M F P	UK		MFP 1260
LENNY DAVIDSON	G B (ALL	GLAD ALL OVER	1964	EPIC	US MON LN24093		STER BN 26093
RICK HUXLEY	G (ALL	AMERICAN TOUR	1964	EPIC	US MON LN24104		STER BN 26117
DENNIS PAYTON	SAX K (ALL	RETURN	1964	EPIC	US MON LN24104		
		COAST TO COAST	1965	EPIC	US		STER BN 26128
		CATCH US IF YOU CAN	1965	COLUMBIA UK			SX 1756
		WILD WEEKEND	1965	EPIC	US MON LN24162		STER BN 26162
		I LIKE IT LIKE THAT	1966	EPIC			
		GREATEST HITS	1966	COLUMBIA UK			SX 6105
		GREATEST HITS	1966	EPIC	US		STER BN 26185
		TRY TO HARD	1966	EPIC	US MON LN24198		STER BN 26198
		SATISFIED WITH YOU	1966	EPIC	US MON LN24212		STER BN 26212
		MORE GREATEST HITS	1966	EPIC	US MON LN24221		STER BN 26221
		5 BY 5	1967	EPIC	US		
		YOU GOT WHAT IT TAKES	1967	EPIC	US		STER BN 26312
		EVERYBODY KNOWS	1968	COLUMBIA UK			SX 6207
		14 TITLES BY DAVE CLARK	1968	COLUMBIA UK			SCX 6309
		WEEKEND IN LONDON	1968	EPIC	US MON LN24139		STER BN 26139
		BEST OF	1970	STARLINE UK			SRS 5037
		IF SOMEBODY LOVES YOU(SOLO)	1971	COLUMBIA UK			SCX 6437
		GOOD OLD ROCK'N'ROLL	1971	STARLINE UK			SRS 5090
		GLAD ALL OVER	1975	EPIC US			33459
		GOOD OLD ROCK'N'ROLL	1975	MFP	UK		MFP 90197
		BEST OF	197	EMI EURO	048 50737		
		25 THUMPING HITS	1978	POLYDOR UK			POLTV 7
		THE VERY BEST OF	19	MFP	EURO 96813/14		
		DAVE CLARK FIVE (DBL)	19	EPIC	US		EG 30434
		BEAT BATTLE OF THE WORLD	19	GROOVEMASTER US			BR 140
		ACROSS CANADA	19	CAPITOL CAN			
		ON STAGE	19	CAPITOL CAN			
		OVER & OVER	19	CAPITOL CAN			
		INSTRUMENTAL ALBUM	1966	CAPITOL CAN 6162			
EPS		DAVE CLARK FIVE	1964	COLUMBIA UK	SEG 8289		
		HITS OF THE D CLARK FIVE	1964	COLUMBIA UK	SEG 8381		
		& FRIENDS	1972	COLUMBIA UK			SCX 6494

DEE CLARK

```
DEE CLARK            (AB      (A) YOUR FRIENDS                    1980 CHARLY    UK    CTD    115
                             (B) KEEP IT UP        (EP)         1980 CHARLEY   UK    CRB    1010
```

C123

GENE CLARK
C123

```
GENE CLARK       G V  (ALL    (A) GENE CLARK & THE GOSDIN BROTHERS  1967 CBS    US 9418  US   CL2618
LEON RUSSELL     K    (A      (B) FANTASTIC EXPEDITION            1969 A&M    US 4159  UK   AMLS 939
BUTCH TRUCKS     D    (F      (C) THROUGH THE MORNING             1969 A&M    US 4203  UK   AMLS 966
RUSS KUNKEL      D    (F      (D) WHITE LIGHT                     1972 A&M    US 4292  UK   AMLS64297
MICHAEL UTLEY    K    (DFH    (D) WHITE LIGHT                     1974 ARIOLA                88172
CRAIG DOERGE     K    (F      (E) ROAD MASTER                     1973 ARIOLA                87584
JOE LALA         PERC (F      (F) NO OTHER                        1974 ASYLUM US 7E1016 UK  SYL  9020
RICHARD GREENE   VLN  (F      (F) NO OTHER                        1974 ELEKTRA   UK        K53005
CHRIS HILLMAN    MAND (AF     (G) KANSAS CITY SOUTHERN            1975 ARIOLA                86436
TED MACHELL      CELLO(F      (H) TWO SIDES TO EVERY STORY        1977 RSO    US 1 3011 UK  2394  176
JESSE ED DAVIS   G    (DF     ( ) COLLECTORS CLASSICS             1976 CBS       US        32998
BILL CUOMO       K    (F      ( ) EARLY L A SESSIONS              1975 CBS       US        31123
JERRY McGEE      G    (FH     ( ) GENE CLARK       (COMP)         19   TOGETHER  US        ST 1001
DANNY KOOTCH     G    (F
STEVE BRUTON     G    (F   BUZZY FEITEN      G   (F   RONNIE BARRON    V    (F   SHIRLEY MATTHEWS  V  (F
CARLENA WILLIAMS V    (F   TIM SCHMIT        V   (F   AL PERKINS       G    (H   JEFF BAXTER       G  (H
DOUG DILLARD          (ABH EMMYLOU HARRIS    V   (H   BYRON BERLINE    FDL  (H   CHRIS ETHRIDGE    B  (D
BOBBYE HALL      PERC (D   GARY MALLABER     D   (D   JOHN SELK        G    (D   BEN SIDRAN        K  (D
BILL RHEINHART   G    (A   CLARENCE WHITE    G   (A   GLEN CAMPBELL    G    (A   JERRY COLE        G  (A
MIKE CLARKE      D    (A   SAMMY CREASON     D   (H   JIM FIELDER      B    (H   STEVE SOLES       V  (H
PEPPER WATKINS   V    (H   JOHN HARTFORD     V   (H   T JEFFERSON KAY PROD V  (HF DANIEL MOORE     V  (H
MATTHEW MOORE    V    (H   LELAND SKLAR      B   (F   CINDY BULLENS    V    (F   VANETTA FIELDS    V  (F
CLYDIE KING      V    (F
```

C124

GUY CLARK
C124

```
GUY CLARK        G V  (ABC    (A) OLD NUMBER ONE                  1976 RCA                 APLI 1303
MIKE LEECH       B    (AB     (B) TEXAS COOKIN'                   1976 RCA    US 1944  UK   RS  1097
JERRY KROON      D    (ABC    (C) GUY CLARK                       1978 WB US 3241    UK   K  56565
JERRY CARRIGAN   D    (A      (D) SOUTH COAST OF TEXAS            1980 WB US 3381    UK   K  56902
PHILLIP DONNELLY G    (C
LARRIE LONDIN    D    (A   CHIP YOUNG        G   (A   PAT CARTER       G V  (A   STEVE GIBSON      G  (A
DICK FELLER      G    (A   JIM COLVARD       G   (A   REGGIE YOUNG     G    (A   HAL RUGG     DOB STEEL(A
DAVID BRIGGS     K V  (ABC CHUCK COCHRAN     PNO  (AB  SHANE KEISTER    PNO  (A   LEA JANE BERINATI K V(ABC
JOHNNY GIMBLE    FDL  (A   BRIAN AHERN       G   (B   DANNY ROWLAND    G V  (B   MICKEY RAPHAEL    HCA (AC
RODNEY CROWELL   V    (ABC EMMYLOU HARRIS    V   (AB  GARY B WHITE     V    (A   FLORENCE WARNER   V  (A
STEVE EARLE      V    (A   SAMMI SMITH       V   (A   STEVE KEITH      FDL  (B   TOMMY WILLIAMS    FDL(A
JACK HICKS       BANJO(BC  PETE GRANT      STEEL(B   CHRIS LAIRD      PERC (B   BYRON BACH  CELLO (BC
JERRY JEFF WALKER G V (B   WAYLON JENNINGS   G V (B   CHIP MOMAN       G    (B   NICOLETTE LARSON  V  (B
SUSANNA CLARK    V    (B   CHARLIE BUNDY     V   (B   TRACY NELSON     V    (B   HOYT AXTON        V  (B
ALBERT LEE       G    (C   B SPEARS          B   (C   CHERYL WHITE     V    (C   DON EVERLY        V  (C
GORDON PAYNE     V    (C   BUCK WHITE   MAND     (C   SHARON HICKS     V    (C   FRANK DAVIS       V  (C
DON BROOKS       HCA  (C   STRING SECTION        (C
```

C124A

LOUIS CLARK
C124A

```
LOUIS CLARK      K    (A      (A) PER-SPEK-IIV                    1979 JET       UK        LP218
```

C125

SANFORD CLARK
C125

```
SANFORD CLARK         (ALL    ( ) THEY CALL ME COUNTRY            19   EMBER          CW   131
                             ( ) MODERN ROMANCE                  1975 DO JA     US
```

C126

CLARK- HUTCHINSON
C126

```
ANDY CLARK       V K  (ABC    (A) A=MH²                           1970 NOVA GER 6 22548 UK  SDNR2
STEPHEN AMAZING  B    (AB     (A) A=MH²                           1970 SIRE       US       97021
MICHAEL HUTCHINSON G  (ABC    (B) RETRIBUTION                     1970 DERAM UK SML1076 GER NOVA 12014
DEL COVERLY      PERC (C      (B) RETRIBUTION                     1970 DERAM US  18055
                             (C) GESTALT                         1971 DERAM      UK       SML 1090
                             (AB)A=MH²/RETRIBUTION               1973 TELDEC    GERM SDM3015/ 2
```

C127

ALLAN CLARKE
C127

```
ALLAN CLARKE     V    (ALL    (A) MY REAL NAME IS 'AROLD          1972 RCA        UK       SF  8283
WITH                         (B) HEADROOM                        1973 EMI        UK       EMA  752
HERBIE FLOWERS   B    (AC     (C) ALLAN CLARKE                    1974 EMI        UK       EMC 3041
GARY BROOKER     K    (A      (D) I'VE GOT TIME                   1976 EMI        UK       EMC 3130
ROGER COULAM          (A      (D) I'VE GOT TIME                   1976 ASYLUM     US       7E 1056
JOE EGAN              (A      (E) I WASN'T BORN YESTERDAY         1978 AURA       UK       AUL  704
JOE MORRETTI          (A      (E) I WASN'T BORN YESTERDAY         1979 ATLANTIC   US       SD 19175
B J COLE         STEEL(C      (F) LEGENDARY HEROS                1979 ELEKTRA UK 52224 US CURB  267
ERIC DILLON           (A
ALAN PARKER           (A   DEE MURRAY        K V (AB  MARGO NEWMAN     V    (B   KIRK DUNCAN     K V (B
TONY NEWMAN      D V  (B   RAY GLYNN         V G (BC  STEVE KIPNER     V    (E   DAVID KEMPER    D   (E
LARRY BROWN      PERC (E   JAY GRAYDON       G   (E   BEN BENAY        G    (E   TOM HENSLEY     K   (E
MIKE PORCARO     B    (E   ROBBIE BUCHANAN   V   (E   DEAN WEBB        MAND (E   TONY BERG       G   (E
RANDY BISHOP     G V  (E   MIKE STATON     STEEL(E   DAVID WOLFER     MAND (E   HERB PEDERSEN   V   (E
TONY NEWMAN      D    (C   MIKE MORAN            (C   PETE ROBINSON    K    (C   JOHN GUSTAFSON  B   (C
LIZA STRIKE      V    (C   MADELINE BELL     V   (C
```

C128

JOHNNY CLARKE
C128

```
JOHNNY CLARKE                 (A) ENTER INTO HIS GATES            1975 ATTACK          ATLP 1015
                             (B) PUT IT ON                       1975 VULCAN          VULP 001
                             (C) ROCKERS TIME NOW                1976 VIRGIN          V    2058
                             ( ) AUTHORISED VERSIONS             1977 VIRGIN          V    2076
                             ( ) UP PARK CAMP                    1977 JUSTICE         JUS  001
                             ( ) DONT STAY OUT LATE              1977 PARADISE        PDL  001
                             ( ) GIRL I LOVE YOU                 1978 JUSTICE         JUS  006
                             ( ) SWEET CONVERSATION              1978 THIRD WORLD     TWS  914
                             ( ) KING OF THE ARENA               1978 THIRD WORLD     TWS  932
                             ( ) SATISFACTION                    1979 THIRD WORLD     TWSD   4
```

STANLEY CLARKE

STANLEY CLARKE	B PNO (ALL	(A) STANLEY CLARKE	1974 NEMPEROR US 431			UK K50101
BILLY COBHAM	D (C	(A) STANLEY CLARKE RI	1980 EPIC US 36973 UK EMBASSY 32042
JEFF BECK	G (BCDE	(B) JOURNEY TO LOVE	1975 NEMPEROR US 433			UK K50187
MILT HOLLAND	PERC (C	(B) JOURNEY TO LOVE RI	1980 EPIC US 36974 UK EMBASSY 32093
CHICK COREA	K (BC	(C) SCHOOLDAYS	1976 NEMPEROR US 900			UK K50296
CHARLES JOHNSON	G (CF	(C) SCHOOLDAYS RI	1980 EPIC US 36975 UK EMBASSY 32094
GEORGE DUKE	K SYN (BCEG	(D) MODERN MAN	1978 NEMPEROR US 35303 EPIC UK 82674
DAVID SANCIOUS	G (BC	(E) I WANNA PLAY FOR YOU	1979			EPIC UK 88331
LENNY WHITE	D (BC	(F) ROCKS PEBBLES & SAND	1980 EPIC US 36506			UK 84342
SIMON PHILLIPS	D (F	(G) STANLEY CLARKE/GEORGE DUKE PROJECT 1981 EPIC US 36918				UK 84848
JON FADDIS	TPT (ABC	( ) CHILDREN OF FOREVER	1972 POLYDOR		US	PD 5531
LEW SOLOFF	TPT (ABC		

CARMINE APPICE	D (D	PETER GORDON	HRNS(ABC	ALAN RUBIN	TPT (BC	DAVID TAYLOR	TROM (ABC
TOM MALONE	TROM (BC	JOHN CLARK	HRNS(BC	EARL CHAPIN	HRNS (BC	WILMER WISE	HRNS (BC
JEFF BAXTER	G (DE	JEFF PORCARO	D (D	RAY GOMEZ	G (CDE	MICHAEL GARSON	K (DE
JAMES TINSLEY	TPT (DE	AL HARRISON	TPT (DE	DEE DEE BRIDGEWATER	V(DE	BOBBY MALACH	TPT (DE
ALFIE WILLIAMS	SAX (DE	DALE DEVOE	TROM(D	MAXINE WILLARD	V (D	JULIA TILLMAN	V (D
GERRY BROWN	D (DEC	JOHN McLAUGHLIN	G (BC	STEVE GADD	D (BCDE	JAN HAMMER	K (A
TONY WILLIAMS	D (A	BILL CONNORS	G (A	AIRTO MOREIRA	PERC (AE	JAMES BUFFINGTON	HRNS(A
GARNET BROWN	HRNS (A	DARRYL BROWN	(E	CATHY CARSON	(E	TODD COCHRAN	K (E
JUANITA CURIEL	(E	RONNIE FOSTER	(E	STAN GETZ	SAX (E	FREDDIE HUBBARD	(E
HARVEY MASON	D (E	GWEN OWENS	V (E	LEE RITENOUR	G (E	PETER ROBINSON	K (E
TOM SCOTT	SAX (E	STEVE BACH	K (F	PHIL JOST	K (E	
JOHN ROBINSON	D (G	JERRY HEY	TPT (G	GARY FOSTER	WIND (G	MICHAEL BODDICKER	SYN (G
STRING SECTION	(G				

THE CLASH

TERRY CHIMES	D (12A	(A) THE CLASH	1977 CBS US 36060			UK 82000
KEITH LEVINE	G (1	(B) GIVE THEM ENOUGH ROPE	1978 CBS	US 35543		UK 82341
MICK JONES	G V (123ABCD	(C) LONDON CALLING (DBL)	1979 CBS	US 36328		UK CLASH3
JOE STRUMMER	G V (123ABCD	(D) SANDINISTA (TRP)	1980 CBS	US 37037		UK FSLN 1
NICKY HEADON	D (3BCD	(E) BLACK MARKET (10")	1980 EPIC US 36846
PAUL SIMONON	B (123ABCD	(F) PEARL HARBOUR	19			JAP
BEN HEGART	(D	( ) COST OF LIVING (EP)	1979 CBS
MICKEY GALLAGHER	K (D	(1) APR/SEP 1976 (2) SEP76/MARCH 77	(3) MAR77/>>
TOMON DOGG	V (D			
MIKE DREAS	V (D	NORMAN WATTROY	(D	J P NICHOLSON	(D
ELLEN FOLEY	(D	DAVID PAYNE	(D	RAY GASCOGNE	(D

CLASSIC NOUVEAUX

(A) NIGHT PEOPLE	1981 LIBERTY UK LBG30325 NL	83143
(A) CLASSIC NOUVEAUX (SAME TRACKS)	1981 LIBERTY	US LT 1104

CLASSICS IV

DENNIS YOST	V (	(A) SPOOKY	19	IMPERIAL	US 12371
JAMES COBB	G (	(B) MAMAS AND PAPAS SOUL TRAIN	19	IMPERIAL	US 12407
WALLY EATON	(	(C) TRACES	19	IMPERIAL	US 12429
JOSEPH WILSON	B (	( ) GOLDEN GREATS	19	IMPERIAL	US 16000
KIM VENABLE	D (	( ) VERY BEST OF	19	UA	US LA446
ALBURN BURRELL	G (	( ) DENNIS YOST & CLASSICS IV	19	M G M	US 702
DEAN DOUGHTRY	G (				
STEVE PULLIAS	G (	SAM ANDERSON SAX (	DANIEL RAMOS	K (WILLIAM GILMORE	B (
MICHAEL HUEY	D (			

LEE CLAYTON

LEE CLAYTON	HCA V G (ABC	(A) LEE CLAYTON	1973	MCA	US 365
COLIN CAMERON	B (B	(B) BORDER AFFAIR	1978	CAPITOL NL85446 US ST 11751
JIMMY DAY	STEEL (B	(C) NAKED CHILD	1979	CAPITOL NL85880 US EST 11942
PHILIP DONNELLY	G (B1	(D) THE DREAM GOES ON	1980	CAPITOL	UK 12139
CARLY SIMON	V (A	(1) 1979 TOUR		
DANNY LANE	D (B			
ANDY McMAHON	K (B	WAYNE JACKSON	TPT (B	ANDREW LOVE	SAX (B
REGGIE YOUNG	G (A	CHIP YOUNG	G (A	JOHN CHRISTOPHER	G (A
RICHARD BOWEN	G (A	LLOYS GREEN	STEEL (A	ED BLACK	STEEL(A
BOBBY WOODS	K (A	SHANE KESTLER	K (A	MIKE LEECH	B (A
TIM DRUMMOND	B (A	DENNIS LINDE	B (A	KENNY MALONE	D (A
MICKY McGEE	D (A	BONNIE BRAMLETT	V (A	BILLY COX	B (1
TONY NEWMAN	D (1			

MERRY CLAYTON

MERRY CLAYTON	V (ALL	(A) GIMME SHELTER	1970 A&M UK AMLS995	US ODE 77001
CAROLE KING	PNO (B	(A) MERRY CLAYTON	1971 A&M UK AMLS67012 US ODE 77012
GARY KING	B (C	(B) MERRY CLAYTON	197 EPIC	US PE 34948
HUGH McCRACKEN	G (C	(C) KEEP YOUR EYE ON THE SPARROW	1975 ODE US 77030	US EPIC 34957
DAVID SPINOZZA	G (C	(D) CELEBRATION	197 ODE US	X 77008
KEN ASHER	K (C	(E) EMOTION	1979 MCA	US 3200
BOB JAMES	K (C			
STEVE GADD	D (C	IDRIS MUHAMMED	D (C		

PETER CLAYTON

PETER CLAYTON	V (A	(A)PEARL HARBOUR BLUES (1 SIDE ONLY)	1970 RCA INT	INT 1176
BLIND JOHN DAVIS	PNO (A				
RANSOM KNOWLING	B (A	WILLIE LACEY	G (A	ALFRED ELKINS	B (A

DAVID CLAYTON THOMAS

DAVID CLAYTON THOMAS	V (ALL	DAVID CLAYTON THOMAS	1969 DECCA	DL 75146
WILLIAM D SMITH	K (*	DAVID CLAYTON THOMAS	1972 CBS US	31000
DOMENIC TROIANO	G (*	DAVID CLAYTON THOMAS	1972 CBS UK	65755
PAUL STALLWORTH	B (*	HARMONY JUNCTION	1973 RCA US	UK SF 8381
KENNETH RICE	D (*	(*) DAVID CLAYTON THOMAS	1973 RCA	US APLI 0173
NEIL LEVANG	BANJ (*	TEQUILA SUNRISE	1972 CBS US 31700	UK 65237
KEN MARCO	G (*	CLAYTON	19 ABC	US 1104
CHUCK RAINEY	B (*			
GABRIEL MEKLER	PNO (*	MOUSE JOHNSON	D (*	KING ERRISSON	PERC (*

CLEAR BLUE SKY

JOHN SIMMONS	G (A	(A) CLEAR BLUE SKY	1971 VERTIGO	UK 6360 013
MARK SHEATER	B (A			
KEN WHITE	D (A			

CLEAN LIVING

C136B

ELLIOT SHERMAN	K	(A	(A) CLEAN LIVING	1972 VANGUARD	US	79318
ROBERT LAMOUNTAIN	G V	(AB	(B) MEADOWMUFFIN	1973 VANGUARD	US	79334
FRANK SHAW	B V	(AB				
PAUL LAMBERT	STEEL	(AB	JEFFREY POTTER	K PERC(B	TIM GRIFFIN	D	(AB
ROBERT LAPALM	G	(AB	NORMAN SCHELL	G V	(AB	K P BURKE	HCA	(A
AL ANDERSON	G	(AB	MIKE MANDEL	PNO	(B	TIM PITT	G	(B
GUILLAUME LAPALM	FDL	(B				

C137

CLEARLIGHT

C137

STEVE HILLAGE   G   (A   (A) CLEARLIGHT SYMPHONY   1975 VIRGIN   V   2029
DIDIER MALHERBE   SAX (AD   (B) FOREVER BLOWING BUBBLES   1975 VIRGIN   V   2039
MARTIN ISAACS   B   (A   (C) LES CONTES DU SINGE FOU   1976 ISADORA   ISA 9009
CHRISTIAN BOULE   G   (ABD   (D) VISIONS   1978 LTM   FR   1005
JACKY BOULADOUX   D PERC(D
GILBERT ARTMAN   D PERC(AB   CYRILLE VERDEAUX   K   (ABCD   TIM BLAKE   SYN   (AC
FRANCOIS JEANNEAU   WIND (B   BOB BOISADAN   K   (B   JOEL DUGRENOT B V   (BC
JEAN CLAUDE AGOSTINI GFLT (B   CHRISTIAN STAPINOPOULOS D (B   BRUNO VERDEAUX SYN   (B
BRIGITTE ROY   V   (B   FRANCIS MANDIN   SYN   (CD   YVES CHOUARD G   (C
IAN BELLAMY   V   (C   DIDIER LOCKWOOD   VLN   (CD   SERGE AOUZI   D PERC(C
DAVID CROSS   VLN (D   GERARD GUSTIN   V   (D   PHILIPPE MELKONIAN   B   (D
LUC PLOUTON   SYN (D   GERARD AUMONT   V   (D   PATRICK DEPAUMANOU   SIT   (D
MOHAMED TAHA   PERC (D

C138

CLEAR LIGHT (US)

C138

CLIFF DE YOUNG	V	(A	(A) CLEAR LIGHT	1967 ELEKTRA	US	EKS 74011
DOUGLAS LUBAHN	B	(A				
MICHAEL NEY	D	(A	BOB SEAL	G	(A	DALLAS TAYLOR	D	(A
RALPH SCHUCKETT	K	(A	DANNY KOOTCH	G	(		

C138A

EDDIE CLEARWATER

C138A

EDDIE CLEARWATER   (A   (A) EDDIE CLEARWATER   1979 MCM   FR   900 296

C138B

VASSAR CLEMENTS

C138B

VASSAR CLEMENTS   (A   (A) VASSAR   1981 FLYING FISH   US   FF232

C138C

CLICKER

C138C

STEVE TRACY   B V   (A   (A) CLICKER   1973 HEMISPHERE   US   5180
JERRY TRACY   D V   (A   (B) HARDE HAR HAR   1975 CLICKER   US   1975
MARK ERVERIST   V   (A
BOB SCMIDTKE   G   (A
LYNN McLAUGHLIN V   (A   DICK WIEGEL   G V   (A   CHRISTINE HESS   V   (A
                                 JEFF EISBERNER   K   (A

C139

JIMMY CLIFF

C139

JIMMY CLIFF   V   (ALL   (A) HARD ROAD   1967 ISLAND   UK   ILPS 962
WITH   (A) HARD ROAD   1967 PHONOGRAM   EUR 9101 675
JACKIE JACKSON   B   (E   (B) JIMMY CLIFF   1969 TROJAN   TRLS   16
WINSTON GRENNAN   D   (E   (B) JIMMY CLIFF   1977 ISLAND   UK   ILPS 9414
RAD BRYAN   G   (E   (C) ANOTHER CYCLE   1971 ISLAND UK ILPS9159 US   9202
HUX BROWN   G   (E   (D) HARDER THEY COME   1972 ISLAND   UK   ILPS 9202
WINSTON WRIGHT   ORG (E   (E) UNLIMITED   1973 EMI   UK   EMA   757
GLADSTONE ANDERSON   K   (E   (E) UNLIMITED   197 EMI FR 05404 US REPRISE 2147
LESLIE BUTLER   K FLT (E   (F) STRUGGLING MAN   1974 ISLAND   UK   ILPS 9235
HEPTONES   V   (E   (G) HOUSE OF EXILE   1974 EMI   UK   EMC 3035
BOBBY ELLIS   TPT (E   ( ) MUSIC MAKER   1974 REPRISE   US   2188
RITA MARLEY   V   (E   (H) BRAVE WARRIOR   1975 EMI   UK   EMC 3078
JUDY MOWATT   V   (E   (H) BRAVE WARRIOR   1975 PATHE   FR   066 05873
NEVILLE GRANT   V   (E   (I) BEST OF JIMMY CLIFF   1975 ISLAND   UK   ICD 6
BINGI BUNNY   PERC (E   (J) FOLLOW MY MIND   1976 REPRISE US 2218 UK   K 54061
TOMMY McCOOK   WIND (E   (K) GOODBYE YESTERDAY   197 ISLAND   IMP   85568
JEAN WATT   V   (E   (L) OH JAMAICA   1976 EMI UK NUT 3 NL 06241
BOB TAYLOR   V   (E   (M) POP CHRONIK   VOL 9 (DBL) 1975 ISLAND   IMP
DENSIL LAING   PERC (E   (N) LIVE IN CONCERT   1976 REPRISE US 2256 UK   K 54086
RALSTON WEBB   V   (E   (O) WONDERFUL WORLD   197 A&M   US   4251
ZOOT SIMS   (E   (P) GIVE THANX   1978 WB US 3240 UK   K 56558
RON WILSON   WIND (E   ( ) SENSE OF DIRECTION   197 SIRE   US   7501
NORA DEAN   V   (E   ( ) CANT GET ENOUGH   197 VEEP   US   VPS 16536
BONGO HERMAN   PERC (E   (O) WONDERFUL WORLD   197 ISLAND   IMP   86488
STICKIE THOMPSON   PERC (E   (P) I AM THE LIVING   1980 WEA US 5153 UK   99089
TESFA McDONALD   V   (E   (Q) GIVE THE PEOPLE   1981 WEA US 5153 UK   99160
GLENTON TAYLOR   V   (E
BARRY BECKETT   K   (C   ROGER HAWKINS   D   (C   DAVID HOOD   B   (C
JIMMY JOHNSON   G   (C   TIPPY ARMSTRONG G   (C   JOSEPH HIGGS   V   (N
EDDIE HINTON   G   (C   ERNEST RANGLIN   G   (N   EARL 'BAGA'WALKER B   (N
NOEL BAILEY   G   (N   SANTA   D   (N   ERNEST McCLEOD K   (N

C139A

BUZZ CLIFFORD

C139A

BUZZ CLIFFORD   V   ((A) BABY SITTIN' WITH BUZZ   19   CBS US 8416 US   1616
                                   (B) SEE YOUR WAY CLEAR   1969 DOT   US   25965

C139B

DOUG CLIFFORD

C139B

DOUG CLIFFORD   (A   (A) DOUG'COSMO' CLIFFORD   1972 FANTASY   US   9411

C140

PAUL CLINCH & CHOYA

C140

PAUL CLINCH   V B G K(A   (A) LIVING LIKE A RICH MAN   1976 BUDDAH   US   5678
GARY GIES   D   (A
BRUCE LEY   K V   (A   DEBBIE SCHALL   V STR (A   JOHN SHAND   G SAX V (A
RICKY YORK   V PERC(A   DAVE MORRISON   G   (A   DON PAVELING B (A
HAL GREER   B   (A   FRED MOLLIN   G   (A   WAYNE ST JOHN V (A
I GUENTHER   FDL   (A   G SEMKIW   G   (A

C140A

CLIMAX

C140A

SONNY GERACI   V   (A   (A) CLIMAX   1972 ROCKY ROAD   US   RR 3506
JOE OSBORN   B   (A
STEVE LAFEVER   B   (A   REINIE PRESS   B   (A   JOE BELLAMY   B   (A
EARL PALMER   D   (A   JON GUTTMAN   D PERC(A   JOHN RAINES   D   (A
WILT NIMS   G   (A   JOHN STEVENSON   K   (A   LARRY KNECHTEL K   (A
NICK D'AMICO   K   (A   ALAN ESTES   PERC (A   LARRY COX   PERC (A
GORDON MacKINNON HRNS (A

```
C140B                          CLINIC                                                        C140B
     GERRY MURPHY      D    (A    (A) NOW WE'RE EVEN            1973  ROULETTE          US   3010
     PHIL TRAINER      B V  (A
     PHIL RIGHAM       G V  (A    ALAN REEVES        K SYN V(A
C140C                         CLOCK DVA                                                      C140C
     CHARLIE COLLINS   WIND (A    (A) THIRST                   1981  FETISH        UK        2002
     ADI NEWTON        V CLAR(A    ( ) WHITE SOULS IN BLACK SUITS 19  CASS ONLY
     ROGER QUAIL       D    (A
     TURNER            B    (A    PAUL WIDGER        G    (A
C141                       CLIMAX BLUES BAND                                                 C141
     ARTHUR WOOD       K    (ABCD  (A) CLIMAX CHICAGO BLUES BAND 1969 PARLOPHONE    UK   PCS  7069
     GEORGE NEWSOME    D    (ABCD  (A) CLIMAX CHICAGO BLUES BAND 1970 SIRE US 4901  US   SES 97013
     PETE HAYCOCK      V G  (ALL   (B) PLAYS ON                 1969 PARLOPHONE    UK   PCS  7084
     COLIN COOPER      SAX  (ALL   (B) PLAYS ON                 1970 SIRE US 6033  US   SES 97023
     RICHARD JONES     K    (BHJK  (C) A LOT OF BOTTLE          1970 HARVEST       UK   SHSP 4009
     JOHN CUFFLEY      D    (EFJHGKLMN (C) A LOT OF BOTTLE       19   SIRE US 6004  US        7518
     DEREK HOLT        B    (ALL   (D) TIGHTLY KNIT             1971 HARVEST       UK   SHSP 4015
     PETER FILLEUL     K V  (KL    (D) TIGHTLY KNIT             197  SIRE US 6008  US        7517
     PETE RILEY        PER  (K     (E) RICH MAN                 1972 HARVEST       UK   SHSP 4024
     COLIN FAIRLEY     V    (K     (E) RICH MAN                 197  SIRE          US        7402
     MADELINE BELL     V    (K     (F) FM/LIVE                  1974 POLYDOR       UK   2383  259
     JOY YATES         V    (K     (F) FM/LIVE                  197  SIRE US  6013 US        7411
     LIZA STRIKE       V    (K     (G) SENSE OF DIRECTION       1974 POLYDOR       UK   2883  291
     HELEN CHAPPELLE   V    (K     (G) SENSE OF DIRECTION       1974 SIRE          SAS  7501
     NICKY HOPKINS     PNO  (MN    (H) STAMP ALBUM              1975 B T M         UK   BTM  1004
     GABRIEL KATONA    SYN  (M     (H) STAMP ALBUM              1975 SIRE          US        6016
     MAXINE WILLARD    V    (M     (H) STAMP ALBUM              19   SIRE          US        7507
     JULIA TILLMAN     V    (M     (I) 1969 72                  1975 HARVEST       UK   SHSM 2003
     CLYDENE JACKSON   V    (M     (J) GOLD PLATED              1976 B T M         UK   BTM  1009
     JOHN RYAN         PROD (M     (J) GOLD PLATED              197  SIRE          US        7523
     HUMPTY FARMER     K    (C     (K) SHINE ON                 1978 WB UK  K 56461 US SIRE   6056
     BOB WALTERS       TPT  (G     (L) REAL TO REEL             1979 WB UK K56642  US        3334
     DAVID CAMPBELL    STGS (N     (M) FLYING THE FLAG          1980 WB UK K56871  US        3493
     MICHAEL BODDICKER SYN  (N     (N) LUCKY FOR SOME           1981 WB UK K56952  US        3623
     GLENN HUGHES      V    (N
C141A                         CLIQUE                                                         C141A
     RANDY SHAW             (A     (A) THE CLIQUE               197  WHITE WHALE   US   WW   7126
     GARY ZEKLEY       PROD (A
     SID                    (A     OSCAR              (A   DAVE           (A
C141B                       CLOCKWORK                                                        C141B
                                   (A) CLOCKWORK                19   GREEN BOTTLE  US        1013
C142                          CLOUDS                                                         C142
     HARRY HUGHES      D    (AB    (A) SCRAPBOOK                1969 ISLAND        UK   ILPS 9100
     IAN ELLIS       G B V  (AB    (A) UP ABOVE OUR HEADS       1969 DERAM         US   DES 18044
     BILLY RITCHIE  K B G V (AB    (B) WATERCOLOUR DAYS         1971 ISLAND        UK   ILPS 9151
                                   (B) WATERCOLOUR DAYS         1971 DERAM         US   DES 18058
C143                          CLOUT                                                          C143
     CINDI ALTER       V    (      (A) SUBSTITUTE               1978 CARRERE            EMC  3279
     INGE HERBST       G V  (      (B) CLOUT                    1979 EPIC          US        35617
     BONES BRETTELL    D    (      (C) SIX OF THE BEST          1980 EPIC          US        36350
     JENNIE GARSON     K    (      (D) THREAT AND A PROMISE     1981 EMI           UK        3363
     SANDIE ROBBIE     G V  (
     LEE TOMLINSON     B V  (
C144                          CLOVER                                                         C144
     JOHN McFEE   VLN G V STEEL(ALL (A) CLOVER         1970 FANTASY US 8395    LIBERTY UK   83340
     JOHNNY CIAMBOTTI   B V  (ALL   (B) FOURTY NINER   1971 FANTASY US 8405    LIBERTY UK   83487
     HUEY LOUIS        HCA V (CDE   (C) CLOVER          1977 MERCURY US SRMI1169
     SEAN HOPPER       K V  (CDE   (D) UNAVAILABLE     1977                   VERTIGO UK 6360 141
     ALEX CALL         V G  (ALL   (E) LOVE ON THE WIRE 1977 MERCURY US SRMI 3708 VERTIGO UK 6360 155
     MICKY SHINE       D V  (CD    (AB) CHRONICLE (COMP AB) 1979 FANTASY              UK   FT550
     ED BOGAS          FDL  (A
     TONY BRAUNAGEL    D    (E     MITCH HOWIE        D    (AB
C144A                        THE CLOVERS                                                     C144A
     JOHN BUDDY BAILEY V    (      (A) THE CLOVERS          19  ATLANTIC US 1248   US   8009
     BILLY MITCHELL    V    (      (B) DANCE PARTY          19  ATLANTIC           US   8034
     BILL HARRIS       G    (      (C) IN CLOVER            19  UA        US 3033 US POPLAR 1001
     HAROLD LUCAS      V    (      (D) LOVE POTION No9      19  UA        US 6099
     MATTHEW McQUATER  V    (      (E) THE ORIGINAL LOVE POTION No9 19 GRAND PRIX US   K428
     HAROLD WINLEY     V    (      (F) THEIR GREATEST RECORDINGS 19 ATCO        US   SD33374
     THOMAS WOODS      V    (      (EP) THE CLOVERS         19  ATLANTIC           US   590
     BILLY SHELTON     V    (      (EP) GOOD LOVIN'         19  ATLANTIC           US   537
                                   (EP) ONE MINT JULEP      19  ATLANTIC           US   504
C145                          CLUSTER                                                        C145
     HANS JOACHIM ROEDELIUS SYN(ALL (A) KLOPFZEICHEN  (KLUSTER) 1970 SCHWANN   GER  STUDIO511
     DIETER MOEBIUS    SYN(ALL   (B) ZWEI OSTEREI (KLUSTER) 1970 SCHWANN      GER  STUDIO512
     CONRAD SCHNITZLER SYN(AB    (C) CLUSTER               1971 PHILIPS       GER  6305 074
     CONRAD PLANK           (D    (D) CLUSTER 2             1972 BRAIN GER 1006 RI  0060 402
     MICHAEL ROTHER    G    (E    (E) ZUCKERZEIT            1974 BRAIN
     HOLGER CZUKAY     B    (GH   (E) ZUCKERZEIT            1980 BRAIN         UK   0040 116
     BRIAN ENO         SYN  (GH   (F) SOWIESO               1976 RCA SKY       GER  005
     ASMUS TIETCHENS   SYN  (G    (G) CLUSTER & ENO         1977 RCA SKY       GER  010
     OKKO BEKKER       G    (G    (H) AFTER THE HEAT        1979 SKY           GER  021
                                   (I) GROSSES WASSER        1979 SKY           GER  027
                                   (J) CLUSTER 71 REISSUE OF(C) 1980 SKY        GER  047
                                   (K) CURIOSUM              1981 SKY           GER  063
```

COAST ROAD DRIVE

LES NICOL	G V	(A	(A) DELICIOUS & REFRESHING		1974	DERAM		UK	SML 1113
STEVE CHAPMAN	D	(A							
CHARLIE HARRISON	G B V	(A	STEVE KRIEGER	G V (A	MICK WEAVER	K	(A		
NICKY HOPKINS	PNO	(A	CHRIS MERCER	SAX (A	HENRY LOWTHER	TPT	(A		
CRAIG AUSTIN	V	(A							

C146 THE COASTERS **C146**

CARL GARDNER	V	THE COASTERS	19	ATCO	US		33101	
BILLY GUY	V	COASTERS GREATEST HITS	19	ATCO	US		33111	
BOBBY NUNN	V	COASTERS GREATEST HITS	19	LONDON	UK	HAE	2237	
LEON HUGHES	V	ONE BY ONE	1961	ATCO	US		33123	
YOUNG JESSIE	V	COASTIN' ALONG	1961	ATCO	US		33135	
RONNIE BRIGHT	V	COASTIN' ALONG	1962	LONDON	UK	HAK	8033	
RALPH HAMILTON	B	COASTIN' ALONG	19	ATLANTIC	UK	588	134	
CORNEL GUNTER	V	GREATEST RECORDINGS	19	ATCO	US		33171	
WILL 'DUB' JONES		THATS ROCK 'N' ROLL	19	CLARION	US		605	
JOE OLIVERA	PERC	ALL TIME GREATEST HITS	1967	ATEANTIC	UK	590	015	
EARL CARROLL	V	THE EARLY YEARS	19	ATLANTIC	UK	K 30031		
JIMMY NORMAN	V	ON BROADWAY	19	KING	US		1146	
WITH		ON BROADWAY	1974	LONDON	UK	SHZ 8460		
FRANCISCO POZO	PERC	16 GREATEST HITS	19	TRIP	US		TOP16/7	
HARRY BREUER		WORLD FAMOUS COASTERS	1976	DJM	UK	DJM22053		
PLAS JOHNSON	SAX	HUNGRY	19	JOY	UK	JOYS 189		
KING CURTIS	SAX	20 GREAT ORIGINALS	1978	ATLANTIC	UK	K 30057		
LLOYD TROTMAN	B	IT AINT SANITARY	19	TRIP	US		8028	
BUDDY LUCAS	SAX HCA	EPS						
SELDON POWELL	SAX	ROCK 'N' ROLL WITH	19	ATCO	US		4501	
HAYWOOD HENRY	SAX	KEEP ROCKIN WITH	19	ATCO	US		4502	
JIMMY POWELL	SAX	THE COASTERS	19	ATCO	US		4506	
PAUL WILLIAMS	SAX	TOP HITS	19	ATCO	US		4507	
NOBLE WATTS	SAX	COASTERS	19	LONDON	UK	REE 1203		
MILT HINTON	B							

ALVA McCAIN	SAX	STEVE DOUGLAS	SAX	GRADY GAINES	SAX	CLIFFORD BURKS	SAX
BARNEY KESSEL	G	KENNY BURRELL	G	AL CAIOLA	G	ALAN HANLON	G
PHIL SPECTOR	G	CORNELL DUPREE	G	THOMAS PALMER	G	CARL LYNCH	G
EVERETT BARKSDALE	G	VINCENT BELL	G	AL GORGONI	G	BILLY BUTLER	G
MIMI ROMAN	G	BUCKY PIZZARELLI	G	JOE RICHARDSON	G	SONNY FORRIEST	G
GEORGE BARNES	G	RENE HALL	G	ART RYERSON	G	ADOLPH JACOBS	G
MICKEY BAKER	G	TONY MOTTOLA	G BAN	DON ARNONE	G	CLIFFTON BEST	G
ALVIN STOLLER	D	JOE MARSHALL	D	FRED BELOW	D	BUDDY SALZMAN	D
RAY LUCAS	D	PANAMA FRANCIS	D	GARY CHESTER	D	EMILE RUSSELL	D
BOB ROSENGARTEN	D	MELVIN POLLAN	D	DON LAMOND	D	ALFRED DREARES	D
JESSIE SAILES	D	WILLIE DIXON	B	MIKE STOLLER	PNO	RED SOLOMAN	TPT
WENDEL MARSHALL	B	LAMAR WRIGHT	TPT	JOE NEWMAN	TPT	BILL BERRY	TPT
BERT KEYES	PNO	BILL WINSTON	B	BOBBY DONALDSON	D	JAMES CLEVELAND	TROM
LEROY GLOVER	ORG	HORACE OTT	PNO	RUSS SAUNDERS	B	ELMON WRIGHT	TPT
GEORGE MATTHEWS	TROM	GEORGE STUBBS	PNO	JIMMY LEWIS	B	ART BUTLER	PNO
DUD BASCOMBE	TPT	HARRY DEVITO	TROM	AL LUCAS	B	OLSIE ROBINSON	B
GARY BELL		SANDY NELSON	D	JAMES DAVIDS		MICHAEL ADAMS	
LLEWELLYN KLASS		ABIE BAKER	B	JEWEL GRANT		ERNIE FREEMAN	PNO
EDDIE WILLIAMS	B	GEORGE DUVIVIER	B	PHIL KRAUS	PERC	WILL RODRIGUEZ	PERC
STICK EVANS	D						

C147 BILLY COBHAM **C147**

BILLY COBHAM	D PERC	(ALL	(A) SPECTRUM	1973	ATLANTIC	UK K40406	US 7268	
TOMMY BOLIN	G	(A	(B) TOTAL ECLIPSE	1974	ATLANTIC	UK K50098	US 18121	
LELAND SKLAR	B	(A	(C) CROSSWINDS	1974	ATLANTIC	UK K50037	US 7300	
JIMMY OWENS	HRNS	(JA	(D) SHABAZZ	1975	ATLANTIC	UK K50147	US 18139	
RON CARTER	B	(A	(E) A FUNKY THIDE OF SINGS	1975	ATLANTIC	UK K50189	US 18149	
JOHN ABERCROMBIE	G	(BCD	(F) LIFE & TIMES	1976	ATLANTIC	UK K50253	US 18166	
RANDY BRECKER	HRNS	(BCDEJ	(G) LIVE IN EUROPE	1976	ATLANTIC	UK K50316	US 19194	
ALEX BLAKE	B	(BDE	(H) MAGIC	1977	CBS	UK 82277		
GLEN FERRIS	TROM	(BDE	(J) INNER CONFLICTS	1978	ATLANTIC		US 19174	
JOHN SCOFIELD	G	(DEFGJ	(K) SIMPLICITY OF EXPRESSION	1978	CBS	UK 82967		
WALT FOWLER	TPT	(E	(L) A LIVE MUTHA FOR YA	1978	CBS	UK 82813		
LARRY SCHNEIDER	SAX	(E	(M) B C	1979	CBS	UK 83641	US 35993	
TOM MALONE	TROM	(E	(N) THE BEST OF	1980	CBS	UK 84235	US 36400	
STEVE KHAN	G	(LJ						

DAWILLI GONGA	K	(F	DOUG RAUCH	B	(F	ALAN ZAVOD	K	(F	PHIL BODNER	REEDS B(F
AL BROWN	VIOLA	(F	KERMIT MOORE	CELLO	(F	GENE ORLOFF	VLN	(F	GARNETT BROWN	TROM (CM
GEORGE DUKE	K V	(CGM	LEE PASTORA	PERC	(C	JOHN WILLIAMS	B	(C	ALFONSO JOHNSON	B V (GL
TOM SCOTT	SAX	(L	JAN HAMMER	K	(A	JOE FARRELL	WIND	(A	JOHN TROPEA	G (A
RAY BARRETO	PERC	(A	JOHN ABERCROMBIE	G	(BCD	MICHAEL BRECKER	HRNS	(BCDEJ	MILCHO LEVIEV	K (BDE
JOACHIM KUHN	PNO	(H	PETE MAUNO	K	(H	MARK SOSKIN	K	(H	RANDY JACKSON	B (H
ALVIN BATISTE	CLAR V	(H	SHEILA ESCOVEDO	CONG	(HJ	RUTH UNDERWOOD		(J	PETE ESCOVEDO	PERC V(HJ
KATHLEEN KAAN	V	(H	DON GROLNICK	K	(J	JOSE NAJEIRA	PERC	(J	DAWILLI GONGO	K (J
ERNIE WATTS	SAX	(JM	JULIAN PRIESTER	TROM	(J	JIM GILSTAP	V	(M	BOOBY LYLE	K (M
NATHANIEL PHILLIPS	B	(M	VANCE TENORT	CONGA	(M	DONNA FEIN	V	(M	MERRY GREENE	V (M
MUFFY HENDRIX	V	(M	JOE CROYLE	V	(M	MICHAEL WRIGHT	V	(M	WAYNE HENDERSON	TROM (M
MICHAEL McGLAIRY	G	(M	ED REDDICK	B	(M	MIKI HOWERD	V	(M	AUGUST JOHNSON	V (M
LOUIS PATTON	V	(M	ALEXANDRA BROWN	V	(M	JON JOYCE	V	(M	STEVE MADAIO	TPT (M
OSCAR BRASHEAR	TPT	(M	ERNIE TACK	TROM	(M	PETER CHRISTLIEB	WIND	(M	BILL GREEN	WIND (M
DAVID DUKE	HRNS	(M								

C147A COBRAA **C147A**

FRIEDEL AHRENS	K SYN	(A	(A) COBRAA	1974	ELECTROLA	GER 29507	
BERND KLIEMT	D PERC	(A					
ROLF SONDERMANN	G B	(A	WOLFGANG HAUSMANN	G (A	KLAUS SEBASTIAN	G (A	

C148 COCHISE **C148**

B J COLE	STEEL G	(ABC	(A) COCHISE	1970	UA	UK	UAS	29117
MICK GRABHAM	G K V	(ABC	(B) SWALLOW TALES	1971	LIBERTY	UK		LBG83428
WILLIE WILSON	D	(AB	(B) SWALLOW TALES	1971	U A	US		5518
STEWART BROWN	V G	(AB	(C) SO FAR	1972	U A	UK	UAS	29286
RICK WILLS	B V	(ABC	(EP) SWALLOW TALES	1971	UA	US		SP 50
ROY OTEMRO	D	(C						
JOHN GILBERT	V	(CB	CALEB QUAYE	PNO	(B	STEVE MARRIOTT	PNO V(B	NIGEL OLSSON	V (B
TIM RENWICK	G	(B	CAL BATCHELOR	G	(B				

```
EDDIE COCHRAN  D G V B   (ALL
GENE VINCENT         V   (*
JOE BROWN            G   (*
```

EDDIE COCHRAN	1960	LIBERTY	US	LST 7172
EDDIE COCHRAN	1960	LIBERTY	US	LRP 3172
CHERISHED MEMORIES	1962	LIBERTY		LBY 1109
CHERISHED MEMORIES	196	LIBERTY		LBS 83072
CHERISHED MEMORIES	1972	SUNSET	UK	SLS 50289
MEMORIAL ALBUM	1963	LIBERTY		LBY 1127
MEMORIAL ALBUM	19	LIBERTY		LBS 83009
MEMORIAL ALBUM	1960	LONDON	UK	HAG 2267
SINGING TO MY BABY	1963	LIBERTY		LBY 1158
SINGING TO MY BABY	19	LIBERTY	MONO	LRP 3061
SINGING TO MY BABY	1958	LONDON	UK	HAG 2093
SINGING TO MY BABY	1968	LIBERTY	UK	LBS 83152
MY WAY	1964	LIBERTY	US	LBY 1205
MY WAY	19	LIBERTY	UK	LBS 83104
NEVER TO BE FORGOTTEN	1963	LIBERTY	US	LRP 3220
SUMMERTIME BLUES	19	SUNSET	GERM	SLS 50094
SUMMERTIME BLUES	19	SUNSET	US	SUS 5123
SUMMERTIME BLUES	19	SUNSET MONO	US	SUM 1123
C'MON EVERYBODY	1970	SUNSET	UK	SLS 50155
10th ANNIVERSARY ALBUM	1970	LIBERTY	UK	LBS 83337
STORY VOL 1	1970	SONOPRESSE	FR	83430
STORY VOL 2	1970	SONOPRESSE	FR	83431
STORY VOL 3	1970	SONOPRESSE	FR	83432
STORY VOL 4	1970	SONOPRESSE	FR	83433
LEGENDARY	1971	U A	UK	UAS 29163
STORY VOL 5	1971	SONOPRESSE	FR	29167
LEGENDARY MASTERS DBL	1972	UA	UK	60017/18
LEGENDARY MASTERS DBL	1972	UA	US	9959
ON THE AIR (*)	1972	UA	UK	UAS 29380
VERY BEST OF(15th ANNIVERSARY)	1975	UA	UK	UAG 29760
MANY SIDES OF	1975	ROCKSTAR		JGR 1001
LEGEND IN OUR TIME	1979	CHARLY		CR 30168
EDDIE COCHRAN DBL	197	SUNSET		55003/4
VERY BEST OF	19	UA	US	LA 428E
A LEGEND IN OUR TIME	19	UNION PACIFIC	US	UP001
COFFRET 5 ALBUMS	19	UA	FR	25003/7
CREST SESSIONS	19	RAVE ON	FR	5001
SINGLES ALBUM	1979	UA	UK	UAK 30244
20th ANNIVERSARY ALBUM	1980	UA	UK	UCSP 20
MANY SIDES OF	1979	ROLLER COASTER		RSRLP1001

EPS

NEVER TO BE FORGOTTEN	1962	LIBERTY	UK	LEP 2052
CHERISHED MEMORIES	19	LIBERTY	UK	LEP 2111
CHERISHED MEMORIES	1961	LONDON	UK	REG 1301
C'MON EVERYBODY	1959	LONDON	UK	REV 1214
C'MON EVERYBODY	19	LIBERTY	UK	LEP 2111
SOMETHIN' ELSE	1960	LONDON	UK	REV 1239
SOMETHIN' ELSE	1963	LIBERTY	UK	LEP 2122
CHERISHED MEMORIES OF EDDIE COCHRAN	1963	LIBERTY	UK	LEP 2123
EDDIES HITS	1960	LONDON	UK	REG 1262
EDDIES HITS	1963	LIBERTY	UK	LEP 2124
C'MON AGAIN	1964	LIBERTY	UK	LEP 2165
STOCKINGS N SHOES	1964	LIBERTY	UK	LEP 2180

```
JACKIE LEE COCHRAN  V(A
```

(A) SWAMP FOX	19	ROLLIN ROCK	US	RR005

```
WAYNE COCHRAN        V    (ALL
ALLYN ROBINSON       D    (E
DENNIS WILSON        WIND (E
HAROLD PIERCE        TPT  (E
SKIP WEISSER         TROM (E
DON CARPON           TPT  (E
BUZZ TROY            TPT  (E
CHARLIE BRENT        G K  (E
BOB SCELLATO         TPT  (E
ARTIE GOLENIAK       B    (E
```

(A) HIGH & RIDIN'	19	BETHLEHEM	US	10002
(B) ALIVE & WELL	19	KING	US	1116
(C) OLD KING GOLD	19	KING	US	16001
(D) WAYNE COCHRAN	19	CHESS	US	1519
(E) COCHRAN	19	EPIC	US	30989
(E) COCHRAN	19	EPIC	UK	64933

```
MICHAEL PALMIERI     SAX  (E    ROBERT GABLE    WIND (E
MIKE KATZ            TROM (E    RANDY EMERICK   SAX  (E
BOB BRAWN            TROM (E
```

```
BRUCE COCKBURN   G DULC V  (ALL
ROBERT BOUCHER        B    (HIJ
PAT GODFREY           PNO V PERC(I
BILL USHER            PERC V(HI
RAY MACKAY            PIPES (I
FRED STONE            HRNS  (H
BEVERLEY COPELAND     V     (J
BRENT TITCOMB         V     (J
BOB DISALLE           D     (HJ
GENE MARTYNEC         G     (J
MARTY NAGLER          V     (J
MICHAEL DONATO        B     (H
KATHY MOSES           WIND  (J
TOMMY GRAHAM          V     (J
```

(A) BRUCE COCKBURN	1970	TRUE NORTH	CAN	TN1
(A) BRUCE COCKBURN	1971	EPIC	US	30812
(B) HIGH WINDS WHITE SKY	1971	TRUE NORTH	CAN	TN3
(C) SUNWHEEL DANCE	1972	EPIC	UK	65187
(C) SUNWHEEL DANCE	1972	TRUE NORTH	CAN	TN7
(C) SUNWHEEL DANCE	1972	EPIC	US	31768
(D) NIGHT VISION	1973	TRUE NORTH	CAN	TN11
(E) HAND DANCING	197	TRUE NORTH	CAN	TN13
(F) SALT SUN AND TIME	1974	TRUE NORTH	CAN	TN16
(G) JOY WILL FIND A WAY	1975	TRUE NORTH	CAN	TN23
(H) IN THE FALLING DARK	197	TRUE NORTH	CAN	TN26
(H) IN THE FALLING DARK	197	ISLAND/TN	US	ILTA 9463
(I) CIRCLES IN THE STREAM DBL	1977	ISLAND/TN	US	ILTA 9475
(J) FURTHER ADVENTURES	197	TRUE NORTH	CAN	TN33
(J) FURTHER ADVENTURES	197	ISLAND/TN	US	ILTA 9528
(K) DANCING IN THE DRAGONS JAW	1979	TRUE NORTH	CAN	TN37
(K) DANCING IN THE DRAGONS JAW	1979	MILLENNIUM	US UK	BXLI 7747
(L) HUMANS	1980	MILLENNIUM	US UK	FL1 7752
(M) RESUME	1981	MILLENNIUM	US UK	17757
(N) INNER CITY FRONT	1981	MILLENNIUM	US UK	17761

C151A — COCKNEY REJECTS

Personnel		
JEFFERSON 'STINKY TURNER	V	(ABCDE
VINCE RIGRDAN	B V	(ABCDE
KEITH 'NIG' WARRINGTON	D	(ABCDE
MICK GEGGUS	G V	(ABCDE

Album	Year	Label		
(A) GREATEST HITS VOL 1	1980	ZONOPHONE	UK	101
(B) GREATEST HITS VOL 2	1980	ZONOPHONE	UK	102
(C) GREATEST HITS VOL 3	1981	ZONOPHONE	UK ZEM	101
(D) THE POWER & THE GLORY	1981	ZONOPHONE	UK	105
(E) WILD ONES	1982	ZONOPHONE	UK	AKA 1

C151B — COCKRELL & SANTOS

BUD COCKRELL	B V	(A		MICHAEL SHELTON	G	(A		JIM ANDERSON	D	(A
PATTIE SANTOS	V	(A		RON STOCKERT	K	(A		VICTOR FELDMAN	PERC	(A
ANGELO ROSSI	G	(A		DAVID GARIBALDI	PERC	(A		STEVE MADAIO	HRNS	(A
JACO PASTORIUS	G	(A		FLORA PURIM	V	(A		ELMO PEELER	K	(A
AIRTO MOREIRA	PERC	(A								
ERNIE WATTS	SAX	(A								

Album	Year	Label		
(A) NEW BEGINNINGS	1978	A&M	US	SP 4712

C151C — CODE BLUE

DEAN CHAMBERLAIN	G V	(A
GARY TIBBS	B V	(A
RANDALL MARSH	D V	(A

Album	Year	Label		
(A) CODE BLUE	1981	WB US 3461	UK	K56868

C151D — DAVID ALLAN COE

DAVID ALLAN COE	G V	(ALL
SKEET PETTY	D	(L
WESLEY TAYLOR	G	(L
ALAN HICKS	B	(L
DALE SEIGFREID	STEEL	(L
PAM ROSE	V	(J
BARBARA SOUTH	V	(L
LINDA HARGROVE	V	(L

Album	Year	Label		
(A) PENITENTIARY BLUES	1968	SSS	US	9
(B) REQUIEM FOR A HARLEQUINN	1969	SSS	US	31
(C) MYSTERIOUS RHINESTONE COWBOY	1974	CBS	US	32942
(D) ONCE UPON A RHYME	1974	CBS UK 80908	US	33085
(E) LONG HAIRED REDNECK	1976	CBS	US	33916
(F) RIDES AGAIN	1977	CBS	US	34310
(G) TATTOO	1977	CBS	US	34870
(H) TEXAS MOON	1977	PLANTATION	US	507
(H) TEXAS MOON	1977	CHARLY	UK	CRL5006
(I) FAMILY ALBUM	1978	CBS	US	35306
(J) HUMAN EMOTIONS	1978	CBS	US	35535
(K) GREATEST HITS	1978	CBS	US	35627
(L) SPECTRUM SEVEN	1979	CBS	US	35789
(M) BUCKSTONE COUNTY PRISON	1979	COE	US	8095
(N) NOTHING SACRED	1979	COE	US	
(O) COMPASS POINT	1980	CBS	US	36277
(P) I'VE GOT SOMETHING TO SAY	1980	CBS	US	36489
(Q) INVICTUS	1981	CBS	US	36970
(R) ENCORE	1981	CBS	US	37352
(S) TENNESSEE WHISKEY	1981	CBS	US	37353

C152 — PETER & CHRIS COE

PETER COE		(AB
CHRIS COE		(AB
DAVE BLAND	V	(A
CLIVE WOOLF	V	(A
DOUG SHERRIFF	V	(A
STEVE ASHLEY	V	(A

Album	Year	Label		
(A) OPEN THE DOOR	1972	LEADER		LER 2077
(B) OUT OF THE SEASON	1976	LEADER		LER 2098
(C) GAME OF ALL FOURS	1979	HIGHWAY		SHY 7007

C152A — COEUR MAGIQUE

CLAUDE OLMOS	G PERC	(A		LAURENT MURINO	B PERC	(A
HARRY SEUR	V	(A				
DIDIER LESSAGE	D	(A				

Album	Year	Label		
(A) WANKAN TANKA	197	BYG	FR	529018

C153 — DENNIS COFFEY & THE DETROIT GUITAR BAND

DENNIS COFFEY	G	(ALL
WITH		
ANDREW SMITH	D	(BC
BOB BABBITT	B	(BC
ERIC MORGANSEN	K	(BC
JACK ASHFORD	PERC	(BCD
EDDY BROWN	PERC	(C
EDDIE WILLIS	G	(G
RUDY ROBINSON	PNO	(G
GARY SCHUNK	PNO	(G
RODERICK CHANDLER	B	(G
LEE NATHAM	D	(G
LORENZO BROWN	PERC	(G

JOHN TRUDELL	TPT	(G		MAURICE DAVIS	TPT	(G		STU SANDERS	TROM	(G		LARRY NOZERO	SAX	(G
BRANDY	V	(G		JAMES BARNES	PERC	(B		TONY NEWTON	B	(B		ART WRIGHT	G	(D
MELVIN WAH WAH RAGIN	G	(D		ED GREENE	D	(D		JAMES GADSON				JOE SAMPLE	K	(D
CLARENCE McDONALD	K	(D		MELVIN MELVOIN	K	(D		STEPHANIE SPRUILL	PERC	(D		KING ERRISON	CONGAS	(D
JOE CLAYTON	CONGAS	(D		JAMES JAMERSON	B	(D		GARY COLEMAN	VIBES	(D		RONALD LANGINGER	HRNS	(D
BUD SHANK	HRNS	(D		LLOYD HILDERBRAND	HRNS	(D		GENE CIPRIANO	HRNS	(D		CHUCK FINDLEY	HRNS	(D
VINCENT DEROSA	HRNS	(D		ARTHUR MAEBE	HRNS	(D		GEORGE BOHANON	HRNS	(D		DICK HYDE	HRNS	(D
BOBBY BRYANT	HRNS	(D		ERNIE WATTS	HRNS	(D		STRING SECTION		(BD				

Album	Year	Label		
(A) EVOLUTION	19	SUSSEX	US	7004
(A) EVOLUTION	19	A&M	UK	AMLS68035
(B) GOIN' FOR MYSELF	1972	SUSSEX	US	7010
(B) GOIN' FOR MYSELF	1972	A&M	UK	AMLS68072
(C) ELECTRIC COFFEY	1972	SUSSEX	US	7021
(D) INSTANT COFFEY	1974	SUSSEX	UK	8031
(E) DANCE PARTY	1974	SUSSEX	US	8152
(F) GETTIN' IT ON	1975	CARRERE	FR	67605
(G) BACK HOME	19	WESTBOUND	US	300
(G) BACK HOME	1977	ATLANTIC	UK	K 50371
(H) SWEET TASTE OF SIN	1978	WESTBOUND	US	6105
(J) FINGER LOOKIN' GOOD	19	WESTBOUND	US	212

C154 — DAVID COHEN

Personnel		
DAVID COHEN	G	(A

Album	Year	Label	
(A) HOW TO PLAY FOLK GUITAR	1976	KICKING MULE	SNKF 118

C155 — JOE COCKER

JOE COCKER	V	(ALL
WITH		
ALAN SPENNER	B	(ACKF
NEIL HUBBARD	G	(FK
CHRIS STAINTON	B K	(ABCDKF
HENRY McCULLOUGH	G	(ABCGH
BRUCE ROWLAND	D	(AC
PAUL HUMPHREY	D	(BC
CAROL KAYE	B	(B
DAVID COHEN	G	(B
LAUDIR DE OLIVIRA	PERC	(B
CLEM CATTINI	D	(B
JIMMY PAGE	G	(B
ALBERT LEE	G	(BJ
B J WILSON	D	(B
MATTHEW FISHER	ORG	(B
STEVE WINWOOD	K	(B

Album	Year	Label		
(A) BACKING BANDS 1968/69 PRE RECORDS				
(B) WITH A LITTLE HELP FROM MY FRIEND	1969	REGAL ZONOPHONE		SLRZ 1006
(B) WITH A LITTLE HELP FROM MY FRIEND	19	A&M	US	AM 4182
(B) WITH A LITTLE HELP FROM MY FRIEND	19	POLYDOR	EURO	2326 015
(B) WITH A LITTLE HELP FROM MY FRIEND	1972	MFP		MFP 52757
(C) JOE COCKER	1969	REGAL ZONOPHONE UK		SLRZ 1011
(C) JOE COCKER	197	A&M	US	AM 4224
(C) JOE COCKER	197	A&M	US	AM 4368
(C) JOE COCKER	197	CUBE POLYDOR	EURO	2326 018
(BC)WITH A LITTLE HELP/JOE COCKER	1972	FLY/CUBE		TOOFA 1/2
(D) MAD DOGS & ENGLISHMEN	1971	A&M	US/UK	AMLD 6002
(E) COCKER HAPPY	1971	FLY UK HIFLY13 EURO CUBE		2338009
(F) SOMETHING TO SAY	1973	CUBE UK HIFLY13	EURO	2338022
(G) I CAN STAND A LITTLE RAIN	1974	CUBE UK HIFLY18	EURO	2338027
(G) I CAN STAND A LITTLE RAIN	1974	A&M	US	AM 3633
(H) JAMAICA SAY YOU WILL	1975	CUBE UK HIFLY20	EURO	2326040
(H) JAMAICA SAY YOU WILL	1975	A&M	US	AM 4529

(CONTINUED)

(CONTINUED)   JOE COCKER

LEON RUSSELL	V K G			(CD (J) STINGRAY	1976	A&M US 4574	UK	AMLH64574	
SNEAKY PETE KLEINOW STEEL(C				(K) LIVE IN L A	1976	CUBE UK HIFLY23	EURO	2326041	
DON PRESTON	G	(D		(L) LUXURY YOU CAN AFFORD	1978	ASYLUM US 6E145	UK	K 53087	
CARL RADLE	B	(D		(L) LUXURY YOU CAN AFFORD	1978	ELEKTRA		K 52092	
JIM GORDON	D	(D		( ) JOE COCKER(BEST OF)	197	IMPACT	FR	6886 554	
JIM KELTNER	D	(DF		( ) GREATEST HITS	19	A&M	US	AM 4670	
CHUCK BLACKWELL	D PERC(D			( ) PLATINUM COLLECTION	1981	DAKOTA	UK	1004	
SANDY KONIKOFF	PER (D								

BOBBY TORRES	PERC (D	JIM PRICE	V K HRNS(DGHK	BOBBY KEYS	SAX	(DKL	STU BLUMBERG	TPT (G
STEVE MADAIO	TPT (GH	JIM HORN	SAX (GHKF	TREVOR LAWRENCE	SAX	(GH	MAYO TIANA	TROM(G
DAVID PAICH	PNO (G	RAY PARKER	G (G	RALPH HAMMER	G	(G	DAVE McDANIEL	B (GH
OLLIE BROWN	D (G	NICKY HOPKINS	PNO (GH	JAY GRAYDON	G	(G	JEFF PORCARO	D (G
RICHARD TEE	K (GHL	CORNELL DUPREE	G (GHJL	CHUCK RAINEY	B	(GHL	BERNARD PURDIE	D (GHL
CHRIS STEWART	B (GH	JIM KARSTEIN	D (GHK	JIMMY WEBB	PNO	(G	PEGGY SANDVIG	GH (GH
GREG MATHESON	PNO (G	RANDY NEWMAN	PNO (G	JEAN ROUSSEL	ORG	(H	BEN BENAY	G HCA(H
SID SHARP	STRINGS(H	DAN SAWYER	G (H	JOE CORRERO	D	(H	DON PONCHER	PERC(H
STEVE GADD	D (JL	GORDON EDWARDS	B (J	ERIC GALE	G	(J	SAM RIVERS	SAX (J
FLACO FALCON	PERC (JKL	ERIC CLAPTON	G (J	CLARENCE WHITE	G	(C	ARTIE BUTLER	PNO (B
TONY VISCONTE	G (B	MIKE KELLIE	D (B	TOMMY EYRE	K	(AB	KENNY SLADE	D (AB
MILT HOLLAND	PERC (C	BARRY BECKETT	K (L	CLIFF GOODWIN	G	(L	HOWIE HERSH	B (L
JOHN RILEY	D (L	GARY BROWN	SAX (L	HANK CRAWFORD	SAX	(L	DAVID NEWMAN	SAX (L
LEROY COOPER	SAX (L	MARCUS BELGRAVE	TPT (L	PHILIP GUILBEAU	TPT	(L	RANDY McCORMICK	K (L
JIMMY JOHNSON	G (L	GEORGE TERRY	G (L	DR JOHN	K	(L	CLYDE KERR	TPT (L
DONNY HATHAWAY	K (L	JOEY MURCIA	G (L	DAVID HOOD	B	(L	ROGER HAWKINS	D (L
LARRY BYROM	G (L	BILLY PRESTON	K (L	CHARLES ROSE	HRNS	(L	WAYNE JACKSON	HRNS (L
HARRISON CALLOWAY	TPT (L	RON EADES	SAX (L	HARVEY THOMPSON	SAX	(L	PETE CARR	G (L
ALLAN TOUSSAINT	K PROD (L	ALAN WHITE	D (F	RICK ALPHONSO	TPT	(F	FRED SCERBO	SAX (F
MILTON SLOANE	SAX (F	REEBOP BAHH	PERC (F	CONRAD ISADORE	D	(F	RICK DANK	B (L
ROSETTA HIGHTOWER	V (B	BRENDA HOLLOWAY	V (B	MERRY CLAYTON	V	(BCG	PATRICE HOLLOWAY	V (BC
MADELINE BELL	V (B	SUE GLOVER	V (B	SONNIE LESLIE	V	(B	BONNIE BRAMLETT	V (CJ
RITA COOLIDGE	V (CD	SHIRLEY MATTHEWS	V (CGH	CLAUDIA LENNEAR	V	(D	DANIEL MOORE	V (DGH
DONNA WEISS	V (D	PAMELA POLLAND	V (D	MATTHEW MOORE	V	(DH	DONNA WASHBURN	V (D
NICOLE BARCLAY	V (D	BOBBY JONES	V (D	CLYDIE KING	B	(GHL	VANETTA FIELDS	V (GH
CAROL STALLINGS	V (H	BUZZ CLIFFORD	V (H	JOANNE BELL	V	(H	CYNTHIA BARCLAY	V (H
LANI GROVES	V (J	DENIECE WILLIAMS	V (J	PHYLLIS LINDSAY	V	(J	MAXINE WILLARD	V (J
BRENDA WHITE	V (J	PATTI AUSTIN	V (J	GWEN GUTHRIE	V	(J	VIOLA WILLS	V (KF
BEVERLY GARDNER	V (KF	VIRGINIA AYERS	V (KF	GLORIA JONES	V	(F	ANN LANG	V (L
MONA LISA YOUNG	V (L	MITCH CHAKOUR	G (L					

LEONARD COHEN

LEONARD COHEN	V (ALL		(A) SONGS OF LEONARD COHEN	1968	CBS	UK 63241	US	9533
JENNIFER WARNES	V (G		(B) SONGS FROM A ROOM	1968	CBS	UK 63587	US	9767
HAL BLAINE	D (G		(B) SONGS FROM A ROOM	1981	EMBASSY		UK	32074
JIM KELTNER	D (G		(C) SONGS OF LOVE & HATE	1970	CBS	UK 69004	US	30103
ART MUNSON	G (G		(D) LIVE SONGS	1973	CBS	UK 65224	US	31724
DAVID KESSEL	G (G		(E) NEW SKIN FOR OLD CEREMONY	1974	CBS	UK 69087	US	33167
DAVID ISAAC	G (G		(F) GREATEST HITS	1975	CBS	UK 69161	US	34077
DAN KESSEL	G K (G		(G) DEATH OF A LADIES MAN	1977	CBS	UK 86042	US WB 3125	
JESSE ED DAVIS	G (G		(H) RECENT SONGS	1979	CBS	UK 86097	US	36364
PHIL SPECTOR	G K (G							

CHARLES LOPER	TROM (G	RAY POHLMAN	G B (G	ALBERT PERKINS	G (G	PETE KLEINOW	STEEL(G
PETE JOLLY	K (G	TOM HENSLEY	K (G	DON RANDI	K (G	BILL MAYS	K (G
BARRY GOLDBERG	K (G	STEVE DOUGLAS	WIND (G	MIKE LANG	K (G	JACK REDMOND	TROM (G
DEVRA ROBITAILLE	SYN (G	TERRY GIBBS	PERC (G	RAY NEOPOLITAN	B (G	EMIL RADOCCHIA	PERC (G
GENE ESTES	PERC (G	BOB ZIMMITTI	PERC (G	BOBBY BRUCE	FDL (G	DON MENZA	WIND (G
CONTE CANDOLI	TPT (G	JAY MIGLIORI	SAX (G	ALAN GINSBERG	WIND (G	BILLY DIEZ	V (G
RONNIE BLAKELY	V (G	VENNETTE FIELDS	V (G	BRENDA BRYANT	V (G	GERRY GARRETT	V (G
CLYDIE KING	V (G	LORNA WILLARD	V (G	JULIA TILLMAN	V (GH	ORNA DRAKE	V (G
BOB DYLAN	V (G	JOHN BILEZIKJIAN	G (H	ABRAHAM LABORIEL	B (H	RANDY WALDMAN	K (H
JENNIFER WARNES	V (H	STEVE MEADOR	D (H	CHARLES BECK	B (H	BILL GINN	K (H
MITCH WATKINS	G (H	PAUL OSTERMEYER	SAX (H	STEPHANIE SPRUILL	V (H	MAXINE WILLARD	V (H
JAMES GILSTRAP	V (H	ROGER ST KENERLY	V (H	JOHN MILLER	B (H	JOHN LISSAUER	K (H
PABLO SANDOVAL	TPT (H	JOSE PEREZ TPT	(H	RICARDO GONZALEZ	G (H	FELIPE PEREZ	(H
EVERADO SANDOVAL	G (H	GARTH HUDSON	(H	EARLE DUMLER	OBOE (H		

COINCIDENCE

JEAN-CLAUDE LLABADOR	(A	(A) COINCIDENCE	1977	DISQUES TROMBLAS	FR	RY1133
JEAN-PIERRE LLABADOR	(A					

MARK COLBY

MARK COLBY	SAX (A	(A) SERPENTINE FIRE	1978	CBS	UK	82668
ERIC GALE	G (A	(A) SERPENTINE FIRE	1978	CBS	US	35298
STEVE KHAN	G (A					
BOB JAMES	(A	STEVE GADD D (A				

COLD BLOOD

CARL LEACH	TPT (A	(A) COLD BLOOD (FIRST BLOOD)	1970	SAN FRANCISCO	US	200	
RAUL MATUTE	K (ABCDEF	(A) COLD BLOOD (FIRST BLOOD)	1970	ATLANTIC	UK	588 218	
LARRY JONUTZ	TPT (AB	(B) SISYPHUS	1971	SAN FRANCISCO	US	205	
ROD ELLICOTT	B (ABDE	(B) SISYPHUS	1971	ATLANTIC	UK	2400 102	
FRANK J DAVIS	D (A	(C) FIRST TASTE OF SIN	1972	REPRISE	US	2074	
DANNY HULL	SAX V(ABF	(D) THRILLER	1973	REPRISE	US	2130	
DAVID PADRON	TPT (A	(E) LYDIA	1974	WB UK K56-47	US	2806	
LYDIA PENSE	V (ABCDEF	(F) LYDIA PENSE & COLD BLOOD	1976	ABC UK 5172	US	ABCD 917	
SANDY McKEE	D (B						

LARRY FIELD	G (AB	MIC GILLETTE	HRNS (AB	JOSE CHEPITO AREAS	PERC(B	POINTER SISTERS	V (BD
MIKE ANDREAS	SAX (D	RIGBY POWELL	TPT (D	MEL MARTIN	SAX (D	HOLLY TIGARD	V(D
GAYLORD BIRCH	D (DE	BILL ATWOOD	TPT FLT(D	MAX HASKETT	TPT V (DEF	SKIP MESQUITE	WIND V(D
BOB FERREIRA	WIND (D	MICHAEL SASAKI	G (DEF	TOMMY CATHEY	B (E	PAT OHARA	TROM (D
PETER WELKER	TPT (D	JOE WILLIAMS	D (E	JOHN MEWBORN	HRNS (D	PAUL CANNON	G (D
STEVE CROPPER	G (E	BENNY MAUPIN	WIND (E	MEMPHIS HORNS	(E	SMITH DOBSON	PNO V(E
DANNY KOOTCH	G (E	BOBBYE HALL	PERC (E	DAVID LUELL	SAX (E	CHUCK BENNETT	TROM(E
PAUL HUBINON	TPT (E	CHUCK FINDLEY	TPT (E	BOBBY SHEW	TPT (E	JIM HORN	WIND(E
DON MENZA	WIND (E	PETER CHRISTLIEB	WIND (E	BROOKS HUNNICUTT	V (E	GWEN EDWARDS	V (E
BRENDA GORDON	V (E	TISH SMITH	V (E	PAT COULTER	V (E	JERRY JONUTZ	SAX (A
HARVEY HUGHES	D (F	DOMINGO BALINTON	B (F	SKIP KONTE	SYN (F		

```
C158A                          COLD CHISEL                                        C158A
    IAN MOSS           G V  (CDF    (A) YOUR'E 13                1978  ELEKTRA      EP 12001
    JIM BARNES         V    (CDF    (B) COLD CHISEL              1978  ELEKTRA
    DON WALKER         K V  (CDF    (C) BREAKFAST AT SWEETHEARTS 1979  ELEKTRA         90001
    PHIL SMALL         B V  (CDF    (D) EAST                     1980  ELEKTRA         90003
    STEVE PRESTWICH    D V  (CDF    (E) SWINGSHIFT               1981  ELEKTRA         90025
    JOE CAMILLERI      SAX  (D      (F) CIRCUS ANIMALS           1982  POLYDOR      POLS 1065
C159                           COLD COMFORT                                       C159
    DAVE PRICE         V G K(A      (A) IN THE CAN               1978 JET UK       JET LP211
    DEREK SODEN        V B G(A
    NIGEL BAGGE        V G  (A  IAN BYRON      D  (A  ROD EDWARDS   K VLN (A  GRAHAM MATTHEWS PERC V(A
    HENRY LOWTHER      TPT  (A  GEOFF DALY     SAX (A  CHRIS MERCER  SAX  (A
C159A                          COLD FIRE                                          C159A
                                (A) TOO COLD                     1981  CAPITOL         12096
C160                           COLD STEEL                                         C160
    DAVID LOVELACE     K    (A      (A) COLD STEEL               1974  ARIOLA      IMP 87736
    GREG ATTAWAY       V D  (A
    RICHARD BOWDEN     G V  (A  MIKE BOWDEN    B V (A  SNEAKY PETE   STEEL (A  GIB GUILBEAU    FDL (A
C160A                          COLDWATER ARMY                                     C160A
    BOBBY GOLDEN       G V  (A      (A) PEACE                    1972  AGAPE        US  2600
    KENNY GOLDEN       B    (A
    RICKY HUGHES       D    (A  BOB SPEARMAN  K V (A  BOB GARRETT V TPT K(A  NICK JONES    TPT V(A
    DALE MILLER        SAX  (A
C161                           B J COLE                                           C161
    B J COLE  STEEL  G K (A      (A) NEW HOVERING DOG            1972  UA          UK  UAS 29418
    ROBERT KIRBY       PNO  (A
    GRAHAM PRESKETT    VLN  (A  TRISTRAM FRY    PERC (A  KEITH BAKER     B   (A
    CRISPIAN STEEL PERKINS TPT(A LAURIE JELLYMAN  D  (A  MICK AUDSLEY    G V (A
    DANNY THOMPSON     B    (A  MIKE GILES      D   (A  FRANCIS MONKMAN K   (A
    ANDY BABYNCHUK     VLN  (A  ROY GILLARD     VLN (A  SUE SHEPPARD    CELLO(A
    BRIAN HAWKINS      VIOLA (A
C161A                          JERRY COLE  (& THE SPACEMEN)                       C161A
    JERRY COLE         G          A GO GO GUITARS             19  CROWN       US     539
                                  OUTER LIMITS               19  CAPITOL     US    2044
                                  HOT ROD DANCE              19  CAPITOL     US    2061
                                  SURF AGE                   19  CAPITOL     US    2112
C161B                          THE COLLECTORS                                     C161B
    CLAIRE LAWRENCE WIND K HCA V(AB (A) THE COLLECTORS        1968  WB US  WS 1746 MIDI  26008
    GLENN MILLER       B V  (AB     (B) GRASS & WILD STRAWBERRIES 1968 WB US WS 1774 MIDI 26024
    ROSS TURNEY        D    (AB
    BILL HENDERSON     V G K(AB  HOWIE VICKERS    V   (BA  LARRY KNECHTEL   K  (A
    NORM JEFFRIES      VIBES(A   JESSE ERLICH     CELLO (A
C161C                          TONY COLE                                          C161C
    TONY COLE          G V  (A      (A) IF THE MUSIC STOPS     1972  20th CENT    T 403
    JOHN FARRAR        G    (A
    TERRY BRITTEN      G V  (A  ALAN TARNEY     B   (A  BARRY MORGAN    D   (A
    BARRIE GUARD       D PERC(A  BOB EFFORD     REC (A  REINER SCHUELEIN REC (A
    KEVIN PEEK         G    (A  DAVE PERKIN     B   (A  TIM KRAEMER    CELLO(A
    HERBIE FLOWERS     B    (A  WALLY SMITH     TROM (A  MIKE CLAYTON        (A
    DAVE McCRAE        K    (A  TOM CAMPO       B   (A  RICK BUSCH     HRNS (A
    SKAILA KANGA       HARP (A  JOHN BURDEN     HRNS (A  DAVID MACKAY    V   (A
C161D                          COLLAGE                                            C161D
    DONNA              (          (A) THE COLLAGE            1967  SMASH       US     101
    JODIE              (
    JERRY              (        RON             (
C161E                          COLLECTIVE HORIZONTAL                              C161E
                                (A) CRAP GAME     (EP)        19  DOLMEN      DO 1
C162                           ALBERT COLLINS                                     C162
    ALBERT COLLINS     G V  (ALL    (A) TRUCKIN               19  BLUE THUMB  US    B7S8
       WITH                         (B) COOL SOUND OF         19  T C F HALL  US    8002
    LARRY BURTON       G    (G      (C) LOVE CAN BE FOUND     1968  IMPERIAL   US   12428
    JIM KELTNER        D    (F      (C) LOVE CAN BE FOUND     19  LIBERTY     UK   83238
    BRIAN GAROFALO     B    (F      (D) TRASH TALKIN'         1969  IMPERIAL   US   12438
    ALAN BATTS         K    (GH     (E) COMPLEAT ALBERT COLLINS 19 IMPERIAL   US   12445
    A C REED           SAX  (GH     (F) THERE'S GOTTA BE A CHANGE 19 TUMBLEWEED UK TW 3501
    CASEY JONES        D    (G      (F) THERE'S GOTTA BE A CHANGE 1971 TUMBLEWEED US TWS 103
    CHUCK SMITH        SAX  (G      (G) ICE PICKIN'           1978  SONET     UK  SNTF 707
    ARON BURTON        B    (G      (G) ICE PICKIN'           197  ALLIGATOR   US   4713
    MARVIN JACKSON     G    (H      (H) FROSTBITE             1980  SONET     UK  SNTF 837
    JOHNNY GAYDEN      B    (H      (H) FROSTBITE             19  ALLIGATOR   US
    PAUL HOWARD        TPT  (H      (J) ALIVE & COOL          197  RED LIGHTNIN UK  RL 004
    JERRY WILSON       SAX  (H      (K) FROZEN ALIVE          1981  SONET     UK  SNTF 874
    BILL McFARLAND     TROM (H      (K) FROZEN ALIVE          1981  ALLIGATOR   US   4725
    HENRI FORD         SAX  (H
    MAC REBENNACK      K    (F  JOE ZAGARINO    K   (F  LARRY DANIELS   D   (F
    MICHAEL ROSSO      D    (F  JAMES DALLAM    K   (F  BUD BRISBOIS   TPT  (F
    PETE CANDOLI       TPT  (F  JIM HORN        SAX (F  ERNIE WATTS    SAX  (F
    PLAS JOHNSON       SAX  (F  JAY MIGLIORI    SAX (F  LEW McCREARY   TROM (F
    BOB KNIGHT         TROM (F  JUDY RODERICK   V   (F  BRENT WILLIAMSON V (F
    BILL SZYMCZYK      V    (F
C163                           DAVE & ANSELL COLLINS                              C163
    DAVE COLLINS                    (A) DOUBLE BARREL         19  TROJAN        TRL 162
    ANSELL COLLINS                  (A) DOUBLE BARREL         19  BLUE THUMB US  2005
                                    (B) IN THE GHETTO         1976  TROJAN       TRLS 124
```

                                   [121]

```
JUDY COLLINS      V G K(ALL  (A)MAID OF CONSTANT SORROW              1962 ELEKTRA      US   EKS 7209
WITH                         (A) MAID OF CONSTANT SORROW            1975 ELEKTRA      UK   K  52032
MICHAEL SAHL      K    (H    (B) GOLDEN APPLES OF THE SUN           1962 ELEKTRA      US   EKS 7222
STEPHEN STILLS    G    (H    (B) GOLDEN APPLES OF THE SUN           1975 ELEKTRA      UK   K
CHRIS ETHRIDGE    B    (H    (C) 3RD ALBUM                          1964 ELEKTRA      US   EKS 7243
JAMES GORDON      D    (H    (C) 3RD ALBUM                          19   CHANT DU MONTE FR      4324
MICHAEL MELVOIN   K    (H    (D) CONCERT                            1964 ELEKTRA      US   EKS 7280
JAMES BURTON      G    (H    (E) FIFTH ALBUM                        1965 ELEKTRA      US   EKS 7300
BUDDY EMMONS      STEEL(H     (E) FIFTH ALBUM                       19   CHANT DU MONTE FR     74333
VAN DYKE PARKS    K    (H    (F) WILD FLOWERS                       1968 ELEKTRA      US   EKS 74012
FRED HELLERMAN    G    (A    (F) WILD FLOWERS                       197  ELEKTRA      UK   K  42014
ERIK DARLING      BANJO(A    (F) WILD FLOWERS                       19   VOGUE        FR        217
WALTER RAIM       G BANJO(BC (G) IN MY LIFE                         1967 ELEKTRA      US   EKS 74027
ROGER McGUINN     G BANJO(C  (G) IN MY LIFE                         197  ELEKTRA      UK   K  42009
BILL TAKAS        B    (CE   (G) IN MY LIFE                         1968 ELEKTRA      US       7320
CHUCK ISRAELS     B CELLO(DE (G) IN MY LIFE                         19   VOGUE        FR        155
STEVE MANDELL     G BANJO(D  (H) WHO KNOWS WHERE THE TIME GOES      1969 ELEKTRA      US   EKS 74033
RICHARD FARINA    DULCIMER(E (H) WHO KNOWS WHERE THE TIME GOES      197  ELEKTRA      UK   K  42044
ERIC WEISSBERG    G V  (E    (H) WHO KNOWS WHERE THE TIME GOES      197  VOGUE        FR        322
JERRY DODGION     FLT  (E    ( ) RECOLLECTIONS(BEST OF)            1969 ELEKTRA      US       74055
BOB SYLVESTER     CELLO (E   ( ) RECOLLECTIONS(BEST OF)            197  ELEKTRA      UK   K  42035
BILL LEE          B    (E    (I) BOTH SIDES NOW                     1971 ELEKTRA US75030 UK K 42098
JOHN SEBASTIAN    HCA  (E    (J) WHALES & NIGHTINGALES              1971 ELEKTRA US75010 UK K 42059
DANNY KALB        G    (E    (K) LIVING                             1972 ELEKTRA US75014 UK K 42102
GEORGE MARGE      HRNS (M    ( ) COLOURS OF DAY    (BEST OF)        1972 ELEKTRA           US    75030
BILL SLAPIN       FLT  (M    ( ) AMAZING GRACE     (BEST OF)        1972 ELEKTRA      UK   K  42110
ROMEO PENQUE      FLT  (M    (L) TRUE STORIES & OTHER DREAMS        1973 ELEKTRA US75053 UK K 42132
EMANUEL VARDI     VLA  (M    (M) JUDITH                             1975 ELEKTRA US 1032 UK K 52019
GENE ORLOFF       VLN  (M    (N) BREAD & ROSES                      1976 ELEKTRA US 1076 UK K 52039
KEN ASCHER        K    (M    (O) SO EARLY IN SPRING                 1977 ELEKTRA US 6007 UK K 52019
HUCH McCRACKEN    G    (M    (P) SAVE THE CHILDREN                  197  WOMAN        US       W001
DAVID SPINOZZA    G    (M    ( ) MOST BEAUTIFUL SONGS OF            1979 ELEKTRA      UK   K  62006
STEVE BURGH       G    (M    (R) HARD TIME FOR LOVERS               1979 ELEKTRA US6E171 UK K 52121
STEVE GADD        D    (M    (S) RUNNING FOR MY LIFE                1980 ELEKTRA US6E253 UK K 52205
TONY LEVIN        D    (M
RALPH McDONALD  PERC (M  KEN BISCHEL      SYN (M  CHARLIE BROWN   G    (M  ERIC WEISSBERG   G    (M
PAT REBILLOT    K    (M  DON BROOKS       HCA (M  SELDON POWELL   HRNS (M  ARTHUR CLARKE    HRNS (M
TONY STUDD      HRNS (M  FRANK WESS       HRNS (M  GARNETT BROWN   HRNS (M  RANDY BRECKER    HRNS (M
PAUL GRIFFIN    K    (M  STEVE GOODMAN    V   (M  DENVER COLLINS  V    (M  CISSY HOUSTON    V    (MR
SYLVIA SHEMWELL V    (M  EUNICE PETERSON  V   (M  CORKY HALE      HARP (M  DOMINIC CORTES   ACC  (M
JOEL KAYE       WIND (M  BOB STEEN        WIND(M  GEORGE RICCI    CELLO(M  LES SCOTT        WIND (M
JERRY SMITH     WIND (M  SIDNEY WEINBERG  WIND(M  LARRY WECHSLER  HRNS (M  ALBERT RICHMOND  WIND (M
WAYNE ANDRE     TROM (M  VINNIE FAMUELE   TROM(M  THOMAS PEARSON  K    (M  ABE ROSEN        HARP (M
CLIFF MORRIS    G    (M  HANK JARAMILLO   PERC(M  JOHN BEAL       B    (M  CHARLIE McCRACKEN CELLO(M
KERMIT MOORE    CELLO(M  DENNIS BUDIMIR   G   (R  LEE RITENOUR    G    (R  DAVID HUNGATE    B    (R
JAI WINDING     K    (R  JIM KELTNER      D   (R  DEAN PARKS      G    (R  MIKE LANG        K    (R
FRED TACKETT    G    (R  JEFF BAXTER    G STEEL(R  DAVID WOLFERT   G    (R  NORTON BUFFALO   HCA  (R
MAERETHA STEWART V   (R  HILDA HARRIS     V   (R  SID SHARP       STR  (R  HARRY BLUESTONE  STR  (R
VINCE DEROSA    HRNS (R  DAVID DUKE       HRNS(R  BOB HENDERSON   HRNS (R  BILL LANE        HRNS (R
LEW McCREARY    TROM (R  DICK HYDE        TROM(R  LOUISE DITULLIO FLT  (R  SHERIDON STOKES  FLT  (R
CHARLES GOULD   WIND (R  JACK MARSH       WIND(R  JOHN ELLIS      WIND (R  EARL DUMLER      WIND (R
TED NASH        CLAR (R  DICK SPENCER     CLAR(R  JACK NIMITZ     CLAR (R  GARRY COLEMAN    PERC (R
LOU VOLPE       G    (S  WARREN DOZE      D   (S  BOB CRANSHAW    B    (S  TOM BARNEY       B    (S
BOB CHRISTIANSON SYN (S  THOMAS BOGOAN    V   (S  LESLIE DORSEY   V    (S  DAVID SMITH      V    (S
STEVE CLAYTON   V    (S  JUNE MAGRUDER    V   (S  HELEN MILES     V    (S  CHARLES MAGRUDER V    (S
LENNY ROBERTS   V    (S  THOMAS TEXTOR    V   (S  STRING SECTION       (M
```

```
PAUL COLLINS      G V  (A    (A) PAUL COLLINS BEAT                  1979 CBS          UK       83895
STEVEN HUFF       B V  (A
LARRY WHITMAN     G V  (A    MICHAEL RUIZ     D   (A
```

```
PHIL COLLINS    D V K PERC(AB (A) FACE VALUE                        1981 VIRGIN UK 2185 ATLANTIC US 16029
JOHN GIBLIN     B      (AB    (B) HELLO I MUST BE GOING             1982 VIRGIN UK 2252
DARYL STEURMER  G BAN(AB
STEPHEN BISHOP  V    (A  ALPHONSO JOHNSON  B   (A  DON MYRICK      SAX  (AB  LOUIS SATTERSFIELD TROM(AB
RAHMLEE MICHAEL DAVIS TPT(AB MICHAEL HARRIS TPT (AB JOE PARTRIDGE  G    (A   RONNIE SCOTT     SAX  (A
ERIC CLAPTON    G    (A  PETER ROBINSON    K   (AB CHOIR                (A   MO FOSTER        B    (B
```

```
SHIRLEY COLLINS   V G BANJO(ALL (A) FALSE TRUE LOVERS              1959 FOLKWAYS          FG3564
TONY ENGLE        (K         (B) FOLK ROOTS                        1964 DECCA        UK        4652
PAUL NIEMAN       HRNS (K     (C) THE SWEET PRIMEROSES             1967 TOPIC        UK   12TS 170
MICHAEL GREGORY   PERC (K     (D) POWER OF THE TRUE LOVE KNOT      1968 POLYDOR      UK   583 025
DOLLY COLLINS     V    (EFGH  (E) ANTHEMS IN EDEN                  1969 HARVEST      UK   SHVL 754
CHRIS HOGWOOD     K    (FJ    (F) LOVE DEATH & THE LADY            1970 HARVEST      UK   SHVL 771
ALLAN LUMSDEN     SACK (FGJ   (G) NO ROSES                         1971 PEGASUS UK PEG 7 US ANTILLES7017
ADAM SKEAPING     VLN  (FJ    (G) NO ROSES                         1974 MOONCREST    UK   CREST 11
ROD SKEAPING      VLN  (FJ    (H) ADIEU TO  OLD ENGLAND            1974 TOPIC        UK   12T  238
ELEANOR SLOAN     REBEC(F      (I) A FAVOURITE GARLAND  (BEST OF)  1975 DECCA US 1017 UK  SML 1117
JOHN FORDHAM      REC  (FJ    (J) AMARANTH                         1976 HARVEST      UK   SHSM2008
TERRY COX         PERC (F     (K) FOR AS MANY AS WILL              1978 TOPIC        UK   12T  380
PETER WOOD        CONC (F
SIMON NICOL     V G  (GHJ IAN WHITEMAN    PNO (G  DAVE BLAND      CONC (G  ASHLEY HUTCHINGS B    (G
ROGER POWELL    D    (G  RICHARD THOMPSON G   (G  LOL COXHILL     SAX  (G  ALAN CAVE      BASSOON (G
TONY HALL       MEL  (G  DAVE MATTACKS    D   (GJ JOHN KIRKPATRICK ACC  (GJ NIC JONES     V FDL (G
BARRY DRANSFIELD V FDL(GK TIM RENWICK     G   (G  FRANCIS BAINES  G    (G  COLIN ROSS    PIPES   (G
MADDY PRIOR     V    (G  LAL WATERSON     V   (G  ROYSTON WOOD    V    (G  STEVE MIGDEN    HRNS (G
MIKE WATERSON   V    (G  GREGG BUTLER     SERP(G  TREVOR CROZIER  V    (G  JOHN WATCHAM    CONC(HJ
TERRY POTTER    HCA  (HJ BILL MOLAN       V MEL(H GEOFF SINGLETON V FDL(H  JOHN HARRINGTON V CONC(H
IAN HOLDER      ACC  (H  BOB STEWART      PSALT(H ROGER SWALLOW   D   (H  JOHN RODD       CONC(J
PAT DONALDSON   B    (H  ROGER BRENNER    SACK(J  COLIN SHEEN     SACK(J  PAUL BEER       SACK(J
MARTIN NICHOLLS SACK (J  JOHN SOTHCOTT    VIELL(J DAVID MURROW    WIND(J  STEVE ASHLEY    V   (J
RAY WORMAN      V    (J  JOHN MORGAN      V   (J  DAVID BUSBY     V   (J  MIKE CLIFTON    V   (J
DOTS DAULTREY   V    (J  STUART HOLLYER   V   (J  ROGER RIGDEN    V   (J  ADA TURNHAM     V   (J
OLIVER BROOKES  VLN  (J  MICHAEL LAIRD    CORNET(J RICHARD LEE    REC (J  GILLIAN REID    BELL(J
PHIL PICKETT    WIND (K  DAVEY GRAHAM     G   (K
```

C165A COLONEL BAGSHOT C165A

```
KEN PARRY          G K V(A     (A) OH! WHAT A LOVELY WAR        1971  CADET CONCEPT  US        50010
DAVE DOVER         B K V (A
BRIAN FARRELL      G V   (A     TERRY McCUSKER      D V   (A
```

C166 COLOSSEUM C166

```
JON HISEMAN             D      (ALL    (A) THOSE WHO ARE ABOUT TO DIE   1969  FONTANA                UK   STLS 5510
DICK HECKSTALL SMITH SAX       (ALL    (A) THOSE WHO ARE ABOUT TO DIE   1969  DUNHILL                US        50062
TONY REEVES             B      (ABFD   (B) VALENTYNE SUITE              1969  VERTIGO UK VO1 BRONZE        HELP4
JAMES LITHERLAND        G      (ABDF   (B) VALENTYNE SUITE              1     BRONZE                 UK   BRNA 214
DAVE GREENSLADE         K      (ALL    (C) DAUGHTER OF TIME             1970  VERTIGO                UK   6360 017
MARK CLARKE             B      (CEF    (C) DAUGHTER OF TIME             1970  DUNHILL                US        50101
HARRY BECKETT           TPT    (C      (D) GRASS IS GREENER(BEST OF)    1970  DUNHILL                US        50079
DAVE CLEMPSON           G      (CEFD   (E) LIVE                         1971  BRONZE                 UK   ICD 1
CHRIS FARLOWE           V      (CEF    (E) LIVE                         197   WB                     US   2XS 1942
LOUIS CENNAMO           B      (C      (F) COLLECTORS COLOSSEUM         1971  BRONZE                 UK   ILPS 9173
BARBARA THOMPSON        WIND   (BC     (G) POP CHRONIK                  1975                              VO12
DAVE GELLY              SAX    (B
JIM PHILLIP             SAX    (B      DEREK WADWORTH      TROM    (C    STRING SECTION               (C
JIM ROCH                G(PRE LP
```

C167 COLOSSEUM II C167

```
JON HISEMAN        D    (ABC     (A) STRANGE NEW FLESH       1976  BRONZE             UK   ILPS 9356
NEIL MURRAY        B    (A       (A) STRANGE NEW FLESH       1976  WB                 US        2016
JOHN CARY          K    (        (B) ELECTRIC SAVAGE         1977  MCA                UK   MCF  2800
DON AIREY          K    (ABC     (B) ELECTRIC SAVAGE         1977  MCA                US        2293
MIKE STARR         V    (A       (C) WARDANCE                1977  MCA UK MCF2817 UL RI    1603
GARY MOORE         G    (ABC     (C) WARDANCE                1977  MCA                US        2310
JOHN MOLE          B    (BC
```

C168 COLOURS C168

```
CARL RADLE         B    (A       (A) COLOURS                 19    DOT                US        25854
CHUCK BLACKWELL    D    (A       (B) ATMOSPHERE              19    DOT                US        25935
GARY MONTGOMERY    PNO  (A       (AB) COLOURS /ATMOSPHERE    19    PARAMOUNT          US        81030
JACK DALTON        G    (A
ROB EDWARDS        G    (A
```

C168A P J COLT C168A

```
PJ COLT            V    (A       (A) P J COLT                1976  POLYDOR UK 2489 011 US 244 043
FRANCISCO SERRANO  B    (A
JIM WILKINS        D    (A    JEFF BAXTER      G    (A    VALERIE ROBINSON  V    (A   CYNTHIA OUTLAW   V    (A
GWEN ROGERS        V    (A    ROSALIND ROGERS  V    (A    ED COSTA          K    (A   PEE WEE ELLIS    HRNS (A
HANK CRAWFORD      HRNS (A    BARRY ROGERS     HRNS (A    JULIAN PRIESTER   HRNS (A   JOANNE BENNETT   V    (A
MONICA WILLIAMS    V    (A
```

C169 JESSI COLTER C169

```
JESSI COLTER       V K (ALL      (A) A COUNTRY STAR IS BORN       1970  RCA       US   LSP 4333
WITH                             (B) I'M JESSI COLTER             1975  CAPITOL   US   ST11363
WAYLON JENNINGS    G V  (BCDEF   (C) JESSI                        1975  CAPITOL   US   ST11477
JOHN LESLIE HUG    G    (D       (D) DIAMOND IN THE ROUGH         1976  CAPITOL   US   ST11543
RITCHIE ALBRIGHT   D    (BCDEF   (D) DIAMOND IN THE ROUGH         1976  CAPITOL   US   SM11822
SHERMAN HAYES      B    (CDEF    (E) MIRRIAM                      1977  CAPITOL   US   ST11583
RALPH MOONEY       STEEL(BCDEF   (F) THATS THE WAY A COWBOY ROCKS 1978  CAPITOL   US   ST11863
BILLY GRAHAM       FDL MAND(D
CRAIG WARE         HRNS (D    ROBERT WARE      HRNS (D    TODD MILLER   HRNS (D   DON ROBERTSON   K    (D
BARNEY ROBERTSON   K V  (DEF  CARTER ROBERTSON V    (DEF  JOHN BUCK WILKIN G  (B   REGGIE YOUNG    G    (BC
LARRY MUHOBERAC    PNO  (BC   DUKE GOFF        B    (BC   TOMMY COGBILL  B    (B   WELDON MYRICK   STEEL(B
JOHNNY GIMBLE      FDL  (BF   JIM GORDON       HRNS (BCE  RANDY SCRUGGS  G BANJ(C  DICK HYDE       TROM (BCE
MAC JOHNSON        TPT  (CE   LARRY MURRAY     DULC (C    GORDON PAYNE   G    (EF  G MERLIN   DULC      (E
JOHN CHRISTOPHER   G    (E    GAYLE LEVANT     HARP (E    RANCE WASSON   G    (E   FRED CARTER     G    (F
TONY JOE WHITE     G HCA(F    J J CALE    G    (
```

C171 CHI COLTRANE C171

```
CHI COLTRANE       V PERC K(ALL    (A) CHI COLTRANE       1972  CBS US 31275  UK   65043
JIM GORDON         D    (BC        (B) LET IT RIDE        1973  CBS US 32463  UK   65639
BARRY DE SOUZA     B    (B         (C) ROAD TO TOMORROW   1977  TK                 82501
JIM KELTNER        D    (B         (D) SILK & STEEL       1981  CBS                85277
STEVE PARSONS      D    (B
CHRIS KARAN        D    (B    KENNY EDWARDS    B    (C    WILLIE WEEKS    B    (C   LARRY KNECHTEL  B    (B
EMORY GORDY        B    (B    KLAUS VOORMAN    B    (B    CHRIS LAURENCE  B    (C   MARK CIPOLA     B    (B
JOE PUERTA         B    (B    BOBBYE HALL      PERC (B    PAUL BUCKMASTER SYN  (B   JOHN GUSTAFSON  B    (B
LEE RITENOUR       G    (B    BEB BENAY        G    (BD   LARRY BYROM     G    (B   ALAN ESTES      PERC (B
PAUL ESSARD        CLAR (B    MERRY CLAYTON    V    (B    JEFF PORCARO    D    (C   STEPHANIE SPRUILL V  (B
CLYDIE KING        V    (C    MICHAEL BOTTS    D    (C    ABE LABORIEL    B    (C   VICTOR FELDMAN  PERC (C
GREG PRESTOPINO    V    (C    JENNIFER WARNES  V    (C    IAN UNDERWOOD   SYN  (C   BRIAN RUSSELL   V    (C
JIM HORN           HRNS (C    CHUCK FINDLEY    HRNS (C    QUITMAN DENNIS  HRNS (C
```

C172 COLWELL WINFIELD BLUES BAND C172

```
MIKE WINFIELD      B    (A       (A) COLD WIND BLUES       1968  VERVE       US   3056
BILL COLWELL       G    (A
MOOSE SORRENTO     V    (A    CHUCK PURRO      D    (A    JACK SHROER     SAX  (A
COLLIN TILTON      WIND (A
```

C172A JEFFREY COMANOR C172A

```
JEFFREY COMANOR    G V  (AB      (A) JEFFREY COMANOR           1975  EPIC   US      32832
DON FELDER         G    (B       (B) A RUMOR IN HIS OWN TIME   1976  EPIC   US      34080
COLIN CAMERON      B    (B       (C) SURE HOPE YOU LIKE IT     19    A&M    US  SP  4237
AL KOOPER          ORG  (B
DAVID GARLAND      PNO  (B    GARY MALLABER    D    (B    HUGH McCRACKEN  G    (B
TIM SCHMIT         V    (B    RICHARD BELL          (C    DANNY COHEN          (C
TOXEY FRENCH            (C    BONES HOWE            (C    GERY ILLINGSWORTH    (C
LARRY KNECHTEL     K    (C    JOE OSBORNE      B    (C    RED RHODES      STEEL(C
HOMER WILLIS            (C
```

C172B COMFORTABLE CHAIR C172B

```
BERNIE SCHWARTZ    V    (A       (A) THE COMFORTABLE CHAIR     1968  ODE            44005
BARBARA WALLACE    V WIND(A
GENE EARFIN        G    (A    TAD BACZEK       K    (A    GARY DAVIS      B G  (A
GREG LEROY         D    (A    JOHN DENSMORE    PROD (A    ROBBY KRIEGER   PROD (A
```

[123]

```
     GEORGE FRAYNE      K V  (ALL         (A) LOST IN THE OZONE              1971  PARAMOUNT    US   PAR  6017
     BILLY C FARLOW     HCA V(ABCDEFG      (A) LOST IN THE OZONE              197   PARAMOUNT         SPFL  276
     LANCE DICKERSON    D V  (ABCDEFG      (A) LOST IN THE OZONE              197   CARRERE      FR         68020
     ANDY STEIN         FDL SAX(ABCDEFG    (A) LOST IN THE OZONE              1976  ANCHOR       UK   ABC  5074
     BILL KIRCHEN       G V  (ABCDEFG      (B) HOT LICKS COLD STEEL           1972  PARAMOUNT    US   PAS  6031
     BRUCE BARLOW       B V  (ABCDEFGJ     (B) HOT LICKS COLD STEEL           197   PARAMOUNT         SPFL  281
     BOBBY BLACK        STEEL V(BCDFGJK    (B) HOT LICKS COLD STEEL           197   CARRERE      FR         68019
     JOHN TICHY         G    (ABCDEF       (B) HOT LICKS COLD STEEL           1976  ANCHOR       UK   ABCL 5079
     ERNIE HAGAR        STEEL(E            (C) COUNTRY CASANOVA               1973  PARAMOUNT    US   PAS  6054
     RICK HIGGINBOTHAM  G    (G            (C) COUNTRY CASANOVA               197   PARAMOUNT         SPFL  287
     MIC GILLETTE       TPT  (EF           (C) COUNTRY CASANOVA               197   CARRERE      FR         68002
     GREG ADAMS         TPT  (EF           (C) COUNTRY CASANOVA               1976  ANCHOR       UK   ABCL 5083
     DAVID BROMBERG     G    (F            (D) LIVE DEEP IN THE HEART OF TEXAS 1974 PARAMOUNT    US   PAS  1017
     HOYT AXTON         G V  (F            (D) LIVE DEEP IN THE HEART OF TEXAS 197  PARAMOUNT         SPFL  295
     RONEE BLAKLEY      B V  (F            (D) LIVE DEEP IN THE HEART OF TEXAS 197  CARRERE      FR         68001
     MIMI FARINA        B V  (F            (D) LIVE DEEP IN THE HEART OF TEXAS 1976 ANCHOR       UK   ABCL 5088
     NORTON BUFFALO     HRNS V(GK          (E) COMM' CODY HIS LOST PLANET AIRMEN 1975 WB         US   BS   2847
     FRED MYER          D    (J            (E) COMM' CODY HIS LOST PLANET AIRMEN 1975 WB         UK   K  56108
     DARIUS JAVAHER     G    (J            (F) TALES FROM THE OZONE           1975  WB           US   BS   2883
     ROB GREER          B    (J            (F) TALES FROM THE OZONE           1975  WB           UK   K  56158
     CISCO G            SAX  (J            (G) WEVE GOT A LIVE ONE HERE        1976  WB           US   BS   2939
     CRAIG CHAQUICO     G    (J            (G) WEVE GOT A LIVE ONE HERE        1976  WB           UK   K  66043
     RENEE ARMAND       V    (F            (H) MIDNIGHT MAN    (CODY SOLO)    19    ARISTA       US   AB   4125
     MARC EDELSTEIN     V    (F            (J) ROCK'N'ROLL AGAIN              1977  ARISTA       UK   SPART1018
     NICOLETTE LARSON   V    (FJK          (J) ROCK'N'ROLL AGAIN              1977  ARISTA       US   AL   4135
     GRAHAM BROAD       PERC (J            (J) ROCK'N'ROLL AGAIN              1977  PATHE        FR   068 99251
     DEBORAH ANDERSON   V    (F            (K) FLYING DREAMS                  1978  ARISTA       UK   AB   4183
     CHARRA PENNY       V    (J            (K) FLYING DREAMS                  1978  ARISTA       US   SPART1067
     TOM FLYE           PERC (J
     KEVIN FARRELL      V    (F   SCOTT EDWARDS    B  (K   JEFF BAXTER    G  (K   NEIL LARSON      K  (K
     JENNIFER WARNES    V    (K   ED GREENE        D  (K   BUZZ FEITON   G  (K   LEE MONTGOMERY   V  (K
     ERNIE WATTS        SAX  (K   SHIRLEY MATTHEWS V  (K   ABRAHAM LABORIEL B (K  RICHARD BOWDEN   G  (K
     JOHN HUG H HARP K  D    (K   DAVID HUNGATE    B  (K   JOE ENGLISH    D  (K   VENETTA FIELDS   V  (K
     CLYDIE KING        V    (K   DANNY GATTON     G  (K   DELANEY BRAMLETT V (K  STEVE BECKMEYER  G  (K
     BUZZ BUCHANEN      PERC (K   GARY COLEMAN        PERC (K   WEST VIRGINIA CREEPER STEEL(A
```

C173A   THE COMMERCIALS   C173A

```
     LOYD GROSSMAN      G V  (A            (A) COMPARE & DECIDE               1980  EAT          US   EAT1
     JOHN DEELP         B SYN(A
     NEAL GROSSMAN      SYN  (A   GARY LONG           IAN DUCK      G   (A
```

C174   COMMODORES   C174

```
     LIONEL RICHIE                         (A) MACHINE GUN                    1974  MOTOWN US M7 798 UK STML11273
     WILLIAM KING                          (A) MACHINE GUN                    1981  MOTOWN US M5 121 UK        5002
     WALTER ORANGE                         (B) CAUGHT IN THE ACT              1975  MOTOWN US M7 820 UK STML11286
     RON LAPRAED                           (C) HOT ON THE TRACKS              1976  MOWTOWN          UK STM 12031
     MILAN WILLIAMS                        (D) MOVIN ON                       197   MOTOWN US M7 848 UK STML12001
     TOMMY McCLARY                         (D) MOVIN ON                       1981  MOTOWN US M5 178
                                           (E) ZOOM                          1977  MOTOWN           UK STML12057
                                           (F) COMMODORES                    197   MOTOWN US M7 884
                                           (G) LIVE                          1978  MOTOWN US M9 894 UK TMSP 6007
                                           (H) NATURAL HIGH                  1978  MOTOWN US M7 902 UK STML12087
                                           (I) GREATEST HITS                 1978  MOTOWN US M7 912 UK STML12100
                                           (J) MIDNIGHT MAGIC                1979  MOTOWN US   926 UK STMA 8032
                                           (K) HEROS                         1980  MOTOWN US   939 UK STMA 8034
                                           (L) IN THE POCKET                 1981  MOTOWN US   995 UK STML12156
                                           (M) LOVE SONGS                    1982  MOTOWN US  1171
```

C174A   COMMON PEOPLE   C174A

```
     DANNY REBINETT     G V  (A            (A) OF THE PEOPLE BY THE PEOPLE FOR.. 1969 CAPITOL     US        266
     JOHN BARTLEY       G    (A
     JERRALD REBINETT   D    (A   MICHAEL McCARTHY    B  (A
```

C174B   COMSAT ANGELS   C174B

```
     MIC GLAISHER       D    (ABC          (A) WAITING FOR AN MIRACLE         1980  POLYDOR      UK   2383 578
     STEPHEN FELLOWS    G V  (ABC          (B) COMSAT ANGELS                  19    METRONOME    GER       60357
     KEVIN BACON        B    (ABC          (EP) EYE OF THE LENS +3            1981  METRONOME    GER  930 031
     ANDY PEAKE         K V  (ABC          (C) SLEEP NO MORE                  1981  POLYDOR      UK   POLS 1038
```

C174C   BOBBY COMSTOCK   C174C

```
     BOBBY COMSTOCK     V    (A            (A) BOBBY COMSTOCK                 19    ASCOT        US   13026
```

C174D   COMPANYIA ELECTRICA DHARMA   C174D

```
     ESTEVE FORTUNY     G    (AB           (A) DIUMENGE                       1975  ZELESTE EDIGSA FR      2018
     JORDI SOLEY        K    (AB           (B) L'OUCEMBALLA                   1976  ZELESTE EDIGSA FR      2026
     JEAN FORTUNY       SAX  (AB
     CARLES VIDAL       B    (AB   JOSEP FOTUNY        D  (AB
```

C175   COMUS   C175

```
     ROGER WOOTTON      G V  (AB           (A) FIRST UTTERANCE                1971  DAWN         UK   DNLS 3019
     BOBBIE WATSON      V PERC(AB          (B) TO KEEP FROM CRYING            1974  VIRGIN       UK   V    2018
     COLIN PEARSON      VLN  (A
     ROB YOUNG          PERC (A   KEITH HALE       K  (B   ANDY HELLABY  B  (B
     LINDSAY COOPER     WIND (B   GORDON CAXON     D  (B   PHIL BARRY   PERC (B
     DIDIER MALHERBE    SAX  (B   TIM KRAEMER    CELLO (B
```

C175B   CONGO ASHANTE ROY   C175B

```
                                           (A) SIGN OF THE STAR               1981  CHARISMA UK PREX 8 NL6302 147
```

C176   CONGO   C176

```
                                           (A) HEART OF THE CONGO             1978  BLACK ART
                                           (B) CONGO                          1979  CBS                83796
```

C176A   CONGRESS OF WONDERS   C176A

```
                                           (A) REVOLTING                      19    FANTASY      US   7016
```

C176B   ARTHUR CONLEY   C176B

```
     ARTHUR CONLEY      V    (ALL          ( ) SWEET SOUL MUSIC               19    ATCO         US   33215
                                           ( ) SHAKE RATTLE & ROLL            19    ATCO         US   33220
                                           ( ) SOUL DIRECTION                 19    ATCO         US   33243
                                           ( ) MORE SWEET SOUL                19    ATCO         US   33276
```

CONTINIUM

YOEL SCHWARCZ	G HCA(A	(A) CONTINIUM	1970	RCA	US	8157
HARVEY TROUPE	D (AB	(B) AUTUMN GRASS	1971	RCA	US	8196
TIM RICE	K (B					
PETER BILLAM	B G (AB					

C177   BILLY CONNOLLY   **C177**

BILLY CONNOLY	LIVE	1972	TRANSATLANTIC	UK	TRA 258
	LIVE RI	1981	TRANSATLANTIC	UK	TRS 103
	SOLO CONCERT	1974	TRANSATLANTIC	UK	TRA 279
	WORDS & MUSIC	1975	TRANSATLANTIC	UK	TRASAM 32
	COP YER WHACK FOR THIS	1974	POLYDOR	UK	2383 310
	GET RIGHT INTAE HIM	1975	POLYDOR	UK	2383 368
	ATLANTIC BRIDGE	1977	POLYDOR	UK	2383 419
	RAW MEAT FROM THE BALCONY	1977	POLYDOR	UK	2383 464
	BILLY CONNOLLY	1977	HALLMARK	UK	SHM 927
	B C COLLECTION	1978	PICKWICK		PDA 035
	THE BIG YIN	1976	TRANSATLANTIC	UK	TRASAM 38
	GOLDEN GIFT BOX	1976	TRANSATLANTIC	UK	GAR1
	ANTHOLOGY	1978	TRANSATLANTIC	UK	MTRA 2008
	RIOUTOUS ASSEMBLY	1979	POLYDOR	UK	2383 543

C177A   ROBERT CONNOLLY   **C177A**

ROBERT CONNOLLY	G B K (A	(A) PLATEAU	1978	TUBE		TSH 352
GREG McILVEEN	D (A					
DAVE BEATLY	G (A	PETER CROLLY B V FLT (A	FRANK RUSSELL	D (A	
HOWIE STRUTT	V (A	SHEILA WILLICK V (A	SANDRA WILLICK	V (A	

C177B   BILL CONNORS   **C177B**

BILL CONNORS	G (AB	(A) THEME TO THE GUARDIAN	1975	ECM	1057
JAN GARAREK	SAX (B	(B) OF MIST & MELTING	1978	ECM	1120
GARY PEACOCK	B (B				
JACK DEDOHNETTE	D (B				

C177C   CONTOURS   **C177C**

BILLY GORDON		(A) DO YOU LOVE ME	19	GORDY	US	901
JOE BILLINGSLEA		(B) BABY HIT & RUN	1974	M F P	UK	50054
SYLVESTER POTTS						
BILLY HOGGS	HUBERT JOHNSON	HUEY DAVIS	G			

C177D   CONTORTIONS   **C177D**

JAMES CHANCE/WHITE	V K SAX(ALL	(A) BUY	1979	ZE	CAN	33002
GINGER LEE	D (CD	(B) SECOND CHANCE	1980	PVC	US	7918
RICHARD HARRISON	D (C	(C) LIVE AUX BAINS DOUCHES	1980	INVISIBLE	FR	10008
DON CHRISTENSEN	G (D	(D) JAMES WHITE & THE BLACKS	1980	ZE	GER	202 452
VIVIENNE DICK	VLN (D					
AL MACDOWELL	B (C	PATRICK GEOFFROIS	G (C	LORENZO WYCHE	TPT (C	
FRED WELLS	G (C	LYDIA LUNCH	G (D	RAY MANTILLA	PERC (D	
GEORGE SCOTT	B (D	ADELE BERTEI	PNO (D	PAUL COLIN	SAX (D	
PAT PLACE	V (D	JODY HARRIS	V (D	CHRISTIAN HOFFMAN	PNO (D	
BOB QUINE	G (D					

C178   CONTRABAND   **C178**

MAE McKENNA	G V (A	(A) CONTRABAND	1974	TRANSATLANTIC	UK	TRA 278
PETER CAIRNEY	G B (A					
JOHN MARTIN	VLN (A	ALEC BAIRD	D G (A	GEORGE JOHNSON MAND K KG	(A	
BILLY JOHNSON	B (A					

C178A   CONTRABAND (US)   **C178A**

DAVID PRITCHARD	G (A	(A) TIME & SPACE	1971	EPIC	US	30814
CHARLES ORENA	WIND (A					
PETE ROBINSON	K (A	BRUCE CALE	B VLN (A	BRIAN MOFFATT	D PERC(A	

C178B   CONTRABAND (AUSTR)   **C178B**

MARK EVANS	B V (A	(A) NOTHING TO HIDE	1978	PORTRAIT	US	35450
GRAHAM KENNEDY	G V (A					
PETER McFARLANE	D V (A	OWEN ORFORD	V (A	CHRIS JONES	G (A	
KERRIE BIDDELL	V (A	RALPH WHITE	HRNS (A			

C179   RY COODER   **C179**

RY COODER	G V B MAND (ALL	(A) RY COODER	1971	REPRISE	US 6402	UK K44093
JIM KELTNER	D (BCDEHIJK	(B) INTO THE PURPLE VALLEY	1972	REPRISE	US 2052	UK K44142
MILT HOLLAND	PERC (ABCDEFHJ	(C) BOOMERS STORY	1972	REPRISE	US 2117	UK K44224
ROGER HAWKINS	D (C	(D) PARADISE & LUNCH	1974	REPRISE	US 2179	UK K44260
CHARLES LAWING	CLAR (C	(E) CHICKEN SKIN MUSIC	1976	REPRISE	US 2254	UK K54083
RANDY NEWMAN	PNO (C	(F) SHOWTIME	1977	WB	US 3059	UK K56386
GEORGE BOHANON	HRNS (BCEGJ	(G) JAZZ	1978	WB	US 3197	UK K56488
ATTA ISAACS	G (E	(H) BOP TILL YOU DROP	1979	WB	US 3358	UK K56691
TOMMY McCLURE	B (C	(I) BORDERLINE	1980	WB	US 3489	UK K56864
GENE FINNEY	HCA (C	(J) LONG RIDERS(SOUNDTRACK)	1980	WB	US 3448	UK K56826
CHUCK RAINEY	B (K	(K) THE SLIDE AREA	1982	WB	US 3651	
SLEEPY JOHN ESTES	G V (C	(1) NOV 1980 TOUR(UK)				
JIM DICKINSON	PROD PNO(BCJK					

ISAAC GARCIA	D (F	HENRY BIG RED OJEDA	B (EF	FRANK VILLAREAL	SAX (F	ELDRIDGE KING	V (F
BOBBY KING	V(1DEFHIK	TERRY EVANS		SAX (EF	PAT RIZZO	SAX (EFG	JESSE PONCE BANJO	(F
EARL HINES	PNO (DG	RITCHIE HAYWARD	D (A	ROY ESTRADA	B (A	JOHN BARBEDA	(A
MAX BENNETT	B (A	BOBBY BRUCE		V (A	GEORGE McCURN	V (D	WALTER COOK	V (D
RICHARD JONES	V (D	KARL RUSSELL	V (D	TOM PEDRINI	B (G	RANDY ALLCROFT	TROM(G
DAVID SHERR	CLAR (G	HARVEY PITTEL	WIND (G	TOM COLLIER	PERC (G	BARBARA STARKEY	K (G
CHUCK DOMANICO	B (G	MARIO GUARNERI	CORNET(G	RED CALLENDER	B TUBA (DEG	MARK STEVENS	D (G
DAVID LINDLEY	G MAND(GHJ	CHRIS ETHRIDGE	B (ABCED	FRITZ RICHMOND	B (B	JERRY JUMONVILLE	HRNS(B
JOE DAVIS	HRNS (B	IKE WILLIAMS	HRNS (B	JOHN CRAVIOTTO	D (B	VAN DYKE PARKS PROD K(AB	
GLORIA JONES	V (AB	DONNA WASHBURN	V (B	DONNA WEISS	V (B	CLAUDIA LENNEAR	V (B
SIMON PICO PAYNE	V (DG	BILL JOHNSON	V (DG	JIMMY ADAMS	V (GH	CHUCK BERGHOFFER	B (G
WILLIE SCHWARTZ	CLAR (G	BILL HOOD	SAX (G	JOHN RODBY	K (G	FRED JACKSON	SAX(E
STUART BROTMAN	CYMB (G	OSCAR BRASHEAR CORNET(DEGJ		CLIFF GIVENS	V (EGH	RUSS TITELMAN PROD B V(DE	
BENNY POWELL	TROM (G	GABBY PAHINUI	STEEL(E	RONNIE BARRON	K (DH	HERMAN JOHNSON	V (EHK
JOHN DUKE	B (D	PLAS JOHNSON	SAX (D	GENE MUMFORD	V (D	RANDY LORENZO	V (H
TIM DRUMMOND	B (HIK	PATRICK HENDERSON K (H		PICO PAYNE	V (HJ	GREG PRESTOPINO	V (H

(CONTINUED)

FLACO JIMINEZ	ACC	(EF	CHAKA KHAN	V	(H	GEORGE McFADDEN	V	(HK	GEORGE PIERRE	PERC(IJK
REGGIE McBRIDE	B	(HIK	WILLIAM D SMITH	K V	(IK	JOHN HIATT	G V	(IK	JESSE HARMS	SYN(I1
WILLIE GREEN	V	(1IK	CURT BOUTERSE	DULC	(J	BILL BRYSON	B	(J	TOM SAUBER	BAN G	(J
MITCH GREENHILL	G V	(J	JOE CHAMBERS	V	(J	JIM KEACH	V	(J	LESTER CHAMBERS	V	(J
HARRY CAREY JRN	V	(J	DAN PENN	V	(C	DARRELL VERDUSCO	D	(1	JAMES ROLLESTON	B	(1
JOSEPH BYRD	PROD	(G	LENNY WARONKER	PROD(ABCD		PICO PAYNE	V	(G	BOBBY BAKER	V	(K
KAZU MATSUI		(K	NICK DECARO	SRT	(K					

COOKES TOUR	1960	RCA		2221
HITS OF THE 50s	1960	RCA	US	2236
ONE & ONLY	196	RCA	US	2264
SAM COOKE	19	CAMDEN	US	2433
SAM COOKE	196	RCA	US	2293
MY KIND OF BLUES	1961	RCA	US	2392
GOLDEN SOUND	19	TRIP	US	28030
TWISTIN THE NIGHT AWAY	1961	RCA	US	2555
TWISTIN THE NIGHT AWAY	1976	STARCALL	UK	1034
BEST OF SAM COOKE VOL1	1962	RCA	US	2625
MR SOUL	1962	RCA	US	2673
3 GREAT GUYS(ANKA SEDAKA)	196	RCA	US	2720
NIGHT BEAT	1963	RCA	US	2709
SOUL STIRRERS	1964	SAR	US	105
SOUL STIRRERS	1964	LONDON		
AINT THAT GOOD NEWS	1964	RCA	US	2899
AINT THAT GOOD NEWS	1964	SPECIALTY		2115
GOSPEL SOUL OF SAM COOKE	196	SPECIALTY	US	2116
2 SIDES	19	SPECIALTY	US	2119
2 SIDES	1971	SONET	UK	SNTF5009
GOSPEL SOUL VOL 2	196	SPECIALTY	US	2128
AT THE COPA	1964	RCA	US	2970
ORIGINAL SOUL STIRRERS	196	SPECIALTY	US	2137
THATS HEAVEN TO ME	196	SPECIALTY	US	2146
GOLDEN SOUND	196	TRIP	US	8030
16 GREATEST HITS	196	TRIP	US	15 2
SHAKE	1965	RCA	US	3367
BEST OF VOL 2	1965	RCA	US	3373
SAMS SONGS	196	FAMOUS	US	502
ONLY SIXTEEN	196	FAMOUS	US	505
SO WONDERFUL	196	FAMOUS	US	508
YOU SEND ME	196	FAMOUS	US	509
YOU SEND ME	19	CAMDEN US		ACL10445
CHA CHA CHA	196	FAMOUS	US	512
RIGHT ON	196	CHERIE	US	1001
TRY A LITTLE LOVE	1965	RCA	US	3435
HIT KIT	196	KEEN	US	86101
I THANK GOD	196	KEEN	US	86103
SAM COOKE	196	KEEN	US	2001
ENCORE	196	KEEN	US	2003
TRIBUTE TO THE LADY	196	KEEN	US	2004
ENCORE VOL 2	196	KEEN	US	2008
WONDERFUL WORLD(50s)	1966	IMMEDIATE		UKIMLP002
WONDERFUL WORLD(50s	1966	KEEN	US	86106
UNFORGETTABLE SAM COOKE	1966	RCA	US	3517
UNFORGETTABLE SAM COOKE	196	CAMDEN	US	2610
MAN WHO INVENTED SOUL	1968	RCA	US	3991
GOLDEN AGE	196	RCA	UK	1054
THE LATE SAM COOKE	1969	RCA INT		UKINT1080
THIS IS SAM COOKE	1971	RCA	UK	2007
THIS IS SAM COOKE	197	RCA	US	6027
SINGS BILLIE HOLIDAY	1976	STARCALL	UK	1030
SINGS BILLIE HOLIDAY	197	UPFRONT	US	160
INTERPRETS BILLIE HOLIDAY	19	RCA		APLI0899
INTERPRETS BILLIE HOLIDAY	1976	RCA	UK	HY1030
FOREVER	1976	RCA		7194
ANOTHER SATURDAY NIGHT	19	RCA	US	4375
WHEN I FALL IN LOVE	1979	NUT		UK NUTM23

| CALVIN COOL | | (A) THE SURFERS BEAT | 19 | CHARTER | US | 103 |

| DOUG COOK | (A | (A) LATE NIGHT BAR FIGHTS | 1978 | ROCKING HORSE | US | 5520 |

ROGER COOK	V	(ALL	(A) STUDY	1970 COLUMBIA		UK	SCX 6388
LES HURDLE		(B	(B) MEANWHILE BACK AT THE WORLD	1972 REGAL ZONO UK8508 US KAMASUTRA 2056			
JIMMY HOROWITZ FLT K		(B	(C) MINSTREL IN FLIGHT	1973 REGAL ZONO UK1935 US KAMASUTRA 2069			
VICKI BROWN	V	(B	(D) ALRIGHT	1976 POLYDOR UK 2383357 US WB			2909
LIZA STRIKE	V	(B					

ROSETTA HIGHTOWER	V	(B	LESLEY DUNCAN	V	(B	NEIL LANCASTER	V	(B	TONY BURROWS	V	(B
JOHNNY GOODWIN	V	(B	ALAN BRANSCOMBE	SAX	(B	BARRY DESOUZA	D	(B	ALAN PARKER	G	(B
CHRIS SPEDDING	G	(BC	CALEB QUAYE	G	(B	MIKE EGAN	G	(B	TONY NEWMAN	D	(C
HERBIE FLOWER	B	(CD	RAY COOPER	PERC	(C	BRIAN PARRISH	G	(C	FRANK RENSHAW	G V	(C
TONY KELLY	G	(C	PAUL YOUNG	V	(C	B J COLE	STEEL(C		PETE ROBINSON	K	(C
DAVE WILKINSON	ORG	(C	HUGH BURNS	G	(D	RAY GLYNN	G	(D	JOHNNY CHRISTOPHER	G(D
REGGIE YOUNG	G	(D	MARY HOPEFINGER	HARP	(D	DENNIS GOOD	TROM	(D	GEORGE TIDWELL	TPT	(D
JILL HUTTON	V	(D	SANDY MASON	V	(D	MADELINE BELL	V	(D	DOREEN CHANTER	V	(D
IRENE CHANTER	V	(D	SAM LORBER	V	(D	RICHARD BRANNON	V	(D	RICHARD LEIGH	V	(D
KENNY MALONE	D	(D	BARRY MORGAN	D	(D	JOE ALLEN	B	(D	BILLY PUETT	WIND(D
BOBBY WOOD	K	(D	CHARLES COCHRAN	K	(D	MIKE MORAN	K	(D		

```
RITA COOLIDGE      V  (ALL      (A) RITA COOLIDGE          1971 A&M US 4291   UK  AMLS 2015
WITH                           (B) NICE FEELIN'           1971 A&M US 4325   UK  AMLS64325
LEON RUSSELL       K  (A        (C) LADY'S NOT FOR SALE    1972 A&M US 4370   UK  AMLS64370
DANIEL TIMMS       V  (F        (C) LADY'S NOT FOR SALE    1981 M F P         UK      50500
SPOONER OLDHAM     K  (A        (D) FALL INTO SPRING       1974 A&M US 3627   UK  AMLS63627
CLARENCE WHITE     G  (A        (E) ITS ONLY LOVE          1975 A&M US 4531   UK  AMLS64531
MARC BENNO         G  (ABC      (F) ANYTIME ANYWHERE       1977 A&M US 4616   UK  AMLH64616
CHRIS ETHRIDGE     B  (A        (G) LOVE ME AGAIN          1978 A&M US 4699   UK  AMLH64699
JIM KELTNER        D  (ACH      (H) SATISFIED              1979 A&M US 4781   UK  AMLH64781
FRED TACKETT       G  (HI       (I) HEARTBREAK RADIO       1981 A&M US 3727   UK  AMLK63727
STEPHEN STILLS     G  (A        ( ) GREATEST HITS(VERY BEST OF) 1980 A&M US 4836 UK AMLH68520
BOOKER T JONES     B K(ACDEFGH  (FH) ANYTIME/SATISFIED     1980 A&M        CASS UK CAM CR5
BOBBY WOMACK       G  (A
DONALD DUNN    B  (A    BOBBYE HALL     PERC(ADEF  LARRY LEE      V  (G   JERRY McGEE    G (ACDEFG
PLAS JOHNSON   SAX (A   RY COODER       G  (A      FUZZY SAMUELS  B  (A   JIM HORN       SAX (AC
JOHN KELSO     SAX (A   DON MENZA       SAX (A     CLIFFORD SCOTT SAX (A  PETER CHRISTLIEB   (A
GEORGE BOHANON HRNS (A  LEW McCREARY    TROM (A    ERNIE TACK     TROM (A JACK REDMAN    TROM (A
DICK HYDE      TROM (A  OLLIVER MITCHELL HRNS (A   CHUCK FINDLEY  TPT (A  AL AARONS      TPT (A
DALTON SMITH   HRNS (A  VINCE DE ROSA   HRNS (A    BILL HENSHAW   HRNS (A ARTHUR MAEBE   HRNS (A
DAVID DUKE     HRNS (A  CLYDIE KING     V  (AEF    VANETTA FIELDS V  (AF  SHIRLEY MATTHEWS V(ACEF
PRISCILLA COOLIDGE V (ACDH DONNA WEISS  V  (AC     GRAHAM NASH    V  (A   BOB SEGARINI   V  (A
RANDY BISHOP   V  (A    MIKE UTLEY      K (BCDCEFGHI CARL RADLE   B  (C   AL PERKINS     G  (CE
RUSS KUNKEL    D  (DI   JAY GRAYDON     G  (G      JIM HAAS       V  (G   STEPHEN BRUTON V G (GH
BERNIE LEADON  G  (C    LEE SKLAR       B  (CDEF   AL KOOPER      G  (C   JOHN SEBASTIAN HCA (C
CHARLIE FREEMAN G (BC   TOMMY McCLURE   B  (BCH    SAMMY CREASON  D (BCDEFH SNEAKY PETE   STEEL(C
BROOKS HUNNICUTT D (DE  JENNIFER WARNES V  (DE     PETSYE POWELL  V  (E   STEVE FORMAN   PERC (G
MAXINE WILLARD V  (CG   KRIS KRISTOFFERSON V  (C   BARBARA CARROLL PNO (E CHUCK DOMANICO B  (E
COLIN BAILEY   D  (E    MIKE BAIRD      D  (FG     DENNIS BELFIELD B (G   JULIA TILLMAN  V  (G
ORRIN WATERS   V  (G    LUTHER WATERS   V  (G      CORY WELLS     V  (G   DEAN PARKS     G (DFHI
BOB GLAUB      B  (HI   DOROTHY ASHBY   HARP (H    JOHN SEITER    V  (H   MICHAEL McDONALD V (H
RICHIE CANNATA HRNS (H  DONNY GARRARD   V  (H      RITA JEAN BODINE V (D  LINDA DILLARD  V  (D
KEN EDWARDS    V  (DI   ANDREW GOLD  G K PER V (DID DANIEL TIMMS  V  (F   GAYLE LEVANT   HARP (F
JEFF PORCARO   D  (I    WADDY WACHTEL   G  (I      NICOLETTE LARSON V (I  BILL PAYNES    K  (I
LENNY CASTRO   V  (I    KIM CARNES      V  (F      BROCK WALSH    V  (I   MAUREEN McDONALD V (I
MIKE BOTTS     D  (I    J D SOUTHER     V  (I      WILLIAM SMITH  V  (I   GIB GUILBEAU   FDL (D
GEOFF LEVIN    G  (D    DAVID CAMPBELL  STR (DI    NICK DE CARO   ACC (BDI RUSTY YOUNG   STEEL(B
HERB PEDERSEN  BAN (D   MILT HOLLAND    PERC (D    DON BROOKS     HCA (B
```

C182   ALICE COOPER   C182

```
ALICE COOPER    ⌐ V  (ALL   (1) SPIDERS (2) EARWIGS(EARLY GROUPS)
VINCENT FURNIER ⌐            (A) PRETTIES FOR YOU        1969  STRAIGHT US STS1051 WB 1840
GLEN BUXTON      G (123ABCDEFGH (B) EASY ACTION          1969  STRAIGHT US 1061   WB  1845
MICHAEL BRUCE    K G(123ABCDEFGH (AB)SCOOLDAYS(PRETTIES/EASY ACTION 1973 STRAIGHT UK K 66021
STEVE HUNTER     G  (FJKLM   (C) LOVE IT TO DEATH       1971  STRAIGHT           STS 1065
PRAKASH JOHN     B  (JLM     (C) LOVE IT TO DEATH       1971  WB US 1883    UK K 46177
JOSEF CHIROWSKI  K  (JL      (C) LOVE IT TO DEATH       197   MIDI               20633
DICK WAGNER      G (EFGJKLMOR (D) KILLER                1971  WB GER 46121  UK K 56005
NEAL SMITH       D (123ABCDEFGH (D) KILLER              1971  WB        US        2567
DENNIS DUNAWAY   B (123ABCDEFGH (E) SCHOOLS OUT         1972  WB US 2623   UK K 56007
DAVID BRIGGS     PNO (B      (F) BILLION DOLLAR BABIES  1973  WB US 2685   UK K 56013
JULIA TILLMAN    V  (L       (G) MUSCLE OF LOVE         1974  WB US 2748   UK K 56018
ALLEN SCHWARZBERG D  (KL     (H) GREATEST HITS          1974  WB US 3107   UK K 56043
AL McMILLAN      PNO (KL     (J) WELCOME TO MY NIGHTMARE 1975 ANCHOR UK 2011 CARRERE FR 68051
AL KOOPER        K  (L       (J) WELCOME TO MY NIGHTMARE 1975 ATLANTIC   US    19130
DAVEY JOHNSTONE  G  (OP      (K) GOES TO HELL           1976  WB US 2896   UK K 56171
TONY LEVIN       B  (JKL     (L) LACE & WHISKEY         1977  WB US 3027   UK K 56365
JIM KELTNER      D  (O       (M) ALICE COOPER SHOW      1977  WB US 3138   UK K 56439
DONOVAN          G  (F       (N) ALICE COOPER           19    CHARTERLINE     CTR 46177
JOHNNY BADANJEK  D  (J       (O) FROM THE INSIDE        1978  WB US 3263   UK K 56577
REGGIE VINCENT   G V (E      (P) FLUSH THE FASHION      1980  WB US 3436   UK K 56805
SHARON LEE WILLIAMS V(K      (Q) SPECIAL FORCES         1981  WB US 3581   UK K 56927
JAN UVENA        D  (R       (R) ZIPPER CATCHES SKIN    1982  WB           UK K 57021
CRAIG KRAMPF     D  (R       (S) LIVE IN TORONTO        1982  WB
COLINA PHILLIPS  V  (K
DENNY VOSBURGH   V  (K   JIM GANNON      V  (K  BILL MISENER    V  (K   JIM MAELEN    PERC(K
JOHN TROPEA      G  (K   MICHAEL SHERMAN V  (K  SHAUN JACKSON   V  (K   SHEP GORDON    V  (K
LAUREL WARD      V  (K   DENNIS CONWAY   B  (P  JOHN LOPRESTI   B  (P   PENTTI GLAN   D  (JM
FRED MANDEL      K  (MP  VANETTA FIELDS  V  (L  LORNA WILLARD   V  (L   ERNIE WATTS   SAX (L
JIM GORDON       D  (KL  RICK NIELSEN    G  (O  BOB BABBITT     B  (LK  BOB EZRIN  PROD K V (DJKL
GERRY LYONS      V  (J   STU DAY         V  (G  DAVE LIBERT     V  (FG  RONNIE SPECTOR V  (G
NONA HENDRYX     V  (G   MICK MASHBIR    G  (G  LIZA MINNELLI   V  (G   SARAH DASH     V  (G
POINTER SISTERS  V  (G   DENNIS FERRANTE V  (G  MARK VOLMAN     V  (P   HOWARD KAYLAN  V  (P
RICKY TIERNEY    V  (P   KEITH ALLISON   V  (P  MIKE PINERA     G  (QR  DUANE HITCHINGS G (QR
DANNY JOHNSON    G  (Q   CRAIG KRAMPF    D  (Q  ERIK SCOTT      B  (Q   JOHN TATUM        (1
JOHN SPEAR          (1   JOHN NITZINGER  V  (R  BILLY STEELE    G  (R
```

C182 A   D B COOPER   C182A

```
D B COOPER       V  (ABC   (A) EVERY MAN A KING       1980  BLUE CELLAR   US   001
JON CHAPMAN      D  (C     (B) BUY AMERICAN           1980  WB UK K 56831 US 3444
MICHAEL TOWERS   G V (C    (C) DANGEROUS CURVES       1981  WB            US 3544
BOB IRVING       K  (C
ROGER HEATH      G  (C   ROBBY SCHARF     B  (C
```

C183   MIKE COOPER   C183

```
MIKE COOPER      V  (ALL   (A) INVERTED WORLD        1968  MATCHBOX        SDM 159
WITH                      (B) OH REALLY              1969  PYE UK NSPL18281 US JANUS3004
ALAN COOK        K  (      (C) DO I KNOW YOU          1970  DAWN UK NLS 3005 US JANUS3021
TIM RICHARDSON   PERC (    (D) TROUT STEEL            1970  DAWN         UK DNLS 3011
LES CALVERT      BASS (    (E) PLACES I KNOW          1971  DAWN         UK DNLS 3026
STEFAN GROSSMAN  G  (D     (F) MACHINE GUN COMPANY    1972  DAWN         UK DNLS 3031
THE HERON        V  (D     (G) LIFE & DEATH IN PARADISE 1974 FRESH AIR    UK 6370 500
ALAN SKIDMORE    SAX (D
```

(CONTINUED)

C183 (CONTINUED)

MIKE COOPER

JOHN TAYLOR	PNO	(D	GERRY FIELDS	VLN	(D
BILL BOAZMAN	G	(D	MIKE OSBORNE	WIND	(DG
ROY BABBINGTON	B	(D	NICK PICKETT	VLN	
HARRY MILLER	DBL B	(CG	IAN A ANDERSON		(A
LOUIS MUHOLO	D	(G	COLIN BOYD	B	(A
ALAN GOWER	PNO	(G	TERRY EVERETT	SYN	(G

ALAN JACKSON   D   (D
GEOFF HAWKINS   WIND (D
POOR LITTLE ANN V   (C
TERRY CLARKE   G V (G
IAN FOSTER   D   (G

C183A

COOPER BROTHERS

BRIAN COOPER   B V   (A
RICHARD COOPER   G V   (A
TERRY KING   STEEL V (A
GLEN BELL   D V   (A
KEITH JOLLIMORE SAX   (A
LENNY SOLOMON   STRINGS(A

(A) THE DREAM NEVER DIES   1978   CAPRICORN US 0206 UK 2429 171

DON BREGG   V   (A
DARRYL ALGUIRE   PERC V (A
GLOVES McGUINTY   PNO (A
CHARLIE ROBERTSON FLT (A

AL SERWA   K V   (A
JOHN SAUNDERS   BANJO(A
AL BRISCOE   DOBRO(A
STEVE HOLLINGWORTH D V (A

C184

JOHN COOPER-CLARKE

JOHN COOPER CLARKE V   (ALL
PAUL BURGESS   D   (AD
LYN OAKLEY   G   (DA
BILL NELSON   G   (AD
PETE SHELLEY   G   (AD
STEVE HOPKINS   K   (AD
MARTIN HANNETT   B   (AD
JOHN SCOTT   G   (AD
DAVE HASSELL   D   (D

(A) DISGUISE IN LOVE   1978   CBS   UK   83132
(B) OU EST LA MAISON DE FROMAGE   197   EPIC   US
(B) OU EST LA MAISON DE FROMAGE   197   RABID   UK   NOZE1
(C) WALKING BACK TO HAPPINESS(LIVE) 1979 CBS 10" UK   JCC1
(D) SNAP CRACKLE BOP   1980   EPIC   UK   84083
(E) ME & MY BIG MOUTH   1981   EPIC   UK   84979

TREVOR SPENCER   (D   KARL BURNS   (D
STEPHANIE FORMULA V (D   TOBY   (D

C184A

GREG COPELAND

GREG COPELAND   V   (A
IAN WALLACE   D   (A
BOB GLAUB   B   (A
JACKSON BROWNE   G   (A

(A) REVENGE WILL COME   1982   GEFFEN   US   2010

DANNY KORTCHMAR   G   (A
JIM EHRINGER   K   (A

RICK VITO   G   (A
BILLY PAYNE   K SYN(A

C184B

COPPERPENNY

RICH WAMIL   V B K G(A
KEN HOLLIS   V   (A
BERT HAMER   D V (A

(A) COPPERHEAD   1970   RCA   US   LSP 4291

LAVERNE McDONALD   G V   (A   PAUL REIBLING   B V   (A

C185

COPPERHEAD

JOHN CIPOLLINA   G   (A
GARY PHILIPPET   V G K (A
JIM McPHERSON   V G B (A
HUTCH HUTCHINSON   V B (A

(A) COPPERHEAD   1973   CBS UK 65715 US   32250
(A) COPPERHEAD   1980   CBS   NL   84483

DAVID WEBER   D   (A

C185A

JOHN COPPIN

JOHN COPPIN   V G K (A
PHIL BEER   VLN G V (A
TONY BENNETT   G V (A
MICK DOLAN   G   (A
REGINE CANDER   V   (A
DIK CADBURY   V   (A

(A) NO GOING BACK   1979   ROLA   R002

MICK CANDLER   D   (A
BIMBO ACOCK   SAX (A
GILLY ELKINS   V   (A

STEVE HUTT   B V   (A
ANTHONY HEAD   V   (A
GILLY DARBEY   V   (A

C185B

PHIL CORDELL

PHIL CORDELL   G B (A
BARRY DE SOUZA D   (A
CHRIS HUNT   D   (A
PAUL KENDRICK   B V (A
REV STOCKDALE   K   (A
DOREEN CHANTER V   (A
JIMMY HELMS   V   (A

(A) BORN AGAIN   1977   PRODIGAL   PDL   2006

CHAS O'BRIEN   D   (A
DAVE MARKEE   D   (A
MADELINE BELL   V   (A
LIZA STRIKE   V   (A
TONY BURROWS   V   (A

RAY FENWICK   G   (A
LENNIE WATTS   K   (A
R & J STONE   V   (A
GEORGE CHANDLER V   (A
WESLEY McGOOGAN SAX (A

C185C

CORNELLS

(A) BEACH BOUND   196   GAREX   US   LPGA 100

C185D

CORONARIAS DAN

KENNETH KNUDSEN   K   (AB123
CLAUS BOHLING   G   (3B
OLE STREENBERG   D   (B23
PETER FRIIS NIELSEN   B   (123AB
CLAUS BOJE   D   (A1

(1) 1969 71   (2) 71 72   (3) 73+
(A) BREATHE   1971   PARLOPHONE   EUR   MOCK 1018
(B) VISITOR   1975   STEEPLECHASE   SCS 1032

C185E

JERRY CORBETTA

JERRY CORBETTA   K V (A
MIKE BAIRD   D   (A
MIKE PORCARO   B   (A
CINDY BULLENS   V   (A
JIM HAAS   V   (A

(A) JERRY CORBETTA   1978   WB   US   3230

JAY GRAYDON   G   (A
JON JOYCE   V   (A
BOB WEBBER   G   (A

GREG MATHIESON   PNO   (A
RUSTY BUCHANAN   B   (A
MYREN POLLOCK   D   (A

C185F

MIKE CORBETT & JAY HIRSH

MIKE CORBETT   FLT PERC (A
JAY HIRSH   (A
HUGH McCRACKEN G   (A
SCOT McCRACKEN V   (A
PAUL GRIFFIN   K   (A
AL ROGERS   D   (A
MICHAELLE PROSKY V   (A

(A) MIKE CORBETT & JAY HIRSH   1972   ATCO   US   33361

JOHN SIOMOS   D   (A
CHRISTIE THOMPSON K   (A
ERIC WEISBERG   STEEL (A
JANET SAPADIN   V   (A

JODI McCRACKEN   V   (A
LEO WARRINGTON   HRNS (A
RUSSELL GEORGE   FDL   (A
MARIA BRAY   V   (A

C185G

CORBIN / HANNER

(A) FOR THE SAKE OF THE SONG   1981   ALFA   US   10003

C185H

CORPORATION

KENNETH BERDOLL   B V   (A
JOHN KONDOS   G V K FLT   (A
NICHOLAS KONDOS   D V   (A
GERARD SMITH   G V   (A
PATRICK McCARTHY   K TROM(A

(A) THE CORPORATION   1969   CAPITOL   US   175
(B) GET ON OUR SWING   19   AGE OF AQUARIUS US   4150
(C) HASSELS IN MY MIND 19   AGE OF AQUARIUS US   4250

DANIEL PEIL   V   (A

C185J

HUGH CORNWALL/ROBERT WILLIAMS

HUGH CORNWALL   G B V (A
ROBERT WILLIAMS D B V SYN (A
A N RUSSIAN   V   (A
IAN UNDERWOOD   SAX SYN (A

(A) NOSFERATU   1979   LIBERTY   UK   UAG 30251

DAVID WALLDROOP   G   (A
MARK MOTHERBAUGH SYN V (A

BOB MOTHERSBAUGH   G V   (A

Personnel	Inst		Album	Year	Label	Country	Cat
CHICK COREA	K	(ALL	(A) TONES FOR JOANS BONES	1968	VORTEX	IMP	2004
FLORA PLURIM	V PERC	(INj	(A) TONES FOR JOANS BONES	1978	ATLANTIC	UK	K50302
AIRTO MOREIRA	D PERC	(INTj	(B) IS	1969	SOLID STATE	US	18055
JOE FARRELL	WIND	(AJNThj	(C) NOW HE SINGS	1969	SOLID STATE	US	7011
STANLEY CLARKE	B	(JKONTUWahj	(D) SONG OF THE SINGING	1971	BLUENOTE	US 84353 RI 78 40030
ANTHONY BRAXTON	WIND	(Tf	(E) COREA	19	BLUENOTE		39542
DAVE HOLLAND	B	(DFTf	(F) ARC	1971	ECM	1009
BARRY ALTSCHUL	D	(DFT	(G) PIANO IMPROVISATIONS	1972	ECM	1014
BILL CONNORS	G	(K	(H) CRYSTAL SILENCE	1972	ECM	1024
LENNY WHITE	D	(KOUWh	(I) LIGHT AS A FEATHER	1972	POLYDOR US 5525 uk 2310 247
BENNY MAUPIN		(BQ	(I) LIGHT AS A FEATHER	1981	POLYDOR RI 2482 497
AL DIMEOLA	G	(OUWh	(J) CHILDREN OF FOREVER	1972	POLYDOR	UK	2310 267
GAYLE MORAN	V	(Yah	(K) HYMN OF THE SEVENTH GALAXY	1972	POLYDOR US 5536 UK 2310 286
STEVE GADD	D	(ah	(K) HYMN OF THE SEVENTH GALAXY	1972	POLYDOR	EURO	2302 028
EDDIE GOMEZ	B	(Y	(L) PIANO IMPROVISATIONS 2	1972	ECM	1020
ANTHONY JACKSON	B	(Y	(M) BLISS	1973	MUSE	5011
BILL WATRONS	TROM	(Y	(N) RETURN TO FOREVER	1972	ECM	1022
WAYNE ANDRE	TROM	(Y	(O) WHERE HAVE I KNOWN YOU BEFORE	1974	POLYDOR US 6509 UK 2310 354
DANNY CAHN	TPT	(Y	(O) WHERE HAVE I KNOWN YOU BEFORE	197	POLYDOR EURO 2302 030 2482502
BOB MILLIKAN	TPT	(Y	(P) ROUND TRIP	1974	EPIC	UK	65559
JOHN GATCHELL	TPT	(Y	(Q) SUNDANCE	1974	PEOPLE UK 09 US G MERCHANT2202
JEAN LUC PONTE	VLN	(a	(R) INNER SPACE	1974	ATLANTIC US 2305 uk K60081
DON ALIAS	PERC	(aj	(S) WITH UNDERSTANDING	1975	MUSE	5083
JOHN THOMAS	TPT	(a	(T) LIVE IN NEW YORK 74	1975	OXFORD	US	3005
JOHN ROSENBURG	TPT	(a	(U) NO MYSTERY	1975	POLYDOR US 6512 UK 2310 378
RON MOSS	TPT	(a	(V) CAPTAIN MARVEL	1975	VERVE		2304 225
NARADA MICHAEL WALDEN	D	(a	(W) ROMANTIC WARRIOR	1976	CBS US 34076 UK 81221
WOODY SHAW	TPT	(A	(X) CIRCLING IN	1976	BLUENOTE BLNAD 472
STEVE SWALLOW	B	(A	(Y) LEPRECHAUN	1976	POLYDOR	UK	2391 217
JOE CHAMBERS	D	(A	(Z) MUSIC MAGIC	1977	CBS US 81959
GERRY BROWN	D	(	(a) MY SPANISH HEART	1977	POLYDOR	UK	2672 031
PETE LE ROCCO	D	(M	(b) MAD HATTER	1978	POLYDOR US 16130 uk 2490 114
STAN GETZ	SAX	(V	(c) LIVE	1978	CBS UK 82808
SADAO WATANABE		(P	(d) SECRET AGENT	1979	POLYDOR	UK	2391 381
STUART BLUMBERG	TPT	(A	(e) DELPHI VOL 1	1979	POLYDOR	UK	2490 150
HERBIE HANCOCK	K	(g	(f) CIRCLES PARIS CONCERT (DBL)	197	ECM 1018/19
JIM PUGH	TROM	(h	(g) COREA HANCOCK	1979	POLYDOR	UK	2672 049
LAUDIR DE OLIVEIRA	PERC	(j	(h) BEST OF RETURN TO FOREVER	1980	CBS UK 84292
HUBERT LAWS	FLT	(j	(j) TAP STEP	1980	WB	US 3425	UK	K 56801
BUNNY BRUNEL	B	(j	(k) 3 QUARTETS	1981	WB	U 3552	UK	K 56908
TOM BRECHTLEIN	D	(j	(m) BLISS	1981	MUSE	5011
AL VIZZUTTI	TPT	(j	(n) CHICK & LIONEL	1982	GATEWAY	UK	7005
JAMIE FAUNT	B	(j					
JOE HENDERSON	SAX	(j	STRING SECTION	(aY	LIONEL HAMPTON	VIBES	(n
JOHN GILMORE	SAX	(m	WALTER BOOKER	B (m	PETE LA ROCA	D (m

Personnel	Inst		Album	Year	Label	Country	Cat
DAVE 'BABY' CORTEZ	ORG	(ALL	RINKY DINK	19	CHESS	US	1473
			ORGAN SHINDIG	19	ROULETTE	US	25298
			GOLDEN HITS	1964	LONDON	UK	HAU 8142
			MUSIC AROUND THE CLOCK	19	CLOCK	US	CX201
			IN ORBIT WITH	19	ROULETTE	US	25328
			HAPPY ORGAN	19	RCA	US	2099
			FABULOUS ORGAN	19	METRO	US	550
			& JERRYS HOUSE ROCKERS	19	CROWN	US	357
			DAVE BABY CORTEZ	19	CLOCK	US	331

Personnel	Inst		Album	Year	Label	Country	Cat
JEREMY VALENTINE	V	(A	(A) TRUE ROMANCES	1978	CBS	UK	82831
MIKE FEWINGS	G	(A					
NICK SHEPPARD	G	(A	DEXTER DALWOOD	B (A	DAN SWAM	D (A

Personnel	Inst		Album	Year	Label	Country	Cat
LARRY CORYELL	K G SYN	B(ALL	(A) FREE SPIRIT	1967	ABC 062 90593
BILLY COBHAM	D	(DJN	(B) LADY CORYELL	1969	VANGUARD VSD 6509+19051 MUSIDISC 23017
CHICK COREA	K	(DJN	(C) CORYELL	1969	VANGUARD VSD 6547 19059 MUSIDISC 23020
JACK BRUCE	B	(	(D) SPACES	1970	VANGUARD VSD 6558 79345 MUSIDISC 23002
WILL LEE	B	(N	(D) SPACES	1974	VANGUARD 6359 005
JOHN MARSHALL	D	(	(E) FAIRYLAND	1971	FLYING DUTCHMAN 51500 MEGA US 607
MICHAEL LAWRENCE	TPT	(DNOXY	(E) FAIRYLAND	1972	PHILIPS 6369 411
MIROSLAV VITOUS		(BN	(F) AT THE VILLAGE GATE	1971	VANGUARD VSD 6573 MUSIDISC 23024
JOHN LEE	B	(OQUY	(G) BAREFOOT BOY	1972	FLYING DUTCHMAN 10139 PHILIPS 6369 407
MIKE MANDEL	K	(CGHIJNOPQXY	(H) OFFERING	1972	VANGUARD 79319 MUSIDISC 23001
ALPHONSE MOUZON	PERC	(JORUXYN	(I) THE REAL GREAT ESCAPE	1973	VANGUARD 79329 MUSIDISC 23019
STEVE KHAN	G	(OQNV	(J) INTRODUCING 11TH HOUSE	1974	VANGUARD 79342
PHILIP CATHERINE	G	(STU	(K) ESSENTIAL	1975	VANGUARD VSD 75/76
TAWATHA AGEE	V	(U	(L) RESTFUL MIND	1975	VANGUARD 79353 MUSIDISC 23013
DANNY TRIFAN	B	(JRXN	(M) THE OTHER SIDE OF	1975	VANGUARD 79360
MICHAEL BRECKER	HRNS	(IQW	(N) PLANET END	1976	VANGUARD 79367 MUSIDISC 23022
MERVIN BRONSON	B	(FCHIJ	(O) LEVEL ONE	1976	ARISTA US 4025 UK ARTY 113
HARRY WILKINSON	D	(FGIJ	(P) BASICS (68/69)	1976	VANGUARD 79375
JULIE CORYELL	V	(FI	(Q) ASPECTS	1976	ARISTA US 4077 UK ARTY 133
MITCH MITCHELL	D	(	(R) LION & THE RAM	1976	ARISTA US 4108 UK ARTY 154
JIM PEPPER	SAX	(AC	(S) TWIN HOUSE	1976	ATLANTIC UK K50342
CHRIS HILLS	B	(A	(T) SPLENDID	1976	ELEKTRA UK K52086
BOB MOSES	D	(AB	(U) BACK TOGETHER AGAIN	1977	ATLANTIC US 18220 UK K50382
CHIP BAKER	G	(A	(V) TWO FOR THE ROAD	1977	ARISTA UK SPART1050
RON CARTER	B	(CP	(W) DIFFERENCE	1978	EGG EURO 900 558
BERNARD PURDIE	D	(CEP	(X) AT MONTREUX(74)	1978	VANGUARD 79410
STEVE HAAS	D	(P	(Y) LIVE IN EUROPE	1978	LC IMP IC1
RAY MANTILLA	PERC	(Pc	(Z) STANDING OVATION	1978	MOOD 22888 ARISTA UK 3024
TERUMASA HINO	TPT	(Q	(a) EUROPEAN IMPRESSIONS	1978	ARISTA US 3005
MTUME	PERC	(Q	(b) BETTER THAN LIVE	1978	DIRECT DD109
DAVID SANBORN	SAX	(QW	(c) RETURN	1979	VANGUARD 79426

(CONTINUED)

[129]

LARRY CORYELL   (CONTINUED)

```
DANNY TOAN           G    (QR        (d) FREE SMILE              1979   ARISTA    US
ARTHUR RHAMES        G    (W         (e)TRIBUTARIES             1980   NOVIS     US 3017
GLEN MOORE           B    (W         (f) LARRY CORYELL          1982   BOLERO        33850
STEVE GADD           D    (W
CHERYL ALAXANDER     V    (U   RANDY BRECKER    HRNS (JQ CHUCK RAINEY     B   (CEP GERRY BROWN    D    (Q
TONY WILLIAMS        D    (W   DON GROLNICK     K    (W  L SUBRUMANIUM   VLN  (Z   LAWRENCE KILLIAN CONGA(G
STEVE MARCUS         SAX  (GHI ROY HAYNES       D    (G  ALBERT STINSON  B    (C   JIM GARRISON     B    (B
ELVIN JONES          D    (B   JOE BECK     SYN G B  (Rc MICHEL URBANIAK VLN  (R   RALPH TOWNER     G    (L
COLIN WALCOTT        CONGA (L  GLEN MOORE       B    (L  JOHN McLAUGHLIN G    (DN  DARIUS BRUBECK   PNO  (c
CHRIS BRUBECK        B    (c   DAN BRUBECK      D    (L  JOACHIM KUHN    PNO  (T   JOHN SCOFIELD    G    (e
```

COS

```
BOB DARSCH           D    (A         (A) VIVA BOMMA             1976   IBC       BEL    23605
MARC MOULIN          SYN  (A         (B) SWISS CHALET           19     IBC       NL     23902
DENIS VAN HECKE      CELLO (A
PHILIPPE ABLAERT     D    (B   PASCALE SON      V OBOE (AB  ALAIN GOUTIER   B    (AB
DANIEL SCHELL        G FLT (A   MARC HOLLANDER   K    (A   GUY LONNEUX     D    (B
PIPOU PITOU          PERC (A   JIB HAESEVEETS   PERC (A   CHARLES LOOS    K    (B
MUTSARI              B    (B
```

COSMIC EYE

```
AMANCIO D'SILVA      G    (A         (A) DREAM SEQUENCE         1972   REGALZONOPHONE UK  SLRZ 1030
V JASANI             SIT  (A
JOHN MAYER           VLN  (A   RAY SWINFIELD    FLT  (A   DAVE GROSSMAN   FLT  (A
C TAYLOR             FLT  (A   ALAN BRANSCOMBE  SAX  (A   TONI CAMPO      B    (A
KESHAV SATHE         TABLA (A  D WRIGHT         D    (A
```

COSMIC JOKERS

```
DIETER DIERKS                        (A) COSMIC JOKERS         1974   METRONOME    KM  58008
JURGEN DOLLASE                       (B) PLANET SIT IN         1974   METRONOME    KM  58013
MANUEL GOETTSCHING
HARALD GROSSKOPF                 KLAUS SCHULZE            STERNEN MADCHEN GILLE
```

COSMIC SOUNDS

```
PAUL BEAVER          SYN ELEC(A        (A) THE ZODIAC            1967   ELEKTRA      EKS  74009
CYRUS FARYAR         V    (A
```

ELVIS COSTELLO

```
ELVIS COSTELLO       G V  (ALL      (A) MY AIM IS TRUE       1977   STIFF JAP 6581            UK     SEEZ 3
JOHN McFEE           G V  (AFGJ     (A) MY AIM IS TRUE       1977   CBS  US 35037 BARCLAY FR  940566
HUEY LOUIS           HCA V (AFG     (B) THIS YEARS MODEL     1978   RADAR JAP 10538          UK     RAD 3
JOHNNY CIAMBOTTI     B V  (AFG      (B) THIS YEARS MODEL     1978   CBS  US 35331 SMASH SWED SLEPT2
DAVE EDMUNDS         V    (FG       (B) THIS YEARS MODEL     1981   F BEAT UK XXLP4
SEAN HOPPER          K V  (AFG      (C) ARMED FORCES         1979   RADAR JAP 10627          UK     RAD14
ALEX CALL            G V  (AFG      (C) ARMED FORCES         1979   CBS  US 35709 SMASH SWED SLEPT5
STEVE GOULDING       D    (G        (C) ARMED FORCES         1981   F BEAT UK XXLP5
MICKY SHINE          D V  (AFG      (D) LIVE AT MOCAMBO      1978   CBS  CAN PROMO
STEVE MASON (NAIVE)  K    (BCFGHJK  (E) GET HAPPY            1980   F BEAT UK XXLP 1
NICK LOWE            B V  (1FGJ     (E) GET HAPPY            1980   CBS  US 36347 SMASH SWED SLEPT7
BRUCE THOMAS         B    (BCEFGHJK (F) TAKING LIBERTIES     1980   CBS  US 36839
ANDREW BODMAR        B    (G        (G) 10 BLOODY MARYS (CASS)1980  F BEAT UK XXC6
PETER THOMAS         D    (BCDEFGHJK (H) TRUST               1981   F BEAT UK XXLP 11        EURO   WEA58260
GLENN TILBROOK       V    (F        (H) TRUST               1981   CBS  US 37051
MARTIN BELMONT       G    (F        (J) ALMOST BLUE          1981   F BEAT UK XXLP13         EURO   WEA58392
NASHVILLE STRINGS         (J        (J) ALMOST BLUE          1981   CBS  US 37562
NASHVILLE SINGERS         (J        (K) IMPERIAL BALLROOM    1982   CBS  US 38157
BILLY SHERRILL       PROD (J        (EP)HIGH FIDELITY        1980   F BEAT UK XX3
TOMMY MILLER         VLN  (J
```

GENE COTTON

```
GENE COTTON          G V  (ALL      (A) GRAY OF THE MORNING   1974   MYRRH      US MST 6511
WITH                                (B) LIBERTY               1974   MYRRH      US MST 6524
PETE WADE            G    (BA       (C) FOR ALL THE YOUNG WRITERS 1976 ABC      US AB  933
BILLY SANFORD        G    (AB       (D) RAIN ON               1976   ABC UK ABCL5213 US AB  983
JOHNNY CHRISTOPHER   G    (BC       (E) SAVE THE DANCER       1978   ARIOLA US50031  UK ARL 5015
SANDY COTTON         FLT  (B        (E) SAVE THE DANCER       1978   EMI INT          INS 3018
CHARLIE McCOY        HCA  (B        (F) NO STRINGS ATTACHED   1979   ARIOLA     US     50070
JACK WILLIAMS        B    (ABCDF    (G) ECLIPSE OF THE BLUE MOON 1981 KNOLL      US     1001
KENNY BUTTREY        D    (ABCF
SHANE KEISTER        K SYN(DF  JIM COLVARD     G    (C  RON OATES      K    (D  LARRIE LONDIN    D    (D
KENNY MALONE         D    (DF  JOE OSBORN      B    (C  TED REYNOLDS   B G  (D  STEVE GIBSON     B G MAND(CDF
FARRELL MORRIS       PERC (DF  DIANNE DARLING SYN PERC V(F MARC SPEER  G STEELV(F TOMMY WELLS     D    (F
JAMES OWNBY          K SAX V(F MIKE JOYCE      B V  (F  BOBBY OGDIN    K SYN(F  BUDDY SKIPPER    SYN  (F
MIKE LAWLER          SYN  (F   GUNNAR SCRIVENOR AUTOHARP(F DOYLE GRISHAM STEEL(F BILL JONES      SAX  (F
BOBBY THOMPSON       G BANJ(C  CHARLIE CRINO   PNO  (A  JOE ALLEN      B    (A  JERRY CARRIGAN   D    (A
WELDON MYRICK        STEEL(A   JERRY WASLEY    D    (A  BEEGIE CRUSER  K    (A
```

JAMES COTTON BLUES BAND

```
JAMES COTTON         V HCA(ALL      (A) JAMES COTTON BLUES BAND 1967 VERVE FVS9507 US    3023
WITH                                (B) PURE COTTON            1968   VERVE FVS9512 US    3038
MATT MURPHY          G    (EFG      (C) COTTON IN YOUR EARS    1968   VERVE         US    3060
JAMES BOOKER         PNO  (         (D) CUT YOU LOOSE          1968   VANGUARD 19035       79283
BOB ANDERSON         B    (         (E) TAKING CARE OF BUSINESS 19    CAPITOL             SM814
ALBERT GIANQUINTO    PNO  (         (F) 100% COTTON            1974   BUDDAH              BDS5620
FRANCIS CLAY         D    (         (G) HIGH ENERGY            1978   BUDDAH 5650         BDLP 4048
MARTIN FIERRO        SAX  (D        (H) LIVE & ON THE MOVE     1977   BUDDAH              5661
MIKE FENDER          TPT  (D
EDDIE ADAMS          B    (D   JOE RODRIGUEZ   D    (D  LITTLE BO      SAX  (F  CHARLES CALMESE  B  (FG
KENNY JOHNSON        D    (FH  LENNY KING  SAX     (F  PHIL JEKANOWSKI PNO  (F JAMES COOK       G  (D
MIKE BLOOMFIELD      G    (E   TODD RUNDGREN PERC G V (E DOMENIC TROIANO G   (E  JOHNNY WINTER    G  (E
MARK KLINGMAN        V K  (E   RALPH SCHUCKETT PNO  (E  STU WOODS      B V  (D  RITCHIE HAYWARD  D  (E
JOEL BISHOP OBRIEN   D    (E   N D SMART       D V  (E  TOM COSGROVE   V    (E  CISSY HOUSTON    V  (E
VENERIT SIMMS        V    (E   RONELLE STAFFORD V    (E  DEIRDRE TUCK   V    (E  GENE DINWIDDIE   HRNS(E
TREVOR LAWRENCE      HRNS (D   DAVE SANBORN    HRNS (E  STEVE MADAIO   HRNS (E  LUTHER TUCKER    G  (
WAYNE TALBERT        K    (D   ALLEN TOUSSAINT K    (G  STEVE HUGHES   G    (G  TEDDY ROYAL      G  (G
CLYDE KERR           TPT  (G   SHAVIS SHERRIFF SAX  (G  ALVIN THOMAS   SAX  (G  LON PRICE        SAX(G
NANCEE SEHORN        FLT  (G   MIKE ZAITCHIK   K    (H  GEORGE T GREGORY III (H
```

C195A   COTTONWOOD   C195A
    GARY ROWLES   (A   (A) CAMARADERIE   1971 ABC   US   ABC 729
    RICK ALLEN   (A
    DAVID WEYER   (A   DOUG PHILLIPS   (A DAVID FARRELL   (A
C195B   COTTONWOOD SOUTH   C195B
                                    (A) COTTONWOOD SOUTH   19   CBS   US   33009
C195C   COUCHIS   C195C
    CHRIS COUCHIS   G V D (AB   (A) COUCHIS   1979 WB   US   3289
    PAT COUCHIS   G V   (AB   (B) NASTY HARDWARE   1980 WB UK K56829 US   3420
    MIKE COUCHIS   D V   (AB
    HOWARD MESSER   B V   (AB   CHAS CARLSON   K V   (AB
C196   JOHNNY COUGAR   C196
    JOHNNY COUGAR MELLENCAMP (ALL   (A) CHESTNUT ST INCIDENT   1977 MCA   US   2225
    MIKE BOYER   G   (A   (B) BIOGRAPHY   1978 RIVA   RVLP6
    JIMMY HOROWITZ   (C   (C) JOHNNY COUGAR   1979 RIVA   RVLP9
    ROBERT FRANK   B   (BC   (D) NOTHING MATTER'S & WHAT IF IT DID 1980 RIVA   RVLP10
    TOM KNOWLES   D   (BC   (E) NIGHT DANCIN'   1980 RIVA   US   7401
    JOHN SMITH   (C
    ANDY MACKAY   SAX   (B   LARRY CRANE   G   (BC MIKE RANCHIE   G   (AC
    BRIAN BEC VAR   (C   JOE LALA   PERC (C   PAUL HARRIS   K   (C
    BLUE WEAVER   K   (C   MIKE LEWIS   (C   RICHARD KELLY   G   (A
    DAVID PARMAN   G   (A   MICK RONSON   G   (A   MICHAEL KAMEN   K   (A
    STEVE LINDEMAN   K   (A   TOM WINCE   K   (A   BILLY BERGMAN   D   (A
    JERRY DEUPREE   D   (A   HILLY MICHAELS   D   (A   WAYNE HALL   SAX (A
    KIRK BUTLER   SYN PERC (A   DAVID MANSFIELD STEEL MAND VLN(A
C197   DENNIS COULSON   C197
    DENNIS COULSON   (A) DENNIS COULSON   1973 ELEKTRA 75067 US K 42148
C198   CLIFFORD COULTER   C198
    CLIFFORD COULTER   K V G (ALL   (A) EAST SIDE SAN JOSE   1971 IMPULSE   US   9197
    JOHN TURK   TPT   (AB   (B) DO IT NOW WORRY ABOUT IT LATER 1872 IMPULSE US 9216
    CORNELIUS BUMPUS   SAX   (A   (C) BETTER PART OF ME   1980 CBS   US   35786
    GINO LANDRY   SAX   (A
    MEL BROWN   G   (AB   JERRY PEREZ   G   (A   JIMMY CALHOUN   B   (AB
    JOE PROVOST   D   (A   BILLY INGRAM   D   (A   RON BECK   D   (B
    RAY MacCARTY   G   (B   HARRY EDISON   TPT   (B   BILL PERKINS   SAX (B
    MARSHALL ROYAL   SAX   (B   PLAS JOHNSON   SAX   (B   JIMMY CLEVELAND TROM(B
    WILLIE RUFF   HRNS (B   SONNY GLAZE   G   (B   LUCY WILKINS   V   (B
    MARLENE WILKINS   V   (B   DONNIE ROGERS   V   (B   SHANNE COULTER V   (B
C199   COUNT BISHOPS   C199
    JOHNNY GUITAR   G V   (ABCD   (A) THE COUNT BISHOPS"GOOD GEAR" 1977 DYNAMITE HOLL 33001
    PAUL BALBI   D   (ABCD   (B) COUNT BISHOPS   1977 CHISWICK   UK   WIK1
    STEVE LEWINS   B   (AB   (C) LIVE   12"   1978 CHISWICK   UK   CH7
    ZEN DEFLEUR HIEROWISKI G V(ABCD   (C) LIVE   10"   1978 CHISWICK   UK   CHT7
    MIKE SPENCER   V   ((C) LIVE   12"   1979 CHISWICK   RIUK CWK 3006
    DAVE TICE   V   (BCD   (C) LIVE   10"   1979 CHISWICK   UK CWM 2001
    PAT McMULLEN   B   (CD   (D) CROSSCUT(BISHOPS)   1979 CHISWICK   UK CWK 3009
    JULIAN HOLLAND   PNO   (BD   (E) SPEEDBALL   1979 CHISWICK EP   UK   SW1
    RUAN O'LOCHLAIN   HRNS (D
    NOEL NORRIS   HRNS (D
C199A   COUNT FIVE   C199A
    KENN ELLNER   V HCA 'A   (A) PSYCHOTIC REACTION   1966 DOUBLE SHOT US DSM 1001
    SEAN BYRNE   G   (A
    JOHN MICHALSKI   G   (A   ROY CHANEY   B   (A   CRAIG ATKINSON D   (A
C199B   COUNTS   C199B
    LEROY EMANUEL   G V   (B   (A) IT'S WHATS UP THAT COUNTS 1972 WESTBOUND US   2011
    MOSE DAVIS   K V   (B   (B) LOVE SIGN   1973 AWARE   US   2002
    DEMO CATES   WIND V(B   (C) FUNK PUMP   1975 AWARE   US   2006
    ANDREAU GIBSONT   D V   (B   (D) LOVE SIGNS   197 GRC   US   2002
C199C   COUNTRY COOKING   C199C
    RUSS BARENBERG   G MAND(ALL   (A) COUNTRY COOKING   1971 ROUNDER   US   006
    KENNY KOSEK   FDL K (ALL   (B) FRANK WAKEFIELD WITH C C 1972 ROUNDER   US   007
    JOHN MILLER   B G   (ALL   (C) BARREL OF FUN   1973 ROUNDER   US   033
    HARRY GILMORE   MAND (A
    TONY TRISCHKA   BAN STEEL(ALL PETER WERNICK   BAN   (ALL FRANK WAKEFIELD G MAND (B
    ANDY STATMAN   MAND (C   NONDI LEONARD   V   (BC
C200   COUNTRY GAZZETTE   C200
    BYRON BERLINE   FDL V (ABCDELK (A) TRAITOR IN OUR MIDST   1972 U A US 5596 UK UAG 29404
    ROGER BUSH   B V   (ABCDELM (B) LIVE IN AMSTERDAM   1972 BUMBLE   GEXD 301
    ALAN MUNDE   BANJ V(ALL   (C) DONT GIVE UP YOUR DAY JOB 1973 U A US 090 UK UAS 29491
    KENNY WERTZ   G V   (ABCDEHL (D) BLUEGRASS SPECIAL   1973 ARIOLA   86 501HT
    HERB PEDERSEN   V G   (AC   (E) BANJO SANDWICH   197 ARIOLA   NL   27239
    SKIP CONOVER   DOBRO (AFK   (F) LIVE   1975 TRANSATLANTIC UK TRA 291
    CHRIS SMITH   G   (A   (F) LIVE   1975 ARIOLA   NL   88558
    CLARENCE WHITE   G   (C   (G) MILESTONES   1975 EMI INT   COPS7418D1/2
    AL PERKINS   STEEL (CH   (H) SUNNY SIDE OF THE MOUNTAIN 1976 TRANSATLANTIC UK TRA 318
    ROLAND WHITE   (FHKMN   (J) OUT TO LUNCH   197 FLYING FISH US   FF027
    LEE SKLAR   B   (C   (K) WHAT A WAY TO EARN A LIVING 1977 TRANSATLANTIC UK TRA 347
    DAVE FERGUSON   FDL   (HM   (K) WHAT A WAY TO EARN A LIVING 1977 RIDGE   US   008
    BILL BRYSON   B V   (K   (L) FROM THE BEGINNING   1978 SUNSET   UK SNS 50414
    RICHARD GREENE   FDL   (K   (M) ALL THIS AND MONEY TOO 1979 RIDGE RUNNER US RRR 017
    MIKE RICHEY   G   (KMN   (AC)TRAITOR/DONT GIVE UP   19   UA   184 52064/5
    MICHAEL ANDERSON   B V   (MN   (N) AMERICAN & CLEAN   1981 FLYING FISH US   252
    JOE CARR   G V   (MN
    TOMMY SPURLOCK   STEEL(M   MIKE McCARTY   D   (M   MICHAEL J DOHONEY D (M
    SAM BUSH   FDL   (N   DATTRELL NORRIS   D   (N
C201   PIERRE COURBOIS   C201
    PIERRE COURBOIS   D   (A   (A) ASSOCIATION   1970 MUNICH   6802634
    JASPER VANTHOF   PNO   (A
    SIGGI BUSCH   B   (A   PETER KRIJNEN   B   (A   TOTO BLANKE   G   (A

[131]

C201A   DAVID COURTNEY   C201A
```
DAVID COURTNEY   V PNO (A        (A) FIRST DAY                    1975 EMI UK EMC3094 US UA  LA 553G
BARRY MORGAN     D     (A
BRIAN ODGERS     B     (A  STEVE GAY        PNO (A  PAUL KEOGH    G   (A  ALAN PARKER    G (A
SKAILA KANGA     HARP  (A  TONY BURROWS     V   (A  MIKE MORAN    K   (A  BARRY DE SOUZA D (A
ANDREW POWELL    B K   (A  FRANCIS MONKMAN  SYN K(A  JEAN ROUSSEL  PNO (A  RUSS BALLARD   G (A
FRANK RICOTTI    PERC  (A  BRUCE LYNCH      B   (A  AIXA COURTNEY V   (A  JANE POWELL    V (A
B J COLE         STEEL G(A  MORRIS PERT     PERC (A FLEXATONE(A PILOT         V (A
RICHARD HARVEY   WIND  (A  BERNARD THOMAS   WIND (A DAVE GILMOUR  G   (A  ENGLISH CORALE V (A
```
C202   DAVE COUSINS   C202
```
DAVE COUSINS     PER V G PNO(AB   (A) TWO WEEKS LAST SUMMER      1972 A&M         UK   AMLS68118
ROGER GLOVER     B     (A        (B) OLD SCHOOL SONGS            1980 O SCHOOL UK 1 US PVC 8901
TOM ALLOM        ORG   (A
MILLER ANDERSON  G     (A  DAVE LAMBERT     G   (A  JON HISEMAN   D   (A  RICK WAKEMAN   K (A
LAMPOON                (A  KIDDINGTON COSSACKS  (A  ROBERT KIRBY  WIND (A  BRIAN WILLOUGHBY G(B
```
C203   DON COVAY   C203
```
DON COVAY        V     (ALL       (A) MERCY                      1964 ATLANTIC    US        8104
WITH                             (B) SEE SAW                     1966 ATLANTIC    US        8120
JOE RICHARDSON   G V   (C        (C) HOUSE OF BLUE LIGHT         1969 ATLANTIC    US        8237
MARGARET WILLIAMS G V  (C        (C) HOUSE OF BLUE LIGHT         1969 ATLANTIC    UK   K 50225
JOHN HAMMOND     HCA G (C        (D) DIFFERENT STROKES           1970 JANUS       US        3038
BUTCH VALENTINE  B     (C        (E) SUPERDUDE                   1973 MERCURY     UK   6338 211
DANNY JONES      D     (C        (E) SUPERDUDE                   1973 MERCURY     US   SRM1 653
JERRY JEMMOTT    B     (CF        (F) HOT BLOOD                   1975 MERCURY     UK   9100 010
CHARLES OTIS     D     (C        (G) TRAVELLIN' IN HEAVY TRAFFIC 1976 PHILAD INT   PIR 81492
SREDNI VOLLNER   HCA   (F        (G) TRAVELLIN' IN HEAVY TRAFFIC 1976 PHILAD INT        33957
TONY VON COVAY   D     (F        ( ) COUNTRY FUNK                19   POLYDOR          2482 018
RODNEY BEYTHAM   K     (F
BILLY CADIEUX    G     (F  LEMON JEFFERSON  (D  DENNIS HARRIS   G  (G  NEIL LARSEN    K (G
ROLAND CHAMBERS  G     (G  T J TINDALL      G  (G  MICHAEL FOREMAN B  (G  RON KERSEY     K (G
LARRY WASHINGTON CONGA(G  CHARLES COLLINS  D  (G  KARL CHAMBERS   D  (G  BARBARA INGRAM V (G
CARLA BENSON     V     (G  EVETTE BENTON    V  (G
```
C203A   COVEN   C203A
```
JINX DAWSON      V     (C        (A) WITCHCRAFT                  1970 MERCURY     US       61239
CHRISTOPHER NIELSEN G V (C       (B) COVEN                       19   MGM         US        4801
JOHN HOBBS       K     (C        (C) BLOOD ON THE SNOW           1974 BUDDAH 5614     BDLH 5011
OZ OSBORNE       B     (C
STEVE ROSS       D     (C  FRANK SMITH      SAX (C  ALAN ESTES        CONGA(C
```
C204   DAVID COVERDALE & WHITESNAKE   C204
```
DAVID COVERDALE  V     (ALL       (A) WHITESNAKE                 1977 PURPLE      UK   TPS 3509
MICK MOODY       G     (ABCDEFGHIJ(A) WHITESNAKE                 1977 VOGUE       FR       20257
SIMON PHILLIPS   D     (A        (B) NORTHWINDS                 1978 PURPLE      UK   TPS 3513
TIM HINKLEY      K     (A        (C) TROUBLE                    1978 SUNBURST         INS 3022
HELEN CHAPPELLE  V     (A        (C) TROUBLE                    1980 UA US 937 UK      30305
RON ASPERY       SAX   (AB        (D) SNAKEBITE (EP)             1978 SUNBURST        INEP 751
DELISLE HARPER   B     (A        (E) SNAKEBITE (LP)             1978 SUNBURST NL 61290 US/UA 915
ROGER GLOVER     K B PERC (AB     (F) LOVEHUNTER                 1979 UA US 981 UK    UAG 30264
DAVID DOWLE      D     (CDEFI     (G) LIVE IN THE HEART OF THE CITY 1980 UA          SNAKE  1
BERNIE MARSDEN   G     (CDFGHIJ   (H) READY & WILLING            1980 UA               UAG 30302
BRIAN JOHNSTON   K     (         (I) LIVE AT HAMMERSMITH        1978 SUNBURST    1288
DOREEN CHANTER   V     (B        (J) COME AN' GET IT            1981 LIBERTY     UK   LBG 3023
IREENE CHANTER   V     (B
NEIL MURRAY      B     (CDEFGHJI  JON LORD         K   (CH  BARRY ST JOHN  V  (A
IAN PAICE        D     (EFGHIJ    PETE SOLLEY      K   (D   ALAN SPENNER   B  (B
TONY NEWMAN      D     (B        LEE BRILLEAUX    HCA (B   HENRY LOWTHER  HRNS (B
MALCOLM GRIFFITHS TROM (B        GRAHAM PRESKETT  K   (B   LIZA STRIKE    V  (AB
```
C205   JOEY COVINGTON   C205
```
JOEY COVINGTON   D V   (A        (A) FAT FANDAGO                 1973 GRUNT            BFL1 0149
PATRICK CRAIG    K     (A
STEVE MIDNITE    G     (A  JACK PRENDERGAST     B (A
```
C206   JULIE COVINGTON   C206
```
JULIE COVINGTON  V     (AB        (A) BEAUTIFUL CHANGES          1971 COLUMBIA    UK   SCX 6466
RICHARD THOMPSON G     (B        (B) JULIE COVINGTON            1978 VIRGIN      UK   V 2107
NEIL LARSEN      K     (B
WILLIE WEEKS     B     (B  RAY COOPER       PERC (B  JOHN KIRKPATRICK ACC (B  TREVOR LUCAS   G (B
SIMON NICOL      G     (B  CHRIS SPEDDING   G   (B  RUSS TITELMAN    G   (B  STEVE WINWOOD  K (B
ANDY FAIRWEATHER LOW V (B  IAN MATTHEWS     V   (B  GARY TRAVERS     V   (B  GREG PRESTOPINO V (B
PLAS JOHNSON     SAX   (B  ANDY NEWMARK     D   (B  JOHN CALE        K   (B
```
C207   COWBOY   C207
```
SCOTT BOYER      G     (ALL       (A) REACH FOR THE SKY          1971 ATLANTIC    UK   2466 022
JOHNNY SANDLIN   D     (CD        (A) REACH FOR THE SKY          1970 CAPRICORN   US      33351
TOMMY TALTON     G V   (CD        (B) 5'LL GET YOU TEN           1972 ATLANTIC    UK   K 40312
BILL SYEWART     D     (CD        (B) 5'LL GET YOU TEN           1971 CAPRICORN   US        864
BILL PILLMORE    K G V (A        (AB) WHY QUIT WHEN YOU'RE LOSING 1975 CAPRICORN  US   2CX  0121
TOMM WYNN        D PERC(A        (C) BOYER & TALTON             1975 CAPRICORN   US        0127
GEORGE CLARK     B V   (AB        (D) HAPPY TO BE ALIVE          1976 CAPRICORN   US        0167
PETE KOWALKE     G V   (AB        (E) COWBOY                     1977 CAPRICORN   US        0194
DUANE ALLMAN     G DOBRO(B
CHUCK LEAVELL    PNO   (BCD CHARLIE HAYWARD  B   (C  PAUL HORNSBY   K  (C  JIMMY NALLS    G (C
RANDALL BRAMBLETT SAX V(CE DAVID BROWN      SAX V(C  DONNA HALL     V  (C  TOY CALDWELL   G (C
DREW LOMBAR      BANJ  (C  JAIMOE           PERC (CE JOHN HUGHEY    G  (C  ELLA BROWN     V (C
JOYCE KNIGHT     V     (C  BONNIE BRAMLETT  V   (D  CHIP CONDON    K V (E  CHIP MILLER    D PERC(E
ARCH PEARSON     B V   (E  TOPPER PRICE     HCA (E  HAROLD WILLIAMS SAX (E
```
C207A   COWBOYS INTERNATIONAL   C207A
```
TERRY CHIMES     D     (A        (A) THE ORIGINAL SIN           1979 VIRGIN UK V2136 US 13138
KEN LOCKE        V     (A
JIMMY HUGHES     B     (A  EVAN CHARLES     PNO (A  RICK JACKS    G  (A  KEITH LEVINE   G (A
```

STANLEY COWELL

```
STANLEY COWELL          (A      (A) NEW WORLD                 1981 GALAXY          GXY 5131
```

C208
BILLY COX
C208

```
BILLY COX          B    (A      (A) NITRO FUNCTION           1971 PYE         UK NSPL25158
CHAR VINNEDGE      G    (A
ROBERT TARRANT     D    (A
```

C208A
DANNY COX
C208A

```
DANNY COX          G V  (AB     (A) BIRTH ANNOUNCEMENT        1969 TOGETHER    US   ST1011
RICHARD RUSHER     G    (A       (B) DANNY COX                 1971 DUNHILL     US    50114
DOUG RHODEN        B    (A       (C) FEEL SO GOOD              197  CASABLANCA  ?     ?
JOHN KAHN          B    (B
MERL SANDERS       K    (B   RED RHODES      STEEL(A   PAT SHANAHAN    D   (A  STEVE LEFEVER   B  (A
BILL VITT          D    (B   JOSE CHEPITO AREAS PERC(B  TIM BARNES      G   (B  WALTER HAWKINS  V  (B
LYNNETTE HAWKINS   V    (B   TRAMAINE HAWKINS V   (B   SKIP MESQUITE   WIND (B  STEVE KUPKA   SAX  (B
EMILIO CASTILLO    SAX  (B   MIC GILLETTE    TPT (B   GREG ADAMS      WIND (B
```

C208B
MICK COX
C208B

```
MICK COX           G V PERC(A    (A) MICK COX BAND            1973 CAPITOL         ST11175
TONY O'MALLEY      V    (A
MICK WEAVER        K    (A   PETE ARNESON    K   (A   CHRIS STEWART   B   (A  ANDREW STEELE   D  (A
ALAN SKIDMORE      SAX  (A
```

C209
LOL COXHILL
C209

```
LOL COXHILL        SAX  (ALL     (A) EAR OF THE BEHOLDER      1971 DANDELION  69001      8008
STEVEN MILLER      PNO  (A       (A) EAR OF THE BEHOLDER      1971 AMPEX      US        10132
DAVID BEDFORD      ORG  (A       (B) TOVERBAL SWEET           1972 MUSHROOM          150MR 23
MIKE OLDFIELD      G    (A       (C) COXHILL MILLER           1973 CAROLINE   UK        C1503
ROBERT WYATT       PERC V(AD     (D) STORY SO FAR...OH REALLY ½LP 1974 CAROLINE UK     C1507
PIERRE COURBOIS    D    (AB      (E) LOL COXHILL & WELFARE STATE 1975 CAROLINE UK      C1514
JASPER VANT HOF    PNO  (AB      (F) FLEAS IN THE CUSTARD     1975 CAROLINE   UK        C1515
PIP PYLE           PERC(C        (G) DIVERSE                  1976 OGUN             OG 510
RICHARD SINCLAIR   B    (C       (H) THE JOY OF PARANOIA      1978 OGUN             OG 525
PHIL MILLER        G    (AD      (I) MOOT                     1978 ICTUS              0008
LAURIE ALLEN       CYMB(CD       (J) LID                      1978 ICTUS              0011
ARCHIE LEGGETT     BASS(CD       (K) MURDER IN THE AIR (EP)   1978 CHILTERN SOUND    CS 100
KEVIN AYERS        G    (AD      (L) DIGSWELL DUETS           1979 RANDOM RADAR     RRR 005
JOHN FOX           SAX  (E       (M) SLOW MUSIC               1980 PIPE             PIPE 1
MORGAN FISHER G B K V   (M
LOU GLANDFIELD     TROM(E   PHIL MINTON     TROM (E   COLIN WOOD      CELLO(EG TED SPEIGHT    G   (A
CATHY KIDDLE       CLAR(E   STEVE GUMBLEY   PERC (E   PENNY GLANFIELD PERC (E  WARNER VEN WELY V   (E
JANE DURRANT       SAX  (E   PETER KIDDLE    WHIST(E   JOHN CHAPMAN    WHIST(E  LIZ LOCKHART  FLT(E
SUE FOX            V    (E   DIANA DAVIES    ORG  (E   BORIS HOWARTH   VLN G(E  MICK AUDSLEY  V   (F
KEN ELLIS          V    (F   G F FITZGERALD  G    (F   DAVE GREEN      B    (G  ANDREA CEMTAZZO D (I
JOHN MITCHELL      D    (G   MICHAEL GARRICK PNO  (H   PAUL MITCHELL DAVIDSON B (H  KEN SHAW   G   (H
VERYAN WESTON      PNO  (H   RICHARD WRIGHT  G    (H
```

C210
KEVIN COYNE
C210

```
KEVIN COYNE        V G  (ALL     (A) CASE HISTORY            1972      DANDELION    2310 228
WITH                             (B) MARJORY RAZORBLADE      1973      VIRGIN EURO 87742 UK  VD 2501
GORDON SMITH       G    (BCDK    (C) BLAME IT ON THE NIGHT   1974      VIRGIN       UK   V2012
JEAN ROUSSEL       K    (BK      (D) MATCHING HEAD & FEET    1975      VIRGIN EURO 88919 UK  V2033
TONY COUSINS       B    (BCK     (E) HEARTBURN               1976      VIRGIN EURO 27265 UK  V2047
CHILI CHARLES      D    (BCK     (F) IN LIVING BLACK & WHITE (DBL) 1976 VIRGIN      UK   VD2505
STEVE VERROCA      PERC K(BK     (F) IN LIVING BLACK & WHITE (DBL) 1976 POLYDOR  EUR 2676 710
RUAN O'LOCHLAINN   SAX G K(CK    (G) DYNAMITE DAZE           1978      VIRGIN       UK   V2095
FI TRENCH          K    (C       (G) DYNAMITE DAZE           1978      POLYDOR   EUR 2933 746
RICK DODD          SAX  (C       (H) MILLIONAIRES & TEDDY BEARS 1978   VIRGIN EURO 200215 UK  V2110
TERRY SLADE        D    (C       (I) BEAUTIFUL EXTREMES      1978      VIRGIN       UK   V2527
ARCHIE LEGGET      B    (DK      (J) BABBLE                  1979      VIRGIN EURO 200596 UK  V2128
PETER WOOLF        D    (DEFK    (K) LETS HAVE A PARTY       19        VIRGIN EURO 89800
TIM PENN           K    (DK      (L) BURSTING BUBBLES        1980      VIRGIN EURO 201654 UK  V2151
ANDY SUMMERS       G    (DEFK    (M) SANITY STOMP            1980      VIRGIN EURO 301427 UK  V3504
LISA STRIKE        V    (C       (N) BOXED SET               1980      BUTT              BOX1
JOANNE WILLIAMS    V    (C       (O) POINTING THE FINGER     1981      CHERRY RED   UK   RED23
BARRY ST JOHN      V    (C
ZOOT MONEY         K V(EFGJ  STEVE THOMPSON  B    (EF  BOB WARD        G    (HJM PAUL WICKENS    K  (GHJM
VIC SWEENEY        D    (GHJL  AL JAMES       B    (GHJM DAGMAR KRAUSE   V    (J  MICK SWEENEY    G  (A
NICK CUDWORTH      G    (J   DAVE CLAGUE      G    (AB  MALCOLM HEALEY   K   (B  TIM RICE       K  (G
JERRY DECADE       K    (J   BRIAN GODDING    G    (LMO CHRIS HUNTER    SAX  (L  PAUL FOX       G  (M
DAVE RUFFY         D    (M   GARY BARNACLE    SAX  (M  ROBERT WYATT     G V K(M  DAVE SHEEN   D V  (O
STEVE LAMB         B    (O   STEVE BULL       K    (O  SEGS            B    (M
```

C211
CRABBY APPLETON
C211

```
MICHAEL FENNELLY   G V  (AB     (A) CRABBY APPLETON          1970 ELEKTRA         EKS 74067
PHIL JONES         D    (AB     (B) ROTTEN TO THE CORE       1971 ELEKTRA         EKS 74106
CASEY FOUTZ        K    (AB
FLACO FALCON       PERC (AB  HANK HARVEY       B   (AB  DAVID GRISMAN   MAND (B
BYRON BERLINE      FDL  (B   CLYDIE KING       V   (B   OMA DRAKE       V   (B
JESSICA SMITH      V    (B   DON GALLUCCI      PROD (A
```

C212
CRACK THE SKY
C212

```
JOHN PALUMBO       K V  (ABCEFG  (A) CRACK THE SKY           1975 LIFESONG            6000
RICK WITKOWSKI     G    (ABCDEF  (A) CRACK THE SKY    (RI)   197  LIFESONG   US      34994
JIM GRIFFITHS      G V  (ABCDEF  (B) ANIMAL NOTES            1976 LIFESONG            6005
JOE MACRE          B V  (ABCDEF  (B) ANIMAL NOTES     (RI)   197  LIFESONG   US      34996
JOEY D'AMICO       D V  (ABCDEF  (C) SAFETY IN NUMBERS       1978 LIFESONG            6015
GARY LEE CHAPPELL  V    (CDE     (C) SAFETY IN NUMBERS (RI)  19   LIFESONG   US      35041
ROB STEVENS        K    (C       (D) LIVE SKY                1978 LIFESONG           35620
CAREY ZIEGLER      B    (G       (E) WHITE MUSIC             1980 LIFESONG            8028
JOHN TRACEY        D    (G       (F) CLASSIC CRACK           1980 LIFESONG            8029
VINCE DEPAUL       K    (DEG     (G) PHOTOFLAMINGO           1981 LIFESONG            8133
MICHAEL TAYLOR     G K  (G
```

[133]

CRACKERS

STEVE ALMAAS	B V	(A	(A) THE CRACKERS	1980	TWIN TONE	US	TTR 8122
KAREN INDIANA	G V	(A					
JAY PECK	D V	(A					

CRAMPS

BRYAN GREGORY	G	(AB	(A) GREATEST HITS (EP)	1979	ILLEGAL UK ILS 12013		
CONGO POWERS	G	(C	(B) SONGS THE LORD TAUGHT US	1980	ILLEGAL UK 005 US IRS	007	
IVY RUHRSCHACH	V	(ABC	(C) PSYCHEDLIC JUNGLE	1981	ILLEGAL UK 009 US IRS	10016	
LUX INTERIOR	B	(ABC					
NICK KNOX	D	(ABC	BOOKER C	K	(B	ALEX CHILTON	PROD (B

CRAMPLE

ARMIN CHRISTOPH	V K SYN(A	(A) RIGHT IN TIME		1980	?	GER	91155
UWE HOFFMEISTER	V SAX (A						
MARKUS MAYER	B	(A	WOLFGANG	D	(A	GUNTER KREMPL	G	(A
HANS PRITACHET	TPT PERC(A	EBERHARD STOIBER	G V	(A			

CRACKIN'

PETER BUNETTA	D	(BC	(A)CRACKIN	1975	POLYDOR UK2391 187 US	6044	
JERRY MARTINI	SAX	(A	(B) MAKINGS OF A DREAM	1977	WB	US	BS2989
RICK CHUDACOFF	B	(ABC	(C) CRACKIN	1977	WB	US	BS3123
ARNO LUCAS	V PERC(ABC	(D) SPECIAL TOUCH	1978	WB	US	3235
LESLIE O SMITH	V PERC(ABC						
GT CLINTON	K	(ABC	BOB BORDY	G	(BC	LESTER ABRAMS	V K (ABC
BRIAN RAY	G	(C	GENE DINWIDDIE	HRNS (BC	VICTOR FELDMAN	PERC (B
MILT HOLLAND	PERC	(B	DAVID SANBORN	HRNS (B	STEVE MADAIO	HRNS (C
CHUCK FINDLEY	HRNS	(C	JACKIE KELSO	HRNS (C	FRED SELDON	STRGS(C
MICHAEL OMARTIAN	K	(C	STEMSY HUNTER	SAX (C	CHEPITO AREAS	PERC (C

CRASS

STEVE IGNORANT	V	(A	(A) STATION OF CRASS	(DBL)	1979	CRASS	52 1984
PENNY RIMBAUD	D	(A	(B) FEEDING THE 5000		1980	CRASS	
EVE LIBERTINE	V	(A	(C) PENIS ENVY		1981	CRASS	321984/1
JOY DE VIVRE	V K G	(A					
N A PALMER	G V	(A	PETE WRIGHT	V B	(A	PHIL FREE	G V	(A

CRAVATS

ROB DALLAWAY	G V	(A	(A) IN TOYTOWN	1980	SMALL WONDER	UK	CRAVAT1
DAVE BENNETT	D	(A					
THE SHEND	B V	(A	RICHARD LONDON(SVOR NAAN) SAX(A				

THE CRAWDADDYS

STEVE POTTERF	G V HCA(A	(A) CRAWDADDY EXPRESS	1979 VOX/BOMP US 200001 UK	28541			
MARK ZADERNOWSKI	B	(A	(A) CRAWDADDY EXPRESS	1980 LINE	GER	LLP 5012	
RON SILVA	G V	(A	(B) STILL STEAMIN'	1980 LINE	GER	LSLP 4005	
DAN McCAIN	D	(A					

HANK CRAWFORD

HANK CRAWFORD	SAX	(ALL	(A) MORE SOUL	1961	ATLANTIC	US	1356
MILT TURNER		(AG	(B) SOUL CLINIC	1961	ATLANTIC	US	1372
DAVID NEWMAN	SAX	(ABCI	(C) FROM THE HEART	1962	ATLANTIC	US	1387
JOHN DUKE	B	(R	(D) SOUL FROM THE BALLAD	1963	ATLANTIC	US	1405
CARL LETT JR	D	(R	(E) TRUE BLUE	1964	ATLANTIC	US	1423
SONNY FORRIEST		(CE	(F) DIG THESE BLUES	1965	ATLANTIC	US	1436
MARTY PAICH		(D	(G) AFTER HOURS	1967	ATLANTIC	US	1455
WENDELL HARRISON		(G	(H) Mr BLUES	1967	ATLANTIC	US	1470
JOE NEWMAN		(I	(I) DOUBLE CROSS	1968	ATLANTIC	US	1503
JACK McDUFF		(I	(J) Mr SOUL PLAYS LADY SOUL	19	ATLANTIC	US	1523
RICHARD TEE	K	(LMN	(K) HELP ME MAKE IT THROUGH THE NIGHT	19	KUDU	US	06
BOB CRANSHAW	B	(L	(L) WILDFLOWER	1973	KUDU	US	15
IDRIS MUHAMMAD	D	(LM	(M) DONT YOU WOORY 'BOUT A THING	1974	KUDU	US	19
JOE BECK	G	(L	(N) I HEAR A SYMPHONY	1975	KUDU	US	26
BOB JAMES	K	(M	(O) HANK CRAWFORDS BACK	19	KUDU	US	33
GARY KING	B	(MN	(P) TICO RICO	19	KUDU	US	35
HUGH McCRACKEN	G	(M	(Q) CAJUN SUNRISE	19	KUDU	US	39
RALPH McDONALD	PERC	(MN	(R) 1959 LINE UP				
JOE FARRELL	WIND	(M					
ERIC GALE	G	(N	BERNARD PURDIE	D	(N	PHIL BODNER	WIND (M	PEPPER ADAMS	SAX (M
RANDY BRECKER	TPT	(M	JON FADDIS	TPT	(M	ALAN RUBIN	TPT (LM	ROMEE PENQUE	SAX (M
BERNIE GLOW	TPT	(L	MARVIN STAMM	TPT	(L	WAYNE ANDRE	TROM (L	TONY STUDD	TROM (L
PAUL FAULISE	TROM	(L	JIMMY BUFFINGTON	HRNS (L	BROOKS TILLOTSON	HRNS (L	BILL EATON	V (L
RANDY PEYTON	V	(L	HILDA HARRIS	V	(L	MAERETHA STEWART	V (L

RANDY CRAWFORD

RANDY CRAWFORD	V	(ALL	(A) EVERYTHING MUST CHANGE	1976 WB	UK K56328	US	2975
JEROME RICHARDSON	SAX	(A	(B) MISS RANDY CRAWFORD	1977 WB	UK K56882	US	3083
DICK SPENCER	SAX	(A	(C) RAW SILK	1978 WB	UK K56592	US	3283
RAY PIZZI	WIND	(A	(D) NOW WE MAY BEGIN	1980 WB	UK K56791	US	3421
LEW TABAKIN	WIND	(A	(E) SECRET COMBINATION	1981 WB	UK K56904	US	3541
BILL HOOD	WIND	(A	(F) WINDSONG	1982 WB	UK K57011		
MICHAEL SEMBELLO	G	(F					
BOBBY BRYANT	HRNS	(A	SNOOKY YOUNG	HRNS (A	BILL BERRY	HRNS (A	BUDDY CHILDERS	HRNS(A
JACK RAINES	HRNS	(A	DICK NASH	HRNS (A	BRITT WOODMAN	HRNS (A	GARNET BROWN	TROM(A
MAURICE SPEARS	TROM	(A	DON GRUSIN	PNO (AC	JOHN WILLIAMS	B (A	RALP HUMPHREY	D (A
MUNDELL LOWE	G	(A	JOE SAMPLE	K (AD	ROBERT POPWELL	B (A	JAMES GADSON	D (AC
LARRY CARLTON	G	(A	JAY GRAYDON	G (A	RALPH MACDONALD	PERC (A	ERIC GALE	G (A
HUGH McCRACKEN	G	(A	ANTHONY JACKSON	B (A	RICK MAROTTA	D (AC	PAT REBILLOT	K (A
DEAN PARKS	G	(ADEF	HAROLD VICK	SAX (A	HUGH MASEKELA	HRNS (A	RANDY McCORMICK	K (B
KEN BELL	G	(B	LARRY BYROM	G (B	ROGER CLARK	D (B	BOB WRAY	B (B
HARRISON CALLAWAY	HRNS	(B	RONNIE EADES	HRNS (B	DENNIS GOOD	HRNS (B	HARVEY THOMPSON	HRNS(B
BILL PUETT	FLT	(B	MAXINE WILLARD	V (BD	JULIA TILLMAN	V (BD	PAT HENDERSON	V (B
DONNA RHODES	V	(B	SANDRA CHALMERS	V (B	GREG POREE	G (C	ABRAHAM LABORIEL	B (CDE
LEON PENDARVIS	PNO	(CEF	JOHN TROPEA	G (C	WILL LEE	B (C	JOE PORCARO	PERC (C
WILLIAM D SMITH	K	(C	PHYLLIS STJAMES	V (C	ROLAND BAUTISTA	G (D	TIM MAY	G (D
DAVID T WALKER	G	(D	WILTON FELDER	B SAX(D	STIX HOOPER	D (D	MIKE BAIRD	D (D
PAULINHO DACOSTA	PERC	(D	EDDIE BROWN	PERC (D	OSCAR BRASHEAR	TPT (D	GWEN OWENS	V (D
MELVIN FRANKLIN	V	(D	JEFF PORCARO	D (EF	STEVE LUKATHER	G (EF	LENNY CASTRO	PERC(EF
ROBBEN FORD	G	(E	ERNIE WATTS	FLT (E	NEIL LARSEN	K (E	LARRY WILLIAMS	HRNS(EF
BILL REICHENBACH	HRNS	(E	GARY HERBIG	HRNS (EF	JIM HORN	HRNS (EF	CHUCK FINDLEY	HRNS(E

(CONTINUED

```
C213E                    RANDY CRAWFORD            (CONTINUED)                    C213E
   TOMMY LIPUMA    PROD (EF  BUZZY FEITEN    G   (F  DAVID SANBORN  SAX (F  GARY GRANT      HRNS(F
   LEW McCREARY    HRN (F    PAUL JACKSON    G   (F  RICHARD PAGE   V   (F  CARMEN TWIDLIE  V (F
   LPAULETTE BROWN V (F      STEVEN GEORGE   V   (F  BILL CHAMPLIN  V   (F  MARTY WALSH     G  (F
   NEIL STUBENHAUS B (F      JERRY HEY       HRN (F  CHARLES LOPER  HRNS (F ROBBIE BUCHANAN SYN(F
   STRING SECTION      (B
C214                          CRAWLER                                                C214
   TONY CARR         PERC (A   (A) CRAWLER                   1977  EPIC US 34900  UK  EPC 82083
   TERRY WILSON SLESSER V (AB  (B) SNAKE RATTLE & ROLL       1979  EPIC US 35482  UK  EPC 82965
   TERRY WILSON      B V (AB
   TONY BRAUNAGEL    D V (AB   JOHN BUNDRICK     K   (AB   TED BUNTING      SAX (A
   CHRIS WOOD        FLT (A    STEVIE LANGE      V   (A    GEOFF WHITEHORN  G   (A
C214A                     PEE WEE CRAYTON                                            C214A
   PEE WEE CRAYTON             PEE WEE CRAYTON              1975  BULLDOG        BDL  1004
                              PEE WEE CRAYTON              197   CROWN    US   CLPS 5175
                              THINGS WE USED TO DO         1976  VANGUARD US   VSD  6566
                              THINGS WE USED TO DO         197   CHARLY   UK   CR   30014
                              BLUE GUITAR GENIUS VOL 1 (10") 19  ACE      UK   10CH 23
C214B                     ROBERT CRAY BAND                                           C214B
   ROBERT CRAY       G V (A    (A) WHO'S BEEN TALKIN'        1980  TOMATO   US        7041
   CURTIS SALADO     HCA V (A
   RICHARD COUSINS   B (A      DAVE OLSON       D   (A
C214C                          CRAZE                                                 C214C
                               (A) SPARTANS                 1980  HARVEST  UK   SHSP 4114
C215             CRAZY CAVAN & THE RHYTHM ROCKERS                                     C215
   CRAZY CAVAN GROGAN V (*     CRAZY RHYTHM                 19    ROCKHOUSE          7510
   LYNDON NEEDS      G (*      ROCKABILITY                  1976  CHARLY   UK   CR   5001
   TERRY WALLEY      G (*      ROCKABILITY                  1976  POLYDOR       2445 210
   GRAHAM PRICE      B (       IS STILL ALIVE               19    CHARLY   UK   CR   5002
   MICK COFFEY       D (*      IS STILL ALIVE               19    POLYDOR       2445 211
   STEVE VINCENT     B (*      OUR OWN WAY OF ROCKIN'       1977  CHARLY   UK   CR   5004
   GERAINT WATKINS   K (*      OUR OWN WAY OF ROCKIN'       1977  POLYDOR       2933 214
                               LIVE AT THE RAINBOW          1978  CHARLY   UK   CR   30139
                               CRAZY RHYTHM                 19    CHARLY   UK   CR   30156
                               RED HOT 'N' ROCKABILLY       1979  CHARLY   UK   CR   30174
                               (*) MR COOL                  1979  CHARLY   UK   CR   31203
                               ROCKABILLY IN PARIS          1981  MAGNUM FORCE UK  003
                               (EP) BOPPIN & SHAKIN         1978  CHARLY   UK   CEP  118
C215A                      CRAZY ELEPHANT                                            C215A
   LARRY ALUFER      K V (A    (A) CRAZY ELEPHANT           19    BELL     US        6034
   BOB AVERY         D (A
   RONNIE BRETONE    B (A      KENNY COHEN    K SAX V (A    HAL HING     V   (A
C216                          CRAZY HORSE                                            C216
   BILLY TALBOT      B (ALL    (A) CRAZY HORSE              1971  REPRISE  US   RSLP 6438
   RICK CURTIS       G V (C7   (A) CRAZY HORSE              1980  REPRISE RI GERM REP 24026
   RALPH MOLINA      D (ALL    (A) CRAZY HORSE              1972  REPRISE  UK   K  44114
   DANNY WHITTEN     G V (A123456 (B) LOOSE                 1972  REPRISE  US   MS 2059
   BOBBY NOTKOFF     VLN (CD1234  (B) LOOSE                 1972  REPRISE  UK   K  44171
   LEON WHITSELL     G V (1    (C) AT CROOKED CREEK         1973  EPIC     US   KE 31710
   GEORGE WHITSELL   G V (B17  (C) AT CROOKED CREEK         1973  EPIC     UK   EPC 65223
   NILS LOFGREN      G V (A4568 (D) CRAZY MOON              1978  RCA           AFL1 3054
   JACK NITZSCHE     K (A6
   GREG LEROY        G V (BCD67 (1) 1962 68 ROCKETS
   JOHN BLANTON      K (B67    (2) 69  +NEIL YOUNG LP(EVERYBODY)
   MICHAEL CURTIS    G K V (CD7 (3) 1969
   BEN KEITH         STEEL (8  (4) 1969 70
   FRANK SAMPEDRO    G (D9     (5) MID 70 + NEIL YOUNG LP(GOLDRUSH)
   PACHECO           CONGA (C  (6) JULY70 DEC71
   SNEAKY PETE KLEINOW STEEL (C (7) 1972 73
   PATTI MOAN        V (C      (8) LATE 73 + NEIL YOUNG LPs(TONIGHTS +ON THE BEACH)
   STEVE LAWRENCE    SAX (C    (9) FEB 75 + NEIL YOUNG LP (ZUMA)
   KIRBY             PNO (D
   NEIL YOUNG        G V (D2589 RY COODER       G    (A   GIB GUILBEAU    FDL (A
   BARRY GOLDBERG    K (D      TOM BRAY        TPT  (D   JOEL TEPP       HCA (B
   JAY GRAYDON       G (D      KENNY WALTER    TROM (D   MICHAEL KOWALSKI D  (D
C217                        PAPA JOHN CREACH                                         C217
   PAPA JOHN CREACH  VLN V(ALL (A) PAPA JOHN CREACH         1971  GRUNT          FTR 1003
   BIG JOE TURNER    V (B      (B) FILTHY                   1972  GRUNT          FTR 1009
   HARMONICA FATS    HCA (B    (C) ZULU ( PLAYING MY FIDDLE FOR YOU 1974 GRUNT    BFL1 0418
   CARL BYRD         D (B      (D) IM THE FIDDLE MAN        1975  BUDDAH UK 4039 US    5649
   JACK CASADY       B (AB     (E) ROCK FATHER              1976  BUDDAH US 5660 FR VOGUE 60007
   JOHN PARKER       K (BE     (F) THE CAT & FIDDLE         1977  DJM DJM11     DJF 20515
   SAM WILLIAMS      B (B      (G) INPHASION               1978  DJM DJM18  UK  DJF 20545
   HENRY COKER       TROM(B
   SAMMY PIAZZA      D (AB   JOHN EWING    TROM (B  BLUE MITCHELL    TPT (B  JOE LANE DAVIS  SAX(B
   JERRY JUMONVILLE  SAX (B  MAURICE SIMON SAX (B  MAXINE WILLARD   V (B   VANETTA FIELDS  V (B
   SHIRLEY MATTHEWS  V (B    MARTI McCALL  V (B    LUTHER WATERS    V (B   ORRIN WATERS    V (B
   GREG ADAMS        TPT (A  JACK BONUS    SAX (A  JOHN CIPOLLINA   G (A   JOEY COVINGTON  D (A
   MIC GILLETTE      TROM(A  MIKE LIPSKIN  K   (A  PETE SEARS       B (A   GRACE SLICK     V (
   STAN MONTEIRO     CLAR(A  BOB WILSON    G   (A  NICK BLACK       PNO (A  BRUCE CONTE     G (A
   DOUGLAS RAUCH     B (A    STEVE HABERMAN K  (FG BRIAN TILFORD    B V (EFG MARK LEON      D V(E(FG
   JOE BRASLER       G (FG   REID KING     V G (FG TONY SMITH       D (A   CARLOS SANTANA  G (A
   ART HILLERY       PNO (A  PAUL KANTNER  G   (A  BOBBY HAYES      B (A   AL STAEHELY     V (F
   SCOTT CUSHNIE     K (F    BOB ZIMMITTI  D   (G  JOHNNY GUITAR WATSON G (G CHARLIE DANIELS FDL (G
   DR JOHN           K (G    DAVID LAFLAMME FDL (G RUFUS ANDERSON   G (A   DAVID BROWN     B (A
   JERRY GARCIA      G (A    GREGG ROLIE   ORG (A  KEVIN MOORE      G (BE  JORMA KAUKONEN  G (AB
   HOLDEN RAPHAEL    PERC(BC DAVID BROWN   B   (A  TRACY RICHARDSON V (F   RACHEL OLDFIELD V (F
   ROY SCIACCA       V (F    ERNESTINE GOLDSTEIN V (G
```

```
ERIC CLAPTON          G V    (ALL
JACK BRUCE            HCA K B V (ALL
GINGER BAKER          D V    (ALL
FELIX PAPPALARDI B K VLA PROD G(*

FRESH CREAM              1966 REACTION  UK   594  001      BEST OF CREAM          1969 POLYDOR    UK   583  060
FRESH CREAM              1966 ATCO      US        33206    BEST OF CREAM          1969 POLYDOR    GERM 184  298
FRESH CREAM              1966 POLYDOR   GERM 623  031      BEST OF CREAM    (DBL) 19   RSO        FR   2675 087
FRESH CREAM              197  RSO       US     1 3009      I FEEL FREE            1969 KARUSSELL  GERM 2499 002
FRESH CREAM              1978 RSO       GER  2479 180      BEST OF          (DBL) 1969 KARUSSELL  GERM 2499 010
FULL CREAM               1966 REACTION  UK   2447 010      SWLABR                 19   KARUSSELL  GERM 2499 013
DISRAELI GEARS           1967 REACTION  UK   594  003      ROCK SENSATION         1969 KARUSSELL  GERM 2499 112
DISRAELI GEARS           1967 POLYDOR   GERM 184  105      CREAM LIVE             1970 POLYDOR    UK   2383 016
DISRAELI GEARS           1967 ATCO      US        33232    CREAM LIVE             1970 ATCO       US        33328
DISRAELI GEARS           19   POLYDOR   UK   2442 114      CREAM LIVE             197  RSO        US     1 3014
DISRAELI GEARS           197  RSO       US     1 3010      CREAM LIVE 2           1972 POLYDOR    UK   2383 119
DISRAELI GEARS           197  RSO            2394 129      CREAM LIVE 2           197  RSO        US     1 3015
WHEELS OF FIRE (DBL)*    1968 POLYDOR   UK   583 031/2     CREAM LIVE 2           1972 ATCO       US        7005
WHEELS OF FIRE (DBL)*    1968 ATCO      US      2/700      OFF THE TOP            1972 POLYDOR    US        5529
WHEELS OF FIRE (DBL)*    1972 POLYDOR   UK   2612 001      HEAVY CREAM            1973 POLYDOR    UK   2659 022
WHEELS OF FIRE (DBL)*    1972 POLYDOR        2658 110      HEAVY CREAM            1973 POLYDOR    US        3502
WHEELS OF FIRE (DBL)*    197  RSO       US     2 3802      CREAM                  1975 POLYDOR    UK   2384 067
WHEELS OF FIRE (DBL)*    19   RSO            2671 109      PORTRAIT OF CREAM      1975 POLYDOR    UK   2482 142
WHEELS OF FIRE(STUDIO)*  1968 POLYDOR   UK   583  033      THE BEST VOL 2         1975 POLYDOR    UK   2675 087
WHEELS OF FIRE (LIVE)    1968 POLYDOR   UK   583  040      POP GIANTS             19   BRUNSWICK       2911 528
GOODBYE                  1969 POLYDOR   UK   583  053      BEST OF CREAM LIVE     19   POLYDOR         2674 018
GOODBYE                  1969 ATCO      US        7001     POP HISTORY            197  POLYDOR         2675 014
GOODBYE                  1969 POLYDOR   GERM 184  203      CREAM VOL 2            1978 RSO        UK   2479 701
                                                           EARLY CREAM            19   SPRINGBOARD US   4037
                                                           BEST                   19   ATCO       US        33291
                                                           CREAM (6LPS)           1981 POLYDOR    NL   2658 142
```

```
JACK JONES      D  (ABC      (A) WE ARE THE PAINTERMEN   1967 SONET DK       SLPS 1251
KENNY PICKETT   V  (ABC      (A) WE ARE THE PAINTERMEN   1970 SONET RI    DK 1933
EDDIE PHILLIPS  G  (ABC      (A) WE ARE THE PAINTERMEN   1967 HIT TON   GERM 340  037
BOB GARNER      B  (ABC      (B) BEST OF CREATION        1968 POP   GERM  ZS 10 168
                            (C) 1966 67 CREATION        1973 CHARISMA  UK    CS8
                            ( ) SUPER ROCK              19   TOSHIBA   US    95016
                            ( ) THIS IS CREATION        19   TOSHIBA   US    95024
                            ( ) CREATION                1975 ATCO      US    7041
```

```
(A) STARSHIP AFRICA        1980 4D RHYTHMS      4DLP 1
(B) PSYCHOTIC JUNKANOO     1981 STATIK          9994
```

```
HEIKO STEINSIEK        D PERC(AB      (A) GORILLA     1973 BRAIN    1017
M M MAASS            B G K V (AB      (B) LADY PIG    1974 BRAIN    1061
APOSTOLOS PAPANIKOLAOU G(B
RUDIGER STREMMEL   SAX V(AB  HUBERTUS KREUTNER TPT V(AB  RAINER ERBEL  V (AB  KLAUS WEBER  G PERC(A
GUNTER SCHMEIDE    G B (A
```

```
MELVIN RAGIN     G    (B      (A) CREATIVE SOURCE       1974 SUSSEX         LPSX6
RAY PARKER       G    (B      (A) CREATIVE SOURCE       1974 SUSSEX    US   8027
JAMES JAMESON    B    (B      (B) MIGRATION             1974 SUSSEX         LPSX7
KENNETH RICE     D    (B      (B) MIGRATION             1974 SUSSEX    US   8035
CLARENCE McDONALD K   (B      (C) PASS THE FEELING ON   1976 POLYDOR        2391 196
SKIP SCARBOROUGH K    (B      (C) PASS THE FEELING ON   1976 POLYDOR   US   6052
BOBBYE HALL      PERC (B      (D) CONSIDER THE SOURCE   1976 POLYDOR        2391 221
MIKE STOKES      K    (B      (D) CONSIDER THE SOURCE   1976 POLYDOR   US   6065
CARL AUSTIN      STINGS(B
RALPH TERRANA    SYN  (B      JOHN TRADEL       HRNS  (B
```

```
MONSTER RALLY     19 RCA   US   1923
```

```
MICHAEL McKEAN  G V   (      A GREAT GIFT IDEA   1973 REPRISE  US   2154
LOWELL GEORGE   G     (
RON ELLIOTT     G     (      RICHARD HAYWARD  D    (      HARVEY MASON    PERC (
MILT HOLLAND    PERC  (      JOE PORCARO      PERC (      KENNY GRADNEY   B    (
RAY POHLMAN     B     (      DAVID HERSCHER   B    (      HARRY SHEARER   K V  (
MARK LEVINE     K     (      NICK DECARO      K    (      TOMMY MORGAN    HCA  (
PENNY NICHOLS   V     (      RICHARD BEEBE    V    (      DAVID LANDER    V    (
```

```
(A) CREED       1980 ASYLUM   US   146
```

```
                                                 FANTASY  FANTASY  LIBERTY  MUSIDISC
                                                 UK       US       UK       FR
TOM FOGERTY   G V  (ALL
JOHN FOGERTY  G V  (ALL
STU COOK      D    (ALL
DOUG CLIFFORD B    (ALL
              (A) CREEDENCE CLEARWATER REVIVAL 1969 506   8382     83259    6049
              (B) BAYOU COUNTY                 1969 507   8387     83261    6048
              (C) GREEN RIVER                  1969 504   8393     83273    6047
              (D) WILLIE & THE POOR BOYS       1970 503   8397     83338    6046
              (E) COSMOS FACTORY               1970 502   8402     83388    6043
              (F) PENDULUM                     1971 508   8410     83400    6042
              (G) MARDI GRAS                   1972 505   9404              6036
              (H) CREEDENCE GOLD               1973 501   8402              6029
              (H) CREEDENCE GOLD               197        9418  NL MFP 58089
              (I) MORE CREEDENCE GOLD          1973 512   9430              6019
              (J) LIVE IN EUROPE               1974 520   FCCR 1            6009
              (K) MASTERS OF ROCK              1975 EMI IMP SC054
              (L) CHRONICLE                    1976 528   FCCR 2             235
              (L) CHRONICLE                    1978 FESTIVAL ALB 235 IMP
              (M) LIVE AT THE ALBERT HALL (70) 1981 FANTASY US 4501 NL 614 173
              (AB) C C R/ BAYOU COUNTRY        1978 FANTASY SWE CCR68
              (CD) GREEN RIVER/WILLIE          1978 FANTASY SWE CCR69
              (EF) COSMOS/PENDULUM             1978 FANTASY SWE CCR70
```

(CONTINUED)

```
                        ( ) LIVE IN GERMANY        197   FANTASY GER 15200
                        ( ) 20 GREATEST HITS        19   FANTASY      558
                        ( ) CREEDENCE COUNTRY      1981   MFP 4509
                        (EP) C C R                 1981   FANTASY NL  64441
```

C221A   CREEPY JOHN THOMAS   C221A

```
  CREEPY JOHN THOMAS  G V  (A    (A) CREEPY JOHN THOMAS       1969  RCA          UK  SF 8061
  PAUL ROGERS           V  (A
  ANDY MARX           B V  (A    HELMUT POHL        D     (A
```

C222   LOL CREME & KEVIN GODLEY   C222

```
  LOL CREME    G B V K PERC (ALL   (A) CONSEQUENCES      1977 MERCURY CONSO17     6641658
  KEVIN GODLEY  D V PERC B K(ALL   (A) CONSEQUENCES      1977 MERCURY       US   SRM31700
  PHIL MANZANERA      G      (D    (B) "L"              1978 MERCURY UK9109611 US POLYDOR 6177
  JONATHAN HANDELSMAN SAX    (B    (C) MUSIC FROM CONSEQUENCES 1978 MERCURY       9109 615
  ANDY MACKAY         SAX    (B    (D) FREEZE FRAME     1979 POLYDOR UK 2442 166 +5027 US 6257
  PAUL GAMBACCINI     V      (B    (E) ISMISM           1981 POLYDOR UK 2442 193 +5043
  PAUL McCARTNEY      V      (D
```

C222A   CRESCENDOS   C222A

```
  DALE WARD           V      (A    (A) OH JULIE            196   GUEST STAR   US       1453
```

C222B   MARSHALL CRENSHAW   C222B

```
  MARSHALL CRENSHAW  G V PROD(A    (A) MARSHALL CRENSHAW   1982  WB US 3673   UK K57010
  CHRIS DONATO       B V     (A
  MICHAEL OSBORNE    PERC    (A    ROBERT CRENSHAW    D V    (A    TONY GARNIER      B     (A
  RICHARD GOTTEHRER  PROD    (A
```

C223   CRESSIDA   C223

```
  ANGUS CULLEN        V G  (AB    (A) CRESSIDA             1970  VERTIGO              V07
  PETER JENNINGS      K    (AB    (B) ASYLUM               1971  VERTIGO           6360 025
  KEVIN McCARTHY      B    (AB
  IAIN CLARK          D    (AB    HAROLD McNAIR      FLT  (B    JOHN CULLEY *      G     (B
                                  *SAME PERSON??   JOHN HEYWORTH *    G     (A
```

C223A   CRESTS   C223A

```
  JOHNNY MAESTRO      V    (      CRESTS SING              19   POST        US       3000
  JAY CARTER          V    (      CRESTS SING ALL BIGGIES  19   COED        US        901
  HARROLD TORRES      V    (      BEST OF THE CRESTS       19   COED        US        904
  TOMMY GOUGH         V    (
```

C223B   CRETONES   C223B

```
  STEVE BEERS         D    (A     (A) SNAP SNAP            1981  PLANET          P15
  PETER BERNSTEIN   B V    (A
  MARK GOLDENBERG   G V    (A     STEVE LEONARD     K    (A    PHIL KANZIE     SAX   (A
```

C224   CRICKETS   C224

```
  BUDDY HOLLY        G V  (A      (A) CHIRPIN CRICKETS     1958  CORAL      UK   LVA 9081
  JERRY ALLISON      D    (ALL    (A) CHIRPIN CRICKETS     1969  CORAL      UK   CP    20
  LARRY WELBORN      B    (       (A) CHIRPIN CRICKETS     1974  MCA        UK   CRLM 1023
  NIKI SULLIVAN      G    (A      (A) CHIRPIN CRICKETS     1975  MCA        UK   CDLM 8035
  JOE MAULDIN        B    (ALL    (A) CHIRPIN CRICKETS      19   BRUNSWICK  US        54038
  JERRY NAYLOR              (A    (A) CHIRPIN CRICKETS      19   BRUNSWICK  US        71036
  GLEN D HARDIN     G K            (B) BOBBY VEE MEETS THE CRICKETS 196  LIBERTY UK  SLBY 1086
  SONNY CURTIS      G V   (       (B) BOBBY VEE MEETS THE CRICKETS 1974 SUNSET  UK  SLS 50357
  RICK GRECH         B    (JK     (C) IN STYLE WITH        196   CORAL     UK   LVA 9142
  BOBBY VEE          V    (B      (C) IN STYLE WITH        196   CORAL            57320
  ALBERT LEE         G    (JK     (D) CALIFORNIA SUN        19   LIBERTY   US        7372
  NICKY HOPKINS      K    (       (E) SOMETHING OLD SOMETHING NEW ... 19 LIBERTY UK SLBY 1120
  BOB MONTGOMERY     PROD  (K     (E) SOMETHING OLD SOMETHING NEW     19 LIBERTY US      7272
  CAROL MONTGOMERY   V    (K      (F) WE GOTTA GET TOGETHER 19   LIBERTY   US        55742
  STEVE KRIKORIAN   V HCA (JK     (G) ROCKIN 50s ROCK'N'ROLL 1971 CBS      UK        64301
  NICK VANMAARTH    G V   (JK     (G) ROCKIN 50s ROCK'N'ROLL 1971 BARNABY  US        30268
                                  (H) ROCK REFLECTIONS     1971  SUNSET    UK   SLS 50207
                                  (I) BUBBLEGUM, POP , BALLADS & BOOGIE 1973 PHILIPS UK 6308 149
                                  (J) REMNANTS             1973  VERTIGO 1020 NL  6360 104
                                  (J) REMNANTS             1973  MERCURY          1 695
                                  (K) LONG WAY FROM LUBBOCK 1974 MERCURY   UK   6310 007
                                  (L) BACK IN STYLE        1975  M C A     UK   MCFM 2710
                                  EPS
                                  STRAIGHT NO STRINGS       19   LIBERTY   UK   SLEP 2094
                                  THE CRICKETS              19   CORAL     US        81192
                                  CHIRPING CRICKETS         19   BRUNSWICK US        71036
                                  SOUND OF THE CRICKETS     19   BRUNSWICK US        71038
                                  BOBBY VEE & THE CRICKETS  19   LIBERTY   UK   LEP 2084
                                  A FOREVER KIND OF LOVE    19   LIBERTY   UK   LEP 2089
                                  BOBBY VEE MEETS THE CRICKETS  19 LIBERTY UK   LEP 2116
                                  BOBBY VEE MEETS THE CRICKETS 2 19 LIBERTY UK  LEP 2149
                                  COME ON                   19   LIBERTY   UK   LEP 2173
```

C225   CRISIS   C225

```
  TONY WAKEFIELD     B    (A      (A) NO TOWN HALL    (EP)  1979  C A G     UK
  DOUG PEARCE        G    (A      (B) HYMNS OF FAITH  (EP)  1980  ADRCOR    UK
  LESTER JONES       G    (A
  INSECT ROBIN       D    (A      PHRAZER           V    (A
```

C226   CRISPY AMBULANCE   C226

```
                                  (A) UNSIGHTLY & SERENE  (EP) 1980 FACTORY 10"  UK  FAC 32
                                  (B) LIVE ON HOY AUGUST NIGHT (EP) 1981 FACTORY 12" BELG FACBN 4
```

C227   PETE CRISS   C227

```
  PETE CRISS         D V  (ABC    (A) PETE CRISS          1978  CASABLANCA      NBLP 7122
  STEVE LUKATHER     G    (ABC    (B) OUT OF CONTROL      1980  CASABLANCA      NBLP 7240
                                  (B) OUT OF CONTROL      1980  MERCURY   UK   6302 065
                                  (D) LET ME ROCK YOU     1981  MERCURY   UK   6302 194
```

C227A   CRISTINA   C227A

```
  CRISTINA MONET     V    (A      (A) CRISTINA            1980  ZE        UK   ILPS 7004
  CAROL COLEMAN      B    (A
  MICKEY MARTINEZ    D    (A      DUANE ROGERS      G   (A    BERNARD HAVEN    K   (A
  RALPH SHUCKETT     K    (A      MILTON CARDONS    PERC (A
```

CRITICAL MASS

(A) ITS WHATS INSIDE THAT COUNTS 19 MCA US 3260

CRITTERS

CHRIS DARWAY	AUTOHARP	(	( ) TOUCH'N GO WITH THE CRITTERS	196	PROJECT 3	US	PB 4001
KENNY GORKA	B	(	( ) THE CRITTERS	1966	PROJECT 3	US	PB 4002
BOB SPINELLA	K	(	( ) YOUNGER GIRL	1966	KAPP	US	1485
JIM RYAN	G	(	( ) YOUNGER GIRL	1966	KAPP	US STEREO	3485
JEFF PELOSI	D	(					

JIM CROCE

JIM CROCE	G V	(ALL	(A) CROCE	19	CAPITOL	US	ST315
INGRID CROCE		(AI	(B) YOU DONT MESS AROUND WITH JIM	1971	VERTIGO UK 6360700 US ABC		756
GARY CHESTER	D	(BC	(B) YOU DONT MESS AROUND WITH JIM RI	19	COMMAND US 40006 LIFESONG US 34993		
H J BOYLE	G	(B	(B) YOU DONT MESS AROUND WITH JIM RI	1981	ROADRUNNER 9996		
ELLIE GREENWICH	V	(BCD	(C) LIFE & TIMES	1973	VERTIGO UK 6360 701 US ABC		769
TASHA THOMAS	V	(BCD	(C) LIFE & TIMES	197	COMMAND US 40007 LIFESONG US 35008		
JOE MACHO	B	(BCD	(C) LIFE & TIMES	1981	ROADRUNNER 9997		
TERRY CASHMAN	V	(BC	(D) I GOT A NAME	1973	VERTIGO UK 6360 703 US ABC		797
JIM RYAN	B	(B	(D) I GOT A NAME	197	COMMAND US 40008 LIFESONG US 35009		
MAURY MUEHLEISEN	G V	(BCD	(D) I GOT A NAME	1981	ROADRUNNER 9998		
TOMMY WEST	K V B	(BCD	(E) PHOTOGRAPHS & MEMORIES	1975	LIFESONG UK 500 US ABC		835
ALAN ROLNICK	G V	(CD	(E) PHOTOGRAPHS & MEMORIES	197	COMMAND US 40020 LIFESONG US 35010		
KENNY ASCHER	ORG	(C	(F) THE FACES I'VE BEEN	1975	LIFESONG	UK US	ELSDP900
RICK MAROTTA	D	(D	(G) JIM CROCE COLLECTION	197	TEE VEE	US	TVLP77024
STEVE GADD	D	(D	(H) TIME IN A BOTTLE	197	LIFESONG	US	35000
MARTY NELSON	V	(D	(I) ANOTHER DAY	1977	PICKWICK	US	3332
TERENCE MINOGUE	STR V	(D	(J) BAD DAB LEROY BROWN	1979	LIFESONG	US	35571
ERIC WEISSBERG	FDL	(C	(K) ZIJN GROOTSHE SUCCESSEN (NL)	19	ROADRUNNER	NL	9999
MICHAEL KAMEN	SYN	(CD	(L) HIS GREATEST SONGS	1980	K TEL	UK	NE 1059
GEORGE DEVENS	PERC	(D					
STU WOODS	B	(D	BOBBY MATOS	PERC	(D LEROY BROWN	V	(D

CROCODILES

(A) NEW WAVE GOODBYE 1981 AURA UK AUL 716

CROMAGNON ORGASM

(A) CROMAGNON ORGASM 1969 ESP US 2001

CROME SYRCUS

LEE GRAHAM	B V FLT	(A	(A) THE LOVE CYCLE	196	COMMAND	RS	925
DICK POWELL	K V HCA	(A					
ROD PILLOUD	D	(A	TED SHREFFLER	K	(A JOHN GABORIT	G	(A

ANDREW CRONSHAW

ANDREW CRONSHAW	G ZITHER	(ALL	(A) A IS FOR ANDREW	1974	TRANSATLANTIC	UK	XTRA 1139
MARTIN SIMPSON	G	(C	(B) EARTHED IN CLOUD VALLEY	1977	TRAILER	UK	LER 2104
RIC SAUNDERS	VLN	(C	(C) WADE IN THE FLOOD	1978	TRANSATLANTIC	UK	LTRA 508
JOHN GILLESPIE	K	(C					
HOLLY TANNEN	DULC	(C	RICK KEMP	B	(C		

CROOKS

DINO DEAN	V G K	(A	(A) JUST RELEASED	1980	BLUEPRINT	UK	5002
CHRIS BRODERICK	B V	(A					
JIM FINGERS	G V	(A	MICHAEL SPARROW	D	(A SIMON BOSWELL	K	(A

STEVE CROPPER

STEVE CROPPER	G	(ALL	(A) WITH A LITTLE HELP FROM MY FRIENDS	1971	STAX	UK	SXATS1008							
WITH			(A) WITH A LITTLE HELP FROM MY FRIENDS	1971	VOLT	US	VOS 6006							
ALBERT KING	G	(B	(B)JAMMED TOGETHER	1971	STAX	UK	STX 3009							
POP STAPLES	G	(B	(C) PLAYING MY THANG	1980	MCA	US	5171							
DUCK DUNN	B	(C	(D) NIGHT AFTER NIGHT	1982	MCA	US	5340							
JERRY HAY	TPT	(C												
RAYFORD GRIFFIN	D	(D	NEAL STUBENHAUS	B	(C	RICK SCHLOSSER	D	(C	CRAIG KRAMPF	D	(C
WILLY HALL	D	(C	DAVID PAICH	K	(C	ANDREW LOVE	HRNS	(C	JIM HORN		HRNS(CD
JACK HALE	TROM	(C	DAN FERGUSON	G	(C	STEVE FOREMAN	PERC	(CD	JOHN JARVIS	K	(C
KRON	SYN	(C	TREVOR VEITCH	G	(C	WILLIAM D SMITH	K	(CD	BILL PAYNE	K	(C
BOBBY KIMBALL	V	(CD	BRUCE ROBB	V	(DC	JOE ROBB	V	(C	STEVE ROBB	V	(C
ROGER HAWKINS	D	(D	SCOTT EDWARDS	B	(D	DAVID HOOD	B	(D	CLAYTON IVEY	K	(D
BARRY BECKETT	K	(D	RUSSELL FARENTE	G	(D	CHARLES FEARING	G	(D	JIM JOHNSON	G	(D
WAYNE PERKINS	G	(D	JEFF BAXTER	G	(D	CHUCK FINDLEY	HRNS	(D	JULIA TILLMAN	V	(D
MAXINE WILLARD	V	(D	CLYDENE JACKSON	V	(D	TIM SCMIDT	V	(D	BURTON CUMMINGS	V	(D
BONNIE BRAMLETT	V	(D									

DAVID CROSBY

DAVID CROSBY	G V	(A	(A) IF I COULD ONLY REMEMBER MY NAME	1971	ATLANTIC UK 2401 005	K40320					
GRAHAM NASH	G V	(A	(A) IF I COULD ONLY REMEMBER MY NAME	1971	ATLANTIC US		7203			
BILL KREUTZMANN		(A									
PHIL LESH	G	(A	DAVID FREIBERG	(A	ETHAN CROSBY	(A	MICKEY HART	(A
HENRY DILTZ		(A	LAURA ALLEN	(A	PAUL KANTNER	(A	JERRY GARCIA	(A
MICHAEL SHRIEVE		(A	JACK CASADY	(A	JORMA KAUKONEN	(A	GRACE SLICK	(A
GREGG ROLIE		(A	JONI MITCHELL	(A	GARY BURDEN	(A	STEPHEN BARNCARD	(A
ROBERT HAMMER		(A	DAVID GEFFEN	(A	RONALD STONE	(A	ELLIOT ROBERTS	(A
NEIL YOUNG		(						

CROSBY & NASH

DAVID CROSBY	G V	(ALL	(A) CROSBY & NASH	1972	ATLANTIC UK K50011 US 7220						
GRAHAM NASH	G V K	(ALL	(B) WIND ON THE WATER	1975	POLYDOR	UK	2310 428				
TIM DRUMMOND	B	(BCDE	(B) WIND ON THE WATER	1975	POLYDOR	EUR	2302 038				
DANNY KORTCHMAR	B G	(ABCDE	(B) WIND ON THE WATER	1975	ABC US 902 MCA RI 37007						
CRAIG KINLERS	G	(C	(C) WHISTLE DOWN THE WIRE	1976	POLYDOR	UK	2310 468				
DAVID LINDLEY	VLN G	(BCDE1	(C) WHISTLE DOWN THE WIRE	1976	ABC US		956				
CRAIG DOERGE	K	(ABCDE1	(D) LIVE	1977	POLYDOR	UK	2310 565				
JOEL BERNSTEIN	G	(BC	(D) LIVE	1977	ABC US		1042				
BEN KEITH	G	(BC	(E) BEST OF	1978	POLYDOR UK 2310 626 RI 2482490						
RUSS KUNKEL	D	(ABCDE	(E) BEST OF	1977	ABC US 1102						
STAN SZELESTE	K	(BC	(1) 1976 BRITISH TOUR								
LEE SKLAR	B	(ABCE									
BILL KREUTZMANN	D	(AE	LEAH KUNKEL	V	(E	JERRY GARCIA	G STEEL(AE	JACKSON BROWNE	(BE
JOHN BARBATA	D	(AE	JONI MITCHELL	V	(E	JAMES TAYLOR	V	(BCE CAROLE KING	K	(BCE
GREG REEVES	B	(A	CHRIS ETHRIDGE	K	(A	DAVE MASON	G	(A PHIL LESH	B	(A
LEVON HELM	D	(B	ARTHUR MAEBE	HRN	(A	DAVID DUKE	HRN	(A GEORGE PRICE	HRN	(A
DANA AFRICA	FLT	(A			[138]			LAURA ALLEN	ZITHER(C

```
DAVID CROSBY        G V  (ABCDE1234FG  (A) CROSBY STILLS & NASH      1969 ATLANTIC UK 588  189 RI K40033
GRAHAM NASH         G V  (ABCDE1234FG  (A) CROSBY STILLS & NASH      1969 ATLANTIC US            8229
NEIL YOUNG          G V  (BCD234       (B) DEJA VU                   1970 ATLANTIC UK 2401 001 RI K50001
STEPHEN STILLS    B G V K(ABCDE1234FG  (B) DEJA VU                   1970 ATLANTIC US 7200    RI 19118
CALVIN SAMUELS      B    (C2           (C) FOUR WAY STREET           1972 ATLANTIC UK 2657 007 RI K60003
JOE LALA            PERC (4G           (C) FOUR WAY STREET           1972 ATLANTIC US 2/902
TIM DRUMMOND        B    (4E           (D) SO FAR                    1974 ATLANTIC UK            K50023
RUSS KUNKEL         D    (4EG          (D) SO FAR                    1974 ATLANTIC     US  18100
JERRY GARCIA        STEEL(B            (E) C S N                     1977 ATLANTIC US19104 UK   K50369
DALLAS TAYLOR       D    (AB12         (F) REPLAY                    1980 ATLANTIC US 16082 UK  K50766
TIM SCHMIDT         V    (G            (G) DAYLIGHT AGAIN            1982 ATLANTIC US 19360 UK  K50896
JOHN SEBASTIAN      HCA  (B            (1) 1968/1969  (2) 1969/70 (3) 1970   (4) 1974/75
GREG REEVES         B    (B2
JOHN BARBATA        D    (C3  CRAIG DOERGE   K   (EG GEORGE PERRY    B   (EG JOE VITALE D K FLT (EG
JIMMY HASLIP        B    (EG  RAY BARRETTO   PERC (E  TIM DRUMMOND   B   (E  GERALD JOHNSON B   (E
MIKE FINNIGAN       K    (G   MICHAEL STERGIS G V (G  WAYNE GOODWIN  FDL (G  LEE SKLAR     B   (G
GERRY TOLMAN        G    (G   ROBERLEIGH BERNHART CELLO(G ERNIE EKHART CELLO (G  BOB GLAUB    B   (G
JOEL BERNSTEIN      G    (G   RICHARD T BEAR  K  (G  DEAN PARKS     G   (G  JAY FERGUSON  K   (G
MIGUEL MARTINEZ     CELLO(G   ART GARFUNKEL      V  (G
```

```
JAY SIEGEL      V PERC(A        (A) CROSS COUNTRY         1973 ATLANTIC    UK     K 40516
MITCH MARGO     V PERC K G (A   (A) CROSS COUNTRY         1973 ATCO        US     SD 7024
BOB MANN         G    (A
PHIL MARGO      V PERC(A  AL GORGONE   G       (A HUGH McCRACKEN  G   (A  JERRY FRIEDMAN G  (A
LOREN KOREVEC    V    (A  ERIC WEISSBERG  STEEL(A RICK McGRATH   STEEL(A  KIRK HAMILTON  B  (A
STU WOODS        B    (A  GREG WALKER   D      (A ALLEN SCHWARZBERG D (A  JIM MAELEN    PERC(A
GEORGE DEVENS    PERC (A  MAX HOLLANDER   STRINGS(A
```

```
                                 (A) EAST OF WHERE   1981   HEADFIRST   US          9704
```

```
HOWARD KAYLAN    SAX V(A        (A) CROSSFIRES         1981 RHINO US          019
MARK VOLMAN      SAX V(A
AL NICHOL        G V  (A  DON MURRAY   D     (A CHUCK PORTZ  B    (A  JIM TUCKER    G    (A
TOM STANTON      G    (A  TERRY HAND   D     (A
```

```
CHRISTOPHER CROSS G V (A        (A) CHRISTOPHER CROSS    1979 WB  US 3383   UK  K56789
TOMMY TAYLOR      D   (A         (B) ANOTHER PAGE        1983 WB
ANDY SALMON       B   (A
DON ROBERTS       SAX (A  MICHAEL OMARTIAN  SYN K V(A STORMIE OMARTIAN V  (A  JAY GRAYDON   G   (A
LENNY CASTRO      PERC(A  NICOLETTE LARSON  V   (A  ROB MEURER      K SYN(A  MYRNA MATTHEWS V  (A
MARTY McCALL      V   (A  VICTOR FELDMAN    PERC(A  CHUCK FINDLEY   HRNS(A  VALERIE CARTER V  (A
MICHAEL McDONALD  V   (A  LARRY CARLTON     G   (A  DON HENLEY      V  (A  J D SOUTHER   V   (A
ERIC JOHNSON      G   (A  TOMAS RAMIREZ     SAX (A  JIM HORN        SAX(A  JACKIE KELSO  SAX (A
LEW McCREARY      TROM(A
```

```
KEITH CROSS      G V  (A        (A) BORED CIVILIANS     1972 DECCA    UK  SKL 5129
PETER ROSS       G V  (A
SID GARDNER           (A  JENNY MASON       (A  BILLY RANKIN    (A  CHRIS STEWART  B  (A
PETER ARNESSON        (A  STEVE CHAPMAN     (A  JIMMY HASTINGS  (A  DEE MURRAY        (A
TONY SHARP            (A  TONY CARR         (A  BRIAN COLE      (A  NICK LOWE         (A
LEA NICHOLSON         (A
```

```
DAVE WAGNER      V    (ABCDE      (A) CROW MUSIC         1969 AMARET                5001
DICK WIEGAND     G    (ABCD       (A) CROW MUSIC         1969 STATESIDE   UK  SSL 10301
LARRY WIEGAND    B    (ABCD       (B) CROW BY CROW       1970 AMARET      1970      10306
KINK MIDDLEMIST  K    (ABCD       (B) CROW BY CROW       1970 STATESIDE   UK  SSL 10310
DENNY CASSWELL   D    (BCD        (C) MOSAIC             1981 AMARET      US        5009
BROOKS HUNNICUTT V    (B          (D) BEST OF            1972 AMARET      US        5012
MAXINE WILLARD   V    (B          (E) DAVID WAGNER,CROW  1972 AMARET      US        5-13
JULIA TILLMAN    V    (B
MARK'CHICO' PEREZ PERC(B  JIM GORDON    D    (E JOHN GUERIN        (E  LARRY BROWN   (E
BOBBY HALL       PERC (E  JOE OSEBORNE       (E MIKE DEASY         (E  DON PEAKE     (E
DEAN PARKS       G    (E  MICHAEL OMARTIAN   (E JACKIE KELSO       (E  BUD BRISBOIS  (E
BUDDY CHILDERS        (E  OLLIE MITCHELL     (E RON HICKLIN        (E  STAN FARBER   (E
GENE MORFORD          (E
```

```
SONNIE BERNARDI   D    (ABCDEF  (A) OFFICIAL MUSIC(KING BISCUIT BOY) 1970 PARAMOUNT  US  PAS 5030
JOZEF CHIROWSKI FLT PERC K(ABCDEF (B) BAD MANORS        1970 CAPITOL          SBA 16004
JOHN 'GHETTO'GIBBARD G V(ABCDEF (B) BAD MANORS          1971 PARAMOUNT   UK  SPLA 272
KELLY JAY        K V  (ABCDEF   (B) BAD MANORS          1971 PARAMOUNT   US  PAR 6007
ROLAND GREENWAY  B V  (ABCDEF   (C) LARGER THAN LIFE    1971 PARAMOUNT        SPLA 7002
RHEAL LANTHIER   G V  (ABCDE    (D) HEAVY DUTY          1972 DAFFODIL   AUST DDL 34665
RAY FENNELL      PERC (C        (D) HEAVY DUTY          1973 PARAMOUNT        SPFL 283
SKIP PROKOP      PERC (C        (E) CROWBAR             1973 EPIC        UK        80046
LEIGH ROBINSON   PERC (C        (E) CROWBAR             1973 EPIC        US  KE 32746
KING BISCUIT BOY V    (B        (F) CROWBAR CLASSICS    1972 CAPITOL          16030
BOB BRYDEN       V    (B
RITCHIE YORK     PERC (B  BRUCE FLYNN     HRNS (C BRIAN LE BLANC  HRNS (C STEVE KENNEDY  HRNS K(BC
BRUCE CASSIDY    HRNS (B  GREG MUDRY      HRNS (C KEITH JOLLIMORE HRNS (C HOWARD SHORE   HRNS (C
PETE SIMPSON     HRNS (C  LARRY GREEN     HRNS (C MICHAEL BRECKER HRNS (E THE ROCK           (E
PAUL PRESTOPINO       (E  RANDY BRECKER   HRNS (E STEVE HUNTER    G    (E SNEAKY PETE KLEINOW STEEL(E
HUGH McCRACKEN   G    (E  WADE MARCUS          (E JAY MESSINA          (E ED SPRIGG          (E
JOHN PEARSON          (E  TERRY BERRY CHOIR V (BC LARRY SMITH          (E JANEY DICKENSON V  (D
BARRY TALLMAN    HRNS (D  DAVID DOBBS     HRNS (D JEAN PIERRE GALIPEAU HRNS(D
```

```
                                 (A) A WORLD APART     1981 POSHBOY    US          108
```

```
J D CROWE        BAN V (A        (A) THE NEW SOUTH      19   ROUNDER    US          0044
TONY RICE        G V  (A
RICKY SKAGGS     MAND FDL(A  BOBBY SLONE     B    (A  JERRY DOUGLAS  DOB G(A
```

RODNEY CROWELL

RODNEY CROWELL	GV	(A	(A) AINT LIVING LONG LIKE THIS	1978	WB US BSK3228	UK	K 56564
LARRY LONDIN	D	(BC	(B) BUT WHAT WILL THE NEIGHBORS THINK	1980	WB US BSK3407	GERM	56776
EMORY GORDY	B	(ABC	(C) RODNEY CROWELL	1981	WB US BSK3587	UK	K 56934
ALBERT LEE	G V PNO	(ABC					

JAMES BURTON	G DOBRO(A	AMOS GARRETT	G	(AB	RY COODER	G	(A	JOHN WARE D	(A
HAL BLAINE	D	(A	JIM KELTNER	D	(A	EMMYLOU HARRIS	V G	(A	MAC REBENNACK K	(A
RICKY SKAGGS	FDL V(A	BYRON BERLINE	FDL	(A	BRIAN AHERN	G PERC(A	GLEN D HARDIN	PNO (A
JERRY JUMONVILLE	HRNS (A	RICHARD GREENE	STRINGS(A	HANK DEVITO	STEEL	(ABC MICKEY RAPHAEL HCA (A
NICOLETTE LARSON	V	(A	WILLIE NELSON	V	(A	LARRY WILLOUGHBY V	(ABC DONIVAN COWART V	(A
TOM SAUBER	BANJO(A	TONY BROWN	V	(BC	FRANK RECKARD	G	(B	STEVE WOOD	K V (B
DON WHALEY	G	(B	CRAIG LEON	PNO FLT(B	TOWER OF POWER	HRNS	(B	BOOKER T JONES K	(C
RICHARD BENNETT	G	(C	PHIL KENZIE SAX	(C	ROSEMARY BUTLER	V	(C	VINCE GILL	G V (C
ROSANNE CASH	V	(C	BILL LAMB	HRNS	(C				

CROWFOOT

RUSSELL DASHIELL	G K B V	(AB	(A) CROWFOOT	1970	PARAMOUNT	US	265
SAM McGUIRE	G V	(B	(B) FIND THE SUN	1971	ABC US ABCS745 UK PROBE 1042
DON FRANCISCO	D PERC V	(B					
RICK JAEGER	D	(A					

ARTHUR 'BIG BOY' CRUDUP

ARTHUR'BIG BOY' CRUDUP	(ALL	(A) LOOK ON YONDERS WALL	1968	DELMARK		DS	614
RANSOM KNOWLING	B	(AC	(B) MEAN OLE FRISCO	1969	TRIP	US	7501
EDWARD EL		(AC	(B) MEAN OLE FRISCO	1969	BLUE HORIZON	UK	763855
DAVE MYERS	B	(AC	(C) CRUDUPS MOOD	1970	DELMARK		DS	621
LAWRENCE 'JUDGE' RILEY	D(AC	(D) FATHER OF ROCK'N'ROLL	1971	RCA	UK	RD 8224
WILLIE DIXON	B	(C	(D) FATHER OF ROCK'N'ROLL	1971	RCA	US	573
			(E) ROEBUCK MAN	1974	LIBERTY	UK	UAS 29092
			(F) THATS ALL RIGHT MAMA	1976	DJM	UK	22025
			HARPIN' ON IT	197	POLYDOR		2941 001
			ARTHUR BIG BOY CRUDUP	19	FIRE	US	103

R CRUMB & THE CHEAP SUIT SERENADERS

R CRUMB	BANJO(AB	(A) CHEAP SUIT SERENADERS VOL 1	1974	BLUE GOOSE		BG 2014
ROBERT ARMSTRONG	G	(AB	(B) CHEAP SUIT SERENADERS VOL 2	1976	BLUE GOOSE		BG 2019
ALLAN DODGE	FDL MAND(AB	(C) CHEAP SUIT SERENADERS VOL 3	1978	BLUE GOOSE		BG 2025
TERRY ZWIGOFF	CELLO	(AB					

CRUSADERS

WILTON FELDER	SAX	(ALL	FREEDOM SOUND	1961	PACIFIC JAZZ		PJ 27
			LOOKING AHEAD	1962	PACIFIC JAZZ		PJ 43
JOE SAMPLE	K	(ALL	AT THE LIGHTHOUSE	1963	PACIFIC JAZZ		PJ 57
			TOUGH TALK	1963	PACIFIC JAZZ		PJ 58
LARRY CARLTON	G	(ABCDEFGHIN	HEAT WAVE	1965	PACIFIC JAZZ		PJ 87
STIX HOOPER	D	(ABCDEFGHIJKLNY	CHILE CON SOUL	1966	PACIFIC JAZZ		PJ 20092
			LIGHTHOUSE 66	1966	PACIFIC JAZZ		PJ 20098
WAYNE HENDERSON	TROM	(ABCDEFGY	TALK THAT TALK	1966	PACIFIC JAZZ		pj 20106
ROY GAINES	G	(	FESTIVAL JAZZ	1967	PACIFIC JAZZ		PJ 20115
JIMMY BOND	B	(Y	LIGHTHOUSE 68	1968	PACIFIC JAZZ		PJ 20131
JOE PASS	G	(Y	UH HAH	1968	PACIFIC JAZZ		PJ 20175
MONK MONTGOMERY	B	(Y	POWERHOUSE	1969	PACIFIC JAZZ		PJ 20136
LARRY GOSKIN		(	LIGHTHOUSE 69	1969	PACIFIC JAZZ		PJ 20165
BILLY ROGERS	G	(JK	BEST OF THE JAZZ CRUSADERS	1969	PACIFIC JAZZ		PJ 20175
POPS POPWELL	B	(GHIJ	GIVE PEACE A CHANCE	19	LIBERTY		LIB11005
ARTHUR ADAMS	G	(ABCGHK	(Y) YOUNG RABBITS	1976	BLUE NOTE UK BND4028 BNLA 530
MAX BENNETT	B	(C	OLD SOX NEW SHOES	19	CHISA		804
DAVID T WALKER	G	(ABN	OLD SOX NEW SHOES	1971	RARE EARTH	SRE	3001
DEAN PARKS	G	(JHLN	PASS THE PLATE	19	CHISA		807
PAULINHO DA COSTA	PERC	(JHLNK	HOLLY WOOD	1973	MOWEST		118
ROLAN BAUTISTA	G	(JHLK	HOLLYWOOD	1973	MOWEST		7004
CHUCK RAINEY	B	(A	AT THEIR BEST	19	MOWEST		796
BILL WITHERS	V	(L	(A) CRUSADERS (DBL)	1971 ABC		US	ABCD 609
RANDY CRAWFORD	V	(K	(A) CRUSADERS (DBL)	1971 BLUE THUMB US BTS6001 UK	ILPS 9218
VICTOR GASKIN	B	(Y	(B) SECOND CRUSADE (DBL)	1972 ABC ABCD 610	BTS 7000
LEROY VINNEGAR	B	(Y	(C) UNSUNG HEROES	1973 ABC ABCL 5180 BLUE THUMB BTS 6007
CHARLES WILLIAMS	B	(Y	(D) SCRATCH	1975 ABC ABCL 5181 BLUE THUMB BTS 6010
BOBBY HAYNES	B	(Y	(E) SOUTHERN COMFORT (DBL)	1975 ABC ABCD 607 BLUE THUMB BT 9002
CLARE FISCHER	K	(Y	(F) CHAIN REACTION	1975 ABC ABCL 5144 BLUE THUMB BT 6022
JOE COCKER	V	(N	(F) CHAIN REACTION	1981 MCA US 37147
CARLOS VIDAL	CONG	(Y	(G) THOSE SOUTHERN KNIGHTS	1976 ABC ABCL 5164 BLUE THUMB BTS 6024
BARRY FINNERTY	G	(NK	(G) THOSE SOUTHER KNIGHTS	1981 MCA US 37147
RALPH MACDONALD	PERC	(H	(H) FREE AS THE WIND	1977 ABC ABCL 5226 BLUE THUMB BT 6029
REGGIE YOUNG	G	(N	(H) FREE AS THE WIND	1981 MCA US 37073
ALPHONSO JOHNSON	B	(LK	(I) BEST OF THE CRUSADERS(DBL)	1976 ABC ABCD 612 BLUE THUMB BT 6027
STEVE GIBDON	G	(N	(I) BEST OF THE CRUSADERS(DBL)	1981 MCA US 26006 UK MCLD 602
BOB MANN	G	(L	(J) IMAGES	1978 ABC ABCL 5250 BLUE THUMB BT 6030
JON GOIN	G	(N	(J) IMAGES	1981 MCA UK 1625
HUBERT LAWS	FLT	(Y	(K) STREET LIFE	1979 MCA UK MCF 3008
AL McKIBBON	B	(Y	(L) RHAPSODY & BLUES	1980 MCA UK MCG 4010
HUNGRIA GARCIA	PERC	(Y	(M) ONGAKU KAI/LIVE IN JAPAN	1981 CRUSADERS US 16002
PHIL UPCHURCH	G	(L	(N) STANDING TALL	1981 MCA UK 3122 US 5254
JAMES JAMERSON	B	(K	(O) ROYAL JAM	1982 MCA UK 455
SHEILA ESCOVEDO	PERC	(L					

ABRAHAM LABORIEL	B	(L	RALF RICKERT	TPT	(L	MARCUS MILLER	B	(N
LOUIS JOHNSON	B	(N	BILLY PRESTON	K	(N	MAXINE WILLARD	V	(N
JULIA TILLMAN	V	(N	STEPHANIE SPRUILL	V	(N	ROBERT OBRYAN	TPT	(K
OSCAR BRASHEAR	TPT	(K	JEROME RICHARDSON	SAX	(K	BILL GREEN	SAX	(K
GARNETT BROWN	TROM	(K	PAUL M JACKSON	G	(K			

(NOTE) RECORDS BEFORE (A) ARE BY THE JAZZ CRUSADERS

C241A   CRYAN SHAMES   C241A
    JIM FAIRS   G B FLT(AB (A) A SCRATCH IN THE SKY   1967 CBS   US   2786
    DENNIS CONROY   D   (AB   (A) A SCRATCH IN THE SKY   1967 CBS   US   9586
    TOM DOODY   V   (AB   (B) SUGAR & SPICE   1966 CBS   US 2589 9389
    LENNY KERLEY   G B V (A   (C) SYNTHESIS   1968 CBS   US   9719
    ISAAC GUILLORY B G K (A
    J C HOOKE   PERC V(A   JIM PILSTER   TAMB (B   JERRY STONE   G   (B
    DAVE PURPLE   K B   (B
C241B   CRYSTAL MANSION   C241B
    ERIC FAULKNER   V   (A   (A) CRYSTAL MANSION FEATURING J CASWELL19 CAPITOL   US   SKAO 227
    JOHNNY CASWELL V PNO (A   (B) CRYSTAL MANSION   1971 RARE EARTH US   R540L
    JERRY MARLOW   B   (A
    RONNIE GENTILE G B   (A   RICKEY MORLEY   D   (A   DAVE WHITE   PNO V   (A
    SAN ROTA   K   (MARIO SANCHEZ   V PERC (BILL CRAWFORD B   (
C241C   THE CRY   C241C
    ROBBO MACPHERSON K V (A   (A) THE CRY   1980 RCA   0368
    GARY SCROTTON   G   (A
    KIMALL FOX   V   (A   BILL WADE   D   (A   BRIAN WHITTY   B   (A
C241D   CRY FREEDOM   C241D
    GERHARD BILLMAN K SYN (ABC (A) VOLCANO   1976 ?   GER   66 21313
    DIETER URBASSIK SAX   (A   (B) SUNNY DAY   1979 ERLKONIG   GER 148 408
    RUDI MADSIUS   G V   (ABC (C) NOBODY'S FOOL   1980 ERLKONIG   GER 148 416
    KLAUS KUKLA   B   (A
    HELMUT KORBER   B   (BC   KLAUS BRAUN   D   (ABC JAMES T DURHAM SAX PERC(BC
    OLDERS FRENZEL PERC (C
C241E   CRYERS   C241E
                            (A) CRYERS   1979 MERCURY   US   3734
                            (B) TELL ME YOUR DREAMS   1980 MERCURY   US   3785

C241F   CRYSTAL GRASS   C241F
                            (A) CRYSTAL WORLD   1974 POLYDOR US PD6516 UK 2391 185
C242   CRYSTALS   C242
    MARY THOMAS   V   (WALL OF SOUND VOL3 THE CRYSTALS 1975 PHIL SPECTOR   2307 006
    DEE DEE KENNIEBREW V   (HES A REBEL   196   LONDON 8120 PHILLES   4001
    LALA BROOKS   V   (TWIST UPTOWN   196   PHILLES   4000
    BARBARA ALSTON   V   (GREATEST HITS   196   PHILLES   4003
    VICKI ALSTON   V   (
    PAT WRIGHT   V   (
C242A   CUBAN HEELS   C242A
    LUURIE CUFFE   (A   (A) WORK OUR WAY TO HEAVEN   1981 VIRGIN UK2210 GER   204064
    NICK CLARK   (A
    JOHN MILARKY   (A
    ALI MACKENZIE   (A
C243   CUBY & THE BLIZZARDS   C243
    HARRY'CUBY'MUSKEE PROD V HCA(ALL (A) DESOLATION   1966 PHILIPS UK SBL7874 NL 6440 309RI
    EELCO GELLING   G   (ABDGHIKMQ (B) WITH REGARDS FROM GROLLO 1967 PHILIPS NL 6343 227 6440 310RI
    HANS KINDS   G   (AFMBQ   (B) WITH REGARDS FROM GROLLO 1967 PHILIPS   855 040
    WILLY MIDDEL   B   (ABDFMQ   (B) GROETEN UIT GROLLO   1967 PHILIPS   9286 131
    HENK HILBRANDIE PNO (AQ   (C) TRIPPIN'THRU' A MIDNIGHT BLUES 1967 PHILIPS   NL 6343 228
    EDDIE BOYD   PNO (D   (D) PRAISE THE BLUES   1968 PHILIPS NL 6440 308RI
    HERMAN BROOD   K V (BCSFGMOPQ (D) PRAISE THE BLUES   1968 PHILIPS   US   665 033
    JAAP VAN EIK   B   (CDFGPQ   (E) SOUL   1968
    DICK BEEKMAN   D   (CFGPQ   (F) BEST OF (66 68)   1968 PHILIPS   NL 6677 023
    EDWARD NINCK BLOK TPT (C   (G) LIVE   1968 PHILIPS NL 6440 091 6440 307RI
    ROEL HEMMES   SAX (C   (G) LIVE   1968 PHILIPS US   600   307
    JEUNE MEINEMA   SAX (C   (H) APPLEKNOCKERS FLOPHOUSE   1969 PHILIPS   UK SBL 7918
    ALEXIS KORNER   G V (G   (H) APPLEKNOCKERS FLOPHOUSE   1969 PHILIPS   NL 6430 0167
    HELMIG VANDER VEGT K (HIKLPQ (I) TOO BLIND TO SEE   1969 PHILIPS RI   NL 6440 312
    HERMAN DEINUM   B   (BHIKLPQ (I) TOO BLIND TO SEE   1969 PHILIPS   NL 6413 002
    BAS MUNNINKSNA WIND (I   (J) KING OF THE WORLD   1970 PHILIPS   NL 6314 002
    RUDI VAN DIJK   SAX (J   (J) KING OF THE WORLD   1970 PHILIPS US   600 331
    FRANK NUYENS   G   (NO   (K) SIMPLE MAN   1971 PHILIPS   NL 6413 014
    LOURENS LEEUW   B   (NO   (K) SIMPLE MAN   1971 PHILIPS   NL 6440 306
    HERMAN VAN BOEYEN D (N   (L) SOMETIMES   1972 PHILIPS   NL 6413 026
    GEORGE KOOYMANS G V (N   (L) SOMETIMES   1972 PHILIPS   NL 6440 311
    ROBERT JAN STIPS K   (N   (M) AFSCHEIDSCONCERT   1974 PHILIPS   NL 6343 229
    EGON JANSEB   PERC (N   (N) RED WHITE BLUE   1975 POLYDOR   NL 2925 034
    MELS BOL   D   (O   (N) RED WHITE BLUE   1975 VERTIGO   NL 6360 631
    MAGGIE McNEAL   V   (O   (O) KID BLUE   1976 CNR   NL   660 002
    JAN GROENONK   D   (R   (O) KID BLUE   1976 INTERCORD   GER 145 604
    MARGRIET ESHUIS V   (O   (P) OLD TIMES GOOD TIMES   1977 PHILIPS   NL 6416 111
    NEPPY NOYA   PERC (O   (Q) FORGOTTEN TAPES   1977 PHILIPS   NL 6401 107
    JAN SCHUURMAN   PERC (O   (R) LOVE VENDETTA(HARRY MUSKEE BAND) 1977 NEGRAM   NL   NN3
    ROB HOEKE   PNO (P   (S) LIVE FEATURING HERMAN BROOD 1979 MELODY EXPRESS NL ME1
    MARTIN VAN DIJK PNO (R
    BERNARD PEINKE G   (R   PIET VAN BLAUW   D   (R   HANS WATERMAN D   (AQ
    HANS LAFAILLE   D   (HIKQ
C243A   RON CUCCIA   C243A
    RON CUCCIA   (A   (A) MUSIC FROM THE BIG APPLE 1981 ARMAGEDDON UK 10 US OBLIQUE 10
C243B   CUDDLY TOYS   C243B
                            (A) GUILLOTINE THEATRE   1980 FRESH   UK   LP 1
                            (EP) CUDDLY TOYS   1981 FRESH
                            (B) TRAILS & LOSSES   1981 ?
C243C   CULPEPER   C243C
    GARY CY NICKLIN G V PERC(AB (A) CULPEPER'S ORCHARD   1971 POLYDOR   GER   2380 006
    NIELS HENDRIKSEN G K V(A   (B) ALL DRESSED UP & NOWHERE TO GO 1977 SONET   SLP 1558
    MICHAEL FRILE   B K FLT(A
    RODGER BARKER   D   (A   TOM MCEWAN   D   (B   TOM PUGGAARD-MULLER G   (B

[141]

CULT

THE MAIL MUST GO THROUGH   19   STARBURST   US   SLT   500

CULTURE

```
JOSEPH HILL          V   (ABCDE    (A) 2 7S CLASH            1978 LIGHTNING         UK        LIP1
KENNETH LLOYD DAYES  V   (ABCDE    (B) AFRICA STAND ALONE    1978 APRIL             ADI       735
ALBERT WALKER        V   (ABCDE    (C) HARDER THAN THE REST  1978 FRO'T LINE        UK        FL1016
ROBBIE SHAKESPEARE   B   (ACD      (D) CUMBOLO               1979 FRONT LINE        UK        FL1040
ANSEL COLLINS        K   (CD       (E) INTERNATIONAL HERB    1979 FRONT LINE        UK        FL1047
EARL WIRE LINDO      K   (CD       (F) BALDHEAD BRIDGE       1980 LASER             UK        LASL 7
WILLIE LINDO         G   (CD       (G) VITAL SECTION         1981 VIRGIN            UK        V 1001
RANCHIE              G   (CD       ( ) CULTURE               1981 JOE GIBBS         US        6038
SLY DUNBAR           D   (ACD
STICKY               PERC (ACD DAVID MADDEN    TPT (CD  VIN GORDON      TROM (ACD ERROL NELSON     K(A
CEDRIC BROOKS        SAX (CD  ERIC LAMONT    G   (A   FELIX HEADLEY   SAX (CD  LENNOX GORDON   (A
LLOYD PARKS          B   (A   HERMAN MARQUIS SAX (A   FRANKLIN WAUL   K   (A   BOBBY ELLIS     TPT(A
TOMMY McCOOK         SAX (A   KEN PALEY      V   (D   MICHAEL RICHARD D   (D   RADCLIFFE BRYAN G  (D
HAROLD BUTLER        K   (D   CLIVE HUNT              SAX (D
```

BURTON CUMMINGS

```
BURTON CUMMINGS      K V (ALL     (A) BURTON CUMMINGS      1976 PORTRAIT UK 81573  US 34261
DICK WAGNER          G   (C       (B) MY OWN WAY TO ROCK   1977 PORTRAIT UK 82012  US 34698
RANDY BACHMAN        G V (BC      (C) DREAM OF A CHILD     1978 PORTRAIT UK 82962  US 35481
TREVOR LAWRENCE      SAX (B       (D) SWEET SWEET          1981 ALFA              US 11007
IAN GARDINER         B   (BC
JIM GORDON           D   (C   JEFF BAXTER     G   (C   BOBBY KING       V   (B   E L KING        V (B
RICK SCHLOSSER       (BC  TERRY EVANS     V   (B   PHYLLIS ST JAMES PERC (BC  STEVE MADAIO    HRNS(C
BECKY LOPEZ          V   (C   VANETTA FIELDS  V   (B   PLAS JOHNSON    SAX (C   SHIRLEY MATTHEWS V (C
JIMMY PHILLIPS       K SYN(BC  JEFF PORCARO    D   (BC  JIM HORN        SAX (BC  DANNY WEIS      G (B
LENNY CASTRO         PERC (B   RAY PARKER      G   (B   SCOTT EDWARDS   B   (B   OLLIE E BROWN   D (B
```

RICK CUNHA

```
RICK CUNHA           G V (AB      (A) CUNHA SONGS         1973 GRC               US  GA  5004
JERRY CARRIGAN       D   (A       (B) MOVING PICTURES     1977 CBS               US      33697
TOMMY COGBILL        B   (A
JOE OSBORN           B   (A   BILL CUNNINGHAM (A   LARRY MUHOBERAC  (A   REGGIE YOUNG    G (A
LARRY CARLTON        G   (A   JEFF GILKENSON  (A   DON BROOKS      HCA (A   DAVID BRIGGS    K (A
JOHN GUERIN          (A   WAYLON JENNINGS (A   CATES SISTERS   (A   WELDON MYRICK     (A
GARY SCRUGGS         (A   NASHVILLE EDITION (A  DAVID DAWSON    (A   RANDY SCRUGGS     (A
STEVE NORMAN         (A   DONNA WEISS     (A   DONNA WASHBURN  (A
```

CURE

```
ROBERT SMITH         G   (ABCD    (A) THREE IMAGINARY BOYS      1979 FICTION         UK       FIX001
MATHIEU HARTLEY      K   (B       (B) SEVENTEEN SECONDS        1980 FICTION         UK       FIX004
LAURENCE TOLHURST    D   (ABCD    (C) BOYS DONT CRY           1980 FICTION UK FIX005 US PVC 7916
SIMON GALLUP         B   (B       (D) FAITH                   1981 FICTION UK FIX006 US 2383 605
MICHAEL DEMPSEY      B   (ACD     (BD) HAPPILY EVER AFTER (DBL) 1981 A&M      US 6020
CHRIS PARRY          K   (CD
MIKE HEDGES          PROD (B
```

CURFEW

(A) LET THERE BE DARK   19   UA   US   6746

CURLY CURVE

```
MARTIN KNADEN        G   (A       (A) CURLY CURVE        1974 BRAIN        GER      1040
KURT HERKENBERG      B V (A
CHRIS AXEL KLOBER    K   (A   HANNO BRUHN  G V (A  HANS WALLBAUM     D   (A
```

PAT CUPP & HIS FLYING SAUCERS

PAT CUPP   (A   (A) MODERN ROCKABILLY   1981 ACE 10"   CH 32

CHERIE CURRIE

```
CHERIE CURRIE        V   (A       (A) BEAUTY'S ONLY SKIN DEEP   197 MERCURY
MARIE CURRIE         K V (A
STEPHAN T            (G V (A   SAL MAIDA    B   (A   MIKE BAIRD      D   (A   WILLIE ORNELAS  D (A
MOOSE McCAINS        B V (A   BILLY THOMAS D   (A   THOM ROTELLA    G   (A   DAN FERGUSON    G (A
DAVID HUNGATE        B   (A
```

CHERIE & MARIE CURRIE

```
CHERIE CURRIE        V   (A       (A) MESSIN' WITH THE BOYS     1980 CAPITOL        ST  12022
MARIE CURRIE         V   (A
MIKE BAIRD           D   (A   MIKE PORCARO    B   (A   STEVE LUKATHER  G   (A   JOEY BRASLER    G (A
JAI WINDING          K SYN(A   TREVOR VEITCH   G   (A   BOBBY KIMBALL   V   (A   BILL CHAMPLIN   V (A
TOM KELLY            V   (A   MICHAEL BODDICKER SYN (A TOM WERMAN      TAMB (A  KEITH LANDRY    V (A
TOM FUNDERBUNK       V   (A   BILLY BIZEAU    G   (A   WADDY WACHTEL   G   (A   JON PIERCE      B (A
MIKE LANDAU          G   (A
```

TIM CURRY

```
TIM CURRY            V   (ABC     (A) READ MY LIPS       1978 A&M US 4717  UK  AMLH64717
DICK WAGNER          G   (B       (B) FEARLESS          1979 A&M US 4773  UK  AMLH64773
MICHAEL KAMEN        K   (B       (C) SIMPLICITY        1981 A&M US 4830  UK  AMLH64830
BOB BABITT           B   (B
JIN MAELEN           PERC (B   CHARLES COLLINS D   (B   DAVID LASLEY    V   (B   ARNOLD McCULLER V (B
ULA HEDWIG           V   (B   BOB KULICK      G   (B   BETTE SUSSMAN   K   (B   MICHAEL TSCHUDIN SYN(B
DAVE SANBORN         SAX (B   ALLEN SCHWARZBERG D  (B
```

LITTLE JOE CURTIS

```
LITTLE JOE CURTIS    V   (A       (A) LITTLE JOE CURTIS  19   MARBLE ARCH       MAL 772
                                  (B) SOUL              19   ALSTON            5082
```

MAC CURTIS

```
MAC CURTIS           V   (ALL     (A) GOOD ROCKIN TOMORROW  19   ROLLIN ROCK   US   LP007
                                  (B) RUFFABILLY           19   ROLLIN ROCK   US   LP002
                                  (C) SUNSHINE MAN         19   EPIC          US   26419
                                  (D) ROCKABILLY KINGS     1974 POLYDOR       UK   2310 293
                                  (E) ROCKIN' MOTHER       1979 RADAR         UK   RAD22
```

SONNY CURTIS

```
SONNY CURTIS         G V (ALL     (A) BEATLE HITS FLAMENCO STYLE GUITAR 1964 IMPERIAL   US      12276
                                  (B) 1ST OF SONNY CURTIS       1968 VIVA      US  V  36012
                                  (c) SONNY CURTIS STYLE        1969 VIVA      US  V  36021
                                  (D) SONNY CURTIS             1979 ELEKTRA   US UK   6E227
                                  (E) LOVE IS ALL AROUND       1980 ELEKTRA   US       6E283
```

CURTISS A

CURTISS A — C250C

| | | | (A) COURTESY | | | 1980 | TWIN TONE | US | | 8015 |

```
CURTISS A            V    (A
TOM BURNEVIK         SAX  (A
DALE STRENGTH        G V  (A       DAVE AHL        D    (A    MARK GOLDSTEIN    K   (A
FRANK BERRY          G    (A       BILLY STEINER   HCA  (A    BOB STRENGTH      V   (A
RENALDO TORO         B    (A       BART HAZLETT    D    (A    BUZZ BARKER       G   (A
```

CURVED AIR — C251

```
SONJA KRISTINA          V    (ABCDEFG   (A) AIR CONDITIONING        1970  WB US 1903    UK  K   56004
FLORIAN PILKINGTON MIKSA D(ABCE        (A) AIR CONDITIONING        1970  WB PIC DISC           3012
FRANCIS MONKMAN         K    (ABCE      (B) SECOND ALBUM           1971  WB US 1951    UK  K   46092
DARYL WAY               VLN  (ABCEFG    (C) PHANTASMAGORIA         1972  WB US 2628    UK  K   46158
KIRBY                   G    (D         (D) AIR CUT               1973  WB            UK  K   46224
JIM RUSSELL             PERC (D         (E) LIVE                  1975  DECCA UKSML119 US  BTM  5001
STEWART COPELAND        D    (FG        (F) MIDNIGHT WIRE         1975  BTM           UK  BTM 1005
MIKE JACQUES            G    (FG        (G) AIRBORNE              1976  BTM           UK  BTM 1008
PHILIP KOHN             B G  (E         ( ) BEST OF               1976  WB                K   36015
TONY REEVES             B    (G         ( ) CURVED AIR            197   MIDI          UK      20021
HENRY LOWTHER           HRNS (G
COLIN CALDWELL          PERC (C     ALEX RICHARDSON   K     (      JEAN AKERS       PERC (C
MAL LINWOOD ROSE        PERC (C     STEVE SAUNDERS    TROM  (C     DAVID PARKER     TROM (C
ALAN GOUT               TROM (C     CHRIS PYNE        TROM  (C     FRANK RICOTTI    PERC (CG
JACK EMBLOW             ACC  (G     BOB SARGEANT      K     (C     ANNIE STEWART    FLT  (C
CRISPIAN STEEL PERKINS TPT(C        JIM WATSON        TPT   (C     PAUL KOSH        TPT  (C
GEORGE PARNABY          TPT  (C     JOHN PERRY        B     (F     PETER WOOD       K    (F
DEREK DAMAIN            V    (F     ROBIN LUMLEY      PNO   (G     ALAN SKIDMORE    SAX  (G
IAN EYRE                B    (AB    MIKE WEDGEWOOD    B     (CD
```

CURVES — C251A

| | | | (A) CURVES | | | 1981 | LIBERTY | US | | LT 1111 |

IAN CUSSICK — C251B

| | | | (A) IAN CUSSICK | | | 1978 | METRONOME | GER | | 60101 |

```
IAN CUSSICK          B V  (A
PETER FRANKEN        D    (A
PETER WEIHE          G    (A       CLAUS KRUSE     K    (A    LEMMY LEMBRECHT   PERC (A
SIGURD SCHMIDT       G    (A       WOLFGANG SCHLUTER PERC (A    GARY L TODD      B   (A
```

IVOR CUTLER — C252

			WHO TORE YOUR TROUSERS			19	DECCA			LK 4405
			LUDO			19	DECCA			
			DANDRUFF			1974	VIRGIN		V	2021
			VELVET DONKEY			1975	VIRGIN		V	2037
			JAMMY SMEARS			1976	VIRGIN		V	2065
			LIFE IN A SCOTCH SITTING ROOM			1978	HARVEST			SHSP4084

```
IVOR CUTLER          V K  (ALL
```

CYANIDE — C253

| | | | (A) CYANIDE | | | 1978 | PYE | UK | | NSPL18554 |

```
BOB DE VRIES         V    (A
DAVE STEWART         G    (A
DAVE THOMPSON        B    (A       MICK STEWART    D    (A
```

JOHN L CYBORG — C253A

| | | | (A) SATORI & THE FLOWER TRAVELLING BAND | 198 | GTR | CAN | 9230 1005 |

```
JOHN L CYBORG        SYNS (A
AKISI YAMANAKA       V    (A
MASANI WADA          D    (A       HIDEKI SHIMA    G    (A    SHIGEYUKI KOBAYASHI B  (A
```

CYMANDE — C254

			(A) CYMANDE			1973	JANUS	US	JSL	3044
			(A) CYMANDE			1973	ALASKA		ALKA	100
			(B) SECOND TIME AROUND			1973	JANUS	US	JLS	3054
			(C) PROMISED HEIGHTS			1974	CONTEMPO		CLP	508

```
RAY KING             V PERC(A
PETER SERREO         SAX  (A
MIKE ROSE      WIND PERC  (A
PABLO GONSALES       CONGA (A
SAM KELLY            D    (A
JOEY DEE             V PERC(A
PATRICK PATTERSON    G    (A       DEREK GIBBS     SAX  (A    STEVE SCIPIO      B  (A
```

CYMARRON — C254A

| | | | (A) RINGS | | | 1971 | ENTERPRISE | US | | 30962 |

CYMBELINES — C254B

| | | | (A) CYMBELINES   (EP) | | | 19 | TORCH | UK | | TOR07 |

CYRKLE — C255

			(A) RED RUBBER BALL			1966	CBS MONO	US		2544
			(A) RED RUBBER BALL			1966	CBS	STEREO		9344
			(B) NEON			1967	CBS MONO	US		2632
			(B) NEON			1967	CBS	STEREO		2977
			(B) NEON			1967	CBS	UK		62977

```
TOM DAWES       SITAR G B (AB
MICHAEL LOSEKAMP     K    (AB
MARTY FRIED          D PERC(AB
DON DANNEMAN         G    (AB
BOBBY GREGG          PERC (B
BUDDY SALZMAN        PERC (B
JOHN SIMON           K    (B       RAY BARRETTO    PERC  (B
```

CYRUS — C255A

| | | | (A) CYRUS | | | 1971 | ELEKTRA | US | | 74105 |

HOLGER CZUKAY — C256

			(A) MOVIES			1979	HARVEST		EUR	45754
			(A) MOVIES			1979	EMI	UK	EMC	3319
			(B) ON THE WAY TO THE PEAK OF NORMAL	19	WELT	GER		46400

```
HOLGER CZUKAY   V G K SYN(AB
JAKI LIEBEZEIT       D    (AB
MICHAEL KAROLI       G    (A
IRMIN SCHMIDT        PNO  (A
REBOP KWAKU BAAH     PERC (A       JAH WOBBLE      B    (B
```

CZUKAY, WOBBLE & LIEBEZEIT — C257

| | | | (A) 4 TITLE EP | | | 1981 | EMI | GER | | 64419 |

```
HOLGER CZUKAY        G K HRNS(A
```

D C NIGHTHAWKS — D1

| | | | (A) THE D C NIGHTHAWKS | | | 1980 | MERCURY | | | 6337 111 |

D F K BAND — D1A

| | | | (A) SPECIAL TOUR SAMPLER | | | 1978 | CBS | US | | AS430 |
| | | | (B) DFK BAND | | | 1979 | CBS | US | | 35770 |

```
LES DUDEK            G    (AB
MIKE FINNIGAN        K    (AB
JIM KRUEGER          G    (AB
MAX GRONENTHAL       K    (AB    TREY THOMPSON   B    (AB   MIKE HOSSACK      D  (A
BILL MEEKER          D    (AB    BOBBYE HALL     PERC (B    JAMES NEWTON HOWARD K (B
```

D M Z

RICK CORACCIO	B	(A	(A) DMZ	1978 SIRE SRK 6051
PAUL MURPHY	D	(A	(1) 1976	
JAY RASSLER	G	(A1		
PETER GREENBERG	G	(A1	DAVE ROBINSON D (1	MONO MANN V K PERC(1
MIKE LEWIS	B	(1		

DBs

PETER HOLSAPPLE	G V	(AB	(A) STANDS FOR DECIBELS	1981 ALBION UK 105
CHRIS STAMEY	G V	(AB	(B) REPERCUSSION	1981 ALBION CASS 109
WILL RIGBY	D	(AB		
GENE HOLDER	B	(AB	JOHN EARLE SAX (B	ANDY CLARK K (B
DICK HANSEN	TPT	(B	CHRIS GOWER TROM (B	ALAN BETROCK PROD(A
SCOTT LITT	PROD	(B		

D V C

JOHN BOLIN	D	(A	(A) DVC	1981 ALFA US AAB 11005
MAX PADILLA	B V	(A		
JOHN BARTLE	G V	(A	ROB FOREST G V (A	

MICHAEL D'ABO

MICHAEL D'ABO	V K	(ALL	(A) D'ABO	1970 UNI 6369 601
WITH			(A) D'ABO	1970 MCA MAPS 2040
GRAHAM NASH	V	(C	(B) DOWN AT RACHEL'S PLACE	1972 A&M US 4363 UK AMLH68097
DENNY SEIWELL		(C	(B) DOWN AT RACHEL'S PLACE	1972 RCA FR SP 4346
MIKE BLOOMFIELD	G	(C	(C) BROKEN RAINBOWS	1974 A&M US 3634 UK AMLH63634
TEDDY IRWIN		(C	(D) SMITH & D'ABO	1976 CBS uk 81583
RAB NOAKES		(C	(1) TOURING BAND 1971 ??	
JACK LANCASTER	SAX	(D	(E) GULLIVERS TRAVELS	19 INSTANT INLP 003
TONY	V	(A		
GARY TAYLOR	B	(C	MARK NAFTALIN K (C	JORDANAIRES V (C
BOBBY THOMPSON		(C	BEN KEITH (C	MO FOSTER B (B1
GRANT SERPELL	D	(B1	JIMMY ROBERTSON ACC (B	MIKE MORAN K (B
MIKE JOPP		(B1	JOHN KONGOS G (B	RAY COOPER PERC (B
LYN DOBSON	HCA FLT SAX	(B	MIKE LENTIN G (B	KEITH CHRISTIE TROM (B
ALBERT LEE	G	(A	CHRIS SPEDDING G (A	PAT DONALDSON B (A
ROY BABBINGTON	B	(A	GERRY CONWAY D (B	JOHN MARSHALL D (A
MATTHEW	HCA	(A	LEW WARBURTON STRINGS	MIKE LEANDER STRING(A
SUE GLOVER	V	(A	SUNNY LESLIE V (A	DORIS TROY V (A
NANETTE	V	(A	HUGH V (A	JOHN NEIL V (A

PAULINHO DACOSTA

PAULINHO DACOSTA	PERC V	(A	(A) AGORA	1977 POLYDOR UK 2335 747
			(B) HAPPY PEOPLE	1979 POLYDOR UK 2312 102

DADA

ELKIE BROOKS	V	(A	(A) DADA	1970 ATCO 2400 030
ROBERT PALMER	V	(		
PAUL KORDA	V	(A	JIMMY CHAMBERS V PERC (A	MARTYN HARRYMAN D (A
ERNIE LAUCHLAN	HRNS	(A	PETE GAGE G B (A	BARRY DUGGAN WIND (A
STEVE YORK	B	(	DON SHINN K (A	MALCOLM CAPEWELL WIND (A

DADDY COOL

ROSS WILSON	HCA G V	(ABC	(A) DADDY COOL	1971 REPRISE US 6471
ROSS HANNAFORD	G V	(ABC	(B) TEENAGE HEAVEN	1972 REPRISE US 2088
WAYNE DUNCAN	B V	(ABC	(C) LIVE	1972 WIZARD US 202
GARY YOUNG	D V	(ABC		
IAN WINTERS	G	(BC	DAVE BROWN WIND (A	ROBIE PORTER K STEEL(A
JERRY NOONE	SAX K	(B		

DADDY LONGLEGS

KURT PALOMAKI	B V CLAR	(ABC	(A) DADDY LONGLEGS	1970 WB UK 3004
CLIFF CARRISON	D	(ABCD	(B) OAKDOWN FARM	1971 VERTIGO UK 6360 038
STEVE HAYTON	G V	(AC	(C) THREE MUSICIANS	1972 POLYDOR UK 2371 261
MOE ARMSTRONG	V	(A	(D) SHIFTING SANDS	1972 POLYDOR UK 2371 323
STEVE MILLER	K	(AC		
IVAN CHANDLER	K	(C	GARY NORTON HOLDERMAN G V (BD	PETER ARNESEN K (BC

PATTI DAHLSTROM

PATTI DAHLSTROM	V	(ABCD	(A) THE WAY I AM	1973 20th CENTURY US T 421
LARRY KNECHTEL	K	(BC	(A) THE WAY I AM	1973 20th CENTURY CAN 9209 421
MICHAEL UTLEY	K	(B	(B) YOUR PLACE OR MINE	1975 20th CENTURY US T 461
ANDY CAHAN	K	(B	(C) LIVIN' IT THRU'	1976 20th CENTURY US T 521
GEORGE CLINTON	K	(B		
JACK CONRAD	B	(BC	DAVID HUNGATE B (B	KLAUS VOORMANN B (B
DAVID KEMPER	D	(B	GARY MALLABER D (B	JIM KELTNER D (B
DEAN PARKS	G	(B	AL STAEHELY G (B	ART MUNSON G (B
FRED TACKETT	G	(B	STEVE CROPPER G (B	JAY GRAYDON G (B
AL CASEY	G	(B	DAVID LINDLEY BANJ FDL L (B	NICK DE CARO ACC (B
JIM HORN	HRNS	(BC	CHUCK FINDLEY HRNS (BC	JACKIE KELSO HRNS (BC
LON VAN EATON	HRNS	(B		

DON DAILEY

DON DAILEY		(A	(A) SURF STOMPIN'	19 CROWN US CST 314

DAKOTA

JERRY HLUDZIK	G V	(A	(A) DAKOTA	1980 CBS US 36261
BILL KELLY	G V	(A		
JEFF MITCHELL	K V	(A	BILL McHALE B V (A	LOU COSSA K V (A

DAKOTAS

ROBIN McDONALD	G	(	(A) MEET THE DAKOTAS (EP)	196 PARLOPHONE GEP 888
MIKE MAXFIELD	G			
RAY JONES	B		TONY MANSFIELD D	

WES DAKUS & THE REBELS

WES DAKUS		WES DAKUS REBELS	19 KAPP US 3536
		WES DAKUS ALBUM	19 CAPITOL US 6120

DALEK 1

ALAN GILL	V SYN B	(A	(A) COMPASS	1980 BACK DOOR UK OPEN1
DAVE HUGHES		(A		
CHRIS HUGHES	B	(A	HUGH JONES D (A	DAVE BATES V (A

EARL DALEY

EARL '16' DALEY   (A   (A) REGGAE SOUND   1981   DREAD AT CONTROL   DCLP3
D7   MICHAEL D'ALBUQUERQUE   D7
MICHAEL D'ALBUQUERQUE G V K(AB   (A) WE MAY BE CATTLE BUT WEVE ALL GOT NAMES 1974 RCA   UK   SF 8383
FRANK RICOTTI   PERC SAX(AB (B) STALKING THE SLEEPER   1976 WB   UK   K 56276
OLLIE HALSALL   G V K (A
GORDON BECK   K   (A   CHRIS LAWRENCE   B   (A   BRIAN BENNETT   D   (A
B J COLE   STEEL (A   GERRY CONWAY   D   (A   STAN SALZMAN   SAX (A
CHRIS PINE   TROM (A   JOHN UCKERIDGE   TPT (A   HENRY LOWTHER   TPT (A
DAVID KATZ   STR (A   ROBIN SYLVESTER   B   (A   JOHN TAYLOR   K   (A
ALAN SKIDMORE   SAX (A
D7A   DALLAS COUNTY   D7A
                                 (A) DALLAS COUNTY   19   ENTERPRISE   US   1011
D8   KATHY DALTON   D8
KATHY DALTON   V   (A   (A) AMAZING   1973   DISCREET UK K59202 US DS2168
WITH   (A) BOOGIE BANDS & ONE NIGHT STANDS 1974 DISCREET   US   DS2208
LOWELL GEORGE   G V (A   (ONE TRACK DIFFERENT)
PAUL BARRERE   G   (A
BILL PAYNE   K   (A   SAM CLAYTON   PERC (A KENNY GRADNEY   B   (A RICHIE HAYWARD   D   (A
VAN DYKE PARKS   PNO V(A   SNEAKY PETE   STEEL(A CLYDIE KING   V   (A JIMMY GILSTRAP   V   (A
LOULIE JEAN NORMAN   V   (A   BILLY HINSCHE   V   (A CARL WILSON   V   (A JEAN JUDSON   V   (A
TONY MARTIN   V   (A   VANILLA GRITS   V   (A JOHN RAYFORD   HRNS (A GABRIEL FLEMMING HRNS(A
LARRY WILSON   HRNS (A   JIMMY REED   HRNS (A JAY MIGLIORI   HRNS (A ERIC HORD   G   (A
STAN AYEROFF   G   (A
D8A   DALTON BROTHERS   D8A
SCOTT ENGEL   V   (A   I ONLY CAME TO DANCE   1964 TOWER   UST5026
JOHN'MAUS' STEWART   V
D9   ROGER DALTREY   D9
ROGER DALTREY   V   (ALL   (A) DALTREY   1973   TRACK   UK   2406 207
WITH   (A) DALTREY   1973   POLYDOR   2409 202
RUSS BALLARD   V G (AB   (A) DALTREY   1973   MCA US 328 RI   37052
PADDY McHUGH   V   (B   (B) RIDE A ROCK HORSE   1975   POLYDOR   UK   2442 135
DYAN BIRCH   V   (B   (B) RIDE A ROCK HORSE   1975   MCA US 2147 RI   37030
FRANK COLLINS   V   (B   (C) ONE OF THE BOYS   1977   POLYDOR   UK   2441 146
DAVE WINTOUR   B   (AB   (C) ONE OF THE BOYS   1977   MCA US 2271 RI   37031
PHILIP GOODHAND TAIT PNO(B   (D) BEST OF   1981   POLYDOR   UK   2490 162
CLEM CLEMPSON   G   (B   (E) McVICAR(SOUNDTRACK)   19   POLYDOR GER 2303 102 US 6284
HENRY SPINETTI   D   (B
ALAN BROWN   (B   STEWART FRANCIS   D   (B DAVE COURTNEY PNO (A BOB HENRIT   D   (A
DAVE ARBUS   VLN (A B J COLE   STEEL   (A ROY YOUNG BAND HRNS (A BRIAN ODGERS B   (C
JOHN ENTWISTLE   B   (CE STUART TOSH   D   (C JIMMY McCULLOCH G   (C PAUL KEOGH   G   (C
ROD ARGENT   K   (C PHIL KENZIE   SAX (C JIMMY JEWELL   SAX (C TONY RIVERS   V   (C
JOHN PERRY   V   (C STUART CALVER   V   (C KENNY JONES   D   (E STUART ELLIOTT D (E
DAVE MATTACKS   D   (E HERBIE FLOWERS   B   (E DAVE MARKEE   B   (E RICKY HITCHCOCK G (E
BILLY NICHOLS   G   (E KEN FREEMAN K SYN   (E FRANK RICOTTI PERC (E TONY CARR   PERC (E
RON ASPERY   FLT (E
D9A   DAMNATION   D9A
ADAM BLESSING   V   (ABC   (A)WHICH IS THE JUSTICE   1971   UA US   UAS 5533
JIM QUINN   G V PERC(ABC (B) SECOND DAMNATION   19   UA US   UAS 6773
BOB KAFAMASZ   G V (ABC   (C) THE DAMNATION OF ADAM BLESSING 19 UA US   UAS 6738
RAY BENICK   B   (ABC
BILL SCHWARK   D   (ABC KEN CONSTABLE   (A
D10   DAMNED   D10
DAVE VANIAN   V   (ABCD   (A) DAMNED DAMNED DAMNED   1977   STIFF   UK   SEEZ1
BRIAN JAMES   G V (AB   (B) MUSIC FOR PLEASURE   1977   STIFF   UK   SEEZ5
CAPTAIN (RAY BURNS)SENSIBLE GB(ABCD (C) MACHINE GUN ETIQUETTE   1979   CHISWICK   UK   CWK 3011
RAT SCABIES(CHRIS MILLAR)D (ABCD (D) THE BLACK ALBUM   1980   CHISWICK UK 3015 IRS NL 70012
PAUL GREY   B   (D   (E) BEST OF   1981   ACE   UK   DAM1
NICK LOWE   PROD(A
ROBERT 'LU'EDMUNDS   G   (B LOL COXHILL SAX   (B JOHN MOSS   D   (ALGY WARD   B (C
ROMAN JUGG   K   (
D10A   DANCE BAND   D10A
LOU STONEBRIDGE   V G (A   (A) FANCY FOOTWORK   1980   DOUBLE D   UK   DDLP1
STEVE VANDELLER   G   (A
ROB TOWNSEND   D   (A STEVE MULLENS   B   (A PETER HOPE EVANS HCA (A
DICK HANSON   TPT (A JOHN IRISH EARLE SAX (A
D10B   THE DANCE   D10B
                                 (A) IN LUST   1981   STATIK   UK   LP 3
D11   DANDO SHAFT   D11
MARTIN JENKINS   V MAND VLN(ABCD (A) AN EVENING WITH DANDO SHAFT 1970 YOUNGBLOOD UK   SSYB6
POLLY BOLTON   V   (BCD   (A) AN EVENING WITH DANDO SHAFT 1970 DECCA   US   75217
DAVE COOPER   G V (ABCD   (B) DANDO SHAFT   1971   NEON   UK   NE5
KEVIN DEMPSEY   G V B(ABCD   (C) LANTALOON   1972   RCA UK   SF   8256
TED KAY   PERC(ABCD   (D) KINGDOM   1977   RUBBER   RUB RUB 034
ROGER BULLEN   B   (AB
PAUL DUNMALL   SAX (D TOMMY KEARTON   K   (D DANNY THOMPSON B   (D JON STEVENS   D (D
ROD CLEMENTS   B   (D
D11A   BARBARA DANE   D11A
BARBABRA DANE   V   (AB   (A)& THE CHAMBERS BROTHERS   19   FOLKWAYS   US   2468
                                 (B) SINGS THE BLUES   19   FOLKWAYS   US   2471
D11B   RODNEY DANGERFIELD   D11B
RODNEY DANGERFIELD   (AB   (A) NO RESPECT   1980   CASABLANCA US   7229
                                 (B) THE LOSER   1980   RHINO   US   012

CHARLIE DANIELS

```
CHARLIE DANIELS  G FDL V  (ALL      (A) TE JOHN,GREASE & WOLFMAN      1970  KAMA SUTRA   US        2060
WITH                                (A) TE JOHN,GREASE & WOLFMAN      1978  EPIC    RI   SU        34665
JOEL DIGREGORIO K V (ABCDEFGHIJKL1   (B) CHARLIE DANIELS             1970  CAPITOL US ST11414 RI 8116039
EARL'TE JOHN' GRIGSBY  B V(ABC       (C) HONEY IN THE ROCK          1970  KAMA SUTRA   US        2071
JEFF 'WOLFMAN' MYER  D    (AB        (D) WAY DOWN YONDER             1970  KAMA SUTRA   US        2076
BUDDY DAVIS       D       (CD        (D) WHISKEY                     1977  EPIC    RI   US        34664
FRED EDWARDS      D (CDEFGHI*JKL1    (E) FIRE ON THE MOUNTAIN        1975  KAMA SUTRA   US        2603
HOLLADAY SISTERS  V       (C         (E) FIRE ON THE MOUNTAIN        1975  KAMA SUTRA   UK        7007
TIM DRUMMOND      B       (B         (E) FIRE ON THE MOUNTAIN        1979  EPIC    RI   US        34365
MYLON LEFEVRE     V PERC(*           (E) FIRE ON THE MOUNTAIN        1981  EMBASSY      UK RI     31830
BILLY COX         B       (BD        (F) NIGHTRIDER                 1975  KAMA SUTRA   US        2607
KARL HIMMEL       D       (B         (F) NIGHTRIDER                 1975  KAMA SUTRA   UK        7009
BOB WILSON        K       (B         (F) NIGHTRIDER                 197   EPIC         US        34402
BEN KEITH         STEEL   (B         (G) SADDLE TRAMP               1976  EPIC         UK        81335
JERRY CORBITT     V G     (B         (G) SADDLE TRAMP               1976  EPIC         US        34150
BARRY BAINES      G V     (D         (H) UNEASY RIDER               197   EPIC         UK        34369
GARY ALLEN        D       (DE        (I) HIGH & LONESOME            1977  EPIC         US        34377
MARK FITZGERALD   B V     (DE        (I) HIGH & LONESOME            1977  EPIC         UK        81666
LEA JANE BERINATI V       (DK        (J) MIDNIGHT WIND              1977  EPIC         US        34970
TED REYNOLDS      D       (D         ( ) ESSENTIAL CHARLIE DANIELS  197   KAMA SUTRA   US      2/2612
CHARLIE HAYWARD   B    (FGHIJ*1KL    (*) VOLUNTEERS JAM             1976  CAPRICORN    UK   2429 143
DICKIE BETTS      G       (E*        ( ) VOLUNTEERS JAM 3/4         1978  EPIC         US   E2 35368
TOY CALDWELL      G STEEL (FGI*      ( ) VOLUNTEERS JAM    (EP)     197   KAMA SUTRA   US        EP10
JAMES MARSHALL    D       (1KL       (1) NOV 1979 GIG
MARIE CAIN        D                  (K) MILLION MILE REFLECTIONS   1979  EPIC US 35751 UK       83446
TOM CRAIN         G V  (FGHI*KL      (L) FULL MOON                  1980  EPIC US 36571 UK       84461
PAUL HORNSBY      K       (FG        ( ) VOLUNTEERS JAM VI          1980  EPIC         UK        22107
DON MURRAY        D       (FGHI
SHARON VAUGHN     D       (D    JAIMIE NICHOLS      PERC  (E*   GEORGE McCORKLE    G   (I*
BANJO BANJO       G       (E    JAI JOHNNY JOHANSON D    (FG   TOM CALDWELL       B   (*
DOUG GRAY         V PERC(*      JERRY EUBANKS       SAX   (*    PAUL RIDDLE       D   (*
CHUCK LEAVELL     PNO     (*    JIMMY HALL          HCA   (*    DAVID BROWN       B   (*
GARY PEACEMAKER   D       (*    RONNIE STONEMAN     BANJO (*
(*) NOT STRICTLY CHARLIE DANIELS ALBUMS BUT HES ON EVERY TRACK.
```

PHIL DANIELS & THE CROSS

```
PHIL DANIELS      G V     (A         (A) PHIL DANIELS & THE CROSS   1980  RCA          UK  PL 25259
JOHN McWILLIAMS   D       (A
BARRY NEIL        B       (A         PETER HUGODALY      K     (A
```

RICK DANKO

```
RICK DANKO        B G     (A         (A) RICK DANKO                1978  ARISTA       UK  SPARTY1057
WITH                                 (A) RICK DANKO                1977  ARISTA US 4141 EURO     63173
DENNY SEIWELL     D       (A
TERRY DANKO       D       (A    LEVON HELM        V    (A    ROBBIE ROBERTSON  G   (A    MICHAEL DE TEMPLE G  (A
LEWIS BUSTOS      HRNS    (A    ROCKY MORALES     HRNS (A    DOUG SAHM         G   (A    ROB FRABONI     PERC (A
GERRY BECKLEY     V G     (A    JIM ATKINSON      G    (A    BLONDIE CHAPLIN   G B (A    WAYNE NEUENDORF   V   (A
WALT RICHMOND     PNO     (A    RON WOOD          G    (A    TIM DRUMMOND      B   (A    JIM GORDON       K HRNS(A
ERIC CLAPTON      G       (A    KEN LAUBER        PNO  (A    JIM PRICE         HRNS (A   JOE LALA        PERC (A
GEORGE WEBER      ORG     (A    CHARLIE McBURNEY  HRNS (A    RICHARD MANUEL    K   (A    DAVID PAICH      K   (A
GARTH HUDSON      ACC     (A
```

DANNY & THE JUNIORS

```
DANNY RAPP                          ( ) ROCK AND ROLL IS HERE TO STAY  19  SINGULAR    US         569
DAVE WHITE
BILL CARLUCCI           FRANK MAFFEI              JOE TERRANOVA
```

BOBBY DARIN

```
BOBBY DARIN     V  (ALL                              US               UK        UK
                                                                      STEREO    MONO
                     BOBBY DARIN           195  ATCO   33102  LONDON            HAE 2140
                     THATS ALL             195  ATCO   33104  LONDON            HAE 2172
                     THIS IS               1959 ATCO   33115  LONDON  SAH 6067  HAE 2235
                     AT THE COPA           19   ATCO   33122  LONDON  SAH 6103  HAE 2291
                     FOR TEENAGERS ONLY    19   ATCO   1001   LONDON            HAE 2311
                     TWO OF A KIND         196  ATCO   33124  LONDON            HAK 2363
                     25TH DAY OF DECEMBER  1961 ATCO   33123
                     BOBBY DARIN STORY     196  ATCO   33131  LONDON            HAK 2372
                     LOVE SWINGS           196  ATCO   33134  LONDON  SAHK 6193 HAK 2394
                     TWIST WITH            1962 ATCO   33138
                     SINGS RAY CHARLES     1962 ATCO   33140  LONDON  SAHK 6243 HAK 2456
                     THINGS & OTHER THINGS 196  ATCO   33148  LONDON            HAK 8030
                     ITS YOU OR NO ONE     196  ATCO   33124  LONDON            HAK 8192
                     OH LOOK AT ME NOW     196  CAPITOL 1791                    1791
                     EARTHY                196  CAPITOL 1826
                     YOU'RE THE REASON     1963 CAPITOL 1866
                     18 YELLOW ROSES       196  CAPITOL 1942
                     GOLDEN FOLK HITS      1964 CAPITOL 2007
                     HELLO DOLLY           1964 CAPITOL 2194
                     VENICE BLUE           1965 CAPITOL 2322
                     BEST OF               196  CAPITOL 2571
                     I WANNA BE AROUND     196  CAPITOL 2322
                     SHADOW OF YOUR SMILE  19   ATLANTIC 8121 ATLANTIC 588 014
                     DR DOOLITTLE          196  ATLANTIC 8154
                     IF I WERE A CARPENTER 196  ATLANTIC 8135 ATLANTIC 588 051
                     WINNERS               196  ATLANTIC 33167 ATLANTIC ATL5014
                     STORY                 196  ATLANTIC 33187 ATLANTIC         587 065
                     IN A BROADWAY BAG     196  ATLANTIC 8126 ATLANTIC 588 020
                     SOMETHING SPECIAL     196            ATLANTIC         587 073
                     GREATEST MOMENTS      196            ATLANTIC         K40547
                     BOBBY DARIN           1973 MOTOWN  B 753
                     1936/73               1975 MOTOWN    813
                     BOBBY DARIN           19   DIRECTION 1936
                     COMMITMENT            19   DIRECTION 1937
```

[146]

DARK DAY

    ROBIN LEE CRUTCHFIELD V K PERC(A   (A) EXTERMINATING ANGELS   1980 LUST   US   JMB 229
    PHIL KLINE   G SYN B   (A
    BARRY FRIAR   D   (A   STEVEN BROWN SAX (A   MYSTERY WOMAN   V (A
DARK STAR
    RIK STAINES   K V   (A   (A) DARK STAR   1981 AVATAR   AALP 5003
    DAVE HARRISON   G V   (A
    BOB KEY   G V   (A   MARK OSELAND   G V (A STEVE ATKINS   D V (A
DARLING
    ALICE SPRINGS   V   (A   (A) PUT IT DOWN TO EXPERIENCE   1979 CHARISMA US 2204 UK   CAS 1144
    MICK HOWARD   B   (A
    PAUL VARLEY   D   (A   HAL LINDES   G   (A
JENNY DARREN

    JENNY DARREN   V   (ABC   (A) CITY LIGHTS   1977 DJM   UK DJF20497
    CLIFF WADE   G B V(ABC   (B) JENNY DARREN   1978 DJM   UK DJF20523
    GEOFF GILL   PERC V(ABC   (C) QUEEN OF FOOLS   1978 DJM   UK DJF20547
    WILL MALONE   PNO V(A   (D) JENNY DARREN   1980 DJM   UK DJF20569 NL 64122
    STUART BUCKLEY   SAX (C   MIKE ASHCROFT   G   (BEAU CHEMIN   K   (
    BRIAN JONES   SAX (A   TONY SPATH   G   (LEE PATRICK   G V (BC DES TONGUE   B   (BC
    COLIN ELLAR   B   (KELLY CONOVER   D   (
CHRIS DARROW
    CHRIS DARROW BAN G V MAND VLN(ALL   (A) CHRIS DARROW   1973 UA UK UAG29453 US   UALA 048
    WITH   (B) UNDER MY OWN DISGUISE   1974 UA UK UAG29634 US   UALA 242
    CALEB QUAYE   PNO G(A   (C) FRETLESS   1979 PACIFIC ARTS US PAC7 132
    CLIVE CHAMAN   B   (A   (D) ARTIST PROOF   1978 FANTASY   US   9403
    ROGER POPE   D   (A   (E) SOUTHERN CALIFORNIA DRIVE   1980 LINE GER 5060
    DAVID JONES   PERC (C   (F) EYE OF THE STORM   1981 TAKOMA US 7092
    TITO LLOYD   PERC (C
    STEVE CAHILL G V AUTOHARP(AC   EARL DANN   G   (A   SONNY BINNS   K   (A   TREVOR WHITE   B   (A
    DANNY SMITH   D   (A   DAVE PEGG   B   (A   DAVE MATTACKS   D   (A   ALAN STIVELL HARP FLT (A
    DOLLY COLLINS   K   (A   ALAN LUMSDEN   SACK (A   RODERICK SKEAPING VLA (A JOSEPH SKEAPING REBEC(A
    THERESA CAUDLE   WIND (A   ANDREW VANDER BEEK HRNS(A RANDY STERLING B   (C   JOHN RUSSELL   D   (C
    LOREN NEWKIRK   PNO (C   STEVEN DARROW PERC (C   JERRY WALLER   TPT K (C   BOB SIGGINS   V STEEL(C
    MAX BUDA   HCA (C   ROBB STRANDLUND G V (C   FRANK RECKARD   G   (C   STEVE MORK   HRNS (C
    CINDY EDWARDS   V   (C   CORKY CARROLL V   (C   EARL SHAKELFORD V   (C   GREG PRESTOPINO V   (C
    BABATUNDE OLATUNJI CONGA(C
PHIL D'ARROW
    PHIL D'ARROW   G V (A   (A) SUB ZERO   1980 POLYDOR   US   PD6271
    ROGER MURDOCK   D   (A
    BILL COMMAROTA   K V   (A   JOSEPH JAMES   G   (A   BRIAN STANLEY   B   (A   KATHERINE PHOENIX V (A
    SAMMY FIGUEROA   PERC (A   JAMES E MONROE SAX (A   JON PARIS   HCA (A   CURTIS FIELDS   SAX(A
DARTS
    HORATIO HORNBLOWER SAX (AB   (A) DARTS   1977 MAGNET UK MAg 5020 US UA 1977
    GEORGE CURRIE   G   (AB   (B) EVERYBODY PLAYS DARTS   1978 MAGNET   UK MAG 5022
    GRIFF FENDER   V   (AB   ( ) AMAZING DARTS   1978 MAGNET   062 61889
    JOHN DUMMER   D   (AB   ( ) AMAZING DARTS   1978 K TEL   UK   DLP 7981
    DEN HEGARTY   V   (AB   (C) DART ATTACK   1979 MAGNET UK MAGL5030 US   63186
    RITA RAY   V   (AB   ( ) GREATEST HITS   1980 MAGNET   UK MAGL 5037
    THUMP THOMPSON   B   (AB   ( ) DARTS   1980   US   6250
    MIKE DEACON   K   (( ) DOUBLE TOP   1981 HALLMARK   SHM 3087
    HAMMY HOWELL   K   (AB
    BOB FISH   V   (AB
    KENNY EDWARDS   V   (DAVE KELLY   G   (
DARTS(US)
                                          ( ) HOLLYWOOD DRAG   19   DELFI   US   DFST 1244
RUSSELL DASHIELL
    RUSSELL DASHIELL V G K PERC(A   (A) ELEVATOR   1978 EPIC UK 82637 US   35074
    STU COOK   B   (A
    DOUG CLIFFORD   D   (A   JOHN TANNER   PNO   (A
DAS DRITTE OHR
    UDO WOLF   V HCA (A   (A) BLUE & BOOGIE   19   PUR OHNE POLITUR   FR   7701
    HELMUT MEYER   B   (A
    TOM SCHRADER   G V   (A   FERDI PETERS   D   (A
DAUGHTERS OF THE ALBION
    GREG DEMPSEY   (A   (A) DAUGHTERS OF THE ALBION   1968 FONTANA   67586
    KATHLEEN YESSE   (A   (A)   "   "   "   1968 FONTANA NL 887806 UK STL 5486
WOLFGANG DAUNER
    WOLFGANG DAUNER   K FLT (ALL   (A) DREAM TALK   1964
    EBERHARD WEBER   B CELLO(DGHKM   (B) FREE ACTION   1967
    FRED BRACEFUL   D   (HKLMNQ   (C) PSALMUS SPEI   1969
    ROLAND WITTICH   D   (KGM   (D) FUR   1969 CALIG   GER   30603
    SIGFRIED SCHWAB   G   (KM   (E) OLMELS   1970
    LARRY CORYELL   G   (L   (F) BEO BACH TUNGEN   1970
    GUNTER LENZ   B   (L   (G) MUSIC ZOUNDS   1970 MPS   GER   15270
    JON HISEMAN   D   (L   (H) OUTPUT   1970 ECM   1006
    RICHARD KETTERER   V   (L   (J) DAUNER SATO   1971
    JURGEN SCHMIDT-OEHM VLN FLT(N   (K) ET CETERA   1971 INTERCORD   GER   26001
    MATHIES THUROW   B   (N   (L) KHIRSH   1972 MPS   GER   2 121 432
    LACA KOVACEV   D   (N   (M) RISCHKAS SOUL   1972 BRAIN   GER   1016
    ZBIGNIEW SEIFERT   V SAX (P   (N) ET CETERA LIVE   1973 MPS   GER   2 921 754
    HANS KOLLER   SAX   (P   (O) THIS IS   1974 BRAIN   GER   200 150
    ABELHARD ROIDINGER B   (P   (P) KUNSTKOPFINFIANER   1974 MPS   GER   2 122 019
    JANUS STEFANSKI   D   (P   (Q) GIRL FROM MARTINIQUE   19   ECM   1008
    ROBIN KENYETTA   (Q   (R) CHANGES   1979 MOOD   GER   23333
    ARILD ANDERSON   (Q
DAVE DEE, DOZY, BEAKY, MICK , & TITCH
    DAVE DEE(HARMAN)   V   (ALL   DAVE DEE, DOZY, BEAKY, MICK & TITCH 1966 FONTONA   STL 5350
    TREVOR'DOZY' DAVIES B   (IF MUSIC BE THE FOOD OF LOVE   1966 FONTANA   STL 5388
    JOHN'BEAKY' DYMOND G D (IF MUSIC BE THE FOOD OF LOVE   1967 FONTANA   858 030
    MICHAEL'MICK' WILSON D   (GOLDEN HITS   1967 FONTANA   STL 5441
    IAN 'TITCH' AMEY   G   (WHATS IN A NAME   1967 FONTANA   858 000
    PETER LUCAS   G   ((CONTINUED)

                                              [147]

(CONTINUED)   DAVE DEE, DOZY, BEAKY, MICK , & TITCH

PETER LUCAS	G	(	IF NO ONE SANG	1968	FONTANA		886 478
			IF NO ONE SANG	1968	FONTANA		STL 5471
			GREATEST HITS	1968	FONTANA		SFL 13002
			TOGETHER	1969	FONTANA		701 751
			TOGETHER	1969	FONTANA		SFL 13173
			LEGEND OF	1969	FONTANA		SFL 13063
			FRESH AIR	1970	PHILIPS		6308 029
			ATTENTION	19	FONTANA		6438 058
			GREATEST HITS	1971	PHILIPS		6382 018
			GREATEST HITS	19	FONTANA	US	67567
			GREATEST HITS	19	FONTANA	US	27567
			GREATEST HITS	1976	PHILIPS	UK	SON =!%

DAVEY & THE BADMEN

			WANTED	19	KRW US		63 054

DAVID & JONATHAN

DAVID			(A) MICHELE	19	CAPITOL		T2473
JONATHAN							

DIANNE DAVIDSON

DIANNE DAVIDSON	V G (AB		(A) BABY	1971	JANUS	US	3031
WITH			(B) BACKWOODS WOMAN	1972	JANUS UK 6310	209 US	3043
MAC GAYDEN	G V (ABC		(C) MOUNTAIN MAMA	1972	JANUS	US	3048
JOHN HARRIS	PNO (BC						

TIM DRUMMOND	B (ABC	KARL HIMMEL	D (BC	KENNETH BUTTREY	D (AC	KENNY MALONE	D (C
WELDON MYRICK	STEEL(BC	RUTH PFAU	VIOLA(C	BRENT DAVIDSON STEEL DRUM(C		ANITA BALL	G V (C
TRACY NELSON	V (BC	CHARLIE McCOY	G B (AB	BOBBY THOMPSON	K (B	VASSAR CLEMENTS FDL	(B
BUDDY SPICHER	FDL (B	LAUREL CANYON	V (B	JANIS SIEGEL	V (B	JOHN DRUMMOND	G (A
DR JOHN HARRIS	K (A	LINDA RONSTADT	V (A	PHIL ROYSTER	CONGA (B	HONEY COMBS	V (B

ALUN DAVIES

ALUN DAVIES	V G (A		(A) DAYDO	1972	CBS US 31469	UK	65108
JEREMY TAYLOR	G (A						

CAT STEVENS	K (A	CHARLIE GAINSFORD BANJO(A	GERRY CONWAY	D (A	CHRIS LAURENCE B (A
JEAN ROUSSEL	K (A	LARRY STEELE B (A	HARVEY BURNS	D (A	

CYRIL DAVIES

CYRIL DAVIES	HCA V(A		(A) THE LEGENDARY CYRIL DAVIES	1957	PRIVATE PRESSING UK		
WITH			(A) THE LEGENDARY CYRIL DAVIES	1970	FOLKLORE	UK	FLEUT 9
ALEXIS KORNER	V G (A		(EP) THE SOUND OF DAVIES	19	PYE INT	UK NEP 44025	
LISA TURNER	V BANJ(A		( ) CYRIL DAVIES	19	ACE OF CLUBS	UK	ACL 1130
MIKE COLLINS	PERC (A						
TERRY PLANT	B (A	JEFF BRADFORD G MAND(A	REG TURNER	JUG (A			

RON DAVIES

RON DAVIES	G (AB		(A) SILENT SONG THROUGH THE LAND	1970	A&M	UK	AMLS 933
MIKE DEASY	G (A		(B) I DONT BELIEVE IT	1980	FIRST AMERICAN		7714
DIMITRI CALLAS	G (A						

MIKE LANG	PNO (A	LARRY KNECHTEL	ORG (A	CHAD STUART	B (A	JIM KELTNER	D (A
VICKI DAVIES	V (A	LEON RUSSELL	PNO (A	DOUG DILLARD	BANJO (A	BYRON BERLINE	MAND(A
MERRY CLAYTON	V (A	CLYDIE KING	V (A	VANETTA FIELDS	V (A		

BETTY DAVIS

BETTY DAVIS	V (ALL		(A) BETTY DAVIS	1973	JUST SUNSHINE		JSS5
WITH			(B) THEY SAY IM DIFFERENT	1974	JUST SUNSHINE	US	JSS 3500
GREGG ERRICO	D (A		(B) THEY SAY IM DIFFERENT	1974	POLYDOR	UK	2933 402
HERSHALL KENNEDY	K V (AB		(C) NASTY GAL	1975	ISLAND	UK	ILPS 9329
VICTOR PANTOJA	PERC (AB						

DOUG RODRIGUES	G (A	NEAL SCHON	G (A	BUDDY MILES	G (B	MERL SAUNDERS	K (A
LARRY GRAHAM	B (A	RICHARD KERMODE	K (A	DOUG RAUCH	B (A	PETE SEARS	PNO (A
GREG ADAMS	HRNS (A	SKIP MESQUITE	SAX (A	MIC GILLETTE	TROM (A	JULES BROUSSARD SAX	(A
POINTER SISTERS	V (A	KATHI McDONALD	V (A	PATRYCE BANKS	V (A	WILLY SPARKS	D V (AB
LARRY JOHNSON	B (BC	FRED MILLS K V	(B	CARLOS MORALES	G V (B	NICKY NEAL	D V (B
ERROL BENNETT	PERC (A	JAMES ALLEN SMITH K	(B	DEBBIE BURRELL	V (B	ELAINE CLARK	V (B
TRUDY PERKINS	V (B	MARY JONES	V (B	TONY VAUGHN	K V (B	CORDELL DUDLEY	V G (B
PETE ESCOVEDO	PERC (B	MIKE CLARKE	D (B	JIMMY GODWIN	G (B	SYLVESTER	V (A
ANNIE SAMPSON	V (A						

EDDIE DAVIS

EDDIE DAVIS			LIVE AT MINTONS	1964	STATESIDE	UK	SL 10102
JOHNNY GRIFFIN	SAX (		LIVE AT MINTONS	196	PRESTIGE	US	7309
SHIRLEY SCOTT	K (		COOKBOOK	1974	PRESTIGE		PR 24039
			LEAPIN' ON LENNOX	1976	BLACK'N'BLUE		33072
			TOUGHESS TENORS	1976	MILESTONES	M	47135
			EDDIE LOCKJAW DAVIS	1976	MAHOLNY		558 104

FRANK DAVIS

FRANK DAVIS			METAMORPHOSIS (UNRELEASED)				

JESSE ED DAVIS

JESSE ED DAVIS	G V (ALL		(A) JESSE ED DAVIS	1971	ATCO US 33346	UK	2400106
ALBHY GALUTEN	PNO (A		(B) ULULU	1972	ATCO US 33382	UK ATLANTIC	K40329
LEON RUSSELL	PNO (AB		(C) KEEP ON COMING	1973	EPIC US 32133	UK CBS	65649
LARRY KNECHTEL	K (AB						

DONALD DUNN	B (B	BILLY RICH	B (AB	ARNOLD ROSENTHAL	B (B	JIM KELTNER	D (B
MAXINE WILLARD	V (A	GRAM PARSONS	V (A	MERRY CLAYTON	V (AB	VANETTA FIELDS	V (AB
CLYDIE KING	V (AB	CHUCK KIRKPATRICK	V (B	CHARLES CHALMERS SINGERS(B		ERIC CLAPTON	G (A
JOEL SCOTT HILL	G (A	LARRY PIERCE	K (A	BEN SIDRAN	K (A	JOHN SIMON	K (A
STEVE THOMPSON	B (A	CHUCK BLACKWELL	D (A	STEVE MITCHELL	D (A	BRUCE ROWLAND	D (A
ALAN WHITE	D (A	PATT DALEY	PERC (A	SANDY KONIKOFF	PERC (A	JACKIE LOMAX	PERC(A
PETE WADINGTON	PERC (A	JOHNNIE WARE	PERC (A	ALAN YOSHIDA	PERC (A	JIM GORDON	HRNS(A
JERRY JUMONVILLE	HRNS (A	DARRELL LEONARD	HRNS (A	FRANK MAYES	HRNS (A	NIKKI BARCLAY	V (A
BOBBY JONES	V (A	GLORIA JONES	V (A	MAC REBANNACK	PNO (B	STAN SZELESTE	PNO (B

MILES DAVIS	TPT	(ALL
WITH		
WAYNE HENDERSON	TROM	(
JOE ZAWINUL		(
TONY WILLIAMS	D	(
HERBIE HANCOCK	K	(
KEITH JARRETT	K	(
JOHN McLAUGHLIN	G	(
CHICK COREA	K	(
LARRY CORYELL	G	(
GEORGE PAULIS	K	(
AL FOSTER	D	(
T M STEVENS	B	(
MASUBUMBI KIKUCHI	K	(
WAYNE SHORTER	SAX	(
DAVE HOLLAND	B	(
RON CARTER	B	(
JOHN COLTRANE	SAX	(
DIZZY GILLESPIE	TPT	(
CHARLIE PARKER	SAX	(
GIL EVANS		(
CANNONBALL ADDERLEY	SAX	(
TADD DAMERON	PNO	(
RED GARLAND	K	(
OSCAR PETERSON	KB	(
PAUL CHAMBERS	B	(
PHILLY J JONES	D	(
MILT JACKSON	VIBES	(
THELONIUS MONK	PNO	(
PERCY HEATH	B	(
KENNY CLARKE	D	(
CHARLES MINGUS	PNO B	(
MAX ROACH	D	(
JOHN LEWIS	PNO	(
SONNY ROLLINS	SAX	(
HORACE SILVER	PNO	(
ART BLAKEY	D	(
WYNTON KELLY	PNO	(
BILL EVANS	PNO	(
JIMMY COBB	D	(
VICTOR FELDMAN	PNO	(
GEORGE COLEMAN	SAX	(
FRANK BUTLER	D	(
HANK MOBLEY	SAX	(
BOB DOROUGH	V	(
GEORGE BENSON	G	(
LENNY WHITE	D	(
BENNY MAUPIN	CLAR	(
JIM RILEY	PERC	(
JACK DEJOHNETTE	D	(
HARVEY BROOKS	B	(
CHARLES ALIAS	D	(
LARRY YOUNG	PNO	(
STEVE GROSSMAN	SAX	(
BILLY COBHAM	D	(
MICHAEL HENDERSON	B	(
AIRTO MOREIRA	PERC	(
GARY BARTZ	SAX	(
HERMETO PASCAL	PNO	(
KHAUL BALAKRISHNA	SITAR	(
REGGIE LUCAS	G	(
SEAK LAWSON	ORG	(
MTUME	PERC	(
BADAL ROY	TAB	(
CARLOS GARNETT	SAX	(
BIHARI SHARMA	SITAR	(
LONNIE SMITH	D	(
WILLIAM HART	D	(
SONNY FORTUNE	WIND	(
HAROLD WILLIAMS JR	K SITAR	(
DAVID LIEBMSN	FLT	(
PETE CASEY	G	(
DOMINIQUE GAUMONT	G	(
CEDRIC LAWSON	PNO	(
JOHN STOBBLEFIELD	SAX	(
BERNARD PURDIE	D	(,
CORNEL DUPREE	G	(
WALLY CHAMBERS	HCA	(
ELVIN JONES	D	(
BUSTER WILLIAMS	B	(
JOE BECK	B	(
DAVE SCHILDKRAUT	SAX	(
J J JOHNSON	TROM	(
LUCKY THOMPSON	SAX	(
SAMMY FIGUEROA	PERC	(
BILL EVANS	SAX	(
MARCUS MILLER	B	(
BARRY FINERTY	G	(
MIKE STERN	G	(
RANDY HALL	SYN V	(
ROBERT IRVINE	K	(
FELTON CREWS	B	(
VINCENT WILBURN	D	(

MUSSINGS OF MILES	1955	PRESTIGE US 7007			
MILES	1955	PRESTIGE US 7014			
BAGS GROOVE	195	PRESTIGE US 24012			
COOKIN	195	PRESTIGE 24053			
RELAXIN'	195				
MILES DAVIS DBL	195	PRESTIGE 24001			
SOULIN	195				
WORKIN'	195	PRESTIGE 7166			
STEAMIN'	195	PRESTIGE 7200			
WORKIN' & STEAMIN'	1974	PRESTIGE US 24034			
ODYSSEY	19	PRESTIGE US 7540			
MODERN JAZZ GIANTS	19	PRESTIGE US 7650			
CONSEPTION	19	PRESTIGE US 7744			
MILES AHEAD	19	PRESTIGE US 7822			
OLEO	19	PRESTIGE US 7847			
WALKIN'	195	PRESTIGE US 7608			
KIND OF BLUE	1959	CBS	US 8163		UK 62066
PORGY & BESS	1959	CBS	US 8085		UK 62108
SKETCHES OF SPAIN	1959	CBS	US 8271		UK 62327
ROUND ABOUT MIDNIGHT	1962	CBS	US 8649		UK 62323
FRIDAY AT THE BLACKHAWK	19	CBS			UK 62306
FRIDAY AT THE NIGHTHAWK VOL2	19	CBS			UK 62307
IN PERSON AT THE BLACKHAWK	19	CBS	US C2S 820(DBL)		
MILESTONES	1959	CBS	US 9428		UK 62308
MILES & MONK AT NEWPORT	19	CBS	US 8978		UK 62389
SOMEDAY MY PRINCE WILL COME	1962	CBS	US 8465		UK 62104
AT CARNEGIE HALL	19	CBS	US 8612		
SEVEN STEPS TO HEAVEN	19	CBS	US 8851		UK 62170
QUIET NIGHTS	1964	CBS	US 8906		
IN EUROPE	1964	CBS	US 8983	EMBASSY UK 31103
MY FUNNY VALENTINE	1965	CBS	US 9106		UK 62510
FOUR & MORE	1966	CBS	US 9253		UK 62655
MILES AT ANTIBES	19	CBS			UK 62390
MILES AHEAD	19	CBS	US 8633		UK 62496
FACETS	19	CBS			UK 62637
IN BERLIN	19	CBS			UK 62976
TRUMPET GIANTS	1964	NEWJAZZ S 8296	STATESIDE UK 10103
PLAYS RICHARD RODGERS	1964			STATESIDE UK 10111
PLAYS RICHARD RODGERS	1976	PRESTIGE US 7332		CBS UK 88029
ESP	1965	CBS	US 9150		UK 62577
PLAYS FOR LOVERS	1966	PRESTIGE US 7352	STATESIDE UK 10168
GREATEST HITS	1966	PRESTIGE US 7457			
MILES SMILES	1967	CBS	US 9401		UK 62933
THE SORCERER	1967	CBS	US 9532		UK 63097
NEFERTITI	1968	CBS	US 9594		UK 63248
MILES IN THE SKY	1968	CBS	US 9628		UK 63352
AT NEWPORT	19	CBS			UK 63417
FILLES OF KILIMANJARO	1968	CBS	US 9750		UK 63551
GREATEST HITS	1969	CBS			UK 63620
IN A SILENT WAY	1969	CBS	US 9857		UK 63630
BITCHES BREW	1970	CBS	US PG26		UK 66236
BITCHES BREW	197	CBS			30997
LIVE AT THE FILLMORE(DBL)	1971	CBS			UK 66257
JACK JOHNSON(SOUNDTRACK)	1971	CBS	US 30455		UK 70089
LIVE EVIL(DBL)	1972	CBS	US 30954		UK 67219
ON THE CORNER	1973	CBS	US 31906		UK 65246
IN CONCERT(DBL)	1973	CBS			UK 68222
ESSENTIAL MILES DAVIS	1973	CBS			UK 66310
AT NEWPORT	197	CBS			UK 66417
TALLEST TREES(DBL)	1973	PRESTIGE			24012
COLLECTORS ITEMS (DBL)	1973	PRESTIGE			24022
BASIC MILES	197	CBS	US 32025		UK 65343
JAZZ AT THE PLAZA	1974	CBS	US 32470		UK 65778
BIG FUN	1974	CBS	US 32866		UK 88024
BLACK BEAUTY	1974	CBS			
GET UP WITH IT	1974		33236		UK 88092
CLASSICS (DBL)	1975	CBS			UK 88138
AGHARTA (DBL)	1975	CBS	US 33967		UK 88159
BIRD & MILES	1975	DJM	DJB26062		DJML 062
EARLY MILES	1975	PRESTIGE US 7674		UK PR7674
MILES DAVIS	1975	BLUENOTE			81501/2
ALL STARS	1976	BEPPO			BEP 502
AT THE BIRDLAND	1976	BEPPO			BEP 501
DAVIS PARKER GILLESPIE	1976	VOGUE			VKD5529
GREEN HAZE	1976	PRESTIGE			24064
WATER BABIES	1977	CBS	US 34396		
DIRECTIONS	197	CBS			UK 88514
WITH JOHN COLTRANE	197	CBS			UK 88029
TUNE UP	19	PRESTIGE PRESTIGE 24077
WITH LEE KOWITZ,TEDDY CHARLES	197	EZZTHETIC 7013
PARIS FESTIVAL	197	CBS			
PRE BIRTH OF THE COOL	197	JAZZLIVE BLJ 8003
AT BIRDLAND	197	JAZZLIVE BLJ 8023
STAN GETZ & MILES DAVIS	197	KINGS OF JAZZ		KLJ 20013
& JOHN COLTRANE	197	UNIQUE JAZZ UJ 19
ARCHIVES OF JAZZ VOL 3	19	PATHE		FR 062 95819
BIRTH OF THE COOL	19	CAPITOL			40678
BLUE HAZE	19	PRESTIGE			054 10134
COMPLETE BIRTH OF THE COOL	19	PATHE		FR 062 80798
DIG	19	PRESTIGE			24054
MILES OF JAZZ	19	TRIP			5015
SOMETHING ELSE	19	CBS			81595
LIVE AT THE PLUGGED NICKEL	19	CBS			

(CONTINUED)

```
    LEE KONITZ         SAX    (        PONGAEA                              19    CBS
    SAL MOSCA          PNO    (        JAZZ TRACK                           19    CBS        US 1268
    BILLY BAHER        G      (        MOUNTAINS IN THE SKY                 19    ATCO       US SD1622
    ARNOLD FISHKIN     B      (        CIRCLE IN THE ROUND                  1979  CBS        US 36278
    JIMMY RANEY        G      (        THE MAN WITH HORN                    1981  CBS        US 36790
    DICK MINESON       B      (
    ED SHAUGHNESSY     D      (    TEDDY CHARLES    VIBES(     JAMES MOODY      SAX  (   KAI WINDING TROM (
    JUNIOR COLLINS     HRNS   (    GERRY MULLIGAN   SAX  (     AL HAIG      PNO      (   JOE SCHULMAN     B(
    SANDY SIEGELSTEIN  HRNS   (    NELSON BOYD      B    (     GUNTHER SCHULLER HRNS (   AL McKIBBON      B(
    MIKE ZWERIN              (     JOHN LEWIS            (     KENNEYH HAGOLD        (   BREW MOORE       (
    GENE RAMAY         B      (    STAN GETZ        SAX  (     BILL EVANS   PNO      (   PAUL CHAMBERS    B(
    ART TAYLOR         D      (    BILL BARBER      TUBA (     DANNY BANK   CLAR     (   JIMMY BUFFINGTON HRNS(
    RONEO PENQUE       WIND   (
```

D27A   PAUL DAVIS   D27A

```
    PAUL DAVIS         V      (ALL   (A) LITTLE BIT OF P D              197    BANG          US        223
    JIMMY JOHNSON      G      (D     (B) PAUL DAVIS                     1974   BANG          US        226
    DAVID HOOD         B      (D     (C) RIDE 'EM COWBOY                1975   BANG          US        401
    BARRY BECKETT      K      (D     (D) SOUTHERN TRACKS & FANTASIES    1976   BANG          US        405
    ROGER HAWKINS      D      (D     (E) SINGER OF SONGS                1977   BANG US 410   UK SHOT   002
    BARRY BAILEY       G      (C     (F) PAUL DAVIS                     1980   BANG          US        36094
    CHARLIE OWEN       STEEL  (C     (G) COOL NIGHT                     1981   ARISTA        US        9578
    TOM ROBB           B      (C
    CHRIS ETHRIDGE     B      (C     ROY YEAGER         D    (C   AUBURN BURRELL   G    (C
```

D27B   SANDY DAVIS   D27B

```
    PAUL 'SANDY' DAVIS V G K B D(AB   (A) INSIDE EVERY FAT MAN           1974   EMI           UK        EMC 3029
    PETER SKELLERN     PNO    (A     (B) BACK ON MY FEET AGAIN          1975   EMI           UK        EMC 3070
    ALAN CAWDEROY      G      (A
    MARTIN BRILEY      G      (AB    ANDREW PRYCE JACKMAN K     (A   GORDON HUNTE    G    (B
    DELISLE HARPER     B      (B     ROY DAVIES           K     (B   STEVE FERRONE   D    (B
    CHRIS MERCER       SAX    (B     AVERAGE WHITE BAND   V     (B
```

D28   SPENCER DAVIS   D28

```
    SPENCER DAVIS      G V    (ALL   (A) EVERY LITTLE BIT HURTS         1965   WING          UK  WL    1165
    MUFF WINWOOD       G V B(ABCDEFGHIKNO  (A) THEIR FIRST LP           1965   SONET SW1401 FONTANA TL 5242
    STEVE WINWOOD      K G V(ABCDEFGHIKNO  (A) THEIR FIRST LP           19     ISLAND  RI GER 201658
    PETER YORK         D (ABCDEFGHIJKLMNO  (B) SECOND ALBUM             1966   FONTANA       UK  TL    5295
    EDDIE HARDIN       K      (JLM   (C) AUTUMN 66                      1966   FONTANA       UK  STL   5359
    PHIL SAWYER        G      (1967  (D) GIMME SOME LOVIN'              1967   UA            US        3578
    RAY FENWICK        G      (JLM1  (D) GIMME SOME LOVIN'              1967   UA            US        6578
    NIGEL OLSSON       D      (69/70 (E) I'M A MAN                      1967   UA            US        3589
    DEE MURRAY         B      (68/70 (E) I'M A MAN                      1967   UA            US        6589
    GARY COOPER        G      (L     (F) THE BEST OF SPENCER DAVIS      1967   ISLAND        UK  ILPS  9070
    CHARLIE McCRACKEN  B      (LM    (G) VERY BEST OF                   1968   UA            US        443E
    TONY COE           CLAR   (M     (H) HERE WE GO ROUND THE MULBERY BUSH 1968 UA UK SULP1186 FR RI   29637
    BRIAN DEXTER       ACC    (M     (I) GREATEST HITS                  1968   UA            US        3461
    MARTYN FORD        HRNS   (M     (I) GREATEST HITS                  1968   UA            US        6641
    DORIS TROY         V      (M     (J) WITH THEIR NEW FACE ON         1968   UA            US        6652
    LIZA STRIKE        V      (M     (J) WITH THEIR NEW FACE ON         1968   UA                      1192
    RUBY JAMES         V      (M     (J) LETS DANCE WITH                19     SUNSET        GERM      50141
    DAVE HYNES         D      (68/69 (K) HEAVIES                        1969   UA            US        6691
    TRAFFIC                   (H     (L) GLUGGO                         1973   VERTIGO UK 6360088 GER6360102
    ANDY ELLISON              (H     (L) GLUGGO                         1973   VERTIGO       US        1015
    PETER JAMESON             (X     (M) LIVING ON A BACK STREET        1974   VERTIGO       UK  6360. 105
    SNEAKY PETE        STEEL  (Y     (M) LIVING ON A BACK STREET        197    VERTIGO UK 6499 978 US  1021
    LARRY KNECHTEL     K      (YX    (N) GIMME SOME LOVIN'              1973   ISLAND        GER       85897ZT
    KENNY SALMON       ORG    (A     (O) SOMEBODY HELP ME               1973   ISLAND        GER       85925 ET
    TRET FURE          G      (Y     ( )POP CHRONIK (DBL)               1975   ISLAND        IMP       VOL4
    ANDY WAY           B      (Y     ( ) POP CHRONIK (DBL)              1977   ISLAND        IMP       87213
    GIB GILBEAUX       FDL    (Y     ( ) SPENCER DAVIS GROUP            19     SONET                   GP 9916
    LEE SKLAR         B       (Y     ( ) BEST OF                        19     SONET                   GP 9992
    CHUCK FINDLEY      HRNS   (Y     (EP) SPENCER DAVIS KEEP ON RUNNING 1978   ISLAND        UK        1EP10
    ERNIE WATTS        SAX    (Y     (EP) EVERY LITTLE BIT HURTS        1965   FONTANA       UK
    GEORGE BOHANNON    TROM   (Y     (EP) YOU PUT THE HURT ON ME        1965   FONTANA       UK        TF17444
    HARRY EDISON       TPT    (Y     (EP) SITTIN' & THINKIN'            1966   FONTANA       UK        TF17463
    BARRY HESSEL              (X     (X) ITS BEEN SO LONG  (S DAVIS SOLO) 1971 UA  34416     UK        UAS 29177
                                     (X) ITS BEEN SO LONG               1971   MEDIARTS      US        4111
    RICHARD LANDIS            (X     (Y) MOUSETRAP       (S DAVIS SOLO)  1972   UA            UK        UAS 29361
                                     (Z) NOSTALGIA VOL 2                197    UA            FR        29629
```

D29   BRIAN DAVISON   D29

```
    BRIAN DAVISON      D V    (A    (A) EVERY WHICH WAY          1970   CHARISMA UK CAS1021 MERCURY US 61340
    GRAHAM BELL        V K    (A
    GEOFF PEACH        WIND   (A    ALAN CARTWRIGHT    B    (A   JOHN HEDLEY    G    (A
```

D29A   TIM DAWE   D29A

```
    TIM DAWE           G V'   (A    (A) PENROD                   1970   STRAIGHT       US        S1058
    ARNIE GOODMAN      K      (A
    CHRIS KEBECK       G      (A    DON PARRISH       B    (A   CLAUDE MATHIS   D    (A
```

D29B   DAWN PATROL   D29B

```
    DAWN               V      (A    (A) DAWN PATROL (EP)         198    DINOSAUR                 DD005
    STEVE                     (A
    REBECCA            B V    (A    NEON IAN          G V   (A
```

D30   JIMMY DAWKINS   D30

```
    JIMMY DAWKINS      G V    (ALL  (A) TRANSATLANTIC 770        1972   BLUE HORIZON  UK
    WITH                            (A) TRANSATLANTIC 770        1975   CONTEMPO          CLP   513
    JOE JAMMER         G      (A    (A) TRANSATLANTIC 770        1978   SONET             SNTF  758
    ROSA DOTSON        V      (A    (A) TRANSATLANTIC 770        197    EXCELLO       US        8024
    BOB BRUNNING       B      (A    (B) FAST FINGERS             19     DELMARK               DS 623
    CECIL MOSS         TPT    (A    (C) ALL FOR BUSINESS         1971   DELMARK               DS 634
    MIKE VERNON        PERC   (A    (D) BLISTERING               1977   DELMARK       US        641
    PETE WINGFIELD     K      (A    (E) I WANT TO KNOW           1977   MCM           IMP   900 290
    TONY STEVENS       B      (A    (F) COME BACK BABY           19     MCM           FR    900 295
    BILLY GRAHAM       TROM   (A    (G) TRIBUTE TO ORANGE        1971   BLACK & BLUE            33538
            (CONTINUED)
```

NOVELLE WILLIAMS	V K	(A
REG ISADORE	D	(A
OTIS RUSH	G	(C
ERNEST GATEWOOD	B	(C
CLARENCE 'GATEMOUTH' BROWN	G(G
TED HARVEY	D	(G
DICK PARRY	SAX	(A

JIMMY DAWKINS

A G'BUBBLES' WHITE	G	(A	ANDREW'BIG VOICE' ODOM	V	(C
JIM CONLEY	SAX	(C	SONNY THOMPSON	PNO	(C
ROBERT CROWDER	D	(C	CHARLES HICKS	D	(C
COUSIN JOE	PNO	(G	MAC THOMPSON	B	(G
VELMA SMITH	V	(A	CHRIS MERCER	SAX	(A

D30A — BOBBY DAY

BOBBY DAY	V	(A

(A) ROCKIN' ROBIN   19   CLASS   US   LP 5002

D30B — DAY BLINDNESS

DAVE MITCHELL	V D	(A
GARY PIHL	G V	(A
FELIX BRIA	V B K	(A

(A) DAY BLINDNESS   19   STUDIO 10   DBX 101

D31 — DAY OF THE PHOENIX

HANS LAURIDSEN	V	(AB
ERIK RASMUSSEN	B V	(AB
HENRIK FRIIS NIELSEN	D	(AB
KARSTEN LYNG	G	(AB
OLE PREHN	G V	(AB
KENNETH KNUDSEN	PNO	(A

(A) WIDE OPEN N WAY   1970 SONET   SLPS 1510
(A) WIDE OPEN N WAY   197   GREENWICH   UK   GSLPR1002
(B) THE NEIGHBOUR'S SON   1972 SONET   SLPS 1541
(B) THE NEIGHBOUR'S SON   197   CHAPTER ONE   UK   CNSR 812

PETER FRIIS NIELSEN   B   (A   TONY REEVES   B   (B

D31A — DAYLIGHT

MIKE SILVER	G V	(A
STEVE HATTON	G MAND V	(A
CHRISSIE QUAYE	G	(A
LYN DOBSON	WIND	(A

(A) DAYLIGHT   1971 RCA   UK   SF 8194

TONY CARR   D   (A   SPIKE HEATLEY   B   (A

D31B — STU DAYE

STU DAYE		(A

(A) FREE PARKING   1976 CBS   US   33936

D31C — DAYSHIFT

(A) LIVING IN THE UK (EP)   1980 WOT   WOT1

D31D — DAYTON

(A) CUTIE PIE   1981 LIBERTY   US   LT 1093

D32 — DEAD BOYS

STIV BATORS	V	(AB
JOHNNY BLITZ	D	(AB
CHEETAH CHROME	G	(AB
JIMMY ZERO	G	(AB
JEFF MAGNUM	B	(AB
FELIX PAPPALARDI	V	(B

(A) YOUNG LOUD & SNOTTY   1977 SIRE   UK   9103 329
(A) YOUNG LOUD & SNOTTY   1978 SIRE   UK   SRK 6038
(B) WE HAVE COME FOR YOUR CHILDREN 1978 SIRE   UK   SRK 6054
(B) WE HAVE COME FOR YOUR CHILDREN 1978 SIRE   GER 28 387

JOEY RAMONE   V   (B   DEE DEE RAMONE   V   (B

D33 — DEAD FINGERS TALK

BOBO PHOENIX	V	(A
ANDY LINKLATER	B	(A
JEFF PARSONS	G	(A

(A) STORM THE REALITY STUDIOS 1978 PYE   UK   NSPH 24

TONY CARTER   D   (A

D33A — DEAD KENNEDYS

EAST BOY RAY	G	(A
TED	D	(A
KLAUS FLOURIDE	B V	(A
JELLO BIAFRA	V	(A
ROCKY MOUNTAIN ARSENAL CHOIR	(A

(A) FRESH FRUIT FOR ROTTING VEGETABLES 1980 CHERRY REDUK RED10 FAULTY US70014
(EP) CALIFORNIA   198   FAST UK FAST12

PAUL ROESSLER   K   (A   NINOTCHKA   K   (A

D33B — DEAD SEA FRUIT

DAVE'BEANO'LASHMAR	G V	(A
CLIVE KENNEDY	V	(A
CHRISTOPHER HALL	B G V	(A

(A) DEAD SEA FRUIT   1967 CAMP   UK   603001

JOHN TOWNSEND   PERC V (A   SI CLIFFORD   K   (A

D33C — DEADLY EARNEST & THE HONKY TONK HEROES

(A) DEADLY EARNEST   1979 PACIFIC ARTS 7134+ WHEELER 80

D33D — DEADLY NIGHTSHADES

HELEN HOOKE	G V FDL K SYN	(AB
ANNE BOWEN	G V PERC	(AB
PAMELA BRANDT	V B	(AB

(A) THE DEADLY NIGHTSHADES   1975 RCA   US   BPLI 0955
(B) F & W   1976 RCA   US   BPLI 1370

D33E — DEAF AIDS

CRAIG WAITES		(A
JOHN O'ROURKE		(A
GRAHAM HOGGARD		(A

(A) HEROES   EP   1980 CONSPIRACY   UK CONS 1 12

TERRY GAMWELL   (A

D34 — DEAF SCHOOL

TIM WHITTAKER	D	(BC
ENRICO CADILLAC	V	(ABC
CLIVE LANGER	G	(ABC
MAX RIPPLE	K	(ABC
ERIC SHARK	V	(CB
BETTE BRIGHT	V	(ABC
PAUL PILNICK	G B ACC	(B

(A) DONT STOP THE WORLD   1975 WB   UK   K 56364
(B) SECOND HONEYMOON   1976 WB   UK   K 56280
(AB) DONT STOP/2ND HONEYMOON   197   WB   US   2LS 3011
(C) ENGLISH BOYS WORKING GIRLS 1978 WB   UK   K 56450
(C) ENGLISH BOYS WORKING GIRLS 197   WB   US   3169

IAN RITCHIE   SAX   (BC   STEVE LINDSEY   B   (BC

D34B — TONE DEAF & THE IDIOTS

TONE DEAF	V	(A
BEAN HOWARD	G V	(A
LEW KNEE	B V	(A
BUNK DOGGER	G V	(A

(A) CATASTROPHE ROCK   1979 BLUE ANGEL   UK   BLISS 1

HARRY 'DEAD' TREES   D V (A   NIGEL BROMLEY   D   (A
ROGER WYATT   G   (A

D34C — CHRISTOPHER DEAN

CHRISTOPHER DEAN		(

(A) IMAGES   197   MAINSTREAM   US   302

D35 — ELTON DEAN

ELTON DEAN	SAX	(ALL
PHIL HOWARD	D	(A
MARK CHARIG	CORNET	(A
NEVILLE WHITEHEAD	B	(A
MIKE RATLEDGE	K	(A
ROY BABBINGTON	B	(A
ALAN SKIDMORE		(D
HUGH HOPPER	B	(CE
KEITH TIPPETT	PNO	(CB
JOE GALLIVAN		(CF
KENNY WHEELER	TPT	(F

(A) ELTON DEAN   1971 CBS   UK   64539
(B) THEY ALL BE ON THIS OLD ROAD 1977 OGUN   OG 410
(C) CRUEL BUT FAIR   1977 COMPENDIUM   NOR FID 4
(D) EL SKID   1978 VINYL   VS 103
(E) ROGUE ELEMENTS   1978 OGUN   UK   OG 527
(F) CHEQUE IS IN THE POST   1977 OGUN   UK   OG 610
(G) NINESENSE   1977 OGUN   UK   OG 900
(H) HAPPY DAYS   1978 OGUN   UK   OG 910

CHRIS LAURENCE   B   (BD   JOHN MARSHALL   D   (D
LOUIS MOHOLO   D   (B

DEBRIS

(A) DEBRIS		19	STATIC DISPOSAL	PIGO000

CHRIS DE BURGH

```
CHRIS DE BURGH    G V  (ALL    (A) FAR BEYOND THESE CASTLE WALLS   1975  A&M US 4516   UK  AMLH68284
RAY JACKSON  MAND/HCA  (A     (B) SPANISH TRAIN & OTHER STORIES    1975  A&M US 4568   UK  AMLH68343
CHRIS LAURENCE    B    (AB    (C) AT THE END OF A PERFECT DAY      1977  A&M US 4647   UK  AMLH64647
LIZA STRIKE       V    (A     (D) CRUSADER                        1979  A&M US 4746   UK  AMLH64746
JOY YATES         V    (A     (E) EASTERN WIND                    1980  A&M US 4815   UK  AMLH64815
KEN FREEMAN      SYN   (AB    (F) BEST MOVES                      1981  A&M          UK  AMLH68532
MADELINE BELL     V    (A     (G) THE GETAWAY                     1982  A&M          UK  AMLH68549
RUPERT HINE      SYN   (G
TONY REEVES       B    (B   CHRIS MERCER    SAX  (B   MICK EVE       SAX (B   IAN BAIRNSON       G (B
DAVID PATON       B    (D   STUART ELLIOTT  D    (A   MIKE MORAN     K   (D   ANDREW POWELL    PNO (D
BARRY DE SOUZA    D    (AB  BRIAN ODGERS    B    (A   LENNOX LAINGTON PERC(AB  RONNIE LEAHY       K  (A
RAY GLYNN         G    (B   B J COLE   STEEL     (A   TONY HYMAS     K   (B   PHILIP GOODHAND TAIT K(AB
TIM WYNVEEN      G V   (E   GLENN MORROW    K    (E   AL MARNIE      B V (E   JEFF PHILLIPS      D (E
JOHN HELLIWELL   SAX   (E   DICK SMITH      PERC (E   ERIC ROBERTSON K   (E   LISA DELBELLO      V (E
COLLEENA PHILLIPS V   (E   SHARON LEE WILLIAMS V (E   DAVID HENTSCHEL SYN (B   PHIL PALMER        G (G
JOHN GIBLIN       B    (G   STEVE NEGUS     D    (G   DAVID CADDICK  PNO (G
```

MIKE DEASY

```
MIKE DEASY      V G K B(A    (A) LETTERS TO MY MIND           1973  CAPITOL       US   1170
JIM GORDON        D   (A
JIM KELTNER       D   (A
LEE SKLAR         B   (A   JERRY SCHEFF     B    (A   MAX BENNETT     B   (A   MIKE MELVOIN     K (A
LARRY KNECHTEL    K   (A   JAY DEE MANESS   STEEL(A   ART MANSON      G   (A   GARY COLEMAN     PERC(A
JIM HORN        HRNS  (A   CHUCK FINDLEY    HRNS (A   JACKIE KELSO    HRNS(A   OLLIE MITCHELL   HRNS(A
PAUL HUBINON    HRNS  (A   SLYDE HYDE       HRNS (A   LEW McCREARY    HRNS(A   PLAS JOHNSON     HRNS(A
VANETTA FIELDS    V   (A   KATHY DEASY      V    (A   ANNIE HENING    V   (A   STEVE ADLER      V (A
KATH WARD         V   (A   CHARLES MERRIAM  V    (A   TRIS JONS       V   (A   MICHAEL CLOUGH   V (A
```

DECAMERON

```
DAVE BELL       G B  (ABCDE   (A) DECAMERON              1973  VERTIGO      UK   6360 097
DIK CADBURY   B G V(BCDE     (B) MAMMOTH SPECIAL         1974  MOONCREST    UK   CREST 19
JOHNNY COPPIN   G K  (ABCDE   (C) THIRD LIGHT            1975  TRANSATLANTIC UK  TRA  304
AL FENN       HCA G B (ABCDE  (D) BEYOND THE LIGHT       1975  MOONCREST    UK   CREST 28
GEOFF MARCH     K V SAX(ABCDE (E) TOMORROWS PANTOMIME    1976  TRANSATLANTIC UK  TRA  325
JOHN HALSEY     D    (BC
FRANK RICOTTI   PERC (B   JOHN MEALING    K    (C   DUDU PUKWANA    PERC (B  MONGEZI FEZA     PERC(B
MIKE WINFIELD   HRNS (C   GASPAR LAWAL    PERC (B   SHAMSI SARUMI   PERC (B  BOB CRITCHLEY      D (E
ANDY ROBERTS    G    (A   B J COLE   STEEL(A   IAN WHITMAN     K    (A  TIMI DONALD        D (A
```

DECEMBERS CHILDREN

DECEMBERS CHILDREN		19	MAINSTREAM	US	6128

DECCENNIUM

```
GER BRANDS      D    (AB    (A) SONG OF SAD TIMES        1974                NR  501
FRITS VAN UDEN  ORG V(A     (B) HIGHWAY SONG             1980  KILLROY   NL  19923
JACQUE KESSELS  G V  (AB
```

DEDRINGER

```
J J HOYLE       V    (A     (A) DIRECT LINE             1981  DINDISC   UK  DID  7
LEE FLAXINGTON B V K (A     (B) MAXINE        (DBL)     1982  DINDISC   UK  DID 11
NEIL HUDSON     G    (A   KENNY JONES     D    (A   AL SCOTT        G   (A
```

DE DANANN

```
ALEC FINN            (       (A) DE DANANN               1977  DECCA     UK  SKL 5287
FRANKIE GAVIN        (       (B) MIST COVERED MOUNTAIN   1980  GAELLIN   IR  CEF  087
DOLORES KEANE        (
JOHNNY McDONAGH      (
JACKIE DALLY         (   CHARLIE PIGGOTT      (   JOHNNY MOYNIHAN    ( TIM LYONS       (
```

JOEY DEE & THE STARLIGHTERS

```
JOEY DEE         V   (ALL   PEPPERMINT TWISTERS          196   SCEPTER    US       503
CARLTON LATIMORE K SAX(     DOIN' THE TWIST              196   ROULETTE   US   RS25166
WILLIE DAVIS    D V  (      HEY LETS TWIST               196   ROULETTE   US   RS25168
LARRY VERNIERI   V   (      ALL THE WORLD IS TWISTIN'    196   ROULETTE   US   RS25171
DAVID BRIGATI   V SAX(      BACK AT THE PEPPERMINT LOUNGE 196  ROULETTE   US   RS25173
JIMI HENDRIX     G   (1     TWO TICKETS TO PARIS         196   ROULETTE   US   RS25182
                           JOEY DEE    (SOLO)            19    ROULETTE   US   RS25197
                           DANCE DANCE DANCE (SOLO)      19    ROULETTE   US   RS25221
                           (1) LIVE 1966
```

GRAHAM DEE

```
GRAHAM DEE      G V  (A      (A) SOMETHIN' ELSE          197   PYE       UK   NSPL 18570
FRANK RICOTTI   PERC (A
RAY WARLEIGH    WIND (A   RICHY HITCOCK   G    (A   SIMON MORTON    PERC (A  FRANK GIBSON       D (A
JEAN GILBERT    V    (A   PAUL HART  K VLN     (A   LAWRENCE JUBER  G    (A  KEVIN PEEK         G (A
PAUL WESTWARD   B    (A   GARRY TRAVERS   V    (A   JOY YATES       V    (A
```

KIKI DEE

```
KIKI DEE        V    (ALL    (A) I'M KIKI DEE            1968  FONTANA       UK   STL 5455
BIAS BOSHELL    K    (GDJK   (B) GREAT EXPECTATIONS      1970  TAMLA US TS303 UK  STM 11158
ROGER POPE      D    (D      (C) LOVING & FREE           1973  ROCKET US 3040 UK  PIGL  5
JO PARTRIDGE    G    (D      (C) LOVING & FREE           1973  MCA           US        395
BRIAN HOLLAWAY  G    (G      (D) IVE GOT THE MUSIC IN ME 1974  ROCKET US 3042 UK  PIGL 10
ANDY DALBY      G    (G      (D) IVE GOT THE MUSIC IN ME 1974  MCA           US        458
B J COLE        STEEL(CD     (E) KIKI DEE                1974  SOUNDS SUPERB UK   SPR 90030
ROGER BALL      SAX  (C      (F) PATTERNS                1974  PHILIPS       UK   6382 079
DAVEY JOHNSTONE G    (CG     (F) PATTERNS                1974  LIBERTY       US   LST  763
NIGEL OLSSON    D    (C      (G) KIKI DEE                1977  ROCKET US 2257 UK  ROLA  3
DOREEN CHANTER  V    (C      (H) STAY WITH ME            1979  ROCKET US 3011 UK  TRAIN 3
DAVE MATTACKS   D    (C      (I) GREATEST HITS           1980  WARWICK    UK WW  5092
DEE MURRAY      B    (C      (J) PERFECT TIMING          1981  ARIOLA UK 5050 US RCA  14180
KAY GARNER      V    (CD
PAUL KEOGH      G    (C   JIMMY HALL      K    (C   IRENE CHANTER   V   (CD  JIM RYAN         G (C
JOHN McBERNIE   G    (C   GERRY CONWAY    D    (C   ELTON JOHN      K   (C   LESLEY DUNCAN    V (C
RONNIE LEAHY    K    (C   LIZA STRIKE     V    (C   PETE CLARKE     D   (D   MIKE DEACON      K (D
```

(CONTINUED)

KIKI DEE (CONTINUED) D39

CISSY HOUSTON	V	(D	JOSHIE ARMSTEAD	V	(D	MAERETHA STEWART	V	(D	BARRY MORGAN	PERC (D
JEFF TITMUS	PERC	(D	CLIVE FRANKS	V	(D	STUART EPPS	V	(D	BARRY ST JOHN	V (D
BILLY LAWRIE	V	(D	PAUL VIGRASS	V	(D	GARY OSBORNE	V	(D	PHIL CURTIS	B (DG
MELVIN GALE	PERC	(G	HUGH McDOWELL	CELLO(G	RAY COOPER	PERC	(G	DAVID SANBORN	HRNS(G
MICHAEL BRECKER	HRNS	(G	RANDY BRECKER	HRNS (G	R & J STONE	V	(G	SUNNY LESLIE	V (G
STEVE HOLLY	D	(GJ	JAMES NEWTON HOWARD	(G	RICHARD TANDY	SYN	(G	TONY BURROWS	V (G
BOB JENKINS	D	(J	GARY TWIGG	B	(J	FRANK RICOTTI	PERC	(J	PIP WILLIAMS	G (J
PATRICK MORAZ	K	(J								

DEEP D39A

PSYCHEDELIC MOODS	196	PARKWAY	US	7051

DEEP FEELING (1) D39B

JOHN POLI PALMER	VIBES(A	(A) ROCK GENERATION VOL 8(2 TRACKS)	1971	BYG	FR	529708
GORDON JACKSON	G V	(A				
LUTHER GROSVENOR	G V	(A	JIM CAPALDI	D V	(A	DAVE MASON	B V (A

DEEP FEELING (2) D39C

JOHN SWAIL'GUY DARRELL' V(A	(A) DEEP FEELING	1971	DJM		DJLPS419
DEREK ELSON	K	(A				
MARTIN JENNER	G V	(A	DAVID GREEN	B V FLT(A

DEEP FREEZE D39E

SHERRIE LAWRENCE	PNO	(A	(A) MY GERANIUMS ARE BULLETPROOF	1979	MOLE EMBARKING UK	MOLE1
ALAN JENKINS	G B CLAR(A					
GRAHAM SUMMERS	D	(A	ERICA STOCK	PERC	(A	MICK BUNNAGE	V (A

DEEP PURPLE D40

JON LORD	K	(ALL	(A) SHADES OF DEEP PURPLE	1968	PARLOPHONE	UK	PCS	7055
IAN PAICE	D	(ALL	(A) SHADES OF DEEP PURPLE	1977	HARVEST	UK	AHSM	2016
		(ABCDEFGHIJ	(A) SHADES OF DEEP PURPLE	19	PATHE	FR	066	04175
RITCHIE BLACKMORE	G	[(KLNOPQST*VW	(A) SHADES OF DEEP PURPLE	1968	TETRAGRAMMATON US			102
NICK SIMPER	B	(ABC*SIT	(B) BOOK OF TALIESYN	1969	HARVEST	UK	SHVL	751
ROD EVANS	V	(ABCTSI	(B) BOOK OF TALIESYN	196	TETRAGRAMMATON US			107
ROGER GLOVER	V	(DEFGHIJNOQ*STW(B) BOOK OF TALIESYN	19	PATHE	FR	066	04000
IAN GILLAN	V	(DEFGHIJNOQ*STW(C) DEEP PURPLE	1969	HARVEST	UK	SHVL	759
DAVID COVERDALE	V	(KLMPRW	(C) DEEP PURPLE	19	TETRAGRAMMATON US			119
GLEN HUGHES	B	(KLMPRTW	(C) DEEP PURPLE	19	PATHE	FR	066	90505
TOMMY BOLIN	G	(MRT	(D) CONCERTO FOR GROUP & ORCHESTRA	1970	HARVEST	UK	SHVL	767
$ RANDY CALIFORNIA	G		(D) CONCERTO FOR GROUP & ORCHESTRA	1970	PATHE FR 90749 US WB			1860
			(E) DEEP PURPLE IN ROCK	1970	HARVEST UK SHVL777 US WB			1877
$ REPLACED BLACKMORE IN US 1 NIGHT			(F) FIREBALL	1971	HARVEST UK SHVL793 US WB			2564
			(G) MACHINE HEAD	1972	PURPLE	UK	TPSA	7504
			(G) MACHINE HEAD	1972	PATHE FR 83261		US WB	2607
			(H) MADE IN JAPAN	1972	PURPLE UK TPSP351	US		2701
			(H) LIVE IN JAPAN	197	PURPLE			55067
			(I) BEST OF	1972	SCEPTER	US		18010
			(J) WHO DO WE THINK WE ARE	1973	PURPLE UK TPSA7508 US WB			2678
			(J) WHO DO WE THINK WE ARE	1973	PATHE	FR	066	94140
			(K) BURN	1974	PURPLE UK TPS3505 US WB			2766
			(L) STORMBRINGER	1974	PURPLE	UK	TPS	3508
			(L) STORMBRINGER	197	PATHE FR 96004		US WB	2832
			(*) Mk 1 & 2	1974	PURPLE	UK	188	94865
			(M) COME TASTE THE BAND	1975	PURPLE	UK	TPSA	7515
			(M) COME TASTE THE BAND	1975	PATHE FR 97044		US WB	2895
			(N) 24 CARAT PURPLE	1975	PURPLE UK TPSM2002 FR			96424
			(O) PURPLE PASSAGES	1972	WB		US	2644
			(P) MADE IN EUROPE	1976	PURPLE UK		TPSA	7517
			(P) MADE IN EUROPE	197	PATHE FR 98181 US	WB		2995
			(Q) POWER HOUSE	1977	PURPLE UK TPS3510 FR			60072
			(R) LAST CONCERT IN JAPAN	1977	PURPLE	UK	P	10370
			(S) THE SINGLES A's & B's	1978	HARVEST	UK	SHSM	2026
			(T) WHEN WE ROCK WE ROCK	1978	WB		US	3223
			(V) DEEP PURPLE Mk 2 SINGLES	1979	PURPLE	UK	TPS	3514
			(W) DEEPEST PUPLE	1980	HARVEST UK EMITV25 US			3486
			(X) IN CONCERT (DBL)	1980	HARVEST UK SHDW412			
			(EP) NEW LIVE & RARE	1978	PURPLE	UK	PUR	137

DEEP SIX D40A

( ) DEEP SIX	19	LIBERTY	US LRP	3475

DEF LEPPARD D40B

STEVE CLARK	G	(ABC	(A) GETCHA ROCKS OFF (EP)	1979 BLUDGEON 001	RI VERTIGO 6059240
RICK SAVAGE	B	(ABC	(B) ON THROUGH THE NIGHT	1980 VERTIGO UK 9102040 US MERCURY 3828
PETE WILLIS	G	(ABC	(C) HIGH & DRY	1981 VERTIGO UK 6359045 US MERCURY 4021
RICK ALLEN	D	(ABC		
JOE ELLIOTT	V	(ABC		

DEFENDERS D40C

( ) PLAY THE BIG ONES(WILD WEEK END)	19	WORLD PACIFIC	US	WP	1810
( ) DRAG BEAT	19	DEL FI	US	DFLP	1242

JACK DeJOHNETTE D40D

JACK DeJOHNETTE D G K SYN (ALL	(A) THE DE JOHNETTE COMPLEX	1968	MILESTONE			9022
JOHN ABERCROMBIE	G	(GHJK	(B) HAVE YOU HEARD	19	MILESTONE			9029
GARY PEACOCK		(I	(C) SORCERY	19	MILESTONE			9061
KEITH JARRETT	PNO	(EI	(C) SORCERY	19	PRESTIGE			10081
MIROSLAV VITOUS	B	(	(D) COSMIC CHICKEN	1975	PRESTIGE			10094
EDDIE GOMEZ	B	(K	(E) RUTS AND DAITYA	1975	ECM			1021
LESTER BOWIE	TPT	(K	(F) GATE WAY	1975	ECM			1061
ALEX FOSTER	SAX	(J	(G) UNTITLED	1976	ECM		ECM	1074
MIKE RICHMOND	B	(GJ	(H) PICTURES	1977	ECM		ECM	1079
WARREN BERNHARDT	K	(G	(I) TALES OF ANOTHER	1977	ECM			1101
JOHN PURCELL	WIND	(N	(J) NEW RAGS	1977	ECM		ECM	1103
CHICO FREEMAN	WIND	(N	(K) NEW DIRECTION	1978	ECM		ECM	1128
PETER WARREN	B	(N	(L) SPECIAL EDITIONS	1980	ECM			1152
			(M) NEW DIRECTIONS IN EUROPE	1980	ECM			1157
			(N) TIN CAN ALLEY	1980	ECM			1189

DEFUNKT

		Year	Label	Country	Cat.
(A) DEFUNKT		1981	HANNIBAL	UK	1301

DESMOND DEKKER

DESMOND DEKKER V (ALL
WITH
BARRY HOWARD V
SAMMY JONES V

	Year	Label	Country	Cat.
(A) ISRAELITES	1975	CACTUS		CTLP 111
(A) ISRAELITES	19	UNI	US	73059
(B) DOUBLE DEKKER	1973	TROJAN		TRLD 401
(C) YOU CAN GET IT	1970	TROJAN		TRL 146
(D) SWEET 16 HITS	1978	TROJAN	UK	TRLS 154
( ) THIS IS	1969	TROJAN		TTL4
( ) BLACK & DEKKER	1980	STIFF	UK	SEEZ 26
( ) COMPASS POINTS	1981	STIFF	UK	SEEZ 36

DELEGATES

	Year	Label	Country	Cat.
(A) THE DELEGATES	197	MILESTONE	US	100

DELFONICS

WILLIAM HART V (ALL
WILBERT HART V (ALL
RANDY CAIN V (
RITCHIE DANIELS V (
MAJOR FARRIS V (
BRUCE PETERSON V (

	Year	Label			Country	Cat.
(A) LA MEANS I LOVE YOU	1968	BELL	UK	SBLL106	US	1150
(B) SOUND OF SEXY SOUL	1969	BELL	UK	SBLL121	US	1151
(C) DELFONICS	1971	BELL	UK			SBLL 137
(D) SUPER HITS	1972	BELL	UK			BELLS 204
(D) SUPER HITS	197	PHILLY GROOVE	US			1152
(E) TELL ME THIS IS A DREAM	1973	BELL	UK	BELLS217	US	1154
(F) ALIVE & KICKING	1974	BELL	UK	BELLS245	US	1501
(G) LET IT BE ME	1975	SOUNDS SUPERB	UK			SPR 90078
( ) DIDN'T I BLOW YOUR MIND	19	PHILLIES				1153

DEL VIKINGS

NORMAN WRIGHT V (
CORINTHIAN JOHNSON V (
DONALD BAKUS V (
DAVID LERCHEY V (
CLARENCE E QUICK V (

	Year	Label	Country	Cat.
COME GO WITH ME	19	DOT	US	DLP 3695
COME GO WITH ME	19	LUNAVERSE	US	LP 1000
COME GO WITH ME	19	CONTOUR	UK	2870 388
AND THE SONNETS	19	CROWN	US	CLP 5368
NEWIES & OLDIES	19	FEE BEE	US	205
SWINGING SINGING RECORD SESSION	19	MERCURY	US	MG 20353
THEY SING THEY SWING	19	MERCURY	US	MG 20314
(EPS)				
COME GO WITH US	19	DOT	US	DEP 1058
DEL VIKINGS	19	MERCURY	US	MEP 35A
THEY SING THEY SWING	19	MERCURY	US	EP1 3362

DELIVERANCE

DAVE McSPARREN B (A
JACQUES BELZING G (A
DANNY JANZ V (A
KEN JANZ V (A
SCOTT NEWTON TPT (A

	Year	Label		Cat.
(A) TIGHTROPE	1979	GLOBAL		0063 215

GUY ROELLINGER B (A   PAUL JANZ V (A
ELMER LOUIS PERC (A   LEE HARPER TPT (A
BOBBY STERN SAX (A   HORST MULLER PROD (A

DELLS

MARVIN JOHNSON V (
CHUCK BARKSDALE V (
VERNE ALLISON V (
JOHNNY CARTER V (
MIKE McGILL V (
JOHNNY FUNCHES V (

		Year	Label		Country	Cat.
THERE IS		19	CADET		US	804
GREATEST HITS		19	CADET		US	824
MUSICAL MENU		19	CADET		US	822
LOVE IS BLUE		1969	CADET		US	829
LIKE IT IS		19	CADET		US	837
FREEDOM MEANS		197	CADET		US	50004
SING DIONNE WARWICK		19	CADET		US	50017
SWEET AS FUNK CAN BE		1974	CADET		US	50021
GREATEST HITS		1974	CADET		US	50036
GIVE YOUR BABY		1974	CADET		US	50037
DELLS		1974	CADET		US	50046
CORNERED	DBL	1977	DJM		UK	DJD 28032
BEST OF		1973	CHECKER		US	6467 303
MIGHTY MIGHTY		1975	CHESS US 60030	UK		9109 100
WE GOT TO GET TOGETHER		1975	CADET		US	6044
OH WHAT A NITE		19	VEE JAY		US	1010
OH WHAT A NIGHT		19	JOY UK JOYS186	US		BUDDAH5053
NO WAY BACK		19	MERCURY		US	SRM 11084
ITS NOT UNUSUAL		19	VEEJAY		US	1141
FACE TO FACE		19	ABC		US	AA 1113
LOVE CONNECTION		1978	mERCURY		US	SRM1 3711
THEY SAID IT COULN'T BE DONE BUT WE DID			MERCURY		US	SRM1 1145
NEW BEGINNINGS		1978	ABC		US	1100
I TOUCHED A DREAM		1980	20TH CENT		UK	T 618
WHATEVER TURNS YOU ON		1981	20th CENT			T 633
(EP) STAY IN MY CORNER		1980	CHARLY			CTD 110

DELMORE BROTHERS

	Year	Label	Country	Cat.
(A) BEST	19	KING	US	1C90

DELTA CROSS BAND

BILLY CROSS G V (A
TROELE JENSEN G K V (A
PREBEN FEDDERSEN D (A
SOREN ENGEL B HRN(A
SVEND ASMUSSEN HRNS (A

	Year	Label	Country	Cat.
(A) RAVE ON	1979	MEDLEY	EURO	6031
(B) UP FRONT	198	ARIOLA	GER	203 942

BOB CURLAN HRNS (A   JORGEN LANG HRNS (A
ANNE GRETHE HRNS (A

DELTA FIVE

	Year	Label	Country	Cat.
(A) SEE THE WHIRL	1981	PRE	UK	PREX 6

DEMIAN

ROD PRINCE
ROY COX B V (A
TODD POLTER G V (A

	Year	Label	Country	Cat.
(A) DEMIAN	1971	ABC	US	718

DAVID FORE D (A

DEMIAN

	Year	Label		Cat.
(A) ROCK STAR FARM	19	STARBURST		ARC 3301

MAX DEMIAN BAND

PAUL ROSE G V (A
KIRT PENNEBAKER B V (A
JIM LEFEVRE K G V (A

	Year	Label		Cat.
(A) TAKE IT TOO THE MAX	1979	RCA		PL 13273

DANIEL HOWE G K V (A   PETE SIEGEL D (A

D45D   **DELUXE BLUES BAND**   D45D

(A) LIVE AT HALF MOON PUTNEY 1981 HOT BOX UK HOT1

D46   **DEMICK & ARMSTRONG**   D46

| HERBIE ARMSTRONG | V G | (AB | (A) LITTLE WILLIE RAMBLE | 1971 | MAM | UK | MAM 1001 |
| ROD DEMICK | V G STEEL HCA | (AB | (B) LOOKING THROUGH | 1972 | A&M 2504 | UK | AMLH68098 |

WITH

GORDON SMITH	G V	(AB	HENRY SPINETTI	D PERC	(B	TONY KNIGHT	D	(A
DAVID WATKINS	PNO	(A	ALICE PEPPER	V	(	SUE GLOVER	V	
SUNNY LESLIE	V	(	KAY GARNER	V	(			

D46A   **DEMICS**   D46A

JIMMY WEATHERSTONE	D	(AB	(A) TALKS CHEAP	(EP)	1979	READY	CAN	RROO1
LAIN ATKINSON	B	(AB	(B) THE DEMICS		1980	INTERCAN	CAN	IC 1010
ROB BRENT	G	(A						
STEVE KOCH		(B	TOM TRUMUTH	K	(B	KEITH WHITTAKER	V	(AB
STEVE KOCH		(B						

D46B   **DEMON**   D46B

DAVE HILL	V	(	(A) NIGHT OF A DEMON	1981	CARRERE	UK	CAL 126
MAL SPOONER	G	(	(B) THE UNEXPECTED GUEST	1982	CARRERE	UK	CAL 129
LES HUNT	G	(					
CHRIS ELLIS	B	(	JOHN WRIGHT	D	(		

D47   **DEMON FUZZ**   D47

SMOKEY ADAMS	V	(A	(A) AFREAKA	1971	JANUS	US	JLS 3029
STEVEN JOHN	D	(A	(A) AFREAKA	1971	DAWN	UK	DNLS 3013
RAY RHODES	K	(A	(EP) I PUT A SPELL ON YOU	1970	DAWN	UK	DNX 2504
SLEEPY JACK JOSEPH	B	(A					
W RAPHAEL JOSEPH	G	(A	CLARENCE BROOMS CROSDALE TROM (A	PADDY COREA	WIND (A		
AYINDE FOLARON	CONGA	(A					

D48   **DEMON THOR**   D48

TOMMY'DEMON'FORTMAN	V	(AB	(A) ANNO 1972	1974	UA	UK	UAS 29393
STEPHEN NUESCH	K	(B	(B) WRITTEN IN THE SKY	1974	UA	UK	UAS 29496
GEFF HARRISON	V	(					
VEIT MARCUS	K	(	CLAUDE THOMAN	D	(B	PETER BISCHOF	V	(B
OLIVER FREYTAG	V	(B	GEFF HARRISON	V	(B			

D48A   **DEMONS**   D48A

MARTIN RAPPOPORT	D PERC	(A	(A) DEMONS	1977	MERCURY	US	SRM1 1164
MARTIN BUTLER	G	(A					
ELIGT KIDD	G V PERC	(A	ROBBIE TWYFORD	B V	(A	BOB JONES	G V	(A
LIZA BURNS	V	(A	CRAIG LEON	PROD K	(A			

D49   **SANDY DENNY**   D49

SANDY DENNY	V	(ALL	(A) ALL GUR OWN WORK	1968	PICKWICK	UK	SHM 813
TONY HOOPER	G V	(A	(B) FOTHERINGAY	1970	ISLAND UK ILPS9125 US A&M4269		
DAVE COUSINS	G V K	(A	(C) SANDY DENNY	1970	SAGA	UK	8153
RON CHESTERMAN	B	(A	(C) SANDY DENNY	1977	NOVA	GERM 6 22968AK	
KEN GUDMAND	D	(A	(C) SANDY DENNY (*)	1978	MOONCREST	UK	CREST 28
TREVOR LUCAS	G V	(BDF	(D) NORTHSTAR GRASS MAN & THE RAVENS	1971	ISLAND UK ILPS9165 US A&M4317		
GERRY CONWAY	D	(BDF	(E) SANDY	1972	ISLAND UK ILPS9207 US A&M4371		
LINDA (THOMPSON) PETERS	V	(BE	(F) LIKE AN OLD FASHIONED WALTZ	1973	ISLAND UK ILPS9258 US	9340	
IAN WHITEMAN	K	(D	(G) RENDEZVOUS	1977	ISLAND	UK	ILPS 9433
TONY REEVES	B	(D	(*) HAS 1 TRACK EXTRA				
BARRY DRANSFIELD	V	(D					

ROBIN DRANSFIELD	V	(D	ROYSTON WOOD	V	(D	ROGER POWELL	D	(D	LADYBIRDS	V	(G
BUDDY EMMONS	STEEL	(D	TIMI DONALD	D	(EG	DAVE SWARBRICK	VLN	(E	JERRY DONAHUE	G V	(BDFG
SNEAKY PETE KLEINOW	STEEL	(E	RABBIT BUNDRICK	K	(EFG	DAVE PEGG	B	(FG	DAVE MATTACKS	D	(FG
DANNY THOMPSON	B	(F	ALAN SKIDMORE		(F	PAT DONALDSON	B V	(BDEFG	STEVE WINWOOD	K	(G
IAN ARMIT	B	(F	JEAN ROUSSEL	K	(F	DIZ DISLEY	G	(F	FRANK RICOTTI	G	(G
JUNIOR MARVIN	G	(G	BROTHER JAMES	G	(G	JIMMY HAINES		(G	BOB WESTON	G	(G
JOHN GILLASPIE		(G	DICK CUTHELL		(G	BILLIE LIVSEY	K	(G	BOB WESTON	G	(G
JESS RODEN	V	(G	SUE GLOVER	V	(G	SUNNY LESLIE	V	(G	KAY GARNER	V	(G
CLAIRE TORRY	V	(G	BENNIE GALLAGHER	V	(G	GRAHAM LYLE	V	(G			

D50   **DEODATO**   D50

EUMIR DEODATO	K	(ALL	(A) PRELUDE	1973	CTI CTL 10	US	6021
RON CARTER	B	(AB	(B) DEODATO 2	1973	CTI CTL 17	US	6029
STANLEY CLARKE	B	(AB	(C) IN CONCERT	1974	CTI CTL 21	US	6041
BILLY COBHAM	D	(ABD	(D) WHIRLWINDS	1974	MCA UK MCG3518 US	410	
AIRTO MOREIRA	PERC	(AC	(E) VERY TOGETHER	1976	MCA UK MCG2774 US	2219	
JOHN FROSK		(A	(E) VERY TOGETHER	19	BARCLAY FR 414004		
RUBENS BASS NI	PER	(BD	(F) LOVE ISLAND	1978	WB UK K56416	US BSK 3132	
MARVIN STAMM	TPT	(ABD	(G) ARTISTRY	1975	MCA MCF2587	US	457
GARNETT BROWN	TROM	(AB	(H) FIRST CUCKOO	1975	MCA MCF 2728	US	491
WAYNE ANDRE	TROM	(AB	(H) FIRST CUCKOO	197	BARCLAY	FR	410039
GEORGE STRAKEY	TROM	(A	(I) 2001	1972	CTI	CTI 7081	
MARKY MARKOWITZ	TPT	(A	(J) NIGHT CRUISER	1980	WB US BSK3467 GERM	56848	
BILL WATRONS	TROM	(A	(K) KNIGHTS OF FANTASY	1979	WB US 3321		
PAUL FAULISE	HRNS	(A					

JOE SHEPLEY	TPT	(AB	BILL BUFFINGTON	HRN	(ABDF	JOHN TROPEA	G	(ABCED	PETER GORDON	HRNS	(A
JOHN GUILING	B	(BD	GERRY CHAMBERLAIN	TROM	(F	TONY LEVIN	B	(D	HUBERT LAWS	FLT	(AB
PHIL BODNER	WIND	(AD	GEORGE MARGE	WIND	(ABD	ROMEO PENQUE	WIND	(ABDF	BURT COLLINS	HRNS	(B
JAY BERLINER	G	(A	RICK MAROTTA	D	(BF	GILMORE DEGAP	PERC	(BD	RAY BARRETTO	CONGA	(A
JON FADDIS	HRNS	(BD	VICTOR PAZ	HRNS	(BD	ALAN RUBIN	HRNS	(B	TONY STUDD	HRNS	(B
BROOKS TILLOTSON	HRNS	(BFD	JOE TEMPERLEY	HRNS	(BD	LARRY CARLTON	G	(F	RAY GOMEZ	G	(FJ
POPS POPWELL	B	(F	HARVEY MASON	D	(F	JIMMY MAELEN	PERC	(FJ	CHARLIE CONRAD	PERC	(F
VICTOR FELDMAN	PERC	(F	RAY ARMANDO	PERC	(F	JOE CORRERO	D	(F	AL McKAY	G	(F
VERDINE WHITE	B	(F	PHILIP BAILEY	PERC	(F	GORDON EDWARDS	B	(F	JERRY DODGION	FLT	(F
JOEL KAYE	FLT	(F	WALLY KANE	FLT	(F	JOHN GATCHELL	TPT	(F	RANDY BRECKER	TPT	(F
BOB MILLIKAN	TPT	(D	SAM BURTIS	TROM	(DF	TONY PRICE	TUBA	(DF	NICK REMO	D	(D
JOHN ECKERT	TPT	(D	LARRY SPENCER	TPT	(D	URBIE GREEN	TROM	(D	ARTIE KAPLAN	WIND	(D
GARY GRANGER	B	(J	STEPHEN DANIELS	PERC	(J	GEORGE PARRISH	G	(J	PLATINUM HOOK	V	(J
SERGIO DIAS	G	(J	DAVID BRAVO	K	(J	SKIPP INGRAM	B	(J	VICTOR JONES	G	(J
RONALD BELL	SAX	(J	KEITH O'QUINN	TROM	(J	HARVEY ESTRIN	FLT	(J	LOU MARINI	SAX	(J
STRING SECTION		(DJ									

D50A
DEPECHE MODE
(A) SPEAK & SPELL   1981   MUTE   UK   STUMM 5   D50A

D51
DEPRESSIONS
'AMMER SMITH	G	(A	(A) THE DEPRESSIONS		1978	BARN	UK	2314 105
RICO THE KNIFE	G	(A	(B) IF YOU KNOW WHAT I MEAN(AS D Ps)	1978	BARN	UK	2314 107
DAVE BARNARD	B V	(AB					
KROBAR GARVEY	D	(AB	ERIC WRIGHT	G V	(B	TONY MAYBERRY	G V	(B

D51A
LOUIS DEPRESTIGE
LOUIS DEPRESTIGE	G	(A	(A) LE MONDE EST ROCK	1980	MOTORS	FR	77017
FRANCOIS AUGER	D	(A					
DOMINIQUE PERRIER	PNO	(A	GEORGE RODI	SYN	(A	ALAIN HATOT	SAX	(A
PATRICK JOUASSIN	G	(A					

D51B
ROBERT DERBY
ROBERT DERBY   (A   (A) I'M NORMAL   1980   CATCHALOT   US   111   D51B

D52
DEREK & THE DOMINOES
ERIC CLAPTON	G V	(AB	(A) LAYLA & OTHER ASSORTED LOVE SONGS	1971	ATCO	US	SD2 704
CARL RADLE	B	(AB	(A) LAYLA & OTHER ASSORTED LOVE SONGS	1971	POLYDOR	GER	2625 005
BOBBY WHITLOCK	K	(AB	(A) LAYLA & OTHER ASSORTED LOVE SONGS	1977	RSO US 3801	UK	2671 110
JIM GORDON	D	(AB	(A) LAYLA & OTHER ASSORTED LOVE SONGS	1977	RSO	US	3801
DAVE MASON	G V	(LIVE	(A) LAYLA & OTHER ASSORTED LOVE SONGS	197	POLYDOR		2612 014
DUANE ALLMAN	G	(A	(B) LIVE IN CONCERT	1973	POLYDOR	UK	2659 020
			(B) LIVE IN CONCERT	1973	POLYDOR	GER	2671 101
			(B) LIVE IN CONCERT	197	RSO	US	SO 28800

D53
RICK DERRINGER
RICK DERRINGER	G V	(ALL	(A) ALL AMERICAN BOY	1973	BLUE SKY	US 32481	UK	EPC 65831
VINNY APPICE	D	(CDEI	(B) SPRING FEVER	1975	BLUE SKY	US 33423	UK	SKY 80733
DANNY JOHNSON	G	(CDEI	(C) DERRINGER	1976	BLUE SKY	US 34181	UK	SKY 81458
KENNY AARONSON	B	(CDEFGI	(D) SWEET EVIL	1977	BLUE SKY	US 34470	UK	SKY 81847
MYRON GROMBACHER	D	(FG	(E) LIVE	1977	BLUE SKY	US 34848	UK	SKY 82130
TASHA THOMAS	V	(C	(F) IF YOU WEREN'T SO ROMANTIC	1978	BLUE SKY	US 35075	UK	SKY 82464
MAERETHA STEWART	V	(C	(G) GUITARS & WOMEN	197	BLUE SKY	US 36092	UK	SKY 83746
NEIL GERALDO	PNO	(G	(H) FACE TO FACE	1980	BLUE SKY	US 36551	UK	SKY 84462
JIMMY WILCOX	D V	(H	(I) LIVE IN CLEVELAND	1977	BLUE SKY	US PRO265		
BENJY KING	K V	(H						

ROGER POWELL	SYN	(G	DONNIE KISSELBACH	B V	(H	KASIM SULTON	B V	(G	TODD RUNDGREN	V (G
BOBBY CALDWELL	D	(AB	LANI GROVES	V	(A	CARL HALL	V	(A	KENNY PASSERELLI	B (A
PAUL HARRIS	SYN K	(A	EDGAR WINTER SAX	SYN K	V(AB	JOHN SIOMOS	D	(B	PAUL PRESTOPINO MAND	V(B
DAN HARTMAN	V	(BF	DORIS STILL	V	(B	DAVID JOHANSEN	HCA	(B	JOE LALA	PERC(A
TASHA THOMAS	V	(A	JOE WALSH	G	(A	JOE VITALE	D	(A	DAVID BROMBERG	G (A
TOOTS THIELMAN	HCA	(B	JOHN SIEGLER	B	(B	ALLEN NICHOLS	V	(B	CHICK COREA	SYN(B
JOHNNY WINTER	G	(B	MARK CUNNINGHAM	G	(F					

D53A
MICHAEL DESBARRES
MICHAEL DESBARRES	G V	(A	(A) I'M ONLY HUMAN	1980	DREAMLAND	US 15001	UK 2394 279
PAUL DELPH	K V	(A					
NIGEL HARRISON	B	(A	JOHN GOODSALL	G	(A	RIC PARNELL	D V	(A

D53B
DESERTERS
(A) THE DESERTERS   1981   CAPITOL   US   ST 12164   D53B

D53C
JACKIE DESHANNON
JACKIE DESHANNON	V G	(ALL	(A) JACKIE DESHANNON	1963	LIBERTY	US	7320
RON TUTT	D	(S	(B) THIS IS	196	IMPERIAL	US	12286
LARRY KNECHTEL	K SYN	(S	(C) YOU WON'T FORGET ME	196	IMPERIAL	US	12294
JOHN KHAN	B	(S	(D) IN THE WIND	196	IMPERIAL	US	12296
MIKE DEASY	G	(SP	(E) BREAKING IT UP	1965	LIBERTY	US	7390
WADDY WACHTEL	G	(S	(F) ARE YOU READY FOR THIS	196	IMPERIAL	US	12328
JESSE ED DAVIS	G	(S	(G) NEW IMAGE	196	IMPERIAL	US	12344
MICHAEL STEWART	G	(S	(H) FOR YOU	196	IMPERIAL	US	12352
JOE CLAYTON	PERC	(S	(I) ME ABOUT YOU	196	IMPERIAL	US	12386
LAURA CREAMER	V	(S	(J) WHAT THE WORLD NEEDS NOW	1965	IMPERIAL	US	12404
BOB CLAIR	FLT	(S	(K) LAUREL CANYON	196	IMPERIAL	US	12415
MARK CREAMER	V	(S	(L) C'MON LOVE A LITTLE	1967	LIBERTY	US	7430
SUSAN STEWART	V	(S	(M) LONELY GIRL	1968	SUNSET	US	5225
KENNY RANKIN	G	(S	(N) PUT A LITTLE LOVE IN YOUR HEART	1969	IMPERIAL	US	12442
BRIAN WILSON	V	(S	(O) TO BE FREE	1970	IMPERIAL	US	12453
MARILYN WILSON	V	(S	(P) SONGS	1971	CAPITOL	US	ST 772
RANDY EDELMAN	V	(SP	(Q) JACKIE	1972	ATLANTIC	US	7231
PETER MARSHALL	B	(S	(R) YOUR BABY IS A LADY	1973	ATLANTIC	US	7303
GARY DALTON	G	(S	(S) NEW ARRANGEMENT	1975	CBS	US	33500
BUDDY EMMONS	STEEL	(S	(T) YOU'RE ONLY THE DANCER	1977	AMHERST	US	1010
LEE SKLAR	B	(S	( ) JACKIE DE SHANNON	19	SUNSET	US	5322
BARRY FASMAN	SYN	(S	( ) THE VERY BEST OF	19	UA	US	LA434
VICTOR FELDMAN	VIBES	(S	( ) HERES JACKIE	19	SUNSET	US	1029
DANNY KOTCH	G	(P					

DICK ROSSMINI	G	(P	BRYAN GAROFALO	B	(P	RUSS KUNKEL	D	(P		
JERRY JUMONVILLE	SAX	(P	CLYDIE KING	V	(P	ALBHY GALUTEN	K	(Q		
CHARLES CHALMERS	V	(Q	SANDRA RHODES	V	(Q	DONNA RHOADS	V	(Q		
CISSY HOUSTON	V	(Q	DEIDRE TUCK	V	(Q	VANETTA FIELDS	V	(P		
RENELLE STAFFORD	V	(Q	REGGIE YOUNG	G	(Q	MAC REBBENACK	PNO	(K		
JOHN CHRISTOPHER	G	(Q	HAROLD BATTISTE	PNO	(K	BOBBY WOODS	PNO	(Q		
RUSS TITLEMAN	G	(K	MIKE LEACH	B	(Q	CRAIG TARWATER	B	(K		
BISHOP HEYWOOD	D	(Q	PAUL HUMPHREY	D	(K	LARRY McDONALD	PERC	(Q		
BARRY WHITE	V	(K	DENZIL LAING	G	(Q	BRENDA DAVIES	V	(K		
JOHN STEWART	XYLO	(Q	DON McALLISTER	V	(K	BWIA SUNSET BAND		(Q		
ARIF MARDIN	ACC	(Q	SEYCHELLES SINGERS		(S					

D54
ANDY DESMOND
ANDY DESMOND	V G	(AB	(A) LIVING ON A SHOE STRING	1975	KONK		KONK 103
RON LAWRENCE	B	(B	(B) ANDY DESMOND	1978	ARIOLA		ARL 5001
NICK TREVISICK	D	(B					

TOM KING	V G	(B	MICK WEAVER	K	(B	LOZ NETTO	G	(B	PAUL CARTWRIGHT	PERC(AB
DYAN BIRCH	V	(B	FRANK COLLINS	V	(B	BONNIE WILKINSON	V	(B	NICKY PAYN	HCA SAX (B
KEITH NELSON	BANJO	(B	DEBI DOSS	HCA	(B	JACK EMBLOW	ACC	(B	IAN LYNN	SYN V (B
BARRY ST JOHN	V	(B	DAVE MARKEE	B	(B	TERRY JONES	HRNS	(B	GRAHAM COLLYER	G (B

(CONTINUED)

[156]

ANDY DESMOND (CONTINUED)

NOEL McCALLA	V (B	GRAHAME SMITH	VLN (B	SHIRLEY RODEN	V	(AB IAIN WHITMORE	V (B
LUCY KLEE	V (B	GINNY KLEE	V (B	NEIL McBAIN	D	(A EDDY SPENCE	K (A
PHIL PALMER	G (A	RICK LLOYD	MAND G (A	RICHARD GARRETT	V	(A PAMELA TRAVIS	V (A
ALAN HOLMES	WIND (A	JOHN GOSLING	K (A	DAVE DAVIES	G V	(A	

DESPARADOS

(A) THE DESPARADOS	1981	CHARISMA	UK	CLASS11	

DESPERATE BYCYCLES

DANNY WIGLEY	V K (A	(A) REMORSE CODE	1980	REFILL	UK	RR6
NICKY STEPHENS	B HCA	(A			
DAN ELECTRO	G	(A	JEFF TITLEY	D (A	

JIMMY DESTRI

JIMMY DESTRI	G V (A	(A) HEART ON A WALL	1981	CHRYSALIS	CHR 1368		
CLEM BURKE	D	(A					
JOHN SIEGLER	B	(A	TOMMY MORRONGIELLO G	(A	EARL SLICK	G	(A CARLOS ALOMAR	G V(A
MICHAEL KAMEN	K V	(A	CHRIS STEIN	G HCA(A	DONNA DESTRI	V	(A DEBBIE HARRY	V (A
SASHA KAMEN	V	(A	JOEY WILSON	V (A				

JIMMY DESTRY & DESTINY

JIMMY DESTRY	(A	(A) GIRLS ROCK'N' ROLL & CARS	1980	MILLENIUM	7753

DETECTIVE

BOBBY PICKETT	B	(ABC	(A) DETECTIVE	1977	SWANSONG	US SS8417 UK 59405
TONY KAYE	K	(ABC	(B) IT TAKES ONE TO KNOW ONE	1978	SWANSONG	US SS8504 UK 59406
MICHAEL DES BARRES	V	(ABC	(C) LIVE	1978	SWANSONG	US LAAS 002
JON HYDE	D V	(ABC				
MICHAEL MONARCH	G	(ABC				

DETERGENTS

(A) THE MANY FACES OF THE DETERGENTS	19	ROULETTE	US	25308	

DETONATORS

(A) NEED YOU LOVE EP	197	LOCAL	LP1		

DETROIT EMERALDS

ABE TILLMAN	V (ALL	(A) YOU WANT IT YOU GET IT	1972	JANUS	UK 6310 207
JAMES MITCHELL	V (ALL	(B) ABE JAMES & IVORY	1973	WESTBOUND	UK 6309 101
IVORY TILLMAN	V (ALL	(C) LET'S GET TOGETHER	1978	ATLANTIC	UK K 50452
		(D) FEEL THE NEED	1977	WESTBOUND	UK K 50372

DEUTSCH AMERIKANISCHE FREUNDSCHAFT(D A F)

ROBERT GORL	D	(BCD	(A) EIN PRODUKT DAR D.A.F.	19		
W SPELMANS	G SYN V(B	(B) DIE KLEINEN UND DIE BOSEN	1980	MUTE	STUMM1
GABI DELGADOOLOPEZ	V	(BCD	(C) ALLES IST GUT	1981	VIRGIN UK V2202 GER 203 644
C HAAS	B SAX SYN(B	(D) GOLD UND LIEBE	1981	VIRGIN UK 2218 GER 204 165

HARI DEUTER

HARI DEUTER	(A	(A) SILENCE IS THE ANSWER	1981	KUCKUCK	049/050

DEVIANTS

MICK FARREN	V	(AB	(A) DISPOSABLE	1968	STABLE	UK SLP 7001
SID BISHOP		(A1	(A) DISPOSABLE	1969	SIRE	US 97005
DUNCAN SANDERSON		(A1C	(B) PTOOFF	1969	UNDERGROUND IMPRESARIOS	IMP1
RUSS HUNTER	D	(AB1C	(B) PTOOFF	1969	SIRE	US 97001
M J McDONNELL		(A	(B) PTOOFF	1969	DECCA	UK SKLR 4993
DENNIS HUGHES		(A	(C) DEVIANTS	1969	TRANSATLANTIC	UK TRA 204
PAUL RUDOLPH	G	(AC	(C) DEVIANTS	1978	LOGO	UK MOGO 4001
STEPHEN SPARKES		(A	(C) No3	197–	SIRE	US 97016
DICK HECKSTALL SMITH	SAX	(A	( ) SCREWED UP(EP)	19	STIFF	UK LAST 4
GEORGE		(A				
PETE BROWN		(A	TONY FERGUSON	(A	JIMMY ASHWORTH	(A
KARL DALLAS		(A	ANDREW JOHNS	(A	CORD REES	B G V(A

DEVILS ANVIL

(A) HARD ROCK FROM THE MIDDLE EAST	19	CBS	US	9464	

KARLA DEVITO

KARLA DEVITO	(A	(A) IS THIS A COOL WORLD OR WHAT	1981	EPIC US 37014 UK 84841

DEVO

MARK MOTHERSBAUGH	G V K(ALL	(A) Q.ARE WE NOT MEN A. WE ARE DEVO	1978	VIRGIN UK 2106 US WB BSK 3239
BOB MOTHERSBAUGH	G V (ALL	(B) DUTY NOW FOR THE FUTURE	1979	VIRGIN UK 2115 US WB BSK 3337
BOB CASALE	G K V(ALL	(C) FREEDOM OF CHOICE	1980	VIRGIN UK 2162 US WB BSK 3435
GERALD CALE	K V (ALL	(D) DEVO LIVE(MINI LP)	1981	VIRGIN UKOVED1 US WB BSK 3584
ALAN MYERS	D (ALL	(E) NEW TRADITIONALISTS	1981	VIRGIN UK 2191 US WB BSK 3595
BRIAN ENO	PROD (A				

DEXY'S MIDNIGHT RUNNERS

KEVIN ROWLAND	V	(	(A) SEARCHING FOR THE YOUNG SOUL REBELS 1980 PARLOPHONE	UK PCS 7213
GROCK	D	(			
PETE WILLIAMS	B	(	STEVE SPOONER	HRNS (	J B HRNS (
JIMMY PATERSON	HRNS	(			

CLIFF DE YOUNG

CLIFF DE YOUNG	V (A	(A) CLIFF DE YOUNG	1975	MCA	US 432
JOE OSBORN	B (A				
VICTOR FELDMAN	PERC (A	DENNIS BUDIMIR	G (A	BEN BENAY	G (A
LARRY MUHOBERAC	PNO (A	BROOKS HUNNICUTT	V (A	NORMAN KURBAN	PNO V(A
DAVID KEMPER	D (A	DAVID HUNGATE	B (A	ART MUNSON	G (A
GEORGE BOHANON	TROM (A	OSCAR BRASHEAR	TPT (A	JACKIE KELSO	SAX (A
VALERIE CARTER	V (A				

DIAMOND

(A) DIAMOND	1974	PARAMOUNT	US	1021	

DHARMA BLUES BAND

MIKE KING	K (A	(A) DHARMA BLUES	1969	MAJOR MINOR	SMCP5017
JOHN HILLARY	G V (A				
GARY COMPTON	HCA (A				

DYAN DIAMOND

DYAN DIAMOND	V G	(A	(A) IN THE DARK		1978	MCA US 3053		UK	MCF 2875
CRAIG MAGEE	G	(A							
JERRY ACKERMAN	B	(A	JOSEPH FITZGERALD	K	(A	RANDY WHELPLEY	D	(A	
CHRIS DARROW	G MAND	(A							

DIAMOND HEAD

SEAN HARRIS	G V	(AB	(A) LIGHTNING & THE NATIONS	198	FAN CLUB ONLY?
BRIAN TATLER	G	(AB	(B) LIVING ON BORROWED TIME	1982	MCA UK DH1001
COLIN KIMBERLEY	B	(AB	(EP) DIAMOND LIGHTS	19	
DUNCAN SCOTT	D	(AB	(EP) FOUR CUTS	1982	MCA UK DH101

DIAMOND REO

NORM NARDINI	G B V	(A	(A) DIAMOND REO	1975	BIG TREE US 89507
BOB McKEAG	G V	(A			
ROB JONES	D V	(A	FRANK JOHNS	D V	(A

THE DIAMONDS

DAVE SOMERVILLE	V	(AB	POP HITS	19	WING	CAN	12178
MIKE DOUGLAS	V	(B	AMERICA'S No 1 SINGING STYLISTS	19	MERCURY	US MG	20309
JOHN FELTON	V	(B	MEET PETE RUGOLO	19	MERCURY	US MG	20368
EVAN FISHER	V	(B	OLD WEST	19	MERCURY	US MG	60159
BILL REED	V	(A	STROLL	19	MERCURY	US EP	13390
TED KOWALSKI	V	(Z	DIAMONDS	19	BRUNSWICK	US EP	71031
PHIL LEAVITT	V	(C	(A) 1955/58 (B) 1959>				

MANU DIBANGO

MANU DIBANGO SAX PERC V K	(ALL	(A) SOUL MAKOSSA		1972	ATLANTIC	US	7267
JOBY JOBS	D	(A	(B) OBOSO	1973	LONDON	UK SH	8451
ROBBIE SHAKESPEARE B		(J	(C) MAKOSSA MAN	1974	ATLANTIC	US	7276
MALEKANI GERRY	G	(J	(D) MAKOSSA MUSIC	1975	CREOLE	UK	CRLP 503
VAL DOUGLAS	B	(J	(E) MANU 76	1976	DECCA	FR	362 001
GEOFF CHUNG	B G K	(J	(F) SUPER KUMBA	1976	DECCA	FR	360 052
CLYDE BULLARD	B	(J	(G) AFROVISION	1976	DECCA	UK SKLR	5296
SLY DUNBAR	D	(J	(G) AFROVISION	1978	ISLAND	US	9526
MIKEY BOO RICHARDS	D	(J	(H) A L'OLYMPIA DBL	1978	FIESTA	FR 360 099/100
CRUSHER BENNETT	PERC	(J	(I) SUN EXPLOSION	1978	DECCA	UK SKLR 5303
STICKY	PERC	(J	(J) GONE CLEAR	1980	ISLAND	UK ILPS 9539
MIKEY MAO CHUNG	G	(J	(K) ABASSADOR	1981	ISLAND	UK ILPS 9658
WILLIE LINDO	G	(J					

ANSEL COLLINS	K	(J	BARRY ROGERS	TROM (J	LOU MARINI	SAX (J	RANDY BRECKER TPT (J
JON FADDIS	TPT	(J	ED BYRNE	TROM (J	WAYNE ARMOND	G (J	PETER ASHBOURNE K (J
MIKE LAWRENCE	TPT	(J	ROBBIE LYN	K (J	CLIVE HUNT	K (J	GWEN GUTHRIE V (J
YOLLANDA McCULLOUGH	V	(J	BRENDA WHITE	V (J	YVONNE LEWIS	V (J	FRANK FLOYD V (J
JOCELYN BROWN	V	(J	LONG MANFRED	B 'AC	PATRICE GALAS	PNO (C	SLIM PEZIN G (C
HARRY GATIBELZA	ORG	(J	LUCIEN DOBAT	D (C	FREEDY N'KOUNKOU	PERC (C	MANU RODANET (AC
FREDDY MARS	PERC	(A	PIERRE ZOGO	G (A	GEORGES ARVANITAS	PNO (A	JERRY MALEKANY G (C
PHILIPPE NEVEU	B	(C	CLAUDE VAMUR	D (C			

DICK & DEE DEE

DICK ST JOHN	V	(	YOUNG & IN LOVE	19	WB	US	1500
DEE DEE SPERLING	V	(	TURN AROUND	19	WB	US	1538
			THOU SHALT NOT STEAL	19	WB	US	1586
			SONGS WEVE SUNG	19	WB	US	1623
			TELL ME	19	LIBERTY	US	7236

DICKEY DOO & THE DONTS

GERRY'DICKEY DOO'GRANAHAN	V	(	( ) THE MADISON	196	UA	US UAS 6094
JERRY GRANT	V	(	( ) TEEN SCENE	196	UA	US UAS 6097
HARVEY DAVIS	V	(				
AL WAYS	V	(	RAY GANGI	V	(	

TOM DICKIE & DESIRES

TOM DICKIE	G V	(A	(A) COMPETION	1981	MERCURY US 14918 .EURO 6337 168
MICHAEL ROY	G V	(A			
MICKY CURRY	D	(A	JON MACEY	B V (A	GARY CORBETT K (A
RONNIE BELL	PERC	(A	JOE MARTINO	G (A	

DICKIES

LEONARD PHILIPS	K V	(AB	(A) THE INCREDIBLE SHRINKING DICKIES	1979	A&M UK AMLH64742
STAN LEE	G V	(AB	(B) DAWN OF THE DICKIES	1979	A&M UK AMLE68510
BILLY CLUB	V B	(AB			
KARLOS KABALLERO	D	(AB	CHUCK WAGON	K G (AB	BONITA BUTTER V (A
JOHN HEULETT	PROD	(B			

JAMES LUTHER DICKINSON

JAMES LUTHER DICKENSON		(A	(A) DIXIE FRIED	19	ATLANTIC US 8299

DICTATORS

HANDSOME DICK MANITOBA	V	(ABC	(A) GO GIRL CRAZY	1975	EPIC	US 33348 UK 80767
ANDY SHERNOFF	B K V	(ABC	(B) MANIFEST DESTINY	1977	ASYLUM US 7E1109 UK 53061
SCOTT KEMPER	G	(	(C) BLOOD BROTHERS	1978	ASYLUM US 147 UK K53083
ROSS FUNICELLO	G V	(ABC	(D) LIVE,FUCK 'EM IF THEY CANT TAKE	1981	REACH OUT US 102
RITCHIE TEETER	D V	(BC				
MARK MENDOZA	B	(B	STU BOY KING	D (A	SCOTT'TOP TEN' KEMPER G (A
PETRONIUS WOOCS	K	(B	MURRAY KRUGMANN	PROD (ABC	
SANDY PEARLMAN	PROD	(ABC	ALAN GLOVER	K (A	

BO DIDDLEY

BO DIDDLEY'ELIAS McDANIELS' G V(ALL
JEROME GREEN MARACAS

OTIS SPANN	PNO	(	BILLY BOY ARNOLD	HCA (	FRANK KIRKLAND	D (	THE DUCHESS	G (
CHUCK BERRY	G	(	HOWLIN' WOLF	V HCA(*	MUDDY WATERS	G V (*	COOKIE VEE	V (X
RICHARD EVANS	B	(X	CLIFFORD DAVIS	SAX (X	WILLIE HENDERSON	SAX (X	GENE BARGE	SAX (X
STEVE GALLOWAY	TROM	(X	FRANK GORDON	TPT (X	MURRAY WATSON	TPT (X	ARTHUR HOYLE	TPT (X
PHILIP UPCHURCH	G	(X	GERALD SIMS	G (X	TENNYSON STEPHENS	PNO (X	DERF REKLAW RAHEEM	CONGA(X
ROBERT CROWDER	D	(X	BRIAN GRICE	D (X	MARY ANN STEWART	V (X	MARYLYN HAYWOOD	V (X
VIVIAN HARRELL	V	(X	ROY WOOD	B (X	EDDIE HARDIN	ORG (X	RAY FENWICK	G (X
KEITH SMART	D	(X	CHARLES GRIMAR	CONGA(X	NIGEL GRAINGE	PERC (X	GREGORY TAYLOR	V (X
CHARISE TAYLOR	V	(X	JUANITA BUCKNER	V (X	CRYSTAL BRAKE	V (X	ANGELA SMITH	V (X
LYNN MOORE	V	(X	TOM THOMPSON	G (Z	RICHARD DAVIS	B (Z	ED O'DONNELL	D (Z

(CONTINUED)

SHUGGIE OTIS	G	(Z	DAVE ARCHULETTA	ORG	(Z	TERRY GOTTLIEB	B	(Z	JOHNNY OTIS	D	(Z
CARMINE APPICE	D	(V	TIM BOGERT	B	(V	BILLY JOEL	K	(V	ALBERT LEE	G	(V
ROGER McGUINN	G	(V	DANIEL MOORE	V	(V	TED NEELEY	V	(V	ELVIN BISHOP	G	(V
JOE COCKER	V	(V	CARKY LAING	PERC	(V	ALVIN LEE	G	(V	KEITH MOON	D	(V
MATTHEW MOORE	V	(V	LESLIE WEST	G	(V	JOHN TROPEA	G	(V	CARL LYNCH	G	(Z
ERNEST HAYES	K	(Z	WILBUR BASCOMB	B	(Z	JIMMY JOHNSON	D	(Z	MONTEGO JOE	PERC	(Z
ESMOND EDWARDS	PERC	(Z	JOE NEWMAN	TPT	(Z	JOHN BELLO	TPT	(Z	MARVIN STAMM	TPT	(Z
JON FADDIS	TPT	(Z	IRWIN MARKOWITZ	TPT	(Z	HARRY DIVITO	TROM	(Z	GARNETT BROWN	TROM	(Z
DOMICK GRAVINE	TROM	(Z	WILLIS JACKSON	SAX	(Z	JOHN LEONE	SAX	(Z	TONY PRICE	TUBA	(Z
MICHAEL PICKETT	HCA	(Z	GENE BIANCO	V	(Z	J R BAILEY	V	(Z	KEN WILLIAMS	V	(Z
MELVIN KENT	V	(Z									

HAVE GUITAR WILL TRAVEL	196	CHECKER	US	2974
IN THE SPOTLIGHT	196	CHECKER	US	2976
IN THE SPOTLIGHT	1964	PYE	UK	NPL 28034
IS A GUNSLINGER	1963	PYE INT	UK	280
IS A GUNSLINGER	196	CHECKER	US	2977
A LOVER	196	CHECKER	US	2980
IS A TWISTER	196	CHECKER	US	2982
BO DIDDLEY	1963	PYE	UK	28026
BO DIDDLEY	196	CHESS	UK	704
BO DIDDLEY	196	CHECKER	US	2984
BO DIDDLEY	196	CHECKER	US	1431
BO DIDDLEY RIDES AGAIN	1963	PYE	UK	28029
BEACH PARTY	1963	PYE	UK	28032
(**)TWO GREAT GUITARS	1964	PYE	UK	28047
(**)TWO GREAT GUITARS	1964	CHECKER	US	2991
HEY GOOD LOOKING	1964	CHESS	UK	CRL 4002
BO DIDDLEY & COMPANY	196	CHECKER	US	2985
SURFIN' WITH BO DIDDLEY	196	CHECKER	US	2987
SURFIN' WITH BO DIDDLEY	196	MARBLE ARCH UK	MAL	751
ROAD RUNNER	196	CHECKER	US	2988
16 ALL TIME HITS	1964	PYE INT	UK	28049
16 ALL TIME HITS	196	CHECKER	US	2989
LET ME PASS	1965	CHESS	UK	CRL 4507
HEY BO DIDDLEY	196	PYE	UK	28025
HEY BO DIDDLEY	1967	GOLDEN GUINEA UK	GGO358	
HEY BO DIDDLEY	1968	MARBLE ARCH	UK	MAL814
HEY BO DIDDLEY	196	CHECKER	US	2992
500% MORE MAN	196	CHECKER	US	2996
ORIGINATOR	196	CHECKER	US	3001
GO BO DIDDLEY	196	CHECKER	US	3006
GO BO DIDDLEY	196	CHECKER	US	1436
GO BO DIDDLEY	1959	LONDON	UK	HAM 2230
BOSS MAN	196	CHECKER	US	3007
(*) SUPER BLUES BAND	1968	CHECKER	US	3010
BLACK GLADIATOR	196	CHECKER	US	3013
BLACK GLADIATOR	196	CHECKER	US	50004
(X) LONDON SESSIONS	1972	CHECKER	UK	6499 476
(X) LONDON SESSIONS	197	CHESS	US	50029
GOT ANOTHER BAG OF TRICKS	1973	CHECKER	UK	6467 304
GOT ANOTHER BAG OF TRICKS	1973	CHESS	US	2CH60005
GOLDEN DECADE	1973	CHESS	UK	6310 123
ANOTHER DIMENSION	1975	CHESS	US	50001
(V) 20thANNIVERSARY	1976	RCA		1042
(V) 20thANNIVERSARY	1976	RCA		APLI 1225
(W) WHERE IT ALL BEGAN	197	CHESS	US	50016
(Z) BIG BAD BO	197	CHECKER	US	50047
I'M A MAN(DBL)	1977	M F		202/2
CHESS MASTER	1981	CHESS	UK	4003
EPS				
CHUCK & BO	1963	PYE	UK	NEP 44009
HEY BO DIDDLEY	1963	PYE	UK	NEP 44014
THE STORY OF BO DIDDLEY	1964	PYE	UK	NEP 44019
IS A LUMBERJACK	1964	PYE	UK	NEP 44031
DIDDLING	1964	PYE	UK	NEP 44036
IM A MAN	1965	CHESS	UK	CRE 6008
ROOSTER STEW	1966	CHESS	UK	CRE 6023
BO DIDDLEY	19	CHESS	US	5125

D66A DIESEL D66A				
ROB VUNDERLINK	G V	(A		
MARK BOON	G V	(A	(A) WATTS IN A TANK	1980 REGENCY 19315 POLYDOR 2925 092
FRANK PAPENDRECHT	B V	(A		
			PIM KOOPMAN	D K V(A

D66B   DIESEL SMOKE   D66B

(A) DIESEL SMOKE	1963	STARDAY	US	250

D66C   DIESTELMANN   D66C

STEFAN DIESTELMANN	G V	(A	(A) FOLK BLUES BAND	19 AMIGA 855633
BERND KLEINOW	HCA	(A		
DIETRICH PETZOLD	V	(A	RUDIGER PHILLIP	B	(A	WOLFGANG FIEDLER	PNO	(A
MEMPHIS SLIM	PNO V	(A	VOLKER SCHLOTT		(A			

D66D   DIF JUZ   D66D

(A) HUREMICS	1981	4AD	UK	BAD 109

D67   DIGA RHYTHM BAND   D67

MICKEY HART	D	(A	(A) DIGA RHYTHM BAND	1976 UA ROUND UK UAS 29975
JIM LOVELESS	PERC	(A	(A) DIGA RHYTHM BAND	1976 UA ROUND US RXLA 600G
RAY SPIEGEL	PERC	(A		
JOY SCHULMAN	PERC	(A	ZAKIR HUSSAIN	PERC	(A	PETER CARMICHAEL	PERC (A
ARSHAD SYED	PERC	(A	JORDAN AMARANTHA	PERC	(A	VINCE DELEACHO	PERC (A
TOR DIETRICHSON	PERC	(A	ASHIM CHAUDHURI	PERC	(A		

RICHARD DIGANCE

RICHARD DIGANCE	G V	(ALL	(A) PISCES	1971	TRAILER	UK	LER 2025
JOHN O'CONNOR	G V	(ACF	(B) IN CONCERT 74	1976	TRANSATLANTIC	UK	TRASAM 35
BARRIEMORE BARLOW	D V	(F	(C) ENGLANDS GREEN & PLEASANT LAND	1974	TRANSATLANTIC	UK	TRA 277
RICK KEMP	B V	(F	(D) HOW THE WEST WAS LOST	1975	TRANSATLANTIC	UK	TRA 289
DOUG MORTER	G V	(CDF	(E) TREADING THE BOARDS	1975	TRANSATLANTIC	UK	TRA 306
MIKE LEWIS	K	(F	(F) LIVE AT QUEEN ELIZABETH HALL	1978	CHRYSALIS	UK	CHR 1187
DAVE COOKE	PNO	(C	(G) COMMERCIAL ROAD	1979	CHRYSALIS	UK	CHR 1262
ENGLISH TAPESTRY	V	(D	( ) RICHARD DIGENCE	1975	MERCURY	US	1 1042
PETER CURTIS	B K	(C					
ALAN BROOKS	D	(C	PHIL MILNER	B V	(D	NIGEL PEGRUM	PERC (D
MICHAEL CHAPMAN	G	(D	MARTIN JENKINS	BANJO FDL (D	ALEX ATTERSON V HARMONIUM (D		
DIK CADBURY	B V	(D	GERRY MORRIS	B	(D	PAUL RODRIGUEZ	K (D
MIKE BIEVENEU	PNO	(D	JOHN REDPATH	D	(D		

DOUG DILLARD

DOUG DILLARD	BANJO G	(ALL	(A) THE BANJO ALBUM	1969	TOGETHER	US	1003
BERNIE LEADON	G	(A	(B) DUELLING BANJOS	1973	20th CENTURY	US	T 409
ANDY BELLING	K	(ABC	(C) DOUGLAS FLINT DILLARD	1974	20th CENTURY	US	T 426
MILT HOLLAND	PERC	(A	(D) HEAVEN	1979	FLYING FISH	US	FF086
RED MITCHELL	B	(A	(E) JACKRABBIT	1980	FLYING FISH	US	208
GENE CLARK	HCA	(A					
DON BECK	G	(A	JOHN HARTFORD	FDL	(A	BILL BRYSON	B (E
SKIP CONOVER	G	(E	SAM BUSH	MAND	(A	PAUL BREIDENBACH	G (E
DAN CRARY		(D	JEFF GILKINSON	B	(DB	JOHN HOBBS	(D
MARK SORGER		(D	ROD DILLARD	G V	(CDB	COLIN CAMERON	B (C
VASSAR CLEMENTS	FDL	(C	RAY PACK	G V	(E	PAUL YORK	D (CDB
JOHN RAINES	D	(CD	MARK DAWSON	HCA	(D	DICK ROSINI	G (EB
BUDDY EMMONS	STEEL	(BC	DOUG BOUNSALL	G	(D	BILLY CONSTABLE	G (DE
RICK RUSKIN	G	(C	DAVID JACKSON	B	(D	COLIN CAMERON	B (B
BYRON BERLINE	FDL	(BDE	SNEAKY PETE KLEINOW STEEL		(C	RON STARR	SAX (C
BILLY RAY LATHAM	G	(B	LINDA DILLARD	V	(CD	RICK CUNHA	G (B
DONNA WASHBURN	V	(CD	PEPPER WATKINS	V	(C	DAVID JACKSON	B (CD
JOE OSBORNE	B	(C	HERB PEDERSEN	GV	(C		

DILLARD & CLARK

DOUG DILLARD	BANJO G	(ALL	(A) FANTASTIC EXPEDITION	1968	A&M	US	AMLS 939
GENE CLARK	G V	(ALL	(A) FANTASTIC EXPEDITION	1975	A&M	US	SP 4158
DAVID JACKSON	B V	(ABC	(B) THROUGH THE MORNING	1969	A&M	UK	AML 966
BERNIE LEADON	G V	(AC	(B) THROUGH THE MORNING	1975	A&M	US	SP 4203
JON CORNEAL	D	(BC	(C) GENE CLARK & DOUG DILLARD	1975	ARIOLA		86027
BYRON BERLINE	FDL	(BC	(D) KANSAS CITY SOUTHERN	1975	ARIOLA		86436
MICHAEL CLARK	D	(A	( ) GRASS ROOTS (½ ALBUM ½BURRITOES)	1972	MAYFAIR	UK	AMLB51038
DON BECK	G HCA	(AC					
DONNA WASHBURN	V G	(BC	ANDY BELLING	K	(C	SNEAKY PETE	STEEL (C
CHRIS HILLMAN	MAND	(C					

DILLARD HARTFORD DILLARD

DOUG DILLARD	BAN	(ABCD	(A) DILLARD HARTFORD DILLARD	1977	SONET	UK	SNTF 730
ROD DILLARD	G V	(AD	(B) GLITTER GLASS	1977	FLYING FISH	US	FF036
JOHN HARTFORD		(AD	(C) DILLARD HARTFORD DILLARD	19	FLYING FISH	US	036
SAM BUSH	MAND	(A	(D) PERMANENT WAVE	1980	FLYING FISH	US	233
AMOS GARRETT	G	(D					
IM COLVARD	G	(A	BUDDY EMMONS	STEEL	(A	PEPPER WATKINS	G (A
HARGUS ROBBINS	PNO	(A	HENRY STRZELECKI	B	(A	JEFF GILKENSON	HCA (A
KENNY MALONE	D	(A	BENNY MARTIN	V	(A	MICHAEL MELFORD	MAND (AD
PHIL AABERG	K	(D	MAC CRIDIN	B	(D	SCOTT MATHELOS	D (D
SAMM BENNETT	CONGA	(D	GREG SELKER	MARIMBA	(D	LINDA DILLARD	V (D
GINGER BLAKE	V	(D	LAURA CREAMER	V	(D		

THE DILLARDS

DOUG DILLARD	BAN G	(ABCM	(A) BACK PORCH BLUE GRASS	1963	ELEKTRA	US	EKS 7232
ROD DILLARD	G	(ABCDEFGJLKM	(B) LIVE ALMOST	1964	ELEKTRA	US	EKS 7265
DEAN WEBB	MAND	(ABCDEFGJLKM	(C) PICKIN' & FIDDLIN'	1965	ELEKTRA	US	EKS 7285
MITCH JAYNE	B V	(ABCDEFGM	(D) WHEATSHEAF SUITE	1968	ELEKTRA US 74035 UK		K 42045
HERB PEDERSEN	BANJO	(DELKM	(E) COPPERFIELDS	1970	ELEKTRA US 74054 UK		K 42034
ANDREW BELLING	K	(G	(F) ROOTS & BRANCHES	1972	UA UK UAS29366 US ANTHEM 5091		
COLIN CAMERON	B	(G	(G) TRIBUTE TO THE AMERICAN DUCK	1973	UA UK UAS29516 US POPPY		175
JOHN HARTFORD	FDL	(GM	(H) BEST OF THE DILLARDS	1976	ELEKTRA	UK	K 52035
BUCK GRAVES	DOBRO G	(G	(J) Vs THE INCREDIBLE L A TIME MACHINE 77		SONET	UK	SNTF 743
DON GALLESE	PERC	(G	(J) Vs THE INCREDIBLE L A TIME MACHINE 77		FLYING FISH	US	FF040
BUDDY EMMONS	STEEL	(D	(K) DECADE WALTZ	1979	FLYING FISH	US	FF082
JOE OSBORNE	B	(D	(L) MOUNTAIN ROCK	1980	CRYSTAL CLEAR		5007
TOXEY FRENCH	D	(D	(M) HOMECOMING & FAMILY REUNION	1980	FLYING FISH	US	215
JIM GORDON	D	(D					
JOHN RAINES	D	(G	IRV DUGAN	G	(G	LINDA DILLARD	V (GM
JEFF GILKENSON	B V	(JKLM	DOUG HAYWOOD	B V	(J	JOEY SCARBURY	V (J
JEFF SILVERMAN	G	(J	GABRIEL KATONA	K	(J	BYRON BERLINE	FDL (CE
BILLY RAY LATHAM	G	(FGL	PAUL YORK	D	(EFGJLK	GARY ITRI	B (G
DOUG BOUNSALL	G V	(LKM	RAY PARKS	FDL	(LK	RICHARD GODFREY	D (M
HOMER DILLARD SNR	FDL V	(M	BILL BRYSON	B	(M	GLENN HARDIN	K (K
HOMER DILLARD JR	ACC	(M	EMORY GORDY	B	(K	BRIAN DILLARD	TAMB (M
MARK SORGER		(K	EARLING DILLARD	G	(M	CHUCK FLORE	(K
EARL DILLARD	BAN	(M					

DILLINGER

DILLINGER		(ALL	(A) CB 200	1975	MANGO	US	9385
SLY DUNBAR	D	(A	(B) BIONIC DREAD	1977	MANGO/ISLAND		9455
EARL CHINNA SMITH	G	(A	(C) TALKING BLUES	1977	MAGNUM		DEAD 1001
ASTON BARRETT	B	(A	(D) TOP RANKING	1977	THIRD WORLD		919
STICKY	PERC	(A	(E) ANSWER ME QUESTION	1978	THIRD WORLD		928
TOMMY McCOOK	HRNS	(A	(F) MARIJUANA MY BRAIN	1978	JAMAICA SOUND		002
NOEL BENBOW	D	(A	(G) LIVE AT THE MUSIC MACHINE	1978	JAMAICA SOUNS		004
VIN GORDON	HRNS	(A	(H) BABYLON FEVER	19	UA	US	795
TRINITY	V	(A	(I) LIVE IN LONDON	1981	ECHO	UK	020
BOBBY ELLIS	HRNS	(A	(J) CORNBREAD	1981	ECHO	UK	021
CLINT EASTWOOD	V	(I	(K) BADDER THAN THEM	1981	A&M	UK	AMLH68528

```
D71B                    DIMEOLA, McLAUGHLIN , DELUCIA                      D71B
      AL DIMEOLA        G  (A      (A) FRIDAY NIGHT IN SAN FRANCISCO  1980  PHILIPS GER 302137 CBS UK 84962
      JOHN McLAUGHLIN   G  (A
      PACO DELUCIA      G  (A
D71C                         DILLMAN BAND                                  D71C
      PAT FREDERICK     V VLN(A     (A) LOVIN THE NIGHT AWAY       1981  RCA
      DANNY FLAHERTY    D V (A
      STEVE SOLMONSON   G V (A   STEVE SEAMANS      STEEL(A  DIK SHOPTEAU      B   (A
D72                           AL DIMEOLA                                    D72
      AL  DIMEOLA       G  (ALL    (A) LAND OF MIDNIGHT SUN       1976  CBS  US 34074      UK 81220
      PETER CANNAROZZI  K  (D       (A) LAND OF MIDNIGHT SUN       1981  EMBASSY RI         UK 32027
      MINGO LEWIS       PERC K(ABCDE (B) ELEGANT GYPSY            1977  CBS  US 34461      UK 81845
      STEVE GADD        D  (ABCDE   (C) CASINO                    1978  CBS  US 35277      UK 82645
      ANTHONY JACKSON   B  (ABCDE   (D) SPLENDIDO HOTEL           1979  CBS  US 36270      UK 88468
      PHILLIPE SAISSE   K  (DE1     (E) ELECTRIC RENDEZVOUS       1982  CBS               UK 85431
      ROBBIE GONZALES   D  (1D      (1) 1978 UK TOUR
      CHICK COREA       K  (AD
      LENNY WHITE       D  (AB  BARRY MILES      K   (AC  EDDIE COLON   PERRC (CD1 STANLEY CLARKE   B (A
      JAN HAMMER        K  (BDE PATTI BIYAKAS    V   (A   PACO DE LUCIA  G    (BE ALPHONSE MOUZON  D (A
      JACO PASTORIUS    B  (A   WILODEK GULGOWSKI K   (1   LES PAUL       G    (D  TIM LANDERS      B (D1
D72A                          MICHAEL DINNER                                D72A
      MICHAEL DINNER    G V (AB     (A) PRETENDER               1974 FANTASY          US       9454
      WADDY WACHTEL     G V (B      (B) TOM THUMB               1976 FANTASY UK 3006 US       9512
      DAVID FOSTER      K   (B
      BILL CHAMPLIN     K V (B  LAURA ALLEN     V  (B  CHUCK FINDLEY  TPT (B   LENNY PICKETT  SAX (B
      GARY ROWLES       V   (B  DEE MURRAY      B V (B  NIGEL OLSSON   D V (B   TIM SMITH(TIM SCHMIT)? V(B
      ALAN ESTES        PERC (B  DICK HYDE       TROM(B  RICHIE HAYWARD V   (B   BOB WARFORD         G  (A
      ED BLACK          STEEL(A  JOHN BOYLAN     K  (A   MIKE BOWDEN    B   (A   MICKEY McGEE        D  (A
      SNEAKY PETE       STEEL(A  DON FELDER      G  (A   MICK UTLEY     ORG (A   GAIL DAVIES         V  (A
      RUSS KUNKEL       D   (A  LINDA RONSTADT  V  (A   DOUG HAYWOOD   V   (A   HERB PEDERSEN       V  (A
      ROBERT GRINNEDGE  STEELDRUM(A  MILT HOLLAND    PERC(A  ANDREW GOLD    PNO (A   GARY MALLABER       D  (A
      LARRY KNECHTEL    PNO (A  RONEE BLAKLEY   V  (A   NICK DE CARO   ACC (A
D72B                            DINGOES                                     D72B
      BRODERICK SMITH   V HCA(AB    (A) FIVE TIMES THE SUN      1977 A&M US 4636    UK   AMLH64636
      CHRIS STOCKLEY    G  (A       (B) ORPHANS OF THE STORM    1979 A&M US 4733    AUST    36721
      KERRYN TOLHURST   G MAND(AB
      JOHN DU BOIS      B  (AB  JOHN LEE       D  (AB  NICKY HOPKINS  PNO (A   GARTH HUDSON    K  (A
      ANDREW HARDIN     G V (B   HOLLY SHERWOOD V  (B   CHERRI GRASSO  V  (B   JAMES McLAIN    V  (A
      SMIGGY            V  (B
D73                             DIODES                                     D73
      PAUL ROBINSON     V   (ABC    (A) THE DIODES            1978 CBS   NL             82681
      JOHN CATTO        G   (ABC    (B) RELEASED             1978 EPIC  CAN            80002
      IAN McKAY         B V K(ABC    (C) ACTION/REACTION      1980 ORIENT       CAN      001
      JOHN  HAMILTON D V K SAX(AB
      MIKE LENGYELL     D V (BC
D74                        DION & THE BELMONTS                              D74
      DION DI MUCCI     V    (ALL   PRESENTING DION & THE BELMONTS   196  LAURIE      US    2002
      FRED MILANO       V   (        DION ALONE                      196  LAURIE      US    2004
      ANGELO D'ALEO     V   (        TOPPERMOST VOL 1                1960  TOP RANK    UK   25/027
      CARLO MASTRANGELO V   (        WISH UPON A STAR                196  LAURIE      US    2006
      RON FRANGIPANE    PNO (S       RUNAROUND SUE                   196  LAURIE      US    2009
      JOE MACK          B   (S       RUNAROUND SUE                   196  HMV         UK   CLP 1539
      AL ROGERS         D   (S       LOVERS WHO WONDER               196  LAURIE      US    2012
      SAL DITROIA       G   (S       LOVERS WHO WONDER               196  STATESIDE   UK   SL 10034
      GEORGE DEVENS     PERC (S      DIONS GREATEST HITS             196  LAURIE      US    2013
      DAVE BROMBERG     G   (S       LOVE CAME TO ME                 196  LAURIE      US    2015
      SELDON POWELL     SAX (S       TOGETHER WITH BELMONTS          196  LAURIE      US    2016
      MIKE OMARTIAN     K V (*       SONGS TO SANDY                  1966  LAURIE      US    2017
      LEE SKLAR         B   (*       15 MILLION SELLERS              1966  LAURIE      US    2019
      DAVID KEMPER      D   (*       MORE GREATEST HITS DION         19   LAURIE      US    2022
      DEAN PARKS        G   (*       RUBY BABY                       1963  CBS         US    2010
      BEN BENAY         G   (*       DONNA THE PRIMA DONNA           19   CBS         US    2107
      VICTOR FELDMAN    PERC (*      DONNA THE PRIMA DONNA           19   CBS         US    8907
      GARY COLEMAN      PERC (*      WONDER WHERE IM BOUND           19   CBS         US    9773
      STEVE BARRI       PERC (*      TOGETHER AGAIN                  1967  ABC         US    599
      CHUCK FINDLEY     TPT (*       TOGETHER AGAIN                  1967  HMV         UK   CSD 3618
      STEVE MADAIO      TPT (*       TOGETHER AGAIN                  19   B+C         UK   CAS 1007
      NINO TEMPO        SAX (*       DION                            1969  LONDON      UK   SHP 8390
      ERNIE WATTS       SAX (*       DION                            196  LAURIE      US    2047
      STEVE DOUGLAS     SAX (*       SIT DOWN OLD FRIEND             1970  WB          US   WS 1826
      DICK HYDE         TROM (*      YOU'RE NOT ALONE                1971  WB          US   WS 1872
      SID SHARP         STRINGS(*    (S)SANCTUARY                    1972  WB          US   WS 1945
      PHIL EVERLY       V   (*       (S)SANCTUARY                    1972  WB          UK   K 46122
      ORRIN WATERS      V   (*       SUITE FOR LATE SUMMER           1972  WB  US 2642 UK   K 46199
      ANN WHITE         V   (*       LIVE AT MADISON SQUARE GARDENS 1972  1972  WB     US    2664
      LUTHER WATERS     V   (*       REUNION                         1973  WB  US 2664 UK   K 46208
      CAROLYN WILLIS    V   (*       BORN TO BE WITH YOU             1975  PHILLES     UK   2307 002
      KERRY CHATER      V   (*       BORN TO BE WITH YOU             197  PHIL SPECTOR US    002
      MYRNA MATTHEWS    V   (*       (*) STREET HEART                1976  WB          UK   K 56279
      JIM HAAS          V   (*       (*) STREET HEART                197  WB          US   BS 2954
      STORMIE OMARTIAN  V   (*       PICK OF THE RADIO GOOD GUYS VOL 1  1976  SONIC    UK   SON ?
                                     PICK OF THE RADIO GOOD GUYS VOL 2  197   SONIC    UK   SON 004
                                     PICK OF THE RADIO GOOD GUYS  VOL 3  197   SONIC   UK   SON 019
                                     RETURN OF THE WANDERER          1978  LIFESONG    US         35356
                                     60 HITS BOX SET                 19   LAURIE      US   SLP 6000
                                     DOOWOP                          19   PICKWICK    US   VSP 3521
                                     EVERYTHING YOU WANTED TO HEAR BY DION 19  LAURIE US    4002
                                     20 HITS                         19               US   ENY 8
                                     DIONS GREATEST HITS             1973  CBS         US    31942
                                     OLDIES BUT GOODIES              1979  TELDEC      GER  623646
                                     REUNION                         1981  WB          UK   K26049
                                     INSIDE JOB                      1981  STRINGDAY   UK    4006
```

DIRE STRAITS

D75									D75
MARK KNOPFLER	G V	(ALL	(A) DIRE STRAITS	1978	VERTIGO	UK	9102 021	US WB	3266
DAVID KNOPFLER	G V	(AB	(B) COMMUNIQUE	1979	VERTIGO	UK	9102 031	US WB	3330
JOHN ILLSLEY	B V	(AB1CD	(C) MAKING MOVIES	1980	VERTIGO	UK	6359 034	US WB	3480
PICK WITHERS	D	(AB1CD	(1) 1980 TOUR						
B BEAR	K	(B	(D) LOVE OVER GOLD	1982	VERTIGO	UK	6359 109		
HAL LINDES	G	(1							
ALAN CLARK	K	(1	ROY BITTAN	K	(C	ED WALSH		SYN (D	
MIKE MAINIERI	VIBES (D								

DIRECTIONS

D75A			D75A
(A) THREE BANDS TONIGHT(EP)	1979	TORCH	UK	TOR004

DIRTY ANGELS

D76							D76
CHARLIE KARP	V G	(AB	(A) KISS TOMORROW GOODBYE	1977 PRIVATE STOCK UK 1019 US	2020
DAVID HULL	K B V MANS	(AB	(B) DIRTY ANGELS	1978 A&M	US	4716
GEORGE MAHER	G	(AB			
JIMMY MAHER	D V	(AB	RICHARD GOTTEHRER	K V	(A	ARTIE KAPLAN	SAX (A
JACK KRAFT	K	(B	PAT ELLINGTON	V	(B	JUDY ELLINGTON	V (B
JOAN ELLINGTON	V	(B	DICKY SIMMONS	HCA	(B	MONTEGO JOE	PERC (B

DIRTY BLUES BAND

D77								D77
ROD PIAZZA	V HCA	(AB	(A) DIRTY BLUES BAND	1967	BLUESWAY	US	BLS	6010
GLEN ROSS CAMPBELL	G	(A	(A) DIRTY BLUES BAND	196	STATESIDE	UK	SSL	10234
ROBERT SANDELL	STEEL	(A	(B) STONE DIRT	1969	BLUESWAY	US	BLS	6020
PAT MALONE	K	(AB	(B) STONE DIRT	1969	STATESIDE	UK	SSL	10268
LES MORRISON	B	(A						
JOHN MILLIKEN	D	(A	DAVE MITER	D	(B	RICK LUNETTA	G	(B
GREGG ANDERSON	B	(B	JIMMY FORREST	SAX	(B	WILLIE GREEN	SAX	(B
FREDDIE HILL	TPT	(B						

DIRTY DOG

D77A				D77A
(A) LET GO OF MY HAND	1977	LIGHTNING	UK	GIL 511

DIRTY DOGS

D77B			D77B
(A) 7 LIVES FOR ROCK'N'ROLL	1979	CBS	UK	83929

DIRTY JOHNS HOT DOG STAND

D77C~			D77C
(A) RETURN FROM THE DEAD	19	AMSTERDAM	US	12004

DIRTY LOOKS

D77D						D77D
PATRICK BARNES	G V	(A	(A) DIRTY LOOKS	1980	STIFF UK SEEZ22 US	36434
MARCO SIN	B V	(A	(B) TURN IT UP	1981	STIFF UK SEEZ 38	
PETER PARKER	D V	(A				
CHARLIE GIORDANA	K	(A				

DIRTY TRICKS

D78							D78
TERRY HORBURY	B	(ABC	(A) DIRTY TRICKS	1975	POLYDOR	UK	2383 351
ANDY BEIRNE	D	(C	(B) NIGHT MAN	1976	POLYDOR US 16082 UK 2383 398	
KENNY STEWART	V	(ABC	(C) HIT & RUN	1977	POLYDOR US 16104 UK 2383 466	
JOHN FRASER BINNIE	G K	(ABC					
JOHN LEE	D	(A					

DIXIE CUPS

D78A					D78A
(A) CHAPEL OF LOVE	1964	REDBIRD	US	20100
(B) IKO IKO	196	REDBIRD	US	20103
(C) RIDIN' HIGH	196	PARAMOUNT	US	525
(D) TEENAGE ANGUISH VOL1	197	CHARLY	UK	CRM 2004

DISCHARGE

D78B					D78B
(A) DECONTROL(EP)	1980	CLAY	UK	CLAY5
(B) REALITIES OF WAR(EP)	19	CLAY	UK	
(C) FIGHT BACK (EP)	1980	CLAY	UK	

DISLOCATED DANCE

D78C				D78C
(A) SLIP THAT DISC	1981	NEW HORMONES	UK	ORG10

DISTRACTIONS

D78D						D78D
MIKE FINNEY	V	(A	(A) YOU'RE NOT GOING OUT DRESSED LIKE THAT 1979 TJM (EP) UK TJM2
STEVE PERRIN	G	(A	(B) NOBODY'S PERFECT	1980	ISLAND	UK	ILPS9604
PIP NICHOLLS	PNO	(A					
ADRIAN WRIGHT	G K	(A	ALEC SIDEBOTTOM	D	(A		

DIVERSIONS

D78E					D87E
LENE LOVICH	V SAX	(A	(A) SOUL SURVIVORS	1977	POLYDOR(NOT RELEASED)
GLENN CARTLIDGE	G	(A			
JEFFREY RAY SMITH	K	(A	DAVE QUINN	B	(A	LES CHAPPELL	G (A
GREG SHEEHAN	D	(A	STEVE SAXON	SAX	(A	MIKE VERNON	PROD (A

DIXIE BELLES

D78F			D78F
(A) DOWN AT PAPA JOES	1964	SAVAGE STAGE US 7 UK LONDON8152

DIXIE DREGS (The DREGS)

D79						D79
ROD MORGENSTEIN	D	(ABCDEF	(A) FREE FALL	1977	CAPRICORN US 0189 UK 2429 154
ANDY WEST	B	(ABCDEF	(B) WHAT IF	1978	CAPRICORN US 0203 UK 2429 165
ALLEN SLOAN	VLN	(ABCDE	(C) NIGHT OF LIVING DREGS	1979	CAPRICORN US 216 UK 2429 181
STEVE MORSE	G	(ABCDEF	(D) DREGS OF THE EARTH	1980	ARISTA	US 9528 NL 202 207
STEVE DAVIDOWSKI	K	(A	(E) UNSUNG HEROES (DREGS)	1981	ARISTA	US 9548 NL 203 630
MARK PARRISH	K	(BC	(F) INDUSTRY STANDARD (DREGS)	1982	ARISTA	US 9588 GER 204 559
T LAVITZ	K	(DEF				
PATRICK SIMMONS	V	(F	STEVE HOWE	G	(F	ALEX LIGERTWOOD	V (F

ERROL DIXON

D79A				D79A
ERROL DIXON		(A	(A) BLUES IN A POT	19	LONDON	US	PS550

FLOYD DIXON

D80					D80
FLOYD DIXON		(ALL	(A) OPPORTUNITY BLUES	1978	ROUTE 66		KIX1
			(B) ROCKIN' THIS JOINT TONITE	1978	JSP	UK	1002
			(C) HOUSTON JUMP	1979	ROUTE 66	SWED	KIX11

WILLIE DIXON

D80A					D80A
WILLIE DIXON	B V	(ALL	(A) WILLIES BLUES	19	PRESTIGE	US	1003
MEMPHIS SLIM	PNO	(AE	(B) I AM THE BLUES	1976	CBS	US	9987
			(C) AUX TROIS MAILOTS	19	POLYDOR	US	658148
			(D) CATALYST	19	PATHE	FR	064 9603
			(D) CATALYST	1976	OVATION	UK	1433

(CONTINUED)

[162]

WILLIE DIXON (CONTINUED)

(E)	AT THE VILLAGE GATE		19				
(F)	WHAT HAPPENED TO MY BLUES		1978	OVATION			QD 1441
(G)	EARTHQUAKE & HURRICANE		19	SPOONFUL	US		
(H)	EVERY WHICH WAY		19	VERVE	US		3007
(J)	SONGS		19	FOLKWAYS	US		2385

D81 LYN DOBSON **D81**

LYN DOBSON

(A) JAM SANDWICH   1974   FRESH AIR   6370 501

D81A DOC HOLLIDAY **D81A**

(A) RIDES AGAIN   1982   A&M   UK   AMLH64882

BRUCE BROOKSHIRE	G V	(A				
EDDIE STONE	K V	(A				
JOHN SAMUELSON	B V	(A	RICK SKELTON	G V	(A	HERMAN NIXON	D	(A
BOB BROOKSHIRE	HCA	(A	TOM ALLOM	K PERC V(A	ERNEST C CHARLES	V	(A

D82 DR ALIMANTADO **D82**

GREGORY ISAACS	V	(A	(A) BEST DRESSED CHICKEN IN TOWN	1978	GREENSLEEVES	UK	GREL1
HORACE ANDY	V	(A	(B) SONS OF THUNDER	1981	GREENSLEEVES	UK	GREL22
JACKIE EDWARDS	V	(A					
JAH WOOSH	V	(A	JIMMY RADWILL	V	(A	DROPPY V	(A

D83 DR BUZZARD'S ORIGINAL SAVANNAH BAND **D83**

CORY DAYE	V B	(AB	(A) DR BUZZARD'S ORIGINAL SAVANNAH BAND	1976	RCA	RS 1072 US APLI 1504
AUGUST DARNELL	V B	(AB	(B) DR BUZZARD MEETS KING PENETT	1978	RCA	APLI 2402
ANDY HERNANDEZ	ACC PERC(AB	(C) GOES TO WASHINGTON	1980	ELEKTRA	US	218
MICKEY SEVILLA	D	(AB					
SANDY LINGER	PROD	(A	PAULINHO DA COSTA	PERC	(B	SUSANDRA MINSKY	V	(B
DON ARMANDO BONILLA	PERC	(A	STONY BROWDER	V G K	(AB			

D83A DR DOPO JAM **D83A**

K POMMER	K G V	(A	(A) FAT DOGS & DANISHMEN	1974	ZEBRA	DENM 2949 012
J KNUDSEN	G	(A					
S SNITKER	HRNS	(A	A GAARDMAN	WIND	(A	J NORDAL	TROM	(A
B C LAUSEN D G VIBES	(A	E WEISGARD	D PERC	(A	V HANSEN	B	(A
LARS BISGAARD	V	(A	BORGE LYSHOLMORTENSEN V	(A	BIRGIT SMIDT	V	(A
BIRGITE HOLM SORENSEN	V	(A					

D84 DR FEELGOOD **D84**

LEE BRILLEAUX	V G HCA(ALL	(A) DOWN BY THE JETTY	1975	UA	UK	UAS 29727
JOHN B SPARKS	B	(ALL	(B) MALPRACTICE	1975	UA	UK	UAS 29880
FIGURE MARTIN	D	(ALL	(B) MALPRACTICE	1975	CBS	US	34098
WILKO JOHNSON	G V	(ABCD	(C) STUPIDITY	1976	UA	UK	UAS 29990
HENRY McCULLOUGH	G	(1	(D) SNEAKIN' SUSPICION	1977	UA	UK	UAS 30075
JOHN MAYO	G	(EFGHJ	(D) SNEAKIN' SUSPICION	1977	CBS	US	34806
TIM HINKLEY	K	(D	(E) BE SEEING YOU	1977	UA	UK	UAS 30123
BOB ANDREWS	K SAX	(AB	(F) PRIVATE PRACTICE	1978	UA	UK	UAG 30184
BRINSLEY SCHWARZ	SAX	(A	(G) AS IT HAPPENS	1979	UA	UK	UAS 30239
			(H) LET IT ROLL	1979	UA	UK	UAS 30269
			(J) CASE OF SHAKES	1980	UA UK 30311 US STIFF USE 12
			(K) ON THE JOB	1981	LIBERTY	UK	LBG 30328
			(L) CASEBOOK	1981	LIBERTY	UK	LBG 30341
			(M) FAST WOMEN & SLOW HORSES	1982	CHISWICK	UK	TOSS 4
			(1) 1977 TOUR				

D85 DR HOOK & THE MEDICINE SHOW **D85**

RAY SAWYER	V G	(ALL	(A) DR HOOK & THE MEDICINE SHOW	1971	CBS	US	30898
			(A) DR HOOK & THE MEDICINE SHOW	1971	CBS	UK	65754
DENNIS LOCORRIERE	V G	(ALL	(B) SLOPPY SECONDS	1972	CBS	US	31622
			(B) SLOPPY SECONDS	1972	CBS	UK	65132
WILLIAM FRANCIS	K	(ALL	(C) BELLY UP	1973	CBS	US	32270
			(C) BELLY UP	1973	CBS	UK	65560
RICHARD ELSWIT	G	(B>P	(D) FRIED FACE	1974	CBS	UK	80372
GEORGE CUMMINGS	STEEL	(ABCD	(E) BALLAD OF LUCY JORDAN	1975	CBS	UK	80114
JANCE GARFAT	B	(B>O	(F) BANKRUPT	1976	CAPITOL		11397
JOHN DAVID	D	(ABCD	(G) A LITTLE BIT MORE	1976	CAPITOL		11522
JOHN WOLTERS	D	(EFGHIJKLNOP	(H) MAKIN' LOVE & MUSIC	1977	CAPITOL		11632
BOB HENKE		(EFGHIJK	(I) STREET PEOPLE	197	CBS	US	32920
ROD SMARR	G	(MOP	(J) REVISITED	197	CBS	US	34147
BILL EMERSON	G	(C	(K) PLEASURE & PAIN	1978	CAPITOL		11859
EDWARD ADAMS	B	(C	( ) SYLVIAS MOTHER	1977	EMBASSY	UK	31458
JOCK SCHROER	HRNS	(C	( ) BEST OF	197	CBS	US	34147
JULES BROUSSARD	HRNS	(C	( ) BEST OF (DBL)	1980	CBS		22102
JOHN WILMETH	HRNS	(C	(L) GREATEST HITS	1980	CAPITOL		26037
FOREST BUCHTEL	HRNS	(C	(M) RISING	1980	MERCURY		6302 076
TOMMY WILLIAMS	FDL	(C	(N) SOMETIMES YOU WIN	1990	CAPITOL		12023
SHERRY FOX	V	(C	(O) LIVE IN THE UK	1981	CAPITOL		26706
ELLEN SCHROER	V	(C	(P) PLAYERS IN THE DARK	1982	MERCURY		MERS 002
NANCY PARIS	V	(C					

D86 DR JOHN **D86**

Dr JOHN(MAC REBENNACK) K V (ALL	(A) DrJOHN AND HIS NEW ORLEANS CONG	19	ACE	US	2020
WITH		(B) GRIS GRIS	1968	ATLANTIC GER 30045 UK 588 147
ERIC CLAPTON	G	(E	(B) GRIS GRIS	1968	ATCO	US	33234
SHIRLEY GOODMAN	V	(EF	(B) GRIS GRIS	1972	ATLANTIC	UK	K 40168
RONNIE BARRON	V K	(EFLT	(C) BABYLON	1969	ATLANTIC	UK	228 018
VICTOR BROX	HRNS K(E	(C) BABYLON	1969	ATCO	US	33270
P P ARNOLD	V	(E	(D) REMEDIES	1970	ATLANTIC	UK	2400 015
DORIS TROY	V	(E	(D) REMEDIES	1970	ATCO	US	33316
STEVE YORK	B	(E	(E) SUN MOON & HERBS	1971	ATLANTIC	UK	2400 161
CALVIN SAMUELS	PERC	(E	(E) SUN MOON & HERBS	1971	ATCO	US	33362
GRAHAM BOND	SAX	(E	(E) SUN MOON & HERBS	1971	ATLANTIC	UK	K 40250
JIM PRICE	TPT	(E	(F) GUMBO	1972	ATLANTIC	UK	K 40384
JOHN BOUDREAUX	D	(ELA	(F) GUMBO	1972	ATCO	US	7006
TAMMY LYNN	V	(EFLT	(G) IN THE RIGHT PLACE	1973	ATLANTIC	UK	K 50017
ALVIN BISHOP ROBINSON G	(FLT	(G) IN THE RIGHT PLACE	1973	ATCO	US	7018
ROBBIE MONTGOMERY	V	(FJL	(H) TRIUMVIRATE(BLOOMFIELD HAMMOND)	1974	CBS US 32172 UK	65659
TOMMY FERRONNE	G	(E	(J) DESITIVELY BONAROO	1974	ATLANTIC	UK	K 50035
RAY DRAPER	TUBA V(E	(J) DESITIVELY BONAROO	1974	ATCO	US	7043

(CONTINUED)

[163]

DR JOHN

FRED STAEHLE	D PERC(EFT	(K) CUT ME WHILE I'M HOT					1975	DJM UK DJM22019			DJSLM 019	
MICK JAGGER	V (E	(L) HOLLYWOOD KNOW THY NAME					1975	UA		UK	UAG 29902	
JONI JONZ	FLT (E	(L) HOLLYWOOD KNOW THY NAME					1975	UA		US	UALA 552	
KEN TERROADE	FLT (E	(M) ONE NIGHT LATE					19	KARATE		US	5402	
CHRIS MERCER	SAX (E	(N) Dr JOHN SUPERPAH					19	TRIP		US	3507	
WALTER DAVIS	PNO (E	(O) ZU ZU MAN					19	TRIP		US	9518	
BOBBY WHITLOCK	V (E	(O) Dr JOHN					19	SPRINGBOARD		US	4018	
JIM GORDON	PERC (E	(Q) 16 GREATEST HITS					19	TRIP		US	TOP 16/1	
JESSIE BOYCE	B (E	(R) CITY LIGHTS					1978	HORIZON		US	AMLJ 732	
WAYNE JACKSON	HRNS (E	( ) ANYTIME ,ANYPLACE					19	BAROMETER		US	BRM67001	
BOB EZRIN	K V (L	( ) MARDI GRAS					19	ATLANTIC			40554	
ROGER HOPPS	TPT (E	( ) NITE TRIPPER AT HIS BEST					1975	RARE BID			8014	
FREEMAN BROWN	PERC (E	(T) TANGO PALACE					1979	HORIZON		US	740	
ANDREW LOVE	SAX (E											
BOBBY KEYS	SAX (E	CARL RADLE	B (E	JULIUS FARNER	B (L	JACK HALE	TROM(E					
ED LOGAN	SAX (E	JAMES MITCHEL	SAX (E	RON JOHNSON	(E	ED HOERNER	TPT (E					
JERRY JUMONVILLE	SAX (E	MELVIN LASTIE	CORN(F	SIDNEY GEORGE SAX HCA	(F	LEE ALLEN	SAX (F					
DAVID LASTIE	SAX (F	MOE BECHAMIN	SAX V(F	HAROLD BATTISTE	WIND (F	KEN KLIMAK	G (F					
JIMMY CALHOUN	B (F	RICHARD WASHINGTON PERC(F	JESSIE SMITH	V (FJ	ALLEN TOUSSAINT	K (GJ					
DAVID SPINOZZA	G (G	RALPH McDONALD	PERC(G	GARY BROWN	SAX (GJ	LEO NOCENTELLI	G (GJ					
ARTHUR NEVILLE	K (GJ	GEORGE PORTER	B (GJ	JOSEPH MODELISTE	D (GJ	STEVE HUNTER	G (L					
THE METERS	(J	MARK COLBY	WIND(J	WHIT SIDENER	SAX (J	KEN FAULK	HRNS(J					
PETER GRAVES	HRNS (J	JOHNNY BADANJEK	D (L	LEROY COOPER	SAX (L	ERNIE WATTS	SAX (L					
CHAUNCEY WELSH	TROM (L	BOBBY TORRES	CONGA (L	VENETTA FIELDS	V (L	WARREN LUENING	TPT (L					
JAMES SMITTY SMITH	G (L	CLIFFORD SOLOMON	SAX (L	KENNY ASCHER	K (L	TOMMY VIG	PERC(L					
STEVE GADD	D (RT	WILL LEE	B (R	RICHARD TEE	K (RT	HUGH McCRACKEN	G (RT					
JOHN TROPEA	G (R	ARTHUR JENKINS	PERC(R	POO PAH DOO	PERC (A	? DITMUS	PERC(A					
? MANN	G (A	BATTISTE OF SCORPIO B	(A	? McLEAN	MAND (A	? BOLDEN	FLT (A					
DIDO	(A	? RONYARDS	(A	?CHINA	(A	GONCY O'LEARY	(A					
SHIRLEY LAVEAUX	(A	? DURDEN	(A	PLAS JOHNSON	WIND (AT	WEST BROWNING	(A					
JEAN FREUNX	(A	JOHN GUMBO	(A	CECILIA LA FAVORITE	(A	KARLA LE JEAN	(A					
ALVIN 'RED' TYLER	SAX (A	HUEY SMITH	PNO (A	FRANKIE FORD	V (A	ROLAND STONE	V (A					
ABRAHAM LABORIEL	B (T	HERMAN ERNEST	D PERC(T	ANDRE FISCHER	D (T	PAULINHO DACOSTA PERC(T						
NEIL LARSEN	PERC (T	CHARLIE MILLER	HRNS(T	OSCAR BRASHEAR	HRNS (T	WARREN LUENING	HRNS(T					
BENNY POWELL	TROM (T	HERMAN RILEY	SAX (T	JACKIE KELSO	WIND (T	GARY HERBIG	SAX (T					
TOMMY JOHNSON	TUBA (T	LARRY WILLIAMS	WIND(T	KIM HUTCHCROFT	SAX (T	STEPHANIE ?	(A					
THERESA	(A											

DR K's BLUES BAND

GEOFF KRIVIT	G B (A	(A) DR K'S BLUES BAND		1968 WORLD PACIFIC US 21903			
ROGER ROLT	G (A	(A) DR K'S BLUES BAND		1968 SPARK		UK 101	
DR K(RICHARD KAY)	PNO (A						
HAROLD VICKERS	B (A	ERIC PEACHEY	D (A	MICK HASSE	V HCA (A		

DR KOCK VENTILATOR

DR KOCK	G (A	(A) DR KOCK VENTILATOR		1980	REFLEKTOR	GER 0060272
KLAUS BLUMENTHAL	K (A					
CHRIS CHAOS	K (A	ALFRED E WAGNER	SAX (A	SCHMITT MARTIN	B (A	

DR MARIGOLDS PRESCRIPTION

DAVE MORRIS	D (	(A) PICTURES OF LIFE		1969	MARBLE ARCH	UK MALS 1222
FRED RADLEY	G V (	(B) HELLO GIRL		1973	SANTA PONSA	UK PNL 501
ALAN FRENCH	K (					
BILL FRENCH	B (					

DR MIX & THE REMIX

ERIC DEBRIS	V (B	(A) PSYCHEDELIC DESERT		19	CELLULIOD	(EP) CEL 6585
PAT VINCENT	G V (B	(B) WALL OF NOISE		19	ROUGH TRADE	ROUGH 6
CHARLIE H	K G D V(B					

DR STRUT

DAVID WOODFORD	WIND (AB	(A) DR STRUT		1979	MOTOWN US 924	UK STML 12120	
KEVIN BASSINSON	K (AB	(B) STRUTTIN'		1980	MOTOWN US 931	UK ATML 12432	
TIM WESTON	G (AB						
PETER FREIBERGEL	B (AB	CLAUDE PEPPER	D (AB	EVERETT BRYSON		PERC (A	

DR STRANGELY STRANGE

TIM GOULDING	V K (B	(A) KIP OF THE SERENES		1969	ISLAND	UK ILPS 9106	
TIM BOOTH	V G (B	(B) HEAVY PETTING		1970	VERTIGO	UK 6360 009	
IVAN PAWLE	V B K (B						
JOHNNY MOYNIHAN	BAZ (B	DAVE MATTACKS	D (B	GARY MOORE	G (B		
JAY MYRDAL	GLOCK (B	HEATHER WOOD	V (B	ANDY IRVINE	MAND (B		
LINUS	PERC (B	JOHANNA	V K (B	ANNIE CHRISTMAS	V K (B		
BRENDAN SHIELS	B (B						

DR WEST'S MEDICINE SHOW & JUNK BAND

NORMAN GREENBAUM	V (A	(A) THE EGGPLANT THAT ATE CHICAGO		19	GREGEOR	US 001	
BONNIE WALLACH	G V (A						
JACK CARRINGTON	G PERC V(A	EVAN ENGBER		PERC (A			

DR 'Z'

KEITH KEYES	K V (A	(A) THREE PARTS TO MY SOUL		1971	VERTIGO	UK 6360 048
ROB WATSON	B (A					
BOB WATKINS	D (A					

DOCTORS OF MADNESS

DAVE VANIAN	V (2	(1) 1978 (2) 1978 APRIL (3) MAY 1978>					
RICHARD'KID' STRANGE G V	(ABCD123	(A) LATE NIGHT MOVIES		1976	POLYDOR	UK 2383 378	
COLIN'STONER' BROWN B	(123ABCD	(B) FIGMENTS OF EMANCIPATION		1976	POLYDOR	UK 2383 403	
PETER DILEMMA	D (ABC123D	(C) SONS OF SURVIVAL		1978	POLYDOR	UK 2383 472	
JILL MACKINTOSH	V (B	(D) DOCTORS OF MADNESS		1978	UA	US 871	
URBAN BLITZ	G VLN (ABC	(E) REVISIONISM		1981	POLYDOR	UK 2478 146	
CLAIRE TORRY	V (B						
STEPHANIE DE SYKES	V (B						

DODGERS

JOHN WILSON	G B V (A	(A) LOVE ON THE REBOUND		1978	POLYDOR	UK 2391 379	
ROGER LOMAS	G B V (A	(A) LOVE ON THE REBOUND		1978	POLYDOR	US PD1 6174	
BOB JACKSON	K V G (A	(A) LOVE ON THE REBOUND		1978	POLYDOR	UK 2383 513	
PAUL HOOPER	D V (A						

ERNIE K DOE D90A

D90A	ERNIE K DOE	V	(A	(A) ERNIE K DOE	1972	JANUS	US 3030

DOG SOLDIER D91

D91							
KEEF HARTLEY	D	(A	(A) DOG SOLDIER	1975	UA US UALA405	UK	UAS 29769
MILLER ANDERSON	G V	(A1	(1) LATER LINE UP				
PAUL BLISS	B	(A1					
MEL SIMPSON	K	(A1	DEREK GRIFFITHS	G	(A1	ERIC DILLON	D (1

BUNK DOGGER D92

D92

BUNK DOGGER	V G SYN	(AB	(A) FIRST OFFENCE	1978	RCA	UK	PL 25138
ANDY ROBERTS	G	(A	(B) GREAT DETECTIVE	1980	RCA	UK	PL 25298
JIMMY JEWELL	SAX	(A					
LESLEY DUNCAN	V	(A	TONY BURROWS	V	(A	DAVE QUINN	B V (B
PETE WINGFIELD	K	(A	ALAN HODGE	G	(AB	IAN WILSON	G (A
NACHUM HEIMAN	ACC	(A	RUSSELL STONE	V	(A	TOM WILDY	SAX (AB
PHIL CURTIS	B	(A	JOHN ATKINSON	B	(A	MARY CARROLL	V (A
FRANK RICOTTI	PERC	(A	LUIS JARDIM	PERC	(A	ALUN EDEN	D (AB
TONY COX	PNO	(A	GERRY CONWAY	D	(A	RICKY WORTHY	G V (B
STEVE THUNDER	B V	(B	LESLEY DUNCAN	V	(B	JOHN WOOLLAMS	SAX (B
FOXY	D	(B	STEVE HENDERSON	PERC	(B	BARRIE GUARD	PERC (B
ANDY ROBERTS	G	(B	BILLY LIVSEY	K	(B	GAYLE CUNNINGHAM	V (B
GEOFF WESTLEY	PNO	(B	TREVOR HARGREAVES	HRNS	(B		

DOGGEREL BANK

D93

WILLIAM BEALBY WRIGHT	V	(AB	(A) SILVER FACES	1973	CHARISMA	UK	CAS 1079
SUSAN BAKER VLN MAND HCA		(AB	(B) MISTER SKILLICORN DANCES	1975	CHARISMA	UK	CAS 1102
GARY BOYLE	G	(AB					
ANDREW STEELE	D	(A	TONY CAMPO	B	(A	RAY COOPER	PERC (A
JIM PARKER	K	(AB	TOM PARKER	K	(AB	RICHARD MORCOMBE	G (B
DAVE OLNEY	B	(B	MARTIN FRY	TUBA	(B	JONATHAN ADAMS	V (B
JOE CASTALDINI	BASSOON	(B	TINA CHARLES	V	(B	CLAIRE TORRY	V (B
MARTIN JAY	V	(B					

DOGFEET D93A

D93A							
TREVOR POVEY	G V	(A	(A) DOGFEET	1970	REFLECTION		REFL 8
ALAN PEAVE	G V	(A					
DUCK PERRY	D	(A	DAVE NICHOLS	B	(A	ANDREW CAMERON MILLAR PROD	(A

BILL DOGGETT D93B

D93B							
BILL DOGGETT	ORG	(ALL	WOW	1965	HMV UK CLP1884 US	ABC	507
			HONKY TONK	19	CBS	US	1814
			PRELUDE TP THE BLUES	19	CBS	US	1942
			FINGERTIPS	19	CBS	US	2082
			HONKY TONK	19	HARMONY	US	11237
			MOONDUST	19	KING	US	502
			HOT DOGGETT	19	KING	US	514
			AS YOU DESIRE	19	KING	US	523
			EVERYBODY DANCE THE HONKY TONK	19	KING	US	531
			DAME DREAMING	19	KING	US	532
			A SALUTE TO ELLINGTON	19	KING	US	533
			DOGGETT BEAT FOR DANCING FEET	19	KING	US	557
			CANDLE GLOW	19	KING	US	563
			SWINGIN' EASY	19	KING	US	582
			DANCE AWHILE	19	KING	US	585
			CHRISTMAS SONGS	19	KING	US	600
			HOLD IT	19	POWER US 269	US KING	609
			HIGH & WIDE	19	KING	US	633
			BIG CITY DANCE PARTY	19	KING	US	641
			ON TOUR	19	KING	US	667
			FOR REMINISCENT LOVERS	19	KING	US	706
			BACK AGAIN WITH MORE	19	KING	US	723
			MANY MOODS	19	KING	US	778
			PLAYS AMERICAN SONGS	19	KING	US	830
			IMPRESSIONS	19	KING	US	868
			THE BEST OF	19	KING	US	908
			BONANZA OF 24 HIT SONGS	19	KING	US	959
			HONKY TONK POPCORN	19	KING	US	1078
			THE NEARNESS OF YOU	19	KING	US	1097
			RAM BUNK SHUSH	19	KING	US	1101
			SENTIMENTAL MOOD	19	KING	US	1104
			SOFT	19	KING	US	1108
			HONKY TONK A LA MOD	19	ROULETTE	US	25330
			3046 PEOPLE DANCED TILL 4am	19	W B	US	1404
			THE BAND WITH THE BEAT	19	W B	US	1421
			SWINGS	19	WB	US	1452
			PRESENTS	1977	WHOS		21002
			16 BANDSTAND FAV'S	19	STAR		3-23
			MIDNIGHT SLOWS 9	1981	BLACK & BLUE		33145

DOGS D93C

D93C							
? HUGHES	B	(B	(A) DOGS	1979	PHILIPS	CAN	9120 412
DOMINIQUE	G V	(B	(B) WALKING SHADOWS	1980	PHILIPS	FR	6313 058
MICHEL	D	(B					

DOGWATCH D93D

D93D							
ROY WEARD	V	(A	(A) LIVE	1979	BRIDGEHOUSE	UK	002
ROGER GLYNN	G	(A					
NICK SACK	D	(A	TONY MORLEY	B V	(A	LINDA KELSEY	K (A
JOHN TRELAWNEY VLN TROM		(A					

DANE DOHERTY D93E

D93E							
DANE DOHERTY	V	(A	(A) DANE DOHERTY	1978	CBS	US	34278

DENNY DOHERTY

DENNY DOHERTY	V G	(AB	(A) WHAT'CHA GONNA DO		1971	DUNHILL	US	50096
EDDY FISCHER	G	(A	(B) WAITING FOR A SONG		1973	EMBER	UK	5080
RUSS KUNKEL	D	(A					
BRIAN GAROFALO	B	(A	GABE LAPANO	K V	(A	ERIC HORD	G SIT	(A
BARRY McGUIRE	G HCA	(A	BUDDY EMMONS	STEEL	(A	JIMMIE HASKELL	ACC	(A
BILL SZYMCZYK	PERC	(A					

D93F (right)

KLAUS DOLDINGER

D93G

KLAUS DOLDINGER	SAX	(A	(A) BLUES HAPPENING	19	WORLD PACIFIC	20167
INGFRIED HOFFMAN	PNO	(A			
HELMUT KANDELBURGER	B	(A	CEES SEE	D	(A

D93G (right)

DON DOKKEN

D93H

DON DOKKEN	G V	(A	(A) BREAKIN' THE CHAINS		1982	CARRERE	UK	CAL 136
JUAN CROCIER	B V	(A					
GEORGE LYNCH	G	(A	MICK BROWN	D V	(A		

D93H (right)

DOLL

D94

MARION VALENTINE	V G	(A	(A) LISTEN TO THE SILENCE		1979	BEGGARS BANQUET	UK	BEGA12 NL 660055
DENNIS HAINES	K	(A					
JAMES WEST-ORAM	G	(A	CHRISTOPHER YIANNI	B	(A	PAUL TURNER	D	(A

D94 (right)

DOLL BY DOLL

D95

JACKIE LEVEN	V G	(ABC	(A) REMEMBER		1979	AUTOMATIC		K	56618
JO SHAW	V G K	(ABC	(B) GYPSY BLOOD		1979	AUTOMATIC		K	56755
TONY WAITE	V B	(BC	(C) DOLL BY DOLL		1981	MAGNET UK 5039	UK		5269
ROBIN SPREAFICO	B	(A	(D) DXD	(EP)	1981	MAGNET	NL		64587
DAVID McINTOSH	V D	(ABC	(E) GRAND PASSION		1982	MAGNET	UK		5047
GRAHAM PRESKETT	VLN K	(B							
B J COLE	STEEL G	(B	GEOFF WESTLEY	PNO	(C	SHELLEY MORRIS	PERC	(C	
NINA SPENCER		(C	ROD BEDDALL	ACC	(C	PETE GIBSON	HCA	(C	
TOM NEWMAN		(C	FIONA PRENDERGAST		(C	SUSIE O'LIST	V	(C	

D95 (right)

DOLPHIN

D95A

ROY DAVIES	K	(A	(A) GOODBYE		1977	PRIVATE STOCK		PVLP 1055
GERRY CONWAY	D	(A	(B) MOLECULES		1980	GALE		LP 02
JOHN GIBLIN	B	(A					
JIMMY JEWELL	SAX	(A	ROGER CHURCHYARD	VLN	(A	PAUL CARMAN	B BANJO V	(A
GLEN LEFLEUR	D	(B	DAVE ROSE	SYN	(B	PRESTON HEYMAN	D	(B

D95A (right)

DOME

D95B

B C GILBERT	V B G D PERC	(ABC	(A) DOME1		1980	DOME	UK	DOME1
G LEWIS	V B G SYN PERC	(ABC	(B) DOME 2		1980	DOME	UK	DOME2
ERIC RADCLIFFE	G	(C	(C) DOME 3		1981	DOME	UK	DOME3
D O MILLER	SAX	(C					
NISSELL MILS	V PERC	(C	PETER PRICE	D	(C		

D95B (right)

FATS DOMINO

D96

ANTOINE 'FATS' DOMINO PNO V(ALL
WITH

LEE ALLEN	SAX	DAVE BARTHOLOMEW	TPT	SMOKEY JOHNSON	D	JOE HARRIS	SAX
HERB HARDESTY	SAX	ALVIN RED TYLER	SAX	CLARENCE HALL	SAX	ERNEST McLEEN	G
FRANK FIELDS	B	EARL PALMER	D	WENDEL DUCONGE	SAX	ROBERT BUDDY HAGANS	SAX
WALTER NELSON	G	BILLY DIAMOND	B	CORNELIUS COLEMAN	D	HARRISON VERRETT	G
JUSTIN ADAMS	G	CHARLES WILLIAMS	D	WALDRON JOSEPH	TROM	CLARENCE FORD	SAX
ROY MONTRELL	G	JIMMY DAVIS	B	FREDRICK KEMP	SAX	FRED SHEPPARD	SAX
WALTER LASTIE	D	WALTER KIMBLE	SAX	ROGER HAYWARD LOUIS	SAX	DAVID DOUGLAS	B
MORRIS SIMON	SAX	THOMAS JOHNSON	TPT	CARLTON MACWILLIAMS	B	JOSEPH JOHNSON	D

LP's

		US	US	US RI	UK		UK
CARRY ON ROCKIN		19	IMPERIAL 9004		LONDON		2041
ROCK AND ROLLIN'		19	IMPERIAL 9009	12387	LONDON		2028
THIS IS FATS DOMINO		1956	IMPERIAL 9028	12389	LONDON		2073
HERE STANDS FATS DOMINO		1957	IMPERIAL 9038	12390	LONDON		2052
THIS IS FATS		1958	IMPERIAL 9040	12391	LONDON		2087
FABULOUS MR D		1958	IMPERIAL 9055	12394	LONDON		2135
FATS DOMINO SWINGS		19	IMPERIAL 9062	12091			
LETS PLAY FATS DOMING		1959	IMPERIAL 9065		LONDON		2223
FATS DOMINO SINGS		1960	IMPERIAL 9103	12103			
A LOT OF DOMINO'S		1960	IMPERIAL 9127	12066	LONDON		2312
I MISS YOU SO		1961	IMPERIAL 9138	12398	LONDON		2364
LET THE 4 WINDS BLOW		1961	IMPERIAL 9153	12073	LONDON		2420
WHAT A PARTY		1961	IMPERIAL 9164		LONDON		2426
TWISTIN' THE STOMP		1962	IMPERIAL 9170		LONDON		2447
JUST DOMINO		1963	IMPERIAL 9206		LONDON		8039
LETS DANCE		1963	IMPERIAL 9239				
HERE HE COMES AGAIN		1963	IMPERIAL 9248				
WALKING TO NEW ORLEANS		1963	IMPERIAL 9227	12227	LONDON		8084
HERE COMES FATS		1963	ABC 455		HMV		1690
FATS ON FIRE		1963	ABC 479		HMV		1740
GETAWAY WITH FATS		1966	ABC 510		HMV		1821
FANTASTIC FATS		196	ABC		STATESIDE		10240
FATS DOMINO		196	SUNSET 5103				
AINT THAT A SHAME		19	SUNSET 5130				
WHEN IM WALKING		19	HARMONY 11343				
BIG ROCK SOUNDS		19	SUNSET 1011				
GOLDEN GREATS		19	LIBERTY 8668				
STOMPIN'		1967	SUNSET 5158				
WHEN MY DREAMBOAT		19	PICKWICK 3165				
FATS DOMINO		19	GRAND AWARD 267				
FATS DOMINO		19	EVEREST 280				
TROUBLE IN MIND		196	SUNSET 5200				
FATS IS BACK		1968	REPRISE 6304		VALIANT		107
FATS		1970	REPRISE 6439				
MILLION SELLERS		1962	IMPERIAL 9195	12195	LIBERTY 3303		83023
MILLION SELLERS VOL 2		19			LIBERTY 3046		83024
MILLION SELLERS VOL 3		19			LIBERTY		83101

(CONTINUED)

		US	US		UK	UK
FAT SOUND		19			LIBERTY	83142
'65		1965	MERCURY	20070(M) 62039		
VERY BEST OF		19	UA	223 380	LIBERTY	83331
SOUTHWIND USA		19	MERCURY	21065 (M)61065(S)		
RARE DOMINO'S		19			LIBERTY	83174
30 HITS		19	UA	104		
COOKING WITH FATS		1966	UA	122	UA	60061/2
BE MY GUEST		1971			SUNSET	50252
RARE DOMINOS VOL 2		1972			UA	29152
LEGENDARY MASTERS (DBL)		1972	UA	9958	UA	60015/6
PLAY IT AGAIN FATS		1973			UA	29467
LIVE IN LAS VEGAS		1973			PHILIPS	6336 217
LIVE AT MONTREUX		1974			ATLANTIC	K 50107
FATS DOMINO STORY (DBL)		1974			LIBERTY	83456/7
LIVE IN NEW YORK		1976			PHILIPS	6336 275
20 GREATEST HITS		1976			UA	29967
STAR COLLECTION		19			WB MIDI	MD2 4006
BLUEBERRY HILL		19	PICKWICK	3111		
MY BLUE HEAVEN		19	PICKWICK	3295		
STORY VOL1		1977			UA	30067
STORY VOL2		1977			UA	30068
STORY VOL 3		1977			UA	30069
STORY VOL 4		1977			UA	30070
STORY VOL 5		1977			UA	30117
STORY VOL 6		1977			UA	30118
LIVE IN EUROPE		1978			UA	30121
SLEEPING ON THE JOB		1979	POLYDOR	PD 3215	SONET	SNTF 793
GOLDEN GREATS		1979			HAMMER	HMR 9002
WHEM IN WALKING		1979	CBS	35996		
EP's						
BLUES FOR LOVE		196			LONDON	1022
BLUES FOR LOVE 2		196			LONDON	1062
FATS		196			LONDON	1073
HERE COMES FATS		196			LONDON	1079
HERE COMES FATS		196			LONDON	1080
CARRY ON ROCKIN'		19			LONDON	1115
CARRY ON ROCKIN' 2		19			LONDON	1116
BLUES FOR LOVE 3		19			LONDON	1117
BLUES FOR LOVE 4		19			LONDON	1121
HERE COMES FATS 3		19			LONDON	1138
THE ROCKIN Mr D		19			LONDON	1206
THE ROCKIN Mr D		19			LONDON	1207
BE MY GUEST		19			LONDON	1261
THE ROCKIN Mr D 3		19			LONDON	1265
WHAT A PARTY		19			LONDON	1340
RED SAILS IN THE SUNSET		19			HMV	7EG 8862

DON 'SUGARCANE' HARRIS	VLN(AB		(A) DON & DEWEY		19	SPECIALTY	UK	SNTF 5006
DEWEY TERRY	K V	(AB	(B) THEY'RE ROCKIN TILL MIDNIGHT		19	SPECIALTY	US	SPS 2131
PLAS JOHNSON	SAX							
JACKIE KELSO	SAX	(	RENE HALL	B	(	EARL PALMER	D	(
PETE SMITH	B	(	SONNY GILLETTE	D	(			

LOU DONALDSON	SAX	(AB	(A) SASSY SOUL STREET			1973	BLUE NOTE	US	109
HORRACE OTT	PNO	(AB	(B) SWEET LOU			1974	BLUE NOTE	US	259
DAVID SPINOZZA	G	(AB							
JIMMY YOUNG	D	(B	PAUL GRIFFIN	K	(AB	JOHN TROPEA	G	(A	ERNIE ROYAL	TPT (B
JOE SHEPLEY	TPT	(B	DANNY MOORE	TPT	(B	GARNETT BROWN	TROM	(B	SELDON POWELL	WIND(B
ARTHUR CLARKE	WIND	(B	BUDDY LUCAS	HCA	(B	CORNELL DUPREE	G	(B	HUGH McCRACKEN	G (B
WILBUR BASCOMBE	B	(B	BERNARD PURDIE	D	(B	BARBARA MASSEY	V	(B	HILDA HARRIS	V (B
EILEEN GILBERT	V	(B	CARL WILLIAMS	V	(B	WILLIAM SAMPLE	V	(B	BILL DAVIS	V (B
ERIC FIGUEUOA	V	(B								

PETER DONATO		(A	(A) PETER DONATO			1974	CAPITOL	CAN	6423
MICHAEL HEYDON		(A							
DENNIS PENDRITH	B	(A	BARRY KEANE	D	(A	BERT HERMISTON	SAX	(A	DAVID McLEY	(A
BRUCE PENNYCOOK		(A	JAMES ATKINSON		(A	ERIC ROGERTSON	K	(A	JANIS CRAMER	(A
RUSS LITTLE	TROM	(A	MOE KOFFMAN	HRNS	(A	BOB VAN EVERA		(A		

RAL DONNER	V	(ALL	( ) TAKIN CARE OF BUSINESS	196	GONE	US	5012
			( ) TAKIN CARE OF BUSINESS VOL1	19	RONDO	US	RLP 22436
			( ) TAKIN CARE OF BUSINESS VOL2	19	RONDO	US	RLP 22437
			( ) ELVIS SCRAPBOOK	1977	GONE US		5033
			( ) YOU DONT KNOW WHAT YOU GOT	1978	PYE UK		NSPL 28269

DONOVAN LEITCH	V G HCA (ALL	(A) WHAT'S BIN DID	1965	PYE	UK	NPL 18117
WITH		(A) WHAT'S BIN DID	1968	MARBLE ARCH	UK	MAL 795
LESLEY DUNCAN	V	(QL	(B) CATCH THE WIND	1965	HICKORY	US	123
SUZI QUATRO	V	(Q	(B) CATCH THE WIND	1971	HALLMARK	UK	HMA 200
VALERIE CARRINGTON	V	(Q	(C) FAIRYTALE	1965	PYE	UK	NLP 18128
JILL UTTING	V	(Q	(C) FAIRYTALE	1965	HICKORY	US	127
NICK CURTIS	V	(Q	(C) SONGS FOR SUNSHINE (1 DIFF TRACK)	1965	PYE	UK	2053
CARY WILSON	V	(Q	(C) FAIRYTALE	1969	MARBLE ARCH	UK	MAL 867
GAYNOR STEWART	V	(Q	(D) SUNSHINE SUPERMAN	1967	PYE	UK	NPL 18181
JULIE FORSYTHE	V	(Q	(D) SUNSHINE SUPERMAN	1966	EPIC	US	BN 26217
LESLYE ASH	V	(Q	(E) THE REAL DONOVAN	1966	HICKORY	US	LP 135
JOHN McCARTHY	V	(Q	(F) MELLOW YELLOW	1967	EPIC	US	BN 26239
LESLIE FYSON	V	(Q	(G) FOR LITTLE ONES	1967	EPIC	US	BN 26350

(CONTINUED)

CHRIS SPEDDING	V	(Q
COZY POWELL	D	(Q
ALAN WHITE	D .	(Q
CLIVE CHAMAN	B	(Q
DENNIS WALL	B	(Q
PHIL CHEN	B	(Q
JOHN BUNDRICK	K	(Q
BOBBY KEYS	SAX	(Q
JIM HORN	SAX	(Q
PETE HALLING	VLN	(Q
JACK EMBLOW	ACC	(Q
TONY CARR	PERC	(GJLQ
RONNIE LEAHY	K	(V
NICK SOUTH	B	(V
COLIN ALLEN	D	(V
ISAAC GUILLORY	G	(V
JOHNNY CHRISTOPHER	G	(T
DAVID BRIGGS	K	(T
HARVEY THOMPSON	HRNS	(T
HARRISON CALLOWAY	HRNS	(T
BEN CAULEY	HRNS	(T
CHARLIE ROSE	HRNS	(T
RONNIE EADES	HRNS	(T
BUFFY ST MARIE	V	(T
LEA JANE BERINATI	V	(T
GINGER HOLLADAY	V	(T
DAVID HUNGATE	B	(U
MARY HOLLADAY	V	(T
FLORENCE WARNER	V	(T
BYRON WARNER	V	(T
WILTON FELDER	B	(U
KLAUS VOORMANN	B	(U
LELAND SKLAR	B	(U
JIM KELTNER	D	(U
DOUG DAVIS	CELLO	(U
TOM SCOTT	WIND	(U
DAVID FOSTER	K	(U
EMIL RICHARDS	PERC	(U
BOBBYE HALL	PERC	(U
CHUCK FINDLEY	HRNS	(U
PHILIP DONNELLY	G	(U
JESSE ED DAVIS	G	(U
LEW McCREARY	HRNS	(U
B J COOK	V	(U
DONNY GERRARD	V	(U

ED WHITTING	V	(U	JENNETTE CLINGER	V	(U	STACY JO CLINGER V (U	ALLAN DELORY	V	(U
RON HICKLIN	V	(U	JENNIFER HICKLIN	V	(U	SUSIE IVES	V	(U	JOHN MERLINO	V	(U
MAXINE WILLARD	V	(U	JULIA TILLMAN	V	(U	CLIFF BARTON	B	(HM	JACK BRUCE	B	(HM
MIKE O'NEIL	K	(HMO	KEITH WEBB	D	(HM	CANDY JOHN CARR PERC(GHMO	HAROLD McNAIR	FLT	(GHJLM
MIKE CARR	VIBES(HM	ERIC LEESE	G	(HM	BRIAN LOCKING	B	(AB	SKIP ALLEN	D	(AB
GYPSY DAVE	KAZOO (AB	DANNY THOMPSON	B	(L	ALAN HAWKSHAW	PNO(L	MADELINE BELL	V	(L
JEFF BECK	G	(L	KEN BALDOCK	B	(GM	RON WOOD	G (L	ROD STEWART	V	(L
NICKY HOPKINS	K	(L	AYNSLEY DUNBAR	D	(L	MIKE THOMPSON	V G(O	JOHN PAUL JONES	K	(F
SHAWN PHILLIPS	G	(C	JOHN CAMERON							

(H) WEAR YOUR LOVE LIKE HEAVEN	1967	EPIC	US	BN	26349
(I) UNIVERSAL SOLDIER	1967	MARBLE ARCH	UK	MAL	718
(J) IN CONCERT	1968	PYE		NSPL18237
(J) IN CONCERT	1968	EPIC	US	BN	26386
(DJ) IN CONCERT/SUNSHINE SUPERMAN(DBL)19		EPIC	US		33734
(K) HURDY GURDY MAN	1968	EPIC	US	BN	26420
(L) BARABAJAGAL	1968	EPIC	US	BN	26481
(KL) HURDY GURDY/BARABAJAGAL(DBL)	19	EPIC	US		33731
(M) A GIFT FROM A FLOWER TO A GARDEN	1968	PYE (DBL)	UK	NSPL20000
(M) A GIFT FROM A FLOWER TO A GARDEN	1968	EPIC(DBL)	US	B2N	171
(N) LIKE IT IS	1968	HICKORY	US		143
( ) GREATEST HITS	1969	PYE	UK	NSPL18283
( ) GREATEST HITS	1969	EPIC	US	BN	26836
( ) GREATEST HITS	19	EPIC	US		26439
( ) BEST OF DONOVAN	19	HICKORY	US		149
( ) DONOVAN P LEITCH	19	JANUS	US		3022
( ) WORLD OF DONOVAN	1969	MARBLE ARCH	UK	MAL	1168
( ) WORLD OF DONOVAN	19	EPIC			66289
( ) WORLD OF DONOVAN	19	EPIC			64494/5
( ) WORLD OF DONOVAN	19	EPIC	US		31210
(O) OPEN ROAD	1970	DAWN	UK	DNLS 3009
(O) OPEN ROAD	1970	EPIC	US		30125
( ) GOLDEN HOUR	1971	PYE	UK	GH	506
(P) H M S DONOVAN (DBL)	1971	DAWN	UK	DNLD 4001
( ) COLOURS	1972	HALLMARK	UK	HMA	241
(Q) COSMIC WHEELS	1973	EPIC US 32156	UK		65450
(R) ESSENCE TG ESSENCE	1973	EPIC US 32800	UK		69050
(S) LIVE IN JAPAN	1973	EPIC SONY		ECPM	25
(T) 7 TEASE	1974	EPIC US 33245	UK		69104
(T) 7 TEASE	1974	EPIC	NL		80531
( ) DONOVAN	1974	JOKER	IT		13730
( ) DONOVAN	197	ARISTA	US		4143
( ) DONOVAN	19	VOGUE	FR		687
(U) SLOW DOWN WORLD	1976	EPIC US 33945	UK		86011
(U) SLOW DOWN WORLD	1976	EPIC	NL		81371
(V) DONOVAN	1977	RAK EURO 9929	UK	SRAK	528
(W) DONOVAN FILE	1977	PYE	UK	FILD	004
( ) TROUBADOUR	19	MODE	IMP	MD	9034
( ) HEAR ME NOW	19	JANUS	US		3025
( ) HISTORY OF POP	1976	PYE	UK		502
( ) SPOTLIGHT	1981	PRT	UK		1017
( ) 4 SHADES 4 lps	19	PYE	UK	11PP	102

LONNIE DONEGAN BANJ V G	(ALL
WITH		
DENNY WRIGHT	G	(A
MICKY ASHMAN	B	(A
NICK NICHOLLS	D	(A
DAVE WINTOUR	B	(T
RAY COOPER	PERC	(T
HENRY SPINETTI	D	(T
RINGO STARR	D	(T
NICKY HOPKINS	K	(T
BRUCE GARY	D	(T
GARY BROOKER	K	(T
FRANK GIBSON	D	(T
PETE WINGFIELD	K	(T
JIM KELTNER	D	(T
ALAN JONES	B	(T
KLAUS VOORMANN	B	(T
MICK RALPHS	G B	(T
PETER JAMESON	G	(T
RORY GALLAGHER	G	(T
ROGER McKEW	G B	(T
ALBERT LEE	G	(T
PETER BANKS	G	(T
BRIAN MAY	G	(T
RON WOOD	G	(T
LEO SAYER	HCA V	(T
ZOOT MONEY	PNO	(T
ELTON JOHN	PNO	(T
WILLIAM D SMITH	ORG	(T
COLIN FAIRLEY	D	(T
MICHELLE PHILLIPS	V	(T
REV JAMES CLEVELAND PNO	(T

(A) SHOWCASE	1956	PYE NIXA	UK	NPT 19012
(A) SHOWCASE	1968	MARBLE ARCH	UK	MAL	797
(B) LONNIE	1958	PYE NIXA	UK	NPT 19027
(C) TOPS WITH LONNIE	1957	PYE	UK	NPL 18034
(D) RIDES AGAIN	1959	PYE	UK	NPL 18043
(D) RIDES AGAIN	1969	MARBLE ARCH	UK	MAL	1153
(E) MORE TOPS WITH LONNIE	1961	PYE	UK	NPL 18063
(F) SING HALLELUJAH	1962	PYE	UK	NPL 18073
(F) SING HALLELUJAH	19	ABC	US		433
(G) GOLDEN AGE OF DONEGAN	1962	GOLDEN GUINEA	UK	GGL 0135
(G) GOLDEN AGE OF DONEGAN	1965	MARBLE ARCH	UK	MAL	636
(H) GOLDEN AGE OF DONEGAN VOL 2	1963	GOLDEN GUINEA	UK	GGL 0170
(H) GOLDEN AGE OF DONEGAN VOL 2	1967	MARBLE ARCH	UK	MAL	698
(I) FOLK ALBUM	1965	PYE	UK	NPL 18126
(I) FOLK ALBUM	1967	GOLDEN GUINEA	UK	GGL 0382
(J) AN ENGLISHMAN SINGS AMERICAN FOLK	19	MERCURY	US		20229
( ) HITS OF LONNIE DONEGAN	1978	MFP	UK		50389
(K) LONNIE POPS	19'=	DECCA	UK	SKL 5068
(L) GOLDEN HOUR	197	PYE	UK	GH	514
(M) GOLDEN HOUR VOL2	1973	PYE	UK	GH	564
(N) GREATEST HITS	19	RONCO	UK	RTL 2017
(O) MY OLD MANS A DUSTMAN	1971	HALLMARK	UK	HMA	204
(P) LONNIE DONEGAN	19	HALLMARK	UK	HMA	252
(Q) LONNIE DONEGAN	19	DOT	US		3394
(R) SKIFFLE FOLK MUSIC	19	ATLANTIC	US		8038
(S) LONNIE DONEGAN FILE (DBL)	1977	PYE	UK	FILD 0111/2
(T) PUTTIN' ON THE STYLE	1977	CHRYSALIS	UK	CHR 1158
(T) PUTTIN' ON THE STYLE	1977	UA	US	UALA 827
(T) PUTTIN' ON THE STYLE	197	PHONOGRAM	EUR	6367 618
(U) SUNDOWN	1978	CHRYSALIS	UK	CHR 1205

DOOBIE BROTHERS

JOHN HARTMAN	D	(ABCDEFH*J	(A) DOOBIE BROTHERS	1971	WB US 1919	UK K	46090
TOM JOHNSTON	G V	(ABCDEFH*J	(B) TOULOUSE STREET	1973	WB	US 2634	UK K	46183
DAVE SHOGREN	K B V (A		(C) THE CAPTAIN & ME	1974	WB	US 2694	UK K	46217
PAT SIMMONS	G V	(ABCDEFGHJK	(D) WHAT WERE ONCE VICES	1974	WB	US 2750	UK K	56026
MICHAEL HOSSACK	D	(BCD	(E) STAMPEDE	1975	WB	US 2835	UK K	56094
TIRAN PORTER	B	(BCDEFGHJK	(F) TAKING IT TO THE STREETS	1976	WB	US 2899	UK K	56196
KEITH KNUDSEN	D V	(DEFGHJK	(G) BEST OF	1976	WB	US 2978	UK K	56308
JEFF BAXTER	G STEEL (CDEFGHJ		(H) LIVING ON THE FAULT LINE	1977	WB	US 3045	UK K	56383
BILL PAYNE	K	(CDEJ	(J) MINUTE BY MINUTE	1979	WB	US 3193	UK K	56486
MILT HOLLAND	PERC	(D	( ) STAR COLLECTION	1974	MIDI			26022
MIKE McDONALD	K V	(FGHJK	(K) ONE STEP CLOSER	1980	WB	US 3452	UK K	56824
BOBBY LAKIND	CONGA (FHJK		(*) 1970 LINE UP NO ALBUMS					
MARIA MULDAUR	V	(EF	( ) BEST OF THE DOOBIES	1980	WB	US 3112		
WAYNE JACKSON	HRNS	(DF	( ) BEST OF VOL 2	1981	WB	US 3612	UK K	56956
ANDREW LOVE	HRNS	(DF						

NOVI	VLA	(D	JAMES MITCHELL	HRNS	(DF	LEWIS COLLINS	HRNS	(F	JACK HALE	TROM (DF
RITCHIE HAYWARD	D	(F	JESSE BUTLER	ORG	(F	DAN ARMSTRONG	SITAR(H		NORTON BUFFALO	HCA(H
VICTOR FELDMAN	PERC	(EH	ROSEMARY BUTLER	V	(H	MAUREEN McDONALD V		(H	RY COODER	G (E
KARL HIMMEL	D	(E	BOBBYE HALL	PERC	(E	SHIRLEY MATTHEWS	V	(E	VANETTA FIELDS	V (E
JESSICA SMITH	V	(E	CONTE CONDOLI	TPT	(E	PETE CONDOLI	TPT	(E	EDDIE GUZMAN	PERC(D
ARLO GUTHRIE	HCA	(D	WILLIE WEEKS	B	(	TED TEMPLEMAN	PERC	(K	JOEL PESKIN	SAX (K
CHRISTOPHER THOMPSON V		(K	LEE THOMBERG	TPT	(K	PAT HENDERSON K		(K	BYRON BERLINE	FDL (K
NICOLETTE LARSEN	V	(JK	BEN CAULEY	TPT	(J	CHET McCRACKEN	D	(K	JIMMY HASKELL	STR (K
JERRY JUMONVILLE	SAX	(K	BILL ARMSTRONG	TPT	(K	HERB PEDERSEN	BAN	(J	JAMES BOOKER	PNO (D
LESTER ABRAMS	PNO	(J	JOHN McFEE	G V	(K	CORNELIUS BUMPUS SAX V(K				

DOOMED

DAVE VANIAN	(A) NO RECORDS
RAT SCABIES	
CAPT SENSIBLE	HENRI BADOWSKI

DOOR & THE WINDOW

	(A) FIRST EP	19	NB	UK NB 1
	(B) SECOND EP	19	NB	UK NB 2
	(C) DETAILED TWANG(LIM EDITION)	19	NB	UK NB 5

THE DOORS

JIM MORRISON	V	(ABCDEFGJMNO	(A) THE DOORS	1967	ELEKTRA	US UK	74007
RAY MANZAREK	K V	(ALL	(A) THE DOORS	1971	ELEKTRA	UK	K 42012
ROBBIE KRIEGER	G	(ALL	(B) STRANGE DAYS	1968	ELEKTRA	US	74014
JOHN DENSMORE	D	(ALL	(B) STRANGE DAYS	1971	ELEKTRA UK K42016 RI		22008
DOUGLAS LUBAHN	B	(BCDN	(C) WAITING FOR THE SUN	1968	ELEKTRA	US	74024
HARVEY BROOKS	B	(DN	(C) WAITING FOR THE SUN	1971	ELEKTRA	UK	K 42041
JERRY SCHEFF	B	(GHMN	(D) SOFT PARADE	1969	ELEKTRA	US	75005
MARC BENNO	G	(GN	(D) SOFT PARADE	1971	ELEKTRA	UK	42079
CURTIS AMY	SAX	(DN	(E) MORRISON HOTEL	1970	ELEKTRA	US	75007
GEORGE BOHANON	TROM	(D	(E) MORRISON HOTEL	1971	ELEKTRA	UK	K 42080
CHAMP WEBB	HRNS	(D	(F) ABSOLUTELY LIVE (DBL)	1970	ELEKTRA	US	2 9002
JESSE McREYNOLDS	MAND	(D	(F) ABSOLUTELY LIVE (DBL)	1971	ELEKTRA	UK	K 62005
JIMMY BUCHANAN	FDL	(D	(G) LA WOMAN	1971	ELEKTRA	US	75011
REINOL ANDINO	PERC	(D	(G) LA WOMAN	1971	ELEKTRA	UK	K 42090
KERRY MAGNESS	B	(C	(H) OTHER VOICES	1971	ELEKTRA	US	75017
LEROY VINEGAR	B	(C	(H) OTHER VOICES	1971	ELEKTRA	UK	K 42104
RAY NEAPOLITAN	B	(EH	(J) WEIRD SCENES INSIDE THE GOLDMINE	1971	ELEKTRA (DBL)	US	2 6001
LONNIE MACK	B	(EN	(J) WEIRD SCENES INSIDE THE GOLDMINE	1971	ELEKTRA (DBL)	UK	K 62009
G PUGLESE (J SEBASTIAN) HCA(E			(K) DOORS 13	197	ELEKTRA	US	74079
JACK CONRAD	B	(HL	(K) DOORS 13	1971	ELEKTRA	UK	K 42062
WILLIE RUFF	B	(H	(L) FULL CIRCLE	1972	ELEKTRA	US	75038
FRANCISCO AQUABELLA PERC		(H	(L) FULL CIRCLE	1972	ELEKTRA	UK	K 42116
EMIL RICHARDS	PERC	(H	(M) AN AMERICAN PRAYER	1978	ELEKTRA	US	5E502
WOLFGANG MELTZ	B	(H	(M) AN AMERICAN PRAYER	1978	ELEKTRA	UK	K 52111
CHRIS ETHRIDGE	B	(L	( ) GREATEST HITS	1980	ELEKTRA US 515 uk		52254
CHARLES LARKEY	B	(L	( ) BEST OF	1974	ELEKTRA	US	EQ 5035
BOBBYE HALL	PERC	(L	( ) BEST OF	1974	ELEKTRA	UK	K 42143
CHARLES LLOYD	WIND	(L	( ) STAR COLLECTION	1975	MIDI	UK	22001
LELAND SKLAR	B	(L	( ) STAR COLLECTION 2	1975	MIDI	UK	22019
CHICO BATERA	PERC	(L	(AB) DOORS /STRANGE DAYS (DBL)	1975	ELEKTRA	GERM	621013
CLYDIE KING	V	(L					

VANETTA FIELDS	V	(L	MELISSA MACKAY	V	(L	BOB GLAUB	B (M
JOHN SEBASTIAN	HCA	(N	JOHN HARVEY		(M	FRANK LUSCIANDRO	(M
PAUL ROTHCHILD	PROD(ABCDEFGHM		BRUCE BOTNICK	PROD	(M	REIND ANDINA	PERC (M
ARTHUR BARROW	SYN	(M					

CHARLIE DORE

CHARLIE DORE	V	(AB	(A) WHERE TO NOW	1979 ISLAND	UK	ILPS 9559
ALAN TARNEY	G K B V(A		(B) LISTEN	1981 CHRYSALIS	UK	CHR 1225
TREVOR SPENCER	D	(A				

MEL COLLINS	SAX	(A	GARY TAYLOR	B V	(A	CLIFF HALL	K	(A	DALE SELLARS	G (A
REGGIE YOUNG	G	(A	SONNY CURTIS	G	(A	JULIAN LITTMAN G MAND V		(A	BOBBY WOOD	K (A
DAVID BRIGGS	K	(A	TOMMY COGBILL	B	(A	MIKE LEECH	B	(A	JERRY CARRIGAN	D (A
KARL HIMMEL	D	(A	CHARLIE McCOY	HCA	(A	LARRY SASSER	STEEL(A		JERRY ROBERTS	ACC (A
FARRELL MORRIS	PERC	(A	SHELLY KURLAND	STR	(A	ROY CHRISTIANSEN	STR	(A	JOHNNY CHRISTOPHER	V(A
JEFF PORCARO	D	(B	STEVE LUKATHER	G	(B	MIKE PORCARO	B	(B	ROBBIE BUCHANAN	K SYN(B
STEWART LEVINE	PROD	(B								

RAY DORSET

RAY DORSET	G V	(A	(A) COLD BLUE EXCURSION	1972 DAWN	UK	DNLS 3033
MIKE McNAUGHT	PNO	(A				
DAVE MARKEE	B	(A	MIKE TRAVIS	D	(A	JOE RUSH	PERC (A	SUNNY LESLIE	V (A
SUE GLOVER	V	(A	COLIN EARL		(A	JOHN GODFREY	B	(A

LEE DORSEY

LEE DORSEY	V	(ALL	(A)	LEE DORSEY	1966	AMY	US 8010 UK STATESIDE	10177
ALLEN TOUSSAINT	PNO	(	(B)	NEW LEE DORSEY	1966	AMY	US 8011 UK STATESIDE	10192
CHARLES WILLIAMS	D	(	(C)	YES WE CAN	1970	POLYDOR 2482 280 +		2489 006
ROY MONTRELL	G	(	(C)	YES WE CAN	1970	POLYDOR	GERM	244042
NAT PERILLAT	SAX	(	(D)	GREATEST HITS	19	SUE /ISLAND		UK ILP924
			( )	GREATEST HITS	1974	SOUNDS SUPERB	UK	SPR 90045
			( )	BEST OF	19	STARLINE	UK	SRS 5023
			( )	NIGHT PEOPLE	1978	ABC	US	1048
			( )	GONNA BE FUNKY	1980	CHARLY	UK	CRB 1001
			( )	WORKING IN A COALMINE	1980	CHARLY EP	UK	CTD 101

DOUCETTE

JERRY DOUCETTE	V G B(A		(A)	MAMA LET HIM PLAY	19	MUSHROOM	US	5009
DURIS MAXWELL	D K	(A	(B)	THE DOUC IS LOOSE	1979	MERCURY	GER	9124 410
DONNIE CUMMINGS	B	(A						
MARK OLSON	K	(A IRA HIRSCHEL	SYN (	PETER HOORELBEKE	D	(A		

EARLE DOUD

EARLE DOUD	V PERC(ALL		(A)	LYNDON JOHNSONS LONELY HEARTS CLUB BAND	19	ATCO	US	SD33230
ALEN ROBIN			(B)	HONEST TO GOD WE REALLY MEANT IT	19	BRUNSWICK	US	754201
			(C)	WELCOME TO L B J RANCH	19	CAPITOL	US	2423

STEVE DOUGLAS & THE REBEL ROUSERS

STEVE DOUGLAS	(A		(A)	TWIST	19	CROWN	US	5254

DOVELLS

LEN BARRY	V	(	(A)	BRISTOL STOMP	1961	PARKWAY	US	7006
JERRY SUMMERS	V	(	(B)	ALL THE HITS	1962	PARKWAY	US	7010
MIKE DENNIS	V	(	(C)	FOR YOUR HULLY GULLY PARTY	1962	PARKWAY	US	7020
ARNIE SATIN	V	(	(D)	YOU CANT SIT DOWN	1962	PARKWAY	US	7025
DANNY BROOKS	V	(	(E)	BIGGEST HITS	196	WYNCOTE	US	9114
			(F)	DISCOTHEQUE	19	WYNCOTE	US	9052
			(G)	CAMEO PARKWAY SESSIONS	1979	LONDON	UK	HAU 8515

KENNY DOSS

KENNY DOSS	(A		(A)	MOVIN ON A FEELING	1980	BEARSVILLE		202224

DOUG & THE SLUGS

DOUG BENNETT	G V	(A	(A)	COGNAC & BOLOGNA	1981	RCA	US	AFL 13387
SIMON KENDALL	K	(A						
JOHN BURTON	G V	(WALLY WATSON	D	(A RICHARD BAKER	G	(A STEVE BOSLEY	B	(A

DANNY DOUMA

DANNY DOUMA	G V	(A	(A)	NIGHT EYES	1979	WB	US	3326
PETER FRIEBERGER	B	(A						
TODD SHARP	G	(A ERIC CLAPTON	G	(A JOHN McVIE	B	(A AMOS GARRETT	G	(A
LINDSEY BUCKINGHAM	G	(A MICHELLE GRUSKA	V	(A CLAUDE PEPPER	D	(A NICK VAN MAARTH	G V(A
JAY GRUSKA	K	(A MICK FLEETWOOD	D	(A CHRISTINE McVIE	K V	(A DAVID WOODFORD	SAX(A
GARTH HUDSON	ACC	(A						

BRENTON DOWE

BRENTON DOWE	V	(A	(A)	BUILD ME UP	19	TROJAN	UK	TRLS 76

JOHN DOWIE

JOHN DOWIE	(A		(A)	ANOTHER CLOSE SHAVE	1977	VIRGIN	UK	VEP 1004

BOB DOWNES

BOB DOWNES	V WIND(ALL		(A)	DREAM JOURNEY	1970	PHILIPS		SBL 7922
CHRIS SPEDDING	G	(ABC	(B)	ELECTRIC CITY	1970	VERTIGO	UK	6360 005
RAY RUSSELL	G	(BCF	(C)	DEEP DOWN HEAVY	1970	M F P	UK	MFP 1412
PETER BILLAM	G	(C	(D)	DIVERSIONS	1974	OPENIUM		BDOM 001
ROBERT COCKBURN	V	(C	(E)	EPISODE AT 4 AM	1974	OPENIUM		BDOM 002
DEREK HOGG	D	(AC	(F)	HELLS ANGELS	1975	OPENIUM		BDOM 003
JOHN STEVENS	D	(AF	(G)	OPEN MUSIC	19			
ALAN RUSHTON	D	(BC						
HARRY MILLER	D	(ABCF LAURIE ALLEN	D	(C DAVE BROOKS	SAX	(BF HERBIE FLOWERS	B	(BF
DARRYL RUNSWICK	B	(B DENNIS SMITH	D	(ABDF JIM GREGORY	FLT	(A CLEM CATTINI	D	(B
DOM FAY	SAX	(BF NIGEL CARTER	TPT	(AB KENNY WHEELER	TPT	(B BUD PARKES	HRNS	(B
HAROLD BECKETT	HRNS	(BF IAN CARR	HRNS	(B ROBIN JONES	PERC	(B JOHN WARREN	SAX	(A
CHRIS PYNE	TROM	(A BUTCH HUDSON	TPT	(A LAURIE BAKER	SYN	(DF WENDY BENKA FLT PER	(E
TONY ROBERTS	SAX	(F CLIVE STEVENS	SAX	(A HENRY LOWTHER	TPT	(AF BARRY GUY	B	(DF
JEFF CLYNE	B	(DF MARC CHARIG	TPT	(F				

DOWNLINER SECT

DON CRAINE	V	(ALL	(A)	THE SECT	1964	COLUMBIA	UK	33SX 1658
PAUL TITLER	HCA V	(D	(A)	THE SECT	1977	CHARLY GER 3014 UK		CR 30122
KEITH GRANT	V B	(ALL	(B)	THE COUNTRY SECT	1965	COLUMBIA	UK	33SX 1745
TERRY GIBSON	G	(ALL	(B)	THE COUNTRY SECT	1979	CHARLY GER 3021 UK		CR 30137
JOHN SUTTON	D	(ABC	(C)	THE ROCK SECTS IN	1966	COLUMBIA	UK	SCX 6028
PIP HARVEY	V	(	(C)	THE ROCK SECTS IN	1978	CHARLY GER 3035 UK		CR 30140
JOHN PAUL JONES	PNO	(	(D)	SHOWBIZ	1979	SKY GER 301		UK RAW RWLP106
MICHAEL SUTTON	PERC D(		(E)	THE DOWNLINERS SECT	19	HMV		SWED SGLP 534
RAY SONE	HCA	(A	(EP)	NITE AT GT NEWPORT STREET	1964	RBC	UK	001
PAUL HOLM	D	(DE	(EP)	SECT SING SICK SONGS	1965	COLUMBIA	UK	SEG 8438
			(EP)	SHOWBIZ	1979	SKY	GER	103
			(EP)	I WANT MY BABY BACK	1978	CHARLY	UK	CEP 119

DOWNTRIP

JEAN PAUL GOSSENS	V	(A	(A)	DOWNTOWN	1979	PHILIPS	NL	6410 976
PAUL VANDER GOOSSENS	V	(A						
JOHN HASTRY	B	(A JOS CUISSET	G	(A				

LAMONT DOZIER

LAMONT DOZIER	V	(ALL	(A)	OUT HERE ON MY OWN	1974	ABC	US	804
			(B)	BLACK BACH	1975	ABC	US	839
			(C)	LOVE & BEAUTY	1975	INVICTUS	US	33134
			(D)	RIGHT THERE	1976	WB	US	2929
			(E)	PEDDLIN'	1977	WB	US	3039
			(F)	BITTERSWEET	1979	WB	UK	K56594
			(G)	WORKING ON YOU	1981	ARC	US	37129

PETER DOYLE

```
    PETER DOYLE         G V   (A    (A) SKIN DEEP                1977  RCA                PL 25113
    ALAN TARNEY V G B K       (A
    GEOFF WHITEHORN     G     (A    PAUL KEOGH          SLIDE (A   TREVOR SPENCER    D   (A
    SIMON PHILLIPS      D     (A    B J COLE            STEEL (A   TONY HYMAS        K   (A
    MAC TONTOH          TPT   (A    JOY YATES           V     (A   JEAN GILBERT      V   (A
    VAL STOKES          V     (A
```

DRAGON

```
    NEIL STORY          D     (     ( ) SCENTED GARDENS FOR THE BLIND  19  PHONOGRAM          6360 903
    IVAN THOMPSON       K     (     ( ) SAME OLD BLUES             19    PORTRAIT           32636
    MARC HUNTER         V     (     ( ) RUNNING FREE               1977  CBS          UK    33005
    ROBERT TAYLOR       G V   (     ( ) DRAGON                     1977  PORTRAIT     UK    PRT 82636
    KERRY JACOBSON      D     (
    PAUL HEWSON         K V   ((    TODD HUNTER         B V   (
```

DRAGONFLY

```
                                   (A) ALMOST ABANDONED          1974  RETREAT UK 6002 US METROMEDIA ?
```

NICK DRAKE

```
    NICK DRAKE     V G PNO  (ALL    (A) FIVE LEAVES LEFT         19    ANTILLES     US    AN   7010
    DORIS TROY          V     (B    (A) FIVE LEAVES LEFT         1969  ISLAND       UK    ILPS 9105
    PAUL HARRIS         PNO   (AB   (B) BRYTER LAYTER            1970  ISLAND       UK ·  ILPS 9134
    RICHARD THOMPSON    G     (AB   (B) BRYTER LAYTER            1977  ANTILLES     US    AN   7028
    DANNY THOMPSON      B     (AD   (C) PINK MOON                1972  ISLAND US 9318 UK  ILPS 9184
    ROCKY DZIDZORNU     PERC  (AD   (ABC)FRUIT TREE(+ EXTRA TRACKS)  1979  ISLAND   US    NDSP 100
    CLARE LOWTHER       CELLO (AD   (D) NICK DRAKE               19    ISLAND       US    ILPS 9307
    TRISTAN FRY         D VIBES(A
    DAVE PEGG           B     (BD   DAVE MATTACKS       D     (B   RAY WARLEIGH      SAX (B
    ED CARTER           B     (BD   MIKE KOWALSKI       D     (BD  LYN DOBSON        FLT (B
    JOHN CALE           VLA K (BD   CHRIS McGREGOR      V     (B   P P ARNOLD        V   (B
```

PETE DRAKE

```
    PETE DRAKE          STEEL (ALL  FOREVER                      1964  SMASH        US    SRS 67053
                                    PETE DRAKE & HIS TALKING GUITAR  19  MOUTAIN DEW US   S   7042
                                    AMAZING                      19    STARDAY      US        319
                                    THE HITS I PLAYED ON         1969  AMBASSADORE  US    S  98061
                                    PLAYS ALL TIME COUNTRY FAVOURITES  19  HOLLYWOOD  US  HLP  506
                                    STEEL AWAY                   1973  CANAAN       UK    CGS 8502
                                    PETE DRAKE SHOW              19    STOP         US       1011
                                    FABULOUS STEEL GUITAR        19    STARDAY      US        180
```

DRAMATIS

```
    CHRIS PAYNE         K V   (A    (A) FOR FUTURE REFERENCE     1981  ROCKET       UK    TRAIN 18
    DENNIS HAINES       K V   (A
    RUSSELL BELL        G     (A    CEDRIC SHARPLEY     D     (A
```

THE DRANSFIELDS

```
    ROBIN DRANSFIELD    V G  (ABDEG (A) ROUT OF THE BLUES        1970  TRAILER      UK    LER  2011
    BARRY DRANSFIELD  V G FDL (ABCDEF (B) LORD OF ALL I BEHOLD   1971  TRAILER      UK    LER  2026
    BRIAN HARRISON      D     (D    (C) BARRY DRANSFIELD         1972  POLYDOR      UK    2383 160
    CHARLIE SMITH       V B K (D    (D) THE FIDDLERS DREAM       1976  TRANSATLANTIC UK   TRA   322
                                    (E) POPULAR TO CONTRARY BELIEF  1977  FREE REED UK    FRR   018
                                    (F) BOWIN' & SCRAPIN'        1978  TRANSATLANTIC UK   TRA   386
                                    (G) TIDEWAVE                 1981  TOPIC        UK    12TS  414
```

MIKEY DREAD

```
    MIKEY DREAD         V     (AB   (A) DREAD AT THE CONTOLS     1979  TROJAN       UK    TRLS 178
    EARL"BAGGA" WALKER  B     (A    (B) WORLD WAR THREE          1980  DREAD AT THE CONTROLS TNT 1
    ROBBIE SHAKESPEARE  B     (A
    FRANKLYN WAUL       K     (A    SLY DUNBAR          D     (A   LARRY"HORSE MOUTH"WALLACE D  (A
    SANTA               D     (A    EARL"CHINNA"SMITH   G     (A   RAD"DOUGGIE"BRYAN  G   (A
    BOO PEE BROWN       G     (A    WINSTON BROWN       G     (A   AUGUSTO PABLO     K   (A
    ANSEL COLLINS       PNO   (A    STICKY              PERC  (A   SKULLY            PERC (AB
    LATTY GOURZONG      PERC  (A    FRANKLYN"BLUBBER"WAUL SYN  (A  VIN GORDON        TROM (A
    FELIX"DEADLEY" HEADLEY WIND(AB  GLADSTONE ANDERSON  PNO   (A   ERROL"FLABBA"HOLT B   (B
    LINCOLN"STYLE"HOLT  D     (B    NOEL"SOWELL"BAILEY  G     (B   BONGO HERMAN      PERC (B
    ANTHONY"STEELIE"NELSON ORG(B    EDI FITZROY         V     (B   EARL SIXTEEN      V   (B
    MICHAEL CAMPBELL    V     (B    WALTY BURNETT       V     (B
```

DREAM

```
    DEKE LEONARD        G V   (A    (A) 1967/ 68    NO ALBUMS
    MARTIN ACE          G V   (A
    WES REYNOLDS        B     (A    TERRY WILLIAMS      D     (A
```

DREAMS

```
    JEFF KENT         K G V   (A1   (1) 1969    (2) LATER LINE UPS
    DOUG LUBAHN        B V    (A1   (A) DREAMS                   1970  CBS US 30225       UK  64203
    MARK WHITTAKER     D      (1    (B) IMAGINE MY SUPRISE       1971  CBS US 30960       UK  64597
    RANDY BRECKER      HRNS   (AB
    MICHAEL BRECKER    HRNS   (AB   BILLY COBHAM        D     (AB  JOHN ABERCROMBIE  G   (A
    BOB MANN        G WIND V  (B    EDWARD VERNON       V     (AB  WILL LEE          B   (B
    BARRY ROGERS       TROM   (AB   DON GROLNICK        K     (A   STEVE CROPPER     G   (B
    TONI TORRENCE      V      (B    ANGEL ALLENDE       CONGA (A   ALLEN SCHWARZBERG D   (2
    STEVE GADD         D      (2    CHUCK RAINEY        B     (2
```

DRIFTERS

```
    CLYDE McPHATTER     V     (     ( ) CLYDE McPHATTER & THE DRIFTERS  1958  ATLANTIC  US    8003
    BEN E KING          V     (     ( ) ROCKIN' & DRIFTIN'       1958  ATLANTICO    US       8022
    DAVID BAUGHN        V     (     ( ) DRIFTERS GREATEST HITS   1960  ATLANTIC     US       8041
    ELSBERRY HOBBS      V     (     ( ) SAVE THE LAST DANCE FOR ME  1962  ATLANTIC   US      8059
    RUDY LEWIS          V     (     ( ) SAVE THE LAST DANCE FOR ME  1962  ATLANTIC   UK    587 063
    BILLY LEWIS         V     (     ( ) I'LL TAKE YOU WHERE THE MUSIC'S..  1965  ATLANTIC  US  8113
    CLYDE BROWN         V     (     ( ) I'LL TAKE YOU WHERE THE MUSIC'S..  1965  ATLANTIC  UK  587 061
    DIONNE WARWICK      V     (     ( ) I'LL TAKE YOU WHERE THE MUSIC'S..  1971  ATLANTIC  UK RI  K40009
    JO BLUNT            V     (     ( ) GOLDEN HITS              1966  ATLANTIC     US       8153
                                    ( ) GOLDEN HITS              1966  ATLANTIC     UK    588 013
                                    ( ) GOLDEN HITS              1972  ATLANTIC     UK    K40018

                                                                     (CONTINUED)
```

D116 (CONTINUED)   **DRIFTERS**   **D116**

DEE DEE WARWICK	V	(	( ) THE DRIFTERS	197	ATLANTIC	UK	K40412
CISSY HOUSTON	V	(	( ) STAR COLLECTION	197	MIDI	UK	20027
DORIS TROY	V	(	( ) THE DRIFTERS NOW	1973	BELL	US	219
JIMMY OLIVER	G	(	( ) LOVE GAMES	1975	BELL UK BELLS246	US	246
TOMMY EVANS	V	(	( ) THERE GOES MY FIRST LOVE	1975	BELL UK BELLS280	US	260
CHARLES HUGHES	V	(	( ) 24 ORIGINAL HITS	1975	ATLANTIC	UK	K60106
ANDREW THRASHER	V	(	( ) THE DRIFTERS STORY	1975	ATLANTIC	UK	K40565
			( ) SAVE THE LAST DANCE	1975	SOUNDS SUPERB	UK	SPR 90083
			( ) EVERY NIGHT IS SATURDAY NIGHT	1976	ARISTA	AB	4140
BOBBY HENDRICKS	V	(	( ) UP ON THE ROOF	1963	ATLANTIC	US	8073
JOHNNY MOORE	V	(	( ) UP ON THE ROOF	1963	ATLANTIC	UK	588 160
BILL PINKNEY	V	(	( ) OUR BIGGEST HITS	196	ATLANTIC	US	8093
GERHARD THRASHER	V	(	( ) OUR BIGGEST HITS	196	ATLANTIC	UK	587 038
CHARLIE THOMAS	V	(	( ) UNDER THE BOARDWALK	1964	ATLANTIC	US	8099
DOC GREEN	V	(	( ) GOOD LIFE	1965	ATLANTIC	US	8103
			( ) GREATEST RECORDINGS	19	ATCO	US	33375

D117   **DRIFTWOOD**   **D117**

NEIL ALFORD	G V	(A	( ) DRIFTWOOD	1970	DECCA	UK	SKL 5069
NICK HARRISON	G V HCA	(A					
NEIL HARRISON	K V	(A					

D118   **JULIE DRISCOLL**   **D118**

JULIE DRISCOLL (TIPPETS)	V(ALL		(A) JULIE DRISCOLL	1971	POLYDOR		2480 074
WITH			(A) JULIE DRISCOLL	1971	POLYDOR	GER	2383 077
KEITH TIPPETT	K	(A	(B) STARPORTRAIT	197	POLYDOR		2625 008
CHRIS SPEDDING	G B	(A	(C) SUNSET GLOW	1976	UTOPIA	UTS	601
BOB DOWNES	FLT	(A	(D) JULIE DRISCOLL	19	SPRINGBOARD	US	SPB 4043
JEFF CLYNE	B	(A					
ELTON DEAN	SAX	(AC	NICK EVANS	TROM	(AC	TREVOR TOMKINS	D	(A
KARL JENKINS	OBOE	(A	BUD PARKES	TPT	(A	STAN SULZMANN	SAX	(A
DEREK WADSWORTH	TROM	(A	BRIAN GODDING	V G	(AC	BRIAN BELSHAW	B V	(CA
JIM CREGAN	G	(A	BARRY REEVES	D	(A	MARC CHARIG	HRNS	(AC
HARRY MILLER	B	(C	LOUIS MOHOLO	D	(C			

D119   **DRIVER**   **D119**

PETER GLIDEMAN	G V	(A	(A) NO ACCIDENTS	1977	A&M	US	4545
DENNIS COATS	B V	(A					
STEVE ROXFORD	D	(A					

D120   **DRONES**   **D120**

M J DRONE	V G	(A	(A) FURTHER TEMPTATIONS	1977	VALER	UK	VLRP1
PETE PURRFECT	D	(					
STEVE CUNDALL	B	(A	GUS CALLENDER	G	(	P LAMBERT HOWELLS	D	(A
SIMON HUMPHREY	PROD	(A					

D120A   **DRUG ADDIX**   **D120A**

(A) FROM NEW ADDINGTON(EP)	1978	CHISWICK	UK	SW 39

D120B   **JOE DROUKAS**   **D120B**

JOE DROUKAS		(A	(A) SHADOWBOXING	1975	SOUTHWIND	US 6400

D121   **DRUICK & LORANGE**   **D121**

DWIGHT DRUICK	(A) DRUICK & LORANGE 1974 GOODEAR EARLH5001
KIRK LORANGE	

D122   **DRUID**   **D122**

NEIL BREWER	B	(AB	(A) TOWARDS THE SUN	1975	EMI	UK	EMC 3081
ANDREW McCRORIE SHAND	K	(AB	(B) FLUID DRUID	1976	EMI	UK	EMC 3128
CEDRIC SHARPLEY	D PERC	(AB					
DANE	G V	(AB					

D122A   **DRUIDS OF STONEHENGE**   **D122A**

(A) CREATION	19	UNI	US	73004

D122B   **DRY CITY SCAT BAND**   **D122B**

( ) DRY CITY SCAT BAND	19	ELEKTRA	US	7292

D122C   **DUCKS**   **D122C**

BRUCE BRYMEN	D V	(A	(A) DUCKS	1973	JUST SUNSHINE	US	JSS6
KENT HOUSEMAN	G V	(A					
DENNIS LANIGAN	V K SAX FLT	(A	DONALD LUTHER	B V	(A	JIM GORDON	D	(A

D123   **DUCKS DELUXE**   **D123**

SEAN TYLA	G V K	(ABCDE12	(A) DUCKS DELUXE	1974	RCA		PI 5008
MARTIN BELMONT	G	(ABCDE12	(B) TAXI TO THE TERMINAL ZONE	1974	RCA	UK	SF 8402
NICK GARVEY	B HCA	(AB1	(C) JUMPIN' (EP)	1975	SKYDOG		005
TIM ROPER	D	(ABC1	(D) DONT MIND ROCKIN' (COMPILATION)	1978	RCA US 3025	PL	25132
BOB ANDREWS	K V	(AE	(1) 1974 (2) FINAL LINE UP 1975				
GEORGE LARNYOH	SAX	(A	(E) LAST NIGHT OF A PUB ROCK BAND(DBL)	1979	DYNAMITE	NL	3303
PETER VANDER PUIJE	SAX	(A					
EDDIE QUANSAH	TPT	(A	DAVE EDMUNDS	G	(BD	ANDY McMASTERS	K V	(1
BILLY RANKIN	D	(2E	BRINSLEY SCHWARZ	G V	(2E	MICK GROOM	B	(2CE
NICK LOWE	G	(E	MARTIN STONE		(E	KEN WHALEY		(
LEE BRILLEAUX	V	(E					

D124   **LES DUDEK**   **D124**

LES DUDEK	G V	(ALL	(A)LES DUDEK	1976	CBS US 33702		UK 81380
WITH			(B)SAY NO MORE	1977	CBS US 34397		UK 81758
JEFF PORCARO	D	(ABC	(C)GHOST TOWN PARADE	1978	CBS US 35088		UK 82562
MARL HUDSON	V	(D	(D)GYPSY RIDE	1981	CBS US 36798		NL 84611
GERALD JOHNSON	B	(ABC					
DAVID PAICH	K	(ABC	MAXINE GREEN	V	(A	PEPPER SWENSON	V	(A
JERI STEVENS	V	(A	JIM HUGHART	B	(A	CAROLYN WILLIS	V	(A
MYRNA MATTHEWS	V	(A	DAVID HUNGATE	B	(A	REBECCA LOUIS	V	(AB
CHUCK RAINEY	B	(AB	BOZ SCAGGS	V	(A	DAVID FOSTER	K	(A
MAILTO CORREA	CONGA	(A	GLEN CHRONCHITE	PERC	(A	JIM KELTNER	D	(C
ALAN FEINGOLD	K	(B	JOACHIM YOUNG	K	(B	TED STRAON	K	(B
DAVID SANCIOUS	K	(B	TONY WILLIAMS	D	(B	KEVIN CALHOUN	PERC	(B
SHIRLEY MATTHEWS	V	(B	CLYDIE KING	-V	(B	REYMONDO	PERC	(B
PAT MURPHY	PERC	(BC	JIM KRUEGER	G	(C	MIKE FINNIGAN	K V	(CD
GARY MALLABER	D	(C	JACK BRUCE	V	(C	ROBERT 'POPS' POPSWELL	B	(BC

LES DUDEK

```
D124
    MAX GRONENTHAL        K V  (CD    CARMINE APPICE        D     (C    (CONTINUED)
    JERRY KNIGHT          V    (D     PETER SCHLESS         K     (D    TOM SCOTT         LYRICON (A
    MAX NOLAND            B    (D     JAMES NEWTON HOWARD   K     (D    TREY THOMPSON     B       (D
    CLIFF NEWTON          G V  (D     MARK STEIN            SYN   (D    GARY FERGUSON     D       (D
```

DUDES

```
D125                                                                                              D125
    BRIAN GREENWAY        G V  (A     (A) WERE NO ANGELS            1975   CBS             US   33577
    DAVID HENMAN          G V  (A     (EP) WANNA DANCE             19     CBS             US   156
    WAYNE CULLEN          D V  (A
    BOB SEGARINI          G V  (A     RITCHIE HENMAN        D V  (A     KOOTCH TROCHIM   B V  (A
```

DUFFO

```
D125A                                                                                             D125A
    DUFFO                 V    (AB    (A) DUFFO                     1979   BEGGARS BANQUET UK BEGA5
    TIM WHEATLEY          B    (C     (A) DUFFO                     1979   BEGGARS BANQUET GER 146512
    MIKE HOWLETT          B    (A     (B) THE DISAPPEARING BOY      1980   PVK UK PVK 2 NL DURECO 66012
    NICHOLAS COLA         PNO  (AB    (C) BOB THE BIRDMAN           1981   PVK UK DUF1 FR   2801
    DAVID HERZOG          G    (A
    PETER DOBSON          D    (AB    ROB ADAMS             D     (C    DICK MIDDLETON   G     (C
    LEW SEVARINI KOWICZ   K SYN(B     CHRIS PASKALEDES      B     (B    TIM GRAPPELLI    VLN   (B
    JIMMY PURSEY          V    (B     BRIAN ARMSTEAD        (
```

DUESENBERG

```
D125B                                                                                             D125B
                                      (A) CHAPTER IV               1981   VERTIGO         NL   6435077
```

DUFFY

```
D126                                                                                              D126
    DUFFY                      (AB    (A) SCRUFFY DUFFY             1973   CHAPTER ONE     UK   CHSR 814
                                      (B) JUST IN CASE YOU'RE INTERESTED  19  ARIOLA            85846
```

LARS DUGGAN

```
D126A                                                                                             D126A
    LARS DUGGAN               (A     (A) FROM THE LAKE STUDIOS      1980 PHILO           PH 9002
```

DORIS DUKE

```
D126B                                                                                             D126B
    DORIS DUKE            V    (AB    (A) IM A LOSER               19     CANYON 7704  CONTEMPO 101
    PAUL HORNSBY          K    (A     (B) LEGEND IN HER OWN TIME   19     MANKIND          200
    JERRY WILLLIAMS       K    (AB
    ROBERT POPWELL        B    (AB  JESSE CARR    G    (AB  JASPER GUARINO   D  (B  CHARLIE CHALMERS V (B
    SANDRA RHODES         V    (AB  DONNA RHODES  V    (B   JEANIE GREEN     V  (B  JOHNNY SANDLIN     (A
    CHUCK LEAVELL         K    (B
```

GEORGE DUKE

```
D127                                                                                              D127
    GEORGE DUKE           K V  (ALL   (A) GEORGE DUKE QUINTET      19     MPS                  68233
    JEROME RICHARDSON     WIND (Q     (B) SAVE THE COUNTRY(1969)   1978   LIBERTY 11004 PICKWICK 3588
    JOHN HEARD            B    (ABCEF (C) GEORGE DUKE    (1969)    1978   PACIFIC JAZZ  UK   891
    DAVID SIMMONS         TPT  (A     (D) LIVE IN L A              1971   SUNSET               50232
    GEORGE WALKER         D    (A     (E) FEEL                     1974   MPS US 25355  GER 212 23124
    JAY GRAYDON           G    (BC    (F) FACES IN REFLECTION      1975   MPS US 22018
    ERNIE WATTS           SAX  (BC    (G) I LOVE THE BLUES         1975   MPS US 25671  GER   5071
    RICHARD BERK          D    (BCQ   (H) THE AURA WILL PREVAIL    1975   BASF US 25613 GER   5064
    ERNIE TACK            TROM (BC    (I) LIBERATED FANTASIES      1976   BASF          GER   22835
    JAY DAVERSA           TPT  (BC    (J) LIVE IN EUROPE           1976   ATLANTIC US 18194 UK K50316
    CHARLES FINDLEY       TPT  (BC    (K) FROM ME TO YOU           1977   EPIC  US 34469 UK  81850
    GLENN FERRIS          TROM (BC    (L) REACH FOR IT             1977   EPIC  US 34883 UK  82216
    LEON NDUGU CHANCLER D PERC(EFGHIK (M) DONT LET GO              1978   EPIC  US 35366 UK  82821
    AIRTO MOREIRA         PERC (EGHI  (N) FOLLOW THAT RAINBOW      1979   EPIC  US 35701 UK  83336
    JOHNNY GUITAR WATSON  G    (G     (O) MASTER OF THE GAME       1979   EPIC  US 36263 UK  83951
    FLORA PURIM           V    (EGNO  (P) BRAZILIAN LOVE AFFAIR    1980   EPIC  US 36483 UK  84311
    FRANK ZAPPA           G    (E     (Q) INNER SOURCE             19     MPS               88031/2
    TOM FOWLER            B    (G     (R) POLYRHYTHM               19     LISTENING HOUSE   91003
    LEE RITENOUR          G    (G
    BYRON MILLER          B (GKNO  GEORGE JOHNSON    G    (GI  DARYL STUERMER   G    (GI  EMIL RICHARDS  PERC (G
    JOHN WITTENBERG       VLN  (G   JANET FERGUSONHOFF V   (GI  LUIS GASCA       TPT  (Q   ARMANDA PERAZA PERC (Q
    RUTH UNDERWOOD        PERC (GI  BRUCE FOWLER     TROM (G   ALPHONSO JOHNSON B    (HJS  SYLVIA ST JAMES V   (H
    KATHY WOEHRLE         V    (H   GEE JANZEN       V    (H   EMBAMBA          B    (I   NAPOLEON MURPHY BROCK V (INO
    DAVID AMARO           G    (I   RASHID DUKE      V    (I   BILLY COBHAM     D    (J   JOHN SCOFIELD  G    (J
    STANLEY CLARKE        B    (K   MIKE SEMBELLO    G    (K   DIANE REEVES     V    (K   MAXINE WILLARD V    (K
    JULIA TILLMAN         V    (K   JESSICA SMITH    V    (K   RICKY LAWSON     D    (NO  CHARLES JOHNSON G   (N
    SHEILA ESCOVEDO       PERC (NO  LYNN JAMES       V    (NO  JOSIE JAMES      V    (NO  ROLAND BAUTISTA    (O
    GARY GRANT            (O   GARY HERBIG      SAX  (O   JERRY HEY        HRNS (O   DAVID MYLES        (O
    RAY OBIEDO            G    (O   BILL REICHENBACH TROM (O   FRED WASHINGTON  (O   JOHN HERD        B  (Q
    JAMES LEARY           (Q   PETE MAGANINI    D    (R   DAVE YOUNG       B    (R   DON MENZA          (R
```

DUKE & THE DRIVERS

```
D127A                                                                                             D127A
    RHINESTONE MUDFLAPS V SAX (AB    (A) CRUISIN'               19     ABC             US   911
    MAD MISSISSIPPI BUFFALO V K(AB   (B) ROLLIN ON             1975   ABC             US   942
        (TOM SWIFT)
    SAM DELUXE           G V  (AB   CADILLAC JACK     G V  (AB  BOBBY BLUE SKY   D V  (B
    DR FEELGOOD FUNK     D V  (A    KOKO DEE          B V  (AB  EDDIE KRAMER     PROD  (A
```

DUKE JUPITER

```
D127B                                                                                             D127B
    GEORGE BARAJAS       B V  (ALL   (A) SWEET CHEEKS          1978   MERCURY              91IO 064
    DON MARACLE          G    (ALL   (B) TASTE THE NIGHT       1979   MERCURY         US   SRM 13756
    GREG WALKER          G V  (ALL   (C) BAND IN BLUE          1980   MERCURY         US   SRMI 3815
    MARSHALL STYLER      K V  (ALL
    DAVID HANLON         D PERC(BC  YVONNE M LEWIS    V    (B   JANET WRIGHT     V    (B
    DIVA GRAY            V    (B    CHUCK LEAVELL     K    (A   STEVE KATZ       HCA  (C
    EARL JETTY           D    (A    JAI JOHANNY JOHANSON PERC (A  RANDALL BRAMBLETT SAX (A
    HAROLD WILLIAMS      HRNS (A    RONNIE EADES      HRNS (A   HARVEY THOMPSON  HRNS (A
    HARRISON CALLOWAY    HRNS (A    DENNIS GOOD       HRNS (A
```

THE DUKES

```
D127C                                                                                             D127C
    MILLER ANDERSON      G V  (A12   (A) THE DUKES            1979   WB US BSK 3376  UK K56710
    RONNIE LEAHY         K    (A12   (1) 1979      (2) 1980
    JIMMY McCULLOCH      G V  (A1
    CHARLIE TUMAHAI      B V  (A12   STUART ELLIOTT    D    (A   BARRY DE SOUZA   D    (A
    MORRIS PERT          PERC (A     GREG JACKMAN      D    (A   MICK GRABHAM     G    (2
    NICK TREVISICK       D    (12
```

DULCIMER

JEM NORTH	B PERC(A	(A) DULCIMER	1971	NEPENTHA		6437 003
DAVE EVES	G HCA REC(A					
PETE HODGE	G DULC(A	RICHARD DODD	V	(A		

JOHN DUMMER

JOHN DUMMER	D	(ALL	(A) CABAL	1969	MERCURY	UK SMCL20136
BOB HALL	PNO	(AB	(B) JOHN DUMMERS BLUES BAND	1969	MERCURY	UK SMCL20167
DAVE KELLY	G V	(ABH12E	(B) JOHN DUMMERS BLUES BAND	1969	MERCURY	NZ MCY138166
ADRIAN PIETRYGA	G	(2BDHAC	(C) FAMOUS MUSIC BAND	1970	PHILIPS	UK 6382 040
CHRIS TRENGROVE	SAX	(C	(C) FAMOUS MUSIC BAND	1970	FONTANA	GER 6309 008
IAIN THOPSON	B V	(AB12DHC	(D) BLUE	1972	VERTIGO	UK 6360 055
NICK PICKETT V VLN	G K	(1BCDE	(E) THIS IS(COMP)	1972	PHILIPS	6382 039
KINGSLEY WARD	PNO	(H	(F) TRY ME ONE MORE TIME (COMP)	197	PHILIPS	UK 6382 040
MIKE EVANS	VLN	(H	(G) VOL 2 (COMP)	1973	PHILIPS	6382 083
JO ANN KELLY	V	(ABH1	(H) OOBLEEDOOBLEEJUBILEE	1973	VERTIGO	UK 6360 083
MIKE COOPER	G	(1	(H) OOBLEEDOOBLEEJUBILEE	1974	MERCURY	2360 083
ELLIOTT JACKSON		(1	(1) 1968 (2) 1969			
ROGER BROWN	V	(H				
KEITH TILLMAN	B	(A	TONY McPHEE G V (AE	JOHN O'LEARY	HCA	(A1
STEVE MILLER	PNO	(H	JOHN FAIRWEATHER HARMONIUM(C			

AYNSLEY DUNBAR

AYNSLEY DUNBAR	D	(ALL	(A) AYNSLEY DUNBAR RETALIATION	1969	BLUE THUMB	US BTS 4
VICTOR BROX HRNS K	G V	(ABCD1	(A) AYNSLEY DUNBAR RETALIATION	1968	LIBERTY	UK LBL 83154
JOHN MOORSHEAD	G V	(ABCD1	(A) AYNSLEY DUNBAR RETALIATION	19	BYG	FR 529501
ALEX DMOCHOWSKI	B	(ABCD	(B) DOCTOR DUNBARS PRESCRIPTION	1969	LIBERTY	UK LBS 83223
TOMMY EYRE	K	(CE	(B) DOCTOR DUNBARS PRESCRIPTION	1969	BLUE THUMB	US BTS 6
PETER GREEN	G	(	(B) DOCTOR DUNBARS PRESCRIPTION	1969	BYG	FR 529504
ANNETTE BROX	V	(D	(C) TO MUM FROM AYNSLEY & THE BOYS	1969	LIBERTY	UK LBS 83223
KEITH TILLMAN	B	(1	(C) TO MUM FROM AYNSLEY & THE BOYS	19	BYG	FR 529506
CHARLES GREETHAM	WIND	(E	(C) RETALIATION	1976	BLUE THUMB	US BTS 14
PAUL WILLIAMS	B	(E	(D) REMAINS TO BE HEARD	1970	LIBERTY	UK LBS 83316
PETER FRIEDBERG	V	(E	(E) REMAINS TO BE HEARD	1970	BYG	FR 529506
PAT HICKS	TPT	(E	(E) BLUE WHALE	1970	WB	K 46062
IVAN ZAGNI	G	(E	(E) BLUE WHALE RI	1978	CHARLY GER 3038 UK	CR 30142
NORMAN LEPPARD	SAX	(E	( ) CLASSIC BRITISH ROCK	19	SONOPRESSE	2978889
ROGER SUTTON	B	(E	( ) JOY TO THE WORLD	19	CAPITOL	US SMAS 788
EDWARDS REAY-SMITH	TROM	(E	(1)1967 LINE UP			
JACK BRUCE		(	( ) HISTORY OF BRITISH BLUES(COMP)	1973	SIRE	3701
ROD STEWART	V	(?				

SLY DUNBAR

SLY DUNBAR	D	(AB	(A) SIMPLE SLY MAN	1978 FRONT LINE	UK	1008
ROBBIE SHAKESPEARE	B	(B	(B) SLY WICKED & SLICK	1979 FRONT LINE	UK	1042
MIKEY CHUNG	K G B(B					
ANSEL COLLINS	K	(B	KEITH STERLING K (B	RAD BRYAN	G (B	ROBERT LYN K (B
DEAN FRASER	SAX	(B	TOMMY McCOOK SAX (B	VIN GORDON	TROM (B	HERMAN MARQUIS SAX(B
ELNATHAN BRACKENRIDGE TPT(B			BERES HAMMOND V (B	CALMAN SCOTT	V (B	TAMLINS V (B
TOUTER	V	(B	STICKY PERC (B	SCULLY	PERC (B	BARNABAS PERC(B

LESLEY DUNCAN

LESLEY DUNCAN V G MAND		(ALL	(A) SING CHILDREN SING	1971	CBS	UK 64202
WITH			(B) EARTH MOTHER	1972	CBS	UK 64807
ELTON JOHN	PNO	(A	(C) EVERYTHING CHANGES	1974	GM	GML 1007
TERRY COX	D	(A	(D) MOONBATHING	1975	GM UK GML 1017 US MCA 2207	
TRISTAN FRY	PERC	(A	(E) MAYBE IT'S LOST	1977	GM UK GML 1019 US MCA 2274	
TONI CAMPO	B	(A				
JOE MORETTI	G	(A	RAY COOPER PERC (A	DAVID KATZ STR (A	CHRIS SPEDDING G BOUZ (ABDE	
BOB COHEN	G	(C	LARRY STEELE B (C	LIZA STRIKE V (CD	JIMMY HOROWITZ K (ABCDE	
SUE GLOVER	V	(C	ANDY BOWN B (BC	PETER FRAMPTON G (C	PETE DENNIS B (DE	
GLEN LEFLEUR	D	(DE	BARRY DE SOUZA D (BC	JOANNA NEWMAN V (D	DEREK GROSSMITH WIND(D	
JACK ROTHSTEIN	STR	(B	ROBERT AHWAI G (E	NICO RAMSDEN G V (E	ALAN MURPHY G (E	
BOBBY KEYS	SAX	(E	LAURIE ANDREW V (E	JOHN PERRY V (E	MADELINE BELL V (E	

DAVID DUNDAS

DAVID DUNDAS	V K	(AB	(A) DAVID DUNDAS	1977	CHRYSALIS	UK CHR 1141
WITH			(B) VERTICAL HOLD	1978 CHRYSALIS UK		CHR 1197
ALAN TARNEY	B	(B				
GERRY CONWAY	D	(B	GRAHAM PRESKETT K MAND V(B	FRANK RICOTTI	PERC (B	KEN FRIEDMAN SYN(B
JIMMY JEWELL	SAX	(B	RON ASPERY SAX (B	DOREEN CHANTER	V (B	JOHN GREEN HRNS(B
IRENE CHANTER	V	(B	RICKY HITCHCOCK G (B	EDDIE HOWELL	V (B	

KEVIN DUNN

KEVIN DUNN		(A	(A) THE JUDGEMENT OF PARIS	1981 ARMAGGEDON	UK	ARM3
DEBBI HEIDEL		(A				
LEONORE THOMPSON		(A	TERRY COBURN (A			

CORNELL DUPREE

CORNELL DUPREE	G	(A	(A) TEASIN'	1975 ATLANTIC UK K50071	US	7311
RICHARD TEE	K	(A				
CHUCK RAINEY	B	(A	BERNARD PURDIE D (A	RALPH McDONALD	PERC (A	
PAUL GRIFFIN	K	(A	GEORGE STUBBS K (A	DAVID NEWMAN	SAX (A	
JOE FARRELL	SAX	(A	SELDON POWELL SAX (A	ERNIE ROYAL	TPT (A	
JOE NEWMAN	TPT	(A	GARNETT BROWN TROM (A	MARK MEYERSON	PROD (A	
MICHAEL CUSCUNA	PROD	(A	TREVOR KOEHLER SAX (A	JON FADDIS	TPT (A	

CHAMPION JACK DUPREE

CHAMPION JACK DUPREE V K D (ALL			SINGS THE BLUES	19	KING	US 735
WITH			CHAMPION JACK DUPREE	19	STORYVILLE	SLP 107
MICKEY BAKER	G	(EFJ	CHAMPION JACK DUPREE	19	EVEREST	US 217
HAL SINGER	SAX	(J	BLUES FOR EVERYONE	19	KING STARDAY	US KS 1084
MICHEL CARRAS	ORG	(M	(A)CHAMPION JACK DUPREE	19	STORYVILLE	SLP 824
LARRY MARTIN	G	(ML	PLAYS & SINGS THE BLUES	19	STORYVILLE	SLP 145
PAUL PECHANAERT	G	(M	BEST OF THE BLUES	19	STORYVILLE	SLP 151
ZOX	B	(LM	BARREL HOUSE BLUES	19	STORYVILLE	SLP 155
JACQUES MAHIEUX	D	(LM	CHAMPION JACK DUPREE	19	STORYVILLE	SLP 161
RICHARD STUDT	VLN	(H	BOOGIE BLUES & BARRELHOUSE BLUES	19	STORYVILLE	SLP 183
REG COLE	VLN	(H	PIANO BLUES VOL 2	19	STORYVILLE	SLP 187

(CONTINUED)

PETER OXER	VLN	(H	JACK DUPREE		19	STORYVILLE		SLP 193
TERRY NOONAN	HRNS	(H	JACK DUPREE		19	STORYVILLE		SLP 194
BUD PARKES	HRNS	(H	BLUES IN EUROPE		19	STORYVILLE		SLP 214
ALAN SKIDMORE	SAX	(H	CHAMPION JACK DUPREE		19	STORYVILLE		SLP 216
LES WINGFIELD	SAX	(H	FROM NEW ORLEANS TO CHICAGO		1966	DECCA	UK	LK 4747
JIM CHESTER	SAX	(H	FROM NEW ORLEANS TO CHICAGO		196	LONDON	US	553
WALLACE TRING	B	(H	(E)& HIS BLUES BAND		1967	DECCA	UK	SKL 4871
MIKE VERNON	PERC	(H	BLUES FROM THE GUTTER		196	ATCO	US	8019
BIG CHIEF DRUMSTICK	D PERC	(H	BLUES FROM THE GUTTER		1975	ATLANTIC	UK	K 40526
CHRISTOPHER TURNER	HCA	(G	CHAMPION OF THE BLUES		19	ATLANTIC	US	8056
STAN WEBB	G	(G	(F)ANTHOLOGIE DU BLUES		1968	VOGUE	FR	CLVLX 271
MICK TAYLOR	G	(H3	(G)WHEN YOU FEEL THE FEELING		1968	BLUE HORIZON	UK	763206
EDUARDO GIVEZANO	B	(H	(G) WHEN YOU FEEL THE FEELING		1968	CBS	US	7702
HARRIS DUNDEE	D	(G	(H)SCOOBY DOOBY DOO		1969	BLUE HORIZON	UK	763214
PAUL KOSSOFF	G	(12G	HEAVY BLUES		1969	SIRE	US	97010
STUART BROOKS	B	(12G	NATURAL & SOULFUL BLUES		196	ATLANTIC	US	8045
SIMON KIRKE	D	(12G	CHAMPION OF THE BLUES		196	ATLANTIC	US	8056
GARY THAIN	B	(3	TRICKS		19	GNP		10001
KEEF HARTLEY	D	(3	(J)IM HAPPY TO BE FREE		1971	GNP		10005
DUSTER BENNETT	HCA	(3G	CHAMPION JACK DUPREE		1971	FESTIVAL		FLD 653
HORST LANGE	G	(A	INCREDIBLE		1970	SONET		SNTF 614
MOGENS SEIDELIN	B	(A	LEGACY OF THE BLUES VOL 3		197	GNP		10013
KING CURTIS	SAX	(N	LEGACY OF THE BLUES VOL 3		1972	SONET	UK	SNTF 626
			(N) BLUES FROM MONTREUX		19	ATCO	US	1637
			(N) BLUES FROM MONTREUX		1972	ATLANTIC	UK	K 40434
			CHAMPION JACK		1972	BLUE HORIZON	US	4610
			WALKING BLUES		19	KING		1084
			LOWDOWN BLUES		19	CONTINENTAL		16002
			CHAMPION JACK DUPREE		19	OKEH	US	14103
(1) 1968 APRIL			WOMAN BLUES		19	FOLKWAYS		3825
(2) 1968 LIVE BAND			TROUBLE TROUBLE		19	MUSIDISC	FR	ST 21001
(3) 1969 SESSION			FINE & MELLOW		19	MUSIDISC	FR	ST 21009
			HAMBURG SESSIONS		1974	HAPPYBIRD		HAPB 5011
			BLUES OF C J DUPREE		1976	STORYVILLE		SLP 240
			(L)SHAKESPEARE SAYS		1976	SARAVAH		SH 10065
			(M)1977		1977	ISADORA		ISL 6405

D133A   **ROBBIE DUPREE**   D133A

ROBBIE DUPREE	V HCA PERC	(AB	(A) ROBBIE DUPREE		1980	ELEKTRA US 6E273	UK K52235
BILL ELLIOTT	SYN K	(A	(B) STREET CORNER HEROES		1981	ELEKTRA US 6E344	UK K52290
ROBERT PALMER	G	(A					
RICK CUDACOFF	K B	(AB	PETER BUNETTA	D PERC	(AB	MIGUEL RIVERA	PERC	(A
BILL LABOUNTY	K V	(A	BRIAN RAY	G	(AB	DENNIS HERRING	G	(AB
BOB BORDY	G	(A	JERRY PETERSON	SAX	(AB	MICHAEL BODDICKER	SYN	(AB
ALAN ESTES	PERC	(A	KAL DAVID	SITAR V	(AB	LESLIE SMITH	V	(AB
ARNO LUCAS	PERC V	(AB	MATTHEW WEINER	V	(AB	JOE TURANO	V	(AB
JOE LALA	PERC	(B	DAVID ANDERSON	V	(B	DAVID WOODFORD	HRNS	(B
LEE THORNBURG	TPT	(B	DARREL LEONARD	TPT	(B	BILL ARMSTRONG	TPT	(B
BILL McWHIRTER	TROM	(B						

D134   **SIMON DUPREE & THE BIG SOUND**   D134

DEREK SHULMAN	V	(	(A) WITHOUT RESERVATIONS		1967	PARLOPHONE	UK	PCS 7029
PHIL SHULMAN	SAX	(A	(A) WITHOUT RESERVATIONS		1967	CAPITOL	US	T 5097
RAY SHULMAN	B G V	(A						
PETER O'FLAHERTY	B	(A	TONY RANSLEY	D	(A	MARTIN SMITH	D (
GEARY KENWORTHY		(	ERIC HINE		(		

D134A   **VAN DUREN**   D134A

VAN DUREN G K B SYN	V	(AB	(A) STARING AT THE CEILING		1978 LONDON UK SHY8530 US BIGSOUND3816
HILLY MICHAELS	D	(A	(B) ARE YOU SERIOUS		1978 US BIGSOUND 019
DOUG SNYDER	PERC	(A			
JON TIVEN	G SAX	(A			

D134B   **DURAN DURAN**   D134B

SIMON LE BON	V	(AB	(A) DURAN DURAN		1981	EMI UK EMC3372 US HARVEST 12158
JOHN TAYLOR		(AB	(B) RIO		1982	EMI UK EMC3411
NICK RHODES		(AB			
ROGER TAYLOR		(AB	ANDY TAYLOR		(AB

D135   **TERRY DURHAM**   D135

TERRY DURHAM			(A) CRYSTAL TELEPHONE		1969	DERAM	UK	SML 1042
WITH								
EVAN PARKER	SAX	(A	CHRIS KARAN	D	(A	ALAN PARKER	G	(A	JOHN COLEMAN	PNO(A

D135A   **DUROCS**   D135A

RON NAGLE	V K	(A	(A) DUROCS		1979	CAPITOL	US	11981
SCOT MATTHEWS D B G	K SAX	(A						
LARRY REID	V	(A	MAURICE GRIDLIN	ACC	(A	JOHN BLAKELEY	G B	(A
STEVE DOUGLAS	SAX	(A	PHIL AABERG	K B SYN	(A	CHRIS RICHIE	G	(A
ERIC STEIN	SYN	(A	LARRY BLACKSHIRE	VIBES	(A		

D136   **DURUTTI COLUMN**   D136

TONY BOWERS	B G	(	(A) RETURN OF DURUTTI COLUMN		1980	FACTORY	UK	FAC14
VINNIE RILEY	G K	(ABC	(B) 2 TRIANGLES		1981	FACTORY	BEL	10
DAVE ROWBOTHAM	G B	(	(C) LC		1981	FACTORY	UK	FACT 44
CHRIS JOYCE	D	(						
PHIL RAYNHAM	V	(	BRUCE MITCHELL	PERC	(C	PETE CROOKS	B	(A
TOLY	D	(A						

IAN DURY & THE BLOCKHEADS

IAN DURY	V	(ALL	(A) NEW BOOTS & PANTIES	1977	STIFF	US	0002	UK SEEZ4
CHARLEY CHARLES	D	(ABC	(B) DO IT YOURSELF	1979	STIFF	US	36104	UK SEEZ14
NORMAN WATT ROY	B	(ABC	(C) LAUGHTER	1980	STIFF	US	36998	UK SEEZ30
CHAZ JANKEL	G K	(ABD	(D) LORD UPMINSTER	1981	POLYDOR US 16337 UK 5042			NL 2383 617
DAVEY PAYNE	SAX	(ABC	(E) JUKE BOX JURY	1981	STIFF			UK SEEZ41
EDWARD SPEIGHT	G	(A						
GEOFF CASTLE	K	(A	MICK GALLAGHER	K	(BC	JOHN TURNBULL	G	(BC
SLY DUNBAR	D	(D	ROBBIE SHAKESPEARE	B	(D	DON CHERRY	TPT	(D
RAY COOPER	PERC	(C	IVOR RAYMOND	STR	(C	TYRONE DOWARE		(D
WILKO JOHNSON	G V	(C						

RICHIE WISE	G V	(AB	(A) DUST		19	POLYDOR UK 2319 014 US MYRRH6504		
MARC BELL	D	(A	(A) DUST		19	KAMA SUTRA	US	KSBS 2041
KENNY AARONSON	B STEEL G(AB		(B) HARD ATTACK		19	KAMA SUTRA	US	KSBS 2059

(A) HONKY TONK MUSIC		197	CAPITOL	US	11614
(B) DOMINO JOE		197	CAPITOL	US	11755

BOB DYLAN HCA V G   (ALL
WITH

ROBBIE ROBERTSON	G V(GKOPR	RICK DANKO	B V VLN (GKOPR	LEVON HELM	D V MAND (KOPR	RICHARD MANUEL	K V D (GKOPR
GARTH HUDSON	K SAX(GKOPR	AL KOOPER	G K HRNS (KLGFN	CHARLIE McCOY	G HCA(GHJKF	KENNY BUTTREY	D (GHJKN
JOHNNY CASH	V (J	JIM KELTNER	D (MXY	EMMYLOU HARRIS	V (S	MICK RONSON	G (T
ROGER McGUINN	G (M	PETE DRAKE	STEEL(HJKN	CHARLIE DANIELS	B G(JKLN	NORMAN BLAKE	(JKN
BOB WILSON	(JK	TONY BROWN	B (Q	BUDDY CAGE	STEEL(Q	PAUL GRIFFIN	K (EFQ
ERIC WEISSBERG	BAN (J	DELIVERANCE	(Q	STEVEN SOLES	VG (STUV	ALAN PASQUA	K (UV
CAROLYN DENNIS	V (UWXY	WAYNE MOSS	G V (G	BILLY CROSS	G (UV	JERRY SCHEFF	B (U
IAN WALLACE	D (U	JO ANN HARRIS	V (U	DAVID MANSFIELD MAND G(TUV		STEVE DOUGLAS	SAX (UVY
BOBBYE HALL	PERC (U	HELENA SPRINGS	V (UW	JOAN BAEZ	G V(	PAUL BUTTERFIELD	HCA (U
JESSE ED DAVIS	G (	FRED KATZ	CELLO(M	DAVID BROMBERG	G (KLN	BILLY DAVENPORT	D (
ROB STONER	B (STV	ALBERT W BUTLER	V (M	RINGO STARR	D (Y	RONNIE BLAKELY	V (S
FRED CARTER	(KN	MARK NAFTALIN	(	LUTHER RIX	PERC (S	MARVIN D CHANTRY	VIOLA(K
MIKE BLOOMFIELD	G (F	HOWARD WYETH	D PNO (ST	RON CORNELIUS	G (KLN	BILLY PRESTON	K (
GARY BURKE	D (T	DOTTIE DILLARD	V (K	ELVIN BISHOP	G (	SCARLET RIVERA	VLN (ST
DELORES EDGIN	(KN	LEON RUSSELL	K (	TED MICHEL	CELLO(M	SOLIE J FOTT	(K
JEROME ARNOLD	(	DOM CORTESE	MAND (S	BUBBA FOLLER	G (KN	KLAUS VOORMANN	B (
GEORGE BARNES	B. (B	DENNIS A GOODE	TROM (M	SAM LAY	D (	DICK WELLSTOOD	PNO (B
EMANUEL GREEN	VLN (K	GEORGE HARRISON	G V (	HERB LOVELL	D (B	HILDA HARRIS	K (KLN
ERIC CLAPTON	G (S	HOWIE COLLINS	G (B	FREDRICK HILL	TPT(K	BYRON BERLINE	FDL (M
LEONARD GASKIN	B (B	KARL HIMMEL	D (K	TERRY PAUL	B (M	BRUCE LANGHORNE	G (BME
LILIAN HUNT	(K	BRENDA PATTERSON	V (M	BYRON BACH	VLN(K	MARTIN KATAHN	V (K
CARL FORTINA	K (M	BRENTON BANKS VLN SYN(K		DOUG KERSHAW	VLN(K	GARY FOSTER	WIND (M
GEORGE BINKLEY	VLN (K	MILLIE KIRKHAM	(KN	MARTHA McCRORY CELLO (K		BARRY McDONALD	(K
SHELDON KURLAND	VLN (K	OLIVER MITCHELL TPT (K		CAROL MONTGOMERY	(KN	BOB MOORE	B (KN
GENE A MULLINS	(K	JUNE PAGE	V (KN	REX PEER	(K	GARY VAN OSDALE	VIOLA(K
BILL PURSELL	(KN	ALBERTINE ROBERTSON	V(KLN	ALVIN ROGERS	D (KN	FRANK C SMITH	(K
MAERETHA STEWART V (KLONPR		ANTHONY FERRON	(K	STU WOODS	B (KN	STEVE MADAIO	TPT (U
HAPPY TRAUM B G V BANJ(*		HARVEY BROOKS	B (FL	BUZZY FEITEN	G (L	RUSS KUNKEL	D (LMN
BILL MUNDI	D (L	BOOKER T JONES	B (M	CAROL HUNTER	G V(M	DONNA WEISS	V (M
PRISCILLA JONES	V (M	VINCENT BELL	BAZ (S	T BONE BURNETT	G PNO(T	JOE SOUTH	(G
HENRY STRZELECKI	B (G	BILL ATKINS	K (G	JERRY KENNEDY	G (G	HARGUS ROBBINS	K (G
HARVEY GOLDSTEIN	B (F	NEIL YOUNG	G V (U	BEN KEITH	STEEL(+	JOLLY ROGER	BAN (M
AL GORGONI	G (E	KEN RANKIN	G (E	JOHN SEBASTIAN	B (E	JOHN BOONE	B (E
BOBBY GREGG	D (E	FRANK OWENS	PNO (EF	JOE MACHO	B (E	WILLIAM LEE	B (E
JOHN HAMMOND JR	G (E	RUSS SAVAKUS	B (F	MICKEY JONES	D (E	FRED FOSTER	G (K
BARRY CORNFIELD	G (Q	RICHARD CROOKS	G (Q	CHARLIE BROWN	G (Q	KEN ODEGUARD	G (Q
CHRIS WEBER	K (Q	BILL PRESTON	B (Q	GREG INHOFER	G (Q	BILL BERG	D (Q
LUTHER RIX	CONGA(S	DEBBIE DYE	V (V	MARK KNOPFLER	G (W	BARRY BECKETT	K PERC(W
TIM DRUMMOND	B (WXY	PICK WITHERS	D (W	MUSCLE SHOALS HORNS	(W	MICKEY BUCKINS	PERC (W
REGINA HAVIS	V (WX	FRED TACKETT	G (XY	SPOONER OLDHAM	K (X	TERRY YOUNG	K (X
CLYDIE KING	V (XY	MONA LISA YOUNG V (X		REGINA MACCREY	V (Y	MADELYN QUEBEC	V (Y
STEVE RIPLEY	G (Y	CARL PICKHARDT PNO (Y		BENMONT TENCH	K (Y	DANNY KORTCHMAR	K (Y
WILLIAM SMITH	ORG (Y	DONALD DUCK DUNN	B(Y	RON WOOD	G (Y	BOB NEUWIRTH	G (
RAMBLIN JACK ELLIOTT	G(	JERRY GARCIA	G (	CARLOS SANTANA	G (		

LP's

	DATE	US	STEREO	MONO	JAPAN				UK	
(A) BOB DYLAN	1962	CBS	8579	1779	CBS SONY	25AP 268	CBS		62022
(A) BOB DYLAN							RI EMBASSY		32001
(B) FREEWHEELIN' BOB DYLAN	1963	CBS	8786	1986	CBS SONY	25AP 269	CBS		62193
(C) TIMES THEY ARE A CHANGIN'	1964	CBS	8905	2105	CBS SONY	25AP 270	CBS		62251
(D) ANOTHER SIDE OF BOB DYLAN	1964	CBS	8993	2193	CBS SONY	25AP 271	CBS		62429
(E) BRINGING IT ALL BACK HOME	1965	CBS	9128	2328	CBS SONY	25AP 272	CBS		62515
(F) HIGHWAY 61 REVISITED	1965	CBS	9189	2389	CBS SONY	25AP 273	CBS		62572
(G) BLONDE ON BLONDE (DBL)	1966	CBS	C2S841	C2841	CBS SONY	40 AP 274/5	CBS		66012
(H) JOHN WESLEY HARDING	1968	CBS	9604	2804	CBS SONY	25AP 277	CBS		63252
(J) NASHVILLE SKYLINE	1969	CBS	9825		CBS SONY	25AP 278	CBS		63601
(K) SELF PORTRAIT (DBL)	1970	CBS	30050		CBS SONY	40AP279/80	CBS		66250
(L) NEW MORNING	1970	CBS	30290		CBS SONY	25AP 281	CBS		69001
(M) PAT GARRETT & BILLY THE KID	1973	CBS	32460		CBS SONY	25AP 284	CBS		69042
(N) DYLAN	1973	CBS	32747		CBS SONY	25AP 285	CBS		69049
(O) PLANET WAVES	1974	ASYLUM	7E1003				ISLANDILPS9261		
(P) BEFORE THE FLOOD (DBL)	1974	ASYLUM	AB 201				ISLAND	IBD 1	
(Q) BLOOD ON THE TRACKS	1974	CBS	33235		CBS SONY	25AP 286	CBS		69097
(R) BASEMENT TAPES (DBL)	1975	CBS	33682		CBS SONY	40AP287/8	CBS		88147
(S) DESIRE	1976	CBS	33893		CBS SONY	25AP 289	CBS		86003
(T) HARD RAIN	1976	CBS	34349		CBS SONY	25AP 290	CBS		86016
(U) STREET LEGAL	1978	CBS	35453		CBS SONY	25AP 1099	CBS		86067
(V) AT BUDOKAN (DBL)	1978	CBS	36067		CBS SONY	40AP 2200	CBS		96004
(W) SLOW TRAIN COMING	1979	CBS	36120				CBS		86095
(X) SAVED	1980	CBS	36553				CBS	UK 83113	
(Y) SHOT OF LOVE	1981	CBS	37496				CBS		85178

(CONTINUED)

BOB DYLAN (CONTINUED) D139

( ) GREATEST HITS	1967	CBS	9463	2663	CBS SONY 25AP 276	CBS	62847
( ) GREATEST HITS VOL 2	19	CBS	31120			CBS	62911
( ) GREATEST HITS VOL 3	19	CBS				CBS	63111
(*) MORE GREATEST HITS (DBL)	1972	CBS				CBS	67239
( ) NOBODY SINGS LIKE BOB DYLAN	19	CBS				CBS	62694
( ) 11 YEARS IN THE LIFE OF BOB DYLAN	197				SOPI 11/12	
(+) S N A C K	1975	VIBRATOR 160					
( ) BOB DYLAN	197	JOKER ITALY T63					
( ) BROADSIDE BALLADS	19	BROADSIDE BR301					
( ) BROADSIDE REUNION	1972	FOLKWAYS	5315				
( ) NEWPORT BROADSIDE	1964	VANGUARD	79144			FONTANA	6038
( ) EVENING CONCERTS AT NEWPORT	1964	VANGUARD	79148			FONTANA	6138
( ) TRIBUTE TO WOODY GUTHRIE	19					CBS	64861
( ) WE SHALL OVERCOME	1964	FOLKWAYS	5592				
( ) MASTERPIECES(TPL)	197	CBS AUSTRALIA	220502				
(EP) I WANT YOU	19	CBS	43683			CBS	6051
(EP) ONE TOO MANY MORNINGS	1965	CBS				CBS	6070
(EP) Mr TAMBOURINE MAN	1966	CBS					

D140   DYNAMIC ROCKERS D140

(A) THE DYNAMIC ROCKERS	1980	DURECO		NL	44019

D141   DYNAMIC SUPERIORS D141

(A) GIVE	1977	MOTOWN		US	879
(B) PURE PLEASURE	1977	MOTOWN		US	841
(C) YOU NAME IT	1977	MOTOWN		US	875

D142   DYNASTY D142

(A) YOUR PIECE OF THE ROCK	1980	SOLAR		UK	3398
(B) ADVENTURES IN THE LAND OF MUSIC	1980	SOLAR		UK	3576

D143   DZYAN D143

JOCHEN LEUSCHNER V PERC(A	(A) DZYAN	1972	ARONDA	10006
REINHARD KARWATKY B (ABC	(B) TIME MACHINE	1973	BACILLUS	19161
GERD EHRMANN SAX (A	(C) ELECTRIC SILENCE	1975	BACILLUS	19202
HARRY KRAMER G (A				
LUDWIG BRAUM D PERC(A EDDY MARRON G (BC PETER GIGER D (BC				

E1   EAGLE E1

WAYNE ULAKY B (A	(A) COME UNDER NANEY'S TENT	19	JANUS	US	JLS 3011
JOHN WRIGHT V (A					
ROBERT RHODES K HRNS (A J JAMES G V (A					

E2   EAGLES E2

				US	UK	UK
RANDY MEISNER V B G(ABCDE	(A) THE EAGLES	1972	ASYLUM	5054	SYTC101 +	K 53009
GLENN FREY V G (ABCDEFG	(B) DESPARADO	1973	ASYLUM	5068	SYLA9011+	K 53008
DON HENLEY D V (ABCDEFG	(C) ON THE BORDER	1974	ASYLUM	7E1004	SYL9016 +	K 43005
BERNIE LEADON G V BAN(ABCD	(D) ON OF THESE NIGHTS	1975	ASYLUM	7E1039	SYLA 8759+	K 53014
DON FELDER G V (CDEFG	(E) HOTEL CALIFORNIA	1976	ASYLUM	7E1084 RI 103		K 53051
JOE WALSH G V (EFG	(F) THE LONG RUN	1979	ASYLUM	6 508		K 52181
TIM SCHMIT B V (FG	(G) EAGLES LIVE	1980	ASYLUM	705		K 62032
J D SOUTHER V G (G	( ) GREATEST HITS	1975	ASYLUM	6E105		K 53017
JOE VITALE K D (G						
PHIL KENZIE SAX (G	VINCE MELAMED K (G	JAGE JACKSON G (G				
ALBHY GALUTEN SYN (D	JIM ED NORMAN PNO (D	DAVID SANBORN SAX (F				
AL PERKINS STEEL (C	DAVID BROMBERG FDL (D	JIMMY BUFFET V (F				

E3   BOBBY EAGLESHAM E3

BOBBY EAGLESHAM G V (A	(A) BOBBY EAGLESHAM	1974	XTRA	UK	XTRA 1137
SID CAIRNS B (A					

E3A   SNOOKS EAGLIN E3A

SNOOKS EAGLIN G V (ALL	(A) NEW ORLEANS STREET SINGER	19	FOLKWAYS	US	2476
ELLIS MARSHAL PNO (C	(B) LEGACY VOL2	19	GNP	US	10012
CLARENCE FORD SAX (C	(C) DOWN YONDER	1978	SONET	UK	SNTF 752
GEORGE FRENCH B (C					
BOB FRENCH D (C					

E3B   RICHARD EARL E3B

RICHARD EARL (A	(A) EGG STORE ILK	1981	PILOT	UK	PILOT1

E3C   EARLY BIRD E3C

ALBERT VELD (A	(A) FLY AWAY	1980	KILLROY	NL	16963
HENDRIK WARINGA (A					
KARINA HENSON-KLOK (A	MEINE BRUINSMA (A LEO ROODHOF (A				
HARRY ZIJLSTRA (A					

E3D   EARLY FROST E3D

(A) EARLY FROST	1978	VANGUARD	US	79392

E4   EARTH & FIRE E4

JERNEY KAAGMAN V (ALL	(A) EARTH & FIRE	1971	NEPENTHAL	NL 6437 004	POLYDOR NL 2441011
GERARD KOERTS V FLT VIBES K(ALL	(A) EARTH & FIRE	197	REDBULLET	US 3000	
HANS ZIECH B (ABCG	(B) SONG OF MARCHING CHILDREN	197	POLYDOR	NL 2925 003	
THEO HURTS G B (DE	(B) MEMORIES	1975	POLYDOR	GER 2310 209	
CHRIS KOERTS G V (ABCD	(C) ATLANTIS	1973	POLYDOR	NL 2419 059	NL 2925013
TON VANDER KLEIJ D V (ALL	(C) ATLANTIS	1975	POLYDOR	GER 2310 262	
BERT RUITER B (EG	(D) TO THE WORLD A FUTURE	1975	POLYDOR	NL 2925 033	2374121
RONNIE MAYES G (G	(E) GATE TO INFINITY	1977	POLYDOR	NL 2925 065	
AD TAMBOER D (G	(F) REALITY FILLS FANTASY	1979	VERTIGO	NL 6413 501	
	(G) ANDROMEDA GIRL	1981	VERTIGO	NL 6399 271	
	( ) SUPERSTARSHINE VOL1 COMP	19	POLYDOR	NL 2419 029	
	( ) ROCK SENSATION	19	POLYDOR	GER 2499 109	
	( ) BEST OF	1975	POLYDOR	NL 2491 004	
	( ) BEST OF	1979	POLYDOR	NL 2426 012	
	( ) THE STORY OF	1976	POLYDOR	NL 2925 044	
	( ) THE HITS OF	1980	ORION	NL	
	( ) GREATEST HITS	1980	POLYDOR	NL2475 206	

EARTH OPERA

```
PETER ROWAN    V SAX G   (AB      (A) EARTH OPERA                        1968  ELEKTRA              74016
DAVID GRISMAN  K SAX (AB          (B) THE GREAT AMERICAN EAGLE TRAGEDY   1969  ELEKTRA              74038
JOHN NAGY      B     (AB
BILL STEVENSON K     (A     BILL KEITH        STEEL     (B   BILL MUNDI        PERC (A
PAUL DILLON    D G V (AB    DAVE HOROWITZ     K         (B   JOHN CALE         G V  (B
RICHARD GRANDO SAX   (B     HERB BUSHLER      B         (B   BOB ZACHARY       PERC (B
JACK BONUS     WIND  (B
```

EARTH QUAKE

```
ROBBIE DUNBAR   G V   (ALL    (A) EARTHQUAKE              1971  A&M                US  SP   4308
JOHN DOUKAS     V PNO (ALL    (B) WHY DO YOU TRY ME       1972  A&M                US       4337
STAN MILLER     B V   (ALL    (C) EARTHQUAKE LIVE         1975  U A                UK  UAS 29853
STEVE NELSON    D     (ALL    (C) ROCKIN' THE WORLD       1975  BESERKLEY USO045 RI     34752
GARY PHILLIPS   G V   (CDE    (C) ROCKIN' THE WORLD       197   BESERKLEY          GER      23356
PETE SEARS      K     (B      (C) ROCKIN' THE WORLD       1978  BESERKLEY     UK       BSERK 3
LENNY PICKETT   SAX   (B      (D) 8.5                     197   BESERKLEY US 0047 RI 34754
CHUCK FINDLEY   TPT   (B      (D) 8.5                     1976  BESERKLEY         UK       BSERK5
JIM HORN        SAX   (B      (E) LEVELED                 197   BESERKLEY US 0054 RI  34801
MATTHEW KAUFMAN PROD  (C      (E) LEVELED                 1977  BESERKLEY UK BSERK7 GER 23311
                              (F) 2 YEARS IN A PADDED CELL 1979 BESERKLEY        US       10065
```

EARTH WIND & FIRE

```
MAURICE WHITE   D V   (ALL      (A) EARTH WIND & FIRE                    1971  WB    US   1905
VERDINE WHITE   B V   (FKMDNPJ  (B) THE NEED OF LOVE                     1972  WB    US   1958
FRED WHITE      D PERC(KMNPJ    (C) ANOTHER TIME                        1972  WB    US   2798
ANDY WOOLFOLK   WIND  (FKMNPJ   (D) LAST DAYS & TIME                    1973  CBS   US 31702        UK 65208
DICK HYDE       TROM  (PJ       (D) LAST DAYS & TIME                    1979  EMBASSY                UK 31761
PHILIP BAILEY   V PERC(FKMNDPJ  (E) HEAD TO THE SKY                     1973  CBS   US 32194        UK 65604
LEW McCREARY    TROM  (PJ       (E) HEAD TO THE SKY                     1981  EMBASSY                UK 32017
RONALD BATTISTA G     (DP       (F) OPEN YOUR EYES                      1974  CBS   US 32712        UK 65844
CHARLES LOPER   TROM  (PJ       (F) OPEN YOUR EYES                      1981  EMBASSY                UK 32033
LARRY DUNN      K SYN (DFMKNPJ  (G) THATS THE WAY OF THE WORLD          1975  CBS   US 33280        UK 80575
GARY GRANT      TPT   (G        (G) THATS THE WAY OF THE WORLD          1981  EMBASSY                UK 32054
RON WAYNE LAWS  WIND  (D        (H) GRATITUDE                          1975  CBS   US 33694        UK 88160
RALPH JOHNSON   D PERC(FKMDNPJ  (J) SPIRIT                             1977  CBS   US 34241        UK 81451
AL McKAY        G PERC(FKMND     (K) ALL AND ALL                       1978  CBS   US 34905        UK 86051
JOHNNY GRAHAM   G     (FKMNPJ    (L) BEST OF VOL 1                     1978  CBS   US 35647        UK 83284
DAVID FOSTER    K     (MNP       (M) I AM                              1979  CBS   US 35730        UK 86084
EDDIE DEL BARRIO PNO  (KM        (N) FACES (DBL)                       1980  CBS   US 36795        UK 88498
MARLO HENDERSON G     (MNP       (O) EARTH WIND & FIRE (TRIPLE BOX)GJK 1979  CBS                    UK 66350
SKIP SCARBOROUGH PERC (K         (EP) SING A SONG(PROMO EP)            1977  CBS              EWF1
BELOYD TAYLOR   G     (P         (P) RAISE                             1981  CBS   US 37548        UK 85272
PAULINHO DA COSTA PERC (KMNP
DONALD MYRICK   SAX   (KMPJ   LOUIS SATTERFIELD   TROM   (KMNPJ  MICHAEL HARRIS      TPT   (KMNPJ
RAHMLEE DAVIS   TPT   (MNP    JESSICA CLEAVES     V      (D      STEVE LUKATHER      G     (MN
BILLY MYERS     K     (MP     SHEILA WHITT        V      (M      BENJAMIN POWELL     TROM  (M
STEVE PORCARO   SYN   (M      JEANETTE HAWES      V      (M      BILL REICHENBACH    TROM  (MNP
WANDA HUTCHINSON V    (M      ELMER BROWN         TPT    (M      MAURICE SPEARS      TROM  (M
OSCAR BRASHEAR  TPT   (MDNPJ  FRED JACKSON        SAX    (MN     BOBBY BRYANT        TPT   (MDN
HERMAN RILEY    SAX   (M      JEROME RICHARDSON   SAX    (M      JERRY HEY           TPT   (MNP
BARBARA KORN    HRNS  (M      DOROTHY ASHBY       HARP   (MJ     RICHARD LEPORE      PERC  (M
STEVE MADAIO    TPT   (MNJ    GEORGE BOHANON      TROM   (MNPJ   GARNETT BROWN       TROM  (M
SIDNEY MULDREW  HRN   (M      RICHARD PERISSI     HRNS   (M      MARILYN ROBINSON    HRN   (MNJP
WAYNE VAUGHN    K     (P      MICHAEL BODDICKER   K      (P      LARRY HULL          TPT   (P
CHUCK FINDLEY   TPT   (PNJ    80 PIECES STRING SEC       (N      HARVEY MASON        PERC  (J
GARRY GLEN      K     (N      NOLAN SMITH         TPT    (N      JEFF CLAYTON        TROM  (N
FRED WESLEY     TROM  (N      ARTHUR MAEBE        HRN    (NJ     ALAN ROBINSON       HRN   (N
JOHN JOHNSON    TUBA  (N      REGGIE ANDREWS             (D      MARTIN YARBOUGH            (D
JERRY PETERS    K     (NJ     GARY GRANT          TPT    (N      LAWRENCE WILLIAMS   WIND  (N
VINCENT DEROSA  HON   (N      GEORGE PRICE        HRN    (N      TOM JOHNSON         HRNS  (J
```

EARTHQUIRE

```
TATA VEGA      V     (A      (A) EARTHQUIRE                    1972  NATURAL RESOURCES  NR  106L
GREG MATHESON  K     (A
MARK KOFSTEIN  WIND  (A      BOB CROSBY      WIND  (A    LAURIE ANNE BALL   V   (A
JIM VARLEY     D     (A      MIKE GORFAINE   V     (A    CHARLIE STEPHENS   B   (A
BRIE BRANDT    V     (A
```

EARTHSTAR

```
DENNIS REA         G     (AB     (A) FRENCH SKYLINE           1979  SKY              SKY  031
TIM FINNEGAN       FLT   (A      (B) ATOM KRAFT ? NEIN DANKE  1981  SKY                   051
CRAIG WUEST        K     (AB
NORMAN PEACH       B     (A      DARYL TRIVIERI    VLN   (AB   MARLA THOMSON     HRNS (A
DIRK SCHMALENBACH  SITAR (A      LOUIS DEPONTE     TAPES (B    DAN ZONGRONE      PNO  (B
RAINER BOHM        VLN   (B      CHRISTOPHER LAGEMANN CELLO (B MELANIE LOIRE     PERC (B
JOHN BUNKFELDT     HCA   (B      MARTY BURDETTE    G     (B
```

CHRIS EAST

```
CHRIS EAST      G     (A     (A) HOTEL IN THE COUNTRY       1978  GTO              UK  GTLP 034
MO WITHAM       G B   (A
PAUL THOMPSON   D     (A     KEVIN MORRIS    D     (A    IAN GIBSONS        (K
B J COLE        STEEL (A     ALAN HAWKSHAW   K     (A
```

EAST OF EDEN

```
DAVE ARBUS    WIND VLN  (12ABCEGDJ (A) MERCATOR PROJECTED          1969  DERAM US 18023 UK  SML  1038
RON CAINES    V SAX (12ABE         (B) SNAFU                       1970  DERAM US 18043 UK  SML  1050
PETER FILLEUL K     (F             (AB)SNAFU/MERCATOR              1975  DERAM              UK  SDM3013 1/2
DAVE DUFORT   D     (AE            (C) EAST OF EDEN                1971  HARVEST US 806 UK  SHVL  792
STEVE YORK    B     (AE            (D) NEW LEAF                    1971  HARVEST            UK  SHVL  796
ANDY SNEDDON  B     (12BE          (E) WORLD OF        (COMP)      1971  DECCA              UK5PA34+SPA157
JEFF ALLEN    D     (2DEFGJKL      (F) HERE WE GO AGAIN            1976  EMI                EURO 062 98065
JOE O'DONNELL VLN   (J             (G) MASTERS OF ROCK  (COMP)     1975  EMI                EURO 062 95117
DAVID JACKS   B     (CEFGDKL       (H) THINGS           COMP AB    1976  NOVA               GER      628367
JIM ROCHE     G     (CDH           (I) JIG A JIG                   197   DECCA                   210006
DAVE WELLER   SAX   (DFKL          (J) ANOTHER EDEN               1975  EMI                GER       97101
LES DAVIDSON        (FKL           (K) IT'S THE CLIMATE           1976  EMI                GER       61810
GEOFF NICHOLSON G V (ABE12         (L) SILVER PARK                1978  EMI                GER       62639
      (CONTINUED)
```

[178]

```
E8                                   EAST OF EDEN        (CONTINUED)                              E8
    GEOFF BRITTON      D    (BE1    (1) 1969    (2) 1970
    BARRY ST JOHN      V    (K
    BIMBO ACOCK        B    (K      THEO THUNDER            (K      GARTH WATT ROY         (J
    DYL KATTS          B    (KL     MARTIN FISHER           (J      BRENDA LYNN            (K
    DAVE ROSE          B    (K      GEORGE HOWDEN           (K
E8A                                 EAST SIDE KIDS                                                E8A
    DAVE POTTER        B    (A      (A) TIGER & THE LAMB            19     UNI                73032
    JOE MADRID         V    (A
    DAVID DOUD         G    (A      MIKE DOUD          B    (A
E8B                                 CLINT EASTWOOD                                                E8B
    CLINT EASTWOOD     V    (A      (A) SEX EDUCATION               1980   GREENSLEEVES    UK GREL11
E9                                  EASY STREET                                                   E9
    PETER MARSH        G    (AB     (A)EASY STREET                  1976   POLYDOR         UK  2383 415
    KEN NICOL          G    (AB     (B) UNDER THE GLASS             1977   POLYDOR         UK  2383 444
    JIM HALL           B    (AB     (B) UNDER THE GLASS             1977   CAPRICORN       US      0184
    KEVIN SAVIGAR      K    (B
    JOHN WALTERS       SAX  (A      PETE ZORN          B SAX (A     CHRISTOPHER       PNO (A
    RICHARD BURGESS    D    (AB     ROD ARGENT         K      (A    DICK PEARCE       HRNS (A
    PETER THOMS        HRNS (A      ROGER WILLIAMS     HRNS   (A    KENNY KING        HRNS (A
E10                                 EASYBEATS                                                     E10
    GEORGE YOUNG       G V  (CG     (A) FRIDAY ON MY MIND           1967   UA              US  UAS 6588
    DICK DIAMONDE      B    (CG     (B) GOOD FRIDAY                 1967   UA              UK  SULP 1167
    HARRY VANDA        G V  (CG     (B) GOOD FRIDAY                 1967   UA              US  UA 29627
    STEVE WRIGHT       V    (CG     (C) FALLING OFF THE EDGE OF THE WORLD 1968 UA          US  UAS 6667
    GORDON FLEET       D    (CG     (D) VIGIL                       1968   UA              UK  SULP 1199
    TONY CAHILL        D    (        (E) FRIENDS                     1970   POLYDOR         UK  2482 010
                                    (F) ABSOLUTE ANTHOLOGY (DBL)    19                     AUST
                                    (G) NOSTALGIA                   19     UA              FR     29627
                                    (H) THE SHAME JUST DRAINED      1978   ALBERT                 026
E11                                 EATER                                                         E11
    ANDY BLADE         V    (A      (A) THE ALBUM                   1977   THE LABEL       UK  TLRLP 001
    BRIAN CHEVETTE     G    (A      (B) GET YER YO YO'S OUT(EP LIVE) 1978  THE LABEL       UK  TLR  007
    IAN WOODCOCK       B    (A
    DEE GENERATE       D    (A
E11A                         EBERSON. GRAF. HOVENSJO. CHRISTENSEN                                  E11A
    JON EBERSON        G    (A      (A) BLOW OUT                    1977   COMPENDIUM      NOR  FID 10
    HAKON GRAF         K    (A
    SVEINUNG HOVENSJO  B    (A      JOHN CHRISTENSEN   D    (A      MIKI NDOYE        CONGA  (A
    FRODE HOLM         (
E11B                                ECHO & THE BUNNYMEN                                           E11B
    WILL SARGEANT      G    (ABC    (A) CROGODILES                  1980   KOROVA UK KODE1 US SIRE 6096
    IAN McCULLON       G V  (C      (B) SHINE SO HARD               1981   KOROVA UK ECHO1 NL WEA 28223
    LES PATTERSON      B    (C      (C) HEAVEN UP HERE              1981   KOROVA UK KODE3US SIRE 3569
    LESLIE PENNY       WIND (C      (EP) A PROMISE                  1981   KOROVA UK 15T
    PETER DE FREITAS   D    (C
    HUGH JONES         PROD (C
E12                                 ECLECTION                                                     E12
    KERRILEE MALE      V    (A      (A) ECLECTION                   1968   ELEKTRA           EKS 74023
    MICHAEL ROSEN      V G TPT(A
    TREVOR LUCAS       G V  (A      GERRY CONWAY       D V  (A      GEORG HULTGREEN   V G  (A
    DORRIS HENDERSON   V    (        POLI PALMER        V VIBES(     MICK WOODS        D    (
    KEVIN WESTLAKE     PERC G(       GARY BOYLE         G    (       ERIC JOHNS        G    (
E12A                                ECLIPSE                                                       E12A
    PIERRE GAUTHIER    K V  (A      (A) NIGHT & DAY                 1977 CASABLANCA US NBLP7097
    JESSE OTTEN        G V  (A
    MIKE DINARDO       D PERC(A     CLAUDE LAFERRIERE  B G  (A
E13                                 EDDIE & THE HOT RODS                                          E13
    BARRY MASTERS      V    (ABCDE  (E) LIVE AT THE MARQUEE   (EP)  1976   ISLAND          UK     IEP  2
    DAVE HIGGS         G K  (ABCDE  (B) TEENAGE DEPRESSION          1976   ISLAND          UK  ILPS 9457
    STEVE NICOL        D    (ABCDE  (B) TEENAGE DEPRESSION          1976   PHONOGRAM       EURO 9101 671
    PAUL GRAY          B    (ABCDE  (C) LIFE ON THE LINE            1977   ISLAND US/UKILPS9509
    GRAEME DOUGLAS     G V K (CD     (C) LIFE ON THE LINE            1977   PHONOGRAM       EURO 9123 025
    AL KOOPER          K G V (E      (EP) AT THE SOUND OF SPEED      1977   ISLAND          IEP5
    RUFUS JENKINS      ACC  (E      (D) THRILLER                   1979   ISLAND          UK  ILPS 9563
    MARTIN AUBREY      V    (E      (E) FISH & CHIPS               1980   EMI UK 3344      US     17037
    KEITH COTTON       V    (E
    PATTI HELD         V    (E      GEORGE PAGE        V    (E
E13A                                EDDIE BOY BAND                                                E13A
    JOSH LEO           G V  (A      (A) EDDIE BOY BAND        1975 MCA US 2153 UK MAPS 8150+MCF 2735
    MARK GOLDENBERG    V G K (A
    TIM WALKOE         B V  (A      JOHN PARUDO        K V  (A      DAVID WOLINSKI    SYN (A
    DENNIS EBERT       D PERC(A     JON CARSON         G    (A      MIKE LERNER       D PERC(A
    DICK CAINE         G    (A
E14                                 DUANE EDDY                                                    E14
    DUANE EDDY   G
    WITH
    AL CASEY       B G       LARRY KNECHTEL       K          STEVE DOUGLAS  SAX    IKE CLANTON   B
    BUDDY WHEELER  B         BOB TAYLOR           D          CORKY CASEY    G      JIM HORN      SAX
    DON OWEN       G         JIMMY TROXEL         D          BEN DEMOTTO    V

    HAVE TWANGY GUITAR WILL TRAVEL        1958   JAMIE  US  3000     LONDON UK (M) HAW 2160
    ESPECIALLY FOR YOU                    1958   JAMIE  US  3006     LONDON UK (M) HAW 2191 (S) SAHW 6045
    TWANGS THE THANG                      1959   JAMIE  US  3009     LONDON UK (M) HAW2236  (S) SAHW 6068
    SONGS FOR OUR HERITAGE                1960   JAMIE  US  3011     LONDON UK (M) HAW 2285 (S) SAHW 6119
    1,000,000 DOLLARS OF TWANG            1961   JAMIE  US  3014     LONDON UK (M) HAW 2325
    GIRLS GIRLS GIRLS                     1961   JAMIE  US  3019     LONDON UK (M) HAW 2373 (S) SAHW 6173
    1,000,000 DOLLARS OF TWANG            1964   JAMIE  US  3021     LONDON UK (M) HAW 2435
    TWISTIN' & TWANGIN'                   1962   RCA    US  LSP2525
    TWANGY GUITAR SILKY STRINGS           1962   RCA    US  LSP2576  RI CAMDEN CDS 1072

                                                                    (CONTINUED)
```

TWISTIN'	196	JAMIE	US	3022				
SURFIN'	1964	JAMIE	US	3024				
IN PERSON	196	JAMIE	US	3025				
16 GREATEST HITS	196	JAMIE	US	3026				
DANCE WITH THE GUITAR MAN	1963	RCA	US	LSP2648				
PURE GOLD	19	RCA	US	ANL2671				
TWANGS A COUNTRY SONG	1963	RCA	US	LSP2681	RCA	UK	SF	7560
TWANGIN' UP A STORM	1963	RCA	US	LSP 2700	RCA	UK	RD	7568
LONELY GUITAR	1964	RCA	US	LSP2798				
WATERSKIING	196	RCA	US	LSP2918				
TWANGIN' GOLDEN HITS	196	RCA	US	LSP2993	RCA INT	UK	INT	1057
DUANE A GO GO	1965	COLPIX	US	PXL490				
DUANE DOES DYLAN	1965	COLPIX	US	PXL494				
TWANGSVILLE	1965	RCA	US	LSP3432				
BEST OF	1965	RCA	US	LSP3477	CAMDEN	UK	CDS	1109
BIGGEST TWANG OF ALL	1966	REPRISE	US	6218	VALIANT	UK	VS	108
ROARIN' TWANGIES	1967	REPRISE	US	6240				
MOVIN' & GROOVIN'	1970				LONDON	UK	ZGW	105
MOVIN' & GROOVIN'	1980	LONDON	NL	6399093				
LEGEND OF ROCK	1974				DERAM		DLL5033/4	
LEGEND OF ROCK 2	1974				TELDEC	GER	LS	3259
LEGEND OF ROCK 3 RARE ITEMS	1974				LONDON		LS	3281
YESTERDAYS POP SCENE	1975				TELEFUNKEN	AF	622002	
GUITAR MAN	1975				GTO		GTLP	002
GUITAR MAN	197				HALLMARK			947
VINTAGE YEARS	1975	SIRE	US	3707/2				
PURE GOLD	1978	RCA	US	2671				
DUANE EDDY	1979				RCA UKAPL	12671		
GREATEST HITS	1979				RONCO	UK	RTL	2035
OLDIES BUT GOODIES	1979				TELDEC	GERM	623647	
DUANE EDDY COLLECTION	1978				PICKWICK	UK	PDA	043
20 TERRIFIC TWANGIES	1980				RCA INT		5056	
(EPS)								
MOVIN' & GROOVIN' 19		JAMIE	US	JEP 100				
YEP	19	JAMIE	US	JEP 300				
DETOUR	19	JAMIE	US	JEP 301				
SHAZAM	19	JAMIE	US	JEP 303				
BECAUSE THEY'RE YOUNG 19		JAMIE	US	JEP 304				

RANDY EDELMAN	K V	(ALL	(A) RANDY EDELMAN	1972	SUNFLOWER	US	5005
NIGEL OLSSON	D V	(DEG	(B) LAUGHTER & TEARS	1973	LION	US	1012
REINIE PRESS	B	(D	(C) PRIME CUTS	1976	20TH CENT	US UK	448
GARY COLEMAN	PERC	(D	(D) FAIRWELL FAIRBANKS	1976	20th CENT		494
DEAN PARKS	G	(DEG	(E) IF LOVE IS REAL	1977	20th CENT		542
LEE RITENOUR	G	(D	(E) IF LOVE IS REAL	1977	ARISTA	US	4139
AL KOOPER	G	(D	(F) UPTOWN UPTEMPO	1979	20th CENT		601
JEFF PORCARO	D	(E	(G) YOU'RE THE ONE	1979	20th CENT		581
LEE SKLAR	B	(EG	(G) YOU'RE THE ONE	1979	ARISTA	US	4210
TOMMY VIG	PERC	(E					

STEVE CROPPER	G	(D	ART MUNSON	G	(D	BEN BENAY	G	(DG		
ANDREW GOLD	G	(D	DEE MURRAY	V	(ED	JIMMY HAAS	V	(DE		
TOM BAHLER	V	(D	MELISSA MANCHESTER	V	(D	JACKIE DeSHANNON	V	(D		
VINI PONCIA	V	(D	VICTOR FELDMAN	PERC	(E	DOUG MASEK	SAX	(E		
JOHN JOYCE	V	(E	JOHN GUERIN	D	(B	LYLE RITZ	B	(BG		
JAY GRAYDON	G	(G	MIKE PORCARO	B	(G	MATTHEW McCAWLEY	SYN	(G		
RICK MAROTTA	D	(G	FRED MOLLIN	PERC	(G	DAVID PAICH	K	(G		
ERICA GOODMAN	HARP	(G	NICK BAIRD	D	(G					

RICHARD SCHAMACH	G	(AB	(A) EDENS CHILDREN	1968	ABC	US	ABCS 624
JIMMY STURMAN	D	(AB	(A) EDENS CHILDREN	1968	STATESIDE	UK	SSL 10235
LARRY KILEY	B	(AB	(B) SURE LOOKS REAL	1969	ABC	US	ABCS 652

JOHN MOSS	D	(A	(A) SQUARE ONE	1980	HURRICANE UK FLAK102 NL 55019		
LU EDMUNDS	G	(A	(B) EDGE	1981	CASABLANCA		7214
GAVIN POVEY	K	(A					
GLYN HAVARD	B	(A					

(A) UNEASY PEACE	1975	INTERN	NSPL 41037	

GRAEME EDGE	D V	(AB	(A) KICK OFF YOUR MUDDY BOOTS	1974 THRESHOLD UK US THS15	NOVA GER 22281		
ADRIAN GURVITZ	G V K	(AB	(B) PARADISE BALLROOM	1977 DECCA UK TXS 121	NOVA GER 23087		
PAUL GURVITZ	B V	(AB	(B) PARADISE BALLROOM	1977 LONDON US PS 686			
MICK GALLAGHER	K	(A					
BRIAN PARRISH	V	(B	RAY THOMAS	V	(A	SUNNY LESLIE	V	(A
RUBY JAMES	V	(B	NICKY JAMES	V	(A	LESLEY DUNCAN	V	(A
BARRY ST JOHN	V	(A	JOANNE WILLIAMS	V	(A	GINGER BAKER	D	(A
ANN ODELL	K	(B	TONY HYMAS	K	(B	BLUE WEAVER	K	(B
REBOP	PERC	(B	LAWRIE McMILLAN	HRNS	(B	B J COLE	STEEL	(B
BILL EASLEY	HRNS	(B	KEN SPAIN	HRNS	(B	BEN CAULEY	HRNS	(B
EDGAR MATTHEWS	HRNS	(B						

DAN 'FREEBO' FRIEDBERG	G B	(A	(A) BLESS YOU, DR WOODWARD	1970	COTILION	US	SD 9022
T J TINDALL	G V	(A					
MARK JORDAN	K G	(A	RIP STOCK	V D	(A	MICHAEL ZIEGLER	G	(A
NORMAN PRIDE	CONGA	(A	BROOKMEAD MUMBLE CHOIR	V	(A			

ANN BALLISTER	K	(	ALLEE DES TILLEULS	19	SONOPRESSE	FR	UAS 29965
MIMI LORENZINI	G V	(	ALIQUANTE	19	RCA	PL	37069
JOSQUIN TURENNE B G V	(					
J J BOUCHET D'ANGELY	D	(					

EDITH NYLON

```
    MYLENE KHASKI          V SYN  (A      (A) EDITH NYLON                         1979   CBS                    CAN      90571
    KARL MORMET            B      (A
    ALBERT T               D      (A      CHRISTOPHE BOUTIN    G      (A      ZAKO                   G      (A
```
DAVE EDMUNDS
(& ROCKPILE)

```
    DAVE EDMUNDS       G K V B PROD(ALL
    MICKEY GEE             G     (HJ      (A) ROCKPILE                          · 1971   REGAL ZONOPHONE UK SLRZ 1026
    B J COLE           STEEL     (A       (A) ROCKPILE                           1972   MAM US MAM3 EURO EMI 93282
    ANDY FAIRWEATHER LOW G       (A       (B) STARDUST (SOUNDTRACK 1 SIDE)(DBL) 1974   RONCO            UK   RG2009/10
    BILLY RANKIN           D     (D       (C) SUBTLE AS A FLYING MALLET          1975   ROCKFIELD        UK   RRL  101
    STEVE GOULDING         D     (D       (C) SUBTLE AS A FLYING MALLET          1978   RCA UK PL 25129  RI INTS 5131
    PAUL RILEY             B     (D       (C) SUBTLE AS A FLYING MALLET          1975   RCA US APLI5003 GER    21505
    GERRY HOGAN        STEEL     (E       (D) GET IT                             1977   SWANSONG UK 59404 US    8418
    PETE KELLY         PNO       (E       (E) TRACKS ON WAX                      1978   SWANSONG UK 59407 US    8505
    IAN GOMM           G V       (C       (F) REPEAT WHEN NECESSARY              1979   SWANSONG US 59409 US    8507
    PICK WITHERS           D     (C       (G) SECONDS OF PLEASURE(ROCKPILE)      1980   F BEAT UK XXLP7 GER    58218
    ALBERT LEE            G       (FJ      (H) TWANGIN'                           1981   SWANSONG UK 59411 US   16034
    BOB ANDREWS           K       (CD      (I) BEST OF                            1981   SWANSONG          US    8510
    BILLY RANKIN         D V      (C       (J) D E 7                              1982   ARISTA           GER   204508
    NICK LOWE      PROD B V       (CDEFGH  ( ) COLLEGE RADIO PRESENTS (PROMO)     198    SWANSONG         PR 230
    JOHN WILLIAMS         B       (H
    BILLY BREMNER        G V(CDEFGH        TERRY WILLIAMS       D      (ACDEFGH   BRINSLEY SCHWARZ     G     (C
    STRAY CATS                   (H        HUGHIE LEWIS         HCA    (F        ROGER BECHINAN       PNO   (F
    CHESTERFIELD KINGS  HCA      (H        DAVE PEACOCK         B      (J        BOBBY IRWIN          D     (J
    NEIL KING           TPT      (J        LIAM GRUNDY          PNO    (J        DAVE CHARLES         D     (J
    JOHN DAVID          B        (J        GERAINT WATKINS      K      (J        DICK HANSON          TPT   (J
    JOHN'IRISH' EARLE   SAX      (J
```
EDWARD BEAR

```
                                          ( ) EDWARD BEAR                        19     PENNYFARTHING          UK   PELS 532
```
EDWARD BEAR

```
    LARRY EVOY           D V     (BD       (A) BEARINGS                          1969   CAPITOL                US   SKAO  426
    DANNY MARKS          G V BAN(B         (B) ECLPSE                            1970   CAPITOL CAN 6349       US        580
    GENE MARTYNEC        SYN     (D        (C) EDWARD BEAR                       197    CAPITOL                US   ST 11157
    PAUL WELDON          K B V   (B        (D) CLOSE YOUR EYES                   1973   CAPITOL                CAN  SMAS11192
    ROGER ELLIS          G V     (D
    BOB KENDALL          K V     (D        DENNY DEPORTER       G V    (D        RANDY GULLIVER       K V   (D
    BILL LOOP            B V     (D        TIM WYNVEER          G V    (D
```
JACKIE EDWARDS

```
    JACKIE EDWARDS       V       (ALL      ( ) STAND UP FOR JESUS                1964   ISLAND                 UK   ILP 912
                                          ( ) COME ON HOME                      1965   ISLAND                 UK   ILP 931
                                          ( ) THE BEST OF                       1966   ISLAND                 UK   ILP 936
                                          ( ) PLEDGING MY LOVE                  1966   ISLAND                 UK   ILP 941
                                          ( ) BY DEMAND                         1966   ISLAND                 UK   ILP 940
                                          ( ) PREMATURE GOLDEN SANDS            1967   ISLAND                 UK   ILP 960
                                          ( ) PUT YOUR TEARS AWAY               19     VEEP                   US   PS 16533
                                          ( ) I DO LOVE YOU                     1972   TROJAN                 UK   TRL   47
                                          ( ) DO YOU BELIEVE IN LOVE            1976   KLIK                   UK   KLP 9009
                                          ( ) BEFORE THE NEXT TEARDROP          1977   THIRD WORLD                 TWS 928
                                          ( ) LET'S FALL IN LOVE                1978   THIRD WORLD                 TDWD    3
                                          ( ) COME TO ME SOFTLY                 1979   THIRD WORLD                 TDWD   10
```
JANG EDWARDS

```
    JANG EDWARDS                 (AB       (A) CLOWN POWER                       19     ARIOLA                 NL   202 144
                                          (B) LIVE IN EUROPE                    19     POLYDOR                NL   2925 113
```
JONATHAN EDWARDS

```
    JONATHAN EDWARDS B G HCA V(ALL         (A) JONATHAN EDWARDS                  1971   CAPRICORN US               821
    STUART SCHULMAN      B VLN K(ABCD       (A) JONATHAN EDWARDS                  1971   ATLANTIC               UK   K 40282
    BILL KEITH       STEEL BANJO (ABCD      (B) HONKY TONK STARDUST COWBOY        1972   ATCO                   US   SD  7015
    BILL ELLIOTT      PNO ORG(CD           (C) HAVE A GOOD TIME FOR ME           1973   ATCO                   US   SD  7036
    GEORGE GRANTHAM   D V      (C          (D) LUCKY DAY                         1974   ATCO                   US   SD 36104
    R DAVIES          B        (C          (E) ROCKIN' CHAIR                     1976   REPRISE                US        2238
    DAVID BROMBERG G MAND DOBRO(C          (F) SAILBOAT                          1977   WB                     US   BS  3020
    AL ANDERSON       G        (D
    ERIC LILLEQUIST   G V      (ABD        DEAN ADRIAN          PERC   (BD       BOB CHOUINARD        D     (D
    DAVE CONRAD       B        (D          JOHN WARE            D      (EF       GLEN D HARDIN        PNO   (EF
    JAMES BURTON      G        (E          HANK DE VITO         STEEL  (EF       EMORY GORDY          B MAND(EF
    EMMYLOU HARRIS    V G      (EF         JEFF LABES           K      (A        RICHARD ADELMAN      D     (AB
    CHANDLER TRAVIS   MARACAS(B            BILL PAYNE           PNO    (E        BRIAN AHERN          G     (EF
    RODNEY CROWELL    G        (EF         BYRON BERLINE        FDL    (E        HERB PEDERSEN        BANJ V(EF
    DAVID GRISMAN     MAND     (E          DIANNE BROOKS        V      (EF       LYNNIE (DALL) EDWARDS V   (DE
    MIKE AULDRIDGE    DOBRO    (F          ALBERT LEE           G MAND (F
```
STONEY EDWARDS

```
    STONEY EDWARDS       V       (AB       (A) MISSISSIPPI, YOU'RE ON MY MIND    197    CAPITOL                     11401
    GEORGE KIRIAKIS      G       (B        (B) BLACKBIRD                         1976   CAPITOL                     11499
    JOHN PLATANIA        G       (B
    CRAZY JOE RENDA      K       (B        PHIL TRIMBLE         FDL    (B        DON BROOKS           HCA   (B
    DAVID KAPELL         B       (B        BEAU SEGAL           D      (B        DAVID MANSFIELD K STEEL G  (B
    CHIP TAYLOR          G       (B
```
EDWARDS HAND

```
    ROY EDWARDS          K V     (ABC      (A) EDWARDS HAND                      1969   GRT                    US        10005
    ROGER HAND           G V     (ABC      (B) STRANDED                          1971   RCA                    UK   SF 8154
    JAMES LITHERLAND     G       (B        (C) RAINSHINE                         1973   REGAL ZONOPHONE UK SRZA 8513
    JOHN WETTON          B       (B
    CLEM CATTINI         D       (B
```

E21A — EELA CRAIG

Personnel			Albums	Year	Label		Cat.	
HUBERT BOGNERMAYR	K V	(A	(A) ONE NITER	1976	VERTIGO		6360	635
HUBERT SCHNAUER	K	(	(B) HATS OF GLASS	1977	VERTIGO		6360	638
HARALD ZUSCHRADER	K G	(	(C) MISSA UNIVERSALIS	1978	PHILIPS		6360	639
WILL ORTHOFER	V	(	(D) ONE NIGHTER	1981	ARIOLA	NL	202	311
FRITZ RUDELBERGER	G K V	(						
GERHARD ENGLISCH	B PERC	(	FRANK HUEBER	D	(			

E21B — EFENDI'S GARDEN

Personnel			Albums	Year	Label		Cat.
CURTIS EFENDI	V	(A	(A) EFENDI'S GARDEN	19	BABYLON	GER	80004
FRANK MEIER	B	(A					
WOLFGANG KRANTZ	K G	(A	WOLFGANG SCHREINER	D PERC (A	KLAUS HESS	G	(A
HEINZ ALBERDING	SAX	(A					

E22 — JOE EGAN

Personnel			Albums	Year	Label			Cat.	
JOE EGAN	G V	(A	(A) OUT OF NOWHERE	1979	ARIOLA	US 50064	UK	ARL	5021
HENRY SPINETTI	D	(A	(B) M A P	1981	ARIOLA		UK	ARL	5052
DAVE MARKEE	B	(A							
BILLY LIVSEY	K	(A							
ALAN PARKER	G	(A	PAUL PILNICK	G	(A	PHIL PALMER	G	(A	
GRAHAM LYLE	MAND	(A	CHARLES SPITTERI	PERC	(A	BENNY GALLAGHER	ACC	(A	
VICKY BROWN	V	(A	SYLVIA	V	(A	JOY YATES	V	(A	
			GEORGE CHANDLER	V	(A	JIMMY ELLIS	V	(A	

E23 — WALTER EGAN

Personnel			Albums	Year	Label			Cat.	
WALTER EGAN	V	(ALL	(A) FUNDAMENTAL ROLL	1977	POLYDOR	UK		2310	614
WITH			(A) FUNDAMENTAL ROLL	1977	UA	UK	UAG	30032	
ANNIE McCLOONE	V	(BCD	(A) FUNDAMENTAL ROLL	1977	CBS	US			34679
TOM MONCRIEFF	G V	(BCD	(B) NOT SHY	1978	CBS	US			35077
LINDSEY BUCKINGHAM	G	(ABCD	(B) NOT SHY	1978	POLYDOR	UK		2310	609
MICK FLEETWOOD	D	(B	(C) HI FI	1979	CBS	US			35796
EARL SHAKLEFORD	V PERC	(BCD	(D) THE LAST STROLL	1981	EDGE UK HOG 3	US CBS			36513
JOHN SELK	B V G	(ABCD							
MIKE HUEY	D PERC	(BCD	STEVE HAGUE	K V	(B	STEVIE NICKS	V	(BA	
DEAN TORRANCE	V	(B	JOHN ZAMBETTI	V	(BCD	SKIP EDWARDS	K G V	(CD	
LEE KIX	D V	(D	DEKE LEONARD	G V	(D	JEAN ANNE CHAPMAN	V	(D	
EARLE MANKEY	PROD	(D	GARY ROWLES	V	(A	DENNID MANSFIELD	D	(A	
BILL CUOMO	K	(A	JOHN WARE	D	(A				

E24 — EGG

Personnel			Albums	Year	Label			Cat.	
HUGH MONTGOMERY CAMPBELL	K	(ABC	(A) EGG	1970	NOVA		SDN		14
DAVE STEWART	K	(ABC	(A) EGG	1970	DERAM	US			18039
CLIVE BROOKS	D	(ABC	(B) POLITE FORCE	1970	DERAM	UK	SML		1074
ANN ROSENTHAL	V	(C	(B) POLITE FORCE	1970	DERAM	US			18056
AMANDA PARSONS	V	(C	(C) CIVIL SURFACE	1974	CAROLINE	UK	C		1510
STEVE HILLAGE	G	(C							
BARBARA GASKIN	V	(C	JEREMY BAINES	FLT	(C	LINDSAY COOPER	WIND	(C	
TIM HODGKINSON	CLAR	(C	HENRY LOWTHER	TPT	(B	MIKE DAVIS	TPT	(B	
BOB DOWNES	SAX	(B	TONY ROBERTS	SAX	(B	MAURICE CAMBRIDGE	CLAR	(C	
STEPHEN SOLLOWAY	FLT	(B	CHRIS PALMER	WIND	(B				

E24A — EGGS OVER EASY

Personnel			Albums	Year	Label		Cat.
AUSTIN DELONE	K G V	(A	(A) GOOD'N' CHEAP	1972	A&M	US	4366
BRIEN HOPKINS	K B G V	(A					
JACK OHARA	G B HCA V	(A	BILL FRANZ	D	(A		

E24B — EGO

Albums	Year	Label		Cat.
(A) ON THE ROCKS	1981	JUPITER	NL	624692

E24C — EIGHT O ONE (801)

Personnel			Albums	Year	Label		Cat.
PHIL MANZANERA	G V	(A	(A) 801 LIVE	1976	ISLAND UK ILPS 9444	US POLYDOR	6178
BRIAN ENO	K	(A	(A) 801 LIVE	1977	POLYDOR RI UK		2302 044
LLOYD WATSON	G	(A					
FRANCIS MONKMAN	K	(A	BILL MACCORMICK	B	(A	SIMON PHILLIPS	D (A

E25 — EIGHTEEN CARAT GOLD

Personnel			Albums	Year	Label		Cat.
KLAUS EBERTS	G		( ) ALL BUMM	1974	UA UK UAS29559	TELEFUNKEN	NL624853
JURG EVERS	G	(					
LOTHER MEID	B	(	KEITH FORSEY	D	(		

E25A — ALF EMIL EIK

Personnel			Albums	Year	Label		Cat.
ALF EMIL EIK	D G V K B	(A	(A) JOYS AND BREATH OF ETERNITY	1979	RVEST	NOR	37377
IRIS REUTZ	V	(A					
ANNE ENGH	V	(A	SVEND UNDSETH	WIND (A	JOHN ERIK HOLTAN	PNO	(A

E26 — EIRE APPARENT

Personnel			Albums	Year	Label		Cat.
MICHAEL COX	G	(A	(A) SUNRISE	1969	BUDDAH 203 021	US	5031
DAVE LUTTON	D	(A	(B) ROCK'N'ROLL BAND	19	POLYDOR		
ERNIE GRAHAM	B	(A					
JIMI HENDRIX	G	(A	CHRIS STEWART	B	(A	HENRY McCULLOUGH	G (
NOEL REDDING	B	(A	ROBERT WYATT	D	(A	MITCH MITCHELL	D (A
TERRY TAYLOR	G V	(	VIC BRIGGS	PNO	(A	PETE TOLSON	G (A

E27 — EKSEPTION

Personnel			Albums	Year	Label			Cat.	
RICK VAN DER LINDEN	K	(ABCDEJKLP	(A) EKSEPTION	1969	PHILIPS	NL	873		003
REIN VAN DER BROEK	HRNS	(ALL	(A) EKSEPTION	1970	PHILIPS	UK	6314		005
PETER DE LEEUWE	D V	(ACDEAOP	(A) EKSEPTION	1970	PHILIPS		600		344
COR DEKKER	B	(ADEGOBC	(B) BEGGAR JULIA'S TIME TRIP	1969	PHILIPS 6314001	US	600	348	
DICK REMELINK	WIND	(BCDEOP	(C) 3	1972	PHILIPS		6423		005
PETER VOOGT	D	(G	(D) 00.04	1971	PHILIPS		6423		019
JAN VANNIK	WIND	(	(E) EKSEPTION 5	1972	PHILIPS		6423		042
DENNIS WHITBREAD	D	(B	(E) EKSEPTION 5	197	PHILIPS	US	700		002
TONY VASSA	SAX	(OP	( ) BEST OF	197	PHILIPS		6423		053
STEVE ALLEN	V	(BP	(F) TRINITY	1973	PHILIPS	NL	6423		056
ROB KRUISMAN	WIND G V	(AP	(G) NEW FORMULA	1974	BINGO		6413		501
HANS JENSEN	K	(G	(H) CLASSICS IN POP	197	PHILIPS		6423		079
HUIB VAN KAMPEN	G SAX	(AP	(I) MIND MIRROR	1975	PHILIPS	NL	6423		082
TONY VOS	SAX	(O	(J) CLASSICS	1975	PHILIPS		6410		044
MICHEL VAN DIJK	V PERC	(B	(K) REFLECTION SERIES	1976	PHILIPS	NL	6428		111
LINDA VAN DYCK	V	(B	(L) GREATEST HITS	197	PHILIPS		6677		025
			(M) BACK TO THE CLASSICS	197	POLYDOR		2393		167

(CONTINUED)

E27			EKSEPTION	(CONTINUED)			E27

```
E27                        EKSEPTION           (CONTINUED)                          E27
                  (N) LA CINQUIEME            197     PHILIPS              6440  217
                  (O) EKSPETION 78            1978    MERCURY      NL      665  081
                  (P) SENSATIONAL             19      PHILIPS              928  857
                  (Q) DANCE MACABRE           1981    ARIOLA               203  629
                  (R) GREATEST HITS           1982    PHILIPS      NL      6423 490

E28                        ELASTIC BAND                                             E28
   ANDY SCOTT             (A) EXPANSIONS ON LIFE   1969   NOVA                   SND 6
   DAVE SCOTT
   TED YEADON      SEAN JENKINS

E29                        DONNIE ELBERT                                            E29
   DONNIE ELBERT   V  (ALL  ( ) ROOTS OF DONNIE ELBERT  1973  EMBER       UK  EMB 3421
                         ( ) STOP IN THE NAME OF LOVE    1976  D J M UK 22014 US TRIP 9524
                         ( ) WHERE DID OUR LOVE GO       19    ALL PLATINUM US     3007
                         ( ) DONNIE ELBERT SINGS         19    KING        US      629
                         ( ) HAVE I SINNED               19    DELUXE      US  DLP 12003
                         ( ) DANCING THE NIGHT AWAY      1978  ALL PLATINUM US     3019

E30                        EL CHICANO                                              E30
   BOBBY ESPINOSA  K V (CDEFGJ  (A) VIVA TIRADO          1970  MCA US 548    KAPP US 3632
   MICKEY LESPRON  G   (CDEFGJ  (B) REVOLUTION           1971  MCA UK MCA 2654 KAPP US 3640
   ENRIQUE BAEZA   PERC (CDEFGJ (C) CELEBRATION          1972  MCA UK MUPS456 KAPP US 3663
   DANNY LAMONT    D   (C       (C) CELEBRATION          1974  MCA UK MCA 2659
   HECTOR REGALADO D PERC(CDEG  (D) EL CHICANO           1973  MCA UK MUPS 445 MCA US  312
   BRIAN MAGNESS   B   (E       (D) EL CHICANO           1974  MCA UK MCA 69
   JERRY SALAS     G V (DEG      (E) CINCO                1974  MCA UK MAPS7262MCA US   401
   EDDIE RODRIGUEZ D PERC(E      (E) CINCO                1974  MCA US MCF 2556
   SHERRY WILLIAMS V   (DJ       (F) LOOK OF LOVE         197   MUSIDISC       CU   1183
   FREDDIE SANCHEZ B V (C        (G) PYRAMID OF LOVE & FRIENDS 1975 MCA     US     2150
   JOHN DE LUNA    D   (CJ       (H) THE BEST OF EVERYTHING    1975 MCA     US      437
   MAX GARDUNE     G V PERC(C    (J) THIS IS EL CHICANO   1976  SHADYBROOK  US    33005
   STEVE SALAS     V   (C
   JAMES ESPINOZA  B   (D   JOESEPH PERREIRA   B SYN V(J  JERRY ANGELO    WIND (J
   DANNY LAMONT    D   (D   DICK HENDERSON     B    (D    BOBBY LOYA      TPT  (D
   CRUZ BACA       V   (D   DAVID BATTEAU      V    (J    MARK GREEN      SYN  (J

E31                        EL COCO                                                 E31
   W MICHAEL LEWIS K SAX (ABC  (A) LET'S GET IT TOGETHER 1976  PYE         UK  NSPL28235
   LAURIN RINDER  V D SAX (ABC  (B) COCOMOTION           1978  PYE         UK  NSPL28237
   JOE BELLAMY     B   (A       (C) DANCING IN PARADISE   1978  PYE         UK  NSPL28268
   JOHN HUNT       G   (A
   HARRY KIM       TPT (ABC  DOUG RICHARDSON    WIND (ABC  DAVE CAHOUN     PNO  (A
   JACK WEBER      G   (A    CHRIS BOCCHINO     V    (A    JERRI BOCCHINO  V    (A
   MARSHA THACKER  V   (AB   ADRIENNE WILLIAMS  V    (AB   KATHY NIXON     V    (B
   MERRIA ROSS     V   (ABC  PAT POWDRILL       V    (A    CLEO KENNEDY    V    (B
   BILL HENDERSON  VLN (B    PAM TOMPKINS       VLN  (B    JIMBO ROSS      VIOLA(B
   MIKE JACOBSEN   CELLO (B  DAVID STOUT        TROM (C    BOB ETOLL       G    (C
   SHAMSI SARUMI   PERC (C   ALEX BROWN         V    (C    MORTONETTE JENKINS V (C

E31A                       COON ELDER BAND                                         E31A
   COON ELDER      G V  (A   (A) THE COON ELDER BAND    1977  MERCURY      US  SRM11140
   BRENDA PATTERSON V  (A
   PHIL BLACK    G FDL V(A  BILL MARSHALL D PERC V(A   MARK SALLINGS WIND HCA V(A  ROCKY BERETTA    B (A

E31B                       ELDERS                                                  E31B
                  (A) LOOKING FOR THE ANSWER  1972  AUDIO FIDELITY        6247

E31C                       FRANKIE ELDORADO                                        E31C
   FRANKIE ELDORADO V PERC(A (A) FRANKIE ELDORADO      1980  EPIC UK 84128 US  36291
   MARK ROCKET     D K  (A
   THOMAS MORRANGELO V PERC(A  JACK LESLIE       SYN   (A    KASIM SULTAN    B    (A'
   JOE MAURI       G   (A

E31D                       ELECTRA                                                 E31D
   RAINER UEBEL    K SYN (A  (A) ADAPTIONEN           19    AMIGA       GER     855501
   WOLFGANG RIEDEL B   (A    (B) 3                    19    AMIGA       GER     855762
   PETER LUDEWIG   D   (A
   GISBERT KORENG  G   (A    BERND AUST         WIND  (A    MANUEL V SENDEN  V K PERC(

E31E                       ELECTRA FIVE                                            E31E
   TOM FERRARA     G V  (A   (A) PICTURE            1981  TELDEC      GER  24949
   TOM GRAVES      K   (A
   ALAN CHILDS     D   (A    KELVYN HALLIFAX    G V  (A    MIKE TOMASIO    B V  (A

E31F                       ELECTRIC BANANA                                         E31F
   PHIL MAY        G B V(ALL  (A) ELECTRIC BANANA        1967  DE WOLFE    UK   3040
   DICK TAYLOR     G B V(ABCG  (B) MORE ELECTRIC BANANA  1968  DE WOLFE    UK   3069
   SKIP ALLAN      D V  (A     (C) EVEN MORE ELECTRIC BANANA 1969 DE WOLFE UK   3123
   JOHN POVEY      K D  (ABCDFG (D) HOT LICKS           1973  DE WOLFE    UK   3284
   WALLY ALLEN WALLER G B V(ABCG (E) RETURN OF THE ELECTRIC BANANA 1979 DE WOLFE UK 3381
   PETER TOLSON    G B  (DF    (F) ELECTRIC BANANA  THE 70's 1979 BUTT     UK  NOTT001
   GORDON EDWARDS  V G B (DF   (G) ELECTRIC BANANA  THE 60's 1980 BUTT     UK  NOTT003
   TWINK(JOHN ALDER) D  (G
   MICKY FINN      G   (F   BRIAN JOHNSON   K (F   BILLY LOVEDAY   MAND (F   CHICO GREENWOOD  D (F

E32             WAYNE/JAYNE COUNTY & THE ELECTRIC CHAIRS                           E32
   WAYNE/JAYNE COUNTY V  (ABCDEFG (A) EP THE ELECTRIC CHAIRS 1977 ILLEGAL UK       ILO02
   GREG VAN COOK   G   (B       (B) ELECTRIC CHAIRS     1978 SAFARI UK LONG1 GER   26308
   VAL HALLER      B   (BCD     (B) ELECTRIC CHAIRS     1978 SAFARI       UK  SPA 20308
   J J JOHNSON     D   (BCD     (C) STORM THE GATES OF HEAVEN 1978 SAFARI UK GOOD1 GER 61847
   JOOLS HOLLAND   K   (B       (D) THINGS YOUR MOTHER NEVER TOLD 1979 SAFARI UK GOOD2 GER 62853
   ELLIOT MICHAELS G   (DG      (E) EP BLATANTLY OFFENSIVE 1978 SAFARI UK WC   2
   HENRI PADOVANI  G   (CDEF    (F) MAN ENOUGH TO BE A WOMAN 1978 SAFARI   GER     61986
   DAVID CUNNINGHAM SYN (D      (G) R'N'R RESERUCTION     LIVE 1980 SAFARI UK LIVE 1
   SHARON C        HCA (C
   DARRYL WAY      VLN (C   MORGAN FISHER      K    (C    PETER JORDAN    B    (F
   SAMMY MINELLI   D   (F
```

```
NICK GRAVENITES      V G    (ABCD    (A) A LONG TIME COMIN'           1968  CBS           UK        63294
MIKE BLOOMFIELD      G V    (ACD     (A) A LONG TIME COMIN'           1968  CBS           US     CS 9597
BUDDY MILES          D V    (ABCD    (A) A LONG TIME COMIN'           1974  EMBASSY       UK RI     31061
BARRY GOLDBERG       K      (ACD     (B) ELECTRIC FLAG                1969  CBS           UK        63462
HARVEY BROOKS        G B V  (ABD     (B) ELECTRIC FLAG                1969  CBS           US     CS 9714
HERBIE RICH      SAX K G V  (ABD     (C) THE BAND KEPT PLAYING        1974  ATLANTIC      UK      K 50090
MARCUS DOUBLEDAY     TPT    (ABD     (C) THE BAND KEPT PLAYING        1974  ATLANTIC      US        18112
STEMSY HUNTER        V SAX  (AB      (D) THE BEST OF                  1971  CBS US 10169  US        30422
PETER STRAZZA        SAX    (A       (D) THE BEST OF                  1971  CBS           UK        64337
SIVUCA               G      (A       (E) THE TRIP SOUNDTRACK          19    SIDEWALK      ST      ST 5908
MIKE FONFARA         K      (A
JOHN COURT           V PERC (A       RICHIE HAVENS      PERC  (A       ALBHY GALUTEN     K     (C
JOE CHURCH           PERC   (A       PAUL BEAVER        K     (A       ROGER TROY        B     (BC
JOHN SIMON           PNO    (B       HOSHAL WRIGHT      G     (B       TERRY CLEMENTS    SAX   (B
VIRGIL GONSALVES     WIND   (B       GEORGE TERRY       G     (C       BARRY BECKETT     K     (C
NICK MARRERO         PERC   (C       RICHARD NEWELL     HCA   (C       RICHARD TEE       K     (C
```

```
ROY WOOD                 G V     (A        (A) ELECTRIC LIGHT ORCHESTRA        1971  HARVEST        UK    SHVL 797
RICK PRICE                       (         (A) ELECTRIC LIGHT ORCHESTRA        197   SONOPRESSE     FR        69670
JEFF LYNNE   SYN K G V           (ALL      (A) ELECTRIC LIGHT ORCHESTRA        197   UA             US         5573
BEV BEVAN                D V     (ALL      (A) NO ANSWER(RI OF(A)              1978  JET            US        35524
RICHARD TANDY SYN V K            (B>R      (A) NO ANSWER(RI OF (A)             1972  UA             US    UALA 040
MICHAEL D'ALBUQUERQUE B V        (BCDEFG   (B) ELO 2                           1973  HARVEST        UK    SHVL 806
MIKE EDWARDS             CELLO   (BCDEFG   (B) ELO 2              RI           1978  JET US 35533   US        LA040
COLIN WALKER             CELLO   (B        (B) ELO 2                           197   SONOPRESSE     FR        69671
WILF GIBSON              VLN     (B        (C) ON THE THIRD DAY                1973  WB             UK    K 56021
HUGH McDOWELL            CELLO   (EFGHIJK  (C) ON THE THIRD DAY                197   SONOPRESSE     FR        30091
MIK KAMINSKI             VLN     (CDEFGHIJ (C) ON THE THIRD DAY                1978  JET UK LP202   US        35525
MELVYN GALE              CELLO   (FGHIJK   (C) ON THE THIRD DAY                1973  UA             US    UALA 188
KELLY GROUCUTT           B       (FGIJKNPQR(D) SHOWDOWN                        1974  HARVEST        UK    SHSP 4037
BILL HUNT                HRNS    (A        (E) THE NIGHT THE LIGHTS WENT IN    1974  WB             UK    K 56058
STEVE WOOLAM             VLN     (A        (E) THE NIGHT THE LIGHTS WENT IN    197   UA             US    UALA 318
TED BLIGHT               CELLO   (CD       (F) FACE THE MUSIC                  1975  JET            UK       LP 11
SANDI                    V       (R        (F) FACE THE MUSIC                  1978  JET            UK      LP 201
GHISLAINE                V       (R        (F) FACE THE MUSIC                  197   SONOPRESSE     FR        30034
                                           (F) FACE THE MUSIC                  1975  UA             US    UALA 546
                                           (F) FACE THE MUSIC                  197   POLYDOR        GREECE 2310 414
                                           (F) FACE THE MUSIC                  1978  JET            US        35526
                                           (G) ELDORADO                        1975  WB             UK    K 56090
                                           (G) ELDORADO                        197   SONOPRESSE     FR        30092
                                           (G) ELDORADO                        1978  JET UK LP203   US        35526
                                           (G) ELDORADO                        1975  UA             US    UALA 339
                                           (H) OLE' ELO                        1976  JET            UK       LP 19
                                           (H) OLE' ELO                        1978  JET            US        35528
                                           (H) OLE' ELO                        1978  JET            NL       LP 903
                                           (H) OLE' ELO                        1976  UA             US    UALA 630
                                           (J) NEW WORLD RECORD                1976  JET            UK        30034
                                           (J) NEW WORLD RECORD                1977  UA             US    UALA 679
                                           (J) NEW WORLD RECORD                1978  JET UK LP200   US        35529
                                           (J) NEW WORLD RECORD                197   SONOPRESSE     FR        30017
                                           (K) OUT OF THE BLUE                 1977  JET            UK    UAR 100
                                           (K) OUT OF THE BLUE                 1978  JET                     DP 400
                                           (K) OUT OF THE BLUE                 1978  JET            US        35530
                                           (K) OUT OF THE BLUE                 1978  JET            US    JTLA 823
                                           (L) THE LIGHT SHINES ON            1977  HARVEST        UK    SHSM 2015
                                           (M) THE LIGHT SHINES ON VOL2        1979  HARVEST        UK    SHSM 2027
                                           (N) DISCOVERY                       1979  JET                     LX500
                                           (N) DISCOVERY                       1979  JET            US        35769
                                           (N) DISCOVERY                       1979  CBS SONY       JAP   25AP 1600
                                           (O) GREATEST HITS                   1979  JET            UK       LX525
                                           (O) GREATEST HITS                   1979  JET            US        36310
                                           (P) XANADU          (SOUNDTRACK)    1980  JET            UK          526
                                           (P) XANADU                          1980  MCA            US         6100
                                           (Q) BOX OF THEIR BEST               1980  JET            US        36966
                                           (R) TIME                            1981  JET            UK          236
                                           (R) TIME                            1981  JET            US        37371
                                           (EP) E L O                          1978  JET                      ELO1
```

```
JORG OHLERT          G K    (A       (A) ELECTRIC SANDWICH           1973
KLAUS LORMANN        B      (A
JOCHEN CARTHAUS      V SAX  (A       WOLF FABIAN        D     (A      DAVID AXELROD          (D
```

```
ULI ROTH             G      (AB      (A) EARTHQUAKE                  1979  BRAIN         GER   0060 196
CLIVE EDWARDS        D      (AB      (B) FIREWIND                    1979  BRAIN                    6410
ULE RIGEN            B      (AB
```

```
                                     (A) CURRENT EVENTS              1981  CAPITOL             12093
                                     (B) STATE SHOCK                 1981  CAPITOL             12162
```

```
DAVE HALL            G V    (A       (A) IN THE HANDS OF KARMA       1970  NASCO         US    NASCO 9004
MONT  ?              (A
? RAISIN             (A       ? WILLARD       (A
```

E35   ELECTRIC PRUNES   E35

```
JIM LOWE    AUTOHARP V G  (AB      (A) ELECTRIC PRUNES            1967  REPRISE       US   RLP  6248
JOHN HERREN          K    (CDE     (A) ELECTRIC PRUNES            1967  REPRISE       GER       24033
MARK TULIN           B    (AB      (B) UNDERGROUND                1967  REPRISE       US   RLP  6262
KEN WILLIAMS         G    (AB      (C) MASS IN F MINOR            1968  REPRISE       US   RLP  6275
PRESTON RITTER       D    (A       (C) MASS IN F MINOR            1972  REPRISE       UK   K    34003
WEASEL SPAGNOLA      G    (AB      (C) MASS IN F MINOR            197   MIDI UK            24010
DAVE HASSINGER       PROD (AB      (C) MASS IN F MINOR            1980  REPRISE       NL        44057
RON MORGAN           G    (CDE     (D) RELEASE OF AN OATH         1968  REPRISE       US   RLP  6316
MARK KINCAID         G V  (CDE     (E) JUST GOOD OLD ROCK'N'ROLL  1969  REPRISE       US   RSLP 6342
RICHARD WHETSTONE    D G V (CDE
BRETT WADE        B V FLT  (CDE    QUINT              D      (B
```
E35A   ELECTRIC STRING BAND   E35A
```
DENNY LAINE          V G  (
ANDY LEIGH           B V  (
VIV PRINCE           D    (         JOHN STEIN         VLN    (    CLIVE GILLINSON    CELLO    (
ANGUS ANDERSON       VLN  (         HAFLIDR HALYNISSON CELLO  (
```
E35B   ELECTROPHON   E35B
```
BURT ALCANTARA            (A        (A) ZYGOAT                     1974  POLYDOR            2383 270
                                    ( ) FURTHER THOUGHTS ON THE CLASSICS 1977 POLYDOR      2482 335
```
E35C   BIG MOJO ELEM   E35C
```
BIG MOJO ELEM        V B  (A        (A) MOJO BOOGIE                1978  MCM           FR        900303
FRED BELOW           D    (A
WAYNE BENNETT        G    (A        WILLIE JAMES LYONS  G     (A
```
E36   ELEPHANT   E36
```
DICK GLASS           V G  (AB       (A) ELEPHANT                   1973  CAPITOL            SMAS11154
RUSS KUNKEL          D    (A        (B) THE ELEPHANT               1974  MOONWATCHER   US        20001
CHARLES LARKEY       B    (A
GEOFF LEVIN          G    (AB       AMBROSE CAMPBELL    PERC  (A   HAROLD COWART      B    (B
RONALD ZEIGLER       D    (B
```
E37   ELEPHANTS MEMORY   E37
```
RICK FRANK           D V  (ABCDE    (A) ELEPHANTS MEMORY           1969  BUDDAH                 5033
STAN BRONSTEIN       V SAX (ABCDE   (A) ELEPHANTS MEMORY           1969  BUDDAH             203  022
GARY VAN SCYOC       B V  (ABCDE    (B) MIDNIGHT COWBOY (SOUNDTRACK) 1969 BUDDAH               5038
WAYNE TEX GABRIEL    G V  (D        (C) TAKE IT TO THE STREETS     1971  METRONOME     MD   1052
JOHN LENNON     V G K PERC (D       (C) TAKE IT TO THE STREETS     1971  METRONOME          1035
CHRIS ROBISON        V K G (E       (D) ELEPHANTS MEMORY           1972  APPLE         US   SMAS 3389
ADAM IPPOLITO     K TPT V (D        (D) ELEPHANTS MEMORY           1972  APPLE              SAPCOR.22
THUNDERTHIGHS        V    (E        (E) ANGELS FOREVER             1974  POLYDOR            2383 260
TERRY & THE PIRATES V    (E        (E) ANGELS FOREVER             1974  RCA                APLI 0569
YOKO ONO             V    (D
MARTHA VELEZ         V    (D
HILDA HARRIS         V    (D        KEITH JOHNSON      TPT    (D   DAVID PEEL         V    (D
TONI WINE            V    (D        LINDA NOVEMBER     V      (D   MYRON YULES        V    (D
JON SACHS            G V  (D        JOHN WARD          B      (    RICHARD SUSSMAN    K    (
```
E37A   ELEVATORS   E37A
```
TOM MYERS            K    (A        (A) FRONTLINE                  1980  ARISTA        US        4270
JOHN CLARK           G    (A
JERRY ELLIS          B    (A        ZONDER KENNEDY      G     (A   WILLIAM BENJAMIN   D    (A
```
E38   ELF   E38
```
RONNIE JAMES DIO ]SAME V B(ABC      (A) ELF                       19    EPIC          US        31789
RON PADAVONA                        (B) CAROLINA COUNTRY BALL      1974  PURPLE        UK   TPSA 3506
MICKEY LEE SOULE    K G   (ABC      (B) L A /59                    1974  MGM           US   M3G  4974
GARY DRISCOLL       D     (ABC      (C) TRYING TO BURN THE SUN     1975  MGM           US   M3G  4994
DAVE FEINSTEIN      G     (A
GRAIG GRUBER        B     (BC       STEVE EDWARDS      G      (BC  MARK NAUSEEF       PERC (C
CHRIS PYNE          TROM  (B        HENRY LOWTHER      TPT    (B   HELEN CHAPPELL     V    (B
LIZA STRIKE         V     (B        BARRY ST JOHN      V      (B
```
E38A   ELIAS HULK   E38A
```
PETER THOPE         V     (A        (A) ELIAS HULK UNCHAINED       1970  YOUNGBLOOD    US   SSYB 8
GRANVILLE FRAZER    G     (A
NEIL TATUM          G     (A        JAMES HAINES       B      (A   BERNARD JAMES      D    (A
```
E39   ELI ZABETH   E39
```
STEVE WEINGARTEN    G ORG (A        (A) ELIZABETH                  1968 VANGUARD UK SVRL 19010 US VSD6501
JIM DAHME           V FLT G(A
BOB PATTERSON       G V   (A        STEVE BRUNO        B K    (A   HANK RANSOME       D G B(A
```
E40   YVONNE ELLIMAN   E40
```
YVONNE ELLIMAN      V     (ALL      (A) I DON'T KNOW HOW TO LOVE HIM 1972 POLYDOR 2383141 US DECCA 75341
WITH                                (B) FOOD OF LOVE               1973  PURPLE        UK   TPS  3504
DAVID SPINOZZA      G     (A        (B) FOOD OF LOVE               1973  MCA  US            356
HUGH McCRACKEN      G     (A        (C) RISING SUN                 1975  RSO  UK      2393 149 US 4808
STU WOODS           B     (A        (D) LOVE ME                    1977  RSO  US  3018     UK 2394 182
RICK MAROTTA        D     (A        (E) NIGHT FLIGHT               1978  RSO  US  3031     UK 2394 197
MICHAEL OMARTIAN    K     (F        (F) YVONNE                     1979  RSO  US  3038     UK RS   16
JIM KELTNER         D     (FE
JEFF PORCARO        D     (F   STEVE CROPPER    G    (FE  JAY GRAYDON      G   (F  RICHIE ZETO      G   (F
MARTY WALSH         G     (F   DAVEY JOHNSTONE  G SITA(EF MIKE PORCARO     B   (F  LEE RITENOUR     G   (F
VICTOR FELDMAN      PERC  (F   PAUL STALLWORTH  B    (FE  STEVE BARRI      PERC(F  LEE SKLAR        B   (FE
JIM HORN            WIND  (FE  BUELL NEIDLINGER B    (F   MAXINE WILLARD   V   (FE DAVID PAICH      K   (F
JULIA TILLMAN       V     (F   TOM SNOW         K    (F   JIM HAAS         V   (F  TOM CANNING      K   (F
JON JOYCE           V     (F   BILL PAYNE       K    (F   STAN FARBER      V   (F  CRAIG DOERGE     K   (FE
JOHN HENRY KURTZ    V     (F   DR JOHN          K V  (F   GARY COLEMAN     PERC(DEF JOE PORCARO     PERC(F
FRED STAEHLE        PERC  (F   CHUCK FINDLEY    HRNS (FE  ERIC CARMEN      V K (EF JACKIE KELSO     HRNS(EF
MATTHEW MOORE       V     (F   KATHY COLLIER    V    (FE  CARMEN TWILLIE   V   (EF VENNETTE GLOUD   V   (EF
MIKE BAIRD          D     (E   SONNY BURKE      K    (E   BOB BOWLES       G   (ED JAMES GADSON     D   (ED
JAMES NEWTON HOWARD K (E  LOWELL GEORGE    G    (E   RITCHIE HAYWARD  D   (E  WILLIAM SMITH    K   (E
STEVE HUNTER        G     (E   RUSS KUNKEL      D    (E   KIKI DEE         V   (E  DANNY KORTCHMAR  G   (E
BABOO PIERRE        PERC  (E   DONNY GERRARD    V    (E   DEAN PARKES      G   (E  PAULINHO DA COSTA PERC(ED
SCOTT EDWARDS       B     (ED  HENRY KAPONO     V    (E   BOB ZIMITTI      PERC(DE DEE MURRAY       B   (E
```

(CONTINUED)

E40 (CONTINUED) — YVONNE ELLIMAN

MARTI McCALL	V (E	FRED PERREN	SYN (ED	BEN BENAY	G (E	CECILIO RODRIGUEZ	V (E
BRUCE EPSTEIN	G (A	FRANK CARILLO	G (C	MARK WARNER	G (A	PETER GORDON	HRNS(A
RALPH MacDONALD	PERC (A	GARY STARBUCK	G (D	JOHN BARNES	K PERC(D	PETER ROBINSON	K (A
ALAN WEIGHALL	B (A	KENNY ASCHER	K (A	LOUIS STEWART	G (A	BRUCE ROWLAND	D (A
GEORGE BUTCHER	PNO (A	GEORGE YOUNG	FLT (A				

E41 — MARC ELLINGTON

MARC ELLINGTON V G BAGPIPES(ALL	(A) MARC ELLINGTON	1969 PHILIPS UK SBL7883 US APMEX 10131
WITH	(B) RAINS/ REINS OF CHANGE	1971 B&C UK CAS 1133
KAREN ELLINGTON V (ABC	(C) A QUESTION OF ROADS	1972 PHILIPS UK 6308 120
RICHARD THOMPSON G (ABE	(D) RESTORATION	1972 PHILIPS UK 6308 143
DAVE PEGG B (B	(E) MARC TIME	1972 XTRA UK XTRA 1154
CHRIS HILLMAN V MAND(B		

DAVE MATTACKS D (BDE	IAN MATTHEWS V (BD	SNEAKY PETE KLEINOW STEEL(B	TONY COX K (BDE
MIKE DIEGHAN G BANJO(BCD	PAT DONALDSON B (BDE	GERRY CONWAY D (BE	GORDON HUNTLEY B (AB
RAY DUFFY D (BC	SANDY DENNY V (B	FRITZ FRYER V (B	STEVE RYE HCA (B
MICK FRENCH VLN(B	RICK ROBERTS V (B	GERRY FIELD VLN (B	TIM RENWICK G (C
BRUCE THOMAS B (C	ANDY LEIGH B (C	JOHN WILSON D (C	DAVE RICHARDS B PNO(CDE
ANDY ROBERTS G K(CDE	ERIC ELLINGTON V (D	JERRY DONAHUE G (DE	DAVE PEACOCK B (D
DAVE HEPBURN B (D	TIMI DONALD D (DE	BARRY DE SOUZA D (D	PHIL CHESTERTON D (D
TOM PARKER PNO(D	ZOOT MONEY K (D	DOLLY COLLINS PNO (D	BOB RONGA G (D
SIMON NICOL G (ADE	PHIL PICKETT G (D	RAY WARLEIGH SAX (D	IAN WHITEMAN K (DE
SUE DRAHEIM VLN(D	MAC KISSOON V (DE	SANDY ROBERTSON G (E	LONGDANCER V (D
KATHY KISSOON V (DE	ROGER SWALLOW D (AE	LINDA THOMPSON V (E	B J COLE STEEL(E
STEVE ASHLEY HCA(E	REG POWELL K (A	JAMIE OGILVY FORBES PIPES(D	MARK GRIFFITHS B (AB

E42 — CASS ELLIOT

CASS ELLIOT V (ALL	(A) CASS ELLIOT	1968 RCA US LSP 4619
DAVE MASON G V(F	(B) DREAM A LITTLE DREAM	1968 DUNHILL US 50040
HARVEY BROOKS (B	(B) DREAM A LITTLE DREAM	1968 STATESIDE UK 5004
JAMES BURTON G (B	(C) BUBBLE GUM LEMONADE & SOMETHING	1969 DUNHILL US 50055
CYRUS FARYAR (B	(C) BUBBLE GUM LEMONADE & SOMETHING	1969 STATESIDE UK 5014
JIM GORDON D (B	(D) MAKE YOUR OWN MUSIC	19 DUNHILL US 50071
STEPHEN STILLS G V(B	(E) MAMA'S BIG ONES	1971 PROBE UK SPB1020 RI ABC 50113
JOHN SIMON (B	(E) MAMA'S BIG ONES	1974 DUNHILL US 50093
DON RANDI PNO(A	(F) DAVE MASON & CASS ELLIOT	1971 PROBE UK SPB6259 US BTHUMB8825
JOHN GUERIN D (A	(G) ROAD IS NO PLACE FOR A LADY	1974 RCA US LSA 3194 UK SF 8306
LOUIE SHELTON G (A	(G) ROAD IS NO PLACE FOR A LADY	1972 RCA US 4753
AL CASEY G (A	(H) DON'T CALL ME MAMA ANYMORE	1974 RCA UK APLI 0303
JULES GREENBERG VIBES(A		

BRUCE JOHNSTON K V(A	CAROL KAYE B (A	REGGIE COLSON PERC (A	LARRY CARLTON G (A
DENNIS BUDIMIR G (A	EDWIN CARTER G (A	CARL FORTINA K (A	JOE OSBORN B (A
ED GREENE D (A	MICHAEL LANG PNO(A	EDWARD KUSBY TROM (A	GROVER MITCHELL TROM (A
MAURICE TROM(A	WILLIAM ANDERSON TPT(A	GINO BOZZACCO TPT (A	MOACIR SANTOS SAX (A
JACK NIMITZ SAX(A	JERGME RICHARDSON SAX(A	JAN GASSMAN V (A	BENNY COLSON V (A
CLARK BURROUGHS V (A	MARILYN MESSINA V (A	CARL WILSON V (A	CLYDIE KING V (A
SHIRLEY MATTHEWS V (A	VENETTA FIELDS V (A		

E43 — COLONEL ELLIOT

COLONEL ELLIOT	(A) INTERSTELLA REGGAE DRIVE	1974 RHINO SRNP 9001

E44 — DAVE ELLIOTT

DAVID ELLIOTT G V B(AB	(A) DAVID ELLIOTT	1972 ATLANTIC UK K 40374
CALEB QUAYE G PNO (A	(A) SOLID GROUND	1973 ATLANTIC UK K 40527
DEE MURRAY B (A		

NIGEL OLSSON D (A			
FRANCIS MONKMAN K (A	CHRIS KARAN D (AB	DAVE MATTACKS D (A
RICK WILLS B (A	ROY O TEMRO D (A	MICK GRABHAM G (AB
B J COLE STEEL (AB	ALBERT LEE G (A	JOHN PERRY B (B
DAVID HOOD B (B	GASPER LAWAL CONGAS (B	TERRY STANNARD D (B
PETE CARR DOB (B	ROGER HAWKINS D (B	BARRY BECKETT K (B
	JIMMY JOHNSON G (B	

E45 — RON ELLIOTT

RON ELLIOTT G V (A	(A) CANDELESTICK MAKER	19 WB WS 1833
MARC McCLURE G V (A		

CHRIS ETHRIDGE B (A	DENNIS DRAGON D (A	BUD SHANK FLT (A
SAL VALENTINO TAMB (A	DAN LEVITT G V (A	RY COODER G (A
LYLE RITZ B (A	PAUL HUMPHREY D (A	

E46 — ELLIS

STEVE ELLIS V (AB	(A) RIDING ON THE CREST OF A SLUMP	1972 EPIC US 31945 UK 64878
ZOOT MONEY K V (AB	(B) WHY NOT?	1973 EPIC UK 65650
ANDY GEE G (AB		

DAVE LUTTON D (AB			
JIM LEVERTON B (A	COLIN ALLEN D PERC (B	GARY FARR HCA (
NICK SOUTH B (B	MAGGIE BELL V (AB	MICK WEAVER K (
MIKE PATTO V (B	JULIE TIPPETTS V (B	ROGER CHAPMAN V (B
	MAGGIE NICHOLLS V (B	

E47 — DAVE ELLIS

DAVE ELLIS G (A	(A) ALBUM	1973 SONET UK SNTF 646
GORDON GILTRAP G (A		

E48 — MATTHEW ELLIS

MATTHEW ELLIS V G K (ALL	(A) MATTHEW ELLIS	1971 REGAL ZONOPHONE UK SRZA 8501
CHRIS SPEDDING g (B	(B) AM I	1971 REGAL ZONOPHONE UK SRZA 8505
TONI CAMPO B (B		

CLEM CATTINI D (B	BARRY MORGAN D (B	CHRIS WALKER K (B	REX MORRIS SAX (B
PAUL SCHERMAN VLN (B	TOMMY REILLY HCA (B	SUNNY LESLIE V (B	KAY GARNER V (B
LESLEY DUNCAN V (B			

E49 — PEE WEE ELLIS

PEE WEE ELLIS SAX K V PERC(A	(A) HOME IN THE COUNTRY	1977 SAVOY IMP SJL 3301
ROLAND HANNA K (A		

JON SCHOLLE G (A	JEFF BERLIN B (A	IDRIS MUHAMMAD D (A	JIMMY STRASSBURG D (A
JUMMA SANTOS CONGA (A	CHARLOTTE CROSSLEY V (A	LILLIAN TYNES V (A	CHARLES BROWN G (A
ANTHONY JACKSON B (A	BABATUNDE CONGA (A	GORDON EDWARDS B (A	MELANIE JORDIN V (A
JOHN GATCHELL TPT (A	BARRY ROGERS TROM (A	ERNIE HAYES K (A	CORNELL DUPREE G (A
ERIC GALE G (A	BERNARD PURDIE D (A	RAY MANTILLA PERC (A	LEON THOMAS V (A
LANI GROVES V (A	WAYMON REED TPT (A	GEORGE BENSON G (A	CHRIS PARKER D (A
VIVIAN CHERRY V (A	DWAIN JONES V (A	DAVE LIEBMAN SAX (A	ELEANA STEINBERG V (A

LORRAINE ELLISON

LORRAINE ELLISON	V	(ALL	(A) HEART & SOUL/STAY WITH ME	1970	WB	US 1821	UK	K46037	
RICK JAEGER	D	(B	(B) LORRAINE ELLISON	1974	WB	US 2780			
MARC JORDON	K	(B	(C) BEST OF PHILADELPHIAS QUEEN	1976	WB		UK K	56230	
TOM RUTLEY		(B							
WILTON FELDER	B	(B	KENNY GRADNEY	B	(B	ARTHUR ADAMS	G	(B	

E50   ELMER GANTY'S VELVET OPERA   E50

ELMER GANTRY	V G	(AB	(A) ELMER GANTRY'S VELVET OPERA	1968 DIRECTION UK 863300	US EPIC 26415	
COLIN FORSTER	G	(A	(B) 1968 LIVE LINE UP			
JOHN FORD	B	(AB				
RICHARD HUDSON	D	(AB	PAUL BRETT	G	(B	

E50A   ELOY   E50A

FRANK BORNEMANN	V G	(ALL	(A) INSIDE	1973	ELECTROLA	GERM	29479
KLAUS PETER MATZIOL	V B	(DJK	(A) INSIDE	1973	JANUS	US	3062
FRITZ RANDOW	D G	(ABK	(B) FLOATING	1974	ELECTROLA	GERM	29521
HANNES ARKONA	G K	(JK	(B) FLOATING	1974	JANUS	US	7018
DETLER SCHMIDTCHEN	K SYN	(D	(C) POWER & THE PASSION	1975	ELECTROLA	GERM	29602
JURGEN ROSENTHAL	D	(D	(D) DAWN	1976	ELECTROLA	GERM	31787
MANFRED WIECLORKE	K G V	(AB	(E) OCEAN	1977	ELECTROLA	GERM	32596
WOLFGANG STOCKER	B	(B	(F) SILENT CRIES AND MIGHTY ECHOES	1978	ELECTROLA	GERM	45269
LUITJEN JANSSEN	B	(B	(G) LIVE	1978	ELECTROLA	GERM	32934
HANNES FOLBERTH	K	(JK	(H) COLOURS	1980	ELECTROLA	GERM 064	45936
JIM McGILLIVRAY	D	(J	(J) PLANETS	1982	HEAVY METAL		HM LP1
			(K) TIME TO TURN	1982	ELECTROLA	GER	46548

E50B   ELUSION   E50B

(A) ALL TOYS BREAK	1981	ATLANTIC	US	16040

E51   JOE ELY   E51

JOE ELY	G V	(ALL	(A) JOE ELY	1977	MCA US 2242	UK MCF	2808	
WITH			(A) JOE ELY	1981	MCA RI		1604	
LLOYD MAINES	STEEL V	(BCE	(B) HONKY TONK MASQUERADE	1978	MCA US 2333	UK MCF	2832	
JESSE TAYLOR	G V	(BCE	(C) DOWN IN THE DRAG	1979	MCA US 3080	UK MCG	3532	
GREGG WRIGHT	B V	(BC	(D) LIVE SHOTS	1980	MCA US 5262	UK MCF	3064	
STEVE KEETON	D	(BC	(E) MUSTA NOTTA GOTTA LOTTA	1981	MCA US 5183	UK MCA	3099	
PONTI BONE	K	(BCE						
SMOKEY JOE MILLER	SAX	(E	CHIP YOUNG	G	(B	SHANE KEISTER	K	(B	
FARRELL MORRIS	PERC	(B	ED CIZARD	SAX	(C	RICHARD BOWDEN	FDL	(C	
DAVID MASON	K	(C	DINK THOMAS	WHISTLE	(C	PETER WEST	V	(C	
LEA JANE BERINATI	V	(B	GINGER HOLLADAY	V	(B	LISA SILVER	V	(B	
BUTCH HANCOCK	V	(B	MICHAEL BROVSKY	PROD	(E	MICHAEL ROBBERSON	B	(E	
ROBERT MARQUAM	D	(E	REESE WYNAMS	K	(E	JAMES FENNER	PERC	(E	
MARK HALLMAN	V	(E	JUDY PRICE	V	(E				

E52   EMBRYO   E52

CHRISTIAN BURCHARD	V D K	(ALL	(A) OPAL	1970	OHR	GERM OMM 56003	
EDGAR HOFFMANN	VLN V WIND	(12ABCD	(B) EMBRYO'S RACHE	1971	LIBERTY	GERM UAS 29239	
MAL WALDRON	K	(DE	(C) FATHER SON HOLY GHOST	1972	LIBERTY	GER UAS 29344	
JOHN KELLY	G V	(1A	(D) STEIGAUS	1973	BRAIN	GERM	1023
UWE MULLRICH	B	(2	(E) ROCK SESSION	1973	BRAIN	GERM	1036
ROMAN BUNKA	G V CLAR	(2BDGH	(E) ROCK SESSION	197	BRAIN		201190
RALPH FISCHER	B V	(1A	(F) THIS IS EMBRYO	1974	BRAIN	GER	200152
JIMMY JACKSON	K	(DE	(G) WE KEEP ON	1974	BASF	US/ GERM 21865/1	
SIEGFRIED SCHWAB	G	(CE	(H) SURFIN'	1975	BASF	US/ GER	22385/3
JORG EVERS	B	(E	(J) EMBRYO LIVE	1976	TRIKONT		0003
BETTSY ALLEN	V	(A	( ) CLASSIC GERMAN ROCK SCENE	1975	UA	GER UAS 29774	
ROBERTO DETREE		(A	(1) 1969 (2) 1977				
DIETER MIEKAUTSCH	K	(G					
UWE MULLRICH	B	(D	FRANZ BONTGEN	V	(B	HERMAN BREUKERK	(B
DAVE KING	B FLT V	(DE	HOLGER TRULZSH	PERC	(A	HANSI FISCHER	FLT PERC(B
CHARLIE MARIANO	WIND	(GH	LOTHER MEID		(1	ALFRED JONES	(
JORG EVERS		(	KLAUS GOTZNER		(	MULLAH STILETTI	(
MARIA ARCHER		(	BUTZE FISCHER		(	MICHAEL WEHEMEYER	(

E52A   EMERGENCY   E52A

HANUS BERKA	WIND PERC	(ABCDE	(A) EMERGENCY	1971	CBS	GER	64381
JOHN REDPATH	D	(D	(B) ENTERANCE	1972	CBS	GER	64928
FRANK DIEZ	G B	(DE	(C) GET TO THE COUNTRY	1973	BRAIN	GER	1037
HANS STOER	G B	(D	(D) GOLD ROCK	1973	BRAIN	GER 201104	
PETER BISCHOF	B	(CD	(E) NO COMPROMISE	1974	BRAIN	GER	1052
RICHARD PALMERJAMES	G	(D					
MARTIN HARRISON			ELMAR SCHMIDT	D	(	RALF TOURSEL	K SYN(
UDO LIDENBERG	D PERC	(A	JIRO MATOUSEK	K	(A	OTTO BEZLOJA	B	(A
BARRIE NEWBY	G	(A	REDDY	V PERC	(A	DUSKO GOYKOVIC	TPT	(A
RICHARD PALMER-JAMES	G	(C	VEIT MARVOS	K	(C	BERND KNAAK	D	(C
YERZY ZIEMBROWSKI	B	(C					

E52B   BILLY THE KID EMERSON   E52B

BILLY THE KID EMERSON	V PNO	(A	(A) LITTLE HEALTHY THING	19	CHARLY	UK CR 30187			
EUGENE FOX	SAX	(A							
OLIVER SAIN	SAX	(A	IKE TURNER	G	(A	JESSE KNIGHT	B	(A	CHARLES SMITH TPT (A
MOSES REED	SAX	(A	CALVIN NEWBORN G		(A	ROBERT PRINDELL D		(A	WILLIE SIMS D (A
BOBBY FIELD	SAX	(A	LUTHER TAYLOR SAX		(A	JEWEL BRISCOE	SAX	(A	KENNETH BANKS B (A
RAYMOND HILL	SAX	(A	BENNY MOORE	SAX	(A	ELVEN PARR	G	(A	PHINEAS NEWBORN D (A

E52C   KEITH EMERSON   E52C

KEITH EMERSON	K	(AB	(A) INFERNO(SOUNDTRACK)	1980 ARIOLA NL 202079 WB UK	K50753			
FRANK SCULLY	D	(AB	(B) NIGHTHAWKS	1981 MCA NL 203 453	UK MCF 3107			
KENDAL STUBBS	B	(AB						
NEIL SYMONETTE	D	(B	TRISTAM FRY	PERC	(B	JEROME RICHARDSON	SAX	(B
GREG BOWEN	TPT	(B	PAULETTE McWILLIAMS	V	(B	STRINGS & ORCH		(AB

KEITH EMERSON	K	(ALL	(A) EMERSON LAKE & PALMER	1970	ISLAND	UK	ILPS 9132
GREG LAKE	PROD B G V	(ALL	(A) EMERSON LAKE & PALMER	1973	MANTICORE	UK	K 43503
CARL PALMER	D	(ALL	(A) EMERSON LAKE & PALMER	1970	COTILLION	US	9040
WITH			(A) EMERSON LAKE & PALMER	197	MANTICORE	US	19120
LONDON SYMPHONY ORCH		(GH	(A) EMERSON LAKE & PALMER	197	ARIOLA	GERM	87 224ET
JOE WALSH	G	(G	(B) TARKUS	1971	ISLAND	UK	ILPS 9155
ORCH DE L'OPERA DE PARIS		(GH	(B) TARKUS	1973	MANTICORE	UK	K 43504
JAMES BLADES	PERC	(G	(B) TARKUS	1971	COTILLION	US	9900
			(B) TARKUS	197	MANTICORE	US	19121
			(B) TARKUS	197	ORRIZONTE	IT	8214
			(B) TARKUS	197	ARIOLA	GERM	87225XOT
			(C) PICTURES AT AN EXHIBITION	1971	ISLAND	UK	HELP1
			(C) PICTURES AT AN EXHIBITION	1973	MANTICORE	UK	K 33501
			(C) PICTURES AT AN EXHIBITION	197	MANTICORE	US	66666
			(C) PICTURES AT AN EXHIBITION	197	MANTICORE	US	19122
			(C) PICTURES AT AN EXHIBITION	197	ARIOLA	GERM	87 226.ET
			(C) PICTURES AT AN EXHIBITION	1981	MOBILE	US	031
			(D) TRILOGY	1972	ISLAND	UK	ILPS 9186
			(D) TRILOGY	1973	MANTICORE	UK	K 43505
			(D) TRILOGY	1972	COTILLION	US	9903
			(D) TRILOGY	197	MANTICORE	US	19123
			(D) TRILOGY	197	ARIOLA	GERM	87 227XOT
			(E) BRAIN SALAD SURGERY	1973	MANTICORE	UK	K 53501
			(E) BRAIN SALAD SURGERY	1973	MANTICORE	US	66669
			(E) BRAIN SALAD SURGERY	197	ATLANTIC	US	19124
			(E) BRAIN SALAD SURGERY	197	ARIOLA	GERM	87 302XOT
			(F) WELCOME MY FRIENDS	1974	MANTICORE	UK	K 63500
			(F) WELCOME MY FRIENDS	1974	MANTICORE	US	MC3 200
			(F) WELCOME MY FRIENDS	197	ARIOLA	GERM	88 150XET
			(G) WORKS	1977	MANTICORE	UK	K 80009
			(G) WORKS	1977	ATLANTIC	US	SD2 7000
			(G) WORKS	197	ARIOLA	GERM	28 614XDU
			(H) WORKS VOL 2	1977	ATLANTIC	UK	K 50422
			(H) WORKS VOL 2	1977	ATLANTIC	US	19147
			(H) WORKS VOL 2	197	ARIOLA	GERM	25 553XOT
			(J) LOVE BEACH	1978	ATLANTIC	UK	K 50552
			(J) LOVE BEACH	1978	ATLANTIC	US	19211
			(J) LOVE BEACH	1978	ARIOLA	GERM	200249320
			(K) IN CONCERT	1979	ATLANTIC	UK	K 50757
			(K) IN CONCERT	1979	ATLANTIC	US	19255
			(L) BEST OF	1980	ATLANTIC	US	19283
			(L) BEST OF	1980	ATLANTIC	UK	K 50652

WILLI MORRISON	G V	(A	(A) EMIGRE	1979	CHRYSALIS	US	CHR 1228
IAN GUENTHER	VLN	(A					
BARRY KEANE	D	(A	JOHN SHAND	G	(A	MITCHELL LEWIS	G	(A
CHRIS VICKERY	B	(A	BRUCE LEY	K	(A	DICK SMITH	PERC	(A
JIM CAMPBELL	V	(A					
BOB BONNELL	V	(A	GEORGE SEMKIW	PROD	(A

BOBBY EMMONS	K	(A	(A) BLUES WITH A BEAT AND AN ORGAN	19	HI	US	32024

BUDDY EMMONS	STEEL	(ALL	(A) 2 ACES BACK TO BACK(I SIDE)	1971	K ARK	US	K6028
BUDDY SPICHER	FDL	(E	(B) EMMONS GUITAR INC	197	EMMONS	US	
LENNY BREAU		(	(C) STEEL GUITAR	1975	FLYING FISH	UK	SNTF 708
JOHNNY GIMBLE	FDL	(C	(C) STEEL GUITAR	1975	FLYING FISH	US	FF 007
BUNKY KEELS	PNO	(C	(D) SINGS BCB WILLS	1976	FLYING	UK	SNTF 706
BUD LOGAN	B	(C	(D) SINGS BOB WILLS	1977	FLYING FISH	US	FF 017
MICHAEL MILFORD	MAND	(C	(E) BUDDIES	1977	FLYING FISH	US	FF 041
LEON RHODES	G	(C	(E) BUDDIES	1977	FLYING FISH	UK	SNTF 741
KARL HIMMEL	D	(C	(F) EMMONS LIVE VOL 1	197	MIDLAND	US	ISGC1
MIKE LEECH	B	(C	(G) EMMONS LIVE VOL 2	197	MIDLAND	US	ISGC2
KENNY MALONE	D	(C	(H) MINORS ALOUD	1979	FLYING FISH	US	FF 088
RON OATES	PNO	(C	(H) MINORS ALOUD	1979	FLYING FISH	UK	SNTF 799
DALE SELLERS	G	(C					

JEANETTE HAWES	V	(E	(A) SO I CAN LOVE YOU	1970	VOLT	4110	US	6008
SHEILA HUTCHINSON	V	(EFG	(B) SONGS OF LOVE	19	VOLT		US	6921
WANDA HUTCHINSON	V	(EFG	(C) UNTOUCHED	1972	VOLT	4112	US	6015
PAMELA	V	(F	(D) CHRONICLE	19	STAX		US	4121
THERESA DAVIS	V	(G	(E) FLOWERS	1976	CBS US 34163		UK	81639
VERDINE WHITE	B	(EFH	(F) REJOICE	1977	CBS US 34762		UK	82065
LARRY DUNN	K	(EF	(G) SUNSHINE	1977	STAX US 4100		UK	3003
AL McKAY	G	(EFH	(H) SUNBEAM	1978	CBS US 35385	UK	82864
JOE HUTCHINSON	G	(E	(J) BEST OF	1979	STAX US 4121		UK	3008
BAR KAYS		(C	(K) COME INTO OUR WORLD	1980	CBS US 36149	UK	83483
MICHAEL HARRIS	TPT	(EH	(L) CHRONICLE	1980	STAX		NL	62752
SOUL SPACEMEN		(C	(M) NEW AFFAIR	1981	CBS US 37456	UK	85172
FRED WHITE	D	(EFH						

WILLIE HALL	D	(G	DON MYRICK	D	(EFH	OSCAR BRASHEAR	TPT	(EFH	RICHARD BROWN SAX	(E
DAVID SHIELDS	B	(F	JAMES GADSON	D	(F	MAURICE WHITE	D	(F	JERRY PETERS K	(F
PAULINHO DACOSTA	PERC	(FH	SKIP SCARBOROUGH	K	(FH	MARLO HENDERSON	G	(FH	CLARENCE McDONALD K	(F
LOUIS SATTERFIELD	TROM	(EFH	MICHAEL TOLES	G	(G	BOBBY MANUEL	G	(G	MARVELL THOMAS K	(G
LESTER SNARE	K	(G	RONNIE WILLIAMS	K	(G	EARL THOMAS	B	(G	DONALD DUCK DUNN B	(G
AL JACKSON	D	(G	TERRY MARSHALL	K	(H	CHARLES HOSCH	B	(H	BARBARA KORN HRNS	(H
ALAN ROBINSON	HRNS	(H	MARILYN ROBINSON	HRNS	(H	GEORGE PATTERSON SAX		(H	GARY GRAINGER B	(H
KEITH HENDERSON	G	(H	JON LIND	G	(H	DOUZELL DAVIS	D	(H	EARL DE ROVEN PERC	(H
CHUCK FINDLEY	HRNS	(H	GEORGE BOHANON	TROM	(H	MAURICE SPEARS	TROM	(H	SID MULDROW HRNS	(H
GALE ROBINSON	HRNS	(H								

EMPEROR

```
    JOE ALEXANDER      G V   (A      (A) EMPEROR                 1977  PRIVATE STOCK           2029
    JOE MARQUES        B V   (A
    MIKE LOBETT        K V   (A      STEVE WATTS      D V   (A   RANDY BUDIHAS      D V   (A
```
END
```
    DAVE BROWN         B V   (A      (A) INTROSPECTION           1969  DECCA UK SKL5015 US LONDON 505
    TERRY TAYLOR       G     (A
    NICK GRAHAM        K V   (A      HUGH ATTWOOL     D     (A   COLIN GRFFIN       STEEL V(A
    BILL WYMAN         B     (A      CHARLIE WATTS    D     (A   NICKY HOPKINS      K   (A
```
ENGLAND
```
    MARTIN HENDERSON   B V   (A      (A) GARDEN SHED             1977  ARISTA          UK   ARTY 153
    FRANC HOLLAND      G V   (A
    ROBERT WEBB        K V   (A      JODE LEIGH       B V   (A
```
ENGERLING BLUES BAND
```
    WOLFRAM BODAG      K V HCA(A      (A) ENGERLIND BLUES        197   AMIGA           GER  855 597
    JENS SALEH         B     (A
    MICHA ARNOLD       B     (A      HEINER WITTE     G     (A   BERND KUHNERT      G   (A
    GOTTFRIED KLIER    SAX   (A      RAINER LOJEWSKI  G     (A
```
ENGLAND DAN & JOHN FORD COLEY
```
    ENGLAND DAN SEALS  V G   (ALL    (A) ENGLAND DAN & JOHN FORD COLEY 197  A&M  US 4305   UK AMLS64305
    JOHN FORD COLEY    V G K (ALL    (B) FABLES                 197   A&M   US 4350   UK AMLS64350
    WITH                             (C) I HEAR MUSIC            1976  A&M   US 4616   UK AMLH64613
    BOBBY THOMPSON  G BAN   (DEF     (D) NIGHTS ARE FOREVER      1976  BIG TREE US 89517 UK K 50297
    JOHNNY CHRISTOPHER G(F           (E) DOWDY FERRY ROAD        197   BIG TREE US 76000 UK K 50362
    STEVE GIBSON  G MAND(FDEG        (F) SOMETHINGS DONT COME EASY 1978 BIG TREE US 70006 UK K 50470
    LEE RITENOUR    G   (G           (G) DR HECKLE & MR JIVE     1979  BIG TREE US 76015 UK K 50602
    GINGER HOLLADAY V   (D           (H) BEST OF                 1980  BIG TREE US 76018
    LARRY LONDIN    D   (DDE         (I) JUST TELL ME IF YOU LOVE ME 1980 BIG TREE US
    STEVE LUKATHER  G   (G
    DAN FERGUSON    G   (G     WAH WAH WATSON    G (G    DOYLE GRISHAM   STEEL (FD  JACK WILLIAMS  B   (F
    JOE OSBORN      B   (FDCE  WILTON FELDER     B (G    DEE MURRAY      B    (G   DAN GORMAN     D   (G
    JOHN LELAND     B   (G     LEE SKLAR         B (G    SHANE KEISTER   K    (FG  JOEY CARBONE   PNO (G
    BOBBY EMMONS    ORG (F     GREG PHILLINGANES PNO (G  MICHAEL BODDIKER SYN (G   STEVE PORCARO  SYN (G
    MICHAEL VERNACCHIO K(G     BILL PAYNE        SYN (G  FARRELL MORRIS  PERC (F   CYNDI REYNOLDS HARP(F
    MIKE MILLER     SAX (F     BILLY PUETT      WIND(FDE GUNNAR SCRIVENER AUTOHARP(F HARRISON CALLOWAY HRNS(F
    HARVEY THOMPSON HRNS(F     RONNIE EADES     HRNS(F   DENNIS GOODE    HRNS (FDE SHELLEY KURLAND STR(F
    LISA SILVER     V   (FDE   SHERI KRAMER      V (FD   DIANE TIDWELL   V    (FDE VICKI LEHNING  V   (F
    DENISE PERALTA  V   (F     STEVE FORMAN     PERC(G   ERNIE WATTS     SAX  (G   GARY MALLABER  D   (G
    RALPH HUMPHREY  D   (G     JEFF PORCARO      D (G    RICHIE ZETO     G    (G   JIM GILSTRAP   V   (G
    JAI WINDING     PNO (G     LESLIE BULKIN     V (G    KELLY BULKIN    V    (G   OVID STEVENS   G   (G
    ED GREENE       D   (G     BUBBA KEITH      HCA(G    GARY TORPS      G    )G   TED REYNOLDS   D   (G
    KYLE LEHNING    B   (D     SHANE KEISTER     K (DE   JIM SEALS       G FDL(DE  GEORGE CUNNINGHAM TPT(D
    DON DHEFFIELD   TPT (D     DENIS SOLEE      WIND(D   JANIE FRICKIE   V    (D   RUSS KUNKEL    D   (B
    LARRY MOHOBERAC K   (B     JACK CONRAD       B (B    CLARENCE McDONALD K  (B   MAX BENNETT    B   (BC
    JOHN GUERIN     D   (B     BOBBIE HALL  PERC  (B    MARTY PAICH     STR  (B   JEFF PORCARO   D   (C
    DAVID HUGATE    B   (C     MARK STEVENS     PERC(C   WENDY SUITS     V    (E   REINEE PRESS   B   (B
    LOUIE SHELTON   G B SIT(BC JIM GORDON        D (BC   HAL BLAINE      D    (B   PAUL HUMPHREY  D   (B
    LARRY KNECHTEL  K   (B     DON RANDI         K (B    RON TUTT        D    (C   DAVID PAICH    K   (C
    ALLAN ESTES     PERC(C     TOMMY MORGAN     HCA(C    DOYLE GRISHAM   STEEL(DE  GEORGE TIDWELL TPT(E
    BUDDY SKIPPER   WIND(E
```
THE ENID
```
    ROBERT GODFREY     K    (ABCD    (A) THE ENID               1976  BUK UK BULP 2014 US 52001
    FRANCIS LICKERISH  G    (ABCD    (A) IN THE REGION OF THE STARS 1977 EMI INS3005 BUK GER 6 22929
    STEPHEN STEWART    G    (ABCD    (B) AERIE FAERIE NONSENSE   1977  EMI INS3012
    GLEN TALLETT       B K HRNS(A    (B) AERIE FAERIE NONSENSE   1977  BELLAPHON       GER    44005
    DAVID STOREY       D    (BC      (C) TOUCH ME                1979  PYE        UK  NSPH18593
    CHARLIE ELSTON     K    (B       (D) SIX PIECES              1979  PYE        UK   N   116
    TERRY PACK         B    (BC      (E) RHAPSODY IN ROCK        1980  PYE        UK       18619
    WILLAIM GILMOUR    K    (CD      (NB) SOME OF ABOVE HAVE BEEN REISSUED ON THE ENID LABEL
    TONY FREER         HRNS (C
    MARTIN RUSSELL     K B  (D       ROBBIE DOBSON  D    (AD
```
BRIAN ENO
```
    BRIAN ENO        V K SYN (ALL    (A) NO PUSSYFOOTIN'        1973  ISLAND UK HELP16 US ANTILLES7001
    WITH                             (A) NO PUSSYFOOTIN'        197   PHONOGRAM       EURO 9101  629
    ROBERT FRIPP     G   (ABEFHJ     (B) HERE COME THE WARM JETS 1973  ISLAND UK ILPS9268 US    87665
    KURT SCHWITTERS  V   (H          (B) HERE COME THE WARM JETS 1974  PHONOGRAM       EURO 6396  032
    FREDDIE SMITH    D   (D          (C) JUNE 1ST 1974          1974  ISLAND UK        ILPS 9291
    SHIRLEY WILLIAMS PERC (H         (D) TAKING TIGER MOUNTAIN BY STRATEGY 1974 ISLAND UK US  ILPS 9309
    JAKI LIEBEZEIT   D   (H          (D) TAKING TIGER MOUNTAIN BY STRATEGY 197  POLYDOR   UK   2302 068
    RHELL DAVIES     PERC (H         (D) TAKING TIGER MOUNTAIN BY STRATEGY 197  ISLAND US       1-3001
    PAUL RUDOLPH     G   (BEHJ       (E) ANOTHER GREEN WORLD    1974  ISLAND UK US     ILPS 9351
    FRED FRITH       G   (HJ         (E) ANOTHER GREEN WORLD    1974  POLYDOR    UK    2302 069
    PERCY JONES      B   (EHJ        (F) EVENING STAR           1975  ISLAND UK HELP22 US ANTILLES7018
    BILL McCORMICK   B   (HJB        (G) DISCREET MUSIC         1975  OBSCURE UK  OB 4 US ANTILLES7030
    PHIL COLLINS     PERC (HJDE      (H) BEFORE & AFTER SCIENCE 1977  POLYDOR    UK    2302 071
    DAVE MATTACKS    PERC (HJ        (H) BEFORE & AFTER SCIENCE 1977  POLYDOR EURO 2310 547 2344 087
    ROD MELVIN       K   (EJ         (H) BEFORE & AFTER SCIENCE 1977  ISLAND US          9478
    ANDY FRASER      B   (H          (J) MUSIC FOR FILMS        1978  POLYDOR    UK    2310 623
    JOACHIM ROEDELIUS K  (HK         (K) AFTER THE HEAT         1978  SKY        GER     021
    MOBI MOEBIUS     K   (HK         (L) MUSIC FOR AIRPORTS     1979  AMBIENT UK  001 US PVC    7908
    BRIAN TURRINGTON B   (DEH        (M) POSSIBLE MUSIC         1980  EDITIONS          EGED7
    RABBIT BUNDRICK  K   (C          (N) THE PLATEAUX OF MIRRORS 1980  EDITIONS         EGAMB 002
    EDDIE SPARROW    D   (C          (O) FOURTH WORLD           1980  EG    UK EGED 7
    MIKE OLDFIELD    G   (C          (P) MY LIFE IN THE BUSH    1981  EG    UK EGED 48 US SIRE  6093
    JOHN CALE      VIOLA K(CE        (Q) EMPTY LANDSCAPES       1981
    OLLIE HALSALL    G PNO(C         (R) ON LAND                1982  EG    UK EGED 20
    ARCHIE LEGGET    B   (C
    KEVIN AYERS      B   (C   ROBERT WYATT   PERC(CDL  NICO      V HARMONIUM(C  JOHN HASSEL          (M
    HAROLD BUDD      (N       INGE ZEININGER  V  (L    NICK JUDD      K    (B   ANDY MACKAY   SAX K(BD
    PHIL MANZANERA   G   (BD  SWEETFEED       V  (B    CHRIS THOMAS   B    (B   LLOYD WATSON   G   (B
    PAUL THOMPSON    PERC (B  MARTY SIMON    PERC(B    SIMON KING     PERC (B   JOHN WETTON    B   (B
    BUSTA CHERRY JONES B (B   CHRIS SPEDDING   G (B    CHRISTA FAST    V   (L   CHRISTINE GOMEZ V  (L
```

(CONTINUED)

E59 (CONTINUED)   BRIAN ENO   E59

PORTSMOUTH SINFONIA (D   POLLY ELTES   V   (D   SIMPLISTICS   V (D   RANDI & PYRAMIDS V (D
DAVID BYRNE   (P   DAVID VAN TIEGHAM D   (P   JOHN COOKSOY   D (P   CHRIS FRANTZ   D (P
DENNIS KEELEY   (P   MINGO LEWIS   PERC(P   PRAIRIE PRINCE   D (P   JESSE ROSSY   G (P
STEVE SCALES   SONGA(P   BUSTA JONES   B   (P   TIM WRIGHT   B (P   DUNYA YUSIN   V (P
SAMIRA TEWFIK   V   (R   MICHAEL BEINHORN SYN (R   MICHAEL BROOKS   G (R   AXEL GROS   G (R
BILL LASWELL   B   (R   JON HASSELL   TPT (R

E60   JOHN ENTWISTLE   E60

JOHN ENTWISTLE   B V K (ALL   (A) SMASH YOUR HEAD   1971 TRACK   UK   2406 005
GRAHAM DEACON   D PERC(CD   (A) SMASH YOUR HEAD   1971 MCA US 2024 GER POLYDOR 2480033
TONY ASHTON   PNO (D   (A) SMASH YOUR HEAD   (DIFF MIX) 1971 DECCA   US   79183
JIM RYAN   G   (D   (B) WHISTLE RHYMES   1972 TRACK   UK   2406 104
HOWIE CASEY   SAX (CD   (B) WHISTLE RHYMES   197 DECCA US79190 US MCA   2027
JIMMY McCULLOCH G   (B   (B) WHISTLE RHYMES   1972 POLYDOR   GER   2480 202
DAVE CASWELL   TPT (D   (C) RIGOR MORTIS SETS IN   1973 TRACK   UK   2406 106
JOHN MUMFORD   TROM (D   (C) RIGOR MORTIS SETS IN   1972 MCA   US   321
DICK PARRY   SAX (D   (D) MAD DOG   1975 TRACK   UK   TX   5114
DOREEN CHANTER   V   (D   (D) MAD DOG   197 MCA US 2129 GER NOVA 622212
BRYAN WILLIAMS   TROM K(CB   (D) MAD DOG   197 LONDON JAP LAX   1034
IRENE CHANTER   V   (D   (E) BACKTRACK 14 (THE OX)   1971 TRACK   UK   2407 014
MIKE WEDGEWOOD   G   (D   (F) TOO LATE THE HERO   1981 WEA UK 99179 US ATCO   38142
EDDIE JOBSON   K   (D
NEIL SHEPPARD   K   (B   JOHN MEALING   PNO (D   JUANITA FRANKLIN   V (D
ALAN ROSS   G   (C   LADYBIRDS   V   (C   ROD COOBES   D (B
PETER FRAMPTON   G   (B   JERRY SHIRLEY   D   (A   VIV STANSHALL   PERC(B
NEIL INNES   PERC((B   KEITH MOON   PERC (B   CYRANO   G (A
DAVE LAYSTON   G   (A   JOHN WEIDER   VON (D   JOE WALSH   G K SYN(F
JOE VITALE   D K FLT(F   BILLY NICHOLLS   V   (F

E60A   EON   E60A

                             EON   1976 SCEPTER   US   5122
                             EON   1977 ARIOLA   US   50038
E60B   EPITAPH   E60B

CLIFF JACKSON   G V (C   (A) EPITAPH   1971
KLAUS WALZ   G   (C   (B) STOP LOOK LISTEN   1972
BERND KOLBE   B   (C   (C) OUTSIDE THE LAW   1974 BRAIN 22 1311 BILLINGSGATE US 1009
BILLY SHAW   ORG (C   (D) SEE YOU IN ALASKA   1980 BRAIN NL 760 274
ACHIM WIELERT   D   (C   (E) LIVE   1981 BRAIN 50038
FRED KAZ   PNO (C

E61   EPISODE SIX   E61

SHEILA CARTER DIMMOCK K V (1234   (1) 1965 (2) 1965/7   (3) 1967   (4) 1967/8
GRAHAM CARTER DIMMOCK G V (1234
TONY LANDER   G V (1234   HARVEY SHIELD   D V (12   IAN GILLAN   V   (234
ANDY ROSS   V G (1   JOHN KERRISON   D   (3   MICK UNDERWOOD D   (4
ROGER GLOVER   B V (1234

E61A   PRESTON EPPS   E61A

                              BONGOLA   19   TOP RANK   US RM   349
                              BONGO ROCK   1959 ORIGINAL SOUND US   1001
                              SURFIN' BONGOS   19   ORIGINAL SOUND US 5009M+8872S
                              BONGO   1966 ORIGINAL SOUND US   8851
E61B   EPSILON   E61B

MICHAEL WINZKOWSKI G V (ABC   (A) EPSILON   1971 BELLAPHON   GER BLPS19070
HARTMUT PFANNMULLER D PERC(ABC (B) MOVE ON   197 BELLAPHON   GER BLPS19078
WALTER ORTEL   K   (AB   (C) EPSILON OFF   1974 PHILIPS   GER 6305 216
MICHAEL ERTL   B   (AB
CURT CRESS   D PERC(B   CHRISTIAN FELKE   FLT (B   HIENRICH MOHN   G   (C
JOHAN DAANSEN   G K V (C   PETE BENDER   V   (B   RAINER MARS   G V (B
E62   EQUALS   E62

DERVIN GORDON   V   (1234   UNEQUALLED   1967 PRESIDENT   PTL 1006
DAVE MARTIN   G   (CD   UNEQUALLED   196 LAURIE   US   2045
LINCOLN GORDON   G   (1234   EQUAL SENSATION   1968 PRESIDENT   PTL 1015
EDDIE GRANT   G   (1   SENSATIONAL EQUALS   1968 PRESIDENT   PTLS 1020
PAT LLOYD   G   (1234   EQUALS SUPREME   1968 PRESIDENT   PTLS 1025
JOHN HALL   D   (123   BABY COME BACK   1968 RCA   US LSP 4078
JIMMY HAYNES   G   (B   EQUALS STRIKE BACK   1969 PRESIDENT   PTLS 1030
NEIL McBAIN   D   (4   BEST OF THE EQUALS   1969 PRESIDENT   PTLS 1050
                              BEST OF THE EQUALS   1969 JOY PRESIDENT   JOYS 137
                              AT THE TOP   1970 PRESIDENT   PTLS 1038
(1) 1966   (2) 1971   EQUALS ROCK AROUND THE CLOCK 1974 PRESIDENT   PTLS 1054
(3) 19673 (4) 1975   GREATEST HITS   1974 M F P   UK MFP 50153
                              DOIN' THE 45's   1975 RHAPSODY   RHAS 9017
                              BORN YA   1976 MERCURY   UK 9109 601
                              MYSTIC SYNSTER   1978 ICE   UK ICEL 1002
E62A   ERGO SUM   E62A

LIONEL LEDISSEZ V   ((A) MEXICO   19   THELEME   FR 6332 500
JEAN GUERIN   K   (
MAX TOUAT   B   (ROLAND MEYNET   VLN (MICHEL LEONARDI G   (
BRUTUS   D   (
E62B   ROKY ERICKSON & THE ALIENS   E62B

ROKY ERICKSON   G V (AB   (A) ROKY ERICKSON & THE ALIENS 1980 CBS   UK   84463
DUANE ASLAKSEN   G   (AB   (B) THE EVIL ONE   1981 415   US   415A
BILL MILLER   AUTOHARP (AB
JEFF SUTTON   D   (B   BOBBY GORMAN   B   (STEVE BURGESS   B   (AB
BRIAN MARNELL   V   (A   FUZZ FURIOSO   D   (AB   LINK DAVIS   ORG (A
SCOTT MATTHEWS   D   (A   STU COOK   B   (B   ANDRE LEWIS   SYN K (AB
E62C   EQUATORS   E62C

                              (A) HOT   1981 STIFF   UK SEEZ 35

[190]

E63

JOACHIM H EHRIG	K SYN G D VLN (ABCD				
CARLOS BOTTICH	G	(C			
KASI KLASSEN	B V HCA(C				
VOLKER KAHRS	K	(C			
WOLFGANG JAEGER	B	(C			
GERD KUHN	G V	(C			
BERNHARD UHLEMANN	B V	(C			

EROC   E63

(A) EROC	1975	BRIAN	EURO	1069
(A) EROC	1977	BRAIN	UK	201 109
(B) ZWEI	1976	BRAIN		006 0007
(C) 3 (RECORDED 1969 79)	1979	BRAIN		0060 197

STEPFAN DANIELAK   G V   (C   EDD HUBER   B   (C

E63A

KING ERRISSON

KING ERRISSON	PERC	(
WITH		
PRESTON LOVE	WIND	(A
FREDDIE HILL	TPT	(A
JACK WALRATH	TPT	(A
GEORGE BOHANON	TROM	(A
CLARENCE McDONALD	PNO	(A
DAVID T WALKER	G	(A
CHARLES CLARK	V	(C
PAMELA VINCENT	V	(C

E63A

(A)THE KING ARRIVES	197	CANYON	US	7703
(B) MAGIC MAN	197	WESTBOUND	US	224
(C) L A BOUND	1977	WESTBOUND	US	WT 307
(C) L A BOUND	1977	WEA		50426

BENNY PARKS	D	(A	WASHINGTON RUCKER	D	(A	
JYMM YOUNG	PNO	(A	CALVIN KEYS	G	(A	
WILTON FELDER	B	(A	BILL UPCHURCH	B	(A	
CLEVELAND HORNE	V	(C	DONNA DAVIS	V	(C	
CYNTHIA DOUGLAS	V	(C	MAURICE SPEARS	TROM	(A	

ERUPTION   E64

(A) ERUPTION	1978	ATLANTIC US 50033 UK	K	50454
(B) LEAVE A LIGHT	1979	ATLANTIC	UK	K 50595
(C) FIGHT FIGHT FIGHT	1980	HANSA	NL	201 716
(D) BEST OF	1981	HANSA	NL	203 490

E64A

ESCORTS   E64A

(A) 3 DOWN 4 TO GO   1973   ALIGATOR   US   9106

E65

COKE ESCOVEDO

COKE ESCOVEDO	PERC	(ALL
WITH		
ERROL KNOWLES	V	(B
FRANK MERCURIO	K	(B
GLEN SYMMONDS	D	(B
JOE HENDERSON	SAX	(B

COKE ESCOVEDO   E65

(A) COKE	1975	MERCURY	US	SRM1 1041
(B) COMIN' AT YA	197	MERCURY	US	SRM1 1085
(C) DISCO FANTASY	1977	MERCURY	US	SRM1 1132

MARG PHILLIPS   B   (B   ABEL ZAPATE   G   (B
GABOR SZABO   G   (B

E66

RAYMOND VINCENT	VLN	(ABC
TONY MALISAN	D	(ABC
GINO MALISAN	B	(ABC
TONY HARRIS	VIOLA	(ABC
BRUNO LIBERT	K V	(AB
TIMOTHY KRAEMER	CELLO	(ABC
BRIGETTE DU DOIT	V	(ABC
KIM MOORE	V	(C

ESPERANTO ROCK ORCHESTRA   E66

(A) ESPERANTO ROCK ORCHESTRA	1973	A&M US 4399	UK	AMLH68175
(B) DANSE MACABRE	1974	A&M US 3624	UK	AMLH63624
(C) LAST TANGO	1975	A&M US 4524	UK	AMLH68294

KEITH CHRISTMAS	V	(B	GODFREY SALMON	VLN V	(ABC
GLEN SHORROCK	V	(ABC	BRIAN HOLLAWAY	G	(AB
JANICE SLATOR	V	(A	ROGER MEAKIN	G	(C

E66A

ESSENTIAL LOGIC   E66A

RICH TEA	(A	(A) BEAT RHYTHM NEWS	1979	ROUGH TRADE	UK	ROUGH 5
LORA LOGIC	(A			
ASHLEY BUFF	(A	MARK TURNER	(A	DAVE WRIGHT	(A

E67

SLEEPY JOHN ESTES   E67

SLEEPY JOHN ESTES	G V	(ALL
WITH		
HAMMIE NIXON	HCA	(ABDCI
YANK RACHELL	G	(BD
ED WILKENSON	B	(AD
RANSOM KNOWLING	B	(D
SUNNYLAND SLIM	PNO	(F
JIMMY DAWKINS	G	(F
ODIE PAYNE	D	(F
CAREY BELL	HCA	(F
EARL HOOKER	B	(F
JOE HARPER	B	(F

(A) LEGEND OF	1963	DELMARK		DL 603
(A) LEGEND OF	19	TRIO	JAP	PA 6212
(B) BROKE & HUNGRY	19	DELMARK		DL 608
(C) IN EUROPE	1966	DELMARK		DL 611
(D) BROWNSVILLE BLUES	1965	DELMARK		DL 613
(E) ELECTRIC SLEEP	19	DELMARK		DL 619
(F) 1929 1940	1967	FOLKWAYS		RF8
(G) DOWN SOUTH BLUES	1974	MCA		510 091
(H) SLEEPY JOHN ESTES	19	COLLECTORS CLASSICS		CC.24
(I) & HAMMIE NIXON	19	STORYVILLE		SLP 172

MIKE BLOOMFIELD   G   (B   JOHN'KNOCKY' PARKER   PNO   (A

E67A

ETERNITYS CHILDREN   E67A

(A) ETERNITYS CHILDREN   19   TOWER   US   ST 5223

E67B

ETHEL THE FROG   E67B

(A) ETHEL THE FROG   1980   EMI   UK   EMC 3329

E68

ETHIOPIANS   E68

(A) WOMAN CAPTURE MAN	1970	TROJAN		TBL 112
(B) SLAVE CALL	1977	THIRD WORLD		TWS 15

E69

CHRIS ETHRIDGE   E69

CHRIS ETHRIDGE	B V	(A
JOEL SCOTT HILL	G V	(A
JOHN BARBATA	D	(A

(A) L A GETAWAY   1971   ATLANTIC US 33357 UK K 40310

E69A

GUIGOU CHENEVIER	D	(AB1234
JEAN BAPTISTE MOULU	K	(1
MOREY	B	(1
CHRIS(EULALIE RYNAT)CHANET	SAX	(123A
FERDINAND RICHARD	B	(34AB
FRANCIS'PICHENETTE' GRAND	SAX	(B4
JEAN PIERRE GRASSET	G	(B

ETRON FOU LELOUBLAN   E69A

(A) BATELAGES	1976	GRATTE CIEL	FR	CIEL 2001
(B) LES TROIS FOUS PERDEGAGNENT	1978	9H17 RECORDS	FR	7001
(B) LES TROIS FOUS PERDEGAGNENT	197	TAPIOCA		TP 10020
(1) 1971 (2) 1972 (3) 1973 (4) 1977				
(C) LIVE IN AMERICA	1981			

MICHAEL GREZES   (B

E69B

BART LIBBY	K	(A
STEVE TRACY	G V	(A
GARY VIOLESTTI	B V	(A

EUPHONIOUS WAIL   E69B

(A) EUPHONIOUS WAIL   19   KAPP   US   3668

SUZANNA REY   V   (A   DOUG HOFFMANN   D   (A

E69C

EUPHORIA   E69C

(A) EUPHORIA   19   HERITAGE   US   HTS35.005

E69D

EUCLID BEACH BAND   E69D

(A) EUCLID BEACH BAND   1981   CLEVELAND INT   US 35619

CHRIS EVANS & DAVID HANSELMANN

```
    CHRIS EVANS              (A     (A) STONEHENGE                1980   WEA                      58092
    DAVE HANSELMANN          (A
```

E70

EVEN DOZEN JUG BAND

E70

```
    MARIA D'AMATO(MULDAUR) V (A     (A) EVEN DOZEN JUG BAND       1964   ELEKTRA        US  EKS  7246
    STEVE KATZ         G V   (A     (A) JUG BAND SONGS OF SOUTHERN MOUNTAINS  LEGACY  US  LEG  119
    PETE SIEGEL        G V   (A
    JOHN SEBASTIAN     G V   (A   JOSHUA RIFKIN      PNO    (A   STEFAN GROSSMAN   G V  (A
```

E71

BETTY EVERETT

E71

```
    BETTY EVERETT      V     (ALL  (A) THERE'LL COME A TIME      1974   MCA            UK  MCF  2676
    JOE SAMPLE         K     (B    (A) THERE'LL COME A TIME      197    UNI US 73048   UNLS 109
    GENE PAGE          K     (B    (B) HAPPY ENDINGS             1975   FANTASY            FT   524
    GARY COLEMAN       PERC  (B    (B) HAPPY ENDINGS             1975   FANTASY        US       9480
    RAY PARKER         G     (B    (C) ITS IN HIS KISS           19     JOY                JOYS 106
    DEAN PARKS         G     (B    (C) ITS IN HIS KISS           1976   DJM                DJM  22042
    MELVIN WAH WAH RAGIN G  (B     (D) THEY'RE DELICIOUS TOGETHER 197   JOYS 123       VEEJAY   1099
    DAVID T WALKER     G     (B    (E) BETTY EVERETT STARRING    197    TRADITION      US       2073
    SCOTT EDWARDS      B     (B    (F) & KETTY LESTER            19     GRAND PRIX     US       K 125
    KETTY LESTER       V     (F    ( ) LOVE RHYMES               1973   FANTASY                 9447
    BOBBYE HALL        PERC  (B    ( ) HOT TO HOLD               1980   CHARLY         UK  CRB  1006
    CAROLYN WILLIS     V     (B    ( ) BETTY EVERETT             1968   SUNSET                  5220
    ED GREENE          D     (B    ( ) TOGETHER                  19     BUDDAH         US       7507
    MARTI McCALL       V     (B    ( ) YOU'RE NO GOOD            19     VEEJAY                  1077
    EDNA WRIGHT        V     (B    ( ) VERY BEST OF              19     VEEJAY                  1122
    JACKIE WARD        V     (B    ( ) GETTING MIGHTY CROWDED    1980   CHARLY         US  CTD  1011
    JERRY BUTLER       V     (B
```

E71A

EVERGREEN BLUES BAND

E71A

```
    MANNY ESPARZA      V     (A    (A) 7 DO ELEVEN               19     MERCURY        US  SR   61157
    KEN WALTHER        TROM  (A
    RICK BARRIO        G     (A   SAM LOMBADO     D     (A   JOE McSWEYN        B   (A
    STEVE LAWRENCE     K     (A   TOM BRAY        TPT   (A
```

E72

EVERGREEN BLUESHOES

E72

```
    SKIP BATTIN        B V   (A    (A) THE BALLAD OF EVERGREEN BLUESHOES 1969  LONDON   UK  SHU  8399
    LANNY MATHIJSSEN   G     (A    (A) THE BALLAD OF EVERGREEN BLUESHOES 1969  AMOS     US       7002
    AL ROSENBERG       G     (A
    KEN KLEIST         K     (A   CHESTER McCRACKEN  D    (A
```

E72A

EVERY MOTHERS SON

E72A

```
    BRUCE MILNER       K     (A    (A) EVERY MOTHER'S SON        19     MGM            US  SE   4471
    DENNIS LARDEN V G BANJO  (A    (B) BACK                      1968   MGM            US  SE   4504
    LARRY LARDEN       G V   (A
    CHRISTOPHER AUGUSTINE  D (A   SCHUYLER LARSEN   B    (A   DON KERR           B   (
```

E73

DON EVERLY

E73

```
    DON EVERLY         G V   (ALL  (A) DON EVERLY                1971   ODE US 77005  A&M UK   2007
    JEAN ROUSSEL       B    (B     (B) SUNSET TOWERS             1974   ODE            US/UK    77023
    BUDDY EMMONS       STEEL(BC    (C) BROTHER JUKE BOX          1977   DJM            UK       20501
    PETE GAVIN         D PERC(B    (C) BROTHER JUKE BOX          1977   HICKORY        US       44003
    ALBERT LEE         G B K(B
    JOE OSBORN         B     (BC  RAY SMITH       G     (B   LANI GROVES     V     (B   JUNE WILLIAMS        V (B
    SHIRLEY BREWER     V     (B   STEPHANIE SPRUILL V   (B   JESSICA CLEAVES V     (B   CYNTHIA BULLENS      V (B
    REGGIE YOUNG       G     (C   JOHN LEE CHRISTOPER G (C   JERRY STEMBRIDGE G    (C   LOUIS NUNLEY         V (C
    BOBBY R WOOD       PNO   (C   MICHAEL LEECH     B   (C   KENNY MALONE    D     (C   LEA JANE BERINATI  V (C
    JANIE FRICKE       V     (C   GINGER HOLLADAY   V   (C   BOBBY HARDEN    V     (C   J ALAN MOORE      V K STR(C
    DAVID VANDERPOOL   STR(C       MARILYN SMITH    STR  (C   PAUL YANDELL    G     (C   TONY MIGLIORE      PNO(C
    RALPH GALLANT      D     (C   THOMAS MARTIN     G   (C   HARGUS ROBBINS  PNO   (C   JEANINE WALKER       V (C
    WILLIAM WRIGHT     V     (C   DOROTHY DILLARD       (C
```

E74

PHIL EVERLY

E74

```
    PHIL EVERLY        V G   (ALL  (A) STAR SPANGLED SPRINGER    1973   RCA            UK  SF   8370
    WITH                           (A) STAR SPANGLED SPRINGER    1973   RCA            US  APLI 0092
    WARREN ZEVON       G K   (AC   (B) NOTHINGS TOO GOOD FOR MY BABY 1974 PYE          UK  NSPL 18448
    JAMES BURTON       G     (A    (B) PHILS DINER               197    PYE            US       12104
    DUANE EDDY         G     (A    (C) MYSTIC LINE               1975   PYE            UK  NSPL 18473
    DONNIE LANIER      G     (A    (C) MYSTIC LINE               1975   PYE            US       12121
    NEIL LEVANG        G     (A    (D) PHIL EVERLY (LIVING ALONE) 1979  ELEKTRA        US       6E213
    JOE MORETTI        G     (B    (E) PHIL EVERLY               1983   CAPITOL        UK
    KENNY CLAYTON      PNO   (B
    SAMMY McCUE  G K STEEL(A       DEAN PARKS       G    (A   BUDDY EMMONS    STEEL (A   JAY DEE MANESS   STEEL(A
    REINIE PRESS       B     (A    LYLE RITZ        B    (A   JOHN GUERIN     D     (A   EARL PALMER        D (A
    VICTOR FELDMAN     PERC  (A    JIM HORN         SAX  (A   MARTIN KERSHAW  G     (A   FOGGY LITTLE       G (BC
    FRANK McDONALD     B     (C    RONNIE VERRELL   D    (C   CLEM CATTINI    D     (C   RICHARD BENNETT    G (A
    BARRY MORGAN       D     (B    TONY CAMPO       B    (B
```

E75

THE EVERLY BROTHERS

E75

```
    DON EVERLY         G V   (ALL  (EP)
    PHIL EVERLY        G V   (ALL  THE EVERLY BROTHERS           1958 CADENCE US CEP104 LONDON UK 1113
    WITH                           THE EVERLY BROTHERS 2         1958 CADENCE US CEP105 LONDON UK 1148
    CHET ATKINS        G     (*    THE EVERLY BROTHERS 3         1958 CADENCE US CEP107 LONDON UK 1149
    PAUL YANDELL       G     (*    THE EVERLY BROTHERS 4         1959 CADENCE US CEP111 LONDON UK 1174
    DALE SELLERS       G     (*    THE EVERLY BROTHERS 5         1960 CADENCE US CEP118 LONDON UK 1229
    PETE WADE          G     (*    THE EVERLY BROTHERS 6         1961 CADENCE US CEP121 LONDON UK 1311
    BOBBY THOMPSON   G BANJ(*      SONGS OUR DADDY TAUGHT US     1959 CADENCE US CEP108 LONDON UK 1195
    WELDON MYRICK      STEEL (*    SONGS OUR DADDY TAUGHT US     1959 CADENCE US CEP109 LONDON UK 1196
    HAROLD RUGG        STEEL (*    SONGS OUR DADDY TAUGHT US     1959 CADENCE US CEP110 LONDON UK 1197
    HARGUS ROBBINS     PNO   (*    ROCKIN WITH                   1960 CADENCE MINI LP US    CLLP 333
    DAVID BRIGGS       PNO   (*    ROCKIN WITH                   1960 CADENCE MINI LP US    CLLP 334
    STEVE SCHAFFER     B     (*    ESPECIALLY FOR YOU            1961 CADENCE US CEP1381/1 WB UK 6034
    RALPH GALLANT      ]  D  (*    ESPECIALLY FOR YOU            1961 CADENCE US CEP1381/2
    LARRY LONDIN                   ITS EVERLY TIME               1961 WB   ED 1381/1      WB UK 6056
    JOHNNY GIMBLE    FDL MAN(*     BOTH SIDES OF AN EVENING(FOR DANCING) 1963 WB  ED 1418/1   UK 6115
    DELANEY BRAMLETT   G V   (S    BOTH SIDES OF AN EVENING(FOR DREAMING)1964 WB  UK 6117
    JEFF KENT          G V   (S    BOTH SIDES OF AN EVENING(FOR FUN)  1965 WB  UK 6138
    DENNIS LINDE       G     (S    FOR EVERLY YOURS              1962 WB   UK 6049
        (CONTINUED)
```

GEOFF MULDAUR	G	(S
WAYNE PERKINS	G	(S
JOHN SEBASTIAN	G HCA V	(S
WADDY WACHTEL	G	(S
DANNY WEISS	G	(S
CLARENCE WHITE	G	(S
RY COODER	G	(S
BUDDY EMMONS	G	(S
JERRY McGEE	G	(S
SPOONER OLDHAN	K	(S
WARREN ZEVON	K	(S
JOHN BARBATA	D	(S
JIM GORDON	D	(S
RUSS KUNKEL	D	(S
GEORGE BOHANNON	HRNS	(S
TOMMY JOHNSON	HRNS	(S
JIMMY HASKEL	STR	(S
BONNIE BRAMLETT	V	(S
DAVID CROSBY	V	(S
DOUG LEBAHN	V	(S
GRAHAM NASH	V	(S
CHRIS ETHRIDGE	B	(S

Title		Year	Label	Country	Cat No		
(EP)EVERLY BROTHERS(MUSKRAT+2		19	WB	US	5501		
A DATE WITH VOL1		1963	WB	UK	6107		
A DATE WITH VOL2		1963	WB	UK	6109		
INSTANT PARTY 1		1963	WB	UK	6111		
INSTANT PARTY 2		1963	WB	UK	6113		
GREAT COUNTRY HITS 1		1964	WB	UK	6128		
GREAT COUNTRY HITS 2		1964	WB	UK	6131		
GREAT COUNTRY HITS 3		1964	WB	UK	6132		
THE PRICE OF LOVE		1965	WB	UK	WEP604		
ROCK'N'SOUL		1965	WB	UK	WEP608		
ROCK'N'SOUL		1965	WB	UK	WEP609		
LOVE IS STRANGE		1966	WB	UK	WEP610		
PEOPLE GET READY		1966	WB	UK	WEp612		
WHAT AM I LIVING FOR		1966	WB	UK	WEP618		
LEAVE MY GIRL ALONE		1967	WB	UK	WEP622		
SOMEBODY HELP ME		1967	WB	UK	WEP623		
THE EVERLY BROTHERS		1971	WB	UK	K16124		
THE EVERLY BROTHERS		1972	WB	UK	K 16209		
(LP)							
THE EVERLY BROTHERS		1958	LONDON	UK	HA A 2081		
THE EVERLY BROTHERS		1958	CADENCE	US	CLP 3003		
SONGS OUR DADDY TAUGHT US		1958	LONDON	UK	2150		
SONGS OUR DADDY TAUGHT US		1958	CADENCE	US	CLP 3016		
SONGS OUR DADDY TAUGHT US		1975	PHILIPS		6467 500		
FOLK SONGS BY THE EVERLY BROTHERS	RI	19	CADENCE	(M)CLP3059	(S) 25059		
THEIR BEST		1959	CADENCE	US	CLP 3025		
FABULOUS STYLE OF THE EVERLY BROTHERS		1960	CADENCE	US CLP3040	(S) 25040		
FABULOUS STYLE OF THE EVERLY BROTHERS		1960	LONDON	UK	2266		
ITS EVERLY TIME		1960	WB	US	1381		
ITS EVERLY TIME		1960	WB	UK(M)4012	(S) 8012		
A DATE WITH THE EVERLY BROTHERS		1960	WB	US	1395		
A DATE WITH THE EVERLY BROTHERS		1960	WB	UK(M)4028	(S) 8028		
BOTH SIDES OF AN EVENING		1961	WB	US	1418		
BOTH SIDES OF AN EVENING		1961	WB	UK(M)4052	(S) 8052		
INSTANT PARTY		1962	WB	US	1430		
INSTANT PARTY		1962	WB	UK(M)4061	(S) 8061		
GOLDEN HITS		1962	WB		1471		
GOLDEN HITS		1962	WB	UK	8108		
CATHYS CLOWN(GOLDEN HITS)		1980	PICKWICK		3030		
GOLDEN HITS		1971	WB	UK RI	1471		
GOLDEN HITS		1971	WB	UK RI K	46005		
CHRISTMAS WITH		1962	WB	US 1483	UK 8116		
CHRISTMAS WITH		1969	HARMONY	US 11350			
15 HITS		1962	CADENCE	US CLP3062	(S) 25062		
SING GREAT COUNTRY HITS		1963	WB	US 1513	UK 8138		
VERY BEST OF		1965	WB	US 1554	UK 8163		
VERY BEST OF		1972	WB		UK K46008		
ROCK'N'SOUL		1965	WB	US 1578	UK 8171		
ROCK'N'SOUL		1965	WB	RI	UK 1578		
GONE GONE GONE		1965	WB	US 1585	UK 8169		
GONE GONE GONE		1965	WB	RI	UK 1585		
GONE GONE GONE		1970	VALIANT	UK VS	109		
BEAT & SOUL		1965	WB	US 1605	UK 1605		
IN OUR IMAGE		1965	WB	US 1620	UK 1620		
TWO YANKS IN ENGLAND		1965	WB	US 1646	UK 1646		
HIT SOUNDS OF		1967	WB	us 1676	UK 1676		
THE EVERLY BROTHERS SING		1967	WB	US 1708	UK 1708		
ROOTS		1968	WB	US 1752	UK 1752		
ROOTS		1971	WB	UK RI	K 46128		
ROOTS		1973	WB	UK RI	K36002		
WAKE UP LITTLE SUSIE		1969	HARMONY	US	11304		
CHAINED TO A MEMORY		1970	HARMONY	US	11388		
THE EVERLY BROTHERS SHOW	(DBL)	1970	WB	US 1858	UK 1858		
THE EVERLY BROTHERS SHOW	(DBL)	1971	WB	UK RI	K 66003		
MOST BEAUTIFUL SONGS		1973	WB	UK	66016		
ORIGINAL GREATEST HITS	(DBL)	1970	BARNABY	US 6006	UK CBS 66255		
END OF AN ERA	(DBL)	1970	BARNABY	US 30260	UK CBS 66259		
(S) STORIES WE COULD TELL		1972	RCA	US 4620	UK SF 8270		
(S) STORIES WE COULD TELL		1974	RCA	INT 1474			
(S) THE EVERLY BROTHERS		1975	CAMDEN	UK	1142		
HISTORY OF THE EVERLY BROTHERS		1972	BARNABY	US	15008		
(*)PASS THE CHICKEN		1973	RCA	US 4781	UK SF 8332		
(*)EXCITING EVERLY BROS(PASS THE CHICKEN)		1975	CAMDEN RI	CDS	1136		
FABULOUS 50s TREASURY		1974	JANUS		6310 300		
EVERLYS		1975	RCA		7507		
WALK RIGHT BACK		1975	WB	UK	K 56168		
BYE BYE EVERLYS		1975	MIDI		66032		
NEW ALBUM		1977	WB	UK	K 56415		
EVERLY BROTHERS		197	GTE	US	GTR 7702		
ORIGINAL HITS		197	MUSIDISC		256		
20 SUPERHITS		197	TELDEC	GERM	AP6 23484		
LIVING LEGENDS		1977	WARWICK	UK	WW 5027		
GREATEST HITS 1		1978	BARNBY	US	4004		
GREATEST HITS 2		1978	BARNABY	US	4005		
GREATEST HITS 3		1978	BARNABY	US	4006		
GREATEST HITS COLLECTION DBL		1979	PICKWICK	US	063		
THE EVERLY BROTHERS	(PROFILE)	19	TELDEC	GER	6 24003		
ROCK'N'ROLL FOREVER		1981	WB	UK	26003		
THE EVERLY BROTHERS		1981	WB	UK	26010		

EVERYONE

```
    ANDY ROBERTS   G V VLN (A      (A) EVERYONE                      1971   B&C          UK   CAS  1028
    BOB SARGEANT G V K HCA(A        (A) ANDY ROBERT WITH EVERYONE    1971   AMPEX        US        10117
    JOHN PEARSON        D(A
    DAVE RICHARDS    VB K (A    JOHN PORTER    G
```
E76A   EXCITERS   E76A
```
    BRENDA REID      V  (          (A) TELL HIM               19   UA US MONO 3264  US STER  6264
    CAROL JOHNSON    V  (          (B) EXCITERS               19   ROULETTE US               25326
    LILIAN WALKER    V  (          (C) CAVIAR & CHITLINS      19   RCA      US          LSP  4211
    HERBERT ROONEY   V  (          (D) BLACK BEAUTY           19   TODAY    US          TLP  1001
```
E76B   EX   E76B
```
                                   (A) DISTURBING DOMESTIC PEACE   1980   VERRECORD      NL     005
```
E76C   EXHIBIT A   E76C
```
                                   (A) NO ELEPHANTS THIS SIDE OF WATFORD GAP(EP)19 IRRELEVANT WAMBAT
```
E77   EXILE   E77
```
    J P PENNINGTON  G V (BCD       (A) EXILE                  1973   WOODEN NICKEL US          1020
    JIMMY STOKEY    V   (BC        (B) MIXED EMOTIONS         1978   RAK UK SRAK 533 WB US     3205
    BUZZ CORNELISON K V (BC        (C) ALL THERE IS           1979   RAK UK SRAK 535 WB US     3323
    MARLON HARGIS   K V (BCD       (D) STAGE PASS             1979   RCA US      3087
    SONNY LEMAIRE   B V (BCD       (E) DONT LEAVE ME THIS WAY 1981   WB  US      3437
    STEVE GOETMAN   D   (BCD       (F) HEART & SOUL           1982   WB  US      3588
    SUE RICHMAN     V   (C
    RUSTY BUCHANAN  V  (C    LYNDA LAWLEY  V    (C    ANDREA ROBINSON V   (B  DANNY WILLIAMS   V B(B
    LEY TAYLOR     G V (D    MACK GRAY K V      (D
```
E77A   EXILED   E77A
```
    SVOLTA          V   (A         (A) EXILED                 1980   RCA             PL 25297
    SEICO BROTHERS  V   (A
    LESLEY DUNCAN   V   (A   TERRY CASSIDY   V  (A   DAN McCAFFERTY  V (A   FRANCIS ROSSI  V  (A
    BERNIE FROST    V   (A   COLIN BLUNSTONE V  (A   NIGEL MARTINEZ  D (A   STUART ELLIOTT D  (A
    PAUL THOMPSON   D   (A   DELISLE HARPER  B  (A   JOHN GIBLIN     B (A   ANDY PASK      B  (A
    JOE JAMMER      G   (A   PAUL KEOGH      G  (A   RAY RUSSELL     G (A   MITCH DALTON   G  (A
    LAWRENCE JUBER  C   (A   STEVE COE       K  (A   DAVE LAWSON     K (A   ROBIN LUMLEY   K  (A
    CHRIS PARREN    K   (A   CRAIG PRUESS    K  (A   TOMMY EYRE      K (A   LUIS JARDIM PERC(A
    JOHN EARLE     SAX  (A   ROBERT POWELL NARRATIVE(A
```
E77B   EXMAGMA   E77B
```
    FRED BRACEFUL  D PERC(A        (A) GOLDBALL               1974   DISJUUCTA      FR  000 00009
    ANDY GOLDNER   G B SAX(A
    THOMAS BALLUFF K TPT WIND(A
```
E77C   EXPERIMENTS WITH ICE   E77C
```
    DAVID JIGGENS   K   (A         (A) EXPERIMENTS WITH ICE   1981   UNITED DARIES  UK     EX001
    ROBIN KNAPP     D   (A
    NICKY PATRIACHAEOS G V SYN(A   PHIL ROSE        B  (A
```
E77D   EXPRESSO   E77D
```
                                   (A) PROMISES & TIES        1981   WEA                  58303
```
E77E   EXPLOITED   E77E
```
    WATTIE          V   (A         (A) PUNKS NOT DEAD         1981   SECRET       UK   SEC  1
    BIG JOHN       G V  (A
    GARY           B V  (A   DRU STIX       D V  (A   CAROLE       V (A           V      (A
```
E78   EXUMA   E78
```
    EXUMA         G V PERC(ALL     (A) EXUMA                  19     BARCLAY           920    208
    YOGI BEN MAUSEL V PERC   (     ( ) EXUMA                  1973   BARCLAY           920    291
    O'NEIL GUIMUNGIE   SAX V (     ( ) EXUMA                  19     VERTIGO          6338   018
    KESTER SMITH    D    (         ( ) EXUMA II               1973   MERCURY      US        61314
    BARON SAMEDI    PERC(          ( ) SNAKE                  19     POLYDOR 2319016 KAMA SUT US 2052
    R WISE          G    (         ( ) REINCARNATION          19     POLYDOR          2319  026
    KENNY AARONSON  D    (         ( ) REINCARNATION          1973   KAMA SUTRA   US        2062
    PAUL CARPENTER  K    (         ( ) LIFE                   1974   KAMA SUTRA   US        2074
    F GUMBS         D    (         ( ) THE OBEAH MAN          19     MERCURY      US       61265
                                   ( ) DO WAH NANNY           1973   KAMA SUTRA   US        2040
                                   ( ) PENNY SAUSAGE          1980   INAGUA       US         999
```
E78A   EYELESS IN GAZA   E78A
```
    MARTYN BATES  V ALL   (AB      (A) PHOTOGRAPHS AS MEMORIES 1980  CHERRY RED    UK   BRED 13
    PETE BECKER   V ALL   (AB      (A) CAUGHT IN THE FLUX     1981   CHERRY RED    UK   BRED 18
```
E78B   TIM EYERMANN & EAST COAST OFFERING   E78B
```
    TIM EYERMANN   WIND   (A       (A) ALOHA                  1980   INNER CITY    US        1095
    PHIL McCUSKER  G     (A
    WADE MATTHEWS  B     (A    BRUCE HARRISON K   (A    JOHN MOLO   D (A   LOUIS SCHERR   K  (A
```
E79   EYES   E79
```
    NEIL MERRYWEATHER B V (A       (A) RADICAL GENES          1980   RCA           NL       44019
    KEN SPENCE     G SAX  (A
    CEES MEERMAN   D     (A    MICHAEL WILLIS   G  (A
```
E80   EYES OF BLUE   E80
```
    GARY PICKFORD HOPKINS V (B1    (A) CROSSROADS OF TIME     1968   MERCURY US 61184  UK 20134
    JOHN WEATHERS    F    (B       (A) CROSSROADS OF TIME     1968   MERCURY NL           134 087
    RITCHIE FRANCIS  G    (B1      (B) IN FIELDS OF ARDATH    1969   MERCURY US 61220  UK 20164
    WYNDHAM REES     D    (1       (B) IN FIELDS OF ARDATH    1969   MERCURY NL           134 224
    R BENNETT        B    (B       (1) 1967
    PHIL RYAN        K    (AB1
    RAY WILLIAMS     B    (1
```
FI   F B I   F1
```
    BONNIE WILKENSON  V   (A       (A) F B I                  1976   GOODEARTH     UK   GDS 802
    ROOT JACKSON      V   (A
    JOANE BLACK       V   (A    HERSCHEL HOLDER    PERC  (A  LLOYD SMITH    HRNS (A
```
F1A   F M   F1A
```
    BEN MINK      VLN G  V(CD       (A) F M                    19
    MARTIN DEKER   D     (BCD       (B) BLACL NOISE           1979   PASSPORT US 7007 NL WEA 58198
    CAMERON HAWKINS V SYN B(D       (C) SURVEILLANCE          1980   PASSPORT US 2001 NL WEA 58197
    NASH THE SLASH  VLN V (B        (D) CITY OF FEAR          1981   PASSPORT US 6004 UK LOGO 1031
```

```
        DUTCH SCHULTZ      D   (A     (A) F WORD LIKE IT OR NOT      1978   PBS              US      101
        RICK L RICK        V   (A
        DIM WANKER         G   (A     STEVE EFFETE        B     (A
F2A                                   FABIAN                                    F2A
        FABIAN             V   (ALL   ( ) HOLD THAT TIGER          19     CHANCELLOR       US      5003
                                      ( ) FABULOUS FABIAN          19     CHANCELLOR       US      5005
                                      ( ) GOOD OLD SUMMERTIME      19     CHANCELLOR       US      5012
                                      ( ) ROCKIN' HOT             19     CHANCELLOR       US      5019
                                      ( ) 16 GREATEST HITS        19     CHANCELLOR       US      5024
                                      ( ) 16 GREATEST HITS        1974   ABC              US      806
                                      ( ) 16 GREATEST HITS        19     TRIP             US      TOP 1620
                                      ( ) VERY BEST OF FABIAN     19     UA               US      UA LA 449
                                      ( ) FACADE                  19     CHANCELLOR       US      68902
                                      ( ) FABIAN                  1974   EMI              NL      95031
F2B                                   FABLE                                     F2B
        PETER GAOLBY   G V MAND  (A   (A) FABLE                    1973   MAGNET           UK      MAG 5002
        PAUL ROBBINS     K B V (A
        PETER MACKIE     B V   (A     KEITH TULLY        D PERC(A    MAC BAILEY          G     (A
F3                                    FABULOUS POODLES                          F3
        TONY DE MEUR       G V (ABCD  (A) FABULOUS POODLES         1977   PYE              UK      NSPL18530
        BOBBY VALENTINO    VLN (ABCD  (B) UNSUITABLE               1978   PYE              UK      NSPH  25
        RICHIE ROBERTSON   B   (ABCD  (C) THINK PINK               1979   BLUEPRINT        UK      BLUP 5001
        CHRIS SKORNIA      K   (C     (C) THINK PINK               1979   EPIC             US      36256
        BRYN B BURROWS     D   (ABCD  (D) MIRROR STARS             1979   EPIC             US      35666
        JOHN PARSONS           (C
        IAN TRIMMER        SAX (C     MARY ANN MORGENTHALER V    (C
F3A                                   FABULOUS RHINESTONES                      F3A
        MARTY GREBB SAX K V G  (AB    (A) THE FABULOUS RHINESTONES 1972  JUST SUNSHINE US      JS1
        HARVEY BROOKS      B V (ABC   (B) FREEWHEELIN'             1973   JUST SUNSHINE US      JSS9
        KAL DAVID        G V  (ABC    (C) THE RHINESTONES          1975   JUST SUNSHINE US
        TERRY EATON        SAX (B
        GREG THOMAS        D   (AB    BOB LEINBACK       K HRNS (C   ARTIE FUNARO        G V (C
        DAVE SANBORN       SAX (B     REINOL ISAAC ANDINO CONGA (AB  RANDY BRECKER       HRNS (B
        MICHAEL BRECKER    HRNS (B    BARRY ROGERS       TROM    (B   DENNIS WHITTED      D   (B
        JEAN'TOOTS' THIELEMANS HCA(B  TITO PUENTE        PERC    (B   KAT McCORD          V   (B
        ERIC PARKER        D   (C
F3B                                   FABULOUS THUNDERBIRDS                     F3B
        JIMMY VAUGHAN      G   (ABCD  (A) FABULOUS THUNDERBIRDS    1979   CHRYSALIS        UK      CHR 1250
        DENNY BRUCE        PROD (ABC  (A) FABULOUS THUNDERBIRDS    1979   TAKOMA           US      7068
        KIM WILSON       V HCA (ABCD  (B) WHATS THE WORD           1980   CHRYSALIS        UK US CHR 1287
        KEITH FERGUSON     B   (ABCD  (C) BUTT ROCKIN             1981   CHRYSALIS        UK US CHR 1319
        NICK LOWE          PROD (D    (D) T BIRD RHYTHM            1982   CHRYSALIS        UK US CHR 1395
        MIKE BUCK          D   (AB
        FRAN CHRISTINA     D PERC(BC  AL COPLEY          PNO     (C   DOUG JAMES          SAX (C
        GREG PICOLO        SAX (C     ANSON FUNDERBURGH  G       (C
F3C                                   FACE DANCER                               F3C
        SCOTT McGINN     B SYN V(AB   (A) THIS WORLD              1979   CAPITOL          EST 11934
        JEFF ADAMS         G   (AB    (B) ABOUT FACE              1980   CAPITOL          EST 12082
        BILLY TRAINOR      D   (AB
        MICHAEL MILSAP     K V (B     CAREY KRESS             (A    DAVID UTTER         G V (A
F4                                    FACES                                     F4
        RONNIE LANE        B   (ABCDE (A) FIRST STEP              1970   WB  US           UK K 46053
        IAN MACLAGAN       K   (ABCDE (B) LONG PLAYER             1971   WB  US  1892     UK K 46064
        KENNY JONES        D   (ABCDE (C) A NODS AS GOOD AS A WINK 1972  WB  US  2574     UK K 56006
        ROD STEWART        V   (ABCDE (D) OOH LA LA               1973   WB  US  2665     UK K 56011
        RON WOOD           G   (ABCDE (E) OVERTURE /COAST TO COAST 1974 MERCURY US 1 697  UK 9100 011
        TETSU YAMAUCHI     B   (E     (AB) FIRST STEP/LONG PLAYER 1977   WB               UK K 66027
        BOBBY KEYS         SAX (B     ( ) BEST OF                 1977   RIVA             UK RVLP.3
        HARRY BECKETT      TPT (B     ( ) SNAKES & LADDERS (BEST OF) 1976 WB   US2897      UK K 56172
                                      ( ) ROD STEWART & THE FACES 19     SPRINGBOARD      US      4030
                                      (EP) STAY WITH ME           1977   RIVA             RIVA8
F4A                                   FAD GADGET                                F4A
        FAD GADGET       V SYN WIND(A (A) FIRESIDE FAVOURITES     1980   MUTE             UK  STUMM  3
        ERIC RADCLIFFE   G B BAN  (AB (B) INCONTINENT             1981   MUTE UK STUMM 6  GER 146802
        JOHN FRYER         PERC  (AB
        NICK CASH        D V ACC  (AB DANIEL MILLER      PERC SYN (AB  PHIL WAUQUAIRE      B     (A
        PETER BAHNER       G B   (B   DAVID SIMMONDS     PER SYN V (B   BIJI FROST          V     (B
        ANNE CLIFT         V     (B   ROBERT GOTOBED             D  (B
F4B                                   FACTORY                                   F4B
        YVES MATRAT        V     (AB  (A) BLACK STAMP             1977   COBRA            FR      37010
        DENIS FUSI         D     (A   (B) CACHE TA JOIE           1979   PATHE            FR      14828
        LAHMI "PUCE" SAIBI G     (AB
        FOURMI             B     (B   BAPS               D       (A   RIDO BAYONNE        B PERC (A
        HERVE DUCLOS       K     (B   ALAIN GUILLARD            (B    YVES GUILLARD           (B
        ARIANE CADDIER     V     (B   ELISABETH WIENER   V      (B
F4C                                   DONALD FAGEN                              F4C
        DONALD FAGEN     K V HRNS(A   (A) THE NIGHTFLY            1982   WB               UK      923696
        GREG PHILLINGANES K SYN(A
        ROB MOUNSEY    SYN HEN(A  ROGER NICHOLS    PERC (A   JEFF PORCARO     D  (A   DEAN PARKS         G(A
        CHUCK RAINEY     B   (A   MICHAEL OMARTIAN K   (A   MARCUS MILLER    B  (A   ABE LABORIEL       B  (A
        STEVE JORDON     D   (A   LESLIE MILLER    V   (A   RANDY BRECKER    TPT(A   MICHAEL BRECKER    SAX (A
        DAVE BARGERON    TROM (A   ZACK SANDERS     V   (A   GORDON GRODY     V  (A   DAVE TOFANI       SAX (A
        VALERIE SIMPSON  V   (A   LARRY CARLTON    G   (A   ED GREEN         D  (A   STEVE KAHN        G   (A
        WILL LEE         B   (A   GARY KATZ        PROD (A   HUGH McCRACKEN   G HCA(A  STARZ VANDERLOCKET PERC(A
        ANTHONY JACKSON  B   (A   RON CUBER        SAX (A   FRANK FLOYD      V  (A   RICK DERRINGER    G   (A
F4D                                   RICHARD FAGAN                             F4D
        RICHARD FAGAN        (A      (A) RICHARD FAGAN            1980   MERCURY          US      3811
```

JOHN FAHEY	G	(ALL	JOHN FAHEY	1966	US VANGUARD VSD 79259					
WITH			TRANSFIGURATION OF BLIND JOE DEATH	1967	US TAKOMA	9015	UK 19	/ SONET SNTF 607		
JAY FERGUSON	K	(Y	TRANSFIGURATION OF BLIND JOE DEATH	1970	US TAKOMA	1002	UK 19	SONET SNTF 774		
MARK ANDES	B	(Y	TRANSFIGURATION OF BLIND JOE DEATH	19	US RIVER	RB1		UK TRANSATLANTIC TRA173		
MATT ANDES	G	(Y	DEATH CHANTS & BREAKDOWNS	1968	US TAKOMA	1003	UK 1969 SONET SNTF 608			
KEVIN KELLEY	D	(Y	(Y)YELLOW PRINCESS	1968	US VANGUARD VSD 79293		UK 19	SVRL 19033		
WOODROW MANN	G	(O	REQUIA	19	VANGUARD		UK	SVRL 19055		
JACK FEIERMAN	TPT	V(O	DANCE OF DEATH	196	US TAKOMA	1004				
ALLAN REUSS	G BANJO(O		GREAT SAN BERNADINO BIRTHDAY PARTY	196	US TAKOMA	1008				
JOE DARENSBOURG	CLAR(O		DAYS HAVE GONE BY	1967	US TAKOMA	1014				
IRA WESTLEY	TUBA(O		VOICE OF THE TURTLE	1968	US TAKOMA	1019				
JOHN ROTELLA	SAX(O		NEW POSSIBILITY	19	US TAKOMA	1020				
BRITT WOODMAN	TROM(O		FARE FORWARD VOYAGERS	1974	US TAKOMA	1035	UK 1974 SONET SNTF 656			
DICK CARY	PNO (O		FAHEY, LEO KOTTKE , PETER LANG	19	US TAKOMA	1040	UK 197 SONET SNTF 675			
NICK FATOOL	D (O		(O)OLD FASHIONED LOVE	1975	US TAKOMA	1043	UK 1975 SONET SNTF 688			
BOBBY BRUCE	V VLN(O		CHRISTMAS ALBUM	19	US TAKOMA	1045	UK 1976 SONET SNTF 702			
			BEST OF 1959 77	1977	US TAKOMA	1058	UK 197 SONET SNTF 733			
			OF RIVERS & RELIGION	1972	US REPRISE	2089	UK 197 REPRISE K 44213			
			AFTER THE BALL	1973	US REPRISE	2145	UK 197 REPRISE K 44246			
			FAHEY,KELLY ,MANN,MILLER,SEIDLER	19	US BLUE GOOSE BG 2009					
			ESSENTIAL JOHN FAHEY	1979	VANGUARD VSD 55/56					
			VISITS WASHONGTON DC	1980	US TAKOMA	7069				
			YES JESUS LOVES ME	1980	US TAKOMA	7085				
			LIVE IN TASMANIA	1981	US TAKOMA	7089	UK	SONET SNTF 861		

PETER DALTREY	V K (A	(A) FROM HOME TO HOME	1970	VERTIGO UK 6360 001	
EDDY PUMER	V K G(A				
STEVE CLARK	B FLT(A	DAN BRIDGMAN V D (A	DVAID SYMONDS	PROD (A	

(A) 1966(ETHNIC SHUFFLE ORCH)	(1) FAIRPORT CONVENTION	1968	POLYDOR	UK	583	035
(B) 1967 SPRING (1 GIG)	(1) FAIRPORT CONVENTION	1968	COTILLION	US	SD	9024
(C) 1967 JULY NOV	(1) FAIRPORT CONVENTION	1975	POLYDOR RI	UK	2384	047
(D) 1967 NOV/MAY 1968	(1) FAIRPORT CONVENTION	197	POLYDOR	EURO	2383	355
(E) 1968 MAY/FEB 1969	(1) FAIRPORT CONVENTION	197	POLYDOR	NL	2485	211
(F) 1969 FEB/JUNE 1969	(2) WHAT WE DID ON OUR HOLIDAYS	1969	ISLAND	UK	ILPS 9092	
MOTORWAY ACCIDENT KILLED	(2) WHAT WE DID ON OUR HOLIDAYS	19	ARIOLA		88 183XAT	
MARTIN LAMBLE.	(2) FAIRPORT CONVENTION	1969	A&M	US		4185
(G) 1969 SEPT/NOV	(3) UNHALFBRICKING	1969	ISLAND	UK	ILPS 9102	
(H) 1969 DEC/JAN1971	(3) UNHALFBRICKING	1976	ISLAND	IT		8088
(i) 1971 JAN/DEC	(3) UNHALFBRICKING	19	A&M	US		4206
(J) 1971 DEC RAINBOW GIG	(4) LIEGE AND LIEF	1969	ISLAND	UK	ILPS 9115	
(K) 1971 DEC/FEB 1972	(4) LIEGE AND LIEF	19	A&M	US		4257
(L) 1972 FEB /JUNE	(5) FULL HOUSE	1970	ISLAND	UK	ILPS 9130	
(M) 1972 JUNE/AUTUMN. RECORDED	(5) FULL HOUSE	1970	A&M	US		4265
MANOR ALBUM NOT RELEASED.	(6) ANGEL DELIGHT	1971	ISLAND	UK	ILPS 9162	
(N) 1972 AUTUMN/SUMMER 1973	(6) ANGEL DELIGHT	1976	ISLAND	IT		8338
(O) 1973 SUMMER/MARCH 1974	(6) ANGEL DELIGHT	1971	A&M	US		4319
(P) 1974 MARCH/ JAN 1975	(7) BABBACOMBE LEE	1971	ISLAND	UK	ILPS 9176	
(Q) 1975 JAN/FEB	(7) BABBACOMBE LEE	1971	A&M	US		4333
(R) 1975 FEB /DEC	(7) BABBACOMBE LEE	1980	ISALND	NL	200	572
(S) 1976 JAN/FEB	(8) HISTORY OF (DBL)	1972	ISLAND	UK		ICD 4
(T) 1976 MARCH	(8) HISTORY OF (DBL)	197	PHONOGRAM	EURO	6405	004
(U) 1976 MARCH	(9) ROSIE	1973	ISLAND	UK	ILPS 9208	
(V) 1976 APRIL/SEPT. SHORTENED	(9) ROSIE	197	ISLAND	GER		88106
NAME TO 'FAIRPORT'.	(9) ROSIE	1973	A&M	US		4386
(W) 1976 SEPT/AUG 1979 RESTORED	(10) FAIRPORT NINE	1973	ISLAND	UK	ILPS 9246	
NAME TO 'FAIRPORT CONVENTION'	(10) FAIRPORT NINE	1973	A&M	US		4407
(X) 1979 AUG GROUP ABANDONED	(10) FAIRPORT NINE	197	A&M	US		3603
APART FROM ANNUAL REUNIONS	(11) FAIRPORT LIVE A MOVEABLE FEAST	1974	ISLAND US	UK	ILPS 9285	
	(12) RISING FOR THE MOON	1975	ISLAND US	UK	ILPS 9313	
	(13) FAIRPORT CONVENTION(TOUR SAMPLER)1975	ISLAND		UK		ISS2
N.B. (13) MARKED	(14) GOTTLE O' GEER	1976	ISLAND	UK	ILPS 9389	
"FOR RADIO USE ONLY" ALSO USED	(14) GOTTLE O' GEER	1976	PHONOGRAM	EURO	9101	665
AS A PRIZE IN N.M.E. COMPETITION.	(15) CHRONICLES	1976	A&M	US		3530
	(16) LIVE AT L A TROUBADOUR	1976	ISLAND	UK	HELP	28
	(17) HEYDAY (CASSETTE ONLY)	1976				
	(18) BONNY BUNCH OF ROSES	1977	VERTIGO	UK	9102	015
	(18) BONNY BUNCH OF ROSES	1977	PHONOGRAM	EURO	6360	152
	(19) TIPPLERS TALES	1978	VERTIGG	UK	9102	022
	(20) FAREWELL FAREWELL	1979	SIMONS	UK	GAMA 1	
	(20) FAREWELL FAREWELL	1979	WOODWORM	UK	BEAR22	

DAVE SWARBRICK VLN V MAN (GHiJKLMNOPQRSTUVWX3.4.5.6.7.8.9.10.11.12.13.14.15.16.17.18.19.20.	
DAVE PEGG B V (HiJKLMNOPQRSTUVWX 5.6.7.8.9.10.11.12.13.14.15.16.17.18.19.20.	
SIMON NICOL V G (ABCDEFGHiJWX 1.2.3.4.5.6.7.8.13.14.15.16.17.18.19.20. TONY COX PNO (15.	
DAVE MATTACKS D (GHiJKOPN 4.5.6.7.8.9.10.11.12.13.15.16. PAT DONALDSON B (15.	
RICHARD THOMPSON V G(ABCDEFGHJ 1.2.3.4.5.8.9.13.15.16.17. IAN WHITEMAN PNO (15.	
ASHLEY HUTCHINGS B V (ABCDEFG 1.2.3.4.8.13.15.17. IAN WILSON V (14.	
SANDY DENNY V G PNO(EFGJPQR 2.3.4.8.9.11.12.13.15.17. ERIC JOHNS G (14.	
JERRY DONAHUE G V(NOPQR 9.10.11.12.13.15. HENRY LOWTHER HRNS (14.	
TREVOR LUCAS V G PERC (NOPQR 3.8.9.10.11.12.13.15. JIMMY JEWELL SAX (14.	
BRUCE ROWLAND D (RSTUVWX 12.13.14.18.19.20. NICK JUDD PNO (14.	
MARTIN LAMBLE D VLN (CDEF 1.2.3.8.13.15.17. GRAHAM LYLE V G ACC (14	
IAN MATTHEWS V PERC(DE 1.2.3.8.13.17. MARTIN CARTHY G (14.	
JUDY DYBLE V AUTOHARP (BCD1 CLARE LOWTHER CELLO(1.2.8.	
IAN FRATER D (B BENNY GALLAGHER V G ACC (14. DAN AR BRAS G (V	
MARC ELLINGTON V (3 ROGER BURRIDGE V VLN (TUV 14. PAUL WARREN D (Q	
A L LLOYD V (7 TIMI DONALD D (9 GERRY CONWAY D (9.13.15.	
PHILIP STIRLING WALL V (7 ROGER HILL G V (KL TOM FARNELL D (LM	
DAVID REA V G BANJO (M LINDA THOMPSON V (9.13.15. RALPH McTELL G (9	
BOB BRADY K V (UV 14.	

ANDY FAIRWEATHER LOW	G V	(ALL	(A) BEGINNING FROM AN END(FAIRWEATHER	1971	NEON		UK US	NE1
WITH			(B) SPIDER JIVING	1974	A&M US 3646		UK	AMLH68263
HENRY McCULLOUGH	G	(B	(C) LA BOOGA ROOGA	1975	A&M US 4542		UK	AMLH68328
MARK NAFTALIN	K	(B	(D) BE BOP & HOLLA	1976	A&M US 4602		UK	AMLH64602
MICK WEAVER	K	(BD	(E) ANDY FAIRWEATHER LOW (COMP)	1976	RCA			HY 1033
BLUE WEAVER	K	(A	(F) MEGA SHEBANG	1980	WB US BSK3450		UK	K 56820
CHRISSY STEWART	B	(B						

DENNY SEIWELL	D	(B	JOHN KAHN	G	(B	JIMMY JEWELL	SAX (C	CHARLIE McCOY	HCA (B				
WELDON MYRICK	STEEL(B		BUDDY SPICHER	FDL	(B	VASSAR CLEMENTS	FDL (B	BOBBY THOMPSON	BANJ(B				
LEA JANE BERINATI	V	(B	MEMPHIS HORNS		(B	JOHN DAVID	B V (CDF	B J COLE	STEEL (ACD				
GERRY RAFFERTY	V	(C	JOE EGAN	V	(C	EDDIE THORNTON	TPT (CD	STEVE GREGORY	HRNS(CDF				
BUD BEADLE	SAX (CDF		NEIL JONES	G	(A	CLIVE TAYLOR	B (A	GEORGIE FAME	K (CD				
BENNY GALLAGHER	V	(C	GRAHAM LYLE	V	(C	DAVE MATTACKS	D (C	BRUCE ROWLAND	D (C				
BERNIE LEADON	G	(CD	DOREEN CHANTER	V	(C	IRENE CHANTER	V (C	BARRY ST JOHN	V (C				
LIZA STRIKE	V	(C	JOANNE WILLIAMS	V	(C	HENRY SPINETTI	D (DF	KENNY BUTTREY	D (B				
MARY HOLLADAY	V	(B	GINGER HOLLADAY	V	(B	DIANE DAVIDSON	V (B	DENNIS BRYON	D (A				
JULIAN DIGGLE	PERC(D		RABBIT BUNDRICK	K	(CD	KENNY JONES	D (CD	TUNJI OMOSHETI	PERC(D				
MALCOLM GRIFFITHS	TROM(D		MARTIN DROVER	TPT	(D	GLYN JOHNS	PERC (D	BRYN HAWORTH	G (D				
BUD PARKES	TPT (A		TERRY NOONAN		(A	DEREK WADSWORTH	HRNS(F	DAVE CHARLES	B (F				
LINCOLN CARR	D	(F	GERAINT WATKINS	K	(F	MICKEY GEE	G (F	GEORGE CHISHOLM	HRNS(F				
MEL COLLINS	SAX (F												

HEINZ MIKUS	G V	(A	(A) FADING BEAUTY	1973	CADE	GER	10002
MANFRED VON BUTTLAR	K	(ABC	(B) BACK ON MY HILL	1980	SKY	SKY	038
HORST STABENOW	B	(AB	(C) ROCK LIONS	1981			
JURGEN WERITZ	D	(AB					
RENATE HEEMANN	V	(A					

ADAM FAITH	V	(ALL	(A) ADAM	196	PARLOPHONE UK	PCS 3010	PMC 1128
RUSS BALLARD	G K	(HJ	(B) BEAT GIRL	196	COLUMBIA UK		33SX 1125
JOHN BARRY		(B	(C) ADAM FAITH	196	PARLOPHONE UK	PCS 3025	PMC 1162
BOB HENRIT	D	(HJ	(D) FROM ADAM WITH LOVE	196	PARLOPHONE UK	PCS 3038	PMC 1192
PETE SALT	G	(HJ	(E) FOR YOU	106	PARLOPHONE UK		PMC 1213
MOD ROGAN	B	(H	(F) ON THE MOVE	196	PARLOPHONE UK		PMC 1228
CHRIS ANDREWS	V	(H	(G) FAITH ALIVE	196	PARLOPHONE UK		PMC 1249
DAVE WINTOUR	G	(J	(H) THE TWO BEST SIDES OF ADAM FAITH	196	EMI UK		NUT 16
DAVE COURTNEY	PNO	(J	(J) I SURVIVE	1976	WB US 2791 UK		K 56054
MARTIN BIRCH	D	(J	(K) BEST OF	1974	STARLINE UK		SRS 5067
RICHIE BLACKMORE	G	(J	(EP)				
MIM	ACC	(J	(ADAMS HIT PARADE	196	PARLOPHONE UK		GEP 8811
ROYSTON WILLOCK	SAX	(J	ADAM No1	196	PARLOPHONE UK	SGE 2014	GEP 8824
			ADAM No2	196	PARLOPHONE UK	SGE 2015	GEP 8828
			ADAM No3	196	PARLOPHONE UK	SGE 2018	GEP 8831
			BEAT GIRL	196	COLUMBIA UK	SEG 8138	
			ADAM'S HIT PARADE No 2	196	PARLOPHONE UK		GEP 8841
			ADAM FAITH No1	196	PARLOPHONE UK		GEP 8851
			ADAM FAITH No2	196	PARLOPHONE UK		GEP 8852
			ADAM FAITH No3	196	PARLOPHONE UK		GEP 8854
			ADAMS HIT PARADE No3	196	PARLOPHONE UK		GEP 8862
			LATEST HITS	196	PARLOPHONE UK		GEP 8877
			TOP OF THE POPS	196	PARLOPHONE UK		GEP 8893
			FOR YOU ADAM	196	PARLOPHONE UK		GEP 8904
			A MESSAGE FROM ADAM	196	PARLOPHONE UK		GEP 8929
			SONGS AND THINGS	196	PARLOPHONE UK		GEP 8939

CARL STORIE	V HCA (BC		(A) FAITH	1973	BROWN BAG	US	BB 085
DAVID BENNETT	G	(BC	(B) ROCK'N' ROMANCE	1978	MERCURY		
JOHN CASCELLA	K SAX V(BC		(C) FACE TO FACE	1979	MERCURY	US	3770
MARK CAWLEY	B V	(BC	(D) VITAL SIGNS	197)	MERCURY	US	
DAVID BARNES	D	(BC					

MARIANNE FAITHFULL	V	(ALL	(A) COME MY WAY	1965	DECCA UK LK 4688		
WITH			(B) MARIANNE FAITHFULL	1965	DECCA UK LK 4689	US LONDON 3423	
THE GREASE BAND		(*	(C) GO AWAY FROM MY WORLD	1965		US LONDON 3452	
JOE MAVERTY		(KL	(D) NORTH COUNTRY MAID	1966	DECCA UK LK 4778		
BARRY REYNOLDS		(KL	(E) FAITHFULL FOREVER	1966		US LONDON 3482	
STEVE YORK	B	(KL	(F) LOVE IN A MIST	1967	DECCA UK LK 4854		
TERRY STANNARD		(KL	(G) GREATEST HITS	196	DECCA UK LK	US LONDON 3547	
FRANKIE COLLINS	V	(KL	(H) WORLD OF	1969	DECCA UK SPA 17		
JULIAN DIGGLE		(L	(*I) DREAMIN' MY DREAMS	1976	NEMS UK NEL 6007		
MARTIN DROVER		(L	(*J) FAITHLESS	1978	NEMS UK NEL 6012		
DENNIS HAINES		(L	(K) BROKEN ENGLISH	1979	ISLAND UK+US	ILPS 9570	
NEIL HUBBARD	G	(L	( ) AS TEARS GO BY (COMP)	1981	DECCA UK TAB 13		
JIM LEVERTON		(	(L) DANGEROUS ACQUANTANCES	1981	ISLAND UK	ILPS 9648	
ISABELLA DULANEY		(K	(EP) MARIANNE FAITHFULL	1965	DECCA UK DFE 8624		
FUZZY SAMUELS	B	(L					
DIANE SPENNER		(L	CHRIS STAINTON	K	(L	PICKFORD SYKES	(L
PETER VEITCH		(L	STEVE WINWOOD	K	(KL	TONY CALDER	PROD (AB
MARK MILLER MUNDAY	PROD	(K	DIANE BIRCH		(K	MORRIS PERT	PERC (K
JIM CUOMO		(K	GUY HUMPHRIES		(K	DARRYL WAY	(K

BILLY FALCON	G V	(ABC	(A) BILLY FALCONS BURNING ROSE	1978	PHILIPS	UK	9103 450
RICHIE MEADE	V	(A	(A) BILLY FALCONS BURNING ROSE	1978	MANHATTAN	US	832
MICHAEL VISAGGIO	K FLT V(A		(B) IMPROPER ATTIRE	1979	UA	US	967
RICK ZOLLO	G V	(A	(C) FALCON AROUND	1980	MCA US 3238	UK	MCF 3065
BILLY MILNE	D V	(A					
GLENN EICHLER	B HCA	(A	GREG MEADE	V	(A	PAGE TO THE WIND CHOIR(A	

RODERICK FALCONER

RODERICK FALCONER	SYN V G(AB	(A) NEW NATION			1976	UA US 651	UK	UAG 29992
HIRAM BINGHAM	B (A	(B) VICTORY IN ROCK CITY			1977	UA US 777	UK	UAG 30100
MIKE KELLIE	D (A							
MIKE JAPP	G (AB	MATTHEW FISHER	K	(A	BRUCE GARY	D	(B	
REGGIE McBRIDE	B (B	BRIE HOWARD	V	(B	WENDY HAAS	V	(B	
JIMMIE GREENSPOON	K (B	PATTI QUATRO	V	(B	PETER IVERS	PROD (B	

TAV FALCO'S PANTHER BURNS

TAV FALCO	G V (A	(A) BEHIND THE MAGNOLIA CURTAIN		1982	FRENZI 400 ROUGH TRADE	16
ALEC CHILTON	G D (A					
JIM DUCKWORTH	G D (A	RON MILLER	B (A	TATE COUNTY DRUM COROS	(A	

FALCKENSTEIN

MONIKA MARIE DOMIN	G V (A	(A) FALCKENSTEIN		1979	NATURE	GER 60 175
WENDELIN WERNER	G (A				
JOACHIM LUHRMANN	D PERC(A	PETER LOWNER	B (A	MICK FRANKE	G (A
THOMAS KAGERMANN	VLN G(A				

FALCONS

1950s EARLY 60S	
JOE STUBBS	V
MACK RICE	V LANCE FINNIE V WILLIE SCHOFIELD V EDDIE FLOYD V WILSON PICKETT V

FALL

KARL BURNS	D (345ABCDEFG	(A) LIVES AT THE WITCH TRIALS		1979	STEP ORWARD UK 1 US A&M SPOO3		
MARK SMITH	V (12345ABCDEFG	(B) DRAGNET		1979	STEP FORWARD		SFLP 4
ERIC	B (4	(C) TOTALES TURNS		1980	ROUGH TRADE	UK	ROUGH10
MIKE LEIGH	D (BCDE	(D) GROTESQUE		1980	ROUGH TRADE	UK	ROUGH18
YVONNE PAWCETT	K (AE	(E) SLATES		1981	ROUGH TRADE	UK	RT073
STEVE HANLEY	B (5BCDEFG	(F) EARLY YEARS (1977/1979		1981	STEP FORWARD	UK	SFLP 6
PAUL HANLEY	G D (G	(G) HEX EDUCATION		1982	LINE	GER	LLP 5194
MARTIN BRAMAH	G (A1234	(1) 1976 (2) 1977 (3) 1978 (4) 1978 (5) 1979					
UNA BAINES	K (234						
JONNIE BROWN	B (3	TONY FRIEL	B (12E	MARC RILEY	G B(A5BCDEFG	
CRAIG SCANLON	G (5BCDFG	KAY CARROLL	V PERC (G			

FALL MOUNTAIN

JIM KATZIN	VLN (A	(A) EARLY FALL		1979	PARACHUTE	P 009
BOB OSTERTAG	SYN (A				
NED ROTHENBERG	WIND (A	RICHARD ROGERS	PNO (A	DAVID WILES	PERC (A

FALLENROCK

LARRY KEITH	(A) WATCH FOR FALLENROCK	1974	CAPRICORN US 0143 UK 2429 122
STEVE PIPPIN			
RAFE VAN HOY			

FAMILY

ROGER CHAPMAN	V HCA (ALL	(A) MUSIC IN A DOLLS HOUSE		1968	REPRISE	UK/US 6312
CHARLIE WHITNEY	G (ALL	(A) MUSIC IN A DOLLS HOUSE		1971	REPRISE RI UK K44057 GER 24018
ROB TOWNSEND	D (ALL	(B) FAMILY ENTERTAINMENT		1969	REPRISE	UK/US 6340
JIM KING	WIND V(ABH	(B) FAMILY ENTERTAINMENT		1971	REPRISE	UK RI K 44069
JOHN WEIDER	B V (CDHJ	(C) A SONG FOR ME		1970	REPRISE	US 6384
		(C) A SONG FOR ME		1970	REPRISE	UK 9001
POLI PALMER	K VIBES(CDEFHJ	(C) A SONG FOR ME		1971	REPRISE	UK RI K 44104
JOHN WETTON	B V (EF	(D) ANYWAY		1970	REPRISE	UK 9005
RICK GRECH	B V VLN (ABHJ	(D) ANYWAY		1971	REPRISE	UK RI K 54002
JIM CREGAN	G D (G	(D) ANYWAY		1970	UA	US 5527
TONY ASHTON	K (G	(E) FEARLESS		1971	REPRISE	UK K 54003
CHARLIE McCRACKEN	G (G	(E) FEARLESS		1971	UA	US 5562
PETER HOPE EVANS	(G	(F) BANDSTAND		1972	REPRISE	UK K 54006
ROY DYKE	(G	(F) BANDSTAND		1972	UA	US 5644
LADBROKE HORNS	(E	(G) ITS ONLY A MOVIE		1973	RAFT	UK RA 58501
DAVE MASON	PROD (A	(G) ITS ONLY A MOVIE		1973	UA	US UALA 181
JIMMY MILLER	PROD (A	(H) OLD SONGS NEW SONGS		1971	REPRISE US 6413 UK K 34001
GEORGE CHKIANTZ	PROD (E	(J) BEST OF FAMILY		1974	REPRISE	UK K 54023

FAMILY DOGG

STEVE ROWLAND	(	(A) A WAY OF LIFE		1969	BELL	SP 22122
ALBERT HAMMOND	G V (B	(B) VIEW FROM ROWLANDS HEAD		1972	POLYDOR	UK 2318 061
MIKE HAZELWOOD	(B	(B) VIEW FROM ROWLANDS HEAD		197	BUDDAH	US BDS 5100
JIMMY PAGE	G (A				
JOHN PAUL JONES	(	CHRISTINE HOLMES	B (IRENE SHERR	B V (B
ANDREW STEEL E	D (B	ALAN PARKER	G (B B J COLE	DOB G (B BARRY MORGAN	D (B
LIZA STRIKE	V (B	DORIS TROY	V (B MIKE MORGAN	K (B CHRIS SPEDDING G (B
MADELINE BELL	V (B	PHIL DENNYS	PNO (B TONY CARR	PERC (B SUE LYNN	V (B
PAT ARNOLD	V (B	CLAIRE TORRY	V (B	

FAMILY TREE

BOB SEGARINI	G V (A	(A) MISS BUTTERS		1968	RCA	US LSP 3955
VANN SCATER	(A				
MICHAEL DURE	(A	BILL TROCHIM	B (A JIMMY DE COCQ	G K (A

FAMILY FODDER

ALIG	G K B SAX(ABC	(A) SUNDAY GIRLS	EP	1980	FRESH	UK 9
MARTIN	B G V(BC	(B) MONKEY BANANA KITCHEN		1980	FRESH	UK LP3
NINA	V (B	(C) SCHIZOPHRENIA PARTY	EP	198	FRESH	UK 37
FELIX	K VLN V(B				
DOMINIQUE	V (B	RICK	D PERC(B IAN	K V HCA(B MICK	B PERC(B
CHARLES	D G V(B	JUDY	V (B NARESH	V (B GRAHEME	CELLO (B
MARK	PERC (B	MIKE	G (B IAN HILL	V PERC (C BAT SMITH	PERC (C
GRAHAM PAINTING	V G B(C	LYNN ALICE	V (B		

```
GEORGIE FAME(CLIVE POWELL) K V(ALL   (A) R& B AT THE FLAMINGO           1964 COLUMBIA          UK   SX  1599
WITH                                 (B) FAME AT LAST                   1964 COLUMBIA          UK   33SX 1638
COLIN GREEN        G    (CDR1         (C) SWEET THING                   1966 COLUMBIA          UK   SX  6043
TED MAKINS         B    (             (D) SOUND VENTURE                 1966 COLUMBIA          UK   SX  6076
GEORGE KISH        G    (G            ( ) YEH YEH                       1966 IMPERIAL          US       12282
JOHN McLAUGHLIN    G    (G            ( ) GET AWAY                      1966 IMPERIAL          US       12331
RED PREECE         D    (             (E) HALL OF FAME                  1967 COLUMBIA          UK   SX  6120
AL WATSON          SAX  (             (F) TWO FACES OF FAME             1967 CBS               UK       63018
CLIFF BARTON       B    (C            (G) THIRD FACE OF FAME            1968 CBS               UK       63293
PHIL BATES         B    (DFG          (H) SEVENTH SON                   1969 CBS               uk       63786
RICK BROWN         B    (F            (J) GEORGIE FAME                  1969 STARLINE          UK   SRS 5002
FRANK CLARKE       B    (G            (K) DOES HIS OWN THING WITH STRINGS 1970 CBS             UK       63650
RONNIE SEABROOK    B    (G            (L) GOING HOME                    1971 CBS               UK       64350
JEFF CLYNE         B    (F            (M) FAME & PRICE                  1971 CBS               UK       64392
JOHN MITCHELL      D    (C            (N) ALL ME OWN WORK               1972 REPRISE           UK   K  44183
PHIL SEAMAN        D    (D            (O) FAME AGAIN                    1972 STARLINE          UK   SRS 5107
BILL EYDEN         D    (DFG          (P) BALLAD OF BONNIE & CLYDE      1973 EMBASSY UK 31033 EPIC US  26368
HUGHIE FLINT       D    (F            (Q) GEORGIE FAME                  1974 ISLAND            UK   ILPS 9293
HAYDEN JACKSON     D    (G            (R) RIGHT NOW                     1979 PYE               UK   NSLP18600
SPEEDY ACQUAYE     D    (CRS          (S) THATS WHAT FRIENDS ARE FOR    1979 PYE               UK       N 119
J SCOTT            D    (F            (T) CLOSING THE GAP               1980 PICCADILLY        UK       N 137
JIM MULLEN         G    (S            (1) 1969 LIVE BAND
TONY OXLEY         D    (F            (U) IN HOGLAND                    1981 BALD EAGLE        UK   BELP 181
ANNIE ROSS         V    (U
TERRY SMITH        G    (GR    ARTHUR GREENSLADE K   (G    GORDON BECK      K   (DFG ERNIE SHEARS    G    (G
STAN TRACY         K    (D     PETER COE          SAX (C    GLEN HUGHES      SAX (C   ROY WILCOX      SAX (D
RAY WARLEIGH       SAX  (DR    RONNIE SCOTT       SAX (DFG  TUBBY HAYES      SAX (D   HARRY KLEIN     SAX (DFG
ALAN BRANSCOMBE    SAX  (DF    TONY COE           SAX (DFG  DICK MORRISSEY   SAX (DFS LYN DOBSON      SAX (F
TOMMY WHITTLE      SAX  (G     ART ELLEFSON       SAX (G    CYRIL REUBENS    SAX (G   JOHNNY MARSHALL SAX(FG
PETER KING         SAX  (F     ED THORNTON        TPT (CFST GREG BOWEN       TPT (DFG BERT COURTLEY   TPT (D
IAN HAMMER         TPT  (DFGS  JIMMY DEUCHER      TPT (D    LES CONDON       TPT (DGH KENNY WHEELER   TPT (DF
TONY FISHER        TPT  (D     DEREK WATKINS      TPT (FG   DEREK HEALEY     TPT (G   ALBERT HALL     TPT (G
BOB HAUGHEY        TPT  (G     KEITH CHRISTIE     TROM (DF  ALAN PARKER      G   (RS  CHRIS SMITH     TROM(DF
KEN GOLDE          TROM(D      GIB WALLACE        TROM (DFG DEREK WADSWORTH  TROM (F  MORRIS PLATT    TROM(G
BERNIE HOLLAND     G    (R     BRIAN ODGERS       B   (RS1  BARRY MORGAN     D   (RS  HENRY LOWTHER   TPT (R
STEVE GREGORY      SAX  (SR    MALCOLM GRIFFITHS  TROM(RS   FRANK RICOTTI PERC SAX (1 ALAN SKIDMORE   SAX (1
JOHN WARREN        SAX  (1     HAROLD BECKETT     TPT (1    CHRIS PYNE       TROM (1  HARVEY BURNS    D   (1
HENRY SPINETTI     D    (S     MIKE DAVIS         TPT (S    BRIAN SMITH      WIND (S  REGGAE PHILHARMONIC ORCH(T
JAMES LASCELLES    HRNS(T      GUARDIAN ANGELS    V   (T    JACKIE SHARP     SAX (D
```

```
JILL JOHNSON         V G  (AB    (A) SUNSHINE POSSIBILITIES        1969 LIBERTY    UK  LBS 83263
PETE BERRYMAN        G V  (AB    (B) CHAMELEON                     1970 LIBERTY    UK  LBS 83355
CLIVE PALMER         G V  (A
HENRY VIII BARTLETT  V JUG (AB
```

```
RAY  FENWICK       G   (C    (A) FANCY MEETING YOU HERE        19   POISON RING  US       2238
MO FOSTER          B   (CB   (B) WILD THING                    1974 ATLANTIC     UK  K 51502
LES BINKS          D   (CB   (B) WILD THING                    1974 BIG TREE     US       89502
ANNIE KAVANAGH     V   (CB   (C) SOMETHING TO REMEMBER         1975 ARISTA       US  ARTY 102
MARLON             G V (CB   (D) TURNS YOU ON                  1976 RCA          US  APLI 1482
```

```
NICK SIMPER        B   (AB   (A) SLIPSTREAMING                 1979 GULL         UK  GULP 1033
PETE PARKS         G   (AB   (B) FUTURE TIMES                  1980 SHARK        GER     148 506
JIM PROOPS         V   (AB
RON PENNEY         D   (A    NEIL McARTHUR        ORG    (A
```

```
JOE LYN TURNER     G V (ALL  (A) FANDANGO                      1978 RCA          US
RICK BLAKEMORE     G   (ALL  (B) LAST KISS                     1979 RCA          US
BOB DANYLS         B   (ALL  (C) ONE NIGHT STAND               1979 RCA          US
ABE SPELLER        D   (ALL  (D) CADILLAC                      1980 RCA          US  AFLI 3591
```

```
JOHNNY PACHECO     FLT PERC(CDEHJ  (A) LIVE AT THE RED GARTER       1968 FANIA     US       355
STEVE WINWOOD      G      (K        (B) LIVE AT THE RED GARTER 2     1968 FANIA     US       364
RAY BARRETTO       PERC   (CDEHJ    (C) LIVE AT THE CHEETA VOL 1     1971 FANIA     US       415
BOBBY VALENTIN     B      (CDEHJ    (D) LIVE AT THE CHEETA VOL 2     1973 FANIA     US       416
NIKKY MARRERO      PERC   (CDEHJ    (E) LATIN SOUL ROCK             1973 FANIA     US       470
ROBERTO ROENA      PERC   (CDEHJ    (F) SALSA                       1975 ISLAND    UK  HELP 20
PAPO LUCCA         PNO    (K        (G) FANIA ALL STARS             1975 ISLAND    UK  ILPS 9331
WILLIE COLON       TROM   (CDEHJ    (H) SALSA LIVE                  1976 ISLAND    UK  HELP 21
LARRY HARLOW       K      (CDEHJ    (H) LIVE AT YANKEE STADIUM VOL1  1976 FANIA    US       476
RICHARD RAY        K      (CDEHJ    (J) LIVE AT YANKEE STADIUM VOL2  1976 FANIA    US       477
MONGO SANTAMARIA   PERC   (EHJ      (K) DELICATE & JUMPY            1976 ISLAND    UK  ILPS 9447
CELIA CRUZ         V      (HJ       (K) DELICATE & JUMPY            1976 CBS       US       34283
JUSTO BETANCOURT   V      (HJ       (L) RHYTHM                      1977 CBS       US       34711
SANTOS COLON       V      (CDEHJ    (H) SPANISH FEVER               1978 CBS       US       35336
BOBBY CRUZ         V      (CDEHJ    (N) CROSSOVER                   1979 CBS       US       36109
CHEO FELICIANO     V      (CDEHJ
PETE RODRIGUEZ     V      (CDEHJ  LEWIS KAHN       TRGM (EHJ   HECTOR LAVOE     V    (CDEHJ
RAY MALANALDO      TPT    (EHJ    BARRY ROGERS     TROM (CDEHJ ISMAEL MIRANDA   V    (CDEHJ
LUIS ORTIZ         TPT    (EHJ    YOMO TGRO        TRES (CDEHJ ISHMAEL QUINTANA V    (HJ
VICTOR PAZ         TPT    (EHJ    LOU SOLOFF       TPT  (E     BILLY COBHAM     D    (E
JAN HAMMER         K      (E      JORGE SANTANA    G    (E     MANU DIBANGO     SAX  (EJ
ROBERTO RODRIGUEZ  TPT    (CD     HECTOR ZARZUELA  TPT  (CD    RARRY SPENCER    TPT  (CD
RENALDO JORGE      TROM   (CD     ORESTES VILATO   PERC (CD    ADALBERTO SANTIAGO V  (CD
```

```
F18                              FANNY                                              F18
    JEAN MILLINGTON    G B V (ABCDE12  (A) FANNY                    1970   REPRISE US 6416    UK  6416
    JUNE MILLINGTON    G V   (ABCD2    (B) CHARITY BALL             1971   REPRISE US 6456    UK K44144
    NICOLE BARCLAY     K V   (ABCDE    (C) FANNY HILL               1972   REPRISE US 2058    UK K44174
    ALICE DE BUHR      D V   (E1       (D) MOTHERS PRIDE            1973   REPRISE US 2137    UK K44233
    PATTI QUATRO       B     (E1       (E) ROCK'N'ROLL SURVIVORS    1975   CASABLANCA US 7007 UK  4001
    BRIE HOWARD        D     (E2       (E) ROCK'N'ROLL SURVIVORS    19     PATHE FR    064 96062
    CAM DAVIES     D       (1          (1) 1974  (2) 1975
    BOBBY KEYS     SAX     (C
    JIM PRICE     WIND    (C      JAMES NEWTON HOWARD K    (E
F18A                          FANNY ADAMS                                           F18A
    TED TOI        B     (A            (A) FANNY ADAMS              1971   KAPP   US  3644
    VINCE MELANEY  G     (A
    DOUG PARKINSON G     (A       JOHNNY DICK        D    (A
F18B                       FANTASTIC BAGGIES                                        F18B
    PHIL SLOAN          (A            (A) TELL 'EM I'M SURFIN'      196    IMPERIAL   US       12270
    STEVE BARRI        (A
F18C                            FANTASY                                            F18C
    DAVID REED    B V   (A            (A) PAINT A PICTURE           1973   POLYDOR            2383 246
    PAUL LAWRENCE G V   (A
    DAVID MATCALFE K V  (A        PETER JAMES  G V  (A     JON WEBSTER   D V  (A
F19                      RICHARD & MIMI FARINA                                      F19
    MIMI FARINA        V    (ALL      (A) RICHARD & MIMI FARINA      1965 VVANGUARD              79174
    RICHARD FARINA     V    (ABCDE    (B) CELEBRATIONS FOR A GREY DAY 1965 FONTANA 6060 VANGUARD VSD 79281
    RUSS KUNKEL        D    (F        (C) REFLECTIONS IN A CRYSTAL WIND 1965 FONTANA 6075 VANGUARD VSD 79204
    TOM JANS          V    (F        (D) MEMORIES                   1968 VANGUARD19047       VSD 79263
    JOAN BAEZ         G V  (D        (E) RICHARD FARINA             1968 VANGUARD            VSD 79281
    RUSS SAVAKUS      B    (D        (F) MIMI FARINA & TOM JANS     1971 A&M  US 4310  UK  AMLS64310
    BRUCE LANGHORNE   G    (D        ( ) THE BEST OF RICHARD & MIMI FARINA 70 VANGUARD      VSD 21/2
    CHARLES SMALL    PNO   (D
    AL ROGERS        D    (D        JOHN HAMMOND        HCA   (D      FRITZ RICHMOND    B   (D
    KYLE GRAHAN      HCA   (D        EMIL RICHARDS       PERC  (F      GRADY MARTIN      G   (D
    CRAIG DOERGE     K    (F        LEE SKLAR           B     (F      EDGAR LUSTGARTEN  PPNO (F
    SNEAKY PETE     STEEL (F
    JIM KELTNER      D    (F        (RICHARD DIED 1966,MIMI IS JOAN BAEZ SISTER)
F19A                            FAR CRY                                            F19A
    JERE WHITING      V HCA (A       (A) FAR CRY           19 VANGUARD US VSD 6510 UK SVRL 19041
    PAUL LENART       G    (A
    DICK MARTIN      SAX PERC(A      DAVID PERRY        G V   (A     LARRY LUDDECKE     K   (A
    SEAN HUTCHINSON   B    (A        VICTOR McGILL      D PERC (A
F20                           FAR CRY (2)                                          F20
    PETER THAN        V    (A        (A) THE MORE THE BETTER        1980   CBS       US    36286
    PHIL GALDSTON     K V  (A
F20A                    FAR EAST FAMILY BAND                                       F20A
    FUMIO MIYASHTA V G K SYN (       (A) NEPPORJIN                  1975   VERTIGO           6370 850
    HIROHITO FUKUSHIMA G V  (        (B) THE CAVE DOWN TO EARTH     1975   MULAND          CD 7139M
    YUJIN HARADA     D PERC(        (C) PARALLEL WORLD             1976   MULAND          LQ 7002M
    AKIRA FUKAKUSA   B    (        (D) TENKEYIN                   1977   ALL EARS   US       11479
F20B                          DON FARDON                                          F20B
    DON FARDON        V    (A        (A) LAMENT OF THE CHEROKEE     1968   GNP       US       2044
                                     (B) IVE PAID MY DUES          1970   DECCA     US       75225
                                     (C) RELEASED                  1970   YOUNGBLOOD US      YB13
F20C                          LEE FARDON                                          F20C
    LEE FARDON              (A        (A) STORIES OF ADVENTURE      1981   AURA             AUL  713
F21                         CHRIS FARLOWE                                         F21
    CHRIS FARLOWE     V    (ALL       (A) CHRIS FARLOWE & THE THUNDERBIRDS 1966 COLUMBIA  UK  SCX  6034
    ALBERT LEE        G    (AB        (B) STORMY MONDAY             1966 M F P      UK MFP 1186
    IAN HAGUE         D    (          (B) CHRIS FARLOWE & THE THUNDERBIRDS 1978 CHARLY UK CR 30021
    DAVE GREENSLADE   K    (          (C) OUT OF TIME              1966 IMMEDIATE      Z12 52010
    BRUCE WADDELL     B    (H         (C) OUT OF TIME              1976 IMMEDIATE UK RI IML 1002
    PAT DONALDSON     B    (J         (C) GREATEST HITS            1977 IMMEDIATE UK   IML 2002
    RICKY CHARMAN     B    (          (D) 14 THINGS TO THINK ABOUT 1966 IMMEDIATE UK   IMLP 005
    PAUL CARSON      SAX   (          (E) THE ART OF CHRIS FARLOWE 1966 IMMEDIATE UK   IMLP 006
    CARL PALMER       D    (          (F) THE BEST OF CHRIS FARLOWE 1968 IMMEDIATE UK   IMCP 010
    PETE SHELLEY      D    (          (G) THE LAST GOODBYE         1969 IMMEDIATE UK   IMLP 021
    STEVE HAMMOND     G    (H         (H) FROM HERE TO MAMA ROSA   1970 POLYDOR  UK     2425 029
    JOANNE WILLIAMS   V    (J         (H) FROM HERE TO MAMA ROSA   1970 POLYDOR  US   20 4041
    COLIN DAVY        D    (H         (J) CHRIS FARLOWE BAND LIVE  1975 POLYDOR  UK     2460 259
    PETER ROBINSON    K    (H         (K) OUT OF TIME/PAINT IT BLACK 1976 CHARLY UK  CR 300020
    PAUL BUCKMASTER  CELLO (H         (C) GREATEST HITS            1977 IMMEDIATE UK   IML 2002
    JEAN ROUSSEL      K    (J         ( ) PAINT IT BLACK           19  IMMEDIATE     SHZEL  9
    GERRY CONWAY      D    (J         (EP) AIR TRAVEL              19  DECCA     UK DFE 8665
    CHRIS MERCER     SAX   (J         (EP) FARLOWE IN THE MIDNIGHT HOUR 19 IMMEDIATE UK IMEP 001
    MADELINE BELL     V    (J         (EP) HITS                    19  IMMEDIATE UK   IMEP 004
    RON CARTHY       HRNS  (J         (EP) THE IMMEDIATE CATALOGUE 19  VIRGIN    UK   SV  102
F22                          MARK FARNER                                         F22
    MARK FARNER      G V   (AB        (A) MARK FARNER              1978   ATLANTIC US 18232 UK K50419
    PHIL AABERG       K    (A         (B) NO FRILLS                1979   ATLANTIC US 19196
    ANDY NEWMARK      D    (B
    BOB BABITT        B    (A        BOB KULICK         G    (A    AL WOTTON     D   (A
    JIM MAELEN       PERC  (A        DICK WAGNER        G    (A    RICKY FARNER  V   (A
    DENNIS BALLINGER  V    (AB       KAREN LAWSON       V    (B
F22A                           FARQUAHR                                          F22A
    BARNSWALLOW FARQUAHR G V (AB      (A) FABULOUS FARQUAHR        19   VERVE FORECAST   FTS 3053
    HUMMINGBIRD FARQUAHR G V (AB      (B) FARQUAHR970   ELEKTRA    US   EKS 74083
    CONDOR FARQUAHR   G V  (AB
    FLAMINGO FARQUAHR G V  (AB        JERRY RAGOVOY      K    (B    GARY CHESTER   D   (B
    ERIC WEISSBERG   BANJO (B         JOE MACK           B    (B    LOU MAURO          (B
```

```
F23                                    GARY FARR                                    F23
    GARY FARR          V G   (ALL    (A) TAKE SOMETHING WITH YOU        1969  MARMALADE     UK   608  013
    MIKE STEPHENS      G   (A        (B) STRANGE FRUIT                  1971  CBS           UK        64138
    ROGER POWELL       D   (A        (C) ADDRESSED TO THE CENSORS OF LOVE 1973 ATCO        US   SD   7034
    IAN WHITEMAN     WIND K (A        (D) LONDON 1964/65                 1977  CHARLY        UK   CR 300015
    ANDY LEIGH         B   (A        (E) ROCK GENERATION VOL 7 (1 SIDE)  19   BYG           FR   529  707
    MARTIN STONE       G   (A
    BRIAN BELSHAW      B   (A    NICK JONES PERC     (A    RICHARD THOMPSON   G   (B    VINCE WETHERALL    G   (D
    MICHAEL EVANS      B   (A    ANDY McKECHNIE G    (D    STU PARKS          B   (D    BRIAN WALKELEY     D   (D
    ANDY STEELE        D   (D    HARVEY THOMPSON WIND(C    MIKE LEWIS       WIND (C    RONNIE EADES     SAX (C
    HARRISON CALLOWAY TPT(C     BEN CAULEY     TPT  (C    CHARLES ROSE     TROM (C    GEORGE TERRY       G   (C
    JIMMY JOHNSON      G   (C    PETE CARR      G    (C    BARRY BECKETT      K   (C    DAVID HOOD         B   (C
    GERRY MASTERS      B   (C    ROGER HAWKINS  D    (C
F23A                                   JOHN FARRAR                                   F23A
    JOHN FARRAR        G V K   (A     (A) JOHN FARRAR                    1980  CBS UK 84324 US        36475
    MICHAEL BOTTS      D       (A
    TOM SNOW           PNO     (A     ED GREENE        D    (A  MICHAEL BODDICKER         SYN (A
    MICHAEL PORCARO    B       (A     DAVID McDANIELS  B    (A
F24                                    MICK FARREN                                   F24
    MICK FARREN        V   (AB        (A) CARNIVOROUS CIRCUS(MONA)       1970  TRANSATLANTIC UK  TRA   212
    WILKO JOHNSON      G   (B         (B) VAMPIRES STOLE MY LUNCH MONEY  1978  LOGO          UK  LOGO 1010
    ALAN POWELL        D   (B
    WILL STALLIBRASS HCA(B      ANDY COLQUHOUN B    (B    CHRISSIE HYNDE   V   (B    SONJA KRISTINA     V   (B
    SUSIE              V   (B    MARIA          V    (B    TWINK            D   (A    STEVE TOOK         B   (A
    VICTOR BROX        K   (A    PETE ILLINGWORTH    (     FRANK NEWBOLD        (A    JOHN GUSTAFSON     B   (A
    STEVE HAMMOND      G   (A    PAUL BUCKMASTER CELLO(A
F24A                                   FASHION                                       F24A
    DIK        PERC HCA V(A     (A) PRODUCT PERFECT               1979  FASHION UK FML1 US  IRS  002
    LUKE           G V    (A
    MULLIGAN       B SYN V (A
F25                                    FAST                                          F25
    PAUL ZONE          (A            (A) THE FAST FOR SALE              1980  RECCA              2000
    MIKI ZONE          (A
    ARMAND ZONE        (    PETER HOFFMAN     (    TOMMIE MODNIL      (    JOE POLISENO       (A
    LOUIS BOVA         (A
F26                                    FAST BUCK                                     F26
    DAVID KERR CLEMSON (            (A) FAST BUCK                       1976  JET       UK   JETLP 16
    ANDREW LOCKE       (
    MIKE BARON         (    EDWIN HAMILTON     (    MIKE HOUGH     ( JAMIE PEARCE  (  STEPHEN FORREST  (
F26A                                   FAST LANE                                     F26A
                                 (A) FAST LANE EP                   19    ACE       UK        006
F27                                    FAT                                           F27
    PETER NEWLAND    V HCA (A        (A) FAT                           1970  RCA LPS 4368  LSA3009
    JAMES KAMINSKI     G V  (A
    MICHAEL BENSON     G   (A    GUY DE VITO         V   (A    WILLIAM BENJAMIN   D V  (A
F27A                                   FAT CITY                                      F27A
    WILLIAM DANOFF     G V  (AB       (A) REINCARNATION                1969  PROBE     US   CPLI 4508
    TAFFY DANOFF       V    (AB       (B) WELCOME TO FAT CITY          19    PARAMOUNT US        6308
    EVERETT BARKSDALE  B    (A
    JIM PARKER         G    (AB   TED SOMMER          D    (A    HUBERT LAWS      FLT (A
    DAVE APPEL         G    (A    MARGARET ROSE     HARP  (A    BOB JAMES        K   (A
    ARTIE TRAUM        G    (A    BERNARD PURDIE      D    (A    RONNIE ZITO      D   (A
    HOWARD COLLINS     G    (A    BUCKY PIZZARELLI  G BAN (A    ERNIE HAYES      K   (A
    RICHARD GREENE     VLN  (B    ERIC WEISSBERG    STEEL  (B    DICK WEISSMAN    BAN (B
    FRANK OWENS        K    (B    CLIVE STEVENS      FLT   (B    CHRIS SARANDON   V   (B
    SUE SARANDON       V    (B    TIMMY JEROME        (B        ELIZABETH LINDSAY V  (B
F27B                                   FAT CHANCE                                    F27B
    FAT CHANCE                       1972  RCA           US        4626
F28                              FAT MAN RIDDIN SECTION                              F28
                                 (A) ISRAEL TAFARI                 1978  TOP RANKING  UK
F29                                    FAT MATTRESS                                  F29
    NOEL REDDING  G B V  (A1         (A) FAT MATTRESS       1969 POLYDOR UK 583  056  ATCO US 33309
    STEVE HAMMOND      G    (2        (B) FAT MATTRESS 2     1970 POLYDOR UK 2383 025  ATCO US 33347
    NEIL LANDON        D    (12A      (1) 1969   (2)1970
    JIM LEVERTON     K B V  (12A
    ERIC DILLON        D    (12A    CHRIS WOOD     FLT    (A    MICK WEAVER    K   (
F29A                                   FAUN                                          F29A
                                 (A) FAUN                          19    GREGAR    US   GG 7000
F29B                                   FATAL MICROBES                                F29B
                                 (A) MEET THE POISON GIRLS        1979  SMALL WONDER UK  WEENY 3
F29C                                   FAT WATER                                     F29C
                                 (A) FAT WATER                     19    MGM       US        4660
F30                                    FAUST                                         F30
    WERNER DIERMAIER        (ABC      (A) FAUST                        1971  POLYDOR      UK   2310 142
    JEAN HERVE PERON        (ABC      (A) FAUST                        1979  RECOMMENDED          RR1
    RUDOLF SOSSNA           (ABC      (B) SO FAR                       1972  POLYDOR      UK   2310 196
    TONY CONRAD             (C        (B) SO FAR                       1972  RECOMMENDED          RR2
    HANS JOACHIM IRMLER     (AB       (C) OUTSIDE DREAM SYNDICATE      1973  CAROLINE     UK   C1501
    GUNTHER WUSTHOFF        (AB       (D) FAUST 4                      1973  VIRGIN UK V2004 GER   87739
    ARNULF MEIFERT          (A        (E) FAUST TAPES                  1973  VIRGIN       UK   VC501
    UWE NETTLEBECK     PROD  (        (F) FAUST TAPES                  198   RECOMMENDED  UK   RR6
                                      (G) CASABLANCA MOON             198   RECOMMENDED  UK   RR5
```

BILL FAY

BILL FAY	V PNO (AB	(A) BILL FAY	1970	DERAM NOVA		SDN..12
GEORGE BIRD	B (A	(B) TIME OF LAST PERSECUTION	1971	DERAM		SML1079
JOHN MARSHALL	D (A					
TREVOR TAYLOR	D (A	RICHARD MILLS	G (A	RAY RUSSELL	G (A
ALAN RUSHTON	D (B	DARYL RUNSWICK	B (B	TONY ROBERTS	WIND (B
NICK EVANS	TROM (B	BUD PARKES	TPT (B		

FEAR ITSELF

(A) FEAR ITSELF	19	DOT	US	DLP 25942

FAY RAY

OWEN HUGHES	D (A	(A) FAY RAY	1982	WEA	GER	99188
JOHN LOVERING	G (A					
SHEILA McCARTNEY	V L PERC(A	JEFF TAYLOD	WIND ACC(A	TONY TRAVIS	B V (A

CHARLIE FEATHERS

CHARLIE FEATHERS	G V (ALL	(A) ROCKABILLY KING	1974	POLYDOR	UK	2310 293
QUINTON CLAUCH	G (C	(B) CHARLIE FEATHERS (EP)GONE GONE	1977	CHARLY	UK	CEP 116
BILL CANTRELLI	FDL (C	(C) ROCKABILLY MAN	1978	CHARLY	UK	CR 30161
STAN KESTER	STEEL (C	( ) GOOD ROCKIN' TONIGHT	19	BARRELHOUSE	US	BH 03
BILL BLACK	B (C	( ) LIVE IN MEMPHIS TENNESSEE	197	BARRELHOUSE	US	BH.06
JEFF TODD	B (C	( ) THAT ROCKABILLY CAT	1979	BARRELHOUSE	US	BH014
BILLY RILEY	B (C	( ) CHARLIE FEATHERS VOL 1	1979	FEATHERS	US	FR101
MARCUS VAN STORY	B (C	( ) CHARLIE FEATHERS VOL 2	1979	FEATHERS	US	FR102
BUBBA FEATHERS	G (C	( ) ROCK'N'ROLL	19	STAR	US	
MACK SELF	V (C					
JIMMY VAN EATON	D (C	JACK SMITH D (C WILLIAM DIEHL	B (C BRAD SUGGS	G (C

DR FEELGOOD

WILLIAM 'DR FEELGOOD' PERRYMAN (ALL	( ) R& B WITH DR FEELGOOD(EP)	196	COLUMBIA	UK	SEG 8310
AKA PIANO RED	( ) PERCUSSIVE PIANO	19	EUPHONIC	US	1212
	( ) JUMPIN' THE BOOGIE	19		US	1 2821
	( ) PIANO RED	19	BLACK LION		BLP 30171

FEELIES

BILL MILLION	PERC G V(A	(A) CRAZY RHYTHMS	1980	STIFF	UK	SEEZ 20
KEITH CLAYTON	D B V (A					
GLENN MERCER	G V D (A	ANTON FIER	D (A		

WILTON FELDER

WILTON FELDER	HRNS B(AB	(A) WE ALL HAVE A STAR	1978	ABC UK ABCL5265 US MCA		1109
DEAN PARKS	G (B	(B) INHERIT THE WIND	1980	MCA UK MCG 4013 US MCA		5144
ARTHUR ADAMS	G (B					
ROLAND BAUTISTA	G (B	JOE SAMPLE	K SYN (B	ABRAHAM LABORIEL B (B	NDUGU CHANCLER	D (B
RICKY LAWSON	D (B	PAULINHO DA COSTA PERC (B	BOBBY WOMACK	V (B	MERRY CLAYTON	V (B
PAT POWDRILL	V (B	GWEN EVANS	V (B	GERRY GARRETT	V (B	ALEX BROWN	V (B
JIM GILSTRAP	V (B	ZEDRIC TURNBOUGH	V (B	AUGIE JOHNSON	V (B

VICTOR FELDMAN

VICTOR FELDMAN PERC PNO VIBES(ALL	(A) ROCKAVIBABE	1977	DJM	UK	DJM 22058
JOHN GUERIN	D (A	( ) SUITE 16	19			C3541
TOM SCOTT	SAX (AY	( ) THE ARRIVAL OF VICTOR FELDMAN	1958	CONTEMPORARY S7549 +	LAC 12172
CHUCK DOMANICO	B (A	( ) LATINSVILLE	1960	COMTEMPORARY		LAC 580
TERRY GIBBS	(*	(D) ARTFUL DODGER	1976	CONCORD JAZZ	US	.38
LARRY BUNKER	(*	(*) VIBES TO THE POWER OF 3	1960	TOP RANK	UK	30 007
JACK SHELDON	(D	(*) VIBES TO THE POWER OF 3	19	INTERLUDE	US	
		( ) IN MY POCKET(DIRECT CUT)	1978	COHEARANT	US	CER 1001
		(Y) YOUR SMILE	1975	CHOICE	US	1005

JULIE FELIX

JULIE FELIX	V G (ALL	(A) JULIE FELIX	1964	DECCA	UK	SKL 4626
WITH		(B) SINGS DYLAN & GUTHRIE	1965	DECCA	UK	LK 4683
STEVE HAYTON	G V (P	(C) 2ND ALBUM	1965	DECCA	UK	LK 4724
DANNY THOMPSON	B (P	(D) 3RD ALBUM	1967	DECCA	UK	LK 4820
BILLY STEVENS	HCA (P	(E) CHANGES	1966	FONTANA	UK	TL/STL 5368
KESH SATHIE	TABLA (P	(F) FLOWERS	1967	FONTANA	UK	TL/STL 5437
TED LAZER	ACC (P	(F) FLOWERS	1974	CONTOUR	UK	6870 507
		(G) THIS WORLD GOES ROUND & ROUND	1968	FONTANA	UK	TL/STL 5473
		(H) THE WORLD OF JULIE FELIX	1969	DECCA	UK	SPA 6
		(I) GOING TO THE ZOO	1969	DECCA		SFL 13117
		(J) THE WORLD OF VOL 2	1970	DECCA	UK	SPA 76
		(K) THIS IS JULIE FELIX	1970	PHILIPS	UK	6382 019
		(L) CLOTHO'S WEB	1972	RAK US 31609	UK	SRKA 6752
		(M) THIS IS JULIE FELIX VOL 2	1974	PHILIPS	UK	6382 049
		(N) LIGHTNING	1974	EMI	UK	EMC 3030
		(O) LONDON PALLADIUM	1974	RCA		LSP 6021
		(P) HOT CHOCOLATA	1979	GULL	UK	GULP 1032

DICK FELLER

DICK FELLER	V (ALL	( ) NO WORDS ON ME	1974	ASYLUM	US	CM1
CHARLIE McCOY	HCA (	( ) SOME DAYS ARE DIAMONDS	1975	ASYLUM	US	7E 1044
JOHNNY GIMBLE	FDL (	( ) THEN I WROTE	1973	UA	US 094	349
PETE DRAKE	STEEL (					

NARVEL FELTS

NARVEL FELTS	V (ALL	(A) DRIFT AWAY	19	CINNAMON	US	5000
		( ) RECONSIDER ME	1975	DOT	US	DOSD 2025
		( ) GREATEST HITS	19	DOT	US	DOSD 2036
		( ) NARVEL THE MARVEL	1976	DOT	US	2033
		( ) THIS TIME	1976	HI	US	32098
		( ) DOIN WHAT I LIKE	1977	DOT	US	2065
		( ) TOUCH OF FELTS	1977	DOT	US	2070

FENDERMEN

JIM SUNDQUIST	(A	( ) MULE SKINNER BLUES	196	SOMA	US	MG 1240
PHIL HUMPHREY	(A					

MICHAEL FENNELLY

```
    MICHAEL FENNELLY    G V  (ALL   (A) LANE CHANGER                    1974  EPIC     UK 80230    US 32703
    CASEY FOUTZ       K (A          (B) STRANGERS BED                   1975  MERCURY             US 1-1043
    NICK NEWELL       SAX(A
    JIM RODFORD       B (A   ROBERT HENRIT    D   (A    HENRY SPINETTI  D  (A  DAVE WINTOUR   B  (A
    MIKE COTTON       TPT(A   JOHN BEECHAM    TROM  (A    ALAN HOLMES   SAX (A  ROD ARGENT     V  (A
    RUSS BALLARD      V (A    GASPAR LAWAL    PERC  (A    MIKE GILES    D  (A
```

SHANE FENTON & THE FENTONES

```
    SHANE FENTON      V (A   (A)    GOOD ROCKIN TONIGHT               1974  CONTOUR   UK   2870 409
    (BERNARD JEWRY)                 IM A MOODY GUY            EP      1977  EMI       UK        2696
    (LATER ALVIN STARDUST)
```

RAY FENWICK

```
    RAY FENWICK       G V   (A     (A) KEEP AMERICA BEAUTIFUL        1971  DECCA     UK   SKL 5090
    CALEB QUAYE       G     (A
    DEE MURRAY        B (A   (A     NIGEL OLSSON    D   (A   PETE YORK        D  (A
    EDDIE HARDIN      K     (A      ROGER POPE      D   (A
```

FERGUS

```
    FERGUS            G V   (A      (A) FERGUS                        1978  RONDERCREST    ROND LP1
```

JAY FERGUSON

```
    JAY FERGUSON      K V(ALL       (A) ALL ALONE IN THE END ZONE    1976  ASYLUM  US  1063  UK K53040
    JOE WALSH         G  (ABCDE     (B) THUNDER ISLAND               1977  ASYLUM  US  1115  UK K53066
    JOE VITALE        D PERC (AC    (C) REAL LIFE AINT THIS WAY      1979  ASYLUM  US 6E 158 UK K53086
    JOEY MURCIA       G  (AB        (D) TERMS & CONDITIONS           1980  CAPITAL        US 12083
    MARK ANDES        B  (E         (E) WHITE NOISE                  1982  CAPITOL        US 12196
    GEORGE PERRY      B V(A
    JOE LALA          PERC(A  STAN SKIPPER   D   (AC    TONY BATTAGLIA  B  (BCD ED BROWN    B  (B
    HAROLD COWART     B  (B   BILL SZYMCZYK  PERC PROD)BC BOB WEBB     G  (BCDE ROBBIE ALBERT K (D
    DAVID WHITE       B V(D   CURLY SMITH    D    (DC    HARRY STINSON  V  (D  JIM HORN     SAX (D
    TERRY NELSON      PERC(D  JUAN PEREZ     PERC  (C    COL CLESSER   SAX (C  MARK COLBY   SAX (C
    SCOTT CHAMBERS    B  (C   MIKE HAMILTON  G    (E     TRIS IMBODEN   D  (E  TOM KELLY    V  (E
    RANDY CALIFORNIA  G  (E   KEVIN VALENTINE D   (E     TOM FERGUSON  VLN (E DAVID TOLEGIAN HRNS (E
```

ANDY FERNBACH

```
    ANDY FERNBACH     G V   (A1     (A) IF YOU MISS YOUR CONNEXION   1969  LIBERTY   UK   LBS 83233
    DAVE FERNBACH     K (A          (1) 1969 BAND CALLED CONNEXION
    PETE CRUICKSHANK  B (A
    KEN PUSTELNIK     D (A    CHRIS ELVIN    HCA   (A    J D FANGER    G  (A1 BOB ROWE    B  (1
    PHILLIP CROWTHER  D (1
```

AL FERRIER & HIS BOPPIN' BILLIES

```
    AL FERRIER                      (A) BIRTH OF ROCKABILLY          19    GOLDSTAR   US
                                    (B) SOUND OF ROCKABILLY          19    SHOWTIME   US         1000
                                    (C) BOPPIN' TONIGHT              1977  FLYRIGHT   UK       LP525
```

FERRIS WHEEL

```
    MICHAEL SNOW V K G (AB          (A) CANT BREAK THE HABIT         1967  PYE       UK  NPL 18203
    LINDA LEWIS       V  (AB        (B) FERRIS WHEEL                 1970  POLYDOR   UK   588 066
    DAVID SWEETNAM/FORD SAX (AB
    GEORGE SWEETNAM/FORD B V(AB  DENNIS ELLIOTT  D  (AB    TERRY EDMUNDS  G  (B   BERNIE HOLLAND  G  (B
    DIANA FERREZ      V  (A   MICKY LISTON       (A    KEITH ANTHONY  (A
```

BRIAN FERRY

```
    BRIAN FERRY       V PNO (ALL    (A) THESE FOOLISH THINGS   1973 ISLAND   UK ILPS9249 ATLANTIC US 7304
    WITH                            (A) THESE FOOLISH THINGS   1977 POLYDOR RI2302 046         2310 507
    ROBBIE MONTGOMERY V    (A       (A) THESE FOOLISH THINGS   1973 ISLAND   GER                  87266
    ANN ODELL         V    (1       (B) ANOTHER TIME ANOTHER PLACE 1974 ISLAND UK ILPS9284 ATLANTIC US18113
    CHRIS SPEDDING  G  (CD1         (B) ANOTHER TIME ANOTHER PLACE 1977 POLYDOR RI 2302 047     2310 508
    ANGELETTES        V    (A       (B) ANOTHER TIME ANOTHER PLACE 1974 ISLAND GER                86067
    JOHN WETTON       B    (BCD1    (C) LET'S STICK TOGETHER   1976 ISLAND   UK ILPS9367 ATLANTIC US18187
    PHIL MANZANERA    G    (ACD1    (C) LET'S STICK TOGETHER   1977 POLYDOR RI 2302 045         2310 045
    JESSIE DAVIS      V    (A       (C) LETS STICK TOGETHER    1976 ISLAND   GER                  27953
    DYAN BIRCH        V    (D1      (D) IN YOUR MIND           1977 POLYDOR RI 2302 055 ATLANTIC US18216
    PADDY McHUGH      V    (D1C     (E) BRIDE STRIPPED BARE    1978 POLYDOR  POLD 5003 ATLANTIC US19205
    MALCOLM DUNCAN    SAX  (A       (E) BRIDE STRIPPED BARE    1978 POLYDOR NL 2344 110
    FRANK COLLINS     V    (D1      (EP) PRICE OF LOVE         1976 ISLAND    UK IEP 1
    PAUL THOMPSON     D    (ABCD1   (1) 1977 LIVE TOUR
    MARTIN DROVER     HRNS (BCD1
    NEIL HUBBARD      G    (CED  ALAN SPENNER    G    (E   WADDY WACHTEL K G (E  RICK MAROTTA   D  (E
    CHRIS MERCER   SAX (BCD  MEL COLLINS   SAX  (CD   EDDIE JOBSON  VLN K (AC MORRIS PERT  PERC(BC
    JOHN GUSTAFSON B  (C     RICK WILLS    B    (C    JOHN PORTER   G B   (ABCD DAVID O'LIST  G  (BC
    HENRY LOWTHER HRNS (BA   RUAN OLOCHLAINN SAX (BA   CHRIS PYNE    TROM (B   TONY CARR     (B
    TONY CHARLES      (B     PAUL KOSH          (B    GEOFF DALEY        (B   BOB EFFORD    (B
    MALCOLM GRIFFITHS (B     JIMMY HASTINGS     (B    JOHN PUNTER   D   (AB  ALF REECE     (B
    PETER ROBINSON    (B     RONNIE ROSS        (B    BRUCE ROWLAND      (B   STEVE SAUNDERS (B
    ALAN SKIDMORE     (B     WINSTONE STONE     (B    DAVID SKINNER PNO (AD  VICKI BROWN   V (BC
    RAY COOPER    PERC (D    MARK WARNER        (B    JACQUIE SULLIVAN V (DC HELEN CHAPPELLE V (BCD
    DOREEN CHANTER  V (DC    PRESTON HAYWARD    (D    BARRY ST JOHN V   (B   LIZA STRIKE   V (B
    DON CIRILO        V (A   ROGER BALL    SAX  (A    MARTHA WALKER V   (C
```

FEVERTREE

```
    E E WOLFE      B    (ABCD        (A) FEVER TREE               1968  UNI UK UNLS 102 US   73024
    JOHN TUTTLE    PERC(ABCD         (A) FEVER TREE               19    MCA RI US  551 NL EMI 99191
    ROB LANDES     WIND K (ABCD      (B) ANOTHER TIME ANOTHER PLACE 1968 UNI US 73040 UK MCA MUPS 347
    DENNIS KELLER  V    (ABCD        (C) CREATION                 19    UNI           US   73067
    MICHAEL        G    (ABCD        (D) FOR SALE                 1970  AMPEX         US  A 10113
    KEVIN KELLEY   D    (D
    GRANT JOHNSON  K    (D   HAL BLAINE    D    (D    DAVID COHEN   G  (D  WALT MESCAL  G (D
    JOE OSBORNE    B    (D   LARRY KNECHTAL K   (D
```

KAREL FIALKA

```
    KAREL FIALKA   V SYN (A         (A) STILL LIFE               1980  BLUEPRINT  U  BULP 5003
    ROBERT LANGRIDGE K  (A
    MARTIN DEEGAN  D    (A   HAMTONES   V    (A  ANDY BROWN  B (A   DEREK TULLOCH       SAX (A
```

```
F44                          FIELDS                                    F44
   GRAHAM FIELD    K  (A        (A) FIELDS              1971   CBS    UK 69009   US EPIC 31154
   ALAN BARRY G V B SYN(A
   ANDY McCULLOCH  D  (A    FRANK FARRELL  B  (
F44A                         FIELDS (2)                                 F44A
   STEVE LAGAN     D  (A        (A) FIELDS              1969   UNI    US      73050
   PATRICK BURKE   B  (A
   RICHARD FORTUNATO  G(A
F44B                      FIFTY FOOT HOSE                               F44B
   CORK MARCHESCHI    (AB       (A) CAULDRON            1968   LIMELIGHT    86062
   DAVID BLOSSOM  G   (AB       (B) I'VE PAID MY DUES   1970   DECCA        75225
   LARRY EVANS   G V  (AB
   KIM KIMSEY     D   (AB    TERRY HUNSLEY  B   (AB     NANCY BLOSSOM  V   (AB
F44C                      FIFTH AVENUE BAND                             F44C
   KENNY ALTMAN  G B (A         (A) FIFTH AVENUE BAND   1969   REPRISE      RSLP 6369
   JERRY BURNHAM   B FLT(A
   PETER GALLWAY G V (A    PETE HEYWOOD   D  (A    JON LIND   V   (A    MURRAY WEINSTOCK K  (A
F45                          FINCH                                      F45
   JOOP VAN NIMWEGEN G  (CD     (A) FINCH              19
   AD WAMMES      K    (D       (B) BEYOND EXPLOSION   19
   HANS BASBOOM   D    (D       (C) GLORY OF THE INNER FORCE  1975 ATCO   US      36124
   PETER VINK     B    (CD      (D) GALLEON OF PASSION  1977  ROCKBURGH   UK   ROC 103
   BEER KLAASSE   D    (CD
   CLEEM DETETMEIJER K (CD
F45A                         FINE WINE                                  F45A
   BOB MOSLEY    B V  (A        (A) FINEWINE           1976   POLYDOR   GER    2310  438
   JERRY MILLER  G V  (A
   MICHAEL BEEN   G V (A    JOHN CRAVIOTTA   D  (A
F46                       PETER FINGER                                  F46
   PETER FINGER    G   (ALL     (A) DETLEF & FINGER    197  KICKING MULE UK 104
                               (B) BOTTLENECK GUITAR SOLOS  1975 KICKING MULE UK 105  US  116
                               (C) ACCOUSTIC ROCK GUITAR   1977 KICKING MULE UK 144  US  149
F47                       FINGERPRINTZ                                  F47
   JIMME O'NEIL  G V  (ABCD     (A) THE VERY DAB       1979   VIRGIN UK 2119   GER  201 048
   CHA BURNZ     G V  (ABCD     (B) DISTINGUISHING MARKS 1980 VIRGIN UK 2170   GER  202 284
   KENNY ALTON   B V  (ABCD     (B) DISTINGUISHING MARKS 1980 VIRGIN US 13136
   BOB SCHILLING  D   (ABC      (C) DANCING WITH MYSELF  12" EP  1979 VIRGIN UK 23512
   STEP LANG      V   (C        (D) BEAT NOIR          1981   VIRGIN UK 2201
   BOGDAN WICZLING    (D
   STEVE KING     K   (D    SADIE THE CAT    V   (D    RON FRANCOIS   B   (D   DON SNOW   K   (D
   KRZYSTOF KAFKA ACC (D    JOHN EARLE  SAX    (D    DICK HANSON   TPT (D
F48                       MIKE FINNIGAN                                 F48
   MIKE FINNIGAN  B V (AB       (A) MIKE FINNIGAN      1976   WB  US  2944   UK  K56257
   ROGER HAWKINS  D   (A        (B) BLACK & WHITE      1978   CBS      US     35258
   DAVID HOOD     B   (B
   BARRY BECKETT  K   (A    PETE CARR       G   (A    JIMMY JOHNSON   G  (A    AMOS GARRETT   G  (B
   TOM ROADY     PERC (A    JOHNNY GIMBLE  FDL   (A    TEX WEX      PERC (A    HARRISON CALLOWAY HRNS(A
   RON EADES      SAX (A    CHARLES ROSE   TROM  (A    PEE WEE ERWIN  TPT (A    BUDDY MORROW   TROM(A
   BOB WILBUR     CLAR(A    DON BUTTERFIELD TUBA (A    ED SAUTER     STR (A    STAMPS QUARTET  V  (A
   FRANCES BARNETTE V (A    PRISCILLA THOMAS V   (A    JACKIE DIXON   V  (A    SUZY STORM     V  (A
   BARBARA WYRICK  V  (A    AVA ALDRIDGE     V   (A    JAMES GRIFFIN  V  (A    MARIA MULDAUR  V  (A
F48A                      FINNIGAN & WOOD                               F48A
   MIKE FINNIGAN V K HCA(A      (A) CRAZED HIPSTERS    1972   BLUE THUMB  US  BTS  .35
   JERRY WOOD    V G  (A
   DON CLAREY     D   (A    RAY BAGBY     D  (A       DAVE GATES  B   (A   RAY LOECKLIE   SAX (A
F48B                         FIRE                                       F48B
   DAVID LAMBERT V G K(A        (A) MAGIC SHOEMAKER    1970   PYE      UK  NSPL18343
   BOB VOICE     D V  (A
   DICK DUFALL   B V  (A
F48C                      FIRE ESCAPE                                   F48C
   HANK LEVINE   PROD  (A       ( ) PSYCHOTIC REACTION 19     GNP CRESENDO   US   2034
   LARRY GOLDBERG      (
F48D                      FIRE & RAIN                                   F48D
                               (A) FIRE & RAIN        1973   MERCURY  US    1 654
F48E                      FIRE ENGINES                                  F48E
   RUSSELL BURN   G   (A        (A) LUBRICATE YOUR LIVING ROOM  1980 ACCESSORY  UK   ACCOOL
   DAVID HENDERSON G V (A       (B) AUFGELADEN UND BEREIT FUR ACTION  1981 FAST  GER
   GRAHAM MAIN    B   (A
   MURRAY SLADE   G   (A
F48F                      FIREBALLET                                    F48F
   JIM COMO     V D PERC(AB     (A) NIGHT ON BALD MOUNTAIN  1975 PASSPORT  US   98010
   BRYAN HOWE   K V SAX(AB      (B) TWO TOO           1976   PASSPORT  US   98016
   RYCHE CHLANDA G V MAN(AB
   MARTIN BIGLIN  G B (AB   FRANK PETTO   K SYN V(AB  IAN McDONALD   WIND(A JOHN ZANGRADO  WIND (B
   BRIAN CUOMO    K   (B    MARY ELLEN DURKA  V  (B   IRENE CONRAD   V   (B JUDY ELLINGTON  V   (B
   JOAN ELLINGTON V   (B    PAT ELLINGTON     V  (B   ALPHONSE ROCQUE PEC (B
F49                        FIREBALLS                                    F49
   JIMMY GILMER   K   (        (A) VAQUERO           1961 TOP RANKUK35 105 US(M)343(S)643
   GEORGE TOMSCO  G   (        ( ) TORQUAY           1963   DOT      US     25512
   STAN LARK      B   (        ( ) SUGAR SHACK       196    DOT      US     25545
   ERIC BUDD      D   (        ( ) FIREWATER         196    DOT      US     25856
                               ( ) SUGER SHACKERS    19     CROWN    US
                               ( ) JIMMY GILMER & FIREBALLS  19  CROWN  US     5376
                               ( ) HERE WE ARE       19     WARWICK  US     W2042
                               ( ) BOTTLE OF WINE    1968 STATESIDEUK10237 US ATCO 33239
                               ( ) COME ON REACT     1969 LONDON UK  8396  US ATCO 33275
                               ( ) CAMPUSOLOGY       19     DOT      US
```

```
RICK ROBERTS    G V   (ABCDEF      (A) FIREFALL                           1976   ATLANTIC US 18174 UK K  50260
MIKE CLARKE     D     (ABCDF       (B) LUNA SEA                           1977   ATLANTIC US 19101 UK K  50355
MARK ANDES      B     (ABCDF       (C) ELAN                               1978   ATLANTIC US 19183 UK K  50494
JOCK BARTLEY    G     (ABCDEF      (D) UNDERTOW                           1980   ATLANTIC US 16006 UK K  50665
LARRY BURNETT   V G   (ABCDEF      (E) CLOUDS ACROSS THE SUN              1981   ATLANTIC US 16024 UK K  50767
DAVID MUSE      K WIND(ABCDEF      (F) BEST OF                            1981   ATLANTIC US 19316 UK K  50839
PETER GRAVES    TROM  (A
WHIT SIDENER    SAX  (A   ANDREW LOVE     SAX  (B   KEN FAULK       TPT  (A   WAYNE JACKSON HRNS  (A
JACK HALE       TROM (A   LEWIS COLLINS   SAX  (B   JAMES MITCHELL  SAX  (B   CLYDIE KING    V   (B
VANETTA FIELDS   V   (B   SHIRLEY MATTHEWS V  (B   JOE LALA       PERC(B   FLACO PADRON   PERC(B
ALAN ESTES      PERC(B   SKIP EDWARDS    PNO  (B   TIM SCHMIT      V   (B   JERRY AIELLO   ORG(B
LAURA TAYLOR     V   (C   STEVE FOREMAN   PERC (C   JIM KELTNER     D   (C   TRIS IMBODEN   D    (EF
TOM KELLY        V   (D   CHRISTOPHER DENNIS PERC(D   SANDRA RHODES   V   (D   DONNA RHODES   V   (D
CHARLIE CHALMERS V  (D   GEORGE HAWKINS B V  (EF   PAUL HARRIS  K       (D   ANDY NEWMARK   D   (D
BILL PAYNE      K   (D   DAVID MUSEL     WIND K(EF   LISA MENZO      V   (EF   MARY ANN KENNEDY V(E
FARRELL MORRIS  PERC(E   KYLE LEHNING    K   (E    PAM ROSE        V   (E
```

F50A   FIREFLIES   F50A
```
RITCHIE ADAMS                 ( ) YOU WERE MINE             19         TAURUS         US   1002
LEE REYNOLDS
JOHNNY VISCELLI    PAUL GIACOLONE
```

F50B   FIREPOINT   F50B
```
BOB HALL        K   (A      (A) FIREPOINT                   1969   SPARK      UK    SRLM 2003
MIKE COOPER     G   (A
SAM MITCHELL    G   (A   DAVE KELLY    G    (A    DUFFY POWER  HCA (A  TOM ROBINSON
GERALD HARP         (
```

F51   FIRESIGN THEATRE   F51
```
DAVID OSSMAN    V PERC(ALL      (A) WAITING FOR THE ELECTRICIAN OR SOMEONE   1968 CBS UK 65129 US  9518
PHILIP AUSTIN   G K V (ALL      (B) HOW TO BE IN TWO PLACES AT ONCE         1968 CBS UK 65130 US  9884
PHILIP PROCTOR  VLN V FLT (ALL  (C)DONT CRUSH THAT DWARF HAND ME THE PLIERS 1972 CBS        US 30102
PETER BERGMAN   SAX V G B (ALL  (D) I THINK WERE ALL BOZOS ON THIS BUS      1972 CBS        US 30737
DAVID GRIMM     ORG  (B         (E) DEAR FRIENDS                      DBL    1972 CBS        US 31099
THE GRATEFULL BOOGIES K(B       (F) NOT INSANE OR ANY THING YOU WANT        1972 CBS        US 31585
WILLIAM F MAAOCH     (B         (G) IN THE NEXT WORLD YOU'RE ON YOUR OWN    1972 CBS US 31383 RI 33475
CATHE COZZI          (B         (H) TV OR NOT TV                            1973 CBS        US 32199
ANNA LEE AUSTIN      (B         (J) THE TALE OF THE GIANT RAT OF SUMATRA    1974 CBS        US 32370
JANE DANSIE     V    (B         (L) EVERYTHING YOU KNOW IS WRONG            1975 CBS        US 33141
ELIZABETH PLUMB V    (B         (M) FORWARD INTO THE PAST                   1977 CBS        US 34391
JOHN KINICK     V    (B         (N) JUST FOLKS                              197  BUTTERFLY  US   001
CATHLEEN O'MARA V    (B         (O) FIRESIGN WORLD                          197  WRMB       US   512
THE ANDROID SISTERS V (B        (P) NICK DANGER THE CASE OF THE MISSING SHOE 1979 RHINO    US   506
LITTLE BUBBLES  SAX  (B         (Q) FIGHTING CLOWNS                         1980 RHINO      US   018
AMBIENTS NOYES CHORAL V(B
OONA ELLIOTT    V   (C   C D TAYLOR    G     (F   MICHAEL GWYNNE   D FLT(F   BO MAY       SAX (F
CYRUS FARYAR    B   (FH  RICHARD PARKER K    (Q   JEFF BAXTER     G   (Q   ED ROSCETTI    D  (Q
JOHN MITCHELL   SAX (T   DICK SPENCER WIND   (Q   RICHARD COOPER  TPT (Q
```

F51A   FIRST AID   F51A
```
ALAN WORMALD    G V  (A      (A) NOSTRADAMUS                    1977   DECCA      UK   TXS 117
KEITH PARKINSON K    (
DAVE FREEMAN    PERC (A   NORRIE TENNENT   B    (A
```

F53   FIRST CLASS   F53
```
CHAS MILLS      V    (       ( ) FIRST CLASS                1974   UK 53109 US   UK  UKAL 1008
TONY BURROWS    V    (       ( ) S S T                      1976   UK           UK  UKAL 1022
JOHN CARTER     V    (       ( ) GOING FIRST CLASS          1978   ALL PALTINUM US      3018
DEL JOHN        V    (       ( ) FIRST CLASS                1981   SUGARHILL    US       255
SPENCER JAMES   G V  (
EDDIE RICHARDS  D V  (
ROBIN SHAW      B V  (       CLIVE BARRETT     K V  (
```

F54   WILD MAN FISCHER   F54
```
LARRY 'WILD MAN' FISCHER V(ALL   (A) AN EVENING WITH WILD MAN FISCHER 1970 REPRISE 6332 BIZARRE  6332
DON BUCHANAN    G    (B          (B) WILDMANIA                         1977 RHINO          RNLP  001
JOE STODDARD    D    (B
STUART DEAL     B    (B          LEONARD SAMARTINO    G V   A(B   SANDRA SAMARTINO   V   (B
FRANK ZAPPA     PERC (A          ART TRIPP         PERC   (A   KIM FOWLEY         V   (A
RODNEY BINGENHEIMER  (A          G T O's           (A
```

F54A   FISCHER Z   F54A
```
JOHN WATTS      G V  (ABC     (A) WORD SALAD                  1979   UA US 975       UK   UAG 30232
STEVE SKOLNIK   K V  (AB      (B) GOING DEAF FOR A LIVING     1980   UA US 1048      UK   UAG 30295
STEVE LIDDLE    D PERC(ABC    (C) RED SKIES OVER PARADISE     1981   LIBERTY NL83100 UK   UAG 30326
DAVID GRAHAM    B    (ABC     (EP) OVER GERMANY               1981   LIBERTY        GER       83101
```

F55   FISHBAUGH FISHBAUGH ZORN   F55
```
GARY FISHBAUGH V G PERC  (A     (A) FISHBAUGH FISHBAUGH & ZORN   1972   CBS        UK       64783
PAULA FISHBAUGH V PNO PERC(A
PETE ZORN     V B G WIND PERC(A   RICK WEST        G    (A   BRIAN DALY      G    (A
JUNIOR CAMPBELL  G K  (A          STUART COWELL    G    (A   TERRY COX       D    (A
RAYMOND DUFFY    D    (A          REG GUEST        K    (A   GORDON HUNTLEY  STEEL(A
GRAHAM PRESKETT  VLN  (A          MIKE STONE       PERC (A
```

F55A   SONNY FISHER   F55A
```
SONNY FISHER        (A       (A) TEXAS ROCKABILLY 10"        19     ACE        UK   10CH14
```

F56   MATTHEW FISHER   F56
```
MATTHEW FISHER PERC V K G HCA(ABC   (A) JOURNEYS END          1973   RCA  UK SF8380    APLI 0195
GEOFF SWETTENHAM D   (A             (B) I'LL BE THERE         1974   RCA              APLI 0325
MICK HAWKSWORTH  B   (A             (C) MATTHEW FISHER        1980   VERTIGO UK 9198652 US A&M4801
BOBBY HARRISON   V   (A             (D) STRANGE DAYS          1981   MERCURY     NL   6302 108
TONY BURROWS     V   (A
JOHN CARTER      V   (A   MIKE JAPP     G      (B   ALAN COULTER    D PERC (B   STEVE BINGHAM   B (BC
JIM RYAN       B G(B      JAMES FRANK   D      (B   DAVE MATTACKS   D   (C   HENRY SPINETTI  D (C
BARRY DE SOUZA  D (C      DILL KATZ     B      (C   PAUL WESTWOOD   B   (C   TIM RENWICK     G (C
MICK GRABHAM    V (C      JIM DEWAR     V      (C   PETE ZORN       V   (C   JOHN VERITY     V (C
ROD ARGENT      V (C      KEN LEWIS     V      (B
```

FIST

```
F56A
      HARRY HILL         D     (A      (A) TURN HELL ON          1980  MCA             UK    MCF 3082
      KEITH SATCHFIELD   G V   (A      (B) HOT SPIKES            1981  A&M             US        4823
      JOHN WYLIE         B V   (A
      DAVE IRWIN         G V   (A
F56B                             PATRIK FITZGERALD                                              F56B
      PATRIK FITZGERALD  V     (ALL    (A) SAFETY PIN STUCK IN MY HEART EP  1978  SMALL WONDER  UK  SMALL4
                                       (B) PARANOID WARD      EP  1979  SMALL WONDER   UK    WEENY1
                                       (C) BACK STREET BOYS   EP  1979  SMALL WONDER   UK    SMALL6
F57                                G F FITZGERALD                                              F57
      G F FITZGERALD     G B K V (A    (A) MOUSEPROOF             1970  UNI                 UNLS 115
      ALAN PLACE         G     (A
      ROD HERMAN         G     (A      B J COLE         STEEL (A    RIK KENTON       B    (A
      IAN ANDREWS        B     (A      GEOFF LEIGH      SAX   (A    SAM GOPAL        TABLA  (A
      TED TETLAN         D     (A      TONY TURNBULL    D     (A
F57A                              FIVE AMERICANS                                               F57A
                                       ( ) I SEE THE LIGHT       19    ABNAK           US        8503
                                       ( ) WESTERN UNION         19    ABNAK           US        2067
                                       ( ) PROGRESSIONS          19    ABNAK           US        2069
                                       ( ) NOW & THEN            19    ABNAK           US        2071
F57B                               FIVE BY FIVE                                                 F57B
                                       (A) NEXT EXIT             1968  PAULA           US    LPS 2202
F58                              FIVE DOLLAR SHOES                                              F58
      GREGG DIAMOND      D V   (A      (A) FIVE DOLLAR SHOES     1972  NEIGHBORHOOD    UK    NH 3001
      TOM GRAVES         K V   (A
      JIM GREGORY        B V   (A      MIKE MILLIUS     V HCA (A    SCOTT WOODY      G V  (A
F59                              FIVE HAND REEL                                                 F59
      BOBBY EAGLESHAM    V G   (ABCD   (A) FIVE HAND REEL        1976  RUBBER G19 RCA  PL 25065
      DICK GAUGHAN       G V   (ABC    (B) FOR A' THAT           1977  RCA             PL 25066
      TOM HICKLAND     K VLN V (ABCD   (C) EARL O'MORAY          1978  RCA             PL 25150
      BARRY LYONS      PERC B K (ABCD  (D) BUNCH OF FIVES        1979  TOPIC           12TS 406
      DAVE TULLOCH       D     (ABCD   (E) NOTHING BUT THE BEST  1980  RCA             UK   25267
      SAM BRACKEN        V G   (D
F59A                        FIVE MAN ELECTRICAL BAND                                            F59A
      LES EMMERSON       G V   (       ( ) FIVE MAN ELECTRICAL BAND  1969  CAPITOL     US      ST165
      BRIAN RADING       V B   (       ( ) FIVE MAN ELECTRICAL BAND  19    PICKWICK    US  SPC 3289
      RICK BELANGER      D V   (       ( ) COMING OF AGE         197   LIONEL              1101
      TEDDY GEROW       SAX K V(       ( ) GOODBYE & BUTTERFLIES 19    LIONEL 1100 US MGM 4725
      MIKE BELANGER      V PERC(       ( ) SWEET PARADISE        19    LIONEL              1009
                                       ( ) FIND THE ONE          1972  LIONEL          US
F59B                               FIVE ROYALES                                                F59B
      LOWMAN PAULING     V     (       ( ) DEDICATED TO YOU      19    KING                580
      CLARENCE PAULING   V     (       ( ) FIVE ROYALES          19    KING                678
      JOHNNY MOORE       V     (       ( ) ALL TIME HITS         19    KING                955
      OBEDIAH CARTER     V     (       ( ) ROCKIN'               19    APOLLO              488
      JOHNNY TANNER      V     (
F59C                               FIVE OR SIX                                                 F59C
                                       (A) POLAR EXPOSURE        1981  CHERRY RED      UK   CHERRY23
F59D                              FIVE SPECIAL                                                 F59D
                                       (A) SPECIAL EDITION       1980  ELEKTRA US 270      K52230
F60                               ROBERTA FLACK                                               F60
      ROBERTA FLACK    V PNO(ALL       (A) FIRST TAKE            1969  ATLANTIC US 8230   UK588 204
      WITH                             (A) FIRST TAKE            1971  ATLANTIC        RI UK K40040
      JOHN PIZZARELLI    G     (A      (B) CHAPTER TWO           1970  ATLANTIC US 1569  UK 2400 023
      RON CARTER         B     (A      (B) CHAPTER TWO           1971  ATLANTIC        RI UK K40097
      RAY LUCAS          D     (A      (C) QUIET FIRE            1971  ATLANTIC US 1594   UK K40297
      FRANK WESS         SAX   (A      (D) & DONNIE HATHAWAY     1972  ATLANTIC US 7716   UK K40380
      SELDON POWELL      SAX   (A      (E) KILLING ME SOFTLY     1973  ATLANTIC US 7271
      BENNIE POWELL      TROM  (A      (E) KILLING ME SOFTLY     1973  ATLANTIC US 19154  UK K50021
      JOE NEWMAN         TPT   (A      (F) FEEL LIKE MAKIN LOVE  1975  ATLANTIC US 18131  UK K50049
      JIMMY NOTTINGHAM   TPT   (A      (G) BLUE LIGHTS IN THE BASEMENT 1977 ATLANTIC US 19149 UK K50040
      REGGIE LUCAS       G     (GHJ    (H) ROBERTA FLACK         1978  ATLANTIC US 19186  UK K50495
      HOWARD KING        D V   (GHJ    (J) FEATURING DONNIE HATHAWAY 1980 ATLANTIC US 16013 UK K50696
      JIM GILSTRAP       V     (G      (K) LIVE & MORE           1981  ATLANTIC US 2/7004
      DAVID SPINOZZA     G     (GH
      HARRY WHITTAKER    K     (GHJ    (AB) FIRST TAKE / CHAPTER TWO  1975  ATLANTIC   RI UK K60062
      RONNIE FOSTER      K     (GHJ    ( ) FIRST TIME I SAW YOU  19    PICKWICK          SHM 3022
      DAVE CAREY         PERC  (GH
      GARY KING          PERC (G   DON GROLNICK      K   (G    PAUL GRIFFIN    K   (GH   MICHAEL KAMEN       OBOE (G
      ROB MOUNSEY        K    (GH  LEON PENDARVISK   V   (GH   GWEN GUTHRIE    V   (GHJ  ANTHONY JACKSON     B    (GHJ
      BRENDA WHITE       V    (GHJ BASIL FEARRINGTON B   (GHJ  WILL LEE        B   (GH   LANI GROVES         V    (GH
      JIMMY MAELEN       PERC (G   STEVE GADD        D   (GH   JIMMY WONG      D   (G    IDRIS MUHAMMAD      D    (G
      ALLEN SCHWARZBERG  D    (G   MTUME             PERC (GH  ERROL BENNETT  PERC (GHJ  DONNY HATHAWAY      V PNO(DJ
      EUGENE McDANIELS   V    (G   ZACK SANDERS      V   (GH   HIRAM BULLOCK   G   (HJ   CLIFF MORRIS        G    (H
      MONTY ALEXANDER    K    (H   HOWARD SCHNEIDER  K   (H    BRIAN ALLSOP    B   (H    ULLLANDA McCULLOUGH V    (H
      ELEANORE MILLS     V    (J   JOCELYN SHAW      V   (J    ERIC MERCURY    V   (J    ED WALSH            SYN  (J
      HUBERT EAVES       SYN  (J   STEVE FERRONE     D   (H    GARY MURE       D   (H    WARREN CHIASSON     PERC (H
      ANGELO DIBRACCIO   SAX  (H   LARRY ALEXANDER   PERC (H   SHERRY WILSON   FLT (H    FRANK LLOYD         V    (H
      LUTHER VANDROSS    V    (HJ  YVONNE LEWIS      V   (GH   TOMMY SMITH     V   (H    ELURIEL BARFIELD    B    (J
      RAY JONES          K    (J   RAY CHEW          K   (J    HUGH McCRACKEN  G   (GH   JEFF MIRONOV        G    (GHJ
      JOHN TROPEA        G    (GJ  DENIECE WILLIAMS  V   (G
F60A                                 FLAME                                                     F60A
      JIMMY CRESPO       G     (A      (A) QUEEN OF THE NEIGHBOURHOOD  1977  RCA        PL 12160
      FRANK RUBY         G     (A      (B) FLAME                 1978  RCA             US       2690
      MARGE RAYMOND      V     (A
```

FLAIRCK

```
                              ( ) GEVECHT MET DE ENGEI            1980  POLYDOR        NL   2925 097
                              ( ) VARIATIONS ON A LADY            1980  POLYDOR        NL   2480 508
                              ( ) LIVE IN AMSTERDAM        DBL    1980  POLYDOR        NL   2646 103
```

F61   FLAMIN' GROOVIES   F61

```
   CYRIL JORDAN      G V  (123ABDEGJK   (A) SNEAKERS        10" LP  1969  SNAZZ         US        2371
   GEORGE ALEXANDER  B    (123ABCEGJK   (A) SNEAKERS        10" LP  1975  SKYDOG        US   FGG  803
   TIM LYNCH         G    (ABDE         (B) SUPER NAZZ              1970  EPIC          US        26487
   DANNY MIHM        D    (12ABDE       (D) FLAMINGO               1971  KAMA SUTRA    US   KSBS 2021
   RON GRECO         D    (             (D) THIS IS (FLAMINGO)     1975  METRONOME     EURO 201 707
   JAMES FARRELL     G    (23G          (E) TEENAGE HEAD           1971  KAMA SUTRA    US   KSBS 2031
   CHRIS WILSON      G V  (23GJK        (DE)FLAMINGO/HEAD          1976  KAMA SUTRA    UK   KSMD101/1
   JEAN CHARLES COSTA   V(E             (DE)COLLECTORS ITEMS (HEAD/FLAMINGO) 1976 KAMA SUTRA  940 106/7
   JIM DICKINSON     PNO  (E            (DE) FLAMIN' GROOVIES  DBL  19    POLYDOR       UK   2683 003
   TERRY RAE         D    (             (F) GREASE      (EP)       197   SKYDOG        US        66001
   DAVID WRIGHT      D    (3KGJ         (G) SHAKE SOME ACTION      1976  SIRE          UK   9103 251
   MIKE WILHELM      G    (KJ           (G) SHAKE SOME ACTION      197   SIRE US  7521 GER       26464
   ROY A LONEY       V    (1ABDE        (G) SHAKE SOME ACTION      197   PHILIPS       EURO 6370 804
   STEPHEN GOLDMAN   PROS (B            (H) MORE GREASE(EP)        19    SKYDOG US 66202 FR      FG13
   RICHARD ROBINSON  PROD (DE           (I) STILL SHAKIN'          1976  BUDDAH        US        5683
   DAVE EDMUNDS      G PROD(GJ          (I) STILL SHAKIN'          1976  PHILIPS       EURO      940541
   KANN BERG         V    (E            (J) NOW                    1978  SIRE   US 6059 UK       7059
   R MELTZER         V    (             (J) NOW                    1978  SIRE               9103 333
   ROGER BECHINAN    PROD (K            (J) NOW                    1978  SIRE               7222 103
                                        (K) JUMPIN IN THE NIGHT    1979  SIRE          UK   SRK 6067
                                        (EP) SLOW DEATH            197   UA            UK   406
                                        (EP) SHAKE SOME ACTION     197   SIRE          UK   6198 086
                                        (EP) ABSOLUTELY SWEET MARY 197   SIRE          UK   SIR 4018
                                        (EP) FEEL A WHOLE LOT BETTER 1978 SIRE         UK   6078 619
```

F61A   FLAMIN' OH'S   F61A

```
   ROBERT WILKINSON  G V  (A            (A) FLAMIN' OH'S           1980  FAT CITY      US   2504
   BOB MEIDE         PNO  (A
   JODY RAY          B    (A   JOSAF H BEHREND    K V (A
```

F62   FLAMING YOUTH   F62

```
   RONNIE CARYL      B    (A            (A) ARK 2                  19    UNI                73075
   GORDON SMITH      G    (A            (A) ARK 2                  1969  FONTANA       UK   STL 5533
   PHIL COLLINS      D    (A
   BRIAN CHATTON     K    (A
```

F62A   TOMMY FLANDERS   F62A

```
   TOMMY FLANDERS    V    (A            (A) THE MOONSTONE          1969  VERVE US 3075 UK   SVLP 6020
   JERRY SCHEFF      (A
   BRUCE LANGHORN    (A    DICK ROSMINI      (A    MICHAEL BOTTS        (A DENNIS McCARTHY    (A
```

F63   FLASH   F63

```
   TONY KAYE         K    (A            (A) FLASH                  1972  SOVEREIGN UK SVNA 7251 US CAPITOL 11040
   PETER BANKS BAN G V SYN (ABC         (B) FLASH IN THE CAN       1972  SOVEREIGN UK SVNA 7255 US CAPITOL 11115
   COLIN CARTER      V D  (ABC          (C) OUT OF OUR HANDS       1973  SOVEREIGN UK SVNA 7260 US CAPITOL 11218
   RAY BENNETT K B G V SYN(ABC          (C) OUT OF OUR HANDS       1973  SOVEREIGN              IMP XHVL 1026
   MIKE HOUGH        D PERC (ABCD
```

F64   FLASH CADILLAC   F64

```
   FLASH CADILLAC    GV   (ABCD         (A) FLASH CADILLAC & THE CONTINENTAL 1973 EPIC US 31787 UK 65438
   WARREN'BUTCH'KNIGHT B V(ABC          (B) NO FACE LIKE CHROME    1974  EPIC US 32488       UK 65870
   SAM McFADIN       G V  (A            (C) SONS OF BEACHES        1975  PRIVATE STOCK      US   2003
   WALLY STEWART     D    (C            (C) SONS OF BEACHES        1975  PRIVATE STOCK UK 1002 +2012
   ANGELO MOE        K V  (A C          (D) ROCK'N'ROLL FOREVER    19    EPIC US 33465
   GEORGE ROBINSON   SAX  (A
   JOHN MASION       D V  (A    LINN PHILLIPS    G V (    TOXEY FRENCH   PROD  (C SPIDER BEMENT   SAX (C
```

F65   FLASH FEARLESS   F65

```
   ELKIE BROOKS      V    (A     (A) FLASH FEARLESS Vs THE ZORG WOMEN  1975  CHRYSALIS    UK   CHR 1081
   FRANKIE MILLER (US) V (A
   ALICE COOPER      V    (A    JAMES DEWAR     V   (A    JIM DANDY      V    (A   KAY GARNER    V  (A
   MADDY PRIOR       V    (A    DOREEN CHANTER  V   (A    LESLEY DUNCAN  V    (A   KEITH MOON    K  (A
   THUNDERTHIGHS     V    (A    JOHN ENTWISTLE  V B (A    MICK GRABHAM   G    (A   CARMINE APPICE D  (A
   NICKY HOPKINS     K    (A    MIKE DEACON     K   (A    GRAHAM DEACON  PERC (A   ROBERT JOHNSON G  (A
   JOHN WEIDER       G    (A    BILL BRUFORD    D   (A    JUSTIN HAYWARD G    (A   JIM FRANK     HCA (A
   EDDIE JOBSON      K VLN(A    STEVE PETTICAN  G   (A    CHICK CHURCHILL K   (A   HOWIE CASEY   SAX (A
   JILL MACKINTOSH   V    (A    KIRK DUNCAN     PNO (A    KENNEY JONES   D    (A
```

F65A   FLASH AND THE PAN   F65A

```
   GEORGE YOUNG      SYN V(AB           (A) FLASH AND THE PAN      1979  ENSIGN  UK ENVY6 US EPIC 36018
   HARRY VANDA       G V  (AB           (A) FLASH AND THE PAN      1979  MERCURY         EURO 6310 956
   WARREN MORGAN     PNO  (B            (B) LIGHTS IN THE NIGHT    1980  ENSIGN  UK ENVY13 US EPIC 36432
   RAY ARNOTT        D    (B            (B) LIGHTS IN THE NIGHT    1980  MERCURY         EURO 6359 012
   LES KARSKI        B    (B
```

F65B   STEVE FLASHMAN   F65B

```
   STEVE FLASHMAN    G K V(AB           (A) FREEFALL               1980  KINGSWAY       UK   KMR313
                                        (B) SIGNWRITER             1981  KINGSWAY       UK   KMB349
```

F65C   FLASHMAN   F65C

```
                                        (A) FLASHMAN               1979  VANGUARD       US   VSD79403
```

F65D   F LATLANDERS   F65D

```
   JIMMY GILMORE     G V  (A            (A) ONE MORE ROAD(1972 REC) 1980 CHARLY         UK   CR 30189
   JOE ELY           G V  (A
   BUTCH HANCOCK     V    (A    TOMMY HANCOCK   FDL (A    SYLVESTER RICE B    (A   STEVE WESSON  SAW?(A
```

F65E   FLAVIUM   F65E

```
                                        (A) NO KIDDING            1980  POLYDOR        NL   2925 096
                                        (B) FLAVIUM LIVE          1980  POLYDOR        NL   2925 170
                                        (C) BEST OF               1980  ELF            NL   9586
```

MICK FLEETWOOD

```
     MICK FLEETWOOD    G PERC V(A      (A) THE VISITOR                    1981   RCA US AFLI 4080 UK      5044
     GEORGE HAWKINS    V B K G(A
     PETER GREEN       G V (A      LORD TIKI        PERC(A      TODD SHARP      G      (A    GEORGE HARRISON G V(A
     IAN BAIRNSON      G    (A      MIKE MORAN SYN      (A      EBALI GBIKO ENSEMBLE   (A    ACCRO R C CHOIR  V(A
     ADJO & SUPERBRAINS     (A      GHANA FOLKLORE GROUP (A
```

F66   FLEETWOOD MAC   F66

```
     MICK FLEETWOOD    D    (ALL      (A) FLEETWOOD MAC            1968   BLUE HORIZON  UK 7 63200 US EPIC   26402
     JOHN McVIE        B    (ALL      (A) FLEETWOOD MAC            1973   EMBASSY                  31036 +   31494
     CHRISTINE McVIE   V K(BGHJKLMNOPQR XY (B) MR WONDERFULL       1968   BLUE HORIZON  UK 7 63205
     PETER GREEN       G V (ABCDEGWXYZV (C) BLUES JAM AT CHESS     1969   BLUE HORIZON  US 3801      UK    7 66227
     JEREMY SPENCER    G V (ABCDEFGXYZV (C) FLEETWOOD MAC IN CHICAGO 1969 SIRE     US 3715+2XS            6009
     BOB BRUNNING      B    (A       (D) THEN PLAY ON              1969   REPRISE US 6368           UK MIDI24001
     BOB WELCH         G V (HKLMJ     (D) THEN PLAY ON             1970   REPRISE                   UK  K 44103
     STEVE GREGORY     SAX  (B       (E) PIOUS BIRD OF GOOD OMEN   1969   BLUE HORIZON  (COMP)      UK  7 63215
     RAY LINDSAY       G    (RQ       (E) PIOUS BIRD OF GOOD OMEN  1981   EMBASSY                   UK     32050
     JOHNNY ALMOND     SAX  (B       (F) KILN HOUSE               1970   REPRISE US 6408 UK 9004 +  UK K 54001
     ROLAND VAUGHAN    SAX  (B       (G) ORIGINAL FLEETWOOD MAC    1971   SIRE    US 6045       UK CBS 63875
     DUSTER BENNETT    HCA  (B       (H) FUTURE GAMES              1971   REPRISE UUS6465           UK  K 44153
     DAVE HOWARD       SAX  (B       (J) BARE TREES                1972   REPRISE US 2080+2278      UK  K 44181
     DANNY KIRWAN      V    (CDEFHXV  (K) PENGUIN                  1973   REPRISE US 2138           UK  K 44235
     BOB WESTON        G    (LK       (L) MYSTERY TO ME            1973   REPRISE US 2158+2279      UK  K 44248
     MARTIN BIRCH      G    (L        (M) HEROES ARE HARD TO FIND  1974   REPRISE US 2196  UK        K 54026
     DAVE WALKER       HCA V(K        (N) FLEETWOOD MAC            1975   REPRISE US 2225 +2281     UK  K 54043
     STEVE NYE         K    (K        (O) RUMOURS                  1977   WB      US 3010           UK  K 56344
     RALPH RICHARDSON  PERC (K        (P) TUSK        DBL          1980   WB      US 3350           UK  K 66088
     RUSSEL VALDEZ     PERC (K        (Q) LIVE        DBL          1980   WB      US 3500           UK  K 66097
     FRED TOTESANT     PERC (K        (R) MIRAGE                   1982   WB      US   23607
     WADDY WACHTEL     G    (N
     STEVE NICKS       V    (NOPQR    (U) ENGLISH ROSE             1969   EPIC  US26446 75 RI 33740  UK CBS 22025
     LINDSEY BUCKINGHAM G  V(NOPQR    (V) BLACK MAGIC WOMAN        197    EPIC    US 30632           UK     31798
     OTIS SPANN        PNO  (C        (W) GREATEST HITS            1971   CBS                       UK CBS 69011
     WILLLIE DIXON     B    (C        (X) VINTAGE YEARS            1975   SIRE 3706+ 6006           UK CBS 88227
     WALTER HORTON     HCA  (C        (Y) ALBATROSS                1977   EMBASSY                   UK     31569
     GUITAR BUDDY      G    (C        (Z) MAN OF THE WORLD         1978   CBS                       UK     83110
     HONEYBOY EDWARDS  G    (C        ( ) BEST OF                  1978   REPRISE                   UK  K 44138
     SP LEARY          D    (C        ( ) BLACK MAGIC WOMAN        1980   EMBASSY                   UK     31798
     SNEAKY PETE       STEEL(M
     J T BROWN         V SAX(K   EDDIE BOYD V PNO (E   TONY TORARO PERC (Q    JEFFREY SOVA      K   (Q
```

JOY FLEMING

```
     JOY FLEMING       V    (ALL      (A) JOY FLEMING             1973   INTERCORD               26011/7
     GARY UNWIN        B    (ABC      (B) LIVE                    1974   ATLANTIC                40566
     KEITH FORSEY      D    (ABC      (C) THIS IS MY LIFE         1974   ATLANTIC                50056
     RALF NOWY         FLT  (ABC
     THOR BALDURSSON   K    (BC   DON ANDERSON    PERC (B   SYLVESTER LEVAY K   (ABC  PAUL VINCENT  G   (ABC
     BERNIE PROCK      PERC (A    RALPH SIEGEL    K    (A   MARTIN HARRISON D   (B    VICTOR BEHRENS   TPT (C
     ANDY MARX         G    (A
```

FLESH EATERS

```
                                 (A) NO QUESTIONS ASKED          1980   UPSETTER   US      34
                                 (B) A MINUTE TO PRAY A SECOND TO DIE 1981 INITIAL      IRC 007
```

FLESHTONES

```
     PETER ZAREMBA     V K HCA(A      (A) BLAST OFF               1982   ROIR  CASS              A107
     KEITH STRONG      G V (A
     JAN MAREK PAKULSKI B V (A    LENNY CALDERONE  D V (A    ALAN VEGA     V   (A    MARTY THAU   PROD (A
```

ROBERT FLEISCHMAN

```
     ROBERT FLEISCHMAN      (A      (A) A PERFECT STRANGER        1979   ARISTA     US           4220
```

FLICKS

```
     TOMMY WILLIS      G    (A      (A) GO FOR THE EFFECT         1979   ARIOLA           ARL  5024
     JOHN BUTLER       G V (A
     DAVE SMITH        D V (A    JOHNNY KAPP G V (A       LEE STRZELCZYK  B   (A
```

FLIGHT

```
                                 (A) FLIGHT                      1976   CAPITOL    US          11458
                                 (B) INCREDIBLE                  1976   CAPITOL    US          11536
```

FLINT

```
     DON BREWER        D V (A      (A) FLINT                     1979   CBS
     MEL SCHACHER      B G V(A
     CRAIG FROST       K    (A    BILLY ELWORTHY   G V (A
```

FLO & EDDIE

```
     FLO(MARK VOLMAN) V    (ALL     (A) PHLORESCENT LEECH & EDDIE 1972   REPRISE US 2097    UK K44201
     EDDIE (HOWARD KAYLAN)V(ALL     (B) FLO & EDDIE               1973   REPRISE US 2141    UK K44234
     JIM PONS          B    (AB      (C) IMMORAL ILLEGAL & FATTENING 1974 CBS    US 33554
     AYNSLEY DUNBAR    D    (ABC     (D) MOVING TARGETS           1976   CBS    US 33262    UK  81509
     GARY ROWLES       G    (AB      (E) ROCK STEADY WITH FLO & EDDIE 1981 EPIPHANY   US  ELP 4010
     DON PRESTON       K    (A
     DANNY KOOTCH      G    (C    LEE SKLAR     B    (C   IAN UNDERWOOD K   (C    JOHN HERREN    K   (B
     LYNN BLESSING          (A    CLAUDE WILLIAMS (A    ERIC SCOTT    B   (C    ANDY CAHAN   D K (CE
     PHILL REED        G    (C    EARL CHINNA SMITH G(E  AUGUSTOS PABLO K   (E  LEASLIE BUTLER K   (E
     ASTON BARRETT     B    (E    SANTA DAVIS   D    (E   STICKY THOMPSON PERC (E  ALBERT WING  SAX (E
     JIMMY'SENYA' HAYNES B (E    PHIL RAMOCAN   K   (E   ARNOLD BRACKENRIDGE HRNS(E  ELNATHAN BRACKENRIDGE HRNS(E
     ENROY GRANT       SAX (E    NAMBO        TROM (E   DEAN FRAZIER  SAX (E   WALT FOWLER   TROM (E
```

FLOATING BRIDGE

```
     RICK DANGEL       G    (A      (A) FLOATING BRIDGE           1969   LIBERTY    UK  LPS 83271
     JOE JOHANSEN      G    (A      (A) BROUGHT UP WRONG          1970   VAULT      US          124
     JOE JOHNSON       B    (A
     MIKE MARINELLI    D    (A
```

FLOATING HOUSE BAND

```
                                 (A) FLOATING HOUSE BAND         1972   TAKOMA     US          1029
```

```
F69B                            FLOATING OPERA                                  F69B
    STEVE WELKOM      G   (A         (A) THE FLOATING OPERA      1971  EMBRYO        US       730
    JOHN NEMEROVSKI   PNO (A
    CAROL LEES        K   (A    GARY MUNCE   B   (A   ARTIE ALINKOFF      D   (A
F69C                            FLOCK OF SEAGULLS                               F69C
    A SCORE           D   (A         (A) A FLOCK OF SEAGULLS    1982  ARISTA        US       6600
    M SCORE           V G K(A
    P REYNOLDS        G   (A    F MAUDSLEY  B V  (A
F70                                  FLOCK                                      F70
    JERRY GOODMAN     VLN (AB        (A) FLOCK                  1969  CBS    US 9911  UK    63733
    FELIX PAPPALRDI   V   (C         (A) FLOCK                  1981  EMBASSY RI     UK    31910
    FRED GLICKSTEIN   G V (ABC       (B) DINOSAUR SWAMPS        1971  CBS    US30007  UK    64055
    JAMES L HIRSEN    K V (C         (C) INSIDE OUT             1975 MERCURY US 11035 UK 9100 016
    JERRY SMITH       D V (ABC       (AB) FLOCK (DBL)           1972  CBS    NL 67278
    RON KARPMAN       D V (ABC
    MIKE ZYDOWSKY     VLN (C    RICK CANOFF SAX   (AB  TOM WEBB     (AB  FRANK POSA        (A
F70A                            FLOH DE COLOGNE                                 F70A
    BRITTA BATTRUSCHAT    (A        (A) VIETNAM                 1968  PLANE               33101
    HANSI FRANCHI     D   (ABC      (B) FLIESSBANDBABYS BEAT SHOW 1970 OHR       GER OMM556000
    DIETER KLEMM      V   (ABCD     (C) ROCKOPER PROFITGEIER LIVE 1971 OHR       GER OMM556010
    MARKUS SCHMIDT    G K (ABCD     (D) GEYER SYMPHONIE         1973  OHR        GER OMM556033
    DICK STADTLER     B   (ABCD     (E) LUCKY STREIK LIVE       1973  OHR        GER OMM556029
    GERD WOLLSCHON    V   (ABCD     (F) MUMIEN                  1974  PLANE             99201
    DIETER SUVERKRUP      (A
    THEO KONIG            (D
F70B                            HERBIE FLOWERS                                  F70B
    HERBIE FLOWERS    B   (AB       (A) PLANT LIFE              1975  PHILIPS         9109 204
    JACK COLLIER      B   (A        (B) A LITTLE POTTY          1980  NOTE            NTS 216
    TONY NEWMAN       D   (A
    RONNIE VERRELL    D   (A    ANDY WHITE  D   (A     MARK SINGER D   (A    FRANK RICOTTI PERC (A
    RAY COOPER        PERC (A    CHRIS SPEDDING G(A     ALAN PARKER G    (A    BRYAN DALY  G   (A
    JACK EMBLOW       ACC  (A    DAVID SNELL HARP (A    ALBERT HALL HRNS(A    GREG BOWEN  HRNS (A
    ALAN DOWNEY       HRNS (A    TED BARKER HRNS  (A    DUNCAN LAMONT HRNS(A  F GABARRO   CELLO(A
    W DEMONT          CELLO(A    JOANNE WILLIAMS V(A    MADELINE BELL  V (A   KAY GARNER  V    (A
    GILLIAN LINDSAY   V   (A    SUE CHAPMAN V    (A    CATHERINE FAULKNER V (A GEORGE FENTON V  (A
    ROSSETTA HIGHTOWER V(A      EDDIE LESTER  V  (A    NICK CURTIS    V (A   FRANK HOLMES V    (A
    TONY MANSELL      V   (A
F71                                  FLOW                                      F71
    JOHN WINTER       SAXK (A        (A) FLOW                   1970  CTI           US       1003
    DON FELDER        G   (A
    CHUCK NEWCOMB     V B (A    MIKE BARNETT     D   (A   ED SHAUGHNESSY PERC  (A   ANGEL ALLENDE PERC (A
    JOHNNY PACHECO    PERC (A
F71A                        FLOWER TRAVELLING BAND                             F71A
    JOE YAMANAKA      V HCA(BCDE     (A) CHALLENGE (as 'THE FLOWERS') 1969 CBS     JAP   10063
    GEORGE WADE       D   (ALL       (B) ANYWHERE               1970  PHILIPS       JAP   8507
    HIDKI ISHIMA      G   (BCDE      (C) SATORI                 1971  ATLANTIC      JAP   8056
    JUN KOZUKI        G B (BCDE      (D) MADE IN JAPAN          1972  ATLANTIC      JAP   8187
    YUCA UCHIDA       V PERC(AB      (E) MADE UP DBL            1973  ATLANTIC      JAP   5073/74
    REMI ASOH         V   (A
    KATSUHIKO KOBAYASHI STEEL(A  KEN HASHIMOTO        B   (A
F72                                  EDDIE FLOYD                               F72
    EDDIE FLOYD       V   (ALL       ( ) KNOCK ON WOOD          1967  ATCO          UK    228 014
    ISAAC HAYES       V   (X         ( ) KNOCK ON WOOD          1967  STAX          US    714
    DAVID PORTER      V   (X         ( ) NEVER FOUND A GIRL     19    STAX          US    2002
    JOHNNIE TAYLOR    V   (X         ( ) RARE STAMPS            19    STAX          US    2011
    BOOKER T JONES    G K B(X        ( ) YOU'VE GOT TO HAVE EDDIE 197 POLYDOR UK 2363010 US STAX2017
    AL JACKSON        D   (X         ( ) CALIFORIA GIRL         19    STAX          US    2029
                                     ( ) DOWN TO EARTH          19    STAX          US    2041
                                     ( ) THINK ABOUT IT         19    ATCO          US    7023
                                     ( ) SOUL STREET            1974  STAX US 5512  UK    1002
                                     ( ) BABY LAY YOUR HEAD     1975  STAX          US    3016
                                     ( ) EXPERIENCE             1977  MALACO              6352
                                     (X) CHRONICLE              1978  STAX   US 4122  UK   7005
F73                                  FLYING ACES                               F73
    MARTIN ACE        G B V(AB       (A) 1975 (B) 1977
    GEORGINA ACE      G B V(AB
    RICHARD TREECE    G   (B    MICK GIBBON D     (B
F74                         FLYING BURRITO BROTHERS                            F74
    CHRIS ETHRIDGE    K B V(AFE      (A) GILDED PALACE OF SIN   1969  A&M    US  4175  UK   931
    CHRIS HILLMAN     G V B (ABCDEKO (B) BURRITO DELUXE         1970  A&M    US  4258  UK   983
    JON CORNEAL       D   (AE        (C) FLYING BURRITO BROTHERS 1971 A&M    US  4295  UK   64295
    GRAM PARSONS      G V MAND (ABEFKO (D) LAST OF THE RED HOT BURRITOS 1971 A&M  US 4343 UK 64343
    PETE KLEINOW      STEEL(ABCEFJKMOPK (E) CLOSE UP THE HONKY TONKS (COMP) 1974 A&M US 3631 UK 63631
    BERNIE LEADON     G V (BCDEKO    (F) FLYING AGAIN           1975  CBS    US  33817  UK   61984
    RICK ROBERTS      G V (CDEHLO    (G) HOT BURRITO            1975  ARIOLA US 9379  NL   85272
    MIKE CLARKE       D   (BCDEKO    (H) LIVE IN AMSTERDAM      1975  BUMBLE US 301 ARIOLA NL 86439
    BYRON BERLINE     FDL (ABDELK    (H) LIVE IN AMSTERDAM      1975  PHONOGRAM          6641 144
    ROGER BUSH        B   (DHL       (J) AIRBORNE               1976  CBS    US  34222  UK   81433
    KENNY WERTZ       G V (DEHL      (K) SLEEPLESS NIGHTS       1976  A&M    US  4578   UK   64578
    AL PERKINS        D   (DEK       (L) BLUEGRASS SPECIAL      19    ARIOLA             NL   86501
    ALAN MUNDE        G   (HL        (M) LIVE FROM TOKYO        1978  REGENCY            US   79001
    HERB PEDERSEN     G V (EOK       (M) CLOSE ENCOUNTERS TO THE WEST COAST 78 BETTERDAYS JAP Yx 7218
    ERIC DALTON       G   (HL        (N) POP CHRONIK      (DBL) 19    ARIOLA             NL   89136
    DON BECK          STEEL(HL       (O) HONKY TONK HEAVEN (DBL) 19   ARIOLA             NL   87585
    JAMES BURTON      G   (K         (P) HEARTS ON THE LINE     1980  CURB          US    37004
    SKIP BATTIN       B   (JMP
    GENE PARSONS      D   (FJ   EDDIE HOH    D    (AE   SAM GOLDSTEIN D    (AE   POPEYE PHILLIPS    D  (AE
    SPOONER OLDHAM    K   (F    GIB GUILBEAU G FDL(FJMP JOEL SCOTT HILL G V (FJ   ED PONDER         D  (
    LEON RUSSELL      PNO (BE   LEOPOLD CARBAJAL ACC(B  FRANK BLANCO. PERC (B    TOMMY JOHNSON     HRNS(B
                                              (CONTINUED)
                                                [209]
```

(CONTINUED)   FLYING BURRITO BROTHERS

```
        BUDDY CHILDERS   HRNS (B    GREG HARRIS G BAN V(M   GENE CLARK    V      (EO   JOHN BELAND         G V (P
        RON TUTT         D    (K    EARL BALL    PNO   (C   BOB GIBSON         G  (C   MIKE DEASY      G       (C
        STEVIE WONDER    K    (J    JIMMI SEITER    PERC(J  LUIS CABAZA        K  (J   JAMIE FAUNT     B       (J
        WARREN PEMBERTON D    (J    MICK McGEE      D   (P  KIM CARNES      V    (P    CHARLES HARWOOD     K   (P
        MARK HUDSON           (P    ALAN ESTES          (P  TOM HENSLEY          (P    RON KRASINSKI          (P
        JOHN HOBBS            (P    DOLLY PARTON V      (P  DAVID WHEATLEY       (P    GLEN D HARDIN  PNO      (K
        HENRY LEWY       PROD (B    JIM DICKSON PROD    (P  EMORY GORDY     B    (K
```

FLYING CIRCUS
                        (A) PREPARED IN PEACE   1970 CAPITOL US ST11147 HARVEST UK SHSP4010

FLYING ISLAND

```
        JEFF BOVA     K TPT(       (A) FLYING ISLAND              19   VANGUARD    US     79359
        RAY SMITH     G   (        (B) ANOTHER KIND OF SPACE      1976 vANGUARD    US     79368
        BILL BARON    D   (
        FAITH FRAIOLI VLN (   THOM PREL      B   (A
```

FLYING LIZARDS

```
        PATTI PALLADIN     V      (B      (A) FLYING LIZARDS        1980  VIRGIN US 13137    UK V2150
        STEVE BERESFORD    K G B(A        (A) FLYING LIZARDS        1980  VIRGIN GER 201426
        JJ JOHNSON         D PERC(B       (B) FOURTH WALL           1981  VIRGIN             UK V2190
        DAVID CUNNINGHAM   G VLN K V(B     (B) FOURTH WALL           1981  VIRGIN GER 203204
        PETER GORDON       SAX   (B
        ROBERT FRIPP       G     (B   GARETH SAGER     SAX    (B   JULIAN MARSHALL K V    (B   CHERYL LEWIS   V    (B
        V HALLER           B     (B   MICHAEL NYMAN    PNO    (B   LUCY SKEAPING          (B   NICK HAYLEY         (B
        BEN GROVE          B     (B   EDWARD PILLINGER K      (B   RORY ALLAM      K      (B   ANNE BARNARD   HRN  (B
        STEVE SAUNDERS     TROM  (B   KEITH THOMPSON   SAX    (B
```

FLYING MACHINE

```
        TONY NEWMAN     G   (A         (A) DOWN TO EARTH            19   PYE   NSPL 18328
        STUART COLEMAN  B V (A
        STEVE JONES     G V (A   PAUL WILKINSON    D V   (A
```

FLYING SAUCERS

```
        SANDY FORD      G V (A         (A) KEEP ON COMING          1978  ALASKA UK 101 CHARLY UK CR30207
        NIGGSY OWEN     G             (B) SOME LIKE IT HOT        1981  EMI   UK EMC3366
        PETE PRITCHARD  B   (         (EP) BALLAD OF JOHNNY RED    19   CHARLY             UK CEP121
        ROLLIN' DANNY   D   (
```

FLYING SAUCERS
                        ( ) WATERGATE   19   IX CHAINS   US   9000

FLYING SQUAD

```
        IAN MUIR          G   (A      (A) FLYING SQUAD            1978  EPIC        UK     82875
        MONTY McMONAGLLE  G   (A
        GEORGE CROSSAN    B K V(A   ALEX CALDER G V   (A     JIM KELLY     D      (A
```

FLYIN' SPIDERZ

```
        GUUS     G V (A         (A) FLYIN' SPIDERZ        1977  EMI   NL      25725
        AAD      B V (A         (B) LET IT CRAWL          1977  EMI   GER     26049
        KOOS     G V (AB
        HENRI    D PERC V(AB
        JOHN     B V (B   APPIE BAARS    SAX    (B
```

FLYS

```
        NEIL O'CONNOR   G V K(AB       (A) WAIKIKI BEACH REFUGEES  1978  EMI    UK  EMC  3249
        DAVID FREEMAN   G V (AB        (B) OWN                    1979  EMI    UK  EMC  3316
        JOE HUGHES      B   (AB        (EP) BUNCH OF FIVES        1977  ZAMA   UK  BSS  209
        PETE KING       D   (A
        GRAHAM DEACON   D   (B   VANCE ANDERSON   V PERC(A   MIKE FINESILVER V PERC(A   WILLY BARRETT FDL(A
        LYNN DOBSON     SAX (A   KEN FREEMAN SYN STR(A
```

FOCUS

```
        THIJS VAN LEER FLT SYN K V(ABCDEFGHI (A) IN & OUT OF FOCUS   1971  POLYDOR UK 2344 003    US SIRE  97027
                                             (A) IN AND OUT OF FOCUS 197                    RI   US SIRE   7404
        JAN AKKERMANN   G PERC  (ABCDEFG      (B) MOVING WAVES        1971  BLUE HORIZON UK 2931 002
                                             (B) MOVING WAVES        1971  POLYDOR UK RI 2931 002  US SIRE   7401
        HANS ERIC CLEUVER     D(AE            (C) FOCUS THREE         1972  POLYDOR UK 2659 016    US SIRE   3901
        MARTIN DRESDEN        B(AE            (D) AT THE RAINBOW      1973  POLYDOR UK 2443 118    US SIRE   7408
        PIERRE VAN DER LINDEN D(BCEF          (E) HAMBURGER CONCERTO  1974  POLYDOR UK 2442 124    US ATCO  36100
        CYRIL HAVERMANS       B(B             (F) SHIP OF MEMORIES    1974  HARVEST UK SHSP4068    US SIRE   7531
        BERT RUITER      PERC B(CDEFG         (G) MOTHER FOCUS        1975  POLYDOR UK 2302 036    US ATCO  36117
        COLIN ALLEN      PERC D(EFG           (G) MOTHER FOCUS        197   POLYDOR     ABCR 266        2310  408
        DAVID KEMPER          D(FG            (H) FOCUS               1975  POLYDOR UK 2384 070
        PHILIP CATHERINE      G(I             (I) FOCUS CON PROBY     1978  HARVEST IS 11721   IMP EMI 064 25713
        STEVE SMITH           D(I             (J) DUTCH MASTERS       19                        US SIRE   7505
        P J PROBY             V(I             ( ) MASTERS OF ROCK     1975  EMI                     054 25130
        EEF ALBERS            G(I
        MIKE VERNON      PROD (BCDE    HUBERT TEREGGEN      PROD(AG
```

DAN FOGELBERG

```
        DAN FOGELBERG    V K G(ALL      (A) HOME FREE              1973  CBS  US 31751 UK 81   31847
        WITH                           (B) SOUVENIRS             1975  EPIC US 33137    UK   80623
        NORBERT PUTNAM   B    (ABCD     (C) CAPTURED ANGEL        1975  EPIC US 34499    UK   69189
        DON HENLEY       V    (BDE      (D) NETHERLANDS           1977  EPIC US 34185    UK   81574
        KENNY BUTTREY    D    (ADF      (E) TWIN SONS OF DIFFERENT MOTHERS 1978 EPIC US 35339 UK  82774
        JOE WALSH        G    (BD       (F) PHEONIX               1980  EPIC US 35634    UK   83317
        GAYLE LEVANT     HARP (F        (G) THE INNOCENT AGE      1981  EPIC US 37393          88533
        FRANK MAROCCO    ACC  (D
        WELDON MYRICK STEEL G (A   BUDDY SPICHER    FDL (A   GLENN FREY       V    (B   DAVID BRIGGS   PNO (A
        GLEN SPREEN    STRINGS(A   RUSS KUNKEL      D   (BCD FARRELL MORRIS  PERC (A   AL PERKINS     STEEL(BC
        JOE VITALE       D    (D   JOHN DAVID SOUTHER V (DC  JOE LALA        PERC (CDE  TIM WEISBERG   FLT (DE
        JOHN STRONACH    PERC (D   HOT DAMN BROTHERS V  (C   KENNY PASSARELLI B    (B   GRAHAM NASH    V   (B
        JIMMY HASKELL    ACC  (B   PAUL HARRIS      K   (F   BRYAN GAROFALO  G    (B    NEIL LARSEN    K   (E
        BOBBYE HALL      PERC (E   ANDY NEWMARK     D   (E   WILLIE WEEKS    B    (E    JIM KELTNER    D   (E
        EARL DUMLER      HRNS (E   DAVID BREINENTHAL BASSOON(E JOHN HUG      G     (E    ANN MASON STOCKTON HARP(E
        JOHN ELLIS       OBOE (E   VINCENT DE ROSA  HRNS(E   GARY COLEMAN    PERC (E    FLORENCE WARNER   V (E
        RANDY MEISNER    V    (B   JODY BOYER       V   (B   MARIE OUHRABKA  V    (B    MIKE UTLEY     K   (F
        GERRY BECKLEY    G    (B   JODY LINSCOTT    CONGA(F  MARTY LEWIS     PERC (F    TOM SCOTT      SAX (F
        JERRY HEY        HRNS (F
```

```
JOHN FOGERTY    G V  (ALL      (A) BLUE RIDGE RANGERS          1973 FANTASY UKFT511   US  9415
                               (B) JOHN FOGERTY               1975 FANTASY UKFT526
                               (B) JOHN FOGERTY               1975 ASYLUM           US7E 1046
                               (C) HOODOO                     1976 ASYLUM           US 7E1081
```

```
TOM FOGERTY     G V  (ALL      (A) TOM FOGERTY               1972 FANTASY       US  9407
STU COOK     B G V SYN (C       (B) EXCALIBUR                 1973 FANTASY       US  9413
DOUG CLIFFORD   D V  (C        (C) ZEPHYR NATIONAL           1974 FANTASY       US  9448
J C FOGERTY     G V  (C        (D) MYOPIA                    1975 FNTASY        US  9469
MERL SAUNDERS   K V  (AB       (E) DEAL IT OUT               1981 FANTASY       US  9611
JOHN KAHN       B    (AB
JERRY GARCIA    G    (B    BILL VITT     D PERC  (AB    RUSS GARY       G V  (AD   BILLY MUNDI    PERC (A
ROGER COLLINS   V    (A    TOM PHILLIPS  G    (C    GARY POTTERTON  G    (C    STEPHEN MILLER K(D
STEPHEN FUNK    K    (C    JEFF NERELL  STEEL DR(C   REV RON STALLINGS SAX (C   JOHN BLAKELEY  G(E
GREG DOUGLAS    G    (C    BILL SWARTZ   G    (E    JOHN ALLAIR     K SYN(E   MARC RUSSO     K(E
MARK ISHAM      K    (E    PEEWEE ELLIS   SAX (E    TOM LILIENTHAL  B    (E    DAVID HAYES    B V(E
JEFF MYER       D    (E    SCOTT MORRIS  D    (E    DANNY KOPELSON  V    (E    MARK SPRINGER  V(E
JEANIE TRACY    V    (E    LILLIAN,NETTA & JO=THE STOVELLS V(D
```

```
ROD PRICE  V DOBRO G (ABCDEFGHJK   (A) FOGHAT                      1972 BEARSVILLE US 2077 UK K45503
DAVE PEVERETT   V G  (ABCDEFGHJKL  (B) FOGHAT ROCK'N'ROLL         1973 BEARSVILLE US 2136 UK K 45514
NICK JAMESON K G B V (E            (C) ENERGISED                  1974 BEARSVILLE US 6950 UK K 55500
ROGER EARL      D    (ABCDEFGHJKL  (D) ROCK'N'ROLL OUTLAWS        1974 BEARSVILLE US 6956 UK K 55502
TONY STEVENS    B    (ABCD         (E) FOOL FOR THE CITY          1975 BEARSVILLE US 6959 UK K 55507
CRAIG MACGREGOR B    (FGHJKL       (F) NIGHT SHIFT                1977 BEARSVILLE US 6962 UK K 55511
DAVE EDMUNDS    G    (A            (G) LIVE                       1977 BEARSVILLE US 6971 UK K 55518
TODD RUNDGREN        (A            (H) STONE BLUE                 1978 BEARSVILLE US 6977
JOHN WILLIAMS        (A            (J) BOOGIE MOTEL               1979 BEARSVILLE US 6990
ANDY FAIRWEATHER LOW V(A           (K) TIGHT SHOES                1980 BEARSVILLE US 6999 UK ILPS9637
ALTO REED      SAX   (K            (K) TIGHT SHOES                1980 BEARSVILLE         EURO 202457
ERIK CARTWRIGHT B    (L            (L) GIRLS TO CHAT,BOYS TO BOUNCE 1981 BEARSVILLE US 3578 EURO 203917
JIMMY AMBROSIA  K    (K
COLIN EARL      K    (K
```

```
ELLEN FOLEY     V    (A            (A) NIGHT OUT                 1979 EPIC          UK      83718
KERRYN TOLHURST G    (A            (B) SPIRIT OF ST LOUIS        1981 EPIC US 36984 UK      84809
IAN HUNTER K V PERC  (A
TOM MANDEL      K    (A    HILLY MICHAELS  D    (A   MARTIN BRILEY   B    (A   RORY DODD     V   (A
MICK RONSON G V K PERC(A
```

```
WOLF MAAHN      V G  (A            (A) FOODBAND                  1979 ELECTRIC               TRIX10
AXEL MANRICO HEILHECKER G V(A
MATHIAS KEUL B K V   (A    JUMPY ZERLETT K V  (A   JAN DIX         D V  (A   WOLFGANG BULLMEYER B(A
LYN DOBSON     SAX   (A    ZWIEBEL       B    (A   PACO SAVAL      V    (A   MIDNIGHT HANDCLAP SEC V(A
```

```
SEEMON POSTHUMA      (A            (A) FOOL                      1969 MERCURY US 61178   UK 20138
MARIJKE KOGER        (A
JOSJE LEEGER         (A    BARRY FINCH (A
```

```
RICK BARTLETT   G    (B            (A) SOLD OUT                  1980 EMI US 17024   UK  AML 3008
DOUG FORMAN     B    (B            (B) HEAVY MENTAL              1981 EMI US 17046
CHRIS PEDRICK   D    (B
STACEY PEDRICK  G    (B    MIKE GIRARD V    (B
```

```
TOM KELLY     V G B(AB             (A) FOOLS GOLD                1976 ARISTA US 5500 UK  ARTY 131
DENNY HENSON   G V   (AB            (B) MR LUCKY                  1977 CBS    US 34828 UK     82148
DOUG LIVINGSTON G K  (AB
RON GRINEL      D    (A    KEITH OLSON    PERC  (A   TOM SCOTT      SAX (A   ANDREW GOLD    G   (B
DAN FOGELBERG  STEEL(B     DAVID FOSTER   K    (B   DON FELDER   G MAND(B   COLIN TULLY   SAX (B
MIKE PORCARO    N    (B    JEFF PORCARO   D    (B   JOE WALSH      G    (B   DUNCAN CAMERON G V(B
DAVID PAICH     K    (B    BILL CHAMPLIN  K    (B   WADDY WACHTEL  G    (B   MEL COLLINS    SAX(B
```

```
BOB HORNE       K    (AC           (A) A FOOT IN COLD WATER      1972 DAFFODIL CAN 16012
HUGHIE LEGGAT  B G V(AC            (B) SECOND FOOT IN COLD WATER 1973 DAFFODIL CAN 16028
ALEX MACHIN     V    (AC           (C) OR ALL AROUND US          1974 ELEKTRA  US 7 1025
PAUL NAUMANN   G B   (AC           (C) A FOOT IN COLD WATER      1974 ELEKTRA  UK  52011
DANNY TAYLOR   D V   (AC           (D) BREAKING THROUGH          1976 ANTHEM   CAN 1 1008
```

```
STEVE FORBERT HCA G V (ALL         (A) ALIVE ON ARRIVAL         1978 NEMPEROR US 35538 UK EPIC 83308
SID McGINNIS    G    (D            (A) ALIVE ON ARRIVAL         1980 EMBASSY   UK 32053
STEVE BURGH     G    (AD           (B) JACKRABBIT SLIM          1979 NEMPEROR US 36191 UK EPIC 83879
BARRY LAZAROWITZ D   (ACD          (C) LITTLE STEVIE ORBIT      1980 NEMPEROR US 36595 UK EPIC 84501
HUGH McDONALD  G B   (ACD          (D) STEVE FORBERT            1982 NEMPEROR US 37434
CLAY BARNES     G    (D
ROBBIE KONDOR   K    (ACD  HARVEY SHAPIRO  STEEL (A  DAVID SANBORN  SAX (AD  BRIAN TORFF    B(A
BOBBY OGDIN    PNO   (B    PAUL ERRICO    K   (BC   JOHN GOIN      G   (B   GUNNAR GELLOTE D(B
BOB WRAY        B    (B    ALAN FREEDMAN  G   (B    JACK WILLIAMS  B   (B   ROGER CLARK    D(B
JERRY BRIDGES   B    (B    BILL JONES    SAX  (BC   MIKE LEECH     B   (B   RON KELLER     TPT(B
DENNIS GOODE   TROM  (A    AVA ALDRIDGE   V   (B    CINDY RICHARDSON V  (B   MARIE TOMLINSON V(B
SHANE FONTAYNE  G    (C    KEN KOSEK     FDL  (C    BOBBY LLOYD HICKS D (C   LARRY CAMPBELL STEEL(D
LENNY PICKETT  SAX   (D    CHUCK WILSON  SAX  (D    GORDON STOKER  V   (D   DWAYNE WEST    V  (D
NEIL MATTHEWS   V    (D    RAY WALKER     V   (D    YVONNE LEWIS   V   (D   LARITA GASKINS V  (D
CHRISTINE WILSHIRE V (D    RORY DODD      V   (D    ERIC TROYER    V   (D   PETER ECKLUND  HRNS(D
CRIS CIOE      SAX   (D    JOSH SHNEIDER  SAX (D    ROGER ROSENBERG SAX (D   JOE HELLENY    TROM  (D
```

```
FRANKIE FORD    V    (ALL          (A) ON A SEA CRUISE          19   ACE        US   1005
                               (B) FRANKIE FORD             19   BRIARMEADE US   5002
                               (EP) BEST OF                 19   ACE        US   EP 105
```

FORCE 10

    GRIFF STEVENS   V SAX(A   (A) FORCE 10   1981   WB UK K56932   US   3557
    LARRY TUTTLE   B V (A
    RICK WHITE   K V (A   THOMAS BRIGHTON G V   (A JEFF SWISSTACK D   (A
F83D   JIM FORD   F83D
    JIM FORD   (A   (A) HARLAN COUNTY   19   WHITE WHALE US   1002
F83E   NEAL FORD & THE FANATICS   F83E
    NEAL FORD   V   (A   (A) NEAL FORD & THE FANATICS   19   HICKORY US   LPS141
    JON PARELES   G V (A
    W JOHNSON   B   (A   LAMIER GREIG   K   (A JOHN CRAWLEY D   (A
F83F   ROBBEN FORD   F83F
    ROBBEN FORD   G V (A   (A) THE INSIDE STORY   1981   ATLANTIC   US   16999
    ROLAND   K   (A
    RUSSELL FERANTES   K   (A   JIMMY HASLICK   B   (A RICK LAWSON D PERC(A
F84   FOREIGNER   F84
    MICK JONES   K V G (ABCD   (A) FOREIGNER   1977   ATLANTIC US 18215   UK K50356
    IAN McDONALD   K G D V (ABC   (B) DOUBLE VISION   1978   ATLANTIC US 19999   UK K50476
    LOU GRAMM   V   (ABCD   (C) HEAD GAMES   1979   ATLANTIC US 29999   UK K50651
    TOM DOLBY   SYN (D   (D) '4'   1981   ATLANTIC US 16999   UK K50796
    DENNIS ELLIOTT   D   (ABCD   (EP) FEELS LIKE THE FIRST TIME 1978   ATLANTIC   UK K11086
    AL GREENWOOD   SYN K(ABC
    ED GAGLIARDI   V B (AB   IAN LLOYD   V   (BD MUTT LANGE   V   (D BOB MAYO   K (D
    RICK WILLS   G V (D   MARK RIVERS SAX (D   HUGH McCRACKEN   G   (D JUNIOR WALKER SAX (D
    LARRY FAST   SYN (D   MICHAEL FONFARA K (D
F85   FOREST   F85
    MARTIN WELHAM G V K PERC(AB   (A) FOREST   1969   HARVEST   UK   SHVL 760
    DEREK ALLENBY K V HCA PERC(AB   (B) FULL CIRCLE   1970   HARVEST   SHVL 784
    HADRIAN WELAHM G K V HCA PERC(AB
    GORDON HUNTLEY   STEEL   (B
F85A   FOREVER MORE   F85A
    STEWART FRANCIS D V (AB   (A) YOURS FOREVER MORE   1970   RCA US LSP 4272   UK SF8016
    ALAN GORIE   K B (AB   (B) WORDS ON BLACK PLASTIC   1971   RCA US LSP 4435   UK 3015
    ONNIE MAIR   G V B(AB
    MICK TRAVIS   G   (AB
F85B   DAVID FORMAN   F85B
    DAVID FORMAN   (A   (A) DAVID FORMAN   1976   ARISTA   US   4084
F85C   FORMERLY FAT HARRY   F85C
    PHIL GREENBERG   V G (A   (A) FORMERLY FAT HARRY   1971   HARVEST   UK   SHSP 4016
    GARY PETERSON V G K PERC(A   (A) FORMERLY FAT HARRY   1971   CAPITOL   US   877
    BRUCE BARTHOL   B   (A
    LAURIE ALLEN   D   (A   NISAR AHMAD GEORGE KHAN SAX (A
F86   SHARON FORRESTER   F86
    SHARON FORRESTER V   (A   (A) SHARON   1974   ASHANTI SHAN105+ VULCAN
    GEOFFREY CHUNG   K V G(A
    ROBERT BAILEY   K   (A   PHIL CHEN   B   (A RICHARD BAILEY D   (A WINSTON DELANDRO G (A
    ALLAN SHARP   PERC (A   DEL RICHARDSON HCA (A MIKE MORAN   K   (A HENRY LOWTHER TPT (A
    RON CARTHY   TPT (A   RAY WARLEIGH HRNS (A GRAHAM PRESKETT MAND (A VAL DOUGLAS   B   (A
    MICHAEL RICHARDS D   (A   ROBERT LYN   PNO   (A EARL LINDO   K   (A MALCOLM GRIFFITHS TROM(A
    CHRIS MERCER   SAX (A   MEL COLLINS   SAX (A MARTIN DROVER TPT (A MARTYN FORD   HRNS (A
    38 PIECE ORCHESTRA   (A   NINE BACKING SINGERS   (A
F86A   FORT MUDGE MEMORIAL DUMP   F86A
    CAROLINE STRATTON   (A   (A) FORT MUDGE MEMORIAL DUMP   197   MERCURY   61256
    DAN KEADY   (A
    JAMES DEPTULA   (A   DAVID AMARAL   (A RICHARD CLERICI   (A
F86B   FORTRESS   F86B
    DONNY VOSBURGH   D   (A   (A) HAND IN THE TILL   1981   ATLANTIC US 19282 UK K50782
    ERIC TURNER   G   (A
    JIM WEST   V   (A   CHARLES SAUZA   B   (A
F87   FORTUNES   F87
    BARRY PRITCHARD G V ((A) FORTUNES   1965   DECCA   LK 4736
    DAVID CARR   K   ((B) FORTUNES   1972   CAPITOL   ST 21891
    ROD ALLEN   B   ((C) REMEMBER ING THE FORTUNES 1976   DECCA   REM2
    ANDY BROWN   D   (( ) HERE COMES THAT RAINY DAY 1973   CAPITOL   809
    GLEN DALE   G V (( ) STORM IN A TEACUP   1972   CAPITOL   11041
    SHEL McCRAE   (
F88   FOSTER BROTHERS   F88
    GRAHAM FOSTER G V SYN(A   (A) ON THE LINE   1977   ROCKET   UK   ROLL10
    MALCOLM FOSTER G V   (A
    EDDIE WILLIAMS D PERC(A   ROB McINTOSH   V K   (A PETE WINGFIELD K   (A STEVE GREGORY HRNS (A
    BUD BEADLE   SAX   (A   GEORGE CHISHOLM TPT (A MALCOLM GRIFFITHS TROM(A
F88A   RONNIE FOSTER   F88A
    RONNIE FOSTER   V K (AB   (A)CHESHIRE CAT   1975   BLUE NOTE   US   LA425
    DENNIS DAVIS   D   (AB   (B) LOVE SATELLITE   1978   CBS   UK   83037
    LEON CHANCLER   PERC (B
    ALPHONSO JOHNSON B   (B   PAULINHO DA COSTA PERC(B HARVEY MASON   D   (B BYRON MILLER B (B
    JERRY PETERS   V PNO (B   STEVE WONDER   D   (B   ROY AYERS   VIBES (B JOE BECK   G (A
    GEORGE BENSON   G   (A   WILLIAM ALLEN B   (A   GARY KING   B   (A JAMES MTUME PERC(A
F89   FOTHERINGAY   F89
    SANDY DENNY   V   (A   (A) FOTHERINGAY   1970   ISLAND UK ILPS9125 US A&M4269
    TREVOR LUCAS   G   (A
    JERRY DONAHUE   G   (A   PAT DONALDSON   B   (A GERRY CONWAY D   (A LINDA THOMPSON V (A
    TOD LLOYD   V   (A
F90   FOTOMAKER   F90
    WALLY BRYSON   G V (A   (A) FOTOMAKER   1978   ATLANTIC US 19165 UK K50450
    GENE CORNISH   B V (A   (B) VIS A VIS   1978   ATLANTIC US 19208
    DINO DANELLI   D   (A   (C) TRANSFER STATION   1979   ATLANTIC US 19246
    LEX MARCHESI   G V (A
    FRANKIE VINCI   K V (A   EDDIE KRAMER   PROD (A

CLEM CURTIS	V	(A	(A) FROM THE FOUNDATIONS	1967	PYE		UK	NPL	18206
COLIN YOUNG	V	(D	(A) BABY NOW THAT IVE FOUND YOU	1967	UNI		US		73016
ALAN WARNER	G	(AD	(B) ROCKING THE FOUNDATION	1968	PYE		UK	NPL	18227
ERIC ALLENDALE	TROM	(AD	(C) BUILD ME UP BUTTERCUP	1968	UNI		US		73043
TONY GOMEZ	ORG	(AD	(D) DIGGING THE FOUNDATIONS	1969	PYE		UK	NPL	18290
TIM HARRIS	D	(AD	(D) DIGGING THE FOUNDATIONS	1969	UNI		US		73058
PETER MACBETH	B	(AD	( ) THE FOUNDATIONS	1968	MARBLE ARCH		UK	MALS	11571
PAT BURKE	WIND	(AD	(EP) ITS ALL RIGHT	1968	PYE		UK	NEP	24297
MIKE ELLIOTT	SAX	(A	( ) GOLDEN HOUR	1973	PYE		UK		GH574
			( ) ROCK FROM BRITAIN VOL 2	1979	MODE		US		9040

DAN LOWE	G	(A	(A) 451`	1981	INTERCORD			1009
HAL WHITFORD	V	(A						
BRAD STECKEL	G V	(A	JIM CLENCH B V (A STEVE NELSON D (A					

JEFF SEVERSON	V G K	(A	(A) 4 OUT OF 5 DOCTORS	1980	NEMPEROR	US	36575
CAL EVERETT	B V	(A					
GEORGE PITTAWAY	G V	(A	TOM BALLEW D V (A PATRICE CARROLL V (A JEFF KIRK WIND(A				

FRANKIE VALLI	V	(XSV	SHERRY	1963	VEE JAY	US	1053	UK STATESIDE		10033
TOMMY DEVITO			GREETINGS	1963	VEE JAY	US	1055	UK STATESIDE		10051
NICK DEVITO			BIG GIRLS	1963	VEE JAY	US	1056			
NICK MASSI			AINT THAT A SHAME	1963	VEE JAY	US	1059	UK STATESIDE		10042
BOB GAUDIO	K V	(SV	STAY	1964	VEE JAY	US	1082			
JOEY LONG			GOLDEN HITS	196	VEE JAY	US	1088			
GERRY POLCI	D V	(XSV	WE LOVE GIRLS	196	VEE JAY	US	1121			
DON CICCIONE	B	(XSV	LIVE ON STAGE	196	VEE JAY	US	1154			
LEE SHAPIRO	K	(SV	DAWN	1964	PHILIPS	US	600124		BL	7621
JOHN PAIVA	G V	(SV	BORN TO WANDER	1964	PHILIPS	US	600129		BL	7611
JERRY CORBETTA	K V	(X	RAG DOLL	1964	PHILIPS	US	600146		BL	7643
LARRY LINGLE	G V	(X	SING BIG HITS	1965	PHILIPS	US	600150		BL	7687
REX ROBINSON	K	(X	ENTERTAIN YOU	1965	PHILIPS	US	600164		BL	7663
ROBBY ROBINSON	K	(X	BIG HITS BY BACHARACH,DAVID & DYLAN	PHILIPS	US	600193				
RICHARD GARCIA	PERC	(X	GOLD VAULT HITS	1965	PHILIPS	US	600196		BL	7719
TOBEE TYLER	V	(X	WORKING MY WAY BACK TO YOU	1965	PHILIPS	US	600201		BL	7699
TONY WALTHERS	V	(X	2ND VAULT	196	PHILIPS	US	600221			
			LOOKING BACK	196	PHILIPS	US	600222		BL	7752
			CHRISTMAS ALBUM	1966	PHILIPS	US	600223		BL	7753
			NEW GOLD HITS	196	PHILIPS	US	600243			
			GENUINE IMITATION LIFE GAZETTE	1968	PHILIPS	US	600290			
			HALF & HALF	196	PHILIPS	US	600341			
			EDIZIONE D'ORO	1969	PHILIPS	US	2 6501		UK	6640 002
			SEASONED HITS	1968	FONTANA				UK	SFJL 952
			BIG ONES	1971	PHILIPS				UK	6336 208
			CHAMELEON	1972	MOWEST	US	108		UK	MWAS 5501
			CHAMELEON	1975	MOWEST				UK RI	MWS 7006
			GOLD	1975	PRIVATE STOCK					
			OUR DAY WILL COME	1975	PRIVATE STOCK					
			CLOSE TO YOU	1975	PRIVATE STOCK				UK	PVLP 1001
			FALLEN ANGEL	1975	PRIVATE STOCK				UK	PVLP 1005
			(S)WHO LOVES YOU	1975	WB	US	2900		UK	K 56179
			INSIDE STORY	1976	MOWEST				UK	MWS 7007
			STORY	1976	PRIVATE STOCK	US	7000			
			(V) HELICON	1977	WB	US	3016		UK	K 56350
			FRANKIE VALLI IS THE WORD	1978	WB	US				
			(X) REUNITED	1981	WB	US	3497		UK	K 66098
			GREATEST HITS	1976	K TEL				UK	952
			GREATEST HITS 4 ALBUM SET	19	LONGINES	US	95883			
			BROTHERHOOD OF MAN	19	PICKWICK	US	3223 + SEARS US 609			
			(EP)							
			GENUINE IMITATION LIFE GAZETTE	19	PHILIPS	US	2704			
			FOUR SEASONS SING	19	VEE JAY	US	902			
			PEANUTS	19	VEE JAY	US	901			

LEVI STUBBS	V	(ALL	(A)FOUR TOPS	1965	TAMLA MOTOWN	US	622		UK	STML11010
RENALDO BENSON	V	(ALL	(B)SECOND ALBUM	1966	TAMLA MOTOWN	US	647		UK	STML 11021
LAWRENCE PAYTON	V	(ALL	(B)SECOND ALBUM	199	TAMLA MOTOWN				UK RI	STMR9007
ABDUL FAKIR	V	(ALL	ON TOP	1966	TAMLA MOTOWN	US	634		UK	STML 11037
WITH			LIVE	1967	TAMLA MOTOWN	US	654		UK	STML 11041
ED GREENE	D	(*SU	REACH OUT	1967	TAMLA MOTOWN	US	660		UK	STML 11056
MAX BENNETT	B	(*	ON BROADWAY	1967	TAMLA MOTOWN	US	657		UK	STML 11046
WILTON FELDER	B	(*QRSU	GREATEST HITS	1968	TAMLA MOTOWN	US	662		UK	STML 11061
BEN BENAY	G	(*RSU	YESTERDAYS DREAM	1969	TAMLA MOTOWN	US	669		UK	STML 11087
DAVID T WALKER	G	(*R	FOUR TOPS NOW	1969	TAMLA MOTOWN	US	675		UK	STML 11113
LEE RITENOUR	G	(*	SOUL SPIN	1970	TAMLA MOTOWN	US	695		UK	STML 11138
DEAN PARKS	G	(*SU	STILL WATERS RUN DEEP	1970	TAMLA MOTOWN	US	704		UK	STML 11149
JAY GRAYDON	G	(*	CHANGING TIMES	1971	TAMLA MOTOWN	US	721		UK	STML 11173
MICHAEL OMARTIAN	K	(*RSU	MAGNIFICENT SEVEN	1971	TAMLA MOTOWN				UK	STML 11179
CLIFFORD CARTER	K	(*UV	RETURN OF THE MAGNIFICENT SEVEN	71	TAMLA MOTWON				UK	STML 11192
VICTOR FELDMAN	PERC	(*Q	GREATEST HITS VOL 2	1971	TAMLA MOTOWN	US	740		UK	STML 11195
KING ERRISSON	PERC	(*QRSU	DYNAMITE (SUPREMES)	1972	TAMLA MOTOWN	US	745		UK	STML 11203
ERNIE WATTS	HRNS	(*U	(P)NATURE PLANNED IT	1972	TAMLA MOTOWN	US	748		UK	STML 11206
CHUCK FINDLEY	HRNS	(*	BEST OF	197	TAMLA MOTOWN	US	764			
PAUL HUBINON	HRNS	(*	(Q) KEEPER OF THE CASTLE	1972	DUNHILL	US	50129	PROBE	UK	SPB 1064
JACKIE KELSO	HRNS	(*	(Q) KEEPER OF THE CASTLE RI	1974	ABC UK ABCL5023			1976 MFP	UK	50253
LEW McCREARY	HRNS	(*	FOUR TOPS STORY	1973	TAMLA MOTOWN				UK	TMSP 1124
FRED SELDON	HRNS	(*	(R) MAIN STREET PEOPLE	1973	DUNHILL	US	50144	PROBE	UK	SPBA 6277
SID SHARP	STRINGS	(*	(R) MAIN STREET PEOPLE	1974	ABC				UK	ABCL 5037
GINGER BLAKE	V	(*	(S) MEETING OF THE MINDS	1974	DUNHILL	US	50166	PROBE	UK	SPBA 6283
LEONARD CASTON	K	(P	(S) MEETING OF THE MINDS	1974	ABC				UK	ABCL 5046

(CONTINUED)

ANDREW SMITH	D	(P	SHAFT IN AFRICA(SOUNDTRACK)	1974	PROBE	UK SBP1077 ANCHOR UK ABCL	5035
EDDIE BONGO BROWN	PERC	(PV	(U)LIVE IN CONCERT	1974	DUNHILL	US 50188 ANCHOR UK ABCL	5062
EDDIE WILLIS	G	(PV	(*) NIGHT LIGHTS HARMONY	1974	ABC	US 862 ANCHOR UK ABCL	5130
JAMES JAMERSON	B	(P	SUPER HITS	1976	TAMLA MOTOWN	UK STML	8028
LARRY CARLTON	G	(QRS	(W)CATFISH	1976	ABC	US 968 UK ABCL	5197
JOE SMITH	G	(QTV	MILESTONES	1977	EMI	UK	50207/8
CHIP CRAWFORD	K	(QR	ANTHOLOGY	197	TAMLA MOTOWN	US M9809	
JIMMIE HASKELL	SYN	(Q	MOTOWN SPECIAL	1977	TAMLA MOTOWN	UK STMX	6004
MICHAEL WOFFORD	K	(R	SHOW MUST GO ON	1977	ABC	US 1014 ANCHOR UK ABCL	5223
SCOTT EDWARDS	B	(S	(Z) AT THE TOP	1978	ABC	UK ABCL	5262
RAY PARKER	G	(S	ITS ALL IN THE GAME	1979	MFP	UK	50416
JEROME RICHARSON	HRNS	(U	REACH OUT 20 GOLDEN GREATS	1981	TAMLA MOTOWN	UK EMTV	26
SIHAB SHIHAB	HRNS	(U	TONIGHT	1981	CASABLANCA	US 7258	
JULIUS BROOKS	HRNS	(U	(EP) FOUR TOPS HITS	1967	TAMLA MOTOWN	UK TMA	2018
CHARLES LOPER	HRNS	(U					
MAURICE SPEAR	HRNS	(U					

GENE ESTES	PERC	U	MARION CHILDERS	HRNS	(U	HERMAN RILEY	HRNS	(U	GEORGE BOHANON	HRNS	(U
EUGENE YOUNG	HRNS	(U	LAWRENCE PAYTON	K	(V	RICHARD ALLEN	D	(P	JACK ASHFORD	PERC	(P
DENNIS COFFEY	G	(PV	MELVIN RAGIN	G	(P	PAUL HUMPHREY	D	(QR	RONNIE BROWN	B	(Q
DAVID COHEN	G	(Q	RICHARD BENNETT	G	(Q	DENNIS LAMBERT	K	(QRS	GARY COLEMAN	PERC	(QRS
BRIAN POTTER	PERC	(QR	STEVE BARRI	PERC	(S	RICHARD BUDSON	K	(V	EARL VAN DYKE	K	(V
JOE GUASTELLA	G	(V	ROBERT WHITE	G	(V	URIEL JONES	D	(V	JOHNNY TRUDELL	HRNS	(V
GREG COLES	B	(V	DAVE PENNEY	PERC	(V	NORMAN HARRIS	G	(Z	EDWARD MOORE	G	(Z
BRUCE GRAY	K	(Z	LARRY WASHINGTON	PERC	(Z	T J TINDALL	G	(Z	CARETON H KENT	K	(Z
KEITH BENSON	D	(Z	HENRI SMITH	PERC	(Z	STRINGS		(VZ			

BRIAN O'HARA	G V	(A	(A) FIRST & FOURMOST	1965	PARLOPHONE	UK PMC	1259
MIKE MILLWARD	G V	(A	(EP)FOURMOST SOUND	1964	PARLOPHONE	UK GEP	8892
BILLY HATTON	B	(A	(EP)FOURMOST	1964	PARLOPHONE	UK GEP	8917
DAVE LOVELADY	D	(					

KIM FOWLEY	V K	(ALL	(A) LOVE IS ALIVE AND WELL	1967	TOWER	US DT	5080
MIKE ALLSUP	G	(D	(B) IN THE UNDERGROUND	1968			
EDDIE HOH	PERC	(D	(C) BORN TO BE WILD	1968	IMPERIAL	US LP	12413
MARS BONFIRE	G	(DGP	(D) OUTRAGEOUS	1969	IMPERIAL	US LP	12423
JIMMY GREENSPOON	K	(D	(E) GOOD CLEAN FUN	1969	IMPERIAL	US LP	12443
JOE SCHERMIE	B	(D	(F) IHE DAY THE EARTH STOOD STILL	1970	MNW	SWED MNWL	7P
ORVILLE RHODES	STEEL	(G	(G) I'M BAD	1972	CAPITOL US ST11075 GER 81208		
WAYNE TABERT	K	(D	(H) OUTLAW SUPERMAN (NOT RELEASED	1971	RCA		
CARMAN RIALE	B	(D	(I) INTERNATIONAL HEROES	1973	CAPITOL US ST11159 GER 81385		
BEN BENAY	G	(DG	(J) SUNSET BOULEVARD	1978	ILLEGAL UK 002 US PVC	7906	
JOE TORRES	PERC	(D	(K) AUTOMATIC	197	CAPITOL		11248
PETE SEARS	B K	(GP	(L) LIVING IN THE STREETS	1977	SONET	UK SNTF	755
WARREN KLEIN	G	(G	(M) ANIMAL GOD OF THE STREETS	1979	CAPITOL		24636
DRACHEN THEAKER	D	(GP	(N) LEGENDARY DOG DUKE SESSIONS	19	B F D	BFD	5012
KERRY SCOTT	G VIBES	(IP	(O) SNAKE DOCUMENT MASQUERADE	1979	ISLAND ILPS 9572 EURO 201217		
GLEN TURNER	G V	PERC(IP	(O) SNAKE DOCUMENT MASQUERADE	1979	ANTILLES	US	7075
CHARLIE McCRACKEN		B(IP	(P) VISIONS OF THE FUTURE	19	CAPITOL		24626
TONY MAC	D	PERC(IP	( ) VAMPIRES FROM OUTER SPACE	19	BOMP	US	40050
TONY MARSH	PNO	(IP					
JUSTIN CHEEN	PERC	(IP	RON BURNS	PERC	(IP	RON CHARLES	V	(IP	JOHN ELSTAR	HCA	(IP
PETER MOSS	BAN HCA K	VLN(IP	MADELINE BELL	V	(IP	PETER LION		(P	JIM MOON	D	(P
CARLOS BERNAL		(P	CHRIS DARROW		(P	TORNADO TURNER		(P			

NOOSHA FOX	V	(AB	(A) FOX	1975	GTO UK GTLP001 ARIOLA US50001		
HERBIE ARMSTRONG	G V	(A	(A) TALES OF ILLUSION	1975	GTO	UK GTLP	006
KENNY YOUNG	G V	(A	(C) BLUE HOTEL	1977	GTO	UK GTLP	020
GARY TAYLOR	B V	(A					
JIM FRANK	D PERC V	(A	PETE SOLLEY	K V	(A	JIM GANNON	G V	(A

STEVE BRAYNE	G	(A	(A) FOR FOX SAKE	1970	FONTANA	UK	6309 007
WINSTON WEATHERILL	G SITAR	(A					
TIM REEVES	D	(A	DAVID WINDCROSS	B PNO(A	ALEX LANE	K	(A

		(A) REVOLT OF EMILY YOUNG	1971	MCA UK MUPS419 US DECCA 75193	

CHARLES FOXX	V	(ALL	(A) MOCKINGBIRD	1964	SUE	US 1027 UK ILP911	
INEZ FOXX	V	(ALL	(A) MOCKINGBIRD	1969	UA	29025	
WITH			(B) INEZ & CHARLES FOXX	196	SUE	US 1037 LONDON UK	8241
WILLIE HALL	V	(C	(C) AT MEMPHIS	1973	VOLT	US 6022	
DEBORAH MANNING	V	(C	(D) COME BY HERE	1968	DYNAMO 8000 DIRECTION UK863085		
BENNY MABONE	V	(C	(E) GREATEST HITS	19	DYNAMO 8002 PYE UK	4406	
WILLIAM BROWN	V	(C	( ) HITS	1968	DIRECTION	UK	863281
JOYCE THARP	V	(C					
WILLIAM MURPHY	B	(C	CHARLES PITT	G	(C	BOBBY MANUEL	G	(C	MICHAEL TOLES	G	(C
LESTER SNELL	K	(C	MARVEL THOMAS	K	(C						

JOHN FOXX	G D SYN	(ALL	(A) METAMATIC	1980	VIRGIN UK V2146		
JOHN BAKER	SYN	(A	(B) THE GARDEN	1981	VIRGIN UK V2194 GER 204 096		
JAKE DURANT	B	(AB	(C) JOHN FOXX(COMP)	1981	VIRGIN CAN		
GARETH JAMES	PERC	(B					
DUNCAN BRIDGEMAN	B	(B	JO DVORNIAK	B	(B	PHILIP ROBERTS	D	(B

CARL DRIGGS	V PERC	(A	(A) GET OFF	1978	TK	TKR	82544
ISH LEDESMA	G V	(A	(B) HOT NUMBERS	1979	TK	UK TKR	83353
ARNOLD PASEIRO	B	(A					
RICHIE PUENTE	PERC K	(A	CHARLIE MURCIANO	K V WIND(A	JOE CALDO	D V	(A	PETER BROWN	B	(A
WAYNE THALER	VIBES	(A	BONAROO HORNS	HRNS	(A	WILDFLOWER	V	(A

F99 GARLAND FRADY F99

GARLAND FRADY   (A) PURE COUNTRY   1973   COUNTRYSIDE   US   CS101

F99A RENZO FRAESE F99A

(A) FILALMENTE   1978   PYE   UK   NSPL28267

RENZO FRAESE	K SYN(A						
BOB DAUGHERTY	B (A						
DAVE WILLIAMS	B (A	CHET McCRACKEN	D (A	DOUG RICHARDSON	PERC (A	SANFORD RICHMOND	PERC(A
DALTON SMITH	TPT (A	BOB PAYNE	TROM (A	DAVE ROBERTS	HRNS (A	ANDY MACKINTOSH	WIND(A
JOE IZEN	G V (A	BILL LAMB	TPT (A	LOU KORELL	HRNS (A	LON NORMAN	TROM(A
STEVE KRAVITZ	WIND (A	PHIL AYLING	WIND (A	TOM JUSTIN	G (A	BILL STAPLETON	TPT(A
JOE KRUGER	HRNS (A	ERNIE CARLSON	TROM (A	HOWARD FALLMAN	WIND (A	DOUG WINTZ	TROM(A
DON RADER	TPT (A						

F100 PETER FRAMPTON F100

PETER FRAMPTON	G V B K(ALL	(A) WIND OF CHANGE	1972	A&M	US 4348	UK	AMLS68099
RICK WILLS	B V (BC	(B) FRAMPTONS CAMEL	1973	A&M	US 4389	UK	AMLH68150
MICK GALLAGHER	K (B	(C) SOMETHINGS HAPPENING	1974	A&M	US 3619	UK	AMLH63619
MIKE KELLIE	D (A	(D) FRAMPTON	1975	A&M	US 4512	UK	AMLH64512
JOHN SIOMOS	D (BDEF	(E) COMES ALIVE	1975	A&M	US 3703	UK	AMLG63703
ANDY BOWN	K (AD	(F) I'M IN YOU	1977	A&M	US 4704	UK	AMLK64704
BOB MAYO	V K G(EFG	(G) WHERE I SHOULD BE	1979	A&M	US 3710	UK	AMLK63710
STANLEY SHELDON	B (EFG	(H) BREAKING ALL THE RULES	1981	A&M	US 3722	UK	AMLK63722
MARK GOLDENBERG	V G K(A	(J) THE ART OF CONTROL	1982	A&M		UK	AMLH64905
STEVIE WONDER	HCA (F						
JAMIE OLDACKER	D (G	FRANK CARILLO	G V PERC(AB	POLI PALMER	VIBES (D	RITCHIE HAYWARD	PERC(F
JOHN HEADLEY DO::N D	(C	NICKY HOPKINS	PNO (C	STEVE FORMAN	PERC (G	CHRIS KARAN	PERC(A
FRANK RICOTTI	PERC (G	MICKEY JONES	G (A	RINGO STARR	D (F	JOE VITALE	V (G
STEVE CROPPER	G (G	DONALD DUNN	B (G	DAVID ALLEN DUKE	HRNS (G	JIM PRICE	HRNS(A
KLAUS VOORMANN	B (H	TOWER OF POWER	HRNS (G	ED MANTELEONE	G (H	STEVE LUKATHER	G (H
JEFF PORCARO	D (H	JOHN REGAN	B (HJ	WATERS FAMILY	V (G	HARRY STINSON	D(J
IAN LLOYD	V (J	EDDIE KRAMER	V (J	JOHN DWORKOW	V (J		

F101 RITCHIE FRANCIS F101

(A) SONGBIRD   1971   PEGASUS UK PEG 1+ INTERCORD 26006-7U

RITCHIE FRANCIS	PNO V(A						
MIKE KELLIE	D (A						
BARRY MORGAN	D (A	WILL MALONE	D (A	PHIL CURTIS	B (A	JOHN ROSTILL	B (A
TAFF WILLIAMS	G (A	JIM SULLIVAN	G (A				

F101A BOB FRANK F101A

BOB FRANK   G V (A   (A) BOB FRANK   19   VANGUARD   US   6582

F101B STANLEY FRANK F101B

(A) PLAY TILL IT HURTS   1980   A&M   AMLH 64828

STANLEY FRANK	G K V PERC(A						
PAUL HANNAH	D (A						
BILL WADE	D (A	ANTON EVANS	B V (A	WOODY WEST	G V (A	MARK RUTTER	ORG (A
DAVE WILCZEWSKI	SAX (A	DOC FINGERS	PNO (A	ROBIN CABLE	PROD (A		

F101C FRANKE AND THE KNOCKOUTS F101C

(A) FRANKE AND THE KNOCKOUTS   1981   MILLENIUM LP5026   BXLI7755

FRANKE PREVITE	V (A						
BILLY ELWORTHY	G (A						
BLAKE LEVINSON	K (A	LEIGH FOXX	B (A	CLAUDE LEHENAFF	D (A	TOMMY AYERS	K SYN V(A
CHARLIE DOMINICI	V (A	JIMMY MAELEN	PERC (A	BROOKLYN DREAMS	V (A		

F101D FRANKFURT CITY BLUES BAND F101D

(A) ...IS IN TOWN   1979   TRION CASS   GER   7901
(B) SECOND STEP   1979   MOONSHINE CASS GER   5001

ANDREUS AUGUST	V G K(AB						
MANFRED HAEDER	G (AB						
TSCHO THOMAS SCHILLING	B(AB						
GEORGE VIEL	D (AB	BERNARD DILL	HCA G (AB	ACHIM FAHR	SAX(AB	HELMUT SCHICK	HRN(B
CONNY KELLER	V (B	DORIS TANGEL	V (B	THOMAS GOERTEN	PERC(B	LOTHAR KRELL	K (B
EVA MITTMANN	G (B						

F102 FRANKIE & JOHNNY F102

(A) SWEETHEART SMPLER   1973   WB   US   2675

FRANK RUBY	G V (A						
JOHN PAUL FETTA	B V (A						
BARRY BAILEY	G (A	EDDIE BARBATO	G (A	AL KOOPER	GK (A	J R COBB	G (A
DEAN DAUGHTRY	K (A	ROBERT NIX	D (A	MIKE GATELY	V (A		

F103 ARETHA FRANKLIN F103

ARETHA FRANKLIN	PNO V (ALL	ARETHA	1961	CBS	US 8412	FONTANA	UK TFL5173
WITH		ELECTRIFYING	1962	CBS	US 8561		
CORNELL DUPREE	G (*	TENDER,MOVING & SWINGING	1962	CBS	US 8676		
JACK CAVARI	G (*	LAUGHING ON THE OUTSIDE	1963	CBS	US 8897		
TOM HANLON	G (*	UNFORGETTABLE	1964	CBS	US 8963		
RICHARD TEE	K (*	SONGS OF FAITH	1964	CHECKER	US 10009	ATLANTIC UK'67 588066	
KEN ASCHER	K (*	RUNNING OUT OF FOOLS	1964	CBS	US 9081		
PAUL GRIFFIN	K (*	YEAH	1965	CBS	US 9151	UK	62556
VAN McCOY	V K (*	SOUL SISTER	1966	CBS	US 9321	UK	62744
GORDON EDWARDS	B (*	QUEEN OF SOUL	196	HARMONY	US 11274	CBS UK	52562
BRIAN ALLSOP	B (*	TAKE IT LIKE YOU GIVE IT	1967	CBS	US 9429	UK	62969
CHRIS PARKER	D (*	LEE CROSS	1967	CBS		UK	63160
CRUSHER BENNETT	PERC (*	GREATEST HITS	1967	CBS	US 9473	UK	64536
GEORGE DEVENS	PERC (*	TAKE A LOOK	1967	CBS	US 9554	UK	63269
KEN BISCHEL	SYN (*	I NEVER LOVED A MAN	1967	ATLANTIC	US 8139	UK	588 066
DESTRY	V (*	I NEVER LOVED A MAN	1972	ATLANTIC		UK	K 40134
ZULEMA CUSSEAUX	V (*	ONCE IN A LIFETIME	196	HARMONY	US 11349		
ALBERT BAILEY	V (*	GREATEST HITS 1960/65	196	HARMONY	US 30606		
BRENDA HILLIARD	V (*	ARETHA ARRIVES	1967	ATLANTIC	US 8150	1972 UK	K 40157
JEROME JACKSON	V (*	GREATEST HITS VOL 2	1968	CBS	US 9601+31355	UK	63064
RICHARD HARRIS	V (*	LADY SOUL	1968	ATLANTIC	US 8176	UK	588 099
PETE MARSHALL	V (*	LADY SOUL	1972	ATLANTIC		UK RI	K40016
CAROLYN FRANKLIN	V (*	ARETHA NOW	1968	ATLANTIC	US 8186	UK	588 114
SHARON BROWN	V (*	LIVE AT PARIS OLYMPIA	1968	ATLANTIC	US 8207	UK	588 149
PAT WILLIAMSON	V (*	LIVE AT PARIS OLYMPIA	1972	ATLANTIC		UK	K49924
CURTIS MAYFIELD	G (Z	BEST OF	1968	ATLANTIC	US 8305		
GARY THOMPSON	G (Z	SOUL 69	1969	ATLANTIC	US 8212	UK	588 163
DONNEL HAGAN	D (Z	TODAY I SING THE BLUES	1969	CBS	US 9956		
ALFONZO SURRET	V (Z	SOFT & BEAUTIFUL	196	CBS	US 9776		
DICKI LINTON	V (Z	ARETHA GOLD	1969	ATLANTIC	US 8227	UK	588 192
RICH TUFO	K (Z	ARETHA GOLD	1972	ATLANTIC		UK	K 40036
JOSEPH SCOTT	B (Z	SATISFACTION	19	ATLANTIC	US 8215		

(CONTINUED)

ARETHA FRANKLIN

HENRY GIBSON	PERC (Z						
MATTIE BUTLER	V (Z						
DERNESE HEARD	V (Z						

I SAY A LITTLE PRAYER	1969	ATLANTIC		UK	2464 002
THIS GIRLS IN LOVE WITH YOU	1970	ATLANTIC US 8248		UK	2400 004
SPIRITS IN THE DARK	1970	ATLANTIC US 8265	1972 UK	K 40095
DONT PLAY THAT SONG	1970	ATLANTIC		UK	2400 021
LIVE AT FILLMORE WEST	1971	ATLANTIC US 7205		UK	2400 136
LIVE AT FILLMORE WEST	1972	ATLANTIC		UK	K 40222
YOUNG GIFTED & BLACK	1971	ATLANTIC US 7213		UK	2400 188
YOUNG GIFTED & BLACK	1972	ATLANTIC		UK	K 40323
ARETHAS GREATEST HITS	1971	ATLANTIC US 8295		UK	K 40279
AMAZING GRACE	1972	ATLANTIC US 2 906		UK	K 60023
HEY HEY NOW	1973	ATLANTIC US 7265		UK	K 40504
COLLECTION	1973	MIDI		UK	30035
FIRST 12 SIDES	1973	CBS	US 31953	EMBASSY UK	31006
LET ME INTO YOUR LIFE	1974	ATLANTIC US 7292		UK	K 50031
WITH EVERY THING I FEEL IN ME	1975	ATLANTIC US 18116		UK	K 50093
TWO ORIGINALS	1975	ATLANTIC		UK	K 80007
YOU	1975	ATLANTIC US 18151		IL	K 50159
SPARKLE	1976	ATLANTIC US 18176		UK	K 56248
TEN YEARS OF GOLD	1976	ATLANTIC US 18204		UK	K 50326
SWEET PASSION	1977	ATLANTIC US 19102		UK	K 50368
MOST BEAUTIFUL SONGS	1977	ATLANTIC		UK	K 60030
(Z) ALMIGHTY FIRE	1978	ATLANTIC US 19161		UK	K 50445
STAR COLLECTION	1978	MIDI		UK	K 20017
STAR COLLECTION 2	1978	MIDI		UK	K 20079
(*) LA DIVA	1979	ATLANTIC US 19248		UK	K 50637
ARETHA	1980	ARISTA		UK SPART 1147
LOVE ALL THE HURT AWAY	1981	ARISTA		UK SPART 1170
GREATEST HITS	1982	ATLANTIC		UK	K 40279
JUMP TO IT	1982	ARISTA		GER	204 742

F103A   CAROLYN FRANKLIN   F103A

CAROLYN FRANKLIN V (ALL						

(A) BABY DYNAMITE	1969	RCA	US		LSP 4160
( ) I'D RATHER BE LONELY	1975	RCA	US		LSP 4411
( ) CAROLYN FRANKLIN	1976	RCA		UK	APLI 0420
( ) CHAIN REACTION	19	RCA		US	LPS 4317
( ) FIRST TIME I CRIED	19	JOY		UK	JOYS 180

F103B   ERMA FRANKLIN   F103B

ERMA FRANKLIN V (	

(A) SOUL SISTER	1975	BRUNSWICK			754147
( ) HER NAME IS ERMA	19	EPIC	US		3824

F103C   RODNEY FRANKLIN   F103C

RODNEY FRANKLIN K B V (AB			
VINCENT SPAULDING G (AB			
HAROLD FOREMAN B (A			
IAN UNDERWOOD SYN (A			
TONY ST JAMES D (AB	KENNETH NASH PERC (A	DEAN HOLZKAMP WIND(a	MEL MARTIN WIND (A
RANDY MERRITT D (A	PAUL JACKSON B (A	RAY PIZZI CLAR(A	PHYLLIS ST JAMES V(AB
LISA ROBERTS V (A	BROOKS HUNNICUTT V (A	AUDREY FRANKLIN V (A	OSCAR BRASHEAR HRNS(B
DAVID LUELL HRNS (B	SEAWIND HRNS (A	PHIL UPCHURCH G (B	NATHAN EAST B(B
BOBBY BRYANT HRNS (B	PAULINHO DA COSTA PERC (B	MARTI McCALL V (B	CARMEN TWILLIE V)B
DENNIS BUDIMIR G (B	DAVID SHIELDS B (B	JEFF PORCARO D (B	VICTOR FELDMAN PERC(B
ERNIE WATTS SAX (B	LEONARD GIBBS PERC (B	DON MYRICK SAX (B	FREDDIE HUBBARD HRNS(B

(A) YOU'LL NEVER KNOW	1980	CBS	US 36122	UK	83812
(B) RODNEY FRANKLIN	1980	CBS	US 36747	UK	84528
(C) ENDLESS	1981	CBS	US 37154	UK	84945

F103D   MICHAEL FRANKS   F103D

MICHAEL FRANKS (ALL				
JOE SAMPLE K (C				
WILTON FELDER (C				
JOHN GUERIN (C				
LARRY CARLTON G (C				
RICK ZUNIGAR (F				
DAVID SANBORN (C				
MICHAEL BRECKER HRNS (C				
LARRY BUNKER (C				
RAY ARMANDO (C	JOAO PALMA (C	JOAO DONATO (C	HELIO DELMIRO (C
DENNIS BELFIELD (F	LENNY CASTRO (F	ANDRE FISHER (F	ERIC GALE G (F
EDDIE GOMEZ (F	DON GROLNICK K (F	JERRY HEY HRNS (F	NEIL JASON B (F
RICK MAROTTA D (F	HUGH McCRACKEN G (F	GEORGE SOPUCH (F	LARRY WILLIAMS (F
DAVID SPINOZZA G (F	TENNISON STEPHENS (F	TOM SCOTT SAX (	LOUIE SHELTON G (
LARRY BUNKER PERC (	WENDY WALDMAN V DULC(	ED GREENE D (	JERRY McGEE G (
CAROLE KAYE B (A				

(A) MICHAEL FRANKS	1973	BRUT	US		6005
(B) THE ART OF TEA	1976	REPRISE	US		2230
(C) SLEEPING GYPSY	1977	WB	US 3004	UK	K 56346
(D) BURCHFIELD NINES	197	WB	US 3167		
(E) TIGER IN THE RAIN	1979	WB	US 3294	UK	K 56612
(F) ONE BAD HABIT	1980	WB	US 3427	UK	K 56814
(G) LIVE	1981	WB			56922
(H) OBJECTS OF DESIRE	1982	WB	US 3642	UK	K 56975

F103E   FRANTIC   F103E

(A) FRANTIC	19	LIZARD	US	20103

FRANZ   F103F

MICK HANNES G (AB		
STEFAN JOSEFUS D (AB		
PETER JOSEFUS B V (AB		
WERNER BECKER K (B		

(A) SENSEMANN	1972	RUHR	GER	007
(B) ROCK IN DEUTSCH	1973	ZEBRA	GER	2949 014

F104   ANDY FRASER   F104

ANDY FRASER B V (AB1	
NICK JUDD K (A1	
KIM TURNER D (A	
FRANKIE MILLER V (1	
HENRY McCULLOUGH G (1	MIKE KELLIE D (1

(A) ANDY FRASER BAND	1975	CBS	UK	80731
(B) IN YOUR EYES	1975	CBS	UK	81027
(1) 1974 MILLER FRASER BAND				

F104A   FRATERNITY OF MAN   F104A

ELLIOT INGBER G (AB	
WARREN KLEIN G SITAR (AB	
RICHIE HAYWARD D V (AB	
MARTIN KIBBEE B (AB	LAWRENCE WAGNER G V (AB

(A) THE FRATERNITY OF MAN	19	ABC	US	ABCS 647
(B) GET IT ON	19	DOT	US	25955

JOHN FRED & HIS PLAYBOYS

JOHN FRED	V HCA(ALL	(A) JOHN FRED & HIS PLAYBOYS		1968	PAULA	US	2191
ANDREW BERNARD	SAX (	(B) 34.40 OF JOHN FRED		196	PAULA	US	2193
RONNIE GOODSON	TPT (	(C) AGNES ENGLISH		19	PAULA	US	2197
CHARLIE SPIN	TPT (	(C) JUDY IN DISGUISE		19	PAULA	US	
JIMMY O'ROURKE	G (	(D) PERMANENTLY STATED		1968	PAULA	US	2201
HAROLD COWART	B (	(E) LOVE IN MY SOUL		19	UNI	US	73077
TOMMY DE GENERES	ORG (						
JOE MICELY	D (						

FRED BANANA COMBO

NICOLLE MEYER	D V (AB	(A) FRED BANANA COMBO	1980	ARIOLA	GER	201722
BILL BROWN	B (AB	(B) THE INCREDIBLE FRED BANANA COMBO	1981	GEEBEEDEE	GER	0647
GODFREY TOLLMAN	G B V(AB					
DIZZY FISCHER	TROM (B	HORDT GLAESKER	K (B	GERD POSNY	D SAX (A	RAY McENTHUN D (A
PETER RUEBSAM	PIPES(B	CHRIS BOLLMANN	HRNS (B	KAI WOLF	D (A	THE ORDINAIRES V(A

FREDDIE & THE DREAMERS

FREDDIE GARRITY	V (ALL	FREDDIE & THE DREAMERS	1963	COLUMBIA	UK	33SX 1577
ROY CREWSDON	G (	YOU WERE MADE FOR ME	1964	COLUMBIA	UK	33SX 1663
PETE BIRRELL	D (	SING ALONG	1965	COLUMBIA	UK	SX 1785
BERNIE DWYER	D (	IN DISNEYLAND	1966	COLUMBIA	UK	SCX 6069
DEREK QUINN	G (	FREDDIE & THE DREAMERS	1966	MERCURY	US	61017
		DO THE FREDDIE	196	MERCURY	US	61026
		SEASIDE SWINGERS	1966	MERCURY	US	61031
		FRANTIC FREDDIE	196	MERCURY	US	61053
		FUN LOVIN'	196	MERCURY	US	61061
		KING FREDDIE & DREAMING KNIGHTS	1967	COLUMBIA	UK	SX 6177
		I'M TELLING YOU	19	TOWER	UK	5003
		OLIVER IN OVERWORLD	1970	STARLINE	UK	SRS 5019
		BEST OF	1977	EMI UK NUT11 US CAPITOL 11896		
		EPs				
		IF YOU MAKE A FOOL	1963	COLUMBIA	UK	SEG 8275
		CRAZY WORLD	1964	COLUMBIA	UK	SEG 8287
		YOU WERE MADE FOR ME	1964	COLUMBIA	UK	SEG 8302
		FREDDIE & THE DREAMERS	1965	COLUMBIA	UK	SEG 8323
		READY FREDDIE GO	1965	COLUMBIA	UK	SEG 8403
		JUST FOR YOU	196	COLUMBIA	UK	SEG 8349
		FREDDY GARRITY	1974	BUSSTOP	BUS	5002
		I'M TELLING YOU NOW	1977	EMI	UK	2694

BILL FREDERICKS

BILL FREDERICKS	(A) LOVE WITH YOU	1978	POLYDOR	UK	2382 470

FREE

PAUL RODGERS	V (ABCDEGH13456	(A) TONS OF SOBS	1969	A&M US 4198	UK ISLAND	ILPS 9089
PAUL KOSSOFF	G (ABCDEFGH1235	(B) FREE	1969	A&M US 4204	UK ISLAND	ILPS 9104
ANDY FRASER	B (ABCDEG13	(C) FIRE & WATER	1970	A&M US 4268	UK ISLAND	ILPS 9120
		(C) FIRE & WATER	1970	ISLAND GER 6339007 RI EURO 200 563		
SIMON KIRKE	D (ABCDEFGH123456	(D) HIGHWAY	1970	A&M US 4287	UK ISLAND	ILPS 9138
		(D) HIGHWAY	1970	ISLAND GER 6339028		
TETSU YAMAUCHI	B (FH2456	(E) LIVE	1971		UK ISLAND	ILPS 9160
RABBIT BUNDRICK	K (FH2456	(F) KOSSOFF,KIRKE,TETSU & RABBIT	1971		UK ISLAND	ILPS 9188
SNUFFY WALDEN	G (H	(G) FREE AT LAST	1972	A&M US 4349	UK ISLAND	ILPS 9192
		(G) FREE AT LAST	1972	ISLAND GER 86171		
WENDEL RICHARDSON	G(6	(H) HEARTBREAKER	1972	ISLAND US 9324	UK ILPS 9217	
B J COLE	STEEL (F	(H) HEARTBREAKER	19	ISLAND RI EURO	200 561	
STEVE MILLER	PNO(A	(J) THE FREE STORY	(DBL) 1973		UK ISLAND	ISLD4
REBOP	PERC (H	(K) BEST OF FREE	1975	A&M US 3663		
		(L) FREE & EASY ROUGH READY	1976		UK ISLAND	ILPS 9453
(1) 1968/71	(2) MAY71/JAN72	(M) POP CHRONIK	(DBL) 1977	EURO ISLAND	89236	
(3) 71 /72	(4) JUL72/SEP72	(EP) ALL RIGHT NOW	1978	ISLAND UK IEP 6		
(5) SEPT 72	(6) JAN73/JUNE73					

FREE BEER

SANDY ALLEN	V G B(ABC	(A) FREE BEER	1975	SOUTHWIND	US	SWS 6402
MICHAEL PACKER	V G B(ABC	(B) HIGHWAY ROBBERY	1976	RCA		APLI 1733
CALEB POTTER V G PERC (ABC		(C) NOUVEAU CHAPEAU	1977	RCA		APLI 2072
NED ALBRIGHT	PNO (A					
RICHARD CROOKS	D (A	JOE X DUBE	D (A	LARRY GONSKY K SYN (A	RICHARD HARBERT	PNO(A
BRENDAN HARKIN	G V (A	PATTIE DARDY HARKIN V (A	JACK JENNINGS PERC (A	GEORGE MARGE	SAX(A
JON HARRIS	HCA (A	BERNARD PURDIE	D (A	RONNIE RENNINGER G (A	PAUL SCHWARZ	D (A
ERIC WEISSBERG FDL DOB(A		DANIEL BEN ZEBULON PERC (AB	MARKY MARKOWITZ HRNS (A	BOB MINTZER	SAX(A
JERRY MAROTTA	D (B	DAN DALEY	STEEL (A	WERNER FRITZSCHING G (B	RALPH SCHUCKETT	K (BC
HUGH McCRACKEN	G (C	STEVE KHAN	G (C	KEN ASCHER	K (C	WILL LEE	B (C
CHRISTOPHER PARKER D (C		STU WOODS	B (C			

FREE CREEK

TODD RUNDGREN	G (A	(A) MUSIC FROM FREE CREEK	1973	CHARISMA	UK	CADS 101
ROY MARKOWITZ	D (A	(A) SUMMIT MEETING	1976	CHARISMA		CS3
MOOGY KLINGMAN	ORG (A					
STU WOODS	B (A	LEW DELGATTO	TROM(A	BOBBY KELLER	TROM(A	MECO MONARDO	TROM(A
LEW SOLOFF	TPT (A	ALAN RUBIN	TPT (A	BILL CHASE	TPT (A	BUZZY FEITEN	G (A
ERIC CLAPTON	G (A	KEITH EMERSON	ORG (A	MITCH MITCHELL D (A	CHUCK RAINEY	B (A
DELANEY BRAMLETT	G (A	CHRIS WOOD	FLT (A	JOE FARRELL FLT (A	TOM MALONE	TROM(A
ELLIOTT RANDALL	G (A	RED RHODES	STEEL(A	JOHN LONDON B (A	JOHN WARE	D (A
MAERETHA STEWART	V (A	HILDA HARRIS	V (A	VALERIE SIMPSON V (A	HARVEY MANDEL	G (A
JACK WILKINS	G (A	JIMMY GREENSPOON K (A	LARRY TAYLOR B (A	LARRY PACKER	VLN (A
FITO DE LA PARRA	D (A	BILLY CHESBORO CONGA(A	EARLE DOUD V CONGA(A	DIDYMUS	PERC(A
CAROL HUNTER	G (A	RICHARD DAVIS	B (A	DOCTOR JOHN PNO (A	KING COOL	G (A
RICHARD CROOKS	D (A	TOMMY COSGROVE	B (A	DOUGIE RODRIGUEZ G (A	BOBBY DEAN	TROM(A
HARRY HALL	TPT (A	LINDA RONSTADT	V (A	BERNIE LEADON G (A	CHRIS DARROW	VLN (A
TIMMY HARRISON	V (A	ERIC MERCURY	V (A	BOB SMITH ORG (A	GERI MILLER	V (A

```
F109A                            FREE SPIRIT                                              F109A
    LARRY CORYELL    G    (A       (A) OUT OF SIGHT & SOUND      19      ABC           US        593
    JIM PEPPER       SAX  (A
    CHRIS HILL       B V  (A       CHIP BAKER    G  (A    BOB MOSES D  (A
F110                             FREEDOM                                                  F110
    BOBBY HARRISON   V D  (ALL     (A) FREEDOM                  1970    PROBE         UK    SPBA 6252
    STEVE JOLLY      G    (ALL     (B) AT LAST                  1970    METRONOME     UK    MLP 15371
    PETER DENNIS     V B K(ALL     (C) THROUGH THE YEARS        1971    COTILLION     US    SD  9048
    ROGER SAUNDERS   V G K(ALL     (D) FREEDOM                  1971    VERTIGO       UK    6360 049
                                   (E) IS MORE THAN A WORD      1972    VERTIGO       UK    6360 072
F110A                            BOBBY FREEMAN                                            F110A
    BOBBY FREEMAN    V    (ALL     (A) DO YOU WANNNA DANCE      1958    JOSIE US             1086
                                   (B) C'MON & SWIM             1964    AUTUMN        US        102
                                   (C) GET IN THE SWIM          1959    JOSIE         US        4007
                                   (D) TWIST WITH               19      JUBILEE       US        5010
                                   (E) LOVABLE SIDE OF          1960    KING          US        930
F110B                            FREEPORT                                                 F110B
    CRAIG HOLT       G V  (A       (A) FREEPORT                 1969    MAINSTREAM    US        6130
    KEVIN RALEIGH    K V  (A
    ROGER LEWIS      G V  (A       BILL STALLING   D V (A    DENNIS STADNEY   G    (A
F110C                            FREEWAY                                                  F110C
    JOHN HOBBS K B G      (A       (A) FREEWAY                  1979    DECCA         UK    TXS  131
    J D MANESS       STEEL(A
    TERRY MELCHER    V PNO(A       MEL COLLINS SAX  (A    RICKY FATAAR D PERC(A    JIM SEITER    PERC (A
F111                             ACE FREHLEY                                             F111
    ACE FREHLEY V B G SYN (A       (A) ACE FREHLEY              1978    CASABLANCA    UK/US NBLP 7121
    ANTON FIG        D    (A
    WILL LEE         B    (A       CARL TALLARICO   D    (A    LARRY KELLY   V    (A    DAVID LASLEY  V  (A
    BILL SCHENIMAN   V    (A       SUSAN COLLINS    V    (A
F112                             FRESH                                                    F112
    MILO MARTIN      B    (A       (A) GET FRESH                1977    MCA     US 2241   UK MCF 2797
    BILL PRATT       V    (A       (B) FRESH - FELLIN' FRESH    1978    PRODIGAL      US        10024
    FRED ALLEN       D    (A       (C) OMNIVERSE                1979    PRODIGAL      US        10028
    ELAINE MAYO      G    (A
    PAUL MARSHALL    G    (A       DAVID KAFFINETTI K(A
F113                             FRESH                                                    F113
    BOB GORMAN       G V  (AB      (A) FRESH OUT OF BORSTAL     1970    RCA   US 4328    UK   8122
    KEVIN FRANCIS    B V  (AB      (B) FRESH TODAY              1971    RCA   US 3027
    ROGER CHANTLER   D    (AB
F113A                            FRESH START                                             F113A
                                   (A) FRESH START             1975    DUNHILL       US        50175
F113B                            FRESHIES                                                F113B
                                   (EP) BAISER                 19      RAZZ          UK        EP1
                                   (EP) STRAIGHT IN AT No 2    197     RAZZ          UK        EP2
                                   (EP) WRAP UP THE ROCKETS    1980    MCA           UK    MCAT 693
F114                             FRESHLY LAYED BAND                                      F114
    TIM HOLT         G V  (A       (A) A LOW VOLUME(200??) CASSETTE RELEASED BY THE GROUP THEMSELVES
    BOB PENDRY       G V  (A
    RICHARD FURTER   B    (A       NICK BUCKLER    D    (A    ROGER HUNT    V    (A
F114A                            GLENN FREY                                              F114A
    GLENN FREY G V K B SYN(A       (A) NO FUN ALOUD            1982    ASYLUM        US        60129
    MICHAEL HUEY     D    (A
    JOHN ROBINSON    D    (A       ROGER HAWKINS    D    (A    BRIAN GAROFALO B    (A    BOB GLAUB     B    (A
    ROBERTO PINON    B    (A       DAVID HOOD       B    (A    JOSH LEO     G    (A    DAN KORTCHMAR G    (A
    DUNCAN CAMERON   G    (A       DAVID WOLINSKI   SYN  (A    "HAWK"       K    (A    ALLAN BLAZEK  K    (A
    AL GARTH         SAX  (A       ERNIE WATTS      SAX  (A    JIM HORN     SAX  (A    BILL BERGMAN  SAX (A
    JIM COILE        SAX  (A       GREG SMITH       SAX  (A    HARVEY THOMPSON SAX  (A   RONNIE EADES  SAX (A
    JIM ED NORMAN    STR  (A       LEE THORNBURG    TPT  (A    JOHN BERRY   TPT  (A    MARCY LEVY    V    (A
    TOM KELLY        V    (A       BILL CHAMPLIN    V    (A    OREN WATERS  V    (A    JULIA TILLMAN V  (A
    MAXINE WILLARD   V    (A
F114B                            JAMES FREUD                                             F114B
    JAMES FREUD      V    (A       (A) BREAKING SILENCE        1980    MUSHROOM      AUST      37309
    ROGER MASON      V SYN K(A
    MICK PRAGUE      B    (A       TOMMY HOSIE D    (A    PETER COOK G V    (A
F115                             DEAN FRIEDMAN                                           F115
    DEAN FRIEDMAN    G K V(AB      (A) AN FRIEDMAN             1978    LIFESONG US 35001  UK  6008
    DON SARLIN       G V  (B       (B) WELL WELL SAID THE ROCKING CHAIR 1978 LIFESONG   UK  6019
    JONNY MANN       B    (B
    BILL WARD        D    (B       GEORGE YOUNG     SAX  (B    ANDY GOLDMARK V    (B    HOLLY SHERWOOD   V (B
    JIM RYAN         G    (B       MARK RIVERA      SAX V (B    JOSEPH SHEPLEY TPT  (B   DAVID TAYLOR  TROM (B
    DENISE MARSA     V    (B       STU NUNNERY      V    (B    ROB STEVENS  VIBES (B    MICHELE LAMB     V (B
    LORRAINE REBIDAS V    (B       TONY LEVIN       B    (B    RON McCLURE  B    (B
F116                             KINKY FRIEDMAN                                          F116
    KINKY FRIEDMAN   V    (ALL     (A) SOLD AMERICAN          1974    VANGUARD      US        79333
    JIM ATKINSON     G    (C       (B) KINKY FRIEDMAN         1975    ABC     US 829 UK ANCHOR 5134
    T BONE BURNETT   G    (C       (C) LASSO FROM EL PASO     1976    EPIC    US 34304       81640
    MICK RONSON      G    (C
    TOM CULPEPPER    G    (C       BILL HAM     D    (C    LEVON HELM    G    (C    RON WOOD       G    (C
    STEVE SOLES      G    (C       ERIC CLAPTON DOBRO(C    MICHAEL DE TEMPO G (C   BRIAN CLARKE   B    (C
    TERRY DANKO      B    (C       ROB STONER B    (C    IRA WILKES    B    (C    MAJOR BOLES    D    (C
    GARY BURKE       D    (C       TEDDY JACK EDDY D (C   RICHARD MANUEL   D (C   DARRELL NORRIS D  (C
    HOWIE WYETH      D    (C       DR JOHN      K    (C    KEN LAUBER    K    (C    JEWFORD SHELBY K  (C
    RED YOUNG        K    (C       DAVID MANSFIELD STEEL(A RUSTY YOUNG   STEEL(C   SNAKEBITE JACOBS HRNS(C
    ROGER McGUINN    BANJO(C        AL GARTH     FDL  (C    FRENCHIE BOURKE FDL (C  RINGO STARR    D    (C
    TERRY BALIN      V    (C       RICK DANKO B V  (C    RONNIE HAWKINS V  (C    ROSCOE WEST    V    (C
```

BRIAN FRIEL

```
    BRIAN FRIEL      V G  (ABC      (A) BRIAN JOSEPH FRIEL         1974   DAWN      UK 3054
    COLIN PINCOTT    G    (B        (A) ASHES & MATCHSTICKS        1976   PYE       US 12102
    DELISLE HARPER   B    (B        (B) ARRIVEDERCI ARDROSSAN      1975   DAWN      UK 3064
    MICK DEVONPORT   G    (B                                          /
    TIM RENWICK      G    (B     ANDY ROBERTS     G    (B   ARTHUR RODMAN   G    (B   ZOOT MONEY     K    (AB
    CRAIG PRUESS     K(B          PAUL FRANCIS     D    (B   BILLY LAWRIE    V    (A   PAUL VIGRASS   V    (AB
    STEVE THOMPSON   B    (A      GARY OSBORNE     V    (A   COLIN ALLEN     D    (A   THE PHANTOM    G    (A
    B J COLE       STEEL(A        MAGS McGLINT     V    (A
```
TERRY FRIEND

```
    TERRY FRIEND                    (A) COME THE DAY              1978   TRAMP
```
FRIENDS

```
    MARC COHEN       SAX  (A        (A) FRIENDS                   1975   CAROLINE    UK     C1511
    CLINT HOUSTON    B    (A
    JOHN ABERCROMBIE G    (A     JEFF WILLIAMS    D    (A
```
FRIENDSHIP

```
    ALEX ACUNA       D    (A        (A) FRIENDSHIP                1979   ELEKTRA US 6E 241  UK K52185
    ERNIE WATTS      WIND (A
    DAVE GRUSIN      K    (A     ABRAHAM LABORIEL B    (A   LEE RITENOUR   G (A
```
FRIJID PINK

```
    TOM BEAUDRY      D    (ALL      (A) FRIJID PINK               1970   DERAM  UK 1062 US PARROT 71033
    RICH STEVERS     D    (ALL      (B) DEFROSTED                 1970   DERAM  UK 1077 US PARROT 71041
    GARY THOMPSON    G    (ALL      (C) EARTH OMEN                1973   LIONEL     US       1004
    KELLY GREEN      V    (         (D) IN THE BEGINNING          1973   TELDEC     GER    621 681
                                    (E) ALL PINK INSIDE           1975   FANTASY    US       9464
```
FRINGE BENEFIT

```
    JOHN JONES       G V  (A        (A) FRINGE BENEFIT            1977   CAPRICORN  US     CP 0183
    CHRIS HAINES     B    (A
    DAVE GRAY        G    (A     STEVEN LAURIE    D    (A   MIKE MORAN     K    (A
```
ROBERT FRIPP

```
    ROBERT FRIPP     G    (ALL      (A) NO PUSSY FOOTIN'          1972   ISLAND UK HELP16 US ANTILLES 7007
    BRIAN ENO        K    (ABC      (A) NO PUSSY FOOTIN'          1977   POLYDOR EG    UK    2343 095
    BARRY ANDREWS    K    (C        (B) EVENING STAR              1975   ISLAND UK HELP22 US ANTILLES 7018
    PETER HAMMILL    V    (C        (B) EVENING STAR              1977   ISLAND GER 89867 EG UK   2343094
    PHIL COLLINS     D PERC(C       (C) EXPOSURE                  1979   EG UK EGLP 101   GER    2302 092
    PETER GABRIEL    V    (C        (C) EXPOSURE                  1979   POLYDOR US 6201
    MICHAEL WALDEN   D    (C        (D) GOD SAVE THE QUEEN/MANNERS 1980   EG UK EGLP 105   GER    2302 098
    DARYL HALL       V    (C        (D) GOD SAVE THE QUEEN/MANNERS 1980   POLYDOR US 6288
    TERRE ROCHE      V    (C        (E) FRIPPERTRONICS/LET THE POWER FALL 1981 EG UK EGED 10  GER  2311 073
    TONY LEVIN       B    (C
    DAVID BYRNE      V    (D     PAUL DISKIN      D    (D   BUSTA CHERRY JONES  B (D
```
LLORRAINE FRISAURA

```
    LORRAINE FRISAURA V G(A         (A) BE HAPPY FOR ME           1976   RCA              PL  13034
    STEVE KHAN       G    (A
    DON GROLNICK     K    (A     MICHAEL BRECKER  HRNS (A   MERLE MILLER   V    (A   ERIN DICKINS   V    (A
    WILLIAM F LEE    B    (A     MIKE MANDEL      SYN  (A   GAIL KANTOR    V    (A   CHRIS HILLS    D    (A
    MTUME            PERC (A     KAY T OSLIN      V    (A
```
FRISKY

```
                                    (A) FRISKY                    1980   VANGUARD     US     79430
```
FRED FRITH

```
    FRED FRITH   SYN G B K D (ALL   (A) GUITAR SOLS              1974   CAROLINE    UK      C1508
    DEREK BAILEY         (B         (B) GUITAR SOLOS 2           1976   CAROLINE    UK      C1518
    HANS REICHEL         (B         (C) GUITAR SOLOS 3           1979   RIFT                RIFT1
    HASSE BRUNIUSSON HRNS (E        (D) WITH FRIENDS LIKE THIS   1979   METALANGUAGE          107
    HENRY KAISER         (C         (E) GRAVITY                  1980   RALPH       US      8057
    G F FITZGERALD       (B         (F) SPEECHLESS               1981   RALPH       US      8106
    CHIP HANDY           (C
    PETER CUSACK         (C      DAVEY WILLIAMS       (C   KEITH ROWE       (C   EUGENE CHADBURNE    (C
    AKIRA HIJIMA         (C      EINO HAAPALA     G MAND (E   LARS HOLLMER  K ACC(E   CHRIS CUTLER   PERC  (E
    OLIVIA BUYNHOOGHE PERC(E     MARC HOLLANDER   WIND (E   TINA CURRAN    B WIND(E   CATHERINE JAUNIAUX PERC(E
    FRANK WUYTS      PERC D(E    MICHEL BERKMANS  PERC (E   STORM          V    (F   ETIENNE CONOD   PERC(E
    DENIS VAN HECKE  PERC (E     VERONIQUE VINCENT PERC (E  ASHA SWANSON   V    (E   FRED MAHER     D    (F
    DAVE NEWHOSE     SAX K(F     BILLY SWAN       B    (E   PAUL SEARS     D    (E   GUIGON CHEVENIER D SAX(F
    MARGOT MATHIEU   SAX V(F     FERDINAND RICHARD B V (F   JO THIRION     K    (F   TOM SCOTT      SAX  (E
    ROGER PARSONS    PIPES(F     BILL LASWELL     B    (F   STEVE BUCHANAN SAX  (F   GEORGE CARTWRIGHT SAX (F
    MARS WILLIAMS    SAX  (F
```
DONNIE FRITTS

```
    DONNIE FRITTS    V PNO(A        (A) PRONE TO LEAN             1974   ATLANTIC    US   SD 18117
    PETE CARR        G DOB(A
    JIMMY JOHNSON    G    (A     EDDIE HINTON     G HCA(A   BARRY BECKETT K VIBES(A  MIKE UTLEY     ORG(A
    DAVID HOOD       B    (A     ROGER HAWKINS    D    (A   SAMMY CREASON   D    (A  JERRY McGEE    G   (A
    TONY JOE WHITE   G B V(A     JERRY MASTERS    B    (A   SPOONER OLDHAM VIBES (A  MICKEY RAPHAEL HARP(A
```
EDGAR FROESE

```
    EDGAR FROESE  MULTI INST(ALL    (A) AQUA                     1974   VIRGIN US 13111 UK  V2016
    KLAUS KRIEGER    D    (C        (B) EPSILON IN MALAYSIAN PALE 1975  VIVGIN      UK      V2040
                                    (C) AGES                     1977   VIRGIN      UK      V2507
    CHRIS FRANK      SYN  (A        (D) MACULA TRANSFER           19     IMP
    GUNTHER BRONSCHEN     (A        (E) STUNT MAN                 1979   VIRGIN      UK      V2139
                                    (F) ELECTRONIC DREAMS         197    BRAIN       GER   0040 148
```
WYNDER K FROG

```
    WYNDER K FROG(MICK WEAVER) K (ALL  (A) SUNSHINE SUPER FROG   1967   ISLAND      UK      ILPS 944
    CHRIS MERCER     SAX  (BC       (B) OUT OF THE FRYING PAN    1968   UA US 6695 UK ISLANDILPS 9082
    REBOP            PERC (B         (C) INTO THE FIRE            1970   UA US 6740
    NEIL HUBBARD     G    (BC
    ALAN SPENNER     B    (BC    BRUCE ROWLAND    D    (BC  DICK HECKSTALL SMITH SAX(B  HENRY LOWTHER HRNS    (B
    ROCKY DZIZORDNU  PERC (C     SHAWN PHILLIPS   G V  (C
```

```
   RAYMOND FROGGATT   V    (ABCD        (A) VOICE AND WRITING OF           1969   POLYDOR        UK    583   044
   LOUIS CLARK        K    (A           (B) BLEACH                         1972   BELL           UK    BELLS 207
   LEONARD ABLETHORPE D    (A           (C) ROGUES & THIEVES               1974   REPRISE        UK    K  44257
   HARTLEY CAIN       G    (A           (D) SOUTHERN FRIED FROG            1978   JET            UK    JATLP 209
   JOHN FIDDY         B    (A.          (E) CONVERSATIONS                  1979   JET            US 35729
   JORDANAIRES        V    (D
   BILLY SANFORD STEEL (D   PETE DRAKE STEEL  (D       BUDDY HARMON     D      (D   LARRY BUTLER  PNO (D
   JAMES CAPPS        G    (D   TOMMY ALSUP B    (D
```

```
   JOHN TROIA         V    (A           (A) FROM THE POND                  19     FROGGIE BEAVER US        7301
   JOHN FISCHER       V G B(A
   ED STASZKO         K V  (A   RICK BROWN        D V(A    CHRIS STOVALL   VIBES  (A   MIKE McKEEN  PERC  (A
```

```
   MIKE SMITH         G V  (A           (A) FROGMORTON AT LAST             1976   PHILIPS        UK    6308  261
   LUCY SHARPE G PERC V    (A
   CHRIS TULLOCH K MAND V(A   DAVE HARDY ACC PERC(A        BILL LYNN       B      (A   TERRY NEWBURY  D   (A
```

```
   FRANK FROST        (A                (A) HEY BOSS MAN                   1980   CHARLY         UK    CRM 2011
```

```
   STEVEN FROMHOLZ G V (ALL             (A) FROMMOX                        1969   PROBE          US    CPLP45115
   JOHN BEAL          B    (A           (B) HOW LONG IS THE ROAD TO KENTUCKY 1973 NOT RELEASED
   DON BROOKS         HCA  (A           (C) A RUMOR IN MY TIME             1976   CAPITOL        US        11521
   BOB JAMES          PNO  (A           (D) FROLICKING IN THE MYTH         1977   CAPITOL        US        11611
   OMAR CLAY          D    (A           (E) MUSIC FROM OUTLAW BLUES(3SONGS) 1977  CAPITOL        US        11691
   EVERETT BARKSDALE B     (A           (F) JUS' PLAYIN' ALONG             1978   LONE STAR      US    L4601
   ERIC WEISSBERG FDL G STEEL B(A       (G) FROMHOLZ LIVE                  1979   FELICITY RECORDS US   FR001
   KENNY ALTMAN       B    (A
   GARY BARRY              (C     RANDY BEAVERS        (A   BILL BROWDER     (C   MICHAEL CAMPBELL   (C
   DOUG DILLARD  BANJO G(CE   DONNY DOLAN      D PERC (C   KELLY DUNN  K SYN (C   DAVE FERGUSON    K (C
   PAUL HARRIS        PNO  (C     ROGER HARRIS         (C   JOHN INMON  G V   (C   MICHAEL JEFFREY  G (C
   FRED KRC    D PERC (C     ROBERT LIVINGSTON G B V (C   REX LUDWICK      (C   WILLIE NELSON    V (C
   GARY NUNN G K B V SYN (C     JODY PAYNE           (C   GARY PELFRY      (C   JOE PORCARO  PERC (C
   MICKEY RAPHAEL     HCA  (C     RED RHODES      STEEL (CD   JOHN SEBASTIAN G V (C   BEE SPEARS     B (C
   B W STEVENSON  G V (C     CASSELL WEBB     V   (C   KIRK BRUNER   D    (D   MIKE McKINNEY  B V(D
   STEVE FORMAN       PERC (C     JIM SCHULMAN    PERC G V(D   STANLEY SCHWARTZ PNO (D   LARRY NYE   G (D
   JOE RENZETTI       G    (D     JAY GRAYDON     G    (D   JOHN BARNES  K SYN (D   DAVID LUELL  SAX  (D
   ANDY MUSON         B    (D     JIM KELTNER     D    (E   JEFF BAXTER  G    (E   ROBBEN FORD   G(E
   GEORGE CLINTON     PNO  (E     ARNIE MOORE     B    (E   RICHARD GREENE FDL (E   J J WALKER  PERC (E
   MARK DAWSON        HCA  (E     PETE GRANT     STEEL (E   BAMBI ROBERTS K    (E
```

```
   DICK WAGNER        G V  (ABC         (A) FROST MUSIC                    19     VANGUARD       US        6520
   DON HARTMAN        G V  (ABC         (B) ROCK'N' ROLL MUSIC             19     VANGUARD       US        6541
   GERDY GARRIS D K V (ABC         (C) THROUGH THE EYES OF LOVE            19     VANGUARD       US        6556
   BOB RIGGS          D    (ABC
```

```
   CARSTEN BOHN     B PERC(ABCDE        (A) ALL WILL BE CHANGED            1970   VERTIGO              6305  067
   KARL HEINZ SCHOTT    B(ABCDE         (B) FRUMPY 2                       19     VERTIGO              6305  098
   RAINER BAUMANN G STEEL (BCDE         (C) BY THE WAY                     19     VERTIGO              6360  604
   ERWIN KANIA        K(C               (C) BY THE WAY                     1974   BILLINGSGATE         BG 1003
   INGA RUMPF         V G  (ABCDE       (D) LIVE                           19     VERTIGO              6623  022
   JEAN JACQUES KRAVETZ K(ABCDE         (E) ATTENTION                      19     FONTANA              6434 163
```

```
   PETER FARELLY    B G V(ABCD          (A) FUTURE LEGENDS                 1973   DAWN           UK    DNLS 3053
   STEPHEN HOUSTON K OBOE V(ABC         (B) PRINCE OF HEAVENS EYES         1974   DAWN           UK    DNLH   2
   MARTIN FOYE      D PERC(ABCD          (C) SEVEN SECRETS                 1974   DAWN           UK    DNLS 3058
   VINCE McCUSKER   G V  (ABCD          (D) MODERN MASQUERADES             1975   DAWN           UK    DNLS 3070
   JOHN MASON         K    (D
   IAN McDONALD       SAX  (D
```

```
   TONY DURANT        G V  (A           (A) FUCHSIA                        1971   PEGASUS              PEG 8
   MADELINE BLAND  CELLO K V(A
   MICHAEL GREGORY   D    (A   VANESSA HALL-SMITH  VLN V(A   JANET ROGERS  VLN V (A MICHAEL DAY   B  (A
```

```
                                        (A) FUGITIVES AT DAVES HIDEOUT     19     HIDEOUT        US    HLP 1001
```

```
   GERD FUHRS       D SYN V(AB          (A) AMMERLAND                      1978   BRAIN          GER   60 105
   HEINZ FROHLING  G V PERC(AB          (B) STRINGS                        1979   BRAIN          GER   60 223
   JAN GROENING       D    (B           (C) DIARY                          1981   BRAIN          GER   60 333
   DETLEF WIEDEKE   B D V(B
   KOOS BLOESMA       PERC(B
```

```
   ED SANDERS         V    (CEDFG       (A) FIRST ALBUM                    1965   ESP US  1018 UK FONTANA 5513
   JIM PEPPER         FLT  (ACEDGF      (A) FIRST ALBUM                    1965   ESP EXPLOSIVE  FR       538114
   KEN WEAVER         V D  (ACEDGF      (B) THE FUGS( KILL FOR PEACE)      1966   ESP            US       1028
   DAN HAMBURG        G    (G           (B) THE FUGS                       1966   ESP EXPLOSIVE  FR       538115
   PETER STAMPFEL G BAN HCA (ABC        (B) THE FUGS                       1970   FONTANA        UK    STL 5524
   TULI KUPFERBERG  V PERC(ABCDEFGH     (C) VIRGIN FUGS                    1966   ESP US  1028 UK FONTANA 5501
   JULIUS WATKINS    HRNS (F            (C) VIRGIN FUGS                    1966   ESP EXPLOSIVE  FR       538116
   KEN PINE          G V  (EDGF         (D) TENDERNESS JUNCTION            1966   TRANSATLANTIC  UK    TRA 180
   CHARLES LARKEY     B    (EDGF        (D) TENDERNESS JUNCTION            1968   REPRISE        US       6280
   BOB MASON          D    (EF          (E) IT CRAWLED INTO MY HAND HONEST 196    TRANSATLANTIC  UK    TRA 181
   BETSY KLEIN             (            (E) IT CRAWLED INTO MY HAND HONEST 19     REPRISE        US       6305
   PETE KEARNEY           (            (F) GOLDEN FILTH                    1968   REPRISE        US       6396
   LU CRABTREE           (ABC          (G) BELLE OF AVENUE A               1969   REPRISE        US       6359
   STEVE WEBER        G    (ABC         (H) FUGS 4 ROUNDERS SCORE          1975   ESP            US       2018
   VINNY LEARY        G    (ABC
   JOHN ANDERSON    B V  (ACB   DOUG FRANKLIN     V (E   JENNIFER BROWN  V (E   EARL BAKER     V (E
   KENNETH BATES      K    (E   BILL WOLF         B (E   LESLIE DORSEY   V (E   BOB DOROUGH    V (E
   BARBARA CALABRIA V     (E   MARLYS TRUNKHILL  V (E   BOB HANSON      V (E   JAMES JARVIS   B (E
   ALLEN GINSBERG   V HCA(D   DANNY KORTCHMAR   G (ED   MARETTA GREER   V (D   CARL LYNCH     G (F
   RICHARD LEE        K    (     HOWARD JOHNSON   HRNS( F
```

```
F133A                           FULL MOON                                        F133A
   LUCAS AMOR        VLN  (AB      (A) MOON FOOLS                    1976  FULL MOON        FM001
   JOHANNES LUTTICK  G V  (AB      (B) NOTHING VENTURED NOTHING GAINED 1977 FULL MOON       FM002
   NORMAN HASSALL    PERC (A
   BERT KLEYN        D PERC(B    MAX BRUNET  G SYN (AB    GERARD AMMERLAAN    B STRINGS(AB
F133B                       BOBBY FULLER FOUR                                     F133B
   BOBBY FULLER           (ALL     (A) I FOUGHT THE LAW              196   MUSTANG    US       901
   JIM REESE              (         (A) I FOUGHT THE LAW             1981  LINE       GER      5133
   RANDY FULLER           (         (B) K R L A KING OF THE WHEELS    196   MUSTANG    US       900
   WAYNE QUIRICO          (         (B) K R L A KING OF THE WHEELS   1981  LINE       GER      5146
                                    (C) CIVIL DEFENSE                19    ?          US
                                    (D) MEMORIAL ALBUM              1966  PRESIDENT  US       1003
F134                            LOWELL FULSON                                     F134
   LOWELL FULSON     G V  (ALL     (A) BLUES MASTERS        (DBL)   1977  CHESS UK US       205
   TOMMY CATHEY           (E        (B) HUNG DOWN HEAD               19    CHESS      US       408
   STEVE CROPPER     G    (E        (C) IN A HEAVY BAG              1972  POLYDOR UK 2384038 US JEWEL5003
   AL JACKSON        D    (E        (D) LOWELL FULSON (EARLY RECORDINGS) 1975 ARHOOLIE  US      2003
   MARVELL THOMAS         (E        (E) THE OL' BLUES SINGER        1975  JET UK LP9 GRANITE US  1006
   MICHAEL TOLES          (E        (F) SOUL                        19    KENT    US 516 UNITED US 7737
   BEN BENAY         G    (E        (G) TRAMP                       19    KENT  US 520 UNITED US 7741
   REINIE PRESS           (E        (H) NOW                         19    KENT  US 531 UNITED US 7752
   MIKE HENDERSON         (E        (J) LETS GO GET STONED          19    KENT  US 558 UNITED US 7768
   DONALD MENZA           (E        (K) IVE GOT THE BLUES           1973  JEWEL      US       5009
   DALTON SMITH           (E        (L) EVERYDAY I HAVE THE BLUES   19    NASHVILLE  US       2030
   LEONARD MALARSKY       (E        (M) LOWELL FULSON               19    KENT       US       5020
   JULIA TILLMAN     V    (E        (N) SAN FRANCISCO BLUES         19    VOGUE      FR       512508
   CARL LAMAGNA           (E        (O) MAN OF MOTION               1980  CHARLY     UK   CRB 1018
   BILLY AADNOT      B    (A        (P) LOVEMAKER                   1978  BIG TOWN             1008
   EDDIE CHAMBLEE    SAX  (EAB
   RAY KELLEY             (E     MAXINE WILLARD    V     (E   JOHN KELSO    HRNS (E    BUD BRISBOIS       (E
   LOU McCREARY           (E     THOMAS SHEPARD          (E   CAROLYN WILLIS V (E     BOBBYE HALL     PERC(E
   JAMES GETZOFF          (E     HARRY WESTONE           (E   LOU KLASS        (E     MURRAY ADLER       (E
   BONNIE DOUGLAS         (E     GARETH NUTTYCOMBE       (E   SAM BOGHOSSIAN   (E     JAN KELLEY         (E
   HARRY BLUESTONE   SAX         EARL BROWN SAX          (AEBN LLOYD GLENN  PNO (ABEN ELDRIDE McCARTHY PNO(N
   BIG DAD           B    (N     RUFUS J RUSSELL  PNO    (N   ARTHUR ROBINSON N (N    ASAL CARSON    D   (N
   ELLIS SOLOMON     PNO  (E     RALPH HAMILTON  B       (E   BOB HARVEY    D  (N     ROGER HAWKINS D    (C
   EDDIE HINTON      G    (C     BARRY BECKETT   K       (C   DAVID HOOD    B  (C     ROBERT SIMS   D    (A
   LOUIS WILLIAMS    SAX  (A     JIM WYNN        SAX     (A
F135                               FUMBLE                                        F135
   DES HENLY         G V  (B       (A) FUMBLE                       1972  SOVEREIGN UK SVNA7254 US 11125
   DAVE CHRISTOPHER  G V  (B       (B) POETRY IN LOTION             1974  RCA UK  SF 8403    US 5082
   SEAN MAYES        V PNO(B
   MARIO FERRARI     B V  (B     BARRY PIKE  D      (B
F135A                           FUN & GAMES                                      F135A
                                    (A) ELEPHANT CANDY              19    UNI        US       73042
F135B                              FUNERAL                                       F135B
   MIKE MARTT        G V  (A       (A) FUNERAL                      1981  AZRA (EP)
   MATT DORSETT      G    (A
   JOHN NEFF         B    (A     D THUM      D     (A
F136                               FUNGUS                                        F136
   FRED PIEK         G V  (A       (A) LIEF ENDE LEID               1975  NEGRAM     NL       NR 115
   BOB DEKENGA       K    (A
   KOOS PAKVIS       B V  (A     LOUIS DEBIJ     D     (A   RENS VANDER ZALM  VLN G(A   SIDO MARTENS       G(A
F136A                           FUNK FACTORY                                     F136A
                                    (A) FUNK FACTORY                1976  ATCO       US       36116
F137                             FUNKADELIC                                      F137
   GARY SHIDER       G V  (FK      (A) FUNKADELIC                   1970  WESTBOUND  US 216  PYE UK 28137
   MIKE HAMPTON      G    (K       (B) FREE YOUR MIND YOUR ASS WILL FOLLOW 71 WESTBOUND US 2001 PYE UK 28144
   BOBBY LAVIS       G    (K       (C) MAGGOT BRAIN                 1971  WESTBOUND  US 2007   UK6310200
   WALTER MORRISON   K SYN(K       (D) COSMIC SLOP                  1973  WESTBOUND  US 2022
   BERNARD WORRELL   K V  (KF      (E) AMERICA EATS ITS YOUNG       1973  WESTBOUND  US 2020
   TYRONE LAMPKIN    D    (FK      (F) STANDING ON THE VERGE OF TIME 19   WESTBOUND  US  208
   BOOTSY COLLINS    D    (K       (G) LETS TAKE IT TO THE STAGE    1975  WESTBOUND  US  215
   JEROME BRAILEY    D    (K       (G) LETS TAKE IT TO THE STAGE    1975  20TH CENTURY UK 215
   JIMMY CALHOUN     B    (F       (H) GREATEST HITS                1975  WESTBOUND  US 1004
   LARRY FRATANGELO  D    (K       (I) TALES OF KIDD FUNKADELIC     197   WESTBOUND  US  227
   RAYMOND DAVIS     V    (KF      (J) HARDCORE JOLLIES             1978  WB         US 2973  UK K56299
   LYNN MABRY        V    (K       (K) ONE NATION UNDER A GROOVE    1978  WB         US 3209  UK K56539
   RON FORD          V    (K       ( ) BEST OF THE EARLY YEARS      197   WESTBOUND  US  303
   DAWN SILVA        V    (K       (M) UNCLE JAM  WANTS YOU         1979  WB         US 3371  UK K56539
   LEON PATILLO      PNO  (F       (N) ELECTRONIC SPANKING OF BABIES 1980 WB         US 3482  UK K56874
   GARY BRONSON      D    (F       (O) CONNECTIONS & DISCONNECTIONS 1981  LAX        US 37987
   RON BRYLOWSKI     G    (F
   DEBBIE WRIGHT     V    (K     GARY SHIDE       V    (K  JEANETTE WASHINGTON V (K  MULLIN FRANKLIN  V  (K
   CORDELL MOSSON    V B  (KF    GEORGE CLINTON        (KF GRADY THOMAS       V (KF  CALVIN SIMON     V PERC(K
   CLARENCE HASKINS  V    (F     R FULWOOD     V PERC  (F
F137A                 FUNKY COMMUNICATION COMMITTEE                              F137A
                                    (A) BABY I WANT YOU             1979  FREE FLIGHT  US  AHLI 3405
F138                             FUNKY KINGS                                     F138
   JACK TEMPCHIN   V G HCA(A       (A) FUNKY KINGS                  1976  ARISTA       US  AL  4078
   RICHARD STEKOL  V G PNO(A
   JULES SHEAR     G V(A         FRANK COTINOLA   D    (A  BILL BODINE    B V (A  GREG LEISZ  G STEEL V (A
   MIKE FINNIGAN   V K(A         BARRY BECKETT   PNO   (A  KATY MOFFATT   V   (A
```

RICHIE FURAY

```
RICHIE FURAY       V G  (ALL      (A) I'VE GOT A REASON          1976 ASYLUM  US 7E1067 UK    K 53043
JAY TRUAX          B V  (A        (B) DANCE A LITTLE             1978 ASYLUM  US 6E115  UK    K 53074
JOHN MEHLER        D    (AB       (C) I STILL HAVE DREAMS        1981 ASYLUM  US 6E213
TOM STIPE          K V  (A
MICHAEL OMARTIAN   K V  (A   STORMIE OMARTIAN V  (A   AL PERKINS        G   (AB  STEVE CROPPER   G  (A
ANN WADE           V    (A   MYRNA MATTHEWS   V  (A   CAROLYN WILLIS    V   (AB  AL MacDOUGALL   PERC(A
DON BARBER         BANJO(A   BILLY BATSTONE   B V(BC  GABRIEL KATONA    K   (B   JIM MASON       PERC(B
WILLIAM SMITH      K    (C   DAN DUGMORE      G  (C   VIRGIL BECKHAM    G V (B   JIM HORN        HRNS(B
TIM SCHMIDT        V    (BC  JIM LOILLE       HRNS(B  DAVID CASSIDY     V   (B   JACK REDMAN     HRNS(B
CRAIG FULLER       V    (C   JIM MESSINA      G  (B   CHUCK FINDLEY     HRNS (B   ED COBB         V  (B
STEVE MADAIO       HRNS (B   CHRIS HILLMAN    V  (B   VICTOR FELDMAN    PERC (B   GEORGE GRANTHAM V(B
RUSTY YOUNG        STEEL(B   TOM KUBIS        HRNS(B  RANDY MEISNER     V   (C   RUSS KUNKEL     D  (C
ROSEMARY BUTLER    V    (C   LEE SKLAR        B  (C   VANETTA FIELDS    V   (C   WADDY WACHTEL   G  (C
J D SOUTHER        V    (C
```

BILLY FURY

```
BILLY FURY         V    (ALL      (A) THE SOUND OF FURY 10"      1960 DECCA   UK (RI 1981) LF 1329'
JOE BROWN          G    (A        (B) BILLY FURY                 1960 ACE OF CLUBS UK      ACL 1047
ARTHUR GREENSLADE  K    (A        (C) HALFWAY TO PARADISE        1961 ACE OF CLUBS UK      ACL 1083
                                  (D) BILLY                      1963 DECCA   UK          LK  4533
                                  (E) WE WANT BILLY              1963 DECCA   UK     SKL  4548
                                  (F) BEST OF                    1967 ACE OF CLUBS UK      ACL 1229
                                  ( ) WORLD OF                   1972 DECCA   UK     SAA  108
                                  ( ) THE BILLY FURY STORY  DBL  1977 DECCA   UK     DPA 3033
                                  ( ) GOLDEN YEARS               1979 K TEL   UK     NE  1020
```

FUSE

```
RICK NIELSEN       G K  (A        (A) FUSE                       1968 EPIC    US               26502
CRAIG MEYERS       G    (A
CHIP GREENMAN      D    (A   JOE SUNDBERG  V  (A   TOM PETERSON   B  (A
```

FUSION ORCHESTRA

```
COLIN DAWSON       G    (A        (A) SKELETON IN ARMOUR         1973 EMI     UK      EMA  758
DAVE BELL          D    (A
JILL SAWARD G SYN FLT V (A  STEN LAND G SYN PERC HCA(A  DAVE COWELL  B HCA(A
```

FUSE ONE

```
                                  (A) FUSE ONE                   1981 CTI  UK 2406 012    US 9003
```

FUSION

```
REG WEBB           K V  (A        (A) TILL I HEAR FROM YOU       1980 TELEPHONE      TEL 101
NICK KERSHAW       G V  (A
ALAN CLARKE        D    (A   KENN ELSON  B  (A
```

FUTURE FLIGHT

```
                                  (A) FUTURE FLIGHT              1981 CAPITOL  US           12154
```

FUZZY DUCK

```
MIKE HAWKSWORTH    B    (1        (A) FUZZY DUCK                 1971 MAM     UK      MAM 1005
PAUL FRANCIS       D    (1        (1) POST LP LINE UP  DIFFERENT GUITARIST ON LP
GARTH WATT ROY     G V  (1
ROY SHARLAND       ORG  (1
```

FYNN McCOOL

```
CHRIS STONE        G V  (A        (A) FYNN McCOOL                1970 RCA     UK      SF 8112
MICK CARTER        D    (A
ALAN ESCOMBE       B    (A   MICK FOWLER K V  (A
```

JOHNNY G

```
JOHNNY G           G V  (A        (A) G SHARP G NATURAL          1979 BEGGARS BANQUET  UK    BEGA 6
GRAHAM HINE        G    (A        (B) G BEAT                     1980 BEGGARS BANQUET  UK    BEGA6
TAFFY DAVIES       K    (A        (C) WATER INTO WINE            1981 BEGGARS BANQUET  UK    BEGA30
PAUL HUGHES        B V  (B
KEITH TRUSSELL     V    (A   JOHN RANDALL    D PERC(A  CHAS AMBLER   V   (AB  MALCOLM BENNETT  B  (A
CHRIS GOWER        TROM (A   DICK HANSON  HRNS   (A  RAY BEAVIS    SAX  (A  JOHN EARLE       SAX (A
DAVE BELLOTTI      (A   ANGUS GAYE       V  (A  TERRY BARKHAM  B   (A  NICK HOWELL      D  (A
STEVE LILLYWHITE   B    (A   NICK GLENNIE SMITH PNO (A  MARK HOLLIS   V   (A  JOHN SPENCER     (A
JOHN EVERY         HCA  (B   BRETT            V  (B  FIN           V   (B
```

G FORCE

```
GARY MOORE         G K V(A        (A) G FORCE                    1980 JET     UK      JETLP 229
MARK NAUSEEF       D PERC(A
WILLIE DEE         B K V(A   TONY NEWTON  V  (A
```

GABRIEL

```
FRANK BUTORAC      G V  (A        (A) THIS STAR ON EVERY HEEL    1975 ABC     US      ABCD 885
MICHAEL KINDER     D PERC(A        (B) SWEET RELEASE              1976 ABC     US      AB   972
STACY CHRISTENSON  K V  (A        (C) GABRIEL                    1978 EPIC    US           35454
GARY RUHL          B    (A
TERRY LAUBER G STEEL V (A    MARK PENNICK CONGA(A
```

BB GABOR

```
B B GABOR                         (A) BB GABOR                   1980 BLUEPRINT    UK      5004
```

PETER GABRIEL

```
PETER GABRIEL      V K  (ALL      (A) PETER GABRIEL              1977 CHARISMA    UK  CDS  4006
ALLEN SCHWARZBERG  D    (A        (A) PETER GABRIEL              1977 PHONOGRAM   EURO 9103 115
TONY LEVIN         B V  (ABC      (A) PETER GABRIEL              1977 ATCO       US        36147
JIM MAELEN         G    (A        (B) PETER GABRIEL              1978 CHARISMA    UK  CAS  4013
STEVE HUNTER       G    (A        (B) PETER GABRIEL              1978 ATLANTIC    US        19181
ROBERT FRIPP       G    (ABC      (B) PETER GABRIEL              1978 PHONOGRAM   EURO 9103 123
DAVID RHODES       V    (C        (B) PETER GABRIEL              1978 CHARISMA    GER  )!"$ 025
JOSEF WAGNER       G    (         (C) PETER GABRIEL              1980 CHARISMA    UK  CAS  4019
JERRY MAROTTA      V D  (BC       (C) PETER GABRIEL              1980 MERCURY     US         3848
SIDNEY McGINNIS    G V  (B        (C) PETER GABRIEL              1980 CHARISMA    GER 9124 054
LARRY FAST         SYN  (ABC
TIM CAPELLO        SAX  (B   BAYETE           K  (B  ROY BITTAN    K   (B  GEORGE MARGE RECORDERS(B
JOSEF CHIROWSKI    K    (A   JOHN GIBLIN      B  (C  PAUL WELLER   V   (C  DAVE GREGORY    V  (C
KATE BUSH          V    (C   PHIL COLLINS     D  (C
```

```
                              GABRIEL BONDAGE
G2A                                                                            G2A
   REX BUNDY         G V (         (A) ANOTHER TRIP TO EARTH      1978 DHARMA        US       808
   TONY STRAM        B V (
   L JAMES BIERACKI  G MAND V( RON SCHWARTZ  K SYN(  BILL WISNIEWSKI  WIND V (  NOEL LEVITT D V      (
G2B                              GADGETS                                        G2B
   ? TUCKER            (A         (A) GADGETREE               1980 FINAL SOLUTION  UK    001
   ? JOHNSON           (A         (B) LOVE CURIOSITY FRECKLES & DOUBT 1980 FINAL SOLUTION  UK    002
   ? HYDE              (A
G2C                              GAFFA                                          G2C
                                  (A) NEITHER USE NOR ORNAMENT   19  GAFFA           ZZZZ001
G3                               GAGS                                           G3
   GERRY MacLOUGHLIN G  (A        (A) DEATH IN BUZZARD GULCH    1978 GAG
   BREN GORE         K V  (A
   JOHN KELLY        B  (A    NIGEL COATMAN    D  (A
G3A                       GALACTIC SUPERMARKET                                  G3A
   GILLE                          (A) GALACTIC SUPERMARKET      1974 KOMISCHE      KM  58010
   ROSI
   DIETER DIERKS        (      JURGEN DOLLASE      (A  MANUEL GOETTSCHING (   HARALD GROSSKOPF     (
   KLAUS SCHULZE        (
G3B                              ARLYN GALE                                     G3B
   ARLYN GALE        G V (A        (A) BACK TO THE MIDWEST NIGHT  1978 ABC      UK     ABCL 5261
   ALONA TUSEL       K SYN(A
   OMAR HAKIM        D V (A    IVAN ELLIS    B        (A  STEVE CAVARETTA   G    (A
G4                               ERIC GALE                                      G4
   ERIC GALE         G   (ALL      (A) FORECAST            1973 KUDU   US 11  UK      KUL .8
   BOB JAMES         K   (B        (B) GINSENG WOMAN       1977 CBS    US 34421 UK      82958
   RICHARD TEE       K   (BD       (C) MULTIPLICATION      1978 CBS    US 34938 UK      82283
   ANTHONY JACKSON   B   (BD       (D) PART OF YOU         1979 CBS    US 35715
   HARVEY MASON      D   (D        (E) TOUCH OF SILK       1980 CBS    US 36570 UK      84509
   STEVE GADD        D   (BD       (F) BEST OF             1980 CBS    US 36363 UK      84201
   RALPH MACDONALD   PERC (BD
   GROVER WASHINGTON SAX (BDE ALLEN TOUSSAINT  K   (E   ROBERT DABON   K   (E   GARY KING      B   (B
   ANDREW SMITH      D   (B   GEORGE YOUNG SAX     (B   GARY BROWN    SAX  (E   ARTHUR BLYTHE  SAX (E
   HAROLD VICK       SAX (E   WAYNE ANDRE  TROM    (B   DAVE TAYLOR   TROM (B   LOU SOLOFF     TPT (B
   BILL EATON        V   (B   ZACK SANDERS  V      (B   RAY SIMPSON    V   (B   FRANK FLOYD    V   (B
   VIVIAN CHERRY     V   (B   LANI GROVES    V     (B   PATTI AUSTIN   V   (B   RANDY BRECKER  TPT (B
   ALAN RUBIN        TPT (B   JON FADDIS    TPT    (B   EDDIE DANIELS SAX  (B   MICHAEL BRECKER SAX (B
   CHARLES EARLAND   K   (E   IDRIS MUHAMMAD   D   (DE  KENNETH WILLIAMS PERC (E  JAMES BLACK    D   (E
   DAVID BARARD      B   (E   BERNADETTE RANDLE PNO (D  NEIL JASON    B    (D   DAVE CRUSIN PNO    (D
G4A                          GALE FORCE                                         G4A
                                  (A) GALE FORCE            1978 FANTSAY      US       9527
                                  (B) TIRO                  1978 FANTASY      US       9551
G5                           RORY GALLAGHER                                     G5
   RORY GALLAGHER    G V (ALL      (A) RORY GALLAGHER       1971 POLYDOR      UK    2383 044
                                  (A) RORY GALLAGHER       1971 ATLANTIC     US       33368
                                  (A) RORY GALLAGHER       198  CHRYSALIS          CHR 1258
   GERRY McAVOY      B (ABCDEFGHIJKLMNO (A) RORY GALLAGHER 1975 POLYDOR      UK    2384 066
   WILGAR CAMPBELL   D   (ABCJLZ    (B) DEUCE              1971 POLYDOR      UK    2383 076
                                  (B) DEUCE               1971 ATLANTIC     US       7004
                                  (B) DEUCE               198  CHRYSALIS          CHR 1254
                                  (B) DEUCE               19   CHRYSALIS    NL   511 254
   ROD DeATH         D   (EDFJK    (C) LIVE IN EUROPE      1972 POLYDOR US 5513 UK 2383 112
                                  (C) LIVE IN EUROPE      19   CHRYSALIS    NL   202 647
   LOU MARTIN        K   (EDFJKZ   (D) BLUEPRINT          1973 POLYDOR US 5522 UK 2383 189
                                  (D) BLUEPRINT          198  CHRYSALIS          CHR 1253
   TED McKENNA       D   (MNO      (E) TATTOO             1973 POLYDOR US 5539 UK 2383 230
                                  (E) TATTOO             198  CHRYSALIS          CHR 1259
   VINCENT CRANE     K   (A        (F) IRISH TOUR 1974    1974 POLYDOR US 9501 UK 2659 031
                                  (F) IRISH TOUR 1974    1974 POLYDOR      GER   2679 030
   BOB ANDREWS       K   (P        (G) IN THE BEGINNING   1974 EMERALD GEM  UK    GES1 101
   RICHARD McCRACKEN B   (ZY       (G) IN THE BEGINNING   197  SPRINGBOARD         4056
   JOHN WILSON       D   (ZY       (H) AGAINST THE GRAIN  1975 CHRYSALIS    UK/US CHR 1098
   RAY BEAVIS        SAX  (P        (H) AGAINST THE GRAIN  1975 POLYDOR     EURO 6307 563
   DICK PARRY        SAX  (P        (I) SINNER ......& SAINT 197 POLYDOR US 6510   2383 315
   BRENDAN ONEIL     D   (P        (J) THE STORY SO FAR   1975 POLYDOR US 6519 UK 2383 376
   ERIC KITTERINGHAM B   (G        (K) CALLING CARD       1976 CHRYSALIS    UK/US CHE 1124
   NORMAN DAMERY     D   (G        (K) CALLING CARD       1976 PHONOGRAM    EURO 6307 586
                                  (L) THE BEST YEARS     1976 POLYDOR            2664 303
                                  (M) PHOTO FINISH       1978 CHRYSALIS    UK    CHR 1170
                                  (M) PHOTO FINISH       1978 CHRYSALIS    GER   6307 620
                                  (N) TOP PRIORITY       1979 CHRYSALIS    UK/USCHR 1235
                                  (N) TOP PRIORITY       1979 CHRYSALIS    NL    511 235
                                  (O) STAGE STRUCK       1980 CHRYSALIS    UK/US CHR 1280
                                  (O) STAGE STRUCK       1980 CHRYSALIS    GER   202 884
                                  ( ) LIVE  TRACKS FROM (C) (F) 1977 POLYDOR      2384 079
                                  (P) JINX               1982 CHRYSALIS    UK    CHR 1359
                                  (P) JINX               1982 MERCURY      US    SRM1 4051
                                  (W) TAKE IT EAST BABY  1976 SPRINGBOARD  US       4056
                                  (X) RORY GALLAGHER     1980 HALLMARK     UK       3041
                                  (Y) FIRST & BEST       19   BELLAPHON    GER   29385
                                  (Z) STORY OF R G       197  POLYDOR      GER   2664 377
```

GALLAGHER & LYLE

BENNY GALLAGHER	G V	(ALL	(A) GALLAGHER & LYLE	1972	CAPITOL	US	11016	UK	21906
GRAHAM LYLE	G V	(ALL	(A) GALLAGHER & LYLE	1972	A&M				AMLS68125
WITH			(B) WILLIE & THER LAP DOG	1973	A&M	US	4384	UK	AMLH68148
JIMMY JEWELL	SAX	(1DEF	(C) SEEDS	1973	A&M	US	4425	UK	AMLS68207
JOHN MUMFORD	HRN	(1EF	(D) LAST COWBOY	1974	A&M	US	3665	UK	AMLS68273
IAIN RAE	K	(1F	(E) BREAKAWAY	1976	A&M	US	4566	UK	AMLH68348
ALAN HORNALL	B	(12EFG	(F) LOVE ON THE AIRWAVES	1976	A&M	US	4620	UK	AMLH64620
CHRIS STEWART	B	(A	(F) LOVE ON THE AIRWAVES	1981	MFP	UK RI			50497
RAY DUFFY	D	(12EFG	(G) SHOWDOWN	1978	A&M	US	4675	UK	AMLH68461
BILLY LIVSEY	K	(2DEG	(H) LONESOME NO MORE	1979	MERCURY		UK		9109 628
STEVE GREGORY	WIND	(2	(I) BEST OF	1980	WARWICK		UK		WW 5080
PAUL NIEMAN	TROM	(2	(1) 1977 TOUR (2) 1978 TOUR						
PHIL RYAN	K	(2	(EG) BREAKAWAY/SHOWDOWN	1981	A&M	CASS CR6			
BRYN HAWORTH	G	(2							
PETE TOWNSHEND	HCA	(B	RAY COOPER PERC (G BRUCE ROWLAND		D PERC(ABD	HUGHIE FLINT D		(B	
JIM HORN	SAX	(G							

GALLIARD

RICHARD PANNELL	G	(	(A) STRANGE PLEASURE	1969	NOVA		UK		SDN4
GEOFF BROWN	V	(	(B) NEW DAWN	1970	DERAM		UK	SML	1075
ANDREW ABBOTT	B	(							
LESLIE PODRAZA	D	(	JOHN SMITH WIND (DAVE CASWELL	WIND (					

GAMBLER

NATHAN SHAFFER	V G	(A	(A) TEENAGE MAGIC	1979	LIBERTY			AML	3005
WARREN MAYS	G V	(A	(B) LOVE AND OTHER CRIMES	1980	U A AML 3010	EMIUS		17017	
DEL BRECKENFELD	B V	(A							
CHUCK SCHWARTZ	D	(A	BRUCE BRECKENFELD K V (A						

GAMMA

RONNIE MONTROSE	G	(CA	(A) 1	1980	ELEKTRA	US 6E 129	UK K 52163		
JIM ALCIVAR	SYN	(A	(B) 2	1980	ELEKTRA	US 6E 228	UK K 52245		
DAVEY PATTISON	V	(CA	(C) 3	1980	ELEKTRA	US 60034			
ALAN FITZGERALD	B	(A							
SKIP GILLETTE	PERC	(A	MITCHELL FROMM K (C DENNY CARMASSI	D	(C GLENN LEITSCH	B	(C		

GANG OF FOUR

JOHN KING	V	(A	(A) ENTERTAINMENT	1979	EMI	UK EMC 3313 US WB	3446		
ANDY GILL	G	(A	(B) SOLID GOLD	1981	EMI	UK EMC 3364 US WB	3565		
HUGO BURNHAM	D	(A	(EP) GANG OF FOUR	1981	MINI	UK 3494			
DAVE ALLEN	B	(A							

GANGSTERS

RICHARD HOLGARTH	G V	(A	(A) GANSTERS	1979	STORTBEAT		BEAT2
BILL MEADOWS	G V	(A					
TERRY HANDS	D	(A	MARTIN HOLDEN B (A STEVE HORTON	K	(A	

GAME

CHUCK FITZPATRICK	G V B(B		(A) GAME	19	EVOLUTION	US	2021
GEORGE TERRY	G B	(B	(B) LONG HOT SUMMER	19	EVOLUTION	US	3008
SCOTT KIRKPATRICK	D TPT(B						
EDDIE KEATING	B V	(B	LES LUHRING K VIBES V(B				

CECIL GANT

CECIL GANT	PNO V(ALL		(A) INCOMPARABLE	19	SOUND	US	601
			(B) ROCK LITTLE BABY	1974	FLYRIGHT	UK	4710
			(C) CECIL BOOGIE	1976	FLYRIGHT	UK	4714
			(D) KILLER DILLER BOOGIE	1979	MAGPIE	UK	PY1816

JERRY GARCIA

JERRY GARCIA	G V	(ALL	(A) GARCIA	1972	WB	US	2582	UK K46139	
HOWARD WALES	K	(B	(B) HOOTEROLL	1972	DOUGLAS	US	30859	69013	
JOHN KAHN	B	(BCEF	(C) LIVE AT THE KEYSTONE	1973	FANTASY			79002	
CURLY COOKE	G	(B	(D) GARCIA	1974	GARCIA/ROUND 59301			102	
BILL VITT	D	(BC	(E) REFLECTIONS	1976	UA/ROUND	US LA565	UK	29921	
MICHAEL MARINELLI	D	(B	(F) CATS UNDER THE STARS	1978	ARISTA UK SPART1053 US			AB4160	
KEN BALZALL	TPT	(B							
MARTIN FIERRO	WIND	(B	KEITH GODCHAUX V K (FE DONNA GODCHAUX	V K	(FC BRIAN GODCHAUX VLN (F				
CANDY GODCHAUX	VLN	(F	RON TUTT D (FE MERL SANDERS	K	(FC MARIA MULDAUR V (FD				
STEVE SCHUSTER	WIND	(F	BOB WEIR G (E PHIL LESH	B	(E BILL KREUTZMANN D (AE				
MICKEY HART	D	(E	NICKY HOPKINS K (E LARRY KNECHTEL	PNO	(E LARRY CARLTON G (A				
MICHAEL O'MARTIAN	K	(D	BOBBYE HALL PERC (D RICHARD GREENE	VLN	(D CLYDIE KING V (D				
BEN BENAY	G	(D	AMOS GARRETT G (D MERRY CLAYTON	V	(D TERRY ADAMS CELLO(D				
ROBERT HUNTER	G	(A							

ART GARFUNKEL

ART GARFUNKEL	V	(ALL	(A) ANGEL CLARE	1973	CBS	US	31474	UK	69021
JAMES GILSTRAP	V	(D	(A) ANGEL CLARE	1981	EMBASSY			UK	32076
LARRY CARLTON	G	(A	(B) BREAKAWAY	1975	CBS	US	33700	UK	86002
DEAN PARKS	G	(AF	(C) WATERMARK	1977	CBS	US	34975	UK	86054
STEVE CROPPER	G	(B	(D) FATE FOR BREAKFAST	1979	CBS	US	35780	UK	86082
MAX BENNETT	B	(B	(E) ART GARFULKEL	1979	CBS		TRIPLE	UK	66351
LON VAN EATON	G	(B	(F) SISSORS CUT	1981	CBS	US	37392	UK	85259
MAXINE ANDERSON	V	(D							

LOUIE SHELTON	G	(ABD	MIKE OMARTIAN	K	(A	JIM GORDON	D	(A	JOE CLAYTON	PERC (B
PETE CARR	G	(BCF	LARRY KNECHTEL	K	(ABDF	RUSS KUNKEL	D	(BF	TOM ROADY	PERC (C
PAUL SIMON	G V(ABCF		BRUCE JOHNSTON	PNO	(B	DENNY SEIWELL	D	(B	THOMAS LA TONDRE	PERC (C
JIMMY JOHNSON	D	(C	BILL PAYNE	K	(BC	JIM KELTNER	D	(B	CRAIG KRAMPF	PERC (C
HUGH McCRACKEN	G	(DC	NICKY HOPKINS	K	(B	RICK SCHLOSSER	D	(BC	TOMMY VIG	VIBES(CF
ANDREW GOLD	G V	(BF	JIMMY WEBB	K	(CF	JOHN GUERIN	D	(B	DEREK BELL	HARP (C
STEPHEN BISHOP	G V	(BCD	RICHARD TEE	K	(CD	ROGER HAWKINS	D	(BC	MICHAEL TUBRIDY	FLT (C
JOE OSBORN	B	(ABCF	BARRY BECKETT	PNO	(BC	STEVE GADD	D	(CD	SEAN KEANE	FDL (C
LEE SKLAR	B	(B	JOHN JARVIS	PNO V	(BF	HAL BLAINE	D	(A	PADDY MOLONEY	WIND (C
KLAUS VOORMANN	B	(B	PAUL DESMOND SAX		(C	RALPH McDONALD	PERC (C		JOE FARRELL WIND	(C
DAVID HOOD	B	(B	MARTIN FAY	FDL	(C	GRAHAM NASH	V	(B	DAVID CROSBY	V (BC
REINIE PRESS	B	(B	TONI TENNILLE	V	(B	JAN JOYCE	V	(B	JAY CLAYTON	V (C
TONY LEVIN	B	(CF	SHELLEY HIRSCH	V	(C	ED HASSELBRINK	V	(C	FRED FARELL	V (C

(CONTINUED)

G10   ART GARFUNKEL   (CONTINUED)   G10

```
CAROL FLAMM        V    (C   ALEXANDRA STAVROU  V    (C   JAMES TAYLOR      V    (C   BOB DOROUGH       V    (C
LEAH KUNKEL        V    (CDF RICHIE ZITO        G    (D   MICHAEL BAIRD     D    (D   NEIL JOHNSON      B    (D
MICHAEL BRECKER    SAX  (DF  BOB MOUNSEY        STR  (D   PENNY NICHOLS     V    (D   LYLE FORMAN       PERC (D
CHRIS SPEDDING     G    (D   LES HURDLE         B    (D   EDWIN ROXBURGH    B    (D   JEFFREY STATON    G V  (DF
MICHAEL BODDICKER  SYN  (F   LISA GARBER        V    (F   GRAHAM LYLE       G    (F   RICK MAROTTA      D    (F
LEWIS SOLOFF       HRNS (F   CAROLYLN DENNIS    V    (D   LARRY ROLANDS     V    (D   DENNIS BELFIELD   B    (D
ALAN ESTES         PERC (D   DEL NEWMAN         STR  (DF  CRUSHER BENNET    PERC (DF  ALESSI BROTHERS   V    (D
TOM SCOTT          SAX  (D   SIMON PHILLIPS     D    (D   ROLAND HARKER     G    (D   ROY MORGAN        D    (F
RAY COOPER         PERC (D   LEE RITENOUR       G    (D   DAVID CAMPBELL    STR  (F   SCOTT CHAMBERS    B    (F
RICK SCHLOSSER     D    (F   MICHAEL STATON     G    (F   MARK FRIEDMAN     REC  (A   JIMMY HASKELL     STR  (A
JJ CALE            G    (A   JERRY GARCIA       G    (A   CARL RADLE        B    (A   JULES BROUSSARD   SAX  (A
JORGE MILCHBERG    PERC (A   MILT HOLLAND       PERC (A   SALLY STEVENS     V    (A   ERNIE FREEMAN     STR  (A
PETER MATZ         STR  (A   FRED CARTER        G    (A   TOMMY TEDESCO     MAND (A   JACK SHROER       SAX  (A
DOROTHY MORRISON   V    (A   ST MARYS CHOIR     V    (A   LYLE HARPER       B    (D   NEIL JASON        B    (D
OKLAHMA UNI CHORALE     (C
```

G10A   GARRISON & VAN DYKE   G10A

```
MICHAEL GARRISON   V    (A             (A) GARRISON & VAN DYKE       1979  ATCO          US        38119
RINUS VAN DYKE     G B K HCA(A
SHELL SHELLEKENS   D    (A   EELCO GELLING      G    (A   DANNY LADEMACHER  G    (A   KOKO KAUWSOLEA    PERC (A
```

G10B   AMOS GARRETT   G10B

```
AMOS GARRETT       G V UKE(A           (A) GO GO CAT GO             1980  WATERFRONT              UK   006
MAC DRIDLIK        B    (A
BILL SLAIS         SAX  (A   MICHAEL MILFORD    MAND (A   DARYL COLEY       V    (A   KYLE WRIGHT       V    (A
PHIL AABERG        K SYN(A   SCOTT MATTHEWS     D PERC(A  HIROSHI SATO      SYN  (A   DAVE BERGEN       HCA  (A
LARRY ROBERSON     V    (A
```

G10C   MICHAEL GARRISON   G10C

```
MICHAEL GARRISON   V    (A             (A) IN THE REGIONS OF SUN RETURN   1979  ARIOLA         202 864
```

G11   GARUDA   G11

```
TONY COE           WIND (A             (A) GARUDA       1977                EMI      UK    EMC  3174
JEFF DALEY         WIND (A
HENRY LOWTHER      HRNS (A   DAVE HORTER   TROM (A   ZACK LAWRENCE    K    (A   TONI CAMPO    B G  (A
BARRY MORGAN       D    (A   HAROLD FISHER      D    (A   FRANK RICOTTI    PERC (A
```

G11A   GAS   G11A

```
             (A) EMOTIONAL WARFARE       1981  POLYDOR        UK   POLE 1052
```

G11B   GAS MASK   G11B

```
ENRICO RAVA        TPT  (A             (A) THEIR FIRST ALBUM       1970  TONSIL   US            4001
BOBBY OSBOURNE     V    (A
DAVID GROSS        WIND (A   NICK OLIVA         K    (A   RAY BROOKS       B    (A   RICHARD GRANDO   WIND(A
BILL DAVIDSON      G    (A   JAMES STRASSBURG   D    (A
```

G11C   GAS WORKS   G11C

```
JOHN BROWN         V G B(A             (A) GAS WORKS       1973  REGAL ZONOPHONE  UK   SRLZ1026
MICK DRAPER        VLN MAN HCA (A
```

G11D   GASKIN   G11D

```
             (A) END OF THE WORLD       1981  RONDELET               ABOUT4
```

G12   GASOLIN   G12

```
FRANZ BECKERLEE  G K SYN V (ALL  (A) ANGAENDE LONE (EP)     1970  SONET                 T 7259
WILI JONSSON       B K V  (ALL  (B) GASOLIN                1971  CBS                   64685
KIM LARSEN         G V    (ALL  (C) GASOLIN 2              1972  CBS                   65229
TOM BAILEY         G      (      (D) GASOLIN 3              1973  CBS                   65798
TOM McEWAN         D      (      (E) GASOLIN                1974  CBS             UK    80099
NIELS HARRIT       SAX    (E    (F) STAKKELS JIM (LAST JIM) 1974  CBS      80549  UK    80470
BJORN UGLEBJERG    D      (A    (G) GAS 5                  1975  CBS                   80993
SOREN BERLEV       D      (ALL  (H) LIVE SADAN       DBL   1976  CBS                   88207
KLAUS AGERSCHOU    K      (M    (J) LEMON (US GASOLIN)     1976  CBS US 34149   UK    81436
FELIX PAPPARDI     B G K  (N    (K) EFTER ENDNU EN DAG     1976  CBS                   81650
                                (L) GOR DET NOGET          1977  CBS                   82378
                                (M) KILLIN' TIME           1978  CBS                   82900
                                (N) LIVE IN EUROPE         1978  CBS                   83240
                                (O) SUPERMIX               1980  CBS                   84154
```

G12A   GASOLINE BAND   G12A

```
BRIAN BEVAN        G V    (A             (A) THE GASOLINE BAND      1972  CUBE      UK    HI FLY9
GEORGE THOMPSON    B      (A
FRED SCHWARTZ      K      (A   JEROME JOHNSON   TROM (A   MAJOR WILBURN    SAX  (A   CHARLES BOWEN   SAX  (A
RONALD PHILLIPS    TPT    (A   JIM DVORAK       TPT  (A   WILLIAM GOFFIGAN D    (A   JOE OGE         PERC(A
```

G13   GASS   G13

```
BOB TENCH          B V    (A             (A) GASS                   1979  POLYDOR   UK    2383 022
GODFREY McLEAN     D      (A
ERROL McLEAN       PERC   (    FRANK CLARK      K    (    HUMPHREY OKAN    SAX  (    ALAN ROSKAMS    G    (
DELISLE HARPER     B PERC(A    MICHAEL PIGGOTT  VLN (A    DEREK AUSTIN     K    (A   PETER GREEN     G    (A
MEL COLLINS        PROD   (A
```

G14   DAVID GATES   G14

```
DAVID GATES        V G    (ALL  (A) FIRST ALBUM       1973  ELEKTRA US 75066  UK K 42150
MIKE BOTTS                (ACE  (B) NEVER LET HER GO   1975  ELEKTRA US 1028   UK K 52012
LARRY CARLTON      G      (AC   (C) GOODBYE GIRL       1978  ELEKTRA US 6E148  UK K 52091
JAMES GETZOFF      STRING(A     (D) SONGBOOK           197   ELEKTRA US 6002
RUSS KUNKEL        D      (ACE  (E) FALLING IN LOVE AGAIN 1980 ELEKTRA US 251  UK K 52206
JOHN GUERIN        D      (ACE  (F) TAKE ME NOW        1081  ARISTA  US 9563   UK SPART1175
DAVID LINDLEY      FDL    (E
JIM GORDON         D      (AC   JIM HORN    SAX (ACE   LARRY KNECHTEL   K    (ACE LOUIE SHELTON   G   (A
HUDLEY HOCKENSMITH G      (EF   ROBIN WILLIAMSON (E    DEAN PARKS       G    (C   DAN DUGMORE     STEEL(CE
DAVID MINOR        G      (E
```

G15   GATOR CREEK   G15

```
ALLAN BEUTLER      WIND   (A             (A) GATOR CREEK        1970  MERCURY           6338 085
DEE BARTON         V K    (A
MIKE DEASY         G V    (A   RAY NEAPOLITAN   B    (A   MERRY CLAYTON    V    (A   LOUIE SHELTON   V   (A
CHUCK FINDLEY      TPT    (A   NICK CEROLI      D    (A   LARRY KNECHTEL   G    (A   VANETTA FIELDS  V   (A
MIKE OMARTIAN      K      (A   KATHY DEASY   V PERC (A    KENNY LOGGINS    G V  (A   GENE PELLO      D   (A
CLYDIE KING        V      (A   LOUIS GASCA TPT  (A    JOHN BANISTER    K    (A
```

　　　　　　　　　　GATE　　　　　　　　　　

```
    MANOS TSANGARIS    D G  (AB      (A) LIVE                    1977 BRAIN          GER    60 043
    ANGELOS TSANGARIS  K B  (AB      (B) RED LIGHT SISTER        1978 BRAIN          GER    60 093
    MARTIN KOHMSTEDT   G    (AB
    MANFRED SCHROPFER  G B V(A   HORST KAMP   V   PERC(AB LOTHAR KRELL   K   (B   STAFAN LANG    PERC(B
    OLIVER PETRY       SYN  (B
```

　　　　　　　　　　MAC GAYDEN　　　　　　　　　　

```
    MAC GAYDEN V G BANJO MAND(ALL    (A) McGAVOCK GAYDEN         1973 EMI            UK     EMA  760
    BILL CHEATHAM      G    (C       (B) SKYBOAT                 1976 ABC US 927     UK     ABCL 5169
    VIC MASTRIANNI     D    (C       (C) HYMN TO THE SEEKER      1976 ABC US 960
    MIKE MILLER        WIND V(CB
    BILL AIKENS        K    (C   NELSON M PADRON   PERC (C   BUZZ CASON      V   (CB RANDY MEISNER   V  (C
    ANITA BALL         V    (C   KEN BUTTREY       D    (A   PHILLIP ROYSTER CONGA(A KARL HIMMEL     PERC (AB
    BOB JOHNSTON       HCA  (A   JAMES MOON        V    (A   CHARLES MYERS   V   (A  PAUL EASLEY     V  (A
    JAMES CLEMMONS     V    (A   JIM ALTHOUSE      B    (B   JAMI NICHOLS    SONGA(B PETER KEEBLE       (B
    QUITMAN DENNIS     SAX  (B   ANDY McMAHAN      K    (B   JACK LEE        B   (B  WASUNT PUNDANT  TABLA  (B
    KRISTY KARSON      V    (A   BOBBY OGDIN       K    (B   JACL WILLIAMS   B   (B  DANNY SPERRY    CELLO V(B
    CINDY REYNOLDS     HARP (B   TAMMY CASON       V    (B   KIM GAYDEN      V   (B  VIVKIE HATNIE   V  (B
    JANIE FRICKE       V    (B   GINGER HOLLADAY   V    (B   ROBERT KNIGHT   V   (B  FARRELL MORRIS  PERC(B
    STEVE GIBSON       G    (B   TOMMY COGBILL     B    (B   JERRY CARRIGAN  D   (B
```

　　　　　　　　　　MARVIN GAYE　　　　　　　　　　

```
    MARVIN GAYE    V K D(ALL     SOULFUL MOOD                1961 TAMLA US 221THAT STUBBORN KINDA
    WITH                        FELLOW   1963 TAMLA US 239
    KIM WESTON         V         LIVE ON STAGE               1963 TAMLA US 242
    DIANA ROSS         V         WHEN I'M ALONE I CRY        1964 TAMLA US 251
    TAMMY TERRELL      V         GREATEST HITS               1964 TAMLA US 252
    MARY WELLS         V         HOW SWEET IT IS             1964 TAMLA US 258   UK     STML11004
    RAYMOND CROSSLEY   K    (Z   HOW SWEET IT IS             1973 MFP            UK       90006
    GORDON BANKS       G    (Z   HOW SWEET IT IS             1979 MFP            UK       50423
    CURTIS NOLEN       G    (Z   HELLO BROADWAY              1964 TAMLA US 259   UK     STML11015
    ROBERT AHWAI       G    (Z   TOGETHER (MARY WELLS)       1964 TAMLA US 613 STATESIDE UK 10097
    SUNSHIP            PERC (Z   MARVIN GAYE                 1964              STATESIDE UK 10100
    JOE MAYO          PERC (Z   TRIBUTE TO NAT KING COLE    1965 TAMLA US 261   UK     STML11022
    NOLAN SMITH        TPT  (Z   MOODS OF MARVIN GAYE        1966 TAMLA US 266   UK     STML11033
    GEORGE SHAW        TPT  (Z   TAKE TWO                    1966 TAMLA US 270   UK     STML11049
    KENNY MASON        TPT  (Z   UNITED   (TAMMY TERRELL)    1966 TAMLA US 277   UK     STML11062
    RAY BROWN          TPT  (Z   GREATEST HITS               196  TAMLA             UK     STML11065
    FRANK BLAIR        D B  (Z   YOU'RE ALL I NEED TO GET BY 1968 TAMLA US 284   UK     STML11084
    BUGSY WILCOX       D    (Z   IN THE GROOVE               1968 TAMLA US 285   UK     STML11091
    NIGEL MARTINEZ     D    (Z   M.P.G.                      1969 TAMLA US 292   UK     STML11119
    ELMIRA COLLINS    VIBES(Z   & HIS GIRLS(TERRELL WELLS KIM WESTON) 1969 TAMLA US 293 UK  STML11123
    GARY JONES        PERC (Z   EASY                        1969 TAMLA US 294   UK     STML11132
    FLEECY JOE JAMES  PERC (Z   THATS THE WAY LOVE IS       1969 TAMLA US 299   UK     STML11136
    SIDNEY MULDREW     HRNS (Z   SUPERHITS                   19   TAMLA US 300
    RAPHAEL RAVENSCROFT SAX(Z   GREATEST HITS               1970 TAMLA US 302   UK     STML11153
    FRANK BATES            (Z   WHATS GOING ON              1971 TAMLA US 310   UK     STML11190
    LEE KENTLE              (S   HITS OF MARVIN GAYE         1972 TAMLA             UK     STML11201
    WILTON FELDER      B    (S   TROUBLED MAN    (SOUNDTRACK) 1972 TAMLA US 322  UK     STML11225
    JAMES JAMERSON     B    (ST  (S) LETS GET IT ON         1973 TAMLA US 329   UK     STMA 8013
    EDDIE BROWN        D    (S   MARVIN ' DIANA              1974 TAMLA US 803   UK     STMA 8015
    BOBBYE HALL       PERC (S   (T) LIVE                    1974 TAMLA US 333   UK     STML 8018
    MELVIN RAGIN       G    (S   ANTHOLOGY                   1974 TAMLA US 790/1 UK     TMSP 1128
    PAUL HUMPHRIES     D    (S   I WANT YOU                  1976 TAMLA US 342   UK     STML12025
    URIEL JONES        D    (S   THE BEST OF                 1976 TAMLA US 348   UK     STML12042
    LOUIS SHELTON      G    (S   LIVE AT LONDON PALLADIUM    1977 TAMLA US 352   UK     TMSP 6006
    DAVID T WALKER     G    (ST  HERE MY DEAR                1978 TAMLA US 364   UK     TMSP 6008
    ROBERT WHITE       G    (S   LOVE MAN (WITHDRAWN)???     1979 TAMLA US 369   UK     STML12126
    EDDIE WILLIS       G    (S   EARLY 1961/64               1980 TAMLA US       UK     STML 9004
    EMIL RICHARDS     PERC (S   (Z) IN OUR LIFETIME         1981 TAMLA             UK     STML12149
    MARVIN JENKINS     PNO  (S   (EP)
    JOE SAMPLE         PNO  (ST  MARVIN GAYE                 1966 TAMLA             UK     TME  2016
    VICTOR FELDMAN    VIBES(S   ORIGINALS FROM              1967 TAMLA             UK     TME  2019
    ED GREEN           D    (T
    RAY PARKER         G    (T
    JOHN ARNOLD       PERC (T
    JOE CLAYTON       CONGA(T   JAMES GETZOFF   SRT  (T   JACK SHULMAN    STR (T   PAUL HUBINON   TPT(T
    GEORGE BOHANON     TROM (T   ERNIE WATTS     SAX  (T   WILLIAM GREEN   SAX (T   ERIC DOLEN  V  (T
    CHARLES BURNS      V    (T   DWIGHT OWENS    V    (T   MICHAEL TORRENCE V (T   WALLY COX       V  (T
```

　　　　　　　　　　GAYLADDS　　　　　　　　　　

```
                               (A) UNDERSTANDING           1979 BALLISTIC   UK UAG30236
```

　　　　　　　　　　GEARS　　　　　　　　　　

```
                               (A) ROCKIN' AT GROUND ZERO  1980 PLAYGEMS       US    6471
```

　　　　　　　　　　RON GEESIN　　　　　　　　　　

```
    RON GEESIN V K SYN BANJO(ALL    (A) THE BODY             1970 HARVEST    UK   SHSP 4008 SW751
    ROGER WATERS        (A       (B) ELECTROSOUND          197  KPM                      1102
                                 (C) AS HE STANDS          197  GEESIN         UK   RON   28
                                 (D) PATRUNS               197  GEESIN         UK   RON   31
                                 (E) RIGHT THROUGH         197  GEESIN         UK   RON  323
```

　　　　　　　　　　J GEILS BAND　　　　　　　　　　

```
    J GEILS          G    (ALL    (A) J GEILS BAND          1971 ATLANTIC US 8275 UK  K 40108
    PETER WOLF       V    (ALL    (B) MORNING AFTER         1972 ATLANTIC US 8297 UK  K 40293
    SETH JUSTMAN     K V  (ALL    (AB) J GEILS /MORNING AFTER 1975 ATLANTIC       UK  K 60061
    MAGIC DICK   TPT HCA  (ALL    (C) LIVE FULL HOUSE       1972 ATLANTIC US 7241 UK  K 40426
    DANNY KLEIN      B    (ALL    (D) BLOODSHOT             1973 ATLANTIC US 7260 UK  K 40479
    STEPHEN BLADD    D V  (ALL    (E) LADIES INVITED        1974 ATLANTIC US 7286 UK  K 40536
    BARBARA INGRAM   V    (J      (F) NIGHTMARES            1974 ATLANTIC US 18107 UK K 50073
    EVETTE BENTON    V    (J      (G) HOT LINE              1975 ATLANTIC US 18147 UK K 50175
    HARRIET THARPE   V    (J      (H) BLOW YOUR FACE OUT    1976 ATLANTIC US 2/507 UK K 60115
    LUTHER VANDROSS  V    (JN     (J) MONKEY ISLAND         1977 ATLANTIC US 19130 UK K 50381
    G DIANE SUMLER   V    (J      (K) SANCTUARY             1978 EMI      US 17006 UK AMS 2004
    MICHELLE COBBS   V    (J      (L) LOVE STINKS           1980 EMI      US 17016 UK AML 3004

                    (CONTINUED)
```

J GEILS BAND

```
                                                                    (CONTINUED)
THERESA REED        V    (J      (M) BEST OF                 1980 ATLANTIC US 19284 NL      50762
GEORGE YOUNG        HRNS (N      (N) FREEZE FRAME            1981 EMI      US 17062 UK       3020
LOU MARINI          HRNS (N
MICHAEL BRECKER     HRNS (J   RON CUBER      SAX (JN LEW DEL GATTO    SAX (J   FRANK VICARI    SAX (J
RANDY BRECKER       HRNS (JN  ALAN RUBIN     TPT (JN LEW SOLOFF       TPT (J   JUKE JOINT JIMMY G (H
TOM MALONE          HRNS (N   KENNY WILLIAMS V  (N  TAWATHA AGEE      V   (N   CISSY HOUSTON   V (JN
FONZI THORNTON      V    (N   GEOFFREY HASLEM PROD (A BRAD SHAPIRO    PROD (A  BILL SZYMEZYK   PROD(EF
SETH JUSTMAN        PROD (L
```

GENERATION X

```
BILLY IDOL          G V  (ALL     (A) GENERATION X             1978 CHRYSALIS UK/US 1169 GER6307623
BOB ANDREWS         G V  (AB1     (B) VALLEY OF THE DOLLS       1979 CHRYSALIS UK/US 1193 NL  511193
TONY JAMES          B    (ABC1    (C) KISS ME DEADLY            1981 CHRYSALIS UK   1327 NL  203259
JOHN TAOWE          D    (1       (1) 1976/77
MARK LAFF           D    (AB
TERRY C CHIMES      D    (C   JOHN McGEOGH    G    (C   JAMES STEVENSON  G  (C  STEVE JONES   G (C
```

GENESIS

```
JOHN MAYHEW         D    (AB      (A) FROM GENESIS TO REVELATION  1969 US LONDON 643   UK DECCA      4990
ANTHONY PHILLIPS    G    (AB      (A) IN THE BEGINNING            1974 US LONDON 50006 UK DECCA      4990
TONY BANKS          K    (ALL     (B) TRESPASS                    1970 US ABC'74 816  UK CHARISMA CAS 1020
                                  (B) TRESPASS                    1970 US IMPULSE 9295
MIKE RUTHERFORD     G B  (ALL     (C) NURSERY CRYME               1971              US/UK CHARISMA CAS 1052
                                  (C) NURSERY CRYME               1971      PHILIPS  GER          6369916
PETER GABRIEL V FLT PERC(ABCDEFG  (BC) TRESPASS/NURSERY CRYME     1975              US/uK CHARISMA CGS 102
PHIL COLLINS  D PERC V(CDEFGHJKLMN12o(D) FOXTROT                  1972              US/UK CHARISMA CAS 1058
                                  (CD) NURSERY/FOXTROT            1976 CHARISMA US 2701 RI BUDDAH US 5659
STEVE HACKETT       G B  (CDEFGHJKL (E) SELLING ENGLAND BY THE POUND 1973 CHARISMA US 6060 UK        CAS 1074
                                  (E) SELLING ENGLAND BY THE POUND 1973 CHARISMA      GER  6369 944
BILL BRUFORD        D PERC(K       (DE)FOXTROT /SELLING ENGLAND   1975              UK CHARISMA CGS 103
CHESTER THOMPSON    D PERC(12 K    (F) LIVE                       1973 CHARISMA  US 1066      UK CLASS 1
                                  (F) LIVE                        1973 CHARISMA      GER     6499 593
DARYL STUERMER      G    (12      (G) THE LAMB LIES DOWN ON BROADWAY 1974 US ATCO  2401   UK CHARISMA CGS 101
                                  (G) THE LAMB LIES DOWN ON BROADWAY 1974 CHARISMA      GER  6641 226
CHRIS STEWART       D    (*       (H) TRICK OF THE TAIL           1976 US ATCO 36129   UK CHARISMA CDS 4001
                                  (H) TRICK OF THE TAIL           1976 CHARISMA      GER    6369 974
DAVID HITCHCOCK     PROD (B       (H) TRICK OF THE TAIL           19   US ATCO RI 38101
JIM SILVER          D    (*       (J) WIND & WUTHERING            1977 US ATCO 36144   UK CHARISMA CDS 4005
EARTH WIND & FIRE HRNS (O         (J) WIND & WUTHERING            197  US ATCO RI 38100
DAVE HENTSCHEL      V    (N       (K) SECONDS OUT                 1977 ATLANTIC 20002 UK CHARISMA GE 2001
                                  (K) SECONDS OUT                 1977 CHARISMA      GER     6641 697
                                  (L) SPOT THE PIGEON (EP)        1977 ATLANTIC US 1800 UK CHARISMA GEN 001
                                  (M) AND THEN THERE WERE THREE   1978 ATLANTIC 19173 UK CHARISMA CDS 4010
                                  (M) AND THEN THERE WERE THREE   1978 CHARISMA      GER     9124 024
                                  (N) DUKE                        1980 ATLANTIC 16014 UK CHARISMA BRA 101
                                  (N) DUKE                        1980 CHARISMA      GER     9124 053
                                  (O) ABACAB                      1981 ATLANTIC US 19313 UK CHARISMA CBR102
                                  (O) ABACAB                      1981 VERTIGO      NL       6302 162
                                  ( ) ROCK ROOTS                  1975              UK DECCA    ROOTS.1
                                  ( ) REFLECTION                  1975                  FONTANA 9299 515
                                  ( ) THE BEST OF                 1976 US BUDDAH 56592
                                  ( ) STORY OF GENESIS            1978                  JAP FLYOVER 10061/2
                                  (1) 1978 TOUR   (2) 1980 TOUR  (*) PRE RECORDING MUSICIANS
```

GENOCIDE

```
                                  (A) GENOCIDE               1979    SAFARI    UK        SAP 2
```

AX GENRICH

```
AX GENRICH        G V B (A        (A) HIGHDELBERG         1975    HAPPY BIRD    GER      5015
JAN FRIDE         D    (A
MANI NEUMEIER     D PERC(A HELMUTH HATTLER  B V  (A DIETER MOEBIUS SYN (A ACHIM ROEDELIUS PNO(A
PETER WOLFBRANDT  V G PERC(A
```

GENTLE GIANT

```
PHIL SHULMAN       SAX  (ABCD     (A) GENTLE GIANT              1970                    UK VERTIGO 6360 020
DEREK SHULMAN  V G B    (ALL      (B) ACQUIRING THE TASTE       1971 US VERTIGO 1005    UK VERTIGO 6360 041
RAY SHULMAN  V B VLN PERC(ALL     (C) THREE FRIENDS             1972 US CBS 31649       UK VERTIGO 6360 070
                                  (AC)THREE FRIENDS/GENTLE GIANT 1972 GER                  VERTIGO 6685 016
KERRY MINNEAR      K V  (ALL      (D) OCTOPUS                   1973 US CBS 32022       UK VERTIGO 6360 080
GARY GREEN         G V  (ALL      (E) IN A GLASS HOUSE          1973 GER VERTIGO 6366100 UK WWA WWA 002
MARTIN SMITH       D    (AB       (F) THE POWER & THE GLORY     1974 US CAPITOL 11337 UK W W A   WWA 010
CLAIRE DENIZ       CELLO   (A     (F) THE POWER & THE GLORY     1976 US CAPITOL 16044
JOHN WEATHERS      D V  (DEFGHJKLMNO (G) FREE HAND              1975 US CAPITOL 11428 UK CHRYSALIS  1093
                                  (G) FREE HAND                 197  US CAPITOL 16048
MIKE VICKERS       SYN  (D        (H) A GIANT STEP  (DBL) (COMP) 1975              UK VERTIGO 6641 334
MARTIN RUSHENT     SYN  (D        (J) INTERVIEW                 1976 US CAPITOL 11532 UK CHRYSALIS  1115
TONY VISCONTI      PROD (A        (J) INTERVIEW                 19   US CAPITOL 16047
CHRIS THOMAS       SYN  (B        (K) PLAYING THE FOOL (LIVE DBL) 1976 US CAPITOL 11592 UK CHRYSALIS 1133
                                  (K) PLAYING THE FOOL (LIVE DBL) 1976 GER CHRYSALIS        6641 579
PAUL KOSH          TPT  (B        (L) THE MISSING PIECE         1977 US CAPITOL 11696 UK CHRYSALIS 1152
                                  (L) THE MISSING PIECE         1977 GER CHRYSALIS        6307 604
MALCOLM MORTIMER   D    (         (M) PRETENTIOUS   DBL(COMP)   1977              UK VERTIGO 6641 629
                                  (N) GIANT FOR A DAY           1978 US CAPITOL 11813 UK CHRYSALIS 1186
                                  (O) CIVILIAN                  1980 US CBS      36341 UK CHRYSALIS 1285
                                  (O) CIVILIAN                  1980 NL CHRYSALIS         511 285
                                  ( ) GREATEST HITS             1981 PHILIPS 6381 045
```

GENTLEHOOD

```
HAL BLAINE        D    (A         (A) GENTLEHOOD            19    CBS         US    32032
JOE OSBORNE       B    (A
GENE PELLO        D    (A   DANN MATHER  B  (A   JANET LAING  VLA (A  PHIL SAWYER PNO (A
KATHI GRANDE      V    (A
```

GENTRYS

```
LARRY RASPBERRY   V    (A         (A) KEEP ON DANCING      1965 MGM          US    4336
BRUCE BOWLES      V    (          (B) TIME                 1966 MGM          US    4346
LARRY WALL        D    (          (C) GENTRYS              1970 SUN          US    117
JIMMY HART        V    (
PAT NEAL          B    (   JIMMY JOHNSON  TPT (  BOBBY FISHER    G  (
```

RON GEODERT

```
    RON GEODERT      K V (A        (A) BREAKING ALL THE RULES        1980 POLYDOR                6265
    JERRT RUNYAN     G   (A
    RIFF WEST        B   (A    JACK WEST       D   (A    JOHN ANTONY      K   (A
G23                                  GEORDIE                                        G23
    BRIAN JOHNSON    V   (A        (A) HOPE YOU LIKE IT               1973 EMI         UK   EMC  3001
    TOM HILL         B   (         (B) MASTERS OF ROCK               1974 EMI         UK   054 95689
    BRIAN GIBSON     D   (         (C) DONT BE FOOLED BY THE NAME    1974 EMI         UK   EMA   764
    VIC MALCOLM      G   (         (D) SAVE THE WORLD                1976 EMI         UK   EMC  3134
                                   (E) FEATURING B JOHNSON           1981 REDBUS      UK   RBMP 5001
G24                                LOWELL GEORGE                                     G24
    LOWELL GEORGE    G V (A        (A) THANKS I'LL EAT IT HERE       1979 WB US 3194  UK   K 56487
    JIM GORDON       D   (A
    JIM KELTNER      D   (A    JIM PRICE      HRNS (A    MIKE BAIRD      D   (A    DARRELL LEONARD  HRNS(A
    CHUCK RAINEY     B   (A    FRED TACKETT    G   (A    BILL PAYNE      K   (A    DAVID FOSTER     K   (A
    JIMMY GREENSPOON PNO (A    JEFF PORCARO    D   (A    BONNIE RAITT    V   (A    CHILLI CHARLES   D   (A
    DENNIS BELFIELD  B   (A    GORDON DE WITTE K   (A    JAMES HOWARD    K   (A    NICKY HOPKINS    K   (A
    PAUL STALLWORTH  B   (A    JERRY JUMONVILLE HRNS (A  STEVE BRUTON    G   (A    DEAN PARKS       G   (A
    FLOYD SNEED      D   (A    ROBERTO GUTIERREZ   (A    LUIS DAMIAN     G   (A    RICHIE HAYWARD   D   (A
    HERB PEDERSEN    V   (A    J D SOUTHER     V   (A    MAXINE WATERS   V   (A    BOBBY BRUCE      FDL (A
    PEGGY SANDVIG        (A    BRUCE PAULSON       (A    MAXAYN LEWIS    V   (A    JOEL PESKIN      SAX (A
    JOHN PHILLIPS    SAX (A
G24A                                  GERMS                                         G24A
    DARBY CRASH      V   (A        (A) G I                           1979 SLASH      US   SR103
    LORNA            B   (A        (B) THE DECLINE    (VAR ARTIST)   1980 SLASH      US   SR105
    DON              D   (A
    PAT              G   (A
G25                               GERONIMO BLACK                                    G25
    JIMMY CARL BLACK D   (AB       (A) GERONIMO BLACK                1972 UNI 127 1974 MCA MCF 2683
    TJAY CANTRELLI   G   (AB       (B) WELCOME BACK GERONIMO BLACK   19   HELIOS US 704
    DENNY WALLEY     G   (AB
    BUNK GARDNER     WIND (AB   ANDY CAHAN      K   (AB   TOM LEAVEY      B   (AB   BUZZ GARDNER        (AB
    DON PRESTON      K   (B     RAY COLLINS     V   (B    MEATBALL        D   (B    JOE LALA    PERC   (B
    JAMES HARMON     HARP (B    JERRY McGEE     G   (B    MURRAY ROMAN    V   (A    KEITH OLSON V      (A
    STRING SECTION       (A
G25A                              DENNY GERRARD                                     G25A
    DENNY GERRARD        (A        (A) SINISTER MORNING              1970 DERAM NOVA      SDN10
    TONY HILL        G   (A
    SIMON HOUSE      VLN (A    PETER PAVLI  B  (A    ROGER HADDEN    D   (A
G26                           GERRY & THE PACEMAKERS                                G26
    GERRY MARSDEN    G V (ALL    HOW DO YOU DO IT                    1963 COLUMBIA  1546(M) SCX 3492(S)
    FREDDIE MARSDEN      (ALL    FERRY ACROSS THE MERSEY             1964 COLUMBIA  SCX3544 US UA3387
    LES McGUIRE      B V (ALL    DONT LET THE SUN CATCH YOU CRYING   196  LAURIE    US       2027
    LES CHADWICK     PNO (ALL    SECOND ALBUM  (US)                  196  LAURIE    US       2037
                                 I'LL BE THERE                       196  LAURIE    US       2030
                                 GREATEST HITS                       196  LAURIE    US       2031
                                 GIRL ON A SWING                     196  LAURIE    US       2037
                                 BEST OF                             1977 EMI UK NUT 1o CAPITOL US 11898
    EPS
    HOW DO YOU DO IT          19663  COLUMBIA    SEG 8257    YOU'LL NEVER WALK ALONE  1964 COLUMBIA  SEG8295
    I'M THE ONE        1964     COLUMBIA    SEG 8311    DONT LET THE SUN         1964 COLUMBIA  SEG8346
    IT'S GONNA BE ALL RIGHT1964 COLUMBIA    SEG 8367    GERRY IN CALIFORNIA      1964 COLUMBIA  SEG8388
    FERRY ACROSS THE MERSEY1965 COLUMBIA    SEG 8397    RIP IT UP                1965 COLUMBIA  SEG8426
G26A                              RENEE GEYER BAND                                  G26A
    RENNE GEYER      V   (ALL      (A) IT'S A MAN'S WORLD            1974 RCA UK SF8450 AUST MVP1 0024
    MARK PUNCH       G V (BE!      (B) READY TO DEAL                 1975 RCA          AUST VPL1 0105
    GREG TELL        D   (BC       (C) REALLY REALLY LOVE ME         1976 RCA          AUST VPL1 0120
    MAL LOGAN        K   (BCDE1    (D) MOVING ALONG                  1977 RCA          AUST VPL1 0140
    RUSSELL SMITH    TPT (BC       (E) BLUES LICENSE                 1978 RCA          AUST VPL1 0214
    TONY BUCHANAN    WIND (BE1     (1) 1977 TOUR BAND
    BARRY SULLIVAN   B   (B
    TWEED HARRIS     K   (A    GARRY HYDE      PERC (A    JULIE McKENNA   V   (A    WENDY REECE V     (A
    BOBBY BRIGHT     V   (A    MIKE BRADY      V   (A    BRUCE SANDELL   SAX (C    MIGUEL CARRANZA   TROM(C
    OTIS KEVINAGH    V   (C    DOUGLAS WILLIAMS V  (C    STANLEY BROWN   V   (C    PHIL LAWSON       B  (1
    RUSSEL DUNLOP    (1      JOHN PUGH        G   (C    ERNIE WATTS     SAX (d    NICA REJTO FLT    (D
    CHARLES VEAL     STRING(D  JACK ASHFORD    PERC (D    REG BURKE       PNO (D    HARRY BOOKER     K  (D
    STEPHEN BECKMEIER G (D    FREDERICK LEWIS  PERC (D    JAMES JAMERSON  B   (D    RAY E PARKER     G  (D
    JERRY PETERS     K   (D    GREGG POREE      G   (D    RAYMOND POUNDS  D   (D    NATHAN WATTS     B  (D
    VENETTA FIELDS   V   (D    PAT HENDERSON    B   (D    SHIRLEY MATTHEWS V  (D    TIEMEYER McCAIN  V  (D
    OTIS STOKES      V   (D    FRANK WILSON     V   (D    KEVIN BORICH    G   (E    JOHN ANNUS       D  (E
    TIM PARTRIDGE    B   (E    JOHN WATSON      D   (E    KERRI BIDELL    V   (E    RON KING         HCA(E
    TIM PIPER        G   (E    STEVE HOPES D    (E
G26B                                GIANT CRAB                                      G26B
    E RNIE OROSCO    V G (A        (A) A GIANT CRAB COMES FORTH      1968 UNI        US        73037
    RAY OROSCO       B K (A        (B) COOL IT HELIOS                196  UNI        US        73057
    RUBEN OROSCO     B D SAX(A
    DENNIS FRICIA   D HRNS (A    KENNY FRICIA    K HRNS VIBES(A
G26C                                  GIANTS                                        G26C
    KARL RUCKER      B   (A        (A) THANKS FOR THE MUSIC          1976 CASABLANCA US   NBLP 7027
    JOHN COHEN           (A
    JOHN PLATANIA    G V (A    LAURIE COHEN     V   (A   BRUCE GARY    B PERC (A RON ELLIOTT G    (A
G26D                                 GIANTS 2                                       G26D
    GREG ERRICO      D SYN(A        (A) GIANTS                       1978 MCA        UK MCF 3058
    CARLOS SANTANA   G   (A        (  ) GIANTS                       1980 MCA        US 3188
    HERBIE HANCOCK   PNO (A
    LEE OSKAR        HCA (A    NEAL SCHON      G   (A    MIKE CARABELLO  K   (A    BIANCA THORNTON-ODEN V(A
    COKE ESCOVEDO    V   (A    GREGG ROLLIE    K   (A    CHEPITO AREAS   PERC (A   RICO REYES   PERC  (A
    DOUG RAUCH       B   (A    MIKE GARCIA VIBES   (A    WENDY HAAS      K V (A    GENE WASHINGTON   V (A
    JODY MOREING     V   (A    VICTOR PANTOJA  CONG (A   ROBERT VEGA     B   (A    DOUG RODRIGUEZ    G (A
    FREDDIE POOL     V   (A    LINDA TILLERY   V   (A
```

```
STEVE GIBBONS   G V  (ALL        (A) SHORT STORIES         1971 WIZARD              UK   SWZA 5501
TREVOR BURTON   B V G(BCDEFGH     (B) ANY ROAD UP          1976 MCA      US 2183    POLYDOR UK 2383 381
BOB WILSON      G K V(BCDEF       (C) ROLLING ON           1977 MCA      US 2243    POLYDOR UK 2383 433
DAVE CARROLL    G    (BCDEF       (D) CAUGHT IN THE ACT    1977 MCA      US 2305    POLYDOR UK 2478 112
CHRIS BARBER    TPT  (H           (D) CAUGHT IN THE ACT    1977 POLYDOR  EURO                2460 276
BOB LAMB        D    (BCDEF       (E) DOWN IN THE BUNKER   1978 POLYDOR  US 6154    UK   2391,358
MIKE COTTON     TPT  (H           (E) DOWN IN THE BUNKER   1978 POLYDOR  EURO                2383 502
GARY WRIGHT     K    (A           (G) STREET PARADE        1980 RCA      US 6293    UK   LP 5005
MIKE KELLIE     D    (A           (H) SAINTS & SINNERS     1981 RCA                 UK   PL25387
P J WRIGHT      V G K(H
DORIS TROY      V    (A    PAT DONALDSON     B  (A   MADELINE BELL V  (A   JERRY DONAHUE    G   (A
JIMMY MILLER    PERC (A    GREG RIDLEY  B    (A   HUGH McCRACKEN G  (A   NICK PENTELOW   SAX(EH
TONY VISCONTI   SYN B(A    LONDON SYMPHONY ORCH  (E   HARRY RIX   D V  (G   BILL PAUL       SAX (G
GINGER JOHNSON  PERC (A    IAN WHITEMAN PNO   (A   LARRY FALLON WIND (A   ALAN WHITE PERC FLT (A
GERRY CONWAY    STEEL(A    ROCKY DZIDZORNU    PERC (A   JOHNNY VAN DERRICK (A   CLAIRE DENIZ   CELLO(A
BILL POVEY      CLAR (A    DEREK WOOD        B V (H   ALAN WICKETT D V  (H   AL SHACKLOCK    K   (H
GERAINT WATKINS K ACC(H
```

```
UWE PATZKE      B V  (AB          (A) GIFT                 1972 TELEFUNKEN                   14680
RAINER BAUR     G    (AB          (B) BLUE APPLE           1974 NOVA GER                     8002
HELMUT TREICHEL G    (AB
HERMANN LANGE   D PERC(AB  DIETER ALTARER   G V (B   DIETER FREI K SYN(B
```

```
NICK GILDER     V    (ABCD        (A) YOU KNOW WHO YOU ARE  1977           CHRYSALIS UK  CHR 1147
JAMES McCULLOCH G    (ABCD        (B) CITY NIGHT           1978           CHRYSALIS UK  CHR 1202
JAMES HERNDON K SYN G V(BCD       (C) FREQUENCY           1979           CHRYSALIS UK  CHR 1219
ERIC NELSON     B V  (ABCD        (D) ROCK AMERICA        1980           CASABLANCA UK 7243 EURO 6302066
STEVE KALTER    K    (A
CRAIG KRAMPF    D PERC V  (BC  CHET McCRACKEN   D  (A   KEN MANSFIELD PROD(D   JIMMY HUNTER    D (D
```

```
MIKE GILES      D    (A           (A) CHEERFUL INSANITY   1968 DERAM SML 1022 UK  SPA  423
PETER GILES     B    (A
ROBERT FRIPP    G    (A    JUDY DYBLE       V   (    CLIFF HARDIE TOM  (A   T BARKER   TROM  (A
THE BREAKAWAYS  V    (A    STRING SECTION       (A   NICKY HOPKINS K   (A   MIKE HILL  K     (A
```

```
PHIL LEE        G    (AB          (A) GILGAMESH                     1975 CAROLINE   UK   CA 2007
ALAN GOWEN      K    (AB          (B) ANOTHER FINE TUNE YOU'VE GOT ME INTO 1978 CHARLY  UK   CRL 5009
JEFF CLYNE      B    (A
MICHAEL TRAVIS  D    (A    HUGH HOPPER  B   (B   AMANDA PARSONS   V  (A   TREVOR TOMKINS  D  (B
```

```
CONNY VEIT  SYN G V  (A           (A) GILA                 1971 BASF            GER  20 21109/6
DANIEL ALLUNO   D PERC(A          (B) BURY MY HEART AT WOUNDED KNEE 1973 WB     GER  46234
FRITZ SCHEYHING G K  (A
SABINE MERBACH  V    (B    WALTER WIEDERKEHR B  (A   FLORIAN FRICKE   K  (B   DANIEL FIECHELSCHER D(B
```

```
IAN GILLAN      V    (ALL         (A) CHILD IN TIME       1976 OYSTER UK 2490   136 US 1602
MARK NAUSEEF    D PERC(ABCDEF     (A) CHILD IN TIME       1976 POLYDOR          UK  ACBR 261
JOHN GUSTAFSON  B V  (ABCDEF      (B) CLEAR AIR TURBULENCE 1977 ISLAND          UK  ILPS 9500
RAY FENWICK     G V  (ABCDEF      (C) SCARABUS            1977 ISLAND UK ILPS9511 US ANTILLES 7066
BERNIE TORME    G    (HJKLM       (D) LIVE AT BUDOKAN VOL 1 1978 EAST WPRLD     JAP       81112
COLIN TOWNS     K(BCDEFGHIJKLM    (E) LIVE AT BUDOKAN VOL 2 1978 EAST WORLD     JAP       81113
MICK UNDERWOOD  D    (HJKLM       (F) LIVE AT BUDOKAN (DBL) (DE) 1978 EAST WORLD JAP
JANICK GERS     G    (M           (G) GILLAN              1978 EAST WORLD       JAP       8112-
MIKE MORAN      K    (A           (H) MR UNIVERSE   (DIFF) 1979 INTERFUSION     AUST      37135
STEVE BYRD      D    (GJ          (J) MR UNIVERSE         1979 ACROBAT          UK        ACRO 3
PHIL KENZIE     SAX  (B           (K) GLORY ROAD          1980 VIRGIN  US 13146 UK        V 2171
LIAM GENOCKEY   D    (GJ          (K) FOR GILLAN FANS ONLY FREE WITH ABOVE     UK        VDJ32
JOHN HUCKRIDGE  TPT  (B           (L) FUTURE SHOCK        1981 VIRGIN           UK        V 2196
DEREK HEALEY    TPT  (B           (M) DOUBLE TROUBLE      1981 VIRGIN           UK        VGD 3506
MALCOLM GRIFFITHS TROM (B         (EP) NO LAUGHING IN HEAVEN 1981 VIRGIN        UK        VS 425
MARTIN FRITH    SAX  (B
ROGER GLOVER    SYN V(A    STEVE TOWNES     K   (    JOHN McCOY       B(GHJKLM PETER BARNACLE  D  (
```

```
DANA GILLESPIE  V G SYN(ABC1      (A) BOX OF SURPRISES    1969 DECCA            UK   SKL 5012
BRIAN ODGERS    B    (B           (A) FOOLISH SEASONS     1969 LONDON           US        540
DAVE WINTOUR    B    (B           (B) WERE'NT BORN A MAN  1973 RCA              UK/us APLI0354
PAT DONALDSON   B    (B           (C) AIN'T GONNA PLAY NO SECOND FIDDLE 1974 RCA UK/US APLI0682
MIKE MORAN      K    (B           (1) 1978 TOUR
PAUL KEOGH      G    (B    CHRIS RAY       G   (B   RONNIE LEAHY K  (B   RAY GLYNN       K  (B
JIM RYAN        G    (B    RICK WAKEMAN    K   (B   BARRY DE SOUZA D )B   TERRY COX       D  (B
BOBBY KEYS      SAX  (B    RAY COOPER      PERC(B   FRANK RICOTTI PERC (B   ROSETTA HIGHTOWER V (B
LIZA STRIKE     V    (B    JOANNE WILLIAMS V   (B   JOHN HAWKEN  K  (1   JOHN KNIGHTSBRIDGE G(1
BARBARA SPITZ   G    (1    NEIL KORNER     B   (1   JOHN BARKER  D  (1   TONY HALL       SAX(1
JOHN PORTER     G    (C    BRYN HAWORTH    G   (C   DAVE SKINNER K  (C   PHIL CHEN       B  (C
BOB WESTON      G    (C    SIMON PHILLIPS  D   (C   MEL COLLINS  SAX (C   ROBIN SYLVESTER B  (C
EDDIE JOBSON    SYN VLN(C  JOHN TURNBULL   G   (C   MICK GALLAGHER PNO (C   JODY LINSCOTT   CONGA(C
RABBIT BUNDRICK K    (B    FRANK COLLINS   V   (C   DYAN BIRCH   V  (C   PADDY McHUGH    V  (C
MALCOLM DUNCAN  HRNS (C    ROGER BALL      HRNS (C   HENRY LOWTHER    HRNS(C
```

```
STEVE GILLETTE                    (A) STEVE GILLETTE      1967 VANGUARD         US   VSD79251
                                  (B) ALONE               1980 SIERRA           US        1001
```

```
MICKEY GILLEY            (AB      (A) THATS ALL THAT MATTERS TO ME 1980 EPIC    UK        84391
(JERRY LEE LEWIS COUSIN)          (B) DOWN THE LINE       1981 CHARLY           UK        30192
```

G34   **DAVE GILMOUR**   G34

```
    DAVE GILMOUR      G V (A        (A) DAVID GILMOUR          1978 US CBS 35388 UK HARVEST SHVL817
    MICK WEAVER       K   (A
    WILLIE WILSON     D   (A   RICK WILLS       B (A
```

G35   **GORDON GILTRAP**   G35

```
    GORDON GILTRAP    G   (ALL      (A) TESTAMENT OF TIME      1971 MCA    MKPS 2020 +    MCF  2688
    CLIVE BUNKER      D   (E        (B) GILTRAP                1973 PHILIPS               6308  175
    JOHN G PERRY      B   (CE       (C) VISIONARY              1976 ELECTRIC       UK     TRIX.2
    ROD EDWARDS       K V (EC       (D) PERILOUS JOURNEY       1977 ELECTRIC       UK     TRIX.4
    ROGER HAND        G V (E        (E) FEAR OF THE DARK       1978 ELECTRIC       UK     TRIX.7
    EDDIE SPENCE      K   (         (F) PEACOCK PARTY          1980 PVK            UK     GIL  1
    RIC SANDERS       VLN (F        (G) EARLY DAYS             1968 ALLEGRO        UK     4052
    IAN MOSLEY        D   (F
    SIMON PHILLIPS    D   (EC   GRAHAM PRESKETT    VLN (E   SHIRLEY RODEN    V (E  RICHARD HARVEY   RECORDER(EF
    TONY CARR         PERC (E   JOHN BAILEY        G   (C   BIMBO ACOCK    WIND (F  JOHN GUSTAFSON   B (F
    MORRIS PERT       PERC (F
```

G35A   **GINA X PERFORMANCE**   G35A

```
    G IN A KIKOINE    V   (A        (A) GINA X PERFORMANCE     1979 EMI            UK     EMC  3314
    ZEUS B HELD       K   (A        (B) X TRA ORDINAIRE        1980 EMI            UK     EMC  3336
    LASZLO CXIGANY    D   (A
    HEINZ TREWER      SYN (A   MARTIN HAMBERG   SYN (A
```

G35B   **GIPSY LOVE**   G35B

```
    CHARLY RATZER     G V (A        (A) GIPSY LOVE             197  BASF       GER        21115
    KURT HAUENSTEIN   B V K(A
    GEORG DOGGETTE    V   (A   PETER WOLF       K   (A   JANO STOJKA    D (A  RICHARD SCHONHERZ  K  (A
```

G36   **GINHOUSE**   G36

```
    GEOFF SHARKEY     G V (A        (A) GINHOUSE               1971 B&C            UK     CAS 1031
    STEWART BURLISON  B V (A
    DAVE WHITAKER     D   (A
```

G36A   **GIRL**   G36A

```
    SIMON LAFFY       G   (AB       (A) SHEER GREED            1980 JET US 36490 UK     JETLP224
    GERRY LAFFY       B V (AB       (B) WASTED YOUTH           1982 JET          UK     JETLP238
    PHILIP LEWIS      V   (AB
    PHIL COLLEN       G   (AB   DAVE GAYNOR    G   (A   PETE BARNACLE    G  (B
```

G37   **GIRLS SCHOOL**   G37

```
    ENID WILLIAMS     B V (A        (A) DEMOLITION             1980 BRONZE         UK     BRONX 525
    KELLY JOHNSON     G V (A        (B) HIT & RUN              1981 BRONZE     GER        203 556
    KIM McAULIFFE     G V (A        (C) WILDLIFE  EP           198
    DENISE DUFORT     D   (A
    KIM WESTON        B V (
```

G37A   **GIRLS AT OUR BEST**   G37A

```
    JUDY EVANS        V   (A        (A) PLEASURE              1981 HAPPY BIRTHDAY UK    RULP 1
    JAMES ALAN        G V (A
    D CARL HARPER     D   'A   GERARD SWIFT     B V (A   ROD JOHNSON    D (A  ALAN WAKEMAN   CLAR(A
    DAVE FISHEL       K   (A   THOMAS DOLBY     SYN (A   LAWRENCE DIANA PROD (A
```

G38   **GIRLS TOGETHER OUTRAGEOUSLY**   G38

```
    MISS PAMELA       V   (A        (A) PERMANENT DAMAGE       1969 STRAIGHT       UK     STS  1059
    MISS MERCY        V   (A
    MISS CHRISTINE    V   (A   MISS CINDERELLA  V   (A   MISS SANDRA    V (A  JIMMY CARL BLACK D (A
    ROY ASTRADA       B   (A   IAN UNDERWOOD    K   (A   CRAIG DOERGE   K (A  JEFF BECK    G   (A
    NICKY HOPKINS     K   (A   ROD STEWART      V   (A   FRANK ZAPPA  TAMB (A  DON PRESTON     SYN(A
```

G38A   **GLACIER**   G38A

```
G38B                                (A) FROM SEA TO SKY19      MERCURY       US    MG    20895
                                    GLAD                                                       G38B
G38C                                (A) FEELIN' GLAD           19   ABC         US         665
                                    GIZMO                                                      G38C
    STEVE WISE        D   (A        (A) JUST LIKE MASTER BATES 1979 ACE                   001
    MAURICE MEMMOTT   K VLN(AB       (B) VICTIMS                1981 CLEEP'N'EAT             1
    DAVE RADFORD      G V (AB
    BRIAN GOULD       SYN K(AB  GRAME QUINTON JONES  G   (B
```

G39   **GLADIATORS**   G39

```
    CLINTON FEARON    B V (ABCDE     (A) TRENCH TOWN MIX UP    197  VIRGIN         UK     V 2062
    ALBERT GRIFFITHS  V G (ABCDE     (B) PROVERBIAL REGGAE     1978 FRONT LINE     UK     FL1002
    LLOYD PARKS       B   (AC        (C) NATURALITY            1978 FRONT LINE     UK     FL1035
    GALLIMORE SUTHERLAND V G(ABCDE   (D) SWEET SO TILL         1979 FRONT LINE     UK     FL1048
    SCULLY            PERC (C        (E) GLADIATORS            1980 VIRGIN         UK     V 2161
    ANSEL COLLINS     K   (Bd
    STICKIE THOMPSON  PERC (BCD  EARL LINDO     K   (B   SLY DUNBAR     D (B  PABLO BLACK K   (D
    RICHARD ACE       K   (D    EARL BAGGA     B   (D   BONGO HERMAN PERC (D  SKY JUICE   PERC  (D
    TOMMY McCOOK      WIND (D    HEADLEY BENNETT HRNS (D  LEROY WALLACE  D (CD  ERNEST RANGLIN G (D
    JIMMY BECKMAN     HCA (D     SOJIE          PERC (D  BOBBY ELLIS  HRNS (D  RANCHIE McLEAN  G (C
    WINSTON WRIGHT    K   (C     ANGUS GAYE     D   (E   EDDIE GRANT  K G (E  DONALD BENJAMIN G (E
    TONY ZAP EDMUNDS  K   (E     TONY KING      K   (E   MARK JAMES     B (E  COACH HOUSE HORNS (E
```

G40   **GLADSTONE**   G40

```
    H L VOELKER       V   (BA       (A) GLADSTONE              1972 PROBE UK SPBA6264 ABC US751
    DOUG RHONE        G V (BA       (B) LOOKIN' FOR A SMILE    1973 ABC            US     ABCX 778
    JERRY SCHEFF      B   (BA
    RON TUTT          D   (AB   RANDY FOUTS      K   (BA  BOBBY TUTTLE  STEEL(B  MICK RAPHAEL   HCA (B
    ROBIN BRIANS      V PERC(BA  DAVID STANLEY    B   (B   PAUL LEIM      D (B  GARY CRAPSTER  D  (B
    LARRY WHITE       DOBRO(BA  A D WASHINGTON   CONG (B   LYNN GROOM     K (B  TOM RUSSELL    V  (B
    DALE BAKER        V   (B    DAHRILL RHONE    B   (A   MICHAEL RABON  G (A  ALAN ESTES   CONGA(A
    GARRY MOORE       BAN (A
```

G41   **GLASS FAMILY**   G41

```
    RALPH PARRETT     G V (A        (A) A ELECTRIC BAND
    DAVID CAPILOUTO   K B (A                                  1967 WB             US            1776
    GARY GREEN        D PERC(A
```

GLASS MOON

(A) GLASS MOON	1980	RADIO	UK	2003

G42

GLASS PRISM

(A) ON JOY & SORROW	1970	RCA	US	LSP 4270
( ) POE THROUGH THE GLASS PRISM	1969	RCA	US	LSP 4201

G43

GLASSHARP

PHIL KEAGGY	G V (A	(A) GLASSHARP	1972 MCA UK MUPS431 US DECCA 75261
JOHN SFERRA	D V G(A	(B) SYNERGY	1972 MCA UK MUPS449 US DECCA 75306
DAN PECCHIO	B V (A	(C) IT MAKES ME GLAD	1973 MCA UK MUPS470 US DECCA 5358

G44

GLASSHOUSE

(A) THANKS I NEEDED THAT	19	INVICTUS	US	T9810

G45

GLENCOE

GRAHAM MAITLAND	K V (AB	(A) GLENCOE	1972 EPIC US 31901 UK 65207
NORMAN WATT ROY	B V (AB	(B) THE SPIRIT OF GLENCOE	1973 EPIC us 32353 UK 65717
STEWART FRANCIS	D (AB		
JOHN TURNBULL	G V (AB GERALD JOHNSON G (B KOFI AYIVOR PERC (B BEN SIDRAN K (B		

G46

GLOBAL VILLAGE TRUCKING COMPANY

JON OWEN	G V (AB	(A) GREASY TRUCKER LIVE AT DINGWALLS	1973 GREASY TRUCKERS UK GT 4997
JOHN McKENZIE	B (AB	(B) GLOBAL VILLAGE TRUCKING COMPANY	1976 CAROLINE UK C 1516
JIMMY LASCELLES	K (AB		
SIMON STEWART	D (AB MIKE MEDORA HCA G V (AB PETE KIRTLEY G V (B CAROMAY DIXON V (B		
JIM CUOMO	SAX (B JEREMY LASCELLES PERC (B MONICA GARELTS V (B		

G47

GLOBE UNITY

ENRICO PAVA	TPT (G	(A) LIVE IN WUPPERTAL	1973 FMP	0160
MANFRED SCHAF	HRNS (G	(B) EVIDENCE	1976 FMP	0220
PETER BROTZMANN		(C) INTO THE VALLEY	1976 FMP	0270
EVAN PARKER		(D) PEARLS	1977 FMP	0380
KENNY WHEELER	HRNS (G	(E) JAHRMARKET	1977 POTORCH	JWB3
TONY BRAXTON		(F) IMPROVISATIONS	1978 JAPO	60021
GERK DUDEK	SAX (G	(G) COMPOSITIONS	1979 JAPO	60027
MICHEL PILZ	CLAR (G			
BOB STEWART	HRNS (G BUSCHI NIEBERGALL B (G PAUL LOVENS D (G ALBERT MANGELSDORFF TROM (G			
ALEXANDER V SCHLIPPENBACH (G GRUNKI CHRISTMANN TROM (G PUAL RUTHERFORD TROM (G STEVE LACY SAX (G				
EVAN PARKER S	SAX (G			

G48

GLORIA MUNDI

EDDIE MAELON	V (AB	(A) I INDIVIDUAL	1978 RCA	UK PL 25157
MIKE NICHOLLS	D (AB	(B) WORD IS OUT	1979 RCA	UK PL 25244
SUNSHINE	K V (AB			
BEETHOVEN	G (A KIRBY G (B CC SAX (AB NIGEL ROSS SCOTT B (B			
ICE	B (A			

G48A

GLORY

(A) A MEST MUSIC	1969 TEXAS REVOLUTION	US	69

G49

JOHN GLOVER

JOHN GLOVER	G V (A	(A) MIDNIGHT OVER ENGLAND	1978 ELECTRIC UK TRIX9
PETE VAN HOOKE	D (A		
PAUL WESTWOOD	B (A JOHN MEALING K (A STEVE O'DONNELL K (A PETER ARNESEN PNO (A		
TONY HICKS	G (A JOHN IRISH EARLE SAX (A STEVE GREGORY WIND (A GEOFF RICHARDSON VLA (A		
COLIN JENNINGS	PERC (A DICK HANSON TPT (A JACQUIE SULLIVAN V (A JOY YATES V (A		
B J COLE	STEEL(A ROGER SAUNDERS G (A		

G50

ROGER GLOVER

ROGER GLOVER	B V (AB	(A) BUTTERFLY BALL	1974 PURPLE UK TPSA 7514
SIMON PHILLIPS	D (B	(A) BUTTERFLY BALL(ROGER GLOVER)	1974 OYSTER US 1605
GRAHAM PRESKETT	VLN (B	(B) ELEMENTS	1978 OYSTER US 1637 UK POLYDOR 2391 306
RONNIE ASPERY	WIND (b		
MICKY LEE SOULE	K V (AB MARTIN BIRCH (B LIZA STRIKE V (AB HELEN CHAPPELLE V (AB		
EDDIE HARDIN	K SYN(A LES BINKS D (A RAY FENWICK G (A MO FOSTER B (A		
MIKE MORAN	K (A BARRY ST JOHN V (A JUDY KUHL V (A KAY GARNER V (A		
JOANNE WILLIAMS	V (A ANN ODELL PNO (A MIKE GILES D (A NIGEL WATSON SAX (A		
EDDIE JOBSON	VLN (A JACK EMBLOW ACC (A CHRIS KARAN TABLA(A ROBIN THOMPSON BASSOON (A		
GLENN HUGHES	V (A NEIL LANCASTER V (A JOHN GOODISON V (A DAVID COVERDALE V (A		
RONNIE DIO	V (A		

G51

SUE GLOVER

SUE GLOVER	V (A	(A) SOLO	1976 DJM DJF 20469 + DJLPS 469
EDDIE BAIRD	G (A		
TONY BRAUNAGEL	D (A IRENE CHANTER V (A DOREEN CHANTER V (A MICK FEAT B (A		
PAUL KOSSOFF	G (A DAVE MATTACKS D (A RABBIT BUNDRICK K (A TONY WILLIAMS D (A		
TERRY WILSON	B (A SUNNY LESLIE V (A		

G51A

GLAXO BABIES

ROB CHAPMAN	V (C	(A) THIS IS YOUR LIFE (EP)	1979 HEARTBEAT 12PULSE3
DAN CATSIS	G V (C	(B) NINE MONTHS TO THE DISCO	1980 HEARTBEAT HB2
TONY WRAFTERS	SAX (C	(C) PUT ME ON THE GUEST LIST	1980 HEARTBEAT HB3
TOM NICHOLS	B V (C		
GEOFF ALSOPP	D (C CHARLES LLEWELLYN D (C		

G51B

GNAGS

HENNING STAERK	D PER(B	(A)	
JENS J NEILSEN	D PRC(B	(B) BURHONS	1979 GENLYD LP114
PETER AG NIELSEN	B V (B	(C) INTERCITY	1980 GENLYD LP122
IVAN SORENSEN	K G SYN(B		
JACOB RIIS-OLSEN	G V (B PER FROST G SYN K V(B		

G52

GNIDROLOG

STEWART GOLDRING	G (AB	(A) IN SPITE OF HARRY'S TOENAIL	1971 RCA UK SF8261
COLIN GOLDRING	G V SAX (AB	(B) LADY LAKE	1972 RCA UK SF8322
NIGEL PEGRUM	D FLT OBOE(B		
JOHN EARLE	V WIND(B PETER COWLING B CELLO(B CHARLOTTE FENDRICH PNO (B		

G52A

GOBLIN

CLAUDO SIMONETTI	K (A	(A) SUSPIRIA(SOUNDTRACK)	1979 EMI UK 3222
MASSIMO MORANTE	G V (A		
FABIO PIGNATELLI	B G PERC V(A AGNOSTINO MARANGOLA D V (A		

GO GOS

CHARLOTTE CAFFEY	G K V(A	(A) BEAUTY & THE BEAT	1981	IRS		70021
BELINDA CARLISLE	V (A	(B) VACATION	1982	IRS		70031
GINA SCHOCK	D PERC(					
KATHY VALENTINE	B V (A	JANE WIEDLIN	G V (			

KEITH & DONNA GODCHAUX

KEITH GODCHAUX	K V ((A	(A) KEITH & DONNA GODCHAUX	1975	ROUND	UK/US	RX 104
DONNA GODCHAUX	V (A					
JERRY GARCIA	G V (A	BRIAN GODCHAUX VLN (A JOHN KAHN B (A DENNY SEIWELL D (A				
MERL SAUNDERS	ORG (A	JIM BRERETON D (A CHRISSY STEWART B (A BERNARD PURDIE D (A				
BILL WOLF	B (A					

GODDO

GREG GODOVITZ	V B (ALL	(A) GODDO	1976	POLYDOR		2424 901
GINO SCARPELLI	G (BD	(B) WHO CARES	1978	POLYDOR		2424 902
DOUG INGLIS	D (BD	(C) AN ACT OF GODDO	1979	POLYDOR		2424 189
ROSEMARIE TEDESCO	PNO (B	(D) LIGHUE	1981	ATTIC		1107
PETER SCHENKMAN	CELLO(B					
DR JOHN BJARNASON	HCA (B	MARTIN MELHUISH G (B PAUL IRVINE SAX (B				

STEVE GODDARD

STEVE GODDARD	G V K(A	(A) WAITING FOR GODDARD	1981	KINSWAY	UK	KMR 310

ROBERT JOHN GODFREY

ROBERT JOHN GODFREY	(A	(A) FALL OF HYPERION	1974	CHARISMA	UK	CAS 1084

GODIEGO

YUKIHIDE TAKEKAWA	G (A	(A) WATER MARGIN	1978	SATRIL	UK	SATL 4009
MICKIE YOSHINO	K (A	(B) ROAD OF BROODY CLAP	197		UK	
TAKAMI ASANO	G (A	(C) MONKEY	1980	BBC	UK	384
TAKAHIKO ISHIKAWA	G (A					
MEGUNI SAKAMOTO	V (A	JUNKO KAMIMURA V (A STEVE FOX B (A RYOJI ASANO D (A				
YUJIN HARADA	D (A					

GODS

KEN HENSLEY	K G V PERC (ABC1	(A) GENESIS	1968	COLUMBIA	UK	SCX 6286
LEE KERSLAKE	D (ABC1	(B) TO SAMUEL A SON	1970	COLUMBIA	UK	SCX 6372
JOE KONAS	G V (ABC1	(C) GODS	1976	HARVEST	UK	SHSM 2011
JOHN GLASCOCK	B V (ABC	(1) PRE LP LINE UP				
GREG LAKE	B V (1					

THE GODZ

ERIC MOORE	B V (AB	(A) GODZ	1978	MILLENNIUM 8003 + RCA XL13051
GLEN CATALINE	D V (AB	(B) NOTHING IS SACRED	1979	CASABLANCA 7134 + RCA XL13072
MARK CHATFIELD	G V (AB				
BOB HILL	G K V(AB				

THE GODZ

PAUL THORNTON	D (ABCD	(A) CONTACT HIGH	1967	ESP US 1037 NL FONTANA 858108
JAY DILLON	K (ABD	(B) GODZ TWO	1968	ESP US 1047 RI BASE II 1077
LARRY KESSLER	G VLN(ABCD	(B) GODZ TWO	1969	FONTANA UK STL5512
JIM McCARTHY	G V (ABCD	(C) THIRD TESTAMENT	19	ESP US 1077
CHARLES CAZALET	G (D	(D) GODZHUNHEIT	19	ESP US 2017
MORTY KALB	(C				
THE GREAT PAHENE	PNO (D	HERB ABRAMSON (C BILLY PAYNE D (D BOB UNGER B (D			
SMOKEY HEAD	G (D	JIMMY NORWOOD G (D LESLIE FRADKIN G B V(D PATTIE THORNTON V (D			
U E GLASS	G (D	GEORGE CAMERON D V (D BOB GALLAGHER G (D ROBERT FRIEDMAN B (D			
GIOVANNI ROSARIO	D (D				

GERRY GOFFIN

GERRY GOFFIN		(A) IT AINT EXACTLY ENTERTAINMENT	19	ADELPHI	US	4102

HERBIE GOINS

HERBIE GOINS		(A) NO ONE IN YOUR HEART	1967	PARLOPHONE	UK	PMC 7026

ANDREW GOLD

ANDREW GOLD	G V K B D(ALL	(A) ANDREW GOLD	1975	ASYLUM US 7E 1047	UK	SYL 9028
KENNY EDWARDS	G VB(ABDC	(A) ANDREW GOLD	1975	ASYLUM	UK	K 53020
DON FRANCISCO	V (A	(B) WHAT'S WRONG WITH THIS PICTURE	1976	ASYLUM US 7E 1086	UK	K 53052
GENE GARFIN	V D (A	(C) ALL THIS & HEAVEN TOO	1978	ASYLUM US 6E 116	UK	K 53072
MIKE BOTTS	D (ABD	(D) WHIRLWIND	1980	ASYLUM US 6E 264	UK	K 52219
LINDA RONSTADT	V (AB					
TREVOR LAWRENCE	HRNS (A	BOBBY KEYS HRNS (A PETER BERNSTEIN B (A DAVID KEMPER D (A				
DAN DUGMORE	G STEEL (A	BROCK WALSH K V (BDC WADDY WACHTEL G (BDC RUSS KUNKEL D (BC				
LEE SKLAR	B (BC	DONALD MENZA SAX (B DANNY KORTCHMAR G (B PETER ASHER V PERC(B				
VAL GARAY	V (B	TESSE COEN PERC (B CLARENCE McDONALD K (B BRYAN GAROFALO B (D				
RICK MAROTTA	D (DC	DON GROLNICK K (D ERNIE WATTS SAX (C JEFF PORCARO D (C				
MARK SAFAN	V (C	BEAU SEGAL D (C J D SOUTHER V (C STIX AKIMBO PERC(C				
JENNIFER WARNES	V (C	BRAD PALMER B (C				

JIM GOLD

JIM GOLD	V (ALL	(A) JIM GOLD & GALLERY	1976	WESTBOUND	US	225
JOHN STEVENSON	B V (C	(B) I CANT FACE	1977	TABU	US	1 2308
DAVE THOMPSON	K (C	(C) HOMETOWN HERO	1978	TABU	US	35520
MIKE EVERSOLE	G (C					
DAVE EVERSOLE	B STEEL V(C	SCOTT THOMPSON D (C MIKE IRISH G MAND(C				

BARRY GOLDBERG

BARRY GOLDBERG	V G K (ALL	(A) CHICAGO ANTHOLOGY	1966	TOGETHER	US	ST1024
DAVID HOOD	B (HJK	(B) BLOWING MY MIND	1966	EPIC	US	26199
ROGER HAWKINS	D (J	(C) REUNION	1968	BUDDAH	US	5012
PETE CARR	G V (J	(D) TWO JEWS BLUES	1969	BUDDAH	US	5029
JIMMY JOHNSON	G (EJ	(D) TWO JEWS BLUES	1969	BUDDAH	UK	203 020
EDDIE HINTON	G (DHJ	(E) STREETMAN	1970	BUDDAH	US	5051
RULE YARBOROUGH	BANJO(J	(F) BARRY GOLDBERG AND	1972	RECORD MAN	US	CR5105
HARVEY THOMPSON	WIND (J	(G) IVAR AVENUE REUNION(N MERRYWEATHER)	197	RCA	US	LSP 4442
WAYNE HILL	TPT (J	(H) BLAST FROM MY PAST	1974	BUDDAH	US	5081
ARTHUR JENKINS	PERC (J	(H) BLAST FROM MY PAST	1974	POLYDOR	UK	2318 938
TEX BERNFELD	V (J	(J) BARRY GOLDBERG	1974	ATCO	US	7040
MARGARET BRANCH	V (J	(K) &FRIENDS RECORDED LIVE	1976	BUDDAH	US	5684

(CONTINUED)

```
GEORGE TERRY        G    (J    BARRY BECKETT     K    (J    JIMMY EVANS      CONGA(J   RONNIE EADES       SAX  (J
AL LESTER           FDL  (J    CHARLES ROSE      TROM (J    RALPH MACDONALD  PERC (J   BOB DYLAN          V PERC(J
HARRISON CALLOWAY   TPT  (J    TOM BERNFIELD     V    (J    BRENDA BRYANT    V    (J   PAT SMITH          V    (J
JERRY WEXLER        PERC (J    DANNY WHITTED     G    (H    DUANE ALLMAN     G    (DH  HARVEY MANDEL      G(ABCDFHK
MIKE BLOOMFIELD     G   (DFHK  DON McCALLISTER   B    (CDH  PETE STRAZZA     SAX  (H   CHARLIE MUSSELWHITE HCA(ABCDGHK
MARKEYS             HRNS (H    EDDY HOH          D    (CDK  RON WOODS        PERC (C   RONALD MINSKY       PERC(C
NETTIE'MAMA' GOLDBERG K(CH     GREAT             G HRNS(D   NEIL MERRYWEATHER B   (GK  LYNN CAREY         V    (G
SOULVILLE HORNS          (D    ROBIN BOERS       D    (G    RON RUBY         B    (AB  BOBBY JONES        G    (A
JOHN RICHARDSON     G    (G    MAURICE McKINLEY  D    (B    BILLY BUTLER     G    (E   ERIC GALE          G    (E
VINNIE BELL         G    (K    BOBBY GREGG       D    (E
JERRY JEMMETT       B    (E
```

G61A   STU GOLDBERG   G61A

```
STU GOLDBERG        K    (A    (A) SOLOS/DUOS/TRIO              1978 MPS           GER    61400
LARRY CORYELL       G    (A
L SUBRAMANIAM       VLN  (A
```

G62   GOLDBRIARS   G62

```
                               (A) GOLDBRIARS             19   EPIC        US     BN  26087
                               (B) STRAIGHT AHEAD         19   EPIC        US     BN  26114
```

G62A   GOLDEN DAWN   G62A

```
TOM RAMSEY          (           (A) POWER PLANT            1967 INTERNATIONAL ARTISTS US IA 4
GEORGE KINNEY       (
BILL HALLMARK       (           BOBBY RECTOR     (A    BIRD        (
```

G62B   JOHN GOLDING   G62B

```
JOHN GOLDING        G V  (A    (A) PHOTOGRAPHS             1974 ATLANTIC      UK    K50085
GEORGE VAN RISTELL MAND(A
DAVE DODDINGTON     G DULC(A   JIMMY JEWELL     SAX  (A   PETE COSKER      B    (A   PAUL GARRETT       K    (A
PAUL MIDDLETON     B STEEL(A   RODGER NARRWAY   PERC (A   PETE SAGE        VLN  (A   ROY WEBBER       V    (A
```

G64   GOLDEN EARRING   G64

```
GEORGE KOOYMANS    G V  (ALL   (A) JUST EARRING         1964              POLYDOR NL   736 007
RINUS GERRITSEN    B K  (ALL   (B) WINTER HARVEST       196  CAPITOL US 2823 POLYDOR NL   736 068
BARRY HAY          V FLT(C>W   (C) MIRACLE MIRROR       196  CAPITOL US 164 POLYDOR NL  1236 283  + 2459 330
ROBERT JAN STIPS   K    (MNQTV (D) ON THE DOUBLE        196              POLYDOR NL  2653 001 +2236 823/4
CESAR ZUIDERWIJK   D    (C>W   (E) EIGHT MILES HIGH     1969 MAJ/MIN UKSM 65 POLYDOR NL 1656 015 UK 658  900
TONY BRITNEL       SAX  (TV    (E) EIGHT MILES HIGH     1969 POLYDOR GER 184 356   ATLANTIC US  8244
EELCO GELLING      G    (LPQSFM (F) GOLDEN EARRING      197  CAPITOL US11315 POLYDOR    2499 009 + 2482 329
PAT PAAY           V    (LQ    (F) GOLDEN EARRING       197  DWARF   US 200 POLYDOR GER 2488 308
BERTUS BORGERS     SAX  (FLMN  (G) SING MY SONG         197  KARUSSELL GER          2499 009
KEVIN NANCE        K    (S     (H) SEVEN TEARS          1971 POLYDOR              2344 008 UK 2310 135
LANI GROVES        V    (ST    (I) TOGETHER             1972 POLYDOR NL           2925 009 UK 2310 210
JIM MAELEN         PERC (ST    (J) BEST OF              1973 KARUSSELL 2499053    POLYDOR  2459 259
JOHN ZANGRANDO     SAX  (ST    (K) HEARING EARRING      1973 TRACK UK 2406109
JOAP EGGERMONT     D    (ABCDE (L) MOONTAN              1974 MCA US 2354    POLYDOR         UK 2310 288
NEPPIE NOYA        PERC (Q     (L) MOONTAN              1973 MCA US 396     TRACK          UK 2406 112
FRANS KRASSENBURG  V    (ABC   (M) SWITCH               1975 MCA US 2139   POLYDOR        UK 2310 381
SIEB WARNER        D PERC(E    (M) SWITCH               1975 TRACK UK 2406117
JOHN LEGRAND       HCA  (U     (N) TO THE HILT          1976 MCA US 2183   POLYDOR         2430 330
CHRIS MERCER       SAX  (N     (O) MAD LOVE             1977 MCA US 2254
PETER DE PONDE     G    (AB    (P) LIVE (DBL)           1977              POLYDOR          2625 034
                               (Q) CONTRABAND           1977              POLYDOR 2344 059 UK 2310 491
                               (R) STORY                1977              POLYDOR          2664 372
                               (S) POTRAIT OF           1977              POLYDOR  EURO   2482 192
                               (T) GRAB IT FOR A SECOND 1979              POLYDOR        UK 2310 639
                               (U) NO PROMISES          1979              POLYDOR        US   6223
                               (V)  PRISONER OF THE NIGHT1980             POLYDOR        NL 2344 161
                               (V) LONG BLOND ANIMAL    1980             POLYDOR        US 1 6303
                               (W) 2ND LIVE             1981 POLYDOR 2335 222VERTIGO 2625 042
```

G64A   GOLIATH   G64A

```
JOSEPH ROSBOTHAM   WIND(A      (A) GOLIATH              1970  CBS UK 64229   US   ABC702
MALCOLM GRUNDY     G    (A
LINDA ROTHWELL     V    (A     JOHN WILLIAMSON  B    (A   ERIC EASTMAN    D PERC(A
```

G64B   GOLLIWOGS   G64B

```
JOHN FOGERTY       G V  (A     (A) GOLLIWOGS(PRECREEDENCE)  1975 FANTASY US F9474   FAN 5996
TOM FOGERTY        G V  (A
STU COOK           B    (A     DOUG CLIFFORD    D    (A
```

G64C   RAY GOMEZ   G64C

```
RAY GOMEZ  G V K B PERC (A     (A) VOLUME               1980  CBS US 36243 UK      84134
CHRIS PALARO       K VIBES(A
JIMMY HASLIP       B    (A     WILL LEE         B    (A   GREG MANN               (A   NARADA MICHAEL WALDEN D(A
RONNIE ST GERMAIN       (A     RANDY BRECKER    TPT  (A   MICHAEL BRECKER  SAX  (A   GEORGE YOUNG       SAX (A
SAMMY FIGUEROA     CONGA(A     RAFAEL CRUZ      PERC (A   DIVA GRAY        V    (A   ULLANDA McCULLOUGH V (A
LANI GROVES        V    (A     DAVID SANCIOUS   K    (A
```

G65   IAN GOMM   G65

```
IAN GOMM           V G  (AB    (A) GOMM WITH THE WIND ]SAME 1978 STIFF US 36103 ALBION UK DAI1
HERBIE FLOWERS     B    (AB    (A) SUMMER HOLIDAY     ]      1978 ALBION         UK   ALBG 100
CHRIS PARREN       K    (AB    (B) WHAT A BLOW          1980 STIFF US 36433 ALBION UK  102
BARRY DE SOUZA     D    (AB
RAY TAFF WILLIAMS G V  (B      ROD DEMICK   B V  (B   NICK GLENNIE SMITH  K V  (B   B J COLE   STEEL  (B
ALAN COULTER       D V  (B     MARTIN RUSHENT V (B    MALCOLM MORLEY      K    (B   RAPHAEL RAVENSCROFTBRASS(B
```

```
FRANCIS MOSE        B    (DG        (A) MAGICK BROTHER         1970  BYG FR 5293 305  GER METRONOME MLP 15372
DI BOND STEWART     D    (M         (A) MAGICK BROTHER         1977  AFFINITY  UK AFF 4
CHRISTIAN TITSCH    G B  (BCDEJ     (B) CAMEMBERT ELECTRIQUE   1971  BYG FR 529353 1974 CAROLINE UK    1052
DELMELZA            PERC (O         (B) CAMEMBERT ELECTRIQUE   197   VIRGIN UK VG502
IDIER MALHERBE  WIND(ABCDEFGHIJLN   (C) CONTINENTAL CIRCUS     1971  PHILIPS 6332 330
DAEVID ALLEN        G V  (CDEFIJ    (D) THE FLYING TEAPOT      1973  VIRGIN  UK 2002 +  BYG    FR    529027
GILLI SMYTH         V    (ABCDEFIJ  (E) ANGELS EGG             1973  VIRGIN  UK 2007
PIP PYLE            D    (BC        (F) YOU                    1974  VIRGIN  UK 2019  GER          88424
CHARLES HAYWARD     D    (A         (G) SHAMAL                 1976  VIRGIN UK 2046 US 34156 GER VIRGIN 28423
LAURIE ALLEN        D    (E         (H) GAZEUSE                1977  VIRGIN  UK 2074 + POLYDOR   2473 711
BOB TAIT            D    (I         (I) LIVE ETC               1977  VIRGIN   UK 3501  POLYDOR   2676 723
STEVE HILLAGE       G    (DEFGIJ    (J) GONG EST MORT  DBL     1977  TAPIOCA 10002/3     LTM 1003/4
TIM BLAKE           K    (DEFIJ     (K) EXPRESSO 2             1978  VIRGIN  UK 2099  POLYDOR   2473 742
RACHID HOUARI       D    (AD        (K) EXPRESSO               1980  ARISTA US 4204 VIRGIN GER     25856
MIKE HOWLETT        B V  (DFGIJ     (L) DOWNWIND               1979  ARISTA UK 1080 US 4219  NL     62272
BILL BRUFORD        D    (          (M) TIME IS THE KEY        1979  ARISTA UK SPART 1105      US   4255
BRIAN DAVISON       D    (          (N) P MOERLENS GONG LIVE   1979  ARISTA UK SPART 1130  NL    202 205
MIREILLE BAUER  D   PERC (EGHILK    (O) LEAVE  T OPEN          1981  ARISTA                NL    202 955
PIERRE MOERLEN  D   (EFGHIKLMNO
PATRICE LEMOINE     K    (GI  JORGE PINCHEVSKY  VLN (G   EARL FREEMAN     (A  SANDY COLLEY       (G
DARRYL WAY          VLN  (LKM FRANCOIS CHAUSSE  PERC(LKNO ALLAN HOLDSWORTH  G(HLKM MICK TAYLOR  G (LK
HANNY ROWE          B    (LKMNO MIKE OLDFIELD    G B (LN  BENOIT MOERLEN PERC(HKLN STEVE WINWOOD  K (L
MAC POOLE           D    (    ROSS RECORD        G   (L   MINO CINELON   PERC(H  DIETER GEWISSLER  (A
BURTON GREEN             (A   JAMSIN                 (A   MIQUETTE GIRAUDY V K(GI FRANCIS BACON    (D
DIDIER LOCKWOOD      VLN  (L   FRANCOIS COUSSE CONGA(LK  BON LOZAGA        (KMNO PERE CUSHION DE D (J
MISTER T BEING      B    (J   TERRY OLDFIELD     FLT (L   JOE KIRBY   B    (M   PETE LEMER     K  (M
NICO RAMSDEN        G    (M   CHARLES MARIANO    SAX (O   BRIAN HOLLOWAY G (O   PHIL NEWELL    PROD (I
JOHN WALTERS        PROD (I   BARE PHILLIPS       B  (A   PIERRE LATTES PROD (D SIMON HEYWORTH PROD (F
```

```
MICK EVE          SAX (ABCDE     (A) GONZALEZ                   1974 EMI        UK        EMC  3046
BUD BEADLE        SAX (ABCDE     (B) OUR ONLY WEAPON IS OUR MUSIC 1975 EMI      UK        EMC  3100
RON CARTHY        TPT (ABCDE     (B) OUR ONLY WEAPON IS OUR MUSIC 197  CAPITOL  US        ST  11644
ROY DAVIES        K   (ABCDE     (C) HAVEN'T STOPPED DANCIN'    1979 CAPITOL US 11855 SIDEWALK UK2001
STEVE GREGORY     SAX (ABCE      (D) MOVE IT TO THE MUSIC       1979 CAPITOL US 11995 SIDEWALK UK2003
GORDON HUNTE      G   (ABCE      (E) SHIPWRECKED(SOME TRACKS AS C) 1977 CAPITOL US     SW  11855
SERGIO CASTILO    D   (D         (F) WATCH YOU STEP            1980 CAPITOL    12103
CHRIS MERCER      SAX (ABCDE
BOBBY STIGNAC     D   (BCDE  COLIN JACAS     TROM (CDE  STEVE WALLER    G V (CE  GEORGE CHANDLER  V (A
JOHN GIBLIN       B   (CE   DE LISLE HARPER B   (A    GLEN LE FLEUR   D   (AB  PRESTON HEYMAN   D (B
ALLAN SHARPE      PERC (AB   RICHARD BAILEY  D   (ACE  LENNY ZAKATEK   B   (BCE BOBBY JOHN      PERC(A
LINDA TAYLOR      V   (CDE   MARTIN DROVER   HRNS (CDE LARRY STEELE    B   (B   ROBERT AHWAI     G (B
KEN FREEMAN       SYN (B     MALCOLM GRIFFITHS TROM(D  LANCE DIXON     SYN (B   GODFREY McLEAN   PERC(B
VIOLA WILLS       V   (D     ALAN MARSHALL   V   (D    TIM CANSFIELD   V G (D   HUGH BULLEN      B (D
```

```
MARK PERRY        G K V(A         (A) FIRE FROM HEAVEN          1979  DEPTFORD FUN CITY  UK DLP 04
GILLIAN HANNA     V REC(A
DAVE GEORGE       G FLT V(A DENNIS BURNS   B   (A   HENRY BADOWSKI  D SAX (A GLYN COLLINS    FLT (A
PAUL REEKIE       B   (A   SOOZE              V   (A
```

```
PATRICK CAMPBELL  B   (AB         (A) PISTOL PACKIN' MAMA       1976  UA UK UAS 29951 US ROUND LA57G
DAVID NELSON      G V (AB         (B) BLUEGRASS                 1978  FLYING FISH     US    FF  049
DON RENO          BAN V(AB
FRANK WAKEFIELD   MAND V(AB  CHUBBY WISE      FDL (AB
```

```
JOE FRANCO        D   (BCDEFG     (A) GOOD RATS                 1968  KAPP          US        3580
LENNY KOTKE       B   (BCDEFG     (A) TASTY                     1974  WB US 2813 RI 78 RAT CITY8002
PEPPI MARCHELLO   V   (BCDEFG     (C) RAT CITY IN BLUE          1976  PLATINUM      US      RCR 8001
MICKEY MARCHELLO  G V (BCDEFG     (C) RAT CITY IN BLUE          1976  PHILIPS              6310 625
TOM JULIANO       SAX (D          (D) RATS TO RICHES            1978  RADAR UK RAD5 PATHE FR 606<5
BRIAN CUOMO       PNO (DE         (D) RATS TO RICHES            1978  PASSPORT  US 9825 NL  062
HOWARD KAYLAN     V   (D          (E) BIRTH COMES TO US ALL     1979  PASSPORT    US 9830
MARK VOLMAN       V   (D          (F) LIVE AT LAST              1980  RAT CITY 998 PASSPORT NL 68032
JOHN GATTO        K G(BCDEF       (G) GREAT AMERICAN MUSIC      1981  RAT CITY 8003 LOGO UK   1027
MANFRED MANN      K   (E
RICHARD TEE       K   (E    JOHN TROPEA     G   (E   JIMMY MAELIN    PERC(E JANIS PENDANVIS   V (E
JOSHIE ARMSTEAD   V   (E    ZEPHRYN         V   (E   JOE ZANGRANDO   FLT (E MEL COLLINS SAX   (E
PETER WOODS       K   (E    LARRY FAST      SYN (E   STEPHEN GALFAS  K   (E MAX MIDDLETON   K (E
JOHN GATTI        WIND K(F   SCHUYLER DEALE  B   (G   BRUCE KULICK    G   (G
```

```
JAMES CAHOON LINDSAY V PERC(A    (A) GOOD THUNDER         1972 ELEKTRA UK K 42123 US EKS 75041
JOHN DESAUTELS    D   (A
DAVID HANSON      G V (A   BILL RHODES     B   (A   WAYNE COOK    K(A
```

```
                                  (A) SIDEWALK SURFING   19   GNP CRESCENDO      US   2001
```

```
PHILLIP GOODHAND TAIT K V(ALL     (A) REHEARSAL              1971  DJM       UK    DJLPS 411
ANDY LATIMER      G   (B           (B) I'LL WRITE A SONG      1971  DJM       UK    DJLPS 416
DOUG FERGUSON     B   (B           (C) SONGFALL              1972  DJM       UK    DJLPS 425
ANDY WARD         D   (B           (D) PHILIP GOODHAND TAIT  1973  DJM       UK    DJLPS 432
                                   (D) PHILIP GOODHAND TAIT  1973  20TH CENTURY US      424
                                   (E) JINGLE JANGLE MAN     1975  DJM       UK    DJLPS 453
                                   (F) OCEANS AWAY           1976  CHRYSALIS UK    CHR  1113
                                   (G) TEACHING AN OLD DOG   1977  CHRYSALIS UK    CHR  1146
                                   (H) GOOD OLD PHIL'S       1980  GUNDOG          GUN LP1
```

GOODIES

```
BILL ODDIE          V PERC(ALL      (A) THE GOODIES LP                    1976 BRADLEYS        UK      BRAOL 1012
TIM BROOKE-TAYLOR  V    (ALL        (B) NOTHING TO DO WITH US             1976 ISLAND          UK      ilps9452
GRAEME GARDEN       V    (ALL
DAVE McRAE          K    (B    JEFF SEOPARDIE    D    (B   BILLY KRISTIAN   B    (B   CHRIS RAE        G   (B
RAY FLACK           G    (B    BERNIE HOLLAND    G    (B   DEREK WATKINS    TPT  (B   HENRY LOWTHER    TPT (B
JOHN HUCKRIDGE      TPT  (B    PAUL COSH         TPT  (B   CHRIS PYNE       TROM (B   GEOFF WRIGHT     TROM(B
RON ASPREY          SAX  (B    GEOFF DAILEY      SAX  (B   TONY CARR        D    (B   ALAN PARKER      G   (B
BRIAN ODGES         B    (B    GRAHAM PRESCOTT   FDL  (B   JOY YATES        V .  (B   JACQUIE SULLIVAN V   (B
STEVIE LANGE        V    (B    RUSSELL STONE     V    (B   CHAS MILLS       V    (B   TONY BURROWS     V   (B
CHARLIE DORE        V    (B    DAVID KATZ        STR  (B
```
GOODNESS

```
                               (A) GOODNESS                               1977 AUDIO FIDELITY  US      6284
```
GOODNESS & MERCY

```
DAVE TALISMAN       V    (A         (A) GOODNESS & MERCY                  19   MGM             US      SE 4730
PETER MARTIN        K V  (A
JOE BELLAMY         B V  (A    RIC MILLER        D    (A   ELVIS DITTA      PERC (A   JOHN TROMBATORE  G   (A
HARRY KIM           TPT  (A    JERRY GRANT       SAX  (A   STEVE DAVIS      TROM (A
```
STEVE GOODMAN

```
STEVE GOODMAN       G V  (ALL      (A) STEVE GOODMAN                      1971 BUDDAH          US      BDS 5096
DONNIE FRITTS       ORG  (A        (A) STEVE GOODMAN                      1972 BUDDAH          US      BDLH 5007
NORBERT PUTNAM      B    (A        (B) SOMEBODY ELSE'S TROUBLE            1973 BUDDAH UK4019   US      5121
DAVID BRIGGS        PNO  (A        (C) JESSIE'S JIG & OTHER FAVOURITES    1975 ASYLUM          UK      SYL 9017
CHARLIE McCOY       HCA  (A        (C) JESSIE'S JIG & OTHER FAVOURITES    1975 ASYLUM UK K53025 US   7E 1037
BILLY SANFORD       G BAN(A        (D) WORDS WE CAN DANCE TO              1976 ASYLUM UK K53038 US   7E 1061
BUCKY WILKIN        V    (A        (E) THE ESSENTIAL (AB)                 1975 BUDDAH US 5665
BEN KEITH           STEEL(A        (F) SAY IT IN PRIVATE                  1977 ASYLUM UK K53067 US   7E 1118
BRIAN RAY           G    (J        (G) HIGH & OUTSIDE                     1979 ASYLUM          US      174
JEFF BAXTER         G    (J        (H) GATHERING                          1980 MOUNTAIN RAILWAY US    670
AMOS GARRETT        G    (J        (J) HOT SPOT                           1980 ASYLUM          US      297
BILL ELLIOTT        G    (J
STEPHEN BRUNTON     PERC (A   GRADY MARTIN      (A   VASSAR CLEMENTS  FDL (A   PETE WADE        G  (A
GEORGE TIDWELL      TPT  (A   WILLIAM PUETT    CLAR (A   GENE MULLINS    TROM (A   DENNIS GOODE     TROM(A
MARTHA McCRORY      CELLO(A   STEVE BURGH      G    (BCD STEVE MOSLEY    D   (BD  SID SIMS         B  (D
SAUL BROUDY         HCA  (A   WINNIE WINSTON BAN STEEL(DC JEFF GUTCHEON  K   (BCD BILL SWOFFORD   V  (DC
HUGH McDONALD       B    (BCD RUAN MacKINNON   V    (DC DIANE HOLMES     V   (DC  MARK GAFFNEY     V  (D
JIM ROTHERMEL       SAX  (DJ  PETER ECKLUND    CLAR (D   JETHRO BURNS    MAND (DC  KENNY KOSEK      FDL(D
LEW LONDON          DOBRO(D   TOM RADTKE TIMBALES  (D   JOHN FRIGO      B VLN(D   BOBBY ROSSI      ACC(D
KEN BUTTREY         PERC (A   RICK CHUDACOFF   B    (J   PETER BUNETTA   D   (J   ARNO LUCAS       PERC(J
MATTHEW WERNER      V    (A   ALAN ESTES       PERC (J   BILL LABAMTY    V   (J   PHOEBE SNOW      V  (J
JACK McGANN         G ACC(B   HUGH McCRACKEN   G    (B   EDDIE BRIGATI   V   (B   DAVID NEWMAN     SAX (B
WILLIE BRIDGES      SAX  (B   MARK HOROWITZ    G BAN(B   JERRY BARNHAM   FLT (B   ARIF MARDIN      PNO (B
DAVID BRIGATI       V    (B   CHARLES McCRACKEN CELLO(B  LARRY PACKER    FDL (B   DAVID BROMBERG   G MAND(B
ROBERT THOMAS       PNO V(B   MARIA MULDAUR    V    (B   SHELDON PLOTKIN D PERC(C  VASSAR CLEMENTS  FDL (C
JOHN BURNS          G    (C   ABBY NEWTON CELLO     (C   VIEN BLOOM      WIND(C   TED BOGAN        G  (C
HOWARD ARMSTRONG    FDL  (C   BONNIE KOLAC     V    (C   SAUL BROUDY     HCA (C   JACK THE BEAR    TPT (C
CARL MARTIN         MAND V(C
```
GOOSE CREEK SYMPHONY

```
RITCHIE HART        V G  (A        (A) GOOSE CREEK SYMPHONY               19   CAPITOL US M444
PAUL HOWARD         G V  (A        (B) WORDS OF EARNEST                   1972 CAPITOL                 EST 11044
BOB HENKE           G K V(A        (C) WELCOME TO GOOSE CREEK             1973 CAPITOL US 690
ELLIS SCHWEID       FDL  (         (D) DO YOUR THING                      1974 CBS             US      32918
DENNIS KENMORE      D    (
DAVE BIRKETT        B    (A   MIKE McFADDEN    G    (A   CHARLES GEARHART G   (B   PAUL SPRADLIN    G  (B
JIM TOLLES          VLN  (B   FRED             VLN  (B   FROGGY          B   (B   FLASH            D  (B
WILLARD             G    (B   RANDALL          SAX  (B   HAROLD          SAX (B   PAT MOORE        B  (
CHRIS MOSTERT       SAX  (
```
SAM GOPAL

```
SAM GOPAL           PERC (AB       (A) SAM GOPAL                          1969 STABLE          UK      SLE 8001
IAN 'LEMMY'WILLIS   G V  (AB       (B) ESCALATOR
ROGER DIELIA        G    (AB
PHIL DUKE           B    (AB  SUNNY LESLIE     V    (A   SUE GLOVER       V (A
```
GORDIAN KNOT

```
PAT KINCADE         G V  (A        (A) TONES                              1968 VERVE           US      V6 5062
DULIN COMMODORE LANCASTER D(A
J D LOBUE           K V  (A   LELAND RUSSELL   B V(A    JAMES WEATHERLY  G V (A
```
JIM GORDON

```
JIM GORDON              (A        (A) PLAYS HEAVY                         19   CREAM           US      9007
```
ROBERT GORDON

```
ROBERT GORDON       V    (ALL      (A) ROBERT GORDON & LINK WRAY          1977 PRIVATE STOCK PVLP1027+PS  2030
JORDANAIRES         V    (B        (A) ROBERT GORDON & LINK WRAY          19   RCA RI 3296
LINK WRAY           G    (AB       (B) FRESH FISH SPECIAL                 1978 PRIVATE STOCK PVLP1038+ 7008
CHRIS SPEDDING      G    (C        (B) FRESH FISH SPECIAL                 19   RCA RI 3299
HOWIE WYETH         D    (ABC      (C) ROCK BILLY BOOGIE                  1979 RCA                     APLI 3294
ROB STONER          B PNO(ABC      (D) LIVE AT DJ PARADISE BOSTON         197  RCA                     3411
CHARLIE MESSING     G    (A        (E) BAD BOY                            1980 RCA                     3523
RICHARD GOTTEHRER   PNO  (A        (G) ARE YOU GONNA BE THE ONE           1980 RCA       UK 5033  us   3773
BILLY CROSS         G    (AB
TERRY VERNON        V    (C   PAUL EVANS       V    (C   MARTIN NELSON   V   (C   ROBIN GREAN      V  (C
```
GORILLAS

```
ALAN BUTLER         B    (A        (A) MESSAGE TO THE WORLD               1978 RAW             UK      RWLP 103
GARY ANDERSON       D    (A
JESSE HECTOR        G V  (A
```
GOSPEL OAK

```
JOHN RAPP           G    (A        (A) GOSPEL OAK                         1970 UNI                     UNLS 113
BOB DEGATE          G V  (A
KERRY GAINES        D    (A   MATTHEW KELLY  HCA G(A   GORDON HUNTLEY  STEEL (A
```

GRAHAM GOULDMAN
```
   GRAHAM GOULDMAN   G V B G(AB    (A) GRAHAM GOULDMAN THING          1978  RCA            LSP3954
   RICK FENN          G V  (B      (B) ANIMALYMPICS                  1980  MERCURY UK 9109630 A&M US4810
   DUNCAN MACKAY      K   (B
   PAUL BURGESS       D   (B   STUART TOSH      V   (B  MIKE TIMONY   ACC (B
```
GOTHAM
```
                               GOTHAM                              1978 DREAM          US     3501
```
BARRY GOUDREAU
```
   BARRY GOUDREAU     G V (A       (A) BARRY GOUDREAU               1980 PORTAIT US 36542 UK   84449
   JESSE ERLICH       CELLO(A
   JOY LYLE           VLN (A   SID SHARP     VLN (A  DAVID SCHWARTZ  VLA (A
```
GOTHIC HORIZON
```
   ANDY DESMOND       V G B(AB      (A) THE JASON LODGE POETRY BOOK  1979 ARGO
   RICHARD GARRETT    V   (AB       (B) TOMORROW IS ANOTHER DAY      1972 ARGO          UK  ZDA 150
```
MICK GRABHAM
```
   MICK GRABHAM       G V (A        (A) MICK THE LAD                 1972  U A    UK     UAS 29341
   NIGEL OLSSON       D   (A
   MIKE STOREY        PNO (A   DICK PARRY      SAX (A  CALEB QUAYE   G  (A
```
GRACIOUS
```
   PAUL DAVIS         G V (A        (A) GRACIOUS!                   1970 VERTIGO UK 6360 002 CAPITOL US 602
   MARTIN KITCAT      K   (A        (B) THIS IS                     1972 PHILIPS UK 6382 004
   ALAN COWDEROY      G V (A
   TIM WHEATLEY       B   (A   ROBERT LIPSON    D   (A
```
GRADUATE
```
   CURT SMITH         B V (A        (A) ACTING MY AGE               1980   PRECISION      UK PART 001
   STEVE BUCK         K FLT(A
   ANDY MARSDEN       D   (A   ROLAND ORZABAL    G V (A   JOHN BAKER  G V (A
```
GRAFFITI
```
   GEORGE STRUNZ      G   (A        (A) GRAFFITI                    1968  ABC       US   ABCS 663
   JOHN ST JOHN       G   (A
   RICHIE BLAKIN      D   (A   STEVE BENDEROTH   K B (A  TONY TAYLOR  V  (A
```
GRACE
```
                                    (A) GRACE                       1981 MCA       UK     MCF 3102
```
DAVEY GRAHAM
```
   DAVEY GRAHAM       G V  (ALL     (A) GUITAR PLAYER               1963 GOLDEN GUINEA  UK  GGL 0224
   WITH                             (B) FOLK ROOTS NEW ROUTES       1964 DECCA UK LK4652 RI RIGHTEOUS001
   SHIRLEY COLLINS    BANJO(B       (C) FOLK BLUES & BEYOND         1965 DECCA       UK   LK  4649
   EDDIE TRIPP        B   (G        (D) MIDNIGHT MAN                1966 DECCA       UK   LK  4780
   TONY KINSEY        D   (G        (E) LARGE AS LIFE & TWICE AS NATURAL 1968 DECCA  UK   SKL 4969
   KESHAU SATHE       TABLA(G       (F) HAT                         1969 DECCA       UK   SKL 5011
                                    (G) GODINGTON BOUNDARY          1970 PRESIDENT        PTLS 1039
                                    (H) 3/4 AD                      19   TOPIC       UK   TOP  70
                                    (I) HOLLY KALEIDOSCOPE          1970 DECCA       UK   SKL 5056
                                    (J) COMPLETE GUITARIST          1978 KICKING MULE UK  SNKF 138
                                    (K) DANCE FOR TWO PEOPLE        1979 KICKING MULE UK  SNKF 158
```
ERNIE GRAHAM
```
   ERNIE GRAHAM       G V  (A       (A) ERNIE GRAHAM               1971  LIBERTY     UK   LBS 83485
   BOB ANDREWS        G V K(A
   C CUNNINGHAM       VLN (A   J EICHLER        V   (A  IAN GOMM    G V (A  NICK LOWE  B V (A
   MALCOLM MORLEY     D V (A   BILLY RANKIN     D   (A  BRINSLEY SCHWARZ G (A  RICHARD TREECE G (A
   DAVE CHARLES       D V (A   KEN WHALEY       B   (A
```
LARRY GRAHAM
```
   LARRY GRAHAM B D G K V (ALL      (A) STAR WALK                  1979  WB US    3322
   ERIC DANIELS       K V  (B       (B) ONE IN A MILLION           1980  WB US    3447    NL 56843
   WILTON RABB        G V  (B       (C) JUST BE MY LADY            1981  WB               UK 56909
   TINA GRAHAM        V    (B
```
TOMMY GRAHAM
```
   TOMMY GRAHAM  G SITAR (A         (A) PLANET EARTH               1972  CAPITOL         EAST21956
   SKIP BECKWITH      B    (A
   JOSH COLLINS       D    (A   RON BULLY        D   (A  EUGENE AMARO  FLT (A  MIKE LEWIS PNO (A
   BILLY SPEER        PNO  (A   BUDDY CAGE    STEEL  (A  KATHY MOSES   FLT (A  MILES WILKINSON (A
   JENNY BABOOLA      TAMB (A   BRIAN AHERN      G   (A
```
GRAHAM CENTRAL STATION
```
   LARRY GRAHAM       V B G (ALL    (A) GRAHAM CENTRAL STATION     1974  WB  UK K 46286    US   2763
   PATRYCE BANKS      D V  (ABD     (B) RELEASE YOURSELF           1974  WB  UK K 56062    US   2814
   HERSHALL KENNEDY   WIND (ABDE    (C) AINT NO BOUT ADOUT IT      1975  WB  UK K 56147    US   2875
   WILLIE SPARKS      D   (AB       (D) MIRROR                     1976  WB  UK K 56235    US   2937
   DAVID VEGA         G   (ABDE     (E) NOW DO U WANNA DANCE       1977  WB  UK K 56359    US   3041
   ROBERT SAM         K V  (ABDE    (F) MY RADIO SURE SOUNDS GOOD  1978  WB               US   3175
   MILT HOLLAND       PERC (A
   LENNY WILLIAMS     V    (A   FREDDIE STONE    G   (A  GAYLORD BIRCH   D  (DE  GAIL MULDROW   G V (E
   GREG ADAMS         HRNS (D   EMILIO CASTILLO  HRNS (D  MICK GILLETTE  HRNS (D  STEVE KUPKA    HRNS(D
   LENNY PICKETT      HRNS (D
```
BILLY GRAMMER
```
   BILLY GRAMMER      G V (A        (A) TRAVELLIN' ON              1959 MONUMENT    US     4000
```
GRAND FUNK RAILROAD
```
   MARK FARNER K G V HCA(ALL        (A) ON TIME                    1969  CAPITOL  EURO 80249 EST 307
   MEL SCHACHER       V B(A>M       (B) GRAND FUNK                 1970  CAPITOL  EURO 80357 EST  406
   DON BREWER         D V  (ALL      (C) CLOSER TO HOME            1970  CAPITOL  EURO 80456 EST  471
   CRAIG FROST        K V  (LK       (D) LIVE                      1971  CAPITOL UK ESTDW1/2 EST  633
   TODD RUNDGREN      G    (K        (E) SURVIVAL                  1971  CAPITOL  EURO 80783 ESW  764
   FRANK ZAPPA        G    (P        (F) E PLURIBUS FUNK           1972  CAPITOL            EAS  853
   DENNIS BELLINGER   V B  (R        (G) MARK,DON & MEL  1969 71(COMP) 1972 CAPITOL UK ESTSP10   11042
   DOUG KERSHAW       FDL  (H        (H) PHOENIX                   1973  CAPITOL            11099
                                     (J) WE'RE JUST AN AMERICAN BAND 1973 CAPITOL EURO 81469   11207
                                     (K) SHININ' ON               1974  CAPITOL            11278
                                     (L) MASTERS OF ROCK (COMP)   1975  EMI    054 81479 EMI  81580
                                     (M) ALL THE GIRLS IN THE WORL BEWARE 1975 CAPITOL      11356
```
             (CONTINUED)

GRAND FUNK RAILROAD   (CONTINUED)
                                          (N) CAUGHT IN THE ACT (DBL)   1975   CAPITOL UK ESTSP 15   11445
                                          (O) BORN TO DIE   1976   CAPITOL EURO 82107   11482
                                          (P) GOOD SINGING, GOOD PLAYING   1976   EMI   UK 1503 MCA US 2216
                                          (Q) HITS   (COMP)   1977   CAPITOL US 12010   11579
                                          (R) GRAND FUNK LIVES   1981   WEA   UK 99191

GRAND HOTEL
  COL CAMPSIE   V   (A   (A) DO NOT DISTURB   1979   CBS   UK 83134
  IVAN PENFOLD   G K V(A
  ROB GREEN   G V (A   MEL COLLINS   SAX (A   GEORGE McFARLANE   B K V(A   GRAHAM BROAD   D PERC(A
  DANNY McINTOSH   G   (A   NICKY GRAHAM STRINGS (A
GRAND PRIX
  PHIL LANZON   K V (AB   (A) GRAND PRIX   1980 RCA   UK PL 25321
  MICHAEL O'DONAGHUE G V (AB   (B) THERE FOR NONE TO SEE   1982 RCA   UK RCALP6027
  RALPH HOOD   B V (AB   ANDY BEIRNE D PERC(AB   BERNIE SHAW   V (A   ROBIN McAULEY   V (B
GRANNY'S INTENTION
  PAT NASH   D   (A   (A) HONEST INJUN   1970   DERAM   UK   SML 1060
  PETE CUMMINGS B FLT   (A
  JOHN RYAN   K   (A   JOHNNY DUHAN V   (A   JOHNNY HOCKEDY   G MAND(A
GRANATI BROTHERS
  BERNIE GRANATI   K V (A   (A) G FORCE   1979 A&M   US   4748
  RICKY GRANATI   D V (A
  JOEY GRANATI   K B V(A   DAVID GRANATI   G B V(A   TONY LEE BONOMO   D V (A
GRANFALLOON
                                          (A) LASER PACE   197   TAKOMA   US   9021
GRANDMOTHERS
  JIMMY CARL BLACK V   (ALL   (A)ANTHOLOGY OF PREVIOUSLY UNRELEASED MATERIAL 1980 RHINO US 302 LINE GER 5101
  DON PRESTON   K   (ALL   (B)OFFICIAL GRANDMOTHERS FAN CLUB TALK ALBUM   1981 PANDA 001
  ELLIOT INGBER   G   (ALL   (C)LOOKING UP GRANNY'S DRESS   1982 RHINO US 804 LINE GER 5186
  BUNK GARDNER   WIND (ALL
  BUZZ GARDNER   HRNS (ALL   JAMES SHERWOOD   SAX (ALL RAY COLLINS   V (C   TOM FOWLER   B VLN (C
  CHRIS PARLATA   D   (A   TJAY CONTRELLI WIND (AC JOHN BALKIN   (A   IRA INGBER PERC   (AC
  RAW MILK   D   (A   CHR'STY RUNDQUIST SYN (A ANDY CAHAN   D (AC DENNY WALLEY   G (A
  TOM LEAVEY   B   (AC EMIL RICHARDS PERC (A ERIC LINDERMAN   PNO (A DAVE PARLATA   G B (A
  JOHNNY DYRE   HARP (A   KEITH OLSEN   D (A MEATBALL   D (A   RICHIE HAYWARD D (A
  SANDY REINER   D   (A   PHIL DAVIS   SYN (A WALT FOWLER   TPT K V(C LARRY TAYLOR B (A
  LIL' JOHNNY   G   (A   PAUL HUFF   (C DON K MATIC   TROM (C   JOHN LASONIO   B (C
  DAVID TRENT   D PERC(C DANNY NEWMARK   K (C SID THE KID   SAX (C   DUSTY WAKEMAN   B (C
  STEELFINGER   G   (C   TOM BROWN   G (C FRANK SARKIN   SAX (C   FRANK ZAPPA   D (C
EDDIE GRANT
  EDDIE GRANT   (ALL   (A) WALKING ON SUNSHINE   1979 ICE UK 4   EPIC US 36244
                                     (B) LOVE IN EXILE   1980 ICE UK 19   EPIC US 36522
                                     (C) CANT GET ENOUGH   1981 ICE UK 21
GRAPEFRUIT
  GEOFF SWETTENHAM D   (AB   (A) DEEP WATER   1969   RCA US LSP4215   ST 8030
  GEORGE ALEXANDER B   (AB   (B) AROUND GRAPEFRUIT   1969   DUNHILL   US   50050
  JOHN PERRY   G   (AB   (B) AROUND GRAPEFRUIT   1969   STATESIDE   UK   SSL 5008
  PETE SWETTENHAM   G   (B
  BOB HALE   (MICK FOWLER   (
GRASS ROOTS
  JOEL LARSON   D   (J   (A) GRASS ROOTS   19   HAVEN   US   9204
  BONES HOWE   PERC (B   (B) WHERE WERE YOU WHEN I NEEDED YOU 19   DUNHILL   US   50011
  WARREN ENTNER   G   (ABCDEFGHI (C) LETS LIVE FOR TODAY   19   DUNHILL   US   50020
  ROB GRILL   V   (ABCDEFGHI (D) FEELINGS   19   DUNHILL   US   50027
  VIRGIL WEBER   (J   (E) GOLDEN GRASS   1969 DUNHILL   US   50047
  REED KAILING   (J   (F) LOVIN' THING   1969 DUNHILL   US   50052
  ERIK MICHAEL COONCE D (ABCDEFGH (G) LEAVING IT BEHIND   1969 DUNHILL   US   50067
  CREED BRATTON   G   (ABCDEF   (G) LEAVING IT BEHIND   1969 STATESIDE   UK   SSL 5012
  DENNIS PROVISOR   V   ((H) MORE GOLDEN GRASS   1970 DUNHILL   US   50087
  TERRY FURLONG   G   ((I) 16 GREATEST HITS   1971 DUNHILL   US   50107
  LARRY KNECHTEL   K   (B   (J) MOVE ALONG   1972 DUNHILL   US   50112
  JOE OSBORNE   G   (B   (K) A LOT OF MILEAGE   197   DUNHILL   US   50137
  BOBBY RAY   G   (B
  P F SLOAN   G   (B
GRATEFUL DEAD
  JERRY GARCIA   G V(All   (A) GRATEFUL DEAD   1967 WB   US 1689
  ROD'PIGPEN'McKERNAN K V(ABCDEFGHI (B) ANTHEM FOR THE SUN   1968 WB   US 1749   UK K 46021
                                    (AB) GRATEFUL/ANTHEM   1976 WB   GER 66040
  BOB WEIR   G   (ALL   (C) AOXOMOXOA   1969 WB   US 1790   UK K 46027
  PHIL LESH   B V   (ALL   (D) LIVE/DEAD(DBL)   1970 WB   US 1830   UK K 66002
  MICKEY HART   D   (BCDFPRTUVW (E) WORKINGMANS DEAD   1970 WB   US 1869   UK K 46049
  BILL KREUTZMANN D (ALL   (F) AMERICAN BEAUTY   1971 WB   US 1893   UK K 46074
                                    (F) AMERICAN BEAUTY   1980 MOBILE US 014
  TOM CONSTANTEN   K (CD   (G) GRATEFUL DEAD LIVE(DBL) 1971 WB   US 1935   UK K 66009
  ROBERT HUNTER   (EFGHPT   (H) EUROPE 72   (TRIPLE) 1972 WB   US 3X2662 UK K 66019
  KEITH GODCHAUX   K (HPRTUV   (I) VINTAGE DEAD   1972 POLYDOR   UK 2310 172
  DONNA GODCHAUX   V (HPRTUV   (I) VINTAGE DEAD   197 SUNFLOWER   US SNF 5001
  DAVE NELSON   G (F   (J) HISTORY OF(BEARS CHOICE) 1973 WB   US 2721   UK K 46246
  DAVE TORBERT   B (F   ( ) HISTORY OF   197 PRIDE US 0016
  DAVE GRISMAN   MAND(F   (L) HISTORIC DEAD   197 POLYDOR   UK 2310 171
  BRENT MYDLAND   (UVW   (IL) POP HISTORY   1972 POLYDOR 2612 019 GER 2335 059
  HOWARD WALES   K (F   ( ) HISTORIC DEAD   197 SUNFLOWER   US   5004
  NED LAGIN   K (F   (M) WAKE OF THE FLOOD   1973 G DEAD US 01   UK K 49301
  MERL SAUNDERS   K (G   (M) WAKE OF THE FLOOD   1976 UA   UK RI   29903
  JOHN DAWSON   G V ((N) FROM MARS HOTEL   1974 G DEAD US 102   UK K 59302
  BOB MATTHEWS   G V ((N) FROM MARS HOTEL   1976 UA   UK RI29904   GER 63826
  STEVEN SCHUSTER   (P   (MN) WAKE /MARS HOTEL   1977 UA   UK UDM103/4
  BILL ATWOOD   TPT (MN   (O) SKELETONS FROM THE CLOSET 1974 WB US 2764   UK K 56024
  VASSAR CLEMENTS VLN(MN   (P) BLUES FOR ALLAH   1975 G DEAD US 494   UK UAS 29895
  PAT OHARA   TROM (MN   (Q) STEAL YOUR FACE(DBL)   1976 G DEAD US 62   UK UAD60131/2
  JOE ELLIS   TPT (MN   (R) TERRAPIN STATION   1977 ARISTA US 7001   UK   1016

                                                            (CONTINUED)

(CONTINUED)   GRATEFUL DEAD

```
    MARTIN FIERRO   SAX (MN      (S) WHAT A LONG STRANGE TRIP(COMP)1978 WB     US  3091    UK     K 66073
    SARAH FULCHER   V   (MN      (T) SHAKEDOWN STREET              1978 ARISTA US 4198 UK ARTY159 GER  62101
    MATTHEW KELLY   HCA (MNT     (U) GO TO HEAVEN                  1980 ARISTA US 9508    UK         1115
    DOUG SAHM       G(MN         (V) RECKONING                     1981 ARISTA US 8604 UK DARTY GER 301 621
    BENNY VELARDES  PERC(MN      (W) DEAD SET LIVE                 1981 ARISTA        UK ARTY 11 GER 301738
    JORDAN AMARANTHA PERC (T
    FRANK MORIN     SAX (MN
```

G84A   NICK GRAVENITES   G84A

```
    NICK GRAVENITES G V  (ALL      (A) MY LABORS                   1969 CBS     US 9899    UK 63818
    PETE SEARS      B K  (C        (B) JUNKYARD IN MALIBU          1980 LINE            GERM 6 24264
    JOEY COVINGTON  D    (C        (C) BLUE STAR                   1980 LINE            GERM LLP 5039
    HUEY LOUIS      HCA  (C        (D) STEEL YARD BLUES(SOUNDTRACK)1973 LIBERTY US 352662
    MIKE BLOOMFIELD G    (AD
    GREG DOUGLAS    G    (C   WILLY TROST    G    (C   ROGER TROY     B V  (C   JOHN CIPOLLINA  G   (C
    MARLA HUNT      V    (C   DIANE HURST    V    (C   JOB JONES      D    (A   MARK NAFTALIN   PNO (A
    DINO ANDINO     CONGA(C   IRA KAMIN      ORG       (A   JOHN KAHN      B    (AD  JOHN WILMETH    TPT (A
    NOEL JENKINS    SAX  (A   GERALD OSHITA  SAX  (A   MERL SAUNDERS  ORG  (D   PAUL BUTTERFIELD HCA(D
    MARIA MULDAUR   V    (D
```

G84B   GRAUZONE   G84B

```
    MARTIN EICHER   G B V(A      (A) GRAUZONE                      1981 OFF COURSE      GER    46 500
    MARCO REPETTO   D G V(A
    STEPHAN EICHER  G V B K(A   ERIENNE CONOD  PNO (A
```

G85   GRAVY TRAIN   G85

```
    NORMAN BARRETT  V G  (ABCD     (A) GRAVY TRAIN                 1970 VERTIGO UK 6360 023
    BARRY DAVENPORT D    (AB       (B) BALLAD OF A PEACEFUL MAN    1971 VERTIGO UK 6360 051
    J D HUGHES WIND K V  (ABCD     (C) SECOND BIRTH               1973 DAWN    UK DNLS 3046
    LES WILLIAMS    B V  (ABCD     (D) STAIRCASE TO THE DAY       1974 DAWN    UK DNLH   1
    GEORGE LYNON    G    (D
    PETE SOLLEY     SYN  (D   MARY ZINOVIEFF   SYN VLN(D
```

G85A   DOBIE GRAY   G85A

```
    DOBIE GRAY      V    (ALL      (A) DRIFT AWAY                  1973 DECCA      US   7 5397
    DAVID BRIGGS    K    (ABC      (B) LOVING ARMS                 1973 MCA        US     371
    MIKE LEECH      B    (ABC      (C) HEY DIXIE                   1974 MCA        US     449
    KENNY MALONE    D    (ABC      (D) NEW RAY OF SUNSHINE         197  CAPRICORN  US    0163
    TROY SEALS      G    (ABC      (E) MIDNIGHT DIAMOND            1978 INFINITY   US    9001
    REGGIE YOUNG    G BAN(ABC      (F) DOBIE GRAY                  1978 INFINITY   US    9016
    WELDON MYRICK   STEEL(A
    BUDDY SPICHER   FDL  (AB  MENTOR WILLIAMS  G    (A   CHARLIE McCOY     HCA  (B   TOMMY COGBILL    B   (C
    LONNIE MACK     G    (C   NORBERT PUTNAM   B    (C   HERSHEL WIGINTON  B V  (C   HARVEY THOMPSON  HRNS(C
    BEN CAULEY      HRNS (C   CHARLES ROSE     HRNS (C   HARRISON CALLOWAY HRNS (C   RONNIE EADES     HRNS(C
    RANDY McCORMICK K    (EF  ROGER CLARK      D    (EF  LARRY BYROM       G    (EF  KEN BELL    G    (EF
    BOB WRAY        B    (EF  MICKEY BUCKINS   PERC (E   LENNY LEBLANC     V    (EF  EDDIE STRUZICK   V   (EF
    THOM FLORA      V    (E   STEVE NATHAN     K    (EF  OWEN HALE         D    (F   JIMMY ENGLISH    G   (F
    WALT ALDRIDGE   G    (F   RALPH EZELL      B    (F   DANNY KIRSCH      SAX  (F   CHUCK GODWIN     FLT (F
    CHALMERS DAVIS  K    (F   MARK GRAY        K V  (F   DONNA RHODES      V    (F   CHARLIE CHALMERS V   (F
    SANDRA RHODES   V    (F
```

G86   GREASE BAND   G86

```
    HENRY McCULLOUGH G   (AB       (A) THE GREASE BAND            1971 HARVEST UK SHVL790 SHELTER US 8904
    MICK WEAVER     K    (B        (A) THE GREASE BAND            1981 LINE RI GER      LLP 5005
    ALAN SPENNER    B    (AB       (B) AMAZING GREASE             1975 GOODEAR  UK 2902 RI CHARLY 30166
    BRUCE ROWLAND   D    (AB       (B) AMAZING GREASE             1981 LINE RI GER      LLP 5008
    NEIL HUBBARD    K    (AB
    CHRIS STAINTON  K    (B   TERRY STANNARD   D    (B   MEL COLLINS    SAX (B   TOMMY EYRE    K   (
    JOHN WEATHERS   D    (
```

G86A   GREAT BEAR   G86A

```
                                   (A) GREAT BEAR                 1971 WAND       UK     WNS8
                                   (A) GREAT BEAR                 197  SCEPTER    US SPS 585
```

G86B   GREAT BUILDINGS   G86B

```
    DANNY WILDE     G V K(A        (A) APART FROM THE CROWD       1981 CBS        US     36920
    RICHARD SANFORD D PERC(A
    PHILLIP SOLEM   G V  (A   IAN AINSWORTH    B K V(A
```

G87   GREAT JONES   G87

```
    BILLY CADIEUX   G    (A        (A) ALL BOWED DOWN            197  TONSIL     US   T 4002
    GARY KOLLARUS   D    (A
    DAVID TOLMIE    B    (A   JEFF GUTCHEON    K    (A   MERRY CLAYTON    V   (A   VANETTA FIELDS   V   (A
    CLYDIE KING     V    (A
```

G87A   GREAT METROLPOLITAN STEAM BAND   G87A

```
                                   (A) GREAT METROPOLITAN STEAM BAND 1969 MCA  UK MUPS 403 + MAPS 2162
```

G88   GREAT SOCIETY   G88

```
    GRACE SLICK     V    (AB       (A) GREAT SOCIETY             196  CBS US 30459 UK      63476
    PETER VANDERGELD B   (B        (A) GREAT SOCIETY             197  EMBASSY      UK      31800
    JERRY SLICK     D    (B        (B) CONSPICUOUS ONLY IN ITS ABSENCE 1968 CBS US  9624
    DARBY SLICK     G    (B        (C) HOW IT WAS                1968 CBS US  9702          30461
    DAVID MINOR     G    (B        (D) SOMEBODY TO LOVE          19   HARMONY US             30391
                                   (ABC) COLLECTORS ITEM         19   CBS     US 30459
```

G89   GREATEST SHOW ON EARTH   G89

```
    COLIN HORTON JENNINGS V G D(AB (A) HORIZONS                  1970 HARVEST UK SHVL769 GER  04310
    GARTH WATT ROY   VG  (AB       (B) THE GOING'S EASY          1970 HARVEST UK SHVL783 GER  04570
    NORMAN WATT ROY  V B (AB       (AB) GREATEST SHOW ON EARTH   1975 HARVEST      UK  SHSM 2004
    MIKE DEACON     K    (AB
    RON PRUDENCE    CONGA D(AB DICK HANSON  HRNS    (AB TEX PHILPOTTS   SAX  (   IAN AITCHISON   SAX (
```

G90   JOHN GREAVES & PETER BLEGVAD   G90

```
    JOHN GREAVES    B V K PERC(A   (A) KEW RHONE                 1977 VIRGIN UK V2082 US    34758
    PETER BLEGVAD   V G SAX(A
    LISA HERMAN     V    (A   ANDREW CYRILLE   D PERC(A  MIKE MANTLER   HRNS (A CARLA BLEY      V SAX(A
    MICHAEL LEVINE  VLN V(A   VITO RENDACE WIND     (A   APRIL LANG     V    (A DANA JOHNSON    V   (A
    BORIS KINBERG   CLAVE (A
```

RICK GRECH

RICK GRECH	B VLN V(A		(A) THE LAST FIVE YEARS(COMP)	1973 RSO	US	876		UK	2394 111		

GREEN

GARY CASEBEER K HRNS V(A (A) GREEN 1969 ATCO UK 33282
RICHARD GARDZINA K V HRNS(A
WILSON FISHER V HCA(A JOHN MARTIN K V (A JAMES NEEL V K WIND (A BOBBY BLOOD HRNS (A

AL GREEN

AL GREEN	V (ALL	(A) BACK UP TRAIN	19	HOT LINE	US	1500			
WAYNE JACKSON	TPT (H	(B) GREEN IS BLUES	1970	HI	US	32055			
ANDREW LOVE	SAX (H	(C) GETS NEXT TO YOU	1971	HI	US	32062	LONDON UK	8424	
ED LOGAN	SAX (H	(D) LETS STAY TOGETHER	1972	HI	US	32070	LONDON UK	8430	
JAMES MITCHELL	SAX (H	(E) I'M STILL IN LOVE WITH YOU	1972	HI	US	32074	LONDON UK	8443	
JACK HALE	TROM (H	(F) CALL ME	1973	HI	US	32077	LONDON UK	8457	
HOWARD GRIMES	D PERC(H	(G) LIVING FOR YOU	1974	HI	US	32082	LONDON UK	8464	
LEROY HODGES	B (H	(H) EXPLORES YOUR MIND	1974	HI	US	32087	LONDON UK	8479	
CHARLES HODGES	K (H	(I) AL GREEN IS LOVE	1975	HI	US	32092	LONDON UK	8488	
TEENIE HODGES	G (H	(J) FULL OF FIRE	1976	HI	US	32097	LONDON UK	8493	
ARCHIE TURNER	PNO (H	(K) HAVE A GOOD TIME	1976	HI	US		LONDON UK	8505	
MICHAEL ALLEN	PNO (H	(L) BELLE ALBUM	1977	HI	US	6004	CREAM UK	6004	
MEMPHIS STRINGS	(H	(M) TRUTH & TIME	1978	HI	US	6009			
REUBEN FAIRFAX	B (L	(N) CREAM OF	1980	CREAM	US	HLP101			
JAMES BASS	G (L	( )=AL GREEN	19	BELL	US	6076			
MARGARET FOXWORTH	V (L	( ) GREATEST HITS	1981	TELDEC	GER	622217			
LINDA JONES	V (L	( ) HITS VOL 2	1979	HI	US	32105			
HARVEY JONES	V (L	( ) TOKYO LIVE	1981	HI			UK	5001	
LEON THOMAS	K (L	( ) HIGHWAY TO HEAVEN	1981	MYRRH	US	6661			
DARRYL NEELY	HRNS (L								
JOHNNY BROLIN	K (L	FRED JORDAN TPT K (L	JOHN TONEY		D	(L	RON ECHOLS	SAX (L	
ROB PAYNE	PERC (L	ARDIS HARDIN D	(L	BUDDY JARRETT	SAX	(L			

BUNKY GREEN

BUNKY GREEN	(ALL	(A) THE LATINIZATION OF..	19	CADET	US	LP 780	
		(B) TESTIFYIN' TIME	19	CADET	US	LP 753	
		(C) PLAYING FOR KEEPS	19	CADET	US	LP 766	

DANNY GREEN

DANNY GREEN	G V (A	(A) NIGHT DOG	1978 ABC UK ABCL5259 MCA US 1085				
DON BARRETT	B (A						
GINO ZIMMERMAN	G (A	CARSON WHITSETT	K (A	KAREN TAYLOR	V (A	JOE HARDY	V (A
JAMES STROUD	D PERC(A	ED FORESMAN	B V (A	WALTER POLK	D (A	JUDY RODMAN	V (A
JERRY McKINNEY	HRNS (A	DR JOHN	PNO (A	WILLIAM C BROWN	V (A	DUNCAN SISTERS	V (A
JOE MULHERIN	HRNS (A	MIKE PLUNKETT	K (A				

IAN GREEN

IAN GREEN (A (A) REVELATION 1970 CBS UK 63840
ROSSETTA HIGHTOWER V (A
MADELINE BELL V (A

JACK GREEN

JACK GREEN	G B V(AB	(A) HUMANESQUE	1980 RCA RCAALP 5004 APL1 3639				
RICHIE BLACKMORE	G (A	(B) REVERSE LOGIC	1981 RCA AFLI 4122				
BRIAN CHATTON	K (AB						
MEL COLLINS	SAX (AB	ANDY DALBY	G (AB	IAN ELLIS	B (AB	SIMON FOX D (B	
MAC POOLE	D (A	PETE TOLSON	G (AB	GEORGE SERGHI	(B		

PETER GREEN

PETER GREEN	G V (ALL	(A) THE END OF THE GAME	1970 REPRISE UK RSLP9006+RI K44106	
ZOOT MONEY	PNO (A	(A) THE END OF THE GAME	1970 REPRISE US 6434	
GODFREY MACLEAN	D (A	(B) IN THE SKIES	1979 PVK UK 101 LOTUS EURO 4063	
JEFF DALY	SAX (D	(B) IN THE SKIES	1979 CREOLE GER 6 23793	
NICK BUCK	K (A	(C) LITTLE DREAMER	1980 PVK UK 102 LOTUS EURO 4090	
MO FOSTER	SAX (D	(C) LITTLE DREAMER	1980 CREOLE GER 6 24300	
ALEX DMOCHOWSKI	B (A	(D) WHATCHA DONNA DO?	1981 PVK UK PET 1 NL POLYDOR 2925119	
JOHN EDWARDS	B (CE	(E) BLUE GUITAR	1981 CREOLE CRX 5	
KUMA HARADA	B (BCE			
REG ISADORE	D (A	RON JOHNSON G (CDE	PAUL WESTWOOD B (CDE	DAVE WILKEY PNO (C E
SNOWY WHITE	G (BE	LENNOX LAINGTON D (CDE	PETER BARDENS K (BE	ROY SHIPSTON K (CDE
PETER VERNON KELL	PNO (CE	DAVE MATTACKS D (CDE	MORRIS PERT PERC (CE	CAROL INGRAM V (CE
PAM DOUGLAS	V (CE			

GREEN BULLFROG

RICHIE BLACKMORE	G (A	(A) GREEN BULLFROG	19 MCA MKPS 2021 RI 74 MCF 2689		
ALBERT LEE	G (A	(A) GREEN BULLFROG	19 ECY STREET 16 DECCA 75269		
ROGER GLOVER	B (A				
IAN PAICE	D (A	BIG JIM SULLIVAN G (A	CHAS HODGES	B (A	ROD ALEXANDER G (A
MATTHEW FISHER	K (A	TONY ASHTON K (A	EARL JORDON	V (A	

NORMAN GREENBAUM

NORMAN GREENBAUM	V G K (ALL	(A) SPIRIT IN THE SKY	1969	REPRISE US 6365	
DAN HICKS	PERC (B	(B) BACK HOME AGAIN	1972	REPRISE US 6422	
DAN PAIK	MAND (B	(C) PETALUMA	1973	REPRISE US 2084	
STEVE BUSFIELD	G (B				
LYNN ELDER	(B	RUSSEL DASHIELL G (BA	BILL DOUGLAS	B (B	DOUG KILLMER B (BA
NORMAN MAYELL	D. (BA	JOHN McFEE STEEL(B	BILL MEEKER	D (B	STOVAL SISTERS V (B
WILLIAM TRUCKAWAY	SYN (BA	ROBBIE ROBINSON G (A	CHUCK PETERSON	(A	DAN PADIRIS (A
JOHN COPPOLA	(A	BILL SABATINI (A			

JEANIE GREENE

JEANIE GREENE	K V (A	(A) MARY CALLED JEANNIE GREENE	1971 ELEKTRA	74103	
MARLIN GREENE	B (A				
ROGER HAWKINS	D (A	BARRY BECKETT K (A	WAYNE PERKINS	G SIT(A	LEO LEBLANC STEEL (A
CLAUDIA LENNEAR	V (A	MARY PEDERSON V (A	CHRIS ETHRIDGE	B (A	TIM SCHMIT V (A
DAVID HOOD	B (A	LARRY NICHOLSON G (A	JIMMY JOHNSON	G (A	

MARLIN GREENE

MARLIN GREENE	G V (A	(A) TIPTOE PAST THE DRAGON	1972 ELEKTRA	UK K 42111	
WAYNE PERKINS	G (A				
LARRY NICHOLSON	G (A	EDDIE HINTON G (A	ROGER HAWKINS	D (A	FRED PROUTY D (A
LOU MULLENIX	D (A	BARRY BECKETT K (A	CHUCK LEAVELL	K (A	JERRY MASTERS B (A
DAVID HOOD	B (A	LEO LE BLANC STEEL(A	JEANIE GREENE	PNO (A	CASEY KELLY G (A

MIKE GREENE

```
MIKE GREENE V K WIND  (AB        (A) PALE PALE MOON              1975 GENERAL REC              10013
RANDE POWELL      D    (AB        (B) MIDNIGHT MIRAGE            1976 MERCURY       US        SRM1 1100
DAVID MICHAEL          (AB
MIKE HOLBROOK     K    (AB  NEIL LARSEN    K    (A  CARLOS MARTINEZ  PERC (A   GURU VIR    PERC (A
DEAN BROTHERS     V    (A   SKIP LANE     STR (B  FARRELL MORRIS   PERC (B
```

GREENSLADE

```
DAVE GREENSLADE   K    (ABCD       (A) GREENSLADE               1973 WB UK K 46207+ PHILIPS 6325 500
TONY REEVES       B    (ABC        (B) BEDSIDE MANNERS ARE EXTRA 1973 WB UK K 46259+
DAVE LAWSON       K    (ABCD       (C) SPYGLASS GUEST           1974 WB UK K 56055+ MERCURY US  1015
ANDY McCULLOCH    D    (ABCD       (D) TIME & TIDE             1975 WB UK K 56126+ MERCURY US  1025
ANDY ROBERTS      G    (C          (D) TIME & TIDE             1975 VERTIGO EURO  6370 113
MARTIN BRILEY     G B  (D
DAVE CLEMPSON     G    (C   GRAHAME SMITH   VLN (C  MICK ROGERS    G V (   BARRY MORGAN   PERF (D
JILL MACKINTOSH   V    (D   DAVE MARKEE   B    (   ANN SIMMONS    V   (D   TREVERVA MALE CHOIR (D
JEREMY ENSOR EFFECTS   (C   GREG JACKMAN  EFFECTS(C
```

DAVE GREENSLADE

```
DAVE GREENSLADE   K    (AB         (A) CACTUS CHOIR            1976 WB          UK    K 5630&
TONY REEVES       B    (A          (B) PENTATEUCH OF THE COSMOGONY(DBL) 1979 EMI  UK  EMC3321/2
SIMON PHILLIPS    D    (A
JOHN PERRY        B    (A   STEVE GOULD  V  (A  BILL JACKMAN   WIND (A  MICK GRABHAM    G (A
JOHN LIGERTWOOD   PERC (B   PHIL COLLINS PERC (B
```

ELLIE GREENWICH

```
ELLIE GREENWICH   V    (A          (A) LET IT BE WRITTEN,LET IT BE SUNG 1973 MGM VC5091  2315 243
RICK MAROTTA      D    (A
STEVE GADD        D    (A   AL ROGERS    D    (A  RUSSELL GEORGE  B  (A  CHARLIE BROWN  G (A
VINNIE BELL       G    (A   ERIC WEISSBERG G  (A  SAL DITROIA    G  (A  JOHN ABBOTT    G (A
STEVE FLEDMAN     K    (A   ARTIE BUTLER K    (A  STEVE TUNANGER  PERC (A
```

MICK GREENWOOD

```
MICK GREENWOOD  V G K(ABC          (A) LIVING GAME            1971 MCA UK 8003+RI MCA 74 MCG 3520
JIMMY HELMS       V    (B          (A) LIVING GAME            1971 DECCA    US  75318
JERRY DONAHUE    G V   (AB         (B) TO FRIENDS            1972 MCA UK 2026+RI MCA UK MCF 8692
DORIS TROY        V    (B          (B) TO FRIENDS            1972 MCA      US  307
TONY COX        K V   (AB          (C) MIDNIGHT DREAMER      1974 WB UK            K56059
PAT DONALDSON     B    (A
GERRY CONWAY      D    (A   LYN DOBSON WIND SITAR(A  DAVE PEGG    B   (A  ANDY SMITH BANJO (A
CHRISTINE QUAILE  V    (A   DUDU PUKWANA   SAX (A  KARL JENKINS SAX (A  BUD PARKES TPT  (A
DEREK WADSWORTH   TROM (A   NED BALEN   PERC (A  BARRY DE SOUZA  D  (A  DAVE PEACOCK B V VLN (B
BARRY ST JOHN     V    (B
```

NICK GREENWOOD

```
NICK GREENWOOD         (A          (A) COLD CUTS             1972 KINGDOM    UK        KVLP 9002
```

GREEZY WHEELS

```
CLEVE HATTERSLEY  V G  (AB         (A) JUST LOVE DEM 'OL GREEZY WHEELS 1975 LONDON  US  PS 657
LISSA HATTERSLEY  G V  (AB         (B) RADIO RADIALS        1976 LONDON US 667 UK  SHU 8497
MARY EGAN         FDL  (AB
PAT PANKRATZ      G    (AB  TONY AIROLDI   G   (AB MIKE PUGH    B  (AB TONY LAIER D  (AB
MADRILLE WILSON   CONGA(AB  JIMMY DAY   STEEL (A  ALFRED ROBERTS  PERC (A  RILEY OSBORNE PERC(A
```

ZAINE GRIFF

```
ZAINE GRIFF       SYN  (A          (A) ASHES & DIAMONDS     1980 AUTOMATIC US 34834 UK K56834
ANDY DUNCAN       D    (A
STEVE BOLTON      G    (A   ANDY CLARK   K   (A  TONY VISCONTI B V PERC(A HANS ZIMMER  SYN (A
```

GRIFFIN

```
GRAHAM BELL       V    (1          (1) 1969
ALAN WHITE        D    (1
COLIN GIBSON      B    (1   PETE KIRTLEY   G   (1  KEN CRADDOCK   K   (1
```

JAMES GRIFFIN

```
JAMES GRIFFIN    G V   (A          (A) JAMES GRIFFIN        1978 POLYDOR    UK   2391 274
DAVID PAICH       K    (A          (B) EAGLE               197  POLYDOR    US      6018
DAVE BUDAMEYER    B    (A          ( ) BREAKING UP IS EASY  1974 POLYDOR    UK   2391 113
JIM GORDON        D    (A
JACK HALE        TROM  (A   DEAN PARKS   G   (A  JIM HORN      HRNS (A  LARRY KNECHTEL  B(A
MIKE BOTTS        D    (A   CAROL CARMICHAEL V (A  DAVID GATES  D  (A  JOE LAMANO     B (A
ED LOGAN          SAX  (A   BARRY BURTON   G   (A  ANDREW LOVE   SAX (A  JAMES MITCHELL SAX (A
WAYNE JACKSON    HRNS  (A
```

ROB GRILL

```
ROB GRILL         V    (A          (A) UPROOTED             1979 MERCURY 9111 055  US SRM1 3798
ROBBIE BUCHANAN   K    (A
STEVE HUNTER      G    (A   JOHN McVIE   B   (A  MICK FLEETWOOD  D  (A  MARK LEONARD   B (A
LINDSEY BUCKINGHAM G   (A   MIKE HUEY   D    (A  DENNIS PROVISOR K  (A  ANNIE McCLOONE V (A
DONNIE GERRARD    V    (A   BILL CHAMPLIN  V   (A  JAY GRUSKA   V  (A  CARL GRAVES    V (A
KATHY COLLIER     V    (A   BRIAN NAUGHTON G   (A
```

CAROLE GRIMES

```
CAROL GRIMES      V    (ALL        (A) FOOLS MEETING(WITH DELIVERY) 1970 B+C CAS 1023 PHILIPS GER 6369 004
STEVE MILLER      PNO  (A          (B) WARM BLOOD          1974 CAROLINE    UK  CA 2001
ROY BABBINGTON    B    (A          (C) CAROLE GRIMES       1976 DECCA      UK  SKLR5258
GARY TWIGG        B    (2          (C) CAROLE GRIMES       1979 CHARLY     UK  CR 30164
PHIL MILLER       G    (A          (1) MAY 1978 TOUR
PIP PYLE          D    (A          (2) 1980 F.A. RECORDING IN SWEDEN
LOL COXHILL       SAX  (A          (C) CAROLE GRIMES       1979 CHARLY              30164
TONY HICKS        D    (2
BOB WILSON        K    (B   RON CORNELIUS   G   (BC MAC GAYDEN   G   (B  KENNY BUTTREY  D (B
TOMMY COGBILL     B    (B   KARL HIMMEL   D   (B  GRAHAM BELL   HCA V(B  SAM MITCHELL   G (B
RABBIT BUNDRICK   K    (B   TOMMY EYRE   K   (B  ARCHIE LEGGET  V  (B  JESS RODEN     V (B
ROGER BALL        SAX  (B   MALCOLM DUNCAN SAX (B  HENRY LOWTHER  TPT (B  JOHN McKENZIE  B (1
NIGEL WATSON      D    (1   COLIN FLETCHER  G   (1  ANDY WINFIELD  G  (1  TINO TURVILLE  K (1
MICHAEL BRECKER   HRNS (C   MEMPHIS HRNS        (C  WESTETTES    V  (C  GINGER HOLLADAY V (C
MARY HOLLADAY     V    (C   BOB MANUEL   G   (C  BUDDY DAVIES  G  (C  HUGH McCRACKEN  G (C
NEIL HUBBARD      G    (C   DONALD DUNN   B   (C  JOE DAVIES   B  (C  WILLIE HALL    D (C
LLOYD PERRATA     D    (C   BOBBY EMMONS PNO (C  JAY SPELL    PNO (C  BOB CLAIRE HRNS PNO (C
FREDERICK KNIGHT       (C   OLLIE MALLARD K V (2  PETE KIRTLEY  G V (2
```

GRIMMS

NEIL INNES	G K V(ABC	(A) GRIMMS	1973	ISLAND UK HELP1 US ANTILLES 7012
ROGER McGOUGH	V (ABC	(B) ROCKING DUCK	1973	ISLAND	UK	ILPS 9248
JOHN GORMAN	V (ABC	(C) SLEEPERS	1976	D J M	UK	DJLPS 470
ANDY ROBERTS	G (BC					
DAVE RICHARDS	B V (BC JOHN MEGGINSON B V K(ABC OLLIE HALSALL		G V (B ZOOT MONEY K (AC
MIKE McGEAR	V (AB GERRY CONWAY D (B ADRIAN HENRI		V (A BRIAN PATTEN V(AB
TIMI DONALD	D (C MIKE GILES D (A			

GRINDERSWITCH

DRU LOMBAR	G V (ABCDE	(A) HONEST TO GOODNESS	1974	CAPRICORN	US	CP 0135
STEPHEN MILLER	K V (CDE	(B) MACON TRACKS	1975	CAPRICORN	US	CP 0150
LARRY HOWARD	G V (ABCD	(C) PULLIN' TOGETHER	1977	CAPRICORN UK2429 144 US CP 0173
JOE DAN PETTY	B V (ABCDE	(D) REDWING	1977	ATCO	US	36152
RICK BURNETT	D (ABCDE	(E) GRINDERSWITCH	1981			
PAUL HORNSBY	K (ABE					
CHARLIE DANIELS	FDL (B JIMMY HALL HCA (C JEROME JOSEPH		CONGA(C DICKIE BETTS G (A
JAIMOE JOHNANNY	CONGAS(A			

GRINGO

JOHN G PERRY	B V (A	(A) GRINGO	1971	MCA US 75314 UK MKPS 2017
CATHY SYNGE	V (					
SIMON BYRNE	D V (HENRY MARSH G K V(CASEY		V (A

GROBSCHNITT

JOACHIM H EHRIG(EROC)D V SYN(ALL		(A) GROBSCHNITT	1972	BRAIN		1008
AXEL HARLOS(FELIX) D PERC (A		(B) BALLERMANN	1974	BRIAN 2/1050 BRAIN 0021 050
STEFAN DANIELAK(WILDSCHWEIN) G V(ALL		(C) JUMBO ENGLISH LYRICS	1975	BRAIN		1076
BERNARD UHLEMANN(BAER) B FLR PERC(AB		(C) JUMBO GERMAN LYRICS	1976	BRAIN		1081
GERD KUHN (LUPO)	G V (ALL	(D) ROCKPOMMELS LAND	1977	BRAIN		0060 041
HERMANN QUETTING(QUECKSILBER)K PERC(A(E) SOLAR MUSIC LIVE			1978	BRAIN		0060 139
WOLFGANG JAEGER(PEPE) B (CDEFG (F) MERRY GO ROUND			1979	BRAIN		0060 224
VOLKER KAHRS(MIST) K V (BCDEFG (G) VOLLE MOLLE			1980	BRAIN		0060 291
MILLA KAPOLLKE	B (HJ	(H) ILLEGAL	1981	BRAIN		0060 510
TONY MOFF MOLLO	V (J	(J) RAZZIA	1982	BRAIN		0060 510

MAX GRONENTHAL

MAX GRONENTHAL	K V (AB	(A) WHISTLING IN THE DARK	1979	CHRYSALIS	UK/us CHR1231
BILLY MEEKER	D (A	(B) MAX	1980	CHRYSALIS	UK/US CHR1278
TREY THOMPSON	B (A					
TIMMY GOODMAN	G (A WILL McFARLANE G (A MICHAEL O'NEILL		G (A JAMES N HOWARD SYN (A
ROCKE GRACE	V (A KENNY LOGGINS V (A GERARD McMAHON		V (A MICHAEL McDONALD V (A
PATRICK SIMMONS	V (A RICKY FATAAR D PERC V G(B JERRY WILSON		B V (B RICK BEILKE G V (B
RENEE GEYER	V (B MIKE FINNIGAN V (B MARCY LEVY		V (B RUSTY ANDERSON G (B

GROOTNA

ANNA RIZZO	V (A	(A) GROOTNA	1972	CBS	US	31033
KELLY BRYAN	B (A					
SLIM CHANCE	G (A GREG DEWEY DA GREASE D (A RICHARD SUSMAN		PNO (A VIC SMITH G (A
JACK BONUS	SAX (A TERRY ADAMS STR (A CAROL GARNETT		STR (A MICHAEL LAFFERTY TROM(A
BENNET FRIEDMAN	CLAR (A					

WINSTON GROOVY

WINSTON GROOVY	(A	(A) PRESENTING WINSTON GROOVY	1974	TROJAN	UK	TRLS 88
		(B) WINSTON GROOVY	1978	LIGHTNING	UK	PIL 6

HENRY GROSS

HENRY GROSS	V G (ALL	(A) HENRY GROSS	1969	ABC	US	ABCX 747
JERRY McGEE	G (A	(B) PLUG ME INTO SOMETHING	1970	A&M	US 4502 UK AMLS 64502
CARL WILSON	V (B	(C) HENRY GROSS	1974	A&M	US 4426 UK AMLH 64416
RICKY FATAAR	V (B	(D) SHOW ME THE STAGE	197	LIFESONG	US 6016 RI	35002
CARLOS MUNOZ	V (B	(E) RELEASE	1976	LIFESONG	6002 RI	34995
TERRY CASHMAN	V (BE	(E) LOVE IS THE STUFF	197	LIFESONG		35280
TOMMY WEST	V (BCE					
STEVE GADD	D (CE WARREN NICHOLS B (BE PHIL AABERG		K (BE ALLEN SCHWARZBERG D (BE
ANN E SUTTON	V (BE MICHAEL KAMEN SYN (BC MARTY NELSON		V (BCE RICHIE SCHMIERER V (B
TASHA THOMAS	V (BCE DAVE SANBORN SAX (E ELLIE GREENWICH		V (E HUGH McCRACKEN G (E
GEORGE DEVENS	PERC (BE BUCKY PIZZARELLI G (E LARRY PACKER		FDL (E MIKE CORBETT V (E
STU WOODS	B (C ARNIE LAWRENCE FLT (C TYRONE BABBOZZA		V (C JOE MACHO B (C
ERIC WEISSBERG	VLN (C RONDO RAPPONE V (C ZELDA GROSS		V (C EUGENE BIANCO HARP (C
JIM KELTNER	D (A MAX BENNETT B (A SNEAKY PETE		STEEL(A SPOONER OLDHAM PNO (A
PAUL HARRIS	K (A WILTON FELDER B (A STRINGS		(A

HARALD GROSSKOPF

HARALD GROSSKOPF		(A) SYNTHESIST	1980	SKY	GER	043

STEFAN GROSSMAN

STEFAN GROSSMAN	G (ALL	(A) YAZOO BASIN BOOGIE	1970	TRANSATLANTIC	UK	TRA 217
WITH		(A) YAZOO BASIN BOOGIE	197	KICKING MULE	UK	SNKF 134
DANNY KALB	(U	(A) YAZOO BASIN BOOGIE	1975	KICKING MULE	US	102
PAUL ROWAN	HCA (Q	(B) RAGTIME COWBOY JEW	1970	TRANSATLANTIC	UK	TRA 223
EDDIE HOUSE	V (Q	(C) HOW TO PLAY BLUES	1971	TRANSATLANTIC	UK	XTRA 1113
JO ANN KELLY	V (Q	(C) HOW TO PLAY BLUES	197	KICKING MULE US 109 UK SNKF 150
PAT DONALDOSN	B (B	(C) HOW TO PLAY BLUES	1971	ELEKTRA	US 324
MIKE COOPER	G (KQ	(D) THOSE PLEASANT DAYS	1971	TRANSATLANTIC	UK	TRA 246
SAM MITCHELL	G (QT	(E) HOT DOGS	1972	TRANSATLANTIC	UK	TRA 257
DUCK BAKER	G (TU	(E) HOT DOGS	197	KICKING MULE	US	131
TONY ROBERTS	WIND (U	(F) GRAMERCY PARK SHEIK	1972	SONET	UK	SNTF 627
JOHN RENBOURN	G (RT	(G) ANN MOLLY'S MURRAY FARM	1973	SONET	UK	SNTF 640
RORY BLOCK	G (C	(H) LIVE	1973	TRANSATLANTIC	UK	TRA 264
GERRY DONAHUE	G (B	(I) MEMPHIS JELLYROLL	1973	TRANSATLANTIC	UK	TRA 274
TREVOR LUCAS	G (B	(I) MEMPHIS JELLYROLL	1973	KICKING MULE	US	118
LINDA PETER	V (B	(J) FINGER PICKIN'	1974	TRANSATLANTIC	UK	XTRA 1138
GERRY CONWAY	D (B	(K) BOTTLENECK SERENADE	1975	TRANSATLANTIC	UK	TRA 293
PETER BARDENS	K (B	(K) BOTTLENECK SERENADE	1975	KICKING MULE	US	121
BERNIE HOLLAND	G (B	(L) HOW TO PLAY RAGTIME GUITAR	1975	TRANSATLANTIC	UK	XTRA 1151
TODD LLOYD	V (B	(M) MY CREOLE BELLE	1976	TRANSATLANTIC	UK	TRA 326
RICHARD THOMPSON	G (D	(N) ACOUSTIC MUSIC FOR BODY & SOUL	1976	KICKING MULE	US	105
DANNY THOMPSON	B (D	(O) BOX SET (TRIPLE)	1977	TRANSATLANTIC	UK	GRS 6

(CONTINUED)

[241]

G110	(CONTINUED)		STEFAN GROSSMAN					G110
HARVEY BURNS	D	(D	(P) HOW TO PLAY RAGTIME	197	KICKING MULE	US		115
THE KAERNES	V	(D	(Q) COUNTRY BLUES GUITAR	1977	KICKING MULE	UK	SNKF	129
ALAN WHITE	D	(E	(Q) COUNTRY BLUES GUITAR	1977	KICKING MULE	US		145
BIG JIM SULLIVAN	G	(E	(R) AND JOHN RENBOURN	1978	KICKING MULE	UK	SNKF	139
HOWRD BUZZ FEITEN	G	(W	(R) AND JOHN RENBOURN	197	KICKING MULE	US		152
BARRY FINNERTY	G	(W	(S) HOW TO PLAY BLUES VOL2	197	KICKING MULE			148
ONAJE ALLEN GUMBS	K	(W	(T) UNDER THE VOLCANO	1979	KICKING MULE	UK	SNKF	161
MASABUNI KIKUCHI	K	(W	(U) THUNDER ON THE RUN	1980	KICKING MULE	UK	SNKF	170
MARK EGAN	B	(W	(V) CROSSCURRENTS	19	COTILLION	US	SD	9007
MARCUS MILLER	B	(W	(W) PERSPECTIVE	1979	ATLANTIC	US		19230
STEVE JORDON	D	(W						
VICTOR LEWIS	D	(W	RAPHAEL CRUZ PERC(W SAMMY FIGUEROA CONGA(W LENNY WHITE D (W					

G111			LUTHER GROSVENOR				G111
LUTHER GROSVENOR	B G V	(A	(A) UNDER OPEN SKIES	1971	ISLAND		ILPS 9168
MIKE KELLIE	D	(A					
JOHN HAWKEN	PNO	(A	JIM CAPALDI V (A MICK RALPHS V (A MIKE GILES D (A				
TREVOR BURTON	B	(A	TREVOR LUCAS V (A PAUL BENNETT V (A				

G111A		<	GROUP 87			G111A
			(A) FIRST	1980 CBS	84397	

G111B			GROUP THERAPY			G111B
			(A) YOU'RE IN NEED OF...	19 PHILIPS	UK SBL 7883	

G112			GROUNDHOGS					G112
TONY McPHEE	G B SYN V	(A11	(A) SCRATCHING THE SURFACE	1968	LIBERTY	UK	LBS 83199	
PETER CRUICKSHANK	B	(ABCDEFGH	(A) SCRATCHING THE SURFACE	197	WORLD PACIFIC	US		21892
DAVE BOORMAN	D	(	(B) BLUES OBITUARY	1969	LIBERTY UK 83253			
BOB HALL	PNO	(	(B) BLUES OBITUARY	196	IMPERIAL	US		12452
KEN PUSTELNIK	D	(ABCDEH	(C) THANK CHRIST FOR THE BOMB	1970	LIBERTY UK 83295 US			7644
STEVE RYE	HCA	(A	(C) THANK CHRIST FOR THE BOMB	1975	SUNSET UK			50376
DAVE WELLBELOVED	G	(KL	(D) SPLIT	1971	LIBERTY UK 83401 US			UA5513
			(D) SPLIT	19	UA RI 1017			
MARTIN KENT	B	(KL	(E) LIVE AT LEEDS	1971	(LTD ED? OR BOOT?)			
MICK COOK	K	(KL	(F) WHO WILL SAVE THE WORLD	1972	UA UK 29237	US UA5570		
CLIVE BROOKS	D	(GH	(G) HOGWASH	1972	UA UK 29419	US UA 008		
RICK ADAMS	G	(K	(H) SOLID	1974	WWA UK 004			
			(I) GOT TO GET ENOUGH	1972	TURBO US 7005			
			(J) BEST OF 1969 72	1974	UA UK 60063/4			
			(K) CROSSCUT SAW	1976	UA UK 29917 US	LA 603		
			(L) BLACK DIAMOND	1976	UA UK 29994 US	LA 680		
			( ) JOHN LEE HOOKER, JOHN MAYALL	19	CLEVE US	82871		
			(BF) BLUES ORBITUARY/WHO WILL SAVE	1975	UA GER 29794/95 DBL			

G112A			GROWL				G112A
MICK SMALL	G	(A	(A) GROWL	1974	DISCREET .	US	DS 2209
DENNIS RODRIGUEZ	V	(A					
RICHARD MANUPUTI	V	(A	DANNY McBRIDE D (A HARRY BRENDER BRANDIS G V(A GENO LUCERO B (A				

G112B			GROW UP			G112B
STEVEN WESTWOOD	D	(A	(A) THE BEST THING	1979 OBJECT	UK	OBJ005
BILLY JOHN McDONALD	D V(A					
JOHN BISSET-SMITH	G B K V(A	ROGER BLACKBURN G B (A RICHARD WESTWOOD WIND (A ANN BISSET-SMITH V (A				

G112C			GROWING CONCERN			G112C
RALPH WILLIAMS	D	(A	(A) GROWING CONCERN	196 MAINSTREAM	US	6108
PETE GUERINO	G V	(A				
RALPH TOMS	G	(A	JOHN PEDLEY B (A DON PASSAGLIA K V (A BONNIE McDONALD V (A			
MARY GARSTKI	V	(A				

G112D			JACK GRUNSKY				G112D
JACK GRUNSKY	V G K(ALL		(A) MY SHIP	1969			
MIKE ROSEN	K	(B	(B) TORONTO	1970			
ANNETTE BROX	V	(B	(C) BUFFALO BRAIN	1971	KUCKUCK	2375	007
MICK TAYLOR	G	(B	(D) NEWBORN MAN	1972	KUCKUCK	2375	011
ALEXIS KORNER	G	(B	(E) JACK GRUNSKY	1972	KUCKUCK	2375	015
THEO BINA	G B	(CDE					
ULRIKE BISCOFF		(C	FRANK DIEZ G (D OLDERS FRENZEL D (CD MUCK GROH (C				
SONNY HENNINIG	K	(CD	TOMMY ROEDER B (CD GEORGE MEYER FLT (CD ERNST SCHULTZ (E				
WALTER SCHNEIDER	B	(D	GUNTHER STORCH D (E JIMMY WOODE (E THOMAS HOLM (E				

G113			GRUPPO SPORTIVO				G113
HANS VANDENBURG	G V	(ABC	(A) 10 MISTAKES	1977 ARIOLA NL 25464+1978 EPIC UK 82793			
ANN MARTIN		(C	(A) 10 MISTAKES	1978 SIRE US 6066 BELLAPHON GER 2548			
MAX MOLLINGER	D	(ABC	(B) BACK TO 78	1978 ARIOLA NL 26472 EPIC UK 83263			
ERIC WEHRMEYER	B	(ABC	(C) COPY COPY	1980 ARIOLA EURO 202 327			
MARTIN BAKKER	G V	(C	(EP) RARE TRACKS	1977 POLYDOR 2454 120			
PETER CALICHER	K	(ABC					
EDWIN THEUERZEIT	TPT	(C	JOSEE VAN IERSEL V (AB MEIKE TOUW V (AB JANKEES TANS SAX (B				
ROB KRUISMAN	HRNS	(B	REIN VANDER BROEK HRNS (B MAARTEN VAN NORDEN HRNS (B JAN DE LIGT SAX (C				
LAURENS DE JONGE	SAX	(C					

G113A			DAVE GRUSIN				G113A
DAVE GRUSIN	K	(AB	(A) MOUNTAIN DANCE	1980 ARISTA		5010	
STANLET TURRENTINE		(B	(A) A FLIP OF THE COIN	1980 MANHATTAN	UK	5008	
HARVEY MASON	D	(A					
MARCUS MILLER	B	(A	JEFF MIRONOV G (A ED WALSH SYN (A IAN UNDERWOOD SYN (A				
RUBENS BASSINI	PERC	(A					

G114			GRYPHON					G114
BRIAN GULLAND	REC HRNS (ALL		(A) GRYPHON	1973	TRANSATLANTIC	UK	TRA 262	
RICHARD HARVEY	WIND HRNS(ALL		(B) MIDNIGHT MUSHRUMPS	1974	TRANSATLANTIC	UK	TRA 282	
GRAEME TAYLOR	G	(ABCD	(C) RED QUEEN TO GRYPHON 3	1974	TRANSATLANTIC	UK	TRA 287	
DAVID OBERLE	PERC	(ALL	(C) RED QUEEN TO GRYPHON 3	197	ARISTA US 4018 BRAIN GER		1071	
MALCOLM BENNETT		(CD	(D) RAINDANCE	1975	TRANSATLANTIC	UK	TRA 302	
BOB FOSTER	G	(E	(E) TREASON	1977	HARVEST	UK	SHSP 4063	
ALEX BAIRD	D	(E						
JON DAVIE	B	(E	PHILIP NESTOR B (BC PETER AIREY G (GRAEME GULLAND G (A					
DAVID BRIAN	PERC	(A	RICHARD BRIAN K (A PETE REDDING G B (BC ERNEST HART K (A					

```
BURTON CUMMINGS    V K  (ALL        ( ) SHAKIN ALL OVER            1968 SCEPTER US 533+ SPRINGBAORD4022
GARRY PETERSON     D    (A>V        (A) GUESS WHO                  19   MGM     US    4654
RANDY BACHMAN      G V  (ABCDE      (B) PLAY THE GUESS WHO         1976 PIP     US    6804
CHAD ALLEN         V    (R          (C) WHEATFIELD SOUL            1969 RCA     US LSP 4141    ANLI 1171
                                    (C) WHEATFIELD SOUL            1969 RCA            UK  SF  8037
JIM KALE           B    (CDEFGHIOPSW (D) CANNED WHEAT              1969 RCA     US LSP 4157 RI ANLI 0986
KURT WINTER        G    (FGHIJKLPS  (E) AMERICAN WOMAN             1970 RCA     US LSP 4266 UK  SF  8107
GREG LESKIW        G    (FGHOPS     (F) SHARE THE LAND             1970 RCA     US LSP 4359 UK  SF  8153
BILLY WALLACE      B    (JKLMNOPS   (G) SO LONG BANNATYNE          1971 RCA     US LSP 4574 UK  SF  8216
DOMENIC TROIANO    G    (NM         (H) ROCKIN'                    1972 RCA     US LSP 4602 UK  SF  8269
DON McDOUGAL       G    (IJKLW      (H) ROCKIN'                    1978 RCA                  ANLI 2683
ALLAN McDOUGALL    V    (W          (I) LIVE AT THE PARAMOUNT      1972 RCA     US LSP 4779 UK  SF  8329
DAVID PARASZ       HRNS (w          (J) TEN                        1973 RCA     US APLI 0130
DAVID INGLIS       G    (W          (K) ARTIFICIAL PARADISE        1973 RCA     US LSP 4830 UK  SF  8349
VANCE MASTERS      V D  (W          (L) ROAD FOOD                  1974 RCA     US APLI 0405
                                    (M) FLAVOURS                   1975 RCA     US APLI 0636 UK  SF  8399
                                    (N) POWER IN THE MUSIC         1975 RCA     US APLI 0995 UK  RS  1017
                                    (O) BEST OF THE GUESS WHO      1971 RCA     US LSPX 1004 UK  AFLI2594
                                    (P) BEST OF VOL 2              1974 RCA     US APLI 0269
                                    (Q) GREATEST                   19   RCA     US APLI 2253
                                    (R) BORN IN CANADA             1976 WAND          691
                                    (S) HISTORY OF                 1973 PRIDE         0012
                                    (T) WILD ONE                   19   PICKWICK US   3246
                                    (U) GUESS WHO                  19   PICKWICK US   3240
                                    (W) ALL THIS FOR A SONG        1979 AQUARIUS US 3246 HILLTAK 19299
```

```
GIB GUILBEAU       FDL  (ALL        GIB GUILBEAU                   1973 ALSHIRE      US   AS 209
                                    CAJUN COUNTRY                  197  ALSHIRE      US   S 5121
                                    CAJUN COUNTRY                  1975 ARIOLA            87147
                                    TOE TAPPIN' MUSIC             1979 SHILOH       US   4085
```

```
ISAAC GUILLORY G V B K (A          (A) ISAAC GUILLORY             1974 ATLANTIC US 7307  UK 40521
SAM GOPAL          TABLAS(A          (B) SOLO                      1980 CBS     NL 84568
JIM CAREY          D    (A
FRED GANDY         B    (A  MOX       HCA (A  JIM COLE             B V (A  CATHY HALL     FLT (A
JIM FAIRS          G DULC(A  JOHNSE HOLT G  (A  PETE GAVIN          D   (A  ROGER POPE  D   (A
```

```
JAMES(GUITAR SLIM) STEPHENSON G V(ALL (A) THINGS I USED TO DO      19   SPECIALTY   US    2120
ALSO  USED NAME GUITAR SLIM GREEN     (B) STONE DOWN BLUES         19   UNITED      US    7764
                                      (C) GREENSBORO ROUNDER       1977 FLYRIGHT    UK  LP 538
                                      ( ) CAROLINA BLUES           19   ARHOOLIE    US    2005
```

```
CAROL BREVAL            (A           (A) GUILLOTINE                19   AMPEX       US   10122
JOE TREVSONNO           (A
PAUL MORIN              (A  JEAN MORIN      (A  PAUL DALONZO        (A  ANDRE MORIN     (A
FRANCOIS                (A  PIERRE NADEAU   (A  ROBERT TURMEL       (A
```

```
DARYL HALL         K V  (A           (A) GULLIVER                  1969 ELEKTRA US 74070+1970 UK 2410006
JIM HELMER         D    (A
TIM MOORE          G V  (A  TOM SELLERS     B K (A
```

```
ADRIAN CURTIS(GURVITZ) G (AB         (A) GUN                       1968 CBS  US 26468  + UK  63552
PAUL CURTIS(GURVITZ)   B (AB         (B) GUNSIGHT                  1969 CBS  US 26551  + UK  62683
LOUIS FARRELL      D    (A
PETER DUNTON       D    (  TIM MYCROFT    (
```

```
WARD DOTSON        G V  (A           (A) FIRE OF LOVE              1981 NEW ROSE         ROSE8
JEFFREY LEE PIERCE G V  (A
ROB RITTER         B    (A  TERRY GRAHAM    D   (A  TITO LARNIA    VLN (A  LOIS GRAHAM     V  (A
```

```
GLENN LEOPOLD      V G K(A           (A) GUNHILL ROAD              19   KAMA SUTRA  US  KSBS 2061
STEVEN GOLDRICH    V PNO(A
GIL ROMAN          G V  (A  KENNY ROGERS B V  (A  LARRY BROWN       D  (A  BILL PERRY  B   (A
JIM RYAN           B    (A  ANDY NEWMARK    D  (A  PAUL COTTON       G  (A  GENE LORENZO    K  (A
GEORGE GRANTHAM    D    (A  REINIE PRESS    B  (A  DENNIS LEPRI      G  (A
```

```
ARTHUR GUNTER                        (A) BLACK & BLUES             19   CONTEMPO UK119+EXCELLO US 8017
                                     (B) BLUES AFTER HOURS         19   BLUE HORIZON      2431 012
```

```
MANI NEUMEIER PROD D K (ALL         (A) UFO                        1970 OHR       GER   556005
ULI TREPTE         B    (ABC         (B) HINTEN                    1971 OHR       GER   556027
AX GENRICH         G    (ABCDEG      (C) KAN GURU                  1972 BRAIN     GER   1007
SEPP JANDRISITS    G    (GHI         (D) GURU GURU                 197  BRAIN           1025
TOMMY GOLDSCHMIDT PERC (GHI          (E) DONT CALL US WE CALL YOU  1973 ATLANTIC        50022
JAN FRIDE          K    (G           (F) DANCE OF THE FLAMES       1974 ATLANTIC  UK   K50044
INGO BISCHOF       K    (GHIK        (G) MANI UND SEINE FREUNDE    1975 ATLANTIC  GER  K50157
MOEBI MOEBIUS      K    (G           (H) TANGO FANGO               1976 BRAIN     GER    1089
JOACHIM RODELIUS   K    (G           (I) GLOBETROTTER              1977 BRAIN           0060 039
JOGI KARPENTIEL    B    (GHI         (J) LIVE DBL                  1978 BRAIN     GER  0080 018
GERD DUDECK        WIND (G           (K) HEYDU                     1979 BRAIN           0060 187
HELMUT HATTLER     B    (GI          ( ) THIS IS    (COMP)         1973 BRAIN     GER  200 145
PETER WOLBRANDT    G    (G           ( ) DER ELEKTROLURCH (COMP DBL) 1974 BRAIN   GER  2 1057
CHAMPION JACK DUPREE K  (G
CHRISTA FAST            (G  PETER KUHMSTEDT    B   (ILK  ROLAND SCHAEFFER SYN G(HIJK  HOUSCHANG NEJADEPOUR G(F
CONNY PLANK        G K  (CDG HANS HARTMANN     B   (EF  GERALD LUCIANO HARTWIG B(K  MICHAEL PITZ    CLAR(
KARLA VON SINNEN  B     (K  BUTZE FISCHER   D PERC(K  BRUNO SCHABB   B   (D  LARRY           CONGA (I
DIETER BORNSCHLRGEL G   (J
```

ADRIAN GURVITZ

```
ADRIAN GURVITZ    G V  (A                             (A) SWEET VENDETTA              1979   JET US 35782 UK   JETLP   220
JOE PORCARO       PERC (A                             (B) IL ASSASSINO               1980   JET          UK   JETLP 226
JEFF PORCARO      D    (A
ED GREENE         D    (A   RICK SCHLOSSER   D   (A   DAVID HUNGATE        G   (A   DAVID SHIELDS    B  (A
FRED TACKETT      G    (A   STEVE PORCARO    K   (A   DAVID PAICH          PNO (A   STEVE LEEDS  SAX FLT(A
DICK HYDE         TROM (A   CHUCK FINDLEY    TPT (A   STEVE MADAIO         TPT (A   JERRY HEY    TPT     (A
EARL LON PRICE    SAX  (A   PAUL GURVITZ     V   (AB
```

ARLO GUTHRIE

```
ARLO GUTHRIE      G V  (ALL                           (A) ALICES RESTAURANT          1967   REPRISE    US 6267    UK K44045
KEVIN BURKE       FDL  (H                             (B) ARLO                       1968   REPRISE    US 6299    UK K44052
JIM KELTNER       D    (HI                            (C) RUNNING DOWN THE ROAD      1969   REPRISE    US 6346    UK K44071
BOB GLAUB         B    (HK                            (D) WASHINGTON COUNTY          1970   REPRISE    US 6411    UK K44099
JESSE ED DAVIS    G    (HI                            (E) ALICES RESTRAURANT (SOUNDTRACK) 1969 UA      US 5195    UK 29061
JIM GORDON        D    (HI                            (F) ARLO GUTHRIE    (COMP)     1972   CHARTER LINE          IT 24003
GEORGE BOHANON    HRNS (H                             (G) HOBOES LULLABYE            1972   REPRISE    US 2060    UK K44169
DICK HYDE         TROM (H                             (H) LAST OF THE BROOKLYN COWBOYS 1973 REPRISE    US 2142    UK K44236
GENE COE          HRNS (H                             (I) ARLO GUTHRIE               1974   REPRISE    US 2183    UK K54019
NICK DECARO       ACC  (HIK                           (J) TOGETHER  (DBL) LIVE)      1975   REPRISE    US 2214    UK K64023
JERRY WIGGINS     D    (H                             (K) AMIGO                      1975   REPRISE    US 2239    UK K54077
DOYLE SINGER      B MAND(H                            (L) THE BEST OF                1977   WB         US 3117    UK K56431
STAN FREE         K    (B                             (M) ONE NIGHT                  1978   WB         US 3232
PETE SEEGER       G V  (J                             (N) OUTLASTING THE BLUES       1978   WB         US 3336    UK K56658
DON RICH          G FDL(H                             ( ) STAR COLLECTION            197    MIDI                  UK   4003
BOB ARKIN         B    (H                             (P) POWER OF LOVE              1981   WB         US 3558    UK K56910
BUDDY ALAN        G    (H
BOB MORRIS        G    (H   JIM SHAW       PNO         (H   DON CHRISTLIEB    WIND (H   BUDDY COLLETTE  CLAR (H
JERRY BRIGHTMAN STEEL  (H   WILLIAM GREEN  OBOE  (H   ERNIE WATTS       FLT  (H   LEE SKLAR      B    (H
RY COODER         G    (HI  JOHN PILLA     G    (HIN GENE PARSONS      D    (H   THAD MAXWELL   B    (H
DOUG DILLARD      BANJO(HI  GIB GUILBEAU   FDL  (H   CLARENCE WHITE    G    (H   GRADY MARTIN   G    (H
RICHARD HAYWARD   D    (H   CHUCK RAINEY   B    (H   MIKE UTLEY        ORG  (H   JESSIE SMITH   V    (HI
CLYDIE KING       V    (HI  VANETTA FIELDS V    (H   GENE MERLINO      V    (H   THURLE RAVENSCROFT V (HI
ROBERT TEBOW      V    (H   BILL COLE      V    (H   TERRY A LA BERRY       (N   STEVE IDE           (N
DAVID GROVER           (N   DAN VELIKA          (N   CAROL IDE              (N   ED SHAUGHNESSY D    (B
LINDA RONSTADT    V    (K   STRINGS             (K   BYRONE BERLINE    FDL  (L   ROGER BUSH     B    (L
BUDDY EMMONS      STEEL(L   CHRIS ETHRIDGE B    (L   WILTON FELDER     B    (L   DARRYL HARDY   V    (L
MILT HOLLAND      PERC (LK  MARTY McCALL   V    (L   SPOONER OLDHAM    PNO  (L   GREG PRESTOPINO G K (L
SOUTHERN CAL COMM CHOIR(L   LEAH KUNKEL  K V    (K   RUSS KUNKEL       D    (K   WADDY WATCHELL  G   (K
JAI WINDING       K    (K   GAYLE LEVANT   HARP (K   RICK JAEGER       D    (K   BILLY GREEN    G    (K
DAVID GROVER      G BAN(MN  CAROL IDE      G    (MN  STEVE IDE         G TROM(MN DON VELIKA     B    (K
TERRY ALA BERRY   D    (N   PETER ADAMS    STEEL(N   JOHN SAVER        K    (N   JOHN CULPO     ACC  (N
RON SLOAN         HCA  (N
```

BUDDY GUY

```
BUDDY GUY         G V  (ALL                           (A) HOODOO MAN BLUES           1966   DELMARK               612
JUNIOR WELLS      HCA V(JKM                           (B) ITS MY LIFE BABY           1966   VANGUARD   VSD 79231
ERIC CLAPTON      G    (J                             (C) COMING AT YOU              1968   VANGUARD SVRL19001  VSD 79262
DR JOHN           PNO  (J                             (D) A MAN AND HIS BLUES        1968   VANGUARD SVRL19002  VSD 79272
J GEILS BAND           (J                             (E) I LEFT MY BLUES IN SAN FRANCISCO 1968 CHESS  1527 BELLAPHON 4069
LONNIE TAYLOR     D    (DH                            (F) BLUES TODAY                1968   VANGUARD SVRL 19004
MIKE UTLEY        K    (J                             (G) THIS IS BUDDY GUY          196    VANGUARD SVRL 19008 VSD 79290
TIM KAIHATSU      G    (GH                            (H) HOT & COOL                 1979   VANGUARD            VSD 79290
JACK MYERS        D    (DHJKLM                        (I) HOLD THAT PLANE            1972   VANGUARD            VSD 79323
GLENWAY McTEER    D    (GH                            (J) & JUNIOR WELLS PLAY THE BLUES 1972 ATLANTIC          K 40240
NORMAN SPILLER    TPT  (GH                            (K) I WAS WALKING THROUGH THE WOODS 19 CHESS            LP 409
BOBBY FIELD       SAX  (DGH                           (L) IN THE BEGINNING(58/64)    1971   RED LIGHTNING      RL  001
JUNIOR MANCE      PNO  (H                             (M) GOT TO USE YOUR HEAD       1979   BLUES BALL         2005
GARY BARTZ        SAX  (HI                            (N) DOLLAR DONE FELL           1980   JSP                1009
MARK JORDAN       K    (I                             (EP) CRAZY MUSIC               1965   CHESS    CRE 6004
LEROY STEWART     B    (J                             (EP) WITH THE BLUES            1965   CHESS    CRE 6009
BARRY ALTSCHUL    D    (IJ                            ( ) BUDDY & THE JUNIORS        19     BLUE THUMB  -8820
BILL WYMAN        B    (O                             (O) DRINKIN' TNT SMOKIN' DYNAMITE 1981 RED LIGHTNIN'  UK  0034
PINETOP PERKINS   PNO  (O                             (P) BREAKIN' OUT               1981   JSP            UK  1017
TERRY TAYLOR      V    (O
JUKE JOINT JIMMY       (J   LESLIE CRAWFORD SAX (GH   SETH JUSTMAN      PNO (J   GEORGE ALEXANDER   TPT(GH
J W WILLIAMS      B    (N   ERNEST JOHNSON   B  (HM   WAYNE BENNETT     G  (DG   AL DUNCAN          D  (M
CLIFTON JAMES     D    (M   ROBERT NIGHTHAWK G  (M    FRED BELOW        D (DKLHM SONNY BOY WILLIAMSON HCA(LM
FREEBO            B    (L   ROOSEVELT SHAW   D  (J    CARL RADLE        B  (JL  STEPHEN BLADD      D  (J
MAGIC DICK        HCA  (J   LAFAYETTE LEAKE  PNO (MKL A C REED         SAX (GHIJ PHILIP GUY         G  (HJN
JESSE LEWIS       D    (HI  OTIS SPANN       PNO(DHKLM AARON CORTHEN   SAX (DH   PHIL THOMAS        D  (LM
DAVID RIP STOCK   D    (I   BILL FOLWELL     B  (I    JIM GORDON        D  (J   DANNY KLEIN        B  (J
GERRY GIBSON      SAX  (KLM BOB NEELY        SAX (LM   MACK EASTER      B  (L    OTIS RUSH          G  (L
WILLIE DIXON      B    (L   ODIE PAYNE       D  (L    DONALD HANKINS   SAX(DHLM SONNY TURNER       TPT(LM
MURRAY WATSON     TPT  (LM  ABE LOCKE        SAX (LM   LEFTY BATES      G (LM   LITTLE PHIL SMITH   G  (N
RAY ALLISON       D    (N   DALLAS TAYLOR    D  (O
```

DENNY GUY

```
DENNY GUY         V    (A                             (A) DENNY GUY                  1972   DAY BREAK US   DR  2008
RANDALL ATON      B    (A
JOHN MILLIKEN     D    (A   JAMES JEFFERS    G   (A   THOMAS GUY        G   (A   EMPERADOR ATON D  (A
```

GWENDAL

```
BRUNO BARRE       VLN  (AB                            (A) GWENDAL                    1974   PATHE      FR   064 12725
JEAN MARIE RENARD G    (AB                            (B) GWENDAL 2                  1975   PATHE      FR   064 13075
YOUENN LEBERRE    WIND (AB
PATRICE GRUPALLO MAND PERC(AB   ROGER SCHAUB  B G  (AB
```

GYPSY

```
ROBIN PIZER       G V  (AB                            (A) GYPSY                      1971   UA         UK   UAS 29155
MOTH SMITH        D    (AB                            (B) BRENDA & THE RATTLESNAKE   1972   UA         UK   UAS 29420
ROD READ          G V  (A
DAVID McCARTHY    B V  (AB   JOHN KNAPP    V G K (AB   RAY MARTINEZ     G V  (B   RAY COOPER     PERC (B
```

H P LOVECRAFT

```
    GEORGE EDWARDS     V G B(AB          (A) H P LOVECRAFT              1967 PHILIPS   BL 7830+6336210+600252
    DAVE MICHAELS      K V  (AB          (B) H P LOVECRAFT2            1968 PHILIPS   SBL7872+6336213+600279
    TONY CAVALLARI     V G  (AB
    JERRY McGEORGE     V B  (A    MICHAEL TEGZA V D     (AB  JEFF BOYAN      B   (B   LEN DRUSS        HRNS(A
    RALPH CRAIG        TROM (A    HERB WEISS   TROM     (A   CLYDE BACHAND   TUBA (B   BILL TRAUB       WIND(A
    EDDIE HIGGINS      VIBES(A    PAUL TERVELT HRNS     (A   JACK HENNINGBAUM HRNS (A
```

HABIBIYYA

```
    ROGER POWELL       (A                (A) IF MAN BUT KNEW           1972  ISLAND   US 9305 UK HELP 7
    IAN WHITEMAN       (A
    MIKE EVANS         (A
```

HACKAMORE BRICK

```
    CHICK NEWMAN       (A                (A) ONE KISS LEADS TO ANOTHER 1970 KAMA SUTRA     US      2025
    ROBBIE BIEGE       (A
    BOB ROMAN          (A    TOMMY MOONLIG      (A
```

HACKENSACK

```
    PAUL MARTINEZ      B  (A              (A) UP THE HARDWAY            1971   POLYDOR        2383 263
    RAY SMITH          G  (A
    NICKY MOORE        V  (A    SIMON FOX    D     (A
```

STEVE HACKETT

```
    STEVE HACKETT      V G K(ALL          (A) VOYAGE OF THE ACOLYTE    1975 CHARISMA UK CAS1111   US 1176
    PHIL COLLINS       D V  (A            (A) VOYAGE OF THE ACOLYTE    1975 CHARISMA EURO 9103106 GER 6369970
    JOHN HACKETT       FLT K(ABC1EF       (B) PLEASE DONT TOUCH        1978 CHARISMA UK CAS4012   US 1112
    JOHN ACOCK         K    (AB           (B) PLEASE DONT TOUCH        1978 CHARISMA EURO 9103122
    MIKE RUTHERFORD    B    (A            (C) SPECTRAL MORNINGS        1979 CHARISMA UK CDS4017   US 1223
    KIM POOR           V    (F            (C) SPECTRAL MORNINGS        1979 CHARISMA GER  9124 039
    SALLY OLDFIELD     V    (A            (D) DEFECTORS               1980 CHARISMA UK CDS4018   US 3103
    NICK MANUS         K    (CDEF         (D) DEFECTORS               1980 CHARISMA GER 9124 058
    GRAHAME SMITH      VLN  (B            (E) CLOCKS EP               1979 CHARIAMA UK 34112
    TOM FOWLER         B    (B            (F) CURED                  1981 CHARISMA UK CDS4021 EPIC US 37632
    JAMES BRADLEY      PERC (B            (F) CURED                  1981 CHARISMA GER 6302 153
    PETER HICKS        V    (1CE          (1) 1978 TOUR
    DIK CADBURY        B    (1CE
    ROBIN MILLER       WIND (A    NIGEL WARREN-GREEN CELLO(A  PERCY JONES     B   (A   JOHN GUSTAFSON   B  (A
    RANDY CRAWFORD     V    (B    RICHIE HAVENS     V PERC(B  STEVE WALSH     V   (B   DAVE LEBOLT      K  (B
    JOHN SHEARER       D    (C1E  HUGH MALLOY    CELLO(B   CHESTER THOMPSON PERC(B   PHIL EHART      PERC(B
```

SAMMY HAGAR

```
    SAMMY HAGAR        G V  (ALL          (A) NINE ON A TEN SCALE      1976   CAPITOL         EST 11489
    JERRY SHIRLEY      D    (A            (A) NINE ON A TEN SCALE      1981   GREENLIGHT          2017
    BILL CHURCH        B    (ABCDEFGH     (B) SAMMY HAGAR              1977   CAPITOL         EST 11599
    MARK JORDAN        K    (E            (B) SAMMY HAGAR              1981   GREENLIGHT          2007
    ALAN FITZGERALD    K    (ABCDG        (C) MUSICAL CHAIRS           1978   CAPITOL      UK EST 11706
    STEVE DOUGLAS      SAX  (E            (C) MUSICAL CHAIRS           1981 GREENLIGHT           2021
    DENNIS CARMASSI    D    (CD           (D) ALL NIGHT LONG(LIVE)     1978   CAPITOL      UK EST 11812
    SCOTT QUICK        G    (A            (E) STREET MACHINE           1979   CAPITOL      UK EST 11983
    JIM HODDER         D    (A            (F) DANGER ZONE              1979   CAPITOL      UK EST 12069
    AYNSLEY DUNBAR     D    (A            (G) LOUD & CLEAR   (COMP)    1980   CAPITOL      UK EST 25330
    DALLAS TAYLOR      D    (A            (H) STANDING HAMPTON         1981 GEFFEN             85456
    DAVID LAUSER       D    (H
    VANETTA FIELDS     V    (A    SHIRLEY MATTHEWS   V  (A  MAXAYN LEWIS    V  (A   WIZARD STAN     K  (A
    JOE CRANE          K    (A    DAVID LEWARK       G  (B  JOHN BLAKELEY   G  (A   MIC GILLETTE    HRNS(A
    GREG ADAMS         HRNS (A    EMILIO CASTILLO  HRNS (A  STEVE KUPKA     HRNS(A   LENNY PICKETT   HRNS(A
    SCOTT MATTHEWS     D    (B    GARY PIHL          G  (ALL CHUCK RUFT    D V (EF   NEAL SCHON      G  (EF
    STEVE PERRY        V    (F    GEOFF WORKMAN      K  (F
```

NINA HAGEN BAND

```
    NINA HAGEN         V    (             (A) NINA HAGEN BAND          1978   CBS          UK    83136
    REINHOLD HEIL      K V  (AB           (B) UNBEHAGEN                1979   CBS          UK    84159
    HERWIG MITTEREGGER D V (AB           (C) NINA HAGEN BAND  10"     1980   CBS          US    36817
    BERNNARD POTSCHKA  G    (AB
    MANNE PRAEKER      B G V(AB
```

HAIR

```
    PETER ROINAES      D    (A            (A) PIECE                    1970   COLUMBIA        SCX 6452
    ALLEN SORENSEN     B    (A
    BENNY DYHR         G    (A    PADDY GYTHFELDT  K G  (A
```

THE HAGERS

```
    JIM HAGER          (A                 (A) THE HAGERS               1974 ELEKTRA      US 7E 1021
    JOHN HAGER         (A
    PETE JOLLIE        K    (A    SNEAKY PETE      STEEL(A  JOHN GUERIN     D  (A   RON TUTT        D  (A
    LYLE RITZ          D    (A    CAROL KAYE         B  (A  JAMES BURTON    G  (A   BEN BENAY       G  (A
    AL CASEY           G    (A    JOHN MORRELL       G  (A
```

JERRY HAHN

```
    JERRY HAHN         G BAN V(AB         (A) JERRY HAHN'S BROTHHOOD   19   CBS US         1044
    GEORGE MARSH       D    (AB           (B) MOSES                    19
    MIKE FINNIGAN      K HCA V(A
    CLYDE GRAVES       B    (A    MEL GRAVES    B    (B   MERL SAUNDERS   K SYN(B
```

BILL HALEY

```
    BILL HALEY         G V  (             EPS
    RUDY POMPELLI      SAX  (             DIM DIM THE LIGHTS         1955  BRUNSWICK UK  9129
    FRANCIS BEECHER    G    (             ROCK'N'ROLL               1955  LONDON    UK  1031
    JOHN GRANDE        K    (             LIVE IT UP 1              1956  LONDON    UK  1049
    BILLY WILLIAMSON   STEEL(             LIVE IT UP 2              1956  LONDON    UK  1050
    AL REX             B    (             ROCK'N'ROLL               1956  BRUNSWICK UK  9214
    DON RAYMOND        D    (             ROCK AROUND THE CLOCK     1956  BRUNSWICK UK  9250
                                          LIVE IT UP 3              1956  LONDON    UK  1058
                                          ROCK 'N'ROLL STAGE SHOW 1 1956  BRUNSWICK UK  9278
                                          ROCK'N'ROLL STAGE SHOW 2  1956  BRUNSWICK UK  9279
                                          ROCK'N'ROLL STAGE SHOW 3  1956  BRUNSWICK UK  9280
                                          ROCKIN THE OLDIES  1      1958  BRUNSWICK UK  9349
                                          ROCKIN' THE OLDIES        1958  BRUNSWICK UK  9350
                                          ROCKIN THE OLDIES         1958  BRUNSWICK UK  9351
```

                                                                    (CONTINUED)

EPs

ROCKIN AROUND THE WORLD	1959	BRUNSWICK	UK		9446
BILL HALEY & HIS COMETS	1959	BRUNSWICK	UK		9459
HALEY & HIS COMETS	1960	WB	UK		6001
HALEY'S JUKE BOX	1961	WB	UK		6025
BILL HALEY	1964	WB	UK		6133
BILL HALEY 2	1964	WB	UK		6136

LPs

LIVE IT UP 10"	1955	LONDON	UK		1042
BILL HALEY & THE COMETS	19	DECCA	US		2670
" " " "	19	WB	US		1378
HALEYS JUKE BOX	1960	WB	US		1391
SHAKE RATTLE & ROLL 10"	19	DECCA	US		5560
ROCK AROUND THE CLOCK	1956	BRUNSWICK	UK		8117
" " " "	1956	DECCA	US		8225
" " " "	1970	HALLMARK	UK	SHM	668
" " " "	1971	CORAL		CP	55
" " " "	1974	CORAL		CDL	8017
" " " "	1974	CORAL	UK	CRLM	1039
" " " "	1961	ACE OF HEARTS	UK	AH	13
" " " "	1981	WB	UK	K	26007
ROCK 'N' ROLL STAGE SHOW	1956	DECCA	US		8345
" "	1956	BRUNSWICK	UK		8139
TWISTING KNIGHTS	1962	ROULETTE	US		25174
" "	1962	COLUMBIA	UK	33sx	1460
ROCKIN' THE OLDIES	1957	BRUNSWICK	UK		8219
" " "	1962	ACE OF HEARTS	UK	AH	35
" " "	19	DECCA	US		8569
ROCKIN' AROUND THE WORLD	19	DECCA	US		8692
ROCKIN' THE JOINT 10"	1957	DECCA	US		8775
" " " "	1957	BRUNSWICK	UK		8268
" " " "	1964	GOLDEN GUINEA	UK		0282
" " " "	1966	MARBLE ARCH	UK		817
" " " "	1979	ROLLERCOASTER	UK		2002
" " "	1957	LONDON	US	HAF	2037
CHICKS	1964	ACE OF HEARTS	UK	AH	66
"	1959	BRUNSWICK	UK	STA	3011
"	1959	DECCA	US		8821
HE DIGS ROCK'N'ROLL	19	DECCA	US		8315
STRICTLY INSTRUMENTAL	1960	BRUNSWICK	UK	LAT	8326
" " "	196	DECCA	US		8964
GREATEST HITS	1968	MCA	US		161
ON STAGE	1970	HALLMARK	UK	SHM	694
ROCK'N'ROLL	19	GNP	US		2077
ROCK AROUND THE COUNTRY	1971	SONET	UK	SNTF	623
" " " "	197	GNP CRESCENDO	US		2097
" " " "	1974	HALLMARK	UK	SHM	837
GOLDEN KING OF ROCK'N'ROLL	1972	HALLMARK	UK	SHM	773
KING OF ROCK	1973	EMBER	UK	EMB	3396
" "	197	ALSHIRE	US		5313
BILL HALEY & THE COMETS	19	VALIANT	UK	VS	103
RIP IT UP	19	MCA	UK	MUPS	318
Mr ROCK'N'ROLL	19	EMBER	UK	EMB	3401
TRAVELLING BAND	19	JANUS	US		3035
RAZZLE DAZZLE	19	JANUS	US		7003
ROCK 'N' ROLL DANCE PARTY	19	SUMMERSET	US		4600
ROCK WITH	19	TRANSWORLD	US		202
JUST ROCK'N'ROLL MUSIC	1973	SONET	UK	SNTF	645
KING OF ROCK'N'ROLL MUSIC	1973	MUSIDISC		ALB	137
LIVE IN LONDON 74	1974	ATLANTIC	UK	K	51501
RARE ITEMS	1975	MCA		COPS72741/2
SCRAPBOOK	19	KAMA SUTRA			2014
ROCK	19	ESSEX	US		202
COLLECTIONS	1976	PICKWICK		PDA	006
ROCK ROCK ROCK	1975	MUSIDISC		CV	1072
GOLDEN HITS	1974	MCA	UK	MCF	2555
" "	197	DECCA	US		7211
R O C K	1976	SONET	UK	SNTF	710
ARMCHAIR ROCK'N'ROLL	1978	MCA	UK	MCF	2838
GOLDEN COUNTY ORIGINS	1978	GRASS ROOTS			1001
20 GOLDEN PIECES OF	1979	BULLDOG	UK	BDL	2002
EVERYONE CAN ROCK'N'ROLL	1979	SONET	UK	SNTF	808
TRIBUTE TO BILL	1981	MCA	UK	MCF	3105
ROCK'N'ROLL REVIVAL	1981	WB	US		1831
ROCK'N'ROLL FOREVER	1981	WB	UK	K	40555

HALF JAPANESE

(A) HALF JAPANESES (BOX SET)	19	ARMAGEDDON	UK	ABOX1
(B) LOUD	1981	ARMAGEDDON	UK	ARM7

HALFBREED

MICK WHITTAKER	V	(A	(A) HALFBREED	1975	U A	UK	UAG 29877
TOM FARRIER	G	(A				
JIM LOWERY	K	(A	GEOFF HUTCHINSON D (A FRANKIE GIBBON B (A			

DARYL HALL

DARYL HALL	V K	(A	(A) SACRED SONGS	1980	RCA	UK US	3573
ROBERT FRIPP	G	(A				
KENNY PASSARELLI	B	(A	ROGER POPE D (A CALEB QUAYE G (A CHARLIE DRACHEN SAX(A
DAVID KENT	V	(A				

BOBBYE HALL

BOBBYE HALL(PORTER) V PERC(A	(A) BODY LANGUAGE FOR LOVERS	1977	20TH CENTURY	US	534

```
CAROL HALL              (AB        (A) IF I BE YOUR LADY          19   ELEKTRA        UK    74078
                                   (B) BEADS & FEATHERS           19   ELEKTRA        UK    75018
```

```
JIMMY HALL V HCA SAX PERC(AB        (A) TOUCH YOU                  1980 EPIC           US    36516
JACK HALL          B V  (A          (B) CADILLAC TRACKS            1982 EPIC           US    37701
GUNNAR GELOTTE     D PERC(A
BONNIE BRAMLETT    V    (A    MIKE DUKE        PNO  (A   MIKE EUBANK      PNO (A   SHELLY KURLAND   STR (A
FARRELL MORRIS     PERC (A    GREG TAYLOR      HCA  (A   NORBERT PUTNAM   STR (A   DONNA HALL       V   (A
ANITA HALL         V    (A    STEVE BRANTLEY   V    (A   DAVE LOGGINS     V   (A   LARRY BERWALD    G   (AB
JON GOIN           G    (A    KENNY MINS       G    (B   BILL SANFORD     G   (B   LARRY BYROM      G   (B
RANDY McCORMICK    K    (B    MIKE HANNA       K    (B   SHANE KEISTER    K   (AB  BOB WRAY         B   (B
JAMES TSROUD       D    (B    KENNY MALONE     PERC (B   HARRISON CALLOWAY HRNS(B  RONNIE EADES     HRNS(B
CHARLES ROSE       HRNS (B    HARVEY THOMPSON  HRNS (B   ROGER BISSELL    HRNS(B   QUITMAN DENNIS   HRNS(B
RON KELLER         HRNS (B    DENIS SOLEE      HRNS (B   GEORGE TIDWELL   HRNS(AB
```

```
JOE HALL V G HCA PERC(A              (A) JOE HALL & THE CONTINENTAL DRIFT  1978 POSTERITY     CAN   13009
TONY QUARRINGTON  G K PERC(A
PAUL QUARRINGTON  B V  (A    GEORGE DOBO      K G  (A   MARTIN WORTHY    D   (A   STEVE HUTT       SAX (A
PETER STRYNIAK    VLN  (A    ART JANSEN       VLA  (A   JOEY QUARRINGTON B   (A
```

```
JOHN HALL          G V  (ALL        (A ACTION                     1973 CBS            US        1043
WELLS KELLY        D    (A          )B) JOHN HALL                 1978 ASYLUM  US 6E 117 UK K 53075
MICHAEL BRECKER    HRNS (B          (C) POWER                     1979 CBS        US 35790
PAUL HARRIS        K    (A          (D) DOUBLE OR NOTHING         1979 A&M        US   4760
RICHARD GREENE     VLN  (A          (E) ALL OF THE ABOVE          1981 EMI AM     US 17058
LYNN PITNEY        V    (BC
GARLAND JEFFREYS   V    (B    JOEL TEPP        HCA  (B   JERRY LAWSON     V   (B   CHUCK RAINEY     B   (B
STEVE GADD         D    (B    JOE SAMPLE       K    (B   JIMMY HAYES      V   (B   BILL PAYNE       K   (B
SONNY BURKE        K    (B    DAVID LASLEY     V    (B   ARNOLD McCULLER  V   (B   TUBO             V   (B
ED GREENE          D    (B    PHILIP BALLOU    V    (BC  DAVID SANBORN    SAX (B   DAVID HUNGATE    B   (B
JAMES TAYLOR       V    (BC   CARLY SIMON      V    (B   WILTON FELDER    V   (B   MILT HOLLAND     PERC(B
DAVID PAICH        PNO  (A    LOWELL GEORGE    G V  (B   JAY OTIS WASHINGTON V (B  BONNIE RAITT     V   B(B
JOSEPH RUSSELL     V    (B    JOHN SEBASTIAN   G HCA(A   ELLIOTT ZIGMUND  D   (A   JIM COLGROVE     B   (A
HARVEY BROOKS      B    (A    SHARON ALEXANDER V    (A   BOB LEINBACH     K V (E   JODY LINACOTT    PERC(C
LOUIS LEVIN        K    (C    JOHN POUSETTE DART V  (A   TONY LEVIN       B   (C   CARLY SIMON      V   (C
ERIC PARKER        D    (CE   DAVID SCHWARTZ   B    (C   BRYAN CUMMINGS   SAX G(C  JOHN TROY        V   (CE
MICHAEL MARNION    VIBES(C
```

```
LANI HALL          V    (ALL        (A) SUNDOWN LADY              1974 A&M   US 4359   UK  AMLS64359
CHARLES LOPER      TROM (C          (B) HELLO ITS ME              1975 A&M   US 4508   UK  AMLS64508
LEW McCREARY       TROM (C          (C) SWEETBIRD                 1977 A&M   US 4617   UK  AMLH64647
TONY TERRAN        TPT  (C          (D) DOUBLE OR NOTHING         1979 A&M   US 4670   UK  AMLH64670
JOHN PISANO        G    (B          (E) BLUSH                     1981 A&M   US 4829
PAPITO HERNANDEZ   B    (B
STEVE SCHAEFFER    D    (B    CLARENCE McDONALD K  (B   VINCE CHARLES    PERC(B
LARRY CARLTON      G    (BC   BOB FINDLEY      TPT  (B   WILTON FELDER    B   (B   MARK STEVENS     D   (B
PETE JOLLY         ACC  (B    HERB ALPERT  TPT PNO (BC  JIM HUGHART      B   (B   MICHEL COLOMBIER B   (BC
EMIL RICHARDS      PERC (B    JULIUS WECHTER   PERC (B   DAVE FRISHBERG   PNO (B   BOB EDMONDSON    TROM(B
MIKE MELVOIN       PNO  (B    JIM GORDON       D    (B   ERNIE McDANIELS  B   (B   NICK CEROLI      D   (B
JOHN AUDINO        TPT  (C    BOBBY SHEW       TPT  (C   LEE RITENOUR     G   (C   DENNIS BUDIMIR   G   (C
CHUCK DOMANICO     B    (CD   STAN CLARKE      B    (C   JIM KELTNER      D   (C   MILT HOLLAND     PERC(C
MICHAEL BODDICKER  SYN  (C    GAYLE LEVANT     HARP (C   DAVID DUKE       HRNS(C   NEIL LARSEN      K   (D
BUZZ FEITEN        G    (D    PETER DONALD     D    (D   MANOLO BADRENA   PERC(C   JERRY KNIGHT     B   (D
LERRY TOLBERT      D    (D    VINCENT DEROSA   HRNS (C   ROBERT HENDERSON HRNS(C   EARL DUMLER      OBOE(C
LANNY MORGAN       WIND (C    CLIFFORD SHANK   FLT  (C   JEROME RICHARDSON FLT (C  STRING SECTION
```

```
DARYL HALL         K V G(ALL        (A) WHOLE OATES               1972 ATLANTIC  US 7242 UK 76 K50306
JOHN OATES         G V K(ALL        (B) ABANDONED LUNCHEONETTE    1973 ATLANTIC  US 7269 UK    K40534
CHRIS BOND         G K  (BDEG       (B) ABANDONED LUNCHEONETTE    197  ATLANTIC  RIUS 19139
TOM SCOTT          SAX  (EG         (C) WAR BABIES                1974 ATLANTIC  US 18109  UK K50086
GARY COLEMAN       PERC (DEG        (D) HALL & OATES              1975 RCA APLI1144 UK RI 80 INTS 5010
GORDON EDWARDS     B    (B          (E) BIGGER THAN BOTH OF US    1976 RCA APLI1467 UK RI 81 INTS 5088
LELAND SKLAR       B    (DEG        (F) NO GOODBYES               1977 ATLANTIC US 18213  UK K50347
JIM GORDON         D    (DE         (F) NO GOODBYES               197  RCA  RI US/UK  I/2802
ED GREENE          D    (DE         (G) BEAUTY ON A BACK STREET   1977 RCA      US/UK  I/2300
EDDIE ZYNE         D    (           (H) ALONG THE RED LEDGE       1978 RCA      US/UK  I/2894
DAVE KENT          K V  (JH         (I) PAST TIME BEHIND          1977 CHELSEA         US    547
TODD SHARP         G    (           (J) LIVE TIME                 1978 RCA      US/UK  I/2802
STEPHEN DEAN       B    (           (K) X STATIC                  1979 RCA      US/UK  I/3494
JIM GETZOFF        K    (E          (L) VOICES                    1980 RCA      US/UK  I/3646
TOM HENSLEY        PNO  (E          (M) PRIVATE EYE               1981 RCA  AFLI4028   UK  RCALP6001
TODD RUNDGREN      G    (C          (N) H²O                       1982 RCA                UK  RCALP6056
TOM WOLK           B    (N
ROGER POPE         D    (HJ   DON YORK         K    (C   JOHN SIEGLER     B   (C   JOHN WILCOX      D   (C
MIKE McCARTY       B    (A    JIM HELMER       D    (A   HUGH McCRACKEN   G   (B   BERNARD PURDIE   D   (B
RALPH McDONALD     PERC (B    LARRY PACKER     FDL  (B   JOE FARRELL      SAX (B   RICK MAROTTA     D   (B
RICHARD TEE        K    (B    GLORIA AGOSTINI  HARP (B   JOHN BLAIR       VLN (B   CLARENCE McDONALD K (D
SCOTT EDWARDS      B    (DEG  STEVE GELSAND    G B  (B   JERRY RICKS      G   (B   PANCHO MORALES   D   (B
PAT REBILLOT       K PERC(B   MARK HORWITZ BANJO   (B   MARVIN STAMM     HRNS(B   MIKE BAIRD       D   (D
C O B              SYN  (     SANDY ALLEN      V    (D   JEFF PORCARO     D   (G   TONI MOTTOLA     V   (G
GAIL BOGGS         V    (C    KENNY PASSARELLI B    (JHK CALEB QUAYE      G   (JH  RALPH SCHUCKETT  K   (K1
CHARLES DE CHANT   K V(HJKMN  YOGI HORTON      D    (K   NEIL JASON       B   (K   WERNER FRITZSCHING G(K
STEVE LOVE         G    (K    GEORGE BITZER    H    (H   ROBERT FRIPP     G   (H   JAY GRAYDON      G   (HK
RICK NIELSON       G    (H    DICK WAGNER      G    (H   JOHN SIEGLER     B   (KLM CHUCK BURGI      D   (LM
LARRY FAST         SYN  (M    RAY GOMEZ    G       (H   DAVID FOSTER     K   (HK  STEVE LUKATHER   G   (H
GEORGE HARRISON    G    (H    STEVE PORCARO    G    (H   LES THOMPSON         (H   G E SMITH        (KLMN
JERRY MAROTTA      D    (KLM  JEFF SOUTHWORTH  G    (LM  MIKE KLVANA      SYN (L   MICKET CURRY     D   (M
JIMMY MAELIN       PERC (MK   JOHN JARRETT     V    (M
```

FERGUS HAMBLETON

FERGUS HAMBLETON V K G B SAX(A	(A) ALL THE RIGHT NOISES		1971	CAPITOL		CAN	ST	6370
GREG HAMBLETON	V	(A						
ALVIN FALL	HRNS (A	JACK TAYLOR	HRNS (A	STAN THERIAULT	B	(A	PAUL CLINCH D	(A
STRINGS								

PETER MICHAEL HAMEL

PETER MICHAEL HAMEL	K(AB	(A) HAMEL	1972	VERTIGO	GER	6641 055
ANATOL ARKUS	(	(B) VOICE OF SILENCE	1973	VERTIGO	GER	6360 613

CHICO HAMILTON

CHICO HAMILTON	PERC D(ALL	(A) PASSIN' THRU	1963	IMPULSE	AS	29
BILL PAYNE	PNO (I	(B) MAN FROM TWO WORLDS	1964	IMPULSE	AS	59
LOWELL GEORGE	G (I	(C) CHIC CHIC CHICO	1965	IMPULSE	AS	82
KENNY GRADNEY	B (I	(D) EL CHICO	1966	IMPULSE	AS	9102
GEORGE BOHANON	TROM (K	( ) FURTHER ADVENTURES OF EL CHICO	1966	IMPULSE	AS	9114
PAUL BARRERE	G (I	(E) THE DEALER	1967	IMPULSE	AS	9130
STU GARDNER	K (I	(F) BEST OF	1975	IMPULSE	AS	9174
SAM CLAYTON	D (I	(G) HIS GREAT HITS	19	IMPULSE		AS9213/2
JERRY AIELLO	K (I	(H) WITH GERRY MULLIGAN	19	FANTASY		8082
ERIC DOLPHY	WIND (K	(I) CHICO THE MASTER	1973	STAX/ENTERPRISE		ENS 7501
DENNIS BUDIMIR	G (K	(J) MONTREUX FESTIVAL	1975	STAX		STX 1029
CHARLES LLOYD	SAX (K	(K) THAT'S JAZZ	1976	WB	UK	K 56239
ALBERT STINSON	B (K	( ) HEAD HUNTER	1969	SOLID	US	18050
WYATT RUTHER	G (K	( ) & PLAYERS	1976	BLUE NOTE		622
GABOR SZABO	G (K	( ) PEREGRINATIONS	1976	BLUE NOTE		520
NATHAN GERSHMAN	CELLO(K	( ) CAT WALK	1976	MERCURY		1163

HAMILTON, JOE FRANK (& REYNOLDS)

DAN HAMILTON	G V (ALL	(A) HAMILTON JOE FRANK & REYNOLDS	1970			
JOE FRANK CAROLLO	B V (ALL	(B) DON'T PULL YOUR LOVE OUT	1971	ABC	US	3555
JOE CARRERO	D (ALL	(C) HALWAY SYMPHONY	1972	ABC	US	
ALAN DENNISON	K V (DE	(D) FALLIN' IN LOVE	1975	PLAYBOY	US	407
TOMMY REYNOLDS	V FLT G(ABC	(E) LOVE & CONVERSATION	1976	PLAYBOY	US	414

CLAIRE HAMILL

CLAIRE HAMILL	V G K(ALL	(A) ONE HOUSE LEFT STANDING		1971	ISLAND US 9316 UK		ILPS9182
JOHN MARTYN	G (A	(B) OCTOBER		1973	ISLAND	UK	ILPS9225
PAUL BUCKMASTER	CELLO(A	(C) STAGE DOOR JOHNNIES		1974	KONK	UK	101
DAVID LINDLEY	G (A	(D) ABRACADABRA		1975	KONK	UK	104
JOHN HAWKEN	K (A						
RAY WARLEIGH	FLT (A	JACK EMBLOW ACC	(A	JOHN PIGNEGNY	HRNS (A	AUBREY JOHNSON	OBOE(A
PHIL BATES	B (A	TERRY REID	G V (A	SIMON KIRKE	D (A	TETSU YAMAUCHI	B (A
RABBIT BUNDRICK	K (A	WAYNE PERKINS	G V (B	JEAN ROUSSEL	K (B	TIM SMITH	G V (B
STEVE SMITH	K V (B	CHRIS LAURENCE	B (B	ALAN WHITE	D (B	GERRY CONWAY	D (B
PAT DONALDSON	B (B	HENRY SPINETTI	PERC (B	NICK SOUTH	B (C	PHILIP CHEN	B (CD
PAUL WESTWOOD	B (C	DAVE ROWEBERRY	K (C	TIM HINKLEY	K (C	JIM FRANKS	D (C
CLEM CATTINI	D (C	NEIL McBAIN	D (C	PHIL PALMER	G (CD	DIZ DISLEY	G (C
ROY NEVE	G (C	LAURIE BROWN TPT	(C	ALAN HOLMES	FLT (C	JOHN HARTMANN	K (D
GARY RAY	D (D	MEL COLLINS SAX	(D	DOREEN CHANTER	V (D	VICKY BROWN	V (D
TOM ROBINSON	V (D	RAPHAEL DOYLE	V (D	HEREWARD KAYE	V (D	ALEX WELSH BAND	(A

HAMILTON FACE BAND

LENNY LAKS	V (A	(A) AIN'T GOT NO TIME	1970	BELL	US 6042	UK SBLL132
RUTH UNDERWOOD	V (A					
STEVEN MARGOSHES	PNO (A	RONNIE SELDIN	G (A	ALAN COOPER	B (A	

JAN HAMMER

JAN HAMMER	K (ALL	(A) LIKE CHILDREN	1974	ATLANTIC	UK K 50092 US NEMPEROR 430
JERRY GOODMAN	VLN (A	(B) FIRST SEVEN DAYS	1975	ATLANTIC	UK K 50184 US NEMPEROR 432
JEFF BECK	G (E	(C) OH YEAH	1976	NEMPEROR	UK K 50276 US	437
STEVE KINDLER	VLN G(BCG	(D) MAKE LOVE	1976	BASF	GERM 20688
FERNANDO SAUNDERS	B V (CHG	(E) LIVE WITH JEFF BECK	1977	CBS	UK 86025 US EPIC 34433
TONY SMITH	D V (CHG	(F) TIMELESS	197		US ECM 1047
DAVID EARLE JOHNSON PERC(B		(G) MELODIES	1979	EPIC	UK 82405 US NEMPEROR35003
COLIN HODGKINSON	V (H	(H) BLACK SHEEP	1979	ASYLUM	UK K 53089 US ASYLUM 6E173
BOB CHRISTIANSON	V (H					
GREGG GEYA CARTER	V (H					

HAMMER

JACK O'BRIEN	G (A	(A) HAMMER	1971	SANFRANCISCO	US	SD 203
NORMAN LANDSBERG	K (A					
JOHN DEROBERTS	V (A	RICHIE McBRIDE	B (A	JOHN GUERIN	D (A	

HAMMERSMITH

	(A) HAMMERSMITH	197	MERCURY	US	SRM11040
	(B) IT'S FOR YOU	197	MERCURY	US	SRM11102

PETER HAMMILL

PETER HAMMILL	V G K(ALL	(A) FOOLS MATE	1972	CHARISMA US/UK CAS1037 NL	9199 190
GUY EVANS	D (ABCDEFL	(B) CHAMELEON IN THE SHADOW	1973	CHARISMA US/UK CAS1067 NL	9124 051
DAVID JACKSON	SAX (ABCEGJKL	(C) THE SILENT CORNER	1974	CHARISMA US/UK CAS1083 NL	9198 771
HUGH BANTON	K (ABCE	(D) IN CAMERA	1974	CHARISMA US?UK CAS1089 NL	9198 770
NIC POTTER	B (ABF	(E) NADIRS LAST CHANCE	1975	CHARISMA US/UK CAS1099 NL	9198 772
PAUL WHITEHEAD	D (AD	(F) OVER	1977	CHARISMA US/UK CAS1125 NL	9124 008
RANDY CALIFORNIA	G (C	(G) FUTURE NOW	1978	CHARISMA UK CAS1137 US	2202
GRAHAME SMITH	VLN (FJG	(H) VISION(COMP)	1978	GTR	US	9211 1016
CHRIS SMITH	PERC V (D	(J) P H 7	1979	CHARISMA UK CAS1146 US	2205
ROD CLEMENTS	B VLN(A	(J) P H 7	1979	CHARISMA GER	9124 044
ROBERT FRIPP	G (A	(K) BLACK BOX	1980	MERCURY EURO	6302 067
MARTIN POTTINGER	D (A	(L) SITTING TARGETS	1981	VIRGIN UK 2205 GER MERCURY 6203 130
RAY JACKSON	HCA MAND (A	( ) BETWEEN CONTEMPLATION	19	AURAL	US	5067
PAUL WHITEHEAD	D (A					
DAVID FERGUSON	SYN (K	PHIL HARRISON	SYN (L	MORRIS PERT	PERC(L DAVID HENTSCHEL	SYN (D

ALBERT HAMMOND

```
ALBERT HAMMOND      G V (ALL      (A) IT NEVER RAINS IN SOUTHERN CALIFORNIA   1973 MUM US 31905 UK    65320
MIKE OMARTIAN       K   (B        (B) FREE ELECTRIC BAND                      1973 MUM US 32267 UK    65554
JIM GORDON          D   (B        (C) ALBERT HAMMOND                          1974 MUM US 32834 UK    80026
JOE OSBORN          B   (B        (D) 99 MILES FROM LA                        1975      EPIC           80961
JAY LEWIS           G   (B        (E) WHEN I NEED YOU                         1977      EPIC           81983
LARRY CARLTON       G   (B        (F) GREATEST HITS                          1978      EMBASSY        31643
CAROL CARMICHAEL    V   (B        (G) YOUR WORLD IS MY WORLD                 1980 CBS US 36964 UK   84824
SID SHARP           STRING(B
```

LAWRENCE HAMMOND

```
LAWRENCE HAMMOND   G K V(A        (A) COYOTES DREAM                          1976 TAKOMA                1047
ALAN McSHANE       D    (A
BILL WEINGARDEN    STEEL(A   BYRON BERLINE    FDL (A  LENI ISAACS    FLT (A  LEROY DEWEY    D (A
DAVID ROBINSON     G    (A   2 BUTTON GREENE  PERC (A  JAMES LOUIS PARBER G  (A
```

JOHN HAMMOND

```
JOHN HAMMOND   HCA G V (ALL      (A) JOHN HAMMOND                    1963      VANGUARD    US         2148
BILLY BUTLER       G   (BEQ      (B) BIG CITY BLUES                  1964      VANGUARD    US     VSD 79153
JAMES SPRUILL      G   (BEQ      (B) BIG CITY BLUES                  1964      FONTANA     UK     TFL 6046
JIMMY LEWIS        B   (BCEFQ    (C) SO MANY ROADS                   1965      VANGUARD    US     VSD 79178
BOBBY DONALDSON    D   (BEQ      (C) SO MANY ROADS                   1965      FONTANA     UK     TFL 6059
CHARLIE MUSSELWHITE HCA(CEQ      (D) COUNTRY BLUES                   1965      VANGUARD    US     VSD 79198
JAIME R ROBERTSON  G   (CEFQ     (E) MIRRORS                         1968      VANGUARD    US     VSD 79245
LEVON HELM         D   (CEQ      (F) I CAN TELL                      1968      ATLANTIC    US     SD  8152
MIKE BLOOMFIELD  G PNO (CEQL     (G) SOONER OR LATER                 1968      ATLANTIC    US     SD  8206
DR JOHN            K   (0        (H) SOUTHERN FRIED                  1970      ATLANTIC    US     SD  8251
BILLY NICHOLS      B   (K        (K) SOURCE POINT                    1971      CBS US 30458    UK      64365
EDDIE HINTON     G PNO(R         (L) LITTLE BIG MAN   (SOUNDTRACK)   197       CBS US 30545
RANDALL BRAMBLETT  K   (R        (M) WHEN I NEED                     197       CBS US 30549
KENNY BUTTREY      D   (R        (N) I'M SATISFIED                   1972      CBS             UK      65051
TOMMY COGBILL      B   (R        (O) TRIUMVIRATE                     1973      CBS             UK      65659
SPOONER OLDHAM     PNO (R        (P) SPIRITUALS TO SWING             19        VANGUARD           VRS8523/4
LEONARD FEATHER    G   (F        (Q) BEST OF   (SOUTHERN FRIED)      1974      VANGUARD           VSD 11/2
ROGER HAWKINS      D   (R        (R) CANT BEAT THE KID               1975      CAPRICORN   US     CP 0153
RICK DANKO         B   (F        (S) MY SPANISH ALBUM                19        CAYTRONICS  US         1493
BILL WYMAN         B   (F        (T) JOHN HAMMOND SOLO               197       VANGUARD    US     VSD 79380
JAN ZUKOWSKI       B   (V        (U) FOOTWORK                        197       VANGUARD    US     VSD 79400
JIMMY THACKERY     G   (V        (V) HOT TRACKS                      197       VANGUARD    US     VSD 79424
MARK WEINER        HCA (V        (W) MILEAGE                         1979      SONET UK SNTF835 US  ROUNDER3032
PETE RAYUSA        D   (V
ERIC 'GARTH' HUDSON ORG(CEQ  CHARLES OTIS     D     (FKW  BOB MONTALTO     PNO (W  ROBBIE KONDOR   PNO (W
SHERMAN HOLMES     B   (W        SEE MIKE BLOOMFIELD ENTRY FOR FULL LINE UP ON(O)
```

HANGMEN

```
                                 (A) BITTER SWEET                    19        MONUMENT    US     MLP 8077
```

HANK THE KNIFE

```
                                 (A) BEST OF                         1980 MFP             NL         58095
                                 (B) CRAZY GUITAR                    1980 MERCURY         NL     6423 343
```

HANNIBAL

```
ALEX BOYCE         V   (A        (A) HANNIBAL                        1970      B&C         UK     CAS 1022
BILL HUNT          K HRNS(A
ADRIAN INGRAM      G   (A   JACK GRIFFITHS   B   (A   JOHN PARKES    D  (A
```

RANDY HANSEN

```
RANDY HANSEN       G V (A        (A) RANDY HANSEN                    1980      CAPITOL            EST 12119
SCOTT ROSBURG      B V (A
CHARLES TAPP       D V (A
```

HANS A PLAST

```
                                 (A) HANS A PLAST                    1978 LLAVA               79 449
```

JUNIOR HANSON

```
JUNIOR HANSON      G V (AB       (A) NOW HEAR THIS                   1973      MANTICORE US 66670 UK K43507
JEAN ROUSSEL       K   (A        (B) MAGIC DRAGON                    1974      MANTICORE    US   MC 66672
CLIVE CHAMAN       B   (A
CONRAD ISADORE     D   (A   LISLE HARPER     B   (A  REBOP KWAKU BAAH PERC (A  JIMMY THOMAS   V (A
KEN CUMBERBATCH    PNO (A   CHRIS WOOD       FLT (A  BOB TENCH       G V (A  GODFREY MACLEAN D V(A
NEIL MURRAY        B   (B   BROTHER JAMES    PERC (B  GLEN LEFLEUR    D   (B  ANDRE LEWIS    K (B
MARLO HENDERSON    G   (B   CASSANDRA        V   (B
```

BO HANSSON

```
BO HANSSON         G K B (ALL    (A) LORD OF THE RINGS              1972 PVC US 7907  CHARISMA UK 1059
RUNE CARLSSON      D   (ABC      (B) MAGICIANS HAT                  1973 CHARISMA UK 1073 . US  6062
GUNNAR BERGSTEN    WIND (ABC      (C) ATTIC THOUGHTS                 1975 SIRE US 7525 CHARISMA UK   1113
STEN BERGMAN       FLT (ABC      (D) WATERSHIP DOWN                 1977 SIRE US 6044 CHARISMA UK   1132
KENNY HAKANSSON    B G (BCD
ROLF SCHERRER      G   (BC  BOBO STENSSON    K   (B  OWE GUSTAVSSON  B   (B  PELLE EKMAN    D (B
GORAN FREESE       SAX (B   BILL OHRSTROM    CONGA(B  GORAN LAGERBERG B G (CD  THOMAS NETZLER B (CD
MATS GLENNGARD     VLN (C   BO SKOGLUND      D   (D  TORBJORN EKLUND FLT (D  FREDRIK NOREN  D (D
PONTUS OLSSON      PNO (D
```

HANSSON & KARLSSON

```
BO HANSSON         ORG (AB       (A) SWEDISH UNDERGROUND            1967      POLYDOR            184 196
JAN KARLSSON       D   (AB       (B) GOLD (COMPILATION)             19        KARUSSELL          2468 009
```

HANUMAN

```
AOLF-RUDIGER UHLIG  K V (A       (A) HANUMAN                        1972 KUCKUCK      GER    2375 012
JORG HAHNFELD      B   (A
PETER BARTH        WIND (A   THOMAS HOLM      D   (A
```

HERBIE HANCOCK

```
HERBIE HANCOCK      K V  (ALL      (A) TAKIN' OFF                      1963 BLUENOTE                    84109
EDDIE HENDERSON     TRP PERC(JLOd   (B) MY POINT OF VIEW               1963 BLUENOTE                    84126
BILLY HART          D PERC(JLQ      (C) INVENTIONS & DIMENSIONS        196  BLUENOTE                    84147
JULIAN PRIESTER     TROM (JLd       (D) EMPYREAN ISLES                 1964 BLUENOTE                    84175
BUSTER WILLIAMS     B PERC(JLQd     (E) HERBIE HANCOCK                 1964 BLUENOTE                    84190
BENNY MAUPIN   WIND PERC(JLMNdhlm   (F) MAIDEN VOYAGE                  1966 BLUENOTE  US 40020          84195
JACO PASTORIUS      B   (L          (G) SPEAK LIKE A CHILD             1968 BLUENOTE      40025         84279
PATRICK GLEASON     SYN (L          (H) PRISONER                      19   BLUNOTE                     84321
VICTOR PONTOJA      CONGA(L         (I) THE BEST OF                    19   BLUNOTE   US 33199          80546
CANDY LOVE          V   (L          (J) MWANDISHI                      1971 WB        US 1898   UK K46077
SANDRA STEVENS      V   (L          (K) CROSSING                       1972 WB        US 2617   UK K46164
DELTA HORNE         V   (L          (L) SEXTANT                        1972 CBS       US 33212  UK 65582
VICTOR DOMAGALSKI   V   (L          (M) HEAD HUNTERS                   1974 CBS       US 32731  UK 65928
SCOTT BEACH         V   (L          (N) THRUST                         1974 CBS       US 32965  UK 80193
RON CARTER          B   (Gcde       (O) TREASURE CHEST                 1974 WB        US 2/2807
TONY WILLIAMS       D   (cde        (P) BLOW UP    (SOUNDTRACK) VAR ARTIST)197 MGM   US 4447
FREDDIE HUBBARD     TPT (d          (Q) FAT ALBERT ROTUNDA             1974 WB        US 1834   UK K46039
WAYNE SHORTER       SAX (d          (R) DEATH WISH                     1975 CBS       US 33199  UK 80546
WAH WAH WATSON      G   (Xdehmn      (S) MAN CHILD                     1975 CBS       US 33812  uk 69185
RAY PARKER          B   (Xdmnh      (T) LIVE IN JAPAN  (DBL)           1975 CBS/SONY  JAP 98/99
JOHNNY COLES        HRNS (Qe        (U) SUCCOTASH                      1975 BLUENOTE  US LA152
PAUL JACKSON        B   (MYdelm     (V) WATER BABIES                   197  CBS                 UK 81741
FREDDIE WASHINGTON  B   (eh         (W) HANCOCK                        1975 BLUENOTE  US LA399
SHEILA ESCOVEDO     V   (e          (X) SECRETS                        1976 CBS       US 34280  UK 81591
JAMES LEVI          V   (Xdh        (Y) KAWAIDA                        1976 DJM                 UK 22008
KENNETH NASH        PERC (Xdm       (Z) LIVE UNDER THE SKY             1976 CBS/SONY  JAP 1037/875
LEON CHANCLER       D   (Jom        (b) FLOOD                          1977 cbs
JOSE AREAS          PERC (J         (c) HERBIE HANCOCK TRIO            1977 CBS       JAP 25AP650
RONNIE MONTROSE     G   'J          (d) V S O P                        1977 CBS       US 34976  UK 88235
GARNETT BROWN       TROM (Q         (e) QUINTET                        1977 CBS                 UK 88273
TOOTIE HEATH        D   (Q          (f) SUNLIGHT                       1978 CBS       US 34906  UK 82240
HARVEY MASON        D   (Mo         (g) TEMPEST IN THE COLOSSEUM       1978 CBS/SONY  JAP 40AP771/2
ALPHONSE MOUSON     D   (nlh        (h) FEETS DONT FAIL ME NOW         1979 CBS       US 35764  UK 83491
BILL SUMMERS        PERC (Mhlmo     (j) AN EVENING WITH                1979 CBS                 UK 88329
BYRON MILLER        B   (ml         (k) IN CONCERT(DUETS)              1979 CBS       US 35663
BYRON DAVIS         PERC (h         (l) DIRECT STEP                    1979 CBS/SONY  JAP 30AP1032
DON KERR            V   (Xm         (m) BEST OF                        1979 CBS                 UK 84106
BILL CHAMPLIN       V   (n          (n) MONSTER                        1980 CBS                 UK 84237
RANDY HANSEN        G   (n          (o) MR HANDS                       1980 CBS                 UK 84638
LUTHER WATERS       V   (hmn        (p) HANCOCK ALLEY                  1980 MANHATTAN           UK 5021
OREN WATERS         V   (HMN        (q) MAGIC WINDOWS                  1981 CBS                 UK 85144
MICHAEL CLARK       D   (m
EDDIE WATKINS       B   (hm
GREG WALKER         V   (n    FRED DOBBS      V(Xm    WEBSTER LEWIS   K   (lh  GAVIN CHRISTOPHER  V(n
MAXINE WILLARD      V   (hmn  JULIA TILLMAN   V(Xmn   CHICK COREA     K   (k   COKE ESCOVEDO    PERC (hm
RAUL RAKOW          PERC (m   ART BALDACCI V  (Xm  FREDDIE WASHINGTON B   (n   JERRY DODGION        (G
CARLOS SANTANA      G   (n    JAMES GADSON D  (Xm  PETER PHILLIPS    TROM (G   THAD JONES HRNS      (G
MICKEY ROKER        D   (G    CHRIS MANCINI V  (Xm  RAY OBIEDO       G   (1hm
```

HAPPY THE MAN

```
KIT WATKINS  SYN K   (AB         (A) HAPPY THE MAN        1976   ARISTA US 4120 UK  SPART1057
MICK BECK        PERC (A         (B) CRAFTY HANDS         1978   ARISTA US 4181
RICK KENNELL     B   (AB
STANLEY WHITAKER G V (AB FRANK WYATT WIND K V (AB RON RIDDLE  D PERC(B
```

HAPSHASH & COLOURED COAT

```
TONY McPHEE      G V (AB         (A) HAPSHASH & COLOURED COAT     1967 MINIT      US       40001
GUY STEVENS          (A          (B) WESTERN FLYER                1969 LIBERTY    UK       83212
MICHAEL RAMSDEN  V   (B          (B) WESTERN FLYER                1969 IMPERIAL   US   LP 12430
ANDY RENTON      D   (B          (C) HUMAN HOST & THE HEAVY METAL KIDS 19 LIBERTY UK     40001
MICHAEL MAYHEW   G   (a
HEAVY METAL KIDS PERC (B  EDDIE TRIOO B   (AB FREDDIE BALLERINI   VLN(AB  MIKE BATT   K   (AB
MICKEY FINN
```

HARDCAKE SPECIAL

```
ANDY KIRNBERGER   G K  (A         (A) HARDCAKE SPECIAL            1974 BRAIN      GERM     1060
REINHART BOPP     G    (
RON SCHEEPMAKER   K    (A  JOCHEN LEUSCHNER G  (A  GUNTER BOPP  B V  (A  HANS HARBRECHT  D  (A
```

HARCOURTS HEROS

```
CHARLIE HARCOURT  G V  (A         (A) 1977 LINE UP
RAY JACKSON       V    (A
MARTIN CRAGGS SAX PERC (A  COLIN MASON      D    (A  BARRY SPENCE  B V  (A  LES DODDS     G  (A
```

HARD ROAD

```
JOHN SPENCER      G    (A         (A) NO PROBLEM         1979   GOODSTUFF   UK   LP1002
KRIS GRAY         G V  (A
HEANOR HUCKNALL   B    (A  RORY O'CARROLL       (A
```

HARD STUFF

```
JOHN GUSTAFSON    B    (A         (A) BULLET PROOF       1972   PURPLE UK 7505 MERCURY US 663
JOHN CANN         G    (A         (B) BOLEX DEMENTIA     1973   PURPLE UK 7507
PAUL HAMMOND      D    (
```

EDDIE HARDIN

```
EDDIE HARDIN     V K  (A     (A)YOU CANT TEACH AN OLD DOG NEW TRICKS 1977 ATTIC   UK  LAT 1023
LIZA STRIKE      V    (A     ( ) HOME IS WHERE YOU FIND IT  1972 DECCA      UK  TXS 106
HENRY SPINETTI   D    (A
IAN PAICE        D    (AB B J COLE     STEEL   (A  MO FOSTER    B   (A  HELEN CHAPELLE  V  (A
BARRY DE SOUZA   D    (A  ROGER GLOVER  PERC V (A  DORIS TROY   V   (A  RAY FLEMING     G V(A
DEE MURRAY       B    (AB BOBBY KEYS    SAX   (B  JIM PRICE    HRNS (B  RAY FENWICK G V    (B
PETE YORK        D    (B
```

TIM HARDIN

```
TIM HARDIN        K V G(ALL    (A) TIM HARDIN 1              1966 VERVE   UK 5018 US 3004 GER 9501
WARREN BERNHARDT  K     (F     (B) TIM HARDIN 2              1967 VERVE   UK 6002      US    3022
BOB COHEN         G     (K     (C) THIS IS TIM HARDIN        1967 ATCO    UK 588 082   US   33210
GARY KLAIN        K     (F     (D) LIVE IN CONCERT           1968 VERVE   UK 6010      US    3049
DONALD McDONALD   D     (F     (E) TIM HARDIN 4              1969 VERVE   UK 6016      US    3064
MONTE DUNN        G     (F     (F) SUITE FOR SUSAN MOORE & DAMIAN 1970 CBS UK 63571    US    9787
KEITH             TPT   (F     (G) THE BEST OF               1970 VERVE   UK 2317003   US    3078
DAVID             SAX   (F     (H) BIRD ON A WIRE            1970 CBS     UK 64335     US   30551
BUZZ              CELESTE (F    (I) PAINTED HEAD             1973 CBS     UK 65209     US   31764
ANDY BOWN         B     (K     (J) ARCHETYPES                1973 MGM                  US    4952
PHILIPE           CONGA(F      (K) NINE                      1974 ANTILLES US 7023 GM UK  1004
WALTER YOST       B     (A     (K) NINE                      1974 PHILIPS    GER     6370 105
JOHN MEALING      K     (K     (AB) TIM HARDIN 1&2           1974 VERVE   UK 2683 048
EARL PALMER       D     (A     (L) STATE OF GRACE            1981 CBS     US 37164
BOB BUSHWELL      B     (A
MIKE DRISCOLL     D     (K  JIMMY HOROWITZ  K   (K  PETER FRAMPTON   G   (K  LESLEY DUNCAN   V  (K
LIZA STRIKE       V     (K  MADELINE BELL   V   (K  SUSAN GLOVER     V   (K  DAVID KATZ    STRINGS(K
JOHN SEBASTIAN    HCA   (A  GARY BURTON VIBES (A  PHIL KRAUSS      VIBES(A  BUDDY SALZMAN   D  (A
```

HARDIN & YORK

```
EDDIE HARDIN      K V   (ALL   (A) TOMORROW TODAY            1969 BELL    US 6043      UK SBLL 125
PETER YORK        D     (ALL   (B) WORLDS SMALLEST BIG BAND  1970 BELL                 UK SBLL 136
HERBIE FLOWERS    B     (A     (C) FOR THE WORLD             1971 LONDON US 602 DECCA UK SKL 5095
MIKE HURST        G     (A     (AB)POP HISTORY               1972 POLYDOR              2625 021
MEL THORPE        HRNS  (AE    (D) AIN'T NO BREEZE           197  PHONOGRAM            6360 622
VIC FLICK         G     (A     (E) HARDIN & NEW YORK         1981 TELDEC      GER     6 24595
ROGER MENNS       K SYN(E
STEVE RICHARDSON  B V   (E
```

HARDMEAT

```
MICK CARLESS      D PERC(A     (A) HARDMEAT                  1970 WB                   WS 1852
MICK DOLAN  G HCA V (AB        (B) THROUGH A WINDOW          1970 WB WS 3008 US  UK    WS 1879
STEVE DOLAN       B G V(AB
IAN WHITEMAN  PNO FLT(A  BRUCE HOWARD     PNO  (A  PETE WESTBROOK  FLT (B  PHIL JUMP  K  (B
```

LINDA HARGROVE

```
LINDA HARGROVE    G V   (ALL   (A) MUSIC IS YOUR MISTRESS    1973 ELEKTRA     US  EKS 75063
BUDDY HARMON      D     (BA    (B) BLUE JEAN COUNTRY QUEEN   1974 ELEKTRA     US     7E1013
KENNY MALONE      D     (B     (C) LOVE,YOU'RE THE TEACHER   1975 CAPITOL     US  ST 11463
JERRY CARRIGAN    D     (BA    (D) JUST LIKE YOU             1976 CAPITOL     US  ST 11564
BOB MOORE         B     (BA    (E) IMPRESSIONS               1977 CAPITOL     US  ST 11685
TOMMY COGBILL     B     (B
LARRY BUTLER   PNO  (AB  HARGUS'PIG'ROBBINS PNO (AB  BOBBY WOOD     PNO (B  PETE DRAKE  STEEL  (AB
BOBBY BLACK    STEEL(B  PETE WADE       G    (B  JIMMY CAPPS      G   (B  DAVE KIRBY      G  (AB
REGGIE YOUNG   G     (B  RONNIE LIGHT    G    (B  LARRY BLACK      G   (B  GRADY MARTIN    G  (AB
JIMMY COLVARD  G     (BA  BUDDY SPICHER   FDL  (B  BOBBY THOMPSON BANJO(BA  MARY HOLLADAY   V  (B
GINGER HOLLADAY  V  (B  LEA JANE BERINATI V   (B  JERRY SMITH      PNO (A  JOE ALLEN      B  (A
MELBA MONTGOMERY V  (A  GARY S PAXTON SINGERS (B  CHIP YOUNG       G   (A  JACK SOLOMAM    G  (A
EARL BALL      K     (A  HENRY STRZELECKI B   (A  ANITA GROUP SINGERS  (A  KARL HIMMEL     D  (A
HAROLD BRADLEY G     (A  SHELLEY KURLAND STRINGS(A
```

STEVE HARLEY & COCKNEY REBEL

```
STEVE HARLEY       V    (ALL      (A) THE HUMAN MENAGERIE    1974 EMI  US 11294 UK  EMA  759
STUART ELLIOTT     D    (ABEDFGHKL1 (B) PSYCHOMODO           1974 EMI  US 11330 UK  EMC 3033
JEAN PAUL CROCKER  VLN  (ABEFK     (C) BEST YEARS OF OUR LIVES 1975 EMI US 11394 UK EMC 3068
PAUL JEFFREYS      B    (ABFK      (D) TIMELESS FLIGHT       1976 EMI  US 11500 UK  EMA  775
MILTON REAME JAMES K    (ABFK      (E) LOVE IS A PRIMA DONNA 1976 EMI  US 11596 UK  EMC 3156
JIM CREGAN         G V  (ECFKD     (F) A CLOSER LOOK         1976 EMI  US 11456
GEORGE FORD        B    (CEFGHKD    (G) FACE TO FACE         1977 EMI  US 11661 UK  EMSP  320
DUNCAN MACKAY      K    (CEFGKHD    (H) HOBO WITH A GRIN     1978 EMI  US !!''= UK  EMC 3254
LINDSAY ELLIOTT    PERC (DEGK1      (J) CANDIDATE            1979 EMI           UK  EMC 3311
JO PARTRIDGE       G    (EK1        (K)BEST OF STEVE HARLEY & COCKNEY R 1980 EMI UK EMC 3345
STUART CALVER      V    (G         (1) 1979 OCT CONCERT LINE UP
TONY RIVERS        V    (G
JOHN PERRY         V    (G   BILL PAYNE      PNO  (K  BOBBY KIMBALL   V  (K  JIMMY HOROWITZ  K (1
BOB GLAUB          B    (K   GREG POREE      G    (K  BILL CHAMPLIN   V  (K  TOMMY KELLY     V (K
JOHN GIBLIN        B    (1   NICO RAMSDEN    G    (1  LINDA LEWIS     V  (C  YVONNE KEELY    V (CDH
TINA CHARLES       V    (C   MARTIN JAY      V    (C  LIZA STRIKE     V  (CD BARRY ST JOHN   V (D
PATRICIA PAAY      V    (D   JOY YATES       V    (D  MADELINE BELL   V  (D  GEORGE FORD     V (D
PETER CLARKE       V    (D   LEROY WIGGINS   V    (D  LARRY STEEL     V  (D
```

HARLIS

```
CHARLY MAUCHER    B V   (AB    (A) HARLIS                    1975 SKY                  001
WERNER LOHR       D V   (AB    (B) NIGHT MEETS THE DAY       1976 SKY                  008
WOLFGANG KRANTZ   G     (AB
ARNDT SCHULZ      G     (AB
```

HARLEQUINN

```
GEORGE BELANGER   V     (A     (A) LOVE CRIMES               1981 A&M
GARY GOLDEN       K V G(A
RAPLH JANES       B     (A   GLEN WILLOWS     G V  (A  DAVID BUDZAK    D V (A
```

HARMONIA

```
DIETER MOEBIUS    K  V  (AB    (A) HARMONIA                  1973 BRAIN                1044
JOACHIM ROEDELIUS K  V(AB      (B) DE LUXE                   1975 BRAIN                1073
MICHAEL ROTHER    K G V(AB     ( ) DINO                      197  BRAIN       GER    0040 116
MANI NEUMEIER     D PERC(B
```

HARMONIUM

```
                               (A) L'HEPTADE                 19   CBS                  88234
```

ROY HARPER

```
ROY HARPER      G V B K SYN(ALL   (A) SOPHISTICATED BEGGAR                1967 STRIKE              JHL 105
BILL BRUFORD         D   (J        (A) SOPHISTICATED BEGGAR                1970 YOUNGBLOOD               SYB.7
HENRY McCULLOUGH     G   (K        (A) SOPHISTICATED BEGGAR                1972 BIRTH RAB.3 1977 BIGBEN 502
KEITH MOON           D   (         (B) COME OUT FIGHTING GHENGIS SMITH     1967 CBS            UK      63184
DAVE COCHRAN             (JK       (C) FOLKJOKEOPUS                        1969 LIBERTY        UK      LBS 83231
JIMMY PAGE           G   (RFH      (C) FOLKJOKEOPUS                        1975 SUNSET         UK      SLS 50373
JOHN HALSEY          D   (K        (C) FOLKJOKEOPUS                        19   WORLD PACIFIC  US      21888
RONNIE LANE        G B   (K        (D) FLAT BAROQUE & BERSERK              1970 HARVEST US 418 UK  SHVL 776
BRIAN HODGES         B   (RF       (D) FLAT BAROQUE & BERSERK              1978 CHRYSALIS      US      1160
DAVE LAWSON          K   (KQ       (E) STORMCOCK                           1971 HARVEST        UK  SHVL 789
LAURIE ALLEN         D   (BF       (E) STORMCOCK                           1978 CHRYSALIS      US      1161
CHRIS SPEDDING           (J        (F) LIFE MASK                           1973 HARVEST        UK  SHVL 808
IAN ANDERSON       FLT   (H        (F) LIFE MASK                           1978 CHRYSALIS      US      1162
ANDY ROBERTS         G   (KQ       (G) VALENTINE                           1974 HARVEST        UK  SHSP 4027
KEITH EMERSON        K   (D        (G) VALENTINE                           1974 PATHE          FR  062 05531
TONY CARR                (RF       (G) VALENTINE                           1978 CHRYSALIS      US      1163
BRIAN DAVISON        D   (DR       (H) FLASHES FROM THE ARCHIVES           1974 HARVEST        UK  SHDW 405
LEE JACKSON          B   (D        (H) FLASHES FROM THE ARCHIVES           197  PATHE          FR  162 05736
RAY WARLEIGH      WIND   (JR       (H) FLASHES FROM THE ARCHIVES           1978 CHRYSALIS      US      1164
WINGS                    (K        (J) WHEN AN OLD CRICKETER               1975 CHRYSALIS      US      1105
TONY VISCONTI  RECORDER(D          (J) HQ                                  1975 HARVEST        UK  SHSP 4046
STEVE BROUGHTON  K G V(KJRQ        (J) HQ                                  1975 PATHE          FR  066 05883
B J COLE          STEEL(KQ         (K) BULLINAMINGVASE                     1977 HARVEST        UK  SHSP 4060
HERBIE FLOWERS       B   (K        (K) BULLINAMINGVASE                     1977 PATHE          FR  068 06336
RUSS                 B   (C        (K) ONE OF THOSE DAYS IN ENGLAND        1977 CHRYSALIS      US      1138
BRIAN GOFF               (K        (L) COMMERCIAL BREAK                    1977 HARVEST        UK  SHSP 4077
PERCY JONES          B   (K        (M) THE EARLY YEARS                     1977 EMBASSY        UK      31544
JIMMY McCULLOCH      G   (K        (N) ROY HARPER 70/75                    1978 HARVEST        UK  SHSM 2025
DAVID BEDFORD        K   (EGJQ     (Q) UNKNOWN SOLDIER                     1980 HARVEST        UK  SHVL 820
MOX                      (C        (R) LIFE MASK                           1981
CLEM                 D   (C        (K) AFTER LEGAL ACTION(FEB 1979)        ONE TRACK REMOVED
NICKY              PNO   (C
```

```
JOHN PAUL JONES          (J   SKAILA KANGA       (A   ALVIN LEE          (A   MAX MIDDLETON      K   (K
DAVE PLOWMAN             (K   DAVID GILMOUR      (JQ  JANE               (C   S FLAVIUS MERCURIUS    (E
GRIMETHORPE COLLIERY BAND(Q   SARA POZZO         (Q   JIM CUOMO          (Q   HAYDN BENDALL          (Q
NEIL JASON               (Q   WILL LEE           (Q   DAVE SCANCE        (Q   SAL DiTROIA            (Q
TONY LEVI                (Q   DON GROLNICK       (Q   HUGH BURNS         (Q   TIM DONALD             (Q
JIM BAIN                 (Q   ANDY NEWMARK       (Q   JIMMY MAELIN       (Q   PETE WINGFIELD     K   (Q
GEORGE CONSTANTINO       (Q   JO PARTRIDGE       (Q   KATE BUSH        V (Q
```

HARPERS BIZARRE

```
TED TEMPLEMAN     G V  (ABCDE   (A) FEELIN' GROOVY                  1967 WB              US   WS 1693
DICK SCOPPETTONE  G    (ABCDEF  (B) ANYTHING GOES                   1967 WB              US   WS 1716
EDDIE JAMES       G    (ABCDEF  (C) SECRET LIFE OF HARPERS BIZARRE  1968 WB              US   WS 1739
JOHN PETERSON     D    (ABCDE   (D) HARPERS BIZARRE 4               1969 WB              US   WS 1784
DICK YOUNT        B    (ABCDEF  (E) BEST OF                         1974 WB              UK   K56044
VAN DYKE PARKS  PNO    (E       (F) AS TIME GOES BY                 1976 FOREST BAY CO   US   7545
```

SLIM HARPO

```
SLIM HARPO V HCA G(DIED 1970)ALL  (A) A LONG DRINK OF THE BLUES   1965 STATESIDE    UK   SL 10135
GUITAR GABLE       G   (DF        (B) HE KNEW THE BLUES            19   BLUE HORIZON UK   763844
WARREN STORM       D   (F         (B) HE KNEW THE BLUES            19   EXCELLO      US   8013
FATS PERRODIN      B   (DF        (B) HE KNEW THE BLUES            1978 SONET        UK   SNTF 769
JERRY WEST         D   (D         (C) TIP ON IN                    19   PRESIDENT    US   PTS 1017
BOBBY McBRIDE      B   (F         (C) TIP ON IN                    19   EXCELLO      US   8008
JAMES JOHNSON      G   (D         (D) TRIGGER FINGER               1971 BLUE HORIZON UK   2431 013
SAMMY K BROWN      D   (D         (E) BLUES HANGOVER               1976 FLYRIGHT     UK   LP 520
RUDOLPH RICHARD    G   (D         (F) GOT LOVE IF YOU WANT IT      1980 FLYRIGHT     UK   FLY 558
GEESE AUGUST       D   (D         (G) BABY SCRATCH MY BACK         19   EXCELLO      US   8005
CLARENCE ETIENNE   D   (F         (H) RAINING IN MY HEART          19   EXCELLO      US   8003
AUSTIN BROUSSARD   D   (F         (I) THE BEST OF                  19   EXCELLO      US   8010
AL FOREMAN         G   (F
MERTON THIBODEAUX PNO  (F   RUFUS THIBODEAUX  B   (F
```

GEORGE HARRASMENT

```
GEORGE HARRASMENT       (A      (A) MASAI SLEEP WALKING     19   BLACK NOISE   UK   12 6
MICHELLE                (A
L VOAG              B   (A   THE HOMOSEXUALS  (A   ZOE   (A   VIDA   (A
```

CAREY BELL HARRINGTON

```
CAREY BELL HARRINGTON V HCA(AB  (A) BLUES HARP    19   DELMARK     DS 622
DAVE MYERS       B   (B         (B) LAST NIGHT    1973 BLUESWAY    BLS 6079
WILLIE SMITH     D   (B
EDDIE TAYLOR     G   (B   JOE PERKINS K  (B
```

DERRICK HARRIOTT

```
DERRICK HARRIOTT        (ALL    (A) UNDERTAKER        19   TROJAN    TBL 114
                                (B) PSYCHEDELIC TRAIN  19   TROJAN    TBL 141
                                (C) REGGAE HITS        1975 TROJAN    TRLS 116
```

DON 'SUGARCANE' HARRIS

```
DON SUGARCANE HARRIS V FDL(ALL  (A) KEEP ON DRIVING          19   MUSIDISC 15060 +   MPS 68027
VOLKER KRIEGEL    G    (AFGI    (B) FIDDLER ON THE ROCK      1970 BASF878  POLYDOR   20878
TERJE RYPDAL      G    (C       (B) FIDDLER ON THE ROCK      19   MUSIDISC 15062 +   MPS 68028
NEVILLE WHITEHEAD B    (C       (C) GOT THE BLUES            19   POLYDOR            21283
ROBERT WYATT           (C       (C) GOT THE BLUES            19   MUSIDISC 15079 +   MPS 68029
PAUL LAGOS        D    (BDEJ    (D) CUPFUL OF DREAMS         1973 POLYDOR            21792
HARVEY MANDEL     G    (BDJ     (D) CUPFUL OF DREAMS         1973 BASF US            MPS 68030
LARRY TAYLOR      B    (BD      (E) I'M YOUR CASE            19   MPS  21912         MPS 68031
JOHNNY OTIS            (H       (F) FLASHIN' TIME            19   SONOPRESSE 60204   MPS 68032
SHUGGIE OTIS    G B    (H       (G) SUGARCANE                1971 EPIC US 26524  +     30027
CLIFTON EDDIE     D    (E       (H) DON'SUGARCANE 'HARRIS    1970 EPIC  26286
DEWEY TERRY       K    (EDFI    (I) KEY STOP                 19   BASF               MPS 68032
JAMES BRADSHAW    G    (E       (J) CHOICE CUTS              1972 EPIC US 31401
RANDY RESNICK     G    (EDJ     (K) NEW VIOLIN SUMMIT        1971 METRONOME          22720
RICHARD APLANALP SAX  (E   JEAN LUC PONTE   FDL  (K   MICHAEL URBANIAK  VLN (K
BILL SPRAGUE     TPT  (E   DALNE VAIL       V    (E   ELSIE LEWIS           (E   TONY OXLEY   D (A
WOLFGANG DAUNER    K  (C   GUNTER LENZ           (FI  TODD CANADY           (FI  VICTOR CONTE B (DJ
```

EMMYLOU HARRIS

```
     EMMYLOU HARRIS      V G  (ALL       (A) GLIDING BIRD                        1969 JUBILEE          US    JGS  0031
     BEN KEITH           STEEL(BCG       (A) GLIDING BIRD                        1979 PYE              UK    PKL  5577
     BYRON BERLINE FDL MAND (BC          (A) GLIDING BIRD                        19   AMOS             US         12052
     JAMES BURTON        G    (BCDEGL     (B) PIECES OF THE SKY                   1975 REPRISE US 2213  UK    K 54037
     GLEN D HARDIN       K    (BCDEGL     (B) PIECES OF THE SKY                   197  WB RI   US 2284
     EMORY GORDY         B    (CDEGLK     (C) ELITE HOTEL                         1976 REPRISE US 2236  UK    K 54060
     JOHN WARE           D    (CDEGLK     (D) LUXURY LINER                        1977 REPRISE US 2998
     HANK DE VITO        STEEL(CDEGL      (D) LUXURY LINER                        1977 WB      US 3115  UK    K 56334
     RODNEY CROWELL      G V  (CDEGL      (E) 1/4 MOON IN A TEN CENT TOWN         1978 WB      US 3141  UK    K 56443
     ALBERT LEE          G V  (DEGLK      (F) PROFILE          (COMP)             1978 WB      US 3258  UK    K 56570
     RAY POHLMAN         B    (B          (G) BLUE KENTUCKY GIRL                  1979 WB                UK    K 56627
     RON TUTT            D    (BCG        (H) CHRISTMAS ALBUM(LIGHT IN THE STABLE)79 WB        US 3484
     HERB PEDERSEN G BANJ V (BCD1         (J) HER BEST SONGS                      1980 K TEL             UK    NE 1058
     DON EVERLY          V    (G          (K) ROSES IN THE SNOW                   1980 WB      US 3422  UK    K 56796
     BERNIE LEADON V G BANJ (BC           (L) EVANGELINE                          1981 WB      US 3508  UK    K 56880
     BRIAN AHERN         B G (BCDEGLK
     RICK CUNHA          G    (BCD  RICHARD GREENE   FDL  (B  FAYSSOUX STARLING  V (BCDEG  BILL PAYNE       K  (BC
     BRUCE ARCHER        G    (AB   TOM GUIDERA       B   (B  DANNY PENDLETON    STEEL(B  RICKY SKAGGS FDL MAND(BDGLK
     DUKE BARDWELL       B    (BG   AMOS GARRETT      G   (BCL MARK CUFF          D  (B  LINDA RONSTADT    V  (BCGLK
     DIANNE BROOKS       V    (CDE  JOHN STARLING     V   (C  JONATHAN EDWARDS   V  (C  MIKE AULDRIDGE    G  (CD
     DOLLY PARTON        V    (DGLK NICOLETTE LARSON  V   (DE MICK RAPHAEL       HCA(CDEGL CHERYL WARREN    V  (GL
     FRANK RICKARD       G    (L    TONY RICE         G V (LK SHARON WHITE       V  (LK DON JOHNSON      K V(L
     DAVID BRIGGS        K    (L    HAL BLAINE        F   (L  BRYAN BOWERS       AHARP(K BUCK WHITE       K V (K
     TONY BROWN          K    (GL   MIKE BOWDEN       B   (GL LINCOLN DAVIS      ACC (G TANYA TUCKER     V  (G
     SHARON HICKS        V    (G    CRAIG SAFAN      STR  (L  JERRY DOUGLAS      DOB G(LK WAYLON JENNINGS  V  (L
     BARRY TASHIAN       V    (L    LARRIE LONDIN     D   (L  STEVE FISHELL      DOB G(L MAC REBBENACK    K  (L
     LYNN LANGHAM        SYN  (L    WILLIE NELSON     V   (K  JOHNNY CASH        V  (K
```

HI TIDE HARRIS

```
     HI TIDE HARRIS      V G  (AB        (A) CELEBRATING WITH HI TIDE HARRIS     1978 RCA              JAP   RVL 8031
     JUNJI YAMAGISHI     G    (A         (B) GENTLEMANS BLUES                    197  RCA              JAP   RVL
     OSAMU ISHIDA        G    (A
     SHINJI SHIOTSUGU    G    (A    TADASHI KOBORI    B   (A  YU FUJII           B  (A  TERUO MATSUMOTO  D  (A
     CHARLES SHIMIZU     K    (A    YASUHARU NAKANISHI K  (A  TATSURO KONDO      K  (A  SHUICHI CHINO    D  (A
     RYUICHIRO SENOO     HCA  (A    TETSU NAKAMURA   SAX  (A  JUNICHI KANEKAZI   TPT(A  ICHIRO ARAI     HRNS (A
```

GENE HARRIS

```
     GENE HARRIS         G V  (A         (A) ASTRAL SIGNAL                       1974 BLUENOTE         US    LA 313
     HARVEY MASON        D    (A
     JERRY PETERS        K V  (A    CHUCK RAINEY      B   (A  JOHN ROWEN         G  (A  DAVID T WALKER   G  (A
     KEG JOHNSON         V    (A    JIM SIFFLETT     HRNS (A  GEORGE BOHANNON    HRNS(A OSCAR BRASHEAR  HRNS(A
     SIDNEY MULDROW      HRNS (A    ERNIE WATTS      HRNS (A  MAXINE WILLARD WATERS V(A JULIA TILLMAN WATERS V(A
     OREN WATERS         V    (A    TRISHA CHAMBERLAIN V (A  LYNN MACK          V  (A
```

JET HARRIS

```
     JET HARRIS          B    (A         (A) REMEMBERING                         1976 DECCA            UK    REM.1
     TONY MEEHAN         D    (A
```

JOHNNY HARRIS

```
     JOHNNY HARRIS            (A         (A) ALL TO BRING YOU MORNING            1973 WB               UK    K56185
     JON ANDERSON        V    (A
     STEVE HOWE          G    (A
```

SHAKEY JAKE HARRIS

```
     SHAKEY JAKE HARRIS HCA V(ABC        (A) FURTHER ON UP THE ROAD              1969 LIBERTY          UK        83217
     JOHN MAYALL         G K  (B         (A) FURTHER ON UP THE ROAD              19   WORLD PACIFIC    US    21886
     KENNY COURTNEY      HCA  (A         (B) THE DEVIL'S HARMONICA               1972 POLYDOR US 5014  UK    2391 015
     ELLIOT INGBER       G    (B         (C) GOOD TIMES                          19   BLUESVILLE       US        1008
     PHIL PARKER         D    (B         (D) MOUTH HARP BLUES                    19   BLUESVILLE       US        1027
     WANDERING JOHN      PNO  (A
     LUTHER ALLISON      G    (A    ROBERT MOJO ELEM  B   (A  SUNNYLAND SLIM     PNO(A  DENNY BRUCE     PERC(A
     FRANCIS CLAY        D    (A    STEVE CUMMINS    PERC (A  FREDDY ROBINSON    G  (B  LARRY TAYLOR    B  (B
     RON SELICO          D    (B
```

SHAUN HARRIS

```
     SHAUN HARRIS        G V B(A         (A) SHAUN HARRIS                        1973 CAPITOL          ST    11168
     DAN HARRIS          G V  (A
     BEN BENAY           G    (A    DEAN PARKS        G   (A  BOBBY PHILLIPS     G  (A  HAL BLAINE      D  (A
     JIM GORDON          D    (A    JOHN GUERIN       D   (A  JOHANNA HARRIS     K  (A  LARRY KNECHTEL  K  (A
     MICHAEL OMARTIAN    K    (A    CAROL KAYE        B   (A  JOE OSBORN         B  (A  BRUCE JOHNSTON   V  (A
```

BILLY HARRISON

```
     BILLY HARRISON      V G  (A         (A) BILLY WHO?;                         1980 VAGABOND  GERM VRLP 8 80001
     NIELS TABY          D    (A
     PETER URBAN         K    (A    MARTIN TIEFENSEE  B   (A  HANNES BAUER       G  (A  RAINER BAUMANN   G  (A
```

WYNONIE HARRIS

```
     WYNONIE HARRIS      G V  (A         (A) GOOD ROCKIN' BLUES                  19   KING       US         1086
```

DON HARRISON BAND

```
     DON HARRISON        V G  (ABC       (A) DON HARRISON BAND                   1976 ATLANTIC US 18171 UK   K 50263
     STU COOK            B V  (ABC       (B) RED HOT                             1976 ATLANTIC US 18208 UK   K 50340
     DOUG CLIFFORD       D V  (ABC       (C) NOT FAR FROM FREE                   1977 MERCURY  US SRM11185 UK9100 044
     RUSSELL DASHIELL    G V  (ABC
     JOHN TANNER         K    (B    MICHAEL CARROLL   B   (C  JEFF MORROW        K  (C  JOEL PESKIN SAX (C
     GARY GOSSETT        D    (C    KAREN FRIEDMAN    V   (C  NOVI NOVAG         VILA(C DAN STICKLER    G  (C
     PAT MATA            V    (C    MEMPHIS HRNS          (A
```

GEFF HARRISON

```
     GEFF HARRISON       V    (A         (A) TOGETHER                            19   JUPITER               25595
     PETER OEHLER        G V  (A
     ALAN WROE           B V  (A    ASTOR ASTOR       D V (A  CHRIS KLOBER       K V (A
```

```
GEORGE HARRISON    G V  (ALL       (A) WONDERWALL                        1968 APPLE   FR 90490 US 3350 UK SAPCOR 1
ERIC CLAPTON       G    (CDFK       (B) ELECTRONIC SOUNDS                 1969 APPLE   US 3358      UK ZAPPLE2
JESSE ED DAVIS     G    (DG         (C) ALL THINGS MUST PASS              1971 APPLE   STCH639+PATHE FR  040789
RINGO STARR        D    (CDFE       (D) CONCERT FOR BANGLA DESH           1972 APPLE   STCX3385
JIM KELTNER        D    (DFEG       (E) LIVING IN A MATERIAL WORLD        1973 APPLE   PAS10006         US   3410
KLAUS VOORMANN     B    (CDFEG      (F) DARK HORSE                        1974 APPPLE  PAS 10008        US   3418
BILLY PRESTON      K    (CDFGH      (F) DARK HORSE                        1974 PATHE            FR 068 05774
RICHARD TEE        K    (GH         (F) DARK HORSE                        1980 M F P        UK        50510
LEON RUSSELL       K B V(DG         (G) EXTRA TEXTURE                     1975 APPLE   PAS 10009        US   3420
STEVE WINWOOD      K V  (K          (G) EXTRA TEXTURE                     1975 PATHE            FR 068 05952
WILLIE WEEKS       B    (FKGH       (H) 33 1/3                            1976 DARK HORSE K 56319+  US DH3005
ANDY NEWMARK       D    (FKG        (J) BEST OF                           1976 PARLOPHONE       UK  10011
GARY WRIGHT        K    (CFEGH      (J) BEST OF                           1976 PATHE            FR 068 06249
MICK JONES         G    (F          (J) BEST OF                           1976 CAPITOL          US  11578
DEREK TAYLOR            (G          (J) BEST OF                           1981 M F P        UK        50523
CHUCK FINDLEY      HRNS (FG         (K) GEORGE HARRISON                   1979 DARK HORSE K 56562+  US   3255
ALI AKBAR KHAN         (D          (L) SOMEWHERE IN ENGLAND               1981 DARK HORSE US 3492  UK  56870
DERREK VAN EATON   V    (F
ROGER KELLAWAY     PNO  (F  NICKY HOPKINS    PNO  (FEG DAVE MASON     G V  (C  JIM PRICE              (C
BOBBY KEYS         SAX  (C  GINGER BAKER     D    (C  RON WOOD       G    (F  JIM HORN      FLT     (FEDG
ROBBEN FORD        G    (F  PATTI HARRISON   V    (F  TOM SCOTT      SAX  (FG LON VAN EATON  V  (F
EMIL RICHARDS      PREC(FGHK MAX BENNETT B        (F  ALAN WHITE     D    (C  ALVIN LEE      G   (F
JOHN GUERIN        D    (F  PAUL STALLWORTH  B    (G  LEGS LARRY SMITH V  (G  NORM KINNEY PERC   (G
GAYLE LEVANY       HARP (K  JIM GORDON       D    (EG ZAKIR HASSIEN  TABLA(E  CARL RADLE      B  (DG
ALLA RAKAN         TABLA(D  BOB DYLAN    V HCA(D  DON PRESTON    V    (D  RAVI SHANKAR    SITAR   (D
KAMBLA RAVARTY     PERC (D  PETER HAM        G    (D  JOHN BARNHAM   STR  (E  DAVID FOSTER    K  (GH
PETER SELLERS           (G  DON AIRALI            (G  DENNIS KILLEEN      (G  ALVIN TAYLOR    D  (H
ERIC IDLE               (G  CHUCK TRAMELL         (G
```

```
JERRY HARRISON     V G B K(A       (A) THE RED AND BLACK                 1981 SIRE     UK        SRK 3631
YOGI HORTON        D    (A
JOHN COOKSEY       D    (A  STEVE SCALES     D PERC(A GEORGE NURRAY  B    (A  TINKER BARFIELD    B    (A
BERNIE WORRELL     K    (A  ADRIAN BELOW     G    (A  NONA HENDRYX   V    (A  DOLETTE McDONALD   V    (A
KOKO MAE EVANS     G    (A  DAVE JERDEN PROD      (A
```

```
MIKE HARRISON      V K HCA(ABC      (A) MIKE HARRISON                    1971 ISLAND US 9313   UK   ILPS 9170
KEN IVERSON        D V  (A          (B) SMOKESTACK LIGHTNING             1972 ISLAND US 9321   UK   ILPS 9209
PETER BATEY        B    (A          (C) RAINBOW RIDER                    1975 GOODEAR UK 7002+SONOPRESSE37007
NORBERT PUTNAM     B    (C          (C) RAINBOW RIDER                    1975 ISLAND US 9359
IAN HERBERT        G V K(A
FRANK KENYON       G V  (A  ARTHUR BELCHER   SAX  (A  PETER CARR     G    (B  JIMMY JOHNSON   G  (B
WAYNE PERKINS      G    (B  LUTHER GROSVENOR G    (B  BARRY BECKETT  K    (B  CLAYTON IVEY    K  (B
DAVID HOOD         B    (B  HARRISON CALLOWAY TPT (B  MIKE STACEY    TPT  (B  HARVEY  THOMPSON SAX (B
RONNIE EADES       SAX  (B  CHARLES ROSE     TROM (B  MORGAN FISHER  K    (C  KENNY BUTTREY   D  (C
MICKY JONES        G    (C  BOB COHEN        G    (C  WAYNE JACKSON  HRNS (C  KIRK LORANGE    G  (C
MEMPHIS HRNS            (C  20TH CENTURY SINGERS  (C  CORONA STAGE SCHOOL V(C
```

```
NEIL HARRISON      V K G (A        (A) ALL DRESSED UP WITH NOWHERE TO GO 1974 DERAM           SML 1115
JULI LANDO         V    (A
ADE COOKE          G SYN(A  ROB WRIGHT    G V    (A  MIKE FREEMAN   B    (A  JOHN MEYDAM     D PERC(A
GRAHAM PRESCETT    B K HCA(A B J COLE          STEEL(A PIP WILLIAMS  G    (A  PAUL KEOUGH     G  (A
JOHN RICHARDSON    D    (A  JIM LAWLESS      PERC (A  CHRIS LAWRENCE B    (A  PAUL NIEMAN     TROM(A
RICK KENTON        K    (A  KEITH WHITING    PROD (A
```

```
WILBERT HARRISON   V G  (ALL        (A) LETS WORK TOGETHER               1969          SUE US 8801 LONDON UK SH8415
                                    (B) BATTLE OF THE GIANTS(1 SIDE)     1962          JOY                 JOYS191
                                    (C) KANSAS CITY                      19            SPHERE       US   7000
                                    (D) WILBERT HARRISON                 1972          BUDDAH       US   5092
                                    (E) SOUL FOOD MAN                    19            CHELSEA      US    523
                                    (F) ANYTHING YOU WANT                19            WET SOUL     US   1001
                                    (G) SHOOT YOU FULL OF LOVE           19            JUGGERNAUT   US   8803
```

```
MELANIE HARROLD    V    (AB         (A) FANCY THAT(AS JOANNA CARLIN)     1977 DJM          DJF 20508
JERRY DONAHUE      G    (A          (B) BLUE ANGEL                       1979 DJM          DJF 20550
PAT DONALDSON      B    (A
JOHNNY VAN DERRICK VLN (A  TOMMY EYRE       K    (A  BOB HIRSCHMAN  TROM (A  HENRY SPINETTI  D  (A
GLEN LE FLEUR      D    (A  PETE ZORN    SAX FLT (A  KEITH NELSON   BANJO(A  PETE SOLLEY     K  (A
MICK MOODY         G    (A  MARTIN JAY       V    (A  GRAHAME SMITH  FDL  (B  JULIAN LITTMAN  G  (B
PAUL DI VINCI      V    (B  RICHARD BRUNTON  G    (B  BILL SKEAT     K FLT(B  SIMON MORTON    PERC(B
MALCOLM GRIFFITHS  TROM (B  BETSY COOKE      V    (B  ALBERT WING    SAX  (B  LIAM GENOCKEY   D  (B
GARY TAYLOR        B    (B
```

```
DEBBIE HARRY       V    (A          (A) KOO KOO                          1981 CHRYSALIS 1347  GER      203810
NILE RODGERS       G V  (A
BERNARD EDWARDS    B    (A  ROBERT SABINO    K    (A  TONY THOMPSON  D    (A  RAYMOND JONES   K  (A
CHRIS STEIN        G    (A  VINCENT DE ROSA  HRNS (A  RAY MALDONADO  HRNS (A  SAMMY FIGUEROA  PERC(A
MANUEL BADRENA     PERC (A  ROGER SQUITERO   PERC (A  SPUD & PU DEVO V    (A  GORDON GORDY    V  (A
FONZI THORNTON     V    (A  CHUCK MARTIN          (A
```

```
MARK GRIFFITHS     G    (A          (A) HEAVEN & HELL                    1969 PHILIPS          SBL  7891
CARL BARNWELL      G    (A
ROGER SWALLOW      D    (A  CLIFF JENKINS         (A STEVE MILLER        (A
```

```
BILLY HART              (A          (A) ENCHANCE                         1978 HORIZON          AMLJ 725
```

```
MICKEY HART       D V  (A       (A) ROLLING THUNDER                    1972 WB   US 2635    UK    K 46182
STEPHEN STILLS    G V  (A
JOHN CIPOLLINA    G    (A    JERRY GARCIA      G    (A   CARMELO GARCIA TIMBALES (A    BOB WEIR     G V (A
STEVE SHUSTER     FLT  (A    BARRY MELTON      G    (A   BILL CHAMPLIN   K    (A       ALLA RAKHA        (A
TOWER OF POWER    HRNS (A    DAVID FREIBERG K G V B(A   ROBBIE STOKES   G    (A       GRACE SLICK  V   (A
PHIL LESH         V    (A    MIKE HINTON  MARIMBA (A    ZAKIR HUSSAIN  TABLA(A       SAM ANDREW   G   (A
PAUL KANTNER      V    (A    GREG ERRICO       D    (A   TERRY HAGGERTY  B    (A       NANCY HINTON MARIMBA(A
```

```
MIKE HART         G V  (AB      (A) MIKE HART BLEEDS                   1970  DANDELION    UK          63756
NEIL FORD         G K  (A        (B) BASHER CHALKY PONGO & ME          1972  POLYDOR      UK     2310 211
JAN SCHELLHAS     K    (A
DAVE PAULL        B    (A    JOHN SKORSKY      D    (A   RICK SANDERS    G    (A       ANDY DONALDSON HCA (A
VIVIAN STANSHALL  V REC(B    MORAY SLADEN      BAN  (B   ROBIN PARK      K    (B       ED JONES     B    (B
JOHN RAMSEY       D V  (B    DAVE MURRICANE    K    (B   JOHN COMMING    V    (B       BOB HAMILTON V    (B
MIKE HARRIGAN     V    (B    TONY HAYGARTH     V    (B   DEREK O'CONNOR  V    (B       JOHN SHRAPNEL V   (B
```

```
TIM HART          G V  (A        (A) TIM HART                         1979 CHRYSALIS UK CHR1218  GER 6307658
RICK KEMP         B    (A
NIGEL PEGRUM      D    (A    VIC EMERSON       SYN  (A   STEWART GOLDRING K   (A       ASHLEY MULFORD  G  (A
MADDY PRIOR       V    (A    STEVE BROOMHEAD   G    (A   DES TONGUE      B    (A       PETE GLENNON    B  (A
DAVE HASSEL       PERC (A    ALAN FAWKES       WIND (A
```

```
TIM HART          G V  (ALL     (A) FOLK SONGS OF OLDE ENGLAND 1      1968  B&C              TEPEE105
MADDY PRIOR       V    (ALL     (A) FOLK SONGS OF OLDE ENGLAND 1      19    ADRHYTHM         ARP 53
ANDY IRVINE       MAND (C        (A) FOLK SONGS OF OLDE ENGLAND 1      1974  MOONCREST        CREST 23
JOHN RYAN         B    (  C      (B) FOLK SONGS OF OLDE ENGLAND 2      19    ADRHYTHM         ARP 54
GERRY CONWAY      D    (C        (B) FOLK SONGS OF OLDE ENGLAND 2      1976  MOONCREST        CREST 26
PAT DONALDSON     B    (C        (B) FOLK SONGS OF OLDE ENGLAND 2      1968  TE PEE
                                  (C) SUMMER SOLSTICE                  1972  B&C              CAS 1035
                                  (C) SUMMER SOLSTICE                  1974  MOONCREST        CREST 12
```

```
JOHN HARTFORD  G FDL BAN(ALL    (A) LOOKS AT LIFE                     1967  RCA       US  LSP  3687
BENNY MARTIN      FDL  (KM       (B) EARTHWORDS & MUSIC                1967  RCA       US  LSP  3796
KENNY MALONE      D    (KM       (C) THE LOVE ALBUM                    1968  RCA       US  LSP  3884
DALTON DILLINGHAM B    (K        (D) HOUSING PROJECT                   1968  RCA       US  LSP  3998
ROY HUSKY JR      B    (MK       (E) GENTLE ON MY MIND                 1968  RCA       US  LSP  4068
JIMMY COLVARD     G    (MK       (F) JOHN HARTFORD                     1969  RCA       US  LSP  4156
DALE SELLERS      G    (K        (G) IRON MOUNTAIN DEPOT               1970  RCA       US  LSP  4337
DAVID BRIGGS      K    (KM       (H) AERO PLAIN                        1971  WB        US       1916
BUDDY EMMONS      STEEL(KM        (I) MORNING BUGLE                     1972  WB        US       2651
SAM BUSH          V MAND(KM       (J) MARK TWANG                        1976  FLYING FISH US     FF 020
MAC WISEMAN       V    (K         (J) MARK TWANG                        1976  SONET     UK  SNTF 700
LARRIE LONDIN     D    (M         (K) NOBODY KNOWS WHAT YOU DO          1976  FLYING FISH US     FF 028
CURLY SECKLER     V    (M         (K) NOBODY KNOWS WHAT YOU DO          1977  SONET     UK  SNTF 727
HENRY STRZELECKI  B    (M         (L) DILLARD HARTFORD DILLARD  (*)     1977  FLYING FISH US     FF 036
PIG ROBBINS       PNO  (M         (L) DILLARD HARTFORD DILLARD  (*)     1977  SONET     UK  SNTF 730
JACK GREENE       V    (N         (M) ALL IN THE NAME OF LOVE           1977  FLYING FISH US     FF 044
JEANNIE ELLEY     V    (N         (M) ALL IN THE NAME OF LOVE           1978  SONET     UK  SNTF 747
DIANE TIDWELL     V    (N         (N) HEADING DOWN INTO THE MYSTERY BELOW 78 FLYING FISH US     FF 063
BILLY RAY REYNOLDS V   (N         (O) SLUMBERIN' ON THE CUMBERLAND      1979  FLYING FISH US     FF 095
LISA SILVER       V    (N         (P) YOU AND ME AT HOME               1981 FLYING FISH US        228
PAT BURTON            (A
                                (*) FULL LINE UP IN DILLARD HARTFORD DILLARD ENTRY)
```

```
KEEF HARTLEY      D    (ALL      (A) HALFBREED                        1969 DERAM  UK SML 1037   US  18024
MILLER ANDERSON   G V  (ABCDE    (B) BATTLE OF N W 6                  1970 DERAM  UK SML 1054   US  18035
PETER DINES       K    (AD        (C) THE TIME IS NEAR                 1970 DERAM  UK SML 1071   US  18047
SPIT JAMES        G    (AB        (D) OVERDOG                          1971 DERAM  UK DSL    2   US  18057
GARY THAIN        B    (ABCDEF    (E) LITTLE BIG BAND                  1971 DERAM  UK SDL    4
HENRY LOWTHER     VLN TPT(ABC     (F) SEVENTY SECOND BRAVE             1972 DERAM  UK SDL    9   US  18065
HARRY BECKETT     TPT  (ABE       (G) LANCASHIRE HUSTLER               1973 DERAM  UK SDL   13   US  18070
LYN DOBSON        WIND (ABE       (H) THE BEST OF       (DBL)          1974 DERAM  UK DPA 3011/2
CHRIS MERCER      SAX  (ABEF      (I) THROUGHOUT THE YEARS (DBL)       197  LONDON               US 2 6001
MICK WEAVER       K    (BDFG
RAY WARLEIGH      FLT  (B     MICK TAYLOR      G    (B   MIKE DAVIS      TPT  (BE DAVE CASWELL  TPT (CD
LYLE JENKINS      SAX  (CD    BARBARA THOMPSON WIND (BE  STUART WICKS    K    (C  DEL ROLL      PERC(C
JOHNNY ALMOND     FLT  (D     JON HISEMAN      D    (D   INGRID THOMAS   V    (D  JOAN KNIGHTON V   (D
VALERIE CHARRINGTON V  (D     PETE WINGFIELD   K V  (F   JUNIOR KERR     G V  (FG NICK NEWELL WIND  (F
JESS RODEN        V    (G     JEAN ROUSSEL     K    (G   PHIL CHEN       B    (G  PETE GAGE     G   (G
ELKIE BROOKS      V    (G     ROBERT PALMER    V    (G   JIMMY JEWELL    SAX  (BC PETE YORK     PERC(E
DEREK AUSTIN      K    (E     ROGER WADE       SAX  (E   MIKE ROSEN      TPT  (E  TERRY NOONAN  TPT (E
MARTIN DROVER     TPT  (E     DANNY ALLMARK    TROM (E   DEREK WADSWORTH TROM (E  JOHN MAYALL   V   (A
```

```
DAN HARTMAN  V K G B  (ALL       (A) IMAGES                           1976  BLUE SKY US 34322
EDGAR WINTER      HRNS (ABC       (B) INSTANT REPLAY                   1978  BLUE SKY US 35641   UK  83265
HILLY MICHAELS    D    (BC        (C) RELIGHT MY FIRE                  1979  BLUE SKY US 36302   UK  84073
BLANCHE NAPOLEON  V    (BC
G E SMITH         G    (BC    LARRY WASHINGTON CONGA(BC  VINNIE CUSANO   G V  (B  JOHN WILCOX   D   (A
JOHN SIEGLER      B    (A     RONNIE MONTROSE  G    (A   RICK DERRINGER  G    (A  CARL HARTMAN      (A
CLARENCE CLEMONS  SAX  (A     REVELATION       V    (A   TOM STROHMAN    FLT  (A  RANDY BRECKER HRNS(A
GEORGE YOUNG      HRNS (A     TONY POGANO  HRNS     (A   LARRY SADLER    D    (A  JOE ABBONDANZA B  (A
JIMMY MAELEN      PERC (C     STEVIE WONDER    HCA  (C   PHIL HOUGHTON   CONGA(C  LOLEATTA HOLLOWAY V (C
BRIAN BRAKE       D    (C     CRAIG PEYTON     VIBES(C   OOGAH BUNCH     V    (C  SCHOOLHOUSE KIDS V (C
```

ALEX HARVEY	G V	(ALL	(A) ALEX HARVEY SOUL BAND	1964	POLYDOR 237624	KARUSSEL	GER	635 049
ZAL CLEMINSON	G	(EFGHIJKLMO	(B) THE BLUES	1964	POLYDOR			5LPHM237641
CHRIS GLEN	B	(EFGHIJKLMO	(C) ROMAN WALL BLUES	1969	FONTANA		UK	STL 5534
MICKEY KEENE	G	(C	(D) JOKER IS WILD	1972	METRONOME	GER		15429
LESLIE HARVEY	G	(C	(D) THIS IS	19	METRONOME RI	GER		2001
HUGH McKENNA	K	(EFGHIJKLM	(E) FRAMED	1972	VERTIGO		UK	6360 081
TED McKENNA	D	(EFGHIJKLMO	(F) NEXT	1974	VERTIGO	US 1017	UK	6360 103
TOMMY EYRE	K	(10R	(G) IMPOSSIBLE DREAM	1974	VERTIGO	US 2000	UK	6360 112
PHIL KENZIE	SAX	(E	(H) TOMORROW BELONGS TO ME	1975	VERTIGO	US 2004	UK	6360 120
BUD BEADLE	SAX	(E	(I) LIVE	1975	ATLANTIC	US18184 VERTIGO	UK6360 122
DAVID BATCHELOR	V	(F	(J) PENTHOUSE TAPES	1975	VERTIGO EURO 9103 205		UK 9102 007
VICKI SILVA	V	(G	(K) STORIES	1976	MOUNTAIN		UK	TOPS 112
VICKY BROWN	V	(H	(L) BIG HITS & CLOSE SHAVES	1977	VERTIGO		UK	6360 147
LIZA STRIKE	V	(H	(M) FOURPLAY	1977	MOUNTAIN 4		UK	TOPC5006
BARRY ST JOHN	V	(H	(N) PRESENTS THE LOCK NESS MONSTER	1977	K TEL		NE	984
B J COLE	STEEL	(I	(O) ROCK DRILL	1978	MOUNTAIN		UK	TOPS 114
SIMON CHATTERTON	D	(1R	(P) VAMBO ROOLS	197	VERTIGO EURO 6370422			
MATTHEW CANG	G	(1R	(Q) COLLECTORS ITEMS	1980	MOUNTAIN		UK	TOPS 129
DON WELLER	SAX	(1R	(R) MAFIA STOLE MY GUITAR	1979	RCA		UK	PL 25257
GORDON SELLARS	B	(1R	(1) LIVE LINE UP					
MAURICE COCKERILL	K	(C	( ) ATTENTION	19	FONTANA GER			9199 091
PETER WOLFE	D	(C						
BUD PARKS	TPT	(C	DEREK WATKINS TPT (C ASHTON TOOTLE WIND (C LAURIE BAKER B ELEC(C					

ALEXANDER HARVEY	V	(ALL	(A) ALEX HARVEY	1971	CAPITOL		US	789
CRAIG DOERGE	PNO	(A	(B) SOUVENIRS	1973	CAPITOL	US EST 11128		
PETE SEARS	K B	(B	(C) ALEXANDER	1974				
HONEY COMBS	V	(A	(D) PRESHUS CHILD	197	KAMA SUTRA		US KSBS 2618
AYNSLEY DUNBAR	D	(B	(E) PURPLE CRUSH	1978	BUDDAH	US		5696
JOHN HOBBS	PNO	(A						
DAVID JACKSON	B	(A	DENNIS ST JOHN D (AB KEN VASSEY G (A DANNY ROWLAND G (A					
RANDY STERLING	B G	(A	AL PERKINS STEEL (A KENNY ROGERS V (A CAROL CARMICHAEL V (A					
LARRY CANSLER	STRING	(A	VANGIE CARMICHAEL V (A JOHN HARRIS PNO (A KENNETH BUTTREY D (A					
MAC GAYDEN	G	(A	WELDON MYRICK STEEL (A WAYNE MOSS G (A BROOKS HUNNICUTT V (A					
KIM GARNES	V	(A	DAVID ELLINGTON V (A BUDDY SPICHER VLN (A JOE ALLEN B (A					
JIMMY ISBELL	D	(A	KEN MALONE D (A JOHN DARNALL G (A BOBBY THOMPSON G (A					
TRACY NELSON	V	(A	DIANNE DAVIDSON V (D NEIL SCHON G (B ROBBIE MONTGOMERY V (B					
RUSSEL DASHIELL	G	(B	BRUCE GARY D (B STEVE LEFEVER B (B EMORY GORDY B (B					
VANETTA FIELDS	V	(B	RICHARD BENNETT G (B BETTY GOUCHE V (B DELORES PATTERSON V (B					
DENISE ERWIN	V	(B	CLYDIE KING V (B SHIRLEY MATTEWS V (B					

RICHARD HARVEY	WIND	(A	(A) DIVISION ON A GROUND	1975	TRANSATLANTIC		TRA	292

GORDON HASKELL	G V	(AB	(A) SAIL IN MY BOAT	1969	CBS	UK		63741
JOHN WETTON	B K V	(B	(B) IT IS AND IT ISN'T	1974	ATLANTIC US 33378	UK K40311		
DAVE KAFFINETTI	K	(B						
BILL ATKINSON	D	(B	ALAN BARRY G (B ARIF MARDIN K (B DAVID SPINOZZA G (B					
NEAL ROSENGARDEN	PNO	(B	EDDIE BRIGATI V (B DAVID BRIGATI V (B					

ANNIE HASLAM	V	(A	(A) ANNIE IN WONDERLAND	1978	SIRE US 6046	WB UK	K 56453
JON CAMP	G B	(A						
DAVE DONOVAN	D	(A	LOUIS CLARK SYN (A ROY WOOD G B K D WIND(A					

JOHN EDWARD DIZEK	V PERC	(AB	(A) HASSLES	19	US	US	UAS 6631
BILLY JOSEPH JOEL	V K	(AB	(B) HOUR OF THE WOLF	19	UA	US	UAS 6699
HOWARD ARTHUR BLAUVELT	B	(A						
JONATHAN SMALL	D	(AB	RICHARD McKENNER G (A					

TORU HATANO	ALL INST	(A	(A) LOVE FOR YOU	1976	MULAND		LX 7024M

GEORGE HATCHER	V	(ABC	(A) DRY RUN	1976	UA		UK UAG 29997
JOHN THOMAS	G	(ABC	(B) HAVE BAND WILL TRAVEL(10")	1977	UA		UK EXP 100
STEVE WREN	K	(ABC	(C) TALKIN' TURKEY	1977	UA		UK UAS 30090
JAMES MORGAM	G	(D	(D) RICH GIRL	1978	SHARK		GER 148 502
HARRIS JOANNOU	B V	(ABC						
PHIL SWAN	G	(ABC	TERRY SLADE D (ABC JOHN McFEE STEEL (C HUEY LOUIS HCA (C					
TONY CARR	PERC	(C	DYAN BIRCH V (C FRANK COLLINS V (C PADDY McHUGH V (C					
PETE GOSHING	G	(D	GERAINT WATKINS K (D RENATE MAUERER V (D CLAUDIA SCHWARZ V (D					
GITTA WALTHER	V	(D	VIC YOUNG B (D MAC POOLE D (D					

JAMES LACEY	G	(A	(A) HATE KILLS	1970	FAMOUS		US	5752
LEONARD GRAHAM	B	(A						
ALAN PRATT	D	(A	NEIL BRUCE K (A ROBERT MUNRO V (A					

RICHARD SINCLAIR	B V	(AB	(A) HATFIELD & THE NORTH	1974	VIRGIN	UK	V2008
PIP PYLE	D	(AB	(B) THE ROTTERS CLUB	1975	VIRGIN	UK	V2030
STEVE MILLER	K	(	(C) AFTERS	1979	VIRGIN	UK	VR5
PHIL MILLER	G	(AB						
DAVID SINCLAIR	K	(	DAVE STEWART K (AB AMANDA PARSONS V (AB BARBARA GASKIN V (AB					
ANN ROSENTHAL	V	(AB	GEOFF LEIGH WIND (A JEREMY BAINES WIND (A ROBERT WYATT V D(A					
JIMMY HASTINGS	WIND	(B	MONT CAMPBELL HRNS (B LINDSAY COOPER WIND (B TIM HODGKINSON CLAR(B					

HELMUT HATTLER

```
HELMUT HATTLER    B V  (A        (A) BASEBALL                    1977 EMI      GER          32523
INGO BIRSCHOF     K    (A
PETER WOLFBRANDT  G    (A  TRUC SSERC    D  (A  GERD DUDEK     SAX (A  ANDY GOLDNER    V (A
NOPS NOPPENEY     VLA  (A  JAN FRIDE     D  (A  JOEY ALBRECHT  G   (A  ROLAND SCHAEFFER SAX(A
ELMER LOUIS       PERC (A
```

DONNIE HATHAWAY

```
DONNIE HATHAWAY   V    (ALL      (A) EVERYTHING IS EVERYTHING   1970 ATLANTIC US 33332 UK 2465 019
ROBERTA FLACK     V    (DF       (A) EVERYTHING IS EVERYTHING   1971 ATLANTIC        UK  K40063
ERIC GALE         G    (F        (B) DONNIE HATHAWAY            1970 ATLANTIC US 33360 UK 503 068
DAVID SPINOZZA    G    (F        (B) DONNIE HATHAWAY            1971 ATLANTIC US       UK  K40241
CORNELL DUPREE    G    (BFC      (C) LIVE                       1972 ATLANTIC US 33386 UK  K40369
PHIL UPCHURCH     B G  (FCB      (D) FLACK & HATHAWAY           197  ATLANTIC         UK  K40380
MIKE HOWARD       G    (FC       (E) EXTENSION OF MAN           1973 ATLANTIC US  7029 UK  K40487
KEITH LOVING      G    (F        (F) BEST OF                    1980 ATLANTIC US 38107 UK  K50525
DAVE SANBORN      WIND (F        (G) IN PERFORMANCE             1980 ATLANTIC US 19278 UK  K50742
HERB SMITH        B    (F
CHUCK RAINEY      B    (FB  DEREK GRAVES    B  (F  BERNARD PURDIE   D  (F  STEVE NOVOSEL   B  (FB
WILLIE WEEKS      B    (FC  BILLY COBHAM    F  (F  AL JACKSON       D  (FB MORRIS JENNINGS D  (F
FRED WHITE        D    (FC  RAY LUCAS       D  (F  BILLY JOHNSON    D  (F  RALPH McDONALD  PERC(F
EARL DEROUEN      PERC (FC  JACK JENNINGS   PERC (FB LEONARD GIBBS  PERC (F  JOE GENTLE     WIND(F
KING CURTIS       SAX  (FB  I STONE         V  (B  L TYNES          V  (B  CISSY HOUSTON   V  (B
SYLVIA SHEMWELL   V    (B   DEIDRE TUCK     V  (B  J R BAILEY       V  (B  MYRNA SUMMERS   V  (B
S WHITE           V    (B   JOE NEWMAN      TPT (B MYRNA SMITH      V  (B  JUDY CLAY       V  (B
SAMMY TURNER      V    (B   RONALD BRIGHT   V  (B  THE INTERDENOMINATIONAL SINGERS V(B
```

HAVE MERCY

```
STEVE BAKER    G V  HCA(A     (A) BOODLAM                 1977 ANTAGON          3209
BRIAN BARNETT  V G  DOB(A
DICK BIRD      V G  DOB(A  JON ECHOLLS  V HCA PERC(A  HENRY HEGGEN  V HCA PERC(A RORY McLEOD V HCA PERC(A
```

RICHIE HAVENS

```
RICHIE HAVENS G V SITAR(ALL   (A) RICHIE HAVENS RECORD 1965 TRANSATLANTIC 199UK US DOUGLAS   779
JERRY FRIEDMAN    G    (L     (B) ELECTRIC HAVENS      1966 TRANSATLANTIC 187  US DOUGLAS   780
ERIC WEISSBERG    STEEL(L     (C) MIXED BAG            1967 VERVE  UK 2317002 US MGM        4698
ERIC OXENDINE     B    (JLK   (D) SOMETHING ELSE AGAIN 1968 VERVE  UK 2317030 US VERVE      3034
ARNIE MOORE       B    (E     (D) SOMETHING ELSE AGAIN 1968 MGM US 4699
PAUL WILLIAMS     G    (CDEJLOK(E) RICHARD D HAVENS 1983 1969 VERVE  UK 2620001 US VERVE     3047
CARTER COLLINS    CONGA(E     (E) RICHARD D HAVENS 1983 1969 MGM US 4700
DANIEL BEN ZEBULON D   (DEL   (F) STONEHENGE           1970 POLYDOR UK 2317004 US STORMY FOREST 6001
PAUL HOFFERT      ORG  (L     (G) A STATE OF MIND       1971 VERVE  UK 2304050
BILLIE MITCHELL   G    (L     (H) ALARM CLOCK           1971 POLYDOR UK 2310080 US STORMY FOREST 6005
WARREN BERNHARDT  K    (DE    (J) GREAT BLIND DEGREE    1972 POLYDOR UK 2480049 US STORMY FOREST 6016
JEREMY STEIG      FLT  (DE    (K) LIVE ON STAGE         1972 POLYDOR UK 2659015 US STORMY FOREST 6012
DONALD MACDONALD  D    (DE    (L) PORTFOLIO             1973 POLYDOR UK 2480166 US STORMY FOREST 6013
EDDIE GOMEZ       B    (D     (M) MIXED BAG 2           1974 POLYDOR UK 2310356 US STORMY FOREST 6201
DON PAYNE         B    (D     (N) END OF THE BEGINNING  1976 A&M  UK AMLH64598 US A&M         4598
ADRIAN GUILLERY   G    (D     (O) MIRAGE                1977 A&M  UK AMLH64641 US A&M         4641
JOHN BLAIR        VLN  (D     (P) RICHIE HAVENS         19   POLYDOR UK 2482273
SKIP PROKOP       D    (DE    (Q) POP HISTORY           197  POLYDOR UK 2612017
DARRYL JOHNSON    G K  (ON    (R) CONNECTIONS           1980 ELEKTRA US 242 NL 52186
JUMM FAIRS        B    (E
HERMAN ERNEST     D    (ON  TONY BROUSSARD  B   (O  DAVID LEBOLT   K  (O  .WILLIAM SMITTY SMITH K V (O
TOM SCOTT         WIND (O   GARY COLEMAN    PERC (O DUITCH HELMER  V  (O  CHRISTOPHER BOND   G  (O
DENNY GERRARD     B    (F   EMILE LATIMER   CONGA(JK BOB MARGOULEFF SYN (J  MALCOLM CECIL    SYN (J
PAUL HARRIS       K    (C   HARVEY BROOKS   B   (C  BILL LAVORGNA  D  (C  HOWARD COLLINS    G  (C
JOE PRICE         PERC (C   JOHN ORD        K   (E  BRAD CAMPBELL  B  (E  KEN LAUBER        K  (E
TEDDY IRWIN       G    (E   WELDON MYRICK   STEEL(E CAROL HUNTER   B  (E  BRUCE LANGHORNE   G  (E
COLLIN WALCOTT    SITAR(E   CHARLIE SMALL   K   (E  STEVE STILLS   B  (E  MARK ROTH            (E
BOB CHASE         PERC (E   DIANE COMINS HARP   (E  CHARLES HOWALL V  (E  JOEY OLIVER       K  (N
TESSIE COEN       PERC (N   BRENDA RUSSELL  V   (N  JULIA TILLMAN  V  (N  MIKE BAIRD        D  (N
DUCK DUNN         B    (N   DANNY MOORE     V   (N  WILLIAM SMITH  K V (N JEFF BAXTER       G  (N
BRIAN RUSSELL     V    (N   DIANNE BROOKS   V   (N  BOOKER T JONES K  (N  STEVE CROPPER     G  (N
MATT MOORE        V    (N
```

CYRIL HAVERMANNS

```
CYRIL HAVERMANS     V G B(AB     (A) CYRIL             1973 MGM 2315 261  + MGM SE  4926
PIERRE VANDER LINDEN D(A         (B) MIND WAVE         1974 MGM 2315 311
THIJS VAN LEER      K FLT(A
JACKIE WARD         V    (A  ANDREA WILLIS  VLN (A  MAXINE WILLARD V  (A  CHUCK DOMANICO   B  (A
EMIL RICHARDS       PERC (A  BOBBY BRUCE    VLN (A  JOHN D'ANDREA  PERC (AB HERMAN DEINUM B PERC(B
RUDY DE QUELJOU     G    (B  HANS LAFAILLE  PERC (B CAROLYN WILLIS V  (A
```

DALE HAWKINS

```
DALE HAWKINS   V    (ALL   ( ) LETS TWIST AT THE PEPPERMINT LOUNGE 196  ROULETTE   US  25175
JAMES BURTON   G    (      ( ) DALE HAWKINS                        19   CHESS           703
                           ( ) SUSIE Q                             19   CHECKER    UK6467310
                           ( ) SUSIE Q                             1958 CHESS      US   1429
                           ( ) LA MEMPHIS & TYLER TEXAS            1970 BELL       US   6036
```

RONNIE HAWKINS

```
RONNIE HAWKINS    V    (ALL   (A) RONNIE HAWKINS            1959 ROULETTE   US    R25078
KING BISCUIT BOY  HCA  (J     (B) Mr DYNAMO                1960 ROULETTE   US    R25102
BYRON BACH        STR  (L     (B) Mr DYNAMO                1960 COLUMBIA   UK  SX 1238
ROBBIE ROBERTSON  G    (G     (C) FOLK BALLADS             1960 COLUMBIA   UK  SX33 1295
BARRY BECKETT     K    (J     (C) FOLK BALLADS             1960 ROULETTE   US    R25120
SCOTT CUSHNIE     K    (J     (D) SINGS HANK WILLIAMS      1961 ROULETTE   US    R25137
DUANE ALLMAN      G    (J     (E) SINGS HANK WILLIAMS      19   GRAND PRIX SWED GP 9970
EDDIE HINTON      G    (J     (F) THE BEST OF              1963 ROULETTE   US    R25255
JIMMY JOHNSON     G    (J     (F) THE BEST OF(EITH THE BAND) 19  ROULETTE   US    SR42045
DAVID HOOD        B    (J     (G) MOJO MAN                 1964 ROULETTE   US    R25390
ROGER HAWKINS     D    (J     (H) RRRRACKET TIME           1965 WLW        CAN   WLW101
JAMES COTTON      HCA  (H     (H) RRRRACKET TIME           1980 CHARLY     UK  CR 30180
LEVON HELM        D    (ABCDGH (I) RONNIE HAWKINS          1968 YORKVILLE  US  YVS 33002
FRED CARTER       G    (HL    (I) HAWK IN WINTER(REISSUE OF ABOVE) 1976 POLYDOR CAN 2424 121
```

(CONTINUED)

RONNIE HAWKINS

```
        (CONTINUED)
DAVE KIRBY          G    (L        (J) RONNIE HAWKINS              1970  COTILLION    US   SD  9019
JERRY CARRIGAN      D    (L        (J) RONNIE HAWKINS              1970  ATLANTIC     UK   2400 009
DAVID BRIGGS        ORG  (L        (K) THE HAWK                    1971  COTILLION    US   SD  9039
BOOTS RANDOLPH      SAX  (L        (L) ROCK & ROLL RESURRECTION    1972  MONUMENT     US   KZ  31330
DON SHEFFIELD       TPT  (L        (L) ROCK & ROLL RESURRECTION    1972  MONUMENT     UK       65122
DAVID DARLING   STRINGS(L          (M) GIANT OF ROCK'N'ROLL        1974  MONUMENT     US   KZ  32940
JAMES CASON         V    (L        (N) ROCKIN                      197   MODE         FR   MO  9028
MARY HOLLADAY       V    (L        (N) ROCKIN                      1977  PYE          UK   NSPL28238
TIM DRUMMOND        B    (L        (O) THE HAWK                    1979  UA  US LA968  UAG 30283
STAN SZELESTE       PNO  (LO       (LM) GIANT /RESURRECTION        1976  MONUMENT     US       33855
RAY PAULMAN         G    (AB       ( ) ARKANSAS ROCKPILE           196   ROULETTE     US       1003
CHARLIE McCOY       HCA  (L        (EP) ROCKIN' WITH RONNIE        196   COLUMBIA     UK   ESG 7792
NORMAN RAY          SAX  ((L       (EP) ROCKIN' WITH RONNIE 2      196   COLUMBIA     UK   ESG 7795
MARVIN CHANTRY  STRINGS(L
JUNE PAGE       V  (L   GINGER HOLLADAY  V  (L   GRADY MARTIN      G  (L   KENNETH BUTTREY  D  (L
FARRELL MORRIS  PERC (L  PETE DRAKE   STEEL(L   BILL PUETT     SAX  (L   GARY VANOSDALE STRINGS(L
D BERGEN WHITE  V  (L   JEANNIE GREENE   V  (A   KEITH ALLISON V G B  (O   JAMES BURTON   G  (O
WADDY WACHTEL   G  (O   DEE MURRAY       B  (O   JERRY SOMMERS    D  (O   RICK SSHLOSSER   D  (O
GARTH HUDSON ACC SYN (O  GABRIEL KATONA  SYN (O   CARL MATHERS   FDL  (O   JERRY PETERSON SAX (O
PAUL BUTTERFIELD HCA (O  RYELAND ALLISON PERC (O  BOBBY LAKIND  CONGAS(O   BROOKS HUNNICUTT V  (O
LISA ROBERTS    V  (O   PHYLLIS ST JAMES  V  (O   TERRY DANKO      V  (O   JAMES G EVANS    B  (B
```

SCREAMING JAY HAWKINS

```
JALACY 'JAY' HAWKINS  V(ALL      (A) AT HOME WITH                 1957  EPIC          US   3448
GINNY HAWKINS          V  (F      (B) THE NIGHT & DAY OF           19    PLANET        US   1001
RED PRYSOCK           SAX  (H     (C) A NITE AT THE FORBIDDEN CITY 19    SOUND OF HAWAII US 50158
TINY GRIMES            G  (H      (D) WHAT THAT IS                 1969  PHILIPS       US 600319
LEROY KIRKLAND BAND       (H      (E) SCREAMIN' JAY HAWKINS        1970  PHILIPS       US 600336
TEDDY McRAE ORCHESTRA     (H      (F) PORTRAIT OF A MAN & HIS WOMAN 1972 HOT LINE      US 10024
SAMMY LOWE'S ORCHESTRA    (H      (G) I PUT A SPELL ON YOU         1969  EPIC          US 26457
WALTER YOUNG ORCHESTRA    (H      (H) SCREAMIN' THE BLUES          1979  RED LIGHTNING UK RL0025
GRAHAM BOND            K  (
EARL PALMER   D  (D   PLAS JOHNSON    SAX  (D   LYLE RITZ        B  (D   MIKE ANTHONY    G BAN(D
EDDIE HOH     D  (D   RON JOHNSON      B  (D   ERNEST McLEAN    BAN  (D   HERB ELLIS      G  (D
BILLY WATKINS SINGERS V(D  CARL GOTTLIEB   V  (D   CHRISTOPHER ROSS V  (D   SAL VALENTINO   V  (D
DEIRDRE LA PORTE  V  (D   TOM REID        V  (D   THEA MARCUS      V  (D
```

THE HAWKS

```
DAVE HEARN     K V  (A       (A) THE HAWKS                        1980  CBS           US   36922
LARRY ADAMS    D    (A
FRANK WIEWEL   B V  (A   KIRK KAUFFMAN   G V  (A   DAVE STEEN   G V  (A
```

HAWKWIND & HAWKLORDS

```
DAVE BROCK  HCA V G V K(ABCDEFGHJKLPQ(A) HAWKWIND             1970  LIBERTY  US  5519 UK LBA 83348
TIM BLAKE        K       (PQ       (A) HAWKWIND              1980  LIBERTY  RI        UK     1012
NIK TURNER      V SAX(ABCDEFGHJ    (A) HAWKWIND              1975  SUNSET             UK SLS 50374
TERRY OLLIS      D       (ABJG      (B) IN SEARCH IN SPACE    1971  U A   US  5567 UK UAG 29202
DAVE ANDERSON    B       (J         (C) DOREMI FARSOLATIDO    1972  U A   US LA 001 UK UAG 29364
BOB CALVERT              (DHJKLG    (D) SPACE RITUAL          1973  U A   US LA 120 UK UAD600378
DIKMIK           K       (ABCDJG    (E) HALL OF THE MOUNTAIN GRILL 1974 U A  US 328  UK UAG 29672
HENRY LOWTHER    TPT     (L         (E) HALL OF THE MOUNTAIN GRILL 1981 LIBERTY RI
ADRIAN SHAW      B       (K         (F) WARRIOR ON THE EDGE OF TIME 1975 U A         UK UAG 29766
MARTIN GRIFFIN   D       (L         (F) WARRIOR ON THE EDGE OF TIME 1975 ATLANTIC US 36 115
LLOYD LANGTON    G       (AJPQG     (G) ROAD HAWKS           1976  U A     US 624 UK UAK 29919
IAN'LEMMY' KILMISTER B G V(CDEFJ    (H) ASTOUNDING SOUNDS    1976  CHARISMA          UK CDS  4004
SIMON KING       D       (CDEFHJKLPG (J) MASTERS OF THE UNIVERSE 1977 U A            UK UAG 30025
DEL DETTMAR      K       (BCDEJG    (K) QUARK STRANGENESS & CHARM 1977 CHARISMA US 4008 US SIRE 6047
SIMON HOUSE      K       (EFHJKL    (L) 25 YEARS (HAWKLORDS)  1978  CHARISMA US 2203 UK CDS 4014
PAUL RUDOLPH     B       (H         (M) HAWKWIND(ROCKFILE)   197   LIBERTY           UK LBR  1012
ALAN POWELL      D       (FHG       (N) PXR 5                1979  CHARISMA          UK CDS  4016
JOHN HARRISON    B       (AJG       (O) REPEAT PERFORMANCE (COMP) 1980 CHARISMA      UK      BG2
MICHAEL MOORCOCK V       (F         (P) LIVE 79              1980  BRONZE            UK BRON 527
HARVEY BAINSBRIDGE B V  (LOP       (Q) LEVITATION           1980  BRONZE            UK BRON 530
LES McCLURE      B       (H         (R) SONIC ATTACK         1981  BRONZE
STEVE SWINDELLS  K V     (L
```

BRYN HAWORTH

```
BRYN HAWORTH     G V   (ALL       (A) LET THE DAYS GO BY     1974  ISLAND     UK  ILPS 9287
BRUCE ROWLAND    D     (AB        (B) SUNNY SIDE OF THE STREET 1975 ISLAND     UK  ILPS 9332
TERRY STANNARD   D     (AB        (C) GRAND ARRIVAL          1978  A&M        UK  AMLH68462
FRAN BYRNE       D     (1         (D) KEEP THE BALL ROLLING  1979  A&M        UK  AMLH68507
STU CALVER       V     (D         (E) GAP                    1980  CHAPEL     UK       8004
BUGS PEMBERTON   D     (A         (1) 1978 TOUR
KARL HIMMEL      D     (C
BUDDY HARMON     D  (C   ALAN SPENNER   B  (AB   CHRIS STAINTON  K  (BD   BUDDY EMMONS   G  (C
DAVE MATTACKS    D  (B   JOHN COWAN     B  (C    RABBIT BUNDRICK K  (A    JIM MULLEN     G  (B
KEVIN KELLEY     D  (A   DAVE PEGG      B  (B    PETE WINGFIELD  K  (ABD  JOHN PORTER    G  (A
JERRY CARRIGAN   D  (C   PAT DONALDSON  B  (C    TONY O'MALLEY   K  (B    BILLY SANFORD  G  (C
HENRY SPINETTI   D  (D   FREEBO         B  (A    MICK WEAVER     K  (1    HAROLD BRADLEY G  (C
DAVE SWARBRICK   FDL(C   GORDON HASKELL B  (C    BOBBY WOOD      K  (C    BAM KING       G  (1
SHELLEY KURLAND STRINGS(C JESSIE BOYCE  B  (C    RON OATES       K  (C    RONNY LIGHT    G  (C
COURTNEY JOHNSON BANJO(C  TEX COMER     B  (1    PIG ROBBINS     K  (C    CURTIS BURCH   G  (C
ALAN MUNDE       BANJO(B  JOE OSBORN    B  (C    GRAHAM MAITLAND K  (A    TERRY HELLYER  TROM (D
FARRELL MORRIS   PERC (C  NICK RATHER   B  (C    BILLY PUETT    SAX (C    DENNIS GOODE   TROM (C
SAM BUSH         MAND (C  TOMMY COGBILL B  (C    ANDREW LOVE    SAX (C    GEORGE TIDWELL TPT(C
SIMON MORTON     PNO  (D  DAVE MARKEE   B  (C    MEL COLLINS    SAX (ABD  WAYNE JACKSON  TPT(C
IMPERIALS        V    (B  MADELINE BELL V  (B    STEVE GREGORY SAX FLT(D  MARTIN DROVER  TPT(D
LEE VANDERBILT   V    (B  JOANNE WILLIAMS V (B   BUD BEADLE     SAX (D    PADDY McHUGH   V  (B
FRANK COLLINS    V    (B  MARY HOLLADAY  V  (C   GINGER HOLLOWAY V (C     JIM CUOMO  SAX    (D
DYAN BIRCH       V    (B  DON EVERLY     V  (C   CLIFF RICHARD   V  (C    JOHN PERRY     V  (D
TONY RIVERS      V    (D
```

ISAAC HAYES

ISAAC HAYES	K V	(ALL	(A) PRESENTING	1967 ENTERPRISE	US		13 100
LESTER SNELL	K	(FMN	(A) IN THE BEGINNING	1972 ATLANTIC	US		1599
WILLIE HALL	D	(FMN	(B) HOT BUTTERED SOUL	1969 ENTERPRISE	US 1001 RI STAX	5002
RONALD HUDSON	B	(F	(C) ISAAC HAYES MOVEMENT	1970 ENTERPRISE	US		1010
MICHAEL TOLES	G	(FMN	(D) TO BE CONTINUED	1970 ENTERPRISE	US 1014 RI		4133
ANTHONY SHINAULT	G	MN	(E) SHAFT	1971 ENTERPRISE	US	2 5002
WILLIE COLE	D	(MN	(F) BLACK MOSES	1972 ENTERPRISE	US		5003
TOMMY WILLIAMS	SAX	(MN	(G) AT SAHARA TAHOE	1973 ENTERPRISE	US		5005
LEWIS COLLINS	SAX	(M	(H) JOY	1973 ENTERPRISE	US		5007
BILL EASLEY	SAX	(MN	(I) TOUGH GUYS	1974 ENTERPRISE	US		7504
WILLIAM TAYLOR	TPT	(MN	(J) TRUCK TURNER	1974 ENTERPRISE	US		7507
RICHARD DOLPH	HRN	(MN	(K) CHOCOLATE CHIP	1975 ABC	US		874
JOHNNY DAVIS	TPT	(M	(L) DISCO CONNECTION	1975 ABC	US		923
BILL FLORES	TROM	(M	(M) GROOVE A THON	1976 ABC	US		925
GARY RUSSELL	TROM	(MN	(N) JUICY FRUIT	1976 SBC	US		953
KIM PALUMU	G	(N	(O) A MAN AND A WOMAN	1977 ABC	US		966/2
KEN SPAIN	TROM	(N	(P) HOT BED	1977 STAX	US		4102
CHARLE SPITTS	G	(FMN	(Q) NEW HORIZON	1978 POLYDOR	US		6120
GARY JONES	PERC	(F	(R) FOR SAKE OF LOVE	1979 POLYDOR	US		6146
SIDNEY KIRK	PNO	(FMN	(S) DONT LET GO	1980 POLYDOR	US		6224
WILLIAM VAUGHN	G	(M	(T) AND ONCE AGAIN	1980 POLYDOR	US		6269
ERROLL THOMAS	B	(NM	(U) ENTERPRISE GREATEST HITS	1980 STAX	UK		88003
JIMMY THOMPSON	PERC	(MN	(V) LIFETIME THING	1981 POLYDOR	UK		2311 074
DARNELL SMITH	SAX	(MN					
EMERSON ABLE	SAX	(MN					
FLOYD NEWMAN	SAX	(MN BEN CAULEY	TPT (MN BRYANT MUNCH	HRNS (MN EDGAR MATTHEWS	TPT (MN
JACKIE THOMAS	TROM (MN JAZZMO	PERC (N DEREK GALBREITH	B (N NICK VERGOS HRN	(N

HAYSTACKS BALBOA

MARK MAYO	(A	(A) HAYSTACK BALBOA	1970 POLYDOR US 24 4032 GER 2425 032
MARK POLITT	(A		
BRUCE SCOTT	(A DEBORAH MAYO	(A MARK BABABI	(A LARRY WEST	(A
LLOYD LANDESMAN	(A		

JUSTIN HAYWARD

JUSTIN HAYWARD	G V	(AB	(A) SONGWRITER	1977 DERAM US 18073 DECCA UK SDL 15
AJ WEBBER		(A	(B) NIGHT FLIGHT	1980 DERAM US 4801 DECCA UK TXS 138
KEN FREEMAN		(A		
CLEM CATTINI	D	(A TERRY ROWLEY	(A PETE MORGAN	(A MEL GALLEY G (A
DAVE HOLLAND		(A DAVID SNELL	HARP (A	

TONY HAZZARD

TONY HAZZARD	G V	(ALL	(A) TONY HAZZARD SINGS	1969 CBS U 63608
B J COLE	STEEL	(BC	(B) LOUDWATER HOUSE	1971 BRONZE UK ILPS 9174
CHRIS SPEDDING	G	(B	(C) WAS THAT ALRIGHT THEN	1973 bronze UK ILPS 9222
ROY O'TEMRO	D	(B		
CHRIS SLADE	D	(B CLEM CLEMPSON	G (B CALEB QUAYE	G (B TONI CAMPO B (BC
MIKE BATT	PNO	(B DAVE GREENSLADE	K (BC LAGHTY AMAO	CONGAS(B RAY COOPER PERC(BC
SUE GLOVER	V	(B SUNNY LESLIE	V (B LESLEY DUNCAN	V (B KAY GARNER V (B
JACKIE LEE	V	(B RUSSELL STONE	V (B RICHARD BARNES	V (B ROGER McKEW G (C
MICK WEAVER	PNO	(C TEX MARSH	D (C GLENN LEFLEUR	D (C HELEN SCOTT V (C
TONY CHARLES STEEL BAND(C				

HAZZARD & BARNES

TONY HAZZARD	G	(A	(A) HAZZARD & BARNES	1977 WB US 4670 UK k56233
RICHARD BARNES	G	(A		
HERBIE FLOWERS	B	(A BARRY DE SOUZA	D (A TONY HYMAS	K (A ROGER McKEW G BAN(A
PETER SWETTENHAM	K	(A JACK EMBLOW	ACC (A JOHNNY VAN DERRICK FDL	(A CHRIS NEILL HCA (A
TONY ASHTON	K	(A DAVE LAWSON	SYN (A FRANK RICOTTI	PERC (A LESLEY DUNCAN V (A
LIZA STRIKE	V	(A +HRNS & STRINGS		

EDDIE HAZEL

EDDIE HAZEL	(A	(A) GAMES, DAMES & GUITAR THANGS	1977 WB US BS 3058
		(B) SUGAR DONT YOU KNOW	1979 AUDIOFILE US 137
		(C) TAKE YOUR SHOES OFF	1979 MONMOUTH US 7075

HEAD

BILL KYLE	D	(ABC	(A) F F T	1973 SRT 72254
HOWARD COPLAND	SAX	(AB	(B) RED DWARF	1975 CANNON UK 5970
CHARLES ALEXANDER	G	(AB	(C) BLACKPOOL COOL	1978 HEAD HSLP 330
JOHN DAVIES	TPT K(ABC		
GORDON CRUICKSHANK	SAX (C LACHLAN McCOLL	G (C GRAHAM MINCE	B (ABC

HEAD (US)

(A) HEAD	19 BUDDAH BDS 5062

MURRAY HEAD

MURRAY HEAD	G V	(ALL	(A) NIGEL LIVED	1973 CBS US 31947 UK 65503
BOB WESTON	G V	(B	(B) SAY IT AINT SO	1975 ISLAND FR 9101 655 UK ILPS 9347
BRIAN BROCKLEHURST	B	(B	(B) SAY IT AINT SO	1975 A&M US 4558
GINNY CLEE	V PERC(E		(C) BETWEEN US	1979 PHILIPS GER 9198 177
ALUN DAVIES	G V	(B	(D) JOKES/VOICES	1980 MERCURY NL 6313 045
GEOFF RICHARDSON	G VLA(E		(E) FIND THE CROWD	1981 MERCURY FR 6313 179
JIM CREGAN	G	(B		
BRUCE LYNCH	B	(B		
TONY KAYE	PNO	(B GLENN LE FLEUR	D (B PAM KEEVIL	V (B JOHN ALTMAN CLAR(B
ARTHUR WATTS	B	(B LIZA STRIKE	V (B PETE THOMPSON	D (B BROTHER JAMES CONGA(B
CHILLI CHARLES	PERC	(B MICKY FINN	G (B NICKY SOUTH	B (B SIMON PHILLIPS D (B
P J CROTTY	WIND	(B BILLY DAY	K (B MORRIS PERT	PERC (B BRIAN JOHNSTON K (B
CHAS JANKEL	K	(B ANN O'DELL	K (B GERRY CONWAY	D (B SUE LYNCH V (B
ANTHONY HEAD	K	(B VICKY BROWN	V (B GRAHAM PRESKETT	MAND (B TROPIC ISLES STEEL BAND(B
NOEL NORRIS	TPT	(B MARK WARNER	G (A CLIVE CHAMAN	B (A DAVE WINTOUR B (A
PETER GILES	B	(A MIKE GILES	D (A COZY POWELL	D (A BARRY DESOUZA D (A
PETE ROBINSON	K	(A FIACHRA TRENCH	K (A TONY COE	SAX (A JIMMY HASTINGS SAX (A
TOMMY WHITTLE	SAX	(A JIM CHESTER	SAX (A CHRIS MERCER	SAX (AD CHRIS NEIL HCA (A

(CONTINUED)

MURRAY HEAD

(CONTINUED)

SUE GLOVER	V	(A	SUNNY LESLIE	V	(A	KAY GARNER	V	(A	FRIENDLY SISTERS	V	(A
FRANK RICOTTI	PERC	(A	RAY COOPER	PERC	(A	SPIKE HEATLEY	B	(A	JOHN DONNELLY		HRNS(A
HENRY LOWTHER	HRNS	(A	DAVE CHAMAN	HRNS	(A	MARTIN FRY	HRNS	(A	RALPH HO		HRN (A
JAMES HARPHAM	REC	(A	NICK DECARO	ACC	(A	SKAILA KANGA	HARP	(A	CHRIS KARAM TABLA		(A
MIGUEL BARADOS	STEEL DRUM(A		JACK ROTHSTEIN	VLN	(A	MIKE RENNIE	VLN	(A	PETE VEITCH K		VLN (E
PHIL PALMER	G	(E	ALAN SPENNER	B	(E	TREVOR MORIAS	D	(CE	BOB WESTON	G	(C
JOHN PERRY	B	(C	JEFF BECK	G	(D						

HEAD EAST

ROGER BOYD	K V	(ABCDEFG	(A) FLAT AS A PANCAKE		1975	A&M US 4537	UK AMLH64537		
DAN BIRNEY	B V	(ABCDE	(B) GET YOURSELF UP		1976	A&M US 4579	UK AMLH64579		
MIKE SOMERVILLE	G V	(ABCDE	(C) GETTIN' LUCKY		1977	A&M US 4624	UK AMLH64624		
JOHN SCHLITT	V	(ABCDE	(D) HEAD EAST		1978	A&M US 46680	UK AMLH64680		
STEVE HUSTON	D V	(ABCDE	(E) LIVE	(DBL)	1979	A&M US 6007	UK AML 66007		
RICHARD PODOLOR	G	(C	(F) A DIFFERENT KIND OF CRAZY		1980	A&M US 4795			
STAN GILL	ORG	(E	(G) US1		1980	A&M US 4826			
KEN KRUEGER	V	(G							
DEDE TOWNSEND	G	(G	FLOYD BROWN	D	(G	STEVE HUTTON	D V	(FG	TONY GATES G V (FG
MACK BOATMAN	V	(FG	DAN ODUM	V PERC(FG		JIMMY GREEN	SAX	(G	JESSE HENDERSON D (G
CHRIS HARWOOD	G	(G							

HEADBOYS

LOU LEWIS	G V	(A	(A) HEADBOYS		1980	RSO US 3968 GER 2394 244 UK 13		
GEORGE BOYTER	B V	(A						
CALUM MALCOLM	K V	(A	DAVY ROSS	D V	(A	ROBIN MORTON	PERC (A	ALY BAIN FDL (A
BOB HEATLIE	SAX	(A						

HEAD MACHINE

		(A) ORGASM	19	VOGUE	522

HEADBANK

EDDIE COLTON	B	(A	(A) LETTIN EVERYTHING GO		1981	MADDOG	106077
DINO FASANO	V	(A					
SIMON GANNETT	K	(A	EDDIE WISCONSIN G (A	ANDY RUBBO	D (A		

HEADHUNTERS

BENNIE MAUPIN	WIND V(DF	(A) HEADHUNTERS	1973	CBS	US	32731
MICHAEL CLARK	D (F	(B) THRUST	1974	CBS	US	32965
PAUL JACKSON	B V (F	(C) DEATH WISH	1974	CBS	US	33199
OBSIDIKTION BLACKBYRD	JG B V(F	(D) SURVIVAL OF THE FITTEST	1975	ARISTA US 4038 UK	ARTY 116	
DWAYNE McKNIGHT		(E) MAN CHILD	1976	CBS	US	33812
PAUL PORTYEN	K V (F	(F) STRAIGHT FROM THE GATE	1977	ARISTA US 4146 UK APART1048		
DERRICK YOUMAN	V (F					
BILL SUMMERS	PERC(F					

HEADSTONE

MARK ASHTON	G V	(AB	(A) BAD HABITS	1974	EMI UK EMA766 US DUNHILL 50176	
STEVE BOLTON	G	(AB	(B) HEADSTONE	1975	EMI UK	EMC 3073
PHILIP CHEN	B	(A	(B) HEADSTONE	19	20TH CENTURY US	T483
CHILLI CHARLES	D	(A				
JOE O'DONNELL	VLN G(AB	STEVE GOULD	V (A	SPARKIE	V (A	JUANITA FRANKLIN V(AB
CARL DOUGLAS	V	(A	TONY LUKYN SYN	(A	DAVE KAFFINETTI	K (A	PETER VAN HOOKE D (B
JEROME RIMSON	B	(B				

HEADS HANDS & FEET

ALBERT LEE	G V	(ABC	(A) HEADS HANDS & FEET	1971	CAPITOL US 608	UK ISLAND ILPS9149
PETE GAVIN	D V	(ABC	(B) TRACKS	1972	CAPITOL US11051 UK ISLAND ILPS 9185	
CHAS HODGES	B G FDL V	(ABC	(C) OLD SOLDIERS NEVER DIE	1973	ATLANTIC US 7025 UK	K40465
MIKE O'NEIL	K	(A				
RAY SMITH	B G V(BAC	JERRY DONAHUE	V (BC	RAY OSBORNE	V (B	BARRY ST JOHN V (B
LINDA THOMPSON	V	(C	GERRY HOGAN STEEL	(B	LINDA LEWIS	V (C	NORMA WINSTONE V (C
JIM DONNELLY	V	(C	DAVE SWARBRICK	V (C	JACKIE LYNTON	V (C	PAM SUILICON V (C
SYLVIA KING	V	(C	ELTON DEAN	SAX (A	TONY COLTON	V (ABC	

HEART

NANCY WILSON	V G	(ALL	(A) DREAMBOAT ANNIE	1976	MUSHROOM US 5005 ARISTA UK ARTY139	
ANN WILSON	K V	(ALL	(B) LITTLE QUEEN	1977	PORTRAIT US 34799	UK 82075
MICHAEL DEROSIER	D	(ABCDEFGH	(C) MAGAZINE	1978	MUSHROOM US 5008 ARISTA UK	1024
HOWARD LEESE	G K SYN	(ABCDEFGH	(D) DOG AND BUTTERFLY	1978	PORTRAIT US 35555	UK 83080
STEVE FOSSEN	B PERC(ABCDEFGH		(E) BEBE LE STRANGE	1980	EPIC US 36371	UK 84135
ROGER FISHER	STEEL G	(ABCDG	(F) GREATEST HITS LIVE	1981		UK 84829
KAT HENDRIKSE	D	(A	(G) GREATEST HITS LIVE (DBL)	1980	EPIC US 36888	
BRIAN NEWCOMBE	B	(A	(H) PRIVATE AUDITION	1982	EPIC US 38049	
DURIS MAXWELL	D	(A				
ROB DEANS	K SYN(A	MIKE FLICKER PERC	(A	DAVE WILSON	D (A	ROY AYOTTE PERC (A
GEOFF FOUBERT	BANJO(A	SUE ENNIS	G V (E	CHRISSY SHEFTS	G (E	LYNN WILSON/KEAGLE V (BH
GARY HUMPHREY	V	(E	DON WILHELM	V (E	TOWER OF POWER HRNS(E	SEAL DUNNINGTON V (E
LENNY PICKETT	HRNS	(EFG	GREG ADAMS	HRNS (EFG	STEVE KUPKA	HRNS(E	MIC GILLETTE HRNS (EFG
EMILIO CASTILIO	HRNS	(EFG				

HEARTBREAKERS

JOHNNY THUNDERS	G V	(AB	(A) L.A.M.F.	1977	TRACK	2400 218
JERRY NOLAN	V D	(A	(B) LIVE AT MAX'S KANSAS CITY	1979	BEGGARS BANQUET	BEGA9
WALTER LURE	G	(AB				
RICHARD HELL	B V	(A	BILLY RATH B (AB	TY STYX	D (B	PETE CRAWLEY PROD (B
SPEEDY KEEN	PROD (A		DANIEL SECUNDA PROD(A			

HEARTS & FLOWERS

DAVE LAWSON	V AUTOHARP	(AB	(A) NOW IS THE TIME	1967	CAPITOL	US ST 2762
LARRY MURRAY	G V	(AB	(B) OF OLD HORSES,KIDS & FORGOTTEN	1968	CAPITOL	US ST 2868
RICK CUNHA	G V	(AB				
BERNIE LEADON	G	(B	DAVID JACKSON B (			

HEARTSFIELD

```
ARTIE BALDACCI D SYN K V(ABCD      (A) HEARTSFIELD                 1973  MERCURY       US   SRM1 688
GREG BIELA       B V (ABCD          (B) WONDER OF IT ALL            1974  MERCURY       US   SRM1 1003
FRED DOBBS     G BAN V (ABCD        (C) FOOLISH PLEASURES           1975  MERCURY       US   SRM1 1034
J C HARTSFIELD G MAN FDL V(ABCD     (D) HEARTSFIELD COLLECTORS ITEM 1977  CBS           US        34456
PHIL LUCAFO      G STEEL V(ABCD
PERRY CORDELL JORDAN  G V(ABCD
FLACO FALCON      PERC (A   TOM GEVING SAX PNO   (AC  BRIAN PRICE     FDL (C   CHEPITO AREAS   PERC (C
KURT McGETTRICK   HRNS (A   TED ASHFORD PNO      (D   TERRY ADAMS     CELLO(D  JACK KRAMMER    TPT  (B
BILL DINWIDDIE    TROM (B   BRANDON LEAVITT  PERC (B
```

HEARTWOOD

```
BYRON PAUL          G V  (A       (A) NOTHING FANCY               1975  GRC       US        GA 10008
CARTER MINOR V HCA PERC(A
T M HILDEBRANDT   G V  (A   JOE McGLOHON STEEL SAX(A  BUDDY BLACKMAN  BANJO(A  JERRY JOSEPH    CONGA (A
BILL BUTLER     V G K(A     DAVID BLACKMAN   MAND (A  ROBERT HUDSON  V B (A   PAUL HORNSBY      K   (A
DAVIS CAUSEY      G   (A    GARY JOHNSON     V B (A
```

HEAT

```
JEFF FORMOSA     D    (          (A) HEAT                        1980  MCA       US        3225
JEFF LI        B G    (
DWYTT DAYAN    V D    (   ALVIN ROBERTSON  D   (   TALLY TALIOFERRO  G   (
```

HEATERS

```
MERCY BERMUNDEZ  V SAX(          (A) THE HEATERS                 1978  ARIOLA            50032
MAGGIE CONNELL   K    (          (B) ENERGY TRANSFER             1980  CBS   US 36486    UK 84454
MISSY CONNELL    B V  (
```

HEATWAVE

```
JOHNNY WILDER    V CONGA(ABCD    (A) TOO HOT TOO HANDLE          1976  GTO UK GTLP 013  EPIC US 34761
ROD TEMPERTON    K    (ABC       (B) CENTRAL HEATING             1978  GTO UK GTLP 027  EPIC US 35260
KEITH WILDER     V    (ABD       (C) HOT PROPERTY                1979  GTO UK GTLP 039  EPIC US 35970
J D NICHOLAS     V    (D         (D) CANDLES                     1980  GTO UK GTLP 047  EPIC US 36873
MARIO MANTESE    B    (AB
ERIC JOHNS       G    (AB   ERNEST BERGER    D   (ABD  ROY CARTER    B PNO (A  CALVIN DUKE K      (D
DEREK BRAMBLE D  (D         WILLIAM L JONES  G V (D
```

HEAVEN & EARTH

```
                                 (A) HEAVEN & EARTH              1978  MERCURY       US        3722
                                 (B) FANTASY                     1979  MERCURY       US        3763
```

HEAVEN 17

```
GLENN GREGORY      V   (A        (A) PENTHOUSE & PAVEMENT        1981  VIRGIN UK V2208 GER 204 017
IAN CRAIG MARSH   SYN SAX (A
MARTIN WARE     K SYN V (A   JOHN WILSON    G B SYN(A  JOSIE JAMES     V   (A   STEVE TRAVELL   PNO (A
BOYS OF BUDDAH    HRNS (A
```

HEAVEN

```
TERRY SCOTT      V G K(A         (A) BRASS ROCK 1    (DBL)       1971  CBS           UK        66293
EDDI HARNETT     G V  (A
JOHN JAMES GORDON V B (A   VIC GLOVER       D   (A   DAVE GAUTREY   HRNS (A  BUTCH HUDSON    HRNS(A
DAVID HORLER     TROM K(A   RAY KING        HRNS (A   DEREK SOMERVILLE HRNS (A
```

HEAVY JELLY

```
JOHN MOORSHEAD   G (ABCDEFG  JIM CAPALDI   D (BC   STEVE THOMPSON  B (GF   CHRIS WOOD    WIND  (BC
ALEX DMOCHOWSKI  B (ABCDE    JACKIE LOMAX  V G(CDEFG DAVEY LUTTON   D (G    BARRY JENKINS   D   (D
BRUCE ROWLAND  D (EF         ROCKY         (A        CARLO LITTLE  D (A

(A) EARLY 1969    (B)    1969   (C) JULY 1969   (D) JAN 1970   (E) MARCH 1970   (F) MID 1970  (G) LATE 1970.


(NB) THE HEAVY JELLY ON THE ISLAND SAMPLER(NICE ENOUGH TO EAT'( I KEEP SINGING THAT SAME OLD SONG) WAS REALLY
SKIP BIFFERTY.  THE NAME HEAVY JELLY BEGAN AS A REVIEW HOAX BUT WAS REGISTERED BY JOHN CURD OF HEAD RECORDS AND
APPLIES TO THE LINE UPS HERE.
ONE SINGLE 'CHEWN IN/TIME OUT' ON HEAD 4001. AN ALBUM WAS PREPARED BUT WAS NOT RELEASED. ALSO A SESSION FOR THE
B.B.C. WAS RECORDED  MID 1970.
```

HEAVY METAL KIDS

```
GARY HOLTON      V   (AB12       (A) HEAVY METAL KIDS            1974  ATLANTIC  US 7047 UK K50047
RONNIE THOMAS  B V   (AB12       (B) ANVIL CHORUS                1975  ATLANTIC      UK    K50143
KEITH BOYCE      D   (ABC12      (C) KITSCH                      1977  RAK           UK   SRAK 523
JOHN SINCLAIR  K V   (1          (1) 1976       (2) 1977/78
BARRY PAUL     G V   (12
JAY WILLIAMS         (2   MICKEY WALLER    G   (A   DANNY PEYRONEL  K V (AB  PHIL KENZIE SAX     (B
MADELINE BELL    V   (B   IRENE CHANTER    V   (B   DOREEN CHANTER  V (B   COSMO        G     (2
```

DICK HECKSTALL SMITH

```
DICK HECKSTALL SMITH SAX(A       (A) A STORY ENDED               1972  BRONZE UK ILPS 9196 US WB 2650
PAUL WILLIAMS    V   (A
CALEB QUAYE      G   (A    DAVE GREENSLADE  K   (A   JON HISEMAN    D   (A   MARK CLARKE B   (A
GORDON BECK     PNO  (A    CHRIS SPEDDING   G   (A   ROB TAIT       D   (A   GRAHAM BOND K V (A
CHRIS FARLOWE    V   (A
```

DASHIELL HEDAYAT

```
DASHIELL HEDAYAT G V K(AB       (A) MELMOTH  LA DEVANTURE DES IVRESSES1969  ARION     FR     30 T079
RICHARD RAUX    WIND (A          (B) OBSOLETE                   1971  SHANDAR FR 10009 CBS UK 83512
ROBERT BALESTER  D   (A
JOSE B FADLA     G   (A    DIDIER DE ST JORES  K (A   DAEVID ALLEN    G   (B   WILLIAM BURROUGHS  V(B
DIDIER MALHERBE WIND (B    PIP PYLE      G D (B   GILLI SMYTH     V   (B   CHRISTIAN TRITSCH  G B(B
SAM WYATT        V   (B
```

HEDGEHOG PIE

```
MARGI LUCKLEY    V   'BC         (A) HIS ROUND                   1972  RUBBER        UK   RUB 002
JED GRIMES       G   (BCD        (B) HEDGEHOG PIE                1975  RUBBER        UK   RUB 009
MARTIN JENKINS V MAND VLN(BC     (C) GREEN LADY                  1975  RUBBER        UK   RUB 014
STU LUCKLEY    V B   (BC         (D) JUST ACT NORMAL             1978  RUBBER        UK   RUB 024
DIK              D   (C          (EP) WONDERFUL LEGEND OF LAMBTON 1977  RUBBER        UK   TUB 12
WALTER FAIRBAIRN G   (D
TONY CAPSTICK    (A   TOM DUFFY       B   (D   DAVE BURLAND        (D   MICHAEL DOONAM   FLT (BCD
PHIL MURRAY    B   (
```

[261]

HEE BEE GEE BEES

(A) 439 GOLDEN GREATS   1981 HEEBEEGEEBEE   TWITS 101

HEINSIGHT

(A) THE GREAT WHITE   1978 churchill   us   67233

HEINZ

(A) TRIBUTE TO EDDIE   1964 DECCA   UK   LK   4599
(B) REMEMBERING   1977 DECCA   UK   REM.7

ZEUS B HELD

ZEUS B HELD

(A) ZEUS AMUSEMENT   1978 BRAIN   0060 120

HELDON

RICHARD PINHAS	G K	(ALL	(A) ELECTRONIC GORILLA	1974	DISJUNCTA	000	001
PATRICK GAUTHIER	K SYN	(ACDEFJ	(A) ELECTRONIC GORILLA	1979	COBRA		37019
GEORGES GRUNBLATT	SYN K	(ABC	(B) ALLEZ TEIA	1975	DISJUNCTA	000	002
PIERROT ROUSSEL	B	(A	(C) ITS ALWAYS ROCK AND ROLL	1975	DISJUNCTA	000	006/7
COCO ROUSSEL	PERC	(AD	(D) AGNETA NILSSON	1976	URUS	000	011
GILLES DELEUZE	V	(A	(E) UN REVE SANS CONSEQUENCE SPECIALE	1976	COBRA	60008	37002
ALAIN BELLAICHE	G	(BD	(F) INTERFACE	1976	COBRA		37013
KLAUS BLASQUIZ	V	(J	(G) A DREAM WITH OUT	1978	INNER		1021
JANIK TOP	B	(E	(H) HELDON IV	1979	AURAL	US	5001
ALAIN RENAUD	G	(ABC	(J) STAND BY	1979	EGG	900	578
JEAN MY TRUONG	D	(C					
GILBERT ARTMAN	D	(C	ARIEL KALMA	K	(C	PHILIBERT ROSSI	SYN (D MICHEL ETTORI G (D
GERARD PREVOST	B	(D	FRANCOIS AUGER	D PERC	(EFJ	DIDIER BATARD	B (EJC
AURORE	V	(C					

H89B

ERWIN HELFER

ERWIN HELFER   PNO (A   (A) BOOGIE PIANO CHICAGO SYTLE   1976 BIG BEAR   BEAR 11

H89C

HELIX

BRAIN DOERNER	D V	(A	(A) BREAKING LOOSE	1979 HANDS		101
BRENT DOERNER	G	(A	(B) WHITE LACE & LEATHER	1981		
PAUL HACKMAN	G	(A				
BRAIN VOLLMER	V	(A	KEITH ZURBRIGG B (A			

RICHARD HELL

RICHARD HELL	B V	(ALL	(A) BLANK GENERATION	1976	STIFF	UK		BUY7
MARC BELL	D	(B1	(B) BLANK GENERATION	1977	SIRE	US 6037	UK	9103 327
IVAN JULIAN	G	(B1	(1) MAY 1978					
ROBERT QUINE	G	(B1						
JERRY ANTONIUS	K B	(1	FRANK MAURO D (1					

HELL PREACHERS

RUMOURED TO BE   (A) SUPREME PSYCHEDELIC UNDERGROUND 1968 MARBLE ARCH   UK MAS 1169
RITCHIE BLACKMORE G
JON LORD   K   IAN PAICE   D   IN PRE DEEP PURPLE DAYS BUT ALWAYS DENIED BY THEM ALL.

HELLFIELD

RICK LAMB	K G V	(A	(A) HELLFIELD	1979	EPIC	US	36005
MITCH HELLFIELD	D G V	(A	(B) NIGHT MUSIC	1979	EPIC	UK	80028
JAMIE LARSEN	B V	(A					
DICK SMITH	D	(A	DAVE HOVEY G (A				

HELLO PEOPLE

N D SMART	D V	(A	(A) THE HANDSOME DEVILS	1974	DUNHILL	US	50184
LAURENCE TASSE		(A	(B) BRICKS	19	ABC	US	883
ROBERT SEDITA		(A	(C) THE HELLO PEOPLE	19	PHILIPS		PHS 600165
GREGORY GEDDES		(A	(D) FUSION	19	PHILIPS		PHS 600276
			(E) HAVE YOU SEEN THE LIGHT	19	MEDIARTS	US	41/8

LEVON HELM

LEVON HELM	D V	(AB	(A) LEVON HELM & THE RCO ALL STARS	1977	ABC US 1017	UK	ABCL 5236
PAUL BUTTERFIELD	HCA	(A	(B) LEVON HELM	1978	ABC US 1089		
FRED CARTER	G	(AC	(C) AMERICAN SON	1980	MCA US 5120		
HAROLD ROBBINS	K	(C					
DONALD DUNN	B	(A	STEVE CROPPER	G	(AB	BOOKER T JONES	K (A JOHN FLAMINGO V (A
JEANETTE BAKER	V	(A	ROBBIE ROBERTSON	G	(A	GARTH HUDSON	ACC (A CHARLES MILLER SAX (A
ALAN RUBIN	TPT	(AB	LOU MARINI	SAX	(AB	WILLIE HALL	D (B TOM MALONE TROM(B
HOWARD JOHNSON	HRNS	(AB	ROGER HAWKINS	D	(B	DR JOHN	K G (A EMMARETTA MARKS V (A
BARRY BECKETT	K	(B	RANDY McCORMICK	K	(B	ERNIE CATE	V (B DAN FERGUSON G (B
LARRY BYROM	B	(B	EARL CATE	V	(B	JIMMY JOHNSON	G (B SCOTT EDWARDS B (B
DAVID HOOD	B	(B	LOU DEL GATTO	SAX	(B	MARY BERRY	V (B BOBBY OGDEN K (C
BILLY SANFORD	G	(C	HENRY STRZELECKI	B	(C	JERRY CARRIGAN	D (C MITCH HUMPHRIES K (C
STEVE SCHAFFER	B	(C	BUDDY EMMONS	STEEL	(C	JERRY SHOOK	K (C STEVE GIBSON G (C
KENNY BUTTREY	D	(C	BUSTER PHILIPS	D	(C	CLIFFORD ROBERTSON	K (C BEEGIE ADAIR K (C
BUZZ CASON	V	(C	TODD CERNEY	V	(C		

H92A

HELMET BOY

(A) HELMET BOY   1980 ELEKTRA US 280 uk K 52249

HELP YOURSELF

MALCOLM MORLEY	G V	(ABCDE	(A) HELP YOURSELF	1971	LIBERTY	US 5583 UK	83484
RICHARD TREECE	G V	(ABCDE	(B) STRANGE AFFAIR	1972	U A	US 5591 UK	UAS 29287
KEN WHALEY	B	(ADE	(C) BEWARE OF THE SHADOW	1972	U A	US 079 UK	UAS 29413
DAVE CHARLES	D V	(ABCDE	(D) RETURN OF KEN WHALEY	1973	U A	UK	UAS 29487
PAUL BURTON	B G	(BCDE	(E) HAPPY DAYS	1973	U A	UK	FREE1
MARTIN ACE	V B	(E	(DE) RETURN/HAPPY DAYS	1973	U A	UK	UDG 4001
GEORGINA ACE	V G	(E					
VIV MORRIS	G V	(E	ERNIE GRAHAM	V G (B JOJO GLEMSER G (B			

HEMLOCK

MILLER ANDERSON	G V	(A	(A) HEMLOCK	1973	DERAM	UK	SML 1102
JIM LEVERTON	B V	(A					
ERIC DILLON	D	(A	MICK WEAVER	K (A PETER DINES K G V(A CHRIS MERCER SAX (A		
PETE WILLSHER	STEEL	(A	CHRIS STEWART	V (A		

BUGS HENDERSON

BUGS HENDERSON	G V	(A	(A) AT LAST	1978	ARMADILLO	US ARLP78	
RON THOMPSON	D	(A					
ROBERT CHITWOOD	B	(A					

H87A

H87B

H88

H89

H89A

H89B

H89C

H90

H91

H91A

H91B

H92

H92A

H93

H94

H94A

DORRIS HENDERSON

DORRIS HENDERSON	ACC V	(ABC	(A) THERE YOU GO	1965	COLUMBIA	UK	SX	6001
JOHN RENBOURN	G	(AB	(B) WATCH THE STARS	1967	FONTANA	UK	STL	5385
TIM WALKER	G	(B	(C) ROTTERDAM BLUES(EP)	196	SHR	NL	VR	108
DANNY THOMPSON	B	(B					

WAYNE HENDERSON

WAYNE HENDERSON TROM (AB   (A) LIVING ON A DREAM   1978 POLYDOR US 16145   UK 2391 343
RONNIE LAWS   SAX (A   (B) FREEDOM SOUNDS   19   ATLANTIC US 1512
DEBORAH SHOTLOW V (A   ( ) AT BIG DADDY'S PLACE 1977 ABC   US
ALEXANDRA BROWN V (A   ( ) STEP INTO YOUR LIFE   1978 POLYDOR POLS 1004 UK 2391 380
AUGIE JOHNSON   V (A   ( ) EMPHASISED   1979 POLYDOR
BOBBY LYLE   K (A
ROLAND BAUTISTA G (A   STEVEN GUITIERREZ D (A   DON BECK   B (A   MARLON McLAIN   G (A
NATHANIEL PHILLIPS B (A   BRUCE CARTER   D (A   VANCE TENORT   PERC (A   DEAN GANT   SYN (A
VICTOR FELDMAN PERC (A   JAY GRAYDON   G (A   GEORGE DEL BARRIO K (A   GEORGE BOHANON TROM(A
DONALD COOKE   TROM (A   JOHN ERVIN   WIND (A   EARL DUMLER   OBOE (A   JACK MARSH WIND   (A
OSCAR BRASHEAR TPT (A   STEVE MADAIO   TPT (A   DAVE GROVER   TPT (A   BOB GREVE   WIND (A
CHUCK BROOKE   WIND (A   SYLVIA ST JAMES V (A   SAUNDRA ALEXANDER   (A   JIM GILSTRAP   V (A
MYRNA MATTHEWS V (A   SYREETA WRIGHT   V (A

EDDIE HENDERSON

EDDIE HENDERSON HRNS (ALL   (A) INSIDE OUT   1974 CAPRICORN US CPO122 UK 2429 106
PATRICE RUSHEN   B K (E   (A) INSIDE OUT   1974 CAPRICORN   UK K 57504
GEORGE CABLES   K   (E   (B) REALIZATION   1974 CAPRICORN US CPO118 UK K 57505
CHARLES MIMMS   K   (E   (C) SUNBURST   1975 BLUENOTE   BNLA 464
MTUME   K V PERC (E   (D) HERITAGE   197 BLUENOTE   BNLA 636
LEE RITENOUR   G   (E   (E) COMIN' THROUGH   1977 CAPITOL   EST 11671
AL McKAY   G   (E   (F) MAHAL   1978 CAPITOL   EST 11846
MANI BOYD   WIND (E   (G) RUNNING TO YOUR LOVE 1979 TOWER   EST 11984
CONNIE HENDERSON WIND (E
JULIAN PRIESTER   TROM (E   PHILIP BAILEY   V PERC(E HOWARD KING   D (E   PAUL JACKSON   B (E
SKIP DRINKWATER   PERC (E   DIANE REEVES   V (E

MICHAEL HENDERSON

             (A) SOLID   1976 BUDDAH   BDS5662
MICHAEL HENDERSON V B K(ALL   (B) GOIN' PLACES   1977 BUDDAH   BDLH 5018
ROZ RYAN   V   (E   (C) IN THE NIGHT TIME   1978 BUDDAH   BDLH 4055
ELI FONTAINE   SAX (E   (D) DO IT ALL   1979 BUDDAH US 5719 UK BDLP 4062
KATHY KOSINS   V   (E   (E) WIDE RECEIVER   1980 BUDDAH US 6004 UK BDLP 4065
SHEILA HORNE   V   (E
CAROL HALL   V   (E   JEANETTE McFRUDER V (E   VENNA KEITH   V (E   RANDALL JACOBS G PNO(E
RAY PARKER   G   (E   OLLIE E BROWN   D (E   CORY HEATH   D (E   BOBBY FRANKLIN   D (E
CHERYL NORTON   V   (E   ERIK WALLACE   D (E   RON PANGBORN   D (E   ERNESTRO WILSON K (E
GARY NESTER   K   (E   MANON SAULSBY   K (E   SYLVESTER RIVERS PNO (E   MICHAEL IACOPELLI SYN (E
LORENZO BROWN   PERC (E   MIGUEL FUENTES   PERC (E

JIMI HENDRIX

JIMI HENDRIX   G V (ALL   (A) ARE YOU EXPERIENCED 1967 TRACK   2407 004
NOEL REDDING   B (ABCDIMN (A) "   "   "   1967 POLYDOR GER 184 085
MITCH MITCHELL   D (ABCDHIKLMNU (A) "   "   "   1970 BACKTRACK   2407 010
BILLY COX   B (GHIJKLNOU (A) "   "   "   19   REPRISE US   RS6261
JACK CASADY   B ((A) "   "   "   19   TRACK   612 001
BUDDY MILES   D (FLWU   (B) AXIS BOLD AS LOVE   1967 REPRISE US   RS6281
AL KOOPER   K (D   (B) "   "   "   " 1967 TRACK   UK 2407 011
JIM MORRISON   V HCA(W   (B) "   "   "   " 19   POLYDOR GER 184 110
JIM McCARTY   G (W   (B) "   "   "   " 19   TRACK   GER 239 000
ROLAND ROBINSON B (U   (AB) ARE YOU/AXIS   19   POLYDOR   2383 031
LARRY YOUNG   K (U   (C) SMASH HITS   1968 REPRISE US   MS2025
LARRY LEE   G (U   (C) "   "   1968 TRACK   UK 613 004
STEVE WINWOOD   K (H   (C) "   "   1973 POLYDOR UK ACD 219
JEFF MIRANOV   G (OS   (C) "   "   1968 POLYDOR GER 184 138
ALLEN SCHWARZBERG D (OS   (D) ELECTRIC LADYLAND(DBL)1968 TRACK   UK 2657 001
LANCE QUINN   G (S   (D) "   "   1968 REPRISE US   2RS 6307
JIMMY MAELEN   PERC(OS   (D) "   "   1968 POLYDOR GER 2612 002
MAERETHA STEWART V (S   (D) "   "   197 POLYDOR   2657 012
HILDA HARRIS   V (S   (D) "   "   19   BARCLAY FR 80583/4
VIVIAN CHERRY   V (OS   (D) "   "   PT1 1968 TRACK   UK 613 010
BUDDY LUCAS   HCA (S   (D) "   "   PT1 1974 POLYDOR UK 2310 271
CHRIS WOOD   WIND (H   (D) "   "   PT2 1968 TRACK   UK 613 017
LINDA NOVEMBER   V (O   (D) "   "   PT2 1968 POLYDOR UK 2310 272
JUMA EDWARDS   PERC (I   (E) ELECTRIC HENDRIX***** 1968 TRACK   UK 2856 002
RONETTES   V (I   (F) MONTEREY   1970 REPRISE UK K40430
GHETTO FIGHTERS V (HI   (F) "   "   1970 REPRISE US   MS 2029
EMERETTA MARKS   V (H   (G) BAND OF GYPSYS   1970 TRACK   UK 2406 002
BUZZY LINHART   VIBES(H   (G) "   "   "   1970 CAPITOL US   STAO472
BARBARA MASSEY   V (O   (G) "   "   "   1970 BARCLAY FR 92922
JOHNNY WINTER   G (W   (G) "   "   "   1974 POLYDOR UK 2480 005
RANDY HOBBS   B (W   (H) CRY OF LOVE   1971 POLYDOR UK 2302 023
RANDY ZEHRINGER D (W   (H) "   "   1971 BARCLAY FR 80433
BOB BABBIT   B (OS   (H) "   "   1971 REPRISE US   RS 2034
LONNIE YOUNGBLOOD V SAX(A   (H) "   "   197 POLYDOR   2406 002
HERMAN HITSON   ((H) "   "   197 POLYDOR   2408 101
DAVE MASON   G (D   (I) RAINBOW BRIDGE   1971 REPRISE UK K44159
ROCKY DZIDZORNU   PERC((I) "   "   1971 REPRISE US   RS 2040
CURTIS McTEARA   B ((J) ISLE OF WIGHT   1971 BARCLAY FR 80462
RONNETTES   V (T   (J) "   "   "   1971 POLYDOR UK 2302 016
CURTIS KNIGHT   ((K) IN THE WEST   1972 POLYDOR UK 2302 018
MIKE EPHON   K ((K) "   "   "   1972 BARCLAY FR 80448
LEE MOSES   G ((K) "   "   "   1972 REPRISE US   RS 2049
MICHAEL WATSON   G ((L) WAR HEROES   1973 POLYDOR UK 2302 020
NURTE EDMONDS   K ((L) "   "   1973 BARCLAY FR 80448
JEANETTE JACOBS   V (D   (L) "   "   1973 REPRISE US   RS 2103
EDDIE KRAMER   V (N   (M) JIMI HENDRIX(COMP) 1973 REPRISE UK K64017
KEN WEAVER   V (N   (N) LOOSE ENDS   1973 POLYDOR UK 2310 301
STEVE STILLS   PNO (H   (N) "   "   1973 BARCLAY FR 80491

(CONTINUED)

PAUL CARUSO	HCA (H	
LITTLE RICHARD	V K (	
DEWEY TERRY	G (	
DON SUGARCANE HARRIS	VLN(	
EDDIE BROWN	D (	
MIKE FINNIGAN	B (D	
FREDDIE SMITH	SAX (D	
LARRY FAUCETTE	CONGA(D	
GARY LEEDS	(B	
ROY WOOD	V (B	
TREVOR BURTON	V (B	
GRAHAM NASH	(B	
MIKE MANDEL	PNO (D	

***** THIS ALBUM WITHDRAWN BEFORE
        PUBLIC RELEASE A FEW DJ COPIES
        CAN BE BOUGHT.

(O) CRASH LANDING	1975	POLYDOR	UK	2310 398
(O) " " "	1975	REPRISE	US	RS 2204
(P) JIMI HENDRIX(SPECIAL)	1975	POLYDOR	UK	2343 080
(Q) JIMI HENDRIX 2(COMP)	1975	POLYDOR	UK	2343 086
(R) LEGACY (COMP)	1971	POLYDOR	UK	MP9357/8
(S) MIDNIGHT LIGHTNING	1976	POLYDOR	UK	2310 415
(S) " "	197	POLYDOR		2302 039
(S) " "	1976	REPRISE	US	RS 2229
(T) THE ESSENTIAL	1978	POLYDOR	UK	2612 034
(T) THE ESSENTIAL	1978	REPRISE	US	2245
(U) 9 TO THE UNIVERSE	1980	POLYDOR		POLS1023
(U) " " " "	1980	POLYDOR	UK	2344 155
(U) " " " "	1980	REPRISE	US	2299
(V) STONE FREE	1981	POLYDOR	UK	2343 114
(W) WOKE UP THIS MORNING	1980	RED LIGHTNIN'		0015
(W) SKY HIGH(BOOTLEG ?)	1972	SKYDOG		SGSH20/7378
(W) SKY HIGH(BOOTLEG ?)	197	KUSTOM		SJSH 1
(X) ESSENTIAL II	1979	REPRISE	US	2293
(X) ESSENTIAL II	1979	POLYDOR	UK	2311 014
( ) BOX SET 13 LP	1980	POLYDOR	UK	2625 040
( ) BOX SET 13 LP	1980	POLYDOR	NL	2625 038
( ) LEGENDARY	1980	POLYDOR	NL	2490 156
( ) CONCERTS	1	1982		
JIMI HENDRIX	1968	SAGA		6307
AT HIS BEST 1	1972	SAGA		6313
AT HIS BEST 2	1972	SAGA		6314
AT HIS BEST 3	1972	SAGA		6315
LOOKING BACK	1974	EMBER		EMB3428
EXPERIENCE (SOUNDTRACK)	1971	EMBER		NR 5057
EXPERIENCE (SOUNDTRACK)	1971	VOGUE		30148
EXPERIENCE (SOUNDTRACK)	1978	MODE		9011
MORE EXPERIENCE	197	EMBER		NR 5061
MORE EXPERIENCE	1972	VOGUE		782
MORE EXPERIENCE	1972	BULLDOG		BDL4003
JIMI HENDRIX	197	TRIP		3505
JIMI HENDRIX	197	TRIP		3509
ROOTS OF HENDRIX	197	TRIP		9501
IN THE BEGINNING	1973	EMBER		NR 5068
IN THE BEGINNING	197	SHOUT		502
IN THE BEGINNING	197	T NECK	US	3007
THE EARLY YEARS	19	MFP		
BIRTH OF SUCCESS	1970	MFP		50053
FRIENDS(LITTLE RICHARD)	1977	EMBER		EMB3434
JIMI HENDRIX	1973	BOULEVARD		41060
JIMI HENDRIX VOL1	1973	PAN		6313
JIMI HENDRIX VOL2	1973	PAN		6314
JIMI HENDRIX VOL3	1973	PAN		6315
HENDRIX 66	197	ENTERPRISE		1030
VERY BEST OF	1975	UA		LA 505
FOR REAL	1976	DJM		DJLMD8011
THE BEST OF	19	MUSIDISC		CV 1208
RARE HENDRIX	1975	ENTERPRISE		3000
RARE HENDRIX	1981	AUDIO FIDELITY		1016
RARE HENDRIX	1975	EXPLOSIVE		558002
RARE HENDRIX	1973	TRIP	US	9500
HENDRIX STORY	197	WB		K64017
SUPER HENDRIX	197	MUSIDISC		1354
ETERNAL	197	HALLMARK		732
IN CONCERT	197	SPRINGBOARD		4031
THE WILD ONE	1973	HALLMARK		SHM 791
GET THAT FEELING(C KNIGHT)	1968	LONDON		SH 8349
GET THAT FEELING	1968	CAPITOL	US	2856
JIMI HENDRIX	19	BELLAPHON		1552
FACE & PLACE	19	BYG	FR	529912
VOODOO CHILE	19	KARUSSEL	GER	2999012
STAR PORTRAIT	19	KARUSSEL	GER	2672002
BEFORE THE DELUGE	19	EMI		50780
JIM	19	PICKWICK		3528
STRANGE THING	1968	LONDON		SH 8369
BACKTRACK 4(1 SIDE)	19	TRACK		2407 004
BACKTRACK 5(1 SIDE)	19	TRACK		2407 005
GENIUS OF HENDRIX	1978	FESTIVAL		ALB 204
STAR PORTRAIT	197	POLYDOR		2672 002
POP HISTORY	197	POLYDOR		2675 013
JIMI HENDRIX	19	SPRINGBOARD		4010
HIGH LIVE & DIRTY	19	NUTMEG	US	1001
COSMIC TURN AROUND	19	AUDIO FIDELITY		1002
TOGETHER	19	PICKWICK	US	3347
FREE SPIRIT	19	ACCORD	US	7101
BEFORE LONDON	1981	ACCORD	US	7101
SUPER PACK	19	TRIP	US	3509
GENIUS	19	TRIP	US	9523
ROOTS OF ROCK	19	EVEREST	US	296
GREATEST SEESIONS	1980	SAAR	IT	2506
MOODS	19	TRIP	US	9512
2 GREAT EXPERIENCES	1971	PLATINUM	UK	6004
2 GREAT EXPERIENCES	1971	MAPLE	US	6004
DAY TRIPPER	19	QUALITY		1814
LIVE VOL1	19	STATESIDE		SL155
WHAT'D I SAY	1972	M F P	UK	5278

JIMI HENDRIX   (CONTINUED)

GET THAT FEELING	19	FLASHING	US	659
FLASHING	1968	CAPITOL	US	2894
LAST NIGHT	19	ALSTAN	GER	201016
SECOND TIME AROUND	19	ALSTAN	GER	201018
MR PITIFUL	19	ALSTAN	GER	201019
WELCOME HOME	19	ALSTAN	GER	201020
HUSH NOW	19	ALSTAN	GER	201021

SONNY HENNIG

FRANK DIEZ	G	(A	(A) TRANENGAS	1971 KUCKUCK	GER	237 5008
WALTI SCHNEIDER	B	(A				
GUNTHER STORCH	D	(A	TOMMI ROEDER SAX (A ERNST SCHULTZ G (A ELKART RAHN B (A			

HENRICH & HOCHSTETTER

CHRISTIAN HOCHSTETTER	G SIT(A	(A) HENRICH & HOCHSTETTER	19	PHILIPS	GER	6305 149
UDO HENRICH	G V	(A				
DAGMAR DECKERS	V	(A HANS ESSERS HCA (A PETE SMITH D PERC (A RALPH KLEINE-TELBE B (A				

PIERRE HENRY

PIERRE HENRY	K SYN(A	(A) MESSE DE LIVERPOOL	19	PHILIPS		6510 001
(LINE UP FOR (B) SEE SPOOKY TOOTH		(B) CEREMONY (WITH SPOOKY TOOTH)	1969	ISLAND	UK	ILPS9107
		(C) MESSE POUR LE TEMPS	19	PHILIPS		836 893

HENRY COW

TIM HODGKINSON SAX K V (ALL	(A) LEGEND	1973	VIRGIN US 13107 UK	V 2005
ROBERT WYATT	V	(DE	(A) LEGEND	1973	VIRGIN GER 87738	
FRED FRITH	G VLN K	(ALL	(B) UNREST	1974	VIRGIN	UK	V 2011
JOHN GREAVES	B PNO(ABCD	(C) IN PRAISE OF LEARNING	1975	VIRGIN	UK	V 2027
PETER BLEGVAD	G V CLAR(C	(D) CONCERTS	1976	CAROLINE	UK	CAD 3002
CHRIS CUTLER	V	(ALL	(D) CONCERTS	1978	COMPENDIUM	FIDARO 1
ANTHONY MOORE	K	(C	(E) WESTERN CULTURE	1978	BROADCAST	BC 1
LINDSAY COOPER	WIND (ABCDE			
GEOFF LEIGH	SAX (CA MONGEZI FEZA TPT (C DAGMAR KRAUSE (ACD GEORGIE BORN B (BE
ANNEMARIE ROELOFS TROM (E LOL COXHILL   (B HENK WELIEVRED   (B D J PERRY   (B
JACK BALCHIN   (B MIKE OLDFIELD   (B CHARLES FLETCHER (B

HENSKE YESTER

JUDY HENSKE	V	(AB	(A) FAREWELL ALDEBARAN	1969	STRAIGHT GER 90928 UK STS 1052
ZAL YANOVSKY	PROD (A	(A) FAREWELL ALDEBARAN	1969	RERPISE US 6388
JERRY YESTER	G B V(AB	(B) ROSEBUD	1971	REPRISE	RS 6426
GRAIG DOERGE	K V (B			
JOHN SEITER	D V (B DAVID VAUGHT B (B RAY BROWN B (B BUDDY EMMONS STEEL(B
BARRY ZWEIG	G (B MIKE DEASY G (B

JUDY HENSKE

JUDY HENSKE	V	(ALL	(A) JUDY HENSKE	1963	ELEKTRA		EKS 7231
JOHN FORSAY	G	(BC	(B) HIGH FLYING BIRD	1964	ELEKTRA		EKS 7241
TOM TEDESCO	G	(C	(C) DEATH DEFYING	1965	REPRISE	UK	RS 6203
JIMMY BOND	B	(A	(D) A LITTLE BIT OF SUNSHINE	1965	MERCURY	US	SR 61010
JOHN EWING	TROM (A					

KEN HENSLEY

KEN HENSLEY	V G K(AB	(A) PROUD WORDS ON A DUSTY SHELF	1973	BRONZE UK ILPS 9223+RI BRON 223
B J COLE	STEEL(B	(A) PROUD WORDS ON A DUSTY SHELF	1973	MERCURY US 1 661
DAVE PAUL	B(A	(B) EAGER TO PLEASE	1975	BRONZE UK ILPS 9307+RI BRON 307
GARY THAIN	B(A	(B) EAGER TO PLEASE	197	WB	US	2863
LEE KERSLAKE	D(A	(C) FREE SPIRIT	1980	BRONZE UK 533
MARK CLARKE	B(B			
BUGS PEMBERTON	D(B			

HEPTONES

EARL MORGAN	G V	(D	(A) HEPTONES & FRIENDS	1972	TROJAN		TBL 183
LEROY SIBBLES	B V	(D	(B) NIGHTFOOD	1976	ISLAND		ILPS 9381
BARRY LLEWELLYN	V	(	(C) COOL RASTA	1976	TROJAN		TRLS 128
WILLIE LINDO	G	(D	(D) PARTY TIME	1977	ISLAND		ISPS 9456
PHILL	G	(D	(E) IN LOVE WITH YOU	1978	UA		LA 805
R WILLIAM	G	(D	(F) BETTER DAYS	1978	THIRD WORLD		TDWD 1
SKULLY	PERC (D	(F) BETTER DAYS	1981	MERCURY		6302 037
DAVID MADDEN	HRNS (D	(G) HEPTONES & FRIENDS VOL 2	197	ATTACK		ATLP 1001
GLEN DA COSTA	HRNS (D	(H) GOOD LIFE	1979	GREENSLEEVES		GREL 6
VIN GORDON	HRNS (D	(J) KING OF MY TOWN	1980	MERCURY		9103 565
BORIS GARDINER	B	(D				
KEITH STERLING	PNO (D WINSTON WRIGHT K (D MIKEY BOO D (D

HERD

PETER FRAMPTON	G V	(A	(A) PARADISE LOST	1968	FONTANA	UK	STL 5458
ANDY BOWN	K	(A	(B) LOOKIN' THRU YOU	1968	FONTANA	US	67579
GARY TAYLOR	B	(A	(C) NOSTALGIA	1972	BUMBLE	US	GEMP 5001
ANDREW STEELE	D	(				
RIC ROTHWELL	D	(HENRY SPINETTI D (TONY CHAPMAN D (TERRY CLARKE G (
LEWIS RICH	V	(MICK UNDERWOOD D (LOUIS CENNAMO B (

HERE & NOW

STEFFY SHARPSTRING	G V(ABC	(A) WHAT YOU SEE (½ LP WITH A'TV)1	178	DEPTFORD FUN CITY		DLP 02
GAVIN DA BLITZ	K SYN V(ABC	(B) GIVE & TAKE	1978	CHARLY	UK	NOW 1
KEITH DAMISSILEBASS	B V(ABC	(C) ALL OVER THE SHOW	1979	CHARLY	UK	NOW 2
KIF KIF LE BATTER	D G V (AB	(EP) A DOG IN HELL	1978	CHARLY	UK	CEP 122
SUZE DA BLOOZ	V	(AB				
ANNE WOMBAT	V	(AB ROB BOUGIE D (C BERNIE ELLIOTT G (C

```
        PETER NOONE         V G K(ALL
        DEREK LECKENBY      G V  (    KEITH HOPWOOD      G V  (   KARL GREEN  B V  (   BARRY WHITWAM  D  (
        FRANK RENSHAW       G  (      CHRIS FINLEY       G  (     DAVE BARROW        (

        HERMANS HERMITS              1965 COLUMBIA  UK  33SX1727   X15                        1967 COLUMBIA  GERM SMC74317
        HERMANS HERMITS              1965 MGM       US      4382   BLAZE                      1967 MGM       US  SE  4478
        HERMANS HERMITS              1965 COLUMBIA  GERM C 73994   BLAZE                      1967 COLUMBIA  UK  SCX    35
        HERMANS HERMITS              196  H M V     SW  SGLP 532   MRS BROWN (SOUNDTRACK)     1968 COLUMBIA  UK  SCX 6303
        HERMANS HERMITS              197  M F P     AUST A 8148    MRS BROWN (SOUNDTRACK)     1968 MGM       US  SE  4548
        HERMANS HERMITS              1968 REGAL     UK  SREG1117   BEST OF VOL 3              1968 MGM       US  SE  4505
        THE BEST OF                  1965 COLUMBIA  UK  SCXC  27   THE BEST OF UK             1969 COLUMBIA  UK  SCX 6332
        THE BEST OF                  1965 MGM       US  SE  4315   THE MOST OF                1972 M F P     UK  MFP 5216
        HERMANS HERMITS HITS         1965 COLUMBIA  GERM C 74030   MOST OF VOL 2              1973 M F P     UK  MFP50000
        BRITISH GOGO (ANIMALS)       1965 MGM       US  SE  4306   XX THEIR GREATEST HITS     1973 ABKOC     US  AB  4227
        INTRODUCING                  1965 MGM       US  SE  4282   20 GREATEST HITS           1977 K TEL     UK  NE  1001
        INTRODUCING                  1965 ODEON     JAP     7282   GREATEST HITS              1980 CRYSATAL  GER     50727
        ON TOUR                      1965 MGM       US  SE  4295   A WHALE OF A TALE (HERMITS)     RCA NOT RELEASED
        WHEN THE BOYS MEET THE GIRL  65 MGM        US  SE  4334   ROCK'N'ROLL PARTY          1969 MGM NOT RELEASED
        WHEN THE BOYS MEET THE GIRL  65 MGM        UK      8006   ROCK'N'ROLL BEST           1977 RAK       JAP    90062
        BOTH SIDES OF                1966 COLUMBIA  UK  SX  6084   VERY BEST OF               1980 MFP       GER    97206
        BOTH SIDES OF                1966 MGM       US  SE  4386   (EP) HERMANIA              1965 COLUMBIA      SEG 8380
        AGAIN                        1966 COLUMBIA  GERM SMC74150   (EP)MRS BROWN             1965 COLUMBIA      SEG 8440
        LUCKY 13                     1966 COLUMBIA  GERM SMC74232   (EP) HITS                 1965 COLUMBIA      SEG 8442
        HOLD ON(SOUNDTRACK)          1966 MGM       US  SE  4342   (EP) A MUST TO AVOID      1965 COLUMBIA      SEG 8477
        BEST OF VOL 2                1966 MGM       US  SE  4416   (EP) HOLD ON              1966 COLUMBIA      SEG 8503
        BEST OF VOL 2                1966 COLUMBIA  UK SCX    32   (EP) DANDY                1966 COLUMBIA      SEG 8520
        THERE'S A KIND OF HUSH       1967 COLUMBIA  UK  SCX 6174   (EP) LONDON LOOK          1968 YARDLEY (PROMO) SLE15
        THERE'S A KIND OF HUSH       1967 COLUMBIA  UK SCXC  34
        THERE'S A KIND OF HUSH       1967 MGM       US  SE  4438
```

H108A   HERO   H108A
```
        JEFF JONES          D   (B     (A) HERO                    1977 MERCURY      US      1137
        MARK HOULE          B   (B     (B) BOYS WILL BE BOYS       1978 20 CENTURY   US       573
        NEIL CITRONS        G V (B
        CUT HOULE           K V (B     SCOTT PHARES       V    (B
```
H108B   HEROES   H108B
```
                                       (A) BORDER RAIDERS          1980 POLYDOR US 6254  NL  2442 171
```
H109   HERON   H109
```
        ROY APPS            V G K(B     (A) HERON                   1970 DAWN     UK   DNLS 3010
        STEVE JONES         K   (B      (B) TWICE AS NICE          1972 DAWN     UK   DNLS 3025
        TONY POOK           V PERC(B
        GERALD T MOORE      V G K(B  MIKE FINESILVER    B   (B  TERRY GITTINS     D  (B  MIKE COOPER G V  (B
        WILLIE BOAZMAN      G V (B
```
H110   MIKE HERON   H110
```
        MIKE HERON          G G K (ABC  (A) SMILING MEN WITH BAD REPUTATIONS   1971 ISLAND UK ILPS9146 GER 85381
        DUDU PUKWANA        SAX  (A      (A) SMILING MEN WITH BAD REPUTATIONS   197  ELEKTRA       US   EKS74093
        MALCOLM LE MAISTRE  C(AB          (B) MIKE HERONS REPUTATION            1975 NEIGHBOURHOOD UK   NBH 80637
        SIMON NICOL         G   (A        (C) DIAMOND OF DREAM                  1977 BRONZE UK ILPS9460+RI BRON460
        BETSY COOK          V   (D        (C) DIAMOND OF DREAM                  1977 BRONZE        GER  28571
        DAVE PEGG           B   (A        (D) MIKE HERON                        1980 CASABLANCA US 7186
        JOE BOYD            PROD(A
        MIKE KOWALSKI       D   (A  RICHARD THOMPSON  G  (AB  GERRY CONWAY   D   (A  SUE GLOVER   V   (A
        SUNNY LESLIE        V   (A  LIZA STRIKE       V  (A   VEMU MUKUNDA       (A  MOHANA LAKSHMIPATHY  (A
        VSHAILENDRA             (A  P R MONEY            (A   HEATHER WOOD   V   (A  DR STRANGELY STRANGE V(A
        PAT DONALDSON       B   (A  TONY COX         SYN (A   FRANK USHER    G   (C  DAVID SAMS     K   (C
        MIKE TOMICH         B   (C  JOHN GILSTON      D  (CB  SUSIE WATSON-TAYLOR V (CB  DAVID BARKER  K  (C
        PETE TOWNSHEND      G   (A* JOHN ENTWISTLE    B  (A*  KEITH MOON     D   (A* KRYSIA KOCJAN  V   (CB
        ROSE SIMPSON        B   (A  DAVE MATTACKS     D  (A   JOHN CALE B G K V VLN (A GRAHAM FORBES  G  (B
        TIM HINKLEY         K   (B  AMIN MONAMMED     B  (B   RON LEAHY      K   (B  ULF RONQUIST    G  (B
        BARRY HARWOOD       G   (B  JOHN MULKEY       B  (B   ROY YEAGER     PERC (B EDDIE JOBSON   VLN (B
        ROBIN WILLIAMSON    V WHIS(B MELANIE          V  (B   LINDA THOMPSON V   (B  BENNY KING  PERC   (B
        DUNCAN BROWNE       G   (B  JOE BAVIN   B V K (D   STEVE LIPSON   G V (D  DON WELLER SAX     (D
        JOHN GORDON         B   (D  PETE WINGFIELD    K  (D   HUGH MURPHY    PNO (D  LIAM GENOCKEY   D  (D
        RICHARD HARVEY      WIND(D  MEL COLLINS     SAX (D   FRANK USHER        (D  FRANK RICOTTI  PERC(D
        GRAHAM PRESKETT     VLN (D  NIK ROWLEY      STR (D   RICHARD BRUNTON  G (D  PHIL BODGER     V (D
```
                         *CREDITS ON ALBUM AS TOMMY & THE BIJOUX
H111   GARTH HEWITT   H111
```
        GARTH HEWITT        G V  (ALL    (A) THE LION & THE RAM     1973 MYRRH        MYR1001
        GRAHAM JARVIS       D PERC(A      (B) I NEVER KNEW LIFE     1974 MYRRH        MYR1017
        DAVE WINTOUR        B   (A        (C) LOVE SONGS T THE EARTH 1976 MYRRH       MYR1051
        JO PARTRIDGE        G   (A        (D) I'M GRATEFUL          1979 MYRRH        MYR1078
        MIKE MORAN          K   (A        (E) DID HE JUMP OR DID HE FALL  1979 PATCH  UK WOOF1001
        KEVIN PEEK          G   (A        (F) UNDER THE INFLUENCE   1981 MARSHALL ART    1002
        CLIFF RICHARD       V   (AE       (G) BEST OF               1980 MYRRH           1093
        DAVE LAWSON         K   (A
        ADRIAN LEE          SYN (A  BRYN HAWORTH G      (AF  PETE WILLSHER  STEEL(F  VICKI BROWN   V  (F
        TOM BLADES          G   (F  JAN PULSFORD    K V (F  LUIS JARDIN    PERC (F  RON ASPERY    SAX(F
        NETWORK 3           V   (F  STEVE BRUCE      D  (F  BOB HADDRELL   K   (F  ROB BURNS      B  (B
        CLIFF HALL          K   (B  LAURA WARMUN     V  (B
```
H111A   JOHN HIATT   H111A
```
        JOHN HIATT          VG  (ALL     (A) HANGING ROUND THE OBSERVATORY  197  EPIC    US
        JON PARIS           B G (C        (B) OVERCOATS             1975 EPIC    US          33190
        DOUG YANKUS         G   (C        (C) SLUG LINE             1979 MCA     US 3088 UK  MCF3005
        BRUCE GARY          D   (C        (D) TWO BIT MONSTERS      1980 MCA     US 5123 UK  MCF3078
        B J WILSON          D   (C        (E) ALL OF A SUDDEN       1982 GEFFEN  US          2009
        GERRY CONWAY        D   (C
        JESSE HARMS         K V (C  THOM MOONEY       D  (C  TODD COCHRAN   K   (C  ETAN McELROY  PNO V(C
        VEYER HILDEBRAND    B   (C  HOWARD EPSTEIN       (D  SHANE KEISTER      (D  DARYL VERDUSCO V D (DE
        JAMES ROLLESTON     B V (E
```

JIMMY HIBBERT
```
   JIMMY HIBBERT      PERC (A          (A) HEAVY DUTY                 1980 LOGO  UK LOGO 1021 NL   63871
   MANFRED MANN       SYN  (A
   GEOFF WHITEHORN  G V  (A   PAT KING      B V (A   JOHN LINGWOOD  D V (A   GRAHAM PRESKETT  SYN (A
   ED CROSS           V    (A   LAURIE CATHAM   V PERC(A  DAVE PHEE     V   (A   STEVE WALLER     V  (A
   STEVE BOLTON       V    (A
```
H111C   HIFI   H111C
```
   LARRY BERRIDGE   G V K(AB        (A) TOWNS & BARS                  1980 WEA          GER    58105
   BYRON CONTOSTAULOS B V (AB       (B) SING SONG                     1981 WEA          GER    58270
   STEVE GOODWIN      PERC (B
   TERRY JENKINS    G V  (AB  STEVE JONES    D PERC(A  HERBERT BOHME  V  (B   JACKSON      CONGAS(B
```
H111D   HI TEK   H111D
```
                                    (A) HI TEK                       1981 ORIGINAL            ORA105
```
H111E   HI TENSION   H111E
```
   PAUL PHILLIPS      G  (A          (A) HI TENTION                  1978 ISLAND      UK     ILPS 9564
   PAUL McLEAN        G  (A
   DAVID PHILIPS      K  (A   KEN JOSEPH     B   (A   DAVID REID     D  (A   LEROY WILLIAMS  CONGA(A
   JEFFREY GUISHARD  PERC (A  PATRICK McLEAN   SAX  (A
```
H112   DAN HICKS & HIS HOT LICKS   H112
```
   DAN HICKS  V G HCA    (ALL        (A) ORIGINAL RECORDINGS         1969 EPIC       US      26464
   JON WEBER          G   (A         (B) WHERES THE MONEY            1971 BLUE THUMB US      BTS29
   SID PAGE       V  VIOLA(ABCDF     (C) STRIKING IT RICH           1972 BLUE THUMB US 36 UK ILPS 9204
   SHERRY SNOW        V   (A         (D) LAST TRAIN TO HICKSVILLE    1973 BLUE THUMB US 51 RI US MCA 671
   CHRISTINA GANCHER V K  (A         (E) HEY GOOD LOOKIN'           1975 WB         UK      K 56157
   JAIME LEOPOLD    VLN B(ABCD       (F) IT HAPPENED ONE BITE       1978 WB         US      BSK  3158
   MARYANN PRICE    V PERC(BCDF
   NAOMI EISENBERG V VLN PERC(BCD JOHN L GIRTON  G   (CDF GERRY STEINHOLTZ D PERC(F  BOB SCOTT     D (D
   MICHAEL FRANKS   BANJO(F   LYLE RITZ       B   (F  CLARENCE McDONALD  K  (F  BILL DICKENSON  B (F
   JOHN PISANO      G   (F   RICHARD BORD D PERC(E
```
H113   JOE HIGGS   H113
```
   JOE HIGGS          (A            (A) LIFE OF CONTRADICTION       1976   VULCAN          GROL 508
                                    (B) UNITY IS POWER              1979   ISLAND          ILPS 9535
```
H113A   HIGH INERGY   H113A
```
                                    (A) HIGH INERGY                 1981 MOTOWN    UK   STML12157
```
H113B   HIGH COTTON   H113B
```
                                    (A) HIGH COTTON                 1975   ISLAND   US    9395
```
H114   HIGH COUNTRY   H114
```
                                    (A) HIGH COUNTRY                19   RACOON  US 1937   UK 7
                                    (B) DREAMS                      19   RACOON  US 2608
```
H114A   HIGHWIND   H114A
```
                                    (A) HIGHWIND                    1979 EMI      UK     INS 3025
```
H115   HIGH TIDE   H115
```
   TONY HILL          G   (AB        (A) SEA SHANTIES               1969 LIBERTY US 7638 UK LBS 83264
   SIMON HOUSE        VLN (AB        (B) HIGH TIDE                  1970 LIBERTY         UK LBS 83294
   PETER PAVLI        B   (AB
   ROGER HADDEN       D   (AB
```
H116   HIGHWAY   H116
```
   DARYL BRAITHWAITE V   (A          (A) HIGHWAY 1                  1979 EPIC       UK   83760
   GARTH PORTER     K V   (A
   TONY MITCHELL    B V   (A  HARVEY JAMES G V   (A  ALAN SANDON   D   (A  JIM HORN    SAX (A
   DAVID FOSTER     SYN   (A  JAY LEWIS      G SIT(A  BILL CUOMO    K   (A  STEVE FORMAN PERC(A
   MICHAEL BODDICKER SYN  (A  CARMEN TWILLIE  V   (A  VENNETTE GLOUD  V (A  SHARON ROBINSON V(A
```
H116A   HIGHWAY (UK)   H116A
```
   RAY MINHINNIT    G V  (AB         (A) HIGHWAY                    1974 EMI          UK  EMA 3019
   JIM HALL         K V  (AB         (B) SMOKING AT THE EDGE        197  EMI          UK  EMA  770
   JOHN GORDON      B G V(AB
   JON ELSTAR       V HCA PERC(AB  IAN BYRON    D V  (AB
```
H116B   HIGHWAY ROBBERY   H116B
```
   DON FRANCISCO    D V   (A         (A) FOR LOVE OR MONEY          1972 RCA      US     LSP 4735
   MICHAEL STEVENS  G V   (A
   JOHN LIVINGSTON TUNISON B V(A
```
H116C   ROSSETTA HIGHTOWER   H116C
```
   ROSSETTA HIGHTOWER    V   (A      (A) HIGHTOWER                  1971 CBS          UK   64201
   HENRY McCULLOUGH  G   (A
   RICK GRECH        B   (A  KEN CRADDOCK    K   (A  GORDON BECK   K   (A  JIM PRICE    TPT (A
   BOBBY KEYS       SAX  (A  COLIN GREEN     G   (A  HAROLD McNAIR  WIND(A  HENRY LOWTHER TPT(A
   BRUCE ROWLANDS    D   (A
```
H117   DAN HILL   H117
```
   DAN HILL       G V  (ALL          (A) DAN HILL                   1976 20th CENTURY     BTH  500
   LARRY LONDIN     D   (BC          (B) HOLD ON                    197  20th CENTURY     BTH  526
   RICK HOMME       B   (ABC         (C) LONGER FUSE                1978 20th CENTURY BTH 8005+BT  547
   DON POTTER     V G   (ABC         (D) FROZEN IN THE NIGHT        1978 20th CENTURY     BT   558
   JOHN CAPEK       K   (BC          (E) IF DREAMS HAD WINGS        1980 EPIC US 36411 UK 84273
   FRED MOLLIN    G V   (ABC         (F) BEST OF                    1980 20TH CENTURY          614
   MATTHEW McAULEY  V K  (ABC        (G) PARTIAL SURRENDER          1981 EPIC
   CATHY SMITH      V   (B
   BOB MANN         G   (BC
   BRIAN RUSSELL    G   (AB  BOBBY OGDIN   PNO      (C  BEN MINK     MAND (C  ERICA GOODMAN  HARP(C
   TOM SZCZESNIAK   B   (ABC JORN ANDERSEN   D   (BC DENNIS PENDRITH  B (C  RON LAURIE CELLO  B(C
   BOB BOUCHER      B   (B   BRIAN LEONARD   D   (A  BARRY KEANE    D  (A  STEPHANIE TAYLOR V (C
   ERIC ROBINSON    K   (ABC
```
H117A   JESSE HILL   H117A
```
   JESSIE HILL      V   (A           (A) NATURALY                   197  BLUE THUMB  US    BTS31
   DAVE LASTIE          (A
   BUCK BLACK           (A   SHINE ROBINSON     (A
```

ROY HILL

```
ROY HILL            V    (A12        (A) ROY HILL                   1978   ARISTA           UK   SPART1034
MIKE TAYLOR         K    (12         (1) 1978 (2) 1979
JAMIE WEST ORHAM    G    (1
STEVE SHONE         B    (1   COLIN WILKINSON   D    (1   JOHN KNIGHTSBRIDGE G    (2   CHAS CRONK      B   (2
PETE ACOCK          WIND (2   PETE THOMAS       WIND (2   TONY FERNANDEZ     D    (2
```

STEVE HILLAGE

```
STEVE HILLAGE G SYN V (ALL       (A) FISH RISING            1975 ATLANTIC US 13118   VIRGIN UK V2031
MIQUETTE GIRAUDY    K    (BCDEFGA  (B) "L"                   1975 ATLANTIS US 18205   VIRGIN UK V2066
PIERRE MOERLEN      PERC (B        (B) "L"                   1975 VIRGIN GER 28023
DON CHERRY          HRNS (B        (C) MOTOVATION RADIO      1977 ATLANTIC US 19144   VIRGIN UK V2777
MIKE HOWLETT        B    (A        (C) MOTOVATION RADIO      1977 VIRGIN GER 25469
ROGER POWELL        K    (B        (D) GREEN                1978 VIRGIN GER 25875     UK V2098
JOHN WILCOX         D    (B        (E) LIVE HERALD (DBL)     1978 VIRGIN GER 200 273    UK  3502
KASIM SULTON        B    (B        (F) OPEN                 1979 VIRGIN            UK V2135
LARRY KARUSH        PERC(B         (G) RAINBOW DOME MUSICK   1979 VIRGIN EURO 2445301   UK VR1
SONJA MALKINE       K    (B        ( ) AURA                 1980 AURA US 1   GER 202 799
LINDSAY COOPER      WIND (A
COLIN BASS          B    (E   PHILIP HODGE    K    (E   BASIL BROOKS    K   (E   JAHIB           PERC   (E
CHRISTIAN BOULE     G    (EA  CLIVE BUNKER    D    (E   CURTIS ROBERTSON B  (DE  JOE BLOCKER   D  (BCDE
CHUCK BYNUM         K G  (    JOHN McKENZIE   B    (E   ANDY ANDERSON   D   (DEF  DAVE STEWART   G V  (F
JEAN PHILIPPE RYKIEL SYN(F    REG McBRIDE     B    (C   MALCOLM CECIL   SYN (C  DAVE STEWART   SYN  (AFG
PAUL FRANCIS        B    (F   TIM BLAKE       SYN  (A   DIDIER MALHERBE WIND(A  GILLI SMYTH    V    (A
NICK MASON          D    (D   RUPERT ATWILL        (G
```

CHRIS HILLMAN

```
CHRIS HILLMAN       G V B(ALL       (A) CHRIS HILLMAN       1974   TOG                  1012
LARRY SIMS          B V  (C         (B) SLIPPIN' AWAY       1976   ASYLUM US 7E 1062 UK   K 53041
AL GARTH            SAX FDL(C        (C) CLEAR SAILIN'       1977   ASYLUM US 7E 1104 UK   K 53060
MEREL BREGANTE      D    (C
FUZZY SAMUELS       B    (     RICHARD MARS    G V  (BC  SKIP EDWARDS K  SYN STE(C  JOHN BRENNEN   G     (C
JOE LALA            PERC (BC   JIM GORDON      D    (B   PAUL HARRIS   K     (B   GEORGE TERRY   G     (B
STEVE CROPPER       G    (B    TIM SCHMIT      V    (BC  HERB PEDERSEN V     (B   MARK VOLMAN    V     (B
HOWARD KAYLAN       V    (B    JIM FIELDER     B    (B   RUSS KUNKEL   D     (B   LEE SKLAR      B   (B
AL PERKINS          STEEL(B    ALBHY GALUTEN   SYN  (B   DONNIE DACUS  G     (B   RICK ROBERTS   V     (B
DONALD DUNN         B    (B    SAM BROUSSARD   G    (B   DAVID GARIBALDI D   (B   HOWARD ALBERT  PERC(B
IVORY JOE HARRIS    K    (B    BYRON BERLINE   V FDL(B   BERNIE LEADON G V   (B   JOCK BARTLEY   G     (C
MICHAEL CLARKE      TAMB (C    BOBBY LAKIND    PERC (C   RON ALBERT    PROD(C   HOWARD ALBERT  PROD (B
```

RUPERT HINE

```
RUPERT HINE G V HCA (AB       (A) PICK UP A BONE       1971   PURPLE US 879        UK TPSA 7502
SIMON JEFFES        G    (A        (B) UNFINISHED PICTURE  1973   PURPLE               UK   TPSA 7509
DAVID MACIVER       G    (A        (C) IMMUNITY           1981   A&M   US 4858   UK   AMLH68519
BARRY DE SOUZA      D    (A
PETER ROBINSON      K    (A    PETE MORGAN     B    (A   TERRY COX     D    (A   CLIVE HICKS G    (A
RAUL MAYORA         PERC (A    ERIC FORD       G    (A   JOE MORETTI   G    (A   STEVE HAMMOND G BAN(A
PAUL BUCKMASTER     CELLO(A    EDDIE MORDUE    WIND (A   ROY WILCOX    WIND (A   ROGER GLOVER    PERC(A
GEOFF RICHARDSON    VLA  (A    PHIL COLLINS    PERC (C   PHIL PALMER   G    (C   OLLIE W TAYLOR  WIND(C
MARIANNE FAITHFULL  V    (C    TREVOR MORAIS        D PERC(C
```

JUSTIN HINES

```
JUSTIN HINES        V    (AB       (A) JEZEBEL             1976   ISLAND          UK   ILPS 9416
                                   (B) JUST IN TIME        1979   MANGO           UK   MLPS 9532
```

MARCIA HINES

```
MARCIA HINES        V    (A        (A) OOH CHILD           1980   LOGO            UK   LOGO 1023
MIKE PORCARO        B    (A
DAVID HUNGATE       B    (A    LEE RITENOUR    G    (A   TIM MAY       G    (A   FRED TACKETT   G    (A
ROBBIE PORTER       PERC (A    RICK SPRINGFIELD G   (A   BOB MACK      G    (A   PAUL SABY    G    (A
WILLIE ORNELAS      D    (A    ED GREENE       D    (A   STEVE FORMAN  PERC (A   JAI WINDING    K    (A
AL CAPPS            K    (A    TERRY YOUNG     K    (A   JULIUS WECHTER PERC (A   BOB CONTI    PERC   (A
CARL FRIBERG        PERC (A
```

HINKLEYS HERO'S

```
TIM HINKLEY         K    (12       PICK UP BAND WHICH FORMS FROM TIME TO TIME FOR ODD GIGS PERSONNEL VARIES
MIKE PATTO          V    (1        (1) 1976/JAN 77
BOZ BURRELL         B    (12       (2) JULY 1980
HENRY McCULLOUGH    D    (12
POLI PALMER         VIBES(12  CHARLIE WHITNEY  G    (1   BRIAN ROBERTSON G  (1   MICK RALPHS    G    (1
JOHN HALSEY         D    (12  BERNIE HOLLAND   G    (1   BOB TENCH     G V  (1   ROGER CHAPMAN  V    (12
STEVE SIMPSON       G    (2   MITCH MITCHELL   D    (12  MEL COLLINS   SAX  (12  JIM CREGAN     G    (1
ERIC BURDON         V    (1   KIKI DEE        V    (2
```

HIROSHIMA

```
                                   (A) HIROSHIMA           19     ARISTA          US      4252
```

HITCH HIKERS

```
                                   (A) HITCH HIKERS        1977   ABC             ABCL 5209
```

HITMEN

```
BEN WATKINS         G V  (A        (A) AIM FOR THE FEET    1980   URGENT UK ZIP84888 CBS US 36874
PETE GLENISTER      G.V  (A
NEIL BROCKBANK      B    (A    STAN SHAW       K    (A   MIKE GAFFEY     D V  (A
```

ROBYN HITCHCOCK

```
ROBYN HITCHCOCK     V K B G (A       (A) BLACK SNAKE DIAMOND ROLE  1981 ARMAGEDDON   UK     ARM4
MORRIS WINDSOR      D V  (A
GARY BARNACLE       SAX  (A    MATTHEW SELIGMANN  B  (A   VINCE ELY      D    (A   KIMBERLEY REW   G    (A
KNOX                G    (A    ROBB APPLETON   V    (A   HOWIE GILBERT  V    (A   TOM DOLBY      SYN(A
```

HOBO

```
STUART HARRISON     V G  (A        (A) HOBO                1976   ROCKFIELD       UAS 29909
COLIN DUGGAN        V G  (A
JOHN MORRIS         V G  (A    PAUL COBBOLD    B K  (A   STEVE BULL    D    (A   ROGER DAVIES   V    (A
```

TOMMY HOEHN

```
TOMMY HOEHN         V K G (A        (A) LOSING YOU TO SLEEP  1978   LONDON US 719   UK SHU 8536
GENE NUNEZ          G B  (A
JOHN HAMPTON        D PERC(A    KEITH YOUNG          B    (A
```

HOELDERLIN

JOACHIM GRUMBKOW	G K	(AF	(A) HOELDERLIN TRAUM	1972			
CHRISTIAN GRUMBKOW	G V	(AF	(B) HOELDERLIN	1975 SPIEGELEI	GER	160601	
NANNY DE RUIG	V	(A	(C) CLOWN & CLOUDS	1976 SPIEGELEI	GER	160607	
CHRISTOPH NOPPENEY	WIND(A		(D) RARE BIRDS	1977 SPEGELEI	GER	160608	
PETER KASEBERG	B G V(A		(E) HOELDERLIN LIVE	1978 SPEGELEI	GER	160602	
MICHAEL BRUCHMANN	D	(A	(F) NEW FACES	1979 SPEGELEI	GER	145605	
PETER BURSCH	SIT	(A					
MIKE HELLBACK	TABLA(A	WALTER WESTRUPP FLT (A HANS BAR		B V (F EDWARD SCHICKE D PERC(F			
TOMMY LONE	K G V(F	RUDIGER ELZE G (F					

H126   MICHAEL HOENIG   H126

MICHAEL HOENIG	K SYN(A	(A) DEPARTURE FROM THE NORTHERN WASTELAND 1978 WB US BSK3152	UK K56464			
LUTZ ULBRICH	G	(A				
MICKY DUWE	V	(A USCHI V (A				

H126A   HOG HEAVEN   H126A

PETER LUCIA	D V	(A	(A) HOG HEAVEN	1971 ROULETTE	US	42057
MIKE VALE	B V	(A				
RON ROSMAN	K V	(A EDDIE GRAY G (A				

H127   SILAS HOGAN   H127

SILAS HOGAN		(A) TROUBLE AT HOME	19	CONTEMPO	CRM	117
		(A) TROUBLE AT HOME	1971 BLUE HORIZON		2431	008

H128   SMOKEY HOGG   H128

SMOKEY HOGG	(A) SINGS THE BLUES	19	EMBER	EMB	3405
	(B) JOHN LEE HOOKER,LIGHTNING HOPKINS	1973 SPECIALTY		SNTF	5013
	(C) U BETTER WATCH THAT JIVE	1974 SPECIALTY		SNTF	5018
	( ) SMOKEY HOGG	19	TIME	US	6
	( ) ORG FOLK BLUES	19	UNITED	US	7745
	( ) ORG FOLK BLUES	19	KENT	US	5024
	( ) SINGS	19	CROWN	US	5226

H128A   HOGS HEAD   H128A

COLIN DAVIDSON	G V	(A	(A) ROCKIN(IN THE COUNTRY	1979 ROLLERCOASTER	ROLL 2003	
D G ELVIN	G	(A				
KEN CLEAVE	G	(A DAVID VAUGHAN HCA (A JERRY ALLSFORD		FDL (A DAVE HATFIELD B (A		
RICHIE BULL	BAN PROD(A					

H129   HOKUS POKE   H129

CLIVE BLENKHORN	G V	(A	(A) EARTH HARMONY	1972	VERTIGO	UK 6360 064
SMITH CAMPBELL	B	(A				
ROGER CLARKE	G STEEL(A	JOHNNIE MILES D (A				

H129A   HOKUS POKUS   H129A

MICHAEL MONARCH	(	(A) HOKUS POKUS	19
JON HYDE	(		
SCOTT THURSTON	(BILLLY CIOFFI (DANNY GORMAN		(

H129B   RANDOM HOLD   H129B

RANDOM HOLD	V	(ABC	(A) RANDOM HOLD (EP)	1979 POLYDOR	UK RHX 1	
DAVE FERGUSON	K	(AB	(B) THE VIEW FROM HERE	1980 POLYDOR	POLS1015 2383 564	
DAVID RHODES	G	(AB	(C) ETCETERAVILLE	1980 PASSPORT	US	9847
BILL MACCORMICK	B	(AB				
PETER PHIPPS	D	(AB DAVID LEECH D (SIMON AINLEY		G V (		

H130   RAM JAM HOLDER   H130

RAM JAM HOLDER	(ALL	(A) BOOTLEG BLUES	1974 BEACON	BEA.	17
		(B) BLACK LONDON BLUES	1974 BEACON	BEA	2
		(C) YOU SIMPLY ARE	1975 FRESH AIR	9299	470

H131   ALLAN HOLDSWORTH   H131

ALLAN HOLDSWORTH	G	(A	(A) VELVET DARKNESS	1977 CTI	6068
ALPHONSE JOHNSON	B	(A			
ALAN PASQUE	K	(A NARADA MICHAEL WALDEN D (A		

H131A   MARC HOLLANDER   H131A

MARC HOLLANDER	K CLAR SAX(A	(A) ONZE DANSES POUR COMBATTRE LA MIGRAINE1977 KAMIKAZE	KAM1		
PAOLO RADONI	G	(A			
JEANNOT GILLIS	VLN	(A VINCENT KENIS ACC (A CATHERINE JAUNIAUX V (A LUCY GRAUMAN V (A			
CHRIS JORIS	K SAX(A DAVID LEE SCHLOSS SAX (A				

H131B   HOLLANDER   H131B

	(A) SIDE KICKS	1980 CBS 84567

H131C   JOOLS HOLLAND   H131C

JOOLS HOLLAND	V K (A	(A) AND THE MILLIONAIRES	1981 A&M UK AMLH 68534

H131D   BRENDA HOLLOWAY   H131D

BRENDA HOLLOWAY	V	(ALL	(A) EVERY LITTLE BIT HURTS	19 TAMLA	US 257
			(B) ARTISTY OF	19 TAMLA	UK STML11083

H132   THE HOLLIES   H132

TONY HICKS	G	(ALL	(A) STAY WITH THE HOLLIES	1964 PARLOPHONE UK (S)3054	(M) 1220
			(A) STAY WITH THE HOLLIES	1964 WORLD RECORDS	1035
ALLAN CLARKE	V	(ABCDEFGHIJX	(B) IN THE HOLLIES STYLE	1965 PARLOPHONE UK	(M) 1235
TERRY SYLVESTER	G V	(X	(C) HERE I GO	1965 IMPERIAL US	12265
MICHAEL RICKFORS	B	(	(D) HEAR HERE	1965 IMPERIAL US	12299
GRAHAM NASH	G/V	(ABCDEFGHIJ	(E) THE HOLLIES	1965 PARLOPHONE UK	(M) 1261
DON RATHBONE	D	(	(E) THE HOLLIES	1965 IMPERIAL US	12312
ERIC HAYDOCK	B	(	(F) WOULD YOU BELIEVE	1966 PARLOPHONE UK	7008
BOBBY ELLIOTT	D	(X	(G) FOR CERTAIN BECAUSE	1966 PARLOPHONE UK	7011
BERNIE CALVERT	B	(X	(H) EVOLUTION	1967 EPIC US 26315 PARLOPHONE UK7022	
			(H) EVOLUTION	1978 PARLOPHONE UK RI	7175
PETE WINGFIELD	K	(XYZ	(I) BUTTERFLY	1967 PARLOPHONE UK	7039
PETER ARNESEN	K	(YZ	(I) BUTTERFLY	1978 PARLOPHONE UK RI	7177
JIMMY JEWELL	SAX	(Y	(J) HOLLIES GREATEST	1968 EPIC US 32061 PARLOPHONE UK7057	
TONY COE	SAX	(Y	(J) HOLLIES GREATEST	19 ODEON	SM074 236
REG BROOKS	HRNS	(Z	( ) KING MIDAS	1968 EPIC US	26344
SOL AMARFIO	CONGA(Y		( ) SING DYLAN	1969 EPIC US 26447 PARLOPHONE UK7078	
HOWIE CASEY	HRNS	(Z	( ) SING HOLLIES	1969 PARLOPHONE UK	7092
DON HARPER	VLN	(Z	( ) GREATEST HITS	1969 IMPERIAL US	12350
DAVE CASWELL	HRNS	(Z	( ) MOVING FINGER	196 EPIC US	30255
RON ASPERY	HRNS	(Z	(E) REFLECTION	1969 STARLINE UK	SRS 5008

                                                              (CONTINUED)

[269]

THE HOLLIES

( ) HE AINT HEAVY	1970 EPIC US 26538			
( ) CONFESSIONS OF THE MIND	1970 PARLOPHONE UK 7116+RI 1978 7178			
( ) BUS STOP	19 IMPERIAL US 12330			
( ) BUS STOP	19 EMIDISC EURO 048 50732			
( ) DISTANT LIGHT	1971 EPIC US 30950 PARLOPHONE 10005			
( ) STOP STOP STOP	1971 IMPERIAL US 12339 STARLINE 5088			
( ) ROMANY	1972 EPIC US 31992 POLYDOR 2383 144			
(H) HOLLIES	1972 M F P UK 5252			
( ) GREATEST HITS VOL 2	1972 PARLOPHONE 7148			
( ) GREATEST HITS VOL 2	1974 BOVEMA EURO 054 05432			
( ) THE HOLLIES	1974 EPIC US 32574 POLYDOR 2383 262			
(f) I CANT LET GO	1974 M F P 50094			
( ) ANOTHER NIGHT	1975 EPIC US 33387 POLYDOR 2441 128			
( ) HISTORY OF THE HOLLIES DBL	1975 EMI EMSP 650			
( ) WRITE ON	1976 POLYDOR 2442 141			
( ) RUSSIAN ROULETTE	1976 POLYDOR 2382 421			
( ) VINTAGE RARE	19 WRC US 979			
( ) VERY BEST OF	1975 UA US GERM LA 329			
( ) POP CHRONIK	19 POLYDOR GERM			
(X) LIVE HITS	1977 POLYDOR UK2383 428+GERM2374 123			
( ) BEST OF THE HOLLIES	1978 PARLOPHONE UK 7174			
( ) THE OTHER SIDE OF	1978 PARLOPHONE UK 7176			
( ) 20 GOLDEN GREATS	1978 EMI UK EMTV 11			
(Y) CRAZY STEAL	1978 E½IC US 35334 POLYDOR 2383 474			
( ) DOUBLE SEVEN 0 FOUR	1979 POLYDOR UK 2442 160			
(Z) HOLLIES SING HOLLY	1980 POLYDOR UK POLTV 12			
( ) THE AIR THAT I BREATH	1980 POLYDOR UK 2384 115			
( ) LONG COOL WOMAN	1980 MFP UK 50450			
( ) THE BEST OF THE HOLLIES EPS	19 PARLOPHONE UK PMC 7174			
( ) THE BEST OF THE HOLLIES EPS RI	19 EMI UK NUT 30			
( ) THE OTHER SIDE OF THE HOLLIES	19 PARLOPHONE UK PMC 7186			

EPS

( ) ROCKIN ROBIN	19 PARLOPHONE UK GEP 8909			
( ) JUST ONE LOOK	19 PARLOPHONE UK GEP 8911			
( ) HERE I GO AGAIN	19 PARLOPHONE UK GEP 8915			
( ) WERE THROUGH	19 PARLOPHONE UK GEP 8927			
( ) IN THE HOLLIES STYLE	19 PARLOPHONE UK GEP 8934			
( ) I'M ALIVE	19 PARLOPHONE UK GEP 8942			
( ) I CANT LET GO	19 PARLOPHONE UK GEP 89			

LAURIE HOLLOWAY

LAURIE HOLLOWAY	K	(A	(A) CUMULUS
DAVE MARKEE	B	(A	
HUGH BURNS	G	(A	

1979 HOBO   HO503

NORMA WINSTONE   V   (A   JOHN GIRVAN   G   (A   BARRY MORGAN   D   (A

LOLEATTA HOLLOWAY

LOLEATTA HOLLOWAY	V	(A	(A) QUEEN OF THE NIGHT
EARL YOUNG	D	(A	( ) LOLAETTA
MADELINE STRICKLAND	V	(A	( ) LOVE SENSATION
SCOTTY MILLER	D	(A	
GORDON EDWARDS	B	(A	
DENNIS RICHARDSON	K	(A	
KIM MILLER	G	(A	
JIMMY SIGLER	K	(A	
LARRY WASHINGTON	CONGA	(A	
MOTO	PERC	(A	

1978 SALSOUL UK1509 GOLDMINE US 9501
1977 SALSOUL UK5513 GOLDMINE US 9504
1980 GOLDMINE   US 9506

STEVE GADD	D	(A	JIMMY WILLIAMS	B	(A	RAYMOND EARL	B	(A
NORMAN HARRIS	G	(A	T J TINDALL	G	(A	EDWARD MOORE	G	(A
MIKKI FARROW	V	(A	CORNELL DUPREE	G	(A	ERIC GALE	G	(A
BUNNY SIGLER	K	(A	RON KERSEY	K	(A	BRUCE GARY	K	(A
RICHARD TEE	K	(A	GEORGE BUSSEY	K	(A	RON TYSON	V	(A
JAMES WALKER	CONGA	(A	EMANUEL WILLIAMS	CONGA	(A	BUNNY HARRIS	PERC	(A
CARLA BENSON	V	(A	EVETTE BENTON	V	(A	BARBARA INGRAM	V	(A

HOLLY & THE ITALIENS

HOLLY VINCENT	V	(A	(A) THE RIGHT TO BE ITALIan 1981 VIRGIN UK 2186 US 37359 EURO 203 434

BUDDY HOLLY

BUDDY HOLLY	G V	(ALL						
BOB MONTGOMERY		(						
TOMMY ALSUP	G	(	JERRY ALLISON	D	(	NIKI SULLIVAN	G	(	JOE MAULDIN	B(
SONNY CURTIS	G FDL	(	LERRY WELBORN	B	(	GRADY MARTIN	G	(	FARIS COURSEY	D (
RAMONA TOLLETT	V	(	BILL PICKERING	V	(	BOB LATHAM	V	(	NORMAN PETTY	K (
BOB LINVILLE	V	(	DAVID BIGHAM	V	(	PANAMA FRANCIS	D	(	BO CLARKE	D (
WAYLON JENNINGS	V	(	PHIL EVERLY	V	(	DON GUESS	B	(	BOOTS RANDOLPH	SAX(
OWEN BRADLEY	PNO	(	GARY TOLLETT	V	(	JOHN PICKERING	V	(	VI PRTTY	V (
G W KENDALL	PNO	(	RAY RUSH	V	(	RAY RUSH	V	(	SAM TAYLOR	SAX(
HELEN WAY SINGERS	V	(	GEORGE ATWOOD	B	(	KING CURTIS	SAX	(	LOU GIORDANO	V (

CHIRPIN CRICKETS	1957 BRUNSWICK US 54038	GREATEST HITS	1967 ACE OF HEARTS AH148
CHIRPIN CRICKETS	1958 CORAL UK 9081	GREATEST HITS	1969 CORAL UK CP8
CHIRPIN CRICKETS	1969 CORAL UK CP 20	GREATEST HITS	1974 MCA UK CDLM 8007
CHIRPIN CRICKETS	1975 MCA UK CD 8035	GREATEST HITS	1974 CORAL UK CRLM 1001
BUDDY HOLLY	1958 CORAL UK 9085	GREATEST HITS	1974 CORAL UK CRL 1005
BUDDY HOLLY	19 CORAL US 57210	GREATEST HITS 2	1970 CORAL UK CPS 47
BUDDY HOLLY	1975 MCA UK CP 8034	LISTEN TO ME	1968 MCA UK MUPS 312
BUDDY HOLLY STORY	1959 CORAL UK 9105	LISTEN TO ME	1974 MCA UK MCF 2613
BUDDY HOLLY STORY	19 CORAL US 57279	THE GREAT BUDDY HOLLY	196 CORAL US 57492
BUDDY HOLLY STORY	19 CORAL US 81182	THE GREAT BUDDY HOLLY	196 VOCALION UA VL 3811
BUDDY HOLLY STORY 2	1960 CORAL UK 9127	RAVE ON	1968 MCA UK MUPS 313
BUDDY HOLLY STORY 2	196 CORAL US 57326	RAVE ON	1974 MCA UK MCF 2614
THAT'LL BE THE DAY	1961 ACE OF HEARTS AH3	RAVE ON	1975 M F P 50176
THAT'LL BE THE DAY	1974 CORAL UK CP 24	BROWN EYED HANDSOME MAN	1968 MCA UK MUPS 314
THAT'LL BE THE DAY	197 DECCA US 8707	BROWN EYED HANDSOME MAN	1974 MCA UK MCF 2615
THAT'LL BE THE DAY	1974 CORAL UK CRL1024	HE'S THE ONE	1968 MCA UK MUPS 315
REMINISCING	1963 CORAL UK LVA 9212	TRUE LOVE WAYS	1968 MCA UK MUPS 319
REMINISCING	1963 CORAL US 57426	TRUE LOVE WAYS	1974 MCA UK MCF 2616
REMINISCING	1974 MCA UK MCF2615	WISHIN'	1968 MCA UK MUPS 320
SHOWCASE	1964 CORAL UK LVA 9222	GIANT	1969 MCA UK MUPS 371
SHOWCASE	1964 CORAL US 57450	GIANT	196 CORAL US 57504
HOLLY IN THE HILLS	1965 CORAL UK LVA 9227	GIANT	1974 MCA UK MCF 2625
HOLLY IN THE HILLS	1965 CORAL US 57463	REMEMBER	1971 CORAL UK CPS 71
BEST OF	1966 CORAL US CXB 8	REMEMBER	1974 CORAL UK CRL 1087
		GOOD ROCKIN'	1971 VOCALION US 73923

(CONTINUED)

BUDDY HOLLY (CONTINUED)

ROCK'N'ROLL COLLECTION	1972	MCA		2 4009	E Ps			
ROCK'N'ROLL COLLECTION	1972	DECCA	US	DSXE 7207	LISTEN TO ME	1958	CORAL	UK	2002
LEGEND	1974	MCA	UK	CDMSP 802	SOUND OF THE CRICKETS	1958	CORAL	UK	2003
COMPLETE B H (9LP SET)	1974	MCA UK	COPS 7100H1/9	RAVE ON	1958	CORAL	UK	2005
NASHVILLE SESSIONS	1975	MCA	UK	CDLM 8038	ITS SO EASY	1959	CORAL	UK	2014
STORY	1975	WORLD RECORDS	301/5	HEARTBEAT	1959	CORAL	UK	2015
PORTRAIT IN MUSIC	1975	TELDEC	EURO	4408	IT DOESN'T MATTER ANY MORE	1959	CORAL	UK	2032
PORTRAIT IN MUSIC (DBL)	1975	CORAL	UK	5616/7	BUDDY HOLLY 1	1959	BRUNSWICK	UK	9456
WESTERN & BOP	1978	MCA	UK	CDLM 8055	BUDDY HOLLY 2	1959	BRUNSWICK	UK	9457
20 GREATEST HITS	1978	MCA	UK	CMTV8	LATE GREAT	1960	CORAL	UK	2044
20 GOLDEN GREATS	19	MCA	UK	3040	4 MORE	1960	CORAL	UK	2060
BUDDY HOLLY (6LP SET)	1979	CORAL		CDMSP 807	THAT'LL BE THE DAY	1960	CORAL	UK	2062
BUDDY HOLLY LIVES	1978	MCA		EMTV 8	BY REQUEST	1964	CORAL	UK	2065
BUDDY HOLLY STORY	1979	WARWICK		WW 5064	TEX MEX SOUND	1964	CORAL	UK	2066
BUDDY HOLLY	1980	PICKWICK	UK	3070	WISHING	1964	CORAL	UK	2067
ROCK ON WITH BUDDY HOLLY	1980	M F P	UK	54495	SHOWCASE	1965	CORAL	UK	2068
					SHOWCASE 2	1965	CORAL	UK	2069
					SINGS	1965	CORAL	UK	2070

H134A HOLLYWOOD ARGYLES H134A

GARY PAXTON	V	(		(A) ALLEY OOP	196	LUTE	US		L9001
BOBBY REY	V	(						
TED MARSH	V	(	GARY WEBB	D (	DEANY WEAVER	G (TED WINTERS	B (A

H135 HOLLYWOOD BRATS H135

ANDREW MATHESON	V	(AB	(A) GROWN UP WRONG	1975		US	
EUNON BRADY	G	(AB	(B) HOLLYWOOD BRATS (RECORDED 73)	1980	CHERRY RED	UK	ARED 6
WAYNE MANOR	B	(AB					
LOUIS SPARKS	D	(AB	CASINO STEEL G V K (AB				

H135A HOLLYWOOD STARS H135A

TERRY RAE	V D	(A	(A) HOLLYWOOD STARS	1977	ARISTA		AL4119
RUBEN DE FUENTES	G	(A					
BOBBY DRIER	D	(A	MARK ANTHONY V G (A NICKY HOPKINS	PNO (A	MICHAEL RUMMANS	B (A
STEVE DeLACY	G	(A	OLLIVER E BROWN CONGA(A				

H135B HOLLYWOOD FATS BAND H135B

HOLLYWOOD FATS	G	(A	(A) HOLLYWOOD FATS BAND	1979	PBR		7008
FRED KAPLAN	PNO	(A					
LARRY TAYLOR	B	(A	AL BLAKE V HCA (A RICHARD INNES	D (A

H136 JAKE HOLMES H136

JAKE HOLMES	G K V(ALL	(A) JAKE HOLMES	1969	POLYDOR	UK	583 578
TED IRWIN	G	(A	(B) SO CLOSE SO VERY FAR TO GO	1970	POLYDOR UK 2425036	US 244 034
WELDON MYRICK	STEEL(A	(C) HOW MUCH TIME	1972	CBS US 30996	UK	64905
DAVID BRIGGS	PNO	(A	( ) ABOVE GROUND SOUND OF JAKE HOLMES	19	TOWER	US	ST 5079
KENNY BUTTREY	D	(A					

H136A NICK HOLMES H136A

NICK HOLMES	G V	(A	(A) THE SOULFUL CROONER	1973	JUST SUNSHINE US	JSS 3
DONALD McDONALD	D	(A					
TONY LEVIN	B	(A	MICHAEL MAINIERI K VIBES(A HUGH McCRACKEN	G (A DAVID BROMBERG	DOB (A
JON PIERSON	V	(A	DAVID SPINNOZA G (A RANDY BRECKER	HRNS (A JEREMY STEIS	FLT (A

H137 RUPERT HOLMES H137

RUPERT HOLMES V K SYN	(ALL	(A) RUPERT HOLMES	1975	EPIC UK 80942	US 33443
DEAN BAILIN	G	(F	(B) WIDESCREEN	1975	EPIC UK 80323	US 32864
BENNY GRAMM	D PERC(F	(C) PURSUIT OF HAPPINESS	1978	PRIVATE STOCK UK1034	US 7006K
ALAN SCHWARZBERG	D	(C	(C) PURSUIT OF HAPPINESS	1980	MCA RI US 3241	
JOHN CARUSO	B	(F	(D) SINGLES	197	EPIC	US 34283
CHRISSY FAITH	V	(F	(E) PARTNERS IN CRIME	1979	MCA UK MCF3051 INFINITY US 9020
PHIL BUDHOS	PNO	(F	(F) ADVENTURE	1980	MCA UK MCF3088 MCA US 5129
SETH GLASSMAN	B	(F	(G) FULL CIRCLE	1981	ELEKTRA US 560 UK K52328
JIMMIE YOUNG	D	(C				
JIMMY MAELEN	PERC (C	WILBUR BASCOMB B (C WILL LEE	B (C JOE MACK	B (C
STEVE KHAN	G	(C	ELLIOTT RANDALL G (C HILDA HARRIS	V (C CARTER CATHEART	K (C
PAT REBILLOT	K	(C	MICHAEL BRECKER SAX (C RANDY BRECKER	HRNS (C MEL DAVIS	TPT (C
MARVIN STAMM	TPT	(C	PETER GORDON HRNS (C VIVISN CHERRY	V (C LANI GROVES	V (C
MAERETHA STEWART	V	(C				

H137A HOLOCAUST H137A

	(A) THE NIGHTCOMERS	1981	PHOENIX	UK	PSLP1

H137B GARY HOLTON & CASINO STEEL H137B

GARY HOLTON	V	(AB	(A) GARY HOLTON & CASINO STEEL	1981	POLYDOR	SCAN	2382 124
CASINO STEEL	(PNO (AB	(B) PART 2	1982	POLYDOR	SCAN	2382 130
GEIR WADE	(						
BARD SVENDSEN	(	BARD FREDRIKSEN (CARL H WAADELAND	(IVAR GAFSETH	(
J P WEST	(	EUNAN BRADY (JOHN CHIVERS	(GUNNAR BERG	(
BJORN NESSJOE	(	SEXY BERIT (TRONDHEIM SYM ORCH	(

H138 ROOSEVELT HOLTS H138

ROOSEVELT HOLTS	G V	(	(A) PRESENTING THE COUNTRY BLUES	19	BLUE HORIZON UK 763201+US 7704
			(B) AND HIS FRIENDS	1974	ARHOOLIE	US 1057

H138A HOLY MACKEREL H138A

PAUL H WILLIAMS	V	(A	(A) HOLY MACKEREL	1968	REPRISE	US 6311
GEORGE HILLER G K V	(A					
RALPH WILLIAMS	G V	(A	JEREMIAH SCHEFF B V (A MIKE CANNON	D V (A CYNTHIA FITZPATRICK FLT(A

H139 HOLY MODAL ROUNDERS H139

JOHN WESLEY ANNIS	B	(	(A) INDIAN WAR HOOP	1967	ESP	US	1068
ASTEVE WEBER	G V	(A	(B) MORAY EELS EAT	1968	ELEKTRA	US	74026
RICHARD TYLER	PNO	(A	(C) HOLY MODAL ROUNDERS	1968	PRESTIGE	US	7720
SAM SHEPARD	D	(A	(D) HOLY MODAL ROUNDERS 2	1968	PRESTIGE	US	7410
PETER STAMPFEL FDL BANJ V(A	(E) GOOD TASTE IS TIMELESS	1969	METROMEDIA	US	740
ROBIN REMAILLY	(		(F) STAMPFEL & WEBER (COMP DBL)	1972	FANTASY	US	24711
MICHAEL HURLEY	(		(G) ALLEGED IN THEIR OWN TIME	1975	ROUNDER	US	3004
LUKE FAUST	(		(H) LAST ROUND	1979	ALDELPHI	US	1030
KEN CRABTREE	K	(A	(I) HOLY MODAL ROUNDERS	19	TRANSATLANTIC	UK	7451
ANTONIA	V	(A					
BARBARA	V	(A	WENDY V (A				

```
    BILLY BATSON        K V  (A      (A) HOLY MOSES                 1971 RCA  UK SF 8204  US  LSP4523
    DAVID VITTEK        G BV(A
    TEDDY SPEDEDS       G V  (A   MARTY DAVID B SAX V(A      CHRISTOPHER PARKER  PERC(A
```
H139B   HOMBRES   H139B
```
    JOHN W HUNTER       D    (A      (A) LET IT OUT                 19   VERVE      US        3036
    JERRY LEE MASTERS   B    (A
    GARY W McEWEN       G    (A   B B CUNNINGHAM    K    (A
```
H140   HOME   H140
```
    LAURIE WISEFIELD    G V  (ABC     (A) PAUSE FOR A HOARSE HORSE  197  EPIC US 31146  UK     64365
    MICK STUBBS         K V  G(ABC    (B) HOME                      1972 CBS            UK     64752
    CLIFF WILLIAMS      B V  (ABC     (C) ALCHEMIST                 1973 CBS            UK     65550
    MICK COOK           V D  (ABC
    JIMMY ANDERSON      K    (C   DAVID SKILLIN LYRICS  (C   WILL WEIDER   FDL  (A  CLIVE JOHN  K    (A
```
H141   HOMETOWN BAND   H141
```
    SHARI ULRICH V VLN FLT (AB       (A) FLYING                    1976  A&M  US 4605  UK  AMLH 64605
    CLAIRE LAWRENCE    WIND  (AB      (B) HOMETOWN BAND             1977  A&M  US 4671
    GEOFF EYRE          D V  (AB
    ROBBIE KING         K V  (AB  DOUG EDWARDS  K B V G(AB    EDWARD PATTERSON  G V  (B
```
H142   HONEY BOY   H142
```
                                    (A) SWEET CHERRIES             1974  CACTUS          CTLP  101
                                    (B) A TASTE OF HONEY           1975  CACTUS          CTLP  105
                                    (C) LOVERS                     1977  THIRD WORLD     TWLP  108
                                    (D) STRANGE THOUGHTS           1977  TROJAN          TRLS  125
                                    (E) DARK END OF THE STREET     1978  DIAMOND         DMLP  402
                                    (F) ARISE                      1981  DIAMOND   UK    DMLP  403
```
H143   HONEYBUS   H143
```
    PETER DELLO         V    (        (A) STORY                     1970  DERAM    UK    SML   1056
    JIM KELLY           G V  (A
    RAY CANE V G K V     (A   PETE KIRCHER     (        COLIN HARE    V G B  (A
```
H143A   HONEYCOMBS   H143A
```
    HONEY LANTREE       D V  (A       (A) ALL SYSTEMS GO            1965 PYE     UK    NPL 18132
    DENIS D'ELL         V HCA(A
    MARTIN MURRAY       G    (A   ALAN WARD        G    (A   JOHN LANTREE    B    (A
```
H144   HONEYDEW   H144
```
                                    (A) HONEYDEW                   1971  ARGO                ZFB  15
```
H144A   HONK   H144A
```
                                    (A) HONK                       1974 20TH CENT          406
                                    (B) HONK                       1975 EPIC       US      33094
```
H145   HONKY   H145
```
    RAY OTHEN           V PERC(A       (A) HONKY                     1978  CREOLE    UK    CRLP513
    BOB WHITE           D    (A
    TREVOR CUMMINS      G    (A   CLIFF BARKS  B    (A   MALCOLM BAGGOTT   SAX (A  CLARK NEWTON  SAX (A
    RON TAYLOR          SAX  (
```
H146   HOODOO RHYTHM DEVILS   H146
```
    JOHN REWIND         G    (ABC     (A) BARBEQUE OF THE DEVILLE   197  BLUE THUMB     US   BTS 42
    JOE CRANE           V    (ABCE    (B) RACK JOBBERS BLUES        1972 CAPITOL       US   ST 842
    BOB PLUMES          G    (C       (C) WHAT THE KIDS WANT        1973 BLUE THUMB BTS 57+VOGUE FR 10029
    GLENN WALTERS PERC V (ABCE    (D) SAFE IN THEIR HOMES          1976 FANTASY 9522+WORLD JAZZ   9201
    DEXTER C PLATES     B    (ABC     (E) ALL KIDDING ASIDE        1978 FANTASY FTC 540 +       F 9543
    SKIP MESQUITE       SAX  (        ( ) TOO HOT TO HANDLE        1973
    JEROME              D    (C
    BOB WRAY            B    (E   MUSCLE SHOALS HRNS     (E    CLAYTON IVEY    K   (E    BARBARA WYRICK  V  (E
    ROGER CLARK         D    (ABE  LARRY BYROM      G   (E    SUZY STORM      V   (E    TOM ROADY     PERC(E
    MARTIN FIERRO       HRNS  (B   MEL MARTIN       HRNS (B   BOOTS HUGHSTON  HRNS(B    MIC GILLETTE  HRNS(B
    CHESTER CRILL       HCA  (B   POINTER SISTERS    V    (B
```
H146A   HOOK   H146A
```
    BOBBY ARLIN         G    (AB      (A) THE HOOK WILL GRAB YOU    19   UNI          US    73023
    LEE 'BUDDY' SKLAR B  (AB      (B) HOOKED                    19   UNI          US    73038
    DENNIS PROVISOR     K    (A
    DALE LOYALE         D    (A   CRAIG BOYD       D    (B
```
H147   EARL HOOKER   H147
```
    EARL HOOKER         G    (ALL     (A) DON'T HAVE TO WORRY       1969 BLUESWAY      US         6032
    REGGIE BOYD         G    (J       (B) SWEET BLACK ANGEL         1970 BLUE HORIZON  UK       763850
    JOHNNY'BIG MOOSE'WALKER K V(JJ    (B) SWEET BLACK ANGEL         1970 BLUE THUMB    US       BT8812
    LILLIAN OFFITT      V    (J       (C) THERES A FUNGUS           1972 RED LIGHTNING UK     RL  009
    RICK ALLEN          V    (J       (D) DO YOU REMEMBER           1973 BLUESWAY      US     BLS6072
    A C REED            V    (J       (E) 2 BUGS & A ROACH          1975 ARHOOLIE           F  1044
    STEVE MILLER        PNO V(G       (G) HOOKER & STEVE            1975 ARHOOLIE      US   F  1051
    LOUIS MYERS         HCA  (G       (H) FIRST & LAST              1975 ARHOOLIE      US   F  1066
    GENO SKAGGS         B V  (AG      (J) LEADING BRAND             1977 RED LIGHTNING UK     RL 0018
    BOBBY JOHNSON       D    (G       (K) THE LAST OF THE GREAT EARL HOOKER 1977 ANTILLES  US    7024
    ROOSEVELT SHAW      D    (A       (L) THE GENIUS                197  CUCU          US        3400
    ANDREW OLDHAM       V    (A       (M) MEMORIAL ALBUM            19   BLUE FLAME               102
    JEFFREY M CARP      HCA  (A       (N) IF YOU MISS HIM           19   BLUESWAY      US        6038
    PAUL ASBELL         G    (A       (O) BLUE GUITAR               1981 P VINE        JAP       9015
```
H148   HOOKFOOT   H148
```
    CALEB QUAYE         G V K(ALL     (A) HOOKFOOT                  1971  DJM UK DJLPS413 US A&M    4316
    DAVE GLOVER         B    (ABE     (B) GOOD TIMES A COMIN'       1972 A&M US SP4338  UKDJM DJLPS 422
    IAN DUCK            HCA V(ALL     (C) COMMUNICATIONS            1973  DJM UK DJLPS428 US A&M   4380
    ROGER POPE          D V  (ALL     (D) ROARING                  1974  DJM UK DJLPS435 US A&M   3608
    PETER ROSS          HCA V(AE      (E) HEADLINES (DBL)(COMP)     1975  DJM DJLPS28013+   DJLMD 8013
    FREDDY GANDY        B V  (CDE
    BOB KULICK          G V  (BE
```

```
MARSHALL HOOKS    G V  (A        (A) MARSHALL HOOKS & CO          1970 BLUE HORIZON      2431  003
JOHN GOINES       D    (A
RON SIMPKINS      K    (A   JIM SUARD      B   (A
```

```
JOHN LEE HOOKER      V    (ALL
ROBERT HOOKER        K    (DH
CLIFF COULTER        K    (DH  BENNY ROWE        G    (DH  LUTHER TUCKER    G    (DEH GINO SKAGGS B        (DBH
RON BECK             D    (DH  KEN SWANK         D    (DEH CHARLIE MUSSELWHITE HCA(D  CHUCK GRIMMELL   D    (DH
MICHAEL WHITE        VLN  (DH  MARK NAFTALIN     K    (DH  PAUL WOOD        G    (DH  MEL BROWN        G    (DH
RAY McCARTY          G    (DH  ELVIN BISHOP      G    (DH  VAN MORRISON     V    (DH  EDDIE KIRKLAND   G    (J
MEMPHIS SLIM         PNO  (DH  JIMMY REED      V G    (AK  ALAN WILSON  G HCA PNO  (C  HENRY VESTINE    G    (C
ANTONIO BARRADA      B    (C   ADOLFO DE LA PARRA D  (C   EDDIE TAYLOR     B    (K  GEORGE WASHINGTON B(K
TOM WHITEHEAD        D    (K   OTIS FINCH       SAX  (K   QUINN WILSON     B    (K  FRANKIE BRADFORD PNO (K
EVERETT McCRARY      B    (K   RICHARD JOHNSON   D   (K   JOE HUNTER       PNO  (K  EARL PHILLIPS    D    (K
OSCAR BRASHEAR       HRNS (H   GEORGE BOHANON   TROM (H   JOHN KLEMMER     SAX  (H  DON MENZA        SAX      (H
STEVE MILLER         PNO  (H   DON SUGARCANE HARRIS VLN(H  JOHN KAHN        B    (H  MARTI McCALL     V    (H
BLINKY WILLIAMS      V    (H   OMA DRAKE         V      (H  TONY McPHEE      G    (G  GROUNDHOGS            (G
CHARLIE GRIMES       G    (E   LEX SILVER        B    (E   EARL HOOKER      G    (B  PAUL ASBELL      G    (B
JOHNNY WALKER        K    (B   JEFFREY CARP     HCA  (B   ROOSEVELT SHAW   D    (B
```

```
HOUSE OF THE BLUES          1960  CHESS      US 1454      NO FRIEND AROUND              1970 RED LIGHTNIN' RL 003
HOUSE OF THE BLUES          19    MARBLE ARCH   663       NO FRIEND AROUND              1979 CHARLY  UK   CR30170
PLAYS & SINGS THE BLUES     1961  CHESS      US 1454      COAST TO COAST               1971 U A              29235
TUPELO BLUES               1962  RIVERSIDE     673020     COAST TO COAST               1971 U A      US      5512
FOLKLORE OF JOHN L HOOKER  1962  STATESIDE UK  10014      (C) HOOKER & HEAT            1971 LIBERTY  UK   103/4
FOLKLORE OF JOHN L HOOKER  1962  VEE JAY   US  1033       (C) HOOKER & HEAT            19   TRIP     US      3501
FOLKLORE                    19    JOY       JOYS133       (C) HOOKER & HEAT            1971 U A      US   3500/2
(A) PREACHIN THE BLUES      1964  STATESIDE UK  10053      WHISKEY & WIMMEN             19   TRIP     US    X 9504
(A) BIG SOUL                1964  VEE JAY   US  1088       REAL BLUES                   19   TRADITION US      2089
(A) BIG SOUL                19    JOY       JOYS147       BOOGIE CHILLIN'              1971 FANTASY  US     24706
I WANT TO SHOUT THE BLUES  1964  STATESIDE UK  10074      ENDLESS BOOGIE               1971 PROBE    UK SPB1034
I WANT TO SHOUT THE BLUES  1964  VEE JAY   US  1066       ENDLESS BOOGIE               1971 ABC      US       720
SEVEN NIGHTS                1966                           (D) NEVER GET OUT OF BLUES  1972 PROBE    UK SPB1057
IT SERVES YOU RIGHT         1966  HMV    UK   CSD3542      (D) NEVER GET OUT OF BLUES  1972 ABC      US       736
IT SERVES YOU RIGHT         1966  IMPULSE US   9103       (E) LIVE AT SOLEDAD PRISON 72 ABC      UK       716
LIVE AT CAFE AU GO GO       1966  HMV    UK   CSD3612      DETROIT SPECIAL              197  ATLANTIC UK  K40405
LIVE AT CAFE AU GO GO       1973  BLUESWAY     BLS6002     DETROIT SPECIAL              197  ATLANTIC US    7228
REAL FOLK BLUES            1968  CHESS    US   1508       SLIMS STOMP                  197  POLYDOR  UK 2310256
REAL FOLK BLUES            19    TRADITIONAL US  2089     JOHN LEE HOOKER              19   XTRA       XTRA114
URBAN BLUES                1968  STATESIDE     10246      JOHN LEE HOOKER              19   EVEREST  US       222
URBAN BLUES                1973  BLUESWAY     BLS6012     JOHN LEE HOOKER              19   KENT     US       525
(B) IF YOU MISS 'IM         1969  BLUESWAY     BLS6038     JOHN LEE HOOKER              1963 GALAXY   (US 8201
SIMPLY THE TRUTH           1969  STATESIDE     10280      JOHN LEE HOOKER              1966 VERVE    US      3003
SIMPLY THE TRUTH           1969  BLUESWAY US  BLS6023     JOHN LEE HOOKER              19   ARCHIVE  US       222
I'M JOHN LEE HOOKER        196   JOY       JOYS101       GREATEST HITS                19   KENT     US       559
I'M JOHN LEE HOOKER        19    VEE JAY   VJLP1007      JOHN LEE HOOKER              1975 NEW WORLD NW 6003
BURNIN'                     196   JOY       JOYS124       (F) DUSTY ROAD (DBL)         19   BELLAPHON BLS 5523
BURNIN'                     19    VEE JAY   1043          (G) DON'T WANT NOBODY        19   INTERCORD  128607
TRAVELLIN'                  19    JOY       JOYS129       KABUKI WUKI                  1973 BLUESWAY     BLS6052
TRAVELLIN'                  19    VEE JAY   1023          (H)BORN IN MISSISSIPPI        1973 ABC      ABCX  768
CONCERT AT NEWPORT         196   JOY       JOYS142       MADMAN BLUES                 19   CHESS    US    68011
CONCERT AT NEWPORT         196   VEE JAY   1078          JOHN LEE VOL 1               1973 GREENBOTTLE GN4002
IN PERSON                  196   JOY       JOYS152       THE BLUES                    197  MUSIDISC   AM 6078
BEST OF                    196   JOY       JOYS156       LIVE AT SUGAR HILL           19   MUSIDISC   AM 6094
BEST OF                    196   VEE JAY   1049          LIVE AT SUGAR HILL           19   US GALAXY      8205
THATS WHERE ITS AT         1970  STAX      2362   017     I WANNA DANCE ALL NIGHT     19   MUSIDISC   AM 6101
THATS WHERE ITS AT         197   STAX      US   2013      LIVING WITH BLUES           19   MUSIDISC   CV  955
THATS WHERE ITS AT         19    STAX RI US  4343        KING OF FOLK BLUES          19   MUSIDISC   AM 6074
FOLK BLUES                  19    CROWN    US   CLP5295    GREAT BLUES SOUND OF         19   MUSIDISC   AM 6077
MOANIN' & STOMPIN THE BLUES 19   KING     US   SK 1085    BLACK R&B                    1975 MUSIDISC   ALB 186
I FEEL GOOD                1972  JEWEL    US   5005       (J) MAD MAN BLUES            1973 CHECKER  6467  305
NO FRIEND AROUND           1970  RED LIGHTNIN' RL 003     (J) MAD MAN BLUES            197  CHESS    US  2 60011
DRIFTIN THE BLUES          19    UNITED   US   7710       BEST OF                      1974 CRESCENDO    210007
THE BLUES                  19    UNITED   US   7725       FREE BEER & CHICKEN          1974 ABC      ABCL 5059
FOLK BLUES                  19    UNITED   US   7729       FREE BEER & CHICKEN          1974 ABC      US       838
GREAT BLUES SOUNDS         19    UNITED   US   7731       ALONE                        1974 SPECIALTY SNTF 5005
IN THE MOOD                19    UPFRONT  US   104        ALONE                        197  SPECIALTY US      2125
IS HE REALY THE WORLDS GREAT     VEE JAY  US   8502       ALONE                        1980 LABOR    US         4
VERY BEST OF               19    BUDDAH   US   4002       DONT TURN ME FROM YOUR DOOR 74 ATLANTIC UK  K40507
BIG RED BLUES              19    BUDDAH   US   7506       DONT TURN ME FROM YOUR DOOR 74 ATCO     US SD33151
GOING DOWN HIGHWAY 51       19    SPECIALTY US 2127       BIG MACEO MERRIWEATHER       19   FORTUNE  US      3002
BURNIN HELL                19    RIVERSIDE               BLUES BEFORE SUNRISE         1976 BULLDOG         1011
THATS MY STORY             19    RIVERSIDE    321        (K) DIMPLES                  1977 DJM      DJD 28026
FOLK BLUES                  19    RIVERSIDE    838        BLACK SNAKE                  1978 FANTASY  US    24722
HOOKED ON BLUES            19    ARC FOLK     347        LIVE                         1978 LUNARZ   LZS 2008
BLUES MEN                  19    BATTLE   US   6113       THE CREAM (DBL)              1978 TOMATO   US 2 7009
HOW LONG BLUES             19    BATTLE   US   114        THIS IS HIP                  1980 CHARLY         1004
SINGS THE BLUES            19    CROWN    US   5232       SITTIN HERE THINKING         1980 MUSE     US      5205
BLUES                      19    CROWN    US   5157       EVERYBODY ROCKIN'            1980 CHARLY   UK  CRB1014
SINGS THE BLUES            19    KING     US   727
FRIEND AROUND              1979  CHARLY   UK   CR30170
```

```
STIX HOOPER          D    (A        (A) WORLD WITHIN              1979 MCA  MCF3042 UK     US   3180
ALPHONSO JOHNSON     B    (A
BOBBY HUTCHERSON     PERC (A   PAULINHO DA COSTA PERC V(A  DEAN PARKS      G    (A  BARRY FINNERTY   G  (A
ROLAND BAUTISTA      G    (A   KIM HUTCHCROFT    HRNS (A   LARRY WILLIAMS  HRNS (A  JERRY HEY        HRNS(A
OSAMU KITAJIMA       KOTO (A   KAZU MATSUI      PERC (A   TODD COCHRAN    SYN  (A  FRANK MAROCCO MUSETTE(A
```

```
                               (A) HOOVER                   1969 EPIC             US   26537
```

   (A) HOPE   1973 A&M   US   4329

MARY HOPKIN V G HCA	(ALL	(A) POSTCARD	1969	APPLE SW 3351	US	UK SAPCOR	5
KEVIN PEEK	G	(B	(B) EARTH SONG	1971	APPLE SW 3381	US	UK SAPCOR	21
BRIAN DALY	G	(B	(C) THOSE WERE THE DAYS	1972	APPLE SW 3395	US	UK SAPCOR	23
RALPH McTELL	G	(B	(D) WELSH WORLD OF (RECORDED 1968)	1979	DECCA	UK	SPA	546
TERRY WEIL	CELLO(B	(E) KIDNAPPED	19	AIR	US	1042
DAVE COUSINS	G BAN(B
CLIVE ANSTEE	CELLO(B	DANNY THOMPSON	B	(B	TONY VISCONTI	V	(B

SAM LIGHTNIN' HOPKINS G V(ALL
EARL PALMER   D   (
JIMMY BOND   B   (

CALIFORNIA MUDSLIDE	19	VOLT	US	129	FIRST MEETING	1964	WORLD	US	1817
KEEPS ON RAININ'	19	SUPERSCOPE	US	047	GOTTA MOVE YOUR BABY	19	PRESTIGE	US	7831
LIGHTNING STRIKES	1963	STATESIDE	UK	10031	SOMETHING BLUE	19	VERVE	US	3013
LIGHTNING STRIKES	196	VERVE		5014	SINGS THE BLUES	19	CROWN	US	5224
LIGHTNING STRIKES	196	TRADITION	US	2013	IN TOWN	19	FOLKART	US	5003
KIGHTNING STRIKES	19	VEE JAY	US	1044	AT THE BIRD LOUNGE	19	GUEST STAR		1459
LIGHTNING STRIKES	19	MAYFAIR		4000	LIGHTNING HOPKINS	19	GUEST STAR		1909
LIGHTNING STRIKES	19	JOY		5115	COUNTRY BLUES	1960	TRADITION		1035
COFFEE HOUSE BLUES	19	JOY		5175	LAST OF THE GREAT BLUES	19	TIME	US	70004
BLUES HOOT	1964	STATESIDE		10076	MOJO HAND	19	FIRE	US	104
BLUES HOOT	196	HORIZON	US	1617	ON STAGE	19	IMPERIAL	US	9180
HOOTIN' THE BLUES	1965	STATESIDE	UK	10110	SOUL BLUES	19	PRESTIGE	US	7377
HOOTIN' THE BLUES	196	PRESTIGE	US	14021	LIGHTNIN' HOPKINS	19	TRIP		8015
HOOTIN' THE BLUES	196	PRESTIGE		7806	LIGHTNIN' HOPKIN	19	ARCHIVES		241
DOWN HOME BLUES	1965	STATESIDE	UK	10155	GOTTA MOVE YOUR BABY	19	PRESTIGE		7831
DOWN HOME BLUES	1965	PRESTIGE	US	1086	LIGHTNIN HOPKINS	19	HORIZON	US	1617
& SPIDER KILPATRICK	196	ARHOOLIE		F1011	REALLY THE BLUES	19	MUSIDISC	AM	6080
& BARBARA DANE	1965	ARHOOLIE		F1022	PENITENTIARY BLUES	19	CHANT DU MONDE	53822
TEXAS BLUES MAN	1965	ARHOOLIE		F1034	LIGHTNIN' HOPKINS	19	PATHE	FR	40005
LIGHTNIN' HOPKINS	1966	SAGA		ER08001	LIGHTNIN' HOPKINS	19	VOGUE		68130
THE BLUES	1969	ACE OF HEARTS		183	LIGHTNIN' HOPKINS	19	TRIUMPH		240036
LIGHTNIN' VOL 1	1970	POPPY		11000	& JOHN LEE HOOKER	19	STORYVILLE	SLP 174
LIGHTNIN'	197	POPPY	US	60002	ROOTS OF	19	XTRA	XTRA 1127
IN NEW YORK	19	BARNABY	US	30247	ROOTS OF	19	FOLKWAYS	US	31011
SHAKE IT BABY	19	VOGUE		891	ROOTS OF	19	VERVE		5003
BLUES UNDERGROUND	19	"D"		8000	ROOSTER CROWED IN ENGLAND	19	77	LA 12/200
LIGHTNIN' HOPKINS VOL 1	19	TIME	US		LEGACY OF THE BLUES	19	SPECIALTY	SNTF 672
LETS WORK AWHILE	1971	BLUE HORIZON	2431005	LEGACY OF THE BLUES	19	GNP	US	10022
EARTH BLUES	19	UA		40006	LONESOME LIGHTNIN'	1972	CARNIVAL	2941005
FAST LIFE WOMAN	19	VERVE	US	8453	BLUE LIGHTNIN'	197	JEWEL		5000
SINGS THE BLUES	19	CROWN	US	5224	BLUE LIGHTNIN'	197	DISCODIS	155 505
AT HIS NATURAL BEST	19	RHAPSODY	US	RHAP8	TALKING SOME SENSE	197	JEWEL		5001
FREE FORM PATTERNS	19	INT ARTISTS		AT6	TALKING SOME SENSE	197	PATHE FR		C240842
BURNIN' IN L A	19	FONTANA	688	801ZL	GREAT ELECTRIC SHOW	1973	MUSIDISC	FR AM013/4
BLUE BIRD BLUES	19	FONTANA	688	803ZL	GREAT ELECTRIC SHOW	197	JEWEL		5002
AUTOBIOGRAPHY	1960	TRADITION		1040	DIRTY BLUES	1973	MAINSTREAM	MSL1001
BEST	19	TRADITION		2056	DIRTY BLUES	197	MAINSTREAM	US	326
GREATEST HITS	19	PRESTIGE		7592	THE BLUES	1974	MAINSTREAM	MSL1020
BEST OF TEXAS BLUES BAND	19	PRESTIGE		7714	THE BLUES	197	MAINSTREAM	US	311
DOUBLE BLUES	19	FANTAGE		24702	THE BLUES	197	PRESTIGE	US	7811
GOIN' AWAY	19	PRESTIGE		1073	LOWDOWN DIRTY BLUES	1975	MAINSTREAM	MSL1031
HIS GREATEST HITS	19	BLUESVILLE	US	1084	LOWDOWN DIRTY BLUES	197	MAINSTREAM	US	405
AND THE BLUES	19	IMPERIAL	US	12211	IN BERKELEY	1975	ARHOOLIE		F1063
AND THE BLUES	19	HERALD	US	1012	EARLY RECORDINGS	1975	ARHOOLIE		F2007
FREEFORM PATTERNS	19	INT ART	US	6	EARLY RECORDINGS 2	1975	ARHOOLIE		F2010
ORIGINAL FOLK BLUES	19	KENT	US	525	LEGEND IN HIS OWN TIME	1976	BLUE ANTHOLOGY	5608
LEGEND IN HIS OWN TIME	19	KENT	US	9008	ALL THEM BLUES	1976	DJM		28016
SOUTHERN MEETING	19	KIMBERLEY	US	2017	KING OF DOWLING STREET	19	PATHE		83254
BLUES IN MY BOTTLE	19	XTRA	UK	5036	GOT TO MOVE YOU BABY	19	XTRA	UK	5044

NICKY HOPKINS	K	(ALL	(A) REVOLUTIONARY PIANO	1966	CBS		UK	62679
			(B) TIN MAN WAS A DREAMER	1973	CBS US 32074	UK	65416
			(C) NO MORE CHANGES	1975	MERCURY	US	SRM1 1028

HUGH HOPPER	B PNO(ALL	(A) 1984	1973	CBS		UK	65466
JOHN MARSHALL	D	(A	(A) 1984	1980	ATMOSPHERE	US	IRI 5010
PYE HASTINGS	G	(A	(B) CRUEL BUT FAIR	1976	COMPENDIUM		FIDARDO 4
LOL COXHILL	SAX	(A	(C) HOPPER TUNITY BOX	1977	COMPENDIUM		FIDARDO 7
GARY WINDO	SAX	(AC	(D) ROUGE ELEMENT	197	OGUN		OG 527
MALCOLM GRIFFITHS	TROM	(A	(E) MONSTER BAND	1979	ATMOSPHERE		IRI 5003
NICK EVANS	TROM	(A
ELTON DEAN	SAX	(BCDE	KEITH TIPPETT	PNO	(B	JOE GALLIVAN	D SYN(B	MARK CHARIG	CORNET(C
FRANK ROBERTS	PNO	(C	DAVE STEWART	ORG	(C	MIKE TRAVIS	D	(CE	RICHARD BRUNTON G	(C
NIGEL MORRIS	D	(C	ALAN GOWAN	ORG	(D	SHEEN		(D	JEAN PIERRE CAROLFI K	(E
JEAN PIERRE WEILLER	B	(E

ONNIE McINTYRE	V G	(A	(A) 1967
STEWART FRANCIS	D	(A
GRAHAM MAITLAND	K	(A	ALAN GORRIE V B (A

RICHARD ACCART	WIND (A	(A) GESTATION SONORE	1971	FUTURA	FR	SON 003
FRANCKY BOURLIER	HARP VIBES(A
JACQUES FASSOLA	B BAN G(A	GIL STERG D PERC	(A

JIM HORN

```
H155B                              JIM HORN                                      H155B
   JIM HORN        FLT SAX(AB       (A) THROUGH THE EYE         1972 SHELTER      US      8906
                                    (B) JIM'S HORN             1973 SHELTER      US      8918
H156                               PAUL HORN                                     H156
   PAUL HORN       HORNS(ALL        (A) IN KASHMIR              19   LIBERTY              83084
   JIM KELTNER     D    (J          (B) INSIDE                  1969 EPIC    US 26466  UK 65201
   ABRAHAM LABORIEL B   (J          (C) INSIDE TWO              19   EPIC    US 31600
   DEAN PARKS      G    (J          (D) VISIONS                 1974 EPIC    US 32837
   ERNIE WATTS     SA   (J          (E) SPECIAL EDITION         1974 ISLAND       UK      ISLD 6
   JIM HORN        SAX  (J          (F) PAUL HORN & NEXUS       1976 EPIC        UK      69219
   CHARLES LOPER   HRNS (J          (G) IN INDIA  (1967)        1976 BLUENOTE    UK      BNLAD 519
   CHUCK FINDLEY   HRNS (J          (H) ALTURA                  1977 EPIC    US 34231
   OSCAR BRASHEAR  HRNS (J          (J) DREAM MACHINE           1978 MUSHROOM            5010
   MIKE MELVION    K SYN     (J     (K) CONCERT ENSEMBLE        19   OVATION  US 1405
   JOE SAMPLE      K SYN(JD
   CLARK SPANGLER  K    (J  LALO SCHIFRIN   K SYN(J  EMIL RICHARDS   PERC(J  PAULINHO DACOSTA PERC(J
   ROBIN HORN      PERC (J  LYN BLESSING    VIBES(E  ART JOHNSON     G   (E  DAVE PARLATO     B  (E
   BART HALL       D    (E  TOM SCOTT       K?   (D  JOHN GUERIN     D   (D  MAX BENNETT      B  (D
   LARRY CARLTON   G    (D  ROGER JOHNSON   G    (D  RUBENS BASSINI  PERC(D  JONI MITCHELL    V K(D
   CARMEN KNEDDY   V    (D  KATHY COLLIER   V    (D
H157                             JIMMY BO HORNE                                   H157
   JIMMY BO HORNE  V    (A          (A) DANCE ACROSS THE FLOOR  1978 TK                  TKR82533
   HARRY CASEY     K    (A          (B) BEST OF                 1980 TK                  TKR83391
   SNOOPY DEAN     G    (A
   MIKE LEWIS      SAX  (A  ROBERT JOHNSON  D    (A  RONALD ZIEGLER  D   (A  RICHARD FINCH    B  (A
   WHIT SIDENER    SAX  (A  VINNIE TANNO    TPT  (A  KEN FAULK       TPT (A  FERMIN GOYTISLO PERC(A
   JEROME SMITH    G    (A
H157A                              HORSE                                         H157A
   ROD ROACH       G    (A          (A) HORSE                   1970 RCA    GER 10308    UK SF8109
   COLIN STANDRING B    (A
   RIC PARNELL     D    (A  ADRIAN HAWKINS  V    (A
H157B                              HORSES                                        H157B
                                    (A) HORSES                  19   WHITE WHALE US  WW 7121
H157C                             HORSESHOE                                      H157C
   ARTO BORG       G    (A          (A) FIRST KICK              19   BASF     GERM 20 25727.4
   TIMO JUUTI      B PERC(A
   HANS RANTIO     D PERC V (A  ARI TALKAMO   V G PNO(A
H158                              HORSLIPS                                       H158
   EAMONN CARR     D V  (ABDEFGHIJKL (A) HAPPY TO MEET          1973 OATS                M003
   CHARLES O'CONNOR VLN (ABCDEFGHIJKL (A) HAPPY TO MEET         197  ATLANTIC    GER 20119
   DECLAN SINNOTT  G    (J          (A) HAPPY TO MEET           197  ATCO         US    7030
   GUS GUEST       G    (J          (A) HAPPY TO MEET           1978 DJM      UK DJF 20544
   JIM LOCKHART FLT VLN K (ABCDEFGHIJKL (B) THE TAIN            1973 OATS                M005
   BARRY DEVLIN    V B  (ABCDEFGHIJKL (B) THE TAIN             197  ATLANTIC    GER 50034
   DEC O'DOHERTY   PNO  (K          (B) THE TAIN                197  ATCO         US    7039
   JOHN FEAN       V G  (ABCDEFGHIJKL (B) THE TAIN              1978 DJM      UK DJF 20543
   STEVE KATZ      TAMB (K          (C) DANCEHALL SWEETHEARTS   1974 OATS                M007
                                    (C) DANCEHALL SWEETHEARTS   1974 RCA             APLI0709
                                    (D) UNFORTUNATE CUP OF TEA  1975 OATS                M008
                                    (D) UNFORTUNATE CUP OF TEA  1975 RCA              SF 8432
                                    (E) DRIVE THE COLD WINTER AWAY 1976 OATS            M009
                                    (F) HORSLIPS                1976 OATS                M0010
                                    (G) CELTIC SYMPHONY/BOOK OF INVASIONS 1977 DJM DJM10 US UK DJF 20498
                                    (H) ALIENS                  1977 DJM   DJM16 US UK DJF 20519
                                    (H) ALIENS                  1977 ATLANTIC    GER 64202
                                    (I) TRACKS FROM THE VAULTS  1978 OATS                M0013
                                    (J) MAN WHO BUILT AMERICA   1979 DJM   DJM20 US UK DJF 20546
                                    (K) SHORT STORIES –TALL TALES 1980 MERCURY US 3809 UK 9100  070
                                    (L) THE BELFAST GIGS        1980 OATS           UK    M0020
                                    (L) THE BELFAST GIGS        1980 MERCURY     US    3842
H159                            WALTER HORTON                                    H159
   WALTER HORTON   V HCA(ALL        (A) SOUL OF BLUES HARMONICA 1964 ARGO        US      4037
   ROBERT NIGHTHAWK G   (B          (B) AN OFFER YOU CANT REFUSE(1SIDE) 1972 RED LIGHTNIN' UK RL008
   JIMMY DE BERRY  G    (C          (C) COTTON PATCH HOTFOOTS  (1SIDE) 1973 POLYDOR   2383 200
   WILLIE NIX      D    (C          (D) AND HOT COTTAGE         1974 EXTRA               1135
   CAREY BELL HARRINGTON HCA(E      (E) WITH CAREY BELL         1972 ALLIGATOR 4702+UK SONET SNTF677
   EDDIE TAYLOR    G    (E          (F) FINE CUTS               19   BLIND PIG   US      006
   JOE HARPER      B    (E          (G) SOUTHERN COMFORT        19   SIRE              97011
   BUDDY GUY       G    (A          (H) LITTLE BOY BLUE         1980 JSP         UK      1019
   BOBBY BUSTER    ORG  (A
   JACK MYERS      B    (A  WILLIE SMITH   D    (A  FRANK SWAN      D   (E  LEFT HAND FRANK G  (H
   RONNIE HORVATH  G    (H  OLA DIXON      D    (H  MICHAEL WARD    B   (H
H159A                          HOT CHOCOLATE                                     H159A
   ERROL BROWN     V    (ALL        (A) CICERO PARK             1974 RAK         UK   SRAK 507
   PAT OLIVE       B    (           (B) HOT CHOCOLATE           1975 RAK         UK   SRAK 516
   LARRY FERGUSON  K    (           (C) MAN TO MAN              1976
   TONY CONNOR     D    (           (D) 20 GREATEST HITS        1976 RAK         UK   SRAK 524
   HARVEY HINSLEY  G    (           (E) EVERY 1's A WINNER      1978 RAK         UK   SRAK 531
   TONY WILSON     B V  (           (F) GOING THROUGH THE MOTIONS 1979 RAK       UK   SRAK 536
                                    (G) CLASS                   1980 RAK         UK   SRAK 536
                                    (H) 20 HOTTEST HITS         1980 EMI         UK   EMTV 22
H160                              HOT DOGS                                       H160
   BILL RENNIE     V    (A          (A) SAY WHAT YOU MEAN       1973 ARDENT            ADS 2805
   GREG REDING     PNO G V(A
   TERRY MANNING   G    (A  JACK HOLDER    G    (A  ROBERT JOHNSON  G   (A  FRED PROUTY      D  (A
   STEVE HOLT      D    (A  RICHARD ROSEBROUGH D (A  STEVE SMITH    K   (A  CARGOE           V  (A
```

```
    JORMA KAUKONEN   G V  (ALL      (A) HOT TUNA                          1970 RCA   UK SF 8125  US    LSP  4353
    JACK CASADY      B V  (ALL      (B) FIRST PULL UP(ELECTRIC)LIVE       1971 RCA               US    LSP  4550
    WILL SCARLETT    HCA  (AB       (C) BURGERS                           1972 GRUNT UK 1004 US 0921 GER 2591
    PAPA CREACH      V VLN(CB       (D) PHOSPHORESCENT RAT                1974 GRUNT            UK US BFLI  0348
    JOEY COVINGTON   D    (         (E) AMERICA'S CHOICE                  1975 GRUNT UK FTR2003 US   BFLI  0820
    SAMMY PIAZZA     D V  (CDB      (F) YELLOW FEVER                      1975 GRUNT             US   BLFI  1238
    NIKKI BUCK       K SYN(CFGH     (G) HOPPKORV                          1976 GRUNT UK FTR2006 US   BFLI  1920
    BOB STEELER      D    (EFGH     (H) DOUBLE DOSE    (DBL LIVE)         1977 GRUNT UK FLO2545 US   CYL  22545
    JOHN SHERMAN     G    (FG       (I) FINAL VINYL                       1979 GRUNT UK FL13357
    MARTY BALIN      G    (
    PAUL ZEIGLER     G    (     DAVE CROSBY      V   (C   RICHARD TALBOTT   V G (C  KAREN TOBIN    V (G
    ANDREW NARVELL PERC    (D
```

```
    IAN A ANDERSON   G V  (AB       (A) CARRION ON                        1976 RED RAG          UK       RRR 005
    MAGGIE HOLLAND   B V  (AB       (B) EAST ST SHAKES                    1978 RED RAG          UK       RRR 015
    MARTIN SIMPSON   G BAN(B
    RAGGY FARMER    PERC V(B    DAVE GRIFFITHS VLN MAND(A  AL JONES        G   (A   JOHN PILGRIM   PERC(A
    DAVE PEABODY     HCA  (A    SIMON MAYOR    FDL MAND(B  HILARY JONES    V   (B
```

```
    TOMMY CALTON     G V  (AB       (A) HOTEL                             1979   MCA US 3158    UK    MCF  3036
    MARC PHILLIPS    K V  (AB       (B) HALFMOON SILVER                   1980   MCA US 5113
    MICHAEL REID     G V  (AB
    GEORGE CREASMAN  B V  (AB   LEE BARGERON      K V  (AB  MICHAEL CADENHEAD D PERC(AB  FARRELL MORRIS  PERC    (A
    SHANE KEISTER    SYN  (AB   JOHN NUCKOLS      D    (A
```

```
    ERIC STEWART   G B V(ABC        (A) THINK SCHOOL STINKS               1971 PHILIPS 6308 057+      6308  047
    KEVIN GODLEY     D V  (ABC      (A) THINK SCHOOL STINKS               1971 CAPITOL                US ST 378
    LOL CREME    G B K V  (ABC      (B) SONGS                             197  PHILIPS                 6308  080
    BAZ BARKER       VLN  (C        (C) YOU DIDN'T LIKE IT                1976 SONIC                   SON  009
    GRAHAM GOULDMAN  B    (C
    MIKE TIMONEY     ORG  (C
```

```
    GREGG ALLMAN     K V  (ALL      (A) HOURGLASS                         1968 LIBERTY US 7536 UK  LBL 83219
    PAUL HORNSBY     K    (A        (B) POWER OF LOVE                     19   LIBERTY US 7555
    DUANE ALLMAN     G    (ALL      (AB) HOURGLASS     (DBL)              1973 UA      US 013G2 UK  USD 303/4
    JESSE WILLARD CARR (
    MABRON McKINNEY    (       JOHNNY SANDLIN     (    PETE CARR         B   (A
```

```
    DIXON HOUSE      K V  (A        (A) FIGHTING ALONE                    1979 INFINITY             INS  2006
    CHRISSY SHEFTS   G    (A
    HOWARD LEESE     G    (A    CHUCK GARDNER     G    (A   JAMES KENFIELD  B   (A   FRED ZEUFELDT   B(A
```

```
    BEE HOUSTON      G V  (A        (A) BEE HOUSTON                       19   ARHOOLIE             US  1050
```

```
    CISSY HOUSTON    V    (ALL      (A) CISSY HOUSTON                     1971 JANUS        UK      6310 205
    RICK MAROTTA     D    (B        (B) CISSY HOUSTON                     1977 PRIVATE STOCK UK PVLP 1030
    STEVE JORDAN     D    (B        (C) THINK IT OVER                     1978 PRIVATE STOCK UK PVLP 1044
    LEON PENDARVIS   K    (B        (D) STEP ASIDE FOR A LADY             !)(= EMI            UK  EMC 3327
    RICHARD TEE      K    (B
    DONNY HARPER     B    (BC   BOB BABBIT        B    (B   LANCE QUINN     G   (B   VOICES OF HOPE   V   (B
    ARNOLD McCULLER  V    (B    YOLANDA McCULLOUGH V    (B  DAVID LASLEY    V   (B   MAERETHA STEWART V   (B
    KEN WILLIAMS     V    (B    WHITNEY HOUSTON   V    (C   ALVIN FIELDS    V   (C   LANI GROVES      V   (C
    ALLEN SCHWARZBERG D   (CD   FRANCISCO CENTENO B    (CD  JEFF MIRANOV    G   (BCD ROB MOUNSEY      K   (BCD
    RUBENS BASSINI  PERC (BCD   LUTHER VAN DROSS  V    (D   WILL LEE        B   (BD  STEVE LOVE       G   (D
    GERALD CHAMBERLAIN TROM(D   RONNIE CUBER     SAX   (D   JOHN GATCHELL   TPT (D   JOCELYN BROWN    V   (D
    JERRY NNIEWOOD   WIND (D    ELTESA WEATHERSBY V    (D   STRINGS             (D   BEVERLY INGRAM   V (C
```

```
                                    (A) DEMOLITION ROCK                   1974 CONTOUR           UK    2870  160
```

```
    CHUCK HOWARD     V    (A        (A) CHUCK HOWARD                      1977 CREAM              US    CR1005
    KEN PARK         D    (A
    JERRY COLE       G    (A    BEN BENAY        G    (A   ROB WALSH       G   (A   DAVE McDANIELS   B (A
    MARK GIBBONS     K    (A    RAY PIZZI       WIND  (A   JONATHAN LEE    HCA (A   JEFF TWEED       V (A
    JOHN NICOLS      V    (A
```

```
    CATHERINE HOWE   V K  (ALL      (A) HARRY                             1975 RCA LPI 5091  +         SF 8407
    PETER BOITA      D    (C        (B) SILENT MOTHER NATURE              1976 RCA                     RS 1041
    ALAN PARKER      G    (C        (C) DRAGONFLY DAYS                    1977 ARIOLA                  ARL 5013
    CHRIS REA        G    (C        (EP) TRUTH OF THE MATTER              1977 RCA                     PE  5004
    FOGGY LITTLE     G    (C
    PAUL KEOGH       G    (C    LES HURDLE        B    (C   MELT KINGTON    B   (C   CHRIS KARAN PERC    (C
    RICHARD HEWSON   SYN  (C    DAVID HANCOCK    HRNS  (C   PETE WINGFIELD  K   (C   DICK HOLMES      K (C
```

```
    STEVE HOWE G V B K SYN PERC(AB  (A) BEGINNINGS                        1977 ATLANTIC US 18514 UK K 50151
    PATRICK MORAZ    K    (AB       (B) STEVE HOWE ALBUM                  1979 ATLANTIC US 19243 UK K 50621
    ALAN WHITE       D    (AB       (C) THE BODAST TAPES                  1980 CHERRY RED        UK  RED12
    DAVID OBERLE     D    (A
    JOHN MECK        VIOLA(A    PATRICK HALLING   VLN  (A   WILLIAM REID    VLN (A   PETER HALLING CELLO  (A
    CHRIS LAURENCE   B    (A    JAMES GREGORY    FLT   (A   MALCOLM BENNETT FLT (A   BUD BEADLE       SAX (A
    SIDNEY SUTCLIFFE OBOE (A    BILL BRUFORD      D    (AB  MICK EVE        SAX (A   GWYN BROOKE  BASSOON(A
    COLIN GIBSON     B    (A    RONNIE LEAHY      K    (B   CLIVE BUNKER    D   (B   CLAIRE HAMILL    V (B
    GRAHAM PRESKETT  VLN  (B
    GRAEME TAYLOR    G    (A        * SEE 'BODAST' FOR LINE UP OF (C)
```

```
EDDIE HOWELL      G V K(A      (A) GRAMOPHONE RECORD              1975  WB                    UK   K 56154
PHIL COLLINS      D   (A
JOHN GOODSALL     G   (A   PERCY JONES      B   (A  GARY MOORE      G  (A  ROBIN LUMLEY     K  (A
JACK LANCASTER    WIND (A   GASPAR LAWAL    PERC (A  TONY SADLER     G  (A  CHARMING LEMMINGS PERC(A
DAVID MINNS       V   (A   MARTIN KITCAT     V  (A  JEROME RIMSON   B  (A
```

```
RUEBEN HOWELL     V   (A      (A) REUBEN HOWELL                   1973 MOTOWN              US    771
CLAYTON IVEY      K G PERC(A
GEORGE SOULE      B V   (A   KEN BELL         G   (A  CHARLES CHALMERS STR V(A  HARRISON CALLOWAY HRNS (A
HARVEY THOMPSON   SAX   (A   TERRY WOODFORD   V   (A  SANDRA RHODES    V   (A  PHILLIP MITCHELL  V   (A
LAURA STRUZICK    V   (A   JIMMY EVANS  B PERC (A  PETE CARR        G   (A  MIKE LEWIS       STR   (A
BEN CAULEY        HRNS  (A   RONNIE EADES    SAX   (A  CHARLES ROSE     TROM (A  SUE RICHARDS      V   (A
DONNA RHODES      V   (A   JEANNIE GREENE    V   (A
```

```
HOWLIN' WOLF(CHESTER BURNETT)V G HCA (A) MOANING IN THE MOONLIGHT  1964 CHESS UK 4006     US       1434
HUBERT SUMLIN     G    (MNPQUVWZY    (A) "   "   "   "              196  MARBLE ARCH       UK   MAL 665
WILLIE JOHNSON    G    (EFQSTUWX    (A) EVIL                        196  CHESS            US       1540
WILLIE DIXON      B    (QUVWY       (B) POOR BOY                    1965 CHESS            UK   CRL4508
SAM LAY           D    (UVXY        (C) REAL FOLK BLUES             1966 CHESS            US       1502
HOSEA LEE KENNARD PNO  (QTUVWXY     (D) BIG CITY BLUES             1966 EMBER UK 3370 UNITED US  7717
EARL PHILLIPS     G D  (QTUVXYW     (E) CITY BLUES                  19   UNITED US 7717 + US CUSTOM 2055
JODY WILLIAMS     G    (QXYW        (F) ORIGINAL FOLK BLUES         19   UNITED US 7747 + US KENT   526
SP LEARY          D    (NUVXY       (G) SINGS THE BLUES             19   CROWN            US       5240
FRED BELOW        D    (NWX         (H) MORE REAL FOLK BLUES        1967 CHESS            US       1512
IKE TURNER        PNO  (EFSTWVX     (I) SUPER SUPER BLUES BAND      1968 CHECKER UK 3010 + US CHESS 4537
HENRY GRAY        PNO  (VWY         (J) THE HOWLIN' WOLF ALBUM      1969 CADET   UK LPS319+US CHESS 4543
WILLIE STEEL      D    (EFQSTVWX    (K) AKA CHESTER BURNETT         1974 CHESS            US       60016
JAMES COTTON      HCA  (TVW         (L) MESSAGE TO THE YOUNG        1971 CHESS UK 6310108 +US CHESS 50002
JOHNNY JONES      PNO  (UVY         (M) LONDON SESSIONS             1971 ROLLSTONES 49101 +US CHESS 60008
J T BROWN         SAX  (UXY         (N) LIVE & COOKIN' AT ALICES REVISITED1972 CHESS     US       50015
BILLY DOBKINS     SAX  (TUV         (O) BACK DOOR WOLF              1973 CHESS US 50045 GER    928  008
OTIS SMOTHERS     G    (TUWX        (P) LONDON REVISITED            1974 CHESS            US       60026
DON HANKINS       SAX  (UY          (Q) BLUES MASTERS              1977 CHESS            UK   2ACBM 201
JUNIOR BLACKMAN   D    (XY          (R) SAM'S BLUES                 197  CHARLY           UK   CR  30102
BUDDY GUY         G    (V           (S) LEGENDARY SUN PERFORMERS    197  CHARLY           UK   CR  30134
WILLIE WILLIAMS   D    (WX          (T) HEART LIKE A RAILROAD STEEL 19   BLUES BALL       US       2001
L D McGHEE        D    (VYU         (U) CANT PUT ME OUT             19   BLUES BALL       US       2002
LAYFAYETTE LEAKE  PNO  (MU          (V) FROM EARLY TO LATE          19   BLUE NIGHT           BN 0731667
DAVE MYERS        B    (N           (W) GOIN' BACK HOME             19   SYNDICATE CHAPTER US    SC  003
JEROME ARNOLD          (X           (X) HOWLIN' WOLF               19   PYTHON           US   PLP KM 13
ALBERT LUANDREW   PNO  (N           (Y) CHANGIN MY WAY              1977 CHESS                CHV  418
OTIS SPANN        PNO  (Q           (Q) CHESS MASTERS               1981 CHESS            UK       4004
IAN STEWART       PNO  (M
BRYCE ROBERSON    G    (L   SONNY THOMPSON  PNO  (L  ALFRED ELKINS   B   (UT ERIC CLAPTON    G  (M
STEVE WINWOOD     K    (M   BILL WYMAN       B   (MP CHARLIE WATTS   D   (MP JEFFREY M CARP  HCA(MP
KLAUS VOORMAN     B    (M   JOHN SIMON       K   (M  PHIL UPCHURCH   B   (MJ DENNIS LANSING  HRNS(M
DONALD MYRICK     FLT  (J   GENE BARGE      HRNS  (J  JOE MILLER      HRNS (M  JORDON SANDKE   HRNS(M
MORRIS JENNINGS   D    (J   ROLAND FAULKNER  G   (J  JOHN STOCKLIN   G   (L  TYRONE SMITH     D  (L
LOUIS SATTERFIELD B    (J   MUDDY WATERS    G V  (I  PETE COSEY      G   (J  BOB CROWDER      D  (L
ALBERT WILLIAMS   PNO  (Q   JOHN JERIMIAH   ORG  (L  BO DIDDLEY      G V (I  JIMMY ROGERS     G  (Y
ABE LOCKE         SAX  (WY  LV WILLIAMS      B   (U  ERNIE SHAW      SAX (U  ANDREW PALMER    B  (Y
ARNOLD ROGERS     SAX  (Y   ADOLPH DOLLINS  SAX  (W  ERNIE SHAW      SAX (U
```

```
LINDA HOYLE       V    (A      (A) PIECES OF ME                    1971 VERTIGO          UK   6360   060
CHRIS SPEDDING    G    (A
JOHN MARSHALL     D    (A   JEFF CLYNE       B   (A  KARL JENKINS   OCBE K (A  COLIN PURBROOK  PNO(A
```

```
                               (A) HUB                             1975 CAPITOL          US       11439
```

```
ALAN VON BUR      G V  (AB     (A) HUBBLE BUBBLE                   198  SINUS            BEL 120 330 036
DANNY JOAN        G V  (B      (B) FAKING                          198  SINUS            BEL 120 330 045
ROGER JUNIOR      D V  (A
DEE MASSART       B V  (A   JERRY            D   (B  J L U BOAT      B   (B  LIPSTICK         D  (B
```

```
KEITH HUDSON                   (A) TOUCH OF FREEDOM                1975 ATRA                  1001
SLY DUNBAR         D    (C      (B) TOO EXPENSIVE                   1976 VIRGIN           UK   V 2056
ERIC CLARKE        D    (C      (C) RASTA COMMUNICATIONS           1978 JOINT                JT0003
ROBBIE SHAKESPEARE G    (C      (D) RASTA COMMUNICATION            1979 GREENSLEEVES     UK   GREL 5
EARL SMITH         G    (C
RANCHIE McLEAN    B G   (C   DONALD GITS      G   (C  PAGET KING     K V (C  TONY BROTHER    PERC (C
STICKMAN           V    (C   LAZA STRIKE      V   (C  THEO BECKFORD  K   (C  TARZAN NELSON    K  (C
KEITH STIRLING     K    (C   WILLY BARRETT    G   (C  KEN ELLIOT     K   (C
```

```
BILL HUDSON       G V  (ALL     (A) HUDSON                         197  PLAYBOY          US   PB 102
MARK HUDSON       G V  (ALL     (B) HOLLYWOOD SITUATION            1974 CASABLANCA US 9008 UK    4002
BRETT HUDSON      V B  (ALL     (C) TOTALLY OUT OF CONTROL         1975 MCA US 406 JAP ROCKET   80363
CRAIG KRAMPF      D    (B       (D) BA FA                          1975 ROCKET    US PIG2169
PHIL'REED         K    (B       (E) HUDSON                         1977 PLAYBOY   US 34734
MIKE PARKER       K    (B       (F) PEOPLE LIKE US                 1978 ARISTA    US
BARRY PULMAN      SYN  (B       (G) HUDSON BROTHERS                1978 FIRST AMERICAN US      7708
                                (H) TRUTH ABOUT US                 1979 ARISTA    US 4199
```

```
RICHARD HUDSON V G PERC  (ABCD  (A) NICKELODEON                    1973 A&M US 3616     UK   AMLH 68208
JOHN FORD         G B  (ABCD    (B) FREE SPIRIT                    1974 A&M US 3652     UK   AMLH 68274
KEN LAWS          D    (D       (C) WORLDS COLLIDE                 1975 A&M US 4535     UK   AMLH 64535
BRENT FORBES      B    (D       (D) DAYLIGHT                       1977 CBS             UK       82027
CHRIS PARREN      K    (D
DAVE MARKEE       B    (D   IAN BAIRNSON     G   (D  GRAHAM PRESKETT VLN K(D  MARTIN DROVER   TPT (D
RAY RUSSELL       G    (D
```

LEON HUFF

LEON HUFF		(A	(A) HERE TO CREATE MUSIC		1980 PHILADELPHIA US 36758 UK 84530		

H174
HUG
H174

MIKE HUGG	V K	(A	(A) NEON DREAM		1975 POLYDOR	UK	2383 330
RON TELEMACQUE	D V	(A					
MARCUS JAMES	D V	(A	JOHN KNIGHTSBRIDGE	G V	(A		

H175
MIKE HUGG
H175

MIKE HUGG	V K	(AB	(A) SOMEWHERE		1972	POLYDOR	UK	2383 140
MICKY WALLER	D	(AB	(B) STRESS & STRAIN		1973	POLYDOR	UK	2383 213
KIM GARDNER	B	(B					
DAVE KING	G	(AB	SONNY CORBETT	HRNS (B	DAVID HEATH HADFIELD G	(B	EDDIE GRANT	G (B
LYN DOBSON	HRNS (B		PAUL WESTWOOD	B (B	KEVIN PEEK	G	(AB	ELTON DEAN	SAX(AB
IAN CARR	HRNS (B		TONY RIVERS	K V (B	ANDY BOWN	B	(A	TOM McGUINESS	G (A
LIZA STRIKE	V	(A	JUDITH POWELL	V (A	ALAN TARNEY	B	(A	BRIAN HUGG	V (A
MANFRED MANN	ORG	(A	TWEED HARRIS	STRINGS(A	ROGER POPE	D	(A	BARRY ST JOHN	V (A
GRAHAM PRESKETT	B	(A	TERRY BRITTEN	G (A	CALEB QUAYE	G	(A	MICK ROGERS	G (A
HENRY SPINETTI	D	(A	GERRY BECKLEY	G (A				

H176
GLENN HUGHES
H176

GLENN HUGHES V G B K(A			(A) PLAY ME OUT		SAFARI 1977 LONG2 +1978 6/23085		
MEL GALLEY	G	(A					
BILL BOWMAN	G	(A	PAT TRAVERS	G (A	DAVE HOLLAND	D	(A	TERRY ROWLEY	PNO (A
ROBERT BAILEY	PNO	(A	RON ASPERY	SAX (A	HENRY LOWTHER	TPT	(A	MARK NAUSEEF	PERC(A
LIZA STRIKE	V	(A	JOY WRIGHT	V (A	HELEN CHAPPELLE	V	(A		

H176A
JIMMY HUGHES
H176A

JIMMY HUGHES		(A	(A) A SHOT OF RHYTHM & BLUES		1980	CHARLY	CTD 103

H177
ALAN HULL
H177

ALAN HULL V G PERC K	(ABC		(A) PIPEDREAM		1973	CHARISMA	UK	CAS 1069
KEN CRADDOCK G V K PERC(ABC			(B) SQUIRE		1975	WB US WS4587 UK	K 56121
COLIN GIBSON	B PERC(ABC		(C) PHANTOMS		1979	ROCKET	UK	TRAIN 6
RAY LAIDLAW	D	(ABC					
MICK MOODY	G	(B	LESLEY DUNCAN	V (BC	JOHN TURNBULL	G	(A	RAY JACKSON HCA MAND (AB
BRIAN CHATTON	K	(B	JO NEWMAN	V (BC	DAVE BROOKS	SAX	(A	TERRY POPPLE	D (B
ALBERT LEE	G	(B	JEAN ROUSSEL	K (B	PETER KIRTLEY	G	(C	STEVE GREGORY	HRNS(C
BUB BEADLE	HRNS (C		LIZA STRIKE	V (C	RAB NOAKES	V	(C		

H178
HUMAN BEAST
H178

GILLIES BUCHAN	G V	(A	( ) HUMAN BEAST		1970	DECCA	UK	SKL 5053
EDWARD JONES	B V	(A					
JOHN ROMSEY	D	(A	DAVID McNIVEN	CLAR (A				

H178A
HUMAN LEAGUE
H178A

IAN CRAIG MARSH	SYN V(AB		(A) REPRODUCTION		1979	VIRGIN	UK	V 2133
PHILIP OAKLEY	SYN V(ALL		(B) TRAVELOGUE		1980	VIRGIN	UK	V 2160
MARTIN WARE	SYN V(AB		(C) DARE		1981	VIRIGN	UK	V 2192
PHILIP ADRIAN WRIGHT SYN(ABC			(EP)THE DIGNITY OF LABOUR		1979	FAST	UK	V F 1
JO CALLIS	SYN	(C					
IAN BURDEN	SYN	(C	JOANNE CATHEDRALL V	(C	SUSANNE SULLEY	V	(C	COLIN THURSTON	PROD	(A
MARTIN RUSHANT	PROD (C						

H178B
HUMAN SEXUAL RESPONSE
H178B

(A) FIGURE 14	1980 DONT FALL OF THE MOUNTAIN UK 1	
(A) FIGURE 14	1980 PASSPORT	US 9851
(B) IN A ROMAN MOOD	1981	UK K11

H179
HUMBLE PIE
H179

STEVE MARRIOTT G V K HCA(ALL			(A) AS SAFE AS YESTERDAY IS	1969 IMMEDIATE US 101 UK	IMSP025	
PETER FRAMPTON	G V	(ABCDELKMN	(B) TOWN & COUNTRY	1969 IMMEDIATE	UK	IMSP027
JERRY SHIRLEY	D	(ALL	(B) TOWN & COUNTRY	1978 CHARLY	UK	CR 300016
GREG RIDLEY	B	(ABCDEFGHJKLMN(C) HUMBLE PIE	1970 A&M US 4270	UK	AMLS 986
DAVE CLEMPSON	G	(FGHJN	(D) ROCK ON	1971 A&M US 4301	UK	AMLS 2013
B J COLE	STEEL(CDGN		(E) ROCKIN' AT FILLMORE (DBL)	1971 A&M US 3506	UK	AMLH 63506
WILLIE WILSON	D	(C	(F) SMOKIN'	1972 A&M US 4342	UK	AMLS 64342
ALEXIS KORNER	V	(DF	(G) EAT IT	1973 A&M US 3701	UK	AMLS 6004
BOBBY KEYS	SAX	(D	(H) THUNDERBOX	1974 A&M US 3611	UK	AMLH 63611
DORIS TROY	V	(DF	(J) STREET RATS	1975 A&M US 4514	UK	AMLS 68282
P P ARNOLD	V	(D	(K) CRUST OF(COMP)	1975 EMI	IMP	C048 50720
CLAUDIA LENNEAR	V	(D	(L) BACK HOME AGAIN	1976 IMMEDIATE	UK	IML 1005
MADELINE BELL	V	(F	(M) GREATEST HITS(COMP)	1977 IMMEDIATE	UK	IML 2005
STEPHEN STILLS		(F	(N) POP CHRONIK (COMP)	19 A&M	IMP	80771
RICKY WILLS		(F	(O) FAMOUS POP GROUPS OF THE 60s(+NICE 19 MFP	GERM 14694319/2	
SYDNEY GEORGE	SAX	(GN	(P) ON TO VICTORY	1980 JET UK 231 US ATLANTIC 38122	
BILLIE BARNUM	V	(GHN	(AB) LOST & FOUND (DBL)	1973 A&M US 3513	
MAXINE DIXON	V	(Q	(AB) LOST & FOUND (DBL)	1975 CHARLY GER CR 3002	
TIM HINKLEY	K	(J	(Q) GO FOR THE THROAT	1981 ATLANTIC UK 38131	
BOB TENCH	G V	(PQ	(D+) SHINE ON	1971 CLUB GER	92982
DANA KRAL	V	(Q			
ROBYN BECK	V	(Q	ANTHONY JONES	B V (PQ	LYN DOBSON	WIND (ALM	CLYDIE KING	V (GN
CARLENA WILLIAMS	V	(H	VANETTA FIELDS	V (GHN	MEL COLLINS	HRNS (HJ	GLYNN JOHNS	PROD(D

H180
HUMBLEBUMS
H180

BILLY CONNOLLY	V G	(ABC	(A) FIRST COLLECTION....	1969 TRANSATLANTIC	UK	TRA 186
TAM HARVEY V G MAND		(A	(B) HUMBLEBUMS	1969 TRANSATLANTIC	UK	TRA 201
RONNIE RAE	B	(A	(B) HUMBLEBUMS	1969 LIBERTY	US	7636
GERRY RAFFERTY	G V	(BC	(C) OPEN UP THE DOOR	1970 TRANSATLANTIC	UK	TRA 218
BERNIE HOLLAND	G	(C	(C) OPEN UP THE DOOR	1970 LIBERTY	US	7656
TERRY COX	D	(C	(ABC) THE COMPLETE..	1974 TRANSATLANTIC	UK	TRAT288
JIMMY TAGFORD		(C	( ) HUMBLEBUM	1981 TRANSATLANTIC	UK	TRS 107
BARRY DRANSFIELD	FDL	(C			
REG GUEST		(C			

HUMMINGBIRD

```
H181                                    HUMMINGBIRD                                              H181
    BOB TENCH         G V  (ABC              (A) HUMMINGBIRD                      1975 A&M  US 4536   UK  AMLS 68292
    MAX MIDDLETON     K    (ABC              (B) WE CANT GO ON MEETING LIKE THIS  1976 A&M  US 4595   UK  AMLH 68383
    CLIVE CHAMAN      B    (ABC              (C) DIAMOND NIGHTS                   1977 A&M  US 4661   UK  AMLH 64661
    BERNIE HOLLAND    G    (AB
    BERNARD PURDIE    D    (BC  ROBERT AHWAI      G   (BC  CONRAD ISADORE    D    (A   JIM HORN      WIND (C
    QUITMAN DENNIS    HRNS (C   CHUCK FINDLEY     HRNS (C  AIRTO MOREIRA     PERC (C   PANCHO MORALES PERC(C
    VANETTA FIELDS    V    (C   MAXINE WILLARD    V   (C   JULIA TILLMAN     V    (C   STEPHANIE SPRUILL V(C
    PAULETTE McWILLIAMS V  (C   LISA FREEMAN ROBERTS V (C  LINDA LEWIS       V    (A   SANDRA ISADORE   V  (A
    GODFREY MACCLEAN  CONGA(A   MADELINE BELL     V   (B   JOANNE WILLIAMS   V    (B   LIZA STRIKE      V  (B
```

HUNGRY CHUCK

```
H182                                    HUNGRY CHUCK                                             H182
    PETER ECKLUND     WIND (A              (A) HUNGRY CHUCK                      1972 BEARSVILLE          BR 2071
    N D SMART         V D  (A
    JIM COLGROVE      B G V(A   BEN KEITH        STEEL(A  AMOS GARRETT  G TROM V(A  JEFFREY GUTCHEON   K  V(A
```

HUNGRY WOLF

```
H183                                    HUNGRY WOLF                                              H183
    ALAN HAWKSHAW     K    (A              (A) HUNGRY WOLF                       1970 PHILIPS          6308  009
    ALAN PARKER       G    (A
    CLEM CATTINI      D    (A   BOBBY HAUGHEY    TPT (A   DEREK WATKINS    TPT (A   HERBIE FLOWERS  B  (A
    PETER LEE STIRLING V   (A   TONY FISHER      TPT (A   CLIFF HARDY      TROM(A   KEN GOULDIE TROM   (A
    JOHNNIE EDWARDS   TROM (A
```

HUNT

```
H183A                                   HUNT                                                     H183A
    PAUL DICKINSON    G V  (AB             (A) HUNT                             1975        CAN
    PAUL KERSEY       D   'AB             (B) BACK ON THE HUNT                  1980  VISA 7013 US UK LOGO 1028
    BRIAN GAGREN      B V K G (AB
```

MARSHA HUNT

```
H184                                    MARSHA HUNT                                              H184
    MARSHA HUNT       V    (A             (A) WOMAN CHILD                       1971 TRACK UK 2410 101 GERM  2383081
                                          (A) ATTENTION WOMAN CHILD)            1974 FONTANA         GERM RI
```

HUNTER

```
H184A                                   HUNTER                                                   H184A
    LES HUNT          G V  (A             (A) ROCK ON                          1978  PATHE         FR  068 61882
    LES CRITCHLOW     D    (A
    P G CORNELL  VLN TROM K(A   NICK EGAN        B  (A  CHRIS ELLIS      K  (A
```

CHRIS HUNTER

```
H184B                                   CHRIS HUNTER                                             H184B
                                          (A) EARLY DAYS                       1981 ORIGINAL        UK   ORA 104
```

IAN HUNTER

```
H185                                    IAN HUNTER                                               H185
    IAN HUNTER        G V  (ALL           (A) IAN HUNTER                       1975 CBS US 33480   UK       80710
    EARL SLICK        G    (C             (B) ALL AMERICAN ALIEN BOY           1976 CBS US 34142   UK       81310
    MICK RONSON       G V  (ABDEFG        (C) OVERNIGHT ANGELS                 1977 CBS US 34721   UK       81993
    ROB RAWLINSON     B    (C             (D) SHADES OF (COMP DBL)             1978 CBS US 36251   UK       88476
    CURLY SMITH       D    (C             (E) YOU'RE NEVER ALONE WITH A SCHIZO 1979 CHRYSALIS      UK   CHR 1214
    PETER OXENDALE    K    (C             (F) LIVE WELCOME TO THE CLUB(DBL)    1980 CHRYSALIS US 1269  UK  CJT6
    DENNIS ELLIOTT    D    (AC            (G) SHORT BACK & SIDES               1981 CHRYSALIS           CHR1326
    JOHN HOLBROOK
    AYNSLEY DUNBAR    D    (B   PETER ARNESEN    K   (A  DAVID SANBORN    SAX  (B   FREDDIE MERCURY V  (B
    CHRIS STAINTON    K    (B   GEOFF APPLEBY B HCA V (A  BRIAN MAY        V    (B   ROGER TAYLOR    V  (B
    MILLER ANDERSON   V    (CG  ROY BAKER        PERC (C  LEM LUBIN        V    (C   ROY BITTAN      K  (E
    GARRY TALLENT     B    (E   MAX WEINBERG     D   (E  JOHN CALE        K    (E   GEORGE YOUNG    SAX (E
    LEW DEL GATTO     SAX  (E   ELLEN FOLEY      V   (EFG RORY DODD        V    (E   ERIC BLOOM      V  (E
    ERIC PARKER       D V  (FG  MARTIN BRILEY    B V (FG  TOMMY MORRONGIELLO G B V(FG TOMMY MANDEL   K V(FG
    GEORGE MEYER      K V  (FG  SUSIE RONSON     V   (F   BO SEGARINI      V    (F   JOHN GUSTAFSON  B  (A
    PACO PASTORIOUS   G B  (B   MOTT THE HOOPLE  D   (B   GARY WEEMS       G    (D   DOMINIC CORTESE SAX (B
    CORNELL DUPREE    G    (B   DON ALIAS        PERC (B  ARNIE LAWRENCE   CLAR (B   DAVE BARGENIN   TROM  (B
    LEW SOLOFF        TPT  (B   ANN SUTTON       V   (B   MICK BARAKEN     G    (G   TODD RUNDGRAN   B V (G
    ROGER POWELL      V    (G   GARY WINDO       SAX (G   WELLS KELLY      D    (G   MICK JONES      G V (G
    TOPPER HEADON     D    (G   TYMON DOGG       VLN (G
```

ROBERT HUNTER

```
H186                                    ROBERT HUNTER                                            H186
    ROBERT HUNTER     V G  (ABC           (A) TALES OF GREAT RUM RUNNERS       1974 ROUND             RX  101
    MICKEY HART       D    (AB            (B) TIGER ROSE                       1975 ROUND             RX  105
    BARRY MELTON      B    (A             (C) JACK O' ROSES                    1980 DARK STAR        DSLP 8001
    JERRY GARCIA      G K SYN(AB
    DAVID FREIBERG B K SYN(AB   PETER ALBIN      B   (A   KEITH GODCHAUX   K    (A   DONNA GODCHAUX   V (AB
    STEVEN SCHUSTER   SAX  (A   SNOOKY FLOWERS   SAX (A   MARIO CIPOLLINA       (A   BRUCE GAPINSKI   (A
    MILT FARROW       (A      JOHN FAREY       (A   DAVID KESSNER         (A   RAY SCOTT      (A
    JEFF SLATTERY     (A      RANDALL SMITH        (A   BILL STEELE           (A   HADI EL SADOON TPT(A
    RODNEY ALBIN      V FDL(A   T WILL CLAIRE    V   (A   MAUREEN AYLETT   SPOONS(A   BUDDY CAGE STEEL (A
    RICKY SHUBB       BANJ (A   MARKEE SHUBB     MAND (A  ROBBIE STOKES    G    (A   JAMIE PARIS      (A
    PETE SEARS        B K  (AB  CHRISTIE BOURNE  PERC (A  DAVE TORBERT     B    (B   B D SHOT     D  (B
    DAVID GRISMAN     MAND (B
```

STEVE HUNTER

```
H187                                    STEVE HUNTER                                             H187
    STEVE HUNTER      G V  (A             (A) SWEPT AWAY                       1977 ATCO US    SD  36148
    PRAKASH JOHN      B    (A
    JIM GORDON        D    (A   BOB EZRIN        K PERC V (A  JIM MAELEN    PERC (A   JOSEF CHIROWSKI K  (A
    C EZRIN           B    (A   CAROL POPE       V   (A  JOANNE BROOKS     V    (A   TONY D'AMICO   V  (A
```

HUNTER MUSKETT

```
H188                                    HUNTER MUSKETT                                           H188
    DANNY THOMPSON    B    (A             (A) EVERYTIME YOU MOVE               1970 DECCA NOVA        SND 20
    DOUG MORTER       G V  (AB            (B) HUNTER / MUSKETT                 1973 BRADLEYS          BRADL 1003
    CHRIS GEORGE      G HCA V(AB
    TERRY HISCOCK     G K V(AB  MIKE GILES       D   (B   KEN FREEMAN      SYN  (B   JIM McCARTY PERC (B
    ROGER TREVIT      B V PER(B
```

MICHAEL HURLEY

```
H189                                    MICHAEL HURLEY                                           H189
    MICHAEL HURLEY  G V FDL(ABC           (A) ARMCHAIRBOOGIE                   1971 WB          US  WS 1915
    JEFFREY FREDERICKS V PERC(B           (B) HAVE MOICY                       1976 ROUNDER     US     3010
    ROBERT IWASKIEWICZ  G V B(BC          (C) LONG JOURNEY                     19   ROUNDER     US     3011
    ROBERT NICKSON    D    (BC            ( ) HI FI SHOCK UPTOWN               19   RACCOON     US     2625
    PAUL PRESTI       G V  (B             ( ) SNOCKGRASS                       1980 ROUNDER     US     3043
    DAVE REISCH       B V  (BC            ( ) FIRST SONGS                      19   FOLK        US     3581
    ROBIN REMAILLY V FDL MAND(B
    PETER STAMPFEL V BAN FDL(BC  JOHN NAGY     MAND (B  MORGAN HUBER      B PNO(C   DEREK SEMLER   B V (C
    ROB HYKYS         STEEL(C   AL ZANZLER       TPT (C   ELVIN WOODS      FDL  (C   CHRISTOPHER L'ESTRANG G  (C
    MEDULLA           V    (C   JOHN KEYES      V   (C
```

HURRIGANES

REMU AALTONEN	D V	(CDEF	(A) ROCK & ROLL ALL NIGHT LONG	19	LOVE		SW	LRLP 84
CISSE HAKKINEN	B V	(CDEF	(B) ROAD RUNNER	19	LOVE		SW	LRLP 117
RICHARD STANLEY	F	(F	(C) CRAZY DAYS	1975	LOVE SW 141		SONET	3018
ILE KALLIO	G	(C	(D) HOT WHEELS	19	LOVE		SW	LRLP 206
			(E) HURRIGANES	1977	SONET FR STA 20311 UK		SNTF	732
			(F) USE NO HOOKS	1978	SONET FRSTA20345UK		SNTF754	
			(F) ISUGU WAY	1977	LOVE		SCAN	LRLP250
			(G) STRANDED IN THE JUNGLE	1978	SONET			SLP 3039
			(H) 16 GOLDEN GREATS	1977	LOVE		SCAN	LRLP 230

PHIL HURTT

PHIL HURTT	V PNO(AB		(A) GIVING IT BACK	1978	FANTASY US 9552		F 546
EVETTE BENTON	V	(AB	(B) P H FACTOR	1979	FANTASY US 9582		FT 561
BARBARA INGRAM	V	(AB					
CARLA BENSON	V	(AB	BABBS STEWART	V	(A	RICHIE ROME	K	(A	GREG POREE	G	(A
DAVID WILLIAMS	G	(A	GREG MIDDLETON	B	(A	LARRY TOLBERT	D	(A	SHONDON AKIEM	PERC(A
CARL HELM	V	(B	RON TYSON	V	(B	ANN S CLARK	PNO	(B	LARRY WASHINGTON PERC(B
MIGUEL FUENTES	PERC (B						

HUSTLER

TONY BEARD	D	(A	(A) HIGH STREET	1974	A&M US 4504		UK AMLS 68276
HENRY SPINETTI	D	(B	(B) PLAY LOUD	1975	A&M US 4556		UK AMLH 33001
STEVE HAYNES	V	(AB					
MICKEY LLEWELYN	G V	(AB	KENNY DAUGHTERS	K	(AB KENNY LYONS	B V	(AB

HUSTLER (2)

		(A) JUKEBOX QUEEN ·	19	REFINED	UK	RR1

WILLIE HUTCH

WILLIE HUTCH	G V	(ALL	(A) FULLY EXPOSED	1973	MOTOWN US 784	UK	STML11247
LAWRENCE DICKENS	B	(A	(B) FOXY BROWN	1975	MOTOWN	UK	STML11269
TOMMY MYLES	WIND	(A	(C) MARK OF THE BEAST	1975	MOTOWN	UK	STML11280
KING ERRISON	PERC	(A	(D) ODE TO MY LADY	1975	MOTOWN	UK	STML12015
JOE SAMPLE	PNO	(A					
ALAN ESTES	PERC (A	JULIA TILLMAN	V	(A	OREN WATERS	V	(A	MILTON HAYES	V (A
TIM LAWSON	G	(A	FRED WHITE	D	(A	SAM CLAYTON	CONGA(A	GENE ESTES	PERC(A
MAXINE WILLARD	V	(A	CAROL WILLIS	V	(A	RICHARD HUTCH	V (A	DENNIS ALBERT	V (A

ASHLEY HUTCHINGS

ASHLEY HUTCHINGS	V B	(ALL	(A) MORRIS ON	1972	ISLAND	UK HELP 5
RICHARD THOMPSON	G V	(A	(B) COMPLEAT DANCING MASTER	1974	ISLAND UK HELP 17	US ANTILLES7003
BARRY DRANSFIELD	G V VLN(A		(C) RATTLEBONE & PLOUGHJACK	1976	ISLAND	UK HELP24
JOHN KIRKPATRICK	V ACC(AB		(D) SON OF MORRIS ON	1976	HARVEST	UK SHSM 2012
DAVE MATTACKS	D	(ABD	(E) KICKIN' UP THE SAWDUST	1977	HARVEST	UK SHSP 4073
SHIRLEY COLLINS	V	(AD				
BERT CLEAVER	PIPE (AB	PHIL PICKETT	WIND (BD	SIMON NICOL	G)BD	ROGER SWALLOW	D (B
ROD SKEAPING	VLN (B	JEREMY MONTAGU	PERC (B	SUE HARRIS	OBOE (B	RICHARD HARVEY	CLAR(B
ADAM SKEAPING	VLN (B	ALAN LUMSDEN SERPENT (B	TERRY POTTER	HCA (BE	DAVE KETTLEWELL	WIND(B
ALAN WARD	CELLO(A	FANNY WARLOCK SPINET (B	PETER KNIGHT	VLN (B	RAY WARLEIGH	SAX (B
FRANCIS BAINES	VLN (B	ELIZABETH BAINES VLN (B	LONI PATT	VLN (B	PETER VEL	VLN (B
JOHN WATCHAM	CONC (D	MICHAEL GREGORY D PERC (DE	MARTIN CARTHY	G (D	JOHN TAMS	CONC V (DE
JAMES PLESTER	VLN (D	JOHN RODD CONC (DE	IAN CUTLER	VLN (D	BOB CANN	MELODEON (E
JIMMY COOPER	DULC (E	MICHAEL HEBBERT CONC K(E	PETER BULLOCK	WIND SYN (E	GRAEME TAYLOR	G (E

J B HUTTO

J B HUTTO	V G	(ALL	(A) HAWKSQUAT	1973	DELMARK	US	DS 617
BREWER PHILLIPS	G V	(C	(B) SLIDEWINDER	1974	DELMARK	US	DS 636
MARK HARRIS	B	(C	(C) LIVE VOLUME ONE	1977	CHARLY	UK	CR 30182
TED HARVEY	D	(C	(D) BLUES FOR FONESSA	1979	AMUGO		AMLP 823
MIKE ALLEN	PNO	(C	(E) LIVE AT SANDY'S JAZZ REVUE	1979	BARON		101
SUNNYLAND SLIM	PNO	(A	(F) MASTER OF MODERN BLUES	19	TESTAMENT	US	2213

HYBRID KIDS

LOL COXHILL	SAX	(B	(A) A COLLECTION OF CLASSIC MUTANTS	1980	CHERRY RED	UK	ARED 5
MORGAN FISHER	K	(AB	(B) CLAWS	1980	CHERRY RED	UK	BRED 11
MAGGIE NICHOLS	V	(B					
JOEL CUTRARA	V	(B	IAIN MONEY	V	(A	CHRIS ROSS	V	(B	VALERIE ROSS	V (B

HYDRA

WAYNE BRUCE	V K	(AB	(A) HYDRA	1974	CAPRICORN US 0130	UK 2429120
SPENCER KIRKPATRICK G	(AB		(B) LAND OF MONEY	1975	CAPRICORN US 0157	UK 2429130
ORVILLE DAVIS	B	(AB	(C) ROCK THE WORLD	1977	CAPRICORN US 6096	
STEVE PACE	D	(AB				
DAN TURBEVILLE	K	(A	RANDALL BRAMBLETT SAX (A	WILL BOULWARE	K (B	EARL FORD	TROM(A
JOHNNY SANDLIN	PERC (B	OSCAR JACKSON SAX (A	TODD LOGAN	TPT (A	CHUCK LEAVELL	K (B
BILL STEWART	PERC (A					

HYDRAVION

PHILIPPE BESOMBES	K G V(A	(A) HYDRAVION	1978	SONET UK SNTF766 GER DECCA 69068
PIERRE BATTAILLET	D	(A			
DOMINIQUE ESNAULT	D	(A	PATRICK VERBEKE	G	(A	COOKY RHINOSCEROS	G	(A	CHRIS SAINT ROCK B	(A
CHRISTIAN WERBROUCK EFFECT(A					

PHYLLIS HYMAN

PHYLLIS HYMAN		(ALL	(A) PHYLLIS HYMAN	1977	BUDDAH US 5681	BDLP 4046
			(B) SING A SONG	1979	BUDDAH	BDLP 4058
			(C) SOMEWHERE	1979	ARISTA US 4202	
			(D) YOU KNOW HOW TO LOVE ME	1980	ARISTA US 9509 UK	1114
			(E) CANT WE FALL IN LOVE	1981	ARISTA	UK SPART 1154

HYPSTRZ

ERNEST BATSON	G	(A	(A) HYPSTRIZATION	1980 LINE GERM 5093 US VOXX	200003
RANDY WIESS	B	(A			
BILL BATSON	V	(A	JOHN HAGA	D	(A

I DON'T CARE

GARY BOGGESS	K SYN(A	(A) ASK ANYONE	1976	BUDDAH	KSBS 2617
FRANK PELLINE	G K V(A				
PETER KNAPP	HRNS V(A	JOSE ORTIZ	D V	(A	TIM GRAZIANO	B	(A	PAUL McDONALD	WIND(A
FRANK BONZIE	V	(A	DOUG THOMAS	V	(A			

```
I ROY REED        (ALL        (A) PRESENTING I ROY          19   TROJAN                  TRLS 63
ROBBIE SHAKESPEARE  B  (I      (B) HELL & SORROW             19   TROJAN                  TRLS 71
LEROY WALLACE     D  (I        (C) I ROY                     1974 TROJAN                  TRLS 91
EARL LINDO        K  (I        (D) VERSIONS GALORE           19   TROJAN                  TBL 161
EARL SMITH        G  (I        (E) DREAD BALDHEAD            1976 KLIK                    KLP  9020
CARLTON DAVIS     D  (I        (F) CRISUS TIME               1976 CAROLINE      UK        CA   2011
SCIENTIST         PERC (I      (G) CANT CONQUER RASTA        1977 JUSTICE                 JUSTLP 008
SCULLY            PERC (I      (H) MUSICAL SHARK ATTACK      1977 VIRGIN        UK        V  2075
PABLO BLACK       SYN (I       (I) HEART OF A LION           1978 FRONT LINE    UK        FL 1001
                               (J) TEN COMMANDMENTS          1978 FRONT LINE    UK        FL 1028
                               (K) DREADLOCKS IN JAMAICA     1978 LOVE & LIVE             05
                               (L) GODFATHER                 1978 THIRD WORLD             930
                               (M) THE GENERAL      (DBL)    1978 FRONT LINE    UK        FLD6002
                               (N) WORLD ON FIRE             1978 FRONT LINE    UK        FL 1033
                               (O) CANCER                    1979 FRONT LINE    UK        4001
                               (P) WHAP'N BAP'N              1980 VIRGIN        UK        2164
                               (Q) MANY MOODS                1981 TROJAN        UK        TRLS91
```

```
JANIS IAN       G V (ALL    (A) JANIS IAN                1967 VERVE FORECAST      US FTS3017
AL ROGERS       D   (D      (A) JANIS IAN                1976 POLYDOR            PD 6058
WILL LEE        B   (A      (A) JANIS IAN                1967 POLYDOR    GER 2391 202 RI   9506
JEFF MIRANOV    G   (A      (A) JANIS IAN                1982 VERVE           UK RI 2482  572
B BUSHNELL      B   (D      (B) FOR ALL THE SEASONS      1968 VERVE              US FTS3024
DICK HYMAN      ORG (D      (C) SECRET LIFE OF EDDIE FINK 1968 VERVE             US FTS3048
HUGH McCRACKEN  G   (D      (D) WHO REALLY CARES         1969 VERVE   MGS 1850   US FTS3063
MARVIN STAMM    VLN (D      (E) PRESENT COMPANY          1971 CAPITOL     SM683     VMP 1014
STU SCHARF      G   (D      (F) STARS                    1974 CBS      US 32857   UK   80224
STEVE GADD      D   (AM     (F) STARS                    1981 CBS              UK RI   32049
RALPH CASALE    G   (D      (G) BETWEEN THE LINES        1975 CBS      US 33394   UK   80635
TONY STUD       TROM (DA    (H) AFTERTONES               1975 CBS      US 33919   UK   69220
WAYNE ANDRE     TROM (A     (H) AFTERTONES               1981 CBS              UK RI   32018
BERNIE GLOW     TPT (D      (J) MIRACLE ROW              1977 CBS      US 34440   UK   81879
RAY ALONGE      HRNS (D     (K) JANIS IAN                1978 CBS      US 35325   UK   82700
GEORGE YOUNG    SAX (A      (L) JANIS IAN        (COMP)  1978 CBS          JAP   26AP  1327
BRAD SPINNEY    PERC (D     (M) NIGHT RAINS              1979 CBS      US 36139   UK   83802
GENE ORLOFF     VLN (DA     (N) BEST OF                  1980 CBS              UK   84711
HAROLD COLETTA  VIOLA(DA    (O) MY FAVOURITES            1980 CBS          NL         84188
GEORGE RICCI    CELLO(DFG   (P) RESTLESS EYES            1981 CBS      US 37360   UK   85040
CLAIRE BAY      V   (HJA
PHIL BODNER     WIND (FGH   GONZALO FERNANDEZ   (H   RON FRANGIPANE    STR(K  GLORIA AGOSTINI  HARP    (M
LARRY HARLOW    K   (H      ODETTA              (H   JEFF LAYTON     G  (HJ  AL GORGONI       G(AGH
BUCKY PIZZARELLI G  (H      STU WOODS       B   (HJ  RICHARD DAVIS   B  (AFGH BARRY LAZAROWITZ PERC(FGHJ
JOE FARRELL     SAX (D      ROMEO PENQUE    SAX (DFH  MANNY GREEN     VLN (D   JOE MALIN        VLN (D
AARON ROSAND    VLN (D      JULES SCHACTER  VLN (D    ARTIE BUTLER    K  (A    VINNIE BELL      G  (A
SAL DE TROIA    G   (AGM    JOE MARK        B   (A    ARTIE KAPLAN    FLT (A   KEN KOSEK        FDL (G
RUSSELL GEORGE  B   (G      BUDDY SALZMAN   D   (A    ALAN RAPH       TROM (G  JESSE LEVY       STRINGS(H
PHOEBE SNOW     V   (H      RAY BECKENSTEIN WIND (F   JOE SHEPLEY     HRNS (F  DON PAYNE        B  (G
BURT COLLINS    TPT (H      RUBENS BASSINI  CONGA(J   PHIL KRAUS      PERC (J  CLARENCE CLEMONS SAX(M
MIKE MAINIERI   VIBES(M     RICHARD CROOKS  D   (M    JIM MAELEN      PERC (MA JOHN CROWDER     B V (M
RON GETMAN      G   (M      STEVE LOVE      G   (M    GARY HERBIG     SAX (M   CHICK COREA      PNO (M
LES HURDLE      B   (M      STEVE MADAIO    TPT (M    KEITH FORSEY    D  (M    HAROLD FACTERMEYER K(M
STEPHANIE SPRUILL V (M      LISA ROBERTS    V   (M    FRANK OWENS     K  (M    BOB KULICK       G  (M
SCOTT ZITO      G   (M      MATS BJOERKLUND G   (M    GORDON GRODY    V  (M    FRANK FLOYD      V  (M
ALLAN SCHWARZBERG D (M      NEIL JASON      B   (M    JOE D'ELIA         (M    JOCELYN BROWN    V  (M
LANI GROVES     V   (M      DINO SOLERA     SAX (M
```

```
IAN TYSON       G V (ALL)   (A) IAN & SYLVIA             1962 VANGUARD US 79215   + VSD 2113
SYLVIA TYSON AUTOHARP V(ALL (B) FOUR STRONG WINDS        1964 VANGUARD             VSD  2149
MONTE DUNN      G   (D      (C) NORTHERN JOURNEY         1964 VANGUARD             VSD 79154
RUSS SAVAKUS    B   (D      (D) EARLY MORNING RAIN       1965 VANGUARD US 79175 FONTANA TF6053
AMOS GARRETT    G   (R      (E) PLAY ONE MORE            1966 VANGUARD             VSD 79215
BUDDY CAGE      STEEL(R     (F) SO MUCH DREAMING         1967 VANGUARD             VSD 79241
N D SMART       D   (R      (G) NASHVILLE                1968 VANGUARD             VSD 79284
KEN KALMUSKY    B   (R      (H) FULL CIRCLE              1968 MGM                       4550
DAVID BRIGGS    PNO (R      (I) BEST OF                  1968 VANGUARD UK SVRL19004 VSD 79269
                            (J) IAN & SYLVIA (GREATEST HITS) 19 VANGUARD           VSD 5/6
                            (K) BEST OF                  19   CBS      US 32516   UK  64634
                            (L) LOVIN' SOUND             19   POLYDOR 2353 063 US MGM  4388
                            ( ) OL'OEN(SOLO IAN)         19   A&M                  SP  9017
                            ( ) WOMANS WORLD (SOLO SYLVIA) 19 CAPITOL             ST 11434
                            ( ) ONE JUMP AHEAD OF THE DEVIL(IAN) 1979 BOOT   CAN BOS 7189
                            ( ) YOU WERE ON MY MIND      19   CBS          US        31337
                            ( ) GREATEST HITS            19   VANGUARD             23/4
                            ( ) IAN & SYLVIA             1971 CBS          US        30736
                            (R) GREAT SPECKLED BIRD      19   AMPEX        US        10103
```

```
JIMMY IBBOTSON  G V (A      (A) NITTY GRITTY IBBOTSON    1977 FIRST AMERICAN   US   7718
LARRY THOMPSON  D   (A
STEVE SYKES     G   (A      JOHN MACY      STEEL(A  PAUL VASTOLA   SYN (A  RAY BONNEVILLE   HCA   (A
STAN ROGERS     HRNS (A     RENE ULIBARRI  V   (A   MIKE MARTIN    V  (A   HILLIARD WILSON  B    (A
DIK DARNELL     PNO (A      ALBERT CAMPBELL K  (A   GERARD McMAHON K  (A   PHILIP McLOURD   SAX (A
PAM ADDINGTON GRAZIER V(A   PAM MARTIN     V   (A
```

```
JOHN CARTER     (          (A) ICE                      1974 PASSPORT      US        10075
STEVE TURNER    B   (      (B) IMPORT/EXPORT             1975 PASSPORT      US        10096
GLYN JAMES      (
LYNTON NAIFF    K   (      GRANT SERPELL   D   (
```

```
                            (A) PLANET MARS DUB          1978 FRONT LINE    UK        FL 1010
```

ICEHOUSE

```
IVA DAVIES          G V  (A         (A) ICE HOUSE              1981 CHRYSALIS  GER 203 845 UK   1350
KEITH WELSH         B V  (A
GEOFF OAKES         SAX  (A    JOHN LLOYD   D V  (A      ANTHONY SMITH   K V  (A   IAN MOSS    G    (A
MICHAEL HOSTE       K    (A
```

IDEAL

```
F J KRUGER          G V  (A         (A) IDEAL                 1980  IC            GERM       80004
ANNETTE             K V  (A
ULI DENKER          B V  (A    HANS BEHRENDT        D V  (A
```

IDES OF MARCH

```
JOHN LARSON         TPT  (A         (A) VEHICLE              1970  WB            US   WS1863
RAY HERR            G B V(A         (B) COMMON BOND          1971  WB            US   WS1896
JAMES PETERIK       G V  (ABCD      (C) WORLD WOVEN          1972  RCA           US   LSP  4812
LARRY MILLAS G B FLT V (ABCD        (D) MIDNIGHT OIL         1973  RCA           US   APLI 0143
MIKE BORCH          D VIBES (ABCD
BOB BERGLAND        B V  (ABCD  CHUCK SOUMAR PERC HCA V(ABCD  DAVE ARELLANO    K (D  RUSTY YOUNG STEEL/DOB(D
```

IDLE RACE

```
JEFF LYNE           G V  (1AB       (A) BIRTHDAY PARTY       1968 LIBERTY US 7603    UK LBS 83132
GREG MASTERS        B    (1ABC      (A) BIRTHDAY PARTY       1976 SUNSET           UK SLS 50381
DAVE WALKER         (C             (B) IDLE RACE            1969 LIBERTY          UK LBS 83221
BOB WILSON          (                (C) TIME IS             1971 REGAL ZONOPHONE    SLRZ  1017
BOB LAMB            (                (D) IMPOSTERS OF LIFE MAGAZINE 1974 DAFFODIL    CAN   10046
RITCHIE WALKER      (                (E) ON WITH THE SHOW    1973 SUNSET           UK SLS 50354
DAVE PRITCHARD      G    (1ABC          (1) 1967
MIKE HOPKINS        (C
ROGER SPENCER       D    (1ABC
```

BILLY IDOL

```
BILLY IDOL          V    (A         (A) BILLY IDOL           1982 CHRYSALIS    UK       CHr1377
```

IF

```
TERRY SMITH         G    (ABCDI     (A) IF                   1970 CAPITOL US 539   UK ISLAND ILPS 9129
DICK MORRISSEY      SAX  (ALL       (B) IF2                  1970 CAPITOL US 676   UK ISLAND ILPS 9137
JOHN MEALING        K    (ABCDI     (C) IF3                  1971 CAPITOL US 820   UK U A    UAG 29158
JIM RICHARDSON      B    (ABCDI     (D) IF4                  1972                  UK U A    UAG 29315
DENNIS ELLIOTT      F    (ABCDI     (E) NOT JUST A BUNCH OF PRETTY.. 1974 CAPITOL US 11299 UK GULL GULP 1004
J W HODGKINSON      (ABCDI     (F) TEA BREAK IS OVER    1975 CAPITOL US 11344 UK GULL GULP 1007
DAVE QUINCY         SAX  (ABCDI     (G) THIS IS IF          1973 BRAIN              201  005
DAVE GREENSLADE     K    (          (H) GOLDROCK            1974 BRAIN              201  103
DAVE WINTOUR        B    (I         (I) WATERFALL           1971 METROMEDIA    IMP       1057
CLIFF DAVIS V D SYN (EHIFJ     (J) DOUBLE DIAMOND      1973 METROMEDIA              1 0174
WALT MONAGHAN       V B  (EHIF
FI TRENCH           K    (J    KURT PALOMAKI     PERC (J    PETE ARNESEN    K   (J   GEOFF WHITEHORN  G   (EHIF
GABRIEL MAGNO       K    (EFHI STEVE ROSENTHAL  G V  (J    CARLOS MARTINEZ  PERC (F
```

IGGINBOTTOM'S WRENCH

```
ALLAN HOLDSWORTH  G V  (A          (A) IGGINBOTTOM'S WRENCH   1969   DERAM        UK       SML1051
DAVE FREEMAN        D    (A
STEVE ROBINSON    G V  (A    MICK SKELLY         B    (A
```

IGGY POP & THE STOOGES

```
IGGY POP            V    (ALL       (A) THE STOOGES         1969 ELEKTRA US EKS74051 UK  K 42032
SCOTT THURSTON B V G K(EGHJ     (B) FUN HOUSE           1970 ELEKTRA            UK  K 42055
SCOTT ASHETON       D    (ACEBL     (C) RAW POWER           1973 CBS    US  32111 UK    65586
FRED SONIC SMITH    G    (          (C) RAW POWER           1977 EMBASSY            UK    31464
TONY SALES          B    (FGH       (D) IDIOT               1976 RCA                   PL12275
RICKY GARDINER      G    (FH        (E) METALLIC K O        1976 SKYDOG            US   IMP1015
GARY RASMUSSEN      B    (          (F) LUST FOR LIFE       1977 RCA                   PL12488
HUNT SALES          D    (FGH       (G) KILL CITY           1978 BOMP US 4001 RADAR UK K56467+RAD2
DAVID BOWIE         PNO V(FH        (H) T V EYE             1978 RCA                   PL12796
STACEY HAYDEN       G    (H         (J) NEW VALUES          1979 ARISTA US 4237    UK APART1092
ROBERT DUPREE       G    (M         (J) NEW VALUES          1979 ARISTA            GER 62 699
DAVE ALEXANDER      B    (AB        (K) SOLDIER             1980 ARISTA US 4259    UK SPART1117
STEVE TRANIO        B    (G         (L) NO FUN   (COMP)     1980 ELEKTRA US EF 7095 UK  K 52234
JAMES WILLIAMSON  G V  (CEGJ     (M) PARTY               1981 ARISTA GER 203 806 UK SPART1158
RON ASHETON       V B G(ACE       (N) ZOMBIE BIRDHOUSE    1982 ANIMAL            UK   CHR1399
CARLOS ALOMAR     G V  (F          (EP) JESUS LOVES THE STOOGIES 1977 LINE      GER       3006
GAYNIA              V    (G
BRIAN GLASCOCK      D    (G
JOHN HARDEN         SAX  (GJ    DAVE BROCK    STRINGS (J   GLEN MATLOCK   G V(K  IVAN KRAL     K G  (KM
STEVE NEW           (K    BARRY ANDREWS        (K   EARL SHAKELFORD  V  (J  ALFONO SISTERS  V   (J
KLAUS KRUGER        D    (JK   JACKIE CLARK    B    (J   DOUGLAS BROWNE   D (M  MICHAEL PAGE   B    (M
```

IGUANA

```
BRUCE ROBERTS     G V  (A          (A) IGUANA              1974 POLYDOR UK 2383 108 US LION 1011
PETE HUNT           D    (A
JOHN CARTWRIGHT     B    (A    RON TAYLOR         SAX (A    CHRIS GOWER   TROM (A   DON SHINN     PNO (A
```

IHRE KINDER

```
SONNY HENNIG        V G K(ALL       (A) IHRE KINDER          1969 PHILIPS        GER 844393
WALTI SCHNEIDER     G V B(ABF       (B) LEERE HANDE          1970 KUCKUCK        GER 237 5001
JUDITH BRIGGER      V PERC(A        (C) 2375004              1970 KUCKUCK        GER 237 5004
OLDHAM FRENZEL      D    (ABCDE      (D) WERDOHL              1971 KUCKUCK        GER 237 5013
MUCK GROL           G    (ABE        (E) POP HISTORY VOL 24   19   POLYDOR        GER 2634 018
GEORGIE MEYER       V FLT(ABCDE      (F) ANFANG OHNE ENDE     1972 KUCKUCK        GER 237 5016
ERNST SCHULTZ       V FLT(BCDE
TOMMI ROEDER      B SAX(CDE WOLF STUMM       G    (F   GUNTHER STORCH   D  (F
```

IJAHMAN

```
IJAHMAN             V G(AB          (A) HAILE I HYMN         1978   ISLAND              ILPS 9521
JONI                G    (A         (B) ARE WE A WARRIOR     1979   ISLAND              ILPS 9557
BO PEE              G    (A
WILLIE LINDO        G    (A    EARL SMITH    G    (A   DEL RICHARDSON   G   (A   GEOFFREY CHUNG  K G (A
STEVE WINWOOD       K    (A    EARL LINDO    K    (A   ERROL NELSON     PNO (A   ROBERT LYN PNO     (A
OSSIE HIBBERT       PNO  (A    VAL DOUGLAS   B    (A   ROBBIE SHAKESPEARE B (A   LLOYD PARKS    B   (A
MICKY RICHARDS      D    (A    SLY DUNBAR    D    (A   BOBBY ELLIS      TPT (A   HERMAN MARQUIS SAX (A
RICHARD HALL        SAX  (A    EDDIE BLAIR   HRN  (A   ADRIAN BRETT     WIND (A  ALAN BEEVER FLT   (A
HI HO SILVER        PERC (A    SONS OF NEGUS PERC (A   GROCO            PERC (A
```

ILLINOIS SPEED PRESS

PAUL COTTON	G V	(AB	(A) ILLINOIS SPEED PRESS	1969	CBS	US 9792	UK	63691
FRED PAGE	D	(A	(B) DUO	1970	CBS	US 9976		
MICHAEL ANTHONY	K	(A						
KAL DAVID	G V	(AB ROB LEWINE	B (A					

ILLUSION (US)

MIKE RICCIARDELLA	D	(ALL	(A) ILLLUSION	1969	STEED US 37033	UK SLPD531
RICHIE CERNIGLIA	G	(ALL	(B) TOGETHER	19	STEED	US 37005
CHUCK ADLER	B	(ALL	(C) IF IT'S SO	19	STEED	US 37006
MIKE MANISCALCO	G K	(ALL				
JOHN VINCI	V	(ALL				

ILLUSION

JANE RELF	V	(AB	(A) OUT OF THE MIST	1977	ISLAND ILPS9489	GER	28663
JIM McCARTY	G V	(AB	(B) ILLUSION	1978	ISLAND		ILPS 9519
JOHN HAWKEN	K	(AB					
EDDIE McNEIL	D	(AB LOUIS CENNAMO	B (AB JOHN KNIGHTSBRIDGE G (A	PAUL SAMWELL SMITH	V(B		

ILLUSTRATION

BILL LEDSTER	V	(A	(A) ILLUSTRATION	1970	PYE INTERNATIONAL	NSPL28140
JOHN RANGER	K	(A	(A) ILLUSTRATION	1970	JANUS	US 3010
BENOIT HARINEN	TPT	(A				
GARY BEATTIE	G	(A NORMAN BURGESS	SAX (A ROGER HOMEFIELD	TPT (A RICHARD TERRY	B (A	
DONALD SANDERS	SAX	(A CLAUDE RAY	D (A			

IMAN CALIFATO INDEPENDIENTE

KIKO GUERRERO	D	(A	(A) CAMUNO DEL AGIULA	19	CBS	SPAIN S84277
MARCOS MANTERO	K	(A				
MANUEL RODRIGUES	G V	(A URBANO MORALES	B (A			

IMPALAS

JOE FRAZIER	V	(	(A) SORRY(I RAN ALL THE WAY HOME)	19	CUB	US 8003
TONY CARLUCCI	V	(				
LENNY RENDA	V	(RICHIE WAGNER	V (A			

ILMO SMOKEHOUSE

KEITH RAND	G	(A	(A) ILMO SMOKEHOUSE	19
FREDDIE TIEKEN	SAX V	(A		
GERRY GABEL	K FLT V	(A DENNIS TIEKEN	D V (A	

IMPERIALS

TIME TO GET IT TOGETHER	1974	KEY		KL 012
FOLLOW MAN WITH MUSIC	1974	KEY		KL 025
THE IMPERIALS NOW	19	IMPACT	US	HWS1990
WHO'S GONNA LOVE ME	1978	POWER EXCHANGE		PXL 029
HEED TO CALL	1979	DAYSPRING		4003
SAIL ON	1978	DAYSPRING	UK	DAY4001
PRIORITY	1981	DAYSPRING		4005
ONE MORE SONG	1982	DAYSPRING		4004

IMPROVED SOUND LIMITED

JOHNNY FICKERT	V SAX	(B	(A) IMPROVED SOUND LIMITED	1971		
AXEL LINSTADT	G V K	(B	(B) CATCH A SINGING BIRD	1973	CBS	65619
ULI RUPPERT	B	(B				
ROLF GROSCHNER	D	(B FRANK BAUM	STEEL (B RALF NOWY	SAX (B		

IMPRESSIONS

JERRY BUTLER	V	THE IMPRESSIONS	1963	ABC	US	450		
CURTIS MAYFIELD	V	NEVER ENDING IMPRESSIONS	1963	ABC	US	468	HMV	UK CLP 1743
SAMUEL GOODEN	V	KEEP ON PUSHING	1964	ABC	US	493		
FRED CASH	V	PEOPLE GET READY	1965	ABC	US	505		
LEROY HUGHES	V	GREATEST HITS	1965	ABC	US	515		
REG TORAIN	V	ONE BY ONE	1965	ABC	US	523		
RALPH JOHNSON	V	BIG 16	1965	HMV	UK	(M) CLP 1935		(S)CSD1642
		RIDIN' HIGH	1966	ABC	US	545	UK HMV	CSD3548
		FABULOUS IMPRESSIONS	1967	ABC	US	606	UK HMV	CSD3631
		WE'RE ON A WINNER	1968	ABC	US	635	UK STATESIDE	10239
		THIS IS MY COUNTRY	1968	CURTOM	US	8001		
		YOUNG MOD'S FORGOTTEN STORY	1969	CURTOM	US	8003	UK POLYDOR	2359 003
		BEST IMPRESSIONS	196	CURTOM	US	8004		
		BIG 16 VOL 2	1969				UK STATESIDE	10279
		AMEN	196				UK POLYDOR	2359 009
		BEST OF	19	ABC	US	654		
		VERSATILE	19	ABC	US	668		
		CHECK OUT YOUR MIND	197	CURTOM	US	8006	UK POLYDOR	2318 017
		TIMES HAVE CHANGED	1972	CURTOM	US	8012	UK POLYDOR	2310 059
		16 GREATEST HITS	197	ABC	US	727		
		EARLY YEARS	1973				UK PROBE	GTSP 201
		PREACHER MAN	1973	CURTOM	US	8016		
		FINALLY GOT MYSELF TOGETHER	1974	CURTOM	US	8019	UK BUDDAH	4003
		FIRST IMPRESSIONS	1975	CURTOM	US	0103	UK	K 56143
		FIRST IMPRESSIONS	1979	RSO			RI	RSS 009
		BIG 16 RI	1975	ABC			UK	ABCL5104
		SOONER OR LATER	1975	CURTOM	US	5003		
		FOR YOUR PRECIOUS LOVE	1976	VEE JAY	US1075		UK DJM	DJB26086
		FOR YOUR PRECIOUS LOVE	197	JOY				JOYS104
		IT'S ABOUT TIME	1976	COTILLION	US 9912			
		ORIGINALS (DBL)	1976	ABC	US	303		
		LOVING POWER	1976	CURTOM	US	5009	UK	K 56211
		VINTAGE YEARS	197	SIRE	US	3717		
		THREE THE HARD WAY	197	CURTOM	US	8602		
		COLLECTION	197	ABC	US	30009		
		COME TO MY PARTY	197	20TH CENTURY	596			
		FANS THE FIRE	1981	20TH CENTURY	624			
		LOVING POWER	19	RSO	US	RSS 10		

IN TRANSIT

(A) IN TRANSIT	1980	RCA	US	3607

INCREDIBLE BONGO BAND

```
                                (A) BONGO ROCK              1973 PRIDE US 028  UK DJM 76  20452
                                (B) RETURN OF               1974 PRIDE US 6010
```

INCREDIBLE HOG

```
KEN GORDON      G HCA V(A      (A) VOLUME ONE             1973   ?          ?
JIM HOLMES      B V  (A
TONY AWIN       D    (A
```

INCREDIBLE STRING BAND

```
ROBIN WILLIAMSON G V K VLN+(ALL  (A) INCREDIBLE STRING BAND  1966 ELEKTRA              EKS 7322
MIKE HERON K G V B HCA FLT+(ALL  (B) THE 5000 SPIRITS         1967 ELEKTRA EKS 74010+RI K 42001
CLIVE PALMER   V G BANJO   (A    (C) HANGMANS BEAUTIFUL DAUGHTER 1968 ELEKTRA EKS 74021+RI K 42002
ROSE SIMPSON     B PERC(CDEGJFH   (D) THE BIG HUGE          1968 ELEKTRA EKS 74037+RI K 42022
LICORICE McKECHNIE VLN K(BCDGFHJK (E) WEE TAM               1968 ELEKTRA EKS 74036+RI K 42021
MALCOLM LeMAISTRE V K B+(KLMN    (F) CHANGING HORSES        1969 ELEKTRA EKS 74057+RI K 42037
GERALD DOTT     CLAR K (LM       (G) I LOOKED UP            1970 ELEKTRA EKS 74061+RI K 42046
GREG HEAT        SITAR(H         (G) I LOOKED UP            1970 ELEKTRA UK 2460 002
JOHN GILSTON    D    (           (H) 'U'                    1970 ELEKTRA EKS 7E2003    K62002
STAN LEE    B V STEEL (KMN       (I) RELICS OF I S B        1970 ELEKTRA     K62008+   K 42060
WALTER GRUNDY    HCA  (K         (I) RELICS OF I S B        1970 ELEKTRA     US7E2004
GRAHAM FORBES    G   (N          (J) BE GLAD FOR THE SONG   1970 ISLAND              ILPS 9140
MIKE TOMICH          (           (K) LIQUID ACROBAT         1971 ISLAND GER 85749 UK ILPS 9172
DAVID BARKER         (           (K) LIQUID ACROBAT         1971 ELEKTRA US 74112
IVAN PAWLER     K    (F          (L) EARTH SPAN             1972 ISLAND          UK   ILPS 9211
JACK INGRAM     V D  (MN         (M) NO RUINOUS FEUD        1973 ISLAND          UK   ILPS 9229
JANET SHANKMAN  V    (H          (M) NO RUINOUS FEUD        1973 REPRISE         US   2139
DANNY THOMPSON  B·   (BN         (N) HARD ROPE & SILKEN TWINE 1974 ISLAND        UK   ILPS 9270
JOHN GIMBRI     FLT  (G          (N) HARD ROPE & SILKEN TWINE 1974 REPRISE       US   2198
JOHN HOPKINS    PNO  (B          (O) SEASONS THEY CHANGE    1976 ISLAND          UK   ISLD  9
SUSIE WATSON TAYLOR FLT(M
B J WILSON      D    (M   STAN SCHNIER    B V (M   ALUN EDEN      D  (M   JANET WILLIAMSON FLT (M
SOMA   SITAR TAMBOURA (B' GERRY CONWAY    D   (K   JOE BOYD       PROD (B  DAVE MATTACKS   D  (G
PETER GRANT     BAN  (H
```

INCREDIBLES

```
                                (A) HEART & SOUL           1974 CONTEMPO           CLP  512
                                (A) HEART & SOUL           19   AUDIO ARTS         AAS 7000
```

INDIAN SUMMER

```
BOB JACKSON     K V   (A         (A) INDIAN SUMMER          1971 NEON             NE  3
COLIN WILLIAMS  G V   (A
PAUL HOOPER D PERC V  (A   MALCOLM HARKER B VIBES V   (A
```

INDUSTRIALS

```
DANNY STAG     V G K B (A        (A) INDUSTRIALS            1980 EPIC         UK    84399
J B FRANK      V G K D (A
JAN MACKENZIE   V     (A   MIKE BOLT     V G K(A  CALVIN TEARDROP  B  (A  CYCLOPS  D  (A
```

INFERNAL BLUES MACHINE

```
WARREN RAY      V     (A         (A) INFERNAL BLUES MACHINE  1976 LONDON US 666 UK  SHU 8496
GREG MIDDLETON  B     (A
MIKE CAVANAUGH  K     (A   GREGG PARKER    G   (A
```

INDIGO

```
                                (A) INDIGO                 1977 WB           US    2991
```

INFA RIOT

```
                                (A) STILL OUT OF ORDER     1982 SECRET       UK    SEC 7
```

INMATES

```
PETER GUNN      G V  (AB         (A) FIRST OFFENCE     1979 RADAR UK 25 GER 56743 US POLYDOR6241
BILL HURLEY     V    (AB         (B) SHOT IN THE DARK  1980 RADAR UK 28          US POLYDOR6302
BEN DONNELLY    B    (AB
TONY OLIVER     G V  (AB  LAURIE GARMAN   HCA (A   JOHN BULL   D  (A  EDDIE       D (A
JOHN EARLE      SAX  (A   DICK HANSON     TPT (A   RAY BEAVIS  SAX (A  GAVIN POVEY K (A
JIM RUSSELL     D V  (AB  VIC MAILE      PROD (AB
```

INNER CIRCLE

```
ROGER LEWIS     G    (           (A) ROCK THE BOAT          1974 TROJAN         TRLS  93
JACOB MILLER         (           (B) BLAME IT ON THE SUN     1975 TROJAN         TRLS  114
BERNARD 'TOUTER' HARVEY K(        (C) REGGAE THING           1976 CAPITOL        EST  11574
IAN LEWIS       B    (           (D) READY FOR THE WORLD     1977 CAPITOL        EST  11664
LESTER ADDERLEY G V  (           (E) KILLER DUB              1978 TOP RANKING        8364  182
CALVIN McKENZIE D    (           (F) EVERYTHING IS GREAT     1979 ISLAND         ILPS  9558
CHARLES FARQUHARSON K (           (G) NEW AGE MUSIC          1980 ISLAND         ILPS  9608
EVERALD 'BLACKSPY' JAHSON PERC(   (H) SOMETHING SO GOOD      1982 CARRERE         CAL  143
JOE ORTIZ            (
```

INNER CITY UNIT

```
NIK TURNER      V SAX(AB         (A) PASS OUT               1980 RIDDLE          RID   002
TREN THOMS      G V  (AB         (B) MAXIMUM EFFECT         1981 AVATAR          AALP 5004
DEAD FRED       V K  (AB         (C) PUNKADELIC             1982 FLICKKNIFE      SHARP 103
BAZ MAGNETO     B V  (A
MICK STUPP      D    (A   DINO FERARI  D   (B   CAPTAIN SENSIBLE  G  (B  BILL BOSTON HRN (B
MAX WALL        V    (B
```

INNER LIFE

```
                                (A) I'M CAUGHT             1980 PRELUDE      US    12175
```

INNER SOUND OF THE ID

```
                                (A) THE INNER SOUND OF THE ID 1967 RCA       US    LSP 3805
```

NEIL INNES

```
NEIL INNES  G V HCA K (ABCD      (A) LUCKY PLANET (WORLD)   1970 LIBERTY        LBG 83419
IAN WALLACE     D    (A          (B) HOW SWEET TO BE AN IDIOT 1973 U A          UAG 29492
ROGER McKEW     G    (A          (C) RUTLAND TIMES          1976 BBC            REB  233
ROGER ROWAN     B    (A          (D) TAKING OFF             1977 ARISTA         SPARTY1004
JOHN HALSEY     D    (CD         (E) INNES BOOK OF RECORDS  1979 POLYDOR       2383 556
TIMMI DONALD    D    (D          (F) NEIL INNES A GO GO     1980 LIBERTY    UK  LBR 1018
ROGER SWALLOW   D    (C
JON FIELD     CONGA(D  BRIAN HODGSON   B  (CD  ALAN JAMES   B  (D  BILLY BREMNER   G (CD
ROGER RETTIG  G STEEL(CD JOHN MEGGINSON K  (D  JULIAN SMEDLEY VLN V(D KEITH NELSON BANJO(D
WILLIE FAHEY  WIND (D  BRIAN BOWLES    V  (D  SUE JONES DAVIS V (D  GERRY CONWAY   D (B
```

```
        (CONTINUED)
```

NEIL INNES   (CONTINUED)

```
ANDY ROBERTS      G   (BC  MIKE KELLIE     D    (B   DAVE RICHARDS    B    (BC  OLLIE HALSALL    G   (B
ERIC IDLE         V   (C   DAVE BALLBY     V    (C   STUART ELLIOTT   D    (E   PETE VAN HOOK    D   (E
BRUCE LYNCH       B   (E   HARVEY WESTON   B    (E   BILLY LIVESY     K    (E   BRIAN HOLLOWAY   G   (E
RICHARD BRUNTON   G   (E   MITCH DALTON    G    (E   BRIAN LEMON      PNO  (E   JOHN MUMFORD     TROM(E
SHARON CAMPBELL   V   (E   YVONNE KEELEY   V    (E   ANNIE KAVANAGH   V    (E   PAUL TRAVIS      V   (E
KENNY DUKAYNE     V   (E   GARY TRAVERS    V    (E   HENRY LOWTHER    TPT  (E   DIGBY FAIRWEATHER TPT(E
MARTIN DROVER     TPT (E   DAVE SPENCE     TPT  (E   PAUL NIEMAN      TROM (E   PETE STRANGE     TROM  (E
BILL SKEAT        SAX (E   RANDY COLVILLE  SAX  (E   TOMMY WHITTLE    SAX  (E   KEITH GEMMELL    SAX (E
PAT KYLE          SAX (E
```

INSECT TRUST

```
LUKE FAUST   HCA G V   (AB         (A) INSECT TRUST             1968  CAPITOL     US   SKAO  109
TREVOR KOEHLER WIND D  (AB         (B) HOBOKEN SATURDAY NIGHT   1970  ATCO        US   SD  33313
ROBERT PALMER  WIND    (AB
NANCY JEFFRIES    V    (AB  BILL BARTH  G STEEL(AB  HUGH McCRACKEN   G    (AB  ELVIN JONES      D   (B
BERNARD PURDIE    D    (AB  BUDDY SOUTHMAN   D   (A  CHARLES NEALY    D    (B   DONALD McDONALD  D (B
WILLIAM FOLWELL   B TPT(B   JOE MACHO        B   (B  BOB BUSHNELL     B    (B   CHARLIE MACEY    G B(B
WARREN GARDNER    TPT  (B   RALPH CASALE     G   (B
```

INSTRUCTIONS

```
OWEN SMITH        V    (A          (A) INSTRUCTIONS            1980  QUALITY     CAN        2067
MARTIN WALL       K    (A
PETER CROLLY      B    (A   REGAN MYERS     K    (A   ALAN WEBSTER     D    (A   DAVE BEATTY      V   (A
DOMENIC TROIANO   G    (A   LARRY           V    (A   JANET WILLIAMSON V    (A   KIMBERLEY JOHNSTON V  (A
```

INTERGALACTIC TOURING BAND

```
DAVID SCANCE      G    (A          (A) INTER GALACTIC TOURING BAND  1977  CHARISMA  UK  CDS  4009
BRIAN CUOMO       K    (A
STEVE BARTH       V    (A   ROD ARGENT      V    (A   PETER SABEL      B    (A   LARRY FAST       K SYN(A
RYCHE CHLANDA     G    (A   PERCY JONES     B    (A   DAVE COUSINS     V    (A   JEFFREY LEYNOR   V   (A
JIM CUOMO         V    (A   MR SNIPS        V    (A   JOHN TROPEA      G    (A   MARGE RAYMOND    V   (A
PAUL MARCHETTI    PERC (A   FRANCIS ROSSI   V    (A   ANNIE HASLAM     V    (A   JOEL KRATZ       V   (A
ANTHONY PHILLIPS  G    (A   FRANK PRESCOD   B    (A   DAVID BEDFORD         (A   MIGHTY JOE YOUNG     (A
FRANK D'AGOSTINO       (A   CLARENCE CLEMONS SAX (A   RICK PARFITT          (A   ARTHUR BROWN         (A
MEATLOAF          V    (A   BEN E KING      V    (A   WILL MALONE           (A
```

INTERNATIONAL SUBMARINE BAND

```
GRAM PARSONS      G V  (A          (A) SAFE AT HOME   1968  LHI US LHIS12001 SHILOH RI 4087
BOB BUCHANAN      G V  (A
IAN DUNLOP        B    (A   JOHN NUESE      G    (A   JON CORNEAL      D    (A   JAYDEE MANESS    STEEL (A
EARL BALL         PNO  (A
```

INTERVIEW

```
JEFF STARRS       V    (AB         (A) BIG OCEANS            1979  VIRGIN US 13131  UK        V2123
PETE ALLERHAND  G V K(AB           (B) SNAKES & LADDERS      1980  VIRGIN US 13141  UK        V2157
ALAN BRAIN      G V    (AB
MANNY ELIAS       D    (AB  PHIL CROWTHER   B    (A   MARLIS DUNKLAN   V    (B   PETE WINGFIELD   K   (B
```

INVISIBLE MANS BAND

```
                                   (A) INVISIBLE MANS BAND   1980  ISLAND      UK   ILPS 9537
```

INVADERS

```
SOO LUCAS         V    (A          (A) TEST CARD            1980  POLYDOR      UK   2383  589
```

IONA

```
MICHAEL STOREY  V K HCA(A          (A) CUCKOO              1978  SILVERSCALES     KOO 13913
JAMES LASCELLES  K V   (A
DAVE SHEEN       D V   (A   JOHN McKENZIE   B    (A   PETE KIRTLEY     G    (A   COLIN GIBSON     B   (A
DARRYL LEE QUE   PERC  (A   KUMA HARADA     B    (A   JOHN PORTER      G B  (A
```

DONNIE IRIS (& THE CRUISERS)

```
DONNIE IRIS      G V   (AB         (A) BACK ON THE STREETS  1980  MCA              US  3272
MARK AVSEC        K    (A          (B) KING COOL            1981  MCA
MARTY LEE         G    (A
ALBRITTON McLAIN  D    (A   KEVIN VALENTINE   B V (A   KENNY BLAKE           (A
```

IRON BUTTERFLY

```
RON BUSHY         D   (ABCDEFH   (A) HEAVY                1967  ATCO      US 33227 US 2465  015
MAXINE WILLARD    V   (F         (A) HEAVY                1973  ATLANTIC GER 20050
DOUG INGLE      K V   (ABCDEH    (B) IN A GADDA DA VIDA   1968  ATCO      US 33250 UK 588  116
JERRY PENROD         (          (B) IN A GADDA DA VIDA   196   ATCO      UK K40022 FR    WE341
DANNY WEIS           (          (C) BALL                 1969  ATLANTIC US 33280 UK 228  011
DARRYL DELOACH       (          (D) LIVE                 1970  ATLANTIC US 33318 UK 2400  014
DENIECE WILLIAMS  V   (F         (D) LIVE                 1970  ATLANTIC GER 20095 UK RI K40086
ERIC BRANN      G V   (BCFGHD    (E) METAMORPHOSIS        1970  ATLANTIC US 33339 UK 2401  003
MIKE PINERA       G   (E         (F) METAMORPHOSIS        1972  ATLANTIC         UK  K 40294
LARRY RHEINHART   G   (E         (F) SUN & STEEL          1975  MCA       US  2164 UK MCF 2738
PHIL KRAMER       B   (FG        (F) SUN & STEEL          1975  MCA       IMP 32869
HOWARD REITZES    K   (G         (G) SCORCHING BEAUTY     1975  MCA       US   465 UK MCF 2694
LEE DORMAN        B   (BCDEH     ( ) EVOLUTION (BEST OF)  1970  ATLANTIC US 33369 UK  K 40298
BILL DEMARTINES K V   (F         ( ) STAR COLLECTION      1973  ATLANTIC  30038    +     20021
RICHARD PODOLOR G SITAR(E        (CE) BALL METAMORPHOSIS (DBL)  1975  ATLANTIC     UK  K 80003
BILL COOPER       G   (E
JEROME JUMMONVILLE HRNS(F   JULIA TILLMAN      V    (F
```

IRON CITY HOUSEROCKERS

```
JOE E GRUSHECKLY G V  (ABC        (A) LOVES SO TOUGH      1979  MCA          UK  MCF  3031
NED E RANKIN      D   (ABC        (B) HAVE A GOOD TIME    1980  MCA          US        5111
GIL SNYDER        K   (ABC        (C) BLOOD ON THE BRICKS 1981  MCA          US        5252
BILLY CROSS       G   (A
RICHARD REISING   V   (A   SUSAN LYNCH     V    (A   RODNEY PSYKA     V    (A   MARC REISMAN    HCA  (ABC
PAUL GLANZ       PNO  (A   ART NADINI      B    (ABC GARY SCALESE     G    (A   DENNY MARTIN    ACC  (A
TAMPA LANN        V   (A   EDDIE BRITT   G V    (BC  TOMMY MANDEL     K    (B   MICK RONSON    K MAND(B
JOEY MISCULIN    ACC  (B   IAN HUNTER  G V K    (B   ROY MARTIN       V    (B   ELLEN FOLEY      V   (B
STEVE CROPPER     G   (C   JIM HORN        SAX  (C   STEVE FORMAN     PERC (C   STEVE MADIAO    TPT (C
```

IRON MAIDEN

PAUL DI'ANNO	V	(ABCD	(A) IRON MAIDEN	1980 EMI UK EMC3330 US HARVEST	12094
DAVE MURRAY	G	(ABCD	(B) KILLERS	1981 EMI UK EMC3357 US HARVEST	12141
ADRIAN SMITH	G	(BCD	(C) SOUNDHOUSE TAPES	1979 ROCKHARD ROK1	
STEVE HARRIS	B V	(ABCD	(D) MAIDEN IN JAPAN	1981	
DENNIS STRATTON	G V	(AC	(E) NUMBER OF THE BEATS	1982 EMI UK EMC3400	
CLIVE BURR	D	(ABD			
BRUCE DICKINSON	V	(E			

IRONHORSE

RANDY BACHMAN	G SYN V	(AB	(A) IRONHORSE 1979	SCOTTI BROS US 7103 UK K 50598	
TOM SPARKS	G V	(AB	(B) EVERYTHING IS GREY	1980 SCOTTI BROS US 7108 UK K 50730	
JOHN PIERCE	B	(A			
MIKE BAIRD	D	(A	FRANK LUDWIG V K (B RON FOOS	B (B CHRIS LEIGHTON D (B	
MAVIS McCAULEY	V	(A	BARRY ALLEN V (A		

WELDON IRVINE

WELDON IRVINE	K SAX	V(A	(A) COSMIC VORTEX	1974 RCA US APLI0703	
NALO	V	(A			
BOB CRANSHAW	B	(A	WESLEY WATSON D (A HENRY GRATH	G (A NAPOLEON REVELS PERC (A	
BUD JOHNSON	CONGAS	(A	JIMMY OWENS TPT (A ROY ROMAN	TPT (A BILL BARNWELL FLT (A	
GENE JEFFERSON	SAX	(A	OJULEBA V (A GORDON EDWARDS	B (A JIM YOUNG D (A	
CORNELL DUPREE	G	(A	EVERETT HOLLINS TPT (A GEORGE MURRAY	B (A LENNY WHITE D (A	
JOE CARO	G	(A	CHIPPER LYLES D (A		

GREGORY ISAACS

GREGORY ISAACS	(ALL	( ) IN PERSON	1975	TROJAN RI 82	TRLS 102
SLY DUNBAR	(	( ) ALL I HAVE IS LOVE	1976	TROJAN	TRLS 121
ROBBIE SHAKESPEARE	(	( ) COOL RULER	1978	FRONT LINE UK	FL 1020
		( ) BEST OF	1978	CHANNEL	GO 30
RADICS	(	( ) LONELY LOVER	1980	PRE/CHARISMA	001
		( ) SOON FORWARD	1979	FRONT LINE UK	FL 1044
		( ) FOR EVERYONE	1980	SUCCESS	102
		( ) THE EARLY YEARS	1981	TROJAN UK	TRLS!)&
		( ) MORE GREGORY	1981	POE UK	PREX9
		( ) EXTRA CLASSICS	1981	ECHO	1003
		( ) ALL I HAVE IS LOVE	1982	TROJAN UK	TRLS121
		( ) NIGHT NURSE	1982	ISLAND UK	ILPS 9721

ISHMAEL

PETER 'ISHMAEL' SMALE	G V	(ALL	(A) CHARGE OF THE LIGHT BRIGADE	1980 KINGSWAY UK	335
DEREK MOON	K SYN	(B	(B) LAND OF HOPE & GLORIES	1981 KINGSWAY UK	340
NEIL COSTELLO	G	(B	(C) IF YOU CANT SHOUT'SAVED'	19 KINGSWAY UK	DOVE60
LES MOIR	B	(B			
TIM SMALE	B	(B	CHAS O'BRIAN D (B		

ISIS

CAROL MACDONALD	G V	(AB	(A) ISIS	1974 BUDDAH BDS5605 + BDLP 4002	
GINGER BIANCO	D	(AB	(B) AIN'T NO BACKIN' UP NOW	1975 BUDDAH BDS5626	
STELLA BASS	B	(AB			
LIBERTY MATA	PERC	(AB	JEANIE FINEBERG WIND (AB LOLLIE BIENENFIELD TROM V(A JUNE MILLINGTON G (B		
EDITH DANKOWITZ	WIND	V(B	ELLEN SEELING TPT (B RENATE FERRIER G (B LEWIS SOLOFF TPT(B		
MARGO LEWIS	K V	(B	LAUREN DRAPER HRNS (A SUZI GHEZZI G (A		

ISLEY BROTHERS

RUDOLPH ISLEY	V	(ALL	SHOUT	1959 RCA US LSP 2156	
RONALD ISLEY	V	(ALL	TWIST & SHOUT	1962 WAND US 653 UK DJM 76 2628	
KELLY ISLEY	V	(ALL	TWISTING & SHOUTING	196 UA US 6313 UK UA ULP 1064	
MARVIN ISLEY	B	(ABCDEFGH	TAKE SOME TIME OUT	1966 T NECK US 552 UK MARBLEARCH 894	
ERNIE ISLEY	G D	(ABCDEFGH	THIS OLD HEART OF MINE	1966 TAMLA US 269 UK STML 11034	
JIMI HENDRIX	G	(*	THIS OLD HEART OF MINE	1981 MOTOWN UK RI STMS 5026	
CHRIS JASPER	K	(ABCDEFGH	SOUL ON THE ROCKS	1966 TAMLA US 275	
			TAMLA MOTOWN PRESENTS	1967 TAMLA US 37080	
ROCKY DZIDZORNU	CONGA	(A	DOIN' THEIR THING	1969 TAMLA US 287 UK SUNSET 5257	
TRUMAN THOMAS	K	(A	IT'S OUR THING	1969 TNECK US 3001	
GEORGE MORELAND	D	(A	THE BROTHERS ISLEY	1969 TNECK US 3002 UK STATESIDE10300	
			LIVE AT YANKEE STADIUM	1970 TNECK US 3004	
			GET INTO SOMETHING	1970 TNECK US 3006	
			(*) IN THE BEGINNING	1970 TNECK US 3007	
			GIVING IT BACK	1971 TNECK US 3008	
			ROCK ON BROTHER	1971 RCA CAMDEN US 0126	
			BROTHER BROTHER BROTHER	1972 TNECK US 3009	
			LIVE	197 TNECK US 3010	
			GREATEST HITS	197 TNECK US 3011 UK STARLINE 5043	
			ROCK AROUND THE CLOCK	19 CAMDEN US ACLI0861	
			(A)THREE + THREE 1973	TNECK US 32453 UK EPIC 65740	
			BEST OF	19 BUDDAH US 2 5652	
			VERY BEST OF	19 UA US LA 500G	
			LIVE IT UP	1974 TNECK US 33070 UK EPIC 80317	
			(B)THE HEAT IS ON	1975 TNECK US 33536 UK EPIC 69139	
			(C)HARVEST FOR THE WORLD	1976 TNECK US 33809 UK EPIC 81268	
			SUPER HITS	1976 UK TAMLA STMA8024	
			(D) GO FOR YOUR GUNS	1977 TNECK US 34432 UK EPIC 86027	
			(E)FOREVER GOLD (COMP)	1977 TNECK US 34452 UK EPIC 86040	
			(F) SHOWDOWN	1978 TNECK US 34930 UK EPIC 86039	
			TIMELESS	1978 TNECK US 36650 UK EPIC 88327	
			(G) WINNER TAKES ALL	1979 TNECK US 36077 UK EPIC 88460	
			(H) GO ALL THE WAY	1980 TNECK US 36035 UK EPIC 65740	
			INSIDE YOU	1981 UK EPIC 85252	
			GRAND SLAM	1981 TNECK US 37080 UK EPIC 84914	
			SUPER HITS	1981 MOTOWN UK STMA 8024	
			THE REAL DEAL	1982 TNECK US UK EPIC 85790	
			SOUL SHOUT	19? PICKWICK CAN 3331	
			AND MARVIN & JOHNNY	19 CROWN US 643	

```
   GARY BOYLE        G    (ABCD    (A) ISOTOPE              1974 POLYDOR FR 2933 701 UK GULL 1002
   BRIAN MILLER      K    (A       (B) ILLUSION             1974 POLYDOR FR 2933 704 UK GULL 1006
                                   (B) ILLUSION             1974                  US GULL  402
   JEFF CLYNE        B    (A       (C) DEEP END             1976                  UK GULL 1017
   LAURENCE SCOTT    K    (BC      (D) BEST OF              1978                  UK GULL 1024
   HUGH HOPPER       B    (BC
   ZOE KRONBERGER    K V  (C    FRANK ROBERTS    K   (C  NIGEL MORRIS     D    (ABC AUREO DE SOUZA   D   (
   DAN K BROWN       B    (C    MORRIS PERT    PERC (C  NEVILLE WHITEHEAD B    (C
```

```
                                   (A) SAME SONG            1978 TOP RANKING IMP+HARVEST UK SHSP4099
```

```
   DAVID LAFLAMME F FLT VLN V(ALL   (A) ITS A BEAUTIFUL DAY  1968 CBS  US  9768    UK       63722
   DON WALDROP       HRNS (E        (A) ITS A BEAUTIFUL DAY  1980 CBS UK RI 83787
   LINDA LA FLAMME K (A             (A) ITS A BEAUTIFUL DAY  196  ALLIED PRODUCTION (PROMO)  364
   PATTI SANTOS      V PERC(ABCDE   (B) MARRYING MAIDEN      1970 CBS  US  1058    UK       64065
   GREG BLOCH     VLN MAND  (E      (B) MARRYING MAIDEN      1980 CBS  NL RI 83905 UK RI 82  32132
   BILL GREGORY      G    (CDE      (C) CHOICE QUALITY STUFF 1971 CBS  US 30734    UK       64314
   JERRY GARCIA      G BAN(B        (C) CHOICE QUALITY STUFF 1980 CBS  NL RI 83904
   TOM FOWLER        B    (CD       (D) LIVE AT CARNEGIE HALL 1972 CBS US 31338    UK       64929
   HAL WAGENET       G V  (ABC      (D) LIVE AT CARNEGIE HALL 1979 CBS NL RI 83907
   MITCHELL HOLMAN HCA V B(ABC      (E) TODAY               1973 CBS  US 32181    UK       65483
   RICHARD OLSEN     CLAR (B        (E) TODAY               1980 CBS  NL RI 83908
   ROLF STUART       FLT  (C        (F) 1001 NIGHTS         1974 CBS  US 32660    UK       65812
   BUD COCKRELL      B V  (E        (F) 1001 NIGHTS         1982 CBS  UK RI 32133
   JOSE AREAS        PERC (C
   FRED WEBB         K V  (BCDE VAL FUENTES   D V(ABCDE COKE ESCOVEDO    PERC (C  SID PAGE        VLN (BC
   BRUCE STEINBERG   HCA  (AC  VAN HUGHES    TROM(C    BILL ATWOOD      TPT  (C  ROBERT FERREIRA SAX (C
   CHARLES PETERSON  SAX  (C  GREGG ROLIE      K   (C
```

```
   PETER IVERS       V HCA   (A     (A) TERMINAL LOVE        1974 WB          US        2804
   ALICE DE BUHR     D    (A
   BUELL NEDLINGER   B    (A   PAUL LENART    G   (A  MARTY KRYSTALL   SAX  (A  KATHY APPLEBY   VLN (A
   BEN BENAY         G    (A   DAVID COHEN    G   (A  ELLIOT INGBER    G    (A  BILLY OSBORNE   PERC(A
   SHIRLEY MATTHEWS  V    (A   MARTI McCALL   V   (A  LISA ROBERTS     V    (A  ANDRA WILLIS    V   (A
   JACKIE WARD       V    (A   DEAN ROD       V   (A
```

```
   RON WOOD          G    (A       (A) MAYBE TOMORROW        1969 APPLE          SAPCOR  8
   PETE HAM          V G  (A
   TOM EVANS         B V  (A   MIKE GIBBONS   D   (A
```

```
   KENNY THOMURE          (A       (A) IVORY                 1968 TETRAGRAMMATON US  104
   MIKE McCAULEY          (A
   CHRIS CHRISTMAN   V    (A
```

```
                                   (A) LIFE IS A FIGHT      1976 MAGNET        MAG  5017
                                   (B) JUST ANOTHER LONELY NIGHT 1977 MAGNET   MAG  5018
                                   (C) MOVIN' CITY HIGH     1978 MAGNET        MAG  5023
                                   (EP)  NOTHING EVER COMES THAT EASY 1977 MAGNET MAG 901
```

```
                                   (A) FOOD FOR THOUGHT     1972 PEOPLE US 5601 POLYDOR UK 2391 034
                                   (B) DAMN RIGHT I AM SOMEBODY 1974 PEOPLE US 6602 POLYDOR UK 2391 125
```

```
   GARCIA MORALES    D V  (A       (A) J J BAND            1971 CBS           UK       64396
   FRANCIS WEYER     G V  (A
   GUY DELO          K TPT(A   RALPH BENATAR  WIND (A  MIKE LOVELL      HRNS (A  YVAN DE SOUTER  B V (A
   BRUNO CASTELLUCCI D V  (A   DOUGLAS LUCAS  HRNS (A  JEAN CLEMENT CLEMENT SAX (A
```

```
   JAN PIET DEN TEX       (A       (A) HEARTBEAT           1980 BUBBLE        NL   202 852
   MICHIEL JANSEN    G    (A
   JAAP VENDERSLUYS  B    (A   KEES MEERMAN   D   (A  WILLEN ENNES     K    (A
```

```
   DES COFFIELD MAND G K V(ABCD    (A) COUNTRY OF THE BLIND 1971 REGAL ZONOPHONE UK SLRZ 1018
   SEAN O'ROURKE G V FDL  (ABCD    (B) TAKE OFF YOUR HEAD(VAR ART) 1972 RUBBER  UK RUB  001
   JIM DIVERS B CELLO V   (ABCD    (C) J S D BAND         1972 'FLY UK HIFLY11 CUBE GER 07269
   CHUCK FLEMING     FDL MAND(DA   (D) TRAVELLING DAYS    1973 CUBE UK HIFLY14 GER 26608/9
   COLIN FINN        D    (CDA
   LINDSAY SCOTT     VLN V(C
```

```
   VICKY BUSISWE MHLONGO V(A       (A) JABULA              1975 CAROLINE      UK       CA 2004
   GRAHAM MORGAN     D    (AB      (B) THUNDER INTO OUR HEARTS 1976 CAROLINE   UK       CA 2009
   KEN ELY           SAX  (AB      (C) IN AMSTERDAM        1979 JABULA               JBL2003
   MADUMETJA RANKU   G PERC(AB
   EDDI QUANSAH      TPT  (A   WILLIE CHEETHAM PERC V(A GEORGE LARNYOH   WIND (A  JEAN ROUSSEL    K   (A
   SEBOTHANE BAHULA  PERC (AB  SPARTACUS R    B   (B  MIKE ROSE        FLT  (B  MAUREEN KOTO LEMBEDE V(A
   FRANK ROBERTS     K    (B   BOB HOWSE     WIND (B  JIM CHAMBERS     V    (B  DUDU PUKWANA    SAX (AB
   PETER VANDER PUIJE SAX (A   MOGOTSI MOTHLE B V (AB NICK EVANS       TROM (B  JIM DVORAK      TPT (B
   JIM THOMAS        V    (B
```

```
   ALAN JACK         K V  (A       (A) BLUESY MIND        19   BYG                  529011
   CLAUDE OLMOS      G V  (A
   RICHARD FONTAINE  B V  (A   JEAN FALISSARD D V (A
```

```
   JOHN WETTON       B V K(A       (A) I WISH YOU WOULD    1979 POLYDOR UK POLS1010 GER 2302 094
   RICHARD PALMER-JAMES G (A
   JOHN HUTCHESON    K V  (A   CURT CRESS     D PERC(A PETER BISCHOF    V    (A  MICHAEL LOHMANN SAX (A
   KRISTIAN SCHULZE  K    (A
```

JACK THE LAD

RAY LAIDLAW	D V	(ABC	(A) JACK THE LAD			1974	CHARISMA	UK	CAS	1085
PHIL MURRAY	B V	(BCD	(B) OLD STRAIGHT TRACK			1974	CHARISMA	UK	CAS	1094
BILLY MITCHELL	G V	(ABCD	(C) ROUGH DIAMONDS			1975	CHARISMA	UK	CAS	1110
WALTER FAIRBAIRN	G V	(BCD	(D) JACKPOT			1976	UA	UK	UAS	29999
RAY JACKSON	HCA	(CD	( ) ITS JACK			1975	ASYLUM	US		1014
TOM ALLOM		(D								
MADDY PRIOR	V	(A	TOMMY EYRE	K	(A	CHRIS MERCER	HRNS (D	JOHN KIRKPATRICK	ACC (C
JIMMY WRIGHTSON	CONC (A		STEVE GREGORY	HRNS (D	ROD CLEMENTS		(A	ANDY BOWN	K	(D
BUD BEADLE	HRNS (D		SIMON COWE	G V	(AB					

BRIAN JACKSON

BRIAN JACKSON		(ALL	(A) ITS YOUR WORLD	1976	ARISTA	UK	DARTY1
			(B) SECRETS	1978	ARISTA	UK	SPARTY 1073
			(C) WINTER IN AMERICA	19	STRAT EAST	US	19742

BULLMOOSE JACKSON

BULLMOOSE JACKSON		(A	(A) SINGS HIS HITS	19	AUDIO LAB	US	12RY

CHARLES JACKSON

CHARLES JACKSON	V	(AB	(A) PASSIONATE BREEZES	1978	CAPITOL		11775
BRUCE CONTE	G	(B	(B) GONNA GETCHA LOVE	1979	TOWER	EST	12002
MICHAEL McGLOIRY	G	(B					
COLEMAN HEAD	G	(B	VICTOR CONTE	B	(B	JERRY KNIGHT	B V	(B	JULIA TILLMAN	V	(B
MELVIN BRITT	V	(B	WELTON GITE	B	(B	HARVEY HUGHES	D	(B	DENNIS DAVIS	D	(B
GAVIN CHRISTOPHER	K V	(B	GREG LEVIAS	K	(B	MAXINE WILLARD	V	(B	JUDY JONES	V	(B
NATE GINSBERG	K	(B	CHESTER THOMPSON	K	(B	RONNIE FOSTER	K	(B	ROBERT THE ROOK	HCA(B
SYLVIA COX	V	(B	LUTHER WATERS	V	(B					

J J JACKSON

J J JACKSON	V K PERC(ALL	(A) WITH THE GREATEST LITTLE SOUL BAND	1967	STRIKE	UK		104
DICK MORRISSEY	SAX	(BC	(B) THE GREATEST LITTLE SOUL BAND	1969	MCA		SKA100
TERRY SMITH	G	(BC	(C) J J JACKSONS DILEMMA	1971	RCA UK SF8093	US PERCEPTION 3
ROY EDWARDS	TPT	(BC					
JOHN MARSHALL	SAX	(B	STU HAMMER	TPT	(B	RICO RODIGUEZ	TROM (B	BRIAN HENDERSON	K	(B
JEFF WHITTAKER	CONGA(A		LARRY STEELE	B	(BC	BILL EGDEN	D	(B	RONNY STEPHENSON	D	(B
TERRY JENKINS	D	(B	IAN HAGUE	D	(C	CHRIS PARREN	K	(C	JOHN BENNETT	TROM(C
GEORGE JONES	TPT	(C	DAVE QUINCY	SAX	(C	JEFF McCARTHY	B	(C	GEORGE BARKER	TPT	(C
DICK PARRY	SAX	(C								

GORDON JACKSON

GORDON JACKSON G V SITAR(A	(A) THINKING BACK	1969	MARMALADE	UK		608 012
(NOT THE ACTOR)							
REMI KABAKA	PERC (A	STEVE WINWOOD	B K	(A	POLI PALMER	V K	(A	JIM CAPALDI	V	(A
LUTHER GROSVENOR	V	(A	ROCKY DZIDZORNU	PERC (A	RICK GRECH	B	(A	CHRIS WOOD	WIND (A
JULIE DRISCOLL	V	(A	DAVE MASON	B	(A	ROB BLUNT	SITAR G	(A	JIM KING	SAX	(A
REG KING	V	(A								

LEE JACKSON

LEE JACKSON	G V	(A	(A) LONELY GIRL	197		
CAREY BELL	HCA	(A				
PHIL UPCHURCH	B	(A	BRIAN GRICE	D	(A	GERALD SIMS	G	(A	BRAD FIELD	K	(A

JOE JACKSON

JOE JACKSON	V K HCA	(ALL	(A) LOOK SHARP	1979 A&M US 4743	UK	AMLH 64743
PETE THOMAS	SAX	(D	(A) LOOK SHARP	1982 RI A&M AMID120		
GARY SANFORD	G	(ABC	(A) LOOK SHARP (10" DOUBLE)	1979 A&M	US	SP 3666
GRAHAM MABY	B	(ABC	(B) I'M THE MAN	1979 A&M US 4794	UK	AMLH 64794
DAVE HOUGHTON	D	(ABC	(C) BEAT CRAZY	1980 A&M US 4837	UK	AMLH 64837
DAVID KERSHENBAUM	PROD (AB	(D) JUMPIN' JIVE	1981 A&M	UK	AMLH 68530
RAUL OLIVERIA	TPT	(D	(E) NIGHT & DAY	1982 A&M	UK	AMLH 64609
NICK WELDON	PNO	(D				
DAVE BITELLI	WIND (D	LARRY TOLFREE	D	(D			

MICK JACKSON

MICK JACKSON	V	(A	(A) MICK JACKSON	1979	ATLANTIC	UK	K 50605
KEITH FORSEY							
CURT CRESS	PERC (A	MATS BJOERKLUND	G	(A	GUNTHER GEBAUER	B	(A	SYLVESTER LEVAY	K	(A
PATRICIA SHOKLEY	V	(A	TIM TOUCHTON	V	(A	ERIK THONER	V	(A	GABOR CRISTIF	TPT	(A
GUISEPPE SOLERA	SAX	(A	GEOFF BASTOW	K	(A	PATRICK GAMMON	K V	(A	MAX GREGOR	K	(A
KRISTIAN SCHULZE	SYN	(A	TOOTS THIELEMANS	HCA (A	VICTORIA MILES	V	(A	JERRY RIX	V	(A
WOLFGANG EMPERHOFF	V	(A	BOBBY STERN	SAX	(A	BENNY GEBAUER	SAX	(A	HERMANN BREUER	TROM(A

MICHAEL JACKSON

MICHAEL JACKSON	V	(ALL	(A) GOT TO BE THERE	1972 MOTOWN US 747	UK STML 11205
GREG PHILLINGANES	K	(J	(A) GOT TO BE THERE	1981 MOTOWN RI	UK STMS 5005
BILL WOLFER	K	(J	(B) BEN	1973 MOTOWN US 755	UK STML 11220
MICHAEL BODDICKER	K	(J	(B) BEN	1981 MOTOWN RI	UK STMA 5008
DAVID WILLIAMS	G	(J	(C) MUSIC & ME	1974 MOTOWN US 767	
LOUIS JOHNSON	B	(J	(D) FOREVER	1975 MOTOWN US 825	UK STMA 8002
PAULINHO DACOSTA	PERC (J	(E) BEST OF M JACKSON	1975 MOTOWN UK STML12005 RI STMR9009
JERRY HEY	TPT	(J	(F) OFF THE WALL	1979 EPIC US 35745 UK 83468
GARY GRANT	TPT	(J	(G) SUPERSTAR	1980 MOTOWN US 107
LARRY WILLIAMS	WIND (J	(H) ONE DAY IN YOUR LIFE	1981 MOTOWN UK STMC 12158
EDDIE VAN HALEN	G	(J	(J) THRILLER	1982 EPIC UK 85930
JULIA WATERS	V	(J		
BILL REICHENBACH	TROM (J	MAXINE WATERS	V	(J	OREN WATERS	V	(J	JAMES INGRAM	K V	(J
BUNNY HULL	V	(J	BECKY LOPEZ	V	(J	DAVID PAICH	SYN K(J	STEVE PORCARO	SYN (J
NDUGO CHANCLER	D	(J	DAVID FOSTER	SYN	(J	DEAN PARKS	G	(J	STEVE LUKATHER	B G(J
JEFF PORCARO	D	(J	VINCENT PRICE	V	(J	ROD TEMPERTON	SYN (J	BRIAN BANKS	SYN (J
TOM BAHLER	K	(J	GREG SMITH	K	(J	PAUL JACKSON	G (J	HOWARD WEWETT	V	(J
JANET JACKSON	V	(J	LATOYA JACKSON	V	(J					

MILLIE JACKSON	V	(ALL	(A) MILLIE JACKSON		1972	POLYDOR UK 2391 025	US	SPRING 5703
JIMMY JOHNSON	G	(DEJFKMLP	(B) IT HURTS SO GOOD		1972	POLYDOR UK 2391 091	US	SPRING 5706
PETE CARR	G	(EFK	(C) MILLIE		197		US	SPRING 6701
BARRY BECKETT	K	(DFJKML	(D) CAUGHT UP		197	POLYDOR UK 2391 147	US	SPRING 6703
DAVID HOOD	B	(DFJKMLP	(E) STILL CAUGHT UP		197	POLYDOR UK 2391 183	US	SPRING 6708
ROGER HAWKINS	D	(DEJFKMLP	(F) FREE & IN LOVE		197	POLYDOR UK 2391 215	US	SPRING 6709
BRAD SHAPIRO	PERC	(D	(G) BEST OF		1976	POLYDOR UK 2391 247		
TOM ROADY	PERC	(DEJFKML	(H) LOVINGLY YOURS		197	POLYDOR UK 2391 252	US	SPRING 6712
CHARLES CHALMERS	V	(EF	(J) FEELIN' BITCHY		1977	POLYDOR UK 2391 301	US	SPRING 6715
SANDY RHODES	V	(EF	(K) GET IT OUTCHA SYSTEM		1978	POLYDOR UK 2391 336	US	SPRING 6719
DONNA RHODES	V	(EF	(L) ROYAL RAPPIN'S		1979	POLYDOR UK 2480 516		
ISAAC HAYES	V	(L	(M) MOMENTS PLEASURE		1979	POLYDOR UK 2391 395	US	SPRING 6722
KEN BELL	G	(JFP	(O) LIVE		1980		US	SPRING 6725
SPIDERMAN HARRISON		V(JK	(P) FOR MEN ONLY		1980	POLYDOR UK 2391 460		
MARY LOU VAN DE PITTE	V	(K	(Q) I HAD TO SAY IT		1980	POLYDOR UK 2391 495		
RANDY McCORMICK		(MLP	(R) LIVE & OUTRAGEOUS		1982	POLYDOR UK 2391 540		
MICKY BUCKINS		(P						

RON EADES	HRNS	(FP	CYNTHIA DOUGLAS		(K	THE MOMENTS	V	(H	HARRISON CALLOWAY	HRNS(FP
DONNA DAVIS	V	(K	STEVE MELTON		(K	HARVEY THOMPSON	HRNS	(FP	SHELDON KIRKLAND	STRINGS(K
BRANDYE	V	(JHML	TIM HENSON	K	(J	PAM VINCENT	V	(K	CHARLES ROSE	HRNS(F
LARRY BYROM	G	(JML	MIKE MEYERS		(K	BEN CAULEY	HRNS	(P	CLAYTON IVEY	(LMP
JANE FRICKE	V	(E								

WANDA JACKSON	V	(ALL	ROCKIN WITH WANDA	1960	CAPITOL	US	TS	1384
BILLY SANFORD	G	(*	ROCKIN WITH WANDA	1977	CAPITOL	UK	CAPS	1007
RAY EDENTON	G	(*	RIGHT OR WRONG	1061	CAPITOL	US	ST	1596
RUSSELL HICKS	G	(*	WONDERFUL WANDA	1962	CAPITOL	US	ST	1776
JERRY SHOOK	G	(*	THERE'S A PARTY GOING ON	19	CAPITOL	US	ST	1511
JAMES CAPPS	G	(*	WANDA JACKSON	19	CAPITOL	US	T	1041
WELDON MYRICK	STEEL	(*	LOVE ME FOREVER	19	CAPITOL	US	ST	1911
CHARLIE McCOY	HCA	(*	I GOT TO SING	19	CAPITOL	US	ST	669
JERRY SMITH	PNO	(*	2 SIDES OF WANDA	19	CAPITOL	US	ST	2030
JACK WILLIAMS	B	(*	WANDA JACKSON	19	PICKWICK	UK		2053
HENRY STRZELECKI	B	(*	BLUES IN MY HEART	19	CAPITOL	US	ST	2306
KENNY MALONE	D	(*	SINGS COUNTRY SONGS	1966	CAPITOL	US	ST	2438
JERRY CARRIGAN	D	(*	COUNTRY MUSIC HALL OF FAME	1967	CAPITOL	US	ST	2606
FARRELL MORRIS	PERC	(*	YOU'LL HAVE MY LOVE	19	CAPITOL	US	ST	2812
DELORES EDGIN	V	(*	CREAM OF THE CROP	1969	CAPITOL	US	ST	2976
JUNE PAGE	V	(*	BEST OF	19	CAPITOL	US	ST	2883
BERGEN WHITE	V	(*	BEST OF	19	CAPITOL	UK	ST	11166
HURSHAL WIGGINTON	V	(*	A PORTRAIT OF	1970	CAPITOL	US	ST	21530
JOSEPH BABCOCK	V	(*	A WOMAN LIVES TO LOVE	1970	CAPITOL	US	ST	554
			COUNTRY	1970	CAPITOL	US	ST	434
			PRAISE THE LORD	1972	CAPITOL	US	ST	11023
			PIONEERS OF ROCK	1972	STARLINE	UK	SRS	5120
			COUNTRY KEEPSAKES	1973	CAPITOL	US	ST	11161
			I WOULD'NT WANT YOU ANY OTHER WAY	1973	CAPITOL	US	ST	11096
			COUNTRY CLASSICS	1973	CAPITOL EURO		5C 052 81215
			WHEN IT'S TIME TO FALL IN LOVE AGAIN	1974	CAPITOL	US	ST	6513
			COUNTRY GOSPEL	1974	WORD US (UK82) WST		9514
			NOW I HAVE EVERYTHING	1975	MYRRH US 6533	MYR	1021
			MAKE ME A CHILD AGAIN	1976	MYRRH		MYR	1043
			MY TESTAMENT	1982	WORD			9617
			(*)I'LL STILL LOVE YOU	1976	DJM	UK	DJF	20493
			LEAVE MY BABY	19	HILLTOP	US	JS	6074
			PLEASE HELP ME I'M FALLING	19	HILLTOP	US	JS	6058
			WE'LL SING IN SUNSHINE	19	HILLTOP	US	JS	6116
			BY THE TIME I GET TO PHOENIX	19	HILLTOP	US	JS	6123
			TEARS AT GRAND OLE OPRY	19	HILLTOP	US	JS	6184
			NOBODY'S DARLIN'	19	VOCALION	US	VL	73861
			CLOSER TO JESUS	1978	WORD	(UK82) WST	9580
			ROCK'N'ROLL HISTORY	1979	CAPITOL	US	038 82098
			GREATEST HITS	1979	CAPITOL	US	134 53025/6

LEE JACKSON	B V G	(ABCD	(A) KING PROGRESS	1970	CHARISMA	UK	CAS	1018
CHARLIE HARCOURT	G K V	(A	(A) KING PROGRESS	197	MERCURY	US	SR	61331
TOMMY SLOANE	D	(A	(B) 5TH AVENUE BUS	1972	VERTIGO	UK	6360	067
MARIO ENRIQUE	B	(A	(C) RAGAMUFFINS FOOL	1973	VERTIGO	UK	6360	077
COVARRURAS TAPIA		(A	(C) JACKSON HEIGHTS	1973	VERVE	US	V6	5089
PATRICK MORAZ	K	(	(D) BUMP & GRIND	1973	VERTIGO	UK	6360	092
MIKE GILES	D	(BCD						

BRIAN CHATTON	K V	(BCD	JOHN McBURNIE	G V K	(BCD	TONY CONNOR		(C	LAWRIE WRIGHT	PNO (B
DAVE WATTS	PNO	(B	IAN WALLACE	D	(D	ROGER McKEW	G	(D	JOHNNY VAN DERRICK	FDL(D
BILLY BELL	BANJO	(D	CHRIS LAURENCE	B	(D	JOHNNY TOOGOOD	SAX	(C	RACE McCLEOD	D(C
MO FLETCHER	B	(C	MOX	HCA	(C	KEITH HARRIS	BANJO	(C	OLI OLIVER	FDL (C
LAURIE JAY	D	(C								

DENNIS GULLEY	V G K	(A	(A) JACKSON HIGHWAY	1980	CAPITOL	US	ST	12044
BRITT MEACHAM	G V	(A						

TOMMY PATERSON	K V	(A	RUSSELL GULLEY	B V	(A	RONNIE VANCE	D V	(A	ROGER HAWKINS	D (A
DAVID HOOD	B	(A	JIMMY JOHNSON	G	(A	RANDY McCORMICK	K	(A	RICKY MEDLOCKE	D (A
GREG T WALKER		(A	DUNCAN CAMERON		(A					

MICHAEL JACKSON	V	(	I WANT YOU BACK	1969	TAMLA US		
JACKIE JACKSON	V	(	DIANA ROSS PRESENTS	1970	TAMLA US 700	UK	STML 11142
TITO JACKSON	V	(	A B C	1970	TAMLA US 709	UK	STML 11156
BILL CROSBY		(	A B C	1982	TAMLA	UK RI STMS 5068
JERMAINE JACKSON	V	(	CHRISTMAS ALBUM	1970	TAMLA	UK	STML 11168
MARLON JACKSON	V	(	THIRD ALBUM	1971	TAMLA US 718	UK	STML 11174
TOMMY SMOTHERS		(	THIRD ALBUM	1982	TAMLA	UK RI STMS 5037

(CONTINUED)

[289]

```
J15      (CONTINUED)                    THE JACKSONS                                                          J15
    RANDY JACKSON      V   (        MAYBE TOMORROW                1971  TAMLA  US 735    UK    STML 11188
    ROSEY GRIER            (        GREATEST HITS                 1972  TAMLA  US 741    UK    STML 11212
    JON MOFFETT        D   (        GREATEST HITS                 1982  TAMLA            UK RI STMS  5032
    DAVID WILLIAMS     G   (        LOOKIN' THROUGH WINDOWS       1972  TAMLA  US 750    UK    STML 11214
    MICHAEL McKINNEY   B   (        SKYWRITER                     1973  TAMLA  US 761    UK    STML 11231
    BILL WOLFER        K   (        DANCING MACHINE               1973  TAMLA  US 780    UK    STML 11275
    WESLEY PHILLIPS    HRNS (       GET IT TOGETHER               1973  TAMLA  US 783    UK    STML 11243
    GLORIS GRIMES      HRNS (       MOVING VIBRATIONS             1975  TAMLA  US 829    UK    STML 11290
                                    JACKSONS                      1976  EPIC   US 34229  UK        86009
                                    JACKSONS                      1982  EPIC             UK RI     32101
                                    MOTOWN SPECIAL                1977  TAMLA            UK    STMX  6006
                                    ANTHOLOGY                     1977  TAMLA  US M7868  UK    TMSM  6004
                                    JOYFUL JUKEBOX MUSIC          1977  TAMLA  US 865    UK    STML 12046
                                    GOIN' PLACES                  1977  EPIC   US 34835  UK        86035
                                    DESTINY                       1978  EPIC   US 35520  UK        83200
                                    ZIP A DEE DOO DAH             1979  MFP              UK        50418
                                    20 GOLDEN GREATS              1979  TAMLA            UK    STML 12121
                                    JACKSON 5                     19    PICKWICK US 2080
                                    TRIUMPH                       1980  EPIC   US 36424  UK        86112
                                    LIVE (DBL)                    198   EPIC             UK        88562
J15A                                   DALE JACOBS                                                           J15A
    DALE JACOBS        K   (A       (A) COBRA                     1979  EPIC US 36100    UK        83761
    JOEL WADE          B   (A
    BRETT WADE         G   (A   JIM VALLANCE    D   (A  JIM McGILLEVRAY  PERC(A   DOUG LOUIE      K  (A
    WAYNE KOSAK        WIND (A  LOU HOOVER      D   (A  TOM LAVIN       G   (A   BRIAN HARRISON  B  (A
    KAT HENDRIKSE      D   (A   DOUG CUTHBERT   D   (A  RALPH DYCK      VIBES(A
J15B                                   JADD FAIR                                                             J15B
                                    (A) ZOMBIES OF MORA TAM       1980  ARMAGEDDON       UK    AEP  003
J16                                    JADE WARRIOR                                                          J16
    TONY DUHIG         G B K(ALL     (A) JADE WARRIOR             1971  VERTIGO US 1007  UK    6360  033
    JON FIELD  PERC G K FLT(ALL      (B) RELEASED                 1971  VERTIGO US 1009  UK    6360  062
    COLERIDGE GOODE    (DF           (C) AUTUMNS DREAM            1972  VERTIGO US 1012  UK    6360  079
    GLYN HAVARD        B G V(ABC      (D) FLOATING WORLD          1974  ISLAND    US /UK  ILPS 9290
    DAVID DUHIG        G   (CDE       (E) WAVES                   1975  ISLAND    US /UK  ILPS 9318
    ALAN PRICE         D   (BC        (F) KITES                   1976  ISLAND    US /UK  ILPS 9393
    SKAILA KANKA       HARP(DG        (G) WAY OF THE SUN          1978  ISLAND UK ILPS9552 US ANTILES7068
    CHRIS KARAN        D   (D         (H) REFLECTIONS  (COMP)     1980  BUTT             BUTT  001
    GRAHAM DEACON      D   (D
    MARTHA MDENGE      V   (D   STEVE WINWOOD    K   (E  CLODAGH SIMMON   V   (F  ROGER BRYSON   PNO (F
    JOE O'DONNELL      VLN (F   GOWAN TURNBULL   SAX (FG DAVE CONNERS   WIND (B  GRAHAM MORGAN  D  (FGE
    DEBBIE HALL        VLN (F   GEOFF WESTLEY    PNO (F  JOHN DENTITH   D   (G  DICK CUTHELL   HRNS(G
    PETE GIBSON        HRNS (F  WILLIE           PERC (F FRED FRITH     VLA (F  BILL SMITH     B   (G
J16A                                   JAGS                                                                  J16A
    NICK WATKINSON     G V (ABC      (A) BACK OF MY HAND (EP)     1979  ISLAND      UK    12SWIP6501
    JOHN ALDER         G V (ABC      (B) EVENING STANDARD         1980  ISLAND UK ILPS9603 EURO 201 291
    ALEX BAIRD         B V (ABC      (C) NO TIE LIKE A PRESENT    1981  ISLAND UK ILPS9655 EURO 203 379
    STEVE PRUDENCE     B V (AB
    CHRIS HUNTER       HRNS (B  GUY BARKER   HRNS    (B  MICHAEL COTTON  B V (C  PADDY O'TOOLE   K  (C
J16B                                   CHRIS JAGGER                                                          J16B
    CHRIS JAGGER       V K FLT(AB     (A) CHRIS JAGGER            1973 G M          UK   GML1003
    ROGER EARLE        D   (A         (B) THE ADVENTURES OF VALENTINE VOX...1974 ASYLUM   US   7E1009
    JOHN URIBE         B V G(A
    DAVID PIERCE       G K  (AB  BOBBY KEYS    SAX (A  MICK JAGGER    V   (A  MICHAEL OMARTIAN  K   (A
    DON PONCHER        D PERC(A   OLIVER TOBIAS V   (A  PAT VEGAS      B   (A  PAT ARNOLD        V   (A
    ELAINE             V   (A   CLAUDIA LENNEAR  V   (A  BOB DENT     CELLO(A  DIANE           PERC(A
    BOB GRIFFITH       B   (A   IAN STEWART   PNO (A  MIKE KELLIE    D   (A  BRIAN BELSHAW    B   (A
    KEVIN WESTLAKE     G   (A   DAVE FARREL   B   (A  PICK WITHERS   D   (B  ANDY BOWN        B V (B
    JOHN MEALING       K   (B   BOB COHEN     G   (B  JIM RYAN       G   (B  CHRIS STAINTON   K   (B
    BUSTER CHERRY JONES B  (B   NEIL HUBBARD  G   (B  TERRY STANARD  D   (B  PETER FRAMPTON   G   (B
    PETE SEARS         B   (B   MICKY WALLER  D   (B  STEVE DARRINGTON ACC (B  JOHN ROUSSEAU  K WIND(B
    DAVE EDMUNDS       G   (B   ALAN SPENNER  B   (B  STEVE SMITH    V PERC(B
J16C                                   JAGGERZ                                                               J16C
    JIMMY ROSS         HRNS B V(A     (A) WE WENT TO DIFFERENT SCHOOLS  1970  KAMA SUTRA     US 2017
    BENNY FAIELLA      G BV (A
    DOMINIC LERACE     G B V(A  THOM DAVIS    K HRN   (A  BILLY MAYBRAY  B D V  (A JIM PUGLINRO  D V (
J17                                    JAGUAR                                                                J17
    ROY HOWELL   G MAND B  (A        (A) JAGUAR                   1977  RCA              APLI 2420
    ED FORESMAN        B V  (A
    WALTER POLK        D PERC(A  RANDY COPELAND  B   (A  DREW HAYS    V PERC(A  PAT TAYLOR     G V (A
    DOUG MAYO          K PERC(A  BEVERLEY BAXTER V   (A
J17A                                   JAH LION                                                              J17A
    JAH LION               (A        (A) COLUMBIA COLL            1976  ISLAND/MANGO UK/US ILPS 386
J17B                                   JAH LLOYD                                                             J17B
    JAH LLOYD          V   (AB        (A) THE HUMBLE ONE          1978  FRONT LINE   UK      1005
    SLY DUNBAR         D   (B         (B) BLACK MOSES             1979  FRONT LINE   UK      1031
    ROBBIE SHAKESPEARE B   (B
    ANSEL COLLINS      K   (B   BOBBY KALPHAT   PNO (B  ERIC LAMONT    G   (B  RAD BRYAN       G   (B
    STICKY THOMPSON    PERC (B  HUNTLEY         FLT (B
J17C                                   JAH STITCH                                                            J17C
    JAH STITCH         V   (ALL       (A) MY PRECIOUS LOCKS       1978  CANCER              002
    CARLTON'SANTA' DAVIS D(BC         (B) NO DREAD CAN'T DEAD     19    THIRD WORLD         401
    ROBBIE SHAKESPEARE     B(BC       (C) WATCH YOUR STEP YOUTH MAN 1979 THIRD WORLD        701
    LLOYD PARKS        B   (BC
    TOUTER HARVEY      K   (BC  TARZAN      K PREC(BC  SKULLY        PERC(BC  EARL SMITH      G  (BC
    TONY CHINN         G   (BC  AUSSIE'NOGO' HERBERT K(BC JOHNNIE CLARKE PNO (BC BARNABAS    PERC(BC
    DOPEPEA            G   (BC  ANSEL COLLINS  K   (BC  SLY DUNBAR    D   (BC

                                          [290]
```

JAH THOMAS

JAH THOMAS	V	(AL	(A) STOP YU LOAFIN		1978	GREENSLEEVES	UK	GREL3
DUGGIE	G	(A	(B) DANCE HALL STYLE		1980	DADDY KOOL		P16
SLY DUNBAR	D	(A						
BARNABAS	PERC	(A	RANCHIE	B	(A	SKULLEY	PERC (A	STICKY	PERC	(A
TOUTER HARVEY	K	(A	ROBBIE SHAKESPEARE B	(A	ANSEL COLLINS	K	(A

JAH WOOSH

JAH WOOSH		(ALL	(A) THE WORLD MARIJUANA TOUR	1977	CARIB GEMS	
ERROL NELSON		(D	(B) LICK HIM WITH THE DUSTBIN	1977	KAB	
TARZAN		(G	(C) JAH WOOSH	1974	CACTUS	CTLP 103
TOUTER HARVEY	D	(G	(D) JAH JAH DEY DEY	1976	CACTUS	CTLP 116
FULLY	B	(G	(E) DREADLOCK AFFAIR	1976	TROJAN	TRLS 113
RANCHIE	B	(G	(F) PSALMS OF WISDOM	1977	BLACKWAX	LP2
STICKY	PERC	(G	(G) RELIGIOUS DREAD	1979	TROJAN	TRLS 157
CHINNA	G	(G				

JAKE & THE FAMILY JEWELS

| JAKE(ALLAN JACOBS) V G | (AB | (A) JAKE & THE FAMILY JEWELS | 1970 POLYDOR US 24 4029 UK 2425 027 |
| MIKE ROSA | D | (AB | (B) BIG MOOSE CALLS HIS BABBY | 1971 POLYDOR US 5024 |
| JEREMIAH BURNHAM FLT B V(A |
ROB ROTHSTEIN	B	(B	DAN MANSOLINO	K V	(A	DANIEL BEN ZEBULON PERC(A	KENNY PINE	G V(A
KATHLEEN WHELEN	PERC (A	VITO JACOBS	G V	(A	MYLES ARONOWITZ JEWSHARP(A	JON LIND	G V(A
JIM STARSES	G	(A	BOB SMITH	PNO	(A	PERRY ROBINSON	CLAR(A	LARRY PACKER	FDL(A
CHARLIE CHIN	BANJ (A	DON BROOKS	HCA	(A	BUZZY LINHART	V	(A	BUNKY ROCHELLE SKINNER V(A
DANNY MANSELINO	K	(B

THE JAM

PAUL WELLER	G V	(ALL	(A) IN THE CITY	1977	POLYDOR US 6110	UK	2383 447
RICK BUCKLER	D	(ALL	(B) THIS IS THE MODERN WORLD	1977	POLYDOR US 6129	UK	2383 475
BRUCE FOXTON	B V	(ALL	(C) ALL MOD CONS	1978	POLYDOR US 6118	UK	2442 155
MICK TALBOT	PNO	(D	(C) ALL MOD CONS	1978	POLYDOR	UK	POLD 5008
STEVE RUDI	SAX	(D	(D) SETTING SONS	1979	POLYDOR US 6249	UK5018 2442 168
			(E) SOUND AFFECTS	1980	POLYDOR US 6315	UK5035
			(F) THE GIFT	1982	POLYDOR	UK 5055
			(AB) IN THE CITY/MODERN WORLD	1980	POLYDOR	UK	2683 074
			(EP) THE JAM	1981	POLYDOR

BOB JAMES

BOB JAMES	K	(ALL	( ) BOB JAMES TRIO	1965	ESP	US 1009
RON TOOLEY	TPT	(L	(A) ONE	1975	CTI	6043
LUTHER VANDROSS	V	(L	(A) ONE	1981	CBS	UK	84820
GARY KING	B	(ABCDEFGHIKL	(B) TWO	1975	CTI	6057
BABI KLOYD	V	(L	(B) TWO	1981	CBS	UK	84821
STEVE GADD	D	(ABDEFIK	(C) THREE	1976	CTI	6063
MILT GRAYSON	V	(L	(C) THREE	1981	CBS	UK	84822
RALPH McDONALD	PERC (ABCDEFGHIKL	(D) FOUR	1977	CTI	7074
JOHN ROBINSON	D	(L	(D) FOUR	1981	CBS	UK	84823
GROVER WASHINGTON SAX	(ACEHIL	(E) HEADS	1977	CBS US 34896	UK	82271
JON FADDIS	HRNS (ACEHIKL	(F) TOUCHDOWN	1978	CBS US 35594	UK	83175
LEW SOLOFF	TPT	(ABCDEI	(G) ONE ON ONE	1979	CBS US 36241	UK	83931
WAYNE ANDRE	TROM (ABCEIK	(H) 'H'	1980	CBS US 36422	UK	84238
EDDIE DANIELS	WIND (BCDEHIL	(I) BEST OF	1978	CTI	UK	630.34
GEORGE MARGE	WIND (ADEHIGL	(J) EXPLOSIONS	1975	ESP	US	1009
ROMEO PENQUE	WIND (ADHIG	(K) LUCKY SEVEN	1979	CBS US 36056	UK	83729
ERIC GALE	G	(BCDEGIKL	(L) SIGN OF THE TIMES	1981	CBS	UK	85181
ARTHUR JENKINS PERC	(BI	(M) ALL AROUND THE TOWN	1981	CBS	UK	88509
HUBERT LAWS	FLY	(BCDEI	(N) HANDS DOWN	1982	CBS	UK	85848
RANDY BRECKER HRNS (BEHIK
MARVIN STAMM	TPT (ABCI	DANNY CAHN	TPT (H	MICHAEL LAWRENCE TPT (HKL	IDRIS MUHAMMAD D (AEHK
RICHIE RESNICOFF	G	(ABIK	ERIC WEISSBERG STEEL(AI	DAVE FRIEDMAN	VIBES(AI	HUGH McCRACKEN	HCA(ACI
THAD JONES	HRNS (AI	VICTOR PAZ	TPT (ABI	ALAN RUBIN	TPT (ABI	PAUL FAULISE	TROM (AHI
JACK GALE	TROM (AFI	ALAN RAPH	TROM (AI	ANDREW SMITH	D (BI	JOHN FROSK	HRNS(BCDEI
JIMMY BUFFINGTON	HRNS (BEIGK	PETER GORDON	HRNS (BIEK	AL RICHMOND	HRNS (BI	EDDIE BERT	TROM (BI
TOM MITCHELL	TROM (BEI	TONY STUDD	TROM (BI	PATTI AUSTIN	V (BEIKL	FRANK FLOYD	V (IBL
LANI GROVES	V	(BEI	ZACHARY SANDERS V	(BI	SIDNEY WEINBERG	WIND (DI	EARL KLUGH	G (FG
BARRY ROGERS	TROM (H	LIBERTY DE VITO D	(H	DAVID BROWN	G (H	HIRAM BULLOCK	B (HFK
BUDDY WILLIAMS	D	(HL	HARVEY MASON	D (CGI	ANDY NEWMARK	D (CE	WILL LEE	B (CE
JEFF MIRANOV	G	(CE	JERRY DODGION FLT (CHI	DAVE BARGERON	HRNS (CI	DAVE TAYLOR	TROM (CEIKL
GLORIA AGOSTINI	HARP (CEI	ART FARMER	HRNS (DI	JOHN GATCHELL	TPT (D	JIM PUGH	TROM (HL
DOUG STEGMEYER	B	(HL	LEONARD GIBBS PERC (HL	AIRTO MOREIRA	PERC (HL	BRUCE DUNLAP	G (HL
MICHAEL MAINERI	VIBES(E	DAVE SANBORN	SAX (EFK	VIVIAN CHERRY	V (EL	GWEN GUTHRIE	V (E
ALLEN SCHWARZBERG	D	(E	ALPHONSO JOHNSON B	(E	STEVE KHAN	G (EKL	JEFF LAYTON	G (E
BROOKS TILLOTSON	HRNS (E	PHIL BODNER	WIND (EHGL	MICHAEL BRECKER	SAX (EK	GERRY NIEWOOD	WIND (E
RON CARTER	B	(FG	NEIL JASON	B (GK	MONGO SANTAMARIA	(F	JIMMY MAELIN	PERC (K
RICK MAROTTA	D	(L	WALLY KANE	WIND (GL	JAY BECKENSTEIN	SAX (L	MARCUS MILLER	B (L
MAJOR HOLLEY	B	(L	CASEY CYSCK	V (L	HILLARY JAMES	V (L	YVONNE LEWIS	V (L
WHIT SIDENER	WIND (L

ELMORE JAMES

ELMORE JAMES	G V	(ALL	(A) TOUGH	197	BLUE HORIZON	UK	7 63204
JOHN BRIM		(AK	(B) TO KNOW A MAN	1969	BLUE HORIZON	UK	7 66230
JOHNNY JONES	PNO	(DELMN	(C) LEGEND OF	1970	UA	UK	UAS 29109
HOMESICK JAMES WILLIAMSON(E	(D) COTTON PATCH(1 SIDE)	1973	POLYDOR	UK	2383 200
J T BROWN	SAX	(DELMN	(E) ALL THEM BLUES	1975	DJM	UK	DJLMD 8008
ODIE PAYNE	D	(DE L	(F) RESURRECTION OF ELMORE JAMES	1976	BLUES ANTHOLOGY UK	AB 5610
BOYD ATKINS	SAX	(D	(F) RESURRECTION OF ELMORE JAMES	197	KENT	US	9010
IKE TURNER	PNO	(D	(G) LEGEND OF ELMORE JAMES	1976	BLUES ANTHOLOGY UK	AB 5601
JAMES PARR	TPT	(D	(G) THE LEGEND OF ELMORE JAMES	1976	KENT US 9001	UNITED US	7778
MAXWELL DAVIS	SAX	(D	(H) BEST OF	19	SUE	UK	ILP 918
JEWELL GRANT	SAX	(D	(J) MEMORIAL ALBUM	19	SUE	UK	ILP 927
JESSE SAILES	D	(D	(K) WHOSE MUDDY SHOES	19	CHESS 1537	RI UK 82	2007
EDDIE TAYLOR	G	(M	(L) THE BLUES IN MY HEART	19	CUSTOM US 1054 UNITED US	7716
WILLARD McDANIEL	(	(M) STREET TALKIN'	19	MUSE	MR 5087
BUSHY HEAD	PNO	(B	(N) DUST MY BLUES	19	GLOBE	VIP 5004M
CHUCK HAMILTON	(	(O) ELMORE JAMES	19	KENT	US	522

(CONTINUED)

ELMORE JAMES

(P) HISTORY OF VOL 1	1975	TRIP	US			8007
(Q) HISTORY OF VOL 2	19	TRIP	US			9511
(R) ONE WAY OUT	1980	CHARLY	UK		CRB	1008
(S) SKY IS CRYING	19	SPHERE SOUND	US			7002
(T) SCREAMING BLUES	19	HARLEM HIT PARADE				5014
(U) BLUES MASTERS VOL 1	19	BLUE HORIZON	US			46021
(V) I NEED YOU	19	SPHERE SOUND	US			7008
( ) ELMORE JAMES	19	BELL	US			6037
( ) BLUES AFTER HOURS	19	CROWN	US			5168
( ) ORIGINAL FOLK BLUES	19	KENT US 522	US	UNITED	7743
( ) THE GREAT ELMORE JAMES	19	UPFRONT	US			122
( ) GOT TO MOVE	1981	CHARLY	UK		CRB	1017
( ) BEST OF	1981	ACE	UK			CH31

ETTA JAMES

ETTA JAMES	V	(ALL	AT LAST	1961	CADET	US		4003
WITH			SECOND TIME AROUND	1961	CADET	US		4011
JEFF PORCARO	D	(*	ETTA JAMES	1963	CADET	US		4013
CHUCK RAINEY	B	(*	SINGS FOR LOVERS	1963	CADET	US		4018
LARRY CARLTON	G	(*	TOP TEN	1963	CADET	US		4025
CORNELL DUPREE	G	(*	ROCKS THE HOUSE	1963	CADET	US		4032
BRIAN RAY	V	(*	QUEEN OF SOUL	1965	CADET	US		4040
RICHARD TEE	K	(*	CALL MY NAME	196	CADET	US		4055
KEITH JOHNSON	PNO	(*	(X)TELL MAMA	1969	CADET	US		802
ALEXANDER HAMILTON	V	(*	(X)TELL MAMA	1969	CHESS		CRL	4536
MERRY CLAYTON	V	(*	FUNK	1970	CADET	US		
JOYCE AUSTIN	V	(*	MISS ETTA JAMES	19	CROWN	US	CLP	5209
GILBERT IVEY	V	(*	BEST OF	19	CROWN	US	CLP	5234
REUBEN FRANKLIN	V	(*	TWIST WITH	19	CROWN	US	CLP	5250
HENRY JACKSON	V	(*	GOLDEN DECADE	1972	CHESS	UK		6310 126
THE SNAKES	V	(*	ETTA JAMES	1973	CHESS			50042
TOM ROADY	PERC	(*	COME A LITTLE CLOSER	1974	CHESS			60029
RICK SCHLOSSER	D	(*	ETTA IS BETTA THAN EVAH	1975	CHESS			19003
JIM HORN	SAX	(*	PEACHES	1973	CHESS		2CH	60004
RON STOCKERT	K	(*	LOOSERS WEEPERS	1974	CADET	US		847
CARL BANKS	ORG	(X	SINGS	19	UNITED	US		7712
BARRY BECKETT	ORG	(X	BEST OF	19	UNITED	US		7727
CHARLES CHALMERS	V	(X	(*) DEEP IN THE NIGHT	1978	WB	US BSK 3156	UK K	56492
GEORGE DAVIS	K	(X	CHESS MASTERS	1981	CHESS	UK		2000
ROGER HAWKINS	D	(X	GOOD ROCKIN MAMA	1981	ACE	UK		CH33
DAVID HOOD	B	(X						
JIMMY RAY JENKINS	G	(X	ALBERT LOWE	G	(X	GENE MILLER	TPT	(X	JAMES MITCHELL	SAX	(X
FLOYD NEWMAN	SAX	(X	DEWEY L OLDHAM	K	(X	MARVELL THOMAS	PNO	(X	AARON VARNELL	SAX	(X
ALIMASH SHANANDA	PERC	(*	STEVE CROPPER	G	(*	PLAS JOHNSON	SAX	(*			

GARY JAMES

GARY JAMES	(A) THIRDS	19	ABC DUNHILL	US	ABCX 721

JIMMY JAMES & THE VAGABONDS

JIMMY JAMES	V	(ABC	(A) NEW RELIGION	1966	PICCADILLY		NPL 38027
COUNT MILLER	V	(A	(B) OPEN UP YOUR SOUL	1968	PYE		NSPL 18231
WALLACE WILSON	G	(A	(C) THIS IS JIMMY JAMES	1968	MARBLE ARCH		MAL 823
RUPERT BALGOBIN	D	(A	(D) LONDON SWINGS (1SIDE)	1968	PYE		NSPL 18156
NAT FREDERICK	SAX	(A	(E) YOU DONT STAND A CHANCE	1975	PYE US 12111	UK	NSPL 18457
PHIL CHEN	B	(A	(F) NOW	1976	PYE		NSPL 18495
PAT GRAVESEND	SAX	(	(G) COME SOFTLY TO ME	19	ATCO	US	SD33222
ARTHUR REGIS	ORG	(A	(H) LIFE	1977	CASABLANCA	US	7054
CARL NOEL	ORG	(A	(J) DANCIN' TILL DAWN	1979	PYE	UK	N101
MILTON JAMES	SAX	(A	(K) GOLDEN HOUR	1979	PYE		GH 679

JOHN JAMES

JOHN JAMES	G V	(ALL	(A) MORNING BRINGS THE LIGHT	1970	TRANSATLANTIC	UK	TRA 219
PETE BERRYMAN	G	(C	(B) JOHN JAMES	1971	TRANSATLANTIC	UK	TRA 242
JOHN RENBOURN	G	(DEF	(C) SKY IN MY PIE	1972	TRANSATLANTIC	UK	TRA 250
CHRIS BILLINGS	G	(F	(D) HEAD IN THE CLOUDS	1975	TRANSATLANTIC	UK	TRA 305
DUCK BAKER	G	(E	(E) DESCRIPTIVE GUITAR INSTRUMENTALS	1977	KICKING MULE UK 128	US	143
			(F) IN CONCERT	1978	KICKING MULE	UK	SNKF 136

KEEF JAMES

KEEF JAMES	(A	(A) ONE TREE OR ANOTHER	1973	RARE EARTH US 539 UKSRE 3007

NICKY JAMES

NICKY JAMES	V PERC G	(ABC	(A) NICKY JAMES	1971	PHILIPS		6308 069
KIRK DUNCAN	PNO V	(AC	(B) EVERY HOME SHOULD HAVE ONE	1973	THRESHOLD	UK	THS 10
MIKE WEDGWOOD	B V	(AC	(C) THUNDERTHROAT	1976	THRESHOLD	UK	THS 19
GRAHAM DEACON	D	(AC					
LYNDON GREEN	G	(C	RAY GLYNN	G	(AC	RAY THOMAS	FLT	(C	GERRY HOFF	V	(C
DAVID KATZ	STRINGS	(C	NASHVILLE KATZ	STRINGS(C	JUSTIN HAYWARD	G	(C	MOX	FLT HCA	(C
B J COLE	STEEL(C	ALAN FELDMAN	K	(C	BROTHER FATAAR	B	(C	CHICO GREENWOOD	D	(C
BARRY MARTIN	WIND V(C	JOHN WEIDER	G VLN	(C	MAGGIE CAIRNES	V	(C	HIROSHI KATO	G	(C
IRENE CHANTER	V	(C	DOREEN CHAMTER	V	(C						

RICK JAMES

RICK JAMES	(A	(A) COME GET IT	1978	MOTOWN UK STML12085	
STONE CITY BAND		( ) BUSTIN' OUT OF L SEVEN	1979	MOTOWN UK STML12104	GORDY US 894
		( ) FIRE IT UP	1979	MOTOWN UK STML12128	GORDY US 990
		( ) 3 TIMES IN LOVE	1980		GORDY US 995
		( ) GARDEN OF LOVE	1981	MOTOWN UK STML12141	
		( ) STREET SONGS	1981	MOTOWN UK STML12153	
		( ) THROWING DOWN	1981	MOTOWN UK STML12167	

SKIP JAMES

SKIP JAMES	G V	(ALL	A TRIBUTE	19	BIOGRAPH	BLP	12016
			THIS OLD WORLD	1974	BIOGRAPH	BLP	12027
			EARLY RECORDINGS	19	BIOGRAPH	BLP	12029
			THEY SANG THE BLUES	19	HISTORICAL	HLP	22
			SKIP JAMES TODAY	1965	VANGUARD SVRL 19001+VSD		79219
			DEVIL GOT MY WOMEN	1968	VANGUARD	VSD	79273
			GREATEST OF THE DELTA BLUES SINGERS	19	MELODEON	US	7321
			GREATEST OF THE DELTA BLUES SINGERS	19	STORYVILLE	GER	670185
			I'M SO GLAD	1978	VANGUARD	VPD	20001

```
TOMMY JAMES      V   (ALL    (A) HANKY PANKY                    1966 ROULETTE      US        25336
RONNIE ROSMAN    K   (K      (B) ITS ONLY LOVE                  196  ROULETTE      US        25344
PETER LUCIA      D   (K      (C) I THINK WE'RE ALONE NOW        196  ROULETTE      US        25353
MIKE VALE        B   (K      (D) SOMETHING SPECIAL              196  ROULETTE   US 25355      42005
EDDIE GRAY       G   (K      (E) GETTING TOGETHER               196  ROULETTE      US        25357
PETE DRAKE       STEEL   (N  (F) MONY MONY                      1968 ROULETTE      US        25012
DALE SELLERS     G   (N      (G) CRIMSON & CLOVER               1969 ROULETTE      US        42023
DAVE KIRBY       G   (N      (H) CELLOPHANE SYMPHONY            1969 ROULETTE      US        42030
LINDA HARGROVE   G   (N      (J) BEST OF                        1970 ROULETTE      US        42040
RAY EDENTON      G   (N      (K) TRAVELIN'                      1970 ROULETTE      US        42044
HARGUS ROBBINS   K   (N      (L) TOMMY JAMES                    197  ROULETTE      US        42051
GEORGE RICHEY    K   (N      (M) CHRISTIAN OF THE WORLD         1972 ROULETTE   US 3001       42062
BUDDY HARMON     D   (N      (N) MY HEAD,MY BED & MY RED GUITAR 1973 ROULETTE   US 3007 UK 2432 005
D J FONTANA      D   (N      (O) AT THE SATURDAY HOP            19   LOUISIANNE    US
RUSS LESLIE      D   (N      (P) IN TOUCH                       19   FANTASY       US        9509
BOB KING         B   (N      (Q) MIDNIGHT RIDER                 1979 FANTASY       US        9532
BUDDY SPICHER    FDL (N      (R) 20 GENUINE US CHARTBUSTERS     1977 PYE           UK        NSPL 28260
NASHVILLE EDITION V  (N      (S) 3 TIMES IN LOVE                1980 RCA           US        7748
CHARLIE McCOY    HCA (N      (T) EASY TO LOVE                   1980 MILLENIUM     US        7758
```

```
JIM FOX          D V(ABCDEFHJLMEGH (A) YER ALBUM                1969 STATESIDE UK 10295   ABC US     688
DALE PETERS      B V. (BCDFGHLME   (A) YER ALBUM                1969 BLUESWAY              US         6034
GLENN SCHWARTZ   G    (            (B) JAMES GANG RIDES AGAIN   1970 PROBE     UK 6253    ABC US     711
TOM KRISS        B    (A           (B) JAMES GANG RIDES AGAIN   1970 ABC       UK 5009    MCA GERM   52075
DOMENIC TROIANO  G    (EF          (C) THIRDS                   1971 PROBE     UK 038     ABC US     721
ROY KENNER       V    (EHJF        (D) LIVE IN CONCERT          1971 PROBE     UK 1045    ABC US     733
TOMMY BOLIN      G    (HJ          (D) LIVE IN CONCERT          1974 ABC       UK 5016
BUBBA KEITH      G V  (L           (E) STRAIGHT SHOOTER         1972 PROBE     UK 1056    ABC US     741
RICHARD SHACK    G    (L           (F) PASSIN' THROUGH          1972 PROBE     UK 1065    ABC US     760
ALBHY GALUTEN    K    (J           (G) BEST OF                  1972 PROBE     UK 1070    ABC US     774
RUSTY YOUNG      STEEL(B           (G) BEST OF                  1973 ABC       UK 5027    MCA US     1615
SHELLY KURLAND   VLN  (E           (H) BANG                     1973 ATLANTIC  UK K50028  ATCO US    ')£)
DAVID BRIGGS     ORG  (LF          (I) GOLD RECORD              1973 ABC                  EURO  68303
TOM DOWD         K    (L           (J) MIAMI                    1974 ATLANTIC  UK K50068  US         36102
KEN HAMANN       SYN  (L           (K) 16 GREATEST HITS         1974                      ABC US     801/2
GEORGE RICCI     CELLO(L           (L) NEWBORN                  1975 ATLANTIC  UK K50148  US         36112
DONNY BROOKS     HCA  (L           (M) JESSE COME HOME          1976 ATCO                 US         36141
AL PERKINS       STEEL(L           (N) LAST RIDE                1976 ATCO
BOB WEBB         V G  (M
PHIL GIALLOMARDO K V  (M   JOE WALSH     G V(ABCD  FLACO PADRON   PERC (M   CHARLIE McCOY   HCA (F
WELDON MYRICK    STEEL(F   WILLIAM SMITH    K    (F  CRAIG SAPPHIN  STR (F
```

```
NICK JAMESON  V G B K D(A  (A) ALREADY FREE            1977 BEARSVILLE US 6972   UK K 55519
ERIC PARKER      D    (A
PAUL BUTTERFIELD HCA (A
```

```
                          (A) JAMESTOWN SHEIKS        19   CHAPTER ONE    UK   CMS 1001
```

```
D ADEY           (A        (A) JAMME                  197  DUNHILL        US   50072
K ADEY           (A
P DOWNEY         (A
```

```
JOE JAMMER    G V (A       (A) BAD NEWS               1973 REGAL ZONOPHONE UK  SRZA 8515
TONY STEVENS     B (A
REG ISADORE      D (A  SAPPHO KORNER    V  (A  JEAN ROUSSEL   K  (A  CHRIS MERCER   HRNS (A
DANNY LEWINSON   V (A
```

```
MICK JAGGER      V (A       (A) JAMMING WITH EDWARD    1972 ROLLING STONES   COC 39100
NICKY HOPKINS    K (A
RY COODER        G (A  BILL WYMAN   B  (A  CHARLIE WATTS   D  (A
```

```
JAN BERRY        V (ALL     GOLDEN HITS                1962 LIBERTY US (M) 3248    (S)7248
DEAN TORRENCE    V (ALL     GOLDEN HITS                1962 LIBERTY UK LBY 1279
WITH                       TAKE LINDA SURFIN'         1963 LIBERTY US (M) 3294    (S)7294
HAL BLAINE       D (*   (*) SURF CITY                  1963 LIBERTY US (M) 3314    (S)7314
RAY POHLMAN      (*     (*) SURF CITY                  1963 LIBERTY UK            LBY 1163
LEON RUSSELL     K (*       DRAG CITY                  1963 LIBERTY US (M) 3339    (S)7339
LARRY KNECHTEL   B (*       DEAD MANS CURVE/NEW GIRL IN SCHOOL 1964 LIBERTY US (M) 3361  (S)7361
STEVE DOUGLAS    SAX (*     RIDE THE WILD SURF         1964 LIBERTY US (M) 3368    (S)7368
                           RIDE THE WILD SURF         1981 GREENLIGHT UK 2011
TOMMY TEDESCO    G (*       LITTLE OLD LADY FROM PASADENA 1964 LIBERTY US (M) 3377  (S)7377
BILL PITMAN      (*         COMMAND PERFORMANCE        1965 LIBERTY US (M) 3403    (S)7403
BILLY STRANGE    (*         GOLDEN HITS VOL 2          1965 LIBERTY US (M) 3417    (S)7417
GLEN CAMPBELL    G V (*     FOLK & ROLL                1965 LIBERTY US (M) 3431    (S)7431
                           FILET OF SOUL              1966 LIBERTY US (M) 3441    (S)7441
                           MEET BATMAN                1966 LIBERTY US (M) 3444    (S)7444
                           POPSICLE                   1966 LIBERTY US (M) 3458    (S)7458
                           GOLDEN HITS VOL 3          1966 LIBERTY US (M) 3460    (S)7460
                           SAVE FOR A RAINY DAY       1967 J &D   US JDS101 + CBS US 9461
                           JAN & DEAN                 1968 SUNSET US (M) 1156     (S)5156
                           JAN & DEAN                 1968 SUNSET UK 50001
                           LEGENDARY MASTERS          1971 UA                 UAS  9961
                           REMEMBER (EP)              1973 UA    US REM401
                           VERY BEST OF               19   SUNSET UK 50165
                           GOTTA TAKE THAT ONE LAST RIDE 1974 UA   US        UALA 341H2
                           JAN & DEAN (DBL)           197  SUNSET NL          12860020/1
                           20 ROCK'N'ROLL HITS        1979 UA       SWED ROCK10
                           STORY                      1980 CREOLE UK PAST 1   US KTEL502
                           DEAD MANS CURVE            1980 UA   US 10011
                           BEST                       1981 LIBERTY US 10115
```

JAN & LORRAINE

```
JAN HENDIN        G K V(A      (A) GYPSY PEOPLE                    1969 ABC          US           691
LORRAINE LEFEVRE  V G  (A
KAESHAW SATHE     TABLA(A  CLEM CATTINI    D   (A  BRIAN ODGERS   B   (A   NAZIR JAIR AZBHOY  TAM (A
TERRY COX         PERC (A  ROAD MINFIELD       PERC (A
```
JAN DUKES DE GREY

```
DEREK NOY G TPT TROM(B      (A) SORCERERS                         1970 NOVA         UK           SDN  8
DENIS CONLAN      D (B      (B) MICE & RATS IN THE LOFT           1971 TRANSATLANTIC UK           TRA234
MICHAEL BAIRSTOW  WIND(B
```
JANE

```
BERND PULST       V    (A      (A) JANE TOGETHER                  1972 BRAIN        GER             1 002
KLAUS HESS        G V  (ABCDEFGHJK (B) HERE WE ARE                1973 BRAIN        GER             1 032
WERNER NADOLNY    K FLT(AB      (C) JANE 3                        1974 BRAIN GER 1048 CAPITOL US 11425
CHARLY MAUCHER    B V  (AC      (D) LADY JANE                     1975 BRAIN        GER             1 066
PETER PANKA       D V  (ABCDEFGHJK (E) FIRE, WATER , EARTH & WIND 1975 BRAIN        GER             1 084
MARTIN HESSE      B    (DEFGHJK (F) LIVE                          1976 BRAIN        GER           0080 001/2
GOTTFRIED JANKO   K V  (D       (G) BETWEEN HEAVEN & HELL         1977 BRAIN        GER           0060055
WOLFGANG KRANTZ   G PNO(BC      (H) AGE OF MADNESS                1978 BRAIN GER 60124 LOGO UK 1005
DIETER DIERKS     SYN  (B       (J) SIGN No NINE                  1979 BRAIN        GER           0060 218
PEDJA             V STR(K       (K) JANE                          1981 BRAIN        GER           0060 354
MIRAIM KALENBERG  V    (B
ARIANE GOTTBERG   V    (B   BRIGITTE BLUNCK   V  (B  ANGELIKA WINKLER V  (B  PETER HEINEMANN  V  (B
GUNTER KORBER     V    (B   WERNER ADOLUNG        (E  MANFRED WIECZORKE K V (FG  A ZCCHENKER     HARP  (G
```
LU JANIS

```
LU JANIS          V K  (A      (A) OR DURVS                       1978 INPHASION                 3900
AL CINER          G    (A
JOEY BRASLER      G    (A   PHIL REED      G    (A  DENNIS BELFIELD V B (A  BUTCH RILLERA  D  (A
BOBBY RUFFINO     D    (A   CRAIG KRAMPF   D    (A  ROY BRAVERMAN   K   (A  BECKY LEWIS    V  (A
VINCE POULOS      EFFECTS (A SILKY MAYER   G    (A
```
JANUARY

```
JANUARY TYME      K V PERC(A     (A) FIRST TIME FROM MEMPHIS      19   ENTERPRISE        US   1004
ALLEN COOLEY      D V  (A
STEVE CIANTRO     B    (A   WILLIAM BRANCACCIO   G K V(A ANTHINY IZZO  G V  (A
```
CHAS JANKEL

```
CHAS JANKEL V K PERC G (A      (A) CHAS JANKEL                    1980 A&M US 4862 UK       AMLH 68518
PETER VAN HOOKE   D    (A      (B) CHASANOVA                      1981 A&M US       UK       AMLH 68533
CHRIS WARWICK     SYN  (A
MARK ISHAM TPT SAX SYN(A   KUMA HARADA  B   (A  CHRIS HUNTER   SAX (A  PAUL WESTWOOD   B  (A
```
JANUS

```
                               (A) GRAVEDIGGER                    1974 ELECTROLA         IC062 29433
```
NOEL JANUS

```
NOEL JANUS        (A           (A) HEROES OF THE WORLD            1977 DJM          UK       DJF 20509
KIRBY             G    (A
JEFF RICH         D    (A   STEVE EMERY      B   (A  JOHN COOK   K SYN(A
```
JAPAN

```
DAVID SYLVIAN     V G  (ABCDEF (A) ADOLESCENT SEX                1978 ARIOLA US 50037 UK AHAL 8004
                               (A) ADOLESCENT SEX                1978 HANSA        GER          26091
MICK KARN         B V  (ABCDEF (B) OBSCURE ALTERNATIVES          1979 ARIOLA US 50047 UK AHAL 8007
                               (B) OBSCURE ALTERNATIVES          1979 HANSA        GER      200 166
STEVE JANSEN      D V  (ABCDEF (C) QUIET LIFE                    1979 ARIOLA                AHAL 8011
                               (C) QUIET LIFE                    1979 HANSA        GER      201 261
                               (C) QUIET LIFE                    1982 FAME         UK            3037
ROB DEAN          G V  (ABC    (D) GENTLEMEN TAKE POLAROIDS      1980 VIRGIN       UK       V  2180
RICHARD BARBIERI  K V  (ABCDEF (E) ASSEMBLAGE                    1981 ARISTA       UK       HANLP1
RAY SINGER        V    (AB     (F) TIN DRUM                      1981 VIRGIN       UK       V 2209
SIMON HOUSE       VLN  (F      (EP) LIVE IN JAPAN                1980 HANSA        GER      600242
YUKA FUJII        V    (F
```
BERT JANSCH

```
BERT JANSCH       G V PNO(ALL  (A) BERT JANSCH                   1965 TRANSATLANTIC UK      TRA 125
JAY LACY          G    (NM     (B) IT DON'T BOTHER ME            1965 TRANSATLANTIC         TRA 132
JIM BAKER         G V  (N      (C) JACK ORION                    1966 TRANSATLANTIC UK      TRA 143
DON WHALEY        B V  (N      (C) JACK ORION                    196  VANGUARD      US      VSD 6544
ERNIE McDANIELS   B    (N      (D) BERT & JOHN RENBOURN          1966 TRANSATLANTIC UK      TRA 144
DAVID HUNGATE     B HRNS(N     (E) LUCKY THIRTEEN                1966 VANGUARD              VSD79212
DANNY R LANE      D    (NM     (F) NICOLA                        1967 TRANSATLANTIC UK      TRA 157
TRIS IMBODEN      D    (N      (G) BIRTHDAY BLUES                1968 TRANSATLANTIC UK      TRA 179
RED RHODES        STEEL(M      (G) BIRTHDAY BLUES                1968 REPRISE       US           6343
ROBERT GREENIDGE  D    (N      (H) STEPPING STONES               1969 VANGUARD US 6506 UK   VSD79292
CRAIG BULHER      HNRS (N      (I) SAMPLER                       1969 TRANSATLANTIC UK      TRASAM 10
DARREL LEONARD    HRNS (N      (J) ROSEMARY LANE                 1971 TRANSATLANTIC UK      TRA 235
DUFFY POWER       HCA  (G      (J) ROSEMARY LANE                 1971 REPRISE       US           6455
JIM GORDON        HRNS (N      (K) BOX OF LOVE (COMP)            1972 TRANSATLANTIC UK      TRASAM 27
BILL SMITH        K    (N      (L) MOONSHINE                     1973 REPRISE US 2129      UK K44225
DAVID BARRY       K    (N      (M) L.A. TURNAROUND               1974 CHARISMA      UK      CAS  1090
GEORGE SEYMOUR    K    (N      (N) SANTA BARBARA HONEYMOON       1975 CHARISMA      UK      CAS  1107
RAY WARLEIGH      FLT  (KG     (A) EARLY BERT                    1976 XTRA         UK       XTRA 1163
BETH FICHET       V    (N      (B) EARLY BERT VOL 2              1976 XTRA         UK       XTRA 1164
RON McGUIRE       V    (N      (F) EARLY BERT VOL 3              1976 XTRA         UK       XTRA 1165
STEVE WOOD        V    (N      (J) EARLY BERT VOL 4              1977 XTRA         UK       XTRA 1170
MICHAEL NESMITH   G    (M      (O) A RARE CONUNDRUM              1977 CHARISMA      UK      CAS  1127
TERRY COX         D    (G      (O) A RARE CONUNDRUM              1977 KICKING MULE  US           302
RALPH McTELL      HCA  (OL     (P) ANTHOLOGY                     1978 TRANSATLANTIC UK      MTRA 2007
DAVE BAINBRIDGE   K    (O      (Q) AVOCET                        1979 CHARISMA      UK      CLASS   6
PICK WITHERS      D    (O      (R) 13 DOWN                       1980 KICKING MULE US 309 UK      162
ROD CLEMENTS  G B MAND (O      (S) BEST OF                       1980 KICKING MULE                334
DANNY THOMPSON    B    (GLQ    (T) HEARTBREAK                    1982 LOGO         UK      1035
MIKE PIGGOTT      VLN  (O
JOHN RENBOURN     G    (BCDKH
NIGEL PORTMAN SMITH B K(   LUCE LANGRIDGE  D   (  JACQUI McSHE  V  ( MARTIN JENKINS FLT VLN MAND(KQ
TONY VISCONTE     B    (L  MARY VISCONTE   V   (L DAVE MATTACKS  D  (L SKAILA KANDA    HARP   (L
ALI BAIN          FDL  (L  LAURIE ALLAN    D   (L RICHARD ADENEY FLT (L THEA KING       CLAR   (L
MARILYN SANSON    CELLO(L  GARY BOYLE      G   (L DANNY RICHMOND D  (L MIKE COHEN      PNO    (M
KLAUS VOORMANN    B    (M  JESSE ED DAVIS  G(M    BYRON BERLINE  FDL (M
```
[294]

JEAN MICHEL JARRE

JEAN MICHEL JARRE	K SYN(ALL	(A) OXYGENE	1977	POLYDOR US 6112	UK 2310 555
		(B) EQUINOXE	1978	POLYDOR US 6175	UK POLD 5007
		(B) EQUINOXE	1978	POLYDOR	EURO 2310 636
		(C) MAGNETIC FIELDS	1981	POLYDOR US 6325	UK POLS 1033
		(D) CONCERTS IN CHINA	1982	POLYDOR	UK PODV 3

AL JARREAU

AL JARREAU	V	(ALL	(A) WE GOT BY	1975	WB US 2224	UK K 54045
TOM CANNING	K	(AB	(B) GLOW	1976	WB US 2248	UK K 54073
JOE CORRERO	D	(AB	(C) LOOK TO THE RAINBOW(DBL) LIVE	197	WB US 3052	UK K 66059
WILTIN FELDER	B	(B	(D) ALL FLY HOME	1979	WB US 3229	UK K 56546
LARRY CARLTON	G	(B	(E) THIS TIME	1980	WB US 3434	UK K 56804
LARRY NASH	K	(B	(F) BREAKING AWAY	1981	WB	UK K 56957
JOE SAMPLE	PNO	(B				

LARRY BUNKER	VIBES(A	STEVE FORMAN	PERC (B	RALPH MACDONALD	PER (B	DAVE GRUSIN	K (A
WILLIE WEEKS	B	(B	PAUL STALLWORTH	B	(AB	ABE LABORIEL	B (E	GREG MATHIESON	K SYN(E
MICHAEL OMARTIAN	SYN	(E	RALPH HUMPHREY	D	(E	CARLOS VEGA	D (E	STEVE GADD	D (E
TOM CANNING	PNO	(E	DAVID FOSTER	PNO	(E	LARRY WILLIAMS	PNO (E	GEORGE DUKE	PNO (E
JAY GRAYDON	G	(E	OSCAR NEVES	G	(E	DEAN PARKS	G (E	EARL KLUGH	G (E
JERRY HEY	HRNS(E	CHUCK FINDLEY	HRNS (E	BILL REICHENBACH	TROM (E	LON PRICE	SAX (E
LES THOMPSON	HCA (E	ARTHUR ADAMS	G (A			

JASPER

STEVE RADFORD	G	(A	(A) LIBERATION	1969 SPARK	SRLP 103
ALAN FELDMAN	K	(A			
JON TAYLOR	B	(A	NICK PAYN	V HCA FLT(A	CHICO GREENWOOD	D (A

JASPER WRATH

MICHAEL SOLDAN	(A	(A) JASPER WRATH	19	MGM	US	SNF5003
CHRISTOPHER HAWKE	(A					
ROBERT GENNETTE	(A	PHILLIP STOLTIE	(A			

JAY & THE AMERICANS

JAY BLACK V	(ALL	(A) SHE CRIED	1962	UA	US	6222
KENNY VANCE	(	(B) AT THE CAFE WHA	1963	UA	US	6300
SANDY YAGUDA	(	(C) COME A LITTLE BIT CLOSER	1965	UA	US	6407
MARTY SANDERS	(	(D) BLOCKBUSTERS	1965	UA	US	6417
WALTER BECKER	B G (	(E) GREATEST HITS VOL 1	1965	UA	US	6453
DONALD FAGEN	K (	(F) SUNDAY & ME	1966	UA	US	6474
HOWIE KANE	G (	(G) LIVING ABOVE YOUR HEAD	1966	US		6534
JAY TRAYNOR	V (A	(H) GREATEST HITS VOL 2	1967	UA	US	6555
		(J) TRY SOME OF THIS	1967	UA	US	6562
		(K) SAND OF TIME	1969	UA	US	6671
		(L) WAX MUSEUM VOL 1	1970	UA	US	6719
		(M) WAX MUSEUM VOL 2	197	UA	US	6751
		(N) VERY BEST OF(COMP)	1975	UA UK LBR1000	US>	UALA 357
		(O) CAPTURE THE MOMENT	19	UA	US	6762
		( ) EARLY AMERICAN HITS	19	SUNSET	US	5278
		( )GOOD TIMES	19	SUNSET	US	1001
		( ) GREATEST HITS	1980	UA	US	1010

JAZZ ROCK EXPERIENCE

(A) JAZZ ROCK EXPERIENCE	1970	NOVA	SDN 19

JEBADIAH

(A) ROCK'N'SOUL	1978 EPIC US 35592	NL KILLROY 19912

JEFFERSON AIRPLANE & STARSHIP

PAUL KANTNER G V		(A) JEFFERSON AIRPLANE TAKES OFF	1966	RCA US LSP 3584	UK SF 8195
(ABCDEFGHJKLMNOPQRSTV		(A) JEFFERSON AIRPLANE TAKES OFF	1974	RCA INTERNATIONAL	INT 1476
JORMA KAUKONEN	G V	(B) SURREALISTIC PILLOW****	1967	RCA US LSP 3766	UK SF 7889
(ABCDEFGHJKLP		(B) SURREALISTIC PILLOW****	1975	RCA YLI3738 RI 81 UK INTS5030	
MARTY BALIN G V		(C) AFTER BATHING AT BAXTERS	1967	RCA US LSO 1511	UK SF 7926
(ABCDEFJLMNOPQR		(C) AFTER BATHING AT BAXTERS	197	RCA	AFLI 4545
SIGNE ANDERSON	V (ALP	(D) CROWN OF CREATION	1968	RCA US LSP 4058	UK SF 7976
SKIP SPENCE D	(ALP	(E) BLESS ITS POINTED LITTLE HEAD	1969	RCA US LSP 4133	UK SF 8019
SPENCER DRYDEN	D (BCDEFJLP	(E) BLESS ITS POINTED LITTLE HEAD	197	TELDEC SR 3012 +RCA AFLI 4133	
BOB HARVEY	B (	(F) VOLUNTEERS	1969	RCA US LSP 4238	UK SF 8076
JACK CASADY B	(ABCDEFGHJKLP	(G) BARK	1971	GRUNT	FTR 1001
GRACE SLICK K V		(H) LONG JOHN SILVER	1972	GRUNT	FTR 1007
(BCDEFGHJKLMNOPQV		(J) THE WORST OF (COMP)	1970	RCA US LSP 4459	UK SF 8164
JOEY COVINGTON	D (FGHL	(K) 30 SECONDS OVER WINTERLAND	1973	GRUNT	BFLI 0147
JERRY GARCIA	G (FL	(L) EARLY FLIGHT	1974	GRUNT	APLI 0437
PAPA JOHN CREACH	VLN V(GHKMNR	(M) DRAGONFLY	1974	GRUNT	BFLI 0717
JOHN HAMMOND HCA	(LF	(N) RED OCTOPUS	1975	GRUNT FTR 2002	BFLI 0999
NICKY HOPKINS	K (F	(N) RED OCTOPUS	1980	GRUNT US RI	3660
JOHN BARBATA	D (HKMNOQR	(O) SPITFIRE	1976	GRUNT	BFLI 1557
SAMMY PIAZZA D	(H	(P) FLIGHT LOG	1977	RCA US LSP 3766	UK SF 7889
DAVID FREIBERG	V (KMNOQRSV	(P) FLIGHT LOG	1976	GRUNT	US/UK 1255
IRV COX	SAX (N	(Q) EARTH	1978	GRUNT	US/UK 2515
PETER KAUKONEN	B (	(R) GOLD (COMP)	1979	GRUNT	US/UK 13247
BOBBYE HALL PERC (N		(S) FREEDOM AT POINT ZERO	1979	GRUNT	US/UK 13452
CRAIG CHAQUICO	G (MNOQRSV	(T) BEST OF	1980	RCA INT US 42727	UK 5030
PETER SEARS B K	(MNOQRSV	(AB) SURREALISTIC AIRPLANE (DBL)	19		
AYNSLEY DUNBAR	D (SV	(DF) CROWN/VOLUNTEERS	1980	RCA NL 43302	
MICKEY THOMAS	V (SV	( ) ELEPHANT MOUNTAIN	1975	GRUNT	US 4510
DAVID CROSBY	V (F	(V) MODERN TIMES	1980	GRUNT US 3848 UK 3050 RI INT5027	
STEVE STILLS	ORG (F				
RICK JARRARD PROD	(B	AL SCHMITT	PROD (F	MARY GANNON	V (F	MARILYN HUNT	V (F
DEANE HURSH	V (F	DENISE JEWKES	V (F	BILL LANDER	V (G	MATTHEW KATZ	PROD(A
TOMMY OLIVER	PROD (A						

```
GARLAND JEFFREYS  PERC G V  (ALL    (A) GARLAND JEFFREYS           1973 ATLANTIC US SD 7253
STEVE GADD          D    (BC         (B) GHOST WRITER              1977 A&M US  4629      UK AMLH 64629
DON GROLNICK        K    (BC         (C) ONE EYED JACK             1978 A&M US  4681      UK AMLH 64681
DR JOHN             K    (ABC        (D) AMERICAN BOY & GIRL       1979 A&M US  4778      UK AMLH 64778
JEFF MIRANOV        G    (C          (E) ESCAPE ARTIST             1980 EPIC US 36983     UK     84808
RICHARD TRIFAN      K    (C          (F) ROCK'N' ROLL ADULT        1982 EPIC              85307
DAVID SANBORN       SAX  (BC
LUTHER VANDROSS     V    (C   HUGH McCRACKEN G HCA  (BC  G E SMITH         G B (E  ANDREW BODNER     B  (E
MICHAEL BRECKER     SAX  (BCE PHOEBE SNOW     V    (C   PAUL PRESTOPINO   MAND (D  DAVID SPINOZZA K G  (BC
RANDY BRECKER       TPT  (BCE DAVID LASLEY    V    (BC  ALAN FREEDMAN     G   (ABDE PAT AUSTIN     V    (A
DAVID BROMBERG      DOBRO(A  DONALD BROOKS    HCA  (A   HUX BROWN         G   (A  LORI BURTON       V    (A
GEOFFREY CHUNG      G    (A   RICHARD DAVIS   B    (A   WINSTON GRENNAN   D   (A  PAUL GRIFFIN      K    (A
NEVILLE HINDS       ORG  (A   JACKIE JACKSON  B    (A   JIMMY JOHNSON     D   (A  DENZIL LAING      PERC (A
RALPH MACDONALD     PERC (A   MIKE MAINIERI   VIBES(A   ADAM MILLER       V   (A  DAVID NEWMAN      SAX  (A
CHRIS OSBORNE       G    (A   LARRY PACKER    VLA VLN(A THE PERSUASIONS   V   (A  BERNARD PURDIE    D    (A
CHUCK RAINEY        B    (A   ALBERTINE ROBINSON V (A   JOHN SIMON        PNO (A  MAERETHA STEWART  V    (A
WINSTON WRIGHT      PNO  (A   ANTHONY JACKSON B    (BC  RUBENS BASSINI    PERC (B  ARNOLD McCULLER  V    (B
JAMES TAYLOR        V    (B   JOHN BOUDREAUX  D    (B   PHIL MESSINA      TROM (B  SUGARBEAR        G    (B
DANNY CAHN          TPT  (B   LYNNE PITNEY    V    (B   AL COHN           SAX  (B  LEON PENDARVIS   K    (B
DAVID PEEL          V    (B   BURT COLLINS    TPT  (B   ROBERT ATHAS      G B (D  TIMMY CAPELLO  K SAX V(D
ANTON FIG           D    (D   RAFAEL GOLDFARB B    (D   RORY DODD         V   (D  ERIC TROYER       V    (D
HERB ALPERT         TPT  (B   MICHAEL CUSCUNA PROD (A   STEVE GOULDING    D   (E  DANNY FREDERICI  K ACC(E
ROY BITTAN          PNO  (E   LINTON KWESI JOHNSON V (E ARTY FUNERO       G K (E  LARRY FAST       SYN  (E
ADRIAN BELEW        G    (E   ROBERT ATHAS    G    (E   EARL LINDO        ORG (E  JIMMY MAELIN      PERC(E
LOU REED            V    (E   DIANE GRASSELLI V    (E   MYRIAM VALLE      V   (E  MARIA VIDAL       V  (E
BOB CLEARMOUNTAIN   E    (E   JOHN KPIAYE     G    (E   EATON BLAKE       B   (E  DENNIS BOVELL    K G (E
WEBSTER JOHNSON     K PERC(E   ERROL MELBOURNE D    (E   SEYOUM NET FA     MEL (E  PATRICK TENYRE   HRNS(E
AUGUSTOS TENYRE.    HRNS (E
```

```
FRED BLIFFERT       V    (A          (A) TRUE STORY               1977 ASYLUM      US      7E 1096
JESSE ROE           V    (A
AMY MADIGAN         V    (A
```

```
                                     (A) JELLY BEANS              1976 BAAL       UK      89002
```

```
PAUL BUTLER         G V  (ABC        (A) FIRST SLICE              1969 BLUE HORIZON US 4801 UK 7 63853
PETE WINGFIELD      K V  (AB         (B) 65 PARKWAY               1970 BLUE HORIZON         2431 002
JOHN BEST           B    (ABC        (C) BACK TO BEGIN AGAIN      1972 BLUE HORIZON         2931 004
CHRIS WATERS        D    (AB
RICK HAYWARD        G    (C   KENNY LAMB   D PERC   (C
```

```
BOB THRONE          TROM (A          (A) JELLYROLL                1971 MCA UK MUPS 420 + US KAPP 3626
LES ASCH            SAX  (A
DAVE PARKINSON      SAX  (A   TIM HEDDING   K   (A  ED SETGER    G   (A  ROGER TROY       B  (A
STU PERRY           D    (A
```

```
JOHNNY JENKINS  V G HCA   (A         (A) TON TON MACOUTE          1970 ATLANTIC UK 2400 033+ RI K40105
DUANE ALLMAN        G    (A          (A) TON TON MACOUTE          1970 ATCO     US SD 33331+ FR 503056
PETE CARR           G    (A          (B) TON TON MACOUTE          1974 CARRI    US RI        0136
PAUL HORNSBY        G K  (A
ROBERT 'POPS' POPWELL B(A   BERRY OAKLEY    B    (A BUTCH TRUCKS D   (A  ELLA BROWN       V  (A
JOHNNY SANDLIN      D    (A   JAI JOHANNY JOHANSON PERC(A EDDIE HINTON PERC (A  JOHNNY WYKER     PERC(A
TIPPY ARMSTRONG     PERC (A   SOUTHERN COMFORT V    (A
```

```
BILL JENNINGS            (A          (A) GUITAR MOODS             19   KING       US      KEP 342
```

```
WAYLON JENNINGS     G V  (ALL    FOLK COUNTRY               1965 RCA              US LSP  3523
BILLY SANFORD       G    (OM     LEAVIN TOWN                1966 RCA              US LSP  3620
DALE SELLERS        G    (O      NASHVILLE REBEL            1966 RCA              US LSP  3736
REGGIE YOUNG        G    (OPZX   SINGS OL' HARLAN           1966 RCA              US LSP  3660
GERRY GROPP         G    (O      JEWELS                     1969 RCA              US LSP  4085
EDDIE HINTON        G    (O      LOVE OF THE COMMON PEOPLE  1967 RCA              US LSP  3825
BILLY REYNOLDS      G    (OQMUS  HANGIN' ON                 1968 RCA              US LSP  3918
RANDY SCRUGGS       G    (OQS    ONLY THE GREATEST          1968 RCA   UK SF 8003 US LSP  4023
LARRY WHITMORE      G    (OPQUS  COUNTRY FOLK               1969 RCA              US LSP  4180
STEVE YOUNG         G    (O      JUST TO SATISFY YOU        1969 RCA              US LSP  4137
RALPH MOONEY STEEL G (OPMSTUXZ   WAYLON JENNINGS            1969 VOCALION         US VL   73873
JOE ALLEN           B    (OQ     BEST OF                    1970 RCA   UK LSA 3000 US LSP 4341
BEE SPEARS          B    (OZ     WAYLON                     1970 RCA              US LSP  4260
HENRY STRZELECKI    B    (OM     SINGER OF SAD SONGS        1970 RCA   UK LSA 3025 US LSP 4418
TOMMY WILLIAMS      B    (O      SINGER OF SAD SONGS        1980 RCA INT UK INTS5020
BYRON BACH          CELLO(       DONT THINK TWICE           1969 A&M              US S    4238
MARTHA McCRORY      CELLO(O      COUNTRY STYLE OF           1970 A&M              AMLB    1006
DAVID BRIGGS        PNO  (O      THE TAKER                  1970 RCA              US LSP  4487
ANDY McMAHON        ORG  (OQ     THE ONE & ONLY WAYLON      1967 CAMDEN           CAS     2183
DON BROOKS          HCA  (OPZ    CEDARTOWN GEORGIA          1970 RCA   UK LSA 3053 US LSP 4567
WILLIE ACKERMAN     D    (O      (M)LADIES LOVE OUTLAWS     1971 RCA   UK LSA 3142 US LSP 4751
RICHIE ALBRIGHT     D    (OPQSTUXZ GOOD HEARTED WOMAN       1972 RCA              US LSP  4647
BUDDY HARMON        D    (OM     HEARTACHES BY THE NUMBER   1972 CAMDEN           CAS     2556
FRED NEWELL         G    (PQ     LONESOME ON'RY & MEAN      1972 RCA              US LSP  4854
WILLIE NELSON       V B  (P      (O ) HONKY TONK HEROES     1973 RCA              US APL1 0240
JESSI COLTER        K    (P      RUBY DONT TAKE YOUR LOVE TO TOWN 1973 CAMDEN     CAS     2608
DEE MOELLING        K    (P      (P) THIS TIME              1974 RCA              US APLO539
DUKE GOFF           B    (OPQSTU (Q ) RAMBLING MAN          1974 RCA   UK LSA 3136 US APL1 0734
KYLE LEHMING        K TPT(OPQ    NED KELLY                  1975 U A              US UALA 3066
CHARLIE McCOY       HCA  (S      OUTLAWS                    1976 RCA   UK RS 1078 US APL1 1321
ROGER CRABTREE      HCA  (QSU    (S)DREAMING MY DREAMS      1975 RCA   UK LSA 3247US APL1 1062
CHARLES LOCHRAN     PNO  (S      (T)ARE YOU READY FOR COUNTRY 1976 RCA UK RS 1067 US APL1 1816
MERLE WATSON        V B  (       ARE YOU READY FOR THE COUNTRY 1981 RCA 3663
JOHN WILKIN         G    (MRS    (U)LIVE                    1976 RCA   UK PL 11108 US APL1 1108
```

(CONTINUED)

[296]

WAYLON JENNINGS (CONTINUED)

JOE PALLEN	G	(S	MACKINTOSH & TJ (SOUNDTRACK)	1976	RCA	US	APL1 1520
JIMMY COLVARD	G	(S	HITS OF	1977	RCA UK PL 42211		
KENNY MALONE	D	(S	(X)OL' WAYLON	1977	RCA UK PL 12317 US		APL1 2317
BUDDY SPICHER	FDL	(S	WAYLON & WILLIE	1978	RCA UK PL 12686 US		APL1 2686
STRING SECTION		(S	(Z) I'VE ALWAYS BEEN CRAZY	1978	RCA UK PL 12959 US		APL1 2959
DAVE KIRBY	G	(MQ	WAYLON AT JDs	1978	BEAR FAMILY	GERM	JD 1001
BUNKY KEELS	PNO	(Q	A SOUVENIR OF ARIZONA	19			LJR 114
LARRIE LONDIN	D	(MQ	ONLY DADDY THAT'LL WALK THE LINE	19	RCA		ACLI 0306
THOMAS JACKSON	FDL	(Q	DARK SIDE OF FAME	19	RCA		ACLI 7019
LEON RHODES	B	(Q	GREATEST HITS OF WAYLON	1979	RCA UK PL 13378		
CARL GAY	G	(Q	WHAT GOES AROUND	1979	RCA UK PL 13493		
SHERMAN HAYES	B	(Q	EARLY YEARS	1979	CORAL CDL 8501		
JOHN LESLIE HUG	G	(T	WAYLON MUSIC	1980	RCA UK PL 43166		
BARNEY ROBERTSON	PNO/V	(T	MUSIC MAN	1980	RCA	US	3602
GRAHAM NASH	V	(T	GREATEST HITS	1981	RCA UK LP 3031		
JIM GORDON	HRNS	(T	LEATHER & LACE	1981	RCA UK LP 3931		
MAURICE SPEARS	HRNS	(T	BLACK ON BLACK	1982	RCA UK 3072		
MACK JOHNSON	HRNS	(T					
CARTER ROBERTSON	V	(TXZ					
GORDON PAYNE	V	(ZX	RANCE WASSON V (TXZ JERRY STEMBRIDGE G (M FRED CARTER (Z				
TONY JOE WHITE		(Z	STAN REECE (Z CLIFF ROBERTSON K (XZ JOHNNY GIMBLE G (S				
KENNY BUTTREY	D	(M	NORBERT PUTNAM B (M HARGUS 'PIG' ROBBINS PNO(M JIM PIERCE PNO (M				
JOHN CHRISTOPHER	G	(X	BOBBY DYSON B (N BILLY GRAHAM FDL (T DON ROBERTSON (T				
BOBBY THOMPSON	G	(Q	QRICK POWELL SYN (M				

JENSON INTERCEPTOR

CHARLOTTE WIEBE	K V	(A	(A) JENSON INTERCEPTOR	1980	HOUSE OF LORDS		1002
DOUG JENSON	G V	(A`					
KENNY JENSON	K	(A	ALBERT BLAINE D (A JOHN FYNN D (A				

JEREMY & THE SATYRS

JEREMY STEIG	FLT	(A	(A) JEREMY & THE SATYRS	1968	REPRISE	US RS	6282
DONALD McDONALD	D	(A					
EDDIE GOMEZ	B	(A	ADRIAN GUILLERY G (A WARREN B BERNHARDT K (A				

JERICHO

ROBB HUXLEY	G	(AB	(A) JUNKIES MONKEYS AND DONKEYS	1971	A&M	UK	AMLH 68050
AMI TRIEBICH	D	(AB	(B) JERICHO	1972	A&M	UK	AMLS 68079
DANNY SHOSHAN	V	(AB					
MICHAEL GABRIELLOV	B	(AB	HAIM ROMANO G (AB				

JERONIMO

RINGO FUNK	D V	(A	(A) TIME RIDE	1972	BELLAPHON		BLPS 19095
MICHAEL KOCH	G V K	(A					
GUNNAR SCHAEFER	V B G	(A	DIETER DIERKS V (A PETER HAUKE V (A				

JACK JERSEY

JACK JERSEY		(A	(A) FOREVER	19	EMI	IMP 064 25560	

JERUSALEM

LINDEN WILLIAMS	V	(A	(A) JERUSALEM	1972	DERAM	UK	SDL 6
BOB COOK	G	(A					
BILL HAYDEN	G	(A	PAUL DEAN B (A RAY SPARROW D (A				

JET

DAVY O'LIST	G	(A	(A) JET	1975	CBS	UK	80699
CHRIS TOWNSON	D	(A					
PETER OXENDALE	K	(A	MARTIN GORDON B (A ANDY ELLISON V (A				

JETHRO TULL

IAN ANDERSON	FLT G V	(ALL	(A) THIS WAS JETHRO TULL	1968	ISLAND	UK	ILPS 9085
CLIVE BUNKER	D	(ABCDE	(A) " " " "	1973	CHRYSALIS	UK	CHR 1041
MICK ABRAHAMS	G	(AE	(A) " " " "	1969	REPRISE	US	6336
GLEN CORNICK	B	(ABCE	(A) " " " "	197	PHONOGRAM	EURO	6307 517
JEFFREY HAMMOND HAMMOND	B	(DEFGHJ	(B) STAND UP	1969	ISLAND	UK	ILPS 9103
MARTIN BARRE	G	(1BCDEFGHJKLMNOPQRS	(B) " "	1973	CHRYSALIS	UK	CHR 1042
ANGELA ALLEN	V	(K	(B) " "	1973	CHRYSALIS	GER	202 057
TONY IOMMI	G	(	(B) " "	197	REPRISE	US	6360
BARRIEMORE BARLOW	D	(1FHMOPQGJK	(B) " "	197	PHONOGRAM	EURO	6307 519
JOHN EVAN	K	(1CDEFGHJMPOQ	(C) BENEFIT	1970	ISLAND	UK	ILPS 9123
JOHN GLASCOCK	B	(MOPQK	(C) " "	1973	CHRYSALIS	UK	CHR 1043
STRING SECTION		(J	(C) " "	1973	ISLAND	GER	6339 009
HARRY HUGHES	D	(	(C) " "	197	REPRISE	US	6400
DAVID PALMER	K	(1MOPQHJ	(C) " "	197	PHONOGRAM	EURO	6307 516
TONY WILLIAMS	B	(1M	(D) AQUALUNG	1971	ISLAND	UK	ILPS 9145
FRANCIS WILSON	V	(Q	(D) " "	1973	CHRYSALIS	UK	CHR 1044
DAVE PEGG	B	(RS	(D) " "	197	REPRISE	US	2035
MARK CRAWEY	D	(R	(D) " "	197	PHONOGRAM	EURO	6307 515
EDDIE JOBSON	K VLN	(R	(E) LIVING IN THE PAST	1972	CHRYSALIS	UK	CJT1
DAVY OLIST	G	(	(E) " " " "	197	CHRYSALIS	US	1035
STEVE CROPPER	G	(D	(E) " " " "	197	CHRYSALIS	US	2106
DARRYL WAY	VLN	(0	(F) THICK AS A BRICK	1972	CHRYSALIS	UK	CHR 1003
JAMES ANDERSON		(R	(F) " " " "	197	REPRISE	US	2071
MADDY PRIOR	V	(K	(F) " " " "	197	PHONOGRAM	EURO	6307 502
TERRY ELLIS	PROD	(AB	(G) PASSION PLAY	1973	CHRYSALIS	UK	CHR 1040
PETER JOHN VETTES	K V	(S	(G) " " " "	197	PHONOGRAM	EURO	6307 518
GERRY CONWAY	D	(S	(H) WAR CHILD	1974	CHRYSALIS	US+UK	CHR 1067
			(H) " " " "	197	PHONOGRAM	EURO	6307 537
			(J) MINSTREL IN THE GALLERY	1975	CHRYSALIS	US+UK	CHR 1082
			(J) " " " "	197	PHONOGRAM	EURO	6307 559
			(K) TOO OLD TO ROCK'N'ROLL	1976	CHRYSALIS	US+UK	CHR 1111
			(K) " " " "	197	PHONOGRAM	EURO	6307 572
			(L) THE BEST OF JETHRO TULL	1976	CHRYSALIS	UK	CHR 1078
			(M) SONGS FROM THE WOOD	1977	CHRYSALIS	US+UK	CHR 1132
			(M) " " " "	197	PHONOGRAM	EURO	6307 591
			(N) REPEAT (BEST OF VOL 2)	1977	CHRYSALIS UK CHR1135 GER		6307611
			(O) HEAVY HORSES	1978	CHRYSALIS	US+UK	CHR 1175
			(O) " " " "	197	PHONOGRAM	EURO	6307 622

(CONTINUED)

(CONTINUED)   **JETHRO TULL**

                              (P) LIVE BURSTING OUT   1978   CHRYSALIS US 21201 UK   CJT4
                              (Q) STORMWATCH   1979   CHRYSALIS UK CDL1238 GER 6307670
                              (R) "A"   1980   CHRYSALIS UK CDL1301 GER 202834
                              (S) BROADSWORD & BEAST   1982   CHRYSALIS   CDL 1380
                              (1) LIVE TV SHOW VIA SATELLITE
                              (EP) LIFE IS A LONG SONG   1971   CHRYSALIS   UK   WIP 6106
                              (EP) RING OUT SOLSTICE BELLS   1976   CHRYSALIS   UK   CFX2

JETS (UK)

   BOBBY COTTON   V B (AB   (A) JETS   1981   EMI   UK   3356
   TONY COTTON   V D (AB   (A) JETS   1982   FAME   RI   UK   3036
   RAY COTTON   G V (AB   (B) 100% COTTON   1982   EMI   UK   3399
   JOHNNY PARIS   SAX (A
   DAVEY PAYNE   SAX (A   MICK GALLAGHER   K   (A
JETS
                                 (A) ROCK'N'ROLL MUSIC   1974 SEVEN SUN   SBLP   100
JOAN JETT
   JOAN JETT   V   (ALL   (A) JOAN JETT   1980   ARIOLA   ARL   5058
                                 (B) BAD REPUTAION   1981 BOARDWALK US 37065 EPIC UK 85045
                                 (B) I LOVE ROCK 'N' ROLL   1982 BOARDWALK US 33245 EPIC UK 85686
JIMMY JEWELL
   JIMMY JEWELL   SAX (AB   (A) I'M AMAZED   1977   AFFINITY   AFF2
   JOHN MUMFORD   TROM (AB   (B) FROM THE FIRST TIME I MET YOU 1978 AFFINITY   AFF5
   BILLY LIVSEY   PNO (AB
   RICHARD BRUNTON   G   (AB STEVE BINGHAM   B   (AB RAY DUFFY   D   (AB
JIG SAW
   DES DYER   V D (A   (A) SKY HIGH   1975 SPLASH   1001
   CLIVE SCOTT   K V (A   (B) JIGSAW   1977
   BARRIE BERNARD   B   (A
   TONY CAMPBELL   G   (A
JIVA
   MICHAEL LANNING   G V (A   (A) JIVA   1975 DARK HORSE/A&M   UK AMLH 22003
   JAMES STRAUSS   B V (A
   THOMAS HILTON   G V (A   MICHAEL REED   D PERC(A
JIVE BUREAUX
   TONY MESSENGER G V HCA (A   (A) STICK IT   1978 GULL   UK GULP 1025
   SHAM   V   (A
   TIM MATTHEWMAN   B V (A   BOB WILSON   K   (A   IAN STEPHENSON   PERC (A JOE SLYTHE   D   (A
   ROGER QUESTED   PERC (A   SUE GLOVER   V   (A   SUNNY LESLIE   V (A J STONE   V (A
   GARY WINDO   SAX (A   HARRY BECKETT   TPT (A   NICK EVANS   TROM (A BARRY MORGAN PERC (A
   FRANK RICOTTI   VIBES(A
JO JO GUNNE
   MARK ANDES   B V (A   (A) JO JO GUNNE   1972 ASYLUM US SD 5053 UK SYLA 8752
   JOHN STRONACH   PROD (D   (A) JO JO GUNNE   1976 ASYLUM UK RI K53034
   JAY FERGUSON   K V (ABCD   (B) BITE DOWN HARD   1973 ASYLUM US SD 5065 UK SYL 9005
   MATT ANDES   G V (ABC   (C) JUMPIN' THE GUNNE   1973 ASYLUM US 5071 UK SYL 9015
   CURLY SMITH   D   (ABCD   (D) SO...WHERE'S THE SHOW   1974 ASYLUM US 7E 1022 UK SYL 9019
   JIMMIE RANDALL   B   (BCD
   JOHN STAEHELY   G V (D
JO JO ZEP & THE FALCONS
   JOE CAMILLERI   SAX V(ALL   (A) DON'T WASTE IT   1976   EMI AUSTRALIA   062 61153
   JEFF BURSTIN   G   (ALL   (B) WHIP IT OUT   1977   OZ AUSTRALIA   OZS 1004
   JOHN POWER   B V (ALL   (C) SO YOUNG   1978   OZ "   "   OZS 1002
   GARY YOUNG   D   (ALL   (D) LIVE IN CONCERT   1978   OZ "   "   OZS 1013
   TONY FAEHSE   G   (BCDEFGH (E) SCREAMING TARGETS   1979   MUSHROOM UK K99094 US CBS 36442
   WILBUR WILDE   SAX (BCDEFGH (F) JO JO ZEP & THE FALCONS   1979   ROCKBURGH   UK   ROC 108
   WAYNE BURT   G V (ABEFG   (G) TAKIN' THE WRAPS OFF (DBL) 1979 ROCKBURGH   UK   ROCD 110
   ROSS WILSON   PROD (G   (H) HATS OFF, STEP LIVELY   1980   MUSHROOM   UK   K37321
JO MAMA
   BOB WILLIAMS   TPT (A   (A) JO MAMA(O SOLE MIO)   1971 ATLANTIC US SD 8269 UK 2400 129
   MICHAEL DUBKIN   SAX (A   (B) J IS FOR JUMP   1971 ATLANTIC US SD 8288 UK 2400 174
   OLLIE MITCHELL   TPT (A
   MAYO TIANA   TROM (A   ABIGALE HANESS   V   (AB CHARLES LARKEY   B   (AB CAROLE KING V (B
   JOEL BISHOP-O'BRIEN D (AB RALPH SCHUCKETT   K V (AB DANNY KOOTCH   G V (AB
JOBRIATH
   BARDEN JOBRIATH   (AB   (A) JOBRIATH   1973 BARCLAY FR 80514 ELEKTRA US 75070
   STEVE LOVE   G   ((B) CREATURES OF THE STREET   1974 ELEKTRA   US   7E 1010
   ANDY MUSON   B   (
   JOHN SIOMOS   D   (
JO'BURG HAWK
   BRAHAM MALBERBE   G PERC(A   (A) JO'BURG HAWK   1973 CHARISMA   UK   CAS 1064
   JULIAN LAXTON   G   (A
   DAVE ORNELLAS   V   (A   LES GOODE   B   (A SPOOK KAHN   G   (A IVOR BACK   D (A
   BILLY KNIGHT   PERC V(A   AUDREY MOTAUNG   PERC V(A PETE KUBHAKA   PERC V(A
J JOCKO
   J JOCKO   (A) THAT'S THE SONG   19   KAMA SUTRA   US KSBS 2604
JODY GRIND
   TIM HINKLEY   K V (AB   (A) ONE STEP ON   1969   UA   US   UAS 6774
   PETE GAVIN   D   (B   (A) ONE STEP ON   1969   TRANSATLANTIC UK   TRA 210
   BARRY WILSON   D   (A   (B) FAR CANAL   1970   TRANSATLANTIC UK   TRA 221
   IVAN ZAGNI   G   (A   (B) FAR CANAL   1970   METRONOME   EURO MLP15 388
   BERNIE HOLLAND   G   (B
   LOUIS CENNAMO   B   (A

```
BILLY JOEL          V K  (ALL      (A) COLD SPRING HARBOUR    1972 PHONOGRAM 6269 150 US FAMILY  2700
RICHIE CANNATA      K WIND(EF      (B) PIANOMAN              1973 CBS           US 32544 JAP 25AP952  UK 80719
PHIL RAMONE         PROD (G        (B) PIANOMAN              1981 CBS RI UK 32002
LIBERTY DEVITO      D    (DEFGH    (C) STREET LIFE SERENADE  1975 CBS           US 33146 JAP 25AP1078 UK 80766
HIRAM BULLOCK       G    (E        (C) STREET LIFE SERENADE  1981 CBS RI UK 32035
DOUG STEGMEYER      B    (DEFGH    (D) TURNSTILES            1976 CBS           US 33848 JAP 25AP953  UK 81195
PHIL WOODS          SAX  (E        (D) TURNSTILES            1981 CBS RI UK 32057
RUSSEL JAVORS       G    (DGH      (E) STRANGER              1977 CBS           US 34987 JAP 25AP843  UK 82311
STEVE KHAN          G    (FE       (F) 52nd STREET           1978 CBS           US 35609 JAP 25AP1152 UK 83181
HOWIE EMERSON       G    (D        (G) GLASSHOUSES           1980 CBS           US 36384            UK 86108
JAMES SMITH         G    (D        (H) SONGS IN THE ATTIC    1981 CBS           US 37461            UK 85273
DEAN PARKS          G    (B        (DEF) BOX SET       *     1980 CBS                                UK 66356
RON TUTT            D    (BC
ERIC WEISSBERG      BANJ (B   LAURA CREAMER      V   (B   LARRY CARLTON      G   (B   WILTON FELDER        K   (BC
RHYS CLARK          D    (B   FRED HEILBRUN      BANJO(B   MARK CREAMER       V   (B   RICHARD BENNETT  G   (ABC
EMORY GORDY         B    (ABC MIKE OMARTIAN      ACC  (B   BILLY ARMSTRONG    FDL (B   SUSAN STEWARD    V   (B
LARRY KNECHTEL      B    (C   TOM WHITEHORSE     STEEL(C   GARY DALTON        G   (C   MINGO LEWIS PERC     (D
JOE CLAYTON         CONGA(C   MIKE DEASY         G    (C   ROJ RATHOR         G   (C   AL HERTZBERG     G   (C
DON EVANS           G    (C   ART MUNSON         G    (C   MICHAEL STEWART    G   (C   WILLIAM SMITH    K   (C
FREDDIE HUBBARD     TPT  (F   MIKE MAINIERI      PERC (F   ZACK SANDERS       V   (F   MILT GRAYSON     V   (F
RAY SIMPSON         V    (F   GEORGE MARGE   RECORDER(F   DAVID SPINOZZA     G   (F   DONNIE DACUS     V   (F
PETER CETERA        V    (F   DAVID FRIEDMAN     PERC (F   RALPH MACDONALD    PERC (FE  ERIC GALE        G   (F
FRANK FLOYD         V    (F   BABI FLOYD         V    (F   HUGH McCRACKEN     G   (EF  RICHAR TEE       ORG     (E
LANI GROVES         V    (E   PATTI AUSTIN       V    (E   STEVE BURGH        G   (E   DOMINIC CORTESE  ACC (E
PHOEBE SNOW         V    (E   GWEN GUTHRIE       V    (E   DAVID BROWN        G   (E
```

```
DAVID JOHANSEN      V K  (AB       (A) DAVID JOHANSEN        1978 BLUE SKY US 34926 UK        82335
JOHNNY RAO          G    (A        (B) IN STYLE              1979 BLUE SKY US 36082 UK        83745
THOMAS TRASK        G    (A        (C) HERE COMES THE NIGHT  1981 BLUE SKY US 36589 UK        84504
BUZ VERNO           B    (A
SARA DASH           V    (A   SCARLET RIVERA     VLN  (A   STAN BRONSTEIN     HRNS(A   TONY MACHINE     PERC (A
FELIX CAVALIERE     ORG  (A   BOBBIE BLAIN  ORG      (A   NONA HENDRYX       V   (A   JOE PERRY        K   (A
FRANKIEN LAROCKA    D    (A
```

```
ANDREW JOHN V G B K D WIND(A       (A) THE MACHINE STOPS     1972   CBS               UK        64835
MIKE WOODS          G B  (A
CLIVE SARSTEDT      B    (A   RIC LEE            D    (A   CARSTEN SMEDEGAARD D   (A
```

```
CLIVE JOHN(CLINT SPACE)G K V(A     (A) YOU ALWAYS KNOW WHERE YOU STAND WITH A BUZZARD 1975 UA  UK UAS 29733
MARTIN ACE          B    (A
DAVE CHARLES        D    (A   TOMMY RILEY        D    (A   PHIL RYAN          K   (A   BRIAN BREEZE     G   (A
ANDY FAIRWEATHER LOW G V(A   PETE HURLEY        B    (A   JOHN WILLIAMS      V   (A   TED CROOK        HCA (A
```

```
ELTON JOHN          V K  (ALL      (A) EMPTY SKY             1969 MCA    US  2130 UK DJM DJLPS 403
STEVE WRATHER       G    (R        (A) EMPTY SKY             19   MCA RI US 3008 RI UK 80      22086
CALEB QUAYE         G    (ABCFMO   (B) ELTON JOHN            1970 UNI   US 93090  UK DJM DJLP  20406
DAVID PAICH         K    (R        (B) ELTON JOHN            1970 MCA   US 3000 RI 37067 RI UK 22087
DAVEY JOHNSTONE     G    (FGHJKMO  (C) TUMBLEWEED CONNECTION 1970 UNI   US 73096    UK DJM DJLPS410
STEVE LUKATHER      G    (RQ       (C) TUMBLEWEED CONNECTION 19   MCA RI US 3001 UK RI DJM     22088
TIM SCHMIT          V    (R        (D) 17.11.70              1971 UNI   US 93105  UK DJM DJLPS 414
FRANK CLARK         G    (B        (D) 17.11.70              1971 MCA   US      2015+3002
COLIN GREEN         G    (R        (E) FRIENDS               1971 PARAMOUNT 6004  +    SPFL 269
GLEN FREY           V    (R        (F) MADMAN ACROSS THE WATER 1971 UNI US 93120  UK DJM DJH 20420
CLIVE HICKS         G    (B        (F) MADMAN ACROSS THE WATER 1971 MCA US 3003 RI
ROLAND HARKER       G    (B        (G) HONKY CHATEAU         1972 MCA   US  3004 UK  DJM DJLPH  423
DON HENLEY          V    (R        (G) HONKY CHATEAU         19   MCA RI US 37063 UK RI UK     22090
ALAN PARKER         G    (F        (H) DONT SHOOT ME, I'M ONLY THE PIANO 1973 MCA US 3005 UK DJM DJLPH 427
RICHIA CARNATA      SAX  (R        (H) DONT SHOOT ME, I'M ONLY THE PIANO 19 MCA US 2100  US RI 37113
MAX GROENTHAL       V    (RS       (H) DONT SHOOT ME, I'M ONLY THE PIANO 1981 DJM UK RI 22091
LES THATCHER        G    (F        (J) GOODBYE YELLOW BRICK ROAD 1973 MCA US 2/10003 UK DJM LP 1001
CHRIS SPEDDING      G    (F        (J) GOODBYE YELLOW BRICK ROAD 1976          UK DJM DJE29001
TIM RENWICK         G    (P1       (K) CARIBOU               1974 MCA   US  3006 UK  DJM DJLH   439
PAT SIMMONS         V    (Q        (K) CARIBOU               197  MCA   US RI 37065 UK   2116
LARRY HALL          WIND (R        (K) CARIBOU               1980 DJM UK RI 22092
B J COLE            STEEL(F        (L) CAPTAIN FANTASTIC     1974 MCA   US  3009 UK  DJM DJLPX    1
CLIVE FRANKS        PERC (R        (L) CAPTAIN FANTASTIC     19   MCA   US RI 2142 +  B1 RI 37066
ALLAN TAYLOR        D    (RS       (L) CAPTAIN FANTASTIC     1981 UK DJM RI 22094
RICHIE ZITO         G    (RST      (M) ROCK OF THE WESTIES   1975 MCA   US  3010 UK  DJM DJLPH  464
BILL CHAMPLIN       V    (RS       (M) ROCK OF THE WESTIES   19   MCA   US 2163     US RI 80  621
JERRY HEY           WIND (R        (M) ROCK OF THE WESTIES   1980 DJM     UK RI 22093
TONY MURRAY         B    (A        (N) HERE & THERE          1976 MCA   US 2197  UK  DJM DJH  20473
DAVE RICHMOND       B    (B        (O) BLUE MOVES            1976 MCA   US211004 UK ROCKET   ROLL12
CHUCK FINDLEY       HRNS (R        (O) BLUE MOVES            197  ROCKET UK DJM ROSP1
LES HURDLE          B    (B        (P) SINGLE MAN            1978 MCA   US  3065 UK ROCKET TRAIN 1
VICTOR FELDMAN      PERC (RS       (P) SINGLE MAN            1978 ROCKET EURO    9103 500
BRIAN ODGERS        B    (F        (Q) VICTIM OF LOVE        1979 ROCKET EURO 9103 509 UK HISPD125
HERBIE FLOWERS      B    (F        (R) 21 AT 33              1980 ROCKET EURO 9103 511+UK HISPD126
CHRIS LAURENCE      B    (F        (S) THE FOX               1981 ROCKET EURO 6302 106 UK TRAIN 16
DEE MURRAY          B    (CFGHJKRST(S) THE FOX               1981 GEFFEN US 2002
JIM HORN            SAX  (RS       (T) JUMP UP               1982 GEFFEN US
BILL REICHENBACH    TROM (R
VENNETTE GLOUD      V    (RS       ( ) GREATEST HITS         1974 MCA US 2128 3007 UK DJM     442
KENNY PASSARELLI    B    (MO       ( ) POP CHRONIK           1975 DJM     EURO          VOL7
DAVID GLOVER        B    (GF       ( ) GREATEST HITS         1977 MCA UA 3027     UK DJM    20520
ALAN WEIGHELL       B    (BF       ( ) LIVE COLLECTION (DBL) 1979 PICKWICK  US  PDA       047
BARRY MORGAN        D    (BF       ( ) LIVE (NEW YORK 1970)  1978 HALLMARK   UK       SHM 942
TERRY COX           D    (BF       ( ) LONDON & NEW YORK     1978 HALLMARK   UK       SHM 966
ROGER POPE          D    (ACFMO    ( ) LADY SAMANTHA (COMP)  1980           UK DJM    22085
STEVE HOLLY         D    (PT       ( ) VERY BEST OF          1980 K TEL      UK       NE 1094
DENNIS LOPEZ        PERC (B        (EP) FOUR FROM FOUR EYES  1977           UK    DJM  18001
RAY COOPER          PERC (FGJKMO   ( ) GREATEST HITS  1&2 DBL 1981          UK    DJM  DJLP1
```

(CONTINUED)

```
NIGEL OLSSON          D(ACFGHJKRS)
JAN JOYCE         V    (O    GENE MORFORD       V    (O    BRIAN DEE         K    (BD   DIANA LEWIS      SYN  (EF
RICK WAKEMAN      K    (F    DAVID HENTSCHEL    K    (GJK  CHESTER THOMPSON  K    (K    JAMES NEWTON HOWARD K (MO1
JACK EMBLOW       ACC  (F    CARL FORTINA       ACC  (O    MARTYN FORD ORCHESTRA   (O    DON FAY          WIND (A
LEROY GOMEZ       SAX  (J    STEVE KUPKA        SAX  (K    EMILIO CASTILLO   SAX  (K    MIC GILLETTE     HRNS (K
GREG ADAMS        HRNS (K    RANDY BRECKER      HRNS (O    MICHAEL BRECKER   HRNS (O    BARRY ROGERS     HRNS (O
DAVID SANBORN     HRNS (O    LENNY PICKETT      WIND (K    LESLEY DUNCAN     V    (BCF  TONY HAZZARD     V    (BG
BARRY ST JOHN     V    (F    TERRY STEELE       V    (F    SHIRLEY MATTHEWS  V    (K    CARL WILSON      V    (K
BILLY HINSCHE     V    (K    ANN ORSON          V    (M    JOE CHEMAY        V    (O    CINDY BULLENS    V    (O
CURT BOETCHER     V    (O    KAY GARNER         V    (B    ROGER COOK        V    (BF   LIZA STRIKE      V    (FG
KIKI DEE          V    (JM   JESSIE MAY SMITH   V    (K    BRUCE JOHNSTON    V    (KO   LABELLE          V    (M
DAVID CROSBY      V    (O    CLARK BURROUGHS    V    (O    RON HICKLIN       V    (O    CORNERSTONE CHIOR V  (G
JACQUES BOLOGNESI TROM (G    IVAN JULIAN        TPT  (G    JEAN LOUIS CHAUTEMPS SAX(G   ALAIN HATOT      SAX  (G
JEAN LUC PONTY    VLN  (G    LEGS LARRY SMITH   V    (G    LARRY STEELE      V    (G    GUS DUDGEON  V WHISTLE(G
TEX NAVARRA       PERC (B    IAN DUCK      HCA       (C    SKAILA KANGA      HARP (B    GRAHAM VICKERY   HCA  (A
PAUL BUCKMASTER   CELLO(O    GENE PAGE          STR  (O    MICHAEL HURWITZ   CELLO(O    MADELINE BELL    V    (BG
TONY BURROWS      V    (BF   SUE GLOVER         V    (F    SUNNY LESLIE      V    (F    CLYDIE KING      V    (K
DUSTY SPRINGFIELD V    (K    TONI TENNILLE      V    (KO   CLIVE FRANKS      V    (MP   GRAHAM NASH      V    (O
CARMAN TWILLEY    V    (R    LENNIE CASTRO      PERC (R    STEPHANIE SPRUILL V    (QRS  BYRON BERLINE    FDL  (R
GARY OSBORNE      V    (T    PETE TOWNSHEND     G    (T    JEFF PORCARO      D    (T    KEITH FORSEY  D    (Q
MARCUS MILLER     B    (Q    CRAIG SNYDER       G    (Q    TIM CANSFIELD     G    (Q    THOR BALDURSSON  K    (Q
ROY DAVIES        K    (Q    PAULINHO DACOSTA   PERC (Q    JULIA TILLMAN     V    (Q    MAXINE WILLARD   V    (Q
MIKE McDONALD     V    (Q    TAMARA MATOESIAN   V    (S    REGGIE McBRIDE    B    (S    RONALD BAKER     V    (S
CHUCK CISSEL      V    (S    GARY OSBORNE       V    (S    MICKEY RAPHAEL    HCA  (S    JAMES GILSTRAP   V    (S
JOHN LEHMAN       V    (S    CARL CARWELL       V    (S    ROY GALLOWAY      V    (S    OREN WATERS      V    (S
CLARENCE FORD     V    (S
```

```
JOHNNY LITTLE JOHN  G V(ALL     (A) JOHNNY LITTLE JOHN & CHICAGO BLUES BAND 197  ARHOOLIE        F 1043
DAVE MYERS         B    (B      (B) FUNKY FROM CHICAGO                    1973  BLUESWAY      BL 6069
EDDIE TAYLOR       G    (B      (C) JOHNNY LITTLE JOHN                    197   MCM       FR  900 300
FRED BELOW         D    (B
MONROE JONES       G    (A  ALVIN NICHOLS    B   (A  ROBERT PULLIAM   SAX (A  WILLIE YOUNG SAX    (A
BOOKER SIDGROVE    D    (A
```

```
ROBERT JOHN        V    (ALL    (A) ON THE WAY UP                        1971  HARMONY     US 31353
GEORGE TOBIN       V    (B      (B) ROBERT JOHN                          1979  EMI AMERICA     AML 3003
ED GREENE          D    (B      (C) BACK ON THE STREET                   1980  EMI UK 3014   US  17027
HAL BLAINE         D    (B
H LEE WOLEN      D PERC(B  SCOTT EDWARDS    B   (B  DAVID SHIELDS    B   (B  DENNIS BELFIELD B   (B
MIKE PICCIRILLO    G V  (B  BILL NEALE    G      (B  STEWART LEVIN    K   (B  MIKE THOMPSON K     (B
EDNA WRIGHT        V    (B  DARLENE LOVE     V   (B  GEORGE TOBIN     V   (B
```

```
JOHNNY PARIS       SAX  (      JOHNNY & HURRICANES                       1960  WARWICK      US        W2007
PAUL TESLUK        ORG  (      STORMSVILLE                               1960  WARWICK US W2010 +LONDON UK 2269
DAVE YORKO         G    (      BIG SOUND                                 1960  LONDON  HAX 2322 BIG TOP US 1302
LIONEL MATTICE     B    (      BEATNIK FLY                               19    TWIRL        US        5002
DON STACZEK        D    (      BEST OF                                   196   LONDON       UK   HA   2227
BILL SAVICH        D    (      RED RIVER ROCK                            19    BIRCHMOUNT   US        565
TONY KAYE          D    (      PROFILE                                   19    TELDEC       GERM      624008
                               LIVE AT THE STAR CLUB HAMBURG             196   ATILA        US        1030
                          (EP)REMEMBER                                   1973  UA                     REM 401
                               VERY BEST OF                              1975  CONTEMPO               CRMD 1002
                               LEGEND OF ROCK VOL 1 (DBL)                19    LONDON                 DP628 329
                               LEGEND OF ROCK VOL 2 (DBL)                19    LONDON                 DP628 318
                          (EP) JOHNNY & THE HURRICANES                   19    WARWICK      US        700
                               JOHNNY & THE HURRICANES                   1981  LONDON       UK    TAB 32
```

```
                               (A) OUT ON BAIL                           19    CHARLY       UK   CR   30184
```

```
ANDY ELLISON       V    (A     (A) ORGASM                                19    WHITE WHALE  US        WW 7128
MARC BOLAN         G V  (       (A) THE LEGENDARY ORGASM ALBUM(+TRACKS)1982  CHERRY RED    UK        BRED31
JOHN HEWLETT       B    (A
CHRIS TOWNSON      D    (A
```

```
ALPHONSO JOHNSON   B V  (AB    (A) MOONSHADOWS                           1976  EPIC         US        34118
DAWILLI GONGA      K V  (A     (B) YESTERDAYS DREAMS                     1976  EPIC         US        34364
PATRICE RUSHEN     K    (AB    (C) SPELLBOUND                            1978  EPIC         US 34369 UK 82197
GEORGE BOHANON     TROM (B     ( ) BEST OF                               1980  EPIC         US 36521
CHRIS BOND         G    (A
IAN UNDERWOOD      K    (AB  FLORA PURIM      V   (AB  BENNIE MAUPIN  WIND (A  NARADA MICHAEL WALDEN D K(A
LEON CHANCLER      D    (A   BLACKBIRD McKNIGHT G (A   ALEJANDRO ACUNA PERC(A  AIRTO MOREIRA    PERC   (A
GARY BARTZ         SAX  (A   ALPHONSE MOUZON  K   (A   GROVER WASHINGTON SAX(B  RAY GOMEZ      G       (B
LEE RITENOUR       G    (AB  MARK JORDAN      KRG (B   DAVID FOSTER   ORG (B   RUTH UNDERWOOD   PERC   (B
CHESTER THOMPSON   D    (B   MIKE CLARK       G   (B   SHEILA ESCOVEDO PERC(B  GARNETT BROWN    TROM   (B
JON LUCIEN         V    (B   PHILIP BAILEY    V   (B   DIANE REEVES   V   (B   ERNIE WATTS      SAX    (B
ERNIE FIELDS       SAX  (B   CHUCK FINDLEY    TPT (B   GARY GRANT     HRNS (B
```

```
BOB JOHNSON        (A          (A) KING OF ELFLAND'S DAUGHTER            1977  CHRYSALIS    UK CHR1137
PETER KNIGHT       (A
CHRISTOPHER LEE    V    (A   MARY HOPKIN      V   (A   FRANKIE MILLER  V   (A   ALEXIS KORNER   V   (A
P P ARNOLD         V    (A   DEREK BRIMSTONE  V   (A   CHRIS FARLOWE   V   (A
```

```
DAVID EARL JOHNSON (A           (A) TIME IS FREE                         1978  VANGUARD          VSD 79401
JAN HAMMER         K    (A
```

```
JIMMY JOHNSON      (AB          (A) JIMMY JOHNSON & LUTHER JOHNSON       1977  MCM               900  294
LUTHER JOHNSON     G    (A      (B) JIMMY JOHNSON                        1978  MCM               900  302
                               (C) JOHNSONS WHEELS                       1980  DELMARK      UK        644
```

LARRY JOHNSON

```
LARRY JOHNSON      G V  (ALL    (A) PRESENTING THE COUNTRY BLUES   1970  BLUE HORIZON          7 63851
                                (B) COUNTRY BLUES                 197   BIOGRAGHICAL    US   BLP 12028
JOHN PAUL HAMMOND       (B      (C) FAST & FUNKY                  19    BLUE GOOSE          BG  2001
```

LINTON KWESI JOHNSON

```
LINTON KWESI JOHNSON V (ALL    (A) FORCES OF VICTORY             1979  ISLAND          UK   ILPS 9566
                                (B) BASS CULTURE                  1980  ISLAND          UK   ILPS 9605
                                (c) L K J IN DUB                  1980  ISLAND          UK   ILPS 9650
                                (D) BEST OF                       1980  EPIC            US 36521
                                (E) DREAD BEAT & BLOOD            1981  VIRGIN          UK      1002
```

LONNIE JOHNSON

```
LONNIE JOHNSONG K VLN (ALL    (A)LONNIE JOHNSON                 1974  STORYVILLE            SLP  162
ELMER SNOWDEN      G   (         LONNIE JOHNSON                  19    COLLECTORS CLASSICS  CC   30
VICTORIA SPIVEY    V   (         BLUES GUITAR VOL 2              1970  PARLOPHONE           PMC 7106
OTIS SPANN         PNO (K        ANOTHER NIGHT TO CRY            19    BLUESVILLE      US    1062
JOHN HUGHES        PNO (K        TOMORROW NIGHT                  196   STARDAY/KING SK1083+ GD  5039X
ROY COULTER        B   (K        MR JOHNSONS BLUES               197   MAMUSH               3807
ALLEN SMITH        PNO (K        BLUES & BALLADS                 19    PRESTIGE        US    1011
MONTE MORRISON     B   (K        BLUES BY LONNIE JOHNSON         19    PRESTIGE        US    1007
HERMAN SMITH       PNO (K        IDLE HOURS                      19    PRESTIGE        US    1044
JAMES JOHNSON      G   (T        WOMAN BLUES(AS VICTORIA SPIVEY) 19    PRESTIGE        US    1054
JACK ERBY          PNO (T     (K)LONESOME ROAD                   19    KING            US    520
LAZY HARRIS        G   (T        SINGS 24 12 BAR BLUES           19    KING            US    958
PORTER GRAINGER    PNO (T        LOSING GAME                     19    PRESTIGE        US    1024
JOSHUA ALTHEIMER   PNO (S        (S) BLUEBIRS No 13              19    RCA             PM   42390
ALFRED ELKINS      B   (S        (T) WOKE UP THIS MORNING        1980  ORIGINAL JAZZ   OJL  23
LIL ARMSTRONG      PNO (S
BLIND JOHN DAVIS   PNO (S  ANDREW HARRIS   B  (S
```

LUTHER 'GEORGIA BOY SNAKE' JOHNSON

```
LUTHER JOHNSON     G V  (ABC   (A) WITH THE MUDDY WATERS BLUES BAND 1969 TRANSATLANTIC  UK   TRA 188
GEORGE 'MOJO' BUFORD HCA(A     (A) WITH THE MUDDY WATERS BLUES BAND 1969 DOUGLAS        US   SD 781
MUDDY WATERS       G   (A      (B) BORN IN GEORGIA              1974  BLACK & BLUE    FR   33503
OTIS SPANN         PNO (A      (C) ON THE ROAD AGAIN            1976  BLACK & BLUE    FR   33509
SAMMY LAWHORN      G   (A      ( ) COME ON HOME                 19    DOUGLAS         US   SD 789
FRANCIS CLAY       D   (A      ( ) LUTHER JOHNSON               1975  MUSE           US   5021
```

ROBERT JOHNSON

```
ROBERT JOHNSON     G V  (ALL      KING OF THE DELTA BLUES SINGERS  1966  CBS US CL1654   UK   62456
                                  KING OF THE DELTA BLUES SINGERS VOL 2 1970 CBS US 30034 UK  64102
                                  LEGACY                         19    CBS US 33904
```

ROBERT JOHNSON

```
ROBERT JOHNSON     G V  (AB    (A) CLOSE PERSONAL FRIENDS       1979  ENSIGN UK ENVY4 INFINITY  9000
DAVID COCHRAN      V B D(AB    (B) MEMPHIS DEMOS                 1980  ENSIGN              ENRJ 12
BLAIR CUNNINGHAM   V D  (AB
```

WILKO JOHNSON & SOLID SENDERS

```
WILKO JOHNSON      G V  (A     (A) SOLID SENDERS                1978  VIRGIN          UK   V 2105
JOHN POTTER        K   (A      (A) LIVE  (FREE WITH V 2105)     1978  VIRGIN          UK  VDJ 26
STEVE LEWINS       B   (A      (B) ICE ON THE MOTORWAY          1981  FRESH           UK   LP 4
MICKEY GALLAGHER   K   (B
ALAN PLATT         D   (A  DAVE BROOKS    SAX (A    JOHN DENTON    PNO (A   RUSSELL STRUTHER B  (B
ALEX BINES         D   (B
```

BROTHERS JOHNSON

```
                               (A) LOOK OUT FOR NO 1            1976  A&M             UK   AMLH 64567
                               (B) RIGHT ON TIME                1977  A&M             UK   AMLH 64644
                               (C) BLAM                         1978  A&M             UK   AMLH 64714
                               (D) LIGHT UP THE NIGHT           1980  A&M             UK   AMLK 62716
                               (E) WINNERS                      1981  A&M             UK   AMLK 63724
```

ADRIENNE JOHNSTON

```
ADRIENNE JOHNSTON V  (A      (A) ADRIENNE JOHNSTON OF THE JOHNSTONS 1975 RCA     UK   SF 8416
DON FRASER        PNO  (A
PAT DONALDSON     B   (A   BARRY MORGAN    D   (A   GERRY CONWAY     D   (A   GREG BARON CELLO  (A
MICHAEL HURWITZ   CELLO(A  BARRY CASTLE    HRNS(A   CHRIS ANDREETY   V   (A   TOM MADDEN   V    (A
WILF GIBSON       VLN (A   HOWARD DAVIS    VLN (A   GEORGE ROBERTSON VLA (A   CLIVE ANSTEE CELLO (A
JOHN HORNET       HRNS(A   FRANK RYECROFT  HRNS(A   MIRIAM KEOGH     HARP(A   SIMON NICOL  G    (A
```

BRUCE JOHNSTON

```
BRUCE JOHNSTON     G V  (ABC   (A) SURFIN' PAJAMA PARTY         196   DELFI           US      634
                               (B) SURFIN' AROUND THE WORLD     196   CBS  US 2057  +     8857
                               (C) GOING PUBLIC                 1977  CBS  US 34459   UK   81854
```

TOM JOHNSTON

```
TOM JOHNSTON      V G  (A     (A) EVERYTHING YOU'VE HEARD IS TRUE 1979 WB   US BSK 3304  UK K 56632
JIM KELTNER       D   (A      (B) STILL FEELS GOOD TO ME        1981  WB   US 9SK 3527
TOWER OF POWER    HRNS(A
RICK SCHLOSSER    D   (A   DAVID GARIBALDI  D   (A   KEITH KNUDSEN    D   (A   PAUL STALLWORTH B  (A
BOB GLAUB         B   (A   RICK CHUDACOFF   B   (A   PAUL BARRERE     G   (A   BILL PAYNE   K    (A
DAVID PAICH       K   (A   MARK JORDAN      K   (A   MICHAEL McDONALD K   (A   NICOLETTE LARSON V (A
TED TEMPLEMAN     V   (A   ANDREW LOVE      SAX (A   LEWIS COLLINS    HRNS(A   BEN CAULEY   HRNS(A
JERRY JUMONVILLE  SAX (A   JACK HALE        HRNS(A   LENNY PICKETT    HRNS(A   EMILIO CASTILLO HRNS (A
STEVE KUPKA       HRNS(A   MIC GILLETTE     HRNS(A   GREG ADAMS       HRNS(A
```

DAVEY JOHNSTONE

```
DAVEY JOHNSTONE   G V  (A     (A) SMILING FACE                  1973  ROCKET UK PIGL2 RI ROLA 2
DAVE HENTSCHEL    SYN  (A     (A) SMILING FACE                  1973  MCA     US     340
JOAN ARMATRADING  PNO  (A
GUS DUDGEON       PERC (A   B J COLE     STEEL(A  MOHAMMED AMIR    HCA (A   RICK BATEMAN  HCA (A
CHRIS LAURENCE    B   (A    MICHAEL HINTON TPT(A  GRAHAM MORGAN    D   (A   MICK FLYNN    WHISTLE(A
JO PARTRIDGE      G   (A    CHRIS KARAN  TABLA(A  RAY COOPER       PERC (A  DEE MURRAY  B    (A
DI JOHNSTONE      V   (A    ELTON JOHN   HCA (A   NIGEL OLSSON     D   (A   DEL NIEWMAN SAX  (A
```

JOLLIVER ARKANSAW

```
LESLIE WEST       G   (A     (A) HOME                           1969  BELL            US      119
FELIX PAPPALARDI      (A
```

```
      JIM DOAK          B V  (A        (A) JOLT                           1978 POLYDOR        UK   2383 504
      ROBERT COLLINS    G V  (A
      IAIN SHEDDEN      D    (A
```

```
      JON BLAIR         G    (AB       (A) SURF BEAT '80                  1980 VOXX US 200002 LINE GER  LLP5088
      DAVE WRONSKI      G    (B        (A) SURF BEAT                      1981 CHARLY UK CR30213
      DDIE B GIANNI     G    (A        (B) LIVE AT THE WHISKY             1981 VOXX US 200005 LINE GER  LLP5118
      NIKI SYXX         B    (AB
      DUSTY WATSON      D    (AB
```

```
      JON ANDERSON      V    (AB       (A) SHORT STORIES                  1980  POLYDOR  UK 5030    US 6072
      VANGELIS          K SYN (AB      (B) FRIENDS OF MR CAIRO            1981  POLYDOR  UK 5039    US 6326
      RAPHAEL PRESTON   G    (B
      DAVID COKER       V    (B    SALLY GRACE   V   (B    DICK MORRISEY      WIND (B   CAROL KENYON    V  (B
      CLAIR HAMILL      V    (B
```

```
      ROBERT GENGO      G V  (A        (A) JONAH                          1974 20TH CENT      T   456
      MICHAEL GREGORIO  PERC V(A
      VINCENT LA FATA   G V  (A    JOE GENGO      PERC (A   DON GROLNICK       ORG  (A   BOB MANN        G  (A
      EDDIE BRIGATI     PERC (A    TOMMY WEST     K    (A   TONY SANTARELLA    B    (A   MIKE BRECKER    SAX (A
      ALLEN SCHWARZBERG D    (A
```

```
      BOOKER T JONES    K V  (A        (A) TRY AND LOVE AGAIN             1978 A&M            UK   AM   64720
      PATRICIA HENDERSON V   (A        (B) THE BEST OF YOU                1980 A&M US 4798    UK   AMLK 64789
      JAY GRAYDON       G    (A
      DENNIS BELFIELD   B    (A    MIKE BAIRD     D    (A   MIKE UTLEY         K    (A   JIM GILSTRAP    V  (A
      JOHN LEHMAN       V    (A    MARLENA TETER  V    (A
```

```
      BRIAN JONES            (A        (A) PRESENTS THE PIPES OF PAN AT JOUJOUKA 1971  ROLLING STONES  COC  49100
```

```
      BUSTA JONES            (A        (A) BUSTA JONES                    19   SPRING         US        6728
```

```
      CASEY JONES       V    (AB       (A) DONT HA HA                     1964 GOLDEN              12 106
      ROGER HOOK        G    (AB       (B) SECOND ALBUM                   1965 GOLDEN              12 108
      DAVID COLEMAN     G    (AB
      JIM REDFORD       B    (AB   PETER RICHARDS  D    (AB
```

```
      CHRISTOPHER JONES      (A        (A) NO MORE RANGE TO ROAM          1978 TRANSATLANTIC   UK   TRA 503
      MICK LINNARD      G B  (A
      PICK WITHERS      D    (A    GERALD MOORE    G   (A   JEFFREY JONES      HCA G K(A
```

```
      CURTIS JONES      PNO V(AB       (A) NOW RESIDENT IN EUROPE         1968 BLUE HORIZON    UK   7 63207
      BRIAN BROCKLEHURST  B(A          (B) TROUBLE BLUES                  19   PRESTIGE        US        1022
      DOUGIE WRIGHT     D    (A        (C) LONESOME BEDROOM BLUES         1979 DELMARK              DL 605
      ALEXIS KORNER     G    (
```

```
      GLORIA JONES      V    (A        (A) WINDSTORM                      1977 CAPITOL 11854      SIDEWALK 1002
      DAN FERGUSON      G    (A        (A) WINDSTORM                      1979 EMI RI UK  EMC3291
      ROBERT WHITE           (A        (B) GLORIA JONES                   1978 MOTOWN      US   790
      LAWRENCE HILL     V    (A
      DARRYL MOORE           (A    PAUL HUMPHREY   D    (A   OMA DRAKE          V    (A   T YOUNG         V    (A
      M YOUNG           V    (A    RAY PARKER      G    (A   JOE SAMPLE         K    (A   SCOTT EDWARDS   B    (A
      JACK ASHFORD      PERC (A    EDDIE BROWN          (A   JAMES GADSON       D    (A   EMANUEL GREEN   VLN (A
      SYLVESTER RIVERS  K    (A    WAH WAH WATSON  G    (A   TIM MAY                 (A   RON COLEMAN          (A
      GARY COLEMAN      PERC (A    J SINGLETON     V    (A   JOE GREEN          V    (A   JESSE KIRKLAND  V    (A
      SHARON MINGUS     V    (A    NANIS NORMAN    V    (A
```

```
      GRACE JONES       V    (ALL      (A) PORTFOLIO                      1977 ISLAND          UK   ILPS 9470
      JOHN DAVIS        K    (B        (B) FAME                           1978 ISLAND          UK   ILPS 9525
      PIGGY PIGERINO    VLN  (B        (C) MUSIC                          1979 ISLAND          UK   ILPS 9538
      JIMMY WALKER      PERC (B        (D) WARM LEATHERETTE               1980 ISLAND          UK   ILPS 9592
      LARRY WASHINGTON  PERC (AB       (E) NIGHT CLUBBING                 1981 ISLAND          UK   ILPS 9624
      CRAIG SNYDER      G    (B
      JIMMY WILLIAMS    B    (B    CARLA BENSON      V    (AB  SWEETHEARTS OF SIGMA V(AB BARBARA INGRAM V    (AB
      EVETTE BENTON     V    (AB   ALLAN SCHWARZBERG D    (A   WILBUR BASCOMB     B  (A   LANCE QUINN     G    (A
      CLIFF MORRIS      G    (A    BOBBY ELI         G    (A   CARLTON KENT       (A     RON KERSEY      K    (A
      VINCE MONTANA     VIBES(A    MOTO              TAMB (B   DON RENALDO        STR(AB   KEITH BENSON    D    (B
      SLY DUNBAR        D    (D    ROBBIE SHAKESPEARE B   (D   BARRY REYNOLDS     G (D    MICHAEL CHUNG   G    (D
      WALLY BADAROU     K    (D    STICKY THOMPSON   PERC (D
```

```
      JOHNNY JONES      K V  (A        (A) LIVE IN CHICAGO                1979 ALLIGATOR US 4717 SONET UK  821
      BILLY BOY ARNOLD  V HCA(A
```

```
      LINDA JONES       V    (A        (A) YOUR PRECIOUS LOVE             19   TURBO                7007
```

```
      MICKY JONES       G V  (
      TWEKE LEWIS       G    (
      STEVE DIXON       D    (    STEVE GURL    K    (A   ALAN McKENNA    B      (
```

```
      NIGEL MAZLYN JONES  G V(A        (A) SHIP TO SHORE                  1976 ISLE OF LIGHT        IOL 666/1
                                       (B) SENTINEL                       1978 AVADA                AVA 105
```

```
      PAUL JONES        V G HCA(ALL    (A) MY WAY                         1966 HMV          UK   CLP 3586
                                       (B) PRIVILEGE                      1966 HMV          UK   CLP 3523
                                       (C) LOVE ME LOVE MY FRIENDS        1967 HMV          UK   CSD 3602
                                       (D) CRUCIFIX IN A HORSESHOE        1971 VERTIGO UK 6360 059 LONDON US605
                                       (E) SINGS PRIVILEGE & OTHERS       19   CAPITOL      US   ST 2795
                                       (F) HITS & BLUES                   1980 ONE UP       UK        2231
```

RICKIE LEE JONES

```
RICKIE LEE JONES G K V PERC(AB    (A) RICKIE LEE JONES          1979   WB  US BSK 3296      UK K 56628
STEVE GADD          D     (AB     (B) PIRATES                   1981   WB  US      3432     UK K 56816
JERRY HEY           HRNS (B
ANDY NEWMARK        D     (A   VICTOR FELDMAN PERC K D(AB  MARK STEVENS   D PERC(A  JEFF PORCARO     D  (A
TOM SCOTT           HRNS (A    ARNO LUCAS         V   (AB  MATTHEW WIENER   V   (A  WILLIE WEEKS     B  (A
RED CALLENDER       B     (A   BUZZY FEITEN       G   (AB  FRED TACKETT     D   (A  NEIL LARSEN      K  (AB
CHUCK FINDLEY       HRNS (A    LESLIE SMITH       V   (AB  MICHAEL McDONALD V   (A  RANDY KERBER     K  (AB
RALPH GRIERSON      K     (A   DR JOHN            K   (A   RANDY NEWMAN     SYN (A  MICHAEL BODDICKER SYN(AB
ERNIE WATTS         HRNS (A    JOE TORANO         V   (AB  NICK DE CARO     ACC (A  CHUCK RAINEY     B  (B
ART RODRIGUEZ       D     (B   DEAN PARKS         G   (B   STEVE LUKATHER   G   (B  DAVID KALISH     G  (B
RUSSELL FERRANTE    K     (A   CLARENCE McDONALD K (B  LENNY CASTRO     PERC (B  DONALD FAGEN    SYN (B
ROB MOUNSEY         SYN   (A   RANDY BRECKER     TPT (B  DAVID SANBORN    SAX (B  SAL BERNARDI    HCA V(B
```

JONESES

```
HAROLD TAYLOR       V SAX     (A    (A) KEEPIN' UP WITH THE JONES   1974 MERCURY  US         1021
REGGIE NOBLE        SAX   (A
GLENN DORSEY        B     (A   WENDELL NOBLE      SAX (A  SAM WHITE      SAX (A  RICHARD TEE     K  (A
PAUL GRIFFIN        K     (A   CORNELL DUPREE     G   (A  CARL LYNCH     G   (A  LEE VALENTINE   G  (A
WILBUR BASCOMBE     B     (A   WARREN SMITH      PERC(A  BILL LA VORGNA D   (A  STEVE GADD      D  (A
RICK MAROTTA        D     (A   DOODIE LONDIN      D   (A  ALAN SCHWARZBERG D (A  SAL SCHLINGER   HRNS(A
CRAWFORD PERRY      D     (A   RICHARD PRATT    CONGA(A  RALPH McDONALD CONGA(A  SELDON POWELL   HRNS(A
JON FADDIS          HRNS (A   ERNIE ROYAL        HRNS (A  GARNETT BROWN  HRNS (A  DANNY MOORE     HRNS   (A
GEORGE COLEMAN      HRNS (A   HELENE MILES V      (A  ADRIENNE ALBERT  V  (A  MAERETHA ALBERT  V  (A
```

JONESY

```
ALAN BOWN           TPT PERC(BC    (A) NO ALTERNATIVE     1972   DAWN          UK   DNLS 3042
PLUG THOMAS         D V     (BC    (B) KEEPING UP         1973   DAWN          UK   DNLS 3048
JAMIE KALETH        K V     (ABC   (C) GROWING           1973   DAWN          UK   DNLS 3055
JOHN EVAN JONES     G V     (ABC1  (1) JONESY 1978
GYPSY JONES         G V     (BC
JACK JONES          (1   MORRIS PERT      PERC (C  PAUL STARK      (1   DAVID PAULL     B V (A
JIM PAYNE           D     (A   PHIL CLARKE      (1   KEN ELLIOT    SYN (C  CLIVE LONIE     (1
BERNIE HAGLEY       SAX   (C
```

JOOK

```
                                    (A) WATCH YOUR STEP(EP)  197   CHISWICK      UK    SW30
```

JANIS JOPLIN

```
JANIS JOPLIN        G V     (ALL   (A) I GOT DEM OL' KOZMIC BLUES AGAIN 1969  CBS US 9913   UK  63546
BRAD CAMPBELL       B     (ABCF   (B) PEARL                 1971   CBS US 30322  UK  64188
CLARK PIERSON       D     (BCF    (C) IN CONCERT (DBL)      1972   CBS US 31160  UK  67241
KEN PEARSON         ORG     (BCF  (D) GREATEST HITS         1973   CBS US 32168  UK  65470
DAVE GETZ           D     (CF     (D) GREATEST HITS         1982   CBS           UK RI32190
JOHN TILL           G     (BCF    (E) JANIS (SOUNDTRACK)(DBL) 1974  CBS US 33345  UK  88115
RICHARD BELL        PNO     (BCF  (F) ANTHOLOGY (DBL)       1980   CBS US 88492  UK  22101
SANDRA CROUCH       TAMB (B        (G) JANIS JOPLIN          19     SUPRAPHON     IMP  1 13 2215
BOBBYE HALL         PERC (B
BOBBY WOMACK        G     (B   VINCE MITCHELL     V   (B  PHIL BADELLA    V  (B  JOHN COOKE    V  (B
SAM ANDREW          G V     (ACF  RICHARD KERMODE    K   (AF GABRIEL MEKLER  K  (AF MAURY BAKER   D  (A
LONNIE CASTILLE     D     (AF  SNOOKY FLOWERS     SAX (AF TERRY CLEMENTS  SAX (AF LUIS GASCA   TPT (AF
JAMES GURLEY        G     (CF  PETER ALBIN        B   (CF
```

LONNIE JORDAN

```
LONNIE JORDAN       K B D V(A    (A) DIFFERENT MOODS OF ME   1978   MCA US 2329   UK Mcg 3526
EUGENE PALMER       V     (A
DAROLD MATHEW       V     (A   MOSES WHEELOCK    PERC (A  CAMEO ROSS      V  (A  LARRY BROWN      G  (A
ANDY SHAPHIN        SYN   (A   TOM LETONDRE       TPT (A  JOE ROBB        SAX (A  SUSAN BUCKNER    V  (A
DEBORAH PRATT       V     (A   LEM TAYLOR         V   (A  MILTON MYRICK   V  (A  DOUGLAS PARKS    V  (A
DAWN PARKS          V     (A   MICHAEL PARKS      V   (A  GREGORY PARKS   V  (A  CAROL WILSON     V  (A
KEVIN FARMER        V     (A   KIMBERLY FARMER    V   (A  ROBIN PARKS     V  (A
```

LOUIS JORDAN

```
LOUIS JORDAN        V SAX(ALL   (A) SOMEBODY UP THERE LIKES ME  19  WING US 16126+MERCURY US 20242
SHUGGIE OTIS        G B K(I     (B) GREATEST HITS          19   MCA US 274 + DECCA    US 75033
JOHNNY OTIS         D PNO(I     (C) LOUIS JORDAN VOL 1     19   DECCA                 US   2029
IRV COX             SAX   (I     (D) LOUIS JORDAN VOL 2     19   DECCA                 US  A645
BOB MITCHELL        TPT   (I     (E) MAN WERE WAILIN'       19   MERCURY               US 20331
CHRIS BARBER        (N     (F) & HIS TYMPANI FIVE   19   JAZZ CLUB US 123+ PERFORMANCE 3001
BUD JOHNSON         (     (G) HALLELUJAH             1964 TANGERINE                    1503
ERNIE ROYAL         (     (H) LET THE GOOD TIMES ROLL 1970 CORAL CP 59 +CP 54 + CRLM  1042
JIMMY CLEVELAND     (     (H) LET THE GOOD TIMES ROLL 19  DECCA                    US 8551
SAM TAYLOR          (     (I) GREAT RHYTHM & BLUES   1973 BULLDOG     RI 82       BDL 1000
TEDDY EDWARDS       SAX   (     (J) BEST OF               1975 MCA  US 2 4079     +UK MCFM 2715
                                (K) I BELIEVE IN MUSIC     1975 BLACK & BLUE             33059
                                (L) CHOO CHOO CH BOOGIE    1975 PHILIPS          6336 246
                                ( ) CHOO CHOO CH BOOGIE    1982 MFP                   50557
                                (M) IN MEMORIAM            1975 MCA              PCO 7837
                                (M) IN MEMORIAM            1975 CORAL                622175
                                (N) LOUIS JORDAN SWINGS    1976 BLACK LION       BLP 30175
                                (O) & HIS ORCHESTRA        1976 M C A            PCO 8332
                                (P) COLLATES               1979 SWINGHOUSE    UK    SWH2
                                (Q) JUMPIN' STUFF          1981 RARITIES              46
                                (R) BEST OF                1981 MCA              MCL 1631
```

JORDANAIRES

```
HOYT HAWKINS        V     (1    WE'D LIKE TO TEACH THE WORLD TO SING 1972 EMBER    UK CW 141
NIAL MATTHEWS       V     (1    SPOTLIGHT ON THE JORDANAIRES  19   CAPITOL      US ST 1742
LOVIS NUNLEY        V     (1    BIG COUNTRY HITS          19   CBS          US  9258
GORDON STOKER       V     (1    MONSTER MAKERS            19   STOP         US 10010
                                CHURCH IN THE WILDWOOD    19   VOCALION     US 73854
                                THE JORDANAIRES           19   CBS          US
                                (1)1978
```

JOSEFUS

```
DOUG TULL           PERC (A    (A) JOEFUS               19   MAINSTREAM  US   6127
PETE BAILEY         V HCA(A
RAY TURNER          B     (A   DAVE MITCHELL      G   (A
```

                                    (A) PINCER MOVEMENT   1981 HEDONICS   HEDON5 UK
J99   JOURNEY   J99

GREGG ROLIE	G V (ABCDEFGHJ	(A) JOURNEY	1975 CBS	US 33388	UK	80724
NEAL SCHON	G (ALL	(B) LOOK INTO THE FUTURE	1976 CBS	US 33904	UK	69203
JONATHAN CAIN	K G V(K	(B) LOOK INTO THE FUTURE	198 CBS		UK	32102
AYNSLEY DUNBAR	D (ABCDF	(C) NEXT	1977 CBS	US 34311	UK	81554
GEORGE TICKNER	G (AF	(D) INFINITY	1978 CBS	US 34912	UK	82244
ROSS VALORY	B (ALL	(E) EVOLUTION	1979 CBS	US 35797	UK	83566
ROBERT FLEISHMAN	V (	(F) IN THE BEGINNING(DBL) (COMP)	1979 CBS	US 36324	22073	
STEVE PERRY	V (DEGHJK	(G) DEPARTURE	1980 CBS	US 36339	UK	84101
STEVE SMITH	D (EGHJK	(H) DREAM AFTER DREAM	1980 CBS	JAP 27AP1950		
		(J) ESCAPE	1981 CBS	US 37406	UK	85138
		(K) CAPTURED	1981 CBS	US 37016	UK	88525
		(L) TRON (SOUNDTRACK Part)	1982 CBS		UK	85669

J99A   JOY DIVISION   J99A

IAN CURTIS	V (ABC	(A) UNKNOWN PLEASURES	1979 FACTORY		UK FACT 10
BERNARD ALBRECHT	G K (ABC	(B) CLOSER	1980 FACTORY GER 60361		UK FACT 25
PETER HOOK	B (ABC	(C) STILL (DBL)	1981 FACTORY		UK FACT 40
STEVE MORRIS	D (ABC				

J100   JOY OF COOKING   J100

TONI BROWN	V K G(ABC	(A) JOY OF COOKING	1970 CAPITOL		EST	661
TERRY GARTHWAITE	V G (ABC	(B) CLOSER TO THE GROUND	1971 CAPITOL		EST	828
FRITZ KASTEN	D SAX(ABC	(C) CASTLES	1972 CAPITOL		EST	11050
JEFF NEIGHBOR	B TROM (BC					
RON WILSON	PERC HCA (ABC	JIM HORN SAX (C DAVID GARTHWAITE	B G (A			

J100A   JOY UNLIMITED   J100A

KLAUS NAGEL	G FLT(AB	(A) OVERGROUND	1970	PILZ	GER
ROLAND HECK	K (ABCD	(B) SCHMETTERLINGE	1971	PILZ	GER 20 21090/1
HANS HERKENNE	PERC (ABCD	(C) REFLECTIONS	1973	BASF	GER 20 21686/1
ALBIN METZ	B TPT(ABCD	(D) MINNE	1975	BASF	GER 12 22 331/0
DIETER KINDL	G (AB				
JOY FLEMING	V (A	HANS LINGENFELDER G (D JOSCHI DINIER	G B V (D KEN TRAYLOR		G (C
GERD KOTHE	FLT (D				

J101   JUBAL   J101
DENNIS LINDE   G V (A   (A) JUBAL   1972 ELEKTRA   US   75033
J101A   JUDAS JUMP   J101A

ALAN JONES	WIND (A	(A)SCORCH	1970 PARLOPHONE UK PAS 10001
ANDT BOWN	K G (A	(A) SCORCH	1972 PRIDE US 0003
CHARLIE HARRISON	B (A		
HENRY SPINETTI	D (A	TREVOR WILLIAMS G (A ADRIAN WILLIAMS	V (A

J102   JUDAS PRIEST   J102

K K DOWNING	G (ALL	(A) ROCKA ROLLA	1974 GULL UK GULP1005 VISA	7001
GLEN TIPTON	G (ALL	(B) SAD WINGS OF DESTINY	1976 GULL	UK GULP 1015
ROB HALFORD	V (ALL	(B) SAD WINGS OF DESTINY	1976 JANUS US 7019 OVATION RI	1751
IAN HILL	B (ALL	(C) SIN AFTER SIN	1977 CBS US 34587 UK	82008
JOHN HINCH	D (AD	(D) THE BEST OF	1978 GULL	UK GULP 1026
ALAN MOORE	D (BD	(E) STAINED CLASS	1978 CBS US 35296 UK	82430
SIMON PHILLIPS	D (C	(F) KILLING MACHINE	1978 CBS	UK	83135
		(F) KILLING MACHINE	1982 CBS	UK	32218
LES BINKS	D (FG	(G) UNLEASHED IN THE EAST	1979 CBS US 36179 UK	83852
DAVE HOLLAND	D (HK	(H) BRITISH STEEL	1980 CBS US 36443 UK	84160
		(J) POINT OF ENTRY	1981 CBS US 37052 UK	84834
		(K) SCREAMING TO VENGENCE	1982 CBS	UK	85941
		(CEF) BOX SET	1980 CBS	UK	66357

J102A   JUDD   J102A

TAT MEAGER	D (A	(A) JUDD	1970 PENNY FARTHING U K PEL 504
ROGER FLAVELL	B (A		
ROGER McKEW	G (A	MARK WIRTZ K (A SUE GLOVER	V (A SUNNY LESLIE V (A
DORIS TROY	V (A	MADELINE BELL V (A	

J103   JUDE   J103

ROBIN TROWER	G (		
FRANKIE MILLER	V (		
JIMMY DEWAR	B (	CLIVE BUNKER D (	

J104   JUDGE DREAD   J104

JUDGE DREAD		(A) DREADMANIA	1973 TROJAN		TRLS	60
		(B) WORKING CLASS 'ERO	1974 TROJAN		TRLS	100
		(C) BEDTIME STORIES	1975 CACTUS		CTLP	1130
		(D) LAST OF THE SKINHEADS	1976 CACTUS		CTLP	123
		(E) BEST OF	1976 KLIK		KLP	9008
		( ) 40 BIG ONES	1980 CREOLE	UK	BIG 1	
		(EP) JAMAICA JERK	1977 CACTUS		CT	98

J104A   JUDITH NYLON   J104A

ERIC VANDER BRINK	G V (A	(A) THIS IS FEEDBACK	1980 LINK NL 80002
BOB BARNEVELD	B (A		
RENE VAN BARNEVELD	G(A	JOS SMULDERS D V (A MARCUS NIJSSEN	PNO (A HAROLD SCHELLINCK SYN (A

J104B   JUICE   J104B
                                   (A) DOMESTIC REGGAE   1981 FULL CIRCLE UK   8002
J104C   JUICE ON THE LOOSE   J104C

RON KAVANA	G V (A	(A) JUICE ON THE LOOSE	1981 JUICE UK JJOS1 LINE GER LLP5151
FRAN BYRNE	D (A		
BAM KING	G V B(A	CHARLIE HART B V K(A NICK PENTELOW	SAX (A GERAINT WATKINS K (A
ED DEANE	G (A	PETER THOMS TROM (A MARTIN DROVER	TPT (A CRAIG MACKIE K (A
TWINKI	V (A		

J104D   JUICY GROOVE   J104D

RAINBOW NEAL	G V (A	(A) FIRST TASTE	1978 PAYOLA US
MERCURY FLYER	G (A		
MARS BONFIRE	G (A	MAGIC MARKER B (A THUNDERCLOUD	D (A VICTORIA REID V (A
RON BUSHY	D (A	LARRY LAZAR B (A GARY MORELL	D (A

JUICY LUCY

```
    RAY OWEN          V    (A        (A) JUICY LUCY            1969 VERTIGO UK 847 901 US ATCO 33367
    ROD COMBES        D    (BC       (A) JUICY LUCY            1969 BRONZE    GER 26323
    GLENN CAMPBELL    V G  (ABC      (B) LIE BACK & ENJOY IT   1970 VERTIGO UK 6360014 US ATCO 33345
    PAUL WILLIAMS V K PERC (BCD      (B) LIE BACK & ENJOY IT   1970 BRONZE    GER 200 411
    CHRIS MERCER      SAX K(ABC      (C) GET A WIFF A THIS     1971 BRONZE UK ILPS9157 US ATCO 33367
    NEIL HUBBARD      G    (A        (D) PIECES                1972 POLYDOR       UK 2310 160
    KEITH ELLIS       B    (AB       (E) BEST OF               19   ISLAND EURO 85814 BRONZE GER25842
    PETE DOBSON       D    (A
    MICK WEAVER       K    (D   IAN McLAGAN  K       (D   REMI KABAKA    PERC (A   JEAN ROUSSEL   K  (D
    RON BERG          D    (D   LOUGHTY AMAO PERC    (A   ANDY PYLE      B    (D   JIM LEVERTON   B  (C
    MICK MOODY        G    (BCD
```

JULES & THE POLAR BEARS

```
    JULES SHEAR       G V  (AB       (A) GOT NO BREEDING       1978 CBS              US 35601
    JIM GORDON        D    (A        (A) PHONETICS/FENETIKS    1979 CBS US 36138     UK 83865
    RICHARD BREDICE   G    (AB
    STEPHEN HAGUE     K SYN(AB  DAVID BEEBE      D     (AB DAVID WHITE     B    (B   KENNY ALTMAN   B  (B
    LARRY HIRSCH      PERC  (A  JERRY PETERSON  SAX    (A  JERRY JUMONVILLE SAX (A   MIKE HENDERSON SAX (A
    LEE THORNBERG     TPT   (A  DARRELL LEONARD  TPT   (A  BILL EDWARDS    TROM (A   MARK UNDERWOOD TPT (A
    JAY PRUITT        TPT   (A  SKIP WIESNER TROM (A  LINDA SMALL    TROM (A
```

JULVERNE

```
    PIERRE COULON       FLT  (A       (A) A NEUF              19   CRAMMED DISCS       CRA 274
    MICHEL DURET        CLAR (A       (B) COULONNEUX          19   IBC/EMI             058 99069
    MICHEL BERCKMANS BASSOON(A
    JEAN PAUL LAURENT PNO (AB  CHARLES LOOS    PNO  (A  BAUDOUIN DEHAYE  VIBES(A  JOSE BEDEUR    B  (A
    DENIS VAN ECKE    CELLO(AB  JEAN FRANCOIS LACROIX SAX(A JEANNOT GILLIS VLN (AB  MICHEL DAYEZ   G  (B
    RICHARD ROUSSELET TPT (B   ANNE DENIS      VLN (B  JEAN COULON     TROM (B
```

JUKIN' BONE

```
    JOE WHITING         V    (A       (A) WAY DOWN EAST        1972 RCA         US       LSP 4768
    MARK DOYLE          G K V(A
    GEORGE EGOSARIAN    G    (A  JOHN DEMASO  B PERC V(A   DANNY COWARD   D PERC(A  KEVIN SHWARYK  D  (A
```

JULY

```
    TOM NEWMAN          V    (A       (A) JULY                 1968 MAJOR MINOR      SMLP 29
    CHRIS JACKSON       K    (A
    TONY DUHIG          G    (A  JON FIELD   FL  (A  ALAN JAMES     B  (A
```

JUMBO

```
                                      (A) CITY GIRLS          1978 PYE INT     UK       28234
```

JUNCO PARTNERS

```
    RONNIE BARKER        (1        (A) JUNCO PARTNERS      197  BARCLAY    FR      920193
    JOHN WOODS      D    (1BA      (B) JUNCO PARTNERS      1971 PHILIPS            6308 032
    DAVE SPROAT     B    (1BA      (1) 1978 REFORMED
    KENNY BARKER         (1
    BOB SARGEANT    K V  (BA  NEIL PERRY    SAX     (1   MAV LANDERS    V    (1   CHARLES HARCOURT G (AB
```

JUNIORS EYES

```
    MICK WAYNE           (         (A) JUNIOR'S EYES        196  A&M       US       SP 4189
    JOHN REDFERN         (         (B) BATTERSEA POWER STATION 1969 REGAL ZONOPHONE UK SLRZ 1008
    STEVE CHAPMAN        (
    GROM KELLY           (    TIM RENWICK  G      (   JOHN CAMBRIDGE      (
```

JUNKYARD ANGELS

```
    KEN IVERSON     D V  (A        (A) APPEARED ON  MIKE HARRISON LP   1971 ISLAND  UK    ILPS 9170
    PETER BATEY     B    (A
    IAN HERBERT     G V K(A   FRANK KENYON G V  (A
```

MICKEY JUPP

```
    MICKEY JUPP     G V K(ABC      (A) JUPPANESE           1978 STIFF GER 6.23055 UK SEEZ  10
    ROBIN TROWER    G    (B        (A) JUPPANESE           1980 LINE    GER 5095
    DAVE EDMUNDS    G V  (A        (B) LEGEND (COMP OF 'LEGEND'TRACKS) 1978 STIFF GER 6 23442 UK GET 2
    BILLY BREMNER   G    (A        (C) LONG DISTANCE ROMANCER 1979 CHRYSALIS GER 6307 686 UK CHR1261
    TONY VISCONTI        (B        (C) LONG DISTANCE ROMANCER 1080 LINE GER 5099
    SANDY ROBERTSON      (B        (D) OXFORD              1980 LINE    GER 5083
    IAN DUCK        G HCA(D        (E) SOME PEOPLE CANT DANCE 1982 A&M UK AMLH 68535 GER LINE 5148
    NICK LOWE       B    (A        (1) 1975 BAND
    TERRY WILLIAMS  D    (A
    GARY BROOKER    K    (AB  BRUCE LYNCH    B   (A  CHRIS SPEDDING  G   (A  DAVE MATTACKS  D  (A
    MO WITHAM       G    (B   BOB CLOUTER    D   (B1D BILL FIFIELD  D   (B  CHRIS EAST     G  (B
    STEVE GEERE     B    (B   NIGEL DUNBAR   D   (B  CHRIS COPPING   B   (B  B J WILSON     D  (B
    TIM RENWICK     G    (B   MICK MOODY     G   (B  COLIN GIBSON    B   (B  HENRY SPINETTI D  (B
    JIMMY JEWELL    SAX  (B   PETE SOLLEY PROD PNO (B  GLEN LE FLEUR PERC (B  KEVIN GODLEY  D V (C
    GARY TIBBS      B    (C   LOL CREME      G V (C  ANDY MACKAY    SAX (C  PETRINA LORDAN V  (C
    ERIN LORDAN     V    (C   JOHN PUGH      SAX (1  BOB FISH        V   (1  COLIN MAXWELL  D  (1
    PETE ZEAR       G    (1   JOY SARNEY     V   (1  PAUL MITCHELL   B   (1  FRANK MEAD    SAX (1
    PETE THE HAT    V    (1   RON TELEMACQUE D   (   JOHN GORDON     B   (   MICK GRABHAM   G  (
    DAVE BRONZE     B    (D
```

BILL JUSTIS

```
    BILL JUSTIS     SAX  (      RAUNCHY & OTHER GUITAR INSTRUMENTALS 1974 SUN  UK    6467 010
    SID MANKER      G    (      RAUNCHY              19   SUN        US        109
                               ENCHANTED SEA        1972 HARMONY    US        31189
                               SOLID & RAUNCHY      19   PHILIPS INTERNATIONAL US 1950
```

JUSTWATER

```
    GUSKIN MARTIN   D    (A        (A) THE RIFF          1977 BRANDED           2027
    TOM KORBA       B    (A
    MITCHELL DANCIK V G  (A   DANNY RUBIN    G     (A
```

JUSTINE

```
    JOHN McBURNIE   G    (A        (A) JUSTINE           1970 UNI    UK    UNLS 111
    VALERIE COPE    V PERC(A
    LAURIE STYVERS  V    (A   KEITH TROWSDALE  G V (A  JERRY HOVELL   B  (A  CHRIS GIBB    D  (A
```

PATRICK JUVET

```
PATRICK JUVET     V K  (ALL      (A) PARIS BY NIGHT          1977   BARCLAY                        90098
SONNY BURKE       K    (A        (B) PATRICK JUVET           1978 CASABLANCA US 7107 UK  CAL 2028
HENRY DAVIS       B    (A        (C) LADY NIGHT              1979   CASABLANCA           CAL 2049
SCOTT EDWARDS     B    (A        (D) STILL ALIVE             1980   BARCLAY                96112
JIM GORDON        D    (A        (E) I LOVE AMERICA          19     BARCLAY                91003
JAMES GADSON      D    (A
ED GREENE         D    (A  GARY COLEMAN    PERC(A  KEITH FORSEY   D    (D  BARRY FINNERTY   G    (C
PARKER            G    (A  LEE RITENOUR    G    (AD ERNIE WATTS   HRNS (A  JIM HORN         SAX  (A
MIKE BODDIKER     K    (AD K SCHAEFFER   STRINGS  GEORGES RODI   SYN  (A  RUSSELL DABNEY   D    (AC
ALFONSO CAREY     B    (BC JIMMY LEE      G    (BC ROGER LEE     G    (BC NATHANIEL WHITE  K    (B
ERROL BENNETT     CONGA(B  M GRILLO       PERC (B  PHIL KRAUS    PERC (B  BABATUNDE OLATUNJI PERC(B
GEORGE DEVENS     PERC (B  JEFF BAXTER    G    (D  TOM POLITE    PNO  (C  NATHANIEL WICKIE K    (C
JIMMY MAELEN      PERC (C  TREVOR WHITEHEAD PERC (C TREVOR VEITCH G   (D  LES HURDLE       B    (D
THOR BALDURRSON   K    (D
```

K C & THE SUNSHINE BAND

```
HARRY WAYNE 'KC'CASEY  K(ALL   (A) DO IT GOOD            1974   JAYBOY JSL  9   + US TK  500
ROBERT JOHNSON     D    (GH    (A) DO IT GOOD            197    TK    UK TK 82505 + US TK  600
RICHARD FINCH    B D    (GH    (B) K C & THE SUNSHINE BAND 1975  JAYBOY JSL  9   + US TK  603
JEROME SMITH       G    (GH    (C) SOUND OF SUNSHINE     1975                  US TK  604
FERMIN GOYTISOLO PERC  (GH    (D) PART THREE            1977   TK    UK TK 82507 + US TK  605
MIKE LEWIS       SAX   (G     (E) THE BEST OF           197    JAYBOY UK JSB 101
VINNIE TANNO     TPT   (G     (F) I LIKE TO DO IT       1977   PRESIDENT             JRE 500
KEN FAULK        TPT   (G     (G) WHO DO YA LOVE        1978   TK    UK TK 86100 + US TK  607
WHIT SIDENER     SAX   (G     (H) DO YOU WANNA PARTY    1979   TK    UK 83369
BEVERLEY CHAMPION V    (G     (I) GREATEST HITS         1980   TK    UK 83385
JEANETTE WILLIAMS V    (G     (J) SPACE CADET           1980   TK    UK
                              (K) THE PAINTER           1981   EPIC  UK 85219
```

JOSEF K

```
JOSEF K                 (A     (A) ONLY FUN IN TOWN      1981   POSTCARD      UK      811
```

K G B

```
RAY KENNEDY       V    (AB     (A) K G B                1976 MCA  UK  MCF 2749   US   2166
MIKE BLOOMFIELD   G    (A      (B) MOTION               1976 MCA  UK  MCF 2773   US   2221
RICK GRECH        B    (A
CARMINE APPICE    D    (AB  BARRY GOLDBERG   K   (AB BEN SCHULTZ  G   (B  GREG SUTTON   B    (B
```

KAJANUS / PICKETT

```
GEORG KAJANUS          (A      (A) HI HO SILVER         1973 SIGNPOST UK SGZ500 MCA  US  304
PHIL PICKETT           (A
```

HARRY KAKOULLI

```
HARRY KAKOULLI V B SYN G D(A   (A) EVEN WHEN I'M NOT    1980   OVAL          UK      OVLP 505
GARRELL REDFEARN  SYN   (A
NIGEL SHARPE      G    (A   NICK ROBBINS    D    (A
```

**** KAK

```
DELMER C PATTEN   G V  (A      (A) KAK                  19     EPIC          US      26423
GARY L YODEN      G V  (A
JOSEPH DAMRELL    B SIT(A   CHRISTOPHER LOCKHEED  D K V(A
```

KALA

```
JOHNNIE MILES     D V  (A      (A) KALA                 1973   BRADLEYS      UK      BRADL 1002
PERRY SINCLAIR    G V  (A
SID GARDNER       B V  (A   DAVE CODLING    G V  (A  DAVE SKINNER  PNO  (A  PAUL BENNETT  V    (A
LES NICOL         G V  (A   JACK STEVENSON  PERC (A  PETER ARNESEN PNO  (A  SHIVA JONES   V K  (A
CAROL GRIMES      V    (A   JOHN BARHAM     CELLO (A
```

KALEIDOSCOPE

```
PETE DALTREY      K    (       (A) TANGERINE DREAM      1967   FONTANA       UK      TL 5448
EDDIE PUMER       G    (       (B) FAINTLY BLOWING      1969   FONTANA       UK      STL 5491
DANNY BRIDGMAN    F    (
STEVE CLARK       B    (
```

KALEIDOSCOPE(US)

```
FENRUS EPP    VLN K(ABCDE ****  (A) SIDE TRIPS          1967   EPIC          US      26304
JOHN VIDICAN     PERC (AB      (B) BEACON FROM MARS     1968   EPIC          US      26333
SOLOMON FELDTHOUSE G V (ABCDE  (C) INCREDIBLE KALEIDOSCOPE 1969 EPIC         US      26467
DAVID LINDLEY  VLN G V(ABCD    (D) BERNICE              1970   CBS      UK 64005 US   26508
CHRIS DARROW   FDL G V (ABE    (E) WHEN SCOPES COLLIDE  1976   ISLAND UK       ILPS  9462
STUART BROTMAN   B V  (CDE     (E) WHEN SCOPES COLLIDE  1976 PACIFIC ARTS     US      102
PAUL LAGOS       D V  (CDE     (F) BROTHER MARY (ZABRISKIE POINT) 19 POLYDOR         2315 002
RICHARD APLAN    FLT  (
JEFF KAPLAN      G V  (D   BARRY FRIEDMAN    PROD  (A PETE MADLIN  G   (B  JOHN WARE    D    (E
RON JOHNSON      B    (D   DE PARIS LETANTE  G    (E
                          ****CONNIE CRILL/MAX BUDA/TEMPLETON PARCELY ARE ALL FENRUS EPP
```

KALEIDOSKOP

```
HARDY WRIEDEN     V    (A      (A) 100% LIVE            1982 ROCKFARM     ROLP 8101
HANNO BONSDORF    G    (A
NORBERT WESCH     G V  (A   GUNTER BLENDERMANN  B  (A  DIETER SCHMIDT  D  (A
```

KALYAN

```
                               (A) ALL THE WAY    LIVE  1980   RCA                    3514
```

AMORY KANE

```
AMORY KANE        G V  (AB     (A) MEMORIES OF TIME UNWOUND 1968 MCA      UK      MUPS 348
DAVE PEGG         B    (B      (B) JUST TO BE THERE    1970   CBS           UK      63849
NED BALEN         D    (B
```

KANGAROO

```
JOHN HALL         B    (A      (A) KANGAROO             1968   ?             US
TEDDY SPELEOD     G    (A
N D SMART II      D    (A   BARBARA KEITH   V    (A
```

KANSAS

```
    PHIL EHART           D    (ABCDE      (A) MASQUE                      1975  KIRSHNER US 33806
    STEVE WALSH          K V  (ABCDE      (B) KANSAS                      1975  KIRSHNER US 32817   UK  80174
    ROBBIE STEINHARDT  VLN V  (ABCDE      (C) SONG FOR AMERICA            1976  KIRSHNER US 33385   UK  80740
    DAVE HOPE            B    (ABCDE      (D) LEFTOVERTURE                1976  KIRSHNER US 34224   UK  81728
    RICH WILLIAMS        G    (ABCDE      (E) POINT OF KNOW RETURN        1977  KIRSHNER US 34929   UK  82234
    KERRY LIVGREN      G K    (ABCDE      (F) TWO FOR THE SHOW            1978  KIRSHNER US 35560   UK  88318
                                          (G) MONOLITH                    1979  KIRSHNER US 36008   UK  83644
                                          (H)AUDIO VISIONS                1980  KIRSHNER US 36588   UK  84500
```
K10   PAUL KANTNER   K10
```
    PAUL KANTNER        G V  (ABC        (A) ITS A FRESH WIND THAT BLOWS ....  1970  RCA US LPS 4448   UK SF 8163
    GRACE SLICK         K V  (ABC        (B) SUNFIGHTER                  1971  GRUNT                FTR 1002
    DAVID FREIBERG        V  (AC         (C) BARON VON TOLLBOOTH         1973  GRUNT                BFLI 0148
    JACK CASADY          B   (ABC
    POINTER SISTERS      V   (C    PAPA JOHN CREACH  VLN (BC  JOHN BARBATA    D   (C   CRAIG CHAQUICO      G (C
    MICKEY HART          D   (AC   PETER KAUKONEN      G  (A  PHIL SAWYER         (AB  BILL KREUTZMANN     D (A
    CHRIS ETHRIDGE       B   (C    DAVID CROSBY        V G (ABC JORMA KAUKONEN  G   (ABC RON DUDLEY           (A
    JOEY COVINGTON     D PERC(AB  BILL THOMPSON        (A  JERRY GARCIA    G BAN(ABC JACK TRAYLOR          V (C
    HARVEY BROOKS        B   (A    GRAHAM NASH         V PERC(AB SPENCER DRYDEN    (B
```
K10A   KARAT   K10A
```
    BERD ROMER           G   (           (A) FIRST                        19    AMIGA           GER   855573
    HERBERT DREILICH     V   (           (B) UBER SIEBEN BRUCKEN          19  * AMIGA           GER   855695
    HENNING PROTZMANN    B   (           (C) SCHWANENKONIG                19    AMIGA           GER   855770
    ULRICH ED SWILLMS  V K   (
    MICHAEL SCHWADT      D   (
```
K10B   JURGEN KARG   K10B
```
    JURGEN KARG              (           (A) ELEKTRONISCHE MYTHEN         1976  MOOD            23 555
```
K10C   BILLY KARLOFF   K10C
```
    BILLY KARLOFF        V   (ALL        (A) THE MANIAC                   1978 JUPITER    GER     26373
    CHRIS PYE          G V   (A          (B) LET YOUR FINGERS DO THE TALKING  1981  WB    56894
    JULIAN               G   (A
    ED DUANE             B   (A    PEDRO ORTIZ  D V (A   PAUL JELLIMAN    G   (B   NEIL HAY      G V   (A
    GLEN BUGLASS         B   (B    DOLPHIN TAYLOR D V(B  CHUCK LEAVELL    PNO (B   STEVE NATHAN  SYN   (B
    RICK KURTZ           G   (B
```
K10D   KAROLINE   K10D
```
    SERGE TAFINI         V   (A          (A) KAROLINE                     1980  WEA  NL 58141
    JEFF CASTALDI      G V   (A
    VINCENT CASTALDI   B V   (A    DANIEL APROSIO   PERC V(A
```
K10E   CHRIS KARRER   K10E
```
    CHRIS KARRER       G V SAX(A         (A) CHRIS KARRER                 1980 VINYL      GER    6 24328
    CURT CRESS           D   (A
    GEORGE INCHL         K   (A    GERRARD CARBONNEL  B   (A   JORG EVERS   G B V  (A
```
K11   KARTHARGO   K11
```
    JOEY ALBRECHT      V G   (ABCDE      (A) KARTHARGO                    1971  BASF            GERM 2021/185/1
    GLENN CORNICK        B   (C          (B) SECOND STEP                  1973  BASF US 217 80  GERM 2021/180/1
    INGO BISCHOF       K V   (ABCDE      (C) ROCK'N'ROLL TESTAMENT        1974  BELLAPHON       GERM BLPS 19201
    TOMMY GOLDSCHMIDT  D     (ABCDE      (D) LIVE AT THE ROXY             1976  BELLAPHON       GERM BDA  7506
    NORBERT LEHEMANN   D     (B          (E) LIVE                         1976  BELLAPHON       GERM B   15190
    KONNI BOMMARIUS      D   (C
    GERALD HARTWIG B V PERC(ABD  WOLFGANG BROCK    D PERC (A   RINGO FUNK     D   (D   REINHARD BOPP     G V  (D
    VICKI BROWN          V   (C    BARRY ST JOHN       V   (C   JOANNE WILLIAMS  V  (C   TOM CUNNINGHAM    V  (C
```
K11A   NICK KATZMAN   K11A
```
    NICK KATZMAN       G V   (ALL        (A) MISSISSIPPI RIVER BOTTOM BLUES 1975 KICKING MULE    US   !!!
    RAY GOLDSTEIN        G   (B          (B) SPARKLING RAGTIME & HARDBITTEN BLUES80 KICKING MULE US   167
    TERRY GARTHWAITE   V(AB
```
K12   JORMA KAUKONEN   K12
```
    JORMA KAUKONEN     G V   (ALL        (A) QUAH                         1975  GRUNT      US     BLFI 0209
    TOM HOBSON           V   (A          (B) JORMA                        1979  RCA 13446
    DENNY DECORIO        B   (C          (C) BARBECUE KING                1980  RCA 13727
    JOHN STENCH          D   (C
    HILARY STENCH        B   (C    MIKE BUTERA      SAX (C   LARRY WHITMAN    V   (C   STEVE HUFF  V (C
```
K13   PETER KAUKONEN   K13
```
    PETER KAUKONEN     G V   (A          (A) BLACK KANGAROO               1971  GRUNT      US     FTR 1006
    SHELLEY SILVERMAN  D     (A
    TERRY ADAMS        CELLO (A    DIANE EARL        V   (A   LARRY WEISBERG   B   (A   NICK BUCK   K (A
    PETER MARSHALL       B   (A    MARK RYAN         B   (A   JOEY COVINGTON   D V (A
```
K13A   RYO KAWASAKI   K13A
```
    RYO KAWASAKI         G   (AB         (A) JUICE                        19    RCA  US      1855
    ALEX BLAKE           B   (B          (B) NATURES REVENGE              1978 MPS          61332
    BUDDY WILLIAMS       D   (B
    DAVE LIEBMAN        SAX  (B    TOM COSTER       K   (A
```
K14   JOHN KAY   K14
```
    JOHN KAY         V G HCA  (ALL       (A) FORGOTTEN SONGS & UNSUNG HEROES 1972 DUNHILL US 50120 UK PROBE  1054
    KENT HENRY           G   (AB         (B) MY SPORTIN' LIFE             1973 DUNHILL US 50147 UK PROBE  8011
    GEORGE BIONDO        B   (AB         (B) MY SPORTIN' LIFE             1973                   UK PROBE  6274
    PENTTI GLAN          D   (AB         (C) ALL IN GOOD TIME             1978 MERCURY US 1 3715 UK  9110 054
    HUGH SULLIVAN        K   (AB         (D) JOHN KAY & SPARROW           19    CBS             UK      63564
    LARRY KNECHTEL       K   (B
    BILL COOPER          B   (B    ALAN O'DAY        K   (B   DANNY KORTCHMAR  G   (B   RUSS KUNKEL      D (B
    LEE SKLAR            B   (B    MIKE UTLEY       PNO (B   DARRYL DRAGON    K   (B   RICHARD PODOLOR K MAND(B
    SHIRLEY MATTHEWS     V   (B    GLORIA JONES      V   (B   VANETTA FIELDS   V   (B   STAN FARBER      V (B
    GENE MORFORD         V   (B    JOAN SLIWIN       V   (A   MARSHA TEMMER    V   (A   ALEXANDRA SLIWIN V (A
```

[307]

KAYAK

```
CEES VAN  LEEUWEN B    (AB        (A) SEE SEE THE SUN         1973 HARVEST  UK SHSP4033 US 11305 NL 24933
TON SCHERPENZEEL  K    (ABCDEFGHI (B) KAYAK                   1974 HARVEST  UK SHSP4036          NL 24993
MAX WERNER    V D K((ABCDEFGHI    (C) THE LAST ENCORE         19
JOHAN SLAGER      G    (ABCDEFGH  (D) ROYAL BED BOUNCER       1975 VERTIGO UK  6360 530 US JANUS7023
PIM KOOPMAN       D    (ABD       (D) ROYAL BED BOUNCER       1975 EMI                N 0625271
CHARLES SCHOUTEN  D    (e         (E) STARLIGHT DANCER        1977 VERTIGO UK 6360 856 US JANUS7034
BERT VELDKAMP     B    (DI        (F) THE BEST OF             1978 EMI                NL      25828
THEO DEJONG       B    (E         (G) PHANTOM OF THE NIGHT    1978 VERTIGO NL 6413 507 US JANUS7039
GERRIT JAN LEENDERS V  (A         (H) PERISCOPE LIFE          1980 VERTIGO EURO 6413 960 MERCURY US SRM13824
ERNST REIZIGER  CELLO(A           (I) MERLIN                  1981 VERTIGO EURO 6399 115
GINNY BUSCH       VLN  (A
MARTIN KOEMAN     VLN  (A   RIJN PETER DE KLERK    (A   EDWARD REEKERS  V   (GHI IRENE LINDERS V (HGI
JIM PRICE         HRNS (H   KATHERINE LAPHORN  V   (GHI PETER SCHERPENZEEL B   (GHI LEE THORNBURG HRNS(H
JIM GORDON        SAX  (H   JACK LANCASTER    PROD (E  G PERLEE BARRELORGAN    (A  REIN VANDER BROCK WIND(I
BENNY BEHR        STR  (I
```

THOMAS JEFFERSON KAYE

```
THOMAS JEFFERSON KAYE G V(AB      (A) THOMAS JEFFERSON KAYE    1973              PROBE UK SPB 1074
MICHAEL OMARTIAN  K    (B         (B) FIRST GRADE             1974 DUNHILL US 50142 ABC UK ABCL5048
DONALD FAGEN      K    (AB
WALTER BECKER     B    (AB  JOE OSBORNE     B    (B   JIM GORDON    D    (B   VIC FELDMAN   PERC  (AB
RICK DERRINGER    G    (AB  DEAN PARKS      G    (B   RICHIE FURAY  V    (B   TIM SCHMIT    V    (B
JEFF BAXTER       G    (AB  DUSTY SPRINGFIELD V  (B   CLYDIE KING   V    (AB  SHIRLEY MATTHEWS V (AB
JIM MASON         V    (A   JIMMY HASKEL HRNS    (B   RICK SLOSSEN  D    (A   JOE FRANK CORROLA  B (A
TOM SALISBURY     PNO  (A   RANDY HOBBS     B    (A   VENETTA FIELDS V   (A   DAVID PALMER  V    (A
DOROTHY MORRISON  V    (A   DIANE MORRISON  V    (A   CHRIS WILLIAMSON V (A   MARK SPRINGER V    (A
MICKI ST CLAIR    V    (A
```

ERIC KAZ

```
ERIC KAZ  V G K HCA SYN (ABC      (A) IF YOU'RE LONELY         1972 ATLANTIC UK K 40468 US  SD 7246
BOB BABITT        B    (B         (B) CUL DE SAC              1973 ATLANTIC           US  SD 7290
PAUL BARRERE      G    (B         (C) FULLER/KAZ              1978 CBS               US     35324
MALCOLM CECIL     SYN  (B
GORDON EDWARDS    B    (B   BOOKER T JONES HRNS K G(B   JOHN KELSO    HRNS (B   JIM KELTNER   D    (B
RAY LUCAS         D    (B   TIM MOORE       D    (B   BERNARD PURDIE D   (B   JEROME RICHARDSON SAX (B
ROCKY DZIDZORNU   PERC (B   SNEAKY PETE KLEINOW STEEL(B DAVID T WALKER G   (B   CRAIG FULLER  G V  (C
DAN DUGMORE       G    (C   LEE SKLAR       B    (C   RUSS KUNKEL   D PERC(C   CRAIG DOERGE  K    (C
DON GROLNICK      K    (C   STEVE LUKATHER  G    (C   CHARLES VEAL  VLN  (C   ROLLICE DALE  VLA  (C
DENNIS KARMAZYN  CELLO(C    LEAH KUNKEL     V    (C   LEO SAYER     V    (C   JAMES NEWTON HOWARD K (C
```

LINDA KEEL

```
LINDA KEEL        V    (A         (A) LADY ROCK'N'ROLL        1978 PYE           UK    NSPL 28273
JACKY CHALARD     B    (A
PATRICK VERBEC    G    (A   MOREAU SERRI    G    (A   JEAN PIERRE PREVOTAT  D (A JEAN YVES D'ANGELO  K (A
ROLLY             HCA  (A   RENE MORIZURE   SAX  (A   PIERROT PLOQUIN    TPT(A FREDDY OMEZIAN      TPT(A
ERIC BAMI         V    (A
```

JOHN 'SPEEDY' KEEN

```
JOHN'SPEEDY'KEEN V G K D(AB       (A) PREVIOUS CONVICTIONS     1971  TRACK UK 2406 105 US MCA  331
JIMMY McCULLOCH   G    (B         (B) Y' KNOW WOT I MEAN      1975  ISLAND    /  UK    ILPS 9338
DAVE McDOUGALL    K    (
BUTCH SANDFORD    G    (B   TERRY WILSON    B    (B   EMANUEL RENTZOS  K  (B   TONY BRAUNAGEL D   (B
RABBIT BUNDRICK   K    (B   B J COLE      STEEL(B   PETER VANDER PUIJE HRNS (B   LIZA STRIKE   V    (B
GEORGE LEE        HRNS (B   EDDIE QUANSAH   HRNS (B
```

ACE KEFFORD

```
ACE KEFFORD       B    (1         (1) ACE KEFFORD STAND 1969
COZY POWELL       D    (1
DAVE BALL         G    (1   DENNIS BALL         (1
```

KEITH

```
DAVID JIMINEZ     G    (A         (A) THE ADVENTURES OD KEITH 1969  RCA US      LSP 4143
JOE COYLE         G    (A
DAVE FIEBRT       B    (A   RICK FOX      D    (A
```

CASEY KELLY

```
CASEY KELLY  V G HCA  (AB         (A) CASEY KELLY             1972 ELEKTRA US 75040     UK K 42121
LEE SKLAR         B    (A         (B) FOR SALE                197  ELEKTRA
RUSS KUNKEL       D    (A
CRAIG DOERGE      K    (A   SNEAKY PETE KLEINOW STEEL(A  AL GARTH      FDL  (A   DANNY COHEN  ACC   (A
JIM MESSINA       G    (A
```

DAVE KELLY

```
DAVE KELLY     G V PERC(ALL       (A) KEEPS IT IN THE FAMILY  1969 MERCURY       UK    20151
STEVE GURL        K    (DE        (B) DAVE KELLY              1971 MERCURY       UK 6310 001
BOB HALL          PNO  (ABDE      (C) SURVIVORS               1979 APPALOOSA     ITALY  AP 001
PAUL JONES        HCA  (DE        (D) WILLING                 1979 APPALOOSA     ITALY  AP 003
GARY FLETCHER     B    (DE        (E) FEELS RIGHT             1981 COOLKING      UK    CKLP1
JO ANN KELLY      V    (AB
ANDY RYGA         G V  (A   KEITH TILLMAN   B    (A   PETER GEE     G    (A   BOB BRUNNING  B   (B
ALAN HAWKSHAW     K    (B   BARRY GUARD     D    (B   RANDY JONES   D    (B   STEVE RYE  · HCA(B
ALAN PARKER       G    (B   HERBIE FLOWERS  B    (B   CLEM CATTINI  D    (B   JOHN ALTMAN  WIND(B
JOHNNY DEAN       PERC (B   KENNY WHEELER   HRN  (B   PETER SNELL   HARP (B   TOM McGUINNESS G B (E
LOU STONEBRIDGE   K V  (E   ROY MORGAN      D    (E   GRAHAM PRESKETT VLN (E   KEITH NELSON  BJO (E
JOHN EARLE        SAX  (E   STEVE BENNETT   V    (E
```

JO ANN KELLY

```
JO ANN KELLY      G V  (ABCD      (A) SAME THING ON THEIR MINDS 1971 SUNSET     UK   SLS 50209
JOHN FAHEY        G    (B         (B) WITH FAHEY,MANN & MILLER 1972 BLUE GOOSE  US     2009
ALAN SEIDLER      B    (B         (C) JO ANN KELLY            1969 CBS UK 63841 US EPIC  26491
WOODY MANN        B    (B         (D) DO IT                   1976 RED RAG           RRR 006
PETE EMERY        D    (D
TONY McPHEE       G V  (A   JOHN MILLER     G V  (A
```

JONATHAN KELLY

```
JONATHAN KELLY  V G K D(ALL       (A) JONATHAN KELLY                1970 PARLOPHONE    UK    PCS 7114
BRIAN GASCOIGNE MARIM  (E          (B) TWICE AROUND THE HOUSES      1972 RCA           UK    SF 8262
MARK GRIFFITHS    B    (C          (C) WAIT TILL THEY CHANGE+THE BACKDROP 73 RCA       UK    SF 8353
ROY BABBINGTON    B    (C          (D) WAITING ON YOU              1974 RCA           UK    LPL 15022
RAY DUFFY         D    (C          (E) TWO DAYS IN WINTER          1865 RCA           UK    SF 8415
PETER WOOD        K    (BC
THUNDERTHIGHS     V    (BC  BARRY DESOUZA    D   (C   BRUCE THOMAS   B   (C   WILLIE WILSON    D   (C
TIM RENWICK G FLT V    (BC  IAIN SUTHERLAND  V   (C   GAVIN SUTHERLAND V (C   MICHAEL OLIVER   D   (C
LENNOX JAMES    PERC  (C    LUCIANO BRAVO    D   (C   KEN SCOTT    PERC (C   TREVOR WILLIAMS  B   (D
CHAS JANKEL       G   (D    DAVE SHEEN       D   (DE  SNOWY WHITE    G   (D   LARRY STEELE     D   (B
GERRY CONWAY      D   (B    RICK KEMP        B   (B   HARVEY BURNS   D   (B   DONAL LUNNY      G   (B
DAVE BALL         G   (B    JIM TOOMEY       D   (B   BYRON LYEFOOT  D   (B   JERRY DONAHUE    G   (B
KUMA HARADA     B G PERC(E   DARRYL LEE QUE  CONGA(E  PIZZA QUARTET      (E
```
TONY KELLY

```
TONY KELLY        G V  (A          (A) BRING ME BACK               1972 POLYDOR       UK    2383  123
PAUL MILLINS      K    (A
JACK MILLS        G    (A   KEITH EVANS      B   (A   CODY      PERC HCA(A   TERRY STANNARD D PERC (A
CLAUDIA LENNEAR   V    (A   KATHI MacDONALD  V   (A   LINDA NOVEMBER V (A    HELEN MILES    V    (A
HILDA HARRIS      V    (A
```
EDDIE KENDRICKS

```
EDDIE KENDRICKS   V    (ALL         (A) ALL BY MYSELF             1971 TAMLA US  309   UK STML 11186
                                    (B) PEOPLE HOLD ON            1973 TAMLA US  315   UK STML 11213
                                    (C) EDDIE HENDRICKS           1973 TAMLA US  327   UK STML 11245
                                    (D) BOOGIE DOWN               1974 TAMLA US  330   UK STML 11266
                                    (E) FOR YOU                   1975 TAMLA US  335   UK STMA  8020
                                    (F) THE HIT MAN               1975 TAMLA US  338   UK STML 12001
                                    (G) HE'S A FRIEND             1976 TAMLA US  343   UK STML 12016
                                    (H) GOING UP IN SMOKE         1976 TAMLA US  346   UK STML 12043
                                    (J) SLICK                     1977 TAMLA US  356   UK STML 12071
                                    (K) AT HIS BEST               1978 TAMLA US  354   UK STML 12080
                                    (L) VINTAGE 78                1978 ARISTA US 4170  UK SPART 1040
                                    (M) SOMETHING MORE            1981 ARISTA US 4250
                                    (N) LOVE KEYS                 1981 ATLANTIC        UK   K 50779
```
GRAHAM KENDRICK

```
GRAHAM KENDRICK   G V  (AB          (A) FIGHTER                   1980 KINGSWAY       DOVE 55
DAVE McSPARFAN    D    (B
SPUD SPURLING     B    (B   LES MOIR         B   (B   ANDY BILLUPS   G   (B   NEIL COSTELLO    G   (B
CHRIS EATON       PNO  (B   BASIL MEADE      K V (B   JOHN PANTRY    SYN (B   MAXINE SIMPSON   V   (B
```
RAY KENNEDY

```
RAY KENNEDY       V    (A          (A) RAY KENNEDY                19   CBS  US 36395
```
CHRIS KENNER

```
CHRIS KENNER      V    (A          (A) LAND OF A THOUSAND DANCES  1963 ATLANTIC   US          SD 8117
```
KENNY & THE KASUALS

```
KENNY DANIELS   V G HCA B(ABC       (A) IMPACT                    1965 MARK  US
TOMMY NICHOLS     B    (B           (B) LIVE AT THE STUDIO CLUB   1966 MARK  US          MARK  5000
LEE LIGHTFOOT     B    (AB
DAVID BLACKLEY    D    (AB  PAUL ROACH       K  (AB   JERRY SMITH    G   (AC  ROSEBUD        B   (C
WALLY WILSON      K    (C   GREGG DANIEL     B  (C    RON MASON    K PERC(C   MAX BALL       SAX     (C
JACK MORGAN       G    (C   KARL TOMORROW    K  (C    TONY VINSEY    VLN (C   CAIN SISTERS   V   (C
```
KENSINGTON MARKET

```
ALEX DAROU        B    (           (A) KENSINGTON MARKET, AVENUE ROAD 1968 WB    US       WS   1754
LUKE GIBSON       V    (           (B) AARDVARK                  1969 WB    US
GENE MARTYNEC   V G PNO(
KEITH McKIE     G V    (    JIMMY WATSON     D  (
```
KLARK KENT

```
KLARK'STEWART COPELAND'KENT        (A) KLARK KENT 10"             1980 A&M UK AMLE68511 IRS US 70600
```
PAUL KENT

```
PAUL KENT         V K  (AB          (A) P C KENT                  1970 RCA           UK    SF 8083
DAVID RICHARDS  V G K (A            (B) PAUL KENT                 1971 B&C           UK    CAS 1044
GAVIN WATSON    V G B (AB
JOHN WARD         D    (A   PAT DONALDSON    B  (B    TIM RENWICK    G   (B   TONY REEVES     B   (B
KATHY KISSOON     V    (B   MIKE LONDON      V  (B    GERRY CONWAY   D   (B   RAY WARLEIGH  WIND (B
ROGER POWELL      D    (B   CHRIS TURNER   HCA (B    MAC KISSOON    V   (A   ANDY ROBERTS    G   (B
```
KENTUCKY COLONELS

```
CLARENCE WHITE    G V  (ALL         (A) NEW SOUND OF BLUEGRASS    1963 BRIAR       US   M109
ROLAND WHITE    V MAND(BCDEFGH      (B) APPALACHIAN SWING         1964 WORLD PACIFIC US 1821
BILLY LEE LATHAM  BAN  ABCDEF       (B) KENTUCKY COLONELS         1974 UA RI 29514  US ROUNDER  0070
ERIC WHITE        B    (EFG         (C) LIVING IN THE PAST (1961/65) 1975 BRIAR     US   4202
LEROY MACK        DOB  (ABC         (D) LIVE IN L.A. WITH SCOTTY STONEMAN 1975 BRIAR US   4206
DENIS MORRIS      G    (EG          (E) KENTUCKY COLONELS (1965)   1977 ROUNDER    US        070
BOBBY SLONE       FDL  (ABC         (F) CLARENCE WHITE & KENTUCKY COLONELS1980 ROUNDER US   098
SCOTT STONEMAN    FDL  (CDE         (G) KENTUCKY COLONELS 66       1978 SHILOH     US        4084
BOB WARFORD       BAN  (EFG         (H) THE WHITE BROTHERS LIVE IN SWEDEN 1979 ROUNDER US   073
ROGER BUSH      B V    (ABCDEF
BOBBY CRANE       FDL  (G   ALAN MUNDE       BAN (H
```
WOODY KERN

```
JOHN SANDERSON  WIND VLN(A          (A) THE AWFUL DISCOSURES OF MARIA MONK 1967  PYE  UK NSPL 18273
RICK KENTON       K    (A
MIKE WHEAT        B    (A   STEVE HARRIS     D  (A
```
SARAH KERNOCHAN

```
SARAH KERNOCHAN V PNO(AB           (A) HOUSE OF PAIN             1973 RCA    US 10343
BOB MANN          G    (A           (B) BEAT AROUND THE BUSH      1974 RCA    US 10671
JOE BECK          G    (A
JOE COCUZZO     PERC   (A   VINNIE BELL      G  (A    TONY LEVIN     B   (A   LYN CHRISTIE    B   (A
RALPH SCHUCKETT   K    (A   TOM KEENE        K  (B    ROBERT WACHTEL G   (B   EARL PALMER     D   (B
LYLE RITZ         B    (B   DAN DUGMORE    STEEL(B    LINCOLN MAYORGA K  (B   BOB JAMES       K   (B
ED SUMMERLIN      SYN  (B   PETER JAMESON    G  (B    RON TUTT       D   (B   PAUL HUMPHREY   D   (B
MIKE DEASY        G    (B   BOB BRUCE        FDL(B    FRANK MAROCCO  ACC (B
```

DOUG KERSHAW	G V (ALL	(A) THE CAJUN WAY	1969 WB	US	WS 1820
JOHN CHRISTOPHER	G (EF	(B) SPANISH MOSS	1970 WB	US	WS 1861
JIMMY COLVARD	G (E	(C) DOUG KERSHAW	1971 WB	US	WS 1906
TROY SEALS	G (E	(D) SWAMP GRASS	1972 WB	US	BS 2581
BUDDY KILLEN	PERC (E	(E) DEVILS ELBOW	1972 WB UK K 46196	US	BS 2649
WILLIE ACKERMAN	D (E	(F) DOUGLAS JAMES KERSHAW	1973 WB UK K 46264	US	BS 2725
STU BASORE	STEEL(E	(G) MAMA KERSHAWS BOY	1974 WB	US	BS 2793
CURLY CHALKER	STEEL(E	(H) ALIVE & KICKIN'	1975 WB	US	BS 2851
BOBBY EMMONS	K (EF	(I) RAGIN' CAJUN	1976 WB	US	BS 2910
BOBBY WOOD	K (EF	(J) FLIP FLOP FLY	1977 WB	US	BS 3025
KARL HIMMEL	D (E	(K) LOUISIANA MAN	1978 WB	US	BS 3166
JOE ALLEN	B (EF	(L) LOUISIANA CAJUN COUNTRY	1979 STARFLITE	US	2003
JERRY CARRIGAN	D (E	(A) M) INSTANT HERO	1981 SCOTTI BROS	US 37428	

HARRISON CALLOWAY	TPT (J							
CHARLIE McCOY	HCA (E	TOMMY COGBILL	B (E	KENNY MALONE	D (EF	JORDANAIRES	V (EF
CHIP MOMAN	G (F	RICHARD MAINEGRA	G V (F	REGGIE YOUNG	G (F	MIKE LEECH	B (F
LARRIE LONDIN	D (F	DON SHEFFIELD	TPT (F	DWAYNE WEST	V (F	GORDON STOKER	V (F
RAY WALKER	V (F	HOYT HAWKINS	V (F	DOTTIE DELEONIBUS	V (F	BILL STEWART	D (J
MARTY VADALABENE	D (J	CALVIN ARLINE	B (J	MAX PAUL SCHWENNSEN	G V (J	JOHNNY SANDLIN	G (J
JIMMY NALLS	G (J	ELVIN BISHOP	G (J	NEIL URPEN	K (J	JOHN HUGHEY	STEEL(J
BONNIE BRAMLETT	V (J	RONNIE EADES	SAX (J	CHARLES ROSE	TROM (J	PETE PENDRAS	G (J
AL KAATZ	G (J	DR JOHN	K (J	ANNIE ROSE DEARMAS	V (J	RANDALL BRAMBLETT	SAX (J
HARVEY THOMPSON	SAX (J						

RUSTY KERSHAW	(A	(A) CAJUN IN BLUES COUNTRY	1970 COTILLION	US	SD 9030

DOUG KERSHAW	FDL V(ABC	(A) LOUISIANA MAN 1971	LONDON	UK LGE 114
RUSTY KERSHAW	G V (ABC	(B) LOUISIANA MAN 1976	DJM	UK DJB 26080
TOMMY JACKSON	FDL (B	(C) CAJUN COUNTRY ROCKERS	1979 BEAR FAMILY	GERM BRX 15036

HOWARD JOHNSON	G (B							
CHET ATKINS	G (B	EDDIE HILL	G (B	HAROLD RAY BRADLEY	G (B	HANK GARLAND	G (B
RAY EDENTON	G (B	FLOYD CHANCE	B (B	WOODY WOODHAMS	B (B	ERNIE NEWTON	B (B
JIMMY DAY	STEEL(B	BOB FOSTER STEEL	(B	PETE DRAKE	STEEL(B	CHARLES THERIOT	STEEL(B
LOUIS FOURNERAT	STEEL(B	FLOYD CRAMER PNO	(B	WILEY BARKDULL	PNO V(B	MARK H HARMAN	D (B
CAROLEE COOPER	V (B						

DAVE BLACK	G V (A	(A) KESTREL	1975 CUBE	HIFLY 19
JOHN COOK	G V SYN (A			
DAVID WHITAKER	D PERC(A	FENWICK MOIR B (A	TOM KNOWLES	V (A

VOLKER LANGEFELD	V(MULTI INST)A	(A) FIT ME IN	1978 ELECTROLA	EURO IC 064 45137
ALAN WARREN	D (A			

KEES MAAS	(A	(A) LIFE IS LIKE A PENGUIN	1980 IDIOTEN	NL 7777
WILLEM WISSELIWK	(A			
JOHAN VISSER	G B (A	FRED BONTHUIS D (A		

PAT McAULIFFE	V (A	(A) KEY LARGO	1970 BLUE HORIZON	UK 7 63859
LAURENCE GARMAN	HCA (A			
BOB SAVAGE	K (A	LAURIE SANFORD G (A	TOM STEAD B (A	KENNY LAMB D (A

TROYCE KEY	(A	(A) I'VE GOTTA NEW CAR	1980 RED LIGHTNIN' UK 0028
J J MALONE	(A		

BOBBY KEYS	SAX (A	(A) BOBBY KEYS	1972 WB	UK K46141
JIM PRICE	HRN K(A			
JIM GORDON	D (A	RINGO STARR D (A	CORKY LAING D (A	JACK BRUCE B (A
CARL RADLE	B (A	FELIX PAPPALRDI B (A	KLAUS VOORMANN B (A	MIKE UTLEY K (A
NICKY HOPKINS	K (A	JOHN URIBE G (A	DAVE MASON G (A	LESLIE WEST G (A
CHARLIE FREEMAN	G (A	GEORGE HARRISON G (A		

	(A) THE KEYS ALBUM	1981 A&M US 4868	UK AMLH 68526

STEVE HILLAGE	G (12A	(A) SPACE SHANTY	1972 BRAIN GER	UK DERAM SDLR11
ERIC PEACHEY	D (12A	(A) SPACE SHANTY	1978 PVC US 7902
NICK GREENWOOD	B (A1	(1) APRIL 1971 JULY 1972 (B) JULY 1972 NOV 1972	
NIGEL SMITH	B (2		
DICK HENNINGHAM	K (1	DAVE STEWART K (2A	

CHAKA KHAN	V (A	(A) CHAKA	1978 WB US BSK 3245 UK	K56560
RICHARD TEE	K (AC	(B) NAUGHTY	1980 WB US BSK 3385 UK	K56713
KERMIT MOORE	CELLO(A	(C) WHAT CHA GONNA DO FOR ME	1981 WB US 3526 UK	K56888

TERRI GONZALES	V (A							
STEVE FERRONE	D (AC	PHIL UPCHURCH	G (A	HAMISH STUART	G V (AC	WILL LEE	B V (A
ANTHONY JACKSON	B (AC	BROOK TILLOTSON	HRNS (A	JIM BUFFINGTON	HRNS (A	ARTHUR JENKINS	K (A
ONNIE McINTYRE	G (A	MARK STEVENS	B V (AC	SAMMY FIGUEROA	CONGA(A	TONY MAIDEN	G (A
RICHARD BOCK	CELLO(A	CISSY HOUSTON	V (A	DAVID LASLEY	V (A	RANDY BRECKER	TPT (AC
GEORGE YOUNG	SAX 'A	MICHAEL BRECKER	SAX (AC	GENE BIANCO	HARP (A	ALAN GORRIE	V (A
GEORGE BENSON	V (A	RAFAEL CRUZ	CONGA(A	DAVID SANBORN	SAX (A	JOHN CLARK HRNS	(A
PAUL FAULISE	TROM (A	JESSE LEVY	CELLO(A	BARRY ROGERS	TROM (A	RONNIE CUBER SAX	(A
LEON PENDARVIS	K (A	RICK MAROTTA	D (A	CORNELL DUPREE	G (A	KEN BISCHEL	SYN (A
EDDIE DANIELS	FLT (A	PHIL BODNER	FLT (A	GEORGE MARGE	FLT (A	AIRTO MOREIRA	PERC (A
ANDREW KASTNER	G (A	LARRY WILLIAMS	K SAX(C	DAVID WILLIAMS	G (C	GREG PHILLINGANES	K (C
MIKE SEMBELLO	G (C	RAY POUNDS	D (C	PAULINHO DA COSTA	PERC (C	DIZZY GILLESPIE	TPT (C
HERBIE HANCOCK	K (C	RONNIE FOSTER	K (C	ABRAHAM LABORIEL	B (C	CASEY SCHELIERELL	D(C
CHRUSHER BENNETT	PERC (C	JERRY HEY	TPT (C	DAVID RICHARDS	SYN (C	HIRAM BULLOCK	G (C

```
K37                          STEVE KHAN                                    K37
   STEVE KHAN        G  (ALL     (A) TIGHTROPE              1978  CBS  US 34857    UK  82230
   JEFF MIRANOV      G  (C       (B) BLUE MAN               1978  CBS  US 35539    UK  83146
   WILL LEE          B  (C       (C) ARROWS                 1979  CBS  US 36129
   CRUSHER BENNETT   PERC (C      (D) BEST OF                1980  CBS  US 36406    UK  84234
   DAVID SANBORN     SAX  (C
   ROB MOUNSEY       SYN  (C  ELLIOT SCHEINER   PROD(C  DON GROLNICK     K   (C  STEVE GADD    D  (C
   RANDY BRECKER     HRNS(C  MICHAEL BRECKER  HRNS (C  RICK MAROTTA     D  (C
K38                   KID CREOLE & THE COCONUTS                           K38
   AUGUST DARNELL    B V  (AB     (A) OFF THE COAST OF ME   1980 ISLAND UK 7012 ANTILLES US 7078
   BROOKSIE WELLS    V    (A      (B) FRESH FRUIT IN FOREIGN PLACES 1981 ISLAND UK 7014 SIRE  US  3534
   LOURDES COTTO     V    (A      (B) FRESH FRUIT IN FOREIGN PLACES 1981 ISLAND EURO 203 805
   ADRIANA KAEGI     V    (AB     (C) TROPICAL GANSTERS     1982 ISLAND UK 7016
   FONDA RAE         V    (A
   PETER SCHOTT      PNO  (AB  FRANZ KRAUNS   G   (A  COATIMUNDI    VIBES (AB  ANDREW LLOYD   PERC(AB
   WINSTON GRENNAN   D    (AB  TOMMY BROWDER  B   (A  MARC MAZUR          (B  CAROL COLMAN        (B
   YOGI HORTON       D    (B   LORI EASTSIDE      (B  STEVE KROON         (B  CHERYL POIERER  V   (B
   DON ARNONE        D    (B   DAVE CHARLES       (B  DOMINICK CORTESE    (B  SAL GALLINA        (B
   SATN BROWDER      K    (AB  FREDDIE HARRIS     (B  MICKEY SEVILLA  D   (A  SUGAR COATED ANDY  (A
   SAM TURNER        D    (B   JILL JAFFE'S   STR (B  DON ARMANDO BONILLA V (A
   RONNIE RODGERS    SYN  (A   GICHY DAN      V   (A  FREDDIE HARRIS  D   (AB  JAY ATOYALL    G   (A
   MIA MARTINEZ      V    (A   DURCH ROBINSON     (B  DON HAMILTON        (B  BEVERLY BROWN      (B
   ANGELINA DE LA LANA    (B   ARROLL CORUN       (B  RUBIN BASSINI       (B CHARLES LAGROND  HRNS (B
K39                   JOHNNY KIDD & THE PIRATES                           K39
   JOHNNY KIDD(FRED HEATH) V(ALL  (A) SHAKIN' ALL OVER      1971  STARLINE       UK    SRS 5100
   ALAN CADDY        G  (12      (B) YOUR CHEATIN' HEART    197   PATHE      IMP 2C062 04731
   TOMMY DOCHERTY    G  (1       (C) MEMORIAL ALBUM         197   PATH       IMP 2C062 04422
   JOHNNY GORDON     B  (1       (D) BEST OF                1978  EMI        UK    NUT M12
   CLEM CATTINI      D  (1       (EP) PLEASE DONT TOUCH     1960  HMV        UK    7EG 8628
   KEN McKAY         D  (2       (EP) I'LL NEVER GET OVER YOU 1963 HMV       UK    7EG 8834
   BRIAN GREGG       B  (2       (1) 1958/9   (2) 1959   (3) 1962  (4) 1962/65
   JOE MORETTI       G  (2       (5) 1965    (6) 1966   (7) 1966  (8) 1966/67
   THUNDERCLAP JONES PNO (2
   JOHNNY PATTO      G  (3   JOHNNY SPENCER   B   (345  FRANK FARLEY    D  (345  MICK GREEN    G   (345
   JOHN WEIDER       G  (5   ROGER TRUTH      D   (678  NICK SIMPER     B  (678  JOHNNY CARROL ORG  (8
   RAY SOAPER        ORG (6   MICKY STEWART    G   (678
K40                          GREG KIHN                                     K40
   GREG KIHN         G V  (ALL     (A) GREG KIHN           1976 BESERKLEY US 0046 UK BSERK 4 GER 623358
   STEVE WRIGHT      B V  (ABCDEFGH (B) GREG KIHN AGAIN    1977 BESERKLEY US 0052 UK BSREK 8 GER 623467
   LARRY LYNCH       D V  (ABCDEGH  (C) NEXT OF KIHN       1978 BESERKLEY US 0056 UK BSERK13
   ROBBIE DUNBAR     V K G(A       (D) GREG KIHN /RUBINOOS LIVE 1978 BESERKLEY      UK GIG1
   DAVE CARPENDER    G V  (BCDEGH   (E) WITH THE NAKED EYE 1979 BESERKLEY US 10063 UKBSERK20 GER 623865
   GARY PHILLIPS     K V  (AGH      (F) POWERLINES         1980 BESERKLEY      UK BSERK20
   MARK JORDAN       K    (A       (G) GLASSHOUSE ROCK     1980 BESERKLEY US 10068       GER 624361
   JOHN DOUKAS       K    (A       (H) ROCKIHNROLL BAND    1980 BESERKLEY US 10069 UK 85213
K41                  KILBURN & THE HIGH ROADS                             K41
   IAN DURY          V    (A       (A) HANDSOME            1975  DAWN       UK DNLS  3065
   KEITH LUCAS       G    (A       (A) HANDSOME            1977  PYE        UK NSPL 18541
   DAVEY PAYNE       SAX  (A       (B) WOT A BUNCH         1978  WB         UK  K  56513
   RODERICK MELVIN   PNO  (A       (EP) KILBURN & THE HIGH ROADS 19 BONAPARTE  UK   BONE1
   CHARLES SINCLAIR  B    (A
   CLAIRE TORRY      (A   MARIO GIBBINGS      (A  CLYDE DIAS      (A  MATTHEW EMMANUEL   (A
   DAVID NEWTON ROHOMAN D (A  PETE WILLSHER    (A  LES THATCHER    (A  DAVE MATTACKS    D (A
   JON FIELD         (A   ROD KING            (A  MARTIN JAY      (A  TONY CHARLES      (A
   TREVOR CUMBERBATCH (A  TINA CHARLES    V   (A
K42                          KILLERS                                       K42
   SUCHARD THITTICHAI G  (A       (A) KILLER              1978  ARIOLA        ARL  5003
   JOHN CLAY         G V  (A
   TONY MAYBERRY     B    (A  STUART GREEN    D   (A  PHIL KENZIE   SAX (A
K43                          KILLING FLOOR                                 K43
   MICK CLARKE       (          (A) KILLING FLOOR        1970  SPARK  SRLP 102+1973 SRLM 2004
   BILL THORNYCROFT  (          (A) KILLING FLOOR        1970  SIRE   US          97019
   STU McDONALD      (          (A) KILLING FLOOR        1970  PINK ELEPHANT       855 009
   BAS SMITH         (          (B) OUT OF URANUS        197 PENNY FARTHING  UK    PELS 511
   LOU MARTIN        (
K43A                         KILLING JOKE                                  K43A
   JAZZ COLEMAN      K V  (A       (A) KILLING JOKE       1980 EG  UK 5 45   US EDITIONS 109
   PIG YOUTH         B V  (A       (B) WHATS THID FOR...  1981 EG  UK 550    US EDITIONS 111
   PAUL              D    (A       (B) WHATS THIS FOR...  1981 POLYDOR NL 2302 109
   GEORDIE           G    (A
K43B                         KILO                                          K43B
                                   (A) KILO              1979  STAX       US  4125
K44A                  KIND HEARTS & ENGLISH                                K44A
   TONY BIRD         V    (        (A) A WISH FOR A SEASON 1976  DJM       UK DJF 20490
   JOHN TIPPET       G PNO(        (B) BEACHCOMBER        1977  DJM       UK DJM 20512
   PAUL KEOGH        G    (
   LEE FOTHERGILL    G    (   PAUL BIRCHIL   G   (   FRANK MacDONALD   B   (   KEVIN WELLS D (
   DOUGLAS KEAN      SYN  (
K44B                         KIN PING MEH                                  K44B
   KALLE WEBER       D    (BC      (A) KIN PING MEH       1971
   TORSTEN HERZOG    B V  (B       (B) KIN PING MEH 2     1972  ZEBRA      GER  2944 005
   FRIEDER SCHMITT   K V  (BCD     (C) KIN PING MEH 3     1973  ZEBRA      GER  2949 011
   WILLIE WAGNER     G V  (A       (D) VIRTUES & SINS     1974  NOVA       GER  6/22015
   WERNER STEPHAN    G V  )BC
   ULI GROSS         G.   (BC  GERHARD MROZECK    (BCD ALAN WROE     B  (CD GEFF HARRISON  V  (CD
   CHARLY WEBER      D    (D   JEAN JACQUES KRAVETZ K (D

                                     [311]
```

```
    GLORIA GAIONE      V    (AB      (A) KINDRED                    19
    MARTY RODGERS      V    (AB      (B) NEXT OF KIN                19      WB   US  2640
    BOBBY COCHRAN      G V  (AB
    BERNIE MYSIOR      B    (AB  DAVID BLUEFIELD  K  (AB  RON GRINEL      PERC (A   OLIVER BROWN  CONGA  (A
    JIMMY ERICKSON     PERC (B
```

```
B B KING  G V PNO(ALL                                  (A)LIVE AT THE REGAL        1975 ABC      US ABCS 724
KENNY SANDS      TPT  (A   HENRY BOOZIER    TPT  (A   (A) "   "    "             1965 ABC      US ABCD 509
PLUMA DAVIS      TROM (A   LAWRENCE BURDINE SAX(A      (A) "   "    "             1965 HMV      UK
JOHNNY BOARD     SAX  (A   BARNEY HUBERT    SAX  (ADFH (B) BLUES ON TOP OF BLUES 1967 BLUESWAY US BLS 6011
MILLARD LEE      PNO  (A   MAYALL YORK      B    (A    (B) "   "    "             1968 STATESIDE UK    10238
SONNY FREEMAN    D   (ADFHI JOHN BROWNING   TPT  (DF   (B) "   "    "             19   ABC      US ABC  709
BROOKER WALKER   SAX  (DL  RON LEVY     SYN PNO(DFLHI  (C) INDIANOLA MISSISSIPPI 1970 PROBE    UK SPB 6255
ALEXIS KORNER    G    (E   RINGO STARR      D    (E    (C) "   "    "             197  ABC      US     713
JIM PRICE        HRNS (E   BOBBY KEYS       HRNS(E     (D) LIVE AT COOK COUNTY   1971 PROBE    UK SPB 1032
GARY WRIGHT      K    (E   KLAUS VOORMANN   B    (E    (D) "   "    "             197  ABC      US     723
DUSTER BENNETT   HCA  (E   STEVE MARRIOTT   G    (E    (E) B B KING IN LONDON    1971 PROBE    UK SPB 1041
GREG RIDLEY      (E        JERRY SHIRLEY    (E         (E) "   "    "             197  ABC      UK ABC 5015
PETE WINGFIELD   K    (E   PAUL BUTLER      (E         (E) "   "    "             197  ABC      US     730
JOHN BEST        (E        JIM GORDON       D    (E    (F) L A MIDNIGHT          1972 PROBE    UK SPB 1051
BILL PERKINS     (E        OLLIE MITCHELL   (E         (F) "   "    "             1977 ABC      US     743
CHUCK FINDLEY    HRNS (EJ  JIM KELTNER      D    (E    (G) FRIENDS               1974 ABC      UK ABCL5051
MAC REBENNNACK   PNO  (E   JOHN URIBE       (E         (G) "   "    "             1977 ABC      US AB  825
BARRY FORD       (E        RICK WRIGHT      (E         (H) TOGETHER              1974 DUNHILL  US 751096
DAVID SPINOZZA   (E        CARL HALL        (E         (H) "   "                 1974 ANCHOR   UK ABCD 605
JOE SAMPLE       K    (J   WILTON FELDER    SAX  (J    (I) GUESS WHO             1973 PROBE    UK    1063
STIX HOOPER      D    (J   POPS POPWELL     B    (J    (I) "   "                 1973 ABC      US     759
DR RAGOVOY       (E        JOSHIE ARMSTEAD  V    (E    (I) "   "                 197  ABC      US    5021
TASHA THOMAS     V    (E   CAROLE KING      PNO  (C    (J) MIDNIGHT BELIEVER     1978 ABC      UK ABCL5246
BRYAN GAROFALO   B    (CF  RUSS KUNKEL      D    (C    (K) KINGSIZE              1977 ABC      US     977
LEON RUSSELL     PNO  (C   JOE WALSH        G    (FC   (K) KINGSIZE              1977 EMI EUROIC   95148
PAUL HARRIS      K    (FC  HUGH McCRACKEN   G    (C    (L) LUCILLE TALKS BACK    1975 ABC      UK    5149
JERRY JEMMOTT    B    (CI  HERB LOVELL      D    (C    (L) LUCILLE TALKS BACK    197  ABC      US     898
SHIRLEY MATTHEWS V    (C   MERRY CLAYTON    V    (C    (M) NOW APPEARING AT O'MISS 80 MCA     MCA28016
CLYDIE KING      V    (C   VANETTA FIELDS   V    (C    (N) TO KNOW YOU IS TO LOVE1973 PROBE   UK    1083
BOBBY BRYANT     TPT  (FK  PLAS JOHNSON     SAX  (F    (N) "   "    "             1973 ABC      US    5083
BOB MORIN        D    (F   MEL BROWN        G    (FH   (N) "   "    "             1974 ABC      US     794
JOHN TURK        ORG  (F   EARL PALMER      D    (F    (O) TAKE IT HOME          1979 MCA      US    3151
RONNIE BAKER     B    (GN  ELLI TARKESTY    G    (GN   (P) MUST BE A BETTER WORLD1981 MCA      UK    3095
WILL BOULWARE    K    (G   VINCE MONTANA    VIBES (GN  B B KING STORY           1968 BLUE HORIZON 7 63216
MEMPHIS HRNS     HRNS (GN  MELVIN JACKSON   (H         B B KING STORY VOL 2     1969 BLUE HORIZON 7 63226
CATO WALKER      (H        CHARLES POLK     (H         LIVE & WELL              1970 STATESIDE UK   10297
THEODORE ARTHUR  (H        JOSEPH HARDIN    (H         "   "                    1973 BLUESWAY US BLS6031
DEAN PARKS       G    (J   ROLAND BAUTISTA  G    (J    "   "                    19   ABC      US     819
KURT McGETTRICK  SAX  (J   LUTHER WATERS    V    (J    COMPLETELY WELL          1970 STATESIDE UK   10299
JULIA TILLMAN    V    (J   RED CALLENDER    TUBA (F    "   "    "               19   ABC          868
JESSE ED DAVIS   G    (F   STEVIE WONDER    K    (N    "   "    "               1974 BLUESWAY US BLS6037
CLIFF COULTER    K PERC(F  RANDY WOLFE      G    (F    "   "    "               19   NEW WORLD   NW6005
SANDY KONIKOFF   PERC (F   DERYLL INMAN     G    (G    BACK IN THE ALLEY        1973 BLUESWAY US    6050
ROLAND CHAMBERS  G    (GN  RON KERSEY       K    (G    "   "                    1977 ABC      US     878
ANDREW LOVE      SAX  (G   DON RENALDO STRINGS   (G    GREATEST HITS            1973 PROBE    UK    1069
BEN BENAY        G    (H   BOBBY FORTE      SAX  (HLI  GREATEST HITS VOL 1      19   UNITED   US    7766
TOMMY PUNKSON    (H        THEODORE REYNOLDS (H        "   "    "               19   KENT     US     552
ALFRED THOMAS    (H        JAMES GADSON     D    (J    LUCILLE                  1969 STATESIDE UK   10272
GEORGE BOHANON   HRNS (J   GARY HERBIG      FLT  (J    "   "                    1973 BLUESWAY US    6016
ORRIN WATERS     V    (J   MAXINE WILLARD   V    (J    "   "                    1977 ABC      US     712
RED HOLLOWAY     SAX  (F   VICTOR FELDMAN PERC K(F     MR BLUES                 19   ABC      US     456
EARL TURBINTON   SAXI (FI  TAJ MAHAL      HCA G (F     BEST OF                  1973 ABC          5026
RON BROWN        B    (F   EARL YOUNG       D    (GN   "   "                    19   ABC          767
NORMAN HARRIS    G    (GN  DAVE CRAWFORD    K    (GN   "   "    "               1981 MCA      UK    1612
LARRY WASHINGTON PERC (GN  WAYNE JACKSON    TPT  (GN   B B KING                 19   NEW WORLD    6004
PHILADELPHIA STRINGS  (GN  MILTON HOPKINS   G    (KHLI B B KING VOL 2          19   NEW WORLD    6006
EDWARD ROWE      HRNS (HLI HAROLD POTIER JR (H         CLASSIC REVISITED        1977 ABC      US     724
LEO PENN         (H        MICHAEL OMARTIAN K    (H    SOUL OF B B KING         19   FESTIVAL     532
STEVE MADAIO     TPT (JI   QUITMAN DENNIS   HRNS(J     "   "    "               19   KENT     US   5-16
ABE MOST         CLAR (J   LEE RITENOUR     G    (K    "   "    "               19   KENT     US     516
JAMES TONEY      ORG  (KL  RONNIE BARRON    ORG  (K    "   "    "               19   CUSTOM   US    2052
SONNY BURKE      K    (K   JOE TURNER       B    (K    "   "    "               19   CUSTOM   US    1052
SCOTT EDWARDS    B    (K   JOHN STARKS      D    (KL   "   "    "               19   UNITED   US    7714
ED GREENE        D    (K   EARL NASH        PERC (K    BLUES IS KING            19   ABC      US     704
EDDIE BROWN      PERC (K   AL AARONS        TPT  (K    "   "    "               196  HMV      UK    3608
ROY POPER        TPT  (K   GARNETT BROWN    TROM (KI   "   "    "               19   BLUESWAY US    6001
JIMMY FORREST    SAX  (K   FRED JACKSON     WIND (K    CONFESSIN' THE BLUES     19   ABC      US     528
ERNIE WATTS      SAX  (K   JEROME RICHARDSON SAX (K    "   "    "               19   HMV      UK    3514
JOE LIGON        V    (K   JOHNNY MARTIN    V    (K    THE ELECTRIC B B KING    1977 ABC      US     813
ELMEO FRANKLIN   V    (K   RICHARD WALLACE  V    (K    "   "    "               19   ABC      US    1061
CALVIN OWENS     TPT  (M   CALEP EMPHREY    D    (M    "   "    "               1969 STATESIDE UK   10284
EDGAR SYNIGAL    SAX  (M   LEONARD GILL     G    (M    "   "    "               1969 BLUESWAY US    6022
STEVE SHERARD    TROM (M   HILTON JOSEPH    SAX  (M    KING OF THE BLUES        1976 M F P   UK   50259
PHIL BLACKMAN    K    (M   JOHN WILLIE COOK TPT  (M    "   "    "               19   CROWN    US    5167
JON JONES        G    (M   NANA VASCONCELOS PERC (M    "   "    "               19   UNITED   US    7730
RUDY AIKELS      B    (L   MARCUS BARNETT   PERC (L    TOGETHER AGAIN           1976 IMPULSE       8027
JOSEPH BURTON    TROM (LI  JESS DANIELS     G    (L    "   "    "               1976 IMPULSE  US    9317
HERBERT HARDESTY SAX  (L   RUSSELL JACKSON  B    (M    TAKE A SWING WITH ME     19   BLUE HORIZON2431 004
WILBERT FREEMAN  B (DFMHI  EDDIE MILLER     WIND(J     B B KING ANTHOLOGY       1976 ABC          5611
DAVID SANBORN    SAX  (I   LOUIS HUBERT     SAX  (I    "   "    "               19   KENT     US    9011
GENE DINWIDDIE   SAX  (I   CORNELL DUPREE   G    (I    FEELING THEY CALL THE BLUES 19 TRIO    JAP PA 6220
FRANK OWENS      PNO  (I   BERNARD PURDIE   D    (I    FEELING THEY CALL VOL2   19   TRIO     JAP PA 6221
ERNIE ROYAL      TPT  (I   TREVOR LAWRENCE  SAX(I      B B KING LIVE            19   KENT     US     565
HOWARD JOHNSON   SAX  (I   RON KERSEY       K    (N    LIVE                     19   KENT     US     515
CHARLIE MANN     K V  (N   ANDREW LOVE      HRNS(N     LIVE                     19   UNITED   US    7771
```

                (CONTINUED)

ON STAGE LIVE	19	UNITED	US	7736	LET ME LOVE YOU	19	KENT	US	513
ON STAGE LIVE	19	KENT	US	5015	LET ME LOVE YOU	19	UNITED	US	7734
SING SPIRITUALS	19	CROWN	US	5119	ORIGINAL SWEET 16	19	KENT	US	568
SWING LOW	19	UNITED	US	7721	ORIGINAL SWEET 16	19	UNITED	US	7773
BETTER THAN EVER	19	KENT	US	561	PURE SOUL	19	KENT	US	517
BOSS OF THE BLUES	19	KENT	US	529	THE JUNGLE	19	KENT	US	521
BOSS OF THE BLUES	19	UNITED	US	7750	THE JUNGLE	19	UNITED	US	7742
DOING MY THING LORD	19	KENT	US	563	TURN ON WITH B B KING	19	KENT	US	548
FROM THE BEGINNING	19	KENT	US	533	TURN ON WITH B B KING	19	UNITED	US	7763
INCREDIBLE SOUL OF	19	KENT	US	539	UNDERGROUND BLUES	19	KENT	US	535
INCREDIBLE SOUL OF	19	UNITED	US	7756	9 X 9,5	19	UNITED	US	7788
B B KING STORY	19	JOKER	ITALY	3727	WAILS	19	CROWN	US	5115
SINGIN' THE BLUES	19	CROWN	US	5020	WAILS	19	CROWN	US	147
SINGIN' THE BLUES	19	UNITED	US	7726	BLUE FOR ME	19	UNITED	US	7708
MORE	19	CROWN	US	5230	BLUE FOR ME	19	CUSTOM	US	2046
MY KIND OF BLUES	19	CROWN	US	5188	BLUES IN MY HEART	19	CROWN	US	309
MY KIND OF BLUES	19	UNITED	US	7724	EASY LISTENING BLUES	19	CROWN	US	5286
SPANISH HARLEM	19	ATCO	US	33133	EASY LISTENING BLUES	19	UNITED	US	7705
THE BLUES	19	CROWN	US	5063	GREAT B B KING	19	CROWN	US	5143
THE BLUES	19	UNITED	US	7732	THE GREAT	19	UNITED	US	7728
ROCK ME BABY	19	KENT	US	5012	HEART FULL OF BLUES	19	UNITED	US	7703
ROCK ME BABY	19	UNITED	US	7733	I LOVE YOU SO	19	CUSTOM	US	2049
TWIST WITH B B KING	19	CROWN	US	5248	I LOVE YOU SO	19	UNITED	US	7711

ALBERT KING	G V	(ALL	(A) THE BIG BLUES	1962	KING	US		852
DONALD 'DUCK' DUNN	B	(FHO	(B) TRAVELLING TO CALIFORNIA	1967	KING	US		K1060
STEVE CROPPER	G	(F	(B) TRAVELLING TO CALIFORNIA	1967	POLYDOR	UK		2343 026
AL JACKSON	D	(EFGO	(C) BORN UNDER A BAD SIGN	1967	STAX/ATLANTIC	US	7723	
JIM KELTNER	D	(H	(D) KING OF THE BLUES GUITAR	1968	ATLANTIC	UK	588 173	US	SD8213
ROGER HAWKINS	D	(H	(D) KING OF THE BLUES GUITAR	197	ATLANTIC	UK RI		K40494
WILLIE HALL	D	(O	(E) LIVE WIRE BLUES POWER	1968	STAX	US	2003	UK	1002
EDDIE WILLIS	G	(R	(E) LIVE WIRE BLUES POWER	1980	STAX	US RI	4128	
JAMES GADSON	D	(L	(F) DOES THE KINGS THING	1968	STAX	US	2015	UK	1017
DAVID HOOD	B	(H	(G) YEARS GONE BY	1969	STAX	US	2010	UK	1022
EARL THOMAS	B	(O	(H) LOVEJOY	1971	STAX	US	2040	UK	2325
HENRY DAVIS	B	(L	(I) I'LL PLAY THE BLUES FOR YOU	1972	STAX	US	3009	UK	1019
CHUCK RAINEY	B	(L	(I) I'LL PLAY THE BLUES FOR YOU	197	POLYDOR			UK 2325089
JESSE ED DAVIS	G	(H	(J) I WANNA GET FUNKY	1974	STAX	US	5505	UK	1003
TIPPY ARMSTRONG	G	(H	(K) MONTREUX FESTIVAL	197	STAX	US	5520	
WAYNE PERKINS	G	(H	(L) TRUCKLOAD OF LOVIN'	1976	UTOPIA	US 1	1387	UK UTS 602
MICHAEL TOLES	G	(H	(M) LIVE (DBL)	1977	UTOPIA	US 2	2205	
VERNON BURCH	G	(O	(N) ALBERT	1977	UTOPIA	US 1	1731	
BOBBY MANUEL	G	(O	(O) THE PINCH	1978	STAX	US	4101	UK	3001
WAH WAH WATSON	G	(L	(P) DOOR TO DOOR	19	CHESS			1538
BILLY FENDER	G	(L	(Q) CHRONICLE (1 SIDE)	1979	STAX	US	4123	
GREG POREE	G	(L	(R) KING ALBERT	1977	TOMATO	US	6002	
RONALD WRIGHT	D	(R	(S) ALBERT LIVE	1979	TOMATO	US	7009	
LESTER SNELL	K	(O	(T) NEW ORLEANS HEAT	1979	TOMATO	US	7022	
GLEN GOINS	G	(R						
JOE SAMPLE	K	(L	SANDY KONIKOFF	PERC (H	KING ERRISSON	PERC (L	DENIECE WILLIAMS	V (L
JEANIE ARNOLD	V	(L	OTIS RUSH	G V (P	JOHN GALLIE	K (H	WINSTON STEWART	K (O
BERT DECOTEAUX	K	(L	JEANNE GREENE	V (H	LANI GROVES	V (L	JULIA TILLMAN	V (L
MEMPHIS HORNS		(O	BARRY BECKETT	K (H	MARVELL THOMAS	K (O	JERRY PETERS	K (L
WILLIAM C BROWN	V	(O	MAXINE WILLARD	V (L	DEE IRVIN	V (L	MOUNT ZION SINGERS	V (H
RUDY ROBINSON	K	(R	ANTHONY WILLIS	B (R	AARON WILLIS	G (R	RAY TINI JR	G (R
DWAYNE LOMAX	D	(R	BARBARA HUBY	PERC (R	LARRY FRATANGELO	PERC (R	BRANDYE	V (R
JOHN FRAGA	B	(R	JAMES McCARTY	G (R	DENNIS ROBBINS	G (R	JOHN BADANJEK	D (R
FRED WESLEY	HRNS (R							

BEN E KING	V	(ALL	(A) WHAT IS SOUL	196	ATCO	UK 587 072	
GWEN GUTHRIE	V	(I	(B) SPANISH HARLEM	1961	ATCO	US 33133	UK 590 000
JEFF MIRANOV	G	(OI	(C) SINGS FOR SOULFUL LOVERS	1962	ATCO	US 33137	UK LONDON 8026
KEN HATFIELD	G	(O	(D) DONT PLAY THAT SONG	1962	ATCO	US 33142	UK LONDON 8012
KEN KIRKLAND	K	(O	(E) GREATEST HITS	1964	ATCO	US 33165	UK 2464 010
JIMMY YOUNG	D	(O	(F) SEVEN LETTERS	1965	ATCO	US 33174	
BEN E KING JR	B	(O	(G) BEGINNING OF IT ALL	1971	MANDALA	US 3007	UK CBS 64570
MARCUS MILLER	B	(O	(H) ROUGH EDGES	197	MAXWELL	US 88001	UK CREWE 203
SAMMY FIGUEROA	PERC	(O	(I) SUPERNATURAL THING	1975	ATLANTIC	US 18132	UK K50118
YVONNE LEWIS	V	(O	(J) BEN E KING STORY	1975	ATLANTIC	UK	K50139
JANET PENDARVIS	V	(O	(K) I HAD A LOVE	1976	ATLANTIC	US 18169	UK K50264
RICKY WILLIAMS	K	(I	(L) BENNY & US (A W B)	1977	ATLANTIC	US 19105	UK K50384
CRYSTAL DAVIS	V	(O	(M) LET ME LIVE IN YOUR LIFE	1978	ATLANTIC	US 19200	UK K50527
DEIRDRE TUCK-COREL	V	(O	(N) STAR COLLECTION	197	MIDI	GERM	20040
RODNEY PHELPS	G	(I	(O) MUSIC TRANCE	1980	ATLANTIC	US 19269	UK K50713
KEVIN DOUGLAS	B	(O	(P) STREET TOUGH	1980	ATLANTIC	US 19300	UK K50787
JERRY FRIEDMAN	G	(I	(Q) YOUNG BOY BLUES	19	CLARION	US 606	
CARLOS ALOMAR	G	(I					
RICARDO WILLIAMS	D	(O	EMMANUEL REDDING	D (O	TYRONE WILLIAMS	K (O	GREGORY McCOY	K (O
JAMES DRUMGOLE	TPT	(O	RONNELLE STAFFORD	V (O	JAMILLAR MUHAMMAD	V (O	DEREK SMITH	K (I
BERT DE COTEAUX	K	(I	BOB BABBIT	B (I	JERRY JEMMOTT	B (I	GEORGE DEVENS	PERC(I
PHIL KRAUS	PERC	(I	TED SOMMERS	PERC (I	JACK JENNINGS	PERC (I	CARLOS MARTIN	CONGA(I
YVONNE GUTHRIE	V	(I	BRENDA GUTHRIE	V (I	LANI GROVES	V (I	LYNN WEIPPERT	V (G
KATHY ALSON	V	(G	LESLIE ZIMEI	V (G	RONNIE CANGRO	D (F	DON OLSEN	B (F
JOHN BRIGANTI	D	(G	CARE SCICKLER	G (G	MIKE MATTIA	K (G		

BOBBY KING		(A	(A) CHASER	197	MCM	FR	900 292

CAROLE KING	G PNO V	(ALL	(A) NOW THAT EVERYTHINGS BEEN SAID	1969	ODE	Z1244 012(BY GROUP CITY)		
RALPH SCHUCKETT	K	(BCDL	(B) WRITER	1970	ODE	US 77006	US RI EPIC 34944	
CHARLES LARKEY	B	(BCDEFGLN	(B) WRITER	1970	A&M UK		AMLS 996	
DANNY KOOTCH	G V	(BCDEFGIL	(C) TAPESTRY	1972	ODE	US 77009	US RI EPIC 34956	
JAMES TAYLOR	G V	(BCDIL	(C) TAPESTRY	197	A&M UK	2025	US RI EPIC 82308	
BOBBYE HALL	PERC	(DEFL	(D) MUSIC	197	ODE	US 77013	US RI EPIC 34949	
THERESA CALDERONE	PERC	(DL	(D) MUSIC	197	A&M UK		AMLH 67013	
ABIGALE HANESS	V	(BDG	(E) RHYMES & REASONS	1972	ODE	77016	US RI EPIC 34950	
MERRY CLAYTON	V	(CDL	(F) FANTASY	1973	ODE	77018	US RI EPIC 34962	
WILLIAM GREEN	WIND	(DL	(G) WRAP AROUND JOY	1974	ODE	77024	US RI EPIC 34953	
WILLIAM COLLETTE	WIND	(DL	(H) REALLY ROSIE	1975	ODE	77027	US RI EPIC 34955	
ERNIE WATTS	WIND	(DEFGJKL	(I) THOROUGHBRED	1976	ODE	77034	US RI EPIC 34963	
DEBORAH NORTH	V	(N	(I) THOROUGHBRED	1980	EMBASSY UK RI	31841		
PLAS JOHNSON	WIND	(DL	(J) SIMPLE THINGS	1977	CAPITOL		11667	
MIKE ALTSCHUL	WIND	(DFG	(K) WELCOME HOME	1978	CAPITOL		11785	
OSCAR BRASHEAR	WIND	(DJ	(L) GREATEST HITS	1978	ODE	86043	US EPIC 34967	
CURTIS AMY	WIND	(CDFL	(M) TOUCH THE SKY	1979	CAPITOL		11953	
OSCAR FORD JR	V	(N	(N) PEARLS	1980	CAPITOL		12073	
DON KNAUB	TROM	(N						
BILL INN	STR	(N	MARK MANISCALE	BAN (N	ERIC JOHNSON	G (N	STEVE MEADOR	D (N
GLORIA HINES	V	(N	LYDIA NORTH	V (N	MICHAEL MUNDAY	TROM (N	BOBBY MEYER	TPT (N
RAY CRISARA	TPT	(N	BETTY WHITLOCK	FDL (N	CHRISTOPHER GROSS	G (N	RICK EVERS	PERC(K
GEORGIA KELLY	HARP	(K	ANNE GOLIA	TAMB (K	BOB HARRINGTON	DULC (K	ANN WHITE	V (K
HARVEY MASON	D	(EFL	DAVID T WALKER	G (DEL	RED RHODES	STEEL(E	HARRY EDISON	HRNS (E
ROBERT BRYANT	HRNS	(E	GEORGE BOHANON	TROM(EFGJKL	CHARLIE LOPER	TROM (EL	DICK HYDE	TROM (FGL
OLLIE MITCHELL	HRNS	(F	CHUCK FINDLEY	TPT (FGL	ALBERT AARONS	TPT (EL	TOM SCOTT	SAX (FGJL
ANDY NEWMARK	D	(GL	DEAN PARKS	G (GL	FRED JACKSON	HRNS (G	GENE COE	HRNS (G
JIM HORN	SAX	(G	EDDIE KENDRICKS	SINGERS(F	LOUISE GOFFIN	V (GJL	SHERRY GOFFIN	V (GLJ
WADDY WACHTEL	G	(IL	RUSS KUNKEL	D (CIL	LEE SKLAR	B (LI	RALPH MACDONALD	PERC(IL
DAVID CROSBY	V	(I	GRAHAM NASH	V (I	J D SOUTHER	V (I	ROBERT McENTEE	V G K(JK
MARK HALLMAN	G V K(JKMN		ROB GALLOWAY	B (KJ	MICHAEL WOOTEN	D (JK	MIGUEL RIVERA	PERC (JKM
RICHARD HARDY	WIND(JKMN		CLARK SPANGLER	SYN (JK	NOLAN SMITH	HRNS (JK	MAURICE SPEARS	TROM (J
TERRY HARRINGTON	SAX	(J	JOEL O'BRIEN	D (CL	PENN STEINBERG	B (C	JULIA TILLMAN	V (BL
JOHN FISCHBACK	SYN	(B	DOLORES HALL	V (B	LEO LEBLANC	G V (M	REESE WYNANS	K (MN
FRED KRC	D V	(M	DAVE PERKINS	G V (M	BOBBY RAMBO	G V (M	TOMAS RAMIREZ	WIND V(MN
STEPHANIE SPRUILL	V	(K	ALEXANDRA BROWN	V (K	STRING SECTION	(CEFK		

CLYDIE KING	V	(A	(A) BROWN SUGAR	1974	POLYDOR	UK	2310 231

DENNY KING	G V B(A		(A) EVIL WIND IS BLOWING	1973					
ALEX ST CLAIR	G B TPT(A								
JESSE BRIONES	B	(A	GREG HAMPTON	D (A	AL CARR	CONGA (A	DOUGLAS MOON	HCA (A
PETE DOLAN	FLT	(A							

DON KING	(AB	(A) LONELY HOTEL	19	EPIC	US 36469	
		(B) WHIRLWIND	19	EPIC	US 37105	

EARL KING	(AB	(A) NEW ORLEANS ROCK'N'ROLL	1978	SONET	UK	SNTF 719
		(B) EARL KING	19	VIVID	JAP	1012

FREDDIE KING	G V	(ALL	(A) FREDDIE KING SINGS	196	KING US 762		
SONNY THOMPSON	PNO	(ABCDE	(B) LETS HIDEAWAY & DANCEAWAY	196	KING US 773		
CLIFFORD SCOTT	SAX	(ABCDE	(C) GIRL BOY GIRL	196	KING US 777		
GENE REDD	SAX	(ABCDE	(D) BOSSA NOVA & BLUES	196	KING US 821		
FRED JORDAN	G	(ABC	(E) FREDDIE KING GOES SURFIN'	196	KING US 856		
WILLIAM WILLIS	B	(ABCDE	(F) BONANZA OF INSTRUMENTALS	196	KING US 928		
BENNY TURNER	B	(F	(G) VOCALS & INSTUMENTALS	196	KING US 964		
PHILIP PAUL	D	(ABC	(H) HIDEAWAY	196	KING US 1059+ 1977 RI STARDAY 5033		
BUD BEADLE	SAX	(PRT	(I) KING OF R&B VOL 2	1969	POLYDOR UK	2343 009	
RON CARTHY	TPT	(PRT	(J) IS A BLUES MASTER	1969	ATLANTIC UK 588 186 + RI	K 40496	
ROY DAVIES	K	(PRT	(J) IS A BLUES MASTER	1969	COTILLION	US SD9004	
MICK EVE	SAX	(PRT	(K) HIS EARLY YEARS	197	POLYDOR	UK 2343 047	
STEVE FERRONE	D	(PRT	(L) MY FEELING FOR THE BLUES	1970	COTILLION	US SD9016	
STEVE GREGORY	SAX	(PRT	(L) MY FEELING FOR THE BLUES	1975	ATLANTIC	UK RI K 40947	
DELISLE HARPER	B	(PRT	(M) GETTING READY	1971	A&M UK AMLS65004	US SHELTER 8905	
CHRIS MERCER	SAX	(PRT	(N) TEXAS CANNONBALL	1972	A&M UK AMLS68113	US SHELTER 8905	
BOB TENCH	G V	(PRT	(O) WOMAN ACROSS THE WATER	1973	A&M UK AMLS68919	US SHELTER 8919	
MIKE VERNON	PERC	(RT	(P) BURGLAR	1974	RSO UK 2394 140	US RSO 4803	
PETE WINGFIELD	K	(PRT	(Q) BEST OF FREDDIE KING	1974	A&M UK AMLS68313	US SHELTER 2140	
LONNIE MACK	G	(F	(Q) BEST OF FREDDIE KING	1974	SHELTER	US 52021	
BRIAN AUGER	ORG	(p	(R) LARGER THAN LIFE	1975	RSO UK 2394 163	US RSO 4811	
MISTY BROWNING	V	(P	(S) ORIGINAL HITS	1977	STARDAY/KING	US 5012	
P P ARNOLD	V	(P	(T) 1934 TO 1976	1977	RSO UK 2394 192	US RSO 1 3025	
VIE	V	(P	(U) REST OF FREDDIE KING	1976	ISLAND	UK ISA 5001	
ERIC CLAPTON	G V	(PT	(V) 17 HITS	1978	KING US 5012		
JOHN THOMAS	TPT	(R					
JAMIE OLDAKER	D	(PT	CARL RADLE	B (OPNT	DICK SIMS	K (PT	GEORGE TERRY	G (PT
SERGIO PASTORA	PERC	(T	MELVIN JONES	ORG (T	LOUIS STEPHENS	PNO (RT	KING CURTIS	SAX (L
JERRY JEMMOTT	B	(L	ERNIE ROYAL	TPT (L	FRANK WESS	SAX (L	JOHN GALLIE	K (MN
DON PRESTON	G V(MNO		CLAUDIA LENNEAR	V (M	SONNY BURKE	K (R	JIM KELTNER	D (O
HENRY DAVIS	B	(R	JIM GORDON	K SAX (R	ANDREW JONES	G (R	MIKE O'NEILL	G (N
BENNY TURNER	B	(RT	KENNY PASSARELLI	B (T	ROBERT WILSON	B (R	WILLIE BRIDGES	SAX (L
GEORGE COLEMAN	SAX	(L	TREVOR LAWRENCE	SAX (L	KENNY RICE	D (L	CHUCK BLACKWELL	D(MNO
JIM GORDON	D	(N	LEON RUSSELL	K (MNO	KATHI McDONALD	V (M	SAM CLAYTON	PERC(N
O'NEILL TWINS	V	(R	BIG JOHN ETHOMASSIE	D (R	ALVIN HEMPHILL	K (R	DARRYL LEONARD	TPT (N
MELVIN WAH WAH RAGIN	G	(R	K O THOMAS	PNO (R	SAM WYLE	G (T	CHARLES ROBINSON	D(T
MARTIN BANKS	TPT	(L	CORNELL DUPREE	G (L	HUGH McCRACKEN	HCA (L	GEORGE STUBBS	PNO (L
DONALD DUCK DUNN	B	(MN	AL JACKSON	D (N	JOEY COOPER	V (M	CHARLES MYERS	D (MR
JOE DAVIS	SAX	(R	REV PAT HENDERSON	K (O	JAMES GADSON	D (R	JERRY JUMONVILLE	SAX(R
DAVID NEWMAN	SAX	(R	JOHN THOMAS	TPT (R				

REG KING

REG KING	G V	(A		(A) REG KING			1971	UA		UK	UAS 29157
MICK EVANS	B	(A									
ROGER POWELL	D	(A	IAN WHITEMAN	K B FLT	(A	BRIAN GODDING	G V	(A	DORIS TROY	V	(A
PETER DALE	V	(A	NICK JONES		PERC (A	MARTIN STONE	G	(A	BRIAN BELSHAW	B V	(A
PETER SWALES	V	(A	BRENDA FRENCH		V (A	ALAN KING	G	(A	KEVIN WESTLAKE	D G	(A
DICK THOMAS	D	(A	FRANK FARRELL	B	(A	JO WRIGHT	G	(A	GEORGE BARKER		TPT (A
PAUL NIEMAN	TROM	(A	BARRY JENKINS	D	(A	MICK TAYLOR	G	(A	BRIAN AUGER	K	(A
DANNY McCULLOCH	B	(A	ELTON DEAN		SAX (A	MARK CHARIG	TPT	(A	STEVE WINWOOD	K	(A

KING BISCUIT BOY

KING BISCUIT BOY	HCA G V	(ALL		(A) GOOD UNS			1971	PARAMOUNT	US PAS 6023	+SPFA	7001
(RICHARD NEWELL)				(A) GOOD UNS			19	DAFFODIL		IMP	934 505
LARRY ATAMANUIK	D	(AB		(B) OFFICIAL MUSIC			1971	PARAMOUNT	US PAS 5030	+SPFL	270
ROLY GREENWAY	B	(AB		(C) KING BISCUIT BOY			1974	EPIC	US		32891
SONNIE BERNARDI	D	(A									
DIANNE BROOKS	V	(A	BRIAN RUSSELL	V	(A	RHONDA SILVER	V	(A	RICK BELL	K	(AB
RHEAL LANTHIER	G	(AB	KELLY JAY	K	(AB	STEVE KENNEDY	HRNS	(AB	SLIDE TALLMAN		HRNS (A
ALLEN TOUSSAINT	PROD K V	(C	ARTHUR NEVILLE	K	(C	LEO NOCENTELLI	G	(C	GEORGE PORTER JR	B	(C
JOSEPH MODELISTE	D	(C	ALFRED ROBERTS		CONGA (C	CLYDE KERR JR	HRNS	(C	LESTER CALISTE		HRNS (C
CARL BLOUIN	HRNS	(C	ALVIN THOMAS	HRNS	(C	JOAN HARMON	V	(C	DR JOHN	G	(C
DANNY McBRIDE	G	(C	JOHN GIBBARD	G	(B	DOUG RILEY	K	(B	MOE KOFFMAN		HRNS)B
GREGG MUDRI	HRNS	(B									

KING CRIMSON

ROBERT FRIPP	G K	(ALL	(A) IN THE COURT OF THE CRIMSON KING	1969	ISLAND	UK	ILPS9111		
MIKE GILES	D	(ABK	(A) IN THE COURT OF THE CRIMSON KING	1969	ATLANTIC	US	8245	+RI	SD19155
GREG LAKE	B V	(AB	(A) IN THE COURT OF THE CRIMSON KING	1969	POLYDOR	UK	2302 057	+FR	2310 516
IAN McDONALD FLT	K	(AHK	(B) IN THE WAKE OF POSEIDON	1970	ISLAND	UK	ILPS9127	+US ATLANTIC	8266
MEL COLLINS	SAX	(BCDEH	(B) IN THE WAKE OF POSEIDON	197	POLYDOR	UK	2302 058	+FR	2310 517
PETE SINFIELD LYRICS		(ABCDE	(C) LIZARDS	1970	ISLAND	UK	ILPS9141	+US ATLANTIC	8278
PETE GILES	B	(BK	(C) LIZARDS	197	POLYDOR	UK	2302 059	+FR	2310 518
TONY LEVIN	B	(M	(C) LIZARDS	1977	POLYDOR	GER	2344 071		
GORDON HASKELL	B V	(BC	(D) ISLANDS	1971	ISLAND	UK	ILPS9175	+US ATLANTIC	7212
ANDY McCULLOCH	D	(C	(D) ISLANDS	1971	POLYDOR	UK	2302 060	+FR	2310 519
BOZ BURRELL	B V	(DE	(E) EARTHBOUND	1972	ISLAND	UK	HELP 6		
IAN WALLACE	D V	(DE	(E) EARTHBOUND	1977	POLYDOR	UK	2343 092	+FR	2344 074
BILL BRUFORD	D	(FGHJM	(F) LARKS TONGUES IN ASPIC	1973	ISLAND	UK	ILPS9230	+US ATLANTIC	7263
JOHN WETTON	B	(FGHJ	(F) LARKS TONGUES IN ASPIC	1977	POLYDOR	UK	2302 061	+FR	2310 520
DAVID CROSS	VLN K	(FGHJ	(G) STARLESS & BIBLE BLACK	1974	ISLAND	UK	ILPS9275	+US ATLANTIC	7298
KEITH TIPPETT	K	(BCD	(G) STARLESS & BIBLE BLACK	1977	POLYDOR	UK	2302 065	+FR	2310 521
ADRIAN BELEW	G V	(M	(G) STARLESS & BIBLE BLACK	1977	POLYDOR	GER	2459 348		
OBIN MILLER	WIND	(CDH	(H) RED	1974	ISLAND	UK	ILPS9308	+US ATLANTIC	18110
MARK CHARIG	CORNET	(CDH	(H) RED	1977	POLYDOR	UK	2302 066	+FR	2310 522
HARRY MILLER	B	(D	(J) U S A	1975	ISLAND	UK	ILPS9316	+US ATLANTIC	18136
JON ANDERSON	V	(C	(J) U S A	1977	POLYDOR	UK	2302 067	+FR	2310 523
JAMIE MUIR	PERC	(F	(J) U S A	1977	POLYDOR	GER	2344 075		
NICK EVANS	TROM	(C	(K) YOUNG PERSONS GUIDE TO K C DBL	1975	ISLAND	UK	ISLD	7 GER	89497
EDDIE JOBSON	K VLN	(J	(K) YOUNG PERSONS GUIDE TO K C	1977	POLYDOR	UK	2612 036	+FR	2625 035
PAULINA LUCAS	V	(D	(L) GREATEST	197	PHONOGRAM		FR		6641 356
TONY LEVIN	B V	(M	(M) DISCIPLINE	1981	EG UK EGLP49 GER 2302 112 US WB BSK3429				

KING CURTIS

KING CURTIS	SAX	(ALL	HAVE TENOR WILL BLOW	1959	ATCO	US			33113
(CURTIS OUSLEY)			SAX IN MOTION	1963	US	RI CAMDEN 2242			
WILLIE BRIDGES	SAX	(L	SOUL SERENADE	1964	CAPITOL	US			2095
MELVIN LASTIE	CORNET	(L	PLAYS HITS OF SAM COOKE	1965		US			
CHARLES RAINEY	B	(L	THAT LOVIN' FEELIN'	1966	ATCO US 33189				
CORNELL DUPREE	G	(L	(L) LIVE AT SMALLS PARADISE	1966	ATCO US 33198	UK ATLANTIC		K30029	
PAUL GRIFFIN	PNO	(L	PLAYS GREAT MEMPHIS HITS	1967	ATCO US 33211	UK ATLANTIC 588 067			
RAY LUCAS	D	(L	KINGSIZE SOUL	1967	ATCO US 33231	UK ATLANTIC 587 043			
NOBLE KNIGHTS		(S	SWEET SOUL	1968	ATCO US 33247	UK ATLANTIC 588 115			
SHIRELLES	V	(E	BEST OF KING CURTIS	1968	ATCO US 33266	+US PRESTIGE		7709	
			BEST OF KING CURTIS	19	ATLANTIC	UK 228 002	+ K40067		
CHAMPION JACK DUPREE	V K	(B	INSTANT GROOVE	1968	ATCO US 33292	UK ATLANTIC 2228027			
			ONE MORE TIME(BEST OF)	196	PRESTIGE	US		7775	
			GET READY	196	ATCO US 33338				
			LIVE AT FILLMORE	19	ATCO US 33359	UK ATLANTIC		K40214	
			EVERYBODY'S TALKIN'	19	ATCO US 33385	UK ATLANTIC		K40360	
			(E) ETERNALLY SOUL	1970	WAND		WNS4		
			(S) SOUL SERENADE	1972	EMBER		SPE 6600		
			MR SOUL	1972	EMBER		SPE 6607		
			(B) BLUES AT MONTREUX	197	ATLANTIC US 1637	UK K40430			
			SOUL TWIST	19	ENJOY	US		2001	
			SOUL TIME	19	UPFRONT	US		UPF 157	
			KING SOUL	19	PRESTIGE	US		7789	
			SOUL MEETING	19	PRESTIGE	US		7833	
			JAZZ GROOVE	1974	PRESTIGE	US		24033	
			STAR COLLECTION	1974	ATLANTIC	UK		K30049	
			SAX ROCK	1976	MUSIDISC	EURO		CV 1334	

KING EARL BOOGIE BAND

COLIN EARL		(A	(A) TROUBLE AT MILL		1972	DAWN		DNLS 3040	
PAUL KING		(A							
DAVE LAMBERT	G	(A	RUSSELL JOHN BROWN D (A	JOE RUSH	PERC (A				

KING HARRY

HAROLD KING	D	(A	(A) DIVIDED WE STAND		1977 EMI UK EMC 3188 US CAPITOL 11753		
JOHN DICKERSON	K V	(A					
ALAN BOWERY	G B V	(A	TINO LICINIO G B V	(A			

KING HARVEST

PETER CETERA		(B	(A) DANCING IN THE MOONLIGHT			1973 PYE UK NSPL28174 US PERCEPTION36				
MIKE LOVE		(B	(B) KINGHARVEST			1975 A&M	US	SP 4540		
CARL WILSON		(B								
LANCE HOPPEN	B V	(A	WELLS KELLY	D	(A	DAVID ROBINSON	V B HCA(B	EDDIE TULEJA	G	(B
RON ALTBACK	K	(B	ROD NOVAK	SAX	(B	BOBBY FIGUERA	D	(B	DAVID MONTGOMERY	D(B
TONY CAHILL	B	(B	SHERMAN KELLY	K	(B					

KING OF HEARTS

ROBERT FITOUSSI	V	(A	(A) CLOSE BUT NO GUITAR			1978 CAPITOL		11873		
MARC TOBALY	V G	(A								
ELLIOTT RANDALL	G	(A	STEVE PORCARO	K	(A	STU WOODS	B	(A	RICK SCHLOSSER	D (A
JAI WINDING	K	(A	MICHAEL BRAUN	D	(A	PEPPI CASTRO	B	(A	DEAN KRAUS	K (A
JEFF LAYTON	G	(A	TONY WELLS	V	(A	LENNY ROBERTS	V	(A	JIM HAAS	V (A
LEE SKLAR	B	(A	IVAN ELIAS	B	(A	DAVID BROWN	G	(A	JIM MAELEN	PERC (A
PAUL GRIFFIN	ORG	(A	MARTY NELSON	V	(A	JON JOYCE	V	(A	LOREN FARBER	V (A
RICHARD LANDIS	PROD(A									

KING PEACH

DONNIE McCUTCHEON	B V	(A	(A) FAIR WARNING		1981 FLYING HIGH	US	6504
JOE COPELAND	G V	(A				
DANNY HAYNES	K V	(A	RANDY DEHART	D V	(A	

KINGBEES

JANIE JONES	G V	(AB	(A) KINGBEES	1980 RSO
REX ROBERTS	D	(AB	(B) THE BIG ROCK	1981 RSO
MICHAEL RUMMANS	B	(AB		

KINGFISH

DAVE TORBERT	V B	(ABC	(A) KINGFISH			1976 ROUND US LA 564 UK UAG 29922				
MATTHEW KELLY	V G	(ABC	(B) LIVE & KICKIN'			1977 JET US LA 732 UK UAG 30080				
BOB WEIR	G	(AB	(C) TRIDENT			1978 JET US 35479 UK JETLP 215				
ROBBY HODINOTT	G	(AB								
CHRIS HEROLD	D	(AB	DAVE PEPPER	D V	(AC	MICHAEL O'NEILL	G V	(C	BOB HOGINS	K V (C
BARRY FLASH	PNO	(A	JOE ENGLISH	D	(C	JOHN HUG	G	(C	JOHNNY SANDLIN	B (C

KINGS

ARYAN ZERO	G V	(AB	(A) THE KINGS ARE HERE		1980 ELEKTRA US 6E274 UK K 52250	
DAVID DIAMOND	B V	(AB	(B) AMAZON BEACH		1981 ELEKTRA US 5E543	
SONNY KEYES	K	(AB				
MAX STYLES	D	(AB	BOB EZRIN	PNO	(B	

KINGSMEN

(A) IN PERSON	1963 WAND 657
(B) VOLUME II	1964 WAND 659 PYE INT UK 28054
(C) VOLUME III	196 WAND 662
(D) ON CAMPUS	196 WAND 670
(E) 16 GREAT HITS	1966 WAND 674
(F) BEST OF	1972 SCEPTOR 18002

KINKS

RAY DAVIES	V G	(ALL	(A) THE KINKS	1964 PYE UK NPL 18096(M) 83021(S)
DAVE DAVIES	G V	(ALL	(B) YOU REALLY GOT ME	1965 REPRISE US 6143
MICK AVORY	D	(ALL	(C) KINKSIZE	1965 REPRISE US 6158
PETER QUAIFE B		(ABCDEFGHIJKL	(D) KINDA KINKS	1965 PYE UK NPL 18112 REPRISE US 6173
JOHN DALTON	B	(OPRSTUVYbcfh	(D) KINDA KINKS	1969 MARBLE ARCH UK MAL1100
JOHN GOSLING	K	(PRSVYjbcfh6	(E) KINKS KINGDOM	1966 REPRISE US 6184
ALAN HOLMES	HRNS	(VYbcf	(F) KINKS KONTROVERSY	1966 PYE UK NPL 18131 REPRISE US 6197
LAURIE BROWN	HRNS	(Ybc	(G) KINKS GREATEST HITS	1966 REPRISE US 6217
JOHN BEECHAM	HRNS	(VYbc	(H) FACE TO FACE	1966 PYE UK NPL 18149 REPRISE US 6228
ANDY PYLE	B	(hj	(I) THE KINKS (COMP)	1966 GOLDEN GUINEA UK GGL0357
JIM RODFORD	B	(ns	(J) WELL RESPECTED KINKS	1966 MARBLE ARCH UK MAL 612
GORDON EDWARDS	K	(	(K) LIVE AT KELVIN HALL	1967 PYE UK NSPL18191 REPRISE US 6260
NICK TREVISIK	D	(j	(L) SOMETHING ELSE	1967 PYE UK NSPL18193 REPRISE US 6279
RON LAWRENCE	B	(j	(M) SUNNY AFTERNOON (COMP)	1967 MARBLE ARCH UK MAL 716
PAMELA TRAVIS	V	(Yc	(N) VILLAGE GREEN PRESERVATION SOC	1968 PYE UK NSPL18233 REPRISE US 6327
SHIRLEY RODEN	V	(c	(O) ARTHUR OR DECLINE OF BRITISH EMP	1969 PYE UK NSPL18317 REPRISE US 6366
LYNDSEY MOORE	V	(c	(P) KINKS PART 1 (LOLA Vs POWERMAN	1970 PYE UK NSPL18359 REPRISE US 6423
JUNE RITCHIE	V	(c	(Q) THE KINKS (COMP DBL)	1970 PYE UK NPL 18326
NICK NEWELL	K SAX	(fn	(R) PERCY (SOUNDTRACK)	1971 PYE UK NSPL18365
LEE PAVEY	V	(Y	(S) MUSWELL HILLBILLIES	1971 RCA UK SF 8423 US LSP4644
KRYSIA KOCJAN	V	(Y	(T) GOLDEN HOUR	1971 PYE UK GH 501
MIKE COTTON	TPT	(SV	(U) LOLA	1971 HALLMARK UK HMA 201
SUE BROWN	V	(Y	(V) EVERYBODY'S IN SHOWBIZ	1972 RCA UK DPS 2035 US 6065
DAVEY JONES	WIND	(V	(W) KINK KRONIKLES	1972 REPRISE US 6454
LEWIS RICH	V	(Y	(X) GREAT LOST KINKS ALBUM	1973 REPRISE US 2127
IAN GIBBONS	K	(n	(Y) PRESERVATION ACT 1	1973 RCA UK SF 8392 US LPL5002
SHEL TALMY	PROD	(K	(Z) ALL THE GOOD TIMES	1973 PYE UK
A GIRTON	V	(b	(a)GOLDEN HOUR VOL 2	1973 PYE UK GH 558
			(b) PRESERVATION ACT 2	1974 RCA UK 5040 US CPL5040
			(c) SOAP OPERA	1975 RCA UK SF 8411 US LPI5081
			(d) POP CHRONIK	1975 PYE VOL1
			(e) CELLULOID HEROES (COMP)	1976 RCA UK RS 1059 US LPI1743
			(f) SCHOOLBOYS IN DISGRACE	1976 RCA UK RS 1028 US FLI5102
			(g) KINKS (FILE DBL)	1977 PYE UK FILD 001-1/2
			(h) SLEEPWALKER	1977 ARISTA UK 1002 US AL 4106
			(i) ALL THE GOOD TIMES	197 PYE UK ILPP 100/4
			(j) MISFITS	1978 ARISTA UK 1055 US AL 4167
			(k) 20 GOLDEN GREATS	1978 RONCO UK RPL2031
			(m) LOW BUDGET	1979 ARISTA UK 1099 US AB 4240
			(n) ONE FOR THE ROAD (LIVE DBL)	1980 ARISTA UK DARTY6
			(o)YOU REALLY GOT ME (COMP)	1980 PYE UK NSPL18615 FR MODE 9017
			(p)ALL DAY & ALL OF THE NIGHT	19 FR MODE 9054
			(q) KINKS COLLECTION	1980 HALLMARK UK 072
			(r) 2ND TIME AROUND	1980 RCA US 3520
			(s) SPOTLIGHT	1981 PRT UK 1009
			(t) GIVE THE PEOPLE WHAT THEY WANT	1981 ARISTA US 3549 UK SPARTY1171
			(u) 100 MINUTES (CASSETTE)	1982 PRT UK ZCTON 102

(CONTINUED)

                        (EPS)
                        KINKSIZE HITS   1964 PYE   UK   NEP 24203
                        KWIETKINKS   1965 PYE   UK   NEP 24221
                        FOUR TIMES FOUR   1965 PYE   UK   NEP 24228
                        KINKSIZE SESSION   1966 PYE   UK   NEP 24200
                        DEDICATED KINKS   1966 PYE   UK   NEP 24258

K61A   STEVE KIPNER   K61A
    STEVE KIPNER   (A   (A) KNOCK DOWN THE WALLS   1980 E+ELTRA   US   202
K62   KIPPINGTON LODGE   K62
    BARRY LANDERMAN   K V   1965/69
    BOB ANDREWS   K V
    NICK LOWE   B V   BRINSLEY SCHWARZ   G V   PETER WHALE   D
K63   KIRBY   K63
    KIRBY   G   (A   (A) COMPOSITION   1978 HOT WAX   HW2
    FRAN BYRNE   D   (A
    IAN PAICE   D   (A   STEVE EMERY   B   (A   JOHN COOK   K   (A   CHRIS FLETCHER   PERC(A
    ROBIN JAMES   PERC   (A   NIGEL WATSON   G   (A   TONY RIVERS   V   (A   STUART CALVER   V   (A
    JOHN PERRY   V   (A   MICK EVE   HRNS (A   NORMAN NEWELL HRNS (A   BUD BEADLE   HRNS (A
    COLIN JACAS   HRNS   (A   MIKE BAILEY   HRNS (A   RON ASPERY   SAX (A
K64   BASIL KIRCHIN   K64
    BASIL KIRCHIN   (AB   (A) A WORLD WITHIN WORLDS 1971 COLUMBIA   UK   SCX 6463
                                  (B) WORLDS WITHIN WORLDS 3/4 1974 ISLAND   UK   HELP18
K64A   RICHARD H KIRK   K64A
    RICHARD H KIRK   (A   (A) DISPOSABLE ½ TRUTHS   1981 INDUSTRIAL   CASS   34
K64C   JOHN KIRKBRIDE   K64C
    JOHN KIRKBRIDE   V G (A   (A) TRACKS   1976 EMI/SONGBIRD GER   31138
    HERMAN VAN DER VLAG STEEL G (A
    JAN THEELEN   K   (A   NICO VERHOEVEN   B   (A   MITCH CAHNEN D   (A   JOKE VAN HOUT V   (A
    MARIETTE VIEVERMANNS   V(A
K65   JOHN KIRKPATRICK & SUE HARRIS   K65
    JOHN KIRKPATRICK K WIND V(ABCDEFG   (A) JUMP AT THE SUN   1972 TRAILER   LER 2033
    SUE HARRIS WIND DULC V (ABCDEFG   (B) ROSE OF BRITAINS ISLE 1974 TOPIC   12TS 247
    TONY ROSE   WIND V(A   (C) AMONG THE ATTRACTIONS...... 1976 TOPIC 12TS 295
    MARTIN BRINSFORD   V (F   (D) PLAIN CAPERS   1976 FREE REED   FRR 010
    BERI CROWE   V (A   (E) SHREDS & PATCHES   1977 TOPIC   12TS 355
    ROB LENNOX   V (A   (F) GOING SPARE   1978 FREE REED   FRR 030
    ANGELA McNEILL   V (A   (G) FACING THE MUSIC   1980 TOPIC   12TS 408
    FI FRASER   V (F
    TERRY ROBINSON   V (A   DAVE WIGHT   V   (A   DENIS SHEEHAN V   (A   AGNES MIRREN   G   (A
    ASHLEY HUTCHINGS   B (A   PENNIE HARRIS   DULC (E   TUFTY SMITH MELOD(E   DEREK PEARSE BAN PERC(EF
    GEOFF HARRIS   G (E   STEWART GOLDRING G   (F   ALAN HARRIS   BAN (F   BILL CADDICK   G   (F
    COLIN GOLDRING   B (F   NIGEL PEGRUM   D   (F
K66   DANNY KIRWAN   K66
    DANNY KIRWAN   V G (ALL   (A) SECOND CHAPTER   1975 DJM UK DJLPS 454 US   DJM 1
    GEOFF BRITTON   D (A   (B) MIDNIGHT IN SAN JUAN 1976 DJM UK   DJF 20481
    JIM RUSSELL   D (A   (C) HELLO THERE BIG BOY   1979 DJM UK   DJF 20555 US DJM 22
    ANDY SYLVESTER   B (A   (D) DANNY KIRWAN   1971 DJM   US   DJM 9
    PAUL RAYMOND   K (A
    JOHN COOK   PNO (BC   TEX COMER   B   (C   STUART CALVER V   (C   JOHN PERRY   V   (C
    STEVE EMERY   B (B   KIRBY   G   (C   FRAN BYRNE   D   (C   KEVIN KITCHEN K   (C
    DANA GILLESPIE   V (C   JEFF RICH   D   (B   BOB WESTON   G   (C   TONY RIVERS   V   (C
    CHRIS FLETCHER   PERC (C
K67   KISS   K67
    ACE FREHLEY   G (ALL   (A) KISS   1975 CASABLANCA US 7001 UK   CBC 4003
    PAUL STANLEY   G (ALL   (A) KISS   1977 CASABLANCA   UK RI CAL 2006
    GENE SIMMONS   B (ALL   (B) HOTTER THAN HELL   1974 CASABLANCA US 7006 UK 77 CAL 7007
    PETE CRISS   D (A>N   (C) DRESSED TO KILL   1975 CASABLANCA US 7016 UK   CBC 4004
    BRUCE FOSTER   PNO (A   (C) DRESSED TO KILL   1977 CASABLANCA   UK RI CAL 2008
    ERIC CARR   D (0   (D) ALIVE   197 CASABLANCA US 7020 UK RI CAS 5001
                                 (E) DESTROYER   1976 CASABLANCA US 7025 UK 77 CAL 2009
                                 (F) THE ORIGINALS   197 CASABLANCA US 7032
                                 (G) ROCK'N'ROLL OVER   197 CASABLANCA US 7037 UK 77 CAL 2001
                                 (H) LOVE GUN   197 CASABLANCA US 7057 UK 77 CAL 2027
                                 (J) ALIVE 2   1978 CASABLANCA US 7076 UK   CAL 5004
                                 (K) DOUBLE PLATINUM (DBL) 1978 CASABLANCA US 7100-2 UKCALD5005
                                 (L) DYNASTY   1979 CASABLANCA US 7152 UK   CALH2051
                                 (M) UNMASKED   1980 MERCURY   US 7225 UK   6302 032
                                 (N) THE BEST OF THE SOLO ALBUMS 1981 CASABLANCA UK 6302 060
                                 (O) MUSIC FROM THE ELDER 1981 CASABLANCA   UK   6302 163
                                 (P) ROCK'N'ROLL OVER   1982 CASABLANCA   UK   6399 060
K67A   KITE   K67A
                             (A) KITE   19 SOLENT   SS 050
K67B   THE KITCHEN CINQ   K67B
                             (A) EVERYTHING BUT ..... 19 L H I   US   12000
K67C   KITTYHAWK   K67C
                             (A) KITTYHAWK   19 EMI   US   17029
                             (B) RACE FOR THE OASIS   19 EMI   US   17053
K67D   KIX   K67D
    DONNIE PURNELL   B (A   (A) KIX   1981   ATLANTIC US
    JIMMY CHALFANT   D (A
    STEVE WHITEMAN   V (A   RONNIE YOUNKINS G   (A   BRIAN FORSYTHE G   (A
K68   KLAATU   K68
                             (A) KLAATU   1976 CAPITOL   11542
                             (B) HOPE   1977 CAPITOL   11633
                             (C) SIR ARMY SUIT   1978 CAPITOL   11836
                             (D) ENDANGERED SPECIES   1980 CAPITOL   12080

KLEER

```
WOODY CUNNINGHAM   D V (ABC                (A) I LOVE TO DANCE        1979 ATLANTIC US SD 19237    UK K50614
MELANIE MOORE        (C                    (B) WINNERS               1980 ATLANTIC US    19262
RICHARD LEE        G (ABC                  (C) LICENSE TO DREAM      1981 ATLANTIC US SD 19288
YVETTE FLOWERS       (C
PAUL CRUTCHFIELD   PERC V(ABC NORMAN DURHAM      B V  (ABC   ISABELLE COLES    V    (AC   RANDY BRECKER   HRNS (A
MARVIN STAMM       HRNS (A   TERRY DOLPHIN     PNO  (AC   RICHARD CUMMINGS K    (A    ANGEL NATER     PERC (A
LOUISE FISCHER     V   (A    ERIC ROHRBAUGH         (C
```
SNEAKY PETE KLEINOW

```
SNEAKY PETE        STEEL(AB               (A) SNEAKY PETE           1979 CHILOH         SLP 4086
GENE PARSONS       D    (A                (B) COLD STEEL            19   ARIOLA             87736
MICKEY McGEE       D    (A
ED PONDER          D    (A   GREG HARRIS       G   (A    BOBBY COCKRAN     G    (A    SKIP BATTIN     B     (A
JAMIE FAUNT        B    (A   CONNIE WILLIAMS   V   (A    CHARLIE HARWOOD   PNO  (A    GIB GUILBEAU    V FDL (A
R BOWDEN           G    (B   D LOVELACE    PNO       (B    GREG ATTAWAY   V D   (B    M A BOWDEN      B  (B
```
MARK KLINGMAN

```
MARK 'MOOGY' KLINGMAN K V (A            (A) MARK MOOGY KLINGMAN      197   CAPITOL        ST11072
RALPH SCHUCKETT      (A
JOHNNY SIOMOS      D   (A   JOHNNY SEIGLER    B   (A    JOEL BISHOP O'BIEN MAN(A  DOUG RODRIGUEZ  G   (A
PETE LABARBA       VIBES(A  COLIN WILCOX      HRNS (A    TERRY EATON       HRNS (A  KEITH JOHNSON   HRNS(A
MARK ROSENGARTEN   CONGA(A  AMOS GARRETT      G   (A    TODD RUNDGREN     G K  (A  N D SMART       D   (A
STU WOODS          B   (A   TOMMY COSGROVE    G   (A    RICK DERRINGER    G    (A  BEN KEITH       STEEL DOBR(A
ROBBIE KOGEL       G   (A   BUZZY LINHART     G   (A    RICHARD COREY     FDL  (A  JOHNNY MILLER   B   (A
```
KLYMAXX

```
LORENA PORTER      V   (A              (A) NEVER UNDERESTIMATE THE POWER... 1981 SOLAR S21    52304
```
EARL KLUGH

```
EARL KLUGH         G   (ALL             (A) EARL KLUGH              1976 BLUENOTE          US LA 596
GREG PHILLINGANES  K   (E               (B) LIVING INSIDE YOUR LOVE 1977 UA UK UAG 20009 BLUENOTE US 667
CHARLES MEEKS      B   (E               (C) FINGER PAINTING        1977 UA UK UAG 20011 BLUENOTE US 737
RALPH MACDONALD    PERC (E              (D) MAGIC IN YOUR EYES      1978 UA UK UAG 30171      US  877
VICTOR LEWIS       D   (E               (E) HEART STRING           1979 UA UK UAG 30233      US  942
PHIL UPCHURCH      G   (E               (F) DREAM COME TRUE         1980 UA UK UAG 30092 LIBERTY US 1026
GLORIA AGOSTINI    HARP (G              (G) LATE NIGHT GUITAR       1980 UA UK UAG 30332 LIBERTY US 1079
DR GIBBS           PERC (G              (H) CRAZY FOR YOU           1981 LIBERTY UK 30329
DAVID SPINOZZA     G   (G
PHIL BODNER        WIND (G   WALTER KANE     WIND (G    DAVID FRIEDMAN    PERC (G   JOSEPH SHEPLEY  TPT (G
SAM BURTIS         TROM (G   JOSE MADERA     PERC (G    LEWIS PEAR        B   (G   JACK KULOWITCH  B   (G
JAY ELFENBEIN      B   (G   RON CUBER       SAX  (G    KEN ASCHER        PNO  (G   MICHAEL COLLAZO PERC(G
GINO BIONDO        B   (G   MARCUS MILLER   B    (G    JOHN GATCHELL     TPT  (G   DAVID TOFANI    SAX (G
```
THE KNACK

```
DOUG FIEGER        G   (ABC             (A) GET THE KNACK           1979 CAPITOL           11948
BERTON AVERRE      G   (ABC             (B) BUT THE LITTLE GIRLS UNDERSTAND 1980 CAPITOL    12045
BRUCE GARY         D   (ABC             (C) ROUND TRIP             1981 CAPITOL
PRESCOTT NILES     B   (ABC
```
KNICKERBOCKERS

```
JOHN CHARLES       B   (                (A) LLOYD THAXTON PRESENTS... 196 CHALLENGE      US  12664
BEAU CHARLES       G   (                (B) JERK & TWINE           196  CHALLENGE US 621 RI GER LINE5082
BUDDY RANDALL      SAX (                (C) LIES                   1966 CHALLENGE US 622 LONDON UK 8294
JIMMY WALKER       D   (A               (C) LIES                   198  LINE GER  5056
                                        (D) STICK WITH US          198  LINE GER  5155
```
CURTIS KNIGHT

```
CURTIS KNIGHT      G V (ALL             (A) DOWN THE VILLAGE       19   PARAMOUNT          US5023
JIMI HENDRIX       G   (BCD             (B) GET THAT FEELING       1968 LONDON UK SH 8349 DECCA US195002
EDDIE CLARKE       G   (E               (C) STRANGE THINGS         1968 LONDON UK SH 8369 DECCA US185005
NICKY HOPKINS      K   (E               (D) THE WILD ONE           1973 HALLMARK          UK  791
CHRIS PERRY        PERC (E              (E) SECOND COMING          1974 DAWN   UK          DNLS3060
JOHN WEIR          B   (E
```
JEAN KNIGHT

```
JEAN KNIGHT                             (A) Mr BIG STUFF           1977 STAX   US ST2045 UK  STX 1004
```
GLADYS KNIGHT & THE PIPS

```
GLADYS KNIGHT      V   (ALL   EVERYBODY NEEDS LOVE         1967 SOUL   US 706  TAMLA UK STML 11058
WITH                          FEELIN BLUESY                1968 SOUL   US 707
THE PIPS                      TASTIEST HITS                1968 BELL   US 6013
MERALD KNIGHT      V   (      SILK & SOUL                  1969 SOUL   US 711  TAMLA UK STML 11100
BRENDAN KNIGHT     V   (      NITTY GRITTY                 1970 SOUL   US 713  TAMLA UK STML 11135
WILLIAM GUEST      V   (      GREATEST HITS                1970 SOUL   US 723  TAMLA UK STML 11148
ELENOR GUEST       V   (      ALL IN A KNIGHTS WORK        197  SOUL   US 730
EDWARD PATTEN      V   (      IF I WERE YOUR WOMAN         1971 SOUL   US 731  TAMLA UK STML 11187
DEAN PARKS         G   (X     STANDING OVATION             1972 SOUL   US 736  TAMLA UK STML 11208
DAVID T WALKER     G   (X     HELP ME MAKE IT THROUGH THE NIGHT 1973   TAMLA UK STML 11226
BOB BABBITT        B   (X     NEITHER ONE OF US            1973 SOUL   US 737  TAMLA UK STML 11230
REINI PRESS        B   (X     ALL I NEED IS TIME           1974 SOUL   US '39  TAMLA UK STML 11264
JOE SAMPLE         K   (X     ANTHOLOGY                    1974 TAMLA  US 792        UK TMSP  1127
VICTOR FELDMAN     PERC (X    GLADYS KNIGHT & THE PIPS     1974 HALLMARK      UK SHM   833
PLAS JOHNSON       HRNS (X    IMAGINATION                  1974 BUDDAH US 5141    UK BDLP  4005
DAVID LUELL        HRNS (X    CLAUDINE                     1974 BUDDAH US 5602    UK BDLP  4010
GARY GRANT         TPT (X     I FEEL A SONG                197  BUDDAH US 5612    UK BDLP  4030
RANDY ALOSCROFT    TROM (X    2ND ANNIVERSARY              1975 BUDDAH US 5639    UK BDLP  4038
JIM GILTRAP        V   (X     2ND ANNIVERSARY              1975 BUDDAH          UK  2318  111
DAN FERGUSON       G   (X     KNIGHT TIME                  1975 SOUL   US 741  TAMLA UK STML 11279
DAVID HUNGATE      B   (X     A LITTLE KNIGHT MUSIC        1975 SOUL   US 744  TAMLA UK STML 12013
BOB GLOUB          B   (X     BEST OF                      1975 STAX           UK STX   1042
DAVID FOSTER       PNO (X     GLADYS KNIGHT & THE PIPS     1975 DJM            UK DJMLD 8010
ED GREENE          D   (X     SUPER HITS                   1976 TAMLA          UK STMA  8026
JIM HORN           HRNS (X    PIPE DREAMS                  1976 BUDDAH US 5676    UK BDLP  5017
MIKE ALTSCHUL      HRNS (X    TAKE ME IN YOUR ARMS         1976 MFP            UK      50304
RAY PIZZI          HRNS (X    STILL TOGETHER               1977 BUDDAH US 5689    UK BDLP  5014
GENE GOE           TPT (X     BEST OF                      1977 BUDDAH          UK BDLP  5013
BILL WATROUS       TROM (X    BLESS THIS HOUSE             1978 BUDDAH US 5651    UK BDLP  4050
                              GLADYS KNIGHT                1979 CBS            UK      83341
                          (X) MISS GLADYS KNIGHT           1979 BUDDAH US 5714    UK BDLP  4056
                          (X) MISS GLADYS KNIGHT           1979 BUDDAH   GER 6 23694
```

        (CONTINUED)

GLADYS KNIGHT & THE PIPS (CONTINUED)

LETTER FULL OF TEARS	19	FURY	US	1003
VERY BEST OF	19	UA	US	LA503
EARLY HITS	19	SPRINGBOARD	US	4035
HOW DO YOU SAY GOODBYE	19	SPRINGBOARD	US	4050
BEST OF	19	MODE	FR	9021
GLADYS KNIGHT & THE PIPS	19	TRIP	US	3500
" " " " "	19	UP FRONT	US	130
" " " " "	19	UP FRONT	US	185
" " " " "	19	SPHERE SOUND	US	7006
" " " " "	19	MAXX	US	3000
20 GOLDEN GREATS	1979	MOTOWN	UK STML	12122
30 GREATEST HITS	1979	K TEL	UK	NE1004
MEMORIES	1979	BUDDAH	BLD	2004
A TOUCH OF LOVE	1980	K TEL	UK	1090
SPOTLIGHT	1980	PRT	UK	1006
ABOUT LOVE	1980	CBS US 36387	UK	84178
TAKE ME BACK	1980	MANHATTAN	UK	5000
NIGHTFUL	1980	MANHATTAN	UK	5001
FIRST SHOT	1980	MANHATTAN	UK	5002
FUNKY	1980	MANHATTAN	UK	5003
I HEARD IT THROUGH THE GRAPVINE	19	PICKWICK	US	3534
POW	19	PICKWICK	US	3374
GOLDEN HITS	19	FIRST RECORD	US	1001

REGGIE KNIGHTON

REGGIE KNIGHTON	G V	(AB	(A) REGGIE KNIGHTON		1977	CBS US 34685		
BRIAN RAY	G	(B	(B) REGGIE KNIGHTON BAND		1978	CBS US 35286	UK 82627	
GLENN SYMMONDS	D	(B						
JOHN STAEHELY	G	(B	KURTIS TEEL	B (B	GEOFF WORKMAN	STRINGS(B	JON LIND	V (B
RICHARD HOVEY	V	(B						

BUDDY KNOX

BUDDY KNOX	G V	(ALL	BUDDY KNOX	1957	ROULETTE US		25003
DON LANIER	G	(	BUDDY KNOX & JIMMY BOWEN(1 SIDE EACH 19		ROULETTE US		25048
DAVE ALLDRED	D	(	BUDDY KNOX	19	POINT US		201
JIMMY BOWEN	B	(	BUDDY KNOX IN NASHVILLE	19	POINT US		289
			GOLDEN HITS	196	LIBERTY US	LST	7251
			GYPSY MAN	1970	U A US	UAS	6689
			ROCK REFLECTIONS	1971	SUNSET UK	SLS	50206
			BUDDY KNOX ROCKS	1973	SWEETWATER CAN	SW	1001
			PARTY DOLL	1978	PYE INT UK	NSPL	28243
			FOUR ROCK LEGENDS (8 TRACKS)	1978	HARVEST HERITAGE UK	SHSM	2024

KRYSIA KOCJAN

KRYSIA KOCJAN	G V	(A	(A) KRYSIA			1974	RCA		UK	LPLI 5052
STEVE HAYTON	G	(A								
JERRY DONAHUE	G	(A	RABBIT BUNDRICK	K (A	ALAN SHEARER	VLV (A	JOHN McLEVY	TPT (A		
ROY SIDWELL	SAX	(A	DAVE PEGG	B (A	RAY COOPER	PERC(A	ROGER CHURCHYARD	VLN (A		
DAVE SHARMAN	TROM	(A	DAVE MATTACKS	D (A	MOX	FLT (A	TONY COE	CLAR (A		
HARRY KLEIN	SAX	(A								

JOHN KOERNER

'SPIDER' JOHN KOERNER	(ALL	(A) MUSIC IS JUST A BUNCH OF NOTES	19		SWEETJANE	US	SJL 5872
		(B) SONGS LIKE THEY USED TO	19		SWEETJANE	US	1074
WILLIE MURPHY	(D	(C) SPIDER BLUES	19		ELEKTRA	US	7290
		(D) RUNNING JUMPING STANDING STILL	19		ELEKTRA US 74041	UK K42026	

KOERNER, RAY & GLOVER

JOHN KOERNER	G	(ALL	(A) BLUES RAGS & HOLLERS	19	ELEKTRA	US	240
DAVE RAY	G	(ALL	(B) GOOD OLD KOERNER, RAY & GLOVER	19	MILL CITY	US	MCR 172
TONY GLOVER	HCA	(ALL	(C) LOTS MORE BLUES RAGS & HOLLERS	19	ELEKTRA	US	7267
			(D) RETURN OF KOERNER ,RAY & GLOVER	19	ELEKTRA	US	7305

KOKOMO

TONY O'MALLEY	V K	(ABC	(A) KOKOMO		1975	CBS US 33442	UK	80670		
PADDY McHUGH	V	(ABC	(B) RISE & SHINE		1975	CBS US 34031	UK	69229		
DYAN BIRCH	V	(ABC	(C) KOKOMO		1982	CBS	UK	85604		
FRANK COLLINS	V	(ABC								
MEL COLLINS	SAX	(ABC	TERRY STANNARD	D (A	JIM MULLEN	G (A	ALAN SPENNER	V B (ABC		
JOHN SUSSEWELL	D	(B	NEIL HUBBARD	G (ABC	JODY LINCOTT	PERC(C	STEVE BERRY	TROM (C		
TONY BEARD	D	(C	JAMES MACK	K (C	BOB WESSBERG	PERC(C	BOBBY LEWIS	TPT (C		
PAUL HOWARD	TPT	'C	FRANK TESUINSKY	TROM (C	PAT FERRERI	G (C	TERRY FRYER	SYN (C		

MARTIN KOLBE UND RALF ILLENBERGER

MARTIN KOLBE	(AB	(A) COLOURING THE LEAVES	19	MOOD	23 700	
RALF ILLENBERGER	(AB	(B) WAVES	1980	MOOD	22 900	

KOLLEKTIV

JURGEN KARPENKIEL	B	(A	(A) KOLLEKTIV	1973 BRIAN	GER	1034
JURGFN HAUIX	G	(A				
WALDERMAR KARPENKIEL	D(A	KLAUS DAPPER WIND (A				

BONNIE KOLOC

BONNIE KOLOC	G V	(ALL	(A) AFTER ALL THIS TIME	1971	LONDON UK 8432 OVATION	US	14 21
NORMAN CHRISTIAN	D	(ABC	(B) HOLD ON TO ME	1972	LONDON UK 8440 OVATION	US	14 26
RON SCROGGIN G HCA B V	(ABC	(C) BONNIE KOLOC	1973	OVATION		US	14 29
STU HEISS	G	(A	(D) YOU'RE GONNA LOVE YOURSELF	1974	OVATION		US	14 38
PHIL UPCHURCH	B G	(AB	(E) CLOSE UP	1976	EPIC		US	34184
ALLEN BARCUS	PNO	(AB	(F) WILD RECLUSE	1978	EPIC		US	35254
SID SIMMS	B	(A	(G) AT HER BEST	1977	OVATION		US	1701
TREVOR VEITCH	G DOB(B						

BOB LEWIS	G	(B	BOBBY CHRISTIAN	PERC (BC	PHIL THOMAS	CONGA(B	WALLY PILLICH	B (B		
CHUCK DE MEYER	K V	(C	JONATHAN PEARTHREE	G V(C	HAROLD KRITZ	B (C	DAVID VAN DELINDER	G (C		
LONNIE KNIGHT	G	(C	DANNY LONG	PNO (C	DAVID BRIGGS	PNO (D	MIKE LEECH	B (D		
NORBERT PUTNAM	B	(D	HENRY STRZELECKI	B (D	REGGIE YOUNG	G (D	JOHNNY CHRISTOPHER	G (D		
BILLY SANFORD	G	(D	JIMMY COLVARD	G (D	PETE WADE	G (D	STEVE GOODMAN	G (DE		
KENNY MALONE	D	(D	LARRY LONDIN	D (D	JERRY CARRIGAN	D (D	FARRELL MORRIS PERC	(D		
RUSTY YOUNG	STEEL(E	DAVID LINDLEY	G (E	PAUL HARRIS	K (E	BRYAN GAROFALO	B (E		
GARY MALLABER	D	(E	GUILLE GARCIA	CONGA(E	PHILIP DONNELLY G	(E	JAI WINDING	PNO(E		
DONNIE FRITTS	PNO	(E	CHUCK DOMANICO	B (E	CORKY SIEGEL	HCA (E	MIKE CAMPBELL	G (E		
DON MENZA	WIND (E	RAY NEOPOLITAN	B (E							

```
     SERGE CATTALANO    D     (A     (A) LE BAL DU RAT MORT           1971 HARVEST PATHE FR    2C 062 11774
     RICHARD AUBERT     VLN   (A
     OLIVIER ZDRZALIK B G V (A    FRANCIS LEMONNIER SAX V(A    MICHEL MUSAC    G (A    PASCAL CHASSIN    G (A
```

```
     JOHN KONGOS     V G PERC (AB    (A) CONFUSIONS ABOUT GOLDFISH    1969 JANUS   US 3032 DAWN UK DNLS 3002
     CALEB QUAYE     G       (B      (B) JOHN KONGOS                  1971 ELEKTRA US 75019 FLY UK HIFLY  7
     DAVE GLOVER     B       (B
     ROGER POPE      D       (B    RAY COOPER    PERC (B    MIKE NOBLE    PERC(B    DAVID CHAMBERS    HRNS (B
     LOL COXHILL     SAX     (B    MIKE MORAN    K    (B    RALPH McTELL    G (B    GUS DUDGEON       PERC(B
     SUE GLOVER      V       (B    SUNNY LESLIE  V    (B    CLAIRE DENIZ  CELLO(B
```

```
     ROY MORRIS            (A      (A) KOOBAS                        1969 COLUMBIA      UK         SCX 6291
     STU LEATHERWOOD       (A
     KEITH ELLIS     B     (A    TONY O'RILEY       (A
```

```
     ROBERT 'KOOL' BELL B V(ALL    (A) KOOL & THE GANG         19    DE LITE US 2003
     CHARLES'CLAYDES'SMITH G V(QQRCF (B) MUSIC IS THE MESSAGE  19    DE LITE US 2011 POLYDOR   2347 004
     GEORGE BROWN     D V K(OQRCF    (C) LIVE AT THE SEX MACHINE 19   DELITE  US 2008 POLYDOR   2343 083
     ROBERT MICKENS   TPT V(QQRCF    (D) BEST                   19    DE LITE US 2009
     OTHA NASH        V HRNS(O       (E) LIVE AT PJs            19    DE LITE US 2010
     DENNIS THOMAS    WIND K V (OQRCF (F) GOOD TIMES            19    DE LITE US 2012
     RON'KHALIS BAYYAN'BELL WIND K V(OQRCF(G) WILD & PEACEFUL   1974 DE LITE US 2013 POLYDOR UK 2310 299
     DONAL BOYCE      V       (O      (H) LIGHT OF WORLDS       1974 DE LITE US 2014 POLYDOR UK 2310 357
     KEVIN LASSITER   K V     (O      (J) GREATEST HITS         1975 DE LITE US 2015 POLYDOR UK 2310 401
     RENEE CONNEL     V       (O      (K) SPIRIT OF THE BOOGIE  1975 DE LITE US 2016 POLYDOR UK 2310 416
     ARTHUR CAPEHART  TPT     (O      (L) LOVE & UNDERSTANDING  1976 DE LITE US 2018 POLYDOR UK 2310 441
     BEVERLEY OWENS   V       (O      (M) BEHIND THE EYES       197             POLYDOR
     CYNTHIA HUGGINS  V       (OQ     (N) OPEN SESAME           197  DE LITE US 2025
     M.F.S.B.   STRINGS       (O      (O) THE FORCE             1977 DE LITE US 9501 MERCURY   6372 700
     JOAN MOTLEY      V       (OQ     (P) SPIN THEIR TOP HITS   1978 DE LITE US 9507
     CHRIS ALBERT     TPT     (Q      (Q) LADIES NIGHT          1979 DE LITE US 9513         UK 6372 763
     JON FADDIS       TPT     (Q      (R) CELEBRATE             1980 DE LITE US 9518         UK 6359 029
     EARL TOON        K V     (RQ     ( ) KOOL JAZZ             1975 DE LITE US 4001
     DIANE CAMERON    V       (Q      (T) EVERYBODYS DANCIN'    1979 DE LITE US 9509
     CEDRIC TOON      V       (RQ     (U) SOMETHING SPECIAL     1981 DELITE                  UK  DSR 001
     KEVIN BELL       K       (R
     JAMES J T TAYLOR V       (QR  MEEKAEEL MUHAMMAD V   (R    ADAM IPPOLITO    K (RQ  EUMIR DEODATO    K (Q
     CLIFF ADAMS      TROM    (Q   STRINGS              (F    SHARON MOE    HRN(F  BILLY BROWN      HRN (F
     ASSUNTA DELL AQUILA HARP(F  RICKY WESTFIELD    K     (CF
```

```
     AL KOOPER        K G V(ALL    (A) SUPER SESSION               1969 CBS  US  9701    UK 63396
     MIKE BLOOMFIELD  G     (ACL   (A) SUPER SESSION               1973 EMBASSY RI       UK 31029
     STEPHEN STILLS   G     (AL    (B) I STAND ALONE               1969 CBS  US  9718    UK 63538
     HARVEY BROOKS    B     (AGL   (C) LIVE ADVENTURES  (DBL)      1969 CBS  US  PG6     UK 66216
     EDDIE HOH        D     (AL    (D) YOU NEVER KNOW WHO YOUR FRIENDS...1969 CBS US 9855 UK 63651
     BARRY GOLDBERG   K     (AL    (E) KOOPER SESSIONS             1970 CBS  US  9951    UK 63797
     SHUGGIE OTIS     G     (EL    (F) EASY DOES IT                1970 CBS  US 30031    UK 66252
     WELLS KELLY      D     (EGL   (G) LANDLORD                    1971 U A              UK 29120
     STU WOODS        B     (ELF   (H) NEW YORK CITY               1971 CBS  US 30506    UK 64340
     MARK KLINGMAN    K     (E     (J) POSSIBLE PROJECTION OF FUTURE 1972 CBS US 31159   UK 64208
     CARLOS SANTANA   G     (C     (K) NAKED SONGS                 1973 CBS  US 31793    UK 65193
     RALPH CASALE     G     (D     (L) AL'S BIG DEAL(UNCLAIMED FREIGHT)DBL)1975 CBS US 33169  UK 88093
     ERIC GALE        G     (DG    (N) ACT LIKE NOTHINGS WRONG     1976 UA               UK 30020
     ERNIE HAYES      K     (D     (O) AL KOOPER & STEVE KATZ      19   VERVE        UK 2304010
     PAUL GRIFFIN     K     (D
     FRANK OWENS      K     (DG  CHUCK RAINEY     B    (DG  JERRY JEMMOTT   B   (D   JOHN MILLER     B (DGF
     BERNARD PURDIE   D     (D   AL RODGERS       G D  (DFG BERNIE GLOW    TPT  (DG  ERNIE ROYAL     TPT(D
     MARVIN STAMM     TPT   (DG  RAY DESIO        TROM (D   JIMMY KNEPPER  TROM (D   BILL WATRONS    TROM(D
     TONY STUDD       TROM  (D   GEORGE YOUNG     SAX  (DG  SOL SCHLINGER  SAX  (D   SELDON POWELL   SAX (D
     JOE FARRELL      SAX   (DG  MANNY GREEN      VLN  (D   JERRY KUSHNICK STRINGS(D STAN POLLEY  STRINGS(D
     AARON SCHECTER   STRING(D  HILDA HARRIS      V    (DEL CONNIE ZIMET    V   (D   ALBERTINE ROBERTSON V(DELK
     MIKE GATELY      V     (DJK ROBERT JOHN      V    (DJK LOU CHRISTIE    V   (D   CHARLIE CALELLO V(D
     MAERETHA STEWART V(    (GLK LORRAINE ELLISON V    (G   STAPLES SINGERS V   (G.  JOHN HALL       G(G
     PHIL BODNER      WIND  (G   PAUL HARRIS      PNO  (G   JOE BECK        G   (G   STEVE KATZ      G(LO
     FRED LIPSIUS     SAX   (LF  BOBBY COLOMBY    D V  (FL  JERRY WEISS    HRNS (L   RANDY BRECKER   HRNS(L
     DICK HALLIGAN    HRNS  (L   JIM FIELDER      B    (L   AL GORGONI      G   (L   JOHN SIMON      PNO (L
     VALERIE SIMPSON  V     (LE  MELBA MOORE      V    (L   BOB DYLAN      G V  (L   RON CORNELIUS   G(L
     CHARLIE DANIELS  G B   (BLF RUSS KUNKEL      D    (L   JOHN KAHN       B   (LC  SKIP PROKOP     D(L
     PAUL SIMON       V     (LC  J R COBB         G    (LK  BARRY BAILEY    G   (LK  DEAN DAUGHTRY   PNO(LK
     PAUL GODDARD     B     (L   ROBERT NIX       D    (LK  EILEEN GILBERT  V   (LK  LINDA NOVEMBER  V(LK
     TASHA THOMAS     V     (LK  PATTI AUSTIN     V    (LK  JERRY KENNEDY   G   (LK  WAYNE MOSS      G (LBF
     CHARLIE McCOY    HCA   (BFL KENNY BUTTREY    D    (LBF RICK MAROTTA    D   (LF  HERBIE FLOWERS B (LHJ
     KEN SCOTT        (L   BLOSSOMS               V    (LBF DON ELLIS      HRNS (B   ELVIN BISHOP    G (B
     STEVEN MILLER    K     (B   DAVE BROWN       B    (B   JOE OSBORNE     B   (F   LYLE RITZ       B (F
     STU SCHAFF       G     (FJ  KEITH ALLISON    G    (F   FREDDIE WELLER  G   (F   LOUIE SHELTON   G (FH
     TOMMY TEDESCO    G     (F   TOM COSGROVE     G    (F   DAVID BROMBERG STEEL(F   PETE DRAKE      STEEL(F
     EARL PALMER      STEEL (F   MILT HOLLAND     PERC (F   GEORGE DEVENS  PERC (F   LARRY KNECHTEL  K (F
     CALEB QUAYE      G     (H   SNEAKY PETE      STEEL(H   CAROL KAYE      B   (H   BOBBY WEST      B (HJ
     BOBBIE HALL      PERC  (HJ  ROGER POPE       D    (H   PAUL HUMPHRIES  D   (HJ  RITA COOLIDGE   V (H
     VANETTA FIELDS   V     (HJ  CLYDIE KING      V    (HJ  DONNA WEISS     V   (HJ  JULIA TILLMAN   V (H
     DOROTHY MORRISSON V    (H   CLAUDIA LENNEAR  V    (HJ  EDNA WRIGHT     V   (HJ  LORNA WILLARD   V (H
     EDNA WOODS       V     (H   MAXINE WILLARD   V    (H   ROBBIE MONTGOMERY V (H   JESSIE SMITH    V (H
     ROBERT JOHN      V     (H   MIKE GATELY      V    (H   JAY SEIGAL      V   (H   ALAN PARKER     G (J
     BARRY MORGAN     D     (J   LINDA LEWIS      V    (J   OMA DRAKE       V   (J   CHARLIE BROWN   G (K
     JOHN PAUL FETTA  B     (J   PAUL GODDARD     B    (J   JUNIOR HANLEY   D   (J   RICHARD GREEN   FDL (J
     MARUGA           PERC  (J
```

PAUL KORDA

| PAUL KORDA | V K G(A | | (A) PASSING STRANGER | | 1971 | MAM | | MAM AS 1003 |

```
PAUL KORDA       V K G(A      (A) PASSING STRANGER        1971 MAM          MAM AS 1003
ALAN GORRIE      B K G V(A
ROB TAIT         D    (A  ONNIE McINTYRE  G   (A  RAY RUSSELL   G   (A  DORIS TROY      V (A
MADELINE BELL    V    (A  NANETTE NEWMAN  V   (A  ANDY ROBERTS  G   (A  CHRIS SPEDDING G (A
JONATHAN COUDRILLE K  (A  MIKE STOREY     K   (A
```

KORGIS

```
ANDY DAVIS V K D MAND (A   (A) THE KORGIS         1979 RIALTO UK TENOR 101 US WB 3349
JAMES WARREN     V B  (A   (B) DUMB WAITERS       1980 RIALTO UK TENOR 104 US ASYLUM290
PHIL HARRISON    K PERC(A   (C) STICKT GEORGE      1981 RIALTO UK ALTO 103
GLENN TOOMEY     K    (A
DAVID LORD       K    (A  BILL BIRKS   D   (A  AL POWELL        D   (A  STUART GORDON VLNMAND(A
KEITH WARMINGTON HCA  (A  KENNY LACEY  PERC (A  JO MULLEY            V (A  JO POMEROY    V  (A
```

ALEXIS KORNER

```
ALEXIS KORNER    G V   (ALL   (A) R & B AT THE MARQUEE          1962 ACE OF CLUBS   UK    ACL  1130
ERIC CLAPTON     G     (V     (A) R & B AT THE MARQUEE          196  DECCA                846039
ZOOT MONEY       K     (HNPQV (B) AT THE CAVERN                 1964 ORIOLE         UK
CHRIS FARLOWE    V     (V     (C) RED HOT FROM  ALEX            1964 TRANSATLANTIC  UK    TRA  117
IAN STEWART      V     (VY    (D) BLUES INC                     1965 ACE OF CLUBS   UK    ACL 1187
PAUL JONES       V     (V     (D) BLUES INC                     196  DECCA          GER        419
ART THEMAN       WIND  (CHDRV (E) BLUES INC                     1967 POLYDOR        UK    236  206
MEL COLLINS      HRNS  (NOPQV (F) I WONDER WHO                  1967 FONTANA        UK    STL5381
DICK MORRISSEY   SAX   (VT    (G) NEW GENERATION OF BLUES       1968 SONET               SLP   64
DICK HECKSTALL SMITH SAX(DHMVX (G) NEW GENERATION OF BLUES      1968 LIBERTY             LBS 83147
JOHN SURMAN      SAX   (MVI   (G) NEW GENERATION OF BLUES       1968 PHILIPS             6401 901
MIKE ZWERIN      TROM  (V     (H) ALEXIS KORNERS  ALL STARS BLUES INC 69 TRANSATLANTIC UK TRASAM  7
COLIN HODGKINSON B     (IMPQSTV (I) BOTH SIDES                  1969 METRONOME            MLP 15364
STU SPEAR        (V           (J) THE NEW CHURCH                1970 METRONOME
JIMMY LITHERLAND G     (V     (K) ALEXIS                        1971 RAK            UK    SRAK  501
GUS JOHNSON            (V     (L) WHATS THAT SOUND I HEAR       1971 SUNSET         UK    SLS 50245
IAN WALLACE      D     (NOPQ  (M) BOOTLEG HIM                   1972 RAK UK SRAKSP 51 US WB   1966
BOZ BURRELL      B     (NOPQ  (N) ACCIDENTALLY BORN IN NEW ORLEANS 1973 TRANSATLANTIC UK TRA 269
STEVE MARRIOTT   ORG   (NS    (N) ACCIDENTALLY BORN IN NEW ORLEANS 1973 WB         US         2647
DAVE CASTLE      WIND  (CHR   (N) THE ACCIDENTAL BAND           1973 BRAIN          GER       1022
HERBIE GOINS     V     (CHMR  (O) SNAPE LIVE ON TOUR            1974 BRAIN               2/ 1039
RON EDGEWORTH    K     (CHR   (P) ALEXIS KORNER                 1974 POLYDOR        GER  2374 109
DANNY THOMPSON   B     (CEHM  (Q) MR BLUES                      1974 TOADSTOOL            35434
BARRY HOWTEN     D     (CHR   (R) BLUES INC                     1974 JUST SUNSHINE  US    JUST13
CYRIL DAVIES     HCA V(CMX    (S) GET OFF MY CLOUD              1975 CBS   US 33427 UK    69155
KEITH SCOTT      PNO   (MA    (T) JUST EASY                     1978 INTERCORD           INT 60099
COLIN BOWDEN     D     (M     (U) ME     (DIRECT CUT)           1979 JETON               100  3305
DAVE STEVENS     PNO   (M     (V) THE PARTY LP                  1980 INTERCORD      GER  170 000
CHARLIE WATTS    D     (MY    (W) TELL                          1980 TELDEC              623075
JACK BRUCE       B     (MXY   (X) PROFILE                       1981 TELDEC              624425
TERRY COX        D     (ME    (Y) ROCKETT 88                    1981 ATLANTIC             50776
CHRIS PYNE TROM PNO    (MEI   (Z) THE ORIGINAL                  1980 TRANSATLANTIC  NL    44014
RAY WARLEIGH     SAX   (MI    (a) WHITE & BLUE                  1980 BLUE SILVER    FR    3008
DAVE HOLLAND     B     (M
ALAN SKIDMORE    SAX   (ME
GINGER BAKER     D     (MX
GRAHAM BOND      SAX   (MX   JOHNNY PARKER PNO  (MXD  NIGEL STANGER  SAX (M    BRIAN SMITH   SAX (M
PETER THORUP     V G(MNOPQI  PAUL RODGERS   V   (MI   ANNETTE BROX   V   (MI   ANDY FRASER   B  (MI
LOL COXHILL      SAX   (M    JOHN MARSHALL  D   (MI   MALCOLM GRIFFITHS TROM(M  HAROLD BECKETT TPT(IQPM
HENRY LOWTHER    TPT   (MI   VICTOR BROX PNO TPT V(M  ROBERT PLANT   V HCA(M   STEVE MILLER  PNO (MG
PETER FENSOME    V     (M    ROY BABBINGTON  B  (M    CHRIS McGREGOR PNO (M    LARRY POWER   G  (M
JACK BROOKS      D     (M    JOHN CAMERON   K   (MP   ALAN PARKER    G   (M    HERBIE FLOWERS B (M
BARRY MORGAN     D     (M    TONY CARR      D   (MQP  SPIKE HEATLEY  B   (AMX  JIM LAWLESS   PERC(M
BILL LESAGE      PERC  (M    HAROLD McNAIR  FLT (M    TONY COE       WIND (M    PETE KING    WIND(M
DANNY MOSS       WIND  (M    BOB EFFORD     WIND (M    RON ROSS      WIND (M    NEIL SANDERS HRNS(M
KENNY WHEELER    TPT   (MI   GREG BOWEN     TPT (M    TONY FISHER    TPT (M    LES CONDON   TPT (M
DON LUSHER       TROM  (M    JOHN MARSHALL  TROM(M    BRIAN PERRIN   TROM (M    BILL GELDARD TROM(M
SAPPHO GILLETT KORNER V(JSTV GRAHAM BURBRIDGE D (M    LONG JOHN BALDRY V  (AX   MIKE SCOTT   (D
PHIL SEAMAN      D     (D    MIKE PATTO     PNO (QP   ELTON DEAN     SAX (QP   NICK EVANS    TROM (QP
CAROL MORGAN     V     (Q    RON ASPERY     SAX (QP   RICK MISHLEN   V   (Q    EDDIE MORDUE  SAX (QP
DUSTER BENNETT   HCA   (QP   PADDY McHUGH   V   (S    DYANE BIRCH    V   (S    MORRIS PERT  PERC(S
GEORGE CALDWELL  PERC  (S    JASON CAINE    PERC (S    TONY O MALLEY PNO (S    NICKY HOPKINS PNO (S
TERRY STANNARD   D     (S    RICK WILLS     D   (S    ALAN SPENNER   D   (S    PETER FRAMPTON G (S
GASPAR LAWAL     PERC  (O    DUFFY POWER    HCA (EV   TIM HINKLEY    P(ONPQ    NEIL HUBBARD  G(S
KEITH RICHARD    G     (S    NEIL FORD      G   (T    GEORGE GREEN   PNO (Y    COLIN SMITH  TPT (Y
FRANK COLLINS    V     (S    IRENE CHANTER  V   (S    SUNNY LESLIE   V   (S    LISA STRIKE   V(S
BARRY ST JOHN    V     (S    JOANNE WILLIAMS V  (S    JIM DIAMOND    V   (T    DAVE WINTOUR  B  (T
HENRY SPINETTI   D     (T    GRAHAM DEAKIN  D   (T    GRAHAM BROAD   D   (T    MICK WEAVER   K  (T
RICHIE ZITO      G     (T    PETER WARD     G   (T    DANNY McKINTOSH G  (T    RONNIE JONES  V (X
JIM BRAY         B     (X    MIKE COLLINS   PERC (X    CHRIS CAPON   B   (X    DAVE STEVENS PNO (X
HAL SINGER       SAX   (Y    JOHN PICARD    TROM (Y    DON WELLER    SAX (Y
```

ARTIE KORNFELDS TREE

```
TONY LEVIN       B     (A    (A) A TIME TO REMEMBER           1970 DUNHILL 50092 UK PROBE SPB 1022
HUGH McCRACKEN   G     (A
FRANK HARRIS     K     (A   MIKE MENICCI   PERC (A   DONALD McDONLD  D   (A
```

KORONA

```
BRUCE BLACKMAN   K V   (A    (A) KORONA                       1980 UA        US           1020
BOB GAUTHLER     G V   (A
```

KORPS

```
                             (A) HELLO WORLD                  1979 LIMP      IMP          1002
```

DANNY KORTCHMAR

```
DANNY KORTCHMAR  G V   (A    (A) KOOTCH                       1973 WB            US   BS 2711
WILLIAM SMITH    K     (A    (B) INNUENDO                     1980 ASYLUM US 250 NL     52207
CRAIG DOERGE     K     (A
JIM HORN         WIND  (A   DOUG RICHARDSON SAX (A   ABIGALE HANESS  V   (A   DAVID KEMPER  D  (B
BOB GLAUB        B     (B   LOUISE GOFFIN   V   (B   DAVID LASBY     V   (B   JIM KELTNER   D  (B
LEE SKLAR        B     (B   WADDY WACHTEL  G V  (B   MICHAEL BODDICKER SYN (B KENNY EDWARDS B  (B
JULES SHEAR      V     (B   ARNOLD McCULLER V   (B   RICK MAROTTA  PERC (B    PAUL STALLWORTH B(B
```

TONY KOSINEC

TONY KOSINEC	G V	(A	(A) PROCESSES			19	CBS	US	9832
SKIP PROKOP	D	(A							
PAUL HOFFERT	K	(A	HARVEY BROOKS	B (A	RALPH COLE	G (A	PATTI LABELLE	V (A	
BLUEBELLES	V	(A							

PAUL KOSSOFF

PAUL KOSSOFF	G	(AB	(A) BACK STREET CRAWLER			1973	ISLAND	UK/US	ILPS 9264
ALAN WHITE	D	(A	(B) KOSS (COMP DBL)			1977	DJM	US 300	UK 29002
EDDIE QUANSAH	HRNS	(B	(C) THE HUNTER			1981	STREET TIMES	UK	STLP 001
RABBIT BUNDRICK	K	(AB							
ALAN SPENNER	B	(A	JEAN ROUSSEL	K (A	JESS RODEN	V (A	TETSU YAMAUCHI	B (AB	
SIMON KIRKE	D	(AB	JOHN MARTYN	G (AB	PAUL RODGERS	V (AB	ANDY FRASER	B (AB	
CONRAD ISADORE	D	(A	CLIVE CHAMAN	B (A	TREVOR BURTON	B (A	DAVID HOOD	B (B	
ROGER HAWKINS	D	(B	BARRY BECKETT	K (B	PETE CARR	G (B	JIMMY JOHNSON	G (B	
MIKE KELLIE	D	(B	DAVID ELLIOTT	PNO (B	TONY BRAUNAGEL	D (B	TERRY WILSON	B (B	
MIKE MONTGOMERY	PNO	(B	PETER COX	V (B	JIM CAPALDI	V (B	SUE GLOVER	V (B	
EDDIE BAIRD	G K V	(B	TERRY WINCOTT	G V (B	WILLY MURRAY	D (B	SUNNY LESLIE	D (B	
MICK FEAT	B	(B	TERRY WILSON SLESSER	V (B	GEORGE LARNYOH	HRNS (B	PETER VANDER PUIJE	HRNS(B	
EDDIE QUANSAH	HRNS	(B							

LEO KOTTKE

LEO KOTTKE	G	(ALL	(A) CIRCLE AROUND THE SUN	1970	SYMPOSIUM			2001
MIKE JOHNSON	G	(G	(B) MUDLARK	1971	CAPITOL			682
BILL BERG	PERC	(FGI	(C) LEO KOTTKE 6 & 12 STRING GUITAR	1972	SONET UK SNTF 629 TAKOMA US1024			
BILL PETERSON	B	(FGI	(D) GREENHOUSE	1973	CAPITOL			11000
BILL BARBER	SYN	(FGI	(E) MY FEET ARE SMILING	1973	CAPITOL			11164
CAL HAND	STEEL	(FG	(F) ICE WATER	1974	CAPITOL			11262
HERB PILHOFER	PNO	(G	(G) DREAMS & ALL THAT STUFF	1974	CAPITOL			11335
JOHN FAHEY	G PROD	(BH	(H) LEO KOTTKE, JOHN FAHEY & PETER LANG	1974	SONET UK SNTF 675			
JACK SMITH	PNO	(GI	(I) CHEWING PINE	1975	CAPITOL			11446
ROY ESTRADA	B	(B	(J) BEST OF	1976	CAPITOL		UK	CAPS1003
PAUL LAGOS	D	(B	(K) LEO KOTTKE	1976	CHRYSALIS		UK	CHR 1106
WAYNE MOSS	B	(B	(L) BURNT LIPS	1978	CHRYSALIS		UK	CHR 1191
PETER LANG	G	(H	(L) BURNT LIPS	1978	CHRYSALIS		EURO 6307 631	
KEN BUTTREY	D	(BO	(M) THE BEST	1978	CAPITOL US 11867 UK		ESTSP 21	
JOHN HARRIS	PNO	(BO	(N) LEO KOTTKE 1971/76	1976	CAPITOL			11576
MIKE LEECH	B	(O	(O) BALANCE	1979	CHRYSALIS		UK	CHR 1234
BOBBY OGDIN	PNO	(O	(P) LIVE IN EUROPE	1980	CHRYSALIS		UK	CHR 1284
LARRY TAYLOR	B	(B	(Q) GUITAR MUSIC	1981	CHRYSALIS		UK	CHR 1328
KIM FOWLEY	V	(B						
DENNY BRUCE	PROD	(BDEFIL KERRY FAHEY PROD (H PAT SMITH			B (B	JEFFREY KAPLAN	PNO (B	

KRAAN

PETER WOLBRANDT	G V	(ABCDEFGH	(A) WINTHRUP	1972	SPIEGELEI		28523/9
HELLMUT HATTLER	B	(ABCDEFGH	(B) KRAAN	1973	SPIEGELEI		28778/9
JAN FRIDE	D	(ABCDEF	(C) ANDY NOGGER	1975	GULL UK 1009 PASSPORT US	98006	
JOHANNES PAPPERT	SAX	(ABCDE	(D) KRAAN LIVE	1975	GULL UK		2001/2
INGO BISCHOF	K	(EFGH	(D) KRAAN LIVE	1975	SPIEGELEI		26440/8
TOMMY GOLDSCHMIDT	PERC	(F	(E) LET IT OUT	1975	GULL UK 1013 PASSPORT US	98015	
UDO DAHMEN	D	(G	(E) LET IT OUT	1975	SPIEGELEI		24548/1
			(F) WIEDERHOREN	1977	HARVEST ELECTROLA GER	064 32110	
			(G) FLYDAY	1978	HARVEST ELECTROLA		064 45210
			(H) TOURNEE	1980	EMI GER		064 45931

KRACKER

KARL DRIGGS	V PERC	(B	(A) LA FAMILIA	1972	DUNHILL US		50134
BOBBY KEYS	SAX	(B	(B) KRACKER BRAND	1973	ROLLING STONES		COC 49102
CHUCK FRANCOUR	K V	(B	(B) KRACKER BRAND	1973	DUNHILL US		50154
VICTOR ANGULO	G V	(B	(C) ROCKIN THE NATION	1980	PS US 0001		
CARLOS GARCIA	B V	(B					
ARTHUR CASADO	D	(B	MALCOLM CECIL	SYN(B ROBERT MARGOULEFF	SYN(B		

KRACQ

(A) CIRCUMVISION	1978	UAP		003

KRAFTWERK

RALF HUTTER	V K D	(ABCDEFGHIJK	(A) KRAFTWERK 1 .	1971	PHILIPS		6305 058
FLORIAN SCHNEIDER	D K	(ABCDEFGHIJK	(B) KRAFTWERK 2	1972	PHILIPS		6305 117
KLAUS ROEDER	VLN G	(E	(AB) KRAFTWERK DBL	1973	VERTIGO	UK	6641 077
WOLFGANG FLUR	PERC	(EFGHIJK	(D) RALF & FLORIAN	1973	VERTIGO	UK	6360 616
FLAK KUEBLER		(J	(D) RALF & FLORIAN	1973	WB	US	2006
MARTIN TEWIS		(J	(E) AUTOBAHN	1974	VERTIGO US 2003 UK		6360 620
CAROL MARTIN		(J	(E) AUTOBAHN	1974	MERCURY US 1 3704		
KARL BARTOS	PERC	(FGHIJK	(F) RADIOACTIVITY	1975	CAPITOL		11457
CONRAD PLANK	PROD	(C	(G) EXCELLER 8	1975	VERTIGO	UK	6360 629
BOB KRASNOW		(J	(H) TRANS EUROPE EXPRESS	1977	CAPITOL		11603
MARVIN KATZ		(J	(I) MAN MACHINE	1978	CAPITOL		11728
IAN FLOOKS		(J	(J) COMPUTOR WORLD	1980	EMI UK 3776	US WB	3549
DOREEN D'AGOSTINO		(J	(K) ELECTROKINETIK	1981	VERTIGO	UK	6449 066
TOM LANIK		(J					
TAKESHI SHIKVRA		(J					

BILLY J KRAMER & THE DAKOTAS

BILLY J KRAMER	V	(ALL	LISTEN TO	1963	PARLOPHONE UK (M) 1209 (S) 3047		
MIKE MAXFIELD	G	(	I'LL KEEP YOU SATISFIED	196	IMPERIAL US (M) 9273 (S)12273		
ROBIN McDONALD	G	(	LITTLE CHILDREN	196	IMPERIAL US (M) 9287 (S)12267		
RAY JONES	B	(	TRAINS BOATS & PLANES	196	IMPERIAL US (M) 9291 (S)12291		
TONY MANSFIELD	D	(	THE BEST OF	1977	EMI UK NUT 9 US CAPITOL		11897
			(EP) HITS	1963	PARLOPHONE UK		GEP 8885
			(EP) I'LL KEEP YOU SATISFIED	1964	PARLOPHONE UK		GEP 8895
			(EP) LITTLE CHILDREN	1964	PARLOPHONE UK		GEP 8907
			(EP) FROM A WINDOW	1964	PARLOPHONE UK		GEP 8921
			(EP) PLAYS FROM THE STATES	1965	PARLOPHONE UK		GEP 8928

BERNIE KRAUSE

BERNIE KRAUSE		(A	(A) CITADELS	1981	TAKOMA	US	7074

JEAN JACQUES KRAVETZ

```
JEAN JACQUES KRAVETZ   K    (A     (A) KRAVETZ                    1972  VERTIGO            6360 605
UDO LINDENBERG         D V  (A
THOMAS KRETZSCHMER     G(A  CARL G STEPHAN    B   (A   INGA RUMPF        V   (A   ROGER HOOK      G  (A
```

K94 KRAZY KAT K94

```
GRAHAME WHITE          G V  (AB    (A) CHINA SEA                 1976  MOUNTAIN           TOPC 5004
TONY FERGUSON          G V  (AB    (B) TROUBLED AIR              1977  MOUNTAIN           TOPC 5009
ROGER BRADLEY-WILLIS   D(AB
RAY LEWIS              B V  (AB    HENRY MACDONALD  K V  (AB
```

K94A ROBBIE KRIEGER K94A

```
ROBBIE KRIEGER        G V K(A    (A) ..AND FRIENDS             1977  BLUE NOTE          LA 664
ED GREENE             D    (A
REGGIE McBRIDE        B    (A    RON STOCKERT    K   (A  SAL MARQUEZ   HRNS K  (A  JOCK ELLIS      TROM (A
JOEL PESKIN           SAX  (A    BRUCE GARY      D   (A  KENNY WILD      B    (A  GREG MATHESON   ORG  (A
SHARON ROBINSON       V    (A    AFREEKA TREES   V   (A  JIMMY SMITH     ORG  (A  JOHN DENSMORE   D   (A
STU GOLDBERG          SYN K(A    PERICO        CONGA(A  EDDIE TALAMANTES TIMBS(A  GARY BARONE     TPT  (A
BOB GLAUB             B    (A
```

K94B SONJA KRISTINA K94B

```
SONJA KRISTINA        V    (A    (A) SONJA KRISTINA            1980  CHOPPER            CHOPE5
LIAM GENOCKEY         D    (A
ALFIE AGIUS           B    (A    STEVE BYRD      G    (A  COLIN TOWNS    FLT K (A  GASPAR LAWAL    PERC (A
NIGEL GRAY            SYN  (A    DARRYL WAY      VLN  (A  ALEXANDER SKEAPING  K(A  LAWRENCE JUBER  G  (A
IAIN DUNNET           SYN  (A    DAVE SMITH      B    (A  TONY HENDRICKS  D   (A  BOB BARNETT     G  (A
DAVID WALKER          K    (A    BRIAN DEVITO    B    (A  PETER VAN HOOKE D   (A  DAVE OLNEY      B  (A
IAN MILNE             K    (A    PETE ACOCK      SAX  (A  TONY CARR      PERC (A  CORONA STAGE SCHOOL V(A-
```

K94C VOLKER KRIEGEL K94C

```
VOLKER KRIEGEL  G SIT (ALL    (A) SPECTRUM                  1971  MPS       GER 21/20874/5
JOHN TAYLOR           K  (ABC  (B) MISSING LINK              1972  MPS       GER 3321431/1
CECS SEE            PERC (ABC  (C) LIFT                      1973  MPS       GER 2121753/1
ALBERT MANGELSDORFF      (B    (D) MILD MANIAC               1974  MPS       GER 2122020/6
HEINZ SAUER          SAX  (B
JOHN MARSHALL        D    (B   ZBIGNIEW SEIFERT VLN (C  JOE NAY       D   (D  PETER TRUNK   B CELLO(A
PETER BAUMEISTER     D    (A   ALAN SKIDMORE   SAX  (B  EBERHARD WEBER B   (BCD  STAN SULZMANN WIND   (C
RAINER BRUNINGHAUS   K    (D   PETER GIGER     PERC (D
```

K95 KRIS KRISTOFFERSON K95

```
KRIS KRISTOFFERSON V G (ALL   (A) KRISTOFFERSON              1970  MONUMENT UK 5042
WITH                          (A) HELP ME MAKE IT THROUGH THE NIGHT 1980 EMBASSY        UK  31839
JERRY KENNEDY        G  (ACD  (A) ME & BOBBY McGEE(RI)       1973  MONUMENT UK 64631  US  30817
NORBERT PUTNAM       B  (CE   (B) CISCO PETE                 197   CBS                US   9154
JERRY CARRIGAN       D  (CD   (C) SILVER TONGUED DEVIL & I   1971  MONUMENT UK 64636  US  30679
DAVID BRIGGS         K  (CE   (D) BORDER LORD                1972  MONUMENT UK 64963  US  31302
JERRY SHOOK          G  (CED  (E) JESUS WAS A CAPRICORN      1973  MONUMENT UK 65391  US  31909
NORMAN BLAKE         G  (C    (F) SPOOKY LADY'S SIDESHOW     1974  MONUMENT UK 69074  US  32914
BOBBY DYSON          B  (C    (G) WHO'S TO BLESS & WHO'S TO BLAME 1975 MONUMENT UK 69158 US 33379
CHARLIE McCOY        HCA K(CD  (H) SURREAL THING             1976  MONUMENT UK 81496  US  35254
FARRELL MORRIS       PERC (CD  (J) SONGS OF KRISTOFFERSON    1977  MONUMENT UK 82002  US  34254
BILLY SWAN           B V  (CDEGH (K) A STAR IS BORN  (SOUNDTRACK) 1977 CBS   UK 86021
CHRIS GANTRY          G  (C    (L) EASTER ISLAND             1978  MONUMENT UK 86056  US  35310
DONNIE FRITTS        K V  (CDG  (M) MR SHAKE HANDS           1979  CBS                US  36135
JERRY SHOOK          G  (D    (N) TO THE BONE                1981  CBS       UK 84818  US  36885
RITA COOLIDGE        V  (CDFHG
LARRY GATLIN         V    (E    BENNY WHITEHEAD  V  (E   RANDY CULLERS  V    (E   ALAN RUSH      V  (E
TERRY DEARMORE       V    (E    ALLEN WALD       V  (H   TERRY PAUL     V   (HGD  GARY BUSEY     V  (H
KENNY BUTTREY        D   (ED    ANDY NEWMARK     D  (E   JOSH GRAVES    G    (E   JERRY McGEE    G V(FH
LEE SKLAR            B   (FHG   BARBARA STREISLAND V (K   SAMMY CREASON D   (FHG  BOBBYE HALL    PERC(FG
JIM HORN            SAX  (F     JACKIE KELSO    SAX (F   CHUCK FINDLEY  TPT  (F   DICK HYDE      TROM(F
HERB PEDERSEN        V  (FHG    LARRY MURRAY     V  (F   JOHN BELAND    V    (F   BOBBY NEUWIRTH V  (H
CLYDIE KING          V  (HG     SHIRLEY MATTHEWS V  (H   BYRON BERLINE  V    (H   JACK SKINNER   V  (H
CHARLES CHALMERS     V  (E      SANDRA CHALMERS  V  (E   DONNA RHODES   V    (E   D BERGEN WHITE V  (E
JAMES E CASON        V  (E      JUNE PAGE        V  (E   JORDANAIRES    V    (E   RAYMOND WALKER V  (E
HOYT HAWKINS         V  (E      JOHN HARRIS      K  (E   GORDON STOKER  V    (E   DON GANT       V  (E
MILDRED KIRKHAM      V  (E      STEPHEN BRUTON  G V (ED  DENNIS LINDE   G    (ED  TOM COGBILL    B  (E
MAC GAYDEN           G  (E      CHIP YOUNG       G  (E   JOHN BUCK WILKIN G  (E   JAMES COLVARD  G  (E
GRADY MARTIN         G  (E      FRED CARTER      G  (E   JOHN L CHRISTOPHER G (E  WELDON MYRICK  STEEL(E
MIKE UTLEY           K V (EG     BOBBY WOOD       K  (E   BOBBY EMMONS   K    (E   PETE DRAKE     STEEL(D
TOMMY JACKSON        FDL (G      BENNY WHITEHEAD  V  (G   FRED TACKETT   G    (G   NICK DECARO    ACC (G
MENTOR WILLIAMS      V  (G       WARREN OATES     V  (G
```

K96 KRIS KRISTOFFERSON & RITA COOLIDGE K96

```
KRIS KRISTOFFERSON   V  (ABC    (A) FULL MOON                1973  A&M      US 4403  UK  AMLH64403
RITA COOLIDGE        V  (ABC    (B) BREAKAWAY                1974  MONUMENT US 33278 UK    80547
STEPHEN BRUTON       G V (AC     (C) NATURAL ACT             1978  A&M      US 4690  UK  AMLH64690
CHIP YOUNG           G  (B
JIM COLVARD          G  (B      JOHN L CHRISTOPHER G (B   JERRY SHOOK    G    (B   WELDON MYRICK  STEEL(B
MIKE UTLEY           K  (ABC    BOBBY WOOD       K  (B   BOBBY EMMONS   K    (B   TOMMY COGBILL  B  (B
JOSH GRAVES          G  (A      JERRY McGEE      G  (AC   LEE SKLAR      B    (A   SAMMY CREASON  D  (ABC
BOBBYE HALL          PERC (A     TERRY PAUL       V  (A   GENE CHRISMAN  D    (B   BUDDY SPICHER  FDL  (B
REGGIE YOUNG         G  (B      RAY EDENTON      G  (B   SHANE KEISTER  K    (B   FARRELL MORRIS PERC (B
CHARLIE McCOY        HCA  (B     RON EADES      HRNS (B   HARRISON CALLOWAY HRNS(A  CHARLES ROSE  HRNS (B
DON SHEFFIELD        HRNS (B     DAVID BROMBERG   G  (A   NICK DE CARO   V    (A   DAVID SMITH        (A
GARY SCRUGGS         V  (B       RANDY SCRUGGS    V  (A   VASSAR CLEMENTS FDL (A   BOOKER T JONES K   (A
HERB ALPERT          TPT  (A     BILLY SWAN       V  (C   DONNIE FRITTS  K    (C   JERRY JUMONVILLE SAX(C
DENNIS BELFIELD      B  (C
```

K96A KROKUS K96A

```
MARC STORACE         V  (AB     (A) METAL RENDEZVOUS          1980  ARIOLA            ARL 5056
TOMMY KIEFFER        G V (AB     (B) HARDWARE                 1981  ARIOLA UK ARL5064 GER 203322
FERNANDO VON ARB     G V (AB     (C) PAINKILLER               1981  MERCURY  NL  6326 800
CHRIS VON ROHR       B V (AB
FREDDY STEADY        D V (AB    JUERG NAEGELI    K V (A
```

JIM KRUEGER

JIM KRUEGER	(A	(A) SWEET SALVATION	1978	CBS	US	35295	

KROKODIL

TERRY STEVENS	G B V(ABEF	(A) KROKODIL	1969	LIBERTY		LBS 83306
HERDY HEPP	K VLN(ABF	(B) SWAMP	1970	LIBERTY		LBS 83417
DUDE DURST	PERC D(ABEF	(AB) CLASSIC GERMAN ROCK SCENE	197	UA	GER DBL UAS 29776/77
MOJO WEIDELI	FLT HCA (ABEF	(C)				
WALTY ANSELMO	B V SIT(ABEF	(D) MUSIC				
RAINER MARZ	G (F	(E) GETTING UP FOR THE MORNING	1972	BELLAPHON	GER	19117
VEIT FEIDEN	K VIBES(F	(F) SWEAT & SWIM	1973	BELLAPHON	GER	7502

DAVID KUBINEC

DAVID KUBINEC	G V PNO (A	(A) SOME THINGS NEVER CHANGE	1978	A&M	US 4766	UK	AMLH68501
CHRIS SPEDDING	G (A						
JIM BAIN	B (A	JOHN CALE	K (A	OLLIE HALSALL	G (A	ALAN MACLEOD PIPES (A
TIMI DONALD	D (A	PAT DONALDSON	B (A			

JOACHIM KUHN

JOACHIM KUHN	K (ALL	(A) BOLD IS WONDERFUL	19	MPS		15239
PHILIP CATHERINE	G (L	(B) CINEMASCOPE	1976	MPS BASF		2122270 5
JOHN LEE	B (L	(C) IMPRESSION OF NEW YORK	19	IMPULSE		9158
GERRY BROWN	D (L	(D) INTERCHANGE	19	MPS		21328 5
ZBIGNIEW SEIFERT	VLN (L	(E) PARIS IS WONDERFUL	19	BYG		529 346
CURT CRESS	D (L	(F) PIANO	1971	MPS BASF		2121330 7
ROLF KUHN	(CK	(G) SOLOS	1974	FUTURA	GER	18
PETER WARREN	(J	(H) SOUNDS OF FEELING	19	BYG		519 317
DANIEL HUSSAIN	(J	(J) THIS WAY OUT	19	BASF		2921752 3
GERD DUDEK	(J	(K) TRANSFIGURATION	19	MPS		15118
JAN AKKERMAN	G (O	(L) SPRING FEVER	1977	ATLANTIC US 1695 UK	K50280
		(M) CHARISMA	19	ATLANTIC		K50352
		(N) MONDAY MORNING	19	ELECTROLA		SHZE 909B
		(O) SUNSHOWER	1978	ATLANTIC	US 19193	

STEVE KUHN

STEVE KUHN	PNO (ALL	(A) CHILDHOOD IS FOREVER	1969	BYG		529136
JACK DEJOHNNETTE	D (B	(B) TRANCE	1974	ECM		1052
SUE EVANS	PERC (B	(C) ECSTASY	1974	ECM		1058
STEVE SWALLOW	B (B	(D) RAINDROPS	1975	MUSE	US	5106
HARVEY SCHWARZ	B (EFH	(E) MOTILITY	1977	ECM		1094
MICHAEL SMITH	D (E	(F) NON FICTION	1978	ECM		1124
STEVE SLAGLE	WIND (EF	(G) WATCH WHAT HAPPENS	19	MPS		15193
BOB MOSES	D (FH	(H) PLAYGROUND	197	ECM		1059
SHEILA JORDAN	V (H					

LEAH KUNKEL

LEAH KUNKEL	V K(AB	(A) LEAH KUNKEL	1979	CBS	US	35778
RUSS KUNKEL	D (A	(B) I RUN WITH TROUBLE	1980	CBS	US	36398
LELEAND SKLAR	B (A					
DANNY KORTCHMAR	G (A	JIM HORN	FLT (A	STEVEN BISHOP G (A	DAN DUGMORE G (A
ROSEMARY BUTLER	V (A	ANDREW GOLD	G (A	JACKSON BROWNE V (A	DOUG LIVINGSTONE G(A
MIKE PORCARO	B (B	JEFF PORCARO	D (B	GRAHAM NASH V (B	STEPHEN BISHOP G (B
JOHN GUERIN	D (B	MATT MURPHY	K STR(AB	PENNY NICHOLS V (B	PAMELA STANLEY V (B
DAVID HUNGATE	B (B	BERNARD FLEISCHER FLT (B	BOBBY SHEW HRN (B	WILLIAM SMITH K V (B
DAVID DUKE	HRNS (B	CRAIG DOERGE PNO (B	JOHN JARVIS PNO (B	STEVE LUKATHER G (AB
LENNY CASTRO	PERC (B	TOM SCOTT SAX (B	STEVE FOREMAN PERC (B	IAN FAIRBAIRN-SMITH V(B
JAMES LEE STANLEY	V (B	PAUL FANERSO K (B	MITCH HOLDER G (B	JAMES SELF HRNS(B
ERNEST CARLSON	TROM (B	DAVID LASLEY V (B	HARLAN COLLINS V (B	RONALD LEONARD (B

TOLI KUPPERBERG

TULI KUPPERBERG	(A	(A) NO DEPOSIT NO RETURN	19	ESP	US	1035

KURSAAL FLYERS

PAUL SHUTTLEWORTH	V (ALL	(A) CHOCS AWAY	1975 UK UK UKAL1011	UK	2330 101
BOB ANDREWS	SAX (B	(A) CHOCS AWAY	1975 UK EURO 2330 106		
RICHIE BULL	B V (ALL	(B) GREAT ARTISTE	1975 UK UK UKAL1018		
GRAEME DOUGLAS	G (ABC	(C) GOLDEN MILE	1976 CBS	UK	81622
VIC COLLINS G V STEEL	(ALL	(D) FIVE LIVE KURSAALS	1977 CBS	UK	82253
WILL BIRCH	D (ALL				
BARRY MARTIN	G V (D	DIGBY FAIRWETHER TPT (B	BRINSLEY SCHWARZ SAX (B

KWAME

	(A) FOLLOW I	1980	POLYDOR	US	6310

JIM KWESKIN

JIM KWESKIN	G V (ALL	(A) UNBLUSHING BRASSINESS	1963	VANGUARD		VSD 2158
MARIA(D'AMATO) MULDAUR V(FB		(B) JUG BAND MUSIC	1965	VANGUARD		VSD 79163
GEOFF MULDAUR	G V (FB	(C) RELAX YOUR MIND	1966	VANGUARD		VSD 79188
BILL KEITH	BAN STEEL(FB	(D) SEE REVERSE SIDE FOR TITLE	1966 VANGUARD VSD 79234 FONTANA 6080
MEL LYMAN	HCA (FB	(E) JUMP FOR JOY	1967	VANGUARD		VSD 79243
FRITZ RICHMOND	B (FB	(F) GARDEN OF JOY	1967	REPRISE	US	6266
RICHARD GREENE	FDL (F	(G) BEST OF	1968	VANGUARD		VSD 79270
REX RAKISH	V PERC(B	(H) WHATEVER HAPPENED TO THOSE DAYS	1968	VANGUARD		VAS 79278
BRUNO WOLF	V (B	(J) AMERICAN AVIATOR	1969	REPRISE	US	6353
		(K) GREATEST HITS(DBL)	1970	VANGUARD		VSD 13/14
		(L) JIM KWESKIN'S AMERICA	1971	REPRISE	US	6464
		(M) JIM KWESKIN	1978	MOUNTAIN RAILROAD	MR	52780
		(N) LIVES AGAIN	1978	MOUNTAIN RAILROAD	MR	52782
		(O) SIDE BY SIDE	1980	MOUNTAIN RAILROAD US	52790
		(P) SWING ON A STAR	1980	MOUNTAIN RAILROAD US	52793

KWICK

	(A) KWICK	1981	EMI	US	17025

L A EXPRESS

DAVID LUELL	SAX (AB	(A) L A EXPRESS		1976 CARIBOU	US 33940	UK 81267
ROBBEN FORD	G (A	(B) SHADOW PLAY		1976 CARIBOU	US 34355	UK 81671
VICTOR FELDMAN	PERC K (AB					
PETER MAUNU	G (B	MAX BENNETT	B (AB	JOHN GUERIN	D K (AB	JONI MITCHELL V (B
PAULETTE McWILLIAMS V (B						

L A JETS

KAREN LAWRENCE	V (A	(A) L A JETS	1976 RCA	US	APLI 1547
HARLIN McNEES	G V (A				
RON CINDRICH	B (A	JOHN DESAUTELS	D (A	SILVER HANSON	G (A	WAYNE COOK	K(A
JAMES LINDSEY	PERC (A				

L A BOPPERS

(A) L A BOPPERS	1980 MERCURY	US	3816
(B) BOP TIME	1981 MERCURY	US	4006

L T D

BILLY OSBORNE	K (C	(A) LOVE TOGETHERNESS & DEVOTION	197 A&M	US 3602	
JEFF OSBORNE	D V (C	(B) GITTIN' DOWN	1975 A&M	US 3660	UK AMLS63660
HENRY DAVIS	B V (C	(C) LOVE TO THE WORLD	1976 A&M	US 4589	UK AMLH64589
JIMMIE DAVIS	K V (C	(D) SOMETHING TO LOVE	1977 A&M	US 4646	UK AMLH64646
ROBERT SANTIEL	PERC (C	(E) TOGETHERNESS	1978 A&M	US 4705	UK AMLH64705
JOHN McGEE	G (C	(F) DEVOTION	1979 A&M	US 4771	UK AMLH64771
ABRAHAM MILLER	SAX V(C	(G) SHINE ON	1980 A&M	US 4819	UK AMLH64819
CARLE VICKERS	HRNS (C				
LORENZO CARNEGIE	SAX (C	JAKE RILEY	TROM(C	TOBY WYNN	SAX (C

JOAN LA BARBARA

JOAN LA BARBARA	V (A	(A) VOICE IS THE ORIGINAL INSTRUMENT	1976 WIZARD	US	RVW 2266

SLEEPY LA BEEF

SLEEPY LA BEEF	G V (ALL	(A) BULLS NIGHT OUT	1976 SUN	US	130
TERRY DUNCAN	PNO (E	(B) EARLY RARE & ROCKIN	19 BARON	US	102
LONNIE SEABOLT	B (E	(B) EARLY RARE & ROCKIN	1979 CHARLY RI	UK	CR 30181
CLETE CHAPMAN	D (E	(C) WESTERN GOLD	1977 SUN	US	138
BUCKY MEADOWS	G ORG(E	(D) ROCKABILLY 77	1977 SUN	US	1004
CLIFF PARKER	G (E	(E) BEEFY ROCKABILLY	1978 CHARLY	UK	CR 30145
GORDON TERRY	FDL (E	(F) DOWN HOME ROCKABILLY	1979 CHARLY	UK	CR 30172
		(F) DOWN HOME ROCKABILLY	197 SUN	US	1014
RUFUS THIBODEAUX	FDL (E	(G) ROCKABILLY HEAVYWEIGHT	1979 CHARLY	UK	CRL 5017
		(H) SLEEPY LA BEEF & FRIENDS(10")	1979 ACE		10 CH16
		(J) SLEEPY LABEEF	1981 SONET	UK	SNTF 843
		(EP) TORE UP	1978 CHARLY	UK	CEP 123

LABELLE

PATTI LABELLE	V (ALL	(A) OVER THE RAINBOW(BLUEBELLS)	196	ATLANTIC	US SD8119
SARAH DASH	V (HAJ	(B) DREAMER	1967	ATLANTIC	US 8147
NONA HENDRYX	V (HAJ	(C) LA BELLE	1971	WB	US 1943
ALLEN TOUSSAINT	K (H	(D) MOON SHADOWS	1972	WB	US 2618
JAMES ELLISON	K (H	(E) MERRY CHRISTMAS	19	MISTLETOE	US 1204
JAMES BOOKER	K (H	(F) PRESSURE COOKIN'	1974	RCA US LSA 3223 UK APLI0205	
HERMAN ERNEST	D (H	(G) NIGHT BIRDS	197	EPIC US 33075	
GEORGE PORTER	B (H	(H) PHOENIX	1975	EPIC US 33579	UK 69167
CARMINE ROJAS	B (H	(J) C'EST LA VIE	1975	DJM	UK DJSL 050
LEO NOCENTELLI	G (H	(K) CHAMELEON	1976	EPIC US 34189	UK 81422
TEDDY ROYAL	G (H	(L) PATTI LABELLE	1977	EPIC US 34847	UK 82226
LON PRICE	WIND (H	(M) EARLY HITS	19	TRIP US 800	9525
JOHN LONGO	TPT (H	(N) TASTY (PATTI SOLO)	197	EPIC US 35335	
CINDY BIRDSONG	V (AJ	(O) ITS ALL RIGHT WITH ME	1979	EPIC US 35772	UK 83524
EDWARD BATTS	G (H	(P) GREATEST HITS	19	TRIP US 8000	
JEFFREY SHANNON	PERC (H	( ) THE APPOLLO PRESENTS THE BLUEBELLS	19	NEWTOWN US 631	
JIM MOORE	WIND (H	( ) SLEIGHBELLS RING	19	NEWTOWN US 632	
LESTER CALISTE	TROM (H	( ) ON STAGE	19	PARKWAY US 7043	
STEVE HUGHES	G (H	( ) LIVE AT THE APPOLLO	19	UPFRONT US 129	
STEVE HOWARD	HRNS (H	( ) PATTI LABELLE (SOLO)	19	EPIC US 34847	
CARL BLOUIN	SAX (H	( ) ALRIGHT WITH ME	19	EPIC US 35772	
		( ) RELEASED	1980	EPIC US 36381	UK 84190
		( ) GONNA TAKE A MIRACLE	19	CBS US 30987	

JERRY LACROIX

JERRY LACROIX	V (A	(A) SECOND COMING		1974 MERCURY	US	SRM 1 701			
LAUREL ANNE MASSE	V (A	(A) LA CROIX		1972 EPIC	US	31555			
DAVID SPINOZZA	G (A								
JOHNNY WINTER	G (A	BOB MANN	G (A	EDGAR WINTER	K (A	JERRY FRIEDMAN	G (A
BOB ROSE	G (A	HUGH McCRACKEN	G (A	STU WOODS	B (A	JOHN TROPEA	G (A
PAUL GRIFFIN	K (A	RICK MAROTTA	D (A	RALPH MACDONALD PERC (A	TASHA THOMAS	V (A
CARL HALL	V (A	HILDA HARRIS	V (A	CHARLOTTE GILBERT V (A	RALPH SCHUCKETT K (A
RICHARD CROOKS	D (A	RANDY BRECKER	HRNS(A	ROBERT MILLIKAN HRNS (A	DAVID SANBORN	HRNS(A
LEW DELGATTO	HRNS (A	JAMES MAELIN	PERC (A	RICK DERRINGER	G (A	GAIL KANTOR	V (A
MERLE MILLER	V (A								

LADEMACHER

DANNY LADEMACHER	G V (A	(A) INNER SLEEVE		1981 ARIOLA	NL	203 383
ROGER WOLLAERT	D (A					
JAAP VAN DER SLUYS	B V(A	EMILE DEN TEX	V (A			

LA DUSSELDORF

KLAUS DINGER	G V (AB	(A) LA DUSSELDORF	1976 DECCA UK SKLR3252 NOVA GER 22550		
THOMAS DINGER	PERC V (AB	(A) LA DUSSELDORF	1978 RADAR	UK	RAD 7
HANS LAMPE	PERC SYN K(AB	(B) VIVA	1978 RADAR UK RAD10 STRAND GER 23626		
NIKOLAUS VAN RHEIN K (AB		(C) INDIVIDUELLOS	1980 TELDEC	GER 24524	
HARALD KONIETZKO	B (AB				
ANDREAS SCHELL	PNO (B				

LADY JUNE

LADY JUNE	V (A	(A) LINGUISTIC LEPROSY	1974 CAROLINE	UK	C1509
KEVIN AYERS	G B SYN(A				
BRIAN ENO	K G V(A	KIM SOLOMON	PNO (A	DAVID VORHAUS	(A	MARTHA	V (A
PIP PYLE	D (A	JAKOB KLAASE	PNO (A			

LAFAYETTE AFRO ROCK BAND

```
                                  (A) SOUL MAKOSSA          1973   MUSIDISC      FR    CV1269
                                  (B) MALIK                 19     AMERICA             30AM6137
```

DENNY LAINE

```
DENNY LAINE        G K V(ABC      (A) AAH LAINE             1973   WIZARD US 2190   UK   2001
PAUL McCARTNEY V B G D K(BC       (B) HOLLY DAYS           1976   CAPITOL US 11588  UK EMI781
LINDA McCARTNEY  K V  (B          (C) JAPANESE TEARS       1980   SCRATCH           UK   5001
JOHN MOORSHEAD      G   (A
STEVE THOMPSON      B   (A   MACEY McCREARY     V   (A   PHOEBE LAOB    V  (A   COLIN ALLEN    D  (A
JO JO LAINE         V   (C   STEVE HOLLY      D V  (C   BUDDY EMMONS   STEEL(C   THADIUS RICHARDS FLT(C
LAWRENCE JUBER      G   (C   GORDON SELLAR        (C   ANDY RICHARDS     (C   MIKE PIGGOTT      (C
HOWIE CASEY       SAX   (C   DENNY SEIWELL    D   (C   HENRY McCULLOUGH G  (C
```

DAVID LAFLAMME

```
DAVID LAFLAMME    V VLN(AB        (A) WHITE BIRD           1977 AMHERST     US       AMH 1007
MITCHELL FROOM K TPT VIBES(AB     (B) INSIDE OUT           1978 AMHERST     US       AMH 1012
JAMES RALSTON       G   (AB
DOUG KILMER         D   (AB   MICHAEL BAIRD     D   (B   DOMINIQUE DELLACROIX (AB   PETER MILIO    D  (AB
MITCHELL HOLMAN     B   (A    TOM MARKEN      D   (A   JEFF DAMBRAU    BANJO(A   ROGER GLENN    FLT (A
CARL TASSI       PERC   (A    GREG ADAMS      HRNS (A   MIC GILLETE    HRNS (A   EMILIO CASTILLO SAX(A
LENNY PICKETT     SAX   (A    STEVE KUPKA     SAX  (A
```

CORKY LAING

```
CORKY LAING      V D G(A         (A) MAKIN' IT ON THE STREET  1977   ELEKTRA      US    7E 1097
CLYDIE KING         V   (A
PETE CARR           G   (A    NEIL LARSEN     K   (A   HARVEY THOMPSON HRNS (A   RANDALL BRAMBLETT HRNS(A
VANETTA FIELDS      V   (A    TOMMY TALTON    G   (A   CHARLES ROSE   HRNS (A   FRANK VICARI   HRNS (A
SHIRLEY MATTHEWS    V   (A    CALVIN ARLINE   B   (A   RON EADES      HRNS (A   HARRISON CALLOWAY HRNS(A
MIKE MONTGOMERY     K   (     DONNY KRIETER   B   (   BOB KULICK     G   (    TUPPER LIENICE PNO   (
```

GREG LAKE

```
GREG LAKE         G V   (A       (A) GREG LAKE            1981 CHRYSALIS         CHR 1357
TOMMY EYRE          K   (A
BILL CUOMO          K   (A    GREG MATHIESON  K   (A   GARY MOORE     G   (A   STEVE LUKATHER G  (A
DEAN PARKS          G   (A    SNUFFY WALDEN   G   (A   TRISTIAN MARGETTS   B (A   DAVID HUNGATE  B  (A
TED McKENNA         D   (A    MICHAEL GILES   D   (A   JODE LEIGH     D   (A   JEFF PORCARO   D  (A
CLARENCE CLEMONS  SAX   (A    WILLIE COCHRANE PIPES(A   DAVID MILNER   PIPES(A
```

LAKE

```
JAMES HOPKINS-HARRISON V(ABC     (A) LAKE               1976   CBS US 34763   UK 81661
DEITER AHRENDT    D V  (ABC      (B) LAKE 2             1978   CBS US 35289   UK 82651
GEOFF PEACEY     G K V(ABC       (C) PARADISE ISLAND    1979   CBS US 35817   UK 83480
ALEX CONTI       G V  (ABC       (D) OUCH               1980   CBS US 37083      84310
CARL WILSON          (B
DETLEF PETERSEN   K V  (BC  MARTIN TIEFENSEE B  (ABC   OTTO WAALKEN   CONGA(C   JAMES WILLIAM GUERCIO(B
```

LAKESIDE

```
FRED ALEXANDER      D   (C       (A) LAKESIDE            197  ABC           US    AB 999
NORMAN BEAVERS      K   (C       (B) SHOT OF LOVE        1979 RCA           UK    12937
MARVIN CRAIG        B   (C       (C) ROUGH RIDERS        1979 SOLAR US 3490  UK    13490
FRED LEWIS       PERC   (C       (D) FANTASTIC VOYAGE    1980 SOLAR US BXLI3720
TIEMEYER McCAIN  PERC V(C
MARK A WOOD       K V  (C   THOMAS SHELBY    V   (C   STEPHEN SHOCKLEY G K  (C   OTIS STOKES    K B GV(C
```

LAMB

```
BARBARA MAURITZ  G V K(ALL       (A) A SIGN OF CHANGE    1970   CBS    NL       63954
BOB SWANSON      G BAN(ALL       (B) CROSS BETWEEN       1971   WB     US       1920
BILL DOUGLASS       B   (AB      (C) BRING OUT THE SUN   1971   WB     US       1952
DAVID LITURIN    WIND SYN(A
WALTER RAPAPORT      (A    DIVA GOODFRIEND-KOVEN FLT(A   ED BOGAS     VLA  (ABC   ROBERT HUBBARD HRNS(A
DOUGLAS BLUMENSTOCK CELLO(A  TOM SALISBURY        (C   RICHARD SCLOSSER D   (C   MARK SPRINGER  G  (C
JOHN McFEE       STEEL(C   MICHAEL PRENDERGRASS G(C   ED JANG            (B   EDDIE LEE CHARLTON D(C
CLYDE FLOWERS       B   (C   WARREN GALE     TPT (C   DWIGHT HALL    TPT (C   MEL MARTIN     SAX (C
CHARLES PETERSON  SAX   (C   BILL ATTWOOD    TPT (BC   ELLEN DESSIER      (B   PATRICK GLEASON SYN(C
JOHN VIERA        SYN   (C   VINCE DELGRADO  TABLA (C   LAWRENCE DUCKLES   (B   LEONARD LASHER B  (C
MYRON MU          HRNS  (C   STEPHEN FURRE   TROM (C   DAVID HAYES    B   (BC   JERRY GARCIA      (B
STEVIE LANGE        V   (A   JUNIOR MARVIN   G   (A
```

KEVIN LAMB

```
KEVIN LAMB        G V   (A       (A) SAILIN' DOWN THE YEARS   1978 ARISTA US  AB 4166 UK SPART1026
STEVE GOULD         G   (A
MICK FEAT           B   (A   BILLY LIVSEY    K   (A   DAVID DOWLE    D   (A   RAY COOPER     PERC (A
ANDY SUMMERS        G   (A   B J COLE     STEEL(A   GEOFF DALY     SAX (A   CHRIS THOMPSON V  (A
```

DAVE LAMBERT

```
DAVE LAMBERT      G V   (A       (A) FRAMED             1979 POLYDOR  PD 1 6193 UK 2391  391
JOHN ENTWISTLE      B   (A
RICHARD BENNETT     K   (A   LEE SKLAR       B   (A   TOM HENSLEY    K   (A   LARRY BROWN    PERC(A
DENNY SEIWELL       D   (A   ROBBIE BUCHANAN PNO (A
```

LAMBRETTAS

```
JEZ BIRD          G V   (A       (A) BEAT BOYS IN THE JET AGE   1980 ROCKET US PIG 3257 UK  TRAIN 10
DOUG SANDERS      G V   (A       (A) BEAT BOYS IN THE JET AGE   1980 PHONOGRAM NL   6302 034
MARK ELLIS          B   (A       (B) AMBIENCE           1981 ROCKET UK TRAIN 14
PAUL WINCER      PERC   (A
DICK HANSON      HRNS   (A   PETE THOMS     HRNS (A   RONNIE ASPERY   HRNS(A   MARTIN DOBSON  HRNS (A
```

LAMBERT & NUTTYCOMBE

```
DENNIS LAMBERT   G V   (A        (A) AS YOU WILL        19   20TH CENT     US    415
CRAIG NUTTYCOMBE G V   (A
WADDY WACHTEL       G   (A   HOPPY HODGES    D   (A   PEGGY SANDVIG  K   (A   JOE LAMANNO    B  (A
GAIL LEVANT   HARP PERC(A    LEE ALLEN      SAX   (A   LINDSEY BUCKINGHAM G (A   DOMENIC TROIANO G(A
WILLIE WEEKS       BV   (A    JORGE CALDERON  V   (A   TESSIE COHEN   V   (A
```

ROBERT LAMM

```
ROBERT LAMM          (A         (A) SKINNY BOY         1975   CBS US 33095   UK 80359
TERRY KATH       G B   (A
ROSS SALOMONE       D   (A   JAMES VINCENT   G   (A   ALAN DE CARLO  G   (A   POINTER SISTERS V  (A
GUILLE GARCIA    PERC  (A   STRING SECTION      (A   WILLIAM COLLETTE WIND(A
```

LAMONT CRANSTON BAND

PAT HAYES	HCA (A	(A) LAMONT CRANSTON BAND	19	SHADOW	US	3346
LARRY HAYES	G V (A	(B) SPECIALS	19	SHADOW	US	3348
JIM NOVAK	D (E	(C) EL CEE NOTES	19	WATERHOUSE US		6
RICK O'DELL	SAX (E	(D) UP FROM THE ALLEY	19	WATERHOUSE US		10
JIM GREENWELL	SAX (E	(E) SHAKEDOWN	1981	WATERHOUSE US		15
TERRY GRANT	B (E					
CHARLIE BINGHAM	G (E	BRUCE McCABE	K V (E	STEVE KILBRIDE	K G (E	TOM HEINIG	B (E
DAVE SALISBURY	G (A	MIKE NELSON	TROM (E				

JACK LANCASTER

JACK LANCASTER	WIND (AB	(A) MARSCAPE	1976	RSO	US	3020 UK	2394 170
ROBIN LUMLEY	K (A	(B) WILD CONNECTIONS	1979	ACROBAT		UK	ACRO 2
RICK VAN DER LINDEN	K (B						
JOHN GOODSALL	G (A	SIMON JEFFES	KOTO (A	PERCY JONES	B (A	BERNIE FROST	V (A
PHIL COLLINS	D (A	MORRIS PERT	PERC (A	BARRY MORGAN	D (B		

ROBIN LANE & THE CHARTBUSTERS

ROBIN LANE	V (ABC	(A) 5 LIVE	EP	1980	WB	US MINI	3494
LEROY RADCLIFFE	G V (ABC	(B) ROBIN LANE & THE CHARTBUSTERS		1980	WB	EURO 56813 US	3424
ASA BREBNER	G V (ABC	(C) IMITATION LIFE		1981	WB	US	3537
SCOTT BAERENWALD	B V (ABC						
TIM JACKSON	D (ABC	PETER WOOD	K (C				

LANDSCAPE

JOHN WALTERS	WIND K(AB	(A) LANDSCAPE	1979	RCA	UK	PL 25248	RI 81 3034
RICHARD BURGESS	D (Ab	(B) FROM THE TEAROOMS OF MARS	1981	RCA	UK	PL 25328	RI 81 5003
ANDY(CAPT WHORLIX)PASK	B(AB	(C) MANHATTEN BOOGIE WOOGIE	1982	RCA	UK	LP 6037	
CHRIS HEATON	K(B						
PETER THOMAS	TROM (AB						

RONNIE LANE & SLIM CHANCE

RONNIE LANE	V B G(ALL	(A) ANYMORE FOR ANYMORE	1974	GM GML 1017 US +		UK 1024	
CHARLIE HART	VLN K(BC	(B) RONNIE LANE'S SLIM CHANCE	1975	ISLAND UK ILPS 9321 US A&M 3638			
BRIAN BELSHAW	B (C	(C) ONE FOR THE ROAD	1976	ISLAND UK ILPS 9366			
COLIN DAVY	D (C	(D) SEE ME	1979	GEM		UK GEM107	
STEVE SIMPSON	G K (BC						
RUAN O'LOCHLAINN	SAX (B	KEVIN WESTLAKE	G (A	KEN SLAVEN	FDL (A	GLEN LEFLEUR	D (B
BENNY GALLAGHER	G B ACC(A	BILLY LIVSEY	K (A	THE TANNERS	V (A	BRUCE ROWLAND	D (A
GRAHAM LYLE	G BAN MAND (A	STEVE BINGHAM	B (A	JIMMY JEWELL	SAX (A		

PETER LANG

PETER LANG	G V (ALL	(A) LYCURGUS	19	FLYING FISH	US	FF014	
JOHN BOBLETT	TROM (C	(B) THE THING AT THE NURSERY WINDOW	19	TAKOMA	US	1034	
MARK BRUNNER	TPT (C	(C) BACK TO THE WALL	1978	WATERHOUSE	US	7	
JEFF DAYTON	STEEL(C						
BRAD GRAPP	D (C	JAMES HAUCK	MARACAS (C	GARY LOPAC	B (C	JIM PRICE VLN	(C
TED UNSETH	SAX (C	PRUDENCE JOHNSON	V (C	TOM LIEBERMAN	V (C	TIM SPARKS	V (C

CLIVE LANGER & THE BOXES

CLIVE LANGER	G V (AB	(A) I WANT THE WHOLE WORLD	1978	RADAR	UK	RDR 2	
BUDGIE	B D (A	(B) SPLASH	1980	F BEAT	UK	XXLP2	
STEVE ALLEN	V (AB						
BETTE BRIGHT	V (AB	BEN BARSON	K (AB	JAMES ELLER	B (B	MARTIN HUGHES	D (B
RUMOUR BRASS	HRNS (B	ALAN WINSTANLEY	PROD (B	WILL STALLIBRASS	(B	IAN BROWDIE	(B
ALAN JONES	(B	PAUL RILEY	(B	ELVIS COSTELLO	(B		

HIP LANKCHAN

HIP LANKCHAN	G V (A	(A) I AM ON MY WAY	197	MCM	FR	900299
JIMMIE MILLER	G (A					
ERNEST GATEWOOD	B (A	TYRONE CENTURY	D (A			

LA PERVERSITA

HAMILTON BARCLAY	D V (A	(A) LA PERVERSITA	1979	INVISIBLE	FR	10005
JEANNE FOLY	V (A					
LAY JEAME	G V (A	HENRY KAISER	G (A	JACK KASPIER	V (A	MEDOR MADER	G B (A
MARTIN MESONIER	G (A	JOHN SINDLER	VLN (A	HECTOR ZAZU	PNO (A		

LARD FREE

GILBERT ARTMAN	D K (ABC	(A) LARD FREE	1973	VAMP	FR	VP 59500
PHILIPPE BOLLIET	SAX (A	(B) I'M AROUND ABOUT MIDNIGHT	1975	VAMP	FR	VP 59502
FRANCOIS MATIVET	G (A	(C) LARD FREE	1977	COBRA	FR	37007
HERVE EYHANI	B SYN(A					
RICHARD PINHAS	G SYN(B	JEAN JACQUES MIETTE	B (A	ALAIN AUDAT	SYN SAX(B	ANTOINE DUVERNET	WIND(B
XAVIER BAULLERET	G (C	YVES LANES	SYN (C	JEAN PIERRE THIRAUT	CLAR (C		

LARRY & THE MOVERS

LARRY	G V K(A	(A) THE BEST OF LARRY & THE MOVERS	1981	LINE	GER	5094
IAN CUSSICK	B V (A					
PETER	(A	WERNER BECKER	K (A	HANS UWE REINERS SAX (A		JOACHIM WITT	V (A

NEIL LARSEN

NEIL LARSEN	K (AB	(A) JUNGLE FEVER	1978	HORIZON	AMLJ733 +	3116
BUZZ FEITEN	G (AB	(B) HIGH GEAR	1979	HORIZON	738 +	3117
LARRY WILLIAMS	WIND (A					
RALPH MACDONALD	PERC (A	JERRY HEY	HRNS (A	WILLIE WEEKS	B (A	MICHAEL BRECKER	HRNS(AB
ANDY NEWMARK	D (A	RICKIE LEE JONES	V (B	ABRAHAM LABORIEL	B (B	LENNY CASTRO	V (B
STEVE GADD	D (B	TOMMY LIPUMA	PROD (B	PAULINHO DACOSTA	PERC (B	JOE FARRELL	FLT (B

LARSEN/ FEITEN BAND

NEIL LARSEN	K (A	(A) LARSEN/FEITEN BAND	1980	WB	nl 56849 US	BSK 3468
BUZZ FEITEN	G (A					
WILLIE WEEKS	B (A	KIM HUTCHCROFT	SAX (A	LENNY CASTRO	V PERC(A	ART RODRIGUEZ	D (A
BILL REICHENBACH	HRNS (A	LARRY WILLIAMS	SAX (A				

KIM LARSON

KIM LARSON	G V (A	(A) SITTING ON A TIME BOMB	1982	EPIC	US	37677
RICK BLAKEMORE	(A					
JOE DELIA	(A	ABE SPELLER	(A	DENNIS ESPANTMAN	(A		

NICOLETTE LARSON

NICOLETTE LARSON	V G PERC(ALL	(A) NICOLETTE	1978	WB	US BSK 3243	UK	K56569	
BILL PAYNE	K (AC	(B) IN THE NICK OF TIME	1979	WB	US BSK 3370	UK	K56750	
JAMES BURTON	G (A	(C) RADIOLAND	1980	WB	US BSK 3502	UK	K56878	
BOB GLAUB	B (AC							

PAUL BARRERE G (AC HERB PEDERSEN V G (A RICK SCHLOSSER D (AC MARK JORDAN K (AC
DAVID KALISH G (A ANDREW LOVE SAX (A PLAS JOHNSON FLT (A TED TEMPLEMAN V (AC
JIM HORN HRNS (A CHUCK FINDLEY HRNS (A STEVE MADAIO HRNS (A VALERIE CARTER V (A
MIKE McDONALD V (AC LINDA RONSTADT V (AC KLAUS VOORMANN B (AC FRED TACKETT G (AC
ALBERT LEE MAND (AC PATRICK SIMMONS G (AC KEITH KNUDSEN D (C TIRAN PORTER B (C
JOHN McFEE G (C ANDREW KASTNER G (C DOUG LIVINGSTONE K (C MARK JORDAN K (C
BOBBY LAKIND PERC (C MAUREEN McDONALD V (C JERRY JUMONVILLE SAX (C GENE MEROS SAX (C
LEE THORNBURG TPT (C

D C LARUE

D C LARUE	(ALL	(A) CATHEDRALS	19	PYRAMID	US	9003
		(B) TEN DANCE	19	PYRAMID	US	9006
		(C) CONFESSIONS	19	CASABLANCA	US	7098
		(D) FORCES OF THE NIGHT	1980	CASABLANCA	US	7160
		(E) STAR BABY	1981	CASABLANCA	US	7247

LA SEINE

TOM SEUFERT G V (A (A) LIKE THE RIVER 1976 ARIOLA UK AAA752 US 50008
DON WHALEY B (A
TRIS IMBODEN D (A STEVE HAGUE K (A BOB EASTON G SYN (A MARK CREAMER V (A
LAURA CREAMER V (A

LASO

FRANK OWENS K (A (A) LASO 1977 MCA US 2247 UK MCF 2804
GORDON EDWARDS B (A
ALLEN SCHWARZBERG D (A GEORGE DEVENS VIBES(A EUGENE BIANCO HARP (A GERRY CHAMBERLAIN TROM(A
RAY CADLE G)A JOE BATAAN PNO (A ADRIAN ALBERT V (A MAERETHA STEWART V (A
HILDA HARRIS V (A JIM MAELEN CONGA (A PETER QUINTERO CONGA(A BOB PORCELLI SAX (A
LOU MARINI WIND (A LEW SOLOFF TPT (A VICTOR PAZ TPT (A BARRY ROGERS TROM (A
LOUIE DEVIS B (A JULIAN LLANOS V (A JOCELYN SHAW V (A BIG B V (A

LAST

JOE NOLTE G V (A (A) L A EXPLOSION 1979 BOMP US 4004 LONDON UK SHZ8540
MIKE NOLTE V (A
DAVID NOLTE B V (A VITUS MATARE K FLT (A JACK REYNOLDS D (A

LAST NIKEL

LENNY McDANIEL B V (A (A) THE LAST NIKEL 19 MAINSTREAM US 6122
WALLY McDANIEL K (A
ROGER BERTRAND G (A MIKE SCORSONE SAX (A GORDON SCHUMERT TPT (A CLAY MUSACCHIA TROM(A
JERRY ROUSELLE D (A

LAST TOUCH

LADIES OF GREY 1981 ZILCH RIEN 3

THE LAST POETS

ALAFIA PUDIM	V (	THE LAST POETS	1970	DOUGLAS	US	30811
OMAR BEN HASSEN	V (	THIS IS MADNESS	1971	DOUGLAS UK 69012	US	30583
NILIJAH	PERC (	CHASTISEMENT	1972	BLUE THUMB	US	539
ABIO DUN OYEWOLE	V (	RIGHT ON	19	JUGGERNAUT	US	8802
SULIAMAN EL HADI	V (	THE REVOLUTION WILL NOT BE TELEVISED	197			
		JAZZOETRY	197			
		DELIGHTS OF THE GARDEN	19	CASABLANCA	US	7501

LAST WORDS

JOHNNY IOMBARDO V (A (A) LAST WORDS 1968 ATCO US SD 33235
MIKE BYRNES G (A
STEVE SECHAK K (A RICKY COOK D (A

LAST WORDS (2)

MALCOLM BAXTER V (A (A) THE LAST WORDS 1980 ARMAGEDDON UK ARM2
ANDY GROOME G (A
JOHN DUNN D (A RICKY LEIGH KENDALL B (A STEVE BERESFORD K (A DICK NIGHTDOCTOR SAX(A

LATE SHOW

BILL CLIFT G V (A (A) SNAP 1979 DECCA UK TXS134
DAVE HEAD G V (A
MIKE JELLY G V VLN(A TIM JOYCE B V (A NIX F PLONK K (A BRUIZER CLIVE (A
DON WELLER SAX (A GEORGE CHISHOLM TPT (A MALCOLM GRIFFITHS TROM(A ALAN PRICE G (

LAUGHING CLOWNS

ROBERT FARRELL SAX (A (A) LAUGHING CLOWNS 1980 MISSING LINK AUS MLB001
DAN WALLACE-CRABBE K (A
BEN WALLACE-CRABBE B (A JEFFREY WEGENER D PER(A EDMUND KUEPPER G V (A

LAUGHING HANDS

(A) DOG PHOTOS 1980 ADHESIVE UK 2

LAURIE & THE SIGHS

LAURIE BEECHMAN V (A (A) LAURIE & THE SIGHS 1980 ATLANTIC US 19268 GER 50706
TONY SALINAS G (A
DAVID WOFFORF B (A DEMO RAY AGCAOLI D (A DEREK FOX K (A

LATIMORE

BENNY LATIMORE	PNO (ABC	(A) LATIMORE	1974	PRESIDENT UK 1058	GLADES	US6502
FREDDIE SCOTT	D (A	(B) IT AIN'T WHERE YOU BEEN	1977	TK UK XL14034	GLADES	US7509
VAN OLANDER	D (A	(C) LATIMORE 3	1977	PRESIDENT UK 1065	GLADES	US7505
BOBBY RADELOFF	D (A	(D) MORE MORE MORE	19		GLADES	US6503
BETTY WRIGHT	V (A	(E) DIG A LITTLE DEEPER	19		GLADES	US7515
MIKE LEWIS	FLT (A					

RON BOGDON B (A GWEN McCRAE V (A AL KOOPER K (A JOEY MURCIA G (A
GEORGE McCRAE V (A

LAUGHING DOGS

MOE POTTS D V (A (A) LAUGHING DOGS 1979 CBS 36033 UK 83807
RONNIE CARLE B HCA V(A (B) LAUGHING DOGS MEET THEIR MAKER 1980 CBS 36429 UK 84328
CARTER CATHCART K G V(A
JAMES LEONARD G V (A

LAVA

    THOMAS KARRENBACH   K V (A   (A) TEARS ARE GOING HOME   1973   BRAIN GER 1031
    STEFAN OSTERTAG   G V (A
    JURGEN KRAAZ G B FLT B K(A CHRISTIAN OSTERTAG B   (A   ARCHER WEAVER D HCA V(A   PETER MOSES   PERC(A
LAVA (2)

    TOR VISTER   V   (A   (A) CRUSIN'   1981 POLDOR 2382 120
    ROLF GRAF   B   (A
    SIGURD KOHN   SAX (A   MARCUS MILLER   G   (A   PER HILLESTAD   PERC (A   TERJE BAKKO   V (A
    SIDSEL ENDRESEN   V   (A   JAN ERIK AASLAND V (A   PER KALSTAD   K (A   SVEIN DAG HAUGE G (A
    NINA ASKELAND   V   (A
LAVENDER HILL MOB

    NICKY CRIGENO   V B (A   (A) LAVENDER HILL MOB   1977   UA UK UAS30043
    RONNY JONES   G V (A
    GERRY HARDY   V WIND(A HECTOR JACOB   G V (A   CHUCK CHANDLER K V (A   VITO FIORY   D (A
BETTY LAVETTE

    BETTY LAVETTE   V   (A   (A) EASIER TO SAY (THAN DO)   1980 CHARLY UK CTD107
LAW

    TOM POOL   D   (A   (A) LAW   1975 GRC US GA10017
    RONNIE LEE CUNNINGHAM K V(AB   (B) BREAKIN' IT   1977 MCA US 2240   UK   2785
    STEVE ACKER   G V (AB   (C) HOLD ON TO IT   1978 MCA US 2306
    JOHN McIVERS   B   (AB
    JOE LALA   PERC (A   ALBHY GALUTEN   SYN (A   MEMPHIS HRNS   (A   STEVE LAWRENCE D V (B
    ROY KENNER   V   (B   JOEY MURCIA   G   (B   MIAMI HRNS   (B   BILL COLANTONE PERC(B
    FLACO PADRON   PERC (B
DOMINIQUE LAWARLEE

    DOMINIQUE LAWARLEE K   (ALL   (A) INFINITUDES   197 WALRUS WLS001
    MARC HOLLANDER   PNO (C   (B) LE CHOIX DU TITRE EST UN FAUX 1977 WALRUS WLS003
    CHARLES LOOS   PNO (C   (C) TRACES   1978 WALRUS WLS004
                                     (D) BRINS D'HERBE   1978 WALRUS WLS005
                                     (E) VIS A VIS   1979 WALRUS WLS006
CLAIRE LAWRENCE

    CLAIRE LAWRENCE   V WIND(A   (A) LEAVING YOU FREE   1973   HAIDA CAN HL5103
    JIM GORDON   D   (A
    MAX BENNETT   B   (A   LARRY CARLTON   G   (A   DEAN PARKS   G   (A   BRETT WADE   G (A
    CLARENCE McDONALD PNO   (A   RON TUTT   D   (A   LOUIS SHELTON   G   (A   KATHY STACK   V (A
    STEPHANIE SPRUILL V   (A   BEVERLEY JACKSON V   (A   LISA ROBERTS   V   (A   STRING SECTION (A
LAWLER & COBB

                                     (A) MEN FROM NOWHERE   1981 ASYLUM US 279
BILLY LAWRIE

    BILLY LAWRIE   V   (A   (A) SHIP IMAGINATION   1973 RCA UK SF8395
    RONNIE LEAHY   K   (A
    JIMMY McCULLOCH   G   (A   COLIN ALLEN   D   (A   TIM RENWICK   G   (A   STEVE THOMPSON B (A
    WILLIE WILSON   D   (A   BRUCE THOMAS   B   (A   GARY OSBORNE   G V (A   PAUL VIGRASS V (A
    ROGER BALL   HRNS (A MALCOLM DUNCAN   HRNS (A   RAY COOPER   PERC (A   LULU   V (A
    LIZA STRIKE   V   (A   MAGGIE BELL   V   (A   KIM GARDNER   B   (A   KENNY JONES   D (A
    BARRY CLARKE   G   (A   LUIS JARDIM   PERC (A   JUANITA FRANKLIN V (A   PETER WOOD   K (A
    LES HARVEY   G   (A   JOHN COLEMAN   PNO (A   JO PARTRIDGE   G   (A
RONNIE LAWS

    RONNIE LAWS   G   (ALL   (A) PRESSURE SENSITIVE   1975 BLUENOTE 452   UK 76 UAG20002
    MARLOW THE MAGICIAN G   (B   (B) FEVER   1976 UA   US 628   UAG20007
    NATHANIEL PHILLIPS B   (BD   (C) FLAME   1978 UA   UAG30204
    BRUCE CARTER   D   (B   (D) EVERY GENERATION   1980 LIBERTY US LT 1001 UK UAG30289
    DONALD HEPBURN   K   (B
    MICHAEL HEPBURN   K   (B   BRUCE SMITH   PERC (B   BOBBY LYLE   K   (BD   STEVE GUITIERREZ D(AB
    WILTON FELDER   B   (AB   TONY BEN   CONGA(B   STRING SECTION   (BD   ELOISE LAWS   V (D
    ALEXANDRA BROWN   V   (D   JEAN THOMPSON   V   (D   MIKE HOWARD   V   (D   DOROTHY ASHBY HARP(D
    PAT KELLY   G   (D   BARNABY FINCH   SYN (D   LARRY DUNN   (CD   RONNIE FOSTER   (D
    HUBERT LAWS   (D   PATRICE RUSHEN   (D   JOE SAMPLE   K   (AD   PHILIP BAILEY   (C
    ROLAND BAUTISTA   (AC   JOHN W ROWIN   G   (A   CLINT MOSLEY   B   (A   MICHAEL WILLARS D(A
    MIKE CAVANAUGH   K   (A   JERRY PETERS   K   (A   JOE CLAYTON   PERC (A
LAZARUS

    SHELBY SINGLETON   (A   (A) LAZARUS   1970 AMAZON   US   AM 1001
    STEVE McNICOL   (A   (A) LAZARUS   197   BEARSVILLE US   2004
    THOMAS BOMBACI   (A   (B) FOOLS PARADISE   1974 BEARSVILLE US   2135
    RAYMOND CICHON   (A
    RONALD STABLINI   (A   TONY BERTOLLOTTI   (
KEN LAZARUS

    KEN LAZARUS   V   (ALL   REGGAE SCORCHERS   1970 LONDON   UK   ZGJ102
                                     REGGAE GREAT HITS VOL1   1970 LONDON   UK   ZGJ107
                                     REGGAE GREAT HITS VOL 2   1970 LONDON   UK   ZGJ108
LAZY RACER

    TIM RENWICK   G V (AB   (A) LAZY RACER   1979 A&M US 4768 UK AMLH64768
    HENRY SPINETTI   D   (AB   (B) FORMULA 2   1980 A&M US 4808 UK AMLH64808
    DAVE MARKEE   B   (A
    TIM GORMAN   V K (AB BILL LAMB   G V (AB   KELLY HARLAND   V   (AB PAT DONALDSON D (B
BERNIE LEADON & MICHAEL GEORGIADES

    BERNIE LEADON   G V BAN(A   (A) NATURAL PROGRESSION   1977 ASYLUM US 7E1107   UK K53063
    MICHAEL GEORGIADES G V (A
    BRYAN GAROFALO   B   (A   DAVID KEMPER   D   (A   STEVE GOLDSTEIN K   (A   BOBBYE HALL   PERC(A
    IRVING AZOFF   V   (A   JOHN BANDINI BRENNAN G(A   ED SILVERS   V   (A   JOE SMITH   V (A
    BARON STEWART   V   (A
LEAFHOUND

                                     (A) GROWERS OF MUSHROOMS   1971 DECCA   UK   SKLR 5094
                                     (A) GROWERS OF MUSHROOMS   1971 TELEFUNKEN GER   14604
LEAGUE OF GENTLEMEN

    ROBERT FRIPP   G   (A   (A) LEAGUE OF GENTLEMEN   1981 EG UK EGED9   GER 2315 215
    BARRY ANDREWS   K   (A   (A) LEAGUE OF GENTLEMEN   1981 POLYDOR   US   16317
    JOHNNY TOOBAD   D   (A
    SARAH LEE   B   (A

[329]

LEATHER COATED MINDS   L33

J J CALE	G	(A	(A) TRIP DOWN SUNSET STRIP	19	FONTANA UK 5412	VIVA US 36003

L33A
LEATHER NUN   L33A

		(A) SLOW DEATH (EP)	19	INDUSTRIAL	IR 0006

L34
LEAVES   L34

JIM PONS	B V	(AB	(A) HEY JOE	1966	MIRA US 3005 RI LINE GER 5144	
BILL RHEINHART		(A	(B) ALL THE GOOD THAT'S HAPPENING	1967	CAPITOL US	ST 2638
JOHN BECK	G V	(				
BOBBY ARLIN	G V	(	TOM RAY D (ROBERT REINER	(		

L34A
LENNIE LEBLANC   L34A

LENNIE LEBLANC	G V	(ALL	(A) LENNY LEBLANC	1976	BIG TREE US	89515
PETE CARR	G	(A	(B) HOUND DOG MAN	1977	BIG TREE US	76003
BUTCH LEADFORD	B	(A	(C) BREAKTHROUGH	1980	CAPITOL	
ROGER CLARK	D	(A				
EDDIE STRUZICK	V	(A	LAURA STRUZICK V (A HARVEY THOMPSON SAX (A JIMMY EVANS D (A			
RANDY McCORMICK	PNO	(A	STEVE HERBERT D (A			

L35
LEBLANC & CARR   L35

LENNIE LEBLANC	G V	(AB	(A) MIDNIGHT LIGHT	1978	BIG TREE US 89521	UK K50474
PETE CARR	G V	(AB	(B) LIVE FROM THE ATLANTIC STUDIOS	1978	BIG TREE US 003	
BUTCH LEADFORD	B	(A				
BOB WRAY	B	(A	RANDY McCORMICK K (A TIM HENSON K (A CLAYTON IVEY K (A			
ROBERT BYRNE	G	(A	RICK POWELL K (A STEVE NATHAN K (B LEON SHERRILL G (B			
THOM FLORA	K	(B	GARY BAKER B V (B			

L36
LED ZEPPELIN   L36

JIMMY PAGE	G	(ALL	(A) LED ZEPPELIN	1968	ATLANTIC US 8216	UK 588171
ROBERT PLANT	V HCA	(ALL	(A) LED ZEPPELIN	1971	ATLANTIC US 19126	UK K40031
JOHN BONHAM	D	(ALL	(B) LED ZEPPELIN 2	1969	ATLANTIC US 8236	UK 588198
JOHN PAUL JONES	B K	(ALL	(B) LED ZEPPELIN 2	1971	ATLANTIC US 19127	UK K40037
WITH			(C) LED ZEPPELIN 3	1970	ATLANTIC US 7201	UK2401002
VIRAM JASANI	TABLAS	(A	(C) LED ZEPPELIN 3	1971	ATLANTIC US 19128	UK K50002
SANDY DENNY	V	(D	(D) LED ZEPPELIN 4	1971	ATLANTIC US 7208	UK2401012
			(D) LED ZEPPELIN 4	1971	ATLANTIC	UK K50008
			(E) HOUSES OF THE HOLY	1973	ATLANTIC US 7255	UK K50014
			(F) PHYSICAL GRAFFITI	1975	SWANSONG US SS2 200	UK K89400
			(G) PRESENCE	1976	ATCO US 7255	
			(G) PRESENCE	1976	SWANSONG US SS 8416	UK K59402
			(H) THE SONG REMAINS THE SAME	1976	SWANSONG US SS2 201	UK K89402
			(I) LIVE	197	JOKER ITALY	SM3721
			(J) IN THROUGH THE OUT DOOR	1979	SWANSONG US 16002	UK K59410

L36A
ALBERT LEE   L36A

ALBERT LEE	V G K MAND	(A	(A) HIDING	1979	A&M US 4750 UK AMLH64750 NL 271
JOHN WARE	D	(A			
EMORY GORDY	B	(A	HANK DEVITO STEEL V (A GLEN D HARDIN PNO (A RICKY SKAGGS V FDL (A		
EMMYLOU HARRIS	V	(A	MICKEY RAPHAEL HCA (A BRIAN AHERN G (A DON EVERLY V (A		
PETE GAVIN	D	(A	DAVE PEACOCK B (A CHAS HODGES PNO (A BRUCE GARY D (A		
BUDDY EMMONS	STEEL	(A	GERRY CONWAY D (A PAT DONALDSON B (A JERRY JUMONVILLE HRNS (A		
RODNEY CROWELL	V	(A	DONIVAN COWART (A		

L37
ALVIN LEE   L37

ALVIN LEE	G V	(ALL	(A) ROAD TO FREEDOM	1973	CHRYSALIS UK 1054 US CBS 32729	
MYLON LEFEVRE	G V PERC	(A	(B) IN FLIGHT (DBL)	1974	CHRYSALIS UK 1069 US CBS 33187	
STEVE WINWOOD	K	(A	(C) PUMP IRON	1975	CHRYSALIS UK 1094 US CBS 33796	
JIM CAPALDI	D	(A	(D) LET IT ROCK	1978	CHRYSALIS UK 1190	
MICK HAWKSWORTH	B	(EF	(E) ROCKET FUEL	1978	POLYDOR UK 2344 103 RSO US 3033	
REBOP BAAH	PERC	(A	(F) RIDE ON	1979	POLYDOR UK 2310 678 RSO US 3049	
CHRIS STAINTON	K	(H	(G) FREE FALL	1980	AVATAR UK AALP5002	
MIKE PATTO	V	(A	(H) RX5	1981	ATLANTIC US 19306	
TIM HINKLEY	K	(ABC				
GEORGE HARRISON	G	(A	RON WOOD G B D (A MICK FLEETWOOD G (A PETER THOMS TROM (G			
ANDY STEIN	FDL	(A	IAN WALLACE D (ABC BOBBY BLACK STEEL (A BOZ BURRELL B (AC			
MEL COLLINS	SAX	(A	ALAN SPENNER B (B NEIL HUBBARD G (B DYAN BIRCH V (B			
FRANK COLLINS	V	(B	PADDY McHUGH V (B BRYSON GRAHAM D (C JACK LANCASTER HRNS (C			
HAROLD BURGON	K	(C	RONNIE LEAHY K (C STEVE THOMPSON B (C BROTHER JAMES PERC (C			
RON BERG	D	(C	ANDY PYLE B (C COLIN GIBSON B (C STEVE GOULD V G (GH			
MICK FEAT	B V	(GH	TOM COMPTON D PERC (EFGH DEREK AUSTIN K (GH AL KOOPER ORG (G			
RAPHAEL RAVENSCROFT	SAX	(G	BERNIE CLARKE K (E MICK WEAVER K (E			

L38
ARTHUR LEE   L38

ARTHUR LEE	G V	(A	(A) VINDICATOR	1972	A&M US 4356 UK AMLS64356
DON PONCHER	D	(A	(B) ARTHUR LEE	1981	BEGGARS BANQUET UK BEGA 26
CHARLES KARP	G	(A	(B) ARTHUR LEE	1981	LINE GER LLP5120
DAVID HULL	B	(A			
CRAIG TARWATER	G	(A	FRANK FAYAD B (A CLARENCE McDONALD K (A		

L39
BRENDA LEE   L39

BRENDA LEE	1960	DECCA US	74039	THATS ALL	1962	BRUNSWICK UK STA	8516
GRANDMA WHAT GREAT SONGS		BRUNSWICK UK LAT	8319	ALL ALONE AM I	1962	DECCA US	74370
" " "	"	DECCA US	78873	" " "	1962	DECCA US STA	8530
MISS DYNAMITE	196	BRUNSWICK UK LAT	8347	LOVE YOU	1963	ACE OF HEARTS UK AH59	
THIS IS BRENDA LEE	1961	BRUNSWICK UK LAT	8360	LET ME SING	1964	DECCA US	74439
" " "	1961	DECCA US	74082	" "	1964	DECCA US	8548
EMMOTIONS	1961	DECCA US	74104	BY REQUEST	1964	DECCA US	74509
" "	1961	BRUNSWICK UK LAT	8376	" " "	1964	DECCA US	8576
	1961	BRUNSWICK UK STA	3044	MERRY CHRISTMAS	1964	DECCA US	74583
ALL THE WAY	1961	DECCA US	74176	" " "	1964	BRUNSWICK UK STA	8590
" "	1961	BRUNSWICK UK LAT	8383	TOP TEEN HITS	1965	DECCA US	74626
" "	1961	BRUNSWICK UK STA	3048	" " "	1965	BRUNSWICK UK STA	8603
SINCERELY	1961	DECCA US	74216	VERSATILE	1965	DECCA US	74661
" "	1961	BRUNSWICK UK LAT	8396	" "	1965	BRUNSWICK UK STA	8614
" "	1961	BRUNSWICK UK STA	3056	TOO MANY RIVERS	1965	DECCA US	74684
" "	197	MCA US	477	" " "	1965	BRUNSWICK UK STA	8622
THAT'S ALL	1962	DECCA US	74326	BYE BYE BLUES	1966	DECCA US	74755
				" " "	1966	BRUNSWICK UK STA	8649

(CONTINUED)

10 GOLDEN YEARS	1966	DECCA	US	74757
" " "	19	MCA	US	107
COMING ON STRONG	1967	DECCA	US	74825
" " "	1967	BRUNSWICK	UK	8672
REFLECTIONS IN BLUE	1967	DECCA	US	74941
"	19	MCA	UK	MUPS 306
CALL ME BRENDA	196	MCA	UK	MUPS 321
GOOD LIFE	196	MCA	UK	MUPS 322
HERE'S BRENDA LEE	1967	VOCALION	US	VL 7 3795
LET IT BE ME	19	VOCALION	US	VL 7 3890
" " "	19	CORAL	US	CB 20044
FOR THE FIRST TIME	1968	MCA	UK	MUPS 332
" " "	196	DECCA US		74955
JOHNNY ONE TIME	1969	DECCA	US	75111
" " "	1970	MCA	UK	MUPS 396
" " "	1974	MCA	UK	MCF 2633
MEMPHIS PORTRAIT	1970	DECCA	US	75232
" " "	1971	MCA	UK	MUPS 423
" " "	1974	MCA	UK	MCF 2519
MISS DYNAMITE	1979	MCA	FR	414030

A WHOLE LOTTA	1972	MCA	UK	MUPS 460
" "	1974	MCA	UK	MCF 2660
BRENDA	197	MCA	US	305
"	1973	MCA	UK	MUPS 485
"	1974	MCA	UK	MCF 2507
BRENDA LEE STORY	1974	MCA	UK	MCDW 428
" " "	197	DECCA	US	74012
NEW SUNRISE	1974	MCA	US	373
"	1974	MCA	UK	MCF 2527
NOW	1975	MCA	US	433
"	1975	MCA	UK	MCF 2593
SINCERELY	1975	MCA	US	477
" "	1975	MCA	UK	MCF 2709
FUNNY HOW TIME SLIPS	1975	SOUNDS SUPERB	UK	90067
LITTLE MISS DYNAMITE	1976	MCA	UK	MCF 2729
LET IT BE ME	19	VOCALION	US	73840
L A SESSION	1977	MCA	UK	MCF 2783
"	1977	MCA	US	2233
LEGENDS OF ROCK (DBL)	19	CORAL	US	61141/2
LITTLE MISS DYNAMITE	1980	WARWICK	WW	5083

BYRON LEE   (ALL

SOUNDS OF JAMAICA	19	TOWER HALL	US	LP 006
REGGAE	19	TROJAN		TRLS 18
REGGAE SPLASH DOWN	19	TROJAN		TRL 28
REGGAE HOT COOL EASY	19	TROJAN		TRLS 40
REGGAE BLASH OFF	19	TROJAN		TBL 110
REGGAE FEVER '	1974	POLYDOR		2460 229
DISCO REGGAE	1975	MERCURY	US	SRMI 1063
MIDAS TOUCH	1975	DRAGON		DRLS 5006
& MIGHTY SPARROW	1976	DYNAMIC		DYLP 3002
THIS IS CARNIVAL	1976	DYNAMIC		DYLP 3006
REGGAE INTERNATIONAL	1976	DYNAMIC		DYLP 3008
ART OF MAS	1977	DYNAMIC		DYLS 1002
BYRON LEE & THE DRAGONAIRES	19	JAD	US	JAS 1004
MORE CARNIVAL	1978	DYNAMIC		DYLP 3012
CARNIVAL EXPERIENCE	1979	DYNAMIC		DYLP 3014
JAMAICA'S GOLDEN HITS VOL 1	1979	STATE		ETMP 14
JAMAICA'S GOLDEN HITS VOL 2	1979	STATE		ETMP 17
DANCE THE SKY	19	B M N		BLP 004
JUMP UP	19	ATCO	US	33 182
REGGAE BLAST OFF	1980	TROJAN	UK	110
SOUL SKA	1981	ECHO	UK	1001

FREDDY FINGERS LEE   (AB

(A) FREDDY FINGERS LEE	1978	CHARLY		CR 30160
(B) OL' ONE EYE IS BACK	1979	CHARLY		CR 30178

JOHN LEE	K B PERC (ABC	(A) STILL CAN'T SAY ENOUGH		1976 BLUENOTE US BNLA 701				
GERRY BROWN	D PERC(ABC	(B) MANGO SUNRISE		1976 BLUENOTE US BNLA 541 UK 20004				
PHILIP CATHERINE	G (B	(C) CHASER		1979 CBS US 36212				
EEF ALBERS	G (BC							

ERIC TAGG	K (B	JASPER VANT HOF	K (B	ROB FRANKEN	K (AB	MIKE MANDEL	K (B
WAH WAH WATSON	G (B	DARRYL THOMPSON	G (C	PALLE MIKKELBORG	TPT PERC(C	KENNETH KNUDSEN	K (C
BOBBY MALACH	SAX (C	REGGIE LUCAS	G (A	RAY GOMEZ	G (A	HUBERT EAVES	K (A
MTUME	V PERC (A	TAWATHA AGEE	V (A	RANDY BRECKER	HRNS (A	MICHAEL BRECKER	SAX(A
DAVID SANBORN	SAX (A	BARRY ROGERS	TROM (A	HAROLD WILLIAMS	K (A	IAN UNDERWOOD	SYN (A
DONALD SMITH	V (A	C P ALEXANDER	V (A	JON FADDIS	TPT (A	ERNIE WATTS	SAX (A
GARY BARTZ	SAX (A	RON CUBER	SAX (A				

RANDY LEE	V (A	(A) SOAKIN' WITH TEARS		1974 ELEKTRA US EKS 75081			
PETE DRAKE	STEEL(A						
LARRY SASSER	STEEL(A	JERRY CARRIGAN	D (A	PIG ROBBINS	PNO (A	JAMES M JOHNSON	G (A
DON TWEEDY	HRNS (A	GEORGE CUNNINGHAM	HRNS (A	WENDELLYN SUITS	V (A	TOMMY COGBILL	B (A
KENNY BUTTREY	D (A	EARL BALL	PNO (A	JIMMY COLVARD	G (A	BOB PHILLIPS	HRNS (A
LEA JANE BERINATI	V (A	GARY S PAXTON SINGERS	(A	HOYET HENRY	B (A	KEN MALONE	D (A
JACK SOLOMAN	G (A	BILLY SANFORD	G (A	LOUIS BROWN	HRNS (A	SHARON VAUGHN	V (A

ROBERT LEE	G V (A	(A) LEE RIDERS		1972 UA		UAS 29312	
MIKE O'CONNOR	K (A						
MATT PRESBY	G (A	MIKE REILLY	B V (A	ROY OTEMRO	D PERC G (A	B J COLE	STEEL (A

THOMAS LEER	V SYN G (A	(A) THE BRIDGE	1979 INDUSTRIAL UK 1R0007
ROBERT RENTAL	V G SYN B(A		

THOMAS LEER	V ANST (A	(A) CONTRADICTIONS	1982 CHERRY RED RED 26

JOHN LEES	(A	(A) A MAJOR FANCY		1973 HARVEST UK SHVL 811			
SKIP ALLEN	D (A	(A) A MAJOR FANCY		1977 HARVEST RI UK SHSM 2018			
ROD ARGENT	K (A						
ERIC STEWART	G (A	WALLY WALLER	B (A	KEVIN GODLEY	(A	GORDON EDWARDS	PNO(A
REX MORRISON	SAX (A						

MYLON LEFEVRE

```
MYLON LEFEVRE      G V  (ALL    (A) MYLON                           1971 ATLANITC          2400 104
PIERCEFEVRE             (CE     (A) MYLON                           197  COTILLION     US  SD  9026
AUBURN BURRELL     G   (AB      (B) OVER THE INFLUENCE              1972 CBS           US    31472
ALVIN LEE          G V (D       (C) PIERCE & MYLON LEFEVRE         1972 CANAAN        UK  CAS 9673
J P LAUZON         G   (B       (D) ROAD TO FREEDOM                1973 CHRYSALIS     UK  CHR 1054
MARTY SIMON        D   (B       (E) LEFEVRES GREATEST HITS         197  STARDAY       US  SD  3006
LESLIE WEST        G   (B       (F) WEAK AT THE KNEES              1977 WB US 3070    UK    K56407
DR JOHN            K   (B       (G) RUSTLER                        1978 WB US 3216
TINA BLOUNT        V   (B       (H) ROCK'N'ROLL RESURRECTION       1980 MERCURY       US      3799
TOM ROBB           B   (A
SHRILEY MATTHEWS   V   (A   CLYDIE KING       V   (A   ALLEN TOUSSAINT K   (B   BARRY BAILEY    G (AB
RENAY GARVIN       V   (A   LESTER LANGDALE   K   (B   RICHARD PENNIMAN V  (B   STEVE SANDERS   V (B
PAT CUMMINGS       V   (B   KIM VENABLE       D   (A   DEAN DAUGHTRY   K   (A   RON GRAYBEAL    B (A
MERRY CLAYTON      V   (A   VANETTA FIELDS    V   (A   ** FOR FULL LINE UP OF D SEE ALVIN LEE ENTRY
```

LEFT BANKE

```
RICK BRAND         G BAN(A      (A) WALK AWAY RENEE               1967 PHILIPS            SBL 7773
STEVE MARTIN       V   (AB      (A) WALK AWAY RENEE               1967 SMASH US (M)27088  (S) 67088
TOM FINN           B   (AB      (B) TOO                           1969 SMASH US           (S) 67113
MIKE BROWN         K   (A
GEORGE CAMERON     D   (AB  HARRY LOOKOSKY    PROD (A
```

LEGAL WEAPON

```
KAT                V   (A       (A) NO SORROW        (EP)         1981 ARSENAL       UK  LW68
PATRICIA           B V (A
CHARLIE VARTAHIAN  D   (A   BRIAN HANSEN      G   (A
```

JOHNNY LEGEND & THE SKULLCAPS

```
JOHNNY LEGEND          (A       (A) ROCKABILLY RUMBLE             1981 RONDELET      UK  ABOUT 1002
```

LEGEND

```
MICKEY JUPP        G K V(ALL     (A) LEGEND                        1969 BELL          UK  SBLL 115
NIGEL DUNBAR       D   (A        (A) LEGEND                        1969 BELL          US      6027
STEVE GEARE        B V (A        (B) RED BOOT ALBUM                1971 VERTIGO       UK  6360 019
CHRIS EAST         G V (A        (C) MOONSHINE                     1972 VERTIGO       UK  6360 063
MO WITHAM          G   (BCD      (D) MICKEY JUPPS LEGEND (COMP)    1978 STIFF         UK  GET2
JOHN BOBIN         B   (BCD
BILL FIFIELD       D   (B   BOB CLOUTER       D   (C   BARNEY JAMES   D   (    TIM RENWICK    G  (D
MICK MOODY         G   (D   COLIN GIBSON      B   (D   HENRY SPINETTI D   (D   JIMMY JEWELL   SAX (D
PETE SOLLEY        K   (D   GARY BROOKER      PNO (D   CHRIS COPPING  B   (D   B J WILSON     D  (D
GLEN LEFLEUR       D   (D
```

LEGOVER

```
RAPHAEL RAVENSCROFT WIND(A       (A) WAIT TILL NIGHTTIME           1978 SMACK         UK  SL1001
DAVID ULM          PERC V(A
LINDSAY SCOTT      VLN V (A   SEAN BYRNE       G V (A   DAVE ROSE      K   (A   MICKEY FEAT    B  (A
DEREK AUSTIN       K   (A    DELISLE HARPER    B   (A   PHIL CHEN      B   (A   THEODORE THUNDER D(A
GLEN LEFLEUR       D   (A    JOHN DENTITH      D V (A   BILL SKEAT     WIND (A  ALAN BOWN      TPT(A
GEORGE HOWDEN      TROM (A   MICK PACE   HCA   (A       JOHN WELLS     V   (A
```

LEGS DIAMOND

```
MIKE PRINCE        K V (A        (A) FIRE POWER                    1978 CREAM         US      1010
JEFF POOLE         D   (         (B) LEGS DIAMOND                  1978 MERCURY       US      1136
MICHAEL DIAMOND    B   (         (C) A DIAMOND IS A HARD ROCK      1979 MERCURY       US      1191
RICK SANFORD       V FLT(
ROGER ROMEO        G V (
```

PETER LEICH

```
PETER LEICH        G   (A        (A) JUMPT STREET                  1981 JAZZ HOUSE        7001
GEORGE McFETRIDGE  K   (A
NEIL SWOINSON      B   (A   TERRY CLARKE      D   (A
```

LEINEMANN

```
GOTTFRIED BOTTGER  K   (ALL      (A) LEINEMANN'S HONKY TONK        1971 BASF     GER      060
JORN SEELENMEYER   G BAN V(ALL   (B) PIANO SKIFFLE ROCK            1972 PHILIPS  GER  630 5141
JURGEN BAHRS       G V HCA(ALL   (C) LAST TRAIN TO SAN FERNANDO    1973 PHILIPS  GER  630 5185
ULRICH SALM        B   (ALL      (D) LONNIE DONEGAN MEETS LEINEMANN 1974 PHILIPS GER  630 5227
ULF KRUGER         PERC (ALL     (E) DAS IST LEINEMANN             1975 PHILIPS  GER  630 5224
LONNIE DONEGAN     G V (D
PETER HESSLEIN     G   (D   BERRY SAARLOUIS   G V (D   BOLLE BURMEISTER G (E   JURGEN MAASS   G(E
WILLIAM SIMPSON    G   (E   FRANK REINKE      G   (E   KARL ALLOUT    G   (E   DIETER ARENDT  D  (E
WOLF SCHMIDTZ          (D   LORENZ WESTPHAL   VLN V(DE  BARRY REEVES   D   (D   CHRIS HERRMANN HRN(D
```

ANDY LEIGH

```
ANDY LEIGH B V G K PERC(A        (A) MAGICIAN                      1970 POLYDOR       UK  2343 034
BRYN HAWORTH       G   (A        (A) MAGICIAN                      197  SIRE          US  SES97025
KEVIN WESTLAKE     D V (A
REG KING           K   V(A   GORDON JACKSON SITAR(A   GARY FARR      HCA G(A   MIKE KELLIE    D  (A
BRIAN GODDING      G·  (A    TONY PRIESTLAND WIND(A   GARY WRIGHT    K   (A
```

LEMON KITTENS

```
KARL BLAKE         G V (A        (A) WE BUY A HAMMER FOR DADDY     1980 UNITED DAIRIES UK UD02
DANIELLE DAX       SAX (A
MIKE BARNES        D   (A   IAN STURGESS      B   (A
```

JO LEMAIRE & FLOUZE

```
JO LEMAIRE         V   (ALL      (A) JO LEMAIRE & FLOUZE          1979 ROCKET UK TRAIN 11
PHILIPPE DEPREUX   D   (AB       (A) JO LEMAIRE & FLOUZE          1979 VERTIGO  EURO 9198 448
DANIEL FRANCOIS    G   (AB       (B) PRECIOUS TIME                1980 VERTIGO  EURO 6299 102
ATTILIO BORTOLIN   C+AR G(A
GIOVANNE BORTOLIN K SAX SYN(AB MARC SANTKIN    B(A   ALAIN PIRE     G   (B   FERDINAND PHILIPPOT B(B
MARC HEROUET           (A   PETRICK GERARD          (A   OSCAR DENAYER      (A   WINNY NUYENS   (A
```

LEMON PIPERS

```
BILL ALBAUGH       D   (A        (A) GREEN TAMBOURINE             1968 BUDDAH        UK  2349 006
REG NAVE           ORG (A        (B) JUNGLE MARMALADE             1968 BUDDAH        US  BDS 5016
BILL BARTLETT      G   (A
STEVE WALMSLEY     B   (A   IVAN BROWNE  G V (A   PAUL LENKA       PROD (A
```

LENINGRAD SANDWICH

```
MIKE LENINGRAD     V   (A        (A) GO EAST                      1980 UP                3001
JOHNNY LENINGRAD   G   (A
D LENINGRAD        B   (A   CHARLIE HONGKOMG       D   (A
```

CLAUDIA LENNEAR

CLAUDIA LENNEAR	V	(A		(A) PHEW			1973 WB	US BS2654	UK	K 46204	
RY COODER	G	(A									
JOHN CRAVIOTTO	D	(A	JIM DICKINSON	G K (A	CHARLES GRIMES	G	(A	MILT HOLLAND	PERC	(A	
MIKE UTLEY	K	(A	DICK HYDE	TROM (A	JIM KELTNER	D	(A	RICK LITTLEFIELD	G	(A	
LEW McCREARY	TROM	(A	SPOONER OLDHAM	K (A	WILLIAM SMITH	K	(A	ARTHUR ADAMS	G	(A	
HAROLD BATTISTE JR	SAX	(A	TESSIE CALDERON	CONGA (A	GENE CIPRIANO	SAX	(A	MARLINE GREENE	G	(A	
PAUL HUBINON	TPT	(A	WARREN LUENING JR	TPT (A	DON MENZA	WIND	(A	CHUCK RAINEY	B	(A	
ALLEN TOUSSAINT	K V	(A									

JOHN LENNON & YOKO ONO

JOHN LENNON	G K V	(ALL	(A) TWO VIRGINS	1968	APPLE	US 5001	UK SAPCOR 2
YOKO ONO	V WIND	(ALL?	(B) LIFE WITH THE LIONS	1969	APPLE	US 3357	UK ZAPPLE 01
KLAUS VOORMANN	B	(DEFHJNO	(C) WEDDING ALBUM	1969	APPLE	US 3361	UK SAPCOR 11
STEVE BRENDELL	B	(H	(D) LIVE PEACE IN TORONTO	1969	APPLE	US 3362	UK CORE 2001
ALAN WHITE	D	(DEFHJ	(E) PLASTIC ONO BAND	1970	APPLE	US 3372	UK SAPCOR 17
GEORGE HARRISON	G	(HJ	(F) PLASTIC ONO BAND	1971	APPLE		UK PCS 7124
NICKY HOPKINS	K	(HJN	(H) IMAGINE	1971	APPLE	US 3379	UK PAS 10004
TED TURNER	G	(H	(J) SOMETIME IN NEW YORK CITY	1972	APPLE	US 3392	UK PCSP 7161
ROD LINTON	G	(H	(K) MIND GAMES	1973	APPLE	US 3414	UK PCS 7165
JOSE FELICIANO	G	(O	(K) MIND GAMES	1980	MFP		UK 50509
JOHN TOUT		(H	(L) APPROXIMATELY INFINITE UNIVERSE	1973	APPLE		UK SAPD01001
JIM KELTNER	D	(HJKNO	(M) FEELING THE SPACE	1973	APPLE		UK SAPCOR 26
JOHN BARHAM	K	(H	(N) WALLS & BRIDGES	1974	APPLE	US 3416	UK PCTC 253
JIM GORDON	D	(H	(O) ROCK'ROLL	1975	APPLE	US 3419	UK PCS 7169
LEON RUSSELL	K	(O	(O) ROCK'ROLL	1975	APPLE	GER 05834	
KING CURTIS	SAX	(H	( ) SINGS ROCK'ROLL (ROOTS)	1975	ADAM	US 8018	
TOM EVANS	G	(H	(P) SHAVED FISH	1975	APPLE	US 3421	UK PCS 7173
JOEY MOLLAND	G	(H	(Q) DOUBLE FANTASY	1980	GEFFEN	US 2001	UK K 99131
NINO TEMPO	SAX	(O	( ) BOX SET(8 LP SET)(DHEKNOJP)	1981	PARLOPHONE		UK JLB8
MIKE PINDER	PERC	(H					

KEN ASCHER	K	(KNO	GORDON EDWARDS	B	(NO	RICK MAROTTA	D	(K	MICHAEL BRECKER	SAX(K
SNEAKY PETE	STEEL	(K	JESSE ED DAVIS	G	(NO	ERIC CLAPTON	G	(DJ	RINGO STARR	D (EF
JULIAN LENNON	D	(N	FRANK ZAPPA	G V	(J	MARK VOLMAN	V	(J	HOWARD KAYLAN	V (J
JIM PONS	B V	(J	STAN BRONSTEIN	SAX	(JL	DON PRESTON	SYN	(J	RICHARD FRANK	D (JL
IAN UNDERWOOD	WIND K V	(J	BOB HARRIS	K V	(J	ADAM IPPOLITO	K	(JL	WAYNE GABRIEL	G (JL
BOBBY KEYS	SAX	(JNO	GARY VAN SCYOC	B	(JL	AYNSLEY DUNBAR	D	(J	BILLY PRESTON	K (JE
KEITH MOON	D	(J	JOHN LA BOSCA	PNO	(J	ARTHUR JENKINS	PERC	(NO	EDDIE MOTTAU	G (NO
ELTON JOHN	K V	(N	LORI BURTON	V	(N	MAY PANG	V	(N	HARRY NILSSON	V (N
STEVE MADAIO	HRNS	(N	HOWARD JOHNSON	HRNS	(N	RON APREA	HRNS	(N	FRANK VICARI	HRNS(N
DAVID SPINOZZA	G	(K	PHIL SPECTOR	PNO	(E	DENNIS MOROUSE	HRNS	(O	FRANK VICARI	HRNS(O
PETER JAMESON		(O	JOE TEMTERLEY		(O	STEVE CROPPER	G	(O	HAL BLAINE	D (O
JEFF BARRY		(O	BARRY MANN		(O	EARL SLICK	G	(Q	TONY LEVIN	B (Q
ANDY NEWMARK	D	(Q	ED WALSH	K	(Q	CASSANDRA WOOTEN	V	(Q	JACK ERIC TROYER	V (Q
ROBERT GREENRIDGE	PERC	(Q	RANDY STEIN	CONC	(Q	GRANT HUNGERFORD	HRNS	(Q	SELDON POWELL	HRNS (Q
ROGER ROSENBERG	HRNS	(Q	RONALD TOOLEY	HRNS	(Q	HUGH McCRACKEN	G	(Q	GEORGE SMALL	K (Q
ARTHUR JENKINS	PERC	(Q	MICHAELLE SIMPSON	V	(Q	CHERYL MASON	V	(Q	BENNY CUMMINGS SINGERS	V(Q
MATTHEW CUNNINGHAM	DULC	(Q	HOWARD JOHNSON	HRNS	(Q	JOHN PARRAN	HRNS	(Q	GEORGE OPALISKY	HRNS(Q
DAVID TOFANI	HRNS	(Q								

LENNY & SQUIGGY

	(A) LENNY & THE SQUIGTONES	1980	CASABLANCA	UK	7149

J B LENOIR

J B LENOIR	G V	(ALL	(A) CRUSADE	1970	POLYDOR	UK	2482 014	
ALEX ATKINS	SAX	(BC	(B) NATURAL MAN	19	CHESS	US	410	
ERNEST COTTON	SAX	(BC	(C) BLUESMASTER	1976	CHESS		2A CMB208	
JOE MONTGOMERY	PNO	(BC	(D) ALABAMA BLUES	1979	L+R		42 001	
LORENZO SMITH	SAX	(BC	(E) DOWN IN MISSISSIPPI	1980	L+R		42 012	
ALFRED WALLACE	D	(BCF	(F) THE TAY MAY CLUB	1980	FLYRIGHT	UK	FLY 564	
WILLIE DIXON	B	(ABCDE						
FRED BELOW	D	(DAE	LEROY FOSTER	G	(BC	J T BROWN	SAX (F	AL GAVIN	D (BC
SUNNYLAND SLIM	PNO	(BCF						

KLAUS LENZ BAND

KLAUS LENZ		(A) WIEGENLIED	1978	VINYL	UK VS001

DEKE LEONARD

DEKE LEONARD	G K V	(ALL	(A) ICEBERG	1973	UA	US LA150 UK	UAG 29464
MARTIN RUSHANT	PROD V	(C	(A) ICEBERG	1980	LIBERTY ROCKFILE UK	LBR 1042	
MARTIN ACE	B	(ABC	(B) KAMIKAZE	1974	UA	US 306 UK	UAG 29544
DAVE CHARLES PROD	D V	(ABC	(C) BEFORE YOUR VERY EYES	1981	UA		UAG 30240
MICKY JONES	G	(AB					

PAUL BURTON	B V	(A	VICKY SILVER	V	(C	DOREEN CHANTER	V	(C	KENNY MOORE	V (C
TOMMY RILEY	D	(AB	BEAU ADAMS	D	(A	RICHARD TREECE	G	(A	DAVE PHILIPS	VLN (A
BRIAN BREEZE	G	(B	KEITH HODGE		(B	LINCOLN CARR	B G	(B	KEN WHALEY	B (B
TERRY WILLIAMS	D V	(BC	BYRON BERLINE	FDL	(AB	BILLY HAYNES	V	(C	JAN STEVENS	(C
VIRGINIA PECK	V	(C	JOHN McKENZIE	B	(C	BILLY BREMNER	V	(C	MALCOLM MORLEY	K V(C
ANTON MATTHEWS	V	(C	DAVE EDMUNDS	V	(C	RON FRANCOIS	B	(C	CHRIS PARREN	K (C
LENNY MACALUSO	G	(C	CHRIS MERCER	SAX	(C	RON ASPERY	SAX	(C	MARTIN DROVER	TPT (C

LEOPARD

	(A) KANSAS CITY SLICKERS	1978	MOON	IMP

LE ORME

ANTONIO PAGLIUCA	K	(ABCDEFGHJ	(A) COLLAGE	1971	PHILIPS	6323 007
ALDO TAGLIAPIETRA	B V G	(ABCDEFGHJ	(B) UOMO DI PEZZA	1972	PHILIPS	6323 013
MIKI DEI ROSSI	PERC	(ABCDEFGHJ	(C) FELONA & SERONA	1973	PHILIPS	6323 023
GERMANO SERAFIN	G	(GHJ	(C) FELONA & SERONA	1973	CHARISMA	CAS 1072
TOLO MORTON	G V	(G	(D) IN CONCERT	1974	PHILIPS	6323 028
			(E) CONTRAPPUNTI	1974	PHILIPS	6323 035
			(F) BEYOND LENG	1975	COSMOS	PILP 9008
			(G) SMOGMAGICA	1975	PHILIPS	6323 041
			(H) VERITA NASCOSTE	1976	PHILIPS	6323 045
			(J) STORIA O LEGGANDA	1977	PHILIPS	6323 052
			(K) FLORIAN	1979	PHILIPS	6323 086
			(L) PICCOLA RAPSODIE DELL APE	1980	PHILIPS	6323 102

LE PAMPLEMOUSSE

W MICHAEL LEWIS	K	(AB	(A) LE SPANK	1978	PYE	NSPL28244
LAURIN RINDER	D V	(AB	(B) SWEET MAGIC	1978	AV	AVLP 501
MORTONETTE JENKINS	V(B		(C) PLANET OF LOVE	1980	AV	6080
DAVE WILLIAMS	B	(AB				

GIL KARSON   B   (A   SHIRLEY JONES   V   (A   BRENDA JONES   V (A   VALORIE JONES   V (A
DOUG RICHARDSON SAX (AB   HARRY KIM   TPT (AB   JEFF SIGMAN   B (B   DAVID STOUT   TROM (A
ALEX BROWN   V   (B   PATTI HALL   V   (B

LE ROUX

JEFF POLLARD	G V	(ABC	(A) LOUISIANA'S LE ROUX	1978	CAPITOL	11734
LEON MEDICA	B	(ABC	(B) KEEP THE FIRE BURNIN'	1979	CAPITOL	11926
DAVID PETERS	B	(ABC	(C) UP	1980	CAPITOL	12092
BOBBY CAMPO	D V	(ABC				
TONY HABELDON	G	(ABC	RON RODDY K (ABC			

MIKE LESLEY

MIKE LESLEY			(A) MIKE LESLEY	1976	BIG TREE	89516

SUNNY LESLIE

SUNNY LESLIE	V	(A	(A) DOCTORS ORDERS	1974	CBS	80219

LESLIE, KELLY & JOHN FORD COLEY

LESLIE BULKIN	V	(A	(A) LESLIE, KELLY & JOHN FORD COLEY	1981	A&M UK	AMLH 64841
KELLY BULKIN	V	(A				
JOHN FORD COLEY	V K	(A	VAN DUNSON (A HARVEY MASON D (A PAULINHO DACOSTA PERC(A			
DASH CROFTS	V	(A	DAVID FOSTER K (A STEVE LUKATHER G (A JEREMY LUBBOCK STR HRN(A			

LES VARIATIONS

ROBERT FITOUSSI	G V	(A	(A) CAFE DE PARIS	1975	BUDDAH	BDS5625
JACQUES GRANDE	B	(A	( ) TAKE IT OR LEAVE IT	1974	PATHE FR	064 12628
JACKY BITTON	D PERC V	(A	(B) MOROCCAN ROLL	1974	BUDDAH	BDS5601
MARC TOBALY	G V	(A				
MAURICE MAIMOUN	VLN	(A	JIM MORRIS K V (A PATRICK ADAMS STRINGS (A JIM MAELEN PERC (A			
MICHAEL MONTGOMERY	K	(A	PHIL BATES (A GARY DORN (A MICHAEL WENDROFF V (A			

LEVI & THE RIPCORDS

LEVI DEXTER	V	(A	(A) CAT FIGHT (EP)	1980	GUN
DANNY B HARVEY	G	(A			
JIMMY REED	G	(A	DAVE CURRY B (A PAT BROWN D (A		

LEVEL 42

PHIL GOULD	D	(A	(A) LEVEL 42	1981	POLYDOR UK	POLS 1036
MIKE LINDUP	K V	(A	(B) STRATEGY	1981	ELITE UK	LEVLP1
BOON GOULD	G SAX	(A				
MARK KING	B V	(A				

LEVIATHAN

SHOF BEAVERS		(A	(A) LEVIATHAN	197	MACH AMA US	12501
WAIN BRADLEY		(A				
PETER RICHARDSON		(A	JOHN SADLER (A DON SWEARINGEN (A GRADY TRIMBLE (A			

LEVITT McCLURE

DAN LEVITT		(A	(A) LIVING IN THE COUNTRY	19	CASABLANCA	WS 1807
DOUG McCLURE		(A				

BARRINGTON LEVY

BARRINGTON LEVY		(A11	(A) ENGLISHMAN	1979	GREENSLEEVES	GREL 9
ERROL 'FLABBA' HOLT	B	(C	(B) BOUNTY HUNTER	1979	JAH LIFE	
CARLTON 'SANTA' DAVIS	D(C		(C) ROBIN HOOD	1980	GREENSLEEVES	GREL 14
GLADSTONE ANDERSON	K	(C	(D) SHINE I GAL	1980	ECHO	1039
ANSEL COLLINS	K	(C				
ERIC LAMONT	G	(C	EARL SMITH G (C CHRISTOPHER BLAKE PERC(C HEADLEY BENNETT TROM(C			
BOBBY ELLIS	TPT	(C				

O'DONEL LEVY

O'DONEL LEVY	G	(ALL	(A) SIMBA	1973	GROOVEMERCHANT US	526
JON FADDIS	TPT	(AB	(B) DAWN OF A NEW DAY	1974	GROOVEMERCHANT US	518
ERNIE ROYAL	TPT	(A	(C) EVERYTHING I DO GONNA BE FUNKY	1974	GROOVEMERCHANT US	535
LEW SOLOFF	TPT	(AD	(D) WINDOWS	1976	GROOVEMERCHANT US	3313
DAVID E SMITH	WIND	(D				
JIMMY WILSON	TPT	(D	ALETA GREENE V (D STAFFORD LEVY D (D GARY GRAINGER B (D			
CHARLES COVINGTON K SYN(BD	LEW DELGATTO WIND (D GEORGE YOUNG WIND (D RANDY BRECKER TPT(D				
BARRY ROGERS	TROM	(D	JOE RANDAZZO TROM (D BURT COLLINS TPT (AB CECIL BRIDGEWATER HRN(AB			
BILL WATROUS	TROM	(AB	EDDIE DANIELS WIND (A WARREN BERNHARDT K (A TONY LEVIN B (A			
STEVE GADD	D	(A	JIM MADISON PERC (A CHESTER THOMPSON D (A GEORGE RUSSEL B (B			
MARVIN STAMM	TPT	(B	WAYNE ANDRE TROM (B EDDIE BURT TROM (B JUDD WATKINS V PERC(C			
HUGH WALKER	D	(C	STRINGS (D			

JONA LEWIE

JONA LEWIE K V D G PNO (AB			(A) ON THE OTHER HAND THERE'S A FIST	1978	STIFF US USE8 UK SEEZ 8	
MALCOLM MORTIMER	D	(A	(A) ON THE OTHER HAND THERE'S A FIST	1980	STIFF UK RI (DIFF TRACKS)	
DORRIS HENDERSON	V	(A	(B) ALIAS JONA LEWIE	1980	SONET UK	SNTF 794
CLIVE CHAPPEL	G B	(A				
TIM BRANSTON	G	(A	MALCOLM HINE G (A JOHN RANDALL PERC (A KEITH TRUSSELL PERC (A			
ROB CAROL	D	(A	MICK SMYTHE D (A KEN BUTCHER SAX (A HELEN ROBINSON V (A			
CATHY CLELAND	V	(A	DENNIS BOVELL V (A DICK HANSON TPT (A JOHN EARLE SAX (A			
JOHN STONE	PNO	(A	MIKE DAY V (A			

DAVE LEWIS

DAVE LEWIS	G K	(ABC	(A) FROM TIME TO TIME	1976	POLYDOR UK	2383 420
PRESTON HEYMAN	D	(B	(B) A COLLECTION OF HIS SHORT DREAMS	1978	POLYDOR UK	2383 522
FELIX KRISH	B	(B	(C) THE LATE SHOW	1978	POLYDOR UK	2383 493
STEVE BRANTLEY B V PERC(B						
BRUCE DEES	G V	(B	JAMIE BRANTLEY G (B ANDY MACMAHON K V (B MAGGIE RYDER V (B			

```
L61
  FURRY LEWIS        G V          PRESENTING THE COUNTRY BLUES    1969  BLUE HORIZON         763228
                                  IN MEMPHIS                      1970  MATCHBOX          SDR  190
                                  FURRY LEWIS                     1971  XTRA              XTRA 1116
                                  FABULOUS FURRY LEWIS            19    SOUTHLAND    US         3
                                  FURRY LEWIS BAND                19    FOLKWAYS              3823
                                  BEALE STREET BLUES              19    BARCLAY      FR   920  352
                                  FOURTH & BEALE                  19    BARCLAY      FR    80602
                                  & FRED McDOWELL                 19    BIOGRAPH           BLP12017
                                  IN HIS PRIME                    19    YAZOO                L 1050
                                  BLUES MASTERS VOL 5             19    BLUE HORIZON US    BM 4605
                                  HOUSE OF BLUES VOL 2            19    BLUE STAR    FR    80 602
                                  ON THE ROAD AGAIN              1969  ADELPHI             1007
                                  BACK ON MY FEET AGAIN           19    PRESTIGE     US     7810
                                  BACK ON MY FEET AGAIN           197   BLUESWAY     US     1036
                                  SHAKE 'EM ON DOWN               19    FANTASY      US    24703
                                  LIVE AT THE GAS LIGHT           19    AMPEX             A10140
                                  WHEN I LAY MY BURDEN DOWN       19    BIOGRAPH     US    12017
                                  DONE CHANGED MY MIND            19    BLUESVILLE   US     1037
```

L61A   HUEY LEWIS & THE NEWS   L61A

```
  HUEY LEWIS        V   (AB    (A) HUEY LEWIS & THE NEWS   1980  CHRYSALIS        CHR 1292
  CHRIS HAYES       G V (AB    (B) PICTURE THIS            1982  CHRYSALIS        CHR 1340
  SEAN HOPPER       K V (AB
  MARIO CIPOLLINA   B   (AB  BILL GIBSON D V   (AB   JOHNNY COLLA  G SAX V(AB  TOWER OF POWER HRNS(B
```

L61B   GARY LEWIS & THE PLAYBOYS   L61B

```
  GARY LEWIS        G V (ALL   (A) THIS DIAMOND RING         1965  LIBERTY   US    7408
  BOBBY KEYS        SAX (L      (B) A SESSION WITH            1965  LIBERTY   US    7419
  BILL BOATMAN      D   (L      (C) EVERYBODY LOVES A CLOWN   1965  LIBERTY   US    7428
  ARNOLD ROSENTHAL  B   (L      (D) SHES JUST MY STYLE        1966  LIBERTY   US    7435
  CHARLIE CAREY     G   (L      (E) HITS AGAIN                1966  LIBERTY   US    7452
  JOHN GALLIE       K   (L      (F) GOLDEN GREATS             1966  LIBERTY   US    7468
  GEORGE BOHANON    TROM (L     (G) PAINT ME A PICTURE        1967  LIBERTY   US    7487
  JIM PRICE         HRNS (L     (H) NEW DIRECTIONS            1967  LIBERTY   US    7519
  JOHN L WEST       K   (P      (I) NOW                       1968  LIBERTY   US    7893
  AL RAMSAY         G   (P      (J) MORE GOLDEN GREATS        1968  LIBERTY   US    7867
  DAVE COSTELL      G   (P      (K) RHYTHM OF THE RAIN        1969  LIBERTY   US    7623
  DAVE WALKER       G   (P      (L) I'M ON THE RIGHT ROAD NOW 1969  LIBERTY   US    7633
                               (M) PLAYBOYS                  196   SUNSET    US    5168
                               (N) RHYTHM                    1969  SUNSET    US    5262
                               (O) AT THEIR BEST             19    SUNSET    US    1026
                               (P) 20 GOLDEN GREATS          1979  LIBERTY   UK LBR1005
```

L61C   GRAHAM LEWIS & BRUCE GILBERT   L61C

```
  GRAHAM LEWIS        (A    (A) DOME   1980  ROUGH TRADE   UK DOME1
  BRUCE GILBERT       (A    (B) 3R4    1980  4AD           UK CAD16
```

L61D   JIMMY LEWIS & THE CHECKERS   L61D

```
  JIMMY LEWIS      G V (A    (A) YEAH RIGHT   1980  BOMP   US   BLP 4014
  JERRY NAIJEH     D V (A
  ODY NEWTON       G   (A  DOUGLAS NELSON   B V (A   MARTY DAVICH   K   (A   BENIMONT TENCH K (A
  MIKE CAMPBELL    G   (A  GORDON SHRYOCK   PROD (A   NOAH SHARK    PROD (A
```

L62   LEW LEWIS & REFORMER   L62

```
  LEW LEWIS       V HCA(A    (A) SAVE THE WAIL         1979  STIFF   UK   SEEZ 16
  PETE ZEAR       G   (1     (1) 1977 LIVE  (2) 1979 REFORMER
  LEE GREEN       G   (1
  JOHNNY OCEAN    B   (1   BOB CLOUTER      D   (1   JOHNNY SQUIRREL  B   (2A   RICK TAYLOR   G  (2A
  BUZZ BARWELL    D   (2A  GAVIN POVEY  PNO        (A
```

L63   LINDA LEWIS   L63

```
  LINDA LEWIS     V G (ALL   (A) SAY NO MORE             1971  REPRISE         UK      K44130
  CHRIS SPEDDING  G   (A     (B) LARK**                 1972  REPRISE US 2120 UK      K44208
  RAY COOPER      PERC (A    (C) FATHOMS DEEP            1973  REPRISE US 2172 RAFT UK 48501
  SHAWN PHILLIPS  G   (A     (D) NOT A LITTLE GIRL ANYMORE 1975 ARISTA US 4047 UK ARTY 109
  IAN McDONALD    FLT (A     (E) WOMAN OVERBOARD         1977  ARISTA          UK SPARTY1003
  MIKE EGAN       G   (A     ( ) HEART STRINGS           1974  REPRISE US 2192
  SKAILA KANGA    HARP (A    (F) HACIENDA VIEW           1970  ARIOLA          UK    ARL 5033
  FIACHRA TRENCH  K   (A     (1) 1975 OCT GIG      **TWO VERSIONS WITH SLIGHTLY DIFFERENT TRACKS
  LOUIS CENNAMO   B   (A
  TONY CAMPO      B   (A   GEORGE FORD     B   (A   TERRY COX      D   (A   PETE GAVIN      D  (A
  JIMMY HOROWITZ  K   (A   JIM CREGAN      G V (BCDE1 EMILE LATIMER PERC (B  PAT DONALDSON   B  (B
  GERRY CONWAY    D   (BD  JEAN ROUSSEL    K   (BDE  ERIC OXENDINE  B   (B  POLI PALMER FLT VIBES(BC
  PAUL WILLIAMS   G   (B   MICK EVE        SAX (BC   BOB TENCH      G   (C  MAX MIDDLETON   K  (CDE
  CLIVE CHAMAN    B   (CD  CONRAD ISADORE  D   (C    ROBERT AHWAI   G   (CD PHIL CHEN       B  (CDE1
  RICHARD BAILEY  D   (CDE ALLAN SHARPE    PERC (C   DANNY THOMPSON B   (C  LARRY STEELE    PERC(C
  STEVE GREGORY   WIND K(CDE1 RON CARTHY   TPT (C    CHRIS MERCER   SAX (C  ANNA PEACOCK    V  (DE
  DEREK SMITH     K   (DE  JEFF MIRANOV    G   (DE   JERRY FRIEDMAN G   (DE LANCE QUINN     G  (DE
  BOB BABITT      B   (DE  PHIL KRAUS    PERC  (DE   TED SOMMERS    PERC (DE JACK JENNINGS  PERC(DE
  CARLOS MARTIN   PERC (DE DUNCAN McKAY    K   (D    CAPABILITY BROWN V (D  TOWER OF POWER HRNS(D
  DOMINO          V   (D1  DARRYL LEE QUE  PERC (DE1 LENNY PICKETT  FLT (D  BERNIE HOLLAND G  (D
  LOWELL GEORGE   G   (D   LISA STRIKE     V   (DE   SNOWY WHITE    B   (DE GEOFF SEOPARDI D  (1
  DEREK AUSTIN    K   (E1  CLYDE TOVAL     B   (E    ALEX BROWN     V   (E  HERMAN ERNEST  D  (E
  JIM GILSTRAP    V   (E   KIM JOSEPH    PERC  (E    PAUL BATISTE   G   (E  TONY RIVERS    V  (E
  WALTER HARRIS   G   (E   STU CALVER      V   (E    JAMES BOOKER   G   (E  JOHN PERRY     G  (E
  ALLEN TOUSSAINT K   (E   TIM RENWICK     G   (E    WINSTON DELANDRO G (E  BARRY ST JOHN  V  (E
  VICKY BROWN     V   (E   ALUN DAVIES     G   (E    WILLIE WEEKS   B   (E  PETER HOPE-EVANS HCA(E
  OLLIE BROWN     D   (E   BOB BARTON      V   (E    BOBBYE HALL    PERC (E RAY PARKER     G  (E
  JUNE D WILLIAMS V   (E
```

JERRY LEE LEWIS

JERRY LEE LEWIS	PNO V	(ALL
LEO LOONER	G	(N
ROLAND JANES	G	(N
JIMMY VAN EATON	D	(N
BILLY RILEY	G B	(N
JACK CLEMENTS	B	(
OTIS JETT	D	(
J W BROWN	D	(
SCOTTY MOORE	G	(N
HANK GARLAND	G	(
KEN LOVELACE	G	(
ROBBY BROWN	D	(
JOEL SHUMAKER	B	(
DELANEY BRAMLETT	G V	(L
ALBERT LEE	G	(L
GARY WRIGHT	K	(L
PETER FRAMPTON	G V	(L
ANDY BROWN	K	(L
TONY ASHTON	K	(L
KENNY JONES	D	(L
KLAUS VOORMANN	B	(L
RORY GALLAGHER	G	(L
MIKE KELLIE	D	(L
BRAD SUGGS	G	(N
CLIFF ACRED	B	(N
CHARLIE RICH	PNO	(N
JEFF DAVIS	D	(N
ALBERT JACKSON	B	(N
R W McGHEE	D	(N
HERMAN HAWKINS	B	(N
GEORGE WEBB	G	(N
WILLIAM RAY FELTS	ORG	(N
MORRIS TARRANT	D	(N
BUDDY HARMAN	B	(N
FLOYD CHANCE	B	(N
LITTLE JOHNNY DEMPSEY	G	(N
CARL PERKINS	G V	(
JOHNNY CASH	V	(
LINDA GAIL	V	(

Title	Year	UK label	UK cat	US label	US cat
JERRY LEE LEWIS	196	LONDON	UK HAS2138	SUN	US 1230
GREATEST	196			SUN	US 1265
JERRY LEE LEWIS VOL 2	196	LONDON	UK HAS2440		
WHOLE LOTTA SHAKIN' GOIN' ON	196	LONDON	UK HAS8251		
BREATHLESS	196	LONDON	UK HAS8323		
GOLDEN HITS	1964	PHILIPS	UK SBL7622+	SMASH	US 67040
LIVE AT THE STAR CLUB HAMBURG	1964	PHILIPS	UK SBL7646		
GREATEST LIVE SHOW ON EARTH	1964	PHILIPS	UK SBL7650	SMASH	US 67056
RETURN OF ROCK	1963			WING	US 16340
RETURN OF ROCK	1967	PHILIPS	UK SBL7668	SMASH	US 67063
COUNTRY SONGS FOR CITY FOLKS	1965	PHILIPS	UK SBL7688	SMASH	US 67071
MEMPHIS BEAT	196	PHILIPS	UK SBL7706	SMASH	US 67079
BY REQUEST	1967	PHILIPS	UK SBL7746	SMASH	US 67086
SOUL MY WAY	196	PHILIPS US	20117	SMASH	US 67097
ANOTHER PLACE ANOTHER TIME	1968	MERCURY UK	21011	SMASH	US 67104
SHE STILL COMES AROUND	1969	MERCURY UK	20147	SMASH	US 67112
COUNTRY HITS	1969	DBL		SMASH	US 67117/8
TOGETHER (LINDA GAIL)	1969	PHILIPS UK	20172	SMASH	US 67126
SHE EVEN WOKE ME UP TO SAY G'BYE	1970			SMASH	US 67128
BEST OF	196			SMASH	US 67131
I'M ON FIRE	1969	MERCURY UK	20156		
COUNTRY MUSIC HALL OF FAME	19	MERCURY UK	20157		
COUNTRY MUSIC HALL OF FAME 2	19	MERCURY UK	20158		
BEST OF	1970	MERCURY UK	6338014		
ORIGINAL GOLDEN HITS	1970	SUN	UK 6467002	SUN	US 102
THERE MUST BE MORE TO LOVE	1971	MERCURY	UK 6338043		US 61323
ORIGINAL GOLDEN HITS VOL 2	1970	SUN	UK 6467008	SUN	US 103
ROCKIN RHYTHM & BLUES	1971	SUN	UK 6467017	SUN	US 107
GOLDEN CREAM OF COUNTRY	1971	SUN	UK 6467011	SUN	US 108
TASTE OF COUNTRY	1971	SUN	UK 6467015	SUN	US 114
MEMPHIS ROCK'N'ROLL	197			SUN	US 116
SUNDAY DOWN SOUTH(JOHNNY CASH)	1971	SUN	UK 6467024	SUN	US 119
MEMPHIS COUNTRY	1971			SUN	US 120
OLD TYME COUNTRY MUSIC	1971	SUN	UK 6464020	SUN	US 121
MONSTERS	1971	SUN	UK 6467019	SUN	US 124
SINGS WITH HANK WILLIAMS	1971	SUN	UK 6467018	SUN	US 125
IN LOVING MEMORIES	1971			MERCURY	US 61338
ORIGINAL GOLDEN HITS VOL3	1972	SUN	UK 6467023	SUN	US 128
ROCKIN' UP A STORM	1972	SUN (DBL)	UK 6641162		
THE KILLER ROCKS ON	1972	MERCURY	UK 6338088		US 1/637
WOULD YOU TAKE ANOTHER CHANCE	1972	MERCURY	UK 6338071		US 61346
WOULD YOU TAKE ANOTHER CHANCE	1975	CONTOUR	UK 6870620		
ROCKIN'	1972	MERCURY	UK 6336300		
LIVE AT THE INTERNATIONAL	1973	MERCURY	UK 6338148		US 61278
WHO'S GONNA PLAY THE OLD PIANO	1973			MERCURY	US 61366
SOLID GOLD ROCK'N'ROLL VOL 2	197			MERCURY	US 61372
SOMETIMES A MEMORY AINT ENOUGH	1973			MERCURY	US 1 677
(L) LONDON SESSION	1973	MERCURY	UK 6672008	MERCURY	US 2 803
TOUCHING HOME	1973	MERCURY			US 61343
1 40 COUNTRY	1974			MERCURY	US 1 710
COUNTRY STYLE	197	MERCURY	UK 6851001		
ROCKIN' & FREE	1974	SUN	UK 6467029		
FAN CLUB CHOICE	1974	MERCURY	UK 6338496		
SOUTHERN ROOTS	1974	MERCURY	UK 6338452		US 1/690
WHOLE LOTTA SHAKIN	1978	IMPACT	UK 6995 401		
JERRY LEE LEWIS	197	IMPACT	UK 6886402		
FOR LOVERS ONLY	19	CAMDEN			US 9030
ROLL OVER BEETHOVEN	19	HILLTOP			US 6110
SUNSTROKE(CARL PERKINS)	1974	EMBER	UK NR 5038		
RARE VOL1	1975	CHARLY	UK CR30006		
RARE VOL2	1975	CHARLY	UK CR30007		
24 ORIGINAL HITS	1975	MUSIDISC FR	ALB 170		
BOOGIE WOOGIE COUNTRY MAN	1975			MERCURY	US 1 1030
ORIGINAL SUPER ROCK	1975	MUSIDISC FR	ALB 184		
I'M A ROCKER	1975	MERCURY	UK 6338602		
ODD MAN IN	197			MERCURY	US 1 1064
EXPLOSIVE	19	CONTOUR	UK 6870533		
GOOD ROCKIN' TONIGHT	1975	HALLMARK	UK SHM 867		
COUNTRY CLASS	1976			MERCURY	US 1 1109
GOLDEN HITS	1976	PHILIPS INT	6336245		
& HIS PUMPING PIANO	1975	CHARLY	UK CR30002		
THE ORIGINAL	1976	CHARLY	UK CR30111		
NUGGETS	1977	CHARLY	UK CR30121		
(N)NUGGETS VOL 2	1977	CHARLY	UK CR30129		
COUNTRY MEMORIES	1977			MERCURY	US 1 5004
BEST OF VOL 2	1978			MERCURY	US 1 5006
KEEPS ON ROCKIN'	1978			MERCURY	US 1 5010
BACK TO BACK	1978	MERCURY	UK 6641869		
SHAKIN' JERRY LEE	1978	ARCADE	UK ADEP 34		
ESSENTIAL JERRY LEE LEWIS	1978	CHARLY	UK CRM2001		
JERRY LEE LEWIS	1978	IMPACT	6995401		
JERRY LEE LEWIS	1978	FESTIVAL	ALB 233		
DUETS	1978	CHARLY	UK SUN1002		
20 GREATEST HITS	1979	ARCADE FR	FR18		
COLLECTORS EDITION	19	SUN NL	NY6		
JERRY LEE LEWIS	1979	ELEKTRA	UK K52132		
FROM THE VAULTS OF SUN	19	STARDAY			US PO 247
HIGH HEELED SNEAKERS	19			PICKWICK	US 3224
ROLL OVER BEETHOVEN	19			PICKWICK	US 6110
RURAL ROUTE No1	19			PICKWICK	US 6120
COLLECTION	19	PICKWICK	UK PDA 007		
BREATHLESS(DBL)	19			PICKWICK	US 2055
BEST OF J L L	19			TRIP DBL	US 8501

JERRY LEE LEWIS (CONTINUED)

GREAT BALLS OF FIRE	19	HALLMARK UK SHM 823		
WHOLE LOTTA SHAKIN'	19	HALLMARK UK SHM 851		
DRINKIN' WINE SPO DEE O DEE	19		PICKWICK US 3344	
GOT YOU ON MY MIND	19	FONTANA UK SFJL964		
JERRY LEE LEWIS	1979	ELEKTRA UK K52132	ELEKTRA US 6E 184	
JERRY LEE LEWIS	19		EVEREST US 298	
GREATEST HITS VOL1	19	IMPACT 6886402		
GREATEST HITS VOL2	19	IMPACT 6886408		
LIVE AT THE STAR CLUB HAMBURG	1980	PHILIPS UK 6336 634		
JERRY LEE'S GREATEST	1980	CHARLY CRM 2008		
WHEN TWO WORLDS COLLIDE	1980	ELEKTRA UK K52113	US 254	
& FRIENDS (DUETS)	1980	SUN UK 1002	US 1018	
KILLER COUNTRY	1980	ELEKTRA UK K52246	US 291	
COUNTRY MEMORIES	1981	MERCURY	US 5004	
BEST OF COUNTRY HALL OF FAME	1981	MERCURY UK 6463 085		
GREAT BALLS OF FIRE	1982	CHARLY UK CFM 516		
PUMPIN' PIANO CAT	1982	CHARLY UK CFM 514		
TRIO PLUS	1980	CHARLY UK SUN 1004		

(EPs)

JERRY LEE LEWIS VOL 1	195	LONDON UK RES 1140
JERRY LEE LEWIS VOL 2	195	LONDON UK RES 1186
JERRY LEE LEWIS VOL 3	195	LONDON UK RES 1187
JERRY LEE LEWIS VOL 4	195	LONDON UK RES 1296
JERRY LEE LEWIS VOL 5	195	LONDON UK RES 1336
JERRY LEE LEWIS VOL 6	195	LONDON UK RES 1351
4 MORE FROM JERRY LEE	19	LONDON UK RES 1378
COUNTRY STYLE	19	PHILIPS UK 12599
LEWIS BOOGIE	1976	CHARLY UK CEP 105

RAMSEY LEWIS

RAMSEY LEWIS	K (ALL	AN HOUR WITH	1959	US CADET	645
ELDEE YOUNG	B ( ]TRIO	STRETCHIN OUT	1962	US CADET	665
ISAAC HOLT	D (	MORE MUSIC FROM SOUL	1962	US CADET	680
JON LIND	V (R	NEVER ON SUNDAY	1962	US CADET	686
MAURICE WHITE	V (R	SOUND OF CHRISTMAS	1964	US CADET	693
PAULINHO DACOSTA	PERC (R	SOUND OF SPRING	1964	US CADET	693
FRED WHITE	PERC (R	POT LUCK	1964	US CADET	715
DON MYRICK	SAX (R	BAREFOOT SUNDAY BLUES	1964	US CADET	723
LOUIS SATTERFIELD	TROM(R	BACK TO THE BLUES	196	US CADET	732
DERF REKLAW RAHEEM	PERC V (O	AT THE BOHEMIAN CAVERNS	1965 PYE UK NJL55	US CADET	741
BYRON GREGORY	G (OQ	MORE SOUNDS OF CHRISTMAS	1965 CHESS UK 4504	US CADET	745
TERRY FRYER	K (OQ	CHOICE	1965 CHESS US 4518	US CADET	755
RON HARRIS	B (OQ	THE IN CROWD	1965 CHESS UK 4511	US CADET	757
KEITH HOWARD	D (O	HANG ON RAMSEY	1966 CHESS UK 4517	US CADET	761
JIMMY BRYANT	K V (O	SWINGIN'	1966	US CADET	771
RAHM LEE	HRNS (OR	WADE IN THE WATER	1966 CHESS UK 4522	US CADET	774
MICHAEL DAVIS	V TPT(OR	GOIN' LATIN	1967 CHESS UK 4528	US CADET	790
MIKE McGLOIRY	G (Q	MOVIE ALBUM	1967 CHESS UK 4531	US CADET	782
ED REDDICK	B (Q	DANCIN' IN THE STREET	1968 CHESS UK 4533	US CADET	794
JAMES GADSON	D (QR	RAMSEY LEWIS TRIO	1968	US CADET	796
VANCE TENORT	PERC (Q	UP PGPS RAMSEY	1968 CHESS UK 4535	US CADET	799
ALEXANDRA BROWN	V (Q	MAIDEN VOYAGE	1968 CHESS UK 4539	US CADET	811
JIM GILSTRAP	V (Q	MOTHER NATURES SON	1969 CHESS UK 4545	US CADET	821
STEPHANIE SPRUILL	V (Q	(K) UPENDO NI PAMOJA	197 CBS UK 64718	US CBS	31096
ANGELA WINBUSH	V (Q	BACK TO THE ROOTS	1971 CHESS UK 6310 106	US CADET	60001
ALLEN TOUSSAINT	K (R	ANOTHER VOYAGE	197	US CADET	827
HERMAN V ERNEST	D (R	PIANO PLAYER	197	US CADET	836
WARREN WEINBERG	V (R	INSIDE	197	US CADET	60018
JOHN REASONS	K G (Q	BEST OF	1972 CHESS UK 6310 114	US CADET	839
SAM HENRY	G (R	THEM CHANGES	197	US CADET	844
BOBBY LYLE	K (Q	TOBACCO ROAD	1972 CHESS UK 6310 124		
MORRIS JENNINGS	D (KLMQ	(L) FUNKY SERENITY	1973 CBS UK 65307	US	32030
KEITH CARTER	V (Q	GREATEST HITS	1973 CBS UK 65759	US	32490
CYNTHIA HARRELL	V (Q	GROOVER	1974 CHESS UK 6467 305	US CADET	50020
KITTY HAYWOOD	V (Q	(M) SOLAR WIND	1974 CBS UK 80083	US	32897
VIVIAN HAYWOOD	V (Q	DON'T IT FEEL GOOD	1975 CBS UK 81006	US	33800
KENNETH WILLIAMS	PERC (R	SUN GODDESS	1975 CBS UK 80677	US	33194
LEO NOCENTELLI	G (R	SOLID IVORY	1975 CHESS UK 6641 328	US CADET	50058
AVID BARARD	B (R	LIVE IN TOKYO	1975	US CADET	SMS7501
ZURI RAHEEM	V (O	SALONGO	1976 CBS UK 81406	US	34173
DARLENE KOLDENHOVEN	V (Q	(O) LOVE NOTES	1977 CBS UK 82024	US	34696
PAT FERRARI	G (Q	(P) TEQUILA MOCKING BIRD	1977 CBS UK 83270	US	35018
LARRY DUNN	K (R	LEGACY	1978 CBS UK 82964		
AL McKAY	G (R	(Q) RAMSEY	1979 CBS UK 83584	US	35815
BYRON MILLER	B (R	(R) ROUTES	1980 CBS UK 84243		
LEON CHANCLER	D (R	DOWN TO EARTH	19	US MERCURY	36150
KENNY BURKE	B (R	3 PEICE SUITE	1981 CBS UK 84980		
ROLAND BAUTISTA	G (R	BEST OF	1981 CBS UK 84911		
CLEVELAND EATON	B (KLM				
ED GREENE	PERC VLN(L				
STEVE CROPPER	G (M				

SMILEY LEWIS

SMILEY LEWIS	V (ALL	SHAME SHAME SHAME	1970 LIBERTY UK	LBS 83308	
		I HEAR YOU KNOCKING	1978 UA UK UAS 30167	US IMPERIAL9141	
		THE BELLS ARE RINGING	1978 UA UK UAS 30186		

WEBSTER LEWIS

WEBSTER LEWIS	K V (A	(A) 8 FOR THE 80's	1980 EPIC UK	EPC 84283

JAMES GADSON	D (A						
NATHANIEL WATTS	B (A	PAUL JACKSON	G (A	WAH WAH WATSON	G (A	TOWER OF POWER HRNS (A	
OSCAR BRASHEAR	HRNS (A	D J ROGERS	V (A	SYLVIA COX V (A	CHERYL PITTS	B (A	
JOHNNY BAKER	V (A	BOBBY BRYANT	HRNS (A	GARNETT BROWN	HRNS (A	BENNY POWELL HRNS (A	
BILL GREEN	HRNS (A	HERBIE HANCOCK	K (A	CARMEN TWILLIE	V (A	YOLANDA HOWARD V (A	
VENETTE GLOUD	V (A	JUDITH JONES	V (A	BILL CHAMPLIN	V (A		

LEYDEN ZAR
```
   PASCAL MAILLOUX   K V  (A          (A) LEYDEN ZAR                    1981 A&M
   SERGE GRATTON     D PERC(A
   BRIAN WILSON      G V  (A   JACQUES NOEL G   (A   PAUL GRONDIN    B V  (A
```
LIAISONS DANGEREUSES
```
   BEATE BARTEL          (A          (A) LIAISONS DANGEREUSES          1981 TIS        GER        22433
   CHRIS HAAS            (A
   KRISTINE GEINEAU  V   (A   JOANNA   V   (A
```
LIAR
```
   CLIVE BROOKS      D   (AB         (A) STRAIGHT FROM THE HIP         1977 DECCA         UK  SKL 5275
   DAVE BURTON       G   (AB         (B) SET THE WORLD ON FIRE         1979 BEARSVILLE US 6982 UK K 55524
   PAUL TRAVIS       G   (AB
   STEVE MANN        G K (AB  DAVID TAYLOR      B    (AB
```
LIBRA
```
                              LIBRA                            1976 MOTOWN    US            M 847
                              WINTER DAYS NIGHTMARE            1976 MOTOWN    US            M 864
```
DAVID LIEBMAN
```
   DAVID LIEBMAN     SAX (ALL        (A) DRUM ODE                     1975 EMC           US  1046
   JOHN ABERCROMBIE  D   (A          (B) LOOKHOUSE FARM               1975 EMC           US  1039
   JEFF BERLIN       B   (F          (C) FATHER TIME                  1976 ENJA          GER 2056
   AL FOSTER         D   (F          (D) SWEET HANDS                  1977 HORIZON       US  SP 702
   RICHARD BEIRACH   PNO (AEF        (E) FORGOTTEN FANTASIES          1977 HORIZON       US  SP 709
   LINK CHAMBERLAND  G   (F          (F) LIGHT'N UP PLEASE            1977 HORIZON       US  SP 721
   PEE WEE ELLIS     PNO (F          (G) IF ONLY THEY KNEW            1980 TIMELESS          151
   SONNY BROWN       PERC (F
   CHRIS HAYES       G   (F  TONY SAUNDERS     B   (F   JIMMY STRASSBURG D  (F   JUMMA SANTOS    CONGAS(F
   LEON THOMAS       V   (F  HAROLD WILLIAMS   K   (F   JOHN SCOFIELD    G  (G   RON McLURE      B  (G
   ADAM NUSSBAUM     D   (G  RICHIE BEIRACH    K   (A   GENE PERLA       B  (A   JEFF WILLIAMS   D  (A
   BOB MOSES         D   (A  PATATO VALDEZ    PERC (A   STEVE SATTAN    PERC (A   BARRY ALTSCHUL  PERC(A
   BADAL ROY         TABLA(A  COLIN WALCOTT    TABLA(A   RAY ARMANDO     PERC (A   ELEANA STEINBERG V(A
   TERUMASA HINO     HRN  (G
```
LIEUTENANT PIGEON
```
   ROBWOODWARD           (          (A) MOULDY OLD MUSIC             1973 DECCA         UK  SKL 5154
   NIGEL FLETCHER        (          (B) PIGEON PIE                   1974 DECCA         UK  SKL 5174
   Mrs FLETCHER          (          (C) PIGEON PARTY                 1974 DECCA         UK  SKL 5196
   STEVE JOHNSON     B   (
```
LIFE
```
   ROGER COTTON      K V  (A         (A) LIFE AFTER DEATH            1974 POLYDOR           2383 295
   IAN GIBBONS       K FLT(A
   RICHARD THORPE    B V  (A  PAUL THORPE       D V(A
```
LIFE(US)
```
   GEORGE TERRY      G V  (A         (A) LIFE                        1981 ELEKTRA       US  6E 339
   KITTY WOODSON     V    (A
   JAMIE OLDAKER     D    (A  GEORGE BITZER     K   (A   JOEY MURCIA     G   (A   HAROLD COWART   B  (A
   RON ZIEGLER       D    (A
```
LIFESTYLE
```
   JERRY JAY FERGUSON K V (A        (A) LIFESTYLE                   1977 MCA UK MCF 2809     US   2246
   JOHNNY MATHIS     V    (A
   WADE 'HOLMES' DAVIS V (A  SHEDRICK SWEET    V   (A   RICHIE ROME     K   (A   DENNIS HARRIS   G  (A
   GEORGE BERG       SAX  (A  JON FADDIS       TPT  (A   CHARLES LEE     V   (A   MICHAEL FOREMAN B  (A
   LARRY WASHINGTON  CONGA(A  ARTHUR CLARKE    SAX  (A   VICTOR PAZ      TPT (A   MEL DAVIS       TPT(A
   PAUL GRIFFIN      SAX  (A  CHARLES COLLINS   D   (A   RICHARD DAVIS   B   (A   BILLY JACKSON   PERC(A
   ROMEO PENQUE      SAX  (A  BUDDY TERRY      SAX  (A   JANICE ROBINSON TROM(A   STRING SECTION     (A
```
(TONY WILLIAMS) LIFETIME
```
   TONY WILLIAMS     D.   (ALL       (A) LIFETIME                   1965 BLUENOTE             84180
                                     ( ) SPRING                     1966 BLUENOTE          UK 84216
   JACK BRUCE        B    (CF        (B) EMERGENCY                  1969 POLYDOR 583 574 US 25/3001
   JOHN McLAUGHLIN   G    (BCF       (B) EMERGENCY                  197  POLYDOR             2673 002
   ALLAN HOLDSWORTH  G    (HG        (C) TURN IT OVER               1970 POLYDOR UK 2425019 US 244021
   ALAN PASQUA       K    (HG        (D) EGO                        197o POLYDOR 2425 070 ++ 2440 065
   TONY NEWTON       B V  (HG        (E) THE OLD BUMS RUSH          1972 POLYDOR 2391 052  US 5040
   RON CARTER        B CELLO (D      (F) LIFETIME                   1975 POLYDOR             2482 179
   KHALID(LARRY YOUNG)YASIN ORG(BDF  (G) BELIEVE IT                 1976 CBS  UK 69201   US 33836
   TOM DUNBAR        G    (D         (H) MILLION DOLLAR LEGS        1976 CBS  UK 81510   US 34263
   DON ALIAS         PERC (D         (J) LIFETIME                   1978 BLUENOTE             40018
   WARREN SMITH      PERC (D         (K) JOY OF FLYING              1979 CBS  UK 83338
```
LIFT
```
   WERTEHR LOHSE     D V  (A         (A) FIRST                      1977 AMIGA         GER 855550
   MICHAEL HEUBACH   K SYN(AB        (B) MEERESFAHRT                1979 AMIGA         GER 855638
   TILL PATZER       WIND V(AB
   WOLFGANG SCHEFFLER K SYN(AB HENRY PACHOLSKI V (AB GERHARD ZACHER  B V  (AB FRANK ENDRICK MOLL   D  (B
```
JOE & JIMMY LIGGINS
```
   JOE LIGGINS           (AB         (A) JOE LIGGINS                1975 BULLDOG           BDL 1005
   JIMMY LIGGINS         (AB         (B) JOE & JIMMY LIGGINS        1976 SONET         UK  SNTF 5020
```
LIGHT
```
   JIM ARMSTRONG     G    (A         (A) LIGHT                      1977 MINT             MINT11
   ALBERT MILLS      B V  (A
   BRIAN SCOTT       K FLT V (A  GEORGE O'HARA     G V (A   BERTIE MACDONALD  D (A
```
LIGHT OF THE WORLD
```
   NEVILLE McKRIETH  G V  (A         (A) ROUND TRIP                 1980 ENSIGN UK ENVY14 US MERCURY 3819
   PATRYCEBANKS      V    (A         ( ) LIGHT OF THE WORLD         1979 ENSIGN UK      ENVY 7
   PAUL WILLIAMS     B V  (A         ( ) THE BEST REMIXED           1981 MERCURY           6350 062
   PETER HINDS       K    (A
   AUGIE JOHNSON     V    (A  EVERTON McCALLA   D   (A   GANIYU BELLO    PERC V(A NATHANIEL AUGUSTIN TROM(A
   CANUTE WELLINGTON HRNS V(A  DAVID BAPTISTE   WIND V(A   WAYNE HENDERSON TROM (A  BOBBY LYLE      PNO(A
   VICTOR FELDMAN    VIBES(A  MIKI HOWARD      TPT  (A   STEVE MADAIO    TPT (A   JOHN ERVIN      TROM (A
   CHUCK BROOKE      SAX  (A  BOB GREAVES      SAX  (A   VANCE TENORT    PERC (A  STEVE BECKMEIER G  (A
   GREG PRECLES      HRNS (A  MEL GAYNOR        D   (A   STRING SECTION       (A
```

```
GORDON LIGHTFOOT  G PNO V(ALL    (A) LIGHTFOOT                      1966 UA      US 6487
TERRY CLEMENTS G   (JLMNORSV      (B) WAY I FEEL                    1967 UA      US 6587SUNSET UK  50231
RICK HAYNES    B   (HJLMNORSVK    (C) LIGHTFOOT                     1968
PEE WEE CHARLES STEEL(NORSV       (D) DID SHE MENTION MY NAME       1968 US      US 6649   UK SULP 1199
BARRY KEANE    D   (LORSV         (E) BACK HERE ON EARTH            1969 UA      US 6672   UK SULP 1239
GENE MARTYNEC  SYN (MR            (F) EARLY LIGHTFOOT               1969 UA               UK UAS 29012
JIM GORDON     D   (MNOR          (G) SUNDAY CONCERT                1969 UA      US 6714   UK UAS 29040
RED SHEA       G   (HJLMNOSBK      (H) SIT DOWN YOUNG STRANGER      1970 REPRISE US 6392   UK K 44091
DAVID BROWN    PERC (LK            (J) DON QUIXOTE                  1972 REPRISE US 2056   UK K 44166
JOHN STOCKFISH B   (BMNO          (K) SUMMERSIDE OF LIFE           1971 REPRISE US 2037   UK K 44132
CATHERINE SMITH V   (M            (L) OLD DANS RECORDS             1972 REPRISE US 2116   UK K 44219
BRUCE GOOD  AUTOHARP (LOV         (M) SUNDOWN                      1974 REPRISE US 2177   UK K 44258
NICK DE CARO   ACC (LMNOV         (N) COLD ON THE SHOULDER         1975 REPRISE US 2206   UK K 54033
MILT HOLLAND   PERC (MNO          (O) GORD'S GOLD                  1975 REPRISE US 2237   UK K 64033
JACK ZAZA      WIND (NS           (P) VERY BEST OF                 1975 UA      US LA445EMI 5C 05096474
SUSIE McCUNE   V   (N             (Q) EARLY MORNING RAIN           1976 SUNSET           UK SLS 50398
TOM SZCZESNIAK B   (S             (R) SUMMERTIME DREAM             1976 REPRISE US 2246   UK K 54067
LARRY GOOD     BAN (LO            (S) ENDLESS WIRE                 1978 WB      US 3149   UK K 56444
MITCH CLARKE   BASSOON (S         (T) CLASSIC LIGHTFOOT            19   UA               UK UAS 5510
OLLIE STRONG   STEEL(LO           (U) GORDON LIGHTFOOD HUDBA A SLOVA 19   SUPRAPHON
DOUG RILEY     PNO (S             (V) DREAM STREET ROSE            1980 WB      US 3426   UK K 56802
DAVID BROMBERG  G  (L            (JK) 2 ORIGINALS OF GORDON LIGHTFOOT 19   REPRISE           UK K 64022
JUNIOR HUSKY   B   (OK            (W) BEST                         19   UA      US 6754
PIG ROBBINS    PNO (OK            (X) SUNDOWN                      1980 MOBILE  US 018
LENNY CASTRO   PERC (V            (Y) THE BEST OF                  1981 REPRISE           UK K 56915
BOB GLAUB      B   (V
KEN BUTTREY   D    (BKO   GAYLE LEVANT      HARP (V    CHARLIE McCOY    HARM (BKO  MICHAEL OMARTIAN  K (V
HERB PEDERSEN BAN    (V   JACKIE WARD   V      (N    CHIP YOUNG       G   (K    HENRY STRZELECKI   B (K
BUDDY HARMON  D    (K     JIMMY ISBELL      D  (K    VASSAR CLEMENTS  FDL (K    JERRY SHOOK    G   (K
RY COODER     G    (H     VAN DYKE PARKS    HCA (H    JOHN SEBASTIAN   G HCA(H   FARRELL MORRIS    PERC(K
JAMES ROLLESTON  B (K     GORDON STOKER     V  (K    NEAL MATTHEWS    V   (K    HOYT HAWKINS    V  (K
RAY WALKER    V    (K     LAVERNA MOORE     V  (K    MILDRED KIRKHAM  V   (K
```

```
PAPA GEORGE LIGHTFOOT V HCA(ALL  (A) RURAL BLUES VOL 2            19   LIBERTY     UK LBL 83214
CARSON WHITSETT  PNO  (B          (B) NATCHEZ TRACE               1969 LIBERTY     UK LBS 83353
RON JOHNSON    B   (B             (B) NATCHEZ TRACE               1969 VAULT       US     130
JERRY PUCKETT  G   (B
TOMMY TATE     D   (B
```

```
SKIP PROKOP    G D V(ABCDEFGHJK   (A) LIGHTHOUSE                  1969 RCA      US LSP4173
PAUL HOFFERT   K   (ABCDEG        (B) PEACING IT ALL TOGETHER     1970 RCA      US LSP4225 UK SF 8121
RALPH COLE     G V (ABCDEFGHJK    (C) SUITE FEELING               1970 RCA      US LSP4241 UK SF 8103
DON DINOVO     VLA (ABCDEFGHJK    (D) ONE FINE MORNING            1971 EVOLUTION US  3007
DICK ARMIN     CELLO(BCDEGJK      (D) ONE FINE MORNING            1971 VERTIGO             UK 6342010
LOUIS YACKNIN  B   (DEG           (E) THOUGHTS OF MOVING ON       197  EVOLUTION US  3010
KEITH JOLIMORE WIND V(DE          (E) THOUGHTS OF MOVING ON       197  VERTIGO             UK 6342011
LARRY SMITH    TROM V (DEGJ       (F) LIVE                        197  EVOLUTION US  3014
HOWARD SHORE   SAX   (BCDGAE      (G) SUNNY DAYS                  1972 EVOLUTION US  3016
DALE HILLARY   SAX V(JK           (G) SUNNY DAYS                  1972 MOONCREST          UK CREST 2
RICK STEPTON   TROM  (JK          (H) ONE FINE LIGHT              1972 RCA      US     6047
PAUL ARMIN     VLN  (BC           (J) CAN FEEL IT                 1974 POLYDOR  US PD 5056 UK 2391088
PAUL ADAMSON   TPT  (C            (K) GOOD DAY                    19   POLYDOR  US     6028 UK 2391133
ARNIE CHYCOSKI TPT  (BA           (L) BEST OF                     19   JANUS    US JXS7025
JOHN CAPON     TROM (B
PETE PANTALUK  TPT  (D   JOHN NASLEN    TPT    (GJ   PINKY DAUVIN   V    (ABC MYRON MOSKALYK    VLN(C
BRUCE CASSIDY  TPT  (BC  BOB McBRIDE    PERC V  (DGE  ALAN WILMOT    B    (GJ  GRANT FULLERTON  B V(ABC
LES SNIDER     CELLO(ABC RUSS LITTLE      TROM (ABC   MIKE MALONE    TPT  (E   FREDDY STONE    TPT (A
IAN GUENTHER   VLN   (A  DON WHITTON      CELLO(A     TERRY WILKINS  B V  (K   BILLY KING      D  (K
SAM SEE        K    (K
```

```
LIGHTNIN' SLIM(OTIS HICK G V (ALL (A) ROOSTER BLUES              196  EXCELLO      US     8000
PETE WINGFIELD K   (E             (A) ROOSTER BLUES              196  BLUE HORIZON UK   7 63863
LAURIE GARMAN  HCA (E             (B) BELL RINGER                196  EXCELLO      US     8004
RICK HAYWARD   G   (E             (C) HIGH & LOW DOWN            196  EXCELLO      US     8018
PAUL BUTLER    G   (E             (C) HIGH & LOW DOWN            197  CONTEMPO           CRM118
KENNY LAMB     D   (E             (C) HIGH & LOW DOWN            1978 SONET        UK   SNTF 770
JOHN BEST      B   (E             (D) A LONG DRINK OF BLUES(1 SIDE) 1964 EMI       UK   SL10135
DICK PARRY     SAX (E             (E) LONDON GUMBO               1972BLUE HORIZON  UK   2931 005
WILL THAKE     HCA (E             (E) LONDON GUMBO               1975 CONTEMPO UK CLP514 US EXCELLO 8023
CECIL MOSS     TPT (E             (E) LONDON GUMBO               1978 SONET        UK   SNTF 757
MIKE VERNON    G D (E             (F) THE EARLY YEARS            1977 FLYRIGHT           CLP 524
ROGER BROOKS   TROM (E            (G) TRIP TO CHICAGO            1978 FLYRIGHT           CLP 533
LAZY LESTER    HCA (A
WARREN STORM   D   (AB   AL FOREMAN      B    (B   BOBBY McBRIDE   G  (B   KATIE WEBSTER   PNO (B
AUSTIN BROUSSARD D (B    RUFUS THIBODEAUX B    (B   JESSE CARR      G  (C   CLAYTON IVEY    K  (C
STACY GOSS     HRNS (C   MIKE STOUGH     HRNS (C   SONNY ROYAL     HRNS(C   CHARLES ROSE    HRNS(C
FRED PROUDLY   D   (C    BOB WARY         B   (C   TIPPY ARMSTRONG HCA (C
```

```
JOE STICK      G K V(A            (A) I'M NOT AFRAID TO SAY YES   1973 DINGERLAND        0949 0211
NAPPES RAPIERSKY D  (A
DET SILVERSTEIN B V (A   HORREX   G V (A
```

```
                                 (A) LILIENTAL                   19   BRAIN            0060 117
```

```
MIKE SCRIMSHAW V B G K(A          (A) LIMELIGHT                   1980 FUTURE EARTH      FER 008
GLENN SCRIMSHAW G K V (A
PAT COLEMAN    D V  (A
```

LIMEY

```
  BRIAN ENGEL          G V  (AB        (A) LIMEY                               1976 RCA              UK     SF 8463
  JOHN KNIGHTSBRIDGE G   (B        (B) SILVER EAGLE                         1977 RCA                     PL 25032
  PAUL KEOGH           G    (B
  GARTH WATT-ROY       G    (B    TOM WILLIS      G     (B    ALAN SPENNER   B    (B   BOB HENRIT      D  (B
  JIM RODFORD          G    (B    TOMMY EYRE      K FLT(B    DAVE BOWKER    B    (AB  IAN KEWLEY      K  (AB
  ROBIN LE MESURIER  G    (AB   MAC McINERNEY   D PERC(A    B J COLE      STEEL (A  PETER GATTEN   PROD(A
  STEPHANIE DE SYKES  V    (A    CLAIRE TORREY   V     (A    SUE VANNER     V    (A
```

PHILAMORE LINCOLN

```
  PHILAMORE LINCOLN      V    (A        (A) NORTH WIND BLEW SOUTH            19  EPIC        US   26497
  THE YARDBIRDS               (A
```

DENNIS LINDE

```
  DENNIS LINDE B G V D K(ALL        (A) LINDE MANOR                        1970 INTREPID        US      IT 74004
  WAYNE MOSS         G B  (AB        (B) DENNIS LINDE                       1973 ELEKTRA US 75062 UK      K42149
  DOODLES LANCASTER  D    (A         (C) TRAPPED IN THE SUBURBS             1974 ASYLUM US 1011 ELEKTRA UK K52013
  BERGEN WHITE       HRNS (A         (D) SURFACE NOISE     (NOT RELEASED)   197  MONUMENT
  BUDDY SPICHER      STRINGS (ABE    (E) UNDER THE EYE                      1977 MONUMENT        US      MG 7608
  FARRELL MORRIS     PERC (AC
  JERRY SMITH        K    (A    BENNY WHITEHEAD  HRN V(B   RANDY CULLERS D B G V(BCE   TERRY DEARMORE  G V (B
  BOBBY OGDIN FDL K FLT  (BCE  ALAN RUSH  V G BANJO  (BCE ROBERT GALBRAITH K V(BC   LLOYD GREEN    STEEL(BC
  CHIP YOUNG         V    (BC   BILLY SWAN       V    (B    JOHN HARRIS     K    (B   KENNY MALONE   D   (B
  WELDON MYRICK      STEEL(B    BOBBY THOMPSON   BANJ (E    RUSS HICKS     STEEL(E   RON EADES      SAX (C
  HARRISON CALLOWAY  HRNS(C    JOHNNY CHRISTOPHER G  (C    JIMMY COLVARD   G    (C   BOBBY EMMONS   K   (CE
  HURSHAL WIGGINTON  V    (C    SHANE KEISTER    SYN K(E    JERRY CARRIGAN  D    (E   THOMAS CAIN    PNO (E
  MAC GAYDEN         G    (E    MARY HOLLADAY    V    (E    GINGER HOLLADAY V    (E
```

UDO LINDENBERG

```
  UDO LINDENBERG      V D PERC(ALL       (A) LINDENBERG                            1971 TELEFUNKEN   GERM  SLE14637
  THOMAS KRETSCHMER G   (HBCD       (B) DAUMEN IM WIND                        1972 TELEFUNKEN  GER         14679
  KARL ALLAUT        G    (HCD       (C) ALLES KLAR AUF DER ANDREA DORIA      1973 TELEFUNKEN   GERM  SLE14719
  HELMUT FRANKE      G    (ABDH      (D) BALL POMPOS                          1974 TELEFUNKEN   GERM  SLE14790
  STEFFI STEPHAN     B    (ABCDH     (E) VOTAN WAHNWITZ                       1975 TELEFUNKEN   GERM  6 22223
  GOTTFRIED BOTTGER K  (    (CDH      (F) DAS SIND DIE HERRN VOM ANDERN STERN 76  TELEFUNKEN   GERM  6 22460
  JEAN JACQUES KRAVETZ K (HCD       (G) SISTER KING KONG                      1976 TELEFUNKEN   GERM  6 22609
  KEITH FORSEY       D PERC(HD       (H) NO PANIC                             1976 DECCA        UK    TXSR116
  DIETER AHRENDT     D PERC (HD
  LONZO WESTPHAL     VLN    (HD  PETER HERBOLZHEIMER HRNS(BD  BOLLE BURMEISTER SAX (D  RAINER REGEL      SAX (D
  PETER HESSLEIN     G   (C    OLAF KUBLER      SAX   (D    CHRIS HERRMANN TPT(D  GIGG SEELENMEYER  BAN (D
  BACKI BACKHAUSEN   D    (D    WOLFGANG SCHMITZ HRNS (D    ANDY MARK      G   (A  ROGER HOOK        G  (B
  MICHAEL NAURA      K    (B    RALE OBERPICHLER V     (B    JO KISSTEN    ACC (B  JOHNNY MULLER       (B
  RAINER RUBINK      BANJ(B
```

BJORN JAYSON LINDH

```
  BJORN JAYSON LINDH FLT(AB       (A) JAYSON LINDH                        1977 ATLANTIC     UK    K50337
  ERNIE WATTS        SAX  (A         (B) DAY AT THE SURFACE                  1980 SONET        UK    SNTF 833
  NAGI EL HABASHI    CELLO(B       ( ) RAMADAM                           19   METRONOME    US    3000
  DON GRUSIN         PNO  (A       ( ) COUS COUS                         19   METRONOME    US    3001
  LEE RITENOUR       G    (A       ( ) SISSEL                            19   METRONOME    US    3002
  KEN WILD           B    (A
  JOE LALA           PERC (A    LARS CARLSSON    SAX  (A    JIM JOHNSON     G    (A   TOM ROADY    PERF   (A
  BERTIL LOVGREN     TPT  (A    JANNE KLING      WIND (A    JIM GILSTRAP    V    (A   AUGIE JOHNSON    V (A
  JAN KOHLIN         TPT  (A    ULF ADAKER       TPT  (A    ULF ANDERSSON   SAX  (A   JOHAN STENGARD   SAX(A
  BARRY BECKETT      K    (A    DAVID HOOD       B    (A    LARS OLOF KYNDEL K   (A   SVEN LARSSON     TROM(A
  PETER SUNDELL      PERC (A    PETE ROBINSON    K    (B    GEORGE WADENIUS B    (B   OKAY TEMIZ       PERC(B
  JAN BANDEL         VLN  (B    LENNART ABERG    SAX  (B    JON CHRISTENSEN D    (B   JANNE SCHAFFER   G  (AB
  STEFAN BROLUND     B    (AB   MALANDO GASSAMA  D    (AB   MATS GLENNGARD  VLN (A   AKE ERIKSSON     D  (A
  KEN BELL           G    (A    ROGER HAWKINS    D    (A    AMERICO BELLOTTO TPT (A   LARS OLOFSSON    TROM(A
  JOE CORRERO        D    (A
```

DAVID LINDLEY

```
  DAVID LINDLEY      V G B FDL(AB       (A) EL RAYO                         1981 ASYLUM UK K52283 US 5E524
  IAN WALLACE        D     (AB        (B) WIN THIS RECORD                  1982 ASYLUM       US 60178
  WILLIAM SMITTY SMITH K (AB
  BOOKER T JONES     K    (B    BILL PAYNE      K     (A    JORGE CALDERON  V    (AB CURT BOUTERSE   DULC(A
  RUS BABOO          V PERC(A    BOB GLAUB       B     (A    JACKSON BROWNE  V    (A  REGGIE McBRIDE  B   (A
  GARTH HUDSON       K    (A    BERNIE LARSEN V G B(B
```

LINDISFARNE

```
  ALAN HULL          V B K G(ALL       (A) NICELY OUT OF TUNE              1970 CHARISMA UK CAS1025 US ELEKTRA 74099
  ROD CLEMENTS       V G K  (ABCDHIJK   (B) FOG ON THE TYNE                1971 CHARISMA UK CAS1050 US ELEKTRA 75021
  RAY JACKSON        V G MAND(ABCDEFGHIJK (C) DINGLY DELL                  1972 CHARISMA UK CAS1057 US ELEKTRA 75043
  SIMON COWE         V G MAND(ABCDGHIJK  (D) LINDISFARNE LIVE              1973 CHARISMA UK CLASS 2
  RAY LAIDLAW        D     (ABCDGHIJK   (E) ROLL ON RUBY                   1973 CHARISMA UK CAS1076 US ELEKTRA 75077
  PAUL NICHOLS       D    (EF        (F) HAPPY DAZE                      1974 WB        UK K56070  US ASYLUM  7018
  TOM DUFFY          B    (EF        (G) FINEST HITS                     1975 CHARISMA UK CAS1108
  KEN CRADDOCK       K G  (EF        (H) LADY ELEANOR                    1976 PICKWICK     SHM 919
  CHARLIE HARCOURT   G    (EF        (I) BACK & FOURTH                   1978 MERCURY UK 9109609 US ATCO    38108
  BUD BEADLE         HRNS (F         (J) MAGIC IN THE AIR                1978 MERCURY UK 6641877
  STEVE GREGORY      HRNS (F         (K) THE NEWS                        1979 MERCURY UK 9109626
  FRANK RICOTTI      PERC (K        ( ) THE SINGLES ALBUM               1981 CHARISMA UK BG5
  PETE WINGFIELD     PERC (K
  NICK ROWLEY        HRNS(K    STRING SECTION      (K
```

LINER

```
  TOM FARMER         V B   (A        (A) LINER                           1979 ATLANTIC US 38113 UK    K50553
  EDDIE GOLGA        G V   (A
  ARIF MASDIN        SYN   (A    IAN LYNN        K     (A    MEL COLLINS SAX  (A  DICK MORRISSEY  SAX (A
  KEN BISCHEL        K     (A    MARVIN STAMM    TPT   (A    JON FADDIS  TPT  (A  GEORGE YOUNG    SAX (A
  FRANK VICARI       SAX   (A    CISSY HOUSTON   V     (A    BARRY ROGERS TROM (A  RONNIE CUBER    SAX (A
  MAERETHA STEWART   V     (A    BEVERLEY INGRAM V     (A
```

LINES

```
  RICHARD CONNING    V    (AB        (A) COOL SNAP (EP)                  1980 RED
  NIKOLAS CASH       D    (AB        (B) THE LINES (EP)                  198  RED                RL12005
  JO 40              B    (AB
  MICK LINEHAM       G    (AB
```

```
    BUZZY LINHART G V D K (ALL    (A) BUZZY                    1969   PHILIPS      UK          SBL 7885
    BIG JIM SULLIVAN  SITAR(A     (B) MUSIC                    1971   BUDDAH UK 2318 028 US ELEUTHERA 3601
    KESHAV SATHE      TABLA(A     (C) THE TIME TO LIVE IS NOW  1971   KAMA SUTRA UK 2319 011
    RAY 'TAFF' WILLIAMS G (A      (D) BUZZY                    1972   KAMA SUTRA UK 2319 024 US        2053
    RITCHIE FRANCIS   B    (A     (E) THE BEST OF              19     KAMA SUTRA              US 2615
    PHIL RYAN         K    (A     (F) PUSSYCATS CAN GO FAR     1974   ATLANTIC   UK K50046
    JOHN WEATHERS     D    (A
    DOUGLAS RAUCH  B G (B    DOUG RODRIGUES  G PERC(B  JOHN SIOMOS     D (B   DAVID BROMBERG    G    (B
    MARK KLINGMAN     K   (BD    LUTHER RIX   D    (CD  BILL TAKAS   B V(C    JEANNIE LINHART        C  (C
    KEN ASHER         K   (C     JEFF BAXTER  G STEEL (C  PETER PONZOL  WIND(D  DANNY TRIFAN B V K PERC (C
    PETER PLANSKY   TAMB  (D     BARRY BECKETT    K   (F  ROGER HAWKINS PERC(F  PETE CARR         G  (F
    JIMMY JOHNSON     G   (F     DAVID HOOD    B     (F  JERRY MASTERS  B (F   HARRISON CALLOWAY    TPT (F
    BEN CAULEY       TPT  (F     CHARLES ROSE  TROM (F  RONNIE EADES   SAX(F   CHARLIE CHALMERS    SAX (F
    KIRBY CAMPBELL   CLAR (F     BARRY GOLDBERG  K   (F  FRANK TABINO   (F     HERBIE MANN       PERC?(F
    PERRY BARBER      V   (F     BARNABY BYE   V     (F  CAROLE BAYER SAGER V(F  PETER ALLEN       V  (F
    JORDON KAPLAN  DRUNK(F   FLORENCE STATE UNI CHOR V(F
```

```
    SNAKE McANDREW    D   (AB    (A) PROUD FLESH SOOTHSEER   1968  MERCURY UK 20142      US 61181
    DINO LONG         D   (AB    (B) FEVER SHOT              1969  MERCURY UK 20165      US 61218
    FRED WALK    SITAR G   (AB    (C) TILL THE BREAK OF DAWN  1970  PHILIPS              US 600326
    LARRY EASTER    WIND (AB
    STEPHEN MILLER  V ORG(AB
```

```
    STEVE WEBB       G V  (A     (A) RUNNING ALL NIGHT       1980  A&M  US 4755 UK  AMLH64755
    ROBIN LE MESURIER G   (A
    GARY FARR        V   (A    ERIC DILLON    D   (A  STEVE HUMPHREYS B (A   JOHN SINCLAIR   K V (A
```

```
    DAVE GRANT     V PERC(AB     (A) INTUITION               1981  CHRYSALIS     UK   CHR 1332
    SKETCH          B    (AB     (B) GO AHEAD                1981  CHRYSALIS     UK   CHR 1358
    BOB CARTER      K G PERC(A
    ANDY DUNCAN     D PERC(A  LARRY TOLFREE   D   (   SPIKE EDNEY  K G HRN(  CHRIS HUNTER    SAX (
    J J BELLE       G   (    JUNIOR GISCOMBE  V   (   CANUTE EDWARDS  G (A
```

```
                                (A) LIPS                     1979  NEMPOER    US         35621
```

```
    CYNTHIA JOHNSON   V   (ABC   (A) MOUTH TO MOUTH          1980  CASABLANCA UK NBLP 7197
    IVAN RAFOWITZ   K SYN(CA     (B) PUCKER UP               1980  CASABLANCA UK NBLP 7242
    STEVEN GREENBERG K SYN (AC    (C) DESIGNER MUSIC          1981  CASABLANCA    NBLP 7262
    SCOTT JONES     K V  (C
    ROGER DUMAS     SYN  (CA  BOBBY SCHNITZER  G   (C  TERRY GRANT   B (AC  BOBBY VANDELL   D   (C
    MELANIE ROSALES  V   (C   ANDRE CYMONE     V   (C  ROCKIE ROBBINS V (C  TOM RIOPELLE    G   (A
    DAVID RIVKIN     G   (A   DALE MENDENHAL  HRNS(A  JACK GILLESPIE HRNS(A  RICHARD JORGENSEN  HRNS(A
    DANA GREENBERG   V   (A   JOYCE LEPINSKY   V   (A  STRINGS       (A
```

```
    SANDY PANTALEO   V   (A     (A) LIQUID SMOKE             1969  AVCO           33005
    VINCE FERSAK     G   (A
    MIKE ARCHELETA   B   (A  CHAS KIMBRELL   D   (A  BENNY NINMANN  K (A
```

```
    JIM KANE       B SYN(AB     (A) DISTORTIONS              196   WARICK      US      671
    DENNY WAITE    V K   (B     (B) $100. FINE               196   HEXAGON     US      681
    TOM CAPLAN       G   (B     (C) EMERGE                   1969  PROBE               4504
    MARK GALLAGHER   V   (C
    TOM MURRAY       D   (BC  DAN RINALDI  G V (BC  RAY MELINA    G V (C
```

```
    BOOKER LITTLE   TPT  (A     (A) THE LEGENDARY QUARTET ALBUM  1977  ISLAND    UK  ILPS 9454
    TOMMY FLANAGAN  PNO  (A
    WYNTON KELLY    PNO  (A  SCOTT LA FARO   B   (A  ROY HAYNES     D  (A
```

```
    KEN LITTLE       V   (A     (A) SOLO                     1973 DHARMA       US   801
    OAK SHULTZ       K   (A
    GORDY JOHNSON    D   (A   RON RAMELLI  K HCA V  (A  FRANK MUSTARI  G  (A  DANNY MARTIN   B (A
    NORMAN WAGNER    G   (A   SUGARCANE HARRIS  VLN V(A  JOHN CAMELOT   K  (A  RICK MACOWSKI  D (A
    DETROIT JR      PNO  (A   HUBERT SUMLIN   G   (A  JOE PARENTI    D  (A
```

```
    MARIE LITTLE     V   (AB    (A) FACTORY GIRL             1972  ARGO           FB 19
    ROBIN DRANSFIELD     (A     (B) MARIE LITTLE             1973  LEADER         LER2084
    BARRY DRANSFIELD     (A
    SMILEY MOSES     G   (A  DAVE MOSES   B RECORDER(A
```

```
    ANTHONY GOURDINE  V   (     (A) OUT OF SIGHT OUT OF MIND  1969 UA   US 6720 RI LIBERTY 10117
    CLARENCE COLLINS      (     (B) FOREVER YOURS             19   ROULETTE US 42007
    TRACY LORD            (     (C) GREATEST HITS             19   ROULETTE US 25292
    ERNEST WRIGHT         (     (D) GOIN' OUT OF MY HEAD      1965 DCP      US  6808 VEEP US 16511
    NAT ROGERS            (     (E) ON A NEW STREET           1974 AVCO     US 11012
    SAM STRAIN            (     (F) WE ARE THE IMPERIALS      19   END      US   303
                                (G) SHADES OF THE 40's        19   END      US   311
                                (H) I'M ON THE OUTSIDE LOOKIN' IN  1964 DCP US  3801
                                (I) PAYIN' OUR DUES           1967 VEEP     US 16513
                                (J) REFLECTIONS               1967 VEEP     US 16514
                                (K) SING THEIR HITS           19   FORUM    US  9107
                                (L) MOVIE GRABBERS            19   VEEP     US 16516
                                (M) BEST OF VOL 1             196  VEEP     US 16512
                                (N) BEST OF VOL 2             196  VEEP     US 15519
                                ( ) HITS OF                   19   PICKWICK US 3029
                                ( ) LITTLE ANTHONY & IMPERIALS 1970 SUNSET  US 5287
                                ( ) ON THE OUTSIDE            19   DCP      US 3801 VEEP US 16510
                                ( ) VERY BEST OF              19   UA       US LA 255
                                (EP) REMEMBER                 1976 UA                UK REM  405
```

```
   WILLIE' LITTLE BEAVER'HALE G V(ABC   (A) LITTLE BEAVER           1974  PRESIDENT          PTLS1060
   RON BAGDON          B    (AB         (B) PARTY DOWN              1975  PRESIDENT          PTLS1063
   EDMUND COLLINS      B    (A          (C) BLACK RHAPSODY          19    CAT                CAT 1602
   FREDDIE SCOTT       D    (A
   ROBERT FERGUSON     D    (AB  BENNY LATIMORE   K   (AB GEORGE PERRY    B   (B  NELSON PADRON    B  (B
   TIMMY THOMAS        K    (B   GLEN HOLMES     PERC (B  WILLIE CLARKE  PERC (B  BETTY WRIGHT     V  (B
```

```
   DERMOT MOUGHAN      K    (A          (A) LITTLE BO BITCH         1979  COBRA  CBR1002 EMI 062 07160
   BOB WAINWRIGHT      B    (A
   STEVE CARROLL       G    (A   TERRY REECE      D   (A TONY WATSON     V   (A
```

```
   BOB PIAZZA          V    (ABCDEF      (A) OFF THE RAILS          1977  CHISWICK UK WIK6 GER    67052
   GUY GREMY           G    (ABCDE       (B) LITTLE BOB STORY       1978  CRYPTO        FR   ZAL6415
   DOMINIQUE GUILLON   G    (AB          (EP) I'M CRYING            1977  CHISWICK      UK       SW7
   DOMINIQUE QUERTIER  D    (ABC         (C) HIGH TIME              1977  ARCANE        FR   913 076
   DOMINIQUE LELAN     B    (ABCDEF      (D) COME ON SEE ME         1978  RCA           FR   PL 37217
   SEAN TYLA           G    (A           (E) LIVE +EP               1979  RCA           FR   PL 37360
   VICO REBIBO         D V  (DEF         (F) LIGHT OF MY TOWN       1980  RCA           FR   PL 37412
   SERGE HENDRIX       V    (DE
   DOMINIQUE COMONT    K V  (F   JOHN EARL        SAX (F LOUP DURET    G V HCA(F
```

```
   MARC COPLAN         V    (A           (A) IN THE WOODLAND OF WEIR  196 FONTANA       US      67578
   BILL MOONEY         D    (A
   PETER POLLACK       G    (A   RAY LEVIN        K B FLT(A      BASIL ACCOLADE   CLAR (A
```

```
   LITTLE EVA           V   (ALL          (A) LLLLLOCOMOTION        1962  DIMENSION     US    6000
                                          (A) LLLLLOCOMOTION        1963  LONDON           UKHAU8036
                                          (A) LOCOMOTION            1972  LONDON           UKSHU8437
```

```
   LOWELL GEORGE       G V  (ALL          (A) LITTLE FEAT           1971  WB US WS 1890    UK K46072
   RITCHIE HAYWARD     D V  (ALL          (B) SAILIN' SHOES         1972  WB US BS 2600    UK K46156
   RY COODER           G    (A            (C) DIXIE CHICKEN         1973  WB US BS 2686    UK K46200
   PAUL BARRERE        G V  (CDEFGH       (D) FEATS DONT FAIL ME NOW 1974 WB US BS 2784    UK K56030
   SAM CLAYTON       V PERC (CDEFGH       (E) LAST RECORD ALBUM     1976  WB US BS 2884    UK K56156
   KEN GRADNEY         B    (CDEFGH       (F) TIME LOVES A HERO     1977  WB US BS 3015    UK K56349
   BILL PAYNE    K V PERC   (ALL          (G) WAITING FOR COLUMBUS(DBL LIVE) 1978 WB US 2 3140 UK K66075
   ROY ESTRADA         B V  (AB           (H) DOWN ON THE FARM      1979  WB US HS 3345    UK K56667
   JEFF BAXTER         G    (F            (AC)TWO ORIGINALS         1975  WB               UK K66038
   FRED TACKETT        G    (ACFH         (J) HOY HOY               1981  WB               UK K66100
   MICK TAYLOR         G    (C
   PAT SIMMONS         G V  (F   MIKE McDONALD    V   (F  GREG ADAMS     TPT  (FG EMILIO CASTILLO SAX (AFG
   MIC GILLETTE       HRNS  (AFG STEVE KUPKA     SAX  (AFG LENNIE PICKETT SAX (AFG ELLIOT INGBER    (AG
   DEBBIE LINDSEY      V    (BC  EMMYLOU HARRIS   V   (D  JOHN HALL      G    (E  DAVID LINDLEY    (H
   RUSS TITELMAN PROD PNO  (AB  MILT HOLLAND    PERC (BC  FRAN TATE      V    (DE VALERIE CARTER  V  (E
   JULIA TILLMAN       V    (H   JERRY JUMONVILLE     (H  SNEAKY PETE   STEEL(ABCH RON ELLIOTT    G  (B
   BONNIE RAITT        V    (DHC FRAN PAYNE      V   (H  EARL PALMER         (H  MAXINE WILLARD   V  (H
   ROBBEN FORD         G    (H   ROSEMARY BUTLER  V   (H  DAN SMITH           (H  LUTHER WATERS    V  (H
   ORRIN WATERS        V    (H   LEE THORNBERG        (H  STEPHANIE SPRUILLE V (C TED TEMPLEMAN  PROD(B
   BONNIE BRAMLETT     V    (C   TRETT FURE      V   (C  GLORIA JONES        (C  MALCOLM CECIL    SYN(C
   DAN HUNTER          V    (C
```

```
   PETER ILLINWORTH    G V  (A            (A) LITTLE FREE ROCK   1969  TRANSATLANTIC   UK   TRA 608
   PAUL VARLEY         D    (A
   FRANK NEWBOLD       B V PERC(A
```

```
   LITTLE MILTON CAMPBELL G V(ALL         (A) WERE GONNA MAKE IT    19    CHECKER       US      2995
   BOBBY MANUEL        G    (F            (B) SINGS BIG BLUES       1968  CHECKER       US      3002
   LESTER SNELL       PNO   (F            (C) GRITS & GROCERIES     1969  CHESS UK 4552 CHECKER US 3011
   MICHAEL TOLES       G    (F            (D) IF WALLS COULD TALK   1969  CHECKER       US      3012
   WILLIAM MURPHY      B    (F            (E) FRIEND OF MINE        19    GLADES        US      7508
   DAVID WEATHERSPOON  B    (F            (F) BLUES & SOUL          1974  STAX   UK STX1013  US  5514
   WILLIE HALL         D    (F            (G) GOLDEN DECADE         1974  PHONOGRAM          6310  120
   MEMPHIS HRNS             (F            (H) MONTREUX FESTIVAL     1974  STAX          UK   STX 1029
   LAWRENCE TAYLOR    SAX   (J            (J) RAISE A LITTLE SAND   1975  RED LIGHTNIN' UK   RL   0011
   EUGENE TURNER      PNO   (J            (K) BLUES MASTERS         1976  CHESS            2A CMB204
   JERRY WALKER        D    (J            (L) SAMS BLUES            1976  CHARLY        UK   CR  30102
   LARRY PROTO        TPT   (J            (M) WAITIN' FOR           1973  STAX          UK   SAS  3012
   FONTELLA BASS      PNO   (J            (N) GREATEST HITS         1973  CHESS            CH 50113
   C W TATE           SAX   (J            (O) CHRONICLE             1979  STAX          UK   STX  4123
   CLEOPHUS ROBINSON  B     (J
   IKE TURNER         PNO   (J   OLIVER SAIN      SAX  (J LONNIE HAYES   D    (J  VERN HARRELL    SAX (J
   JESSE KNIGHT        B    (J   JAMES CARR       SAX  (J
```

```
   LITTLE RICHARD (PENNIMAN)PNO V(ALL     HERE'S LITTLE RICHARD     1958  SPECIALTY US 2100 UK LONDON  2055
   WITH                                   LITTLE RICHARD 2          1958  SPECIALTY US 2103 UK LONDON  2126
   JIMI HENDRIX        G V  (*            THE FABULOUS              1959  SPECIALTY US 2104 UK LONDON  2193
                                          BIGGEST HITS              196   SPECIALTY US 2111
                                          GREATEST HITS             196   SPECIALTY US 2113
                                          WELL ALRIGHT              1959  SPECIALTY US 2136
                                          SINGS GOSPEL              1964  STATESIDE      UK    SL10054
                                          LITTLE RICHARD IS BACK    196   JOY      US 100
                                          LITTLE RICHARD IS BACK    196   FONTANA        UK    TL5235
                                          LITTLE RICHARD IS BACK    196   VEEJAY   US 1107
                                          LITTLE RICHARDS GREATEST HITS 1964 JOY       US 107
                                          MR BIG                    196   JOY      US 195
                                          RIP IT UP                 196   JOY      US 260
                                          SLIPPIN' & SLIDIN'        196   JOY      US 270
                                          GREAT HITS                196              UK FONTANA  5314
                                          ITS REAL                  196              UK FONTANA 13010
                                          LITTLE RICHARD STORY      196   JOY      US 5003/4
                                          COMING HOME               1964  CORAL  US 757446 UK   LVA9220
                                          SINGS FREEDOM SONGS       1963  CROWN    US 5362
```

          (CONTINUED)
                                          [342]

LITTLE RICHARD   (CONTINUED)

GREATEST HITS LIVE	19	MODERN	US	100	
KING OF GOSPEL SONGS	1965	MERCURY	US	12288	
WILD & FRANTIC	1965	MODERN	US	103	
WILD & FRANTIC	19	UNITED	US	7777	
THE EXPLOSIVE	1967	OKEH	US	14117	UK COLUMBIA 6136
GREATEST HITS LIVE	19	OKEH	US	14121	
& ROY ORBISON	1970	RCA		UK	CDS 1077
THE RILL THING	1971	REPRISE	US	6406	
KING OF ROCK 'N' ROLL	1971	REPRISE	US	6462	UK K 44156
SECOND COMING	1971	REPRISE	US	2107	K 44204
THE GREAT ONES	197			UK MFP	50096
GREATEST HITS	1972	TRIP	US 8013		
ALL TIME HITS	1972	SONET		UK	SNTF 5000
ROCK HARD ROCK HEAVY	1972	SONET		UK	SNTF 5001
THE ORIGINAL	1972	SONET		UK	SNTF 5011
LITTLE RICHARD SINGS	19	20TH CENTURY	5010		
LITTLE RICHARD	19	KAMA SUTRA US	2023		
LITTLE RICHARD	19	BUDDAH	US	7501	
BEST OF	19	SCEPTER	US	18020	
RECORDED LIVE	19	EMBASSY		UK	31065
THE INCREDIBLE	19	CONTOUR		UK	2870 150
YOU CANT KEEP A GOOD MAN DOWN	1972	UNION PACIFIC		UK	UP 003
SINGS SPIRITUALS	19	UNITED	US	7723	
GREATEST HITS	19	UNITED	US	7775	
RIGHT NOW	19	UNITED	US	7791	
THE BEST OF	19	UPFRONT	US	123	
KEEP A KNOCKIN	19	RHAPSODY	US	9013	
EVERY HOUR WITH	1970	CAMDEN	US	2430	
KING OF GOSPEL SINGERS	19	WING	US	12288	
CLAP YOUR HANDS	19	SPINORAMA US	S 119		
BIG HITS	19	GNP		US	9033
THE ONE & ONLY	1974	POLYDOR		UK	2482 440
STAR COLLECTION	1975	REPRISE		UK	K24009
THE VERY BEST OF	1975	UA	US LA4976		
DOLLARS DOLLARS & MORE DOLLARS	1975	CHARLY		UK	CR 30009
CAST A LONG SHADOW	197	EPIC		UK	66285
LITTLE RICHARD	197	EPIC	US	26260	
GREATEST HITS	197	EPIC	US	24257	UK EMBASY 31504
& SISTER ROSETTA THARPE	19	MARBLE ARCH		UK	MALS1319
(*) FRIENDS FROM THE BEGINNING	197	EMBER		UK	EMB 3434
GOOD GOLLY MISS MOLLY	19	HALLMARK		UK	SHM 858
22 ORIGINAL HITS	1977	WARWICK		UK	WW5034
20 ORIGINAL HITS	1976	SPECIALTY		UK	SNTF5017
NOW	1977	CREOLE			CRLP 510
GREATEST HITS	1980	SPECIALTY	UK	SNTF 5028	
GEORGIA PEACH	1980	CHARLY	UK	CR 30190	
MODERN SIDES 10"	1981	ACE	UK	CH38	
ROCK'N'ROLL FOREVER	19	REPRISE	UK	K24031	
(EP)					
HERE'S LITTLE RICHARD	195	SPECIALTY US		SEP 400	
" " " "	2	195	SPECIALTY US		SEP 401
" " " "	3	195	SPECIALTY US		SEP 402
LITTLE RICHARD 1	195	SPECIALTY US		SEP 403	
" " "	2	195	SPECIALTY US		SEP 404
" " "	3	195	SPECIALTY US		SEP 405
ROCKS	19	RCA	US	CAE 446	
LITTLE RICHARD	19	RCA CAMDEN US		CAE 4111	
LONG TALL SALLY	1977	SPECIALTY UK		SONE 1	
LITTLE RICHARD	19	SPECIALTY UK		SON 5016	

LITTLE RIVER BAND

GRAHAM GOBLE	G V	(ABCDEFGHJK	(A) LITTLE RIVER BAND	1975 EMI	UK EMC3144 US CAPITOL 11512
DAVID BRIGGS	G	(BCDEFGHJK	(B) AFTER HOURS	1976 EMI	UK EMC2546 US CAPITOL 16072
GLENN SHORROCK	HCA V	(ABCDEFGHJK	(C) DIAMANTINA COCKTAIL	1977 EMI	UK EMC3187 US CAPITOL 11645
GEORGE McARDLE	B	(BCD	(D) SLEEPER CATCHER	1978 EMI	UK EMA 786 US CAPITOL 11782
DEREK PELLICCI	D	(ABCDEFGHJK	(E) IT'S A LONG WAY THERE	1978 EMIIMP	064 82516
BEEB BIRTLES	G	(ABCDEFGHJK	(F) FIRST UNDER THE WIRE	1979 CAPITOL	11954
WAYNE NELSON	B V	(K	(G) BEGINNINGS	1979 CAPITOL	16141
RICK FORMOSA	G	(AC	(H) BACKSTAGE PASS	1980 CAPITOL	12061
IAN MASON	PNO	(AC	(J) BEGINNINGS	1980 CAPITOL	16142
COL LAUGHNAN	SAX	(A	(K) TIME EXPOSURE	1981 CAPITOL GER 40042	12163
PETER SULLIVAN	PNO	(C			
TONY BUCHANAN	SAX	(C	ROGER McLACHLAN B (A	STEPHEN COONEY MAND (A GARY HYDE	PERC (A
EDDIE DENTON		(C	GRAHAM LYALL FLT (C	PETER JONES PNO (AK GEOFF SKEWES	K (A
BILL COUMO	K	(K			

LITTLE SONNY

LITTLE 'LITTLE SONNY'ARRON G G HCA(AB	(A) NEW KING OF BLUES HARMONICA	197	ENTERPRISE	US	1005
	(B) BLACK N BLUE	197	ENTERPRISE	US	1018

LITTLE TINA & FLIGHT 56

(A) THIS GIRL GONNA ROCK	1978	CHARLY	UK	CR 30155

LITTLE WALTER

LITTLE WALTER JACOBS HCA A(ALL	(A) LITTLE WALTER	1964 PYE INT	UK	NPL 28043	
LOUIS MYERS	G	(AGHLMNJ	(A) LITTLE WALTER	1968 MARBLE ARCH	UK RI MAL 815
DAVE MYERS	G	(AGHLMNJ	(B) SUPER BLUES	1967 CHESS	UK CRL 4529
WILLIE DIXON	G	(AGHLMNJ	(C) BEST	196 CHESS US 1428 +CHECKER	3004
FRED BELOW	D	(AGHLMNJ	(D) BOSS OF BLUES HARMONICA	196 CHESS	US 60014
ROBERT LOCKWOOD	G	(GHLMNJ	(E) BLUES MASTERS	196 CHESS	UK 2A CBM 202
FRED ROBINSON	G	(AGHLMNJ	(F) HATE TO SEE YOU GO	19 CHESS	US 1535
OTIS SPANN	PNO	(AGHLMNJ	(G) & HIS JUKES	19 PYTHON	UK PLPKM 20
MUDDY WATERS	G	(AGLMNJ	(H) QUARTER TO TWELVE	1970 RED LIGHTNIN'	UK RL 002
GEORGE HUNTER	D	(AGHLMNJ	(J) THUNDERBIRD	1971 SYNDICATE CHAPTER	SC 004
LUTHER TUCKER	G	(AGHLMNJ	(K) CONFESSIN' THE BLUES	1976 CHESS US 416	EURO CH 50043
JIMMY LEE ROBINSON G	(G		(L) BLUE & LONESOME	19 ROI DU BLUES	CAN 33 2007

                                   (CONTINUED)

LITTLE WALTER

LEONARD CASTON	G	(GJ		(M) SOUTHERN FEELING	19	ROI DU BLUES	CAN	33 2012	
BILL STEPNEY	D	(G		(N) BLUE MIDNIGHT	19	ROI DU BLUES	CAN	33 2017	
THE CORONETS	V	(M		(O) CHESS MASTERS	1981	CHESS		CXMD 4002	
BO DIDDLEY	G	(G							
JIMMY ROGERS	G	(L	ELGIN EVANSIDE	D (L HENRY GRAY	PNO	(L ANDREW STEPHENSON	B	(M	
JARRETT GIBSON	SAX	(MH	JACK MYERS	B (MN J T BROWN	SAX	(N FRANCIS CLAY	D	(M	
LAFAYETTE LEAKE	PNO	(MN	AL DUNCAN	D (MN PAT HARE	G	(M BUDDY GUY	G	(MN	
BILLY EMERSON	K	(MN	ERNEST 'BIG' CRAWFORD B (N						

L94A
LITTLE WILLIE LITTLEFIELD

LITTLE WILLIE LITTLEFIELD	(A) LITTLE WILLIE LITTLEFIELD VOL 1(10")	1980	ACE		1OCH	24	
	(B) IT'S MIDNIGHT	19	ROUTE 66 SWED	KIX	10	
	(C) LITTLE WILLIE LITTLEFIELD	(10"0	1981	ACE		1OCH	34

L94B
LIVERPOOL EXPRESS

BILLY KINSLEY	B	(A		(A) TRACKS	1976	WB UK	K56281
TONY COATES	G V	(A					
DEREK CASHIN	D	(A	ROGER CRAIG	K (A			

L95
LIVERPOOL SCENE

ANDY ROBERTS	G V	(ABCDEF1		(A) INCREDIBLE NEW LIVERPOOL SCENE	1967	CBS 63045 UK EPIC US BN 26336			
ADRIAN HENRI	V	(ABCDEF1		(B) AMAZING ADVENTURES OF	1968	RCA US LSP4189	UK SF 7995		
MIKE EVANS	V SAX(BCDE1			(C) BREAD ON THE NIGHT	1969	RCA US LSP4267	UK SF 8057		
MIKE HART	V G	(BE1		(D) ST ADRIAN & CO	1970	RCA	UK SF 8100		
PERCY JONES	B HCA(BCDE			(E) HEIRLOON	1970	RCA	UK SF 8134		
BRIAN DODSON	D	(BCDE		(F) RECOLLECTIONS	1972	CHARISMA	UK CS 3		
PETE CLARKE		(E		(1) 1974 REFORM					
ROGER McGOUGH		(E							
TOM KEMPINSKI	V	(E	DAVE RICHARDS	B (1 MIKE KELLIE	D (1	FRANK GARRETT		(E	
KARL JENKINS	SAX	(D	IAN CARR	TPT (D JOHN MUMFORD	TROM (D	IAN WHITMAN	K	(D	

L95A
LIVE WIRE

GERMAN GONZALES	D V	(ABC	(A) PICK IT UP	1979	A&M US 4793	UK AMLH 64793	
MIKE EDWARDS	V G	(ABC	(B) NO FRIGHT	1980	A&M US 4814	UK AMLH 64814	
JEREMY MEEK	B V	(ABc	(C) CHANGES MADE	1981	A&M UA 4856	UK AMLH 68502	
CHRIS CUTLER	G V	(A					
SIMON BOSWELL	G K V(BC	JOHN IRISH EARLE SAX (C					

L95B
LIVIN' BLUES

NICKO CHRISTIANSEN V G SAX(ABCDE			(A) HELLS SESSION	1969	PHILIPS	NL 6440 315	
TED OBERG	G	(ABCDEFG	(B) WANG DANG DOODLE	1970	PHILIPS		6440 125
JOHN LA GRAND	HCA	(ABCDE	(C) BAMBOOZLE	1971	PHILIPS		6413 024
HENK SMITSKAMP	B K	(AF	(D) ROCKIN' AT THE TWEEDMILL	1972	PHILIPS	GER 6423 052	
CESAR ZUIDERWIJK	D	(A	(E) RAM JAM JOSEY	1973	ARIOLA	GER 88525	
RUUD VAN BUUREN	B	(BCDE	(F) LIVE '75	1975	ARIOLA		89243
DICK BEEKMAN	D	(B	(G) BLUE BREEZE	1976	ARIOLA	NL 28430	
ARJEAN KAMMINGA	D	(D					
PETE WINGFIELD	PNO	(DE	MIKE VERNON	V (D KENNY LAMB	D (E JOHN FREDRIKSZ	V	(FG
COR VAN DER BEEK	D	(F	ANDRE REIJNEN	B (G JACOB VAN HEININGEN D	(G MARGRIET ESHUYS	V	(G
MAGGIE McNEAL	V	(G	MARTIN AGTERBERG	K (G JONNY LE JEUNE	B (D		

L95C
KERRY LIVGREN

KERRY LIVGREN K G B D V(A			(A) SEEDS OF CHANGE	1980	KIRCHNER US 36567	UK 84453	
STEVE WALSH	V	(A					
BARRIEMORE BARLOW D	(A	PHIL EHART	D (A PAUL GODDARD	B (A BOBBY CAMPO HRNS/PERC(A		
JEFF POLLARD	V	(A	MYLON LEFEVRE	V (A RONNIE JAMES DIO	V (A JOEY JELL V	(A	
DARRYL KUTZ	HCA	(A	JOHN THOMPSON	D (A BARY GILBERT	B (A DONNA WILLIAMS V	(A	
DAVE PACK	V	(A	DAVY MOIRE	V (A VICTORIA LIVGREN	V (A STEVE VENEZIA V	(A	
ROBBIE STEINHARDT VLN	(A	BRAD AARON	V (A JOHN FRISTOE	V (A		

L96
DANDY LIVINGSTONE

DANDY LIVINGSTONE	(ALL	(A) RETURNS	19	TROJAN		TRL 2	
		(B) DANDY LIVINGSTONE	19	TROJAN		TRL 45	
		(C) MORNING SIDE OF THE MOUNTAIN	19	TROJAN		TBL 118	
		(D) CONSCIOUS	19	MOONCREST		CREST 5	
		(E) SOUTH AFRICAN EXPERIENCE	1978	NIGHT OWL NORLP	1001	

L97
CHARLES LLOYD

CHARLES LLOYD	WIND (ALL	(A) MOONMAN	1972	MCA MUPS 421 UK+1974 UK MCF 2643			
MIKE LOVE	(E	(B) LOVE IN	19	ATLANTIC	US SD 1481		
CARL WILSON	(E	(C) IN EUROPE	19	ATLANTIC	US SD 1500		
AL JARDINE	(E	(D) SOUNDTRACK	19	ATLANTIC	US SD 1519		
ROGER McGUINN	(E	(E) WAVES	1972	A&M	US SP 3044		

L98
IAN LLOYD

IAN LLOYD	V PROD(AB		(A) IAN LLOYD	1976	POLYDOR	US 1 6066	
JIM VALLANCE	(BC		(B) GOOSE BUMPS	1979	SCOTTI BROS UK K50655 US SB 7104		
STEVE BUSLOWE	(B		(C) 3 WC	1980	SCOTTI BROS UK K50770 US 7110		
STEVE LOVE	G	(A					
JIMMY CRESPO		(B	MICK JONES G V (ABC LOU GRAMM	(B DENNIS ELLIOTT	(B		
RICK OCASEK		(B	BENJAMIN ORR	(B JIMMY MAELEN PERC (AB DAVID SINCLAIR	(B		
MICHAEL BRECKER	HRNS	(B	LINDSAY MITCHELL	(B LARRY FAST	(B GREGG DIAMOND PROD D	(AC	
IAN McDONALD	SAX	(A	JAMES GREGSON B (A KENNETH BICHEL K	(A DAVE BYRON V	(A		
BRAN ADAMS	G	(C	NANCY NASH	V (C THE ALIENS	(C BRUCE FAIRBAIRN V	(C	

L98A
RICHARD LLOYD

RICHARD LLOYD G V PNO HCA(A			(A) ALCHEMY	1979	ELEKTRA	UK K52196	
MATTHEW MACKENZIE G PNO V(A							
JIM MASTRO	G	(A	FRED SMITH B V (A VINNY DENUNZIO	D V (A MICHAEL YOUNG	G SYN(A		

L99
ANDREW LLOYD WEBBER

ANDREW LLOYD WEBBER	(A		(A) VARIATIONS	1977	MCA	UK MCF 2824
DON AIREY	K	(A				
ROD ARGENT	K	(A	GARY MOORE G (A JON HISEMAN	D (A BARBARA THOMPSON WIND (A		
JOHN MOLE	B	(A	JULIAN LLOYD WEBBER CELLO(A			

L100
LOADING ZONE

LINDA TILLERY V B D HCA(A			(A) LOADING ZONE	1968	RCA	US LSP 3959	
PAUL FAUERSO	V K	(A	(B) ONE FOR ALL	19	UMBRELLA	US 101	
PETER SHAPIRO	G	(A					
TODD ANDERSON	WIND K(A	PAT O'HARA TROM (A STEVE DOWLER	G (A BOB KRIDLE	B (A		
GEORGE NEWCOM	D	(A					

```
L100A                        LOCAL HEROES                                              L100A
   KEVIN ARMSTRONG    V G  (A        (A) DRIP DRY ZONE              1980   OVAL           UK   OVLP 504
   KIM BARTI          D    (A
   MATTHEW SELIGMAN   B    (A
L100B                         KEN LOCKE                                               L100B
   KEN LOCKE    V K SYN SAX(A        (A) THE IMPOSSIBLE            1981   VIRGIN         UK   V2187
   JIM KERR           V    (A
   BOBBY COLLINS      V    (A   SUSIE O'LIST    V  (A   STEVIE SHEARS   G  (A  JOHN McGEOCH    G  (A
   JO DWORNIAK        B    (A   LEE ROBERTSON   B  (A   JOHN DOYLE      D  (A  PRESTON HEYMAN  D  (A
   PAUL SIMON         D    (A   NASH THE SLASH  VLN (A
L101                         GERRY LOCKRAN                                            L101
   GERRY LOCKRAN      V    (ALL       (A) HOLD ON I'M COMING        1967   PLANET            PLL 1002
   KIRK LORANGE       G V  (D        (B) THE ESSENTIAL             1969   SPARK             SRLP104
   NEIL HUBBARD       G    (DC       (C) WUN                       1972   POLYDOR           2383 122
   HENRY McCULLOUGH   G    (DC       (D) RAGS TO GLADRAGS          1976   DECCA          UK  SKLR5257
   ISRAEL ZACUTO      G    (D        (E) BLUES VENDETTA            19     WAVERLEY          ZLP 2091
   CHRIS STEWART      B    (DC       (1) BLUES BAND 1968
   BRUCE ROWLAND      D    (D
   MEL COLLINS        SAX  (D   CLIFF AUNGIER      (1   PHIL CHEN       B  (D  LOUIE MARTIN   PERC (D
   DWIGHT DRUICK      V    (D   HARVEY BURNS    D  (1   TERRY STANNARD  D  (D  PETE WINGFIELD PNO  (D
   JOHNNY PARKER      PNO  (1   BRIAN HOPKINS      (1   RON WOOD        G  (C  ANDY PYLE      G   (C
   JUNIOR HANSON      G    (C   RON BERG        SAX (C   CLIFF AUNGIER      (C  JEAN ROUSSEL   K   (C
   NICK PEARSON       K    (C   MICK RALPHS     G  (C   BRUCE ROWLANDS  D  (C  CHRIS MERCER   SAX (C
L102                         ROBERT LOCKWOOD                                          L102
   ROBERT 'JUNIOR'LOCKWOOD G V(ALL   (A) STEADY ROLLIN' MAN        1976   DELMARK            630
   GENE SCHWARTZ      B    (DF       (B) COUNTRY BLUES CLASSICS    19     BLUES CLASSICS    7
   GEORGE COOK        D    (D        (C) LONESOME ROAD BLUES       19     YAZOO             1038
   MAURICE REEDUS     SAX  (DF       (D) CONTRASTS                 1974   TRIX              330 7
   LOUIS MYERS        G HCA(E        (E) BLUES LIVE                1975   ADVENT US 2807 +TRIO JAP 6024
   DAVE MYERS         B    (E        (F) DOES 12                   1976   TRIX              331 7
   FRED BELOW         D    (E        (G) HANGIN' ON                19     ROUNDER        US   2023
   MARK HAHN          G    (F
   JIMMY JONES        D    (F   JOHNNY SHINES      G V  (G
L103                         LOCOMOTIV GT                                             L103
   TAMAS BARTA G V HCA  (A        (A) LOCOMOTIV GT              1974 ABC ABCX 811   +EPIC UK80229
   JOSEPH LAUX        D    (A        (B) ALL ABOARD               1975 ABC US 860
   GABOR PRESSER      K V  (A
   THOMAS SOMLO B V SAX VLN(A   JACK BRUCE      HCA (A   JIMMY MILLER   PERC (A
L104                         LOCOMOTIVE                                               L104
   MICK HINCKS        B V  (A        (A) WE ARE EVERYTHING YOU SEE 1969   PARLOPHONE     UK   PCS 7093
   MIKE TAYLOR        TPT  (A
   NORMAN HAINES      K V  (A   CHRIS WOOD     WIND (A   BILL MADGE     SAX (A  BOB LAMB       D   (A
   HENRY LOWTHER      TPT  (A   DICK HECKSTAL SMITH SAX(A  LYNN DOBSON  SAX (A  CHRIS MERCER   SAX (A
L104A                        LOCOMOTIVE (US)                                          L104A
                                   (A) LOCOMOTIVE               19     MGM            US   SE4653
L104B                        LOCOMOTIVE KREUZBERG                                     L104B
   ANDREAS BRAUER     V K SYN(AB      (A) KOLLEGE KLATT             1972   PLANE          GER  99 101
   VOLKER HIEMANN     G V  (AB       (B) JAMES BLOND              1973   PLANE          GER  99 103
   UWE HOLZ           V D HCA(AB      (C) FETLE JAHRE              1975   PLANE          GER  99 104
   FRANZ POWALLA      B V  (AB
   KARL HEINZ SCHERFLING V(AB   MANFRED PRAEKER    V B G  (B
L105                         LOCUST                                                   L105
                                   (A) PLAYGUE                  1977   ANNUIT COEPTIS     AC1004
L105A                        LOCUST (2)                                               L105A
   PHIL SPINELLI      V PERC(A        (A) ALPHA WAVES(LOCUST)       1976   BUK 6 22930    UK   BULP 2001
   PETE BONAS         G    (A
   CHRIS PARREN       K    (A   RAY ALLEN SAX V PER(A   BRENT FORBES    B  (A  JOHN DILLON    D   (A
                                  (UK EDITION NOT RELEASED???)
L106                         JOHN LODGE                                               L106
   JOHN LODGE         V G  (A        (A) NATURAL AVENUE   1977 DECCA UK TXS 120 LONDON US  683
   KENNEY JONES            (A
   BRIAN ROGERS            (A   MEL COLLINS    SAX (A   JOHN RICHARDSON    (A  STEVE SIMPSON      (A
   CHRIS SPEDDING     G    (A   MARTIN DOBSON      (A   ALAN WILLIAMS      (A  MICK WEAVER        (A
   JIMMY JEWELL       WIND (A   GARY OSBORNE       (A   BILLY LAWRIE       (A
L107                         NILS LOFGREN & GRIN                                      L107
   NILS LOFGREN       G VK(ALL        (A) GRIN               1971 EPIC UK 64272 US SPINDIZZY 30321
   JERRY PETERSON     SAX  (M        (A) GRIN               1980 EMBASSY UK 31770
   BOB BERBERICH      D V  (ABCDL     (B) ONE PLUS ONE       1972 EPIC UK 64652 US SPINDIZZY 31038
   BOB GORDON         B V  (ABCDL     (C) ALL OUT            1972 EPIC UK 65166
   TOM LOFGREN        G V  (CDFGHJKL1 (D) GONE CRAZY         1975 A&M  UK 64415 US A&M    SP4415
   REV PAT HENDERSON  K    (HJ        (E) NILS LOFGREN       1975 A&M  UK 64509 US A&M    SP4509
   WORNELL JONES      B V  (EFHJ      (F) CRY TOUGH          1976 A&M  UK 64573 US A&M    SP4573
   KATHI McDONALD     V    (CL        (G) BACK IT UP(AUTHORIZED BOOTLEG) 1975 A&M  US A&M  SP8362
   AYNSLEY DUNBAR     D    (EF        (H) I CAME TO DANCE    1977 A&M  UK 64628 US A&M    SP4628
   STU GARDNER        V    (E         (J) NIGHT AFTER NIGHT  1977 A&M  UK 69439 US A&M    SP3707
   CHUCK RAINEY       B    (F         (K) NILS              1979 A&M  UK 64756 US A&M    SP4756
   JIM GORDON         D    (F         (L) NILS LOFGREN & GRIN 1979 CBS  US            31770
   BOB EZRIN     PERC V K  (K        (AB) GRIN/ONE PLUS ONE  1976 CBS  UK 88204
   DOUG RILEY         ORG  (K         (1) LIVE TOUR 1975 LINE UP
   EMIL RICHARDS      PERC (F         (M) NIGHT FADES AWAY    1981 MCA  UK MCF 3121
   AL KOOPER          K    (FG
   CHUCK FINDLEY      HRN  (M   RON HICKLIN SINGERS   (F   P P ARNOLD     V  (F  CLAUDIA LENNEAR  V  (F
   BUDDY MILES        V    (F   RALPH MOLINA     V  (F   MIKE ZACK       D  (1G BOBBYE HALL     PERC (D
   PAUL STALLWORTH    B    (F   SCOTT BALL       B  (F1G DAVID PLATSHON  D  (J  ANDY NEWMARK     D  (H
   HOLDEN RAPHAEL     PERC (F   GRAHAM NASH      V  (B   CLYDIE KING     V  (D  SHIRLEY MATTHEWS V  (D
   MERRY CLAYTON      V    (D   ALLEN SCHWARZBERG D (K   JODY LINSCOTT  PERC (K DAVID SANBORN   SAX (K
   STU DAYE        G V     (K   BOB BABITT       B  (K   JEFF BAXTER    G PROD(M NICKY HOPKINS   K  (M
   RITCHIE HAYWARD         (M   JEFF PORCARO     D  (M   ED GREENE       D  (M  DAVID HUNGATE   B  (M
   NEIL STUBENHAUS    B    (M   ELLIOTT RANDALL  G  (M   BILLY TALBOT    V  (F  TREVOR VEITCH   G  (M
   GREG MATHIESON     K    (M   NEIL JASON       B  (M   DEL SHANNON     V  (M  FABULOUS ROBBS  V  (M
   ELLEN SNORTLAND    V    (M   MIGHTY CLOUD OF LOS SCUMBO(M

                                       [345]
```

L108   DAVE LOGGINS   L108

```
DAVE LOGGINS     G V  (ALL    (A) PERSONAL BELONGINGS        1972  VANGUARD      UK  VSD 6580
JERRY CARRIGAN   D    (B      (B) APPRENTICE                 1974  EPIC US 32833 UK  80622
JOHN GUERIN      D    (B      (C) COUNTRY SUITE              1976  EPIC US 33946
KENNY MALONE     D    (BCD    (D) ONE WAY TICKET TO PARADISE 1977  EPIC US 34713
NORBERT PUTNAM   B    (BA     (E) DAVID LOGGINS              1977  EPIC US 35972
WILLIAM SMITH    PNO  (B
BILLY SANFORD    G    (BA   BYRON BACH    CELLO(B  FARRELL MORRIS   PERC (B   JOHN RAINES      D(B
LEE SKLAR        B    (B    DAVID BRIGGS  PNO  (AB MIKE NOBLE       G   (BC   AL DELEONIBUS    ACC(B
LARRY LONDIN     D    (B    SHANE KEISTER  K   (B  STEVE GIBSON     G   (BD   MAC GAYDEN       FDL G (BC
WELDON MYRICK    STEEL(BC   GREG JOHNSON HCA V (C  LENNY KERLEY     G   (C    SHERRY KRAMER    V  (CD
BOB GELOFFE      V    (C    BERGEN WHITE      V (CD CRAIG LINK      V   (C    YVONE HODGES     V  (D
BUZZ CASON       V    (D    JOHN CHRISTOPHER G (D  JOHNNY GIMBLE    FDL (C    GAIL WHITFIELD   SAX(D
POP BOTTLE       B    (D    REGGIE YOUNG  G    (D  JIM ISABELL      D   (A    CHARLIE McCOY    HCAK(A
GLENN KENNER     G V  (D    JERRY CRUTCHFIELD K V (C RANDOLF GOODRUM K SYN(CD  JACK WILLIAMS    B  (CD
BILLY SANFORD    G    (C    BEN PEDIGOE  BAN   (C  LISA SILVER      FDL (C    DIANE TIDWELL    V  (CD
JIM SALESTROM    V    (C
```

L109   KENNY LOGGINS   L109

```
KENNY LOGGINS    G V  (ALL    (A) CELEBRATE ME HOME    1977  CBS US 34655  UK  81882
ROBBEN FORD      G    (A      (B) NIGHTWATCH           1978  CBS US 35387  UK  82865
STEVE GADD       D    (A      (C) KEEP THE FIRE        1979  CBS US 36172  UK  83869
LAUDIR DE OLIVEIRA PERC(A     (D) ALIVE(DBL)           1980  CBS US 36378  UK  88500
ERIC GALE        G    (A
GEORGE HAWKINS   B V(ABCD  VINCE DENHAM WIND V (ABCD  MIKE HAMILTON   G V (BCD  BRIAN MANN     K V(D
TRIS IMBODEN     D HCA(BCD  JON CLARKE  WIND PERC(ABCD STEVE WOOD     V   (D    RICHARD STEKOL V (C
MIKE McDONALD    V    (C    GWEN GUTHRIE     V (A   STEVE NICKS      V   (B    PATTI AUSTIN   V )A
HUGH McCRACKEN   G    (A    TOMMY TEDESCO  MAND(A  RICHARD TEE       K   (A    BOB JAMES      K, (A
STEVE FORMAN     PERC (A    HIRAM BULLOCK  G   (A  DEAN PARKS        G   (A    LANI GROVES    V (A
STEVE KHAN       G    (A    RALPH McDONALD  D  (A  HARVEY MASON      D   (A    LEE RITENOUR   G (A
MICHAEL JACKSON  V    (C    MICHAEL BRECKER SAX(C  FRED TACKETT      G   (C    MILT HOLLAND   PERC(C
RICHARD PAGE     V    (C    JEFF BOUCHARD   V  (C  PAULINHO DACOSTA  PERC(D    MARK WITTENBERG G (D
ALBHY GALUTEN    STR  (D
```

L110   LOGGINS & MESSINA   L110

```
KENNY LOGGINS    G V  (ALL    (A) SITTIN' IN        1971  CBS  US 31044  UK 64902
JIM MESSINA      G B V(ALL    (B) LOGGINS & MESSINA 1972  CBS  US 31748  UK 65194
LARRY SIMS       B    (ALL    (C) FULL SAIL         1973  CBS  US 32540  UK 65775
AL GARTH         HRNS FDL(ALL (D) ON STAGE          1974  CBS  US 33848  UK 88014
MEREL BREGANTE   D    (ALL    (E) MOTHERLODE        1975  CBS  US 33175  UK 80431
JON CLARKE       HRNS (ALL    (F) SO FINE           1975  CBS  US 33810  UK 69169
MIKE OMARTIAN    K    (ABCHK  (G) NATIVE SONS       1976  CBS  US 33578  UK 69227
JACK LENZ        FLT  (J      (H) BEST OF FRIENDS   1977  CBS  US 34388  UK 81692
VINCE DENHAM     SAX  (JFGK   (J) FINALE            1978  CBS  US 34167  UK 88205
DON ROBERTS      SAX  (JEFGK  (K) BEST OF           1980  EMBASSY  UK 31826
RICHARD GREENE   VLN  (JFGK
STEVE FORMAN     PERC(JFGK  WOODY CHRISMAN   G (J   GEORGE HAWKINS  B V (J   DOUG LIVINGSTON K (J
WILLIE ORNELAS   D    (J    ED SANFORD      V (GK  MARTY PAICH     STR (GK  MIKE RUBIN      PNO (FGK
DAVID PAICH      K    (EK   RUSTY YOUNG     G (B   VICTOR FELDMAN  PERC(EGK STEVE STILLS    V (B
DAVID WALLACE    SYN  (EK   CHRIS BROOKS KOTO (EK  MURRAY MacLEOD  V   (GK  JOHN TOWNSEND   V (GK
MILT HOLLAND PERC(ABCDEFGHK VINCE CHARLES    D (C
```

L110A   LOGIC SYSTEM   L110A

```
                              (A) LOGIC              1981  EMI           UK  EMC 3375
```

L110B   LOLLIPOP SHOPPE   L110B

```
FRED COLE        V    (A      (A) JUST COLOUR        1967  UNI           UK  73019
RON BUZZEL       G V  (A
ED BOWEN         G V  (A    BOB ATKINS       B (A   TIM ROCKSON     D   (A   JOHN THE GREEK  K (A
CARL FORTINA     ACC(A
```

L111   JACKIE LOMAX   L111

```
JACKIE LOMAX     V G          (A) IS THIS WHAT YOU WANT  1969  APPLE US 3354 UK  SAPCOR 6
(AKA RICK RED STREAK)         (B) HOME IS IN MY HEAD     1971  WB    US 1914 UK  K 46091
JOHN BARHAM           (A      (C) THREE                  1972  WB    US 2591 UK  K 46151
HAL BLAINE       D    (A      (D) LIVIN' FOR LOVIN'      1976  CAPITOL           11558
ALAN BRANSCOMBE      (A       (E) DID YOU EVER           1977  CAPITOL           11668
ERIC CLAPTON     G    (A
PETE CLARKE           (A   NICKY HOPKINS   K (A   BISHOP O'BRIEN      (A   RINGO STARR      D V (A
BRYN HAWORTH     G V  (B   PAUL GRIFFIN    K (B   LINDA NOVEMBER  V  (B    BILLY RICH       B (C
ROBBIE ROBERTSON G    (C   RICHARD MANUEL    (B   RON STOCKERT    K V (DE   STEVE BECKMAIER  G (D
HARVEY MASON     D    (D   IAN MATTHEWS    V (D   GEORGE HARRISON G  (A    LARRY KNECHTEL     (A
TONY NEWMAN      D    (D   KLAUS VOORMANN  B (A   BUGS PEMBERTON  D  (BDE  EDDIE BRIGATI    V (B
SELDON POWELL    SAX  (B   MAERETHA STEWART V (A  JOHN HALL       G  (C    LEVON HELM       V D (C
MARTY GREBB      SAX  (B   WILLIAM D SMITH K (A   MARTY DAVID     B  (DE   CHRISTOPHER PARKER D (D
DON WHALEY       V    (D   SPIKE HEATLEY     (A   PAUL McCARTNEY     (A    JOE OSBORN         (A
ISRAEL ZACUTO    G    (B   TOMMY CACCETTA  B (A   DAVID BRIGATI   V  (B    HELENE W MILES   V (B
BERNARD PURDIE   D    (C   RICK DANKO        (C   GARTH HUDSON       (C    JIMMY ROBERTS    SAX (DE
RANDY ZACUTO     G    (D   RITCHIE HAYWARD D (D   JOE CORRERO     D  (D    AL STAEHELY      V (D
ANDRE FISCHER    D    (E   AL CINER        G (E   MAX MIDDLETON   SYN (E   GENE DINWIDDIE   WIND(E
DEBORAH LINDSEY  V    (E   STEVE MADAIO   TPT (E   JIM PRICE       TROM(E   PAT MURPHY       PERC(E
BROOKS HUNNICUTT V    (E   LISA FREEMAN ROBERTS V (E
```

L112   LOMAX ALLIANCE   L112

```
JACKIE LOMAX     V G  (            NO ALBUMS
BUGS PEMBERTON   D    (
TOM CACCETTA     B    (     JOHN CANNING     G (C
```

L113   LONDON   L113

```
RIFF REGAN       V    (A      (A) ANIMAL GAMES       1978  MCA            MCF 2823
STEVE VOICE      B    (A      (B) LONDON (EP)        1977  MCA            MCA 319
JOHN MOSS        D    (A
DAVE WIGHT       G    (A
```

LONE GROOVER   L113A

```
                              (A) WHO CARES (EP)      1978  CHARLY        UK  CEP 124
```

LONE STAR

```
  KEN DRISCOLL        V    (A          (A) LONE STAR                  1976   CBS  US 34475   UK CBS  81545
  TONY SMITH          G    (AB         (B) FIRING ON ALL SIX          1977   CBS  US 34937   UK CBS  82213
  PAUL CHAPMAN        G    (AB
  PETE HURLEY         B    (AB  DIXIE LEE        D   (AB  RICK WORSNOP    K   (AB  JOHN SLOMAN       V  (B
```

LONESOME SUNDOWN

```
  LONESOME SUNDOWN               (A) LONESOME LONELY BLUES       1970  EXCELLO          US         8012
  (CORNELIUS GREEN)   V G  (AB   (A) LONESOME LONELY BLUES       1970  BLUE HORIZON     UK    7  63864
  LIONEL PREVO        SAX  (A    (B) BEEN GONE TOO LONG          1979  JOLIET           US         6002
  AUSTIN BROUSSARD    D    (A
  KATIE WEBSTER       PNO  (A  MERT THIBODEAUX    PNO  (A  LAZY LESTER     HCA (A  DEE DEE GRADNIER   HCA(A
  BOBBY McBRIDE       B    (A  RUFUS THIBODEAUX   B    (A  WARREN STORM    D   (A
```

ROY LONEY & THE PHANTOM MOVERS

```
  ROY LONEY           V    (ABC        (A) PHANTOM TRACKS (EP)        1980   SOLID SMOKE              9002
  DANNY MIHM          D    (A          ( ) OUT AFTER DARK            1979   SOLID SMOKE     US       9001
  JAMES FERRELL       G    (A          (C) CONTENTS UNDER PRESSURE   1981   WAR BRIDE       UK       9003
  MAURICE TANI        B    (AC
  LARRY LEA           G    (AC  MOREY GOLDSTEIN   SAX  (C  JOHN REWIND     G PERC(C  JOHNNY SURRELL    D  (C
  NICK BUCK           K    (C   JOHN KALDOR       GV   (C  RAFAEL MARTINES PERC (C
```

LONG TALL ERNIE

```
                                       (A) DO YOU REMEMBER           197    POLYDOR         GER  2417 113
```

LONGBRANCH PENNYWHISTLE

```
  J D SOUTHER         G V  (A          (A) LONGBRANCH PENNYWHISTLE   1970   AMOS            US    AAS 7007
  GLENN FREY          G V  (A
  JAMES BURTON        G    (A  RY COODER          G    (A  JIM GORDON      D   (A  BUDDY EMMONS     STEEL(A
  LARRY KNECHTEL      PNO  (A  JOE OSBORN         B    (A  DOUG KERSHAW    G V (A
```

LONGDANCER

```
  MATT IRVING         K G V(B          (A) IF IT WAS SO SIMPLE       1973   ROCKET PIGL  1  US MCA 339
  STEVE SPROXTON      G V  (AB         (B) TRAILER FOR A GOOD LIFE   1974   ROCKET PIGL  6
  BRIAN HARRISON      G B V(AB
  DAVE STEWART        G B V(AB  CHARLIE SMITH     D V  (B  JIMMY HALL      PNO (A  ROGER POWELL      D(A
  VIRAM JASANI        SITAR(B  TOMMY McCARTHY    PIPES(B  POPART STRINGS          (B  KAI OLSSON       G V (A
  BOB RONGA           B    (A  ANDY ROBERTS      DULC (A  KESH SATHIE     PERC(A  BONES             V  (B
  DAVE MATTACKS       F    (A  TONY ASHTON       K    (A  DEL NEWMAN      K   (B  JUDD PROCTOR     BANJ(B
  CHARLES YOUNG       CHOIR (B
```

LONG HELLO

```
                                       (A) LONG HELLO               1979   BUTT            NOTT 002
                                       (B) LONG HELLO VOL 2         1981   BUTT            NOTT 004
```

PROFESSOR LONGHAIR

```
  PROFESSOR LONGHAIR   V PNO(ALL  (A) NEW ORLEANS PIANO       1972  ATLANTIC  US 7225 UK  K 40402
  LEE ALLEN           SAX  (A     (A) NEW ORLEANS PIANO       197   PIONEER    JAP      P4582A
  RED TYLER           SAX  (A     (B) ROCK 'N' ROLL GUMBO     1975  BARCLAY 80606  RI IMS 81
  EDGAR BLANCHARD     B    (A     (C) LIVE ON THE QUEEN MARY  1978  HARVEST    UK SHSP 4086
  EARL PALMER         D    (A     (D) CRAWFISH FIESTA         1980  SONET      UK SNTF 830
  ROBERT PARKER       SAX  (A     (D) CRAWFISH FIESTA         1980  ALLIGATOR  US  AL 4718
  DAVID LEE WATSON    B    (D
  CHARLIE BURBECK     SAX  (D  AL MILLER          D    (A  JOHN WOODROW    D   (A  DR JOHN          G  (D
  ANDY KASLOW         SAX  (D  TONY DAGRADI       SAX  (D  JOHN VIDACOVICH D   (D  JIM MOORE        SAX(D
  ALFRED ROBERTS      CONGA(D
```

WILBERT LONGMIRE

```
  WILBERT LONGMIRE    G V  (ABC        (A) SUNNY SIDE UP            1978   CBS             UK 82845
  BOB JAMES           K    (ABC        (B) CHAMPAGNE               1979   CBS             UK 83257
  DAVE SANBORN        SAX  (A          (C) WITH ALL MY LOVE        1980   CBS US 36342    UK 84155
  ERIC GALE           G    (AB
  HARVEY MASON        D    (AB  RICHARD TEE       K    (AB  RANDY BRECKER   TPT (B  JON FADDIS       TPT (B
  WAYNE ANDRE         TROM (BC  RON CUBER         SAX  (B   EDDIE DANIELS   FLT (B  GORDON GRODY      V  (B
  STEVE KHAN          G    (C   GILMORE DIGAP     PERC (C   PETER GORDON    HRNS(C  GLORIA AGOSTINI  HARP(C
  JOCELYN SHAW        V    (C   GARY KING         B    (BC  JIM MAELEN      PERC(BC IDRIS MUHAMMAD    D  (B
  LEWIS SOLOFF        TPT  (B   MIKE LAWRENCE     TPT  (BC  PAUL FAULISE    TROM(B  GEORGE MARGE     WIND(BC
  PHIL BODNER         FLT  (BC  LANI GROVES       V    (BC  BARRY MILES     K   (C  MARVIN STAMM     HRNS(C
  JIM BUFFINGTON      HRNS (C   BABBI B FLOYD     V    (C   EARL McINTYRE   TROM(B  BARRY ROGERS     TROM(B
  MICHAEL BRECKER     SAX  (B   GEORGE YOUNG      SAX  (B   DIVA GRAY       V   (BC ZACK SANDERS      V  (BC
  BUDDY WILLIAMS      D    (C   DAVE TAYLOR       HRNS (C   FRANK FLOYD     V   (C
```

LOOKING GLASS

```
  ELLIOT LURIE        G V  (AB         (A) LOOKING GLASS            1972   EPIC US 31320 UK  EPC 65041
  LARRY GONSKY        K V  (AB         (B) SUBWAY SERENADE          1973   EPIC US 32167
  PIET SWEVAL         B V  (AB
  JEFF GROB           D    (A  BARBARA MASSEY     V    (A  CAROLYN DAVIS   V   (A  TASHA THOMAS      V  (A
  SELDON POWELL       SAX  (B  RALPH MACDONALD    PERC (B  JOE DUBE        PERC(B  MAXINE DIXON      V  (B
  NANCY NALENCE       V    (B  NANCY FARRELL      V    (B  STEVE VON SCHREIBER V (B
```

JEFF LORBER FUSION

```
  JEFF LORBER         K    (ALL        (A) SOFT SPACE              197    INNER CITY      US  IC1056
  TERRY LAYNE         WIND (A          (B) WATER SIGN             1979   ARISTA          US  AB4234
  LESTER McFARLAND    B    (A          (C) WIZARD ISLAND          1980   ARISTA          US  AL9516
  DENNIS BRADFORD     D    (ABC        (D) GALAXIAN               1981   ARISTA
  FREDDY HUBBARD      HRNS (B
  RON YOUNG           PERC (A  DANNY WILSON       B    (BC  DOUG LEWIS      G   (B  KENNY GORELICK   WIND (C
  CHICK COREA         K    (AC  JOE FARRELL       SAX  (B   DENNIS SPRINGER SAX (B  JAY KODER        G  (BC
  PAULINHO DA COSTA   PERC (C  BRUCE SMITH        PERC (AB  DEAN REICHERT   G   (A
```

JON LORD

```
  JON LORD            K    (ALL        (A) GEMINI SUITE            1971   PURPLE     UK TPSA7501
  TONY ASHTON         K V  (AB         (B) WINDOWS                1974   PURPLE     UK TPSA7513
  DAVID COVERDALE     V    (B          (C) SARABANDE              1976   PURPLE     UK  TPSA 7516
  RAY FENWICK         G    (B
  GLENN HUGHES        V G B(B  EBERHARD SCHOENER K    (B  ROGER GLOVER    B   (A  ALBERT LEE       G  (A
  PETE YORK           D    (BC  YVONNE ELLIMAN    V    (A  IAN PAICE       D   (A  ORCHESTRAS           (BC
  PAUL KARASS         B    (C   MARK NAUSEEL      PERC (C  ANDY SUMMERS    G   (C
```

LORDS

```
    ULLI GUNTHER       V    (        (A) BLACK & WHITE           1965 COLUMBIA    GER 83859
    KLAUS PETER LIETZ  G    (        (B) THE LORDS II            1966 COLUMBIA    GER 84013
    RAINER PETRY       G    (        (C) SOME FOLKS              1967 COLUMBIA
    BERND ZAMULA       B    (        (D) GOOD SIDE OF JUNE       1968 COLUMBIA    GER 74244
    PETER DONATH       D    (        (E) ULLEOGAMAXBE            1969 COLUMBIA    GER 74343
    KNUD KUNTZE        B    (        (F) SHAKIN' ALL OVER '70    1970 COLUMBIA    GER 28478
    HEINZ HEGEMANN     B    (        (G) INSIDE OUT              1971 COLUMBIA    GER 28887
                                     (H) BEST OF                 1971 COLUMBIA    GER 29783
                                     (I) THE LORDS (COMP)        1972 M F P           5142
                                     (J) THE LORDS               1974 COLUMBIA    GER 31972
                                     (K) THE BEST OF 1964/71 (COMP) 19 COLUMBIA   GER 64871
```

LOST & FOUND

```
    JAMES HARRELL      (A        (A) EVERYBODY'S HERE         1976  INTERNATIONAL ARTISTS IALP3
    PETE BLACK         (A
    JIMMY FROST        (A  STEVE WEBB     (A
```

LOS BRAVOS

```
                                 (A) LOS BRAVOS              1966 PRESS        83003
                                 (B) BRING A LITTLE LOVIN'   1968 PARROT US 71021
                                 (C) BLACK IS BLACK (COMP)   1974 DECCA     GER 21670
```

LOSEKES BLUES BAND

```
    FALK STEHR      V HCA(AB    (A) BEST WISHES            19  BLIND MAN   WAM 780064
    BERNIE RINGE    V HCA SAX(AB (B) RED HOT MAMA          19  BLIND MAN      062506
    KALLE WEBER     G   (AB
    HERBERT WEBER   D   (AB  UWE BRUCHHAUSER   PNO   (AB  THOMAS PLOG   B   (AB
```

LOST GONZO BAND

```
    GARY NUNN       PNO V B G  (A    (A) LOST GONZO BAND    1975 MCA   UK MCF 2727  US MCA 487
    ROBERT LIVINGTON B K V(B         (B) THRILLS            1976 MCA               US MCA2232
    JOHN INMON      G V   (B         (C) SIGNS OF LIFE      1978 CAPITOL       US    11788
    KELLY DUNN      SYN K(B
    DONNY DOLAN     D PERC(B
```

LOTHAR & THE HAND PEOPLE

```
    JOHN EMELIN   V EFFECTS(A  (A) PRESENTING LOTHAR & THE HAND PEOPLE 1968 CAPITOL  US   2997
    KIM KING      G SYN  (A    (B) SPACE HYMN                19 CAPITOL       US     247
    TOM FLYE      D      (A
    PAUL CONLEY   K      (A  RUSTY FORD      B   (A
```

J D LOUDERMILK

```
    J D LOUDERMILK          LANGUAGE OF LOVE             196  RCA          US LSP 2434
                            12 SIDES OF                  196  RCA          US LSP 2539
                            SINGS A BIZARRE COLLECTION   1966 RCA UK RD7890 US LSP 3497
                            SURBURBAN ATTITUDES          1967 RCA          US LSP 3807
                            COUNTRY LOVE SONGS           1968 RCA          US LSP 4040
                            THE OPEN MIND OF J D LOUDERMILK 1969 RCA       US LSP 4097
                            ELLOREE VOL 1                1971 WB UK K46124 US     1922
                            BEST OF                      1973 RCA          US LSA 3159
                            ENCORES                      1975 RCA          US LSA 3220
                            JUST PASSING THROUGH         1978 MIM          US MIMLP9009
```

LOUDSPEAKERS

```
    RICHIE RAE     D    (A    (A) LOUDSPEAKERS          1978 EBONY       UK EBY 1004
    CHRIS THOMAS   G V  (A
    IAN GAIR       K V  (A  BRIAN ENGEL     V   (A   BRENDAN WALSH   B G  (A
```

JOE HILL LOUIS

```
    JOE HILL LOUIS G V HCA(A   (A) BLUE IN THE MORNING   1973  POLYDOR        2383  214
    WILLIE NIX     D V   (A
    BILLY 'RED' LOVE PNO (A  WILLIE JOHNSON   G   (A
```

LOUISIANA RED

```
    IVERSON'LOUISIANA RED'MINTER G V(ALL (A) SEVENTH SON     1963 CARNIVAL RI       2941 002
    BILL DICEY     HCA  (C    (A) LOW DOWN BACK PORCH BLUES 196  ROULETTE    US      25200
    TOMMY TUCKER   PNO  (C    (C) SINGS THE BLUES          1972 ATLANTIC UK K40436 US 33389
    DAVE'BABY 'CORTEZ ORG (C  (D) SWEET BLOOD CALL         1975 BLUE LABOR   US   BL 104
    ROBERT BANKS   PNO  (C    (E) DEAD STRAY DOG           1976 BLUE LABOR   US   BL 107
    NAPOLEON ALLEN G    (C    (F) RED FUNK & BLUE          1978 BLACK PANTHER UK  BP1001
    EARL WILLIAMS  D    (C    (G) NEW YORK BLUES           1979 L&R              42 002
    PAUL MARTINEZ  B    (C    (H) KING BEE                 1979 JSP              1006
    KEN MIMMS      G    (C    (J) REALITY BLUES            1980 L&R              42 011
    SUGAR BLUES    HCA  (F    ( ) LOUISIANA RED            19   FORUM            9100
    DICK BUNN      B    (C
    DON COOK       PNO  (C  JIM EVANS      D   (C   BOB MALENKY   G   (C   LEONARD GASKIN   B (C
    SID BARNES     D    (C  ELAINE MONK    V   (G   VIVIAN MINTER V   (G   HUBERT SUMLIN    G (J
    SUNNYLAND SLIM PNO  (J  BOB STROGER    B   (J   ODIE PAYNE    D   (J   CAREY BELL HARRINGTON HCA(J
```

LOVE

```
    ARTHUR LEE   PROD G V (ABCDEFG (A) LOVE             1966 ELEKTRA             EKS 74001
    JOHN ECHOLS    G    (ABCE     (B) DA CAPO           1967 ELEKTRA UK K42011  EKS 74005
    BRYAN MACLEAN  G V  (ABCE     (C) FOREVER CHANGES   1967 ELEKTRA UK K42015  EKS 74013
    KEN FORSSI     B    (ABCE     (D) FOUR SAIL         1969 ELEKTRA UK K42030  EKS 74049
    ALBAN PFISTERER D   (ABE      (E) LOVE REVISITITED  1970 ELEKTRA 2469 009   EKS 74058
    DON CONKA      D    (         (E) LOVE REVISITED    1971 ELEKTRA UK K42091
    MICHAEL STUART PERC (BC       (F) OUT HERE          1969 BLUE THUMB   US   BTS 9000
    TJAY CANTRELLI PERC (B        (F) OUT HERE          1969 HARVEST      UK   SHDW 3/4
    JAY DONNELLAN  G    (DF       (G) FALSE START       1970 BLUE THUMB   US   BTS 8822
    FRANK FAYAD    B    (DFG      (G) FALSE START       1970 HARVEST      UK   SHVL 787
    GEORGE SURANOVICH D (DFG      (H) LOVE MASTERS      1972 ELEKTRA UK K32002
    GARY ROWLES    G    (FG       (J) REEL TO REAL      1974 RSO     2394 145  US   4804
    NOONEY RICKETT G V  (G        (K) BEST OF           1980 RHINO         US   800
    JIMI HENDRIX   G    (G        (L) LOVE LIVE         1981 LINE          GER  5153
    DRACHEN THEAKER D   (DF
    JOEY BLOCKER   D    (J   SHERWOOD AKUNA  B   (J   ROBERT ROZELLE   B   (J   MELVAN WHITTINGTON G (J
    BUZZY FEITEN   G    (J   JOEY DEAGUERO  VIBES(J   VANETTA FIELDS   V   (J   CLIFFORD SOLOMON HRNS (J
    WILBER BROWN   HRNS (J   PAUL MARTIN     G   (F   JIM HOBSON       K   (F   JOHN STIRLING    G (J
    ART FOX        G    (J   BOBBY LYLE      K   (J   CARLENE WILLIAMS V   (J   JOHN CLAUDER     HRNS(J
    ALAN DE VILLE  HRNS (J   HERMAN McCORMICK CONGA(J  HARVEY MANDEL   G   (J   GARY BELL        SYN(J
    JESSIE SMITH   V    (J   FRED CARTER    HRNS (J   BILLY SPRAGUE    HRNS(J   PAUL ROTHCHILD   PROD (B
    BRUCE BOTNICK  PROD (C
```

```
L128A                              CLAYTON LOVE                                   L128A
   CLAYTON LOVE      V PNO(A        (A) COME ON HOME BLUES(10")     197 RED LIGHTNING        RL0029
   SID WALLACE       V    (A
   EUGENE WASHINGTON D   (A   GEORGE BRAZIER  B   (A   NAT RIGGINS      G   (A
L129                                MIKE LOVE                                      L129
   MIKE LOVE         V    (A        (A) CELEBRATION                 197
   CHARLES LLOYD     WIND (A
   RON ALTBACH       PNO V(A   ED CARTER      G    (A   DAVE ROBINSON   B   (A   WELLS KELLY    G  (A
   MIKE KOWALSKI     D    (A   GARY GRIFFIN   K    (A
L129A                               LOVE AFFAIR                                    L129A
   LYNTON GUEST      K    (A        (A) EVERLASTING                 19
   MICK JACKSON      B   (AB        (B) NEW DAY                    1970 CBS  UK     64109
   MAURICE BACON     D    (A        (C) GOLDEN ERA OF POP MUSIC    1973 CBS  UK     68255
   REX BRAYLEY       G    (B
   MORGAN FISHER     K    (A   AUGUSTE EADON    V FLT(A   STEVE ELLIS      V  (A
L130                                LOVE COMMITTEE                                 L130
   NORMAN FRAZIER    V    (A        (A) LAW & ORDER               1978 SALSOUL UK 1506 GOLDMINE US9500
   CARLA BENSON      V    (A        (A) LOVE COMMITEE             1970 ELECTRIC       US 3233
   LARRY RICHARDSON  V    (A
   JOE FREEMAN       V    (A   RON TYSON    V PERC(A    EARL YOUNG     D   (A   KEITH BENSON   D  (A
   RON BAKER         B    (A   JIMMY WILLIAMS  B   (A   NORMAN HARRIS  B   (A   BOBBY ELI      D  (A
   ROLAND CHAMBERS   G    (A   T J TINDALL     G   (A   EDDIE MOORE    G   (A   RON KERSEY     K  (A
   COTTON KENT       K    (A   BRUCE GRAY      K   (A   T G CONWAY     K   (A   BRUCE HAWES    K  (A
   LARRY WASHINGTON  CONGAS(A   ALLAN FELDER PERC  (A   DON RENALDO  STRINGS (A   EVETTE BENTON  V  (A
   BARBARA INGRAM    V    (A
L130A                               LOVECRAFT                                      L130A
   MICHAEL TEGZA     D V  (AB       (A) VALLEY OF THE MOON         1970 REPRISE              6419
   LALOMIE WASHBURN  V PERC(B       (B) WE LOVE YOU WHOEVER YOU ARE 1975 MERCURY     US  SRMI 1031
   FRANK CAPEK       G    (B
   JORGE RODRIGUEZ   G    (B   CRAIG GIGSTAD    B   (B   GEORGE AGOSTO    PERC (B   MARK JUSTIN    K SYN(B
   JIM DONLINGER          (A   MICHAEL BEEN         (A   MARTY GREBB      (A
L130B                               LOVERBOY                                       L130B
   MIKE RENO         V    (AB       (A) LOVERBOY                   1980 CBS UK 84798  US     36762
   PAUL DEAN         G V  (AB       (B) GET LUCKY                  1981 CBS          US     37638
   MATT FRENETTE     D    (AB
   DOUG JOHNSON      K    (AB   SCOTT SMITH     B   (AB  NANCY NASH       V   (B
L130C                               LOVE SCULPTURE                                 L130C
   DAVE EDMUNDS      G V  (ALL      (A) BLUES HELPING             1968 PARLOPHONE UK 7059 US RARE 505
   TERRY WILLIAMS    D    (D        (B) FORMS & FEELINGS          1969 PARLOPHONE UK 7090 US PARROT 71035
   B J COLE          STEEL(D        (B) FORMS & FEELINGS          1969 ODEOM       GER      90637
   JOHN WILLIAMS     B V K(AB       (C) CLASSIC TRACKS            1974 ONE UP          2047
   PETE KERR             (B        (D) ROCKERS                   197 PARLOPHONE UK EURO 99546/7
   MIKE FINESILVER       (B        (E) SINGLES                   1980 HARVEST    UK 2032
   BOB JONES         D V  (ABD      (F) DAVE EDMUNDS & LOVE SCULPTURE 198 EMI  EURO          05637
   ANDY FAIRWETHER LOW    G(D
L131                                LENE LOVICH                                    L131
   LENE LOVICH       V SAX(AB       (A) STATELESS                 1978 STIFF  US 36102 UK  SEEZ 7
   LES CHAPPELL      G    (AB       (B) FLEX                      1979 STIFF  US 36308 UK  SEEZ 19
   MARK CHAPLIN      B V  (B        (B) FLEX                      1979 STIFF  GER 6 24228
   JUSTIN HILDRETH   D    (B
   DEAN KLAVETT      K V  (B   NICK PLYTAS  K    (AB CHRIS JUDGE-SMITH     V (B   JEFF SMITH   SYN    (A
   BOBBI IRWIN       D    (A   RON FRANCOIS B    (A
L132                                LOVING AWARENESS                               L132
   CHARLEY CHARLES   D    (A        (A) LOVING AWARENESS          1976 MORE LOVE         ML  001
   NORMAN WATT-ROY   B    (A
   MICK GALLAGHER    K    (A   JOHN TURNBULL     G    (A
L133                                LOVING SPOONFUL                                L133
   JOHN SEBASTIAN    G V  (ALL      (A) DO YOU BELIEVE IN MAGIC   1965 PYE UK 28069 KAMA SUTRA US 8050
   ZAL YANOVSKY      V G  (ABCDEF    (B) DAYDREAMS                1966 PYE UK 28078 KAMA SUTRA US 8051
   JOE BUTLER        D    (ABCDEF    (C) WHATS UP TIGER LILY[SOUNDTRACK] 1966 KAMA SUTRA    US 8053
   STEVE BOONE       B    (ABCDEF    (D) HUMS                     1966 KAMA SUTRA UK   401    US 8054
   JERRY YESTER      G    (         (D) HUMS                     196 KAMA SUTRA GERM       2319 034
   GLEN COVE         D    (         (E) BEST OF VOL 1            1967 KAMA SUTRA UK   403    US 2608
   WOODY ALLEN            (C        (E) BEST OF VOL 1            1967 KAMA SUTRA GERM 620004  US 8056
   ERIK JACOBSEN     PROD (A        (F) YOU'RE A BIG BOY NOW     1967 KAMA SUTRA UK   402    US 8058
   JOEL WISSERT      PROD (G        (G) EVERYTHING PLAYING       1967 KAMA SUTRA UK   404    US 8061
   HENRY DILTZ       CLAR (D        (G) EVERYTHING PLAYING       1967 KAMA SUTRA GERM 620006
   LARRY HANKIN           (D        (H) BEST OF VOL 2            1968 KAMA SUTRA UK   405    US 8064
                                    (H) BEST OF VOL 2            1968 KAMA SUTRA GERM 620007
                                    (J) REVELATION REVOLUTION '69 1969 KAMA SUTRA UK 406    US 8073
                                    (K) THE VERY BEST OF (COMP)  19 KAMA SUTRA          US 2013
                                    (L) GREATEST HITS           1970 KAMA SUTRA        2361 002
                                    (M) POP HISTORY     (DBL)    19 POLYDOR            2625 010
                                    (AG)MORE GOLDEN SPOONFUL     1974 KAMA SUTRA          KSMD 9002
                                    (AG)MORE GOLDEN SPOONFUL     1974 KAMA SUTRA          2683 042
                                    ( ) BEST OF                  196 MARBLE ARCH    UK      MAL1115
                                    ( ) BEST OF VOL 2            196 MARBLE ARCH    UK      MAL1116
                                    ( ) JOHN SEBASTIAN SONGBOOK  1967 KAMA SUTRA US 2011 G
                                    ( ) JOHN SEBASTIAN SONGBOOK  1967 BUDDAH        GER      623133
                                    ( ) ONCE UPON A TIME         19 KAMA SUTRA US 2029
                                    ( ) RUN WITH YOU             196 KAMA SUTRA        8073
                                    ( ) 24 KARAT HITS            1968 KAMA SUTRA        750
                                    (BC) DAYDREAM/TIGER LILY     19 KAMA SUTRA UK 2683 034
                                    (O) GOLDEN HOUR              1975 PYE          UK          GH  838
                                    (P) THE GREAT YEARS          19 MODE           FR       MD  9022
                                    (Q) LOVING SPOONFUL          19 PROFILE        GERM     624  018
                                    (R) FILE                     1977 PYE          UK       FILD009
                                    ( ) GREAT YEARS              1980 VOGUE         NL 9022

                                                                   (CONTINUED)
```

[349]

LOVING SPOONFUL

(E P s)

DID YOU EVER	1966	KAMA SUTRA	KEP 300
JUG BAND MUSIC	1966	KAMA SUTRA	KEP 301
SUMMER IN THE CITY	1966	KAMA SUTRA	KEP 302
DAY BLUES	1967	KAMA SUTRA	KEP 303
NASHVILLE CATS	1967	KAMA SUTRA	KEP 304
LOVING YOU	1967	KAMA SUTRA	KEP 305
SOMETHING IN THE NIGHT	1967	KAMA SUTRA	KEP 306

LOW NUMBERS

HAROLD BRONSON	V	(A	(A) TWIST AGAIN WITH THE LOW NUMBERS	1978	RHINO		RNLP 004		
LOUIS MAXFIELD	G	(A							
DAVE DENNARD	B	(A	DAVID SCHNEIDER	D	(A	MARK LEVITON	(A	PAGE PORRAZZO	(A
MICK ROSEN		(A	PETER DEAL		(A	STUART DEAL	(A	STEVE ROSEN	(A
DON BUCHANAN		(A	ROB LAMPL		(A	DON KRAIG	(A	BARRY SQUIRE	(A

NICK LOWE

NICK LOWE	B V G	(ALL	(A) JESUS OF COOL	1978	RADAR	UK	RAD 1	+ RADAR K56466	
DAVE EDMUNDS	G	(AB	(A) PURE POP FOR NOW PEOPLE	1978	CBS	US	35329	SCAN SMASH	SLEPT1
BILLY BREMNER	G	(ABC	(B) LABOUR OF LUST	1979	RADAR	UK	RAD21	GER RADAR	56676
TERRY WILLIAMS	D	(ABC	(B) LABOUR OF LUST	1979	CBS	US	36087	SCAN SMASH	SLEPT6
MARTIN BELMONT	G	(C	(C) NICK THE KNIFE	1982	F BEAT	UK	XXLP14		
NEIL KING	K	(C							
STEVE NIEVE	K	(C	PAUL CARRACK	K	(C	HUEY LEWIS HCA (C	BOB ANDREWS	K	(C
BOB IRWIN	D V	(C	ALDO BOCCA	G	(C	CARLENE CARTER/LOWE V(C	BEN BARSON	K	(C
JAMES ELLER	B	(C							

HENRY LOWTHER

HENRY LOWTHER	HRNS VLN	(A	(A) CHILD SONG	1970	DERAM	UK	SML 1070		
TONY ROBERTS	WIND	(A							
MIKE McNAUGHT	K	(A	DARYL RUNSWICK	B	(A	MIKE TRAVIS	D	(A	JIMMY JEWELL SAX (A
NEIL SLAVEN	PERC	(A							

SHARALEE LUCAS

SHARALEE LUCAS	V	(A	(A) DAUGHTER OF MUSIC	1978	GREENTREE		R3520		
FARRELL MORRIS	PERC	(A							
SHANE KEISTER	K	(A	LARRY LONDIN	D	(A	JOE OSBORN	B	(A	BOBBY THOMPSON G BAN(A
STEVE GIBSON	G	(A	JOHN THOMPSON	G	(A	JACK WILLIAMS B	(A	BUDDY SKIPPER SAX (A
CINDY REYNOLDS	HARP	(A	BOBBY TAYLOR	HRNS	(A	KATHY THOMPSON V	(A	BOB FARRELL V (A

TREVOR LUCAS

TREVOR LUCAS	V G	(A	(A) OVERLANDER	1966	REALITY		RY1002
ALF EDWARDS	CONC	(A					
CYRIL HARLING	FDL	(A	GEORGE GIBBS	B	(A		

LUCIFER

(A) BIG GUN	19				LLP 1
(B) EXIT	19				LLP 2
(C) MARGRIET	19	EMI	IMP	064 25655	
(D) BLACK MASS	19	UNI	US		73111
(E) LUCIFER	19	INVICTUS	US		7309

LUCIFERS FRIEND

PETER HECHT	K	(ABCDEFGH	(A) LUCIFERS FRIEND	1971	PHILIPS	GER	6305 068
DIETER HORNS	B V	(ABCDEFGH	(A) LUCIFERS FRIEND	1973	BILLINGSGATE	US	1002
JOHN LAWTON	V	(ABCDEH	(B) WHERE GROUPIES KILLED THE BLUES	1972	PASSPORT	US	98008
PETER VAN ASLEN	V	(F	(B) WHERE GROUPIES KILLED THE BLUES	1973	VERTIGO	GER	6360 602
JOACHIM RIETENBACH	D	(ABC	(C) I'M JUST A ROCK'N'ROLL SINGER	1974	BILLINGSGATE	US	1008
PETER HESSLEIN	G V	(ABCDEFGH	(C) I'M JUST A ROCK'N'ROLL SINGER	1974	VERTIGO	GER	6360 611
BOB LANESE	TPT	(CD	(D) BANQUET	1975	PASSPORT	US	98012
HERB GELLER	WIND	(CD	(D) BANQUET	1975	VERTIGO	GER	6360 618
HERBERT BORNHOLDT	PERC V	(CDEFGH	(E) MIND EXPLODING	1976	VERTIGO	GER	6360 633
KARL HERMANN LUER	WIND	(E	(E) MIND EXPLODING	1976	+JANUS	US	7030
DRIAN ASKEW	K V	(GH	(F) GOOD TIME WARRIOR	1978	ELEKTRA		63 159
MIKE STARRS	V	(FG	(F) GOOD TIME WARRIOR	1978	ELEKTRA	GER	52081
			(G) SNEAK ME IN	1980	ELEKTRA	GERM 52203 US	265
			(H) MEAN MACHINE	1981			

LUDUS

(A) THE VISIT (EP)	19	NEW HORMONE		ORG 4
(B) PICK POCKET	1981	NEW HORMONES CASS		CAT1

LULU

LULU(MARIE LAWRIE	V	(ALL	(A) SOMETHING TO SHOUT ABOUT	1965	DECCA	UK	LK	4719
JIM DEWAR	B	(	(B) LULU	1967	ACE OF CLUBS	UK	ACL	1232
ROSS NELSON		(	(C) TO SIR WITH LOVE	1967	EPIC US 26339 FONTANA	UK		5446
ALEC BELL		(	(D) ITS LULU	1970	EPIC US 26536			
JIMMY SMITH		(	(E) LOVE LOVES TO LOVE LULU	1967	COLUMBIA	UK	SCX	6201
TONY TIERNEY		(	(F) LULU'S ALBUM	1969	COLUMBIA	UK	SCX	6365
DAVID MILLER		(	(G) WORLD OF LULU	1969	DECCA	UK	SPA	8
DUANE ALLMAN	G	(J	(H) WORLD OF LULU	1969	DECCA	UK	SPA	94
MAX BENNETT		(M	(J) NEW ROUTES	1970	ATLANTIC US 33310 UK			228031
JOE OSBORN	B	(M	(K) MELODY FAIR	1970	ATLANTIC US 33330 UK	2400	017	
LOUIE SHELTON		(M	(M) MAKE BELIEVE WORLD	1973	CHELSEA US 0144			
DEAN PARKS	G	(M	( ) LULU	19	PICKWICK	US		3237
HAL BLAINE	D	(M	( ) TO LOVE SOMEBODY	19	HARMONY	US		30449
BOB HARDAWAY		(M	( ) FROM LULU WITH LOVE	19	PARROT	US		71016
JEROME RICHARDSON		(M	(P) DONT TAKE LOVE FOR GRANTED	1979	ROCKET UK TRAIN8	US	3073	
TOM SCOTT	WIND	(M	( ) BOY	19	EPIC	US		26396
SLYDE HYDE	TROM	(M	( ) VERY BEST OF	1980	WARWICK	UK	5097	
CHUCK FINDLEY	TPT	(M						
VICTOR FELDMAN	PERC	(M	GARY COLEMAN PERC	(M	MICHAEL O'MARTIAN K	(M	TOM HENSLEY	(M
DAN PEAKE		(M						

```
L141
    BOB LUMAN          G V  (ALL    LETS THINK ABOUT LIVING              1960  WB                     WS1396
                                    AINT GOT TIME                        1968  EPIC                   26393
                                    COME ON HOME                         1969  EPIC                   26463
                                    GETTING BACK TO NORNA                1970  EPIC                   26541
                                    IS IT ANY WONDER THAT I LOVE YOU     197   EPIC             US    30617
                                    A CHAIN DONT TAKE TO ME              19    EPIC LE10187           30923
                                    LIVIN LOVIN SOUNDS                   1971  LONDON UK ZGE115 US HSP 124006
                                    WHEN YOU SAY LOVE                    1972  EPIC                   31375
                                    LONELY WOMEN MAKE GOOD LOVERS        1972  EPIC             US    31746
                                    BOB LUMAN                            1973  HARMONY          US    32006
                                    NEITHER ONE OF US                    1973  EPIC             US    32192
                                    GREATEST HITS                        1974  EPIC             US    32759
                                    RED CADILLAC & BLACK MUSTACHE        197   EPIC             US    33177
                                    STILL LOVING YOU                     1974  HICKORY          US    4508
                                    WHEN YOU SAY LOVE/LONELY WOMEN (DBL) 197   EPIC             US    33755
                                    A SATISFIED MIND                     1976  EPIC             US    33942
                                    ALIVE & WELL                         1977  EPIC             US    34445
                                    BOB LUMAN ROCKS                      1977  DJM              UK    DJM 22057
                                    THE PAY PHONE                        1978  POLYDOR          US    PD16135
                                    THE ROCKER                           1979  BEAR FAMILY      GERM  15037
                                    MORE OF THE ROCKER                   1979  BEAR FAMILY      GERM  15039
```

L141A   LYDIA LUNCH   L141A

```
    PAT IRWIN               (        (A) QUEEN OF SIAM               1980  ZE    US 33006
    JACK RUBY               (
    DOUG BROWNE             (     ROBERT QUINE      (
```

L142   LURKERS   L142

```
    PETE STRIDE        G   (ABC     (A) FULHAM FALL OUT               1978  BEGGARS BANQUET   UK  BEG2
    HOWARD WALL        V   (ABC     (B) GODS LONELY MEN               1979  BEGGARS BANQUET   UK  BEGA8
    MANIC ESSO         D   (ABC     (C) GREATEST HITS LAST WILL & TESTAMENT 80 BEGGARS BANQUET UK BOPA2
    NIGEL MOORE        B   (ABC     (EP) SHADOW                       1979  BEGGARS BANQUET   UK  BACK1
    KYM BRADSHAW       B   (        (EP) I DONT NEED TO TELL HER      1979  BEGGARS BANQUET   UK  BACK3
    PETE EDWARDS       V HCA(A
    JOHN PLAIN         G   (C     ARTURO BASSICK      B   (C
```

L142A   WILLIAM LYALL   L142A

```
    WILLIAM LYALL V PERC K SYN(A     (A) SOLO CASTING                1976  EMI              UK  EMA 780
    PHIL CHEN           B   (A
    RONNIE LEAHY        PNO (A   PHIL COLLINS    D   (A   DAVID PATON     G   (A   ROBERT AHWAI    G   (A
    IAN BAIRNSON        G   (A   PATATO          CONGA(A  CHRIS MERCER    SAX (A   TERRY WALSH     BAN (A
    FRANK MUSKER        V   (A   DICK TATE       PERC (A  DOMINIC BUGATTI G   (A   BARRY DESOUZA   D   (A
    JACK EMBLOW         ACC (A   PAUL BUCKMASTER CELLO(A  RAY RUSSELL     G   (M
```

L143   BOBBY LYLE   L143

```
    BOBBY LYLE         K V (A        (A) NEW WARRIOR                 1978 CAPITOL/TOWER         11809
    WAYNE HENDERSON    PERC V(A      (B) NIGHT FIRE                  1980 CAPITOL               11956
    ANGELA  WINBUSH    V    (A
    NATHANIEL PHILLIPS B   (A   HARVEY MASON      D   (A   STEPHANIE SPRUILL V  (A   JOE BLOCKER    PERC (A
    RON BANKS          V   (A   JIM GILSTRAP      V   (A   VANCE TENORT      V  (A   ALEXANDRA BROWN V  (A
    MIKE BODDIKER      SYN (A   PAULINHO DA COSTA PERC (A   GREGORY MATTA     G  (A   DAVID T WALKER  G  (A
    MARTINETTE JENKINS V   (A   SUNSHIP           PERC (A   ROLAND BAUTISTA   G  (A   AUGIE JOHNSON   V  (A
    STRING SECTION         (A
```

L144   FRANKIE LYMON & THE TEENAGERS   L144

```
    FRANKIE LYMON      V   (ALL      (A) WHY DO FOOLS FALL IN LOVE   1956 GEE  US     + UK PYE 1978 28251
                                     ( ) TEENAGERS                  195  GEE US 701
    SHERMAN GARNES         (         (B) ROCK'N' ROLL PARTY         19   GUEST STAR       US  GS 1406
    JOE NEGRONI            (         (C) AT THE LONDON PALLADIUM     19   ROULETTE         US  R 25013
    HERMAN SANTIAGO        (         (D) GREATEST HITS              19   ROULETTE         US  R 25250
    JIMMY MERCHANT        (          (EP) FRANKIE LYMON WITH THE TEENAGERS 19  SONET       DK  SXP 3025
                                     (EP)AT THE LONDON PALLADIUM     19   ROULETTE         US  EPR 1304
```

L144A   BARBARA LYNN   L144A

```
    BARBARA LYNN       V   (A        (A) HERE IS                    1976 OVAL            UK  OVLM5002
                                     ( ) YOU'LL LOOSE A GOOD THING  19   JAMIE       US 3023
```

L144B   PHIL LYNOTT   L144B

```
    PHIL LYNOTT        V B (AB       (A) SOLO IN SOHO               1980  VERTIGO UK 9102038 US WB 3405
    TONY CHARLES       D   (A        (B) THE PHILIP LYNOTT ALBUM    1982  VERTIGO UK 6359 117
    BRIAN DOWNEY       D   (A
    BOBBY BENBERG      D   (A   SCOTT GORHAM      G   (A   SNOWY WHITE     G   (A   MARK KNOPFLER  G  (A
    FLACHRA TRENCH     STR (A   ANDY DUNCAN       PERC (A  HUEY LEWIS      HCA (A   JEROME RIMSON  B  (A
    JIMMY BAIN         K SYN(A   MIDGE URE        SYN  (A   BILLY CURRIE    SYN (A   MARK NAUSEEF   D  (A
    GARY MOORE         G   (A
```

L145   JACKIE LYNTON   L145

```
    JACKIE LYNTON      V   (ALL      (A) THE JACKIE LYNTON ALBUM    1974  WWA                WWA 012
    TONY LEACH         V PNO(B       (B) JACKIE LYNTON BAND (DBL)   1980  SCRATCH            SCRL 5002
    GRAHAME WHITE      G V (B
    GREG TERRY-SHORT   D V (B   KIRK RIDDLE       B   (B
```

L145A   WILLIE JAMES LYONS   L145A

```
    WILLIE JAMES LYONS G   (A        (A) W J LYONS & W KENT GHETTO  197   MCM       FR       900  291
    WILLLIE KENT           (A
```

L146   LYNYRD SKYNYRD   L146

```
    RONNIE VAN ZANT    V   (ALL      (A) PRONOUNCED LEHNERD SKINNERD 1974 MCA  US 363   NL 201  US RI 3019
    STEVE GAINES       G   (EF       (A) "    "    "    "           1974 MCA  UK 3502 FR BARCLAY  410010
    GARY ROSSINGTON    G   (ALL      (B) SECOND HELPING             1974 MCA  US 413  US RI       3020
    ALLEN COLLINS      G   (ALL      (B) "    "    "                1974 MCA  UK 2547 FR BARCLAY  410020
    LEON WILKESON      B   (ALL      (C) NUTHIN' FANCY              1975 MCA  US 2137 US RI       3021
    BILLY POWELL       K   (ALL      (C) "    "    "                1975 MCA  UK 2700 FR BARCLAY  410042
    ARTIMUS PYLE       D   (ECDF     (D) GIMME BACK MY BULLETS      1976 MCA  US 2170 US RI       3022
    CASSIE GAINES      V   (EGF      (D) "    "    "    "           1976 MCA  UK 2744 FR BARCLAY  410048
    JO BILLINGSLEY     V   (EGF      (E) ONE MORE FROM THE ROAD     1976 MCA  US 2/8001  RI 801
    LESLIE HAWKINS     V   (EGF      (E) "    "    "    "           1976 MCA  UK 279  FR BARCLAY410060/1
    SAM McPHERSON      HCA (E        (F) STREET SURVIVORS           1977 MCA  US                  3029
    JIMMY JOHNSON      G   (G        (F) "    "    "                1977 MCA  UK 3525 FR BARCLAY  511002
    DAVID FOSTER       K   (C        (F) "    "    "    "           1982 MCA  UK RI MCL 1694
```

```
          RICKY MEDLOCKE      D    (GF        (G) SKYNYRDS FIRST & LAST      1978 MCA    US 3047 UK 3529 UK RI 1627
          RANDY McCORMICK     K    (G         (H) GOLD & PLATINUM BAND (DBL) 1979 MCA    US 11008 UK          MCSP 308
          BOBBY KEYS          SAX  (B         (H) GOLD & PLATINUM     (DBL)  1982 MCA             UK RI        MCUW 456
          MERRY CLAYTON       V    (B         (EP) DOWN SOUTH JUKIN'        1978 MCA    UK                    MCEP 101
          TREVOR LAWRENCE     SAX  (B
          ED KING             G  (ABCFG  ROOSEVELT GOOK  B K V(A  BOBBYE HALL     PERC (AC  WAYNE PERKINS  G  (G
          GREG WALKER         B    (GF   TIM SMITH       V   (GF  MIKE PORTER     D    (B   STEVE MADAIO   TPT(B
          ROBERT BURNS        D    (ABG  ROBERT NIX      D   (A   STEVE KATZ      HCA  (A   RON EADES      SAX (GF
          GIMMER NICHOLS      G    (G    CLYDIE KING     B
```

```
          ROB TYNER           HCA V(ABC       (A) KICK OUT THE JAMS         1969 ELEKTRA US 74042 UK 1977 K42027
          FRED SMITH V K G HCA    (ABC        (B) BACK IN THE USA           1970 ATLANTIC US 8247 UK    2400 016
          MIKE DAVIS          B V  (ABC       (B) BACK IN THE USA           1977 ATLANTIC         UK         K50346
          DENNIS THOMPSON     D V  (ABC       (C) HIGH TIME                 1971 ATLANTIC US 8285 UK         K40223
          WAYNE KRAMER        G V K(ABC
          PETE KELLY          K    (B
          CHARLES MOORE       HRN V(C    JOANNE HILL     V   (C   BRENDAN KNIGHT    V   (C   MERLENE DRISCOLL  V (C
          DAVID OVERSTEAK     TUBA (C    LARRY HORTON    TROM(C   BOBBY WAYNE DERMINER PERC(C  BUTCH O'BRIEN  PERC (C
          LEON HENDERSON      SAX  (C    RICK FERRETTI   SAX (C   SKIP KNAPP      ORG  (C   KINKI LE PEW   PERC (C
          DAN BULLOCK         TROM (C    BOB SEGER       PERC(C   SCOTT MORGAN    PERC (C   TERRY TRABANDT PERC (C
          DAVE HELLER         PERC (C    DAVE MORGAN     PERC(C   ELLIS DEE       PERC (C   DANNY JORDAN   K   (C
```

```
          ROBIN SCOTT         G V  (AB        (A) NEW YORK, LONDON ,PARIS ,MUNICH 1979 MCA  US 6084         UK MCF3046
          PHILIP GOULD        D    (AB        (A) NEW YORK, LONDON, PARIS, MUNICH 1979 MCA  GER 62147       NL 201268
          WALLY BADAROU       SYN K(A         (B) OFFICIAL SECRETS ACT      1980 SIRE  US 6099       MCA UK MCF3085
          MARK KING           G B D(B         (B) OFFICIAL SECRETS ACT      1980 MCA                      NL 203071
          JULIAN SCOTT        B    (AB
          DEIRDRIE COSTELLO   V    (AB   DAVID VORHAUS   SYN (B   GARY BARNACLE   WIND (AB  PADDY KEENAN   PIPES(B
          BRIGIT VINCHON      V    (AB   DENIS BLACKHAM  V   (B   MOG AHERNE      V    (B   JOHN KEOGH     V   (B
          BILLY BROWN         V    (B    DES SMITH       V   (B
```

```
          DEXTER WANSEL       K    (J         (A) M.F.S.B.                  1973 T S O P UK 65903    US 32046
          JAMES HERB SMITH    G    (J         (B) T S O P                   1974 T S O P UK 80154
          LARRY MOORE         B    (J         (C) LOVE IS THE MESSAGE       197  T S O P            US 32707
          EVAN SOLOT          TPT  (J         (D) UNIVERSAL LOVE            1975 T S O P UK 80410    US 33158
          LARRY McKENNA       SAX  (J         (E) PHILADELPHIA FREEDOM      1976 T S O P UK 69206    US 33845
          CLIFFORD RUDD       D    (J         (F) SUMMERTIME                1976 T S O P UK 81459    US 34238
          MIGUEL FUENTES      PERC (J         (G) END OF PHASE ONE          1978 T S O P UK 81889    US 34658
          EVETTE BENTON       V    (J         (H) M F S B & GAMBLE HUFF ORCHESTRA 1978 T S O P UK 83010
          JOHN L USRY         K    (J         (J) MYSTERIES OF THE WORLD    1980 T S O P UK 84251
          DENNIS HARRIS       G    (J
          DON RENALDO         VLN  (J    ZAHMU           V   (J   CARLTON KENT    K    (J   DAVID CRUSE    PERC (J
          MARC RUBIN          G    (J    ALPHONSO CAREY  B   (J   QUINTON JOSEPH  D    (J   STEVE GOLD     K    (J
          DERRICK GRAVES      B    (J    BILLY JOHNSON   D   (J   CARLA BENSON    V    (J   BARBARA INGRAM V   (J
          LENNY PAKULA        K    (J    STEVE GREEN     B   (J   BOB MALACH      SAX  (J   JOEL BRYANT    K    (J
          JOHN R FAITH        FLT  (J    LEON HUFF       K   (J
```

```
          DONALD DUNN         B    (A         (A) THE M Gs                  1973     STAX             STS  3024
          AL JACKSON          D    (A
          BOBBY MANUEL        G    (A    CARSON WHITSETT   K   (A
```

```
          STEVE CAREY         K V  (A         (A) M P G                     1981
          KIM SMITH           G V  (A
          DAVID MIKEAL        G V  (A    MICHAEL BOLT    D V  (A   STEVE LOCKLIN   B V  (A
```

```
          BRUCE ANDERSON      G    (ABC       (A) HARD ATTACK               1977     ISLAND GER 25539 UK ILPS9529
          RICH STIM           G K  (ABC       (B) OUT OF THE TUNNEL         1980     RALPH  US 8002
          DALE SOPHIEA        B    (ABC       (C) CROWD CONTROL             1981     RALPH  US 8102
          JEFF ARMOUR         D    (A
          DAVE MAHONEY        D    (ABC
```

```
          PETER NILSSON       G K  (A         (A) ANOTHER FINE MESS         1977 POLYDOR              2380 050
          MIKE KRAMP          G    (A
          ANDY LARSSON        G B  (A    CHRIS HAVE      D   (A
```

```
          WILLIE MABON        V PNO(ALL        (A) THE COMEBACK             196      AMERICA          AM   6126
          MICKEY BAKER        G    (D          (B) CHICAGO 63               1963     AMERICA          AM   6136
          DAN ARMSTRONG       B    (D          (C) WILLIE MABON             19       CHESS        US      1439
          PETE YORK           D    (D          (D) COMEBACK                 1973     BIG BEAR         BEAR  9
          DYAN BIRCH          V    (D          (E) COLD CHILLY WOMAN        1975     BLACK & BLUE        33501
          COLIN SMITH         TPT  (D          (F) SHAKE THAT THING         1975     BLACK & BLUE        33506
          BILL WARREN         D    (EG         (G) SINGS "I DONT KNOW"      1976     ANTILLES     US
          ERNEST SUTTON       B    (AE         (H) CHICAGO BLUES SESSION    1979     L & R               42 003
          JIMMY ROGERS        G    (F
          LOUIS MYERS         G    (F    DAVE MYERS      B   (F   FRED BELOW      D    (F   FRANK COLLINS  V   (D
          JOHNNY BARNES       SAX  (D    PADDIE McHUGH   V   (D   EDDY TULEJA     G    (A   TONY CAHILL    D   (A
          CLIFTON JAMES       D    (B    WILLIE HUDSON   G   (B   AL DUNCAN       D    (B   EARL CROSSLEY  SAX (
          JOHNNIE CAMERON     SAX  (B    BILLY THE KID EMERSON K(B  JIMMY RICHARDS  B   (G   MALCOLM SIMMONS HCA (G
          MIGHTY JOE YOUNG    G    (G    EUGENE PEARSON  G   (G   HUBERT SUMLIN   G    (H   EDDIE TAYLOR   G   (H
          AARON BURTON        B    (H    CASEY JONES     D   (H
```

```
          JACKIE McAULEY      V G K(A         (A) JACKIE McAULEY            1971 DAWN UK DNLS3023 PYE US 3300
          MIKE McNAUGHT       K    (A
          HENRY LOWTHER VLN HRNS (A      MIKE TRAVIS     D   (A   TONY ROBERTS    FLT  (A   ROY BABBINGTON B   (A
          PETE HOSSEL         JUG  (A
```

DAN McCAFFERTY

```
   DAN McCAFFERTY      V    (A         (A) DAN McCAFFERTY      1975   MOUNTAIN UK TOPS108 US AM4553
   MANNY CHARLTON      G    (A
   HUGH McKENNA        K    (A    CHRIS MERCER     SAX  (A   HELEN CHAPPELLE  V  (A   JOHN PERRY       V  (A
   ZAL CLEMINSON       G    (A    TED McKENNA      D    (A   LIZA STRIKE      V  (A   JOANNE WILLIAMS  V  (A
   ROGER GLOVER        B    (A    GRAHAM PRESKETT  VLN  (A   BARRY ST JOHN    V  (A   TONY RIVERS      V  (A
```

NOEL McCALLA

```
   NOEL McCALLA        V PERC(A        (A) NIGHT TIME EMOTION  1979   EPIC         UK          83838
   TREVOR RABIN        G K B(A
   PRESTON HEYMAN      D    (A    NICK PAYN        SAX  (A   TONY BEARD       D  (A   VICKI BROWN      V  (A
   CHRIS THOMPSON      V    (A    DOUG BAINBRIDGE  SAX  (A   MEL COLLINS              SAX  (A   JOHN McKENZIE    B  (A
   GRAHAM BROAD        D    (A    STEVIE LANGE     V    (A
```

JIM McCARTHY

```
   JIM McCARTHY             (A         (A) GUIDE ME TO YOUR LOVE  1974 ESP     US      ESP  3008
```

PAUL McCARTNEY & WINGS

```
   PAUL McCARTNEY B V G K (ALL        (A) McCARTNEY           1970 APPLE UK 7102  US        3363
                                      (A) McCARTNEY           1979 CBS RI         US       36478
   LINDA McCARTNEY     K V     (ALL   (B) RAM                 1971 APPLE UK 10003 US        3375
                                      (B) RAM                 1979 CBS RI         US       36479
   DENNY LAINE         G V K(CDEFGHJKLO (C) WILD LIFE         1971 APPLE UK 7142  US        3386
   DENNY SEIWELL       D    (BCD       (D) RED ROSE SPEEDWAY  1972 APPLE UK  251  US        3409
   HENRY McCULLOUGH    G    (D         (E) BAND ON THE RUN    1974 APPLE UK 10007 US        3415
   JIMMY McCULLOCH     G    (FGHJ      (E) BAND ON THE RUN    1974 EMI EURO 05503 US CAPITOL 11901
   GEOFF BRITTON       D    (F         (F) VENUS & MARS       1975 EMI    UK  254 US CAPITOL 11419
   JOE ENGLISH         D    (GHJF      (G) WINGS AT THE SPEED OF SOUND 1976 EMI  UK 10010 US CAPITOL 11525
   DAVE MASON          G    (F         (H) WINGS OVER AMERICA 1976 EMI    UK  720 US CAPITOL 11593
   AFRO                PERC (F         (J) LONDON TOWN        1978 EMI    UK 10012 US CAPITOL 11777
   TONY DORSEY         TROM (HG        (K) WINGS GREATEST     1978 EMI    UK  256
   HUGH McCRACKEN      G    (B         (L) BACK TO THE EGG    1979 PARLOPHONE UK 257 US CBS  36057
   THADEUS RICHARD     WIND (HG        (M) McCARTNEY 11       1980 PARLOPHONE UK 258 US CBS  36511
   DAVID SPINOZZA      G    (B         (N) McCARTNEY INTERVIEW 1981 EMI    UK CHAT1
   STEVE HOWARD        HRNS (HG        (O) TUG OF WAR         1982 PARLOPHONE UK 259 US CBS  37642
   ALLEN TOUSSAINT     K    (F
   HOWIE CASEY         SAX  (EH   TOM SCOTT        SAX  (F   ERIC STEWART     G V (0   CARL PERKINS    G  (0
   CAMPBELL MALONY     D    (0    STEVE GADD       D    (0   RINGO STARR      D   (0   ADRIAN SHEPARD  D  (0
   DAVE MATTACKS       D    (0    GEORGE MARTIN    PNO  (0   STANLEY CLARKE   B   (0   STEVIE WONDER V K SYN D(0
   ADRIAN BRETT        PIPES(0    ANDY McKAY       LYRICON(0 JACK ROTHSTEIN   VLN (0   BERNARD PARTRIDGE  VLN(0
   IAN JEWEL           VLA  (0    KEITH HARVEY     CLO  (0   JACK BRYMER      CLAR(0   STEVE HOLLY     D  (L
   REMI KABAKA         PERC (E    LAWRENCE JUBER   G    (L
```

BILLY EARL McCLELLAN

```
   BILLY McCLELLAN          (A         (A) VERY EARLY         1978 LECAM       505
                                       (B) ZERO HIND SIGHT    1981 ELEKTRA   US  258
```

DELBERT McCLINTON

```
   DELBERT McCLINTON        (ALL       (A) DELBERT & GLEN     1972 CLEAN     US   CN6010598
   GLEN CLARK               (AB        (B) SUBJECT TO CHANGE  1973 CLEAN     US   CN6020598
   ROGER HAWKINS       D    (IJ        (C) VICTIM OF LIFE'S CIRCUMSTANCES 1975 ABC US  AB  907
   DAVID HOOD          B    (IJ        (D) GENUINE COWHIDE    1976 ABC       US   ABC  959
   BARRY BECKETT       K    (IJ        (E) LOVE RUSTLER       1977 ABC UK ABCL5217 US   AB  991
   JIMMY JOHNSON       G    (IJ        (F) SECOND WIND        1978 CAPRICORN US   CP 0201
   BONNIE BRAMLETT     V    (IJ        (G) VERY EARLY DELBERT McCLINTON 1978 LECAM US LCS 404A
   WAYNE PERKINS       G    (IJ        (H) KEEPER OF THE FLAME 1979 CAPRICORN US CP 0223
   HARRISON CALLOWAY   HRNS (IJ        (I) JEALOUS KIND       1980 CAPITOL        12115
   BILLY SANDERS       G    (IJ        (J) PLAIN FROM THE HEART 1981 CAPITOL      12188
   ROBERT HARWELL      SAX  (IJ
   AVA AULDRIDGE       V    (J    LENNY LEBLANC    V    (IJ  BEN CAULEY      TPT (J   LARRY LANGE      B  (J
   REESE WYMANS        K    (JI   HARVEY THOMPSON  HRNS (J   RONNIE EADES    HRNS(IJ  CINDY RICHARDSON V  (J
   JOHN JARVIS         PNO  (J    CHARLES ROSE     TROM (JI  BARRY FROST      D  (J   JAMES PENNEBAKER G  (J
   ERNIE DURAWA        PERC (J    RANDY McCORMICK  K    (I   ROBERT BYRNE     V  (I   EDDIE STRUZICK   V  (I
   MARY BETH McCLMORE  V    (I    BOB KRUSEN       PERC (I   DICK COOPER     PERC(I
```

MARC McCLURE

```
   MARC McCLURE        G PERC K V(A    (A) MARC McCLURE       1972 CAPITOL    US      11113
   DAVID VAUGHT        B    (A
   DENNIS DRAGON       D    (A    CHARLES FINDLEY  TROM (A   JOHN SEITER      D  (A   CHRIS DARROW   MAND(A
   SPOONER OLDHAM      K    (A    JIM HORN         SAX  (A   ROBIN BATTEAU    VLN(A   BILL PLUMMER     B  (A
   VINCE DEROSA        HRN  (A    RON ELLIOTT      G    (A   DAN LEVITT       G BAN(A
```

DAVID McCLUSKY

```
   DAVID McCLUSKY      V    (A         (A) A LONG TIME COMING 1978 GRT          9230 1081
   JOHN JARVIS         K    (A
   STEVE LUKATHER      G    (A    ANDY NEWMARK     D    (A   BOBBY KIMBALL    V  (A   FRED MOLLIN    V G(A
   TOM SZCZESNIAK      B    (A    BOB MANN         G    (A   BRIAN RUSSELL    G  (A   DAN DUGMORE      G  (A
   ERNIE WATTS         SAX  (A    JIMMY FARAGNER   V    (A   BOB DiSALLE      D  (A   JIM WYNVEEN      G  (A
   RACHEL PALEMENT          (A    LEE SKLAR        B    (A   JIM HORN        SAX (A   MATTHEW McCAULEY V  (A
   DOUG RILEY          K    (A    JORN ANDERSEN    D    (A   JOHN CAPEK       K  (A   MIKE PORCARO     B  (A
   JEFF PORCARO        D    (A    HERB PEDERSEN    V    (A   BOB BOUCHER      B  (A   JON GOLDSMITH K STR(A
```

KIRSTY MacCOLL

```
   KIRSTY MacCOLL      V    (A         (A) DESPERATE CHARACTER 1981 POLYDOR      POLS 1035
   LU                  G    (A
   BILLY BREMNER       G    (A    MALCOLM MORLEY   G    (A   PHIL RAMBOW      G  (A   NICK 'BAZZA'LOWE PROD G(A
   GLYN HAVARD         B    (A    PAUL RILEY       B    (A   GAVIN POVEY      K  (A   LEE PARTISS    D  (A
   BEN MANDELSON       FDL  (A    LEW LEWIS        HCA  (A   JOHN EARLE      SAX (A   RAY BEAVIS   SAX (A
   CHRIS GOWER         TROM (A    DICK HANSON      TPT  (A
```

CHARLIE McCOY

```
   CHARLIE McCOY       HCA V(ALL       (A) HARPIN' THE BLUES  1970 MONUMENT UK 69204  US 33802
   JIM ISBELL          D    (FAJK       (A) HARPIN' THE BLUES  197  MONUMENT           US  6629
   KENNETH BUTTREY     D    (AFJK       (B) CHARLIE McCOY      1972 MONUMENT UK  5034  US 31910
   JERRY WHITE         D    (FA         (B) CHARLIE McCOY      197  MONUMENT           US  6624
   KENNY MALONE        PERC (AF         (C) REAL McCOY         1972 MONUMENT US 6623   US 31329
   SI EDWARDS          PERC (FAJK       (D) GOOD TIME CHARLIE  1973 MONUMENT US 6625   US 32215
   FARRELL MORRIS      VIBES(FAJK       (E) FASTEST HARP IN THE SOUTH 1973 MONUMENT US 6626 US 32749
   BUDDY SKIPPER K V CLAR (FAJ         (F) NASHVILLE HIT MAN  1974 MONUMENT UK 80115  US  6627
   GEORGE BINKLEY      VLN  (F          (G) CHARLIE MY BOY     1975 MONUMENT US 6628   US 33384
   RUSS HICKS STEEL V G (FAJK           (H) CHRISTMAS ALBUM    197  MONUMENT US 6645   US 33176
```

(CONTINUED)

CHARLIE McCOY

```
         (CONTINUED)
BUDDY SPICHER      FDL  (AF                    (I) GREATEST HITS              197  MONUMENT                 US  7622
BRENTON BANKS      VLN  (F                     (J) PLAY IT AGAIN CHARLIE      197  MONUMENT  UK 81559       US  6630
LENNIE HAIGHT      VLN  (F                     (K) COUNTRY COOKIN'            1977 MONUMENT  UK 82444       US  7612
BERGEN WHITE       V    (F                     (L) STONE FOX CHASE            1977 MONUMENT                 UK  81886
WENDY SUITS        V    (F                     (M) APPALACHIAN FEVER          1979 MONUMENT  UK 83516       US  7632
LARRY BUTLER       PNO  (F
DON SMITH          B    (AFJK LEON RHODES      B G  (F   JOHNNY GIMBLE   FDL  (FK BTRON BACH     CELLO (F
BOBBY THOMPSON     G BAN(AFJK RAY EDENTON      G    (AFJK HAROLD BRADLEY  G   (FAJK JIM COLVARD   G     (AF
JOSH GRAVES        DOBRO(FAJK CARL GORODETZKY  VLN  (F   GARY VANOSDALE  VLA  (F   PIG ROBBINS    PNO   (AFJK
BILLY LINNEMAN     B    (FJ   JOE ZINKAN       B    (F   BOBBY DYSON     B    (FA  STEPHANIE WOOLF VLN  (F
MARTHA McCRORY     CELLO(F    DAVE KIRBY       G    (FJ  CHIP YOUNG      G    (F   BILLY SANFORD   G    (F
JIMMY WILKERSON    G    (FA   SHELDON KURLAND  VLN  (F   CAROL MONTGOMERY V   (F   MARVIN CHANTRY  VIOLA (F
JOHN PROBST        PNO  (FA   WAYNE MOSS       B    AFJK JOHNNY JOHNSON  B    (FA  HAL RUGG        STEEL (F
STEVE SMITH        VLN  (FA   TOMMY ALSUP      G    (F   TERRY DEARMORE  G    (AFJK FRED NEWELL    G    (FJ
DALE SELLERS       G    (FA   WELDON MYRICK    STEEL(FAJK
```

VAN McCOY

```
VAN McCOY          V PNO(ALL  ( ) SOUL IMPROVISATIONS          1972 BUDDAH                US  5103
ALBERT BAILEY      V    (E     (A) DISCO BABY                  1975 AVCO                  UK  9109 004
DESTRY             V    (E     (B) DISCO KID                   1975 AVCO                  UK  9109 007
ZULEMA             V    (E     (C) THE REAL McCOY              1976 H&L                   UK  9109 009
BRENDA HILLIARD    V    (E     (D) THE HUSTLE                  1976 H&L                   US  69016
DIANE WILSON       V    (E     (E) MY FAVOURITE FANTASY        1978 MCA   UK MCF 2843 US      3036
BERNIE GLOW        TPT  (E     (F) LONELY DANCER               19   MCA                   US  3071
URBIE GREEN        TROM (E     (G) DANCIN'                     19   SSS                   US  33
MICKEY GRAVINE     TROM (E     (H) FROM DISCO TO LOVE          19   BUDDAH US 5648 FR MODE    9026
PHIL BODNER        FLT  (E     (J) SWEET RHYTHM                1979 H&L                   6467 651
BOB ADAMS          D    (E   SKIP FENSELL     K    (E   DAVID CAREY     PERC (E   ARTHUR JENKINS  PNO (E
CHARLIE KIPPS      G    (E   CORNELL DUPREE   G    (E   STEVE GADD      D    (E   LEON PENDARVIS  K   (E
PRISCILLA BASKERVILLE V(E   MEL DAVIS        TPT  (E   WAYNE ANDRE     TROM (E   TOM MALONE      TROM(E
JIM BUFFINGTON     HRNS (E   DENNIS RICHEY    G D  (E   JAMES FUNCHES   B    (E   PAT REBILLOT    PNO (E
BERT JONES         PERC (E   GORDON EDWARDS   B    (E   RICHARD TEE     PNO  (E   JOHN TROPEA     G   (E
MIKE MAINIERI      PERC (E   JON FADDIS       TPT  (E   VICTOR PAZ      TPT  (E   BOB ALEXANDER   TROM(E
PAUL FAULISE       TROM (E   BROOKS TILLOTSON HRNS (E   ARTHUR LISI     K    (E   JON WARE        PERC(E
STEVE JORDAN       D    (E   CRUSHER BENNETT  PERC (E   CHRIS PARKER    D    (E   GEORGE DEVENS   PERC(E
HUGH McCRACKEN     G    (E
```

McCOYS

```
RICK DERRINGER     G V  (ALL   (A) HANG ON SLOOPY              1965 BANG US 212    JOY  JOYS 196
RANDY ZEHRINGER    D    (ALL   (A) HANG ON SLOOPY              196  IMMEDIATE      UK   IMLP 001
RANDY HOBBS        B    (ALL   (B) YOU MAKE ME FEEL SO GOOD    1966 BANG           US   213
BOBBY PETERSON     K    (ALL   (C) INFINITE McCOYS             1968 MERCURY US 21128    US 61163
PETE DRAKE         STEEL(D     (D) HUMAN BALL                  1968 MERCURY        US   61207
DICK HALLIGAN      TROM (C     (EP) McCOYS                     1966 IMMEDIATE      UK   MEP002
FRED LIPSIUS       SAX  (C     (EP) McCOYS 2                   196  IMMEDIATE      UK   MEP003
RANDY BRECKER      TPT  (C
JERRY WEISS        TPT  (C
```

JIMMY McCRACKLIN

```
JIMMY McCRACKLIN   PNO V(ALL  MY ANSWER                        19   IMPERIAL       US   LP 12306
DAVID BLUNSTON     PNO  (      EVERYNIGHT EVERYDAY             19   IMPERIAL       US   LP 12285
JOHN HENRY         B    (      THINK                           19   IMPERIAL       US   LP 12297
ALRAY KIDD         D    (      I JUST GOTTA KNOW               19   IMPERIAL       US   LP 12219
ROBERT KELTON      D    (      JIMMY McCRACKLIN SINGS          19   CHESS          US   LP 1464
LITTLE RED         D    (      LETS GET TOGETHER               19   MINIT          US   LP 24011
JOE CONWRIGHT      SAX  (      NEW SOUL OF                     19   IMPERIAL       US   LP 12316
CHARLES SUTTER     SAX  (      (H) TWIST WITH                  19   CROWN US CLP5244 US CUSTOM 2057
LAFAYETTE THOMAS   G    (H     ROCKIN' MAN                     19   ROUTE 66       SWED KIX 12
SAN FRISCO JEFF    D    (      AND HIS BLUESBLASTERS           1981 ACE                 CH 2B
JOHNNY PARKER      SAX  (      BEST OF                         19   MINIT          US   24009
                              YESTERDAY IS GONE               1972 STAX           US   2047
                              SINGER MAN                       19   MINIT          US   24017
                              MY ROCKIN SOUL                  19   UNITED         US   7719
```

MARY McCREARY

```
MARY  McCREARY     V    (AB    (A) JEZEBEL                     1973 SHELTER            US 2110
                               (B) BUTTERFLIES IN HEAVEN       1975 MCA                US 347
```

HENRY McCULLOUGH

```
HENRY McCULLOUGH   G V  (A     (A) MIND YOUR OWN BUSINESS      1975 DARK HORSE         UK  AMLH22005
ALAN SPENNER       B    (A
STEVE CHAPMAN      D    (A   MICK WEAVER      K    (A   JOHN HALSEY     D    (A   LLOYD SMITH     SAX (A
NEIL HUBBARD       G    (A   CHARLIE HARRISON B    (A   TIM HINKLEY     K    (A   FRANKIE MILLER  V   (A
LIONEL KINGHAM     SAX  (A   BRUCE ROWLAND    D    (A   JIM LEVERTON    B    (A   JOE O'DONNELL   VLN (A
HERSCHEL HOLDER    TPT  (A   JOHN JANSEN  PROD (A
```

LENNIE McDONALD

```
LENNIE McDONALD    G V  (A     (A) HARD ROAD                   1975 ARISTA             UK ARTY 117
ALAN TARNEY        B    (A
MIKE GILES         D    (A   CLIFF HALL       (A   CHRIS RAINBOW  PERC V (A   MIKE BARKER     G    (A
RAY JACKSON        HCA  (A   WILF GIBSON      VLN (A   DARRELL RUNSWICK  B STR(A   DENNIS LOPEZ    PERC(A
MEL COLLINS        SAX  (A   GORDON HUNTLEY   STEEL(A   KOKOMO SINGERS (A   LONDON CHAMBER CHOIR (A
```

KATHI McDONALD

```
KATHI McDONALD     V    (A     (A) INSANE ASYLUM               1974 CAPITOL            US  ST 11224
NILS LOFGREN       G    (A
PETE SEARS         G B K(A   BOBBYE HALL      PERC (A   RONNIE MONTROSE  G   (A   GREG DOUGLAS    G   (A
NEAL SCHON         G    (A   MARK UNOBSKI     G    (A   PAPA JOHN CREACH FDL (A   JIM McPHERSON   B   (A
JOHN CIPPOLLINA    G    (A   GARY PHILIPPET   G    (A   BOOTS HOUSTON    HRNS(A   AYNSLEY DUNBAR  D   (A
TOWER OF POWER     HRNS (A   SLY STONE        V    (A   POINTER SISTERS  V   (A
```

MICHAEL McDONALD

(A) IF THATS WHAT IT TAKES   1982 WB US 23703

```
MICHAEL McDONALD   K V (A
STEVE GADD         D   (A
JEFF PORCARO       D   (A   WILLIE WEEKS      B   (A   LOUIS JOHNSON     B   (A   MIKE PORCARO      B   (A
DEAN PARKS         G   (A   STEVE LUKATHER    G   (A   ROBBEN FORD       G   (A   EDGAR WINTER      SAX (A
TOM SCOTT          SAX (A   LENNY CASTRO      PERC (A  BOBBY LAKIND      PERC(A   PAULINHO DACOSTA  PERC(A
TED TEMPLEMAN      PERC (A  GREG PHILLINGANES K   (A   MICHAEL O'MARTIAN K   (A   ED SANFORD        V   (A
MAUREEN McDONALD   V   (A   KENNY LOGGINS     V   (A   AMY HOLLAND       V   (A   MICHAEL BODDICKER SYN(A
```

RALPH MACDONALD

(A) SOUND OF A DRUM   1976 MARLIN US 2202+ XL   XL14030
(B) THE PATH   1978 MARLIN UA 2210+ TK   TKR82515
(C) COUNTERPOINT   1979 TK   UK   TKR83373

```
RALPH MACDONALD      PERC (ALL
GROVER WASHINGTON JR SAX(ABC
CHUCK RAINEY         B   (AB
ERIC GALE            G B (ABC
RICHARD TEE          PNO (ABC ARTHUR JENKINS    K   (ABC DAVID FRIEDMAN    VIBES(AB CLINTON THOBOURNE CLAR(AB
JOE FARRELL          HRNS (A  JIMMY OWENS       HRNS (A  PATTI AUSTIN      V   (AB RAYMOND SIMPSON   V   (A
RICK MAROTTA         D   (AB  WILLIAM EATON     V   (A   NICHOLAS MARRERO  PERC (AB URIAS FRITZ       BOTTLE(A
SELDON POWELL        HRNS (A  VERGIL JONES      HRNS (A  ZACHARY SANDERS   V   (AC GWEN GUTHRIE      V  (AB
JEAN THIELEMANS      HCA (AB  BOB JAMES         SYN (AB  WILLIAM SALTER    B   (AB HAROLD VICK       HRNS (AC
KIANE ZAWADI         HRNS (A  VIVIAN CHERRY     V   (A   FRANK FLOYD       V   (AC STEVE GADD        D   (BC
HARVEY MASON         D   (C   ROBERT GREENIDGE  PERC (C  MICHAEL BRECKER   HRNS (CB RANDY BRECKER    HRNS (CB
BARRY ROGERS         HRNS (CB JOE BROWN         B PERC (C WILL LEE         B   (CB TOM SCOTT         WIND (C
JON FADDIS           HRNS (C  RON CUBER         HRNS (C  DAVE SANBORN      HRNS (CB KEN WILLIAMS     V   (C
HOWARD JOHNSON       HRNS (C  TOM MALONE        HRNS (C  STRING SECTION    (ABC
```

COUNTRY JOE McDONALD & THE FISH

```
JOE McDONALD          G HCA C G(ALL   (A) ELECTRIC MUSIC FOR THE MIND    1967 VANGUARD US VSD 79244 UK SVRL19026
JOHN LEHMAN           V     (W        (A) ELECTRIC MUSIC FOR THE MIND    1967 FONTANA               UK STFL 6081
BARRY MELTON          G     (ABCGIXb  (B) I FEEL LIKE I'M FIXIN TO DIE   1967 VANGUARD US VSD 79266 UK SVRL19029
DAVID COHEN           K     (ABCIXb   (B) I FEEL LIKE I'M FIXIN TO DIE   1967 FONTANA               UK STFL 6087
BRUCE BARTHOL         B HCA(ABCQIXb   (C) TOGETHER                       1968 VANGUARD US VSD 79277 UK SVRL19006
CHICKEN HIRSH         D     (ABIJX    (D) HERE WE ARE AGAIN              1969 VANGUARD US VSD79299  UK STVL19048
DAVID GETZ            D     (M        (E) THINKING OF WOODY GUTHRIE      1969 VANGUARD US VSD  6546 UK VRL 19057
PETER ALBIN           B     (M        ( ) GREATEST HITS                  1969 VANGUARD US VSD  6545 UK SVRL19058
JEFF PORCARO          D     (W        (F) TONIGHT I'M SINGING FOR YOU    1970 VANGUARD US VSD  6557 UK 6359 004
MIKE PORCARO          B     (W        (G) C J FISH                       1970 VANGUARD US VSD  6555 UK 6359 002
MAC CRIDLIN           B     (WZ       (H) QUIET DAY IN CLICHY            1971 SONET                 UK SNTF 622
STEVE MADAIO          HRNS (QWX       (I) FROM ASHBURY TO WOODSTOCK (DBL) 1971 VANGUARD               VSD 27/28
JAY GRAYDON           G     (WZ       (J) HOLD ON ITS COMING             1971 VANGUARD US VSD 79314
JOHN BLAKELEY         G     (WQZ      (K) WAR WAR WAR                    1971 VANGUARD US VSD 79315
DAVID FOSTER          K     (W        (L) INCEDIBLE  LIVE                1972 VANGUARD US VSD 79316
BILL CUOMO            K     (W        (M) PARIS SESSIONS                 1973 VANGUARD US VSD 79328
MICHAEL BODDIKER      K     (W        (O) THE BEST OF                    1973 VANGUARD US VSD 79000 UK SVRL19058
CHILI CHARLES         D     (W        (P) COUNTRY JOE                    1975 VANGUARD US VSD 79348
STEPHANIE SPRUILL     V     (W        (Q) PARADISE WITH AN OCEAN VIEW    1975 FANTASY  US       9495 UK FTA 3002
CARL SHRAGER          (b                (Q) PARADISE WITH AN OCEAN VIEW    1975 BELLAPHON GER       19225
MARTI McCALL          V     (W        (R) THE ESSENTIAL   (DBL)          1976 VANGUARD               VSD 85/86
LISA ROBERTS          V     (W        (T) LOVE IS A FIRE                 1976 FANTASY  US       9511 UK FTA 3005
JAN JOYCE             V     (QW       (U) GOLDEN HOUR                    1977 PYE                    UK     GH 865
JIM GILSTRAP          V     (QW       (V) GOODBYE BLUES                  1977 FANTASY  US       9525 UK FT   529
PETE WALSH            V B   (VWZ      (W) ROCK'N'ROLL FROM PLANET EARTH  1978 FANTASY  US       9544 UK FT   539
BILL STEEL            (b                (W) ROCK'N'ROLL FROM PLANET EARTH  1978 BELLAPHON GER       2553
ROGER KENERLY SAINT   V     (W        (X) REUNION                        1977 FANTASY  US       9530
PAUL ARMSTRONG        PERC (b         (X) REUNION                        1977 BELLAPHON GER       2534
ANDREA ROBINSON       V     (W        (Y) TRIBUTE TO WOODY               19   WB       US 2W    3007
CHUCK FINDLEY         HRNS (W         (Z) LEISURE SUITE                  1979 FANTASY  US 9586  UK FT     565
JOHN MITCHELL         HRNS (W         (a) ON MY OWN                      1980 RAG BABY US 147 406
TREVOR LAWRENCE       HRNS (QW        (b) COLLECTORS ITEM(FIRST 3 EPs)   1980 RAG BABY UK 1008
MIKE BEARDSLEE        V     (b         (c) EARLY YEARS                    1981 PICCADILLY  US 33091
JOHN GUNNING          D     (b
NACHO DEWEY           HCA  (b    SAROD ASHISH KHAN TAMB (W   GREG DEWEY        D   (GJIb DOUG METZNER     B   (GI
MARK KAPNER           K    (GI    DAVID HAYES       B   (QZ  PETER MILIO       D   (QV  TED ASHFORD       K   (QV
STEVE GABOURY         PNO  (Q    VANETTA FIELDS    V   (Q   SALLY STEVENS     V   (Q   MARLEENA JETTER   V   (Q
SID SHARP             STRING(Q   PHIL MARSH        G   (MQ  BOBBY KEYS        SAX (QX  CARLENA WILLIAMS  V  (Q
MAXINE ANDERSON       V    (Q    AUGIE JOHNSON     V   (Q   RON MARABUTO      D   (Q   JOHNNY ROTELLA    SAX (Q
SHIRLEY MATTHEWS      V    (Q    MICHAEL IRWIN     V   (Q   GERALD GARRETT    V   (Q   RICHARD CORSELLO  G  (Z
SCOTT LAWRENCE        PNO  (Z    GREG DOUGLAS      G   (Z   JIM HOBSON        PNO (Z   HERB JIMMERSON    SYN (Z
TIP WIRRICK           G    (Z    CHUCK DAY         G   (Z   VIC SMITH         B   (bJ  DAHUD SHAAR D     (Z
BOB KINGSON           B    (Z    JEFFREY MEYER     D   (Z   MICHAEL HERBICK   D   (Z   KELVIN DIXON      D   (Z
PERSUASIONS           V    (Z    FISCHLERS         V   (Z   BILL COLLINS      V   (Z   DANIEL GUNNIP     V   (Z
BOBBI VANDERVOORT     V    (Z    DAVID GUNNIP      V   (Z   SEBASTIAN         CONG(M    JOHN REWIND       G   (Mb
DIANE RASCONIA        V    (Z    DAVID BROMBERG    G   (V   JERRY CORBITT     V   (V   NATHAN RUBIN      VLN (V
MALVINA REYNOLDS      V    (V    BILL SUMMERS      PERC (V  MARTY BALIN       V   (V   ANNE RIZZO STEEL  V (VMb
TERRY ADAMS           CELLO(V   DOROTHY MISKOWITZ V PNO(M   TUCKI BAILEY      WIND (M   JOHN VIERRA       SYN (M
RICHARD SUSSMAN       K    (bJ   PETER KRUG  G V   (b      PAUL ARMSTRONG    REC (I    CARVEL BASS       G  (I
PEREGRINE PICKLE B    (I         MARK RYAN         B   (I   JOHN FRANCIS GUNNING D (I  ROBIN McDONALD    PERC(I
GRADY MARTIN          G SIT (EF  ALEX DMOCHOWSKI   B   (J   SPENCER DAVIS     G V HCA(J RAY EDENTON      G  (EF
NORBERT PUTNAM        B    (EF   HAROLD BRADLEY    G B (EF  HARGUS ROBBINS    PNO (EF   BUDDY HARMON      D  (EF
THE JORDANARIRES      V    (F    PHIL KAFFEL PERC V (       JOHN FULLER       HARP (V   NICK BUCK         PNO(J
ROCKHEAD              G    (J    ED BOGAS          VLN (J   JOHN HUG          G   (T   SIDI SIDDY        D  (J
ERIC WEISSBERG        B    (J    JOHN BLAKELEY     G   (T   JAYDEE MANESS     STEEL(T   DAVID HAYES       (T
RALPH WASH            B    (T    TED ASHFORD       (T       JIM GORDON        D   (T   JIM ED NORMAN     PNO (T
MAGGI PAYNE           WIND (V    CARL PEDERSEN     VLN (V   JOHN OTIS         CONGA(X   SAM CHARTERS      JUG (X
JIM PRICE             HRNS (X
```

SHELAGH McDONALD

(A) SHELAGH McDONALD   1970 B & C   CAS 1019
(B) STARGAZER   1971 B & C   CAS 1043

```
SHELAGH McDONALD    G V K(AB
JOHN RYAN           B   (B
DANNY THOMPSON      B   (B
KEITH CHRISTMAS     G   (AB  HARVEY BURNS      D   (B   RAY WARLEIGH      SAX (B   IAN WHITEMAN      K   (AB
DAVE RICHARDS       B   (B   KATHY KISSOON     V   (B   MAC KISSOON       V   (B   MIKE LONDON       V   (B
RICHARD THOMPSON    G   (B   DAVE MATTACKS     D   (B   PAT DONALDSON     B   (AB  ANDY ROBERTS      G   (A
ROGER POWELL        D   (A   KEITH TIPPETT     PNO (A   GERRY CONWAY      D   (A   MIKE EVANS        B   (A
GORDON HUNTLEY      STEEL(A   TRISTAN FRY       VIBES(A
```

McDONALD & GILES

```
IAN McDONALD        K SAX(A     (A) McDONALD & GILES    1970 ISLAND    UK  ILPS 9126
MIKE GILES          D   (A      (A) McDONALD & GILES    1977 POLYDOR   UK  2302 070
MICHAEL BLAKESLEY   TROM (A      (A) McDONALD & GILES    197  COTILLION US       9042
PETER GILES         B   (A
STEVE WINWOOD           (A    STRINGS        (A
```

MACEO

```
(A) US    1974 PEOPLE US PE6601 UK POLYDOR 2391122
```

KATE & ANNA McGARRIGLE

```
KATE McGARRIGLE   K V G BAN(ALL   (A) KATE & ANNA McGARRIGLE      1975 WB     US BS2862   UK  K 56218
ANNA McGARRIGLE   V K BAN(ALL     (B) DANCER WITH BRUISED KNEES   1977 WB     US BS3014   UK  K 56356
TONY LEVIN        B   (AC         (C) PRONTO MONTO               1978 WB     US BS3248   UK  K 56561
STEPHEN GADD      D   (ABC        (D) KATE & ANNA McGARRIGLE     1980 ISLAND UK 9654
TREVOR LAWRENCE   G   (A

DAVID SPINOZZA    G    (A    GREG PRESTOPINO G V K(A    BOBBY KEYS      SAX (A    TONY RICE        G   (A
JOEL TEPP     CLAR HCA (A    DAVID GRISMAN   MAND (A    RED CALLENDER   B   (A    AMOS GARRETT     G   (A
JANIE McGARRIGLE-DOW V K(AB  PETER WELDON V HCA BAN(ABC DANE LANKEN     V   (ABC  CHAIM TANNENBAUM V G HCA(ABC
JAY UNGAR         FDL  (AB   FLOYD GILBEAU   FDL  (A    ANDREW GOLD     G   (A    DENSIL LANG      PERC(A
PLAS JOHNSON      WIND (A    RUSS KUNKEL     D    (A    NICK DECARO     ACC (A    DIMMY DIMBUSTER  PERC(A
SCOT LANG         G    (A    JOHN CALE       K    (A    MIKE VISCIGLIA  B   (B    GRADY TATE       D   (BC
TOMMY MORGAN      HCA  (B    RICHARD DAVIS   B    (B    PAT DONALDSON   B   (BC   DAVE MATTACKS    D   (B
KENNY PEARSON     K    (BC   WARREN SMITH    PERC (B    RON DOLEMAN     VLN (B    SUSAN EVANS      PERC(BC
GORDIE FLEMING    ACC  (B    GILLES LOSIER   B    (B    ANDREW COWAN    G   (B    GEORGE BOHANON   HRNS(AB
LOWELL GEORGE     G    (A    HUGH McCRACKEN  G V  (B    JEFF MIRANOV    G   (C    JERRY DONAHUE    G   (C
GEORGE YOUNG      CLAR (C    BOB GLAUB       B    (C    VICTOR FELDMAN  PERC(C    BRYAN CUMMING    SAX (C
GEORGE DEVENS     PERC (C    BERNARD PURDIE  D    (C    GORDON EDWARDS  B   (C    JOHN SCHOLLE     G   (C
MICHAEL MOORE     B    (C    FREEBO          TUBA (C    DAVID NICHTERN  B   (C    DAVID WOODFORD   SAX (C
KEN KOSEK         FDL  (C    GARY MALLABER   D    (C    GARY MURE                 MICHAEL SMALL    V   (A
```

MISSISSIPPI FRED McDOWELL

```
MISSISSIPPI FRED McDOWELL G V(ALL  (A) MISSISSIPPI DELTA BLUES       1964 ARHOOLIE      US    F1021
MIKE RUSSO          G   (E         (A) MISSISSIPPI DELTA BLUES       19   POLYDOR       UK    2460 193
JOHN KAHN           B   (E         (B) MY HOME IS IN THE DELTA       1964 TESTAMENT     US    2208
BOB JONES           D   (E         (C) AMAZING GRACE                1964 TESTAMENT     US    2219
FANNIE DAVIS            (           (D) MISSISSIPPI DELTA BLUES VOL 2 1966 ARHOOLIE      US    F 1027
MILES PRATCHER         (           (E) & HIS BLUES BOYS             19   ARHOOLIE      US    F 1046
ANNIE MAE McDOWELL  V   (ABC        (F) LONDON 1                     1970 TRANSATLANTIC UK    TRA 194
                                   (F) LONDON 1                     1970 SIRE          US    97018
ELI GREEN           V   (D         ( ) LONDON 2                     19   TRANSATLANTIC UK    TRA 203
                                   ( ) LONG WAY FROM HOME           19   CBS UK 63735 MILESTONE US 93003
                                   ( ) & FURRY LEWIS                19   BIOGRAPH      BLP 12017
                                   ( ) KEEP YOUR LAMP TRIMMED       19   ARHOOLIE      US    F1068
                                   ( ) I DONT PLAY NO ROCK'N' ROLL  19   CAPITOL       US    409
                                   ( ) 1904 72                      1974 XTRA          UK    XTRA 1136
                                   ( ) MISSISSIPPI FRED McDOWELL    19   EVEREST       US    253
                                   ( ) LIVE IN NEW YORK             19   OBLIVION      US    OBL 1
                                   ( ) SOMEBODY KEEPS CALLIN' ME    19   ANTILLES      US    7022
                                   ( ) MISSISSIPPI FRED McDOWELL    19   ARC FOLK      US    253
                                   ( ) BLUES ROLL ON                19   ATLANTIC      US    590025
                                   ( ) GOING DOWN SOUTH             1970 POLYDOR       US    2365
```

MIKE McGEAR

```
MIKE McGEAR      V    (AB     (A) WOMAN    1972 ISLAND UK  ILPS 9191
ZOOT MONEY       K    (A      (B) McGEAR   1974 WB  US 2825 UK  K 56051
JOHN MEGGINSON   K    (A

NORMAN YARDLEY   HCA  (A    CHRIS PYNE     HRNS (A    MALCOLM DUNCAN      HRNS (A    PAUL KORDA      V    (A
GINGER JOHNSON   PERC (A    DENNY LAINE    G V  (A    PADDY MOLONEY       PIPES(B    ANDY ROBERTS    G    (A
DAVE RICHARDS    B    (A    GERRY CONWAY   D    (AB   CENTIPEDE STRINGS        (A    CECIL MOSS      HRNS(A
MIKE ROSEN       HRNS (A    ROGER BALL     HRNS (A    TONY COE            SAX  (AB   ALAN GORRIE     V    (A
STEVE GOULD      V    (A    BRIAN AUGER    K    (A    LINDA McCARTNEY     V K  (B    JIMMY McCULLOCH G    (B
BRIAN JONES      SAX  (B    DENNY SEIWELL  D    (B
```

DONNA McGHEE

```
DONNA McGHEE    (A     (A) MAKE IT LAST FOREVER    1978 ANCHOR UK  ANCL 2027
```

ROGER McGOUGH

```
ROGER McGOUGH   V    (A     (A) A SUMMER WITH MONIKA    1978 ISLAND UK  ILPS 9551
PAT DONALDSON   B    (A
JOHN MEGGINSON  K    (A    DAVE OLNEY   B   (A    TIMI DONALD   D   (A    JACK EMBLOW  ACC (A
DAVE LAWSON     SYN  (A    ZOOT MONEY   K   (A    ANDY ROBERTS  G   (A
```

BAT McGRATH

```
BAT McGRATH          (ABC     (A) ANTRODUCING          19   EPIC     US   26499
                              (B) FROM THE BLUE EAGLE  1977 AMHERST  US   1005
DON ETHAN POTTER  G  (        (C) THE SPY              1978 AMHERST  US   1011
```

JIMMY McGRIFF

```
JIMMY McGRIFF       ORG(ALL    (A) CHERRY                     196  SOLID STATE   US   SM 17006
ERIC GALE           G   (A     (B) THE BIG BAND               1968 SOLID STATE   US   LAS 1800
ALLAN SCHWARZBERG   D   (R     ( ) BAG FULL OF SOUL           196  SOLID STATE   US   18002
GRADY TATE          D   (A     (C) ELECTRIC FUNK              19   BLUENOTE      US   BST 84350
MILT HINTON         B   (A     (D) SOMETHING TO LISTEN TO     19   BLUENOTE      US   BST 84364
EVERETT BARKSDALE   G   (A     (E) BLACK PEARL                19   BLUENOTE      US   BST 84374
GROOVE HOLMES       K   (KP    (F) GOOD THING DONT HAPPEN.... 1973 GROOVEMERCHANT US  GM 2205
O'DONEL LEVY        G   (K     (G) GROOVE GREASE              19   GROOVEMERCHANT US  GM 503
GEORGE FREEMAN      G   (K     (H) BLACK & BLUES              19   GROOVEMERCHANT US  GM 2203
BERNARD PURDIE      D   (K     (H) BLACK & BLUES              19   PEOPLE        PLED 501
LARRY FRAZIER           (I     (I) ORGAN & BLUES BAND         1968 SOLID STATE   US   18052
BUB ASHTON              (I     ( ) BAG FULL OF BLUES          1968 SOLID STATE   US   18017
BOBBY CRANSHAW      B   (N     ( ) IVE GOT A NEW WOMAN        1968 SOLID STATE   US   18030
RICHARD MITCHELL        (I     ( ) HONEY                      1968 SOLID STATE   US   18036
DON TURNER              (I     ( ) THINGS TO COME             1969 SOLID STATE   US   18060
LAWRENCE KILLIAN    PERC (K    ( ) WORM                       1969 SOLID STATE   US   18045
KWASI JAYOURBA      CONGA(K    (J) FLYDUDE                    1974 GROOVEMERCHANT US  GM 509
ERNEST JONES        SYN (N     (J) FLYDUDE                    1974 PEOPLE        PLEO 14
LEO JOHNSON         SAX (N     (K) COME TOGETHER              1974 GROOVEMERCHANT US  GM 520
JIMMY PONDER        G   (RSN   (K) COME TOGETHER              1974 PEOPLE        PLEO 16
JESSE MORRISON      SAX (N     (L) LETS STAY TOGETHER         1974 PEOPLE        PLEO 19
```

```
FATS THEUS              (I        (L) LETS STAY TOGETHER          1974 GROOVEMERCHANT   US              5000
JOE THOMAS        SAX   (N        (M) IF YOU'RE READY             1974 PEOPLE                 PLEO   23
JESSE KIRKPATRICK       (I        (M) IF YOU'RE READY             1974 GROOVEMERCHANT   US              529
RALPH BYRD        G     (N        (N) STUMP JUICE                 1975 GROOVEMERCHANT   US        GM    3309
ANDREW McCLOUD    B     (N        (O) FLYIN' TIME                 19   GROOVEMERCHANT   US        GM    4403
JR PARKER              (F        ( ) MAIN SQUEEZE                 1976 GROOVEMERCHANT   US              534
HANK CRAWFORD     SAX   (S        ( ) MEAN MACHINE                1976 GROOVEMERCHANT   US              3311
NEIL JASON        B     (S        (P) GIANT OF THE ORGAN          19   GROOVEMERCHANT   US        GM    3300
JEFF MIRANOV      G     (S        (Q) SUPA COOKIN'                19   GROOVEMERCHANT   US        GM    4409
BARRY MILES       K     (S        (R) TAIL GUNNER                 1977 L R C                      LRC   9316
JIMMY YOUNG       D     (RS       (S) OUTSIDE LOOKIN' IN          1978 L R C                      LRC   9330
RON ZITO          D     (RS
PAT REBILLOT      K     (RS  FRANCISCO CENTENO B    (R   JERRY FRIEDMAN    G   (R   JIMMY MAELEN   PERC (RS
LEW DELGATTO      HRNS  (RS  EDDIE DANIELS   HRNS (RS   GEORGE YOUNG     HRNS (R   ALAN RUBIN     HRNS (R
RANDY BRECKER     HRNS  (R   JACK FROSK      HRNS (R    MARVIN STAMM     HRNS (R   JOE SHEPLEY    HRNS (R
DAVE TAYLOR       HRNS  (R   DOMINIC MENARDO HRNS (R    BARRY ROGERS     HRNS (R   JOE RANDAZZO   HRNS (R
PAUL GRIFFIN      K     (R   RALPH SCHUCKETT K    (R    BOB BABITT       B   (RS  WILL LEE       B    (R
LANCE QUINN       G     (RS  RUBENS BASSINI  PERC (R    AL DOWNING       V   (R   DENISE WOOTEN  V    (R
PATRICIA JOHNSON  V     (R
```

```
ROGER McGUINN     G V B(ALL       (A) ROGER McGUINN               1973 CBS  US 31946       UK   65274
BUDDY EMMONS      STEEL (A        (B) PEACE ON YOU                1974 CBS  US 32956       UK   80171
BRUCE JOHNSTON    PNO   (A        (C) ROGER McGUINN & HIS BAND    1975 CBS  US 33341       UK   80877
DAVID CROSBY      G V  (A         (D) CARDIFF ROSE               1976 CBS  US 34154       UK   81369
JOHN GUERIN       D    (A         (E) THUNDERBYRDS               1977 CBS  US 34656       UK   81883
DAVID VAUGHT      B    (A         (1) THUNDERBYRDS 1976 (2) UK TOUR 1974 AUG
LELAND SKLAR      B    (AB
JIM GORDON        D    (A   JERRY COLE       G    (A   CHRIS ETHRIDGE   B    (A   SPOONER OLDHAM  K   (A
SPANKY McFARLANE  V    (A   HAL BLAINE       D    (A   BOB DYLAN        HCA  (A   CHRIS HILLMAN   B   (A
MICHAEL CLARKE    D    (A   CHARLES LLOYD    SAX  (A   GENE CLARK       V    (A   JIMMY JOYCE CHILDRENS CHOIR(A
RICK VITO         G    (E   GREG THOMAS      D    (E   CHARLIE HARRISON B    (E   MICK RONSON    G V K(D
ROB STONER        B V  (D   HOWIE WYETH      D    (D   TIM SCHMIT       V    (D   RICHARD BOWDEN      (2
JAMES SMITH       G    (1   MARTY GREBB      K    (E   JANIS OLIVER     V    (E   DAVID MANSFIELD G K (D
KIM HUTCHCROFT    SAX  (D   GREG ATTAWAY          (2C  DAVID LOVELACE        (2C  STEVE LOVE     B   (2C
BRUCE BARLOW      B    (1E  LANCE DICKERSON  D    (1   TOM SCOTT        SAX  (E   JENNIFER O'NEILL V (E
KRISTINE OLIVER   V    (E   STEVE FORMAN     PERC (E   JOHN BOYLAN      PROD (C   RUSS KUNKEL    D   (B
PAUL HARRIS       K    (B   DONNIE DACUS G V      (B   DAN FOGELBERG    G V  (B   AL PERKINS     STEEL(B
AL KOOPER         K G  (A   MARK VOLMAN      V    (B   HOWARD KAYLAN    V    (B
```

```
ROGER McGUINN     G V  (ABC       (A) McGUINN,HILLMAN & CLARK     1979 CAPITOL                          11910
CHRIS HILLMAN     V G B(ABC       (B) CITY                        1980 CAPITOL EURO 86075              12043
GENE CLARK        V    (AB        (C) McGUINN , HILLMAN           1980 CAPITOL EURO 86237       US    12108
JOE LALA          PERC (AC
DONNA RHODES      V    (A   GREG THOMAS      D    (A   PAUL HARRIS      K    (A   SANDRA CHALMERS V  (A
GEORGE TERRY      G    (A   JOHN SAMBARATO   G V  (ABC CHARLES CHALMERS V   (A   SCOTT KIRKPATRICK D V(BC
CHUCK CRANE       G    (B   SKIP EDWARDS K STEEL (B   WAYNE PERKINS    G    (C   BARRY BECKETT  K   (C
```

```
TOM McGUINNESS    G B V(ABCDEF     (A) McGUINNESS FLINT           1971 CAPITOL US SMAS625     UK EST 22625
HUGH FLINT        D V  (ABCDEF     (B) HAPPY BIRTHDAY RUTHIE BABY 1971 CAPITOL               ST 22794
DENNIS COULSON    K G V(ABC        (C) LO & BEHOLD                1972 DJM UK DJLPS 424  SIRE US SAS 7405
BENNY GALLAGHER   V G  (AB         (D) RAINBOW                    1973 BRONZE  UK ILPS 9244  UK RI  87330
GRAHAM LYLE       V G  (AB         (E) CEST LA VIE                1974 BRONZE  UK ILPS 9302
DIXIE DEAN        V B K(CDE        (F) GREATEST HITS              197  SOUNDS SUPERB         UK SPR 80537
LOU STONEBRIDGE HCA G V K(DE
JIM EVANS  STEEL FDL G (DE  PAUL RUTHERFORD    HRNS (AC  NICKY HOPKINS      K    (B   JOHN MUMFORD       (B
JIMMY JEWELL      SAX  (B   MIKE HUGG             K    (C   HARRY BECKETT    TPT  (C
```

```
BARRY McGUIRE     V G B(ALL        (A) EVE OF DESTRUCTION         1965 DUNHILL US 50003 UK ABC  ABCL 5110
MICHAEL CLARKE    D    (D          (A) EVE OF DESTRUCTION         19   RCA             UK       RD   7751
ERIC HORD         G V  (D          (B) THIS PRECIOUS TIME         1966 DUNHILL US 50005 UK
CHRIS HILLMAN     B    (D          (C) WORLDS LAST PRIVATE CITIZEN 1968 DUNHILL US 50033
BERNIE LEADON     G    (D          (D) BARRY McGUIRE & THE DOCTOR 1971 ODE   US 77004 UK A&M AMLS 2008
ROCKIE HILTON     G    (D          (E) SEEDS                      1974 MYRRH    US  6519 UK MYRRH  1006
BILLY MUNDI       D    (D          (F) NARNIA                     1974 MYRRH            UK       1007
BYRON BERLINE     FDL  (D          (G) LIGHTEN UP                 1975 MYRRH    US 6531 UK MYRRH  1020
SNEAKY PETE KLEINOW STEEL(D        (H) TO THE BRIDE               1976 MYRRH    US 6548 UK MYRRH  1044
RILEY WILDFLOWER  B    (D          (I) EVE OF DESTRUCTION MAN     197  EMBER            UK       EMB 3362
NICKY WOODS       PERC (D          (J) C'MON ALONG                1976 SPARROW          UK     BIRD 105
MERLE BOATMAN     D    (D          (K) HAPPY ROADS                19   DJM              UK DJM   22071
LARRY KNECHTAL    B    (A          (L) HAVE YOU HEARD             1976 SPARROW    BIRD 3+      BIRD 111
HAL BLAINE        D    (A          (M) COSMIC COWBOY              1979 SPARROW          UK     BIRD 117
STEVE BARRI       PERC (A          ( ) INSIDE OUT                 1980 SPARROW                  112
P F SLOAN         G    (A          (N) JUBILATION                 19   MYRRH    US 6555
TOMMY TEDESCO     G    (A          (O) JUBILATION TOO             19   MYRRH    US 6568
LEW ADLER         PROD (A          (P) BARRY McGUIRE ALBUM        19   HORIZON  US 1636 US MIRA US  3000
                                   (Q) FINER THAN GOLD            1981 SPARROW                  132
```

```
MARIO GUCCIO      V    (A          (A) MECHANICAL MOONBEAMS       1978 EMI HARVEST    EURO  064 23805
ROLAND DE GREEF   B    (A          (B) NEW LINES                  1980    HARVEST     EURO  064 23980
MARC YSAYE        D V  (A
ALBERT LETECHEUR  K    (A   JEAN PAUL DEVAUBE    G    (A
```

```
                                   (EP) MACHINES                 19    WAX                     EAR1
```

```
ELLEN McILWAINE   G V  (ABC        (A) HONKY TONK ANGEL           19   POLYDOR     US           5021
DON PAYNE         B    (B          (B) WE THE PEOPLE              19   POLYDOR     US           5044
DON MOORE         B    (A          (C) THE REAL ELLEN McILWAINE   19   KOT'AI      US           3306
JIMMY MADISON     D    (B
JERRY MERCER      D    (B   COLIN TILTON     SAX  (A   CANDIDO          CONGA(A
```

JIMMIE MACK

```
    JIMMIE MACK          (AB        (A) JIMMIE MACK              19    BIG TREE      US           76007
                                    (B) ON THE CORNER           1979  BIG TREE      US           76014
M32                                        LONNIE MACK                                                   M32
    LONNIE MACK      G V (ALL       (A) THE WHAM OF THE MEMPHIS MAN  1964  FRATERNITY    US           1014
    WAYNE BULLOCK    K B (AF        (A) THE WHAM "  "    "    "      1967  PRESIDENT     US     PTL 1004
    TRUMAN FIELDS    K   (A         (A) FOR COLLECTORS ONLY (THE WHAM) 1970 ELEKTRA      US       EKS74077
    RON GRAYSON      D   (AC        (A) THE WHAM                  1973  ELEKTRA                  K 42056
    MARV LIEBERMAN   SAX (A         (B) GLAD I'M IN THE BAND      1969  ELEKTRA  US 74040  UK   K 42025
    IRV RUSSOTTO     SAX (A         (C) WHATEVER'S RIGHT          1969  ELEKTRA  US 74050  UK   K 42031
    BILL JONES       B   (A         (D) THE HILLS OF INDIANA      1972  ELEKTRA  US 74102  UK   K 42097
    DAVID BYRD       K   (AC        (E) HOME AT LAST              1977  CAPITOL  US 11619
    TIM DRUMMOND     B   (CFD       (F) LONNIE MACK WITH PISMO    1978  CAPITOL  US 11703
    IAN WALLACE      D   (F
    TROY SEALS       V   (FD    DAVID LINDLEY    G   (F     BEN KEITH         STEEL(F    DAVID BRIGGS    K  (FD
    BILLY McINTOSH       (F     STAN SZELESTE    K   (F     TERRY ADAMS       CELLO(F    GRAHAM NASH     V  (F
    TIMOTHY HEDDING  ORG (C     DENZIL RICE      PNO (C     JERRY RICE        D   (C     RUSTY YORK      HCA(C
    JACK BRICKLES    HCA (C     ROY CHRISTIANSEN CELLO(C    SHIRLEY MATTHEWS SINGERS(C   Mt ZION SINGERS V  (D
    DON NIX          SAX (D     BUDDY SPIKER FDL     (D     ROGER HAWKINS     D   (D     BARRY BECKETT   K  (D
    WAYNE PERKINS    G   (D     KENNY BUTTREY    D   (D     NORBERT PUTNAM    B   (D     LLOYD GREEN     STEEL(D
M33                                        WARNER MACK                                                   M33
    WARNER MACK      G V (ALL       (A) GOLDEN COUNTRY HITS       1963  LONDON        UK        SHU 8025
    LLOYD GREEN      STEEL(J        (B) DRIFTING APART            1968  BRUNSWICK UK 8684  US DECCA 74883
                                    (C) THE COUNTRY TOUCH         196                    US DECCA 74766
                                    (D) MANY COUNTRY MOODS        196                    US DECCA 74995
                                    (E) THE CONTRY BEAT OF WARNER MACK  1969             US DECCA 75092
                                    (F) WARNER MACK VOL 1         196                    US KAPP    8002
                                    (G) WARMER MACK VOL 2         196                    US KAPP    8025
                                    (H) I'LL STILL BE MISSING YOU 1970                   US DECCA 75165
                                    (I) LOVE HUNGRY               1970                   US DECCA 75219
                                    (J) YOU MAKE ME FEEL LIKE A MAN 1971                 US DECCA 75272
                                    (K) GREAT COUNTRY             197                    US MCA    20001
                                    (L) THE BEST OF THE BEST      1979                   US GUSTO 0042
M34                                        ANDY MACKAY                                                   M34
    ANDY MACKAY  WIND K SYN(AB      (A) IN SEARCH OF EDDIE RIFF   1974  ISLAND        UK     ILPS9278
    PHIL MANZANERA   G   (AB        (A) IN SEARCH OF EDDIE RIFF   1977  POLYDOR       UK     2302064
    JOHN PORTER      B   (A         (B) RESOLVING CONTRADICTIONS  1978  BRONZE UK BRON 510  NL 26448
    JOHN GUSTAFSON   B   (A
    LLOYD WATSON     G   (A     ROGER GLOVER     B   (A     PAUL THOMPSON     D   (AB   EDDIE JOBSON    VLN K(A
    BRIAN CHATTON    K   (A     BRUCE ROWLAND    D   (A     SADIE MACKENZIE   VLN (A    JANE RIFF       VLN (A
    MO FOSTER        B   (B     TONY STEVENS     B   (B     PETER VAN HOOKE   D   (A    TIM WHEATER     FLT (B
    CHRIS PARREN     K   (B     GAVIN WRIGHT     VLN (B     MICHAEL LAIRD     TPT (B    RAY RUSSELL     G   (B
M35                                        DUNCAN MACKAY                                                 M35
    DUNCAN MACKAY    K   (AB        (A) SCORE                     1977  EMI           UK     EMC 3168
    STEVE HARLEY     V   (A         (B) VISA                      1980  EDGE          UK     HOG   2
    JOHN WETTON      B   (A
    CLIVE CHAMAN     B   (A     ANDY McCULLOCH   D PERC(A    MEL COLLINS       WIND (A    YVONNE KEELY    V   (A
    SIMON PHILLIPS   D   (B     ALAN JONES           (B
M35A                                       FREDDIE McKAY                                                 M35A
    FREDDIE McKAY        (A         (A) CREATION                  1979  PLANT MUSIC          PLAN1003
M36                                        JOANNE MACKELL                                                M36
    JOANNE MACKELL   V   (A         (A) JOANNE MACKELL            1978  UA            UK     UAG 30180
    JOE FALSIA       G PERC(A
    JAMES BURTON     G   (A     STEVE CROPPER    G   (A     PETER JAMESON     G   (A    AUBURN BARRY    G   (A
    JIMMY GREENSPOON K   (A     JAI WINDING      K   (A     WAYNE COOK        K   (A    BARRY GOLDBERG  K   (A
    MICHAEL HUEY     D   (A     ED GREEN         D   (A     DONALD DUCK DUNN  B   (A    BOB GLAUB   B       (A
    EMORY GORDY      B   (A     DIANNE BROOKS    V   (A     MARTHA REEVES     V   (A    JULIA WATERS    V   (A
    BARBARA BENNETT  V   (A     MILES WILKINSON  V   (A
M36A                                       RABBIT MACKAY                                                 M36A
    RABBIT MACKAY  G HCA K V(A       (A) BUG CLOTH               1968  MCA           UK     MUPS 351
    MIKE FLEMING     G V (A
    BOB THOMPSON     D   (A     JOHN RAINES      D   (A     DAVID SUEYEREES   K V (A    JOHN PILLA      G   (A
    REJI PEKAR       G   (A     BILL ST PIERRE   FLT (A     WALK KUNNECKE     FLT (A    HARRY HELLINGS  TPT (A
M37                                        MCKENDREE SPRING                                              M37
    FRAN McKENDREE V B G K(ALL       (A) McKENDREE SPRING        1969  DECCA US75104             MCA  277
    FRED HOLMAN      B V (CD         (B) SECOND THOUGHTS         1970  DECCA US75230
    MICHAEL DREYFUSS VLN K(ABCDEFG   (C) SECOND THOUGHTS         1971  MCA  UK MUPS 433  RI 74 MCF 2651
    MARTIN SLUTSKY   D   (ABCDEFG    (C) THREE                   1972  MCA  UK MUPS 454  RI 74 MCF 2658
    HANK DEVITO      STEEL(D         (C) THREE                   1972  MCA  US MCA  44   DECCA US  75332
    ANDY NEWMARK     D   (CD         (D) TRACKS                  1973  MCA  UK MUPS 476  RI 74 MCF 2666
    RAUN MACKINNON   K   (CD         (D) TRACKS                  197   DECCA US 75385
    ARTIE KAPLAN     SAX (D          (E) SPRING SUITE            1973  MCA  US     370
    DAVID WOODS      G   (D          (F) GET ME TO THE COUNTRY   1975  DAWN UK DNLS3076  US PYE 12108
    JO ANN VENT      V   (D          (G) TOO YOUNG TO FEEL THIS OLD  1976               US PYE   12124
    BOB HIPWELL      V   (D
    JOHN MONTGOMERY  V   (D     CARSON MICHAELS  D V (EG    CHRISTOPHER BISHOP B V K(EFG  VALERIE ROSA   V  (F
    HOWARD WYETH     K   (F     CHILLI CHARLES   PERC (F    BOBBY GREGG       D   (C    ELLEN KEARNEY   V  (C
    JERRY BURNHAM    FLT (C     RUSSELL GEORGE   B   (C     JOHN DEVOE        V   (C    SUZANNE FRENCH  V  (C
    WARREN BERNHARDT K   (G     LARRY TUCKER     B   (AB    ADAM MITCHELL     K SYN HCA(B
M38                                        MAE McKENNA                                                   M38
    MAE McKENNA      V   (ABC        (A) MAE McKENNA            1975  TRANSATLANTIC UK TRA297 PYE US 12117
    TREVOR SPENCER   D   (A          (B) EVERYTHING THAT TOUCHES ME  1976  TRANSATLANTIC    UK    TRA 321
    MARTIN BRILEY    G B (A          (C) WALK ON WATER         1977  TRANSATLANTIC     UK    TRA 345
    GRAHAM PRESKETT  B   (A
    B J COLE         STEEL(A     SKAILA KANGA     HARP (A    ISAAC GUILLORY    G   (BC   ELLIOT RANDALL  G(BC
    RONNIE LEAHY     K   (BC     PETE WILLSHER    STEEL(BC   TIMI DONALD       D   (B    PAT DONALDSON   B(B
    RITCHIE GOLD     K   (B      PETE WINGFIELD   K   (C     JOHN GIBLIN       B   (C    GLEN LEFLEUR    D(C
    COLIN BLUNSTONE  V   (C      ROD ARGENT       V   (C     ALAN JAMES        B   (C    GERRY CONWAY    D(C
    MORRIS PERT      PERC (C
```

McKENNA MENDELSON MAINLINE

```
MIKE McKENNA        G   (ABC        (A) STINK                         1969  LIBERTY      UK    LBS 83251
JOE MENDELSON  G V K HCA(ABC        (B) NO SUBSTITUTE                 1975  TAURUS       CAN   TR   103
TONY VOLASCO        D   (AC         (C) CANADA OUR HOME & NATIVE LAND  19
MIKE HARRISON       B   (A
ADAM MITCHELL  MAND V PERC(B   T TOTH    VLN  (B   JØRN ANDERSEN   PERC (B   EDWARD PURDIE   K  (B
ZEKE SHEPPARD       B MAND (C
```

SCOTT McKENZIE

```
SCOTT McKENZIE      V   (AB         (A) VOICE OF SCOTT McKENZIE       1967  ODE          US    44002
                                    (B) STAINED GLASS MORNING         1970  ODE          US    77007
                                    (C) SAN FRANCISCO                  19   EMBASSY      UK    31077
```

IAN McLAGAN

```
IAN McLAGAN     V K G(AB   .        (A) TROUBLEMAKER                  1979  MERCURY      US    SRM 13786
GEOFF WORKMAN      PROD (A           (B) BUMP IN THE NIGHT             1981  MERCURY      US    4007
JOHNNY LEE SCHELL G V (A
RON WOOD            G   (A   KEITH RICHARDS   G   (A   JIM KELTNER   D  (A   RINGO STARR   D  (A
JOSEPH MODELISTE    D   (A   PAUL STALLWORTH  B   (A   STANLEY CLARKE B  (A   FLAP WORKMAN  ACC(A
BOBBY KEYS        HRNS (A   RON WOOD        V HRNS(A   STEVE MADAIO  HRNS (A   JAIME SEGEL   V  (A
```

MURRAY McLAUCHLAN

```
MURRAY McLAUCHLAN G K HCA V(A       (A) HARD ROCK TOWN                1977  TRUE NORTH   US    9466
JØRN ANDERSEN     D V (A
DENNIS PENDRITH   B V (A   BEN MINK    FDL V  (A   GENE MARTYNEC   G  (A   RONNEY ABRAMSON V (A
KETHRYN MOSES     FLT V (A
```

JOHN McLAUGHLIN & THE MAHAVISHNU ORCHESTRA

```
JOHN McLAUGHLIN G   (ALL       (A) EXTRAPOLATION                  1969  MARMALADE  UK 608007 R170 2343 012
TONY OXLEY       D   (A        (A) EXTRAPOLATION                  1972  POLYDOR UK 2310018+ PD6074 US 5510
BRIAN ODGERS     B   (A        (B) MY GOALS BEYOND                1971  DOUGLAS    UK 69014 US CBS   30766
JOHN SURMAN     SAX  (AE       (C) DEVOTION                       1971  DOUGLAS UK 65075 US 31568 NL 64537
JERRY GOODMAN    VLN (BCDFMH   (D) INNER MOUNTING FLAME           1971  CBS        UK 64717 US CBS  31067
BILLY COBHAM     D   (BDFGMH   (E) WHERE FORTUNE SMILES           1972  DAWN       UK DNLS3018
JAN HAMMER       K   (DFGH     (F) BIRDS OF FIRE                  1973  CBS        UK 65321 US      31996
JEAN LUC PONTY   VLN (IJ       (G) LOVE DEVOTION & SURRENDER      1973  CBS        US 59037 US      32034
RICK LAIRD       B   (DFH      (H) BETWEEN NOTHINGNESS & ETERNITY 1974  CBS        UK 69046 US      32766
CARLOS SANTANA   G   (G        (I) APOCALYPSE                     1974  CBS        UK 69076 US      32957
TONY WILLIAMS    D   (ML       (J) VISIONS OF THE EMERALD BEYOND  1975  CBS        UK 69108 US      33411
MILES DAVIS      TPT (         (K) INNER WORLDS                   1976  CBS        UK 69216 US      33908
JACK BRUCE       B   (ML       (L) IN RETROSPECT(DBL)             1976  POLYDOR UK 2675 091 GER 2679 027
CHICK COREA      K   (M        (M) ELECTRIC GUITARIST             1978  CBS        UK 82702
STANLEY CLARKE   B   (M        (N) ELECTRIC DREAMS (ONE TRUTH BAND) 1979 CBS       UK 83256 US      35785
ALPHONSO JOHNSON     (M        (O) BEST OF MAHAVISHNU ORCHESTRA   1980  CBS        UK 84232 US      36394
PATRICE RUSHEN   V   (M        (P) BEST OF JOHN McLAUGHLIN        1980  CBS        UK 84455 US      36355
DAVID SANBORN   SAX  (M        (1) ONE TRUTH BAND 1978 LIVE
FERNANDO SAUNDERS B  (1        (Q) EXTRAPOLATION                 1981  POLYDOR    UK 2310 018
DAVE LIEBMAN    SAX  (B        (R) BELLO HORIZONTE                1981  WB         UK K99185
BUDDY MILES      D   (C
MARSHA WESTBROOK VLA (I   LARRY YOUNG       K   (CGL  BILLY RICH      B   (C  STU GOLDBERG   K (K1
ANTHONY ALLEN SMITH D (1  L SHANKAR   VLN PERC (1  ARMANDO PERAZA CONGA(G  DON ALIAS      D (G
DOUG RAUCH       B   (FG  MINGO LEWIS     PERC (G  RALPH ARMSTRONG B   (KJI GAYLE MORAN    K (JI
NARADA MICHAEL WALDEN D(JKI STU MARTIN       (E  STEVE KINDLER   VLN (J  DAVE HOLLAND   D (E
KARL BERGER          (E   CAROL SHIRE    VLN (IJ  PHILLIP HIRSCHI CELLO(IJ BOB KNAPP      WIND(J
AIRTO MOREIRA   PERC (B   CHARLIE HAYDEN   B  (B  MAHALAKSHMI     SITAR(B  BADAL ROY      PERC(B
KATIA LA BEQUE  PNO K(R   FRANCOIS COUTURIER SYN (R  JEAN PAUL CELEA B  (R  TOMMY CAMPBELL D (R
FRANCOIS JEANNEAU SAX (R  JEAN PIERRE DROUET PERC(R  STEVE SHEMAN  PERC (R  AUGUSTIN DUMAY VLN (R
PACO DE LUCIA    G   (R
```

DON McLEAN

```
DON McLEAN     G V (ALL        (A) TAPESTRY                  1972  UA      UK UAS 29350    US    5522
GEORGE RICCI  CELLO(A          (B) AMERICAN PIE              1972  UA      UK UAS 29285    US    5535
PAUL GRIFFIN   K   (D          (B) AMERICAN PIE              1981  GREENLIGHT UK RI 2004
RALPH MACDONALD PERC³(DC       (C) DON McLEAN                1972  UA      UK UAS 29399    US    5651
DON BROOKS     HCA (DC         (D) PLAYIN' FAVOURITES        1973  UA      UK UAS 29528    US    LA161 G
DICK HYMAN     PNO (DC         (E) HOMELESS BROTHER          1974  UA      UK UAG 29646    US    LA315 G
WARREN BERNHARDT PNO (DBC      (F) SOLO (LIVE DBL)           1976  UA      UK UAD 60139/40 US    LA652H2
TONY LEVIN     B   (DC         (G) PRIME TIME                1977  EMI     UK INS 3011 ARISTA US 4149
ED TRICKETT   DULC (DC         (H) CHAIN LIGHTNING           1979  EMI     UK INS 3025 CASABLANCA US7173
BUZZY FEITEN   G   (DC         (J) VERY BEST OF              1980  UA      UK UAG 30314
CHRIS PARKER   D   (DC
NEIL LARSEN    K   (DC   RUSS SAVAKUS    VLN  (DC  BOB ROTHSTEIN  B V(DBC  YUSEF LATEEF            (E
KENNY VANCE        (E    BOB MOORE       G    (H   KEN ASCHER     K  (G    PAT REBILLOT      K  (G.
JOHN FARRELL   G   (G    ROBBIE STONER   V B  (G   HOWIE WYETH    K V(G    DAVE SANBORN      SAX(G
RONA WYETH     V   (G    CHRISTINE FAITH V    (G   ANGELA HOWELL  V  (G    GENE ORLOFF STRING (GE
RUBENS BASSINI PERC (G   DOM CORTESE ACC      (G   BILLY SANFORD  G  (H    JAMES CAPPS       G  (H
JOSEPH CHRISMAN D  (H    JORDANAIRES     V    (H   RAY EDENTON    G  (H    PETE DRAKE     STEEL (H
TOMMY ALSUP    G   (H    EDDY ANDERSON   D    (H   PIG ROBBINS    PNO(H    CHUCK COCHRAN     PNO(H
BOBBY WOOD     K   (H    JERRY CARRIGAN  D    (H   PERSUASIONS    V  (E    RAY COLCORD K     G  (E
MIKE MARIERI  PERC (B    CHUCK GREEN          (C   ANDREW SMITH   D  (E    DAVID SPINOZZA    G  (E
WILLIE WEEKS   B   (E    GEORGE BARROW   SAX  (E   CHARLES FAWLKES SAX(E   DANNY MOORE       TPT (E
CISSY HOUSTON  V   (E    DEIDRE TUCK     V    (E   NED ALBRIGHT   V  (E    WALLY KING        WIND(E
JONATHAN DORN  TUBA (E   JOEL DORN       V    (E   ARLENE MARTELL V  (E    MARLENE VERPLANCK V(E
GEORGE DUVIVIER B  (E    RICHARD TEE     K    (E   ARTHUR JENKINS K  (E    HUGH McCRACKEN    G  (E
SELDON POWELL  SAX (E    CHARLES WILLIAMS SAX (E   GARNETT BROWN  TROM(E   JOESEPH WILDER    TPT (E
RENNELLE STAFFORD V (E   STEVEN SOLES    V    (E   PETE SEEGER     V  (E   JAMES BUFFINGTON HRN (E
BILLY SLAPIN   WIND (E   LINDA NOVEMBER  V    (E   HELENE MILES   V  (E    JERRY TEIFFER          (E
BROOKS TILLOTSEN HRN (E  GEORGE MARGE    WIND (E   JERRY LAWSON   V  (E    JIMMY HAYES       V  (E
HERBERT RHOAD  V   (E    PETER GORDON    HRNS (E   RAY ALONGE     HRN (E   NORMA HOLMES      V  (E
SWEET JOE RUSSELL V (E   W C DANIELS     V    (E   WILLIS JACKSON SAX (E   RAY MARKOWITZ     D  (B
RAY COLCORD    K   (B
```

SANDY McLELLAND & THE BACKLINE

```
SANDY McLELLAND V   (A         (A) SANDY McLELLAND & THE BACKLINE 1979 MERCURY  UK  9109 620
DAVID BATES    PERC (A         (B) McLELLAND                      1981 ACTION   UK  AL 1000
PAUL KAMOWSKI  G   (A
ROBIN RANKIN   K   (A    ANDY HAMILTON   SAX  (A   ROBERT PATERSON B  (A   PETER COE     D  (A
MARK KNOPFLER  G   (A    JIM MULLEN      G    (A   DICK HANSON   HRNS (A   JOHN EARLE    HRNS(A
CHRIS GOWER   TROM (A    RAY BEAVIS      HRNS (A   FRANK COLLINS  V   (A   DYAN BIRCH    V  (A
COLLETTE WILKINSON V (A  ANDY LUNN       PERC (A   JON ASTLEY     PERRC(A
```

ANDREW McMAHON

ANDREW'BLUEBLOOD' McMAHON (A   (A) GO GET MY BABY   1978   MCM   FR   900 301

OSCAR McLOLLIE & HIS HONEY JUMPERS

(A) ROLL HOT ROD ROLL   1981 ACE   UK   10CH27

HAROLD McNAIR

HAROLD McNAIR	FLT	(ALL	(A) HAROLD McNAIR	1968	RCA	UK	SF 7969
RICK GRECH	B	(B	(B) THE FENCE	1970	B&C	UK	CAS 1016
KEITH TIPPETT	PNO	(B	(C) HAROLD McNAIR(A) DIFF TRACK 1)	1971	B&C	UK	CAS 1045
BILL LESAGE	PNO	(AC	(D) AFFECTION FINK	19	ISLAND	UK	
TONY CARR	D	(ABC	(E) FLUTE & NUT	19	RCA	UK	INTS1096
SPIKE HEATLEY	B	(AC					
COLIN GREEN	G	(B ALAN BRANSCOMBE ORG (B TERRY COX D (B DANNY THOMPSON B (B					

MACONDO

ALBERT HERNADNEZ	G V	(A	(A) MACONDO	1972	ATLANTIC	US	SD 7234
MAX UBALLEZ	G V	(A					
FRED RAMIREZ	K VIBES(A RON CHRETIN B (A FRANK MARTINEZ D (A LEE PASTORE PERC (A					
EDDIE CAICEDO	PERC (A						

BIG JAY McNEELY

BIG JAY McNEELY	(AB	(A) BIG JAY IN 3D	19	KING	US	650
		(B) LIVE AT CISCO'S	19	WB	US	1523

CLYDE McPHATTER

CLYDE McPHATTER	V	(ALL	CLYDE McPHATTER & THE DRIFTERS	195	ATLANTIC	US SD	8003
			LOVE BALLADS	1958	ATLANTIC	US SD	8024
			CLYDE	1959	ATLANTIC	US SD	8031
			BEST OF CLYDE McPHATTER	1963	ATLANTIC	US SD	8077
			TA TA	19	MERCURY	US (M)20597 (S)	60252
			GOLDEN BLUES HITS	19	MERCURY	US (M)20665 (S)	60665
			LOVER PLEASE	19	MERCURY	US (M)20711 (S)	60711
			RHYTHM & SOUL	19	MERCURY	US (M)20750 (S)	60750
			GREATEST HITS	1963	MERCURY	US (M)20783 (S)	60783
			SONGS OF THE BIG CITY	1964	MERCURY	US (M)20902 (S)	60902
			LIVE AT THE APOLLO	1964	MERCURY	US (M)20915 (S)	60915
			MAY I SING FOR YOU	1966	MERCURY	US (M)12224 (S)	16224
			LETS START OVER	19	MGM	US	3775
			GREATEST HITS	19	MGM	US	3866
			WITH BILLY WARD & THE DOMINOES	19	KING	US	559
			18 ORIGINAL HITS	19	KING	US	5006
			WELCOME HOME	1971	MCA UK MCPS 418	RI 74 MCF2642	
			WELCOME HOME	19	DECCA	US	75231
			A TRIBUTE TO CLYDE McPHATTER	19	ATLANTIC UK		K30033

TONY McPHEE

TONY McPHEE	G K V(ALL	(A) ME & THE DEVIL	1968	LIBERTY	UK	LBS83190	
JO ANN KELLY	V G	(ABC	(B) I ASKED FOR WATER(VAR ARTIST)	1969	LIBERTY UK LBS83252	US 12455	
GROUNDHOGS		(B	(C) SAME THING ON THEIR MINDS	1971	SUNSET	UK	SL550209
BRETT MARVIN & THUNDERBOLTS(B			(D) TWO SIDES OF	1973	WWA	UK	WWA 001
			(***) C FEATURES TRACKS FROM A+B				

RALPH McTELL

RALPH McTELL	G V	(ALL	(A) 8 FRAMES A SECOND	1968	TRANSATLANTIC	UK	TRA 165
MIKE PIGGOTT	FDL	(1GH	(B) SPIRAL STAIRCASE	1969	TRANSATLANTIC	UK	TRA 177
NIGEL SMITH	K	(1	(C) MY SIDE OF YOUR WINDOW	1969	TRANSATLANTIC	UK	TRA 209
DAVE PEGG	B	(1HL	(D) REVISITED	1970	TRANSATLANTIC	UK	TRA 227
DAVE MATTACKS	D	(1G	(E) YOU WELL MEANING BROUGHT ME HERE	1971	FAMOUS 5753 UK	+ ABC ABCL 5084	
BRIAN BROCKLEHURST B		(C	(F) NOT TILL TOMORROW	1972	REPRISE US 2121	UK	K44210
FOLK WEAVERS	V	(C	(G) EASY	1973	REPRISE		K54013
HENRY VIII	JUG	(ABC	(H) STREETS	1975	WB	UK	K56105
PETE BERRYMAN	G	(ABH	(I) STREETS OF LONDON	1975	TRANSATLANTIC	UK	TRASAM34
ROD CLEMENTS	B	(HL	(K) STAR COLLECTION	1975	MIDI		MID26030
GOLDRUSHERS	V	(H	(L) RIGHT SIDE UP	1976	WB	UK	K56296
DANNY THOMPSON	B	(GHL	(M) COLLECTION	1977	TRANSATLANTIC	UK	TRASAM39
DANNY LANE	D	(H	(N) RALPH,ALBERT,SYDNEY	1977	WB	UK	K56399
BOB KERR	SAX	(H	(O) MAGINOT WALTZ (EP)	1977	WB	UK	K17008
JERRY DONAHUE	G	(H	(P) RALPH McTELL	1978	PICKWICK		SHM 962
WIZZ JONES	G	(G	(Q) SLIDE AWAY THE SCREEN	1979	WB	UK	K56599
BOB STRAWBRIDGE	MAND	(L	(R) EASY	1979	KICKING MULE	US	303
WHISPERING MICK	PERC	(AB	(S) LIVE	1979	FANTASY	US	571
ANDY CRONSHAW ZITHER		(H					

STEVE BONNETT   MAND (G   JOHN KONGOS   V   (G   RABBIT BUNDRICK   K   (H   LINDSAY SCOTT   VLN (G
SANDY SPENCER   CELLO(H   ALAN HARRIS   PERC (H   ROD EDWARDS   PNO   (H   MADDY PRIOR   V   (H
GERRY CONWAY   D   (H   BERT JANSCH   G   (G   PICK WITHERS   D   (L   JON STEVENS   D   (L
GRAHAM PRESKETT   K   (L   PETER SWETTENHAM   K   (L   SAMMY MITCHELL   DOB(L   TONY RIVERS   V   (L
KEN GOLD   V   (L   JOHN PERRY   V   (L   JOHN MARTYN   V   (L   McGANN   G   (A

DAVID McWILLIAMS

DAVID McWILLIAMS G V	(ALL	(A) DAYS OF PEARLY SPENCER	1971	STARLINE UK SRS5075	
		(B) LORD OFFALY	1972	DAWN UK DNLS3039 PYE US 3302	
		(C) BEGGAR & THE PRIEST	1973	DAWN UK DNLS3047	
		(D) LIVING JUST A STATE OF MIND	1974	DAWN UK DNLS3059	
		(E) DAVID McWILLIAMS	1977	EMI UK EMC 3169	

MAD MAGAZINE

(A) MAD TWISTS ROCK'N'ROLL	19	BIG TOP US 1305	
(B) FINK ALONG WITH MAD	19	BIG TOP US 1206	

MADE IN SWEDEN

GEORGE WADENIUS	G V	(ALL	(A) MADE IN SWEDEN	1969	SONET SLP71
TOMMY BORGUDD	D	(ABCDE	(B) SNAKES IN A HOLE	1969	SONET SLP2504
BO HAGGSTROM	B	(ABCDE	(C) LIVE AT THE GOLDEN CIRCLE	1970	SONET SLP2506
TOMMY KORBERG	V	(G	(D) MADE IN ENGLAND	1970	SONET SLP2512
PEKKA POHJOLA	B	(G	(E) MAD RIVER	1971	SONET UK 621
VESA AALTONEN	D	(G	(F) THE BEST OF	19	GRAND PRIX 9997
WLODEK GULGOWSKI	K	(G	(G) WHERE DO WE BEGIN	1976	POLYDOR 2480 358
PETER SUNDELL	D	(			

```
M45D                          MADISON DYKE                                            M45D
   JURGEN BAUMANN    G K SYN V(A      (A) ZEITMASCHINE              1988 RACKET      GER        15,001
   BURKHARD RITTLER  V FLT      (A
   ANDREAS NEDDE     G V  (A    ROBERT KRAUSE      B   (A   BURKHARD ENGEL     D   (A
M46                             MAD RIVER                                              M46
   TOM MANNING       V    (ALL       (A) MAD RIVER               1968 CAPITOL   ST2985 RI GER 85882
   DAVID ROBINSON    G    (ALL       (B) PARADISE BAR & GRILL    1969 CAPITOL             ST   185
   RICK BOCHNER      G    (ALL       (EP) MAD RIVER              1967 WEE                   10021
   LAURIE HAMMOND    B V K(ALL
   GREG DEWEY        D HCA V(ALL      JERRY CORBITT      STEEL(B   RON WILSON     PERC (B   BANANA    STEEL (B
M46A                            MADNESS                                                M46A
   MIKE BARSON   HCA PERC K(ABC       (A) ONE STEP BEYOND        1979 STIFF UK 17 GER 624174 US SIRE 6085
   CHRIS FOREMAN     G    (ABC        (B) ABSOLUTELY             1980 STIFF UK 29 GER 624511 US SIRE 6094
   GRAHAM 'SUGGS'McPHERSON V PERC(ABC (C) MADNESS 7              1981 STIFF UK 39            US SIRE
   MARK BEDFORD      B    (ABC
   LEE THOMPSON      SAX V(ABC DAN WOODGATE     D   (ABC CHAS SMASH      TPT V(ABC
M46B                            JIMMY MAELEN                                           M46B
   JIMMY MAELEN      PERC V(A         (A) BEATS WORKIN'          1980 CBS   US 36319   UK       84211
   NEIL JASON        V    (A
   FRANK MAELEN      V    (A    RANDY BRECKER    TPT  (A    BARRY ROGERS    TROM(A   ELLIOT RANDALL   G  (A
   LANI GROVES       V    (A    IRENE CARA       V    (A    STEVE LOVE      HRNS (A   ROBIN BECK       V  (A
   VICKI SUE ROBINSON V   (A    ANNIE SUTTON     V    (A    LUTHER VANDROSS V    (A   GEORGE YOUNG     SAX(A
   JOHN TROPEA       G    (A    ROB MOUNSEY      K    (A    PAT REBILLOT    K    (A   JOHN LONGO       TPT(A
   LEW SOLOFF        TPT  (A    KEN ASCHER       K    (A    ALLEN SCHWARZBERG D  (A   PAUL SHAFFER     K  (A
   RONNIE CUBER      SAX  (A    LAWRENCE FELDMAN SAX  (A
M46C                            MADURA                                                 M46C
   ALAN DE CARLO     G V  (A         (A) MADURA                1971 CBS       US         30794
   ROSS SOLOMONE     D V  (A
   HAWK WOLINSKI     K V  (A
M47                             MAGAZINE                                               M47
   HOWARD DEVITO     V G  (ALL       (A) REAL LIFE             1978 VIRGIN  UK V2100       GER  26190
   BARRY ADAMSON     B V  (ABCDE      (B) SECONDHAND DAYLIGHT    1979 VIRGIN  UK V2121       GER 200385
   DAVE FORMULA      K    (ABCDE      (C) CORRECT USE OF SOAP    1980 VIRGIN  UK V2156 GER 202116 US INT 13144
   MARTIN JACKSON    D    (A          (D) PLAY LIVE             1980 VIRGIN  UK V2184       US INT 70015
   SUPER MAGS        V    (B          (E) MAGIC MURDER & THE WEATHER 1981 VIRGIN UK V2200 GER 203776 US INT 70020
   JOHN McGEOCH      G K SAX (ABC     (EP) SWEETHEART CONTRACT  1980 VIRGIN  368
   JOHN DOYLE        D    (BCDE       (EP) ABOUT THE WETHER     1981 IRS US 70404
   LAURA TERESA      V    (CE
   ROBIN SIMON       G    (D    RAY SHELL      V   (E    BEN MENDELSON G VLN(E
M47A                            MAGIC                                                  M47A
                                    (A) MAGIC                 1972      RARE EARTH    US        527
M47B                            MAGIC LANTERNS                                         M47B
   JIMMY BILSBURY    PNO V(A         (A) SHAME SHAME           1969 ATLANTIC      US        8217
   BEV BEVERAGE      G V  (A
   PETER GARNER      G V  (A    MIKE 'OZ' OSBORNE B V  (A   HARRY PAUL WARD    D V  (A
M47C                            MAGIC MIXTURE                                          M47C
   JIM THOMAS        G V  (A         (A) THIS IS              1968 SAGA       FID 2125
   STAN CURTIS       ORG  (A
   MELVYN HACKER     B    (A    JACK COLLINS       D   (A
M48                             MAGIC SAM                                              M48
   MAGIC SAM MAGHETT G V  (ALL       (A) MAGIC SAM 1937/69     1970 BLUE HORIZON  UK          763223
   LITTLE BRO MONTGOMERY K(ADE        (B) BLACK MAGIC           19   DELMARK DS 620  JAP TRIO PA 6216
   MACK THOMPSON     B    (ABCDEF     (C) WEST SIDE SOUL        19   DELMARK DS 615  JAP TRIO PA 6214
   WILLIE DIXON      B    (ADE        (D) MAGIC ROCKER          1980 FLYRIGHT  UK          FL 561
   BILLY STEPNEY     D    (ABE        (E) OTIS RUSH & MAGIC SAM 1980 FLYRIGHT  UK          FL 562
   EDDIE SHAW        SAX  (B          (F) LATE GREAT MAGIC SAM  1980 L&R                   42014
   LAFAYETTE LEAKE   PNO  (B          (G) BLUES MASTERS VOL 3   19   BLUE HORIZON  US         BN 4603
   MIGHTY JOE YOUNG  G    (BC
   ODIE PAYNE        D    (ABCDE SHAKEY JAKE HARRIS V  (ADE SYL JOHNSON     (ADE HARRY BURRAGE   PNO  (
   STOCKHOLM SLIM    PNO  (C    ERNEST JOHNSON     B   (C   ROBERT ST JULIEN D    (EF  BOYD ATKINS    SAX (
   JOHNNY JONES      PNO  (     ODELL CAMPBELL     B   (E   S P LEARY       D    (     FOUR DUCHESSES V   (
   AMMONS SISTERS    V    (
M48A                            MAGIC SAND                                             M48A
                                    (A) MAGIC SAND           1970      UNI       US          73094
M48B                            MAGIC SLIM                                             M48B
   MAGIC SLIM        G V  (ALL       (A) BORN UNDER A BAD SIGN 197  MCM       FR          900 298
   JUNIOR PETTIS     G    (A          (B) VOL 2                197  MCM       FR          900 305
   NICK HOLT         B    (A          (C) LIVE AT THE ZOO BAR  1980 CANDY APPLE   US
   DOUGLAS HOLT      D    (A
M48C                            MAGITS                                                 M48C
                                    (A( FULLY COHERENT (EP)   19   OUTER HIMALAYAN          ?
M49                             MAGMA                                                  M49
   CHRISTIAN VANDER  D PERC V K(ALL   (A) MAGMA (DBL)           1970 PHILIPS            63595 001/2
   JANNIK TOP        B    (CDF         (B) 1001 CENTIGRADE       1971 PHILIPS  9101 286 +    6397 031
   KLAUS BLASQUIZ    V PERC(ABCDEFH    (C) KOHN TARKOSZ          1974 A&M     US 3650 UK   AMLH68260
   TEDDY LASRY       WIND (ABD         (C) KOHN TARKOSZ          1974 VERTIGO         EURO 6325 750
   JEAN LUC VANDERLIER K (D            (D) MEKANIK DESTRUKTIW KOMMANDOH 1974 A&M  US 4397 UK AMLH64397
   RENE GARBES       CLAR V(D          (D) MEKANIK DESTRUKTIW KOMMANDOH 197 VERTIGO EURO 6499 729 LTM 100
   CLAUDE OLMOS      V    (D          (E) LIVE (DBL)           1975 UTOPIA US CYL21245 + SPC 0002
   BENOIT WIDEMANN   K    (HDEF        (F) UDU WUDU             1976 TOMATO  6001     RCA  FPLA 7332
   TONY RUSSO        TPT  (FE          (F) UDU WUDU             1976 UTOPIA US 1 1730
   BERNARD PAGANOTTI B    (FE          (G) EDITS               1977 TAPIOCA
   DOM REINHARDT     V    (D          (H) ATTAHK              197  WEA      EURO 913213 TOMATO US 7021
   LOUIS SARKISSIAN  SAX  (BC          (I) RETROSPECTIVE VOL 1  19   RCA
   LUCILLE CULLAZ    V    (F          (J) RETROSPECTIVE VOL 2  19   RCA
   MURIEL STREISFELD V    (D
   GABRIEL FEDEROW   G    (E    LIZA DELUXE      V   (F   DIDIER LOCKWOOD  VLN (E   JEAN POL ASSELINE  K   (E
   STELLA VANDER     V    (CDEFH EVELYNE RAZYMOVSKI V   (D   MURIEL STREISFELD V   (D   LOUIS TOESCA      TPT(B
   CLAUD ENGEL       G V  (A    FRANCIS MOZE     B   (AB  FRANCOIS CAHEN   K    (AB  JEFF SEFFER       SAX(B
   ALAIN HATOT       FLT  (D    PATRICK GAUTHIER K   (F   PIERRE DU TOUR   TPT (F   RICHARD RAUX      WIND (A
   ALAIN CHARLERY    TPT  (C    GERLAD BIKAILO   K   (C   MICHEL GRAILLIER K    (CF  BRIAN GODDING     G   (C
   MICHELLE SANTHIER V    (     LAURENT THIBAULT PROD (AH ROLAND HULDA     PROD (B   GIORGIO GOMELSKY PROD(CDEF
   DORIS REINHARDT   V    (D    MICHELE SAULNIER V   (D   JACQUES BOLOGNESI TROM(H   CATHERINE SZPIRA V  (F

                                       [361]
```

MAGNA CARTA

CHRIS SIMPSON	G V	(ALL	(A)	MAGNA CARTA	1969	MERCURY		SMCL20166
DAVEY JOHNSTONE	G V	(BEFH	(B)	SEASONS	1970	VERTIGO 6360003 US	DUNHILL	50091
GLEN STUART	V	(ABEFGH	(C)	TIMES OF CHANGE	197	FONTANA	NL	6438 080
LYELL TRANTER		(AB	(D)	BEST OF MAGNA CARTA	197	VERTIGO	NL	9107 100
STAN GORDON	G V	(GH	(D)	BEST OF MAGNA CATRA	197	VERTIGO	NL RI	9199 737
BARRY MORGAN	D	(B	(E)	SONGS FROM WASTIES ORCHARD	1971	VERTIGO	UK	6360 040
TONY CARR		(ABH	(F)	IN CONCERT	1972	VERTIGO	UK	6360 068
TONY VISCONTI	B PERC	(BE	(G)	LORD OF THE AGES	1973	VERTIGO	UK	6360 093
SPIKE HEATLEY	B	(B	(H)	MARTINS CAFE	197	VERTIGO	NL	6360 146
RICK WAKEMAN	K	(BE	(J)	PUTTING IT BACK TOGETHER	1976	POLYDOR 2321 012	GTO	GTLP 012
PICK WITHERS	D	(J	(J)	PUTTING IT BACK TOGETHER	1976	ARIOLA	US	50014
ALASTAIR ANDERSON		(E	(K)	TOOK A LONG TIME	197	GTO		2321 112
RON CHESTERMAN		(E	(L)	SPOTLIGHT ON	1977	PHILIPS		6625 031
GUS DUDGEON		(E	(M)	PRISONERS ON THE LINE	1978	PHILIPS		9109 229
CHRIS LAURENCE		(E	(N)	LIVE IB BERGEN 8/10/78	1978	FONTANA	NL	6438 080
DANNY THOMPSON	B	(AEG	(O)	NO TRUTH IN THE RUMOUR	1979	VERTIGO	NL	201 176
CHRIS KARAN	D	(J						

FRANK HODGES	PERC	(A	PETER WILLISON	CELLO	(E	DAVE ARTHUR	(E	HEATHER CORBETT	(E
HOOKFOOT		(E	NIC POTTER		(E	TIM RENWICK	RECORDER (B	DEREK GROSSMITH	FLT(B
TONI ARTHUR		(E	JOHNNY VAN DERRICK		(E	HAROLD McNAIR	FLT(A	DAVE MARKEE	B (M
GRAHAM SMITH	B V HCA	(H	LES CYRCLE	D	(M	HENNIE BEKKER	K (M	MIKE FINDLEY	G (M
DAVE BARKER		(	TOMMY HOY		(MJ	NIGEL SMITH	ACC(MJ	LEE ABBOT	(O
ROBIN THYNE		(M	TOM McCONVILLE		(O	GEORGE MORRIS	(	AL FENN	(
ROY BABBINGTON	B	(M	ROBIN ELLIS	V	(M	EMIL ZJHBZ	V (M	CHRIS KARAN	(C
GRAHAM STUART		(	GORDON HUNTLEY	STEEL	(G	B J COLE	STEEL(M	DAVE MATTACKS	D (H
JOHN MEALING	K	(H							

THE MAGNIFICENTS

		(A)	DANCING WITH T M	19	VARIETON	1282

MAGNUM

TONY CLARKIN	G V	(ABC	(A)	KINGDOM OF MADNESS	1978	JET US 35811	UK	LP 210
RICHARD BAILEY	K V FLT	(ABC	(B)	MAGNUM 2	1979	JET	UK	LP 222
BOB CATLEY	G V	(ABC	(C)	MARAUDER	1980	JET	UK	LP 230
KEX GORIN	D	(ABC	(D)	CHASE THE DRAGON	1981	JET	UK	LP 235
COLIN LOWE	B V	(ABC						

TAJ MAHAL

TAJ MAHAL	G V HCA BANJ	(ALL	(A)	TAJ MAHAL	1967	DIRECTION	UK		863279	
RY COODER	G	(A	(A)	TAJ MAHAL	1967	CBS US	(M) 2779	(S)	9579	
JESSE ED DAVIS	G	(ABCE	(B)	NATCH'L BLUES	1978	DIRECTION UK 863397	US CBS	9698	
JAMES THOMAS	B	(A	(C)	GIANT STEP/DE OLE FOLKS (DBL)	1969	CBS UK 866226	US CBS	18	
SANFORD KONIKOFF	D	(A	(D)	THE REAL THING (DBL)	1971	CBS UK 66288	US CBS	30619	
BILL BOATMAN	G	(A	(E)	HAPPY JUST TO BE LIKE I AM	1971	CBS UK 64447	US CBS	30767	
GARY GILMORE	B	(ABC	(F)	RECYCLING THE BLUES	1972	CBS UK 65090	US CBS	31605	
EARL LINDO	K	(JK	(G)	THE SOUNDER(SOUNDTRACK)	1972	CBS	70123		
CHUCK BLACKWELL	D	(ABC	(H)	OOH SO GOOD 'N' BLUES	1973	CBS UK 65814	US CBS	32600	
AL KOOPER	K	(B	(I)	MO ROOTS	1974	CBS UK 80346	US CBS	33051	
EARL PALMER	D	(B	(J)	MUSIC KEEPS ME TOGETHER	1975	CBS UK 80972	US CBS	33801	
JAMES CHARLES OTEY	D	(ED	(K)	SATISFIED N TICKLED TOO	1976	CBS UK 81346	US CBS	34103	
JOHN SIMON	K	(ED	(L)	ANTHOLOGY VOL 1 1966/76	1976	CBS		US CBS	34466	
BILL RICH	B	(EIJDPQO	(M)	MUSIC FUH YA	1977	WB UK K56324	US	2994	
HOSHAL WRIGHT	G	(EIJK	(N)	BROTHERS	1977	WB		US	3024	
ROCKY DZIDZORNU	PERC	(EDIJMNKO	(O)	EVOLUTION	1978	WB		US	3094	
HOWARD JOHNSON	HRNS	(EDF	(P)	& INTERNATIONAL RHYTHM BAND LIVE	1979	CRYSTAL CLEAR(DIRECT)		CCX 5011	
BOB STEWART	HRNS	(ED	(Q)	& INTERNATIONAL RHYTHM BAND	1980	MAGNET		MAGL 5035	
ANDY NARELL	STEEL DRUM	(E	(R)	GOING HOME (COMP)	1980	CBS			31844	
MERL SAUNDERS	K	(H	(S)	THE BLUES	19	CBS	63279		
DAVID COLMAN	G	(E	(T)	THE BEST OF	19	CBS		US	36528	
SAM LIGHTNIN HOPKINS		(G							

CLAUDIA LENNEAR	V	(IN	LARRY McDONALD	PERC K(MNJKO	BISMARK FRANCO	PERC (M	JONI HAASTRUP	V (M
RASHAIDA NIROBE	V	(M	JOSEPH DALEY	HRNS (DE	EARL MacINTYRE	HRNS (DE	KESTER SMITH	PERC(IJKMNOPQ
RUDY COSTA	WIND	((MNJKGPQ	ASTON BARRETT	K (I	CAROLE FREDERICKS	V (JKMIO	TOMMY HENDERSON	V (I
MERRY CLAYTON	V	(I	ROBERT GREENIDGE	D V(MNOPQ	RAY FIZPATRICK B G	KV(MNJK	INSHIRAH MAHAL	V (M
MONA RAM	V	(M	YVONNE FIMBRES	V (M	ALISON MILLS	V (N	JOHN HALL	G (D
GREG THOMAS	V	(D	JUMMA SANTOS	PERC (PQ	ELLA JAMERSON	V (PQ	GERI JOHNSON	V(PQ
BIANCA ODEN	V	(PQ	VERLIN SANDLES	V (PQ	OLA MARIE TYLER	V (PQ	CAREY WILLIAMS	V (PQ
POINTER SISTERS	V	(F	JO BAKER	V (JK	ANNIE SWAMPSON	V (JK	ROB MOUNSEY	K (O
LEON PENDARVIS	K	(O	BOB BABBITT	B	MARY MURE	D (O	ERROLL BENNETT	PERC(O
RAFFAEL RAMIREZ	CONGA(K		JOHN TROPEA	G (O	JANICE GADSDEN	V (O	JOSHIE ARMSTEAD	V (O
BILLY BARNES	V	(O	WAYNE GARFIELD	V (O	CLAUDIA SIEFER	V (O	MARK ISHAM TPT	(
ZANE WOODSWORTH	TPT	(	CHARLES McCARTHY	SAX (	STEPHEN KELLER	SAX (	CARL LARKIN	G (K
JOACHIM YOUNG	K	(K	DON MOORS VIBES	(K	SAM COX	D (K	JOHN TURK	K (K
STAN MULELLAND	B	(K	RICK MYERS	SAX (K	GORDON FOWLEY	TROM (K	FRITZ HEILBRON	TROM(K
CLIFF MORRIS	G	(O	WILL LEE	B (O	DAVE CAREY	PERC (O	STEVE JORDON	D (O
BARRY FINERTY	G	(O	VIRGIL JONES	TPT (O	DENNY MOORE	TPT (O	DENNY MAROUSE	TROM(O
JOHN ZANGRANDO	SAX	(O	ALAN RAPH	TROM (O	SELDON POWELL	SAX (O		

MAHOGANY RUSH

FRANK MARINO	G VK	(ALL	(A)	CHILD OF THE NOVELTY	1975	20TH CENTURY		US T 451
PAUL HARWOOD	B	(ALL	(B)	MAXOOM	1975	20TH CENTURY		US T 463
JIMMY AYOUB	D	(ALL	(C)	STRANGE UNIVERSE	1975	20TH CENTURY		US T 482
NANETTE WORKMAN	V	(G	(D)	MAHOGANY RUSH Iv	1976	CBS	UK 81417	US 34190
VINCE MARINO	G	(H	(E)	WORLD ANTHEM	1977	CBS	UK 81978	US 34677
PHIL BEA	K	(E	(F)	LIVE	1978	CBS	UK 82625	US 35257
			(G)	TALES OF THE UNEXPECTED	1979	CBS	UK 83494	US 35753
			(H)	WHATS NEXT	1980	CBS	UK 83897	US 36204
			(I)	POWER OF ROCK'N'ROLL	1981	CBS	UK 84969	

MAILER MACKENZIE BAND

KID VAN ETTINGER	G	(A	(A)	MAILER MACKENZIE BAND	19
PAUL VAN MELZEN	B	(A			
JAAP MOSSEL	D	(A	FOORT VERBRUGGE V HCA(A		

```
M55                              MAINHORSE                                              M55
   PATRICK MORAZ      K   (A   |      (A) MAINHORSE          1971 POLYDOR UK 2383049+VISA IMP   1001
   PETER COCKETT      G VLN V(A
   BRYSON GRAHAM      D   (A   JEAN RISTON B CELLO V(A
M55A                             MIKE MAINIERI                                         M55A
   MIKE MAINIERI      VIBES(A       (A) JOURNEY THRU AN ELECTRIC TUBE  1969 UA            UAS   29051
   JEREMY STEIG       FLT (A
   JOE BECK           G   (A   SALLY WARING      V   (A  SAM BROWN     G   (A  WARREN BERNHARDT  PNO (A
   DONALD MACDONALD   D   (A   HAL TAYLOR        B   (A  CHUCK RAINEY  B   (A
M55B                             MAINLAND                                              M55B
   LES PAYNE          G V (A       (A) EXPOSURE            1979 CHRISTY MUSIC            AMCL 0200
   ANDY NYE           V K (A
   ADE WALKER         B   (A   JAKE JACOBS       G   (A
M56                              MAJOR LANCE                                            M56
   MAJOR LANCE            (ALL    RHYTHM OF           19   OKEH    UK        33SX 1728
                                GREATEST HITS       1973 CONTEMPO          COLP 1001
                                BEST OF             1976 EPIC    UK            81519
                                LIVE AT THE TORCH   1977 CONTEMPO          CLP   523
                                NOW ARRIVING        1978 TAMLA   UK        STMC 12094
M57                              MAJOR SURGERY                                          M57
   JIM ROCHE          G   (A       (A) FIRST CUT          1977 NEXT                NEXT 1
   DON WELLER         SAX (A
   TONY MARSH         D   (A   BRUCE COLLCUT     B   (A
M57A                             MALACHI                                               M57A
   MALACHI            G   (A       (A) CHEVROLET          19   VERVE            ?
   STEVE CUNNINGHAM
M57B                             MALICORNE                                             M57B
   LAURENT VERCAMBE VLN K V(ABCDEH   (A) MALICORNE        1974 HEXAGONE FR 883002 GER ANTIGON 3220
   HUGHES DE COURSON G B V (ABCDEH   (B) MALICORNE TWO    197  HEXAGONE FR 883004 GER ANTIGON 3221
   GABRIEL YACOUB     G V  (ABCDEFGH (C) ALMANACH         1976 HEXIGONE FR 883007
   MARIE YACOUB V DULC  (ABCDEFGH    (D) MALICORNE IV     197  HEXAGONE FR 883015 GER ANTIGON 3223
   OLIVER ZDRZALIK    B K V(CDEFGH   (E) QUINTESSENCE     1977 HEXAGONE FR 883018 GER ANTIGON 3224
   BRIAN GULLAND      HRN V K(h      (F) L(EX TRAORDI NAIZE  1978 BALLON  FR  13006
   ANDRE PROULX       FLT (H         (G) L'EXTRAORDINAIRE TOUR DE'FRANCE 1978 BALLON FR 13003
   DOM REGER          STR V(H        (H) EN PUBLIC A MONTREAL  1979 BALLON  FR  13010
   PATRICK LEMERCIER FDL G V(H       (J) BESHAIRE        1979 BALLON  FR  13012
   JEAN ARNOUX        D   (H
   NIC KINSEY         PROD (ABCE
M57C                             MALIBOOZ                                              M57C
   JOHN ZAMBETI       G V (A         (A) MALIBOOZ RULE   1981 RALPH    US
   WALTER EGAN        G B V(A
   TOM RUDE           G B (A     SCOTT MONAHAN     K    (A  LEE KIX     D   (A TED ZAMBETTI  D   (A
M58                              MALLARD                                               M58
   BILL HARKLEROAD    G   (AB        (A) MALLARD         1976  VIRGIN            UK  V 2045
   MARK BOSTON        G V B(AB        (B) IN A DIFFERENT CLIMATE  1977 VIRGIN US 34489 UK V 2077
   ARTIE TRIPP        D   (A
   SAM GALPIN         V k  (AB   BARRY MORGAN    PERC (A  JOHN THOMAS    K V (B  GEORGE DRAGGOTA  D   (B
   JOHN JAMES         K   (     RABBIT BUNDRICK   K    (A  JOHN McFEE    STEEL(B
M59                              MALO                                                  M59
   JORGE SANTANA      G   (ALL       (A) MALO            1972  WB     US BS 2584  UK K46142
   RON SMITH          HRNS (CD       (B) DOS             1972  WB     US BS 2652  UK K46179
   WILLIE G           V   (D         (C) EVOLUTION       1973  WB     US BS 2702  UK K46221
   TONY SMITH         PERC V(CD      (D) ASCENSION       1974  WB     US BS 2769  UK K56033
   FRANCISCO AQUABELLA PERC V(BCD
   STEVE SHERARD      TROM (CD MIKE FUGATE    TPT (D  ABEL ZARATE     G   (A  RICHARD SPREMICH  D   (AB
   ROY MURRAY         HRNS (A  ARCELIO GARCIA V PERC (ABC FORREST BUCHTEP TPT (BC RICK QUINTANAL  D   (B
   RON DEMASI         K V (CD  LUIS GASCA     TPT (A  PAUL REKOW      PERC (B  COKE ESCOVEDO   PERC (A
   CARLOS FEDERICO    PNO (C   AL ZULAICA      PNO (C  JOHN WATSON     V   (B  PABLO TELLEZ    B PERC (ALL
   RICHARD KERMODE    K   (AB  LEO ROSALES    PERC (B  VICTOR PANTOJA  PERC (A  RICHARD BEAN    V PERC (A
   HADLEY CALIMAN     WIND (B  GEORGE BERMUDEZ CONGA(B BILL ATWOOD     TPT (A  MIKE HEATHMAN   TROM (B
   JOSE SANTANA       VLN (B   TOM POOLE      TPT (B  ALEX RODRIGUEZ  TPT (B
M60                              MAMA LION                                             M60
   LYNN CAREY         V   (AB        (A) MAMA LION      1972  PHILIPS 6369 153 US FANTASY 2702
   NEIL MERRYWEATHER V B (AB
   COFFI HALL         D   (AB  RICK GAXIOLA      G    (A  JIM HOWARD    K V (AB ALAN HUTTZ    G   (B
   ED MIKENAS         B   (B   BOB ROSE
M61                              MAMA'S & THE PAPA'S                                   M61
   CASS ELLIOT        V   (ALL  IF YOU CAN BELIEVE YOUR EYES  1966 DUNHILL US 50006 UK RCA  RD 7803
   MICHELLE GILLIAM PHILLIPS(ALL CASS,JOHN,MICHELLE & DENNY 1966 DUNHILL US 50010 UK RCA  SF 7834
   JOHN PHILLIPS      V   (ALL  DELIVER             1967 DUNHILL US 50014 UK RCA  SF 7880
   DENNY DOHERTY      V   (ALL  BOOK OF SONGS       196  DUNHILL US 50022
                                FAREWELL TO 1ST GOLDEN ERA  1968 DUNHILL US 50025
   HAL BLAINE         D   (     PAPAS & MAMAS       1968 DUNHILL US 50031 UK RCA  SF 7960
   LARRY KNECHTEL     K   (X    GOLDEN ERA VOL 2    1968 DUNHILL US 50038 UK STATESIDE 5002
   JOE OSBORN         B   (X    HITS OF GOLD        1969 ABC (74)    5003 UK STATESIDE 5007
   FAST EDDIE         D   (X    16 OF THE GREATEST  19   DUNHILL US 50064
   ERIC HORDE         G   (X    A GATHERING OF FLOWERS  1970 DUNHILL US 50073 UK PROBE  1003/4
                            (X) MONTEREY INTERNATIONAL POP FESTIVAL 1971 DUNHILL US 50100
                                PEOPLE LIKE US      1972 DUNHILL US 50106 UK PROBE    1048
                                PEOPLE LIKE US      1974          RI UK ABC  ABCL5017
                                20 GOLDEN HITS      1972 DUNHILL US 50145 UK PROBE     200
                                20 GOLDEN HITS      1974          RI UK ABC  ABCL 604
                                BIGGEST HITS        197  PICKWICK     2076
                                MONDAY MONDAY       1973 PICKWICK US 3380 UK MFP    90025
                                CALIFORNIA          1974 PICKWICK US 3357 UK MFP    90050
                                BEST OF             1977 ARCADE        UK
                                20 GREATEST HITS    1980 MFP           UK          50493
```

MAMAS PRIDE

```
     DON LISTON        G V  (AB              (A) MAMAS PRIDE                        1976   ATLANTIC US 36122    UK   K 50197
     PAT LISTON        G V  (AB              (B) UPTOWN..LOWDOWN                     1977   ATLANTIC US 36146    UK   K 50348
     MAX BAKER         K    (AB
     KEVIN SANDERS          (AB   JOE TUREK          B V  (AB  DICKIE STETTENPOHL B V  (B   FRANK GAGLIANO    K SYN (A
     JOE LALA          PERC (B    JIM MASON         HRNS (B   DENNIS DREITH      HRNS (B   PAUL WILLETT     K V  (B
     JERRY JUMONVILLE  HRNS (B
```
MAN

```
     MICKY JONES       G V  (ALL             (A) REVELATION                         1969  PYE                   UK         18275
     CLIVE JONES       G K V(ABCDFGJ         (B) 2OZ OF PLASTIC WITH A HOLE         1969  PYE GER 88003 DAWN    UK          3003
     DEKE LEONARD G V(ABCSEGJKLMNOP          (C) MAN                                1970  LIBERTY UK 83464      US          9803
     TERRY WILLIAMS D V (CDEFHJKLMOPN        (C) MAN 1970                           1976  SUNSET RI             UK         50380
     JEFF JONES        D    (ABG             (D) DO YOU LIKE IT HERE,ARE YOU...     1971  LIBERTY US  1032      UK UA  29236
     RAY WILLIAMS      B    (ABG             (E) LIVE AT THE PADGET ROOMS PENARTH   1972  UA                    UK     USP 100
     MARTIN ACE        B G V(CDEJMP          (F) BE GOOD TO YOURSELF...             1972  UA       US LA 077    UK US  29417
     TWEKE LEWIS       G    (H               (G) GOLDEN HOUR(COMP FROM A &B)        1973  PYE                   UK      GH 569
     WILL YOUATT       B V  (FHJ             (H) BACK INTO THE FUTURE(DBL)          1973  UA US 170 GER 29547   UK    60053/4
     PHIL RYAN         K V  (FHJNO           (J) CHRISTMAS AT THE PATTI(10" DBL)    1973  UA                    UK   UDX205/6
     KEN WHALEY        B    (KL              (K) RHINOS, WINOS & LUNATICS           1974  UA       US LA 247    UK         29631
     MALCOLM MORLEY    K G V(JK              (L) SLOW MOTION                        1974  UA       US LA 345    UK         29675
     JOHN McKENZIE     B V  (NO              (M) MAXIMUM DARKNESS                   1975  UA                    UK         29872
     JOHN CIPOLLINA    G    (M               (N) THE WELSH CONNECTION               1976  MCA US 2190 UK MCF2753 GER 6 22481
     DAVE CHARLES      (J                    (O) ALL'S WELL THAT ENDS WELL          1977  MCA GER 62098         UK  MCF 2815
     GEORGINA ACE      B    (J               (P) ALSO APPEARED ON GREASY TRUCKERS   1972  UA    Uk UDX203/4 GER GAMMA  3265
     PLUM HOLLIS       V    (J               (EP) BANANAS                           1976  UA                    UK  REM 408
     DAVE EDMUNDS      G V  (J               (Z) GOLDEN HOUR OF MAN                 1973  PYE                   UK   GH 567
     VIC MAILE         PROD (H
     MICKEY GEE        G    (J   B J COLE          STEEL(J   STAN PHIFER     V    (J   SEAN TYLA       G V(J
     RICHARD TREECE    G    (J   PAUL BURTON       B    (J   MARTIN BELMONT  G V  (J   TIM ROPER       D   (J
     NICK GARVEY       B    (J   RAY THOMAS BAKER  PROD (K
```
MANASSAS

```
     STEPHEN STILLS    G V K(AB              (A) MANASSAS         (DBL)             1972  ATLANTIC US 2/903    UK K60021
     AL PERKINS        STEEL(AB              (B) DOWN THE ROAD                      1973  ATLANTIC US  7250    UK K40440
     PAUL HARRIS       K    (AB
     ROGER BUSH        B    (A   JOE LALA          PERC    (AB  KENNY PASSARELLI B V  (   JOE WALSH       G   (B
     DALLAS TAYLOR     D    (AB  BOBBY WHITLOCK    K V  (B  SYDNEY GEORGE    FLT  (AB  CALVIN SAMUELS  B   (AB
     JERRY AIELLO      ORG  (AB  CHARLIE GRIMES    G    (B  CHRIS HILLMAN    B G V(AB  GUILLE GARCIA   PERC(B
     LACHY ESPINOL     PERC (B   PAT ARNOLD        V    (B  BILL WYMAN       B    (A   BYRON BERLINE   FDL (A
```
MANCHILD

```
     ANTHONY JOHNSON   B    (A               (A) POWER & LOVE                       1977  CHINA TOWN US LA765  UK UA 30134
     KENNY EDMONDS     G V  (A               (B) FEEL THE PHUFF                     19    CHINA TOWN US LA 872
     DARYL SIMMONS     PERC V(A
     FLASH FERRELL     V    (A   ROBERT PARSON     D    (A   CHUCKIE BUSH     K(A   REGGIE GRIFFIN   SAX G(A
```
MELISSA MANCHESTER

```
     MELISSA MANCHESTER     V  K (ALL        (A) HOME TO MYSELF                     1974  ARISTA US  4006  UK BELL       233
     ALLAN SCHWARZBERG D    (A               (B) BRIGHT EYES                        1974  ARISTA US  4011
     GEORGE DEVENS     PERC (A               (C) MELISSA                            1975  ARISTA US  4031  UK        ARTY104
     BOB MANN          V G BAN(A             (D) BETTER DAYS & HAPPY ENDINGS        1977  ARISTA US  4067  UK        ARTY125
     JOHN STROLL       PNO  (A               (E) HELP IS ON THE WAY                 1977  ARISTA US  4095  UK        ARTY147
     CORKY HALE        HARP (A               (F) SINGIN'                            1977  ARISTA US  4136
     DAVID MANCHESTER  BASSOON(AJ            (G) DONT CRY OUT LOUD                  1978  ARISTA US  4186
     CHRIS DEDRICK     K    (A               (H) MELISSA MANCHESTER                 1978  ARISTA US  9506
     ANDY MUSON        B    (A               (J) FOR THE WORKING GIRL              1980  ARISTA US  9533
     JOHN LOPRESTI     B V  (ACDE
     DAVE APPELL       G    (A   MICHAEL JOHNSON   G    (A   HANK MEDROSS     PERC (A   JAMES NEWTON HOWARD K (CEF
     DAVID WOLFERT     G SIT(CDE KIRK BRUNER  V D   TROM (CDE KING ERRISON     PERC (C   STEVE MADAIO      TPT (CDG
     JOHN ROTELLA      SAX  (C   DAVID LASLEY      V    (C   DON DIEGO GOJU   PERC (C   STANLEY SCHWARTZ SAX K(EFG
     DAVID SPINOZZA    G    (F   SID McGINNIS      G    (F   TONY LEVIN       B    (F   DON GROLNICK     K     (F
     VINI POCIA        V    (CEF TREVOR LAWRENCE   SAX  (C   LEW McCREARY     TROM (CFG GENE DINWIDDIE   SAX   (C
     ARNOLD McCULLER   V    (F   MORTON K SALT     PERC (C   LENNY CASTRO     PERC V(DEFG JEFF MIRONOV   G     (F
     WILL LEE          B    (F   STEVE GADD        D    (F   TOM SAVIANO      WIND (EFG ANDREW MACKINTOSH SAX (EF
     LES WORTH POTTO   FLT  (F   WENDY HAAS        V    (F   CLAUDIA CAGAN    V    (FG  FARAGHER BROTHERS V   (F
     JOE BEAN ESPOSITO V    (E   DOUG WINTZ        HRN  (F   DICK HYDE        TROM (EG  DAVID T WALKER   G    (G
     JAMES GADSON      D V  (G   RICHARD TEE       K    (G   GENE PAGE        STR  (G   HARRY BLUESTONE  VLN  (G
     DENNIS BUDIMIR    G    (G   JIM KELTNER       D    (G   SONNY BURKE      SYN  (G   CHUCK FINDLEY    TPT  (G
     TOMMY MORGAN      HCA  (G   JAY GRAYDON       G    (G   JAMES STROUD     D    (J   TOM ROBB         B    (J
     ALAN FEINGOLD     SYN  (J   TOMMY COOPER      GLOCK(J   STEVE BUCKINGHAM G    (J   DON HENLEY       V    (J
     CHARLES CHALMERS  V    (J   PAUL DAVIS        V    (J   ED SEAY          V    (J   BERNADINE MITCHELL V  (J
     BARRY FASMAN      STR HRN(J RICH FELTO        TPT  (EF  GEORGE BOHANON   TROM (F   MICHAEL CARNAHAN WIND (FG
     BRIE HOWARD       V    (CEF GAIL KANTOR       V    (F   JOHN VASTANO     G V  (E   GARY COLEMAN     VIBES (E
     BILL PETERSEN     HRN  (G   DICK NASH         HRN  (E   CHUCK RAINEY     B    (G   GREG PHILLANGANES PNO (G
     LEON WARE         V    (G   LEE RITENOUR      G    (G   DAVID BLUMBERG   STR  (G   DAVID HUNGATE    B    (G
     BILL PAYNE        PNO  (G   MICHAEL BODDICKER SYN  (G   DAVID LUELL      SAX  (G   ART RODRIGUEZ    D    (G
     ED GREENE         D    (G   LARRY BYROM       G    (J   RANDY McCORMICK  K    (J   AVTAR SINGH KHALSA VIBES (J
     BETH COOPER       HRNS (J   BEABO BRYSON      V    (J   SANDRA RHODES    V    (J   DONNA RHODES     V    (J
     STEVE CARLISLE    V    (J   KATHLEEN JACKSON  V    (J   PATTI ALLINSON   V    (J   STEVEN CAGAN     STR HRN(J
     STEVE NELSON      V    (J   SUNDRAY TUCKER    V    (E   CHARITY McCRARY  V    (E   LINDA McCRARY    V    (E
     THERESA HENDRICKS V    (E   BETTY JONES       V    (E   JAN E JONES      V    (E   BRENDA L GOOCH   V    (E
```
MANDALA

```
     GEORGE OLLIVER    V    (A               (A) SOUL CRUSADE                       1968  ATLANTIC US          SD 8184
     DOMENIC TROIANO   G    (A
     HUGH SULLIVAN     K    (A   ROY KENNER        V    (A   JOEY CHIROWSKI   K    (A   DON ELLIOTT     B  (A
     WHITEY GLAN       D    (A
```

MANDALABAND

```
    DAVID DURANT          V    (A                                    (A) MANDALABAND              1975  CHRYSALIS        UK CHR  1095
    ASHLEY MULFORD        G    (A                                    (B) THE EYE OF WENDOR        1978  CHRYSALIS        UK CHR  1181
    JOHN STIMPSON         B G  (A
    TONY CRESSWELL        D    (A   VIC EMERSON       K    (A   RITCHIE CLOSE       PNO (B   DAVY ROHL          PNO (B
    KIM TURNER            G D  (B   MEL PRITCHARD     D    (B   GRAHAM GOULDMAN     B   (B   PETE GLENNON       B   (B
    ALF TRAMONTIN         B    (B   NOEL REDDING      B    (B   LES HOLROYD         B   (B   STEVE BROOMHEAD    G   (B
    JIMMY McDONNELL       G    (B   JOHN LEES         G    (B   MADDY PRIOR         V   (B   MARK GILBANKS      TPT (B
    ANDY CROMPTON         TROM (B   MIKE CARLTON      TROM (B   ERIC STEWART        V   (B   TONY SPATH         OBOE(B
    JOHN GILSTON          PERC (B   GERRY MURPHY      PIPES(B   RICHARD SCOTT       RECOD(B   MICKY PURTON       HRNS(B
    RUSSELL HAYWARD       HRNS (B   PAUL BRYAN FARR   HRNS (B   ANDY WARDAUGH       TPT (B   MARTIN LAWRENCE    PERC(B
    DAVID HASSALL         PERC (B   PHIL CHAPMAN      WIND (B   JOHN TURNER         K   (B   STEWART WOLSTENHOLME K(B
    NORMAN BARRETT        G    (B   GERALD BROWN SINGERS V (B   DAVE GORTON         TROM (B   KEVIN GODLEY      V   (B
    PAUL YOUNG            V    (B   JUSTIN HAYWARD    V    (B   LOL CREME           V   (B   IAN WILSON         V   (B
    FRIDAY BROWN          V    (B   GILLY ROHL        V    (B   FIONA PARKER        V   (B
```

HARVEY MANDEL

```
    HARVEY MANDEL         G    (ALL                                  (A) CRISTO REDENTOR          1968  PHILIPS UK SBL 7873 RI 70 6336009
    PETE DRAKE            STEEL(A                                    (A) CRISTO REDENTOR          1968  PHILIPS                US   600281
    KENNY BUTTREY         D    (A                                    (B) RIGHTEOUS                1969  PHILIPS UK SBL 7904    US   600306
    BOB MOORE             B    (A                                    (C) GAMES GUITARS PLAY       1970  PHILIPS UK SBL 7915    US   600325
    HARGUS ROBBINS        K    (A                                    (D) BABY BATTER              1971  DAWN    UK DNLS3015 US JANUS 3017
    LARRY TAYLOR          B    (CEGD                                 (E) ELECTRONIC PROGRESS(SAME AS D??) 1971 BELLAPHON GER 15182 JANUS NL 61701
    GRAHAM BOND           K    (A                                    (F)GET OFF IN CHICAGO        1972  LONDON  UK SHO 8426 US OVATION1415
    EDDIE HOH             D    (ABC                                  (G) THE SNAKE                1972  JANUS   UK 6310 210 US       3037
    RICHARD MARTIN        V    (H                                    (G) THE SNAKE                1972  BELLAPHON GER 19170
    CHIP MARTIN           G    (H                                    (H) SHANGRENADE              1973  JANUS   UK 6499 831 US       3047
    BOB JONES             G    (AB                                   (J) FEEL THE SOUND OF        1974  JANUS                  US       3067
    CATHERINE GOTTHOFER HARP(A                                       (K) BEST OF                  1975  JANUS                  US       7014
    BARRY GOLDBERG        K    (A
    ARMANDO PERAZA        CONGA(A   CAROLYN WILLIS    V    (A   JACQUELINE MAY ALLEN V(A   STEVE MILLER       K   (A
    CARTER COLLINS        CONGA(A   DUANE HITCHINGS   K    (A   ART STAVRO          B   (AB  LARRY EASTER       SAX (A
    JULIA TILLMAN         V    (A   FREDDIE FOX       V    (F   VICKI HUBLEY        V   (F   G E STINSON        G   (F
    NORM WAGNER           G    (F   DAVE COOK         K    (F   IRA KART            K   (F   DON CODY           B   (F
    PETER MILIO           D    (F   KEN LITTLE        B V  (F   BOBBY DAVIS         D   (F   JUDY ROBERTS       K V (F
    JOHN BISHOP           G    (F   NICK TOUNTAS      B    (F   RUSTY JONES         D   (F   PHIL JOHNSON       D   (F
    EARL PALMER           D    (BG  BUDDY CHILDERS    TPT  (B   JOHN AUDINO         TPT (B   STAN FISHELSON     TPT (B
    OLLIE MITCHELL        TPT  (B   LEW McCREARY      TROM (B   MIKE BARONE         TROM (B   PETE MYERS         TROM (B
    DICK LEITH            TROM (B   ERNIE WATTS       SAX  (B   PLAS JOHNSON        SAX (B   BILL PERKINS       SAX (B
    GENE CIPRIANO         SAX  (B   JACK NIMITZ       SAX  (B   PETE JOLLY          K   (B   BOB WEST           B   (B
    HOWARD ROBERTS        G    (B   VICTOR FELDMAN    PERC (B   NICK DECARO         K   (A   CHARLIE MUSSELWHITE HCA (A
    CRAIG RASBAND         B    (F   COLEMAN HEAD      G    (HJ  PAUL LAGOS          D   (DGHJ VICTOR CONTE      G   (GHJ
    BOBBY LYLE            K    (    BOBBY NOTKOFF     STR  (H   FRED ROULETTE       STEEL(GH  DON 'SUGARCANE'HARRIS VLN(GH
    HOWARD WALES          K    (ED  BIG BLACK    CONGA     (ED  MIKE MELVOIN        K   (ED  COLIN BAILEY       D   (E
    EMIL RICHARDS         PERC (ED  JOE PORCARO  PERC      (ED  SANDRA CROUCH       TAMB(ED  RUSSEL DASHIEL     G V K(C
    ALDOLFO DELA PERRA D  G    (G   CHUCK DOMANICP    B    (G   ANTONIO DELA BARREDA B (G   RANDY RESNICK      G   (G
    JIM TAYLOR            PNO  (G   KEVIN BURTON      K    (G   CHARLES LLOYD       FLT (G   RAY LESTER         B   (JH
    MARK SKYER            G V  (JH  DANNY KELLER      D    (JH
```

MIKE MANDEL

```
    MIKE MANDEL           K    (A                                    (A) SKY MUSIC                1978  VANGUARD         VSD 79409
    DAVE SANBORN          SAX  (A
    GARY ANDERSON         SAX  (A   DARRYL THOMPSON   G    (A   BURT KHAN           G   (A   WILBUR BASCOMB     B   (A
    JOHN LEE              B    (A   CHRISTOPHER PARKER D   (A   GERRY BROWN         D   (A   CRUSHER BENNETT    PERC(A
    CHRIS HILLS           PERC (A   JON FADDIS        HRNS (A   LOU SOLOFF          HRNS(A   DAVE TAYLOR        HRNS(A
    GEORGE YOUNG          SAX  (A   ALEX FOSTER       SAX  (A   BARRY ROGERS        TROM(A   LOU MARINI         SAX (A
```

MANDRAKE MEMORIAL

```
    KEVIN LALLY           D    (ABC                                  (A) MANDRAKE MEMORIAL        1968                    US POPPY 40002
    RANDY MONACO          V B  (ABC                                  (B) MEDIUM                   1969  RCA  UK  SF 8028 US POPPY 40003
    CRAIG ANDERTON        (ABC                                       (C) PUZZLE                   1970  POPPY UK   11003 US POPPY 40006
    MICHAEL KAC           K V  (AB
```

MANDRAKE PADDLESTEAMER

```
    MARC BRIERLEY         (A                                         (A) 1969 LINE UP
    BRIAN MARTIN          (A
    PAUL RIBB             (A   JOHN WHITEHEAD            (A   PAUL WHITEHEAD      (A
```

MANDRILL

```
    CARLOS WILSON         SAX V(ALL                                  (A) MANDRILL                 1970  POLYDOR UK 2489 028 US 24 4050
    CLAUDE CAVE           K V  (ALL                                  (B) MANDRILL IS              1972  POLUDOR UK 2391 030 US     5025
    ANDRE LOCKE           D V  (F                                    (C) COMPOSITE TRUTH          19    POLYDOR UK 2391 061 US     5043
    BRIAN ALLSOP          B V  (FE                                   (D) JUST OUTSIDE OF TOWN     1973  POLYDOR UK 2391 092 US     5049
    TOMMY TRUJILLO        G V  (F                                    (E) BEST OF                  19    POLYDOR UK 2391 186 US     6047
    RICK WILSON           SAX  (ALL                                  (F) SOLID                    1975  UA      UK UAG29786 US UA LA408
    LOU WILSON       TPT PERC V(ALL                                  (G) BEAST FROM THE EAST      1976  UA      UK UAS29920 US UA LA577
    CHARLES WILSON HRNS PERC V(F                                     (H) MANDRILLAND              1978  POLYDOR UK 2672 023 US     9002
    CHARLES PADRO  D PERC V(                                         (J) WE ARE ONE               1978  ARISTA  UK SPART1035 US   4144
    FUDGIE KAE            B    (BDH                                  (K) NEW WORLD                1978  ARISTA  UK ARTY 162 US     4195
    OMAR MESA             G PERC V(ABD                               (L) GREATEST                 19    ARISTA             US     7000
    BUNDIE CENAS          B PERC (A                                  (M) GETTING IN THE MOOD      1980  ARISTA             US     9527
    CHARLES PADRO         D PERC(AB
    NEFTALI SANTIAGO      D PERC(H   DOUG RODRIGUES    G V  (H
```

MANDRE

```
    ANDRE LEWIS MANDRE    (                                          (A) MANDRE                   1977  MOTOWN UK STML23062 US     882
                                                                     (B) MANDRE 2                 1978  MOTOWN UK STML12084 US    7900
```

GAP MANGIONE

```
    GAP MANGIONE          K    (ALL                                  (A) GAP MANGIONE             1977  A&M     US 4621
    DAN SAWYER            SAX  (B                                    (B) SUITE LADY               1978  A&M                UK  AMLH 64694
    LARRY CARLTON         G    (B                                    (C) DANCIN                   1979  A&M US 4762
    POPS POPWELL          B    (B
    GREG MATHESON         PNO  (B   ABRAHAM LABORIEL  B    (B   RALPH HUMPHREY      D   (B   JEFF PORCARO       PERC (B
    CHUCK FINDLEY         TPT  (B   PETER DONALD D         (B   VINCENT DE ROSA     HRNS(B   JOE PORCARO        PERC (B
    BILL REICHENBACH      TROM (B
```

TIM HAUSER	V	(ABCDEFGH		(A) JUKIN'				1971 CAPITOL	US 778		E ST 11405
MICKEY ROKER	D	(A		(A) MANHATTAN TRANSFER				1978 MFP RI		UK	50387
ERIN DICKINS	V	(A		(B) MANHATTAN TRANSFER				1975 ATLANTIC	US 18133		UK K50138
PAT ROSALIA	V	(A		(C) COMING OUT				1976 ATLANTIC	US 18183		UK K50291
MARTY NELSON	V CLAR (A			(D) PASTICHE				1978 ATLANTIC	US 19163		UK K50444
ALAN PAUL	V	(BCDEFGH		(E) LIVE				1978 MOBILE	US 22	ATLANTIC UK K50540
LAUREL MASSE	V	(BCDE		(F) EXTENSIONS				1979 ATLANTIC	US 19258		UK K50674
JANIS SIEGEL	V	(BCDEGH		(G) MECCA FOR MODERNS				1981 ATLANTIC	US 16036		UK K50789
CHERYL BENTYNE	V	(FG		(H) BEST OF				1981 ATLANTIC			
GENE PISTILLI	V G										
JOHN MAYER	PNO	(D	NORBERT PUTNAM	B	(A	MIKE ROD	SAX	(B	KENNY BUTTREY	D	(A
TOMMY WEST	K	(A	MURRAY WEINSTOCK	K	(B	DAVID BRIGGS	K	(A	GARY CHESTER	D	(A
JERRY FRIEDMAN	G	(B	GEORGE EDWARDS	STEEL	(A	HAYWOOD HENRY	SAX	(A	RICHARD TEE	K	(B
BUDDY SPICHER	FDL	(A	IRA NEWBORN	G	(BCD	MICHAEL BRECKER	SAX	(BC	ADAM MITCHELL	G	(A
DON GROLNICK	K	(BD	JERRY DODGION	SAX	(AB	RANDY BRECKER	TPT	(BCD	ANDY MUSON	B(BCD
DANIEL BEN ZEBULON PERC	(A		AL GIBBONS	SAX	(A	ROY MARKOWITZ	D	(BC	ZOOT SIMS	SAX	(B
EARL WILLIAMS	D	(A	PAUL FAULISE	TROM	(B	SELDON POWELL	WIND	(A	BOB BUSHNELL	B	(A
MICKEY GRAVINE	TROM	(B	LEW GELGATTO	SAX	(BD	BIG AL WILLIAMS	K	(A	QUENTIN JACKSON	TROM(B
MEL DAVIS	TPT	(B	LEW TABACKIN	SAX	(A	ALAN RAPH	TROM	(B	JON FADDIS	TPT	(B
FRANK BEROWSKI	SAX	(A	PHIL BODNER	SAX	(B	BOB McCOY	TPT	(B	BURT COLLINS	TPT	(A
GEORGE DORSEY	SAX	(B	MARKY MARKOWITZ	TPT	(BD	GARNETT BROWN	TROM	(AB	HARVEY ESTRIN	SAX	(B
MARVIN STAMM	TPT	(BD	WAYNE ANDRE	TROM	(ABD	DAVE SANBORN	SAX	(A	ALAN RUBIN	TPT(BD
SABER	G	(A	FRANK VICARI	SAX	(B	GEORGE YOUNG	SAX	(B	RON CARTER	B	(A
WALLY KANE	WIND	(B	PAUL GRIFFIN	K	(C	BOBBYE HALL	PERC	(CD	RINGO STARR	D	(C
MAC REBENNACK	K	(C	DOUG THORNGREN	PERC	(C	JIM GORDON	D	(CD	JOHN BARNES	PNO	(CD
BEN BENAY	G	(CD	STEVE PAIETTA	ACC	(C	JAY MIGLIORI	SAX	(C	RICK SCHLOSSER	D	(C
CLARENCE McDONALD	PNO	(C	RALPH MACDONALD	PERC	(C	JACKIE KELSO	SAX	(C	JIM NELSON	D	(C
BILL PAYNE	PNO	(C	ROGER STEINMAN	PNO	(C	ARTHUR JENKINS	PNO	(C	NICK MARRERO	PERC(C
JOHN RODRIGUEZ	PERC	(CD	DAVID KEMPER	D	(C	BOB BOWLES	G	(C	JIM KELTNER	D	(C
JOHN RODRIGUEZ	PERC	(CD	DAVID KEMPER	D	(C	BOB BOWLES	G	(C	JIM KELTNER	D	(C
DAVID FRISHBERG	K	(C	JOHN GIMBLE	FDL	(C	AL COHN	SAX	(D	JIMMY GUFFRIE	SAX	(D
DAVID TAYLOR	TROM	(D	STU WOODS	B	(D	ART RODRIGUEZ	D	(D	DICK FRANK	G	(D
TOMMY VIG	PERC	(D	LEE KONITZ	SAX	(D	HURBIE GREEN	TROM	(D	STEVE GADD	D(DG
BUDDY EMMONS	STEEL(D		PETE WADE	G	(D	CHARLIE McCOY	HCA	(D	SHORTY LAVENDER	FDL	(D
BRITT WOODMAN	TROM	(D	DAVID WALLACE	K	(D	LARRY EMERINE	PERC	(D	STEVEN SCHAFFER	D	(D
MIKE BODDIKER	K	(DFG	DAVID FRISHBERG	K	(D	MIKE MELVOIN	K	(D	JEANNE ASHBY	HARP (D
JEFF PORCARO	D	(DF	SCOTT EDWARDS	B	(D	DAVID FOSTER	K	(DFG	JAY GRAYDON	G SYN(DFG
VICTOR FELDMAN	PERC K(DG		MICHAEL OMARTIAN	K	(DF	WILLIE HALL	D	(D	DUCK DUNN	B	(D
BOOKER T JONES	K	(D	STEVE CROPPER	G	(D	TOM HENSLEY	K	(D	PETER JOHNSON	D	(D
WAYNE JOHNSON	G	(D	MICHAEL SCHNOEBELEN	B	(DFG	DON ROBERTS	WIND	(DFG	GENE PAGE	STR (D
RALPH HUMPHREY	D	(F	DAVID HUNGATE	B	(F	RICHIE COLE	SAX	(FG	GREG MATHIESON	K SYN(FG
JIMMY WYBLE	G	(F	IAN UNDERWOOD	SYN	(F	CHUCK DOMANICO	B	(F	BILL MAYS	PNO	(F
STEVE LUKATHER	G	(FG	JAI WINDING	PNO	(F	PAULINHO DA COSTA	PERC	(F	ABRAHAM LABORIEL	B	(FG
ALEX ACUNA	D	(FG	DEAN PARKS	G	(FG	MIKE BAIRD	D	(G	JERRY HEY	TPT	)G
TOM SCOTT	HRNS	(G	ANDY NOVELL	D	(G	YARON GERSHOVSKY	PNO	(G	AL VIOLA	G	(G
MILCHO LEVIEV	K	(G	JON HENDRICKS	V	(G	STEVE GEORGE	SYN	(G			

DEDICATED		19 CARNIVAL		US	201
FOR YOU & YOURS		19 CARNIVAL		US	202
WITH THESE HANDS		19		US DELUXE	12000
MILLION TO ONE		1972 LONDON UK SHB 8449	US DELUXE	12004
THERE'S NO ME WITHOUT YOU		19 CBS		US	32444
THATS HOW MUCH I LOVE YOU		19 CBS		US	33064
MANHATTANS		1976 CBS	UK	81513 US	33820
I WANNA BE YOUR EVERYTHING		1976 DJM	UK	26084	
IT FEELS SO GOOD		1978 CBS	UK	84828 US	34450
THERE'S NO GOOD IN GOODBYE		1978 CBS	UK	82567 US	35252
LOVE TALK		1979 CBS	UK	83342 US	35693
AFTER MIDNIGHT		1980 CBS	UK	84223 US	36411
BEST OF		1980 EMBASSY UK	31806	
GREATEST HITS		1980 CBS		US	36861

RAY BOOSTER	G V	(A	(A) MANIACS	197 BLUBBER LIPS	GER	803
MANNY MANIAC	B V	(A				
CHARLIE ENDURE	D	(A	JOHN ROOTBEER	G	(A	

CARL MANN	G V	(ALL	(A) LIKE MANN	1959 PHILIPS INT	US	PLP1960
			(B) CARL MANN	19 SONET	SWED	SPO 13
			(C) LEGENDARY SUN PERFORMERS	1977 CHARLY	UK	CR 30130
			(D) GONNA ROCK 'N' ROLL TONIGHT	1978 CHARLY	UK	CR 5008
			(EP) CARL MANN	1977 CHARLY	UK	CEP 114
			( ) LIKE MANN	1980 CHARLY	UK	CRM 2006

HERBIE MANN	FLT	ALL	WITH JOAO GILBERTO & ANTONIO JOBIM	19 ATLANTIC		US SD 8105
BILL EVANS	PNO	(N	THE COMMON GROUND	1961 ATLANTIC		US SD 1343
CHUCK ISRAELS	B	(N	THIS IS MY BELOVED	19 ATLANTIC		US SD 1367
PAUL MOTIAN	D	(N	FAMILY OF MANN	19 ATLANTIC		US SD 1371
CHICK GANIMIAN	(I		AT THE VILLAGE GATE	1962 ATLANTIC	UK 599 054	US SD 1380
ROY AYERS	VIBES(IM		RIGHT NOW	19 ATLANTIC		US SD 1384
BRUNO CARR	D	(IM	DO THE BOSSA NOVA	19 ATLANTIC		US SD 1397
REGGIE WORKMAN	B	(I	RETURN TO THE VILLAGE GATE	19 ATLANTIC		US SD 1407
CARLOS VALDES	PERC	(IL	(L)LIVE AT NEWPORT	1963 ATLANTIC		US SD 1413
THOMAS KAZANAN	PERC	(I	LATIN FEVER	1964 ATLANTIC		US SD 1422
GERALDINE SWEE	PERC	(I	(N)NIRVANA	1964 ATLANTIC	UK K 50238	US SD 1426
JIMMY OWENS	TPT	(I	MY KINDA GROOVE	196 ATLANTIC		US SD 1433
JULIAN PRIESTER	SAX	(I	THE SMELL OF THE CROWD,ROAR OF G PAINT	196 ATLANTIC		US SD 1437
JOE ORANGE	SAX	(I	STANDING OVATION AT NEWPORT	196 ATLANTIC		US SD 1445 ·
MOHAMED ELEKLAD ZITHER (I			TODAY	196 ATLANTIC		US SD 1454
ATTILA ZOLLER	G	(IL	MONDAY NIGHT AT THE VILLAGE GATE	196 ATLANTIC		US SD 1462
RICHARD DAVIS	B	(I	OUR MANN FLUTE	196 ATLANTIC		US SD 1464

(CONTINUED)

GLORIA AGOSTINI	HARP (I	NEW MANN AT NEWPORT	196	ATLANTIC		US SD 1471
DAVE PIKE	VIBES(L	(I)IMPRESSIONS OF THE MIDDLE EAST	1967	ATLANTIC		US SD 1475
DON FRIEDMAN	PNO (L	BEAT GOES ON	196	ATLANTIC		US SD 1483
BEN TUETHE	B (L	STRING ALBUM	196	ATLANTIC		US SD 1490
BOB THOMAS	(L	WAILING DERVISHES	196	ATLANTIC		US SD 1497
WILLIE BOBO	PERC (L	(U) MEMPHIS UNDERGROUND	1969	ATLANTIC	UK 588 200	US SD 1522
MELVIN LASTIE	HRNS (M	(U) MEMPHIS UNDERGROUND	197	ATLANTIC	UK K 40038	RI UK K50520
IKE WILLIAMS	HRNS (M	LIVE AT THE WHISKY	196	ATLANTIC		US SD 1536
GEORGE BOHANAN	TROM (M	BEST OF	19	ATLANTIC		US SD 1544
AL VESCOVO	G (M	TURTLE BAY	19	ATLANTIC	UK K 50020	US SD 1642
JOHN BARNES	K (M	GLORY OF LOVE	1969	A&M	UK AMLS 944	US 3003
DARREL CLAYBORN	B (M	EVOLUTIONOF MANN	19	ATLANTIC	UK K 60020	US SD 2 300
RICHARD WATERS	D (M	BEST OF	19	PRESTIGE		US 7432
VICTOR PANTOJA	PERC (M	BIG BOSS MAN	19	CBS		US 1068
LARRY CORYELL	G (M	ET TU FLUTE	19	VERVE		68821
REGGIE YOUNG	G (M	LATIN MANN	19	CSP		US JCS 9188
BOBBY EMMONS	K (M	MANN IN SWEDEN	19	PRESTIGE		US 7659
BOBBY WOOD	K (M	SUPER MANN	1973	TRIP		US 5031
MICK LEECH	B (M	WITH FLOOT TO BOOT	19	SPRINGBOARD		US 4055
GENE CHRISTMAN	D (M	CONCERTO GROSSO IN D BLUES	196	ATLANTIC	UK 2465005	
ERIS WEISSBERG	G (M	STONE FLUTE	19	ATLANTIC	UK 2465088	US EMBRYO 520
SONNY SHARROCK	G (M	MUSCLE SHOALS NITTY GRITTY	19	ATLANTIC	UK 2400022	UK RI K40096
CHARLIE BROWN	G (M	MUSCLE SHOALS NITTY GRITTY	19	EMBRYO		US SD 526
MIROSLAV VITOUS	B (M	(M)MEMPHIS TWO STEP	1971	EMBRYO		US SD 531
RON CARTER	B (M	(P)PUSH PUSH	1971	EMBRYO		US SD 532
RICHIE RESNICOFF	G (M	(P)PUSH PUSH	1971	ATLANTIC	UK 2400191	UK RI K40283
PAT REBILLOT	K (G	BRAZIL BLUES	197	UA	UK UAS 5631	US 5638
SAM BROWN	G (G	MISSISSIPPI GAMBLER	1974	ATLANTIC	UK K 40385	US 1610
TONY LEVIN	B (G	HOLD ON IM COMING	197	ATLANTIC	UK K 40467	US 1632
STEVE GADD	D (G	LET ME TELL YOU	1974	MILESTONE		ML 47010
MINURO MURAOKA	(G	(O)LONDON UNDERGROUND	1974	ATLANTIC	UK K 50032	US SD 1648
MODERN SHOMYO STUDY GROUP(G		REGGAE	1974	ATLANTIC	UK K 50053	US SD 1655
ONG GAGAKU SOCIETY	(P	STAR COLLECTION	1975	MIDI	UK K 20018	
DUANE ALLMAN	G (P	DISCOTHEQUE	1975	ATLANTIC	UK K 50128	US SD 1670
CORNELL DUPREE	G (P	WATER BED	1975	ATLANTIC	UK K 50174	US SD 1676
BERNARD PURDIE	D (P	(G) GAGAKU & BEYOND	1976	FINNADAR		SR 9014
JERRY JEMMOTT	B (P	SURPRISES	19	ATCO		US 1682
AL JACKSON	D (P	BIRD IN A SILVER CAGE	1977	ATLANTIC	UK K 50338	US SD 18209
GENE BIANCO	HARP (P	BRASIL	1978	ATLANTIC	UK	
RICHARD TEE	K (P					

CHUCK RAINEY	B (P	RALPH MACDONALD	PERC (P	DONALD DUNN	B (P	RAY BARRETTO	PERC (
BABATHNDE OLATUNJI PERC(		RAY MANTILLA	PERC (	ARMANDO PERAZA	PERC (	MICK TAYLOR	G (O
ALBERT LEE	G (O	PAT REBILLOT	K (O	FUZZY SAMUELS	B (O	AL GORRY	B (O
AYNSLEY DUNBAR	D (O	ROBBIE McINTOSH	D (O	IAN McDONALD	SAX)O	STEPHANE GRAPPELLI	VLN (O

MICHAEL MANTLER	TPT (ALL	(A) JAZZ COMPOSERS ORCHESTRA	1974	VIRGIN	UK	JD 3001
DON CHERRY	HRNS (AB	(B) NO ANSWER	1974	VIRGIN	UK	WATT 2
STEVE LACY	SAX (A	(C) 13 3/4	1975	VIRGIN	UK	WATT 3
AL GIBBONS	SAX (A	(D) THE HAPLESS CHILD	1976	VIRGIN	UK	WATT 4
GENE HULL	SAX (A	(E) SILENCE	1976	VIRGIN	UK	WATT 5
BOB DONOVAN	SAX (A	(F) MOVIES	1978	VIRGIN	UK	WATT 7
LEW TABACKIN	SAX (A					

GEORGE BARROW	SAX (A	CHARLES DAVIS	SAX (A	LLOYD MICHAELS	HRNS (A	RANDY BRECKER	HRNS(A
BOB NORTHERN	HRNS)A	JULIUS WATKINS	HRNS (A	JIMMY KNEPPER	TROM (A	JACK JEFFERS	TROM(A
STEPHEN FURTADO		HOWARD JOHNSON	TUBA (A	EDDIE GOMEZ	B (A	STEVE SWALLOW	B (ADF
CARLA BLEY	K V(ALL	KENT CARTER	B (A	BEAVER HARRIS	D (A	RON CARTER	B (A
ROSWELL RUDD	TROM (A	RICHARD DAVIS	B (A	PHAROAH SANDERS	SAX (A	CHARLIE HADEN	B (A
CECIL TAYLOR	PNO (A	REGGIE WORKMAN	B (A	JIMMY LYONS	SAX (A	ANDREW CYRILLE	D (A
BOB CUNNINGHAM	B (A	LARRY CORYELL	G (A	REGGIE JOHNSON	B (A	STEVE MARCUS	SAX (A
ALAN SILVA	B (A	FRANK WESS	SAX (A	JACK BRUCE	B V (AB	ROBERT WYATT	V (DE
JACK DEJOHNETTE	D (D	TERJE RYPDAL	G (D	KEVIN COYNE	V (E	CHRIS SPEDDING	G (E
RON McCLURE	B (A	CLARE MAHER	CELLO (E	TONY WILLIAMS	D (F		

MANFRED MANN K SYN V(ALL		(A)MANFRED MANN ALBUM	1964			US ASCOT 16015
MIKE HUGG	D (ABCDEFGHIJKLMO37	(B) FIVE FACES OF MANFRED MANN	1964	HMV CLP 1731		US ASCOT 16018
MIKE VICKERS	SAX (ABCD3I	(C) MANN MADE	1964	HMV CLP 1911/1628		US ASCOT 16024
DAVE RICHMOND	B (GI	(C) MANN MADE	1969	STARLINE	UK	SRS 5007
PAUL JONES	V (ABCDHI3	(D) MY LITTLE RED BOOK OF WINNERS	1965			US ASCOT 16021
TOM McGUINNESS	B G(ABCDEFGHIJK37	(E) MANN MADE HITS	1966	HMV CLP 3559		
JACK BRUCE	B (3I	(F) PRETTY FLAMINGO	1966			US UA 6549
MIKE D'ABO	V (GK37	(G) AS IS	1966			US UA 6551
BERNIE LIVING	WIND (NO	(H) GREATEST HITS	1966			US UA 6551
STEVE YORK	B (NO	(I) SOUL OF MANN	1967	HMV CLP 3594		US CAPITOL 6199
CRAIG COLLINGE	D (NO	(J) UP THE JUNCTION	1968	FONTANA STL 5460	UK 6852 005	
SONNY CORBETT	TPT (NO	(K) MIGHTY GARVEY	1968	FONTANA STL 5470		
IAN FENBY	(N	(L) WHAT A MAN	1968	FONTANA SFL13003		
HAROLD BECKETT	TPT (N	(M) MIGHTY QUINN	1968			US MERCURY 61168
DAVID COXHILL	SAX (NO	(N) CHAPTER THREE	1969	VERTIGO UK VO3		US POLYDOR 4013
DEREK WADSWORTH	(GK	(O) CHAPTER THREE VOL 2	1970	VERTIGO UK 6360 012		
CHRIS PYNE	(N	(P) THIS IS MANFRED MANN	1971	VERTIGO UK 6382 020		
DAVE QUINCY	(N	(Q) EARTH BAND	1972	PHILIPS UK 6308 086		US POLYDOR 5015
PHIL KENZIE	(N	(Q) EARTH BAND	1977	BRONZE UK BRON 252		
DAVE POTTER	(N	(R) GLORIFIED MAGNIFIED	1972	PHILIPS UK 6308 125		US POLYDOR 5031
GEOFF DRISCOLL	(N	(R) GLORIFIED MAGNIFIED	1977	BRONZE UK BRON 257		
NICK EVANS	(N	(S) MESSIN'	1973	PHILIPS UK 6360 087	RI 77 BRONZE 261	
MADELINE BELL	V (N	(T) GET YOUR ROCKS OFF	1973			US POLYDOR 5050
SUNNY LESLIE	V (N	(U) SOLAR FIRE	1973	BRONZE UK ILPS9265		US POLYDOR 6019
SUE GLOVER	V (N	(U) SOLAR FIRE	1977	BRONZE UK BRON 265	GER	28778
BRIAN HUGG	G (NO	(V) THE GOOD EARTH	1974	BRONZE UK ILPS9306	US WB	BS 2826
DAVE BROOKS	SAX (N	(V) THE GOOD EARTH	1977	BRONZE UK BRON 306	GER	88369
CLIVE STEVENS	SAX (O	(W) NIGHTINGALES & BOMBERS	1975	BRONZE UK ILPS9337	US WB	BS 2877

(CONTINUED)

　　(CONTINUED)　　　　　　　　　　　　MANFRED MANN　　　　　　　　　　　　　　　　　　　　　　　　

```
  GERRY FIELDS        FDL   (O      (W) NIGHTINGALES & BOMBERS    1977 BRONZE   UK BRON 337    GER       89059
  CONRAD ISADORE      D     (O      (X) ROARING SILENCE          1976 BRONZE   UK ILPS9357    US WB     BS 3055
  ANDY McCULLOCH      D     (O      (X) ROARING SILENCE          1977 BRONZE   UK BRON 357
  COLIN PATTENDEN     B     (QRSUVWZX  (Y) THE BEST OF MANFRED MANN 1977 EMI     UK NUT 7
  CHRIS SLADE         D     (QRSUVWZ1X (Z) THE EARTH BAND 1971 /73 1977 VERTIGO UK 9199 107    GER       200 367
  MICK ROGERS         G V   (QRSUVWZ24X (1) WATCH                 1978 BRONZE   UK BRON 507    US WB     BS 3157
  DAVE FLETT          G     (X1      (2) ANGEL STATION            1979 BRONZE   UK BRON 516    US WB        3302
  LIZA STRIKE         V     (S       (3) SEMI DETATCHED SUBURBAN  1979 EMI      UK EMTV 19
  RUBY JAMES          V     (SW      (4) CHANCE                   1980 BRONZE   UK BRON 529 GER 202 970 US Wb 3498
  GRAHAM ELLIOTT      CELLO(W         (5) THE BEST OF MANFRED MANN 197 CAPITOL              US        11688
  MARTHA SMITH        V     (W       (6) THE BEST OF MANFRED MANN 197 JANUS                US         3064
  VICKY SILVA         V     (1       (7) ONE WAY                  1968 FONTANA             NL        858037
  STEVE WALLER        G V   (24      (8) ATTENTION  (COMP)        19 FONTANA               GER       6438 063
  ANTHONY MOORE       G K   (12      (9) MANNERISMS               1976 SONIC               SON 016
  DAVID BOSWELL-BROWN CELLO(W        (10) ATTENTION VOL 2         197
  DAVID CULPAN        RECORDER(X      (11) HISTORY OF BRIT POP VOL 6 19 EMI   NL 05020
  BARBARA THOMPSON    SAX   (X4      (12) REMEMBER THE GOLDEN YEARS DBL 19 EMI GER 06532/33
  KLAUS VOORMANN      B     (GK7      (EP) GROOVIN' WITH          1964 HMV  UK 7EG8876
  CHRIS THOMPSON      G V   (X124     (EP) MANFRED MANN           1964 HMV  UK 7EG8848
  IRENE CHANTER       V     (1X       (EP) INSTRUMENTAL ASSASSINATION 1967 FONTANA UK TE 17473
  KIM GOODY           V     (2        (EP) INSTUMENTAL ASYLUM     1966 HMV  UK 7EG8949
  JIM O'NEILL         G     (2        (EP) THE ONE IN THE MIDDLE  1965 HMV  UK 7EG8908
  DOREEN CHANTER      V     (W1X      (EP) THERE'S NO LIVING WITHOUT 1965 HMV UK 7EG8922
  DAVID MILLMAN       STRINGS (WX     (EP) MACHINES               1966 HMV  UK 7EG8942
  TONY ROWELL         RECORDER(X      (EP) AS WAS                 1966 HMV  UK 7EG8962
  PAT KING            B     (124
  LAURIE BAKER        (W
  STEVIE LANGE        V     (1
  GEOFF BRITTON       D     (2
  DYAN BIRCH          V     (24   MARGARET WOOD RECORDER(X    CHRIS WARREN-GREEN VLN (W   NIGEL WARREN-GREEN CELLO(W
  JOHN LINGWOOD       D     (4    TREVOR RABIN   G      (4    SUSANNE LYNCH      V   (X   LYN DOBSON         SAX (I
  HENRY LOWTHER       TPT   (I    GRAHAM PRESKETT VLN   (4    ROBBIE McINTOSH    G   (4   GEOFF WHITEHORN    G   (4
  WILLY FINLAYSON     V     (4    PETER MARSH    V      (4    CAROL STOCKER      V   (4
```

　　　　　　　　　　　　　　　　　　　　MANTRA　　　　　　　　　　　　　　　　　　　　　　　

```
                                     (A) MANTRA                   1981 CASABLANCA         NBPL 7256
```

　　　　　　　　　　　　　　　　　　　PHIL MANZANERA　　　　　　　　　　　　　　　　　　　　　

```
  PHIL MANZANERA      G V K(ALL      (A) DIAMOND HEAD            1975   ISLAND ILPS 9315   US ATCO36113
  SIMON PHILLIPS      D PERC(BC      (A) DIAMOND HEAD            1975   ISLAND GER 88 750
  BRIAN ENO           K     (AB      (A) DIAMOND HEAD            1977   POLYDOR UK RI          2302 062
  BILL MACCORMICK     B     (ABC     (B) LISTEN NOW              1977   POLYDOR UK 2302 074
  IAN McDONALD        PIPES(A        (C) K SCOPE                 1978   POLYDOR UK 2302 083 US     6147
  PAUL THOMPSON       D     (AC      (D) PRIMITIVE GUITARS       1981   EDITIONS UK EGED14
  SONNY AXPAN         PERC  (A
  CHYKE MADU          PERC  (A   DOREEN CHANTER    V    (A   JOHN WETTON      PERC (AC  DAVE SKINNER    K V (C
  ROBERT WYATT        (A   BRIAN TURRINGTON B    (A   ANDY MACKAY      WIND (A   EDDIE JOBSON    K VLN(AB
  DANNY HEIBS         PERC  (A   CHARLES HAYWARD  PERC (A   DAVE JARRETT     K    (A   LOL CREME       V GISMO(BC
  KEVIN GODLEY        V PERC(BC  SIMON AINLEY     G V  (BC  MAL COLLINS      SAX  (BC  BILLY LIVSEY    K WIND(B
  IAN MacCORMICK      V     (B   DAVE MATTACKS    D    (B   FRANCIS MONKMAN  SYN  (BC  EDDIE RAYNER    K SYN  (BC
  JOHN WHITE          TUBA  (B   RHETT DAVIES     K    (B   ALAN LEE         V    (B   TIN FINN        V   (BC
  NEAL FINN           (C
```

　　　　　　　　　　　　　　　　　　　RAY MANZAREK　　　　　　　　　　　　　　　　　　　　　　

```
  RAY MANZAREK        K V   (ABC     (A) THE GOLDEN SCARAB       1975   MERCURY UK 6398 007 US SRMI 703
  LARRY CARLTON       G     (A       (B) THE WHOLE THING STARTED WITH R'N'R 1975 MERCURY UK 6338 552 US SRMI1014
  JERRY SCHEFF        B     (A       (C) NITE CITY               1977 20TH CENTURY      US       528
  TONY WILLIAMS       D     (A
  TONY SALES          (C   STEVE FORMAN     PERC (AB  NIGEL HARRISON      (C   HUNT SALES      D (C
  MAILTO CORREA       PERC  (A   OSCAR BRASHEAR   TPT  (A   MARK PINES       G    (B   MILT HOLLAND    PERC(A
  GARY MALLABER       D PERC (A   MIKE FENNELLY    G    (B   TIM DOWNS        D    (A   ERNIE WATTS     SAX (A
  NOAH JONES          V     (C   PAUL WARREN      G V  (C   MARK VOLMAN      V    (B   HOWARD KAYLAN   V   (B
  JOE WALSH           G     (B   GEORGE SEGAL     BANJO(B   JOHN KLEMMER     SAX  (B   PAUL DAVIS      PERC(B
  PATTI SMITH         V     (B
```

　　　　　　　　　　　　　　　　　　　　JOE MAPHIS　　　　　　　　　　　　　　　　　　　　　　

```
  JOE MAPHIS          G     (ALL     (A) GUITARATION GAP         1972 CHART             US      1042
                                     (B) DIM LIGHTS THICK SMOKE  1978 CHM               US      6224
                                     (C) GRASS & JAZZ            1978 CHM               US      6215
                                     (D) BOOGIE WOOGIE FLAT TOP  1979 CHM               US      6239
```

　　　　　　　　　　　　　　　　　　　　MIKE MARAN　　　　　　　　　　　　　　　　　　　　　

```
  MIKE MARAN          (A       (A) FAIR WARNING           1971 BRONZE            ILPS   9221
  KENNY WHEELER       TPT   (A
  BUTCH HUDSON        TPT   (A   HENRY LOWTHER    TPT  (A   CHRIS PYNE       TROM (A   DAVE HORLER     TROM    (A
  GEOFF PEERKINS      TROM  (A   ALAN SKIDMORE    SAX  (A   STAN SULZMAN     SAX  (A   BARBARA THOMPSON WIND   (A
  ROY BABBINGTON      B     (A   FRANK RICOTTI    PERC (A   DAVE MATTACKS    D    (A   DAVE MacRAE     K  (A
  TONY ASHTON         K     (A   JOHN MARSON      HCA  (A   GERRY BRON       PROD (A   STRING SEC      (A
```

　　　　　　　　　　　　　　　MARCUS HOOK ROLL BAND　　　　　　　　　　　　　　　　　　　

```
  HARRY VANDA         (A       (A) MARCUS HOOK ROLL BAND   1973 CAPITOL     US     11991
  GEORGE YOUNG        (A
```

　　　　　　　　　　　　　　　　　　　　　MARCUS　　　　　　　　　　　　　　　　　　　　　　

```
  MARCUS MALONE       V     (A       (A) MARCUS               1978 UA    UK UAS 30000   US UA LA 668
  GENE BLOCH          G     (A
  RANDALL DAVID       G     (A   TIM BOGERT       B    (A   JACK WEBER       G    (A   DANDY HOLMES    D  (A
```

　　　　　　　　　　　　　　　　　　BENNY MARDONES　　　　　　　　　　　　　　　　　　　　　

```
  BENNY MARDONES      V     (ALL     (A) THANK GOD FOR GIRLS    1978 PRIVATE STOCK      US PS 7007
  MICK RONSON         G     (A       (A) NEVER RUN              1980 POLYDOR US 6263
  JERRY SHIRLEY       D     (A       (C) TOO MUCH TO LOOSE      1981 POLYDOR US
  MIKE NEVILLE        B     (A
  HAYDEN WAYNE        K V   (A   RON FRANGIPANE   K    (A   JOEY STANN      SAX  (A   MERLE MILLER    V    (A
  KIMBERLEY CARLSON   V     (A   D L BYRON        V    (A   SANDY GENNARO   D    (B   RON BLOOM       G   (B
  BOBBY MASSANO       G     (B   KINNY LANDRUM    K    (A   LEIGH FOXX      B    (B
```

　　　　　　　　　　　　　　　　　　　　MARIAH　　　　　　　　　　　　　　　　　　　　　　

```
                                     (A) MARIAH                197  UA       US        UALA 493
```

M84C   JON MARK   M84C

JON MARK	G V	(A		(A) SONGS FOR A FRIEND		1975	CBS	US	33339
TOMMY EYRE	K	(A							
SALLI TERRI	V	(A	RON CARTER	B (A	LARRY KNECHTEL	B (A	HAL BLAINE	D (A	
DONALD REINBERG	TPT	(A	GAYLE LEVANT	HARP (A	VÍCTOR FELDMAN	PERC (A	ANDREW NARELL STEEL	D(A	
PATRICK GLEASON	SYN	(A							

M84D   CHARLIE MARIANO   M84D

CHARLIE MARIANO	WIND	(A		(A) HELEN OF TREES		1976 MPS BASF	22941	
ZBIGNIEW SEIFERT	VLN³	(A						
JAN HAMMER	K	(A	JACK BRUCE	B (A	JOHN MARSHALL	D (A	NIPPY NOYA PERC (A	

M84E   MARIE ET LES GARCONS   M84E

(A) MARIE ET LES GARCONS   1080 ZE   FR 2 6564

M84F   FRANK MARINO   M84F

FRANK MARINO   G V SYN   (AB   (A) POWER OF ROCK'N'ROLL   1981 CBS   US   37099

M85   THE MARKEYS   M85

STEVE CROPPER	G	(	(A) THE MARKEYS	1961	ATLANTIC	US	8055	
DONALD DUCK DUNN	B	(	(B) DO THE POPEYE	1962	ATLANTIC	US	8062	
TERRY JOHNSON	D	(	(C) GREAT MEMPHIS SOUND	1965	STAX US 707	UK ATLANTIC587024		
AL JACKSON	D	(	(D) BACK TO BACK	196	STAX US 720			
PACK AXTON	SAX	(	(E) DAMIFIKNEW	1969	COTILLION	US	SD 9014	
DON NIX	SAX	(	(F) MEMPHIS HORNS	1970	COTILLION	US	9014	
BOOMER T JONES	ORG	(	(G) MEMPHIS EXPERIENCE	1970	STAX	US	2036	
WAYNE JACKSON	TPT	(	(H) HIGH ON MUSIC	1976	RCA	US	1056	
ANDREW LOVE	SAX	(	(I) MELLOW JELLY	19	ATLANTIC	UK	587 135	
ISAAC HAYES	PNO	(						
JERRY LEE SMITH	K	(	FLOYD NEWMAN SAX (					

M86   MARK ALMOND   M86

JON MARK	V G B PERC	(ALL	(A) MARK ALMOND	1971 HARVEST UK SHSP 4011	US BLUETHUMB BTS 27					
JOHN ALMOND	SAX V PERC	(ALL	(A) MARK ALMOND	1971 HARVEST GER 92200						
TOMMY TEDESCO	MAND	(H	(B) MARK ALMOND 2	1972 BLUE THUMB US BT 32						
TOMMY EYRE	K G PERC	(AB	(C) RISING	1972 HARVEST UK SHVL 809	US CBS	31917				
JOHN LEFTWICH	B	(H	(C) RISING	1972 NOVA GER 6 22365						
ROGER SUTTON	G V PERC	(AB	(D) MARK ALMOND 73	1973 NOVA GERM 628448	US CBS	32486				
BOBBY VEGA	B	(H	(D) MARK ALMOND 73	1974 KUCKUCK GER 2375 027						
JOHN TROPEA	G	(F	(E) TO THE HEART	1976 ABC UK ABCL 5183	US ABC ABCD 945					
LEON PENDARVIS	K	(F	(F) OTHER PEOPLES ROOMS	1978 HORIZON UK AMLJ 730	US A&M AM 730					
MARK CRANNY	D	(H	(G) BEST OF	1980 KILLROY GER 19955						
BILL BERG	D	(H	(H) TUESDAY IN NEW YORK	1980 LINE GER LLP5040						
RALPH MACDONALD	PERC	(F								
DANNY RICHMOND	D	(BC	JEFF CONDON	FLT V(C	KEN CRADDOCK	K V G(C	COLIN GIBSON	B V PERC(C		
WILL LEE	B	(F	LARRY WILLIAMS	SYN (F	STEVE GADD	D (F	JERRY HEY	HRNS (F		
JEANNIE McLAINE	PERC V(H		JAY LEWIS	G (H	LARRY KNECHTEL	K (H	JIM SALARGIE	PNO (H		
CARLOS RIOS	G	(G	MARK ROSS	SYN K (GH	DAVE MAROTTA	B (GH	ROBERTO PATTACIA	D (G		
BILLY COBHAM	D	(E	WOLFGANG MELZ	B (E	MILT HOLLAND	PERC(E	JOCK ELLIS	TROM (E		
TOMMY EYRE	K	(E	JIM GORDON	D (E	GREG BLOCH	VLN (E	GARY BARONE	HRNS (E		

M86A   BOB MARKLEY   M86A

BOB MARKLEY		(A	(A) MARKLEY	1969	FORWARD	US	STF 1007	
SHAUN HARRIS		(						
DAN HARRIS		(	MICHAEL LLOYD (					

M87   ALAIN MARKUSFELD   M87

ALAIN MARKUSFELD	G V	(ALL	(A) LE DESERT NOIR	1978	EGG	900 528	
JOEL DUGRENEST	B	(	(B) PLATOCK	1978	EGG	900 556	
LAURENT THIBAULT	K	(	(C) LE MONDE EN ETAGES	19	BARCLAY	920 179	
DOMINIQUE FRANCARD	SYN(		(D) LE SON TOMBE DU CIEL	19	BARCLAY	920 327	
GERA FRENZI	D	(	(E) CONTEMPORUS	1979	EGG 900 581	US VISA 7012	

M88   BOB MARLEY   M88

BOB MARLEY	G V	(ALL	(A) SOUL REBEL	1971	TROJAN		TBL 126	
PETER TOSH		(BDN	(B) CATCH A FIRE	1972	ISLAND	UK	ILPS 9241	
BUNNY LIVINGSTONE		(BDN	(C) AFRICAN HERBSMAN	1973	TROJAN		TRL 62	
EARL LINDO	K	(DFQS	(D) BURNIN'	1973	ISLAND	UK	ILPS 9256	
JUNIOR BRAITHWAITE		(	(E) RASTA REVOLUTION	1974	TROJAN	UK	TRLS 89	
BEVERLEY KELSO		(	(F) NATTY DREAD	1975	ISLAND	UK	ILPS 9281	
CARLTON BARRETT	D	(BDFJPTQSGK	(G) LIVE	1975	ISLAND	UK	ILPS 9376	
ASTON BARRETT	G B	(BDFJPTQSGK	(H) JAH LIVE	1975	ISLAND	UK	IDJ 8	
AL ANDERSON	G	(FJTQSG	(J) RASTA MAN VIBRATION	1976	ISLAND	UK	ILPS 9383	
BERNARD HARVEY	K	(FG	(K) EXODUS	1977	ISLAND	UK	ILPS 9498	
TYRONE DOWNIE	K	(QSK	(L) BIRTH OF A LEGEND	1977	EPIC		82066	
ALVIN PATTERSON	PERC	(FJPQSGK	(M) BIRTH OF A LEGEND (DBL)	1977	CALLA		CAS 1240	
CHINNA SMITH	G	(J	(N) EARLY MUSIC	1977	EMBASSY	UK	31584	
JUDY MOWATT	V	(FJPQSGK	(O) REFLECTION	1977	FONTANA	FR		
MARCIA GRIFFITH	V	(FJPTQSGK	(P) KAYA	1978	ISLAND	UK	ILPS9517	
RITA MARLEY	V	(FJPQSGK	(Q) BABYLON BY BUS (DBL)	1978	ISLAND	UK	ILPD 11	
JUNIOR MARVIN	G	(FPQSK	(R) BOB MARLEY & THE WAILERS	1979	HAMMER		MHR 9006	
DONALD KINSLEY	G	(J	(S) SURVIVAL	1979	ISLAND	UK	ILPS9542	
WAYNE PERKINS	G	(B	(T) UPRISING	1980	ISLAND	UK	ILPS9596	
RABBIT BUNDRICK	K	(B	(U) IN THE BEGINNING	1979	PSYCHO		PLP 6002	
WINSTON RILEY	K	(B	( ) BIRTH OF A LEGEND	1980	EMBASSY	UK	31815	
			( ) SOUL SHAKEDOWN	19	ESP	NL	165837	

M88A   RITA MARLEY   M88A

RITA MARLEY   V   (A   (A) RITA MARLEY   1980 TRIDENT   TLP 001

M89   MARMALADE   M89

PAT FAIRLEY	B	(E	(A) THERE'S A LOT OF IT ABOUT	1968	CBS	UK	63414	
JUNIOR CAMPBELL	G	(E	(B) BEST OF	1969	CBS US 26553	UK	SPB36	
DEAN FORD	G HCA V	(EF	(C) REFLECTIONS	1970	LONDON US 575	UK DECCA	SKL5047	
GRAHAM KNIGHT	B V	(EFH	(D) SONGS	1971	DECCA	UK	SKL5111	
ALAN WHITEHEAD	D	(EH	(E) OB LA DI	1973	EMBASSY	UK	EMB31032	
MIKE JAPP	G V K(F		(F) OUR HOUSE IS ROCKING	1974	EMI	UK	EMC 3047	
DOUGLAS HENDERSON	D	(F	(G) THE WORLD OF MARMALADE	1976	DECCA	UK	SPA 470	
JOE BREEN		(F	(H) ONLY LIGHT ON MY HORIZON NOW	1977	TARGET	UK	TGS 501	
HOWIE CASEY	HRNS	(F	(I) DOING IT ALL FOR YOU	1979	SKY		LP1	
SANDY NEWMAN	G K V(H		(J) BACK ON THE ROAD(69/72)	1981	DECCA	UK	TAB 19	
GARTH WATT ROY	G V	(H						

STEVE MARRIOTT

```
STEVE MARRIOTT   G V  (A        (A) MARRIOTT                    1976  A&M       US 4572    UK AMLH64572
GREG RIDLEY      B V  (A
IAN WALLACE      D    (A   MICKEY FINN      G   (A   DAVID FOSTER    K   (A-  DENNIS KOVARIK    B  (A
BEN BENAY        G    (A   MIKE BAIRD       D   (A   RED RHODES      STEEL(A   ALAN ESTES CONGA      (A
ERNIE WATTS      SAX  (A   DAVID SPINOZZA   G   (A   MAXINE WILLARD  V   (A   VANETTA FIELDS    V  (A
CARLEENA WILLIAMS V   (A
```

M90
JOHNNY MARS
M90

```
JOHNNY MARS      HCA V(AB       (A) BLUES FROM MARS             1972  POLYDOR      UK        2460 168
BOB HALL         PNO MAND(A      (B) OAKLAND BOOGIE             1976  BIG BEAR     UK        BEAR  12
BOB BRUNNING     B    (A         (C) MIGHTY MARS               1980  JSP          UK        1023
BOOGIE WOOGIE RED V  (A
PAT GROVER       G    (A   BABY BOY WARREN   V   (A   JOHN HUNT           D  (A
```

M90A
BERNIE MARSDEN
M90A

```
BERNIE MARSDEN   G V  (AB       (A) ABOUT TIME TOO             1979  PARLOPHONE   UK        PCS 7215
DON AIREY        K    (A         (B) LOOK AT ME NOW            1980  PARLOPHONE   UK        PCS 7217
JACK BRUCE       B    (A
IAN PAICE        D    (A   TONY RIVERS       V   (A   COZY POWELL     D   (A   NEIL MURRAY      B  (A
SIMON PHILLIPS   D    (A   DOREEN CHANTNER   V   (A   IRENE CHANTNER  V   (A   JON LORD         K  (A
ALAN CARVELL     V    (A   STUART CALVER     V   (A
```

M91
MARSEILLE
M91

```
PAUL DALE        V    (AB       (A) RED WHITE & SLIGHTLY BLUE   1978  MOUNTAIN UK TOPC5012
NEIL BUCHANAN    G    (AB        (B) MARSEILLE                 1979  MOUNTAIN UK TOPS 125 US RCA  3631
ANDY CHARTERS    G    (AB
STEVE DINWOODIE  B    (AB   KEITH KNOWLES     D    (AB
```

M92
MARSHALL/HAIN
M92

```
                                 (A) FREE RIDE                 1978  HARVEST      UK        SHSP 4087
```

M92A
KEITH MARSHALL
M92A

```
KEITH MARSHALL        (A        (A) KEITH MARSHALL             1981  ARRIVAL      UK        SPIN 1
```

M93
MARSHALL TUCKER
M93

```
TOY CALDWELL     G V  (ABCDEFGHIJ (A) MARSHALL TUCKER BAND      1973  CAPRICORN US 0112  UK 2429 114
TOMMY CALDWELL   B V  (ABCDEFGHIJ (A) MARSHALL TUCKER BAND      197   CAPRICORN UK RI     K  47509
GEORGE McCORKLE  G    (ABCDEFGHIJKLM(B) A NEW LIFE              1974  CAPRICORN US 0124  UK 2429 101
JERRY EUBANKS    SAX  (ABCDEFGHIJKLM(B) A NEW LIFE              1974  CAPRICORN UK         K 57501
PAUL RIDDLE      D    (ABCDEFGHIJKLM(C) SEARCHIN' FOR A RAINBOW 1975  CAPRICORN US 0161  UK 2429 129
DOUG GRAY        G V  (ABCDEFGHIJKLM(D) WHERE WE ALL BELONG     1975  CAPRICORN US 0145  UK 2659 042
PAUL HORNSBY     K    (ABCF       (E) LONG HARD RIDE           1976  CAPRICORN US 0170  UK 2429 140
CHARLIE DANIELS  FDL  (BCEFL      (F) CAROLINA DREAMS          1977  CAPRICORN US 0180  UK 2476 130
JOHN McEUEN      BANJO(E          (G) TOGETHER FOREVER         1978  CAPRICORN US 0205  UK 2476 139
JEROME JOSEPH    PERC (CE         (H) GREATEST HITS            1978  CAPRICORN US 0214
RICHARD BETTS    G    (C          (I) BEST OF                  1978  CAPRICORN         UK 2429 190
CHUCK LEAVELL    K    (CFJ        (J) RUNNING LIKE THE WIND    1979  WB        US 3317  UK  K 56621
AL McDONALD      MAND (C          (K) TENTH                    1980  WB        US 3410  UK  K 56778
FRANKLIN WILKIE  HRNS (LM         (L) DEDICATED                1981  WB        US 3525
NORTON BUFFALO   HCA  (L          (M) TUCKERIZED               1982  WB        US 3684
EARL FORD        HRNS (B
LEO LABRANCHE    HRNS (C   JAIMOE JOHANSON  CONGA(FAB BUDDY THORNTON       (A   FRED WISE       FDL (A
DONNA HALL       V    (A   ERNESTINE JONES  V    (A   ELLA BROWN      V   (A   OSCAR JACKSON   SAX (A
SAM DIXON        TPT  (A   STEVE MADAIO HRNS (J       GARY GRANT      HRNS(J   DAVID LUELL     HRNS(J
GARY HERBIG      HRNS (J   BILL REICHENBACH HRNS (J   TODD LOGAN      HRNS(B   RONNIE GODFREY  K  (M
YOLANDA McCULLOUGH V  (M   SARAH DASH        V   (M   KRYSTAL DAVIS   V   (M
```

M94
JOHN MARTYN
M94

```
JOHN MARTYN  G V K HCA (ALL      (A) LONDON CONVERSATION        1967  ISLAND UK  ILPS  952
HAROLD McNAIR    FLT  (B          (B) THE TUMBLER              1968  ISLAND UK  ILPS 9091
BEVERLEY MARTYN  V G  (CDEH       (C) STORMBRINGER             1970  ISLAND UK  ILPS 9113  US WB 1854
PAUL HARRIS      K    (CD         (D) THE ROAD TO RUIN         1970  ISLAND UK  ILPS 9133  US WB 1882
HARVEY BROOKS    B    (C          (E) BLESS THE WEATHER        1971  ISLAND UK  ILPS 9167  US 9311
LEVON HELM       D    (C          (F) SOLID AIR                1973  ISLAND UK  ILPS 9226  US 9325
WELLS KELLY      D    (D          (G) INSIDE OUT               1973  ISLAND UK  ILPS 9253  US 9335
BILLY MUNDI      D    (C          (H) SUNDAYS CHILD            1975  ISLAND UK  ILPS 9296  US 9296
HERBIE LOVELL    D    (C          (J) SO FAR SO GOOD           1976  ISLAND UK  ILPS 9484  US 9484
JOHN SIMON       K    (C          (K) LIVE AT LEEDS            1975  ISLAND UK  ILPS 9343
MIKE KOWALSKI    D    (D          (L) ONE WORLD                1977  ISLAND UK  ILPS 9492
ROCKY DZIDZORNU  PERC (D          (M) GRACE & DANGER           1980  ISLAND UK  ILPS 9560
DAVE PEGG        B    (DLF        (N) GLORIOUS FOOL            1981  WEA        UK K 99178
DAVE MATTACKS    D    (F
ALAN SPENCER     B    (D   DANNY THOMPSON    B (DEGHLF LYN DOBSON     FLT (D   RAY WARLEIGH    SAX (D
STEVE WINWOOD    K B  (GL  REMI KABAKA PERC      (G   CHRIS STEWART       (G   CHRIS WOOD      WIND(G
KESH SATHIE      TABLA(GHL BOBBY KEYS        SAX  (G   LIAM GENOCHEY   D   (H   TONY BRAUNAGEL  D  (H
TERRY WILSON     B    (H   AL ANDERSON       B    (H   RABBIT BUNDRICK K   (HF  DUDU PUKWANA    SAX (D
JON FIELD        FLT  (L   TRISTRAN FRY      PERC (LF  GEORGE LEE      SAX (L   NEIL MURRAY     B  (L
ANDY NEWMARK     D    (L   MORRIS PERT       PERC (L   RICO RODRIGUES  TROM(L   HANSFORD ROWE   B  (L
BRUCE ROWLAND    D    (L   JON STEVENS       D    (L   PAUL WHEELER    G   (B   DAVE MOSES      B  (B
TONY REEVES      B    (E   IAN WHITEMAN      K    (E   SMILEY DE JONNES PERC(E   RICHARD THOMPSON G (EF
ROGER POWELL     D    (E   PHIL COLLINS PROD D V (MN  TOMMY EYRE      K   (M   JOHN GIBLIN     B  (M
DAVE LAWSON      SYN  (M   TONY COE          SAX  (F   SIMON NICOL         (F   SUE DRAHEIM     VLN (F
SPEEDY ACQUAYE   PERC (F
```

M95
MARSUPILAMI
M95

```
DAVE LAVEROCK    G    (AB        (A) MARSUPILAMI               1970  TRANSATLANTIC  UK TRA 213
LEARY HASSON     K    (AB         (B) ARENA                    1971  TRANSATLANTIC  UK TRA 230
FRED HASSON      V HCA(AB
MIKE FOURACRE    D    (AB   JESSICA STANLEY-CLARKE FLT V(AB  RICHARD LATHAN HICKS B (AB  BOB WEST     V  (B
PETER BARDENS    PERC (B    MANDY RIEDELBANCH     WIND (B
```

M95A
MARTHA & THE MUFFINS
M95A

```
MARTHA JOHNSON   V K  (ABC       (A) METROMUSIC                1980  DINDISC UK DID1  GER VIRGIN 202178
MARTHA LADLY  K V TROM(ABC        (B) TRANCE & DANCE           1980  DINDISC UK DID5  GER VIRGIN 202837
ANDY HAAS        SAX  (ABC        (C) THIS IS THE ICE AGE      1981  DINDISC          GER        204181
CARL FINKLE      B    (AB
MARK GANE        G    (ABC  TIM GANE       D    (ABC   MIKE HOWLETT        (A   JOCELYNE LANOIS  B PERC(C
DANIEL LANOIS    PERC V(C   NICK GANE           (C   ANDY CONDON         (C   SANDY HORNE      V  (C
GORDON DEPPE     V    (C   ALYX SKRIABOW     V(C   GEORGE AXON     PERC(C   CORINNE PLOMISH  V  (C
GLEN SCHELLENBERG PNO (C
```

DEWEY MARTIN

```
    DEWEY MARTIN      D V  (A    (A) DEWEY MARTIN & MEDICINE BALL   19  UNI        US 73088
    BILL DARNELL      G    (A
    PETE BRADSTREET   PNO  (A    BUDDY EMMONS    STEEL(A   RANDY FULLER    G V  (A   STEVEN LEFEVER    B  (A
    HARVEY KAGEN      B    (A    TERRY GREGG       B V  (A
M95C                                      MIKE MARTIN                                  M95C
    MIKE MARTIN            (A    (A) ON THE ROAD               1979 FLYRIGHT          FLY 301
M95D                                      VINCE MARTIN                                 M95D
    VINCE MARTIN      G V K(A    (A) VINCE MARTIN             1973  CAPITOL     US     11181
    DUKE BARDWELL     B    (A
    JEFF COMANOR      G    (A    CHRIS DARROW  G K FDL(A    VENETTA FIELDS   V   (A   SIDNEY GEORGE    SAX (A
    BUDDY HELM        D    (A    ERIC HORD        G  (A    CLYDIE KING      V   (A   CHARLES LARKEY    B  (A
    VAN DYKE PARKS         (A    JOHN SEBASTIAN   HCA (A    KELLY SHANAHAN   D   (A   HANK WILLIAMS    V  (A
M95E                              VINCE MARTIN & FRED NEIL                            M95E
    VINCE MARTIN      G V  (A    (A) TEAR DOWN THE WALLS      196  ELEKTRA      US    EKL.248
    FED NEIL          G V  (A
    FELIX PAPPALARDI  B HCA(A    JOHN SEBASTIAN    HCA G(A
M96                                      MOON MARTIN                                   M96
    JOHN 'MOON'MARTIN G V  (ALL  (A) SHOTS FROM A COLD NIGHTMARE 1979 CAPITOL UK/US 11787 GER 85513
    HOWIE WYETH       D    (B    (B) ESCAPE FROM DOMINATION   1979  CAPITOL UK/US 11933 GER 85944
    GARY VALENTINE    B    (AX   (C) STREET FEVER             1980  CAPITOL UK/US 12099
    CRAIG LEON        K    (AC   (D) MYSTERY TICKET           1982  CAPITOL    US 12200
    PHIL SEYMOUR      D V  (A    (X) EP(VICTIMS OF ROMANCE +4 1978  CAPITOL UK    16076
    DANY WYNN         D    (D
    MICHAEL BOTTS     D    (D    SUSAN HALL      PERC (A    CHARLIE MERRIAM   V   (A   WILLIE ALEXANDER PNO (A
    JIM LEITH         V    (A    JUDE COLE        V   (BC   DENNIS CROY       B   (BC  RICK CROY        D   (BC
    JEFF FARGUS       K V  (C    STEVE DOUGLAS   SAX  (C    DANA FERRIS       G   (C   ROBERT WRIGHT    V   (C
    P ROBINSON        V    (C    P MAROSHEK       V   (C    S HESS            V   (C   ROB STONER       B   (B
    BOB BABBETTE      B    (D    PETER BERNSTEIN  B   (D    MARK CHRISTIAN    G   (D   ANDREW GOLD      G   (D
    CHRIS BROSIUS     G V  (D    JACK WALDMAN     K   (D    GENE TAYLOR       K   (D   JEFF FARGUS      K   (D
    BILL ELLIOTT      K    (D    JOHN HOBBS       K   (D    BILL HOUSE        V   (D
M96A                                     HIRTH MARTINEZ                                M96A
    HIRTH MARTINEZ         (AB   (A) HIRTH FROM EARTH         19   WB             US    B  2867
                                 (B) BIG BRIGHT STREET        19   WB   UK K56400 US    B  3031
M97                                      NIGEL MARTINEZ                                M97
    NIGEL MARTINEZ        (A     (A) BETTER THINGS TO COME    1978 STATE         UK    ETAT  17
M98                                      MARVELETTES                                   M98
    WANDA YOUNG        V   (     (A)PLEASE MR POSTMAN         1961 TAMLA  US TS 228
    KATHERIN SCHAFFNER V   (     (B) MARVELETTES SING         196  TAMLA  US TS 229
    ANN BOGAN          V   (     (C) PLAYBOY                  1963 TAMLA  US TS 231
    GLADYS HORTON      V   (     (D) MARVELOUS MARVELETTES    1963 TAMLA  US TS 237  UK 65  STML11008
    GEORGEANNA TILLMAN V   (     (E) LIVE ON STAGE            196  TAMLA  US TS 243
    KATHY ANDERSON     V   (     (F) GREATEST HITS            196  TAMLA  US TS 253
    JUANITA COWART     V   (     (G) MARVELETTES              1967 TAMLA  US TS 274  UK 67  STML11052
                                 (H) SOPHISTICATED SOUL       1968 TAMLA  US TS 286  UK 69  STML11090
                                 (I) IN FULL BLOOM            1970 TAMLA  US TS 288  UK     STML11145
                                 (J) RETURN OF THE MARVELETTES 197 TAMLA  US TS 305
                                 (K) BEST OF                  1975 TAMLA            UK     STML11258
                                 (L) ANTHOLOGY                197  TAMLA  US M7 827
M99                              BRETT MARVIN & THE THUNDERBOLTS                       M99
    GRAHAM HINE       G V  (AB   (A) BRETT MARVIN & THE THUNDERBOLTS 1970 SONET UK SNTF 616 METRONOME 15380
    DAVE ARNOT        D    (A    (B) 12 INCHES OF             1971 SONET         UK   SNTF  619
    JIM PITTS  G V HCA    (AB    (C) BEST OF FRIENDS          1971 SONET         UK   SNTF  620
    PETE GIBSON PERC V TROM(AB   (D) ALIAS TERRY DACTYL       1972 SONET         UK   SNTF  630
    JOHN LEWIS        K V  (AB   (E) TEN LEGGED FRIEND        1973 SONET         UK   SNTF  651
    KEITH TRUSSELL   PERC  (AB   (F) BRETT MARVIN             19   BARCLAY       FR   920 242
    BIG JOHN RANDALL PERC (AB
    DAVE ELLIS        G    (B
M100                          HANK MARVIN   & (MARVIN WELCH & FARRAH)                 M100
    HANK MARVIN      G V B(ALL   (A) HANK MARVIN              1969 COLUMBIA      UK   SCX 6352
    BRUCE WELCH      G V  (BCD   (B) MARVIN WELCH & FARRAR    1971 REGAL ZONO UK 8502 US CAPITOL 760
    JOHN FARRAR     G V B(BCD    (B) MARVIN WELCH & FARRAR    1971 EMI  NL 04715
    FRANK RICOTTI   PERC  (E     (C) SECOND OPINION           1971 REGAL ZONO UK 8504 US SIRE  7403
    HERBIE FLOWERS   B    (E     (C) SECOND OPINION           1971 EMI  GER 04894
    BRIAN BENNETT    D PERC(CD   (D) MARVIN & FARRAR          1973 EMI  UK  EMA 755 US CAPITOL11403
    DAVE RICHMOND    B    (C     (E) GUITAR SYNDICATE         1977 EMI  UK  EMC3215
    AL HAWKSHAW      K    (C
    JOHNNY VAN DERRICK FDL (C  OLIVIA NEWTON JOHN REC (D   TREVOR SPENCER   D PERC(D  ALAN TARNEY     B  (D
    ALAN PARKER      G    (E     KEVIN PEEK      G   (E    PAUL KEOGH       G    (E  ALAN SPARKES    G  (E
    LES THATCHER     G    (E     VIC FLICK       G   (E    COLIN GREEN      G    (E  RICKIE HITCHCOCK G (E
    CHRIS REA             (E     CLEM CATTINI    D   (E
M100A                                   MARZ & EPERJESSY                              M100A
                                 (A) MARZ & EPERJESSY         1971 BELLAPHON          BLPS19072
M100B                                    CAROLYNE MAS                                 M100B
    CAROLYNE MAS          (AB    (A) CAROLYNE MAS             1979 MERCURY UK 9100 068 US 3783
    CRISPIN CIDE     SAX  (B     (B) HOLD ON                  1980 MERCURY UK 6337 105 US 3841
    DAVID LANDAU     G    (B     (C) MODERN DREAM             1981 MERCURY             US 4022
    CHARLIE GIORDANO K    (B
    BOBBY CHOUINARD  D    (B
                                        MASCARA                                       M100C
M100C                            (A) DESOLATED WORLD (EP)     19   OPTIMISTIC         OPT 006
M100D                                   MASHMAKHAN                                    M100D
    PIERRE SENECAL  K WIND G V(AB (A) MASHMAKHAN              1969 CBS           US   30 365
    RAYBURN BLAKE   G V  (AB     (B) THE FAMILY               197  EPIC          US   30813
    BRIAN EDWARDS   B V  (AB
    JERRY MERCER    D V  (AB
```

MASKED MARAUDERS

(A) THE MASKED MARAUDERS   1969 REPRISE   US   6378

**REPORTED BY ROLLING STONE MAGAZINE THAT BOB DYLAN, LENNON & McCARTNEY GEORGE HARRISON AND MICK JAGGER WAS
INCLUDED IN THE LINE UP BUT WAS IN FACT 'THE GOODLINESS & CLEANLINESS SKIFFLE BAND' DOING IMITATIONS OF THEM

JIMMIE LEE MASLON

JIMMIE LEE MASLON   (A   (A) YOUR WILDCAT WAYS   1981 RONDELET   ABOUT 1003

DAVE MASON

DAVE MASON	G V (ALL	(A) ALONE TOGETHER	1970 HARVEST	UK SHTC251	UK	ABC 197	5191		
LEON RUSSELL	K (A	(A) ALONE TOGETHER	1975 BLUE THUMB	US BTS 29	+	BT	8819		
JIM CAPALDI	D (A	(B) DAVE MASON & CASS ELLIOT	1971 PROBE	UK 6259	US BLUE THUMB	8825			
JOHN SIMON	(A	(C) HEADKEEPER	1072 BLUE THUMB	UK ILPS9203 US		BTS 34			
JIM KELTNER	D (A	(C) HEADKEEPER	1973 ABC RI	UK ABCL5189					
JIM GORDON	D (AF	(D) IS ALIVE	1972 BLUE THUMB		US	BTS 54			
CHRIS ETHRIDGE	(A	(E) SCRAPBOOK	1972 ISLAND	UK ICD 5					
CARL RADLE	B (A	(F) IT'S LIKE YOU NEVER LEFT	1974 CBS	US 31721		UK 65258			
LARRY KNECHTEL	(A	(G) BEST OF	1974 BLUE THUMB BTSD6013						
MICK DE TEMPLE	(A	(H) DAVE MASON	1975 CBS	US 33096		UK 80360			
JOHN BARBATA	D (A	(J) SPLIT COCONUT	1975 CBS	US 33698		UK 69163			
DELANEY BRAMLETT	G V (A	(K) AT HIS BEST	1975 ABC	US TD880	UK	ABCL5122			
BONNIE BRAMLETT	V (A	(L) CERTIFIED LIVE	1976 CBS	US 34174		UK 88293			
CLAUDIA LENNEAR	V (A	(M) LET IT FLOW	1977 CBS	US 34680		UK 81984			
RITA COOLIDGE	V (AC	(N) MARIPOSA DE ORO	1978 CBS	US 35285		UK 82625			
GERRY BECKLEY	V (N	(O) VERY BEST OF	1979 BLUE THUMB 6032						
JACK STORTI	(A	(P) OLD CREST ON A NEW WAVE	1980 CBS	US 36144	UK	83828			
JERRY WILLIAMS	G (A	(Q) BEST OF	1981 CBS	US 37089					
LOU COOPER	(A								

CASS ELLIOT	V (B	MIKE COOLIDGE	(A	MARK JORDAN	K (CJ	BOB NORWOOD	(A			
LONNIE TURNER	B (CF	RICK JAEGER	D (CFHJPN	FELIX FLACO FALCON	PERC (C	SPENCER DAVIS	V (C			
GRAHAM NASH	V G (CJN	KATHY McDONALD	V (C	JIM KRUEGER	G (HJLMPN	CHUCK RAINEY	B (F			
ROCKY DZIDZORNU	PERC (F	MAXINE WILLARD	V (F	CLYDIE KING	V (F	JULIA TILLMAN	V (F			
KATHLEEN SAROYAN	V (F	SON OF HARRY	G (F	CHARLES FLETCHER	B (F	GREG REEVES	B (F			
JOHN BATDORF	V (F	STEVE MADAIO	HRNS (F	DENNIS MOROUSE	HRNS (F	NORMA BELL	HRNS(F			
STEVIE WONDER	HCA (F	NASTYEE	(F	MIKE FINNIGAN	K V (HLMPN	BOB GLAUB	B (HNP			
GARY BARONE	HRNS (H	JERRY JUMONVILLE	HRNS (H	JOCK ELLIS	HRNS (H	SAL MARQUEZ	HRNS(H			
TIM WEISBERG	FLT (H	EMIL RICHARDS	PERC (J	DAVID CROSBY	V (J	GERALD JOHNSON	(LJMN			
JAI WINDING	K (J	MANHATTAN TRANSFER	V (J	DON PRESTON	(A	STEPHEN STILLS	V (MN			
YVONNE ELLIMAN	V (M	ERNIE WATTS	SAX (MN	BOBBYE HALL	PERC (M	BROOKS HUNNICUTT	V (M			
VERNA RICHARDSON	V (M	KAREN PATTERSON	V (M	BRYAN GAROFALO	B (B	RUSS KUNKEL	D PERC(B			
PAUL HARRIS	K (M	MICHAEL JACKSON	V (P.	RAY REVIS	PERC (P.	MARK STEIN	K V (NP			
RON GREENE	PERC (N	JEFF PORCARO	D (N	JOHN SAMBARATO	V (N	JOE WISSERT PROD	(P			

HARVEY MASON

HARVEY MASON	D (ALL	(A) MARCHING IN THE STREETS	1976 ARISTA	US 4054			
JAN HAMMER	K (B	(B) EARTHMOVER	1976 ARISTA	US 4096			
GREG ADAMS	HRNS (C	(C) FUNK IN A MASON JAR	1977 ARISTA	US 4157 UK SPART 1049			
DOROTHY ASHBY	(C	(D) GROOVIN' YOU	1979 ARISTA	US 4227 UK ARTY 166			
STANLEY BANKS	B (C	(E) WORLD CLASS	1981 ARISTA	US 4283			
WILFREDOWILSON	(D						

GEORGE BENSON	G V (C	EMILIO CASTILLO	HRNS (C	MERRY CLAYTON	V (C	JORGE DALTO	K (C			
BOB JAMES	K (CD	KENNY MASON	TPT (CD	AL McKAY	G (C	RAY PARKER	G (CD			
MIKE PORCARO	B (CD	TOM SCOTT	HRNS (C	TOWER OF POWER	HRNS (C	CHARLES VEAL	VLN(CD			
MAXINE WILLARD	V (AB	VANETTA FIELDS	V (C	CHUCK FINDLEY	HRNS (C	DAVID FOSTER	B (CD			
RONNIE FOSTER	K (CD	MIC GILLETTE	HRNS (C	LOUIS JOHNSON	B (C	MARVIN MASON	(C			
PAULETTE McWILLIAMS	V (C	JERRY PETERS	K (ACD	LEE RITENOUR	G (ACD	IAN UNDERWOOD	(C			
DAVID T WALKER	G (C	BILL WATRONS	TROM (C	LARRY WILLIAMS	WIND (C	BILL CHAMPLIN	V (D			
TONY DUMAS	(C	GARY GRANT	HRNS (C	JAY GRAYDON	G (CD	DAVE GRUSIN	K (AC			
JERRY HEY	HRNS (C	KIM HUTCHCROFT	V (C	DICK HYDE	HRNS (C	ANTHONY JACKSON	B (C			
HOPPY MASON	(CD	RALPH McDONALD	PERC (CD	DAVID PAICH	K (C	LENNY PICKETT	HRNS(C			
SEAWIND	HRNS (C	STEPHANIE SPRUILL	V (CD	PHIL UPCHURCH	G (CD	JULIA TILLMAN	V (AC			
NATE WATTS	B (C	ART WILSON	(C	PETER CHAIKIN	(D	SHEILA ESCOVEDO	(C			
JAMES GILSTRAP	V (AD	BUNNY HULL	(D	ROGER ST KENNERLY	V (D	PHIL MOORE	(C			
RICHARD TEE	K (D	JERRY WHITMAN	V (D	JAI WINDING	PNO (D	JIM HAAS	V (D			
NEIL JASON	V B (D	STEVE LUKATHER	G (D	DAVID SHIELDS	B (D	RANDY WALDMAN	(D			
DAVID WILLIAMS	D (D	BOB WERTZ	(DA	RON HICKLIN	(D	MORRIS PAUL KENNEDY	(D			
BILL MEYERS	(D	DAVID SPINOZZA	D (D	WAH WAH WATSON	G (D	CHUCK RAINEY	B (A			
OSCAR BRASHEAR	TPT (A	ERNIE WATTS	SAX (A	GEORGE BOHANNON	TROM (A	BLUE MITCHELL	TPT (A			
RANDY CRAWFORD	V (A	HUBERT LAWS FLT	(A	HERBIE HANCOCK	K (A	PAUL JACKSON	B (A			
BENNY MAUPIN	SAX (A	FRANK ROSOLINO	TROM (A	MELVIN RAGIN	G (A	BOBBY BRYANT	TPT (A			

JAE MASON

JAE MASON	(A	(A) CROSSROADS	196 BUDDAH	US	BDS5604
		(B) TENDERMAN	196 BUDDAH	US	BDS5640

MASON - PROFFIT

JOHN TALBOT	G V (ALL	(A) MASON PROFFIT WANTED	1969 HAPPY TIGER	US	1009
TERRY TALBOT	G V (ALL	(B) MOVING TOWARDS HAPPINESS	1970 HAPPY TIGER	US	1019
TIM AYERS	B (ALL	(AB) COME & GONE (DBL)	1974 WB US 2746 RI LINE GER 8002		
BRUCE KURNOW	K HCA(DE	(C) LAST NIGHT I HAD STRANGEST DREAM	1971 AMPEX US 10138		
BYRON BERLINE	VLN (	(D) ROCKFISH CROSSING	1972 WB US 2657 RI LINE GER 5065		
BILL CUNNINGHAM	FDL G V(E	(E) BAREBACK RIDER	1973 WB US 2704 RI LINE GER 5061		
ART NASH	D (ALL				
RON SCHUETTER	G V (ABC				
RICK DWETT	PNO (A	JOHN FRIGO FDL (A KINKY SCHNITZNER G (E			
TOM RADTRE	PERC (E				

MASON,WOOD,CAPALDI & FROG

DAVE MASON   G B V(A   CHRIS WOOD   WIND (A   JIM CAPALDI   D V (A   MICK WEAVER   K(A

MASQUERADERS

(A) EVERYBODY WANNA LIVE ON	1976 ABC		US ABCD921
(B) LOVE ANONYMOUS	1977 ABC UK ABCL5222		US ABC 962

```
M102E                          NICK MASON                              M102E
   NICK MASON         (A      (A) FICTITIOUS SPORTS    1981 HARVEST UK SHSP4116 CBS US 37307
   ROBERT WYATT     V (A      (A) FICTITIOUS SPORTS    1981 CBS US 37307
   KAREN KRAFT      V (A
   CHRIS SPEDDING   G (A  CARLA BLEY      K  (A  GARY WINDO   WIND (A  GARY VALENTINE  TROM V(A
   MIKE MANTLER     TPT (A HOWARD JOHNSON TUBA (A  STEVE SWALLOW  B  (A  TERRY ADAMS    K HCA(A
   CARLOS WARD      V (A  D SHARP         V  (A  EARL McINTYRE  V  (A  VINCENT CHANCEY V (A
M102F                          MASSACRE                                M102F
   FRED FRITH       G V K(A   (A) KILLING TIME         1981    CELLULOID FR 6597 GER 802 272
   FRED MAHER       D (A
   BILL LASWELL     TPT (A
M103                           MASS PRODUCTION                         M103
                            (A) WELCOME TO OUR WORLD   1977 COTILLION  UK K 50331  US SD9910
                            (B) BELIEVE                1977 COTILLION  UK K 50400  US SD9918
                            (C) THREE MILES HIGH       1978 COTILLION  UK K 50510  US SD5205
                            (D) IN THE PUREST FORM     1979 COTILLION  UK K 50601  US SD5211
                            (E) MASTERPIECE            1980 COTILLION              US    5218
                            (F) GIRLS ALRIGHT WITH ME  1980 WHITFIELD              US    3389
                            (G) TURN UP THE MUSIC      1981 COTILLION  UK K 50784
                            (H) IN A CITY GROOVE       1982 COTILLION  UK K 50877
M103A                          MASTERS                                 M103A
   JIMMY BERICK     G V (A    (A) MASTERS OF THE AIRWAVES  1974 EPIC    UK X598    US 33060
   RANDY RAND       B G (A
   DAVE RADA        D V (A  JON FLAK      V  (A
M103B                          MASTERS APPRENTICES                     M103B
   DOUG FORD        G V (AB   (A) MASTERS APPRENTICES    197
   JAMES KEAYS      V (A      (B) A TOAST TO PANAMA RED 197
   COLIN BURGESS    D V (
   GLENN WHEATLEY   B V (A
M105                           MATCHBOX                                M105
   BOB BURGOS       D (       (A) SETTIN' THE WOODS ON FIRE  1978  CHISWICK  UK    WIK 10
   GRAHAM FENTON    V (       (B) RIDERS IN THE SKY         1978  CHARLY    UK CR 30157
   FRED POKE        B (       (C) MATCHBOX                  1979  MAGNET    UK MAGL5031
   GORDON WATERS    G V (     (D) MIDNIGHT DYNAMO           1980 MAGNET  US  5036
   STEVE BLOOMFIELD G MAND(
   JIMMY REDHEAD    D (
M105A                          MATERIAL                                M105A
   FRED MAHER       F D (BC   (A) TEMPORARY MUSIC        19
   MICHAEL BEINHORN K SYN (BC (B) TEMPORARY MUSIC 2      1980 RED     12 008
   BILL LASWELL     B (BC     (C) TEMPORARY MUSIC (COMP) 198 CELLULOID FR 6576
   CLIFF CULTRERI   G (C
   DON DAVIS        SAX (C
M106                           MATCHING MOLE                           M106
   ROBERT WYATT     D V (AB   (A) MATCHING MOLE          1972  CBS              UK     64850
   PHIL MILLER      K G (AB   (B) LITTLE RED RECORD      1973  CBS   US 32148  UK     65260
   BILL MACCORMICK  B (AB
   DAVE MACRAE      K (AB  ENO            SYN (B  DAVE SINCLAIR  K (A  DAVE GALE      V  (B
   RUBY CRYSTAL     V (B  LITTLE HONEST INJUN V (B
M106A                          ANDREW MATHESON                         M106A
   ANDREW MATHESON  V (A      (A) MONTEREY SHOES        1979 ARIOLA            ARL 5025
   PETE KIRCHER     D (A
   ANDY PASK        B (A  RAPHAEL RAVENSCROFT   SAX (A  TOMMY EYRE   K  (A  NIGEL JENKINS   G (A
   EUNON S BRADY    G (A  HOWIE CASEY           SAX (A  BILL STREET  HRNS (A
M106B                          MATRIX                                  M106B
   NICK ZESSES      (A        (A) MATRIX               1972 RARE EARTH       US  R542L
   DINO FEKARIS     (A
   TOM BAIRD        (A
M106C                          MATRIX  (2)                             M106C
   LARRY DARLING    HRNS SYN V(A  (A) THE WIZARD       1978 WB         US      3260
   KURT DIETRICH    HRNS SYN V(A
   MIKE HALE        HRNS D V(A  JOHN HARMAN   K PERC   (A  JOHN KIRCHBERGER  WIND (A  BRAD McDOUGAL HRNS V(A
   MIKE MURPHY      D PERC(A  JEFF PIETRANGELO  HRNS PERC(A
M107                           DAVE MATTHEWS                           M107
   DAVE MATTHEWS    K (AB      (A) SHOOGIE WANNA BOOGIE  1976 KUDU              KU 30
   DON GROLNICK     K (A       (B) DUNE                  1977 CTI                 5005
   ANDY NEWMARK     D (AB
   BARRY MILES      K (A  JERRY FRIEDMAN     G (A  STEVE KHAN     G (A  ANTHONY JACKSON   B (A
   SUE EVANS        PERC (AB RANDY BRECKER   TPT (AB JON FADDIS   TPT (AB MICHAEL BRECKER SAX (A
   RON CUBER        SAX (A  BURT COLLINS     TPT (AB ALAN RUBIN   TPT (A  JOE SHEPLEY     TPT (AB
   TOM MALONE       TROM (AB SAM BURTIS     TROM (AB DAVE TAYLOR  TROM (AB PATTI AUSTIN    V (A
   VIVIAN CHERRY    V (A  GWEN GUTHRIE       V (A  JIM BUFFINGTON HRNS (A  PETER GORDON   HRNS(A
   JOE FARRELL      SAX (A  FRED WESLEY     TROM (A  LANCE QUINN    G (A  JOHN TROPEA     G (A
   CARLOS MARTIN    PERC (A  KEN ASCHER      K (A  WILL LEE       B (A  NICKY MARRERO   PERC(A
   PAT REBILLOT     K (A  JEFF BERLIN        B (A  CLIFF CARTER   K (B  MARK EGAN        B (B
   GARY KING        B (B  JIM BOSBY         HRNS (B  JOHN GATCHELL  HRNS (B  LEW SOLOFF    HRNS(B
   STEVE GADD       D (B  HIRAM BULLOCK      G (B  ERIC GALE      G (B  GORDON GOTTLIEB PERC(B
   WAYNE ANDRE      TROM (B  GERRY CHAMBERLAIN TROM (B DAVID SANBORN SAX (B  GROVER WASHINGTON SAX(B
   LEW DEL GATTO    WIND (B  DAVID TOFANI    WIND (B  GOOGIE COPPOLA V (B  SANFORD ALLEN STRINGS(B
```

[373]

```
IAN MATTHEWS      G V  (ALL    (A) MATTHEWS SOUTHERN COMFORT  1970 UNI  UNLS108    MCA UK MAPS 1641
ROGER COULAM      K    (AC     (A) "    "     "             1974 MCA RI MCF2675    US DECCA 75191
SIMON NICOL       G    (A      (B) SECOND SPRING            1970 UNI  UNLS112    MCA UK MAPS 2038
ANDY LEIGH        B V  (BC     (B) "    "     "             1974 MCA RI MCF2677    US DECCA 75242
CARL BARNWELL     G V  (BC3    (B) "    "     "             197  UNI  FR 6369 600
KEITH NELSON      BANJO(C      (C) LATER THAT SAME YEAR     1970 MCA MKPS2015       MAPS3976
CAL BATCHELOR     G    (E      (C) "    "     "             1974 MCA MCF2686
BRUCE THOMAS      B    (E      (C) "    "     "  DIFF TRACKS 197  DECCA US 75264    PICKWICK CAN 3698
BILLY GRAHAM      B FDL(FG     (D) IF YOU SAW THROUGH MY EYES 1971 VERTIGO US VEL1002  UK 6360 034
MICHAEL NESMITH   G    (F      (E) TIGERS WILL SURVIVE      1972 VERTIGO US VEL1010  UK 6360 056
BYRON BERLINE     FDL  (F      (E) "    "     "  (POP LEGEND) 1980 VERTIGO         NL 9199 139
JEFF BAXTER       G    (G      (F) VALLEY HI                1973 ELEKTRA US EKS75061  UK K42144
DANNY WEIS        G    (G      (G) SOME DAYS YOU EAT THE BEAR.... 1974 ELEKTRA US EKS75078  UK K42160
B J COLE          STEEL(G      (H) JOURNEYS FROM GOSPEL OAK 1974 MOONCREST          UK CREST18
JERRY DONAHUE     G    (H      (H) "    "     "    "        1979 BOULEVARD          BD 3009
MIKE PORTER       D    (J      (J) GO FOR BROKE             1976 CBS    US  34102   UK 81316
KENNY EDWARDS     B    (J      (K) HIT & RUN                1977 CBS    US  34671   UK 81930
PETER WOOD        K    (J      (L) STEALIN' HOME            1978 ROCKBURGH          UK ROC106
SHANE KEISTER     K    (J      (L) "    "     "             1978 MUSHROOM           MRS 5012
MUSCLE SHOALS     HRNS (J      (M) SIAMESE FRIENDS          1979 ROCKBURGH          UK ROC107
BONNIE MURRAY     V    (K      (N) SHAKE IT (12" EP)        1978 ROCKBURGH          UK ROCS209
MICK WEAVER       K    (1M     (O) SPOT OF INTERFERENCE     1980 ROCKBURGH US 3092  UK 2383582
PETE WINGFIELD    K    (LN     ( ) BEST OF MATTHEWS SOUTHERN COMFORT 1975 MCA NL 201362  UK MCF2574
SIMON MORTON      PERC (LMN    (1) 1978 TOUR  (2) 1979 FEB TOUR  (3) 1970 LIVE
BOB METZGER       K    (2MO    (P) DISCREET REPEAT (DBL)    1979 ROCKBURGH          UK 109
WOLFE J FLYWHEEL  ACC  (E      (ABC) 1 2 3 TOO GOOD DBL     1970 MCA GER MAPS 7290D1/2
GERRY CONWAY      D    (AD
ASHLEY HUTCHINGS  B    (A
RICHARD THOMPSON  G    (AD  GORDON HUNTLEY STEEL(ABC3  PETE WILLSHER   G   (A   DOLLY COLLINS   K   (A
POLI PALMER       FKT  (A   RAY DUFFY        D   (BC  MARK GRIFFITHS B G V(123BCMO TOM PALEY  BAN (B
ROGER CHURCHYARD  FDL  (B   MARTIN JENKINS   MAND (B   TRISTRAM FRY   VIBES(C   PAT DONALDSON   B   (DH
TIM RENWICK       G    (DE  ANDY ROBERTS     G   (DEGH SANDY DENNY    K V (D   TIMI DONALD     D   (EGH
WILLIE WILSON     D    (E   IAN WHITEMAN     K   (E   BOB RONGA      K B (E   RAY WARLEIGH    SAX (E
DANNY LANE        D    (FG  JAY LACY         G   (FGJK BOBBY WARFORD  G   (FG  RED RHODES      STEEL(F
DAVID BARRY       K    (FG  WILLIE LEACOX    D   (G   DAVID DICKEY   B   (G   MICHAEL FONFARA K   (G
STEVE GILLETTE    G    (G   JOEL TEPP  HCA G (12GJM LYN DOBSON       SAX (G   AL GARTH        SAX (G
DAVID LINDLEY     STEEL(G   TRIS IMBODEN     D   (JK  KENNY BUTTREY  D   (J   DON WHALEY      B   (JK
NORBERT PUTNAM    B    (J   MIKE LEECH       B   (J   STEVE WOOD     K   (J   DAVID BRIGGS    K   (J
GLEN SPREEN       K    (LN  REG YOUNG        G   (J   HARRY ROBINSON G   (J   STEVE HOOKS     WIND(K
CHARLIE HARWOOD   K V  (K   PHIL PALMER      G   (1LN JIM RUSSELL    D   (1LMN BRYN HAWORTH   G MAND(LN
RICK KEMP         B    (LN  MEL COLLINS      SAX (LMN DUFFY POWER    HCA (L   PETER WATKINS   B   (3
ROGER SWALLOW     D    (3   CRAIG BUHLER     SAX (M   DAVE WINTOUR   B   (O   ROBERT HENRIT   D   (O
KEITH TIPPETT     K    (D   MARC ELLINGTON   PERC (A
```

MILT MATTHEWS INC
```
M108A                                                                                  M108A
MILT MATTHEWS         (A   (A) MILT MATTHEWS INC           1971  EMBER              NR 5056
NORMAN HARRISON  K   (A
RANDY B WINGY    G   (A   TOMMY BYRD      D   (A   CARL MATTHEWS   B   (A
```

MATUMBI
```
M109                                                                                   M109
DENNIS BOVELL    V G K(BC   (A) BEST OF MATUMBI             1977  TROJAN          TRLS  145
BEVIN FAGAN      B V  (ABC  (B) SEVEN SEALS                1978  HARVEST         SHSP 4090
EUTON JONES      PERC (ABC  (C) POINT OF VIEW              1979  M R  RDC  2001  US EMI 17034
GLAISTER VENN    V    (ABC  (D) AH WHO SEH ? GO GO DEH!    197   RAMA            R
EATON BLAKE      B    (ABC
LLOYD DONALDSON  D    (ABC  WEBSTER JOHNSON  K V (ABC PATRICK TENYUE  HRNS (C  HENRY TENYUE   HRNS  (C
NICK STRAKER     K    (C    ANDY            G   (C   JULIO FINN     HCA (C
```

CHARLIE MAUCHER
```
M109A                                                                                  M109A
CHARLIE MAUCHER  V G B(A    (A) PERFORMANCE                1980  CM      GER  1111
ULI BOTTCHER     G    (A
WOLFGANG KRANTZ  K    (A    PETER PANKA  D PERC(A
```

MAUDS
```
M109B                                                                                  M109B
J ROGERS             (A    (A) HOLD ON                     1967  MERCURY          61135
B WINTER             (A
F FUSCALDO           (A    T CONIGLIO      (A   P WEINBERG      (A
```

BENNIE MAUPIN
```
M110                                                                                   M110
BENNIE MAUPIN    SAX  (ALL  (A) THE JEWEL IN THE LOTUS     1975  ECM             ECM1043
                           (B) MOONSCAPES                 1978  MERCURY
                           (C) SLOW TRAFFIC TO THE RIGHT  197   MERCURY US       SRMI1148
                           (D) AKMANAC                    1978  IMPROVISING     IAI373851
```

JOHN MAYALL & THE BLUESBREAKERS
```
M111                                                                                   M111
JOHN MAYALL G V HCA K (ALL  OA) JOHN MAYALL PLAYS JOHN MAYALL 1964 DECCA  UK LK 4680
JOHN McVIE       B    (ABCDL.Oak (B) BLUESBREAKERS         1965 DECCA  UK SLK4804   US  LONDON PS492
KEITH TILLMAN    B    (GH   (B) BLUESBREAKERS              1965 DECCA  GER           SLK 16547
MICK FLEETWOOD   D    (LO   (C) A HARD ROAD                1967 DECCA  UK SKL4853   US  LONDON PS502
PETE WARD        D    (C    (C) A HARD ROAD                196  DECCA  GER           SLK 16490
HENRY LOWTHER    TPT  (LJOa (BC) BLUESBREAKERS/HARD ROAD(DBL) 19  DECCA  GER         3027
CHRIS MERCER     SAX  (DGHOa (D) CRUSADE                   1967 DECCA  UK SKL4890   US  LONDON PS529
HUGHIE FLINT     D    (BCDLa1 (D) CRUSADE                  196  GER                  SLK 16499
JON HISEMAN      D    (Ja   (E) BLUES ALONE                1967 ACE    UK SCL1243   US  LONDON PS534
ERIC CLAPTON     G    (BOXdp (F) RAW BLUES                 1967 ACE    UK SCL1220   US  LONDON PS543
DICK HECKSTALL SMITH SAX(GHJOa (EP)WITH PAUL BUTTERFIELD   1967 DECCA  UK DFE8673
JIMMY McCULLOCH  G    (Oa   (G) DIARY OF A BAND VOL 1      1968 DECCA  UK SKL4918   GER  SLK 16543
PAUL WILLIAMS    B    (Oa   (H) DIARY OF A BAND VOL 2      1968 DECCA  UK SKL4919
COLIN ALLEN      D    (K    (GH) DIARY OF A BAND VOL 1/2   1970              US  LONDON PS570
JOHNNY ALMOND    SAX  (BCPQOXk (I) BLUES GIANT             1968 DECCA  IMP         3117
ALEX DMOCHOWSKI  B    (k    (J) BARE WIRES                 1968 DECCA  UK SKL4945   US  LONDON PS537
HARVEY MANDEL    G    (RXY  (J) BARE WIRES                 1968 DECCA  GER          SLK 16558
PAUL LAGOS       D    (X    (K) LAUREL CANYON              1969 DECCA  UK SKL4972   US  LONDON PS545
AYNSLEY DUNBAR   D    (CLOa (K) LAUREL CANYON              196  DECCA  GER SLK16573 GER NOVA 6 21413
BERNIE WATSON    G    (OLa  (L) SO MANY ROADS              1969 DECCA  GER SLK16590 GER RI 6835 132
ANDY FRASER      B    (     (M) LIVE                       1969 DECCA  GER          SLK 16615
```

(CONTINUED)

```
    KEEF HATYLEY         D    (GHOEXabce3   (N) BEST OF JOHN MAYALL          1969 DECCA   GER                SLK 16632
    ROGER DEAN           G    (ALOa         (O) LOOKING BACK                 1970 DECCA   UK SKL5010  US     LONDON PS562
    JACK BRUCE           B    (01           (O) LOOKING BACK (DIFF TRACKS)   1969 DECCA   GER 3104 1/2
    MICK TAYLOR          G    (DGHJKOQXad   (P) TURNING POINT                1970 POLYDOR UK 583 571   US     PD 4004
    TONY REEVES          B    (Ja           (P) TURNING POINT                1982 POLYDOR RI UK 2485 222 GER 2459 355
    RIP KANT             HRNS (DO           (Q) EMPTY ROOMS                  1970 POLYDOR UK 583 580   US          4010
    JEFF KRIBBETT        G    (1            (Q) EMPTY ROOMS                  19   POLYDOR GER 2425 051
    PETER GREEN          G    (CLOadK       (PQ)TURNING POINT/EMPTY ROOMS    1974 POLYDOR UK 2683 039
    STEVE THOMPSON       B    (KPQX6nr      (R) USA UNION                    1970 POLYDOR UK 2425 020  US          4022
    JON MARK             ACC G(PQk          (S) LIVE IN EUROPE               1970 LONDON              US     PS5589
    LARRY TAYLOR         B    (RWXZbghik3Qm (T) WORLD OF VOL1                1970 DECCA   UK SPA 47
    DON SUGARCANE HARRIS VLN(RXehik         (U) WORLD OF VOL2                1971 DECCA   UK SPA 138
    JERRY McGEE          G    (WX           (V) DOWN THE LINE                1972 LONDON              US     PS618/9
    BLUE MITCHELL        TPT  (Zbek         (W) MEMORIES                     1971 POLYDOR UK 2425 085  US          5012
    CLIFFORD SOLOMON     SAX  (Zb           (X) BACK TO THE ROOTS            1971 POLYDOR UK 2657 005  US          3002
    RON SELICO           D    (Z            (X) BACK TO THE ROOTS            1971 POLYDOR FR 2673 003
    FREDDY ROBINSON      G V  (Zbe          (Y) BEYOND THE TURNING POINT     1971 POLYDOR UK 2483 016
    VICTOR GASKIN        B    (be           (Z) JAZZ BLUES FUSION            1972 POLYDOR UK 2425 103  US     PD 5027
    RED HOLLOWAY         SAX  (egkm         (Z) JAZZ BLUES UNION             19   POLYDOR GER 2391 032
    ERNIE WATTS          SAX  (b            (a) THROUGH THE YEARS            1971 DECCA   UK SKL5086   US LONDON PS600/1
    CHARLES OWENS        SAX  (b            (b) MOVING ON                    1973 POLYDOR UK 2391 047  US     PD 5036
    HIGHTIDE HARRIS      G    (g            (c) BEST OF                      197  POLYDOR              US     PD 23006
    SOKO RICHARDSON      D    (ghik56nrv    (d) JOHN MAYALL PROFILE          197  TELDEC  GER              624010
    RANDY RESNICK        G    (g            (e) TEN YEARS ARE GONE           1973 POLYDOR UK 2683 036  US     PD 3005
    DEE McKINNIE         V    (hik          (f) STAR PORTAIT                 1973 POLYDOR IMP 2675019
    NOLAN SMITH          TPT  (4m           (f) POP HISTORY                  1973 POLYDOR IMP 2675017
    ANN PATERSON         WIND (4mn          (g) LATEST EDITION               1975 POLYDOR UK 2391 141  US     PD 6030
    JIMMY ROBERTS        SAX  (4m           (h) NEW YEAR NEW BAND NEW COMPANY 1975 ABC     UK ABCL5115  US          6019
    BILL LAMB            TPT  (4m           (i) NOTICE TO APPEAR             1975 ABC     UK ABCL5142  US     ABCD 926
    WARREN BRYANT        PERC (4m           (i) NOTICE TO APPEAR             1975 ABC     GER 25237
    DAVID LI             SAX  (4m           (j) JOHN MAYALL                  1976 POLYDOR UK 2482 272
    FRANK WILSON         D    (4m           (k) BANQUET IN BLUES             1976 UK      UK ABCL5187  US     ABCD 958
    EDMOND LEE           B    (5            (m) LOTS OF PEOPLE               1977 ABC     UK ABCL5126  US     ABCD 992
    BRAD THOELKE         TROM (tn           (n) A HARD CORE PACKAGE          1977 ABC                  US     ABCD 1039
    JESSE ED DAVIS       G    (             (p) PRIMAL SOLOS                 1977 LONDON              US     LC 50003
    ALLAN TOUSSAINT      K    (i            ( ) HIGHLIGHTS                   1977 POLYDOR GER 2674 013
    RICK VITO            G    (hikt         (q) BLUES ROOTS                  1978 DECCA   UK ROOTS 8
    JAY SPELL            K    (hikm         (r) LAST OF THE BRITISH BLUES    1978 ABC                  US     ABCD 1086
    LARRY BLOUIN         SAX  (i            (s) BOTTOM LINE                  1979 DJM     UK DJF20556  US 23 GER 64216
    LON PRICE            WIND (i            (t) NO MORE INTERVIEWS           1979 DJM     UK DJF20564  US 29 GER 63537
    NICK MESSINA         TPT  (i            (v) ROAD SHOW BLUES                   DJM                      GER 64231
    HERMAN ERNEST        D    (i            ( ) BLUESBREAKERS BOX SET (12LP) 1981 TELDEC                   GER 30122
    JAMES CARROLL BOOKER K    (i            ( ) ROOM TO MOVE                 19   MEDIUM 2486041
    TONY BROUSSARD       B    (i            (1) 1969 (2) 1971 (3)1971  (4) 1977   (5) 1977
    KIM JOSEPH           CONGA(i
    STEVE HUGHES         G    (i
    ALAN SKIDMORE        SAX  (BO  DENNIS HEALEY    TPT  (BO  BUCK CLARK     PERC (k  BENNY POWELL    TROM(k
    RONNIE BARRON        K V  (kt  RON McCURDY      D    (k   DOUG BARE      K    (k  MIKE COOLEY     G   (k
    LENNY McDANIEL       B    (k   PHIL DESPOMMIER  D    (k   NOVI NOVAG     VLA  (k  PAT SMITH       V   (m
    PEPPER WATKINS       V(s4mnr    JAMES SMITH     G    (56  LEON PENDARVIS K    (s  BOB BABITT      B   (s
    FRANCISCO CENTENO    B    (s   JEFF MIRANOV     G    (s   SIDNEY McGINNIS G   (s  JOHN TROPEA     G   (s
    STEVE JORDAN         D    (s   ERROL BENNETT    PERC (s   ARTHUR JENKINS PERC (s  ROB MOUNSEY     K   (s
    JON FADDIS           HRNS (s   VERGIL JONES     HRNS (s   STEVE FORMAN   PERC (s  LEE HOLDRIDGE STRING(s
    CHERYL LYNN          V    (s   DELBERT LANGSTON V    (s   ALAN RAPH      TROM (s  HOWARD JOHNSON  HRNS(s
    VIVIAN CHERRY        V    (s   ULLANDA McCULLOUGH V  (s   GORDON EDWARDS B    (s  JANICE PENDARVIS V  (s
    CORNELL DUPREE       G    (s   JEFF LAYTON      G    (s   PAUL SCHAEFFER K    (s  RUBENS BASSINI  PERC(s
    ALEJANDRO ACUNA      PERC (s   JOHN JARVIS      K    (s   JEFF PORCARO   D    (s  STEVE LUKATHER  G   (s
    BEN BENAY            G    (s   RANDY BRECKER    HRNS (s   MICHAEL BRECKER HRNS(s  RON CUBER    WIND   (s
    LEW SOLOFF           TPT  (s   BERNARD KRAUSE   SYN  (s   DAVID SHIELDS  B    (s  TIM DRUMMOND    B   (s
    LEE RITENOUR         G    (s   NIGEL STANGER    SAX  (AL  MARTIN HART    D    (LOa KEVIN NEWELL   SAX (L
    MAGGIE PARKER        V    (t   JAMES QUILL SMITH G (nrtv  CHRIS CAMERON  K    (t  CHRISTIAAN MOSTERT WIND)t
    ANGUS THOMAS         B    (t   RUBIN ALVAREZ    D    (t   BECKIE MORRIS  V    (mnrt BUDDY McDANIELS SAX (tn
    GEORGE SHAW          TPT  (t   RAY WARLEIGH     WIND (t   TONY McPHEE    G    (O  MALCOLM POOL    B   (O
    BILL SHORTT          PERC (O   JACK DUPREE      V    (O   NIGEL STANGER  SAX  (O  GARY ROWLES     (m
    CLIFF ERVIN          TPT  (n   BUDDY McDANIEL   SAX  (n   JODY LINCOTT   PERC (n  JIM PRICE       TROM(n
    TREVOR LAURENCE      SAX  (n   STEVE MADAIO     TPT  (n   MARILYN SCOTT  V    (nr MINDY MICKEL    V   (n
    EDNA RICHARDSON      V    (n   MARTY GWYNN      V    (r   DONNA WASHBURN V    (r  MAUREEN         V   (r
    COLLEEN              V    (r   JUDY BROWN       V         KEVIN McCORMICK B   (v  MAGGIE PARKER   V PERC(v
```

```
M111A                              MAX                                                           M111A
                               (A) MAX                          1980 CHRYSALIS       UK CHR 1278

M112                           MAX WEBSTER                                                       M112
    DAVE MYLES        B V  (DE  (A) MAX WEBSTER                 1975 ANTHEM CAN ANR 1006
    KIM MITCHELL      G V  (DE  (B) HIGH CLASS & BORROWED SHOES 1977 ANTHEM CAN ANR 1007 MERCURY US1160
    TERRY WATKINSON   K V  (ED  (C) MUTINY UP MY SLEEVE         1978 CAPITOL                  11776
    GARY McCRACKEN    D V  (DE  (D) MILLION VACATIONS           1979 CAPITOL                  11937
                               (E) LIVE MAGNETIC AIR           1979 CAPITOL                  12042
                               (F) UNIVERSAL JUVENILES         1980 MERCURY UK 6337 144 US SRM13855
                               (G) HANGOVER                    1977 MERCURY           US     1131

M113                           MAXFIELD PARRISH                                                  M113
    DAVID BIASOTTI        (A    (A) IT'S A CINCH TO GIVE LEGS.... 1972 CURNON        US     CNL 721
    PERRIN MUIR           (A
    DAVID McCLELLAN       (A    RANDY GROENKE      (A  CHRIS DARROW   G    (A  DAVID LINDLEY   FDL V(A
    BERNIE LEADON     G   (A    JOHN LONDON     B  (A  JOHN WARE      D    (A  CHESTER CRILL        (A
M114A                          PHIL MAY                                                          M114A
    PHIL MAY          V   (A    (A) PHIL MAY & THE FALLEN ANGELS 1978 PHILIPS        NL     6410 969
    WALLY WALLER      B V (A
    CHICO GREENWOOD   D   (A    BILLY LOVELADY  G  (A  ED DEAN        G    (A  BRIAN JOHNSTON  K   (
    MICKEY FINN       G   (A    JACK JOHNSTON   K  (A  JOHN POVEY     V    (A  JOHN PORTER     G   (A
    FRAN BYRNE        D   (A    L SHANKA       VLN (A
```

MAY BLITZ

```
    TONY NEWMAN      VIBES D(AB1    (A) MAY BLITZ            1970 VERTIGO UK 6360007 US PARAMOUNT 5020
    REID HUDSON      B V  (AB       (B) SECOND OF MAY        1971 VERTIGO UK 6360037
    JAMES BLACK      G V  (AB1      (1) 1969 LINE UP
    TERRY POOLE      B    (1
    KEITH BAKER      D    (1
```

M115   CURTIS MAYFIELD   M115

```
    CURTIS MAYFIELD  V    (ALL   EARLY YEARS              1973 PROBE    UK GTSP 201 UK ABC ABCD780
    WENDELL STEWART  D    (S     SWEET EXORCIST           1974 BUDDAH   BDLH 5001 RI UK   2318 099
    TOM FERRONE      G    (S     SWEET EXORCIST           1976 CURTOM   US 8601     UK   K 56284
    TIM TOBIAS       K    (S     ROOTS                    1974 BUDDAH   BDLH 5006  UK   2318 045
    RICH TUFO        K    (S     ROOTS                    1976 CURTOM   US 8009     UKRI K 56249
    KEN BURKE        B    (S     CURTIS                   1974 BUDDAH   BDLH 5005  UK   2318 015
    JOE SCOTT        B    (S     CURTIS                   1976 CURTOM   US 8005     UK   K 56252
    ROSS TRAUT       G    (S     BACK TO THE WORLD        1974 BUDDAH   BDLH 5008  UKRI K 56251
    TONY CARPENTER   PERC (S     BACK TO THE WORLD        197  CURTOM   US 8015
    SONNY SEALS      HRNS (S     IN CHICAGO LIVE          1974 BUDDAH   BDLH 5009
    LEN DRUSS        HRNS (S     IN CHICAGO LIVE          1976 CURTOM   US 8018     UK   K 56250
    ART HOYLE        HRNS (S     SHORT EYES               197  CURTOM   US   5017
    PAUL HOWARD      HRNS (S     DO IT ALL NIGHT          197  CURTOM   US   5022
    DALE CLEVENGER   HRNS (S     MOVE ON UP               1974 BUDDAH   BDLP 4015
    BILL PORTER      HRNS (S     SUPERFLY                 1974 BUDDAH   BDLH 4018
    ROBERT LUSTREA   HRNS (S     SUPERFLY                 197  RSO US RSS5      UK 2394 233
    GILL ASKEY       HRNS (S     GOT TO FIND A WAY        1974 BUDDAH   BDLP 4029 CURTOM US   8604
                                 AMERICA TODAY            1974 BUDDAH   BDLP 4033 CURTOM US   5001
                                 GIVE GET TAKE HAVE       1976 BUDDAH   BDLP 4042 CURTOM US   5007
                                 CURTIS LIVE              1974 BUDDAH   BDLD 2001 CURTOM UK K66047
                                 CURTIS LIVE              197  CURTIM   US 8008
                                 NEVER SAY YOU CANT SURVIVE 1977 CURTOM  CU 5013     UK K56352
                                 HEARTBEAT                1979 CURTOM   US   3053
                                 (S)SOMETHING TO BELIEVE IN 1980 CURTOM UK 2393 271 US   3077
```

M116   PERCY MAYFIELD   M116

```
    PERCY MAYFIELD   V PNO(ALL  (A) PERCY MAYFIELD            1969 TANGERINE    UK      TRC 1505
                               (B) BOUGHT BLUES            1969 TANGERINE    US      TRS 1510
                               (C) TIGHTROPE               1969 BRUNSWICK            754145
                               (D) SINGS                   1970 RCA VICTOR   US      4269
                               (E) WEAKNESS IS A THING CALLED MAN 1970 RCA VICTOR US  4444
                               (F) BLUES  & THEN SOME      1971 RCA VICTOR   US      4558
                               (G) THE INCREDIBLE          1972 SPECIALTY  US 5010 UK SNTF 5010
                               (H) BEST OF                 197  SPECIALTY    US      2126
```

M117   MAZE   M117

```
    FRANKIE BEVERLY        (   (A) ARMAGEDDON               197  MTA          US      MTS 5012
                               (B) MAZE                     1977 CAPITOL              11607
                               (C) GOLDEN TIME OF DAY       1978 CAPITOL              11710
                               (D) INSPIRATION              1980 CAPITOL              11912
                               (E) JOY AND PAIN             1980 CAPITOL              12087
```

M118   MEAL TICKET   M118

```
    CHRIS HUNT   D PERC (AB    (A) CODE OF THE ROAD         1977 EMI          UK      INS 3008
    JACK BRAND   B V    (AB    (B) THREE TIMES A DAY        1978 EMI          UK      INS 3010
    RAY FLACKE   G V    (AB    (C) TAKEAWAY                 1978 LOGO         UK      1008
    STEVE SIMPSON FDL G V (ABC
    RICK JONES   K V    (ABC KEITH NELSON    BANJO(BC  DAVE PIERCE    (    WILLY FINLAYSON G V K(ABC
    DON WELLER   SAX    (B   ALAN COULTER     D    (C   ROD DEMICK    B    (C
```

M119   MEAN STREET DEALERS   M119

```
    MARK BRISTOW    G    (A    (A) BENT NEEDLES             1979 MEAN ST DEALERS    MSD  001
    NIGEL DARVILLS  K    (A    (A) BENT NEEDLES             1979 GRADUATE           GRAD LP1
    JAMES LANGSTON  V    (A
    JIM SIMPSON     D    (A  BOB BOUCHER    B    (A
```

M120   MEATLOAF   M120

```
    MEATLOAF       V    (ABC   (A) STONEY & MEATLOAF         1971 RARE EARTH SRE3005 PRODIGAL 62172
    KARLA DEVITO   V    (      (A) MEATLOAF(FEATURING STONEY) 1979 PRODIGAL  US 10029 UK PDL  2010
    ED KING        G    (      (B) BAT OUT OF HELL           1978 EPIC     US 44974   UK    82419
    TODD RUNDGREN K G V (B     (C) DEADRINGER                1981 EPIC     US 36007   UK    83645
    JIM STEINMAN K SONGS (BC
    ELLEN FOLEY         (
    ROY BITAN      K    (ABC KASIM SULTON    B V  (AB  ROGER POWELL     SYN (B   JOHN WILCOX      D(B
    EDGAR WINTER   SAX  (B   MARVIN LEE      V    (B   MAX WEINBERG     D   (BC  RORY DODD  V     (BC
    DAVEY JOHNSTONE G   (C   STEVE BUSLOWE   B    (C   LIBERTY DEVITTO  D   (C   LARRY FAST       SYN(C
    JIMMY MAELEN   PERC (C   LESLIE LOAF     V    (C   JOE DE ANGELIS   G   (C   NICKY HOPKINS    K  (C
    YMMIJ NELEAM   PERC (C   ALAN RUBIN      HRNS (C   LOU MARINI       HRNS(C   LOU DELGATTO     HRNS(C
    TOM MALONE     HRNS (C   CHER            V    (C   TED NEELEY       V   (C   ALLEN NICHOLLS   V  (C
    ERIC TROYER    V    (C   RHONDA COULET   V    (C
```

M121   MEDICINE HEAD   M121

```
    JOHN FIDDLER    G V  (ALL   (A) NEW BOTTLES OLD MEDICINE  1970 DANDELION         UK       63757
    PETER HOPE EVANS HCA V (ABDEFG (B) HEAVY ON THE DRUM      1971 DANDELION  DAN 8005    K 49005
    KEITH RELF      B V  (C     (C) DARK SIDE OF THE MOON     1971 DANDELION         UK     2310 166
    JOHN DAVIES     D    (C     (D) ONE & ONE IS ONE         1972 POLYDOR  US 5532 UK  2310 248
    ROB TOWNSEND    D    (E     (E) THRU A FIVE              1974 POLYDOR         UK     2383 272
    ROGER SAUNDERS  G    (E     (F) MEDICINE HEAD (COMP)     1975 POLYDOR         UK     2384 069
    IAN SAINTY      B    (      (G) TWO MAN BAND             1976 BARN           UK     2314 102
    CHARLIE McCRACKEN B  (      ( ) POP HISTORY VOL XXV      1973 POLYDOR               2625 026
    GEORGE FORD     B V  (E     ( ) BEST OF                  1981 VERTIGO  UK 2485 204
    TONY ASHTON     K    (DE
    CLIVE THACKER   D    (D  ROY DYKE        D    (D  PAT DONALDSON   B    (D   MIKE LIBER  G    (D
    BRIAN PARRISH   G    (D
```

M121A   MEDIUM MEDIUM   M121A

```
                               (A) THE GLITTERHOUSE         1981 CHERRY RED UK BRED19 GER 148 202
```

MEDITATIONS

(A) WAKE UP   1978 THIRD WORLD   TWS 929

BILL MEDLEY

BILL MEDLEY

100% BILL MEDLEY	1968 MGM	US 4583	UK 8091
SOFT & SOULFUL	1969 MGM	US 4603	
GONE	1970 MGM	US 4741	
SOMEONE IS STANDING OUTSIDE	1970 MGM	US 4640	
NOBODY KNOWS	1970 MGM	US 4702	
A SONG FOR YOU	1972 A&M	US 3505	UK AMLH 63505
WINGS	19 A&M	US 3506	
SMILE	1973 A&M	US 3517	
SWEET THUNDER	1980 LIBERTY	US 1024	UK LT 1097

RANDY MEISNER

RANDY MEISNER	G V(ALL	(A) RANDY MEISNER	1978 ASYLUM US 6E140 UK K53079
PATRICK SHANAHAN	D (A	(B) ONE MORE SONG	1980 EPIC US 36748 UK 84531
STEVE EDWARDS	G (A	(C) RANDY MEISNER	1982 EPIC US 38121
DANNY CARMASSI	D (C		

KERRY MORRIS	B	(A	JOHN HOBBS	PNO (A	JERRY SWALLOW	G (A	TITA KERPAN	V (A
BYRON BERLINE	FDL	(A	DONNY ULLSTROM	V (A	ERNIE WATTS	SAX (A	ALAN BRACKETT	V (A
GEOFFREY LEIB	PNO	(A	RICHIE WALKER	V (A	J D SOUTHER	V (A	BILL LAMB	V (A
DAVID CASSIDY	V	(A	DON FRANCISCO	PERC V(B	CRAIG HULL	STEEL(B	BRYAN GAROFALO	B (B
CRAIG KRAMPF	D	(B	STERLING SMITH	K (BC	WENDY WALDMAN	G V (B	BILL CUOMO	SYN (B
MICHAEL JACOBSON	SAX	(B	KIM CARNES	V (B	DON HENLEY	V (B	GLENN FREY	V (B.
JOHN COREY	G K V(C		TOM ERAK	B (C	MITCHELL FROOM	SYN (C	NICKY HOPKINS	K (C
DIXON HOUSE	K V	(C	PHIL KENZIE	SAX (C	HOWARD LEESE	G V SYN(C	MARCY LEVY	V (C
BRIAN SMITH	G	(C	ANN WILSON	V (C	NANCY WILSON	V (C	TOWER OF POWER	HRNS (C

MEKONS

JON LANGFORD	D (	(A) THE QUALITY OF MERCY IS NOT	1979 VIRGIN UK V 2143
ROSS ALLEN	B (	(B) MEKONS	1980 RED RHINO UK 1
ANDY CARRIGAN	V (		
MARK WHITE	V (	KEVIN LYCETT G (	TOM GREENHALGH G (

MELANIE

MELANIE SAFKA	V (ALL	(A) BORN TO BE	1969 BUDDAH 203 019 BDLH 5002
RON FRANGIPANE	K (GJDO	(B) AFFECTIONATELY	1969 BUDDAH 203 028 BDLP 4016
JOE MACK	B (G	(C) CANDLES IN THE RAIN	1970 BUDDAH 2318 009 BDLP 5003
SAL DE TROIA	G (GJVD	(C) CANDLES IN THE RAIN	1970 BUDDAH GER 2318006 US 5060
ERIC WEISSBERG	FDL (G	(D) LEFTOVER WINE	1970 BUDDAH 2318 011 BDLH 5004
BARRY MORGAN	D (C	(D) LEFTOVER WINE	1970 BUDDAH GER 623142 US 5066
VINNIE BELL	G (G	(E) ALL THE RIGHT NOISES	1971 BUDDAH 2319 034
HUGH McCRACKEN	G (GJU	(F) GARDEN IN THE CITY	1972 BUDDAH 2318 054 BDLP 4017
GEORGE DEVENS	D (GD	(F) GARDEN IN THE CITY	1972 BUDDAH US 5095
BUDDY SALZMAN	D (G	(G) GOOD BOOK	1971 BUDDAH 2322 001 BDLH 5010
GEORGE MARCH	WIND (G	(G) GOOD BOOK	197 BUDDAH US 5006 MODE FR MD9024
DAVE SANBORN	SAX (U	(H) GATHER ME	1971 NEIGHBORHOOD US 4700 BUDDAH 4022
RANDY BRECKER	HRNS (U	(I) FOUR SIDES OF (COMP DBL)	1974 BUDDAH UK BDLD 2002 US 9505
MICHAEL BRECKER	HRNS (U	(J) STONEGROUND WORDS	1972 NEIGHBORHOOD US 47005 UK NHTC 251
RICHARD TEE	K (U	(J) STONEGROUND WORDS	1975 ABC RI UK ABCL 5077
WILL LEE	B (U	(K) AT CARNEGIE HALL	1973 NEIGHBORHOOD US 49001 UK NHSP 301
CHRIS PARKER	D (U	(K) AT CARNEGIE HALL	1975 ABC RI UK ABCL 606
JOHNNY PACHECO	CONGA(J	(L) VERY BEST OF	1974 BUDDAH UK BDLP 4001
BILL KEITH	STEEL(J	(M) PLEASE LOVE ME	1974 BUDDAH US 5132 UK BDLP 4021
DON PAYNE	B (J	(N) MADRUGADA	1974 NEIGHBORHOOD US 48001 UK NH 3003
CHUCK DOMANICO	B (J	(N) MADRUGADA	1975 ANCHOR UK ABCL 5085
ROGER KELLAWAY	PNO (J	(O) AS I SEE IT NOW	1975 NEIGHBORHOOD US 3000 UK NBH 80636
DONALD McDONALD	D (J	(P) SUNSET & OTHER BEGINNINGS	1975 NEIGHBORHOOD US 3001 UK NBH 69168
MEL LEWIS	D (J	(Q) FROM THE BEGINNING (COMP)	1975 ABC US 879 UK ABLC 5124
RICHARD DAVIS	B (JO	(R) PROFILE (COMP)	197 TELDEC GER 424022
ROBBIE GEORGIA	(W	(S) GOLDEN HOUR (COMP)	1977 PYE UK GH 861
BOB LEONE	(W	(T) BEST OF (COMP)	197 BUDDAH US 5664 UK BDLP 5705
MARY McCAFFREY	V (W	(U) PHONOGENIC	1978 MIDSONG US 3033 MCA UK MCF 8033
LOUIS CABAZA	(W	(V) PHOTOGRAPH	1979 ATLANTIC US 18190
TONY BATTAGLIA	(W	(W) BALLROOM STREETS	1979 RCA XL 03073 US TOMATO 9003
STAN KIPPER	D (W	( ) MELANIE	19 BUDDAH US 5041
ALAN PARKER	G (C		

ALAN HACKSHAW	K	(C	HAROLD McNAIR	FLT (C	RICO REYES	CONGA (C	EDWIN HAWKINS	K (C
HERBIE FLOWERS	B	(C	AL GORGONI	G (D	JOSEPH MACHO	B (	GREG DIAMOND	D (D
ART KAPLAN	WIND	(O	ROY YEAGER	D PERC V (O	JOHN MULKEY	B V (O	BARRY HARWOOD	G STEEL V(O
FRANK FRANCO	G	(O	STEVE FELDMAN	K V (O	JOHN SHANE KEISTER	K (O	SY MANN	PNO (O
CLIFF NIVISON	V	(O	GEORGE MARGE	WIND(O	GENE BIANCO	HARP (O	TOOTS THIELEMANS	HCA (O
GEORGE RICCI	CELLO(O		HARRY WIMMER	CELLO (O	SUSIE WATSON TAYLOR	V (O	MIKE HERON	V G (O
ROBIN WILLIAMSON	(O		DAVE DORAN	G V (O	DEAN PARKS	G (V	LOUIS SHELTON	G (V
DAVID PAICH	K	(V	JIM DRENNAN	K (V	JAY WOLFE	B V (V	JERRY SCHEFF	B (V
DAVID JACKSON	B	(V	JIM GORDON	D (V	JEFF PORCARO	D (V	JOHN GUERIN	D (V
MILT HOLLAND	PERC	(V	VICTOR FELDMAN	PERC (V	ANGELO MAUCERI	PERC V(V	CAROL PARKS	V (V
DENNY BELL	V	(V	ART PEPPER	SAX (V	RICHAR GREENE	VLN (V	DAVID CAMPBELL	VLA (V

TERRY MELCHER

TERRY MELCHER	V K (ALL	(A) TERRY MELCHER	1974 REPRISE US MS 2185 UK k54016
JIM KELTNER	D (A	(B) ROYAL FLUSH	1976 RCA US 0948
DORIS DAY	V (A		

HAL BLAINE	D	(A	MICHAEL CLARKE	D (A	JOE OSBORN	B (A	CHRIS HILLMAN	B (A
CLARENCE WHITE	G	(A	RY COODER	G (A	MIKE DEASY	G (A	TONY MARTIN JR	G (A
SNEAKY PETE	STEEL(A		J D MANESS	STEEL(A	LARRY KNECHTEL	K (A	SPOONER OLDHAM	K (A
JIM HORN	HRNS	(A	SLYDE HYDE	HRNS (A	CHUCK FINDLEY	HRNS (A	JACKIE KELSO	HRNS(A
JIMMIE HASKELL	STRING(A		BRUCE JOHNSTON	V (A	SPANKY MACFARLANE	V (A		

BARRY MELTON

BARRY MELTON	G V	(ALL		(A) BRIGHT SUN IS SHINING				1970	VANGUARD	US		VSD 6551	
DONNIE HATHAWAY	PNO	(A		(B) MELTON,LEVY & THE DEY BROTHERS				1972	CBS	US		31279	
PHIL UPCHURCH	B	(A		(C) THE FISH				1975	UA	UK	UAS	29908	
JAY LEVY	K V	(B		(D) WE ARE LIKE THE OCEAN				1977	MUSIC IS MEDICINE US		MIM	9007	
RICK DEY	B V	(B		(E) LEVEL WITH ME				1979	RAG BABY US 1004 GER			85001	
JIM BOYES	V	(D		(E) LEVEL WITH ME				198	MUSIC IS MEDICINE		US	9014	
TONY DEY	D	(B											
MORRIS JENNINGS	D	(A	DAVE CHARLES	D	(C	TOMMY EYRE	K	(C	RAY MARTINEZ	G	(CD		
KEN WHALEY	B	(C	ROB PIZER	G	(D	BOB FLURIE	G	(D	ELMO SHROPSHIRE	BAN(D			
PAUL COBBOLD	B	(D	MOTH SMITH	D	(D	BOB HOGINS	PNO	(D	DAVE BRADY	V	(D		
HEATHER BRADY	V	(D	GERALD SIMS	G	(A	HAROLD ACEVES	D V	(E	BILL ASHLEE	B V	(E		
BOB FLURIE	B V	(E	ROBERT HOGINS	K V	(E								

MEMBERS

NICKY TESCO	V	(AB		(A) AT THE CHELSEA NIGHTCLUB				1979	VIRGIN UK V2120		GER 200 480		
NIGEL BENNETT	G V	(AB		(B) 1980 THE CHOICE IS YOURS				1980	VIRGIN UK V 2153		GER 202 099		
CHRIS PAYNE	B V	(AB											
ADRIAN LILLYWHITE	D PERC(AB	STEVE 'RUD' THOMPSON SAX(A	JOE JACKSON		PNO	(B	DICK CUTHELL	HRNS (B					
JEAN CARROLL	G V	(AB	RUPERT HINE	K	(A	ALBE DONNELLY	SAX	(B	RICO RODRIGUES	TROM (B			

MEMPHIS BEND

MICKY GEE	G V	(A		(A) GOOD ROCKIN TONITE		1977	UA	UK	UAS 30036
LINCOLN CARR	B	(A				
TOM RILEY	D V	(A	JOHN JENKINS	PNO (A	B J COLE	STEEL (A JOHN DAVID	B (A
MICK WEAVER	K	(A				

MEMPHIS SLIM

MEMPHIS 'PETER CHATMAN'SLIM PNO V(ALL

CHRIS SPEDDING	G	(B
PETER GREEN	G	(B
DUSTER BENNETT	HCA	(B
PETE WINGFIELD	K	(B
LARRY STEELE	B	(B
CONRAD ISADORE	D	(B
ROOSEVELT SYKES	K G	(N
BUDDY GUY	G	(NS
JUNIOR WELLS	HCA	(N
PHILIP GUY	G	(N
ERNEST JOHNSON	B	(N
ROOSEVELT SHAW	D	(N
A C REED	SAX	(N
JIMMY CONLEY	SAX	(N
ALEXIS KORNER	G	(CF
STAN GRIEG	D	(CF
LEROY BATCHELOR	B	(M
ALFRED ELKINS	B	(M

ALL THEM BLUES	1976	DJM	DJD	28012
AT LAUSANNE	1974	MUSIDISC	EURO CV	1289
AT THE GATE OF HORN	19	BARNABY US 31291 JOY UK		143
AT THE GATE OF HORN	19	VEE JAY		1012
AT THE VILLAGE GATE	19	FOLKWAYS	US	2386
BAD LUCK & TROUBLE	1972	CBS US 31291	UK	67248
BLUE MEMPHIS	1971	BARCLAY FR 920214	US	WB1899
BLUES IN EUROPE	19	STORYVILLE	SLP	188
BLUES IN EUROPE	19	STORYVILLE	SLP	214
BLUES IS EVERYWHERE	19	GNP CRESCENDO	US	10002
BLUES MAN	1975	MUSIDISC	FR	ALB187
BORN WITH BLUES	1972	JEWEL	US	5004
BOOGIE WOOGIE	1978	FESTIVAL		ALB247
BROKEN SOUL BLUES	19	UA	US	LA 3137
BABY PLEASE COME HOME	19	BATTLE	US	6122
BLUES EVERY WHICH WAY	19	VERVE	US	3007
BLUE PORTRAIT	19	SCEPTER	US	536
BLUES & WOMEN	1981	ISABEL	FR	900 506
CHICAGO BLUES	19	FOLKWAYS US 3536	UK	XTRA 1085
CLASSICAL AMERICAN BLUES	1973	BARCLAY	FR	920 407
CHICAGO BOOGIE	1976	BLACK LION		BLP 30196
() FRISCO BAY BLUES	1960	FONTANA	UK 688	315
FATTENIN FROGS FOR SNAKES	1976	MELODISC		MLPS12149
FAVOURITE BLUES	19	FOLKWAYS	US	2387
GREAT MEMPHIS SLIM	19	AMERICA	AM	6076
GOIN' BACK TO TENNESSEE	1975	BARCLAY	FR	90034
HONKY TONK SOUND	19	FOLK	US	3535
HOUSE OF THE BLUES VOL1	19	BLUE STAR	FR	80601
HOUSE OF THE BLUES VOL 7	19	BLUE STAR	FR	80607
JUST BLUES	19	PRESTIGE	US	1018
LEGACY OF THE BLUES	1973	GNP CRESCENDO	US	10017
LEGACY OF THE BLUES	1973	SONET	UK	SNTF 647
LIVE	1974	STORYVILLE	UK	SLP 219
LEGEND OF THE BLUES VOL 2	19	BEACON	BEAS	6
LONESOME BLUES	19	SPINERAMA	US	149
MEMPHIS SLIM	19	B&B		33002
MEMPHIS SLIM	19	ARC FOLK	US	215
MEMPHIS SLIM	19	BARNABY	US	31241
MEMPHIS SLIM	19	STORYVILLE	UK SLP	118
MEMPHIS SLIM	19	BARCLAY	FR	920214
MEMPHIS SLIM	1974	AMERICA	AM	6130
MEMPHIS SLIM	19	KING	US	885
MEMPHIS SLIM	19	EVEREST	US	215
MEMPHIS SLIM	19	CHESS	US	1455
MEMPHIS SLIM	19	BLACK & WHITE	FR	730 581
MEMPHIS SLIM (BLUEBIRD No 3)	19	RCA		FXMI 7215
MEMPHIS SLIM VOL 2	19	EVEREST	US	286
MEMPHIS SLIM & MATTHEW MURPHY	1974	BLACK & BLUE		33 002
MEMPHIS SLIM & WILLIE DIXON(PARIS)19	BATTLE	US	6122
MEMPHIS SLIM & WILLIE DIXON	19	FOLKWAYS	US	2385
MEMPHIS SLIM & S BOY WILLIAMSON	19	GNP CRESCENDO	US	GNP10003
MEMPHIS SLIM STORY	19	VOGUE		LD 58330
MAMPHIS HEAT	1981	IMS	1080 607	
MESSIN' AROUND WITH THE BLUES	19	KING	US	1082
MOTHER EARTH	1972	BUDDAH	BDS	7505
NO STRAIN	19	PRESTIGE	US	1031
OLD TIMES NEW TIMES	1972	BARCLAY	FR	920332 3
PIANO BLUES	19	STORYVILLE	UK SLP	168
RAINING THE BLUES	19	FANTASY	US	24705
REAL FOLK BLUES	19	CHESS	US	1510
REAL HONKY TONK	19	FOLKWAYS	US	3535
REAL BOOGIE WOOGIE	19	FOLKWAYS		3523
RIGHT NOW	19	TRIP	US	8025
ROCK ME BABY	1975	BLACK LION		2460 155
SELF PORTRAIT	19	SCEPTER	US	535
STEADY ROLLIN BLUES	19	PRESTIGE	US	1075

MEMPHIS SLIM (CONTINUED)

SOUL BLUES	1973	EMBER	UK	3422
(S)SOUTH SIDE REUNION	1975	BARCLAY	FR	80501
(S)SOUTH SIDE REUNION	19	WB	US	2646
USA	19	CANDID	US	9024
WORLDS FOREMOST BLUES SINGER	19	STRAND	US	1046
WILLIES BLUES	19	PRESTIGE	US	1003

MEMPHIS HORNS

WAYNE JACKSON	HRNS (ALL	(A) MEMPHIS HORNS	197	COTILLION	US	9014
ROGER HOPPS	HRNS (	(B) HIGH ON MUSIC	1976	RCA	UK 1056	US 1355
ANDREW LOVE	HRNS (C	(C) GET UP & DANCE	1977	RCA		US 2198
ED LOGAN	SAX (	(D) MEMPHIS HORNS BAND 2	1979	RCA		US 2643
JACK HALE	TROM (C	(E) WELCOME TO	1979	RCA		US 3221
JAMES MITCHELL	SAX (C					
LEWIS COLLINS	SAX (C	CLARENCE McDONALD K (C	JAMES GADSON	D (C	MARLO HENDERSON	G (C
DAVID SHIELDS	B (C	JAY GRAYDON G (C	BOBBY EATON	B (C	PATRICK MOTEN	SYN(C
PAULINHO DACOSTA	PERC (C					

MEN AT WORK

COLIN HAY	G V (A	(A) BUSINESS AS USUAL	1982	CBS	US	37978
RON STRYKERT	G V (A	(B) CARGO	1983	CBS		
JERRY SPEISER	D V (A	GREG HAM WIND K V(A	JOHN REES	B V (A		

MENAGE A TROIS

GREG MOORE	G (A	(A) MANAGE A TROIS	1980	ARIOLA	NL	200 148
EDDIE WATKINS	B (A					
LARRY TOLBERT	D (A	PAULINHO DACOSTA PERC (A	MICHAEL DOVE	K SYN(A	SYLVIA COX	V (A
CARL ANDERSON	V (A	CAROLYN DENNIS V (A	ROY GALLOWAY	V (A	KAY McNEELY	V (A
HELENA SPRINGS	V (A	AFREEKA TRESS V (A				

ANDY MENDELSON

ANDY MENDELSON	V K G B(A	(A) ANDY MENDELSON	1978	ARISTA	US	4207
RICHARD MENDELSON	D (A					
FRANK DE FONDA	D (A	DAVID SHAPIRO B (A	GAIL HEIDEMAN	V (A	GWEN OWENS	V (A
GREG HAWKES	WIND (A	TOM SCOTT WIND (A	JOE FARRELL	SAX (A	ERNIE WATTS	SAX (A
ANDY PRATT	V (A	MARY HASLIM V (A	LAURA CREAMER	V (A		

JOE MENDELSON

JOE MENDELSON	V G B D K(AB	(A) MR MIDDLE OF THE ROAD	19	NOBADY	9230 1027
		(B) SOPHISTO JOE MENDELSON	19	TAURUS	

THE MENTAL

(A) GOD FOR A DAY	19	KAMIKAZE

MENTAL AS ANYTHING

MARTIN PLAZA	G V (A	(A) MENTAL AS ANYTHING	1980	VIRGIN UK 2148	EURO 201 435
GREEDY SMITH	V K HCA(A					
REG MOMBASSA	G V (A	WAYNE DELISLE D (A	PETER O'DOHERTY	B V (A		

MEPHISTOPHELES

FRED TACKETT	G K TPT V(A	(A) IN FRUSTRATION	19	REPRISE	US	6355
STEVEN SIMONE	G V (A				
BOB SILLER	G V (A	GORDON GRANT K (A	SKIP MOSHER	B FLT(A	DARYL BURCH	D (A
DAVID HASSINGER	PROD(A				

ERIC MERCURY

ERIC MERCURY	V (A	(A) ERIC MERCURY	19	MERCURY	US SRM 1 1026
WILLIAM SMITH	K (AB	(B) FUNKY SOUNDS NURTURED IN FERTILE SOIL	197	ENTERPRISE	US	1020
JIM JOHNSON	B (B					
JAY MITTHAUER	D (A	PAUL STALLWORTH B (A	DANNY KORTCHMAR	G (A	GARY COLEMAN	PERC (A
LARRY VON NASH	SYN (A	JIM KELTNER D (A	DENNIS COFFEY	G (A	JESSE ED DAVIS	G (A
DAVID FOSTER	PNO (A	KLAUS VOORMANN B (A	ED BROWN	B (A	WADDY WACHTEL	G (A
DAVID PAICH	K (A	ERIC JOHNSON D (A	BOBBY KEYS	HRNS (A	TREVOR LAWRENCE	PERC(A
JEFF BAXTER	STEEL(A	DOUG RICHARDSON HRNS (A	SONNY BURKE	K (A	PAT MURPHY	CONGA(A
GARY HODGES	D (A	VERNON BERCH G (A	LON VAN EATON	G (A	GARY DELORME	G (A
LYNDA LAWRENCE	V (A	VANETTA FIELDS V (A	CARLINA WILLIAMS	V (A	SID SHARP STR	(A
PAUL CANNON	G (B	STEVE CROPPER G (B	JAY SPELL	K (B	MEMPHIS HRNS	(B

BILLY MERNIT

BILLY MERNIT	V K (A	(A) SPECIAL DELIVERY	1973	ELEKTRA	US	EKS 75054
JOHN SEITER	D (A					
PETER KLIMES	G (A	DAVID VAUGHT B (A				

MERGER

BARRY FORD	G V WIND(A1	(A) EXILES IN BABYLON	1977	SUNSTAR	SUN 1001
IVOR STEADMAN	B (A1	(B) ARMAGEDDON TIME	1980	EMERGENCY	UK	010
WINSTON BENNETT	G V (A12	(1) 1978 (2) LATE 1978				
RAS DANJUMA	G (2					
MIKE OSEI	D (12	EVER WELLINGTON B (2	TONY OSEI	K (12 FAR I	PERC(2
MICHAEL DAN	K V (A	ADETOKUMBO ILLORIN G (A	JIMMY THOMAS	V PERC(A EUNICE GREEN	V (A
PAM NESTOR	V (A	STRECKER CATIOUS V (A				

MAX MERRITT & THE METEORS

MAX MERRITT	G V (ALL	(A) A LITTLE CLOSER	1975	ARISTA	UK ARTY 108
STEWART SPEER	D (AB	(B) OUT OF THE BLUES	1976	ARISTA	UK ARTY 134
LANCE DIXON	K SAX V(B	(C) KEEPING IN TOUCH	1978	POLYDOR	UK 2383 514
JOHN GOURD	G (B					
BARRY DUGGAN	WIND V(A	RAY COOPER PERC (A	DEL NEWMAN	PROD (A	DAVE McRAE	K (A
B J COLE	STEEL(A					

MERRY GO ROUND

EMIT RHODES	G K V(A	(A) YOU'RE VERY LONELY WOMAN	1967	A&M	US	4132
BILL RHINEHARDT	G V (A					
GARY KATO	B V (A	JOEL LARSON D V (A				

NEIL MERRYWEATHER

NEIL MERRYWEATHER	B G V(ALL		(A) NEIL MERRYWEATHER & THE BOERS	19	KENT				US KST	546	
MICHAEL WILLIS	G	(EC	(B) WORD OF MOUTH	1969	CAPITOL				US STBB	278	
TIM McGOVERN	D	(EC	(C) IVAR AVENUE REUNION	1970	RCA				US LPS	4442	
ED GEMONT	SYN	(E	(D) VACUUM CLEANER	1971	RCA	UK SF 8210	US LSP	4485			
STEVE MILLER	G V	(B	(E) SPACE RANGERS	1974	MERCURY	UK 9100008	US SRMI 1007				
BARRY GOLDBERG	K	(B	(F) KRYPTONITE	1975	MERCURY				US SRMI	1024	
DAVE MASON	G	(B	(*C) SEE BARRY GOLDBERG FOR C								
BARRY GOLDBERG		(C									
CHARLIE MUSSELWHITE	HCA(B	HOWARD ROBERTS G	(B	DAVE BURT	G V	(B	SIDNEY GEORGE	HRNS	(D		
COFFI HALL	D	(BD	EDWARD ROTH	FDL FLT K(BD	KAL DAVID	G	(D	HUEY SULLIVAN	PNO	(D	
ROBIN BOERS	D	(AD	J J VELKER	K	(D	JOHN RICHARDSON	G	(DA	LYNN CAREY	V	(D
JAMIE HERNDON	K G	(CE	JIM TAYLOR	PNO	(C						

MERSEYBEATS

TONY CRANE	G V	(A	(A) MERSEYBEATS	1964	FONTANA	UK TL	5210
AARON WILLIAMS	G V	(A	(B) MERSEYBEATS	1965	WING	WL	1163
BILLY KINSLEY	B V	(A	(C) ENGLANDS BEST SELLERS	19	ARC INTERNATIONAL	US ARC	834
JOHN BANKS	D	(A	(EP) MERSEYBEATS	1964	FONTANA	UK TE	17423
JOHN GUSTAFSON	B	(	(EP) ON STAGE	1964	FONTANA	UK TE	17422
BOB GARDNER	B	(	(EP) WISHIN' & HOPIN'	1964	FONTANA	UK TE	17432

MERTON PARKAS

MICK TALBOT	PNO V(A		(A) FACE IN THE CROWD	1979	BEGGARS BANQUET	UK BEGA 11 GER 146523
DANNY TALBOT	D	(A				
SIMON SMITH	D	(A	NEIL HURRELL B V (A			

MESSAGE

ALLAN MURDOCH	G	(ABCDEFG	(A) THE DAWN ANEW IS COMING	197	BELLAPHON	GER BLPS19081	
TOM McGUIGAN	V WIND SYN(ABCD		(B) FROM BOOKS AND DREAMS	1973	BELLAPHON	GER BLPS19159	
HORST STACHELHAUS	B	(ABCD	(C) MESSAGE	1975	NOVA	GER 622213	DECCA UKSKLR5213
GERHARD SCHABER	PERC V(A		(D) SYNAPSE	1976	NOVA	GER 622523	
ALLAN'TAFF' FREEMAN	SYN V(AE		(E) ASTRAL JOURNEYS	1978	BRAIN	GER 0060 165	
BILLY TABBERT	G V	(AE	(F) USING THE HEAD	1977	BRAIN	GER 0060 078	
GUNTHER KLINGER	D	(B	(G) MILES OF SMILES	1980	INTERCORD	GER 145 609	
MANFRED VON BOHR	D PERC(CD						
TONY GREAVES	WIND	(D	SAMMY KUNIG V SAX PERC(E	PETER SCHMIDT	D PERC(E	FRITZ GROGER	G PERC(E
JEANETTE MACLEOD	V	(E	MANFRED KNEIL	VIBES(E	REINER NAGEL	B K	(E	UTE NAGEL	V	(E
HELMUT FICHTNER	K	(F	EMIL WIRTH	B	(F	DAVID HANSELMANN	V	(F	TOMMY WAHL	D PERC(F
HERB GELLER	SAX	(F	LAWRENCE ELAM	TPT	(F	WOLFGANG AHLERS	TROM(F	RAB	?	PERC(B
VOLKER KUNSCHER	SYN K(G	PIT LOW	K SYN(G	WERNER		PERC (	ANGELIKA HANSCHEN	V(F
GABI BOROWSKI	V	(F	TINY HAGEN	HARP	(	THOMAS'CHUCK' TSCHESCHNER B(G		

JIM MESSINA

JIM MESSINA	V G	(ALL	(A) JIM MESSINA & THE JESTERS	196	AUDIO FIDELITY	7037 RI THIMBLE3	
BILL BECKMAN	G	(A	(B) OASIS	1979	CBS US 36140 UK	83803	
RON HOUSE	G	(A	(C) MESSINA	1981	WB US 3559 GER	56911	
JIM SHOLSTEDT	B	(A					
DAVE ARCHULETA	SAX	(A	LARRY CUNDIEFF D	(A	WAYNE NELSON	B V	(B	CRAIG THOMAS	WIND	(BC
MILT HOLLAND	PERC	(B	TONY MORENO	D	(B	JIM STUDER	V K SYN(BC	JEFF ELLIOTT	HRNS	(B
MICHAEL BRADY	B V	(B	JOE PORCARO	PERC(C	NEIL LARSEN	K	(C	DAVID GRISMAN	MAND	(C
SILVIA WOODS	HARP	(C	PAULINE WILSON	V	(C	JANNIE LITTLEPAGE	V	(C	JEFF PORCARO	D	(C
VICTOR FELDMAN	PERC	(C	TOM HENSLEY	K	(C	JERRY HEY	HRNS	(C	CHUCK FINDLEY	HRMS	(C
DAROL ANGER	VLN	(C	JIM HOCHANADLE	WIND	(C	ALAN THORNHILL	V	(C		

METAL URBAIN

		(A) LES HOMMES MORT EST DANGEREUX	1981	BYZANTEEN 8101

METABOLIST

ANTON LOACH	K	(	(A) METABOLIST (EP)	19	DROMM	DRO1
MALCOLM LANE	G	(	(B) HANSTEN KLORK	19	DROMM	DRO2
SIMON MILLWARD	B	(	JED KINGSFORD D (			

METEORS

HUGO SINZHEIMER	V	(AB	(A) TEENAGE HEART	1979	EMI UK EMC3315 NL 26235
FERDINAND BAKKER	G V	(AB	(A) TEENAGE HEART	1979	PASSPORT US 7911
JOHN VEE	B	(AB	(B) HUNGER	1980	HARVEST NL 26540 ARIOLA GER 203140
AKE DANIALSON	K	(AB			
ERIC DE ZWAAN	G V	(AB	JOB TARENSKEEN V D SAX(A	KIM HAWORTH	D	(B	GERRIT VEEN	B	(B
MIKE OTTE		(B	FREDDY CAVALLI	B	(B	MONICA	V	(B	MARJAN	V	(B
FLOOR	V	(B			

THE METERS

ART NEVILLE	K	(ABCDEFGHI	(A) THE METERS	1971	JOSIE	US	4010
CYRIL NEVILLE	PERC	(FGHI	(B) LOOK KA PY PY	1972	JOSIE	US	4011
LEO NOCENTELLI	G V	(ABCDEFHIG	(C) CABBAGE ALLEY	1972	REPISE UK K33242	US	MS 2076
GEORGE PORTER	B	(ABCDEFGHI	(D) REJUVENATION	1974	REPRISE UK K54027	US	MS 2200
JOE MODELISTE	D	(EFHIABCDG	(E) CISSY STRUT	1974	ISLAND UK ILPS9250		
EARL KING	V	(H	(E) SECOND LINE STRUT	1980	CHARLY RI CRB 1009		
KURT McGETTRICK	SAX	(I	(F) FIRE ON THE BAYOU	1975	REPRISE UK K54044	US	MS 2228
SWAMP TABERNACLE CHOIR	(I		(G) BEST OF THE METERS	1975	REPRISE UK K54076		
			( ) BEST OF THE METERS	1975	VIRGO		SV12002
			(H) TRICK BAG	1976	REPRISE UK K54078	US	MS 2252
			(I) NEW DIRECTION	1977	WB UK K56378	US	MS 3042
			(J) GOOD OLD FUNKY MUSIC	1979	PYE UK PKL5578		
			(EP) LOOK KA PY PY	1980	CHARLY	UK CTD	113

PAT METHENY

PAT METHENY	G B	(ALL	(A) BRIGHT SIZE LIFE	1975	ECM	1073
JACO PASTORIUS	B	(A	(B) WATERCOLOURS	1977	ECM	1097
BOB MOSES	D	(A	(C) PAT METHENY GROUP	1978	ECM	1114
LYLE MAYS	K	(BCEG	(D) NEW CHAUTAUQUA	1978	ECM	1131
EBERHARD WEBER	B	(B	(E) AMERICAN GARAGE	1979	ECM	1155
DAN GOTTLIEB	D	(BCE	(F) 80 81	1980	ECM	
MARK EGAN	B	(CE	(G) AS WICHITA FALLS SO FALLS WICHITA	1980	ECM	1190
NANA VASCONCELES	D V	(G				
MICHAEL BRECKER	SAX	(F	JACK DEJOHNETTE D (F	CHARLIE HADEN	B	(F

METHOD ACTORS

```
                              (A) RHYTHMS OF YOU              1981 ARMAGEDDON    UK        12005
M139                                    METHOD                                              M139
   MICK BRASSINGTON  V   (A     (A) METHOD                    1976  UK          UK   UKAL1020
   JOHN HUGHES       G   (A
M139A                                                                                       M139A
   BUBU HIFIKER      D V (A     (A) FOR OUR FRIENDS           1979  METHUSALEM        METH7901
   ANDY SABER        G V (A
   RICK HOCHULI      B V (A  FERNANDO PALENCIAS G V (A  ROBY WURGLER  G V (A  MARCO RAUBER  K  (A
M139B                                  METHUSELAH                                            M139B
   JOHN GLADWIN      V VIBES(A    (A) MATTHEW MARK LUKE & JOHN  19  ELEKTRA    US  EKS 74052
   TERRY WINCOTT     G V (A
   CRAIG AUSTIN      B V (A  LESLIE NICOL   G V (A  M J BRADLEY  D  (A
M140                                     METRO                                              M140
   SEAN LYONS        G   (AB     (A) METRO                    1977 TRANSATLANTIC UK TRAG340 US SIRE 6041
   PETER GODWIN  V SAX SYN(AB     (B) NEW LOVE                1979 EMI           UK  EMC 3295
   DUNCAN BROWNE V G K B  (A     (C) FUTURE IMPACT            1980 EMI           UK  EMC 3334
   JOHN LAFORGE      D   (B
   JOHN GIBLIN       B   (A  SIMON PHILLIPS  D   (A  GRAHAM PRESKETT  VLN (A  BARRY HUSBAND  V (A
   TONY ADAMS        B V (B  COLIN WIGHT     G   (B
M140A                                 METROPOLIS                                            M140A
   UTE KANNENBERG    V PERC(A     (A) METROPOLIS              1974 PAN               87439
   THOMAS HILDEBRAND D   (A
   HELMUT BINZER     G   (A  MICHAEL WESTPHAL  B  (A  MICHAEL DUWE  G V (A
M141                                   AUGIE MEYER                                          M141
   AUGIE MEYER    K G V(ALL       (A) YOU AINT ROLLIN YOUR ROLL  1973 PARAMOUNT   US   6065
   DOUG SAHM           (E         (B) WESTERN HEAD MUSIC CO   1973 POLYDOR        US   24 4069
   JIM LOVING        B   (B       (C) LIVE AT THE LONGNECK    197  TEXAS          US   1002
   HARVEY KAGEN      B   (B       (D) CALIFORNIa BLUES        1974 PARAMOUNT      US
   BOB RAFKIN        G   (B       (E) FINALLY IN LIGHTS       1977 TEXAS US TRC1005 SONET UK  SNTF303
   DAVID PRICE       G   (B
   B J JONES         G   (B  DON POUNCHER   D   (B  STEVE ZWIERN   D  (B  JOHN PEREZ D  (B
   MORY BAKER        D   (B  CAROL MEYER    V   (B  SANDIE JONES   V  (B
M141A                                 FREDDI MEYER                                          M141A
   FREDDI MEYER          (A     (A) FREDDI MEYER             19  BARN                NARB 002
M141B                                    MI SEX                                             M141B
   STEVE GILPIN      V   (A     (A) COMPUTOR GAMES           1980 CBS  US 36349  UK 84157
   DON MARTIN        V B (A     (B) SPACE RACE               1980 CBS  US 36744  UK B4446
   KEVIN STANTON     G V (A
   MURRAY BURNS      K V (A  RICHARD HODGKINSON  D  (A
M142                                 STEPHEN MICUS                                          M142
   STEPHEN MICUS               (A) ARCHAIC CONCERTS          1976 CAROLINE     UK  C 1517
                               (B) IMPLOSIONS                1977 JAPO              60017
M143                                GORDON MICHAELS                                         M143
   GORDON MICHAELS V G K (A      (A) STARGAZER               1979 HORIZON      US  SP 737
   HUGH McCRACKEN    G HCA(A
   RICK MAROTTA      D   (A  TONY LEVIN     B   (A  RICHARD TEE    K   (A  MIKE MAINIERI  PERC(A
   GEORGE YOUNG      FLT (A  ED WALSH       SYN  (A  DAVID SANBORN  SAX  (A  GEORGE MARGE  WIND(A
   LISA GILKYSON     V   (A  ARTHUR JENKINS PERC (A  BILL BROWN    HRNS (A  LINDA REDDWOLF  V (A
M143A                                HILLY MICHAELS                                         M143A
   HILLY MICHAELS    D G K(AB     (A) CALLING ALL GIRLS      1980 WB   US 3431  UK K 56837
   DAN HARTMAN       K B G(AB     (B) LUMIA                  1981 WB   US 3566
   JIMMY McALLISTER  G   (A
   G E SMITH         G   (A  MORGAN WALKER  K   (AB  BILLY CROSS  G V (A  GREG HAWKS   G  (A
   T MANDYE          K   (A  GEORGE YOUNG       (A  ELLIOTT RANDALL  G  (A  RICK DERRINGER  G (B
   LARRY RUSSELL     B   (B  TOM MANDEL     K   (B  JEFF BOVA    K  (B
M144                                  LEE MICHAELS                                          M144
   LEE MICHAELS      V B K(ALL     (A) CARNIVAL OF LIFE       1968 A&M                US    4140
   KEITH KNUDSEN     D   (GH       (B) RECITAL                1969 A&M   UK AMLS 928   US    4152
   JOEL CHRISTIE     B   (G        (C) LEE MICHAELS           1969 A&M   UK AMLS 956   US    4199
   DRAKE LEVIN       G   (GBD      (D) BARREL                 1970 A&M   UK AMLS 991   US    4249
   NORMA KINNEY      PERC (E       (E) FIFTH                  1971 A&M   UK AMLS64302  US    4302
   RICHARD MADRID    PERC (E       (F) LIVE                   1972 ARIOLA    86725   US A&M  3518
   HENRY LEWY        PERC (E       (G) SPACE & FIRST TAKES    1972 A&M   UK AMLS64336  US    4336
   JOEL LARSEN       SAX (E        (H) NICE DAY FOR SOMETHING 1973 CBS   UK    65651  US    32275
   BARTHOLOMEW SMITH-FROST D(CDF   (J) TAILFACE               1974 CBS . UK          US    32846
   MURRAY CLAYTON        (        (K) SATURN RINGS           197  ABC              US   ABCD684
   FRANK DAVIS       D   (B
   JOHN BARBATA      D   (B  LARRY KNECHTAL  B   (B
M145                             MAX MIDDLETON & ROBERT AHWAI                                M145
   MAX MIDDLETON     K   (A      (A) ANOTHER SLEEPER          1979 HARVEST        SHSP 4103
   ROBERT AHWAI      G   (A
   RICHARD BAILEY    D   (A  KUMA HARADA     B   (A  DARRYL LEE QUE  PERC (A  STEVE GREGORY  WIND (A
   BUD BEADLE        WIND (A  GEORGE CHISHOLM TPT  (A  TREVOR BARBER   TPT (A  CHRIS RAINBOW  V  (A
   LINDA TAYLOR      V   (A  CHRISTIE THOMPSON V   (A
M146                                  MIDNIGHT OIL                                          M146
   ROB HIRST         D V (A      (A) HEAD INJURIES            1979 POWDER WORKS   AUST  MLF 322
   PETER GARRETT     V   (A
   JAMES MOGINIE     G K (A  ANDREW JAMES    B V (A  MARTIN POTSEY  G  (A
M146A                                MIDNIGHT RAGS                                          M146A
   PAUL ROLAND               (A) WEREWOLF OF LONDON          1980 ARMAGEDDON   UK  ARM1
M146B                                MIDNIGHT FLYER                                         M146B
   MAGGIE BELL       V   (AB     (A) MIDNIGHT FLYER           1981 SWANSONG       US 8509
   ANTHONY GLYNNE    G   (AB     (B) EP ROCK'N'ROLL PARTY     1981 SWANSONG       US
   TONY STEVENS      B V (AB
   DAVID DOWLE       D . (AB  JOHN COOK      K   (AB  CHRIS PARREN  K   (B
```

MIDNIGHT STAR

```
BELINDA LIPSCOMB     V    (A         (A) THE BEGINNING                    1980 RCA    US 3491      UK SOLA 2
REGINALD CALLOWAY V HRNS(A            (B) STANDING TOGETHER               1981 SOLAR                UK K 52305
VINCENT CALLOWAY     HRNS(A
JEFF COOPER      G   (A   BO WATSON          K V  (A   HARVEY MASON    PERC (A   BILL REICHENBACH      HRNS (A
GEORGE BOHANON   HRNS (A  WILLIAM COLLETTE HRNS (A   JEROME RICHARDSON WIND (A   KENNETH GANT         B V (A
WILLIAM SIMMONS  V SAX(A  MICHAEL BODDICKER K   (A   KENNY MASON     HRNS (A   JERRY HEY           HRNS  (A
OSCAR BRASHEAR   HRNS (A  DAVID DUKE       HRNS (A
```

MIDNIGHT SUN

```
BENT HESSELMANN   WIND (ABCD      (A) RAINBOW BAND                 1970 SONET              SLPS 1523
NIELS BRONDSTED   K    (ABCD      (A) RAINBOW BAND (DIFF VOCALS)   1971 SONET              SLPS1523A
CARSTEN SMEDGAARD D    (ABCD      (B) MIDNIGHT SUN                 1972 MCA                MKPS 2019
PEER FROST        G    (ABC       (C) WALKING CIRCLES              1972 SONET SLPS 1536 UK MCA MKPS 2024
BO STIEF          B    (ABC       (D) MIDNIGHT DREAM               1974 SONET              SLPS 1547
LARS BISGAARD     V    (A
HANS LAURIDSEN    V    (C   JENS ELBØL    B    (D  TOM HEATH     G   (D   ALLAN MORTENSEN  V  (B
```

MIGHTY BABY

```
PETE WATSON       G    (1         (A) MIGHTY BABY                  1969 HEAD UK HDLS6002  US 025
MIKE EVANS        B    (12345A    (B) A JUG OF LOVE                1971 BLUE HORIZON  UK         2931 001
ROGER POWELL      D    (12345A    (1) 1963      (2) ACTION 1966 (3) ACTION   (4) ACTION  (5) 1968 71
REG KING          V    (123
ALAN 'BAM 'KING   G    (12345A   IAN WHITEMAN V WIND K(245A  MARTIN STONE   G (345A
```

MIGHTY DIAMONDS

```
DONALD SHAW       V    (BCDEF     (A) RIGHT TIME                   1976 VIRGIN  US 34235  UK      V 2052
FIZTROY SIMPSON   V    (BCDEF     (B) ICE ON FIRE                  1977 VIRGIN  US 34235  UK      V 2078
LLOYD FERGUSON    V    (BCDEF     (C) PLANET EARTH                 1978 VIRGIN            UK      V 2102
DWIGHT RICHARDS   D    (B         (D) STAND UP                     1978 CHANNEL ONE
KENNETH WILLIAMS  PERC (B         (E) DEEPER ROOTS                 1979 FRONT LINE UK FLD 6001
STEVE HUGHES      G    (B         (F) TELL ME WHAT'S WRONG         1980 J&J       US
HERMAN MARQUIS    SAX  (CF
DAVE BARARD       B    (B   ROBERT DABON      PNO  (B   CLYDE KERR JNR    TPT (B   JOHN LONGO     TPT (B
ALVIN THOMAS      SAX  (B   MICHAEL PIERCE    SAX  (B   CARL BLOUIN       SAX (B   THEODORE ROYAL  G  (B
WARDELL QUEZERGUE K    (B   RAYMOND JONES     PNO  (B   ISAAC BOLDEN      PNO (B   CARLTON DAVIS   D  (B
EARL CHINNA SMITH G    (B   SLY DUNBAR        D    (CF  STICKY            PERC(CF  TOMMY McCOOK   SAX (CF
```

MIGHTY FLEA

```
GENE'MIGHTY FLEA'CONNERS V TROM(A    (A) LET THE GOOD TIMES ROLL    1973 BIG BEAR 19  + POLYDOR79 2460185
```

MIGHTY SPARROW

```
                                     (A) PEACE & LOVE               1979 TROJAN  UK     TRLS 159
```

MIGIL FIVE

```
                                     (A) MOCKINGBIRD HILL           1964 PYE       UK    NPL 18093
                                     (B) COME DANCE WITH            1969 JOY             JOYS 138
```

MIKE, SLOT & BUMPER

```
                                     (A) AMAZIN' R&B      (EP)      1979 BLUEPORT        BLU3
```

BUDDY MILES

```
BUDDY MILES V D G K B  (ALL   (A) EXPRESSWAY TO YOUR SKULL  1968 MERCURY  US SR61196   UK SMCL 20137
HERBIE RICH  ORG SAX   (A     (B) ELECTRIC CHURCH          1969 MERCURY  US SR61222   UK SMCL 20163
JIM McCARTY      G     (ABC    (C) THEM CHANGES             1970 MERCURY  US SR61280   UK   6338 016
BILL RICH        B     (A      (D) WE GOT TO LIVE TOGETHER  1970 MERCURY  US SR61313   UK   6338 028
RON WOODS        D     (A      (E) MESSAGE TO THE PEOPLE    1970 MERCURY  US SRM1608   UK   6338 048
TERRENCE CLEMENTS SAX  (A      (F) LIVE                     1971 MERCURY  US SRM7500   UK   6641 033
MARCUS DOUBLEDAY TPT   (A      (G) WITH CARLOS SANTANA      1972 CBS      US   31308   UK     65142
VIRGIL GONSALVES WIND  (A      (H) CHAPTER VII              1973 CBS      US   32048   UK     65406
BILL McPHERSON   WIND  (AD     (J) BOOGER BEAR              1973 CBS      US   32694   UK     65820
DUANE HITCHINGS  ORG   (BCH    (K) ALL THE FACES OF BUDDY MILES1974 EPIC  US   33089   UK     80349
TOBIE WYNN       SAX   (BC     (L) MORE MILES PER GALLON    1975 CASABLANCA US  7019   UK      4006
JAMES TATUM      SAX   (BC     (M) BICENTENNIAL GATHERING   1976 CASABLANCA US  7024
BOBBY ROCK       SAX   (B      (N) SNEAK ATTACK             1981 ATLANTIC  UK K60156
PETER CARTER     TPT   (BC
TOM HALL         TPT   (BCF BOB PARKINS     ORG  (C   WALLY ROSSUNOLO   G   (C   BILLY COX      B   (C
ROBERT PITTMAN   SAX   (C   TEDDY BLANDIN   TPT  (C   CHARLIE KARP      G   (CDEF BOB HOGINS   K TROM(CDF
ROBIN McBRIDE    K     (C   ANDRE LEWIS     ORG  (CDEH MARLO HENDERSON  G   (CDEH DAVID HULL    B   (CDEF
LEE ALLEN        SAX   (CD  PHIL WOOD       HRNS (CD  MARK WILLIAMS     WIND(CD  ROLAND ROBINSON B  (CJ
FRED ALLEN       PERC  (DE  JOE PORTER      TPT  (D   DICK GABRIEL      SAX (D   MICHAEL FUGATE  TPT (E
HANK REDD        SAX   (EF  STEMSY HUNTER   SAX  (EFL DONNIE BECK       ORG (FJM ADRIAN CURTIS  G V (H
RON JOHNSON      B     (H   ROBERT HOGGINS  G V  (H   RICHARD APLANALP  SAX (H   BILLY SPRAGUE  HRNS(H
DAVID DHALSTON   HRNS  (H   DENISE PANTOS MILES D (H  WILLIE BOBO       PERC(H   VICTOR PANTOJA  CONGA(H
JAMES BRADSHAW   G     (H   PAUL GURVITZ(CURTIS) V (H STEVE BUSHFIELD   G   (J   BOB FERREIRA   SAX (J
PAT O'HARA       TROM  (J   PETER WALKER    TPT  (J   BILL ATWOOD       TPT (J   MINGO LEWIS    PERC(J
JERRY PETERS     K     (K   CLARENCE McDONALD K  (K   JAMES JAMERSON    B   (K   EDWARD GREENE   D  (K
KEN HAWKINS      G     (K   RAY PARKER      G    (K   MELVIN RAGIN      G   (K   JOE CLAYTON    PERC (K
GENE ESTES       PERC  (K   ERNIE WATTS     SAX  (K   BEN SCHULTZ       G K (LM  BOBBY BERGE     D  (LM
STEVE LAWRENCE   SAX   (LM  KEN WALTER      TROM (LM  TOM BRAY          TPT (LM  PAUL CACRA     TPT (LM
STEVIE WONDER    K     (L   AL BROWN        D    (L   JOHN MALLER       D   (M   DANNY HULL     SAX (M
RON PERRY        B     (M   BOYD ALBRITTON  G    (M   DICKIE BETTS      G   (M
```

JOHN MILES

```
JOHN MILES    G V K(ALL    (A) REBEL                   1976 DECCA UK SKL 5231 US LONDON 669
BOB MARSHALL  B    (ABCDE   (B) STRANGER IN THE CITY    1976 DECCA UK TXS  118 US LONDON 682
BARRY BLACK   D    (ABCDE   (C) ZARAGON                 1978 DECCA UK TXS  126 US ARISTA4176
GARY MOBERLEY K    (B       (D) MMMMPH                  1979 DECCA UK TXSR 135
BRIAN CHATTON K    (DE      (E) SYMPATHY                1980               US ARISTA4261
ORCHESTRA          (DE      (F) HIGH MILES              1981 EMI   UK EMC 3374
```

MILESTONES

```
BEATRIX NEUNDLINGER    FLT V(B     (A) MILESTONES            1971
CHRISTIAN KOLONOVITS   K B V(B     (B) EMIGRATION            1973 CBS   UK 65738
GUNTHER GROSSLERCHER   G V  (B
NORBERT NIEDERMAYER B G V(B    CHRI VANDER SCHYT    D    (B
```

```
        IAN NORTH          K G  (A            (A) MILK & COOKIES              1977  ISLAND       UK    ILPS 9320
        JUSTIN STRAUSS     V    (A
        SAL MAIDA          B    (A  MIKE RUIZ    D   (A   JIM GREGORY   B    (    MUFF WINWOOD   PROD(A
M155                                        MILKWOOD                                        M155
        BEN ORR            (              (A) MILKWOOD                  1972  PARAMOUNT    US    6046
        RICHARD OCASEK     (              (B) HOW'S THE WEATHER         19    PARAMOUNT    US
M156                                       MILLENIUM                                        M156
        CURT BOETCHER      V   (A         (A) BEGIN                     1968  CBS          US    CS 9663
        MICHAEL FENNELLY   G V (A
        LEE MALLORY        (A   JOE STEC      (A  RED RHODES     STEEL(A   DOUG RHODES       (A
        KEITH OLSEN        (A   PAT SHANAHAN  (A  RON EDGAR           (A   DOUG DILLARD      (A
        JIM RYAN           (A
M157                                      FRANKIE MILLER                                    M157
        FRANKIE MILLER     V G (ALL       (A) ONCE IN A BLUE MOON       1973  CHRYSALIS   UK/US  CHR1036
        ALLEN TOUSSAINT    K   (B         (B) HIGH LIFE                 1974  CHRYSALIS   UK/US  CHR1052
        JOE WILSON         G   (B         (C) THE ROCK                  1975  CHRYSALIS   UK/US  CHR 1088
        BOB ANDREWS        K V (A         (D) FULL HOUSE                1977  CHRYSALIS   UK/US  CHR 1128
        BRINSLEY SCHWARZ   G   (A         (E) DOUBLE TROUBLE            1978  CHRYSALIS   UK/US  CHR 1174
        BILLY RANKIN       D   (A         (F) FALLING IN LOVE/PERFECT FIT  1979  CHRYSALIS  UK/US  CHR 1220
        JOE OSBORN         B   (G         (F) FALLING IN LOVE/PERFECT FIT  1979  CHRYSALIS  EURO   6307 652
        IAN GOMM           G   (A         (G) EASY MONEY                1980  CHRYSALIS   UK/US  CHR 1268
        NICK LOWE          B V (A         (EP) JEALOUS GUY              1977  CHRYSALIS   UK     CHS 2184
        TOM ROBB           B   (B         (1) FEB 1978 TOUR    (2) MARCH 1978 TOUR
        MIKE HUEY          D   (B         (3) MAY 1978 TOUR    (4) SEPT  1978 TOUR
        G C COLEMAN        D   (B
        AUBURN BURRELL     G   (B   BARRY BAILEY      G   (B   LESTER CALISTE    TROM (B   CLYDE KERR JR    TROM(B
        GARY BROWN         SAX (B   JOHN LONGO    TPT     (B   ALVIN THOMAS      SAX  (B   HENRY McCULLOUGH  G   (C
        MICK WEAVER        K   (C   CHRIS STEWART   B(CDE123   STU PERRY         D    (C   RAY MINHINNIT     G   (D
        JAMES HALL         K   (D   GRAHAM DEACON   D    (D   KAREN LAWRENCE     V   (E   HUGH BURNS        G   (3
        FRAN BYRNE         D   (F4  RICHARD SUPA    V    (E   STEPHEN TYLER      V HCA(E  MARTIN DROVER     TPT (E12
        CHRIS MERCER       SAX (E123 PAUL CARRACK   K V(EF12  B J WILSON         D  (E123 RAY RUSSELL       G   (E2
        MICK MOODY         G   (1   LANI GROVES     V    (E   ERIC TROYER        V   (E   CHRIS SLADE       D   (F
        TEX COMER          B   (F4  DAVE WINTOUR    B    (F   BARRIE GUARD       PERC (F  TIM RENWICK       G   (F
        ED DEAN            G   (F4  TERRY BRITTEN   G    (F   STEVE SIMPSON      G   (F4  LINDA TAYLOR      V   (F
        RON ASPERY         HRNS (F  CHRIS HALL      K    (F   CHRIS SPEDDING     G   (D   RABBIT            K   (D
        GARY BROOKER       K V (D   MEMPHIS HORNS   HRNS (D   LARRY LONDIN       D PERC(G   REG YOUNG        G   (G
        BOBBY THOMPSON     G   (G
M158                                       JACOB MILLER                                     M158
        JACOB MILLER            (A         (A) DREAD DREAD              1978  UA           US    UALA 806
                                           ( ) WANTED                   1979
                                           ( ) TENEMENT STEPS           1980  ISLAND       NL    201 087
                                           ( ) JACOB KILLER MILLER      1980  ISLAND       NL    201 088
                                           ( ) MIXED UP MOODS           1980  ISLAND       NL    202 883
M158A                                  STEPHEN MILLER (UK)                                  M158A
        STEPHEN MILLER     K   (AB        (A) MILLER & COXHILL          1974  CAROLINE     UK    C 1503
        LOL COXHILL        WIND (A        (B) STORY SO FAR              1974  CAROLINE     UK    C 1507
        LAURIE ALLEN       PERC (B
M158B                                  STEPHEN MILLER (US)                                  M158B
        STEPHEN MILLER     K V (A         (A) STEPHEN MILLER            197   MERCURY     US
        FRED WALK          G   (A
        LARRY EASTER       WIND (A  CLARK PIERSON   D   (A  DINO LONG       B   (A  ELVIN BISHOP    G   (A
        APPLE JACK         HCA (A   JOHN CHAMBERS   D   (A  KIP MAERCKLIN   B   (A
M159                                   STEVE MILLER BAND                                    M159
        STEVE MILLER     HCA SYN G K V(ALL    (A) CHILDREN OF THE FUTURE   1968  CAPITOL  718  RI US   2920
        LONNIE TURNER    B G(13456ABCDEHJK    (B) SAILOR                  1969  CAPITOL  719  RI US   2984
        TIM DAVIS          B   (12ABCDE       (AB) LIVING IN USA(DBL )    1973  CAPITOL  717  EURO 197/98
        JAMES COOKE        G   (1EJK          (C) BRAVE NEW WORLD         1969  CAPITOL  184  EURO 80117
        JIM PETERMAN       K   (AB            (D) YOUR SAVING GRACE       1970  CAPITOL  331  EURO 80277
        BOZ SCAGGS         G V (AB            (E) NUMBER FIVE             1970  CAPITOL  436  EURO 80570
        BEN SIDRAN         K   (CDEG          (F) ROCK LOVE              1971  CAPITOL  748  EURO 80962
        NICKY HOPKINS      K   (CDE           (G) RECALL THE BEGINNING    1972  CAPITOL 11022 EURO 81099
        JIMMY MILLER       G   (E             (H) THE JOKER              1973  CAPITOL 11235 EURO 81514
        BOBBY THOMPSON     B   (E             (J) FLY LIKE AN EAGLE       1976  MERCURY UK 9286177 US CAPITOL11497
        KENNY LEE LEWIS    G   (M             (J) FLY LIKE AN EAGLE       1976  MERCURY EURO 6303 925
        BOBBY WINKLEMAN    B   (2             (K) BOOK OF DREAMS          1977  MERCURY UK 9286455 US CAPITOL11630
        JOHN MASSARO       G   (M             (K) BOOK OF DREAMS          1977  MERCURY EURO 6303 926
        ROSS VALORY        B   (F             (L) CIRCLE OF LOVE          1981  MERCURY UK 6302 061 US CAPITOL12121
        JOHN KING          D   (45H           (M) ABRACADABRA            1982           US CAPITOL12216
                                              ( ) REVOLUTION(QUICKSILVER,MOTHER EARTH)1968 UA  UK 29069  US UA  UAS5185
        JACK KING          D   (FG3           ( ) TRIPLE SET(QUICKSILVER,BAND)  19  CAPITOL          STCR 288
        GERALD JOHNSON     D   (345GHLM       ( ) ANTHOLOGY              1973  CAPITOL UK ESTSP12 US       11114
        JIM KELTNER        D   (G             ( ) BEST OF                1973  HORVU     EURO     SHZE 901
        DICKY THOMPSON     K   (345GH         ( ) MASTERS OF ROCK        1974  EMI  EURO 054 81583
        GARY MALLABER      D   (GJKLM         ( ) PROFILES               1974  EMI  EURO 81581
        LES DUDEK          G   (6JK           ( ) THE LEGEND             1975  CAPITOL  VMP 1008
        DOUG CLIFFORD      D   (6             ( ) ADVENTURES OF A SPACE COWBOY 1975 CAPITOL EURO 81645
        NORTON BUFFALO     V HCA(K            ( ) BEST OF 1968 73        1977  CAPITOL     EST 24058
        DAVID DENNY        K   (K             ( ) GREATEST HITS 1974/78  1978  MERCURY UK 9199916 US CAPITOL11822
        BYRON ALLRED       K   (KLM
          JOHN McFEE       G   (J             (1) NOV 1966     (2) NOV 1969/70   (3) JAN 1972
        JOACHIM YOUNG      K   (KJ            (4) MAR 1972     (5) OCT   1972    (6) JULY 1975
        BUD BILLINGS       TPT (E
        KENNY JOHNSON      D   (JK  SNEAKY PETE KLEINOW STEEL(H GREG DOUGLAS   G   (K  BUDDY SPICHER   FDL (E
        JAMES COTTON       HCA (J   ROGER CLARK    D   (34G CHARLIE McCOY    HCA  (E  WAYNE MOSS      G B (E
        LEE MICHAELS       K   (E   JIMMY TILLMAN  D   (E  CHARLIE CALMESE    B   (K  BOB GLAUB       B   (K
        JESSE ED DAVIS     G   (G   PAUL McCARTNEY B D V(C  GLYN JOHNS       G V PERC(
```

```
        JEAN MILLINGTON   B V  (A          (A) LADIES ON THE STAGE              1978   UA      US LA 821    UK UAG 30158
        JUNE MILLINGTON   G V  (A
        LEO ADAMIAN       D V  (A    TONY RAMOS       V   (A    IRENE CARA       V   (A    VICKI RANDLE     V  (A
        FAITH FUSILLO     V    (A    GORDON GRODY     V   (A    CHRIS WILLIAMSON V   (A    FLEMING WILLIAMS V  (A
        TOM SCOTT         WIND (A    DEBBY GABER      G   (A    SNEAKY PETE      STEEL(A    RALPH SCHUCKETT  K  (A
        COLLEEN STEWART   K    (A    TOM SELLERS      K   (A    MARGO LEWIS      V   (A    ED GREENE        D  (A
        SCOTT EDWARDS     B    (A    BRIE HOWARD      V   (A    ROLAND ROZZELLE  K   (A    LARRY CARLTON    G  (A
        KENNY NEMIROFF    K    (A    GARY COLEMAN     PERC(A    JUNE ADAMIAN     V   (A    BRYAN PARRIS     D  (A
        ELLEN SHIPLEY     V    (A    NEGRA            V   (A    LEE RITENOUR     G   (A    DEAN PARKS       G  (A
        CHRISTOPHER BOND  G    (A    EARL SLICK       G   (A
```

M160A   MARIO MILLO   M160A

```
        MARIO MILLO       V G K B D (A        (A) EPIC III                       19            AUST
        MARK KENNEDY      D    (A
        JACKIE ORSZACZKY  B    (A    COS RUSSO        K   (A    LAURA CHISLETT   FLT (A    SAFANYA          V  (A
        GERG TELL         D    (A    PETER KENNY  K       (A    DAVID GLYDE      SAX (A
```

M161   GARNET MIMMS   M161

```
        GARNET MIMMS      V    (ALL       WARM & SOUL                           1966   UA      UK ULP 1145
        WITH                             REMEMBER  (EP)                         1973   UA                   UK REM  403
        SAM BELL          V    (         HAS IT ALL                            1978   ARISTA US 4153        UK SPART1032
        ZOLA PEARNELL     V    (         AS LONG AS I HAVE YOU                 1964   UA            US  UAS  6396
        CHARLES BOYER     V    (         CRY BABY                              1963   UA            US  UAS  6305
                                         I'LL TAKE GOOD CARE OF YOU            1966   UA            US  UAS  6498
```

M162   (WAYNE FONTANA) & THE MINDBENDER   M162

```
        WAYNE FONTANA     V    (         (A) WAYNE FONTANA & THE MINDBENDERS   1965   FONTANA       UK     TL 5230
        ERIC STEWART      G V  (         (A) WFATM(SAME AS ABOVE +3 TRACKS)    1967   FONTANA SPEC       SFL 13106
                                         (A) WFATM(SAME AS A +2 TRACKS)        1967   WING                WL 1166
        BOB LAND          B    (         (B) ERIC RICK WAYNE BOB              1966   FONTANA       UK     TL 5257
        RICK ROTHWELL     D    (         (C) WAYNE ONE(WAYNE SOLO)            196    FONTANA       UK    STL 5351
        PAUL HANCOX       D    (         (D) THE MINDBENDERS                  1966   FONTANA UK 5324 RI SFL 13045
        GRAHAM GOULDMAN   G    (         (E) WITH WOMAN IN MIND               1967   FONTANA       UK    STL 5403
        JAMES O'NEIL      G    (         (F) A GROOVY KIND OF LOVE            1967   FONTANA US(M) 27554 (S)  67554
                                         ( ) TO SIR WITH LOVE(ON SOUNDTRACK)  1967   FONTANA       UK    STL 5446
```

M162A   LINCOLN SUGAR MINOTT   M162A

```
        LINCOLN 'SUGAR' MINOTT (AB       (A) BLACK ROOTS                       1980   ISLAND      UK/US    9591
                                         (B) GIVE THE PEOPLE                   1980   BALLISTIC   UK       30310
```

M162B   MINT TATTOO   M162B

```
        BRUCE STEPHENS    G V  (A        (A) MINT TATTOO                       1      DOT      US        25918
        BURNS KELLOGG     B K V(A
        GREGG THOMAS      D    (A
```

M163   MINK DEVILLE   M163

```
        WILLY DE VILLE    V G  (ALL      (A) MINK DEVILLE                      1977   CAPITOL        UK/US  11631
        BOBBY LEONARDS    K    (AB       (B) RETURN TO MAGENTA                 1978   CAPITOL        UK/US  11780
        VAL HERON         V    (A        (C) LE CHAT BLEU                      1980   CAPITOL US 11955 GER 86086 UK25390
        RUBIN SIQUENZA    B SAX(AB       (D) COUP DE GRACE                     1981   CAPITOL
        LOUIE ERLANGER    G V  (ABC
        THOMAS R ALLEN    D    (A   STEVE DOUGLAS PROD SAX (BC RITCH COLBERT   K    (    KENNY MARGOLIS  K V (C
        JACKIE KELSO      SAX  (B   DR JOHN          PNO (B    DAVID FORMAN    V    (B   LEON DOUGLAS    V   (B
        MIKE JOHNSON      V    (C   MAX BOWMAN       V   (AB JAKE              V    (C   JERRY SCHEFF    B D (C
        RON TUTT          D    (C   EVE MOON         V   (C
```

M163A   MIRAGE   M163A

```
        GEORGE KHAN       SAX FLT(A       (A) NOW YOU SEE IT                   1977   COMPENDIUM     NORWAY FIDARO 9
        BRIAN GODDING     G    (A
        STEVE COOK        B    (A   DAVE SHEEN   D    (A
```

M163B   STEVE MIRO & THE EYES   M163B

```
        STEVE MIRO        V G  (A        (A) RUDE INTRUSIONS                   1980   OBJECT                OBJ008
        JIMMY CARTER      B V  (A        (B) SECOND SENTENCE                   1981   OBJECT                OBJ015
        BRIAN MARTIN      D V  (A
        DUNCAN PRESTBURY  K V  (A   STEVE SOLAMAR    HCA (A   FREDRICK BURROWS  TPT (A
```

M163C   MISFITS   M163C

```
        GLENN DANZIG           (A        (A) BEWARE(EP)                        1979   CHERRY RED     UK     PLP9
        MR JIM            D    (A
        JERRY ONLY             (A   BOBBY STEELE     (A        JOEY IMAGE      (A
```

M163D   MISSION OF BURMA   M163D

```
        CLINT CONLEY      B VG (A        (A) SIGNALS CALLS & MARCHES (EP)      19     ACE OF HEARTS  CAN    1006
        ROGER MILLER      G V  (A
        PETER PRESCOTT    D V  (A   MARTIN SWOPE     TAPE (A
```

M163E   MISSUS BEASTLY   M163E

```
        JURGEN BENZ       WIND PERC(A     (A) MISSUS BEASTLY                   19     NOVA     GER     6 22030
        FRIEDEMANN JOSCH  WIND  (A
        NORBERT DOMLING   G B  (A    LUTZ OLDEMEIER   D    (A  DIETER MIEKAUTSCH  K (A
```

M164   MR BIG   M164

```
        JEFF DICKEN  HCA B G V (AB        (A) SWEET SILENCE                    1975   EMI            UK     EMC 3101
        PETE CROWTHER     G B  (AB        (B) MR BIG                           1977   EMI            UK     EMC 3171
        EDDIE CARTER      G V  (B
        VINCE CHAULK      V D  (AB   JOHN MARTER      D V  (    JOHN BURNIP     D    (A  IAN BLUNSDON    K  (A
        JOHN PUNTER       SYN  (A    ROBERT HIRSCHMAN B TROM(A
```

M165   MR BLOE   M165

```
                                         (A) GROOVIN WITH MR BLOE             1973   SILVERLINE 036 + DJM 1974 DJLPS409
```

M165A   Mr FLOOD'S PARTY   M165A

```
        JAY HIRSH              (A        (A) MR FLOODS PARTY                   1969   COTILLION      US 9003
        MIKE CORBETT           (A
        FRED TESCANO           (A   RICK MIRAGE      (A    TOM CASTAHNARA      (A  MARCEL THOMPSON    (A
```

MR FOX

```
    BOB PEGG        V G B K    (AB      (A) MR FOX                    1970 TRANSATLANTIC      UK    TRA226
    CAROLE PEGG     V FDL(AB           (B) THE GYPSY                  1971 TRANSATLANTIC      UK    TRA236
    ALUN EVANS      D     (AB          (AB THE COMPLETE MR FOX        1975 TRANSATLANTIC      UK    TRA303
    BARRY LYONS     B DULC (AB
    ANDREW MASSEY   CELLO(A  JOHN MYATT      WIND(A    RICHIE BULL    B BANJ(   GRIDLEY TABERNACLE ORCH  (B
    NICK STRUTT     MULTI(
```

MISTERS

```
    BERT DECORTE       G V  (A        (A) CHANGE PARTNERS            1978 ARIOLA    GER    200 229
    LUC'LEWIS' VAN RUMST G V(A        (B) SNAKING OUT FROM THE DARK  1980 POLYDOR   FR     2427 931
    KLAUS WAGNER       B    (A
    ROY HARLINGTON     D    (A   PIETRO LACIRIGNOLA SAX (A   DANNY BODDIN   PNO (A   FRANK TOMMELEIN  V (B
    PAUL COWBELL       B    (
```

MISTRESS

```
    CHARLIE WILLIAMS   G V  (A        (A) MISTRESS                   1979    RSO     US 13059     RSS 14
    DAVID BROWN        B    (A
    KENNY HOPKINS      G V  (A   DANNY CHAUNCEY   G V  (A   MIKE UTLEY     K  (A   DOUG DILLARD    BAN (A
    CHRIS PAULSEN      D    (A   JOHN McFEE       STEEL(A   RICK CLARK     V  (A   GREG DOUGLAS    G  (
    DAVE WALKER        V    (    SKIP OLSON          B  (
```

MISTY IN ROOTS

```
                                  (A) LIVE AT COUNTER EUROVISION  1980     PEOPLE UNITE         PU003
                                  (B) WISE & FOOLISH             1981 PEOPLE UNITE            PU101
```

MISTUNDERSTOOD

```
    GLEN FERNANDO CAMPBELL STEEL(AB   (A)MISTUNDERSTOOD 1966 1967   (B) 1969
    TONY HILL          G V  (A
    GREG TREADWAY      G V  (A   RICK BROWN       V  (A   STEVE WHITING   B  (A   RICK MOE    D   (A
    STEVE HOARD        V    (B   DAVY O'LIST      G  (B   NIC POTTER      B  (B   CHRIS MERCER    SAX(B
    NEIL HUBBARD       G    (B   GUY EVANS           D  (B
```

BLUE MITCHELL

```
    BLUE MITCHELL      HRNS (A        THING TO DO                   19   BLUENOTE           BST 84178
                                      BRING IT HOME TO ME           19   BLUENOTE           BST 84228
                                      BOSS HORN                     19   BLUENOTE           BST 84257
                                      HEADS UP                      19   BLUENOTE           BST 84272
                                      COLLISION IN BLACK            19   BLUENOTE           BST 84300
                                      BANTU VILLAGE                 19   BLUENOTE           BST 84324
                                      BLUE MITCHELL                 1972 MAINSTREAM    US     315
                                      VITAL                         197  MAINSTREAM    US     343
                                      BLUE'S BLUE                   197  MAINSTREAM    US     374
                                      GRAFFITI BLUES                1974 MAINSTREAM    US 400  MSL 1026
                                      MANY SHADES OF BLUE           1975 MAINSTREAM    US 402  MSL 1028
                                      STRATO SONIC                  1975 RCA          US 1109
                                      FUNKTION                      1976 RCA          US 1493
```

IAN MITCHELL BAND

```
    IAN MITCHELL   V G K B  (A        (A) LONELY NIGHTS             1979    WB             UK      K 58070
    JON JAY        B V G(A
    NICKY DIAMOND  K V  (A   PAUL JACKSON G K V(A   LINDSAY SIMON HONEY D V K(A
```

JONI MITCHELL

```
    JONI MITCHELL    V G K(ALL        (A) JONI MITCHELL            1968 REPRISE US  6293   UK   K 44051
    TOM SCOTT        WIND (EJFG       (B) CLOUDS                   1969 RERPISE US  6341   UK   K 44070
    WILTON FELDER    B   (EFH         (C) LADIES OF THE CANYON     1970 REPRISE US  6376   UK   K 44085
    RUSS KUNKEL      D    (DE         (D) BLUE                     1971 REPRISE US  2038   UK   K 44128
    BOBBYE HALL      PERC (EJK        (E) FOR THE ROSES            1972 ASYLUM  US  5057   UK SYLA 8753
    GRAHAM NASH      V HCA(EFH        (E) FOR THE ROSES            1975 ASYLUM         RI UK   K 53007
    JAMES BURTON     G    (E          (F) COURT & SPARK            1974 ASYLUM  US 7E1001  UK SYLA 8756
    STEPHEN STILLS   G B  (ABDE       (F) COURT & SPARK            1975 ASYLUM         RI UK   K 53002
    JAMES TAYLOR     G V  (DHN        (G) MILES OF AISLES          1974 ASYLUM  US   202   UK SYSP 902
    SNEAKY PETE KLEINOW STEEL(D       (G) MILES OF AISLES          1975 ASYLUM         RI UK   K 63001
    JOHN GUERIN      D    (FGHJKN     (H) HISSING OF SUMMER LAWNS  1975 ASYLUM  US 7E1051  UK SYLA 8763
    MAX BENNETT      B    (FGHJ       (H) HISSING OF SUMMER LAWNS  1975 ASYLUM         RI UK   K 53018
    JIM HUGHART      B    (F          (J) HEJIRA                   1976 ASYLUM  US 7E1087  UK   K 53053
    MILT HOLLAND     PERC (CF         (K) DON JUANS RECKLESS DAUGHTER 1977 ASYLUM US 101   UK   K 63003
    CHUCK FINDLEY    TPT  (FJH        (L) MINGUS                   1979 ASYLUM  US 5E505  UK   K 53091
    JOE SAMPLE       K    (FH         (M) SHADOWS & LIGHT (DBL)(BEST OF) 1980 ASYLUM US 704 UK    62030
    STEVE LUKATHER   G    (N          (N) WILD THINGS RUN FAST     1982 GEFFEN         UK       25102
    DAVID CROSBY     V    (FH
    SUSAN WEBB       V    (F   WAYNE PERKINS     G  (F   DENNIS BUDIMIR   G  (F   ROBBIE ROBERTSON G  (F
    JOSE FELICIANO   V    (F   ROBBEN FORD       G  (GH  JEFF BAXTER      G  (H   CHEECH & CHONG   V  (F
    VICTOR FELDMAN   PERC K (FJN BUD SHANK    WIND (N   JACO PASTORIUS   B  (JKLM NEIL YOUNG     HCA (J
    ABE MOST         CLAR (J   CHUCK DOMANICO    B  (J   TERESSA ADAMS    CELLO(C  PAUL HORN       WIND(C
    JIM HORN         SAX  (J   SASKATUNES        V  (C   WAYNE SHORTER    SAX (KLN HERBIE HANCOCK  K  (L
    PETER ERSKINE    D    (L   DON ALIAS      CONGA(LKM EMIL RICHARDS    PERC (L   MANOLO BADRENA  PERC(K
    AIRTO MOREIRA    PERC (K   GLENN FREY        V  (K   LYLE MAYS        K  (M   PERSUASIONS      V  (M
    LARRY CARLTON    G (FHJKN  MICHELE COLOMBIER PNO (K   ALEJANDRO ACUNA  PERC (K  CHAKA KHAN      V  (K
    J D SOUTHER      V    (K   PAT METHENY       G  (M   MICHAEL BRECKER  SAX (M   LEE KEEFER      (M
    LARRY NASH       PNO  (G   CHARLIE MINGUS    V  (L   VINNIE COLAIUTA  D  (N   LIONEL RICHIE    V  (N
    HOWARD KINNEY    V    (N   RUSSELL FERRANTE  SYN (N   KENNY RANKIN     V  (N   SKIP COTTRELL    V  (N
    LARRY KLEIN      B    (N   LARRY WILLIAMS  K SAX(N   CHARLES VALENTINO V (N   MIKE LANDAU      G  (N
    ROBERT DE LA GARZA V  (N   KIM HUTCHCROFT    SAX (N
```

SAM MITCHELL

```
    SAM MITCHELL     G V  (AB         (A) BOTTLENECK & SLIDE GUITAR  1978    KICKING MULE        SNKF 121
                                      (B) FOLLOW YOU DOWN            1978    KICKING MULE        SNKF 147
```

WILLIE MITCHELL

```
    WILLIE MITCHELL  TPT  (ALL        (A) ITS WHATS HAPPENING        196  HI US 32007
    MICHAEL TOLES    G K  (K          (B) HOLD IT                    1964 HI US 32021
    AL JACKSON       D    (           (C) HIT SOUND                  196  HI US 32034
    CHARLES HODGES   K    (G          (D) SOUL SERENADE              1968 HI US 32039 UK LONDON SHU 8365
    JAMES MITCHELL   SAX  (G          (E) LIVE                       1968 HI US 32042 UK LONDON SHU 8368
    LEROY HODGES     B    (G          (F) SOLID SOUL                 1969 HI US 32045 UK LONDON SHU 8372
    HOWARD GRIMES    D    (G          (G) ON TOP                     1969 HI US 32048 UK LONDON SHU 8388
    MABON HODGES     G    (G          (H) SOUL BAG                   1970 HI US 32050 UK LONDON SHU 8408
                                      (I) ROBINS NEST                197  HI US 32058
                                      (J) BEST OF                    19   HI US 32068
                                      (K) LISTEN DANCE               1981 BEARSVILLE US BRK 3520
```

HANK MIZELL

HANK MIZELL	G V	(ALL	(A) JUNGLE ROCK			1976	CHARLY	UK	CRL 5000	
JIMMY DEMPSEY	G	(A	(EP) HIGHER			1977	CHARLY	UK	CEP 115	
JAMES BOBO	G	(A								
LEO JACKSON	G	(A	BILL COLLINS	D	(A	JERRY KROON	D	(A	EDDIE	B	(A
JACK ROSS	B	(A	D J FONTANA	D	(A	BOB DEAN		(A	BILL HUMBLE	B	(A
ALAN MOORE	PNO SAX	(A								

MO DETTES

		(A) STORY SO FAR		1980	DERAM	UK	SML 1120

MOBY GRAPE

PETER LEWIS	G	(ABCDEFGH	(A) MOBY GRAPE	1967	CBS	US	CS 9498(S)	CL 2698 (M)	
JOEL SCOTT HILL	V	(	(A) MOBY GRAPE	196	CBS	US	30392	UK	63090
KENT DUNBAR	D	(	(B) WOW	1968	CBS	US	9613	UK	63271
BOB MOSLEY	B	(ABCEF	(B) WOW/GRAPE JAM (FREE LP WITH WOW)	1968	CBS	US	cxs3	UK	66209
SKIP SPENCE	G D	(ABEFH	(C) MOBY GRAPE 69	1969	CBS	US	9696	UK	63430
BOB NEWKIRK	D	(	(D) TRULY FINE CITIZEN	1970	CBS	US	9912	UK	63698
DON STEVENSON	G D	(ABCDEF	(E) 20 GRANITE CREEK	1972	REPRISE	US	6460	UK	K 44152
JERRY MILLER	G	(ABEFCDH	(F) GREAT GRAPE	1974	CBS	US 31098	UK	64743
BOB MOORE	B	(D	(G) BEST OF	1976	CBS		EURO	53371
GORDON STEVENS	VLN G(E		(H) GRAPE LIVE	1979	ESCAPE		IMP ESAIA	
ANDY NARELL	PERC (E		( ) OMAHA	1971	HARMONY US 30392			
DAVID RUBINSTEIN	PNO PERC(E							
JEFFREY COHEN	B	(E	CORNELIUS BUMPUS SAXK(H	JOHN OXENDINE	D	(H	CHRISTIAN POWELL B (H
TOMMY SPURLOCK	G	(	DANNY TIMMS	K	(	FRANK RECARD	G V (	JEFF BLACKBURN G V (
JOHN CRAVIOTTA	D	(						

MODELS

CLIFF FOX	G V	(	(A) YES WITH MY BABY	1980	WINFIELD	US	3642
MARCO PIRRONI	G	(					
MICK ALLEN	B	(	TERRY DAY	D	(		

MODERATES

BOB CARR	G	(A	(A) FETISHES (EP)	19	OPEN EYE		OE1001
TOM GOULD	G	(A					
PHIL ALLEN	D	(A	HEIDI KURE	V	(A	BRADY	K V (A	MARTIN COOPER	B	(A
BOB MORTEN	SAX	(A					

MODERN MAN

DANNY MITCHELL	G SYN(A		(A) CONCRETE SCHEME	1980	MAM		LP 5001
JIM COOK	V	(A					
MIKE MORAN	B	(A	ALI McLEOD	G	(A	COLIN KING	D V (A

MODERNAIRES

PHILLIP BRADLEY	G V SYN(A		(A) WAY OF LIVING	1980	ILLUMINATED	UK JAMS 3
DAVID BAYNTON POWER D V(A						
HUGH HUGHES	B K V(A	LEA MINSHULL WINS V	(	(A		

MODERN ENGLISH

STEPHEN WALKER	K	(A	(A) MESH & LACE	1981	4AD	UK	CAD105
MICK CONROY	B V	(A					
RICHARD BROWN	D	(A	GARY McDOWELL	G V (A	ROBBIE GREY	V	(A

MODERN EON

BOB WAKELIN SYN V PERC(A		(A) FICTION TALES	1981	DINDISC	UK DID11	
CLIFF HEWITT	D PERC(A					
DANNY HAMPSON	B	(A	TIM LEVER	G SAX(A	ALIX G V K HRN(A	

MOEBIUS & PLANK

DIETER MOEBIUS	K SYN	(A	(A) RASTAKRAUT	1980	SKY	039
CONNIE PLANK	K SYN	(A				

MOGUL THRASH

JAMES LITHERLAND	G	(A	(A) MOGUL THRASH	1971	RCA	UK	SF 8156
JOHN WETTON	B	(A					
BILL HARRISON	D	(A	ROGER BALL	SAX (A	MAL DUNCAN	SAX (A	MIKE ROSEN TPT (A

ESSRA MOHAWK

ESSRA(SANDY HURVITZ)MOHAWK K V(ALL		(A) SANDYS ALBUM IS HERE AT LAST	1969	VERVE	US	V6 5064	
JIM PEPPER	SAX	(A	(B) PRIMORDIAL LOVERS	1970	REPRISE	US	RS 6377
LARRY CARLTON	G	(C	(C) ESSRA MOHAWK	1975	MOONCREST UK CREST24 US ASYLUM1023
TOM SELLERS	K B G(C		(D) ESSRA	1977	PRIVATE STOCK PS 2024 + PVLP 1016
WILTON FELDER	B	(V					
DENNIS PARKER	B	(C	KING ERRISSON	PERC (C	ED GREENE	D	(C	GENE ESTES	PERC (C
ZITRO	D	(C	GENE PELLO	D	(C	KENNY JENKINS	FLT	(C	SKIP SWITZER	D	(C
DEAN PARKS	G	(C	TOM HENSLEY	K	(C	ERIC GALE	G	(D	JONATHAN KALB	G	(D
DAVID STONE	G	(D	SONNY BURKE	K	(D	RICHARD DAVIS	B	(D	ANDY NEWMARK	D	(D
BERNARD PURDIE	D	(D	HOWIE WYETH	D	(D	PAUL GRIFFIN	K	(D	JERRY RAGOVOY	K	(D
JEREMY STEIG	FLT	(AD	DAVID LASLEY	V	(D	ULA HEDWIG	V	(D	ARNOLD McCULLER V	(D.
IAN UNDERWOOD	A	(D	RHETTA HUGHES	V	(D					

MOLKIE COLE

BOB STEINMETZ	K SAX(A		(A) MOLKIE COLE	1977	JANUS	US 7031	
TIMOTHY COLE	D	(A					
PHILIP JAMES	G	(A	PAUL POPE	G	(A	PAT COLE	B	(A	JAMES M TESTA	HCA (A

MOJO HANNAH

MIKE STEWART	G V	(A	(A) SIX DAYS ON THE ROAD	1972	KINGDOM UK	KVL 9001
PAUL MACCULLUM	B V	(A				
MIKE FUDGE	MAND VLN	(A	CHRIS HUNT	D	(A	JOE GILLINGHAM	K	(A

MOLLY HATCHET

DUANE ROLAND	G	(ABCD	(A) MOLLY HATCHET	1978	EPIC	US 35347	UK 83250	
DAVE HLUBEK	G	(ABCD	(B) FLIRTIN' WITH DISASTER	1979	EPIC	US 36110	UK	83791
STEVE HOLLAND	G	(ABCD	(C) BEATIN' THE ODDS	1980	CBS	US 36572	UK	84471
BRUCE CRUMP	D	(ABCD	(D) TAKE NO PRISONERS	1981	EPIC	US 37480	UK	85296
JIMMY FARRAR	V	(CD						
BANNER THOMAS	B	(ABCD DANNY JOE BROWN V (AB	JAI WINDING	K	(D	PAULINHO DACOSTA PERC(D
TOM WERMAN	PERC (D	BABY JEAN	V	(A	TOWER OF POWER	HRNS (D	BABY JEAN	V (D
MINDY STERLING	V	(D	LAURIE BONO	V	(D	KATY SAGAL	V	(D

```
M178B                              MOMS APPLE PIE                                            M178B
    TONY GIGLIOTTI      V   (A        (A) MUSIC                1973   BROWN BAG      US  BB LA 073
    BOB FIORINO         V   (A        (B) MOMS APPLE PIE       1973   BROWN BAG      US     14200
    BOB MILLER          G   (A
    DAVE MAZZOCHI     K V   (A   JOE AHLADIS      G   (A   PAT AULIZIA    D  (A   GREG YOCHMAN   B  (A
    ROGER FORCE       WIND  (A   BOB PINTA      TPT   (A   FRED MARZULLA  TROM (A
M178C                                   MONEY                                                M178C
    LARRY PHILLIPS    B V   (A        (A) FIRST INVESTMENT    1979   GULL           UK  GULP1031
    DAVID WEST-MULLEN VPERC (A
    JOHN OVERTON      G V   (A   TONY BODEN  D PERC V  (A   CHRIS TSANGARIDES  K  (A
M178D                                  MOLOCH                                                M178D
    LEE BAKER         G V   (A        (A) MOLOCH              19     ENTERPRISE     ENS 1002
    PHILLIP DURHAM  D V   (A
    FRED NICHOLSON    ORG(A   STEVE SPEAR      B   (A   GENE WILKINS   V  (A
M179                                EDDIE MONEY                                              M179
    EDDIE MONEY       V K SAX(ABC     (A) EDDIE MONEY         1977   CBS    US 34909  UK 82434
    JIMMY LYON        G   (ABC        (B) LIFE IS FOR THE TAKING  1978  CBS  US 35598  UK 83159
    GARY MALLABER     D   (ABC        (C) PLAYING FOR KEEPS  1980   CBS    US 36514  UK 84371
    LONNIE TURNER     B   (ABC
    GENE PARDUE       D   (A   POPS POWPELL     B   (A   ALAN PASQUA    K  (AB  EMILIO CASTILLO   HRNS(C
    STEVE KUPKA       HRNS (C  MAUREEN McCORMICK V  (C   RANDY NICHOLS  K  (ABC FREDDIE WEBB      K  (A
    KEVIN CALHOUN     PERC (A  TOM SCOTT      SAX  (AB   JO BAKER       V  (A   MYRNA MATTHEWS    V  (C
    JULIA TILLMAN     V   (C   MARTI McCALL     V   (C   VALERIE CARTER V  (C   DAVID LEWARK      G  (C
    JOHN NELSON       G   (C   GREG DOUGLAS     G   (C   BOB GLAUB      C  (C   KENNY LEWIS       B  (C
    NICKY HOPKINS     K   (B   LLOYD CHIATE     G   (B   JOHN WHITNEY   G  (B   DAVE DANZA        D  (B
    GREGORY PHILLINGANES K (B  DAVID LINDLEY    G   (B   TIM SHERIDAN   B  (B   STEVE PORCARO     SYN (B
    DARRELL VERDUSCO  V   (B   K WINBUSH        V   (B
M180                                ZOOT MONEY                                               M180
    ZOOT MONEY        K V   (ALL      (A) IT SHOULD HAVE BEEN ME   1965  COLUMBIA  UK  SX 1734
    PAUL WILLIAMS     B V   (2BE      (B) ZOOT                1966   COLUMBIA   UK  SCX 6075
    COLIN ALLEN       D   (12BE       (C) TRANSITION          1968   DIRECTION  UK  863231
    NICK NEWELL       SAX  (23BE      (D) WELCOME TO MY HEAD  1969   CAPITOL    US  318
    ANDY SUMMERS      G   (12BE       (E) ALL HAPPENING AT KLOOKS KLEEK  19  EPIC  US  24241
    CLIVE BURROWS     SAX  (2         (F) ZOOT MONEY          1970   POLYDOR    UK  2482 019
    PAT DONALDSON     B   (1          (G) MR MONEY            1980   MAGIC MOON     LUNE 1
    BARRY WILSON      D   (4          (1) DANTALIONS CHARIOT  (2) BIG ROLL BAND
    JOHNNY ALMOND     SAX  (BE        (3) MUSIC BAND 1969     (4) MUSIC BAND
    BERNIE BYRNES     D   (3
    JOHN DEAN         B   (4   MIKE COTTON    TPT  (3   JOHN BEECHAM   TROM (3  LEN LUBIN    B   (3
    MICK MOODY        G   (34  JIM GORDON       D   (D   DAVID COHEN        (D  LYLE RITZ        (D
    DON PEAKE             (D   MIKE RUBINI          (D   GARY COLEMAN   PERC (D  JIMMY GETZOFF VLN(D
    VINCE DEROSA      HRNS (D   BILL HENSHAS HRNS  (D   ART MAEBE      HRNS (D  HENRY SIGISMONTI HRNS(D
M180A                                 MONGREL                                                M180A
    ROBERT BRADY      K V   (A        (A) GET YOUR TEETH INTO THIS  1973  POLYDOR  UK  2383 182
    STUART SCOTT      G   (A
    RICK PRICE        B   (A   KEITH SMART      D   (A   CHARLIE GRIMA  PERC (A  MEGAN DAVIES    B  (A
    TOM FARNELL       D   (A   ROGER HILL       G   (A
M180B                              MEREDITH MONK                                             M180B
    MEREDITH MONK     V ORG (A        (A) KEY                 1977   LOVELY MUSIC   US  LML 1051
    DANIEL IRA SVERDLIK  (A
    DICK HIGGINS          (A   COLLIN WALCOTT       (A   LANNY HARRISON     (A  MARK MONSTERMAKER  (A
M180C                             FRANCIS MONKMAN                                            M180C
    FRANCIS MONKMAN       (A        (A) ENERGISM            1980   WEA  NL        58133
M181                                THE MONKEES                                              M181
    DAVY JONES        V   (ALL        THE MONKEES             19     RCA UK SF7844  COLGEMS US  101
    MICKEY DOLENZ   G D V K(ALL        MORE OF THE MONKEES    19     RCA UK SF7868  COLGEMS US  102
    PETER TORK      G B V(ALL EX*     (C)HEADQUARTERS         1967   RCA UK SF7886  COLGEMS US  103
    MICHAEL NESMITH G V  (ALL EX *    (D)PISCES,AQUARIUS, CAPRICORN & JONES  1967  RCA UK SF 7912  COLGEMS US  104
                                       THE BIRDS THE BEES & THE MONKEES  1968  RCA UK SF7948  COLGEMS US  109
    TOMMY BOYCE     PROD (*            INSTANT REPLAY         1969   RCA UK SF8016  COLGEMS US  113
    BOBBY HART      PROD (*            GREATEST HITS          1969          COLGEMS US  115
    BILL MARTIN     K   (D             CHANGES                1970                  COLGEMS US  119
    EDDIE HOH       D   (D             HEAD                   1969   RCA UK SF8015  COLGEMS US  5008
    KIM COPLI       D   (D             GOLDEN HITS            19                    COLGEMS US  329
    CHIP DOUGLAS    K B PROD(D         BARREL FULL OF MONKEES  1970                 COLGEMS US  1001
    FAITHLING HATFIELD PROD(D          THE MONKEES        (DBL)  19  LAURIE HOUSE       US  8009
    PAUL BEAVER     SYN (D             THE MONKEES            1973   SOUNDS SUPERB      UK  90032
    DOUG DILLARD    BANJ (D            RE FOCUS               19     BELL              US  6081
    VINCE DEROSA    HRNS (C            GREATEST HITS          19     ARISTA           GERM 201115
    FRED SEYKORA    CELLO(C            GREATEST HITS          19     ARISTA                4089
                                       MONKEES PRESENT        19     COLGEMS      US 117
                                       MONKEES                1973   MFP          UK  90032
                                   (*)JONES DOLENZ BOYCE & HART  1976  CAPITOL           11513
                                       40 TIMELESS HITS       1980   EMI          UK
M181A                               MONKS (1960s)                                            M181A
    GARY BURGER       G   (A        (A) BLACK MONK TIME     1966   POLYDOR    UK      2417129
    LARRY CLARK       ORG (A
    EDDIE SHAW        B   (A   ROGER JOHNSTON   D   (A
M181B                               MONKS(1979)                                              M181B
    JOHN FORD             (A        (A) BAD HABITS          1979   EMI        UK  EMC 3309
    RICHARD HUDSON        (A
    TERRY CASSIDY         (A
M181C                            MONOCHROME SET                                              M181C
    LESTER SQUARE     G V   (AB       (A) STRANGE BOUTIQUE    1980   DINDISC    UK      DID4
    BID               V G   (AB       (B) LOVE ZOMBIES        1980   DINDISC    UK      DID8
    ANDY WARREN       B V   (AB
    J D HANEY         D V   (AB  BOB SARGEANT   K V  (A   ALVIN CLARK   K  (B  TONY POTTS     (B
M181D                                  MONROE                                                M181D
    STEVE BUTLER      V   (A        (A) MONROE              1980   POLYDOR    UK      2383 597
    GARY SHARPE       G   (A
    PETE HUMPHRIES    G   (A   JAN TAYLOR     B   (A   STEVE GIBSON   D  (A
```

```
M182                            MONTAGE                                          M182
    BOB STEURER        V  (A        (A MONTAGE                1969 LAURIE        US    SLP 2049
    VANCE CHAPMAN      D V (A        (B) HOT PARTS            19   KAMA SUTRA    US        2054
    MIKE SMYTH         G V (A
    LANCE CORNELIUS    B V (A   MICHAEL BROWN   K  (A
M182A                         MONTE CAZAZZA                                      M182A
                                 (A) SOMETHING FOR NOBODY (EP) 19   INDUSTRIAL          IR 0010
M183                          CHRIS MONTEZ                                       M183
    CHRIS MONTEZ       V  (ALL      THE MORE I SEE YOU       1966 PYE    UK NPL23080 MAYFAIR AMLB1011
                                    THE MORE I SEE YOU       19   A&M    US 4115
                                    TIME AFTER TIME          1967 PYE    UK NSPL28187 HAMLET AMLP8006
                                    TIME AFTER TIME          19   A&M    US 4120
                                    FOOLIN' AROUND           1967 A&M    US 4128       UK   AML 906
                                    WATCH WHAT HAPPENED      1968 A&M    US 4157       UK   AML 925
                                    LETS DANCE               19   CBS    UK 65408    LONDON UK HAU8079
                                    LETS DANCE               19   MONOGRAM US 100    M F P  UK 50122
M184                      JAMES MONTGOMERY BAND                                  M184
    JAMES MONTGOMERY V HCA(ALL      (A) FIRST TIME OUT       1974 CAPRICORN     US     CP 0120
    BARRY WASHINGTON PERC (A        (B) HIGH ROLLER          1974 CAPRICORN     US     CP 0142
    BILLY MATHER      B V (AB       (C) JAMES MONTGOMERY BAND 1977 ISLAND UK ILPS9419 US ANTILLES 7059
    PETER MALICK G V STEEL (AB      (D) DUCK FEVER           1979 WATERHOUSE    US 5
    DAVE CASE         K V (AB
    CHUCK PURRO       D V (AB  PETER BELL      G V (AB  SKIP DRINKWATER  PROD (A
M185                    LITTLE BROTHER MONTGOMERY                                M185
    EURREAL MONTGOMERY V PNO(ALL    LITTLE BROTHER MONTGOMERY 1960 DECCA         UK     LK  4664
    LEE COLLINS      TPT (          LITTLE BROTHER MONTGOMERY 1960 COLUMBIA      UK     33SX 1289
    OLIVER ALCORN   WIND (          TASTY BLUES              1960 BLUESVILLE US 1012 PRESTIGE 7807
    ERNEST CRAWFORD   B  (          AFTER HOURS BLUES        19   BIOGRAPH             BLP 12010
    JEROME SMITH      D  (          & SUNNYLAND SLIM         19   77                   LA  1211
    ALEXIS KORNER     G  (          FARRO STREET JIVE        19   XTRA XTRA1115 FOLKWAYS   31014
    LAYFAYETTE THOMAS G  (          1972                     1972 MATCHBOX             SDM 223
    JULIAN EULL       B  (          DEEP SOUTH PIANO         1975 STORYVILLE          SLP 228
    KEN COLYER      TPT (           1930/69                  1971 MATCHBOX             SDR 213
    JACK FALCON       B  (          NO SPECIAL RIDER         19   ADELPHI       US         1003
    ROB GUTHRIE        (            BLUES                    19   FOLKWAY       US         3527
    LONNIE JOHNSON    G  (          SPIRITUALS               19   FOLKWAYS      US        31042
    SONNY GREER       D  (          SOUTH SIDE BLUES         19   REV           US         403
    MAMA YANCEY        (            TISHOMINGO BLUES         1980 JSP                     1015
                                    LITTLE BROTHER MONTGOMERY 19   COLLECTORS CLASSICS US CC 35
                                    LITTLE BROTHER MONTGOMERY 19   DELMARK       US        610
M187                            MONTROSE                                         M187
    RONNIE MONTROSE   G  (ALL       (A) MONTROSE             1973 WB     US 2740       UK K46276
    BOB JAMES         V  (CD        (B) PAPER MONEY          1974 WB     US 2823       UK K56069
    JIM ALCIVAR       B  (CDE       (C) WB PRESENTS          1975 WB     US 2892       UK K56170
    ALAN FITZGERALD   B  (BCE       (D) JUMP ON IT           1976 WB     US 2963       UK K56291
    DENNY CARMASSI    D  (ABCD      (E) OPEN FIRE (RONNIE)   1978 WB     US 3134       UK K56451
    BILL CHURCH       B  (A
    SAMMY HAGAR       V  (AB MARK JORDAN   K   (B  NICK DE CARO  K   (B  NOVI NOVAG   VLA (C
    RANDY JO HOBBS    B  (D   RICK SCHLOSSER  D  (E  EDGAR WINTER  K  (E  TED TEMPLEMAN  PROD(A
M188                  MONTY PYTHON'S FLYING CIRCUS                               M188
    JOHN CLEESE        (            (A) MONTY PYTHON'S FLYING CIRCUS 1970 BBC          REB  73M
    ERIC IDLE          (            (b) ANOTHER MONTY PYTHON RECORD 1971 CHARISMA  UK  CAS  1049
    MICHAEL PALIN      (            (C) PREVIOUS RECORD      1972 CHARISMA     UK    CAS  1063
    TERRY WILLIAMS     (            (D) MATCHING TIE & HANKERCHIEF 1973 CHARISMA UKCAS1080 US ARISTA 4039
    GRAHAM CHAPMAN     (            (E) LIVE AT DURY LANE    1974 CHARISMA     UK    CLASS 4
    TERRY GILLIAM      (            (F) MONTY PYTHON & THE HOLY GRAIL 1975 CHARISMA UKCAS1102 US ARISTA 4050
    DOUGLAS ADAMS      (            (G) LIVE AT THE CITY CENTRE 1976 ARISTA     US          4073
    JOHN YOUNG         (            (H) INSTANT RECORD COLLECTION 1977 CHARISMA UK CAS1134
    BEE DUFFELL        (            (I) WORST OF MONTY PYTHON 19   BUDDAH       US        5656/2
    CONNIE BOOTH       (            (J) LIFE OF BRIAN        1979 WB           UK         K56757
    CAROL CLEVELAND    (            CONTRACTUAL OBLIGATION ALBUM 1980 CHARISMA  UK CAS 1152
M188A                          MONUMENT                                         M188A
    STEVEN LOWE     V K (A          (A) MONUMENT             1971 BEACON               BEAS15
    WES TRUVOR        G  (A
    JAKE BREWSTER     D  (A   MARVE FLETCHLEY   B   (A
M189                          MOODY BLUES                                        M189
    DENNY LAINE     G V (AB         (A) GO NOW , THE MOODY BLUES 1965 LONDON      US  LP 428
    CLINT WARWICK   B   (AB         (B) MAGNIFICENT MOODIES  1966 DECCA        UK   LK 4711
    MIKE PINDER   K V(ABCDEFGHJKLMN (C) DAYS OF FUTURE PAST  1967 DERAM UK SML 707 US LONDON 18012
    GRAEME EDGE   D  (ABCDEFGHJKLMN1R(D) IN SEARCH OF THE LOST CHORD 1968 DERAM UK SML 717 US LONDON 18017
    RAY THOMAS   FLT V (ABCDEFGHJKLMN1R(E) ON THE THRESHOLD OF A DREAM 1969 DERAM UK SML 1035 US LONDON 18025
    JUSTIN HAYWARD  G V(CDEFGHJKLMN1R (F) TO OUR CHILDRENS CHILDREN 1969 THRESHOLD  UK/US THS 1
    JOHN LODGE    B V(CDEFGHJKLMN1R (G) QUESTION OF BALANCE  1970 THRESHOLD      UK/US THS 3
    PATRICK MORAZ    K  (1R         (H) EVERY GOOD BOY DESERVES FAVOUR 1971 THRESHOLD UK/US THS 5
                                    (J) SEVENTH SOJOURN     1972 THRESHOLD UK/US THS7 NL 9299139
    (1) 1978 TOUR                   (K) THIS IS THE MOODY BLUES 1974 THRESHOLD US 2 12/13 UK MB1/2
                                    (K) THIS IS THE MOODY BLUES 1974 DECCA           NL 6645 302
                                    (K) THIS IS THE MOODY BLUES 19   TELDEC    GERM     DX6 28316
                                    (L) IN THE BEGINNING     1975 DERAM      US 18051 TELDEC GERM 769
                                    (L) IN THE BEGGINING     197  DECCA           NL 6454  307
                                    (M) CAUGHT LIVE PLUS FIVE 1977 LONDON US 690/1 UK DECCA MB3/4
                                    (M) CAUGHT LIVE PLUS FIVE 1977 TELDEC    GERM     DP& 24812
                                    (N) DREAM               1977 TELDEC     GERM      DP6 28362
                                    (O) OCTAVE              1978 LONDON US PS 708 UK DECCA TXS 129
                                    (P) OUT OF THIS WORLD (COMP) 1979 K TEL            NE1051
                                    (Q) MOODY BLUES (PROFILE) 19  TELDEC    GERM       624004
                                    (R) LONG DISTACE VOYAGER 1981 THRESHOLD UK 139 US 2901
                                    (S) THE GREAT           19   DERAM       BEL 159/60
                                    (T) BOULEVARD DELA MADELEINE 19 DECCA     NL 6454 041
                                    (EP) MOODY BLUES(EP)    1965 DECCA           UK DFE8622
```

EVE MOON

EVE MOON	G V (A		(A) EVE MOON		1981	CAPITOL		ST 12132
JIMMY RIPP	G (A							
TOM WOLK	B (A	BOB RILEY	D (A	ELAINE CASWELL	PERC (A			

M190   MOON(UK)   M190

NOEL McCALLA	V (AB		(A) TOO CLOSE FOR COMFORT		1976	EPIC	UK	81456
LOZ NETTO	G V (AB		(B) TURNING THE TIDE		1977	EPIC	UK	82084
GRAHAM COLLYER	G (AB							
DOUG BAINBRIDGE	WIND (AB	NICKY PAYN	WIND (AB	JOHN SHEARER	(B	RON LAWRENCE	B	(AB
LUIGI SALVONI	D (A	GARY MOBERLEY	K (A	BOB JACKSON	K (A	DAVE DENNIS	V	(A

M190A   MOON(US)   M190A

MATTHEW MOORE	V PNO(A		(A) MOON WITHOUT EARTH		196	IMPERIAL US LP12381 LIBERTY GER 83146		
DAVID MARKS	G (		(B) MOON		196	IMPERIAL US LP12444		
DAVE JACKSON	B (							
LARRY BROWN	D (							

M191   KEITH MOON   M191

KEITH MOON	D V PERC(A		(A) TWO SIDES OF THE MOON		1975 POLYDOR UK 2442 134 MCA US 2136						
CURLY SMITH	D (A										
CAM DAVIES	D (A	MIGUEL FERRER	D (A	MICKEY McGEE	D (A	RON GRINEL	D (A			
JIM KELTNER	D (A	RINGO STARR	D V (A	JIMMIE RANDALL	B (A	PAUL STALLWORTH	B (A			
JEAN MILLINGTON	B (A	DAVID BIRKETT	B (A	KLAUS VOORMANN	B (A	SPENCER DAVIS	G (A			
AL STAEHELY	G (A	MIKE CONDELLO	B (A	DANNY KOOTCH	B (A	JOHN STAEHELY	G (A			
JESSE ED DAVIS	G (A	PATTI QUATRO	G SYN(A	JOE WALSH	G SYN(A	BEAU GUSS	G (A			
JOHN SEBASTIAN	G (A	STEVE ADAMICK	G (A	JAMES ED HAYMER	G (A	DICK DALE	G (A			
PAUL LENART	G (A	JAY FERGUSON	K (A	NICKEY BARCLAY	K (A	BLAIR AARONSON	K (A			
DAVID FOSTER	K (A	NORMAN KURBAN	K (A	HARRY NILSSON	V (A	SHIRLEY MATTHEWS	V (A			
LORNA WILLARD	V (A	JULIA TILLMAN	V (A	JAMES GILSTRAP	V (A	CLYDIE KING	V (A			
MARK VOLMAN	V (A	HOWARD KAYLAN	V (A	DENNIS LARDEN	V (A	JAY WHITE	V (A			
RON HICKLIN	V (A	AUGUST JOHNSON	V (A	GREG MATTA	V (A	IRMA ROUTEN	V (A			
ANDREA WILLIS	V (A	IRA HAWKINS	V (A	GERALD GARRETT	V (A	CAROLYN WILLIS	V (A			
SKIP EDWARDS	STEEL(A	OLLIE MITCHELL	HRNS (A	STEVE DOUGLAS	HRNS (A	BOBBY KEYS	SAX(A			
ROBERT GREENIDGE	PERC (A	RICK NELSON	V (A							

M191A   MOONDOGS   M191A

GERRY McCANDLESS	G V (A		(A) THAT'S WHAT FRIENDS ARE FOR	1981 SIRE	GER	204 061	
AUSTIN BARRETT	D (A						
JACKIE HAMILTON	B V (A						

M192   MOONDOG   M192

LOUIS HARDIN	V PERC HCA(ALL		(A) MOONDOG	19	CBS	US 7335	UK63906
FRITZ STORFINGER	K (D		(B) MOONDOG 2	1971	CBS	US 30897	
			(C) MOONDOG IN EUROPE	19	KOPF		RRF 33014
			(D) H'ART SONGS	19	KOPF	GER	RRF 33016

M192A   JOHN MOONEY   M192A

JOHN MOONEY	G V (A		(A) COMIN' YOUR WAY		19	BLIND PIG	US	BP 779
BRIAN WILLIAMS	B (A							
BOB COOPER	PNO (A	NICK LANGAN	HCA K(A	TOM McDERMOTT	D (A	STEVE NARDELLA	HCA(A	
GREG PICCOLO	SAX (A	DOUG JAMES	SAX (A	RICH LATAILLE	SAX (A	DAVID SWAIN SECTION	(A	

M192B   MOONQUAKE   M192B

HOVANESS HAGOPIAN	G V (B		(A) MOONQUAKE	197	FANTASY	US	9450
JACK AUGUST	B V (B		(B) STARSTRUCK	197	FANTASY	US	9486
DEREK KENDRICK	D V (B						

M192C   MOONGLOWS   M192C

BOBBY LESTER	(		(A) MOONGLOWS	1972	CHESS	US	701
HARVEY FUQUA	(A		(B) RETURN OF THE MOONGLOWS	1972	RCA	US	4722

M192D   MOONRAKERS   M192D

DENNIS FLANNIGAN	K V (A		(A) TOGETHER WITH HIM	1968 SHAMLEY	704		
VAN DORN	G V (A						
JOEL BRANDES	B (A	RANDY WALRATH	G V (A	BOB SAVNAR	D (A	BOB WEBBET G	(A
JERRY CORBETTA	D (A						

M193   MOONRIDER   M193

KEITH WEST	G V (A		(A) MOONRIDER	1975	ANCHOR	US	ANCL2010
CHICO GREENWOOD	D (A						
JOHN WEIDER	G V (A	BRUCE THOMAS	B (A				

M194   MICHAEL MOORCOCK & DEEP FIX   M194

MICHAEL MOORCOCK	G V MAND(A		(A) THE NEW WORLDS FAIR		1975	UA	UK	UAG 29732
STEVE GILMORE	G (A							
DEBI ROSS	V (A	ALAN POWELL	D (A	KUMA HARADA	B (A	GRAHAM CHARNOCK	G (A
SIMON HOUSE	VLN K(A	DAVE BROCK	G (A	PETE PAVLI	CELLO(A	SHIRLEY RODEN	V (A
SIMON KING	D (A	SNOWY WHITE	G (A	HERBERT NORTH	G (A		

M194A   BOBBY MOORE & THE RHYTHM ACES   M194A

BOBBY MOORE	(A		(A) SEARCHING FOR MY LOVE	19	CHECKER	US	3000

M195   G T MOORE & THE REGGAE GUITARS   M195

G T MOORE	G V (AB		(A) G T MOORE & THE REGGAE GUITARS	1974 CHARISMA UK CAS1095 MERCURY US 1065				
TOM WHYTE	B (AB		(B) REGGAE BLUE	1975 CHARISMA UK CAS1105				
MARTIN HAYWARD	G (AB		(C) MOVE IT ON UP	1980 CHARISMA NL 9124 057				
TIM JONES	K (AB							
CHRIS MERCER	SAX (B	TOM ROBINSON V PERC	(A	RABBIT BUNDRICK	K (A	PETER VAN DER PUIJE SAX	(A
TONY HANNAFORD	V PERC(A	EDDIE QUANSAH	TPT (A	TONY REDUNZO	D V (B	MALCOLM MORTIMER	D (A
GEORGE LARNYOH	SAX (A							

M196   GARY MOORE   M196

GARY MOORE	G V (ABC		(A) GRINDING STONE	1973 CBS UK 65527	US PETERS	9004		
PHIL LYNOTT	B V (B		(B) BACK ON THE STREETS	1978 MCA UK MCF2853	US CBS	35991		
BRIAN DOWNEY	D (B		(B) BACK ON THE STREETS	1978 MCA GER 62/122				
MO FOSTER	B (C		(C) CORRIDORS OF POWER	1982 VIRGIN UK 2245				
DON AIREY	K (B							
SIMON PHILLIPS	D (B	JOHN MOLE	B (B	PEARCE KELLY	D (A	JOHN CURTIS	B (A
JAN SCHELLHAAS	K (A	FRANK BOYLAN	B (A	PHILLIP DONNELLY	G (A	JACK BRUCE	B (C
IAN PAICE	D (C	NEIL MURRAY	B (C	TOMMY EYRE	K (C	BOBBY CHOUINARD	D (C

```
M196A                                    PAMELA MOORE                                                   M196A
   PAMELA MOORE      V    (A       (A) TAKE A LOOK                    1981   FIRST AMERICAN   US  FA7754
M197                                     MERRILL MOORE                                                  M197
   MERRILL MOORE     PNO  (ALL     (A) TREE TOP TALL                 1969   B &C                 CAS 1001
                                   (B) BELLYFULOF BLUE THUNDER       1972   EMBER                EMB 3392
                                   (C) ROUGH HOUSE 88                1972   EMBER                EMB 3394
                                   (D) MERRILL MOORE                 19     CAPITOL        US     1 608
M197A                                    SCOTTY MOORE                                                   M197A
   SCOTTY MOORE      G    (A       (A) GUITAR THAT CHANGED THE WORLD 1973   EPIC    US 26103
   BOOTS RANDOLPH    SAX  (A       (B) BIG ELVIS HITS                1976   CBS     NL 53343
   BILL PURSELL      PNO  (A
   JERRY KENNEDY     G    (A  BOB MOORE      B      (A   D J FONTANA       G (A BUDDY HARMAN    D (A
   JORDANAIRES       V    (A
M197B                                    STEVIE MOORE                                                   M197B
   R STEVIE MOORE    G V K (AB      (A) STANCE                        1978 HP MUSIC US  EP      30733
                                    (B) PHONOGRAPHY                   1978 HP MUSIC US          30734
M198                                     TIM MOORE                                                      M198
   TIM MOORE      G B K V (ALL      (A) A FOOL LIKE YOU          1974 MOONCREST        UK         CREST 16
   RUSS KUNKEL          (B          (B) TIM MOORE                1975 POLYDOR 2310 363 UK US  ASYLUM 7E 1019
   ROY MANKOWITZ   D    (B          (C) BEHIND THE EYES          1975 POLYDOR 2310 412 UK US  ASYLUM 7E 1042
   BERNARD PURDIE  D    (B          (D) WHITE SHADOWS            1977 POLYDOR 2310 512 UK US  ASYLUM 7E 1088
   BILL McCORD     D    (B          (E) HIGH CONTRAST            1979                  US  ASYLUM    179
   BILL PAYNE      K    (D
   MARK VOLMAN     V    (D  JEFF PORCARO  D  (D  ELLIOT RANDALL  G  (D  HOWARD KAYLAN   V (D
   FRED TACKETT    G    (D  MIKE UTLEY    K  (D  LEE SKLAR       B  (D  MICHAEL McDONALD V (D
   JOEL BISHOP OBRIEN D (C  FRANK SIMS    V  (C  GEORGE SIMMS    V  (C  DAVE KONDZIELA  V (C
   PAUL GLANZ      V    (C  ANDY ROBINSON V  (C  ALLAN SCHWARZBERG D (C  JOHN WILCOX    D (C
   BENNETT CARLISLE D   (C  DON PAYNE     B  (C  WILL LEE        B  (C  BOB LIZIK       B (C
   JOHN TROPEA     G    (C
M199                                     JOHNNY MOPED                                                   M199
   JOHNNY MOPED(PAUL HALFORD)V(A     (A) CYCLEDELIC          1978 CHISWICK UK WIK8 NL550 108  GER 67 060
   SLIMEY TOAD        G    (A
   FRED BERK          K B  (A  PHIL BURNS     B   (A  DAVE BERK   D (A  RAY BURNS      G (
M200                                     PATRICK MORAZ                                                  M200
   PATRICK MORAZ      K    (A        (A) "I"                       1976   CHARISMA            CDS 4002
   VIVIENNE McAULIFFE V    (A        (A) "I"                       1976   ATLANTIC       US   18175
   JOHN McBURNIE      V    (AB       (B) OUT OF THE SUN            1977   CHARISMA            CDS 4007
   RAY GOMEZ          G    (AB       (B) OUT OF THE SUN            1977   VISA           US    1015
   JEFF BERLIN        B    (A        (C) PATRICK MORAZ            1978  CHARISMA US 2201  UK   CDS4015
   ALPHONSE MOUZON    D    (A        (D) FUTURE MEMORIES LIVE ON TV 1979   CARRERE     FR     67435
   ANDY NEWMARK       D    (AB       (E) CO EXISTENCE             1980   CARRERE            CAL 117
   JEAN RISTORI       B    (A
   VERONIQUE MUELLER V (A  FRANCOIS ZMIROU  V  (B  RICHIE MORALES   D  (E  JEAN LUC BOURGEOIS  PERC (A
   AUGUSTE DE ANTHONY G (A  PHILIPPE STAEHLI  PERC (A  RENE MORAZ   PERC (A  WORNELL JONES    B  (B
   SYRINX             (E  JOHN WOOLOFF   G  (E  JOY YATES     V  (C  DJALMA CORRIEA   PERC(CE
M200A                                    A.MORE                                                         M200A
   A MORE                             (A) FLYING DOESN'T HELP      1979   QUANGO    UK HMG 98   FR 200139
M200B                                    MORE                                                           M200B
                                      (A) WARHEAD                  1981   ATLANTIC    UK  K50775
M201                                     MORGAN                                                         M201
   MORGAN FISHER     K    (ABC       (A) THE SLEEPER WAKES        1979   CHERRY RED      UK   A RED1
   MAURICE BACON     D    (ABC       (B) NOVA SOLIS               19     RCA
   TIM STAFFELL      G V  (ABC       (C) BROWN OUT                1976   IMPORT      US    1006
   BOB SAPSTEAD      B    (BC
M201A                                    GIORGIO MORODER                                                M201A
   GORGIO MORODER            (AB     (A) MIDNIGHT EXPRESS         1978 CASABLANCA      CAL 2030
                                     (B) E=MC²                    19   OASIS              507
M202                                     RON PAUL MORIN                                                 M202
   RON PAUL MORIN    G V  (A         (A) PEACEFUL COMPANY         1972   SOVEREIGN        SVNA 7252
   LUKE P WILSON  G V BAN (A
   GRAHAM TODD       K    (A  JOHNNY VAN DERRICK FDL (A   JOHN PEARSE    G V (A  RICK KEMP   B (A
   CAMILLA DE CRESPIGNY V (A  CHRIS LAURENCE   B   (A  PETE WILLSHER  STEEL(A  SUSAN JAMES  V (A
M202A                                    ROGER MORRIS                                                   M202A
   ROGER MORRIS      G V  (A         (A) FIRST ALBUM              1972   REGAL ZONOPHONE  UK SRZA 8509
   LISLE HARPER      B    (A
   BRUCE ROWLAND     D    (A  TERRY STANNARD   D   (A  ROD COOMBES   D   (A  TOMMY EYRE     PNO (A
   JOHN WEIDER       G    (A  KEITH WEST       G   (A  GLEN CAMPBELL STEEL(A  JOHNNY ALMOND  SAX (A
   CHRIS MERCER      SAX  (A  KEN BURGESS      V   (A
M202B                                    MORRIS & THE MINORS                                            M202B
                                     (A) STATE THE OBVIOUS(EP)    19   ROUND     UK        MOR 1
M202C                                    TOMMY MORRISON                                                 M202C
   TOMMY MORRISON    V    (A         (A) PLACE YOUR BETS          1979   REAL             RAL 2
   PAUL RODGERS      V    (A
   JOHN WATCHMAN          (A  ROD DEATH    D   (A  DAVE RAMSEY     (A  BOB MARSHALL  (A JAMES HONEYMANSCOTT(A
   KUMA HARADA       B    (A  STEWART McDONALD (A  GARY WINDO      (A  LOU MARTIN   K(A PETE FARNDON (A
```

VAN MORRISON V SAX G K(ALL			(A) BLOWIN' YOUR MIND	1967 BANG	US BLB21 LONDON UK	8346			
RICHARD DAVIS	B	(B	(B) ASTRAL WEEKS	1968 WB US WS 1768 UK K46024 RI 26004					
CONNIE KAY	D	(BFG	(C) BEST OF	1970 BANG	US	BLP222			
WARREN SMITH	PERC	(B	(C) BEST OF	1970 PRESIDENT	UK	1045			
JOHN PAYNE	FLT	(B	(D) MOONDANCE	1970 WB	US WS 1835	UK K46040			
JOHN PLATANIA	G	(DEHJ	(E) HIS BAND & STREET CHOIR	1970 WB	US WS 1884	UK K46066			
JOHN KLINGBERG	B	(DE	(F) TUPELO HONEY	1971 WB	US WS 1950	UK K46114			
GARY MALLABER	D PERC	(DFGHS	(G) ST DOMINICS PREVIEW	1972 WB	US BS 2633	UK k46172			
JACK SCHROER SAX PNO		(DEFGHJL	(H) HARD NOSE THE HIGHWAY	1973 WB	US BS 2712	UK K46242			
COLLIN TILTON	WIND	(D	(J) ITS TOO LATE TO STOP NOW	1974 WB	US BS 2760	UK K86007			
JEFF LABES	K	(DHJL	(K) TB SHEETS	1974 BANG US BLP400	LONDON UK HSM5008				
CHRIS MICHIE	G	(S	(K) TB SHEETS	1974 BELLAPHON GER 15103					
EMILY HOUSTON	V	(D	(L) VEEDON FLEECE	!974 WB	US BS 2805	UK K56068			
JUDY CLAY	V	(D	(EF) HIS BAND/TUPELO HONEY	1975 WB	UK	K86009			
JACKIE VERDELL	V	(D	(M) THIS IS WHERE I CAME IN(COMP)	1977 BANG	UK	6467 625			
DAVID SHAW PERC CLAR		(DEJL	(N) PERIOD OF TRANSITION	1977 WB	US BS 2987	UK K56322			
BILL CHURCH	B	(FG	(O) WAVELENGTH	1978 WB	US BSK3212	UK K56526			
KEITH JOHNSON	TPT	K(E	(P) INTO THE MUSIC	197 MERCURY	US 3390 UK 9102 852 JAP7630				
ALAN HAND	PNO SAX	(E	(Q) CHAIRFELLOWS(BOOTLEG)	1978 IMPOSSIBLE	IMP118				
ELLEN SCHROER	V	(EFG	(R) COMMON ONE	1980 MERCURY	UK 6302 021				
CHRIS HAYES	G	(S	(S) BEAUTIFUL VISION	1982 MERCURY	UK 6302 122				
JAY BERLINER	G	(E	(1) 1979 TOUR						
MARTHA VELEZ	V	(E							
LARRY GOLDSMITH	V	(E	ANDY ROBINSON	V	(E	JANET PLANET	V	(EFG	JIM ROTHERMEL	WIND(L
MARK JORDAN	PNO	(FGP	LUIS GASCA	TPT	(F	RONNIE MONTROSE	G V	(FG	TED TEMPLEMAN	ORG (F
JOHN McFEE	STEEL	(FG	BRUCE ROYSTON	FLT	(F	BOOTS STUART HOUSTON	V FLT(F		JULES BROUSSARD	SAX(GH
TOM SALISBURY	K	(G	DOUG MESSENGER	G	(G	MARK SPRINGER	V	(G	PAT O'HARA	HRNS(G
MARK NAFTALIN	PNO	(G	RICK SCHLOSSER	D	(FGH	ROLF HOUSTON		(G	BERNIE KRAUSE	SYN (G
RON ELLIOTT	G	(G	MARTY DAVID		(H	DAVID HAYES	B	(HJLPRS	BILL ATWOOD	HCA (H
JOSEPH ELLIS	HRNS	(H	JACKIE de SHANNON	V	(H	RALPH WASH	G	(L	JAMES TRUMBO	K (L
JOE MACHO	B	(L	NATHAN RUBIN	STRINGS	(HJL	ZAVEN MALIKIAN	VLN	(H	NANCY ELLIS	VLA (HJ
JOHN TENNEY	VLN	(H	MICHAEL GIRLING	VLN	(H	TIM KOVATCH	VLN	(J	TOM HAPLIN	VLN (J
ALLEN SCHWARZBERG	D	(L	JOHN TROPEA	G	(L	DR JOHN	K	(N	REGGIE McBRIDE	B (N
OLLIE BROWN	D	(N	MARLO HENDERSEN	G	(N	JERRY JUMONVILLE	SAX	(N	ROBBIE MONTGOMERY	V (N
JOE POWELL	V	(N	GARY GARRETT	V	(N	CARLENA WILLIAMS	V	(N	GREGORY WRIGHT	V (N
TONY McVEY	V	(N	CANDY NASH	V	(N	PAULETTE PARKER	V	(N	ROGER KENERLY SAINT	V(N
JOEL PESKIN	SAX	(N	MARK UNDERWOOD	TPT	(N	BOB TENCH	G	(1QOQ	JOHN ALTMAN	SAX (1
KATIE KISSOON	V	(1PQ	TONI MARCUS	VLN	(P	PEE WEE ELLIS	SAX	(PRS	MARK ISHAM SYN	TPT (PRS
PETER VAN HOOKE	D	(OPQR	ROBIN WILLIAMSON	WHISTLE(P		KURT WORTMAN	D	(P	MICK COX	G (R
ZAKIR HUSSAIN	PERC	(P	RY COODER	G	(P	JOHN ALLAIR	K	(RS	PETE BREWIS	G (R
GARTH HUDSON	K SYN	(O	MITCH DALTON	G	(O	GINGER BLAKE	V	(O	LAURA CREAMER	V (O
LINDA DILLARD	V	(O	MICKEY FEAT	B	(OQ	ANNA PEACOCK	V	(Q	LEE CHARLTON	D (R
HERBIE ARMSTRONG	G V	(OPQRS	BIANCA THOPNTON	V	(S	TOM DOLLMEYER	D	(S	ROB WASSERLAN	B (S
SEAN FULSOM	PIPES	(S	PAULINE LOSANA	V	(S	MARK KNOPFLER	G	(S	ERIC GALE	G (K
AL GORGONI	G	(K	BOB BUSHNELL	B	(K	HUGH McCRACKEN	G	(K	DONALD THOMAS	G (K
RUSSEL SAVKAS	B	(K	HERBIE LOVELLE	D	(K	GEORGE DEVINS	PERC	(K	PAUL GRIFFIN	K (K
SELDON POWELL	WIND	(K	CISSY HOUSTON	V	(K	MYRNA SMITH	V	(K	BROOKS ARTHUR	V (K
GARY CHESTER	D	(K	ARTIE BUTLER	K	(K	ARTIE KAPLAN	WIND	(K	JEFF BARRY	PERC V(K
DEE DEE WARWICK	V	(K	BERT BERNS	D	(K					

JAY LEWIS	G V	(A	(A) MORNING	1970 LIBERTY UK LBS83463 US VAULT 138						
JIM HOBSON	K V	(A	(B) STRUCK LIKE SILVER	1974 UA UAS29337 US FANTASY 9402						
BARRY BROWN	G D	(A								
BRUCE WALLACE	B	(A	AL PERKINS	STEEL(A		JIM KEHN	D V	(A	TERRY JOHNSON	G B (A
JAY DONNELLAN	G	(								

JOHN SURMAN	SAX	(A	(A) MORNING GLORY	1973 ISLAND	UK	ILPS 9237		
JOHN MARSHALL	D	(A						
TERJE RYPDAL	G	(A	MALCOLM GRIFFITHS TROM (A	CHRIS LAURENCE	B	(A	JOHN TAYLOR K	(A

RICK BACUS	G K V	(AB	(A) MORNING STAR	1978 CBS	US	35316	
JERRY CHAMBERS	G V	(AB	(B) VENUS	1979 CBS	US	35713	
MICHAEL EDMUNDS	G V	(AB					
GREG HARRIS	D PERC	(AB	GREG LEECH	B	(AB		

ALLEN WEHR	D	(A	(A) A TWO SUNS WORTH	1968 FONTANA	67573	
DANNY NU DELMAN	G V	(A				
LARRY GERUGHTY	K V	(A	GINI CRAYBEAL	PERC V(A	BOB BOHANNA B G V (A	

DICK MORRISSEY	SAX	(AB	(A) UP	1977 EMBRYO	US	SD 536				
JIM MULLEN	G	(AB	(B) CAPE WRATH	1979 FUSION	UK	SHSP 4098				
ROBERT AHWAI	G	(B	(C) BADNESS	1981 BEGGARS BANQUET UK	BEGA 27					
MALCOLM DUNCAN	SAX	(A								
HAMISH STUART	G	(A	ONNIE McINTYRE	G	(A	PAT REBILLOT	K	(A	ROGER BALL	K (A
ALAN GORRIE	B	(A	STEVE FERRONE	D	(A	SAMMY FIGUEROA	PERC	(A	RAFAEL CRUZ	PERC (A
RICHARD BAILEY	D	(B	TONY CARR	PERC	(A	MAX MIDDLETON	K	(B	KUMA HARADA	B (B

T SMITH		(A	(A) MORTIMER	19 PHILIPS	US 600 267
G MASSON		(A			
T VAN BENSCHOTEN		(A			

	(A) LOVE BLIND	1980 BELLAPHON BPLP 001

PABLO MOSES	(ALL	(A) REVOLUTIONARY DREAM	1976 SOUNDTRACS	+ DIFF 1978 GETL 104
		(B) I LOVE I BRING	1978 UA	LA 798
		( ) A SONG	19 ISLAND	UK 9541

M208   MOSE JONES   M208

```
    RANDY LEWIS        B V  (AC            (A) MOSE KNOWS                1974 MCA                  MCA   394
    JIMMY O'NEILL      G V  (A             (B) GET RIGHT                 1974 MCA   US 329         MCF  2673
    BRYAN GLENNCOLE    D V  (A             (C) BLACKBIRD                 1978 RCA                  12793
    STEVE McRAY        K V  (AC
    CHRIS SEYMOUR      D V  (C   MARTIN TAYLOR    G V  (C
```

M209   BOB MOSLEY   M209

```
    BOB MOSLEY         G V  (A             (A) BOB MOSLEY               1972  WB        US         MS 2068
    ED BLACK           STEEL(A
    WOODIE BERRY       V    (A   FRANK SMITH     V   (A  WAYNE JACKSON  HRNS (A  ALLEN WEHR     V (A
    ANDREW LOVE        HRNS (A
```

M210   ELTON MOTELLO   M210

```
    ELTON MOTELLO      V    (AB            (A) POP ART                  1980 EDGE UK HOG1 PASSPORT US 9846
    MIKE BUTCHER       G V  (A             (B) VICTIMS OF TIME          1978 PINBALL GER      6 23650
    WALTER METER       D V  (A
    PAUL KIDSLEY       V    (A   ANDREW GOLDBERG  K V  (A   J P MARTINS   G B  (A   NOBBY GAFF    G  (B
    PETER GOFF         G    (B   WILLIE CHANGE    B   (B   JET STAXX     G    (B   TONY BOAST    G  (B
    TWINK              D    (B   DANNY           CELLO(B   PIETRO       SAX   (B   ROBBIE      K    (B
    JEAN               K    (B   MITZI            V   (B   TIME          V    (B   FRISOI        V  (B
    YVONNE             V    (A   HILDE            V   (A   COOKY         K    (A
```

M210A   MOTELS   M210A

```
    JEFF JOURARD       G    (A             (A) MOTELS                   1979 CAPITOL  11996   NL 85999
    MARTHA DAVIS       V G  (AB            (B) CAREFUL                  1980 CAPITOL          EST 12070
    MARTIN JOURARD     K SAX(AB
    TIM McGOVERN       G    (B   MICHAEL GOODROE  B   (AB  BRIAN GLASCOCK  D  (AB
```

M211   MOTHER EARTH   M211

```
    TRACY NELSON       K V  (ALL           (A) REVOLUTION(+ STEVE MILLER ETC)  1968 UA               US   5185
    MARTIN FIERRO      SAX  (AB1           (B) LIVING WITH THE ANIMALS  1968 MERCURY          US SR 61194
    MARK NAFTALIN      K    (AB            (C) MAKE A JOYFUL NOISE      1969 MERCURY UK SMCL20143 US SR61226
    BOB ARTHUR         B V  (ACDB          (D) TRACY NELSON COUNTRY     1969 MERCURY UK SMCL20179 US  61230
    JOHN ANDREWS       G    (ABDEFG        (E) SATISFIED                1970 MERCURY UK 6338 023  SR61270
    GEORGE RAINS       D SAX(AB            (F) BRING ME HOME            1971 REPRISE UK K44133    US   6431
    TIM DRUMMOND       B    (F             (G) POOR MANS PARADISE       1973 CBS                  US  31759
    KARL HIMMEL        D    (EF            (1) EARLY LINE UP
    IRV KANE           TROM (G
    JOHN GIMBLE        FDL  (CDF  SAMMY DODGE     FDL (F   BEN KEITH      G   (CF   TERRY BURNSIDE  SAX (G
    BILLY PUETT        SAX  (G    REV STALLINGS   V   (C   JOSEPH ARNOLD  SAX (C   PETE DRAKE    STEEL(CD
    PIG ROBBINS        K    (C    R P ST JOHN     HCA V(CBA1 CLAYBORNE BROTHER COTTON(C  SHORTY LAVENDER FDL (CD
    ANDREW MACMAHON    K    (EFG  BOB CARDWELL    G   (EF   JAMES DAY    STEEL(E   DAVE ZETTNER    B   (E
    IRMA JEAN ROUTEN   V    (CF   SADIE CANTRELL  V   (CF   LADY CORDER   V   (CF   LONNIE CASTILLE D   (1
    SCOTTY MOORE       G    (D    JORDANAIRES     V   (D   JACK DRAKE    B   (D   DENNIS GOODE   TROM (G
    JACK LEE           G V  (G    STEVE MANDELL   B   (G   BEAU DOLLAR   D   (G   JERRY CARRIGAN  D   (G
    MAC GAYDEN         G    (G    RANDY SCRUGGS   G   (G   TOMMY SMITH   TPT (G   LOUIS GASCA    TPT (B
    LINK DAVIS         SAX  (B    FRANK MORIN     SAX (G   RON TAORMINA  SAX (B   BOB SALISBURY   SAX (B
    LOSELLA FUNQUE     V    (B    SYLVIA CALDWELL V   (B   SHALIMAR SAMUELSON  V (B   MAKAL BLUMFELD  G   (B
    DANY GOLDBERG      ORG  (B    SPENCER PERSKIN VLN (B   JOSE EMILIO RODRIGUEZ D(B
```

M211A   MOTHER GONG   M211A

```
    GILLI SMYTH        V    (A             (A) FAIRY TALES               19  CHARLY          UK   CRL  5018
    HARRY WILLIAMSON   G    (A
    DIDIER MALHERBE    WIND (A   RONNIE WATHEN PIPES    (A  NIC TURNER   WIND (A   TREVOR DARKS    B  (A
    MO VICARAGE        K    (A   EDUARDO NIEBLA   G   (A  MARIANNE OBERASHER HARP (A  CORRINA        V  (A
    ERMANO GHISIO ERBA D    (A
```

M211B   MOTHER GOOSE(AUST)   M211B

```
    STEVE YOUNG        K    (              (A) MOTHER GOOSE             1978 ?
    CRAIG JOHNSTON     V    (              (B) DONT BELIEVE IN FAIRY TALES  1979 ?
    KEVIN COLLINGS     G    (
    MARCEL RODEKE      D    (    DENIS GIBBINS   B   (   JUSTIN McCARTHY  G   (
```

M211C   MOTHER HEN   M211C

```
    CLARENCE WHITE     G    (A             (A) MOTHER HEN               196  RCA          US LSP 4641
    JERRY McGEE        G    (A
    DANNY KOOTCH       G    (A   SNEAKY PETE KLEINOW STEEL(A  JERRY SCHEFF  B  (A   LEE SKLAR      B  (A
    JAMIE FAUNT        B V  (A   RUSS KUNKEL     D   (A   RON TUTT      D   (A   DAVID CAMPBELL  VLN (A
    EMIL RICHARDS      PERC (A
```

M212   MOTHERS FINEST   M212

```
    B B BORDEN         D    (BCDEF         (A) MOTHERS FINEST           1972  RCA    US 4790
    JOYCE BABY         V PERC(BCDEF        (B) MOTHERS FINEST           1976  EPIC   US 34179   UK    81595
    JEAN KENNEDY    ]                      (C) ANOTHER MOTHER FURTHER   1977  EPIC   US 34699   UK    82037
    GLENN MURDOCK      V    (BCDF          (D) MOTHER FACTOR            1978  EPIC   US 35546   UK    83011
    JAMES CUNNINGHAM   PERC (D             (E) LIVE                     1980  CBS    US 35976
    SKIP SCARBOROUGH   PNO  (D             (F) IRON AGE                 1981  EPIC              UK    84424
    MOSES MO           G V  (BCDEF
    WIZZARD            B V  (BCDEF  MIKE          K   (BCD
```

M212A   MOTHERS RUIN   M212A

```
    SYLVIA             V    (A             (A) WANT MORE                1981 OFF COURSE   GER   3303
    RETO               G    (A
    MARKUS             G V  (A   BAYER     D   (A  GULY         B  (A
```

M212B   MOTHERLODE   M212B

```
                                          (A) TUFFED OUT               1973 BUDDAH    US        5108
```

M212C   MOTION   M212C

```
                                          (A) MOTION                   1981 DOUBLE D  UK   DDLP4
```

M213   MOTORHEAD   M213

```
    LEMMY              B V  (ALL           (A) MOTORHEAD                1977  CHISWICK UK  WIK2 + CWK 3008
    LARRY WALLIS       G    (AE            (B) OVERKILL                 1979  BRONZE     UK    BRON 515
    LUCAS FOX          D    (AE            (C) BOMBER                   1979  BRONZE     UK    BRON 523
    PHIL TAYLOR        D    (ABCDEFG       (D) ACE OF SPADES            1980  BRONZE     UK    BRON 531
    GIRLSCHOOL         (X                  (D) ACE OF SPADES            1980  MERCURY    US    4011
    EDDIE CLARKE       G    (ABCDEFG       (E) ON PAROLE (ROCKFILE)     1980  LIBERTY          LBR 1004
                                           (F) NO SLEEP TILL HAMMERSMITH 1981  BRONZE UK BRON535 GER 203 801
                                           (G) IRON FIST               1982  BRONZE           GER 204 636
                                           (X) ST VALENTINES DAY MASSACRE 1981  BRONZE (EP)  UK    BROX116
```

[392]

```
PETE OVEREND WATTS B (ABCDEFGHJKLMN  (A) MOTT THE HOOPLE           1969 ISLAND UK ILPS9108 US ATLANTIC  8258
DALE GRIFFIN    D   (ABCDJKH         (B) MAD SHADOWS              1970 ISLAND UK ILPS9119 US ATLANTIC  8272
MICK RALPHS     G   (ABCD            (C) WILD LIFE                1971 ISLAND UK ILPS9144 US ATLANTIC  8284
VERDEN ALLEN    K   (ABCD            (D) BRAIN CAPERS             1971 ISLAND UK ILPS9178 US ATLANTIC  8304
STAN TIPPENS    V   (CJ              (E) ROCK'N' ROLL QUEEN       1972 ISLAND UK ILPS9215 US ATLANTIC  7297
IAN HUNTER      V K G(ABCDEFGHJLN    (F) ALL THE YOUNG DUDES      1972 CBS UK 65184 US 31750 EMBASSY UK 31205
ARIEL BENDER    G   (JH              (G) MOTT                     1973 CBS  UK    69038 US              32425
BLUE WEAVER     K   (J               (H) THE HOOPLE               1974 CBS  UK    69062 US              32871
MORGAN FISHER   K   (JKH             (J) MOTT THE HOOPLE LIVE     1974 CBS  UK    69093 US              33282
MICK RONSON     G V (                (K) DRIVE ON                 1975 CBS  UK    69154 US              33705
RAY MAJOR       G   (K               (L) POP CHRONIK              1975 ISLAND IMP VOL 11
NIGEL BENJAMIN  V   (KM              (M) SHOUTING & POINTING      1976 CBS  UK    81289 US              34236
STEVE HYMANS    V   (                (N) GREATEST HITS            1976 CBS  UK    81225 US              34368
MICK BOLTON     ORG (J               ( ) SHADES OF                1979 CBS  UK    88476
GUY STEVENS     PNO (BAD             ( ) 2 MILES FROM HEAVEN      198  ISLAND IRSP 8      ARIOLA EURO 202429
JAMES ARCHER    VLN (C
HOWIE CASEY     SAX (H    JOCK McPHERSON  SAX (H   GERRY HOGAN   STEEL (C  JESS RODEN         V (C
JIM PRICE       TPT (D    PAUL BUCKMASTER CELLO(G  GRAHAM PRESKETT VLN  (GH THUNDERTHIGHS     V (G
ANDY MACKAY     SAX (G    BARRY ST JOHN    V   (H   SONNY LESLIE V (H   SUE GLOVER          V (H
```

```
ANDY McMASTER      V B K(ABC         (A) MOTORS 1                 1977 VIRGIN UK V2089 US 34924 GER 25457
NICK GARVEY        G V  (ABC         (B) APPROVED BY THE MOTORS   1978 VIRGIN UK V2101 US 35348
BRAM TCHAIKOVSKY   G V  (AB          (C) TENEMENT STEPS           1979 VIRGIN UK V2151 US 13139 GER 202 022
RICHARD SLAUGHTER WERNHAM D(AB       (C) TENEMENT STEPS           1979 VIRGIN EURO 2473 755
MARTIN ACE         B    (C
TERRY WILLIAMS     D    (C   MICHAEL DESMARAIS    D  (C
```

```
LESLIE WEST      G V  (ALL           (A) MOUNTAIN                 1970 WINDFALL US   4500
FELIX PAPPALARDI PROD B(ALL          (B) MOUNTAIN CLIMBING        1970 WINDFALL US   4501 UK BELL SBLL133
STEVE KNIGHT     K PERC(ABCDH        (C) NANTUCKET SLEIGHRIDE     1971 WINDFALL US   5500 UK ISLAND 9148
CORKY LAING      D    (BCDEFHJ        (D) FLOWERS OF EVIL          1971 WINDFALL US   5501 UK ISLAND 9179
                                     (D) FLOWERS OF EVIL          1971 ISLAND  GER 85549
NORMAN SMART     D    (               (E) MOUNTAIN LIVE           1972 WINDFALL US   5502 UK ISLAND 9199
                                     (E) MOUNTAIN LIVE           1972 ISLAND  FR 6427 014
DAVID PERRY      G    (J              (F) ROAD GOES ON FOREVER    1972 WINDFALL US   5503
BOB MANN         G K  (K              (G) POP HISTORY     (AB)    1972 POLYDOR              2625 022
ALLEN SCHWARTBERG D   (K              (H) BEST OF                 1973 CBS     US 32079 UK ISLAND 9236
                                     (J) AVALANCHE               1974 EPIC    US 33088 UK      80492
                                     (K) TWIN PEAKS      (DBL)    1974 CBS     US 32818 UK      88095
```

```
BILL KEES        G   (A              (A) SUNDANCE                 1974 GOOD                US     G101
LEE SIMS         D   (A
CRAIG TAKEHARA   B BAN(A   TOM JURKENS  V  (A   STEVE KRATER     D (A  ED MOONEY      G (A
```

```
HANS GERD FUCHS  B V  (A              (A) MOMENTS                 1980 NO FUN          GER 80001
THOMAS MANZEL    D    (A
UWE BODEKER      PERC V(A  ECKHARD WAHMANN   K V (A
```

```
BULL             G    (A              (A) HIGH ON MOUNT RUSHMORE  1968 DOT      US   DLP 25898
KIMBALL          B    (A              (B) MOUNT RUSHMORE          1969 DOT      US       25934
TRAVIS           D    (A
SMITTY           V    (A
```

```
                                      (A) LADY KILLER            1974 SOVEREIGN            SVNA 7262
```

```
ALPHONSE MOUZON    D K (ALL           (A) THE ESSENCE OF MYSTERY  1975 BLUENOTE            BNLA 059
TOMMY BOLIN        G   (C             (B) FUNKY SNAKEFOOT         1975 BLUENOTE            BNLA 222
JAY GRAYDON        G K (C             (C) MIND TRANSPLANT         1975 BLUENOTE            BNLA 398
LEE RITENOUR       G   (CD            (D) THE MAN INCOGNITO       1976 BLUENOTE US 584 UA UK  UAG 20005
JERRY PETERS       K   (C             (E) BACK TOGETHER AGAIN     1977 ATLANTIC      UK     K 50382
HENRY DAVIS        B   (C             (F) ALPHONSE MOUZON         19   SONOPRESSE      FR  056 99408
LARRY CORYELL      G   (E             (G) IN SEARCH OF A DREAM    1978 MPS
PHILIP CATHERINE   G   (E             (H) VIRTUE                 197  MPS      15498
JOHN LEE           B   (E             (J) THE DRUM               19   IMPULSE     9272
CHERYL P ALEXANDER V   (E             (K) BY ALL MEANS           1980 MPS      0068 266
TAWATHA AGEE       V   (E
JERRY HEY     HRNS (K  FREDDIE HUBBARD HRNS (K  KIM HUTCHCROFT WIND (K  LARRY WILLIAMS WIND  (K
LARRY TIM     OBOE (K  HERBIE HANCOCK  K    (K  PAUL JACKSON   G    (K  SCOTT EDWARDS  B    (K
DAWILLI GONGA K SYN(D  TIM DEHUFF      G    (D  CHARLES MEEKS  B    (D  DAVE GRUSIN    K    (D
DAVE BENOIT   K    (D  IAN UNDERWOOD   SYN  (D  VICTOR FELDMAN PERC (D  EMIL RICHARDS  PERC (D
TOM SCOTT     HRNS (D  RAY PIZZI       HRNS (D  GEORGE BOHANON TROM (D  GARY GRANT     TPT  (D
MARTY McCALL  V    (D  JACKIE WARD     V    (D  CAROLINE WILLIS V  (D  DAVID T WALKER G    (D
JOHN MALLER   K    (D  RANDY BRECKER   RPR  (B  ANDY GADSDEN   SAX  (B  LEON PENDARVIS K    (B
RICHIE RESNICOFF G (D  GARY KING       B    (B  STEVE BERRIOS  PERC (B  BARRY ROGERS   TROM (B
HARRY WHITAKER K   (B  MIKE MANDEL     K    (B  MARK HAROWITZ  STEEL(B  RAY ARMANDO    PERC (B
ANGEL ALLENDE     (B
```

```
ROY WOOD   WIND G V (ALL              (A) THE MOVE               1966 REGAL ZONOPHONE    UK SLRZ1002
BEV BEVAN       D V(ALL               (A) THE MOVE               1974 M F P             UK    50158
ACE KEFFORD     B G V(ACF             (A) THE BEST OF MOVE (REPACKAGE) 19 A&M           UK   SP3625
TREVOR BURTON   G B V(ACF             (B) SHAZAM                 1970 REGAL ZONOPHONE    UK SLRZ1012
CARL WAYNE      V B  (ABCF            (B) SHAZAM                 197  A&M               US   SP4259
RICK PRICE      B G V (BCD            (B) SHAZAM                 197  POLYDOR               2310 012
JEFF LYNNE      G V K B(DEH           (C) BEST OF                1970 FLY UK TON 3  KARUSSELL 2345020
DENNY CORDELL   PROD (E               (D) LOOKING ON             1971 FLY  UK FLY1 CAPITOL US ST658
RICHARD TANDY   K    (CF              (E) MESSAGE FROM THE COUNTRY 1971 HARVEST        UK SHSP 4013
                                      (E) MESSAGE FROM THE COUNTRY 197  CAPITOL         US    ST811
                                      (E) SHINES ON              1979 HARVEST           UK SHSM 2029
                                      (F) FIRE BRIGADE           1971 M F P            UK      5276
                                      (G) SPLIT ENDS     (COMP)  1972 UA             US UAS 5666
```

                                                (CONTINUED)

THE MOVE

(AB) MOVE /SHAZAM	1972	CUBE UK TOOFA5/6	GER 2635 003
(H) CALIFORNIA MAN	1974	HARVEST	UK SHSP 4035
(I) MASTERS OF ROCK	1974	HARVEST	EURO 054 05696
(EP) SOMETHING ELSE	1968	REGAL ZONOPHONE	UK TR2 2001
(J) GREATEST HITS VOL 1	1978	HALLMARK UK	SHM 952

M220   MOVIES (UK)   M220

JON COLE	G V (ABCD	(A) THE MOVIES	1975	FIREFLY	UK	AMLH33002
GREG KNOWLES	G V (ABCD	(B) DOUBLE A	1977	GTO	UK	GTLP 026
DAG SMALL	K V (A	(C) BULLETS THROUGH THE BARRIER	1978	GTO	UK	GTLP 031
JULIAN DIGGLE	PERC V(ABCD	(D) INDIA	1980	GEM UK LP105 US RCA 3552
JAMIE LANE	D V (ABCD	(E) MOTOR MOTOR	1981	RCA UK 5054	UK 3854
DURBAN LAVERE	B V (A					
STAN SULZMANN	SAX (B MICK PARKER K CLAR(BC DAVE QUINN B V (BC COLIN GIBSON B V (D
RAY WARLEIGH	SAX (B

M221   MOVIES(US)   M221

TED MEDBURY	(A	(A) MOVIES	1976	ARISTA US	AL 4085
PETER BARNES	(A
MICHAEL MORGAN	(A

M221A   MOVING FINGER   M211A

KEN ELLIOT	V K (A	(A) REALITY	1969	POLYDOR	583045
NICK SOUTH	B (A
KIERAN O'CONNOR	D (A BOB GIBBONS G (A

M221B   MOVING GELATINE PLATES   M221B

GERARD BERTRAM	G V (AB	(A) MOVING GELATINE PLATES	19	CBS	64399
MAURICE HELMINGER	K FLT(AB	(B) THE WORLD OF GENIUS HANS	1971	CBS	64146
DIDIER THIBAUT	B V (AB
GERARD PONS	(AB MICHEL CAMICAS TROM (B JEAN PIERRE LAROQUE BASSOON (B GUY BOYER VIBES (B
CLAUDE DELCLOO	V (B

M221C   MOVING SIDEWALKS   M211C

BILLY GIBBONS	G V (A	(A) FLASH	19	TANTARA	US	TS 6919
DON SUMMERS	B (A
DAN MITCHELL	D (A TOM MOORE K (A

M221D   JUDY MOWATT   M221D

JUDY MOWATT	V (A	(A) BLACK WOMAN	1980	GROVE MUSIC	ILPS 9649
FREDDIE McGREGOR	D K V(A
DALTON BROWNE	G (A LEROY WALLACE D (A HOWARD SPREAD BADESSIE B(A TONY CHIN G (A
EWAN LEWIS	B (A EARL SMITH G (A MASKEL I B (A CAT COORE G (A
MIKEY HEWLETTE	K (A GEOFFREY CHUNG K (A TYRONE DOWNIE K (A WIRE K (A
STELLEY	K (A ARNOLD BRACKENRIDGE TPT(A HEADLEY BENNETT SAX (A DONALD GREAVES TPT (A
HERBERT CHANG	FLT (A ENROY GRANT SAX (A SCULLY PERC (A EVERTON CARRINGTON PERC (A
ORVILLE WOOD	PERC (A RAS INEFIRE TROI PERC (A ANICEA BANKS V (A HAROLD BUTLER MELODICA (A
JOY TULLOCH	V (A SHARON TUCKER V (A PAM HALL V (A

M221E   MOVING HEARTS   M221E

DONAL LUNNY	K V (A	(A) DOUBLE SINGLE	1981	WAE LANDFORD	IR	1 8826
DECLAN SINNOTT	G V (A
MICK HANLY	(A EOGHAN O'NEILL B V (A KEITH DONALD SAX V(A BRIAN CALNAN D (A
DANY SPILLANE	PIPES(A CHRISTIE MOORE G V (A

M222   MOXY   M222

BUDDY CAINE	G (BCD	(A) MOXY 1	1976 MERCURY US SRMI1087 UK POLYDOR 2480 460
BILL WADE	D (BC	(B) MOXY 2	1976 MERCURY US SRMI1115 UK POLYDOR 2480 372
BUZZ SHERMAN	V (BC	(C) RIDIN HIGH	1977 MERCURY US SRMI1161 UK POWER EXCHANGE022
TERRY JURIC	B (DBC	(D) UNDER THE LIGHTS	1978 MERCURY US SRMI3723 UK POLYDOR 2480 400
EARL JOHNSON	G (DBC
MICHAEL RYNOSKI	V (D DANNY BELAN D (D JACK RICHARDSON PROD (D TRACY RICHARDSON V (D
COLINA PHILLIPS	V (D SHARONLEE WILLIAMS V (D SCOT CUSHINE PNO (D

M222A   MTUME   M222A

MTUME	V K PERC(A	(A) IN SEARCH OF THE RAINBOW SEEKERS 1980	EPIC US 36017	UK 84629
TAWATHA AGEE	V PERC(A
REGGIE LUCAS	G V (A HOWARD KING D V (A SINCLAIR ACEY HRNS (A DANNY COLEMAN HRNS (A
GWEN GUTHRIE	V (A BRENDA WHITE V (A BASIL FEARRINGTON B V (A ED TREE MOORE G (A
HUBERT EAVES	K V (A ED WALSH SYN (A PETE CANNAROZZI SYN (A LUTHER VAN DROSS V (A

M222B   MU   M222B

MERREL FRANKHAUSER G V (A	(A) MU	19	RTV US 300 + UK UA	UAG29709
JEFF COTTON	SAX G V (A
RANDY WIMER	PERC (A LARRY WILLEY B V (A

M222C   MUCKRAM WAKES   M222C

CHRIS COE	DULC (B	(A) MAP OF DERBYSHIRE	1973	TRAILER	UK	LER 2085
JOHN ADAMS FDL BAN TROM(BC	(B) MUCKRAM WAKES	1976	TRAILER	UK	LER2093
SUZIE ADAMS	D (BC	(C) WARBLES,JANGLES & REEDS	1980	HIGHWAY	UK	SHY7009
PETER COE	DULC (B
HELEN WATSON	K (BC ROGER WATSON CONC (BC BILL LEADER PERC (B SONIA JACKSON CELLO (B

M222D   MUD ACRES   M222D

MARIA MULDAUR	G FDL V(A	(A) MUD ACRES	1972	ROUNDER	US	3001
HAPPY TRAUM	BAN G B V(A
ARTIE TRAUM	G B BAN V(A JIM ROONEY G V (A ERIC KAZ G HCAV(A JOHN HERALD G V (A
BILL KEITH	BAN G B(A TONY BROWN B (A LEE BERG V (A

M223   MUD   M223

LES GRAY	V (ALL	(A) MUD ROCK	1974	RAK	UK	SRAK 508
ROB DAVIS	G (ALL	(B) USE YOUR IMAGINATION	1975	PRIVATE STOCK	UK	PVLP 1003
ROY STILES	B (ALL	(C) GREATEST HITS	1975	RAK	UK	SRAK 6755
DAVE MOUNT	D (ALL	(D) MUD ROCK VOL 2	1975	RAK	UK	SRAK 513
		(E) ITS BETTER THAN WORKING	1976	PRIVATE STOCK	UK	PVLP 1011
		(F) ROCK ON	1978	RCA		PL25170
		(G) MUD PACK	1977	PRIVATE STOCK	UK	PVLP 1022
		( ) AS YOU LIKE IT	1980	RCA	UK	25256

MUFFINS
```
                        (A) MANNA/MIRAGE              19   RANDOM RADAR      RRR003
                        (B) AIR/LIVE                  19
```

M224   MUGWUMPS   M224
```
   CASS ELLIOT      V  (    (A) MUGWUMPS                 1967  WB        US   W 1697
   DENNY DOHERTY    V  (    (B) HISTORICAL RECORDINGS    197   VALIANT   UK   VS 134
   ZAL YANOVSKY        (
   JAMES HENDRICKS     (
```

M225   IDRIS MUHAMMAD   M225
```
   IDRIS MUHAMMAD   D V (ALL  (A) BLACK RHYTHM REVOLUTION  1972  PRESTIGE  US      10005
   JERRY HEY        HRNS (J   (B) YOU TALK THAT TALK       19    PRESTIGE  US      10019
   LARRY HALL       HRNS (J   (C) PEACE & RHYTHM           1973  PRESTIGE  US      10036
   BILL REICHENBACH HRNS (J   (D) POWER OF SOUL            1974  KUDU              KU 17
   CARLBERG JONES   HRNS (J   (E) IDRIS MUHAMMAD           1976  KUDU              KU 27
   HERB JIMMERSON   K (J      (F) TURN THIS MUTHA OUT      1977  KUDU              KU 34
   ROLAND BAUTISTA  G (J      (G) BOOGIE TO THE TOP        1978  KUDU              KU 38
   TIP WIRRICK      G (J      (H) YOU AIN'T NO FRIEND OF MINE 1978 FANTASY         FT 552
   NATHANIEL PHILLIPS B (J    (I) FOX HUNTIN'              1979  FANTASY US 9581 UK F 562
   CLAY TOVEN       V (J      (J) MAKE IT COUNT            1980  FANTASY   US      F 9598
   MAXINE WATERS    V (J
   JULIA TILLMAN    V (J   CLYDENE JACKSON V (J   PAUL SMITH    K V (J   DAVID FRAZIER PERC (J
   PAT HENDERSON    V (J   KEITH HATCHER   B (J   DAVID STONE   FLT (J   WILL LEE      B  (G
   CLIFF CARTER     K (G   DAVID FRIEDMAN VIBES(G  RONNIE CUBER SAX (G   HIRAM BULLOCK G  (G
   DANIEL CAHN      TPT (G JEREMY STEIG   FLT (G   FRANK FLOYD   V  (G   SAM FIGUEROA  PERC(G
   JOHN GATCHELL    HRNS (G HUGH McCRACKEN HCA (G  ZACHARY SANDERS V (G  NICKY MARRERO PERC(G
   RAY DAVIS        SAX (G GLORIA AGOSTINI HARP (G RAY SIMPSON   V  (G   KEN WILLIAMS  V  (G
```

M227   GEOFF MULDAUR   M227
```
   GEOFF MULDAUR    V G K(ALL (A) GEOFF MULDAUR              1964  PRESTIGE        US   14004
   JAMES JAMESON    B (D      (B) SLEEPY MAN BLUES           1965  PRESTIGE        US   7727
   KLAUS VOORMANN   B (D      (C) IS HAVING A WONDERFUL TIME 1975  REPRISE US 2220 UK   K54046
   AMOS GARRETT     G (CEF    (D) MOTION                     1976  REPRISE        US   MS 2255
   DOC CHEATHAM     TPT (C    (E) GEOFF MULDAUR & AMOS GARRETT 197 FLYING FISH     US   061
   JIMMY NOTTINGHAM TPT (C    (F) BLUES BOY                  1979  FLYING FISH     US   FF 201
   TOM PRINEIPATO   G V (G    (G) I AINT DRUNK               1981  ISLAND               203 546
   TAFT JORDON      TPT (C
   RON CARTER       B (C    STEPHEN BRUTON G V (CF  ED DANIELS      FLT (C  JAMES BOOKER   K (C
   DENSIL LANG      V PERC(C BENNY MORTON  TROM (C  QUENTON JACKSON TROM (C BILL BUTLER    G (C
   PETER GORDON     HRNS (C KENNETH BERGER CLAR (C  JOHN CALE       VLN (C  BOB WILBUR     WIND(C
   RUSSELL PROCOPE  SAX (C  BOB SIGGINS    BANJ (C  FRANK WESS      SAX (C  ROMEO PENQUE   CLAR(C
   JOHN CLARK       HRN (C  GEORGE DORSEY  SAX (C   HOWARD JOHNSON  SAX (C  DAVID SIMON    HCA V(C
   HERSCHEL HOLDER  TPT (C  DON BUTTERFIELD TUBA (C JENNY MULDAUR   V (CF   JERRY JEMMOTT  B (C
   MICHAEL AVERY    D (G    RICK HAMMET    TPT (G   KENNY CRANE     HRNS (G JOE CALO     SAX (G
   KAZ KAZANOFF     SAX V(G RICO ROYAL     SAX (G   GEORGE LEH      V (G    DAVE BURGIN HCA V (G
   BARBARA MENDELSOHN DULC(E NICHOLAS TEN BROEK TROM(E TEM NITMAR    SAX (E  SCOTT MATHAOS D SAX(E
   MICHAEL MELFORD  MAND V(E DWIGHT BRAINERD V (E   SAMMY CREASON   D (F    MIKE UTLEY     K (F
   DENNIS WHITTED   D (F    GEORGE LEN     V (F     PIERRE BEAUREGARD HCA (F SARAH BROWN   V (FG
   STEVE BURDETT    V (F    CRIS CIOE      SAX (F   RICH DISHMAN    D (F    PETER ECKLUND  HRNS(F
   WHIT GRISWOLD    V (F    EARL MACINTYRE TROM (A  MARIA MULDAUR   FDL V(C RICHARD THOMPSON G (C
   BERNARD PURDIE   D (C    HAROLD VICK    SAX (C   LLOYD SMITH     SAX (C  MERLE SAUNDERS K (C
   CHARLES WILLIAMS SAX (C  CORNELL DUPREE G (C     JIMMY SHIRLEY   BANJO(C LIONEL KINGHAM SAX (C
   FRITZ RICHMOND   JUG V(CE BILLY RICH    B (CDEF  GRAHAM LYONS BASSOON (C SELDON POWELL  SAX (C
   EDDIE LOCKE      D (C    PAUL HUMPHREY  D (C     CHRIS PARKER    D (C    BILL KEITH   STEEL (C
   GREG PRESTOPINO  V (CD   PATTI BONE     K (C     LEWIS SOLOFF    HRNS (C JOE FARRELL    OBOE(C
   ED GREENE        D (D    MIKE BAIRD     D (D     STEVE MADAIO    HRNS (D BOBBY KEYS     HRNS(D
   TREVOR LAWRENCE  HRNS (D LYNDA LAURENCE V (D     JIM KELTNER     D (D    ABIGAIL HANESS V (D
   DAVID KEMPER     D (D    CINDY BULLENS  V (D     DR JOHN         K (D    DEIRDA ASKEY   V (D
   TOM COSTER       K (D    SUSAN MOORE    V (D     JAMES GETZ      K (D    MARTIN MULL    V (D
   DENNIS COFFEY    G (D    BONNIE RAITT   V (D     JAY GRAYDON     G (D    SID SHARP STRINGS (D
   JESSE ED DAVIS   G (D    DEAN PARKS     G (D     MIKE ANTHONY    G (D    JOHN MORELL G  (D
   DAVID WOLFERT    G (D    MICHAEL BODDICKER SYN (D BOBBYE HALL    PERC (D JIM PRICE      HRNS(D
   GUS BIVONA       CLAR (A
```

M228   GEOFF & MARIA MULDAUR   M228
```
   GEOFF MULDAUR    V G K(AB  (A) POTTERY PIE           1970  REPRISE         US RS 6350
   MARIA MULDAUR    V (AB     (B) SWEET POTATOES        1972  WB              US MS 2073
   BILL KEITH       STEEL (AB
   AMOS GARRETT     G (AB BILLY WOLF     B  (AB RICK MARCUS    D  (A  BILLY MUNDI    D (AB
   BETSY SIGGINS    V (AB HAL GROSSMAN HRNS (A  PETER ECKLUND  TPT (AB JOHN KAHN     B (B
   STU BROTMAN      TROM (B JUNIOR TURLOCK B (B JEFF GUTCHEON  K  (B  PAUL BUTTERFIELD HCA (B
   MUNE BLACKBURN   WIND (B GENE DINWIDDIE SAX (B BOBBY NOTKOFF VLN (B  TREVOR LAWRENCE SAX (B
```

M229   MARIA MULDAUR   M229
```
   MARIA MULDAUR    V (ALL   (A) MARIA MULDAUR           1974  REPRISE UKK44255 US 2148
   DAVID LINDLEY    G (AB    (B) WAITRESS IN A DONUTSHOP 1974  REPRISE UK K54925 US 2194
   JIM KELTNER      D (A     (C) SWEET HARMONY           1976  REPRISE UK K54059 US 2235
   JIM DICKINSON    K (A     (D) SOUTHERN WINDS          1978  WB UK K56463     US 2162
   MARK JORDAN      K (AB    (E) OPEN YOUR EYES          1979  WB UK K56634     US 3305
   KLAUS VOORMANN   B (A     (F) GOSPEL NIGHTS           1980  TAKOma          US 7084
   RY COODER        G (A
   RAY BROWN        B (AB AMOS GARRETT G B V (ABCDE GLORIA JONES  V  (A  DAVID NICHTERN G (ABCE
   CHRIS ETHRIDGE   B (A SPOONER OLDHAM K (AB BILL KEITH BANJ STEEL(A LARRY PACKER VLN (AB
   DAVE HOLLAND     B (A KAREN ALEXANDER V (A ANDREW GOLD   G  (A  ED SHAUGHNESSY D (A
   JAMES CALHOUN    B (A BETTY LAVETTE V (A   GREG PRESTOPINO V K (ABD CHRIS PARKER D (A
   CLARENCE WHITE   G (A DAVID GRISMAN MAND (AB RICHARD GREENE VLN (AE ELLEN KEARNEY V (ABC
   MAC REBENNACK    K (AB JIM GORDON SAX CLAR K(ACE FREEBO     B  (ABE JOHN BOUDREAUX D (A
   JESSIE M SMITH   V (A PAUL BUTTERFIELD HCA (B JEFF GUTCHEON K (B  BOBBYE HALL   PERC(BE
   JIM GORDON       D (B BOBBY KING    V (B   PAUL HUMPHREY D  (B  DENNIS BUDIMIR G (B
   JOHN KAHN        B (B ROSENDO CERVANTES TPT (B RED CALLENDER B (B  DOC WATSON    G (B
   JAMES BOOKER     K (BC BUD SHANK    SAX (B  TERRY LEE EVANS V (B  HARRY SWEETS EDISON TPT(B
   SNOOKY YOUNG     TPT (B GEORGE BOHANON TROM (B KATE McGARRIGLE V (B LOWELL GEORGE G (B
   MILT HOLLAND     PERC (B JOSE ORDAZ DURANTE TPT (B EARL PALMER D (BC MERLE WATSON G (B
   JOHN COLLINS     G (B ABE MOSS      SAX (B  PLAS JOHNSON  SAX (BC SHAHIB SHIHAB SAX (BC
   ROGER KELLAWAY   K (B LINDA RONSTADT V (BC TOM TEDESCO REQUINTO V (B EMIL RICHARDS PERC(B
   PAUL HARRIS      K (B ANNA McGARRIGLE V (B ALVIN BISHOP ROBINSON G (B FRED STAEHLE D (B
```

(CONTINUED)

```
VI REDD          SAX  (C   WADDY WACHTEL     G    (C   BILL PAYNE         K    (CE  WILLIE WEEKS     B    (CE
FRED JACKSON     SAX  (C   HOWARD JOHNSON    SAX  (C   AL AARONS          TPT  (C   BENNY POWELL     TROM(C
JOHN GIRTON      G    (C   MICHAEL FINNIGAN  K V  (CD  MICHAEL MOORE      B    (C   VICTOR FELDMAN   PERC(CE
DAVID WILCOX     G    (C   BILL DICKINSON    B    (C   MARY ANN PRICE     V    (C   TREVOR LAWRENCE  SAX (CE
JOHNNY ROTELLA   WIND (C   STEVE MADAIO      TPT  (C   LEW McCREARY       TROM (CD  MARSHAL ROYAL    SAX (CE
GENE COE         TPT  (C   OSCAR BRASHEAR    TPT  (C   WENDY WALDMAN      V    (CD  ARTHUR ADAMS     V   (C
WILLIAM SMITH    K    (C   J J CALE          G    (C   LARRY GALES        B    (C   JOE HARNELL      PNO (C
KENNY BURRELL    G    (C   BRITT WOODMAN     TROM (C   CHRISTOPHER BOND   G SYN(D   THOM ROTELLA     G   (D
JOHN HUG         G    (DEG ED GREENE         D    (D   SCOTT EDWARDS      B    (D   LES DUDEK        V   (D
GARY COLEMAN     PERC (D   DAVE BURGIN       HCA  (D   PHIL AABERG        K    (D   PEPPER WATKINS   V   (D
ROSEMARY BUTLER  V    (D   JIM ANDERSON      V    (D   ERNIE WATTS        HRNS (D   DON MENZA        HRNS(D
JIM HORN         HRNS (D   CHUCK FINDLEY     HRNS (D   ROBERT BRYANT      HRNS (D   GARY MALLABER    D   (C
STEVIE WONDER    HCA  (D   JUNIOR WALKER     SAX  (E   PAT HENDERSON           (E   TOMMY McCLURE    B   (AB
DOUG LIVINGSTON  STEEL(E   DAVID WODFORD     SAX  (E   RICK VITO          G    (E   MARTY PAICH      STR (E
JIM PETTAWAY     G    (E   ROBBEN FORD       G    (E   DEAN PARKS         G    (E   RON TUTT         D   (E
PETER BUNETTA    D    (E   JAI WINDING       PNO  (E   BRIAN CUMMINGS     SAX  (E   CURT STEVENS     TPT (E
RICK SCHLOSSER   V    (E
```

```
PETER ROWAN      G V  (A        (A) MULESKINNER              1973   WB       US       2787
DAVID GRISMAN    MAND V(A
BILL KEITH       BAN  (A   RICHARD GREENE    VLN  (A   CLARENCE WHITE     G V  (A   JOHN KAHN        B   (A
JOHN GUERIN      D    (A
```

```
MARTIN MULL      G V K(A        (A) MARTIN MULL              1973 CAPRICORN UK       K47506
RICHARD ADELMAN  D    (A
DEAN ADRIAN      CONGA(A   LEVON HELM        D    (A   BILLY ELGART       D    (A   JACK BONE        B   (A
BILL ELLIOTT   V K HRNS (A STUART SHULMAN    STR  (A   PHIL WILSON        TROM (A
```

```
RAY DORSET G V PERC   (ALL      (A) MUNGO JERRY              1970   DAWN UK DNLS3008 JANUS US 7000
COLIN EARL       PNO V(ABCJ     (B) ELECTRONICALLY TESTED    1971   DAWN         UK       DNLS 3020
PAUL KING      BAN G V  (ABC    (C) YOU DONT HAVE TO BE IN THE ARMY 1971 DAWN     UK       DNLS 3028
                                ( ) MEMOIRS OF A STOCKBROKER  1971               JANUS US 3027
MIKE COLE        B    (A        (D) BOOT POWER               1972   DAWN         UK       DNLS 3041
JOHN GODFREY     V G K(BCD      (E) GREATEST HITS            1973   DAWN         UK       DNLS 3045
JOE RUSH         PERC (C        (F) LONG LEGGED WOMAN        1974   DAWN         UK       DNLS 3051
TIM REEVES       D    (D        (G) GOLDEN HOUR              1974   PYE          UK       GH  586
JON POPE         K    (D        (H) IMPALA SAGA              1976   POLYDOR      UK       2383 364
CHRIS WARNES     B    (J        (I) FILE                     1977   PYE          UK       FILD 003
PETE SULLIVAN    D    (J        (J) LOVE IN THE ALLEY        1977   POLYDOR      UK       2383 435
                                (K) IN THE SUMMERTIME        197    PYE                   H121/6
                                (L) RAY DORSET & MUNGO JERRY 1978   POLYDOR      UK       2383 485
```

```
MICHAEL MURPHEY G V HCA PNO(ALL (A) GERONIMO'S CADILLAC      1972 A&M US SP4358  UK REGAL ZON08512
LEONARD ARNOW  G STEEL (A       (B) COSMIC COWBOY SOUVENIR   1973 A&M US SP4388  UK EMI   EMA 754
GARY NUNN    G B K V   (AB      (C) MICHAEL MURPHEY          1974 EPIC US 32835  UK EMI   EMC2037
ROBERT LIVINGSTON B V G (AB     (D) BLUE SKY NIGHT THUNDER   1975 EPIC US 33290  UK EPIC  80741
BOOMER CASTLEMAN  G   (A        (E) SWANS AGAINST THE SUN    1975 EPIC US 33851  UK EPIC  69224
KENNY BUTTREY    D PERC(AC      (F) FLOWING FREE FOREVER     1976 EPIC US 34220  UK EPIC  81713
KARL HIMMEL      D    (A        (G) LONE WOLF                1978 EPIC US 35013
CHARLES JOHN QUARTO V (A        (H) PEAKS, VALLEYS,HONKY-TONKS & ALLEYS 79 EPIC US 35742
MICHAEL McGEARY  D    (B
HERB STEINER     STEEL (BC CRAIG HILLIS      G    (BC  W ALAN RAMSEY      V    (B   TOMMY COGBILL    B   (C
JOHN HILL        D    (C   BILL FARMER       PNO  (C   BUDDY SPICHER      FDL  (C   BOB HOLMES       ORG(C
CLYDIE KING      V    (C   MERRY CLAYTON     V    (C   PATTIE HENDERSON   V    (C   PAT POWDRILL     V   (C
ANDY JOHNSTON    V    (C   CHARLIE DANIELS FDL G V(E   RICHARD DEAN       G    (E   JOHN DENVER      G V(E
JAMES GUERCIO    B    (E   JEFF HANNA        V    (E   JOHN McEUEN BAN FDL G    (EF MICHAEL McKINNEY B V(EF
JERRY MILLS      MAND (E   JAE MURPHY        K SYN(EF  TRACY NELSON       V    (E   WILLIE NELSON    V   (E
EARL PALMER      D    (E   MICKEY RAPHAEL    HCA  (E   STEVE WEISBERG     G    (E   SAM BROUSSARD    G V (FGH
JAI WINDING      K    (GH  HARRY WILKINSON PERC D(EF   BOB GLAUB          B    (GH  JOHN MACY        STEEL(V
RAY BONNERVILLE  HCA  (F   DAVID LUELL       SAX  (F   DEBORAH McCOLL     V    (F   STEVE FROMHOLZ   V   (F
MIKE BOTTS       D    (G   DENNIS CHRISTIANSON HRNS(G  DICK HYDE          HRNS (G   JERRY JUMONVILLE HRNS(G
STEVE MADAIO     HRNS (G   BILL PAYNE      K SYN HRNS(G LON PRICE         HRNS (G   VICTOR FELDMAN   PERC(FG
ROBERT GREENIDGE PERC(G    JOEY DE LAURO     V    (G   JOHN BOYLAN        V    (G   WENDY WEBB       V   (G
ROD PHILLIPS     K    (H   DON BROOKS    HCA (H   BYRON BERLINE      FDL  (H   DAN DUGMORE      STEEL(H
DOUG DILLARD     BANJO(H   GARY COLEMAN      PERC (H   KATY MOFFATT       V    (H   TOM KELLY        V   (H
BOBBY KIMBALL    V    (H   TIM SCHMIT        V    (H
```

```
J F MURPHY     V K G(ALL        (A) J F MURPHY & SALT        19     MGM?
RON ALLARD       V HRNS(ALL      (B) LIVE                     1972 ELEKTRA   US       75024
JOE PARRINO    V G HRNS(ALL      (C) LAST ILLUSION            1973 CBS       US       32539
GEORGE CHRIST  V HCA PERC(ALL    (D) URBAN RENEWAL(MURPHY'S LAW) 1975 DUNHILL US      50194
RUSSELL WARMOLTS B V  (ALL       (E) ALMOST HOME              19   MGM       US       4708
JOHN REILLY      D    (CD
BOB PAVIA        D    (B   DENNIS COOLEY     V    (B   GLORIA GOLDMAN     V    (B   DELORES HALL     V   (B
VICTORIA MEDLIN  V    (B   ALLAN NICHOLLS    V    (B   AL PERKINS         STEEL(B   BOBBY KURTZ      D   (E
```

```
ELLIOTT MURPHY V G K HCA(ALL    (A) AQUASHOW                 1974 POLYDOR US 5061    2391 100
MATTHEW MURPHY   B V  (A        (B) LOST GENERATION          1975 RCA    US          APLI0916
GENE PARSONS     D V  (A        (C) NIGHT LIGHTS             1976 RCA    US          APLI1318
PAT REBILLOT     K    (A        (D) JUST A STORY FROM AMERICA 1977 CBS   US 34653 UK 81881
LINDA NOVEMBER   V    (A
DENNIS FERRANTE  V    (A   JIM MASON         V    (A   EDDIE MOTTAU       V    (A   MAERETHA STEWART V   (A
TEDDY IRWIN      G    (A   FRANK OWENS       K    (A   DICK WAGNER        V    (A   TASHA THOMAS     V   (A
MICK TAYLOR      G    (A   GORDON EDWARDS    B    (B   JACKIE CLARK       G    (B   SONNY LANDRETH   G   (B
JIM GORDON     D PERC(B    WAYNE DEVILLIER   K    (B   RICHARD TEE        K    (B   JON SMITH        SAX (B
BOBBY KIMBALL    V    (B   TERRY HARRISON    K    (C   ANDY PALEY         D    (C   ERNIE BROOKS     B   (C
BILLY JOEL       PNO  (C   MIKE BRAUN        V    (C   RALPH SCHUCKETT    ORG  (C   DOUG YULE        C   (C
RICHARD DAVIS    B    (C   STEVE KATZ        V    (C   MARK HOROWITZ      STEEL(C   LEW SOLOFF HRNS  (C
LOU MARINI       HRNS (C   TOM MALONE        HRNS (C   MICHAEL BRECKER    HRNS (C   HOWARD JOHNSON   HRNS(C
HARRY LOOKOFSY   VLN  (C   PHIL COLLINS      D    (D   DAVE MARKEE        B    (D   PETER OXENDALE   K   (D
CHRIS MERCER     SAX  (D   STEVE GREGORY     SAX  (D   MORRIS PERT        PERC (D   BARRY DE SOUZA   D   (D
MIKE MORAN       K    (D   NICKY HARRISON RECORDER(D   NICK CARAWAY       V    (D   STRINGS              (D
```

PAULINE MURRAY

```
     PAULINE MURRAY       V    (A      (A) & THE INVISIBLE GIRLS   1980  ILLUSIVE           2394 277
     MARTIN HANNETT             (A
     STEVE HOPKINS              (A
```

M234   JUNIOR MURVIN   M234
```
     JUNIOR MURVIN        G    (A      (A) POLICE & THIEVES        1977  MANGO/ISLAND       ILPS 9499
                                       (B) TEDIOUS                1978  MANGO              2009
```

M235   MUSCLE SHOALS   M235
```
     SPOONER OLDHAM       G    (       (A) DOIN' IT TO THE BONE    1971  ARIOLA             ST  50021
     BARRY BECKETT        K    (ABC    (B) CREAM OF MUSCLE SHOALS  197   ATLANTIC      UK   K 50283
     JIMMY JOHNSON        G    (BC     (C) BORN TO GET DOWN        1976  BANG    BLP 403  + SHOT 001
     DAVE HOOD            B    (AB
     CHARLES ROSE      HRNS (ABC ROGER HAWKINS  D  (ABC HARRISON CALLOWAY HRNS (ABC HARVEY THOMPSON HRNS(ABC
     RONNIE EADES      HRNS (ABC CLAYTON IVEY   K  (B   PETE CARR          G    (B  TRAVIS WAMMACK   G   (B
     ROGER CLARK        D   (A  BOB WRAY        B  (AC  TIM HENSON         K    (A  KEN BELL         G  (AC
     LARRY BYROM        G   (A  TOM ROADY     PERC (AC  ANTHONY PARSONS    FLT  (A  RANDY McCORMICK  K   (C
     KATHERINE HILL     V   (C
```

M236   MUSCLES   M236
```
                                       (A) MUSCLES                197   BIG BEAR           BEAR  24
                                       ( ) MUSCLES                1978  BIG BEAR           BBR 1001
```

MUSIC EXPLOSION
```
     JAMES LYONS          V    (A      (A) LITTLE BIT O' SOUL      1967  LAURIE        US   SLLP 2040
     DON ATKINS           G    (A
     RICK NESTA           G    (A  BUTCH STAHL    B ORG(A  BOB AVERY     D HCA(A
```

MUSICAL JANEENS
```
     ORPHEUS ROVERS       D    (A      (A) SELL OUT               1980  PLUREX        1500
```

M237   MUSIC MACHINE   M237
```
     SEAN BONNIWELL       G    (AB     (A) TURN ON THE MUSIC       1966  ORIGINAL SOUND US  OSRLPS8875
     KEITH OLSEN          B    (A      (B) BONNIWELL MUSIC MACHINE 1968  WB            US   1732
     RON EDGAR            D    (A
     DOUG RHODES         ORG   (A  MARK LANDON   G (A
```

HARRY MUSKEE BAND
```
     HARRY MUSKEE       V HCA(A       (A) HARRY MUSKEE BAND       1977  NEGRAM             NN3
     MARTIN VAN DIJK      K    (A
     BERNARD REINKE       G    (A  LOURENS LEEUW   B  (A  JAN GROENINK   D  (A  PETER SCHON    SYN (A
     PIET VAN BLAUW     PERC  (A  CARL KALFF    HRNS (A  FRANS MIJTS  HRNS (A  FRED LEEFLANG  HRNS(A
     BART VAN LIER     HRNS  (A  JAN SCHUURMAN  BELLS(A  MONICA         V  (A  FLOUR          V  (A
     JOSEE VAN IERSEL    V    (A
```

HARRY MUSKEE & EELCO GELLING
```
     HARRY MUSKEE              (A       (A) BALLADS                1973  ?   RI 80 PHILIPS NL 6423 339
     EELCO GELLING             (A
```

M238   CHARLIE MUSSELWHITE   M238
```
     CHARLIE MUSSELWHITE V G HCA(ALL   (A) STAND BACK HERE COMES C M S'SIDE 1966 VANGUARD  US   VSD 79232
     TIM KAIHATSU         G    (BFK    (B) STONE BLUES            1968  VANGUARD     UK   SVRL19012
     CLAY COTTON        K V    (B      (C) CHARLIE MUSSELWHITE    1968  VANGUARD     US   VSD 79287
     CARL SEVEREID        B    (BFK    (D) LOUISIANA FOG          1968  CHERRY RED   US   CR  5102
     EDDIE HOH            D    (B      (E) BLUES FROM CHICAGO      1968  CHERRY RED   US   CR  5104
     ROBBEN FORD        G V    (G      (F) TENNESSEE WOMAN        1969  VANGUARD     US   VSD  6528
     JACK MYERS           B    (H      (G) TAKIN' MY TIME         1971  ARHOOLIE     US        1056
     LANCE DICKERSON      D    (GF     (H) MEMPHIS TENNESSEE      197   PARAMOUNT         PAR  5012
     GERALD PEDERSEN      B    (G      (J) GOIN' BACK DOWN SOUTH  1974  ARHOOLIE     US        1074
     BOB HALL           PNO    (L      (K) LEAVE THE BLUES TO US  1975  CAPITOL      US        11450
     SAM MITCHELL         G    (L      (L) HARMONICA ACCORDING TO CHARLIE 1978 KICKING MULE US 305 UK SNKF
     EUGENE BLACKNELL     G    (M      (M) TIMES GETTIN TOUGHER THAN TOUGH 1978 CRYSTAL CLEAR(DIRECT) US CCS 005
     PEE WEE ELLIS      SAX    (M
     BIG JOHN EVANS       D   (M  BOBBY FORTE    SAX (M  JOHNNY HEARTSMAN   G  (M  STEVEN B JONES   D  (M
     JOHN TURK          TPT   (M  DARRELL BROADNAX B (M  PAT FORD           D  (DG STU FELDMAN      B  (D
     WORIN BELLAS       ORG   (M  MIKE OSBORN      G (D  STAN POPLIN        G  (D  VICTOR VIGEANT   B  (D
     MICHAEL KONCALSKI    D   (D  DARYL DRAGON   PNO (D  ED CARTER          G  (D  SKIP ROSE      PNO (FKM
     FRED ROULETTE     STEEL(F? LARRY MARTIN      D (K  RAY ARBIZU       HRNS (K  MIKE BLOOMFIELD  G  (K
     LYNN CAREY'MAMA LION' V(K  STEVE YORK       B (L  LONNIE CASTILLE    D  (H  JEFF RICH    D   (L
     STEFAN GROSSMAN  G PROD(L  ROD PIAZZA     HCA (F  FRED BELOW         D  (A  BOB ANDERSON   B   (A
     HARVEY MANDEL      G    (A  BARRY GOLDBERG K PROD(ABK LARRY WELKER    G  (BF
```

MYLES & LENNY
```
     MYLES COHEN        G V    (AB     (A) MYLES & LENNY          1974  CBS   US   33366
     LENNY SOLOMON      VLN    (AB     (B) IT ISNT THE SAME       1975  CBS   US   33938
     BOB MANN             G    (
     MICKY ERBE           B    (   RHONDA SILVER    V  (A  SHARON LEE WILLIAMS V  ( DICK SMITH CONGAS (
     DOUG RILEY           K    (   BRIAN LEONARD    D  (   LAUREL WARD         V  ( HAGOOD HARDY  VIB(
     PATRICK McNEILLY   S/D    (   MARIBETH SOLOMON K  (   BRIAN RUSSELL       G  ( BILL MACKAY   D  (
     LAURIE HOOD          V    (   DICK BERG      HRNS (   DAVID BROMBERG    G DOB( PAUL BLANEY   B  (
     CHARLIE McCOY      HCA    (   JUDY TATE        V  (
```

LOUIS MYERS
```
     LOUIS MYERS      V G HCA(A        (A) I'M A SOUTHERN MAN      1978  ADVENT        US        2809
     FREDDY ROBINSON      G    (A
     NATHANIEL DOVE     PNO    (A  DENNIS WALKER   B  (A  BUSTER JONES   D  (A
```

SAM MYERS
```
     SAM MYERS HCA V           (A      (A) DOWN HOME IN MISSISSIPPI 19   TJ            US        1030
     TOMMY LEE THOMPSON   G    (A
```

M239   RICHARD MYHILL   M239
```
     RICHARD MYHILL       V    (AB     (A) RICHARD MYHILL ALBUM    1974  EMI           UK   EMC3024
     PAUL KEOGH           G    (A      (B) 21 DAYS IN SOHO         1974  EMI           UK   EMC3051
     GRAHAM PRESKETT    B MAND(A
     BRIAN COLE       STEEL(A  MIKE MORGAN     G   (A  FRANK RICOTTI  PERC (A  TONY CARR      PERC(A
     HENRY SPINETTI       D    (A
```

```
M240                                    MYOFIST                                              M240
     RON CHENIER      G V  (A           (A) HOT SPIKES              1980  A&M         UK    AMLH64823
     ED EAGAN         K    (A
     JOHN CHENIER     D V  (A   JEFF NYSTROM    B V  (A
M240A                              GARY MYRICK & THE FIGURES                                 M240A
     GARY MYRICK      G V  (AB          (A) GARY MYRICK & THE FIGURES  1980 EPIC US 36524 UK 84450
     DAVID DENNARD    B    (A           (B) LIVING IN A MOVIE       1981  EPIC
     ED BEYER         K    (A
     JACK WHITE       D    (A
M241                                  MYSTERY GIRLS                                          M241
                                        (A) FAMOUS MEN (EP)         19    STRANGE     UK    HAM  001
M242                                    MYSTERYS                                             M242
                                        (A) MYSTERYS (EP)           1979  DEAD GOOD   UK    DEAD  4
M242A                         MYSTIC NUMBER NATIONAL BANK                                    M242A
     GLENN WALTERS    D V  (A           (A) A MYSTIC NUMBER NATIONAL BANK  1969 PROBE  CPLPS 4501
     BOB SEBBO        G    (A
     RUSS BOOTH       B    (A   DAVE LORENZ    G    (A
M243                                     MYTHOS                                              M243
     STEPHAN KASKE V K SYN D G(A        (A) QUASAR                  1980  SKY               SKY 046
M244                            CEDRIC MYTON & THE CONGOS                                    M244
     CEDRIC MYTON          (A           (A) FACE THE MUSIC          1981  GO FEET     UK    BEAT 4
N1                                        N C C U                                            N1
                                        (A) SUPER TRICK            1977  UA          UK    UAS30122
N2                                        N R B Q                                            N2
     TERRY ADAMS K WIND V  (ALL         (A) N R B Q                1969  CBS         UK          63653
     TOM ARDOLINI     D    (D           (B) BOPPIN THE BLUES       1970
     STEVE FERGUSON   G V  (ABC         (C) SCAPS                  1971  POLYDOR UK 2329018 US KAMA S 2045
     AL ANDERSON      G V  (CDE         (D) WORKSHOP               1972                 US KAMA S 2065
     FRANK GADLER     V    (A           (E) AT YANKEE STADIUM      1978  MERCURY     US          3712
   [ JODY ST NICOLAS  B V  (ABCD        (F) ALL HOPPED UP          1978  RED ROOSTER 101 +ROUNDER 3029
   [ JOE SAMPINAIO ]                    (G) KICK ME HARD           1979  ROUNDER     US          3030
     G T STALEY       D    (ABCD
     DON ADAMS        TROM (CDA
N2A                                       N Y C C                                            N2A
     ARTHUR FREEMAN        (A           (A) MAKE EVERY DAY COUNT   1978  RCA               PL12782
     BENNY DIGGS          (A
     JOSEPH JOUBERT       (A   GREG COLE        PNO (A  RICHARD TEE    K  (A  PAUL SCHAEFFER  PNO (A
     LEON PENDARVIS   K    (A   WILL LEE         B   (A  JOHN TROPEA    G  (A  WILLIAM SEADMAN   G(A
     CLIFF MORRIS     G    (A   JEFF MIRANOV     G   (A  STEVE GADD     D  (A  GEORGE DEVENS   PERC(A
     ERROL BENNETT    PERC (A
N2B                                 NA FILI (The POETS)                                      N2B
     THOMAS O CANAINN V PIPES(A         (A) CHANTERS  TUNE         1977  TRANSATLANTIC UK  TRA353
     TOM BARRY        WIND(A
     MATT CRANITCH    FDL  (A
N2C                                   STEVE NARDELLA                                         N2C
     STEVE NARDELLA       (A           (A) ITS ALL ROCK'N'ROLL     1980  BLIND PIG   US    879
N2D                                     NANTUCKET                                            N2D
                                        (A) NANTUCKET              1978  EPIC    US   35253
                                        (B) YOUR FACE OR MINE      1979  EPIC    US   36023
                                        (C) LONG WAY TO THE TOP    1980  EPIC    US   36523
N3                                    NAPOLEON XIV                                           N3
     JERRY SAMUELS    V    (A           (A) THEY'RE COMING TO TAKE ME AWAY 1966 WB  US    W1661
N4                                      GRAHAM NASH                                          N4
     GRAHAM NASH  K HCA G V (AB         (A) SONGS FOR BEGINNERS    1971  ATLANTIC UK 2401 011 US  SD 7204
     JOHN BARBATA     D    (AB          (A) SONGS FOR BEGINNERS    1971  ATLANTIC        UK IR K40237
     CALVIN SAMUELS   B    (A           (B) WILD TALES             1973  ATLANTIC UK K50025 US  SD 7288
     JOEL BERNSTEIN  K V   (ABC         (C) EARTH & SKY            1980  EMI  US UK 12014
     DAVID MASON           (AB
     DALLAS TAYLOR    D    (A   RITA COOLIDGE    V   (A  JOE YANKEE    PNO (AB PAT P ARNOLD    V  (A
     PHIL LESH        B    (A   JERRY GARCIA     G   (A  DAVID CROSBY  G V (ABC DAVID LINDLEY FDL G V(ABC
     CHRIS ETHRIDGE   B    (A   BOBBY KEYS      SAX  (A  VANETTA FIELDS V  (A  SHIRLEY MATTHEWS V (A
     CLYDIE KING      V    (A   DOROTHY MORRISON V   (A  DORIAN RUDNYTSKY CELLO (A LARRY COX      (A
     TIM DRUMMOND     B    (BC  BEN KEITH      STEEL (B  HARRY HALEX   PNO (B  JONI MITCHELL   V (B
     JOE VITALE    D K FLT(C JOE WALSH    G   (C RUSS KUNKEL    PERC (C  CRAIG DOERGE    K  (C
     CECE BULFORD     V    (C   JOHN BRENNAN    G   (C  DANNY KORTCHMAR G (C  JACKSON BROWNE  V  (C
     STEVE LUKATHER   G    (C   ARMANDO HURLEY   V   (C  NICOLETTE LARSON V (C  CLEO KENNEDY    V  (C
     BRENDA EAGER     V    (C   GLORIA COLEMAN   V   (C  JOE LALA      PERC (C GEORGE PERRY    B  (C
     STEPHEN STILLS   G    (C   LEAH KUNKEL      V   (C
N4A                                   NASH THE SLASH                                         N4A
                                        (A) CHILDREN OF THE NIGHT  1980 ARIOLA 203 406 SINDISC UK DID9
N4B                                     JOHNNY NASH                                          N4B
     JOHNNY NASH      V    (ALL         (A) SOUL FOLK              196   JAD   US 1006
                                        (B) HOLD ME TIGHT          196   JAD   US 1207
                                        (C) JOHNNY NASH            19    ABC   US 244
                                        (D) QUIET HOUR             19    ABC   US 276
                                        (E) I GOT RHYTHM           19    ABC   US 299
                                        (F) LETS GET LOST          19    ABC   US 334
                                        (G) TEARDROPS IN THE RAIN  19    CADET US 50034
                                        (H) STARRING JOHNNY NASH STUDIO TIME 19 ABC US 383
                                        (I) I CAN SEE CLEARLY NOW  1972  CBS  US 31607  UK  64840
                                        (J) MY MERRY GO ROUND      1973  CBS  US 32158  UK  65449
                                        (K) CELEBRATE LIFE         1974  CBS  US 32828  UK  80039
                                        (L) GREATEST HITS          1974  CBS             UK  69096
                                        (M) TEARS ON MY PILLOW     197   CBS             UK  69148
                                        (N) WAHT A WONDERFUL WORLD 1977  EPIC            UK  81783
                                        (O) THE JOHNNY NASH COLLECTION 1977 EPIC         UK  10008
                                        (P) LETS GO DANCING        1979  EPIC            UK  83043
                                        (Q) THE JOHNNY NASH ALBUM  1980  CBS             UK  31779
                                        (R) STIR IT UP             1981  HALLMARK        UK  3063
```

NASHVILLE TEENS

```
ARTHUR SHARP       V  (        (A) TOBACCO ROAD            19   LONDON      US           3407
RAY PHILLIPS       V B (        (B) NASHVILLE TEENS        19   NEW WORLD        AW 6002
JOHN ALLEN         G  (        (C) REMEMBERING             19   DECCA
PATER SHANNON      B G (        (D) NASHVILLE TEENS (EP)   1964 DECCA        UK           DFE8600
BARRY JENKINS      D  (
JOHN HAWKEN        K  (   ROGER GROOM    D  (   NEIL KORNER    B  (
```

NASHVILLE WEST

```
CLARENCE WHITE     G V (A       (A) NASHVILLE WEST         178  SIERRA    US   8701
GENE PARSONS       D V (A
GIB GUILBEAU       G V (A   WAYNE MOORE  B V (A
```

NASMAK

```
JOOP VAN BRAKEL    G V (A       (A) NASMAK & INSTUMENTS    1980 PLUREX   NL           1800
TOON BRESSERS      D   (A
HENK JANSSEN       G   (A   THEO VNA EENBERGEN    B  (A    TRUUS DE GROOT   V SYN G(A
```

NASTY POP

```
TONY WILMSHURST    G V (AB      (A) NASTY POP              1975 ISLAND    UK           ILPS 9340
KEITH WILKINSON    B V (AB      (B) MISTAKEN IDENTITY      1977 POLYDOR   UK           2302 056
STEVE GRACE        G HCA(AB
JON FITZPATRICK    V   (AB  STEVE CORDUNER  D   (B    CHRIS MERCER   SAX (B   MARTYN FORD HRNS (B
JOHN HEATH         D   (A
```

NANETTE NATAL

```
NANETTE NATAL      G V (A       (A) THE BEGINNING          19   EVOLUTION      US           3009
JERRY FRIEDMAN     G   (A
KEN ASCHER         K   (A   ANDY MUSON    B  (A    ALLAN SCHWARZBERG  D   (A
```

NATCHEZ TRACE

```
                                (A) TO NASHVILLE           197  PINE RIDGE          6414 104
                                (B) BEST OF                1975 SWEETFOLK          SFA 048
```

NATIONAL HEAD BAND

```
LEE KERSLAKE       D K V(A       (A) ALBERT ONE            1971 WB        UK           K46094
JAN SCHELHAAS      K   (A
DAVE PAUL          B G K V(A NEIL FORD    G V (A
```

NATIONAL HEALTH

```
AMANDA PARSONS     V    (12A      (A) NATIONAL HEALTH      1978 AFFINITY  UK  AFF 6
DAVE STEWART       K    (1345AB   (B) OF QUEUES & CURES    1978 CHARLY    UK  CRL5010
RICK BIDDULPH      B K  (B        (1) 1977 (2) 1977  (3) 1978 (4) 1978 (5) 1978
BILL BRUFORD       D    (1
ALAN GOWAN         K    (12A PHIL MILLER    G    (ALL NEIL MURRAY    B  (123A PIP PYLE    D (AB2345
JOHN GREAVES       B    (45B GEORGE BORN CELLO B V (45B LINDSAY COOPER  WIND (5   JOHN MITCHELL  PERC(A
JIMMY HASTINGS     WIND (AB PAUL NIEMAN    TROM (B   PHIL MINTON      TPT (B    SELWYN BAPTISTE   (B
KEITH THOMPSON     OBOE (B   PETER BLEGVAD      V  (B
```

NATIONAL LAMPOON

```
JOHN BELUSHI            (*       (A) RADIO DINNER          1972 ISLAND UK HELP 8  BLUE THUMB US 38
CHRISTOPHER CERF        (*       (B) LEMMINGS              1973 BLUE THUMB       US    BTS6006
CHEVY CHASE             (*       (C) MISSING WHITE HOUSE TAPES 1974 BLUETHUMB   US    BTS6008
RHONDA COULLET          (*       (D) GOLD TURKEY           1975 EPIC            US    33410
BRIAN DOYLE-MURRAY      (*       (E) GOODBYE POP           1976 EPIC            US    33956
TONY HENDRA             (*       (F) THATS NOT FUNNY THATS SICK 1978 RADAR      UK    RAD 4
MARK HOROWITZ           (*       (G) ANIMAL HOUSE          1979 MCA  UK MCF 2868 US   3046
DAVID HURDON            (*       (*) GREATEST HITS         1978 VISA            IMP
HAROLD RAMIS            (*       (J) WHITE ALBUM           1980 LABEL 21    US        2002
PHIL JACOBS             (*
BILL MURRAY             (*   ALICE PLAYTEN     (*   NORMAN ROSE   (*   MELISSA MANCHESTER   (*
JOSEPH O'FLAHERTY       (*   GILDA RADNER      (*   PAUL SHAFFER  (*   CHRISTOPHER GUEST    (*
```

NATURAL ACCUSTIC BAND

```
KRYSIA KOCJAN      V  (          (A) LEARNING TO LIVE      1972 RCA       UK  SF 8272
TOM HOY            G V (          (B) BRANCHING IN         1974 RCA       UK  SF 8314
ROBIN THYNE        G V (
JEAN CARLIN        V  (      AYMIN MUHAMMED   B  (    GRAHAM MORGAN   D  (
```

NATIVE

```
WAYNE JOBSON       G V (A        (A) 1ST ALBUM            1979 ARISTA    UK    NEW 2
BRIAN JOBSON       G   (A
WARREN MENDES      B   (A   PETER COUCH    K  (A   PERRY TOLE    G  (A   CHRIS LOPEZ   PERC  (A
RICHARD SINCLAIR   D   (A
```

NAUGHTY SWEETIES

```
LAN JACK           G V (A        (A) LIVE (EP)            1981 RHINO     US           RNDP 906
VOLLA SMITH        G V (A
SIMEON PILLICH     B V (A   ANDY DOERSCHUK   D   (A
```

NATURAL GAS

```
JERRY SHIRLEY      D   (A        (A) NATURAL GAS          1976  PRIVATE STOCK US 2011 UK PVLP1007
PETER WOOD         K   (A
MARK CLARKE        B V (A   JOEY MOLLAND G V (A   FELIX PAPPALARDI   V  (A
```

NAVARRO

```
ROBERT McENTEE     G V (B        (A)LISTEN               1977 CAPITOL   US    SW 11670
MARK HALLMAN       G V K(B        (B) STRAIGHT TO THE HEART 1978 CAPITOL US    SW 11784
RICHARD HARDY      WIND (B
MICHAEL WOOTEN     D   (B   STEVE SIROTKIN   K  (B   ROB GALLOWAY   B  (B   MIGUEL RIVERA   PERC  (B
JOEY CONWAY        PNO (B
```

NAVASOTA

```
JEFF BAXTER        G  (A         (A) ROOTIN'             1972 ABC       US           ABCX 757
RAY PAWLIK         G  (A
STEVE LONG         G  (A    PAUL MINTER    B  (A   LINDSEY MINTER  D  (A   DICKY SONY PNO (A
CLYDIE KING        V  (A    SHIRLEY MATTHEWS V (A  JACKIE WARD     V  (A   DONALD FAGEN   K (A
BYRON BERLINE      FDL (A   MARK VOLMAN    V  (A   HOWARD KAYLAN   V  (A
```

NAZARETH

DAN McCAFFERTY	V	(ALL	(A) NAZARETH	1971 PEGASUS UK PEG 10 MOONCREST CREST 10
PETE AGNEW	G B	(ALL	(A) NAZARETH	197 MOUNTAIN TOPC5001 US WB BS 2615
MANNY CHARLTON	G	(ALL	(B) EXERCISES	1972 MOONCREST CREST14
DARRELL SWEET	D	(ALL	(B) EXERCISES	19 MOUNTAIN TOPS103 US WB BS 2639
PETE WINGFIELD	K	(A	(C) RAZAMANAZ	1973 MOONCREST CREST 1
PETE YORK	PERC	(A	(C) RAZAMANAZ	197 MOUNTAIN TOPS104 US A&M SP 4396
B J COLE	STEEL	(A	(D) LOUD & PROUD	1974 MOONCREST CREST 4
DAVE STEWART	K	(A	(D) LOUD & PRO'D	1974 MOUNTAIN TOPS105 US A&M SP 3609
ZAL CLEMINSON	SYN G	(MNO	(E) HAIR OF THE DOG	1975 MOONCREST CREST27
MAX MIDDLETON	K	(E	(E) HAIR OF THE DOG	197 MOUNTAIN TOPS107 US A&M SP 4511
VICKI BROWN	V	(E	(F) RAMPANT	1975 MOONCREST CREST15
SIMON PHILLIPS	PERC	(E	(F) RAMPANT	197 MOUNTAIN TOPS106 US A&M SP 3641
LISA STRIKE	V	(E	(G) GREATEST HITS	1975 MOUNTAIN TOPS108 US A&M 9020
BARRY ST JOHN	V	(E	(H) CLOSE ENOUGH FOR ROCK'N'ROLL	1976 MOUNTAIN TOPS109 US A&M SP 4562
VICKY SILVA	V	(E	(J) PLAY 'N' THE GAME	1977 MOUNTAIN TOPS113 US A&M SP 4610
JEFF BAXTER	SYN	(O	(K) EXPECT NO MERCY	1977 MOUNTAIN TOPS115 US A&M SP 4666
JOHN LOCKE	K	(OP	(L) HOT TRACKS (EP)	1977 MOUNTAIN NAZ 001 US A&M 4643
BILLY RANKIN	G	(P	(M) NO MEAN CITY	1978 MOUNTAIN TOPS123 US A&M SP 4741
PAULINHO DA COSTA	PERC	(N	(N) MALICE IN WONDERLAND	1980 MOUNTAIN TOPS126 US A&M SP 4799
VANETTA FIELDS	V	(N	(O) FOOL CIRCLE	1981 NEMS UK NEL 6019
SHIRLEY MATTHEWS	V	(N	(P) SNAZ	1981 NEMS UK NAL 102 US A&M SP 6703
PAULETTE BROWN	V	(N		
ALAN ESTES	VIBES	(N		

NAZTY

(A) I GOT TO MOVE	197 CONTEMPO CLP 542

NAZZ

TODD RUNDGREN	G	(AB	(A) NAZZ	1968 SCREEN GEMS US SD 5001
THOM MOONEY	D	(AB	(B) NAZZ NAZZ	1969 SCREEN GEMS US SD 5002
ROBERT ANTONI	K V	(AB	(C) NAZZ 3	1969 SCREEN GEMS US SD 5004
CARSON VAN OSTEN	B V	(AB		

TED NEELEY

TED NEELEY	V	(A	(A) 1974 AD	1973 RCA US APLI 0317
MICHAEL OMARTIAN	K	(A		
LEW McCREARY	TROM	(A	JIM GORDON D (A MARK TULIN B (A DEAN PARKS G (A
BEN BENAY	G	(A	KING ERRISSON CONG (A BARRY FASMAN K (A PAUL HUBINON TPT(A
JACKIE KELSO	SAX	(A	DAVID DUKE HRNS (A BARBARA CARLSON HRNS (A CHUCK FINDLEY TPT(A
FRED SELDON	SAX	(A	SID SHARP STR (A

NEGATIVLAND

DAVID WILLS	SYN V	(A	(A) NEGATIVLLAND	1980 SEELAND US 001
MARK HODLER	K CLAR	(A	(B) POINTS	1981 SEELAND US 002
RICHARD LYONS	K CLAR	(A		
PETER DAYTON	G B VLA	(A	(A W KENNEDY G (A BOB JACKSON CLAR (B JAN ALLEN (B

FRED NEIL

FRED NEIL	G V	(ALL	(A) HOOTENANNY LIVE AT THE BITTER END	1964 FM RECORDS US FM 309
PETE CHILDS	(D		(B) WORLD OF FOLK MUSIC	1964 FM RECORDS US FM 319
DOUGLAS HATFIELD	B	(D	(C) TEAR DOWN THE WALLS	1964 ELEKTRA US EKS 7248
FELIX PAPPALARDI	B	(D	(D) BLEECKER & MACDOUGAL	196 ELEKTRA US EKS 7293
JOHN SEBASTIAN	HCA	(D	(D) LITTLE BIT OF RAIN	1970 ELEKTRA US EKS 74073
			(E) FRED NEIL	1966 CAPITOL US ST 2665
			(E) EVERYBODY'S TALKIN'	1969 CAPITOL US ST 2665
			(F) SESSIONS	1971 CAPITOL US ST 2862
			(G) OTHER SIDE OF THIS LIFE	1971 CAPITOL US ST 657

NEKTAR

MICK BROCKETT		(ALL	(A) JOURNEY TO THE CENTRE OF THE EYE	1972 BELLAPHON/BACILLUS BLPS19064
ALLAN FREEMAN	K	(ALL	(B) TAB IN THE OCEAN	1972 BELLAPHON/BACILLUS BLPS19118
ROY ALBRIGHTON	G V	(ABCDEFGHK	(B) " " " "	1974 UA UAS 29499
RON HOWDEN	D	(ALL	(B) " " " "	1976 PASSPORT US 98017
DEREK MOORE	B V	(ALL	(C) REMEMBER THE FUTURE	1973 BELLAPHON/BACILLUS BLPS19164
DAVE NELSON	G V	(JKLMN	(C) " " " "	1974 UA UAS 29545
CHRIS MERCER	SAX	(E	(C) " " " "	1974 PASSPORT US 98002
LARRY FAST		(J	(D) SOUNDS LIKE THIS	1973 BELLAPHON/BACILLUS BDA7506
STEVE GREGORY	SAX	(E	(D) " " " "	1973 UA UAD60041/2
ROBERT CALVERT	V	(E	(E) (E) DOWN TO EARTH	1974 BELLAPHON/BACILLUS BLPS19190
P P ARNOLD	V	(E	(E) " " "	1973 UA UAG29680
KEN COLE	V	(E	(E) " " "	197 PASSPORT 98005
PHIL BROWN	B	(E	(F) LIVE AT THE ROUNDHOUSE	1974 BELLAPHON BLPS19182
STEPHEN WICK	TUBA	(E	(F) " " " "	197 BACILLUS BAC 2028
BUTCH HUDSON	TPT	(E	(G) RECYCLED	1976 BELLAPHON BLPS19219
RON CARTHY	TPT	(E	(G) " "	1976 DECCA UK SKLR5250 PASSPORT US 98011
CHRIS PYNE	TROM	(E	(H) NEKTAR	1976 BELLAPHON BLPS19224
WALT NEKTROID	G	(J	(J) MAGIC IS A CHILD	1977 BELLAPHON BAC 2050
STRING SECTION		(J	(J) " " "	1977 POLYDOR US PD 6115
			(K) LIVE IN NEW YORK	1977 BELLAPHON BAC 2004
			(L) MORE LIVE IN NEW YORK	1978 BELLAPHON BAC 2058
			(M) THRU THE EARS	1978 VISA IMP 9001
			(N) MAN IN THE MOON	19

BILL NELSON

BILL NELSON	G V	(A	(A) NORTHERN DREAM	1971 SMILE LAF 2182
			(A) NORTHERN DREAM	1980 BUTT RI BUTT002

BILL NELSONS RED NOISE

BILL NELSON	G V		(A) SOUND ON SOUND	1979 HARVEST UK SHSP 4095 US ST 11931
ANDREW CLARK	K	(ABC	(B) QUIT DREAMING AND GET ON THE BEAM	1981 MERCURY UK 6359 055
IAN NELSON	SAX	(ABC	(C) SOUNDING OF THE RITUAL ECHO	1981 FREE WITH B
RICK FORD	B	(ABC		
STEVE PEER	D	(ABC	DAVE MATTACKS D (ABC RICHARD BROWN K D (A GARETH EILLEDGE B (A
LEOM ARTHURS	B	(A	TOM KELLICHEN D (BC

JIMMY NELSON (A

RICK NELSON	G V	(ALL
JAMES BURTON	G	(
JOE OSBORN	B	(
JAMES KIRKLAND	B	(
RICHIE FROST	D	(
RAY JOHNSON	PNO	(
JOE MAPHIS	G	(
BARNEY KESSEL	G	(
GENE GARTH	PNO	(
JIM CETERA	B V	(J
TOM BRUMLEY	STEEL	(JKLMN
ALLEN KEMP	G V	(JKL
PATRICK SHANAHAN	D	(JKL
RANDY MEISNER	B V	(K
ANDY BELLING	K	(K
STEPHEN A LOVE	B V	(L
DON NELSON	FLT	(L
DENNIS LARDEN	G	(MN
JAT DE WITT WHITE	B V	(MN
TY GRIMES	D	(M
RICHIE HAYWARD	D	(
SNEAKY PETE KLEINOW	STEEL	(
BUDDY EMMONS	STEEL	(
STEVE DUNCAN	D PERC V	(N
JAI WINDING	K	(N
ROGER BUSH	B	(N

JIMMY NELSON

(A) JIMMY 'Mr T99' NELSON   1981 ACE UK 10CH 35

RICKY NELSON

RICKY	1957 US IMPERIAL 9048	UK LONDON	HAP 2080
RICKY (RI 2 TRACKS LESS)	1979 US IMPERIAL M1004		
RICKY NELSON	1958 US IMPERIAL 9050	UK LONDON	HAP 2119
RICKY SINGS AGAIN	1959 US IMPERIAL 9061	UK LONDON	HAP 2159
SONGS BY RICKY	1959 US IMPERIAL 9082	UK LONSDON	HAP 2206
SONGS BY RICKY	1959 US IMPERIAL 12030		
MORE SONGS BY RICKY	1960 US IMPERIAL 9122	UK LONDON	HAP 2290
MORE SONGS BY RICKY	1960 US IMPERIAL 12059		
RICK IS 21	1961 US IMPERIAL 9152	UK LONDON	HAP 2379
RICK IS 21	1961 US IMPERIAL 12071		
ALBUM SEVEN	1962 US IMPERIAL 9167	UK LONDON	HAP 2445
ALBUM SEVEN	1962 US IMPERIAL 12082		
BEST SELLERS BY RICK NELSON	1963 US IMPERIAL 9218	US IMPERIAL	12218
ITS UP TO YOU	1963 US IMPERIAL 9223	US IMPERIAL	12223
ITS UP TO YOU (DIFF TRACKS)	1963	UK LONDON	HAP 8066
MILLION SELLERS	1963 US IMPERIAL 9232	US IMPERIAL (S)	12232
MILLION SELLERS(DIFF TRACKS)	1964 UK	BRUNSWICK LBY	3027
HELLO MARY LOU (SAME AS ABOVE)	197 NL SUNSET		DA 5026
ROCK 'N' ROLL CLASSICS(AS ABOVE)	197 NL U A		52 92968
STORY OF R'N'R (RI OF IMP 9232)	19 GERM U A		UA 30050
A LONG VACATION	1963 US IMPERIAL 9244	US	(S) 12244
SINGS FOR YOU	1964 US IMPERIAL 9251	US	(S) 12251
FOR YOUR SWEET LOVE	1963 US DECCA DL 74419	UK BRUNSWICK LAT 8545
SINGS FOR YOU	1964 US DECCA DL 74479	UK BRUNSWICK LAT 8562
THE VERY THOUGHT OF YOU	1964 US DECCA DL 74559	UK BRUNSWICK LAT 8581
SPOTLIGHT ON RICK	1964 US DECCA DL 74608	UK BRUNSWICK LAT 8596
BEST ALWAYS	1965 US DECCA DL 74660	UK BRUNSWICK LAT 8615
LOVE & KISSES	1965 US DECCA DL 74678	UK BRUNSWICK LAT 8630
BRIGHT LIGHTS & COUNTRY MUSIC	1966 US DECCA DL 74779	UK BRUNSWICK LAT 8657
ON THE FLIP SIDE (4 TRACK BY RICK)	66 US DECCA DL 74836		
COUNTRY FEVER	1967 US DECCA DL 74837	UK BRUNSWICK LAT 8680
COUNTRY FEVER	197 US MCA RI MCA2		
ANOTHER SIDE OF RICK	1968 US DECCA DL 74944	UK MCA	MUPS 302
PERSPECTIVE	1969 US DECCA DL 75014		
RICK NELSON IN CONCERT	1970 US DECCA DL 75162	UK MCA	MUPS 409
RICK NELSON IN CONCERT	197 US MCA RI MCA 3		
GOLDEN GREATS	19 US LIBERTY 8674		
(J)RICK SINGS NELSON	1970 US DECCA DL 75236	UK MCA	MUPS 442
(J)RICK SINGS NELSON	197 US MCA RO MCA20	UK MCA RI	MCF 2644
(K)RUDY THE FIFTH	1971 US DECCA DL 75297	UK MCA	MUPS 440
(K)RUDY THE FIFTH	197 US MCA RI MCA37	UK MCA RI	MCF 2535
(L)GARDEN PARTY	1972 US DECCA DL 75391	UK MCA	MDKS8009
(L)GARDEN PARTY	1974 US MCA RI MCA62	UK MCA RI	NCG 3515
(M)WINDFALL	1974 US MCA 383	UK MCA	MCG 3516
(N)INTAKES	1977 US EPIC 34420	UK EPIC	81802
VERY BEST OF	1970 SUNSET	UK	SLS 50164
VERY BEST OF (DIFF TRACKS)	197 UA	US	UALA 330E
LEGENDARY MASTERS	1971 UA US 9960	UK UA	UAD 60029/30
POP CHRONICLE (RI OF ABOVE)	197 UA	GERM	UA 29962
RICK NELSON COUNTRY	1973 MCA	US	MCA 24004
RICK NELSON	197 SUNSET	US	SUS 5118
I NEED YOU	197 SUNSET	US	SUS 5205
RICKY NELSON STORY (TRIPLE)	197 ARI	US	ARI 1003
RICKY NELSON SINGLES	1977 MCA US CDL 8053	UK RI MFP	MFP 50411
RICKY NELSON ALBUMS	1979 UK UA		UAK 30246
STARS OF THE 60s	19 NL UA		50 94953
RICK NELSON STORY	19 JAP JET		JET 7070
BIG HITS	19 JAP UA		UA GXH18
RICKY	1980 UA US 1004		
PLAYING TO WIN	1981 CAPITOL		12109

SANDY NELSON   D   (ALL

SANDY NELSON

TEENBEAT	1960 IMPERIAL US (M)9105(S)12044
HES A DRUMMER BOY	1961 IMPERIAL US (M)9136(S)12159
LET THERE BE DRUMS	1961 IMPERIAL US (M)9159(S)12080
LET THERE BE DRUMS	1961 LONDON UK HAP 2425
DRUMS ARE MY BEAT	1962 IMPERIAL US (M)9168(S)12083
COMPELLING PERCUSSION	1962 LONDON UK HAP 8029
DRUMMING UP A STORM	196 IMPERIAL US (M)9189(S)12189
DRUMMING UP A STORM	196 LONDON UK HAP 8009
GOLDEN HITS	196 IMPERIAL US (M)9202(S)12202
ON THE WILD SIDE	196 IMPERIAL US (M)9203(S)12203
AND THEN THERE WERE DRUMS	196 IMPERIAL US (M)9204(S)12204
AND THEN THERE WERE DRUMS	1968 SUNSET US 5224
TEENAGE HOUSE PARTY	1963 IMPERIAL US (M)9215(S)12215
TEENAGE HOUSE PARTY	1963 LONDON UK HAP 8051
BEST OF THE BEATS	196 IMPERIAL US (M)9224(S)12224
BEAT THAT DRUM	196 IMPERIAL US (S)12237
SANDY NELSON PLAYS	196 IMPERIAL US (M)9249(S)12249
SANDY NELSON PLAYS	1964 LIBERTY UK BY 3007
BE TRUE TO YOUR SCHOOL	196 IMPERIAL US (M)9258(S)12258
LIVE IN LAS VEGAS	196 IMPERIAL US (S)12272
LIVE IN LAS VEGAS	196 LIBERTY UK LBY 3035
TEENBEAT 65	196 IMPERIAL US (M)9278(S)12278
DISCOTHEQUE DRUMS	196 IMPERIAL US (M)9283(S)12283
DRUMS A GOGO	196 LIBERTY UK LBY 3061
BOSS BEAT	196 IMPERIAL US (M)9298(S)12298

SANDY NELSON

SUPERDRUMS	196	IMPERIAL US	(M)9314(S)12914
SUPERDRUMS	196	LIBERTY UK	LBY 3080
IN BEAT	196	IMPERIAL US	(M)9305(S)12305
BEAT THAT *?!! DRUM	196	IMPERIAL US	(M)9329(S)12329
SOUL DRUMS	196	IMPERIAL US	(M)9362(S)12362
BOOGALOO BEAT	196	IMPERIAL US	(M)9367(S)12367
ROCK'N'ROLL REVIVAL	196	IMPERIAL US	(M)9400(S)12400
MANHATTAN SPIRITUAL	1969	IMPERIAL US	(M)9439(S)12439
HEAVY DRUMS	1969	SUNSET US	5261
GROOVY	196	IMPERIAL US	(M)9451(S)12451
WALKING BEAT	19	SUNSET US	5114
TEENDRUMS	19	SUNSET UK	SLS50061
DRUMS DRUMS DRUMS	19	SUNSET UK	SLS50060
FATS DOMINO HITS	19	SUNSET US	5291
GOLDEN GREATS VOL 1	19	LIBERTY US	8679
THE BEST OF	1974	LIBERTY UK	LBS83387
HOCUS POCUS	1976	EMI IMP	UAS29509
VERY BEST OF	1974	UA US	LA 440
VERY BEST OF	1978	SUNSET UK	SLS50411

TRACY NELSON

TRACY NELSON	G K (ALL	(A) DEEP ARE THE ROOTS	1966	PRESTIGE US 7393
REGGIE YOUNG	G (BC	(B) TRACY NELSON	1974	ATLANTIC US SDD7310 UK K50091
MAC GAYDEN	G (AB	(C) SWEET SOUL MUSIC	1975	MCA US MCA 494
BOBBY EMMONS	K (B	(D) TIME IS ON MY SIDE	1976	MCA US 2203 UK MCF2765
BOBBY WOODS	K (D	(E) HOMEMADE SONGS	197	FLYING FISH US FF 052
JIM GORDON	D (D	(F) COME SEE ME ABOUT ME	1980	FLYING FISH US FF 209
RON CORNELIUS	G (BC	(G) DOIN' IT MY WAY	1980	AUDIO DYN US 101 ADELPHI 4119
ED GREENE	D (D			

JIM HUGHART	B (D	DAVID FOSTER	K (D	CLARENCE McDONALD	K (D	LARRY MUHOBERAC	K (D
LARRY CARLTON	G (D	DEAN PARKS	G (D	JESSE ED DAVIS	G (D	DANNY KORTCHMAR	G (D
JIM HORN	SAX (D	LAURA CREAMER	V (D	GERALD GARRETT	V (CE	MAXINE WILLARD	V (D
JULIA TILLMAN	V (D	MARK CREAMER	V (D	IRMA ROUTEN	V (D	SUSAN STEWARD	V (D
OMA DRAKE SINGERS	V (D	DARLENE GRONCKI	V (D	LEON PENDARVIS	K (BC	JACK LEE	G V K (B
TOMMY COGBILL	B (B	KENNY MALONE	D (B	STEVE HOWARD	TPT (B	MARSHALL CYR	TPT (B
LON PRICE	SAX (B	MICHAEL PIERCE	SAX (B	CLARENCE FORD	HRNS (B	CLYDIE KING	V (B
BEAU CECCHINO	V (B	MERRY CLAYTON	V (B	JIM GILSTRAP	V (B	JOE GREEN	V (B
PAT POWDRILL	V (B	WILLIE NELSON	V (B	LINDA RONSTADT	V (B	ANDY MACMAHON	K V (F
BILLY PUETT	SAX³ (F	BOB BABITT	B (C	WILLIE HALL	D (C	MYRNA SMITH	V (C
DANNY SANDERS	SAX (E	SYLVIA SHEMWELL	V (C	JOHNNY GIMBLE	FDL (C	RICHARD TEE	K (C
ESTELLE BROWN	V (C	PETE DRAKE	STEEL(C	HARVEY THOMPSON	HRNS (C	CHARLES ROSE	HRNS (C
RON EADES	HRNS (C	HARRISON CALLOWAY	HRNS (C	LANNY BOLES	PERC (EF	LARRY CHANEY	G (F
BARRY CHANCE	G (F	CHRIS LEUZINGER	G (F	LISA SILVER REYNOLDS	V (F	SHERRY KRAMER	V (F
DONNA McELROY	V (F	JAMIE BRANTLEY	V (F	JACK GROCHMAL	V (F	TED REYNOLDS	B (EF
WAYNE JACKSON	HRNS (F	ANDREW LOVE	HRNS (F	PEBBLE DANIEL	V (F	MARCIA ROUTH	V (F
SHERRY GROOMS	V (F	YVONNE HODGES	V (F	STEVE BRANTLEY	V (F	BRUCE DEES	V (F
WAYNE JACKSON	HRNS (E	CARLENE CARTER	V (E	STEVE HOSTACK	G V (E	SWEET INSPIRATION	V (C
JOHN SALEM	K V (A	CHARLIE MUSSELWHITE	HCA(A				

WILLIE NELSON

WILLIE NELSON	G V (ALL	...AND THAN I WROTE	1962	LIBERTY US LST7239
PAUL ENGLISH	D (RSZX	HERE'S WILLIE NELSON	1963	LIBERTY US LST7308
JODY PAYNE	G V (SRXZ	COUNTRY WILLIE	1965	RCA US LSP3418
BUCKY MEADOWS	G (RXZ	HELLO WALLS	1966	SUNSET US SUS5138
MICKEY RAPHAEL	HCA (RSXZ	HELLO WALLS	197	PICKWICK US SPC3584
DAVID ALLEN COE	V (S	COUNTRY FAVOURITES	1966	RCA US LSP3528
TOM MORRELL	STEEL(S	COUNTRY MUSIC CONCERT	1966	RCA US LSP3659
BOBBIE NELSON	PNO (RSX	MAKE WAY FOR	1967	RCA US LSP3748
BILLY ENGLISH	D (R	THE PARTYS OVER	1967	RCA US LSP3858
BILL SPEARS	B (RSXZ	TEXAS IN MY SOUL	1968	RCA US LSP3937 UK RD 7997
GUZENSLAW BROTHERS	V (S	GOOD TIMES	1968	RCA US LSP4057
STEVE FROMHOTZ	V (S	MY OWN PECULIAR WAY	1969	RCA US LSP4111
CHRIS ETHRIDGE	B (XZ	BOTH SIDES NOW	1970	RCA US LSP4294
MOSES CALDERON	K (Z	LAYING MY BURDENS DOWN	1970	RCA US LSP4404
JOHNNY GIMBLE	FD (Z	COLUMBUS STOCKADE	1970	CAMDEN US CAS2444
BOOKER T JONES	K (X	COLUMBUS STOCKADE	197	CAMDEN US ACL7018
RAY PRICE	V (Z	WILLIE NELSON & FAMILY	1971	RCA US LSP4489
GRADY MARTIN	G (Z	YESTERDAYS WINE	1971	RCA US LSP4568
BUDDY EMMONS	STEEL(Z	YESTERDAYS WINE	197	CAMDEN US ANL1102
CRYSTAL GAYLE	V (Z	YESTERDAYS WINE	1980	INTERNATIONAL INT5014
		THE WORDS DONT FIT	1972	RCA US LSP4653
		THE WILLIE WAY	1972	RCA US LSP4760
		COUNTRY WINNERS	1973	CAMDEN US ACLI0326
		THE BEST OF(RI LST7239)	1973	UA US UALA086
		SPOTLIGHT ON	1974	CAMDEN US ACLI0705
		COUNTRY WILLILE	1973	UA US UALA420
		SHOTGUN WILLIE	1973	ATLANTIC US SD 7262
		PHASES & STAGES	1974	ATLANTIC US SD 7291
		WHAT CAN YOU DO TO ME	1975	RCA US APLI1234
		(R)RED HEADED STRANGER	1975	CBS UK 69200 US 33482
		FAMOUS COUNTRY (DBL)	1975	RCA UK DPS2062
		(S)SOUND IN YOUR MIND	1976	CBS UK 81252 US 34092
		(S)SOUND IN YOUR MIND	1980	EMBASSY UK 31828
		TROUBLEMAKER	1976	CBS UK 81565 US 34112
		WANTED THE OUTLAWS	1976	RCA US APLI1321
		WANTED THE OUTLAWS	1976	RCA UK RS 1048
		WILLIE NELSON LIVE	1976	RCA UK APLI1487 US LSA3277
		& FRIENDS	1976	PLANTATION U US PLP214
		& FRIENDS	1976	CHARLY UK CR30120
		WILLIE NELSON 1961	1977	DOUBLE BARREL LT1961
		BEFORE HIS TIME	1977	RCA US APLI2210
		TEXAS COUNTRY (DBL)	1976	U A US LA574H2
		TO LEFTY FROM WILLIE	1977	CBS US 34695
		WAYLON & WILLIE	1978	RCA UK/ US APLI2686
		(X)STARDUST	1978	CBS US35305 UK 82710

WILLIE NELSON   (CONTINUED)

FACE OF A FIGHTER	1978	LONE STAR	US	L4602
THERE'LL BE NO TEARS	1978	UA US LA930	UK	UAS 30215
WILLIE & FAMILY LIVE	1978	CBS US 35642	UK	88333
PRETTY PAPER	1979	CBS US 36189	UK	83877
SWEET MEMORIES	1979	RCA	US	AHLI3243
CLASSIC WILLIE NELSON	1979	SUNSET		SLS50430
ONE FOR THE ROAD	1979	CBS US 36064	UK	88641
ELECTRIC HORSEMAN	1979	CBS US 36327	UK	70177
(Z)SAN ANTONIO ROSE	1980	CBS US 36476	UK	84358
HONEYSUCKLE ROSE	1980	CBS US 36752	UK	22080
FAMILY BIBLE	1980	SONGBIRD	US	MCA 3258
MINSTREL MAN	1980	RCA	US	4045
SOMEWHERE OVER THE RAINBOW	19	CBS	US	36883
ALWAYS ON MY MIND	1982	CBS	UK	85688
GREATEST HITS	1982	CBS	UK	88567

N24   NEON   N24

PETER BRANNIGAN	G V	(A	(A) NEON			19	PARAMOUNT	US PAS 5024
FRANCIS CRABTREE	K V	(A						
FUNG PORTER	V B	(A	RUSSELL LESLIE	V PERC	(A			

N24A   NEON HEARTS   N24A

PAUL RAVEN	B	(A	(A) POPULAR MUSIC	1979	SATRIL	UK SATL4012
KEITH ALLEN	D	(A				
STEVE HEART	SAX	(A	MARTIN RATCLIFFE	G	(A	

N24B   NEON BABIES   N24B

NIKOLAUS POLAK	G	(AB	(A) NEON BABIES	1981	GOOD NOISE	GER 2005
CONNY COOL	B	(AB	(B) HARMLOS	1982	ARIOLA	GER 204 530
REINHARD MEERMAN	SAX	(AB				
TONI NISSL	D	(AB	INGA'DILEMMA'HUMP K V(AB MIKO	V	(A	

N24C   NEON ROSE   N24C

ROGER HOLEGUARD	G V	(AB	(A) NEON ROSE	1973	VERTIGO	6316 250
BENNO MENGARELLI	B V	(AB	(B) RELOAD	1974	VERTIGO	
STANLEY LARSSON	D	(AB				
PIERO MENGARELLI	G	(AB				

N24D   NERVES   N24D

(A) NOTRE DEMO	1981 GOOD VIBRATIONS	UK

N24E   NERVOUS EATERS   N24E

STEVE CATALDO	G V	(A	(A) NERVOUS EATERS	1980	ELEKTRA	6E282
JEFF WILKINSON	D	(A				
JONATHAN PALEY	G V	(A	ROBB SKEEN	B V	(A NICKY HOPKINS K (A ANDY PALEY K (A
HARRY MASLIN	PERC	(A	STEVE CROPPER	G	(A	

N24F   NERVOUS REX   N24F

SHAUN BRIGHTON	V G	(A	(A) NERVOUS REX	1980 DREAMLAND US 5002 UK 2394 270
LAUREN AGNELLI	K V	(A		
DIANNE ATHEY	B	(A	JONATHAN LEE GILDERSLEEVE D (A	

N25   MICHAEL NESMITH   N25

MICHAEL NESMITH	G V	(ALL	(A) WICHITA TRAIN WHISTLE SINGS	1968	DOT	US 25861	SLPD 516
RED RHODES	STEEL	(ABCDEFGH	(A) WICHITA TRAIN WHISTLE SINGS	1978	PACIFIC ARTS	US RI	PACB 7113
JAMES BURTON	G	(AD	(B) MAGNETIC SOUTH	1970	RCA	US LSP4371 UK SF8136	
SHORTY ROGERS	D	(A	(C) LOOSE SALUTE	1970	RCA	US LSP4415	
HAL BLAINE	D	(A	(D) NEVADA FIGHTER	1971	RCA	US LSP4497 UK SF8209	
JOHN AUDINO	TPT	(A	(E) TANTAMOUNT TO TREASON	1972	RCA	US LPS4563 UK SF8276	
CHUCK BERGHOFFER	B	(A	(F) AND THE HITS JUST KEEP ON COMING	1972	RCA	US LSP4695	
MILT BERNHART	TROM	(A	(F) AND THE HITS JUST KEEP ON COMING	1977	ISLAND	UK	ILPS 9439
BUD BRISBOIS	TPT	(A	(F) AND THE HITS JUST KEEP ON COMING	1979	PACIFIC ARTS	UK RI	PAC 116
FRANK CAPP	PERC	(A	(G) PRETTY MUCH YOUR STANDARD STASH	1973	RCA	US	APLI 0164
BUDDY CHILDERS	TPT	(A	(G) PRETTY MUCH YOUR STANDARD STASH	1977	ISLAND	UK	ILPS 9440
GENE CIPRIANO	WIND	(A	(G) PRETTY MUCH YOUR STANDARD STASH	1979	PACIFIC ARTS	US RI	PAC 117
TOM SAVIANO	SAX	(MN	(H) THE PRISON	1975	ISLAND	UK	ILPS9428
GARY COLEMAN	PERC	(A	(H) THE PRISON	1979	PACIFIC ARTS	US RI	PAC 101
BUDDY COLLETTE	WIND	(A	(J) FROM A RADIO ENGINE TO PHOTON WING	1977	ISLAND	UK	ILPS 9486
JIM DECKER	HRNS	(A	(J) FROM A RADIO ENGINE TO PHOTON WING	1979	PACIFIC ARTS	US	PAC 107
DOUG DILLARD	BANJO	(A	(K) BEST OF	1976	RCA	US	RS 1064
VICTOR FELDMAN	PERC	(A	(L) LIVE AT THE PALAIS	1978	PACIFIC	US	PAC 7118
JOHN HOBBS	K V	(MN	(M) COMPILATION	1977	ISLAND	UK	ILPS 9425
JUSTIN GORDON	WIND	(A	(M) COMPILATION	197	PACIFIC ARTS	US PAC106 +PAC 7106	
BILL HINSHAW	HRNS	(A	(N) INFINITE RIDER ON THE BIG DOGMA	1979	PACIFIC ARTS	US	PAC 7130
LENNY CASTRO	PERC	(MN	(EP) & FIRST NATIONAL BAND	1976	ISLAND	UK	IEP4
JOE HOWARD	TROM	(A					

DICK HYDE	TROM	(A	JULES JACOB	TROM	(A	JOHN KITZMILLER	TUBA	(A	MANNY KLAIN	TPT (A
LARRY KNECHTEL	PNO	(A	JOHN LOWE	WIND	(A	LEW McCREARY	TROM	(A	JACK NIMITZ	WIND (A
BARRETT O'HARA	TROM	(A	EARL PALMER	D	(A	LONNIE MACK	G	(J	DICK PERISSI	HRNS (A
DON RANDI	PNO	(A	SAM RICE	TUBA	(A	KENNY SHROYER	TROM	(A	TOMMY TEDESCO	G (A
TONY TERRAN	TPT	(A	JIMMY ZITO	TPT	(A	LOUISE BLACKBURN	TROM	(A	JULES CHAIKEN	TPT (A
JIM HORN	WIND	(A	OLLIE MITCHELL	TPT	(A	JOHN WARE	D	(BCDL	JOHN LONDON	B (BCD
EARL P HALL	K	(B	AL CASEY	G	(D	JACK PANELLI	D	(E	JOHNNY MEEKS	B (E
DAVID MACKAY	B	(JLMN	LARRIE LONDIN	D	(J	JERRY CARRIGAN	D	(J	GLEN D HARDIN	K (CD
JOSE FELICIANO CONGAS	(E		DAVID BRIGGS	K	(J	JOE OSBORN	B	(D	JAY LACY	G (G
JOHN SHANE KEISTER	K	(J	MAX BENNETT	B	(D	DAVID BARRY	K	(G	JOE CHEMAY	V (MN
MICHAEL COHEN	K	(DEH	BILL GRAHAM	B FDL	(G	LISA SILVER	VLN	(J	GREG TAYLOR	HCA (J
DANNY LANE	D	(G	WELDON MYRICK	STEEL	(J	LINDA HARGROVE	V	(J	MARCIA ROUTH	V (J
PEBBLE DANIEL	V	(J	JACK RANELLI		(J	AL PERKINS	STEEL	(LMN	JAMES TRUMBO	K (L
RON TUTT	D	(D	PAUL LEIM	D	(MN					

N25A   NETWORK   N25A

MICHAEL RICCIARDELLA	D V	(A	(A) NETWORK	1977	EPIC 34979
MIKE COXTON	K	(A	(B) NIGHTWORK		
JEAN PAUL GASPAR	PERC	V(A			
GEORGE BITZER	K V	(A	JOHN VINCI	V (A RICHIE	G (A

```
      KLAUS DINGER      G V D K ALL         (A) NEU                       1972 UA UK UAS 29396  BRAIN   000 1004
      HANS LAMPE        D    (C             (A) NEU                       197  BILLINGATE US 1001
      MICHAEL ROTHER    G B K(ALL           (B) NEU 2                     1973 UA UK UAS 29500  BRAIN   000 1028
      THOMAS DINGER     D    (C             (C) NEU 75                    1977 UA UK UAS 29782  BRAIN   000 1062
      CONREAD PLANK     PROD (AC            (D) HALLOGALLO                197                   BRAIN   0040 145
                                            (AB) 2 ORIGINALS              197                   BRAIN   008 0114
```

N26A   RICK NEUFELD   N26A

```
      RICK NEUFELD      G V  (A            (A) PRAIRIE DOG                1974   RCA  UA APLI 0074   UK  SF 8413
      DON ZUEFF FDL MAND V G (A
      HUMPHREY DUMPTRUCK BAN V(A  BURTON CUMMINGS  K FLT V(A  BILL WALLACE  B HRNS V(A  GARY PETERSON D PERC(A
      AL BRISCOE        STEEL(A  TERRY BUSH       G V    (A  TOM JACKSON   V    (A      LORNA HIBBERT   V  (A
      LUCILLE LEPING    V    (A  GRAEME GARD      V      (A
```

N26B   NEUSCHWANSTEIN   N26B

```
                                            (A) BATTLEMENT                19   RACKET    RAK 15002
```

N27   NEUTRONS   N27

```
      WILL YOUATT       G B  (AB           (A) BLACK HOLE STAR            1974   UA US 1010       UK  UAG 29652
      MARTIN WALLACE    G V  (AB           (B) TALES FROM THE BLUE COCOONS 1975  UA              UK  UAG 29726
      PHIL RYAN         K    (AB
      STUART HALLIDAY   D    (B  CAROMAY DIXON      V    (AB  JOHN WEATHERS  D    (A  RAY TAFF WILLIAMS  G   (AB
      STUART GORDON     VLN  (A  DAVID CHARLES      D    (AB  PICK WITHERS   PERC (A
```

N27A   NEVILLE BROTHERS   N27A

```
                                            (A) THE NEVILLE BROTHERS      1979 CAPITOL   UK US          11865
                                            (B) FI YO ON BAYOU            1980 A&M       US              4866
```

N27B   NEW ADVENTURE   N27B

```
      PETER BOOTSMAN    G V  (A            (A) NEW ADVENTURE              1980   POLYDOR US 6278   UK    2925 098
      HARRY DE WINTER   K B V(A
      HENK TORPEDO      D PERC(A
```

N27C   NEW BARBARIANS   N27C

```
      RON WOOD          G V  (A            (A) LIVE 1979  NO RECORDS
      PHIL CHEN         B    (A
      KEITH RICHARDS    G    (A  BOBBY KEYS       SAX (A  SUGAR BLUE  HCA(A  IAN MACLAGAN  K   (A
```

N27D   NEW AGE STEPPERS   N27D

```
      BRUCE SMITH       D SYN   (A          (A) NEW AGE STEPPERS          1980 ONU       UK      LP1
      'STYLE' SCOTT     D    (A             (B) ACTION BATTLEFIELD        1981 STATIK    UK      STAT2
      CECIL             D    (A
      NOBBY TURNER      PERC (A  GEORGE OBAN      B   (A  STEVE BERESFORD  K B  (A  JOHN WADDINGTON  G  (A
      VIV ALBERTINE     G V  (A  'CRUCIAL' TONY   G   (A  SEAN             K    (A  ARI              V  (A
      MARK              V    (A  'SHOES'          D   (A  DAN              D    (A  VIKKI            VLN (A
```

N28   NEW BIRTH   N28

```
      MELVIN WILSON         (C          (A) NEW BIRTH             197  RCA           US  LSP 4450
      ROBIN RUSSELL     D   (E          (B)AINT NO BIG THING      1971 RCA           US  LSP 4526
      LESLIE WILSON     V PERC(E        (C) COMIN TOGETHER        1972 RCA           US  LSP 4697
      LONDIE WIGGINS    V PERC(E        (D) BIRTHDAY              1973 RCA UK SF 8368 US  LSP 4797
      CARL McDANIEL     G V  (C         (D) BIRTHDAY              197  RCA               APLI2145
      JAMES BAKER       K HRNS(C        (D) ITS BEEN A LONG TIME  1974 RCA               ALPI0285
      TONY CHURCHILL    SAX V(CE        (E) BLIND BABY            1975 BUDDAH UK 4034 US     5636
      LEROY TAYLOR      B G  (E         (F) LOVE POTION           1976 WB  US BS2953
      VERNON BULLOCK        (C          (G) COMIN' FROM ALL ENDS  19   RCA           US  APLI0494
      ALAN FREY         V PERC(E        (H) BEST OF               197  RCA           US  AHLI1021
      ROBERT JACKSON    TPT V(CE        (J) REINCARNATION         1977 RCA           US  APLI1801
      AUSTIN LANDER     SAX V(E         (K) DISCO                 1977 RCA           US 1535
      CHARLIE HEARNDON  G    (E         (L) BEHOLD(THE MIGHTY ARMY) 1978 WB          US       BS3071
      JOSEPH PORTER III V   (E          (M) PLATINUM CITY         1979 CAPITOL       US      50062
```

N29   NEW CACTUS BAND   N29

```
      DUANE HITCHINGS K V FLT(A          (A) SON OF CACTUS        1973 ATLANTIC US SD7917 UK    K40488
      ROLAND ROBINSON   B V  (A
      MANNY BERTEMATTI  D V  (A  MIKE PINERA      G V  (A  JERRY NORRIS   D V  (A
```

N29A   NEW ENGLAND   N29A

```
      JOHN FANNON       G V  (ABC         (A) NEW ENGLAND          1979   INFINITY US 9007   UK INS 2005
      JIMMY WALDO       K V  (ABC         (B) EXPLORER SUITE       1980   ELEKTRA  US 6E307
      HIRSH GARDNER     D V  (ABC         (C) WALKING WILD         1981   ELEKTRA  US 6E346
      GARY SHEA         B    (ABC
      TODD RUNDGREN     G    (C
```

N29B   NEW COLONY SIX   N29B

```
      BILLY HERMAN      D V  (D           (A) BREAKTHROUGH         1966 SENTAR    US   101
      CHUCK LOBES       K    (CD          (B) COLONIZATION         1967 SENTAR    US   3001
      LES KUMMEL        B    (BCD         (C) REVELATIONS          1969 MERCURY   US   61165
      JERRY KOLLENBERG  G V  (ABCD        (D) ATTACKING A STRAWMAN 1970 MERCURY   US   61228
      PAT McBRIDE       V    (ABCD
      RAY GRAFFIA       V TAMB(ABCD WALLY KEMP     B   (AB  CRAIG KEMP   ORG  (A  CHICK JAMES    D  (ABC
      RONNIE RICE       V G K B(BCD
```

N29C   NEW GRASS REVIVAL   N29C

```
      SAM BUSH    MAND FDL G V(ALL         (A) FLY THROUGH THE COUNTRY 197 FLYING FISH  US 016
      COURTNEY JOHNSON  BAN V(ALL          (B) THE NEW GRASS REVIVAL   197 STARDAY      US 482
      CURTIS BURCH      G V  (ALL
      JOHN COWAN        B V  (A  CHUCK COCHRAN    PNO (A  EBO WALKER   B V  (B
```

N29D   NEW HEAVENLY BLUE   N29D

```
                                            (A) NEW HEAVENLY BLUE      1972 ATLANTIC   US    7247
```

N29E   NEW MIX   N29E

```
                                            (A) THE NEW MIX           1968   UA   UAS 6678
```

N30A   NEW MUSIK   N30A

```
      TONY MANSFIELD    V G K(B           (A) FROM A TO B(STRAIGHT LINES) 1980 GTO UK GTLP041 EPIC US 36450
      TONY HIBBERT      B    (B           (B) ANYWHERE                    1981 GTO UK GTLP044
      CLIVE GATES       K    (B           (C) SANCTUARY                   1981 GTO UK
      PHIL TOWNER       D    (B           (D) WARP                        1982 EPIC UK 85567
```

NEW ORDER

RON ASHETON	G	(A	(A) NEW ORDER	1978	RCA/FUN	ISL 6443
DENNIS THOMPSON	D	(A	(B) BRADFORD RED LIGHT DISTRICT	1981	COME	UK CARA 12
RAY GUNN	G	(A				
JIMMY RECCA	B	(A	SCOTT THURSTON K (A	JEFF SPREY	V (A	DAVE GILBERT V (A

NEW ORDER

	(A) MOVEMENT	1981 FACTORY	UK FAC 50

NEW RIDERS OF THE PURPLE SAGE

JOHN DAWSON	G V	(ALL	(A) NEW RIDERS OF THE PURPLE SAGE	1971	CBS	US 30888	UK 64843
DAVID NELSON	G V MAND	(ALL	(B) POWERGLIDE	1972	CBS	US 31284	UK 64843
DAVE TORBERT	B G V	(ABCDE	(C) GYPSY COWBOY	1973	CBS	US 31930	UK 65008
SPENCER DRYDEN	D V	(ALL	(D) ADVENTURES OF PANAMA RED	1973	CBS	US 32450	UK 65687
MICKEY HART	D	(	(E) HOME HOME ON THE ROAD	1974	CBS	US 32870	UK 80060
JERRY GARCIA	G	(ABEG	(F) BRUJO	1975	CBS	US 33145	UK 80405
PHIL LESH	B	(	(G) OH WHAT A MIGHTY TIME	1975	CBS	US 33688	UK 69182
COMMANDER CODY	PNO	(	(H) NEW RIDERS	1976	MCA	US 2196	UK MCF2758
BUDDY CAGE	STEEL	(BCDEFGHK	(J) BEST OF	1976	MCA	US 34367	UK 81742
BILLY KREUTZMAN	PERC	(B	(K) WHO ARE THESE GUYS	1977	MCA	US 2248	UK MCF2793
NICKY HOPKINS	K	(B	(L) MARIN COUNTY LINE	1978	MCA	US 2307	UK MCF2830
SKIP BATTIN	B V	(FGH					
NORBERT PUTNAM	B	(	SLY STONE	K V (G	JOHN HUG G (K	BILL STEWART	D (K
JEFF NARELL	PERC	(G	PEPPER WATKINS	V (G	BOOTCHE ANDERSON V (G	MARILYN SCOTT	V (G
RAY PARK	FDL	(G	DONNA GODCHAUX	V (CD	BUFFY ST MARIE	V (G	MEMPHIS HORNS HRNS (D
STEPHEN LOVE	B	(K	PENE BLANCA	V (G	JACK SCHROER HRNS (C	LUCHA CARDENAS	V (C
RICHARD GREENE	VLN	(C	PATTIE SANTOS	V (C	ANDREA AHLGREN	V (G	DARLENE DIDOMENICO V (C
MARK NAFTALIN	PNO	(C	ANDT STEIN	SAX (E			

NEW TWEEDY BROS

	(A) NEW TWEEDY BROS	1966	RIDON US 234

NEW VICTORY BAND

JOHN ADAMS	TROM FDL	(A	(A) ONE MORE DANCE & THEN	1978	TOPIC	12 TS 382
SUZIE ADAMS	BANJO	(A				
CHRIS COE	DULCIMER	(A	PETER COE	MELODEON (A	HELEN WATSON K (A IAN WORDSWORTH PERC (A
ROGER WATSON	TUBA	(A	LINDA WORDSWORTH	(A	

NEW YORK CITY

	(A) I'M DOIN' FINE	19	CHELSEA US 0198
	(B) SOULFUL ROAD	19	CHELSEA US 500

NEW YORK DOLLS

DAVID JOHANSEN	V	(12345ABC	(A) NEW YORK DOLLS	1973	MERCURY UK 6338 270	US SRM1 675
JOHNNY THUNDERS	G	(1234ABC	(B) TOO MUCH TOO SOON	1974	MERCURY UK 6338 498	US SRMI 1001
RICK RIVETS	G	(1	(AB)N Y DOLLS/TOO MUCH	1977	MERCURY UK 6641 631	
TODD RUNDGREN	K	PROD(A	(C) LIPSTICK KILLERS	1981	ROUR A104 CASS	
ARTHUR KANE	B	(123AC	(1) 1972 (2) 1972 (3) 1972/73 (4) 1974 1975 (5) 1975/77			
BILLY MURCIA	d	(12C				
TONY MACHINE		(5	CHRIS ROBINSON	K (5	SYLVAIN SYLVAIN G K(2345GC	JERRY NOLAN D (34AB
PETER JORDAN	B	(45B	BOBBY BLAIN	K (5	MARTY THALL	PROD (C	SHADOW MORTON PROD (B
BUDDY BOWSER	SAX	(A				

NEW YORK GONG

DAEVID ALLEN	G V	(A	(A) ABOUT TIME	1980	CHARLY	CRL 5021
BILL LASTWELL	B	(A				
BILL BACON	D	(A	FRED MAHER	D (A	CLIFF CLIFTON G (A GARY WINDO SAX (A
MICHAEL BEINHORN	SYN	(A	DON DAVIS	SAX (A	MARK KRAMER	ORG (A

NEW YORK MARY

BRUCE JOHNSTONE	WIND	(B	(A) NEW YORK MARY	197	FREEDOM	US 1019
RICK PETRONE	B	(B	(B) A PIECE OF THE APPLE	1977	FREEDOM UK 41035	US 1035
JOE CORSELLO	D	(B				
ROBERT FRIEDMAN	HRNS	(B	GENE BERTONCINI	G (B	DON ELLIOTT SINGERS V(B	PETE LEVIN SYN (B

NEW YORK ROCK & ROLL ENSEMBLE

DORIAN RUDNYTSKY	K H HRNS	(BDE	(A) NEW YORK ROCK AND ROLL EMSEMBLE	1968	ATCO	US 33240
MARTIN FULTERMAN	D OBOE	(BDE	(B) FAITHFUL FRIENDS	1969	ATCO UK 228 932	US 33294
BRIAN CORRIGAN	G V	(B	(C) REFLECTIONS	1970	ATCO	US 33312
CLIFFORD NIVISON	G	(BDE	(D) ROLL OVER	1971	CBS UK 64126	US 30033
MICHAEL KAMEN	K G V WIND	(BDE	(E) FREEDOMBURGER	1972	CBS UK 64324	US 31317
LARRY PACKER	FDL	(				
DAVID SANBORN	SAX	(	HANK DE VITO	STEEL(D	DENNIS WHITTED D (	

MICKEY NEWBURY

MICKEY NEWBURY	G V	(ALL	(A) HARLEQUINN MELODIES	1968	RCA	US LSP 4043
JERRY KENNEDY	S SITAR	(B	(B) LOOKS LIKE RAIN	1969	MERCURY	US SR 61236
CHARLIE McCOY	HCA G	(BEGC	(C) FRISCO MABEL JOY	1971	ELEKTRA UK K42105	US EKS74107
WAYNE MOSS	G	(BEJGC	(D) SINGS HIS OWN	1972	RCA UK SF 8268	US LPS 4675
FARRELL MORRIS	PERC	(BEIJGC	(E) HEAVEN HELP THE CHILD	1973	ELEKTRA UK K42137	US EKS75055
DENNIS LINDE	G V	(EC	(F) LIVE AT MONTEZUMA	1973	ELEKTRA	US 7E 2007
KENNY BUTTREY	D	(B	(BF)LOOKS LIKE RAIN/LIVE AT MONTEZUMA	197	ELEKTRA	US 72001
KENNY MALONE	D	(EG	(G) I CAME TO HEAR THE MUSIC	1974	ELEKTRA UK K42162	US 7E 1007
WELDON MYRICK	STEEL	(Ec	(H) LOVERS	1975	ELEKTRA UK K52017	US 7E 1030
CHET ATKINS	G	(E	(I) RUSTY TRACKS	1977	HICKORY	US AH44002
NORBERT PUTNAM	B	(EI	(I) RUSTY TRACKS	1977	ABC UK ABCL5215	
BOB SEYMOUR		(E	(J) HIS EYE ON THE SPARROW	1978	HICKORY	US HA44011
BUDDY SPICHER	FDL	(EGC	(K) THE SAILOR	1979	HICKORY	US HB44017
VASSAR CLEMENTS	FDL	(E	(L) FUNNY FAMILIAR FORGOTTEN FEELINGS	19	RCA UK	
JAMES CAPPS		(C	(M) AFTER ALL THESE YEARS	1981	MERCURY	US SRMI4024
EMORY GORDY		(E				
RICHARD BENNETT	G	(E	DENNIS ST JOHN	D (E	DON RANDI PNO (E	MARLINE GREENE G (E
JOE OSBORN	B	(E	BOBBY WOOD	K (EIK	BOBBY THOMPSON G BAN (EIJKC	TOMMY COGBILL B (EG
BOB BECKHAM		(EC	DAVID BRIGGS	K (EG	JIMMY HASKELL ACC/STRINGS(E	JIMMY GETZOFF VLN(E
TOM BAYLOR	V	(E	BILLY SANFORD	G (EIK	STAN FARBER V (E	JOE ALLEN B (I
CHARLES NAVARRO		(C	DON GANT	V (CG	DR JOHN HARRIS (C	JOHN MOSS (C
BILLY PUETT	HRNS	(G	BEEGIE CRUISER	(C	WALKER SILL (C	JAMES ISBELL (CI
HENRY STRZELECKI	B	(GI	HAYWARD BISHOP	D PERC(IJ	LARRIE LONDON D PERC(I	BUDDY EMMONS K (IG
ALAN MOORE	K	(IJK	RON OATES	K (I	PHIL BAUGH G (I	JOHNNY CHRISTOPHER G(I
DAVE KIRBY	G	(I	REGGIE YOUNG	G (GI	BUDDY EMMONS STEEL(I	LLOYD GREEN STEEL (IG

(CONTINUED)

(CONTINUED)   MICKEY NEWBURY

TERRY McMILLAN	HCA (IJK	EVERHARD RAMM	HRNS (I	CINDY REYNOLDS	HARP(I	ROBERT S GALBRAITH	K (J
THOMAS C GAIN	K (J	DONALD L POTTER	G (J	STEVE COLLOM	G (J	JESSE BOYCE	B (J
JOHN C WILLIAMS	B (J	DAN ECKLEY	MAND (J	RAFE VAN HOY	G (K	DON ROTH	G (K
RAY EDENTON	G (GK	BARRY BURTON	G (K	JOSEPH PELLECUIA	SAX (K	BOB L MOORE	B (K
JERRY CARRIGAN	D (GK	MARK B MORRIS	PERC (K	MIKE LEECH	B (G	SHANE KEISTER	SYN (G
PETE WADE	G (G	JERRY SHOOK	G (G	GORDON STOKER	V (G	LAVERNA MOORE	V (G
WENDY SUITS	V (G	GEORGE TIDWELL	HRNS (G	BUDDY HARMON	D (G	HOYT HAWKINS	V (G
DOTTIE DELEONIBUS	V (G	BERGEN WHITE	V (G	DENNIS GOODE	HRNS (G	HAROLD BRADLEY	B (G
RAY WALKER	V (G	NEAL MATTHEWS	V (G	DIANE TIDWELL	V (G	CHIP YOUNG	G (G
DON SHEFFIELD	HRNS(G						

ANDY NEWMAN

ANDY NEWMAN	K (A	(A) RAINBOW		1971	track	UK 2406 103

COLIN NEWMAN

COLIN NEWMAN	G V K(ABC	(A) A–Z		1980 BEGGARS BANQUET	UK BEGA20
DESMOND SIMMONS	G B V(AC	(B) PROVISIONALLY ENTITLED		1981 4AD	UK CAD108
ROBERT GOTOBED	D (ABC	(C) NOT TO		1981 4AD UK CAD201 B BANQUET GER 58425	
MIKE THORN	K (A				
BILLY BRAGG	CLAR (A	SIMON GILLHAM	B V (C	BRUCE GILBERT	G (A

DAVID 'FATHEAD' NEWMAN

DAVID FATHEAD NEWMAN	SAX(ALL	(A) BEST OF	1971	ATLANTIC	US SD 1590
IDRIS MUHAMMAD	D (H	(B) LONELY AVE	197	ATLANTIC	US SD 1600
CLAUDE JOHNSON	PNO G(G	(C) THE WEAPON	19	ATLANTIC	US SD 1638
ROGER BOYKIN	G B (G	(D) CAPTAIN BUCKLES	19	ATLANTIC	US SD 18002
GEORGE CABLES	K (H	(E) STRAIGHT AHEAD	19	ATLANTIC	US SD 1366
HILTON RUIZ	K (H	(F) MR FATHEAD	1976	W B US 1304	UK K56201
GEORGE HARMON	G (H	(G) FRONT MONEY	1977	W B	US BS 2984
LEE RITENOUR	G (H	(H) KEEP THE DREAM ALIVE	1978	PRESTIGE	US P10106
BILL SUMMERS	PERC (HJ	(J) SCRATCH MY BACK	1979	PRESTIGE	US P10108
JEFF DAVIS	TPT (H				
LARRY MOSES	TPT (H	JANICE ROBINSON	TROM (H	EARL McINTYRE	TROM (HJ	KENNETH HARRIS	FLT (HJ
ED XIQUES	SAX (H	RENE MANNING	V (H	YVONNE FLETCHER	V (H	RANDY BRECKER	TPT (J
JERRY DODGION	FLT (J	JAMES BUFFINGTON	HRNS (J	BEN CARTER	V (J	KEVIN TONEY	K (J
RICHARD TEE	K (J	ERIC GALE	G (J	CORNELL DUPREE	G (J	RON CARTER	B (J
WILBUR BASCOMB	B (J	HARVEY MASON	D (J	TANYETTE	V (J	BESSIE RUTH SCOTT	V (J
JON FADDIS	TPT (J	GEORGE MARGE	FLT (J	FLAME BRAITHWAITE	V (J	DEBORAH McGRIFF	V (J

JIMMY C NEWMAN

JIMMY C NEWMAN	(ALL	(A) PROGRESSIVE CC	1977	PLANT US 544 CHARLY UK CRL 5005
		(B) HAPPY CAJUN	1979	CHARLY	UK CR 30177
		(C) CAJUN COWBOY	1980	PLANT US 530	

JOE NEWMAN

JOE NEWMAN	(A	(A) I LOVE MY BABY	1981 BLACK & BLUE	UK 33155

RANDY NEWMAN

RANDY NEWMAN	PNO V(ALL	(A) RANDY NEWMAN	1968	REPRISE	US 6286
RY COODER	G (DEFB	(B) 12 SONGS	1970	REPRISE US 6373	UK K44084
RUSS TITELMAN	G B (DE	(C) LIVE	1971	REPRISE US 6459	UK K44151
JIM KELTNER	D (DEF	(D) SAIL AWAY	1972	REPRISE US 2064	UK K44185
GENE PARSONS	D (DB	(E) GOOD OLD BOYS	1974	WB US 2193	UK K54022
EARL PALMER	D (D	(F) LITTLE CRIMINALS	1977	WB US 3079	UK K56404
CHRIS ETHRIDGE	B (D	(G) BORN AGAIN	1979	WB US 3346	UK K56663
WILTON FELDER	B (D				
JIMMY BOND	B (D	MILT HOLLAND	PERC (DEF	ABE MOST	SAX (D	RED CALLENDER	B (E
DON HENLEY	V (EF	J D SOUTHER	V (F	KLAUS VOORMANN	B (F	TIM SCHMIT	V (F
DAVID SHIELDS	B (G	VICTOR FELDMAN	K PERC (G	CHUCK FINDLEY	TPT (G	STEPHEN BISHOP	V (F
VALERIE CARTER	V (G	ARNO LUCAS	V (G	ANDY NEWMARK	D (EFG	BOBBYE HALL	PERC(E
RON ELLIOTT	G (DB	JOHN PLATANIA	G (E	DENNIS BUDIMIR	G (E	AL PERKINS	STEEL(E
WILLIE WEEKS	B (EFG	GLENN FREY	G V (EF	RICK MAROTTA	D (F	WADDY WACHTEL	G (FG
JOE WALSH	G (F	RALPH GRIERSON	PNO (F	MICHAEL BODDICKER	SYN (FG	LENNY CASTRO	PERC(G
TOM SCOTT	HRNS (G	BUZZY FEITEN	G (G	MILT HOLLAND	PERC (B	AL McKIBBON	B (B
CLARENCE WHITE	G (B	LYLE RITZ	B (B	JIM GORDON	D (B	ROY HARTE	PERC (B

TOM NEWMAN

TOM NEWMAN	G V K(ALL	(A) FINE OLD TOM	1975	VIRGIN UK V2022 US ANTILLES 7042
MIKE OLDFIELD	G (A	(B) LIVE AT THE ARGONAUT(NOT RELEASED)197	VIRGIN	UK	V2042
FRED FRITH	G B (A	(C) FAERIE SYMPHONY	1977	DECCA UK	TXS 123
CHRIS BUTLER	D (A				
JOHN VARNOM	G (A	HUGH FLINT	D (A	MIKE STOREY	K (A	DAVID DUHIG	G (A
NED CALLAN	B (A	JON FIELD D WIND PERC V(AC		PETER COOK	HCA (A	LOL COXHILL	SAX(A
SUZI SHUTE	V (A	JOHN OBYTON	V (A	TED MACDOWELL	G (A	NEIL INNES	K G(A
MICK TAYLOR	G (A	TOM NORDEN	G (C	PETE GIBSON	TROM D(C	DEBBIE HALL	VLN(C
TERRY EDWARDS	V (C	JOE O'DONNELL	VLN (C	TINA JONES	V (C	GEOFF WESTLEY	PNO(C
WARD KELLY CONOVER	D (C	JON COLLINS	VLN (C	JANE GIBSON	D (C		

OLIVIA NEWTON–JOHN

OLIVIA NEWTON JOHN	V (ALL	(A)(A) FIRST IMPRESSIONS	1974 EMI	UK EMC 3056
JAHN FARRAR PROD	G B V SYN(GHJL	(B) LONG LIVE LOVE	1974 EMI	UK EMC 3028
LEE SKLAR	B (H	(C) HAVE YOU EVER BEEN LONELY	1975 EMI	UK EMC 3069
MYRNA MATTHEWS	V (H	(D) CLEARLY LOVE	1976 EMI	UK EMA 774
JULIA RINKER	V (H	(E) COME ON OVER	1976 EMI	UK EMC 3124
SNEAKY PETE KLEINOW	STEEL(H	(F) DON'T STOP BELIEVING	1976 EMI	UK EMC 3162
JEFF PORCARO	D (H	(G) GREATEST HITS	1976 EMI	UK EMA 785
GREG MATHIESON	PNO (H	(H) MAKING A GOOD THING BETTER	1877 EMI	UK EMA 789 MFSL US MFSL 01
JOE PORCARO	PERC (H	(J) TOTALLY HOT	1977 EMI	UK EMA 789 MFSL US 1 01
LAURA CREAMER	V (H	(K) MUSIC MAKES MY DAY	1979 PYE	UK 28185
JAMES NEWTON HOWARD	STR(H	(L) PHYSICAL	1981 EMI	UK EMC 3381
BYRON BERLINE	VLN (H			
TOMMY MORGAN	HCA (H	PETER MYERS	STR (H	MARTI McCALL	V (H	PATTIE BROOKS	V (HJ
GEORGE MARGE	WIND (H	DAVID CAMPBELL	STR (H	DOUG LIVINGSTON	STEEL(H	RANDY EDELMAN	K (H
MIKE BOTTS	D (JK	DAVID HUNGATE	B (JK	STEVE LUKATHER	G (J	PHYLLIS ST JAMES	V (J
CARLOS VEGA	D PERC(L	MICHAEL BODDICKER	SYN (L	BILL CUOMO	SYN (L	GARY HERBIG	HRNS(L
VICTOR FELDMAN	PERC (L	TOM SNOW	SYN (L	LENNY CASTRO	PERC (L	JOHN HOBBS K SYN(L

JUICE NEWTON

JUICE NEWTON	G V (ALL	(A) & SILVER SPUR	1975	RCA		APL11004
TOM KEALEY	G B V(AC	(B) AFTER DUST SETTLED	1977	RCA		APL11722
OTHA YOUNG	G V (ACE	(C) COME TO ME	1977	CAPITOL		11682
JEFF PORCARO	D (A	(D) WELL KEPT SECRET	1978	CAPITOL		11811
HAL BLAINE	D PERC(A	(E) TAKE A HEART	1979	CAPITOL		12000
DENNY SEIWELL	D (C	(F) JUICE	1981	CAPITOL		12136
TEDDY IRWIN	G (C					
MIKE MELVOIN	PNO (A	RUSTY YOUNG STEEL(A	R GILLMAN	K V (C	BUZZY BUCHANAN	D (C
SMIGGY	G (C	MICHAEL O'NEILL G (C	TONY SAUNDERS	B (C	BOB HOGINS	K (C
MATTHEW KELLY	HCA (C	MIKE PORCARO B (E	BILLY WALKER	G (E	JOHN HATTON	B (E
MIKE BAIRD	D (E	DOUG LIVINGSTON K (E	ALAN ESTES	PERC (E	RICK SCHLOSSER	D (E
FRED TACKETT	G (E	STEVE FOREMAN PERC (E	WILLIE ORNALES	D (E	THOM ROTELLA	G (E
ALBERT LEE	G (E	JOHN HUNT G (E	JOHN HOBBS	K (E	STANLEY BERENS	HCA (E
JOHN HUG	G (E	JOHN HERRON K (E				

NIAGARA

KLAUS WEISS	D (AB	(A) NIAGARA	1971	UA	GER	UAS 29232
KEITH FORSEY	D (A	(B) S.U.B.	1972	UA	GER	UAS 29343
COTCH BLACKMON	PERC (A	(C) AFIRE	1973			
JUAN ROMERO	PERC (A					
UDO LINDENBERG	D (A	DANNY FICHELSCHER PERC (AB	GEORGE GREEN	D (A	JOE HARRIS PERC (B	
GARY UNWIN	B (B	PAUL VINCENT G (B	CHRISTIAN SCHULZE	K (B	ACK VAN ROOYEN	HRNS(B
FERDINAND	)B	MILAN PILAR B (B				

NICE

KEITH EMERSON	V K (ALL	(A) THOUGHTS OF EMERLIST DAVJACK	1967	IMMEDIATE	IMSP016	US 52004
BRIAN DAVISON	D (ALL	(A) " " " " "	1973	CBS		IMP 11633
LEE JACKSON	B G V(ALL	(A) " " " " "	1978	CHARLY		UK CR300021
DAVY O'LIST	G (AF	(B) ARS LONGA VITA BREVIS	1968	IMMEDIATE	IMSP020	US 52020
SINFONIA OF LONDON	(D	(B) " " " "	1973	CBS		IMP 11634
GORDON LONGSTAFF	G (1	(B) " " " "	1978	CHARLY		UK CR300019
ALAN SKIDMORE	HRNS (D	(C) NICE	1969	IMMEDIATE	IMSP026	US 52022
KENNY WHEELER	HRNS (D	(C) EVERYTHING AS NICE AS MOTHER	1973	CBS		us 11635
JOHN WARREN	HRNS (D	(C) NICE	1978	CHARLY		UK CR300014
PETE KING	HRNS (D	(D) FIVE BRIDGES SUITE	1970	CHARISMA		UK CAS1014
JOE HARRIOT	HRNS (D	(D) " " " "	1970	MERCURY		US SR61295
CHRIS PINE	HRNS (D	(E) ELEGY	1971	CHARISMA		UK CAS1030
		(E) ELEGY	1971	MERCURY		US SR61324
(1) 1968		(F) AUTUMN 67,SPRING 68	1972	CHARISMA		UK CS1
		( ) BEST OF NICE	197	ELECTROLA		IMP 04890674
		( ) IN MEMORIAM	197	PATHE		FR 05491951
		( ) IMMEDIATE STORY 1	1975	SIRE US 3710		
		( ) HANG ON TO A DREAM	197	EMI IMP		04850722
		( ) AMOENI REDIVIVI	1976	IMMEDIATE		IML1003
		( ) NICE WITH KEITH EMERSON	1976	PHONOGRAM		6641 119
		( ) KEITH EMRSON & THE NICE	197	MERCURY		US SRM26500
		( ) AMERICA	1976	PICKWICK		US SHM 917
		( ) POP GROUPS OF THE 60s(WITH H PIE)	197	MFP	GERM	14694319/20
		( ) GREATEST HITS	1977	IMMEDIATE		IML 2003

NICO

NICO	V HARMONIUM (ALL	(A) CHELSEA GIRL	1968	MGM	UK	2353 025
PHIL MANZANERA	G (D	(B) MARBLE INDEX	1968	ELEKTRA	US EKS74029	UK K 42065
BRIAN ENO	SYN (C	(C) DESERT SHORE	1971	REPRISE	US 6424	UK K 44102
JOHN CALE	K B G(BCD	(D) THE END	1974	ISLAND		ILPS9311
ADAM MILLER	V (C	(E) JUNE 1st 1974	1974	ISLAND		ILPS9291
VICKI WOOD	V (C	(F) DRAMA OF EXILE	1981	AURA		AUZ 715
ANNAGH WOOD	V (C					
FRAZIER MOHAWK	PROD (B	JOE BOYD PROD (C				

LEA NICHOLSON

LEA NICHOLSON	CONC V(ALL	(A) HORSE MUSIC	1971	TRAILER	UK	LER 3010
STAN ELLISON	G V (AB	(B) GOD BLESS THE UNEMPLOYED	1972	TRANSATLANTIC	UK	TRA 254
CHRIS NICHOLSON	PERC (A	(C) THE CONCERTINA RECORD	1980	KICKING MULE		SNKF165
RICK KEMP	B (B					
IAN WHITEMAN	K (B	ROD ARGENT K (C	MIKE OLDFIELD	G PERC (C	RUSS BALLARD	G (C
ROBIN DRANSFIELD	G (C					

STEVIE NICKS

STEVIE NICKS	V (A	(A) BELLA DONNA	1981	WEA UK K99169	US MODERN	38139
SHARON CELANI	V (A					
LORI PERRY	V (A	RUSS KUNKEL D (A	WADDY WACHTEL	G (A	DAVEY JOHNSTONE	G (A
BOB GLAUB	B (A	BILL ELLIOTT PNO (A	BOBBYE HALL	PERC (A	BENMONT TENCH	K (A
DAVID ADELSTEIN	SYN (A	ROY BITTAN PNO (A	TOM PETTY	G V (A	MICHAEL CAMPBELL	G (A
DUCK DUNN	B (A	STAN LYNCH D (A	PHIL JONES	PERC (A	BILLY PAYNE	PNO(A
DAN DUGMORE	STEEL(A	DON HENLEY D V (A	TOM MONCRIEFF	B (A	DON FELDER	G (A
RICHARD BOWDEN	B (A					

NICOL & MARSH

KEN NICOL	G V (AB	(A) NICOL & MARSH	1974	EPIC UK 80468	CAPRICORN US 174	
PETER MARSH	G V (AB	(B) NICOL & MARSH	1978	POLYDOR	POLD5012	
RANDY BISHOP	K (B					
DAVID KEMPER	D (B	JEFF EYRICH B (B	BILL PAYNE	K SYN(B	TONY BERG	G (B
VICTOR FELDMAN	VIBES(B	DAVID LUELL SAX (B	MARTY GWINN	V (B	KRYSIA KRISIANNE	V (B
LEE SKLAR	B (B	TOM HENSLEY K (B	CHRIS DOERGE	PNO (B	BARRY DE SOUZA	D (A
PETE ZORN	B SAX(A	B J COLE STEEL(B	FRANK COLLINS	V (A	RAY DUFFY	D (A
GRAHAM SMITH	HCA (A	DYAN BIRCH V (A	DOUG WRIGHT	D (A	PADDIE McHUGH	V (A
BILL ZORN	BANJO(A					

NIELSEN /PEARSON BAND

MARK PEARSON	(AB	(A) NIELSEN PEARSON BAND	1978	EPIC	
REED NIELSEN	(AB	(B) NIELSEN PEARSON	1980	CAPITOL	US 12101

NIGHT

CHRIS THOMPSON	G V	(AB		(A)NIGHT			1979	PLANET	US	P3	UK	K52200	GER	52144

```
         CHRIS THOMPSON     G V  (AB          (A)NIGHT                    1979 PLANET US  P3  UK K52200 GER 52144
         STEVIE LANGE         V  (AB          (B)LONG DISTANCE           1980 PLANET US P10  UK K52251 GER 52251
         NICKY HOPKINS      PNO    (A
         ROBBIE McINTOSH      G   (AB  BILLY KRISTIAN    B   (AB  RICK MAROTTA    D  (A   BOBBY GUIDOTTI   D (B
         BOBBY WRIGHT         K   (B   STEVE PORCARO   SYN   (A   BILL PAYNE     K SYN(A   MICHAEL McDONALD PNO (A
         BOBBY LAKIND      PERC  (A   DEREK AUSTIN     K SYN(A   JAMES ALBERT JOHNSON D (A  VINCE MELAMED   K  (A
         VICKY BROWN          V   (B   KEN SAVIGAR       K   (B   MORRIS PERT   PERC (B   GRAHAM TODD     PNO (B
```
NIGHTCAPS

```
                                       (A) WINE WINE WINE            197   CHARLY            UK CR30183
```
ROBERT NIGHTHAWK

```
         ROBERT NIGHTHAWK  G V  (ALL    (A) BRICKS ON MY PILLOW      19    PEARL        US         P11
         JOHNNY YOUNG        G   (C     (B) MASTERS OF MODERN BLUES  19    TESTAMENT    US         T 2215
         ROBERT WHITEHEAD    D   (C     (C) LIVE ON MAXWELL STREET 1964  1979 ROUNDER  US         2022
         CAREY BELL        HCA   (C
         HOUSTON STACKHOUSE      (C
```
NIGHTHAWKS

```
         JIM THACLERY      G V  (ACE    (A) OPEN ALL NIGHT           1976 ADELPHI   US 4105
         PETE RAGUSA         D   (ACE   (B) LIVE AT THE PSYCHEDELLY  1977 ADELPHI   US 4110
         DAVE MAXWELL      PNO   (CE    (C) SIDE POCKET SHOT         1978 ADELPHI   US 4115
         GUITAR JUNIOR     G V   (E     (D) JACKS & KINGS           1978 ADELPHI   US 4120
         MARK WENNER       HCA V (ACE   (E) JACKS & KINGS FULL HOUSE 1979 ADELPHI   US 4125
         JAN ZUKOWSKI        B   (ACE   (F) TEN YEARS LIVE           1982 CHESAPEAKE US 101
         PINETOP PERKINS   PNO V(E      (G) ROCK'N'ROLL              1982 ALADDIN   US 101
         BOB MARGOLIN        G   (E     ( ) HOT TRACKS               19   VANGUARD    VSD79424
```
NIGHTHAWKS(EURO)

```
         PETER LA BONTE    V PERC(A     (A) SHANK IT UP              1980 ROCKTOPUS  NL 201 428 320
         OLIVER STEPHEN    G V   (A
         HANS GLINKA       K V   (A   SVEN VAN STRAUCH  B V  (A   JORGEN NITSCH   D   (A   MATZI ENSINGER      (A
         FRANZ DIEZ          G   (A   PIT TROJER       PERC (A   DIDI ZILL     PROD (A
```
MAXINE NIGHTINGALE

```
         MAXINE NIGHTINGALE V   (ALL    (A) RIGHT BACK WHERE WE STARTED  1976  UA   US LA 626  UK UAG29953
                                       (B) LOVE HIT ME              1977  UA              UK UAS30076
                                       (C) NIGHT LIFE              1977  UA   UA LA 731   UK UAS30105
                                       (D) LOVE LINES              1978  UA              UK UAG30179
                                       (E) LEAD ME ON              1979 WINDSONG US 3404
                                       (F) BITTERSWEET            1981  LIBERTY        UK LBG30323
                                       (F) BITTERSWEET            1981  RCA   US 3528
```
NIGHTWING

```
         ALEC JOHNSON        G   (B     (A) SOMETHING IN THE AIR     1980 OVATION  UK       1757
                                       (B) BLACK SUMMER            1982 GULL     UK     GULP 1036
```
NIKKI & THE CORVETTES

```
         LORI                V   (A     (A) NIKKI & THE CORVETTES    1980 BOMP US 4012 LINE GER LLP5087
         KRYSTI              V   (A
         NIKKI               V   (A
```
NIGHTRIDERS

```
         MIKE SHERIDAN       V   (      (PRE IDLE RACE CIRCA 1963)
         ALAN JOHNSON        G   (
         BRIAN COPE          B   (    DAVE PRITCHARD   G   (    JEFF LYNNE    G V  ( ROGER SPENCER     D  (
         GREG MASTERS            (    ROY WOOD         G   (
```
WILLIE NILE

```
         WILLIE NILE G PNO V (AB        (A) WILLIE NILE             1980  ARISTA   US AB4260 UK SPART1126
         FRED SMITH          B   (A     (A) WILLIE NILE             1980  ARISTA   GER 201 734
         CLAY BARNES       G V   (AB    (B) GOLDEN DAWN             1981  ARISTA   US AB4284  GER 203 416
         PETER HOFFMAN       G   (A
         TOM ETHRIDGE        B   (A   JAY DEE DAUGHERTY D  (AB MARK JOHNSON     V   (AB   PAUL SCHAEFFER  K   (B
         GERG HUSTED         K   (B   PAUL PRESTOPINO  DULC G(B LOWRY HAMMER     V   (B    TERRE ROCHE     V   (B
         ARNO HECHT        SAX   (B
```
NINE BELOW ZERO

```
         DENNIS GREAVES    G V  (ABC    (A) PACKED FAIR & SQUARE(EP) 1979 M&L         UK          ML1
         PETER CLARK       B V  (ABC    (B) LIVE AT THE MARQUEE      1980 A&M         UK  AMLE68515
         MARK FELTHAM    V HCA  (ABC    (C) DON'T POINT YOUR FINGER  1981 A&M  US 4859 UK AMLH68521
         STIX BURKEY         D   (BC
         KENNY BRADLEY       D   (A  MICKEY MODEM      PROD (B  GLYN JOHN    PROD (C
```
NINE DAYS WONDER

```
         WALTER SEYFFER    V D  (ABC    (A) NINE DAYS WONDER         1971 BACILLUS  GER 19073
         JOHN EARLE      V SAX G(A      (B) WE NEVER LOST CONTROL    1973 BACILLUS  GER 19163
         ROLF HENNING      G K   (A     (C) ONLY THE DANCERS         1975 BACILLUS  GER 19200
         FREDDIE MUNSTER SAX SYN K(B
         KARL MUTSCHLECHNER   B(A  MARTIN ROSCOE    D  (A  MICHAEL BUNDT   B   (BC  HANS FRAUENSCHAH G (B
         HYAZ INTUS          D   (B  SIDHATTA GAUTAMA D  'C  DAVE JACKSON  WIND (C   STEVE ROBINSON   K  (C
```
NINE NINE NINE(999)

```
         NICK CASH         G V  (ABCD   (A) 9 9 9                    1978 UA            UK       UAG 30199
         PABLO LABRITAIN     D   (ABCD  (B) SEPARATES               1978 UA            UK       UAG 30209
         JOHN WATSON         B   (ABCD  (C) BIGGEST PRIZE IN SPORT  1980 POLYDOR UK POLS1013 US 6256
         ED CASE            D V  (C     (C) BIGGEST PRIZE IN SPORT  1980 ALBION GERM201 331
         GUY DAYS            G   (ABD   (D) CONCRETE                1981 ALBION UK ITS 999 GER 203 320
                                       (D) CONCRETE                1981 POLYDOR US 6323
                                       (E) SINGLES ALBUM           1980 ALBION  UK SOS 999
                                       (F) HIGH ENERGY PLAN        1981 PVC US 7999
```
NINE SENSE

```
         ELTON DEAN        SAX   (AB    (A) OH! FOR THE EDGE        1976 OGUN           OG 900
         ALAN SKIDMORE     SAX   (AB    (B) HAPPY DAZE             1977 OGUN           OG 910
         HARRY BECKETT    HRNS   (AB
         NICK EVANS       TROM   (AB  MARK CHARIG  HRNS     (AB KEITH TIPPETT  PNO (AB HARRY MILLER    B   (AB
         LOUIS MOHOLO        D   (AB  RADU MALFATI      TROM (B
```

```
      KAREN LAWRENCE      V    (AB        (A) 1994                    1978  A&M US 4709        UK AMLH64709
      JOHN DESAUTELS      D    (AB        (B) PLEASE STAND BY          1979  A&M US 4769
      STEVE SCHIFF        G    (AB
      BILL RHODES         B G V(AB  BRAD WHITFORD   G   (A   ERIC TROYER     V   (A   RICK ARMOND G K  (B
      TERRY LINVILL       B    (B   JIM ALCIVER     SYN (B   LANCER GREIG    SYN (B   JIM HORNS   SAX  (B
```

90 DEGREES INCLUSIVE

```
      HUGH FRANCIS        G V  (AB        (A) 90' INCLUSIVE            1976  VERTIGO             UK  6360 139
      HENRY BARNES        G V  (AB        (B) FIRE OVER YONDER         1978  ICE                 ICEL 1005
      WEBSTER DYER        K    (AB
      WINSTON HENRY       B    (AB  DELFORD DAVIS   D   (AB  EDDIE GRANT    SYN HCA(A   LLOYD TYRELL     V (B
```

NINETEEN TEN FRUITGUM COMPANY

```
      PAT SORIANO         K V  (E         (A) SIMON SAYS              19  BUDDAH   US      BDS 5010
      RALPH COHEN         TPT  (E         (B) A RED LIGHT             19  BUDDAH   US      BDS 5022
      JERRY ROTH          SAX  (E         (C) GOODY GOODY GUM DROPS   19  BUDDAH   US      BDS 5027
      DON CHRISTOPHER     G V  (E         (D) INDIAN GIVER            19  BUDDAH   US      BDS 5036
      RICHIE GOMEZ        V    (E         (E) HARD RODE               19  BUDDAH   US      BDS 5043
      JIMMY CASAZZA       D    (E         (F) JUCIEST FRUITGUM        19  BUDDAH   US      BDS 5057
```

NINTH CREATION

```
      BILL ERIKSEN        K WIND(A        (A) FALLING IN LOVE          1979  RITE TRACK US 01  PYE US 12138
      J D BURRISE         PERC V(A
      STEVEN RUBIO        SAX V(A   LAURENCE HOLMAN  HRNS(A   A D BURRISE   B V  (A   DON ROY ALLEN   D V (A
      MIKE MICENHEIMER    HRNS(A    W THAD BOURLAND  TPT V(A   HENRY ANADON  HENS(A   ROBERT E CLARK  G   (A
```

NIPS(NIPPLE ERECTORS)

```
                                          (A) ONLY THE END OF THE BEGINNING  19  SOHO    HOHO1
```

NIRVANA

```
      PATRICK CAMPBELL-LYONS (ABC         (A) SIMON SIMOPATH           1967  ISLAND     UK      ILPS9059
      ALEX SPRYOPOULOS    PNO  (ABC        (B) ALL OF US               1968  ISLAND     UK      ILPS9087
      BRIAN HENDERSON     B    (A          (C) DEDICATED TO MARKOS III 1970  PYE                28132
      RAY SINGER          G V  (A          (D) LOCAL ANAESTHETIC       1971  VERTIGO            6360 031
      SYLVIA SCHUSTER     CELLO(A          (E) SONGS OF LOVE & PRAISE  1972  PHILIPS            6308 089
      PETER KESTER        D    (A          ( ) NIRVANA                 19    METROMEDIA US    1018
      BILLY BREMNER       G    (C
      LESLEY DUNCAN       V    (C    SPOOKY TOOTH       (C
```

NITE CITY

```
      RAY MANZAREK        K    (AB         (A) NITE CITY               1977  20TH CENTURY        T 528
      NOAH JAMES          V    (A          (B) GOLDEN DAYS DIAMOND NIGHTS 1978  20TH CENTURY    6370 263
      PAUL WARREN         G V  (AB
      NIGEL HARRISON      B    (AB   JIMMY HUNTER D V  (AB
```

NITS

```
      HENK HOFSTEDE       K V  (A          (A) TENT                    1979  CBS  NL  84051
      ROB KLOET           D V  (A
      ALEX ROELOFS        B V  (A    MICHAEL PETERS    G V  (A
```

NITTY GRITTY DIRT BAND   (DIRT BAND)

```
      JEFF HANNA          G V  (ALL        (A) NITTY GRITTY DIRT BAND   1967  LIBERTY      US      LST 7501
      JIMMIE FADDEN       G HCA(ALL
      BRUCE KUNKEL        (ACE         (C) RICOCHET                1967  LIBERTY      US      LST 7516
      GLEN CROSLOSE       (           (D) RARE JUNK                1967  LIBERTY      US      LST 7611
      STEVE PRYKA         (           (E) PURE DIRT                1968  LIBERTY      UK          83122
      MICHAEL WHITTAKER   (           (F) ALIVE                   1969  LIBERTY      US      LST 7615
      RALPH BARR          G V  (ACDEFG     (G) DEAD & ALIVE(COMP)      1969  LIBERTY              LBS83286
      WILLIAM McEUEN      (           (H) UNCLE CHARLIE & HIS DOG  1970  LIBERTY  US LST7642 UK LBG83345
      LES THOMPSON        B G V(ACDEFGHJK  (J) ALL THE GOOD TIMES     1972  UA       US UAS5553 UK UAS29284
      JACKSON BROWNE      V    (           (K) WILL THE CIRCLE BE UNBROKEN 1973  UA    US UAT9801
      JOHN McEUEN STEEL   G V  (DEFHJKLMNOPQR(L) STARS & STRIPES FOREVER 1974 UA  US LA 184 UK UAS29570
      DUANE ALLMAN        G    (           (M) DREAM                   1975  UA       US LA469  UK UAS29850
      GREGG ALLMAN        K V  (           (N) DIRT SILVER & GOLD(TRIPLE) 1976 UA   US   9802 +   LA 670
      STEVE GILLETTE      (           (O) DIRT BAND (DIRT BAND)   1978  UA       US LA 854 UK UAK30174
      STEVE MARTIN        (           (P) AMERICAN DREAM(DIRT BAND) 1979 UA    US LA 974 UK UAG30271
      JIM IBBOTSON        G V K D (HJKLMN   (Q) GOLD FROM DIRT         1980  UA               UK UAG30275
      CHRIS DARROW        G V VLN (DFG      (R) MAKE A LITTLE MAGIC    1980  UA       US LT1042 UK UAG30308
      JOHN LONDON         (H          (S) JEALOUSY                1981  LIBERTY  US LW1106
      MIKE RUBINI         (H
      BYRON BERLINE       FDL  (H
      RUSS KUNKEL         (H    JOHN CABLE  G V (HJKLMN   JACKIE CLARK   B (AJLMN  BILL CUNNINGHAM      (H
      MAURICE MANSEAU II  (H    AL GARTH    VLN V SAX(OPR  MEREL BREGANTE  D V (OP  RICHARD HATHAWAY B (OPRQR
      MICHAEL McDONALD    V    (O    JAN GARRETT     V   (O   HADEN GREGG    V   (O   ROSEMARY BUTLER    V (OR
      BOB CARPENDER       V K(OPQR  MICKEY THOMAS   V   (O   LEON MEDICA    B   (OP  BRYAN SAVAGE    HRNS(OR
      DENNY CHRISTENSEN   HRNS (O   AL KOOPER       SYN (O   BOBBY MASON    G   (O   GREG TAYLOR     HARP (O
      JEFF POLLARD        G    (P    TONY HASELDON   G   (P   JIM GORDON  HRNS K (H   DAVID PETERS      D(P
      ROD RODDY           K    (P    LINDA RONSTADT  V   (P   LEAH KUNKEL    V   (P   FUNKY LESTER    HRNS(P
      MARTY GUINN         V    (P    BOBBY LAKIND    PERC (P   STEVE SHLOSSER D   (R   STEVE LUKATHER  G  (R
      KAREN SILVER        V    (R    M L BENOIT      PERC (R   JOHN MACY      STEEL(R   KENNY LOGGINS   V  (R
      DAVID HOLSTER       V    (R    LISA SILVER     V   (R
```

NITZINGER

```
      JOHN NITZINGER      G V  (ABC        (A) NITZINGER               1972  CAPITOL          SMAS 11091
      LINDA WARING        V D  (AB         (B) ONE FOOT IN HISTORY     1973  CAPITOL          SMAS 11122
      CURLY BENTON        B V  (AB         (C) LIVE BETTER ELECTRICALLY 1976 20TH CENTURY US 518 UK 6370 251
      BUGS HENDERSON      G    (B
      PAUL LEIM           D    (C    JERRY HARRIS    B   (C   KENNETH WHITFIELD K (C   LAYTON DE PENNING  V (C
      THE AUSTIN SINGERS  (C    DARRELL NORRIS  D   (C   LARRY WHITE    STEEL(C   RANDY REEDE        D (C
      MARIANNE LINDSEY    V    (C    PHYLLIS LINDSEY V   (C   WHITNEY THOMAS  K  (C
```

JACK NITZSCHE

```
      JACK NITZSCHE       K    (ALL        (A) THE LONELY SURFER       1963  REPRISE          US      6101
      DAVID MEASHAM       (E          (B) HITS OF THE BEATLES    1964  REPRISE          US      6115
      LONDON SYPHONY ORCHESTRA(E          (C) CHOPIN' 66              1966  REPRISE          US      6200
                                          (D) PERFORMANCE             1970  WB                    WS 2554
                                          (E) ST GILES CRIPPLEGATE    1972  REPRISE          US      2092
                                          (E) ST GILES CRIPPLEGATE    197   HARVEST RI UK 2031 INITIAL 006
                                          (F) ONE FLEW OVER THE CUCKOO'S NEST 1976  FANTASY   UK    FTA  3004
```

DON NIX

DON NIX		(ALL	(A) IN GOD WE TRUST			1971	SHELTER			SHE 8902
BARRY BECKETT	K	(ABC	(B) LIVING BY THE DAYS			1971	ELEKTRA UK K 42096			US EKS74101
CHRIS STAINTON	K	(B	(C) HOBOS HEROES & STREET CORNER CLOWNS 74				ENTERPRISE			ENS 1032
WAYNE PERKINS	G V	(BC	(D) GONE TOO LONG			1976	CREAM		US	1001
JIMMY JOHNSON	G	(B	(E) SKYRIDER			1979	CREAM		US	1011
LARRY RASPBERRY	G	(AC								
ROGER HAWKINS	D	(BCA	DAVID HOOD	B	(ABC DONALD DUCK DUNN	B	(B LON PRICE			(C
TIPPY ARMSTRONG	G	(B	GIMMER NICHOLSON	G	(B CLAUDIA LENNEAR	V	(B JOEY COOPER	V		(B
MARLINE GREENE	V	(B	KATHI McDONALD	V	(B DON PRESTON	V	(B JEANNIE GREENE	V		(B
FURRY LEWIS	V	(ABC	PETE CARR		(C EDDIE HINTON	G	(CA KLAUS VOORMANN	B		(C
STEVE SMITH	K G	(C	TIM SMITH		(C BOBBY MANUEL		(C J A SPELL	FDL		(A
DARRELL NORRIS	D	(E	ROB KENDRICK	G	(E ERNIE CHAPMAN	B	(E LEN GROOME		K	(E
ROY HALLE	G	(E	JOHN FRY	ACC	(E WILLIAM C BROWN	V	(E ORCHESTRA			(C

NO DICE

ROGER FERRIS	V	(AB1	(A) NO DICE		1977	EMI UK EMC 3198	US CAPITOL11733
DAVE MOORE	G	(AB1	(B) TWO FACED		1979	EMI UK EMC 3282	US CAPITOL11925
DAVE MARTIN	G	(AB1	(1) 1979 SEPT					
GARY STRANGE	B	(AB1						
CHRIS WYLES	D PERC(AB	TONY FERNANDEZ	D PERC(1 STEVE SMITH	HCA PROD(AB JIMMY JEWEL			SAX(AB

NO ENTRY BAND

KENNETH TURLEWICZ	V	(A	(A) COLD & LONELY LIVES(EP)		1978 KUBE ARTS	KA1
ILONA TURLEWICZ	G V	(A				
KENNETH LITTLE	G V	(A	DOUGIE BURNS	D	(A ROBERT KIRK	B	(A

EDDIE NOACK

EDDIE NOACK		(A	(A) EDDIE NOACK		1980 CHISWICK UK	CH21

RAB NOAKES

RAB NOAKES	G V	(ALL	(A) DO YOU SEE THE LIGHT		1970	DECCA	UK SKL 5061
GERRY RAFFERTY	V	(BCD	(B) RAB NOAKES		1972	A&M	UK AMLS68119
JOE EGAN	V	(BCD	(C) RED PUMP SPECIAL		1974	WB US 2777	UK K46284
SID CAIRNS	B	(D	(D) NEVER TOO LATE		1975	WB	UK K56114
DAVIE CRAIG	FDL V(B		(E) RESTLESS		1978	RING O RECORDS UK	2339 201
ROBIN McKIDD	G HCA(AB		(F) RAB NOAKES		1981	MCA US 3082	UK MCA 3251
ALAN NOAKES	G	(B					
RAY JACKSON	HCA	(C	REGGIE YOUNG	G	(C WAYNE JACKSON	TPT (C JACK HALE	TROM (C
TOMMY JACKSON	HCA	(C	ANDREW LOVE	HRNS	(C SHEL TALMY	TAMB (C JOHN CHRISTOPHER G	(C
TEDDY IRWIN	G	(CD	WELDON MYRICK	G	(C JOHN HARRIS	K (CD TOMMY COGBILL	B (C
KENNY BUTTREY	D	(C	ED LOGAN	SAX	(C JAMES MITCHELL	SAX (C DANNY SEIWELL	D (D
CHRISSY STEWART	B	(D	BEN KEITH	V G K D	(D RALPH MOLINA	V (D ARTIE TRAUM	G (D
BOB BERTLES	SAX	(D	MIKE DEACON	K	(D JACK EMBLOW	ACC (D RICKY FATAAR	D PERC (E
JOHN PERRY	B	(E	RICHARD BRUNTON	G	(EF JEFF ALLEN	D PERC(E PETE ZORN	B (E
MARTIN JENNER	G	(E	ALY BAIN	FDL	(E TERRY MELCHER	K V (E MEL COLLINS	HRNS (E
TOMMY McCARTHY	PIPES(E		SUZANNE LYNCH	V	(E BARBARA DICKSON	V (E CHARLIE DORE	V (E
BARRY ST JOHN	V	(E	ROGER BROWN	V	(E TOMMY EYRE	K (F ROD CLEMENTS	B (F
LIAM GENOCKEY	D	(F	KARL HIMMEL	D	(B BILL KEMP	D (A ALLAN TRAJAN	K (A
RONNIE RAE	B	(A					

NOAH

(A) PEACEMAN'S FARM	1972 DUNHILL US 50117

NOBODY'S BUSINESS

BOBBIE HARRISON	V PERC(A	(A) NOBODY'S BUSINESS		1978 CBS	JAP 7210
JOE JAMMER	G	(A			
TONY STEVENS	B	(A	JERRY FRANK	D	(A

NOEL & THE RED WEDGE

NOEL	V	(A	(A) PEER PRESSURE		1982 CBS US 37944
JOHN OTTEN	G V	(A			
THOM MOONEY	D	(A	VEYLER HILDEBRAND B	(A KURT KEARNES	G (A RICKY PHILLIPS B V (A
FRANKIE BANALI	D	(A	MITCHELL FROOM	K	(A

NOIR

BARRY FORD	D V	(A	(A) WE HAD TO LET YOU HAVE IT	1971 DAWN UK DNLS3029
GORDON HUNTE	G V	(A		
TONY COLE	K	(A	ROY WILLIAMS	B (A

STEVE NOONAN

STEVE NOONAN		(A	(A) STEVE NOONAN	196 ELEKTRA US EKS 74017

IAN NORTH

IAN NORTH	G V SYN	(AB	(A) NEO	1979 AURA AUL 706
			(B) MY GIRLFRIENDS DEAD	1981 CACHALOT US CA 900

LARRY NORMAN

LARRY NORMAN	K V	(ALL	UPON THIS ROCK		1969 KINGSWAY UK DOVE 6
JOHN WETTON	B	(C	(B) SO LONG AGO THE GARDEN		1973 PHYDEAUX 7776 MGM 4942
KEITH SMART	D	(C	(C) ONLY VISITING THIS COUNTRY		1974 VERVE US 5092
MICKY KEEN	G	(C	(D) ROLL AWAY THE STONE		1980 PHYDEAUX US 999/2
ROD EDWARDS	K V	(C	(E) SOMETHING NEW UNDER THE SUN		1981 PHYDEAUX US
ROGER HAND	V	(C	(F) ROUGH MIX 2		19 PHYDEAUX US
GORDON GILTRAP	G	(C			
BOB BRADY	K	(C	MIKE GILES	D (B MICKEY KEENE	G (B MALCOLM DUNCAN SAX(B
ROGER BALL	SAX	(B	GRAHAM PRESKETT	VLN (B MARK HEARD	G (D JON LINN G (D
TOM HOWARD	PNO	(D	ALEX MACDOUGAL	D (D DAVID COY	B (D RANDY STONEHILL G V (D
BILLY BATSONE	B	(D			

NEIL NORMAN

NEIL NORMAN	G V	(A	(A) NOT OF THIS EARTH	1978 GNP US 2111
KIRK BUCHANAN	D	(A		
JOHN GUERIN	D	(A	LARRY KLEIN	D (A GARY BRASWELL	B (A SAM TAGLIAVORE B (A
LES BAXTER	K	(A	MAX BENNETT	B (A KEN HOFFMAN	B (A HALL DANIELS K (A
BOB KENT	K	(A	GREG VITO	FLT (A LARRY DUNN	SYN (A

NORTHWIND

```
   HUGH BARR          G    (A          (A) SISTER BROTHER LOVER       1971  REGAL ZONOPHONE    UK SLRZ 1020
   COLIN SOMERVILLE   K    (A
   DAVE SCOTT         D    (A   TOM BRANNAN  B V  (A   BRIAN YOUNG     G V  (A
```
NOTATIONS

```
                          (A) NOTATIONS                1976  GEMIGO   US 5501  UK WB     K56212
```
NOTE FROM THE UNDERGROUND

```
                          (A) NOTES FROM THE UNDERGROUND   19   VANGUARD   US 6502
                          (B) PSYCHEDELIC VISIONS          1967 MERCURY     16337 US
```
NOVA COMBO

```
   STEPHEN DEES       B V  (A          (A) NOVA COMBO               1981 POLYDOR  UK 2391 523
   MICHAEL SHRIEVE    D    (A
   JACK GRIFFITH      (A   PETE HEWLETT      (
```
NOVA

```
   CORRADO RUSTICI  G MARIMBA V(ABCD   (A) BLINK          1976   ARISTA       UK      ARTY 118
   ELIO D'ANNA      WIND (ABCD         (B) VIMANA         1976   ARISTA  US 4110  UK ARTY 138
   RENATO ROSSET    K V  (ABCD         (C) WINGS OF LOVE  1977   ARISTA  US 4150  UK SPARTY 102
   PERCY JONES      B    (B            (D) SUN CITY       1978   ARISTA  US 4203
   NARADA MICHAEL WALDEN G K(BC
   PHIL COLLINS     PERC (B   ZAKIR HUSSAIN     CONGA(B   RICK PARNELL    D    (ACD BARRY JOHNSON     B V  (AC
   LUCIANO MILANESE B V  (A   FRANCO LOPREVITE  D    (A    DANIELO RUSTICI  G    (A   BARRY SUNJON    V B (D
   STATIA QAMAR     PERC (D
   NECLAR SMILE CHOIR    V(C
```
NOVAKS KAPELLE

```
   ERWIN NOVAK       D    (A          (A) NAKED                 1978   ARIOLA        GERM     25 784
   HARRY STOJKA      G V  (A
   WALLA MAURITZ V SAX HCA(A   PAETER TRAVNICEK  B V  (A   PAUL BRAUNSTEINER  G V  (A   GITTA WALTHER    V  (A
   RENATE MAUERER    V    (A   MARIA NEUHAUSE    V    (A
```
NOVA LOCAL

```
   RANDY WINBURN     G    (A          (A) NOVA 1                196
   JOE MENDYK        G    (A
   CAM SCHINHAN      K    (A   JIM OPTON    B    (A    BILL LEVASSEUR   D    (A   PHIL LAMBETH    G  (A
```
NOVALIS

```
   DETLEF JOB        G V  (BFG         (A) BANISHED BRIDGE        1973   BRAIN          0001029
   FRED MUHLBOCK     G V  (F           (B) NOVALIS               1975   BRAIN          0001070
   LUTZ RAHN         K SYN(ABFG        (C) SOMMERABEND           1976   BRAIN          0001087
   HARTWIG BIEREICHEL  D  (ABFG        (D) KONZERTE              1977   BRAIN          0060065
   HEINO SCHUNZEL    B V  (ABF         (E) BRANDUNG              1977   BRAIN          0060094
   CARLO KARGES      K G  (B           (F) VIELLEICHT BIST DU EIN CLOWN  1978  BRAIN   0060164
   JURGEN WENZEL     G V  (A           (G) NEUMOND               1982   VERTIGO   UK   6435150
                                       ( ) FLOSSENENGER          1979   AHORN          6 23980
```
NOYES BROTHERS

```
   STEVE SOLAMAR    V G K SYN B D(A    (A) SHEEP FROM GOATS   (DBL)    1980   OBJECT MUSIC     OBJ009/0010
   STUART PICKERING  G    (A
   STEVE MIRO       V G K(A   JAE BOYER       V    (A
```
NOW

```
   BOBBY ORE         (A              (A) THE NOE              1979 MIDSONG INT      MSI014
   ROBIN DEE         (A
   JEFF LENNON       (A   MANNIE FRANCIS      (A
```
RALF NOWY GROUP

```
   RALF NOWY        WIND (AB           (A) LUCIFERS DREAM    1973 INTERCORD     GER 26 015 8
   PAUL VINCENT     G    (AB           (B) ESCALATION        1974 ATLANTIC      GER 40556
   LOTHAR MEID      B    (A
   DON ANDERSON     K    (A   BERNIE PROCK PERC (A   LIZ VAN NEYENHOFF   SITAR(A   THOR BALDURSON   K  (B
   VIKTOR BEHRENS   TPT V(B   MARTIN HARRISON D V(B  GARY UNWIN          B    (AB  KEITH FORSEY     D  (AB
   SYLVESTER LEVAY  K    (AB  ANDY MARX    G    (A   AL GROMER           SITAR(A   SANKAR CHATTEERJEL TAB(A
```
NUCLEUS

```
   IAN CARR         TPT  (ALL          (A) ELASTIC ROCK            1970 VERTIGO  UK 6360 065 RI 6360 008
   KARL JENKINS     SAX K(ABCK         (B) WE'LL TALK ABOUT IT LATER 1970 VERTIGO  UK       6360 027
   JOHN MARSHALL    D    (ABCK         (C) SOLAR PLEXUS           1971 VERTIGO        UK     6360 039
   CHRIS SPEDDING   G    (ABCK         (D) BELLADONNA             1972 VERTIGO  UK      6360 076
   BOB BERTLES      SAX  (GHJK         (E) LABYRINTH              1973 VERTIGO  UK      6360 091
   KEN SHAW         G    (GHJK         (F) ROOTS                  1973 VERTIGO  UK      6360 100
   GEOFF CASTLE     K    (GHJLMN       (G) UNDER THE SUN          1974 VERTIGO  UK      6350 110
   ROGER SUTTON     B    (GHJFK        (H) SNAKE HIPS ETCETERA    1975 VERTIGO  UK 6360 119 SIRE US 7508
   ROGER SELLERS    D    (HJLM         (J) ALLEY CAT              1975 VERTIGO  UK 6360 124
   KENNY WHEELER    TPT  (CEK          (K) DIRECT HITS    (COMP)  1976 VERTIGO  UK 9286 019
   BRIAN SMITH      WIND (ABCDEFKLM    (L) IN FLAGRANTE DELICTO   1977 CAPITOL  UK 11771 CONTEMP GER 1
   TONY ROBERTS     WIND (CK           (M) OUT OF THE LONG DARK   1979 CAPITOL  UK 11916  GER 85788
   CHRIS KARAN      PERC (CK           (N) AWAKENING              1980 MOOD 24000
   TONY LEVIN       D    (EK
   KEITH WINTER     K    (C   JEFF CLYNE      B (ABCK  DAVE MacRAE     K    (DEFK  ALLAN HOLDSWORTH G  (DK
   RON MATHESON     B    (CK  ROY BABBINGTON  B    (DEK CLIVE THACKER   D    (DEFK  GORDON BECK      K  (DECK
   TREVOR TOMKINS   PERC(DEJK JOCELYN PITCHEN G    (GFK BRYAN SPRING    D    (GK    KIERAN WHITE     V  (G
   HARRY BECKETT    TPT  (C   CHUCHO          B    (N   NIC FRANCE      D    (N     TONY COE         WIND (EK
   NORMA WINSTONE   V    (EK  PADDY KINGSLAND SYN  (E   AUREO DE SOUZA  PERC (FK    JOY YATES        V  (F
   BILL KRISTIAN    B    (LM  NEIL ARDLEY     SYN  (M   RICHARD BURGESS PERC (M     CHRIS FLETCHER   PERC (M
```
NUCLEUS (US)

```
   BOB HORNE        K    (A          (A) NUCLEUS          196  MAINSTREAM   US     6120
   GREG FITZPATRICK B K V(A
   JOHN RICHARDSON  G    (A   HUGHIE LEGGAT    B V  (A   DANNY TAYLOR   D    (A
```

```
        TED NUGENT      G B V(ALL        (A) THE AMBOY DUKES              1968   MAINSTREAM US 6104
        DAVE PALMER     D   (ABCD        (B) JOURNEY TO THE CENTRE OF THE MIND 1968 LONDON          UK      8378
        STEVE FARMER    G   (AB          (B) "    "    "    "             1968   MAINSTREAM US 6112 GER VOGUE7715
        RICK LOBER      K   (A           (C) MIGRATION                    1969   LONDON             UK      8392
        BILL WHITE      B   (A           (C) "    "                       1969   MAINSTREAM US 6118
        JOHN DRAKE      V   (AB          (D) MARRIAGE ON THE ROCKS/ROCK BOTTOM 1970 POLYDOR  US 6073    24 4012
        ANDY JEZOWSKI   V   (FG          (ABC) JOURNEYS & MIGRATIONS (COMP) 1975 MAINSTREAM US 2/ 801
        GREG ARAMA      B   (BCD         (E) SURVIVAL OF THE FITTEST      1974   POLYDOR   US 4035 UK 2675 141
        ANDY SOLOMON    K   (BCE         (DE) MARRIAGE/SURVIVAL           1977   POLYDOR            UK 2664 344
        WALT MONAGHAN   B   (N           (  ) BEST OF AMBOY DUKES         19     MAINSTREAM US 6125
        ROB RRUZGA      B   (E           (F) CALL OF THE WILD             1974   DISCREET  US 2181 UK   K59203
        K J KNIGHT      D   (E           (G) TOOTH FANG & CLAW            1975   DISCREET  US 2203 UK   K59205
        JOHN ANGELOS    V   (            (FG) CALL/TOOTH(2 ORIGINALS)     1977   WB                 UK   K69202
        ROB GRANGE      B   (EFHJKLG     (H) DR SLINGSHOT    (COMP)       1975   MAINSTREAM US 414
        JOE VITALE      D   (            (I) TED NUGENT                   1975   EPIC   US 33692 UK     8119
        CLIFF DAVIES    D V(IJKLMNOP     (J) FREE FOR ALL                 1976   EPIC   US 34121 UK     81397
        DEREK ST HOLMES V G (IJKLR       (K) CAT SCRATCH FEVER            1977   EPIC   US 34700 UK     82010
        VIC MASTRIANNI  D   (FG          (L) DOUBLE LIVE GONZO            1978   EPIC   US 35069 UK     88282
        BRIAN STAFFELD  PERC (I          (M) WEEKEND WARRIOR              1978   EPIC   US 35551 UK     83036
        CHARLIE HUHN    G V (MNOP        (N) STATE OF SHOCK               1979   EPIC   US 36000 UK     86092
        JOHN SAUTER     B   (M           (O) SCREAM DREAM                 1980   EPIC   US 36404 UK     86111
        GABE MAGNO      K FLT(F          (P) INTENSITIES IN TEN CITIES    1981   EPIC   US 37084 UK     84917
        MEATLOAF        V   (J           (Q) GREAT GONZO THE BEST OF      1981   EPIC   US 37667 UK     85408
        STEVE McRAY     K   (IJ          (R) NUGENT                       1982   ATLANTIC           UK   K50898
        BOZ BURRELL     V   (K
        RORY DODD       V   (K    ALAN SPENNER       V(K      MONTEGO JOE  PERC (K   TOM WERMAN      PERC (IJK
        CARMINE APPICE  D   (R    DAVE KISWENEY   B V (OPR     DAVID HULL   B   (M   RUSTY DAY       V PERC(C
        LEAH KILBURN    V   (N    REV ATROCIOUS THEODOSIUS G V(G
```

```
        GARY NUMAN      K V G(ALL        (A) PLEASURE PRINCIPLE           1979 BEGGARS BANQUET UK BEGA10 GER 146522
        JAMES FRIEND    (E              (A) PLEASURE PRINCIPLE           1979 ATCO  US 38120
        PAUL GARDINER   B   (ABCD        (B) TELEKON                      1980 BEGGARS BANQUET UK BEGA19 GER 146603
        JOHN WEBB       SYN (EF          (B) TELEKON                      1980 ATCO  US 32103
        CHRISTOPHER PAYNE K VLA(ABCD     (C) LIVING ORNAMENTS '79         1981 BEGGARS BANQUET UK BEGA24
        GARRY ROBSON    V   (A           (D) LIVING ORNAMENTS '80         1981 BEGGARS BANQUET UK BEGA25
        CEDRIC SHARPLEY D   (ABCD        (CD)BOX SET +SINGLE              1981 BEGGARS BANQUET UK BRX 1
        BILL CURRIE     VLN (A           (E) DANCE                        1981 BEGGARS BANQUET UK BEGA 28
        ROGER TAYLOR    D   (E           (F) I ASSASSIN                   1982 BEGGARS BANQUET UK BEGA 40
        MICK PRAGUE     B   (E
        MIKE KARN       B   (E    ROB DEAN          (E    CONNIE FILLIPLOT  V (E   RUSSELL BELL   G V      (BCDE
        ROGER MASON     SYN (CDF  DENNIS HAINES   K V (EB  JESS LIDYARD    D(E   PINO PALLADINO B   (F
        CHRIS SLADE     D   (F    JAMES FREUD       (B
```

```
        CRAIG NUTTYCOMBE G V (A          (A) ITS JUST A LIFETIME          1978 A&M         US      SP 4683
        HENRY SPINETTI  D   (A
        DAVE PEGG       B   (A    ANDY FAIRWEATHER LOW V G(A  TIM RENWICK    G   (A   DICK MORRISSEY  SAX (A
        DAVE MARKEE     B   (A    GLYN JONES        G   (A  PETER HOPE EVANS HCA (A   DAVE MATTACKS   D   (A
        PAT DONALDSON   B   (A    GEORGIE FAME      K   (A  TONY CARR       PERC (A   STEVE GREGORY   SAX (A
        BUD BEADLE      SAX (A    MALCOLM GRIFFITHS TROM (A  BERNIE LEADON    G   (A
```

```
        COLEMAN YORK    D V (A           (A) ADD UP                       1979 BASE   CAN    6000
        ED BLOCKI       B V (A
        PETER EVANS     V G K(A    JIM KENNEDY       G V (A
```

```
        STEVE NUNNERY   K G V   (A       (A) STEVE NUNNERY                1973 CREST       CREST 6
        RICK MAROTTA    D   (A
        PAUL GRIFFIN    K SYN(A    BUZZY FEITEN G B   (A   AL GORGONI      G   (A HUGH McCRACKEN   G   (A
        ELLIOTT RANDALL G   (A    DAVID SPINOZZA    G   (A   JOHN TROPEA     G   (A STU WOODS        B   (A
        KIRK HAMILTON   B   (A    ANDY MUSON        B   (A   ALAN SCHWARZBERG D  (A
```

```
                                         (A) THE NUNS                     1981 BUTT   UK ALSO 001
```

```
                                         (A) CHANCE MEETING               1979 UNITED DAIRIES   UK 001
```

```
        MICK DEVONPORT  G V (ABCD        (A) NUTZ                         1974 A&M    US 3648 UK AMLS68256
        DAVID LLOYD     G V (ABCD        (B) NUTZ TOO                     1975 A&M            UK AMLS68306
        KEITH MULHOLLAND B  (ABCD        (C) HARD NUTZ                    1977 A&M    US 4623 UK AMLH64623
        JOHN MYLETT     D   (ABCD        (D) NUTZ LIVE CUTZ               1977 A&M            UK AMLH68453
        RABBIT          K   (A
        CHRIS HUGHES    HRNS (A   PAUL CARRACK      K   (B  NEIL KERNON     K   (B  KENNY NEWTON    K   (D
```

```
        STEPHANE ROSSINI D  (A           (A) NYL                          1976 URUS        FR   000 013
        MICHAEL PETEAU  G   (A
        OLIVER PAMELA   B V (A    BERNARD LAVALLE   G   (A  ELIZABETH WIENER V  (A ARIEL KALMA   SAX (A
        PATRICK QUENTIN SAX (A    LOY               K   (A  JANIK TOP       B   (A
```

```
        LAURA NYRO      G V K(ALL        (A) MORE THAN A NEW DISCOVERY    1966 VERVE  US FTS3020
        JOHN TROPEA     G   (GHJ         (B) ELI & 13TH CONFESSION        1968 CBS    US   9626 UK    63346
        MICHAEL MAINIERI VIBES(H         (C) NEW YORK TENDABERRY          1969 CBS    US   9737 UK    63510
        ANDY NEWMARK    D   (HJ          (D) XMAS & THE BEADS OF SWEAT    1970 CBS    US  30259 UK    64157
        RICHARD DAVIS   B   (DGH         (E) GONNA TAKE A MIRACLE         1971 CBS    US  30987 UK    64770
        NYDIA MATA      PERC (EGHJ       (F) THE FIRST SONGS              1973 CBS    US  31410 UK    64991
        ELLEN SEELING   TPT (H           (G) SMILE                        1976 CBS    US  33912 UK    81171
        JEFF KING       SAX (H           (H) SEASON OF LIGHT              1977 CBS    US  34786 UK    82183
        JEANIE FINEBERG WIND (H          (J) NESTED                       1978 CBS    US  35449 UK    82917
        CARTER COLLINS  PERC (GH         (K) IMPRESSIONS     (COMP)       1980 EMBASSY          UK    31864
        LABELLE         V   (E
        JIM HELMER      D   (E    LARRY WASHINGTON PERC (E  RONNIE BAKER    B   (E  ROLAND CHAMBERS  G (E
        NORMAN HARRIS   G   (E    LENNY PAKULA     ORG  (E  VINCE MONTANA   PERC (E  ROGER HAWKINS    D (D
        EDDIE HINTON    G   (D    BARRY BECKETT   VIBES(D  DAVID HOOD      B   (D  FELIX CAVALIERE  K (DJ
```

        (CONTINUED)

LAURA NYRO

STU SHARF	G (D	DINO DANELLI	D (D	CHUCK RAINEY	B (D	CORNELL DUPREE	G (D
RALPH McDONALD	PERC (D	ASHAD GARABEDIAN	OUD (D	MICHAEL SZITTAI	CIM (D	ALICE COLTRANE	HARP(D
JOE FARRELL	WIND (DG	DUANE ALLMAN	G (D	WILL LEE	B (GJ	CHRIS PARKER	D (G
PAUL MESSING	PERC (G	HUGH McCRACKEN	G (G	BOB BABITT	B (G	ALLEN SCHWARZBERG	G (G
JEFF MIRANOV	G (G	JERRY FRIEDMAN	G (G	DAVID FRIEDMAN	VIBES (G	JIMMY MAELEN	PERC(G
MICHAEL BRECKER	WIND (G	RANDY BRECKER	TPT (G	JOE BECK	G (G	GEORGE YOUNG	FLT(G
RUBENS BASSINI	PERC (G	GREG BENNETT	G (G	RICK MAROTTA	D (G	REIKA KAMOTA	KOTO(G
VINNIE CUSANO	G (J	JOHN SEBASTIAN	HCA (J	CYRIL CIANFLONE	B (J	TONY LEVIN	B (J
JACK JENNINGS	PERC (D	NISAKO KOSHIDA	KOTO (G				

NYTRO

RONALD A SMITH	K (B	(A) NYTRO	1977 WHITFIELD US 3019
MARK ENGEL	HCA (B	(B) RETURN TO NYTROPOLIS	1979 WHITFIELD US WHK3275 UK K56614
CHRIS POWELL	SAX (B		
ROBERT JUSTICE	V (B	THEODORE WILLINGHAM B (B JOHN JACKSON	D (B EARNEST REDD G (B
KENNETH SCOTT	TPT (B	LAMORRIS PAYNE TPT (B JAMES GADSON	D (B TREY STONE G (B
TERRY SANTIEL	PERC (B		

'O' BAND

PIX	G V (ABCD	(A) A BAND CALLED O	1974	EPIC UK 80120
PETER FILLEUL	K (AB	(B) OASIS	1975	EPIC UK 80596
MARK ANDERS	B (ABCD	(C) WITHIN REACH	1976	UA UK UAG29942
DEREK BALLARD	D (ABCD	(D) THE KNIFE	1977	UA UK UAG30077
CRAIG ANDERS	G (ABCD			
JEFF BANNISTER	K V (CD			

O LEVEL

(A) WE LOVE MALCOLM McLAREN(EP)	19 KINGS ROAD	002

OAK

SCOTT WEATHERSPOON	G V (A	(A) OAK	1979	MERCURY US 3802
RICK PINETTE	G V K(A	(B) SET THE NIGHT ON FIRE	1980	MERCURY US 4009
GEORGE BORDEN	B V (A			
DAVID STONE	K (A	DANNY CARON D (A		

OAKLAHOMA

STEVE CROSSLEY	G V (A	(A) OAKLAHOMA	1977	CAPITOL US 11646
SAM FLORES	D (A			
BEN BLAKEMORE	B V (A	DON JUNTUNEN G (A		

JOHN O'BANNION

JOHN O'BANNION	V (A	(A) JOHN O'BANNION	1981	ELEKTRA US 6E342 UK K52284
JOEY CARBONE	K V PERC(A			
CARLOS VEGA	D (A	JAMES NEWTON HOWARD STR(A	JIMMY HAAS	V (A STAN FARBER V (A
RICHIE ZITO	G K (A	DENNIS BELLFIELD B (A	LENNY CASTRO	PERC (A JON JOYCE V (A
BOBBY KIMBALL	V (A			

DEKE O'BRIEN

DEKE O'BRIEN	G V (A	(A) NIGHTBUS	1976	MILLIGAN LUN 3
MICK MOLLOY	G (A			
RUAN O'LOCHLAIRN	CLAR (A	BRENDAN BONASS G (A	BOBBY KELLY	G (A FIACHRE FRENCH K (A
ROBBIE BRENNAN	D (A	BRIAN MASTERSON B (A	DONAL LUNNY	BOUZ(A

OAKLEY

RITCHIE OAKLEY	G (A	(A) OAKLEY	1980	NOVA WRCI 957
WAYNE NICHOLSON	V (A			
BRUCE DIXON	B (A	BILL McCAULEY K (A DOUG MACKAY	D (A	

OBSERVER ALL STARS

(A) DUBBING WITH THE OBSERVER	1978 ATTACK	ATLP1017

OCCASIONAL WORD ENSEMBLE

(A) THE YEAR OF THE GREAT LEAP SIDEWAYS	1970 DANDELION UK	63753

PHIL OCHS

PHIL OCHS	G V (ALL	(A) ALL THE NEWS THATS FIT TO SING	1964	ELEKTRA US 7269
VAN DYKE PARKS	(E	(A) " " " "	19	CHARTERLINE ITALY 22016
JACK ELLIOT	(E	(B) I AINT MARCHIN' ANYMORE	1965	ELEKTRA US 7287
LINCOLN MAYORGA	PNO (EH	(C) IN CONCERT	1966	ELEKTRA US 7310
BOB RAFKIN	G (H	(D) PLEASURE OF THE HARBOUR	1967	A&M US 4133 UK AML 913
KENNY KAUFMAN	B (H	(E) TAPE FROM CALIFORNIA	1968	A&M US 4148 UK AMLS 919
KEVIN KELLEY	D (H	(F) REHEARSALS FOR RETIREMENT	1969	A&M US 4181 UK AMLS 934
		(G) GREATEST HITS	1970	A&M US 4253 UK AMLS 973
		(H) GUNFIGHT AT CARNEGIE HALL	1971	A&M US 9010
		(J) CHORDS OF FAME	1974	A&M US 4599 UK AMLM64599
		(K) PHIL OCHS SINGS	19	FOLKWAYS US 5320
		(L) INTERVIEWS	19	FOLKWAYS US 5321
		(M) BROADSIDE TAPES	19	FOLKWAYS US 5362

HAZEL O'CONNOR

HAZEL O'CONNOR	K V (ABC	(A) BREAKING GLASS	1980	A&M US 4820 UK AMLH64820
BOB CARTER	G K V(AB	(B) SONS & LOVERS	1980	ALBION NL 203215 UK ALB 104
WESLEY McGOOGAN	SAX (ABC	(C) COVER PLUS	1981	ALBION GER 204047 UK ALB 108
MARY HOPKIN	V (C			
RICK FORD	B (AB	ANDY QUNTA	K (C NEIL O'CONNOR	G (BC ANDY DUNCAN D (AB
TONY VISCONTI PROD	K V (AB	ED CASE	D (C WILD OSCAR	B (C GARY TIBBS B (C
JESSICA VISCONTI	V (C	STEVE KMCH	B V (C DELANEY VISCONTI	V (C LIZZIE DONOVAN V (C
NICHOLCHAS DONOVAN	V (C			

OCTOBER CHERRIES

PHIL TOWNER	D (A	(A) BAKING HOT	1980	BAAL BAL89014
STEVE COOPER	D (A	( ) WORLD HITS '76	1976	BAAL BE 603
JOHN EDMED	STEEL(A			
CHRIS GOULSTONE	G (A	PETER DIAZ G V (A JAY SHOTAM	V B (A JEREMIAH STAR K VIBES (A	

OCTOPUS

TOM MILLER	SAX V(A	(A) OCTOPUS	1969	ESP DISK US 2000
LANNY BROOKS	B V (A			
TREVOR KOEHLER	SAX (A	DION GRODY G K V(A CRAIG JUSTIN	D (A	

```
O7                              OCTOPUS                                              O7
   WERNER LITTAU    K   (ABC    (A) THE BOAT OF THOUGHTS      1976  SKY              SKY009
   SEPP NIEMEYER    D PERC(B     (B) AN OCEAN OF ROCKS         1978  SKY              SKY016
   JENNIFER HENSEL  V   (ABC    (C) RUBBER ANGEL              1979  SKY              SKY035
   CLAUS D KNIEMEYER B  (ABC    (D) DE 14 BESTE VAN OCTOPUS   1980  GNOME        NL  12563
   PIT HENSE+       G   (ABC
   FRANK EULE       D   (A
O7A                        MARTIN O'CUTHBERT                                        O7A
   MARTIN O'CUTHBERT     (A     (A) NAVIGATOR THROUGH NOWHERE  19   ESOTERIC         EEE3
O7B                              ODDSOCKS                                           O7B
   ROBIN BROOKS     G V (A      (A) MEN OF THE MOMENT         1975  SWEET FOLK   SFA 030
   GERALD CLARIDGE G V BAN(A
   NICK PERROT      D PERC(A  NICK SALOMAN B K(A
O8                             ANN ODELL                                            O8
   ANN ODELL        K V  (A     (A) A LITTLE TASTE            1973  DJM              DJLPS 434
   MADELINE BELL    V   (A
   LIZA STRIKE      V   (A   DORIS TROY      V   (A  BRUCE ROWLAND  D   (A  BARRY DE SOUZA  V   (A
   RAY COOPER       PERC (A  RAY FENWICK     G   (A  GARY BOYLE     G   (A  CALEB QUAYE     G   (A
   JOHN GUSTAFSON   B   (A   CHRISTOPHER NEAL HARP (A  RICHARD TAYLOR REC (A  PETER ROBINSON  K   (A
   ANDREW CAUTHENY  WIND (A
O8A                          ANDREW ODOM                                           O8A
   ANDREW ODOM      V   (AB     (A) GOING TO CALIFORNIA       197   MCM          FR  900 297
   EARL HOOKER      G   (B      (B) FARTHER ON THE ROAD       1973  BLUESWAY     US  6055
   JOHNNY WALKER    K   (B
   JIMMY BOND       B   (B   DAVID FRANCIS    D   (B
O8B                              ODIN                                               O8B
   STUART FORDHAM D PERC (A     (A) ODIN                      1972  VERTIGO        6360 608
   JEFF BEER        K PERC V(A
   RAY BROWN        B V (A   ROB TERSTALL G V (A
O9                       JOE O'DONNELL BAND                                          O9
   JOE O'DONNELL    VLN (A      (A) GAODHAL'S VISION          1978  POLYDOR        2383 465
   THEODORE THUNDER D   (A
   STEVE BOLTON     G   (A   DAVE LENNOX     K   (A  BILL SMITH     B   (A
O9A                            BUDDY ODOR                                           O9A
                             (A) BUDDY ODOR IS A GAS         198  ARIOLA UK 5045 NL 200 931
O10                             ODYSSEY                                             O10
   GENE PELLO       D   (A      (A) ODYSSEY                   1972  MOWEST       US  MW  115
   BILLY PIERCE     V   (A
   KATHLEEN WARREN  K V (A   WARNER SCHWEBKE  B   (A  DON DACUS     G   (A  DON PEAK        G   (A
   ROYCE JONES      V   (A   CHRIS DARROW FDL BANJ (A  BUDDY EMMONS  STEEL(A  DAVID T WALKER  G   (A
   CARTER C C COLLINS CONGA(A ROBERT JAMES   FLT (A
O10A                         OFF BROADWAY                                          O10A
   CLIFF JOHNSON    V   (AB     (A) QUICK TIMES               1980  ATLANTIC     US  SD 19286
   JOHN IVAN        G   (AB     (B) ON                        1980  ATLANTIC NL 50695 US  19263
   ROB HARDING      G   (AB
   KEN HARCK        D   (AB  MIKE GORMAN     B   (AB
O10B                          OFFENBACH                                            O10B
   GERALD BOULEL    V K G(A     (A) NEVER TOO TENDER          1976  A&M      US 4630 UK  AMLH69025
   JEAN GRAVEL      G V (A
   ROGER BELVAL     D V (A   MICHEL LAMOTHE   B V (A
O11                          OHIO EXPRESS                                           O11
   DALE POWERS      G   (      (A) OHIO EXPRESS               1968  BUDDAH       US  BDS 5018
   DEAN KASTRAN     B   (      (A) OHIO EXPRESS               1968  PYE          UK  NSPL28117
   JIM PFAYLER      K   (      (B) SALT WATER TAFFY           1968  BUDDAH       US  BDS 5021
   TIM CORWIN       D   (      (C) CHEWY CHEWY                1968  BUDDAH UK203015 US BDS 5026
   DOUGALAS GRASSEL G   (      (D) MERCY                      1969  BUDDAH       US  BDS 5037
                             (E) VERY BEST OF THE OHIO EXPRESS 196  BUDDAH       US  BDS 5058
                             (F) BEG, BORROW & STEAL         1968  CAMEO        US  20000
O12                            OHIO KNOX                                            O12
   PAUL HARRIS      K   (A      (A) OHIO KNOX                 1971  REPRISE      US  6435
   PETER GALLWAY    V G (A
   RAY NEOPOLITAN   B   (A   DALLAS TAYLOR    D   (A  RUSS KUNKEL  CONGAS (A LYNN BLESSING   VIBES  (A
   JOHN SEBASTIAN G V HCA (A DANNY WEIS      G   (A
O13                          OHIO PLAYERS                                           O13
   CLARENCE 'PEE WEE'SATCHWELL SAX V(MRT FIRST IMPRESSIONS     1968 TRIP        US     8029
   LEROY 'SUGAR'BONNER  G V (MRT  OHIO PLAYERS                 19   TRIP        US     3506
   JAMES WILLIAMS   D V (MRT  OBSERVATIONS IN TIME            1969 CAPITOL     US      192
   MERVIN PIERCE    HRNS (MRT OHIO PLAYERS                    19   CAPITOL            11291
   MARSHALL JONES   B   (MRT  PAIN                            1972 WESTBOUND   US     2015
   RALPH MIDDLEBROOKS TPT (MR PLEASURE                        1973 WESTBOUND   US     2017
   WILLIE BECK      K V (MR   ECSTACY                         197  WESTBOUND   US     2021
   RUBENS BASSINI   PERC (R   PAIN+PLEASURE=ECSTACY           1974 WESTBOUND   UK     6309  103
   CLARENCE WILLIS  G V (R    BEST OF                         19   WESTBOUND   US      304
   AZZEDIN WESTON   PERC (R   SKIN TIGHT                      1974 MERCURY  UK SRM1  705 UK 6338  497
   L DAVID JOHNSON  K   (T    CLIMAX                          1974 WESTBOUND   US     1003
   JIMMY SAMPSON    D V (T    FIRE                            1974 MERCURY  US SRM1 1013 UK 9100  009
   VINCENT THOMAS   PERC V(T  FIRE                            1974 MERCURY  EURO 6338 527
   RENNEE ARMAND    V   (T    HONEY                           1975 MERCURY  US SRM1 1038 UK 9100  014
   DANIELLE FOREMAN V   (T    CONTRADICTION                   1976 MERCURY  US SRM1 1088 UK 9100  024
   ELLEN GOLDMAN    V   (T    RATTLESNAKE                     1976 WESTBOUND US 211
   SUSAN GRINDELL   V   (T  (M) GOLD                          1976 MERCURY  US SRM1 1122 UK 9100  030
   IRENE REVETS     V   (T    ANGEL                           1977 MERCURY  US SRM1 3701 UK 9100  037
   ABBIE RUBIN      V   (T    MR MEAN                         197  MERCURY  US SRM1 3717
   SALLY STEVENS    V   (T    JASS AY LAY DEE                 1978 MERCURY  US SRM1 3730
   ANN WHITE        V   (T  (R) EVERYBODY UP                  1979 ARISTA   US  AB 4226
   VINCE ANDREWS    HRNS (T    YOUNG & READY                  1980 ACCORD US 7120
   BRYAN CUMMINGS   HRNS (T    SKIN TIGHT                     1981 MERCURY US 8009
   GARY PLATT       HRNS (T  (T) TENDERNESS                   1981 BOARDWALK US 37090 UK EPIC 85041
   MARK THOMAS      D   (T    OUCH                            1981 BOARDWALK US 33247 UK EPIC 85562
   CHUCK RICH       STEEL(T
   MIKE McDONOUGH   G   (T  CINCINNATI SYM ORCH     (T
```

OINGO BOINGO

```
     STEVE BARTEK       G    (B              (A) OINGO BOINGO    (10" EP)        1980  IRS      US      70400
     DANNY ELFMAN       G V  (B              (B) ONLY A LAD                      1981  A&M  NL  64863
     RICHARD GIBBS      K TROM(B
     KERRY HATCH        B    (B    JOHN HERNANDEZ  D   (B   DALE TURNER   SAX (B   SAM PHIPPS   SAX (B
     KON SCHNEIDERMAN   SAX  (B
```

O JAYS

```
     EDDIE LAVERT       V    (ALL     COMIN' THROUGH                 1965 IMPERIAL            US   9290
     WALTER WILLIAMS    V    (ALL     SOUL SOUNDS                    1967 MINIT               US  40008
     WILLIAMS POWELL    V    (ALL (C) BACKSTABBER                    1972 EPIC                UK  65257
     BOBBY MASSEY       V    (LEFT 72 (C) BACKSTABBER                1973 PHILADELPHIA US 31712  UK  65932
     BILL ISLES         V    (LEFT 66  BACK ON TOP                   197  BELL US 6014
                                       IN PHILADELPHIA               1973 EPIC               UK  65469
     WITH                              IN PHILADELPHIA               1973 PHILADELPHIA US 32120  UK  65933
     LEON CHANCLER      PERC (MN       LIVE IN LONDON                1974 PHILADELPHIA US 32953  UK  80169
     KENNY GAMBLE       PROD (CFL      LIVE                          1974 MFP                UK  50124
     THOM BELL          PROD STR(CL (F)SHIP AHOY                     1974 PHILADELPHIA US 32408  UK  65860
     EARL YOUNG         D    (C        SURVIVAL                      1975 PHILADELPHIA US 33150  UK  80765
     MTUME              PERC (MN       PEACE                         1975 POWER EXCHANGE          PXL2001
     LEON HUFF          K    (NCFL     FAMILY REUNION                1976 PHILADELPHIA US 33807  UK  69196
     VICTOR CARSTARPHEN K    (N        MESSAGE IN THE MUSIC          1976 PHILADELPHIA US 34245  UK  81460
     DENNIS WILLIAMS    K    (NL       O'JAYS                        1976 DJM                UK  22009
     MIKE JACKSON       K    (N     (L)SO FULL OF SOUL               1978 PHILADELPHIA US 35355  UK  86066
     ROLAND CHAMBERS    G    (CLN      GREATEST HITS                 1978 PHILADELPHIA       UK  86058
     RAYMOND EVIL       B    (N     (M) IDENTIFY YOURSELF            1979 PHILADELPHIA US 36027  UK  83666
     CHARLES COLLINS    D    (NL    (N) YEAR 2000                    1980 PHILADELPHIA US 36416  UK  84221
     SHORTY MILLER      D    (NL       MY FAVOURITE PERSON           1982 PHILLY             UK  85712
     DAVID CRUSE        PERC (NL
     WALTER SIGLER      PNO  (N
     JAMES SIGLER       K    (N
     LENNY PAKULA       K    (NC   DENNIS RICHARDSON  K   (NL  DENNIS HARRIS   G   (NC  KIM MILLER     G   (N
     WILLIE ROSS        G    (N    MICHAEL FOREMAN    B   (NL  JAMES WILLIAMS  B   (NL  QUINTON JOSEPH D   (NL
     LARRY WASHINGTON   PERC(CLN  CHARLES WILLIAMS  CONGA(NL  BUNNY SIGLER   K PROD(CL RONNIE BAKER   B   (C
     NORMAN HARRIS      G    (C    BOBBY ELI          G   (CL  VINCE MONTANA   PERC (C  DON RENALDO  STR HRNS(CL
     CECILLE DUVALLE    PNO  (L    JAMES CARTER       D   (L   ALFRED POLLITT  PNO  (L  DAVID WILLIAMS D   (L
     BOB BABBIT         B    (L    JAMES WALKER       B   (L   KIM SIGLER      G   (L   RICKY HICKS    PERC (L
     RAYMOND EARL       B    (L    MORMAN SMITH       B   (L   ROBERT LE GRAND G   (L   BARBARA INGRAM V   (L
     EVETTE BENTON      V    (L    CARLA BENSON       V   (L
```

DANNY O'KEEFE

```
     DANNY O'KEEFE      G V  (ALL     (A) DANNY O'KEEFE              1971 ATLANTIC           UK  2466001
     DOUG HASTINGS      G    (A       (A) DANNY O'KEEFE              1971 COTILLION          US     9036
     BILL McPHERSON     WIND (A       (B) O'KEEFE                    1972 SIGNPOST           US     8404
     BOB NIXON          K    (A       (B) O'KEEFE                    1972 SIGNPOST           UK     4252
     CHRIS ETHRIDGE     B    (A       (B) O'KEEFE                    1979 CRIMINAL RI        UK   TAKE 1
     RICH CROOKS        D    (A       (C) BREEZY STORIES             1973 ATLANTIC           US SD 7264
     EDDIE HINTON       G    (A       (D) SO LONG HARRY TRUMAN       1975 ATLANTIC           US SD18125
     JIMMY JOHNSON      G    (A       (E) AMERICAN ROULETTE          1977 WB                 US  BS 3050
     ROGER HAWKINS      D    (A       (F) SEATTLE TAPES              1977 FIRST AMERICAN     US     7700
     BARRY BECKETT      K    'A       (G) GLOBAL BLUES               1978 WB                 US  BS 3314
     JOEL TEPP          G    (G       (H) INTRODUCING                1966 PANORAMA           US      105
     MIKE BODDIKER      SYN  (G       (I) SEATTLE TAPES   VOL 2      1978 FIRST AMERICAN     US     7721
     DAVID HOOD         B    (A
     REGGIE YOUNG       G    (B  JOHN CHRISTOPHER  G   (B  BOBBY WOOD      K   (B  SHANE KEISTER   K   (B
     BOBBY EMMONS       K    (B  MIKE LEECH        B   (B  GENE CHRISMAN   D   (B  HAYWARD BISHOP  D   (B
     HOWARD McNATT      VLN  (B  LEO LEBLANC      STEEL(B  MARKIE MARKOWITZ TPT (B  PHIL OLIVELLA   CLAR(B
     EDDIE BRIGATI      V    (B  DAVID BRIGATI     V   (B  HUGH McCRACKEN  G   (C  DONNY HATHAWAY  K   (C
     GORDON EDWARDS     B    (C  BERNARD PURDIE    D   (C  NORMAN PRIDE    PERC(C  AIRTO MOREIRA   PERC(C
     DOMINIC CORTESE    ACC  (C  MONTEGO JOE      CONGA(C  ARIF MARDIN    VIBES(C  DAVID BROMBERG  G   (C
     RICHARD DAVIS      B    (C  CISSY HOUSTON     V   (C  MYRNA SMITH     V   (C  SYLVIA SHEMWELL V   (C
     ANDY STATMAN      MAND  (C  KEN KOSEK        FDL  (C  DR JOHN         K   (C  HUGH McDONALD   B   (C
     STEVE MOSLEY       D    (C  GENE ORLOFF      VLN  (C  EMANUEL GREEN   VLN (C  RICHARD DICKLER VLA (C
     NORMAN FORREST     VLA  (C  CHARLES McCRACKEN CELLO(C  PETR ECKLUND   TPT (D  JOHN PAYNE      SAX (C
     TOM SCOTT          WIND (DE DAVID GRISMAN    MAND (C  LARRY VANOVER   JUG (D  RANDY MEISNER   B   (D
     LARRY KNECHTEL     K B  (D  DON HENLEY        D V (D  BERNIE LEADON   V   (D  LINDA RONSTADT  V   (D
     ANDREW GOLD        K    (D  JIM FIELDER       B   (D  GARY MALLABER   D   (DE SNEAKY PETE    STEEL(D
     JOHN BOYLAN        K    (D  ROGER KELLAWAY    K   (DEG CHUCK DOMANICO B  (D  JOHN GUERIN     D   (D
     JOYCE EVERSON      V    (D  RICHARD GREENE   VLN  (D  JIMMY BOND      B   (D  GLENN FREY      D   (D
     DAVID LINDLEY     STEEL(DE VEYLER HILDEBRAND  B   (D  MIKE MELVOIN    PNO (E  REGGIE McBRIDE  B   (E
     ALVIN TAYLOR       D    (E  OLIVER BROWN     CONGA(E  SCOTT STRONG    G   (E  KING ERRISSON  CONGA(E
     CHARLES IRWIN      K    (EG VINCE MELAMED     K   (EG DAVE PARLATO    B   (E  ROGER BETHELMY  D   (E
     LAUDIR DE OLIVEIRA PERC(E  BOBBYE HALL       PERC (E  STEVE SCHAEFFER D   (E  PETER WOODFORD  G   (E
     JOHN HOBBS         K    (G  THOM MOONEY       D       TONY WILLIAMS   D   (G  BILL CUOMO      PNO (G
     JIM GORDON         D    (G  STEVE FORMAN      PERC (G  VENETTE GLOUD   V   (G  JIM KELTNER     D   (G
     SHARON ROBINSON    V    (G  LARRY MUHOBERAC   PNO (G  CARMEN TWILLIE  V   (G  BOBBY KING      V   (G
     FRANK MAROCCO      ACC  (G  'BIGGY' McFADDEN  V   (G  KAZU MATSUI SHAKAHACHI V (G RONNIE BARRON  V   (G
     JAY LEWIS          G    (G  JOHN EWING       TROM (G  BILL BRAUN      PERC(G  RICHARD NASH   TROM(G
     RUSTY BUCHANAN     V    (G  MIKE BAIRD       CLAR (G  SUE RICHMAN     V   (G  JOHN ROTELLA   CLAR(G
     LYNDA LAWLEY       V    (G  JOHN COAN       CORNET(G  PAUL WOLTZ     TUBA (G
```

OKLAHOMA MAFIA

```
     LEON RUSSELL       K V  (
     LEVON HELM        MAND  V(
     BOBBY KEYS         SAX  (    CARL RADLE    B   (    JESSE ED DAVIS    G   ( JIMMY MARKHAM        (
```

OLD & IN THE WAY

```
     JERRY GARCIA BANJ G V  (A       (A) OLD & IN THE WAY           1975 ROUND              RX  103
     DAVID GRISMAN     MAND  V(A
     PETER ROWAN        G V  (A   JOHN KAHN     B   (A   VASSAR CLEMENTS   VLN (A
```

MIKE OLDFIELD

MIKE OLDFIELD G B K+++(ALL	(A) TUBULAR BELLS	1973 VIRGIN	US 13135	UK	V 2001
STEVE BROUGHTON	D	(A	(B) HERGEST RIDGE	1974 VIRGIN	US 13109	UK	V 2013
MUNDY ELLIS	V	(A	(C) OMMADAWN	1975 VIRGIN	US 33913	UK	V 2043
JON FIELD	FLT	(A	(X) BOXED	(4LP SET)	1976 VIRGIN	UK	VBOX1
VIV STANSHALL	V	(A	(D) INCANTATIONS	1978 VIRGIN	UK	VDT 101
JABULA	PERC	(D	(E) EXPOSED	(LIVE DBL)	1979 VIRGIN	UK	VD 2511
SALLY OLDFIELD	V	(ABDC	(F) PLATINUM	1979 VIRGIN	UK	V 2141
TERRY OLDFIELD	FLT	(BCD	(G) Q E 2	1980 VIRGIN	UK	V 2181
LINDSAY COOPER B OBOE	(AB	(H) AIRBORNE	1980 VIRGIN US 13135
CHRIS CUTLER	PERC	(X	(I) MUSIC WONDERLAND	1981 VIRGIN
WILLIAM MURRAY	D	(XC	(J) FIVE MILES OUT	1982 VIRGIN EURO 204500
PHIL COLLINS	D	(G

JUNE WHITING	OBOE	(B	TED HOBART	TPT	(B	CHILI CHARLES	D	(B	CLODAGH SIMMONDS	V	(BC
PIERRE MOERLEN	D	(CDF	MIKE FRYE	PERC	K	(EGJ	BENOIT MOERLEN	PERC	(E	DAVID BEDFORD	PERC	(EXG
RINGO McDONOUGH	BOD	(E	NICO RAMSDEN	G	(EF	PHIL BEER	G V	(E	PEKKA POHJOLA	B	(E
PETE LEMER	K	(EF	TIM CROSS	K	(EG	MADDY PRIOR	V	(DE	RAY GAY	TPT	(E
RALPH IZEN	TPT	(E	SIMO SALMINEN	TPT	(E	COLIN MOORE	TPT	(E	SEBASTIAN BELL	FLT	(DE
CHRIS NICHOLLS	FLT	(E	DEBRA BRONSTEIN	V	(E	EMMA ACHESON	V	(E	DIANA COULSON	V	(E
MARY ELLIOTT	V	(E	MARY CREED	V	(E	CECILY HAZELL	V	(E	WENDY LAMPITT	V	(E
CLARA HARRIS	V	(E	EMMA SMITH	V	(E	CATHERINE LOEWE	V	(E	MIKE LAIRD	TPT	(D
DAVID HENTSCHEL	SYN	(G	TIM COOK	B	(G	MAGGIE RILEY	V	(G	MORRIS PERT	PERC	(JC
TOM CROSS	K	(J	RICK FENN	G	(G	PADDY MALONEY	WIND	(BJC	CARL PALMER	PERC	(J
GRAHAM BROAD	D	(J	DAVID STRANGE	CELLO	(C	EDDIE TATANE	D	(C	PENRHOS KIDS	V	(C
BRIDGET ST JOHN	V	(C	ERNEST MOTHLE	V	(C	JULIAN BAHULA	V	(C	DON BLAKESON	TPT	(C
LESLIE PENNING	REC	(CX	HERBIE		PIPES	(C	HEREFORD CITY BAND		(C	TOM NEWMAN	G	(A
STRING SECTION		(E	ROYAL PHIL			(X	LUCKY RANKU	D	(C	ALLAN SCHWARTZBERG	D	(F
NEIL JASON	B	(F	HANSFORD ROWE	B	(F	FRANCISCO CENTENO	B	(F	WENDY ROBERTS	V	(F
SALLY COOPER	BELLS	(F	DEMELZA C		CONGA	(F	GUY BARKER	TPT	(G	RAUL D'OLIVEIRA	TPT	(G
PAUL NEIMAN	TROM	(G	PHILIP TODD SAX			(G

SALLY OLDFIELD

SALLY OLDFIELD V G K WIND(ABC	(A) WATER BEARER	1978	BRONZE	UK	BRON 511
DAVE LAWSON	SYN	(A	(A) WATER BEARER	1978	CHRYSALIS	US	1211
FRANK RICOTTI	PERC	(A	(B) EASY	1979	BRONZE	UK	BRON 522
BRIAN BURROWS	SAX	(A	(C) CELEBRATION	1980	BRONZE	UK	BRON 528
JEAN PRICE	HARP	(A
TIM WHEATER	PERC	(A	TREVOR SPENCER	PERC	(A

KAI OLSSON

KAI OLSSON	G V	(A	(A) CRAZY LOVE	1979	CHRYSALIS	UK	CHR 1226
TERRY BRITTEN	G	(A
MICK GRABHAM	G	(A	TAFF WILLIAMS	G	(A	DAVE WINTOUR	B	(A	HERBIE FLOWERS B	(A
COLIN PATTENDEN	B	(A	ALAN COULTER	D	(A	STUART ELLIOTTD	(A	CHRIS SLADE	D	(A
BARRIE GUARD	G K	(A	CLIFF HALL	K	(A	DAVID MACKAY	K	(A	RON ASPERY SAX	(A
STUART BROOKS	TPT	(A	TERRY JOHN	HRNS	(A	STEPHEN NYE	OBOE	(A	ANDREW JACKMAN	MAND	(A
STEVE SIMPSON	VLN	(A	TONY HARRIS	VLA	(A	DIGBY RICHARDS	V	(A	LINDA TAYLOR	V	(A
WAYNE OLSSON	V	(A

NIGEL OLSSON

NIGEL OLSSON	D V PERC(ABC	(A) DRUM ORCHESTRA	1972	DJM	UK DJLPS417 US UNI 73113
		(B) NIGEL OLSSON	1975	ROCKET UK ROLL 2	US PIGL 2158
		(C) DRUMMERS CAN SING TOO	1978	ROCKET	US PIG 1932
		(D) CHANGING TIDES	19	BANG 3649 NL	EPIC 84360
		(E) NIGEL	1979	CBS	US 35792

OLYMPIC

PETR JANDA	G V	(A	(A) HOLIDAY ON EARTH	1979	SUPRAPHON	CZECH	1113 2714
MILAN BROUM	B	(A
MIROSLAV BERKA	K	(A	PETR HEJDUK D V (A

OLYMPIC RUNNERS

PETE WINGFIELD	K V	(BDEFG	(A) PUT YOUR MONEY WHERE YOUR MOUTH IS	1974	LONDON	US PS653
GLEN LEFLEUR	D	(BDEG	(B) OUT IN FRONT	1975	LONDON	US PS658	UK SHU 8483
JO JAMMER	G	(BDEFG	(C) DONT LET UP	1975	LONDON	US PS668
GEORGE CHANDLER	V	(BDEFG	(D) HOT TO TROT	1977	LONDON	US PS678
DELISLE HARPER	B	(BDEFG	(D) HOT TO TROT	1977	CHIPPING NORTON	UK	NOR 1
MIKE VERNON	PERC	(BDEFG	(E) KEEPING IT UP	1978	RCA		PL 25124
PEARLY GATES	V	(B	(F) PUTTIN' IT ON YOU	1978	POLYDOR		POLD5015
JIMMY HAYNES	V	(B	(G) OUT OF THE GROUND	1979	RCA		PL 25195
GLEN PENNISTON	D	(F	(H) ITS A BITCH	1979	POLYDOR		2383 549
STEVE GREGORY	WIND	(F	(I) DANCEALOT	1979 POLYDOR	US 16196
JOY YATES	V	(D
SIMON PHILLIPS	D	(F	JACQUIE SULLIVAN V	(D	GEORGE CHISHOLM	HRNS (F

OLYMPICS

WALTER WARD	V	(ALL	HULLY GULLY	19	ARVEE	US	423
EDDIE LEWIS	V	(ALL	DANCE BY THE LIGHT OF THE MOON	19	ARVEE	US	424
CHARLES FIZER	V	(ALL	PARTY TIME	19	ARVEE	US	429
MELVIN KING	V	(ALL	OLYMPICS	19	JAYBOY		SSX 2008
			DO THE BOUNCE	19	TRIDISC	US	1001
			SOMETHING OLD SOMETHING NEW	19	MIRWOOD	US	7003
			OLYMPICS SING	19	POST	US	8000

OMAHA SHERRIFF

PAUL MUGGLETON	G V	(A	(A) COME HELL OR HIGH WATER	1977	GOODEARTH UK GDS803 US RCA 2022
BOB NOBLE	K	(A
CHRIS BIRKETT	G V PERC(A	TONY VISCONTI	B	(A	MICHAEL SPENCER ARSCOTT D HCA V(A

MICHAEL OMARTIAN

MICHAEL OMARTIAN	K	(ALL	(A) ONWARD	197	ABC	ABC 903
STORMIE OMARTIAN		(D	(B) WHITE HORSE	197	MYRRH MYRA1048 US DUNHILL	50185
			(C) ADAM AGAIN	1979	MYRRH	MYR 1058
			(D) SEASONS OF THE SOUL	1979	MYRRH	MYR 1073

OMEGA

```
JANOS KABOR         V     (ALL      (A) RED STAR                      1963 QUALITON HUN
GYORGY MOLNAR       G     (ALL      (B) FREDDIE THE BUGLER & TERRIBLE 1969 QUALITON HUN
LASLO BENKO K SYN         (ALL      (C) ON THE HIGHWAY AT NIGHT       19   QUALITON HUN  SLPX17426
TAMAS MIHALY        B     (ALL      (C) OMEGA                         1973 BELLAPHON BLP19147 BAC2017
FERENC DEBRECENI  D PERC(ALL        (C) OMEGA                         1975 PASSPORT US 98007
                                    (D) 10000 LEPES                   19   QUALITON HUN LPX17400
                                    (E) ELO                           19   PEPITA   HUN     17443
                                    (E) ON TOUR                       197  BELLAPHON GER     2527
                                    (F) OMEGA 5                       19   PEPITA   HUN     17457
                                    (F) 2000 YEARS                    19   BELLAPHON GER    19175
                                    (G) NEM TUDOM A NEVED             19   PEPITA   HUN     17483
                                    (H) HALL OF FLOATERS IN THE SKY   1976 DECCA UK 5219 BELLAPHON GER 19218
                                    (I) III                          19   BELLAPHON GER    19191 BAC 2030
                                    (J) IDORABLO                      19   PEPITA   HUN     17523
                                    (J) TIME ROBERS                   1976 DECCA UK 5243
                                    (K) SKYROVER                      19   PEPITA   HUN 17570 FANTASY US 9560
                                    (K) SKYROVER                      1978 BELLAPHON GER BAC2052
                                    (L) ELO KISSTADITION              19   PEPITA   HUN     17619/20
                                    (M) GANNAPOLIS                    1978 BELLAPHON GER 2061
                                    (N) WORKING                       1981 WEA   58329
```

ONE (UK)

```
ALAN MARSHALL  G V HCA (A        (A) ONE                          1969   FONTANA           UK    STL 5539
BOBBY SASS       G K   (A
NORMAN LEPPARD   WIND  (A  KEVIN FOGARTY    G    (A  BRENT FORBES  B   (A   CONRAD ISADORE  D    (A
```

ONE (US)

```
MARK BAKER         D    (A        (A) ONE                          1972   GRUNT           US       FTR  1008
REALITY D BLIPCROTCH V PERC(A
ROGER CRISSINGER K      (A  FRANK TREVOR FEE B   (A  DONALD ENSSLIN  G BAN(A  THEODORE TEIPEL FLT HCA K(A
MARV GRANAT  G SITAR DULC(A  SARAH OPPENHEIM AUTOHARP(A LAURIE PAUL   V   (A
```

100% PROOF

```
STEVE WRIGHT       G V  (A        (A) 100% PROOF                   1981   MYRRH           MYR 1007
CHARLIE WILSON     G V  (A
STEVE HANSON       B    (A  PHIL WRIGHT  D    (A
```

ONE O ONERS (101ERS)

```
CLIVE TIMPERLEY    G    (A        (A) ELGIN AVE BREAKDOWN          1981   ANDALUCIA    UK       AND101
RICHARD DUDANSKI   D V  (A
DAN KELLEHER       B K V(A  JOE STRUMMER G V  (A  MOLE        B (A
```

ONLY ONES

```
MIKE KELLIE        D    (ABC      (A) THE ONLY ONES               1978   CBS             UK  82830
ALAN MAIR          B    (ABC      (B) EVEN SERPENTS SHINE         1979   CBS             UK  83451
JOHN PERRY         G K  (ABC      (C) BABY'S GOT A GUN            1980   CBS US 36584    UK  84089
PETER PERRETT      G V  (ABC      (D) SPECIAL VIEW               1979   EPIC US 36199
KOULLA KAKOULLI    V    (AB
ADAM MAITLAND    K SAX(B  RABBIT BUNDRICK  K    (B   ROBERT ASH     PROD (A   MICK GALLAGHER   K(A
GORDON EDWARDS     K    (A  RAPHAEL & FRIENDS HRNS(A
```

YOKO ONO

```
YOKO ONO           V    (AB       (A) FLY            (DBL)        1971   APPLEUS 3380    UK    SPTU 101/2
JOHN LENNON        G V  (A        (B) FEELING THE SPACE           1973   APPLE US 3412   UK    SAPCOR26
ERIC CLAPTON       G    (A        (C) SEASONS OF GLASS            1981   GEFFEN US 2004  UK    K99164
HUGH McCRACKEN     G    (C
RINGO STARR        D    (AB  KLAUSS VOORMANN  B    (A   JIM KELTNER    D    (AB  JIM GORDON D   (A
BOBBY KEYS         SAX  (A  CHRIS OSBORNE    (A   JOE JONES             (A   DAVID SPINOZZA G (A
KEN ASCHER         K    (B  BOB BABITT       B    (B   ANDREW SMITH   D    (B  JEREMY STEIG   FLT(B
GORDON EDWARDS     B    (B  ARTHUR JENKINS  PERC (BC  DAVID FRIEDMAN VIBES(BC  RICK MAROTTA   D  (B
DON BROOKS         HCA  (B  SNEAKY PETE STEEL  K  (B   MICHAEL BRECKER SAX (BC  JOHN OCEAN    G  (B
EARL SLICK         G    (C  GEORGE SMALL     K    (C   ANTHONY DAVILIO G  (C  TONY LEVIN     B  (C
JOHN SIEGLER       B    (C  ANDREW NEWMARK   D    (C   GEORGE'YOUNG'OPALISKY SAX(C  RONNIE CUBER  SAX(C
HOWARD JOHNSON     TUBA (C
```

OPA

```
HUGO FATTORUSO     K V  (AB       (A) GOLDEN WINGS                1976   MILESTONE           M9069
GEORGE FATTORUSO   D V  (AB       (B) MAGIC TIME                  1977   MILESTONE           M9078
RINGO THIELMANN    B V  (AB
HERMETO PASCOAL    FLT  (AB  DAVID AMRO     G    (AB
```

THE OPEN MIND

```
                                  (A) THE OPEN MIND               19     PHILIPS   UK    SBL 7893
```

OPEN ROAD

```
JOHN CARR          D    (A        (A) WINDY DAZE                  1971   GREENWICH          GSLP 1001
MIKE THOMSON       B    (A
SIMON LANZON       K    (A  BARRY HUSBAND    G V  (A
```

OPERATION BASEBALL

```
                                  (A) ON THE CASE                 19     CHESS     US       1549
```

ORAN UTAN

```
                                  (A) ORAN UTAN                   1974   BELL      US       6054
```

ORANGE JUICE

```
EDWYN COLLINS      G V  (A        (A) YOU CANT HIDE YOUR LOVE FOREVER 1982 POLYDOR       POLS 1057
JAMES KIRK         G V  (A
DAVID McCLYMONT    B    (A  STEVEN DALY      D    (A   MIKE McEVOY    K    (A   JACKIE CHALLENOR   V(A
ESTHER BYRD        V    (A  LORENZA JOHNSON   V    (A   ADAM KIDRON   PROD (A
```

ORANGE PEEL

```
PETER BISCHOF    V PERC(A        (A) ORANGE PEEL                  19     BELLAPHON     GER  19036
CURT CRESS         D    (A
LESLIE LINK        G    (A  HEINE MOHN       B    (A   RALPH WILRHEISS  ORG (A
```

ROY ORBISON G V (ALL	LONELY & BLUE	1963	LONDON		SHU2342
	LONELY & BLUE	196	MONUMENT		14002
	GREATEST HITS	196	MONUMENT	US	18000
	CRYING	1963	LONDON		SHU6229
	CRYING	19	MONUMENT	US	14007
	CRYING	19	MONUMENT	US	6620
	IN DREAMS	1963	LONDON	UK	SHU8108
	IN DREAMS	196	MONUMENT	US	18003
	IN DREAMS	196	MONUMENT	US	6620
	EXCITING SOUNDS	1964	EMBER		
	OH PRETTY WOMAN	1964	LONDON	UK	8207
	THERE IS ONLY ONE	1965	LONDON	UK	8252
	THERE IS ONLY ONE	1965	MGM	US	4683
	THE ORBISON WAY	1966	LONDON	UK	8279
	THE ORBISON WAY	1966	MGM	US	4322
	THE CLASSIC	1966	LONDON	UK	8297
	THE CLASSIC	1966	MGM	US	4379
	SINGS DON GIBSON	1967	LONDON	UK	8318
	SINGS DON GIBSON	1967	MGM	US	4424
	CRY SOFTLY LONELY ONE	1968	LONDON	UK	8357
	CRY SOFTLY LONELY ONE	1968	MGM	US	4514
	FASTEST GUITAR ALIVE	1968	LONDON	UK	8358
	ORBISONGS	196	MONUMENT		5004
	ORBISONGS	196	MONUMENT		18035
	EARLY ORBISON	196	MONUMENT		5013
	EARLY ORBISON	196	MONUMENT		18023
	GREATEST HITS	19	MONUMENT		5007
	GREATEST HITS	19	MONUMENT		64663
	GREATEST HITS	19	MONUMENT	US	6619
	GREATEST HITS	19	MONUMENT		14009
	MORE GREATEST HITS	19	MONUMENT		5014
	MORE GREATEST HITS	19	MONUMENT		6621
	MORE GREATEST HITS	19	MONUMENT		18024
	VERY BEST OF	19	MONUMENT		18045
	VERY BEST OF	19	MONUMENT		6622
	AT THE ROCKHOUSE	196	SUN	US	1260
	AT THE ROCKHOUSE	1980	CHARLY	UK	CRM2007
	MANY MOODS OF	1969	MGM	US	4636
	GREAT SONGS	1969	MGM	US	4659
	HANK WILLIAMS SONGS	1969	MGM	US	4683
	THE BIG O	1970	LONDON		8496
	THE ORIGINAL SOUND	1970	SUN	US	113
	THE ORIGINAL SOUND	197	SUN	UK	6467 005
	ROY ORBISON SINGS	1972	LONDON	UK	8435
	ROY ORBISON SINGS	197	MGM	US	4835
	MEMPHIS	1973	LONDON	UK	8445
	MEMPHIS	1973	MGM	US	4867
	THE BEST OF	1973	BOVEMA	EURO	05491411
	THE BEST OF	19	TRIP	US	
	ALL TIME GREATEST HITS	1973	MONUMENT		67290
	ALL TIME GRESTEST HITS	197	MONUMENT		8600
	ALL TIME GREATEST HITS	1973	MONUMENT	US	31484
	THE EXCITING	1974	HALLMARK	UK	SHM 824
	MILESTONES	1974	MGM	US	4934
	IM STILL IN LOVE WITH YOU	1976	MERCURY	US	SRMI1045
	ORBITING	19	DESIGN	US	DLP 164
	STARS OF THE 60s	1974	EMI	EURO	05092542
	THE BIG O	1975	CHARLY UK		CRR300008
	THE BEST OF	1975	ARCADE	UK	ADEP19
	MONUMENTAL HITS	1975	MONUMENT UK		69147
	MONUMENTAL HITS VOL2	1975	MONUMENT UK		69188
	FOCOS ON	1976	DECCA		FOS/U15/6
	REGENERATION	1977	MONUMENT	UK	81809
	REGENERATION	1977	MONUMENT US		7600
	LAMINAR FLOW	1979	ASYLUM	UK	K53092
	LAMINAR FLOW	1979	ELEKTRA	US	6E 198
	AT THE ROCK HOUSE	1980	CHARLY	UK	CRM2007

PAUL HUMPHREYS	V K PERC(ABC	(A) ORCHESTRAL MANOEUVRES IN THE DARK	1980 DINDISC UK DID2 GER 20297
ANDY McCLUSKEY	V G K(ABC	(B) ORGANISATION	1980 DINDISC UK DID6 GER 202971
DAVE FAIRBAIRN	G (A	(C) ARCHITECTURE & MORALITY	1981 DINDISC UKDID12 GER 204016
MALCOLM HOLMES	PERC D(ABC	(C) ARCHITECTURE & MORALITY	1981 CBS US 37721
MARTIN COOPER	SAX (AC		
MIKE HOWLETT	PROD (BC MICHAEL DOUGLAS K (C DAVID HUGHES	TAPES (C CHESTER VALENTINE PROD(A
RICHARD MAINWARING	(C		

LAURIE BELL	D V (A	(A) ORCHIDS	1980 MCA UK MCF3067 US 3235 GER 202177
JAN KING	V G K(A		
LAURIE McALLISTER B V (A	SUNBIE SINN	G PNO V(A CHE ZURO	G K V(A KIM FOWLEY PROD (A

	(A) BAZAAR	1981 SONET	UK SNTF 864

PAUL McCANDLESS	(FG	(A) MUSIC OF ANOTHER PRESENT ERA	1974 VANGUARD	VSD79326
GLEN MOORE	(FG	(B) DISTANT HILLS	1974 VANGUARD	VSD79341
RALPH TOWNER	(FG	(C) WINTER LIGHT	1975 VANGUARD	VSD79350
COLLIN WALCOTT	(FG	(D) IN CONCERT	1975 VANGUARD	VSD79358
ELVIN JONES	(FG	(E) FRIENDS	1975 VANGUARD	VSD 79370
ZBIGNIEW	VLN (G	(F) TOGETHER	1977 VANGUARD	VSD79377
		(G) VIOLIN	197 VANGUARD	VSD79397
		(H) OUT OF THE WOODS	1978 ELEKTRA	K52101
		(I) IN PERFORMANCE	1980 eELEKTRA US	304

ORGANISATION

```
RALF HUTTER          ORG  (A           (A) TONE FLOAT                    1970 RCA                  SF8111
BASIL HAMMOUDI PERC V (A
FLORIAN SCHNEIDER-ESLEBEN FLT(A  BUTCH HAUF   B PERC   (A  FRED MONICKS D PERC(A
```

ORGINAL MIRRORS

```
PETE KIRCHER         D    (AB          (A) ORIGINAL MIRRORS             1980 MERCURY UK 9102 039  6310 050
STEVE ALLEN          V    (AB          (B) ORIGINAL MIRRORS             1980 ARISTA   US 4269
IAN BROUDIE          B    (AB          (B) HEART TWANGO & RAW BEAT      1981 VERTIGO UK 6359 046
JONATHAN PERKINS     K    (AB
PHIL SPALDING        B    (B  JIMMY HUGHES B     (AB MIKE HOWLETT       PROD(B
```

ORIGINALS

```
WALTER GAINES        (              (A) GREEN GROW THE LILACS      1969 SOUL   US  716
C P SPENCER          (A             (B) PORTRAIT                   1970 SOUL   US  724
HENRY DIXON          (              (C) NATURALLY TOGETHER         1971 SOUL   US  729
FREDERICK GORMAN     (              (D) DEFINITIONS                1972 SOUL   US  734
JOE STUBBS           (              (E) GAME CALLED LOVE           1974 SOUL   US  740
TY HUNTER            (              (F) CALIFORNIA SUNSET          1975 MOTOWN US  826  UK     11287
                                    (G) COMMUNIQUE                 1976 SOUL   US  746  UK TAMLA12034
                                    (H) DOWN TO LOVE TOWN          1977 SOUL   US  749  UK TAMLA12054
                                    (J) ANOTHER TIME ANOTHER PLACE 1978 FANTASY US 9546 UK    FT542
                                    (K) COME AWAY WITH ME          1978 FANTASY US 9577
                                    (L) YESTERDAY & TODAY          19   POLYDOR  US  37075
```

ORION

```
                     (A ) SOMETIMES WORDS JUST GET IN THE WAY 75 LONDON      US     44230
                          REBORN                               197  CHARLY         CRL  5020
                          SUNRISE                              1980 SUN       US    1017
                          ROCKABILLY                           1981 SUN       US    1021
                          COUNTRY                              1981 SUN       US    1019
```

ORLEANS

```
LARRY HOPPEN      G V (ABCDEFG    (A) ORLEANS             1975 ABC US 795 UK 5107  NL 27141
LANCE HOPPEN      B V (ABCDEFG    (B) LET THERE BE MUSIC  1975 ASYLUM US 7E  1029  UK SYL 9023
JOHN HALL         G V (ABCDF      (B) LET THERE BE MUSIC  1975 ASYLUM          UK     K53011
WELLS KELLY       D V K(ABCDEF    (C) WAKING & DREAMING   1976 ASYLUM US 7E  1070  UK     K53044
JERRY MAROTTA     D   (CFG        (D) BEFORE THE DANCE    1977 ABC    US       1058 UK ABCL6224
MICHAEL BRECKER   SAX (C          (E) FOREVER             1979 INFINITY US 9006 UK     2004
RICK MAROTTA      D   (F          (F) ORLEANS             1980 MCA US 5110
GERALDO VALEZ     PERC(F          (G) ONE OF A KIND       1982 RADIO US 90012/1
BLUE MITCHELL     TPT (C
LINDA RONSTADT    V   (C   BOB LEINBACH     K V (EF  R A MARTIN    HRNS K V(AEF  JIMMY MAELEN    PERC(EG
RUBENS BASSINI    PERC (E  BASIL TYLER      HRNS (F   PHIL COLLINS  V    (F      MORRIS PERT     PERC(F
LANE HOPPEN       V K (FG  JAY BECKINSTEIN  SAX  (F   BILL BROWN    HRNS (F      MIKE MUGRAGE   G V (G
BEN WISCH         PROD(G   DENNIS AMERO     G    (G   DON SILVER    PROD (G      STRING SECTION  (E
```

ROBERT ELLIS ORRALL

```
ROBERT ELLIS ORRALL  K V (A          (A) FIXATION        1981 WHY      UK WH02
KOOK LAWRY           G V (A
DAVID STEFANELLI     D V (A   DON WALDEN      B V (A  JOHN PAYNE  SAX (A  ED GRENGA         (A
DOUG MILLETT         G V (A   JIMMY MAELEN PERC (A    RANDY ROOS  G   (A  JOSIAH SPAULDING PROD(A
MICHAEL PILLOT       PROD (A
```

ORLONS

```
STEVE CALDWELL       V  (12          ALL THE HITS         19   CAMEO         US    1033
MARLENA DAVIS        V  (12          SOUTH STREET         19   CAMEO         US    1041
ROSETTA HIGHTOWER    V  (12          NOT ME               19   CAMEO         US    1054
AUDREY BRICKLEY      V  (1           BIGGEST HITS         19   CAMEO         US    1061
SHIRLEY BRICKLEY     V  (1           GOLDEN HITS          196  CAMEO         US    1067
                                     DOWN MEMORY LANE     19   CAMEO         US    1073
                                     THE BEST OF          1977 LONDON        UK    HAU 8594
                                     (1) PRE 1959  (2) POST 1959
```

ORPHAN

```
ERIC LILLEQUIST      V G (C          (A) EVERYONE LOVES TO SING    1972 LONDON US PS 614 UK SHU 8438
STUART SCHULMAN      B K V(           (B) ROCK & REFLECTION        1973 LONDON US PS 630 UK SHU 8452
RICHARD ADELMAN      D   (            (C) MORE ORPHAN THAN NOT     1974 LONDON US PS 645 UK SHU 8475
BILL KEITH           STEEL(
DAVE CONRAD          V   (C   BILL ELLIOTT     K    (C   BOB CHOUINARD   D  (C  DEAN ADREN      G V (C
BRUCE McPHERSON      K V (C   DAVID WOODFORD   SAX  (C   KERRY BLOUNT   SAX (C  JAY DEWALD      TPT (C
BILL SEISM           TPT (C   LLOYD BASKIN     ORG  (C   DAN FRYE       K   (C  SANDRA BASKIN   V  (C
SUZANNE SWAN         V   (C   SHARON BROWN     V    (C
```

ORPHAN EGG

```
JIM BATE             V   (A          (A) ORPHAN EGG      1968 CAROLE GER 9621  US  CARS8004
GEORGE LORIX         D   (A
PAT GALLAGHER        G V (A   LARRY SMITH      B    (A  DAVE MONLEY  G K (A
```

ORPHEUS

```
ERIC GULLIKSEN       B V (ABC         (A) ORPHEUS        1967 MGM     US   4524
K P BURKE            HCA (D           (B) ASCENDING      1968 MGM     US   SE4569
JACK McKENES         G V (ABC         (C) JOYFUL         1968 MGM     US   4599
BRUCE ARNOLD         G V (ABCD        (D) ORPHEUS        1969 BELL    US   6061
HARRY SANDLER        D V (ABC
STEVE MARTIN         V   (D   BERNARD PURDIE   D     (D  HOWARD HARSH   B   (D  ELLIOTT SHERMAN K  (D
```

OSANNA

```
ELIO D'ANNA          SAX (ABCDE       (A) L'UOMO           197  FONIT LPX 10 +1976      MF 103
DANIEL RUSTICI       G   (ABCDE       (B) MILANO CALIBRO 9 1974 FONIT LPX 14 +PETER PILPS9001
MASSIMO GUARINO      D   (ABCD        (C) PALEPOLI         197  FONIT LPX 19
LELLO BRANDI         B   (ABCD        (D) LANDSCAPE OF LIFE 197 FONIT LPX 32 +PETER PILPS9007
LINO VAIRETTI        K SYN V(ABCD     (E) UNO              1974 FONIT LPX 26 +MOTORS MT 44027
ENZO VALICELLI       D   (E
```

OZZY OSBOURNE(BLIZZARD OF OZ)

```
OZZY OSBOURNE        V   (ALL         (A) BLIZZARD OF OZ   1980 JET US 36812 UK  JETLP234
BOB DAISLEY          B V (ABC         (B) DIARY OF A MADMAN 1981 JET           UK      237
RANDY RHODES         G   (ABC         (C) MR CROWLEY  (EP)  1981
LEE KERSLAKE         D   (A           (D) TALK OF THE DEVIL 1982 JET           UK      401
BRAD GILLIS          G   (D
RUDI SARZO           B   (DB  (TOMMY ALDRIDGE  D    (AB DON AVERY     K   (A  BERNIE TORME   G  (
```

OSCAR

```
BRIAN McGLADDERY    G V  (A      (A) OSCAR               1975  BUK  UK 2001 US 22301
GARY McDOUGAL       B    (A      (B) TWILIGHT ASYLUM     1976  DJM            UK   DJF 20494
TONY BANFORD        K    (A      (C) COBBLESTONE HEROES  1977  DJM            UK   DJF 20516
KEVIN PARROT        G    (A
ROGER TWEEDALE      PERC (A
```

OSAMU

```
OSAMU KITAJIMA G KOTO V(A        (A) OSAMU               1977 ISLAND  ILPS9426 US ANTILLES7016
JOHN HUG      G MAND    (A
GEOFFREY HALES  D PERC(A  DENNIS BELFIELD   B   (A   BRIAN WHITCOMB G K SYN(A    TATSUYA SANO        (A
GEORGE MARINELLI  G  (A  MINNIE RIPERTON    V   (A
```

WAVIS O'SHAVE

```
WAVIS O'SHAVE       V    (        (A) DENNIS SMOKES TABS(EP)  19  COMPANY          CR  003
                                 (B) ANNA FORD'S BUM         19  ANTI POP         AP  2
```

JEFF OSBORNE

```
JEFF OSBORNE         (A          (A) AYMUK               1982 A&M      UK   AMLH 64896
```

JOHNNY OSBOURNE

```
JOHNNY OSBOURNE     V    (AB      (A) FALLY OVER          1981 GREENSLEEVES  UK   GREL12
                                  (B) IN NAH DISCO STYLE  1981 CHA CHA       UK   0010
```

OSIBISA

```
TEDDY OSEI FLT PERC  (ALL     (A) OSIBISA          1971 MCA      UK MDKS8001 +74 MCG 3508
LOUGHTY AMAO    SAX  (ABCD    (A) OSIBISA          197  DECCA    US    75285 +MCA  MCA32
ROBERT BAILEY   K    (ABCDGK  (B) WOYAYA           1971 MCA      UK MDKS8005 +74 MCD 3506
SPARTACUS R     B    (ABCD    (B) WOYAYA           197  DECCA    US    75327 +MCA  MCA43
WENDEL RICHARDSON G  (ABCDHK  (C) HEADS            1972 MCA      UK MDKS8007 +74 MCG 3514
MAC TONTOH      TPT  (ALL     (C) HEADS            197  DECCA    US 75368 MCA GER MAPS6283
SOL AMARFIO     D    (ALL     (D) BEST OF          1974 MCA      UK            MCF 2575
KIKI GYAN       K    (FH      (E) HAPPY CHILDREN   1973 WB       US  BS 2732 UK  K56022
KOFI AYIVOR     PERC (EFGH    (F) OSIBIROCK        1974 WB       US  BS 2802 UK  K56048
PAUL GOLLY      G    (FH      (G) SUPER FLY TNT    1974 BUDDAH US    5136  UK 2318 087
GORDON HUNTE    G V  (G       (G) SUPER FLY TNT    197  BUDDAH           UK BDLP4020
JEAN ROUSSEL    K    (E       (H) WELCOME HOME     1975 BRONZE UK ILPS9355 RI  BRNA355
MIKE ODUMUSU    B    (HK      (H) WELCOME HOME     1977 ANTILLES         US    7051
JEAN MANDENGUE  B    (EFGHL   (J) OJAH AWAKE       1976 BRONZE UK ILPS9411 RI BRNA 411
DAKU 'POTATO'   K    (KL      (J) OJAH AWAKE       197  ANTILLES         US    7058
SONIA LEKHELA   V    (K       (K) BLACK MAGIC NIGHT 1977 BRONZE UK BRSP 3
NTOBI MDUDU     V    (K       (L) MYSTIC ENERGY    1980 CALIBRE          UK CAB1002
TINY CONCO      V    (K
LINDA CONCO     V    (K  KARI BANNERMAN  G   (L  EMA YAWKOBA RENTZOS K V(L  KATHY T     V  (L
ROBERT ABIA     G B  (L  ALTON EDWARDS   V   (L  REBOP KWAKU BAAH  PERC (L  PAM DOUGLAS V  (L
MIQUEL BROWN    V    (L  CANDY McKENZIE  V   (L
```

LEE OSKAR

```
LEE OSKAR         HCA V  (AB    (A) LEE OSKAR        1976 UA           US    UALA 594
(OSKAR LEVETIN HANSEN)          (B) BEFORE THE RAIN  1978 MCA UK MCF2870 US ELEKTRA 6E150
B B DICKERSON     B    (A       (C) LEE OSKAR        1980 MCA UK MCF3060 US        37114
GREG ERRICO       K D  (A
ROBERT VEGA       B    (A  STEVE BUSFELD   G   (A  CHEPITO AREAS  CONGA(A  WENDY HAAS   V  (A
HERMAN EBERITZSCH PNO  (A  MOSES WHEELOCK  CONGA(A  HAROLD BROWN   D   (A  MONTY STARK  PERC (A
JULIA TILLMAN     V    (A  MAXINE WILLARD  V   (A  LANI GROVES    V   (A  EDNA WRIGHT  V  (A
CHARLES MILLER    SAX  (A  JERRY FISHER    V   (A  CONNIE FISHER  V   (A  NITO MEDINA  G  (A
LONNIE JORDAN     PERC K (A  PAPA DEE ALLEN  PERC (A  HOWARD SCOTT  G V  (A
```

OSMOSIS

```
CHARLIE MARIANT   WIND (A       (A) OSMOSIS          1970  RCA  US LSA3010 LSP 4369
BOBBY KNOW        V    (A
DANNY COMFORT     B    (A  LOU PETERSON    D   (A  BOBBY CLARK    PERC (A  CHARLIE BECHLER K  (A
ANDY STENBORN     G    (A
```

OS MUNDI

```
ANDREAS VILLAIN   B    (A       (A) LATIN MASS       1980 METRONOME  GER 15381
CHRISTOPH BURSE   G D V(A       (B) 43 MINUTEN       1972 BRAIN      GER 1015
CONNY PLANK       G    (B
DIETRICH MARKGRAF WIND (A  HARTMUT SEIDEL  B   (A  UDO ARNDT      G K  (A  DAVID KALCKREUTH K  (A
BUDDY MANDLER     D    (A  MIKRO RILLING   STR V(A  ERIK SPIEKERMAN G  (B
```

OTGER DICE

```
ANTON VERHAGEN    V    (A       (A) GARDEN OF PLEASURE  19  TRIANGLE   150 330020
OTGER COOYMANS    K V  (A
FRED BERGER       G    (A  DAVID KEMPER    D   (A  PAUL HAPPENER  B   (A  EEF ALBERS   G  (A
JAN PIJNENBERG    D    (A  DEAN PARKS      G   (A  VICTOR FELDMAN PERC (A
```

OTHER HALF

```
RANDY HOLDEN      G    (        (A) THE OTHER HALF   19  ATCO  38004
MIKE PORT              (
```

JOHNNY OTIS

```
JOHNNY OTIS      D V PNO(ALL     (A) COLD SHOT             1969 SONET UK SNTF613 US KENT  534
SHUGGIE OTIS     G B  (A         (B) CUTTIN' UP            1970 EPIC           US      26524
MIGHTY MOUTH EVANS V  (A         (C) LIVE AT MONTEREY      1971 EPIC UK  66295 US      30473
AL RIVERA        B    (A         (D) GREAT R & B           19   BLUES SPECTRUM US    BS 103
HOOTIE GALVAN    D    (A         (E) ROCK'N'ROLL HIT PARADE 197 DIG            US       104
DON SUGARCANE HARRIS VLN(A       (F) FORMIDABLE            19   EMBER          UK  SPE 6604
BROADWAY THOMAS  B    (A         (G) THE JOHNNY OTIS SHOW  19   BOVEMA       EURO 052 80676
BUDDY REDD       D    (A         (H) THE JOHNNY OTIS SHOW  19   SAVOY          US      2221
ESTHER PHILLIPS  V    (          (I) THE JOHNNY OTIS SHOW  19   CAPITOL        US       940
MEL WALKER            (          (J) PIONEERS OF ROCK      1973 STARLINE       UK  SRS 5129
CLIFFORD SOLOMON      (          (K) JOHNNY OTIS           1975 BULLDOG           BDL1002
MIGHTY FLEA      TROM (          (L) ROCK'N'ROLL HISTORY   1979 CAPITOL        FR 038 85085
LADY DEE WILLIAMS     (          (M) ROCK'N'ROLL           1979 FLYRIGHT       UK       550
PETE LEWIS            (
ROBINS           V    (  BIG JIM WYNN      (  OTISETTES        V  (  MARGIE EVANS  V  (
BIG DADDY RUCKER      (  EDDIE VINSON  G V (  BIG JOE TURNER   V  (
```

SHUGGIE OTIS

SHUGGIE OTIS	G B V(ALL	(A) AL KOOPER INTRODUCES	1969 CBS US 9951	UK	63797
JOHNNY OTIS	D PNO(BC	(B) HERE COMES SHUGGIE OTIS	1970 CBS US 26511	UK	63996
AL KOOPER	K V (A	(C) FREEDOM FLIGHT	1971 EPIC US 30752		
RAY JOHNSON	K (B	(D) INSPIATION INFORMATION	1975 EPIC US 33059		
LEON HAYWOOD	K (B	(E) OMAHA BAR B Q	19 KENT US 540		
WILTON FELDER	B (BC	(1) 1969 LIVE			
AL McKIBBON	B (B				

STIX HOOPER	D (B	PAUL LAGOS	D (B	ABE MILLS	D (B	PRESTON LOVE	WIND (B1		
PLAS JOHNSON	SAX (B	TANK JERNIGAN	WINS (AB	JIM HORN	SAX (B	JACK KELSO	SAX (BD1		
MELVIN MOORE	TPT (B	BOB MITCHELL	TPT (B	GENE'MIGHTY FLEA'CONNERS(B		WILLIE RUFF	HRNS (B		
WELLS KELLY	D (A	STU WOODS	B (A	MARK KLINGMAN	PNO (A	CLIFFORD SOLOMON	SAX (1		
ED PLEASANCE	SAX (1	WALLACE BRODIE	SAX (1	JOE EPPS	SAX (1	BILL CATER	SAX (1		
RON SELICO	D (1	MIKE KOWALSKI	D (C	GEORGE DUKE	K (C	AYNSLEY DUNBAR	D (C		
JIM BRADSHAW	HCA V(C	RICHARD APLANALP	FLT (C	CLYDIE KING	V (C	VANETTA FIELDS	V (C		
SHIRLEY MATTHEWS	V (C	CURT SLETTEN	TPT (D	RON ROBBINS	TPT (D	DOUG WINTZ	TROM (D		
JIM PRINGLE	TROM (D	JEFF MARTNEY	HRNS (D	STRINGS SECTION		(AD) RICHARD MACKAY	HRNS (B		

JOHN OTWAY

JOHN OTWAY	G V (ALL	(A) JOHN OTWAY & WILD WILLY BARRETT	1977 EXTRACKED ELP1+POLYDOR 2383 453	
WILD WILLY BARRETT	G V (A F	(B) DEEP & MEANINGLESS	1978 POLYDOR	2383 501
PETE TOWNSHEND	G PROD(A	(C) WHERE DID I GO RIGHT	1979 POLYDOR	2383 532
PAUL WARD	(ABD	(D) WAY & BAR	1980 POLYDOR	2383 581
NIGEL PEGRUM	D (ABD	(E) DEEP THOUGHT	198 STIFF US USE5	
BARON ANTHONY	PROD (A	(F) GONE WITH THE BIN	1981 POLYDOR	POLS1039

ROGER CAREY	(D							
PHIL CUTLER	(A	STUART EATON	(A	LYN FLETCHER	(A	FIONA BUTT	(B	
MARTIN LOVEDAY	(A	MILTON REAME JAMES	(A	LISA STRIKE	V (A	MORGAN FISHER	K (C	
OLLIE HALSALL	G (C	PAUL MARTINEZ	B (C	CHARLIE MORGAN	D (C	MAGGIE RYDER	V (CD	
JULIAN SMEDLEY	FDL (C	MARK FREEMAN	(BD	MAURICE BACON	(D	LOL COXHILL	(D	
DAVE HOLMES	(B	YVONNE GRECH	(B	SIMON HANSON	(B			

OUTCASTS

COLIN COWAN	D (A	(A) SELF CONSCIOUS OVER YOU	1979 GOOD VIBRATIONS		BIG 1			
MARTIN COWAN	G V (A							
GREG COWAN	B V (A	GETTY	G (A	SIMON LLOYD	SAX (A	D SMYTH	G (A	
IZZY TURNER	K (A							

OUT OF FOCUS

REMIGIUS DRECHSLER	G (AB	(A) WAKE UP	1971 KUCKUCK	GER 2375 006
MORAN NEUMULLER	SAX (AB	(B) OUT OF FOCUS	1972 KUCKUCK	GER 2375 010
HENNES HERING	K (AB	(C) FOUR LETTER MONDAY AFTERNOON(DBL) 1972		
STEFAN WISHEU	B (AB			
KLAUS SPORI	D (AB			

OUTDOOR PLUMBING CO

(A) MOONSHINE MOUNTAIN	1980 REBEL US 1578

OUTLAW BLUES BAND

LEON RUBENHOLD	(AB	(A) OUTLAW BLUES BAND	1968 BLUESWAY US BLS 6021
JOE WHITEMAN	(AB	(B) BREAKING IN	1969 STATESIDE UK SSL10290
PHILLIP JOHN	(AB	(B) BREAKING IN	1969 BLUESWAY US BLS 6030
VICTOR ALEMAN	(AB		
LAWRENCE DICKENS	(AB		

THE OUTLAWS (UK)

MIKE BERRY	V (	(A) DREAM OF THE WEST	1961 HMV		UK CLP 1489			
CHAS HODGES	B (A							
REG HAWKINS	G (	BILLY KUY	G (A	BOBBY GRAHAM	D (A	DON GROOM	D (	
KEN WINDGREN	G (	ROGER MINGAY	G (	LORNE GREENE	G (	RITCHIE BLACKMORE	G (	
MICK UNDERWOOD	D (	HARVEY HINSLEY	G (					

OUTLAWS(US)

BILLY JONES	G V (ABCDEFG	(A) THE OUTLAWS	1975 ARISTA US AL 4042 UK ARTY 115			
FRANK O'KEEFE	B (AB	(B) LADY IN WAITING	1976 ARISTA US 4070 UK ARTY 126			
HENRY PAUL	G V (ABC	(C) HURRY SUNDOWN	1977 ARISTA US AL 4135 UK SPART1010			
HUGHIE THOMASSON	G V (ABCDEFGH	(D) BRING IT BACK ALIVE	1978 ARISTA US AL 8300 UK DARTY 5			
MONTE YOHO	D (ABCDEF	(E) PLAYING TO WIN	1978 ARISTA US 4205 UK ARTY 156			
JOE LALA	PERC (B	(F) IN THE EYE OF THE STORM	1979 ARISTA US AL 9507			
HARVEY ARNOLD	B V (CDEF	(G) GHOST RIDERS IN THE SKY	1981 ARISTA US 9542 UK SPART1160			
JOE VITALE	SYN STRING(C	(H) LOS HOMBERS MALO	1982 ARISTA US 9584 UK 204558			
MANUAL LABOUR	PERC (C					
DAVID DIX	D PERC(DEFGH	FREDDIE SALEM	G V(DEFGH RICK CUA	B V (GH	J D SOUTHER	V (A
CAROL BRISTOW	V (H	LU MOSS	V (H	GARY LYONS	K V (H	DAVE LANE	FDL (H

OUTSIDERS

ADRIAN BORLAND	G V (AB1	(A) CALLING ON YOUTH	1977 RAW EDGE RER 001
ADRIAN JANES	D V (AB1	(B) CLOSE UP	1978 RAW EDGE RER 003
BOB LAWRENCE	B (AB	(1) 1979	
GRAHAM GREEN	B (1		

OUTSIDERS (US)

TOM KING	G	(A) TIME WONT LET ME IN	19 CAPITOL US 2501
BILL BRUNO		(B) ALBUM 2	19 CAPITOL US 2568
MERDIN MADSEN	B G HCA	(C) IN	19 CAPITOL US 2636
SONNY GERACI	V	(D) HAPPENING LIVE	19 CAPITOL US 2745
RICKY BAKER	D		

OVARY LODGE

KEITH TIPPETT	K (AB	(A) OVARY LODGE	1973 RCA UK SF8372
JULIE TIPPETT	V (B	(B) OVARY LODGE	1976 OGUN OG 600
HARRY MILLER	B (B		
FRANK PERRY	V PERC(AB	ROY BABBINGTON	B (A

OZARK MOUNTAIN DAREDEVILS

JOHN DILLON	G V K(ABCDEFG	(A) OZARK MOUNTAIN DAREDEVILS	1973	A&M	US	4411	UK	AMLH64411
RANDLE CHOWNING G V HCA(ABCD		(B) IT'LL SHINE WHEN IT SHINES	1974	A&M	US	3654	UK	AMLH63654
STEVE CASH	HCA V(ABCDEFG	(B) CAR OVER THE LAKE ALBUM	1975	A&M	US	4549	UK	AMLH64549
BUDDY BRAYFIELD	K (ABCD	(D) MEN FROM EARTH	1976	A&M	US	4601	UK	AMLH64601
LARRY LEE	D G K(ABCDF	(E) DONT LOOK DOWN	1978	A&M	US	4662	UK	AMLH64662
MICHAEL GRANDA	B V (ABCDFG	(F) ITS ALIVE	1978	A&M	US	6006	UK	AMLH66006
NICK DE CARO	ACC (B	(G) OZARK MOUNTAIN DAREDEVILS	1980	CBS	US	36375	UK	84193
WELDON MYRICK	STEEL(C							

FARRELL MORRIS	PERC (C	JODY TROUTMAN	V	(B	NANCY BLAKE	CELLO	(C BILL JONES	WIND K V(CD
GLYN JOHNS	G (B	STEVE CANADY G D V		(D	JERRY MILLS	MAND (DF	RUNE WALLE	G (DFG
RUSSELL CHAPPELL	K V (F	CONNIE CANADAY	V	(D	BOBBYE HALL	PERC (D	STEVE KENNEDY	G (F
MIKE BOTTS	D (G	JOHN GOIN	G	(G	CLINTON THOMPSON	G (G	JAI WINDING	K (G
JOHN BOYLAN	G (G	PAUL GRUUP	PERC	(G	GARY COLEMAN	PERC (G	BUDDY EMMONS	STEEL(G
VANETTA FIELDS	V (G	ROSEMARY BUTLER	V	(G	PAULETTE BROWN	V (G	TOM KELLY	V (G

OZO

JOHN MIZEROLLO	G (AB	(A) LISTEN TO THE BUDDAH	1976	DJM US DJM 4	UK	20488
BETH KUSTRA	V (A	(B) MUSEUM OF THE WORLD	1978	DJM	UK	20517
VAL MACDONALD	D PERC (A					

VERNON CUMMINGS	PERC V(A	EDDIE DAVIES	K V	(A	MARTIN ABRAHAMS	G (A	FRANZ KOCK	WIND(A
TREVOR STEPHENS	B (A	HELEN DENISTON	V	(A	KIM WENDELS	V (A	DEREK MANDL	G (A
HUGH ASHTON	G (A	MICK WAYNE	G	(A	KATHY TONTO	V (B		

OZZ

ALEXIS T ANGEL	V (A	(A) NO PRISONERS	1980	CBS	36198
GREGG PARKER	G V (A				
DONNELL HAGAN	D (A	CRAIG GRUBER	B (A	WILLIE BASS	B (A MICHAEL CAVANAUGH K SYN(A

OZONE

(A) WALK ON	1980	MOTOWN	US 938
(B) JUMP ON IT	1981	MOTOWN	US 950
(C) NO PRISONERS	1980	EPIC	US 36198

P F M

FLAVIO PREMOLI	K V (ALL	(A) STORIA DI UN MINOTO	1972	NUMERO UNO		IT ZSLN55055
FRANZ DI CIOCCIO	D V (CDFGH	(B) PER UN AMICO	1972	NUMERO UNO		IT ZSLN55155
FRANCO MUSSIDA	G V (CFGHD	(C) PHOTO'S OF GHOSTS	1973	MANTICORE 2003 US 66668 UK KK43502
MAURO PAGANI FLT V VLN(CFHD		(D) WORLD BECAME THE WORLD	1974	MANTICORE US 66673	UK K53502
PATRIC DJIVAS	B (FHD	(E) COOK	1975	MANTICORE US 6502	UK K53506
BERNARDO LANZETTI G V (FH		(F) CHOCOLATE KINGS	1976	MANTICORE	UK	K53508
GIORGIO PIAZZA	B (CG	(F) CHOCOLATE KINGS	1976	NUMERO UNO	IT	55684
GREGORY BLOCH	VLN (G	(F) CHOCOLATE KINGS	1976	ASYLUM	US	7E1071
PETE SINFIELD	PROD (C	(G) MARCONI BAKERY	1976	PETERS INT		9014
CLAUDIO FABI	PROD (CE	(H) JET LAG	1977	MANTICORE	UK	K53511
		(H) JET LAG	1977	ASYLUM	US	7E1101
		(J) PASS PARTU	197	ZOO		34032
		(K) SUONARESUONARE	197	ZOO		34092
		(L) LIVE USA	197	NUMERO UNO		55676

P H D

(A) P H D	1981	WEA	UK K99150

P G R S

GEOFFREY STOCKER	K D (A	(A) PHOTOGRAPHS OF SOUND	1979	RISKYDISC	FUNC 1
PAUL RAMSAY	G D (A				
ROBIN WATTS G K PERC(A		SHANE JARVIS	K (A		

P.M.

CARL PALMER	D (A	(A) ONE P M	1980	ARIOLA	UK 5048 GER 201 659
TODD COCHRAN	K V (A				
BARRY FINNERTY	G V (A	JOHN NITZINGER	G V (A	ERIK SCOTT	B V (A

AUGUSTOS PABLO

AUGUSTOS PABLO	V K (ABC	(A) ITAL DUB	1975	TROJAN	TRLS 115
BAGGA	B (B	(B) EAST OF THE RIVER NILE	1978	MESSAGE	
ROBERT SHAKESPEARE B	(B	(C) ORIGINAL ROCKERS	1979	GREENSLEEVES	GREL 8
CARLTON BARRETT	D (B	(D) THRILLER	1981	ECHO	UK STLP1002
EARL 'CHINNA'SMITH G	(B				
NOEL BENBOW	G (B	C DOWNIE	B (B	MAX EDWARDS	D (B EVERTON DA SILVA PERC (B
ASTON BARRETT	B (B				

PABLO CRUISE

DAVE JENKINS	G B V(ABCDEF	(A) PABLO CRUISE	1975	A&M	US 4528	UK AMLH64528
CORY LERIOS	PNO (ABCDEF	(B) LIFE LINE	1976	A&M	US 4575	UK AMLH64575
STEPHEN PRICE	D PERC(ABCDEF	(C) A PLACE IN THE SUN	1977	A&M	US 4625	UK AMLH64625
BRUCE DAY	B V (E	(D) WORLDS AWAY	1978	A&M	US 4597	UK AMLH64697
BUD COCKRELL	B V (ABC	(E) PART OF THE GAME	1980	A&M	US 3712	UK AMLK63712
GENE MEROS	SAX (E	(F) REFLECTOR	1981	A&M	US 3726	UK AMLK63726
BOBBYE HALL	PERC (A					
MIKE PORCARO	B (E	VICTOR FELDMAN	PERC (E	DAVID FOSTER	SYN (E MICHAEL BODDICKER SYN(E
STEVE PORCARO	SYN (E	ANGELO ROSSI G V	(F	JOHN PIERCE	B V (F CAROLYN BRAND V (A
MIKE UTLEY	K (A	DAVID PAICH	STR (E		

TOM PACHECO

TOM PACHECO	(	(A) PACHECO & ALEXANDER	1971		
		(B) SWALLOWED UP IN AMERICAN HEARTLAND	1976	RCA	APLI 1254
		(C) THE OUTSIDER	1977	RCA	APLI 1887

PACIFIC DRIFT

LAWRENCE ARENDS D PERC V(A		(A) FEELIN' FREE	1970	NOVA UK SND13	US DECCA 18040
BARRY REYNOLDS	G V (A				
BRIAN SHAPMAN	K V (A	GRAHAM HARROP	B G (A	JACK LANCASTER	FLT (A DAVE DAVANI HRNS(A
SUE GLOVER	V (A	SUNNY LESLIE			

PACIFIC EARDRUM

DAVE MACRAE	K (AB	(A) PACIFIC EARDRUM	1977	CHARISMA	CAS1133
ISAAC GUILLORY	G (AB	(B) BEYOND PANIC	1978	CHARISMA	CAS1136
GEOFF SEOPARDIE	D (AB				
JOY YATES	V (AB	BILLY KRISTIAN	B (AB	BRIAN SMITH WIND PERC(B	JIM CUOMO SAX (A
MORRIS PERT	PERC (A	SIMON MORTON PERC	(B		

PACIFIC GAS & THE ELECTRIC

CHARLI ALLEN	V (ALL	(A) PACIFIC GAS & THE ELECTRIC	1969 CBS	US	9900	UK	63822
BRENT BLACK	B (AC	(B) GET IT ON	1969 KENT	UK	547	UK B&C CAS1003
FRANK COOK	D (AC	(B) GET IT ON	19 ORANGE US	701	METRONOME15379
TOM MARSHALL	G (AC	(C) ARE YOU READY	1970 CBS	US	1017	UK	64026
GLENN SCHWARTZ	G (AB	(D) P G & E (HARD BURN)	1971 CBS	US 30362	UK	64295
FREDDY HILL	TPT (AC	(E) P G & E WITH CHARLIE ALLEN	1973 DUNHILL US 157
BUD BRISBOIS	TPT (A	(F) BEST	1973 CBS	US 32019
WAYNE HENDERSON	TROM (A	(G) LIVE & KICKING AT LEXINGTON	187 CBS		UK	66264

ALLEN SCHWARZBERG	D (E									
WILTON FELDER	SAX (E	GORDON EDWARDS	B (E	JOHN HILL	K (E	BOB MANN	G (E
CHARLIE BROWN	G (E	JON STROLL	PNO (E	GEORGE YOUNG	SAX (E	ARTIE KAPLAN	SAX(E
JOE GRIMM	SAX (E	SELDON POWELL	SAX (E	MICHAEL BRECKER	SAX (E	PHIL BODNER	SAX(E
CORNELL DUPREE	G (E	ERNIE HAYES	K (E	LOU SOLOFF	HRNS (E	AL DE RISI	HRNS (E
BURT COLLINS	HRNS (E	MICKEY GRAVINE	HRNS (E	RAY ROLLARD	V (E	J R BAILEY	V (E
JIM MADEN	TAMB V (E	TASHA THOMAS	V (E	BARBARA MASSEY	V (E	CARL HALL	V (E
KENNY WILLIAMS	V (E	LOU COURTNEY	V (E	JERRY FRIEDMAN	G (E	SAMMY TURNER	V (E
SHERMAN LEWIS	V (E	TROY KEYES	V (E	BILL FOSTER	V (E	JON LUCAS	V (E
RON MARSHALL	V (E	LANI GROVES	V (E	GLORIA BARLEY	V (E	SHIRLEY BREWER	V (E
MANNY SEYMOUR	V (E	MELVIN KENT	V (E	JOHN BROWN	V (E	CHARLOTTE GILBERT	V (E
JAMES RYAN	V (E	DELORES HARVIN	V (E	ALBERTINE ROBERTSON	V (E	JOSHIE ARMSTEAD	V (E
VANETTA FIELDS	V (C	DELORES HALL	V (C	GINGER SCHACKNE	V (C	RUSTY YOUNG	G (C
SHERRILL ATWOOD	V (C	CLYDIE KING	V (C	LORNA WILLARD	V (C	MERRY CLAYTON	V (C
SHIRLEY MATTHEWS	V (C	ALFRED GALLEROS	SAX (D	KEN UTTERBACK	V (D	RON WOODS	SAX(D
JERRY AIELLO	K (D	JOE LALA	PERC (D	STANLEY ABERNATHY	TPT (D	FRANK PETRICCA	B (D
BLACKBERRIES	V (D						

CLEO PAGE

(A) LEAVING MISSISSIPPI   1979 JSP   UK 1003

THE PACK

JORG EVERS	G V (A	(A) THE PACK	1978 VINYL	GER	6 23450
DASHIEL DYNAMITE	D (A				
GERARD CARBONEL	B V (A				

PACKARDS

PAUL JOHNSON	G (A	(A) PRAY FOR SURF	19	SURFSIDE	001
CHRIS DARROW	B G (A				
JOHN RUSSELL	D (A				

GENE PAGE

GENE PAGE	BLACULA	197	RCA	US	LSP 4806
	HOT CITY	1975	ATLANTIC US 18111 UK	K50105
	LOVELOCK	1976	ATLANTIC US 18161 UK	K50221
	CLOSE ENCOUNTERS	1978	ARISTA	US	4174	SPART1052
	LOVE STARS AFTER DARK	1980	ARISTA	US	4262

JIMMY PAGE

JIMMY PAGE	G (A	(A) DONT SEND ME NO FLOWERS	1969 MARMALADE	UK 608004
SONNY BOY WILLIAMSON	V (A	(A) SONNY BOY WILLIAMSON	1975 SPRINGBOARD	4038
BRIAN AUGER	K (A	(A) JAM SESSION	1975 CHARLY	UK	CR 30011
JOE HARRIOT	SAX (A	(B) FACES & PLACES VOL 8	19 BYG FR	529 908
ALAN SKIDMORE	SAX (A			
MICK WALLER	D (A			

PAGES

RICHARD PAGE	V PNO(ABC	(A) PAGES	1978 EPIC US
JOHN LANG	LYRICS(C	(B) FUTURE STREET	1979 EPIC US 36209
NEIL STUBENHAUS	B (C	(C) PAGES	1981 CAPITOL US 12123

PAULINHO DACOSTA	PERC(C									
RALPH HUMPHREY	D (C	PAUL JACKSON	G (C	JAY GRAYDON	G (C	ABRAHAM LABORIEL	B (C
STEV GEORGE	V K SYN	STEVE KAHN	G (C	JEFF PORCARO	D (C	CHARLES JOHNSON	G (C
VINCE CALAIUTA	D (C	TOM SCOTT	SAX (C	MIKE BAIRD	D (C	AL JARREAU	V (C

PAGLIARO

(A) PAGLIARO   1972 PYE UK   NSPL 18380

PAICE ASHTON & LORD(PAL)

IAN PAICE	D (A	(A) MALICE IN WONDERLAND	1977 WB	JAPAN P10360	US BS3088
JON LORD	K (A	(A) MALICE IN WONDERLAND	1977 OYSTER UK 2391269 RI 80 2482485
TONY ASHTON	K V (A				
PAUL MARTINEZ	B (A	BERNIE MARSDEN	G (A	HOWIE CASEY	SAX (A	REG BROOKS	TROM (A
SHEILA McKINLEY	V (A	DAVE CASWELL	HRNS (A	GILBERT DALL'ENESE	SAX (A	JEANETTE McKINLEY	V (A

PAINTER

(A) PAINTER   1974 ELEKTRA   US 75071

RONNIE PAISLEY BAND

RONNIE PAISLEY	V (A	(A) SMOKING MIRROR	1979	PYE	UK	NSPL18582
ANDY BROWN	(A				
STEVE GREGORY	HRNS (A	JOHN MARK	(A	TONY HILL	(A	KIM HAKINSSON	(A
PETE KELLY	(A	DAVID PAISLEY	(A	ALAN PARK	(A	PETE PAVLI	(A
FRANK RICOTTI	PERC (A	JIM TOOMEY	(A	PAUL TURNER	(A	DIGGER DAVIES	(A
LADYBIRDS	V (A				

PAKALAMEREDITH

(A) PAKALAMEREDITH   1978 ELEKTRA   US 1106

PALACE FLOPHOUSE

CASPAR FALKE	G MAN(A	(A) BONTEBURG	1980 UNIVERSE	NL	DLS30
WILLY EBBES	D V (A				
ANDRE PASMAN	WIND (A	HENNY HEGMAN	PERC (A	HANS HEGMAN	G V (A	WOLF OVERKAMP	VLN G(A
ELINE HARBES	V (A	GERARD HEGMAN	B V(A	ERNST JAN WITKAP	FLT (A	

PALADIN

KEITH WEBB	D (AB1	(A) PALADIN	1971 BRONZE UK ILPS9150 US EPIC 31137
PETE SOLLEY	K V VLN (AB1	(B) CHARGE	1972	BRONZE	ILPS 9190
PETE BECKETT	B V (AB1	(1) 1972			
LOU STONEBRIDGE	K V (AB				
DEREK FOLEY	G V (AB	JOE JAMMER	G (1			

PALEY BROTHERS

```
ANDY PALEY        V G HCA(A      (A) PALEY BROTHERS          1978 SIRE US SRK6052 GER 200 161*
JONATHAN PALEY    G V  (A        * DIFF TRACKS
JEFF LASS         K    (A
ERIC ROSENFELD    G    (A   JAN UVENA       D   (A   LEIGH FOXX      B   (A   JIM HASLIP      B  (A
RAMONES           G B D(         PHIL JUSTICE    B   (    JEFF WILKINSON  D   (
```

BRUCE PALMER

```
BRUCE PALMER      G B   (A       (A) THE CYCLE IS COMPLETE   1971 VERVE FORCAST  US   vrf 3086
ED ROTH           K     (A
RICK MATTHEWS     PERC V(A   BIG BLACK       CONGA(A   PAUL LAGOS      D   (A   JEFF KAPLAN     K  (A
TEMPLETON PARCELY VLN   (A   RICHARD APLAN   WIND (A
```

ROBERT PALMER

```
ROBERT PALMER G B V K D (ALL     (A) SNEAKIN' SALLY THROUGH THE ALLEY 1974 ISLAND  UK   ILPS 9294
SPIDER WEBB       D     (C        (B) PRESSURE DROP              1975 ISLAND  UK   ILPS 9372
JEFF PORCARO      D     (C        (C) SOME PEOPLE CAN DO WHAT THEY LIKE 1976 ISLAND UK ILPS 9420
ALLEN SCHWARZBERG D     (D        (D) DOUBLE FUN                 1978 ISLAND  UK   ILPS 9476
KEITH BENSON      D     (D        (E) SECRETS                    1979 ISLAND  UK   ILPS 9544
CHRIS PARKER      D     (D        (F) CLUES                      1980 ISLAND  UK   ILPS 9595
MICHAEL DAWE      D     (G        (G) MAYBE IT'S ALIVE           1982 ISLAND  UK   ILPS 9665
RITCHIE HAYWARD   D     (BCD
ED GREENE         D     (B   FREDDIE HARRIS   G  (CD  CHUCK RAINEY   B  (C   BILL PAYNE      K V (BCD
SAM CLAYTON       PERC  (C   PAUL BARRERE     G V(BCD PIERRE BROCK   B  (CDE JAMES ALAN SMITH K  (CD
CHILI CHARLES     PERC  (C   CAROL KAYE       B  (C   JAMES JAMESON  B  (B   JEAN ROUSSEL    K  (B
JODY LINSCOTT     CONGA(C   FREDDIE WALL     G  (C   KEN GRADNEY    B  (B   LOUIS JOHN DAVIS K  (D
ROBERT GREENRIDGE PERC (CD  LOWELL GEORGE    G  (B   BOB BABITT     B  (D   STEVE ROBBINS   K  (DE
LENNY CASTRO      PERC (D   JAMES MAHONEY    G  (D   JIMMY WILLIAMS B  (D   RON KERSEY      K  (D
DAVID SNELL       HARP (B   DONOVAN McKITTY  G  (D   ANDY FRASER    B  (F   EDWARD PUTMON   K  (D
DONY WYNN         D    (EFG NEIL HUBBARD     G  (D   PAUL GARDINER  B  (F   GARY NUMAN      K  (F
GREG CARROLL      HCA  (D   T J TINDALL      G  (D   RANDY BRECKER  HRNS(D  WILLIAM SMITH   K  (C
CHRIS FRANTZ      PER  (F   ALAN MANSFIELD   G  (FG  MICHAEL BRECKER HRNS(B JACK WALDMAN    K  (EF
STEVE YORK        HCA  (B   KENNY MAZUR      G  (EFG MEL COLLINS    SAX (B   ART SMITH  OCARINA (C
BRIAN RUSSELL     V    (B   BRENDA RUSSELL   V  (D   MARTIN FRY     TUBA(B   RAY ALLEN       HRNS(B
FRAN TATE         V    (B   VICKI BROWN      V  (B   MONGEZI FEZA   HRNS(B   MUSCLE SHOALS   HRNS(B
GORDON DEWITTE    K    (B   JOE BROWN        BANJO(B CHRIS BISHOP   B  (G   JACK WALDMAN    K  (G
GARY NUMAN        K    (G   ADRIAN BELEW     G  (G   DANNY WILDE    G B(G
```

PAN

```
RON ELLIOTT          (A       (A) PAN                       1973 CBS         US    32062
KEITH BARBOUR     V  (A
JIM HASKELL       K SYN(A   ARTHUR RICHARDS STEEL G V(A DON FRANCISCO D PERC V(A GABRIEL MEKLER K(A
SHERMAN HAYES     B V  (A   VAL GARAY       G V    (A SANDRA KROUCH  TAMB (A BOBBYE HALL    PERC(A
```

PANAMA

```
                    PANAMA                              1978 PETERS      US    9023
```

PANAMA FRANCIS BLUES BAND

```
                           (A) TOUGH TALK             196  STATESIDE    SL 10070
```

PANAMA LIMITED JUG BAND

```
DENNIS PARKER        (A       (A) PANAMA LIMITED JUG BAND  1969 HARVEST  UK   SHVL 753
LIZ HANNS            (A       (B) INDIAN SUMMER            1970 HARVEST  UK   SHVL 779
BRIAN STRACHAN       (A
GARY COMPTON         (A   RON NEEDS       (A
```

PANDEMONIUM

```
JEAN BAPTISTE BARRIERE SYN(AB  (A) VILLE OUVERTE          1979 ATEM         7003
JEAN MARIE BARRIERE  SYN(AB    (B) NON JAMAIS L'ESPERANCE 1979 ATEM         7004
```

PANTHER

```
KLAUS SCULZ       G V  (A      (A) WIR WOLLEN ALLES       1974 PANTHER  GER  2667
GERT LANGE        G V  (A
OLAF LIETZEN      D    (A   KLAUS AHRENS G B V(A  GREGOR AHRENS    D   (A
```

PANIC

```
REINHARD ROFFEL   D    (A      (A) 13                      1978 ARIOLA   NL    26388
PETER PENTHOUSE   V    (A
MIKE DECOURT      G V  (A   PETE PASSION     B V  (A
```

PANIC SQUAD

```
NORMAN NORMAL     G V  (A      (A) PANIC SQUAD    EP       1980 WHIRLED  US NOno
ANDY GRAY         G V  (A
LONIE LONIE       D    (A   MICHAEL MAXWELL  B  (A BILLY GOOD   G K  (A  JIMMIE O'BRIEN  G  (A
```

JOHN PANTRY

```
JOHN PANTRY       K V(ABC      (A) EMPTY HANDED            19 KINGSWAY     UK DOVE 56
TONY COE          WIND (C      (B) NOTHING IS IMPOSSIBLE   19 KINGSWAY     UK KMR 303
BARRY DE SOUZA    D    (C      (C) HOT COALS               19 MARSHALLS    MRT 1003
BILL ELDRIDGE     TPT  (C
RONNIE GOODMAN    PERC (C   GEORGE HALL   SYN (C  TIM HARRIES    B  (C  'FRESH AIR'     V  (C
DAVE MARTIN       G    (C   ROB McKAY     SAX (C  BRUCE NOCKLES  TPT(C  CHRIS NORTON    K  (C
RAY WEHRSTEIN     SAX  (C
```

PAPA NEBO

```
MICHAEL PACKER    G V  (A      (A) PAPA NEBO               197 ATLANTIC  US  SD 8280
BRENDAN HARKIN    G V  (A
SANDY ALLEN       B V  (A   SAL COSTANZO     K  (A ALL LEATHERS  VLN(A BOB MINTZER   WIND (A
KEN ADAMS         D    (A
```

FELIX PAPPALARDI

```
FELIX PAPPALARDI  B V K(A      (A) FELIX PAPPALARDI & CREATION 1976 A&M US 4586 UK AMLH64586
ERIC GALE         G    (B      (B) DONT WORRY MUM?         1979 A&M US 4729 UK AMLH64729
PAUL BUTTERFIELD  HCA  (A
RALPH MOSS        PERC (C   SHIGERU MATSUMOTO B  (A KAZUO TAKEDA  G  (A YOSHIAKI IIJIMA G  (A
MASAYUKI HIGUCHI  D    (A   RICHARD TEE      K  (B CHUCK RAINEY  B  (B BERNARD PURDIE  D  (B
```

JOHANNES 'ALTO' PAPPERT

```
JOHANNES PAPPERT  SAX G(AB     (A) ALTO                    1978 SPIEGELEI GER 160609 JOJO NL19002
ALLEN MEIER       V    (AB
WOLFGANG GRASEKAMP K   (A   HELMUT HATTLER   B  (A GEORG KOCKBECK K V(B MICKI STICKDORN G V (AB
PETER WOLFBRANDT  G BAN(A   ANDY GOLDNER     G V(A LOU MARIGNAN  B(A HEINZ GENBUS    B  (B
JAN FRIDE         D PERC(A   BERND KIEFER     B  (A ZABBA LINDNER  D(A
```

PARADISE EXPRESS

VI ANN	V	(A	(A) PARADISE EXPRESS		1979	FANTASY	US 9574 UK	FT557
HERB JIMMERSON	K	(A	(B) LETS FLY		1980	FANTASY	US 9589	
SHARON HYMES	V	(A						
KENNETH ELLIOTT	D	(A	DAVID PRUITT	G (A	DAVID FRAZIER	PERC (A	ROMEO WILLIAMS	B (A
BRIAN CABANAS	D	(A	FRED BERRY	HRNS (A	AL BENT	HRNS (A	CHARLES McCARTHY	HRNS(A
MARTHA WASH	V	(A	IZORA RHODES	V (A				

PARAFFIN JACK FLASH LTD

(A) MOVERS & GROOVERS	1968 PYE	NSPL18252

PARAGONS

SLY DUNBAR	(A	(A) SLY & ROBBIE MEETS THE PARAGONS	1981 ISLAND UK ILPS 9632
ROBBIE SHAKESPEARE	(A		

PARAMOUNTS

GARY BROOKER	V K	(A12	(A) PARAMOUNTS 'EP)	196	PARLOPHONE GEP8908
B J WILSON	D	(A12	(A) 1962 (2) 1963/66		
ROBIN TROWER	G	(A12			
CHRIS COPPING	B	(1	DIZ DERRICK	B (A2	

PARASITES OF THE WESTERN WORLD

PATRICK BURKE V B G K SYN(A		(A) SUBSTRATA		1980 MATCHBOX US MB 1004
TERRY CENSKY K V G B D HRN(A				
MIKE AUDRY	D	(A	MIKEY CASCADDEN	G V (A

PARIS

HUNT SALES	D V(B	(A) PARIS		1976 CAPITOL UK/US 11464
ROBERT WELCH	G V (AB	(B) BIG TOWNE 2061		1976 CAPITOL UK/US 11560 GER 85010
GLEN CORNICK	K B (AB			
BERNIE MARSDEN	G (	THOM MOONEY	D (A	

PARISH HALL

GARY WAGNER	G PNO V (A	(A) PARISH HALL	1970 LIBERTY UK LBS83374
STEVE ADAMS	D (A	(A) PARISH HALL	1970 FANTASY US 8398
JOHN HADEN	B (A		

DENNIS PARKER

DENNIS PARKER	V	(A	(A) LIKE AN EAGLE		1979	MERCURY UK 9109 622	
RUSSELL DABNEY	D	(A					
ALFONSO CAREY	B V	(A	JIMMI LEE	G (A	RODGER LEE	G (A	BARRY FINNERTY G (A
TOM POLITE	K	(A	NATHANIEL WILKIE	K (A	RICHARD TRIFAN	SYN (A	PHIL HURTT V (A
MILT GREGSON	V	(A	FRANK FLOYD	V (A	ARTHUR WILLIAMS	V (A	TONY WELLS V (A
LENNY ROBERTS	V	(A	MARTY NELSON	V (A			

GRAHAM PARKER & THE RUMOUR

GRAHAM PARKER	V G (ALL	(A) HOWLIN' WIND	1976	MERCURY	US SRM1 1095
STEVE GOULDING	PERC (ABCDEFGH	(A) " "	1976	VERTIGO	UK 6360 129
BRINSLEY SCHWARZ	G (ABCDEFGH	(B) HEAT TREATMENT	1976	MERCURY	US SRM1 1117
ANDREW BODNAR	D B (ABCDEFGH	(B) " "	1976	VERTIGO	UK 6360 137
MARTIN BELMONT	G (ABCDEFGH	(C) AT MARBLE ARCH	1976	VERTIGO	UK GP1
BOB ANDREWS	K (ABCDEFG	(D) STICK TO ME	1977	MERCURY	US SRM1 3706
STEWART LYNAS	SAX (A	(D) STICK TO ME	1977	VERTIGO	UK 9102 017
HERSCHEL HOLDER	TPT (A	(E) PARKERILLA DBL	1978	MERCURY	US SRM 2100
DAVE CONNERS	SAX (A	(E) PARKERILLA DBL	1978	VERTIGO	UK 6641 797
DANNY ELLIS	TROM (AB	(F) SQUEEZING OUT SPARKS	1979	VERTIGO UK 9102030 GER 6360 168	
JOHN EARLE	SAX (ABE	(G) BEST OF	1980	VERTIGO	UK 9102 042
ALBE DONNELLY	SAX (B	(H) THE UP ESCALATOR	1980	STIFF UK SEEZ23 GER 6 24355	
ROBERT JOHN LANGE	PROD (B	(H) UP THE ESCALATOR	1980	ARISTA US 9517	
DAVE EDMUNDS	G (A	(J) ANOTHER GREY AREA	1982	RCA LP6027	
NICK LOWE	PROD (ABD	(EP) PINK PARKER	1977	VERTIGO	UK PARK 001
NOEL BROWN	G (A	(EP) PINK PARKER	1977	MERCURY	US 6831 040
DICK HANSON	TPT (BED				
ED DEAN	G (A	CHRIS GOWER	TROM (ED	RAY BEAVIS	SAX (E NICKY HOPKINS K (HJ
DANNY FEDERICI	K (H	PETER WOOD	SYN (H	JIMMY MAELEM	PERC (H BRUCE SPRINGSTEEN V(H
JOHN EARLE	SAX (D	JOHN ALTMAN	SAX (D	DARRYL LEEQUE	PERC (D HUGH McCRACKEN G (J
DAVID BROWN	G (J	DOUG STEGMEYER	B (J	MICHAEL BROWN	D (J KURT McGETTRICK WIND(J
GEORGE SMALL	K (J	JIM CLOUSE	SAX (J	PAUL PRESTOPINO	BAN (J JACK DOUGLAS PERC(J
KRYSTAL DAVIS	V (J	KAREN LAWRENCE	V (J	ERIC TROYER	V (J FRED HOSTETLER V (J

JUNIOR PARKER

JUNIOR PARKER	HCA V(ALL	DRIVING	19	DUKE	US DLP 76
MATT MURPHY	G (	BLUES CONSOLIDATED	19	DUKE	US
PAT HARE	G (	BEST OF	19	DUKE	US DLP 83
JOHN BOWERS	D (	JUNIOR PARKER	1974	BLUESWAY	US 6066
KENNETH BANKS	B (	OUTSIDE MAN	19	CAPITOL	US ST 564
JAMES WHEELER	SAX (	LIKE IT IS	19	MERCURY	UK SMCL20097
BILL JOHNSON	PNO (	BLUE SHADOWS FALLING	1972	GROOVE MERCHANT	GM 502
RAYMOND HILL	SAX (	(X) GOOD THINGS DONT HAPPEN EVERYDAY	1972	GROOVE MERCHANT	GM2205
HOUSTON STOKES	D (	YOU DONT HAVE TO BE BLACK	1973	PEOPLE	PLEO 4
IKE TURNER	PNO (	LOVE AIN' NOTHIN' BUT BUSINESS	1974	PEOPLE	PLEO18
JIMMY McGRIFF	ORG (X	BLUES FOR MR CRUMP (APPEARED ON)	1974	POLYDOR	UK 2383 257
AL SMITH	B (	BLUESMAN	19	MINIT	US 24024
OTIS JACKSON	B (	BAREFOOT	1975	DU	US
L C DRANES	D (	(EP) JUNIOR PARKER(LOVE MY BABY)	1976	CHARLY	UK CEP 104
FLOYD MURPHY	G (	LEGENDARY SUN PERFORMERS(1 SIDE)	1978	CHARLY	UK CR 30135
JIM STEWART	TPT (	DUDES DOIN	19	CAPITOL	US 569
JOE FRITZ	SAX (	I TELL STORIES	1972	UA US 6823	
JIMMY JOHNSON	SAX (	100% PROOF	19	UA US 6814	
RAY FIELDS	SAX (	BABY PLEASE	19	WING 16401	
JOE SCOTT	TPT (	HONEYDRIPPER	19	BLUE ROCK US 64004	
DALE McJOWN	PNO (				
HAMP SIMMONS	B (	BILL HARVEY SAX (	PLUMA DAVIS	TROM(SONNY FREEMAN D (	

RAY PARKER JR

```
RAY PARKER JR   V G B K PROD(A      (A) THE OTHER WOMAN           1982 ARISTA      GER  204 673
CHARLES GREEN       WIND (A
MICHAEL BODDICKER SYN (A   ANITA SHERMAN     V  (A   J D NICHOLAS      V  (A   LYNN SMITH  V  (A
OLLIE BROWN     PERC (A   LARRY TOLBERT     D  (A   AMELL CARMICHAEL  V  (A   JERRY KNIGHT    V (A
```

ROBERT PARKER

```
ROBERT PARKER     V   (ALL      (A) BAREFOOTIN'          1966 ISLAND        UK    ILP942
                                (B) BAREFOOTIN'          196  NOLA          US    LP1001
                                (EP) BAREFOOTIN'         1980 CHARLY        UK    CTD123
```

VAN DYKE PARKS

```
VAN DYKE PARKS    V  (ALL      (A) SONG CYCLE           1968 WB              US  WS 1727
HUGH BORDE           (C        (B) DISCOVER AMERICA     1972 WB NL26043 GER 46166 US  2589
MALCOLM CECIL        (C        (C) CLANG OF YANKEE REAPER 1975 WB UK K56161 US  BS 2878
CHILLI CHARLES    D  (C
JESSE ED DAVIS    G  (C   HOLLIS DURITY      (C   ROBERT GREENIDGE    (C   FRED TACKETT    G  (C
JIM KELTNER       D  (C   KLAUS VOORMANN  B  (C   BOBBY KEYS     SAX  (C   NOBLE WILLIAMS     (C
GARVIN ADAMS         (B   MURRAY ADLER       (B   LAURINDO ALMEIDA    (B   JOHN AUDINO        (B
ISRAEL BAKER         (B   JOHN BERGAMO       (B   CHARLES BERGHOFER   (B   ROGER BOBO         (B
NORM BOTNICK         (B   GARY COLEMAN       (B   BONNIE DOUGLAS      (B   JESSE EHRLICH      (B
KAREN ERVIN          (B   ROY ESTRADA        (B   GEORGE FIELDS       (B   LOWELL GEORGE   G  (B
ANNE GOODMAN         (B   JIM GORDON     D   (B   RICHIE HAYWARD      (B   KENRICK HEADLEY    (B
MILT HOLLAND    PERC (B   KIRBY JOHNSON      (B   JERRY KESSLER       (B   MYRA KESTENBAUM    (B
GAYLE LEVANT         (B   LEW McCREARY   HRN (B   AL McKIBBON         (B   MALCOLM McNAB      (B
GORDON MARRON        (B   JAY MIGLIORI       (B   BUELL NEIDLINGER    (B   DAN NEUFELD        (B
JEFFREY REYNOLDS     (B   TOM SCOTT    WIND  (B   FREDERICK SCYKORA   (B   PAUL SHURE         (B
DENNIS SMITH         (B   TONY TERRAN        (B   ESSO TRINIDAD STEELBAND (B
```

PARLIAMENT

```
GEORGE CLINTON    V  (ALL      (A) OSMUIM               1970 INVICTUS           US  7302
CALVIN SIMON      V  (BCE      (B) UP FOR THE DOWN STROKE 1974 CASABLANCA UK CAL2011 US 7002
FUZZY HASKINS     V  (BCE      (C) CHOCOLATE CITY       1975 CASABLANCA UK CAL2012 US 7014
RAYMOND DAVIS     V  (BCE      (D) MOTHERSHIP CONNECTION 1976 CASABLANCA UK CAL2013 US 7022
GRADY THOMAS      V  (BCDE     (E) CLONES OF DR FUNKENSTEIN 1976 CASABLANCA UK CAL2001 US 7034
GARRY SHIDER      V  (BCE      (F) GET DOWN & BOOGIE    197  CASABLANCA            US 7042
EDDIE HAZAL     G V  (BCE      (G) LIVE (DBL)           1977 CASABLANCA UK CALD5002 US 7053
MICHAEL HAMPTON  G V (E        (H) FUNKENSTEIN VsTHE PLACEBO SYNDROME 1977 CASABLANCA UK CALN2021 US 7084
GLEN COLLINS    G V  (E        (J) MOTOR BOOTY AFFAIR   1978 CASABLANCA UK CALH2044 US 7125
WILLIAM NELSON    G  (B        (K) GLORY HALLASTOOPID   1980 CASABLANCA UK/US 7195
BERNIE WORRELL    K  (E        (L) TROMBIPULATION       1981 CASABLANCA UK/US 7294
JEROME BRAILEY    D  (E
BOOTSY COLLINS  B D G(BCE GARY COOPER     D  (E   PRAKASH JOHN      B  (C   RON BYKOWSKI    G  (B
GARY BRONSON      D  (B   TIKI FULWOOD    D  (BC  FRED WESLEY    HRNS  (C   MACEO PARKER  HRNS(E
RICK GARDNER    HRNS (E   MICHAEL BRECKER HRNS(E  RANDY BRECKER  HRNS  (E   CORDELL MOSSON   B(BC
PETER CHASE     WHISTLE(B
```

PARLOUR BAND

```
PETER FILLEUL   K V  (A        (A) IS A FRIEND          1972 DERAM         UK    SDL10
PIX               G  (A
CRAIG ANDERS      G  (A   MARK ASHLEY   G  (A   JERRY ROBBINS     D PERC(A
```

PARRISH & GURVITZ

```
BRIAN PARRISH   G V  (A        (A) PARRISH & GURVITZ    1971 REGAL ZONOPHONE SRZA8506
PAUL GURVITZ    G V  (A
MIKE KELLIE       D  (A
```

BRIAN PARRISH

```
BRIAN PARRISH   G V  (A        (A) LOVE ON MY MIND      1976 BARN          UK 2314 101
BRIAN CHATTON     K  (A
PETER VAN HOOKE   D  (A   JEROME RIMSON   A  PETE WHITFIELD    K  (A
```

ALAN PARSONS PROJECT

```
ALAN PARSONS    K V  (ALL      (A) TALES OF MYSTERY & IMAGINATION 1976 CHARISMA CDS 4003 US 20CENT 339
B J COLE       STEEL(ABD       (B) I ROBOT             1977 ARISTA  US 7002   UK SPARTY1012
STUART TOSH       D  (ABD       (C) PYRAMID             1978 ARISTA  US 4180   UK SPART 1054
IAN BAIRNSON      G  (ABCDEF    (D) EVE                 1979 ARISTA  US 9504   UK SPART1100
DAVID PATON     V B G(ABCDEF    (E) TURN OF A FRIENDLY CARD 1980 ARISTA  US 9518   UK DLART   1
STEVE HARLEY     V   (BD        (F) EYE OF THE SKY      1982 ARISTA  US 9599   UK      3484
JOHN PERRY       V   (B
ALLAN CLARKE     V   (BD   ERIC WOOLFSON    K(BCDE   COLIN BLUNSTONE  V  (CF  JACK HARRIS     V  (BCD
DUNCAN MACKAY    K   (BCD  LENNY ZAKATEK    V(BCDEF  DEAN FORD        V  (C   STUART ELLIOTT  D  (BCDEF
JOE PUERTA       B   (A    DARRYL RUNSWICK  B  (A    BURLEIGH DRUMMOND D  (A   DAVID PACK      G  (A
ARTHUR BROWN     V   (A    CHRIS RAINBOW    V  (EDF  ELMER GANTRY     V  (EF  MUNICH CHAM OPERA ORCH(E
JOHN LEACH       (B        LESLIE DUNCAN    V  (D    CLARE TORRY      V  (D   DAVE TOWNSEND   V  (BD
PETER STRAKER    V   (BD   JAKI WHITREN     V  (BD   HILLARY WESTON   V  (B   TONY RIVERS     V  (B
SMOKEY PARSON    V   (B    STUART CALVER    V  (B    ORCH & CHORUS       (B   MEL COLLINS SAX (F
```

GENE PARSONS

```
GENE PARSONS V G B D(A         (A) KINDLING            1974 WB US    2687  UK  K46257
RED CALLENDER   TUBA (A         (B) MELODIES            1979 SIERRA        US     8703
CLARENCE WHITE  G MAND(A
VASSAR CLEMENTS FDL (A    GIB GUILBEAU     FDL (A    ROGER BUSH        B (A
RALPH STANLEY   SAX (A    BILL PYNE        SYN (A    NICK DECARO       ACC (A   ANDY NEWMARK    D  (A
```

GRAM PARSONS

```
GRAM PARSONS    G V  (ALL      (A) G P                 1973 REPRISE US MS 2123 UK K44228
GEORGE WRIGLEY  BAN G(D         (B) GRIEVOUS ANGEL      1974 REPRISE US MS 2171 UK   K54018
PAUL SURRATT    G BAND         (C) SLEEPLESS NIGHTS(BURRITO BROS) 1976 A&M   US   4578 UK AMLH64578
JOE KELLY      V B  (D         (D) EARLY YEARS         1979 SIERRA  US    8702 ARIOLA200750
LEWIS MORFORD    V  (A         (E) & THE FALLEN ANGELS 1982 SIERRA  US    1973
MITCH WRIGLEY    V  (A         (*) GRAM PARSONS        197  SHILOH  US    4088
TOM BAHLER       V  (A         ( ) GRAM PARSONS        1982 WB             UK   K57008
RON HICKLIN      V  (A         ( ) LIVE 1973           1982 REPERTOIRE     UK 6 25106
KYLE TULLIS      B  (E         (*) RI OF INTERNATIONAL SUBMARINE BANDS SAFE OF HOME'
JOCK BARTLEY     B  (E
GLEN D HARDIN    K  (ABC NEIL FLANZ      STEEL(E  RICK GRECH       B  (ABC N D SMART      D  (BE
HERB PEDERSEN    G  (BC  BERNIE LEADON  G V  (BC  JAMES BURTON     G  (ABC AL PERKINS    STEEL (ABC
```

(CONTINUED)

GRAM PARSONS (CONTINUED)

```
BYRON BERLINE    FDL  (ABC STEVE SNYDER    VIBES(B  LINDA RONSTADT   V   (B  CHRIS HILLMAN   B  (C
SNEAKY PETE      STEEL(C  MICHAEL CLARKE   D   (C  EMORY GORDY      B   (BC RONNIE TUTT     D  (ABC
EMMYLOU HARRIS   V (ABCE  JOHN CONRAD      B   (A  JOHN GUERIN      D   (A  SAM GOLDSTEIN   D  (A
BARRY TASHIAN    G V  (A  BUDDY EMMONS     STEEL(A ALAN MUNDE       BANJO(A  HAL BATTISTE   SAX (A
```

PASSAGE

```
JOEY McKECHNIE        (B       (A) PINDROP           1980 OBJECT    UK      OBJO11
ANDREW WILSON         (B       (B) FOR ALL & NONE    1981 VIRGIN    UK      3200
DICK WITTS            (B       (EP) NEW LOVE SONGS   19   OBJECT            OM   02
TERESA SHAW           (B       (EP) ABOUT TIME       19   OBJECT            OM   08
```

PASSIONS

```
BARBARA GOGAN    G V  (12AB    (A) MICHAEL & MIRANDA      1980 FICTION FIXO03 2383573 NL 2442184
DAVID AGAR       B    (2B      (B) 30000 FEET OVER CHINA  1981 POLYDOR 2383 616 POLS1041
CLIVE TIMPERLEY G K V VLN(12AB (1) 1978  (2) 1981
RICHARD WILLIAMS D    (12A
CLAIRE BIDWELL   B    (1A PETE WILSON    PROD (B  NIGEL GRAY    PROD (B
```

ANDY PARTRIDGE

```
ANDY PARTRIDGE        (A       (A) THE LURE OF SALVAGE  1980 VIRAN  UK   2145
```

PARZIVAL

```
LOTHAR SIEMS     G V  (AB      (A) LEGEND     1971 TELDEC  GER  14635
WALTER QUINTUS   B K VLN(AB     (B) BA-ROCK    19   TELDEC  GER  14685
THOMAS OLIVER    D    (AB
MATTHIAS MULLER-MENCKENS K(A JOACHIM REICHOLD  CELLO(A HANS JASPER   VLA (A   WALTER V SEYDLITZ    CELLO(B
MAT McMILLER     K    (B     HARALD KONIETZKO  B V (B
```

NIK PASCAL

```
NIK PASCAL       D SYN(ABC     (A) BEYOND THE END......ETERNITY  1971 NARCO   NR 102
GYPSY FLEMING    ORG  (        (B) SIXTH EAR                     1972 NARCO   NR 666
                               (C) MAGNETIC WEB                  1973 NARCO   NR 321
```

PASSPORT

```
KLAUS DOLDINGER  SAX K(ALL     (A) PASSPORT              1971 ATLANTIC            40299
OLAF KUBLER      WIND (A        (B) SECOND                1972 ATLANTIC            40417
LOTHAR MEID      B    (A        (C) HAND MADE             1973 ATLANTIC            40483
JIMMY JACKSON    ORG  (A        (D) LOOKING THRU          1973 ATLANTIC US  7042  UK K50024
UDO LINDENBERG   D    (A        (E) DOLDINGER JUBILEE(TRIPLE) 1973 ATLANTIC        60073
JOHN MEALING     K    (B        (F) DOLDINGER             1973 ATLANTIC        UK K44243
BRYAN SPRING     D    (B        (G) DOLDINGER JUBILEE CONCERT 1974 ATLANTIC       50070
FRANK ROBERTS    K    (C        (H) CROSS COLLATERAL      1975 ATLANTIC US 36107  50111
VOLKER KRIEGER   G    (G        (J) DOLDINGER JUBILEE 75  1975 ATLANTIC US 18162  50186
ALEXIS KORNER    G    (G        (K) INFINITY MACHINE      1976 ATLANTIC US 36132  UK K50354
BRIAN AUGER      K    (G        (L) IGUACU                1977 ATLANTIC US 36149
WOLFGANG SCHMID  B G  (BCDEGHK  (M) SKY BLUE              1978 ATLANTI  US 19177
CURT CRESS       D    (CDGHKL   (N) ATARAXIA              1978 ATLANTIC        UK K50456
KRISTIAN SCHULTZE K  (DGHK      (O) GARDEN OF EDEN        1979 ATLANTIC US 19233  UK K50586
WILLY KETZER     D    (MONO     (P) OCEANLINER            1980 ATLANTIC US 19265  50688
HENDRIK SCHAPER  K    (MOPN     (Q) LIFELIKE              1980 ATLANTIC        NL 60150
PEDRO SANTOS     PERC (L
ELMER LOUIS      PERC (MNL DIETER PETEREIT  B (MNOP  ROY LOUIS       G  (LMN GUILLERNO MARCHENA V PERC(MN
KEVIN MULLIGAN   G V  (OP  HORST RAMTHOR    HCA (O   KATHY BARTNEY   V  (O  DAVID CRIGGER   D    (P
MATS BJORKLIND   G    (L   JOHNNY GRIFFIN   SAX (G   PETE YORK       G  (G
```

JACO PASTORIUS

```
JACO PASTORIUS   B    (AB       (A) JACO PASTORIUS  1976 EPIC      US 33949  UK 81453
DON ALIAS        CONGA(A         (B) JACO           1978 IMPRO ARTS         IAI373846
DAVE PRATER      V    (A         (C) WORD OF MOUTH  1981 WB UK K 56897      US  3535
RANDY BRECKER    HRNS (A
RON TOOLEY       TPT  (A  PETER GRAVES     TROM (A  DAVID SANBORN   SAX (A  MICHAEL BRECKER  HRNS (A
HOWARD JOHNSON   SAX  (A  HERBIE HANCOCK   K    (A  NARADA MICHAEL WALDEN D (A  SAM MOORE       V  (A
ALEX DAROU       K    (A  LENNY WHITE      D    (A  BOBBY ECONOMOU  D   (A  STRING SECTION     (A
WAYNE SHORTER    SAX  (A  OTHELLO MOLINEAUX PERC (A LEROY WILLIAMS  PERC (A PETER GORDON     HRNS (A
HUBERT LAWS      WIND (A  PAUL BLEY             (B
```

PATAPHONE

```
ANDRE VIAUD      G    (AB       (A) PATAPHONE      19   POLE            003
GILLES ROUSSEAU  D    (AB       LE MATIN BLANC     1978 FEERI           178
PIERRE DEMOURON  B K  (A
```

BRIAN PATTEN

```
BRIAN PATTEN     V    (ABC      (A) BRIAN PATTEN      1970 CAEDMON          TC 1300
ROGER McGOUGH    V    (C        (B) VANISHING TRICK   1971 TANGENT          TGS 116
LINDA THOMPSON   V    (B        (C) PATTEN & McGOUGH  1976 ARGO             ZLP 1190
CLEO LAINE       V    (D        (D) THE SLY CORMORANT 1977 ARGO        UK   ZSW607
DAVE RICHARDS,   B    (B
GERRY CONWAY     D    (B  JOHN TAYLOR      K    (B  NEIL INNES      K   (B  JONNO DELMAR    G  (B
RICHARD THOMPSON G    (B  NORMA WINSTONE   V    (B  ANDY ROBERTS    G   (B  ALAN DALZIEL    CELLO(B
PHIL LEE         G    (B  STAN SULZMANN    FLT  (B  BRIAN GASCOIGNE K   (D  CATHY WEISS     VLN(D
SUKI TOWB        CELLO(D  DAVID LAWRENCE   CLAR (D  JOHN WILLIAMS   G   (D  DAVID VORHAUS   SYN (D
```

BOBBY PATTERSON

```
BOBBY PATTERSON  V    (AB       (A) ITS JUST A MATTER OF TIME     1972 PAULA   US   LPS 2215
                                (B) SHE DONT HAVE TO SEE YOU(EP)  1980 CHARLY       CTD  112
```

PATTO

```
MIKE PATTO       V    (ABC      (A) PATTO           1970 VERTIGO VEL 1001 +  6360 016
OLLIE HALSALL    G K V(ABC      (B) HOLD YOUR FIRE  1971 VERTIGO VEL 1008    6360 032
CLIVE GRIFFITHS  B    (ABC      (C) ROLL EM SMOKE EM 1972 ISLAND UK ILPS9210 US  9322
JOHN HALSEY      D    (ABC
```

HENRY PAUL BAND

```
HENRY PAUL       G V  (ABC      (A) GREY GHOST      1979 ATLANTIC US 19232
BILLY CRAIN      G    (ABC      (B) FEEL THE HEAT   1980 ATLANTIC US 19273
DAVID FIESTER    G V  (ABC      (C) ANYTIME         1981 ATLANTIC US 19325
WALLY DENTZ      B    (ABC
BILL HOFFMAN     D    (ABC BARRY RAPP      K V (ABC JAI WINDING    K  (C  MONTE YOHO      D  (AB
JOE LALA         PERC (B   JOE VITLAE      SYN (B   JON MATHIES    SYN (B  JIM FISH        V  (B
VALERIE WILSON   V    (B
```

BILLY PAUL

BILLY PAUL	V	(ALL	(A) WAR OF THE GODS	1973 PHILADELPHIA	US 32409
NORMAN FARRINGTON	D(A		(B) 360 DEGREES OF	1973 PHILADELPHIA	UK 65930
ANTHONY JACKSON	B	(A	(C) WHEN LOVE IS NEW	1976 PHILADELPHIA	UK 69202
EDDIE GREEN	K	(A	(D) ONLY THE STRONG SURVIVE	1977 PHILADELPHIA	UK 82236
			(E) FIRST CLASS	1979 PHILADELPHIA	UK 83481
			(F) GREATEST HITS	1980 PHILADELPHIA	UK 84169

P38   LES PAUL   P38

LES PAUL	G	(ALL	NEW SOUND	10 INCH	195	CAPITOL	226
MARY FORD	V	(	NEW SOUND VOL2	10 INCH	195	CAPITOL	286
CHET ATKINS	G	(*	BYE BYE BLUES	10 INCH	195	CAPITOL	356
			HIT MAKERS		19	CAPITOL	416
			LES & MARY		19	CAPITOL	577
			TIME TO DREAM		19	CAPITOL	802
			LOVER		19	CAPITOL	1276
			HITS OF LES & MARY		19	CAPITOL	1476
			LES PAUL & MARY FORD		1965	HARMONY	US 11133
			LES PAUL NOW		1968	DECCA	UK LK 4924 + PFS 4138
			LES PAUL NOW		1968	LONDON US	SP44101
			VERY BEST OF		1974	CAPITOL	23321
			LES & MARY		19	PICKWICK	3122
			TIGER RAG		19	PICKWICK	3145
			STORY VOL 1		1974	CAPITOL EURO	052 81050
			STORY VOL 2		1974	CAPITOL EURI	052 81359
			WORLD IS WAITING FOR THE SUNRISE		1974	CAPITOL US	11308
			LES & MARY		1975	CAPITOL	11308
			GUIAR TAPESTRY		19	PROJECT 3	US6-19/20
			(*) GUITAR MONSTERS		1978	RCA	PL 12786
			(*) CHESTER & LESTER		1977	RCA	LSA 3290
			MULTI TRACKIN		1979	LONDON US	50016

P39   PAUPER   P39

SKIP PROKOP	D V G(AB	(A) MAGIC PEOPLE	1967 VERVE	US 3026
ADAM MITCHELL	G K V D(AB	(B) ELLIS ISLAND	1968 VERVE	US 3051
CHUCK BEAL	G MAND (AB			
DENNY GERRARD	B	(A	BRAD CAMPBELL	G B D V(B	AL KOOPER	K (B

P40   PAVLOVS DOG   P40

DAVID SURKAMP	G V	(AB	(A) PAMPERED MENIAL	1975 CBS US 33552	UK 80872
DOUG RAYBURN	FLT B K	(AB	(B) THE SOUND OF THE BELL	1976 CBS US 33694	UK 81163
STEVE SCORFINA	G	(AB			
DAVID HAMILTON	K	(AB	RICHARD STOCKTON B (AB	TOM NICKESON	G V (B	MIKE SAFRON	D (A
SIEGFRIED CARVER	VLN	(A	BILL BRUFORD D (B	MIKE ABEBE	ORG (A	MICHAEL BRECKER	SAX(B
GEORGE GENCH	ORG	(A	ANDY MACKAY SAX (B	LES NICOL	G (B	PAUL PRESTOPINO	MAND(B
ELLIOTT RANDALL	G B	(B	GAVIN WRIGHT VLN (B	MURRAY KRUGMAN	PROD (A	SANDY PEARLMAN	PROD(A

P41   TOM PAXTON   P41

TOM PAXTON	G V	(ALL	(A) RAMBLIN BOY	1964 ELEKTRA US EKS 7277	UK K42003
JACK BONUS	WIND	(E	(B) AIN'T THAT NEWS	1965 ELEKTRA US EKS 7289	UK K42005
ALBERT BOUCHARD	D	(E	(C) OUTWARD BOUND	1966 ELEKTRA US EKS 7317	UK K42007
DAVID BROMBERG	G	(EF	(D) MORNING AGAIN	1968 ELEKTRA US EKS74019	UK K42019
HERB BUSHLER	B	(EFO	(E) THINGS I NOTICE NOW	1969 ELEKTRA US EKS74043	UK K42028
JOHNNY COLES	HRNS	(E	(F) NUMBER 6	1970 ELEKTRA US EKS74066	UK K42047
RICHARD GRAND	WIND	(E	(G) THE COMPLEAT TOM PAXTON	1971 ELEKTRA US 7E 2003	UK K62004
DAVID HOROWITZ	K	(EFH	(H) HOW COME THE SUN	1971 REPRISE US RS 6443	UK K44129
HUBERT LAWS	FLT	(E	(J) PEACE WILL COME	1972 REPRISE US RS 2096	UK K44182
JIMMY MADISON	D	(E	(K) NEW SONGS OLD FRIENDS	1973 REPRISE US RS 2144	UK K44237
MAX POLLIKOFF	VLN	(E	(L) CHILDRENS SONG BOOK	1974 BRADLEYS	UK BRADN601
ROBERT SYLVESTER	CELLO(E		(M) SOMETHING IN MY LIFE	1975 MAM	UK MAM 1002
STEVE GOODMAN	G V	(O	(M) SOMETHING IN MY LIFE	1975 PRIVATE STOCK	US 2002
ANGEL ALLENDE	V	(O	(N) SATURDAY NIGHT	1976 MAM	UK MAMS1003
IAN HUNT	G	(M	(O) NEW SONGS FROM THE BRIAR PATCH	1977 MAM	UK MAMS1005
DAVE WILLIS	B	(KMH	(O) NEW SONGS FROM THE BRIAR PATCH	1977 VANGUARD	US VSD79395
PETER WOOD	K	(M	(P) HEROES	1978 VANGUARD	VSD79411
BARRY DE SOUZA	D	(M	(Q) UP & UP	1980 MOUNTAIN RAILWAY US 52792	
BARRY KORNFIELD	BAN G(A		(Q) UP & UP	1980 EVOLUTION	UK E2
FELIX PAPPALARDI	G	(A			
CHRIS KARAN	PERC (KM	NANCY LEE BAXTER V (P	KENNETH KOSEK VLN (P	ERIC WEISSBERG G MAND (P
GARY CHESTER	D	(P	PETER SARSTEDT V (K	RALPH McTELL G V HCA (K	GARY MURE D (P
TONY VISCONTI	G	(K	MARY VISCONTI V (K	RAYMOND MANTILLA PERC (P	JENNIFER PAXTON V (K
DANNY THOMPSON	B	(K	PAUL PRESTOPINO G (F	TEDDY SOMMER D (F	MARK HOROWITZ G BAN (H
MIKE MORGAN	G	(H	JULIAN CUMMINGS VLN (H	BRIAN ODGERS B (H	SUE EVANS D (H
CHRIS SLADE	D	(H	DIANA CUMMINGS VLN (H	HARRY PITCH HCA (H	LUCIANO JORIO VLN (H
DOUGLAS CUMMINGS	CELLO(H	KATY PAXTON V (K	MIKE BRITTAIN B (H	CHRIS LAURENCE B (H
JEFF CLYNE	B	(H			

P41A   PAYOLAS   P41A

PAUL HYDE	G V K(	(A) IN A PLACE LIKE THIS	1981 A&M UK 70017
BOB ROOK	G V K(		
GARY MIDDLECLASS B K (		TAYLOR NELSON LITTLE D V K(	

P42   JOHN PAYNE   P42

JOHN PAYNE	(AB	(A) BEDTIME STORIES	19 ARISTA	AL 1025
		(B) RAZOR'S EDGE	1977 ARISTA	AL 1036

P42A   PAZ   P42A

BRIAN SMITH	FLT	(A	(A) KANDEEN LOVE SONG	1977 SPOTLIGHT	SPJ 507
GEOFF CASTLE	K	(A			
PHIL LEE	G	(A	RON MATTHEWSON B (A	DICK CROUCH PERC (A	DAVE SHEEN D (A
SIMON MORTON	PERC (A	RAY WARLEIGH FLT (A	CHRIS FLETCHER CONGA(A		

DAVE PEABODY

```
DAVE PEABODY      G HCA(AB        (A) PEABODY HOTEL           1973 VILLAGE THING    VTS 22
HUGH McNULTY      B  (B           (B) KEEP IT CLEAN           1974 MATCHBOX         SDM 261
BILL SHORTT       WASHB(B
DAVE GRIFFITHS    MAND (B   DIZ WATSON     K  (B   IAN A ANDERSON   G  (B   ANDY LEGGETT    JUG(B
```

DAVE PEACE

```
DAVE PEACE        K V (A          (A) GOOD MORNING            1969 saga            FID  2155
MICK WALSH        D  (A
DAVE 'LILLY' LLOYD G (A   DAVE PEGG    B  (A
```

PEACHES & HERB

```
FRANCINE'PEACHES'HURD  V(ALL      (A) LETS FALL IN LOVE       1967 CBS UK  62966   US DATE  4004
HERB FAME         V  (ALL         (B) FOR YOUR LOVE           1967 CBS UK  63119   US DATE  4005
PETE ROBINSON     K SYN(FG         (C) GOLDEN DUETS            19   DATE            US  TES 4007
FREDDIE PERREN PNO VIBES(FG        ( ) GREATEST HITS           1968 DATE            US      4017
JOHN BARNES       K SYN(E          (D) PEACHES & HERB          1977 MCA UK MCF2802  US      2261
EDDIE WATKINS     B  (FG           (E) 2 HOT                   1979 POLYDOR US 1 6172 UK  2391  378
JAMES GADSON      D  (FGE          (F) TWICE THE FIRE          1979 POLYDOR US 1 6239 UK  2391  433
BOB BOWLES        G  (EFG          (G) WORTH THE WAIT          1980 POLYDOR         UK  2391  484
DAVID T WALKER    G  (E            (H) LOVE IS STRANGE         1979 CBS     US 36089
WAH WAH WATSON    G  (FEG
PAULINHO DA COSTA PERC (EFG  BOB ZIMITTI  PERC  (FEG CLARENCE McDONALD  K (G  JOSE FELICIANO  G (G
EDDIE BROWN       CONGA(G   KATIE KIRKPATRICK HARP (G  GARY HERBIG    SAX (G  MAXINE WILLARD  V (G
JULIA TILLMAN     V  (G     LUTHER WATERS     K  (G  OREN WATERS    V (G  LARRY FARROW    K (E
BOB RABATAILLE    SYN (E
```

ANNETTE PEACOCK

```
ANNETTE PEACOCK  V K SYN(ALL       (A) BLEY/PEACOCK SYNTHESIZER SHOW  1971 POLYDOR         2425 043
MICK RONSON       G  (E            (B) I'M THE ONE             1972 RCA     US LSP 4578 UK  SF 8255
BILL BRUFORD      D  (E            (C) IMPROVISE               1973 AMERICA         FR     6121
GEORGE KHAN       SAX (E            (D) DUAL UNITY              1973 FREEDOM UK 40109 GERM 2383 105
DAVE CHAMBERS     HRNS (E           (E) X DREAMS                1978 AURA  UK AUL702 US TOMATO 7025
TOM COSGROVE      G  (ABE           (F) PERFECT DREAMS PERFECT RELEASE 1979 AURA  UK AUL707 US TOMATO 7044
STEVE HAAS        D  (A             (G) SKY SKATING             1982 IRONIC UK IRON2
JEFF CLYNE        B  (E             (1) 1974 TOUR (NO ALBUM)
CHRIS SPEDDING    G  (E
SAM PHIPPS        SAX (1   ROBBIE SCHWIMMER  K  (1   PETE LA ROCCA   D  (1   PAUL BLEY    K (ABCD
STU WOODS         B  (ABE RICK MAROTTA     D  (ABE MICHAEL GARSON  K  (AB   GLEN MOORE   B (AB
LAURENCE COOK     D  (ABD MICHAEL MOSS     SAX (B   BARRY ALTSCHUL D PERC (AB  AIRTO MOREIRA PERC(B
ORESTES VILATO    PERC (B   DOMIUN ROMAO     PERC (B   APACHE BLEY     PNO (B   RICHARD YOUNGSTEIN B(A
BOB MASSON        K  (A   PERRY ROBINSON   CLAR (A   MARK WHITECAGE  SAX (A   HAN BENNINK  PERC(CD
MARIO PAVONE      B  (D   JIM MULLEN       G  (E   BRIAN GODDING   G  (E   PHIL LEE     G (E
KUMA HARADA       B  (E   PETER PAVLI      B  (E   STEVE COOK      B  (E   JOHN HALSEY  D (E
DAVE SHEEN        D  (E   DARRYL LE QUE    PERC (EF  BROTHER JAMES   PERC (E   RAY WARLIEGH SAX (E
PETER LEMER       K  (E   MAX MIDDLETON    K  (F   ROBERT AHWAI    G  (F   RICHARD BAILEY D (F
JOHN MacKENZIE    B  (F   LENNOX LANGTON   PERC (F   A R FOX         V (G
```

PEANUT BUTTER CONSPIRACY

```
JIM VOIGHT        D  (AB           (A) IS SPREADING           1968 CBS             US      9454
AL BRACKETT       B  (AB           (B) GREAT CONSPIRACY        1968 CBS             US      9590
LANCE FENT        G  (AB           (C) FOR CHILDREN OF ALL AGES 196  CHALLENGE   *  US      2000
JOHN MERRILL      G  (AB
SANDI ROBINSON    V  (AB  BILL WOLF     G HCA (AB
```

BOB PEARCE BLUES BAND

```
BOB PEARCE G V HCA(ALL             (1) BLUES CRUSADE  (EP)     1968  AVENUE         BEV 1054
BOB GORMAN        G V (1           (2) LET'S GET DRUNK AGAIN(SOLO) 1974 WESTWOOD     WRS  040
ROGER CHANTLER    D  (1            (3) COLOUR BLIND           1979  FOREST TRACKS   FT 3015
PETE HARRIS       G V K(4Za        (4)I'M A BLUEMAN   (EP)     1981 WHITE ELEPHANT  UK RIOCH 2
PAUL PRY          G V(NOPQRSTUVWXY3 (5) NEW ALBUM              1983  ?
KEVIN FRANCIS     B V (1
DANNY KELLY       D  (C      (A)    68/FEB 69   (B) FEB 69/JUL 70  (C) JUL 70/OCT 70  (D) OCT 70/NOV 70
GLENN'JUDGE'LEE D(ACDEFGHJKLMVWX   (E) NOV 70/NOV 71 (F) NOV 71/FEB 72 (G) FEB 72/OCT 74 (H) OCT 74/NOV 74
TONY BURNETT      D  (NO           (J) NOV 74/DEC 74 (K) DEC 74/FEB 75 (L) FEB 75/NOV 75 (M) NOV 75/APR 76
JOHN PICKEN       D  (PQ           (N) APR 76/JUL 76 (O) JUL 76/AUG 76 (P) AUG 76/OCT 76 (Q) OCT 76/NOV 76
CHRIS NEWMAN      D  (R            (R) NOV 76/JUL 77 (S) JUL 77/AUG 77 (T) AUG 77/SEP 77 (U) SEP 77/JAN 78
BARRY FREEMAN     D  (ST           (V) JAN 78/JUL 78 (W) JUL 78/DEC 78 (X) DEC 78/FEB 79 (Y) FEB 79/MAY 80
HENRY WRIGHT      D  (UY34Zab      (Z) MAY 80/MAY 81 (a) MAY 81/MAY 82 (b) MAY 82/SEPT 82 (c) SEPT82/JAN 83
BIG JOHN McATEE   B  (CD
BOB WILLIAMS      B  (H   PETE 'BALDY' WARD B(MNOPQR  ERNEST FAGG     B  (ST  KEN WHEELER B  (UVW
JOSS JONES        B  (XY34Z CHRIS GODDEN    G  (F   MICK WILLIAMS   G  (H   DEREK GARDENER  G (J
DOUG WALKER       G  (K   VERNON CHUTER    G  (MNOP JOHN MARSHALL   SAX (O   LEE GOODALL SAX (N
PAPA JOHN LIVERMORE GK(3BY  DAVE 'DOMINO'WARD HCA(TUV  JOHN CARTWRIGHT  B  (*   PETE HUNT      D (*
CARL'SONNY'LEYLAND PNO(4Zabc PETE PLASCOTT    B  (abc
MIKE STEEL        G  (bc  DANNY KELLY      D  (c   (*) INVALUABLE ASSISTANCE THROUGH THE YEARS
```

PEARL

```
DEBBIE PEARL      V  (A            (A) PEARL                  1977 LONDON US 692   UK  SHU 8508
LESLIE PEARL      V  (A
DEAN PARKS        G  (A   RUSS KUNKEL      D  (A   MARK LEVINE     B  (A
```

PEARL HARBOUR

```
PEARL E GATES   V PERC (AB         (A) AND THE EXPLOSIONS      1980 WB  US BSK 3404 UK    K56769
PETER BILT        G V (A           (B) DON'T FOLLOW ME, I'M LOST TOO 1980 WB  US BSK 3515 UK    K56885
HILARY STENCH     B V (A
JOHN STENCH       D  (A
```

PEARLS BEFORE SWINE

```
TOM RAPP          G V (ALL         (A) ONE NATION UNDERGROUND  1967 ESP US 1054    NL 858115
WAYNE HARLEY      BAN V(ABC        (B) BALAKLAVA               1968 ESP            US      1075
LANE LEDERER  B G HRNS V(AB        (C) THESE THINGS TOO        1969 REPRISE        RSLP 6364
ROGER CRISSINGER  K  (A            (D) THE USE OF ASHES        1970 REPRISE        RSLP 6405
WARREN SMITH      D  (A            (E) CITY OF GOLD            1971 REPRISE        RSLP 6442
JIM BOHANNON      K  (B            (F) BEAUTIFUL LIES YOU COULD LIVE 1971 REPRISE  RSLP 6467
RICHARD ALDERSON  PROD(A           (AB) BEST OF(DBL)?          1980 ADELPHI        US      4111
JOE FARRELL       WIND (B
LU CRABTREE       K FLT(B   BILL SALTER      B  (BC  AL SHACKMAN     G  (B   DAVID NOYES   V (E
ELIZABETH         V  (CDEF RICHARD GREENE   VLN  (C   MORRIE E BROWN  B  (F   GRADY TATE    D (C
```

                                  (CONTINUED)

[429]

(CONTINUED)   PEARLS BEFORE SWINE

```
    GORDON HAYES       B    (F   MICHAEL KRAWITZ    PNO  (F   BILLY MUNDI        D    (F   BOB DOROUGH        PNO(F
    STU SCHARF         G    (F   AMOS GARRETT       G    (F   HERB LOVELL        D    (F   JOHN DUKE          WIND(D
    JERRY JEMMOTT      B    (F   CHARLIE McCOY    V G B HCA(D  BUDDY SPICHER      VLN  (D   HUTCH DAVIE        WIND(D
    NORBERT PUTNAM     B    (D   BILL PIPPIN        WIND (D   KEN BUTTREY        D    (D   MAC GAYDEN         G    (D
    DAVID BRIGGS       K    (D   JOHN TOOKER        G    (F   JIM FAIRS        G V K(C   STEVE GRABLE       K    (F
```
KEITH PEARSON

```
    KEITH PEARSON    G V BAN(A        (A) RIGHT HAND BAND                 1976    ERON                    014
    PAUL CRASWELL      B V  (A
    DAVE CRASWELL  G V PERC(A  DAVE ARBUS       VLN SAX V  (A
```
PEDDLER

```
    KENNY WEIR       G V PERC(        (A) STREETCORNER STUFF              1976    UA              US   LA665G
    RUSSELLL TAYLOR    D V  (A
    BO GOOLIAK     B G K V(A  JOHN CASCELLA    K SAX(A  RANDY STIERER    K SYN(A
```
HERB PEDERSEN

```
    HERB PEDERSEN      V    (AB       (A) SOUTHWEST                       1976    EPIC            US      34225
    CHRIS SMITH        G    (A        (B) SANDMAN                         1977    EPIC            US      34933
    ED CARTER          (A
    JIM GORDON         D    (A   JOHN GUERIN       D    (A   LARRY CARLTON      G    (A   JOSH GRAVES DOBRO    (A
    AL PERKINS         G    (A   MIKE BAIRD        D    (A   ROY DEAN WEBB      MAND (A   DAVID LINDLEY        (A
    GARY COLEMAN       PERC (A   EMMYLOU HARRIS    V    (A   LEE SKLAR         B    (AB   LINDA RONSTADT    V  (AB
    DOLLY PARTON       V    (B   LOWELL GEORGE     G    (B   JOEY SCARBURY      (B   JOHNNY RIVERS        (AB
```
PEE WEE & SPECIALS

```
                                     PEE WEE & SPECIALS                  1980 ROCKHOUSE         NL    8004
```
ANN PEEBLES

```
    ANN PEEBLES        V    (ALL      (A) THIS IS                        1969 HI     US 32053
    HOWARD GRIMES      D    (DF       (B) PART TIME LOVE                 1971 HI     US 32059
    LEROY HODGES       B    (DF       (C) STRAIGHT FROM THE HEART        1972 HI     US 32065 UK LONDON SHU8434
    CHARLES HODGES     K    (DF       (D) CANT STAND THE RAIN            1974 HI     US 32079 UK LONDON SHU8468
    ED LOGAN           SAX  (DF       (E) TELLIN' IT                     1976 HI     US 32091 UK LONDON SHU8490
    WAYNE JACKSON      TPT  (DF       (F) STAR PORTRAIT                  1977 CREAM US 58100        GER 6002
    JAMES DROY         D    (F        (G) IF THIS IS HEAVEN              1978 HI     US  6002
    JAMES MITCHELL     SAX  (B        (H) HANDWRITING IS ON THE WALL     197  HI     US  6007
    TEENIE HODGES      G    (DF       (J) STRAIGHT                       1970 HI     US  8009
    ANDREW LOVE        SAX  (DF
    JACK HALE          TROM (DF  ARCHIE TURNER     K    (DF  BEN CAULEY        TPT  (F   EDGAR MATTOUS      TPT(F
    BILL EASLEY        SAX  (F   DONNA RHODES      V    (F   SANDRA RHODES/CHALMERS V(F
```
KEVIN PEEK

```
    KEVIN PEEK         G    (A        (A) AWAKENING                      1982 ARIOLA      UK      5065
                                      (B) LIFE & OTHER GAMES             1982 ARIOLA      UK      5067
```
DAVID PEEL   & LOWER EAST SIDE

```
    DAVID PEEL         V G  (ALL      (A) HAVE A MARIJUANA               1968 ELEKTRA              US EKS74032
    HAROLD C BLACK     V TAMB(ABHI    (B) AMERICAN REVOLUTION            1970 ELEKTRA UK 2410 001 US EKS74069
    LARRY ADAM         G    (A        (C) THE POPE SMOKES DOPE           1972 APPLE             US  SW 3391
    TONY BARTOLI       D    (B        (D) SANTA CLAUS ROOFTOP JUNKIE     1974 RLF 001    RI 79 ORANGE    711
    BILLY JOE WHITE    G    (AB       (E) AN EVENING WITH                1976 ORANGE           US ORA 713
    GEORGE CORI        B  . (A        (F) BRING BACK THE BEATLES         1977 ORANGE           US     004
    CHRIS OSBORNE      (C        (G) KING OF PUNK                   1978 ORANGE           US     700
    EDDIE MOTTAU       (C        (H) JOHN LENNON FOR PRESIDENT       1980 ORANGE           US     005
    EDDIE RYAN         (C        (I) DEATH TO DISCO                 1980 ORANGE           US     666
    HERB BUSHLER       B    (B
    DAVID HOROWITZ     ORG  (B   RICHARD GRANDO    SAX  (B   LES FRADKIN  G K B V(DFI  PAUL THORTON     G V PERC(DF
    MICHAEL ANGELO   G V  (DF  ANDY FRIEDMAN     D PERC(D  GRIMES            TPT(D   RON SKOLER     V    (D
    MARK SHATASKY      V    (D   A J WEBERMAN      V    (D   JEFF GILLMAN      G (F   ANDY PIERCE      G    (FI
    TOM DOYLE      B V G (FGHI  MIKE MURRAY       B    (D   FRED KRAMER       D  (F   SCOTT BAILEY     D V (F
    SAL SPICOLLA       SAX  (F   DEREK LIPMAN      PERC (F   DANNY LIPMAN      PERC(F   TOMMY ACOSTA     V    (G
    RON BLOTTER        V    (G   CHRIS BOVASSO   G V  (G   EDDIE CRISS       G    (GHI BOB DELIA      V    (G
    AL DONNELLY        V    (G   STEVE GIORDANO    B    (G   BARRY GUBER       G    (G   SHANE HARRIS     V    (G
    RICHARD HOFFMAN    V    (G   GREG LANNER       G    (G   PHYLISS LEE    PERC V  (GHI MARUGA        D V    (GI
    JOHN MICHAELS      PERC (G   PETE MONTANO      PERC (G   PAT RAMPEY      G V  (G   DAVID A SCHURE  G V (G
    HANK SHUSTER     G V  (G   NICK TRIP         V    (G   PEPE VALENTINE  PERC G V(GH  PAUL S WEISS    PERC V(G
    DAVID YIFRACH      G    (G   MITCH BLOTTER  PERC V K (HI  MARGOT DAY       FLT  (H   GARY DORFMAN     V    (HI
    BILL DOWNING     V PERC(HI  CURTIS FIELDS   PERC SAX(HI  MARK TRUTHE     TAMB V  (H   B B GUN         PERC(H
    JOHN HAGEL         G    (H   ANDY LLOYD        CONGA(HI  YOKO ONO        PERC V(H   ED PERPER        V    (H
    GABRIEL REXACH     V B  (HI  STEVE ROSENTHAL  V K  (HI  NAGED ABELL       V G  (H   FLOYD AVERY FLEMING PERC(H
    JOE BOZZA          PERC (H   ADELE EVANS     G V  (H   BOB GURTLRT       V    (H   ISHMAEL        G V    (H
    YES LEVY         G V  (H   HANK NUESSLEIN    V TAMB(H   DONNA SCHALL      V K  (H   JOHN STASIC     V PERC(HI
    WAYNE KRAMER       G    (I   TERRY MANN        B    (ISACHA NELSON       FLT  (I   CLANCEY MORALES  PERC(I
    DAVID GALE         B    (I   TOM DE GENNO      G    (I   ADELE KRAUS       V    (I   SHEENA MITCHELL  V    (I
    STEVE BENJAMIN     G    (I   HANK WYATT      G V  (I   SCOTT SEVERIN     V    (I   EDDIE RHODES     V    (I
    GARY SCHWARTZ      PERC (I   MICHAEL SUBRIZI   PERC (I   RIK CHEN YOUNG    V    (I   JOEY BELL       G    (I
    MIKE GIRAO         G    (I   ROB BASSO         G    (I   STEVE VICTIM      B    (I   PHIL LOONEY     K    (I
    RODIE KAISER       TPT  (I   FRANKY CADILLAC   B    (I   G G ALLIN         G    (I   ALAN CHAPPLE    G    (I
```
BOB PEGG

```
    BOB PEGG         G V WIND(ABC      (A) BOB PEGG & NICK STRUTT         1973    TRANSATLANTIC      TRA 265
    NICK STRUTT      G MAND(AB      (B) SHIPBUILDER                   1974    TRANSATLANTIC      TRA 280
    STEVE SIMPSON    G VLN(B       (C) ANCIENT MAPS                  1975    TRANSATLANTIC      TRA 299
    RICHIE BULL        B    (B
    DAVE HAMMEL        D    (B   CHRIS TAYLOR  RECORDER(C   RICHARD McNICOL RECORDER  (C ADRIAN BRETT RECORDER(C
    ROGER BRENNER SACKBUT  (C   MALCOLM FISHER SACKBUT (C   JOHN EDNEY        SACKBUT(C DAVID PURSER SACKBUT (C
    TONY COE           CLAR (C   DAVID CROPPER     HRNS (C   MIKE LAIRD      CORNETTO (C IAN WILSON    CORNETTO(C
    BILL STOKES   CORNETTO (C   RAY WARLEIGH      FLT  (C   PAUL HARVEY        CLAR (C NORMAN WEBB      HARP(C
    BRENT FORBES       B    (C   GRAHAM FIELD      K    (C   HAROLD FISHER     D   (C  RICK RUSSELL     G    (C
    B J COLE           STEEL(A   MICK YARROW            (B
```
BOB & CAROLANNE PEGG

```
    BOB PEGG         G V WIND(A       (A) HE CAME FROM THE MOUNTAIN       1971 TRAILER            UK   LER 3016
    CAROLANNE PEGG     V    (A
```

```
    CAROLANNE PEGG    V    (A        (A) CAROLANNE PEGG                    1973 TRANSATLANTIC    UK    TRA 266
    ALBERT LEE        G K  (A
    KEITH NELSON      BANJO(A   MICHAEL LAVELLE  CELLO(A   ALUN EDEN      D   (A   PAUL ROWAN       HCA(A
    DAVE PEACOCK      B G  (A
```

```
    JIM PEMBROKE           (ABC       (A) WICKED IVORY                      19
    RONNIE OSTERBERG  D    (C         (B) PIGWORM                           1974    LOVE  SWED
    REKKU RECHARDT    G    (C         (C) CORPORAL CAULIFLOWERS MENTAL FUNCTION  1977
    CASTE APRETREA    G    (C
    PAAVO MAIJANEN    B V  (C    EERO KOIVISTOINEN    HRNS(C HESSU HIETANEN ACC (C
```

```
    TEDDY PRENDERGRASS V   (ALL       (A) TEDDY PRENDERGRASS                1977 P I R UK 81756
    VICTOR CARSTARPHON K   (A         (B) LIFE IS A SONG WORTH SINGING      1978 P I R UK 82555
    DEXTER WANSEL     K    (AD        (C) TEDDY                             1979 P I R UK 83656
    ROLAND CHAMBERS   G    (AD        (D) T P                               1980 P I R UK 84542
    DENNIS HARRIS     G    (AD        (E) READY FOR TEDDY                   1981 P I R UK 84903
    MICHAEL FOREMAN   B    (A         (F) ITS TIME FOR LOVE                 1981 P I R UK 85220
    JAMES WILLIAMS    B    (ADF       (G) THIS ONES FOR YOU                 1982 P I R UK 85937
    KEITH BENSEN      D    (AD
    KARL CHAMBERS     D    (A    LARRY WASHINGTON CONGA(A   M F S B HRNS STR      (AF  VALERIE SIMPSON  K V (D
    ERIC GALE         G    (D    BARBARA INGRAM    V    (D   FRANCISCO CENTENO B   (D  CHRIS PARKER     D  (D
    RALPH MACDONALD   PERC(D    NICKOLAS ASHFORD  V    (D   STEPHANIE MILLS   V   (D  CECIL WOMACK     G  (D
    THE FUTURES       V    (D    SAM REED          SAX  (F   LENNY PAKULA     ORG   (F  JAMES CARTER     D  (F
    LEON HUFF         K    (F    KENNETH GAMBLE    V    (F
```

```
    ALVARO PENA ROJAS K V B FLT(A     (A) DRINKING MY OWN SPERM             197  SQUEAKY SHOE          SSRDR 1
    ANTONIO NARVAEZ   D V  (A
    CATHY WILLIAMS    V    (A
```

```
    PAULINE MURRAY    V    (ABC       (A) MOVING TARGETS                    1978 VIRGIN UK  V 2109 GER 200170
    FRED PURSER       G K  (ABC       (B) DANGER SIGNS      (EP)            1979 VIRGIN UK  V25712
    GARY SMALLMAN     D    (ABC       (C) COMING UP FOR AIR                 1979 VIRGIN UK  V 2131 GER 200 964
    NEALE FLOYD       G    (ABC       (D) RACE AGAINST TIME(OFFICIAL BOOT)  1980 CLIFDAYN
    ROBERT BLAMIRE    B    (ABC
    STEVE JACOBS      D    (
```

```
    CLEVELAND DUNCAN  V    (          (A) COOL COOL PENGUINS                19   DOOTONE           US   DTE 242
    DEXTER TISBY      V    (
    CURTIS WILLIAMS   V    (    BRUCE TATE       V    (    RANDY JONES      V   ( TEDDY HARPER    V  (
```

```
    ROBB LEVIN        B    (ABC       (A) I LOVE YOU                        1968 CAPITOL        US    2924
    DENNY FRIDKIN     D    (ABC       (B) BOTH SIDE OF PEOPLE               1968 CAPITOL        US    151
    ALBERT RIBISI     ORG  (ABC       (C) THERE ARE PEOPLE                  19   PARAMOUNT      US    5013
    JOHN TRISTAO      V    (ABC
    TOM TUCKER        G V  (C    GENE MASON       V    (AB LAWRENCE        V   (AB JEFF LEVIN  G    (AB
```

```
    CHARLIE WATTS     D    (A         (A) PEOPLE BAND                       1970 TRANSATLANTIC    UK  TRA 214
    MEL DAVIS         (A
    TERRY DAY         (A    LYN DOBSON        (A   EDDIE EDEM         (A   GEORGE KHAN      (A
    TONY EDWARDS      (A    MICK FIGGIS       (A   FRANK FLOWERS      (A   TERRY TALMAN     (A
    RUSS HERNEY       (A
```

```
    FRANKIE BRUSON    K V  (AB        (A) BOOGIE DOWN U S A                 1975 PIR  UK 69175
    DAVID THOMDSON    PERC (AB        (B) WE GOT THE RHYTHM                 1976 PIR  UK 81370
    ROGER ANDREWS     B    (AB
    GUY FISKE         G    (AB BOBBY ELI       G    (A   NORMAN HARRIS    G   (A   VICTOR CARSTARPHEN ORG(AB
    ZACK ZACHERY      SAX  (A   M F S B         HRNS (A   DONALD FORD      K   (B   DARNELL JORDON     G  (B
    LEON HUFF         V SYN(B   JOHN WHITEHEAD  V    (B   GENE McFADDEN    V   (B   SAM PEAKE        SAX (B
```

```
    BERT JANSCH       G V  (ALL       (A) THE PENTANGLE            1968 TRANSATLANTIC UK TRA162 US REPRISE 6315
    JACQUI McSHEE     V    (ALL       (B) SWEET CHILD      (DBL)   1968 TRANSATLANTIC UK TRA178 US REPRISE 6334
    TERRY COX         D PERC(ALL      (C) BASKET OF LIGHT          1969 TRANSATLANTIC UK TRA205 US REPRISE 6372
    JOHN RENBOURNE G V SITAR(ALL      (C) BASKET OF LIGHT          1969 METRONOME     GER 201 051
    DANNY THOMPSON    B    (ALL       (D) CRUEL SISTER             1970 TRANSATLANTIC UK TRA228 GER 44005
                                      (D) RUEL SISTER              197  XTRA          UK  1172 REPRISE US   6430
                                      (E) REFLECTIONS              1971 TRANSATLANTIC UK TRA240 US REPRISE 6463
                                      (F) SOLOMONS SEAL            1972 REPRISE       UK K44197      US    2100
                                      (G) HISTORY BOOK    (COMP)   1972 TRANSATLANTIC UK TRASAM23
                                      (H) PENTANGLING             1973 TRANSATLANTIC UK TRASAM29 RI 81 TRS 106
                                      (J) PENTANGLE COLLECTION(COMP 1975 TRANSATLANTIC UK 89503/4
                                      (K) ANTHOLOGY      (COMP)    1978 TRANSATLANTIC UK MTRA 2013
```

```
    JIM PEPPER        V SAX D(A       (A) PEPPERS POW WOW                   1971 ATLANTIC       UK    2400 149
    RAVIE PEPPER      FLT V(A
    LARRY CORYELL     G    (A    TOM GRANT     PNO V(A   CHUCK RAINEY     B   (A   BILLY COBHAM     D  (A
    JERRY JEMMOTT     B    (A    SPIDER RICE   D   (A   GIB PEPPER       V D (A
```

```
    VICTOR PERAINO    K V  (A         (A) NO MANS LAND                      1975 MKC               5121 N10
    DAVID WILD        D    (A
    EDWARD HOWLEHAN   D    (A    PAUL ROGERSON   B V (A   JON LAFLOTTE FLT G V (A   DAVID CHRISTIAN  G (A
    HERMAN DALDIN     B    (A
```

```
    DAVID THOMAS      V    (1234ABCDEFG (A) MODERN DANCE                    1978 BLANK US 001 UK MERCURY 9100052
    ALLEN RAVENSTINE  K    (134ABCEG    (A) MODERN DANCE      RI            198  ROUGH TRADE       UK    ROUGH 22
    THOMAS LAUGHNER   G    (1234CBEG    (B) DUB HOUSING                     1978 CHRYSALIS UK CHR1207 GER 6307646
    TOM HERMAN        G    (2134ACBEG   (C) DATAPANIK IN THE YEAR ZERO(EP)  1978 RADAR UK RDR1
    TIM WRIGHT        B    (123CG       (D) DATAPANIK IN THE YEAR ZERO(LP)  1979 ATLANTIC     UK        K50587
    SCOTT KRAUSS      D    (1234ABDEG   (E) NEW PICNIC TIME                 1979 CHRYSALIS UK CHR1248 NL 511248
    TONY MAIMONE      B    (ABCEG       (F) ART OF WALKING                  1980 ROUGH TRADE  UK        ROUGH 14
    ALAN GREENBLATT   G    (4C          (G) 390' SIMULATED STEREO           198  ROUGH TRADE  UK        ROUGH "£
    DAVID TAYLOR      K    (2CG         (1) 1975      (2) 1976    (3) 1976  (4) 1977
```

```
      CHRISTINE(McVIE) PERFECT K V(ALL    (A) CHRISTINE PERFECT         1970 BLUE HORIZON      UK      7 63860
      TOP TOPHAM        G     (AC         (B) ALBATROSS (1 SIDE)        1977 EMBASSY           UK        31569
      RICK HAYWARD      G     (AC         (C) THE LENGENDARY CP ALBUM   1978 SIRE                      SASD 7522
      MARTIN DUNSFORD   B     (A
      DANNY KIRWAN      G     (AC JOHN McVIE      B   (AC ANDY SYLVESTER  B  (B   STAN WEBB      G (B
      DAVE BIDWELL      D     (B  CHRIS HARDING   D   (A
```

```
      CARL PERKINS      G V   (ALL        (A) DANCE ALBUM "TEENBEAT"    1959 LONDON UK HA 2202 US SUN  1225
      WES HOLLAND       D     (1          (B) WHOLE LOTTA SHAKIN'       1959 CBS                   US        1234
      JAY PERKINS       G     (1          (C) COUNTRY BOY DREAMS        1968 LONDON UK SHP8366 US DOLLIE4001
      CLAYTON PERKINS   B     (1          (D) ON TOP                    1969 CBS                   US        9931
      STAN PERKINS      D     (2          (E) BLUE SUEDE SHOES          1969 LONDON UK HAS2202 US SUN   112
      GREG PERKINS      B     (2          (E) BLUE SUDE SHOES           1974 SUN    UK                 6467 009
      DAVID SEA         SAX   (2          (F) ORIGINAL GOLDEN HITS      1970 SUN UK    6467 004 US         111
      LEE McALPIN       PNO   (2          (G) KING OF ROCK              19   CBS    UK      63309
      HAROLD BRADLEY    G     (P          (H) BOPPIN THE BLUES(N R B Q) 1970 CBS    UK    63826 US         9981
      RAY EDENTON       G     (P          (I) CARL PERKINS              19   HARMONY           US       11385
      JERRY KENNEDY     G     (P          (J) BROWN EYED HANDSOME MAN   1972 HARMONY           US       31179
      JERRY SHOOK       G     (PV         (K) GREATEST HITS             1973 HARMONY           US       31792
      PETE WADE         G     (P          (K) GREATEST HITS             19   CBS    US 9833   UK       63676
      CHIP YOUNG        G     (P          (L) MATCHBOX                  19   PICKWICK US JS6103 HILLTOP 6103
      BUDDY HARMON      D     (P          (M) MAN BEHIND JOHNNY CASH    1972 CBS                         64892
      BOB MOORE         B     (P          (N) BEST OF                   19   TRIP              US    TLX8503
      HENRY STRZELECKI  B     (P          (O) GREATEST HITS             197  EMBASSY           UK       31527
      PIG ROBBINS       K     (P          (P) MY KIND OF COUNTRY        1974 MERCURY US SRM1691 UK  6338 475
      MICHAEL LEECH     B     (V          (Q) ROCKIN GUITAR MAN         1975 CHARLY           UK   CR30003
      GAYLE WHITFIELD   SAX   (V          (R) ORIGINAL CARL PERKINS     1976 CHARLY           UK   CR30110
      HOYT HAWKINS      V     (V          (S) CARL PERKINS SHOW         1976 SUEDE            UK    NR 6778
      GINGER HOLLADAY   V     (V          (T) LONG TALL SALLY           1977 EMBASSY           UK       31554
      STEVE FERGUSON    G V HCA(H         (U) FROM JACKSON TENNESSEE    1977 LAKE COUNTY       US    LC 505
      PETE DRAKE        STEEL(P           (V) OL' BLUE SUEDES BACK      1978 JET  US JTLA 856  UK       30146
      CHARLIE McCOY     HCA   (P          (W) OL' BLUE SUEDES BACK      1978 JET  US    35604
      HAYWARD BISHOP    D     (V          (X) SUN SOUNDS SPECIAL        1978 CHARLY           UK   CR30152
      DAVID BRIGGS      PNO   (V          (Y) SUN STORY VOL 3           1979 SUN              US   9330 903
      WELDON MYRICK     STEEL(V           (Z) TENNESSEE                 19   DESIGN           US   DLP 611
      HUGH STOKER       V     (V          ( ) ROCKIN' GUITAR MAN        1982 CHARLY           UK       1015
      NEAL MATTHEWS     V     (V
      RAYMOND L WALKER  V     (V  LEA JANE BERINATI V   (V  LISA SILVER    V  (V  JODY STNICHOLAS  B V (H
      TOM STALEY        D     (H  FRANK GADLEY V PERC(H     DONN ADAMS        TROM(H
                                            (1) EARLY BANDS    (2) 1978 TOUR
```

```
      JOE PERRY         G V   (AB         (A) LET THE MUSIC DO THE TALKING  1980 CBS US 36888     UK   84213
      RALPH MORMAN      V     (A          (B) IVE GOT THE ROCK'N'ROLLS AGAIN 1981 CBS US 37374    NL   85145
      DAVID HULL        V B   (AB
      RONNIE STEWART    D     (AB CHARLIE FARREN    G V  (B
```

```
      JOHN PERRY        B V K(A           (A) SUNSET WADING             1976 DECCA            UK   SKL 5233
      RUPERT HINE       K SYN V(A
      MIKE GILES        D     (A  GEOFF RICHARDSON VLA FLT(A BERYL STREETER   V  (A   MORRIS PERT      PERC(A
      ELIO D'ANNA       WIND  (A  CARRADO RUSTICCI G   (A  ROGER GLOVER        SYN  (A   SIMON JEFFES    KOTO(A
      STRING SECTION          (A
```

```
      LEE PERRY               (ALL        AFRICA BLOOD                 19   TROJAN               TBL  166
                                          REVOLUTION DUB               1979 CACTUS              CTLP 112
                                          BEST OF LEE PERRY & UPSETTERS 19  JET STAR           PTLP1023
```

```
      MARK PERRY        G V WIND(A        (A) SNAPPY TURNS             1980 UK    DEPTFORD FUN CITY  DLP06
      DENNIS BURNS      V SAX B(A
      ANNE              VLN   (A  GRANT SHOWBIZ    B   (A  HAG         SYN V(A   TYRONE THOMAS   G  (A
```

```
      PAUL PERSONNE     G V HCA(A         (A) PAUL PERSONNE            1982 EPIC UK 85445
      DANIEL ANTOINE    K     (A
      PHILIPPE FLORIS   D     (A  GINO            B   (A  PHIL MARLO    G  (A   BOBBY BRUNO     PROD(A
```

```
                                          PERSUADERS                   1974 ATLANTIC UK K40476  US    7021
                                          BEST THING THATS HAPPENED TO ME 1976 ATLANTIC        US    7046
                                          THIN LINE BETWEEN LOVE & HATE 1974 ATLANTIC UK K40370 US   33387
                                          ITS ALL ABOUT LOVE           1976 CALLA             US    34802
```

```
      JERRY LAWSON      V     (BDG        (A) WE CAME TO PLAY          19   CAPITOL           US    791
      JIMMY HAYES       V     (BDG        (B) STREET CORNER SYMPHONY   1972 CAPITOL           US    872
      JOSEPH RUSSELL    V     (BDG        (B) STREET CORNER SYMPHONY   1972 ISLAND    UK   ILPS 9201
      WILLIE C DANIELS  V     (D          (C) SPREAD THE WORD          197  CAPITOL           US  11101
      HERBERT RHOAD     V     (BD         (D) MORE THAN BEFORE         1974 A&M    UK AMLS 63835  US SP3635
      BENORCE BLACKMON  G     (D          (E) I JUST WANNA SING        1976 A&M                US SP3656
      HENRY DAVIS       B     (D          (F) ACAPELLA                 19   STRAIGHT STS1062 REPRISE US 6394
      JAY OTIS WASHINGTON V   (B          (G) CHIRPIN'                 1977 ELEKTRA           US 7E1099
      JEFF BARRY        PERC  (D          (H) WE STILL AIN'T GO NO BAND 197 MCA               US    326
      RICK BEILKE       G     (D
      OLLIE BROWN       D     (D  RANDY KOONTZ     B   (D  JOE AGLIO     D  (D   CLARENCE McDONALD  K (D
```

```
                                          (A) ALIVE                    19   COLUMBIA         IMP GES 90037
```

```
                                          (A) EXCLAMATION MARK         1969 PYE              UK NSPL18293
```

```
      JIM PETERIK             (A          (A) DON'T FIGHT THAT FEELING 1976 EPIC             US    34196
```

[432]

COLLEEN PETERSON

COLLEEN PETERSON	V (ALL	(A) BEGINNING TO FEEL LIKE HOME	1976	CAPITOL		
		(B) COLLEEN	1977	CAPITOL	US	ST 11714
		(C) TAKIN' MY BOOTS OFF	1978	CAPITOL		UK/US 11835

PETARDS

KLAUS EBERT	G V (ABC	(A) A DEEPER BLUE	1968	EUROPA	GER	E313
HORST EBERT	G V (ABC	(B) HITSHOCK	1969	LIBERTY	GER	LBS 83325
ARNO DITTRICH	D (ABC	(C) PETARDS	1970	LIBERTY	GER	LBS 83481 (CASS)
ROGER	B (ABC					

PETER & GORDON

PETER ASHER	V (ALL	PETER & GORDON	1964	COLUMBIA	UK	SCX3518
GORDON WALLER	V (ALL	IN TOUCH	1964	COLUMBIA	UK	SCX3532
		PETER & GORDON	1966	COLUMBIA	UK	SCX6045
		HURTIN 'N' LOVIN'	1965	COLUMBIA	UK	SCX3565
		SOMEWHERE	1966	COLUMBIA	UK	SCX6097
		A WORLD WITHOUT LOVE	196	CAPITOL	US	2115
		I DONT WANT TO SEE YOU AGIAN	196	CAPITOL	US	2220
		I GO TO PIECES	196	CAPITOL	US	2324
		TRUE LOVE WAYS	196	CAPITOL	US	2368
		SING & PLAY THE HITS OF NASHVILLE	196	CAPITOL	US	2430
		WOMAN	196	CAPITOL	US	2477
		BEST OF	196	CAPITOL	US	2549
		LADY GODIVA	196	CAPITOL	US	2664
		KNIGHT IN RUSTY ARMOUR	196	CAPITOL	US	2729
		IN LONDON FOR TEA	196	CAPITOL	US	2747
		HOT COLD & CUSTARD	196	CAPITOL	US	2882
		THE BEST OF	1977	EMI	UK	NUT8
		GORDON (SOLO)	1972	VERTIGO	UK	6360 069

PETER PAUL & MARY

PETER YARROW	G V (ALL	(A) PETER PAUL & MARY	196	WB	US	1449
PAUL STOOKEY	V (ALL	(B) MOVING	196	WB	US	1473
MARY TRAVERS	V (ALL	(C) IN THE WIND	196	WB	US	1507
		(D) IN CONCERT	196	WB	US	1555
		(E) A SONG WILL RISE	196	WB	US	1589
		(F) SEE WHAT TOMORROW BRINGS	196	WB	US	1615
		(G) PETER PAUL & MARY ALBUM	196	WB	US	1648
		(H) ALBUM 1700	196	WB	US	1700
		(J) LATE AGAIN	196	WB	US	1751
		(K) PETER PAUL & MOMMY	196	WB	US	1785
		(L) 10 YEARS TOGETHER THE BEST OF	196	WB	US	2552 UK K46051
		(M) REUNION	1978	WB	US	3231

PETS

GREG SUTTON	B V (A	(A) WET BEHIND THE EARS		1978 ARISTA UK SPART 1061 US AB4154		
GREG LEROY	G WIND(A					
VINCE MELAMED	K V (A DEANE HAGEN	D (A	IRA INGBER	G V (A ALAN ESTES	PERC (A	
STEVE FORMAN	PERC (A EDDIE TUDURI	D (A	MIKE BAIRD	D (A SCOTT STRONG	G (A	
JOANNE HARRIS	V (A					

TOM PETTY & THE HEARTBREAKERS

TOM PETTY	G V (ALL	(A) TOM PETTY & THE HEARTBREAKERS	1977	ISLAND UK ISA5014 US SHELTER 52006		
BENMONT TENCH	K V (ABCDEF	(B) YOURE GONNA GET IT	1978	ISLAND UK ISA5017 US SHELTER 52029		
RON BLAIR	B (ABCDEF	(C) OFFICIAL LIVE BOOTLEG	197	US SHELTER 12677		
STAN LYNCH	D K (ABCDEF	(D) DAMN THE TORPEDOES	1979	BACKSTREET US 5105 UK MCF 3044		
MIKE CAMPBELL	G K HCA(ABCDEF	(E) HARD PROMISES	1981	BACKSTREET US 5160 UK MCA MCF 3098		
HOWIE EPSTEIN	B (F	(F) LONG AFTER DARK	1982	UK MCA MCF 3155		
JIMMY LOVINE	PROD (E					
DUCK DUNN	B (E PHIL JONES	PERC (E	STEVIE NICKS	V (E SHARON CEYLANI	V (E	
A BUGS WEIDEL	PNO (E PHIL SEYMOUR	V (B	NOAH SHARK	PERC (B		

PEZBAND

MIMI BETINIS	G K V(ABCDE	(A) PEZBAND	1977	PASSPORT US 98021		
MIKE GORMAN	B V (ABCDE	(B) LAUGHING IN THE DARK	1978	PASSPORT US 9826 UK RADAR RAD 6		
TOMMY GAWENDA	G (ABCDE	(C) COVER TO COVER	1981	PASSPORT US 9837		
MICK RAIN	D V (ABCDE					
MEL COLLINS	SAX(ABCDE TOMMY EYRE	PNO (ABCDE	CLARENCE CLEMMONS SAX (A	JOHN PAYNE	SAX (A	
RANDY BRECKER	TPT (A ALAN RUBIN	TPT (A	LARRY FAST	SYN (A		

PHANTOM BAND

JAKI LIEBEZEIT	D (AB	(A) PHANTOM BAND	1980	SKY		SKY 048
ELEK GELBA	PERC (AB	(B) FREEDOM OF SPEECH	1981	SKY	GER	SKY 065
HELMUT ZERLETT	K (AB					
DOMINIK VON SENGER	G (AB ROSKO GEE	V B (A				

PHEW

	(A) PHEW	1981	PASS	3F28002

GREG PHILLINGANES

	(A) SIGNIFICANT GAINS	1981	PLANET UK	K52299

ANTHONY PHILLIPS

ANTHONY PHILLIPS	G V (ABCD	(A) THE GEESE & THE GHOST	1977	HIT & RUN UK 001 US PASSPORT 98020		
MICHAEL RUTHERFORD	G B K D(A	(B) WISE AFTER THE EVENT	1978	ARISTA UK SPARTY1063 US PASSPORT9828		
PHIL COLLINS	V (A	(C) PRIVATE PARTS AND PIECES	1978	APL UK AFLP 1 PASSPORT US 7905		
ROB PHILLIPS	OBOE (AB	(D) SIDES	1978	ARISTA UK SPART1085 US PASSPORT9834		
LAZA MOMULOVICH	OBOE (A	(D) SIDES	1978	VERTIGO GER 9124 362		
JOHN HACKETT	FLT (A	(E) PRIVATE PARTS 2	1980	PVC 7913		
WIL SLEATH	FLT (A	(F) 1984	1981	RCA UK 5036 US PASSPORT6006		
JACK LANCASTER	FLT (A					
CHARLIE MARTIN	CELLO(A					
KIRK TREVOR	CELLO(A NICK HAYLEY	VLN (A	MARTIN WESTLAKE PERC (A	VIV McAULIFFE	V (A	
THE VICAR	G V K(BD MIKE GILES	D (BD	JOHN G PERRY B (BD	FRANK RICOTTI	PERC (D	
RALPH BERNASCONE	V (DA VIC STENCH	B (BD	JEREMY GILBERT K (B	RUPERT HINE	V PERC (B	
DALE NEWMAN	V (D DAN OWEN	V (D	RAY COOPER PERC (D	MORRIS PERT	PERC (D	
HUMBERT RUSE	PERC HRNS(ABD MEL COLLINS	SAX (BD	PERKIN ALANBECK SYN (B	TOM NEWMAN	(A	

ESTHER PHILLIPS	V	(ALL	(A) AND I LOVE HIM	19	ATLANTIC	US 8102	
DON GROLNICK	K	(N	(B) SINGS	1966	ATLANTIC		UK 587010
JEFF BERLIN	B	(N	(C) ESTHER	19	ATLANTIC	US 8122	
RANDY BRECKER	TPT	(N	(D) COUNTRY SIDE	19	ATLANTIC	US 8130	
MICHAEL BRECKER	SAX	(N	(E) BURNIN	1970	ATLANTIC	US 1565	
SAN BURTIS	TROM	(N	(F) FROM A WHISPER TO A SCREAM	19	KUDU	US 05	UK 2
ANTHONY JACKSON	B	(N	(G) ALONE AGAIN NATURALLY	1973	KUDU	US 09	UK 6
STEVE KHAN	G	(N	(H) BLACK EYED BLUES	1974	KUDU	US	UK 11
BARRY ROGERS	TROM	(N	(J) PERFORMANCE	1975	KUDU	US 18	UK 18
JOHN BLAIR	VLN	(N	(K) WITH JOE BECK	1975	KUDU		UK 23
BOBBY LYLE	K	(N	(L) CONFESSIN' THE BLUES	1976	ATLANTIC	US 1680	UK K50222
ALLAN HOLDSWORTH	G	(N	(M) FOR ALL WE KNOW	1976	KUDU		UK 28
HUGH McCRACKEN	G	(N	(N) CAPRICORN PRINCESS	1977	KUDU		UK 31
BARRY MILES	SYN	(N	(O) YOU'VE COME A LONG WAY BABY	1977	MERCURY	US SRM1187	
ANDY NEWMARK	D	(N	(P) ESTHER PHILLIPS	1978	KUDU		UK SCU001
JOHN TROPEA	G	(N	(Q) ALL ABOUT ESTHER	1978	PHILIPS		UK 6338885
JON FADDIS	TPT	(N	(R) HERE'S ESTHER ARE YOU READY	1979	MERCURY	US 9111030	UK 9100065
RONNIE CUBER	SAX	(N	(S) GOOD BLACK IS HARD TO CRACK	1981	MERCURY	US SRM14005	
MIKE ABENE	K	(N					

STEVE GADD	D	(N	JOHN GATCHELL	TPT	(N	SUE EVANS	V	(N	JOE FARRELL		WIND	(N
CREED TAYLOR	PROD	(N	GORDON EDWARDS	B	(FGJ	RON CARTER	B	(G	BOZ BURRELL	B		(H
WILL LEE	B	(M	AIRTO MOREIRA	PERC	(F	RALPH MACDONALD	PERC	(GJMNK	ARTHUR JENKINS		PERC	(H
CORNELL DUPREE	G	(FG	ERIC GALE	G		(EFN	JOE BECK	G	(KMO	GEORGE BENSON	G		(G
CHARLIE BROWN	G	(HJ	RICHARD TEE	K	(FGJ	RICHARD WYNARDS	K	(G	TIM HINKLEY		K	(H
DON GROLNICK	K	(KM	JOSHIE ARMSTEAD	V	(FH	HILD HARRIS	V	(FM	BILL VATON	V		(N
BARBARA MASSEY	V	(F	TASHA THOMAS	V	(FGHJM	LANI GROVES	V	(GHJ	DENISE WILLIAMS	V		(J
LOUIS ST LOUIS	V	(F	CAL CALDWELL	V	(GHJ	PATTI AUSTIN	V	(JM	ROBIN CLARK	V		(M
BABI FLOYD	V	(N	ZACHARY SARDEN	V	(N	MAERETHA STEWART	V	(M				

GLENN PHILLIPS	G V	(AB	(A) LOST AT SEA	1975 CAROLINE UK C1519 US SNOWSTAR SSR1	
JOHN CARR HARRIMAN	CELLO	(A	(B) SWIM IN THE WIND	1977 VIRGIN UK	V2087
MIKE HOLBROOK	B	(A			

JIM PRESMANES	D	(A	BILL REA	G	(AB	SANT RAM SINGH KHALSA	K	(AB	JERRY FIELDS		D	(AB
DAVID LANDSBERG	D	(B	JANIE GEISER REA	V	(B	BILLY McPHERSON	WIND	(B	CHUCK MOON		V	(B
JOHN CURRIE	K	(B	DANA HOWARD NELSON	K V	(B	BILLY McKINLEY	BANJO	(B	PHOEBE		PNO	(B
DAVID BYRD	STEEL	(B	JIM MARETT	PNO	(B	BILL SHEFFIELD	HCA V	(B				

| JOHN PHILLIPS | G V HCA | (A | (A) WOLFKING OF L A | 1970 STATESIDE UK 5027 US DUNHILL 50077 | |
| LARRY KNECHTEL | K | (A | | | |

DAVID COHEN	G	(A	DARLENE LOVE	V	(A	FANITA JAMES	V	(A	BUDDY EMMONS		STEEL	(A
GORDON TERRY	FDL	(A	HAL BLAINE	D	(A	JOE OSBORNE	B	(A	DR HORD		G	(A
JEAN KING	V	(A	JAMES BURTON	G	(A	RED RHODES	STEEL	(A				

| MICHELLE PHILLIPS | V | (A | (A) VICTIM OF ROMANCE | 1977 A&M US 4651 | UK AMLH64651 |
| JACK NITZSCHE | K PERC | (A | | | |

SCOTT FREE	D G ACC V	(A	DAVID C ALLEN	G	(A	GREGORY LEE	B	(A	TIM DRUMMOND		B	(A
DON RANDI	PNO	(A	JOHN MOON MARTIN	G V	(A	STEVE DOUGLAS	WIND PERC	(A	RON NAGLE		PERC	(A
GENE ESTES	PERC	(A	BEN BENAY	G MAND	(A	JERRY DONAHUE	G	(A	MIKE BODDIKER		SYN	(A
SID SHARP	STRINGS	(A	JERRY JUMONVILLE	WIND	(A	JAY MIGLIORI	WIND	(A	DENNIS DREITH		WIND	(A
JACK NIMITZ	WIND	(A	BOB FINDLEY	TPT	(A	BILL PETERSON	TPT	(A	MARK UNDERWOOD		TPT	(A
TRICIA JOHNS	V	(A	LAURA CREAMER	V	(A	CHERIE ENGLISH	V	(A	MYRNA MATTHEWS		V	(A
MAXINE WILLARD	V	(A	KATHY WARD	V	(A	BILLY GUY	V	(A	GRADY CHAPMAN		V	(A
JEROME EVANS	V	(A										

SHAWN PHILLIPS	V G SITAR	(ALL	(A) I'M A LONER	1965	COLUMBIA UK	33SX 1748	
ADRIAN GAYE	G	(C	(B) SHAWN	1966	COLUMBIA UK	SCX 6006	
MICK WEAVER	K	(C	(C) CONTRIBUTION	1970	A&M US 4241	UK	AMLS 978
SNEAKY PETE	STEEL	(HL	(D) SECOND CONTRIBUTION	1971	A&M US 4282	UK	AMLS 2006
JIM PRICE	HRNS	(H	(E) COLLABORATION	1972	A&M US 4323	UK	AMLS64324
JIM HORN	SAX	(HL	(F) FACES	1973	A&M US 4363	UK	AMLS64363
CRAIG DOERGE		(H	(G) FURTHERMORE	1974	A&M US 3662	UK	AMLH68278
BOBBY KEYS	SAX	(H	(H) BRIGHT WHITE	1974	A&M US 4402	UK	AMLH64402
LEE SKLAR	B	(LF	(J) DO YOU WONDER	1975	A&M US 4539	UK	AMLH64539
RUSS KUNKEL	D	(L	(K) RUMPLESTILTSKIN'S RESOLVE	1976	A&M US 4582	UK	AMLH64582
JOE SAMPLE	K	(L	(L) SPACED	1977	A&M US 4650	UK	AMLH64650
PETER ROBINSON	K	(DKCG	(M) TRANSCENDENCE	1978	RCA US		APLI13028
MICHAEL BAIRD	D	(L					

CHUCK RAINEY	B	(L	MIKE MILLER	G B	(KL	AL WING	SAX	(KL	STEVE NEILEN		D	(L
ANTHONY NEDZA	K	(L	JOSEPH GAETA	G B	(L	DANIEL TIMMS	G	(L	BRUCE ROWLAND		D	(L
BRIAN ODGERS	B	(DFL	CHRIS MERCER	SAX	(CFL	JOHNNY ALMOND	SAX	(L	MIKE CLARKE		D	(KL
PAUL JACKSON	B	(KL	BOBBY LICHTIG	B	(K	STEVE HAMMOND	G	(K	JOHN GUSTAFSON		B	(KG
BARRY DE SOUZA	D	(KG	CALEB QUAYE	G	(KFG	PAUL BUCKMASTER	K	(FKCG	JOHN PULLEN		OBOE	(K
BILL SUMMERS	PERC	(C	STEVE WINWOOD	K	(CF	CHRIS WOOD	WIND	(C	MOX		HCA	(C
JIM CAPALDI	D	(C	CANDY JOHN CARR	D	(C	REMI KABAKA	PERC	(CF	JIMMY COFF		PERC	(C
HARVEY BURNS	G	(D	JIM CREGAN	G	(D	MARTYN FORD	HRNS	(F	GLEN CAMPBELL		STEEL	(F
JACK CONRAD	B	(F	ED GREEN	D	(F	JOHN PIGNEGUY	HRNS	(F	SKAILA KANGA		HARP	(F
SNEAKY PEYE KLEINOW	STEEL	(F	ED MORIN	D	(F	JOE SAMPLE	PNO	(F	DAVID KATZ ORCH			(F
ANN O'DELL	K	(G	RAUL MAYORA	PERC	(G							

ROBERT PHILLIPS	G V	(AB	(A) LE PARTIE DU COCKTAIL	1979 POLYDOR	US PD1 6198
SEAN MacLEOD	G V	(AB	(B) PHILLIPS & MACLEOD	1980 POLYDOR	US PD1 6255
JIM DIVISEK		(A			

| ANDREW STEELE | | (A | BRIAN WHITCOMB | | (A | BOB CONTI | | (A | DAVID KEMPER | | (A |
| ANDY NEWMARK | D | (B | ART WOOD | D | (B | | | | | |

BENSON BLAKE		(A	(A) PHLUPH	196 US VERVE US 5054
JOHN PELL		(A		
JOEL MAISANO		(A		

PHONEY & HARDCORE

    ERIK STRACK   G V   (A   (A) PHONEY HITS   1979 ARIOLA   NL   200 894
    KEES ALKEMA   V D   (A   (B) PHONEY HITS   1980 ARIOLA   NL   202 878
    TOMMY VANDERSCHOOT B   (A
    BURNY REINKE   G   (A   BIEM VISSER K   (A   NEIL MERRYWEATHER   V(A
PHOTOGLO
                                   (A) PHOTOGLO   1980 20 TH CENT UK 604
PHOENIX
    JOHN VERITY   V G G(AB   (A) PHOENIX   1976 CBS US 34476   UK   81621
    ROBERT HENRIT   D   (AB   (B) IN FULL VIEW   1980 CHARISMA   UK   CAS1150
    ROD ARGENT   K   (B
    JIM RODFORD   D   (A   MICHAEL DES BARRES V   (A   RAY MINHINNIT   G V (B   RUSS BALLARD   V (B
    BRUCE TURGON   V   (B   RONNIE LEE CUNNINGHAM K V(B
PHOTOS
    WENDY WU   V   (AB   (A) PHOTOS   1980 EPIC US 36515 UK PHOTO 5
    STEVE EAGLES   G V   (AB   (B) BLACKMAIL TAPES[FREE WITH (A)]
    DAVE SPARROW   B V   (AB
    OILY HARRISON   D   (AB
PICCADILLY LINE
    ROD EDWARDS   V G K(A   (A) HUGE WORLD OF EMILY SMALL 1967   CBS   63129
    ROGER HAND   G V   (A
    NORRIE McLEAN   B   (A   KEITH HODGE D   (A
PIBLIKO
    JIM MULLEN   G   (AB   (A) ART SCHOOL DANCE GOES ON FOREVER 1970 HARVEST   UK   SHVL768
    ROGER BRUNN   B   (A   (B) THOUSANDS ON A RAFT   1970 HARVEST   UK   SHVL782
    DAVE THOMPSON   D   (AB
    ROB TAIT   D   (AB   PETE BROWN   (AB   STEVE GLOVER   PERC(B
PIC & BILL
    CHARLES PICKINS   V   (A   (A) 30 MINUTES OF SOUL   1978 12 O'CLOCK   US   LD 303
    BILL SMITH
BOBBY 'BORIS' PICKETT
    BOBBY 'BORIS' PICKETT V(A   (A) MONSTER MASH   1973 LONDON   UK   ZGU 133
                                       ( ) MONSTER MASH   1962 GARPAX   US SGP 67001
                                       ( ) ORIGINAL MONSTER MASH   1973 PARROT   UK   71063
COURTLAND PICKETT
    COURTLAND PICKETT V B   (A   (A) FANCY DANCER   1973 ELEKTRA UK K42147 US EKS 75060
    DAVID HOOD   B   (A
    ROGER HAWKINS   D   (A   BARRY BECKETT   K   (A   PETE CARR   G   (A   JIMMY JOHNSON   G (A
    CHARLES STRATFORD TROM (A   BOBBY BRUCE   VLN (A   SONNY ROYAL   CLAR (A   WAYNE HILL   TPT(A
    HARVEY THOMPSON   SAX   (A   RONNIE EADES   SAX (A   CHARLES ROSE TROM (A   JO ANN CARR   V (A
    LAURA STRUZICK   V   (A   SUZY STORM   V   (A
WILSON PICKETT
    WILSON PICKETT   V   (ALL   (A) IN THE MIDNIGHT HOUR   196 ATLANTIC UK 587 032   US   8114
    JEAN ROUSSEL   K   (Z   EXCITING WILSON PICKETT   196 ATLANTIC   US   8129
    MARTY SIMON   D   (Z   WICKED PICKETT   196 ATLANTIC UK 588 057   US   8138
    JERRY KNIGHT   B V   (Z   THE SOUND OF   196 ATLANTIC UK 588 050   US   8145
    WALTER ROSSI   G   (Z   THE BEST OF   196 ATLANTIC UK 588 092   US   8151
    GARY BROWN   SAX   (Z   I'M IN LOVE   196 ATLANTIC   US   8175
    CLYDE KERR   TPT   (Z   MIDNIGHT MOVER   196 ATLANTIC   US   8183
    JIMMY TANAKA   PERC (Z   GREAT HITS   196 WAND   US   672
    GARY WILSON   V   (Z   (I) HEY JUDE   196 ATLANTIC UK 588 170   US   8215
    BILLY NELSON   V   (Z   RIGHT ON   196 ATLANTIC UK 2465 002 US 8250
    PETSYE POWELL   V   (Z   (K) IN PHILADELPHIA   1970 ATLANTIC   US   8270
    ROGER HAWKINS   D   (I   BEST OF VOL 2   1971 ATLANTIC   US   8290
    DAVID HOOD   B   (IX   IF YOU NEED ME   19   JOY   JOYS181
    ALBERT LOWE   G   (I   BEST OF   197 ATLANTIC UK K40015   US 2 501
    BARRY BECKETT   K   (I   GREATEST HITS   1973 ATLANTIC UK K60038   US   2501
    JERRY JEMMOT   B   (I   MR MAGIC MAN   1973 RCA   US   4858
    JAMES JOHNSON   G   (I   DONT KNOCK MY LOVE   1974 ATLANTIC UK K40319   US   8300
    DUANE ALLMAN   G   (I   TONIGHT I'M MY BIGGEST AUDIENCE 1974 RCA UK SF 8344   US   4858
    MARVEL THOMAS   ORG   (I   MIZ LENAS BOY   1974 RCA   UK SF 8390   US   0312
    GENE MILLER   TPT   (I   LIVE IN JAPAN   1974 RCA   APL 20669
    JACK PECK   TPT   (I   PICKETT IN POCKET   1974 RCA   APL1 0495
    AARON VARNELL   SAX   (I   JOIN ME & LETS BE FREE   1975 RCA   UK SF8439 USAPL1 0856
    JOE ARNOLD   SAX   (I   PEACE BREAKER   1975 DJM   UK DJSL064   US 26064
    SWEET INSPIRATIONS V   (I   ITS TOO LATE   19   DOUBLE L   US   2300
    UGENE DOZIER   PNO   (K   KEEP THE DREAM ALIVE   19   RCA   VSPX 6097
    LENNY PAKULA   PNO   (X   STAR COLLECTION   1978 WEA   UK MID26001 FR 20017
    THOM BELL   ORG   (X   (X) FUNKY SITUATION   1978 BIG TREE   76011
    NORMAN HARRIS   G   (X   (Z) I WANT YOU   1979 EMI   UK 3007   US 17019
    ROLAND CHAMBERS   G   (X   RIGHT TRACK   1981 EMI   UK 3016   US 17043
    BOBBY ELI   G   (X   BEST OF   1981 ATLANTIC   UK K20017
    RONNIE BAKER   B   (X   BESTS OF 2   1981 ATLANTIC   UK K20078
    EARL YOUNG   D   (X
    VINCE MONTANA   PERC (X   RANDY McCORMICK   K   (X   LARRY BYROM   G   (X   KEN BELL   G   (X
    BOB WRAY   B   (X   ROGER CLARK   D   (X   MICKEY BUCKINS PERC(X   SANDRA RHODES V (X
    DONNA RHODES   V   (X   CHARLES CHALMERS V   (X   AVA ALDRIDGE   V   (X   CINDY RICHARDSON V(X
    CINDY STORM   V   (X   DON DAILY   PERF (X   PETE CARR   G   (X
PIERCE ARROW
    DOUG LUBAHN   B V   (AB   (A) PIERCE ARROW   1977 CBS   US   34805
    JEFF KENT   K G V(AB   (B) PITY THE RICH   1978 CBS   US   35307
    DAVID BUSKIN   G V   (AB
    ROBIN BATTEAU   G V   (AB   WERNER FRITZSCHING G V   (AB   BOBBY CHOUINARD   D   (AB
PIECES
    GEOFFREY LEIB   K SYNU(A   (A) PIECES   1979 UA US UALA 966 UK UAG 30252
    MIKE LINGLE   D V   (A
    KENNY LEE LEWIS   B V   (A   LARRY LINGLE G V   (A

MARIE PIERRE

```
MARIE PIERRE        V    (A          (A) LOVE AFFAIR              1979  TROJAN              TRLS  177
JAH BUNNY           D    (A
DENNIS BOVELL       K B  (A   WEBSTER JOHNSON  PNO (A   JOHN KPIAYE     G    (A   PATRICK TENYUE   TPT (A
HENRY TENYUE        TROM (A
```

PIDGEON

```
BILL STRONG SMITH D V(A          (A) PIDGEON               196  DECCA               US  75103
CHERI GAGE          V    (A
JOBRIATH SALISBURY K G V(A  RICHARD T MARSHALL      (A
```

PIG IRON

```
BILL PETERS         G V  (A          (A) PIG IRON            1970  CBS              NL 64044
GARY VAN SCYOC      B TPT(A
MARTY FOGEL         SAX  (A   ADAM IPPOLITO    K TPT V(A PAUL SQUIRE    HRNS (A
```

PIGSTY HILL LIGHT ORCHESTRA

```
ANDY LEGGETT V G SAX    (A          (A) PIGGERY JOKERY           1971  VILLAGE THING      VTS 8
DAVID CREECH        V TPT(AC         (B) CUSHION FOOT STOMP       197   VILLAGE THING      VTS 1
BARRY BLACK         G V  (A          (C) PIGSTY HILL LIGHT ORCHESTRA 1976 PHLO            001
BILL COLE           B    (A
JON HAYS            PERC V(C  ROBERT GREENFIELD G V  (C   CHRIS NEWMAN    G B  (C
```

PIIRPAUKE

```
SAKARI KUKKO        SAX PNO(ALL      (A) I                    19   LOVE             LRLP  148
HASSE WALLI         G PERC(ALL       (B) II                   19   LOVE             LRLP  192
ANTTI HYTTI         B V  (AB         (C) LIVE                 19   LOVE             LRLP  251
JUKKA WASAMA        D    (ALL
ILLI-PECKA WASAMA B PERC(C
```

PILOT

```
DAVID PATON         B V  (ALL        (A) FROM THE ALBUM OF THE SAME NAME 1974 EMI US 11368    EMC 3045
BILLY LYALL         K V FLT(AB       (B) SECOND FLIGHT        1975  EMI GER 05879  UK  EMC 3075
ALAN PARSONS        PROD (A           (C) MORIN HEIGHTS        1976  EMI              EMA  779
STUART TOSH         D V  (ABC        (D) TWOS A CROWD         1977  ARISTA           SPARTY 1014
IAN BAIRNSON        G    (ABCD       (E) BEST OF              1980  EMI              NUT  29
DAVID MASON         TPT  (A
PETER OXENDALE      K    (C   TREVOR SPENCER    D     (D   HENRY SPINETTI   D   (D   STEVE SWINDELLS  K V (D
```

PILOT (2)

```
BRUCE STEPHENS      G V K(AB         (A) PILOT                1972  RCA         US   LSP 4730
LEIGH STEPHENS      G    (AB         (B) POINT OF VIEW        197   RCA         US   LSP 4825
MICK WALLER         D    (AB
MARTIN QUITTENTON G    (AB  NEVILLEWHITEHEAD  BAN  (AB
```

PILTDOWN MEN

```
ED COBB                              (EP) PILTDOWN RIDES AGAIN    19   CAPITOL       EAP 1 20155
LINCOLN MAYORGA
```

MICHAEL PINDER

```
MICHAEL PINDER      G K V(A          (A) THE PROMISE          1976   THRESHOLD     UK    THS 18
BILL BERG           D    (A
FLYN J JOHNSON      B    (A   MAXINE WILLARD     V    (A   JEANIE KING      V    (A   JULIA TILLMAN   V  (A
JIM DILLAN          G V  (A   FRED BECKMEIER     B    (A   WILLIAM'SMITTY'SMITH ORG(A SUSAN McDONALD  HARP(A
JOEL DiBARTELLO     B    (A   TOM PETERSON      WIND (A   MICHAEL AZEVEDO  CONGA(A   DEAN OLCH       WIND(A
STEVE MADAIO        TPT  (A   BOBBY KEYS        SAX  (A
```

MIKE PINERA

```
MIKE PINERA         G V  (A          (A) ISLA                 1978  CAPRICORN   US   0202
DUANE HITCHINGS     K    (A          (B) FOREVER              1979  SPECTOR     US   0001
TERRY WEISS         K V  (A
DONNY VOSBURGH      D    (A   FLACO      CONGOS(A
```

RICHARD PINHAS

```
RICHARD PINHAS      SYN G    (ALL    (A) RHIZOSPERE           1979  COBRA       FR   COB37005
FRANCOIS AUGER      D    (AB         (B) CHRONOLYSE           1979  COBRA       FR   COB37015
JEAN PHILIPPE GOUDE SYN(C            (C) ICE LAND             1980  PULSE            001
DIDIER BATARD       B    (B          (D) EAST WEST            1980  PULSE            003
```

PINK FAIRIES

```
DUNCAN SANDERSON  B    (ABCD        (A) NEVER NEVER LAND      1971  POLYDOR     UK   2383 045
RUSSEL HUNTER       D    (ABCD        (B) WHAT A BUNCH OF SWEETIES 1972 POLYDOR  UK   2383 132
MARTIN STONE        G    (           (C) KINGS OF OBLIVION    1975  POLYDOR US5537 UK 2383 212
LARRY WILLIS        G V  (CD         (D) PINK FAIRIES  (COMP) 1975  POLYDOR     UK   2384 071
PAUL RUDOLPH        G    (ABD        (1) 1969 70
TWINK               D    (A1D
MICK FARREN         (1   STEVE TOOK        (1   NEIL SLAVEN      PROD (AD  JON ALDER   PROD    (A
PETER KNIGHT        PROD (D   TREVOR BURTON     G    (B   DAVID HITCHCOCK  PROD (D
```

PINK FLOYD

```
ROGER WATERS        B V G(ALL        (A) PIPER AT THE GATES OF DAWN 1967 TOWER  US 5093 UK COLUMBIA SCX 6157
VANETTA FIELDS      V    (K          (A) PIPER AT THE GATES OF DAWN 1967 COLUMBIA GER 04292
RICHARD WRIGHT      K V  (ALL        (B) SAUCERFUL OF SECRETS  1968 TOWER   US 5131 UK COLUMBIA SCX 6258
CARLENA WILLIAMS    V    (K          (B) SAUCERFUL OF SECRETS  1968 COLUMBIA GER 04290
NICK MASON          D    (ALL        (C) MORE                 1969 HARVEST US 11198 UK COLUMBIA SCX 6346
DICK PARRY          SAX  (K          (C) MORE                 1969 COLUMBIA GER 04096
SYD BARRETT         G V  (ABGZX      (D) UMMAGUMMA            1969 HARVEST US 388 UK HARVEST  SHDW 1/2
NORMAN SMITH        PROD (ABG        (D) UMMAGUMMA            1969 HARVEST GER 04222/23
DAVE GILMOUR        G V  (BCDEFGHJKLMXZ(E) ATOM HEART MOTHER  1970 HARVEST US  382 UK HARVEST  SHVL 781
JOE BOYD            PROD (G          (E) ATOM HEART MOTHER    1970 HARVEST GER 297
ROY HARPER          V    (K          (F) MEDDLE              1971 HARVEST US  832 UK HARVEST  SHVL 795
JIM HAAS            V    (M          (F) MEDDLE              1971 HARVEST GER 04917
SNOWY WHITE         G    (M          (G) RELICS    (COMP)    1971 HARVEST US  759 UK STARLINE SRS 5071
PETER WOOD          K    (           (G) RELICS    (COMP)    1971 HARVEST EURO 50740 1978 UK MFP   50397
JOHN'WILLIE'WILSON D    (           (H) OBSCURED BY CLOUDS   1972 HARVEST US 11078 UK HARVEST  SHSP4020
JOE CHEMAY          V    (M          (H) OBSCURED BY CLOUDS   1972 HARVEST GER 05054
ANDY BOWN           B    (           (J) DARK SIDE OF THE MOON 1973 HARVEST US 11163 UK HARVEST  SHVL 804
STAN FARBER         V    (M          (J) DARK SIDE OF THE MOON 19   HARVEST GER 05249 US MOBILE 17
TONI TENNILLE       V    (M          (K) WISH YOU WERE HERE   1976 CBS     US 33453 UK HARVEST  SHVL 814
JON JOYCE           V    (M          (K) WISH YOU WERE HERE   1976 HARVEST GER 06918
LESLEY DUNCAN       V    (J          (L) ANIMALS             1977 CBS     US 34474 UK HARVEST  SHVL 815
BRUCE JOHNSTON      V    (M          (L) ANIMALS             1977 HARVEST EURO 98434
```

(CONTINUED)

PINK FLOYD   (CONTINUED)

CLAIRE TORRY	V	(J	(M) THE WALL	1979 CBS	US 36183 UK HARVEST	SHDW 411
BARRY ST JOHN	V	(J	(M) THE WALL	1979 HARVEST EURO 63410/11		
LIZA STRIKE	V	(J	(N) COLLECTION OF GREAT DANCE	1981 CBS	US 37680 UK HARVEST	SHVL 822
DORIS TROY	V	(J	(O) THE FINAL CUT	1983 HARVEST UK		
ISLINGTON GREEN SCHOOL	V(M		(AB) A NICE PAIR	1973 HARVEST US 11257 UK HARVEST		SHDW 403
			(AB) A NICE PAIR	1973 HARVEST GER 50203/04		
			(X) MASTERS OF ROCK	1970 EMI IMP EURO 054 04299 1976 062 04299		
			(Y) ZABRISKIE POINT (SOUNDTRACK)	*1970 MGM 2315 002		2354 040
			(Z) TONIGHT LETS ALL MAKE LOVE	*1968 INSTANT ANALYSIS		INLP 002
			(*) BOTH SOUNDTRACK LPS WITH OTHER ARTISTS			

PINK MILITARY

JAYNE	V	(A	(A) DO ANIMALS BELIEVE IN GOD	1980 VIRGIN UK ERICS004 GER 202 512
NICKY	G SYN(A			
CHARLIE	K	(A	MARTIN B G (A NEIL PERC (A CHRIS JOYCE D (A	

PINPOINT

ARTURO BASSICK	G	(	(A) THIRD STATE (WITH FREE EP)	1980 ALBION UK ALB 103 GER 203383
A P BILLINGSLEY	G V	(A		
DAVE ALLEN	B	(A	HUGH GRIFFITHS D (A M R RUSHENT SYN (A I P HARTNELL K (A	
MOSLEY	K	(A		

PIONEERS

GEORGE DEKKER(AGARD)	V	(	LONGSHOT	1970 TROJAN	TBL 103
SYDNEY CROOKS	V	(	BATTLE OF THE GIANTS	197 TROJAN	TBL 139
LAUREN 'JACKIE'ROBINSON	V	(	YEAH	1971 TROJAN	TRL 24
			I BELIEVE IN LOVE	1972 TROJAN	TRLS 48
			FREEDOM FELING	1973 TROJAN	TRLS 64
			I'M GONNA KNOCK ON YOUR DOOR	1974 TROJAN	TRLS 98
			FEEL THE RHYTHM	1976 MERCURY	9286 172
			ROLL ON MUDDY RIVER	1877 TROJAN	TRLS 144
			PUSHER MAN	1979 TROJAN	TRLS 156
			GREATEST HITS	1979 TROJAN	TRLS 172

PIPER

BILLY SQUIER	V G PERC(AB	(A) PIPER	1976 A&M	US SP 4615 RI 3194
ALAN LAINE NOLAN	G PERC(AB	(B)CANT WAIT	19 A&M	US SP 4654
TOMMY GUNN	G	(AB	(B) BILLY SQUIER	19 A&M	US RI 3195
DANNY McGARY	B	(AB		
RICHIE FONTANA	D	(AB		

PIPS

| | | | (A) AT LAST THE PIPS | 1978 CASABLANCA US 7081 UK CAL 2022 |
| | | | (B) CALLIN' | 1978 CASABLANCA US 7113 UK CAL 2031 |

PIRANA

JIM YONGE	D	(AB	(A) PIRANA	19 HARVEST	SHVL 603
GRAEME THOMPSON	B	(AB	(B) PIRANA II	1972 HARVEST	SHVL 609
TONY HAMILTON G B V PERC(AB				
STAN WHITE	K V	(A	COL LAUGHNAN FLT (A KEITH GRIEG K PERC(B	

PIRANHAS

DICK SLEXIA	D	(A	(A) PIRANHAS	1980 SIRE	SRK 6098
BOB GROVER		(A		
JOHNNY HELMER	G	(A	ZOOT SAX (A RICHARD MYHILL K (A MIKE COOK VLN (A	
REG		(A	GRAHAM PRESKETT VLN (A	

PIRATES

MICK GREEN	G	(ABC	(A) OUT OF THEIR SKULLS	1977 WB US 3155	UK K56411
JOHN SPENCER	B V	(ABC	(B) SKULL WARS	1978 WB US 3224	UK K56468
FRANK FARLEY	D	(ABC	(C) HAPPY BIRTHDAY ROCK'N'ROLL	1979 CUBE UK HIFLY33
			(C) HARD RIDE	1979 PACIFIC ARTS US 7140

PLAIN SAILING

PAUL STEWART	V HCA(A	(A) DANGEROUS TIMES	1980 CHARISMA UK CHR 1282
ROBERT FREEMAN	G V	(A		
ALAN STEWART	G V	(A	COLIN STEWART K V (A DAVE WINTOUR B (A ALAN COULTER D (A

PLAIN JANE

BARRY RAY	G V	(A	(A) PLAIN JANE	19 HOBBITT US 5000
DON GLEICHER	G V	(A		
DAVID SCHOENFELD	D	(A	JERRY SCHOENFELD B K V(A	

PLAINSONG

IAN MATTHEWS	G V	(AB	(A) IN SEARCH OF AMELIA EARHART	1972 ELEKTRA NL ELK 22013 UK K42120
ANDY ROBERTS	G V	(AB	(B) PLAINSONG III RELEASED AS A WHITE LABEL PROMO ONLY	
DAVE RICHARDS	G V	(AB		
BOB RONGA	B V	(AB	TIMI DONALD D (A DAVE MATTACKS D (A MARTIN JENKINS MAND(A

PLANET EARTH

COLIN GREEN	G	(A	(A) PLANET EARTH	1978 PYE UK NSPL18556
KEVIN PEEK	G	(A		
BILLY CHRISTIAN	B	(A	TREVOR BARTON K (A RONNIE ASPERY SAX (A BARRY MORGAN D (A
MIKE RATLEDGE	K	(A	TRISTRAN FRY PERC (A KARL JENKINS K (A

PLANET GONG

DAEVID ALLEN	G V	(A	(A) FLOATING ARNACHY LIVE 77	1978 CHARLY UK CRM 2000 FR LTM1002
GILLI SMYTH	V	(A		
PEPI MILAN	G V	(A	JUANE BIBLIONI G V (A SAM GOPAL PERC SYN(A

PLANETS

| | | | (A) GOONHILLY DOWN | 1979 RIALTO TENOR102 US MOTOWN 934 |
| | | | (B) SPOT | 1980 RIALTO   TENOR10? |

PLANT

GERRIT VEEN	B V	(A	(A) LIFETIME GUARANTEE	1978 POLYDOR NL 2925 071
RUDY LENTZE	G V	(A		
RUUD BANUS	ORG V(A		HEDDY VANDER LAAN G V (A EDDY KORMA D (A EELCO GELLING G (A
BEA WILLEMSTEIN	V	(A	MARISKA VERES V (A MARTHA HOLLESTELLE V (A OKKIE HUYSDENS V (A

ROBERT PLANT

```
ROBERT PLANT       V    (A     (A) PICTURES AT ELEVEN          1982 SWANSONG   UK SSK 59418
ROBBIE BLUNT       G    (A
PAUL MATINEZ       B    (A     JEZZ WOODROFFE   K    (A  PHIL COLLINS    D   (A  COZY POWELL D   (A
RAPHAEL RAVENSCROFT SAX(A
```

PLANNING BY NUMBERS

```
STEPHEN MILFORD G V SYN(A      (A) '1'                        198 BEGGARS BANQUET UK BEGA 32
TREVOR STEEL       G    (A
IAN CURNOW         SYN K(A     JOHN HOLIDAY    B V  (A  MILAN ZELAVICA   D   (A
```

PLANXTY

```
CHRISTY MOORE      G V  (EF    (A) PLANXTY                    1973 POLYDOR     UK    2383 186
MATT MOLLOY        FLT  (EF    (B) WELL BELOW THE VALLEY      1973 POLYDOR     UK    2383 232
DONAL LUNNY        G SYN(EF    (C) COLD BLOW & THE RAINY NIGHT 1974 POLYDOR    UK    2383 301
PAUL BRADY         (         (D) PLANXTY COLLECTION          1976 POLYDOR     UK    2389 397
ANDY IRVINE        (ALL   (E) AFTER THE BREAK             1979 TARA             3001
LIAM O'FLYNN       WIND (ALL   (F) WOMAN I LOVED SO WELL      1980 TARA             3005
JOHNNY MOYNIHAN    (
NOEL HILL          CONC (F     TONY LINNANE FDL        (F  BILL WHELAN      K (F
```

PLASMATICS

```
WENDY'O' WILLIAMS V    (AB     (A) NEW HOPE FOR THE WRETCHED  1980 STIFF UK 24  US USE9 GER 624496
STU DEUTSCH        D    (A      (B) METAL PRIESTESS           1981 STIFF        US WOW666
RICHIE STOTTS      G    (AB
WES BEACH          G    (AB    JEAN BEAUVIOR   B    (AB JIMMIY MILLER   PERC(A CHRIS ROMANELLI    B (B
JOEY REESE         D    (B     TONY PETRI      D    (A
```

PLASTER CASTER BLUES BAND

```
ART ADAMS          G    (A     (A) PLASTER CASTERS            1969 BLUES TIME BTS 9001
CLIFFORD SOLOMON   SAX  (A
GEORGE SMITH       HCA(A        GILDO MAHONES   K    (A  BOGGY BRYANT    TPT(A  JULES CHAIKIN  V   (A
ELLEN SANDER       V    (A     MAX HARDY       D    (A
```

PLASTIC BERTRAND

```
PLASTIC BERTRAND V    (A       (A) AN 1                      1978 SIRE                9103 258
```

PLASTIC PEOPLE OF THE UNIVERSE

```
VRATISSLAV         WIND (A      (A) EGON BONDY'S HAPPY HEART CLUB BANNED  19 INVISIBLE   SCOPA 10001
MILAN HLAVSA       B    (A
JOSEF JANICEK      G K  (A     JIRA KABES  VLA G(A     JAROSLAV VOZNIAK  D   (A  IVAN JIROUS        (A
```

PLASTIC PENNY

```
PAUL RAYMOND       ORG  (       (A) 2 SIDES OF PENNY          1968 PAGE ONE    UK 005
NIGEL OLSSON       D    (       (B) CURRENCY                  1969 PAGE ONE    UK 014
TONY MURRAY        B    (       (C) HEAD I WIN,TAILS YOU LOOSE 1970 PAGE ONE   UK 611
BRIAN KEITH        V    (
MICK GRABHAM       G    (
```

PLASTICS

```
HAJIME TACHIBANA        (A      (A) WELCOME BACK              1981 ISLAND    GER   203 435
TOSHI NAKANICHI         (A
CHICA SATO              (A     TEKEMI SHIMA        (A  MA-CHAN SAKUMA      (A
```

PLATINUM HOOK

```
STEPHEN DANIELS    D V  (A      (A) PLATINUM HOOK             1978 MOTOWN US 899  UK STML12086
TINA RENNE STANFORD PERC V(A    (B) IT'S TIME                 1979 MOTOWN US 918  UK STML12140
ROBERT DOUGLAS     K V  (A
ELISHA INGRAMS     B V  (A      VICTOR JONES G V     (A ROBIN D CARLEY   WIND V(A GLENN WALLACE   TROM V(A
JEROME JUMONVILLE  HRNS (A      STEVE MADAIO    HRNS (A  DENNIS CHRISTIANSON HRNS (A RONNIE VANN        G (A
TYRELL DEADRICK    PERC (A      MICHAEL BODDICKER SYN (A
```

PLATTERS

```
DAVID LYNCH        V    (ABCDE   ALL TIME MOVIE HITS            19   MERCURY    US      SR  60782
HERB REED          V    (ABCDE   BEST OF VOL 1                  1973 PHILIPS    UK      6336 218
TONY WILLIAMS      V    (ABC     BEST OF VOL 2                  1973 PHILIPS    UK      6336 219
ALEX HODGE         V    (AB      CHRISTMAS WITH THE PLATTERS    19   MERCURY    US      SR 60841
PAUL ROBBI         V    (BCD     COLLECTION                     1976 HALLMARK   UK      PDA 003
ZOLA TAYLOR        V    (CD      DOUBLE GOLD PLATTERS           19   MUSICOR    US         4601
SONNY TURNER       V    (DE      ENCORE OF BROADWAY GOLDEN HITS 19   MERCURY    US      SR 60613
SANDRA DAWN        V    (E       ENCORE OF GOLDEN HITS          19   MERCURY    US      SR 60243
NATE NELSON        V    (E       ENCORE OF GOLDEN HITS OF THE GROUPS 19 MERCURY US      SR 60893
                                 ENCORES                        19   WING       US      SRW 16112
                                 THE FLYING PLATTERS            19   MERCURY    US      MG 20298
(A) 1953                         FLYING PLATTERS AROUND THE WORLD 19 MERCURY    US      SR 60043
(B) 1954                         GOING BACK TO DETROIT          19   MUSICOR    US      MS  3125
(C) 1955                         GOING BACK TO DETRIT           1967 STATESIDE  UK      SSL 10208
(D) 1961                         GOLDEN HOUR                    19   PYE        UK      GH 808
(E) 1963                         GREAT PRETENDER                1974 HALLMARK   UK      SHM  843
                                 HAVE THE MAGIC TOUCH           19   MUSICOR    US         3111
                                 I GET THE SWEETEST FEELING     1968 MUSICOR    US      MS  3171
                                 I LOVE YOU A THOUSAND TIMES    1966 MUSICOR    US      MS  3091
                                 IN THE STILL OF THE NIGHT      19   PICKWICK   US         3120
                                 JUKE BOX GIANTS                1981 AUDIO FIDELITY UK      007
                                 LIVE                           1974 CONTOUR    UK      6870 627
                                 LIFE IS JUST A BOWL OF CHERRIES 19  MERCURY    US      MG 20589
                                 MOONLIGHT MEMORIES             19   MERCURY    US      SR 60759
                                 MORE ENCORE OF GOLDEN HITS     19   MERCURY    US      SR 60252
                                 MUSIC FROM ACROSS THE WAY      1975 PHILIPS    UK      6382 117
                                 MY PRAYER                      1975 HALLMARK   UK      SHM 876
                                 NOW                            1975 CONTOUR    UK      6870 640
                                 NEW GOLDEN HITS OF THE PLATTERS 19  MUSICOR    US      MS  3141
                                 NEW GOLDEN HITS OF THE PLATTERS 1968 STATESIDE UK      SSL 10227
                                 NEW SOUL OF THE PLATTERS       19   MERCURY    US      SR 60983
                                 ONLY YOU                       19   GUEST STAR US      NG  1419
                                 ONLY YOU                       19   MUSICOR    US         1002
                                 OUR WAY                        19   PYE        UK      NSPL28149
                                 PLATTERS                       19   SPRINGBOARD        4059
                                 THE ORIGINAL                   1978 FESTIVAL   UK      ALB 281
                                 THE ORIGINAL                   1978 PHILIPS    UK      9100 049
```

(CONTINUED)

PLATTERS		19	KING	US		LP549
THE PLATTERS		19	STARDAY	US		K5002
THE PLATTERS		19	MERCURY	US		MG 20146
THE PLATTERS		19	IMPACT	UK		6886 401
THE PLATTERS		19	MERCURY	US		SR 60245
PLATTERS HITS		1976	SONIC			SON 002
PLATTERS HAVE THE MAGIC TOUCH		19	MUSICOR	US		MS 3111
REFLECTIONS		19	MERCURY	US		SR 60160
REFLECTIONS		19	WING RI	US		SRW 16672
REFLECTIONS		1968	WING	UK		WL1174
REMEMBER WHEN		19	MERCURY	US		SR 60087
SING LATINO		19	MERCURY	US		SR 60808
SING LATINO		1968	FONTANA	UK		SFL13040
SIXTEEN GREATEST HITS		19	TRIP	US		TOP 1611
SONG FOR THE LONELY		19	MERCURY	US		SR 60669
SPOTLIGHT ON		1974	PHILIPS	UK		6641 202
SUPER HITS		19	PICKWICK	US		3236
SWEET SWEET LOVIN'		19	MUSICOR	US		MS 3156
SWEET SWEET LOVIN'		1968	STATESIDE	UK		SSL 10245
TWO DECADES OF HITS		19	PYE	UK		PKL 4411
TWENTY CLASSIC HITS		1976	MERCURY	UK		9100 048
TEHTH ANNIVERSARY ALBUM		1968	WING	UK		WL 1174
WONDER OF YOU		1976	HALLMARK	UK		SHM 896

P98   PLAYER   P98

J C CROWLEY	K G V(AB	(A) PLAYER	1978	RSO US 1 3036	UK	2394 193
PETER BECKETT	G V (ABC	(B) DANGER ZONE	1978	RSO US 1 3026	UK	2394 208
JOHN FRIESEN	D (ABC	(B) DANGER ZONE	1978	RSO	UK	RSS 3
RON MOSS	B (ABC	(C) ROOM WITH A VIEW	19	CASABLANCA	UK	NBLP7217
WAYNE COOK	K (AB					

JAY LEWIS   G STEEL(A   JIM HORN   SAX   (A   MICHAEL OMARTIAN   SYN (A   REED KAILING   G (A
GARY COLEMAN   PERC (A   JACK WHITE   D   (A

P99   PLAYERS ASSOCIATION   P99

CHRIS HILLS G V K B D	(BD	(A) PLAYERS ASSOCIATION	1978	VANGUARD	VSD 79384
WENDELL MORRISSON V	(D	(B) BORN TO DANCE	1978	VANGUARD	VSD 79398
MICHAEL BRECKER	SAX (B	(C) TURN THE MUSIC UP	1979	VANGUARD	VSD 79421
DAVE SANBORN	SAX (B	(D) WE GOT THE GROOVE	1980	VANGUARD	VSD 79431
MARIAN ROLLE	V (D	(E) LET YOUR BODY GO	1980	VANGUARD	VSD 79434
JON FADDIS	TPT (B				

STEVE KHAN   G   (B   VICTOR PAZ   TPT (D   JOHN DEARTH   TPT (D   TOM HARREL   HRNS   (D
WILBUR BASCCOMB B   (B   MTUME   CONG (B   LORRAINE MOORE V   (B   WAYNE ANDRE TROM(B
MIKE MANDEL   SYN (B   LEON PENDARVIS K   (B   FREDDIE HARRIS G   (B   DANNY TRIFAN B (B
NICKY MARRERO   CONG (B   DAVID EARLE JOHNSON PERC(B ED'EASY' ZANT V   (B   JIM McELWAINE K (D
CALEB MARTIN   G   (D   LUCIO HOPPER   B   (D   RAY MANTILLA   PERC (D   BOB BERG   SAX(D
ONNIE CUBER   SAX (D

P100   COUSIN JOE PLEASANT   P100

COUSIN JOE PLEASANT V PNO(A		(A) BLUESMAN FROM NEW ORLEANS	1974	BIG BEAR	BEAR3
ROGER HILL	G (A				
GRAHAM GALLERY	V (A				
PADDY McHUGH	V (A				

PETE YORK   D (A   DYAN BIRCH   V   (A   FRANK COLLINS   V (A
GEORGE CHISHOLM TROM (A   COLIN SMITH   TPT (A   JOHNNY BARNES   CLAR(A

P102   PLEASURE   P102

(A) DUST YOURSELF OFF	1975	FANTASY		9473
(B) ACCEPT NO SUBSTITUTES	1976	FANTASY		9506
(C) JOYOUS	19	FANTASY		9526
(D) GET TO THE FEELING	1978	FANTASY	FT 543	9550
(E) FUTURE NOW	1979	FANTASY		9578
(F) SPECIAL THINGS	19	FANTASY		9600

P102A   PLUGS   P102A

(A) PLUGROCK (EP)	19	CATHEDRAL	CATH1

P102B   PLIMSOULS   P102B

LOU RAMIREZ	D (A	(A) THE PLIMSOULS	1981	PLANET US	P13
DAVE PAHOA	B V (A				
EDDIE MUNOZ	G (A				
HERMAN RILEY	SAX (A				

PETER CASE   G V (A   JACKIS KELSO   SAX (A   DOUG RICHARDSON SAX (A

P102C   PLUGZ   P102C

TITO LARRIVA	G V (A	(A) ELECTRIFY ME	1979	PLUG	001
BARRY McBRIDE	B V (A				
CHARLIE QUINTANA	D (A	CLIFF ROMAN	SAX (A	

P102D   PLUM NELLY   P102D

RIC PRINCE	K V (A	(A) DECEPTIVE LINES	19	CAPITOL UK	692
JOHN E WALKER	G (A				
STEVE RESS	G V (A	PETER HARRIS B V (A CHRISTOPHER LLOYD D PERC(A			

P103   PLUMMET AIRLINES   P103

DARRYL HUNT	B V (1A	(1) 1977			
RICHARD BOOTH	G V (1A	(A) ON STONEY GROUND (DBL)	1981	HEDONICS UK	HEDON1/2
DUNCAN KERR	G V (1A				
KEITH GOTHERIDGE	D (1A	HARRY STEPHENSON G V (1A GASPAR LAWAL	PERC (A		

P103A   PLUTO(1)   P103A

PAUL GARDNER	G V (A	(A) PLUTO	197	DAWN UK	DNLS 3030
ALLAN WARNER	G V (A				
MICHAEL WORTH	B (A	DEREK JERVIS D (A			

P104   PLUTO (2)   P104

WENCHE KJAERSTAD	V (A	(A) VOYAGE INTO A DREAMERS MIND	1980 STRWBERRY	SRLP 103
GUNNAR BERG-NIELSEN	D(A			

P104A   POACHER   P104A

TIM FLAHERTY	G (A	(A) POACHER	1978	RK	RKLP 5002
PETE ALLEN	STEEL(A			
PETE LONGBOTTOM	BANJ (A	ADRIAN HART G (A ALLAN CROOKES B (A STAN BENNETT D (A		

P105   POCKETS   P105

(A) COME GO WITH US	1977	CBS US 34897	UK	82288
(B) TAKE IT ON UP	1978	CBS US 35384		
(C) SO DELICOUS	1979	CBS US 36001		

[439]

POCO

```
    RUSTY YOUNG    V STEEL G(ALL        (A) PICKING UP THE PIECES      1969 EPIC   US 26460   UK      65327
    GEORGE GRANTHAM D(ABCDEFGHIJKLM     (B) POCO                       1970 EPIC   US 26522   UK      64082
    RICHIE FURAY     G V(ABCDEH         (C) DELIVERIN'                 1971 EPIC   US 30209   UK      64204
    RANDY MEISNER    B V G(A            (D) FROM THE INSIDE            1971 EPIC   US 30753   UK      64543
    JIM MESSINA      G V   (ABC         (E) GOOD FEELIN' TO KNOW       1973 EPIC   US 31601   UK      65126
    TIM SCHMIT       B V(BCDEFGHIJKLM   (F) CRAZY EYES                 1973 EPIC   US 32354   UK      65631
    PAUL COTTON      G V(DEFGHIJKLMNRST (G) SEVEN                      1974 EPIC   US 32895   UK      80082
    CHARLIE HARRISON B V    (ST         (H) CANTAMOS                   1975 EPIC   US 33192   UK      80596
    STEVE CHAPMAN    D     (STN         (I) THE VERY BEST OF POCO      1975 EPIC   US 33537   UK      88135
    MILT HOLLAND     PERC (JL           (J) HEAD OVER HEELS            1975 ABC    US   890   UK ABCL 5137
    STEVE FORMAN     PERC (JMOT         (K) LIVE                       1975 EPIC   US 33336   UK      80705
    DONALD FAGEN     SYN (M             (L) ROSE OF CIMARRON           1976 ABC    US   946   UK ABCL 5166
    KIM BULLARD      K V   (OST         (L) ROSE OF CIMARRON           1982 MCA               UK  MCL 1638
    MARK HENRY HARMAN K PROD(JL         (M) INDIAN SUMMER              1977 ABC    US   989   UK ABCL 5220
    AL GARTH         VLN  (JLG          (N) LEGEND                     1978 ABC    US  1099   UK ABCL 5264
    VICTOR FELDMAN   PERC (J            (O) UNDER THE GUN              1980 MCA    US  5132   UK  MCF 3076
    MICHAEL VON VERDICK V  (J           (P) SONGS OF RICHIE FURAY      1980 EPIC   US 36211
    CHRIS HILLMAN    MAND  (F           (Q) SONGS OF PAUL COTTON       1980 EPIC   US 36210
    PAUL HARRIS      PNO  (F            (R) BLUE & GRAY                1981 MCA    US 5227
    JOE LALA         PERC (F            (S) COWBOYS & ENGLISHMEN       1982 MCA    US 5288
    BILL GRAHAM      FDL (F             (T) GHOST TOWN                 1982 ATLANTIC          UK K50902
    BOBBYE HALL      PERC (G
    SID SHARP STRINGS    (LM  JOHN LOGAN     BANJO(L  STEVE FERGUSON    PNO (L  GARTH HUDSON     K  (J
    JIM HASKELL    STRING(JM BARRY FAST     PNO  (E  JAI WINDING        K   (N  TOM STEPHENSON   K  (N
    PHIL KENZIE      SAX  (NOT MICHAEL BODDICKER SYN (N  BURTON CUMMINGS  K   (G  DENISE SUBOTNIL  G V (T
    ARMAND KAPROFF   CELLO(T  BUELL NEIDLINGER    (T
```

POE

```
                                       (A) UP THROUGH THE SPIRAL      1972 UNI       US  73099
```

POET & THE ONE MAN BAND

```
    TONY COLTON      V PERC(A           (A) POET & THE ONE MAN BAND    1969 VERVE FORECAST UK SVLP6012
    RAY SMITH        G V  (A            (A) POET & THE ONE MAN BAND    1969 PARAMOUNT      US      5010
    BARRY MORGAN     D    (A
    PAT DONALDSON    B V  (A   ALBERT LEE      G V (A   NICKY HOPKINS   PNO (A  ROGER COULAM    ORG (A
    WILLIAM DAVIES   ORG  (A   SPEEDY ACQUAYE  CONGA(A   JERRY DONAHUE   V  (A  JOHN BELL       CLAR (A
    MIKE O'NEIL      K    (    PETE GAVIN      V D (
```

POET & THE ROOTS

```
    LINTON KWESI JOHNSON  V(A           (A) DREAD BEAT AN' BLOOD       1978 FRONT LINE     UK   FL1017
    VIVIAN WEATHERS  B G V(A
    DENNIS BOVELL    G K  (A   WINSTON CURNIFFE D  (A   JAH BUNNY      D   (A  DESMOND CRAIG   K  (A
    EVERALD FORREST  PERC (A   LILA WEATHERS    V  (A   JOHN VARNOM    G   (A
```

PEKKA POHJOLA

```
    PEKKA POHJOLA  B SYN K (ALL         (A) PIHKASILMA KAARNAKORVA     1972 LOVE                LRLP 71
    EERO KOIVISTOINEN SAX (B            (B) HARAKKA BIALOIPOKKU        1975 LOVE                LRLP 118
    PEKKA POYRY      SAX  (B            (B) B THE MAGPIE               1975 VIRGIN         UK   V 2036
    PAVONI PAAKUNAINEN    WIND(B        (C) SKUGGORNAS TJUVSTART       1977 LOVE                LRLP 219
    BERTIL LOFGREN   TPT (B             (C) MATHEMATICIANS AIR DISPLAY 1977 VIRGIN         UK   V 2084
    COSTE APETREA    G   (B             (D) VISITATION                1980 DIG IT              DIGLP 4
    TOMI PARKKONEN   D   (B
    GEORGE WADENIUS  G PERC(C  WLODEK GULGOWSKI SYN K(C   PIERRE MOERLEN  D PERC(C  VESA AALTONEN    D  (C
    MIKE OLDFIELD    G PERC(C  SALLY OLDFIELD   V  (C
```

POINT BLANK

```
    RUSTY BURNS      G V  (ABCDEF        (A) POINT BLANK              1976 ARISTA US AL 4087 UK ARTY 135
    KIM DAVIS        G V  (ABCDEF        (B) SECOND SEASON            1977 ARISTA US AL 4137 UK SPARTY1019
    PETER GRUEN      D    (ABCDEF        (C) AIRPLAY                  1979 MCA    US   3160 UK MCF 3049
    JOHN O'DANIEL    V    (ABCD          (D) THE HARD WAY             1980 MCA    US   5114 GER 202 431
    PHILIP PETTY     B    (AB            (E) AMERICAN EXCESS          1981 MCA    US   5189 GER 203 692
    BILL RANDOLPH    B V  (CDEF          (F) ON A ROLL                1982 MCA    US   5288 UK MCF3141
    STEVE HARDIN K V HCA  (CD
    KARL BERKE       K V  (D   MIKE HAMILTON    K   (EF  BUBBA KEITH       V  (EF
```

POINT OF VIEW

```
                                       (A) POINT OF VIEW             1973 RCA           4825
```

POLECAT

```
    GRAHAM BROAD D PERC V (A            (A) MONEY TALKIN'             1976 DJM           UK DJH 40475
    BERNIE LEE       G V  (A
    GEOFF KNOWLES    G V  (A   DAVE GOODMAN     B   (A STEPHEN COTTON  K V (A  ROGER DELL     PERC V(A
    ROBIN LAWRENCE   SAX  (A   MARTIN HAYES TPT V  (A
```

POLECATS

```
    TIM WORMAN            (A            (A) CULT HEROES   1981        NERVOUS          NERD 001
    BOZ BOORER           (A
    PHIL BLOOMBERG       (A   NEIL ROONEY      (A
```

POLICE

```
    GORDON 'STING'SUMNER  V B(ALL       (A) OUTLANDOS D'AMOUR         1978 A&M US 4753 UK AMLH68502
    ANDY SUMMERS     G V  (ALL          (B) REGATTA DE BLANC          1979 A&M US 4792 UK AMLH64792
    STEWART COPELAND D V  (ALL          (C) ZENYATTA MONDATTA         1980 A&M US 4831 UK AMLH64831
    HENRY PALOVANI   G    (             (D) GHOST IN THE MACHINE      1981 A&M US 3730 UK AMLK63730
    JEAN ROUSSEL     K    (D
    HUGH PADHAM      PROD (D
```

PAMELA POLLAND

```
    PAMELA POLLAND   K V  (A            (A) PAMELA POLLAND            1972 CBS US 31116 UK 64934
    TAJ MAHAL        G    (A
    MARC McCLURE     V    (A   DENNIS LOCORRIERE V  (A RAY SAWYER     V  (A  GEORGE CUMMINGS  V (A
    ROWAN BROS       V    (A   GEORGE DALY      V   (A JIMMY SPHEERIS V  (A  MARC McCALLEN    V (A
    MEMPHIS HRNS         (A   ART ROSCH      PERC (A PAUL FALLERSO  K  (A  ROSCOE HIRSCHBERG PERC(A
    NICKY HOPKINS    K    (A   DAVID BRIGGS     K   (A JOHN SHINE     G  (A  EDDIE HINTON     G (A
    RICHARD SCHLOSSER D   (A   KENNY BUTTREY    D   (A BING NATHAN    B  (A  NORBERT PUTNAM   B (A
    TOMMY COGBILL    B    (A   BOBBY WOOD       K   (A
```

BONNIE POINTER

```
BONNIE POINTER    V   (A     (A) BONNIE POINTER        1978 MOTOWN US M7 911 UK STML12101
TRUMAN THOMAS     K   (A     (B) BONNIE POINTER 2      1980 MOTOWN US    929 UK STML12129
NIGEL OLSSON      D   (A
OLLIE BROWN       G B (A   EDDIE HAZEL G  (A  JACK ASHFORD   PERC (A  JAMES JAMESON  B (A
DONALD BALDWIN    G B (A
```

POINTER SISTERS

```
ANITA POINTER     V    (ALL      (A) THE POINTER SISTERS      1973 BLUE THUMB US BT 48   UK ILPS 9243
RUTH POINTER      V    (ALL      (B) THATS A PLENTY           1974 BLUE THUMB US  6009   UK ILPS 9276
JUNE POINTER      V    (ALL      (C) LIVE AT THE OPERA HOUSE  1974 ABC       US  8002   UK ABCD  608
BONNIE POINTER    V    (ABCDF    (D) STEPPIN'                 1975 BLUE THUMB US  6021 UK ANCHOR   5133
GAYLORD BIRCH     D    (ACDF     (E) BEST OF                  1976 BLUE THUMB US ABC 6026 UK ABC ABCD 611
TOM SALISBURY     K    (ACDF     (F) HAVING A PARTY           1978 BLUE THUMB US  6023 UK ABC ABCL 5163
RON McCLURE       B    (A        (G) ENERGY                   1978 PLANET    US  P1 UK      K52107
WILLIE FULTON     G    (A        (H) PRIORITY                 1979 PLANET    US  9003 UK     K52161
JOHN REWIND       G    (A        (J) SPECIAL THINGS           1980 PLANET    US  P9 UK      K52242
SKIP MESQUITE     SAX  (A        (K) BLACK & WHITE            1981 PLANET         UK        K52300
JOHN NEWMAN       B    (C        (L) SO EXCITED               1982 PLANET         UK        RPLP6001
CHRIS MICHIE      G    (CDF
SONNY BURKE       K    (F   STEVIE WONDER   K  (DF  OLLIE BROWN    D  (J  NATHAN WATTS      B  (JKL
JAMES GADSON      D    (FJ  ED GREENE       D  (F   LOUIS JOHNSON  B  (F  CHUCK DOMANICO    B  (F
JAMES JAMESON     B    (F   WILLIE WEEKS    B  (F   GENE SANTINI   B  (FD WAH WAH WATSON    G  (DF
RAY PARKER        G    (F   DAVID T WALKER  G  (F   ROBERT BOWLES  G  (F  ERNIE WATTS       SAX(F
ANDY NARELL       STEEL(F   ED MARSHAL      D  (A   ROD ELLICOTT   D  (A  NORMAN LANDSBERG  K  (A
JOE CRANE         K    (A   DEXTER C PLATES B  (A   JEROME KIMSEY  D  (A  KENNETH NASH      PERC(F
GERALD JOHNSON    B    (G   MICHAEL BAIRD   D  (G   ABRAHAM LABORIEL B (G RANDY BACHMAN     G  (G
EDDIE WATKINS JNR B    (G   BRYAN CUMMING   SAX(G   JEFF PORCARO   D  (G  DAVID HUNGATE     B  (G
WADDY WACHTEL     G    (GH  DANNY KORTCHMAR G  (G   DAVID PAICH    K  (G  LENNY CASTRO      PERC(G
JIMMY PHILLIPS    K    (G   MIKE PORCARO    B  (G   STEVE PORCARO  K  (G  JAMES NEWTON HOWARD K(G
DAVEY JOHNSTONE   G    (G   JAI WINDING     K  (G   RICHARD PERRY  PERC(G RICK JAEGER       D  (G
FRED TACKETT      G    (G   HERBIE HANCOCK  K  (D   PAUL JOHNSON   B  (D  BILL SUMMERS      PERC(D
JIM ROTHERMEL     CLAR (D   DAVID SPINOZZA  G  (H   RICK MAROTTA   D  (H  DAN DUGMORE       G  (H
BILL PAYNE        PNO  (H   WILLIAM'SMITTY'SMITH K(MKL SCOTT CHAMBERS B (H BOBBY GUIDOTTI    PERC(H
NICKY HOPKINS     PNO  (H   GREG PHILLINGANES K (JKL PAUL JACKSON  G (JKL PAULINHO DACOSTA PERC(JKL
STEVE MADAIO      TPT  (J   JAY HUTSON      FLT(J   HENRY SIGISMONTE HRNS(J TIM MAY         G  (JK
LANCE ONG         SYN  (J   BURT BACHARACH  K STR(J MARLO HENDERSON G (J  GARY GRANT        TPT (JL
JOHN PIERCE       B    (J   CLARENCE McDONALD K (J  RICKY LAWSON   D  (J  DAVID WILLIAMS    G  (J
JOHN ROBINSON     D    (KL  DAVID FOSTER    SYN(K   ED WALSH       SYN(KL LEE RITENOUR      G  (L
NATHAN EAST       B    (L   ROBBIE BUCHANAN K SYN(K JIM HORN       SAX(L  RANDY WALDMAN     K  (L
JOHN PARKER       K SYN(L   CHUCK FINDLEY   TPT(JL  DON MYRICK     WIND(J BILL REOCHENBACH  TROM(J
TREVOR LAWRENCE   HRNS (JK   TOM SNOW       K SYN(J MICHAEL BODDICKER SYN(JL WARREN LOONEY   HRN(J
RAYMOND POUNDS    D    (J   BEN BRIDGES     G  (J   LARRY GITTENS  TPT(J  JOHN BARNES       K  (JKL
MARK GOLDENBURG   G    (J   JAMES JAMERSON  B  (J   RICHARD PERRY  PROD(JLK JAMES NEWTON HOWARD K(K
MIKE PORCARO      B    (K   MIKE COTTON     SYN(K   DANNY FARAGHER G  (L  GEORGE DOERING    G  (L
WADDY WACHTEL     G    (K   GARY HERBIG     SAX(L   DICK HYDE      TROM(L IRA NEWBORN
```

POISON GIRLS

```
VI SUBVERSA        G V (C     (A) FATAL MICROBES MEET THE POISON GIRLS(EP 1979 SMALL WONDER  UK WEENY3
RICHARD FAMOUS     G V (C     (B) HEX    (EP)                           1979 SMALL WONDER  UK WEENY4
BERNHARDT REBOURS  V B K(C    (C) CHAPPAQUIDDICK BRIDGE                  1980 CRASS        UK 421984/2
LANCE D'BOYLE      D V (C
NIL                VLN (C  GEM STONE       V  (C
```

MICHEL POLNAREFF

```
MICHEL POLNAREFF              (A) MICHEL POLNAREFF       1976 ATLANTIC US SD 18153 UK K50195
LEE RITENOUR       G   (A     (B) LIPSTICK               1976 ATLANTIC               UK K502B1
CLIFF GIVENS       V   (A
ANDREW GOLD        G V (A   STEVE CROPPER   G  (A  GARY STOVALL   G  (A  FRED TACKETT    G  (A
DONNIE DACUS       G   (A   DAVID HENSCHEL  K  (A  LEE SKLAR      B  (A  DAVID HUNGATE   B  (A
REINY PRESS        B   (A   WILLIE WEEKS    B  (A  NIGEL OLSSON   D  (A  JIM GORDON      D  (A
JIM KELTNER        D   (A   DAVID KEMPER    D  (A  RUSS KUNKEL    PERC(A STAR RICHARDS   SAX(A
ELLEN KEARNEY      V   (A   LEAH KUNKEL     V  (A  JENNIFER WARNES V (A  VALERIE CARTER  V  'A
BROOKS HUNNICUTT   V   (A   EUGENE GARFIN   V  (A  LEWIS FUREY    V  (A  BOBBY KING      V  (A
TERRY EVANS        V   (A
```

POLLUTION

```
JOHN LAMBERT       B V (A     (A) POLLUTION              19 ATCO    US    6051
RICHARD LEWIS      TPT K V(A
CHRISTIAN MOSERT   WIND K V(A DENNIS KENMORE  PERC V(A  JAMES QUILL SMITH G V (A DOBIE GRAY    V PERC(A
TATA               V   (A   JOE LALA   CONGA    (A  PAUL LEWINTHAL  SYN (A
```

POLYROCK

```
                              (A) POLYROCK               1980 RCA                   3714
```

JEAN LUC PONTY

```
JEAN LUC PONTY          VLN (ALL   (A) SUNDAY WALK             1967 MPS    006B 226           15045
WOLFGANG DAUNER         PNO (AR    (A) SUNDAY WALK             1975 BASF   BAP 5070            20645
NIELS HENNING PEDERSEN  B(AE   (B) ELECTRIC CONNECTION      1968 PACIFIC JAZZ 20156 UK LIBERTY 83262
DANIEL HUMAIR           D   (A    (C) EXPERIENCE              1969 PACIFIC JAZZ 20168 UK RI SUNSET 50232
GEORGE DUKE             PNO (BCD   (C) EXPERIENCE              1980 PAUSA  RI US 7065
WILBERT LONGMIRE        G   (B    (D) KING KONG               1970 PACIFIC JAZZ 20172 UK LIBERTY 83375
BUD SHANK               SAX (B    (E) ASTRORAMA               1970 FAR EAST                   65016
TONY ORTEGA             FLT (B    (F) OPEN STRINGS            1972 MPS        68088  BASF 75 21288
RICHARD ALPAN           SAX (B    (G) LIVE IN MONTREUX        1972 INNER CITY                 IC1003
TONY RISCH              TPT (B    (H) PONTY/GRAPPELLI         1973 AMERICA                    6139
LARRY McGUIRE           TPT (B    (J) UPON THE WINGS OF MUSIC 1975 ATLANTIC US 18138 UK       K50149
WILLIAM PETERSON        TPT (B    (K) IMAGINARY VOYAGE        1976 ATLANTIC US 18195 UK       K50317
PAUL HUBINON            TPT (B    (L) CANTELOUPE ISLAND(1969) 1976 BLUENOTE US BNLA 632 UK BND 4018
THURMAN GREEN           TROM(B    (M) AURORA                  1977 ATLANTIC US 18163 UK       K50228
FRANK STRONG            TROM(B    (N) ENIGMATIC OCEAN         1977 ATLANTIC US 19110 UK       K50409
FRANK WIMBERLEY         TROM(B    (O) COSMIC MESSENGER        1979 ATLANTIC US 29289 UK       K50505
BOB WEST                B   (B    (P) CIVILIZED EVIL          1980 ATLANTIC US 16020 UK       K50744
PAUL HUMPHREY           D   (B    (Q) A TASTE FOR PASSION     1979 ATLANTIC US 19253
SUGARCANE HARRIS        VLN (R    (R) NEW VIOLIN SUMMIT       1972 MPS GER 33 21285/8
MICHAEL URBANIAK        VLN (R    (S) MYSTICAL ADVENTURES     1982 ATLANTIC         UK        K50872
```

(CONTINUED)

P115 (CONTINUED)

JEAN LUC PONTY

JOHN HEARD	B	(CL	DICK BERK	D	(CL	GENE ESTES VIBES PERC	(DL	BUELL NEIDLINGER	B	(DL
ARTHUR TRIPP	D	(DL	IAN UNDERWOOD	SAX	(DL	WILTON FELDER	B (DL	JOHN GUERIN	D	(DL
ERNIE WATTS	SAX	(DL	FRANK ZAPPA	G	(DL	DONALD CHRISTLIEB WIND	(DL	GENE CIPRIANO	WIND	(DL
VINCENT DE ROSA	HRNS	(DL	ARTHUR MAEBE	HRNS	(DL	JONATHAN MEYER	FLT (DL	HAROLD BEMKO	CELLO	(DL
MILTON THOMAS	VLA	(DL	MASAHIKO SATO	PNO	(E	YOSHIAKI MASUO	G (E	MOTOHIKO HINO	D	(E
JOACHIM KUHN	PNO	(FG	PHILIP CATHERINE	G	(FH	OLIVER JOHNSON	D (FG	PETER WARREN	B	(F
J F JENNY CLARKE	B	(G	NANA	PERC	(G	STEPHANE GRAPPELLY	VLN (H	MAURICE VANDER	PNO	(H
NIPSO BRANTHER	VLN	(R	TERJE RYPDAL	G	(R	NEVILLE WHITEHEAD	B (R	ROBERT WYATT	D	(R
TONY BONFILS	B	(H	ANDRE CECCARELLI	D	(M	DARRYL STUERMER	G(KMNP	PATRICE RUSHEN	K	(MJ
TOM FOWLER	B	(KM	NORMAN FEARRINGTON	D	(M	ALLAN HOLDSWORTH	G (N	RALPHE ARMSTRONG	B	(NO
ALLAN ZAVOD	K	(KNPQ	STEVE SMITH	D	(K	MARK CRANEY	D (OP	CASEY SCHEUERELL	D	(OQ
PETER MAUNU	G	(O	JOAQUIN LIEVANO	G	(OPQ	CHRIS RHYNE	K (P	RANDY JACKSON	B	(P

P115A PONY EXPRESS

(A) PONY EXPRESS	1972	REBEL	US	1513

P116 THE POP

DAVID SWANSON	G V	(B	(A) THE POP		1977	ARISTA	ARTY	170
ROGER PRESCOTT	G V	(B	(B) THE POP		1978	AUTOMATIC	SA	101
JOEL MARTINEZ	D	(	(C) GO!		1979	ARISTA US 4243 UK SPART 1107		
TIM HENDERSON	B V	(B						
IVAN KRAL	(	TIM McGOVERN	G (B	DAVID ROBINSON	(	STEPHEN T	(	
DAVID HOSKOT	D	(	TIM HENDERSON	V (				

P117 THE POP GROUP

MARK STEWART	V	(A	(A) THE POP GROUP 'Y'	1979	RADAR	UK	RAD 20
PAUL STEWART	D	(A	(B) FOR HOW MUCH LONGER DO WE TOLERATE	1980	ROUGH TRADE	UK	ROUGH9
BRUCE SMITH	D	(A	(C) WE ARE TIME	1980	ROUGH TRADE	UK	ROUGH 12
GARETH SAGER	G	(A					
SIMON UNDERWOOD	B	(A	JOHN WADDINGTON G (A				

P117A POPOL ACE

ARNE SCHULZE	G	(	(A) POPOL ACE	1973	POLYDOR	2480 270
THOR ANDREASSEN	D	(	(B) STOLEN FROM TIME	1975	POLYDOR	2480 332
TERJE METHI	B	(	(C) CURLY SOUNDS	1978	POLYDOR	2483 498
PETE KNUDSEN G K SYN	(					
JAHN TEIGEN	V	(				

P117B POP RIVETS

WILD BILLY CHILDISH V	(AB	(A) GREATEST HITS		1979	HIPOCRITE	HIP 007
WILL POWER	G V	(AB	(B) EMPTY SOUNDS FROM ANARCHY RANCH	1979	HIPOCRITE	HIP 0
RUSSELL SQUARE	B V	(AB				
VALENTINE LAX	D V	(A	LI'L RUSS D (B			

P117C POPOL VUH (NORWAY)

JOHN TEIGEN	V	(AB	(A) POPOL VUH	19	POLYDOR
TERJE METHI	B	(AB	(B) QUICHE MAYA	19	POLYDOR
PETE KNUDSEN	K G	(AB			
ARNE SCHULTZE	G	(AB	PJOUKEN EIDE TROM (AB	THOR ANDREASSEN	D (AB

P118 POPOL VUH (GERM)

FLORIAN FRICKE	PNO	(ALL	(A) AFFENSTUNDE	1971	LIBERTY GER	LBS 83460
DANIEL FISCHELSCHER	G	(DEFGHJKLMN	(A) AFFENSTUNDE	1980	INNOVATIVE COMMINICATION	58159
TED DE JONG	PERC	(HKL	(B) IN DEN GARTEN PHARAOS	1972	PILZ GER	212769
BOB ELISCU	OBOE	(CDL	(C) HOSIANNA MANTRA	1973	PILZ GER	291431
MATTIAS V TIPPELSKIRCH	FLT	(J	(C) HOSIANNA MANTRA	1981	CELESTRIAL HARMONIES US CEL 004	
HOLGER TRULKSCH	PERC	(AB	(D) SELIGPREISUNG	1974	KOSMISCHE GER	58 009
ALOIS GROMER	SITAR	(FHJKLM	(E) EINSJAGER UND SIEBENJAGER	1975	KOSMISCHE GER	58 017
FRANK FIELDER	SYN	(AB	(F) DAS HOELIED	1975	UA GER	UAS 29781
CONNY VEIT	G	(CD	(G) AGUIRRE	1975	PDA IT	6040
DJONG YUN	SAX	(CEFGHM	(G) AGUIRRE	1975	BARCLAY FR	840103
KLAUS WIESE	PERC	(C	(H) LETZTE TAGE LETZTE NACHTE	1976	UA GER	UAS 29916
FRITZ SONNLEITNER	VLN	(C	(I) YOGA	1976	PDU IT	6060
SHANA KUMA	TABLAS	(F	( ) PERLENKLANGEO THE BEST OF	1977	PDU IT	6073
SUSAN GOETTING	OBOE	(M	(J) HERZ AUS GLAS (HEART OF GLASS)	1977	BRAIN GER	0060 079
RENATE KNAUP	V	(MN	(J) COEUR DE VERRE (" " ")	1977	EGG FR	900536
CHRIS KARRER	SAX	(N	(K) ON THE WAY TO A LITTLE WAY/NOSFERATU	78	EGG FR	900573
			(L) BRUDER DES SCHATTENS-	1978	BRAIN GER	0060 167
			(M) DIE NACHT DER SEELE	1979	BRAIN GER	0060 242
			(N) SEI STILL, WISSE ICH BIN	1981	INNOVATIVE COMMINICATION	80007
			(CE) DISCOVER COSMIC	1973	OHR DBL GER	94011920

P118A POTTER ST CLOUD

DAVE POTTER	(A	(A) POTTER ST CLOUD				
ENDLE ST CLOUD	(A		1971	MEDIARTS	41 7	
JAMES HARRELL	(A	DANNY BAKER	K V (A	BUZZ CLIFFORD	V (A	GENE TREEK G V (A
SNEAKY PETE	STEEL (A	BILLY CALDWELL	ORG (A	LEE KIEFER	(A	MATT MOORE V (A
GARY MONTGOMERY	V (A	EDDIE FISHER	G (A			

P118B POPPEES

(A) IF SHE CRIES	1978	LINE GER EP	3001

P118C PORK DUKES

VILOS STYLES	G V	(A	(A) PORK DUKES	19	WOOD PORK 001
HARRENDUS STYLES	G	(A			
MARK E VALLEY	K	(A	GERMUM LE PIG D (A		

P118D PORTLAND

GARY OGAN	G V	(A	(A) PORTLAND	1972	ELEKTRA US	75048
BILL LAMB	G V	(A				
DAVID BRIGGS	PNO	(A	RUSSELL DASHIEL	G (A	BOB WRAY	B (A FRED PROUDY D (A
EMORY GORDY	B	(A	DENNIS ST JOHN	D (A	BOBBY BRUCE	FDL (A JOHN BERGMAN PNO (A
RICHARD BENELF	STEEL	(A				

P118E POSITIVE NOISE

ROSS MIDDLETON	V K B	(A	(A) HEART OF DARKNESS	1981	STATIC UK STAT LP1
GRAHAM MIDDLETON	K V	(A			
FRASER MIDDLETON	B V	(A	RUSSELL BLACKSTONE G V (A	LES GAFF	D V (A

POT LIQUOR

P118F

GEORGE RATZLAFF	K G V(A	(A) FIRST TASTE	1972				
JERRY AMOROSO	D V (A	(B) LEVEE BLUES	19	JANUS	US	3033	
GUT SCHAEFFER	B V (A	(C) LOUISIANA ROCK'N'ROLL	19	JANUS	US	3036	
LES WALLACE	G V (A						

NIC POTTER & GUY EVANS

P118G

NIC POTTER	(A	(A) LONG HELLO VOL 2	1981	BUTT	UK	NOTT004
GUY EVANS	(A					

POUSSEZ

P118H

(A) LEAVE THAT BOY ALONE	1980	VANGUARD	VSD 79433	

POUSSETTE DART BAND

P119

JOHN POUSSETTE DART	G (ABCD	(A) POUSSETTE DART	1976	CAPITOL	EST 11507	
JOHN CURTIS	G (ABCD	(B) AMNESIA	1977	CAPITOL	EST 11608	
JOHN TROY	B (CBD	(C) 3	1978	CAPITOL	SW 11781	
MICHAEL DAWE	D (CD	(D) NEVER ENOUGH	1979	CAPITOL	11935	
NORMAN PRIDE	PERC (CD					
DAVE APPELL STRINGS	(CD	HANK MEDRESS PERC (C	DAVID LASLEY	V (CD	STAN SCHWARTZ	K (CD
ARNOLD McCULLER	V (CD					

POWDER BLUES BAND

P119A

TOM LAVIN	G V (AB	(A) UNCUT	1980	RCA	PL 10365	
JACK LAVIN	B V (AB	(B) THIRSTY EARS	1981			
WILL MAC CALDER	K V (AB					
DURIS MAXWELL	D (AB	DAVE WOODWARD SAX V(AB	WAYNE KOZAK	SAX (A	GORD BERTRAM	SAX (AB
MARK HASSELBACH	TPT (AB					

COZY POWELL

P119B

COZY POWELL	D (AB	(A) OVER THE TOP	1979	ARIOLA NL201178 UK ARL5038		
JACK BRUCE	B (AB	(A) OVER THE TOP	1979	POLYDOR	US 6312	
DON AIREY	K (AB	(B) TILT	1981	POLYDOR UK5047 US	1 6342	
GARY MOORE	G (AB					
CLEM CLEMPSON	(AB	MAX MIDDLETON K (A	BERNIE MARSDEN G (AB	JEFF BECK	G (B
DAVID SANCIOUS	K (B	CHRIS GLENN B (B	ELMER GANTRY V (B	MEL COLLINS	SAX(B
KIRBY	G (B	NEIL MURRAY B (B	FRANK AIELLO B V (B	JOHN COOK	K (B

ROGER POWELL

P119C

ROGER POWELL	K (A	(A) AIR POCKET	1980	BEARSVILLE US 6994 UK ILPS9607	

DUFFY POWER

P120

DUFFY POWER	V (ALL	(A) INNOVATIONS	1971	TRANSATLANTIC	TRA229		
JOHN McLAUGHLIN	G (A	(B) DUFFY POWER	1973	SPARK	SRLM 2005		
COLIN PINCOTT	G (A	(C) DUFFY POWER	1973	GSF	GS 502		
JACK BRUCE	B (A	(D) POWERHOUSE	1976	BUK	BULP2010		
DANNY THOMPSON	B (A						
TERRY COX	D (A	PHIL SEAMAN D (A	RED REECE D (A	MARTIN KERSHAW	G (D
GRAHAM JONES	G (D	MARY ZINOVIEFF PNO (D	MIKE THOMPSON B (D	RAY COOPER PERC	(D
ALLAN JAMES	G (D	PETER KIRKE B (D	MIKE GILES D (D	PERE AHERN	D (D
BRYSON GRAHAM	D (D	CHRIS BAILEY D (D	DANA GILLESPIE V (D	ALEXIS KORNER	V (D
BOZ BURRELL	V (D	PAM McKENNA V (D	JOY YATES V (D	MISTY BROWING	V (D

POWERHOUSE FOUR

P122

ERIC CLAPTON	G (A	(A) WHAT'S SHAKIN' (3 TRACKS)	1966	ELEKTRA 4002 UK RI UK EUK 260	
STEVE WINWOOD	K V (A				
PAUL JONES	V HCA(A	JACK BRUCE B V (A	BEN PALMER PNO (A	PETE YORK	D (A

PRAGVEC

P122A

NICHOLAS CASH	D (B	(A) NO COWBOYS	1980	SREC	UK
JOHN STUDHOLME	G V (B	(B) PRAGVEC (EP)	198	CELLULOID	FR 1040
DAVID BOYD	V B (B				
SUSAN GOGAN	V SYN(B				

ANDY PRATT

P123

ANDY PRATT	V PNO(ALL	(A) RECORDS ARE LIKE LIFE	1969	POLYDOR	UK 2489 003	
ANDY MENDELSON	K (D	(B) ANDY PRATT	1973	EPIC US 31722	UK 65646	
GARY LINK	B V (D	(C) RESOLUTION	1976	NEMPEROR US NE438	UK K50279	
RICK SCHLOSSER	D (D	(D) SHIVER IN THE NIGHT	1977	NEMPEROR US NE443	UK K50386	
MARK DOYLE	K G V (BCD	(E) MOTIVES	1979	NEMPEROR US 35781		
LUTHER VANDROSS	V (D					
STEVE GADD	D (C	G DIANE SUMLER V (D	DAVID LASLEY V (D	MICHAEL BRECKER	SAX (D
LOUIS MARINI	SAX (D	LEWIS DEL GATTO SAX (D	RANDY BRECKER TPT (D	RUBENS BASSINI	PERC(DC
ANDY NEWMARK	D (DC	HUGH McDONALD B (CD	GENE ORLOFF STRINGS (D	ARIF MARDIN	PERC(C
DIANE SUMLER	V (C	ANDY MENDELSON SYN (C	CARLOS MARTIN PERC (C	TONY LEVIN	B (C
KEN BICHEL	SYN (C	RICHARD MENDELSON D (C	LUTHER VANDROSS V (C	DAVID LASLEY	V (C
THE ROWANS	V (C				

PRAYING MANTIS

P123A

TINO TROY	G V (A	(A) TIME TELLS NO LIES	1981	ARISTA UK SPART1153 GER 203 449	
CHRIS TROY	B V (A				
STEVE CARROLL	G V (A	DAVE POTTS D (A	TIM FRIESE GREENE PNO(A		

PRELUDE

P124

BRIAN HUME	G V (ABCDE	(A) HOW LONG IS FOREVER	1973	DAWN	UK DNLS 3052	
IAN VARDY	G V (ABCDE	(B) AFTER THE GOLDRUSH	1974	ISLAND	ILPS 9282	
IRENE HUME	V PERC(ABCDE	(C) DUTCH COURAGE	1974	DAWN	UK DNLS 3061	
TONY HYMAS	K (E	(D) OWLCREEK INCIDENT	1975	DAWN DNLH 3	PYE 12120	
HUGH BURNS	G (E	(E) BACK INTO THE LIGHT	1976	PYE	NSPL19448	
DAVE MATTACKS	D (E					
DAVE PEACOCK	B (E	ISAAC GUILLORY B K G(D	MIKE DRISCOLL D (D	ALAN CARNEY	B (E
JIM HORNSBY	BANJO(D	PATRICE LEMOINE K (D	ROGER RETTIG G STEEL (D	LINDA CURTIS	PERC (D
STEVE GREGORY	SAX (D	ROD CLEMENTS B (D	PICK WITHERS D (D		

ELVIS PRESLEY	G V	(ALL						
BILL BLACK	B	SCOTTY MOORE	G	D J FONTANA	D	FLOYD CRAMER	PNO	
JAMES BURTON	G	HANK GARLAND	G	CHET ATKINS	G	KENNY BURRELL	G	
HAL BLAINE	D	JORDANAIRES	V	BUDDY HARMON	D	RONNIE TUTT	D	
JOHN WILKINSON	G	JERRY SCHEFF	B	GLEN D HARDIN	K	SONNY BROWN	PNO	
DAVID BRIGGS CLAR	K	CHARLIE HODGES	G V	BOOTS RANDOLPH	SAX	MARVIN HUGHES	PNO	
SHORTY LONG	PNO	NEAL MATTHEWS	SAX	HUGH JARRETT	V	HOYT HAWKINS	V	
DUDLEY BROOKS	PNO	MIKE STOLLER	PNO	MILLIE KIRKHAM	V	KITTY WHITE	V	
H J TUIMBRELL	G	BOB MOORE	B	HAROLD BRADLEY	G	CHIP YOUNG	G	
PETE DRAKE	G	TOM TEDESCO	G	DON RANDI	K	LARRY KNECHTEL	B	
MIKE DEASY	G	TOMMY COGBILL	B G	BOBBY EMMONS	PNO	GLEN SPREEN	ORG	
MIKE LEECH	B	HENRY SLAUGHTER	ORG	CHARLIE McCOY	HCA	GRADY MARTIN	G	
PETE HALLIN	K	JERRY REED	G	DARLENE LOVE	V	FANITA JAMES	V	
JEAN KING	V	JEANNIE GREENE	V	LARRY MUHOBERAC	PNO	NORBERT PUTNAM	B	
JERRY CARRIGAN	D	TEMPLE RISER	V	KEN BUTTREY	D	EMORY GORDY	B	
JOHN CHRISTOPHER	G	KATH WESTMORELAND	V	J D SUMNER	V	STAMPS	V	
RONNIE MILSAP	V	ED LOGAN	HRNS	MARY HOLLADAY	V	GINGER HOLLADAY	V	
BOB TAYLOR	HRNS	WAYNE JACKSON	HRNS	GENE CHRISMAN	V	JUBILEE FOUR	V	
CAROLE LOMBARD QUARTET		BOB WOOD	PNO	REGGIE YOUNG	G	SANDY POSEY	V	

			MONO UK	STER UK	MONO US	STER US	
ELVIS (ROCK'N'ROLL No1)	HMV	1956	CLP 1093				
" " "	RCA				LPM 1254	LSP 1254	
ELVIS (ROCK'N'ROLL No2)	HMV	1956	CLP 1105				
" " "	RCA	1956	RD 7528	SF 7526	LPM 1382	LSP 1382	RI INT 5142 1981
THE BEST OF ELVIS	HMV	1956	DLP 1159				
LOVING YOU	RCA	1957	RC 24001		LPM 1515	LSP 1515	
LOVING YOU RI 12"	RCA	1977		PLG 2358			
ELVIS CHRISTMAS ALBUM	RCA	1957	RD 27052		LOC 1035		
" " "	RCA	195			LPM 1951	LSP 1951	
" " " "	CAMDEN	19	INT 1126		CAS 2428		RI 1980 INT 5060
KING CREOLE	RCA	1958	RD 27088	SF 8231	LPM 1884	LSP 1884	
GOLDEN RECORDS VOL 1	RCA	1958	RD 16069	SF 8129	LPM 1707	LSP 1707	RI 1980 INT 5143
ELVIS FOR LP FANS ONLY	RCA	1959	RD 27120	SF 8378	LPM 1990	LSP 1990	
A DATE WITH ELVIS	RCA	1959	RD 27128		LPM 2011	LSP 2011	
ELVIS GOLDEN RECORDS VOL 2	RCA	1959	RD 27159 ·	SF 8151	LPM 2075	LSP 2075	RI 1981 INT 5144
ELVIS IS BACK	RCA	1960	RD 27171	SF 5060	LPM 2231	LSP 2231	RI 1981 INT 5141
G I BLUES	RCA	1960	RD 27192	SF 5078	LPM 2256	LSP 2256	
HIS HAND IN MINE	RCA	1960	RD 27211	SF 5094	LPM 2328	LSP 2328	
" " " "	RCA RI	19		SF 8207			
SOMETHING FOR EVERYBODY	RCA	1961	RD 27244	SF 5106	LPM 2370	LSP 2370	RI 1981 INT 5135
BLUE HAWAII	RCA	1961	RD 27238	SF 5115	LPM 2426	LSP 2426	RI 1981 INT 5136
" " "	RCA RI	19		SF 8145			
POT LUCK	RCA	1962	RD 27265	SF 5135	LPM 2523	LSP 2523	
GIRLS GIRLS GIRLS	RCA	1963	RD 7534	SF 7534	LPM 2621	LSP 2621	
IT HAPPENED AT THE WORLD FAIR	RCA	1963	RD 7565	SF 7565	LPM 2697	LSP 2697	
" " " " "	RCA RI	19		1025		APLI2568	
FUN IN ACAPULCO	RCA	1963	RD 7609	SF 7609	LPM 2756	LSP 2756	
GOLDEN RECORDS VOL 3	RCA	1964	RD 7630	sf 7630	LPM 2765	LSP 2765	RI 1981 INT 5145
KISSIN COUSINS	RCA	1964	RD 7645	SF 7645	LPM 2894	LSP 2894	
ROUSTABOUT	RCA	1965	RD 7678	SF 7678		LSP 2999	
GIRL HAPPY	RCA	1965	RD 7714	SF 7714	LPM 3338	LSP 3338	
FLAMING STAR	RCA	1965	RD 7723		PRS 279		
" " "	RCA	19		INT 1017			
" " "	CAMDEN	19			CAS 2304		
ELVIS FOR EVERYONE	RCA	1965	RD 7751	SF 7751	LPM 2450	LSP 3450	
" " "	RCA	19		SF 8232			RI 1981 INT 5073
HARUM SCARUM	RCA	1965			LPM 3468	LSP 3468	
HAREM HOLIDAY	RCA	1965	RD 7767	SF 7767			
HAREM HOLIDAY	RCA	19		46 1022			
FRANKIE & JOHNNY	RCA	1966	RD 7793	SF 7793	LPM 3553	LSP 3553	
" " "	RCA	19		46 1024		ACL 7007	
" " "	RCA	19				APLI2559	
PARADISE HAWAIIAN STYLE	RCA	1966	RD 7810	SF 7810	LPM 3643	LSP 3643	
CALIFORNIA HOLIDAY	RCA	1966	RD 7820	SF 7820			
" " "	RCA	19		46 1020			
SPIN OUT	RCA	1966			LPM 3702	LSP 3702	
" "	RCA	197				APLI2560	
HOW GREAT THOU ART	RCA	1967	RD 7867	SF 7867	LPM 3758	LSP 3758	
" " " "	RCA	19		SF 8206			RI 1981 INT 5147
DOUBLE TROUBLE	RCA	1967	RD 7892	SF 7892	LPM 3787	LSP 3787	
" " "	RCA	196				AFLI2564	
CLAMBAKE	RCA	1967	RD 7917	SF 7917	LPM 3893	LSP 3893	
" "	RCA	19		46 1021		APLI2565	
GOLDEN RECORDS VOL 4	RCA	1968	RD 7924	SF 7924	LPM 3921	LSP 3921	RI 1981 INT 5146
SPEEDWAY	RCA	1968	RD 7957	SF 7957	LPM 3989	LSP 3989	
NBC TV SPECIAL	RCA	1968	RD 8011			LSP 4088	
FROM ELVIS IN MEMPHIS	RCA	1969	RD 8029	SF 8029		LSP 4155	
FROM MEMPHIS TO VEGAS	RCA	1970		SF 8080		LSP 6020	
ON STAGE FEB 1970	RCA	1970		SF 8128		LSP 4362	
WORLDWIDE 50 GOLD HITS VOL 1	RCA	1970	LPM 6401		LPM 6401		
IN PERSON AT THE INTERNATIONAL	RCA	1970				LSP 4428	
BACK IN MEMPHIS	RCA	1970				LSP 4429	
LETS BE FRIENDS	RCA INT	1970		INT 1103			
" " "	CAMDEN	1970			CAS 2408		
ALMOST IN LOVE	RCA INT	1970		INT 1023			
" " "	CAMDEN	1970			CAS 2440		
THATS THE WAY IT IS	RCA	1971		SF 8162		LSP 4445	RI 1981 INT 5137
ELVIS COUNTRY I'M 10,000 YEARS OLD	RCA	1971		SF 8172		LSP 4460	
LOVE LETTERS FROM ELVIS	RCA	1971		SF 8202		LSP 4530	
50 GOLD AWARD (THE OTHER SIDES)	RCA	1971	LPM 6402		LPM 6402		

(CONTINUED)

[444]

Title	Label	Year			
C'MON EVERYBODY	RCA INT	1971	INT 1280		
" " "	CAMDEN	1971		CAS 2518	
I GOT LUCKY	RCA INT	1971	INT 1322	CAS 2533	
" "	CAMDEN	1971	CDS 1154	CAS 2611	
YOU'LL NEVER WALK ALONE	CAMDEN	1971	CMD 1088	CAS 2472	
WONDERFUL WORLD OF CHRISTMAS	RCA	1971	SF 8221	LSP 4579	
" " " "	RCA	197		ANI 1936	
ELVIS NOW	RCA	1972	SF 8266	LSP 4671	
LIVE AT MADISON SQUARE GARDENS	RCA	1972	SF 8296	LSP 4776	
HE TOUCHED ME	RCA	1972	SF 8275	LSP 4690	
HITS FROM THE MOVIES	CAMDEN	1972	CDS 1110	CAS 2567	
HITS FROM THE MOVIES VOL2	CAMDEN	1972		CAS 4776	
ALOHA FROM HAWAII	RCA	1973	DPS 2040	VPSX6089	
ELVIS	RCA	1973	PL 10283	APL10283	
BURNING LOVE	RCA INT	1973	INT 1414		
" "	CAMDEN	1973		CAS 2595	
RAISED ON ROCK	RCA	1973	PL 10388	APL10388	
SEPARATE WAYS	CAMDEN	1973	CDS 1118	CAS 2611	
LEGENDARY PERFORMER 1	RCA	1974	LP 10341	CPL10341	
GOOD TIMES	RCA	1974	PL 10475	APL10475	
LIVE ON STAGE IN MEMPHIS	RCA	1974	PL 10606	APL10606	
HAVING FUN ON STAGE	RCA	1974	PM 10828	AFM10818	
40 GREATEST HITS	ARCADE	1975	ADEP 12		
HITS OF THE 70s	RCA	1974	FL 17527		
PROMISED LAND	RCA	1974	PL 10873	APL10873	
PURE GOLD	RCA	1975		ANL10971	
TODAY	RCA	1975	PL 11039	APL11039	
LEGENDARY PERFORMER VOL 2	RCA	1975		CLP11349	
US MALE	CAMDEN	1974	CDS 1150		
PICTURES OF ELVIS	RCA	1975	HY 1023		
DOUBLE DYNAMITE	PICKWICK	1975		DL 25001	
THE SUN COLLECTION	RCA	1975	HY 1001		
THE SUN SESSIONS	RCA	1976	PM 11675	APL11675	
FROM ELVIS PRESLEY BOULEVARD	RCA	1976	PL 11506	APL11506	
WELCOME TO MY WORLD	RCA	1976	PL 12274	APL12274 RI 1981 LP 3020	
MOODY BLUE	RCA	1977	PL 12428	APL12428 RI 1981 LP 3021	
THE SUN YEARS	CHARLY	1977	SUN 1001		
IN DEMAND	RCA	1977	PL 42003		
THE '56 SESSIONS	RCA	1978	PL 42101		
40 GREATEST HITS	RCA	1978	PL 42691		
ELVIS TAPES CHISWICK /ACE		197	RED 1		
ELVIS PRESLEY COLLECTION	PICKWICK	1978	PDA 042		
HE WALKS BESIDE ME	RCA	1978	PL 12772	APL12772	
TV SPECIAL	RCA	1978	PL 42370		RI 19 5093
LEGENDARY PERFORMER VOL 3	RCA	1978	PL 13082		
RETURN TO SENDER	PICKWICK	19	CDS 1200		
ELVIS	PICKWICK	19	CDS 1201		
WONDERFUL WORLD	PICKWICK	19	PDA 073		
THE '56 SESSIONS VOL 2	RCA	1979	PL 42102		RI 1981 INT 3025
OUR MEMORIES OF YOU	RCA	1979	PL 13448		
ELVIS AARON PRESLEY (8 RECORD SET)	RCA	1980	CPL83699	3699	
INSPIRATION	K TEL	1980	NE 1101		
GUITAR MAN	RCA	1980	RCALP5010	3917	
THE '56 SESSIONS VOL 2	RCA	1981	3030		
HEARTBREAK HOTEL	CAMDEN	1981	CDS 1204		
ITS NOW OR NEVER	CAMDEN	1981	CDS 1202		
ARE YOU LONSOME TONIGHT	CAMDEN	1982	CDS 1207		
GREATEST HITS	RCA	1982	INT 5116		
ROCK & ROLL REBEL	K TEL	1982	NE 1170		
SUSPICIOUS MINDS	CAMDEN	1982	CDS 1206		
THE SOUND OF YOUR CRY	RCA	1982	ALP 3060		
OTHER RELEASES					
PORTRAIT IN MUSIC	RCA	1975	SRS 558		
LID ROCKS	RCA	1975	RJS27120		
GOLD THIRTY	RCA	1975	6176 77		
TODAY TOMORROW & FOREVER	RCA	1971	LSP 10220 GER		
ELVIS THE ROCKIN DAYS	RCA	1972	LSP 10204 GER		
ELVIS FOREVER	RCA	1974	PJL 8024		
SONGS FOR CHILDREN	RCA	1978	PL 12901 GER		
CANADIAN TRIBUTE	RCA	1978	KKL 1 7065 GER		
RARE ELVIS	RCA	1980	PL 42935 GER		
JAILHOUE ROCK/TICKLE ME	RCA	1979	PL 42792 GER		
EASY COME/KID GALLAHAD	RCA	1979	PL 42791 GER		
BURBANK SESSIONS	AUDIFON	19	AFNS 62768 GER		
THIS IS ELVIS	RCA	1981	PL 4031 GER		
GOOD ROCKIN' TONIGHT 10"	RCA	19	130 252		
ELVIS GOLDEN RECORDS 10"	RCA	19	HP 50X		
PANEL DELUXE	RCA	19	9201		
ON STAGE FEB 1970	RCA	19	R4P 5009		
GREAT HITS	RCA	19	SR1 9062		
CHRISTMAS ALBUM	RCA	19	5028		
GIRL HAPPY	RCA	19	5436		
GOLDEN BOY	HORZU	19	SHZT521		
GOLDEN BOY	RCA	1981	GER 43559		
ROCKIN' ON VOL 1	RCA	19	135		
ROCKIN' ON VOL 2	RCA	19	141		
MAGICAL ROCKIN' SOUND	JUBILEE	19	MLP1956		
BLUE CHRISTMAS	RCA	19	KNLI7047		
ELVIS PRESLEY 10"	RCA	19	CML 3009		
ELVIS PRESLEY	IMPACT	1978	6886807		
GREATEST HITS (7 RECORD SET)	RCA	19	GELV 6A		

(CONTINUED)

```
         EPS
         ELVIS PRESLEY                   1956   RCA    US 1254
         ELVIS PRESLEY                   1956   RCA    US 747
         ELVIS PRESLEY                   1956   RCA    US 830
         LOVE ME TENDER                  1956   RCA    US 4006
         THE REAL ELVIS                  1956   RCA    US 940
         ELVIS VOL 1                     1956   RCA    US 992
         ELVIS VOL 2                     1956   RCA    US 993
         ANYWAY YOU WANT ME              1956   RCA    US 965
         JUST FOR YOU                    1956   RCA    US 4041
         LOVING YOU VOL 1                1956   RCA    US 1515
         PEACE IN THE VALLEY             1957   RCA    US 4354   UK RCX 101
         ELVIS PRESLEY                   1957   RCA             UK RCX 104
         JAILHOUSE ROCK                  1957   RCA    US 4114   UK RCX 106
         KING CREOLE VOL 1               1958   RCA    US 4319   UK RCX 117
         KING CREOLE VOL 2               1958   RCA    US 4321   UK RCX 118
         CHRISTMAS SONGS                 1958   RCA    US 4108   UK RCX 121
         CHRISTMAS WITH ELVIS            1958   RCA    US 4340
         ELVIS SAILS                     1958   RCA    US 4325   UK RCX 131
         IN A TENDER MOOD                1959   RCA             UK RCX 135
         TOUCH OF GOLD                   1959   RCA    US 5088   UK RCX 1045
         STRICTLY ELVIS                  1959   RCA             UK RCX 175
            "        "                   1957   RCA    US 994
         TOUCH OF GOLD VOL 2             1959   RCA    US 5101   UK RCX 1048
         TOUCH OF GOLD VOL 3             1959   RCA    US 5141
         SUCH A NIGHT                    1960   RCA             UK RCX 190
         FLAMING STAR                    1961   RCA    US 128
         FOLLOW THAT DREAM               1962   RCA    US 4368   UK RCX 211
         KID GALLAHAD                    1963   RCA    US 4371   UK RCX 7106
         VIVA LAS VEGAS                  1964   RCA    US 4382   UK RCX 7141
         ELVIS FOR YOU 1                 1964   RCA             UK RCX 7142
         ELVIS FOR YOU 2                 1964   RCA             UK RCX 7143
         TICKLE ME 1                     1965   RCA    US 4383   UK RCX 7173
            "     " 2                    1965   RCA             UK RCX 7174
         EASY COME EASY GO               1967   RCA    US 4387   UK RCX 7187
```

```
MELVIN ROBINSON    G    (A         (A) PRESSURE                     1979   MCA US 3195    UK     MCF3055
BARNABY FINCH      K    (A
BOBBY VEGAS        (A   PAT KELLY       G V (A   ART RODRIGUEZ   D   (A  RONNIE LAWS SAX V   (A
JOHNNY LAWS        V    (A   SAMUEL MOORE     V   (A   REGGIE ALEXANDER V   (A  SANDRA              V (A
```

```
BILLY PRESTON      K V  (ALL      (A) THE WILDEST ORGAN IN TOWN        1966 CAPITOL    (RI 76)      ST 2532
OLLIE BROWN        D    (PMN      (B) MOST EXCITING ORGAN EVER         1967 SUE  UK ILP 935  US V JAY1123
KEN BURKE          B    (PMN      (B) MOST EXCITING ORGAN EVER         196  JOY  UK JOYS 112
JULIA WATERS       V    (M        ( ) CLUB MEETING                     19   CAPITOL                  2607
TRUMAN THOMAS      K    (P        (C) GOSPEL IN MY SOUL                19   JOY  UK JOYS 174
MANUEL KELLOUGH    D    (HKLP     (D) THE APPLE OF THEIR EYE           1969 PRESIDENT              PTLS1034
BOBBY WATSON       B    (K        (E) THAT'S THE WAY GOD PLANNED IT    1969 APPLE UK SAPCOR 9  US    ST 3359
TONY MAIDEN        G    (MNKP     (F) ENCOURAGING WORDS                1969 APPLE UK SAPCOR14  US    ST 3370
JOE WALSH          G    (K        (G) I WROTE A SIMPLE SONG            1971 A&M  UK AMLH63507   US     3507
ALBERT PERKINS     BANJ (K        (H) MUSIC IS MY LIFE                 1972 A&M  UK AMLS63516   US     3516
KENNETH LUPPER     K    (KL       (J) EVERYBODY LIKES SOME KIND OF MUSIC 1973 A&M UK AMLH63526  US     3526
HUBERT HEARD       K    (HKL      (K) THE KIDS & ME                    1974 A&M  UK AMLH63645   US     3645
ALVIN TAYLOR       D    (PN       (L) LIVE EUROPEAN TOUR               1974 A&M  UK AMLH68265   US     3657
WELTON GITE        B    (P        (M) ITS MY PLEASURE                  1975 A&M  UK AMLH64532   US     4532
WYNELL MONTGOMERY  SAX  (P        (N) BILLY PRESTON                    1976 A&M  UK AMLH64587   US     4587
EUGENE HENDERSON   G    (P        (O) BILLY'S BAG                      1976 DJM  UK DJB 26082
MICHAEL McGLOIRY   G    (P        (P) WHOLE NEW THING                  1977 A&M  UK AMLH64656   US     4656
CHARLES GARNETT    TPT  (GP       ( ) THE GENIUS OF                    1975 SPRINGBOARD        US     4034
KENNETH L MOORE    K    (P        ( ) SIXTEEN YEAR OLD SOUL            19   DERBY              US      701
BOBBYE HALL        PERC (P        ( ) SOUL'D OUT                       1974 GNP                US   2 2071
ANGELO RICHARDS    TPT  (P        ( ) GREAZEE SOUL                     1969 SOUL CITY              SCM 002
GLORIA JONES       V    (P        ( ) ORGAN TRANSPLANT                 19   PICKWICK               SPC 3315
GWEN GUTHRIE       V    (H        (Q) BEHOLD                           1979 MYRRH                  MYR 1070
SYREETA WRIGHT     V    (RM       (R) & SYREETA(FASTBREAK)             1979 MOTOWN US 915   UK   STML12107
JESSE KIRKLAND     V    (G        (S) LATE AT NIGHT                    1979 MOTOWN US 925   UK   STML12116
LUTHER WATERS      V    (M        ( ) BILLY PRESTON                    19   BUDDAH US 7502
STEVIE WONDER      HCA  (M        (U) BILLY & SYREETA                  19   MOTOWN          UK   STML12155
OREN WATERS        V    (M        (V) THE WAY I AM                     19   MOTOWN US 941
SHUGGIE OTIS       G    (M        (W) UNIVERSAL LOVE                   1980 MYRRH                   1080
ROCKY DZIDZORNU    PERC (M        ( ) EARLY HITS                       19   EXODUS         US       304
ANDRE CROUCH       V    (P
ROBERT MARGOULEFF  SYN  (M
FRANKIE SPRING     V    (P   CLYDIE KING       V  (GHP JOE GREEN    V    (P   VANETTA FIELDS    V  (GH
OMA DRAKE          V    (H   TOM SCOTT    HRNS    (H   JIM HORN     HRNS (H   GEORGE BOHANON    HRN(H
BUCK MONARI        HRNS (H   PAUL HUBINON    HRNS (H   LOUIS JOHNSON B   (H   GEORGE JOHNSON    G B (HN
DAVID T WALKER     G    (G   GEORGE HARRISON G  (GM   MERRY CLAYTON V   (G   PATRICE HOLLOWAY  V  (G
MYRNA MATTHEWS     V    (G   KING ERRISSON CONGA(G   ROCKY PEOPLES  SAX (G   SHERRILL ATWOOD   V  (G
EUGENE BRYANT      V    (G   DOUG GIBBS      V  (G   DUANE ROGERS   V    (G   STEVE BECKMEIER   G(N
STEPHANIE SPRUILL  V    (N   OLIVIA FOSTER   V  (N   REGGIE McBRIDE B    (M   MALCOLM CECIL     SYN (M
TOWER OF POWER     HRNS (N   MERRY CLAYTON   V  (N   JEFF BECK      G    (N
```

```
DON PRESTON        G V  (A         (A) SACRE BLUES                     1981 RAG BABY       US   RAG1005
BARRY FROST        B    (A
DAVE JOHNSON       B    (A   JERRY ZARIMBA    G  (A   BUD DEAL       SAX (A   JOHN HOBBS    K    (A
```

PRETENDERS

```
    CHRIS HYNDE        G V  (AB          (A) PRETENDERS              1979 REAL   UK RAL  3   US SIRE6083
    PETE FARNDON       B V  (AB          (B) 2                       1981 SIRE   UK K56924  US        3572
    MARTIN CHAMBERS    D V  (AB
    JAMES HONEYMAN-SCOTT G K V(AB CHRIS THOMAS    PROD K(A NICK LOWE     PROD (A  CHRIS MERCER     SAX (B
    HENRY LOWTHER      TPT (B   JIM WILSON     TPT (B  GEOFF BRYANT      HRNS (B
```

PRETTY THINGS

```
    PHIL MAY           B G V(ALL        (A) THE PRETTY THINGS        1965 FONTANA US 67544     UK TL5239
    DICK TAYLOR        BG V(ABCDEFJKLMNOX (A) THE PRETTY THINGS      1967 WING              RI UK WL1167
    VICTOR UNITT       G   (FL          (B) THE PRETTY THINGS        1965 FONTANA      US       67544
    BRIAN PENDLETON    G   (ABCJKNX      (C) GET THE PICTURE         1965 FONTANA            UK TL5280
    JOHN STAX          B   (ABCJKNX      (C) WE WANT YOUR LOVE       1967 FONTANA              858039
    PETE TOLSON        G B (GHILM        (D) EMOTIONS                1967 FONTANA UK 13140    UK TL5425
    GORDON EDWARD      V G B K (HI       (E) S F SORROW              1968 COLUMBIA  UK        SCX  6306
    WALLY ALLEN WALLER B V(DEFJKLMO      (E) S F SORROW              1969 RARE EARTH         US   506
    JOHN ADLER (TWINK) D   (EL           (E) S F SORROW              1978 COLUMBIA  EURO      062 04004
    STUART BROOKS      B . (G            (F) PARACHUTE               1970 HARVEST UK          SHVL 774
    VIV PRINCE         D   (ABCJKNX      (F) PARACHUTE               1970 RARE EARTH         US   515
                                         (F) PARACHUTE               1982 GI        UK        WAX 6
    JOHN POVEY  PERC V(DEFGHIJKLMO       (EF) SF SORROW/ PARACHUTE   1975 HARVEST UK          SHDW  406
    NICKY HOPKINS      K   (JK           (EF) REAL PRETTY            19   RARE EARTH   US      R7  549
    JIMMY PAGE         G   (C            (EF) MILESTONES             19   COLUMBIA      NL
    SKIP ALLAN         D  V(BCDFGHIJKLMNO (G) FREEWAY MADNESS        1972 W B      US 2680    UK K46190
    GORDON HUNTLEY     STEEL(G           (H) SILK TORPEDO            1974 SWANSONG US 8411 UK  SSK 59400
    JOHN'WILLY' WILSON D   (M            (I) SAVAGE EYE              1975 SWANSONG US 8414 UK  SSL 59401
    STRING SECTION     (G                (J) GREATEST HITS  DBL (COMP) 1975 PHILIPS         6625  015
                                         (K) VINTAGE YEARS           1976 SIRE      US       SASH37132
                                         (L) THE SINGLES A's & B's   1977 HARVEST   UK       SHSM 2022
                                         (M) CROSS TALK              1980 WB      US 3466 UK   K56842
                                         (N) ATTENTION               1971 FONTANA GER 6438059 RI 6438 202
                                         (O) LIVE                    1978 JADE               EURO 6812  728
                                         (X) DONT BRING ME DOWN      1967 FONTANA   NL
                                         (EPs)
                                         PRETTY THINGS               1964 FONTANA   UK        TE 17434
                                         RAINING IN MY HEART         1965 FONTANA   UK        TE 17442
                                         ON FILM                     1966 FONTANA   UK        TE 17472
                                         PRETTY THINGS               1965 WING      UK        WL 1167
```

DORY PREVIN

```
    DORY PREVIN        G V  (ALL        (A) MYTHICAL KINGS & IGUANAS   1972 UA    US 4110    UK UAG 29186
    PETER JAMESON      G    (ACF        (B) REFLECTIONS IN A MUD PUDDLE 1972 UA   US 5536    UK UAG 29346
    DAVID COHEN        G    (ACDF       (C) MARY C BROWN              1972 UA    US 5657    UK UAG 29435
    LAURINDO ALMEIDA   G    (C          (D) ON MY WAY TO WHERE        1973 UA               UK UAG 29176
    BUDDY COLLETTE     WIND (DF         (D) ON MY WAY TO WHERE        1976 SUNSET RI         UKSLS  50385
    BRYAN GAROFALO     B    (C          (E) LIVE AT CARNEGIE HALL(DBL) 1973 UA  US 108 1/2 UK UAD 60045
    JOE OSBORN         B    (ACF        (F) DORY PREVIN               1974 WB    US 5336    UK    K56066
    REINHOLD PRESS     B    (C          (G) WERE CHILDREN OF COINCIDENCE 1976 WB US 2908   UK    K56213
    PEGGY SANDVIG      K    (C          (H) ONE AM PHONE CALLS       1977 UA               UK UAS 30070
    TOM KEENE          K    (ACF
    MICHAEL LANG       K    (CD  EARL PALMER      D   (C   RON TUTT        D   (ACD BRIAN DAVIES    G   (AF
    JOHN P GUERIN      D    (C   CLARK MAFFITT    G   (A   LAWRENCE W KNECHTEL K (AD LOUIE SHELTON   G   (A
    HAMILTON WESLEY WATT G  (A  DENNY BROOKS      V   (A   MICHAEL McGINNIS  V  (A   PETER MORSE      V   (A
    B G DAVIES         V    (A   FLOYD C MAFFITT  V   (A   JUDY MAYHAN       V  (A   WEST VENET       V   (A
    D VERONICA LANGDEN V    (A   JIMMY BOND       (D         JOHN WILKIN    G   (D   BERNIE LEADON    G   (D
    CAROL KAYE         B .  (D   JOE SAMPLE       K   (D   FRANK CAPP      PERC (D   DENNIS BUDIMIR   G   (D
    HERB ELLIS         (D   DON RANDI        K   (D   JOHN MORELL     G   (D   TOM TEDESCO      G   (D
    ROBERT WACHTEL     G    (F   RON TUTT         D   (F   LYLE RITZ       B   (F   DAN DUGMORE STEEL (F
    MARTI McCALL       V    (F   CAROLYN MATTHEWS V   (F   LISA ROBERTS    V   (F   RAY BROWN        B   (F
    LINCOLN MAYORGA    PNO  (F   BOBBY BRUCE      FDL (F   PERRY BOTKIN    STR (F   MYRNA MATTHEWS   V   (F
    PATRICIA HENDERSON V    (F   SHIRLEY MATTHEWS V   (F
```

JIM PRICE

```
    JIM PRICE      V K HRNS (AB         (A) KIDS NOWADAYS AINT GOT NO SHAME 1971 A&M   UK  AMLS64321
    JOHN URIBE         G V  (AB         (B) SUNDEGOS TRAVELLING ORCHESTRA 1974 DUNHILL  US       50126
    DAVE FARRELL       B    (B          (B) SUNDEGOS TRAVELLING ORCHESTRA 1974 CBS      UK       65245
    KLAUS VOORMANN     B    (A
    JIM KELTNER        D    (A   BOBBY KEYS     SAX (AB  NICKY HOPKINS   K   (A   DON PONCHER D   (B
```

JIM PRICE

```
    JIM PRICE      V K HRNS (AB         (A) KIDS NOWADAYS AINT GOT NO SHAME 1971 A&M   UK  AMLS64321
    JOHN URIBE         G V  (AB         (B) SUNDEGOS TRAVELLING ORCHESTRA 1974 DUNHILL  US       50126
    DAVE FARRELL       B    (B          (B) SUNDEGOS TRAVELLING ORCHESTRA 1974 CBS      UK       65245
    KLAUS VOORMANN     B    (A
    JIM KELTNER        D    (A   BOBBY KEYS     SAX (AB  NICKY HOPKINS   K   (A   DON PONCHER D   (B
```

ALAN PRICE

```
    ALAN PRICE         K V  (ALL        (A) THE PRICE TO PLAY        1966 DECCA     UK        LK4839
    CLIVE BURROWS D B WIND (            (B) A PRICE ON HIS HEAD      1967 DECCA     UK        LK4907
    STEVE GREGORY      WIND (JO         (C) THE AMAZING (EP)         1967 DECCA     UK          8670
    JOHN WALTERS       HRNS (           (D) PRICE IS RIGHT           1968 PARROT    US        PAS 71018
    ROD 'BOOTS'SLADE   B    (1          (E) THE WORLD OF ALAN PRICE 1970 DECCA     UK        SPA  77
    LITTLE ROY         WIND (           (F) FAME & PRICE             1971 CBS       UK          64392
    RICK MORCOMBE      G V  (L          (G) O LUCKY MAN             1973 WB  US 2710  UK      K46227
    THEODORE THUNDER   D V  (L          (H) BETWEEN YESTERDAY & TODAY 1974 WB US 2783 UK      K56032
    JOHN GORDON        B V  (LO         (J) METROPOLITAN MAN         1975 POLYDOR   UK        2442  133
    COLIN GREEN        G B  (HJG        (K) PERFORMING PRICE         1975 POLYDOR   UK        2683 062
    DAVE MARKEE        B    (HGJ        (L) SHOUTS ACROSS THE STREET 1976 POLYDOR   UK        2383  410
    GRAHAM SMITH       HCA  (J          (M) RAINBOWS END            1977 JET       UK        UAG 30133
    LYN DOBSON         WIND (1          (N) ENGLAND MY ENGLAND       1978 JET       JET       DL  300
    HARRY BECKETT      TPT  (1          (O) ALAN PRICE              1978 JET  US LA809G UK    JETLP 207
    BERNIE GEORGE      WIND (J          (P) FOCUS ON                1979 DECCA     UK        FOS  65/6
    DAVID ROSE         K SYN(0          (Q) LUCKY DAY               1979 JET US 35710
    BOB HENDRY         G V  (0          (R) RISING SUN              1980 JET US 36510  UK           227
    BILLY SMITH        B    (0          (S) IN A WORD               1980 JET       UK        13/162
    GEORGE CHISHOLM    TROM (0          ( ) PROFILE                  19   TELDEC    GER       624 284
    HUGHIE FLINT       D    (1          (1) FLOATING BAND
```

                                                          (CONTINUED)

(CONTINUED)   ALAN PRICE

DEREK WADSWORTH	HRNS (1								
JOHN MUMFORD	HRNS (1	WILLY PAINE		(1	DENIS ANDRE		(1	TONY CARR	D PERC(J
BARRY MORGAN	D (J	ALAN PARKER	G (J	PAUL KEOGH	G (J	DON WELLER	SAX (O		
CLIVE THACKER	D (JGH	KENNY BAKER	TPT (J	KENNY WHEELER	TPT (J	ALAN DOWNEY	TPT(J		
CHRIS PYNE	TROM (J	CLIFF HARDY	TROM (J	BILL GELDARD	TROM (J	PETER CIVIL	HRNS(J		
FRED CROSSMAN	HRNS (J	VIC ASH	WIND (J	JACQUIE SULLIVAN	V (O	TONY BURROWS	V(O		
CHAS MILLS	V (O	THEODORE THUNDER	D V (O	MARTIN DROVER	TPT (O	GEOFF DRISCOLL	SAX(O		
KAY GARNER	V (O	JOY YATES	V (O	NEIL LANCASTER	V (O				

LLOYD PRICE

LLOYD PRICE	V (ALL	A B C COLLECTION	1976	ABC	US	AC 30006	
		BEST OF	1970	STARLINE	UK	SRS 5025	
		BEST OF	19	TEEM	US	5007	
		COME TO ME	19	GUEST STAR	US	1910	
		COOKIN'	19	ABC	US	382	
		EXCITING LLOYD PRICE	19	ABC	US	277	
		FANTASTIC	19	ABC	US	346	
		FUNKY	19	UPFRONT	US	128	
		JUKE BOX GIANTS	1981	AUDIO FIDELITY	UK	1009	
		LLOYD PRICE	19	SPECIALTY US 2105 UK SNTF5007			
		LLOYD AT ANY PRICE	19	JOY	UK	JOYS 179	
		LLOYD SWINGS FOR SAMMY	1965	MONUMENT	US	8032	
		LLOYD PRICE ORCHESTRA	19	DOUBLE	US	8301	
		MR PERSONALITY	1959	ABC	US	297	
		MR PERSONALITY SINGS THE BLUES	19	ABC	US	315	
		MR PERSONALITYS BIG 15	196	ABC	US	324	
		MISTY	19	DOUBLE	US	8308	
		MISTY	1976	DJM	UK	DJB26074	
		MISTY	19	UPFRONT	US	UPF 126	
		MR RHYTHM & BLUES	19	GRAND PRIX	US	422	
		NOW	19	TURNTABLE	US	5001	
		NOW	19	JAD	US	1002	
		PERSONALITY	1972	INTERCORD	GER	128613	
		ROCK'N'ROLL CLASSICS	1973	PATHE	FR 052	91361	
		SINGS THE MILLIONS SELLERS	19	ABC	US	366	
		SIXTEEN GREATEST HITS	19	ABC	US	AC 30006	
		SIXTEEN GREATEST HITS	19	STRIP	US	TOP16/5	
		STAGGER LEE	19	JOY	UK	JOY 202	
		THIS IS MY BAND	19	DOUBLE	US	2301	

RICK PRICE

RICK PRICE	G B V(A	(A) TALKING TO THE FLOWERS	1971	GEMINI	UK	GME 1017	

PRIMA VERA

JOHN TEIGEN	V (	(A) PRIMA VERA	1977	RCA	NOR	40020
TOM MATHISEN	V (	(B) BRAKARA	1978	RCA	NOR	40029
HERODES FALSK	V (	(C) SALMER OG SANGER VI GERNE HIVER	1979	RCA	NOR	40163
		(D) DEN STE	1981	RCA	NOR	40233

ROLAND PRINCE

ROLNAD PRINCE	G (A	(A) COLOR VISIONS	1976	VANGUARD		VSD 79371
RANDY BRECKER	TPT (A					

JOE FARRELL	FLT (A	KENNY BARON	K (A	FRANK FOSTER	SAX (A	BOB CRANSHAW B (A
AL CHALK	PERC (A	AL FOSTER	D (A	JOHN HICKS	K (A	ART JARDINE D (A
VIRGIL JONES	TPT (A	EDDIE MOORE	D (A	THOMAS NICHOLAS	PER (A	BUSTER WILLIAMS B (A

PRINCE BUSTER

PRINCE BUSTER	V (ALL	FABULOUS GREATEST HITS	19	MELODISC		M 51
		SISTERS BIG STUFF	19	MELODISC		M12156
		BIG 5	19	MELODISC		M12157
		WRECK A PUM PUM	19	BLUE BEAT		BBLP 821
		TEN COMMANDMENTS	19	RCA	US	LSP 3792
		SHE WAS A ROUGH RIDER	1978	BLUE BEAT		BBLP 820

PRINCE FAR I

PRINCE FAR I	PERC V(ALL	(A) MESSAGE FROM THE KING	1978	FRONT LINE	UK	FL1013
CHINNAAS MELCHEZ INICK	G(BE	(B) LONG LIFE	1978	FRONT LINE	UK	FL1021
BINGY BUNNY	G (BDF	(C) CRY TUFF DUB ENCOUNTER	1978	FRONT LINE	UK	
BOBBY KALPHAT	K (BDF	(D) FREE FROM SIN	1979	TROJAN	UK	TRLS 125
TARZAN	K (B	(E) DUB TO AFRICA	1979	HIT & RUN		APLP 9006
SNAPPY	K (BD	(F) SHOWCASE	1979	PRE		PREFIX 3
ROBBIE SHAKESPEARE	B (B	(G) CRY TUFF DUB ENCOUNTER II	1979	FRONT LINE	UK	FL4002
GEORGE FULLWOOD	B (B	(H) CRY TOUGH DUB ENCO UNTER III	1980	DADDY COOL	UK	DKLP 15
SLY DUNBAR	D (B	(J) JAMAICAN HEROES	1980	TROJAN		190
ROY JOHNSON KONGO	PERC(F					

SANTA	D (B	BONGO HERMAN	PERC (BD	DIRTY HARRY	HRNS (B	DON DRUMMOND HRNS (B
STYLE SCOTT	D (DEF	ERROL HOLT	B (DEF	SOWELL	G VLN(DEF	EARL CHINNA SMITH G (D
DEADLY HEADLEY	HRNS (D	RAS MILLINER	PERC (D	SCULLY	PERC (F	GLADSTONE ANDERSON K (F

PRINCE HAMMER

PRINCE HAMMER	(A	(A) BIBLE	1978	FRONT LINE	UK	FL1004
ERROL NELSON	K (A					
FRANKLIN WAUL	K (A	ERIC LAMONT	K (A	BO PEE	G (A	SLY DUNBAR D (A
LLOYD PARKS	B (A	ROBBIE SHAKESPEARE	B (A	STICKY	PERC (A	TOMMY McCOOK HRNS(A
VIN GORDON	HRNS (A	HERMAN MARQUIS	HRNS (A			

PRINCE JAMMY

(A) KAMIKAZI DUB	1979	TROJAN		TRLS 174

PRINCE MOHAMMED

(A) PEOPLE ARE YOU READY	1978	BALLISTIC	UK	UAS 30192

```
   BELINDA BOURQUIN    K VLN V(ABC        (A) SOUNDTRACK                    1969 DANDELION US D9103    UK S63752
   DAVID JONES         PERC (ABC          (B) THE ASMOTO RUNNING BAND       1971 DANDELION             UK DANB002
   JEREMY ENSOR        B    (AB            (C) ROUND ONE                     1974 DERAM                 UK SML1108
   MARTIN STELLMAN     V    (AB
   ROGER SWALLOW       D    (B   JOHN HILL    DANCE     (A   CHRIS RUNCIMAN   LIGHTS(A  ROOTS CARTWRIGHT G  (ABC
   LESLIE ADEY         LIGHTS(A  MONICA NETTLES    V    (A   VIVIENNE McAULIFFE V   (AB  DAVID WEEKS          (
   GILLIAN HADLEY      (     EVA DARLOW    DANCE     (A   HARRY HOSMAN    STAGE(A  LYN EDWARDS PERC     (A
   RICHARD JONES       B V  (C   NICK PALLETT    G V (C   GEOFF NICHOLS    D    (C   NICK MASON      PROD(B
```

```
   JOHN PRINE          G V  (ALL           (A) JOHN PRINE                   1972 ATLANTIC   US SD 8296 UK K40357
   REGGIE YOUNG        G    (ACE           (B) DIAMONDS IN THE ROUGH        1973 ATLANTIC   US SD 7240 UK K40427
   STEVE GOODMAN       G    (BCDEF         (C) SWEET REVENGE                1974 ATLANTIC   US SD 7274 UK K40524
   DAVID BRIGGS        K    (CE            (D) COMMON SENSE                 1975 ATLANTIC   US SD18127 UK K50137
   MIKE LEECH          B    (ACE           (E) PRIME PRINE                  1976 ATLANTIC   US SD18202 UK
   KENNY MALONE        D    (CE            (F) BRUISED ORANGE               1978 ASYLUM     US 6E 139  UK K53084
   JOHN CHRISTOPHER    G    (ACE           (G) PINK CADILLAC                1979 ASYLUM     US 6E 222  UK K52164
   DAVE PRINE          G    (CDE           (H) STORM WINDOWS                1980 ASYLUM     US    280  NL 52248
   GRADY MARTIN        G    (C
   JERRY SHOOK         HCA  (C   STEVE BURGH     G    (C   KENNY ASCHER    K    (C   HUGH McDONALD     B  (C
   STEVE MOSLEY        D    (C   RALPH McDONALD  PERC (C   JOHN BURNS      G V  (FG  DOYLE GRISHAM     STEEL(C
   BOBBY WOOD          K    (ACE BILL SLATER     B    (C   RAUN McKINNON   V    (CE  JUDY CLAY   STEEL     (C
   DEIRDRE TUCK        V    (CE  CISSY HOUSTON   V    (CE  SID SIMS        B V  (F   TOM RADTKE  D PERC    (C
   JIM ROTHERMEL       WIND V(DE RICK VITO       G    (DE  LEN DRESSLAR    V    (F   DON SHELTON       V  (F
   BOB BOWKER          V    (F   LEO LEBLANC  STEEL G(ACDEFG CORKY SIEGEL  HCA  (F   BONNIE HERMAN     V  (F
   JACKSON BROWNE      V    (DF  MIKE UTLEY      K    (F   VICKI HUBLEY    V    (F   KITTY HAYWOOD     V  (F
   DIANE HOLMES        V    (F   BONNIE KOLOC    V    (F   HOWARD LEVY    K SAX(FG  BOB HOBAN       K V (F
   HARRY WALLER        V    (F   MIKE JORDAN     V    (F   STEVE RODBY     V    (F   SAM BUSH      G V   (F
   JETHRO BURNS        MAND V(F  DAN CRONIN      V    (DF  RAMBLIN JACK ELLIOT V (F  JOHN COWAN        V  (F
   FRED HOLSTEIN       V    (F   BRYAN BOWERS    V    (F   TOM HANSON      V    (F   HANK NEUBERGER    V  (F
   EARL PIONKE         V    (F   JAMES TALLEY    V    (F   ED HOLSTEIN     V    (F   ALDO BOTTALLA     V  (F
   MIKE URSCHEL        V    (F   JAMES McNAMARA  V    (F   AL BUNETTA      V    (F   TYLER WILSON      V  (F
   TIM MESSER          V    (F   PETER BUNETTA   D V  (DE  TOMMY CATHEY    B    (F   JAMES BROWN       K  (DE
   PAUL CANNON         G    (DE  WAYNE JACKSON   HRNS (DE  ANDREW LOVE     HRNS (DE  JACK HALE       HRNS(DE
   JAMES MITCHELL      HRNS (DE  LEWIS COLLINS   HRNS (DE  LARRY MUHOBERAC PNO  (DE  JOHN DAVID SOUTHER V(D
   GLENN FREY          V    (D   BONNIE RAITT    V    (DE  HERB PEDERSEN   V    (D   DUCK DUNN         B  (DE
   ALAN HAND           V K  (DE  MAILTO CORREA   PERC (DE  BROOKS HUNNICUTT V   (DE  PAT COULTER       V  (DE
   GWENN EDWARDS       V    (DE  JIM HORN        HRNS (DE  CHUCK FINDLEY   HRNS (D   JACKIE KELSO    HRNS(D
   GREG JACKSON        V    (D   CARL MARSH·     STR  (D   STEVE SPEAR     B    (D   BOBBY EMMONS    K  (A
   TOM PIEKARSK        B    (G   ANGIE VARIAS    D    (G   JERRY PHILLIPS  G    (G   BILLY LEE RILEY G V (G
   PHYLLIS DUNCAN      V    (G   HELEN BERNARD   V    (G   BEVERLEY WHITE  V    (G
```

```
   MADDY PRIOR         V    (AB            (A) WOMAN IN THE WINGS           1978 CHRYSALIS GER 6307627 UK CHR1185
   CHRIS STAINTON      K    (B1            (A) WOMAN IN THE WINGS           1978 TAKOMA    US 7078
   BARBARA DICKSON     V    (B             (B) CHANGING WINDS               1978 CHRYSALIS         UK  CHR 1203
   PHILIP TODD         WIND (B             (B) CHANGING WINDS               1978 TAKOMA    US 7079
   PAT DONALDSON       B    (1             (1) 1978 TOUR
   JOHN LINGWOOD       D    (1B
   KEVIN SAVIGAR       SYN  (1B  ANDY ROBERTS    G    (A   BARRIEMORE BARLOW D  (A   JOHN GLASCOCK     B  (A
   DAVID PALMER        K    (A   DAVID OLNEY     B    (A   MARTIN BARRE    G    (A   IAN ANDERSON    FLT(A
   JOHN HALSEY         D    (A   BARRY BOOTH     PNO  (A   SHONA ANDERSON  V    (A   CHERRY GILLESPIE V (A
   BOB GILL            G    (A   RAY FLACKE      G    (1   RICHIE CLOSE    K    (B   SARAH DECO  V PNO    (B
   DOUG MORTER         G V  (B   JOHN O'CONNOR   G V  (B   RICK KEMP       B V  (B   B J COLE      STEEL  (B
   DAVID HASSALL       PERC (B   GLYN THOMAS     PERC (B   MALCOLM PEET    G    (B
```

```
   RON TABAK           B    (ABCDEF        (A) PRISM                        1978 EMI UK INS 3014 ARIOLA US 50020
   LINDSAY MITCHELL    G V  (ABCDEF        (B) SEE FOREVER EYES             1978 ARIOLA ARL 5014      US 50034
   JOHN HALL           K V  (ABCD          (C) ARMAGEDDON                   1979 CAPITOL UK 12051 ARIOLA US 50063
   ALLEN HARLOW        B G  (BCDEF         (D) YOUNG & RESTLESS             1980 CAPITOL                12072
   ROCKET NORTON       D    (BCDEF         (E) GREATEST HITS                1980 CAPITOL
   A B BRYANT          B    (A             (F) SMALL CHANGE                 1982 CAPITOL UK 12184
   RODNEY HIGGS        K D  (A
   TOM KEENLYSIDE      HRNS (A   BRUCE FAIRBAIRN   HRNS(A   HENRY SMALL     G B  (F
```

```
   JOHNNY BRAGG        V    (A             (A) FIVE BEATS BEHIND BARS       1979 CHARLY    UK        CR 30176
   ED THURMAN          V    (A
```

```
   HUGHIE LEGGAT       G V  (A             (A) PRIVATE EYE                  1979 CAPITOL             EST 11980
   HOWARD WARDEN       B    (A
   GORDY LEGGAT        G    (A   PAUL 'BOOMER' STAMP     D V (A
```

```
                                          (A) I WANNA STAY FREE (EP)       19   TJM        UK        TJM 8
```

```
   CRAIG COLLINGE      D    (A             (A) PROCESSION                   1969 MERCURY    UK SMCL 20132
   TREVOR GRIFFIN      K V  (A
   MICK ROGERS         V G B(A   BRIAN PEACOCK     B G K(A
```

```
   RYCHE CHLANDA       G V  (A             (A) TROUBLE IN SCHOOL            1980 PASSPORT   US   9848
   BILL PANKOW         K    (A
   SPIKE BIGLIN        B    (A   JOHNNY McLAUGHLIN D V  (A
```

```
   PATTY VAN NESS      V    (A             (A) PRIVATE LIGHTNING            1980 A&M US 4791   UK AMLK 64791
   PAUL VAN NESS       G    (A
   STEVE KEITH         B    (A   ERIC KAUFMAN    K    (A   SCOTT WOODMAN   D    (A
```

P J PROBY

```
    P J PROBY          V   (ALL     'A) SOMEWHERE                    1965 LIBERTY           US 7406
    JOHN PAUL JONES    B K (F       (B) P J PROBY                    1965 LIBERTY           US 7421
    CLEM CATTINI       D   (F       (C) ENIGMA                       1967 LIBERTY           US 7497
    JIMMY PAGE         G   (F       (D) PHENOMENON                   1967 LIBERTY           US 7515
    ALAN HAWKSHAW      K   (F       (E) WHAT'S WRONG WITH MY WORLD   1968 LIBERTY           US 7561
    ALAN PARKER       G    (F       (F) THREE WEEK HERO              1969 LIBERTY        UK LBS83219
    ROBERT PLANT      HCA   (F       (G) LETS DANCE                   19 SUNSET          GER 501072
    DENNIS LOPEZ      PERC(F        (H) SOMEWHERE                    1977 SUNSET         UK 50404
    STAN BARRETT      PERC (F
    JOHN BONHAM        D  (F   AMORY KANE        G   (F
```

P139H   SAMUEL PRODY   P139H

```
    TONY SAVVA         G V (A       (A) SAMUEL PRODY                  19   GLOBAL         6306 906
    JOHN BOSWELL       D V (A
    STEPHEN DAY        B   (A   DEREK SMALLCOMBE  GV  (A
```

P140   PROCOL HARUM   P140

```
    GARY BROOKER       K V (ALL    (A) PROCOL HARUM                 1967 REGAL ZONOPHONE   UK  LRZ 1001
    KEITH REID      LYRICS (ABCDEFG1 (A) PROCOL HARUM               1967 DERAM            US      18008
    B J WILSON        D   (ABCDEFGHJK (B) SHINE ON BRIGHTLY         1969 REGAL ZONOPHONE   UK  SLRZ 1004
    CHRIS COPPING     K B (DEFGHJK   (B) SHINE ON BRIGHTLY          1969 A&M             US   SP 4151
    DAVE KNIGHTS      B   (ABC1      (C) A SALTY DOG                1969 REGAL ZONOPHONE   UK  SLRZ 1009
    B J COLE       STEEL(H           (C) A SALTY DOG                1969 A&M              US   SP 4179
    RAY ROYER         G   (1         (C) A SALTY DOG(RI DIFF TRACKS)1972 M F P            UK  MFP 5277
    BOBBY HARRISON    D   (1         (D) HOME                       1970 REGAL ZONOPHONE   UK  SLRZ 1014
    BILL EYDEN        D   (1         (D) HOME                       1970 A&M              US   SP 4261
    MATTHEW FISHER    K   (ABC1      (E) BROKEN BARRICADES          1971 CHRYSALIS UK ILPS 9158  US A&M SP 4294
                                     (E) BROKEN BARRICADES          1971 CHRYSALIS NL 94566
    ALAN CARTWRIGHT   B   (FGHJ      (E) BROKEN BARRICADES          1974 CHRYSALIS UK RI CHR1056 GER 6499 659
    MICK GRABHAM      G   (GHJK      (F) LIVE IN CONCERT            1972 CHRYLALIS UK CHR 1004  US A&M SP 4335
                                     (F) LIVE IN CONCERT            1972 CHRYSALIS        GER 6307 503
    ROBIN TROWER      G   (ED        (G) GRAND HOTEL                1973 CHRYSALIS UK/US CHR 1037 GER 6307 511
    DAVE BALL         G   (F         (H) EXOTIC BIRDS & FRUIT       1974 CHRYSALIS UK/US CHR 1058
    PETE SOLLEY       K   (K         (J) PROCOL NINTH               1975 CHRYSALIS UK/US CHR 1080 GER 6307 555
    CHRISTIANNE LEGRAND V (G         (K) SOMETHING MAGIC            1977 CHRYSALIS UK/US CHR 1130 GER 6307 593
    DA CAMERA SINGERS V  (F          ( ) BEST                       1975 A&M              US      4401
    EDMONTON SYN ORCH    (F          (AC) WHITER SHADE/SALTY DOG    1972 CUBE  UK TOOFA 7   GER  2635 004
                                     (BD) SHINE ON/HOME             1972 CUBE  UK TOOFA 10  GER  2635 012
    (1)  1967                        ( ) WHITER SHADE OF PALE        19   INTERCORD       GER  126 300
                                     ( ) WHITER SHADE OF PALE        19   A&M            US    SP4373
                                     ( ) ROCK ROOTS                 1976 DECCA UK ROOTS 4
                                     ( ) BEST OF                    1971 FLY   UK TON   4
                                     ( ) PORTRAIT                   1975 POLYDOR  2434 059
                                     ( ) HITS (DBL)                 1976 POLYDOR        GER   2647 102
                                     ( ) GREATEST HITS              1977 IMPACT          FR    6886 555
                                     ( ) GREATEST HITS              1978 HALLMARK  UK SHM  956
```

P140A   PRODUCT   P140A

```
                                     (A) STYLE WARS(45 RPM LP)      1981 CLAY RECORDS    UK  PLATE 1
```

P140B   PROLES   P140B

```
                                     (A) CONDEMNED (EP)              19   ROCK AGAINST RACISM
```

P140C   MICHAEL PROPHET   P140C

```
    MICHAEL PROPHET    V   (A       (A) SERIOUS REASONING           1980 GROVE MUSIC     UK   ILPS9606
    SANTA              D   (A
    CLINTON FERRON     B   (A   ALBERT GRIFFITHS G   (A   CHINNA SMITH    G   (A   BERNARD HARVEY  K  (A
    ANSEL COLLINS      K   (A   PATRICK ANDY     V   (A   SCULLY        PERC  (A   TOMMY McCOOK   HRN(A
    BOBBY ELLIS      HRNS (A   TONY TUFF        V   (A   YABBY U(VIV JACKSON) V  (A
```

P140D   PROFFESIONALS   P140D

```
    STEVE JONES        G V  (A      (A) PROFFESIONALS               1980 VIRGIN     UK         V2167
    PAUL COOK          D V  (A      (B) I DIDN'T SEE                1981 VIRGIN     GER  204 234
    PAUL MEYRS         B    (A
    RAY McVEIGH        G V  (A
```

P140E .   PROOF   P140E

```
                                     (A) ITS SAFE                   1981 NEMPORER   US         36546
```

P141   BRIAN PROTHEROE   P141

```
    BRIAN PROTHEROE   V K G(ALL     (A) PINBALL                     1974 CHRYSALIS  UK/US CHR 1065
    BRIAN ODGERS      D   (B        (B) PICK UP                     1975 CHRYSALIS  UK/US CHR 1090
    BARRY MORGAN      D   (B        (C) I.YOU                       1976 CHRYSALIS        CHR 1108
                                     (D) LEAVE HIM TO HEAVEN         1976 CHRYSALIS        CHR 1118
```

P141A   PROVIDENCE   P141A

```
    JIM COCKNEY     VLN V(A         (A) EVER SENSE THE DAWN         1972 THRESHOLD   UK         THS 9
    BARTHOLOMEW BISHOP  K V(A
    TIM TOMPKINS CELLO V PERC(A BOB BARRIATUA     B V  (A    TOM TOMPKINS   VLN V(A  ANDY GUZIE  G V (A
```

P141B   PRUDENCE   P141B

```
    AGE ALEXANDERSEN   G V (A       (A) 11.12.75  LIVE DBL          1975 ARTIC      NORWAY      7602
    TERJE TYSLAND      G K (A
    JOHAN TANGEN     MAND(A   PER ERIK WALLUM  FLT V(A   KARE SKEVIK   D   (A  JAN DEVIK   B  (A
```

P142   JAMES 'SNOOKY' PRYOR   P142

```
    JAMES 'SNOOKY'PRYOR HCA V(ALL   (A) SNOOKY                       19   MAGPIE     US         1813
    HOMESICK JAMES    G V  (C        (B) SNOOKY PRYOR                 19   FLYRIGHT   UK        LP 100
    BOB HALL         PNO  (C         (C) HOMESICK JAMES & SNOOKY PRYOR 1973 CAROLINE  UK        C 1502
    JOHN HUNT         D   (B         (C) HOMESICK JAMES & SNOOKY PRYOR 1979 BIG BEAR  UK        BEAR21
    BOB BRUNNING      B   (C         (D) DO IT IF YOU WANT            19   BLUEWAY    US          6076
    MOODY JONES       G   (E         (E) SNOOKY & MOODY              1980 FLYRIGHT   UK        FLY565
    EARL PHILLIPS     D   (          ( ) SHAKE YOUR BOOGIE           1976 BIG BEAR   UK        BEAR14
    LEE COOPER        G   (          ( ) CHAKE YOUR BOOGIE           1979 INTERCORD  GER       146406
    SUNNYLAND SLIM   PNO  (E
    ALFRED ELKINS     B   (E   ALFRED WALLACE   D   (E   LEROY FOSTER    G   (   EDDIE TAYLOR   G  (
```

```
    ARTHUR PRYSOCK        (ALL     ART & SOUL                      1967 VERVE    US            65009
                                  ARTHUR PRYSOCK'74               1973 OLDTOWN        US       12001
                                  LOVE MAKES IT RIGHT            1974 OLDTOWN        US       12002
                                  ALL MY LIFE                    1974 OLDTOWN        US       12004
                                  ALL MY LIFE                    1977 POLYDOR        UK       2383 441
                                  BEST OF ARTHUR PRYSOCK          19   VERVE              6 5011
                                  THIS IS MY BELOVED              19   VERVE              6 5070
                                  SILK & SATIN                    19   POLYDOR    US       2 8901
                                  DOES IT AGAIN                  1978 POLYDOR    UK       2383 481
                                  UNFORGETABLE                   1978 KING       US            1134
```

```
    NICK ARMSTRONG    G    (123A   (A) STAMP OUT NORMALITY(EP)    1979 DEAD GOOD  UK         DEAD 2
    GES HALL          B    (12     (1) JULY 1978  (2) AUTUMN 1978   (3) DECEMBER 1978
    PAUL STEEL        G V  (123A
    JOHN CARTWRIGHT   V    (1   MARK SIDDY  D  (123A  JOHN LOONAM    G B (23A
```

```
    BUTLER REP        V    (AB    (A) PSYCHEDELIC FURS           1980 CBS   US 36791  UK      84084
    JOHN ASHTON       G    (AB    (B) TALK TALK TALK             1981 CBS   US 37339  UK      84892
    DUNCAN KILBURN    SAX  (AB
    ROGER MORRIS      G    (AB  VINCE ELY     D   (AB  TIM BUTLER   B   (AB
```

```
                                 (A) WHERE'S THE PARTY            19              US
```

```
                                 (A) THE FREAK SCENE             1968   CBS        CS US 9456
```

```
    DAG SMALL         K V  (A     (A) PUBLIC FOOT THE ROMAN      1973 SOVEREIGN      UK   SVNA 7259
    SEAN BYRNE        G V  (A
    JAMIE LANE        D V  (A   GREG KNOWLES     G  (A   WARD      B   (A
```

```
    JOHN LYDON        V    (ALL   (A) PUBLIC IMAGE LTD       1978 VIRGIN UK V2114 GER 200301 US WB 3288
    KEITH LEVINE      G    (AB    (B) SECOND EDITON          1979 VIRGIN UK VD2512 GER300863
    JIM WALKER        D    (A     (B) METAL BOX(3X 12" EPS)  1979 VIRGIN UK METAL1
    JAH WOBBLE        B    (A     (C) PARIS AU PRINTEMPS     1980 VIRGIN UK V2183 GER 203095
    JEANNETTE LEE          (B     (D) FLOWERS OF ROMANCE     1981 VIRGIN       GER 203410  US WB  3536
    DAVE CROWE             (B
```

```
    GARY PUCKETT      V    (ALL   WOMAN WOMAN                    1968 CBS US          9612
    DWIGHT BEMENT     SAX  (ALL   YOUNG GIRL                     1968 CBS US          9664 UK  63342
    KERRY CHATER      B    (ALL   INCREDIBLE                     1968 CBS US          9715 UK  63429
    PAUL WHEATBREAD   D    (ALL   NEW ALBUM                      1970 CBS US 30862    9935 UK  63794
    GARY WITHEM       PNO  (ALL   GREATEST HITS                  1970   CBS               UK  64115
                                  LADY WILLPOWER                 1972 CBS US 31184
```

```
    ARTHUR BROWN      V    (AB    (A) APRIL 1969    (B) JULY 1969
    DRACHEN THEAKER   SYN D(AB
    DENNIS TAYLOR     B    (AB  GEORGE KHAN    SAX (B   JOHN MARSHALL   D   (A   JONAH MITCHELL  ORG (B
    McCULLOCH         ORG  (A   ANDROID FUNNEL   G  (A
```

```
    DUDU PUKWANA SAX V K PERC(ABC  (A) IN THE TOWNSHIPS          1974 CAROLINE          UK    C 1504
    MONGEZI FEZA  TPT PERC V(ABC   (B) FLUTE MUSIC               1975 CAROLINE          UK    CA2005
    LOUIS MOHOLO      D    (AC    (C) DIAMOND EXPRESS            1978 FREEDOM            FLP 41044
    BIZO MNGQIKANA SAX PERC V(A
    HARRY MILLER      B    (A   ELTON DEAN     SAX (C   NICK EVANS    TROM (C   KEITH TIPPETT   PNO (C
    LUCKY RANKU       G    (C   VICTOR NTONI    B  (C   FRANK ROBERTS  K   (C   ERNEST MOTHLE   B   (C
    JAMES MENE        D    (C   VICTOR WILLIAMS K  (B   PETE COWLING   B   (B   JOHN STEVENS    D   (B
    BOB STIGNEC       PERC (B   AUDREY MOTAUNA  V  (B
```

```
    JACQUES ROMAN     K B  (ABC   (A) POLLEN                 1976 DECCA UK SKLR5228 CBS FR 82769
    VICTOR BOSCH      D PERC(ABC   (B) THE STRANDS OF THE FUTURE  1976 DECCA UK TXS 119  CBS FR 82703
    GILBERT GANDIL    G V  (ABC   (C) HALLOWEEN                   1977            CBS FR 82477
    PHILIPPE ROMAN    B V  (A
    ROLAND RICHARD    FLT  (ABc  MICHEL MASSON    B  (BC
```

```
    BARBARA O'MEARA   V    (A     (A) PUNCHIN' JUDY              1973 TRANSATLANTIC   UK   TRA 272
    JOHN PHILLIPS     G V  (A
    KEITH EVANS       B V  (A   ALAN BROOKS     D V  (A   ROBIN LANGRIDGE   K   (A
```

```
    NEVILLE LUXURY    G    (      (A) LAUGHING ACADEMY           1979 UA UK UAG30258   GER  82735
    BRIAN BOND        V    (
    RED HELMIT        G    (    JIMMY GIRO       B   (   LES DENHAM    D   (
```

```
                                 (A) A TRIBUTE TO THE ROLLING STONES  1966  WING      UK   WL 1150
```

```
    BURNARD PURDIE    D V  (ALL   (A) SOUL FINDERS               1968 CAMDEN              CAS 2170
    RALPH McDONALD    CONGA(E     (B) SOUL DRUMS                 1968 DIRECTION           8 63290
    HORACE OTT        K    (E     (C) STAND BY ME                1971 MEGA                51 5001
    CORNELL DUPREE    G    (E     (D) PURDIE GOOD                1971 PRESTIGE     US      10013
    LLOYD DAVIS       G    (E     (E) SOUL IS ... PRETTY PURDIE  1972 PHILIPS 6369 421 FLY US 10154
    GARNETT BROWN     TROM (E     (F) SHAFT                      1974 PRESTIGE     US      10038
    BILLY NICHOLS     G    (E     (G) DELIGHTS OF THE GARDEN      19  CASABLANCA    US      7051
    ARTHUR CLARKE     SAX  (E
    NORMAN PRIDE      PERC (E   MAERETHA STEWART V  (E   RICHARD TEE   K   (E   JAY BERLINER    G  (E
    PAUL MARTINEZ     B    (E   DANNY MOORE     TPT (E   SELDON POWELL SAX (E   JAMES POWELL    SAX(E
    HILDA HARRIS      V    (E   CHARLIE BROWN   SAX (E   GORDON POWELL PERC (E  JERRY JEMMOTT   B  (E
    EILEEN GILBERT    V    (E   PAUL GRIFFIN     K  (E   ERNIE ROYAL   TPT (E   HAROLD VICK     SAX (E
    CARL HALL         V    (E   BARBARA MASSEY   V  (E
```

PURE FOOD & DRUG ACT

HARVEY MANDEL	G	(A			(A) CHOICE CUTS	1972 EPIC US 31401	NL	65197
DON 'SUGARCANE 'HARRIS VLN(A								
PAUL LAGOS	D	(A	VICTOR CONTE B	(A	COLEMAN HEAD	G V	(A	RANDY RESNICK	G V (A

PURE PRAIRIE LEAGUE

CRAIG FULLER	G V	(AB		(A) PURE PRAIRIE LEAGUE	1972 RCA	UK SF 8320	RI 73 SF8453
GEORGE POWELL	G V	(ABCDEFG		(A) PURE PRAIRIE LEAGUE	1972 RCA	US	LSP4650
JOHN CALL	STEEL	(ACDE		(B) BUSTIN' OUT	1972 RCA	UK SF 8417	US LSP 4769
JIM LANHAM	B V	(A		(C) TWO LANE HIGHWAY	1975 RCA	UK SF 8445	US APLI 0933
BILLY HINDS	D	(BCDEGJK		(D) IF THE SHOE FITS	1976 RCA	UK RS 1040	US AFLI 1247
MICK RONSON	G V	(B		(E) DANCE	1976 RCA	UK PL 11924	US APLI 1924
MICHAEL O'CONNOR	K	(CDEGJK		(F) LIVE TAKIN' THE STAGE	1977 RCA		CPLL 2404
JAMES ROLLESTON	B	(B		(G) JUST FLY	1978 RCA	UK PL 12590	US AFLI 2590
LARRY GOSHORN	G	(CDEG		(H) HOLD BACK	1979 RCA	UK PL 13335	US APLI 3335
MICHAEL REILLY	B	(CDEGJ		(J) FIRIN' UP	1980 CASABLANCA		NBLP 7212
AL BRISCOE	STEEL	(B		(K) SOMETHING IN THE NIGHT	1981 CASABLANCA US 7255		
ANDY STEIN	FDL	(E					
CHET ATKINS	G	(C	TIM GOSHORN	G V (G	DAVID SANBORN	SAX (JK	GARY MIELKE SYN (JK
JANIS GILL	V	(JK	KRISTINE ARNOLD	V (JK	VINCE GILL G V FDL BAN (JK	JEFF WILSON G V (JK
JIM CAUGHLAN	D	(A	DIANNE BROOKS	V (B	LITTLE BOBBY RING PERC (B	BOB RING PROD (A
ASHAN ABRAHAMS	PROD (E		CHARLIE VEAL	VLN (E	DON FELDER	MAND (C	JOHNNY GIMBLE FDL (C
EMMYLOU HARRIS	V	(C	JOHN ROTELLA	K (C	VINCE DEROSA	HRNS (C	JOHN BOYLAN PROD (CE

PURIFY BROTHERS

JAMES PURIFY	V	(AB		(A) JAMES & BOBBY PURIFY	1977 MERCURY US 9110 028 US SRM111134	
BOBBY PURIFY	V	(ALL		(B) YOU & MEE TOGETHER FOREVER	1978 CASABLANCA US 7011 UK CAL2025	
				( ) PURE SOUND OF	19 BELL	US 6010

PURPLE GANG

PETE'LUCIFER' WALKER V KAZOO(A				(A) PURPLE GANG STRIKES	1968 TRANSATLANTIC UK SIRE US 97006	
DEL ROBINSON	HCA MAND(A					
ANK LANGLEY	BAN	(A	GEOFF BOURJER	PNO (A	JAMES BEARD G (A	TONY MOSS B (A

PURPLE HEARTS

ROBERT MANTON	V	(A		(A) BEAT THAT	1980 FICTION UK FIX2 GER 60 280
GARY SPARKS	D	(A			
JEFF SHADBOLT	B V	(A	SIMON STEBBING	G V (A CHRIS TSANGARIDES K (A	

JIMMY PURSEY

JIMMY PURSEY	(AB	(A) IMAGINATION CAMOUFLAGE	1980 POLYDOR UK 2442180 GER 2383 600
		(B) ALIEN ORPHAN	1982 EPIC UK 85235

PUSSYCAT

(A) SOUVENIRS	19 EMI NL	064 25565
(B) FIRST OF ALL	1976 SONET	SNTF 725

PUZZLE

JOHN LIVIGNI	D V	(AB		(A) PUZZLE	1973 MOTOWN US 768
ANTHONY SICILIANO	B	(AB		(B) 2ND ALBUM	1974 MOTOWN US 807
JOSEPH SPINAZOLA	K	(AB			
BOBBY VILLALOBOS	G	(B	RALF RICHERT G TPT	(B BOB WILLIAMS	TPT (B LARRY KLIMAS WIND(BA
BOB CULLEN	PROD (B				

PUZZLES

REUS PLASCHEK	G	(A		(A) LETS HAVE A PUZZLEPARTY	1980 METRONOME GER 60350
JOHNNY LITTLEGIRL SAX	(A				
MARIO LUCCI	B	(A	MARCEL MELLEMA	D (A ARNO ARTS	ORG (A

PYLON

(A) GYRATE	1980 ARMAGEDDON UK ARM5

PYRYMYD

(A) PYRYMYD	1980 CAPITOL US 12027

PYTHON LEE JACKOSN

DAVE BENTLEY	K V	(A		(A) IN A BROKEN DREAM	1974 YOUNGBLOOD 3001 US GNP 2066	
DAVE MONTGOMERY	D	(A				
MICK LIBER	G	(A	TONY CAHILL	B (A ROD STEWART	V (A GARY BOYLE G (A

EDDIE QUANSAH

EDDIE QUANSAH HRNS PERC V(A				(A) CHE CHE KULE	1977 ISLAND	UK ILPS 9446
ROSETTA HIGHTOWER V	(A			(B) AWO AWO	1981 ISLAND	UK ILPS 9546
DICK CUTHELL	TPT (A					
MAC TONTOH	TPT (A	GEORGE LARNYOH	SAX (A	RAY ALLEN	SAX (A PETE VANDER PUIJE SAX(A
CHRIS MERCER	SAX (A	GRAHAM MORGAN	D (A	KOFI AYIVOR	D PERC(A TERRY WILSON B (A
COLIN BASS	B (A	WILLY CHEETHAM	CONGA(A	JIMMY CHAMBERS	V (A PATRICE EBIGWE V (A
JOANNA WHYTE	V (A	ESTHER BYRD	V (A	WINSTON DELANDRO	G V (A JUNIOR KERR G (A
JANOS BAJTALA	K (A	KIKI GYAN	K (A	EMMANUEL RENTZOS	K V (A JOE SCOTT K (A
PETE WINGFIELD	K (A	TONY BRAUNAGEL	D (A	REMI KABAKA	D (A SPARTACUS R B (A
JEROME RIMSON	B (A	REEBOP KWAKU BAAH PERC (A		IAN GREEN	SYN (A CLIFFORD MATAYA V (A
PAMELA DOUGLAS	V (A				

'Q'

VAN CROZIER	(		(A) DANCIN' MAN	1977 EPIC US 34691
DON GARVIN	(			
JOHN HOGUE	(	ED JONNET	(ROBERT PECKMAN	(CHRIS PATARINO (
BILL THOMAS	(	BILL VOGEL		

Q65

FRANK NUYENS	G	(A	(A) REVOLUTION	1966 DECCA NL 6440675
PETER VINK	B	(A	(B) GREATEST HITS	196 DECCA NL 6454409
WILLIAM BIELER	HCA V(A			
JOOP ROELOFS	G	(A	JAY BAAR D (A	

'Q TIPS'

PAUL YOUNG	V	(A	(A) Q TIPS	1980 CHRYSALIS UK CHR 1255
BARRY WATTS	D	(A		
MICK PEARL	B	(A	GARTH WATT ROY G V (A IAN KEW	K (A TONY HUGHES TPT (A
STEVE FARR	SAX V(A		STEWART BLANDMER SAX V(A	

QUANTUM JUMP

```
MARK WARNER        G V  (AC        (A) QUANTUM JUMP              1976 ELECTRIC       UK    TRIX1
TREVOR MORAIS      D    (ABC       (B) BARRACUDA                1977 ELECTRIC       UK    TRIX3
JOHN PERRY         B    (ABC       (C) MIXING                   1979 ELECTRIC       UK    TRIX11
ROY ALBRIGHTON     G    (
RUPERT HINE        K V  (ABC GEOFFREY RICHARDSON G VLN(B MORRIS PERT     PERC (A  RAY COOPER  PERC (AB
PAUL KEOGH         G    (B   ELKIE BROOKS       V      (B GEOFF DALY     HRNS (B  HENRY LOWTHER HRNS(B
PENGUIN CAFE STRINGS    (B   GAVIN WRIGHT STRINGS      (B HELEN LIEBMANN STR  (B
```
QUARTZ(FRANCE)

```
LAURENT TAIEB      SYN  (A        (A) CAMEL IN THE CITY         1979 POLYDOR        PD 1 6203
PATRICK LANGLADE   B    (A
DIDIER PLUS        D    (A
```
QUARTZ

```
DEREK ARNOLD       B    (ABCDE     (A) QUARTZ                   1977 JET           UK    UAG 30081
MALCOLM COPE       D    (ABCDE     (B) QUARTZ                   1978 PYE           UK    NSPL28261
MICK HOPKINS       G    (ABCDE     (C) DELETED                  1979 JET           UK    JETLP 223
MIKE 'TAFFY' TAYLOR V   (ABCDE     (D) LIVE COUNT DRACULA       1980 REDDINGTON UK 001 LOGO 4007
GEOFF NICHOLS      G K  (A         (E) STAND UP & FIGHT         1980 MCA           UK    MCF 3080
```
BILL QUATEMAN

```
BILL QUATEMAN      G V  (ALL       (A) BILL QUATEMAN            1972 CBS  US 31761
TOM RADTKE  PERC   (C              (B) NIGHT AFTER NIGHT        1977 RCA UK PL12027 US   AFLI 2027
CALEB QUAYE        G V  (BC        (C) SHOT IN THE DARK         197  RCA           US   AFLI 2434
DENNY SEIWELL      D    (BC        (D) JUST LIKE YOU            1979 RCA           US        2879
JOHN MARSH         B    (BC
IRA KART           PNO  (B  DAVE SHIELDS     B  (C  TERRY REID      V    (B  RICHARD SUPA    V  (B
LENNY CASTRO       CONGA(BCD IAN UNDERWOOD   K  (B  BRUCE JOHNSTON   V    (B  CINDY BULLENS   V  (B
JIMMY HAAS         V    (B  ERNIE WATTS      HRNS (B NOLAN SMITH     HRNS (B  SHIRLEY MATTHEWS V (BD
GEORGE BOHANON     HRNS (B  OSCAR BRASHEAR   HRNS (B VANETTA FIELDS       (BD MAXAYN LEWIS    V  (B
JACKIE KELSO       HRNS (B  JON JOYCE        V  (B  STRING SECTION       (B  BILL PAYNE      SYN (C
NEIL LARSEN        K    (D  RICK SCLOSSER    D  (D  JAMES NEWTON HOWARD SYN(D GARY HERBIG     SAX(D
BUZZY FEITEN       G    (D  DAVID HUNGATE    B  (D  MICHAEL McDONALD V   (D  STEVE PORCARO   SYN (D
JULIA TILLMAN      V    (D  JOHN JARVIS      K  (D  JEFF BAXTER     G    (D
CHUCK RAINEY       B    (C  DAVID SANBORN    SAX (C
```
QUARTER FLASH

```
RINDY ROSS  V SAX         (A        (A) QUARTER FLASH           1982 GEFFEN UK 85438  US   2003
JACK CHARLES       G V    (A
MARV ROSS          G      (A  RICH GOOCH      B  (A  BRIAN WILLIS    D   (A  RICK DIGIALLONARDO K(A
BRUCE SWEETMAN     VLN    (A  TIM SCHMIT      V  (A  JOHN BOYLAN     V   (A  MARCY LEVY      V(A
PAULINHO DACOSTA   PERC   (A
```
QUATERMASS

```
JOHN GUSTAFSON     B V  (A        (A) QUATERMASS               1970 HARVEST UK SHVL 775 US 314
PETE ROBINSON      K    (A        (A) QUATERMASS               1975 HARVEST RI UK  SHSM 2002
MICK UNDERWOOD     D    (
```
QUATRAIN

```
BUFF LINDSAY       B V  (A        (A)QUATRAIN                  1968 TETRAGRAMMATON  US       5002
DON SENNEVILLE     G V  (A
ERIC PEASE         G V  (A
JIM LEKAS          D V  (A
```
MICHAEL QUATRO

```
MICHAEL QUATRO     K V  (ALL       (A) PAINTINGS               1972 EVOLUTION            3011
TED NUGENT  G      (AB             (B) LOOK DEEP IN THE MIRROR 1973 EVOLUTION            3021
PATTI QUATRO       (AB             (C) IN COLLABORATION WITH THE GODS 1975 UA  US LA 420 UK  UAS 29785
TEDDY HALE         G    (CH        (D) DANCERS ROMANCERS & DREAMERS  1976 PRODIGAL   UK  PDL 2001
RICK DERRINGER     G    (C         (E) GETTING READY          197  PRODIGAL        US  P7 10016
DAVE KISWINEY      B V  (C         (F) GOLDEN HITS            1976 RAK        UK   SKRA 6756
KIRK TRACHSEL      D    (BC        (G) LIVE & KICKIN          1977 RAK             JAP 50009/10
HOWARD KAYLAN      V    (C         (H) MICHAEL QUATRO BAND    1980 LOTUS      SWED      4099
MARK VOLMAN        V    (C
TERRY MULLEN       PERC (A
NANCY QUATRO       V    (A  JOHN FINBY      V  (A  STUART LOVE     PROD (D  TOM CLUPAK  G  (H
JOHN THORPE             (H  GREG KOBE          (H  GARY JACKSON        (H  ARTSKI         (H
LYN ROUSKO              (H  JOHN BAUER         (H  DAVID SURKAMP      (H  JOHN MACINTYRE (H
BILL REYNA         D    (H  BELINDA McCLURE V  (H  TRACY RICHARDSON   (H  STEVE ARGY     (H
```
SUZI QUATRO

```
SUZI QUATRO        B V  (ALL       (A) SUZI QUATRO             1973 RAK UK SRAK505 US BELL    1302
KEITH HODGE        D    (          (B) QUATRO                  1974 RAK UK SRAK509 US BELL    1313
LENNIE TUCKEY      G    (ALL       (C) YOUR MAMA WON'T LIKE ME 1975 RAK UK SRAK514 US ARISTA 4035
MIKE DEACON        K    (DE        (D) AGGRO PHOBIA            1977 RAK UK SRAK525
BILL HURD          K    (          (E) IF YOU KNEW SUZI        1978 RAK UK SRAK532 US RSO     3044
ALASTAIR McKENZIE  K    (ABC       (F) GREATEST HITS           1980 RAK UK EMTV24
DAVE NEAL          D    (ABCDE     (G) ROCK HARD               1980 DREAMLAND US 15006 UK 2479 275
MICK EVE           SAX  (C
STEVE GREGORY      SAX  (C  BUD BEADLE      SAX (C  RON CARTHY      TPT(C
```
QUAZAR

```
                                  (A) QUAZAR                  1978 ARISTA US 4187  UK   ARTY 157
```
QUEEN

```
                                                    UK   UK     US      US    JAP    JAP
FREDDIE MERCURY   V PNO(ALL  (A) QUEEN              1973 EMI EMC 3006 ELEKTRA 75064 ELEKTRA P10118E
BRIAN MAY G K V BANJO  (ALL  (B) QUEEN II           1974 EMI EMC  767 ELEKTRA 75082 ELEKTRA P10119E
JOHN DEACON      G B   (ALL  (C) SHEER HEART ATTACK 1974 EMI EMC 3061 ELEKTRA 7E1026 ELEKTRA P10137E
ROGER TAYLOR     D V   (ALL  (D) A NIGHT AT THE OPERA 1875 EMI EMTC 103 ELEKTRA 7E1053 ELEKTRA P10075E
DAVID BOWIE      V     (M    (E) A DAY AT THE RACES 1976 EMI EMTC 104 ELEKTRA 6E 101 ELEKTRA P10300E
                            (F) NEWS OF THE WORLD  1977 EMI EMA  784 ELEKTRA 7E 112 ELEKTRA P10430E
                            (G) JAZZ               1978 EMI EMA  788 ELEKTRA 6E 166 ELEKTRA P10601E
                            (H) LIVE KILLERS       1979 EMI EMSP 330 ELEKTRA      702
                            (J) THE GAME           1980 EMI EMA  795 ELEKTRA      513
                            (K) FLASH GORDON (S TRCK)1980 EMI EMC 3351 ELEKTRA    518
                            (L) GREATEST HITS      1981 EMI TV 30     ELEKTRA 5E 564
                            (M) HOT SPACE          1982 EMI EMC 797   ELEKTRA  60128
                            (EP) GOOD OLD FASHIONED 1977 EMI EMI 2623
```

[453]

QUESTION MARK & THE MYSTERIANS

RUDY MARTINEZ	V	(		(A) 96TEARS		1966 CAMEO	US	C2004
ROBERT MARTINEZ		(		(B) ACTION		1966 CAMEO	US	C2006
BOBBY BALDERAMMA	G	(						
EDDIE SERRATI	D	(	FRANK LUGO	B (	FRANK RODRIGUEZ	ORG (	LARRY BORJAS	(

QUICK

DANNY WILDE	V	(A	(A) MONDO DECO	1977 MERCURY	US	SRM1 1114
DANNY BENAIR	D	(A				
BILLY BIZEAU	K V	(A	IAN AINSWORTH	B (A	STEVE HUFSTETER	G	(A

QUICKSAND

JIMMY DAVIES	(A	(A) HOME IS WHERE I BELONG	1974 DAWN	UK	DNLS 3056
PHIL DAVIES	(A				
ROBERT COLLINS	(A	ANTHONY STONE	(A		

QUICKSILVER MESSENGER SERVICE

GREG ELMORE	D	(ALL	(A) QUICKSILVER MESSENGER SERVICE	1968 CAPITOL	UK/US	2904
GARY DUNCAN	V G B	(ABDEFGHJ1	(B) HAPPY TRAILS	1969 CAPITOL UK/US 120	EURO	80543
BUD BRISBOIS	TPT	(G	(B) HAPPY TRAILS	1981 GREENLIGHT UK 2012		
JOHN CIPOLLINA	G	(ABCDEJ1	(C) SHADY GROVE	1969 CAPITOL	UK/US	391
DAVID FREIBERG	B V G	(ABCDEJ1	(D) JUST FOR LOVE	1970 CAPITOL	UK/US	498
JIM MURRAY	V HCA	(1	(D) JUST FOR LOVE	197 EMI	GERM 038	80543
NICKY HOPKINS	K	(CDEJ	(E) WHAT ABOUT ME	1971 CAPITOL	UK/US	630
DINO VALENTI FLT	G V	(DEFGJ	(E) WHAT ABOUT ME	19 CAPITOL US/RI 16092 GER		80722
JOSE REYES	PERC	(E	(F) QUICKSILVER	1972 CAPITOL	UK/US	819
MARK RYAN	B	(FG	(G) COMIN' THRU'	1972 CAPITOL UK/US 11002 GER		81121
CHUCK STEAKS	K	(FG	(H) ANTHOLOGY (COMP)(DBL)	1978 CAPITOL UK ESTSP 13	US	11165
PETE SEARS	PNO	(J	(J) SOLID SILVER	1975 CAPITOL	UK/US	11462
MICHAEL LEWIS	K	(J	(K) BEST OF	197 CAPITOL	EURO 054	80691
SKIP OLSON	B	(J	(L) HIT ROAD	1976 EMI	EURO 048	51874
MARIO CIPOLLINA	B	(J	(1) 1965/67			
KEN BALZALL	TPT	(EG				
KATHI McDONALD	V	(J	MARK NAFTALIN PNO (E MARTIN FIERRO	WIND (E RON TAORMINA	SAX (E	
FRANK MORIN	SAX	(E	PAT O'HARA TROM (EG DALTON SMITH	TPT (G SONNY LEWIS	SAX (G	
CHARLES CALOPER	TROM	(G	DON MENZE SAX (G			

QUIET SUN

PHIL MAZANERA	G K	(A	(A) MAINSTREAM	1975 ISLAND	UK	HELP19
DAVE JARRETT	K	(A	(A) MAINSTREAM	1977 POLYDOR RI	UK	2343 093
BRIAN ENO	K	(A	(A) MAINSTREAM	1975 ANTILLES	US	7008
IAN MACCORMICK	V	(A				
BILL MACCORMICK	B V	(A	CHARLES HAYWARD D K V(A			

QUIET WORLD

	(A) THE ROAD	1970 DAWN	UK DNLS 3007	

QUILL

JU UNK KHOL	(A	(A) QUILL	1970 COTILLION	US SD	9017
DA ANK KHOL	(A				
R WILLY NORTH	(A	PHIL STAN D'THERE	(A RED ROCKET ROGERS	(A	

QUINAIMES BAND

DAVID PALMER	V	(A	(A) QUINAIMES BAND	1971 ELEKTRA	US	EKS 74096
KENNY PINE	G V	(A				
MIKE ROSA	D	(A	JERRY BURNHAM B V (A DANNY MANSOLINO	K V (A DANIEL BEN ZEBULON CONGA(A		
DANNY KOOTCH	G	(A	ALLAN JACOBS G (A RICHARD GREENE	FDL (A BILL KEITH STEEL	(A	
RICHARD GRANDO	SAX	(A				

QUINTESSENCE

RAJA RAM FLT V PNO	(ALL	(A) IN BLISSFUL COMPANY	1969 ISLAND	UK	ILPS 9110
SHIVA SHANKAR JONES V K	(ABCD	(B) QUINTESSENCE	1970 ISLAND	UK	ILPS 9128
SAMBHU BABAJI B	(ALL	(C) DIVE DEEP	1970 ISLAND	UK	ILPS 9143
JAKE MILTON D	(ALL	(D) SELF	1971 RCA	UK	SF8273
MAHA DEV(DAVE CODLING)G	(ABCD	(E) INDWELLER	1972 RCA	UK	SF8317
ALAN MOSTERT G	(ALL	(F) BAND REFORMED			

QUIVER

TIM RENWICK	G	(AB	(A) QUIVER	1971 WB	US 1939 UK	K46089
WILLIE WILSON	D	(AB	(B) GONE IN THE MORNING	1972 WB	US 2630 UK	K46153
CAL BATCHELOR	V G K	(AB				
BRUCE THOMAS	B	(AB	DICK PARRY SAX (A			

R.A.F.

DAVID VALENTINE	V K	(AB	(A) R.A.F.	1980 A&M US 4816	UK	AMLH64816
DOUGLAS A BOGIE	G	(AB	(B) THE HEAT'S ON	1981 A&M US 4865	UK	AMLH68525
BILLY McGHEE	B	(AB				
TOM ANNAN	PERC	(AB	BOBBY HEATLIE SAX (A ANDY GROSSART	B (A WENDY BOGIE V	(A	
PETER VETTESE	KV	(B	STEVE DONELLY G (B			

REO SPEEDWAGON

TERRY LUTTRELL	V	(ABD	(A) R E O SPEEDWAGON	1971 EPIC US31089 UK 64813 RI 32096	
KEVIN CRONIN	G V	(DEFHJLMN	(B) R E O 2	1972 EPIC US 31745	
ALAN GRATZER	D	(EHJLABDEFGMN	(D) RIDING THE STORM	1973 EPIC US 32378	
GARY RICHRATH	G V	(EHJLMN	(E) LOST IN A DREAM	1974 EPIC US 34143 32948	
NEAL DOUGHTY	K	(EHJLABDFGMN	(F) THIS TIME WE MEAN IT	1975 EPIC US 33338	
MIKE MURPHY	V	(E	(G) R E O	1976 EPIC US 34143	
SLY STONE	G B K	(E	(H) YOU GET WHAT YOU PLAY FOR	1977 EPIC US 34494 UK	88265
LON PRICE	SAX	(J	(J) YOU CAN TUNE A PIANO	1978 EPIC US 35082 UK	82554
BRUCE HALL	B	(JLMN	(K) NINE LIVES	1979 EPIC US 35988 UK	83647
TOM KELLY	V	(MN	(L) DECADE OF ROCK'N'ROLL (DBL COMP)	1980 EPIC US 36444 UK	88488
STEVE FORMAN	PERC	(MN	(M) HI INFIDELITY	1980 EPIC US 36844 UK	84700
RICHARD PAGE	V	(MN	(N) GOOD TROUBLE	1982 CBS US 38100	
N YOLLETTA	V	(MN			

R M O

	(A) BEYOND THE LIMIT	19 BRAIN	0060 115
	(B) GET THE BALL	19 BRAIN	0001 083
	(C) GARUDA	19 BRAIN	0001 072

RABBIT

```
JOHN 'RABBIT' BUNDRICK V K G B(AB    (A) BROKEN ARROWS              1973 ISLAND         UK    ISPS 9238
TETSU YAMAUCHI       B      (AB      (B) DARK SALOON               1974 ISLAND         UK    ILPS 9289
SNUFFY WALDEN        G      (AB
RE BOP          PERC (A     RANDY         D     (A   GEORGE LARNYOH  HRNS (AB  EDDY QUANSAH   HRNS (AB
PETER VANDER PUIJE   (AB     CHRIS LAURENCE B    (A   GERRY MASTERS   B   (A   JIM CAPALDI    D    (A
PETE CARR       G    (A      RICHARD REEVES G    (A   DUNDEE HORNS        (A   ALAN GERRI     G B  (AB
SIMON KIRKE     D    (A      JUNIOR KERR    G    (A   CONRAD ISADORE  D   (A   TERRY WILSON   B    (B
TONY BRAUNAGEL  D    (B      DAVID KEELEY   G    (B   JANNE SCHAFFER  G   (B   OLA BRUNKERT   D    (B
MIKE            B    (B      BRYSON GRAHAM  D    (B
```

RABBITT

```
TREVOR RABIN G V K SYN (AB          (A) BOYS WILL BE BOYS          1976 CAPRICORN      US          0175
RONNIE ROBOT         (AB            (A) BOYS WILL BE BOYS          1976 JET            UK    JETLP 17
NEIL CLOUD  D PERC   (AB            (B) CROAK & GRUNT IN THE NIGHT 1977 CAPRICORN      US          0190
DUNCAN FAURE    K V  (
```

EDDIE RABBITT

```
EDDIE RABBITT   G V  (ALL           (A) EDDIE RABBITT             1975 ELEKTRA        US      CM3
MIKE LEECH      B    (A             (B) ROCKY MOUNTAIN MUSIC      1976 ELEKTRA UK K52037   US 7E1065
JACK WILLIAMS   B    (BC            (C) RABBITT                   1977 ELEKTRA UK K52054   US 7E1105
JOE OSBORN      B    (B             (D) VARIATIONS                1978 ELEKTRA        US 6E 127
LARRY LONDIN    D    (BC            (E) LOVELINES                 1979 ELEKTRA UK K52135   US 6E 181
HARGUS ROBBINS  PNO  (BC            (F) BEST OF                   1979 ELEKTRA NL 52184    US 6E 235
NORBERT PUTNAM  B    (EG            (G) HORIZONS                  1981 ELEKTRA UK K52225   US    276
SHANE KEISTER   PNO  (B             (H) STEP BY STEP              1981 MERCURY UK 6302 152
JAMES STROUD    D PERC(G
DAVID BRIGGS    PNO  (B   MICHAEL SPRIGGS  G   (B   PETE WADE     G   (B   JOHN CHRISTOPHER G (B
BOBBY THOMPSON  G    (B   STEVE GIBSON     G   (BC  REGGIE YOUNG  G   (BC  SONNY GARRISH    STEEL(BC
HAL RUGG        STEEL(B   BUDDY SPICHER    FDL (B   FARRELL MORRIS PERC (BCG LEA JANE SINGERS   (B
NASHVILLE EDITION    (B   KENNY MALONE     D   (E   MIKE SUTTLE   V   (C   DAVID HOOD       D  (E
DENNIS BELFIELD B    (E   ROGER HAWKINS    D   (E   RANDY McCORMICK K  (EG  STEVE FORMAN     PERC (E
MICHELE GRUSKA  V    (E   DAVID HUNGATE    B   (EG  BARRY BECKETT K   (E   LARRY BYROM      G  (EG
JIMMY JOHNSON   G    (E   TIM MAY          V   (E   ERNIE WATTS   FLT (E   SARAH TAYLOR     V  (E
SHERRY GROOMS   V    (EG  DAVID MALLOY     V   (G   DON BARRETT   B   (G   ALAN FEINGOLD    K  (G
PAUL OVERSTREET V    (G
```

RABBLE

```
                                    (A) LEPS & OTHER NEW WORDS    19   M80           US          801
```

TREVOR RABIN

```
TREVOR RABIN G B K V  (ABC1         (A) TREVOR RABIN             1978 CHRYSALIS       UK    CHR 1196
KEVIN KRUGER    D    (AB            (B) FACE TO FACE             1979 CHRYSALIS       UK    CHR 1221
SIMON PHILLIPS  D    (C             (C) WOLF                     1981 CHRYSALIS       UK    CHR 1295
JACK BRUCE      B    (C             (1) 1979 TOUR
MO FOSTER       B    (C
SIMON FOX       D    (1   MANFRED MANN     V   (C   CHRIS THOMPSON V  (C   STEVIE LANGE   V  (C
RABBIT          K    (C   NOEL McCALLA     V   (C   JOHN GALLEY   K   (1   LES GOODE      B  (1
DAVE MATTACKS   D    (B   RENE ARNELL      V   (B
```

RACING CARS

```
RAY ENNIS       G V  (ABC           (A) DOWNTOWN TONIGHT         1976 CHRYSALIS       UK    CHR 1099
GRAHAM WILLIAMS G V  (ABC           (B) WEEKEND RENDEZVOUS       1977 CHRYSALIS       UK    CHR 1149
GARETH MORTIMER G V  (ABC           (C) BRING ON THE NIGHT       1978 CHRYSALIS       UK    CHR 1178
DAVE LAND       B V  (ABC
ROBERT WILDING  D V  (ABC ROY EDWARDS      K   (A   ROGER HAND    K   (A   BOWLES BROTHERS BAND V(A
TONY CARR       PERC (A   GERAINT WATKINS  K   (AB  TIN HINKLEY   K   (C   VEC FELDMAN    PERC(C
JERRY JUMONVILLE SAX (C   JIM MASON        G   (     SKIP EDWARDS  K   (C
```

MAXIM RAD

```
MAXIM RAD       G V  (A             (A) TIMES AINT THAT BAD      1980 DISQUES MOTORS         77016
CLAUDE ANGEL    G    (A
DOMINIQUE PERRIER K  (A   SAUVEUR MALLIA   B   (A   JEAN PAUL PRATT D V (A  RICHARD PRATT  SAX (A
YVONE JONES     V    (A
```

RADIATOR

```
ALAN HULL       G V  (A             (A) ISN'T IT STRANGE         1977 ROCKET         UK    ROLL 14
RAY LAIDLAW     D    (A
KENNY CRADDOCK  K    (A   PETE KIRTLEY     G   (A   COLIN GIBSON  B   (A   TERRY POPPLE   D  (A
```

RADIATOR(AUST)

```
GEOFF TURNER    B    (A             (A) FEEL THE HEAT            1980 WEA                   60059
BRIAN NICHOL    V    (A
CHRIS TAG       D    (A   FESS PARKER      G   (A   BRENDAN CALLINAN K (A
```

RADIATORS FROM SPACE

```
PETER HOLIDAI   G V  (AB            (A) T V TUBE HEART           1977 CHISWICK UK WIK 4     GER 67051
PHILIP CHEVRON  G V SYN(AB          (B) GHOSTOWN                 1979 CHISWICK UK CWK3003   GER 67064
MARK MEGARAY    B V K(AB
JAMES CRASH     D V  (AB  STEVE RAPID      V   (A   TONY VISCONTI PROD SYN V(B   RUAN O'LOCHLAINN SAX (B
```

RADIO BIRDMAN

```
ROB YOUNGER     V    (A             (A) RADIOS APPEAR            1978 SIRE UK 9103 332 US     6050
WARWICK GILBERT B    (A
CHRIS MASNAK    G    (A   DENIZ TEK        G   (A   JOHNNY KANNIS V   (A   RON KEELEY  D  (A
PIP HOYLE       K    (A   JOHN SAGEN       PROD (A   CHARLES FOWLER PROD (A
```

RADIO STARS

```
ANDY ELLISON    V SYN(AB            (A) SONG FOR SWINGING LOVERS 1977 CHISWICK UK WIK 5  RI CWK 3005
PAUL JONES      HCA  (B             (A) SONG FOR SWINGING LOVERS 1977 CHISWICK GER     67061
MARTIN GORDON   B V K(AB            (B) HOLIDAY ALBUM            1978 CHISWICK UK CWK3001 NL 550011
THE STARLETS    V    (B             (C) TWO MINUTES MR SMITH     1982 MOONLIGHT UK 001
STEVE PERRY     D    (A             (EP) STOP IT                19   CHISWICK              SW  17
IAN MACLEOD     G    (AB
STEVE PRATTLE   D    (B   DANNY GOODWIN    V   (B   GRAHAM CHAPMAN V  (B   CHRIS GENT   SAX (B
JANNIE CROMPTON D    (B   QUASIMODO BROS   V   (B   RED ARMY BOY CHOIR V (B
```

GERRY RAFFERTY

```
GERRY RAFFERTY    V G K(ALL    (A) CAN I HAVE MY MONEY BACK      1971 TRANSATLANTIC  UK     TRA 241
ROGER BROWN       G V  (AD1    (A) CAN I HAVE MY MONEY BACK      197  BLUE THUMB US BTS 58 +RI 78 6031
TOM PARKER        K   (A       (A) ?THE ORIGINAL                 1980 TRANSATLANTIC NL 44010
MORRIS PERT       PERC (G       (B) GERRY RAFFERTY REVISITED      1974 TRANSATLANTIC  UK     TRA 270
GARY TAYLOR       B V  (ADE1    (C) GERRY RAFFERTY               1978 LOGO UK MOGO4002  US VISA 7006
HENRY SPINETTI    D   (AD       (D) CITY TO CITY                 1978 UA     US 840     UK  UAS 30104
JOE EGAN          V   (A        (E) NIGHT OWL                    1979 UA     US LA958   UK  UAS 30238
ROD KING          STEEL(A       (F) SNAKES & LADDERS             1980 UA     US 1039    UK  UAS 32098
ALAN PARKER       G   (A        (G) SLEEPWALKING                 1982 LIBERTY           UK  LBS 30352
CHRISTOPHER NEIL D SYN(G        (1) 1978 TOUR BAND
VIV McAULIFFE     V   (D
GLEN LEFLEUR      PERC (D    BARBARA DICKSON    V   (DE  RAB NOAKES         G V  (AD  HUGH MURPHY V     (AD
JOHN VANDERRICK   FDL (A     ANDREW STEELE      D   (A   ANDY FAIRWEATHER LOW G  (D   HUGH BURNS  G     (DEG
GRAHAM PRESKETT K FDL V(DE   TOMMY EYRE         K   (DE1 RAPHAEL RAVENSCROFT SAX(DEF1 LIAM GENOCKEY D   (EF1G
BRIAN COLE        STEEL(D    MICK MOODY         G   (D   NIGEL JENKINS      G  (D   WILLY RAY   ACC   (D
JERRY DONAHUE     G   (DF    PAUL JONES    HCA      (D   JOHN McBURNIE      V  (D   RICHARD BRUNTON G(EF
RICHARD THOMPSON  G MAND(E   PETE WINGFIELD     ORG (EF  MO FOSTER          B  (EFG FRANK RICOTTI PERC(EFG
JOHN KIRKPATRICK  ACC (E     RICHARD HARVEY WIND SYN(EF  BETSY COOKE        V  (EF  LINDA THOMPSON V(E
IAN LYNN          K   (FG    BRYN HAWORTH       G   (F   BILLY LIVSEY       K  (F   PETE ZORN     B  (F
MEL COLLINS       SAX (FG    ALAN CLARK         K   (G   KEN CRADDOCK       K  (G
```

JIM RAFFERTY

```
JIM RAFFERTY      G V  (AB       (A) DONT TALK BACK              1978 DECCA UK SKL8291 US LONDON  722
HENRY SPINETTI    D   (A         (B) SOLID LOGIC                 1979 DECCA UK SKLR5314
PICK WITHERS      D   (A
DAVE MATTACKS     D   (A     PETER VAN HOOKE    D   (A   LYNTON NAIFF    PNO  (A   BRIAN ODGERS    B  (A
GRAHAM PRESKETT   FDL K(AB   ROD CLEMENTS       B   (A   HUGH BURNS      G    (AB  LAWRENCE JUBER  G  (A
FRANK BOGIE       G   (AB    B J COLE           STEEL(A   GARY TAYLOR     B    (A   FRANCIS MONKMAN K  (A
BARRY MORGAN      D   (A     MIKE DAY         D PERC (A   TIM RENWICK     G    (A   GERRY RAFFERTY G V SYN(AB
HERBIE FLOWERS    B   (A     JOHN JAMES         G   (A   MADELINE BELL   V    (A   KAY GARNER      V  (A
PETE SWETTENHAM       (A     CHRIS MERCER      SAX  (A   JOHN NIVEN      CONC (A   GEORGE McCRAE  PIPES(A
FRANK SHERPAS     V   (A     MIKE SHERPAS       V   (A   BILL McGEACHY   V    (A   FIONA McGEACHY  V  (A
RAB NOAKES        V   (AB    PRESTON HEYMAN     D   (B   BEN BARSON      K    (B   DON AIREY       K  (A
JOHN GIBLIN       B   (B     MEL COLLINS       SAX  (B   MORRIS PERT     PERC (B   MARTIN LEVAN   PERC(B
PEPI LEMER        V   (B     RICKY HITCHCOCK    G   (B   TERRY JONES     HRNS (B
```

RAGE

```
KEITH MULHOLLAND  G   (A         (A) NICE 'N' DIRTY              1982 CARRERE          US        CAL 138
JOHN MYLETT       D   (A
DAVE LLOYD        V   (A     TONY STEERS        G V (A   MICK DEVONPORT  B    (A
```

RAH BAND

```
PETER KING        SAX (A         (A) THE CRUNCH & BEYOND         1978 EBONY                      EBY1001
BARRY DE SOUZA    D   (A         (B) THE RAH BAND                1981 DJM       UK DJF 20573
TONY CARR         PERC (A
RICHARD HEWSON K SYN B(A
```

RAICES

```
JUAN MELENDEZ     WIND V(A        (A) RAICES                     1975 NEMPEROR        US     NE 434
CARLOS MELENOEZ   G V  (A
GONCHI SIFRE      D HCA(A     SAMMY FIGUEROA     PERC V(A  AMAURY LOPEZ    K G SYN(A  ROBERT PURAS    B  (A
RAFAEL CRUZ       D FLT(A
```

(RITCHIE BLACKMORES)RAINBOW

```
RITCHIE BLACKMORE G   (ALL       (A) RITCHIE BLACKMORE'S RAINBOW  1975 OYSTER                    OYA 2001
COZY POWELL       D   (BCDEHJ    (A) RITCHIE BLACKMORE'S RAINBOW  1978 POLYDOR US 6049 UK RI 2490 141
GARY DRISCOLL     D   (AHJ       (B) RAINBOW RISING               1976 OYSTER   US 1601  UK     2490 137
CRAIG GRUBER      B   (AHJ       (C) ON STAGE                     1977 OYSTER                    OYA21801
MICKY LEE SOULE   K   (AHJ       (C) ON STAGE                     1977 POLYDOR                   2490 016
TONY CAREY        K   (BCHJ      (D) LONG LIVE ROCK'N'ROLL        1978 POLYDOR US 6143 UK       2490 142
JIM BAIN          B   (BCHJ      (E) DOWN TO EARTH                1979 POLYDOR          UK       POLD5023
RONNIE DIO        V   (BCDHJ     (F) DIFFICULT TO CURE            1981 POLYDOR UK 6316  UK       POLD5036
MARK CLARKE       B   (HJ        (G) JEALOUS LOVER (EP)           1981 POLYDOR US 1/502
GRAHAM BONNET     V   (EHJK      (H) BEST OF                      1981 POLYDOR          UK PODV 2
DAVID STONE       K   (DHJ       (J) BEST OF                      1981 POLYDOR JAP 139/40
BOB DAISLEY       B   (DH        (K) STRAIGHT BETWEEN THE EYES    1982 POLYDOR UK POLD5056
ROGER GLOVER      B(EFGHJK       (K) STRAIGHT BETWEEN THE EYES    1982 MERCURY US 4041
DON AIREY         K(EFGHJK       (AB) RISING/RAINBOW              1980 POLYDOR UK 2683 078
BOB RONDINELLI    D(FGHK
JOE LYNN TURNER   V (FGHJK
```

CHRIS RAINBOW

```
CHRIS RAINBOW     V   (ABC       (A) HOME OF THE BRAVE           1975 POLYDOR          UK        2383 467
SIMON PHILLIPS    D   (BC        (B) LOOKING OVER MY SHOULDER    1978 POLYDOR          UK        2383 338
PETE ZORN         B   (BC        (C) WHITE TRAILS                1979 EMI              UK        EMC 3305
MO FOSTER         B   (BC
DAVE LAWSON       SYN (CB    IAN BAIRNSON      K   (C   LINDA TAYLOR      V   (C   SHUG BARR     G  (C
MART JENNER       G   (BC    MAX MIDDLETON     K   (C   DEREK QUINN       PERC (C   DICK MORRISSEY SAX(C
MARLYN BAIRNSON   V   (C     CHRISTY THOMPSON  V   (C   MALCOLM CECIL     HRN  (A   ROBERT MARGOULEFF  PROD(A
MAXINE WILLARD    V   (A     OREN WATERS       V   (A   JULIA TILLMAN     V    (A   OLLIE BROWN D  (B
DON GRUSIN        K   (A     SEYMOUR DUNCAN    B   (AB  HENRY SPINETTI    D    (B   DAVE MARKEE    B  (B
JOHN HAMILTON     SYN (B     PAT DONALDSON     B   (B   CLIVE CHAMAN      B    (B   PETE BARON     D  (B
DAVE WINTOUR      B   (B     JAN COCHRANE      D   (B   ANDY STEELE       D    (B   CHRIS KARAN    D  (B
JOHN BARHAM       STR(B
```

RAINBOW CANYON

```
                                 (A) ROLLIN'                     1975 CAPITOL         US        11272
```

RAINBOW PRESS

```
DAVE TROUP        B   (A         (A) SUNDAY FUNNIES              1969 MR G            US        9004
MARC ELLIS        G   (A
LARRY MILTON      K G(A     CHARLIE OSBORNE    K   (A   JOE GROFF      PERC(A BILLY YERGIN   PERC(A
```

RAINBOW FFOLLY

```
                                 (A) SALLIES FORTH              1967 PARLOPHONE                 PCS 7050
```

RAINBOW RED OXIDISER

```
    ED CASSIDY        D    (?          (A) RECORDED LIES              1980 LINE      GER        5084
    MARS BONFIRE      G    (A
    LEON RUBINHOLD    G    (A    GARY MARKER      B    (A   NIKKI & THE CORVETTES V (A   JANA LEE DARC       (A
    CHERYL JONES           (A    JIM EPPOLITO          (A        TIPPI CANOE         (A   SPECIAL OCCASIONS   (A
```

A RAINCOAT

```
    ANDY ARTHUR     G V  (A          (A) DIGALONGAMACS               1975 EMI                UK    EMC 3090
    ROD SYERS       B    (A
    PHILLIPE CHAMBON G   (A    DAVE HUDSON      K    (A   JOHN PUNTER       D   (A   ROSS PEARLSTONE  D (A
    STEVE WILSON    D    (A
```

RAINCOATS

```
    JEREMIE FRANK   G V  (123        (A) RAINCOATS                   1979 ROUGH TRADE        UK    ROUGH 3
    RICHARD DUDANSKI D   (3B         (1) 1978      (2) 1978   (3) 1978 JULY  (4) 1979
    NICK TURNER     D    (12         (EP) FAIRYTALE IN THE SUPERMARKET 1979 ROUGH TRADE      UK
    KATE KORUS      G    (1          (B) ODYSHAPE                   1981 ROUGH TRADE        UK    ROUGH13
    ANA DA SILVA    G V(1234AB
    KADIR DURVESH SHEHNAI (B   GINA BIRCH    B V  (1234AB  PALMOLIVE       D (4A  VICKI ASPINALL VLN G B(4AB
    LORA LOGIC      SAX  (A    SHIRLEY O'LOCHLIN     (B   ROBERT WYATT      D (B   CHARLEY HAYWARD     D  (B
    INGRID WEISS    PERC(B    DICK O'DELL           (B   GEORGIE BORN     CELLO(B
```

MARVIN RAINWATER

```
    MARVIN RAINWATER V    (ALL       (A) GONNA FIND ME A BLUEBIRD    196  MGM            US    4046
                                     (B) SONGS                      196  MGM            US    3534
                                     (C) WITH A HEART               19   MGM            US    3721
                                     (D) MARVIN RAINWATER           19   CROWN          US    5307
                                     (E) GETS COUNTRY FEVER         1972 PHILIPS        UK    6414 110
                                     (F) NEW COUNTRY SOUND          1974 GEM            GES 1108
                                     (G) ESPECIALLY FOR YOU         1976 WESTWOOD       WRS 101
                                     (H) ROCKIN' ROLLIN' RAINWATER  1982 BEAR FAMILY    UK    15079
```

RAINY DAZE

```
    BOB HECKENDORF  ORG  (A          (A) THAT ACAPULCO GOLD         1967 UNI                   73002
    KIP GILBERT     D    (A
    MAC FERRIS      G    (A    SAM FULLER    B    (A   TIM GILBERT     G V  (A
```

RAM JAM

```
    PETER CHARLES   D    (A          (A) RAM JAM                    1977 EPIC   US 34885   UK 82215
    BILL BARTLETT   G V  (A          (B) PORTRAIT OF THE ARTIST     19   EPIC   US 35287
    HOWIE BLAUVELT  B V  (A
    MYKE SCAVONE    V PERC(A
```

RAMASES

```
    RAMASES              (AB         (A) SPACE HYMNS                1971 VERTIGO        UK    6360 046
    SEL                  (AB         (A) SPACE HYMNS                1980 VERTIGO        NL    9199 134
    ERIC STEWART    G SYN(A          (B) GLASS TOP COFFIN           1975 VERTIGO        UK    6360 115
    LOL CREME       G SYN(A
    KEVIN GODLEY    D FLT(A    GRAHAM GOULDMAN  G B  (A   MARTIN RAPHAEL  SITAR(A   PETE KINGSMAN    B  (B
    ROGER HARRISON  D    (B    BARRY KIRSCH     K    (B   JO ROMERO       G   (B   SUE GLOVER       V  (B
    BOB BERTLES     SAX  (B    COLIN THURSTON   B    (B   SUNNY LESLIE    V   (B   KAY GARNER       V  (B
    EDDIE LESTER CHORALE V (B
```

RAMSES

```
    WINFRIED LANGHORST K V (         (A) LA LEYLA                   1975  SKY  002  ANNUIT US 003
    HANS KLINKHAMMER  B   (          (B) ETERNITY RISE              1978  SKY  020
    NORBERT LANGHORST G   (
    HERBERT NATHO     V   (    REINHARD SCHROTER     D   (A
```

RAMATAM

```
    APRIL LAWTON G B V HCA(AB        (A) RAMATAM                    1972 ATLANTIC   UK K40415 US SD7236
    TOMMY SULLIVAN K G V WIND(AB     (B) IN APRIL CAME THE DAWNING  1973 ATLANTIC            US SD7261
    MITCH MITCHELL  D    (A
    MIKE PINERA     G V  (A    RUSS SMITH      B V  (A   JIMMY WALKER    V PERC(B  BRUCE MORGENHEIM VLN (B
    SELDON POWELL   HRNS (B    GARNETT BROWN   HRNS (B   ARTHUR KAPLAN   HRNS (B  JOE NEWMAN       HRNS(B
    MARVIN STAMM    HRNS (B    RAYMOND BECKENSTEIN HRN(B JOE SHEPLEY     HRNS (B  DOMINICK GRAVINE HRNS(B
    STRING SECTION       (B
```

BONIE RAITT

```
    BONNIE RAITT    G V  (ALL        (A) BONNIE RAITT               1971 WB   US WS 1953 UK   K56255
    JUNIOR WELLS    HCA  (A          (B) GIVE IT UP                 1972 WB   US BS 2643 UK   K46189
    A C REED        SAX  (A          (C) TAKIN' MY TIME             1973 WB   US BS 2729 UK   K46261
    WILLY MURPHY    V K  (A          (C) TAKIN' MY TIME             1975 WB   RI         UK   K56254
    FREEBO          B V  (ABCDEFG     (D) STREET LIGHTS              1974 WB   US BS 2818 UK   K56075
    PETER BELL      V    (A          (E) HOME PLATE                 1975 WB   US BS 2864 UK   K56160
    DOUGLAS SPURGEON TROM (A         (F) SWEET FORGIVENESS          1977 WB   US BS 2990 UK   K56323
    PETER ASHER     V    (G          (G) THE GLOW                   1979 WB   US    3369 UK   K56706
    JOHNNY LEE SCHELL G V K(H        (H) GREEN LIGHT                1982 WB              UK   K56980
    RUSSELL HAGEN   G    (A
    STEPHEN BRADLEY D    (A    VOYLE HARRIS     TPT (A   MAURICE JACOX   WIND (A  EUGENE HOFFMAN   SAX (A
    PAUL BARRERE    G    (A    JOHN HALL        G  (BCDE BILL PAYNE    K V (CEFG JIM KELTNER      D  (C
    MILT HOLLAND    PERC (C    EARL PALMER      D   (C   TAJ MAHAL     B V HCA(C  GEORGE BOHANON   TROM(CE
    OSCAR BRASHEAR  HRNS (C    ERNIE WATTS      SAX (C   SAM CLAYTON   CONGA(CF  VAN DYKE PARKS   K V (C
    ANTHONY TERRAN  HRNS (C    GLEN FERRIS      HRNS(C   JOEL PESKIN     HRNS (C  MARTIN KRYSTALL  HRNS(C
    ROBERT HARDAWAY HRNS (C    BUD BRISBOIS HRNS    (C   LOWELL GEORGE   G   (C   DON GROLNICK     K  (DG
    STEPHEN GADD    D    (D    DAVID SPINOZZA   G   (D   ARTHUR JENKINS  PERC (D  LEON PENDARVIS   K  (D
    BOB KREINAR     B    (D    CHARLES BROWN    G   (D   JEFF MIRANOV    G   (D   DAVID LASLEY     V  (D
    LOU COURTNEY    V    (D    JERRY FRIEDMAN   G   (D   CARL HALL       V   (D   SHARON REDD      V  (D
    TASHA THOMAS    V    (D    JOHN TROPEA      G   (D   RALPH McDONALD  PERC (D  PAUL GRIFFIN     K  (D
    JOHN MAYER      K    (D    RICHARD DAVIS    B   (D   ROBERT MANN     G   (D   TERRY REID       V  (E
    EMMYLOU HARRIS  V    (E    GREG PRESTOPINO  V   (E   WILLOW VANDER HOEK V (E  JEFF LABES       K  (F
    MICHAEL McDONALD V   (F    CARLENA WILLIAMS V   (E   NATALIE VENABLE V   (E   GARY MALLABER    D  (E
    WILL McFARLANE  G    (EF   FRED TACKETT     K G (EF  JAY WINDING     K   (E   DENNIS WHITTED   D  (BEF
    WILLIAM'SMITTY'SMITH K (EH JOE PORCARO      PERC (E  JEFF PORCARO    PERC (E  JOHN SEBASTIAN A'HARP(E
    JERRY JUMONVILLE SAX (E    JIM GORDON       SAX (E   DICK HYDE       HRNS (E  VANETTA FIELDS   V  (E
    ROBBIE MONTGOMERY V  (E    MAXAYN LEWIS     V   (EFG JACKSON BROWNE  V   (EH  ROSEMARY BUTLER  V  (EFG
    JOHN D SOUTHER  V    (EFG  DEBBIE GREENE    V   (E   JOHN HERALD     V   (E   TOM WAITS        V  (E
    DAVID GRISMAN   MAND (F    LESTER CHAMBERS  V   (F   TERRY EATON     SAX (B   TIM MOORE        V  (B
    PAUL BUTTERFIELD HCA (BG   GENE STASHUK CELLO   (B   MARTY GREBB     SAX (B   MERL SAUNDERS    PNO (B
```

(CONTINUED)

R22 (CONTINUED)

BONIE RAITT

KAL DAVID	G (B	AMOS GARRETT	G (B	ERIC KAZ	VIBES(B	WELLS KELLY	CONGA(B
T J TINDALL	V (B	MARK JORDAN	K (B	JACKIE LOMAX	V (B	JACK VIERTEL	G (B
DAVE HOLLAND	B (B	LOU TERRICIANO	PNO (B	CHRIS PARKER	D (B	JOHN PAYNE	WIND(B
PETER ECKLUND	CORNET (B	WADDY WACHTEL	G V (G	DANNY KORTHCHMAR	G V (G	BOB GLAUB	B (G
RICK MAROTTA	D (G	KEN EDWARDS	V (G	TREVOR LAWRENCE	SAX (G	LARRY WILLIAMS	SAX (G
DAVID SANBORN	SAX (G	STEVE MADAIO	TPT (G	CRAIG FULLER	V (G	JOHN GUERIN	D (G
BOB MAGNUSSON	B (G	RAY CHARA	B (H	DAVID WOODFORD	SAX (H	STEVE RAITT	V (H
BOB FRABONI	PROD (H	RICKY FATAAR	V D (H	MELANIE ROSALES	V (H	RICK VITO	G (H
RICHARD MANUEL	V (H	VINCE GILL	V (H	IAN McLAGAN	G K (H		

R22A

RAMBLERS

FRANK BECKING	G (C		(A) THE KIDS ARE BACK TO ROCK'N'ROLL	1978 CRYSTAL	GER	CRY 45103
RUDIGER BRAUNE	D V (C		(B) STREETHEAT	1979 ANTAGON	GER	ALP3231
RUDIGER ELZE	G (C		(C) STRANGE LIFE	1980 CBS	NL	8456=
JURGEN MEIER	B V (C					
CHRISTIAN SCHNEIDER	V(C	NICK GENNIE SMITH	K (C			

R23

PHIL RAMBOW

PHILIP RAMBOW	G V (ALL		(A) SHOOTING GALLERY		1979	EMI UK EMC3304 US CAPITOL 12074	
MICK RONSON	G (1		(1) 1977 TOUR				
MAGGIE RONSON	V (1		(B) JUNGLE LAW		1981 PARLOPHONE UK PCS7216		
DAVE DRILL	B (1						
LAURIE JELLYMAN	D (1	HUGH BURNS	G (A	DAVE COCHRAN	B (AB	JOHN MACKENZIE	(A
BLAIR CUNNINGHAM	D (AB	PETE WINGFIELD	K V (A	JOE BREEN	(A	JOHN KIRKPATRICK	(A
TONY BEARD	(A	DAVE DONEN	D PERC(	PETER GORIN	B (	TOM SPAHN	K (
JANN NEILSON	V (B	MATT BATT	V (B	JO SUC	V (B	MATT IRVING	B (B
STEVE BOLTON	G (B	JOHN WETTON	B (B	BERNIE CLARKE	K (B	MARK PINDER	D (B
STEVE HOLLY	D (B	LAWRENCE JUBER	G (B	DAVID BENDETH	G (B	DAVEY PAYNE	SAX(B
JAMIE WEST	G (B						

R24

RAMONES

JOHNNY RAMONE	G (ABCDEF	(A) RAMONES	1976 SIRE		UK	9103 253	
JOEY RAMONE	V (ABCDEF	(A) RAMONES	1976 SIRE	US 7520	RI 1977 6020		
DEE DEE RAMONE	B (ABCDEF	(B) RAMONES LEAVE HOME	1976 SIRE		UK	9103 254	
TOMMY RAMONE	D (ABCE	(B) RAMONES LEAVE HOME	1976 SIRE	US 7528	RI 1977 6031		
MARC BELL RAMONE	D (DF	(C) ROCKET TO RUSSIA	1977 SIRE	US 6042	UK 9103 255		
BARRY GOLDBERG	K (F	(D) ROAD TO RUIN	1978 SIRE UK/US 6063 philips 6370810				
STEVE DOUGLAS	SAX (F	(E) ITS ALIVE (DBLE)	1979 SIRE SRK26074	GER	300 504		
		(F) END OF THE CENTURY	1980 SIRE			SRK 6077	
		(G) PLEASANT DREAMS	1981 SIRE UK 357	GER	203 891		

R24A

RAMP

	(A) COME INTO KNOWLEDGE	1977 BLUE THUMB	US 6028

R24B

WILLIS ALAN RAMSEY

WILLIS ALAN RAMSEY	V B G (A	(A) WILLIS ALAN RAMSEY	1972 A&M	UK	AMLS 68158		
NICK DECARO	ACC (A						
ERNEST WATTS	SAX (A	LEON RUSSELL K VIBES(A	TYLLER COLLIE	D (A	LARRY STEDMAN	PNO (A	
ROBERT ABERG	G (A	RED RHODES STEEL (A	CARL RADLE	B (A	JIM KELTNER	D (A	
KENNY BULBEY	D (A	RUSS KUNKEL	D (A	TIM SELF	FDL (A	CATHY PRUITT	CELLO(A
LEE SKLAR	B (A	DUSTY RHODES	FDL (A				

R25

ELLIOTT RANDALL

ELLIOTT RANDALL	G V (ABC	(A) RANDALLS ISLAND	1970 POLYDOR US 24/4044 UK 2489 004				
BOB PIAZZA	B V (A	(B) ROCK'N'ROLL CITY	1973 POLYDOR US 5026				
ALLEN HERMAN	D PERC(AB	(C) RANDALLS NEW YORK	1977 KIRSHNER US 34351				
PAUL FLEISHER	WIND (AB						
GEORGE ANDREWS	PNO (A	ANDY ALISON	B (A	TERRY ADAMS	K (A	RICHARD BOCK	CELLO(A
POT	PNO (AB	BOB BABITT	B (C	RUBENS BASSINI	PERC (C	GENE BIANCO	HARP (C
KEN BISCHEL	K (C	SUZANNE CIANI	K (C	JERRY FRIEDMAN	G (C	STEVE GADD	D (C
PAUL GRIFFIN	K (C	WILL LEE	B (C	TONY LEVIN	B (C	JESSE LEVY	CELLO(C
RALPH MACDONALD	PERC (C	JIMMY MAELEN	PERC (C	MITCH MARGO	V G K(C	LESLIE MILLER	V (C
JEFF MIRANOV	G (C	JEFF PORCARO	D (C	ALLEN SCHWARZBERG	D (C	JAY SIEGEL	V (C
THE TOKENS	V (C	GARY KING	B (C				

R26

BOOTS RANDOLPH

BOOTS RANDOLPH	SAX (ALL	YAKETY SAX (EP)	1960 RCA	GER	9752
WITH		YAKETY SAX	1964 MONUMENT US 18002	US RI MC6600	
MAYBELLE CARTER	(*	HIP BOOTS	19 MONUMENT UK 5002	US RI MC6601	
CHET ATKINS	G (*	HIP BOOTS	1964 MONUMENT US 18015		
JOSH GRAVES	G (*	MORE YAKETY SAX	1965 MONUMENT US 18037	RI MC6602	
		THE YANKIN' SAX MAN	1964 CAMDEN		CAS825
		SWEET TALK	1965 CAMDEN		CAS865
		THE FANTASTIC BOOTS RANDOLPH	1966 MONUMENT UK 5012	US RI MC6603	
		BOOTS WITH STRINGS	1967 MONUMENT US 18066	US RI MC6604	
		BOOTS WITH STRINGS	1967 MONUMENT UK 5003		
		SAX-SATIONAL	1967 MONUMENT US 18079	US RI MC6605	
		SAX SATIONAL	1967 MONUMENT UK 5022		
		VOICES & STRINGS	1968 MONUMENT US 18082	US RI MC6606	
		SUNDAY SAX	1968 MONUMENT US 18092	US RI MC6607	
		THE SOUND OF BOOTS	1968 MONUMENT US 18099	US RI MC6608	
		WITH LOVE	1969 MONUMENT US 18111	US RI MC6609	
		BOOTS & STOCKING	19 MONUMENT	US RI MC6610	
		YAKETY REVISTED	19 MONUMENT US 18128	US RI MC6611	
		YAKETY REVISITED	19 MONUMENT UK 5040		
		BOOTS WITH BRASS	1970 MONUMENT US 18147	US RI MC6613	
		HIT'S	1970 MONUMENT US 18144		
		HOMER LOUIS RANDOLPH	1971 MONUMENT US 30678	US RI MC6614	
		YAKETY SAX	1971 CAMDEN US 9003		
		GREAT HITS OF TODAY	1972 MONUMENT US 31908	US RI MC6615	
		THE WORLD OF	1972 MONUMENT US 30963	UK	68203
		SENTIMENTAL JOURNEY	1973 MONUMENT US 32292	US RI MC6616	
		(*)COUNTRY BOOTS	1974 MONUMENT US 32912	US RI MC6617	
		COOL BOOTS	1976 MONUMENT US 33803	US RI MC6618	
		GREATEST HITS	1976 MONUMENT UK 80548	US RI MG7602	
		PARTY BOOTS (DBL)	1976 MONUMENT US 34082	US RI MP8604	
		COOL BOOTS	1976 MONUMENT US 33803		
		SAX APPEAL	1978 MERCURY	US	MG7611

R26A   ERIC RANDOM   R26A

```
ERIC RANDOM    V K B G SYN(A    (A) THAT'S WHAT I LIKE ABOUT ME    1980 NEW HORMONE      UK      ORG 6
LYN WALTON          K      (A
```

R27   RANDOM ELEMENT   R27

```
                               (A) RAMDOM ELEMENT             1978 ROCKING HORSE   US      5521
```

R28   RANDY PIE   R28

```
DICKY TARRACH    D     (ABCDe   (A) SIGHTSEEING TOUR           1974 POLYDOR                  2371 491
FRANK DIEZ       G     (E       (A) RANDY PIE                  1974 ZEBRA GER 2949 015
MANFRED THIERS   B V   (ABCE    (B) HIGHWAY DRIVER             1974 POLYDOR  US 6515   2371 555
WERNER BECKER    K V   (ABC     (C) KITSCH                     1975 POLYDOR  US 6518   2371 666
PETER FRENCH          (DE       (D) ENGLAND ENGLAND            1976 POLYDOR             2664 160
BERND SCHULZ          (D        (E) FAST FORWARD               1977 POLYDOR  US 6113   2371 807
BERND WIPPICH    G V   (ABC
RAINER BAUMANN   G     (A    JEAN JACQUES KRAVETZ K (BC  JOCHEN PETERSEN V G SAX(BC   GEORGE MEYER      (D
HERBERT HILDEBRAND G V (D    CARL GRAVES       V   (A   LARRY BROWN              PERC(C
                                              (E
```

R28A   RANK STRANGERS   R 28A

```
CHRIS DARROW G V MAND (A       (A) RANK STRANGERS             1977 PACIFIC ARTS   US   PAC7 112
JOHN SELK        V B   (A
ROBB STRANDLUND  G V   (A    CINDY EDWARDS     V   (A   TEMPLETON PARCELY  VLN (A  =FENRUS EPP
POPE TERMAN      B     (A                                MAX BUDA           HCA (A
```

R28B   KENNY RANKIN   R28B

```
KENNY RANKIN     V G K(A        (A) SILVER MORNING            1974 LITTLE DAVID UK K59651
RICHARD BENNETT  V     (A        (B) INSIDE                   1975 LITTLE DAVID UK K 59653
JOHN GUERIN      D     (AB
JOHN SEBASTIAN   HCA   (A    KING ERRISIN    PERC (A   BOBBYE HALL    PERC (AB  WILLIAM SMITH   K  (AB
JIM GORDON       D     (A    PETER MARSHALL  B    (AB  RON TUTT       D    (A   RICHARD GREEN      (A
JIM NICHOLS            (A    JIM GILSTRAP    V    (A   LANI GROVES    V    (A   ANGIE JOHNSON   V  (A
YVONNE RANKIN    V     (A    STEPHANIE SPRUELL V  (A   DENIECE WILLIAMS V  (A   WILLIE WEEKS    B  (B
WADDY WACHTEL    G     (B    YVONNE RANKIN   V    (B   AL CASEY       STEEL(B  GARY BURTON     VIBES(B
WILTON FELDER    B     (B    JULIA TILLMAN   V    (B   ORAN WATERS    V    (B   MICHAEL STEWART G  (B
ROY McCURDY      D     (B    BILL CHAMPLIN   K    (B   MICHAEL O'MARTIAN K (B   PAUL STALLWORTH B  (B
MAYUTO           PERC  (B    MAX BENNETT     B    (B   JAMES GADSON   D    (B   MAXINE WILLARD  V  (B
LUTHER WATERS    V     (B    STEVE CROPPER   G    (B   JIM HORN       SAX  (B   SID SHARP   STR    (B
```

R28C   RANKING DREAD   R28C

```
                               (A) LOTS OF LOVING             1980 STAND FIRM          01
```

R29   RANKING JOE   R29

```
RANKING JOE      V     (ABC     (A) WEAKHEART FADE AWAY       1978 GREENSLEEVES          GREL2
SLY DUNBAR       D     (C       (B) DUB IT IN A DANCE         1980 TROJAN                TRLS 194
SANTA            D     (C       (C) SATURDAY NIGHT JAMDOWN STYLE 1980 GREENSLEEVES       GREL16
STYLE            D     (C       (D) ROUND THE WORLD           1980 STUDENT      UK       009
JIMMY BECKER     HCA   (C
FLABBA           B     (C    STEELIE         K    (C   ANSEL COLLINS    K  (C   GLADSTONE ANDERSON K (C
SOREL            G     (C    BINGY BUNNY     G    (C   BONGO HERMAN   PERC (C   SKY JUICE   PERC   (C
STICKY           PERC  (C    HEADLEY BENNETT SAX  (C   VAL BENNETT    TROM (C   BOBBY ELLIS TPT    (C
```

R30   RANKING TREVOR   R30

```
RANKING TREVOR   V     (ABC     (A) IN FINE STYLE             1978 FRONT LINE   UK   FL1015
SLY DUNBAR       D     (A       (B) 3 PIECE CHICKEN           1978 CHA CHA           CHALP 001
RANCHIE McLEAN   G B   (A
ROBBIE SHAKESPEARE B   (A    ANSEL COLLINS   K    (A   TOUTER HARVEY  K    (A   DUGGIE      G    (A
STICKY           PERC  (A    BARNABAS        PERC (A
```

R30A   RAPED   R30A

```
                               (A) PRETTY PAEDOPHILES(EP)     19   PAROLE       UK   KNIT 1
```

R31   TOM RAPP   R31

```
TOM RAPP         G V   (ABC     (A) TOM RAPP (FAMILIAR SONGS) 1972 REPRISE      US   MS 2069
ART ELLIS FLT CONC V   (BC      (B) STARDANCER               1972 BLUE THUMB   US   BTS 44
BILL ROLLINS     CELLO(BC        (C) SUNFOREST               1973 BLUE THUMB   US   BTS 56
STEVE McCORD     G     (BC
JIM COLVARD    G DOBR(BC  CHARLIE McCOY HCA V G K(BC  BUZZ CASON      B   (C   DIANE HARRIS    V  (C
CHUCK COCHRAN    PNO   (C  BUDDY SPICHER   VLN (BC  DAVID BRIGGS   PNO  (BC  MIKE LEECH      B  (BC
FARRELL MORRIS   PERC  (C  BOBBY WOOD     PERC (BC  REGGIE YOUNG   PNO  (BC  KARL HIMMEL     D  (C
BOBBY THOMPSON  G BANJ(C  CHIP YOUNG      G    (C  BOB MOORE      B    (C   KENNY BUTTREY   D  (C
BOB DOROUGH      PNO   (C  BILL SALTER     B    (C  WARREN SMITH   PERC (C   JIM ISBELL   D PERC(B
WELDON MYRICK    STEEL(B  FLORENCE WARNER V    (B  HARRY ORLOVE  G V MAND (B STRING SECTION        (B
```

R32   RARE EARTH   R32

```
JERRY LA CROIX   V     (H       (1) DREAM ANSWERS         1968 VERVE                      US 5056
GIL BRIDGES FLT V SAX (ABCDEFGHJ1 (A) GET READY           1970 TAMLA UK  STML11156 RARE EARTH US 507
PETE RIVERA      D V   (ABCDEF1 (B) ECOLOGY               1971 TAMLA UK  STML11180 RARE EARTH US 514
PETE HOORELBEKE  D V   (EFJ   ]SAME? (C) ONE WORLD        1971 RARE EARTH UK 4001           US 520
ROD RICHARDS     G V   (AB1     (D) IN CONCERT            1972 RARE EARTH UK 301            US 534
  KENNY JAMES    K     (AB1     (E) WILLIE REMEMBERS      1973 RARE EARTH UK 3008           US 543
RAY MONETTE      G V   (CDEFGH  (F) MA                    1973 RARE EARTH UK 3010           US 546
FRANK WESTBROOK  K     (H       (G) BACK TO EARTH         1975 RARE EARTH                   US 6 548
MIKE URSO        B V   (EFJ     (H) MIDNIGHT LADY         1976 RARE EARTH UK 3013 NL 97575  US 550
ED GUZMAN        PERC  (CEDGHJ  (J) RARE EARTH            1977 PRODIGAL  UK  2007           US 10019
MARK OLSON       K V   (CEFD    (K) BAND TOGETHER         1978 PRODIGAL  UK  2008           US 10025
REGGIE McBRIDE   B     (GH      (L) GRAND SLAM            1978 PRODIGAL  UK  2009
PAUL WARREN      G V   (GH      ( ) DISQUE DO'R           1976 PATHE      FR           064 95295
GABRIEL KATONA   K V   (G       ( ) MASTERS OF ROCK       19   RARE EARTH   .   GER 95926
BARRY FROST      PERC  (G
MAXINE WATERS    V     (H    RON FRANSEN    K    (J   JULIA TILLMAN  V  (H   JESSICA SMITH   V  (H
DANIEL FERGUSON  G     (J
```

R32A   HERMAN RAREBELL   R32A

```
HERMAN REREBELL  D     (A       (A) NIP IN THE BUD         1981 HARVEST      SHSP 4118
D H COOPER       G     (A
GEORGE PHILLIPS  B V   (A
```

RAREBIRD

STEVE GOULD	V SAX B G(ALL	(A) RAREBIRD	1969 CHARISMA	UK CAS1005	PHILIPS GER 6369900
FRED KELLY	D V (CDEF	(B) AS YOUR MIND FLIES BY	1970 CHARISMA	UK CAS1011 US ABC 716
JOHN WETTON	B (D	(B) AS YOUR MIND FLIES BY	1970 PHILIPS GER 6369904
DAVE KAFFINETTI	K SYN(ALL	(C) EPIC FOREST	1972 POLYDOR	UK 2442 101 US5530
ANDY RAE	B (E	(D) SOMEBODYS WATCHING	1973 POLYDOR	UK 2383 211 US 6502
KEVIN LAMB	ORG V(BEG	(E) BORN AGAIN	1974 POLYDOR	UK 2383 274 US 6506
GRAHAM FIELD	ORG (ABG	(F) RAREBIRD	1975 POLYGRAM	UK 9299 008 US 4514
MARK ASHTON	D V (ABG	(G) SYMPATHY	1976 CHARISMA UK	CS 4
ANDY CURTIS	G (CDH	(H) RARE BIRD(POLYDOR SPECIAL)	1977 POLYDOR UK 2384 078
AL MATTHEWS	PERC (D		
NIC POTTER	B (DH SAMMY ABU	PERC (D	PAUL HOLLAND PERC (DC	PAUL KORDA	V (D
PAUL KARAS	B (CH NICKY JAMES	V (D	

RAS MICHAEL & THE SONS OF NEGUS

RAS MICHAEL	V (ALL	(A) NYAHBINGHI	1975 TROJAN	TRS 113
ALVIN JACK HEWITT	V (C	(B) TRIBUTE	1976 TROJAN	TRS A£"
THOMAS MARTIN	V ((C	(C) MOVEMENTS	1978
ISON FUNDE	(C	(D) FREEDOM SUITE	1979 DYNAMIC	3004
SYDNEY WOLFE	D (C		
DENNIS FERRON	ORG (C EARL'CHINNA' SMITH G	(C	MICHAEL MASKIL G B	(C RICA BACA	V (C
S CHUNG CLANNER	V (C PUMA JONES	V (C	

THE YOUNG RASCALS

FELIX CAVALIERE	K V (ALL	(A) THE YOUNG RASCALS	1966 ATLANTIC UK 587974	US SD8123
DINO DANELLI	D (ALL	(B) COLLECTIONS	1966 ATLANTIC	US SD8134
GENE CORNISH	G (ABCDEFGH	(C) GROOVIN'	1967 ATLANTIC	US SD8148
EDDIE BRIGATI	G V (ABCDEFH	(D) ONCE UPON A DREAM	1968 ATLANTIC	UK 588 098 US SD8169
ROBERT POPWELL	B (JK	(E) GREATEST HITS (TIMEPEACE)	1968 ATLANTIC	UK 588 120 US SD8190
ANN SUTTON	V (JK	(F) FREEDOM SUITE	1969 ATLANTIC	UK 588 183 US SD8901
BUZZY FEITEN	G (JK	(G) SEARCH & NEARNESS	1971 ATLANTIC	UK 2400113 US SD8246
HAROLD COWART	B (G	(H) SEE	1969 ATLANTIC	UK 588 183 US SD8246
CHUCK RAINEY	B (GHF	(J) PEACEFUL WORLD	1971 CBS	UK 66292 US 30462
JOE NEWMAN	TPT (GJ	(K) ISLAND OF REAL	1972 CBS	UK 64756 US 31103
JOE FARRELL	SAX (GJ	(L) STAR COLLECTION	1973 MIDI	UK 30049 GERM 20022
SELDON POWELL	SAX (G		
MOLLY HOLT	V (J HUBERT LAWS	FLT (HJ RON CARTER	B (HJ DANNY LABBATE	SAX (H
JOE BUSHKIN	PNO (H KING CURTIS	SAX (F DAVID SHEWMAN	SAX (F RICHARD DAVIS	B (F
GERALD GEMOTTA	B (FJ LINK CHAMBERLAIN	G (J RALPH MACDONALD	PERC (J CYNTHIA WEBB	V (J
GARNETT BROWN	HRNS (J ERNIE ROYAL	TPT (J ERNIE WILKING	SAX (J WILLIAM SALTER	B (J
BRUCE BUONO	V (J BUDDY BUONO	V (J PEPPER ADAMS	SAX (J JOM SMITH	SAX(J
ALICE COLTRANE	HARP(J		

RASPBERRIES

WALLY BRYSON	G (AB	(A) RASPBERRIES	1972 CAPITOL	UK/US 11036
ERIC CARMEN	G V K(ABED	(B) FRESH	1973 CAPITOL	UK/US 11123
DAVE SMALLEY	G B (AB	(C) SIDE THREE	1974 CAPITOL	UK/US 11220
JIM BONFANTI	D (AB	(D) STARTING OVER	1974 CAPITOL	UK/US 11329
SCOTT McCARL	B (D	(E) BEST OF	1975 CAPITOL	UK/US 11524
MIKE McBRIDE	D (D	(E) BEST OF	1976 CAPITOL	CAPS 1026
JEFF HUTTON	K (D		
JIMMY LENNER	PROD (ABD		

RASPUTIN'S STASH

	(A) RASPUTIN'S STASH	19 COTILLION US 9046
	(B) DEVIL MADE ME DO IT	19 GEMIGO US 5500

(ROYAL) RASSES (ROYALS)

LINCOLN THOMPSON	G V (BC	(A) HUMANITY	1979 BALLISTIC	UAG 30227
KEITH PETERKIN	V (B	(B) EXPERIENCE	1979 BALLISTIC	UAG 30259
CLINTON HALL	V (B	(C) NATURAL WILD	1980 BALLISTIC	UAG 30309
LEROY WALLACE	D (BD	(D) HARDER NA RASS	1980 BALLISTIC	LBR 1031
MIKEYBOOTH	D (BCD		
BOBBY ELLIS	TPT (BD STICKY	PERC (BD VAL DOUGLAS	B (BD WIRE LINDO	K (BD
PABLO BLACK	K (BD GEOFFREY CHUNG	K (BD CECIL LLOYD	K (BD BUBBLER	HRNS(BD
BROTHER JOMO	PERC (BD JOE JACKSON	K (C GEORGE MILLER	G (BD DIGGLES	G (BD
ERNEST RANGLIN	G (BD TOMMY McCOOK	HRNS (BD HEADLEY BENNETT	SAX (BD BAGGA	B (BD
GRAHAM MABY	B (C RANCHIE McLEAN	B (C GARY SANFORD	G (C WILLIE LINDO	G (BC
DOUGIE	G (C DAVE HOUGHTON	D (C ANSEL COLLINS	K (C TONY GAD	SYN (C
GEORGE OBAN	PERC (C CRIS ALNE	DUB SOUNDS(C MO	PERC(C	

RASTUS

DANIEL MAGALEN	V SAX (A	(A) LIVE RASTUS	1971 GRT US 30004
MARC ROMAN	V TROM (A	(B) STEAMIN'	1972 NEIGHBORHOOD	NH3002
DAVE SMELKO	D V (A		
TONY CORRAO	G (A ARTHUR APPLETON	TROM (A MIKE GERACI	SAX V (A VIC WALKUSKI	SAX(A
DON NAGY	B TPT(A GEORGE SOPUCH	G (A	

RATIONALS

SCOTT MORGAN	V (A	(A) RATIONALS	1969 CREWE US 1334
STEVE CORREL	G (A		
TERRY TRABANDT	B (A BILL FIGG	D (A	

RATCHELL

LARRY BYROM	(A	(A) RATCHELL	197 MCA US 5330
CHRIS COUCHOIS	(A		
PAT COUCHOIS	(A HOWARD MESSER	(A	

RATS

	(A) RATS FIRST	1974 GOODEAR EARLH5003

[460]

RATTLES

```
    ACHIM REICHEL      G V  (1        (A) TWIST AT THE STAR CLUB      1964 PHILIPS           BL  7614
    HERBERT HILDEBRAND K B (1        (B) THE RATTLES                 1965 FONTANA
    DICKY TARRACH      D   (1        (C) HURRA! DIE RATTLE KOMMEN    1966 FONTANA
    RUGY RUGINSTEIN    G   (1        (D) ATTENTION                   19   FONTANA              6434 162
    AL BROCK           D   (3H       ( ) REMEMBER FINALE LIGURE      1967 STARCLUB    GER      158 031
    DIETER SADLOWSKI   D   (         (E) GREATEST HITS               1969 FONTANA 701707 US MERCURY 61127
    HAJO KREUTZFELD    V             (F) THE RATTLES                 1971 DECCA        UK      SKL  5008
    ZAPPO LUNGREN      B   (23GH     (G) TONIGHT STARRING EDNA       1972 PHILIPS              6305 176
    FRANK MILLER       G   (23GH     (H) GIN MILL                    1974 RCA                 PPLI 4016
    LUDE LAFAYETTE     K   (3GH      (J) THE WITCH                   19   PHILIPS     GER      6305 072
    HERBERT BORNHOLD   D   (2G       ( ) THE BEST OF                 19   LUXOR GOLD GER        41034
    GEORGE MAYER       G V (3        (EP) TEENBEAT                   19   ARIOLA               541174
    EDNA BEJARANO      V   (2G       (EP) TEENBEAT 2                 19   DECCA            DFE 8568
    LINDA FIELDS       V   (3H       (EP) RATTLES                    19   PHILIPS              423 560
                                     (EP) RATTLES                    19   FONTANA              466 030
                                     (1) 1961   (2) 1970   (3) 1975
```

RATTLESNAKE
```
                                     (A) RATTLE SNAKE               1873 KAMA SUTRA      US      2047
```

GENYA RAVAN
```
    GENYA RAVAN  V HCA PERC(ALL      (A) GENYA RAVAN WITH BABY      1972 CBS        UK 64872 US 31001
    BOBBY KEYS         SAX  (C       (B) THEY LOVE ME /THEY LOVE ME NOT 1973 DUNHILL          US 50143
    KENNETH RICE       D    (C       (C) GOLDIE ZELKOWITZ           1974 JANUS             US  3060
    FRED BECKMAIER     B    (C       (D) URBAN DESIRE               1978 20th CENTURY BTH8007  T 562
    KEN MARCO          G    (C       (E) AND I MEAN IT              1979 20th CENTURY           T 595
    DANNY KORTCHMAR    G    (C
    STEVE BECKMAIER    G    (C   LARRY NASH       K    (C   GABRIEL MAKLER    K   (C   TREVOR LAWRENCE K HRNS(C
    WILLIAM SMITH      K    (C   MAILTO CORREA   PERC (C   STEVE MADAIO    HRNS  (C   ABIGALE HANESS    V  (C
    GWENDOLYN EDWARDS  V    (C   C C WILLIAMSON    V  (C   CHARLIE GIORDANO  K  (DE   CONRAD TAYLOR     G  (DE
    RITCHIE FLIEGLER G MAND(D   DON NOSSOV        B  (D   BOBBY CHEN        D  (DE   STUART DAYE       G  (D
    JOEY RIBAUDO       V    (D   PAUL OPALACH     B   (D   JOHN PAUL FETTA   B  (D   DAVID LASLEY      V  (D
    IVAN KRAL          V    (D   LOU REED         V   (D   MITCH STYLES      G  (A   NICK OLIVA        K  (A
    JOHN PLATANIA      G    (A   PETER HODGSON    B   (A   BRIAN KEENAN      D  (A   BERNARD WILLIAMS CONGA(A
    MIKE LOMBARDI      B    (E   IAN HUNTER       V   (E   MICK RONSON       G  (E
```

RAVEN
```
    JOHN CIPOLLINA     G    (AB      (A) 1976
    ANDY KIRBY         D V  (A       (B) JOHN CIPOLLINAS RAVEN      198  LINE       GER      5041
    DAVID WEBER        D    (A
    SKIP OLSEN B       (A    NICKY HOPKINS    K (A   GREG DOUGLAS   G      (A HUTCH HUTCHINSON K (A
    DAVE WALKER        (
```

RAVEN
```
    JOHN WEITZ         G    (AB      (A) LIVE AT THE INFERNO        19   DISCOVERY    US      36133
    TONY GALLA         V HCA(AB      (B) RAVEN                      196  CBS          US       9903
    JAMES CALIRE       K V  (AB
    GARY MALLABER      D    (AB  THOMAS CALANDRA   B    (AB
```

RAPHAEL RAVENSCROFT
```
    RAPHAEL RAVENSCROFT SAX FLT(A    (A) HER FATHER DIDN'T LIKE ME ANYWAY 1979 PORTRAIT  US      35683
    GARY TAYLOR        B    (A
    KUMA HARADA        B    (A   PETE ZORN      B FLT(A   STEVE YORK      B   (A   LIAM GENOCKEY     D  (A
    PRESTON HEYMAN     D    (A   STRETCH        D    (A   GEOFF BRITTON   D   (A   TOMMY EYRE        K  (A
    JEFF BANNISTER     K    (A   BETSY COOKE    K V  (A   PETE SOLLEY     K   (A   NIGEL JENKINS     G  (A
    JULIAN LITTMAN     G    (A   RICHARD BRUNTON G   (A   STEVE WALLER    G   (A   BRIAN HOLLOWAY    G  (A
    FRANK RICOTTI    PERC  (A   DAVID ULM      PERC (A   CHARLES BOROMEO V   (A   PAUL DA VINCI     V  (A
    MAGGIE RYDER       V    (A   VIVIAN         V    (A   DENNIS O'BRIEN  V   (A   ALBERT WING     WIND (A
    BIL SKEAT        WIND  (A   VIC ASH        SAX  (A   MANNY WINTER   SAX  (A   KEITH BIRD       SAX(A
    JOHN WILBRAHAM    TPT   (A   DEREK WATKINS  TPT  (A   EDDIE BLAIR    TPT  (A   KENNY BAKER      TPT(A
    DEREK HEALEY      TPT   (A   JOHN HUCKRIDGE TPT  (A   DON LUSHER     TROM (A   WALLY SMITH     TROM(A
    BOBBY LAMB       TROM  (A   KEN GOLDIE    TROM   (A   JIM BROWN     HRNS  (A   JOHN PIGNEGNY   HRNS(A
```

RAVENNA & THE MAGNETICS
```
                                     (A) ROCKABILLY FOOL           1981 RONDELET     UK    ABOUT1001
```

RAVERS
```
                                     (A) PUNK ROCK CHRISTMAS (EP)  1978 RHINO        RNEP  503
```

RAW HOLLY
```
    IAN CAMPBELL       V    (A       (A) RAW HOLLY                  1971 CORAL 757515    MCA GER MAPS4067
    ZED JENKINS        G SIT(A
```

RAW MATERIAL
```
    DAVE GREEN         (A           (A) TIME IS                    1971 NEON                  NE 8
    COLIN CATT         (A           (B) RAW MATERIAL ALBUM         1970 EVOLUTION   UK       21006
    PAUL YOUNG         (A
    PHIL GUNN CLIFFORD (A    MIKE FLETCHER        (A
```

DAVE'SNAKER' RAY
```
    DAVE RAY           (A           (A) KID MAN                    1977 MONUMENT    US. 52780
```

JAMES RAY
```
    JAMES RAY          V    (A       (A) JAMES RAY                 1961 CAPRICE     US       1002
```

RAY OWEN'S MOON
```
    RAY OWEN         G V PNO(A       (A) RAY OWEN'S MOON           1971 POLYDOR     UK    2425 061
    SID GARDNER     G B K(A
    DICK STUBBS      G    (A    LES NICOL       G   (A   IAN McLEAN     D   (A
```

RAYBEATS
```
                                     (A) GUITAR BEAT               1981 D F O T M             X7
```

```
    RAY PARKER          G    (ABC           (A) RAYDIO                    1978 ARISTA  US 4163  UK SPART  1041
    VINCENT BONHAM           (A             (B) ROCK ON                   1979 ARISTA  US 4212  UK SPART  1087
    JERRY KNIGHT        B    (A             (C) TWO PLACES AT THE SAME TIME 1980 ARISTA US 9515  UK SPART  1121
    NORMA JEAN BELL     SAX  (B             (D) JUST LOVE                 1981 ARISTA  US 9543  UK SPART  1152
    ARNELL CARMICHAEL        (ABC
    CHARLES FEARING     G    (ABC LARRY TOLBERT       (BC  DARREN CARMICHAEL    (BC  OLLIE BROWN D V  (BC
    SYLVESTER RIVERS    PNO  (A   JACK ASHFORD   PERC (BC  KEN PETERSON   V TPT(BC  HORATIO GORDON   SAX (BC
    VALORIE JONES       V    (B   FRANCIS PEARMAN  V  (B   CHERYL BROWN     V   (B  HERBIE HANCOCK   K   (C
    GARY COLEMAN        VIBES(C   DEBORAH THOMAS      (B
```

```
    CHRIS REA  V G K SYN    (ALL           (A) WHATEVER HAPPENED TO BENNY SANTINI 1978 MAGNET UK MAG5021 US UALA 879
    ROD ARGENT         K    (A             (B) DELTICS                    1979 MAGNET UK MAGL5028 US UA 959
    PETE WINGFIELD     K    (ACD           (C) TENNIS                     1980 MAGNET UK MAGL5032 US CBS 36435
    DAVE MATTACKS      D    (AD            (D) CHRIS REA                  1982              US CBS 37664
    PAT DONALDSON      B    (A
    PAUL KEOGH         G    (A  STEVE GREGORY    SAX (A   GUS DUDGEON PROD PERC(A     DAVE MARKEE  B    (A
    FRANK RICOTTI      PERC (A  PHIL CURTIS          (A   NORMAN NOSEBAIT    D  (AC  EDDIE GUY      G   (A
    GEORGE WOODHEAD    PERC (A  STUART EPPS      V   (C   WATSONI            V  (C   STUART ELLIOTT D   (D
    DAVE BURTON        G    (C  MICK HUTCHINSON  B   (C   GRAHAN WATSON      K  (C   MARK REA       PERC(C
    GEOFF DRISCOLL     SAX  (C  RAPHAEL RAVENSCROFT SAX(C LEE THORNBERG    TPT (C   RAOUL GONZALES TROM(C
    IRENE CHANTER      V    (A  DOREEN CHANTER   V  (A    GEORGE CHANDLER    V  (C   JIMMY CHAMBERS V   (C
    BRUCE LYNCH        B    (C  JIM MULLEN       G   (D   SIMON NICOL        G  (D   CAROL KENYON   V   (D
    LINDA TAYLOR       V    (D  KATY KISSOON     V   (D   DAVID PACK         V  (D   JOE PUERTA     V   (D
    BURLEIGH DRUMMOND  V    (D  STEVE LAWRENCE   B   (D   RON ASPERY       SAX  (D   DAVE PATON     B   (D
    ANDREW POWELL      B    (D  ALLAN MURPHY     G   (D   RAY COOPER       PERC (D   MAX MIDDLETON  K   (D
    MIKE MORAN         K    (D  DAVE SKINNER     PNO (D    SKALA KANGA      HARP (D   DAVID SNELL    HARP(D
```

```
    DAVID REA     G V BANJO (AB            (A) MAVERICK CHILD             19
                                           (B) BY THE GRACE OF GOD        19
                                           (C) SLEWFOOT                   1975  CBS      US    32485
```

```
    JOHN DAWSON READ  G V  (AB             (A) A FRIEND OF MINE           1975 CHRYSALIS     UK  CHR  1075
    ALAN HODGE        G    (A              (B) READ ON                    1976 CHRYSALIS     UK  CHR  1102
    B J COLE        STEEL (A
    LES HURDLE        B    (A  TERRY COX        D   (A    ALBERT HALL      HRNS (A   RAY SWINFIELD  FLT (A
    DEAN FORD         V    (A  GUY FLETCHER     V   (A
```

```
    JOHN FELICE       G V  (A              (A) THE REAL KIDS             1977 BRONZE BRON 509  RED STAR  RS2
    ALAN PAULINO      B V  (A              (A) THE REAL KIDS             1977 RED STAR GER 26206
    HOWARD FERGUSON   D    (A
    BILL BORGEOLLI    G    (A  MONO MANN        PNO     (A
```

```
    ROGER C REALE     B V  (AB             (A) RADIO ACTIVE              1978 BIG SOUND          US   028
    MICHAEL CAVADINI  PNO  (B              (B) ROGER C REALE & RUE MORGUE 1979 LONDON/BIG SOUND      SHY 8528
    BILLY MICHAELS    D V  (B
    G E SMITH         G    (B
```

```
    TONY RIVERS       V            STUART ELLIOTT    D    GEORGE FORD       B       DUNCAN MACKAY  K
```

```
                                           (A) GIVE AN INCH   (EP)       1979 WRECKORD          UK   AERO1004
```

```
    STEVE MADDEN      G V  (A              (A) RECKLESS                  1981 EMI          UK   AMC 3362
    JAN MELANSON      V    (A
    GENE STOUT        B V  (A  GIL ROBERTS      D   (A
```

```
    EUGENE RECORD          (ALL            (A) THE EUGENE RECORD         1977 WB           US        3018
                                           (B) TRYING TO GET YOU         1978 WB           US        3097
                                           (C) WELCOME                   1979 WB UK K56639 US        3284
```

```
    FRANCIS LONNEUX   D    (AB             (A) MUSIC OR NOT MUSIC        19  BARCLAY   FR   920 356
    J PAUL VANDER BOSSCHE B(AB             (B) RECREATION                19  BELLAPHON GER  19006
    JEAN JACQUES     ORG   (AB
```

```
    JOHN WICKS        G V  (ABC            (A) SHADES IN BED             1979 VIRGIN US 13130 UK        V2122
    HUW GOWER         G V  (A              (B) CRASHES                   1980 VIRGIN US 13140 UK        V2155
    JUDE COLE         G B  (B              (C) MUSIC ON BOTH SIDES       1982 VIRGIN GER 204464 UK       V2206
    PHIL BROWN        B V  (ABC            (EP) HIGH HEELS( FREE WITH A) 1979 VIRGIN
    WILL BIRCH        D    (ABC
    IAN GIBBONS       K    (AB  ROBERT J LANGE   PROD (A   BARRY MARTIN    G   (B   CLEM CLEMPSON  G  (B
    DAVE WHELAN       G    (C   CHRIS STEIN          (B   CHRIS GENT      V SAX(B
```

```
    BILL HICKS        FDL V(CD             (A) THE RED CLAY RAMBLERS     1975 FOLKWAYS        US  31039
    TOMMY THOMPSON    G V  (CD             (B) STOLEN LOVE               1976 FLYING FISH US 009
    MIKE CRAVER       D K G(CD             (C) TWISTED LAUREL            1977 FLYING FISH US 030 SONET UK 731
    JIM WATSON    MAND G V B(CD            (D) MERCHANTS LUNCH           1978 FLYING FISH US     SONET UK 745
    JACK HERRICK  B V HCA TPT(CD           (E) CHUCKIN' THE FRIZZ        1979 FLYING FISH US 089
    AL McCANLESS      FDL (C
```

```
    MAYO THOMPSON         (ABC             (A) PARABLE OF ARABLE LAND    1967 INTERNATIONAL ARTISTS US IALP 2
    STEVE CUNNINGHAM      (AB              (A) PARABLE OF ARABLE LAND    1978 RADAR              UK RAD12
    TOMMY SMITH      D    (AB              (B) GOD BLESS THE RED CRAYOLA 1968 INTERNATIONAL ARTISTS US IALP 7
    RICK BARTHELME        (A               (B) GOD BLESS THE RED CRAYOLA 1978 RADAR              UK RAD16
    HOLLY PRITCHARD  V    (B               (C) SOLDIER TALK              1979 RADAR              UK RAD18
    JESSE CHAMBERLAIN     (C               (D) KANGAROO                  1981 ROUGH TRADE  UK    ROUGH 19
    DICK CUTHELL          (C
    SCOTT KRAUSS          (C   CHRISTINE THOMPSON   (C   TOM HERMAN           (C  LORA LOGIC     SAX (C
    DAVID THOMAS          (C   TONY MAIMONE         (C   ALLEN RAVENSTINE     (C  LELAN ROGERS   PROD(A
```

RED EYE

```
    DAVE HODGKINS        G V  (AB      (A) REDEYE                    1971 PENTAGRAM    US   PE 10003
    DOUGLAS 'RED' MARK  G V  (AB      (B) ONE MANS POISON           19   PENTAGRAM    US   PE 10006
    BOB BEREMAN          D    (AB
    BILL KIRKHAM         B V  (AB
```
RED HELICOPTER
```
                                      (EP) BRACKNELL               19   PAY FOR
```
RED NOISE
```
    PATRICK VIAN         G V  (A       (A) SARCELLES LOCHERES        1970 FUTURA       FR   RED01
    JEAN CLAUDE CENCU WIND V(A
    DANIEL GEOFFROY      B V  (A    PHILIP BARRY     D G  (A   JOHN LIVENGOOD  ORG (A   AUSTIN BLUE    PERC (A
```
RED RIDER
```
    TOM COCHRANE         G V  (AB      (A) DONT FIGHT IT             1980 CAPITOL            12028
    PETER BOYNTON        K    (AB      (B) AS FAR AS SIAN            1981 CAPITOL            12145
    KIM GREEN            G K  (AB
    ROB BAKER            D    (AB  KEN GREER     STEEL K G V(AB
```
RED WILDER BLUE
```
    MIKE BALLEW          G    (A       (A) RED WILDER BLUE           1972 PENTAGRAM    US   PE 10007
    DANNY WILDER         B K  (A
    LUCKY FLOYD          D    (A   MACK TUBB        G    (A
```
REDBONE
```
    TONY BELLAMY         G V  (ABCDEF  (A) REDBONE                   1970 CBS  US   501  UK   64069
    PAT VEGAS            B    (ABCDEF  (B) POTLATCH                  1971 EPIC US 30109  UK   64198
    LOLLY VEGAS          G V  (ABCDEF  (C) WITCH QUEEN OF NEW ORLEANS 1971 EPIC        UK   64709
    PETER DEPOE          D    (ABCD    (C) MESSAGE FROM A DRUM       1971 EPIC US 30815
    DON BRANKER          (C            (D) ALREADY HERE             1973 EPIC US 31598  UK   65072
    WARREN WINSTON       (C            (E) WOVOKA                   1973 EPIC US 32462  UK   65500
    EDDIE CAICEDO        (C            (F) BEADED DREAMS            1974 EPIC US 33053  UK   80429
    JOHN D'ANDREA        (C            (G) COME & GET YOUR REDBONE   1975 EPIC US 33456  UK   22003
    RASMUSSEN TOWER      (C            (H) CYCLES                   1978 RCA              AFLI 2352
    CLARENCE McDONALD    (C            (J) BEST OF                  19   EPIC        UK   65678
    BUTCH PILLERA        D V  (EF
    RED RHODES      STEEL(D   TERRY FURLONG    G   (D   GORDON DE WITTE  PNO (D   ELIJAH HORN SECTION (D
    CHIPPER LAVERONE PERC (D   RONNIE BARRON    PERC (D   DAVID OLIVER     V   (D   MICHAEL FREDA    V  (D
    BONNIE BRAMLETT      V   (F   MERRY CLAYTON    V   (F   CLYDIE KING      V   (F   ED GREENE           (C
```
NOEL REDDING
```
    NOEL REDDING        G V B(AB        (A) CLONAKILTY COWBOYS       1975 RCA  UK RS 1030  APLI 1237
    ERIC BELL           G V  (AB        (B) BLOWIN'                  1976 RCA  UK RS 1084  APLI 1863
    LES SAMSON          D    (AB
    DAVE CLARKE         K V  (AB  DON MICHAEL YOUNG K   (B   STANLEY SCHNIER   B   (B   ANDY KEELY      V  (B
```
OTIS REDDING
```
    OTIS REDDING        V    (ALL       (A) THE PAIN IN MY HEART      1965 ATLANTIC  US 33161  UK 587042
    (1941/1967)                         (B) OTIS BLUE                 1966 ATLANTIC  US 33284  UK 587036
    STEVE CROPPER       G    (B         (B) OTIS BLUE                 19   ATLANTIC RIUK K40003 US VOLT412
    JOE CURTIS          V    (QS        (C) DICTIONARY OF SOUL        1966 ATLANTIC  US 33284  US VOLT 416
    JIMMY KING          (                (C) DICTIONARY OF SOUL        19                      US VOLT416
    RON CALDWELL        (                (D) LIVE IN EUROPE           1966 ATLANTIC  US 33286  UK 228 017
    PHALIN JONES        (                (D) LIVE IN EUROPE           19   ATLANTIC  UK 589 011 US VOLT416
    CARL CUNNINGHAM      (                (E) DOCK OF THE BAY          1968 ATLANTIC  US 33288  UK 228 022
    BEN CAULEY          (                (E) DOCK OF THE BAY          19   ATLANTIC  UKRI K40076 US VOLT419
    CARLA THOMAS        V    (P         (F) IMMORTAL OTIS REDDING     1968 ATLANTIC  US 33252  UK 588 113
    SAMMIE COLEMAN      TPT  (GZ        (F) IMMORTAL OTIS REDDING     1966 ATLANTIC  UKRIK40019
                                        (G) IN PERSON AT THE WHISKEY  1968 ATLANTIC  UK 588 148 US  33265
    JOHN FARRIS         TPT  (GZ        (H) LOVE MAN                  1969 ATLANTIC  US 33289  UK 228 025
    CLARENCE JOHNSON    TROM (GZ        (H) LOVE MAN                  19   ATLANTIC  UKRI K40078
    BOB HOLLOWAY        SAX  (GZ        (I) HISTORY OF OTIS REDDING   1969 ATLANTIC  US 33261  UK 228 001
    BOBBY PITTMAN       SAX  (GZ        (I) HISTORY OF OTIS REDDING   197  ATLANTIC  UKRI K40066 US VOLT418
    DONALD HENRY        SAX  (GZ        (J) TELL THE TRUTH            1970 ATLANTIC  UK 2400 018 US  33333
    JAMES RANDOLF YOUNG G( (GZ         (K) THE BEST OF               1972 ATLANTIC  UK K 60016  US  31801
    ELBERT WOODSON      D    (GZ        (L) SINGS SOUL BALLADS        1966 ATLANTIC  US 587035  US VOLT411
    RALPH STEWART       B    (Z         (M) SOUL ALBUM               19   ATLANTIC  US 588 011  US  33285
                                        (N) REMEMBERING              19   ATLANTIC  UK 2464 003
                                        (P) KING & QUEEN             19   ATLANTIC  UK 589007 STAX US  716
                                        (Q) HERE COMES SOME SOUL     19   MARBLE ARCH   UK   MAL 772
                                        (R) MONTEREY POP (1 SIDE)    19   REPRISE       US        2029
                                        (S) SOUL AS SUNG BY          19   ALLSHIRE      US        5082
                                        (T) OTIS REDDING STORY (DBL) 19   ATCO          FR       60013
                                        (U) OTIS REDDING STORY VOL 2 19   ATCO          FR       60016
                                        (V) OTIS REDDING VOL 1       1981 ATLANTIC      UK   K20043
                                        (Z) RECORDED LIVE            1982 ATLANTIC             450881
```
THE REDS
```
    RICK SCHAFFER       G V  (          (A) THE REDS                 1979 A&M US 4772   UK  AMLH64772
    TOM GEDDES          D    (          (B) STRONGER SILENCE         1981 KINGDOM    9005
    BRUCE COHEN         K    (
    JIM PETER           B    (
```
REDUCERS
```
                                        (A) MAN WITH GUN(EP)         19   VIBES         UK   VR 003
```
REDWING
```
    RON FLOEGEL         G V  (ABC       (A) REDWING                  1971 FANTASY       US        8409
    ANDREW SAMUELS      G V B(ABC       (A) REDWING                  1971 UA            UK   UAS29188
    GEORGE HULLIN       D V  (ABC       (B) WHAT THIS COUNTRY NEEDS  1972 FANTASY       US        9405
    TOM PHILLIPS G K STEEL (ABC        (C) TAKE ME HOME             1973 FANTASY UK FT518 US      9439
    JOHN MYERS          B    (BC        (D) DEAD OR ALIVE           1974 FANTASY       US        9459
    ED BOGAS         FDL MAND(C         (E) BEYOND THE SUN & STARS  1975 FANTASY       US        9488
    TIM MOORE           FDL  (C
    DAVE FRASER         PNO  (CDE KENNETH NASH       PERC (DE BUDDY HARPHAN    B V  (E  DEBBIE MOORE    V  (D
```

HERB REED		(A	(A) SWEET RIVER	197 PVK	UK	PVK002

JIMMY REED	G V	(ALL	(A)I'M JIMMY REED	19		USVEEJAY1004
PHIL UPCHURCH	B	(KLCEDMR	(B)ROCKIN WITH JIMMY REED	19		US VEEJAY1008
LEFTY BATES	G	(BCEFJKLMDRQ	(C) FOUND LOVE	19		US VEEJAY1022
AL DUNCAN	D	(KMR	(D)NOW APPEARING	19		US VEEJAY1025
JIMMY REED JR	B	(KMR	(E)AT CARNEGIE HALL	1962 STATESIDE UK SL10012		US VEEJAY1035
EDDIE TAYLOR	G	(KLQABEFJMCDNP	(E)AT CARNEGIE HALL	19 BLUESWAY BLX60732	JOY	JOYS 120
WAYNE BENNETT	G	(L	(E) AT CARNEGIE HALL	19 EXODUS US 307		
JIMMY TILLMAN	D	(L	(O) PREACHIN THE BLUES(4 TRACKS)	1963 STATESIDE UK SL10046		
JOHN LEE HOOKER		(O	(F)THE BEST OF	196		US VEEJAY1039
MEMPHIS SLIM		(O	(R)JUST JIMMY REED	1964 STATESIDE UK SL10055		US VEEJAY1050
MORRIS WILKERSON	D	(QABEFJP	(R)JUST JIMMY REED	196	RI JOY	JOYS146
W C DALTON	G	(QACEFM	(G)T'AINT NO BIG THING	196		US VEEJAY1067
HENRY GRAY	PNO	(ACEFMQ	(H)SINGS THE BEST OF THE BLUES	196 STATESIDE UK SL10069		US VEEJAY1072
MILTON RECTOR	B	(QAEFMC	(J)PLAYS 12 STRING GUITAR BLUES	1964 STATESIDE UK SL10086		US VEEJAY1073
EARL PHILLIPS	D	(ACEDFBJMQ	(J)PLAYS 12 STRING GUITAR BLUES	1968	JOY	JOYS132
VERNELL FOURNIER	D	(Q	(M)BOSS MAN OF THE BLUES	1964 STATESIDE UK SL10091		US VEEJAY1080
REMO BIONDI	B	(QABEFM	(N)AT SOUL CITY	196 JOY JOYS 127		US VEEJAY1095
LEE BAKER	G	(QCEFM	(P)THE LEGEND,THE MAN	196 JOY JOYS 111		US VEEJAY8501
WILLIE DIXON	B	(QCEFM	(P) THE LEGEND,THE MAN	19 EXODUS US 324		
MARY LEE REED	V	(QEJM	(K) SOULIN'	1968 STATESIDE UK SL10221		
MARCUS JOHNSON	B	(CEFJM	(K) SOULIN'	19 BLUESWAY	US BLS	6009
CURTIS MAYFIELD	B	(E	JIMMY REED	19 ARC FOLK US 234		
JOHNNY JONES	PNO	(N	VERY BEST	19 BUDDAH US 4003		
HUBERT SUMLIN	G	(N	ROOTS OF THE BLUES	19 KENT US 5037		
SCREAMING JAY HAWKINS	V	(Z	SOMETHING ELSE	19 SUNSET 5218		
			SOUL GREATS	19 UPFRONT US 101		
			SOULFUL SOUND	19 UPFRONT US 108		
			THE BEST	19 UPFRONT US 125		
			NEW JIMMY REED	19 HMV UK CLP 3611 BLUESWAY 6004		
			WAILIN' THE BLUES	19 MUSIDISC FR 6088 TRADITION US2069		
			(L) BIG BOSS MAN	1973 BLUESWAY	US BLS	6015
			DOWN IN VIRGINIA	197 BLUESWAY	US BLS	6024
			I AIN'T FROM CHICAGO	1973 BLUESWAY	US BLS	6054
			THE ULTIMATE	1973 BLUESWAY	US BLS	6067
			THE BEST OF JIMMY REED	1974 G N P CRESENDO	US GNP	10006
			JIMMY REED IS BACK	1976 JOY JOYS 264		
			(Q)MEMORIAL ALBUM VOL 1	1976 DJM 28033		
			LET THE BOSSMAN SPEAK	19 BLUE ON BLUES	US	10001
			AS JIMMY IS	197 ROKER	US	6067
			COLD CHILLS	1976 ANTILLES	US	7007
			HISTORY OF	1972 TRIP	US	8012
			JIMMY REED	19 EVEREST	US	234
			UPSIDE YOUR HEAD	1980 CHARLY UK CRB 1003		
			(Z) FUNKY FNKY SOUL	1981 MANHATTAN 5041		
			HIGH & LONESOME	1981 CHARLY UK CRB 1013		
			GOT ME DIZZY	1982 CHARLY UK CRB 1028		
			SHAME SHAME SHAME (EP)	1980 CHARLY UK CTD 105		

LOU REED	G V k8ALL	(A) LOU REED	1972 RCA US LSP 4701 UK	SF8281
JO'ANNA KAMERON	V	(L	(A) LOU REED	1981 RCA RI UK 43214
CLEM CATTINI	PERC	(A	(B) TRANSFORMER	1972 RCA US LSP4807 UK RI INTS5061
CALEB QUAYE	G PNO	(A	(C) BERLIN	1973 RCA US 10207 UK RS1002
RICK WAKEMAN	K	(A	(C) BERLIN	1981 RCA UK RI INTS5150
STEVE HOWE	G	(A	(D) ROCK'N'ROLL ANIMAL	1974 RCA US APLIO472 UK PL 10472
CHRISTINE WILTSHIRE	V	(L	(D) ROCK'N'ROLL ANIMAL	1981 RCA US 3664 UK INTS 5086
AUL KEOGH	G	(A	(E) SALLY CANT DANCE	1974 RCA US APLIO611 UK PL 10611
LES HURDLE	B	(A	(F) LOU REED LIVE	1975 RCA US APLIO959 UK RS1007
BRIAN ODGERS	B	(A	(G) METAL MACHINE MUSIC	1975 RCA CPL2 1101
DAVID BOWIE	V	(B	(H) CONEY ISLAND BABY	1976 RCA US APLIO915 UK RS1035
MICK RONSON	G	(B	(H) CONEY ISLAND BABY	197 RCA US ANLI2480 GER 21665
THUNDERTHIGHS	V	(B	(J) ROCK'N'ROLL HEART	1976 ARISTA US 4100 UK 142 GER 98284
KLAUS VOORMANN	B	(B	(K) WALK ON THE WILD SIDE (BEST OF)	1977 RCA US APLI2001 UK PL 12001
HERBIE FLOWERS	B	(B	(L) STREET HASSLE	1978 ARISTA US 4169 UK 1045 GER 60445
JOHN HALSEY	D	(B	(M) LIVE TAKE NO PRISONERS(DBL)	1978 ARISTA US 8502 UK 03066
BARRY DE SOUZA	D	(B	(N) VICIOUS	1979 RCA NL 42731
RONNIE ROSS	SAX	(B	(O) THE BELLS	1979 ARISTA US 4229 UK 1093 GER 62630
STEVE HUNTER	G	(CDF	(P) GROWING UP IN PUBLIC	1980 ARISTA US 9522 UK 1131 GER 202120
ALLAN MacMILLAN	K	(C	(Q) ROCK'N'ROLL DIARY(67/80)	1980 ARISTA US 8603 UK DART8
MICHAEL BRECKER	SAX	(C	(R) THE BLUE MASK	1982 RCA UK RCALP6028

RANDY BRECKER	TPT	(C	JACK BRUCE	B	(C	AYNSLEY DUNBAR	D	(C	BOB EZRIN	K V	(C
TONY LEVIN	B	(C	GENE MARTYNEC	G K V	(C	JON PIERSON	TROM	(C	DICK WAGNER	G V	(CDF
BLUE WEAVER	K	(C	B J WILSON	D	(C	STEVE WINWOOD	K	(C	DENNIS FERRANTE	V	(C
STEVE HYDEN	V	(C	ELIZABETH MARSH	V	(C	RAY COLCORD	K	(DF	PENTTI GLAN	D	(DEF
PRAKASH JOHN	B V	(DEF	MICHAEL WENDROFF	V	(EH	DANNY WEIS	G V	(E	MICHAEL FONFARA	K	(EJMPLO
RITCHIE DHARMA	D	(BE	PAUL FLEISHER	SAX	(E	JOANNE VENT	B V	(E	STEVE KATZ	HCA	(C
GODFREY DIAMOND	V	(H	BOB KULICK	G	(H	MICHAEL SUCHORSKY	D	(HJLMOP	BRUCE YAW	B	(HJ
GARLAND JEFFREYS	V	(J	KAY GARNER	V	(A	HELENE FRANCOIS	V	(A	STUART HEINRICH	G V	(PML
CHUCK HAMMER	SYN G	(P	ELLARD BOWLES V SYN G	B	(PMO	MARTY FOGEL	SAX	(MLO	ANGELA HOWELL	V	(ML
CHRISSY FAITH	V	(M	KAY GARNER	V	(A	HELENE FRANCOIS	V	(A	GENYA RAVAN	V	(L
DON CHERRY	TPT	(O									

DAVID MASON		(A	(A) THE REELS	1979 POLYDOR US PD1 6275
COLIN NEWMAN	K	(A		
PAUL ABRAHAMS	B	(A	JOHN BLISS	D	(A	CRAIG HOOPER	G	(A

MARTHA REEVES

```
MARTHA REEVES       V    (ALL    (A) MARTHA REEVES            1974 MCA       US 414    UK MCF2565
RICHARD PERRY       PERC(A         (B) THE REST OF MY LIFE    1977 ARISTA    US 4105   UK SPART1030
JAMES JAMERSON      B    (A        (C) WE MEET AGAIN          1978 MILESTONE US 9549 FANTASY UK544
LON VAN EATON       G    (A
DANNY FARAGHER      K    (A    STEVE MADAIO    HRNS (A   JAMES GADSON    D    (AC RUSS TURNER    V K (A
LEON PATILLO        V K  (A    &LENNY LEE GOLDSMITH K (A  NICKY HOPKINS   K    (A  ARTHUR ADAMS   G  (A
MALCOLM CECIL       SYN  (A    TREVOR LAWRENCE HRNS (A   BOBBY KEYS      HRNS (A  MELVIN RAGIN   G  (A
HENRY DAVIS         B    (A    JIMMIE CALHOUN  B    (A   TRAVIS FULLERTON D   (A  CAROL KAFI     V  (A
KING ERRISSON       PERC (A    DENNIS COFFEY   G    (A   DEAN PARKS      G    (A  WILLIAM SMITH  K  (A
LARRY NASH          K    (A    BILLY PRESTON   K    (A   CLARENCE MACDONALD K (A  JIM KELTNER D     (A
KLAUS VOORMANN      B    (A    JOE SAMPLE      K    (A   CLYDIE KING     V    (A  JAMES TAYLOR   HRNS(A
D LLOYD GREGORY     G    (A    VINI PONCIA  G V     (A   DEREK VAN EATON G    (A  MILT HOLLAND   VIBES(A
BASIL GREEN         B    (A    KENNY ASHER     K    (A   JESSE BUTLER    K    (A  HOYT AXTON     G  (A
JIM GILSTRAP        V    (A    TOM HENSLEY     K    (A   AVALON COMM CHOIR V  (A  RALPH MACDONALD PERC(A
SYLVESTER RIVERS    K    (C    DALE WARREN     K    (C   GEORGE SPENCER  K    (C  GREG LEVIAS    K  (C
CHARLES FEARING     G    (C    CORNELIUS GRANT G    (C   DAVID PRUITT    G    (C  GREG CROCKETT  G  (A
ROMEO WILLIAMS      B    (C    GARNETT BROWN   TROM (C   MAURICE SPEARS  TROM (C  BUBBA CHAMBERS PERC(C
PHILLIP RANELIN     TROM (C    ROBERT BRYANT   TPT  (C   GROVER MITCHELL TROM (C  ANANIAS CHAMBERS CONGA(A
ALBERT AARONS       TPT  (C    BENJAMIN POWELL TROM(C    ROBERT ZIMITTI  PERC (C  BANJAMIN KIRK  TPT (C
WILLIAM PETERSON    TPT  (C    DONALD CHRISTLIEB WIND(C  JOHN ROBERTS    TPT  (C  WILLIAM GREEN  WIND(C
ERNIE FIELDS        FLT  (C    STRING SECTION  (C        FRED JACKSON    FLT  (C
```

REFUGEE

```
LEE JACKSON         B    (A        (A) REFUGEE               1974  CHARISMA    UK   CAS 1087
BRIAN DAVISON       D    (A
PATRICK MORAZ       K    (A    JOHN BURNS   PROD (A
```

REGULARS

```
ALLAN'KINGPIN'KING  V    (A        (A) VICTIM                1978 CBS         UK   83541
ANTHONY ROOKWOOD    V    (A
NORMAN EBANKS       G    (A    PATRICK DONEGAN G    (A   GEORGE CLARKE   K    (A  TREVOR SALMON  B  (A
ERROLL FRANCIS      D    (A    ERROLL   FORREST PERC (A  GEORGE CHISHOLM TPT  (A  DEREK WADSWORTH TROM(A
STEVE GREGORY       SAX  (A
```

JOHN REID

```
                                   (A) FACADE               19   CBS          US   PC 34298
```

ROY REID

```
ROY REID            V    (A        (A) WHAP'N BAP'N          1980  VIRGIN      UK   V2164
ANGUS GAYE          D    (A
JAH BUNNY           D    (A
WEBSTER JOHNSON     PNO  (A    JOHN KPIAYE     G    (A   EUTON JONES     PERC (A  GLAISTER VENN  PERC (A
ZENON               (A         DELROY CLARKE   FLT  (A   BAGGA FAGAN     PERC B V (A  TONY ROBINSON B (A
DENNIS BOVELL       K B G(A    PATRICK TENYUE  HRNS (A   HENRY TENYUE    HRNS (A  PHIL TOWNER    D  (A
NICK BAILEY         K    (A    JANET KAY       V    (A
```

TERRY REID

```
TERRY REID          G V *(ALL     (A) BANG BANG, YOU'RE TERRY REID  1968 EPIC  US    26427
ERIC LEESE          K    (A        (B) MOVE OVER FOR TERRY REID 1969 EPIC US 26477 UK EMI SCX 6370
KEITH WEBB          D    (AB       (B)THE MOST OF TERRY REID  1971 MFP         UK   5220
CONRAD ISADORE      D    (C        (C) RIVER                  1973 ATLANTIC US 7259 UK WB K40340
WILLIE BOBO         PERC (C        (D) SEED OF MEMORY         1976 ABC US 935   UK  ABCL 5162
AL VIOLA            SAX  (D        (E) ROGUE WAVES            1979 CAPITOL      UK   11857
PETE SOLLEY         K    (B
LEE MILES           B    (CDE DAVID LINDLEY   G VLN(CD  SOKO RICHARDSON D    (D  BEN KEITH      STEEL(D
JOEL BERNSTEIN      G    (D    JESSE ERLICH CELLO   (D   BLUE MITCHELL   HRNS (   FRED WESLEY    HRNS(
PLAS JOHNSON        SAX  (      GRAHAM NASH     V    (D   TIM WEISBERG    FLT  (D  CLIFFORD SOLOMON HRNS(
JAMES GADSON        D    (D    AL PERKINS      STEEL(D   DOUG RODRIGUES  G    (E  JOHN SIOMOS    D  (E
STERLING SMITH      (E         JAMES JOHNSON   (E        CHRIS STEWART   B    (
```

RELEASE MUSIC ORCHESTRA

```
NORBERT JACOBSON PNO WIND V(AB    (A) LIFE                   1974  BRAIN   GER      1056
WOLFGANG'ZABBA'INDNER D V (ABC     (B) GARUDA                1975  BRAIN   GER      1072
JOCHEN PETERSON     SAX  (B        (C) GET THE BALL          1977  BRAIN            1083
BERND KIEFER        B V  (A        (D) BEYOND THE LIMIT      1978  BRAIN   GER      60  115
MANNE RURUP         K SYN V(ABCDE  (E) NEWS                  1979  BRAIN   GER      60  194
FRANK FISCHER       B    (CDE
HOLGER DUNKEL       B    (B    MARGIT MAYA HABERLAND PERC V G(BC WOLFGANG THIERFELDT D (DE
JOHANNES'ALTO'PAPPERT SAX(B    JOCHEN PETERSON SAX  (B   ERHARD SCHAFER  TPT  (C  CPT SNATTY STORTEBECKER(B
MIKE GONG           G    (C    CARLOS KARGES   G    (C   TOMMY GOLDSCHMIDT PERC(DE HANS BEHRENDT  PERC(D
NURI EFFENDI        V    (E
```

RELUCTANT STEREOTYPES

```
PAUL KING           V    (          (A) THE LABEL            1980  WEA     UK       K58201
TONY WALL           B    (
COLIN HEANES        D    (     STEVE EDGSON    CLAR (   PAUL SAMPSON    G    (
```

REMA REMA

```
MARK COX            K SYN (A        (A) WHEEL IN THE ROSES(EP) 1980 4AD     UK      BAD5
GARY ASQUITH        G V  (A
MICHAEL ALLEN       B V  (A    MARCO    G    (A  MAX    D    (A
```

REMAINS

```
BARRY TASHIAN       G V  (A        (A) REMAINS              1967 SPOONFED   US      3305
CHIP DAMIANI        D    (A        (A) REMAINS(ADDITIONAL TRACKS) 1978 EPIC US      24214
VERN MILLER         B G HRNS(A
WILLIAM BRIGGS      K    (A
```

REMIPEDS

```
                                   (A) THE TAHITI SYNDROME   1981 BANANA   UK      EAT 1
```

REMO 4

```
COLIN MANLEY        G V  (AB       (A) SMILE                1967 STARCLUB  GER     158 034
TONY ASHTON         V K  (AB       (B) ATTENTION            1973 PHONOGRAM GER     6434 158
ROY DYKE            D    (AB
PHIL ROGERS         B    (AB
```

RENAISSANCE

KEITH RELF	V G HCA	(AB	(A) RENAISSANCE	1969 ISLAND UK ILPS 9114 US ELEKTRA 74068
JIM McCARTY	D	(AB	(B) ILLUSION	19 ISLAND UK HELP 27 EURO 80895
JANE RELF	V	(AB	(C) PROLOGUE	1972 SOVEREIGN UK 7253 US CAPITOL 11116
NEIL KORNER	B	(B	(C) PROLOGUE	1972 SOVEREIGN GER 94663
JOHN HAWKEN	K	(AB	(D) ASHES ARE BURNING	1973 SOVEREIGN UK 7261 US CAPITOL 11216
LOUIS CENNAMO	B	(AB	(E) TURN OF THE CARDS	1975 BTM UK 1000 US SIRE 6015
TERRY SLADE	D	(B	(E) TURN OF THE CARDS	1975 RCA GER 21490 US RI SIRE 7502
ANNIE HASLAM	V PERC	(CDEFGHJLM	(F) SCHEHERAZADE & OTHER STORIES	1975 BTM UK 1006 US SIRE 6017 + 7510
MIKE DUNFORD	G V	(BDEFGHJLM	(G) LIVE AT CARNEGIE HALL(DBL)	1976 BTM UK 2001 US SIRE 6029 + 3902
JON CAMP	V B G	(CDEFGHJLM	(H) NOVELLA	1977 WB UK K56422 US SIRE 6024 + 7526
JOHN TOUT	K V	(CDEFGHJL	(J) A SONG FOR ALL SEASONS	1978 WB UK K56460 US SIRE 6049
TERENCE SULLIVAN	D V	(CDEFGHJL	(K) IN THE BEGINNING	19 CAPITOL US 11871
ROB HENDRY	G V MAND	(C	(L) AZURE D'OR	1979 WB UK K56533 US SIRE 6068
ANDY POWELL	G	(D	(M) CAMERA CAMERA	1981 ILLEGAL UK ILP008 US IRS 70019
FRANCIS MONKMAN	SYN	(C	(EF) ROCK GALAXY (DBL)	1980 RCA NL 25282
TERRY CROWE	V	(B		
DON SHINN	K	(B	PETER GOSLING K (M PETER BARRON D (M BINKY CULLUM V (
RICHARD HEWSON	STR	(D		

RENALDO & THE LOAF

RENALDO M	G MAND D V	(A	(A) SONGS FOR SWINGING LARVAE	1981 RALPH US 8108 UK DOIT RIDE 6
THE LOAF	G WIND B	(A		

RENEGADES

DENYS GIBSON	G	(A	(A) THE RENEGADE STORY	1978 MIDI GER 26070
KIM BROWN	G V	(A		
IAN MALLETT	B	(A	GRAHAM JOHNSON D (A

JOHN RENBOURN

JOHNRENBOURN	G V	(ALL	(A) JOHN RENBOURN	1965 TRANSATLANTIC UK TRA135 US REPRISE 6482
BERT JANSCH	G	(AB	(B) BERT & JOHN	1966 TRANSATLANTIC UK TRA144
JACQUI McSHEE	V	(CLN	(C) ANOTHER MONDAY	1967 TRANSATLANTIC UK TRA149
JENNIFER DE MONTFORTE JONES OBOE	(C		(D) SIR JOHN ALOT OF M ENGLAND	1968 TRANSATLANTIC UK TRA167 US REPRISE 6344
TERRY COX	PERC	(DGE	(E) LADY & THE UNICORN	1970 TRANSATLANTIC UK TRA224 US REPRISE 6407
RAY WARLEIGH	FLT	(DE	(F) JOHN RENBOURN SAMPLER	1971 TRANSATLANTIC UK TRASAM20
DOMINIQUE TREPEAU	G	(K	(G) FARO ANNIE	1971 TRANSATLANTIC UK TRA247 US REPRISE 2082
JOHN JAMES	G	(K	(H) SO CLEAR	1973 TRANSATLANTIC UK TRASAM28
TONY ROBERTS	V WIND	(LNOE	(J) HEADS & TAILS	1974 TRANSATLANTIC UK TRASAM18
SUE DRAHEIM	V FDL	(GL	(K) THE HERMIT	1976 TRANSATLANTIC UK TRA 336
KESH SATHIE	PERC	(LO	(L) MAID IN BEDLAM	1977 TRANSATLANTIC UK TRA 348
DON HARPER	VLA	(E	(L) MAID IN BEDLAM	1977 SHANACHIE 79004 US
GLEN TOMMY	D	(O	(M) JOHN RENBOURN & S GROSSMAN	1978 KICKING MULE UK SNKF139 GER SONET 69081
JOHN MOLINAUX V DULC MAND	(O		(N) BLACK BALLOON	1979 TRANSATLANTIC UK TRA 355
LEE NICHOLSON	CONC	(E	(N) BLACK BALLOON	1979 KICKING MULE US 163
STEFAN GROSSMAN	G	(M	(O) ENCHANTED GARDEN	1980 TRANSATLANTIC UK TRA 356
STUART GORDON	TABLA	(N	(P) UNDER THE VOLCANO	1980 SONET UK SNTF 161
PETE DYER	HCA	(G		
DORRIS HENDERSON	V	(G	DANNY THOMPSON B (G DAVE SWARBRICK VLN (E

RENIA

PETER SUTHERLAND	K V	(A	(A) FIRST OFFENDERS	1973 TRANSATLANTIC UK TRA261
KENNY STEWART	V	(A		
JOHN ROBINSON	G V	(A	MALCOLM SUTHERLAND B K V(A DAVE MATTHEWS D (A

ROBERT RENTAL & THE NORMAL

A) LIVE AT WEST RUNTON PAVILLION 1980 ROUGH TRADE UK ROUGH 17

REPAIRS

PETER McCANN	V G K	(A	(A) REPAIRS	1972 MOWEST US MW1211
SUKIE HONEYCUTT	V K PERC	(A	(B) ALREADY A HOUSEHOLD WORD	1973 RARE EARTH US 532
LARRY TREADWELL	V K G HCA	(A		
MICHAEL KAMEN	HRNS	(A	MIKE FOLEY V B G TROM(A JIM HONEYCUTT B G (A ACE HOLLERAN D PERC(A
DAVID McCANN	FDL	(A	BOB BONEFANT HRNS (A BARRY MARSHALL HRNS (A

KLAUS RENFT COMBO

KLAUS RENFT	B	(ALL	(A) KLAUS RENFT COMBO	19 AMIGA GER 855326
THOMAS SCHOPPE	G V	(A	(B) RENFT	19 AMIGA GER 855396
PETER KSCHENTZ	WIND	(A	(C) ROCK AUS LEIPZIG(LIVE)	19 TELDEC GER 6622093
JOCHEN HOHL	D	(A		
CHRISTIAN KUNERT K TROM G V(A PETER GLASER G V (A

TIM RENWICK

TIM RENWICK	G V	(A	(A) TIM RENWICK	1980 CBS UK 84082

THE RESIDENTS

THE RESIDENTS	V G K B D VLN HRNS		(A) MEET THE RESIDENTS	1974 RALPH US RRO274
WITH			(A) MEET THE RESIDENTS	1977 RALPH US RRO677
PAMELA ZEIBAK	V	(CD	(B) NOT AVAILABLE	1978 RALPH US RR1174
SNAKEFINGER LITHMAN G V VLN	(CGJ		(C) 3RD REICH & ROLL	1976 RALPH US RR1075
DON JACKOVICH	PERC	(DJ	(D) FINGER PRINCE	1977 RALPH US RR1276
A DEKBAR	VLN	(D	(E) DUCK STAB /BUSTER & GLEN	1978 RALPH US RRO278
T LOGAN	PERC	(D	(F) NIBBLES (COMP)	1979 VIRGIN UK VR3 NL 200 598
RUBY	V	(E	(G) COMMERCIAL ALBUM	1980 RALPH UK PREX2 US 6559
PEGGY HONEYDEW	V	(C	(H) MARK OF THE MOLE	1981 RALPH US 8152
DON PRESTON	SYN	(G	(J) THE TUNES OF TWO CITIES	1982 RALPH UK RZ 8202
CHRIS CUTLER	D	(GJ		
FRED FRITH		(J	SANDY SANDWICH (J MUD'S SIS (J

RESISTERS

DAVE OWYNNE-JONES	G	(A	(A) THE RESISTERS	1979 TRIKONT GERM 0052
SUSY BARRY	D	(A		
ILSE ZANBOUINI	B	(A	GEOFF HOLLAND V (A PETE HULLINEAUX G (A KIM PARKER K (A

RETAINERS

PAUL CARRACK	K	(1	(A) MAY 1978
TONY O'MALLEY	K	(1	
ALAN SPENNER	B	(1	NEIL HUBBARD G (1 MEL COLLINS SAX (1

```
R69A                          MARTIN REV                                      R69A
  MARTIN REV        V    (A    (A) MARTIN REV           1980 INFIDELITY US      228
R69B                          REVELATION                                      R69B
  BENNY DIGGS       V    (A    (A) REVELATION           1975 RSO    US 4810   UK    2394 161
                              (B) GET IN TOUCH          1979 RCA              US    3287
R70                   PAUL REVERE & THE RAIDERS                                R70
  PAUL REVERE      ORG  (ALL   (A) PAUL REVERE & THE RAIDERS  19  SANDE            US  1001
  MARK LINDSAY   K SAX V(K     (A) IN THE BEGINNING     1966 JERDEN              US  7004
  DRAKE LEVIN      G    (       (B) HERE THEY COME       1965 CBS                US  9107
  MICHAEL SMITH    D    (       (C) JUST LIKE US         1966 CBS  UK 62406      US  9251
  JOE CORRERO    D V    (M      (D) MIDNIGHT RIDE        1966 CBS    UK 62397     US  9308
  PHILIP VOLK      B    (       (E) SPIRIT OF 67         1967 CBS                US  9395
  CHARLIE COE      B    (       (F) GREATEST HITS        1967 CBS                US  9462
  JIM VALLEY       G    (       (G) REVOLUTION           1967 CBS   UK 63095     US  9521
  FREDDY WELLER  G V    (K      (H) CHRISTMAS PAST & PRESENT 1968 CBS            US  9555
  KEITH ALLISON  G V K(K        (I) GOIN' TO MEMPHIS     1968 CBS   UK 63265     US  9605
                              (J) SOMETHINGS HAPPENING   1968 CBS                US  9665
                              (K) HARD & HEAVY           1969 CBS   UK 63649     US  9753
                              (L) SPIRIT OF 69           1969 CBS                US  GP12
                              (M) ALIAS PINK PUZZ        1967 CBS                US  9905
                              (N) COLLAGE (RAIDERS)      1970 CBS   UK 63973     US  9964
                              (O) PAUL REVERE & THE RAIDERS  19  HARMONY         US  30089
                              (P) GREATEST HITS VOL 2    1967 CBS                US  30386
                              (Q) INDIAN RESERVATION     1971 CBS   UK 64461     US  30768
                              (E+) GOOD THING    (E) + 1 TRACK)  1969 CBS  UK 62963 HARMONY  30975
                              (S) MOVIN' ON              1972 HARMONY            US  31183
                              (T) COUNTRY WINE           19  CBS                 US  31196
                              ( ) PAUL REVERE & THE RAIDERS  1970 CBS NL 52 830
                              ( ) PAUL REVERE & THE RAIDERS  19  PICKWICK   US 3176
                              ( )GREATEST HITS           1979 CBS  35593
                              ( ) LIKE LONG HAIR         196  GARDENA    US 1000
                              ( ) THE FALCONAIRES WITH MARK LINDSAY 19  USAF US  70 3
                              (U) ALL TIME GREATEST HITS 1972 CBS              US  31464
R70A                          REVILLOS                                         R70A
  FAY FIFE         V    (A      (A) REV UP               1980 DINDISC        UK      DID 3
  EUGENE REYNOLDS  K V  (A
  HI FI HARRIS     G    (A    D K SMYTHE      B   (   ROCKY RHYTHM      D   (A  KID KRUPA   G   (A
  BABS & CHERRY HANDJIVE (A  WILLIAM MYSTERIOUS B   (A
R71                          REVOLUTIONAIRES                                   R71
  SLY DUNBAR       D    (A      (A) REACTION IN DUB      1978 CHACHA          CHALP 002
  ERROLL NELSON    PNO  (A      (B) GOLDMINE DUB         1979 GREENSLEEVES    GREL 4
  SCULLY SIMMS     PERC (A      (C) REVOLUTIONAIRES SOUNDS VOL2 1978 BALLISTIC  UAG 30237
  BOBBY ELLIS      TPT  (A      (D) NEGREA LOVE DUB      1979 TROJAN          TRLS 153
  ROBBIE SHAKESPEARE  G B(A     (E) OUTLAW DUB           1979 TROJAN          TRLS 169
  HERMAN MARQUIS   SAX  (A      ( ) LEGGO DUB            19  CASH & CARRY
  RED BRYAN        G    (A      ( ) GREEN BAY DUB        19  BURNING VIBRATIONS  1004
  TOMMY McCOOK     SAX  (A      ( ) BLACK ASH            1980 TROJAN          186
                              ( ) JONKANOO DUB           19
R72                    REVOLUTIONARY BLUES BAND                                R72
  TOM SCOTT        SAX  (A      (A) REVOLUTIONARY BLUES BAND  1970 MCA UK MUPS402 CORAL US 757506
  DAVID COHEN      G    (A
  ARTHUR ADAMS     G    (A   LIGHTNIN' ROD      V   (A
R73                          REX(SMITH)                                        R73
  REX SMITH        V    (AB     (A) REX                  1977 CBS  US 34399   UK   63439
  MIKE RATTI       D    (AB     (B) WHERE DO WE GO FROM HERE  1978 CBS US 34865  UK  82186
  ORVILLE DAVIS    B    (Ab
  LARS HANSON      G    (AB  LOU VANDORA  G    (AB
R73A                         REXY                                             R73A
                              (A) RUNNING OUT OF TIME    1981 ALIEN    UK       BEALIEN2
R74                          REZILLOS                                          R74
  FAY FIFE         V    (AB     (A) CANT STAND THE REZILLOS  1978 SIRE 9103 257  K56530 US  6057
  EUGENE REYNOLDS  V    (AB     (B) MISSION ACCOMPLISHED  1979 SIRE SRK6069   GER 200 654
  ANGEL PATERSON   D    (AB
  LUKE WARM        G    (B    SIMON TEMPLAR   B.   (B   JO CALLIS    G    (A   GAIL WARNING    V   (B
  WILLIAM MYSTERIOUS SAX B(AB D K SMYTHE      B   (    HI FI HARRIS   G   (
R75                          RHINOCEROS                                        R75
  BILL MUNDI       D    (AB     (A) RHINOCEROS           1969 ELEKTRA US 74030 71RI UK K42042
  MIKE FONFARA     K    (ABC    (B) SATIN CHICKEN        1969 ELEKTRA US 74056 71RI UK K42036
  DANNY WEIS     K G    (ABC    (C) BETTER TIMES ARE COMING  1970 ELEKTRA US 74075  UK  2469 006
  DOUG HASTINGS    G    (AB     (C) BETTER TIMES ARE COMING  1971 ELEKTRA        UK RI K42049
  JERRY PENROD     B    (A
  JOHN FINLEY      V    (ABC ALAN GERBER  K V      (AB DUKE EDWARDS        D (C PETER HODGSON   B  (BC
  LARRY LEISHMAN   G    (C
R76                          EMITT RHODES                                      R76
  EMITT RHODES ALL INST (ALL   (A) AMERICAN DREAM        1971 A&M     US SP4254 UK      AMLS64254
  CHUCK BERGHOFFER B    (A      (B) EMITT RHODES         1971 DUNHILL US 50089 UK PROBE SPBA6256
  HAL BLAINE       D    (A      (C) MIRROR               1971 DUNHILL US 50111 UK PROBE SPBA6262
  DAVID COHEN      G .  (A      (D) FAREWELL TO PARADISE  1972 DUNHILL US 50122 UK PROBE SPBA6266
  JIM GORDON       D    (A      (D) FAREWELL TO PARADISE  1974 ABC RI           UK      ABCL 5041
  JOHN GUERIN      D    (A
  PETE JOLLY            (A   LARRY KNECHTEL   K   (A  GARY KATO     (A  MICHAEL RICE    (A
  JOEL LARSON      D    (A   JAMES LEITCH         (A  DRAKE LEVIN   (A  DON PEAK        (A
  JOE PORCARO      PERC (A   EMIL RADOCCHIA       (A  DON RANDI   K (A  TOM REYNOLDS    (A
  BILL RHEINHART        (A   LYLE RITZ       B   (A
```

RED RHODES

ORVILLE J 'RED'RHODES STEEL(ALL		(A) ONCE A DAY	19	CROWN	US	CST	520
JAY LACY	G (F	(B) BLUE BLUE DAY	19	CROWN	US	CST	528
ROBERT K WARFORD	G (F	(C) STEEL GUITAR RAG	19	CROWN	US	CST	535
COLIN CAMERON	B (F	(D) GUITARS GO COUNTRY	19	CROWN	US		
DANNY LANE	D (F	(E) LIVE AT THE PALOMINO	19	HAPPY TIGER US		HT10035	
DAVID BARNY	PNO (F	(F) VELVET HAMMER IN A COWBOY BAND	1973	COUNTRYSIDE US		CS 102	
JIM STALLINGS	B (F						

RHYTHM CATS

		(A) ROCK WITH THE RHYTHM(EP)	19	TYGER	TYG 3

RHYTHM DEVILS

MICKEY HART	D (A	(A) PLAY RIVER MUSIC	1980	PASSPORT	US	PB 9844
BILLY KREUTZMANN	D (A					
AIRTO MOREIRA	PERC (A	MIKE HINTON	(A	JIM LOVELESS	PERC (A	GREGG ERRICO (A
JORDAN AMARANTHA PERC (A		PHIL LESH	(A			

RHYTHM HAWKS

	(A) WALK OUT ON YOU(EP)	19	REDBALL	RR 011

RHYTHM HERITAGE

MICHAEL OMARTIAN	K V (ABC	(A) DISCO FIED	1976	ABC UK ABCL 5174 US ABCD 934		
STEVE MADAIO	TPT (C	(B) LAST NIGHT ON EARTH	1977	ABC	US	987
ED GREENE	D (ABC	(C) SKY'S THE LIMIT	1978	ABC	US	1037
DEAN PARKS	G (A					
SCOTT EDWARDS	B (ABC TONY TERRAN	TPT (A	TOM SCOTT	WIND (A ERNIE WATTS	SAX (AC
FRED SELDON	WIND (AC LEW McCREARY	TROM (A	SID SHARP	STRINGS(ABC LEE RITENOUR	G (A
DAVID DUKE	(A GALE ROBINSON	(A	ORRIN WATERS	V (AC LUTHER WATERS	V (AC
MICHAEL PRICE	V (A MARVIN DEANE	PERC (A	PAT McCOY	PERC (A RAY PARKER	G (A
BEN BENAY	G (A VICTOR FELDMAN	PERC (AC	PAUL HUBINON	TPT (A JAY GRAYDON	G (C
CHUCK FINDLEY	B (C				

CATHERINE RIBEIRO & LES ALPES

CATHERINE RIBEIRO	V (AB	(A) LE RAT DEBILE ET L'HOMME DES CHAMPS	1974	PHILIPS	FR 9101 003
DANIEL MOTRON	K (A	(B) PAIX	19	PHILIPS	6325 019
GERALD RENARD	B (A				
PATRICE MOULLET	G (AB DENIS COHEN	PERC (A	JEAN JACQUES LEURION K (A	JEAN SEBASTIAN LEMORNE B(B	
PATRICE LEMORNE	K (A MICHAEL SANTANGELLI	D(A			

BOYD RICE

BOYD RICE	(A	(A) BOYD RICE	1981	MUTE	UK	STUMM 4

TONY RICE

TONY RICE	G B (A	(A) GUITAR	197	REBEL	US	SLP 1582
J D CROWE	BAN (A					
LARRY RICE	MAND (A BOBBY SLOAN	FDL B(A				

RICH KIDS

GLEN MATLOCK	B V (A	(A) GHOSTS OF PRINCES IN TOWERS	1978	EMI	UK	EMC 3263
RUSTY EGAN	D (A					
MIDGE URE	G V (A STEVE NEW	G (A	IAN McLAGAN	PNO (A MICK RONSON PROD (A	

RICH MOUNTAIN TOWER

DAVID CARR	G (A	(A) RICH MOUNTAIN TOWER	1970
SANDY GARRETT	B V (A		
DANA PAUL	G K V(A BOB TUCCILLO	D (A RANDY HASPEL	G V (A LAMONTE OUSLEY CONGA(A
CHARLIE McCOY	HCA (A WELDON MYRICK	STEEL(A	

CLIFF RICHARD

CLIFF RICHARD(HARRY WEBB) V(ALL		CLIFF	1959	COLUMBIA UK		33SX1147
HANK MARVIN	G (	CLIFF SINGS	1959	COLUMBIA UK		33SX1192
BRIAN BENNETT	D (T	CLIFF SINGS	19	ABC	US	ABC 321
BRUCE WELCH	G V (ST	ME & MY SHADOWS	1960	COLUMBIA UK SCX3330		33SX1261
TONY MEEHAN	D (	LISTEN TO CLIFF	1961	COLUMBIA UK SCX3375		33SX1320
IAN SAMWELL	(	LISTEN TO CLIFF	19	ABC	US	ABC 391
JET HARRIS	B (	THE YOUNG ONES	1961	COLUMBIA UK SCX3397		33SX1384
TERRY SMART	(	21 TODAY	1961	COLUMBIA UK SCX3409		33SX1368
JOHN ROSTILL	B (	32 MINUTES 17 SECONDS	1962	COLUMBIA UK SCX3436		33SX1431
ALAN TARNEY	B PROD(TW	CLIFFS HITS ALBUM	1962	COLUMBIA UK SCX1512		
JOHN FARRAR	G B (	WHEN IN SPAIN	1963	COLUMBIA UK SCX3488		33SX1541
TERRY BRITTEN	G (T	IN SPAIN WITH THE SHADOWS	196	EPIC	US	24115
GRAHAM TODD	K (TZ	SUMMER HOLIDAY	1963	COLUMBIA UK SCX3462		33SX1472
FRANK RICOTTI	PERC (T	SUMMER HOLIDAY	1963	EPIC	US	24063
JOHN PERRY	V (T	WONDERFUL LIFE	1963	COLUMBIA UK SCX3515		33SX1628
RICHAR HURSON	STR (T	HIT ALBUM	1963	COLUMBIA UK		33SX1512
ROGER POPE	D (T	IT'S ALL IN THE GAME	19	EPIC	US	26089
ALAN JONES	B (T	SWINGERS PARADISE	19	EPIC	US	26145
MO WITHAM	G (T	ALADDIN & HIS WONDERFUL LAMP	1965	COLUMBIA UK SCX3522		33SX1676
ALAN HAWKSHAW	K (T	WONDERFUL TO BE YOUNG	19	DOT	US	3474
TONY RIVERS	V (T	CLIFF RICHARD	1965	COLUMBIA UK SCX3546		33SX1709
CRAIG PRUESS	K SYN(Z	WHEN IN ROME	1965	COLUMBIA UK		SX1762
NIGEL PERRIN	V (Z	MORE HITS	1965	COLUMBIA UK SCX3555		SX1737
MART JENNER	G (Z	LOVE IS FOREVER	1965	COLUMBIA UK SCX3569		SX1769
DAVE COOKE	SYN (Z	KINDA LATIN	1966	COLUMBIA UK SCX6039		SX6039
MEL COLLINS	SAX (Z	FINDERS KEEPERS	1966	COLUMBIA UK SCX6079		SX6079
JOHN CLARK	G (Z	CINDERELLA	1967	COLUMBIA UK SCX6103		SX6103
MO FOSTER	B (Z	DON'T STOP ME NOW	1967	COLUMBIA UK SCX6133		
GRAHAM JARVIS	D (Z	GOOD NEWS	1967	COLUMBIA UK SCX6167		
BILL ROBERTS	G (Z	CLIFF IN JAPAN	1968	COLUMBIA UK SCX6244 GER 05553		
DAVE MATTACKS	D (Z	TWO A PENNY	1968	COLUMBIA UK SCX6262		
MARK GRIFFITHS	B (Z	ESTABLISHED 1958	1968	COLUMBIA UK SCX6282		
PAUL WESTWOOD	B (Z	BEST OF	1969	COLUMBIA UK SCX6343		
ANDY PASK	B (Z	SINCERELY	1969	COLUMBIA UK SCX6357		
		IT'LL BE ME	1969	STARLINE UK		5011
		ABOUT THAT MAN	1970	COLUMBIA UK SCX6408		
		ALL MY LOVE	1970	MFP UK 1420 GER RECORD CLUB68/9		
		LIVE AT THE TALK OF THE TOWN	1970	STARLINE UK		5031
		TRACKS & GROOVES	1970	COLUMBIA UK SCX6435		

(CONTINUED)

CLIFF RICHARD

(CONTINUED)

HIS LAND	1970 COLUMBIA UK SCX6443	
BEST OF VOL 2	1972 COLUMBIA UK SCX6519	
CLIFF & THE SHADOWS	197 ELECTROLA EURO	048 04318
HISTORY OF	1973 EMI IMP EURO	052 05019
TAKE ME HIGH	1973 EMI UK	EMC3016
POWER TO ALL MY FRIENDS	1973 EMI IMP EURO	062 05355
EDITION 2000	19 CONTEMPORARY	C2027/8
HELP IT ALONG	1974 EMI	EMA 768
31ST OF FEBRUARY	1974 EMI	EMC 3048
JAPAN TOUR 1974	1975 IRL IMP	EMS67037
WHEN IN FRANCE	19 EMI BELG 06234	
CLIFF RICHARD & THE SHADOWS	19 DIE VOLKSPLATTE GER	6084
HIER IST CLIFF	19 HOR ZU GER	261
FAMOUS POP GROUPS OF THE 60'S	19 MFP GER	05285/6
ICH TRAUME DEINE TRAUME	19 RECORD CLUB GER	27301/1
LIVE	1976 MFP UK	MFP50307
(S)I'M NEARLY FAMOUS	1976 EMI UK	EMC 3122
(S)I'M NEARLY FAMOUS	1976 ROCKET US 2210 RI	3004
(T)EVERY FACE TELLS A STORY	1977 EMI UK	EMC 3172
(T)EVERY FACE TELLS A STORY	1977 ROCKET US	2268
MY KIND OF LIFE	1977 EMI UK	EMI12584
40 GOLDEN GREATS	1977 EMI UK	EMTVS 6
SMALL CORNERS	1978 EMI UK	EMC 3219
GREEN LIGHT	1978 EMI UK	EMC 3231
ROCK'N'ROLL JUVENILLE	1979 EMI UK	EMC 3307
STARS OF R'N'R	1978 EMI EURO	052 04740
THANK YOU VERY MUCH	1979 EMI UK	EMTV 151
20 ROCK'N'ROLL HITS	1979 EMI GER	07145
I'M NO HERO	1980 EMI UK EMA796 US 17039 NL 07342	
WE DONT TALK ANYMORE	1980 EMI US 17018	
WIRED FOR SOUND	1981 EMI UK EMC3377	GER 07541
LOVE SONGS	1981 EMI UK EMTV27	
(Z) NOW YOU SEE ME ...NOW YOU DON'T	1982 EMI UK EMC3415	

DIGBY RICHARDS

DIGBY RICHARDS	G V (AB	(A) DIGBY RICHARDS	1974 RCA	US	UPLI 0001		
RICHARD BENNETT	G (A	(B) WHISKEY SUNDOWN	1978 RCA	UK	PL 25154		
TAFF WILLIAMS	G (B						
PETE KING	STEEL(B	ROGER BARA	K (B	KEVIN DUNN	B (B	MICKEY GIBBONS D	PERC(B
ALAN LINDGREN	K SYN(A	JOE OSBORN	B (A	JIM GORDON	D (A	JIM KELTNER	D (A
DENNIS CONWAY	D (A						

TURLEY RICHARDS

TURLEY RICHARDS	V (ALL	(A) TURLEY RICHARDS	197 WB US 1870				
LEE SKLAR	B (B	(B) EXPRESSIONS	1971 WB US 1918	UK	K46086		
DANNY KORTCHMAR	G (B	(C) WEST VIRGINIA SUPERSTAR	19 EPIC US		34306		
BRYAN GAROFALO	B (B	(D) THERFU	1980 ATLANTIC	US	19260		
RUSS KUNKEL	D (b						
JIM HORN	FLT (b	MICK FLEETWOOD	D (D	KENNY MALONE	D (D	FARRELL MORRIS	PERC(D
JACK WILLIAMS	B (D	BOB WELCH B	(D	DAVID BRIGGS	K (D	TOM SNOW K	(D
JAY GRUSKA	K (D	SHANE KIESTER	K SYN(D	JOHN GOIN	G (D	REGIE YOUNG	G (D
STEVE GIBSON	G (D	DANNY FERGUSON	G (D	PAUL WORLEY	G (D	TODD SHARP	G (D
BILL JONES	SAX (D	ROGER WILLIAMS	SAX (D	MARIE TOMLINSON	V (D	CINDY RICHARDSON	V (D
AVA ALDRIDGE	V (D						

DEL RICHARDSON

DEL RICHARDSON	G B V(A	(A) A PIECES OF A JIGSAW	1973 MCA UK MUPS 491 +RI MCF 2513				
CHILI CHARLES	D (A						
REMI KABAKA	PERC (A	ROSETTA HIGHTOWER V	(A	JEAN ROUSSEL	K (A	ROGER BALL	HRNS (A
DONNY PERKINS	V (A	ALAN SPENNER	B (A	MALCOLM DUNCAN	HRNS (A		

JONATHAN RICHMOND & THE MODERN LOVERS

JONATHAN RICHMAN	G V (ALL	(A) MODERN LOVERS	1977 BESERKLEY US 0048 UK BSERK 1				
ERNIE BROOKS	B (A	(A) MODERN LOVERS	1977 BESERKLEY US 0050 UK BSERK 2				
SKIP DUELKS	V (E	(B) MODERN LOVERS	19 BESERKLEY US 34755				
JERRY HARRISON	K V (A	(C) ROCK'N' ROLL WITH THE MODERN LOVER1977 BESERKLEY US 0053 UK BSERK 9					
DON GLADSTONE	B (E	(C) ROCK'N' ROLL WITH THE MODERN LOVER1977 BESERKLEY US 34800					
DAVID ROBINSON	D V (AB	(D) MODERN LOVERS LIVE	1977 BESERKLEY US 055 UK BSERK12				
LEROY RADCLIFFE	G V (BCDE	(E) BACK IN YOUR LIFE	1979 BESERKLEY US 060 UK BSERK17				
GREG KERANEN	B V (BC	(F) BEST OF	1980 BESERKLEY UK BSERK 19				
ASA BREBNER	B (DE	( ) THE ORIGINAL MODERN LOVERS	1981 BOMP BOM 1				
D SHARPE	D V (CDE						
JOHN FELICE	G (	RALPH ANDERSON	B (	KENNY LAGUNA	K (E	ANDY PALEY G	(E
STEVE TRACEY	V (E						

RICO

RICO RODRIGUES	TROM (A	(A) MAN FROM WAREIKA	1977 ISLAND	UK	ILPS9485		
RAY ALLEN	SAX (A	(B) MIDNIGHT IN ETHIOPIA	1978 ISLAND	UK	ILPS9516		
HERMAN MARQUIS	SAX (A	(C) THAT MAN IS FORWARD	1981 2 TONE	UK	TT 5005		
SLY DUNBAR	D (A						
BUNNY McKENZIE	B (A	ROBBIE SHAKESPEARE B	(A	JACKO	D (A	DUGGIE RAD BRYAN	G(A
KARL PITTERSON G K PERC(A		JUNIOR HANSON MARVIN G	(A	LLOYD PARKS	G (A	PHIL CHEN	G (A
TOUTER HARVEY	K (A	ANSEL COLLINS	K (A	TARZAN NELSON	K (A	TONY WASHINGTON	K (A
SKULLY	PERC (A	TONY UTER	PERC (A	SATCH DIXON	PERC (A	FLICK	PERC(A
CANDY McKENZIE	V (A	DICK CUTHELL	HRNS (A	VIV TALENT HALL	TPT (A	BOBBY ELLIS	TPT(A
EDDIE THORNTON	TPT (A	DIRTY HARRY	SAX (A	GEORGE LEE	SAX (A	KEITH GEMMELL	SAX(A

FRANK RICOTTI

FRANK RICOTTI	PERC SAX(A	(A) OUR POINT OF VIEW	1969 CBS UK	52668
CHRIS LAWRENCE	B (A			
CHRIS SPEDDING	G (A	BRYAN SPRING	D (A	

RICOTTI & ALBUQUERQUE

FRANK RICOTTI	(A	(A) FIRST WIND	1971 PEGASUS UK	PEG 2
MICHAEL D'ALBUQUERQUE	(A			
JOHN TAYLOR	K (A	CHRIS LAWRENCE B	(A TREVOR TOMKINS	D (A MICHAEL KEEN TPT(A
HENRY LOWTHER	TPT (A			

```
R85A                         BOB RIEDY BLUES BAND                                          R85A
    BOB RIEDY        PNO  (A          (A) JUST OFF HALSTED.            1976 FLYING FISH   US        006
    JOHN REDA        G    (A          (B) LAKE MICHIGAN               1977 ROUNDER       US        2005
    MIKE COGAN       SAX  (A
    DAN DRAHER       G    (A    MARK GASTON      TPT  (A   BOB FALVEY     B   (A    RICHARD ROBINSON D  (A
    CAREY BELL HARRINGTON HCA(A  EDDY CLEARWATER   V   (A   MIKE WILLENS  SAX  (A
R85B                         RIDERS IN THE SKY                                             R85B
                                    (A) THREE ON THE TRAIL           1980 ROUNDER       US        0102
R85C                         WOLFGANG RIECHMANN                                           R85C
    WOLFGANG RIECHMANN  G K B(A       (A) WONDERBAR                  1978 SKY           GER       017
    HANS SCHWEISS    D    (A
R86                          RIFF RAFF                                                    R86
    AUREO DE SOUZA   D    (AB         (A) RIFF RAFF                  1973 RCA           UK        SF 8351
    TOMMY EYRE       K V  (AB         (B) ORIGINAL MAN              1974 RCA                     LPLI5023
    PETE KIRTLEY     G V  (AB
    ROGER SUTTON     B V  (AB   BUD BEADLE      SAX  (AB  JOE O'DONNELL    VIOLA(B  STEVE GREGORY    WIND (B
    JO NEWMAN        V    (B
R86A                         RIFF RAFF (2)                                                R86A
    MARK KAUFFMAN    D    (A          (A) VINYL FUTURE              1981 ATLANTIC UK K50819 ATCO US 32108
    WERNER FRITZSCHING G V(A          () COSMONAUT  (EP)            19   CHISWICK      UK        SW 34
    DOUG LUBAHN      B V  (A
    NED LIBER        G V  (A
R86B                         RIGGS                                                        R86B
    JERRY RIGGS      G V  (A          (A) RIGGS                     1982 FULLMOON      UK        FMM3655
    STEPHEN ROY CARLISLE  D(A
    DAVID RIDARICK   B    (A   JEREMY GRAF        K    (A
R87                          RIGHTEOUS BROTHERS                                           R87
    BOBBY HATFIELD   V    (ALL        RIGHT NOW                     1964 MOONGLOW US 1001  UK PYE   NPL 28059
    BILL MEDLEY      V(ALL EXCEPT *?   SOME BLUE EYED SOUL           1965 MOONGLOW US 1002  UK PYE   NPL 28056
    JIMMY WALKER     V    (*          THIS IS NEW                   1965 MOONGLOW US 1003
    WITH                             BEST OF THE RIGHTEOUS BROTHERS 1966 MOONGLOW US 1004
    DAVID PAICH      K    (S          YOU'VE LOST THAT LOVIN FEELIN' 1965 PHILLES  US 4007  UK LONDON HA 8226
    TOM SELLERS      K    (S          JUST ONCE IN MY LIFE          1965 PHILLES  US 4008  UK LONDON HA 8245
    DENNIS LAMBERT   K PERC(S      (G)BACK TO BACK                  1966 PHILLES  US 4009  UK LONDON HA 8278
    DAVID HUNGATE    B    (S       (H)SOUL & INSPIRATION            1966 VERVE    US 65001 UK VERVE  SVLP9131
    DEAN PARKS       G    (S          GO AHEAD & CRY                1966 VERVE    US 65004 UK VERVE  SVLP9140
    ED GREENE        D    (S          IN ACTION                     1966 GNP      US 2029  UK SUE    ILP 937
    GARY COLEMAN     PERC (S          SAYIN' SOMETHIN'              1967 VERVE    US 65010 UK VERVE  SVLP9168
    BRIAN POTTER     PERC (S          GREATEST HITS                 1967 VERVE    US 5020  UK VERVE  SVLP9183
    CHUCK FINDLEY    HRNS (S          GREATEST HITS                 197  VERVE             UK RI     2352 018
    PAUL HUBINON     HRNS (S          GREATEST HITS VOL 2           1967 VERVE    US 65071 UK        SVLP9240
    ERNIE WATTS      SAX  (S          GREATEST HITS VOL 2           1969 VERVE             UK RI     2352 019
    TOM SCOTT        SAX  (S          SOULED OUT                    1967 VERVE    US 5031  UK        SVLP9190
    DON MENZA        HRNS (S          STANDARDS                     1967 VERVE    US 65051 UK        SVLP9204
    DICK HYDE        TROM (S          ONE FOR THE ROAD              1968 VERVE    US 65058 UK        SVLP9228
    GINGER BLAKE     V    (S          (*)REBIRTH                    1970 VERVE    US 65076 UK VERVE  SVLP9249
    JULIA TILLMAN    V    (S          RIGHTEOUS BROTHERS            1970 MGM      US 102
    MAXINE WILLARD   V    (S          2 BY 2                        1973 POLYDOR           UK        2683 033
    CARLENA WILLIAMS V    (S          GIVE IT TO THE PEOPLE         1974 HAVEN    US 9201  UK CAPITOL 9201
    STRING SECTION        (S       (S)SONS OF MRS RIGHTEOUS         1975 HAVEN    US 9203  UK CAPITOL 9203
    MICHAEL PATTERSON K   (H          PORTRAIT                      1975 POLYDOR           UK        2348 119
    BILL BAKER       SAX  (H          UNCHAINED MELODY              1975 METRONOME         200  115
    DREW JOHNSON     D    (H          HISTORY                       1977 MCM      US 4885
    ART MUSON        G    (H
    JIM BOND         B    (H
    DICK SHEARER     TROM (H   BILL KING         TPT  (H   SANDFORD SKINNER  TPT  (H   BOB FAUST     TPT (H
    BARNEY KESSEL    G    (G   CAROL KAYE        G    (G   DON PEAKE    G       (G   DON RANDI     K   (G
    LARRY KNECHTEL   K    (G   HAROLD BATTISTE   K    (G   MIKE RUBINI  K       (G   LYLE RITZ     B(G
    JIMMY BOND       B    (G   PAT SMITH         B    (G   EARL PALMER  D       (G   RITCHIE FROST  D (G
    FRANK CAPP       PERC (G   JULIUS WECHTER    PERC (G   GENE ESTES          PERC (G   JAY MIGLIORI  HRNS(G
    JIM HORN         HRNS (G   LOU BLACKBURN     HRNS (G   ROY CATON    HRNS   (G   MIKE PATTERSON BAND (G
    PHIL SPECTOR     PROD (G
R88           RIKKI & THE LAST      DAYS OF EARTH                                         R88
    RIKI SYLVAN          (A           (A) FOUR MINUTE WARNING       1978 DJM           UK        DJF 20526
R89                          BILLY LEE RILEY                                              R89
    BILLY LEE RILEY     (ALL          FUNK HARMONICA                19   CRESCENDO     US        2020
                                     IN ACTION                     19   CRESCENDO     US        2028
                                     HARMONICA & THE BLUES         19   CROWN         US        5277
                                     HARMONICA BEATLEMANIA         19   MERCURY       US        SR60974
                                     BIG HARMONICA SPECIAL         19   MERCURY       US        SR60965
                                     WHISKEY A GO GO PRESENTS      19   MERCURY       US        SR60985
                                     SOUTHERN SOUL                 19   MOJO          US        1933
                                     LEGENDARY SUN PERFORMER       1978 CHARLY        UK        CR30131
                                     SUN SOUNDS SPECIAL            1978 CHARLY        UK        CR30151
                                     (EP) BILLY LEE RILEY          1977 CHARLY        UK        CEP 112
R89A                         JIMMY RILEY                                                  R89A
                                     (A) TELL THE YOUTHS THE TRUTH 19   TROJAN                  TRLS 167
                                     (B) JIMMY RILEY EXPLOSIVE SHOW 1978 BURNING SOUNDS         BS 1011
R90                          TERRY RILEY                                                  R90
    TERRY RILEY      K    (ALL        (A) REED STREAMS              1967 MASS,ART,INC US        M131
    JOHN CALE            (D           (B) KEYBOARD STUDIES          1969 BYG
    DAVID BEHMAN     PROD(E           (C) IN 'C'                    1970 CBS  US 7178  UK        64565
                                     (D) CHURCH OF ANTHRAX         1971 CBS  US 30131 UK        64259
                                     (E) RAINBOW IN CURVED AIR     1971 CBS  US 7315  UK        64564
                                     (F) PERSIAN SURGERY DERVISHES 1972 SHANDAR                 83501/2
                                     ( ) HAPPY ENDING              1972 WB   FR 46125
                                     (G) LE SECRET DE LA VIE       1975 PHILIPIS               9120 037
                                     (H) SHRI CAMEL                1980 CBS  US 35164           73929
```

LAURIN RINDER & W MICHAEL LEWIS

LAURIN RINDER	D SAX(AB	(A) SEVEN DEADLY SINS	1978 PYE		UK	NSPL28252		
W MICHAEL LEWIS	K SAX(AB	(B) WARRIORS	1979 AVI		US	6073		
ADAM STRANGE	G (B							
DAVID TURNER	G (B	VENETTE GLOUD	V (B	AZAR LAWRENCE	SAX (B	JIMBO ROSS	VLA (B	
CARMEN TWILLIE	V (B							

VICTOR BROX	K V (A	(A) 1970	
ANNETTE BROX	V (A		
JIM KING	SAX (A	ANNIE MATTHEWS PNO (A GERRY FIELDS VLN (A FLOYD LAWSON B (A
RAY DRAPER	V (A	JOHN PEARSON D (A

BOB GIFFIRD	B V (A	(A) THE RINGS	1980 MCA	US	5165	
MARK SUTTON	G (A	(B) RHYTHM METHOD	1981 MCA			
MIKE BAKER	G (A					
MATT THURBER	D (A					

TWINK   D V (PAUL RUDOLPH   G   (SANDY ROBERTSON   B   (RUSSELL HUNTER   D (

ALLAN BLACK	G (A	(A) CAMEO ROLES	1975 HARVEST	US 11438	UK SHSP4047	
NIGEL WARD	K V (A					
JANE HUTCHINSON	V (A	BILL WARD D (A KEN COOK B (A GRAHAM BLYTH K (A
RON ASPERY	SAX (A					

DAVID STANLEY	G B V(A	(A) RIO GRANDE	1971 RCA LSP 4454
RONNY'MOUSE'WEISS	G V (A		
TOM RUSSELL	G B V(A	BOBBY TUTTLE STEEL G V(A KEN MURRAY D (A DALE HAWKINS PROD(A

GUY SPERANZA	V PERC(ABC	(A) RIOT CITY	1978 ARIOLA		ARL 5007	
MARK REALE	G V (ABC	(B) NARITA	1979 CAPITOL US12081	+ATTIC	1067	
PETER BITELLI	D (AB	(C) FIRE DOWN UNDER	1981 ELEKTRA	UK	K 52315	
JIMMY IOMMI	B (AB	(D) RESTLESS BREED	1982 ELEKTRA	UK	K 52398	
RICK VENTURA	G (BC	L A KOUVARIS G (A KIP LEMING B (C SANDY SLAVIN D (C

(A) RIOT ROCKERS   1978 CHARLY   UK   CR 30158

MITCH MITCHELL	(	(A) 1965/67	
JON LORD	(		
TERRY CLIFFORD	(	GRAHAM BONNET (DELL ROLL (ROGER CRISP (
BUTCH DAVIS	(	BOB EVANS (NERO (

PHIL STEWART	(B	(A) HEY LITTLE COBRA	1964	CBS	UK	8951
ARNIE MARKUS	(B	(B) THREE WINDOW COUPE	1965	CBS	UK	9016
RICH ROTKIN	(B					
BERNIE BRINGAS	(A	BRUCE JOHNSON (B TERRY MELCHER (A

(A) GOD   1981 VIRGIN   UK   V2213

MINNIE RIPPERTON	V (	(A) COME TO MY GARDEN	19 JANUS US 7011 GRT US 30001			
JOSE FELICIANO	(E	(B) PERFECT ANGEL	1974 EPIC US 32561 UK		80426	
HUBERT LAWS	FLT (EF	(C) ADVENTURES IN PARADISE	1975 EPIC US 33454 UK		69142	
TOM SCOTT	SAX (EF	(D) STAY IN LOVE	1977 EPIC US 34191 UK		81457	
DAVID HUNGATE	(E	(E) MINNIE	1979 CAPITOL		11936	
CHUCK RAINEY	B (E	(F) LOVE LIVES FOREVER	1980 CAPITOL		12097	
PHIL UPCHURCH	B (E					
HARVEY MASON	D (EF	GERRY VINCI VLN (EF OSCAR NEVES (E CLAUDIO SLOAN (E			
STEVE FORMAN	(E	ART PHILLIPS (E LARRY WILLIAMS HRNS (E KIM HUTCHCROFT HRNS(E			
VICTOR FELDMAN	PERC (E	JERRY HEY HRNS (E ABE LABORIEL B (EF BILL REICHENBACH (E			
MARLO HENDERSON	(E	LEON CHANCLER (E RANDY WALDMAN (E BUDDY COLLETTE (E			
JEREMY LUBBOCK	(E	BILL GREEN (E PAULINHO DA COSTA PERC (EF SHERIDAN STOKES (E			
HENRY GIBSON	(E	VINCE DE ROSA (E RICHARD PERISSI (E DAVID DUKE (E			
LENNY CASTRO	PERC (F	GREG PHILLINGANES K (F PAUL JACKSON G (F LEE RITENOUR G (F			
TENNYSON STEPHENS	PNO (F	GAYLE LEVANT HARP (F MAXINE WILLARD (F. ROBERTA FLACK V (F			
JULIA TILLMAN	V (F	PEABO BRYSON V (F STEPHANIE SPRUILL V (F MICHAEL JACKSON V (F			
MICHAEL BODDICKER	SYN (F	STEVIE WONDER HCA (F GEORGE BENSON. V (F. PATRICE RUSHEN V K(F			

(A) SHE'S A BAD MOTORCYCLE   196   IMPERIAL US 12269

ED CASSIDY	D ('	TAJ MAHAL V (RY COODER G (JESSIE ED DAVIS G (
JESSE LEE KINCADE	PNO (	KEVIN KELLEY D (GARY MARKER B (

LEE RITENOUR	G V SYN(ALL	(A) FIRST CHOICE	1976 EPIC	US	33847	
PATRICE RUSHEN	K (ABC	(B) CAPTAIN FINGERS	1977 EPIC	US	34426	
DAVID GRUSIN	SYN (ABCFGJ	(C) CAPTAINS JOURNEY	1978 ELEKTRA UK K52094	US	136	
STEVE GADD	D (CF	(D) GENTLE THOUGHTS	1978 JVC	JAP	VIDC1	
DAVID NADIEN	STRINGS (C	(E) SUGAR LOAF EXPRESS	1978 JVC	JAP	VIDC2	
ALEX ACUNA	PERC (BCFG HJ	(F) FEEL THE NIGHT	1979 ELEKTRA UK K52141	US 6E192		
CARMEN TWILLIE	V (C	(G) FRIENDSHIP	1979 JVC	JAP	VIDC3	
JOHNNY MANDEL	STR (H	( ) THE BEST	1980 EPIC	US 36527		
DAVID FOSTER	C (BCFH	(H) RIT	1981 ELEKTRA UK K52273	US 6E331		
LARRY WILLIAMS	HRNS (F	(J) RIO	1982 ELEKTRA UK K52350			
SUE EVANS	PERC (C					
LOUIS JOHNSON	B (AH	PAULINHO DA COSTA PERC (CH RAY BECKENSTEIN FLT (C IAN UNDERWOOD SYN (ABFC			
JAY GRAYDON	G (BC	BILL REICHENBACH HRNS (F VENETTE GLOUD V (C STEVE THORNTON PERC(C			
PATTI AUSTIN	V (CF	DAVE VALENTIN FLT (B ABRAHAM LABORIEL B(CFGHJ ANTHONY JACKSON B (BC			
BILL CHAMPLIN	V (BCH	MITCH HOLDER G (BC ERNIE WATTS SAX(ABCFGJ TOM BAYLOR V (C			
EDDY DANIELS	FLT (C	STEVE FORMAN PERC(BCFHJ JERRY STEINHOLTZ PERC (A JERRY PETERS K (A			
LARRY NASH	K (A	MIKE OMARTIAN K (A CHUCK RAINEY B (A GREG PHILLINGANES K(H			

(CONTINUED)

LEE RITENOUR

ED GREENE	D	(A	TOM SCOTT	SAX	(A	JEROME RICHARDSON	SAX	(A	CHUCK FINDLEY	TPT	(AFH
FRANK ROSELINO	TROM	(A	DAWILLI GONGA	K	(B	DENNIS BUDIMIR	G	(B	RAY PARKER	G	(B
ALPHONSO JOHNSON	B	(B	BILL DICKINSON	B	(AB	CHARLES MEEKS	B	(B	MIKE PORCARO	B	(B
HARVEY MASON	D	(ABH	JEFF PORCARO	D	(BH	MIKE BODDICKER	SYN	(FH	VICTOR FELDMAN	PERC	(F
CHARLES LOPER	HRNS	(H	STEVE LUKATHER	G	(F	JOE SAMPLE	PNO	(F	TOM BAHLER	V	(F
JERRY HEY	HRNS	(FH	GARY GRANT	HRNS	(FH	LEW McCREARY	HRNS	(FH	GREG MATHIESON	K	(H
ERIC TAGG	V	(H	JOHN PIERCE	B	(H	RICHARD TEE	K	(H	DAVID HUNGATE	B	(H
RICK SHLOSSER	D	(H	MARCUS MILLER	B	(J	JEFF MIRANOV	G	(J	PAULINHO BRAGO	D	(J
OSCAR NEVES	G	(J	JOSE DA SILVA	PERC	(J	ARMANDO MARCAL	PERC	(J	BUDDY WILLIAMS	D	(J
RUBINS BASSINI	PERC	(J	LUIZAO MAIA	B	(J	CHICO BATERA	PERC	(J	ROBERTO PINHEIRO	PERC	(J
DON GRUSIN	K	(HJ									

SCARLET RIVERA

SCARLET RIVERA	VLN	(AB	(A) SCARLET RIVERA			1977	WB		US	3060	
KRISTIN PIMPINELLA	V	(A	(B) SCARLET FEVER			1978	WB		US	BSK3174	
DOMINIC CARDINALE	K	(A									
BERNARD PURDIE	D	(A	MIKE MAINIERI	VIBES	(A	GARY BURKE	D	(A	FRANCISCO SANTANA	B	(A
URBIE GREEN	TROM	(A	ED MIKENAS	B	(A	PAUL GRIFFIN	K	(A	PAUL PRESTOPINO	MAND	(A
LANI GROVES	V	(A	ULLANDA McCULLOUGH	V	(A	MICHELLE LEWIS	V	(A	JAMIE LEE	V	(A
REGGIE YOUNG	G	(A	VINNIE BELL	G	(A	ELLIOTT RANDALL	G	(A	CLARENCE CLEMONS	SAX	V(A
SREDNI VOLLNER	HCA	(A	DAVE SANBORN	SAX	(A	MICHAEL BRECKER	SAX	(A	RANDY BRECKER	SAX	(A
BURT COLLINS	TPT	(A	ARTIE KAPLAN	WIND	(A	VIVIAN CHERRY	V	(A	DEDE WASHBURN	V	(A
HELENE MILES	V	(A									

JOHNNY RIVERS

JOHNNY RIVERS	V	(ALL	AT THE WHISKY A GO GO	1964	LIBERTY	UK	LBY3031	US IMPERIAL	12264
WITH			AT THE WHISKY A GO GO	1970	SUNSET	UK	50157	US	5157
JIM GORDON	D	(ABLMOP	HERE WE GOGO AGAIN	1964	LIBERTY	UK	LBY3036	US IMPERIAL	12274
JOE OSBORNE	B	(ABHMGP	IN ACTION	1965				US IMPERIAL	12280
LARRY KNECHTEL	PNO	(ABHGNSP	BACK AT THE WHISKY	1965				US IMPERIAL	12284
MICHAEL OMARTIAN	K V	(ABMOP	ROCKS THE FOLK	1965	LIBERTY	UK	LBY3064	US IMPERIAL	12293
JIM WEBB	K STR	(AR	AND I KNOW YOU WANNA DANCE	1966				US IMPERIAL	12307
JERRY ALLISON	D	(A	(C)CHANGES	1967	LIBERTY	UK	LBY3087	US IMPERIAL	12334
MICHAEL GEORGIADES	V	(ABMOPR	GOLDEN HITS	196				US IMPERIAL	12324
HERB PEDERSEN	V	(ABLMOPR	(G)REWIND	1967				US IMPERIAL	12341
KEITH ALLISON	B	(A	REALIZATION	1969				US IMPERIAL	12372
DEAN PARKS	G	(ABLMOP	A TOUCH OF GOLD	1969	LIBERTY	UK	83141	US IMPERIAL	12427
LARRY CARLTON	G	(ABMP	JOHN LEE HOOKER	1970	SUNSET	UK	50025		
BOBBYE HALL	PERC	(A	(S) SLO SLIM SLIDER	19				US IMPERIAL	16001
GARY COLEMAN	PERC	(ABMOP	WILD NIGHT	1976	LIBERTY	UK	83383	US UA	LA486
JIM HORN	SAX	(ABHLMSP	JOHNNY RIVERS	19				US UA	LA593
CHUCK FINDLEY	HRNS	(ABLMOP	(A) LA REGGAE	1973	UA	UK	29298	US	LA5650
JACKIE KELSO	SAX	(ABMP	(H) HOME GROWN	1973				US UA	LA5532
JACK CONRAD	B	(L	HISTORY OF	197	LIBERTY	UK	83461		
MICHAEL MELVOIN	K	(LP	GO JOHNNY GO	19				UA UA	LA3386
MICKEY JONES	D	(L	(B) BLUE SUEDE SHOES	1973	UA	UK	29473	US	LA 075
JAMES HENDRICKS	V	(B	(L) LAST BOOGIE IN PARIS	1974	ATLANTIC	UK	K50033		
RON TUTT	D	(HS	(R)ROAD	1974	ATLANTIC	UK	K50063	US	7301
GLEN TOWNSEND	G	(H	(M) HELP ME RHONDA	1975	EPIC	UK	80987		
RITA COOLIDGE	V	(H	(P)NEW LOVES AND OLD FRIENDS	1975	CBS	UK	80946	US	33681
CLYDIE KING	V	(H	(O) OUTSIDE HELP	1978	POLYDOR	UK	2310603	US SOULCITY	76004
RON MICO DUQUETTE	G V	(H	MR TEENAGE	19				US SEARS	417
CHARLES D HARRIS	V	(H	SENSATIONAL	19				US CAPITOL	2161
MIKE DEASY	G V	(GH	JOHNNY RIVERS	19				US PICKWICK	3191
FRANK KINSEL	V	(H	VERY BEST OF	1975	UA			US	444
CHRIS ETHRIDGE	B	(H	SUPER PAK	1973	UA			UK UX593	
VANETTA FIELDS	V	(H	SWINGING SHINDIG	19				US CORNET	246
KATHY DEASY	V	(H	20 GREATEST HITS	19				CAN TEEVEE	1062
JIM KELTNER	D	(HO	BORROWED TIME	1980	RSO			US	13082
MICHAEL AMILIUS	V	(H							

JAMES BURTON	G	(HS	JERRY SCHEFF	B	(HS	WAYNE MINCY	V HCA	(H	TOMMY COE	G V	(H
MIKE SHANKLIN	G V	(H	GURU RAMDAS SINGERS		(H	SCOTT EDWARDS	B	(MOP	GINGER BLAKE	V	(MOP
JULIA TILLMAN	V	(MOP	MAXINE WILLARD	V	(MOP	JOHN RAINES	D	(MP	JIM HUGHART	B	(MP
TAY UHLER	G	(MOP	BEN BENAY	G	(MP	TOM SCOTT	SAX	(MPO	BRIAN WILSON	V	(MP
MARK BOOKIN	V	(MRP	BARRY BOOKIN	V	(MP	TOM LEADON	V	(MP	ED GREENE	D	(MOP
BOB ALCIVER	HRNS	(S	MARTY PAICH	HRNS	(S	GARY ILLINGSWORTH	PNO	(S	JOE SAMPLE	PNO	(O
WAYNE BERRY	G V	(O	RICHARD CUOMO	K	(O	M L BENOIT	PERC	(O	LUTHER WATERS	V	(O
ORRIN WATERS	V	(O	JERRY JUMONVILLE	HRNS	(O	JOHN PHILLIPS	HRNS	(O	JOEL PESKIN	HRNS	(O
FRED TACKETT	G	(O	HAL BLAINE	D	(OGS	DAVID HUNGATE	B	(O	JON DOUGLAS HAYWOOD	V	(O
JAMES E HAAS	V	(O	DAVID KEMPER	D	(MP	NED DOHENY	G	(MP	DAVID T WALKER	G	(MP
JIM HELMER	D	(MP	SKIP EDWARDS	K	(MP	DUITCH HELMER	V	(MP	MARTY GWINN	V	(MP
PLAS JOHNSON	SAX	(MP	GARY HERBIG	HRNS	(O	GARY GRANT	HRNS	(O	MILT HOLLAND	PERC	(OR
MARC F LEVINE	B	(O	HARLAN ROGERS	K	(O	ROGER HAWKINS	D	(R	DAVID HOOD	B	(R
BARRY BECKETT	G	(R	PETE CARR	G	(R	JIMMY JOHNSON	G	(R	ERNIE FREEMAN	SAX	(R
JORDONAIRES	V	(R	MIKE LEECH	B	(R	JERRY CARRIGAN	D	(R	BOBE SEYMOUR	STEEL	(R
REGGIE YOUNG	G	(R	RON OATES	K	(R	JOHN REID	G	(R			

RIVITS

JESS RODEN	D V	(A	(A) MULTIPLAY	1980	ISLAND UK	ILPS9617	US ANTILLES7072
PETER WOOD	K V	(A					
STEVE DWIRE	B	(A	DOANE PERRY	D	(A	LEE GOODALL	SAX (A

RIVIERAS

BILL DOBSHAW	V	(A	(A) LET'S HAVE A PARTY	1964	?		US LP102		
PAUL DENNERT	D	(A							
OTTO NUSS	ORG	(A	DOUG GEAN	B	(A	JIM BOAL	G	(A	WILLIE GAUT G	(A

ROAD

```
    JERRY HUDSON      G V  (AB                    (A) ROAD                      1972 KAMA SUTRA US 2012 RAREEARTH3006
    NOEL REDDING      B V  (A                     (A) ROAD                      1972 NATURAL RESOURCES    US   105
    PHIL HUDSON       V    (AB                     (B) COGNITION                 1973 KAMA SUTRA US 2032
    JOE HESSE         B    (AB
    NICK DISTEFANO    D V  (AB   JIM HESSE      K    (AB  RALPH PARKER    G    (A  DON JAKE JAKUBOWSKI K(B
    HUGH McCRACKEN    G    (B    KEN KAUFMAN    K    (B   RON BURRANO     K    (B  DAN TURBEVILLE   K (B
    ROD RICHARDS     G V  (A    LES SAMPSON       D V  (A
```
ROADMASTER

```
    BOBBY JOHNS       D    (BAC                    (A) SWEET WORLD               1979 MERCURY     US        SRM13760
    RICK BENICK       G    (ABC                    (B) FORTRESS                  1979 MERCURY     US        SRM13814
    STEPHEN McNALLY   V    (BCA                    (C) HEY WORLD                 1979 MERCURY     US        SRM13774
    TOBY MYERS        B    (BCA
    MICHAEL READ      K    (BCA
```
ROAD HOME

```
    GREG SHANNON      G    (A                      (A) PEACEFUL CHILDREN         196  DUNHILL        US      50104
    WILLY SPROUSE     K PERC V(A
    DEE ARCHER        V    (A    JIMMY SIMS        D    (A   PETER WICKERSHAM  V    (A  JIMMY HASKELL HRNS STR(A
```
HARGUS ROBBINS

```
    HARGUS 'PIG' ROBBINS PNO(ALL                   (A) HARGUS ROBBINS            1969 CHART          US         1011
                                                   (B) COUNTRY INSTRUMENTALIST   1977 ELEKTRA        US       7E1110
                                                   (C) A PIG IN A POKE           1978 ELEKTRA UK K52071 US  6E 129
                                                   (D) UNBREAKABLE HEARTS        1979 ELEKTRA        US     6E 185
```
ROBBS

```
    JOE ROBB              (A                        (A) THE ROBBS                 1966 MERCURY     21130
    BRUCE ROBB           (A
    CRAIG ROBB           (A    DEE ROBB       (A
```
TEX ROBERG BAND

```
    TEX ROBERG        V    (A1                      (A) FIRST PRESSING            1979 ARNIES SHACK     UK      AS 029
    BRUCE ROBERTS     G V  (A1                      (1) 1979 SPRING
    VERNON CHUTER     G    (A
    DAVE NASH        STEEL(A   MICK WILLIAMS     G    (A   BOB PHILLIPS    B    (A   CHRIS BROWN    G V (1
    CHRIS            PNO (A    DAVE WARD        HCA (1   BOB WILLIAMS    B    (1   PETE HUNT      D   (A1
```
AL ROBERTS JR

```
    AL ROBERTS JR         (AB                        (A) ROCKABILLY GUITAR MAN    1978 FROG                    001
                                                     (B) FROGABILLY               1979 FROG                    002
```
ANDY ROBERTS

```
    ANDY ROBERTS G V PERC FLT(ALL                    (A) HOME GROWN               1971 B&C CAS 1034 RCA UK SF 8086
    IAN WHITEMAN    K V  (AB                          (B) HOME GROWN(SOMR DIFF TRACKS) 1971 AMPEX   US   10120
    JOHN PEARSON    D    (BCD                         (C) ANDY ROBERTS WITH EVERYONE 1971 B&C UK CAS1028 AMPEX US 10117
    RAY WARLEIGH    SAX  (BD                          (D) NINA & THE DREAM TREE    1971 PEGASUS UK PEG5 PHILIPS 6303039
    MIKE EVANS      K V  (AB                          (E) URBAN COWBOY             1973 ELEKTRA         UK    K42139
    DAVE RICHARDS   B V  (ABCDE                       (F) & THE GREAT STAMPEDE     1973 ELEKTRA         UK    K42151
    ROGER POWELL    D V  (ABD                         (G) ANDY ROBERTS            1973 CHARISMA        UK     CS6
    GORDON HUNTLEY  STEEL(AB
    MAC KISSOON     V    (ABD  MIKE LONDON       V    (ABD KATHY KISSOON  V    (ABD ZOOT MONEY    K V (DEF
    IAN MATTHEWS    V    (DE   TIMI DONALD      D    (E   BOB RONGA      B V  (E   B J COLE     STEEL(EF
    DICK PARRY      SAX  (E    RICHARD THOMPSON G    (E   NEIL INNES     G    (E   JOHN MEGGINSON K   (E
    MIKE KELLIE     D    (E    MARTIN CARTHY   BANJO(E   GILLIAN NOEL   V    (E   PAUL KENT    V    (E
    KARENE WALLACE  V    (E    GERRY CONWAY    D(ABDEF  MICK KAMINSKI  VLN  (F   PAT DONALDSON  B    (F
    OLLIE HALSALL   G    (F    SONNY FRANCIS   K    (F   RAY WEHRSTEIN  SAX  (F   BOB SARGEANT V G K HCA(C
    JOHN PORTER     G    (C    PAUL KRIWACZEK  ORG  (B   CHARLENE COLLINS V  (BD  CAROL GRIMES   V    (BD
```
BRUCE ROBERTS

```
    BRUCE ROBERTS    K V  (A                         (A) BRUCE ROBERTS            1978 ELEKTRA  US   7E119 UK   K52061
    DAVID FOSTER     K    (A                         (B) COOL FOOL                1980 ELEKTRA  US    262
    GRADY TATE       D    (A
    JIM CREGAN       G    (A    BOBBYE HALL     PERC (A   RON CARTER    B    (A   JOHN JARVIS K    (A
    STEVE CROPPER    G    (A    IAN UNDERWOOD   K    (A   BROOKS HUNNICUTT V  (A   DONALD DUCK DUNN B(A
    JEFF PORCARO     D    (A    FRED TACKETT    G    (A   TOMMY VIG     PERC (A   MIKE PORCARO   B(A
    BOB GLAUB        B    (A
```
HOWARD ROBERTS

```
    HOWARD ROBERTS   G    (ABCD                       (A) THE REAL HOWARD ROBERTS  19   CONCORD        US        53
    DAVE GRUSIN      ORG  (D                          (B) ANTELOPE FREEWAY         19   IMPULSE                AS9207
    MIKE WOFFORD     PNO  (D                          (C) SOUNDS                   1974 CAPITOL               11247
    JERRY SCHEFF     B    (D                          (D) EQUINOX EXPRESS ELEVATOR 1975 IMPULSE US 9299   IMPL 8004
    JOHN GUERIN      D    (D
    MAILTO CORREA    PERC (D    DIANA LEE         V    (D   ED MICHAL      SYN (D
```
LAVADA JUNE ROBERTS

```
    LAVADA JUNE ROBERTS V PNO(A                       (A) LAVADA                   1976 PYE                   12126
    RICHARD CROOKS   D    (A
    WELDON MYRICK    STEEL(A    FRANK OWENS     ORG  (A   DON PAYNE     B    (A   PAUL PRESTOPINO G  (A
    BOB SYLVESTER    CELLO(A
```
RICK ROBERTS

```
    RICK ROBERTS     G V  (ABC                        (A) WINDMILLS                1972 A&M UK AMLH64372 US  SP 4372
    DON HENLEY       D V  (A                          (B) SHE IS A SONG            1973 A&M            US  SP 4404
    BERNIE LEADON    G V  (A                          (C) BEST OF                  19   A&M            US  SP 4744
    RANDY MEISNER    B V  (A
    JACKSON BROWNE   V    (A    AL PERKINS     STEEL(AB  JOE LALA     PERC (AB  CHRIS HILLMAN   B   (A
    DALLAS TAYLOR    D    (A    DAVID CROSBY    V    (A   JANE GETZ    PNO V(A   BYRON BERLINE  FDL(A
    LEE SKLAR        B    (A    MIKE UTLEY     ORG  (A   MARC BENNO   G    (A   PAUL HARRIS    K   (B
    GEORGE GRANTHAM  D V  (B    KENNY PASSARELLI B   (B   JOE WALSH    G    (B   JOE VITALE     D   (B
    RUSTY YOUNG      G    (B    STEVE FROMHOLZ  B V  (B
```
B A ROBERTSON

```
    BRIAN ALEXANDER ROBERTSON V(ABC                   (A) WRINGING APPLAUSE        1973 ARDENT     US    ADS     2804
    GRAHAM JARVIS    D    (B                          (B) INITIAL SUCCESS          1980 ASYLUM         UK      K52216
    ALAN JONES       B    (B                          (C) BULLY FOR YOU            1981 ASYLUM         UK      K52275
    BILLY LIVSEY     K    (B                          (D) R & BA                   1982 ASYLUM         UK      K52383
    TERRY BRITTEN    G    (B
```

ROBINS

BOBBY NUNN	V	(	(A) ROCK'ROLL WITH ROBINS			1976 WHIPPETT		US		703
TY TERRELL	V	(	(B) THE BEST OF			1976 GNP CRESCENDO		US		9034
ROY RICHARDS	V	(								
BILLY RICHARDS	V	(	GRADY CHAPMAN	V	(	CARL GARDNER	V	(	RICHARD BERRY	V	(
PETE LEWIS	G	(	MARIO DELAGARDE	B	(	JOHNNY OTIS	D	(	DEVONIA WILLIAMS PNO(
LEARD BELL	D	(	DON JOHNSON	TPT	(	LEE GRAVES	TPT	(	LORENCE HOLDEN	SAX(
JAMES VON STREETER	SAX	(	WALTER HENRY	B	(	GEORGE WASHINGTON	TROM	(	GIL BERNAL	SAX(
MIKE STOLLER	G	(	BARNEY KESSEL	G	(	CHARLIE NORRIS	G	(	RALPH HAMILTON	B	(
JESSE SAILES	D	(								

ROBEY, FALK & BOD

BILL ROBEY	G V (A	(A) KENTUCKY GAMBLER			19 EPIC		US	31796
DON FALK	B G V(A							
BOD NOUBARIAN	G V (A	KENNETH BUTTREY	D (A	WELDON MYRICK	STEEL(A	RICK POWELL	SYN(A
BUD SPICHER	FDL (A							

ANDY ROBINSON

ANDY ROBINSON	G V (A	(A) PATTERNS OF REALITY			1968 PHILIPS		600289			
ARTIE BUTLER	K (A									
LINCOLN MAYORGA	K (A	JIM GORDON	D (A	EARL PALMER	D (A	CAROL KAYE	B (A
DAVID COHEN	G (A	DENNIS BUDIMIR	G (A	AL CASEY	G (A	KEN WATSON	PERC (A
GENE ESTES	PERC (A	VICTOR FELDMAN	PERC(A	GARY COLEMAN	PERC (A	SID SHARP	VLN (A
BILL NUTTYCOMBE	VLN (A	SAM BOGHOSSIAN	VLA (A	JESS EHRLICH	CELLO(A		

ROBINSON CRUISER

JAN HOLLESTELLE	(A	(A) CATCH A THRILL		1980 CBS	UK 84600
HANS HOLLESTELLE	(A				
ROBIN LENT	V (A	TOMMY BACHMAN	D (A		

FENTON ROBINSON

FENTON ROBINSON	G V (ALL	(A) SOMEBODY LOAN ME A DIME	197	SONET SNTF686 ALLIGATOR 4705 TRIO6218
STEVE DITZELL	G (B	(B) I HEAR SOME BLUES DOWNSTAIRS	1978	SONET SNTF712 ALLIGATOR 4710 TRIO6219
BILL HEID	K (AB	(C) & LARRY DAVIS	19	PYTHON FR PLP 24
LARRY EXUM	B (B	(D) MONDAY MORNING BOOGIE & BLUES	1972	77 US 7200 UK 2001
EARL CROSSLEY	SAX (B	(E) GETAWAY	19	77 US 77 109
D BALDWIN	SAX (A			
ASHWARD GATES	D (B	BILL MACFARLAND TROM (AB	BILL BRIMFIELD	TPT (B	LARRY DAVIS (C
MIGHTY JOE YOUNG	G (A	CORNELIUS BOYSON B (A	TONY GOODEN	D (A	NORVAL D HODGES TPT(A
ELMER BROWN JR	TPT (A				

FREDDY ROBINSON

FREDDY ROBINSON	G V (AB	(A) AT THE DRIVE IN	19	POLYDOR UK 2325 085 US ENTERPRISE1025
AL VESOVO	G (A	(B) BLACK FOX	19	PACIFIC JAZZ 20162
HARVEY MASON	D (A	(C) HOT FUN SUMMERTIME	197	PACIFIC JAZZ 20176
PAUL HUMPHREY	D (A			
JOE SAMPLE	K (A	WILTON FELDER B (A	MONK HIGGINS	ORG (A	BOBBYE HALL	PERC(A
CLYDIE KING	V (B				

L C ROBINSON

L C ROBINSON	G V VLN STEEL(AB	(A) UPS & DOWNS		1972 ARHOOLIE	US	1062
JAMES MADISON	G (A	(B) HOUSE CLEANING BLUES		1974 BLUESWAY	US	BLS 6082
SAMUEL LAWHORN	G (A					
CALVIN JONES	B (A	WILLIE SMITH	D (A	JOE'PINETOP'PERKINS PNO(A	CHARLIE MUSSELWHITE HCA(A
DAVID ALEXANDER	PNO (A	WILLIAM HYATT	B (A	TEDDY WINSTON	D (A	KEN SWANK	D (B
ROBERT HOOKER	PNO (B	LEX BOYD SILVA	B (B	LUTHER TUCKER	G (B		

SMOKEY ROBINSON & THE MIRACLES

SMOKEY ROBINSON	V(ALL EXCEPT **	HI WE'RE THE MIRACLES	1961 TAMLA		US 220
WILLIAM GRIFFIN	V (**	COOKIN' WITH THE MIRACLES	196 TAMLA		US 223
WAH WAH WATSON	G (ZS	SHOP AROUND	1962 TAMLA		US 224
RICHARD LITTLEFIELD	G (Z	I'LL TRY SOMETHING NEW	196 TAMLA		US 230
MARLO HENDERSEN	G (SZ	CHRISTMAS WITH THE MIRACLES	196 TAMLA		US 236
DAVID T WALKER	G (SZ	FABULOUS MIRACLES	1964 TAMLA	UK STML11003	US 238
PHIL UPCHURCH	G (S	MIRACLES ON STAGE	1964 TAMLA	UK STML10055	US 241
MARV TARPIN	D (STZ	DOIN' MICKEY'S MONKEY	1963 TAMLA		US 245
JAMES GADSON	D (SZ	TEARS OF A CLOWN	196 TAMLA		US 246
ED GREENE	D (Z	I LIKE IT LIKE THAT	196 TAMLA		
SCOTTIE HARRIS	D (ZS	GREATEST HITS	196 TAMLA	UK TML11003	
JOSEPH A BROWN	D (T	THE FABULOUS MIRACLES	1964 STATESIDE	UK SL 10099	
CHUCK RAINEY	B (Z	GOING TO A GO GO	1964 TAMLA	UK STML11024	US 267
KENNETH BURKE	B (S	MIRACLES FROM THE BEGINNING	1965 TAMLA	UK TML11031	
JAMES JAMESON	B (Z	AWAY WE GO GO	1965 TAMLA	UK STML11044	US 271
WAYNE TWEED	B (STZ	MAKE IT HAPPEN	1968 TAMLA	UK STML11067	US 276
DAVID SHIELDS	B (Z	GREATEST HITS VOL 2	196 TAMLA	UK STML11233	US 280
SCOTT EDWARDS	B (STZ	LIVE	1969 TAMLA	UK STML11107	US 289
SONNY BURKE	K (ZST	SPECIAL OCCASION	1969 TAMLA	UK STML11089	US 290
SYLVESTER RIVERS	K (Z	TIME OUT	1970 TAMLA	UK STML11129	US 295
MICHAEL B SUTTON	K (Z	FOUR IN BLUE	1970 TAMLA	UK STML11151	US 297
JOHN BARNES	K (Z	WHAT LOVE HAS JOINED TOGETHER	1970 TAMLA		US 301
RODERICK RANCIFER	K (S	POCKETFUL OF MIRACLES	1970 TAMLA		US 306
RONNIE McNEIR	K (Z	ONE DOZEN ROSES	197 TAMLA		US 312
BOB SMITTY	VIBES(Z	FLYING HIGH TOGETHER	197 TAMLA		US 318
FRED SMITH	WIND (STZ	SMOKEY & THE MIRACLES	1971 TAMLA		
PATRICIA HENLEY	V (ZT	1957/1972	1973 TAMLA	UK STML11172	
CLAUDETTE ROBINSON	V (ZS	(**) RENAISSANCE	1973 TAMLA	UK STMA 8008	US 320
JESSIE RICHARDSON	V (Z	SMOKEY	1973 TAMLA	UK STMA 8010	
JAMES BRADFORD	PNO (Z	ANTHOLOGY	1974 TAMLA	UK STMG 8012	US 328
JAMES SLEDGE	CONGA(ZST	PURE SMOKEY	1974 TAMLA		793
PAULINHO DA COSTA	PERC (Z	(**) DO IT BABY	1974 TAMLA	UK STML11265	US 331
IVORY DAVIS	V (ZST	QUIET STORM	1974 TAMLA	UK STML11276	US 334
CAROLYN DENNIS	V (Z	(**) CITY OF ANGELS	1974 TAMLA	UK STML11288	US 337
MELBA JOYCE	V (T	LOVE MACHINE	1975 TAMLA	UK STML12010	US 339
MELBA BRADFORD	V (Z	(T)SMOKEYS FAMILY ROBINSON	1975 TAMLA	UK STML12020	
FREDRICK ROCHE	K (Z	(**) POWER OF THE MUSIC	1975 TAMLA	UK STML12021	US 341
MICHAEL JACOBSEN	CELLO(ZT	DEEP IN MY SOUL	1977 TAMLA	UK STML12038	
ROBERT ZIMMITTI	PERC (Z	BIG TIME(SOUNDTRACK)	1977 TAMLA	UK STML12055	US 350
CHERYL COOPER	V (ZS	(**) LOVE CRAZY	1977 TAMLA	UK STML12068	US 355
	(CONTINUED		1977 CBS	UK 81696	US 34450

[474]

SMOKEY ROBINSON & THE MIRACLES

PAT TALBERT	V	(S	(**) MIRACLES	1977	CBS		US 34910
STEVIE WONDER	PROD	(S	SMOKEY'S WORLD	1978	TAMLA	UK STML12076	
BRENDA SUTTON	V	(Z	(Z) LOVE BREEZE	1978	TAMLA	UK STML12081	US 359
RONNIE WHITE	V	(	SMOKIN' (LIVE)	1978	TAMLA		US 363
BOBBY ROGERS	V	(	WHERE THERES SMOKEY	1979	TAMLA	UK STML12115	US 366
PETE MOORE	V	(	TEARS OF A CLOWN	19	PICKWICK	US	3389
MARV TAMPLIN	G	(	FROM THE BEGINNING	19	BELL	US	1063
			TEARS OF A CLOWN	1979	MFP	UK 50422	
			(S) WARM THOUGHTS	1980	TAMLA	UK STML12134	US 367
			BEING WITH YOU	1981	MOTOWN	UK STML12151	US 375
			YES ITS YOU LADY	1981	TAMLA		US6001
			SHOP AROUND	19	LONDON		US 1295
			PURE SMOKEY	1982	TAMLA	UK STMS 5043	RI
			QUIET STORM	1982	TAMLA	UK STMS 504$	RI

TOM ROBINSON BAND

TOM ROBINSON	B V	(ALL	(A) POWER IN THE DARKNESS	1978	EMI EMC 3226 CAPITOL	US 11778	
DEREK QUINTON	PERC	(C	(A) POWER IN THE DARKNESS	1978	EMI EURO 06687		
DANNY KUSTOW	G V	(AB1	(B) TRB2	1979	EMI EMC 3296 HARVEST	US 11930	
STEVE B	G	(C	(B) TRB2	1979	EMI EURO 06977		
DOLPHIN TAYLOR	D V	(A1	(C) SECTOR 27	1980	FONTANA	6359 039	
JO BURT	B	(C	(C) SECTOR 27	1980	MERCURY	6359 039	
MARK AMBLER	K	(A	(1) MAY 1978				
NICK PLYTAS	K	(1	( ) TOM ROBINSON BAND	1982	FAME UK FA 3028		
IAN 'QUINCE' PARKER K V	(B	PRESTON HEYMAN	D V	(B	KASIM SULTON	V	(B	CAROL GRIMES	V	(B
BARRY ST JOHN	V	(B	NIAMH CHAMBERS	V	(B

VICKI SUE ROBINSON

VICKI SUE ROBINSON	V	(ABC	(A) NEVER GONNA LET YOU GO	1976	RCA	UK RS 1051 US	APLI 1256
			(B) VICKI SUE ROBINSON	1976	RCA	UK RS 1095 US	APLI 1829
			(C) HALF & HALF	1978	RCA	UK PL12294 US	APLI 2294

MAGGIE & TERRE ROCHE

MAGGIE ROCHE	V G	(A	(A) SEDUCTIVE REASONING	1975	CBS		US 33232
TERRE ROCHE	G V	(A					
BARRY BECKETT	K	(A	PETE CARR	G	(A	JOHNNY GIMBLE	FDL	(A	JOHN HALL	G	(A
ROGER HAWKINS	D	(A	DAVID HOOD	B	(A	JIMMY JOHNSON	G	(A	GEORGE MARGE	CLAR(A
JERRY MASTERS	B	(A	OAK RIDGE BOYS	V	(A	PAUL SIMON	G	(A

THE ROCHES

SUZZY ROCHE	G V	(AB	(A) THE ROCHES	1979	WB GER 56683	US 3298	
MAGGIE ROCHE	SYN G V	(AB	(B) NURDS	1980	WB UK K56855	US 3475	
TERRE ROCHE	G V	(AB					
ROBERT FRIPP	G	(A	TONY LEVIN	B	(A	JIM MAELEN	PERC (A	LARRY FAST	SYN	(A
JAY DEE DAUGHERTY	D	(A	FRED SMITH	B	(A	LINCOLN GOINES	B	(B	JON MATHIAS	B	(B
GABRIEL KATONA	SYN	(B	BOB CONTI	PERC (B	BOBBY GORDON	(B

ROCCO

RUSSELL DUNLOP	D	(A	(A) ROCCO	1976	20TH CENTURY	US	T505
TIM PARTRIDGE	B	(A					
LEO DE CASTRO	V	(A	HARRIS CAMPBELL	G V	(A	SUNIL DE SILVA	PERC (A	TONY ANSELL	K	(A
SPOONS BUCHANAN	SAX	(A	MICK KENNY	SYN	(A	MARK PUNCH	G	(A	RALPH WHITE	HRNS(A
TUI RICHARDS	G	(A					

ROCK'N'ROLL ALL STARS

		(A) RED CHINA ROCKS	1972 B+C		BCM 104

ROCK FOLLIES(TV SHOW)

JULIE COVINGTON	V	(AB	(A) ROCK FOLLIES	1976	ISLAND ILPS 9362 POLYDOR 2302054		
CHARLOTTE CORNWELL	V	(AB	(B) ROCK FOLLIES 77	1977	POLYDOR 2302072 GER 2344 067		
RULA LENSKA	V	(AB					
SUE JONES DAVIS	V	(B	RAY RUSSELL	G	(AB	ANDY MACKAY	SAX	(AB	TONY STEVENS	B	(AB
CHRIS PARREN	K	(B	PETER VAN HOOKE	D	(AB	BRIAN CHATTON	K	(A	ROBIN WILLIAMS	VLN(A
SADIE MACKENZIE	V	(A					

ROCK HOUSE

MARTIN STONE	G	(	(A) ROCK HOUSE (EP)		1979	LIMP	KOOL1
PETE SHELLEY	D	(					
KEITH TILLMAN	B	(	DAVID COXHILL	SAX	(	MICK O'NEAL	SAX	(

ROCK ROSE

CHRIS BARR	K V	(A	(A) ROCK ROSE	1979	CBS	US	35819
JACK D'AMORE	D	(A					
FRANK DEMME	B V	(A	CARL JOHNSON	G	(A			

ROCK WORKSHOP

HARRY BECKETT	HRNS	(AB	(A) ROCK WORKSHOP	1970	CBS	UK	64075
BUD PARKES	HRNS	(AB	(B) THE VERY LAST TIME	1971	CBS	UK	64394
TONY ROBERTS	WIND	(AB					
BOB DOWNES	WIND	(AB	DEREK WADSWORTH	TROM	(AB	ROBIN JONES	D	(A	BRIAN MILLER	K	(AB
PHIL WAINMAN	PERC	(B	ALAN RUSHTON	D	(AB	DARYL RUNSWICK	B	(AB	RAY RUSSELL	G	(AB
ALAN GREED	K V	(AB	GINGER HARPER	V	(B	ALEX HARVEY	V	(A	TONY UTER	PERC(B

ROCKET 88

ALEXIS KORNER	G V	(A	(A) ROCKET 88	1981²	ATLANTIC US SD19293 UK K50776		
JACK BRUCE	B	(A					
CHARLIE WATTS	D	(A	IAN STEWART	PNO	(A	BOB HALL	PNO	(A	DON WELLER	SAX	(A
GEORGE GREEN	PNO	(A	COLIN SMITH	TPT	(A	JOHN RICARD	TROM (A

ROCKETS (US)

DAVID GILBERT	V	(ABCDE	(A) LOVE TRANSFUSION	1977	RCA	US/UK	PL 12572
JIM McCARTY	G V	(ABCDE	(B) ROCKETS	1979	RSO US 3047	UK	2394 224
JOHN BADANJEK	D V	(ABCDE	(C) NO BALLADS	1980	RSO US 3071	UK	2394 250
DENNIS ROBBINS	G V	(ABCD	(D) BACK TALK	1981	ELEKTRA US 6E351 UK	K52309	
JOHN FRAGA	B	(AB	(E) ROCKET ROLL	1982	ELEKTRA US 60143		
DONNIE DACUS	PNO V(BCDE						
DAVID HOOD	B	(B	CHUCK LEAVELL	K	(BANITA POINTER	V	(C	RUTH POINTER	V(C
LEE MICHAELS	ORG	(C	DAN KRYLA	B	(C	BOBBY HARALSON	B	(DE	JACK DOUGLAS	PERC(D
JIMMY Z	HCA	(D					

```
R123A                           ROCKETS(60s)                                            R123A
    DANNY WHITTEN      G V  (A        (A) ROCKETS                    1968 WHITEWHALE   US    WWS7116
    LEON WHITSELL      G V  (A
    GEORGE WHITSELL    G    (A    RALPH MOLINA      D  (A  BILLY TALBOT    B   (A  BOBBY NOTKOFF    VLN (A
R123B                           ROCKETS (FRANCE)                                        R123B
    CHRISTIAN LEBARTZ  V    (B        (A) ROCKETS                    19   DORBY              DBR 20005
    ALAIN GROETZINGER  D    (B        (B) ON THE ROAD AGAIN          1978 DORBY 20014 IPG FR 170/008
    GERARD L'HER       B V  (B        (C) PLASTEROID                 19   ROCKLAND            RKL 20137
    ALAIN MARATRAT     G K V(B        (D) LIVE                       19   ROCKLAND            RKL 20197
    FABRICE QUAGLIOTTI K    (B        (E) GALAXY                     1980 ROCKLAND            RKL 20208
    ZEUS B HELD        V    (B
R124                            ROCKIN' BERRIES                                         R124
    ROY AUSTIN              (         IN TOWN                        1964 PICCADILLY          NPL 38013
    TERRY BOND             (*        LIFE IS JUST A BOWL OF BERRIES  1965 PICCADILLY          NPL 38022
    CHUCK BOTFIELD         (*        EP I DIDN'T MEAN TO HURT YOU    1964 PICCADILLY          NEP 34639
    CLIVE LEA             (         EP NEW FROM THE ROCKIN' BERRIES 1965 PICCADILLY          NEP 34043
    GEOFF TURTON           (      (*) BLACK GOLD                     1976 SATRIL             SATL 4002
    KEN RODWAY            (
    BOBBY THOMPSON         (* TERRY WEBSTER     G V  (* HENRY HADAWAY    PROD (*
R124A                  ROCKIN' DOPSIE & THE CAJUN TWISTERS                              R124A
    ROCKIN' DOPSIE RUBIN V ACC(ALL   (A) DOIN' THE ZYDECO           1976 SONET      UK   SNTF 718
    CHESTER ZENO      PERC (ABCD      (B) ZY DE BLUE                 1977 SONET      UK   SNTF 761
    MAJOR HANDY HARRIS G  (ABCD       (C) HOLD ON!                   1979 SONET      UK   SNTF 800
    AUGUST CHARLES     SAX (AB        (D) BIG BAD ZYDECO             1980 SONET      UK   SNTF 851
    JOSEPH EDWARDS     D   (ABC
    MORRIS FRANCES     B V (ABCD JOHN PARKER HART SAX (CD ALTON RUBIN    D   (D
R124C                  ROCKIN' LOUIE & THE MAMMA JAMMERS                                R124C
                                  (A) IT WILL STAND                 19   CHARLY           CR 30185
R124D                           ROCKIN' FOO                                             R124D
    WAYNE ERWIN        G   (A        (A) A ROCKIN' FOO              1971 HOBBIT           5001
    LESTER BROWN       D   (A
    MICHAEL RACOON     PNO (A
R124E              ROCKIN' JIMMY & THE BROTHERS OF THE NIGHT                            R124E
    'ROCKIN' JIM BYFIELD G V (A      (A) BY THE LIGHT OF THE MOON   1981 SONET       UK SNTF 857
    STEVE HICKERSON    G   (A
    CHUCK DEWALT       D   (A    GARY GILMORE      B   (A  WALT RICHMOND   K  (A  DEBBIE CAMPBELL  V (A
    JIM SWENEY         V   (A
R124F                           ROCKSPUR                                                R124F
    RICH TANNUM        B V (A        (A) ROCKSPUR                   1978 DJM             15
    MICHAEL FESTA G STEEL K(AB       (B) GETTING OFF                1979 DJM  GER   64223
    MICK MORAN         G V K(AB
    PETER BRILLON      D   (AB  GREG HOLLISTER     B V (B
R125                            JESS RODEN                                              R125
    JESS RODEN         V   (ALL      (A) JESS RODEN                 1974 ISLAND      UK  ILPS 9286
    ALLEN TOUSSAINT    PNO (A        (B) YOU CAN KEEP YOUR HAT ON   1976 ISLAND      UK  ILPS 9349
    ART NEVILLE        ORG (A        (C) PLAY IT DIRTY PLAY IT CLASS 1977 ISLAND     UK  ILPS 9442
    JOESEPH MODELISTE  D   (A        (D) BLOWIN'                    1977 ISLAND      UK  ILPS 9496
    GEORGE PORTER      B   (A        (E) PLAYER NOT THE GAME        1977 ISLAND      UK  ILPS 9506
    LEO NOCENTELLI     G   (A        (F) STONECHASER                1980 ISLAND      UK  ILPS 9531
    NEW ORLEANS HRNS       (A        (EP) LIVE                      1976 ISLAND      UK  IEP    3
    SIMON KIRKE        D   (A
    JOHN BUNDRICK      K   (A    RICHARD BAILEY    D  (A  MICK FEAT       B  (A  ROY DAVIES      K (A
    GEORGE LEE         SAX (A    ALLAN SHARP  CONGA   (A  STEVE GREGORY   FLT (A RICHARD DIGA SMITH K(A
    REBOP KWAKU BAAH   PERC (A   MICK WEAVER      K   (A  PAT DONALDSON   B  (A  STEVE WEBB     G V(ABCD
    BRUCE ROBERTS      G V (BCD CHRIS GOWER TROM   (BCD RONNIE TAYLOR   SAX (BCD JOHN CARTWRIGHT B G (BCDF
    PETE HUNT          D   (BCD BILLY LIVSEY    K   (BCD LEON PENDARVIS  K  (EF ROB MOUNSEY     K  (EF
    SHIRLEY SCOTT      K   (E    ANTHONY JACKSON  B   (EF FRANCISCO CENTENO B (E MILT HINTON    B  (E
    CLIFFORD MORRIS    G   (EF   JOHN TROPEA      G   (E  LANCE QUINN     G  (E  JEFF MIRONOV    G  (EF
    FRANKLIN MICARE    G   (E    GARY MURE        D   (E  BUDDY WILLIAMS  D  (E  ERROL BENNETT  PERC(EF
    RUBENS BASSINI     PERC (E   DAVID CAREY   VIBES(E  SCOTT HAMILTON  SAX (E  BARRY ROGERS   HRNS(F
    MICHAEL LEE GRAY   V   (E    DOLORES HALL     V   (E  BENNY DIGGS     V  (E  ARNOLD McCULLER V  (E
    LOU MARINI         WIND (E   RAYMOND BECKENSTEIN WIND(EF GEORGE MARGE  HRNS (E  ALAN RUBIN   HRNS(E
    JON FADDIS         HRNS (E   VIRGIL JONES   HRNS (EF BURT COLLINS  HRNS (E  MICHAEL LAWRENCE HRNS(E
    VICTOR PAZ         HRNS (E   ALAN RAPH       TROM (EF TOM MALONE    TROM (E  WAYNE ANDRE    TROM(EF
    HOWARD JOHNSON     WIND (EF  STRING SECTION       (EF PAT REBILLOT   K  (E  GEORGE T CLINTON K (F
    JEFF LAYTON        G   (F    DAVE TAYLOR    HRNS (F  DAVID LANDALL   G  (F  JAKI WHITREN    V  (F
    JANICE PENDARVIS   V   (F    LUTHER VANDROSS  V   (F  JOSHIE ARMSTEAD V  (F  PAT RYAN       SAX (F
    DAVE TOFANI        WIND (F    HAROLD VICK    WIND (FE ALEX FOSTER   WIND (F  BILLY SLAPIN   WIND(F
    ROMEO PENQUE       WIND (F    CHRIS PARKER     D   (F  RICHARD CROOKS D  (F  PETER BUNETTA   D  (F
    NEIL BUNETTA       D   (F    RICK CHUDAKOFF   B   (F  ARNO LUCAS    PERC(F  CHANDRA ARMSTEAD V  (F
    ZACHARY SANDERS    V   (F    BARBARA MASSEY   V   (F  LEE GOODALL   CLAR(F  LEW SOLOFF   HRNS  (F
    ALLAN TOUSSAINT    PROD (A   CHRIS BLACKWELL  PROD (A
R125A                           THE RODS                                               R125A
    DAVID FEINSREIN    G V (AB        (A) THE RODS                  1981 ARISTA UK SPART1182  US 9558
    GARRY BORDONARO    B V (AB        (B) WILD DOGS                 1982 ARISTA UK SPART1196
    CARL CANEDY        D   (AB

                                       [476]
```

TOMMY ROE	G V	(ALL	SHEILA	1963	ABC		US	ABC432
JACK SARGENT	D	(*	SOMETHING FOR EVERYBODY	1963	ABC		US	ABC467
HAL BLAINE	D	(*	SWEET PEA	1966	ABC		US	ABC575
JOE OSBORN	B	(*	ITS NOW A WINTERS DAY	196	ABC		US	ABC594
KEITH ALLISON	B	(*	PHANTASY	1967	ABC		US	ABC610
RICHARD LAWS	G	(*	DIZZY	196	ABC		US	ABC683
MAXINE WILLARD	V	(*	12 IN A ROE	1970	ABC		US	ABC700
BEN BENAY	G	(*	WE CAN MAKE MUSIC	1970	ABC		US	ABC714
LARRY KNECHTEL	K	(*	GREATEST HITS	1970	STATESIDE		UK	SSL10296
DON RANDI	PNO	(*	(*) BEGINNINGS	1971	ABC			ABC732
DAVE BOONE	FDL	(*	16 GREATEST HITS	1971	ABC	UK ABCL5157	US	ABC762
PLAS JOHNSON	SAX	(*	ENERGY	1976	MONUMENT	US 34182		MG 7604
GINGER BLAKE	V	(*	FULL BLOOM	1978	MONUMENT		US	MG 7614
JULIA TILLMAN	V	(*						

HANS JOACHIM ROEDELIUS	K SYN V(ALL	(A) DURCH DIE WUSTE	1978	SKY			SKY014
SCHAGZERIG GREENE	CELLO(B	(B) JARDIN AU FOU	1979	BARCLAY			90291
CONRAD PLANK	PERC G(CA	(C) SELBSTPORTRAIT	1979	SKY	GER		028
JASO CHRISTO	G B (CA	(D) SELBSTPORTRAIT II	1980	SKY	GER		SKY040
DIETER MOEBIUS	SYN (CA	(E) SELBSTPORTRAIT III	1980	SKY	GER		SKY044
WOLFGANG DIUMSHEDE	FLT (B	(F) LUSTWANDEL	1981	SKY			SKY058
ULRIKE LAI	CELLO (B	(G) WENN DER SUDWIND WEHT	1981	SKY	GER		SKY064
HANS BRANDEIS	G (B	(H) OFFENE TUREN	1982	SKY	GER		SKY072

KENNY ROGERS	V	(ALL	(A) ROLLIN	196	JOLLY ROGER	US	5003
TERRY WILLIAMS	G	(	(B) MONUMENTAL	196	JOLLY ROGER	US	5004
MIKE SETTLE	G	(	(C) THE FIRST EDITION	1968	REPRISE US	6276
THELMA CAMACHO	V	(	(D) THE SECOND EDITION	1969	REPRISE US	6328
MARY ARNOLD	V	(	(E) RUBY DONT TAKE YOUR LOVE TO TOWN	196	REPRISE US	6352	UK K44075
KIM VASSY	G B K(	(F) SOMETHINGS BURNIN'	1979	REPRISE US	6385
MICKEY JONES	D	(	(G) TELL IT ALL BROTHER	1972	REPRISE US 6414
BOB MOORE	B	MQ	(H) BALLAD OF CALICO	1972	REPRISE US	6426
DENNIS WILSON	B V	(MR	(I) TRANSITION	1972	REPRISE US	2039
TOMMY ALLSUP	B	(M	(J) DAY TIME FRIENDS	1977	UA		UK UAG 30256
BILLY SANFORD	G	(MQR	(K) EVERYTIME 2 FOOLS COLLIDE	1978	UA		UK UAS 30170
RAY EDENTON	G	(MQ	(L) LOVE OR SOMETHING LIKE IT	1978	UA		UK UAG 30194
JIMMY CAPPS	G	(MQ	(M) THE GAMBLER	1978	UA	US 934	UK UAG 30220
RANDY DORMAN	G V	(MQR	(N) SINGLES ALBUM	1979	UA		UK UAK 30263
JERRY SHOOK	G	(MQ	(O) CLASSICS	1979	UA		UK UAG 30235
RICK HARPER	G	(MQ	(P) SHINE ON	1980	RADAR		UK K24037
TONY JOE WHITE	G	(M	(Q) KENNY	1980	UA	US 979	UK UAG 30273
REGGIE YOUNG	G	(MQ	(R) GIDEON	1980	UA	US 1035	UK UAK 30303
HARGUS ROBBINS	K	(MQ	(S) LOVE LIFTED ME	1980	LIBERTY		UK LBR 1015
GENE GOLDEN	K V	(MQR	(T) RUBY	1981	MFP		UK	50514
STEVE GLASSMEYER	K SAX V(MQR	(U) SHARE YOUR LOVE	1981	LIBERTY		UK	30339
THOMAS CAIN	K	(M	(V) LADY	1981	LIBERTY		UK LBG 30334
JERRY CARRIGAN	D	(MQR					

BOBBY DANIELS	D V	(MQR	BYRON METCALF	D	(M	EDDY ANDERSON	D	(M	PETE DRAKE	STEEL(M
EDGAR STRUBLE	SYN V(M	JORDONAIRES	V	(M	MICKEY NEWBURY	V	(M	BILL MEDLEY	V (M
CHUCK JACOBS	B	(QR	JOE OSBORNE	B	(Q	DAVID BRIGGS	K	(Q	LARRY KEITH	K (Q
CHUCK COCHRAN	K	(Q	SHANE KEISTER	K	(Q	BOBBY WOOD	K	(Q	DAVE KIRBY G	(Q
JOHNNY CHRISTOPHER	G	(Q	BOBBY THOMPSON	BAN	(Q	FARRELL MORRIS	PERC	(Q	LEA JANE BERINATI	V(QR
DONNA McELROY	V	(Q	YVONNE HODGES	V	(Q	BUZZ CASON	V	(QR	TOM BRANNON	V
BERGEN WHITE	V	(Q	DON GANT	V	(Q	KIM CARNES	V	(RV	WILLIAM CUOMO	K (R
LARRY BUTLER	K	(R	PATRICK HARPER	V	(R	DAVID ELLINGTON	V	(R	WENDY SUITS	V (R
DOTTIE WEST	V	(KOV								

R128

JIMMY ROGERS	G V	(ABCD	(A) THATS ALL RIGHT	1974	BLACK & BLUE		33504
FRED BELOW	D	(BCE	(B) CHICAGO BOUND	19	CHESS		407
WILLIE MABRON	PNO	(A	(C) BLUESMASTERS	1976	CHESS		2ACMB207
DAVE MYERS	B	(AE	(D) & LEFT HAND FRANK	1979	JSP	1008
LOUIS MYERS	G	(AE	(E) GOLD TAILED BIRD	19		
FREDDIE KING	G	(E				
LEFT HAND FRANK	G V	(D	BIG CRAWFORD	B	(D	BOB BRUNNING	B	(D	RAY WESTON	D (D
ERNEST COTTON	SAX	(D	EDDIE WARE	PNO	(BC	WALTER HORTON	HCA	(B	LITTLE WALTER	HCA(BC
ELGIN EVANS	D	(BC	MUDDY WATERS	G	(BC	BOB WOODFORK	G	(C	JOHNNY JONES	PNO(C
WILLIE DIXON	B	(BC	A J GLADNEY	D	(C	J T BROWN	SAX	(BC	HENRY GRAY	PNO(BC
OTIS SPANN	PNO	(BC	JOE YOUNG	G	(C	WAYNE BENNETT	G	(C	S P LEARY	D (C
LUTHER TUCKER	G	(C	FRED ROBINSON	G	(C	GEORGE HUNTER	D	(C	BOB REED	PNO (E

R129

TREVOR SPENCER	D	(B	(A) FALLEN ANGEL	1975	EPIC	UK	69235
BARRY MORGAN	D	(ABC	(B) LET IT GO	1977	EPIC	UK	81987
ALAN TARNEY	B	(B	(C) WOULD YOU LET YOUR DAUGHTER	1979	ARIOLA		ARL 5028
LES HURDLE	B	(ABC						
J W HODGKINSON	V	(ABC	GUY FLETCHER	K V	(ABC	TERRY BRITTEN	G	(B	RITCHIE BULL	BANJO(B
AL HODGE	G	(AC	FRANK RICOTTI	PERC	(A	JIMMY JEWELL	SAX	(C	B J COLE	STEEL(AC

R129A

CHRIS ROHMANN	(	(A) THE MAN I AM TODAY	1974	RCA	UK	SF 8364

R129B

SHEL SHAPIRO	(A	(A) THESE WERE THE ROKES	1977	RCA	IT	33037
MIKE ROGERS	(					
BOBBY POWELL	(	JOHNNY CHARLTON	(				

R130

CLEVELAND WALKER	V	(A	(A) ROKOTTO	1977	STATE		ETAT15
SISTER B	V	(A					
STEWART GARDEN	K	(A	HOWARD LLOYD WISDON B	(A	DEREK HENDERSON	G	(A	HUGH PAUL	V (A
HOWARD McLEOD	D	(A					

[477]

ROLL UPS

```
LEA HART JR        G V (A                  (A) LOVE DIVE FOR HIGH BALLS    197 BRIDGEHOUSE          BHLP 004
PAUL AIRE          K V (A
JEFF PETERS        B V (A    RICKY ANDREO      D  (A
```

ROLLERCOASTER

```
RAY WARLEIGH       SAX (A                   (A) WONDERIN'                  1981 CALIBRE        UK  CABLP1006
DICK MORRISSEY     SAX (A
DEREK WATKINS      TPT (A    CHRIS PYNE        TROM (A   ALAN PARKER    G  (A   MIKE PYNE   PNO (A
RON MATTHEWSON     B   (A    BARRY MORGAN      D   (A   KARL JENKINS   K  (A   MIKE RATLEDGE K (A
```

ROLLING STONES

```
MICK JAGGER        G K V(ALL              (A) THE ROLLING STONES       1964 DECCA      UK LK4605 US LONDON  PS375
KEITH RICHARD      G V K(ALL              (A) THE ROLLING STONES       196  DECCA GER 16300 RI 17005 RI70 621695
                                          (B) THE ROLLING STONES 2     1965 DECCA      UK SLK4661 NOVA GER 621393
BRIAN JONES G V(ABCDEFGHJKLMRN            (C) 12X5                     1965            US LONDON  PS402
IAN STEWART        PNO(ABGEPQUZ,JJ,LL     (D) THE ROLLING STONES NOW   1965            US LONDON  PS420
MICK AVORY         D   (                  (E) OUT OF OUR HEADS         1965 DECCA      UK SKL4733 US LONDON  PS429
DICK TAYLOR        G B (                  (F) DECEMBERS CHILDREN       1965            US LONDON  PS451
CHARLIE WATTS      D   (ALL               (G) AFTERMATH                1966 DECCA      UK SKL4786 US LONDON  PS476
BILL WYMAN  V B SYN    (ALL               (H) HIGHTIDE & GREEN GRASS   1966 DECCA      UK TXA 101 US LONDON  NPS 1
RON WOOD           G B V(LL,MM,NN,OO,     (I) GOT LIVE IF YOU WANT IT  1967 LONDON US SL226/7 DECCA UK SLK 4838
MICK TAYLOR        G V  (QUZYN            (J) BETWEEN THE BUTTONS      1967 DECCA      UK SKL4852 US LONDON  PS499
TONY CHAPMAN       D   (                  (K) FLOWERS                  1967 DECCA SKL16487 US LONDONPS509
AL KOOPER          K   (N                 (K) FLOWERS                  19   NOVA    RI 621407
JIM PRICE          HRNS (QU               (L) SATANIC MAJESTIES REQUEST 1967 DECCA    UK TKS 103 US LONDON  NPS 2
BOBBY KEYS         HRNS (QUN,LL,          (M) BEGGARS BANQUET          1968 DECCA      UK SKL4955 US LONDON  PS539
NICKY HOPKINS      K   (LMMQUZ,HH,LL       (N) LET IT BLEED            1969 DECCA      UK SKL5025 US LONDON  NPS 4
LEON RUSSELL       PNO (N                 (N) LET IT BLEED             1970 NONA       GER 621412
ILLY PRESTON       K   (QUZ,HH,JJ         (O) THROUGH THE PAST DARKLY  1969 DECCA      UK SKL5019 US LONDON  NPS 3
RY COODER          G MAND(QN              (P) GET YER YA YAS OUT       1970 DECCA      UK SKL5065 US LONDON  NPS 5
OLLIE BROWN        PERC (HH,JJ,           (Q) STICKY FINGERS          1971 ROLLING STONE              COC 59100
WAYNE PERKINS      G   (HH,               (R) STONE AGE               1971 DECCA      UK SKL5084
HARVEY MANDEL      G   (HH,               (S) GIMME SHELTER           1971 DECCA      UK SKL5101
PAUL BUCKMASTER        (Q                 (T) MILESTONES              1971 DECCA      UK SKL5098
JACK NITZCHE       K   (EGQB              (U) EXILE ON MAIN STREET    1972 ROLLING STONE UK  69100  US           2900
J W ALEXANDER      PERC (E                (V) ROCK'N'ROLLIN' STONES   1972 DECCA      UK SKL5149
JIM DICKINSON      PNO (Q                 (W) HOT ROCKS 1964/71       1972            US LONDON  606/7
JIMMY MILLER       PERC (QUN              (X) MORE HOT ROCKS          1972            US LONDON  626/7
ROCKY DZIDZORNU    PERC (QN               (Y) GOATS HEAD SOUP         1973 ROLLING STONE    59101 US          39106
CLYDIE KING        V   (U                 (Z) ITS ONLY ROCK'N'ROLL    1974 ROLLING STONE UK  59103  US     RS 79101
VANETTA FIELDS     V   (U                 (AA) NO STONE UNTURNED      1973 DECCA      UK SKL5173
JESSE KIRKLAND     V   (U                 (BB) ROLLED GOLD           1975 DECCA  UK ROST 1/2 GER NOVA  628356
TAMMY LYNN         V   (U                 (CC) METAMORPHOSIS         1975 DECCA      UK SKL5212 US ABCKO    ANA 1
SHIRLEY GOODMAN    V   (U                 (CC) METAMORPHOSIS         1975            CAN LONDON PS 573
DR JOHN            V   (U                 (DD) MADE IN THE SHADE     1975 ROLLING STONE UK 59104 US         79102
JOE GREEN          V   (U                 (EE) STONE AGE/GOT LIVE    1975 TELDEC EURO SD3024   GER 6645 400
KATHI McDONALD     V   (U                 (FF) AROUND & AROUND       197  DECCA  UK SLK6315 GER 16315 RI70 621392
BILL PLUMMER       B   (U                 (  ) LIVE                  197  LONDON     JAPAN           SL226/7
AL PERKINS         STEEL(U                (HH) BLACK & BLUE          1976 ROLLING STONE UK  59106 US         79104
RAY COOPER         PERC (Z                (JJ) LOVE YOU LIVE         1977 ROLLING STONE UK  89101 US         2 9001
BLUE MAGIC         V   (Z                 (KK) SOME GIRLS            1978 ROLLING STONE UK/US CUN 39108
MERRY CLAYTON      V   (N                 (LL) EMOTIONAL RESCUE      1979 ROLLING STONE UK CUN 39111
NANNETTE NEWMAN    V   (N                 (MM) TATTOO YOU            1981 ROLLING STONE UK CUN39114 US 16052
MADELINE BELL      V   (N                 (MM) TATTOO YOU            1981 ROLLING STONE GER 64553
DORIS TROY         V   (N                 (NN) STILL LIFE            1982 ROLLING STONE UK CUN 39115
CHARLIE JOLLY      TABLA(Z                (  ) ROLLING STONES SOLID ROCK 19    DECCA   UK  TAB1
MAX ROMEO          V   (LL                (  ) SLOW ROLLERS          1981 DECCA  UK TAB 30
ED LEACH           PERC (Z                (  ) ROLLING STONES (PROFILE) 19  TELDEC     GERM            624001
KENNY JONES        D   (Z                 (  ) DECEMBERS CHILDREN    1981 DECCA  24314
SUGAR BLUE         HCA (KK,               (  ) SUCKING IN THE SEVENTIES 1981 ROLLING STONES UK 39112 US    16028
MICHAEL SHRIEVE    PERC (LL               (  ) 30 GREAT HITS  (DBL)  1970 ABKCO  IT 3042
GENE PITNEY        V   (A                 (  ) GET STONED            1977 ARCADE UK ADE 32
PHIL SPECTOR       PERC (A                (  ) IN CONCERT            1982 POLYGRAM IMP  6640 037
WILLY WEEKS        B   (Z                 (EP) ROLLING STONES        1964 DECCA   UK DFE 8560
IAN MACLAGAN       K   (KK,               (EP) 5X5                   1964 DECCA   UK DFE 8590
MEL COLLINS        SAX (KK,               (EP) GOT LIVE IF YOU WANT  1965 DECCA   UK DFE 8620
```

ROMANTICS

```
MIKE SKILL         G V (AB                (A) ROMANTICS             1980 EPIC US 36273    UK    84095
WALLY PALMAR       G V (ABC               (B) NATIONAL BREAKOUT     1980 EPIC US 36881    UK    84176
RICH COLE          B V (ABC               (C) STRCTLY PERSONAL      1981 EPIC           UK    85721
JIMMY MARINOS      D V (ABC
PETE SOLLEY        PROD (AB MIKE STONE      PROD (C   COZ CANTHER   G  (C
```

MAX ROMEO

```
MAX ROMEO          V   (ALL               (A) REVELATION TIME       1975 SOUNDTRAC       TSL 1000
BARRY LLEWELLYN    V   (B                 (B) WAR IN A BABYLON      1976 ISLAND      UK  ILPS 9392
EARL MORGAN        V   (B                 (C) RONDOS                19   KING KONG       KANT1
MARCIA GRIFFITHS   V   (B                 (D) OPEN THE IRON GATES   1978 UA          US   LA 803
CYNTHIA SCOLAS     V   (B                 (E) RECONSTRUCTION        1978 MANGO       UK  MLPS 9503
BORIS GARDNER      B   (E
MICKY RICHARDS     D   (E    KEITH STERLING   PNO (E   EARL LINDO   K CLAR(E   DAVID MADDEN   TPT (E
BOBBY ELLIS        HRNS (E   GLEN DA COSTA    SAX (E   VIN GORDON   TROM (E   EARL SMITH     G   (E
ERNIE RANGLIN      G   (E    SHEENA            V   (E   JIMMY RILEY  V   (E   RICKY STORME   V   (E
```

ROMEO VOID

```
DEBORA JYALL       V   (A                 (A) ITSACONDITION         1981 415      US  0004
PETER WOODS        G   (A
JOHN STENCH        D   (A    BEN BOSSI      SAX (A   FRANK ZINCAVAGE  B  (A
```

ROMEO'S

```
                   ROCK'N'ROLL & LOVE & DEATH      1980 CBS      US    36544
```

RONETTES

```
VERONICA BENNETT(SPECTOR) V(ALL      (A) TODAYS HITS              1963 PHILLES        US      4004
ESTELLE BENNETT    V    (            (B) CHRISTMAS GIFT           1963 PHILLES US 4005 UK LONDON HAU8141
NEDRA TALLEY       V    (            (C) FABULOUS RONETTES        1964 PHILLES US 4006 UK LONDON HAU8212
CAROL KAYE         B    (            (D) THE RONETTES             1965 COLPIX   US 486
HAL BLAINE         D    (            (E) CHA CHA CHA              1967 ROPER    US 1009
DENISE EDWARDS     V    (            (F) SING THEIR GREATEST HITS 1975 PHIL SPECTOR    UK    2307 003
LEON RUSSELL       K    (
CHIP FIELDS        V    (
```

RONIN

```
WADDY WACHTEL      G    (A           (A) RONIN                    1980 MERCURY      US   1 3832
RICK MAROTTA       D    (A
DAN DUGMORE        G    (A  STANLEY SHELDON   B V  (A  DON GROLNICK    K   (A
```

MICK RONSON

```
MICK RONSON        G V K(AB          (A) SLAUGHTER ON THE TENTH AVENUE 1974 RCA         APLI0353
IAN HUNTER         G V  (            (B) PLAY DONT WORRY          1975 RCA              APLI0681
TREVOR BOLDER      B HRN(AB
DAVID HENTSCHEL    K    (A  AYNSLEY DUNBAR   D   (AB  MIKE GARSON     K   (AB  MARGARET RONSON  V (A
BEVERLY BAXTER     V    (B  RITCHIE DHARMA   D   (B   VICKY BROWN     V   (B   TONY NEWMAN      D (B
PAUL FRANCIS       D    (B
```

LINDA RONSTADT

```
LINDA RONSTADT     V    (ALL         (A) HAND SOWN HOME GROWN     1969 CAPITOL(RI 1975)     ST208
DAN DUGMORE        G    (GJKOPHQ      (B) SILK PURSE              1970 CAPITOL             ST407
WADDY WACHTEL      G V  (JKOPHQ       (C) LINDA RONSTADT          1972 CAPITOL ST635 RI GREENLIGHT 2013
KENNY EDWARDS      B V  (FGJKIOP HQ   (D) DONT CRY NOW            1974 ASYLUM UK SYL9012   US SD5064
RICK MAROTTA       D    (JOPQ         (D) DONT CRY NOW            1974 ASYLUM UK K43002 RI
DON GROLNICK       K    (JKOP         (E) DIFFERENT DRUM          1974 CAPITOL           US 11269
BRIAN AHERN        PROD (Q            (E) DIFFERENT DRUM          1975 CAPITOLUK VMP1010 RI CAPS 1004
PETER ASHER G V PERC (FGJKOPHQ        (F) HEART LIKE A WHEEL      1974 CAPITOL              11358
CHARLES VEAL       VLN  (JH           (G) PRISONER IN DISGUISE    1975 ASYLUM  UK SYL8761  US 7E1045
DAVID CAMPBELL     VLA  (FJH          (G) PRISONER IN DISGUISE    1975 ASYLUM  UK K53015  RI
DENNIS KARMAZYN    CELLO(FJHQ         (H) HASTEN DOWN THE WIND    1976 ASYLUM  UK K53045  US 7E1072
RICHARD FEVES      B    (FJH          (I) GREATEST HITS           1976 ASYLUM  UK K53055  US 6E 106
MIKE AULDRIDGE     G    (JP           (J) SIMPLE DREAM            1977 ASYLUM  UK K53065  US 6E 104
DOLLY PARTON       V    (JQ           (K) LIVING IN THE USA       1978 ASYLUM  UK K53085  US 6E 155
STEVE FORMAN       PERC (JOP          (L) RETROSPECTIVE           1977 CAPITOL UK CAPSP102 US 11629
DON HENLEY         V D  (CFJOH        (M) THE SOUTHERN BELLE      1978 EMI IMP            05085068
LARRY HAGLER       V    (JO           (N) STONE PONEYS FEATURING L.RONSTADT 1975 CAPITOL  11383
JOHN DAVID SOUTHER V    (CFGIJQ       (O) GREATEST HITS VOL 2     1980 ASYLUM  UK K52255  US 5E 516
HERB PEDERSEN      V    (FCGJIH       (P) MAD LOVE                1980 ASYLUM  UK K52210  US    510
EDIE LEHMANN       V    (Q            (Q) GET CLOSER              1982 ASYLUM              960185
DAVID SANBORN      SAX  (KO
ANDREW GOLD   K G V(FGHIKOPQ RUSS KUNKEL      D(FGHKOPQ DAVID LINDLEY    FDL  (FG  JIM CONNOR      HCA (G
LOWELL GEORGE      G    (G  NIGEL OLSSON      D  (G   DANNY KORTCHMAR  G   (GOPQ DAVID KEMPER   D  (GI
DAN FRANCISCO      G    (G  EMMYLOU HARRIS    V  (FGQ GLEN D HARDIN   PNO  (G   DAVID GRISMAN  MAND(GQ
JAMES TAYLOR       G    (GQ MARIA MULDAUR     V  (FG  EDDIE BLACK     G    (FG  PAT HENDERSON  V (GHKO
JULIA TILLMAN      V    (G  MAXINE WILLARD    V  (G   MIKE MAINIERI   VIBES(K   SHIRLEY MATTHEWS V(FIKOH
JIM GILSTRAP       V    (KOH JOHN LEHMAN      V  (KO  DAVID LASLEY    V    (K   ARNOLD McCULLER  V (K
CLYDIE KING        V    (FIH SNEAKY PETE      STEEL(FIC JIMMY FADDEN  HRNS (CFI WENDY WALDMAN   V (FIOH
CHRIS ETHRIDGE     B    (FI BOB WARFORD       G  (F   DENNIS ST JOHN  D    (F   EMORY GORDY     B  (F
CISSY HOUSTON      V    (F  JOYCE NESBITT     V  (F   LLOYD MYERS     V    (F   PAUL CRAFT      G  (F
JOHN STARLING      G    (F  TOM GUIDERA       B  (F   DANNY PENDLETON STEEL(F   JOHN BOYLAN    G  (CFI
GLENN FREY         G    (CF TIM SCHMIT        B  (F   JIM GORDON      D    (I   JIMMY GORDON   HRNS(I/
BERNIE LEADON      G    (IC AL CAIOLA         G  (I   MARK GOLDENBERG G    (OP  BOB GLAUB      B  (OPQ
BILL PAYNE         K    (OPQ ROSEMARY BUTLER  V  (OPQ NICOLETTE LARSON V   (OP  KARLA BONOFF   V  (HO
PETER BERNSTEIN    G    (P  MICHAEL BODDICKER SYN (P  MIKE BOWDEN     B    (CI  RICHARD BOWDEN G  (CI
GIB GUILBEAU       FDL V(CI TIPPY ARMSTRONG   G  (C   WELDON MYRICK   STEEL(C   BARRY BECKETT  K  (C
DAVID HOOD         B    (C  DEAN WEBB         MAND(C   JOHN MARTIN     G V  (C   RANDY MEISNER  B V(C
ROGER HAWKINS      D    (C  MERRY CLAYTON     V  (C   DIANNE DAVIDSON V    (C   MISS ONA       V  (C
JIM HORN           SAX  (C  WESLEY PRITCHETT  B  (C   BUDDY EMMONS    STEEL(C   LYLE RITZ      B  (C
ANDY JOHNSON       G    (I  PETE WADE         G  (I   SPOONER OLDHAM  PNO(I     NORBERT PUTNAM B  (IB
MICKY McGEE        D    (I  MARTI McCALL      V  (I   MICHAEL BOTTS   D    (IH  GAIL MARTIN    TROM(I
DON RANDI          K    (I  NINO TEMPO        SAX (I   MACK JOHNSON    TPT  (I   DARRELL LEONARD TPT(I
BUDDY SPICHER  BAN FDL (I   GINGER HOLLADAY   V  (I   MARY HOLLADAY   V    (I   JERRY PETERSON SAX (Q
DEBBIE PEARL       V    (Q  PATTI AUSTIN      V  (Q   LINDSEY BUCKINGHAM ACC (Q RICK SHLOSSER  D  (Q
KEN YERKE          VLA  (H  RON HICKLAND      V  (H   CLARENCE McDONALD K   (H  BECCI LOUIS    V  (H
BILL THEDFORD      V    (H  GERRY GARRETT     V  (H   PAUL POLENICK   VLA  (H   BEECHWOOD RANGERS (B
ELLIOTT MAZER      (B       ADAM MITCHELL     (B      KEN BUTTREY     D    (B
```

ROOGALATOR

```
DANNY ADLER        G    (A1          (A) PLAY IT BY EAR           1977 DO IT          UK       RIDE 1
NICK PLYTAS        K    (A           (1) 1978
JUSTIN HILDRETH    D    (A1
JULIAN SCOTT       B    (A1
```

ROOMFUL OF BLUES

```
GERG PICCOLO       SAX  (            (A) ROOMFUL OF BLUES         1979 ISLAND              9474
DOUG JAMES         SAX  (            (B) LETS HAVE A PARTY        1980 ANTILLES     US     7071
RICH LATAILLE      SAX  (            (C) HOT LITTLE MAMA          1981 ACE       UK CH39
```

ROOT BOY SLIM & THE SEX CHANGE BAND

```
ROOT BOY SLIM       V(AB            (A) ROOT BOY SLIM & THE SEX CHANGE BAND 1978 WB US 3160 ILLEGAL 79  003
(FOSTER MACKENZIE III)              (B) ZOOM                     1979 ILLEGAL      UK       004
RATTLESNAKE RATTLES B(AB
(BOB GREENLEE)
COSMO GREEK(WALT ANDREWS G(A  ERNIE E LOCKEROOM   G(A  RON HOLLOWAY    SAX (A  TOMMY RUGER     D  (A
MICKI LEE JONNIE   V    (A  CHERIE GRASSO     V  (A  FLACO FALCON    PERC (A KATHE'SPECIAL K'RUSSELL V(A
WINSTON 'SPOTS'KELLY K(A
```

BIFF ROSE

```
BIFF ROSE          V K  (A           (A) CHILDREN OF LIGHT       1968 TETRAGRAMMATON US T116
VAN DYKE PARKS     SYN  (A
NICK WOODS         SYN  (A  BENNY BARTH       D   (A
```

```
R139B                              ROSE                                              R139B
      DAVID ROSE        V VLN    (A          (A) ROSE              1979 RCA   US   XL17749
      SERJE PERATHONER  K SYN(A
      STEVE SHEHAN      PERC (A  CLAUDE SALMIERI  D    (A
R139C                              ROSE                                              R139C
      GARY PALONNE      B V (AB           (A) TASTE OF NEPTUNE     1977 POLYDOR        2424 135
      RON GLATLEY       K V (AB           (B) JUDGEMENT DAY        1977 POLYDOR        2424 168
      JAMES FOX         D V (AB
      BRIAN ALLEN       G V (AB
R140                             TIM ROSE                                            R140
      TIM ROSE          V   (ALL          (A) TIM ROSE                  1967   CBS    UK 63168  US  9577
      BERNARD PURDIE    D   (A            (B) THROUGH ROSE COLOURED SPECS 1969 CBS    UK 63636  US  9772
      FELIX PAPPALARDI  B   (A            (C) LOVE A KIND OF HATE STORY 1970  CAPITOL           US   673
      JAY BERLINER      G   (A            (D) TIM ROSE                  1972   PLAYBOY           US   101
      HUGH McCRACKEN    G   (A            (E) TIM ROSE                  1974   DAWN   UK DNLS3062
      GARY WRIGHT       K   (E            (F) THE MUSICIAN              1975   ATLANTIC UK K50183
      BRYSON GRAHAM     D   (E            (G) RETROSPECTIVE             1977   CAPITOL
      ARCHIE LEGGETT    B   (E
      MICK JONES        G   (     RICHARD HUSSAN   B   (A    ART BUTLER        K  (A   JIM FISCHOFF    PERC(A
      CHARLES SMALLS    PNO (A    PATTI BROWN      K   (A    CHUCK RAINEY      B  (A   ERNEST HAYES    K  (A
      RICHARD KILLGROVE D   (A    ERIC WEISSBERG   B   (A    DAVE CHARLES      D  (E   TOMMY EYRE      K  (E
      B J COLE          STEEL(E   BOBBY JONES     PERC (A    JONATHAN ROWLANDS TAMB(E  PAUL COBBOLD    B  (E
      RAY MARTINEZ      G   (E    KEN FREEMAN  SYN     (E    ROGER SUTTON      B  (E   RICHARD BURGESS D(E
      JOHN VERITY       G   (E    ANDY SUMMERS     G   (E    LEE JACKSON       K  (E
R140A                          ROSE GARDEN                                           R140A
      DIANA DI ROSE     G   (A            (A) ROSE GARDEN            1968   ATCO             SD 33225
      JOHN NORDEN       G   (A
      JAMES GROSHONG    G   (A    WILLIAM FLEMING  B   (A    BRUCE BOUDIN    D   (A
R141                            ROSE ROYCE                                           R141
      ROSE NORWALT      V   (C            (A) CAR WASH               1976 MCA         UK   MCSP 278
      GWEN 'ROSE' DICKEY V  (D            (B) BEST OF CARWASH        1977 MCA UK MCF 2799 UK RI 1609
      TERRY SANTIEL     CONGA(CDH          (C) IN FULL BLOOM         1977 WHITFIELD US 3074 UK  K56394
      HENRY GARNER      D V (CDH          (D) STRIKES AGAIN          1978 WHITFIELD US 3227 UK  K56527
      LEQUEINT JOBE     B V (CDH          (E) RAINBOW CONNECTION IV  1979 WHITFIELD US 3387 UK  K56714
      MICHAEL MOORE     SAX (CDH          (F) GOLDEN TOUCH           1980 WHITFIELD US 3512 UK  K56881
      KENNY COPELAND    TPT V(CDH         (G) GREATEST HITS          1980 WHITFIELD           RRTV1
      KENJI BROWN       G V (CD           (H) JUMP STREET            1981 WHITFIELD      UK   K56958
      RICHIE BENSON     V   (H
      MICHAEL NASH      K   (CDH FREDDIE DUNN     TPT (CDH MARK DAVIS     K  (CD  WAH WAH WATSON  G  (CDEH
      JAMES GADSON      D   (C    JACK ASHFORD     D   (CDE VICTOR NYX     K  (D   CORNELIUS GRANT G  (D
      JIMMY VALDEZ      D   (D    WALTER DOWNING   K   (DE  MARK KENOLY    B  (D   LAFAYETTE TREY STONE G(E
      ISY MARTIN        G   (E    WALTER McKINSEY  G   (H
R141A                          ROSE TATTOO                                           R141A
      'ANGRY ANDERSON TROAT V(AB          (A) ROSE TATTOO            1980 WEA UK 58144     US MIRAGE 19280
      PETER WELLS       G V (AB           (B) ASSAULT & BATTERY      1981 CARRERE UK CAL127 US MIRAGE19342
      DALLAS ROXAL      D   (AB           (B) ASSAULT & BATTERY      1981 WEA  FR 58359
      GEORDIE LEECH     B   (AB
      MICHAEL COCKS     G   (AB
R142                            ALAN ROSS                                            R142
      ALAN ROSS         G V (ABCD          (A) ROSS                  1974 RSO US 878    UK   2394 127
      STEVE EMERY       V B (AB           (B) PIT & THE PENDULUM     1975 RSO US 4802   UK   2394 144
      BOB JACKSON       K V (AB           (C) ARE YOU FREE ON SATURDAY 1977 EBONY            EBY 1000
      TONY FERNANDEZ    D   (AB           (D) RESTLESS NIGHTS        1978 EBONY      UK   EBY 1003
      REUBEN WHITE      PERC (AB
      FRANK WILSON      K V (C    JOHN COOKE       K V (CD  ED SPEVOCK     D  (CD  PETE DENNIS     B V (CD
      TOM COMPTON       D   (C    CHRIS FLETCHER   PERC V(C CRAIG ANDERS   D V (D   STRINGS            (C
R142A                           DIANA ROSS                                           R142A
      DIANA ROSS        V   (ALL          (A) DIANA ROSS            1970 MOTOWN  UK STML11159 US  711
      NICKOLAS ASHFORD  PROD (ACER         (B) EVERYTHING IS EVERYTHING 1971 MOTOWN UK STML11178 US 724
      VALERIE SIMPSON   PROD (ACER         (C) I'M STILL WAITING    1971 MOTOWN  UK STML11193
      DEBE RICHARDS     PROD (CE           (D) DIANA                1971 MOTOWN  UK STMA 8001
      ALBERT AARONS     TPT (G            (E) GREATEST HITS         1972 MOTOWN  UK STMA 8006
      BOBBY BRYANT      TPT (G            (F) TOUCH ME IN THE MORNING 1973 MOTOWN UK STML11239 US  772
      GOERGIE AULD      SAX (G            (G) LADY SINGS THE BLUES  1973 MOTOWN  UK TMSP 1131 US  758
      PLAS JOHNSON      SAX (G            (H) DIANA & MARVIN        1974 MOTOWN  UK STMA 8015
      MARVIN GAYE       V   (H            (I) LIVE AT CAESARS PALACE 1974 MOTOWN UK STML11248 US  801
      MARSHALL ROYAL    SAX (G            (J) LAST TIME I SAW HIM   1974 MOTOWN  UK STML11255 US  812
      GEORGE BOHANON    TROM (G           (K) MAHOGANY              1975 MOTOWN  UK STML12004 US  858
      HENRY COKER       TROM (G           (L) DIANA ROSS            1976 MOTOWN  UK STML12022 US  861
      MAURICE SPEARS    TROM (G           (M) GREATEST HITS         1976 MOTOWN  UK STML12036 US  869
      GEORGE'RED' CALLENDER B(G           (N) AN EVENING WITH DIANA ROSS 1977 MOTOWN UK TMSP 6005 US 877
      EARL PALMER       D   (G            (O) BABY ITS ME           1977 MOTOWN  UK STMA 8031 US  890
      WILLIAM ANDERSON  TPT (G            (P) ROSS                  1978 MOTOWN  UK STML12093 US  907
      HARRY EDISON      TPT (G            (Q) THREE ORIGINALS       1979 EMI        FR    53013
      WILLIAM COLLETTE  SAX (G            (R) THE BOSS              1979 MOTOWN  UK STML12118
      JACK NIMITY       SAX (G            (S) 20 GOLDEN GREATS      1979 MOTOWN  UK EMTV 21
      ERNIE WATTS       SAX (G            (T) DIANA                 1980 MOTOWN  UK STMA 8033
      JIMMY CLEVELAND   TROM (G           (U) TO LOVE AGAIN         1981 MOTOWN  UK STML12152
      GROVER MITCHELL   TROM (G           (V) WHY DO FOOLS FALL IN LOVE 1981 CAPITOL UK    26733
      MAX BENNETT       B   (G            (W) DIANA'S DUETS         1982 MOTOWN  UK STML12163
      JOHN COLLINS      G BAN(G           (X) SICK ELECTRIC         1982 CAPITOL UK    27313
      DON ABNEY         PNO (G
      GERALD WIGGINS    PNO (G    CHESTER LANE     PNO (G  TEDDY BUCKNER  TPT (G ARTHUR EDWARDS  B  (G
      JESSE SAILES      D   (G    JOHN EWING       TROM (G 'LAUGHEY' ROBERTS SAX (G MICHEL LEGRAND STR (G
      GIL ASHEY         STR (G    OLIVER NELSON    STR (G  RICHARD PERRY  PROD (G JEFF PORCARO    D  (O
      DAVID HUNGATE     B   (O    STEVE LUKATHER   G   (O  TOM SNOW       PNO (O TOM SCOTT       SAX (O
      JACK ASHFORD      PERC (O   GENE PAGE   STR      (O  RAY PARKER     G B (O LEE RITENOUR    G  (O
      MICHAEL OMARTIAN  K   (O    LENNY CASTRO     PERC(O  BECKY LEWIS    V   (O PETSYE POWELL   V  (O
      PATTI BROOKS      V   (O    DONALD DUCK DUNN B   (O  DAVID FOSTER   HRNS (O JAMES NEWTON HOWARD K(O
      DEL NEWMAN        STR (O    KEN PETERSON     K SYN(O JIM HORN       HRNS (O CHUCK FINDLEY  HRNS(O
          (CONTINUED)
```

DIANA ROSS (CONTINUED)

```
DAVID PAICH        V ORG K(O  BOBBY KIMBALL    V     (O   CLYDIE KING       V    (O   SHIRLEY MATTHEWS V(O
ED GREENE          D      (O  RICH ZITO        G     (O   IRA NEWBORN       G HCA(O  BOBBYE HALL      PERC(O
BUD SHANK          FLT    (O  RICHARD HEWSON   STR   (O   RICHARD SHLOSSER  D    (OU  BRYAN GAROFALO   B   (O
STANLEY SCHWARTS   PNO    (O  OLLIE BROWN      D     (O   SCOTT EDWARDS     B    (O   BEN BENAY        G   (O
LENNY CASTRO       PERC   (O  RAY CHEW     K         (RVX ERIC GALE        G    (RVX ANTHONY JACKSON  B(R
FRANCISCO CENTENO  B      (RV JOHN SUSSEWELL   D     (R   SAMMY FIGUEROA    PERC (R   ERROL BENNETT    PERC(RX
MICHAEL BRECKER    SAX    (RV ULLANDO McCULLOUGH    V(R   RAYMOND SIMPSON   V    (R   PAUL RISER   STR HRNS(RVX
ROBERT MOUNSEY STR HRNS(RVX   JOHN DAVIS       STR HRN(R  BERNARD EDWARDS   B PROD(T  NILE RODGERS     G PROD(T
RAYMOND JONES      K      (T  ANDY SCHWARTZ    K     (T   TONY THOMPSON     D    (T   EDDIE DANIELS    SAX (T
MECO MONARDO       TROM   (T  BOB MILLIKEN     TPT   (T   ALFA ANDERSON     V    (T   LUCI MARTIN      V   (T
FONZI THORNTON     V      (T  MICHELLE COBBS   V     (T   MICHAEL MESSER    PROD K(U  LARRY KNECHTEL   PNO (U
BILLY PAYNE        K      (U  LEE SKLAR        B     (U   TIM MAY           G    (U   BECKY LOPEZ      V   (U
MAXINE WILLARD WATERS  V(UX   JULIA TILLMAN WATERS V (UX  NEIL JASON        B    (VX  JEFF MIRANOV     G   (VX
YOGI HORTON        D      (VX BURT DE COTEAUX STR HRNS(V  GEORGE MACDONALD  PERC (V   DON BROOKS  HCA  (V
RANDY BRECKER      HRNS   (V  PATRICK REBILLOT PNO   (V   ED WALSH          SYN  (VX  LEON PENDARVIS   K   (V
RON FRANGIPANE     K      (V  MARGARET DORN    V     (V   LEOTA GALLOWAY    V    (V   MILLIE WHITESIDE V   (V
STEVE GOLDSTEIN    SYN    (X  RICK MAROTTA     D     (X   PAUL SHAFFER      K    (X   LUCIO HOPPER     B   (X
JOE BARGER         PNO    (X  NATHAN WATTS     B     (X   JONATHAN MOFFETT  D    (X   DAVID WILLIAMS   G   (X
DENZIL MILLER      K      (X  LUTHER VANDROSS  V     (X   CISSY HOUSTON     V    (X   PAULETTE McWILLIAMS V(X
TAWATHA AGEE       V      (X  PATTI AUSTIN     V     (X   MICHAEL BODDICKER SYN  (X   BILL WOLFER SYN  (X
GREGORY SMITH      SYN    (X
```

DOCTOR ROSS

```
DOCTOR ROSS V HCA G PERC(ALL   (A) HIS FIRST RECORDINGS    19   ARHOOLIE             F1065
BOB HALL         PNO      (C    (B) LIVE AT MONTREUX        19   ATLANTIC 2460 169 BIG BEAR  18
LAFAYETTE LEAKE  PNO      (B    (C) THE HARMONICA BOSS      1974 BIG BEAR             BEAR 2
LOUIS MYERS      G        (B    (D) JIVIN' THE BLUES        197  BIG BEAR             BEAR15
DAVID MYERS      B        (B    (E) CALL THE DOCTOR         19   TESTAMENT            2206
```

ROSSINGTON COLLINS BAND

```
GARY ROSSINGTON  G       (AB    (A) ANY TIME ANYWHERE       1980 MCA UK MCG 4011   US  5130
ALLEN COLLINS    G       (AB    (B) THIS IS THE WAY         1981 MCA UK  MCG 4018
BILLY POWELL     K       (AB
LEON WILKESON    B       (AB  DALE KRANTZ    V    (AB BARRY HARWOOD  G V  (AB DEREK HESS   D (AB
```

ROTARY CONNECTION

```
MINNIE RIPPERTON  V      (       (A) ROTARY CONNECTION       1968 CHESS CRL 4538 CADET LPS 312
SIDNEY BARNES     V      (       (B) ALADDIN                 196  CADET              LPS 317
BOBBY SIMS        V      (       (C) PEACE AT LAST           1969 CADET              LPS 318
JUDY HAUF         V      (       (D) SONGS                   196  CADET              LPS 322
MITCH ALIOTTA     V      (       (E) DINNER MUSIC            19   CADET              LPS 328
KENNY VENEGAS     V      (       (F) TRIP ONE                1973 CHECKER            6467 300
                                 (G) HEY LOVE                19   CADET         US   50006
```

ARLEN ROTH

```
ARLEN ROTH        G V    (AB     (A) HOT PICKUPS             1980 SONET UK SNTF845 ROUNDER  3044
MICHAEL BRAUN     D      (A      (B) GUITARIST               1978 ROUNDER       US 3022
VAN ELIAS         B      (A
DEAN KRAUS        K      (A   STEPHANIE DAVY   V   (A  THE PERSUASIONS  V   (A  KEVIN KELLY V  (A
TONY BROWN        B      (B   TIM CAPPELLO   SAX   (A  RICHARD CROOKS   D   (B  AUBRAY SCHRAM  V (B
RALPH SCHUCKETT   K      (B
```

MICHAEL ROTHER

```
MICHAEL ROTHER   G B SYN (ALL    (A) FLAMMENDE HERZEN        1976 SKY                SKY 007
JAKI LEIBEZEIT   D       (ABCD   (A) FLAMMENDE HERZEN        197  RADAR (UNRELEASED) RAD 8
                                 (B) STERNTALER             1978 SKY                SKY 013
                                 (C) KATZENMUSIK            1979 SKY                SKY 033
                                 (D) FERNWARME              1982 POLYDOR GER        2372 111
```

ROUGH DIAMOND

```
DAVID BYRON       V      (A      (A) ROUGH DIAMOND          1977 ISLAND             ILPS 9490
DAVE CLEMPSON     G      (A
GEOFF BRITTON     D      (A   DAMON BUTCHER   K   (A   WILLIE BATH      B   (A
```

ROUGH TRADE

```
MICHAEL FONFARA   K      (A      (A) LIVE                   1976 UMBRELLA   CAN      DD1
PETER HOGSON      B      (A
CAROLE POPE       V      (A   JOANNE BROOKS V PERC(A KEVAN STAPLES  G K  (A  RICK GRATTON   D (A
```

ROUNDABOUT

```
CHRIS CURTIS      V      (A      (A) 1967
DAVE CURTIS       V      (A
BOBBY CLARK       D      (A   JON LORD        K   (A   RITCHIE BLACKMORE G  (A
```

ROWAN BROTHERS

```
PETER ROWAN       V G MAND(ALL   (A) THE ROWAN BROTHERS     1972 CBS            US    31297
LORIN ROWAN       G V    (ALL    (B) ROWANS                 1975 ASYLUM SYL9026 US    7E1038
CHRIS ROWAN       G V    (ALL    (B) ROWANS                 197  ASYLUM RI K53023
JACK BONUS        WIND   (B      (C) SIBLING RIVALRY        1976 ASYLUM         US    7E1073
BILL ELLIOTT      PNO    (C      (D) JUBILATION             19   ASYLUM         US    7E1114
JOE CARROLL       B      (C
RICHARD GREENE    VLN    (C   PETER WALSH    B    (C  WALLY DROGAS   D    (C  JORDAN AMARANTHA CONGA(C
K DUDLEY GLANZ    D      (C   JIMMY HODDER   D    (C  MARK STEIN     D    (C  DAVID HAYES    B  (B
RUSS KUNKEL       D      (B
```

ROXY

```
BOB SEGARINI    G B V PERC(A     (A) ROXY                   1970 ELEKTRA        US    EKS74063
RANDY BISHOP    G B K V   (A
JIM DE COCQ      K G     (A   JOHN McDONALD  D PERC(A JAMES MORRIS   K    (A  JOHN HAENY   PROD (A
```

ROXY MUSIC

```
BRYAN FERRY      V K (ALL        (A) ROXY MUSIC          1972 UK ISLAND ILPS9200 RI POLYDOR 2302 048
PAUL THOMPSON    D   (ALL        (A) ROXY MUSIC          197  US REPRISE  RS2114 RI ATCO      36133
PETE SINFIELD    PROD (A         (A) ROXY MUSIC          1972 ISLAND EURO 88179
ROGER BUNN       G   (1          (B) FOR YOUR PLEASURE   1973 ISLAND UK ILPS9232
DAVY OLIST       G   (           (B) FOR YOUR PLEASURE   197  US WB 2629 ATCO 36134
RHETT DAVIES     PROD (H         (B) FOR YOUR PLEASURE   1978 UK POLYDOR RI 2302 049
ANDY MACKAY      SAX (ALL        (C)STRANDED             1973 UK ISLAND ILPS9252 RI POLYDOR 2302 050
BRIAN ENO        SYN K(AB12I     (C)STRANDED             1974 US ATCO 7045  ISLAND EURO 63313
PHIL MANZANERA   G   (ALL        (D) COUNTRY LIFE        1974 UK ISLAND ILPS9303 RI POLYDOR 2302 051
GRAHAM SIMPSON   B   (A12        (D) COUNTRY LIFE        197  US ATCO 36106 EURO POLYDOR 2459 344
RIK KENTON       B   (I          (E) SIREN               1975 UK ISLAND ILPS9344 RI POLYDOR 2302 052
JOHN GUSTAFSON   B   (BCEFI      (E) SIREN               1975 US ATCO 36127 EURO POLYDOR 2344 090
JOHN PORTER      B   (CI         (F) VIVA                1976 UK ISLAND ILPS9400 RI POLYDOR 2302 053
JOHN WETTON      B   (F          (F) VIVA                1976 US ATCO 36139 EURO ISLAND 27553
EDDIE JOBSON     K VLN(CDEFI     (G) MANIFESTO           1979 UK POLYDOR POLHOO1 EURO 2310 651
CHRIS LAURENCE   B   (C          (H) FLESH & BLOOD       1980 UK POLYDOR 2302 099          POLH 002
CHRIS THOMAS     PROD (C         (H) FLESH & BLOOD       1980 US ATCO 32102
SAL MAIDA        B   (F          (I) GREATEST HITS       1977 UK POLYDOR 2302 073 US ATCO      38103
RICK WILLS       B   (F          (1) 1970/71   (2) 1971/72
NEIL HUBBARD     G   (H
SIRENS           V   (F    GARY TIBBS       B  (GH PAUL CARRACK    K (GH ALLEN SCHWARZBERG   D (H
ANDY NEWMARK     D   (H    SIMON PHILLIPS   D  (H  ALAN SPENNER    B (H  NEIL JASON         B (H
DEXTER LLOYD     D   (1
```

ROYAL GUARDSMEN

```
                                (A) SNOOPY Vs THE RED BARON     1966 LAURIE   2038
                                (B) RETURN OF THE RED BARON     19   LAURIE   2039
                                (C) SNOOPY & HIS FRIENDS        19   LAURIE   2042
                                (D) SNOOPY FOR PRESIDENT        19   LAURIE   2046
```

THR ROYALS

```
ROY COUSINS      (ALL           (A) PICK UP THE PIECES     1977 MAGNUM DEAD1004 RI UA  LBR1010
LEROY WALLACE    D   (B          (B) ISRAEL    BE WISE     1978 BALLISTIC          UAG 30206
MIKEY            D   (B          (C) TEN YEARS AFTER       1978 UA                 UAS 30189
WINSTON WRIGHT   K   (B
ANSEL COLLINS    K   (B    VIN GORDON      HRNS (B   HEADLEY BENNETT  HRNS (B   LLOYD PARKS B   (B
BAGGA            B   (B    ROBBY SHAKESPEARE B  (B   RANCHIE McLEAN   G    (B   PABLO BLACK G   (B
BUBBLER          G   (B    ROBERT LYN       G   (B   WINSTON          G    (B   SKULLY    PERC (B
STICKY           PERC (B
```

RUBBER CITY REBELS

```
ROD 'FIRESTONE'BENT V G(AB       (A) FROM AKRON(1 SIDE)    1977  CLONE     US   001
BUZZ CLICK       G V (AB         (B) RUBBER CITY REBELS    1980  CAPITOL   US   12100
DONNIE DAMAGE    B   (
MICHAEL VON HAMMER D  (    PETE SAKE      K V (A   STIX PELTEN    D   (A   BRANDON MATHESON D V (B
JOHNNY BETHESDA  B V (B
```

RUBBER DOLLS

```
CHRIS MARCH      B   (A          (A) MEAT THE RUBBER DOLLS  1981 HAFENKLANG    GER 6 24638
MARTIN NEAL      D   (A
J HILBIG         EFFECTS(A PWC HOBSON     V   (A   GOFFO          G V (A
```

RUBEN & THE JETS

```
RUBEN LADRON DE GuEVARA V TAM(AB (A) FOR REAL     1973 MERCURY    SRM 1 659
TONY DURAN       G V K(AB        (B) CON SAFOS    1973 MERCURY    SRM 1694
ROBERT CAMARENA  G V (AB
JOHNNY MARTINEZ  B V ORG(AB ROBERT ROBERTS SAX (AB  BILL WILD    B V (AB  BOB ZAMORA D   (AB
JIM SHERWOOD     SAX (A
```

RUBETTES

```
ALAN WILLIAMS    G FLT K (       (A) WE CAN DO IT           1975 STATE          ETAT 001
TONY THORPE      G K D(          (B) RUBETTES              1975 STATE US 2193   ETAT 004
MICK CLARKE      B   (           (C) SIGN OF THE TIMES     1976 STATE          ETAT 006
BILL HURD        K   (           (D) BEST OF               1976 STATE          ETAT 008
JOHN RICHARDSON  D   (           (E) WHERE ITS AT          1976 POLYDOR        2383 306
PETER ARNESEN    K   (           (F) BABY I KNOW           1977 STATE          ETAT 012
                                 (G) SOMETIME IN OLDCHURCH 1978 POLYDOR        2383 480
                                 (H) STILL UNWINDING       1978 POLYDOR        2383 520
```

RUBICON

```
DENNIS MARCELLINO WIND (AB       (A) RUBICON          1978 20TH CENTURY   BT 552
BRADLEY GILLIS   G   (AB         (B) AMERICAN DREAMS  1980 20TH CENTURY   BT 557
GREG ECKLER      D   (AB
JERRY MARTINI    SAX (AB MAX HASKETT TPT        (AB JIM PUGH    K   (AB JACK BLADES    B  (AB
```

RUBINOOS

```
JOHN RUBIN       G V (A          (A) THE RUBINOOS            1977 BESERKLEY US  0051 UK BSERK10
TOMMY DUNBAR     G   (A          (B) BACK TO THE DRAWING BOARD 1979 BESERKLEY US 0080 UK BSERK18
ROYSE ADER       B   (A
DONN SPINDT      D   (A
```

RUBY (UK)

```
MIKE LENTON      G   (A          (A) RED CRYSTAL FANTASIES   1974  CHRYSALIS     CHR 1061
JOHN ABBOTT      G V (A
DAVID KNIGHTS    V G B(A RAB MUNRO     V PERC    (A  GERRY SHURY  STRINGS(A GEOFF SWETTENHAM  D (A
COLIN FAIRLEY    D   (A
```

RUBY (US)

```
TOM FOGERTY      G V (AB         (A) RUBY                  1977 PBR INT US 7001  UK  PBRL5001
RANDY ODA        G K V(AB        (B) ROCK'N'ROLL MADNESS   1978 PBR INT US 7004  UK  PBRL5003
BOBBY COCHRAN    D V (AB
ANTHONY DAVIS    B V (AB ED BOGAS        B  (A
```

RUBY & THE ROMANTICS

```
                                 (A) GREATEST HITS         19   MCA US         541
```

RUEFREX

JACKIE FORGE	G	(A	(A) ONE BY ONE(EP)	1979	GOOD VIBRATION	GOT 8
ALAN CLARKE	V	(A				
TOM COULTER	B	(A	PAUL BURGESS	D	(A	

DAVID RUFFIN

DAVID RUFFIN	V	(ALL	MY WHOLE WORLD ENDED	1969	TAMLA	US	685
VAN McCOY	V PROD K(H		FEELIN' GOOD	1969	TAMLA	US	695
GORDON EDWARDS	B	(H	DOIN HIS THING	196	TAMLA	US	696
ERIC GALE	G	(H	DAVID RUFFINS	1973	TAMLA UK STML11228	US	762
PAUL GRIFFIN	K	(H	ME & ROCK'N'ROLL IS HERE TO STAY	1975	TAMLA UK STML11283	US	7818
CRUSHER BENNETT	PERC	(H	WHO AM I	1975	TAMLA UK STML12012	US	7849
HUGH McCRACKEN	G	(H	EVERYTHING'S COMING UP LOVE	1976	TAMLA UK STML12030	US	7866
VICTOR PAZ	TPT	(H	(H) IN MY STRIDE	1977	TAMLA UK STML12064	US	7885
MICKEY GRAVINE	TROM	(H	AT HIS BEST	1978	TAMLA UK STML12079	US	7895
WAYNE ANDRE	TROM	(H	SO SOON WE CHANGE	1979	WB	US	3306
PAUL FAULISE	TROM	(H	G ENTLEMAN RUFFIN	1981	WB	US 3416	
CHARLES KIPPS	PROD	(H					
CORNELL DUPREE	G	(H STEVE GADD	D	(H	DON GROLNICK	K	(H	JON FADDIS	TPT (H
MARVIN STAMM	TPT	(H BOB ALEXANDER	TROM	(H	JANIS ROBBINSON	TROM	(H	ALBERT DAILEY	V	(H

JIMMY RUFFIN

JIMMY RUFFIN	V	(ALL	JIMMY RUFFIN	1967	POLYDOR	UK	2383 240
			SINGS TOP TEN	1967	SOUL	US	704
			JIMMY RUFFIN WAY	1967	TAMLA	UK	STML11048
			RUFF & READY	1969	TAMLA	UK	STML11106
			RUFF & READY	1969	SOUL	US	708
			FOREVER	1970	TAMLA	UK	STML11161
			GROOVE GOVERNOR	1970	SOUL	US	727
			I AM MY BROTHERS KEEPER	1970	SOUL	US	728
			JIMMY & DAVID RUFFIN	1971	TAMLA	UK	STML11176
			GREATEST HITS	1974	TAMLA	UK	STML11259
			LOVE IS ALL WE NEED	1975	POLYDOR	UK	2383 337
			20 GOLDEN CLASSIC	1980	TAMLA	UK	9012
			SUNRISE	1980	RSO US 30784	UK	2394 258

RUFUS

CHAKA KHAN	V	(ABCDEFH	(A) RUFUS	1973	ABC UK ABCL5114	US	783
RON STOCKERT	K V	(AB	(B) RAGS TO RUFUS	1974	ABC UK ABCL5952	US	809
KEVIN MURPHY	K V	(ABCDEFGH	(C) RUFUSIZED	1974	ABC UK ABCL5063	US	837
ANDRE FISCHER	D V	(ABCDE	(D) RUFUS FEATURING CHAKA KHAN	1975	ABC UK ABCL5151	US	909
AL CINER	G V	(AB	(E) ASK RUFUS	1977	ABC UK ABCL5203	US	975
DENNIS BELFIELD	B V	(AB	(F) STREET PLAYER	1978	ABC UK ABCL5239	US	1049
ERIC FISCHER	V	(A	(G) NUMBERS	1979	ABC UK ABCL5263	US	1098
TONY MAIDEN	G V	(CDEFGH	(H) MASTERJAM	1979	MCA	MCG 4007	
BOBBY WATSON	B V	(CDEFGH	(J) PARTY TILL YOU'RE BROKE	1981	MCA UK MCF3108	US	5151
DAVE GROVER	HRNS	(G					
TOWER OF POWER	HRNS	(D RON WOOD	G	(E MILT HOLLAND	PERC	(E JERRY HEY	TPT (FH
KIM HUTCHCROFT	HRNS	(FH BILL REICHENBACH	TROM	(FH LARRY WILLIAMS	WIND	(FH HELEN LOWE	V	(F
EVERETT BRYSON	PERC	(FG JOHN ROBINSON	D	(GH DAVID WOLINSKI	K V(EFGH RICHARD CALHOUN	D PERC(F
LEW McCREARY	TROM	(H GARY GRANT	HRNS	(H LARRY HALL	HRNS	(H LOUIS JOHNSON	PERC (H
GEORGE JOHNSON	PERC	(H RICHARD HEATH	PERC	(H FREDDIE HUBBARD	TPT	(G HARVEY MASON	D	(G
TRUMAN THOMAS	K	(G CHUCK BROOKE WIND		(G JOHN ERVIN	TROM	(G RICHARD MIKULS	G	(G
BOB GREVE	WIND	(G MAXAYN LEWIS	V	(G LALOMIE WASHBURN	V	(G BILL LAMB	HRNS(G

RUGBYS

STEVE McNICOL	G	(A	(A) HOT CARGO	1969	AMAZON US	1000
MIKE MORNER	B	(A				
ED VERNON	K	(A	GLENN HOWERTON	D	(A	

RUMOUR

BRINSLEY SCHWARZ	G	(ABC	(A) MAX	1977	VERTIGO	UK	6360149
BOB ANDREWS	K	(AB	(A) MAX	1977	MERCURY	US	SRM1 1174
STEVE GOULDING	PERC	(ABC	(B) FROGS SPROUTS CLOGS & KRAUTS	1979	STIFF UK SEEZ13 GER	6 23756
ANDREW BODNAR	D	(ABC	(B) FROGS SPROUTS CLOGS & KRAUTS	1979	ARISTA US 4235	
ROGER BECHIRAN	PROD	(B | C) PURITY OF ESSENCE	1980	STIFF	UK	SEEZ 27
DAN ELLIS	TROM	(A				
MARTIN BELMONT	G	(ABC ALBIE DONNELLY	SAX	(A BOB ROBERTSON	SAX	(A DICK HANSON TPT	(AB

INGA RUMPF

INGA RUMPF	G V	(AB	(A) MY LIFE IS A BOOGIE	1977	RCA	PL28321
ALAN SPENNER	B	(A	(B) I KNOW WHO I AM	1980	RCA	PL13499
GERRY CONWAY	D	(A				
PAUL CARRACK	K	(A NEIL HUBBARD	G	(A ROBERT AWHAI	G	(A VINCE WEBER	PNO (A

RUMPLESTILTSKIN

PETER CHARLES GREENE	V	(A	(A) RUMPLESTILTSKIN	1969	BELL	US	6047
JEREMY EAGLES	K	(A				
ANDREW BALMAIN	G	(A RUPERT BAER	D	(A JACKSON PRIMROSE	B	(A HUGH MURPHY	(A

RUNAWAYS

LITA FORD	G V	(ABCDEF	(A) THE RUNAWAYS	1976	MERCURY	US SRMI1090
SANDY WEST	D V	(ABCDEF	(B) QUEENS OF NOISE	1977	MERCURY UK 9100 032 US SRMI1126
VICKI BLUE	G V	(DE	(B) " " "	1977	MERCURY GER 6338 780
JOAN JETT	G V	(ABCDEF	(C) LIVE IN JAPAN	1977	MERCURY UK 9100 046
CHERIE CURRIE	K V	(ABF	(C) " " "	1977	MERCURY GER 6338 833
JACKie FOX	B V	(ABF	(D) WAITIN' FOR THE NIGHT	1977	MERCURY UK 9100 047 US SRMI3705
LAURIE McALLISTER	B	(	(D) " " "	1977	MERCURY GER 6338 844
DUANE HITCHINGS	K	(E	(E) AND NOW THE RUNAWAYS	1979	MERCURY 6304 505
			(E) AND NOW THE RUNAWAYS	1979	CHERRY RED ARED 3
			(F) FLAMIN' SCHOOLGIRLS	1980	CHERRY RED ARED 9
			(F) " " "	1980	MERCURY GER 6337 944

TODD RUNDGREN	G V	(ALL	(A) RUNT	1970 BEARSVILLE UK K45505 US 2046	
DAVID LASLEY	V	(H	(A) RUNT	1970 US AMPEX 10105	
KEVIN ELLIMAN	PERC	(EFG	(B) BALLAD OF TODD RUNDGREN	1971 BEARSVILLE UK K45506 US 2046	
DAVID SANBORN		(DG	(B) " " " "	1971 AMPEX US 10116	
MOOGY KLINGMAN	K	(CDEFGH	(C) SOMETHING ANYTHING	1972 BEARSVILLE UK K65501 US 2BX2066	
FROG LABAT	SYN	(DF	(D) A WIZARD A TRUE STAR	1973 BEARSVILLE UK K45513 US 2133	
RALPH SHUCKETT	B	(DEFGH	(D) A WIZARD A TRUE STAR	1980 BEARSVILLE RI IRSP10	
JOHN SIEGLER	CELLO B	(CFJDGHE	(E) TODD	1974 BEARSVILLE UK K85501 US 6952	
ROGER POWELL	K TPT	(FJKOPLGH	(F) TODD RUNDGRENS UTOPIA	1974 BEARSVILLE UK K55501 US 6954	
KASIM SULTON	B	(KOPL	(G) INITIATION	1975 BEARSVILLE UK K55504 US 6957	
JOHN WILCOX	D	(JKOPLGH	(H) ANOTHER LIVE	1976 BEARSVILLE UK K55508 US 6961	
HUNT SALES	D	(CB	(J) FAITHFUL	1976 BEARSVILLE UK K55510 US 6963	
TONY SALES	B	(CB	(K) R A	1977 BEARSVILLE UK K55514 US 6965	
N D SMART	D	(B	(L) OOPS WRONG PLANET	1977 BEARSVILLE UK K55517 US 6970	
JOHN SIOMOS	D	(CD	(M) HERMIT OF MINK HOLLOW	1978 BEARSVILLE UK K55521 US 6981	
STU WOODS	B	(C	(M) HERMIT OF MINK HOLLOW	1980 BEARSVILLE RI IRSP11	
RANDY BRECKER	HRNS	(CDE	(N) BACK TO THE BARS	1978 BEARSVILLE UK K65511 US 6986	
MICHAEL BRECKER	HRNS	(CDE	(O) ADVENTURES IN UTOPIA	1980 BEARSVILLE UK ILPS9602 US 6991	
BARRY ROGERS	TROM	(CDE	(P) DEFACE THE MUSIC	1980 BEARSVILLE UK ILPS9614 US 3487	
RICK DERRINGER	G	(CDG	(Q) HEALING	1981 BEARSVILLE UK ILPS9657 US WB 3522	
EDWARD OLMOS	C	(C			

AMOS GARRETT	G	(C	BEN KEITH	STEEL	(C	ROBBIE KAGALE	G	(C	BUGSY MAUGH	B (C
RALPH WASH	G	(C	BILLY MUNDI	D	(C	GENE DINWIDDIE	SAX	(C	SERGE KAKEN CONGA	(C
JIM COLGROVE	B	(C	RICK VITO	G	(C	CHARLIE SCHONING	PNO	(C	JIM HORN	SAX(C
JOHN KELSO	SAX	(C	HOPE RUFF	V	(C	RICHARD COREY	V	(C	VICKI ROBINSON	V (C
DENNIS COOLEY	V	(C	CECILIA NORFLEET	V	(C	BROOKS BAXES	V	(C	ANTHONY CARRABBA	V (C
HENRY FANTON	V	(C	ARNOLD McCULLER	V	(H	PHILLIP BALLOU	V	(H	WELLS KELLY	D (E
BILL GELBER	B	(E	PETER POROZEL	SAX	(E	TOM COSGROVE		(D	JERRY SCHEFF	B (B
JOHN GUERIN	D	(B	ROY MARKOWITZ	D	(G	BARBARA BURTON	PERC	(G	LEE PASTORA	PERC(G
JOHN MILLER	B	(GE	RICK MAROTTA	D	(G	BERNARD PURDIE	D	(G	CHRIS PARKER	D (E
BARRY LAZAROWITZ	D	(G	DAN HARTMAN	B	(G	EDGAR WINTER	SAX	(G		

STEVE GOULD	G V	(A	(A) RUNNER	1979 ACROBAT ACRO 1 US ISLAND 9536		
MICKIE FEAT	B V	(A				
DAVE DOWLE	D	(A	ALLAN MEWRILL	G K V(A	RAY COOPER	PERC (A JON COLE G (A
IAN LYNN	K	(A	WILLIAM C LYALL	SYN (A		

RAY RUSSELL	G B K V	(A	(A) RUNNING MAN	1972 NEON NE 11	
ALAN GREED	V K	B(A			
ALAN RUSHTON	D	(A	HARRY BECKETT HRNS (A	GARY WINDO SAX (A ROY CAMERON V (A	

SYLVI LILLEGARD	V	(CD	(A) LET YOUR LIGHT SHINE IN	19 BRAIN 0060 031
JAN SIMONSEN	K	(CD	(B) INNER VOICE	1977 BRAIN 0060 060
KJELL LARSON	G	(CD	(C) FLYING COLOURS	197 BRAIN 0060 108
THOR BENEDIKSEN	D	(CD	(D) HOT RHYTHMS AND HIGH NOTES	1978 ELECTRIC TRIX 8
ASLE NILSEN	B	(CD		
TROND VILLA	VLN	(C		

JOHN RUTSEY	D	(A	(A) RUSH	1974 MERCURY US SRMI1011 UK 9100 011
ALEX LIFESON	G	(ABCDEFHJKLMN	(B) FLY BY NIGHT	1975 MERCURY US SRMI1023 UK 9100 013
GEDDY LEE	G K B V	(ABCDEFHJKLMN	(C) 2112	1976 MERCURY US SRMI1079 UK 9100 039
NEIL PEART	D	(BCDEFHJKLMN	(D) CARESS OF STEEL	1977 MERCURY US SRMI1046 UK 9100 018
ERWIG CHUAPCHUADUA	STEEL D(J		(AB) RUSH/FLY BY NIGHT	19 MERCURY GER 9111 065
HUGH SYME	K	(CJ	(E) ALL THE WORLD'S A STAGE	1976 MERCURY US SRM27508 6672 015
			(F) FAREWELL TO KINGS	1977 MERCURY US SRM11184 UK 9100 042
			(G) ARCHIVES (TRIPLE)(ABD)	1978 MERCURY US SRM39200 6641 799
			(H) HEMISPHERES	1978 MERCURY US SRM13743 UK 9100 059
			(I) CLOSER TO THE HEART (12" EP)	1978 MERCURY UK RUSH12
			(J) PERMANENT WAVES	1980 MERCURY US 4001 9100 071
			(K) MOVING PICTURES	1981 MERCURY US 4013 UK 6337 160
			(L) EXIT STAGE LEFT	1981 MERCURY UK 6619 053
			(M) RUSH THROUGH TIME	1981 MERCURY UK 6331 171
			(N) SIGNALS	1982 MERCURY UK 6337 243

BOBBY RUSH	(A	(A) RUSH HOUR	1979 PHILADELPHIA US 35509

OTIS RUSH	G V	(ALL	(A) THIS ONE'S A GOOD UN	1968 BLUE HORIZON UK 763222
WALTER HORTON	HCA	(AKL	(B) MOURNING IN THE MORNING	1969 COTILLION US 9006 UK ATCOK40495
HAROLD ASHBY	SAX	(AKL	(C) SCREAMING & CRYING	1974 BLACK & BLUE FR 33516
LITTLE BRO MONTGOMERY	PNO	(AKL	(D) BLUES LIVE	1975 TRIO JAP PA3086
JESSE GREEN	D	(F	(D) SO MANY ROADS (1 DIFF TRACK)	1978 DELMARK US DS 643
LOUIS MILES	G	(AKL	(E) RIGHT PLACE WRONG TIME	1976 BULLFROG US 301
WILLIE DIXON	B	(AKL	(F) COLD DAY IN HELL	1976 DELMARK DS 638
ODIE PAYNE	D	(AKL	(G) DOOR TO DOOR (1 SIDE)	1976 CHESS US 1538
RONALD EADES	SAX	(B	(H) CHICAGO BLUES TODAY VOL 2	1966 VANGUARD VSD 79217
JIMMY JOHNSON	G	(BD	(J) TROUBLES TROUBLES	1978 SONET UK SNTF 756
AARON VARNELL	SAX	(B	(K) GROANING THE BLUES	1980 FLYRIGHT UK LP 560
BARRY BECKETT	K	(B	(L) OTHER TAKES 1956/58 (1 SIDE)	1980 FLYRIGHT UK LP 562
BOB LEVIS	G	(F	(M) OTIS RUSH	1972 BLUE HORIZON US 4602
GENE MILLER	TOT	(B		

DUANE ALLMAN	G	(B	MARK NAFTALIN	K	(B	JOE ARNOLD	SAX	(B	ROGER HAWKINS	D (B
JERRY JEMMOTT	B	(B	RED HOLLOWAY	SAX	(KL	LAYFAYETTE LEAKE	K	(KL	WAYNE BENNETT	G (KL
AL DUNCAN	D	(KL	LUCIUS WASHINGTON	SAX	(KL	JODY WILLIAMS	G	(KL	REGGIE BOYD	G (KL
FRED BELOW	D	(KL	JACKIE BRENSTON	SAX	(KL	IKE TURNER	G	(KL	JIMMY DAWKINS	G (C
JEROME VAN JONES	K	(C	SUNNYLAND SLIM	PNO	(C	WILLIE MABON	PNO	(C	JAMES GREEN	B (C
BOB PLUNKETT	D	(C	SYLVESTER BOINES	B	(D	TYRONE CENTURY	D	(D	DOUG KILMER	B (E
JOHN KAHN	B	(E	BOB JONES	D	(E	FRED BURTON	G	(E	IRA KAMIN	ORG(E
JOHN WILMETH	TPT	(E	RON STALLINGS	SAX	(E	HART McNEE	SAX	(E	AB LOCKE	SAX(F
CHUCK SMITH	SAX	(F	BIG MOOSE WALKER	K	(F	MIGHTY JOE YOUNG	G	(F	BOB STROGER	B (F

TOM RUSH	V	(ALL	(A) MIND RAMBLIN'	1963 PRESTIGE	US	14003
HERBIE LOVELLE	D	(I	(B) BLUES SONGS & BALLADS	1965 PRESTIGE		7374
TREVOR VEITCH	G	(I	(B) BLUES & FOLK	1965 TRANSATLANTIC	UK	XTRA5024
WARREN BERNHARDT	K	(I	(C) TOM RUSH	1965 ELEKTRA		EKS 7288
DUKE BARDWELL	B	(I	(D) TAKE A LITTLE WALK WITH ME	1966 ELEKTRA		EKS 7308
DAVID BROMBERG	G	(I	(E) I GOT A MIND TO RAMBLE	1968 TRANSATLANTIC	UK	XTRA5053
JOHN SEBASTIAN	HCA	(CD	(E) I GOT A MIND TO RAMBLE	1968 PRESTIGE	US	7536
PAUL GRIFFIN	K	(I	(F) TOM RUSH	19 FANTASY		24709
RED RHODES	STEEL	(I	(G) THE CIRCLE GAME	1968 ELEKTRA EKS74018	UK RI	K42018
ED FREEMAN	G	(I	(H) CLASSIC RUSH	196 ELEKTRA EKS74062	UK RI	K42073
RON CARTER	B	(I	(I) TOM RUSH	1970 CBS	US 9972 UK	63940
FELIX PAPPALARDI	B	(CD	(J) WRONG END OF A RAINBOW	1970 CBS	US 30402 UK	64268
DADDY BONES	G	(CD	(K) MERRIMACK COUNTY	1972 CBS	US 31306 UK	64887
HARVEY BROOKS	B	(D	(L) LADIES LOVE OUTLAWS	1976 CBS	US 33054 UK	80282
AL KOOPER	K	(D	(M) BEST OF	19 CBS	US 33907	
BILL LEE	B	(C				
FRITZ RICHMOND	JUG	(C	JACK ELLIOT G V (C			

JIMMY RUSHING	(ALL	BLUES I LOVE TO SING	1977 ACE OF HEARTS	UK	AH 119
RAY CHARLES	(*	LISTEN TO THE BLUES	1767 VANGUARD		SRV73007
IVORY JOE HUNTER	(*	GOIN' TO CHICAGO	19 VANGUARD		VRS 8518
		THE YOU & ME THAT USED TO BE	19 ·RCA	UK	SF 8234
		EVERY DAY I HAVE THE BLUES	1967 BLUESWAY		BLS 6005
		SENT FOR YESTERDAY	1968 BLUESWAY		BLS 6057
		IF THIS AIN'T THE BLUES	1974 VANGUARD	UK	VRS 8513
		ESSENTIAL JIMMY RUSHING	1976 VANGUARD	VJD	65/66
		(*) THREE OF A KIND	19 DESIGN	US	DLP 909
		GEE BABY	19 MASTER	US	8104
		LIVING THE BLUES	19 BLUESWAY	US 6017	
		WHO WAS IT	19 MASTER	US	8120

RICK RUSKIN	G V	(ABC	(A) RICHARD RUSKIN	1974 TAKOMA	US	1039
DAVID JACKSON	PNO	(B	(B) MICROPHONE FEVER	1975 TAKOMA	US	1044
MIKE BOTTS	D	(B	(C) SIX STRING CONSPIRACY	1976 TAKOMA	US	1057
COLIN CAMERON	B	(B				
DICK ROSMINI	K V B	(B	MARC CHOVER B (B CASSANDRA THOMAS V (B PAULA THOMAS V (B			
CLAUDIA CRUTZINGER	V	(B				

JOHNNY RUSSELL	(ALL	(A) MR & MRS UNTRUE	1972 RCA	US	LSP4588
		(B) CATFISH JOHN	1973 RCA	US	LSP4851
		(C) RED NECKS WHITE SOCKS	1974 RCA	UK	AFLI0345
		(D) SHE'S IN LOVE WITH A RODEO MAN	1974 RCA		AFLI0542
		(E) HERE COMES JOHNNY RUSSELL	1975 RCA		APLI1211

LEON RUSSELL V K G B PERC	(ALL	(A) LOOKING INSIDE (ASYLUM CHOIR)	1968 SMASH 67107	UK MERCURY	20141
CHRIS STAINTON	K	(BD	(B) LEON RUSSELL	1970 A&M AMLS 982	RI ISLAND	ISA 5005
GEORGE HARRISON	G	(B	(B) LEON RUSSELL	1970 SHELTER US 8901 RI		52008
RINGO STARR	D	(B	(C) ASYLUM CHOIR II	1971 SHELTER US 8910 RI		52010
CHARLIE WATTS	D	(B	(C) ASYLUM CHOIR II	1971 SHELTER UK		AMLS 68089
BILL WYMAN	B	(B	(D) AND THE SHELTER PEOPLE	1971 SHELTER US 8903 RI 52008 RI US 2119		
KLAUS VOORMANN	B	(B	(D) AND THE SHELTER PEOPLE	1971 A&M AMLS65003	RI ISLAND	ISA 5006
B J WILSON	D	(B	(E) CARNEY	1972 SHELTER US 8911 RI		52011
ALAN SPENNER	B	(B	(E) CARNEY	1972 A&M AMLH68911	RI ISLAND	ISA 5007
JIM GORDON	D	(BD	(F) HANK WILSON'S BACK	1973 A&M AMLS68923	US SHELTER	8923
BUDDY HARMON	D	(B	(G) LEON LIVE	1973 SHELTER	US	8917
GREG DEMPSEY		(B	(H) STOP ALL THAT JAZZ	1974 A&M AMLS68262	RI ISLAND	ISA 5009
STEVE WINWOOD	K	(B	(H) STOP ALL THAT JAZZ	1974 SHELTER US 2108 RI 52016		
JIM HORN	SAX	(BIJ	(I) WILL O THE WISP	1975 A&M AMLS68309	RI ISLAND	ISA 5008
DELANEY BRAMLETT	G	(B	(I) WILL O THE WISP	1975 SHELTER US 2138 RI		52020
BONNIE BRAMLETT	V	(B	(J) LIVE IN JAPAN	1975 SHELTER		RS 5117
BOBBY WHIPLASH		(B	(K) WEDDING ALBUM	1976 PARADISE US 2943	UK	K56244
CLYDIE KING		(B	(L) BEST OF LEON RUSSELL	1976 SHELTER US 52004	ISLAND	ISA 5013
BOB MOORE	B	(F	(M) MAKE LOVE TO THE MUSIC	1977 PARADISE US 3066		
MERRY CLAYTON	V	(B	(N) AMERICANA	1978 PARADISE US 3172	UK	K56534
JOE COCKER	V	(B	(O) WILLIE & LEON	1979 CBS	UK	88461
J J CALE	G	(FI	(P) LIFE & LOVE	1979 PARADISE US 3341	UK	K56891
BILLY SANFORD	G	(F	(Q) & NEW GRASS REVIVAL LIVE	1981 WB	UK K56891	
DIANNE DAVIDSON	G	(F	( ) LOOKING BACK	1974 OLYMPIC US 7112		

BEN KEITH	DOB	(M								
ERIC CLAPTON	G	(B	CHUCK BLACKWELL	D (EHDG	CARL RADLE	B EFHIDG	JIM KELTNER	B	(EHID
DON PRESTON	G V	(EHIDG	HAROLD BRADLEY	B (F	JOEY COOPER	G V(EHDG	JOHN GALLIE	K	(DEHGO
JOE ZINKAN	B	(F	RAY EDENTON	G (F	PETE DRAKE	STEEL(FH	DAVID BRIGGS	K	(F
PETE WADE	G	(F	CHARLIE McCOY	HCA (F	JOHNNY GIMBLE	FDL (F	BOBBY THOMPSON	BAN	(F
CURLY CHALKER	STEEL	(F	JIM BUCHANAN	FDL (F	BUTCH ROBINS	G (F	TUT TAYLOR		(F
JERRY CARRIGAN	D	(F	PIG ROBBINS	K (F	WELDON MYRICK	STEEL(F	JESSE ED DAVIS	G	(D
BILLY BYRD	G	(F	CHIP YOUNG	G (F	GRADY MARTIN	G (F	HAL RUGG	STEEL	(F
KARL HIMMEL	D	(HM	HENRY BEST	B (H	WILLIAM KENNER	MAND (H	LINDA HARGROVE	G	(H
EDWIN SCRUGGS	G	(H	JOHN CALE	G (H	WILLIE NELSON	G (HO	ODELL STOKES	G	(H
JAMIE OLDAKER	D	(H	ROBERT WILSON	B (HK	CHARLES WILSON	K V (H	RONNIE WILSON	HRNS	(H
TOMMY LOKEY	HRNS	(H	CHRIS CLAYTON	HRNS (H	MARCY LEVY	V (H	ANN BELL	V	(H
PAM THOMPSON	V	(H	LENA STEPHENS	V (H	TEDDY JACK EDDY	D (IKM	MARY RUSSELL	K V(IKM	
MOON CALHOUN	D	(I	MASAKO HIRAYAMA BIWA	(I	AL JACKSON	D (I	STEVE CROPPER	G	(I
BOBBY MANUEL	G	(I	DONALD DUCK DUNN	B (I	TOMMY ALLSUP	G (I	PATRICK HENDERSON K PERC(IG		
AMBROSE CAMPBELL	PERCD	(IKOGO	STEVE DOUGLAS	FLT (K	DENNIS MANSFIELD	G (K	RICHARD TORRANCE	G	(K
ROGER LINN		(KP	DAVID MINER	B (IM	TRUMAN THOMAS	K (K	JULIUS WECHTER	K	(K
MARTY GREBB	SAX	(KNOPM	GREG THOMAS	D (KM	WILLIE WEEKS	B (K	NIGEL OLSSON	D	(K
GARY ROWLES	G	(K	BOBBY WOMACK	G (K	MARC BENNO	(AC	BRENT NELSON	D	(N
JOE CHEMAY	B	(NP	JOHN WOODHEAD	G (N	MIKE MEROS	K (N	LEE LOUGHNANE	TPT	(N
JAMES PANKOW	TROM	(N	WALTER PARAZEIDER SAX	(N	WORNELL JONES	V (NP	PAUL ENGLISH	D	(O
JIM BOATMAN	V	(O	REX LUDWICK	D (O	JODY PAYNE	G V (O	CHRIS ETHRIDGE	B	(O
BEE SPEARS	B	(O	MICKEY RAPHAEL	HCA(OMP	MARIA MULDAUR	V (O	BONNIE RAITT	G	(O
BERNETTA RAND	V	(P	LENA LUCKEY	V (P	CLAUDIA LENNEAR	V (D	KATHI McDONALD	V	(D
BARRY BECKETT	K	(D	JIMMY JOHNSON	G (D	DAVID HOOD	B (D	ROGER HAWKINS	D	(D
JIM PRICE	K	(D							

RAY RUSSELL

```
RAY RUSSELL        G   (ALL      (A) TURN CIRCLE                       1968 CBS                       52586
TONY ROBERTS       SAX (CDF      (B) DRAGON HILL                       1969 CBS                       52663
DARYL RUNSWICK     B   (CDE      (C) RITES & RITUALS                   1971 CBS                       64271
ALAN RUSHTON       D   (CABD     (D) JUNE 11TH 1971                    1971 RCA                    UK SF8214
HARRY BECKETT      TPT (CBDE     (E) SECRET ASYLUM                     1973 BLACK LION BLP12100       2460 207
NICK EVANS         TROM (CB      (F) READY OR NOT                      1977 DJM                       DJH20506
SIMON PHILLIPS     D   (F
PETER VAN HOOKE    D   (F    MO FOSTER       B   (F   TONY HYMAS      K   (F   CHRIS PARREN      K   (F
JOHN PUNTER        PERC (F   KAPLAN KAYE     PERC (F  MARTIN DROVER   TPT (F   MALCOLM GRIFFITHS TROM(F
AL GREED           V   (F    ANNIE KAVANAGH  V   (F   MOON WILLIAMS   V   (F   ANDY MACKAY       SAX (F
TIM WHITEHEAD      SAX (F    DENNY McCAFFREY V   (F   HELEN WRIGHT    CELLO(F  LIZ EDWARDS       VLN (F
LEVINE ANDRADE     VLA (F    GAVIN WRIGHT VLN    (F   MIKE RUTHERFORD (        GARY WINDO        SAX (E
ROY FRY            PNO (AB   RON MATTEWSON   B   (AB  BUD PARKES      TPT (B   LYN DOBSON  SAX   ( B
DONALD BEICHTOL    TROM (B
```

RUSSIA

```
                             (A) RUSSIA                               1980 WB                     US BSK 3414
```

MIKE RUTHERFORD

```
MIKE RUTHERFORD    G B (AB      (A) SMALLCREEPS DAY                   1980 CHARISMA               UK CAS 1149
ANTHONY PHILLIPS   K   (A       (B) ACTING VERY STRANGE               1982 WEA                    UK K99249
NOEL McCALLA       V   (A
SIMON PHILLIPS     D   (A    MORRIS PERT     PERC (A  DARYL STUERMER  G   (B   JOHN ALEXANDER    G   (B
STEWART COPELAND   D   (A    PETE PHIPPS     D   (B   PETE ROBINSON   K   (B   PAUL FISHMAN      K   (B
GARY BARNACLE      SAX (B    LUKE TUNNEY     TPT (B   STEVE GOULD     V   (B   NOEL McCALLA      V   (B
DALE NEWMAN        V   (B
```

RUTLES

```
OLLIE HALSALL      G K (A       (A) THE RUTLES                        1978 WB UK K56459           US 3151
NEIL INNES         G K V(A
RICKI FATAAR       G B V(A   JOHN HALSEY     D V (A   ANDY BROWN      B   (A
```

THE RUTS

```
MALCOLM OWEN       V   (AB      (A) THE CRACK                         1979 VIRGIN UK V2132  GER 200 988
PAUL FOX           G   (ABC     (B) GRIN & BEAR IT                    1980 VIRGIN UK V2188  GER 203 056
DAVE RUFFY         D   (ABC     (C) ANIMAL NOW                        1981 VIRGIN UK V2193  GER 203 705
VINCE SEGS         B   (ABC
BILL BARNACLE      TPT (BC  GARY BANACLE    SAX K V(ABC LUKE TUNNEY   TPT (A   MANNAH            V   (A
MICK GLOSSOP       SYN (A
```

PAUL RYAN

```
PAUL RYAN          K V (A       (A) SCORPIO RISING                    1976 CHARISMA               UK CAS 1121
RAY ROBERTS        K   (A
DAVE CAKEBREAD     B   (A    KEVIN STEPHENSON G  (A   TONY BEARD      D   (A
```

PAUL & BARRY RYAN

```
PAUL RYAN          V   (A       (A) TWO OF A KIND                     1967 DECCA      UK    LK  4878
BARRY RYAN         V   (A
```

MAGGIE RYDER

```
MAGGIE RYDER       V   (A       (A) MAGGIE RYDER                      1978 POLYDOR     UK    2383 496
STEVE JAMES        PROD(A
```

MITCH RYDER

```
MITCH RYDER        V   (ALL     (A) TAKE A RIDE                       1966 NEW VOICE        US    2000
JIM McCARTY        G   (ABCEFI  (A) TAKE A RIDE                       1966 STATESIDE       UK    10178
JOE CUBERT         G   (ABCEFI  (B) BREAKOUT                          1967 NEWVOICE        US    2002
TONY SUEHY         B   (J       (B) BREAKOUT                          1967 STATESIDE       UK    10189
EARL ELIOT         B   (AEFI    (C) SOCK IT TO ME                     1967 NEW VOICE       US    2003
JOHN'BEE' BADANJEK D (ABCEFHI   (D) WHAT NOW MY LOVE                  1967 DYNAVOICE       US    31901
DAVE OPATIK        G   (J       (D) WHAT NOW MY LOVE                  1967 STATESIDE       UK    10229
JIM McCALLISTER    G   (CDEFI   (E) MITCH RYDER SINGS THE HITS        1968 NEW VOICE       US    2005
BOOKER T JONES     K   (G       (F) ALL MITCH RYDERS HITS             196  CREWE          US    1335
DUCK DUNN          B   (G       (G) THE DETROIT MEMPHIS EXPERIMENT    1969 DOT            US    25963
AL JACKSON         D   (G       (H) DETROIT                           1971 PARAMOUNT  SPFL277  +   6010
STEVE CROPPER      G PROD(G     (I) GREATEST HITS                     1972 BELLAPHON            15163
STEVE HUNTER       G   (H       (J) HOW I SPENT MY VACATION           1979 LINE          GERM   5002
JOHN VASS          G   (J       (J) HOW I SPENT MY VACATION           197  SEEDS & STEMS  US    7801
W R COOKE          B   (H       (K) ROCK'N'ROLL LIVE(EP)              1979 LINE          GERM   3004
BRETT TUGGLE       G   (H       (L) NAKED BUT NOT DEAD                1980 LINE          GERM   5046
WAYNE GABRIEL      G   (J       (L) NAKED BUT NOT DEAD                198  SEEDS & STEM   US    7804
DIRTY ED           PERC (H      (M) WE'RE GONNA WIN (EP)              1980 LINE          GERM   3013
HARRY PHILLIPS     K   (H       (N) GOT CHANGE FOR A MILLION          1981 LINE          GERM   5100
BOOT HILL          K HCA(H      (O) LIVE TALKIES   (DBL)              1982 LINE          GER    8001
BILLY CSERNITS     K   (JKLMN   (P) SMART ASS                         1982 LINE          GER    5200
MARK GOUGEON       B   (JKLMN
JOHN SAUTER        B   (H    MARK MANKO      G   (H   RICHARD SCHEIN  G (JKLMN  JOE GUTE    G    (KLMN
WILSON OWENS       D (JKLMN  BILLY LAVERE(ITCH RYDER) V
```

RYE WHISKEY ROAD BAND

```
MIKE WHITE         G V (A       (A) RUNNING KIND   1979              FOLK HERITAGE          FHR 1017
PETE HANDLEY       V B (A
KEN BYNG   V G STEEL (A   MICK WILLIAMS    G   (A   MAI JONES       V   (A   BERYL WATKINS     V  (A
KIP GLADWELL       D   (A
```

TERJE RYPDAL

```
TERJE RYPDAL       G V FLT(ALL  (A) TERJE RYPDAL                     1971 ECM                    ECM 1016
BOBO STENSSON      K   (AX       (B) WHAT COMES AFTER                 1974 ECM                    ECM 1031
TOM HALVERSEN      K   (A       (C) WHENEVER I SEEM TO BE FAR AWAY    1974 ECM                    ECM 1045
ARILD ANDERSEN     B   (A       (D) ODYSSEY    (DBL)                  1975 ECM                    ECM1067/8
BJØRNAR ANDERSEN   B   (A       (E) AFTER THE RAIN                    1976 ECM                    ECM 1083
JON CHRISTENSEN    D   (ABCFH   (F) WAVES                             1978 ECM                    ECM 1110
BARRE PHILLIPS     B   (B       (G) RYDAL,VITOUS,DeJOHNETTE           1979 ECM                    ECM 1125
ERIK NIORD LARSEN  HRNS (B      (H) DESCENDRE                         1980 ECM                    ECM 1144
INGER LISE RYPDAL  V   (AE      (X) SART                              1971 ECM                    ECM1915
JACK DeJOHNETTE    D   (G       (Y) BLEAK HOUSE                       1968 KARUSSEL    GER  2915  053
MIROSLAV VITOUS    B PNO(G      ( ) DREAM                             19   KARUSSEL    GER  2915  068
PALLE MIKKELBORG   HRNS (FH
```

(CONTINUED)

TERJE RYPDAL

SVEIN CHRISTIANSEN D	(D	C M NEUMANN WIND	(Y	HANS KNUDSEN	B	(Y	KNUR RIISNAES	SAX (Y
FRODE THINGNAES	HRNS (Y	ØRVIND WESTBY	SAX	(Y	TORE NILSEN	SAX	(Y	KJELL HANJEN	SAX (Y
DITLEF ECHHAFF	TPT (Y	KARE FUFUHOLMEN	TPT	(Y	JARL JOHANSEN	TPT	(Y	FROYDRS REE HAUFE	HRNS(Y
ODD ULLEBERG	HRNS (Y	CHRISTAIN REIM	K	(Y	TERJE VENAAS	B	(Y	JOHN CHRISTENSEN D	(Y
TOM KARLSEN	D (Y	ECKEHARD FINTL	WIND	(AXY	JAN GARBAREK	WIND	(AXY	SVEINUNG HOVENSJØ	B(BCDF
PETE KNUTSEN	K (C	ODD ULLEBERG HRN	(C	SUDFUNK SYMPHONY ORCH		(C	TORBJØRN SUNDE	IROM(D
BRYNJOLF BLIX	K (D							

S F F   (SCHICKE, FURHS & FROHLING)

EDWARD SCHICKE	D (AB	(A) SYMPHONIC PICTURES	1976 BRAIN		0060 010
GERHARD FUHRS	K SYN(ABCDE	(B) SUNBURST	1977 BRAIN		0060 068
HEINZ FROHLING	G (ABCDE	(C) AMMERLAND	1978 BRAIN	GER	0060 105
EDWARD BRUMUND RUTHER B(ABC		(D) TICKET TO EVERYWHERE	1979 BRAIN		0060 173
		(E) STRINGS	1979 BRAIN	GER	0060 223

S A F T

(A) THE BEST OF	1974 PHILIPS NOR	6478 019

S B B

JOSEF SZRZEK	K V (A	(A) FOLLOW MY DREAM	1978 SPIEGELEI GER	913272
JERZY PIOTROWSKI	D (A			
APOSTOLIS ANTYMOS G	(A			

S R C

SCOTT RICHARDSON	V (ABC	(A) SRC	1968 CAPITOL	US	2991
GLENN QUACKENBUSH K V (ABC		(B) MILESTONES	1969 CAPITOL	US	134
STEVE LYMAN	G V (AB	(C) TRAVELLER'S TALE	1970 CAPITOL	US	273
E G CLAWSON	D V (BC				
ROBIN DALE	B V (A	AL WILMOT	B V (CB RAY GOODMAN	G (C GARY QUACKENBUSH	G (AB

S V T

JACK CASADY	B (A	(A) EXTENDED PLAY (EP)	19 415A US	0002
BILL GIBSON	D (			
NICK BUCK	K (A	BRIAN MARNELL	G V (PAUL ZAHL	D V (A

SUE SAAD & THE NEXT

SUE SAAD	V (A	(A) SUE SAAD & THE NEXT	1980 PLANET	P4
JAMES LANCE	D V (A			
BILLY ANSTATT	G (A	TONY RIPARETTI	G (A BOBBY MANZER	B (A

SABATAGE

(A) SUBTERFUGE(EP)	19 OPTIMISTIC	OPT004

SABREJETS

(A) RADIOLAND (EP)	1979 BLUEPORT	BLU5

SABU

PAUL SABU	G V (A	(A) SABU	1979 MCA	
DAN HOLMES	D (A	(B) SABU	1980 MCA	202209
RICK BOZZO	B (A			
STEFFEN PRESLEY	K (A			

SAD CAFE

PAUL YOUNG	V (BCDEFH	(A) SAD CAFE (MATERIAL USED ON (B)	1976 CHRYSALIS (NOT RELEASED) 1114
ASHLEY MULFORD	G (BCDEFH	(B) FANX TARA	1977 RCA PL25101 RI INTS 5132
TONY CRESSWELL	D (BCD	(C) HUNGRY EYES	1977 RCA PB 5062
JOHN STIMPSON	B V (BCDEFH	(D) MISPLACED IDEALS	1978 RCA PL25133 RI INTS 5133
LENNI ZAKSEN	SAX (FH	(D) MISPLACED IDEALS	1978 A&M US 4737
VIC EMERSON	G V (BCDEF	(E) FACADES	1979 RCA PL25249 RI 80 3033
IAN WILSON	G V (BDEFH	(E) FACADES	1979 A&M US 4779
LENNY SACHS	SAX (D	(F) SAD CAFE	1980 RCA SAD LP4 + PL 25319
DALE IRVING	D (EF	(F) SAD CAFE	1980 POLYDOR US 5045
JOHN PUNTER	PERC (D	(G) LIVE	1981 RCA UK SAD LP5
DOREEN CHANTER	V (D	(H) SAD CAFE	1981 SWANSONG
IRENE CHANTER	V (D		

SADISTIC MIKA BAND

MIKA KATOH	V (ABC	(A) SADISTIC MIKA BAND	1974 HARVEST US 11375 UK SHSP 4029
KAZUHIKO KATOH	G V (ABC	(B) BLACK SHIP	1975 HARVEST UK SHSP 4043
REI OHARA	B (AB	(C) HOT MENU	1976 HARVEST UK SHSP 4049
YUKIHORO TAKAHASHI D	(ABC		
MASAYOSHI TAKANAKA G	(ABC HIROSHI IMAI	K SAX(BC TSUGUTSHI GOTO	B (C

SAGA

MICHAEL SADLER	K V (ABCDE	(A) SAGA	1978 MAZE US 8001 POLYDOR 6209
PAUL RECHON	K (A	(B) IMAGES AT TWILIGHT	1980 MAZE US 8002 POLYDOR 2391 437
STEVE NEGUS	D (ABCDE	(C) SILENT KNIGHT	1980 POLYDOR 2374 166
IAN CRICHTON	G (ABCD	(D) WORLDS APART	1981 MAZE US 8004 PORTRAIT 25054
JIM CRIGHTON	SYB B(ABCDE	(E) IN TRANSIT	1982 MAZE US 8006
JIM GILMOUR	K V (BCDE		
GREG CHADD	K V (B		

SAGITTARIUS

CURT BOETCHER	(AB	(A) PRESENT TENSE	1968 CBS	US	9644
MIKE FENNELLY	(A	(B) THE BLUE MARBLE	1969 TOGETHER	US	1002
LEE MALLORY	(A			
DOUG RHODES	(A	SANDY SALISBURY	(A JOE STEC	(A RON EDGAR	(A
KEITH OLSEN	(AB	GLEN CAMPBELL	(A BRUCE JOHNSTON	(A STEVE CLARK	(A
GARY USHER	(AB			

SAHARA

PAUL VINCENT	G (A	(A) SUBJECT	1972 EPIC GER 64998
MICHAEL HOFMANN WIND SYN(ABC		(B) SAHARA	1973 DAWN UK DNLS 3068
ALEX PITTWOHN	HCA SAX V(ABC	(C) SUNRISE	1974 PAN GER 87306 US PETERS 9006
HARRY ROSENKIND	D PERC(ABC		
STEFAN WISSNET	B V (ABC NICHOLAS WOODLAND G(BC PETER STADLER	K (A

```
DOUG SAHM          G V FDL(ALL    (A) BEST OF SIR DOUGLAS QUINTET      1965 TRIBE    US 37001 UK LONDONHAU8311
MARTIN FIERRO      SAX    (G       (A) BEST OF SIR DOUGLAS QUINTET      1976 CRAZY CAJUN      RI           1003
WAYNE TALBERT      PNO    (        (B) HONKY BLUES(SIR DOUGLAS)         1968 SMASH          US            67108
TERRY HENRY        HRNS   (        (C) MENDOCINO                        1969 SMASH          US            67115
WHITNEY FREEMAN    B      (        (C) MENDOCINO                        1975 OVAL 5001  MERCURY 9279 125
FRANK MORIN    V HRNS  (CKMDI      (D) 1+1+1=4                          1970 PHILIPS                   600  344
MEL MARTIN         SAX    (G       (E) TOGETHER AFTER FIVE              1970 SMASH          US            67130
BILL ATWOOD        SAX    (        (F) RETURN OF DOUG SALDANA           1971 PHILIPS                   600  353
JOHN PEREZ         D      (CDFIMR  (G) DOUG SAHM & THE BAND             1973 ATLANTIC US 7254   UK K40466
AUGIE MEYER        K      (CDGIKMR (H) TEXAS TORNADO                    1974 ATLANTIC US 7287
KEN KOSEK          FDL    (G       (I) ROUGH EDGES                      1973 MERCURY  US SRMi 655
HARVEY KAGAN       B      (CKMDI   (J) GROOVERS PARADISE                1974 WB     US   2810          K56067
JIM STALLINGS      B      (MFI     (K) TEXAS ROCK FOR COUNTRY ROLLERS   1976 DOT    . US 2057 ABC UK    5186
GEORGE RAINS       D      (GK      (L) LIVE LOVE                        1977 TEXAS    US 1007
JACK BARBER        B V    (GOF     (N) SIR DOUG WAY BACK                1979 HARLEM   US 1005
BOB DYLAN    V G K HCA    (G       (O) HELL OF A SPELL                  1980 TAKOMA   US 7075
DR JOHN            K      (G       (O) HELL OF A SPELL                  1980 CHRYSALIS           UK CHR1249
DAVID BROMBERG     G      (G       (P) WAY BACK WHEN HE WAS JUST D SAHM  1980 ROCKHOUSE NL 8001
DAVID NEWMAN       SAX    (G       (Q) BEST OF SIR DOUGLAS QUINTET      1980 TAKOMA   US 7086
WAYNE JACKSON      TPT    (G       (R) BORDER WAVE                      1981 TAKOMA   US 7088 CHRYSALIS 203258
WILLIE BRIDGES     SAX    (G
JACK WALRATH       TPT    (G
CHARLIE OWENS      STEEL( G   ANDY STATMAN     MAND (G   ARIF MARDIN      PNO  (G   FLACO JIMINEZ    ACC (G
ATWOOD ALLEN       G V  (GF  DOUG CLIFFORD    D    (J   STU COOK         D    (J   LINK DAVIS    K FDL V(J
GARY POTTERTON     STEEL(J   RON STALLINGS    SAX  (J   JOE RAE        MARIMBA (J   ROCKY MORALES    SAX (O
LEON BAEBY         (       JOHN OXENDINE    D    (O   KELLY DUNN       K    (O   LOUIE BUSTOS     SAX (O
CHARLES McBURNEY   TPT  (O   ALVIN CROW       G V  (R   SPEEDY SPARKS    B    (R
```

```
COURT PICKETT             (A       (A) MOTORCYCLE MAMMA                 1972 ELEKTRA    US        75029
JOHN WYKER                (A
CHUCK LEAVEL       K      (A
```

```
GRANT SERPELL      D V  (ABCDG     (A) SAILOR                          1974 EPIC US 33248    UK 80337
GEORG KAJANUS      G V K(ABCDG     (B) TROUBLE                         1975 EPIC US 34039    UK 69192
HENRY MARSH        K V  (ABCDFG    (C) THIRD STOP                      1976 EPIC NL 81701    UK 81637
PHIL PICKETT       G K V(ABCFG     (D) CHECK POINT                     1977 EPIC             UK 82256
VIRGINIA TAYLOR           (F       (E) GREATEST HITS                   1978 EPIC             UK 82754
GAVIN TAYLOR              (F       (F) DRESSED TO DROWN                1981 CARIBOU US 36746 UK 84534
PENGUIN CAFE ORCH         (G       (G) HIDEAWAY                        1978 EPIC NL 83249
```

```
ENDLE ST CLOUD            (A       (A) THANK YOU ALL VERY MUCH          19    INT ARTISTS IALP 12
D F POTTER                (A
PETE BLACK                (A   JAMES HARRELL        (A
```

```
JOHN ST FIELD(JACKIE LEVEN) V G K(A (A) CONTROL                        19    MCA
JOE KUCCER         WIND (A
JOHN HAYNES        D    (A   PHIL RYAN        K    (A
```

```
BRIDGET ST JOHN    G V K(ALL       (A) ASK ME NO QUESTIONS             1969 DANDELION US 101    UK 62750
RON GEESIN         G K  (B         (B) SONGS FOR A GENTLE MAN          1971 DANDELION            UK  DAN8007
RICK SANDERS       G    (BC        (B) SONGS FOR A GENTLE MAN          1971 ELEKTRA   US            74104
JOHN MARTYN        G    (C         (C) THANK YOU FOR                   1972 DANDELION           UK 2310 193
RICK KEMP          B    (C         (D) JUMBLE QUEEN                    1974 CHRYSALIS           UK CHR 1062
PIP PYLE           D    (C
GORDON HUNTLEY     STEEL(C   IAN WHITEMAN     K    (C   ANDY ROBERTS      G    (C   DAVE MATTACKS   D (C
TIM RENWICK        G    (C   WILLIE WILSON    D    (C   BRUCE THOMAS      B    (C
```

```
ROY ST JOHN               (A       (A) ROY ST JOHN(EP)                 1977 VIRGIN        UK    VEP 1002
```

```
ROB GRANGE         B V  (A         (A) ST PARADISE                     1979 WB    US BSK 3281    UK K56689
DENNY CARMASSI     D V  (A
DERFK ST HOLMES    G V  (A   JOHN CORY        K V  (A   MARTY CONN      K    (A
```

```
ED BISSOT          B V  (A         (A) ST JOHN GREEN                   19   FLICK    US        45001
SHEL SCOTT         D    (A
VIC SABINO         HCA V(A   BILL KIRKLAND        (A   MIKE BAXTER    K V  (A
```

```
BUFFY ST MARIE     V G  (ALL       (A) IT'S MY WAY                     1964 VANGUARD  VSD79142
CHARLIE McCOY      HCA  (JH        (A) IT'S MY WAY                     196  FONTANA UK TFL 6040
BILLY SANFORD      G    (JH        (B) MANY A MILE                     1965 VANGUARD  VSD79171
DAVID BRIGGS       K    (JH        (B) MANY A MILE                     196  FONTANA UK TFL 6047
NORBERT PUTNAM     B    (JH        (C) LITTLE WHEEL SPIN               1966 VANGUARD  VSD79211
KENNY BUTTREY      D    (JH        (C) LITTLE WHEEL SPIN               196  FONTANA UK TFL 6071
SID SHARP          STRINGS(J       (D) FIRE ,FLEET & CANDLE LIGHT       1967 VANGUARD  VSD79250
MEMPHIS HORNS          (JH         (E) I'M GONNA BE A COUNTRY GIRL AGAIN 1968 VANGUARD  VSD79280
JACK NITZSCHE      PNO  (G         (F) ILLUMINATIONS                   1970 VANGUARD  VSD79300
MERRY CLAYTON      V    (G         (G) SHE USED TO WANNA BE A BALLERINA 1971 VANGUARD  VSD79311
RY COODER          G    (G         (H) MOON SHOT                       1972 VANGUARD  VSD79312
RUSS TITELMAN           (G         (J) QUIET PLACES                    1973 VANGUARD  VSD79330
GAYLE LEVANT       HARP (G         (K) BEST OF        (DBL)            1973 VANGUARD  VSD  3/4
JESSE ED DAVIS     G    (G         (L) NATIVE NORTH AMERICAN CHILD     1974 VANGUARD  VSD79340
BOBBY WEST              (G         (M) BEST OF VOL 2  (DBL)            1974 VANGUARD  VSD33/44
DANNY WHITTEN           (G         (N) BUFFY                           1974 MCA  US 405 MCG 3517
RALPH MOLINA            (G         (O) CHANGING WOMAN                  1975 MCA  US 451  UK   MCF 2594
BILLY TALBOT            (G         (P) GOLDEN HOUR                     1976 PYE  UK          GH 825
NEIL YOUNG              (G         (Q) SWEET AMERICA                   1976 ABC  US 929  UK ABCL5168
CARLOS PARDEIRO         (G
```

(CONTINUED)

BUFFY SAINTE MARIE (CONTINUED)

```
ARIEL GONZALES      (G    BOB BOZINA    G      (F    BRUCE LANGHORN    G    (DC  MONTE DUNN  MAND    (D
BOB SIGGINS     BAN (D    RUSS SAVAKUS  B      (BD   AL RODGERS        D    (D   ERIC WEISSBERG   G    (C
GRADY MARTIN    G   (E    RAY EDENTON   G      (E    VELMA SMITH       G    (E   HARALD RUGG   STEEL(E
LLOYD GREEN     STEEL(E   WAYNE MOSS    B      (E    JERRY SHOOK       B    (E   JUNIOR HUSKY     B    (E
FLOYD CRAMER    PNO (E    GROVER LAVENDER  VLN (E    SONNY OSBORNE     BJO  (E   BUDDY HARMAN     D    (E
BILL ACKERMAN   D   (E    JORDONAIRES   V      (E    BOB BOZINA        G    (F   JOHN CRAVIOTTO   D    (F
RICK OXENDINE   B   (F    GLORIA JONES  V      (H    RHETTA HUGHES     V    (H   OMA DRAKE        V    (H
PATRICE HOLLOWAY V  (H
```

SAINTS

```
CHRIS BAILY     V   (ABCD      (A) I'M STRANDED        1977 HARVEST      UK   SHSP 4065
ED KUEPPER      G   (ABC       (A) I'M STRANDED        1977 SIRE         US        6039
IVOR HAY        D   (ABCD      (B) ETERNALLY YOURS     1978 HARVEST      UK   SHSP 4078
KIM BRADSHAW    B   (A         (C) PREHISTORIC SOUNDS  1978 HARVEST      UK   SHSP 4094
ALASTAIR WARD   B   (BC        (D) MONKEY PUZZLE       1981 NEW ROSE     ROSE 1
MARTIN BRUCE    TPT (C
MARTIN DROVER   TPT (C    PAUL NIEMAN   TROM   (C    ROGER CAWKWELL SAX PNO (C   BARRINGTON       G    (D
JANINE HALL     B   (D    ROD COE       PROD   (A    MARK BIRMINGHAM    D    (D   PATRICE MATHE    HCA (D
```

RIUIDHI SAKAMATO

```
RIUICHI SAKAMATO    (A         (A) B 2 UNIT           1981 ISLAND       UK   ILPS9656
```

FREDDIE SALEM & THE WILDCATS

```
MYRON GROMBACKER    (A         (A) CAT DANCE          1982 EPIC      US   38018
```

SALLYANGIE

```
MIKE OLDFIELD   G V (A         (A) CHILDREN OF THE SUN 1968 TRANSATLANTIC  UK   TRA176
SALLY OLDFIELD  V   (A
TERRY COX       D   (A    REY WARLEIGH FLT  (A
```

SALUKI

```
KJELL RONNINGEN   K   (A       (A) SALUKI             1976 COMPENDIUM   FIN  FIDARO 6
PETER BERG NILSEN V SAX(A
SVERRE BEYER    B   (A    BJORN JENSEN D PERC  (A    FREDDY DAHL   G V  (A
```

SALVATION (ARMY BANNED)

```
AL LINDE        V   (A         (A) SALVATION          1968 ABC  US ABCS 623 UA UK UAS 29062
ARTIE McLEAN    B   (A
JOE TATE        G   (A    TEDDY STEWART  D    (A    TOM SCOTT      WIND (A   BILL PLUMMER   SIT (A
ART RESNICK     K   (A
```

SAM & DAVE

```
SAM DAVID MOORE  V  (ALL       (A) SAM & DAVE         1966 ROULETTE     US             25323
DAVE PRATER      V  (ALL       (B) HOLD ON I'M COMIN' 1966 ATLANTIC     US              8708
                               (C) DOUBLE DYNAMITE    1966 ATLANTIC     US 8712  UK588181
                               (D) SOUL MEN           1967 ATLANTIC     US 8725  UK580185
                               (E) I THANK YOU        1968 ATLANTIC     US 8205  UK588154
                               (F) BEST OF            1969 ATLANTIC     US 8218  UK588155
                               (F) BEST OF            1972 ATLANTIC     RI UK       K40027
                               (F) BEST OF            1982 ATLANTIC     RI UK       K50748
                               (G) STAR COLLECTION    1974 WB           GERM        20073
                               (H) BACK ATCHA         1975 UA           US      LA   524
```

SAM APPLE PIE

```
SAM SAMPSON         (AB        (A) SAM APPLE PIE      1969 DECCA UK SKLR5005  US SIRE 97020
ANDY'SNAKEHIP'JOHNSON (AB      (B) EAST 17            1973 DJM              UK   DJLPS429
MARTIN BELL     D   (
MARK DeMAJO     B   (     DAVE CHARLES   D    (A    ANDY JOHNSON   G    (    BOB RENNIE    B   (AB
MIKE'TINKERBELL'SMITH G(A DENNY BARNES   G    (B    LEE BAXTER HAYES D  (B   MALCOLM MORLEY K(A
REX MORRIS      SAX (A    HARRY KLEIN    SAX  (A    STEVE JOLLY    G    (A   ANDY CLARK    K(A
```

SAM THE SHAM & THE PHARAOHS

```
DOMINGO 'SAM' SAMUDIO V K(ALL  (A) WOOLY BULLY        1965 MGM          US        4297
DAVID MARTIN    B   (ABCDE     (B) THEIR SECOND ALBUM 1965 MGM          US        4314
RAY STINNET     G   (ABCDE     (C) ON TOUR            1966 MGM          US        4347
JERRY PATTERSON D   (ABCDE     (D) 'LIL RED RIDING HOOD 1966 MGM        US        4407
BUTCH GIBSON    SAX (ABCDE     (E) BEST OF            1967 MGM          US        4422
                               (F) NEFERTITI(REVUE)   1967 MGM          US        4479
                               (G) TEN OF PENTACLES   196  MGM          US        4526
                               (H) SAM,HARD & HEAVY   1970 ATLANTIC     US     SD 8271
```

SAMLA MAMMAS MANNA(SWED)

```
HANS BRUNIUSSON  D  (ALL       (A) SAMLA MAMMAS MANNA 1971 SILENCE          SRS  4604
LARS HOLLMER     K  (ALL       (B) MALTID             1973 SILENCE          SRS  4621
LARS KRANTZ      B  (ALL       (C) KLOSSA KNAPITATET  1974 SILENCE          SRS  4627
BEBBEN OBERG     CONGA(A1      (D) SNORUNGARNAS SYMFONI 1976 MUSIKNATET WAXHOLM MNW  70P
COSTE APETREA    G  (BC3D      (E) FOR ALDRE NYBEGYNNARE 1978 SILENCE       SRS  4640
KALLE ERIKSSON   TPT (D        (1) 1970      (2) 1972
ULF ARTAN WALLANDER SAX(D      (3) 1972      (4) 1976
EINO HAAPALA     G  (E5        (5) 1977
GREGORY FITZPATRICK (D
```

JOE SAMPLE

```
JOE SAMPLE      K   (ALL       (A) RAINBOW SEEKER     1978 ABC  US AA1050   UK ABCL5245
JOHN COLLINS    G   (D         (A) RAINBOW SEEKER     1982 MCA RI UK 1624
STIX HOOPER     D   (AC        (B) FANCY DANCE        1979 SONET         UK SNTF 788
ROBERT POPWELL  B   (A         (C) CARMEL             1979 ABC  US AA1126  UK ABCL 5366
JERRY HEY       HRNS(D         (C) CARMEL             1982 CRUSADERS UK RI 16001
PAULINHO DA COSTA PERC (ACD    (D) VOICES IN THE RAIN 1981 MCA           UK MCG 4016
L SUBRAMANIAM   VLN (D         (E) SING STREET CAFE   1982 CRUSADERS UK     16004
GARNETT BROWN   TROM (A
ERNIE WATTS     WIND (A   FRED JACKSON   SAX  (A    WILLIAM GREEN  WIND (A   ROBERT O BRYANT  TPT(A
JAY DAVERSA     TPT (A    STEVE MADAIO   TPT  (A    RAY PARKER     G    (A   RAY BROWN        B   (D
DEAN PARKS      G   (ACD  BARRY FINNERTY G    (A    BILLY ROGERS   B    (A   DAVID T WALKER   G   (AE
FLORA PURIM     V   (D    JOSIE JAMES    V    (D    PAULINE WILSON V    (D   ABRAHAM LABORIEL B   (CD
NIKA REJTO      FLT (D
```

SAMSON

```
    PAUL SAMSON      G V  (ABCD      (A) SURVIVORS              1979 LASER                   LAP  1
    CHRIS AYLMER     B    (AB        (B) HEAD ON                1980 GEM          UK         GEMLP108
    BRUCE BRUCE      V    (AB        (C) SAMSON                 1981 GEM          UK         GEMLP113
    THUNDERSTICKS    D    (AB        (D) SHOCK TACTICS          1981 RCA          UK LP 5031
```
S15   FUZZY SAMUELS   S15
```
    CALVIN'FUZZY' SAMUELS G B V (A   (A) FUZZY SAMUELS          1974 CAROLINE         UK     CA2002
```
S16   SAMURAI   S16
```
    DAVE LAWSON      K V  (A         (A) SAMURAI                1971 GREENWICH        UK     GSLP 1003
    TONY EDWARDS     G V  (A
    JOHN EATON       B    (A    LENNIE WRIGHT  D PERC (A   KENNY BEVERIDGE   D   (A   TONY ROBERTS    WIND(A
    DON FAY          SAX  (A
```
S17   DAVID SANBORN   S17
```
    DAVID SANBORN    SAX K (ALL      (A) TAKING OFF             1975 WB       US 2873    UK   K56148
    HERB BUSHLER     B    (B         (B) SANBORN                1976 WB       US 2957
    HIRAM BULLOCK    G V  (BCE       (C) DAVID SANBORN BAND     1977 WB       US 3051
    ROSALINDA DELEON K    (BC        (D) HEART TO HEART         1978 WB       US 3189
    PAUL SIMON       V    (E         (E) HIDEAWAY               1980 WB       US 3379    NL 56766
    JAMES TAYLOR     V    (E         (F) VOYEUR                 1981 WB                  UK K 56900
    DANNY KORTCHMAR  G    (E         (G) AS WE SPEAK            1982 WB       US 3650
    WADDY WACHTEL    G    (E
    VICTOR LEWIS     D V  (B    PATTI AUSTIN     V    (B   PHOEBE SNOW      V    (B   JUMMA SANTOS     PERC(BC
    LANI GROVES      V    (BC   MICHAEL BRECKER  SAX  (A   RANDY BRECKER    TPT  (A   HOWARD JOHNSON   HRNS(A
    TOM MALONE       TROM (A    STEVE KHAN       G    (A   BUZZY FEITEN     G    (A   JOE BECK         G   (A
    DON GROLNICK     K    (AE   WILL LEE         B    (A   CHRIS PARKER     D    (A   RICK MAROTTA     D   (AE
    RALPH MACDONALD  PERC (AE   PETER GORDON     HRNS (A   JOHN CLARK       HRNS (A   JOSE MADERA      PERC(A
    WARREN SMITH     PERC (A    STEVE GADD       D    (AE  MARK EGAN        B    (C   DALE OEHLER      K   (C
    KAT McCORD       V    (E    CHRISTINE FAITH  V    (    HAMISH STUART    V    (C   STRINGS              (AE
    DAVID SPINOZZA   G    (E
```
S18   DAVID SANCIOUS   S18
```
    DAVID SANCIOUS K G V PERC(ALL    (A) FOREST OF FEELING      1975 EPIC             US     33441
    GERALD CARBOY    B    (ABC       (B) TRANSFORMATION (& TONE) 1976 EPIC            US     33939
    ERNEST CARTER    D V  (ABC       (C) TRUE STORIES  (& TONE) 1978 ARISTA US 4201  UK     SPART1082
    GAIL BOGGS       V    (C         (D) DAVID SANCIOUS         1977 CHELSEA          US     548
    ALEX LIGERTWOOD       (C         (E) JUST AS I THOUGHT      1980 ARISTA US 4247
    GAYLE MORAN      V    (B         (F) DANCE OF THE AGE OF ENLIGHTENMENT 197 ARISTA US     4130
    BRENDA MADISON        (C         (G) BRIDGE                 1981 ARISTA          UK     SPART1162
```
S18A   SAND   S18A
```
    JACK MEUSSDORFFER G V (A         (A) SAND                   1973 BARNABY          US     BR 15006
    DAN ROSS        G V STEEL (A
    DAN WILSON       V    (A    RICH GOOCH       B V  (A   STEVE             (A
```
S18B   SANDALS   S18B
```
                                     (A) ENDLESS SUMMER (SOUNDTRACK)  19  WORLD PACIFIC  US  ST1832
```                                                                                        S18C
S18C                               ED SANDERS
```
    ED SANDERS   (AB   (A) SANDERS TRUCKSTOP   19   REPRISE   US   6374
                                     (B) BEER CANS ON THE MOON 19   REPRISE   US   2105
```
S18D                          SANDII & THE SUNSETZ                                    S18D
```
    SANDII   V   (A   (A) HEAT SCALE   1981 ALFA   ALF 85642
    MAKOTO KUBOTA G V K (A
    KENI INOVE   G V (A   KING CHAMP   B V (A   HIDEO   D   (A   CHARLES   K   (A
```
S19                                 SANTANA                                          S19
```
    CARLOS SANTANA   G V (ALL   (A) SANTANA   1968 CBS US 9781 UK 63815 RI 32003
    WITH   (B) ABRAXAS   1970 CBS US 30130 UK 64087 RI 32032
    GREGG ROLIE   K V (ABDE1234T (C) WITH BUDDY MILES   1971 CBS US 30308 UK 65142
    DAVID BROWN   B   (ABDL235G (D) SANTANA III   1972 CBS US 30595 UK 69015
    MIKE SHRIEVE   D   (ABDEJK34G (E) CARAVANSERAI   1972 CBS US 31610 UK 65299
    MIKE CARABELLO   PERC (ABCD3   (F) LOVE DEVOTION SURRENDER 1973 CBS US 32034 UK 69037
    NEAL SCHON   G   (CDE34   (G) WELCOME   1974 CBS US 32445 UK 69040
    JOSE CHEPITOS AREAS PER(ABDEKGJMN345 (H) ILLUMINATIONS   1974 CBS US 32900 UK 69063
    RICO REYES   PERC (DE34B   (I) GREATEST HITS   1974 CBS US 33050 UK 69081
    TOM COSTER   K V (EJKLH5678MNO (J) BORBOLETTA   1974 CBS US 33135 UK 69084
    ARMANDO PERAZA   G V (EFJKLR56GHOPQRS(K) LOTUS (TRIPLE)   1975 CBS   UK 66325
    LEON PATILLO   V PERC (57JS   (L) AMIGOS   1976 CBS US 33576 UK 86005
    TOM FRAZER   G   (1   (M) FESTIVAL   1977 CBS US 34423 UK 86020
    ROD HARPER   D   (1   (N) MOONFLOWER   1977 CBS US 34914 UK 88272
    GUS RODRIGUES   B   (1   (O) ONENESS   1979 CBS US 35686 UK 86037
    MARCUS MALONE   PERC (2   (P) INNER SECRETS   1979 CBS US 35600 UK 86075
    BOB LIVINGSTONE D   (2   (Q) MARATHON   1979 CBS US 36154 UK 86098
    TOM RUTLEY   B   (34E   (R) SWING OF DELIGHT (DBL) 1980 CBS US 36590 UK 22075
    COKE ESCOVEDO   PERC (3C4D   (S) ZEBOP   1981 CBS US 37158 UK 84946
    VICTOR PANTOJA   PERC (3C   (T) SHANGO   1982 CBS US 38122 UK 85914
    WILLIE BOBO   PERC (3   (1) 1966/67   (2) 1967/69   (3) 1971   (4) 1971
    PHIL FORD   TABLAS (H   (5) 1974/74   (6) 1976   (7) 1976   (8) 1976
    PETE ESCOVEDO PERC(NOP   LEON THOMAS   V   (KG RICHARD KERMODE K   (KG MINGO LEWIS   PNO (CEF
    BYRON MILLER   B   (6   GREG WALKER   V(56JLM LEON CHANCLER   D   (56JLM JULES BROUSSARD   (HGJ5
    FRANCISCO AQUABELLA PERC(R6 TOM CROUCHER   V   (7   RAUL REKOW   PERC (78RQPS PABLO TELLEZ   B V (78MN
    JOHN SANTOS   PERC (7   DAVID PRATER   D   (7   GAYLORD BIRCH   D   (7M LUTHER RABBS   V   (8
    GRAHAM LEAR   D (8NOPQRST   JOEL   (8   DOUGLAS RAUCH   B G(EFJGK TOWER OF POWER   HRNS(D
    LUIS GASCA   TPT (DC   LINDA TILLERY   V   (D   MARIO OCHOA   K   (D   GREG ERRICO   PERC(DC
    HADLEY CALIMAN   SAX (EC   WENDY HAAS   K   (DGE DAVID RODRIGUES G   (E   LENNY WHITE   PERC(E
    JAMES BOND   B   (PHIL BROWNE   PERC (FH DAVID HOLLAND   B   (H   JACK DeJOHNETTE PERC(H
    ALICE COLTRANE K HARP (H   JULIA TILLMAN WATERS V (LM IVORY STONE   B   (L   MAXINE WILLARD WATERS V(LM
    JOHN McLAUGHLIN G   (FG   BILLY COBHAM   D   (F   JAN HAMMER   K   (F   LARRY YOUNG   ORG (F
    DON ALIAS   D   (F   STANLEY CLARKE B   (J   AIRTO MOREIRA   D   (J   FLORA PURIM   V   (JG
    HERBIE HANCOCK   K   (R   WAYNE SHORTER   SAX (R   RON CARTER   B   (R   TONY WILLIAMS   D   (R
    ORESTES VILATO   PERC (R   HARVEY MASON   D   (R   RUSSELL TUBBS   WIND (R   DAVID MARGEN   B(RNOPQRST
    ALEX LIGERTWOOD V   (QRST STRINGS   (H   ALBERTO GIANQUINTO PNO (B BUDDY MILES D V (C
    RON JOHNSON   B   (R   ROBERT HIGGINS ORG (F   PAUL JACKSON   B   (M   FRANCISCO ZAVALA V   (M
    JULES BROUSSARD SAX (G   GREG ADAMS   STR (G   MICHAEL CARPENTER G   (J   ORIN WATERS   V   (M
    FRANCISCO ZAINLA V   (M   CHRIS RHYME   K   (OP RICHARD BAKER   K   (ST ORESTES VILATO   V PERC(ST
    ALAN PASQUA   K V (QS   CHRIS SOLBERG G K V(PQSO BOB LEVY   SYN (O   URMILA SANTANA   V   (O
    SAUNDERS KING   G V (O   CLARE FISHER   PNO (O   NARADA MICHAEL WALDEN K (O TONY SMITH   D   (G
    BOB YANCE   FLT (G   DOUG RODRIGUEZ G   (G
```

S20 SANFORD & TOWNSEND S20

JOHN TOWNSEND	V	(ABCD	(A) SMOKE FROM A DISTANT FIRE	1976	WB	US BS 2966	
ED SANFORD	K V	(ABCD	(B) DUOGLIDE	1977	WB	US BS 3081	UK K56476
STEVE CROPPER	G	(B	(C) NAIL ME TO THE WALL	1979	WB	US BS 3343	
OTIS HALE	G SAX	(ABC					

ROGER JOHNSON	G	(AC	FRED TACKETT	G	(B	PAUL BARRERE	G	(B	DAVID PAICH	K	(B
HERB PEDERSEN	V	(B	JERRY McGEE	G	(B	MIKE UTLEY	PNO	(B	JEFF PORCARO	D	(C
DAVID HUNGATE	B	(B	MILT HOLLAND	PERC	(B	BILL PAYNE	K	(B	RICHARD TORRANCE	V	(B
JERRY RIGHTMER	B	(AC	CHRIS MEYER	D	(C	TOM ROADY	PERC	(AC	DICK HALLIGAN	STRINGS	(B
JIM VARLEY	D	(A	BARRY BECKETT	K	(A	KENNY LOGGINS	V	(A	GEORGE HAWKINS	V	(A
BILLY TOWNSEND	V	(A	JOHN CLARKE	WIND	(A	TEX WEX	V	(A			

S21 VERONIQUE SANSON S21

VERONIQUE SANSON	(AB	(A) AMOUREUSE	1972	ELEKTRA	K42106
		(B) HOLLYWOOD	1978	ELEKTRA	K52063

S22 SANTA BARBARA MACHINEHEAD S22

JON LORD	K	(AB	(A) TRACKS ON(BLUES ANTHOLOGY VOL3)	1968	IMMEDIATE	UK	IMLP019
RON WOOD	G	(AB	(B) TRACKS ON(BEST OF BRITISH BLUES)	19	IMMEDIATE	GERM	048 90677
KIM GARDNER	B	(AB	(C) TRACKS ON(ANTHOLOGY OF BRITISH)	19	IMMEDIATE	UK	IMA 06
TWINK	D	(AB	THE ONLY THREE TRACKS THEY RECORDED ARE ON THE ABOVE COMPILATION ALBUMS				

S23 BOB SARGEANT S23

BOB SARGEANT	G V K	(A	(A) FIRST STARRING ROLE	1975	RCA	LPLI 5076
COZY POWELL	D	(A				

JOHN WOODS		(A	JACK LANCASTER	WIND	(A	JERRY SMITH		(A	CLIVE CHAMAN	B	(A
ROBIN LUMLEY		(A	RITCHIE DHARMA	D	(A	MIKE GARSON		(A	WALT MONAGHAN	B	(A
HERBIE FLOWERS	B	(A									

S23A SARACEN S23A

RICHARD LOWE	K	(A	(A) HEROES SAINTS & FOOLS	1982	NUCLEUS	492

S24 SAROFEEN & SMOKE S24

			(A) DO IT	1971	PYE	UK	NSPL28153
			(B) SAROFEEN & SMOKE	197	GWP	US	2029

S26 SASSAFRAS S26

DAI SHELL	G	(ABC1	(A) EXPECTING COMPANY	1973	POLYDOR		2383 245
TERRY BENNETT	V	(ABC	(B) WHEELIN' & DEALIN'	1975	CHRYSALIS		CHR 1076
RALPH EVANS	G V	(ABC1	(C) RIDING HIGH	1976	CHRYSALIS		CHR 1100
DICK OWEN	D	(B	(D) SASSAFRAS	1978	H&L	US	69027
RICKY JOHN HOLT	B V	(ABC1	(1) MAY 1978				
ROBERT JONES	D V	(AC					

STEVE FINN	D	(B	EDDIE WILLIAMS	G V	(1	CHRIS SHARLEY	D	(B	JEFF JONES	D	(1
ROB REYNOLDS	D	(A									

S26A SATIN WHALE S26A

THOMAS BRUCK	B V	(A	(A) DESERT PLACES	197	BRAIN	GERM	0040 120
HORST SCHATTGEN	D V	(A					
DIETER ROESBERG	G WIND	(A	GERALD DELLMAN	K	(A		

S27 SATISFACTION S27

MIKE COTTON	HRNS	(A	(A) SATISFACTION	1971	DECCA	UK	SKL5075
LEM LUBIN	B	(A					
JOHN BEECHAM	TROM	(A	DEREK GRIFFITHS	G V	(A	NICK NEWELL	SAX (A	BERNIE HIGGINSON	DV(A

S27A SATISFACTION UNLIMITED S27A

			(A) THINK OF THE CHILDREN	19	HOT WAX	US	716

S27B MERL SAUNDERS S27B

MERL SAUNDERS	K V	(ALL	(A) HEAVY TURBULENCE	1971			
JERRY GARCIA	G V	(ABC	(B) FIRE UP	1973			
TOM FOGERTY	G	(AB	(C) LIVE AT KEYSTONE	1973	FANTASY	US	79002
JOHN KAHN	B	(ABC	(D) YOU CAN KEEP YOUR HAT ON	1976	FANTASY	US	9503
BILL VITT	D	(ABC					

EDDIE MOORE	D SAX	(A	SKIP MESQUITE	SAX	(A	MIC GILLETTE	HRNS	(A	PAT O'HARA		TROM(A
DAVID GRISMAN	MAND	(C	MARTIN FIERRO	WIND	(C	ARTHUR ADAMS	G	(D	BILLY FENDER	G	(D
CHRIS HAYES	G	(D	TONY SAUNDERS	B	(D	PAUL HUMPHREY	D	(D	LARRY VANN	D	(D
SHEILA ESCOVEDO	PERC	(D	JACKIE KING	G	(D						

S28 SATURNALIA S28

ALETTA	V	(A	(A) MAGICAL LOVE	MATRIX	1973	TRIX 1
TOM CROMPTON	D	(A				
ROD ROACH	G	(A	ADRIAN HAWKINS	V	(A	RICHARD HOUGHTON	B	(A

S28A SAVAGE GRACE S28A

JOHN SEANOR	K	(AB	(A) SAVAGE GRACE	1970	REPRISE	US	RS6399
LARRY ZACK	D	(AB	(B) SAVAGE GRACE 2	1972	REPRISE	US	RS6434
AL JACQUEZ	B V	(AB					
RON KOSS	G V	(AB					

S29 SAVAGE RESURRECTION S29

BILL HARPER		(A	(A) SAVAGE RESURRECTION	1968	MERCURY	US SR61156 UK SMCL20123
RANDY HAMMON		(A				
JEFF MYER		(A	STEVE LANGE	(A	JOHN PALMER	(A

S30 SAVAGE ROSE S30

ANNISETTE	V	(ALL	(A) SAVAGE ROSE	1968	POLYDOR	543 031	184 144
ANDERS KOPPEL	K	(ALL	(B) IN THE PLAIN	1968	POLYDOR	543051 46292	US 246001
THOMAS KOPPEL	K V	(ALL	(C) TRAVELLIN'	1969	POLYDOR		184 316
ILSE MARIA KOPPEL	K	(ABCEK	(D) YOUR DAILY GIFT	1971	POLYDOR		2380 004
NILS TUXEN	G	(BCDF	(D) YOUR DAILY GIFT	1971	RCA	UK SF8169 US GREGAR	103
ALEX RIEL	D	(BCDEF	(E) REFUGEE	1972	POLYDOR		2380 014
FLEMMING OSTERMANN	G	(E	(E) REFUGEE	1972	RCA	UK SF8250 US GREGAR	104
JOHN URIBE	G	(E	(F) POP HISTORY	1972	POLYDOR		2675 018
KEN GUDMAND	D	(J	(G) DODENS TRIUMF	1972	POLYDOR		2380 016
RUDOLF HANSEN	B	(J	(H) BABYLON	1973	POLYDOR		2380 019
BEN WEBSTER	SAX	(H	(J) WILD CHILD	1973	POLYDOR		2380 021
JENS RUGSTED	V B	(ABCDF	(K) I'M SATISFIED	197	KARUSSEL		2499 010
PEER FROST	G	(J	(L) SOLE VAROGSA DIN	1980	SONET	SLP 1556	

KIM SIMMONDS	G HCA(ALL	(A) SHAKE DOWN	1967 DECCA	UK SKL4883	
BRYCE PORTIUS	V (A	(B) GETTING TO THE POINT	1968 DECCA	UK SKL4925	US PARROT 71024
MARTIN STONE	G (A	(C) BLUE MATTER	1968 DECCA	UK SKL4994	US PARROT 71027
RAY CHAPPELL	B (A	(D) A STEP FURTHER	1969 DECCA	UK SKL5013	US PARROT 71029
LEO MANNING	D (A	(E) RAW SIENNA	1970 DECCA	UK SKL5030	US PARROT 71036
BOB HALL	PNO (ABCD	(F) LOOKING IN	1970 DECCA	UK SKL5066	US PARROT 71042
CHRIS YOULDEN	V (BCDE	(G) STREET CORNER TALKING	1971 DECCA	UK TXS 104	US PARROT 71047
LONESOME DAVE PEVERETT	G(BCDEF	(H) HELLBOUND TRAIN	1972 DECCA	UK TXS 107	US PARROT 71024
RIVERS JOBE	B (BC	(J) LIONS SHARE	1973 DECCA	UK SKL5152	US PARROT 71052
ROGER EARL	D (BCDEF	(K) JACK THE TOAD	1973 DECCA	UK TXS 112	US PARROT 71059
TONY STEVENS	PERC B(CDEF	(L) BOOGIE BROTHERS	1974 DECCA	UK SKL5186	US LONDON PS638
OWEN FINNEGAN	PERC (F	(M) WIRE FIRE	1975		US LONDON PS659
DAVE WALKER	V (GHJ	(N) SKIN'N'BONE	1976 NOVA	GER 622547	US LONDON PS670
ANDY SYLVESTER	B (GH	(O) BEST OF	1977		US LONDON 50000
RALPH MOMAN	V (R	(P) SAVAGE RETURN	1978		US LONDON PS718
DAVE BIDWELL	D (GHJK	(Q) BLUES ROOTS	1978 DECCA	UK ROOTS 7	
KEITH BOYCE	D (R	(R) ROCK'N'ROLL WARRIOR	1981		US CAPITOL 7002
BARRY PAUL	G (R	(S) JUST LIVE	1981 LINE	GER 5122	
JOHN HUMPHREY	B V (R	( ) GREATEST HITS LIVE	1981		US ACCORD
PAUL RAYMOND	V K G(GHJKNM				

JACKIE LYNTON	V (K	STAN WEBB	G V (L	MILLER ANDERSON	G V (L	RON BERG	D PERC(K
ERIC DILLON	D (L	JIMMY LEVERTON	B (L	IAN ELLIS	B V (NOP	TOM FARNELL	D (MNPO
MIKE VERNON	PERC (CD	PHIL REID	VLN (D	DEREK WADSWORTH	TROM (C	BRIAN PERRIN	TROM (C
TERRY FLANNERY	TROM (C	KEITH MARTIN	TROM (C	ALAN MOORE	TROM (C	BUTCH HUDSON	TPT (D
KENNY WHEELER	TPT (D	EDDIE BLAIR	TPT (D	RAY DAVIS	HRNS (D	BOBBY HAUGHEY	HRNS (D
DON LUSHER	TROM (D	JOHN EDWARDS	TROM (D	BOB EFFORD	SAX (D	REX MORRIS	SAX (D
DON HONEYWILL	SAX (D	STAN SULZMAN	SAX (K	SUE GLOVER	V (K	SUNNY LESLIE	V (K
FRANK RICOTTI	PERC (K	ANDY PYLE	B (JK	BARRY MURRAY PERC	(K	ANDY RAE	B (M
JOHN SINCLAIR	K (R	LINDA LAWLEY	V (R	ANDREA ROBINSON	V (R	SUE RICHMAN	V (R
RIBA GLEICH	V (A						

STARR DONALDSON	G V (A	(A) SAWBUCK	1972	
CHUCK RUFF	G D V(A			
NINE YEAR	B (A	STEPHAN HATLEY	K G V(A MOJO	G V (A

RAY SAWYER	G V (A	(A) RAY SAWYER	1977 CAPITOL	11591	
STEVE GIBSON	G (A				
DOYLE GRISHAM	STEEL(A	SHANE KEISTER	K (A	BOBBY OGDIN	PNO (A	LARRY LONDIN	D (A
KENNY MALONE	D (A	TED REYNOLDS	B (A	LISA SILVER	FDL V(A	BUDDY SPICHER	FDL(A
SHERI KRAMER	V (A	DIANE TIDWELL	V (A	STRING SECTION	(A		

PETER'BIFF' BYFORD	V (ABCD	(A) SAXON	1979 CARRERE		CAL110
PAUL QUINN	G (ABCD	(B) WHEELS OF STEEL	1980 CARRERE US 38 126		UK CAL115
STEVE DAWSON	B (ABCD	(B) WHEELS OF STEEL	1980 CARRERE GER 2934 124		
GRAHAM OLIVER	G (ABCD	(C) STRONG ARM OF THE LAW	1980 CARRERE GER 2934 129		CAL120
PETE GILL	D (ABCD	(D) DENIM & LEATHER	1981 CARRERE GER 2934 138 UK CAL 128		

SKY SAXON	(A	(A) FULL SPOON OF SEEDY BLUES	1967 GNP US 2040	RI GER LINE 5033
DARYL HOOPER	K (A			
JAN SAVAGE	G (A	RICK ANDRIDGE	D (A	

LEO SAYER	V HCA G(ALL	(A) SILVERBIRD	1973 CHRYSALIS UK CHR1050 WB US 2738
MIKE GILES	D (ABC	(B) JUST A BOY	1974 CHRYSALIS UK CHR1068 WB US 2836
HENRY SPINETTI	D (A	(C) ANOTHER YEAR	1975 CHRYSALIS UK CHR1087 WB US 2885
BOB HENRIT	D (A	(D) ENDLESS FLIGHT	1976 CHRYSALIS UK CHR1125 WB US 3101
RUSS BALLARD	K G (AC	(E) THUNDER IN MY HEART	1977 CHRYSALIS UK CHR1154 WB US 3089
DAVE WINTOUR	B (A	(F) LEO SAYER	1978 CHRYSALIS UK CHR1198 WB US 3200
DAVE COURTNEY	PNO (ABH	(G) THE VERY BEST OF	1979 CHRYSALIS UK CHR1222
MAX CHETWYN	G (A	(H) HERE	1979 CHRYSALIS UK CDL1240 WB US 3374
CLIFF HALL	PNO (B	(I) SHOW MUST GO ON	1979 PICKWICK UK SHM3035
PAUL KEOGH	G (BC	(J) LIVING IN A FANTASY	1980 CHRYSALIS UK CDL1297 WB US 3483
DAVE MARKEE	B (BC	( ) LEO SAYER	1980 PICKWICK UK 8030
BOBBYE HALL	PERC (EFH	(K) WORLD RADIO	1982 CHRYSALIS UK CHR 1345

DAVE ROSE	PNO (B	JAMES LITHERLAND	G (B	BILL SMITH	B (B	JOHN MEALING	ORG (B
LIZA STRIKE	V (B	THEODORE THUNDER	D (B	BARRY ST JOHN	V (B	KEITH NELSON	BANJ(B
FRANK FARRELL	K (C	TERRY STARR	TPT (C	NICK NEWELL	FLT (C	JOHNNY VAN DERRICK	VLN(C
DAVID KATZ ORCHESTRA	(C	JEFF PORCARO	D (EF	ABE LABORIEL	B (E	LEE RITENOUR	G (E
FRED TACKETT	G (EFH	TOM SNOW	PNO (EFH	LENNY CASTRO	CONGA(EF	MICHAEL OMARTIAN	K (E
LARRY CARLTON	G (E	JAY GRAYDON	G (EF	CLYDIE KING	V (E	BEN ADKINS	B (E
DAVID HUNGATE	B (E	IRA NEWBORN	G (E	TOM SCOTT	SAX (E	SHIRLEY MATTHEWS	V (E
RAY PARKER	G (E	JACK ASHFORD	PERC (E	JAMES NEWTON HOWARD	K (EF	BECKY LEWIS	V (E
DEAN PARKS	G (F	STEVE LUKATHER	G (F	DAVID LINDLEY STEEL	FDL(F	SCOTTY EDWARDS	B (F
DAVID PAICH	K (F	RUSS KUNKEL	D (F	LELAND SKLAR	B (F	WADDY WACHTEL	G (F
GREG PHILLINGANES	K (F	STEVE PORCARO	SYN (F	JIM GILSTRAP	V (F	BOBBY KIMBALL	V (F
BILL CHAMPLIN	V (F	LINDSAY BUCKINGHAM	G (F	BEN BENAY	G (F	CHUCK RAINEY	B (FH
OLLIE E BROWN	PERC (F	TOM SAVIANO	HRNS (F	MIKE CARNAHAN	HRNS (F	RICHARD FELTS	HRNS(F
DAVEY JOHNSTONE	G (F	RICK SHLOSSER	D (H	PAULINHO DACOSTA	PERC (H	MITCH HOLDER	G (H
BILLY LIVSEY	K (H	VICTOR FELDMAN	PERC (H	MICHAEL BODDICKER	SYN (H	ED GREENE	D (H
DUCK DUNN	B (H	STEVE CROPPER	G (H	DAVE LUELL	SAX (H	STEVE MADAIO	HRNS(H
JEFF BAXTER	V (H	AL KOOPER	K (H	CHRIS DESMOND	(H	JOHN BARNES	K(H
JERRY JUMONVILLE	SAX(H	ARNELL CARMICHAEL	V (H	MARK DOYLE	G (H	BILL PAYNE	SYN K(H
BOB GLAUB	B (H	ALAN TARNEY	V G K B(J	TREVOR TARNEY	D (J	NICK GLENNIE SMITH	K(J

(A) LEAVE ME ALONE (EP)   1980 CLUBLAND

SCAFFOLD

```
MIKE McGEAR       V   (ABCDE    (A) McGOUGH & McGEAR(NOT SCAFFOLD)   1967 PARLOPHONE      UK   PCS  7047
ROGER McGOUGH     V   (ABCDE    (B) AN EVENING WITH SCAFFOLD         1968 PARLOPHONE      UK   PCS  7051
JOHN GORMAN       V   (BCDE     (C) LILY THE PINK                    1969 PARLOPHONE      UK   PCS  7077
JOHN MEGGINSON    K   (DE       (D) FRESH LIVER                      1973 ISLAND         UK   ILPS 9234
GERRY CONWAY      D   (DE       (E) SOLD OUT                         1975 WB             UK        K56097
LOL CREME         GYSMO(E       (B) THANK YOU VERY MUCH              1968 BELL           US        6018
HELEN COX         V   (E
ZOOT MONEY        K   (DE  ANDY ROBERTS     G V  (DE  OLLIE HALSALL    G   (DE  BRIAN JONES       SAX (E
FRANK RICOTTI     PERC (E  NEIL INNES       K G  (D   RAY WARLEIGH     FLT (D   ANTHONY WHITE     G   (D
NORMAN YARDLEY    HCA  (D   TIM RICE         V   (D   ROGER BALL       SAX (D   MALCOLM DUNCAN    SAX (D
MIKE ROSEN        TPT  (D   HARRY BECKETT    TPT (D   DORIS TROY       V   (D   PAUL KORDA        V   (D
JIMMY HELMS       V   (D   ALAN GORRIE      V   (D   DAVE RICHARDS    B V (E   ROB TOWNSEND      D   (E
JIMI HENDRIX      G   (A   DAVE MASON       G   (A   MIKE VICKERS         (B
```

BOZ SCAGGS

```
BOZ SCAGGS        G V  (ALL      (A) BOZ                             1965 POLYDOR        LPHM  46253
GEORGE RAINS      D   (CDE       (B) BOZ SCAGGS                      1969 ATLANTIC UK 588 205 US  8239
BOB ARTHUR        B   (          (B) BOZ SCAGGS                    RI 1971 ATLANTIC UK K40419 US 19166
JOHN ANDREWS      G   (          (C) MOMENTS                         1971 CBS           UK   64248 US 30454
DAVID BROWN       B   (CDE       (D) BOZ SCAGGS & HIS BAND           1971 CBS           UK   64431 US 30796
JOACHIM YOUNG     K   (CDE       (D) BOZ SCAGGS & HIS BAND           1981 CBS RI             US 31848
MEL MARTIN        HRNS (CD       (E) MY TIME                         1972 CBS           UK   64975 US 31384
DOUG SIMRIL       G PNO(D        (F) SLOW DANCER                     1974 CBS           UK   65953 US 33760
RAY PARKER        G   (HK        (F) SLOW DANCER                     1981 CBS UK RI 32072
TOM POOLE         HRNS (D        (G) SILK DEGREES                    1976 CBS           UK   81193 US 33920
CAROLYN WILLIS    V   (GH        (G) SILK DEGREES                    1981 CBS UK RI 32036
ART O'HARA        (            (H) DOWN TWO THEN LEFT              1977 CBS           UK   86028 US 34729
PAT O'HARA        HRNS (CD       (J) HITS                            1980 CBS           UK   84706 US 36846
PAUL BECKER       HRNS (         (K) MIDDLEMAN                       1980 CBS           UK   86094 US 36106
ROGER HAWKINS     D   (BE
EDDIE HINTON      G   (BE  JIM JOHNSON      G    (BE  PETER CARR       G   (E   DAVE HOOD  D     (BE
CLAYTON IVEY      K   (E   SID SHARP    STRINGS(     JOE PORCARO      (        JEFF PORCARO     (GHK
FRED TACKETT      G   (G   LES DUDEK        G    (G   DUANE ALLMAN     G DOB(B   JOHN MADRID  HRNS (
ADRIA TAPIA       SAX (K   LENNY CASTRO   PERC (K   SCOTT EDWARDS    B   (E   STEVE LUKATHER    G   (HK
JAI WINDING       K   (H   JOHN McFEE   STEEL   (C   CURLEY COOKE     G   (C   COKE ESCOVEDO   PERC(C
PETE ESCOVEDO     PERC (C  BILL ATWOOD  HRNS    (C   RITA COOLIDGE    V   (CD  BEN SIDRAN    VIBES (C
CHEPITO AREAS     PERC (D  DOROTHY MORRISON V   (DE  MIKE CARABELLO   PERC (D  LEE CHARLTON        (D
BARRY BECKETT     K   (BE  CHARLES CHALMERS SAX (BE  FLOYD NEWMAN     SAX (B   BEN CAULEY      TPT (B
GENE MILLER       TPT (B   JOE ARNOLD       SAX (B   JAMES MITCHELL   SAX (B   JEANNIE GREENE   V   (B
MARY HOLLADAY     V   (B   DONNA THATCHER   V   (B   TRACY NELSON     V   (B   IRMA ROUTEN      V   (B
JOYCE DUNN        V   (B   AL LESTER    FDL     (B   DAVID PAICH    K SYN(GK  LOUIS SHELTON    G   (G
PLAS JOHNSON      SAX (G   JIM HORN     HRNS    (G   CHUCK FINDLEY  HRNS (G   BUD SHANKS       SAX (G
MARTY McCALL      V   (G   AUGIE JOHNSON    V   (G   MAXINE GREEN     V   (G   PEPPER SWENSON   V   (G
JOHN PIERCE       B   (K   RICK MAROTTA     D   (K   DON GROLNICK     K   (K   CARLOS SANTANA   G   (K
JOE VITALE        D   (K   JAMES NEWTON HOWARD K (K  PAULETTE BROWN   V   (K   DAVID LASLEY     V   (K
SHARON REDD       V   (K   CHARLOTTE CROSSLEY V (K   BILI THEDFORD    V   (K   OREN WATERS      V   (K
BILL CHAMPLIN     V   (K   CHARLES IRWIN    V   (K   DAVID HUNGATE    B   (GHK ZEDRIC TURNBOUGH V   (K
VICTOR FELDMAN    K   (H   PHYLLIS ST JAMES V   (H   ELDRIGE KING     V   (H   CHUCK FINDLEY    HRN (GH
JULIA TILLMAN     V   (HK  STAN FARBER      V   (H   ERNIE WATTS  SAX (H   DON MENZA        HRNS(H
MICHAEL OMARTIAN  K   (H   JAY GRAYDON  B       (H   BOBBYE HALL    PERC (H   JIM GILTRAP      V   (H
JOHN LEHMAN       V   (H   VENETTA FIELDS   V   (H   ROY GALLOWAY     V   (H   BOBBY KING   V   (H
TERRY EVANS       V   (H   ALAN ESTES   CONGA (H   MYRNA MATTHEWS   V   (H   JAMES HAAS       V   (H
STEVE MADAIO      HRNS (H  FRED SELDON      HRNS (H   DAVID DUKE   HRNS   (H   BARBARA KORN     HRNS(H
```

SCARECROW

```
JOHN STEWART      G V  (A        (A) SCARECROW LIVE              1978 SPILT MILK               SMFM1127(
DAVE RUMSEY       D   (A
BILL PUPLETT      G   (A   DICK WILLIAMSON  B   (A
```

SCARS

```
PAUL RESEARCH     G   (A        (A) 1979
CALUNN MACKAY     D   (A        ( ) AUTHOR! AUTHOR!             1981 PRE           UK   PREX      5
BOBBY KING        V   (A
JOHN MACKIE       B   (A
```

SCENE STEALER
```
                                 (A) FIRST OFFENCE             1978 EMI             066 60275
```
SCHADEL BROS!

```
EKKI SCHADEL      V   (AB        (A) QUITE LIKE THIS            1978 PHOX          GER  2013
HEINER SCHADEL    K V  (AB        (B) CAN YOU MATCH A SUPRISE    1980 VERTIGO       GER 6360 644
KLAUS PETER REINICKE  (AB
HEINER LURIG      G   (A   RENE GILLY       G    (A   ARNULF'BRETT'SCHULDT G  (H   DIETER AHLERS     G  (A
MATZ STEINKE      B   (AB  DIRK ERDMANN     B    (A   ERWIN GIEBELHAUSEN B  (AB  HAJO HOFFMANN     VLN(A
WOLFGANG STURWOHLD K  (A   BRIGITTE THIELEPAPPE HRNS(A JIM McGILLIVRAY   D   (A   LOTHAR HITZEK     V  (A
GERD WENNEMUTH    D   (AB  WENER LOHR       D    (B   MICKY STICKDORN  D   (B   LOTHAR KRIST      SAX (B
KLAUS LENZ        TPT (B   JENS FISCHER     G    (B   HASSO ANHOECK    G   (B   ACHIM GIESELER    K  (B
ARNDT SCHULZ      G   (B   MICK RAUSCH  G       (B   MICHAEL THIELEPAPPE SAX (A HORST MICHAEL DURING PERC(A
KARSTEN SEIDENBERG PERC(A  RAINER HOLST   PERC (A   WERNER KUCKUCK   PERC (A  MICHAEL MELLENTHIN PERC(A
SEPPL KREUTZFELD  PERC (A  MICHAEL NULLENTHIN PERC (A BILLY KABUS      B   (B   NORBERT DOMLING   B(B
```

JANNE SCHAFFER

```
JANNE SCHAFFER    G V  (ALL      (A) JANNE SCHAFFER             1973 4LEAF         SWED  EFG  7232
BJORN LINDH       K FLT(ABD      (A) THE CHINESE                1974 VERTIGO       UK    6360  107
STEFAN BROLUND    B   (ABD       (B) ANDRA LP                   1974 EUROPA FILM SWED EFG 501 2106
OLA BRUNKERT      D   (AB        (B) SECOND ALBUM               1975 VERTIGO       UK    6360  118
JAN TOLF          PERC (A        (C) KARTHARSIS                 1977 CBS US 34499  UK          81733
JAN BANDEL    PERC VIBES(AB      (D) EARMEAL                    1979 CBS US 35508  UK          83002
MALANDO GASSAMA   PERC (ABD
SLIM NOTINI       V PNO(A   HALAN NYQVIST    TPT  (A   SVEN LARSSON     TROM (A   BENGT KARLSSON    G  (A
LUCAS LINDHOLM    B   (B   PETER OSTLUND    D    (B   PER SAHLBERG     G   (B   PETER ROBINSON    K  (BD
JOHN GUSTAFSON    B   (B   MADS WINDING     B    (B   JEFF PORCARO     D   (B   STEVE PORCARO     K  (D
MIKE PORCARO      B   (D   JOE PORCARO    PERC (D
```

ARMAND SCHAUBROECK

ARMAND SCHAUBROECK	(ALL	(A) A LOT OF PEOPLE WOULD LIKE TO SEE US DEAD	19	MIRROR		
BRIAN ORMOND	K	(DE	(B) SHAKIN' SHAKIN'	1978	MIRROR	MIRROR 5	
JACK BEARCE	G V	(DE	(C) I CAME TO VISIT	19	MIRROR		
BOBBY HUBER	V PERC	(DE	(D) RATF*CKER	1978	MIRROR	7	
JAY PORTER	D	(DE	(E) LIVE AT THE HOLIDAY INN	DBL	1978	MIRROR	4
GENE D'AGOSTINO	V	(D					
BERNARD HEVERON	B	(DE ETHAN PORTER	G	(DE RILEY NEILSON	V	(D	FRANK M DICESARE WIND(D
JERRY PORTER	HCA	(E					

MICHAEL SCHENKER GROUP

MICHAEL SCHENKER	G	(ALL	(A) MICHAEL SCHENKER GROUP	1980 CHRYSALIS	UK	CHR 1302	
GARY BARDEN	V	(AB	(B) M S G	1981 CHRYSALIS	UK	CHR 1336	
SIMON PHILLIPS	D	(A	(C) ASSULT ATTACK	1982 CHRYSALIS	UK	CHR 1393	
MO FOSTER	B	(A	(D) ONE NIGHT AT BUDOKAN	1982 CHRYSALIS	UK	CHR 1375	
DON AIREY	K	(A					
CHRIS GLEN	B	(ABC COZY POWELL	D	(A TED McKENNA	D	(C GRAHAM BONNET	V (C
PAUL RAYMOND	K G	(B					

GUNTER SCHICKERT

GUNTER SCHICKERT		(AB	(A) UBERFALLIG	1979 SKY		SKY 032
CHARLES M HEUZ		(A	(B) SAMTVOGEL	1975 BRAIN	GER	0040 176

TON SCHERPENZEEL

TON SCHERPENZEEL K B (A			(A) LE CARNIVALDES ANIMALS	1978 ARIOLA	NL	26327	
HANS HOLLESTELLE	G	(A					
THEO DE JONG	B	(A FRANS PETERS	HCA (A IRENE LINDERS	V	(A ADDY DE WILDE HCA	(A
CLOUS VAN MECHELEN SAX (A		MAX WERNER	D PERC (A ELLEN NEEFJES	V	(A		

CONRAD SCHNITZLER

CONRAD SCHNITZLER ELECTRONICS(ALL	(A) SCHWARZ	1971 BLOCK	KS 1001
	(B) ROT	1971 BLOCK	KS 1002
	(C) BLAU	1972 BLOCK	KS 1003
	(D) CON	1977 BARCLAY	EGG 90184
	(E) WORK IN PROGRESS	1978 BLOCK	

EBERHARD SCHOENER

EBERHARD SCHOENER	K	(ALL	(A) DESTRUCTION OF HARMONY	1971	
TONY ASHTON	K V	(E	(B) DIE SCHACHTEL	1971	
STING	B V	(N	(C) DAYS LULLABY	1971	
ANDY SUMMERS	G	(N	(D) MEDITATION	1974 ARIOLA	GER 87131
STEWART COPELAND	D	(N	(E) WINDOWS	1974 ELECTROLA	EURO 95634
EVERT FRATERMAN	D	(N	(F) BALI AGUNG	1976 HORZU	GER 29647
OLAF KUBLER	SAX	(N	(G) BASTIEN UND BASTIENNE	1977 EMI	EURO 30231
HANSI STROER	G B	(N	(H) DER SCHAUSPIELDIREKTOR	1977 EMI	EURO 30230
NEPPI NOYA	PERC	(N	(J) TRANCE FORMATION	1977 HARVEST	EURO 32526
ORCHESTRA		(N	(K) THE BOOK	1978 ARIOLA	EURO 28706
DAVID COVERDALE	V	(B	(L) FLASH BACK	1978 HARVEST	EURO 32839
RAY FENWICK	G	(B	(M) VIDEO MAGIC	1978 HARVEST	EURO 45234
GLENN HUGHES	G V B	(B	(N) VIDEO FLASHBACK	1979 HARVEST	UK SHSM2030
JON LORD	K	(B	(O) EVENTS	1980 HARVEST	EURO 45879

SCHOENHERZ

RICHARD SCHOENHERZ K V (A			(A) WHAT A NIGHT	1878 WB	UK	K56504
CHRISTIAN KOLONOVITS	K	(A				
GEORG LISZT	B	(A RAINER MARZ	G (A JOHAN DAANSEN	G	(A JURGEN ZOLLER	D (A
HARTMUT PFANMULLER D		(A CARO	V (A			

NEAL SCHON & JAN HAMMER

NEAL SCHON	G SYN V(A	(A) UNTOLD PASSION	1981 CBS UK 85355 US 37600
JAM HAMMER	D K SYN(A	
COLIN HODGKINSON	B	(A	

JOHN SCHROEDER

JOHN SCHROEDER	(A	(A) PARTY DANCE VIBRATION	19 POLYDOR 2460 145

ERNST SCHULTZ

ERNST SCHULTZ	G V	(A	(A) PARAMOIA PICKNICK	1972 KUCKUCK	GER 2375 014
JACK GRUMSKY	G HCA	(A			
THEO BINO	G	(A TOMMI ROEDER	K (A SONNY HENNIG	K	(A WALTI SCHNEIDER B (A
GUNTHER STORCH	D	(A WOLF STUMM	G (A ALO SCHNURRER	VLN	(A

ROBERT SCHROEDER

ROBERT SCHROEDER	(A	(A) HARMONIC ASCENDANT	1980 WEA 58087

KLAUS SCHULZE

KLAUS SCHULZE	K SYN(ALL	(A) IRRLICHT	1972 OHR	GER	556022
HAROLD GRASSKOPF	D	(FJG	(A) IRRLICHT	1978 ISADORA	FR	9004
ARTHUR BROWN	V	LM	(A) IRRLICHT	1975 BRAIN	GER	1077
WOLFGANG TIEPOLD CELLO (LMO		(B) CYBORG DBL	1973 KOSMISCHE	GER	2 58 005
ERNST WALTER SIEMON	V	(C	(B) CYBORG	1978 ISADORA		9005/6
MICHAEL SHRIEVE	D	(O	(C) BLACKDANCE	1974 BRAIN	GER	1051
			(C) BLACKDANCE	1975 CAROLINE	UK	2003
			(C) BLACKDANCE	1981 BRAIN	GER RI 0060 406	
			(D) PICTURE MUSIC	1974 BRAIN	GER	1067
			(D) PICTURE MUSIC	1976 CLEMENTINE	FR	33007
			(D) PICTURE MUSIC	1977 ISADORA	FR	9007
			(D) PICTURE MUSIC	1980 BRAIN	GER RI 0040 146	
			(E) TIMEWIND	1975 BRAIN	GER	1975
			(E) TIMEWIND	1975 CAROLINE	UK	2005
			(F) MOONDAWN	1976 BRAIN	GER	1008
			(F) MOONDAWN	1976 VIRGIN NOT ISSUED ?		2064
			(F) MOONDAWN	1977 ISADORA	FR	9001
			(G) BODY LOVE	1977 METRONOME	GER	0060 047
			(H) MIRAGE	1977 ISLAND	UK	ILPS9461
			(H) MIRAGE	1977 BRAIN	GER	0060 040
			(I) BODY LOVE II	1977 BRAIN	GER	0060 097
			(I) BODY LOVE II	1977 ISLAND	UK	ILPS9510
			(J) "X"	1978 BRAIN	GER	0080 023
			(K) BLANCHE	1979 LOGO NOT RELEASED UK		1011

(CONTINUED)

```
                              KLAUS SCHULZE     (CONTINUED)                                    S43
                    (L) DUNE                    1979 BRAIN            GER    0060 225
                    (M) ...LIVE        DBL      1980 BRAIN            GER    0080 048
                    (N) DIG IT                  1980 BRAIN            GER    0060 353
                    (O) TRANCEFER               1981 INNOVATIVE COMM  GER    80 014
                    ( ) ROCK ON       DBL       1981 BRAIN            GER    0080 046
```

```
S44                              SCHUNGE                                                       S44
  SCHUNGE           G V (A    (A) BALLAD OF A SIMPLE LOVE   1972 REGAL ZONOPHONE     SLRZ 1033
  BOB RICARDO        V  (A
  CHRIS SPEDDING    G  (A    JEFF CLYNE     B  (A  HAIM ROMANO     G  (A   BARRY DE SOUZA   D  (A
  ROY BABBINGTON    B  (A    DAVE MACRAE    K  (A
S45                              SCIENTIST                                                     S45
  PRINCE JAMMY          (A    (A) BIG SHOWDOWN               1980 GREENSLEEVES   UK   GRE L10
  SOWELL            G  (C    (B) HEAVYWEIGHT DUB CHAMPION    1980 GREENSLEEVES   UK   GRE L11
  BINGY BUNNY       G  (C    (C) SCIENTIST MEETS THE SPACE INVADERS 1981 GREENSLEEVES  UK  GREL 19
  FLABBA HOLT       B  (C    (D) SCIENTIST IN THE KINGDOM    1981 KINGDOM        UK   9004
  STLE              D  (C
  SANTA             D  (C    SKY JUICE    PERC    (C   GLADDIE      K  (C   SKULLY    PERC (C
  STEELY            K  (C    WINSTON WRIGHT   K  (C
```

```
S45A                             SCISSORS FITS                                                 S45A
                    (A) SOON AFTER DARK          19    TORCH           TOR 005
S45B                             SCOPE                                                         S45B
  RIK               SYN K B(AB   (A) SCOPE       1975 ATLANTIC        GER   40553
  HENK ZOMER        D    (AB    (B) SCOPE II     1975 ATLANTIC        GER   50078
  ROB FRANKEN       K SYN(AB
  RENS NIEUWLAND    G    (AB
S45C                             SCOOTERS(US)                                                  S45C
  LARRY LEE         B V G(A     (A) YOUNG GIRLS   1978 EMI  UK AML3011      US   17026
  BOBBY DEAN WICKLAND D  (A
  LUKE ZAMPERINI    G V (A    ROBERT FERRERO    G V  (A   HELLEN TURNER PNO  (A
S46                              ERROL SCORCHER                                                S46
  ERROL SCORCHER         (A    (A) RASTA FIRE     19   BALLISTIC          UAS 30198
S47                              SCORPIONS                                                     S47
  HERMAN RAREBELL   D   (HEFG   (A) LONESOME CROW  1972 BRAIN 0040 023+METRONOME200191
  RUDOLF SCHENKER   G   (ALL    (A) GOLD ROCK      197  BRAIN 00040016
  KLAUS MEINE       V   (ALL    (A) ACTION         197  BRAIN 0040 0150
  ULRICH ROTH       G   (BCDEFH  (A) I'M GOING MAD  1974 BILLINGSGATE            1004
  MICHAEL SCHENKER  G   (AG     (B) FLY TO THE RAINBOW 1974 RCA   US 1023     APL1 4025
  RUDY LENNERS      D PERC(CDH   (C) IN TRANCE      1976 RCA              APL1 4128
  FRANCIS BUCHOLZ   B   (BCDEFGH (D) VIRGIN KILLER  1977 RCA       3659   APL1 4225
  WOLFGANG DZIONY   D   (A      (E) TAKEN BY FORCE  1978 RCA RI3024 PL28309  APL1 2628
  LOTHAR HEIMBERG   B   (A      (F) TOKYO TAPES     1979 RCA       PL28331  APL2 3039
  JURGEN ROSENTHAL  D   (A      (G) LOVE DRIVE      1979 HARVEST SHSP4097 MERCURY US 3795
  MATTHIAS JABS     G   (J      (H) THE BEST        1979 RCA 3035 +3516  US 28356
  ACHIM KIRSCHNING  K SYN(D     (J) ANIMAL MAGNETISM 1980 HARVEST SHSP4113 MERCURY US 3825
  GEORGE SIMPSON    HRNS (J     ( ) ROCK GALAXY     1980 RCA     28390
  BRAD WARNAAR      HRNS (J     (L) BLACKOUT        1982 HARVESTUK SHVL823
S47A                             CALVIN SCOT                                                   S47A
  CALVIN SCOT           (A      (A) I'M NOT BLIND I JUST CANT SEE  19  STAX       2046
S48                              COLIN SCOT                                                    S48
  COLIN SCOT        G V (ALL    (A) COLIN SCOT WITH FRIENDS  1971 UA  EURO 038 60520 UK UAG29154
  RAY GLYNN      MAND G  (C     (B) JUST ANOTHER CLOWN      1973 WB                 K46236
  DAVE ETHRIDGE     B   (C      (C) OUT OF THE BLUE         1974 WB                 K46281
  KIRK DUNCAN       K   (C      (A) COLIN SCOT              197  VISA        IMP    1010
  BARRY DE SOUZA    D   (C
  JUANITA FRANKLIN  V   (C    SPARKIE       V   (C   TARAGON      V   (C   MOX      FLT HCA (C
  BRIAN ODGERS      B   (C    PHILLIP GOODHAND TAIT K(C  TONY LUKYN  SYN (C   ERIC HASTINGS   VLN(C
  JULIA TURNER      VLN (C    KEITH SMITH    VLN (C   GERRY RICH   VLA (C   KEITH THATCHER CELLO(C
  RUTH LOCK         CELLO(C    PETER GABRIEL     (A   PHIL COLLINS  D  (A   PETER HAMMILL     (A
  ROBERT FRIPP      G   (A    JON ANDERSON      V  (A   RICK WAKEMAN K  (A
S48A                             ESTER MAE SCOTT                                               S48A
  ESTER MAE SCOTT   V   (A      (A) MAM AINT NOBODYS FOOL   1976 BOMP       1
S48B                             ISAAC SCOT BLUES BAND                                         S48B
  ISAAC SCOT            (A      (A) ISAAC SCOT BLUES BAND   1979 RED LIGHTNIN'  UK    0023
S49                              JACK SCOTT                                                    S49
  JACK SCOTT        V   (ALL    (A) WHAT IN THE WORLD       1960 TOP RANK UK 12/024  US   626
                                (B) I REMEMBER HANK WILLIAMS 1960 TOP RANK UK 12/034  US  619
                                (C) THE SPIRIT MOVES ME     1961 TOP RANK UK 35/109  US   648
                                (D) JACK SCOTT              19   CARLTON          US  12107
                                (E) WHAT AM I LIVING FOR    19   CARLTON          US  12122
                                (F) BURNING BRIDGES         19   CAPITOL          US ST2035
                                (G) JACK SCOTT GREATEST HITS 197  PONIE           US   563
                                (H) SECOND ALBUM            1977 PONIE            US  7055
S50                              TOM SCOTT                                                     S50
  TOM SCOTT    SYN WIND  (ALL   (A) HONEYSUCKLE BREEZE      1968 IMPULSE      US AS 9163
  ERIC GALE         G   (FKG    (B) RURAL STILL LIFE        1970 IMPULSE      US    AS 9171
  HUGH McCRACKEN  G HCA(FG      (C) GREAT SCOTT             19   A&M          US    AM 4330
  BOB JAMES         K   (F      (D) TOM SCOTT & L A EXPRESS 1974 ODE    87969 US    77021
  RALPH MACDONALD   PERC (FKG   (E) TOM CAT                 1975 ODE          US    77029
  GARY KING         B   (FKG    (F) NEW YORK CONNECTION     1975 ODE          US    77033
  GEORGE HARRISON   G   (F      (G) BLOW IT OUT             1977 EPIC   UK 82285  US 34966
  RICHARD TEE       K   (FKG    (H) TOM SCOTT IN L A        1977 RCA    UK SF8429
  CHUCK FINDLEY     TPT (FKG    (H) TOM SCOTT IN L A        1977 FLYING DUTCHMAN    BXLI 0833
  JACO PASTORIUS    B   (H      (I) INTIMATE STRANGERS      1979 CBS    UK 83309  US 35705
  STEVE GADD        D   (FKG    (J) STREET BEAT             1979 CBS          US       36437
  DICK HYDE         HRNS (FKG   (K) BEST OF                 1980 CBS    UK 84347  US 36352
  MAX BENNETT       B   (DEK
```

(CONTINUED)

```
S50        (CONTINUED)                    TOM SCOTT                                                           S50
    JOHN GUERIN      D (KBDE  LARRY CARLTON    G   (KD  LARRY NASH      K   (KE  RICK MAROTTA    D  (KG
    ROBBEN FORD      G  (KE   JINI MITCHELL    V   (E   CHUCK DOMANICO  B   (B   JOE SAMPLE      K  (D
    CHUCK RAINEY     B  (G    JOHN TROPEA      G   (D   KENNY ASCHER    K   (G   DENNIS BUDIMIR  G  (G
    RAY PARKER       G  (G    WILL LEE         B   (G   CHRIS PARKER    D   (G
S50A                                        TONY SCOTT                                                       S50A
    TONY SCOTT            (A          (A) MUSIC FOR MEDITATION & OTHER JOYS 1968 VERVE     2304 471
S51                                      GIL SCOTT HERON                                                      S51
    GILL SCOTT HERON G PNO(ALL        (A) SMALL TALK AT 125TH & LENNOX      1972 FLYING DUTCHMAN
    BRIAN JACKSON  FLT K  (GJK        (B) FREE WILL                        1972 FLYING DUTCHMAN        10153
    BARNETT WILLIAMS PERC (KJ         (C) PIECES OF A MAN                   1973 FLYING DUTCHMAN BXLI0833 10143
    LEON WILLIAMS  SAX   (K           (D) WINTER IN AMERICA                 1975 STRATA EAST            19742
    HARVEY MASON    D   (K            (E) REVOLUTION WILL NOT BE TELEVISED  1975 RCA             UK     SF8428
    GREG PHILLINGANES K (K            (E) REVOLUTION WILL NOT BE TELEVISED  1975 FLYING DUTCHMAN        BXLI0613
    ALVIN TAYLOR    D   (K            (F) FIRST MINUTE OF A NEW DAY         1975 ARISTA UK ARTY 106   US  4030
    RALPH PENLAND   D   (K            (G) FROM S AFRICA TO S CAROLINA       1976 ARISTA UK ARTY 121   US  4044
    MAXINE WILLARD  V   (K            (H) IT'S YOUR WORLD                   1976 ARISTA UK DARTY 1    US  5001
    JULIA TILLMAN   V   (K            (J) BRIDGES                           1977 ARISTA UK SPARTY1031 US  4147
    MARTI McCALL    V   (K            (K) SECRETS                           1978 ARISTA UK SPARTY1073 US  4189
    MARLO HENDERSON G   (J            ( ) REAL EYES                         1980 ARISTA               US  9540
    DANNY BOWENS    B   (J            ( ) REFLECTIONS                       1981 ARISTA UK SPARTY 1180
    JO BLOCKER      D   (J            ( ) THE BOTTLE                        19   AUDIO FIDELITY  1017
    BILAL SUNNI ALI SAX (J
    DELBERT TAILOR  TPT (J   REGGIE BRUBANE    D   (J   TONY DUNCANSON  PERC (J   FRED PAYNE      G  (J
S52                                   SCOTTSVILLE SQUIRREL                                                    S52
    CHRIS HILLMAN MAND B V (12        (A) BLUEGRASS FAVOURITES              196  CROWN           US  CST  346
    ED DOUGLAS      B   (12           (1) 1958        (2) 1962
    GARY CARR       G   (12
    LARRY MURRAY    G   (12  KENNY WERTZ     BANJO(1    BERNIE LEADON    BANJO(2
S53                                    SCRATCH & UPSETTERS                                                    S53
                                      (A) CLOAK & DAGGER                   1973 RHINO               SRNO 8002
                                      (B) SUPER APE                        1976 ISLAND              ILPS 9417
S53A                                   THE SCRATCH BAND                                                       S53A
    ROBERT ORSI     V HCA G(A         (A) THE SCRATCH BAND                 1977 BIG SOUND US 1009 LONDON UKSHY8529
    CHRISTINE OHLMAN V   (A           (A) THE SCRATCH BAND                 1977 KUCKUCK       GER 2375 043
    G E SMITH       G   (A
    PAUL J OSSOLA   B   (A   MICKEY CURRY      D   V  (A   THOMAS CAVALIER  PROD (A   TOMMY GREGORY   SAX(A
S53B                                    SCREEN IDOLS                                                          S53B
    CHED CHEESMAN   G   (A            (A) PREMIERE                         1979 COBRA              CBR 1001
    TONY SMITH      G   (A
    MICHELLE NIEDDU V   (A   GEOFF APPLEBY     B   (A   WOODY WOODMANSEY  D   (A
S53C                                    SCRITTI POLITTI                                                       S53C
                                      (A) HEGEMONY(4 A SIDES)(EP)          1979 ROUGH TRADE          RT 027
                                      (B) PEEL SESSIONS      (EP)          1979 ROUGH TRADE          RT 034
S53D                                       SCREAMS                                                            S53D
                                      (A) SCREAMS                          1979 INFINITY      US    9009
S54                                      SCROUNGER                                                            S54
    PAUL LEWIS      V   (A            (A) SNAP                             1976 ANCHOR             ANCL 2021
    IAN CURNOW      K V  (A
    PAUL KEOGH      G   (A   RAY RUSSELL     G   (A   MO FOSTER       B   (A   FRANK McDONALD   B(A
    MIKE NICHOLLS   D   (A   PETER VAN HOOKE   D   (A   JOHN CAMERON  STRINGS (A
S55                                      THE SCRUFFS                                                          S55
    DAVE BRANYAN    G V  (A           (A) WANNA MEET THE SCRUFFS           1977 POWERPLAY      US    5050
    STEPHEN BURNS  G V PNO (A
    RICK BRANYAN  B PNO V  (A   ZEPH PAULSON     D V  (A
S55A                                      EARL SCRUGGS                                                        S55A
    EARL SCRUGGS BAN G  (ALL          (A) NASHVILLE ROCK                   19   CBS US 1007
    GARY SCRUGGS        (HJ           (B) HIS FAMILY & FRIENDS             1972 CBS US 30584  uk 64777
    STEVE SCRUGGS       (J            (C) I SAW THE LIGHT                  1972 CBS US 31354  UK 65023
    RANDY SCRUGGS       (J            (D) LIVE AT KANSAS STATE             1972 CBS US 31758
    JODY MAPHIS         (HJ           (E) DUELING BANJOS                   1973 CBS US 32268
    JOAN BAEZ           (J            (F) EARL SCRUGGS REVUE               197  CBS US 32426
    BONNIE BRAMLETT V   (HJ           (G) WHERE LILLIES BLOOM              19   CBS US 32806
    DAVID BRIGGS        (J            (H) ROCKING ACROSS THE COUNTRY       1973 CBS US 32943
    KENNY BUTTREY   D   (J            (J) ANNIVERSARY SPECIAL              197  CBS US 33416  UK 80821
    JOHNNY CASH     V   (J            (K) EARL SCRUGGS REVUE 2             1976 CBS US 34090
    LEONARD COHEN   V   (J            (L) FAMILY PORTRAIT                  1976 CBS US 34346
    RON CORNELIUS       (J            (M) LIVE FROM AUSTIN CITY LIMITS     1977 CBS UK 34464
    CHARLIE DANIELS     (J            (N) STRIKE ANYWHERE                  1977 CBS UK 34878
    RAMBLIN' JACK ELLIOTT (J          (O) BOLD & NEW                       1978 CBS 35319
    DAN FOGELBERG       (J            (P) TODAY & FOREVER                  1979 CBS US 36084
    LARRY GATLIN        (J
    WILLIE HALL         (J   BILLY JOEL        (J   BOB JOHNSON       (J   JIM KELTNER D    (J
    DOUG KERSHAW    FDL (J   ALVIN LEE   G V   (J   KENNY LOGGINS     (J   ROGER McGUINN     (J
    MIRABAI             (J   JIM MESSINA       (J   MICHAEL MURPHY    (J   TRACY NELSON   V (J
    DON NIX             (J   LEON PENDARVIS    (J   POINTER SISTERS V (J   BUFFY ST MARIE V (J
    REGGIE YOUNG        (J   LOUDEN WAINWRIGHT III V(J  TIM WIPPERMAN (J   RUSTY YOUNG      (J
    SHANE KEISTER   K   (H   JOSH GRAVES    DOB (H   TEDDY IRWIN     G (H   LINDA RONSTADT V (H
    DAVID ALLAN COE V   (H
S55B                                    EDDIE SCWARTZ                                                         S55B
    EDDIE SCWARTZ   V   (A            (A) NO REFUGE                        1981 ATCO US    38141
    GARY CRAIG      D   (A
    BOB WILSON      B   (A   DAVE TYSON      K B (A   PETER FOLLET    G   (A   JIM McGRATH     TPT (A
S55C                                      SEA CRUISE                                                          S55C
    JAY                 (A            (A) SEA CRUISE                       1978 LOLLIPOP   GER  623783
    GERMAIN             (A
    NANETTE SAAB    V   (A
```

[496]

SEA DOG

PAUL WESTON	G V (A			(A)SEA DOG		196 BUDDAH	US BDS	5104
JOHN REDMOND	K V (A							
BRIAN KIRKWOOD	B V (A	JIM NORRIS	D V	(A DOUG VARTY	K V (A			

S56 SEA LEVEL S56

CHUCK LEAVELL V PERC K (ABCDE		(A) SEA LEVEL				1977 CAPRICORN	US 0178 UK 2429 150			
LAMAR WILLIAMS	B (ABCDE	(B) CATS ON THE COAST				1978 CAPRICORN	US 0198 UK 2429 158			
JAI JOHANSON	D (AB	(C) ON THE EDGE				1978 CAPRICORN	US 0212			
ED DOWLING	TPT (D	(D) LONG WALK ON A SHORT PIER				1979 CAPRICORN	US 0227			
JIMMY NALLS	G (ABCDE V(BCDE	(E) BALLROOM				1980 ARISTA US 9531	UK SPARTY 1145			
RANDALL BRAMBLETT SAX V(BCDE										
GEORGE WEAVER	D (B	DAVIS CAUSEY	G (BCDE	DON McCLURE	HRNS (A	LEO LABRANCHE	HRNS (A			
EARL FORD	HRNS (A	CHARLES FAIRLEY	HRNS (A	RUDOLPH CARTER	HRNS (A	JOE ENGLISH	D V (CDE			
MATT GREELEY	PERC V(DE	TOMMY TALTON	V (D	DAVID EARLE JOHNSON	PERC(D	CHARLIE BRENT	SAX (D			
TONY DAGRADI	SAX (D	RODNEY LAFON	TPT (C	JON ROBERT SMITH	SAX (D	JOE WOOLIE TPT	(D			
HAROLD WILLIAMS	SAX (D	RONNIE EADES	HRNS (B	DENNIS GOODE	HRNS (B	HARVEY THOMPSON	SAX(B			
HARRISON CALLOWAY TPT (B										

S57 SON SEALS S57

SON SEALS	G V (ALL	(A) THE SON SEALS BLUES BAND			1974 SONET UK SNTF 679 US ALLIGATOR 4703					
JOHNNY WALKER	ORG (A	(B) MIDNIGHT SON			1977 SONET UK SNTF 728 US ALLIGATOR 4708					
JOHN RILEY	B (A	(C) LIVE & BURNING			1978 SONET UK SNTF 782 US ALLIGATOR 4712					
CHARLES CALDWELL	D (A	(D) CHICAGO FIRE			1980 SONET UK SNTF 838 US ALLIGATOR 4720					
A C REED	SAX (C									
LACY GIBSON	G (C	SNAPPER MITCHUM	B (BCD	TONY GOODEN	D (C	ALBERTO GIANQUINTO PNO(BC				
BERT ROBINSON	D (B	REG ALLMON	SAX (B	KEN COOPER	TPT (BD	BILL McFARLAND	TROM (BD			
MARK WEAVER	G (D	PAUL HOWARD	TPT (D	DAVID D ANDERSON	D (D	KING SOLOMON	K (D			

S57A TROY SEALS S57A

TROY SEALS	V (AB	(A) PRESENTING TROY SEALS		1973 ATLANTIC	US SD7281
		(B) TROY SEALS		1977 CBS	US 34271

S58 SEALS & CROFTS S58

JIM SEALS G V SAX FDL (ALL		(A) SEALS & CROFT		1970 TA		US 5001	
DASH CROFTS D MAND V K G(ALL		(B) DOWN HOME		1970 BELL UK SBLL 139	TA US 5004		
LOUIE SHELTON	G V (DEFGIJL	(C) YEAR OF SUNDAY		1972 WB UK K46133	US 2568		
BOBBY LICHTIG	WIND B(DEJ	(D) SUMMER BREEZE		1972 WB UK K46173	US 2629		
WILTON FELDER	B (DEGIJ	(CD) YEAR/SUMMER		1974 WB UK K66033	US 2809		
DAVID PAICH	K (EFGI	(E) DIAMOND GIRL		1973 WB UK K46218	US 2699		
JOHN GUERIN	D (DE	(F) UNBORN CHILD		1974 WB UK K56028	US 2761		
JIM GORDON	D (DE	(G) I'LL PLAY FOR YOU		1975 WB UK K56116	US 2848		
JEFF PORCARO	D (EFGI	(H) GREATEST HITS		1975 WB UK K56176	US 2886		
HARVEY MASON	D (E	(I) GET CLOSER		1976 WB UK K56209	US 2907		
BOBBYE HALL	PERC (EF	(J) SUDAN VILLAGE		1976 WB UK K56307	US 2976		
JOHN FORD COLEY	V (DE	(K) ONE ON ONE		1977 WB UK K56402			
BUDDY EMMONS	STEEL(F	(L) TAKIN' IT EASY		1978 WB UK K56484 US	3163		
ENGLAND DAN SEALS V (CE		(M) LONGEST ROAD		1980 WB UK K56719 US	3365		
DAVID HUNGATE	B (FI						
JACK LENZ	FLT K(G	ED GREENE	D (GIJ	JIM VARLEY	D (G	ANTOINE DEARBORN PERC (G	
LARRY FORD	TPT (G	RON KING	TPT (G	PAUL HUBINON	TPT (G	BOBBY SHEW	TPT (G
BOBBY CROSBY	WIND (G	JIM HORN	WIND (DGI	STEVE LEEDS	WIND (G	GENE CIPRIANO	WIND (G
HENRY SIGISMONTI	WIND (G	DICK HYDE	TROM (G	JOHN LEYS	TROM (G	LEW McCREARY	TROM (G
MIKE PORCARO	B (G	OVID STEVENS	G (G	BILL CUOMO	K (J	RALPH HUMPHREY	D (JL
MARTY WALSH	G (JL	JOE PORCARO	PERC (J	DONNA GIPSON	V (J	SHIRLEY MATTHEWS	V (IJL
MARTY McCALL	V (J	BECKY LOUIS	V (J	CAROLYN WILLIS	V (IJ	DEAN PARKS	G (J
LEE RITENOUR	G (IJ	JOE SAMPLE	K (IJ	RON KRASINSKI	D (L	JIM KELTNER	D (DL
JAMES DIVISEK	D (L	TONY PELUSO	V SYN G (L	LARRY ROLANDO	G (L	DENNIS BELFIELD	B (L
DAVID PARLATO	B (L	DOMINIC GENOVA	B (L	TOM HENSLEY	K (L	DAVID FOSTER	K (L
STEVEN OLITZKY	K (L	DAN FERGUSON	DOBRO(L	BRIAN WHITCOMB	K (L	DANNY DEARDORFF	HCA (L
DON MENZA	SAX (L	ALAN ESTES	VIBES(L	MANOUCHEHR SADEGHI V	(L	SEAN MACLEOD	V (L
BOB PHILLIPS	V (L	GARY SIMS	V (L	DOUG STRAWN	V (L	TANYA TUCKER	V (L
JAMES GILSTRAP	V (L	VANETTA FIELDS	V (L	LARRY LICHTIG	PNO (L	CLARENCE MACDONALD PNO(D	
MIKE LANG	PNO (L	MICHAEL OMARTIAN	PNO (D	RUSS KUNKEL	D (D	HARVEY BROOKS	B (D
JOE OSBORN	B (D	MILT HOLLAND	PERC (DI	KING ERRISSON	CONGA(D	RED RHODES	STEEL(D
JOHN HARTFORD	BANJO(D	DEL HIGGINS	V (D	DONNIE SHELTON	V (DI	LARRY CARLTON	G (I
RAY PARKER	G (I	CAROL CARMICHAEL	V (I	MYRNA MATTHEWS	V (I		

S59 PHIL SEAMAN S59

PHIL SEAMAN	(ABC1	(A) PHIL SEAMAN NOW...LIVE		1968 VERVE	UK	SVLP 9220	
WITH		(B) THE PHIL SEAMAN STORY		1974 DECIBEL		BSM 103	
ERIC CLAPTON	G (1	(C) PHIL ON DRUMS		1975 77		77SEV 12/53	
GINGER BAKER	D (1	(1) AT BLUES FESTIVAL 1968					

S59A SEANOR & KOSS S59A

JOHN SEANOR	K (A	(A) SEANOR & KOSS		1972 REPRISE	US	2091
RON KOSS	G V (A					
KENNY ALTMAN	B (A	KING ERRISSON	PERC (A	JOHN SEBASTIAN	HCA (A JOHN SEITER D (A	

S60 SEARCHERS S60

JOHN McNALLY	G V (ALL	(A) MEET THE SEARCHERS		1963 PYE	UK	NPL18086
MIKE PENDER	G V (ALL	(A) MEET THE SEARCHERS		1963 KAPP	US	3363
CHRIS CURTIS	D V (ABCDEFGHKLM	(A) MEET THE SEARCHERS		1966 GOLDEN GUINEA UK RI	GGL 0349	
TONY JACKSON	B V (ABCDE	(B) SUGAR & SPICE		1963 PYE	UK	NPL18089
FRANK ALLEN	B (FGHIJKLMNOPQRSTU(B) SUGAR & SPICE			1967 MARBLE ARCH UK RI	MAL 704	
BILLY ADAMSON	D PERC(TU	(C) THIS IS		196 KAPP	US	3409
BOB JACKSON	K (T	(D) NEW SEARCHERS LP		196 KAPP	US	3412
MICK WEAVER	K (U	(E) IT'S THE SEARCHERS		1964 PYE	UK	NPL 18092
ED STASIUM	K (U	(E) IT'S THE SEARCHERS		1968 MARBLE ARCH US MAL 798		
MARTIN HUGHES	PERC (U	(F) SOUNDS LIKE THE SEARCHERS		1964 PYE	UK	NPL 18111
DAVE CHARLES	PERC (U	(G) SEARCHERS No4		196 KAPP	US	3449
		(H) TAKE ME FOR WHAT I'M WORTH		1965 PYE	UK	NPL 18120
		(H) TAKE ME FOR WHAT I'M WORTH		196 KAPP	US	3477
		(I) SMASH HITS		1967 MARBLE ARCH	UK MALS 640	
		(J) SMASH HITS VOL 2		1967 MARBLE ARCH	UK MALS 673	
		(K) NEEDLES & PINS		1971 HALLMARK	UK	HMA 203
		(L) GOLDEN HOUR		1972 PYE	UK	GH 541
		(M) SECOND TAKE		1972 RCA	UK	SF 8298

(CONTINUED)

SEARCHERS

(N)	GOLDEN HOUR VOL 2	1973	PYE	UK	GH 564
(O)	NEEDLES & PINS	1974	RCA INT	UK	INTS 1480
(P)	ROCK MUSIC FROM BRITAIN	197	MODE	FR	9029
(Q)	ATTENTION	197	PHONOGRAM	EURO 6434 127	
(R)	HEAR HEAR	19	MERCURY	US	SR 60916
( )	HISTORY OF BRITISH POP	1976	PYE	US	501
( )	HISTORY OF BRITISH POP 2	1976	PYE	US	508
(S)	THE SEARCHER FILE	1977	PYE	UK	FILD002
(T)	THE SEARCHERS	1980	SIRE	UK SRK 6086	
(T)	THE SEARCHERS(DIFFERENT TRACKS)	1980	SIRE GER 200986	UK SRK	6082
( )	ROCK MUSIC FROM 60'S	1980	VOGUE	NL	- 9039
( )	WHEN YOU WALK IN THE ROOM	1980	PYE	18617	
(U)	PLAY FOR TODAY	1981	SIRE	UK SRK 3523	
(V)	LOVE MELODYS	1981	SIRE	UK SRK 3523	
(W)	100 MINUTES	1982	PRT	CASS UK 103	

SEASTONES

NED LAGIN	K	(A	(A) SEASTONES		1975	ROUND	US	RX 106
PHIL LESH	B	(A						
JERRY GARCIA	G	(A	DAVID FREIBERG	V (A	DAVID CROSBY	V (A	MICKEY HART PERC(A	
GRACE SLICK	V	(A	SPENCER DRYDEN	PERC (A				

B B SEATON

-B B SEATON	(ABC	(A) THIN LINE BETWEEN LOVE & HATE	1973	TROJAN	TRLS 59	
		(B) DANCING SHOES	1974	CAROLINE	CA 2002	
		(C) COLOUR IS NOT THE ANSWER	1976	JAMA	JALP 002	

SEATRAIN

RICHARD GREENE	VLN	(ABC	(A) SEATRAIN	1969	A&M US4171 UK AMLS941 GER 212061	
ANDY KULBERG	FLT	B(ABCD	(B) SEATRAIN	1971	CAPITOL US SMAS659 UK EAST 659	
JILL SHIRES	FLT	(D	(B) SEATRAIN	1971	CAPITOL GER 80726	
DON KRETMAR	SAX	(A	(C) MARBLEHEAD MESSENGER	1972	CAPITOL US SMAS829 UK EAST 829	
JOHN GREGORY	G V	(A	(D) WATCH	1973	WB US BS 2692 UK K 46222	
ROY BLUMENFELD	D	(A				
PETER ROWAN	G	(BC	LARRY ATAMANUIK	D (BC LLOYD BASKIN	K V (BCD JULIO CORONADO	D (D
WILLIAM ELLIOTT	K	(D	PETER WALSH	G V (D JIM ROBERTS	(ABC ANDY MUSAR	B (
SANDRA LEE	V	(D	PAUL PRESTOPINO	G (D BOB STUART	TUBA (D BILL KEITH	BAN(D
SHA NA NA	V	(D	PAUL SHURE	VLN (D BONNIE DOUGLAS	VLN (D MYRA KESTENBAUM	VLA(D
DOUG DAVIES	CELLO(D		ALLAN VOGEL	OBOE (D BUELL NEIDLINGER	B (D WAYNE DALEY	V (D

SEAWIND

PAULINE WILSON	V	(ABC	(A) SEAWIND		1976	CTI	5002	
BOB WILSON	D	(ABC	(B) WINDOW OF A CHILD		1977	CTI	5007	
BUD NUANEZ	G V	(AB	(B) WINDOW OF A CHILD		1978	PYE	NSPL18561	
BUD JUANEZ	HRNS	(C	(C) LIGHT THE LIGHTS		1979	HORIZON	US	734
KEN WILD	B V	(ABC	(D) SEAWIND		1980	A&M US SP4824 UK AMLH 64824		
BILL REICHENBACH	TROM	(BC						
JERRY HEY	HRNS	(ABC	KIM HUTCHCROFT	SAX V(ABC LARRY WILLIAMS	K WIND V(ABC PAULINHO DA COSTA	PERC(AC	
RALPH MACDONALD	PERC	(A	IAN UNDERWOOD	SYN (AB HARVEY MASON	PERC V(AB BILL SUMMERS	PERC(B	
CHARLES VEAL	STRINGS	(B	GARY GRANT	HRNS (C BERNARD IGNER	V (C		

JOHN SEBASTIAN

JOHN SEBASTIAN	G V PERC HCA(ALL		(A) JOHN B SEBASTIAN		1970	REPRISE	US 6379	UK K44086
MILT HOLLAND	D	(D	(A) JOHN B SEBASTIAN (WITHDRAWN)		1970	MGM	US 4654	
RUSSELL DASHIELL	G	(D	(B) CHEAPO CHEAPO PRODUCTION PRESENTS		1971	REPRISE	US 2036	UK K44127
AMOS GARRETT	G	(D	(B) CHEAPO CHEAPO (WITHDRWAN)		1971	MGM	US 4720	
KENNY ALTMAN	B	(CDE	(C) FOUR OF US		1971	REPRISE	US 2041	UK K44149
POINTER SISTERS	V	(D	(D) TARZANA KID		1974	REPRISE	US 2187	UK K54028
RITCHIE OLSON	CLAR	(D	(E) WELCOME BACK		1976	REPRISE	US 2249	UK K54074
GREG REEVES	B	(C						
KELLY SHANAHAN	D	(D	DAVID LINDLEY	FDL (D RON KOSS	G (D JIM GORDON	D (D	
JERRY McKUEN	G	(D	LOWELL GEORGE	G V (D BOBBYE HALL	PERC (D BUDDY EMMONS	STEEL (D	
EMMYLOU HARRIS	V	(D	DAVID GRISMAN	MAND (D PHIL EVERLY	V (D PAUL HARRIS	K (ABC	
RY COODER	MAND G(D		RICHARD BELL	K (E DAVID HUNGATE	B (E JEFF PORCARO	D (E	
MICHAEL OMARTIAN	K	(E	JEFF BAXTER	STEEL(E REGGIE KNIGHTON	G (E JON LIND	V (E	
MURRAY WEINSTOCK	PNO	(E	DALLAS TAYLOR	D (C JOHN BARBATA	D (C FELIX PAPPALARDI	B (C	
MAC REBENNACK	PNO	(C	ESSO STEEL BAND	(C PAUL A ROTHCHILD	PROD (D HARVEY BROOKS	B (A	
RAY NEOPOLITAN	B	(A	DALLAS TAYLOR	D (A LUCIAN BARNES	G (B SAN ARMSTRONG	G (B	

SECOND LAYER

(A) FLESH AS A PROPERTY(EP)	197	TORCH	TOR 001		
(B) STATE OF EMERGENCY (EP)	197	TORCH	TOR 006		
(C) WORLD OF RUBBER	1981	CHERRY RED	UK	BRED 14	

SECOND VISION

RIC SANDERS	VLN	(A	(A) FIRST STEPS	1980	CHRYSALIS CHR 1289
DAVE BRISTOW	K	(A			
JONATHAN DAVIE	B	(A	JOHN ETHERIDGE	G (A MICKEY BARKER	D PERC(A

SECOND MOVEMENT

HARALD KESSELHACK	V	(A	(A) BLIND MAN'S MIRROR	1976	CASTLE GER 1003
MANNI GREINER	B	(A			
SIGGI ZEIDLER	K	(A	THOMAS MOECKL	G (A MATTHIAS HELK	D (A MANNI BIERBACH WIND(A

SECONDHAND

KEN ELLIOT	K V	(AB	(A) REALITY	1968	POLYDOR
ROB ELLIOT	V	(AB	(B) DEATH MAY BE YOUR SANTA CLAUS	1971	MUSHROOM MRE 200 6
KIERAN O'CONNOR	PERC	(B			
GEORGE HART	V VLN(B		MOGGY MEAD	G (B NICK SOOTH	B (A BOB GIBBONS G (A
TONY McGILL	G	(B	CHRIS WILLIAMS	WIND (A PAUL GREEDUS	V (B

THE SECRET

(A) THE SECRET	1979	OVAL AMLH68504

SECRET AFFAIR

```
IAN PAGE          V TPT K  (AB      (A) GLORY BOYS              1979 ISPY UK ISPY1 GER 201 179
MAGGIE RYDER      V        (A       (A) GLORY BOYS              1979 SIRE US 6089
DAVID CAIRNS      G V      (AB      (B) BEHIND CLOSED DOORS     1980 ISPY UK ISPY2 GER ARISTA 202862
DENNIS SMITH      B V      (Ab      (C) BUSINESS AS USUAL       1982 ARISTA UK ISPY3
SEB SHELTON       D        (AB
DAVE WINTHROP     SAX      (AB
```

SECRET OYSTER

```
BO THRIGE ANDERSEN    D(A      (A) FURTIVE PEARL                 1976 PETERS INT    US          9003
JESS STAEHR          B   (BE      (A) SECRET OYSTER               1973 CBS          EURO  65769
CLAUS BØHLING        G   (ABE      (B) SEA SON                     1974 CBS  UK 80489  EURO  19009
MADS VINDING         B   (A       (B) SEA SON                     1974 PETERS INT    US          9009
KENNETH KNUDSEN      K   (ABE      (C) VIDUNDERLIGE                1975 CBS          EURO  81044
FINN ZIEGLER         VLN (B       (D) ORLAVER                      1976 CHRISTIANA               P1
ERLIN CHRISTENSEN CELLO(B         (E) STRAIGHT TO THE KRANKENHAUS  1976 CBS          UK    80489
PALLE MIKKELBORG     TPT (E
KASPER WINDING   PERC (BE  KARSTEN VOGEL    SAX K (ABE HANS NIELSEN     VLN  (B   BJARNE BOIE RASMUSSEN VLA(B
OLE STREENBERG       D   (BE
```

SECRET SERVICE

```
                                  (A) OH SUSIE                    1980 SONET     UK    SNTF    823
```

SECTION

```
DANNY KORTCHMAR   G   (ABC       (A) THE SECTION      1972 WB  US 2661    UK      K46191
LELAND SKLAR      B   (AB        (B) FORWARD MOTION   1973 WB            UK      K46251
CRAIG DOERGE      K   (AB        (C) FORK IT OVER     1977 CAPITOL               11656
RUSS KUNKEL       D   (AB
LEE PASTORA     PERC (B  SERGIO         PERC (B  DAVID CROSBY     V   (C  JAMES TAYLOR     V (C
```

SECTION 25

```
                                  (A) ALWAYS NOW       1981 FACTORY     UK    FACT 45
```

SECTOR 27

```
TOM ROBINSON      G V  (A        (A) SECTOR 27        1980 FONTANA UK 6359 039 US IRS 70013
JOE BUTT          B V  (A
STEVE B   G V          (A  GARY       D      (A
```

THE SEEDS

```
SKY SAXON K V HCA    (ABCDE      (A) THE SEEDS                    1966 GNP 2023                  LINE RI 5021
DARYL HOOPER      K V  (BCAE      (B) WEB OF SOUND                 1966 VOCALION 8062 +GNP 2033 LINE RI 5022
RICK ANDRIDGE     D    (BCAE      (C) FUTURE                       1967 VOCALION 8070 +GNP 2038 LINE RI 5030
JAN SAVAGE        G V  (ABCE      (D) MERLINS MUSIC BOX(RAW & ALIVE)1967 GNP 2043                LINE RI 5036
HARVEY SHARPE     B    (BC        (E) FALLIN' OFF THE EDGE         1977 GNP 2107                 LINE RI 5042
COOKER            G    (B         (F) SEEDS                        1978 SONET    UK   SNTF 746
                                  (G) FULL SPOON OF SEEDY BLUES    1967 GNP US 2040 RI GER LINE GER 5033
```

SEEMON & MARIJKE

```
SEEMON        V K(A       (A) SON OF AMERICA    197 A&M      US    SP4309
MARIJKE   V K (A
COLLEEN FORTUNE   V   (A  RICHARD FURTUNE   G   (A  JOHN BARBATA   D  (A  KING CHARLES    STEEL DR(A
RITA COOLIDGE     V   (A  NICK DE CARO    ACC  (A  CHRIS ETHRIDGE B K (A  MARIO JAMES     STEEL DR(A
BOOKER T JONES    K   (A  FRANK MAYES     SAX  (A  JONI MITCHELL  V  (A  GEROLD LAWRENCE STEEL DR(A
GRAHAM NASH     G C   (A  SNEAKY PETE    STEEL(A  MORREEN THORNTON V (A  MAC NILES       STEEL DR(A
KAZEM RAZZAZAN    VLN (A  GEORGE ST JOHN  SAX  (A
```

BOB SEGARINI

```
BOB SEGARINI    G V K(AB      (A) GOTTA HAVE POP     1978 BOMB 7027 UK EPIC    EPC 83806
PET KASHUR       G   (B       (A) GOTTA HAVE POP     198  LINE GER 5096
MIKE ST DENIS   G V  (AB      (B) GOODBYE L A        1979 BOMP 90576 UK EPIC    EPC 84086
WAYNE MILLS    HRNS (B        (B) GOODBYE L A        198  LINE GER 5051
PHIL ANGERS      B   (AB      (C) THE RADIO          1980 BOMP 7030      LINE GER    5085
MARK BRONSON     D   (AB
GARWOOD WALLACE G V  (A  DAVID HENMAN     G   (A  DAVID CLAYTON THOMAS V (A  GORD PATON       PERC (A
GABOR HEGEDUS    G   (A  KIER BROWNSTONE  B   (A  PAUL IRVINE      SAX  (A  DREW WINTERS     V K (AB
DAVID NORRIS ELYE HRNS (B
```

BOB SEGER

```
BOB SEGER           V    (ALL     (A) RAMBLIN' GAMBLIN' MAN   1969 CAPITOL US 172 UKRI177 CAPS 1013
SAM CLAYTON         V    (M       (A) RAMBLIN' GAMBLIN' MAN   1981 GREENLIGHT RI 2018
DREW ABBOTT         G    (KLGJMNH  (B) NOAH                    1969 CAPITOL US 236
ALTO REED         HRNS  (GKLJMN   (C) MONGREL                 1970 CAPITOL US 499 UKRI177 CAPS 1010
LINDA DILLARD       V    (M       (C) MONGREL                 1981 GREENLIGHT RI 2022
CHARLIE ALLEN MARTIN D (GJKLM     (D) BRAND NEW MORNING       1971 CAPITOL US 731
ROBYN ROBBINS       K    (GJKLM   (E) SMOKIN' OPs             1972 REPRISE US 2109  UK      K44214
GLEN FREY           G    (LM      (E) SMOKIN' OPs             1977 CAPITOL RI 11746 GER 85348
CHRIS CAMPBELL      B    (GKLJMNH  (F) BACK IN 72              1973 REPRISE US 2126  UK      K44227
PAUL HARRIS         K    (M       (F) BACK IN 72              197  CAPITOL 11747
DAVID TEEGARDEN     D    (LMN      (G) SEVEN                   1974 REPRISE US 2184  UK      K44262
DON FELDER          G    (L       (G) SEVEN                   1977 CAPITOL RI 11748 GREENLIGHT 2006
BARRY BECKETT       K    (KLM      (H) BEUTIFUL LOSER          1975 CAPITOL              11378
PETE CARR           G    (KLMH     (J) LIVE BULLET             1976 CAPITOL US 11523 UK    ESTSP 16
JIMMY JOHNSON       H    (KLM      (K) NIGHT MOVES             1977 CAPITOL US/UK11557 GER    85027
DAVE HOOD           B    (KLM      (L) STRANGER IN TOWN        1978 CAPITOL US/UK11698 GER    85333
ROGER HAWKINS       D    (KLM      (M) AGAINST THE WIND        1980 CAPITOL US/UK12041 GER 86097
CRAIG FROST         K    (N       (N) NINE TONIGHT            1981 CAPITOL     US UK    12182
BILL PAYNE          K    (L       (EP) GET OUT OF DENVER       1977 REPRISE                K12476
DOUG RILEY          K    (KL
BOB SCHULTZ  K SAX V(B VANETTA FIELDS   V   (L   JAMES LAVELL    V   (L   CLYDIE KING     V (L
EASLEY STANLEY CARTER V(L  SHIRLEY MATTHEWS  V  (L   GEORGE JACKSON  V   (L   LUTHER WATERS   V (L
ORRIN WATERS        V  (L   JULIA TILLMAN    V   (L   MAXINE WILLARD WATERS V (L  BRANDY         V (L
DAN HONAKER    B V G(ABC PEP PERRINE     D   (BC  DAN WATSON     K V (C   JERRY LUCK      ACC(K
JOE MIQUELON        G  (K   SHARON DEE WILLIAMS V (K  LAUREL WARD    V   (K   RICK MANSKA     K (GJ
DAVID BRIGGS      PNO (G   TOMMY COGBILL    B   (G   KENNY BUTTREY  D   (G   DAVE DORAN      G (G
TOM CARTMELL      SAX (G   BILL MUELLER     G   (G   RANDY MEYERS   D   (G   CHARLIE McCOY   G (G
JIM McCARTY         G  (G   JOHN HARRIS    ORG  (G   TOM NEME     V G K(B   SHAUN MURPHY    V (N
KATHY LAMB          V  (N   COLLEN BEATON    V   (N   JUNE TILTON    V   (N   PAM MOORE  V    (N
DON HENLEY          V  (M   TIM SCHMIT       V   (M   DR JOHN        K   (M   LAURA CREAMER   V (M
```

(CONTINUED)

BOB SEGER

S73	(CONTINUED)										
RANDY McCORMICK	K	(M	MIKE ERELWINE	HARP	(A	PEP PERRINE	V	(A	BON SCHULTZ		(A
SKIP KNAPE	K B	(E	PAM TODD	V	(E	CRYSTAL JENKINS	V	(E	JACK ASHFORD	PERC(E
EDDIE BONGO	PERC	(E	JIM BUZZESE	PERC	(E	HARVEY THOMPSON	SAX	(H	HARRISON CALLOWAY	TPT(H
CHARLES ROSE	TROM	(H	CHARLIE MARTIN		(H	RON EADES	SAX	(H	STONEY & ROCKY	V	(H
KENNY BELL	G	(H	ROBIN ROBBINS	K	(H	PAUL KINGERY	G	(H	TOM CARTMELL	SAX	(H

SELDOM SCENE

MIKE AULDRIDGE	G DOB V(ALL	(A) ACT ONE	1972 REBEL	US	SLP1511
BEN ELDRIDGE	BAN G V(ALL	(B) ACT TWO	1973 REBEL	US	SLP1520
JOHN DUFFY	G V MAND(ALL	(C) ACT THREE	1973 REBEL	US	SLP1536
JOHN STARLING	V G	(ABCDEFG	(D) OLD TRAIN	1974 REBEL	US	SLP1538
LINDA RONSTADT	V	(FD	(E) RECORDED LIVE	1975 REBEL	US SLP1547/48
TOM GRAY	B V	(ALL	(F) THE NEW SELDOM SCENE ALBUM	1976 REBEL	US	SLP1561
RICKY SCAGGS	FDL	(CDG	(G) BAPTIZING	1978 REBEL	US	1573
CLAYTON HAMBRICK	G	(C	(H) ACT FOUR	1979 SUGAR HILL	3709
PAUL CRAFT	G	(D	(I) AFTER MIDNIGHT	1981 SUGAR HILL	3721
BOB WILLIAMS	HCA	(D			
MARK CUFF	D	(F	PHIL ROSENTHAL	G V	(GHI	CARL NELSON	VLN	(I

ZBIGNIEW SEIFERT

ZBIGNIEW SEIFERT	VLN	(ALL	(A) MAN OF THE LIGHT	19 MPS	15489
JACK DEJONETTE	D	(A	(B) SOLO VIOLIN	19 MRC 066 45 088
JOHN SCOFIELD	G	(A	(C) PASSION	19 CAPITOL	11923
EDDIE GOMEZ	B	(A	(D) ZBIGNIEW SEIFERT	19 CAPITOL	11618
RICHIE BEIROICH	PNO	(AE	(E) WE'LL REMEMBER ZBIGGY(74 78	19 MOOD	24500
NANA VASCONCELES	PERC	(A			
JOACHIM KUHN	K	(BE	CECIL McBEE	B	(B	HUBERT EAVES	K	(D	PHILIP CATHERINE G	(DE
BILLY HART	D	(B	DWIGHT BREWSTER	K	(D	JOHN TURNER	B	(D	JASPER VAN'THOF	K	(B
MIKE MANDEL	SYN	(D	JOHN LEE	B	(D	JAMES BATRON	K	(D	REGGIE LUCAS	G	(D
HAKIN THOMPSON	PERC(D	GERRY BROWN	D	(D	ROB FRANKEN	SYN	(D	STEFAN DIEZ G	(D
MTUME	PERC V(D	JOE CARO	G	(D	DARYL BROWN	PERC	(D	JOHN FADDIS TPT	(D
MICHAEL BRECKER	SAX	(D	CHRIS HINZE FLT	(D	MICHAEL LAWRENCE	TPT	(D	DAVID TAYLOR	TROM(D
CHERYL ALEXANDER	V	(D	WOLFGANG DAUNER	K	(E	GLEN MOORE	B	(D	TAWATHA AGEE	V	(D
CHARLIE MARIANO	SAX	(E	DAVID DARLING	STR	(D	JOE HAIDER	K	(E	ADELHARD ROIDINGER	B(E
JAM HAMMER	D	(E	ISLA ECKINGER	B	(E	JOCNUSZ STEFANSKI	D	(E	URSZULA DUDZIAK	V	(E
JOHN NAY	D	(E	ALBERT MONGELSOLORFF	TROM(E	LESZEK ZADLO	SAX	(E	HANS KOLLER SAX	(E

SELECTOR

NOEL DAVIES	G	(AB	(A) TOO MUCH PRESSURE	1980 TWO TONE UK 5002 GER 6703 693
NORMAN WATT-ROY	B	(B	(A) TOO MUCH PRESSURE	1980 CHRYSALIS US 1274
DESMOND BROWN	K	(A	(B) CELEBRATE THE BULLET	1981 CHRYSALIS	UK	CHR 1306
PAULINE BLACK	V	(AB		
CHARLEY ANDERSON	B	(AB	RICO RODRIGUES	TROM (A	DICK CUTHELL	TPT	(A	JOE REYNOLDS	SAX (A
CHARLEY H BEMBRIDGE	D	(AB	COMPTON AMANOR	D V	(AB	ARTHUR HENDRICKSON	V	(AB	HILLFIELD BOYS CHOIR (A
ROGER COMAS	B	(B	BARRY JONES	TPT	(B	ADAM WILLIAMS	B V	(B	JAMES MACKIE	SAX K V(B

SENSATION FIX

FRANCO FALSINI SYN G V	(ALL	(A) PORTABLE MADNESS	1974 POLYDOR		2448 034
RICHARD URSILLO	B	(ALL	(B) FRAGMENT OF LIGHT	1974 POLYDOR	IT	2448 023
STEVE HEAD	K D	(CDE	(C) FINEST FINGER	1976 POLYDOR	IT	2448 048
MARCO MARCOVECCHIO	D	(F	(D) BOXES PARADISE	1977 POLYDOR	IT	2448 068
MATT NOBLE	B	(E	(E) FLYING TAPES	1978 POLYDOR	IT	2448 074
KEITH EDWARDS	D	(A	(F) VISION'S FUGITIVES	197 ALL EARS	US	SF 11478

SEMUTA

	(A)SEMUTA	1979 LEE LAMBERT	LAM 101

SERPENT POWER

DAVID MELTZER	G VHCA(A	(A) SERPENT POWER	1967 VANGUARD	US VSD 79252
DENNY ELLIS	G	(A		
JOHN PAYNE	K	(A	J P PICKENS BAN (A	TINA MELTZER	V	(A	DAVID STENSON	B	(A
CLARK COOLIDGE	D	(A		

JOHN SERRY

JOHN SERRY	K V D	(A	(A) EXHIBITION	1979 CHRYSALIS	UK	CHR 1230
BOB SHEPPARD	SAX	(A	(B) JAZZIZ	1981 CHRYSALIS	UK	CHR 1279
BARRY FINNERTY	G	(A		
GORDON JOHNSON	B	(A	FLIM JOHNSON	B	(A	NANCY SHANX	V (A	CARLOS VEGA	D(A
GORDON GOTTLIEB	PERC	(A		

SEVEN O SEVEN(707)

PHIL BRYANT	B V	(ABC	(A) '707'	1980 CASABLANCA US 7213
JIM McCLARTY	D	(ABC	(B) THE SECOND ALBUM	1981 CASABLANCA US 7248
KEVIN RUSSELL	G V	(ABC	(C) MEGAFORCE	1982 BOARDWALK US 33523
DUKE McFADDEN	K G V(A		
DAVID CARR	K	(A	TOD HOWARTH K G V	(C	KEVIN CHALFANT	V	(C	SANDY WELCH	V (C
ZOE FOX	V	(C		

SEVENTH WAVE

KEN ELLIOT	K V	(AB	(A) THINGS TO COME	1974 GULL UK GULP1001 JANUS US 7009
KIERAN O'CONNOR	PERC	(AB	(B) PSI FI	1975 GULL UK GULP1010 US JANUS 7021
TONY UTER	PERC	(B		
BRIAN GOULD	K	(B	PEPI LEMER	V	(B	CHRIS ANSON	SYN	(B	PETER LEMER	K	(B
STEVE COOK	B	(B	HUGH BANTON	K	(B	TONY ELLIOT	PERC	(B

SEX PISTOLS

JOHN ROTTEN LYDON	V	(ABCDE12	(A) NEVER MIND THE BOLLOCKS	1977 VIRGIN UK V2086 US WB	3142
STEVE NEW	G	(1	(A) " " " "	1977 VIRGIN GER 25593
STEVE JONES	G	(ABCDE12	(B) GREAT ROCK'N'ROLL SWINDLE(DBL)	1978 VIRGIN UK VD2510 GER 300 279
PAUL COOK	D	(ABCDE12	(C) SOME PRODUCT	1979 VIRGIN	UK	VR2
SID VICIOUS	B V	(ABCD	(D) FLOGGING A DEAD HORSE	1979 VIRGIN UK V2142 GER 201 165
GLEN MATLOCK	B	(12	(E) GREAT ROCK'N'ROLL SWINDLE	1980 VIRGIN	UK	V 2168
MALCOLM McLAREN	V	(B	( ) BEST OF ...WE DONT CARE	1980 FLYOVER JAP IMP 7247
NICK KENT	G V	(1	(1) 1975 (2) 1976/77	
RONNIE BIGGS	V	(B		
M				

```
PHIL SEYMOUR    G D V(A     (A) PHIL SEYMOUR                                 1980 BOARDWALK US 36996 UK EPIC 85000
BILL PITCOCK    G    (A
EMORY GORDY     B    (A  DUANE HITCHINGS  K   (A  DAVID CROCKETT  D   (A  LARRY BYROM G   (A
ROGER LINN      G    (A  STEVE ALLEN      G   (A  RON FLYNT       B   (A  CARLA OLSON G   (A
WAYNE COOK      K    (A
```

S78   SHA NA NA   S78

```
JOCKO MARCELLINO    D    (BC     (A) IS HERE TO STAY              1969 KAMA SUTRA US   2010 RI 2077
LONNIE BAKER        SAX  (BC     (A) IS HERE TO STAY              1971 KAMA SUTRA    UK     2319 025
SCOTT POWELL             (B      (A) IS HERE TO STAY              197  MODE           FR        9023
JOHNNY CONTARDO     K D  (CB     (A) IS HERE TO STAY              1974 KAMA SUTRA RI         KSLP7003
DENNIS GREENE            (CB     (B) SHA NA NA                    1971 KAMA SUTRA    UK     2319 007
DON YORK                 (CB     (B) SHA NA NA                    1971 KAMA SUTRA    US        2034
RITCH JOFFE         D    (CB     (B) SHA NA NA                    1974 KAMA SUTRA RI         KSLP7002
ELLIOT CAHN         G    (B      (C) THE NIGHT IS STILL YOUNG     1972 KAMA SUTRA    US        2050
CHRIS DONALD        G    (B      (C) THE NIGHT IS STILL YOUNG     1972 KAMA SUTRA    UK     2319 019
BRUCE CLARKE        B    (CB     (C) THE NIGHT IS STILL YOUNG     1974 KAMA SUTRA RI         KSLP8001
SCOTT SIMON         K B  (CB     (D) GOLDEN AGE OF ROCK'N'ROLL    1973 KAMA SUTRA    UK     2623 102
DAVID BROMBERG      G    (B      (D) GOLDEN AGE OF ROCK'N'ROLL    1973 KAMA SUTRA    US        2073
ELLIOTT RANDALL     G    (       (D) GOLDEN AGE OF ROCK'N'ROLL    197  K TEL          NE         495
TONY SARTINI             (       (E) FROM THE STREETS OF NEW YORK 1974 KAMA SUTRA    UK     2319 038
VINNIE TAYLOR       G    (C      (E) FROM THE STREETS OF NEW YORK 1974 KAMA SUTRA    US        2075
GINO                G    (C      (E) FROM THE STREETS OF NEW YORK 1974 KAMA SUTRA    UK     KSLP7004
JOHN BOWZER BAUMAN  K    (CB     (F) HOT SOX                      1974 KAMA SUTRA    US        2605
HENRY GROSS         G    (       (F) HOT SOX                      1974 KAMA SUTRA    UK     KSLP7001
CHICO RYAN               (       (G) SHA NA NA NOW                1975 KAMA SUTRA    US        2603
ERIC WEISSBERG      STEEL(B      (H) BEST OF                      1976 KAMA SUTRA    US     KSLP2609
RICHARD DAVIS       B    (B      (J) ROCK'N'ROLL REVIVAL          1977 PYE           UK     GH  867
                                 ( ) REMEMBER THEN                1981 ACCORD        US        7115
```

```
MARTIN FIERRO   WIND V(A      (A) SHADES OF JOY    1969 FONTANA   UK      STL 5498
JACKIE KING   G SITAR (A      (A) SHADES OF JOY    196  DOUGLAS   UA 30920
EDWARD ADAMS    B    (A
LEE CHARLTON    VLN  (A  JYMM YOUNG    K HRN(A  JOSE RODRIGUEZ   D   (A  MILLIE FOSTER    V (A
```

S78B   SHABBY TIGER   S78B

```
HENDERSON GIBSON  V    (A      (A) SHABBY TIGER    1977 RCA  PL    25046
TONY BAKER      K V    (A
DAVE ALMOND   G FLT V(A MIKE RYAN    B   (A    GRAHAM FIELDEN    D PERC(A
```

S78C   BOBBY SHAD   S78C

```
BOBBY SHAD           (A      (A) ... AND THE BADMEN    196 MAINSTREAM  US   306
```

S78D   SHADES   S78D

```
                             (A) ACE OF SHADES         1981 MAGNUN FORCE  UK  MFLP 005
```

S78E   SHADOW   S78E

```
                             (A) LOVE LIFE             1980 ELEKTRA  US  233
                             (B) SHADOW                1981 ELEKTRA  US  293
```

S79   SHADOWFAX   S79

```
CHICK GREENBERG  WIND (A      (A) WATERCOURSE WAY     1976 PASSPORT     PPSD98013
PHIL MAGGINI     B    (A
DOUG MALUCHNIK   K    (A  STUART NEVITT    D PERC(A GREG STINSON    G V (A
```

S80   THE SHADOWS   S80

```
HANK MARVIN      G V  (ALL    THE SHADOWS               1962 COLUMBIA UK (M)33SX1374 (S)SCX3414
BRUCE WELCH      G V  (ALL    OUT OF THE SHADOWS        1962 COLUMBIA UK (M)33SX1458 (S)SCX3449
IAN SAMWELL      B    (A      GREATEST HITS             1963 COLUMBIA UK (M)33SX1522 (S)SCX1522
TERRY SMART      D    (A      DANCE WITH THE SHADOWS    1964 COLUMBIA UK (M)33SX1619 (S)SCX3511
JET HARRIS       B    (BC     THE SOUND OF THE SHADOWS  1965 COLUMBIA UK (M)33SX1736 (S)SCX3554
TONY MEEHAN      D    (B      MORE HITS                 1965 COLUMBIA UK (M)33SX1791 (S)SCX3578
BRIAN BENNETT    D    (CDEGIJ  SHADOW MUSIC             1966 COLUMBIA UK (M)33SX6041 (S)SCX6041
BRIAN LOCKING    B    (D      JIGSAW                    1967 COLUMBIA UK              SCX6148
JOHN ROSTILL     B    (E      HANK,BRUCE,BRIAN & JOHN   1967 COLUMBIA UK              SCX6199
JOHN FARRAR    G V B(FGH      ESTABLISHED 1958          1968 COLUMBIA UK              SCX6282
ALAN JONES       B    (HIJ    IT'LL BE ME               1969 STARLINE UK              SRS 5011
FRANCIS MONKMAN  K    (H      SOMETHING ELSE            1969 STARLINE UK              SRS 5012
CLIFF HALL       K    (IJ     SHADES OF ROCK            1970 COLUMBIA UK              SCX6420
DAVE LAWSON      SYN  (J      MUSTANG                   1972 MFP      UK              MFP 5266
NORRIE PARAMOUR  STR  (       THE BEST OF               1973 EMI IMP  EURO            14804859
ALAN TARNEY      B    (       I MAESTRI                 1974 COLUMBIA 04532
DAVE RICHMOND                 OUT OF THE SHADOWS 2      19   COLUMBIA GER 04502
GRAHAM TODD      K    (A      THE SHADOWS               19   CRYSTAL  04203
(A)1958                       THE BEST OF               197  EMI IMP  EURO            05404300
(B) 1959                      SHADOOGIE      (TRIPLE)   19   EMI IMP  EURO            154 061 129
(C) 1961                      ROCKIN' WITH CURLY LEADS  1973 EMI                      EMA 762
(D) 1962                      SPECS APPEAL              1975 EMI                      EMC 3066
(E) 1962                      LIVE AT PARIS OLYMPIA     1975 EMI                      EMC 3095
(F) 1970                      RARITIES                  1976 EMI                      NUT 2
(G) 1973                      THE SHADOWS               1975 EMBER                    SE 8031
(H) 1977                      TASTY                     1977 EMI                      EMC 3195
(I) 1979                      20 GOLDEN GREATS          1977 EMI                      EMTV 3
(J) 1980                      BEST OF THE SHADOWS       1977 EMI                      EMTV 33
                              AT THE MOVIES             1978 MFP                      50347
                              CHANGE OF ADDRESS         1980 POLYDOR UK               2442 179
                              STRING OF HITS            1979 EMI                      EMC 3310
                              ANOTHER STRING OF HITS    1980      UK 3339
                              HITS RIGHT UP YOUR STREET 1981 POLYDOR UK 5046
```

```
JIM SOHNS       V    (ABC     (A) GLORIA             1966 DUNWICH  US      666
WARREN ROGERS   G    (ABC     (A) GLORIA    (RI)     1979 RADAR    UK    RAD 11
JERRY McGEORGE  G    (ABC     (B) BACK DOOR MEN      1967 DUNWICH  US      667
TOM SCHIFFOUR   D    (ABC     (C) SHADOWS OF KNIGHT  1968 SUPER K  US     6002
JOE KELLEY      B    (ABC
THE HAWK        K    (B
```

SHAFTESBURY

```
    ROGER GRIGG        D K V(A      (A) THE LULL BEFORE THE STORM   1980  O K RECORDS              OKA001
    DAVE MARTIN        B V  (A
    PETER ROFFEY       G    (A
```
S81B   SHAGGS   S81B
```
    BETTY WIIGINS      D    (A      (A) PHILOSOPHY OF THE WORLD     1972  THIRD WORLD 3001 RED ROOSTER US 103
    HELEN WIGGIN       G    (A      (A)  "     "    "    "          1980  ROUNDER     US 3032
    DOROTHY WIGGIN     G    (A
```
S82   SHAGRAT THE VAGRANT   S82
```
    MICK FARREN        V    (
    STEVE TOOK         V PERC(
    PAUL BUCKMASTER    CELLO(   RUSS HUNTER      B    (    TWINK       D    (    SID BISHOP         G  (
    CORD REES          PNO  (
```
S82A   SHAKATAK   S82A
```
    GEORGE ANDERSON    B    (B      (A) DRIVING HARD               1981  POLYDOR     UK POLS 1030
    NIGEL WRIGHT       K SYN(AB     (B) NIGHTBIRDS                 1982  POLYDOR     UK POLS 1059
    ROGER ODELL        D    (B
    JACKIE RAWE        V    (B   SIMON MORTON    V PERC(B DICK MORRISSEY   SAX (B   BILL SHARPE K   SYN(B
    KEITH WINTER       G    (B   JILL SAWARD     V   (B   LORNA BANNON     V   (B   STUART BROOKS   TPT (B
```
S83   SHAKE   S83
```
    JOHN CALLIS        G    (A      (A) CULTURE SHOCK  (EP)        1979  SIRE        UK     SIR 4016
    SIMON TEMPLAR      B    (A
    ANGEL PATERSON     D    (A   TROY TATE       G   (A
```
S83A   SHAKERS   S83A
```
    JANET SMALL        K V  (A      (A) YANKEE REGGAE              1976  ASYLUM US7E1057      UK    K53036
    CHRIS SOLBERG      G V  (A
    BILL WALLACE       G V  (A   DON FULTON      B   (A   RON RHODES       D   (A
```
S84   SHAKIN STREET   S84
```
    FABIENNE SHINE     V    (Ab     (A) VAMPIRE ROCK               1978  CBS  UK    82610
    DYAN BIRCH         V    (A      (B) SHAKIN' STREET             1980  CBS         UK          84115
    ERIC LEWY          G    (AB     (C) SKIN EM                    1981  VIRGIN UK 2199
    ROSS THE BOSS      G    (B
    MIKE WINTER        B    (AB  JEAN LOU KALONOWSKI    D(AB FRANK COLLINS V   (A   ARMIK TIGRANE     G   (A
    IAN STEWART        PNO  (A   BONNIE         .        V   (A   PATRICE FABIEN PROD (A
```
S84A   SHAKEY LEGS   S84A
```
    NICK LAURITZEN     K V  (A      (A) SHAKEY LEGS                197   PARAMOUNT        US    6022
    TED DEMOS          G    (A
    JACK BRUNO         D    (A   TOM ENRIGHT     B    (A   JOHN MASTORY B   (A
```
S84B   SHAKEY VICK   S84B
```
    GRAHAM VICKERY     HCA V    (A      (A) LITTLE WOMAN YOURE SO SWEET  1969 PYE  UK NSPL18276
    NED BALIN          D    (A
    BRUCE LANGSMAN     G    (A   NIGEL TICKLER     B    (A
```
S84C   SHAKIN' PYRAMIDS   S84C
```
    DAVIE DUNCAN       V HCA PERC(A      (A) SKIN EM UP            1981  VIRGIN UK 2199  GER 802 088
    JAMES G CREIGHTON  G V  (A      (B) CELTS & COBRAS            1982  VIRGIN UK 2216
    RAILROAD KEN       G V  (A
    NICK CLARK         B    (A
```
S85   SHAKTI   S85
```
    JOHN McLAUGHLIN    G    (ABC     (A) SHAKTI                    1976  CBS  US 34162      UK    81388
    L SHANKAR          VLN V(ABC     (B) HANDFUL OF BEAUTY         1977  CBS  US 34372      UK   81664
    ZAKIR HUSSAIN      PERC (ABC     (C) NATURAL ELEMENTS          1978  CBS  US 34980      UK   82329
    T H VINYAKRAM      PERC V(ABC
```
S85A   SHALAMAR   S85A
```
    JODY WATNEY        V    (CD      (A) UPTOWN FESTIVAL           1977  SOUL TRAIN      UK 12289
    JEFF DANIEL        V    (CD      (B) DISCO GARDENS             1978  RCA   UK 12895
    HOWARD HEWITT      V    (CD      (C) BIG FUN                   1979  SOLAR UK 13479
    LEON SYLVERS       B    (C       (D) THREE FOR LOVE            1980  SOLAR US 13577
    ERNEST REED        G    (C       (E) FRIENDS                   1982  SOLAR UK 52345
    FRED LEWIS         PERC (C       (F) GREATEST HITS             1982  SOLAR UK  3001
    STEVE SHOCKLEY     G    (C
    GREG DAWKINS       CONGA(C   FRED RHEIMERT    G    (C   JAMES DAVIS      B   (C   WARDELL POTTS   D  (C
    ERNEST BILES       B    (C   GERALD THOMPSON  D    (C   FREEMAN BROWN    D   (C   JOEY GALLO      K  (C
    JOHN BARNES        K    (C   RON ARTISTS      K    (C   WILLIAM SHELBY   K   (C   GIP NOBELS K    (C
    KEVIN SPENCER      K    (C   GENE DOZIER      K    (C   KOSSI GARDNER    K   (C   STRING SECTION     (C
```
S86   SHAM 69   S86
```
    JIMMY PURSEY       V    (        (A) TELL US THE TRUTH         1978  POLYDOR UK 2383 491 SIRE US  6060
    DAVE TREGANNA      B    (        (B) THATS LIFE                1978  POLYDOR UK POLD5010+2442 158
    MARK CAIN          D    (        (C) HERSHAM BOYS              1979  POLYDOR    UK POLD5025+2442 165
    DAVE PARROS        G    (        (D) THE GAME                  1979  POLYDOR UK POLD5033+2442 173
    ALBIE SLIDER       B    (        (E) FIRST, THE BEST & THE LAST 1980 POLYDOR    UK  2383 596
```
S86A   SHAMROCKS   S86A
```
                                    (A) THE SHAMROCKS              1965  ARIOLA          72151
                                    ( ) THE SHAMROCKS IN PARIS     19    POLYDOR     FR 658032
                                    (EP) CADILLAC                  19    POLYDOR     FR 60122
                                    (EP) CANT SAY                  19    POLYDOR     FR 60124
```
S86B   SHANDI   S86B
```
    SHANDI             V    (A      (A) SHANDI                           1980  DREAMLAND  2394 257
    PAUL HERTZOG       K    (A
    JAMES ROLLENSTON   B    (A   STEVE SYKES  G   (A   TIM PIERCE       G   (A  PAT MASTELLOTTO  D   (A
```
S86C   SHANGHAI (80's)   S86C
```
    ANTON FIG          D V  (A      (A) SHANGHAI                   1982  CHRYSALIS      UK    CHR 1389
    BOB HANLON         SAX  (A
    KEITH LENTIN       G V  (A   GARY VALENTE TROM     (A  JIMMY LOWELL B V  (A  BEAU HILL     K G V  (A
    NEIL BALM          TPT  (A
```

SHANGHAI (70's)

CLIFF BENNETT	V	(B	(A) SHANGHAI		1974	WB	UK	K56093
BRIAN ALTERMAN	G	(B	(B) FALLEN HEROES		1976	THUNDERBIRD		THR 2000
MICK GREEN	G	(AB						
SPEEDY KING	B	(AB	PETE KIRCHER	D	(AB CHUCK BEDFORD V HCA(A	MIKE DEMIAN		K B (A
BARBARA BEDFORD	V	(A						

SHANGO

RICHIE HERNANDEZ	G	(A	(A) TRAMPIN'		1970	DUNHILL	US	D5 50082
JOE BARILE	D	(A						
MALCOLM EVAN	B	(A	TOMMY REYNOLDS	PERC K(A				

SHANGRILAS

MARY WEISS	V	(	LEADER OF THE PACK	1964	RED BIRD	US	RB 20101
MARYANN GANSER	V	(	SHANGRILAS '65	1965	RED BIRD	US	RB 20104
MARGIE GANSER	V	(	I CAN NEVER GO HOME	1966	RED BIRD	US RI	RB 20104
BETTY WEISS	V	(	GOLDEN HITS	1966	MERCURY	US 61099 UK	20096
SHADOW MORTON	PROD	(	GOLDEN HITS	1973	PHILIPS 6336 215	NL 6430 154	
			TEEN ANGUISH VOL 2	197	CHARLY	UK	CRM 2005
			(EP) REMEMBER (WALKING IN THE SAND)	1976	CHARLY	UK	CEP 109

DEL SHANNON

DEL SHANNON	G V	(ALL	HATS OFF TO LARRY	1963	LONDON UK 8071		
MIKE CAMPBELL	B G	(*	RUNAWAY	1963	LONDON UK 2402	US BIG TOP	1303
BENMONT TENCH	K	(*	LITTLE TOWN FLIRT	1963	LONDON UK 8091	US BIG TOP	1308
STAN LYNCH	D	(*	ANDY MAN	1965	STATESIDE UK 10115	AMY US	8003
RON BLAIR	B	(*	SINGS HANK WILLIAMS	1965	STATESIDE UK 10130	AMY US	8004
DAVID WHITE	B	(*	1,661 SECONDS OF	1965	STATESIDE UK 10140	AMY US	8006
HOWIE EPSTEIN	B	(*	THIS IS MY BAG	196	LIBERTY UK SLBY1320	US LST 7452	
PHIL JONES	V	(*	TOTAL COMMITMENT	1966	LIBERTY UK SLBY1335	US LST 7479	
PHIL SEYMOUR	V	(*	FURTHER ADVENTURES OF C WESTOVER	196	LIBERTY	US LST 7539	
MARTY TOUVARD	SAX	(*	BEST OF	1967	DOT	US	25824
KYM WESTOVER	V	(*	VINTAGE YEARS	19	SIRE	US	3708/2
JUDE COLE	V	(*	DEL SHANNON SINGS	19	POST	US	9000
TOM PETTY	HCA V PROS(*		10TH ANNIVERSARY	1971	SUNSET	UK	50211
			LIVE IN ENGLAND	1973	UA	UK UAS29474 US	LA 151
			LIVE IN ENGLAND	1982	FAME RI UK 3020		
			BEST OF	1973	POLYDOR	EURO 2870 323	
			VERY BEST OF	1975	CONTEMPO	CRMD 1001	
			HIT PARADE	1980	LONDON	UK	HAR 8545
			(*) DROP DOWN AND GET ME	1981	ELEKTRA	US	5E568
			AND THE MUSIC PLAYS ON	1978	SUNSET UK	SLS50412	
			(EP) DELS OWN FAVOURITES	196	LONDON UK	REX 1383	
			(EP) No2	196	LONDON UK	REX 1346	

SHANTI

ASHISH KHAN	SAROD(A	(A) SHANTI		1971	ATLANTIC	US	SD 8302
ZAKIR HUSSAIN	TABLA(A						
NEIL SEIDEL	G (A	STEVE HAEHL	G V (A	STEVE LEACH	V D (A	FRANK LUPICA	D (A
PRANESH KHAN	TABLA(A						

SHARKS

CHRIS SPEDDING	G	(AB	(A) FIRST WATER	1973	ISLAND UK ILPS9233	US MCA351	
ANDY FRASER	B	(A	(B) JAB IT IN YOUR EYE	1974	ISLAND UK ILPS9271	US MCA415	
SNIPS	V	(AB					
MARTY SIMON	D	(AB	NICK JUDD	K	(B BUSTA CHERRY JONES B	(B	

DEE DEE SHARP

DEE DEE SHARP	V	(ALL	(A) ITS MASHED POTATO TIME	196	CAMEO	US	C 1018
			(B) SONGS OF FAITH	196	CAMEO	US	C 1022
			(C) ALL THE HITS	196	CAMEO	US	C 1032
			(D) DO THE BIRD	196	CAMEO	US	C 1050
			(E) BIGGEST HITS	196	CAMEO	US	C 1062
			(F) DOWN MEMORY LANE	196	CAMEO	US	C 1074
			(G) 18 GOLDEN HITS	196	CAMEO	US	C 2002
			(H) THE CAMEO PARKWAY SESSIONS	1979	LONDON	UK	HAU 8514
			( ) HAPPY 'BOUT	1976	PHILADELPHIA	US	33839
			( ) WHAT COLOUR IS LOVE	1978	PHILADELPHIA	US	34437
			( ) DEE DEE	1980	PHILADELPHIA	US	36370

BILLY JOE SHAVER

BILLY JOE SHAVER	V	(	(A) OLD FIVE & DIMERS LIKE ME	1974	MONUMENT KZ32293	MG	7621
			(B) WHEN I GET MY WINGS	1976	CAPRICORN	US	CPN 0171
			(C) GYPSY BOY	197	CAPRICORN	US	CPN 0192

ROCKY SHARPE

ROCKY SHARPE	V	(ABC	(A) RAMA LAMA (REPLAYS)	1979	CHISWICK	UK	CWK 3010
			(B) ROCK IT TO MARS	1980	CHISWICK UK CWK3013	GER 67072	
			(C) DRIP DROP (EP) (RAZORS)	19	ACE	UK	SW6

GARY SHEARSTON

GARY SHEARSTON	G V HCA (AB	(A) DINGO		1974	CHARISMA	UK CAS1091	
TOMMY EYRE	K SYN	(A	(A) THE GREATEST STONE ON EARTH & ...	1975	CHARISMA	UK CAS1106	
DAVE OLNEY	B	(A					

ANDREW STEELE	D	(A	GRAHAME SMITH	VLN (A	JOHN TURNBALL	G (A	JON FIELDS	CONGA(A
ROD KING	STEEL(A	PHIL CHAPMAN	K (A	CARL LEVY	K (A	JIM PARKER	K (A
GARY TAYLOR	G	(A	FRANKLYN DUNN	B (B	LOCKSLEY GICHIE	G (B	ROYSTON MITCHELL K (B
MAURICE ELLIS	D	(B	FRANK McDONALD	B (B	CHRIS RAE	G (B	B J COLE	STEEL(B
BARRY DE SOUZA	D	(B	JOHNNY VAN DERRICK VLN (B	HENRY LOWTHER	VLN (B	KEITH NELSON	BAN (B
ROBERT KIRBY	V K	(B	DAVID KATZ	VLN (B	IAN HAMMER	HRNS (B	EDDIE MORDUE	SAX (B
DAVE HORLER	HRNS	(B	DOREEN CHANTER	V (B	MARTHA SMITH	V (B	JON ASTLEY	V SYN(B
DEBORAH WOOD	V	(B	CAMILLA WIGAN	V (B	LATIFA BALSTON	V (B	LYNN GIBSON	V (B
CHRISTIANE KONCZEWSKI	V(B	MICHAEL THOMAS	V (B	JOHN JAMES	V (B	STABLE STEVENS	V (B

SHEENA & THE ROCKETS

SHEENA	V	(A	(A) SHEENA & THE ROSKETS	1980 A&M	US	SP4875	
MAKOTO AYUKAWA	G V	(A					
TAKESHI ASADA	B V	KAZU KAWASHIMA	D	(A			

SHERBET(SHERBS)

DARYL BRAITHWAITE	V	(	(A) HOWZAT	1976 MCA	US	2226	
TONY MITCHELL	B	(	(B) MAGAZINE	1977 MCA	US	2304	
GARTH PORTER	K	(	(C) COLLECTION	1977			
ALAN SANDOW	D	(	(D) PHOTOPLAY	1978 MCA	US	UK EPIC 82251	
HARVEY JANES	G	(	(E) THE SKILL	1981 ATCO 38137	UK	K50783	

SHERIDAN/PRICE

DAVE SHERIDAN	V	(A	(A) THIS IS TO CERTIFY THAT	1970 GEMINI	UK	GME 1002	
RICK PRICE	V B G	(A					

PETE SHELLEY

PETE SHELLEY	V	(AB	(A) SKY YEN	1980 GROOVY		STP2	
			(B) HOMOSAPIENS	1981 GENETICS	GER	204 163	

SHEPPARDS

(A) SHEPPARDS	1980 SOLID SMOKE	US	CS4

SHILOH

JIM ED NORMANS	K G	(A	(A) SHILOH	1970 AMOS/BELL	AAS7015
DON HENLEY	D	(A			
MIKE BOWDEN	B	(A	RICHARD BOWDEN G (A AL PERKINS STEEL G (A		

PLUTO SHERVING

(A) PLUTO	1976 OPAL	PL1002	

DON SHINN

DON SHINN	K	(AB	(A) TEMPLES WITH PROPHET	1969 COLUMBIA	UK	SCX 6319
STAN TRACY	K PERC	(B	(B) DEPARTURES	1969 COLUMBIA	UK	SCX 6355
BARRY MORGAN	PERC	(B				
TREVOR TOMKINS	D	(B				

JOHNNY SHINES

JOHNNY SHINES	G V	(ALL	(A) LAST NIGHTS DREAM	1969 BLUE HORIZON	UK	763212
WALTER HORTON	HCA	(AC	(B) MASTERS OF MODERN BLUES	1969 TESTAMENT	US	2212
WILLIE DIXON	B	(A	(C) JOHNNY SHINES & BIG WALTER HORTON	1969 TESTAMENT	US	2217
CLIFTON JAMES	D	(A	(D) STANDING AT THE CROSSROADS	1969 TESTAMENT	US	2221
OTIS SPANN	PNO	(AC	(E) CHICAGO BLUES FESTIVAL	1972 BLACK & BLUE		33502
LEE JACKSON	B	(C	(F) JOHNNY SHINES & CO	1972 BIOGRAPH	US	12048
PRINCE CANDY	B	(C	(G) SITTING ON TOP	1972 BIOGRAPH	US	12044
RICHARD BAKER	G	(H	(H) COUNTRY BLUES	1974 XTRA	UK	XTRA1142
ROBERT LOCKWOOD		(L	(J) JOHNNY SHINES	1974 ADVENT		2803
PHILIP WALKER	G	(J	(K) HEY BA BA RE BOP	1978 ROUNDER		2020
DAVID II	SAX	(J	(L) DUST MY BROOM	1980 FLYRIGHT	UK	FLY 563
NATHANIEL DOVE	PNO	(J	( ) JOHNNY SHINES	19 BLUE HORIZON	US	4607
CHARLES JONES	B	(J				
DAVID BROMBERG	G	(F	DOWNY MURL D (J FRED BELOW D (C BILL BROWN B (C			
LUTHER ALLISON	G	(C	DON AUDET HCA (H BOB DERKACH B (H			

THE SHIP

SHIP MELSHENKER	G	(A	(A) THE SHIP	1972 ELEKTRA	UK	K42122
MARE NAMBY	K V FLT	(A	(A) A CON FOLK MUSIC JOURNEY	1972 ELEKTRA	USEKS	75036
STEVE COWAN	G V	(A				
TODD BROADSHAW	B	(A	TIM SCOTT CELLO (A STEVE REINWAND G V (A			

ELLEN SHIPLEY

ELLEN SHIPLEY	V	(AB	(A) ELLEN SHIPLEY	1979 RCA	US BXL1 3428 UK	FL13428
RALPH SCHUCKETT	K V	(B	(B) BREAKING THROUGH THE ICE AGE	1980 RCA	US 3626 UK	PL13626
RICHIE CERNIGLIA	G V	(B				
NICHOLAS LYNN	G V	(B	STEVE VITALE B V (B DENNY McDERMOTT D V (B ALFA ANDERSON V (B			
ONY KAYE	V	(B	JEAN PAUL GASPAR V (B ROBIN LUMLEY SYN (B			

SHIRELLES

ADDIE HARRIS	V	(	(A) TONIGHTS THE NIGHT	1961 SCEPTER	US	501
SHIRLEY ALSTON	V	(	(A) TONIGHTS THE NIGHT	1961 WAND	UK	1001
DORIS KENNER	V	(	(B) SHIRELLES SING	1961 SCEPTER	US	502
BEVERLY LEE	V	(	(B) SHIRELES SING	1961 TOP RANK	UK	35 115
			(C) BABY IT'S YOU	1962 SCEPTER	US	504
			(C) BABY IT'S YOU	1962 STATESIDE	UK	10006
			(D) & KING CURTIS TWIST PARTY	196 SCEPTER	US	505
			(E) GREATEST HITS	196 SCEPTER	US	507
			(E) GREATEST HITS	1963 STATESIDE	UK	10041
			(F) FOOLISH LITTLE GIRL	196 SCEPTER	US	511
			( ) ITS A MAD MAD MAD WORLD	196 SCEPTER	US	514
			(G) SING THE GOLDEN OLDIES	196 SCEPTER	US	516
			(H) GREATEST HITS VOL2	196 SCEPTER	US	560
			(J) SPONTANEOUS COMBUSTION	196 SCEPTER	US	562
			(K) REMEMBER WHEN	196 SCEPTER	US	2 599
			(L) REMEMBER WHEN VOL 1	19 WAND		1009
			(M) REMEMBER WHEN VOL 2	19 WAND		1010
			(N) ETERNALLY SOUL	1970 WAND UK WNS 4 US SCEPTER	569	
			(O) HAPPY IN LOVE	197 RCA US LSP4581 UK	SF8237	
			(P)SHIRELLES	1972 RCA US 4698 UK	SF8279	
			(Q) SWINGS THE MOST	19 PRICEWISE	US	4001
			(R) SING THEIR BEST	1972 SPRINGBOARD	US	4006
			(S) VERY BEST OF	19 UA	US	LA 340
			(T) GOLDEN HOUR	1973 PYE		GH 824
			( ) HERE & NOW	19 PRICEWISE	US	4002
			( ) JUKE BOX GIANTS	1981 AUDIO FIDELITY		1008
			( ) LETS GIVE EACH OTHER	1976 RCA APLIO102		
			(EP) WILL YOU LOVE ME TOMORROW	19&" TOP RANK	UK 3012	

SHIRLEY & CO
(A) SHAME SHAME SHAME   1975 PHILIPS UK 6310604 VIBRATION US 218

SHIRLEY & LEE

SHIRLEY GOODMAN	V	(ALL	(A) LET THE GOOD TIMES ROLL	19 JAYBOY JSX 2005
LEONARD LEE	V	(ALL	" " " "	19 ALADDIN 807
			" " " "	19 SCORE US 4023
			" " " "	1960 WARWICK US 2028
			" " " "	19 IMPERIAL 9179
			" " " "	1975 UA US UALA 069
			LEGENDARY MASTERS	19 UA US UALA 026
			RESPECTFULLY YOURS	1980 MANHATTAN UK 5040
			HAPPY DAYS	1980 MANHATTAN UK 5025

SHIRTS

ANNIE GOLDEN	V	(ABC	(A) THE SHIRTS	1978 HARVEST UK SHSP4089 GER 06717
ART LAMONICA	G V K	(ABC	(A) THE SHIRTS	1978 CAPITOL US SW 11791
RONNIE ARDITO	G V K	(ABC	(B) STREET LIGHT SHINE	1979 HARVEST UK SHSP4104 GER 07111
JOHN PICCOLO	G V K	(ABC	(B) STREET LIGHT SHINE	1979 CAPITOL US 11986
JOHN CRISCIONE	D V	(ABC	(C) INNER SLEEVE	1980 CAPITOL UK/US 12085 GER 86184
ROBERT RACIOPPO	G	(ABC		
LYLE DEDRICK	WIND (B	URBIE GREEN WIND	(B DIANA HALPRIN	VLN (B PAUL EISLER WIND(B
HARVEY ESTRIN	FLT (B	DAVID TOFANI	WIND (B	

SHIVA'S HEAD BAND

SPENCER PERSKIN	V VLN G	(ABC	(A) TAKE ME TO THE MOUNTAINS	19 CAPITOL US 538
SUZY PERSKIN	V ORG	(ABC	(B) COMING TO A HEAD	19 ARMADILLO US NO No
BRIAN 'RED' MOORE	B	(C	(C) YESTERDAYS	1978 APE US 1001
JERRY BRAZIL	D	(C		
ROBERT FLYNN JR	G	(C	SHAWN SIEGEL K V (A KENNY PARKER	B G V(A ROBERT GLADWIN G B(C
RICHARD FUNNELL	D	(A		

SHOCKING BLUE

CORNELIUS VAN DER BEEK	D(A		(A) SHOCKING BLUE	1969 PENNY FARTHING UK PELS500 METRONOME 15373
MARISKA VERES	V	(A	(B) SCORPIOS DANCE	1969 PENNY FARTHING UK PELS510
KASSJE VAN DER WAL	B	(A	( ) SHOCKING BLUE	19 COLOSSUS CS 1000 NL GNR 447 009
ROBBY VAN LEEUWEN	G	(A	( ) GREATEST HITS	19 GNR NL 657 574
			( ) POP POWER	1970 POLYDOR

SHOES

GARY KLEBE	G V	(ABC	(A) BLACK VINYL SHOES	1978 PVC 7904 + BLACK VINYL 51477
JEFF MURPHY	G V	(ABC	(A) BLACK VINYL SHOES	1979 SIRE UK SRK 6075
JOHN MURPHY	V B	(ABC	(B) PRESENT TENSE	1979 ELEKTRA US 6E244 UK K52187
SKIP MEYER	D	(ABC	(C) TONGUE TWISTER	1980 ELEKTRA US 6E303 UK K52261

SHOES FOR INDUSTRY

BASSETT DAVIES	V SAX(A		(A) TALK LIKE A WHELK	1980 FRIED EGG FRY 1
JOHN SCHOFIELD	D	(A		
ANDY BOOT	G	(A	TIM NORFOLK G (A STEVE LONNEN	B (A LAZLO K V(A

SHOOT

CRAIG COLLINGE	D	(A	(A) ON THE FRONTIER	1973 EMI US 11229 UK EMA 753
DAVE GREENE	G V	(A		
JIM McCARTY	K V	(A	BILL RUSSELL B (A	

SHOOTER

DAVE MATTHEW	G V	(A ,	(A) SHOOTER	1978 EMI UK INS3026
STEVE ST CLAIR	G V	(A		
JOHN TOWE	D PERC(A	SPENCER SHIRES K G V(A SIMON JAMES DUNN B V(A		

SHOOTING STAR

STEVE THOMAS	D	(ABC	(A) SHOOTING STAR	1979 VIRGIN UK V 2130
RON VERLIN	B	(ABC	(B) HANG ON FOR YOUR LIFE	1981 VIRGIN US 37407
CHARLIS WALTZ	V VLN K	(ABC	(C) III WISHES	1982 VIRGIN UK V 2235
VAN McCLAIN	G	(ABC		
GARY WEST	V K G D(ABC	BILL GUFFEY K (AB		

BRIAN SHORT

BRIAN SHORT	V	(A	(A) ANYTHING FOR A LAUGH	1971 TRANSATLANTIC UK TRA 245
ALAN WHITE	D	(A		
MAX MIDDLETON	K	(A	KEN CRADDOCK G K V (A RAY COOPER	PERC (A ED SPEVOCK PERC(A
PETE KIRTLEY	G MAND V (A	COLIN GIBSON B (A LYN DOBSON	WIND (A COLERIDGE GOODE B (A

SHORTWAVEBAND

STUART GORDON	G K V(A		(A) SHORTWAVEBAND	1975 RCA UK SF 8400
PHIL HARRISON	K G FLT(A			
PICK WITHERS	D	(A	PAUL COBBOLD B (A	

WAYNE SHORTER

WAYNE SHORTER	SAX	(ALL	(A) FREEFORM	196 BLUENOTE US BST 84118
			(B) SEARCH FOR NEW LAND	196 BLUENOTE US BST 84169
			(C) NIGHT DREAMER	1964 BLUENOTE US BST 84173
MICHELIN PRELL	D	(L	(D) SOME OTHER DTUFF	196 BLUENOTE US BST 84177
			(E) JU JU	1964 BLUENOTE US BST 84182
MIROSLAV VITOUS	G	(KO	(F) SPEAK NO EVIL	1965 BLUENOTE US BST 84194
CHICK COREA	K	(KO	(G) ALL SEEING EYE	1966 BLUENOTE US BST 84219
RON CARTER	B	(O	(H) ADAMS APPLE	1966 BLUENOTE US BST 84232
DAVE HOLLAND	B G	(O	(I) SCHIZOPHRENIA	1968 BLUNOTE UK BNS40026 US BST84297
JOHN McLAUGHLIN	G	(KO	(J) ODYSSEY OF ISKA	1970 BLUENOTE US BST84363
AIRTO MORIERA	PERC (K		(K) SUPER NOVA	1970 BLUENOTE UK BNS40028 USBST84332
MILTON NASCIMENTO		(P	(L) SHORTER MOMENTS	19 TRIP US 5009
SONNY SHARROCK	G	(K	(M) SECOND GENESIS	19 VEE JAY US
JACK DE JOHNETTE	D	(K	(N) WAYNE SHORTER	1974 GNP US GNPS22075
MARIA BOOKER	V	(K	(O) MOTO GROSSO FEIO	1975 BLUENOTE US BNLA 014
WALTER BOOKER	G	(K	(P) NATIVE DANCER	1975 EPIC UK 80721 US 33418
			(Q) ETCETERA	1981 BLUENOTE UKLBR 1037 US 1056
			(R) SOOTHSAYER	1980 UA UK LBR 1021

[505]

SHOT GUN

(A) SHOTGUN	1977 ABC	US	ABCD 979
(B) GOOD THE BAD & FUNKY	197 ABC	US	1060
(C) SHOTGUN	197 ABC	US	1118

SHOT IN THE DARK

KRYSIA KRYSTIANNE K V (A   (A) SHOT IN THE DARK   1981 POLYDOR   UK 2394 297
ADAM YURMAN G V (A
BRYAN SAVAGE WIND (A   ROBIN LAMBLE G V B VLN (A   PETER WHITE   G K B V(A HARRY STINSON   D V (A

JAY SHOTAM

JAY SHOTAM B V (A   (A) MANHATTAN SKYLINE   1979 BAAL   BAL89011
PETER DIAZ G (A
JULIAN LINDSAY K (A   PHIL TOWNER   D (A

SHOTGUN EXPRESS

PETER BARDENS K ((A) SHOTGUN EXPRESS (EP)   196 COLUMBIA   FR   ESRF1864
DAVE AMBROSSE B (
PETER GREEN G (MICK FLEETWOOD D (ROD STEWART   V (PHIL SAWYER   G (
JOHN MOORSHEAD G (BERYL MARSDEN   V (

SHOW OF HANDS

RICK CUTLER D (A   (A) FORMERLY ANTHRAX   1970 ELEKTRA   EKS74084
JACK JACOBSEN K (A
JERRY McCANN FLT G V (A

SHOWADDYWADDY

DAVE BARTRAM V (ALL	(A) SHOWADDYWADDY	1974 BELL	UK BELLS 248
ROMEO CHALLENGER D (ALL	(B) STEP TWO	1975 BELL	UK BELLS 256
AL JAMES B (ALL	(C) TROCADERO	1976 BELL	UK SYBKL 8003
BJ COLE STEEL(E	(D) SHOWADDYWADDY	1977 MFP	UK 50353
JEFF DALY SAX (E	(E) RED STAR	1977 ARISTA	UK SPARTY 1023
JOHN ACOCK PNO (AE	(F) GREATEST HITS	1978 ARISTA	UK ARTY 145
MARTYN FORD ORCHESTRA (E	(G) CREPES & DRAPES	1979 ARISTA	UK ARTV 3
RUSS FIELD G (ALL	(H) BRIGHT LIGHTS	1980 ARISTA	UK SPART 1142
ROD DEES B (ALL	( ) SHOWADDYWADDY	1981 HALLMARK	UK SHM 3085
TREVOR OAKLEY G (ALL			
BUDDY CIASK V (ALL MALCOLM ALLURED D (ALL			

SHUSHA

SHUSHA V (ALL   (A) PERSIAN LOVE SONGS & MYSTIC CHANTS1973 LYRICORD LLST7235 +TANGENT 108
G T MOORE G K (CDEF   (B) SONG OF LONG TIME LOVERS   1972 TANGENT   TGS114
MARTIN HAYWARD G (CDE   (C) SHUSHA   1974 UA   UK UAS29575
CHRIS LAURENCE B (DE   (D) THIS IS THE DAY   1974 UA   UK UAS29684
TOM WHYTE B (CE   (E) BEFORE THE DELUGE   1975 UA   UK UAS29879
TERRY WILSON B (E   (F) FROM EAST TO WEST   1978 TANGENT   TGS 138
RICHIE BULL BANJO(E   (G) HERE I LOVE YOU   1980 RHAPSODY   RHAP 2
B J COLE STEEL(E

TONY BRAUNAGEL PERC (E   BRIAN GASCOIGNE K ACC(E   RABBIT BUNDRICK K (E   GERRY CONWAY D(E
DUSTER BENNETT HCA (E   THUNDERTHIGHS V (E   TIM JONES PERC K (E   JACK EMBLOW ACC (E
GEORGE LARNYOH HRNS (E   EDDIE QUANSAH HRNS (E   PETER VANDER PUIJE HRNS (E   BILL POVEY OCCARINA (E
ROY CARTER WIND (E   FRANK CLARKE B (B   MARTIN KERSHAW G (B   DUNCAN LAMONT FLT (AB
DAVID SNELL HARP (B   JOHNNY DEANE D (B   STANLEY MYERS PNO (B   GRAHAM MATTHEWS D(C
PAUL ROBINSON D (F   KUMU HARADA B (F   JAMES LASCELLES K (F   BROTHER JAMES PERC(F
BAGER AMINI (F   BRIAN SMITH FLT (F   CHAKO YAMASHITA VLN (F   PAUL BUCKMASTER SYN(F
MOX HCA (D   BEHBOUDI ZARB (A   PAT DONALDSON B (D   FRANK RICOTTI PERC(D
JOHN KIRKPATRICK ACC (DG   RICHARD BAILEY D (G   DARRYL LE QUE PERC (G   PATRICK TISON G (G
LESLEY DUNCAN V (G   JOHN McKENZIE B (G   J A GARDET K (G   DAVID WINTHROP SAX (G
GAYLE CUNNINGHAM V (G

MORT SHUMAN

MORT SHUMAN V (ALL

(A) MY DEATH	1969 REPRISE	US	6358
(B) MORT SHUMAN	1973 PHILIPS	US	700 005
(C) VOILA COMMENT	1973 PHILIPS	FR	6499 630
(D) DES CHANSONS SENTIMENTALES	1974 PHILIPS	US	6325 172
(E) IMAGINE	1976 PHILIPS	FR	9101 029
(F) MY NAME IS MORTIMER	1977 PHILIPS	FR	9101 107

SUHRS / SHROLING

(A) DIARY   1981 BRAIN   GER/UK 0060 333

SHU BI DUA

BOSSE HALL CHRISTENSEN D V(ABCDE   (A) SHU BI DUA   1974 POLYDOR DK 2380 024
JENS TAGE NIELSEN K V (ABCDE   (B) "2"   1975 POLYDOR DK 2380 040
MICHAEL HARDINGER GV (ABCDE   (C) "3"   1976 POLYDOR DK 2380 046
MICHAEL BUNDESEN V (ABCDE   (D)"4"   1977 POLYDOR DK 2380 053
PAUL MEYENDORF G V (A   (E) 78 EREN   1978 POLYDOR DK 2380 061
NIELS GRONBECH B V (ABCD   (F) LEIF I PARKEN   1979 POLYDOR DK 2444 070
SVEND ASMUSSEN VLN (ABCD   (G) "7"   1980 POLYDOR DK
TOMMY SEEBACH SYN (AB   (H) "8"   1981 POLYDOR DK
MORTEN LANGEBFEK K (A
PER STAN PERC (AB   KASPER WINDING (A   CLAUS ASMUSSEN G B(BCDE   JESPER THILO SAX (B
ALLAN BOTSCHINSKY HRNS (B   FINN MADSEN HRNS (B   VINCENT NIELSSON HRNS (B   MICHAEL ELO V (C
JENS HYLLESTAD CELLO(C   KIM DAUGAARD B V (E   NIELS ERIK CLAUSEN CELLO(E

SIDE EFFECT

(A) SIDE EFFECT	197 FANTASY	US	9491
(B) GOIN' BANANAS	1978 FANTASY FTA 3008 US	9537
(C) WHAT YOU NEED	197 FANTASY	US	9513
(D) RAINBOW VISIONS	1979 FANTASY	US	9569
(E) AFTER THE RAIN	1980 ELEKTRA	US	261
(F) PORTRAITS	1981 ELEKTRA UK K52295	
(G) ALL ABOARD	1982 ELEKTRA UK 160049	

SIDE WINDER

STUART SMITH G ((A) ALL WOUND UP   1979 TANK   UK   332
FRED SCARRET G (
NEIL HARVEY V (STEVE McLAUGHLIN B (YATTA YATES   D (

SIDEWINDERS

ANDY PALEY V HCA (A   (A) SIDEWINDERS   1972 RCA   US LSP 4696
LEIGH LISOWSKI B V (A
MIKE READ G (A   ERIC ROSENFELD G V (A   HENRY STERN   D PERC V(A

BEN SIDRAN

BEN SIDRAN	V PNO	(ALL	(A) FEEL YOUR GROOVE			1971 CAPITOL		US		ST 825			
CLYDE STUBBLEFIELD	D	(BCD	(B) I LEAD A LIFE			1972 BLUE THUMB		US		BTS 40			
GEORGE BROWN	D	(BC	(C) DONT LET GO			1972 BLUE THUMB		US		BTS 6012			
PHIL UPCHURCH	D G B	(BCDEF	(D) PUTTIN' IN TIME ON PLANET EARTH			1973 BLUE THUMB		US		BTS 55,			
CURLEY JAMES COOKE	G	(ABCDE	(E) FREE IN AMERICA			1976 ARISTA		US		AL 4081			
JERRY ALEXANDER	HCA	(C	(F) DOCTOR IS IN			1977 ARISTA SPARTY1022 US				AL 4131			
BUNKY GREEN	SAX	(C	(G) A LITTLE KISS IN THE NIGHT			1978 ARISTA SPART 1064 US				AB 4178			
SONNY SEALS	SAX	(CE											
KIP MERKLEIN	B	(C	RANDY FULLERTON	B	(F	JIM PETERMAN	ORG	(CD	TOM PIAZZA	D	(C
RICHARD DAVIS	B	(F	CHUCK DOMANICO	B	(F	JOHN GUERIN	D	(F	TONY WILLIAMS	D	(DF
BLUE MITCHELL	TPT	(ABFG	LARRY CARLTON	G	(F	RAY ARMONDO	PERC	(F	DAVID WOODFORD		(G
PHIL WOODS	SAX	(G	GARY MALLABER	D PERC	(AF	GAVIN CHRISTOPHER	V	(BE	CHEEBA SWITZER	V	(B
JOHNNY ALMOND	FLT	(B	BRUCE BOTNICK	V	(B	CURT ROADS	SYN	(B	DENNIS OLIVER	B	(B
TIM DAVIS	CONGA	(BD	CHARLES DAVIS	SAX	(B	BOB FOLKEDAHL	HRNS	(B	BOB CORBET	HRN	(B
JIM GORDON	SAX	(B	JIM KELTNER	D	(A	SANDY KONIKOFF	PERC	(A	JUDY SIDRAN	V	(A
BOZ SCAGGS	G	(A	PETER FRAMPTON	G	(A	GREG RIDLEY	B	(A	CHRIS DRISCOE	SAX	(A
DAVID BROWN	B	(A	GEORGE RAINS	D	(A	MIMI FARINA MELVIN	V	(A	CHARLIE WATTS	D	(A
BILL PERKINS	SAX	(D	LAUDIR DE OLIVEIRA PERC	(D		JOSE SOARES	PERC	(D	STEVE MILLER	G	(D
JESSE ED DAVIS	G	(AG	ABE LABORIEL	B	(A	ARTHUR ADAMS	G	(G	GERALD JOHNSON	G	(G
ROSE BUTLER	V	(G	MAX GRONENTHAL	V	(G	MIKE FINNIGAN	K V	(G	JAY GRAYDON	G	(G
GARY COLEMAN	PERC	(G	BOB GLAUB	B	(G	GARY ZAPPA	B	(E	BILL MEEKER	D	(E
HENRY GIBSON	PERC	(E	MARY ANN STEWART	V	(E	RICHARD TEE	K	(E	WOODY SHAW	TPT	(E
RANDY BRECKER	HRNS	(E	MICHAEL BRECKER	HRNS	(E	KITTY HAYWOOD	V	(E	VIVIAN HAYWOOD	V	(E

PAUL SIEBEL

PAUL SIEBEL	G V	(ALL	(A) WOODSMOKE AND ORANGES	1970 ELEKTRA EKS 74064 RI UK K42040
DAVID BROMBERG	G	(C	(B) JACK KNIFE GYPSY	1971 ELEKTRA EKS 74081 RI UK K42076
GARY WHITE		(C	(C) LIVE	1981 RAG BABY	UK 1006

DAN SIEGEL

DAN SIEGEL	K V	(A	(A) THE HOT SHOT	1980 INNER CITY US	1C1111
GARRY HAGBERG					
ROB THOMAS	B VLN	(A	GARY HOBBS	D	(A	JEFF HOMAN	SAX (A	MARC SIEGEL	V (A
EDWARD McMANUS	HRNS	(A	CINDY McMANUS	HRNS	(A	SUE DAVIS	HARP (A

CORKY SIEGEL

CORKY SIEGEL	V K HCA	(A	(A) CORKY SIEGAL	1974 DHARMA	US 806
SHELLY PLOTKIN	D	(A			
VASSAR CLEMENTS	STR	(A			

SIEGEL SCHWALL BAND

CORKY SIEGEL	V K HCA	(ALL	(A) SIEGEL SCHWALL BAND	1966 VANGUARD	VSD 79235
JIM SCHWALL	G V	(ALL	(B) SAY SIEGEL SCHWALL	1967 VANGUARD	VSD 79249
JOS DAVIDSON	B	(ABCDEFGHIJ	(C) SHAKE	1968 VANGUARD UK SVRL19044+VSD 79289
RUSS CHADWICK	D	(ABCDJ	(D) SIEGEL SCHWALL 70	1970 VANGUARD	VSD 6562
JACK DAWSON	B	(BCDJ	(E) THE SIEGEL SCHWALL BAND	1971 WOODEN NICKEL US	WNS 1002
SHELDON IRA PLOTKIN	D	(EFGHIK	(E) THE SIEGEL SCHWALL BAND	1971 RCA	UK SF 8246
			(E) THE SIEGEL SCHWALL BAND	198 LINE GER 5034	
ROLLOW RADFORD	B	(EFGHIK	(F) SLEEPY HOLLOW	1972 WOODEN NICKEL US	WNS 1010
SAN FRANCISCO SYM ORCH		(K	(F) SLEEPY HOLLOW	1972 RCA LSP10394 GER RI 5043	
			(G) 953 WEST	1973 TELDEC 10121 GER RI LINE 5049	
			(H) LIVE LAST SUMMER	1974 TELDEC 6 24215 GER RI LINE 5032	
			(H) LIVE LAST SUMMER	1974 WOODEN NICKEL US	WNS 1 288
			(I) R.I.P. SIEGEL SCHWALL	1974 TELDEC	6 24217
			(I) R.I.P. SIEGEL SCHWALL	1974 WOODEN NICKEL US	WNS 1 554
			(I) R.I.P. SIEGEL SCHWALL	1980 LINE GER 5054	
			(J) BEST OF	1974 VANGUARD	VSD 79336
			(K) THREE PIECES FOR BLUES BAND & ORCH	1974 POLYDOR 2530 309	
			(K) S S B & SYM ORCH	1980 POLYDOR 2344 157	2261 031

SIERRA

SNEAKY PETE	STEEL	(A	(A) SIERRA	1977 MERCURY	US SRM1 1179
GIB GUILBEAU	FDL	(A			
MICKY McGEE	D V	(A	FELIX PAPPALARDI PROD (A THAD MAXWELL	B V (A BOBBY COCHRAN	G V (A

DAVITT SIGERSON

DAVITT SIGERSON	V	(A	(A) DAVITT SIGERSON	1980 ISLAND/ZE	ILPS 7011
KENWOOD DENNARD	D	(A		
RICHARD CROOKS	D	(A	JIMMY RIPPETOE G B (A GORDON JOHNSON	B (A NED ALBRIGHT	PNO (A
MICHAEL DELUGG	PROD	(A		

BUNNY SIGLER

BUNNY SIGLER	K	(A	(A) LET THE GOOD TIMES ROLL	19 PARKWAY US PS 50000
RAYMOND EARL	B	(F	(B) THAT'S HOW LONG I'LL BE LOVING	1974 PHILADELPHIA UK 80253 US 32589
IM MILLER	G	(F	(C) KEEP SMILIN'	197 PHILADELPHIA US 33249
SCOTTY MILLER	D	(F	(D) MY MUSIC	19 PHILADELPHIA UK 81755 US 34267
DENNIS RICHARDSON	K	(F	(E) LET ME PARTY WITH YOU	1978 SALSOUL UK 1502 GOLD US 9500
LARRY DAVIS	PERC V	(F	(F) I'VE ALWAYS WANTED TO SING	1979 SALSOUL UK 1512 GOLD US 9503
JIMMY SIGLER	K V	(F	(G) LET IT SNOW	1980 SALSOUL UK 8531
CHARLES COLLINS	PERC	(F		
CARLA BENSON	V	(F	EVETTE BENTON V (F BARBARA INGRAM	V (F

SILENT TYPES

(A) WAR ECONOMY(EP)	1980 DOUBLE DOSE SHOT 13

SILICON TEENS

DARRYL	V	(A	(A) MUSIC FOR PARTIES	1980 MUTE UK STUMM2 US SIRE 6092
JACKI	SYN	(A		
PAUL	PERC	(A	DIANE SYN (A	

SILENCERS

(A) ROCK'N'ROLL ENFORCEMENT	19 PRECISION US 36529
(B) ROMANIAC	1981 PRECISION US 37083

THE SILKIE

```
KEV SILKIE         B  (A              (A) YOU'VE GOT TO HIDE YOUR LOVE AWAY 1965 FONTANA    US 67548
MIKE SILKIE        G V (A
SILVIE SILKIE      V  (A   IVOR SILKIE      D  (A   JOHN LENNON      G  (A   PAUL McCARTNEY   G (A
GEORGE HARRISON    G  (A
```

JUDEE SILL

```
JUDEE SILL         G V (ABC           (A) JUDEE SILL                1971 ASYLUM         UK        SYLA 8751
CLYDIE KING        V  (A               (B) HEART FOOD                1973 ASYLUM UK SYL9006 US   5063
VANETTA FIELDS     V  (A               (C) TULIPS FROM AMSTERDAM     1979
RITA COOLIDGE      V  (A
DAVID BEARDEN        (B   LYNN BLESSING     (B   GENE CIPRIANO       (B   VINCE DE ROSA     (B
DOUG DILLARD         (B   OMA DRAKE         (B   ASSA DRORI          (B   BUDDY EMMONS      (B
JESSE EHRLICH        (B   CHRIS ETHRIDGE    (B   RON FULSOM          (B   HARRIS GOLDMAN    (B
JIM GORDON           (B   BOBBYE HALL   PERC (B   GLORIA JONES      V (B   RAY KELLY         (B
WILLIAM KURASCH      (B   LEONARD MALARSKY  (B   SPOONER OLDHAM      (B   RICHARD PERISSI   (B
BILL PLUMMER         (B   EMIL RICHARDS     (B   RALPH SCHAEFFER     (B   LOUIE SHELTON     (B
DAVID SCHWARTZ       (B   CAROLYN WILLIS    (B   TIBOR ZELIG         (B
```

SILLY WIZARD

```
JOHNNY CUNNINGHAM FDL MAND(ABC        (A) SILLY WIZARD             1976 XTRA        UK      XTRA 1158
PHIL CUNNINGHAM    K   (ABC            (B) CALEDONIA'S SONS         1978 HIGHWAY     UK      SHY  7004
ANDY STEWART       V BAN(ABC           (C) SO MANY PARTINGS        1979 HIGHWAY     UK      SHY  7007
GORDON JONES       G MAND(ABC
BOB THOMAS         G   (ABC   MARTIN HODDEN      B  (ABC
```

SILVER

```
JOHN BATDORF       G V (A             (A) SILVER                   1976 ARISTA US 4076  UK   ARTY 144
BRENT MYDLAND      V K (A
RICK GILES         (      GREG COLLIER    G V (A   HARRY STINSON   V D(A  TOM LEADON    B V  (A
```

SILVER APPLES

```
SIMEON             BAN V(A            (A) SILVER APPLES            1968 KAPP        US    3562
DAN TAYLOR         PERC V(A            (B) CONTRACT                1969 KAPP        US    3584
```

SILVER CONDOR

```
CLAUDE PEPPER      D  (A              (A) SILVER CONDOR            1981 CBS   US
JOE CERISCNO       V  (A
EARL SLICK         G  (A   JOHN CAREY    G K V(A      JAY DAVIS     B  (A
```

SILVERADO

```
EARL GOODWIN       G V (AB            (A) SILVERADO               1976 RCA         US       APLI 1792
CARL SHILLO        G V (AB            (B) TAKING IT ALL IN STRIDE 1977 RCA         US       APLI 2421
JAY D MANESS       G   (A             (C) READY FOR LOVE          1981 RCA
J F KEITHLINO      B   (B
RON TUTT           D   (A   VICTOR FELDMAN PERC VIBES(A   AL CASEY     G MAND(A  ALAN ESTES     PERC(A
JAMES B GORDON     D   (A   EMORY GORDY     B   (A    TOM HENSLEY   K   (A   MIKE HAYDEN      D  (B
DON ORIOTO         K   (B
```

SILVERBIRD

```
                                     (A) GETTING TOGETHER         1972 CBS         US   31570
```

SILVERHEAD

```
MICHAEL DES BARRES V   (ABC           (A) SILVERHEAD              1972 PURPLE UK TPSA 7506 US MCA  306
NIGEL HARRISON     B   (ABC           (B) SIXTEEN & SAVAGED       1973 PURPLE UK TPSA 7511 US MCA  391
ROD DAVIES PERC  V G   (ABC           (C) LIVE AT RAINBOW         1976 PUPLE JAP 80351
PETE THOMPSON      D K (ABC
ROBBIE BLUNT       G   (B   MARTIN BIRCH       PROD (A   STEVE FOREST    G V  (A   JOHN MUMFORD   TROM(A
LYLE JENKINS       SAX (A
```

SILVERMETRE

```
LEIGH STEVENS      G   (A             (A) SILVERMETRE             1969 NATIONAL GENERAL      2000
MICK WALLER        D   (A
JACK REYNOLDS      V   (A   PETE SEARS    B K (A
```

SHEL SILVERSTEIN

```
SHEL SILVERSTEIN       (ALL           (A) HAIRY JAZZ              1961 ELEKTRA      US       176
PIG ROBBINS        K   (J             (B) INSIDE SHEL SILVERSTEIN 196  ATLANTIC     US       8257
RAY SAWYER         V   (G             ( ) INSIDE FOLK MUSIC       1962 ATLANTIC     US     SD 8072
DENNIS LOCORRIERE  V   (G             (C) IM SO GOOD , I DONT HAVE TO BRAG 196 CADET US      4052
JAY DAVID              (G             (D) DRAIN MY BRAIN          196  CADET        US       4054
GEORGE CUMMINGS        (G             (E) CROUCHING ON THE OUTSIDE 197 JANUS               2JLS 3052
BILLY FRANCIS          (G             (F) A BOY NAMED SUE         1968 RCA          US      LSP 4192
RIK ELSWIT             (G             (G) FREAKIN' AT THE FREAKERS BALL 1973 CBS  UK 65452 US  31119
AMOS GARRETT      G    (J             (G) FREAKIN' AT THE FREAKERS BALL 1979 CBS  RI UK 31766
JANCE GARFAT           (G             (H) SONGS & STORIES         1978 PARACHUTE    US     RRLP9007
MIKE FINNIGAN          (G             (J) GREAT CONCH TRAIN ROBBERY 1980 FLYING FISH US
ART TWAIN              (G
JELLY ROLL TURNER      (G   TURK MURPHY        (G   CHARLES H PETERSON   (G   CHARLES DAY     (G
DELL DUCKWORTH         (G   CLYDE GRAVES       (G   PHILLIP HOWE         (G   JAMES MAIHACH   (G
LEON OAKLEY            (G   RICHARD SHUBB      (G   FRED MERGY           (G   SAM BUSH        (G
JOHN HARTFORD          (J   D J FONTANA     D  (J
```

DENNIS SIMMONDS

```
DENNIS SIMMONDS        (A  (A) ALONE ON PENGUIN ISLAND  1981 DOME        UK   DOM331
```

DAVID SIMMONS

```
DAVID SIMMONS      V   (AB            (A) HEAR ME OUT             1978 FANTASY      US    F9561
WILLIAM INGRAM     G   (AB            (B) THE WORLD BELONGS TO ME 1979 FANTASY      US    F9588
JAMES RAMSEY       G   (A
JAMES INGRAM       G K (AB   JOHN INGRAM      D   (AB  TIMMI INGRAMS   CONGOS(AB BARBARA INGRAM  V  (AB
JAMES MINGRAM      SAX (A    MARK PRATER      K   (B   BUTCH INGRAM    TPT V (B
```

GENE SIMMONS

GENE SIMMONS	G V (A	(A) GENE SIMMONS		CASABLANCA	UK	NBLP 7120	
ALLEN SCHWARZBERG	D (A						
NEIL JASON	B (A	ELLIOTT RANDALL	G (A	SEAN DELANEY	PERC V(A	BOB SEGER	V (A
JOE PERRY	(A	HELEN REDDY	V (A	MITCH WEISSMAN	(A	RICHIE RANNO	(A
GORDON GRODY	V (A	RICK NIELSEN	G (A	MICHAEL DES BARRES	V (A	DIVA GRAY	V (A
KATE SAPAL	V (A	FRAN EISENBERG	V (A	CAROLYN RAY	V (A	ERIC TROYER	PNO(A
JANIS IAN	(A	STEVE LACEY	G (A	JOHN SHANE HOWELL	G (A	RICHARD GERSTEIN	PERC(A
JEFF BAXTER	G (A	DONNA SUMMER	V (A	JOE PECORINO	(A	CHER	(A

JEFF SIMMONS

JEFF SIMMONS	B V K(AB	(A) NAKED ANGELS SOUNDTRACK	1969 STRAIGHT	STS 1056
FRANK ZAPPA	G (B	(B) LUCILLE HAS MESSED UP MY MIND	1969 STRAIGHT STS1057 REPRISE 6391	
CRAIG TARWATER	G (B			
IAN UNDERWOOD	SAX (B	RON WOODS D PERC(B JOHN KEHLIOR	D (B	

SIMMS BROTHERS BAND

GEORGE SIMMS	V PERC(A	(A) SIMMS BROTHERS BAND	1979 ELEKTRA	US	6E220
FRANK SIMMS	G V (A	(B) ATTITUDE	1980 ELEKTRA	US	289
BUDD TUNICK	D (A				
DAVID SPINNER	V CONG(A ROBERT SABINO K A SHIMMY MAKI	B (A MICKEY LEONARD	G (A		

SIMON & GARFUNKEL

PAUL SIMON	G V (ALL	(A) WEDNESDAY MORNING 3 AM	1966 CBS	UK 63370	US 9049
ART GARFUNKEL	V (ALL	(B) THE SOUND OF SILENCE	1966 CBS	UK 62690	US 9269
FRED CARTER	G (F	(C) PARSLEY SAGE ROSEMARY & THYME	1966 CBS	UK 62860	US 9363
HAL BLAINE	D (F	(D) BOOKENDS	1968 CBS	UK 63101	US 9529
JOE OSBORN	B (F	(E) THE GRADUATE(SOUNDTRACK)	1968 CBS	UK 70042	US 3180
LARRY KNECHTEL	K (F	(F) BRIDGE OVER TROUBLED WATERS	1970 CBS	UK 63699	US 9914
JIMMY HASKELL	STRINGS(F	(G) GREATEST HITS	1972 CBS	UK 69003	US 31350
ERNIE FREEMAN	STRINGS(F	( ) SIMON & GARFUKEL	1967 ALLEGRO		ALL 836
STEVE GADD	D (K	( ) SIMON & GARFUkel	19 PICKWICK		US 3059
GRADY TATE	D (K	( ) SIMON & GARFUNFUEL	19 FONTANA		6430 006
DAVID BROWN	G (K	(K) CONCERT IN CENTRAL PARK	1981 GEFFEN	UK 96008	
JOHN GATCHELL	TPT (K	(EP) WEDNESDAY MORNING 3 AM	1965 CBS		
PETE CARR	G (K	(EP) I AM A ROCK	1966 CBS		6034
ANTHONY JACKSON	B (K	(EP) MRS ROBINSON	1968 CBS		6400
RICHARD TEE	K (K	(EP) FEELING GROOVY	1967 CBS		6360
ROB MOUNSEY	SYN (K				
DAVE TOFANI	SAX (K GERRY NIEWOOD SAX (K JOHN ECKERT	TPT (K			

CARLY SIMON

CARLY SIMON	V G PNO (ALL	(A) CARLY SIMON	1971 ELEKTRA	US 74082	UK K42077
JAMES TAYLOR	G V (DEFGHJK	(B) ANTICIPATION	1971 ELEKTRA	US 75016	UK K42101
JIM RYAN	G B (BCDF	(AB) CARLY SIMON /ANTICIPATION	1975 ELEKTRA		UK K62015
JOHN RYAN	B (BF	(C) NO SECRETS	1972 ELEKTRA	US 75049	UK K42127
PAUL KEOGH	G (C	(D) HOTCAKES	1974 ELEKTRA	US 7E1002	UK K52005
KLAUS VOORMANN	B (CDEFG	(E) PLAYING POSSUM	1975 ELEKTRA	US 7E1033	UK K52020
LOWELL GEORGE	G (CG	(F) THE BEST OF CARLY SIMON	1976 ELEKTRA	US 7E1048	UK K52025
ANDREW GOLD	G D (EFG	(G) ANOTHER PASSAGE	1976 ELEKTRA	US 7E1064	UK K52036
WILLIE WEEKS	B (EF	(H) BOYS IN THE TREES	1978 ELEKTRA	US 6E 128	UK K52066
LEE SKLAR	B (E	(J) SPY	1979 ELEKTRA	US 5E 506	UK K52147
JOE MONDRAGON	B (E	(K) COME UPSTAIRS	1980 WB	US BSK3443	UK K56828
JEFF BAXTER	G (EG	(L) TORCH	1981 WB	US 3592	UK K56935
ANTHONY JACKSON	B (L				

PAUL GLANZ	PNO (BF	ANDY NEWMARK	D PERC(BCDEFG	ALVIN ROBINSON	G (E	PETER ROBINSON	PNO (C
JIM GORDON	D (CDEF	TONY LEVIN	B (FJK	NICKY HOPKINS	PNO (CF	JIM KELTNER	D (BDFG
ROBBIE ROBERTSON	G (FD	JAMES NEWTON HOWARD	K (E	RAY COOPER	PERC (CF	PAUL BARRERE	G (G
PAUL GRIFFIN	PNO (F	RINGO STARR	D (E	GLENN FREY	G (G	KIRBY JOHNSON	K (F
RUSS KUNKEL	D (DE	PATRICK SIMMONS	G (G	BILL PAYNE	ORG (G	IVY COTTLER	D (E
LAURINDO ALAMEIDA	G (G	NICK DE CARO	ACC (G	FREDDIE STAEHLE	PERC (E	STEVE BRUTON	G (G
RICHARD TEE	K (HJ	ALAN ESTES	PERC (E	KENNY GRADNEY	G (G	KEN BISCHEL	K (HJ
JIMMY JOHNSON	D (F	BOB GLAUB	B (G	DON GROLNICK	K (HJK	EDDIE BONGO CONGA	(F
TIRAN PORTER	B (G	BILLY MERNIT	PNO (EJK	RALPH MACDONALD	PERC (FD	ERIC GALE	G (H
DR JOHN	K G(DEFG	RICHARD PERRY	PERC (F	CORNELL DUPREE	G (H	DAVE SANBORN	SAX (HJL
RITCHIE HAYWARD	D V(G	GORDON EDWARDS	B (H	HARVEY ESTRIN RECORDER	(H	RICK JAEGER	D V (G
JOHN HALL	G (HJ	GEORGE MARGE RECORDER	(H	ROBERT GREENIDGE	D (G	JEFF MIRANOV	G (H
BOBBY KEYS	SAX (DCF	JOHN HARTMAN	D (G	HUGH McCRACKEN	G (HL	TREVOR LAWRENCE	SAX (E
KEITH KNUDSEN	D (G	WILL LEE	B (HJ	DERREK VAN EATON	FLT (E	MILT HOLLAND	PERC(G
FRED TACKETT MANDOCELLO(G		MICHAEL BRECKER	SAX(DFJL	VICTOR FELDMAN	PERC (G	ANDREW LOVE	SAX (G
STEVE GADD	D (HJK	CRUSHER BENNETT	PERC (HJ	RUBENS BASSINI	PERC (H	TOMMY MORGAN	HCA (E
JOE CARO	G (J	DAVID SPINOZZA	G (JD	IAN McLAUGHLIN	K (J	WARREN BERNHARDT	K (KL
RANDY BRECKER	TPT (J	RICK MAROTTA	D (JKLD	KEN LANDRUM	(K	MIKE MAINIERI	K V (JKL
HUBERT LAWS	FLT (J	FRANK CARILLO	G (G	CLIFF CARTER	SYN (J	RAPHAEL CRUZ	PERC(J
PETER BALLIN	SAX (J	TOM MALONE	TROM (J	LEW DELGATTO	SAX (J	PETE HEWLETT	G V (K
SID McGINNIS	G V (K	ED WALSH	OBERHEIM (K	JERRY GROSSMAN	CELLO(K	NOVI NOVAG	VLA (G
DAVID CAMPBELL	VLA (G	BUD SHANK	FLT (G	PHIL BODNER	OBOE (H	MARGARET ROSS	HARP(K
GLORIA AGOSTINI	HARP (H	RITA COOLIDGE	V (E	RODNEY RICHMOND	(E	LIZA STRIKE	V (CF
VICKI BROWN	V (CF	BONNIE BRAMLETT	V (CF	DORIS TROY	V (CF	PAUL McCARTNEY	V (CF
LINDA McCARTNEY	V (CF	CLYDIE KING	V (E	CAROLYN WILLIS	V (E	CAROLE KING	V (EF
VINI PONCIA	V (E	MAXINE WILLARD	V (E	JULIA TILLMAN	V (E	ABIGALE HANESS	V (EF
KENNY MOORE	V (EF	CARL HALL	V (FD	TASHA THOMAS	V (FD	LANI GROVES	V (FD
MIKE McDONALD	V (G	LUCY SIMON	V (GJ	ALEX TAYLOR	V (GK	ELLEN KEARNEY	V (G
LINDA RONSTADT	V (G	DOOBIE BROTHERS	V (G	JACKSON BROWNE	V (G	LIBBY TITUS	V (G
LEAH KUNKEL	V (K	TIM CURRY	V (J	ULLANDA McCULLOUGH	V (J	LORAINE NEWMAN	V (K
MARIA AGUIAR	V (K	CHRISTINE MARTIN	V (K	GAIL BOGGS	V (J	HUGH TAYLOR	V (K
SARAH MARIA TAYLOR	V (K	LEE RITENOUR	G (K	LON VAN EATON SIT SYN	(E	ANTHONY JACKSON	B (L
MARTY PAICH	STR (L	EDDIE GOMEZ	B (L	JIMMY WISNER	STR (L	JAY BERLINER	G (L
DON SEBESKY	STR (L	ROBERT M FREEDMAN STR	(L	PHIL WOODS	SAX (L	GRADY TATE	D (L
JERRY MAROTTA	D (L	DAVID NADIEN	VLN (L	MICK JAGGER	C (C	KEN ASHER	K (D
RICHARD DAVIS	B (D	GEORGE DEVONS	PERC (D	TODD GRAFF	V (D	LARRY BREAN	D (D
HOWARD JOHNSON	SAX (D	BARRY ROGERS	TROM (D	BILLY COBHAM	D (D	BENNIE DIGGS	V (D
REVELATIONS	V (D	CARL HALL	V (D	BUCKY PIZZARELLI	G (D	PAUL BUCKMASTER	STR (D
STEVE MADAIO	TPT (D						

JOE SIMON

JOE SIMON	V	(ALL	(A) JOE SIMON	19	JOY	UK JOYS 176		
ROLAND CHAMBERS	G	(G	(B) SOUNDS OF SIMON	19	POLYDOR	UK 2918 001		
T J TINDALL	G	(G	(C) POWER OF SIMON	19	POLYDOR	UK 2391 090		
EARL YOUNG	PERC	(G	(D) GREATEST HITS	1973	MONUMENT	UK 65419	US 231916	
VINCE MONTANA	VIBES	(G	(E) MOOD HEART & SOUL	1974	POLYDOR	UK 2391 132		
LEON HUFF	PNO	(G	(F) GET DOWN	1975	POLYDOR	UK 2391 181		
NORMAN HARRIS	G	(G	(G) DROWNING IN THE SEA OF LOVE	1976	POLYDOR	UK 2482 278		
RONALD BAKER	B	(G	(H) CHOKIN' WIND	1976	MONUMENT	UK 22008		
LARRY WASHINGTON	PERC	(G	(I) TODAY	1976	SPRING	UK 2391 216		
LEONARD PAKULA	ORG	(G	(J) EASY TO LOVE	1977	SPRING	UK 2391 260		
THOM BELL	STR	(G	(K) BEST OF	1977	POLYDOR	UK 2391 311		
			(L) BAD CASE OF LOVE	1978	SPRING	UK 2391 307		
			(M) LOVE VIBRATIONS	1979	SPRING	UK 2391 375		

S125
PAUL SIMON
S125

PAUL SIMON	G V	(ALL	(A) THE PAUL SIMON SONGBOOK	1965	CBS		UK 62579
HUX BROWN	G	(BF	(B) PAUL SIMON(MOTHER & CHILD REUNION)	1972	CBS	US 30750	UK 69007
DAVID SPINOZZA	G	(BCF	(C) THERE GOES RHYMIN' SIMON	1973	CBS	US 32280	UK 69035
WALLACE WILSON	G	(B	(D) LIVE RHYMIN'	1974	CBS	US 32855	UK 69059
JERRY HAHN	G	(B	(E) STILL CRAZY AFTER ALL THESE YEARS	1975	CBS	US 33540	UK 86001
STEFAN GROSSMAN	G	(B	(F) GREATEST HITS ETC	197	CBS	US 35032	UK 86047
NEVILLE HINDS	ORG	(BF	(G) ONE TRICK PONY	1980	WEA	US 3472	UK K56846
JACKIE JACKSON	B	(BF					

RON CARTER	B	(B	RUSSELL GEORGE	B	(BF	JOE OSBORN	B	(B	WINSTON GRENNAN	D (BF
HAL BLAINE	D	(B	VICTOR MONTANEZ	D	(B	DENSIL LANG	PERC	(BF	LOS INCAS PERC FLT	(BF
AIRTO MOREIRA	PERC	(BCF	LARRY KNECHTEL	K HCA	(BF	MIKE MAINIERI	VIBES	(B	FRED LIPSIUS	HRNS(B
JOHN SCHROER	HRNS	(B	STEVEN TURRE	HRNS	(B	CHARLIE McCOY	HCA	(B	CISSY HOUSTON	B (BF
RONELLE STAFFORD	V	(BF	DEIRDRE TUCK	V	(BF	VON EVA SIMS	V	(BF	STEPHANE GRAPPELLY VLN(B
PETE CARR	G	(CEF	CORNELL DUPREE	G	(C	ALEXANDER GAFA	G	(CF	JERRY PUCKETT	G (C
DAVID HOOD	B	(CEF	GORDON EDWARDS	B	(CEF	BOB CRANSHAW	B	(CF	RICHARD DAVIS	B (CF
VERNIE ROBBINS	B	(C	ROGER HAWKINS	D	(CEF	RICK MAROTTA	D	(C	GRADY TATE	D (CEF
JAMES STRAUD	D	(C	BARRY BECKETT	K	(CEF	BOB JAMES	K	(CEF	PAUL GRIFFIN	PNO(C
BOBBY SCOTT	PNO	(CF	ONWARD BRASS BAND		(CF	DON ELLIOTT	VIBES(C		CARSON WHITSETT	ORG(C
DIXIE HUMMINGBIRDS	V	(CF	MAGGIE ROCHE	V	(C	TERRE ROCHE	V	(C	JIMMY JOHNSON	G (CF
JESSY DIXON SINGERS		(DEF	URUBAMBA		(D	RICHARD TEE	K V	(GEF	HIRAM BULLOCK	G (G
RALPH MACDONALD	PERC	(GEF	ERIC GALE	G	(G	JEFF MIRONOV	G	(G	JOHN TROPEA	G (GEF
JOE BECK	G	(GEF	STEVE GADD	D	(GEF	TONY LEVIN	B	(G	HUGH McCRACKEN	G (GEF
DON GROLNICK	SYN	(G	JON FADDIS	HRNS	(G	PATTI AUSTIN	V	(GEF	MIKE BRECKER	HRNS(EF
ART GARFUNKEL	V	(E	SIVUKA	V ACC	(EF	TONY LEVIN	B	(EF	PHOEBE SNOW	V (EF
DAVE MATTHEWS	HRNS	(EF	JERRY FRIEDMAN	G	(EF	KEN ASHER	K	(EF	VALERIE SIMPSON	V (EF
TOOTS THIELMANS	HCA	(E	DAVE SANBORN	SAX	(EF	PHIL WOODS	SAX	(EF	EDDIE DANIELS	SAX (E
LEON PENDARVIS	K	(E	ANTHONY JACKSON	B	(F	CHICAGO COMM CHOIR	V	(E	RANDY BRECKER	TPT (F
THE OAK RIDGE BOYS	V	(F	MARVIN STAMM	TPT	(F	IRVIN MARKOWITZ	TPT	(F	LOU DELGATTO	SAX (F
QUINCY JONES	STR	(F	WALLACE WILSON	G	(F	RONELLE STAFFORD	V	(F	VON EVA SIMS	V (F
REV CLAUDE JITER	V	(F								

S126
SIMPLE MINDS
S126

JIM KERR	V	(ABCDE	(A) LIFE IN A DAY	1979	ZOOM	ZULP 001	
CHARLIE BURCHILL	G V	(ABCDE	(B) REAL TO REAL CACOPHONY	1979	ZOOM	SPART1109	
MICHAEL McNEIL	K V	(ABCDE	(C) EMPIRES AND DANCE	1980	ARISTA	SPART1140	
BRIAN McGEE	D V	(ABCD	(D) SONS AND FASCINATION	1981	VIRGIN	V 2207	
DEREK FORBES	B V	(ABCDE	(E) NEW GOLD DREAM	1982	VIRGIN	V 2230	
KEN LOCKIE	V	(D					
JACQUIE	V	(D	MIKE OGLETREE	D PERC(E	MEL GAYNOR	D	(E	KENNY HYSLOP	D (A
SHARON CAMPBELL	V	(E	HERBIE HANCOCK	K	(			

S127
MARTIN SIMPSON
S127

MARTIN SIMPSON	G V BAN(A		(A) GOLDEN VANITY	1976	TRAILER	LER 2099	
AL SCHMIDT	HCA	(A					
PETER THOMPSON	B	(A					

S128
VALERIE SIMPSON
S128

VALERIE SIMPSON	V K	(AB	(A) VALERIE SIMPSON EXPOSED	1971	TAMLA US 311	UK	STML11194
JAMES JAMESON	B	(A	(B) VALERIE SIMPSON	1972	TAMLA US 317	UK	STML11219
ANDREW SMITH	D	(A	(C) KEEP	1977	TAMLA US 351		
ROBERT WHITE	G	(A					
JOE MESSINA	G	(A	DENNIS COFFEY	G	(A	URIEL JONES	D (A	JOHNNY GRIFFITH	PNO (A
LEONARD CASTON	PNO	(A	EDDIE BROWN	PERC	(A	JACK ASHFORD	PERC (A	JACK BROKENSHAW	PERC(A
JOSHIE ASMSTEAD	V	(AB	PAUL RISER	STR	(AB	NAT ADDERLEY	PNO (B	RAY LUCAS	D (B
BUDDY WILLIAMS	D	(B	CHARLES COLLINS	D	(B	FRANCISCO CENTENO	B (B	KEITH ILLIDGE	G (B
RALPH MACDONALD	PERC	(B					

S129
FRANKIE LEE SIMS
S129

FRANKIE LEE SIMS		(A	(A) LUCY MAE BLUES	19	SPECIALTY	UK	SNTF 5004
HUBERT WASHINGTON	D	(A					

S130
SINCEROS
S130

DON SNOW	K V	(AB	(A) SOUND OF SUNBATHING	1979	EPIC US 36134 UK CBS	83632	
BOBBI IRWIN	D	(AB	(B) PET ROCK	1981	EPIC	UK	85003
MARK KJELDSEN	G V	(AB					
RON FRANCIS	B	(AB	GUS DUDGION	PROD (B			

S131
PETE SINFIELD
S131

PETE SINFIELD	G SYN V	(A	(A) STILL	1973	MANTICORE 2001 UKK43501 US 66667		
RICHARD BRUNTON	G	(A					
B J COLE	STEEL	(A	GREG LAKE	G V	(A	SNUFFY WALDEN	G (A	MEL COLLINS	WIND(A
DON HONEYWELL	SAX	(A	CHRIS PYNE	TROM	(A	GREG BOWEN	TPT (A	STAN RODERICK	TPT (A
ROBIN MILLER	WIND	(A	TIM HINKLEY	PNO	(A	PHIL JUMP	K (A	KEITH TIPPETT	PNO (A
BOZ BURRELL	B	(A	STEVE DOLAN	B	(A	JOHN WETTON	B (A	MIN	D PERC (A
IAN WALLACE	D	(A					

S131A
SINS OF SATAN
S131A

		(A) SINS OF SATAN	1977	BUDDAH	US 5673

SIOUXSIE & THE BANSHEES

```
SIOUXSIE           V   (ALL     (A) THE SCREAM            1978 POLYDOR UK POLD5009 US 6207  GER 2383523
SID VICIOUS        D   (1       (B) JOIN HANDS            1979 POLYDOR UK 2442 264           GER 2383551
STEVE SEVERIN  B G K SYN(ABC123DE (C) KALEIDOSCOPE        1980 POLYDOR UK 2442 177           GER 2383568
MARCO PIRRONI      G   (1       (D) JU JU                 1981 POLYDOR UK POLS1034
P FENTON           G   (2       (E) ONCE UPON A TIME      1981 POLYDOR UK POLS1056
STEVE JONES        G   (C       (1) SEPT 1976   (2) NOV 1976 (3) 1977
KENNY MORRIS       D   (23A
JOHN McKAY         G(3A   JOHN McGEOCH    SAX (BC  THE SIRENS    V   (C   BUDGIE    D B V(C
```

SIR LORD BALTIMORE

```
JOHN GARNER        V D (AB      (A) SIR LORD BALTIMORE    19   MERCURY US  1613
GARY JUSTIN        B G V(AB      (B) KINGDOM COME          19   MERCURY US 61328
LOUIS DAMBRA       G K (AB
JOEY DAMBRA        G K V(A
```

SIREN

```
KEVIN COYNE        G V (AB      (A) SIREN                 1969 DANDELION US D9 104      63755
DAVE CLAGUE        G B (AB      (B) STRANGE LOCOMOTION     1971 ELEKTRA   US74087 DANDELION GER 2310152
NICK CUDWORTH      K V G(AB      (B) STRANGE LOCOMOTION     1971 DANDELION           UKDAN8001
TAT MEAGER         D   (AB
JOHN CHICHESTER    G   (A   COLIN WOOD    K FLT(A   MICK GRATTON G    (B
```

SIRKEL & CO

```
ERIC SIRKEL        G V (A       (A) SIRKEL & CO           1976 CHARLY                CRL5003
MICK TAYLOR        G   (A       (A) SIRKEL & CO           1977 AFFINITY              AFF  1
MARC FRENTZEL      D   (A
GORDON RAITT       B   (A   CHRIS MERCER   SAX  (A   JOY YATES    V   (A   RONNIE LEAHY   K   (A
MICK EVE           SAX (A   LIZA STRIKE    V    (A   COLIN ALLEN  D   (A   ROBIN MILLAR   K   (A
RON CARTHY         TPT (A   JACKIE SULLIVAN V   (A
```

SISTER SLEDGE

```
KATHIE SLEDGE          V   (BCD    (A) CIRCLE OF LOVE      1975 ATLANTIC   UK K50097 US  36105
NARADA MICHAEL WALDEN PROD(D       ( ) TOGETHER            1977 COTILLION            US  9919
DEBBIE SLEDGE          V   (BCD    (B) WE ARE FAMILY       1979 COTILLION  UK K50587 US  5209
KIM SLEDGE             V   (BCD    (C) LOVE SOMEBODY TODAY  1980 COTILLION  UK K50693 US 16012
JONI SLEDGE            V   (BCD    (D) ALL AMERICAN GIRLS   1981 COTILLION  UK K50774 US 16072
NILE RODGERS          G   (B       ( ) SISTER SLEDGE       1981 COTILLION  UK K50853 US  5231
ELLEN SEELING         TPT (B       ( ) THE SISTERS         1982 COTILLION  UK K50853
BARRY ROGERS          TROM (B
BERNARD EDWARDS       B   (B   TONY THOMPSON   D  (B   ROBERT SABINO   K   (B   KAREN MILNE STRINGS(B
CHERYL HONG   STRINGS (B   MARIANNE CARROLLSTRINGS(B   ANDY SCHWARTZ   PNO  (B   RAYMOND JONES   K  (B
SAMMY FIGUEROA   PERC (B   ALEX FOSTER    WIND (B   JEAN FINEBERG   SAX  (B   JON FADDIS    TPT(B
```

EARL SIXTEEN

```
EARL SIXTEEN           (A       (A) REGGAE SOUND          1981 DREAD AT THE CONTROLS UK 003
```

6680 LEXINGTON

```
DAVE GARLAND       K V (A       (A) 6680 LEXINGTON        196  MGM  US 4783
ART MUNSON         G V (A
JOE LAMANNO        B   (A   MIKE PATTERSON  K V (A   ERNIE EARNSHAW  D    (A   VIRGIL BECKHAM  G  (A
BONNIE BOWDEN      V   (A   DARLENE LOVE    V   (A   GEORGE POOLE    VLN  (A   TONY McCASHEN   HCA (A
```

64 SPOONS

```
TAM NEAL           K D V(       (A) LADIES DONT HAVE WILLIES(EP)  19   BUSHBABY
LYNDON CANNACH     D V K(
ANDY CRAWFORD  FLT B G (    TED EMMET       TPT K(   JACKO    FLT G V(
```

SIXTY NINE(69)

```
ARMIN STOUWE       K G V(A       (A) CIRCLE OF THE CRAYFISH  19   PHILIPS       6305 164
ROLAND SCHUPP      PERC (A       (B) 69 LIVE              1974 PHILIPS          6623 046
```

SKAFISH

```
KEN BRONOWSKI      G V (A       (A) SKAFISH              1979 ILLEGAL UK ILP007 US A&M 008
JIM SKAFISH        K V (A
JAVIER CRUZ        K V (A   BARBIE GOODNICK  G V (A   LARRY MAZALAN    B V  (A   LARRY MYSLIWIEC  D (A
GAYLE CROWDER      V   (A
```

SKATELITES

```
                                (A) AFRICAN ROOTS         19   UA          US   LA 799
```

SKID ROW

```
GARY MOORE         G V (A       (A) SKID                 1970 CBS          UK        63965
ADRIAN FISHER      (            (B) 34 HOURS             1971 CBS US 30913 UK        64411
ED DEAN            (            (C) ALIVE & KICKING      1976 RELEASE      RRL 8001
KEVIN McALEA       (
NOEL BRIDGEMAN     D V (A   BRENDAN'BRUSH' SHIELS  B V(A
```

SKIDS

```
STUART ADAMSON     G K V(ABC     (A) SCARED TO DANCE      1979 VIRGIN           UK       V2116
RICHARD JOBSON     V   (ABCD     (B) DAYS IN EUROPA       1979 VIRGIN UK V2138 GER 201 049
WILLIE SIMPSON     B   (AB       (C) ABSOLUTE GAME        1980 VIRGIN UK V2174 GER 202 859
RUSSELL WEBB       B   (C        (D) JOY                  1981 VIRGIN           GER 204 167
MIKE BAILLIE       D   (C        (E) FANFARE              1982 VIRGIN UK VM 2
NICK GRIFFITHS     V   (D
TOM FELLICHAN      D   (     MICK GLOSSOP     PROD (C   RUSTY EGAN      D   (B   BILLNELSON    K  (B
JUDE NETTLETON     D   (C    FRANCES LYNCH    V    (D   NICKY HOLLAND   V   (C   MIKE OLDFIELD     (D
DAVE DUNCAN        BOD (D    SALLY NETTLETON  V    (C   JULIUS NEWELL   V   (C   ANDREW SIGSWORTH V (C
TIM CROSS          K   (D    ALAN RANKIN      V    (C   ALISON PIPKIN   V   (C   JOHN SIGSWORTH   V (C
DAVID PIPKIN       V   (C    BILLY MACKENZIE  V    (D   HANNAH YEADON   V   (C   ESTER MARSHALL   V (C
CHLOE DYMOTT       V   (C    KEN LOCKIE   CELLO   (D   MARLIS DUNKLAN   V   (C   GRACIE BENSON    V (C
HARRIET BAKEWELL   V   (C    VIRGINIA ASHLEY  FLT  (C   MARY VOLKE      V   (C   PAUL WISHART  WIND K (D
J J JOHNSON        D   (D    ALAN DARBY       G    (D   DEBBIE MITCHELL V   (D
```

SKIN ALLEY

```
KRZYSZTOF HENRYK JUSKIEWICZ K(ABCD (A) SKIN ALLEY         1969 CBS          UK        63847
BOB JAMES          G SAX(ABCD     (B) TO PAGHAM & BEYOND   1970 CBS          UK        64140
THOMAS CRIMBLE     B K V(AB       (C) TWO QUID DEAL        1972 TRANSATLANTIC UK       TRA 260
FRITZ FREYER       PROD (C        (C) TWO QUID DEAL        1972 STAX         US        3013
ALVIN POPE         D   (AB        (D) SKINTIGHT            1973 TRANSATLANTIC UK       TRA 273
NICK GRAHAM  V K B FLT (BCD       (D) SKINTIGHT            197  STAX         US        STS3022
TONY KNIGHT        D V (DC
MARTIN DROVER      HRNS (D   GEOFF DRISCOLL   SAX (D   PHIL KENZIE    SAX (D   DAVE COXHILL   SAX (D
BUD PARKES         HRNS (D
```

```
S142                          SKIP BIFFERTY                                              S142
    MICK GALLAGHER    K   (A              (A) SKIP BIFFERTY          1967 RCA  US LSP9761 UK   SF7941
    GRAHAM BELL       V   (A
    JOHN TURNBULL     G   (A   COLIN GIBSON    B  (A   TOM JACKMAN        (A
S143                          SKREWDRIVER                                                S143
    IAN STEWART       V   (A              (A) ALL SKREWED UP  (45 RPM LP)   1977 CHISWICK UK WIK3+CH3 GER 550200
    RON HARTLEY       G   (A              (A) ALL SKREWED UP  (33 LP)       1977 CHISWICK GER 67057
    KEVIN McKAY       B   (A              (EP) SKREWDRIVER                  197  TJM                 TJM4
    GRINNY            D   (A
S144                             SKY                                                     S144
    JOHN WILLIAMS     G   (ABC             (A) SKY                 1979 ARIOLA   UK ARLH 5022
    HERBIE FLOWERS    B   (ABC             (B) SKY2                1980 ARIOLA   UK AD SKY  2
    KEVIN PEEK        G   (ABC             (C) SKY 3               1981 ARIOLA   UK ASKY    3
    TRISTAN FRY       D   (ABC             (D) FORTHCOMING         1982 ARIOLA   UK A SKY   4
    FRANCIS MONKMAN   K   (AB  STEVE GRAY     K  (C
S145                          PATRICK SKY                                                S145
    PATRICK SKY           (A              (A) PATRICK SKY            1965 VANGUARD        VSD 79179
                                          (B) HARVEST OF A GENTLE CLANG 1966 VANGUARD SVRL19054  VSD 79207
                                          (C) REALITY IS BAD ENOUGH   1968 VERVE      US FTS  3052
                                          (D) PHOTOGRAPHS            1969 VERVE      US FTS  3079
                                          (E) SONGS THAT MADE AMERICA FAMOUS 1973 ADELPHI  US AR 4101
                                          (F) TWO STEPS FORWARD ONE STEP BACK 1975 LEVIATHAN  US    2006
S146                          SKY BAND                                                   S146
                                          (A) SKYBAND               1975 RCA  US APLI0839  UK SF 8409
S147                          SKYHOOKS                                                   S147
    GRAEME STRACHEN   V   (ABC             (A) EGO IS NOT A DIRTY WORD  1975 MERCURY UK 6306 900 US SRM11066
    ROBERT STARKIE    G   (AB              (B) LIVING IN THE SEVENTIES 19  MERCURY        US SRM11124
    REDMOND SYMONS    G V (AB              (C) GUILTY UNTIL PROVEN INSANE 1979 UA     UK UAG30241
    GREG MACINTOSH    B   (AB
    FREDDIE KABOODLESCHNITZER D(A  PETER JONES   K  (A   COL LOUGHNAN     SAX (A   IMANTS STRAUKS  D V (B
    ROBERT SPENCER    G V (B   WILBUR WILDE  SAX  (A   TONY ANSELL     K  (B  EDDIE LEONETH   K  (B
S147A                         SKYKING                                                    S147A
    CHRIS BRUBECK B K HRNS V(A             (A) SECRET SAUCE          1975 CBS       US    33367
    DAVID ROSS MASON G B V (A
    RICK JACOBS       G V B(A  RICHIE MORALES   D V (A   CHRIS COAN      V  (A  PETER RUTH     HCA V(A
    LEE PASTORA       PERC (A  JERRY BERGONZI SAX PERC(A  PERRY ROBINSON CLAR (A  LENNY PICKETT  WIND (A
    EMILIO CASTILLO   SAX (A   STEPHEN KUPKA   SAX (A   GREG ADAMS      HRNS (A  JOSHIE ARMSTEAD V  (A
    MAERETHA STEWART  V   (A   CISSY HOUSTON    V  (A
S148                          SKYLARK                                                    S148
    DOUG EDWARDS      G   (A              (A) SKYLARK               1972 CAPITOL          11048
    STEVE PUGSLEY     B   (A              (B) 2                     1974 CAPITOL          11256
    ROBBIE KING       K   (A
    BOBBY TORRES      CONGA (A  PAUL BEAVER     SYN (A   PATRICE HOLLOWAY V  (A  KITTY DITTO    V  (A
    DOMENIC TROIANO   G   (
S149                          SKYROCKETS                                                 S149
    STEVE BONNETT     G V (A              (A) 1974
    ANDREW BODNAR     B   (A
    STEVE GOULDING    D   (A   WILL STALLIBRASS HCA (A   NOEL BROWN      G  (A
S149A                         SKYWHALE                                                   S149A
    STEVE ROBSHAW     G K (A              (A) THE WORLD AT MINDS END  1977 FIREBRAND       DM0013
    STAN THEWLIS      HRNS (A
    PAUL TODD         HRNS (A  DOUGALL AIRMOLE  B  (A   MICK AVORY      D  (A  GWYO ZEPIX     K  (A
    JOHN SCHOFIELD    D   (A
S149B                            SKYY                                                    S149B
                                          (A) SKYY                  1981 EPIC UK 85494  US SALSOUL 8548
S150                          SLACK ALICE                                                S150
    ALICE SPRINGS     V   (A              (A) SLACK ALICE           1974 PHILIPS      UK    6308 214
    PETE FINBERG      G V (A
    JOHN COOK         K V (A   EDDIE LEACH     D  (A   MICK HOWARD     B V (A
S151                             SLADE                                                   S151
    NODDY HOLDER      G V (ALL             (A) BEGINNINGS(AMBROSE SLADE) 1969 FONTANA UK STL  5494 US     67592
                                          ( ) BALLZY               1969 FONTANA            US     67598
    JIM LEA B V K VLN     (ALL             (B) PLAY IT LOUD         1970 POLYDOR UK 2383 026 US COTILLION9035
    DAVE HILL         G V (ALL             (C) SLADE ALIVE          1972 POLYDOR UK 2383 101 US POLYDOR  5508
    DON POWELL        D   (ALL             (D) SLAYED              1972 POLYDOR UK 2383 163 US POLYDOR  5524
                                          (E) SLADEST              1973 POLYDOR UK 2442 119 US REPRISE  2173
                                          (F) OLD NEW BORROWED BLUE 1974 POLYDOR UK 2383 261
                                          ( ) STOMP YOU HANDS      1974 WB            US      2770
                                          (G) IN FLAME (SOUNDTRACK) 1975 POLYDOR UK 2442 126 US WB      2865
                                          (H) THE BEST OF SLADE    1975 POLYDOR UK 2664 124
                                          (J) NOBODY'S FOOLS       1976 POLYDOR UK 2383 377 US WB      2936
                                          (K) WHATEVER HAPPENED TO SLADE 1977 POLYDOR UK 2314 103
                                          (L) ALIVE VOL 2          1978 BARN       UK 2314 106
                                          (M) RETURN TO BASE       1979 BARN UK BARN 10 +       NARB  003
                                          (M) RETURN TO BASE       1979 WEA  NL 58192
                                          (N) SLADE SMASHES        1980 POLYDOR UK  POLTV 13
                                          (O) WE'LL BRING THE HOUSE DOWN 1981 CHEAPSKATE UK   SKATE 1
                                          (EP) 6 OF THE BEST       19   S O T B  UK SUPER 45
S152                          SLAPP HAPPY                                                S152
    ANTHONY MOORE     K V (ALL             (A) SORT OF SLAPP HAPPY  1972 POLYDOR UK 2310 204 RI RECOMMENDED
    PETER BLEGVAD     G V CLAR(ALL         (B) SLAPP HAPPY          1974 VIRGIN  UK V2014
    DAGMAR KRAUSE     PNO V(ALL            (C) DESPERATE STRAIGHTS(H COW) 1974 VIRGIN UK V2024
    MARC SINGER       D   (B              (D) IN PRAISE OF LEARNING 1975 VIRGIN  UK V2027
    DAVE WINTOUR      D   (B              (E) CASABLANCA MOON      19   RECOMMENDED     UK
    GRAHAM PRESKETT VLN MAND(B
    JEREMY BAINES     BASSOON(B ROGER WOOTON     V  (B  EDDIE SPARROW   D  (B  CLAIRE DENIZ   CELLO(B
    JEAN HERVE-PERON  B   (B   NICK WORTERS     B  (B  ANDY LEGGETT JUGS (B  CLEM CATTINI   D  (B
    HENRY LOWTHER     TPT (B   KESHAVE SATHE  PERC  (B  GEOFF LEIGH    WIND (BC JOHN GREAVES  B PNO(C
    CHRIS CUTLER      D   (C   TIM HODGKINSON CLAR PNO(C  FRED FRITH   G VLN (C  PIERRE MOERLEN PERC(C
    MONGEZI FEZA      TPT (C   MUCHSIN CAMPBELL HRNS (C  LINDSAY COOPER WIND (C  NICK EVENAS    TROM(C
```

NELSON SLATER

NELSON SLATER		(A) WILD ANGEL 19	RCA US APL1 1306

S153

SLAUGHTER & THE DOGS

S153

WAYNE BARRETT	V (AB	(A) DO IT DOG STYLE	1978 DECCA UK SKL 5292
BRIAN CRANFORD	D (	(B) LIVE	1978 RABID UK HAT 23
HOWARD BATES	B (ABC	(C) BITE BACK	1980 DJM DJM 20566
MIKE ROSSI	G (ABC	(EP) BUILD UP NOT DOWN	19 TJM UK TJM 3
MAD MUFFET	D (A		
EDDIE GARRITY	V (C PHIL ROWLAND D (C MORGAN FISHER		K (C CHRIS GENT SAX (C
MICK RONSON	A		

S154

SLAVE

S154

MARK ADAMS	B (ADE	(A) SLAVE	1977 COTILLION UK K50358 US 5200
FLOYD MILLER	V HRNS(ADE	(A) SLAVE	198 COTILLION US RI 9914
STEVE ARRINGTON	D V (DE	(B) HARDNESS OF THE WORLD	1978 COTILLION UK K50435 US 5201
CHARLES CARTER	SAX (DE	(C) CONCEPT	1978 COTILLION UK K50512 US 5206
JIMMY DOUGLAS	V (E	(D) JUST A TOUCH OF LOVE	1979 COTILLION UK K50684 US 5217
MARK HICKS	G (ADE	(E) STONE JAM	1980 COTILLION UK K50761 US 5224
CURT JONES	G V (DE		
T LOCKETT	SAX V(ADE O WILHOITE SAX (A RAYE TURNER		K (DE S WASHINGTON V TPT(DEA
DANNY WEBSTER	G V (DEA STARLEANA YOUNG V (DE TINY DOZIER		D V (A C BRADLEY K (A

S155

PERCY SLEDGE

S155

PERCY SLEDGE	V (ALL	WHEN A MAN LOVES A WOMAN	1966 ATLANTIC UK 2464 002 US 8125
		WARM & TENDER SOUL	1966 ATLANTIC UK 588 048 US 8132
		THE PERCY SLEDGE WAY	1967 ATLANTIC UK 587 081 US 8146
		TAKE TIME TO KNOW HER	1968 ATLANTIC
		THE BEST OF	1969 ATLANTIC UK 588 153 US 8210
		THE BEST OF	1972 ATLANTIC UK RI K40026
		GOLDEN VOICE OF SOUL	1974 ATLANTIC UK K50169
		I'LL BE YOUR EVERYTHING	197 CAPRICORN US 0147
		STAR COLLECTION VOL 1	197 MIDI 20019
		STAR COLLECTION VOL 2	197 MIDI 20065
		WHEN A MAN LOVES A WOMAN	19 K TEL NL TN1451

S155A

SLEEPLESS NIGHTS

S155A

COR ZWANN	V (A	(A) SLEEPLESS NIGHTS	1980 SLEEPLESS NIGHTS NL SNLP01
JAN VANDER PIAS	G V (A		
GIJSBERT	B V (A JAN VAN EGMOND D (A		

S156

EARL SLICK BAND

S156

EARL SLICK	G (AB	(A) EARL SLICK BAND	1976 CAPITOL UK/US 11493 EURO 82194
JIMMIE MACK	G V (AB	(B) RAZOR SHARP	1976 CAPITOL UK/US 11570
GENE LEPPIK	B V (AB		
BRYAN MADEY	D (AB JAY FERGUSON K (A MICHAEL KAMEN		PNO (A CLAUDE PEPPER PERC (A

S157

GRACE SLICK

S157

GRACE SLICK	V G K(ALL	(A) MANHOLE	1974 GRUNT BFLI 0347
PETER KAUKONEN	G B (A	(B) THE BEST OF(GREAT SOCIETY	1975 CBS 80172
DAVID FREIBERG	G V (AC	(C) DREAMS	1980 RCA PL 13544
DAVID CROSBY	V (A	(D) WELCOME TO THE WRECKING BALL	1981 RCA 5007 PL 13851
RON CARTER	B (A		
JACK CASADY	B (A CRAIG CHAQUICO G (A JOHN BARBATA	D (A DAVID SNELL HARP(A
JACK ELLORY	FLT (A TIMOTHY WALKER G (A PAUL KANTNER	G V (A GARY DUNCAN G (A
SEEDER PEARS	B (A CHRIS TAYLOR FLT (A ANDREW McGAVIN	HRN (A DOUGLAS MOORE HRNS(A
MICHAEL LAIRD	TPT (A GEORGE WHITING TPT (A RAYMOND PREMRU	TPT (A HAROLD NASH TPT (A
PETER HARVEY	TROM (A TERENCE MACDONAGH OBOE (A PHILIP HILL	OBOE (A FRANK REIDY CLAR(A
ALAN HAKIN	PERC (A TERENCE EMERY PERC (A ERIC ALLEN	PERC (A STAN BARRETT PERC(A
FRANK OWEN	K (C SCOTT ZITO G HCA V(AC NEIL JASON	B (C ALLAN SCHWARZBERG D(C
GEOFF FARR	SYN (A GEORGE WADENIUS G (C JIM MAELIN	PERC (C ED WALSH SYN (C
RON FRANGOPANE	SYN (C JOE SHEPLEY TPT (C JOE D'ELIA	PNO (C PHIL BODNER SAX (C
RONNIE CUBER	SAX (C ARTIE KAPLAN SAX (C STEVE PRICE	D (C GEORGE DEVENS PERC(C
DANNY GULINO	G (D PHIL STONE B (D JOE LALA	PERC (D PAUL HARRIS K (D
BOBBY T	D (D		

S158

SLIK

S158

MIDGE URE	G V (A	(A) SLIK	1976 BELL UK SYBEL8004 ARISTA US 4115
BILLY McISAAC	D (A		
JIM McGINLAY	(A KENNY HYSLOP (A		

S158A

SLIME

S158A

DIRK JORN	V (ALL	(A) SLIME	19 RAUBBAU GER 6622277
MICHAEL MAYER	G (ALL	(B) YANKEES RAUS	19 ARP 006
CHRISTIAN MEWS	G (ALL		
SVEN RAETHER	B (ALL PETER WODOK D (A STEPHEN MAHLER		D (B

S159

SLITS

S159

PALMOLIVE	D (12	(A) CUT	1979 ISLAND UK ILPS9573 US ANTILLES7072
BRUCE SMITH	D (C	(A) CUT	1979 ISLAND GER 200874
TESSA POLLITT	B (12C	(B) RETROSPECTIVE	1980 ROUGH TRADE UK Y 3
VIV ALBERTINE	(2C	(C) RETURN OF THE GIANT SLITS	1981 CBS UK 85269
ARI UP	V (12C	(1) 1976 (2) 1977	
KATE KORUS	G (12		
STEVE BERESFORD	K (C		

S160

P F SLOAN

S160

P F SLOAN	G V HCA (ALL	(A) SONGS OF OUR TIME	1965 DUNHILL US 50004
JOE OSBORN	D (D	(B) 12 MORE TIMES	1966 DUNHILL US 50007
HAL BLAINE	D (D	(C) MEASURE OF PLEASURE	1968 ATCO US 33268
MIKE OMARTIAN	K (D	(D) RAISED ON RECORDS	1972 EPIC UK 65179 MUMS US 31260
WAYNE PERKINS	K G (D		
CHRIS ETHRIDGE	B (B JOHN BARBATA D (D ALAN ESTES	CONGA(D BEN BENAY BANJO G (D
LARRY KNECHTEL	PNO (D BARRY BECKETT ORG (D MIKE MELVOIN	B (D JAMES BURTON DOBRO(D
RICHARD BENNETT	STEEL(D BOBBYE HALL PERC (D TONY TERRAN	TPT (D DUANE EDDY G (D
SID SHARP	STRINGS (D ROBERT KRANTZ VLN (D LOREN FARBER	V (D RON HICKLIN V (D
JOHN BAYLOR	V (D TATA VEGA V (D PHYLLIS BROWN	TPT (D JACKIE KELSO WIND (D
JIM HORN	SAX (D OLLIE MITCHELL TPT (D CONTE CANDOLI	TPT (D DICK HYDE TROM (D
MITCH GORDON	V (D SALLY STEVENS V (D IDA McCUNE	V (D EVANGELINE CARMICHAEL V(D

SLOW CHILDREN

(A) SLOW CHILDREN   1981 ENSIGN   UK   ENVY 501

SLY(& THE FAMILY)STONE

SLY STONE	V G K	(ALL	(A)DANCE TO THE MUSIC	1968 EPIC	US 26371	US RI	30334
FREDDIE STONE	G	(DH	(A) DANCE TO THE MUSIC	1968 DIRECTION		UK	8 63412
CYNTHIA ROBINSON	TPT	(DH	(B) LIFE	1968 EPIC	US 26397	US RI	30333
LARRY GRAHAM	B	(D	(C) M'LADY	1968 DIRECTION		UK	8 63461
GREG ERRICO	D	(D	(D) STAND	1969 EPIC	US 26456	UK	63655
ROSE STONE	V PNO	(DH	(E) WHOLE NEW THING	1970 EPIC	US 26456	US RI	30335
JERRY MARTINI	SAX	(DH	(F) THERE'S A RIOT GOING ON	1971 EPIC	US 30986	UK	64613
RUSTY ALLEN	B	(H	(G) GREATEST HITS	1971 EPIC	US 30325	UK	69002
ANDY NEWMARK	D	(H	(H) FRESH	1973 EPIC	US 32134	UK	69039
PAT RIZZO	SAX	(H	(I) SMALL TALK	1974 EPIC	US 32930	UK	69070
LITTLE SISTER VOCAL GROUP		(H	(J) HIGH ENERGY	1975 EPIC	US 22004	US RI	33462
			(K) HIGH ON YOU	1975 EPIC	US 33835	UK	69165
			(L) HEARD YOU MISSED ME	1976 EPIC	US 34348	UK	81641
			(M) 10 YEARS TOO SOON (E REMIXED)	1979 EPIC		UK	83640
			(N) BACK ON RIGHT TRACK	1979 WB	US 3303	UK	K56640
			( ) RECORDED 1964 67	19 SCULPTURE		US	SCP 2001
			( ) LIFE	1979 EPIC	US 30333		

DRINK SMALL

DRINK SMALL	G V	(A	(A) I KNOW MY BLUES ARE DIFFERENT	19 SOUTHLAND	US	SLP 1

SMALL FACES

STEVE MARRIOTT	G V	(ALL	(A) SMALL FACES	1966 DECCA LK4790			
RONNIE LANR	B V	(ALL	(B) FROM THE BEGINNING	1967 DECCA LK 4879			
KENNY JONES	D	(ALL	(C) ODGENS NUT GONE FLAKE	1967 IMMEDIATE IMSP012 IML 1001			
IAM McLAGAN G ORG		V(CDEFLPST	(C) ODGENS NUT GONE FLAKE	1968 IMMEDIATE US Z1252 008			
JIMMY WINSTON	ORG	(A	(C) OGDENS NUT GONE FLAKE	1978 CHARLY	UK	CR 300015	
RICK WILLS	B	(	(C) OGDENS NUT GONE FLAKE	19 OXFORD 3158			
STAN UNWIN	V	(C	(C) ODGENS NUT GONE FLAKE	1980 VIRGIN UK RI V2159			
JOE BROWN	G V	(S	(D) AUTUMN STONE (DBL)	1969 IMMEDIATE IMA101/2			
VICKI BROWN	V	(ST	(D) AUTUMN STONE (DBL)	19 IMMEDIATE GER SMIM2107/8			
P P ARNOLD	V	(JOPRVRS	(E) IN MEMORIAM	1970 IMMEDIATE		IMM	022
DAVE HYNES	V	(S	(E) IN MEMORIAM	1975 EMI IMP	GERM	048 90201	
GREG RIDLEY	V	(S	(F) WHAM BAM	1970 EMI IMP	GERM	048 50719	
TONY WILLIAMS	V	(S	(G) ROCK ROOTS	1976 DECCA	UK	ROOTS 5	
MEL COLLINS	HRNS	(S	(H) AMEN CORNER & SMALL FACES	1975 NEW WORLD		NW 6001	
SAUL SHECKNER		(S	(J) VINTAGE YEARS	1975 SIRE		3709	
HWLWN CHAPPPELLE	V	(T	(K) HISTORY OF SMALL FACES	197 IMMEDIATE		052 05108	
LAVINA ROBERTS	V	(T	(K) HISTORY OF SMALL FACES	197 PRIDE	US	PRD0014	
MADELINE BELL	V	(T	(L) SMALL FACES	19 NEW WORLD		NW6000	
LIZA STRIKE	V	(T	(M) FIRST STEPS	19 WB	UK	1851	
SAM BROWN		(T	(N) ARCHETYPES	1974 MGM	US	4955	
JIMMY McCULLOCH		(T	(O) FAMOUS POP GROUPS (WITH A CORNER)	19 EMI		148 51812/3	
			(P) THERE ARE BUT FOUR SMALL FACES	19 IMMEDIATE	US	Z1252 002	
			(Q) SMALL FACES PROFILE	19 TELDEC	GERM	624002	
			(R) GREATEST HITS	1977 IMMEDIATE		IML 2008	
			(S) PLAYMATES	1977 ATLANTIC US SD19113	UK K50375		
			(T) 78 IN THE SHADE	1978 ATLANTIC US SD19171	UK K50468		
			(U) LIVE UK 1969	1978 CHARLY	UK	CR 300025	
			(V) BIG HITS	1980 VIRGIN	UK	V2166	
			(W) FOR YOUR DELIGHT	1980 VIRGIN	UK	V2178	
			(X) SMALL FACES(DBL)(C+)	19 CHARLY 3001			
			(Y) IMMEDIATE STORY VOL 2(DBL)	1975 SIRE US 3709/2			
			(Z) SHA LA LA LEE	1981 DECCA	UK	TAB 16	
			( ) MAGIC MOMENTS	1976 IMMEDIATE UK	AML1008		
			( ) BIG HITS	1980 VIRGIN	UK	V2166	

SMALL WONDER

JERRY MORIN	G V	(AB	(A) SMALL WONDER	1976 CBS	US	34100
JIMMY PHILLIPS	K V	(AB	(B) GROWIN	19 CBS	US	34425
HENRY SMALL	V VLN	(AB				

LEROY SMART

LEROY SMART		(ALL	(A) SUPERSTAR	1977 THIRD WORLD	TWS 601
			(B) DREAD HOT IN AFRICA	1978 BURNING SOUNDS	BSLP 1004
			(C) IMPRESSIONS	1978 BURNING SOUNDS	BSLP 1005
			(D) JAH LOVES EVERYONE	1978 BURNING SOUND	BSLP 1008

SMIRKS

SIMON MILNER	G V	(A	(A) AMERICAN PATRIOTS(EP)	1979 SMIRKSOUND DHSS 01
NEIL FITZPATRICK	G	(A		
IAN MORRIS	B	(A	MIKE DOHERTY V (A	

A GROUP CALLED 'SMITH'

GAYLE McCORMICK	V	(AB	(A) A GROUP CALLED SMITH	1969 DUNHILL	US	50056
LARRY MOSS	K	(AB	(B) MINUS PLUS	196 DUNHILL	US	50081
JERRY CARTER	B	(AB				
ROBERT EVANS	D	(A	RICK CLIBURN G (A ALAN PARKER G (A JADE HASS (B			

BOB SMITH

BOB SMITH	G V	(A	(A) THE VISIT FROM BOB SMITH	1971
JOHN LATINI	B	(A		
DON PRESTON	SYN	(A	STAN KEISER FLT (A SKIP SCHNEIDER D (A MIKE DEGREVE G (A	
JAMES CURTIS	D	(A	LARRY CHAPMAN VLN (A	

GEORGE 'HARMONICA' SMITH

GEORGE SMITH	HCA	(ALL	(A) NO TIME TO JIVE	1970 BLUE HORIZON	UK 763856	
J D NICHOLSON	PNO	(A	(B) ARKANSAS TRAP	1971 DERAM SML 1082 US	18059	
BUDDY REED	G	(A	(C) GEORGE SMITH OF THE BLUES	1973 BLUESWAY	US BLS 6029	
GREGG SCHAEFER	G	(A	(D) TRIBUTE TO LITTLE WALTER	197 WORLD PACIFIC	US 21887	
MARSHALL HOOKS	G	(A				
PEE WEE CRAYTON	G	(A	JERRY SMITH B (A DICK INNES D (A			

GORDON SMITH	V HCA G (ALL	(A) LONG OVERDUE	1968 BLUE HORIZON	UK	763211
PETER GREEN	HCA (A	(B) TAKIN' TIME	1979 APPALOOSA	ITALY	AP002
DEREK HALL	PNO (A	(C) DOWN ON THE STREETS	1980 APPALOOSA	ITALY	AP005
JOHN McVIE	B (A				
MICK FLEETWOOD	D (A	PAT GROVER	HCA D(BC	BERNIE PALLO	ACC G(BC	CRAIG MACKIE	PNO (C

HUEY SMITH	PNO (ALL	(A) HAVING FUN	19 ACE	US	(EP) 104
		(B) HAVING A GOOD TIME	19 ACE	US	1004
		(C) FOR DANCING	19 ACE	US	1015
DR JOHN	K (D	(D) NIGHT BEFORE CHRISTMAS	19 ACE	US	1027
		(E) ROCK'N' ROLL REVIVAL	19 ACE	US	2021
		(F) ROCKIN' PNEUMONIA	1978 ACE	US	
		(F) ROCKIN' PNEUMONIA	1978 CHISWICK	UK	CH9

JIMMY SMITH	ORG (ALL	(A) THE INCREDIBLE	1962 HMV		CLP 1595
WITH		(B) HOBO FLATS	1963 VERVE		SVLP 9039
RICHARD DAVIS	B (F	(C) ANY NUMBER CAN WIN	1963 VERVE		SVLP 9057
MILT HINTON	B (C	(D) WHO'S AFRAID OF VIRGINIA WOLF	1964 VERVE		VLP 9068
BOB BUSHNELL	B (C	(E) THE CAT	1964 VERVE VLP 9079	RI	2317 010
WES MONTGOMERY	G (Z	(E) THE CAT	19 VERVE US 68587		
ART DAVIS	B (C	(F) MONSTER	1959 VERVE US 68618	UK SVLP 9093
GEORGE DUVIVIER	B (AE	(G) ORGAN GRINDER SWING	1965 VERVE US 68628	UK SVLP 9108
VINCE GAMBELLA	G (A	THE BEST OF	196 VERVE		2304 004
BARCY GALBRAITH	G (A	(J) I GOT MY MOJO WORKING	1966 VERVE US 68641	UK SVLP 9123
JIMMY WARREN	G (A	PETER & THE WOLF	1967 VERVE		SVLP 9159
KENNY BURRELL	G (CEFGJ	RESPECT	1967 VERVE US 68705	UK SVLP 9182
BILLY MURE	G (C	STAY LOOSE	1968 VERVE		SVLP 9182
GRADY TATE	D (EFGJ	CHRISTMAS COOKING	1968 VERVE		SVLP 9218
PHIL KRAUS	PERC (E	FURTHER ADVENTURE	1969 VERVE US 68766	1969 9241
ED SHAUGHNESSY	D (A	THE BOSS	1969 VERVE		SVLP 9247
DON BAILEY	D (A	JAZZ SPECTRUM	19 VERVE		2355 005
HERB LOVELL	D (C	I'M GONNA GIT MYSELF TOGETHER	19 VERVE		2304 020
GEORGE DEVENS	PERC (C	THE OTHER SIDE OF JIMMY SMITH	19 VERVE		2304 021
BOBBY DONALDSON	D (C	THE INCREDIBLE JIMMY SMITH	1967 MFP		MFP 1292
DOUG ALLAN	PERC (C	THE INCREDIBLE JIMMY SMITH	196 BLUENOTE US 81525	1525
ART MAROTTI	PERC (C	FURTHER	19 VERVE		V 68766
MEL LEWIS	D (C	WALK ON THE WILD SIDE	19 VERVE		2682 025
WARREN T SMITH	PERC (F	PORTUGUESE SOUL	1974 VERVE US 8832	2304 167
JOE NEWMAN	TPT (AC	JIMMY SMITH	1975 VERVE		2356 080
DON SEVERINSEN	TPT (A	BLACK SMITH	1975 DJM		DJLPS 451
JOE WILDER	TPT (A	A NEW STAR SOUND	19 BLUENOTE		BST 81512
ERNIE ROYAL	TPT (AE	A NEW STAR SOUND VOL 2	19 BLUENOTE		BST 81514
CHARLIE SHAVERS	TPT (C	AT THE LOWRY ORGAN	1973 DECCA		SKL 5146
JIMMY MAXWELL	TPT (CE	AT THE ORGAN	19 BLUENOTE		BST 81525
SNOOKY YOUNG	TPT (CE	AT THE BABY GRAND(DBL)	19 BLUENOTE	BST 81528/9
BERNIE GLOW	TPT (E	A DATE WITH (DBL)	19 BLUENOTE	BST 81547/8
THAD JONES	TPT (E	AT THE ORGAN VOL 2	1958 BLUENOTE		BST 81551
TOMMY MITCHELL	TROM (A	SOUND OF JIMMY SMITH	1959 BLUENOTE		BST 81556
JIMMY CLEVELAND	TROM (ACE	PLAYS PRETTY FOR YOU	1959 BLUENOTE		BST 81563
URBIE GREEN	TROM (AE	GROOVIN' AT SMALLS PARADISE	1958 BLUENOTE	BST 81585/6
KAI WINDING	TROM (C	GREATEST HITS VOL 2	19 BLUENOTE		BST 83367
MELBA LISTON	TROM (C	SERMON	1960 BLUENOTE		BST 84011
PAUL FAULISE	TROM (C	HOME COOKING	1961 BLUENOTE		BST 84050
BILLY BYERS	TROM (E	CRAZY BABY	1960 BLUENOTE		BST 84030
TONy STUDD	TROM (E	MIDNIGHT SPECIAL	1961 BLUENOTE		BST 84078
BABE CLARKE	SAX (A	PLAYS FATS WALLER	19 BLUNOTE		BST 84100
ROBERT ASHTON	SAX (AF	BACK AT THE CHICKEN SHACK	19 BLUENOTE		BST 84117
GERRY DODGION	SAX (AG	ROCKIN THE BOAT	1963 BLUENOTE		BST 84141
PHIL WOODS	SAX (ACF	PRAYER MEETING	1964 BLUENOTE		BST 84164
GEORGE BARROW	SAX (A	BUCKET	1966 BLUENOTE		BST 84235
OLIVER NELSON	HRNS (Z	(Z) THE DYNAMIC DUO	1967 VERVE	UK	SVLP 9160
MARVIN HOLLADAY	SAX (C	I'M MOVIN' ON	19 BLUENOTE		BST 84255
BUDD JOHNSON	SAX (CF	OPEN HOUSE	1968 BLUENOTE		BST 84269
SELDON POWELL	SAX (C	PLAIN TALK	19 BLUENOTE		BST 84296
JEROME RICHARDSON	SAX (CF	GREATEST HITS	1968 BLUENOTE		BST 89901
DANNY BANKS	WIND (F	JIMMY SMITH	19 BLUENOTE		BNLA 400
RAY BECKENSTEIN	WIND (F	TOMORROWS SOUND TODAY	1978 GROSVENOR		GRS 1065
GEORGE DORSEY	WIND (F				
HARVEY ESTRIN	WIND (F	RAY ALONGE	HRNE (E	JIMMY BUFFINGTON	HRNS (E	EARL CHAPIN	HRNS (
BILL CORREA	HRNS (E	DON BUTTERFIELD	HRNS (E	CREED TAYLOR	PROD (Z	JAMES SEDLAR	TPT (C
MARKY MARKOWITZ	TPT (E	BRITT WOODMAN	TROM (A				

LONNIE LISTON SMITH G V(ALL		ASTRAL TRAVELLING	1974 FLYING DUTCHMAN	BNLI 0163
MARCUS MILLER	B (ELS	EXPANSIONS	1975 RCA UK SF 8434	BXLI 0934
DONALD SMITH	V FLT(BEL	AFRU DESIA	1975 GROOVEMASTER	GM 3308
RONALD D MILLER	G (ESL	REFLECTIONS	1976 RCA UK RS 1053	US 1460
LINO REYES	D (ES	VISIONS OF A NEW WORLD	1976 RCA UK SF 8461	BXLI 1196
STEVE THORNTON	PERC (ES	COSMIC FUNK	1974 FLYING DUTCHMAN	BXLI 0591
DAVE HUBBARD	FLT (BESL	THINK	19 BLUENOTE		BST 84290
AURELL RAY	G (ES	TURNING POINT	19 BLUENOTE		BST 84313
BUTCH CAMPBELL	G (ES	MOVE YOUR HAND	19 BLUENOTE		BST 84326
JIMMY OWENS	TPT (E	DRIVES	19 BLUENOTE		BST 84351
ROBERT FORTUNATO	TPT (E	RENAISSANCE	1977 RCA		APL111822
VIRGIL JONES	TROM (E	(L) LOVELAND	1978 CBS		82837
TOM MALONE	TROM (E	GOTCHA	1978 TK		TKR 83356
SAM BURTIS	TROM (E	(S)SONG FOR THE CHILDREN	1979 CBS		83609
STRING SECTION	(E	(E) EXOTIC MYSTERIES	1979 CBS		83331
GWEN GUTHRIE	V (E	(F) LOVE IS THE ANSWER	1980 CBS US 36373	UK	84365
BRENDA WHITE	V (E	(B) BEST OF	1980 RCA US 36366	UK PL 12897
ULLANDA McCULLOUGH V (ES		BEST OF	1980 CBS		84348

(CONTINUED)

S169 (CONTINUED) LONNIE LISTON SMITH

```
RAY SIMPSON        V  (E
ZACHARY SANDERS    V  (E    JAMES ROBINSON    V  (S    PETER BROWN      B  (S    KEVIN J PERRY     G  (S
YVONNE LEWIS       V  (E    JANET WRIGHT      V  (S    CECIL McBEE      B  (B    LAWRENCE KILLIAN PERC(B
MICHAEL CARVIN   PERC (B    ART GORE          D  (B    LEOPOLDO FLEMING PERC (B  GREG MAKER        B  (B
WILBY FLETCHER     D  (B    RAY ARMANDO     PERC (B    ANGEL ALLENDE  PERC (B    AL ANDERSON       B  (BL
KEN BISCHEL      SYN  (B    LEON PENDARVIS    K  (B    GENE BERTONCINI  G  (B    GUILHERME FRANCO PERC(B
```

S169A MACK ALLEN SMITH

```
MACK ALLEN SMITH        (A    (A) GOTTA ROCK TONIGHT        1981 CHARLY       UK    CR 30201
```

S169B ROBERT CURTIS SMITH

```
ROBERT CURTIS SMITH     (A    (A) ROBERT CURTIS SMITH      19   BLUESVILLE    US 1064
```

S169C TIGER B SMITH

```
HOLGER SCHMIDT     G V(B      (A) TIGER ROCK                1973
CLAUS MEINHARD     B  (B      (B) WERE THE TIGER BUNCH      1974 BACILLUS     GER  19176
KARL HEINZ TRAUT   D  (B
LINDA FIELD        V  (B      RAINER MARZ  G V    PETER TRUNK    B   (B   CURT CRESS    D  (B
VEIT MARROS      K SYN(B      HANUS BERKA       WIND (B
```

S169D T V SMITH'S EXPLORERS

```
TV SMITH           (A    (A) THE WORDS OF THE GREAT EXPLORER   1981 KALEIDOSCOPE 85087
COLIN STONER     B V(A
MEL WESSON         K (A    ERIK RUSSELL G    (A    DAVID SINCLAIR    D   (A
```

S170 PATTI SMITH

```
PATTI SMITH      V G  (ALL     (A) HORSES             1975 ARISTA US 4066 UK ARTY122 EURO 97237
RICHARD SOHL     PNO  (1236ABCD (B) RADIO ETHIOPIA    1976 ARISTA US 4097 UK SPARTY1001 EURO98283
LENNY KAYE     G B V(A1234567BCD (C) EASTER           1978 ARISTA US 4171 UK SPARTY1043 EURO60561
IVAN KRAL      B G K(A234567CD  (D) WAVE              1979 ARISTA US 4221 UK SPARTY1086 EURO62516
J D DAUGHERTY    D  (A34567BCD  (EP) SET FREE         1978 ARISTA       UK ARIST 12197
TOM VERLAINE     G  (A     (1) 1974     (4) OCT 1976 TOUR   (7) SEPT 1977
ANDY PALEY     PNO  (4     (2) EARLY 1975(5) LATE  76
LEIGH FOXX       B  (5     (3) 1975/76   (6) 1977
BRUCE BRODY      K  (C7
ALLEN LANIER   G K  (AC    ANDI OSTROWE PERC (CD    JIM MAXWELL   PIPES(C    JOHN PAUL FETTA B    (C
TODD RUNDGREN    B  (C
```

S170A WARREN SMITH

```
WARREN SMITH     V G  (ABC   (A) FIRST COUNTRY COLLECTION   1961 LIBERTY        US    LRP 3198
                             (B) LEGENDARY SUN PERFORMERS   1977 CHARLY UK CR31132 US LAKE   506
                             (EP) WARREN SMITH              1977 CHARLY UK CEP 113
                             (C) MEMORIAL ALBUM             1982 MAGNUM FORCE UK 001
```

S171 WHISPERING SMITH

```
MOSES SMITH      V HCA(A    (A) OVER EASY        19 EXCELLO EX8020+ CONTEMPO  CRM 116
BOBBY POWELL     K V  (A    (A) OVER EASY        19 BLUE HORIZON    UK       2431 015
MELVIN HILL      G    (A
HARVEY LEXING    G    (A    ALFRED LUCAS    B   (A    GREG 'DOC' JOHNSON PERC (A   NOLAN SMITH      PERC(A
LEROY PERO     HRNS  (A    WILLIE SINGLETON HRNS (A   JOHNNIE CAGE HRNS (A   NAPOLEON MARTIN HRNS(A
REGGIE MORRISON HRNS  (A    TROMBONE OBRY       TROM (A
```

S172 SMITH PERKINS SMITH

```
STEVE SMITH    K G V(A    (A) SMITH PERKINS SMITH   1972 ISLAND US 9317       ILPS 9198
WAYNE PERKINS     (A
TIM SMITH      K G V(A    BARRY BECKETT    K   (A    JAMIE GRANT    V  (A    DAVID HOOD       B   (A
EDDIE HINTON     G  (A    ROGER HAWKINS    D   (A    LARRY NICHOLSON  G  (A
```

S173 CHRIS SMITHERS

```
CHRIS SMITHERS   G V  (A    (A) DON'T IT DRAG ON     1972 POPPY        US       PYS  5704
ERIC KAZ       PNO    (A
BEN KEITH DOBRO STEEL (A    ROD HICKS        B   (A    ROY MARKOWITZ    D  (A    MARIA MULDAUR    V  (A
BONNIE RAITT     V    (A    KATHY ROSE       V   (A    STU SCHULMAN   VLN  (A    HAPPY TRAUM    BAN(A
```

S173A SMOKE (UK)

```
MICK ROWLEY      V    (A    (A) THE SMOKE           1966 GULL       25114
GEOFF GILL       D    (A
MAL LUBEN        G    (A    ZEKE LUND        B   (A
```

S173B SMOKE (US)

```
                    (A) SMOKE                   19   UNI      US  73052
                    (B) AT GEORGES COFFE SHOP   19   UNI      US  73065
                    (C) THE SMOKE               1968 SIDEWALK US 5912
```

S173C SMOKESTACK LIGHTNING

```
RIC EISERLING    G    (A    (A) OFF THE WALL        1969 BELL US 6026     UK SBLL116
RONNIE DARLING   V    (A
ART GUY          D    (A    KELLY GREEN      B   (A    THE BLOSSOMS     V  (A    MIKE DEASEY      G  (A
LARRY KNECHTEL   K    (A    SANDY ZEVON    K G   (A    HAL BLAINE       D  (A    WILD BILL HOLMAN HRNS(A
```

S174 SMOKIE

```
PETER SPENCER  V D SAX(ALL   (A) PASS IT AROUND           1975 RAK        UK         SRAK 510
TERRY UTTLEY     V B  (ALL   (B) CHANGING ALL THE TIME    1975 RAK        UK         SRAK 517
ALAN SILSON    G V    (ALL   (C) MIDNIGHT CAFE            1976 RAK UK SRAK 520 RSO US    13005
CHRIS NORMAN   V G K  (ALL   (D) GREATEST HITS            1977 RAK        UK         SRAK 526
                             (E) BRIGHT LIGHTS & BACK ALLEYS 1977 RAK UK SRAK 530 RSO US  13029
                             (F) MONTREUX ALBUM            1978 RAK        UK        SRKA 6757
                             (G) THE OTHER SIDE OF THE ROAD 1979 RAK       UK         SRAK 539
                             (H) VERY BEST OF              1980 RAK        UK         SRAK 540
```

S174A OTIS 'SMOKEY' SMOTHERS

```
OTIS SMOKEY SMOTHERS    (A    (A) DRIVIN BLUES              19   KING     US   779
                              (B) SMOKEY SMOTHERS 1960/62   19   KRAZY KAT UK  7406
```

```
GILLI SMYTH          V    (A          (A) MOTHER                    1978 CHARLY        UK    CRL  5007
ORLANDO ALLEN        V    (A          (B) FAIRY TALES               1979 CHARLY        UK    CRL  5018
VERA BLUM            VLN  (A
PIP PYLE             D    (A   TONY PASCHAL      K   (A  DIDIER MALHERBE  SAX (A  DAEVID ALLEN    B G V(A
CHRISTIAN TRITSCH B       (A   RAFEL AGUILO      D   (A  TALIESEN ALLEN   V   (A  PETER LEWIS     V   (A
SAM GOPAL        TABLAS(A       ANNIE TRUXELL     V   (A  MARTIN TALLENTS  WHISTLE(A TOM LIPPS      V   (A
MARTI KLARWEIN       V    (A   PEPE MILAN        G   (A  JOAN BIBILON     G   (A  PATRICK MEADOWS V   (A
FRANK FEHLING        V    (A   PHIL SHEPHERD     V   (A  STEPHANIE SHEPHERD V (A  ANDREW PAGE     V   (A
OONA LIND            V    (A
```

S176   SNAFU   S176

```
BOBBY HARRISON    V PERC(ABC         (A) SNAFU                    1974 W W A UK 003 US CAPITOL 11292
MICK MOODY HCA G V       (ABC        (B) SITUATION NORMAL         1974 W W A UK 013 US CAPITOL 11343
PETE SOLLEY        K VLN V(AB         (C) ALL FUNKED UP           1975 CAPITOL              11473
COLIN GIBSON         B    (ABC
TERRY POPPLE        D B   (ABC MEL COLLINS    SAX (BC  STEVE GREGORY  SAX (B  BUD BEADLE   SAX (B
TIM HINKLEY          K    (C   BRIAN CHATTON  K   (C   VIOLA WILLS    V   (C  LIZA STRIKE  V   (C
```

S176A   SNATCH   S176A

```
                                      (A) SHOPPING FOR CLOTHES(EP) 1980 FETISH          FET  004
```

S177   SNAIL   S177

```
BOB O'NEILL          G V  (AB        (A) SNAIL                    1978 CREAM  US 1009
KEN KRAFT            G V  (AB        (B) FLOW                     1979 CREAM  US 1012
BRETT BLOOMFIELD     B V  (AB
DON BALDWIN          D V  (AB
```

S177A   SNAKEFINGER   S177A

```
PHIL 'SNAKEFINGER' LITHMAN           (A) GREENER PASTURES         1980 RALPH       US    8053
THE RESIDENTS            (B          (B) CHEWING THE SOUND        1979 RALPH US 7909 VIRGIN UK 2149
DON JACKOVICH       PERC (B
PHIL CULP            B   (B   STEVEN BROWN SAX (B
```

S177B   SNEAKER   S177B

```
MICHAEL CAREY SCHNEIDER K V (A       (A) SNEAKER                  1981 HANDSHAKE
MITCH OARE           G V  (A
MICHAEL COTTAGE      B    (A   MICHAEL HUGHES   D   (A  TIM TORRANCE   G   (A  JIM KING    K   (A
```

S177C   SNEAKERS   S177C

```
CHRIS STANLEY       V G K(A          (A) IN THE RED               1978 CAR       0398
MITCH EASTER        V B G D(A
WILL RIGBY           V    (A   ROBERT KEELY     B   (A  JAMES SIMS     K   (A  PHIL THOMAS  B   (A
FAYE HUNTER         FLT   (A
```

S177D   ADRIAN SNELL   S177D

```
ADRIAN SNELL       K G V(ALL         (A) FIREFLAKE               1975 KINGSWAY     UK 34
GARRY PAGE           B    (BC        (B) GOODBYE OCTOBER         1976 KINGSWAY     UK 41
JOE KING             K G  (B         (C) LISTEN TO THE PEACE     1978 KINGSWAY     UK 51
KEN PAGE            WIND  (B         (D) SOMETHING NEW UNDER THE SUN 1979 KINGSWAY UK 63
BERNARD SHAW         D    (BC        (E) THE PASSION            1980 KINGSWAY     UK 308
GORDON CARR         HRNS  (B         (F) CUT                    1981 KINGSWAY     UK 324
ELIZABETH KAUFMANN V      ((B
BILL THORP          STR   (C   BRYN HAWORTH    G   (D  B J COLE       STEEL(D  TONY CARR   PERC (D
TONY CARR           PERC  (D   ROGER HAND     PERC V(DE MARK WILLIAMSON V  (E  MICHAEL HARDING TROM(C
GEOFF TURTON         V    (E   TONY HEPWORTH   TPT (C  SHIRLIE RODEN   V  (EF ROB McKAY     WIND(C
RICHARD BARNES       V    (E   MO WITHAM      G   (C  DEBI DOSS       V  (EF FRANCES KELLY HARP(C
SIMON PHILLIPS       D    (E   JULIAN SULLIVAN CONGA(C GORDON GILTRAP  G   (E  JOHN PERRY    B  (DEF
ROD EDWARDS        K STR(D     DAVID MARTIN    G   (EF KEVIN PEEK      G   (DE EDDY SPENCE   K  (F
FRANK RICOTTI      VIBES (F    NICK PENTELOW   SAX (F  IAN MOSLEY      D   (F  MO McCAFFERTY  V  (E
ANNIE McCRAIG        V    (E   LONDON WELSH MALE CHOIR V(E ENGLISH CHAMBER SINGER V(E ROYAL PHIL ORCH (E
```

S178   SNIFF N THE TEARS   S178

```
PAUL ROBERTS        G V  (ALL        (A) FICKLE HEART           1978 CHISWICK WIK9 UK +UK RI CWD3002
NINK SOUTH           B    (BCD        (A) FICKLE HEART           1978 ATLANTIC US 19242
LOZ NETTO            G    (ABC        (A) FICKLE HEART           1982 CHISWICK UK RI SNIP 1
LEW LEWIS           HCA  (D          (B) THE GAMES UP           1980 CHISWICK      UK    CWK3014
MICK DYCHE           G    (A          (B) THE GAMES UP           1980 ATLANTIC US 19272
DEREK WADSWORTH    TROM  (D          (B) THE GAMES UP,          1982 CHISWICK UK SNIP 2
CHRIS BIRKIN         B    (A          (C) LOVE ACTION            1981 CHISWICK UK 2018 RI UK SNIP 3
RON LAWRENCE         B    (A          (D) RIDE BLUE DIVIDE       1982 CHISWICK UK 3020 RI UK TOSS 3
KEITH MILLER        SYN  (A
LUIGI SALVONI        D    (A   NOEL McCALLA     V   (A  ALAN FELDMAN   K   (A  JIM NELLIS   V  (A
MIKE TAYLOR          D    (BCD PAUL ROBINSON    D   (B  RICHARD BAILEY D   (B  RICHARD MARCANGELO D(B
JAMIE LANE           D    (CD  LES DAVIDSON   G V (CD  RICK FENN      G V  (C  MO McCAFFERTY V  (C
ANNIE McCRAIG        V    (C   MARK WILLIAMSON  V   (C  PAT CRUNLEY    SAX  (C  STEVIE LANGE  V  (D
MARTIN JAY           V    (D   JULIAN DIGGLE  CONGA(D  DICK MORRISEY  SAX  (D  MARTIN DROVER TPT (D
```

S179   SNIPS   S179

```
SNIPS                V    (AB        (A) VIDEO KING             1976 JET           UK    LP   212
MICK DYCHE           G    (A          (B) LA ROCCA               1981 EMI           UK    EMC  3359
GRAHAM DEACON        G    (A
JOHN BENTLEY         B    (A   JACKIE BADGER    B   (AB CHRIS SPEDDING  G   (B  BILL NELSON SYN (B
DAVE MATTACKS        D    (B   CLEM CATTINI  D    (B
```

S179A   SNOPEK   S179A

```
                                      (A) THINKING OUT LOUD      1979 MOUNTAIN RAILROAD US 52789
                                      (B) FIRST BAND ON THE MOON 1981 MOUNTAIN RAILROAD US
```

S180   PHOEBE SNOW   S180

```
PHOEBE SNOW          G V  (ALL        (A) PHOEBE SNOW            1974 A&M          UK    AMLS68283
SONNY BURKE          K    (C          (A) PHOEBE SNOW            1974 SHELTER US2109 UK  ISA  5010
DAVID POMERANZ       K    (C          (C) IT LOOKS LIKE SNOW     1976 CBS   US 34387 UK   81794
JAMES GADSON         D    (C          (D) SECOND CHILDHOOD       1976 CBS   US 33952 UK   81162
REGGIE McBRIDE       B    (C          (E) AGAINST THE GRAIN      1978 CBS   US 34456 UK   82195
STEVE BURGH          G    (BCF        (F) NEVER LETTING GO       1978 CBS   US 34875 UK   82224
ED GREENE            D    (C          ( ) ROCK AWAY              1981 ATLANTIC      UK    K50780
STEVE KHAN           G    (F          (H) SNOWBIRD               1974 CAMDEN    US 0124
JEROME RICHARDSON   FLT  (D
```

(CONTINUED)

PHOEBE SNOW

CHUCK DOMANICO	B	(CB	RAY PARKER JR	G	(C	HARVEY MASON	D	(C	DAVID BROMBERG	G (BC
GREG POREE	G	(C	ANDY NARELL	PERC	(C	KURT McGETTRICK	HRNS	(C	MEL MARTIN	HRNS(C
HADLEY CALIMAN	HRNS	(C	BOB YANCE	HRNS	(C	GOLDEN AGE JAZZ BAND		(C	PHIL KEARNS	V (CD
MAXINE WILLARD	V	(C	JULIA TILLMAN	V	(C	ORRIN WATERS	V	(C	HUGH McDONALD	B (B
STEVE MOSLEY	D	(B	PERSUASIONS	V	(B	TEDDY WILSON	PNO	(B	RALPH McDONALD	PERC(BDF
JOHN ZOOT SIMS	SAX	(B	MARGARET ROSS	HARP	(B	DAVE MASON	G	(B	CHUCK ISRAELS	B (B
BOB JAMES	K	(BF	TONY LEVIN	B	(DF	STEVE GADD	D	(B	KEN ASCHER	K (DF
HUGH McCRACKEN	G	(DF	JOHN TROPEA	G	(DF	KEN BISCHEL	SYN	(D	RICHARD TEE	K (DF
DAVID SANBORN	SAX	(D	STUART SCHARF	G	(D	RON CARTER	B	(D	JESSE DIXON SINGERS	(D
JIMMY YOUNG	D	(D	DON GROLNICK	K	(D	GORDON EDWARDS	B	(D	GRADY TATE	D (DF
PHIL RAMONE	V	(D	WILL LEE	B	(DF					

SOCIAL SECURITY

(A) I DONT WANT MY HEART TO RULE MY HEAD(EP) 19 HEARTBEAT   UK PULSE1

SOCRATES

(A) ON THE WINGS	1976	PETERS INT	PILPS9002
(B) PHOS	19	PETERS INT	PILPS9013

SODS

PETER PETER	V	(A		(A) MINUTES TO GO		
KNUD SORENSEN	B	(A			1979 STEP FORWARD	UK SFLP 3
THOMAS ORTVED	D	(A	STEEN JORGENSON	G	(A	

ERROL SOBER

ERROL SOBER	K	(A		(A) DAY DREAMER				1976 CAPITOL	ST11485	
MICHAEL OMARTIAN	K	(A								
BEN BENAY	G	(A	LEE RITENOUR	G	(A	DEAN PARKS	G	(A	ED GREENE	D (A
MAX BENNETT	B	(A	LEE SKLAR	B	(A	VICTOR FELDMAN	PERC(A	STEVE BARRI	PERC(A
JIMMY HASKELL	K	(A	ERNIE WATTS	WIND	(A	JOHNNY ROTELLA	WIND	(A	GINGER BLAKE	V (A
JULIA TILLMAN	V	(A	MAXINE WILLARD	V	(A	DON WALSH	V	(A	MICHAEL PRICE	V (A
SID SHARP	STR	(A								

SOFT BOYS

ANDY METCALFE	B	(1A	(A) CAN OF BEES	1979 TWO CRABS CLAW 101		
TIM MELTON	D HCA	(A	(A) CAN OF BEES	1979 AURAL AUL709 GER 60301		
ROBYN HITCHCOCK	G V B(1ABC		(B) UNDERWATER MOONLIGHT	1980 ARMAGEDDON UK ARM002		
ROB APPLETON	HCA	(C	(C) 2 HALFS FOR THE PRICE OF ONE	1981 ARMAGEDDON UK BYE 1		
KIMBERLY REW	G	(AB1C	(EP) NEAR THE SOFT BOYS	1980 ARMAGEDDON UK ARM001		
MORRIS WINDSOR	D	(B1AC	(1) APRIL 1978			
MATTHEW SELIGMAN	B	(B				
ANDY KING	SITAR(B	GERRY HALE	VLN (B	MATTHEW SELIGMANN	B	(C

SOFT HEAP

HUGH HOPPER	B	(A	(A) SOFT HEAP	1979 CHARLY	UK	CRL 5014
ELTON DEAN	SAX	(A				
ALAN GOWAN	K	(A	PIP PYLE	D	(A	RADU MALFATTI

TROM (A   MARC CHARIG CORN(A

SOFT MACHINE

LARRY NOLAN	G	(1	(A) THE SOFT MACHINE	1968 PROBE	US 4500		
MIKE RATLEDGE	K(12345ABCDEJFGHMN	(B) VOLUME 2	1969 PROBE	US 4505	UK	SPB 1002
KEVIN AYERS	B V	(A1BMN	(B) VOLUME 2	1974 ABC		RI UK	ABCL 5004
DAEVID ALLEN	G	(1MN	(AB) 1&2	1973 PROBE	US 204	RI UK	ABC 602
ROBERT WYATT	D	(123ABCDMN	(C) THIRD	1970 CBS	US 30339	UK	66246
HUGH HOPPER	B	(ABCDE2345FN	(D) FOURTH	1971 CBS	US 30754	UK	64280
ANDY SUMMERS	G	(1	(E) FIFTH	1972 CBS	US 31604	UK	64806
ELTON DEAN	SAX	(2345CDEN	(E) FIFTH	1979 EMBASSY		RI UK	31748
PHIL HOWARD	D	(4EN	(F) SIXTH	1973 CBS	US 32260	UK	68214
JOHN MARSHALL	D	(5EJKLGFHN	(G) SEVENTH	1973 CBS	US 32716	UK	65799
ROY BABBINGTON	B	(DEGHJN	(H) BUNDLES	1975 HARVEST	UK SHSP4044	GER	96356
KARL JENKINS		(5FGHJNO	(J) SOFTS	1976 HARVEST		UK	SHSP4056
ALLAN HOLDSWORTH	G	(HLN	(K) ALIVE & WELL IN PARIS	1978 HARVEST		UK	SHSP4083
ALAN WAKEMAN	SAX	(J	(L) LAND OF COCKAYNE	1981 EMI	UK EMC3348	GER	07439
JOHN ETHERIDGE	G	(JKN	(M) AT THE BEGINNING	1977 CHARLY	GER 3011	UK	CR300014
RICK SANDERS	VLN	(K	(N) TRIPLE ECHO (TRIP)(COMP)	1977 HARVEST		UK	SHTW 800
STEVE COOK	B	(K	FACES & PLACES VOL 7	1971 BYG		FR	529907
NICK EVANS	TROM	(C2DN	ROCK GENERATION 7 (1 SIDE)	197 BYG		FR	529707
MARK CHARIG	HRNS	(2DN	ROCK GENERATION 8 (1 SIDE)	197 BYG		FR	529708
LYN DOBSON	HRNS	(23CDN	RUBBER RIFF	1976 DEWOLFE	UK 3331		
AB SPALL	VLN	(CN	(1) 1967/68 (2) 1969 (3) 1970				
JIMMY HASTINGS	WIND	(CDN	(4) 1971/72 (5) 1972				
JACK BRUCE	B	(L	DICK MORRISEY	SAX (L	ALAN PARKER	G (L	GIORGIO GOMELSKY PROD (
TOM WILSON	PROD	(A	ALAN SKIDMORE	SAX (DN	PERCY JONES	B (	JIMI HENDRIX G(N
BRIAN HOPPER	SAX	(ABN	RAY WARLEIGH	FLT (HL	JOHN TAYLOR	K (L	TONY RIVERS V (L
STU CALVER	V	(L	JOHN PERRY	V (L	WILLIAM BURROUGH	(N	

SOFTIES

KEITH LANE	D	(A	(A) NICE & NASTY		
MIKE SMITH	G V	(A		1979 CHARLY	UK CRL 5012
JACK BOOTHE	B G K V	(A			

MIKE SOFTLEY

MICK SOFTLEY	V G K(ABC		(A) SUNRISE	1970 CBS		UK	64098		
JERRY DONAHUE	G	(ABC	(B) STREET SINGER	1971 CBS		UK	64395		
PAT DONALDSON	B	(ABC	(C) ANY MOTHER DOESN'T GRUMBLE	1972 CBS		UK	64841		
TONY COX	K	(ABC							
GERRY CONWAY	D	(ABC	SUE GLOVER	V	(A	SUNNY LESLIE	V	(A	LYN DOBSON WIND SITAR(AC
LESLEY DUNCAN	V	(A	NED BALEN	TABLAS	(A	BARRY CLARKE	G	(A	MIKE VICKERS K (A
GRINGO	V	(A	TONY CARR	PERC	(B	STEVE HAYTON	G HCA(B	DAVID HOROWITZ K (B
KARL JENKINS	SAX	(B	DUDU PUKWANA	SAX	(B	FRANK RICOTTI	PERC (B	RICHARD THOMPSON G (B
LIZA STRIKE	V	(B	DORIS TROY	V	(B	JIMMY THOMAS	V	(B	BARRY DE SOUZA PERC(C

```
S186                              SOLAR PLEXUS                                                    S186
  TOMMY KORBERG        V    (      (A) CONCERTO GROSSO(SWEDISH)   1972 ODEON      SWED    154 34 573/4
  MONICA GROSSO        ORG         (A) CONCERTO GROSSO(ENGLISH)   1972 ODEON      SWED    154 34 684/5
  CARL AXEL DOMINIQUE  PNO(        (B) SOLAR PLEXUS 2             1973 ODEON      SWED    062 34 797
  BOSSE HAGGSTROM      B    (      (C) SOLAR PLEXUS               1973 POLYDOR    UK      2383 222
  TOMMY BORGUDD        D    (      (D) DET ER INTE BATEN          1974 HARVEST            062 34 975
  GEORG WADENIUS       G    (A     (E) HELLRRE GYCKLARE AN HYCKLARE  1975 HARVEST         062 35 166
S186A                          SOLID GOLD CADILLAC                                                S186A
  BRIAN GODDING        G    (B     (A) SOLID GOLD CADILLAC        1972 RCA        UK SF 8311
  ROY BABBINGTON       B    (A     (B) BRAIN DAMAGE               1973 RCA        UK SF 8365
  MALCOLM GRIFFITHS TROM   (AB
  ALAN JACKSON D PERC    (AB   PHIL MINTON V TPT    (AB  GEORGE AHMAD KHAN WIND K(AB   BUTCH POTTER G B K BAN(B
  MIKE WESTBROOK   PNO  (AB   CHRIS SPEDDING  G   (A   DICK MORECOMBE  G   (A   FIACHA TRENCH   K   (A
S187                               SOLUTION                                                       S187
  TOM BARLAGE      K WIND(ABCD      (A) SOLUTION                  1972 DECCA          UK      SKLR 5124
  WILLEM ENNES     K    (ABCD       (B) DIVERGENCE                1973 EMI            UK      EMC  3002
  GUUS WILLEMSE    B V  (BCD        (C) CORDON BLEU               1975 ROCKET US 2189 UK      ROLL 1
  HANS WATERMAN    D    (ABCD       (D) FULLY INTERLOCKING        1977 ROCKET        UK      ROLL 8
  RAY COOPER       PERC (D          (E) ITS ONLY JUST BEGIN       1980 CBS        NL    84119
  STUART EPPS      V    (D
  PETER VAN DER SANDE B  (A    FRANKIE FISH V     (C   MICHIEL POS     G SAX(C
S187A                          ERWIN SOMER GROUP                                                  S187A
  ERWIN SOMER  VIBES PERC(A         (A) ERWIN SOMER GROUP         1973 UNIVERSE              UP 110
  RUDY VAN DIJK    SAX   (A
  HELMIG VAN DER VEGT K(A      HANS LAFAILLE    D    (A   JAAP VAN EUCKY     B   (A
S187B                               SONICS                                                        S187B
  GEORGE FENCIL WALLACE G V K(A     (A) SINDERELLA                1980 LINE       GERM    LLP5052AP
  TOM KATTICA      PNO  (A          (A) SINDERELLA                1980 BOMP       US    4011
  BILL SHAW        D V  (A          (1) HERE ARE THE SONICS        196 ETIQUETTE  US            024
  MICHAEL GONE     G    (A          (2) SONICS BOOM                196 ETIQUETTE  US            027
  GEORGE CROWE     B    (A          ( ) INTRODUCING THE SONICS     196 JERDEN     US          7007
  GERRY ROSLIE     K V  (A12        ( ) EXPLOSIVES                 196 BUCKSHOT   US            001
  JAMES N BUTSCH   D    (A          ( ) SONICS                    1977 SRT                   77079
  ANDY PARYPA      B V  (12         ( ) ORIGINAL NORTHWEST PUNK   1979 FIRST      US    7715
  LARRY PARYPA     G V  (12         ( ) UNRELEASED                1980 FIRST      US    7719
  ROB LIND         V SAX(12
  LES CLIN KINGBEARD SAX (A    BOB BENNETT  D          (12
S187C                             JOEL SONNIER                                                    S187C
  JOEL SONNIER     G V D HCA(A      (A) CAJUN LIFE                1980 SONET UK SNTF 839 US ROUNDER
  MICHEL DOUCET    G    (A          (A) CAJUN VALENTINE             19 GOLDBAND   US 7742
  MERLIN FONTENOT  FDL  (A          ( ) HURRICANE AVORY             19 GOLDBAND   US 7747
  JAY STUTES       DOB  (A          ( ) SCENE TODAY IN CAJUN MUSIC  19 GOLDBAND   US 7753
  ROY HUSKY        B    (A
  BUDDY HARMON     D    (A
  EARL BALL        PNO  (A    HENRY STRZELECKI  B   (A   KENNY KENNERSON   PNO  (A   GENE O'NEAL   STEEL(A
  PETE DRAKE       STEEL(A    BOB MILSAP        G   (A   JOE ALLEN         B    (A   WILLIE ACKERMAN D  (A
  BOB WHITE        FDL  (A    PHIL BALL         G   (A   VIC JORDAN        G    (A   BILLY REYNOLDS  D  (A
  TOMMY WILLIAMS   FDL  (A
S187D                               SONOMA                                                        S187D
                                    (A) SONOMA                    1974 DUNHILL    US    50156
S188                            SONNY & CHER                                                      S188
  SONNY BONO       V    (ALL        LOOK AT US                   1964 ATLANTIC US UK 5036 US 33177
  CHER BONO        V    (ALL        WONDROUS WORLD OF            1966 ATLANTIC            US 33183
                                    IN CASE YOUR IN LOVE         1967 ATLANTIC            US 33203
                                    GOOD TIMES                   1967 ATLANTIC            US 33214
                                    BEST OF                       196 ATLANTIC UK 588083 US 33219
                                    BEST OF                      1972 ATLANTIC RI         UK K40012
                                    LIVE                          196 KAPP       US 3654
                                    LIVE                         1972 MCA RI     UKMUPS435 US 2009
                                    BEST OF                      1972 CHARTERLINE         ITALY 20024
                                    BABY DON'T GO                  19 REPRISE    US  6177
                                    LIVE IN LAS VEGAS            1974 MCA   UK MCSP 257   US 2/8004
                                    MAMA WAS A ROCK'N' ROLL SINGER 1974 MCA  UK MCF 3672
                                    ALL I EVER NEED IS YOU       1971 KAPP       US  3660
                                    ALL I EVER NEED IS YOU       1974 MCA   UK MCF 2517 US ri  2021
                                    GREATEST HITS                1975 MCA UK MCF2586 US2117 GER 7527
                                    THE BEAT GOES ON             1975 ATCO       US  11000
                                    GREATEST HITS                1981 ATLANTIC   UK K20026
S189                           SONS OF CHAMPLIN                                                   S189
  BILL CHAMPLIN V G K SAX(ALL       (A) LOOSEN UP NATURALLY      1969 CAPITOL    US       SWBB 200
  TERRY HAGGERTY    G V  (ABCDEFGH   (B) THE SONS                 1969 CAPITOL    US       SKAO 322
  GEOFFREY PALMER K B V SAX(ABCDEFGH (C) MINUS SEEDS & STEMS (LIMITED)  1970
  JAMES PRESTON    D    (EFGH        (D) FOLLOW YOUR HEART        1971 CAPITOL    US        ST  675
  DAVID SCHALLOCK  B V  (EFG         (E) WELCOME TO THE DANCE     1973 CBS        US 32341 UK  65663
  ROB MOITOZA      B HCA V  (H       (F) THE SONS OF CHAMPLIN     1975 ARIOLA     US 50002 UK AAS 1501
  STEVE FREDIANI   WIND (GH          (G) CIRCLE FILLED WITH LOVE  1976 ARIOLA US 50007  GER  27690
  JIM HORN         SAX  (H           (H) LOVING IS WHY           1977 ARIOLA     US 50017 UK AAS 1505
  CHRIS BOND       SYN  (H
  DAVID FAREY      HRNS (H     CHUCK FINDLEY    TPT (H   GARY COLEMAN   PERC (H   DON MENZA     SAX (H
  PAUL HUBINON     TPT  (H     AL STRONG         B  (ABCD  TIM CAINE    SAX  (ABC PHIL WOODS    HRNS(E
  BILL BOWEN       D    (ABCD  MARK USHAM      HRNS(EF   MIKE ANDREAS   HRNS (EF  ERNIE WATTS   SAX (H
S190                              SONS OF JAH                                                     S190
  BUNNY McKENZIE   G    (A           (A) REGGAE HIT SHOWCASE      1980 PLASTIC FANTASTIC   PFULP 350
  WIRE LINDO       K    (A           (B) BURNING BLACK           1979 NATTY CONGO   UK     3502
  NEGUS DAWTAS     V    (A
  SANTA DAVIS           (A    T BOW          G   (A   BROTHER NAT    K   (A   RICO       BRASS     (A
  RANKING REUBEN        (A    SPEEGO         G   (A   ASTON BARRETT  B   (A   TUNGA OF SABANDIS G (A
  TONY ROBINSON    K    (A    TAN TAN      HRNS (A   CARLTON BARRETT D  (A   CHINNA SMITH    G  (A
  TENDA I OF ZABANDIS K (A
```

SOPWITH CAMEL

PETER KRAEMER	V WIND K	(AB	(A) SOPWITH CAMEL	1967 KAMA SUTRA	US	KLPS 8060
TERRY MACNEIL	K G	(AB	(A) HELLO HELLO	1973 KAMA SUTRA	US RI KSBS 2063
MARTIN BEARD	B	(AB	(B)MIRACULOUS HUMP RETURNS FROM THE MOON 1973 REPRISE US MS 2108 UK K44251
NORMAN MAYELL	D HCA SITAR	(AB
WILLIAM SIEVERS	G	(A

SORE THROAT

MATT FLOWERS	K	(A	(A) SOONER THAN YOU THINK	1979 HURRICANE	UK	FLAK 101
DAN FLOWERS	B	(A
JUSTIN WARD	V	(A	REID SAVAGE	G	(A	ROBIN KNAPP	D	(	GREGORY MASON	SAX	(A

SORROWS

DON FARDON	V	(A	(A) TAKE A HEART	1965 PYE	UK	NPL38023
WEZ PRICE	G	(A	(A) TAKE A HEART	1982 RAVEN	AUSTR	1004
PHILIP WITCHER	G	(A
PHILIP PACKHAM	B	(A	BRUCE FINLEY	D	(A

SORROWS(US)

ARTHUR ALEXANDER	G V	(AB	(A) TEENAGE HEARTBREAK	1980 PAVILLION	36369
SHEL TALMY	PROD	(B	(B) LOVE TOO LATE	1981 PAVILLION	37015
JOEY COLA	G	(AB
RICKY STREET	B V	(AB	JETT HARRIS	D	(AB ELLIE GREENWHICH	V	(A	ELLEN FOLEY V	(A
KARLA DEVITO	V	(AB	SUSAN HALL	V	(A	MIKEY HARRIS	V	(A

SORRY

J P CECCARELLI	D	(A	(A) OH KATHY	1978 KISWELL	FR	29 33109
CLIVE EDWARDS	D	(A
DOUDON WEISS	D	(A	BUNNY BRUNEL	B	(A	STEVE CARMEN	B	(A	RONNIE DEVILLE	B	(A
MAX MESUMECCI	K	(A	PAUL IVES	K V	(A	DOMINIQUE RUIZ	G	(A	MICKY	V	(A
JOYCE	V	(A	FLO	V	(A	JACKY	V	(A	RAY HENDRIKSEN	V	(A
STRING SECTION		(A

MARK SOSKIN

MARK SOSKIN	K	(A	(A) RHYTHM VISION	1980 PRESTIGE	P10109
BENNIE MAUPIN	WIND	(A
OSCAR BRASHEAR	HRNS	(A	SNOOKY YOUNG	HRNS (A	GEORGE BOHANON	TROM (A	MEL MARTIN	WIND (A
RAY OBIEDO	G	(A	PAUL SOCOLOW	B	(A	HARVEY MASON	D	(A	SAMMY FIGUEROA	CONGA(A

SOUND

GRAHAM GREEN	B	(CDE	(A) PHYSICAL WORLD (EP)	19 TORCH	UK	TOR003
ADRIAN BORLAND	G V	(CDE	(B) THE SOUND	19 TORCH	UK	TOR008
BENITA MARSHALL	K	(C	(C) JEOPARDY	1980 KOROVA	UK	KODE 2
MICHAEL DUDLEY	D	(CDE	(D) FROM THE LIONS MOUTH	1981 KOROVA	UK	KODE 5
MAX MAYERS	K	(E	(E) ALL FALL DOWN	1982 WEA	240019/1

SOUND CEREMONY

RON WARREN GANDERTON	G	(AB	(A) GUITAR STAR	1979 CELESTIAL SOUND	RWG1
			(B) SOUND CEREMONY	1980 CELESTIAL SOUND	RWG2
			(C) PRECIOUS AS ENGLAND	1981 CELESTIAL SOUND	RWG123

SOUNDS INCORPORATED

ALAN HOLMES	SAX	(	(A) SOUNDS LIKE	196 COLUMBIA	UK	SCX 2531
BARRY CAMERON	SAX	(	(B) SOUNDS INCORPORATED	1964 COLUMBIA 33SX1659	UK	SCX 3531
TONY NEWMAN	D	(	(C) TWIST AT THE STAR CLUB HAMBURG	1964 PHILIPS	P48 036L
JOHN ST JOHN GILLARD	G	(	(D) TOP GEAR (EP)	1964 COLUMBIA	UK	SEG 8360
TERRY FOGG	D	(	(E) SOUNDS INCORPORATED	1966 STUDIO TWO	UK	TWO 1449
GRIFF WEST	WIND	(	(F) RINKY DINK	1973 REGAL	UK	SREG1071
WES HUNTER	B	(

SOUP

(A) SOUP	19 BIG TREE	US	2007

SOUNDS NICE

TIM MYCROFT	K	(A	(A) LOVE AT FIRST SIGHT	1969 PARLOPHONE	UK	PCS7089
PAUL BUCKMASTER	STR	(A
HERBIE FLOWERS	B	(A	CHRIS SPEDDING	G	(A	BRIAN ODGES	B	(A	CLEM CATTINI	D	(A

SOUR GRAPES

RICHARD THOMPSON	G V	(A	(A) 1974 NO LPS
LINDA THOMPSON	V	(A
SIMON NICOL	G V	(A	WILLIE MURRAY	D	(A	STEVE BORRILL	B	(A

TIM SOUSTER

TIM SOUSTER	K	(AB	(A) SWIT DRIMZ	1977 TRANSATLANTIC	UK	TRA 343
			(B) THE FUTURE IS NOW(EP)	1977 TRANSATLANTIC	UK	TBG1

JOE SOUTH

JOE SOUTH	G V	(ALL	(A) INTROSPECTIVE	196 CAPITOL	US 108
			( ) DONT IT MAKE YOU WANT TO GO HOME	19 CAPITOL	US 392
			( ) GREATEST HITS	196 CAPITOL	US 450
			( ) SO THE SEEDS ARE GROWING	19 CAPITOL	US 637
			( ) JOE SOUTH	19 CAPITOL	US 845
			( ) YOU'RE THE REASON	19 NASHVILLE	US 2092
			( ) THE JOE SOUTH STORY	19 MINE	US 1100

J D SOUTHER

JOHN DAVID SOUTHER	G V	(ABC	(A) JOHN DAVID SOUTHER	1972 ASYLUM US SD 5055	UK SYL 9003
NED DOHENY	G	(AB	(A) JOHN DAVID SOUTHER	1975 ASYLUM	UK	K53026
BRYAN GAROFALO	B	(A	(B) BLACK ROSE	1976 ASYLUM US 7E1059	UK	K53037
GARY MALLABER	D K	(A	(C) YOU'RE ONLY LONELY	1979 CBS US 36093	UK	83753
GIB GUILBEAU	FDL	(A
DAVID JACKSON	K B	(A	MIKE BOWDEN	B	(A	MICKY McGEE	D	(A	JOEL TEPP	B	(A
JOHN BARBATA	D	(A	WAYNE PERKINS	G	(A	DANNY KOOTCH	G	(BC	WADDY WACHTEL	G	(BC
PAUL STALLWORTH	B	(B	JIM KELTNER	D	(B	DAVID CROSBY	V	(B	ART GARFUNKEL	V	(B
ANDREW GOLD	V G K(B	GLENN FREY	G	(BC	KENNY EDWARDS	B	(BC	RUSS KUNKEL	D	(B
LINDA RONSTADT	V	(B	PETER ASHER	V	(B	STANLEY CLARKE	B	(B	DAVID DUKE	HRNS	(B
VINCENT DEROSA	HRNS	(B	MIKE BOTTS	D	(BC	ROY POPER	HRNS	(B	DONALD BYRD	HRNS	(B
LOWELL GEORGE	G	(B	CHUCK DOMANICO	B	(B	JOHN GUERIN	D	(B	JAMES BOND	B	(B
DON MENZA	FLT	(B	EARL DUMLER WIND	(B	JOE WALSH	G	(B	DON HENLEY	V	(BC
DON GROLNICK	PNO	(C	RICK MAROTTA	D	(C	DAVID SANBORN	SAX	(C	DAN DUGMORE	G	(C
TOM SCOTT	SAX	(C	JACKSON BROWNE	V	(C	JORGE CALDERON	V	(C	PHIL EVERLY	V	(C
JAI WINDING	ORG	(C	DON FELDER	G	(C	FRED TACKETT	G	(C	JOHN SEBASTIAN	HCA(C

SOUTHER HILLMAN FURAY BAND

```
    JOHN DAVID SOUTHER G V (AB        (A) SOUTHER HILLMAN FURAY BAND      1974 ASYLUM US 7E1006  UK  SYLA 8758
    CHRIS HILLMAN      B V (AB        (B) TROUBLE IN PARADISE            1975 ASYLUM US 7E1036  UK  SYLA 8760
    RICHIE FURAY       G V (AB
    PAUL HARRIS        K   (AB  AL PERKINS  G STEEL   (AB  JIM GORDON    D  (A  JAMES GUERCIO     G  (B
    RON GRINEL         D   (B   GLENN FREY        V   (B   JOE LALA    PERC (AB  DON HENLEY      V  (B
```

S198   SOUTHERN COMFORT   S198

```
    GORDON HUNTLEY STEEL V(ABC        (A) FROG CITY                      1971 HARVEST UK SHSP4012 CAPITOL US800
    CARL BARNWELL      G V K(ABC       (B) SOUTHERN COMFORT               1971 HARVEST           UK      SHSP 799
    MARK GRIFFITHS     G V K(ABC       (B) SOUTHERN COMFORT               1971 CBS   NL 64125    US        1011
    ANDY LEIGH         B V  (ABC       (C) STIR DON'T SHAKE               1972 HARVEST           UK      SHSP 4021
    RAY DUFFY          VLN  (C         (D) DISTILLED (COMP)               1976 HARVEST           UK      SHSM 2009
    DON HARPER         VLN  (C
    KEITH CUMMINGS     VLA  (C   PETER MORRIS     K   (C   BOB JONES      D V (B   JOHN WILMETH     TPT (B
    STEVE FUNK         K    (B   ART STAVRO       B   (B   REV RON STALLINGS SAX V(B  FRED OLSON     G  (B
```

S198A   SOUTHROAD CONNECTION   S198A

```
    DELWIN GILLMAN B TROM K V(A       (A) POSITIVE ENERGY                1980 UA    US LT1047    UK    UAG 30316
    STEVEN FIELDS      D    (A
    LINDA WATSON  V PERC K (A   ELLSWORTH FORRESTER K (A  HAROLD HUTTON   SAX (V  LOU BARBARIN    TROM(A
    MAERETHA STEWART   V    (A   KRYSTAL DAVIS    V   (A   YVONNE LEWIS    V   (A  JEFF MEDINA     G V (A
    MICHAEL JONES      V    (A   ALBERT JONES     TPT (A   RAY BLUE        SAX (A
```

S198B   SOUTHERN FRIED   S198B

```
    MAURICE ROGERS     K V PERC(A       (A) SOUTHERN FRIED                1971 MERCURY      6338 058
    PAT ST CLAIR       VPERC(A
    HARRY HOLT         B V  (A   BOB FERGUSON     G V (A   TODD ROBERTS    D   (A  GENE PELLO      D  (A
    KENT SPRAGUE       D    (A   LARRY TAYLOR     B   (A   LARRY KNECHTAL  B   (A  DAVID T WALKER  G  (A
    GERRY McGEE        G    (A   LOUIE SHELTON    G   (A   DENNY WALLY     G   (A  MIKE O'MARTIAN  K  (A
    ALLAN BEUTLER HRNS (A   CHUCK FINDLEY   HRNS (A   JACK REDMAN     HRNS (A
```

S199   SOUTHSIDE JOHNNY & THE ASBURY DUKES   S199

```
    JOHNNY LYON        G V  (ALL      (A) LIVE AT THE BOTTOM LINE        1976 EPIC               AS 275
    TONY PALLIGROSI    TPT V(BC       (B) I DON'T WANT TO GO HOME        1976 EPIC US 34180   UK  81515
    RICKY GAZDA        TPT V(BCDFE     (B) HAVING A PARTY (RI + 1 TRACK)  1979 EMBASSY       RI UK  31772
    CARLO NOVI         SAX V(BC        (C) THIS TIME IT'S FOR REAL        1977 EPIC  US 34668 UK  81909
    RICHIE'LA BAMBA'ROSENBERG TROM(BCDFE (D) HEARTS OF STONE             1978 EPIC US 35488   UK  82994
    KENNY PENTIFALLO   D V  (BC        (E) THE JUKES                      1979 MERCURY US 3793  UK  9100 067
    KEVIN KAVANAUGH    K V  (BCDE      (F) LOVE IS A SACRIFICE            1980 MERCURY US 3836  UK  9111 081
    EDDIE MANION       SAX V(BCDEF     (G) LIVE REACH UP & TOUCH THE SKY  1981 MERCURY US 8602  UK  6619 052
    AL BERGER          B V  (BCDEF
    BILLY RUSH         G V  (EF   STEVE VAN ZANT   G   (D   STEVE BUSLOWE   B   (F  MAX WEINBERG    D  (D
    STEVE BECKER       D    (FE   STAN HARRISON    SAX (DE  BOB MUCKLIN     TPT (DE JOE GRAMILINI   G  (EF
```

S199A   SOUTHWEST   S199A

```
    JOHN FORD COLEY    V    (A        (A) SMELL OF INCENSE               1968 HIP            US         HIS 7001
    ENGLAND DAN SEALS  V    (A
```

S199B   SOUTHWIND   S199B

```
    JOHN MOON MARTIN G V (Bc       (A) SOUTHWIND                       19   VENTURE    US         VTS 4002
    JIM PULTE          B    (BC       (B) READY TO RIDE                  19   BLUE THUMB US         BTS  13
    ERIK DALTON        D    (BC       (C) WHAT A PLACE TO LAND          1973 BLUE THUMB US         BTS  26
    FONTAINE BROWN     K V G(BC
```

S200   BOB B SOXX & THE BLUE JEANS   S200

```
    DARLENE LOVE       V    (A        (A) ZIP A DEE DOO DAH             1963 PHILLES PHLP4002 LONDON  8121
    BOBBY SHEEN        V    (A        (B) WALL OF SOUND VOL 2           1976 PHIL SPECTOR      2307  004
    FANITA JAMES       V    (A
    GLEN CAMPBELL      G    (A   BILLY STRANGE    G   (A   AL DELORY       (A  LEON RUSSELL    PNO (A
    NINO TEMPO         SAX  (A
```

S201   SPACE ART   S201
                                  (A) SPACE ART   1977 ARIOLA   AHAL 8001

S202   SPACE OPERA   S202

```
    BRETT WILSON        D PERC(A       (A) SPACE OPERA                   1973 EPIC US 32117    UK       65557
    PHILIP WHITE B G K V (A
    SCOTT FRASER       G K V(A   DAVID BULLOCK G FLT HCA V(A
```

S203   SPANKY & OUR GANG   S203

```
    ELAINE'SPANKY'McFARLANE V PERC(ALL (A) SPANKY & OUR GANG             1967 MERCURY UK SMCL20114 US SR61124
    NIGEL PICKERING    G B  (ABCDEF    (B) LIKE TO GET TO KNOW YOU       1968 MERCURY UK SMCL20121 US SR61161
    JOHN SEITER        D    (ABCDE     (C) WITHOUT RHYME OR REASON       1968 MERCURY           US SR61183
    MALCOLM HALE       D    (ABCDE     (D) SPANKY'S GREATEST HITS        1970 MERCURY           US SR61227
    KENNY HODGES       B    (          (E) LIVE                          1970 MERCURY           US SR61326
    LEFTY BAKER        G V  (ABCDE     (F) CHANGE                        1975 EPIC              US33580
    GEOFFREY MYERS     B    (
    CARLOS BERNAL      V    (F   GENE GARLIN      D   (F   GAIL LAUGHTON   HARP(F  JOHN LOGAN HCA    (F
    MARC McCLURE       B V G(F   JIM MOON         D   (F   RAY NEAPOLITAN  B   (F  HERB PEDERSEN   BAN (F
    RICK VITO          G    (F   BILL PLUMMER     B V (F   JOHN RHYTHM     HCA (F  RICHARD THOMPSON PNO(F
    BOBBY WOOD         PNO  (F   JERRY YESTER     V   (F   TOWER OF POWER  HRNS(F
```

S203A   SPANDAU BALLET   S203A

```
    JOHN KEEBLE        D V  (AB        (A) JOURNEY TO GLORY              1981 CHRYSALIS UK CHR1331 GER 203428
    MARTIN KEMP        B V  (AB        (B) DIAMOND                       1982 CHRYSALIS UK CHR1353 GER 204514
    GARY KEMP          G SYN(AB
    STEVE NORMAN       K    (AB
    TONY HADLEY        V SYN(AB  CANUTE WEELINGTON  TPT (B  DAVID BAPTISTE SAX (B  NATHANIEL AUGUSTIN TROM(B
```

S204   OTIS SPANN   S204

```
    OTIS SPANN         PNO V(ALL      (A) OTIS SPANN IS THE BLUES       1960 CANDID 8001 + BARNABY US  30246
    BARRY MELTON       G    (O        (B) BLUES ARE WHERE ITS AT        1963 HMV UK CSD3609 BLUESWAY BLS6003
    LUTHER JOHNSON     G    (OBH      (C) PORTRAIT IN BLUES             1963 STORYVILLE              SLP157
    LONNIE JOHNSON     G    (C        (D) PIANO BLUES                   196  STORYVILLE              SLP168
    JOS DAVIDSON       B    (O        (E) BLUES OF OTIS SPANN           1964 DECCA         UK LK 4615
    LONNIE TAYLOR      D    (O        (F) BLUES NEVER DIE               1965 PRESTIGE US 7319
    LUCILLE SPANN      V    (OH       (F) BLUES NEVER DIE               1966 STATESIDE     UK  SL 10169
    MUDDY WATERS       G V  (LBHQT     (G) NOBODY KNOWS MY TROUBLES     1967 POLYDOR 545 030 +BOUNTY BY 6037
    SAMMY LAWHORN      G    (BH        (H) BOTTOM OF THE BLUES          1968 BLUESWAY US              BLS 6013
    MAC ARNOLD         B    (B         (H) BOTTOM OF THE BLUES          1968 STATESIDE     UK  SL 10255
    FRANCIS CLAY       D    (B         (J) FATHERS & SONS              1969 CHESS                    CRLS 4556
    GEORGE SMITH       HCA  (B         (K) BIGGEST THING SINCE COLOSSUS 1969 BLUE HORIZON US4802 UK  763217
```

                                                                    (CONTINUED)

OTIS SPANN

LITTLE WILLIE SMITH D (BC	(L) CRACKED SPANNER HEAD	1969 DERAM	UK SML 1036
RANSOM KNOWLING B (LQ	(M) HEART HEAVY WITH TROUBLE	19 BLUESWAY	BLS 6063
SPIT JAMES G (L	(N) WALKING BLUES	1972 EPIC US 31290	UK 64888
STEVE GREGORY SAX (L	(O) CRYING TIME	1978 VANGUARD	VSD 6514
BUD BEADLE SAX (L	(P) OTIS SPANN	19 EVEREST	US 216
DANNY KIRWAN G (K	(Q) HALF AIN'T BEEN TOLD	19 BLACK CAT	NL 001
ROD M LEE TPT (K	(R) CHICAGO BLUES	19 TESTAMENT	US 2211
S P LEARY D (K	(S) THE EVERLASTING BLUES	19 SPIVEY	US 1013
PETER GREEN G (K	(T) WITH MUDDY WATERS BAND	19 MUSE	US 5008
JOHN McVIE B (K	(U) SWEET GIANT OF THE BLUES	19 BLUESTIME US 9006	
JOHNNY YOUNG G (G	(V) CRY BEFORE I GO	1974 BLUESWAY US 6070	
JAMES COTTON HCA V(FG			
JIMMY LEE MORRIS B (G			
ROBERT WHITEHEAD D (G	GEORGE BUFORD HCA (H	LAWRENCE WIMBERLEY B (H	MEMPHIS SLIM K(Q
PAUL HUMPHREY D (U	MAX BENNETT B (U	LOUIS SHELTON G (U	TOM SCOTT WIND (U

SPARGO

	(A) GOOD TIME SPIRIT	1980 SCREAM	NL 2604

SPARKS

RON MAEL K V (ALL	(A) SPARKS	1971 BEARSVILLE US 2048	UK K45511
RUSSELL MAEL V (ALL	(B) WOOFER IN TWEETERS CLOTHING	1972 BEARSVILLE US 2110	UK K45510
ADRIAN FISHER G (C	(AB) SPARKS/WOOFER	1975 BEARSVILLE	UK K85505
HARLEY FEINSTEIN D (B	(C) KIMONO MY HOUSE	1974 ISLAND	UK ILPS 9272
EARL MANKEY G (B	(D) PROPAGANDA	1974 ISLAND	UK ILPS 9312
JIM MANKEY G B (B	(E) INDISCREET	1975 ISLAND	UK ILPS 9345
TREVOR WHITE G (	(F) BIG BEAT	1976 CBS US 34359 ISLANDUK ILPS 9445	
IAN HAMPTON B (	(G) INTRODUCING SPARKS	1977 EPIC 34901	UK 82284
DINKY DIAMOND D (C	(H) No 1 IN HEAVEN	1979 VIRGIN	UK V2115
PETER OXENDALE (	(J) BEST OF	1979 ISLAND	UK ILPS 9493
MARTIN GORDON B (C	(K) TERMINAL JIVE	1980 VIRGIN	UK V2137
JEFF SAILIN G V (F	(L) WHOMP THAT SUCKER	1981 RCA US 4091	
TODD RUNDGREN PROD (A			
HILLY MICHAELS D (F	SAL MAIDA B (F	THAD JAMES LOWE PROD (F	MUFF WINWOOD PROD(C

SPARROW

	(A) HATCHING OUT	1974 SPARK	US 05

ROGER RUSKIN SPEAR

ROGER RUSKIN SPEAR V K B SAX(AB	(A) ELECTRIC SHOCKS	1972 UA US 097	UK UAS 29508
CHRIS WELCH D (A	(B) UNUSUAL	1973 UA	UK UAG 29381
PETER BANKS G (A			
ROY HOLLINGWORTH G (A	TONY NEWMAN SAX (A	DAVE GLASSON PNO (A	JERRY GARDINER G (A
GRAHAM PRESKETT VLN (A	SAM SPOONS (A	CYRIL JORDAN G (A	ROGER C MITCHELL V (A
JAMES FERRELL G (A	DANNY MIHM D (A	CHRIS WILSON V (A	STEVE WALLER G (A
DAVE CLAGUE B (A	B J COLE STEEL(A	ANDY NEWMAN K V (B	DAVE CHARLES D (B
RICHARD PERSELL G (B	JOE RYAN G (B	RICHARD TREECE G (B	MAGGIE STREDDER SINGERS(B
ARRAN ROE D (AB	KEN WHALEY B (B	JOHN SAWYER B (B	

SPECIALS

TERRY HALL V (AB	(A) THE SPECIALS	1979 TWO TONE UK 5001	
PAUL HESATT SAX (B	(A) THE SPECIALS	1979 CHRYSALIS US 1256 GER 202 685	
LYNVAL GOLDING G V (AB	(B) MORE SPECIALS	1980 TWO TONE UK CHRT5003	
JERRY DAMMERS K (AB	(B) MORE SPECIALS	1980 CHRYSALIS US 1303 GER 202 848	
RODDY RADIATION G (AB			
HORACE GENTLEMAN B (AB	NEVILLE STAPLES V PERC(AB	JOHN BRADBURY D (A	RHODA DAKER V (B
KIX THOMPSON SAX (B	RICO RODRIGUES HRNS (AB	DICK CUTHELL HRNS(AB	THE GO GO'S V (B

SPECKLED RED

RUFUS PERRYMAN V PNO(ALL	(A) DIRTY DOZENS	19 DELMARK	DL 601
	( ) IN LONDON 1960	19 VJM	LC 11
	( ) PIANO BLUES	19 STORYVILLE	SLP 188
	( ) BLUES IN EUROPE	19 STORYVILLE	SLP 187
	( ) BARRELHOUSE BLUES	19 FOLKWAYS 3555	

RONNIE SPECTOR

RONNIE SPECTOR V (A	(A) SIREN	1981 REDSHADOW UK 002 POLISH US 808	

CHRIS SPEDDING

CHRIS SPEDDING G V (ALL	(A) BACKWOODS PROGRESSION	1970 HARVEST UK	SHSP 4004
PAUL ABRAHAMS K (A	(B) SONGS WITHOUT WORDS	1970 HARVEST EURO SHVL776	
STEVE CURRY G (F	(C) ONLY LICK I KNOW	1972 HARVEST UK	SHSP 4017
MICK OLIVER G (F	(D) CHRIS SPEDDING	1976 RAK UK	SRAK 519
DAVE LUTTON D (F	(E) HURT	1977 RAK UK	SRAK 529
HERBIE FLOWERS B (E	(F) GUITAR GRAFFITI	2979 RAK UK	SRAK 534
CLEM CATTINI D (E	(G) I'M NOT LIKE EVERYBODY ELSE	1980 RAK UK	SRAK 542
RAY COOPER PERC (EF	(H) FRIDAY THE 13TH	1981 PASSPORT US 6007	
JACK EMBLOW MUSETTE (E			
CHAS MILLS V (DE	CHRISSIE HYNDE V (E	JOHN CARTER V (E	ROYSTON MITCHELL K HCA(A
NEIL LANCASTER D (DE	TONY NEWMAN D (F	LINDA LEWIS V (C	LAURIE ALLEN D (C
HAROLD FISHER D (E	ALAN HAWKSHAW PNO (C	PAUL FRANCIS D (C	PHIL DENNYS K (C
LES HURDLE B (D	BRIAN BENNETT D (C	DAVE COCHRAN B (D	TONY CARR D (D
TONY BURROWS V (D	BARRY MORGAN D (D	SUE GLOVER V (D	SUNNY LESLIE V (D
DAVE MATTACKS D (G	RICHARD GOWER V (G	PHIL LANZON PNO (G	PAUL WESTWOOD B (G
PHIL FURSDON V (G	CHRIS GREEN CELLO (G	CHRIS MERCER SAX (G	PETE MILLER V (G
PETE WILLIAMSON CELLO(G	TONI CAMPO B (C	ROY BABBINGTON B (A	LAWRIE ALLEN D (A
FRANK RICOTTI PERC (A	PAUL RUTHERFORD TROM (B	JOHN MITCHELL K (B	ROGER POTTER B (B
JOHN MITCHELL D (B	BUSTA JONES B V (H	TONY MACHINE D V (H	

SPEED LIMIT

ACKER APPLEBY V (A	(A) FIRST OFFENCE	1978 SATRIL	SATL 4011
TONY BAYLIS D (A			
DOUGIE DENNIS B (A	BRIAN SMITH G (A	DAVID MORRIS G (A	

SPEEDOMETERS

ROBBIE WATSON B V (A	(A) DAY IN THE LIGHTS	1979 ACROBAT UK	ACRO5
IAN TAYLOR G V (A			
LEE DALLON K (A	TOMMY EYRE K (A	MARTIN FINLEY G V (A	STEVE PARRY D (A
CHRIS GENT SAX V(A	PAUL SPENCER D (A		

```
S210B                           SPEEDWAY BLVD                                                     S210B
  GREGG HOFFMAN       G V (A      (A) SPEEDWAY BLVD            1980 EPIC          US      36533
  DENNIS FELDMAN      B V (A
  ROY HERRING JR V K PERC(A   GLENN DOVE      D  (A  JORDAN RUDES      K  (A
S210C                             SKIP SPENCE                                                     S210C
  ALEXANDER 'SKIP' SPENCE(A      (A) OAR                      1968 CBS           US      CS 9831
S211                            JEREMY SPENCER                                                    S211
  JEREMY SPENCER      G V (ABC    (A) JEREMY SPENCER          1970 REPRISE US RSLP 9002  UK K44105
  MICK FLEETWOOD      D  (A       (B) & THE CHILDREN          1973 CBS      US    31990  UK 65387
  JOHN McVIE         B  (A        (C) FLEE                    1979 ATLANTIC US 19236     UK K50624
  DANNY KIRWAN       G V (A
  PETER GREEN        BAN (A   STEVE GREGORY    SAX (A  PHIL HAM          G FLT(B  BOAZ              B V (B
  MICHAEL            HCA G V (B  GINNETHON    D PERC (B  MICHAEL FOGARTY   K V (C  JEFF SCHOEN       K  (C
  NEAL JASON         B  (C    AL IZZO         D   (C  BUZ BUCHANAN        D  (C  VICTOR SALAZAR    PERC(C
  RAY GOMEZ          G  (C    STEVE THOMPSON   B  (C  SIMON PHILLIPS      D  (C
S212                         JOHN SPENCER'S LOUTS                                                 S212
  JOHN SPENCER       G V K(A      (A) THE LAST LP            1978 BEGGARS BANQUET          BEGA3
  JOHNNY G  G D V HCA(A
  DAVE THORNE        B BAN(A   CHAS AMBLER     K D  (A  ANDY McDONALD      WIND (A  SIAN DANIELS     V  (A
  ADAM SKEAPING      CELLO(A
S213                            JIMMY SPHEERIS                                                    S213
  JIMMY SPHEERIS     V G K(ALL   (A) ISLE OF VIEW           19   CBS  US 30988 UK 64919
  GEOFF LEVIN        G  (ABCD    (B) ORIGINAL TAP DANCING KID 1973 CBS  US 32157
  DAVID CAMPBELL     VLN (ACD    (C) DRAGON IS DANCING       1975 EPIC US 33565
  LEE CALVIN NICOLI G FLT B V(A  (D) PORTS OF THE HEART      1976 CBS  US 34276
  DAVID HAROWITZ     K  (A
  EMIL LATIMER       CONGO(A   BUDDY SALZMAN    D   (A  FELIX CAVALIERE  K V(B  RUSS KUNKEL       D  (B
  LELAND SKLAR       B  (B    DOREEN DAVIS     V   (B  VINNIE JOHNSON   D  (B  BOBBYE HALL       PERC(B
  SNEAKY PETE        STEEL(B   JANE GETZ       K V  (BC  JOHN SUMMERS     B  (B  HARVEY MASON      D  (B
  NOVAR TROTTER      (B    CHARLIE LARKY    B   (B  BART HALL          D  (CD  JOHNNY PIERCE     B V (CD
  HENRY LEWY         PERC (C   MORGAN AMES     V   (C  MIKE KALLEN       G  (C  PAUL LEWINSON     K  (C
  DOROTHY REMSEN     HARP (C   CHICK COREA     K   (DC  STANLEY CLARKE   B  (D  JIM COWGER        WINDB(CD
  JIM CALIGER        FLT (B   JOHN GUERIN     D   (D  EMILE PANDALF     K  (D  JAY ELLINGTON     HARP(D
  RICHARD FEVES      B  (D    JACKSON BROWNE   V   (D  ROBIN WILLIAMSON   (D  DAN ORBACH MAND(D
S214                          SPHERICAL OBJECTS                                                   S214
  STEVE SOLAMAR      V G HCA(AB  (A) PAST & PARCEL           1978 OBJECT   UK   OBJ001
  DUNCAN PRESTBURY   K V (AB     (B) ELIPTICAL OPTIMISM      1979 OBJECT   UK   OBJ004
  ROGER HILTON       D  (ABCD    (C) FURTHER ELLIPSES        1980 OBJECT   UK   OBJ012
  FREDERICK BURROWS B G (AB      (D) NO MANS LAND            1981 OBJECT   UK   OBJ016
  JOHN BISSET-SMITH G V (AB
  MIKE RABBIT        G  (D    MIKE ZEE        B   (D  ROGER BLACKBURNS   G  (D
S214A                             SPIDER                                                          S214A
  AMANDA BLUE        V  (AB      (A) SPIDER                  1980 RSO  2394260
  KEITH LENTIN       G V (AB     (B) BETWEEN THE LINES       18   DREAMLAND
  JIMMY LOWELL       B  (AB
  ANTON FIG          D  (AB   HOLLY KNIGHT    K   (AB
S214B                             SPIDERZ                                                         S214B
  GUUS BOERS         V  (A       (A) PRESSURE                1980 HURRICANE FLAK103
  BART BROUWER       K V (A
  KOOS CORNELISSEN  G   (A    JOHN SNEP       B   (A  HENRI HOEYMANS     D  (A  APPIR BAARS SAX  (A
S214C                         SPIDERS FROM MARS                                                   S214C
  PETE McDONALD      V  (A       (A) SPIDERS FROM MARS       1976 PYE  US 12125   UK   NSPL18479
  WOODY WOODMANSEY   D  (A
  DAVE BLACK         G  (A    TREVOR BOLDER    B   (A  MIKE GARSON        K  (A
S214D                              SPIN                                                           S214D
  REIN VAN DER BROEK HRNS  (A    (A) SPIN                    1976 ARIOLA       US   ST 50013
  JAN VANNIK         WIND (A
  HANS HOLLESTELLE  G   (A    JAN HOLLESTELLE  B SYN(A  HANS JANSEN       K  (A  CEES KRANENBURG    (A
S214E                             SPIDERS                                                         S214E
  SNIFFA             G  (A       (A) ROCK'N' ROLL GYPSIES    1982 RCA  UK RC3101
  COL HARKNESS       G V (A
  ROB BURROWS        D  (A    BRIAN BURROWS    V B (A
S215                           DAVID SPINOZZA                                                     S215
  DAVID SPINOZZA     G V (A       (A) SPINOZZA               1978 A&M          US   SP4677
  JOE CARO           G  (A
  ANTHONY JACKSON    B  (A    RICK MAROTTA     D   (A  MIKE MAINIERI     SYN (A  LEON PENDARVIS    PNO (A
  LUTHER VANDROSS    V  (A    DAVID LASLEY     V   (A  DIVA GRAY         V  (A  STEVE JORDAN      D  (A
  ROB MOUNSEY        PNO (A   ALAN RUBIN       TPT (A  RANDY BRECKER     TPT (A  JOHN FADDIS       TPT (A
  WAYNE ANDRE        TROM (A  BARRY ROGERS     TROM (A  DAVID TAYLOR      TROM (A  TONY PRICE        TUBA(A
  JOHN TREVOR CLARK HRNS (A   SHARON MOE       HRNS (A  GEORGE MARGE      WIND (A  GEORGE YOUNG      WIND(A
  DAVID TOFANI       WIND (A  KIM CARLSON      V   (A  GORDON GRODY      V  (A  WARREN BERNHARDT K  (A
  GARY MURE          PERC (A  DAVID CAREY      PERC (A  RUBENS BASSINI    PERC (A  DON GROLNICK      PNO (A
  MICHAEL BRECKER    SAX (A   LEW SOLOFF       TPT (A  DAVID SANBORN     SAX (A  RONALD CUBER      SAX (A
  STRING SECTION     (A
```

SPIRIT   S216

```
      RANDY CALIFORNIA G V B(ABCDFGHJKLMNOP(A) SPIRIT                          1968 CBS       UK 63278    US    31457
      ED CASSIDY       D (ABCDEFGHJKLMNOP(A) SPIRIT                            1968 ODE                   US Z1244004
      JAY FERGUSON     K V(ABCDF       (A) BEST OF(REPACKAGED)                 1979 EMBASSY UK 31693
      MARK ANDES       B  (ABCDFJ      (AC) SPIRIT/CLEAR   (DBL)               1973 EPIC                  US    31457
      MIKE FONDALIER   D  (            (B) THE FAMILY THAT PLAYS TOGETHER      1968 CBS       UK 63523    US    31461
      ROB ARKIN        B  (            (B) THE FAMILY THAT PLAYS TOGETHER      1968 ODE                   US Z1244014
      JOHN LOCKE       K  (ABCDEFJO    (BE)FAMILY/FEEDBACK(DBL)                1975 EPIC                  US    33761
      MATT ANDES       G  (J           (C) CLEAR SPIRIT                        1969 CBS       UK 63729 ODE   Z1244016
      JOHN ARLISS      B  (            (D) 12 DREAMS OF Dr SARDONICUS          1970 EPIC      UK 64191    US    30267
      AL STAEHELY      B V (E          (E) FEEDBACK                            1971 EPIC      UK 64507    US    31175
      CHRIS STAEHELY   G V (E          (F) BEST OF SPIRIT                      1973 EPIC      UK 65585    US    32271
      LARRY KNIGHT     B  (LMN         (G) SPIRIT OF 76     (DBL)              1975 MERCURY UK 6672 012 US SRM2 804
      MIKE THORNBURGH  HRNS (O         (G) SPIRIT OF 76     (DBL)              1975 MERCURY GER 6641 323
      COZY POWELL      D  (            (H) SON OF SPIRIT                       1975 MERCURY UK 9100 019 US SRM11053
      STU PERRY        D  (            (J) FARTHER ALONG                       1976 MERCURY              US SRM11094
      BARRY KEENE      B  (GH          (K) FUTURE GAMES                        1977 MERCURY UK 9100 036 US SRM11133
      JOHN TERLEP      B  (            (L) LIVE                                1977 ILLEGAL UK ILP 001
      ERNIE WATTS      SAX (J          (M) LIVE (MADE IN GERMANY)              1978 POTATO    172200
      MICHAEL D TEMPLE MAND (J         (N) LIVE                                1978 POTATO    US PR 2001
      IAN UNDERWOOD        (J          (O) POTATOLAND                          1981 LINE               GER 6 24641
      DAVID BLUMBERG   HRNS (J         (O) POTATOLAND                          1981 BEGGARS BANQUET   UK BEGA 23
      NICK  DE CARO    HRNS (J         (O) POTATOLAND                          1981 RHINO                US
      LAWRENCE WEISBERG B (J           (P) INTERVIEW RECORD                    1981 RHINO     US 1984
      TERRY ANDERSON   V  (K
      GEORGE VALUNE    K  (O  MIKE BUNNELL     K  (O    KARI NILE      K  (O    BENJI       K   (O
      JEFF JARVIS      HRNS (O  CHUCK SNYDER    HRNS (O    JOE GREEN      STR  (O    BERYL       K   (G
      AL SCHNUTT       PROD (J  LOU ADLER       PROD(J    PAUL WALKINS   PROD (L    DAVID BRIGGS PROD   (D
      STEVE LARRENCE   PERC (J  MICHAEL LEE     PROD(O    ROBERT LEE     PROD (O
```

****NOTE (L.M.N. ARE DIFFERENT RECORDS BUT OF THE SAME TOUR ,TRACKS & MIX ARE DIFFERENT.)

SPIRIT OF JOHN MORGAN   S217

```
      JOHN MORGAN      K V (ABC        (A) SPIRIT OF JOHN MORGAN               1969 CARNABY           UK  CNLS 6002
      MICK WALKER      D V (ABC        (B) AGE MACHINE                         1970 CARNABY           UK  CNLS 6007
      DON WHITAKER     G V (A          (C) KALEIDOSCOPE(AS JOHN MORGAN)        1972 CARNABY           UK  6302 010
      PHIL SHUTT       B  (ABC
      TREVOR THOMS     G  (BC
```

SPIROGYRA   S218

```
      MARTIN COCKERHAM G V (B          (A) ST RADIGUNDS                        1971 B&C               CAS  1042
      STEVE BORRILL    B  (B           (B) OLD BOOT WINE                       1972 PEGASUS           PEG   13
      MARK FRANCIS     G V K(B         (C) BELLS BOOTS & SHAMBLES              1973 POLYDOR           2310  246
      BARBARA GASKIN   V  (B
      DAVE MATTACKS    D  (B   JULIAN CUSACK VLN K    (B  ALAN LAING   CELLO (B RICK BIDDULPH  MAND(A
```

SPITBALLS   S219

```
                                       (A) SPITBALLS                           1978 BESERKLEY NL 530057 UK BSERK15
```

SPIZZ(SPIZZELS)   S219A

```
      MARK COALFIELD   K  (A           (A) DO A RUNNER                         1980 A&M               UK  AMLE68514
      DAVE SCOTT       G  (A           (B) SPIKEY DREAM FLOWERS                1981 A&M  US 4861      UK  AMLE68523
      C P SNARE        D  (AB
      JIM SOLAR        B  (AB  SPIZZ          V    (B  LU   G   (B
```

SPLIFF   S219B

```
                                       (A) SPLIFF RADIO SHOW                   1981 CBS   UK    84555
                                       (B) 85555                               1982 CBS   UK    85739
```

SPLINTER   S220

```
      BILL ELLIOTT     V  (ABC         (A) THE PLACE I LOVE                    1974 DARK HORSE         AMLH22001
      BOBBY PURVIS     V  (ABC         (B) HARDER TO LIVE                      1975 DARK HORSE         AMLH22006
      BILLY PRESTON    K  (AB          (C) TWO MAN BAND                        1977 DARK HORSE US 3073 UK   K56403
      KLAUS VOORMAN    B  (A           ( ) SLPINTER                            1980 BELLAPHON      UK 002
      EARL PALMER      D  (B
      BILL DICKINSON   B  (B   GEORGE HARRISON    G   (BA  CHRIS SPEDDING   G  (B   JOHN TAYLOR    K  (B
      JIM KELTNER      D  (AB  TOM SCOTT        HRNS (B  RALPH MACDONALD  PERC (B   WADDY WACHTEL  G  (B
      BILL NUTTYCOMBE     (B   GARY WRIGHT        K   (A  WILLIE WEEKS     B  (A   MIKE KELLY     D  (A
      GRAHAM MAITLAND  ACC (B
```

SPLIT ENZ   S221

```
      TIM FINN         V K (ALL        (A) MENTAL NOTES                        1975 MUSHROOM   AUST    35588
      IAN SHARP        CELLO(          (B) MENTAL NOTES                        1976 CHRYSALIS   UK    CHR 1131
      NEIL FINN        G V (FGH         (C) SECOND THOUGHTS                     1976 MUSHROOM   AUST    35981
      MILES GOLDING    VLN (           (D) DIZRHYTHMIA                         1977 CHRYSALIS   UK    CHR 1145
      WALLY WILKINSON  G   (           (D) DIZRHYTHMIA                         1977 MUSHROOM   AUST    36347
      NOEL CROMBIE         (ALL         (E) FRENZY                             1978 MUSHROOM   AUST    36921
      EDDIE RAYNER     K   (AB          (F) TRUE COLOURS                       1980 A&M UK 64822
      JON CHUNN        B   (AB          (G) WAIATA                             1981 A&M UK 64848
      PHIL JUDD        G V (ABC         (H) TIME & TIDE                        1982
      EMLYN CROWTHER   PERC (AB         (I) BEGINNING OF THE ENZ               1980 CHRYSALIS UK 64822
      ROBERT COLES     HRNS (           (J) BEGINNING OF THE ENZ(DIFF TRACKS)  1980     MUSHROOM   AUST
      MAL GREEN        PERC (G
      NIGEL GRIGGS     B   (FG  ROBERT GILLIES    SAX (B   PHIL MANZANERA   PROD (B   DAVID MUSSEL   PROD(A
      MILES GOLDING    VLN (
```

SPLODGENESSABOUNDS   S221A

```
      MAX SPLODGE      V  (A           (A) SPLODGENESSABOUNDS                  1981 DERAM            UK  SML 1121
```

MARK SPOELSTRA   S222

```
      MARK SPOELSTRA      (ALL         (A) 5 & 20 QUESTIONS                    1965 ELEKTRA          EKS  7283
                                       (B) STATE OF MIND                       1966 ELEKTRA          EKS  7307
                                       (C) MARK SPOELSTRA                      1969 CBS                   9793
                                       (D) MARK SPOELSTRA                      197  FOLKWAYS              3572
                                       ( ) SONGS                              197  FOLKWAYS              2449
                                       ( ) THIS HOUSE                          197  FANTASY      US     8412
```

SPONTANEOUS COMBUSTION

GARY MARGETTS	G V (A	(A) SPONTANEOUS COMBUSTION	1972 HARVEST UK SHVL801 US CAPITOL 11021
TRIS MARGETTS	B V (A	(B) TRIAD	1972 HARVEST UK SHVL805 US CAPITOL 11095
TONY BROCK	D (A		

SPOOKY TOOTH

MIKE HARRISON	K V(ABCDEFG	(A) ITS ALL ABOUT SPOOKY TOOTH	1968 ISLAND UK ILPS9080 GER 85682
GARY WRIGHT	K V(ABCDEFG	(B) SPOOKY TWO	1969 ISLAND UK ILPS9098 US A&M 4194
PIERRE HENRY	ELEC (C	(B) SPOOKY TWO	1969 ISLAND 6339 004 RI 85785
LUTHER GROSVENOR	G (ABCD	(C) CEREMONY	1969 ISLAND UK ILPS59107 A&M 4225
VAL BURKE	B V (G	(C) CEREMONY	1969 PHILIPS FR 849 512
BRYSON GRAHAM	D (EFG	(C) CEREMONY	1969 FONTAN GER 6444 540
GREG RIDLEY	G B (AB	(D) THE LAST PUFF	1970 ISLAND UK ILPS9117 US A&M 4266
MICK JONES	G (EFG	(D) THE LAST PUFF	1970 ISLAND GER 85685
MIKE KELLIE	D (ABCDG	(E) YOU BROKE MY HEART.....	1973 ISLAND UK ILPS9227 US A&M 4385
CHRIS STEWART	B (EF	(E) YOU BROKE MY HEART.....	1973 ISLAND GER 86687
ANDY LEIGH	B (C	(F) WITNESS	1973 ISLAND UK ILPS9255 US ∘9255
MIKE PATTO	V D K(G	(F) WITNESS	1973 ISLAND GER 87332
CHRIS STAINTON	K (D	(G) THE MIRROR	1974 ISLAND US 9292
HENRY McCULLOUGH	G (D	(G) THE MIRROR	1974 GOODEAR UK EARL2001
ALAN SPENNER	(D	(G) THE MIRROR	1979 CHARLY UK CR 30167
		(H) POP CHRONIK (DBL COMP)	1975 ISLAND EURO VOL 10 GER 88133
		(I) THE BEST OF	1976 ISLAND UK ILPS9368

SPORTS

ROBERT GLOVER	B (B	(A) RECKLESS	1978 MUSHROOM AUST 36571
STEPHEN CUMMINGS	V (AB	(B) DONT THROW STONES	1978 MUSHROOM AUST 36844
ANDREW PENDLEBURY	G V (AB	(B+) DONT THROW STONES(DIFF TRACKS)	1979 SIRE UK 6001 US ARISTA 4249
ED BATES	G V (B	(B+) DONT THROW STONES	1979 ARIOLA GER 201 020
JIM NIVEN	K V (B	(C) SPORTS	1979 STIFF SEEZ 15
PAUL HITCHINGS	D (AB	(D) SPORTS (EP)	1979 STIFF LAST 5
MARTIN ARMIGER	G V (B	(E) SUDDENLY	1980 ARISTA US 4266
W WILDE	SAX (B		
M BURNS	SYN (B	PETE SOLLEY K (B	G HYDE	PERC (B	HERBIE FLOWERS B (B
CHANTER SISTERS	V (D		

SPOTNICKS

BO LANDER	G (	(A) SPOTNICKS IN LONDON	1961 KARUSSELL GER 1012 UK ORIOLE
BO WINBERG	G (ALL	(B) SPOTNICKS IN PARIS	1963 KARUSSELL GER 1014 UK ORIOLE
BJORN THELIN	B (	(C) SPOTNICKS IN SPAIN	1963 SWEDISC SWELP 1
OVE JOHANNSON	D (	(D) OUTTA SPACE	1963 ORIOLE UK SPS 40037
PETER WIBERG	(P	(E) IN JAPAN	1966 SWEDISC SWELP 38
LENNART HERMENSSON	(P	(F) IN WINTERLAND	1966 SWEDISC SWELP 48
BO MANIEETE	(P	(G) THE SPOTNICKS	1975 POLYDOR 2482 051
JOHAN DIELEMANS	(P	(H) BEST OF	19 POLYDOR 184 151
MATZ NILSSON	(P	(I) POP GIANTS No8	19 BRUNSWICK 2911 519
JAN SVENSSON	BAN (P	(J) VERY BEST OF	1977 AIR CHM 1171
		(K) LE TOUR DE MONDE DES SPOTNICKS	19 PRESIDENT FR 279 (4LP SET)
		(L) BEST	19 KARUSSELL 2499 017 GER
		(M) SPOTNICKS	19 POLYDOR 27501 6 GER
		(N) ON TOUR	19 KARUSSELL 2499 050 GER
		(O) NEVER TRUST ROBOTS	1978 POLYDOR 2344 116 GER
		(P) TODAY	1973 POLYDOR 2480 164 GER
		(Q) SOMETHING IN THE COUNTRY	19 POLYDOR 2480 112 GER
		(R) SATURDAY NIGHT MUSIC	19 M RECORDS MILP1304
		(S) GREAT SNOWMAN	19 M RECORDS MILP1300
		(EP)ON THE AIR	196 ORIOLE UK 7075
		(EP) IN PARIS	196 ORIOLE UK 7078
		(EP) AT THE OLYMPIA	196 ORIOLE UK 7079

SPREADEAGLE

ANDY BLACKFIELD	G V (A	(A) A PIECE OF PAPER	1972 CHARISMA UK CAS 1055
SAM LLEWELLYN	B V PERC(A		
JIM COPLEY	D (A	JOHN FIELD	PERC (A	TIM PHILLIPS	V G K(A	NICK	PERC (A
SHELL	PERC (A		

SPRIGUNS

MANDY MORTON	G V (ABC	(A) REVEL WEIRD & WILD	1976 DECCA SKL 5262
TOM LING	VLN V(AB	(B) TIME WILL PASS	1977 DECCA SKL 5286
DICK POWELL	G V K(AB	(C) MAGIC LADY	1979 BANSHEE BAN 1101
MIKE MORTON	B V (AB		
CHRIS WOODCOCK	D (A	WAYNE MORRISON G MAND V(B	TIM HART	(C	B J COLE	STEEL(A
LEA NICHOLSON CONCERTINA(B	DENNIS DUNSTAN	PERC D(B	GRAEME TAYLOR	(C	GORDON FOLKARD	CONC (C
SARAH FOLKARD	V (C	BYRON GILES	D (C	ALEX COOPER	D (C

SPRING

MARILYN WILSON-POWELL V(A		(A) SPRING	1974 UA UK UAS 29363 US UAS 5577
DIANE POWELL	V (A		
KEITH ALLISON	B (A	RAY POHMAN	B (A	DAVID COHEN	G (A	LARRY CARLTON	G (A
CARL WILSON	G (A	JOHN GUERIN	D (A	LINCOLN MAYORGA	PNO (A	DAVID SANDLER	PNO (A
ALAN BEUTLER	HRNS (A	IGOR HOROSHEFSKY CELLO(A	BRIAN WILSON	(A

DUSTY SPRINGFIELD

DUSTY SPRINGFIELD	V (A	(A) A GIRL CALLED DUSTY	1964 PHILIPS UK BL 7594
RONALD CHAMBERS	G (A	(B) EVERYTHING IS COMING UP DUSTY	1965 PHILIPS UK SBL 1002
DICK HYDE	TROM (b	(B) SHEER MAGIC RI	197 AUDIO CLUB 6856 020
NORMAN HARRIS	G (P	(C) STAY AWHILE	196 PHILIPS US 600 133
VINCE MONTANA	VIBES(P	(D) DUSTY	196 PHILIPS US 600 156
UGENE DOZIER	PNO (P	(E) OOOOOOOWEEEEE1111	196 PHILIPS US 600 174
RONALD BAKER	B (P	(F) YOU DONT HAVE TO SAY YOU LOVE ME	196 PHILIPS US 600 210
EARL YOUNG	D (P	(G) GOLDEN HITS	1966 PHILIPS UK SBL 7737 US 600 220
DON RENALDO	STR (P	(H) THE PEKING MEDALION(SOUNDTRACK)	1967 PHILIPS UK SBL 7782
SAM REED	HRNS (P	(I) WHERE AM I GOING	1967 PHILIPS UK SBL 7820
RICHARD TEE	K (a	(J) STAY AWHILE	1968 FONTANA UK 131189 UK RI WING1211
JOE SAMPLE	K (a	(K) DUSTY DEFINITELY	1968 PHILIPS UK SBL 7864
BILL PAYNE	K (a	(L) THE LOOK OF LOVE	196 PHILIPS US 600 256

(CONTINUED)

(CONTINUED)   DUSTY SPRINGFIELD

```
    DAVID PAICH      K   (a        (M) DUSTY SPRINGFIELD(LTD EDITION)    196  WORLD RECORD CLUB        ST 848
    JAI WINDING      K   (a        (N) DUSTY IN MEMPHIS                  1969 PHILIPS UK SBL 7889
    WILLIAM SMITH    K   (a        (N) DUSTY IN MEMPHIS                  1969 ATLANTIC            US   8214
    JOHN BARNES      K   (a        (O) BEST OF BACHARACH                 1970 FONTANA UK SFL 13193
    JAY GRAYDON      G   (a        (P) FROM DUSTY WITH LOVE              1970 PHILIPS UK SBL 7927
    DAVID T WALKER   G   (a        (P) A BRAND NEW ME                    1970 ATLANTIC            US   8249
    CHARLES FEARING  G   (a        (Q) A GIRL CALLED DUSTY               1970 FONTANA UK 6438024 RI 6870 555
    THOM ROTILLA     G   (a        (R) THIS IS DUSTY SPRINGFIELD         1971 PHILIPS UK 6382 016
    JEFF BAXTER      G   (a        (S) STAR DUSTY                        197  AUDIO CLUB OF GB        6850 002
    BOB GLAUB        B   (a        (U) SEE ALL HER FACES                 197  PHILIPS UK 6308 117
    KENNETH BURKE    B   (a        (V) MAGIC GARDEN(THIS IS VOL 2)       1973 PHILIPS UK 6382 063
    COLIN CAMERON    B   (a        (W) CAMEO                             1973 PHILIPS UK 6308 152
    CHUCK RAINEY     B   (a        (W) CAMEO                             1973 DUNHILL             US  50128
    ED GREENE        D   (a        (X) LONGINGS   (NOT ISSUED)           197  DUNHILL             US  50186
    RICHARD SCHLOSSER D  (a        (Y) SINGS BACHARACH & KING            1975 PHILIPS UK 6382 105
    OSCAR NEVES      PERC (a       (Z) YOU DONT HAVE TO SAY YOU LOVE ME  1976 CONTOUR US 2016
    MR M             PERRC(a       (a) IT BEGINS AGAIN                   1978 MERCURY UK 9109 607
    TIMMY VIG        VIBES(a       (b) LIVING WITHOUT YOUR LOVE          1979 MERCURY UK 9109 629
    JERRY JUMONVILLE SAX (a        (c) GRESTEST HITS                     1979 PHILIPS UK 9109 629
    PATTI BROOKS     V   (ab       (d) DUSTY IN MEMPHIS PLUS             1981 MERCURY UK 6381 023
    DIANE BROOKS     V   (ab       (e) THE VERY BEST OF                  1981 UK KTEL UK NE 1139
    BRENDA RUSSEL    V   (ab       (EP) I ONLY WANT TO BE WITH YOU       1964 PHILIPS UK 12560
    MICHELLE ALLER   V   (a        (EP) DUSTY                            1964 PHILIPS UK 12564
    SCOT EDWARDS     B   (b        (EP) MADEMOISELLE DUSTY               1964 PHILIPS UK 12579
    WILL LEE         B   (b        (EP) DUSTY IN NEW YORK                1965 PHILIPS UK 12572
    NEIL LARSEN      K   (b        (EP) IF YOU GO AWAY                   1967 PHILIPS UK 12605
    LINCOLN MAYORGA  K   (b
    DENNIS BUDMIR    G   (b     DAVID WOLFERT    G   (b   IAN UNDERWOOD   SYN (b   LENNY CASTRO     PERC(b
    GARY COLEMAN     PERC (b    STEVE MADAIO     HRNS (b  TOM SAVIANO     SAX (b   MIKE CANAHAN     SAX (b
    DAVID LUELL      SAX (b     ARIF MARDIN   PROD   (d   TOM DOWD     PROD (d    JERRY WEXLER     PROD (d
```

RICK SPRINGFIELD

```
    RICK SPRINGFIELD V G K B(ABC   (A) WAIT FOR THE NIGHT               1976 CHELSEA US 2306 UK CHL 515
    NIGEL OLSSON     D V (A        (B) WORKING CLASS DOG                1981 RCA      US
    DEE MURRAY       B V (A        (C) SUCCESS HASN'T SPOILED ME YET    1982 RCA           UK   6033
    JOE LAMANO       B   (A
    JIM HAAS         V   (A    LES EMERSON      V   (A   BILL CUOMO     K   (A   GABRIEL KATONA   K   (A
    JIMMIE HASKELL   STR (A
```

BRUCE SPRINGSTEEN

```
    BRUCE SPRINGSTEEN G V HCA B(ALL (A) GREETINGS FROM ASBURY PARK N J  1973 CBS      US 31903   UK 65480
    CLARENCE CLEMONS SAX V(ABCDEX   (B) WILD, INNOCENT & THE EAST STREET 1973 CBS     US 32432   UK 65780
    GARRY TALLENT    B HRN(ABCDEX   (C) BORN TO RUN                     1975 CBS      US 33795   UK 69170
    MAX WEINBERG     D   (CDEX      (D) DARKNESS ON THE EDGE OF TOWN    1978 CBS      US 35318   UK 86061
    ROY BITTAN       K   (CDEX      (E) THE RIVER                      1980 CBS                  UK 88510
    VINI LOPEZ    D V HRNS (AB      (ABC)BRUCE SPRINGSTEEN(TRIPLE)      1979 CBS                  UK 66353
    DANNY FEDERICI   K V (BCDEX     (X) REQUESTED AROUND THE WORLD(PROMO) 1981 CBS US AS978
    HOWARD KAYLAN    V   (E         (F) NEBRASKA                        1982 CBS                  UK 85669
    MARK VOLMAN      V   (E
    DAVID SANCIOUS   K SAX(ABC RICHARD BLACKWELL PERC (B  ALBANY TELLONE  SAX (B  STEVE VAN ZANDT  G  (CEDX
    MIKE APPEL       V   (C     ERNEST CARTER    D   (C  RANDY BRECKER   HRNS (C MICHAEL BRECKER  HRNS(C
    DAVID SANBORN    SAX (C     WAYNE ANDRE      TROM (C RICHARD DAVIS   B   (AC  HAROLD WHEELER   PNO (A
```

SPUD

```
    DON KNOX         V FDL(AB       (A) A SILK PURSE                    1975 PHILIPS               9108 002
    MICHAEL SMITH    V B (AB        (B) THE HAPPY HANDFUL               1975 PHILIPS               9108 003
    AUSTIN KENNY     G V (AB        (C) SMOKING ON THE BOG              1977 SONET                 SNTF 742
    DERMOT O'CONNOR  G SYN(A
    MALCOLM WRAY     V   (A     DON HARRIS       D   (B  DANNY SMITH     PERC (B  JIMMY FAULKNER  G   (B
    RICK EPPING      CONGA(B    STEVE MOORE      PERC (B DONAL LUNNY     G SYN(A
```

SPY

```
    DANNY SEIDENBERG VLN (A        (A) SPY                             1980 KIRSHNER          US   36378
    DAVID NELSON     G V (A
    BOB GOLDMAN      D   (A     MICHAEL VISCEGLIA B  (A  DAVE LEBOLT     K   (A   JOHN VISLOCKY    V   (A
```

SPYRO GYRA

```
    JAY BECKENSTEIN PERC SAX(ALL   (A) MORNING DANCE                  1978 INFINITY   US 9004 UK INS  2003
    TOM SCHUAMAN    K   (ABCD       (A) SPYRO GYRA                    1977 INFINITY   US 9011 UK INS  2008
    STEVE KROON     PERC (D         (B) SPYRO GYRA                    1982 MCA UK MCL 1628
    DAVID SAMUELS PERC VIBES(BD     (C) CATCHING THE SUN              1980 MCA US 5108 UK 4009
    RICK STRAUSS    G   (ABCD       (D) CARNIVAL                      1980 MCA US 5149 UK 3087
    JEREMY WALL     K PERC(ALL      (E) FREE TIME                     1981 MCA US 5238 UK 3119
    STEVE JORDAN    D   (D          (BC) MORNING DANCE/CATCHING (CASS) 1982 MCA       UK 2/100
    JIM KURZDORFER  B   (ABCD
    DAVID WOFFERN   B   (E     TOM WALSH        D   (B  EMILE LATIMER   PERC (B  RICK BELL        TROM(B
    FRED MARSHALL   TROM (B    RUBENS BASSINI   CONGA(B FREDDY RAPILLO  G   (B   GREG MILLAR      G   (B
    TONY GARUSSO    TPT (D     CHET CATALLO     G   (ALL WILL LEE      B   (D   ELI KONIKOFF     D   (ALL
    CRUSHER BENNETT PERC (D    ROB MOUNSEY      SYN (D  MICHAEL BRECKER FLT (D   HIRAM BULLOCK    G   (D
    GERARDO VELEZ   PERC (D    RANDY BRECKER    TPT (D  DAVID DARLING   CELLO(D  JOHN TROPEA      G   (DE
```

SPYS

```
    ED GAGLIARDI     B   (A        (A) SPYS                           1982 EMI  US      ST 17073
    AL GREEN WOOD    K   (A
    JOHN BLANCO      V   (A     BILLY MIKE       D   (A
```

SQUEEZE

```
    CHRIS DIFFORD    G V (ABCDEFG   (A) SQUEEZE                       1978 A&M US 4687 UK AMLH68465
    GLENN TILBROOK   G V (ABCDEFG   (B) COOL FOR CATS                 1979 A&M SU 4759 UK AMLH68003
    JULIAN HOLLAND   K   (ABCD      (C) SQUEEZE (10")                 1979 A&M US SP3413
    GILSON LAVIS     D   (ABCDEFG   (D) ARGY BARGY                    1980 A&M US 4802 UK AMLH64802
    JOHN BENTLEY     B   (CDEFG     (E) EAST SIDE STORY               1981 A&M      UK AMLH64854
    ROGER BECHIRIAN  PROD (E        (F) SWEETS FORM A STRANGER        1982 A&M      UK AMLH64899
    DAVE EDMUNDS     PROD (E        (G) SINGLES 45's & UNDER          1982 A&M      UK AMLH68552
    PHIL McDONALD    PROD (F        (EP) PACKET OF THREE              197  DEPTFORD FUN CITY   DFC 01
    HARRY KAKOULLI   B   (ABC
    DEL NEWMAN       STR (E     ELVIS COSTELLO VPROD(F    DON SNOW      K V  (F   PAUL YOUNG  B   (F
```

BILLY SQUIER

BILLY SQUIER	G V	(ALL	(A) A TALE OF THE TAPE			1980 CAPITOL UK/US 12062	NL 86138		
BRUCE KULICK	G	(A	(B) DONT SAY NO			1981 CAPITOL	12146		
BUCKY BALLARD	B	(A	(C) EMOTIONS IN MOTION			1982 CAPITOL	12217		
BOBBY CHOUINARD	D	(ABC							
DAVID SANCIOUS	K	(A	RICHARD T BEAR	K	(A ERNEST CARTER	PERC (A	MARK CLARKE	B V (B	
ALAN ST JOHN	K	(BC	GARY SHARAF	G	(B DOUG LUBAHN	B (C	JEFF GOLUB	G (C	
KENNY AARONSON	B	(							

CHRIS SQUIRE

CHRIS SQUIRE	B G V(A	(A) FISH OUT OF WATER			1975 ATLANTIC US 18159	UK K50203	
BILL BRUFORD	D	(A					
MEL COLLINS	SAX	(A	JIM HASTINGS FLT (A PATRICK MORAZ	K SYN(A	BARRY ROSE K (A	
ANDREW BRYCE JACKMAN K	(A	ORCHESTRA (A					

STACKRIDGE

ANDREW CRESWELL-DAVIS	V G K D(ALL	(A) STACKRIDGE	1971 MCA UK MDKS8002 UK 74RI MCG3505
BOB LAMB	TROM	(DF	(A) STACKRIDGE	1971 DECCA US 75317
JAMES WARREN	V B G(ABCF	(B) FRIENDLINESS	1972 MCA UK MKPS2025 UK 74RI MCF2504
MARTIN FRY	TUBA	(F	(B) FRIENDLINESS	1972 MCA US 308
MICHAEL SLATER	V FLT K(ABCDEF	(C) MAN IN A BOWLER HAT	1973 MCA UK	MCG3501
MICHAEL EVANS	V VLN(ABCF	(D) EXTRAVAGANZA	1974 ROCKET ROLLA1 +	PIGL 11
BILLY BRENT	D	(A	(D) EXTRAVAGANZA	1974 SIRE US 7509
JIM CRUN WALTER	G B	(BCEF	(E) MR MICK	1976 ROCKET UK ROLL 3
BILLY SPARKLE	D	(BCF	(F) PINAFORE DAYS	1974 SIRE US 7503
REG LEOPOLD	VLN	(CF	(G) DO THE STANLEY(COMP)	1976 MCA UK MCF2747
WILLIAM REID	VLN	(CF		
GRAEME SCOTT	VLN	(CF	VIVIAN JOSEPH CELLO(CF JACK EMBLOW	ACC (CF RAY DAVIS TPT (CF
DEREK TAYLOR	HRNS	(CF	R CHAMBERLAIN HRNS (CF ROD BOWKETT	K (DF KEITH GEMMELL WIND(DEF
PAUL KARAS	B V	(DF	ROY MORGAN D (DF PETER VAN HOOKE	D (E JOANNA CARLIN V (E
DAVE LAWSON	K	(E	RAY RUSSELL G (	

STACKWADDY

JOHN KNAIL	V HCA(1	(A) STACKWADDY	1971 DANDELION DAN 8003 + 2310 154
MICK SCOTT	G	(1	(B) BUGGER OFF	1972 DANDELION 2310 231
STUART BARNHAM	B	(12	(1) 1966/71 (2) 1973 /76	
STEVE REVELL	D	(1		
MIKE SWEENEY	V	(2	WAYNE JACKSON B (2 ROBIN GOODWIN	D (2

STADIUM DOGS

PETE COUSINS	B V	(A	(A) WHAT'S NEXT	1978 MAGNET MAG 5025
PAUL GRIFFITHS	G V	(A		
STAN PEARCE	D	(A	JONATHAN PERKINS K V (A KIRK THORN	G V (A KEVIN WILKINSON D (A

STAINED GLASS

	(A) CRAZY HORSE ROADS	19 CAPITOL ST 154
	(B) AURORA	19 CAPITOL ST 242

STAINLESS STEEL

(A) CAN CAN	1978 EMI UK EMC 3259 WB US 3274

STALLION

WALLY DAMRICK	V K SYN(A	(A) STALLION	1977 CASABLANCA UK CAL2014 US 7040
JORG GONZALEZ	B V	(A	(B) HEY EVERYBODY	19 CASABLANCA US 7083
LARRY THOMPSON	D	(A		
STEVE STEPHENSON	SAX	(A	DON BUZZARD STEEL (A PAUL VASTOLA	SYN (A BRUCE FOWLER TROM(A
STAN ROGERS	TROM	(A	JIM OATTS TPT (A AL WING	SAX (A CHUCK SNEIDENER SAX (A
DIK DARNELL	V	(A	DANNY O'NEIL G V (A BUDDY STEPHENS	V PERC(A JOHN MACY STEEL(A
PATTY GREER	HARP	(A	DAVE KAHN TROM (A WALT FOWLER	TPT (A TOM HOWARD TPT (A
STEVE FOWLER	SAX	(A		

STAIRSTEP

(A) 2ND RESURRECTION	1976 DARK HORSE US 22004

TERRY STAMP

TERRY STAMP	V	(A	(A) EASTSTICKS	1975 A&M UK AMLH 63329
OLLIE HALSALL	K G	(A		
TONY NEWMAN	D	(A	HERBIE FLOWERS B (A MIKE MORAN	K (A ALAN SPENNER B (A
JIM AVORY	B	(A		

STAMPEDERS

RONNIE KING	(ALL	(A) STAMPEDERS	1972 REGAL ZONOPHONE UK SLPZ 1032
BOB ADDUONO	HRNS	(E	(B) SWEET CITY WOMAN	1973 BELL US 6068
RICH DODSON	(ALL	(C) FROM THE FIRE	1974 REGAL ZONOPHONE UK SLRZ 1039
KIM BERLY	(ALL	(D) NEWDAY	1975 EMI UK INS 3003
GIBBY LACASSA	PERC	(E	(E) HIT THE ROAD	1976 QUALITY US QLP 1001
GUY MARCHI	HRNS	(E		
RANDY MARCHI	HRNS	(E		

STANDELLS

LARRY TAMBLYN	K V	(C	(A) DIRTY WATER	196 TOWER US ST5027
TONY VALENTINO	G	(C	(B) WHY PICK ON ME	196 TOWER US ST5044
GARY LANE	(	(C) HOT ONES	196 TOWER US ST5049
DICK DODD	D	(C	(D) TRY IT	196 TOWER US ST5098
DAVE BURKE	G B	(C	(E) LIVE & OUT OF SIGHT	196 SUNSET US 5136
			(F) IN PERSON AT P Js	196 LIBERTY US LST 7384

MICHAEL STANLEY

MICHAEL STANLEY	G V	(ALL	(A) ROSEWOOD BITTERS	1973 TUMBLEWEED TW 3505
RICK BELL	SAX	(J	(B) MICHAEL STANLEY	1974 TUMBLEWEED TW 106
JONAH KOSLEN	G V	(DEFG	(C) FRIENDS & LEGENDS	1975 MCA MCA 372
DANNY PECCHIO	B V	(DEFG	(D) YOU BREAK IT YOU BOUGHT IT	1975 EPIC US 33492
TOMMY DOBECK	D	(DEFGHJ	(E) LADIES CHOICE	1976 EPIC US 33917
BOB PELANDER	K	(FGHJ	(F) STAGE PASS	1977 EPIC US 34661
GARY MARKASKI	G	(GHJ	(G) CABIN FEVER	1978 ARISTA US 4182 UK SPART 1066
KEVIN RALEIGH	K V	(HJ	(H) HEARTLAND	1980 EMI UK AML 3015 US 17040
MICHAEL GISMONDI	B	(HJ	(I) GREATEST HITS	1979 ARISTA US 4236
MUTT LANGE	B V	(G	(J) NORTH COAST	1981 CAPITOL US 17056
DARRYL TOOKES	V	(J		
CURTIS KING	V	(J	YVONNE LEWIS V (J ED KRAMER	V (J

S242   PAUL STANLEY   S242

```
      PAUL STANLEY    V G B(A        (A) PAUL STANLEY              1978 CASABLANCA        NBLP7123
      BOB KULICK      G   (A
      RICHIE FONTANA  D   (A  CRAIG KRAMPF      D   (A  CARMINE APPICE   D   (A  MARIA VIDAL      V   (A
      DIANA GRASSELLI V   (A  MIRIAM NAOMI VALLE V  (A  STEVE BUSLOWE    B   (A  ERIC NELSON      B   (A
      DOUG KATSAROS   PNO (A  STEVE LACEY       G   (A  PEPPI CASTRO     V   (A
```

S243   VIV STANSHALL   S243

```
      VIV STANSHALL   V WIND(AB1     (A) MEN OPENING UMBRELLAS AHEAD 1974 WB            UK  K56052
      BUBS WHITE      G   (A1        (B) SIR HENRY AT RAWLINSON END  1978 CHARISMA      UK  CAS 1139
      STEVE WINWOOD   B ORG(AB       (C) TEDDY BOYS DONT KNIT        1981 CHARISMA      UK  CAS 1153
      JIM CUOMO       WIND (B        (1) BIG GRUNT 1969
      GASPAR LAWAL    PERC V(A
      NEIL INNES      K G  (A  JIM CAPALDI       D   (A  DEREK QUINN      PERC (A  RIC GRECH        VLN (A
      REBOP K BAAH    PERC (A  DORIS TROY        V   (A  MADELINE BELL    V   (A  BARRY ST JOHN    V   (A
      AYUS APE        V   (A  GANI              V   (A  IAN WALLACE      D   (1  DENNIS COWAN     B   (1
      ROGER RUSKIN SPEAR SAX (1 FRED MUNT        (1  ZOOT MONEY       PNO (   JULIAN SMEDLEY   B MAND(B
      JIM FRENCH      V HRNS(B  PETE MOSS        ACC FDL  (B
```

S243A   HOLLY STANTON   S243A

```
      HOLLY STANTON   V    (A        (A) TEMPTATION              1981 SOLIS SMOKE   US  WB 9004
      JOHN REWIND     K G  (A
      BILLY CARMASSI  D    (A  MICKEY RAZOR     D   (A  J D SHARP        K   (A  GREG SMITH       G   (A
      ALEX BENDAHAN   G    (A
```

S244   STAR PARK   S244

```
      COLIN MOULDING  B    (              (NO RECORDS)
      ANDY PARTRIDGE  G    (
      TERRY CHAMBERS  D    (  DAVE CARTNER     G   (   STEVE HUTCHINS  V   ( JOHNNY PERKINS   K  (
```

S245   STARBUCK   S245

```
      BRUCE BLACKMAN  K V  (BC       (A) MOONLIGHT FEELS RIGHT    1976 PRIVATE STOCK US 2013    1008
      JIMMY COBB      B V  (BC       (B) ROCK'N'ROLL ROCKET      1977 PRIVATE STOCK US 2027 UK 1023
      KEN CRYSLER     D    (BC       (C) SEARCHING FOR A THRILL  1978 UA          US LA918 UK UAS 30221
      SLOAN HAYES     K V  (B
      DARRYL KUTZ     G V  (B  DAVID SHAVER     G V (CB BO WAGNER       PNO (B  JOHN WALKER      G V (C
      JOHN FRISTOE    G V  (C
```

S246   STARCASTLE   S246

```
      STEPHEN HAGLER  G V  (ABCD      (A) STARCASTLE            1976 EPIC        US 33914  UK 81347
      GARY STRATER    B V  (ABCD      (B) FOUNTAINS OF LIGHT    1977 EPIC        US 34375  UK 81665
      HERB SCHILDT    K    (ABC       (C) CITADEL               1977 EPIC        US 34935  UK 82232
      STEPHEN TASSTER D V  (ABC       (D) REAL TO REEL          1978 EPIC        US 35441  UK 82916
      MATTHEW STEWART G V  (B
      TERRY LUTTRELL  V    (B
```

S247   STARDRIVE   S247

```
      ROBERT MASON    SYN  (AB       (A) INTERGALATIC TROT      1973 ELEKTRA     US EKS75058 UK K42140
      JAIME AUSTRIA   B    (AB       (B) STARDRIVE             1974 CBS          US    33047
      BRUCE DITMAS    PERC (A
      HARVEY SARCH    G    (AB  MICHAEL BRECKER  SAX (A  STEPHEN GADD     D   (A  HOWARD REGO      D  (B
```

S248   STARDUST   S248

```
                                     (A) STARDUST              1977 SATRIL                 SATL 4008
```

S249   ALVIN STARDUST   S249

```
      ALVIN STARDUST  V    (ALL      (A) UNTOUCHABLE           1974 MAGNET      UK  MAG 5001
                                     (B) ALVIN STARDUST        1974 MAGNET      UK  MAG 5004
                                     (C) ROCK WITH ALVIN       1975 MAGNET      UK  MAG 5007
                                     (D) GREATEST HITS         1977 MAGNET      UK  MAG 4002
                                     (E) ROCK ON WITH ALVIN    1980 MFP         UK    50464
```

S249A   STARFIGHTERS   S249A

```
      STEVE BURTON    V    (A        (A) STARFIGHTERS          1981 JIVE        HOP 200
      STEVE YOUNG     G    (A
      PAT HAMBLY      G    (A  DOUG DENNIS      B   (A  STEVE BAILEY     D   (A
```

S249B   STARF*CKERS   S249B

```
      OLE FRO              (A        (A) VOGT DEM FOR EFTERLIGNINGER 1978 CBS  DK  83511
      THOMAS GRUE          (A
      JESS STAEHR          (A  KIM LARGEN        (A  STIG MOLLER       (A  KEN GUDMAND      (A
```

S249C   STARFYRE   S249C

```
      JOHN W EDWARDS  K V TPT(ABCD    (A) STARFYRE              1977 AI          US 0016
      EUGENE J HOLDT  K V  (ABC       (B) HERE WE GO AGAIN      1978 AI          US 0016
      EDWARD ABRIL    SAX  (ABC       (C) MUSIC AFTER MIDNIGHT  1979 AI          US 0021
      ROSI HOFFNER    V    (A         (D) LAY IT ON THE LINE    1981 AI          US 0028
      HOWARD TAYLOR   SAX G V(A
      SANTOS HERNANDEZ G V (A  JOEY ROSELES     B G V(A TERRY ROSALES   D   (A  ALAN FOSTER K V  (BC
      NEIL McQUEEN    K V  (D  BILL HUDSPETH    SAX (D  KAREN BURGHARD  V VLN(BC KELLY LOVEGROVE  V VLN(D
      STEVE CHRISTIANSEN G CLAR(AB JAMES GIUSTI  G B (BC RUSS McCALLEY   G V (D  BOB CRAVEN       G V (ABC
      CAREY CLELAND   G    (D  JIM CURRENT      G V FLT (CD TUCKER BURLING B G (CD TROY MARHN     B G V(D
      BOB SPRAGUE     D    (BC CURT TANTILLO    D V (D  RICHARD TUCKER  PERC (CD
```

S250   STARGARD   S250

```
      ROCHELLE RUNNELS V K (ABC       (A) STARGARD            1978 MCA  UK MCF2834 US 2321
      DEBRA ANDERSON  V    (ABC       (B) WHAT YOU WAITING FOR 1978 MCA UK MCF2859 US 3046
      JANICE C WILLIAMS V  (ABC       (C) CHANGING OF THE GARD 1979 WB  US BSK3386 UK     K56746
      KENI BURKE      B    (C         (D) BACK TO BACK        1980 WB  US 3456   UK        K56854
      VERDINE WHITE   B    (C
      BEVERLEY ASHBY  HARP (C  BUTCH AZEVEDO    D   (C  LARRY TOLBERT   D   (C  JOSEPH BAKER     G  (C
      CHARLES FEARING G    (C  ROBERT PALMER    G   (C  MARK DAVIS      K   (C  DEAN GANT        K  (C
      ROBERT WRIGHT   K    (C  EDDIE BROWN      PERC (C  PAULINHO DA COSTA PERC (C DON MYRICK     HRNS (C
      LOUIS SATTERFIELD HRNS (C RAHEEM LEE MICHAEL DAVIS(C FRED JACKSON  HRNS (C  OSCAR BRASHAR   HRNS (C
      JEROME RICHARDSON HRNS (C GARNETT BROWN   HRNS (C
```

S250A   STARJETS   S250A

```
      PAUL BOWEN           (A        (A) GOD BLESS THE STARJETS 1979 EPIC US 36245  UK  83534
      TERRY SHARPE         (A
      SEAN MARTIN          (A  LIAM L'ESTRANGE  (A
```

STARK NAKED
```
     PAUL VENIER      V K PERC(A      (A) STARK NAKED                        1971 RCA              US LSP 4592
     LYNE BUNN        V PERC(A
     JIM MONAHAN      G V (A    JOHN FRAGOS      D PERC(A  TOM RUBINS      B   (A   RICHARD BELSKIN  G (A
```
EDWIN STARR
```
     EDWIN STARR      V    (ALL      (A) SOUL MASTER              1969 TAMLA UK STML11094 US GORDY 931
     L MIDDLETON      G    (L        (B) 25 MILES                 197                  US GORDY 940
     J ROBERTS        B    (L        (C) WAR & PEACE              197                  US GORDY 948
     SPIKE            K    (L        (D) INVOLVED                 1972 TAMLA UK STML11199 US GORDY 956
     R REED           D    (L        (E) HITS OF EDWIN STARR      1974 TAMLA UK STML11209
     M SINGER         D    (L        (F) HELL UP IN HARLEM        1974 TAMLA UK STML11210 US TAMLA 802
     E FLETCHER       PERC (L        (G) FREE TO BE MYSELF        1976 GRANITE         US    1005
     K PEACHY         HRNS (L        (H) AFTERNOON SUNSHINE       1977 GTO    UK             GTLP 019
     E HILL           HRNS (L        (J) EDWIN STARR              1977 20THCENTURY UK 538 GTO US 518
     A HAMILTON       HRNS (L        (K) CLEAN                    1979 20TH CENTURY    UK    BT 559
     CURT SLETTEN     HRNS (L        (L) HAPPY RADIO              1979 20TH CENTURY    UK    BT 591
     JOEL PESKIN      FLT  (L        (M) STRONGER THAN YOU THINK I AM 1980 20TH CENTURY UK   BT 615
     HARRY KIM        FLT  (L        ( ) JUST WE TWOO             19   GORDY US 945
     MAURICE YOUNG    V    (M
     H PRESTON        FLT  (L  D STOUT       FLT  (L  DAVID SHIELDS    B   (M  JAMES GADSON    D  (M
     MELVIN D WEBB    D    (M  DAVID T WALKER G    (M  HOWARD FEITEN    G   (M  RALPH E HAMMER  G  (M
     GLENNIS JONES    G    (M  CLARK E SPANGLER SYN (M  JIMMY McAFEE     B   (M  JOHN J BARNES   K  (M
     LARRY FARROW     K    (M  RONALD COLEMAN K    (M  EARL VAN DYKE    K   (M  RICK McAFEE     K  (M
     EDDIE BROWN      PERC (M  LUKE METOYER   PERC (M  LUTHER WATERS    V   (M  CLIFTON CURTIS  V  M
     ORRIN WATERS     V    (LM MAXINE WILLARD V    (LM JULIA TILLMAN    V   (LM JERRY PETERSON  SAX(M
     WILLIAM CLARK    V    (M  MONROE WRIGHT  V    (M
```
RINGO STARR
```
     RINGO STARR V PERC D (ALL      (A) SENTIMENTAL JOURNEY      1970 APPLE   UK PCS  7101 US        3365
     JOHN LENNON      V PNO(CFD      (B) BEACOUPS OF BLUES        1970 APPLE   UK PAS 10002 US        3368
     GEORGE HARRISON  G   (C         (C) RINGO                    1973 APPLE   UK PCTC  252 US        3413
     PAUL McCARTNEY K V SAX (CF      (D) GOODNIGHT VIENNA         1974 APPLE   UK PLS  7168 US        3417
     KLAUS VOORMANN   B   (CFD       (E) BLAST FROM YOUR PAST     1975 APPLE   UK PCS  7170 US        3422
     BILLY PRESTON    K   (CD        (F) ROTOGRAVURE             1976 POLYDOR UK 2302 040  US ATCO    18193
     JIM KELTNER      D   (CDF       (G) RINGO THE FOURTH        1977 POLYDOR UK 2310 556  US ATCO    19108
     MILT HOLLAND     PERC (C        (H) BAD BOY                 1978 POLYDOR UK 2310 599  US PORTRAIT35378
     LON VAN EATON    PERC (CGD      (I) RINGO STARR             1980 MFP 50508
     DERREK VAN EATON PERC (CD       (J) STOP & SMELL THE ROSES  1981
     LEVON HELM       MAND (CF       (NB) RE ISSUES OF APPLE RECORD ARE ON PARLOPHONE/CAPITOL SAME NUMBERS
     HARRY NILSSON    V   (CFD           DIFFERENT PREFIX
     CHARLIE DANIELS  G   (B
     MARTHA REEVES    V   (C    LINDA McCARTNEY  V   (CF  RICHARD PERRY    V   (C  MELISSA MANCHESTER V(FG
     JESSE ED DAVIS   G   (DF   VAN DYKE PARKS   V K (C   JOE ESPOSITO     V   (FG SNEAKY PETE     STEEL(F
     MARC BOLAN       G   (C    TOM SCOTT        HRNS(C   VINI PONCIA      G V (CFG JAMES BOOKER   PNO (C
     NICKY HOPKINS    PNO (CD   JIMMY CALVERT    G   (C   BOBBY KEYS       SAX (CD  ROBBIE ROBERTSON G  (CD
     RICK DANKO       FDL (C    GARTH HUDSON     ACC (C   MERRY CLAYTON    V   (C   STEVE CROPPER  G   (CD
     TOM HENSLEY      PNO (C    CHUCK FINDLEY    HRNS(CD  ROBERT GREENIDGE PERC(F   JOHN JARVIS    K   (F
     COOKER LOPRESTI  B   (F    DUITCH HELMER    V   (FG  ERIC CLAPTON     G V (F   PAUL STALLWORTH B  (F
     DANNY KORTCHMAR  G V (FG   DR JOHN          K V (FD  PETER FRAMPTON       (F   DAVID SPINOZZA G   (G
     JEFF MIRANOV     G   (G    JOHN TROPEA      G   (G   DON GROLNICK     K   (G   TONY LEVIN     K   (G
     HUGH McDONALD    B   (G    STEVE GADD       D   (G   CORNELL DUPREE   G   (G   RICHARD TEE    K   (G
     NICK MARRERO     PERC (G   JEFF GUTCHEON    K   (G   MARIETTA WATERS  V   (G   MAXINE ANDERSON V  (G
     DAVID LASLEY     V   (G    ROBIN CLARK      V   (G   DEBRA GRAY       V   (G   LUTHER VANDROSS V  (G
     JIM GILSTRAP     V   (GD   DICK FEGY    G       (G   DAVID BROMBERG FDL G (CG  CHUCK RAINEY   B   (G
     BRIE HOWARD      V   (G    LYNN PITNEY      V   (G.  ARNOLD McCULLER  V   (G   REBECCA LOUIS  V   (G
     BETTE MIDLER     V   (G    RANDY BRECKER    HRNS(G   MICHAEL BRECKER  HRNS (G  KEN BISCHEL    SYN (G
     DON BROOKS       HCA (G    CHUCK HOWARD     G   (B   SORRELLS PICKARD G   (B   JERRY REED     G   (B
     PETE DRAKE       STEEL(B   CHARLIE McCOY    HCA (B   ROY HUSKY        B   (B   BUDDY HARMAN       (B
     DAVE KIRBY           (B    JERRY KENNEDY        (B   JERRY SHOOK          (B   GEORGE RICHEY      (B
     GROVER LAVENDER      (B    JIM BAUCHANAN        (B   D J FONTANA      D   (B   BEN KEITH          (B
     JEANNIE KENDAL       (B    ALVIN ROBINSON   G   (D   TREVOR LAWRENCE  SAX (D   LOU McCREARY   SAX (D
     STEVE MADAIO     TPT (D    VINI PONCIA      V   (D   CLYDIE KING      V   (D   LINDA LAWRENCE V   (D
     JOE GREENE           (D    RICHARD PERRY        (D   CYNTHIA WEBB     V   (D   IRA HAWKINS    V   (D
     DAVID FOSTER     K   (D    CARL FORTIA  ACC     (D   THE BLACKBERRIES V   (D   TOM HENSLEY    K   (D
     LINCOLN MAYORGA  K   (D    DENNIS COFFEY    G   (D   ELTON JOHN       K   (D   JAMES NEWTON HOWARD SYN(D
```
STARRY EYED & LAUGHING
```
     TONY POOLE       G V K(AB      (A) STARRY EYED & LAUGHING   1974 CBS              UK  80450
     IAIN WHITMORE    B V (AB       (B) THOUGHT TALK             1975 CBS  US 33837    UK  80907
     MIKE WACKFORD    D   (AB
     ROY CARR         BONGO(A   ROSS McGEENEY    G V (AB  PAUL TURNER      D   (   DAVID POMEROY  B V (
     ARTHUR MAY       G V (     B J COLE         STEEL(A  RAY JACKSON      MAND(A   PETER WOODS    K   (A
     RUSS BALLARD     PNO (A    DAN LOGGINS      HCA (B   JEFF BANNISTER   K   (B   MICHAEL GORE   CELLO(B
     COLIN WALKER     CELLO(B   FRANK RICOTTI    VIBES(B  PETE ZORN        SAX (B
```
STARS & STIPS
```
     CESAR ZUIDERWIJK D   (A        (A) NEVERGREEN              1976 POLYDOR          UK  2925 041
     BERTUS BORGERS   SAX V(A
     RINUS GERRITSEN  B   (A    ROBERT JAN STIPS  K PERC(A
```
STARZ
```
     BRENDAN HARKIN   G   (ALL      (A) STARZ                    1976 CAPITOL               11539
     RICHIE RANNO     G   (ALL      (B) VIOLATION                1977 CAPITOL               11617
     MIKE LEE SMITH   V   (ALL      (C) ATTENTION SHOPPERS       1978 CAPITOL               11730
     PETE SWEVAL      B   (ALL      (D) COLISEUM ROCK            1979 CAPITOL               11861
     JOE X DUBE       D   (ALL      (E) STARZ LIVE (PROMO )      1978        US SPRO8857
     BOBBY MESSANNO   G   (D
```

STATES

JIMMY McDONNELL	G	(A	(A) STATES			1979 CHRYSALIS	CHR 1229	
DOMINIC GERMANO	B	(A	(B) PICTURE ME WITH YOU			19 BOARDWALK	US 37180	
STEPHEN CHANDLER	G V	(A						
BARRY SCOTT	G V	(A	ROBERT SCHINDLER K	(A	JIMMY WILKINS	D (A	GARY COLEMAN	PERC(A
JOHN JANSEN	PROD(A		C B	SYN G V	(A			

CANDI STATON

CANDI STATON	V	(ALL	(A) CANDI STATON			19 FAME	US 1800	
CORNELL DIUPREE	G	(F	(B) STAND BY YOUR MAN			19 FAME	US 4202	
RON MILLER	G	(F	(C) YOUNG HEARTS RUN FREE			11976 WB UK	K56360	
CAROL COLMAN	B	(F	(D) MUSIC SPEAKS LOUDER THAN WORDS			1977 WB UK	K56259	
CRUSHER BENNETT	PERC(F		(E) HOSE OF LOVE			1978 WB UK	K56510	
RAY CHEW	K	(F	(F) CHANCE			1979 WB UK	K56641	
CHRISTOPHER PARKER	D	(F	(G) CANDI			1980 WB UK	K56803	
STAN LUCAS	G	(F						
JAMES SMITH	K	(F	OLLIE BROWN	D (E	SCOTT EDWARDS	B (E	TIMMA I	G (E
DERYLL INMAN	G	(E	DAVE CRAWFORD	K V (E	RAY PARKER	G (E	SONNY BURKE	K (E
JIM GILSTRAP	V	(E	CAROLYN DENNIS	V (E				

STATUS QUO

FRANCIS ROSSI	G V	(ALL	(A) PICTURESQUE MATCHSTICKABLE	1968 PYE	NSPL18220
RICK PARFITT	K G V	(ALL	(B) SPARE PARTS	1968 PYE	NSPL18301
JOHN COUGHLAN	D	(ALL	(C) MESSAGES FROM THE STATUS QUO	1968 CADET	LSP 315
ALAN LANCASTER	V B G	(ALL	(D)STATUS QUOTATION	1969 MARBLE ARCH	MAL 1193
			(E) MA KELLYS GREASY SPOON	1970 PYE UK NSPL18344 US JANUS 3018	
			(F) DOG OF TWO HEAD	1971 PYE UK NSPL18371 US JANUS 3301	
			(G) BEST OF STATUS QUO	1972 PYE	NSPL18402
ROY LYNES	K	(PQSTXWY	(I) GOLDEN HOUR	1973 PYE	GH 556
ROB YOUNG	HCA	(FIKORZc	(I) PILE DRIVER	1973 VERTIGO 6360 082 US A&M 4381	
JIMMY HOROWITZ	PNO	(I	(J) HELLO	1974 VERTIGO 6360 098 US A&M 3615	
BRUCE FOSTER	K	(F	(K) QUO	1974 VERTIGO 9102 001 US A&M 3649	
STEWART BLANDMER	SAX	(J	(L) ON THE LEVEL	1975 VERTIGO 9102 002 US CAPITOL11381	
JOHN MEALING	PNO	(J	(M) GOLDEN HOUR	1975 PYE	GH 604
DAVID KATZ	HRNS	(V	(N) STATUS QUO	1975 VERTIGO QUO 13 US CAPITOL11509	
STEVE FARR	SAX	(J	(O) POP CHRONIK VOL 5	1975 PYE	87099
BUD REVO	V	(V	(P) THE REST OF STATUS QUO	1976 PYE	PKL 5546
FRANK RICOTTI	PERC	(UV	(Q) BLUE FOR YOU	1976 VERTIGO 9102 006	
ANDY BOWN	K	(JORUVZc	(R) LIVE	1977 VERTIGO 6641 580 US CAPITOL11623	
BERNIE FROST	V	(c	(S) STATUS QUO FILE	1977 PYE	FLD 005
JOY YATES	V	(V	(T) PICTURES OF MATCHSTICK MEN	1977 HALLMARK	HMA 257
GRASS	V	(F	(U) ROCKIN ALL OVER THE WORLD	1977 VERTIGO 9102 014 US CAPITOL11749	
TOM PARKER	K	(K	(V) IF YOU CANT STAND THE HEAT	1978 VERTIGO 9102 027	
JAQUIE SULLIVAN	V	(V	(W) COLLECTION	1978 PICKWICK	PDA 046
			(X) STATUS QUO	1978 HALLMARK	HMA 260
			(Y) IN MY CHAIR	1979 MODE FR	9018
			(Z) WHATEVER YOU WANT	1979 VERTIGO 9102 037	
			(a) MEAN GIRL	1979 MODE FR	9053
			(b) JUST FOR THE RECORD	1979 PYE	NSPL18607
			(c) JUST SUPPOSIN'	1980 VERTIGO 6302 057	
			(d) GOLD BARS	1980 VERTIGO QUOTV1	
			(e) NEVER TOO LATE	1981 VERTIGO 6302 104	
			( ) STATUS QUO	198= PICKWICK UK 8035	
			( ) SPOTLIGHT	1981 PRT UK 1010	
			( ) NOW HEAR THIS	1981 RIVA US 7402	
			( ) FRESH QUOTE	1981 PRT DOW 2	
			( ) VOL 1 (1972/74)	1981 VERTIGO 7215 038	

STEALERS WHEEL

GERRY RAFFERTY	G V	(ABC	(A) STEALERS WHEEL			1973 A&M US 4377	UK AMLH68121	
JOE EGAN	K V	(ABC	(B) FERGUSLIE PARK			1974 A&M US 4419	UK AMLH68209	
RAB NOAKES	(		(C) RIGHT OR WRONG			1975 A&M US 4517	UK AMLH68293	
ROGER BROWN	(		(D) STUCK IN THE MIDDLE WITH YOU (COMP197			A&M US 4708	UK AMLH64708	
IAN CAMPBELL	B	(	(E) BEST OF			1981 MFP	UK 50501	
STEVE GREGORY	SAX	(B						
PAUL PILNICK	G	(A	ROD COOMBES	D (A	TONY WILLIAMS	B (A	DELISLE HARPER	B (
LUTHER GROSVENOR	G	(	ANDY STEELE	D PERC(BC	DAVE WINTOUR	B (C	CHRIS MERCER	SAX(BC
CHRIS NEILL	HCA	(BC	BERNIE HOLLAND	G (BC	HUGH BURNS	G (C	DAVID BRIGGS	K (C
GERALDINE JOSEPHINE K	G(C		PETER ROBINSON	K (B	GARY TAYLOR	B SYN(B	JOE JAMMER	G (B
MIKE STOLLER	K	(B	CORKY HALE	HARP (B				

STEAMHAMMER

KIERAN WHITE	HCA G V(ABC		(A) STEAMHAMMER		1968 CBS US 26490	UK 63611	
MARTIN PUGH	G V	(ABCD	(A) STEAMHAMMER		1970 REFLECTION REFL1		
PETE SEARS	PNO	(A	(A) STEAMHAMMER		1970 BELLAPHON GER RI	15134	
STEVE DAVY	B V	(ABC	(B) STEAMHAMMER MARK 2		197 CBS	UK 63694	
HAROLD McNAIR	FLT	(B	(B) STEAMHAMMER MARK 2		1970 BELLAPHON GER RI 14012		
MICK BRADLEY	D	(CD	(C) MOUNTAINS		1970 METRONOME	15 376	
LOUIS CENNAMO	B	(CD	(C) MOUNTAINS		1971 BRAIN	201 006	
KEITH NELSON	BAN	(C	(D) SPEECH		1972 BRAIN 1009	0040 054	
MIKE RUSHTON		(A	(E) THIS IS (CD) (DBL)		1972 BRAIN 201 042	0021 043	
MICKY WALLER	(						
MARTIN QUITTENTON	G	(A	STEVE JOLLIFFE WIND V(B				

STEAMPACKET

BRIAN AUGER	K V	(A	(A) FIRST OF THE SUPERGROUPS		1977 CHARLY UK	CR 30020	
JULIE DRISCOLL	V	(A	(B) THE STEAMPACKET		197 BYT FR 529 706		
VIC BRIGGS	G	(A	(C) PLACES & FACES		197 BYG FR 529 906		
RICKY BROWN	B	(A					
MICK WALLER	D	(A	LONG JOHN BALDRY V	(A	ROD STEWART	V (A	PETER GREEN G (
MICK FLEETWOOD	D	(					

WALTER STEDING

WALTER STEDING		(A	(A) WALTER STEDDING			1980 RED STAR	101				
ROBERT FRIPP	G	(A									
CHRIS STEIN		(A	RICHARD LLOYD	G	(A	JOEY PINTER	B G	(A	RICHARD LLOYD	G	(A
JAN MAREK PAKULSKI	B	(A	JERRY RYAN		D	(A					

STEEL MILL

TERRY WILLIAMS	G	(A	(A) GREEN EYED GOD			1975 PENNYFARTHING	UK	PELS 549
JEFF WATTS	B	(A						
CHRIS MARTIN	D	(A	DAVE MORRIS	K V	(A	JOHN CHALLENGER	WIND	(A

STEEL PULSE

DAVID HINDS	G V	(ABC	(A) HANDSWORTH REVOLUTION	1978 ISLAND	UK	ILPS 9502		
BASIL GABBIDON	G V	(ABC	(B) TRIBUTE TO THE MARTYRS	1979 ISLAND	UK	ILPS 9568		
RONNIE McQUEEN	B	(ABC	(C) CAUGHT YOU/REGGAE FEVER	1980 ISLAND	UK	ILPS 9613		
SELWYN BROWN	K V	(ABC						
FONSO MARTIN	V PERC	(ABC	STEVE NESBITT	D	(ABC MICHAEL RILEY	V PERC(A	RICO RODRIGUES	TROM(B
GODFREY MADURA	SAX	(ABC	DICKAGE		HRNS (B			

STEEL RIVER

RAY ANGROVE	D	(AB	(A) A BETER ROAD	19	EVOLUTION	3006	
TONY DUMMING	G	(AB	(B) WHEIGHING HEAVY	19	EVOLUTION	2018	
LAFE BUCKNER	PERC V(A						
ROB COCKELL	B	(AB	JOHN DUDGEON	G V	(AB ROBERT FORRESTER	K	(AB HEDGEHOGS PERC V(A

JAN STEELE/JOHN CAGE

JAN STEELE	K	(A	(A) VOICES & INSTRUMENTS			1976 OBSCURE	UK OBS5		
JANET SHERBOURNE	V	K	(A						
FRED FRITH	G	(A	STUART JONES	G	(A	KEVIN EDWARDS	VIBES(A	ROBERT WYATT	V (A
STEVE BERESFORD	B	(A	PHIL BUCKLE	PERC	(A	UTAKO IKEDA	FLT (A	DOMINIC MULDOWNEY	VLA(A
MARTIN MAYES	K	(A	CARLA BLEY	V	(A	ARTHUR RUTHERFORD	PERC (A	RICHARD BERNAS	K PERC(A

STEELY DAN

WALTER BECKER	B V G(ALL	(A) YOU GOTTA WALK IT(SOUNDTRACK)	1971 VISA	US 7005 UK SPARK 78	124				
DONALD FAGEN	K V	(ALL	(B) CANT BUY A THRILL	1972 ABC	US 758 UK PROBE	SPB1062			
DENNY DIAS	G	(ABCDEFG	(B) CANT BUY A THRILL	1974 ABC	UK	ABCL 5024			
VALERIE SIMPSON	V	(J	(B) CANT BUY A THRILL	1982 MCA US 37040					
JOE DISCEPOLO	D	(A	(C) COUNTDOWN TO ECSTASY	1973 ABC	US 779 UK PROBE	SPB1079			
JIM HODDER	D	(BCD	(C) COUNTDOWN TO ECSTASY	1974 ABC	UK	ABCL 5034			
DAVID PALMER	V K	(BC	(C) COUNTDOWN TO ECSTACY	1982 MCA RI UK 1664 US 37041					
MICHAEL BRECKER	SAX	(J	(D) PRETZEL LOGIC	1974 ABC	US 808 UK PROBE	SPBA6282			
JEFF BAXTER	G	(BCD	(D) PRETZEL LOGIC	1974 ABC	UK	ABCL 5045			
RALPH MACDONALD	PERC	(J	(D) PRETZEL LOGIC	198 MCA RI US 37042					
JEFF PORCARO	D	(DEJ	(E) KATY LIED	1975 ABC	US 846 UK	ABCL 5094			
RON MOUNSEY	PNO	(J	(E) KATY LIED	198 MCA US RI 37043					
MIKE McDONALD	V	(EFGJ	(F) THE ROYAL SCAM	1976 ABC	US 931 UK	ABCL 5161			
ANTHONY JACKSON	B	(J	(F) THE ROYAL SCAM	198 MCA US RI 37044					
RICK DERRINGER	G	(CEJ	(G) AJA	1977 ABC	US 1006 UK	ABCL 5225			
ZACK SANDERS	V	(J	(G) AJA	1981 MOBILE 033					
ELLIOTT RANDALL	G	(BEF	(H) GREATEST HITS	(DBL)	1978 ABC	US 1107	UK ABCD 616		
FRANK FLOYD	V	(J	(H) GREATEST HITS	1982 MCA UK MCLD 608					
DEAN PARKS	G	(DEFG	(I) PLUS FOUR (EP)	1977 ABC	UK	ABE 12003			
HUGH McCRACKEN	G	(EJ	(J) GAUCHO	1980 MCA	US 6102	UK MCF 3090			
LARRY CARLTON	G	(EFGJ	(BG) CANT BUY A THRILL/AJA (CASS ONLY)1982 MCA	UK 101					
BEN BENAY	G	(CD	( ) GOLD	1982 MCA UK MCF 3145					
GORDON GRODY	V	(J							
DIVA GRAY	V	(J	LEE RITENOUR	G	(G STEVE KHAN	G	(GJ JAY GRAYDON		G (G
MICHAEL OMARTIAN	K	(DEG	DAVID PAICH	K	(BDE VICTOR FELDMAN PERC K(BCDEFGJ ROYCE JONES				V (C
CHUCK RAINEY	B	(EFGJ	WILTON FELDER	B	(DE HAL BLAINE	D	(E TIM SCHMIT		B V (DFG
PLAS JOHNSON	SAX	(DFG	OLLIE MITCHELL	TPT	(D JEROME RICHARDSON SAX	(BD LEW McCREARY		HRNS (DG
ERNIE WATTS	SAX	(CD	RAY BROWN	B	(C TOM SCOTT	SAX	(GJ WAYNE SHORTER		SAX (G
PAUL HUMPHREY	D	(G	CLYDIE KING	V	(BFG VANETTA FIELDS	V	(BFG SHIRLEY MATTHEWS		V (BCEFG
REBECCA LOUIS	V	(G	JOE SAMPLE	K	(GJ BERNARD PURDIE	D	(FGJ PETE CHRISTLIEB		SAX (G
JIM HORN	SAX	(FG	BILL PERKINS	HRNS	(EG JACKIE KELSO	HRNS	(G CHUCK FINDLEY		HRNS(FG
SLYDE HYDE	TROM	(FG	RICK MAROTTA	D	(FGJ PAUL GRIFFIN	K V	(FG DON GROLNICK		K (FGJ
GARY COLEMAN	PERC	(FG	ED GREENE	D	(G JIM KELTNER	D	(G SNOOKY YOUNG		HRNS(B
MYRNA MATTHEWS	V	(CE	PATRICIA HALL	V	(C JAMES ROLLESTON	V	(C MICHAEL FENELLY		V (C
LANNY MORGAN	SAX	(C	JOHN ROTELLA	SAX	(C BOB FINDLEY	HRNS	(F TUBBY BRUCE		(D
STEVE GADD	D	(GJ	JOHN KLEMMER	HRNS	(F JIM GORDON	D	(D CAROLYN WILLIS		V (E
JIMMIE HASKELL	HRNS	(E	PHIL WOODS	HRNS	(E ERROL BENNETT	PERC	(J MARK KNOPFLER		G (J
DAVE TOFANI	SAX	(J	DAVID SANBORN	SAX	(J RON CUBER	SAX	(J RANDY BRECKER		HRNS (J
PAT REBILLOT	K	(J	GEORGE MARGE	CLAR	(J HIRAM BULLOCK	G	(J WALTER KANE		CLAR (J
LESLIE MILLER	V	(J	NICHOLAS MARRERO PERC(J		PATTI AUSTIN	V	(J WAYNE ANDRE		TROM (J
TONI WINE	V	(J	LANI GROVES	V	(J				

STEELEYE SPAN

ASHLEY HUTCHINGS	B	(ABCE	(A) HARK THE VILLAGE WAIT	1970 RCA	UK	SF8113	
TIM HART	V G DULCIMER (ALL	(A) HARK THE VILLAGE WAIT	1971 UA	UK	UAG 29160		
MADDY PRIOR	V	(ALL	(A) HARK THE VILLAGE WAIT	1974 MOONCREST	UK	CREST 22	
GAY WOODS	V CONC(A	(A) HARK THE VILLAGE WAIT	1976 CHRYSALIS	US	1120		
TERRY WOODS	G V MAND(A	(B) PLEASE TO SEE THE KING	1971 B&C	UK	CAS 1029		
MARTIN CARTHY	G V	(BCLO	(B) PLEASE TO SEE THE KING	1974 MOONCREST	UK	CREST 8	
PETER KNIGHT K V V VLN	(BCDEFGHJKP	(B) PLEASE TO SEE THE KING	1976 CHRYSALIS	US	1119		
GERRY CONWAY	D	(A	(B) PLEASE TO SEE THE KING	1976 BIG TREE	US	2004	
RICK KEMP	B V	(DEFGHJKLOP	(C) TEN MAN MOP	1971 PEGASUS	UK	PEG 9	
BOB JOHNSON	G V	(DEFGHJKP	(C) TEN MAN MOP	1974 MOONCREST	UK	CREST 9	
NIGEL PEGRUM	D FLT(GHJKLP	(C) TEN MAN MOP	1976 CHRYSALIS	US	1121		
JOHN KIRKPATRICK	V ACC(LO	(D) BELOW THE SALT	1972 CHRYSALIS CHR1008 GER 6307 508				
DAVID BOWIE	SAX	(G	(E) INDIVIDUALLY & COLLECTIVELY(COMP) 1972 CHARISMA	UK	CS5		
PETER SELLERS	V UKE(H	(F) PARCEL OF ROGUES	1973 CHRYSALIS		CHR 1046		
DAVE MATTACKS	D	(A	(G) NOW WE ARE SIX	1974 CHRYSALIS CHR1053 GER 6307 529				
			(H) COMMONERS CROWN	1975 CHRYSALIS CHR1071 GER 6307 543			
			(I) ALMANACK (COMP)	1973 CHARISMA	UK	CS12	
			(J) ALL AROUND MY HAT	1975 CHRYSALIS		CHR 1091	
			(K) ROCKET COTTAGE	1976 CHRYSALIS CHR1123 GER 6307 584			
			(L) STORM FORCE 10	1977 CHRYSALIS CHR1151 GER 6307 615			
			(M) ORIGINAL MASTERS(COMP DBL)	1977 CHRYSALIS US 2 1136 UK CJT	3		
			(M) ORIGINAL MASTERS	1977 CHRYSALIS GER 6441 636			
			(N) TIME SPAN	1977 MOONCREST	UK	CRD 1	
			(O) LIVE AT LAST	1978 CHRYSALIS		CHR 1199	
			(P) SAILS OF SILVER	1980 CHRYSALIS CHR1304 GER 203 003			
			( ) STEELEYE SPAN	1980 HALLMARK UK 3040			

[531]

STEPASIDE

```
PAUL ASHFORD      B V (A        (A) SIT DOWN & RELAPSE           1980 STEPASIDE          STEP 001
BRENNY BONASS     G V (A
ROBBIE BRENNAN    D V (A    DAVE KODAK        K V (A
```

JIM STEINMAN

```
JIM STEINMAN      V K(A        (A) BAD FOR GOOD                 1981 CBS   UK 84361 US 36531
ROY BITTAN        K  (A
JOE STEFKO        D  (A    STEVE BUSLOWE     B   (A    KARLA DEVITO      V  (A    ELLEN FOLLEY      V  (A
DAVEY JOHNSTONE   G  (A    LARRY FAST           (A    ALAN SCHWARTZBERG D  (A    TODD RUNDGREN     G V (A
MAX WEINBERG      D  (A    KASIM SULTAN B V     (A    RORY DODD         V  (A    ERIC TROYER       V  (A
ROGER POWELL      SYN (A    JIMMY MAELEN      PERC(A    NEIL JASON           (A
```

LEIGH STEPHENS

```
LEIGH STEPHENS    G V K(AB       (A) RED WEATHER              1969 PHILIPS           UK    SBL7897
PETE SEARS        B   (B         (B) CAST OF THOUSANDS        1971 CHARISMA          UK    CAS 1040
KEVIN WESTLAKE    D   (AB
MICK WALLER       D   (AB   NICKY HOPKINS    K   (A    IAN STEWART          (A    BOB ANDREWS     PNO (B
DICK MORRISSEY    SAX (B    DAVE CASWELL     TPT (B    CHARLENE COLLINS  V  (B    KIM GARDNER     B   (B
TONY ASHTON       PNO (B    ROY DYKE         D   (B    DAVE QUINCY       SAX (B    NOEL NORRIS     TPT (B
ALIKI ASHMAN      V   (B    GLENN CORNICK    B   (B    JEFF PEACH        SAX (B    LYLE JENKINS    SAX (B
DAVE JACKSON      SAX (B    PETER ROSS       V   (B    PAUL MAINTENANCE  V G (B    TREVOR OP       V G (B
ELIZABETH LEGWORTHY V (B
```

STEPPENWOLF

```
JOHN KAY        G V (123456HDMNO (A) STEPPENWOLF               1968 DUNHILL US 50029 UK STATESIDE  5020
TOM SCOTT       HRNS (N         (A) STEPPENWOLF               19   MCA GER 201 578
GEORGE BIONDO   B V (456HMNO    (A) STEPPENWOLF               1968 RCA                 UK      RD  7974
JERRY EDMONTON  D  (123456HMNOD (B) THE SECOND                1968 DUNHILL US 50037 UK STATESIDE  5003
BOBBY COCHRAN   G  (56MNO       (C) AT YOUR  BIRTHDAY PARTY   1969 DUNHILL US 50053 UK STATESIDE  5011
WAYNE COOK      K  (60          (D) EARLY STEPPENWOLF         1969 DUNHILL US 50060 UK STATESIDE  5015
GOLDY McJOHN    K  (12345HD     (E) MONSTER                  1970 DUNHILL US 50066 UK STATESIDE  5021
JOHN MORGAN     B  (2           (F) STEPPENWOLF LIVE          1970 DUNHILL US 50075 UK STATESIDE  5029
RUSHTON MOREVE  B  (1           (F) STEPPENWOLF LIVE          197  ABC  RI           UK         ABCL5007
NICK ST NICHOLAS B (3D          (G) STEPPENWOLF 7             1970 DUNHILL US 50090 UK PROBE  SPBA6254
LARRY BYROM     G  (34          (H) FOR LADIES ONLY           1970 DUNHILL US 50110 UK PROBE  SPBA6260
MICHAEL MONARCH G  (12          (J) STEPPENWOLF GOLD          1971 DUNHILL US 50099 UK PROBE  SPB 1033
(1) 1967                        (J) STEPPENWOLF GOLD          197  ABC                  UK        ABCL8613
(2) 1967                        (K) REST IN PEACE             1972 DUNHILL US 50124 UK PROBE  SPB 1059
(3) 1969                        (L) 16 GREATEST HITS          1974 DUNHILL US 50135 UK PROBE  SPB 1071
(4) 1970                        (L) 16 GREATEST HITS          197  ABC  RI           UK         ABCL5028
(5) 1974                        (M) SLOW FLUX                 1974 EPIC    US 33093 UK            80358
(6) 1974                        (N) HOUR OF THE WOLF          1975 EPIC    US 33583 UK            69151
GABRIEL MEKLER  PROD (A         (O) SKULLDUGGERY              1976 EPIC    US 34120 UK            81328
KENT HENRY         (H          (P) MASTERS OF ROCK           1975 ABC                  EURO   054 95147
ANDY CHAPIN     K  (N          (Q) THE ABC COLLECTION        197  ABC    US 30008
MARS BONFIRE    G  (D          (R) REBORN TO BE WILD         1977 EPIC    US 34382
                               (S) 16 GREAT PERFORMANCES     197  ABC    US  4001
                               (T) BEST                      1979 PICKWICK US 3603
                               (U) GOLD                      1980 MCA UK 1502
```

STEPSON

```
JEFF HAWKS      V  (A          (A) STEPSON                   197  ABC         826
BRUCE HAUSER    B V (A
JOEY NEWMAN     G V (A    LEN FAGAN       D   (A    JIMMY GREENSPOON  K  (A    JEFF SIMMONS    HCA (A
DON GALLUCI     HCA (A
```

STERLING

```
                              (A) CITY KIDS                 1980 A&M 4807 US  UK AMLH64807
```

CAT STEVENS

```
CAT STEVENS      V G K(ALL     (A) MATTHEW & SON             1967 DERAM UK SML1004 US 18005
ALUN DAVIES      G V  (DEFGJL   (B) NEW MASTERS               1968 DERAM UK SML1018 US 18010
GERRY CONWAY     D V  (FGHLJ    (AB) MATTHEW /NEW MASTERS     197  DERAM           US       18005
JEAN ROUSSEL     K    (GHJLN    (C) WORLD OF CAT STEVENS      1970 DECCA           UK       SPA 93
BRUCE LYNCH      B    (JLN      (D) MONA BONE JAKON           1970 ISLAND UK ISLP 9118 US A&M 4260
JIM RYAN         G    (J        (E) TEA FOR THE TILLERMAN     1971 ISLAND UK ILPS 9135 US A&M 4280
MARK WARNER      G    (J        (F) TEASER & THE FIRECAT      1971 ISLAND UK ILPS 9154 US A&M 4313
ROLAND HARKER    BANJ (J        (G) CATCH BULL AT FOUR        1972 ISLAND UK ILPS 9206 US A&M 4365
JOHN RYAN        B    (DE       (H) FOREIGNER                 1973 ISLAND UK ILPS 9240 US A&M 4391
HARVEY BURNS     D    (DEF      (I) THE BEST OF               1973 TELDEC           EURO   17009
PETER GABRIEL    FLT  (D        (J) BUDDAH & THE CHOCOLATE BOX 1974 ISLAND UK ILPS 9274 US A&M 3623
JACK ROSTEIN     VLN  (E        (K) VIEW FROM THE TOP(A+B)    1974 DERAM  UK DPA3019/20
LARRY STEELE     B PERC(F       (L) NUMBERS                   1975 ISLAND UK ILPS 9370 US A&M 4555
ANDREAS TOUMAZIS (FG            (M) GREATEST HITS             1975 ISLAND UK ILPS 9310 US A&M 4519
ANGELOS HATZIPAVLI (F          (N) IZITSO                    1977 ISLAND UK ILPS 9451 US A&M 4702
ALAN JAMES       B   (G         (O) BACK TO EARTH             1978 ISLAND UK ILPS 9565 US A&M 4735
LINDA LEWIS      V   (G         ( ) CATS CRADLE              1978 LONDON            US     50010
BERNARD PURDIE   D   (H         ( ) VERY YOUNG & EARLY SONGS  19   DERAM            US     18061
DAVID SANBORN    SAX (L         ( ) FIRST CUT IS THE DEEPEST  1981 ROCK ECHOES TAB 25
PHIL UPCHURCH        (H
PAUL MARTINEZ        (H    HERBIE FLOWERS   B   (H    PATTI AUSTIN      V  (H    BARBARA MASSEY   V  (H
TASHA THOMAS         (N    JIM JOHNSON          (N    ANDY NEWMARK         (N    BILL BERG          (N
CHICK COREA      K   (N    ELKIE BROOKS     V   (N    ROGER HAWKINS     D  (N    DAVID HOOD       B  (N
BARRY BECKETT        (N    PETE CARR            (N    TIM HENSON           (N    DAVID CAMPBELL     (N
SUZANNE LYNCH        (N    WELDON MYRICK        (N    REGGIE YOUNG         (N    BARRY MORGAN       (N
BRODERICK SMITH      (N    MARJORIE LAGERWALL   (N    CARLA BENSON         (N    EVETTE BENTON      (N
BARBARA INGRAM       (N    RAY GOMEZ        G   (N    SIMON NICOL       G  (L    CHRIS BATERA   PERC(L
GORDIE FLEMING   ACC (L
```

JOHN STEVENS

JOHN STEVENS	D	(ALL	(A) CHALLENGE	1966 EYEMARK EMPL 1002
ALLAN HOLDSWORTH	G	(P	(B) KARYOBIN	1968 ISLAND UK ILPS 9097
JEFF YOUNG	K	(PO	(C) SPONTANEOUS MUSIC ENSEMBLE(OLIV)	1969 MARMALADE 608 008 + 2384 009
RON MATTHEWSON	B	(PD	(D) SOURCE FROM & TOWARDS	1971 TANGENT UK TNGS 107
NICK STEPHENS	B	(MLO	(E) BIRDS OF A FEATHER	1972 BYG FR 529 023
RON HERMAN	B	(EHLMO	(F) SO WHAT DO YOU THINK	1973 TANGENT UK TGS 118
ROBERT CALVERT	SAX	(MLO	(G) FOR YOU TO SHARE	1974 'A' 001
DAVID COLE	G	(MLO	(H) BOBBY BRADFORD PLUS SME	1974 FREEDOM 24865
EVAN PARKER	SAX	(STB	(J) SMO	1975 'A' 003
NIGEL COOMBES	VLN	(R	(K) JOHN STEVENS AWAY	1976 VERTIGO 6360 131
ROGER SMITH	G	(R	(L) SOMEWHERE INBETWEEN	1976 VERTIGO 6360 135
COLIN WOOD	CELLO	(R	(M) 'MAZIN' ENNIT	1977 VERTIGO 6360 141
TREVOR WATTS	SAX	(QUACDEFGHKNV	(N) CHEMISTRY	1977 VINYL VS 1978
BARRY GUY		(QUV	(O) 'AH	1978 VINYL VS 111
HOWARD RILEY	PNO	(U	(P) TOUCHING ON	1978 VINYL VS 105
BOBBY BRADFORD	TPT	(H	(Q) NO FEAR	1978 SPOTLITE SPJ 556
KENNY WHEELER	HRNS	(ABCDFN	(R) BIO SYSTEMS	1978 INCUS 24
PAUL RUTHERFORD	TROM	(A	(S) LONGEST NIGHT VOL 1	1978 OGUN OG 120
BRUCE COLE	B	(A	(T) LONGEST NIGHT VOL 2	1978 OGUN OG 420
JEFF CLYNE	B	(AN	(U) END GAME	1979 JAPO 600 28
DAVE HOLLAND	B	(BF	(V) APPLICATION	197 SPOTLITE SPJ 513
DEREK BAILEY	G	(BCF	(W) & SME VOL 1	1981 NESSA N17
PETE LEMER	K V	(C		

PETE LEMER K V (C   MAGGIE NICHOLLS (C   ROLAND NICHOLLS (C   RAY WARLEIGH WIND(DN
JOHNNY DYANNI B (C
BRIAN SMITH WIND (D   BOB NORDERN TROM (DH   CHRIS PYNE TROM (D   MIKE PYNE PNO (D
MARCO MATTOS B (D   JULIE TIPPETTS G V (EH   WORKSHOP GROUP (G   STEVE HAYTON G (K
PETE COWLING D (K   NIGEL MOYSE G (0   BRENT D'FORDO PERC (L

SHAKIN' STEVENS

SHAKIN'MIKE BARRATT'STEVENS	V	(ALL	(A) THE LEGEND	1970 PARLOPHONE UK PCS 7112
STEVE PRIOR		(	(A) LEGEND	1979 EMI UK RI NUT 25
DICK BLAND	B	(M	(B) I'M NO D J	1971 CBS UK 52901
BRIAN WILLIAMS		(	(C) ROCKIN'N' SHAKIN'	1972 CONTOUR UK 2870152
CARL PETERSON	G	(A	(D) SHAKIN' STEVENS & THE SUNSETS	1973 EMERALD GES1121
TREVOR HAWKINS	PNO	(A	(E) SHAKIN' STEVENS & THE SUNSETS	1974 PHILIPS UK 6478010
STEVE PERCY	B	(A	(F) SHAKIN STEVENS	1978 TRACK UK 2406011
ROBERT LOU LLEWELLYN	D	(AE	(H) MARIE MARIE	198 EPIC UK 84547
PAUL DALLAS	SAX	(A	(H) THIS OLD HOUSE (ONE TRACK DIFF)	1981 EPIC UK 84985
IAN LAWRENCE	G	(E	(I) AT THE ROCKHOUSE	1981 MAGNUM FORCE UKMFLP004
TONY BRITNALL	SAX	(E	( ) TAKE ONE	1980 EPIC UK 83978
MIKE SKUDDER	PNO	(E	( ) SHAKEY	1981 EPIC UK 10027
GEORGE CHICK	B	(E	( ) MANHATTAN	1981 MINT 29
LLOYD JONES	G	(	( ) SHAKIN STEVENS	19 HALLMARK SHM3065
MATCHBOX		(	(M) GIVE ME YOUR HEART	1982 EPIC UK 10035
PETE WINGFIELD	K	(M	( ) HOT DOG	1982 EPIC UK 32126
ALBERT LEE	G	(H		

STU COLEMAN B (HM   GERAINT WATKINS K (HM   BILLY BREMNER G (M   ROGER McKEW G (A
GAVIN POVEY K ACC(M   CHRIS WYLES D (M   RAY BEAVIS SAX (M   JOHN EARLE SAX (M
CHRIS GOWER TROM (M   DICK HANSON TPT (M   B J COLE STEEL(M   MICKEY GEE G (M
HOWARD TIBBLE D (M

B W STEVENSON

B W STEVENSON	G V	(ALL	(A) B W STEVENSON	1972 RCA US LSP 4685
SID SIMS	B	(A	(B) LEAD FREE	1972 RCA US LSP 4794
DON SIMMONS	D	(A	(C) MY MARIA	1973 RCA US APLI 0088
PAT FERRARI	G	(A	(D) CALABASAS	1974 RCA US APLI 0410
RONALD STEELE	G	(A	(E) WE BE SAILIN'	1975 WB US 2901
MICKEY RAPHAEL	HCA	(AB	(F) LOST FEELING	1977 WB US 3012
ED SHOOK	PERC V	(A	(G) BEST OF	1977 RCA US APLI 2394
RICHARD SILEN	PERC	(A	(H) LIFELINE	1980 MCA US MCA 3215
KITTY APPLING	V	(A		

RAY TATE STEEL(A   SHANE APPLING B (A   BRIAN CHRISTIAN TAMB (A   JIM GORDON D (BCD
DENNIS ST JOHN D (B   LARRY CARLTON G (BCD   DEAN PARKS G (B   EMORY GORDY B (B
RED RHODES STEEL(BD   LARRY MUHOBERAC K (BCD   GIB GUILBEAU FDL (B   LARRY MURRAY V (B
THAD MAXWELL V (B   LINDA DILLARD V (B   JOE OSBORN B (CDF   HERB STEINER STEEL MAND(C
LAYTON DE PENNING G (C   RODNEY GARRISON D (C   DONNIE DOLAN D (C   BOBBY RAMBO G (D
JAY PRUITT K (D   BOBBYE HALL PERC (D   JIMMY HASKELL SYN (D   LINDA RONSTADT V (D
DANIEL MOORE V (DE   ANDREW GOLD V (D   KEN EDWARDS V (D   KIM CARNES V (D
DAVE ELLINGTON V (D   JULIA TILLMAN V (D   DARLA GRISER V (D   CASSELL WEBB V (E
FRED KRC D (E   RILEY OSBORNE PNO G(E   STUART SCHULMAN STEEL G (E   WALLER COLLIE B (E
TREVOR LAWRENCE SAX (E   LARRY BUNKER PERC (E   JIM HORN SAX (E   NICK DE CARO STRINGS(E
REGGIE YOUNG G (F   STEVE GIBSON G (FGH   CASEY KELLY G (F   DENNIS LINDE G (F
LARRY LONDIN D (F   SHANE KEISTER PNO (FGH   BOBBY WOOD PNO (F   RON OATES PNO(F
FARRELL MORRIS PERC (F   BUZZ CASON V (F   BERGEN WHITE V STRINGS(FH   CAROL MONTGOMERY V (F
SANDY POSEY V (F   DOTTIE DELEONIBUS V (F   ROGER CLARK D (H   TERRY McMILLAN PERC HCA(H
STEVE SCHAFFER B (H   CHRIS CHRISTIAN V (H   JON GION G (H   BOBBY OGDIN K (H
DIANE TIDWELL V (H   SHERI CRAMER V (H   LISA SILVER V (H

AL STEWART

AL STEWART	G V K	(ALL	(A) BEDSITTER IMAGES	1967 CBS UK 63087 RI 64023
MARVIN PRESTWICK	G	(B	(B) LOVE CHRONICLES	1969 CBS UK 63460
JIMMY PAGE	G	(B	(C) ZERO SHE FLIES	1970 CBS UK 63848
SIMON BRECKENRIDGE	G	(B	(D) ORANGE	1972 CBS UK 64730
ASHLEY HUTCHINGS	B	(B	(E) PAST, PRESENT & FUTURE	1974 CBS UK 65726 US JANUS 3063
BRIAN ODGERS	B	(BDE	(F) MODERN TIMES	1975 CBS UK 80477 US JANUS 7012
BRIAN BROCKLEHURST	B	(B	(G) YEAR OF THE CAT	1976 RCA UK RS1082 US JANUS 7072
MARK VOLMAN	V	(L	(G) YEAR OF THE CAT	1981 ARISTA 9503 3015
MARTYN FRANCIS	D	(B	(H) THE EARLY YEARS	1978 RCA UK PL25131
HOWARD KAYLAN	V	(L	(H) THE EARLY YEARS (DBL)	1978 US JANUS 2 7026
HARVEY BURNS	D	(B	(J) TIME PASSAGES	1978 RCA UK PL25173 US ARISTA 4190
ROBIN LAMBLE	B V	(JKLM	(J) TIME PASSAGE	1981 RCA UK RI 3026
HIL PHILLIPS	K	(B	(K) 24 VCARROTS	1980 RCA UK PL25306 US ARISTA 9520
STEPHEN GRAY	G	(C	(K) 24 VCARROTS	1981 RCA UK RI 3042
GEORG HULTGREEN	G	(C	(L) INDIAN SUMMER	1981 RCA UK LP 9001 ARISTA US

(CONTINUED)

```
GERRY CONWAY      D    (CF       (M) THE LIVE RADIO CONCERT ALBUM   1979 ARISTA            SP40
ART TRIPP        PERC (J         (N) LIVE INDIAN SUMMER             1981 RCA UK PL 25391
MIKE WOODS            (C

LARRY STEELE      (C     ADAN YURMAN  G V (KLMN   BRYAN SAVAGE   WIND (LKN  HARRY STINSON   D V (LKMN
TIM HINKLEY      K   (CE  DUFFY POWER      (C     LOUIS CENNAMO  B   (C     PETER GAVIN     D  (C
TIM RENWICK      G (DEFGJ CAL BATCHELOR B  (D     TIM WALKER     G   (D     BRINSLEY SCHWARZ G (D
RICK WAKEMAN     K   (DE  BOB ANDREWS   K  (DE    BRUCE THOMAS   B   (DE    JOHN WILSON     D  (DE
ROGER POPE       D   (D   GRAHAM HUNT   D  (D     JOHN DONELLY     V   (DE  MICK WELTON     V  (DE
KEVIN POWERS     V   (DE  PETE BERRYMAN G  (E     ISAAC GUILLORY G   (EF    B J COLE  STEEL    (E
PETER WOOD       K  (EFGJ BOB SARGEANT  K  (E     ALISTAIR ANDERSON CONC (E DAVE SWARBRICK MAND(E
HAIM ROMANO      MAND (E  LUCIANO BRAVO PERC (E   LENNOX JAMES   PERC (E    MICHAEL OLIVER  PERC(E
FRANK RICOTTI    PERC (E  ROGER MEDDOWSTAYLOR PERC(E FRANCIS MONKMAN SYN (E  KRYSIA KOCJAN      (E
DAVE ELLIS       G   (F   SIMON NICOL   G  (F     STUART COWELL  G   (F     PETE WINGFIELD K  (F
GEORGE FORD      B   (FG  PETER MOSS    B  (F     BARRY DE SOUZA V   (F     TONY CARR      PERC(F
GRAHAM SMITH     HCA (FG  CHAS MILLS    V  (F     BRIAN BENNETT  V   (F     NEIL LANCASTER V  (F
PETER WHITE  G K(GJKLM    DON LOBSTER   K  (G     STUART ELLIOTT D   (GJ    BOBBY BRUCE    VLN (G
PHIL KENZIE      SAX (GJ  MARION DRISCOLL PERC (G DAVID PACK     V   (GJ    TONY RIVERS    V  (G
JOHN PERRY       V   (G   PETER ROBINSON K  (J    JEFF PORCARO   D   (J     TREVOR LUCAS   G  (G
STEVE CHAPMAN    PERC (LK JERRY McMILLAN VLN (LK  KEN NICOL      V   (K     ROBERT MARLETTE K (K
RUSS KUNKEL      D   (K   MARK SANDERS  D  (K     JEFF PORCARO   D   (K     BEAU SEGAL     D  (K
LENNY CASTRO     PERC (K  ROBIN WILLIAMSON MAND (K SYLVIA WOODS  HARP (K     PHIL KENZIE    SAX (M
ROBERT ALPERT    K   (M   MARK GOLDENBURG G (J    PETE SOLLEY    K   (J     AL PERKINS     STEEL(J
KRYSIA KRISTIANNE V(HJKLMN JOE PUERTA       (J    JAMES ROBERT WEST V (J    BRIAN HUDDY    V  (J
JEFF BORGESON    V   (J
```

```
BILLY STEWART         (A      (A) CROSS MY HEART                1976 CHESS      US     50059
```

```
GARY STEWART     G V (ALL     (A) YOU'RE NOT THE WOMAN      1975 MCA      US              488
HAROLD BRADLEY   G B (F       (B) OUT OF HAND               1975 RCA LSA 3215     APLI 0900
TERRY McMILLAN   HCA (F       (C) STEPPIN' OUT              1976 RCA LSA 3266     APLI 1225
HAL RUGG         STEEL(F      (D) YOUR PLACE OR MINE        1977 RCA PL12199      APLI 2199
WELDON MYRICK    STEEL(F      (E) LITTLE JUNIOR             1978 RCA             APLI 2779
REGGIE YOUNG     G   (F       (F) GARY                      1979 RCA PL 13288    APLI 3288
BOBBY WOOD       PNO  (F      (G) CACTUS & ROSE             1981 RCA PL 3637
PIG ROBBINS      K   (F       (H) GREATEST HITS             1981 RCA    3981
HENRY STRZELECKI B   (F
MIKE LEECH       B   (F    JERRY SHOOK    G  (F   BUDDY HARMON  D  (F  JERRY CARRIGAN  D (F
HAYWARD BISHOP   D   (F    DALE SELLERS   G  (F   BOB EMMONS    K  (F
```

```
JOHN STEWART     G V (ALL     (A) SIGNALS THROUGH THE GLASS  1968 CAPITOL US ST 2975 RI 1975 SM2975
WENDY WALDMAN    V   (K       (A) SIGNALS THROUGH THE GLASS  1979 CAPITOL 11988
BUFFY FORD       V  (ACDEGIJL (B) CALIFORNIA BLOODLINES      1969 CAPITOL US ST 203    UK     EST203
BLAISE TOSTI     V   (K       (B) CALIFORNIA BLOODLINES      1979 CAPITOL 11987
FRED CARTER      G B (BCD     (C) WILLARD                    1970 CAPITOL US ST 540    UK     EST540
LINDA RONSTADT   V   (K       (C) WILLARD                    1979 CAPITOL 11989
CHARLIE McCOY    HCA (BCF     (D) LONESOME PICKER RIDES AGAIN 1971 WB   US WS1948   UK        K46135
KENNY BUTTREY    D   (BCI     (E) SUNSTORM                   1972 WB   US BS2611
LLOYD GREEN      STEEL(B      (F) CANNONS IN THE RAIN        1973 RCA  US LSP 4827 UK    SF 8359
NORBERT PUTNAM   B   (BC      (G) CANNONS IN THE RAIN        197  RCA  US AYLI 3731
BUDDY HARMON     D   (BF      (G) PHOENIX CONCERTS LIVE      1974 RCA  US CPLZ 0265 UK   PL20265
HARGUS ROBBINS   PNO (BF      (H) WINGLESS ANGELS            1975 RCA  US APLI 0816 UK    SF 8437
JERRY SMITH      K   (B       (I) FIRE IN THE WIND_          1977 RSO  US RS  13027 UK    2394 194
BEEGIE CRUZER    K   (B       (J) BOMBS AWAY DREAM BABIES    1979 RSO  US RS  13051 UK    2394 228
BERGEN WHITE     V  (BF       (K) DREAM BABIES GO HOLLYWOOD  1980 RSO  US RS  13074 UK  RSD 5007
JOHN'BUCK' WILKIN G (BF       (L) IN CONCERT                 1980 RCA  US AFLI 3513
MARI JOHN WILKIN V  (B        (M) FORGOTTEN SONGS...         1980 RCA             UK   PL43155
JAMES TAYLOR     G V (C

JOEL BISHOP O'BRIEN D (C  RUSS KUNKEL    D (CDEHJK BILL MUNDI        PERC (CE PETER ASHER    V PERC(CD
BRYAN GAROFALO B V(CDEIJ CAROLE KING   PNO (C   MICHAEL STEWART G V(CDEGL DOUG KERSHAW  FDL V (C_
BOBBY THOMPSON BANJ (C    RALPH SCHUCKETT K (C  ABIGALE HANESS   V  (C    DANNY KOOTCH   G  (C
CHRIS DARROW FDL DOBRO(CDF PETER FULLERTON V (D HENRY DILTZ   V HCA (DEK RICK CUNHA    V  (D
JENNIFER       V  (D     KATE TAYLOR   V (D    JIMMY HASKELL  ACC STRING(DE LOREN NEWKIRK PNO (DEGL
KING ERRISON   PERC (DE  BUDDY EMMONS STEEL(DE GLEN D HARDIN   PNO (DE LEE SKLAR      B  (D
ARNIE MOORE  B V(DEFGHL  RON TUTT      D  (EH  DAVID KEMPER    D   (E  JERRY SCHEFF   B  (D
LARRY KNECHTEL PNO (E    JAMES BURTON G DOB(E  BILL CUNNINGHAM FDL (E  MIKE DEASY     G  (E
LARRY CARLTON  G   (E    GARY DAVID   PERC (E  JIM HORN        HRNS (E CHARLES FINDLEY HRNS (E
PAUL HUBINSON  HRNS (E   JACK CARONE   V  (E   LAURA CREAMER   V   (E  JONATHAN DOUGLASK PERC(GHL
JIM GORDON     D   (GL   DAN DUGMORE STEEL(GHL MIKE SETTLE     V  (GHL DENNY BROOKS    V (GHIL
JOE OSBORN     B   (H    PETER JAMESON G  (H   ROBERT WACHTEL  G   (H  TOM KEENE      PNO (H
STEPHANIE FORD V   (H    DANIEL MOORE  V  (H   MARTI McCALL    V   (H  JACKIE WARD    V  (H
LISA FREEMAN ROBERTS V (H JON WOODHEAD G (I    TROY SEALS      G   (I  REGGIE YOUNG   G  (I
JOEY HARRIS  G V (IJ     DAVE KIRBY    G  (I   SHANE KEISTER   K   (I  DAVID BRIGGS   K  (I
BILL CUOMO   K   (I      MICKEY RAPHAEL HCA (I GARY WEISBERG D PERC(IJ CHRIS WHALEN   V  (IJK
JOHN WILLIAMS B  (I      HERB PEDERSEN V  (I   LINDSEY BUCKINGHAM G V (J JOEY CARBONE   G  (JK
MIKE BOTTS   D   (J      STEVE NICKS   V  (J   MARY TORREY     V   (J  RICHARD SCHLOSSER D(J
CHRISTINE DE LISLE V (J  MARY KAY PLACE V (J   DAVID JACKSON   B   (J  CROXLEY GUARD  V  (J
DEBORAH TOMPKINS V (J    CATHERINE GUARD V (J  WAYNE HUNT      K   (J  DAVID PLATSHON D  (K
STEVE ROSS   PERC (K     PHIL EVERLY    V (K   SYDNEY FOX      V   (K  NICOLETTE LARSON V (K
```

```
ROD STEWART      V   (ALL     (A) AN OLD RAINCOAT ...       1970 VERTIGO UK VO4       US MERCURY SR61237
CARMINE APPICE   D V (JMQ     (B) GASOLINE ALLEY            1970 VERTIGO UK 6360 500 US MERCURY SR61264
PHIL CHEN        B V (JM      (C) EVERY PICTURE TELLS A STORY 1971 MERCURY UK 6338 063 US   SRM1 609
RICK GRETCH      VLN (F       (C) EVERY PICTURE TELLS A STORY 1977 MERCURY CAN 6336 548
JOHN JARVIS      K   (JH      (D) NEVER A DULL MOMENT       1972 MERCURY UK 6499 153 US   SRMI 646
BILLY PEEK       G   (JMH     (E) SING IT AGAIN ROD         1973 MERCURY UK 6499 484 US   SRMI 680
JIM CREGAN       G  (JMOPQ    (F) SMILER                    1974 MERCURY UK 9104 001 US   SRM11017
GARY GRAINGER    G  (JM       (G) ATLANTIC CROSSING         1975 WB    UK  K56151 US WB    2875
PETE CARR        G   (G       (H) A NIGHT ON THE TOWN       1976 RIVA  UK RVLP 1  US WB    3116
STEVE CROPPER    G  (GH       (I) SHOT OF RHYTHM & BLUES    1976 CRYSTAL 98198 +PRIVATE STOCK PS  2021
KEITH EMERSON    K  (A        (AB) VINTAGE YEARS 1969/70    1976 MERCURY UK 6672 013 GER 6641 414
JESSE ED DAVIS   G  (G        (J) FOOTLOOSE & FANCY FREE    1977 RIVA UK RVLP5 WB US 3092 GER 56423

     (CONTINUED)
```

S273   **ROD STEWART**   (CONTINUED)   S273

```
JIMMY JOHNSON      G   (G        (K) THE BEST OF              1977 MERCURY UK 6643 030 US      SRM27507
FRED TACKETT       G   (GMH      (L) BEST OF VOL 2            1977 MERCURY                US      SRM27509
DAVID LINDLEY VLN MAND (GH       (M) BLONDES HAVE MORE FUN    1978 RIVA UK RVLP8 WB US 3261 PIC DISC 3276
DONALD DUNN        B   (GH       (N) GREATEST HITS            1979 RIVA      UK RODTV1   US WB       3373
BOB CLAN           G   (G        (O) HOT RODS                 1980 MERCURY UK 6463 061
DAVID HOOD         B   (G        (P) FOOLISH BEHAVIOUR        1980 RIVA      UK RVLP 11  US WB 3485
MEMPHIS HORNS          (GH       (Q) TONIGHT I'M YOURS        1981 RIVA UK RVLP14 WB US 3602
ELTON JOHN         K V (F        ( ) MAGGIE MAY               1981 CONTOUR UK 2043
ANDY NEWMARK       D   (FH       ( ) VOL 1                    1981 MERCURY UK 7145 069
WILLIE WEEKS       B   (FH
MICK WALLER        D  (ABCDF  PETE SEARS        PNO(BCDF RON WOOD        B G(ABCF MARTIN QUITTENTON G (ABCDF
IAN McLAGAN      ORG(ABCDF  DANNY THOMPSON    B   (C   ANDY PYLE       B   (C   DICK POWELL     VLN(BCDF
MADELINE BELL      V   (C   KENNY JONES       D   (BDF MARTIN PUGH     G   (A   TOM VIG         PERC(MHQ
LINDA LEWIS        V   (MQ  MIKE FINNIGAN     V   (M   MAX GRONENTHAL  V   (M   SPIKE HEATLEY   B   (DF
GORDON HUNTLEY   STEEL(D    RONNIE LANE       B   (BD  DUANE HITCHINGS K   (MQ  ROGER BETHELMY  D   (M
PAULINHO DA COSTA PERC(MQ   NICKY HOPKINS     K   (M   GARY HERBIG     FLT (M   PHIL KENZIE     HRNS(M
STEVE MADAIO       TPT (M   TOM SCOTT        WIND(M    SAM MITCHELL    G   (BC  DENNIS O'FLYNN  VLN(B
MIKE D'ABO         PNO (A   RAY JACKSON      MAND(F    DUCK DUNN       B   (H   RON GLAUB       B   (H
LEE SKLAR          B   (H   JOE WALSH         G   (H   DAVID FOSTER    K   (H   J SMITH         K   (H
RICK SCLOSSER      D   (H   ROGER HAWKINS     D   (H   AL JACKSON      D   (H   JOE LALA        PERC(H
JIMMY HORDWITZ     STR (H   MEL LEWIS         STR (H   A MARDIN        STR (H   TOWER OF POWER  HRNS(H
JERRY JUMONVILLE   SAX (H   PLAS JOHNSON      SAX (H   TONY BROCK      D V (Q   JAY DAVIS       B   (Q
JEFF BAXTER        G   (Q   KEVIN SAVIGAR     K   (Q   DANNY JOHNSON   G   (Q   ROBIN LEMESURIER G  (Q
BYRON BERLINE      FDL (Q   PENTECOSTAL COMM CHOIR V(Q TROPIC ISLE STEEL BAND (F CHRIS BARBERS JAZZ BAND (F
PENNY JONES        V   (Q
```

S274   **STICKY FINGERS**   S274

```
BARRY KEANE        D   (A        (A) STICKY FINGERS           1978 EPIC UK 83612
ERROL THOMAS       B   (A
MICHAEL TOLES      G   (A   BRIAN RUSSELL     G   (A   CARL MARSH      K   (A   DICK SMITH  PERC (A
GUIDO BASSO        HRNS(A   AL STANWICK       HRNS(A   RUSS LITTLE     HRNS(A   GARY MORGAN HRNS  (A
ROB McCONNELL      HRNS(A   EUGENE AMARO      HRNS(A   PHYLLIS DUNCAN  V   (A   HELEN DUNCAN      V (A
```

S274A   **ARBEE STIDHAM**   S274A

```
ARBEE STIDHAM          (AB       (A) ARBEES BLUES             19   FOLKWAYS  US    3824
                                 (B) TIRED OF WONDERING        19   BLUESVILLE US 1021
```

S275   **STIFF LITTLE FINGERS**   S275

```
BRIAN FALOON       D   (AB       (A) INFLAMMABLE MATERIAL     1979 ROUGH TRADE      UK   ROUGH 1
HENRY CLUNEY       G   (ABCD      (B) NOBODYS HERO             1980 CHRYSALIS UK CHR 1270 NL 511270
JAKE BURNS         G V (ABCD      (C) HANX                     1980 CHRYSALIS UK CHR1300 GER 202916
JIM REILLY         D   (BCD       (D) GO FOR IT                1981 CHRYSALIS UK CHR1339 GER 203645
ALI McMORDIE       B   (ABCD
```

S275A   **STILL LIFE**   S275A

```
                                 (A) STILL LIFE               1971 VERTIGO    UK 6360 026
```

S275B   **STILL ROCK**   S275B

```
DON PRESTON            (A        (A) STILL ROCK               19   ENTERPRISE US   731016
```

S276   **STEPHEN STILLS**   S276

```
STEPHEN STILLS     G V (ALL      (A) STEPHEN STILLS           1970 ATLANTIC UK 2401 004 US      7202
PAUL HARRIS        K   (BG       (A) STEPHEN STILLS           1972 ATLANTIC UK K40341  RI
DALLAS TAYLOR      D   (ABC      (B) STEPHEN STILLS TWO       1971 ATLANTIC UK 2401 013 US      7206
CALVIN SAMUELS     B V (ABC      (B) STEPHEN STILLS TWO       1972 ATLANTIC UK K40249  RI
JERRY AIELLO       K   (CDE      (C) STILLS                   1975 CBS      UK 69146  US     33575
JOE LALA           PERC (CDEG    (D) STILLS LIVE              1975 ATLANTIC UK K50214  US     18156
DONNIE DACUS       G V (CDE      (E) ILLEGAL STILLS           1976 CBS      UK 81330  US     34148
RUSS KUNKEL        D   (CD       (F) THE BEST OF(STILL STILLS) 1976 ATLANTIC UK K50327  US     18201
KENNY PASSARELLI   B   (CD       (G) THOROUGHFARE GAP         1978 CBS      UK 82859  US     35380
RICK ROBERTS       G V (C        (AB) TWO ORIGINALS           1975 ATLANTIC GER            60063
MIKE FINNIGAN      B   (G        (X) SUPER SESSIONS(SEE AL KOOPER)
DAVE MASON         V   (G
NEIL YOUNG         G V (F    GERRY TOLMAN      G   (G   MIKE FINNIGAN   B   (G   VERNA RICHARDSON V(G
GEORGE TERRY       G   (CG   JOE VITALE        D   (EG  DAVID CROSBY    V   (ACD GRAHAM NASH     V  (AC
BETTY WHITE        V   (C    LEE SKLAR         B   (C   TUBBY ZIEGLER   D   (CE  GEORGE PERRY    B  (EG
HOWARD KAYLAN      V   (E    MARK VOLMAN       V   (E   JEFF WHITTAKER  CONGA(A  RITA COOLIDGE   V  (A
PRISCILLA JONES    V   (A    JOHN SEBASTIAN    V   (A   SHIRLEY MATTHEWS V  (A   CONRAD ISADORE  D  (AB
JUDITH POWELL      V   (A    LIZA STRIKE       V   (A   LARRY STEELE    V   (A   TONY WILSON     V  (A
JIMI HENDRIX       G   (A    ERIC CLAPTON      G   (A   JOHN BARBATA    D   (A   CLAUDIA LENNEAR V  (A
CASS ELLIOT        V   (A    RICHIE HAYWARD    D   (A   BOOKER T JONES  K   (A   SYDNEY GEORGE   WIND(AB
GASPAR LAWAL       PERC (B    DR JOHN          K   (B   NILS LOFGREN    G K V(B  JAMES MITCHELL  SAX (B
FLOYD NEWMAN       SAX (B    ED LOGAN          SAX (B   JACK HALE       TROM (B  ANDREW LOVE     SAX (B
ROGER HOPPS        HRNS (B    WAYNE JOHNSON    HRNS (B  ROCKY DZIDZORNU PERC (B  HENRY DILTZ     V  (B
FEARLESS FREDDY    V   (B    DANNY KORTCHMAR   G V (G   ANDY GIBB       V   (G   PAUL LEE        D  (G
AL GOULD           FDL (G    KENNY KIRKLAND    PNO (G   RICHARD O'CONNELL D (G   GERALD JOHNSON  B  (G
ALBY GALUTEN       K   (G    KITTY PRITIKEN    V   (G   BROOKS HUNNICUTT K  (G   LISA ROBERTS    V  (G
JOEY MERCIA        V   (G    JOHN SAMBATERO    V   (G   WHIT SIDENER    FLT (G
```

S276A   **STILLS/ YOUNG BAND**   S276A

```
STEPHEN STILLS     G V (A        (A) LONG MAY YOU RUN         1976 REPRISE    UK K54081 US 2253
NEIL YOUNG         G V (A
JOE LALA           PERC (A   JERRY AIELLO      K   (A   JOE VITALE      FLT D(A  GEORGE PERRY    B  (A
```

S277   **STILLWATER**   S277

```
MIKE CAUSEY        G   (AB       (A) STILLWATER              1977 CAPRICORN US 0186  UK 2429 155
JIMMY HALL         V PERC(AB      (B) I RESERVE THE RIGHT     1979 CAPRICORN US 0210  UK 2429 176
BOBBY GOLDEN       G   (AB
SEBIE LACEY        D V (AB   ALLISON SCARBOROUGH B V(AB ROB WALKER      G V (AB  BOB SPEARMAN    K  (AB
```

S278   **STINGRAY**   S278

```
DENNIS EAST        V   (A        (A) STINGRAY                1979 CARRERE US 38127      CAL 113
ALLAN GOLDSWAIN    K   (A
MIKE PILOT         G V (A    EDDIE BOYLE       B   (A   SHAUN WRIGHT    D   (A   DANNY ANTHILL   ORG (A
```

S279   **STINKY TOYS**   S279

```
ELLI MEDEIROS      V   (A        (A) STINKY TOYS             1977 POLYDOR         UK   2393 174
BRUNO CARONE       G   (A
JACNO              G   (A    ALBIN DERIAT      B   (A   HERVE ZENOUDA   D   (A
```

```
ALAN STIVELL    V FLT PIPES(ALL    (A) RENAISSANCE OF CELTIC HARP      1972 PHILIPS FR 6414406
YANN JAKEZ HASSOLD V   (EG         (B) A L'OLYMPIA                     1972 FONTANA FR 6325321    6399  005
DAN AR BRAS        G   (ABCEFGK     (C) ALAN STIVELL REFLECTIONS       1973 FONTANA              6399  008
RENE WERNEER       FDL (BCEFK       (D) FROM CELTIC ROOTS              1974 FONTANA              6325  304
ALAN KLOATR    FLT BOD(AEF          (E) A LANGONNED                    1975 FONTANA  9101 500    6325  332
LIAM WELDON        BOD (E           (F) IN DUBLIN                      1975 FONTANA              9299  547
YANN-FANCH AR MERDY D(AE            (G) BEFORE LANDING                 1977 FONTANA              9286  999
LOEIZ ROUJON       D   (E           (H) SUZI MACGUIRE                  1978 IMPACT               6886  122
JANNLUG FAUCHON     D  (E           (J) SYMPHONIE CELTIQUE (DBL)       1980 CBS                        88487
JEAN LUC HALLERAU B V  (K           (K) CELTIC ROCK                    19   VERTIGO    GER 6325 251
BERNARD LEVASSELLY B   (C           (L) 3RD INTERNATIONAL TOUR         1979 METRONOME  GER 60 200
YOVENN SICARD      BOMBA(E
GABRIEL YACOUB G DULC (BCK  PASCAL STIVE      K(BCFK   GERARD LEVASSEUR   B    (AB  HENRI DELAGARDE CELLOFLT(ABC
MICHEL SANTANGELI D(BCFK    SERJ PARAYRE      PERC (BC MIKAEL KLEC'H      FLT  (BC  DANIELE BAROLLETTI  V (A
MICHEL DELAPORTE  PERC (AK  GUY CASCALES      D    (A  GERARD SALKOWSKY   B    (A   GILLES TINAYJRE     K (A
MIK AR BIZ        BOMBA(AF  JEAN MARC DOLLEZ  B    (A  ANNE GERMAIN       V    (A   CLAUDE GERMAIN      V (A
JEAN CLAUDE BRION  V   (A   FRANCOISE WALL    V    (A  JACQUES HENDRIX    V    (A   PADRIG KERRE   FDL DULC(A
ANDREW HERVE       K   (G   MIKAEL HERVE      B    (G  JEAN LUC DANNA     D    (G   DAVE SWARBRICK     FDL(G
MARIA POPKIEWICZ   V   (G   CLEMENT BAILLY    D    (G  DOMINIQUE LURO     K    (G   PATRICK KIFFER      B (G
ALAIN HATOT        SAX (G   ADAM SKEAPING     CELLO(G  LYN DOBSON FLT SITAR PERC(G   RICHARD HARVEY     WIND(G
BAGAD BLEIMOR WIND D   (GK  CHRIS HAYWARD FLT PERC(JL  ROBBY FINKEL       K    (J   MICHEL PREZMAN      K (J
DOMINIQUE WIDIEZ   K   (J   MARC PERRU        G    (JL MIKAEL VALY        B    (J   ROGER SECCO         D (J
PADRIG KERRE FDL MAND(JL    ORCHESTRA & CHOIR      (J  MARIE YACOUB       PERC V(K  ELYANE WERNEER      V (K
MIREILLE WERNEER   V   (K   JACKY THOMAS      B    (K  PADRIG SICARD      BOMB (F   DOMINIQUE MOLLARD   D(F
PADRIG MOLLARD    PIPES(F   PIERRE MAYEL      PIPES(F  MIKAEL AR VALY     B    (L   CHRISTIAN PIGET  K (L
UJAN HERVE         D   (L
```

```
ORVILLE STOEBER   G V  (A          (A) ORVILLE STOEBER                1971 UNI                  UNLS  120
HARRY PALMER       G   (A
RAY BARRETT        K   (A   GEORGE DUVIVIER   B    (A
```

```
SIMON STOKES       V   (ALL         (A) SIMON STOKES & THE NIGHTHAWKS  1971 MGM         US      MGM S4677
BUTCH SENNEVILLE   G   (AB          (B) & THE BLACK WHIP THRILL BAND   1973 SPINDIZZY   US            32075
RANDALL KEITH      G   (A           (C) BUZZARD OF LOVE                197  U A
ROBERT LEDGER      B   (A
JOE YUELE          D   (A   JOHN LOCKE        K    (B  HARRY GARFIELD     K    (B   CHRISTIAN PENNICK  G (B
MARTY TRYON        B   (A   BILLY GOODNICK    D    (B  DAVID LUELL        SAX  (C   CLARK GASSMAN     SYN (C
MAX MENNITT        B   (C   JAT GRAYDON       G    (C  JIM SHULMAN        PERC (C   FRANK CAPP       PERC(C
HAL BLAINE         D   (C   PETER MAUFFU      G    (C  STANLEY SCHWARTZ   K    (C   MAXINE WATERS      V (C
JULIA WATERS       V   (C   ORIN WATERS       V    (C
```

```
                                   (A) IN'N'OUT                       1980 GORDY US 991
                                   (A) BOYS ARE BACK                  1981 GORDY US 1001 UK MOTOWN 12150
```

```
LINDA RONSTADT     V   (ABCDE       (A) STONE PONEYS                  1967 CAPITOL     US      ST  2666
BOB KIMMEL         G   (ABCDE       (B) EVERGREEN VOL 2               1967 CAPITOL     US      ST  2763
KEN EDWARDS        G   (ABCDE       (C) STONE PONEYS & FRIENDS VOL 3  1968 CAPITOL     US      ST  2863
BILLY MUNDI        D   (A           (D) STONE PONEYS FEATURING L RONSTADT 1976 CAPITOL US      ST 11383
JOHN T FORSHA      B   (A           (E) STONEY END                    1972 PICKWICK            SPC  3298
JAMES E BOND JR    B   (A
CYRUS FARYAR       G   (A   PETE CHILDS       G    (A
```

```
LES HARVEY         G   (ALL         (A) STONE THE CROWS               1970 POLYDOR US 244019  UK 2425  017
MAGGIE BELL        V   (ALL         (B) ODE TO JOHN LAW               1970 POLYDOR            UK 2425  042
JOHN McGINNIS      K   (ABE         (C) TEENAGE LICKS                 1971 POLYDOR US PD5020  UK 2425  071
COLIN ALLEN        D   (ALL         (D) 'ONTINUOUS PERFORMANCE        1972 POLYDOR US    5037 UK 2391  043
JIM DEWAR          B   (ABE         (E) STONE THE CROWS(COMP)         1976 POLYDOR/FLASHBACK UK 2482  279
RONNIE LEAHY       K   (CDE
STEVE THOMPSON     D   (CDE JIMMY McCULLOCH   G    (DE ROGER BALL         HRNS (D   MALCOLM DUNCAN    HRNS(D
WEE MARIE              (C   DUNDEE HORNS           (C
```

```
BRIAN LOUSLEY      D V  (A          (A) STONEBOLT                     1978 PARACHUTE  US 9006 UK RRL  2006
JOHN WEBSTER       K   (A           (B) KEEP IT ALIVE                 1980 RCA                PL 10357
DAVID WILLS        V   (A           (C) A NEW SET OF CHANGES          1980 RCA        US 1 3825
DANNY AITCHISON    B   (A
RAY ROPER          G V (A
```

```
LOU STONEBRIDGE HCA G K V(A         (A) CORPORATE MADNESS             1980 RCA               UK  PL 25275
TOM McGUINNESS     G   (A
ROY MORGAN         D   (A   PAUL KARAS        B    (A  MO FOSTER         B    (A   MIKE MORAN    PROD K (A
NICKY PAYNE        SAX (A   DICK HANSON       TPT  (A  CHRIS GOWER       TROM (A   JOHN 'IRISH' EARLE SAX(A
RAY BEAVIS         SAX (A   FRANK RICOTTI     PERC (A  CHARLIE FAWN      V    (A   MORRIS PERT PERC(A
```

```
SAL VALENTINO      G V (ABC         (A) STONEGROUND                   1971 WB   US WS 1895    UK K46087
TIM BARNES         G V (ABCDE       (B) FAMILY ALBUM                  1971 WB   US WS 1956    UK K53999
JOHN BLAKELEY      G B (ABC         (C) STONEGROUND THREE             1972 WB   US BS 2645
PETE SEARS         K B (A           (D) FLAT OUT                      1976 FLAT OUT  US       FOR 001
MICHAEL MAU        D   (A           (E) HEARTS OF STONE               1978 WB   US BSK3187 GER      56543
LUTHER BILDT       G V (A           (F) PLAY IT LOUD                  1980 CRYSTAL   US 5009
AMANDO PERAZA      CONGA(D
LYNNE HUGHES       V   (ABC DEIRDRE LAPORTE  V   (ABC ANNIE SAMPSON  V (ABCD LYDIA PHILLIPS   V  (A
RON NAGLE          K   (A   BRIAN CRODULA    V   (B   LYDIA MORERO    V (BC  STEPHEN PRICE      (B
CORY LERIOS        V   (BC  JO BAKER         V   (ED  TERRY DAVIS     B V (ED LENNY LEE GOLDSMITH V(E
SAMMY PIAZZA       D   (D   FRED WEBB        K   (ED  BOB GAUDIO      K  (E   JERRY PETERSON   SAX(D
STEVE FONTANA      PERC (E  TERRY CLEMENTS   HRNS (C  DAVID McCULLOUGH B  (C  DANNY ARMSTRONG  TROM(D
JULES BROUSSARD    SAX (D   CAL LEWISTON     TPT  (D  JACK SCHROER    SAX (D
```

```
PETER SEARING      G V (A           (A) STONEHOUSE CREEK              1971 RCA              UK  SF 8197
JAMES SMITH        V   (A
IAN SNOW           D   (A   TERRY PARKER      B    (A
```

```
ROB STONER             (A           (A) PATRIOTIC DUTY                1980 MCA  US 5118
```

[536]

S284C   PAUL STOOKEY   S284C
    PAUL STOOKEY   (A   (A) PAUL AND....   197 WB US 1912 RI UK MYRRH 1074
    MAKEL LEWIS   G STEEL (A   (B) ONE NIGHT STAND   197 WB US 2674
    DANNY TURBEVILLE V (A   (C) BAND & BODY WORKS   1980 MYRRH   UK   1087
    JIMMY NAILS   G V (A
    MICHAEL EPSTEIN D V (A   BARRY FLAST K   (A EDDIE MOTTAU   V G PERC(A JIM MASON B V (A
    PAUL PRESTOPINO G (A   CAMERON KOTLER CELLO(A
S284D   RONNIE STOOTS   S284D
    RONNIE STOOTS   V (A   (A) ASHES TO ASHES   1972 TMI   US 1002
    STEVE CROPPER   G (A
    PAUL CANNON   G (A   TIM GOODWIN G   (A DAVID MAYO   G V (A JIM JOHNSON B (A
    J A SPELL   K (A   RICHIE SIMPSON   D   (A JOEL WILLIAMS   D   (A PAT TAYLOR V   (A
    JOSE FELICIANO   G (A   BOB LEHNERT V   (A DAVID BREWER   V   (A NASHVILLE EDITION V(A
S285   MIKE STOREY   S285
    MIKE STOREY K V HCA PERC(AB   (A) STOREY   1974 MAM   MAMAS1011
    NEIL HUBBARD   G (A   (B) WHO ARE YOU PLAYING TO 1975 MAM   AS   1013
    WINSTON DELANDRO G (AB
    MICK WEAVER   K (A   MIKE WOODS   G (A STEVE CHAPMAN   D   (AB RICHARD BAILEY   D(A
    CHARLIE HARRISON B V (A SMILEY DEJONNES PERC (A RAY SINGER   PERC V(A CHRIS MERCER   HRNS(A
    RON CARTHY   HRNS (A STEVE GREGORY   HRNS (A MICK EVE   HRNS (A BUD BEADLE   HRNS(A
    FRANK COLLINS   V (A   DYAN BIRCH   V   (A PADDIE McHUGH   V   (A CLIVE SARSTEDT   V (A
    STUART BROOKS   B (B
S286   STORIES   S286
    IAN LLOYD   B V (ABC   (A) STORIES   1972 KAMA SUTRA   US   KSBS 2051
    MICHAEL BROWN   K SYN(ABC   (B) ABOUT US   1973 KAMA SUTRA   US   KSBS 2068
    STEVE LOVE   G V B(ABC   (C) TRAVELLING UNDERGROUND 1973 KAMA SUTRA   US   KSBS 2078
    BRYAN MADEY   D PERC(ABC
    KENNETH BISCHEL K SYN(C   KENNY AARONSON   B   (C RICH RANNO   G   (PETER HOFFMAN   G (B
    PETER BUONCONSIGILIO VLN(B HARRY LOOKAFSLAV VLN (B
S286A   STORMY SIX   S286A
    FRANCO FABBRI   G   (1   (A) L'UNITA   1970
    UMBERTO FIORI   (1   (B) UN BIGLIETTO DEL TRAM 197 L'ORCHESTRA   OLP 10001
    TOMMASO LEDDI   (1   (C) CLICKE   197 L'ORCHESTRA   OLP 10010
    CARLO DE MARTINI   (1   (D) L'APPRENDISTA   197 L'ORCHESTRA   OLP 10012
                                   (1) 1973
S286B   STORM   S286B
    JANNETTE CHASE   V   (A   (A) STORM   1979 MCA US 3179
    LEAR STEVENS   G   (A
    RONNI HANSON   B   (A   DAVID DEVON D   (A
S286C   BILLY STORM   S286C
    BILLY STORM   (A   (A) BILLY STORM & THE VALIANTS 19 FAMOUS   US 504
                                   (B) BILLY STORM   19   VISTA   US 3315
S286D   JOHNNY STORM   S286D
    JOHNNY STORM   (A   (A) FLAME ON   1981 MAGNUM FORCE   MFLP003
S287   STORYTELLER   S287
    CAROLINE ATTARD V   (AB   (A) STORYTELLER   1970 TRANSATLANTIC   UK   TRA220
    RODNEY CLARK   V B (A   (B) MORE PAGES   1971 TRANSATLANTIC   UK   TRA232
    ROGER MOON   G V (AB
    MIKE ROGERS   V   (AB   CHRIS BELSHAW   B V (B TERRY DURHAM   V   (AB HARRY BECKETT   HRNS(B
    HENRY SPINETTI   D   (B
S288   DAVIS STOUGHTON   S288
    DAVIS STOUGHTON   (A   (A) TRANSFORMER   19   ELEKTRA   US 74034
S288A   STRAIGHT EIGHT   S288A
    RICK CASSMAN   G K V(AB   (A) NO NOISE FROM HERE 1979 EEL PIE   UK   EPRP 001
    BOOT KINGSMAN   G V SAX(AB   (B) SHUFFLE & CUT   1980 LOGO UK FLUSH 1UK GER 64026
    STEVE CHERRY   B V (AB
    PAUL SCHOFIELD   B   (A   TIM BEETON   VLN (A RUAN O'LOCHLAINN   SAX (A GARY HOLTON   V (A
    PAUL TURNER   K D (B   ROD BERRIEDALE JOHNSON D(A RABBIT   K   (A ANDY HAAS   SAX(B
S289   STRAIGHT SHOOTER   S289
    GEORG BUSCHMANN V   (AB   (A) MY TIME HOUR TIME   1974 SKY   SKY 034
    FRIEDHELM MISLEJUK D (A   (B) GET STRAIGHT   1978 SKY   SKY 018
    GUNTHER STRIEPLING G (AB   (C) FLYING STRAIGHT   1981 SKY   SKY 054
    HANS PLANKERT   K   (AB
    ROLAND HAASE   B   (AB   PETER KEGLER D PERC   (B
S289A   NICK STRAKER BAND   S289A
    NICK STRAKER   K V (A   (A) A WALK IN THE PARK 1980 CBS   UK   84608
    ANDY MANSFIELD   G   (A
    DAVE McSHERA   G   (A   TONY HIBBERT   B   (A PETER HAMMOND   B   (A PHIL TOWNER   D (A
    FERNANDO BUSTAMENTE D (A
S289B   STRAND   S289B
    RICK CALHOUN   V   (A   (A) THE STRAND   1980 ISLAND   UK   ILPS 9594
    SCOTT SHELLY   G V (A
    PETER REILICH   K V (A   DEAN COTEZ   B V (A KELLY SHANAHAN   D   (A
S290   RICHARD STRANGE   S290
    RICHARD STRANGE   (A   (A) PHENOMENAL RISE OF RICHARD STRANGE 1981 VIRGIN UK 2203 GER 203 763
    ANGUC McLEAN   G   (A   (A) "   "   "   "   " 1981 PVC 7917
    MARTIN GRIFFIN   D   (A
    PETE O'SULLIVAN B   (A   DAVE WINTHROP   SAX (A STEVE BOLTON   G   (A JIM TELFORD   SYN (A
    J L HELLAWELL   K SYN(A   REBOP KWAKU BAAH PERC (A RADIO JONES   V   (A RENE EYRE   V (A
    SUE SHARP   (A   ROSS MIDDLETON   V   (A
S291   STRANGE DAYS   S291
    GRAHAM WARD   G V (A   (A) NINE PARTS TO THE WIND 1975 RETREAT   UK   RTL6005
    PHIL WALMAN   B V (A
    EDDIE McNEIL   D PERC(A   EDDIE SPENCE K   (A
S291A   STRANGER   S291A
                                   (A) STRANGER   1982 EPIC   US   37940

S292

<pre>
                                            STRANGLERS
   HUGH CORNWELL   G V (ABCDEF   (A) RATTUS NORVEGICUS   1977 A&M US 4648 UA UK   UAG30045 S292
   JET BLACK   D   (ABCDEF   (B) NO MORE HEROES   1978 A&M US 4659 UA UK   UAG30200
   DAVE GREENFIELD   K V (ABCDEF   (C) BLACK & WHITE   1978 A&M US 4706 US UK   UAK30222
   JEAN JACQUES BURNEL B V(ABCDEF   (D) LIVE(X CERT)IV   1979 IRS US 70011   UA UK UAG30224
   LORA LOGIC   SAX (C   (D) LIVE(X CERT)   1979 UA GER 62412
   ERIC CLARK   SAX (A   (E) THE RAVEN   1979   UAG30262
   ALAN WINSTANLEY   (F   (F) THE MEN IN BLACK   1981 LIBERTY NL 83084 UK LBG30313
   ALDO BOCCA   (F   (G) THE COLLECTION   1982 LIBERTY   UK   LBG 30353
   LAURENCE DIANA   (F
   MARTIN RUSHENT   PROD (A
</pre>

S292A

<pre>
                                            STRANGELOVES   S292A
   RICHARD GOTTEHRER   (A   (A) I WANT CANDY   1965 BANG US 211 RI GER LOLLIPOP 624341
   BOB FELDMAN   (A
   JERRY GOLDSTEIN   (A
</pre>

S293

<pre>
                                            STRAPPS   S293
   ROSS STAGG   G V (AB   (A) STRAPPS   1976 HARVEST   UK   SHSP 4055
   JOE READ   B V (AB   (B) SECRET DAMAGE   1977 HARVEST US 11621 UK SHSP 4064
   NOEL SCOTT   K V (AB   (C) SHARP CONVERSATION   1978 HARVEST   UK   SHSP 4088
   MICK UNDERWOOD   D   (AB
</pre>

S294

<pre>
                                     STRAWBERRY ALARM CLOCK   S294
   MARK WEITZ   K   (ABCD   (A) INCENSE & PEPPERMINTS   1968 PYE UK 28106 US UNI   73014
   LEE FREEMAN V D WIND B (ABCD   (B) WAKE UP ,ITS TOMORROW   1968 UNI   US   73025
   ED KING   G V (ABCD   (C) WORLD IN A SEA SHELL   1968 UNI   US   73035
   GARY LOVETRO   B V (A   (D) GOOD MORNING STARSHINE   19   UNI   US   73054
   GEORGE BUNNELL   B   (ABC   (E) BEST OF   19   UNI   US   73074
   RANDY SEOL   D V (ABC   (F) PSYCH OUT(3 TRACKS) (SOUNDTRACK) 1968 SIDEWALK US ST 5913
   JIMMY PITMAN   G V (D   (G) CHANGES   19   VOCALION   73915
   GENE GUNNELS   D   (D
</pre>

S295

<pre>
                                            STRAWBS   S295
   DAVE COUSINS   G V(ABCDEFGHIJKLMNO(A) ALL OUR OWN WORK (1968 RECORDING) 1973 HALLMARK   SHM 813
   RICHARD HUDSON   PERC (BCDEFG   (B) STRAWBS   1969 A&M   UK   AMLS 936
   JOHN FORD   B V (BCDEFG   (C) DRAGONFLY   1970 A&M   UK   AMLS 970
   RICK WAKEMAN   K   (BCDEK   (D) JUST A COLLECTION OF ANTIQUES 1970 A&M US 4288 UK   AMLS 994
   TONY HOOPER   G V (ABCDE   (E) FROM THE WITCHWOOD   1971 A&M US 4304 UK   AMLS64304
   DAVE LAMBERT   G V (FGHJKMNLX (F) GRAVE NEW WORLD   1972 A&M US 4344 UK   AMLS68078
   ROD COOMBES   D   (HJKML   (G) BURSTING AT THE SEAMS   1973 A&M US 4383 UK   AMLH68144
   CHAS CRONK   B   (HJKMNLX   (H) HERO & HEROINE   1974 A&M US 3607 UK   AMLH63607
   NICKY HOPKINS   K   (B   (I) STRAWBS BY CHOICE   1974 A&M   UK   AMLH68259
   BLUE WEAVER   K   (FG   (J) GHOSTS   1975 A&M US 4506 UK   AMLH68277
   JOHN HAWKEN   K   (HJ   (K) NOMADNESS   1976 A&M US 4544 UK   AMLH68331
   CLAIRE DENIZ   CELLO(CJ   (L) DEEP CUTS   1976 OYSTER US 1 1603 UK   2391 234
   RON CHESTERMAN   B   (AC   (M) BURNING FOR YOU   1977 OYSTER US 1 1604 UK   2391 287
   SANDY DENNY   V   (A   (N) DEAD LINES   1978 ARISTA US 4172 UK SPART 1036
   KEN GUDMAND   D   (A   (O) BEST OF   1978 A&M   US   6005 UK AMLM66005
   RUPERT HOLMES   K   (L   (BC) EARLY STRAWBS   1974 A&M CAN 9014
   ROY HILL   G V (X   (X) 1980 BAND
   ALAN PARKER   G   (B
   ANDY WEIGHELL   B   (B ANNE COLLINS   V   (F RON VERRALL   D (B TREVOR LUCAS   V(F
   JOHN MEALING   K(MNKL ROBERT KIRBY   K   (MN TONY FERNANDEZ D (NX TONY VISCONTI PROD(F
   JOHN KNIGHTSBRIDGE G (X ANDY RICHARDS   K   (X JACK EMBLOW   ACC(K TOMMY EYRE   K (K
   TONY CARR   PERC (X JOHN LUMLEY-SAVILE K (K MADDY PRIOR   V (X
</pre>

S295A

<pre>
                                            STRAWHEAD   S295A
   GREGG BUTLER   V WIND(A   (A) SONGS FROM THE BOOK OF ENGLAND(DBL)1980 TRADITION UK TRS 0356
   CHRIS POLLINGTON G K V SYN(A
   MALCOLM GIBBONS G V (A PETE ASHWORTH   VLN (A STUART GRILLS   TPT (A LAWRENCE YATES HRNS(A
   IAN DUCKWORTH   TUBA (A EDWARD HOYLE   TROM(A MICHAEL LORMOR HRNS(A
</pre>

S296

<pre>
                                            STRAY   S296
   DEL BROMHAM   G V K(ABCDEFGH   (A) STRAY   1970 TRANSATLANTIC   UK   TRA216
   STEVE GADD   HCA G V (ABCDE   (B) SUICIDE   1971 TRANSATLANTIC   UK   TRA233
   RITCHIE COLE   D   (ABCDEFGH   (C) SATURDAY MORNING PICTURES 1972 TRANSATLANTIC UK TRA248 RI TRS110
   GARY G GILES   B   (ABCDEFGH   (C) SATURDAY MORNING PICTURES 1972 MERCURY   US SRM1 624
   JIMMY HELMS   TPT (E   (D) MUDANZAS   1973 TRANSATLANTIC   UK   TRA268
   PETE DYER   G V (GH   (E) MOVE IT   1974 TRANSATLANTIC   UK   TRA281
   MIKE EVANS   VLN (C   (F) TRACKS   1975 TRANSATLANTIC   UK TRASAM3066
   KEITH BLEASBY CONGAS(C   (G) STAND UP & BE COUNTED   1975 DAWN UK DNLS 3066 US PYE 12017
   ANDY BEARNE   HCA (C   (H) HOUDINI   1976 PYE UK NSPL18482 US   12129
   P P ARNOLD   V   (C   (J) HEARTS OF FIRE   1976 PYE   UK NSPL18512
   LISA STRIKE   V   (C
   BARRY ST JOHN V   (C KAY GARDNER   V   (C
</pre>

S296A

<pre>
                                            STRAY CATS   S296A
   BRIAN SETZER   G V (ABC   (A) STRAY CATS   1981 ARISTA   UK   STRAY 1
   SLIM JIM PHANTOM D   (ABC   (B) GONNA BALL   1981 ARISTA GER 204 019
   LEE ROCKER   B V (ABC   (C) BUILT FOR SPEED   1982 CAPITOL   US 17070
   IAN STEWART   K   (B
   JOHN LOCKE   K   (B STEVE PONCAR   SAX (B BRIAN McDONALD HCA (A LEE ALLEN SAX (B
   GARY BARNACLE   SAX (A
</pre>

S297

<pre>
                                            STRAY DOG   S297
   SNUFFY WALDEN   G V (AB   (A) STRAY DOG   1974 MANTICORE US 66671 UK K43506
   TIM DULAINE   G V (B   (B) WHILE YOU'RE DOWN THERE 1974 MANTICORE US 501s1 UK K53504
   ALAN ROBERTS   B V (AB
   LES SAMPSON   D   (AB LUIS CABAZA   K V(B
</pre>

S298

<pre>
                                            STRAY GATOR   S298
   NEIL YOUNG   G V (
   BEN KEITH   STEEL(JACK NITZSCHE   (JOHN BARBATA   D (KENNY BUTTREY   D (
   TIM DRUMMOND   B   (
</pre>

STREET CORNER SYMPHONY

JAMES GADSON	D	(	(A) HARMONY GRITS	1975 BANG US	406
JAMES JAMESON	B	(	(B) LITTLE FUNK MACHINE	1977 ABC US	ABC 974

STREET

ANYA COHEN   V PERC(A   (A) STREET   19 VERVE   US FTS 3057
MICHAEL LYNNE   G B V(A
JOHN WILLIAMSON   G B V(A   AL CAMARDO   PERC (A   TOM CHAPSON   D (A   WILL BETZ   G   (A

STREETBAND

PAUL YOUNG	HCA K V (AB	(A) LONDON	1979 LOGO UK	1012
ROGER KELLY	G V (AB	(B) DILEMMA	1979 LOGO UK	1017
JOHN GIFFORD	G V (AB			
MICK PEARL	B V (AB	VINCE CHAULK	D (AB CHAZ JANKEL	V K G(A JOOLS HOLLAND K (B
TREVOR RABIN	K (B			

STREETHEART

DARYL GUTHEIL	K V (AB	(A) MEANWHILE BACK IN PARIS	1978 ATLANTIC	KCA 92002
MATTHEW FRENETTE	D V (AB	(B) UNDER HEAVEN OVER HELL	1979 ATLANTIC	KSD 19228
KENNY SHIELDS	V (ABC	(C) STREETHEART	1982 CAPITOL CAN	ST 6491
SPIDER SINNAEVE	B V (AB			
JOHN HANNAH	G V (B	PAUL DEAN	G V (A	

STREETMARK

DOROTHEA RAUKES	K (	(A) NORDLAND	1975 SKY	SKY003
THOMAS SCHREIBER	G (	(B) EILEEN	1978 SKY	SKY011
GEORG BUSCHMANN	V (	(C) DRY	1979 SKY	SKY023
WOLFGANG WESTPHAL	B (	(D) SKY RACER	1981 SKY	SKY050
HANS SCHWEISS	D (			

STREETNOISE

TINA NEWKIRK   V (A   (A) STREETNOISE   19 EVOLUTION   US 2010
TOM TRICKS   D (A
PAUL PATOS   G V (A   TOM GRAVES   K (A   WALLACE   B   (A

STREETWALKERS

ROGER CHAPMAN	HCA V(ALL	(A) STREETWALKERS	1974 REPRISE UK	K54017
CHARLIE WHITNEY	G (ALL	(A) STREETWALKERS	1975 MERCURY US	SRMI 1060
BOB TENCH	G V (BCDE	(B) DOWNTOWN FLIER	1975 VERTIGO UK	6360 123
TIM HINKLEY	K V (A	(C) RED CARD	1976 VERTIGO UK	9102 010
MAX MIDDLETON	K (A	(C) RED CARD	1976 MERCURY US	SRMI 1083
JOHN WETTON	B V (A	(D) VICIOUS BUT FAIR	1977 VERTIGO UK 9102 012 NL 6360 140	
RIC GRECH	B (A	(D) VICIOUS BUT FAIR	197 MERCURY US	SRMI 1135
NEIL HUBBARD	G (A	(E) STREETWALKERS LIVE(DBL)	1977 VERTIGO UK	6641 703
IAN WALLACE	D (A			
MIKE GILES	D (A	GODFREY McLEAN PERC (A POLI PALMER	VIBES(ABD LINDA LEWIS	V (A
PETE WINGFIELD	K (B	BOZ BURRELL V (A JIM CREGAN	V (A NICKO	D (BC
JON PLOTEL	B (BC	MICKEY FEAT B (A BRIAN JOHNSTON	K (DE DAVID DOWLE	D (DE
MEL COLLINS	HRNS (D			

STRETCH

KIRBY	G (ABCD	(A) ELASTIQUE	1975 ANCHOR UK	ANCL 2014
ELMER GANTRY	G V (ABC	(B) CANT BEAT YOUR BRAIN FOR ENTERTAINMENT	1976 ANCHOR UK	ANCL 2016
STEVE EMERY	B (ABCD	(C) LIFE BLOOD	1977 ANCHOR UK ANCL2023 GER 25698	
JEFF RICH	D (BC	(D) FORGET THE PAST	1978 HOT WAX UK	HW1
ROSHI	G (A			
PAUL MARTINEZ	B (A	JIM RUSSELL D (A JOHN COOK	K (AD CHRIS MERCER	HRNS(AD
MICK EVE	HRNS (A	RON CARTHY HRNS (A MIKE BAILEY	HRNS (A NICKO McBAIN	D (D
CHRIS FLETCHER	PERC (D	FRAN BYRNE D (D NIGEL WATSON	G V (A	

WILLIAM R STRICKLAND

WILLIAM R STRICKLAND (A   (A) WILLIAM R STRICKLAND IS ONLT THE NAME 1969 DERAM   UK   SML 1041

PETE STRIDE & JOHN PLAIN

PETE STRIDE   G V (A   (A) NEW GUITAR IN TOWN   1980 BEGGARS BANQUET UK   BEGA 17
JOHN PLAIN   G V (A
TONY BATEMAN   V B (A   JACK BLACK   D (A   PETE EDWARDS   HCA V(A   MICK TALBOT   K (A

STRIDER

JIM HAWKINS	B (A	(A) EXPOSED	1973 G M	GML 1002
IAN KEWLEY	K V (A	(B) MISUNDERSTANDING	1974 G M UK	GML 1012
BOB MURRAY	G (			
GARY GRAINGER	G (BA	ROB ELLIOT V (B LEE STRELLEZYK	B (BA COSMO	G (
JAY WILLIAMS	G (	MALCOLM MORTIMER D (LES OLBINSON	PERC (TONY MILLS	(
MARK PINDER	D (	TONY BROCK D V (B JENNY HAAN	V (B	

STRIFE

JOHN REID	HCA G V (AB	(A) RUSH	1975 CHRYSALIS	CHR 1063
GORDON ROWLEY	B V (AB	(B) BACK TO THUNDER	1978 GULL UK	GULL 1029
PAUL H ELLSON	D (A			
DAVID WILLIAMS	D V (B	DON AIREY K (B		

STRIKER

SCOTT ROSBURG   V B G((A) STRIKER   1978 ARISTA US 4165   SPART1059
RICK TAYLOR   D V (
RICK RANDLE   V K G(RICK RAMIREZ   G (

STRING DRIVEN THING

CHRIS ADAMS	G V (ABE	(A) STRING DRIVEN THING	1972 CHARISMA UK	CAS 1062
PAULINE ADAMS	V (ABE	(B) MACHINE THAT CRIED	1973 CHARISMA US 6063 UK CAS 1070	
GRAHAME SMITH	VLN (ABCDE	(C) PLEASE MIND YOUR HEAD	1974 CHARISMA UK CAS1097 US 20TH 470	
COLIN WILSON	G B (AB	(D) KEEP YER'AND ON IT	1975 CHARISMA UK CAS1112 US 20TH 503	
BILLY FAIRLEY	D (B	(E) STRING DRIVEN THING	19 CONCORD UK	CON 1001
CLARE SEALEY	CELLO(B			
BILL HATJE	B (B	JAMES EXELL B V (CD KENNY ROWE	V (C GRAHAME WHITE	V (C
COLIN FAIRLEY	D V (CD	ALUN ROBERTS G V (CD KIMBERLEY BEACON	V (CD HENRY McDONALD	K (C
ALAN SKIDMORE	SAX (C	PETER WOOD PNO (CD CUDDLY JUDDLY	HCA (D	

STRINGBAND

SUSIE EVERETT   G V PERC(A   (A) STREET SINGERS HEAVEN   1974 INTERCORD   GER 26467
JOHN EVERETT VLN BAN G (A
JOHN BERQUIST B BAN V (A   BOB DOUGLAS G B V   (A

BARRETT STRONG

BARRETT STRONG	V	(A		(A) STRONGHOLD	1975 CAPITOL		EST 11376
				(B) LIVE & LOVE	1976 CAPITOL		11490

STRONGBOW

BILL BENDER	V K HRNS(A		(A) STRONGBOW	1975 SOUTHWIND	UK	SWS 6401
JOHN STELZER	K WIND V(A					
DAVID SMITH	D V	(A	MICHAEL SHORTLAND G V (A JOHN DURZO	B V (A		

BABE STOVALL

BABE STOVALL		(A	(A) BABE STOVALL	19 VERVE	US	

STUD

JIM CREGAN	G V	(A	(A) STUD	1971 DERAM AML1084 POLYDOR 2310 097
RICHARD McCRACKEN	G B	(A	(B) SEPTEMBER	1972 BASF	GERM	20 29054
JOHN WILSON	D	(A	(C) GOODBYE –LIVE AT COMMAND	1973 BASF	GERM	20 29117
JOHN WEIDER	VLN G K V(BC					

STUFF

CORNELL DUPREE	G	(	(A) STUFF	1977 WB	UK K56305	US BS2968
STEVE GADD	D	(	(B) MORE STUFF	1977 WB		US BS3061
ERIC GALE	G	(	(C) STUFF IT	197 WB		US BS3262
RICHARD TEE	K	(	(D) LIVE IN JAPAN	1979 WEA	JAP	10629
GORDON EDWARDS	B	(	(E) LIVE STUFF	1978 WB	GER	56720
CHRIS PARKER	D	(	(F) LIVE IN NY	1980 WB EURO 56833	US	3417

STUMBLEBUNNY

DAVID WHITE	G V	(A	(A) WHILE YOU WERE OUT	1979 MERCURY	GER 9198 135
PETER JORDON	B	(A			
CHRIS ROBINSON	G K V(A	SAMMY BROWN	D V (A STAN BRONSTEIN	SAX (A	

JEFF STURGES & UNIVERSE

DEAN PARKS	G	(A	(A) JEFF STURGES & UNIVERSE	197 MAM US MAM1	UK	MAMAS1002
DENNIS KELLY	B	(A				
DON BALDWIN	B	(A	HAL STESCH	K	(A	ROGER RAMPTON	PERC (A	MIKE LEWIS	PERC(A
JIMMY MANONE	D	(A	BOBBY SHAW	TPT	(A	TOM PORRELLO	TPT (A	JON MURAKAMI	TPT (A
RICH COOPER	TPT	(A	DEREK WATKINS	TPT	(A	JIM TRIMBLE	TROM (A	BILL BOOTH	TROM(A
STAN NISHAMURA	TROM	(A	ARCHIE WHEELER	SAX	(A	BURT ESTERMAN	SAX (A	DON MENZA	SAX (A
JOHN PHILLIPS	SAX	(A	GARY FREYMAN	SAX	(A	ART MAEBE	HRNS (A	DICK PERISSI	HRNS(A
AUBREY BOUCK	HRNS	(A	RALPH POLLACK	HRNS	(A	JEFF STURGES	(A		

STYLISTICS

RUSSELL THOMPKINS JR	V	(E	(A) THE STYLISTICS	1971 H&L US 33023 UK AVCO 6466 008
JAMES SMITH	V	(E	(B) 2	1972 H&L US 11006 UK AVCO 6466 010
JAMES DUNN	V	(E	(C) ROCK'N'ROLL BABY	1973 H&L US 11010 UK AVCO 6466 012
AIRRION LOVE	V	(E	(D) LETS PUT IT ALL TOGETHER	1974 H&L US 69001 UK AVCO 6466 013
HERB MURRELL	V	(E	(E) HEAVY	197 H&L US 69004
			(F) FROM THE MOUNTAIN	197	UK AVCO 9109 002
			(G) THE BEST OF	1975 H&L US 69005 UK AVCO 9109 003
			(H) THANK YOU BABY	1975 H&L US 69008 UK AVCO 9109 005
			(I) YOU ARE BEAUTIFUL	1975 H&L US 69010 UK AVCO 9109 006
			(J) FABULOUS	1976 H&L US 69013 UK	9109 008
			(K) BEST OF VOL 2	1976 H&L	UK	9109 010
			(L) ONCE UPON A JUKE BOX	197 H&L US 69015
			(M) SUN & SOUL	1977 H&L US 69019 UK	9109 014
			(N) SPOTLIGHT ON	1977 H&L	UK	6641 622
			(O) WONDER WOMAN	1978 H&L US 69032 UK	9109 016
			(P) LIVE IN JAPAN	1979 FLYOVER JAP	594
			(Q) BLACK SATIN	1979 H&L	UK	9198 230
			(R) IN FASHION	19 MERCURY US 3727

STYLUS

PETER JONES STRINGS HRNS(A		(A) STYLUS	1978 PRODIGAL		PDL 2011
GRAHAM LYALL	HRNS (A				
MIKE CLARKE	HRNS (A	SAM McNALLY	K	(A	PETER CUPPLES	V K G(A ASHLEY HENDERSON B V (A
RON PEERS	G V (A	TREVOR COURTNEY	D	(A		

POLY STYRENE

POLY STYRENE	V	(A	(A) TRANSLUCENCE	1980 UA		UAG 30320
RICHARD MOORE	G	(A				
KUMA HARADA	B	(A	TED BUNTING	WIND (A DARYL LEE QUE	PERC (A KEVIN McALEA	K (A
RICHARD BAILEY	D	(A	G T MOORE	G	(A		

LAURIE STYVERS

LAURIE STYVERS	K V	(AB	(A) SPILT MILK	1972 CHRYSALIS UK CHR1007 US WB1946
TOM PARKER	K	(AB	(B) COLORADO KID	1973 CHRYSALIS UK CHR1038
ANDREW STEELE	D	(AB				
HENRY SPINETTI	D	(AB	GARY TAYLOR	B	(AB	BRIAN DALY	G	(A	ROD KING	STEEL(A
MIKE RICHARDS	D	(A	ADRIAN LEGG	G	(A	JIM LAWLESS	PERC (A	CLAIRE TORRY	V	(A
SUE LYNN	V	(A	NOELEEN BATLEY	V	(A	ALAN PARKER	G	(A	JERRY DONAHUE	G	(B
DYAN BIRCH	V	(B	FRANK COLLINS	V	(B	PADDY McHUGH	V	(B	RODNEY WYATT	G	(B
TOMMY EYRE	K	(B	TRISTRAM FRY	PERC	(B	BILLY BEHNKE	G	(B	PETE WILLSHER	STEEL(B
CHRISSIE STEWART	B	(B	MICK COX	G	(B	MAL LUKER	SITAR(B	JERRY HOVELL	V	(B
GEORGE LEE	SAX	(B	JON FIELD	CONGA(B			

STYX

JAMES YOUNG	G	(ALL	(A) STYX	1972 WOODEN NICKEL	US	BXLI 1008
DAN BARBER	HRNS(L		(A) STYX	1980 RCA RI UK 3593
DENNIS DE YOUNG	K	(ALL	(B) STYX II (LADY)	1973 WOODEN NICKEL	US	BXLI 1012
MIKE HALPIN	HRNS (L		(B) STYX II (LADY)	1980 RCA RI UK 3694
CHUCK PANOZZO	B	(ALL	(C) SERPENT IS RISING	1973 WOODEN NICKEL	US	BXLI 0287
MARK OHLSEN	HRNS(L		(C) SERPENT IS RISING	1980 RCA RI UK 3595
JOHN PANOZZO	D	(ALL	(D) MAN OF MIRACLES	1974 WOODEN NICKEL	US	BWLI 0638
BILL SIMPSON	HRNS(L		(D) MAN OF MIRACLES	1980 RCA RI UK 3596
JOHN CURULEWSKI	G	(ABCDE	(E) EQUINOX	1975 A&M US 4559	UK	AMLH64559
TOM NARDIN	G	(	(F) CRYSTAL BALL	1976 A&M US 4604	UK	AMLH64604
TOMMY SHAW	G	(FGHJt	(G) GRAND ILLUSION	1977 A&M US 4637	UK	AMLH64637
JOHN HAYNOR	HRNS (L		(G) GRAND ILLUSION	197 MOBILE US 026
BILL THAUT	SAX	(B	(H) PIECES OF EIGHT	1978 A&M US 4724	UK	AMLH64724
STEVE EISEN	SAX	(JL	(J) CORNERSTONE	1979 A&M US 3711	UK	AMLK63711
			(K) BEST OF	1977 WOODEN NICKEL	US	BXLI 2250
			(K) BEST OF	1979 RCA US 3597	UK	PL 13116
			(L) PARADISE THEATRE	1980 A&M US 3719	UK	AMLK63719

SUBURBAN STUDS

    (A) SLAM   1978 POGO   UK   POW 001

SUBURBS

```
HUGO KLAERS         D    (A       (A) IN COMBO            1980 TWINTONE   US   8014
BLAINE JOHN BEEJTAR V    (A
BRUCE B C ALLEN     G V  (A   CHAN POLING     K V  (A  MICHAEL HALLIDAY    B (A
```

SUBWAY SECT

```
VIC GODDARD         V    (123A      (A) WHAT'S THE MATTER BOY   1980 MCA UK 3070
MARK LAFF           D    (2          (1) 1977       (2) 1977        (3) 1978
PAUL MYERS          B    (123
ROBERT MILLER       G    (123 PAUL SMITH      D   (1   ROB WARD      D   (3
```

SUE & SUNNY

```
SUE GLOVER          V    (A       (A) SUE & SUNNY        1970 CBS         UK        63740
SUNNY LESLIE        V    (A
```

SUGARLOAF

```
JERRY CORBETTA    K V  (ABCD     (A) SUGARLOAF                 1970 LIBERTY US LST7640  UK LBS83415
BOB WEBBER        G B  (ABCD     (B) I GOT A SONG              1973 BRUT        US          6006
BOB RAYMOND   SAX G B  (ABCD     (C) SPACE SHIP EARTH          1974 UA UK UAS29165 US LIBERTY 11010
BOB MACVITTIE     D    (AC       (D) DON'T CALL US, WE'LL CALL YOU   1975 POLYDOR      UK    2310  394
ROBERT YEAZEL     G V  (C        (D) DON'T CALL US, WE'LL CALL YOU   1975 CLARIDGE     US          1000
BOB PICKETT       G B  (
MYRON POLLOCK     D    (D   LARRY FERRIS      D   (B
```

SUICIDE

```
ALAN VEGA          V    (ALL      (A) SUICIDE                 1977 BRONZE BRON 508+RED STAR IMP
MARTY REV          INST (ALL      (B) LIVE(LIMITED EDITION)   1979 FRANKI                       1
RIC OCASEK         PROD (C        (C) SUICIDE                 1980 ZE US 7080      UK    ILPS 7007
CRAIG LEON         PROD (A        (D) HALF ALIVE              1981 ROIR A103
MARTY THAU         PROD (A
```

SUICIDE COMMANDOS

    (A) MAKE A RECORD   1978 BLANK US 002 NL MERCURY 6336673

SUICIDE ROMEO

```
PIERRE GODDARD     G V  (A        (A) PICTURES           1980 ZE           UK   ILPS 7010
MICHEL BELLOCQ     G SYN(A
JEAN LOUIS WINBERG      B(A  DANIEL BRUNETTI   SAX (A   FREDERICK      D   (A
```

BIG JIM SULLIVAN

```
BIG JIM SULLIVAN  G    (ABCD     (A) SITAR BEAT              1968 MERCURY US SR61137 UK SML 30001
BUDDY CHILDERS    HRNS (B         (B) JIM SULLIVAN            1972 PLAYBOY    US 103
CHAS HODGES K FDL G V  (C         (C) BIG JIMS BACK           1974 RETREAT             RTA 4001
IAN WALLACE       D V  (C         (D) SULLIVAN PLAYS OSULLIVAN 1977 MAM                RAM 3003
DAVE PEACOCK B BAN V  (C
CHUCK FINDLEY     HRNS (B   DICK HYDE        TROM (B   VINCE DE ROSA   HRNS (B   KEN SHROYER    HRNS(B
GEORGE ROBERTS    HRNS (B   JIM HORN         SAX  (B   TOM SCOTT       WIND (B   JIM HUGHART    B  (B
COLIN BAILEY      PERC (B   MIKE MELVOIN PNO      (B   DAVID COHEN     G BAN(B   ALLEN REUSS    BAZ (B
GENE ESTES        PERC (B
```

JOHN L SULLIVAN

```
JOHN L SULLIVAN    V    (A        (A) WOMAN LEAVE ME ALONE    1972 NUGGET    US   101
```

ROCKY SULLIVAN

```
JOHN CIPOLLINA     G    (A        (A) ILLEGAL ENTRY      1981 RAG BABY 1010   JUPITER US 2006
ROCKY SULLIVAN     V    (A
JOEY COVINGTON     D    (     MARIO CIPOLLINA    G B  (    JARRETT WASHINGTON K  (    MIKE VARNEY      G  (A
STEVE LIND         B    (A    GREG ANTON         D    (A   SCOTT METHEWS      D  (A   MAC CRIDLIN      B  (A
MARK CUMMINGS      SYN  (A    CAROLE STEELE    PERC (A   MARK SHAIMAN       K  (A   JEFF COHEN       G  (A
GREGG DOUGLASS          (A    NICKY HOPKINS      K    (A   JANET MORRISON     V  (A   JEANETTE SARTAIN V  (A
PAM MOORE          V    (A
```

HUBERT SUMLIN

```
HUBERT SUMLIN    G V  (ALL      (A) HUBERT'S AMERICAN BLUES   19   SCOUT                    SC4
LONNIE BROOKS    G    (B         (B) GROOVE                   1976 BLACK & BLUE             33511
FRED BELOW       D    (BC        (C) KINGS OF CHICAGO BLUES VOL 2  19   VOGUE          LDM 30175
SUNNYLAND SLIM   V PNO(AD        (D) BLUES ANYTIME  (1964)    1980 L+R          GERM      42004
WILLIE MABON     PNO  (B         (E) GAMBLIN' WOMAN           1980 L+R          GERM      42008
CLIFTON JAMES    D    (AD
CAREY BELL       V HCA(B   JIMMY DAWKINS      G    (C   JAMES GREEN     B  (C   BILLY BOY ARNOLD  V HCA(C
EDDIE SHAW       SAX  (C   JOE CARTER       G V  (C   DAVE MYERS      B  (B   WILLIE DIXON      B  (D
```

DONNA SUMMER

```
DONNA SUMMER       V    (A        (A) STAR COLLECTION         1977 ATLANTIC UK 20109
PAUL JABARA             (G        (B) LOVE TO LOVE YOU BABY   1977 GTO UK 008 US OASIS   5001
                                  (C) LOVE TRILOGY            1977     US OASIS 5004
                                  (D) FOUR SEASONS OF LOVE    1977 GTO UK 018 US CASABLANCA 7038
                                  (E) I REMEMBER YESTERDAY    1977 GTO UK 025 US CASABLANCA 7056
                                  (F) THE DEEP                1977 CASABLANCA UK 2018
                                  (G) SHUT OUT                1977 CASABLANCA UK 2019
                                  (H) ONCE UPON A TIME        1977 CASABLANCA UK 5003    US 5003
                                  (I) GREATEST HITS           1977 GTO UK 028
                                  (J) LIVE AND MORE           1978 CASABLANCA UK 5006 RI 81 6680030
                                  (K) I REMEMBER YESTERDAY    1979 EMBASSY UK 31718
                                  (L) BAD GIRLS               1979 CASABLANCA UK 5007 RI 81 6635035
                                  (M) ON THE RADIO(GREATEST HITS)  1979 CASABLANCA UK 5008 RI 81 6685049
                                  (N) WANDERER                1980 GEFFEN UK K99124
                                  (O) WALK AWAY               1981 CASABLANCA UK 6302 070
                                  (P) DONNA SUMMER            1982 WB UK 99163
```

SAFFRON SUMMERFIELD

```
SAFFRON SUMMERFIELD V G K(AB     (A) SALISBURY PLAIN     1974 MOTHER EARTH       MUM 1001
GEORGE NORRIS      G V  (A        (B) FANCY MEETING YOU HERE  1976 MOTHER EARTH   MUM 1202
LAURIE RHODES      B    (A
ALISON BAILEY      CELLO(A
```

BILL SUMMERS

```
BILL SUMMERS      V PERC FLT(AB   (A) STRAIGHT TO THE BANK           1978 PRESTIGE              PR  10105
LEO MILLER          V    (A       (B) ON SUNSHINE                    1979 PRESTIGE              PR  10107
VIRGINIA AYERS      V    (A
RAY OBIEDO          G    (AB  FRED WASHINGTON    B   (A   GEORGE BOHANON   TROM (A   BENNY POWELL      TROM(A
DARRYL JACKSON      D    (A   OSCAR BRASHEAR     HRNS (A  JOHN BARNES      K    (A   RAY BROWN         HRNS(A
LEON CHANCLER       D    (A   JERRY HEY          HRNS (AB DICK HYDE        TROM (A   BILL GREEN        SAX (A
PATTIE BROOKS       V    (A   ERNIE WATTS        SAX  (A  MAXINE ANDERSON  V    (A   LORI HAM          V   (B
JOSIE JAMES         V    (A   CALVIN TILLERY     V    (B  PETSYE POWELL    V    (A   TOM POOLE         TPT (B
LARRY BATISTE TROM V PNO(B    BO FREEMAN         B    (B  CLAYTOVEN     SAX PNO V (B  PAUL VAN WAGENINGEN D(B
PAUL SMITH          K    (B   SCOTT ROBERTS      PERC V(B TIM GORMAN       SYN  (B   MARLON McCLAIN    G   (B
GARY GALVIN         B    (B   GREG PHILLINGANES  PNO  (B  LLOYD ADAMS      D    (B   GAYLORD BIRCH     D   (B
DWAYNE SWEET        K    (B   TONY LEWIS         D    (B  PHILLIP RICHARDSON V  (B   WAYNE WALLACE     TROM(B
MARK SOSKIN       /  PNO (B   COLIN PAYNE        ORG  (B  LARRY WILLIAMS   SAX  (B   MAXINE WILLARD    V   (B
MYYA LARK           V    (B   CARLBERG JONES     HRNS (B  JULIA TILLMAN    V    (B   PAT HENDERSON     V   (B
STRINGS                  (B
```

SUN

```
BARON BYRD WIND K V(C        (A) LIVE ON  DREAM ON           1976 CAPITOL              11461
KEITH CHEATHAM    G TROM V(C  (B) SUN POWER                  1977 CAPITOL              11609
KYM YANCEY        D    V(C    (C) SUNBURN                    1978 CAPITOL              11723
CURTIS HOOKS      B SAX(V(C   (D) DESTINATION SUN            1979 CAPITOL              11941
SONNY TALBERT     K G V SYN(C (E) SUN OVER THE UNIVERSE      1980 CAPITOL              12088
NIGEL BOULTON     HRNS V(C    (F) FORCE OF NATURE            1981 CAPITOL              12142
ERNIE KRISLEY     HRNS (C
GARY KING         TROM V(C  ROBERT ARNOLD   TPT V(C
```

SUN ALSO RISES

```
GRAHAM HEMINGWAY G V  (A     (A) SUN ALSO RISES             1970 VILLAGE THING         UK VTS 2
ANNE HEMINGWAY   V DULC(A
JOHN TURNER      B    (A   ANDY LEGGETT WIND    (A
```

SUN RAYS

```
RICKY HENN       D V  (A     (A) ANDREA                     1967 TOWER       US   5017
EDDIE MEDORA     G V  (A
VINCE HOZIER     B V  (A   MARTY DI GIOVANNI  K   (A   BYRON CASE   G D V(A   MURRY WILSON      PROD(A
```

SUNDANCE

```
BOB BOWMAN       G V BAN(A    (A) RAIN STEAM SPEED          1973 DECCA UK TXS111 US KAPP 3659
JOHN LYNAM       G V MAND(A   (B) CHUFFER                   1974 DECCA UK SKL5183
PHIL SAVAGE      B V HCA((A   (C) SUNDANCE                  1975 20TH CENTURY US 477
STEPHEN GRIFFIN  K V  (A
ALAN MOORE       D V  (A
```

SUNDAY FUNNIES

```
RICHARD KOSINSKI K V  (A     (A) SUNDAY FUNNIES            1971 RARE EARTH      US    RS 526
RICHARD MITCHELL D    (A
RICHARD FIDGE    V    (A   RONALD AITKEN    G V (A
```

ROY SUNDHOLM

```
ROY SUNDHOLM     G V  (AB     (A) CHINESE METHOD           1979 ENSIGN     ENVY 10
ALAN PLATT       D PERC(A     (B) EAST TO WEST             1981 ENSIGN     ENVY 503
BRUCE DOUGLAS    G B  (A
GUY HUMPHRIES    G    (A   BRIAN ROBERTSON  G    (A   CARMEN DEMICHI   G   (A   PATRICK BROWNE   K   (A
BOB ANDREWS      K    (A   RAY BEAVIS   HRNS    (A   JOHN EARLE       HRNS (A   DICK HANSON HRNS     (A
CHRIS GOWER      TROM(A     SHARON CAMBELL   V    (A   LINDA TAYLOR     V   (A
```

SUNFOREST

```
                             (A) SOUND OF SUNFOREST       19   NOVA           UK    SDN17
```

SUNNY JIM BAND

```
MARTIN ALLEN     G V  (A      (A) JAY                     1981 VERTIGO    GER  6435 100
JOHN BARRY       B    (A
DIDIER LAGET     G PERC(A   J J VRENEGOOR    D    (A   DOREEN CHANTER   V   (A   JILL MACKINTOSH  V  (A
STEVE NYE        K    (A
```

SUNNYLAND SLIM

```
SUNNYLAND SLIM     V PNO(ALL   (A) SLIM'S GOT THIS THING GOIN' ON  1968 WORLD PACIFIC  US   WPS 21890
ERNEST DONABLE     D    (A     (A) SLIM'S GOT THIS THING GOIN' ON  1969 LIBERTY        UK   LBS 83237
MICKEY BAKER       G    (K     (B) MIDNIGHT JUMP                   1969 BLUE HORIZON   UK     763213
LAYFAYETTE HUDSON  B    (K     (C) PEARL HARBOUR BLUES(1 SIDE)     1970 RCA INT        UK   INT  1176
GEORGE SMITH       HCA  (A     (D) SAD & LONESOME                  1972 JEWEL          US   LPS  5010
LUTHER ALLISON     G    (A     (E) PLAYS RAGTIME BLUES             1973 BLUESWAY             BLS 6068
MICK TAYLOR        G    (A     (F) & LITTLE BROTHER MONTGOMERY     19   77             77LA 1221
CURTIS TILLMAN     B    (A     (G) SUNNYLAND SLIM                  19   STORYVILLE     SLP  169
RANDY FULLERTON    G    (A     (H) LEGACY OF THE BLUES             1975 SONET          UK   SNTF  671
BIG MAMA THORNTON  D    (A     (I) BLUES MASTERS VOL 8             19   BLUE HORIZON   US     4608
ROBERT ELEM        B    (A     (J) DECORATION DAY                  1980 L+R            GERM   42015
FRANCIS CLAY       D    (A     (K) DEPRESSION BLUES                19   FESTIVAL       FLD 648
HENRY VESTINE      G    (A     ( ) PATIENCE LIKE JOB               1979 AIRWAY         UK   LP 4746
ODIE PAYNE        D    (J      ( ) SHE GOT THAT JIVE               19   AIRWAY     US   3220
BOB STROGER       B    (J      ( ) CHICAGO BLUES                   19   SPIVEY     US   1003
CAREY BELL         HCA  (J
AL WILSON          G    (A   LARRY TAYLOR      B    (A   PAUL LAGOS       D    (A   GUS WRIGHT       D   (A
SHAKEY JAKE        HCA  (A   FRED BELOW        D    (E   DAVE MYERS       B    (E   LOUIS MYERS      D   (E
JOHNNY SHINES      G    (B   WILLIE DIXON      B    (B   WALTER HORTON    HCA  (B   CLIFTON JAMES    D   (B
BLIND JOHN DAVIS   PNO  (A   BIG BILL BROONZY  G    (C   RANSOM KNOWLING  B    (C   JUDGE RILEY      D   (C
HUBERT SUMLIN      G    (J   JEFF SWAN         G    (J
```

SUNSHINE

```
JACK GREEN       B G V(A      (A) SUNSHINE                 1972 WB             UK    K46169
GORDON EDWARDS   G K V(A
PETER OLIVER     G V  (A   TERRY SLADE  PERC D(A    JOANNE WHITE    PERC V(A  ETHEL COLEY    PERC V(A
```

```
S329B                                    SUNSHINE                                                              S329B
     JACK GREEN        B G V(A         (A) SUNSHINE                     1972 WB              UK      K46169
     GORDON EDWARDS    G K V(A
     PETER OLIVER      G V (A   TERRY SLADE  PERC D(A      JOANNE WHITE    PERC V(A ETHEL COLEY    PERC V(A
S329C                                 SUNSET BOMBERS                                                           S329C
     NICK ARMAND       V.  (A         (A) SUNSET BOMBERS               1978 ARIOLA          US      50025
     RICK ARMAND       G  (A
     BRENDON MATHESON  D  (A   DOUGLAS FIEGER    B   (A
S330                               SUNSHINE COMPANY                                                            S330
     MARY NANCE        V PERC(ABC      (A) HAPPY IS THE SUNSHINE COMPANY 1967 IMPERIAL      US      12359
     MAURICE MANSEAU   V K G(ABC       (B) SUNSHINE COMPANY            1968 IMPERIAL        US      12368
     LARRY SIMS        G V (ABC        (C) SUNSHINE & SHADOWS          1968 LIBERTY         UK  LBS 83159
     MEREL BREGANTE    D V (ABC        (C) SUNSHINE & SHADOWS          1968 IMPERIAL        US      12399
     DOUGLAS MARK  G VLN V (ABC
     DAVE HODGKINS     G   (C
S331                                  SUNTREADER                                                               S331
     MORRIS PERT       D  (AB          (A) ZIN ZIN                     1973 ISLAND          UK      HELP13
     PETER ROBINSON    K  (AB          (B) MUSIC OF MORRIS PERT        1976 CHANTRY   UK    ABM 21
     ALYN ROSS         B  (A
     ROBIN THOMPSON    SAX  (B   NEVILLE WHITEHEAD B PERC(B  PAUL BUCKMASTER  CELLO (B MARTYN FORD    HRN (B
     VERONICA HAYWARD  V  (B   GEORGIA DOBREE    HRN (B
S331A                                RICHARD SUPA                                                              S331A
     RICHARD SUPA      G V (A          (A) SUPAS JAMBOREE              19   PARAMOUNT PAS 6009
     LIBERTY DEVITTO   D  (A
     IVAN ELIAS        B  (A   JOHNATHAN HIPPS   K   (A DEAN DOUGHTRY    K  (A  HOWIE EMERSON    G  (A
     J R COBB          G  (A   BARRY BAILEY      G   (A ROBERT NIX       D  (A  PAUL GODDARD     D  (A
S332                                  SUPERCHARGE                                                              S332
     ALBIE DONNELLY    WIND V(AB        (A) LOCAL LADS MAKE GOOD        1976 VIRGIN          UK      V 2053
     DALE IRVING       D V (A           (B) HORIZONTAL REFRESHMENT      1977 VIRGIN          UK      V 2067
     IAIN BRADSHAW     K  (A            (C) BODY RHYTHM  1979           VIRGIN   UK          V 2118
     LES KARSKI        G V (A           (D) NOW JUMP     19             CRIMINAL  UK         STEAL 10
     OZZIE YUE         G V (A           (EP) 4 BY 6      1976           VIRGIN   UK   VEP 1001
     TONY DUNMORE      B V (A
     BOB ROBERTSON     SAX V(A   DICK HANSON    TPT (A
S332A                             SUPERFINE DANDELION                                                          S332A
     MIKE McFADDEN V G HCA  (A          (A) SUPERFINE DANDELION         196  MAINSTREAM      US      S6102
     MIKE COLLINS      D V (A
     ED BLACK          G K V(A   RICK ANDERSON    B G (A
S332B                                  SUPERMAX                                                                S332B
     KURT HAVENSTEIN   V B K(A          (A) WORLD OF TODAY              1977 ATLANTIC                K50423
     CYNTHIA ARRICH    V  (A            (B) DONT STOP THE MUSIC         1977 ATLANTIC        GER     50325
     TEBLES REYNOLDS   V  (A            (C) FLY WITH ME                 1979 ELEKTRA  US 193
     RICHARD SCHOENHERZ SYN K(A         (D) TYPES OF SKIN               1980 ELEKTRA  NL 52253
     RAINER MARZ       G  (A
     JUANITA SCHULZ       V(A   JUANITA FORD PERC      (A HARTMUT PFANNMULLER D(A
S332C                                 SUPERSEPFFT                                                              S332C
     DIETER KOLB       SYN (A           (A) ROBOTER WERK  1979          CBS                         83712
     ROBOTERWERKE      D  (A
S332D                                  SUPERSISTER                                                             S332D
     ROBERT JAN STIPS  K  (ALL          (A) PRESENT FROM NANCY(SUPERSISTER) 1970 POLYDOR 2419061 US DWARF 2001
     RON VAN ECK       B  (ALL          (B) TO THE HIGHEST BIDDER       1971 DANDELION 2310 146 POLY2925002
     MARCO VROLIJK     D  (ABC          (C) PUDDING AND GISTEREN        1972 POLYDOR  2925 007 +   2419 058
     SACHA VAN GEEST   WIND (ABCD       (D) ISKANDER                    1973 POLYDOR  2485 134     2925 021
     CHARLIE MARIANO   WIND (D          (E) SUPER STRASHINE 3           197  POLYDOR  2419 030
     HERMAN VAN BOEYEN D  (D            (F) SWEET OKAY                  1974 POLYDOR NL 2441 048
     PIERRE MOERLEN    PERC (D
S333                                  SUPERTRAMP                                                               S333
     ROGER HODGSON     V G (ABCDEFGJ    (A) SUPERTRAMP                  1970 A&M  US 4665   UK  AMLS 981
     RICHARD DAVIES    K V (ABCDEFGJ    (B) INDELIBLY STAMPED           1971 A&M  US 4311   UK  AMLS64306
     RICHARD PALMER    G  (A            (C) CRIME OF THE CENTURY        1974 A&M  US 3647   UK  AMLS68258
     DAVE WINTHROP     SAX (B           (D) CRISIS? WHAT CRISIS?        1975 A&M  US 4560   UK  AMLH68347
     BOB MILLER        D  (A            (E) EVEN IN THE QUIETEST MOMENTS 1977 A&M US 4634   UK  AMLK64634
     KEVIN CURRIE      D  (B            (F) BREAKFAST IN AMERICA        1979 A&M  US 3708   UK  AMLK63708
     FRANK FARRELL     B  (B            (G) PARIS                       1980 A&M  US 6702   UK  AMLM66702
     BOB BENBERG       D  (CDEFGJ       ( ) EXTREMES(SOUNDTRACK)        1973 DERAM          UK  AML 1095
     JOHN HELLIWELL    SAX (CDEFGJ      (DE) CRISIS?/EVEN IN THE (CASS) 1981 A&M UK CAMCR7
     DOUGIE THOMPSON   B (CDEFG         (J) FAMOUS LAST WORDS           1982 A&M            UK  AMLK63732
     DICK HYDE         TROM (F
     KEN SCOTT         PROD(C   ANN WILSON     V   (J  NANCY WILSON     V  (J   CLAIRE DIAMENT   V (J
S333A                                  SUPREMES                                                                S333A
     DIANA ROSS        V  (            MEET THE SUPREMES              1964 TAMLA US 606  UK STATESIDE10109
     MARY WILSON       V  (            LIVE AT THE APOLLO            1964 TAMLA US 609
     FLORENCE BALLARD  V  (            A BIT OF LIVERPOOL            1965 TAMLA US 621
     BARBARA MARTIN    V  (            WHERE DID OUR LOVE GO         1965 TAMLA US 623
     CINDY BIRDSONG    V  (            COUNTRY WESTERN & POP         1965 TAMLA US 625   UK    TML11018
     JEAN TERRELL      V  (            HITS      (EP)                1965 TAMLA         UK    TME 2008
     LYNDA LAURENCE    V  (            MORE HITS                    1965 TAMLA US 627   UK    TML 11020
     SHARI PAYNE       V  (            WE REMEMBER SAM COOKE         1965 TAMLA US 629   UK    TML 11012
     SUSAYE GREEN      V  (            WITH LOVE                    1965 TAMLA         UK    TML 11002
     KAREN JACKSON     V  (            AT THE COPA                  196  TAMLA US 636   UK    STML11026
                                        MERRY CHRISTMAS              1965 TAMLA US 638
     WITH                             I HEAR A SYMPHONY             1966 TAMLA US 643   UK    STML11028
     JAMES GADSON      D  (            " "                          1981 TAMLA         UK RI STMS 5012
     JULIUS WECHTER    B  (            AGO GO                       1966 TAMLA US 649   UK    STML11039
     RAY PARKER        G  (            " "                          1981 TAMLA         UK RI STMS 5013
     EDDIE BONGO BROWN CONGA(          SING MOTOWN                  1967 TAMLA         UK    STML11047
     JOE SAMPLE        K  (            " "                          1981 TAMLA         UK RI STMS 5014
     GARY COLEMAN      PERC (          SING HOLLAND DOZIER HOLLAND  1967 TAMLA US 650

                                                          (CONTINUED)


                                                [543]
```

SUPREMES

S333A (CONTINUED)

SCOTT EDWARDS	B	(	SING RODGERS & HART	1967	TAMLA US 659	UK	STML11054
OLIVER BROWN	CONGA	(	GREATEST HITS	1968	TAMLA US 663	UK	STML11063
JAY GRAYDON	G	(	FUNNY GIRL	1968	TAMLA US 672	UK	STML11288
DAN WYMAN	SYN	(	LIVE AT THE TALK OF THE TOWN	1968	TAMLA US 676	UK	STML11070
HENRY DAVIS	B	(	" " " "	1979	MFP	UK	50449
WAH WAH WATSON	G	(	REFLECTIONS	1968	TAMLA US 665	UK	STML11073
BEN BENAY	G	(	LOVE CHILD	1969	TAMLA	UK	STML11095
JOHN BARNES	G	(	JOIN THE TEMPTATIONS	1969	TAMLA US 679	UK	STML11096
CLARENCE McDONALD	K	(	" " " "	1981	TAMLA	UK RI	STMS 5015
ROBERT ZIMMITTI	PERC	(	T C B	1969	TAMLA US 682	UK	STML11110
CHUCK RAINEY	B	(	LET THE SUN SHINE IN	1969	TAMLA US 689	UK	STML11114
GREG POREE	G	(	TOGETHER(TEMPTATIONS)	1969	TAMLA US 692	UK	STML11122
SONNY BURKE	K	(	CREAM OF THE CROP	1970	TAMLA US 694	UK	STML11137
			ON BROADWAY(TEMPTATIONS)	1970	TAMLA US 699		
			GREATEST HITS VOL 2	1970	TAMLA US 702	UK	STML11146
			FAREWELL	1970	TAMLA US 708	UK	STML11154
			RIGHT ON	1970	TAMLA US 705	UK	STML11157
			NEW WAYS BUT LOVE STAYS	1971	TAMLA US 720	UK	STML11175
			MAGNIFICENT SEVEN	1971	TAMLA US 717	UK	STML11179
			SURRENDER	197	TAMLA US 723		
			TOUCH	1971	TAMLA US 737	UK	STML11189
			RETURN OF THE MAGNIFICENT SEVEN	1971	TAMLA US 736	UK	STML11192
			DYNAMITE	1972	TAMLA US 745	UK	STML11203
			FLOY JOY	1972	TAMLA US 751	UK	STML11210
			BABY LOVE	1973	MFP	UK	SPR 90001
			GREATEST HITS	1974	TAMLA	UK	STML11256
			SUPREMES PRODUCED BY JIM WEBB	1973	TAMLA US 756	UK	STML11222
			ANTHOLOGY	1974	TAMLA	UK	A3/1
			ANTHOLOGY	1975	TAMLA US 794	UK	TMSP 6001
			SUPREMES	1975	TAMLA US 879	UK	STML11293
			HIGH ENERGY	1976	TAMLA US 863	UK	STML12027
			MARY,SHARI & SUSAYE	1976	TAMLA US 873	UK	STML12047
			STOP IN THE NAME OF LOVE	1976	MFP	UK	MFP 50291
			AT THEIR BEST	197	TAMLA US 904	UK	STML12091
			DIANA ROSS & THE SUPREMES	1977	TAMLA	UK	STMX 6001
			SUPREMES & TEMPTATIONS	1977	TAMLA	UK	STMX 6003
			20 GOLDEN GREATS	1977	TAMLA	UK	EMTV 5
			IT'S HAPPENING	19	MCA		734727
			EARLY DAYS	1980	TAMLA	UK	STMR 9008

THE SURF PUNKS

S333B

DENNIS DRAGON   D V   (A   (A) MY BEACH   1980 EPIC   UK   EPC 84346
DREW STEELE   G V K (A
JOHN HUNT   B   (A   JOHNNY MALIBU   G V (A RAY BAN   B (A THE HULK   HCA   (A
SPJNO URCHIN   G   (A

SURFERS

S333C

(A) ALIVE & WELL   1971 DAYBREAK   US   2001

SUPPLY & DEMAND

S333D

GREG BOLAND   G   (A   (A) SUPPLY DEMAND   1976 MULLIGAN   UK   LUN009
PAUL McATEER   D   (A
JOLYON JACKSON   K V (A   BRIAN MASTERSON   B V (A

SURPLUS STOCK

S333E

ROBERT GIDDENS   SYN (A   (A) HOLLAND IN NOT   1980 OUTATUNE   GER 8004
GARY GIDDENS   (A
JOSEF SCHENK   D   (A   PHIL RENSHAW   G   (A ROB RISIKO   (A IAN DERBYSHIRE   (A
PHIL FALSETTO   (A

SURPRISE SISTERS

S334

PATRICIA   V   (A   (A) SURPRISE SISTERS   1976 GOOD EARTH GDS801 US RCA 1404
LINDA   V   (A
SUSAN   V   (A   ELLEN   V   (A RAY RUSSELL   G   (A BRUCE LYNCH   G (A
JEAN ROUSSEL K   (A   BRENT FORBES B   (A RAY WARLEIGH   SAX (A FRANK RICOTTI VIBES(A
BLUE WEAVER   K   (A   GERRY CONWAY D   (A PHIL KENZIE   SAX (A

SURFARIS

S335

PAT CONNOLLY	B V	(	(A) WIPE OUT	1963	DOT US 25535 UK LONDON HAD8110
JIM FULLER	G	(	(B) SURFARIS PLAY	1963	DECCA US 4470 UK BRUNSWICK 8561
BOB BERRYHILL	G	(	(C) HIT CITY '64	1964	DECCA US 4487 UK BRUNSWICK 8567
RON WILSON	D	(	(D) FUN CITY	1964	DECCA US 4560 UK BRUNSWICK 8582
JIM PASH G WIND		(	(E) HIT CITY '65	1965	DECCA US 4614 UK BRUNSWICK 8605
			(F) WHEELS	19	DIPLOMAT US 2309
			(G) YESTERDAYS POP SCENE	1973	CORAL COPS 6354
			(H) WIPE OUT	1973	POLYDOR 2870 335
			(J) SURFERS RULE	1976	MCA US MCF 2761
			(K) GONE WITH THE WAVE	1977	CORAL CDL 8050

SURRENDER

S335A

PETER CURRY   K   (A   (A) SURRENDER   1979 CAPITOL   CAN   11935
PAUL DELANEY   D   (A
ALFIE ZAPPACOSTA G V (A   GEOFF WADDINGTON   B   (A STEVE JENSON   G   (A

SURVIVOR

S336

FRANKIE SULLIVAN   G V (ABC   (A) SURVIVOR   1979 SCOTTI US 7107 UK K50698
DAVE BICKLER   V K (ABC   (B) PREMONITION   1981 SCOTTI US 37549 UK K85289
JIM PETERIK   G   (ABC   (C) EYE OF THE TIGER   1982 SCOTTI US 38062 UK K85845
GARY SMITH   D   (A
DENNIS KEITH JOHNSON B(A   MARC DROUBAY   D   (BC STEPHAN ELLIS   B   (BC DARYL DRAGON   K (B
FERGIE   V   (B

SUSAN

S337

TOM DICKIE   G V (A   (A) FALLING IN LOVE   1979 CHAMP   US 3372
CHARLES LELAND   B V (
JOHN KALISHES   G   (MICHAEL LELAND   D   (

```
    FRANK V HELVOIRT   SAX PERC(A      (A) SUSTAIN                      19   XILOVOX    NL  0105
    HANS GRANDIA       D    (A
    GIEZEL VOORSLUIJS  B V  (A   WALLIE LATUMETEN  G V (A   COERT COEHOORN     V PERC(A
S338                        SCREAMING LORD SUTCH                                    S338
    LORD SUTCH         V   (ABC     (A) LORD SUTCH & HEAVY FRIENDS 1970 ATLANTIC UK 2400 008 US COTILLION 9015
    JIMMY PAGE         G    (A      (B) HANDS OF JACK THE RIPPER   1972 ATLANTIC UK  K40313 US COTILLION 9049
    NICKY HOPKINS      K    (A      (C) ALIVE & WELL              1980 BABYLON       GERM      B 80010
    JOHN BONHAM        D    (A
    NOEL REDDING       B    (A   JEFF BECK         G    (A   DANIEL EDWARDS    G B  (A   CARLO LITTLE     D  (A
    KENT HENREY        G    (A   MARTIN KOHL       B    (A   RICK BROWN        B    (A   BOB METKE        D  (A
    SID PHILLIPS       SAX  (B   MATTHEW FISHER    K    (B   NICK SIMPER       B    (B   ANNETTE BROX     V  (B
    BRIAN KEITH        V TROM(B   RITCHIE BLACKMORE G   (B   KEITH MOON        D    (B   VICTOR BROX      V  (B
    PAT TRAVERS        G    (C   JIM GREEN         G    (C   RICK NIELSEN      G    (C   RICHARD PRUT     SAX (C
    COLIN SOLMAN       D    (C   DETLEV RESHOFT    K    (C   MARS COWLING      B    (C   KLAUS VOORMANN   B  (C
    REINHARD STROEMER  B    (C
S339                     SUTHERLAND BROTHERS (& QUIVER)                              S339
    GAVIN SUTHERLAND   B G V(ALL    (A) THE SUTHERLAND BROTHERS BAND 1972 ISLAND UK ILPS9181 US 9315
    IAIN SUTHERLAND    V G K(ALL    (A) THE SUTHERLAND BROTHERS BAND 1976 CBS    UK RI 82297
    BRIAN BENNETT      PERC (H      (B) LIFEBOAT                 1972 ISLAND UK ILPS9212 US 9326
    RICK WILLS         B    (H      (B) LIFEBOAT                 1977 CBS    UK RI 82298
    TIM RENWICK        G    (CDEFGH  (C) DREAM KID               1973 ISLAND UK ILPS9259 US 8341
    ANDY PYLE          B    (H      (C) DREAM KID                1977 CBS    UK RI 82299
    WILLIE WILSON      D    (2CDEFGH (D) BEAT OF THE STREET      1974 ISLAND UK ILPS9288 RT CBS 82300
    BRUCE THOMAS       K    (C      (E) REACH FOR THE SKY        1975 CBS    UK   69191 US 33982
    KIM LUDMAN         B    (A      (F) SAILING (COMP)           1976 ISLAND UK ILPS9358 US CBS 33982
    NEIL HOPWOOD       D    (A      (G) SLIPSTREAM               1976 CBS    UK   81593 US   34376
    PETE WOOD          K    (CD     (H) DOWN TO EARTH            1977 CBS    UK   82255 US   35293
    MICK GRABHAM       G    (H      (J) WHEN THE NIGHT COMES DOWN 1979 CBS   UK   83427 US 35703
    TEX COMER          B    (D      (1) MARCH 1978   (2) OCT 1977
    ALAN ROSS          G    (2
    MICK WEAVER        K    (2   GLEN SPREEN       K    (J   JIM HORN          HRNS (J   STEVE PORCARO    SYN (J
    STEVE FORMAN       PERC (J   JOHN SHEARER      PERC (2H  BILL SMITH             (J1  BOB GLAUB            (J1
    MIKE BAIRD         (J1   RITCHIE ZETO          D    (J1  ALBHY GALUTEN     K    (G   FLACO PADRON     PERC(G
    JOHN HAWKEN        K    (B   BOB RONGA         B    (B   STEVE WINWOOD     K    (B   DAVE MATTACKS    D   (B
    PAT DONALDSON      B    (B   RABBIT BUNDRICK   K    (B
S339A                            SWALLOW                                            S339A
    GEORGE LEH         V    (A      (A) OUT OF THE NEST          1972 WB  US 2606   UK      K56174
    PARKER WHEELER     V HCA(A
    VERN MILLER        V G B(A   DAVID WOODFORD    WIND K(A   PHIL GREEN        G    (A   MICK ARANDA      D(A
    BOB CAMACHO        K    (A   JAY DEWALD        TPT  (A   ANDY HARP         TPT  (A   KERRY BLOUT      SAX (A
    GEORGE KENNEDY     TROM (A   JEFF BAXTER       STEEL(A
S340                             SWAMP DOGG                                         S340
    JERRY WILLIAMS     V PNO(ALL    (A) TOTAL DESTRUCTION OF YOUR MIND 1970 CANYON   US   LP 7706
    STACY GOSS         HRNS (BG     (B) SWAMP DOGG(RAT ON)       1971 ELEKTRA  UK   EKS 74089
    SONNY ROYAL        WIND (B      (C) CUFFED COLLARED & TAGGED 1972 CREAM    US        9009
    MIKE STOUGH        HRNS (B      (D) FINALLY CAUGHT UP WITH MYSELF 197 MCA           2504
    ROBERT POPS POPWELL B   (B      (E) SWAMP DOGG               19   WIZARD   US        1122
    JESSE CARR         G V  (B      (F) GAG A MAGGOT             1975 PRESIDENT      PTLS 1059
    JASPER GUARINO     D    (B      (F) GAG A MAGGOT             1973 STONEDOGG           3001
    JIMMY EVANS        D    (G      (G) HAVE YOU HEARD THIS STORY 1975 ISLAND  UK   ILPS 9299
    HARRISON CALLOWAY  TPT  (G      (H) NEVER TOO OLD TO BOOGIE  1976 DJM      UK   DJF 20476
    CHARLES ROSE       TROM (G      ( ) UNCUT & CLASSIFIED       19   CHARLY   UK   CRB  1026
    TRAVIS WAMMACK     G HCA(G
    AUDIE WATKINS      PERC (G   RANDY McCORMICK   K    (G   LENNY LEBLANC     B    (G   DAVE'BABY'JOHNSON WIND(G
    HARVEY THOMPSON    WIND (G   RON EADES         SAX  (G
S340A                            SWAMP GAS                                          S340A
    JACK DAVIS         B   ·(A      (A) SWAMP GAS                19   BUDDAH   US   BDS 5102
    BAIRD HERSEY       G    (A
    KIM ORNITZ         V    (A   RICKY SALTER      D    (A
S340B                            SWAMP RATS                                         S340B
    BOB HOCKO          V    (A      (A) DISCO SUCKS              1980 KEYSTONE    US K111541
S341                             SWAMPWATER                                         S341
    THAD MAXWELL       B V  (A      (A) SWAMPWATER          1971 RCA US LSP 4572+ KING US  1122
    STAN PRATT         D V  (A
    GIB GUILBEAU       FDL G V(A  HERB PEDERSEN     G V  (A   JOHN BELAND       G V  (A   GLEN D HARDIN    G  (A
S342                             BILLY SWAN                                         S342
    BILLY SWAN         V    (ALL    (A) I CAN HELP        1975 MONUMENT UK 80615 US CBS  33279
    KRIS KRISTOFFERSON V   (E      (B) ROCK'N'ROLL MOON   1975 MONUMENT UK 69192 US CBS  33805
    RITA COOLIDGE      V    (E      (C) BILLY SWAN         1976 MONUMENT UK 81387 US CBS  34183
    LEO SAYER          HCA  (E      (D) FOUR               1977 MONUMENT UK 81867 US CBS  34473
    JORDANAIRES        V    (E      (E) YOUR OK I'M OK     1978 A&M  UK  AMLH64886  US      4686
    SCOTTY MOORE       G    (E      (F) BILLY SWAN         1978 EMBASSY  UK 31674
    DONALD DUNN        B    (E      (G) AT HIS BEST        1978 MONUMENT      US      MG7629
    ROGER HAWKINS      (D   (D      (H) I'M IN TO YOU      1981 EPIC US 37079
    DAVID HOOD         (D
    PETE CARR          D    (    BARRY BECKETT      (D   JIMMY JOHNSON      (D   TIM HENSON       K  (D
    MIKE UTLEY         K    (E   STEVE BRUTON      G    (E   SAMMY CREASON    D  (E   JERRY McGEE      G  (E
    BOOKER T JONES     K    (E   OTIS BLACKWELL    PNO  (E   DON ROBERTSON    PNO (E   CLYDIE KING      V  (E
    VANETTA FIELDS     V    (E   PAULETTE BROWN    V    (E   NEAL MATTHEWS    V  (E   LOUIS NUNLEY     V  (E
    GORDON STOKER      V    (E
S343                             SWAN ARCADE                                        S343
    DAVE BRADY         V    (A      (A) SWAN ARCADE       1973 TRAILER    UK      LER2032
    HEATHER BRADY      V    (A      (B) MATCHLESS         197  SHANACHIE          MU 7428
    FRANK TOWARD       V    (A
    JIM BOYES          G V  (A   DAVE FARRER       V    (A   RAB NOAKES        G    (A   DAVE BURLAND     G V (A
    JIMMY HUTCHISON    V    (A   DIXIE KIDD        B    (A   ALASDAIR CAMERON  V    (A
```

DAVE SWARBRICK

DAVE SWARBRICK	FDL MAND VLA(ABCD	(A) RAGS, REELS & AIRS	1967 POLYDOR			236 514
BERYL MARRIOTT	K (BCD	(B) SWARBRICK	1976 TRANSATLANTIC	UK	TRA 337
MARTIN CARTHY	G (ABC	(C) SWARBRICK 2	1977 TRANSATLANTIC	UK	TRA 341
SIMON NICOL	G (BCD	(D) LIFT THE LID & LISTEN	1978 SONET	UK	SNTF 763
DAVE PEGG	B (BCD	(E) THE CEILIDH ALBUM	1978 SONET	UK	SNTF 764
BRUCE ROWLAND	PERC (BCD	(F) SMIDDY BURN	1981 LOGO UK	1029
DIZ DIZLEY	G (A			
SAVOURNA STEVENSON CLAR (BCD KATE GRAHAM   FDL (BC ROGER MARRIOTT MELODIAN(BCD ALAN ROBERTSON   ACC(BCD

SWEAT
S344A •

	NO MORE RUNNING	1980 DOUBLE D	UK	DDLP 2

SWEATHOG
S345

LENNY LEE GOLDSMITH K V(B	(A) SWEATHOG	1971 CBS	US 30601	
BOB JONES G V (B	(B) HALLELUJAH	1972 CBS	US31144	UK	64784
DAVID LEONARD JOHNSON B V(B				
BARTHOLOMEW SMITH-FROST D(B				

SWEENEYS MEN
S346

ANDY IRVINE	(AB12	RATTLIN' & ROARIN' WILLY	1968 TRANSATLANTIC	UK TRA 170
JOW DOLAN	(1	(B) TRACKS OF SWEENEY	1969 TRANSATLANTIC	UK TRA 200
TERRY WOODS	(AB234	(B) TRACKS OF SWEENEY	1977 TRANSATLANTIC	UK TRANAM 40
AL O'DONNELL	(4	(C) SWEENEYS MEN	1976 TRANSATLANTIC	UK TRASAM 37
HENRY McCULLOUGH G	(3			
JOE MOYNIHAN	(AB1234			

THE SWEET
S347

BRIAN CONNOLLY	V (*ABCDEFGHIK	(*) GIMME DAT DING (ONE SIDE)	1970 MFP	UK	5248
STEVE PRIEST	HCA V B (ALL	(A) FUNNY HOW SWEET COCO CAN BE	1971 RCA	UK	SF8288
MIKE TUCKER	D V (ALL	(B) SWEETS BIGGEST HITS	1972 RCA	US	SF8316
FRANK TORPY	G (	(C) SWEET	1973 BELL	US	1124
MICK STEWART	G (	(D) SWEET FANNY ADAMS	1974 RCA		LPLI5039
ANDY SCOTT	G SYN V (ALL	(E) DESOLATION BOULEVARD	1975 RCA UK LPLI5080 US CAPITOL11395
GARY MOBERLEY	K (M	(F) STRUNG UP	1975 RCA		SPC 0001
		(G) GIVE US A WINK	1976 RCA UK RS 1036 US CAPITOL11496
		(H) OFF THE RECORD	1977 RCA UK PL25172 US CAPITOL11636
		(I) GOLDEN GREATS	1977 RCA UK PL25111
		(J) LEVEL HEADED	1978 POLYDOR POLD 5001	2302 077
		(J) LEVEL HEADED	1978 CAPITOL US	11744
		(K) THE SWEET	1978 CAMDEN	UK	CDS 1168
		(L) CUT ABOVE THE REST	1979 POLYDOR POLS 5022 US CAPITOL11929
		(M) WATERS EDGE	1980 POLYDOR POLS 1021 US CAPITOL12106
		(O) IDENTITY CRISIS	1982 POLYDOR UK 2311 179

RACHEL SWEET
S348

RACHEL SWEET	V (AB	(A) FOOL AROUND	1978 STIFF US 36101	UK	SEEZ 12
CHARLIE CHARLES	D (A	(B) PROTECT THE INNOCENT	1980 STIFF US 36337	UK	SEEZ 18
NORMAN WATT ROY	B (A	(B) PROTECT THE INNOCENT	1980 STIFF	GER	624251
BRINSLEY SCHWARZ	G (A	(C) AND THEN HE KISSED ME	1981 CBS	UK	85006
MICKEY GALLAGHER	K (A			
PIETRO NARDINI B G K(A LENE LOVICH   V (A MARK SURGEON   D (A PAUL GILLIERON   SAX (A
JOHN EARLE   SAX (A DICK HANSON   TPT (A CHRIS GOWER   TROM (A SIMON CLIMIE   PERC(A
RAY BEAVIS   SAX (A LEAH SWEET   PERC (A STIFF CHORUS   V (A

SWEET 'D BUSTER
S348A

BERTUS BORGERS	V WIND(ABCD	(A) SWEET'D BUSTER	1977 ARIOLA	25177 XOT
PAUL SMEENK	G (ABCD	(B) FRICTION	1978 ARIOLA	25861 XOT
HERMAN DEINUM	B (ABCD	(C) GIGS	1979 ARIOLA	200 337
HANS LAFAILLE	D (ABC	(D) SHOT INTO THE BLUE	1979 ARIOLA	200 651
ROBERT JAN STIPS	K (ABC			
ARNOLD BOGAARL	PERC (A			
FRANS MIJTS	TPT (A JONS PISTOOR K (D PIERRE VAN DER LINDEN D(D

SWEET F.A.
S348B

CAROL GRIMES	V (A	(A) SWEET F.A.	1980 MNW	SWED	103P
PETE KIRTLEY	G V (A			
GARY TWIGG	B (A TONY HICKS D (A OLLIE MALLARD K V (A

SWEET PAIN (US)
S349

DAVID ROIRDAN	(A	(A) SWEET PAIN	1970 UA UK UAS 29161 US	6793
BOB SPALDING	(	(B) SWEET PAIN II	1974 20TH CENTURY US 410
CARL JOHNSON	(		
MARTY FOLTZ	(FRANK DEMME (J C PHILLIPS (

SWEET PAIN (UK)
S349A

JOHN O'LEARY	HCA (A	(A) SWEET PAIN	1969 MERCURY	UK	SMCL20146
KEITH TILLMAN	B (A	(A) ENGLANDS HEAVY BLUES SUPER SESS	19 MERCURY	US	SR 61231
STUART COWELL	G (A			
DICK HECKSTALL SMITH SAX(A ANNETTE BROX   V (A SAM CROZIER   PNO V(A   JUNIOR DUNN   D(A
ALAN GREED	V (A			

SWEET SLAG
S349B

MICK KARANSKY	G V (A	(A) TRACKING WITH CLOSE UPS	1971 TRANSATLANTIC	UK XTRA 1112
PAUL JOLLY	WIND (A			
NOTH O'NEIL   B TROM(A AL CHAMBERS   D (A

SWEET SMOKE
S350

MARVIN KAMINOWITZ G V (C	(A) JUST A POKE	197 HARVEST	IMP IC062 28886
MARTIN ROSENBERG PERC (C	(A) JUST A POKE	197 HARVEST	5C054 24311
ANDREW DERSHIN	B (C	(B) DARKNESS TO LIGHT	197 HARVEST	IMP IC062 29471
JAY DORFMAN	D (C	(C) LIVE	1974 HARVEST	IMP IC062 29513
RICK GREENBERG	G (C			
JOHN CLASSI	PERC (C			

SWEET THUNDER
S351

	(A) SWEET THUNDER	1978 FANTASY		FT 545
	(B) HORIZONS	1979 FANTASY	US	576

SWEET THURSDAY

NICKY HOPKINS	K	(A	(A) SWEET THURSDAY	1969	TETRAGRAMMATON	US	T 12
JON MARK	G V	(A	(A) SWEET THURSDAY	1969	POLYDOR	UK	2310 051
ALUN DAVIES	G V	(A	(A) SWEET THURSDAY	1973	CBS	UK	65573
HARVEY BURNS	D	(A	(A) SWEET THURSDAY	198	LINE	GER	LLP 5044
BRIAN ODGERS	B WIND	(A					

S353

SWEET WATER

S353

FRED HERRERA	B V	(BC	(A) SWEET WATER	19	REPRISE	US	RS6313
ALEX DELZOPPO	K V HCA	(BC	(B) JUST FOR YOU	1970	REPRISE	US	RS6417
ALBERT B MOORE	FLT B(CB		(C) MELON	1971	REPRISE	US	RS6473
ELPIDIO COBIAN	PERC (BC						
NANSI NEVINS	G V	(CB ALAN MALAROWITZ D	(CB AUGUST BURNS	CELLO(CB RICKY FATAAR		D(C	

S354

SWEETBOTTOM

S354

WARREN 'VITO' WIEGRATZ	K WIND V(AB	(A) ANGELS OF THE DEEP	1978	ELEKTRA	UK K52110	US 6E 156
MARK TORROLL	D	(AB	(B) TURN ME LOOSE	1979	ELEKTRA		US 6E 210
DUANE STUERMER	B V	(AB					
MARTIN J APPEL	G	(AB					

S354A

SWELL MAPS

S354A

BIGGLES BOOKS	G K V B'ABC	(A) TRIP TO MARINEVILLE	1979	ROUGH TRADE		ROUGH 2
BARRY	K	(B	(B) IN 'JANE FROM OCCUPIED EUROPE'	1980	ROUGH TRADE		ROUGH 15
NIKKI MATTRESS	K G V(ABC	(C) WHATEVER HAPPENS NEXT	1981	ROUGH TRADE		ROUGH 21
JOWE HEAD	B HCA G V(ABC						
EPIC SOUNDTRACK K D SYN(ABC	PHONES B SPORTSMAN B VLN G(ABC	GORDON	B V (BC GOLDEN COCKRILL	B G V(A
LORA LOGIC	SAX (C						

S355

JONATHAN SWIFT

S355

JONATHAN SWIFT	G V	(AB	(A) INTROVERT	1971	CBS	UK	64412
PETER MORGAN	B	(B	(B) SONGS	1972	CBS	UK	64751
HAROLD FISHER	D	(B					
ALAN SPARKES	G	(B PAT KELLY	K	(A JACK BRAND	B	(A COLIN DAVY D	(A
STEVE HAMMOND	G	(A LAURIE ALLEN	D	(B LES HARVEY	G	(B ANN ODELL	K	(B

S355A

STEVE SWINDELLS

S355A

STEVE SWINDELLS	K V	(A	(A) MESSAGES	1974	RCA UK 5057		
JOHN GUSTAFSON	B	(A	(B) FRESH BLOOD	1980	ATCO UK K50738	US 38128	
BARRY DE SOUZA	D	(A					
CALEB QUAYE	G	(A DAVE WINTOUR	B	(A MIKE GILES	D	(A BRUCE KNAPP	G	(A
MARK WARNER	G	(A DORIS TROY	V	(A ROSETTA HIGHTOWER	V	(A BARRY ST JOHN	V	(A
CHRIS MERCER	SAX	(A MORRIS PERT	PERC	(A DANNY THOMPSON	B	(A MOUNTAIN FJORD ORCH(A
HUW LLOYD-LANGTON	G	(B NIC POTTER	B	(A SIMON KING	D	(A

S355B

SWIMMING POOL Q's

S355B

	(A) THE DEEP END	1981	ARMAGEDDON	UK	ARM 12

S356

SWINGING BLUE JEANS

S356

RAY ENNIS	G	(ALL	(A) TUTTI FRUTTI	1964	REGAL	UK	SREG 1073
RALPH ENNIS	G	(	(B) BLUE JEANS A SWINGING	1964	HMV UK CLP(M)1802 +CSD(S)		1570
LES BRAID	B	(	(C) HIPPY HIPPY SHAKE	1964	IMPERIAL	US	LPS 12261
NORMAN KUHLKE	D	(	(D) SHAKING TIME	1964	EMI EURO 83716	SWE 94823	
			(E) HEY HEY HEY HEY (LIVE)	1965	ELECTROLA	EURO	83927
			(F) THE SWINGING BLUES JEANS	1966	LIVERPOOL SOUND	UK	PSQ030
			(G) THE SWINGING BLUE JEANS	1967	MFP	UK	MFP1163
			(H) HIPPY HIPPY SHAKE	1973	BELLAPHON	EURO	15100
			(J) BRAND NEW & FADED	1974	DART		BULL1001
			(K) SWINGING BLUE JEANS	1978	EMI	UK	NUT 15
			(EP) SHAKE WITH	196	HMV	UK	7EG 8850
			(EP) YOUR NO GOOD	196	HMV	UK	7EG 8868

S356A

SWINGING MEDALIONS

S356A

JOHN McELRATH	V K	(A	(A) DOUBLE SHOT	1966	SMASH	UK	67083
CARROLL BLEDSOE	TPT	(A					
CHARLIE WEBBER	TPT	(A JIM PERKINS	SAX B(A STEVE CALDWELL	SAX D K(A JIMBO DDARES	G (A
JOE MORRIS	D	(A BRENT FORTSON	K WIND(A				

S357

SWITCH

S357

(A) SWITCH	1978	MOTOWN UK STML12096	US GORDY 980
(B) SWITH II	1979	MOTOWN UK STML12112	US GORDY 988
(C) THIS IS MY DREAM	1980		US GORDY 999
(D) REACHING FOR TOMORROW	1980	MOTOWN UK STML12135	

S358

ROOSEVELT SYKES

S358

ROOSEVELT SYKES	PNO V(ALL	(A) BLUES FROM BAR ROOMS	1967	77	UK	77LEU1250
JUSTIN ADAMS	G	(I	(B) BLUE BIRD No10	19	RCA	FR	PM 42028
CLARENCE FORD	SAX	(I	(C) BLUE & RIBALD	1977	SOUTHLAND	US RI	2
GEORGE FRENCH	B	(I	(D) BLUES	19	FOLKWAYS		3827
ALONZO STEWART	D	(I	(E) BARRELHOUSE BLUES & STOMPS	19	EUPHONIC	US	1205
DON LAWSON	D	(F	(F) BIG MAN OF BLUES	1961	EMI	UK	ENC 183
LITTLE BROTHER MONTGOMERY(R		(G) CHICAGO BLUES FESTIVAL	19	BLACK & BLUE	FR	33513
J T BROWN	SAX	(B	(H) COUNTRY BLUES PIANO ACE	1974	YAZOO		L 1033
WILLIE JAMES LACEY	G(B	(I) DIRTY DOUBLE MOTHER	1973	BLUESWAY	US	BL 6077
ARMAND JACKSON	D	(B	(J) FEEL LIKE BLOWING MY HORN	19	DELMARK		DS 632
JOHNNY WALKER	K	(B	(K) HARD DRIVING BLUES	19	DELMARK		DL 607
JOHN FRAZIER	B	(B	(L) HONEYDRIPPER'S DUKE'S MIXTURE	1971	BARCLAY IMP 920 294	+	80604
CHARLES SAUNDERS	D	(B	(M) HONEYDRIPPER	19	FANTASY	US	24717
JOHNNY MORTON	TPT	(B	(N) IN EUROPE	19	DELMARK		DS 616
OETT MALLARD	SAX	(B	(O) MUSIC IS MY BUSINESS	19	BLUE LABOR	US	BL111
LEON WASHINGTON	SAX	(B	(P) ORIGINAL HONEYDRIPPER	19	BLIND PIG	US	005
LEONARD GASTON	G	(B	(Q) ROOSEVELT SYKES	19	STORYVILLE		SLP 189
ALFRED ELKINS	B	(B	(R) URBAN BLUES	19	FANTASY	US	24717
BILL CASIMIR	SAX	(B	( ) SINGS THE BLUES	19	CROWN	US	5287
ERNEST CRAWFORD	B	(B	( ) SINGS THE BLUES	19	UNITED	US	7792
W B NELSON	D	(B	( ) RETURN OF ROOSEVELT SYKES	19	BLUESVILLE 1006	
ROBERT PETE WILLIAMS	G(A	( ) HONEYDRIPPER	19	BLUESVILLE 1014		
HOMESICK JAMES	G B	(K					

S358A

TERRY SYLVESTER

S358A

TERRY SYLVESTER	G V	(AB	(A) TERRY SYLVESTER	1974	EPIC	US	33076
			(B) I BELIEVE	1976	POLYDOR	UK	2383 394

```
S358B                              SYLVAIN SYLVAIN                                        S358B
        SYLVAIN SYLVAIN   G V  (A        (A) SYLVAIN SYLVAIN         1979 RCA       US/UK    13475
        BOBBY BLAIN       K    (A        (B) AND THE TEARDROPS       1981 RCA                3913
        JON GERBER        SAX  (A
        BUZ VERNO         B    (A    JOHNNY RAO    G      (A   LEE CRYSTAL    D   (A
S358C                               RIKKI SYLVAN                                           S358C
        RIKKI SYLVAN      V SYN(A        (A) THE SILENT HOURS       1981 KALEIDOSCOPE    UK   85198
        ANDY PRICE        B    (A
        STEVE WILKIN      G    (A    CHARLIE CHARLES   D   (A   EUGENE MOULE K V   (A
S358D                                   SYLVERS                                            S358D
        OLYMPIA SYLVERS        (        (A) SYLVERS              19   PRIDE       US   007
        JAMES SYLVERS          (        (B) SYLVERS II           19   PRIDE       US   026
        RICKY SYLVERS          (        (C) SYLVERS III          1974 MGM         US   4940
        CHERMAINE SYLVERS      (        (D) SHOWCASE             197  CAPITOL      US   11465
        EDMUND SYLVERS         (        ( ) SOMETHING SPECIAL    197  CAPITOL      US   11580
        LEON SYLVERS          (        ( ) NEW HORIZONS         197  CAPITOL      US   11705
                                       ( ) BEST OF              197  CAPITOL      US   11868
                                       ( ) FOREVER YOURS        197  CASABLANCA US    7103
S358E                                   SYLVESTER                                          S358E
        SYLVESTER         K V  (ALL      (A) SCRATCH MY FLOWER    1973            US   BTS 45
        JAMES Q SMITH     G V HCA(AB      (B) BAZAAR              1973            US   BTS 60
        KERRY HATCH       B V K(AB       ( ) STARS               1979 FANTASY UK 556   US 9579
        TRAVIS FULLERTON  D V  (AB       ( ) MIGHTY REAL         19   FANTASY UK 3009
        CHRIS MOSTERT     WIND (AB       ( ) STEP TWO            19   FANTASY        US 9556
        BOBBY BLOOD       TPT  (AB       ( ) SYLVESTER           19   FANTASY        US 9531
        PETER MINTUN      K    (A        ( ) LIVING PROOF        19   FANTASY UK 573
                                        ( ) SELL MY SOUL        1980 FANTASY        US 9601
S358F                                     SYN                                              S358F
        CHRIS SQUIRE      B    (         (A) THE SYN             1967 DERAM
        ANDREW JACKSON    K    (
        STEVE NARDELLI    V    (    PETER BROCKLAND(BANKS) G(A   GUNNAR HAKARNARSON D   (A   RAY STEELE      D (
        CHRIS ALLEN       D    (A
S358G                                  SYNATHESIA                                          S358G
        DENNIS HOLMES     G VIBES(A      (A) SYNATHESIA          1969 RCA   UK    SF 8058
        JIMMY FRASER      WIND (A
        LESLIE COOK       V VLN MAND(A
S359                                 SYMPHONIC SLAM                                        S359
        TIMO LAINE        SYN G V(A      (A) SYMPHONIC SLAM      1976 A&M            UK    AMLH69023
        JOHN LOWRY        D V  (A
        DAVID STONE       K V  (A
S360                              SYNDICATE OF SOUND                                       S360
        BOB GONZALES      B    (A        (A) LITTLE GIRL         19   BELL US 6001 STATESIDE UK SSL10185
        JOHN SHARKEY      G K  (A
        DON BASKIN        SAX V(A    JOHN DUCKWORTH   D V   (A   JIM'BO' SAWYERS    G V  (A
S361                                    SYNERGY                                            S361
        LARRY FAST             (        (A) SEQUENCER            1976 SIRE UK 9103326 US PASSPORT 98014
        RON HOWDEN            (        (A) SEQUENCER            1979            RI US PASSPORT 6002
        MORTY SCOTT          (        (B) ELECTRONIC REALIZATIONS 1976 SIRE UK 9299752 US PASSPORT 98009
                                       (B) ELECTRONIC REALIZATIONS 1979          RI US PASSPORT 6001
                                       (C) CHORDS               1979              US PASSPORT 6000
                                       (D) GAMES                1979             US PASSPORT 6003
                                       (E) AUDION               1982 LOGO UK 1033
S362                                     SYREETA                                           S362
        SYREETA WRIGHT    V    (ALL      (A) SYREETA             1972 MOWEST US 7001
        BUZZY FEITON      G    (A        (B) STEVIE WONDER PRESENTS 1974 TAMLA        UK    STML11268
        STEVIE WONDER          (AB       (C) SYREETA             1975 TAMLA US 808          M6  84451
        KEITH COPELAND    D    (A        (D) ONE TO ONE          1977 TAMLA US 349    UK    STML12053
        G C CAMERON            (E        (E) RICH LOVE POOR LOVE 1978 TAMLA US 891    UK    STML12073
        LANI GROVES       V    (AB       (F) SYREETA             1980 MOTOWN US 382   UK    STML12137
        JIM GILSTRAP      V    (A        (G) BEST OF             1981 MOTOWN         UK    STMR 9014
        TREVOR LAWRENCE   PERC (A        (H) SET MY LOVE IN MOTION 1982 MOTOWN       UK    ST 12162
        SCOTT EDWARDS     B    (A
        LINDA TUCKER      V    (A    GLORIA BARLEY      V    (A    JULIAN GAILLARD ORCH(A   OLLIE BROWN      D   (B
        MARLO HENDERSON   G    (A    STEVE MADAIO      TPT  (B    DENIECE WILLIAMS   V(B   ANITA SHERMAN    V   (B
        PAUL RISER        STR  (B    REGGIE McBRIDE    B   (B    MIKE SEMBELLO      G(B   DENNIS MOROUSE   SAX (B
        SHIRLEY BREWER    V    (B    MINNIE RIPPERTON   V    (B    DENNIS MORRISON   V(B
T1                                      STEVEN T                                           T1
        STEVEN T          G V K  (A     (A) WEST COAST CONFIDENTIAL  1978 DREAM US DA 3500  GER 6 23359
        WILTON FELDER     B    (A
        DON MENZA         SAX  (A    MIKE BAIRD      D     (A   DAN FERGUSON    G   (A   BECKY HOBBS PNO  (A
        BEN BENAY         HCA  (A    DAVE CARR     K       (A   LEE SKLAR      B   (A   HAL BLAINE      D  (A
        CHRIS DARROW      ACC V(A    RICK HENN     SYN     (A   MIKE MELVOINE   K   (A   EMIL RICHARDS   PERC(A
        MIKE POCARO       B    (A    LEE RITENOUR    G     (A   MARY HYLAN     V   (A   STEVE LUKATHER  G  (A
        WILLIE ORNELAS    D    (A    JAI WINDING    K      (A   DAVID FOSTER   PNO  (A
T2                            T FORD & THE BONE SHAKERS                                    T2
                                        (A) ROCK RATTLE & ROLL  1978 SPLASH              CPLP1004
                                        (B) JUST KEEP IT UP     1979 SPLASH              CPLP 2001
T3                       T.I.M.E.  (TRUST IN MEN EVERYWHERE)                               T3
        LARRY BYROM       G    (B        (A) T.I.M.E.           1968 LIBERTY US LST7558
        BILL RICHARDSON   G    (B        (B) SMOOTH BALL        1969 LIBERTY US LST7605 UK LBS83232
        STEVE RUMPH       D    (
        NICK ST NICHOLAS  B    (    PAT COUCHOIS    D     (B   RICHARD TEPP    B   (B
T4                         T.K.O.  (TECHNICAL KNOCK OUT)                                   T4
        BRAD SINSEL       V    (A        (A) LET IT ROLL        1979 INFINITY          INS 2002
        RICK PIERCE       G    (A
        MARK SEIDENVERG   B    (A    DARRYL SIGUENZA  D    (A   TONY BORTKO    K G  (A
```

T T REUTER

PETER STRAUSS   D   (A   (A) KONTROLL KLUBB KASHBAN   1980 SKAN HEART WORK   01
PETER IVARSS   B V (A
PETER PUDERS   G V (A   HENRIK VANANT   G V (A

KEITH CROSS   G K V(A   (A) IT'LL ALL WORK OUT IN BOOMLAND   1970 DECCA   UK   SKL 5050
PETER DUNTON   D V (A
BERNARD JINKS   B V (A

                                      (A) TV KIDS   197 BRAIN BOOSTER   TA 001

IAN BROUDIE V PERC PROD(A   (A) A THIN RED LINE   1981 DERAM   UK SML 1123
ALAN WINSTANLEY   PROD (A
NEIL BALDWIN   B   (A   DAVE HAMPTON TPT V(A   ALLY PALMERR   G V(A ALI PATERSON   D (A
NORMAN RODGER   G V (A   STEVE BROWN   PERC(A

JUNE TABOR

JUNE TABOR   V   (ALL   (A) SILLY SISTERS   1976 CHRYSALIS   UK   CHR 1101
MADDY PRIOR   V   (A   (B) AIRS & GRACES   1976 TOPIC   UK   12TS 298
TONY HALL   MEL (AC   (C) ASHES & DIAMONDS   1977 TOPIC   UK   12TS 360
BOB DAVENPORT   (D   (D) BEES ON HORSEBACK   1977 FREE REED   UK   FRR 016
MARTIN CARTHY   G PERC(A   (1) 1977 TOUR
NIC JONES   FDL G(A
ANDY IRVINE   MAND (A   DANNY THOMPSON   B   (A   GABRIEL McKEON   PIPES(A JON GILLASPIE K WIND(ABC1
JOHNNY MOYNIHAN   WIND (A   BRIAN GOLBEY   FDL (A   LUIS JARDIM   PERC (A RICK KEMP   B (C
NIGEL PEGRUM   D   (C   DOUG MORTER   G   (A   MARTIN SIMPSON   G   (1

TAGGETT

COLIN HORTON JENNINGS G (A   (A) TAGGETT   1974 EMI UK EMC3015   US UA   UALA407
TIM WHEATLEY   B V (A
TERRY FOGG   D   (A   PETE ARNESON K   (A

TALBOT BROTHERS

TERRY TALBOT   HCA G V (A   (A) TALBOT BROTHERS   1974 WB   US BS2767   UK   K56039
JOHN TALBOT   BAN G V(A
RUSS KUNKEL   D   (A   LEE SKLAR   B   (A   RANDY SCRUGGS   G   (A JOSH GRAVES G DOBRO (A
SNEAKY PETE KLEINOW STEEL(A   CREEPER KURNOW   HCA (A   DON DACUS   G   (A JOHN JARVIS   PNO(A
DAVID LINDLEY   G   (A

WAYNE TALBERT

WAYNE TALBERT   (AB   (A) HOUSTON NICKEL KICKS   196 MERCURY   US   61259
                                       (B) DUES TO PAY   196 MERCURY   US   10603

TALISKER

MARK MEGGIDO   B   (A   (A) DREAMING OF GLENISLA   1975 CAROLINE   CA 1513
LINDSAY COOPER   WIND (A   (B) LAND OF STONE   1977 ECM   JAP060018
DAVE WEBSTER   SAX (ABC   (C) THE LAST BATTLE   1978 VINYL   VS 107
JOHN RANGECROFT   SAX (ABC
KEN HYDER   D   (ABC JOHN LAWRENCE   B

TALKING HEADS

DAVID BYRNE   G V (ALL   (A) TALKING HEADS '77   1977 SIRE US SR6306   UK   9103 328
TINA WEYMOUTH   B   (ALL   (B) MORE SONGS OF BUILDING & FOOD   1978 SIRE US SR6058   UK   K56531
BRIAN ENO SYN K G V (BCD   (B) MORE SONGS OF BUILDING & FOOD   1979 SIRE GER 200 880
CHRIS FRANTZ   D   (ALL   (C) FEAR OF MUSIC   1979 SIRE US SRK 6076 UK/GER K56707
JERRY HARRISON   G V K(ALL   (D) REMAIN IN LIGHT   1980 SIRE   US/UK   SRK 6095
GENE WILDER   PERC (C   (E) THE NAME OF THIS BAND IS T HEADS 1982 SIRE 23590   GER   K66112
ARI   PERC (C   (EP) HOUSE IN MOTION   1981 SIRE UK 4050
ROBERT FRIPP   G   (C
JULIE LAST   V   (C   ADRIAN BELEW   G   (DE   JON HASSELL   HRNS (DE NONA HENDRYX   V (D
ROBERT PALMER   PERC (D   JOSE ROSSY   PERC   (DE   DOLETTE McDONALD   V PERC(E BERNIE WORRELL K V (E
BUSTA JONES   G B (E   STEVE SCALES   PERC (DE   SWEETBREATHES   V   (C TOMMY BONGIOUR PROD(A
LANCE QUINN   PROD (C

JAMES TALLEY

JAMES TALLEY   G V (ALL   (A) GOT NO BREAD,NO MILK NO MONEY   1975 CAPITOL   11416
BYRON BACH   CELLO(C   (B) TRYIN' LIKE THE DEVIL   1976 CAPITOL   11494
RICK DURRETT   PNO (C   (C) BLACKJACK CHOIR   1977 CAPITOL   11605
DAVE GILLON   G   (C   (D) AIN'T IT SOMETHIN'   1978 CAPITOL   11695
JOHNNY GIMBLE   G   (C
JOSH GRAVES   FDL (C   DOYLE GRISHAM   STEEL(C   STEVE HOSTAK   G   (C IRV KANE   TROM(C
B B KING   G   (C   PEBBLE DANIEL   V   (C   MARCIA ROUTH   V   (C MIKE LEECH   B (C
ANDY McMAHON   K   (C   CLARK PIERSON   D V (C   BILLY PUETT   WIND (C JOHN SAYLES   FDL (C
DON SHEFFIELD   TPT (C   JERRY SHOOK   G B HCA (C   TOMMY SMITH   TPT (C KYLE TULLIS   B (C
REGGIE YOUNG   G   (C   MARY JO TALLEY   V   (C

TALTON,STEWART,SANDLIN

TOMMY TALTON   G V (A   (A) HAPPY TO BE ALIVE   1976 CAPRICORN   US   0167
BILL STEWART   D G PERC(A
JOHN SANDLIN   G B (A   SCOTT BOYER   (A   BONNIE BRAMLETT   (A JOE ENGLISH   (A
CHUCK LEAVELL   (A   DRU LOMBAR   (A   STEVE MILLER   (A JOE WALK   (A

TAMPA RED

HUDSON'RED'WHITTAKER G V(ALL   (A) TAMPA RED   19   BLUESVILLE   US   BVLP1030
GEORGIA TOM DORSEY PNO (C   (B) HOW LONG   19   BLUESVILLE   US   BVLP1043
BLACK BOB   PNO (DE   (C) BOTTLENECK GUITAR 1928 1937   1974 YAZOO   US   1039
BIG MACEO   PNO (D   (D) THE GUITAR WIZARD   19   RCA   AMX2 5501
WILLIE WILLIAMSON HCA (DE   (E) THE GUITAR WIZARD 1935 1953   1974 BLUES CLASSICS US   25
WALTER HORTON   HCA (DE
JOHNNY JONES   PNO (
WILLIE LACEY   G   (ODIE PAYNE   D   (SUGARMAN PENIGAR   SAX (BILL CASIMIR   SAX (
JUDGE RILEY   D   (ARMAND JACKSON   SAX (ERNEST CRAWFORD   B   (OETT MALLARD   WIND(
TYRELL DIXON   D   (RANSOM KNOWLING   B   (BLIND JOHN DAVIS   PNO (

NORMA TANEGA

NORMA TANEGA	G V AUTOHARP(AB	(A) WALKING MY CAT NAMED DOG	1966	NEW VOICE 2001	UK	STATESIDE	10182
MIKE MORAN	K B V(B	(B) I DONT THINK IT WILL HURT	1977	RCA	UK		SF8217
DON PAUL	V (B						

TANGERINE DREAM

EDGAR FROESE	SYN K G B (ALL	(A) ELECTRONIC MEDITATION	1970	OHR	GER	OMM556004	
CHRIS FRANKE	SYN K(BCDEFHJKLMNRS	(B) ALPHA CENTAURI	1971	OHR	GER	OMM556012	
PETER BAUMANN	SYN K(CDEFHJKL	(B) ALPHA CENTAURI	1975	POLYDOR		2383 314	
CONRAD SCHNITZLER	FLT (A	(C) ZEIT	1972	OHR	GER	OMM256021	
KLAUS SCHULZE	K (A	(C) ZEIT	1976	VIRGIN	UK	VD 2503	
UDO DENNEBOURG	FLT (B	(D) ATEM	1972	OHR	GER	OMM566031	
ROLAND PAULCYK	SYN (B	(D) ATEM	1974	POLYDOR		2383 297	
STEVE SCHROYDER	ORG (BC	(BD) ATEM /ALPHA	1976	VIRGIN UK VD2504 GER		87761	
MICHAEL HOENIG	K (	(E) PHAEDRA	1974	VIRGIN UK V 2010 GER		81761	
FLORIAN FRICKE	SYN (C	(E) PHAEDRA	1974	VIRGIN US 13108			
STEVE JOLLIFFE	HRNS FLT(M	(F) RUBYCON	1975	VIRGIN UK V 2025 US		13166	
KLAUS KRIEGER	D (MN	(F) RUBYCON	1975	VIRGIN FR 2933 716			
JOHANNES SCHMOELLING	K (PRS	(H) RICOCHET	1976	VIRGIN UK V 2044 GER		89679	
VOLKER HOMBACH	FLT VLN(	(J) STRATOSFEAR	1976	VIRGIN US 34427 UK		V 2068	
JOHANNES LUCKE	CELLO(C	(J) STRATOSFEAR	1976	VIRGIN GER 28146			
LANSE HAPSHASH	D (	(K) SORCERER	1977	MCA UK MCF2806	GER	62085	
KIRT HERKENBERG	B (	(L) ENCORE (DBL)	1977	VIRGIN US 35014 UK		VD 2506	
JOCHEN VON GRUMBCOW	CELLO(A	(L) ENCORE (DBL)	1977	VIRGIN GER 25495			
SVEN JOHANNSON	D (	(M) CYCLONE	1978	VIRGIN UK V 2097 GER		25843	
HANS JOCHEN BRUNE	CELLO(C	(N) FORCE MAJEURE	1978	VIRGIN UK V 2111 GER		200347	
EDUARD MEYER	CELLO(N	(O) 70/80 (4 LP SET)	1980	VIRGIN	UK	V BOX2	
HANS ULRICH WEIGEL	PROD(A	(P) TANGRAM	1980	VIRGIN UK V 2147 GER		202169	
KLAUS FREUDIGMANN	PROD(A	(Q) THIEF	1981	VIRGIN UK V 2189			
		(R) EXIT	1981	VIRGIN UK V 2212 GER		203998	
		(S) WHITE EAGLE	1982	VIRGIN UK V 2226			

TANGERINE PEEL

(A) SOFT THOUGHTS	1970	RCA	US	LSA 3002

TANGERINE ZOO

DONALD SMITH	D (A	(A) TANGERINE ZOO	19	MAINSTREAM	US	6107
TONY TAVARES	B (A	(B) OUTSIDE LOOKING ON	19	MAINSTREAM	US	6116
ROBERT BENEVIDES	G (A					
WAYNE GAGNOH	G (A	RONALD MEDEIROS	K HCA(A			

TANK

(A) FILTH HOUNDS OF HADES	1981	KAMAFLAGE		KAM LP1

MARC TANNER

MARC TANNER	(	(A) NO ESCAPE	1979	ELEKTRA	US 168	
MIKE BAIRD	D (A	(B) TEMPTATION	1980	ELEKTRA	US 240	NL 52192
BOB GLAUB	B (A					

RITCHIE ZITO G (AB GLEN SPREEN K (A WILLIAM SMITH K (A JIM HORN FLT (A
VANETTA FIELDS V (A GARY MALLABER D (A JAY GRAYDEN G (A BEN BENAY G (A
MAX GRONENTHAL V (A TOMMY VIG PERC (A JEFF PORCARO D (A STEVE LUKATHER G (A
MIKE FINNIGAN V (A ROSE BUTTER V (A DAVID PAICH K (A JOE TURANO V (A
DAVID PIET B (AB MICHAEL STEVENS G (B RON EDWARDS B (B JOE ROMERSA D (B
STEVE MANN WIND (B LINDA STEVENS V (B ED TREE G (B IRVIN KRAMER G (B
MARC GREEN SYN (B JOHN JARVIS K (B BILL PAYNE K (B RICHARD PAGE V (B
GARY GRANT HRNS (B BILLY LAMB HRNS (B CHUCK BROOKE HRNS (B

TAPES

ROLF HERMSEN	G V (AB	(A) YOU JUST CANT SLEEP	1978	VERTIGO GER 9198 108	
MICK BRANDES	G V (AB	(B) PARTY	1980	PASSPORT US 9842 NL 58129	
DICK VANDERVAART	D (A				
IGOR ROOVERS	B (AB	PETER MEURIS	D (B		

TANTRUM

BARB ERBER	V (AB	(A) TANTRUM	1978	OVATION US 1735	GER 146 206
BILL SYNIAR	B (AB	(B) RATHER BE ROCKIN'	1979	OVATION US 1747	
SANDY CAULFIELD	V (AB				
VERN WENNERSTROM	D (AB	PAM BRADLEY V (AB	PHIL BALSANO K (AB	RAY SAPKO G (AB	

TAOS

ALBIE CIAPPA	D V (A	(A) TAOS	196	MERCURY US	61257
BURT LEVINE	G BAN(A				
STEVE OPPENHEIM	G K V(A	JEFF BAKER G K V(A	KIT BEDFORD	B K V(A	

TARGET

JIM JAMISON	V (AB	(A) TARGET	1976	A&M	US 4607
DAVID SPAIN	D (AB	(B) CAPTURED	1977	A&M	US 4652
TOM CATHEY	B (AB				
PAUL CANNON	G (AB	BUD DAVIS K (AB			

TARHEEL SLIM

ALLEN 'SLIM' BUNN	V G (A	(A)NUMBER 9 TRAIN(EP)	1980	CHARLY	UK CTD 125
JIMMY SPRUIL	G (A				

TARNEY SPENCER

ALAN TARNEY	G V K(ABC	(A) TARNEY SPENCER	1976	BRADLEYS	UK BRADL1011
TREVOR SPENCER	D (ABC	(B) THREE'S A CROWD	1978	A&M US 4692	UK AMLH68466
LYNTON NAIFF	K (B	(C) RUN FOR YOUR LIFE	1979	A&M US 4757	UK AMLH64757
COLIN COOPER	(B				
JOE POLLARD	(B	PETER HAYCOCK (B	TONY RIVERS	(B JOHN PERRY	(B
STU CALVER	(B	JOHN CUFFLEY (B	PETER FILLEUL	(B DEREK HOLT	(B

TASAVALLAN PRESIDENTTI

JUKKA TOLONEN	G PNO(ABC	(A) TASAVALLAN PRESIDENTTI	1969	EMI 062 34264 LOVE SWEDLRLP 7	
PEKKA POYRY	WIND (BC	(B) LAMBERTLAND	1972	SONET	SWED SLP2533
VESA AALTONEN	D (ABC	(B) LAMBERTLAND	1973	SONET SNTF636 LOVE SWED LRLP 60	
FRANK ROBSON	K V (A	(B) LAMBERTLAND	1974	BRAIN GER 1063	
MANS GROUNDSTROEM	B K (AB	(C) MILKY WAY MOSES	1974	SONET SNTF658 LOVE SWED LRLP102	
JUHANN AALTONEN	WIND (A	(C) MILKY WAY MOSES	1974	BRAIN GER 1058 US JANUS 3065	
HEIKKI VIRTANEN	B (C				
EERO RAITTINEN	V PERC(BC				

```
RORY GALLAGHER      G V HCA(ALL      (A) TASTE                      1969 POLYDOR UK 583042 US ATCO 33296
RICHARD McCRACKEN   B   (ALL         (B) ON THE BOARDS             1970 POLYDOR UK 583083 US ATCO 33322
                                     (B) ON THE BOARDS             1970 POLYDOR EURO 184 366
JOHN WILSON         D   (ALL         (C) LIVE TASTE                1971 POLYDOR      UK    2310 082
                                     (D) FIRST TASTE(1967)         1971 BASF         GERM20 29084 0
                                     (E) LIVE AT I O W             1972 POLYDOR      UK    2383 120
                                     (F) POP HISTORY               197  POLYDOR             2668 003
                                     (G) POP GIANTS No 5           197  BRUNSWICK    EURO  2911 516
                                     (H) MOVIN' ON                 197  KARUSSEL     EURO
                                     (J) TASTE                     1977 POLYDOR             2384 076
                                     (K) TASTE                     19   VIOLENT SYSTEM     PN100001
                                     (L) GREATEST ROCK SENSATION   1977 POLYDOR      GER   2499 115
                                     (M) IN CONCERT AT THE MARQUEE '68  1977 ARIOLA EURO 25001
```

```
JANCE M JOHNSON     B V (A           (A) A TASTE OF HONEY          1978 CAPITOL      UK    11754
PERRY L KIBBLE      K V (A
HAZEL P PAYNE       G V (A   WARE MARCUS   STR     (A  LARRY MIZELL   PROD (A  DONALD JOHNSON  D V (A
FONCE MIZELL        PROD (A
```

```
THOM MOONEY         D   (A           (A) TATTO                     1976 PRODIGAL    US 10014      PDL2003
JEFF HUTTON         K V (A
WALLY BRYSON        G V (A   DAN KIAWON    B    (A  DAVIS THOMAS    G V (A
```

```
BERNIE TAUPIN           (ALL         (A) BERNIE TAUPIN             19   ELEKTRA     US    EKS 75020
CALEB QUAYE         G   (A           (B) TAUPIN                    1971 DJM         UK    DJLPS 415
DAVEY JOHNSTONE     G MAND(A          (C) HE WHO RIDES THE TIGER    1980 ASYLUM US 6E263 UK    K52220
SHAWN PHILLIPS      G SIT V(A
RICHARD COFF        VLN (A   DIANA LEWIS    K    (A
```

```
MAR WAIS            G   (A           (A) SEPPUKU                   1981 VIRGIN      1981 GER 201 899
DANIEL DARC         V   (A
LAURENT SINCLAIR    K   (A
J J BURNEL          V PROD(A  VIVIENNE VOG    V   (A  JET LE NOIR    D   (A  PHILIPPE        B  (A
```

```
PAUL PHILLIPS       G K V(A           (A) HEY MISTER RECORD MAN     1979 LOGO        UK    LOGO 1015
PETE ZORN B G WIND V (A
MATT FINISH         G   (A   ALLEN KEYS     K SYN   (A  RICHARD BURGESS   D   (A  NAPOLEON GLOSS   D PERC(A
JETT SEOPARDIE      CONGA(A  BILL ZORN      V      (A  KEN NICOL         V   (A
```

```
DAVID CUMMING       G V (A           (A) DAY FOR NIGHT             1980 FANTASY     US    9603
COLIN PAYNE         K   (A
JEFF NEAD           D   (A   TIM GORMAN     K     (A  MAC GARDIN      B  (A
```

```
ALEX TAYLOR         V   (AB          (A) WITH FRIENDS & NEIGHBOURS 1971 ATCO 2400 177 US CAPRICORN  860
JOHNNY SANDLIN      B   (AB          (B) DINNERTIME               1972 CAPRICORN     US          0101
PAUL HORNSBY        K   (A           (C) THIRD FOR MUSIC          1974 DUNHILLUS 50151
TOMMY TALTON        G   (A
STEVE SMITH         V   (B   BILL STEWART    D   (AB  SCOTT BOYER   G V (AB  JAMES TAYLOR    G  (A
KING CURTIS         SAX (A   FRANK WESS      SAX (A   WILLIE BRIDGES SAX (A  RONNIE CUBER    SAX(A
DANNY MOORE         TPT (A   P KOWALKE       G   (A   JOE RUDD      G   (A  LOU MULLENIX    PERC(B
CHARLES HAYWARD     B   (B   ROGER HAWKINS   PERC (B  CHUCK LEAVELL K   (B  WAYNE PERKINS   G B(B
JOHN HUGHEY         STEEL(B  JAI JOHANNY JOHANSON PERC(B EARL SIMS  PERC (B  CHARLES CHALMERS V  (B
SANDY RHODES        V   (B   DONNA RHODES     V   (B   GINGER HOLLADAY V (B  MARY HOLLADAY   V  (B
TEMPLE RISER        V   (B
```

```
ALLAN TAYLOR        G V (ALL          (A) SOMETIMES                1971 LIBERTY US 5529     LBG 83483
DAVE MATTACKS       D   (A           (B) THE LADY                 1972 UA               UAS 29275
DAVE PEGG           B   (A           (C) AMERICAN ALBUM           1973 UA               UAG 29408
DAVE SWARBRICK      VLN (A           (C) AMERICAN ALBUM           1977 MOONCREST   UK    CREST  28
D KELSO HERSTON         (C           (C) AMERICAN ALBUM           1978 ROCKBURGH   UK    ROC   101
SPANKY McFARLANE    V   (C           (D) TRAVELLER               1978 RUBBER      UK    RUB   026
BILLY SANFORD       G   (C           (E) ROCK ON THE DAY         1979 RUBBER      UK    RUB 040
MARY CASLIN             (C
MIKE LEECH              (C   BILLY RILEY     (C   PETE WADE     G   (B  JOHN BUCK WILKIN G  (C
DAVID BRIGGS        PNO (C   JERRY CARRIGAN  (C   BUDDY SPICHER FDL (C  JOHNNY GIMBLE   FDL (C
TOMMY COGBILL       B   (C   LARRY BUTLER   K (C   REGGIE YOUNG  G   (C  STEVE MILLER    K  (C
JAMES COLVARD       G   (C   KARL HIMMEL    D (C   DON GRANT         (C  JAMES CASON     B  (C
D BERGEN WHITE          (C   PETER JAMESON  G (C   MIKE OMARTIAN K   (C  JOHN GUERIN     D  (C
WADDY WACHTEL       G   (C   BRYAN GAROFALO B (C   NICK VAN MAARTH   (C  JAMES E BOND JR    (C
MAX HOCH                (C
```

```
CHIP TAYLOR V G FDL    (ALL          (A) GASOLINE                 1972 POLYDOR 2318074 US BUDDAH  5118
GEORGE KIRIAKIS     G V (BCDF        (B) LAST CHANCE              1974 WB   UK K56036 US WB      2718
JOHN PLATANIA       G   (BCDF        (C) SOME OF US               1974 WB   UK K56077 US WB      2824
JOE RENDA           K   (BCDF        (D) THIS SIDE OF THE BIG RIVER 1975 WB  UK K56152 US WB     2882
TOM REILLY          STEEL(C          (E) ANGEL OF THE MORNING (CASSETTE) 1975 BUDDAH  UK    CBDS 4026
JOHN REGAN          B   (C           (F) SOMEBODY SHOOT OUT THE JUKEBOX 1976 CBS      US      34345
CHUCK FIORE         B   (C           (G) SAINT SEBASTIAN         1979 CAPITOL     US      11909
ERIK'RICK' NELSON D (BC
CHARLIE POWERS      D   (CD  LEE HARRISON    V    (C  JOHN NAGY     PERC (BC MARGARET McGUINN  V (C
ANN McGUINN         V   (C   ANN HEIMBUCH    V    (C  DAVE KAPELL   B    (BDF PETE DRAKE    STEEL(BD
BUDDY SPICHER       FDL (D   DAVID MANSFIELD FDL  (DF KEN GARRETSON WIND (D  SANDY BULL      WIND(D
VIC SERMAN          HRNS (DF  JOE STELLITTI   HRNS (DF RON CARRAN   HRNS (DF DAVE GRISMAN   MAND(B
THE JORDANAIRES     V   (B   BEAU SEGAL       D   (F  'THUMBS' TAYLOR PNO (F
```

```
DAVE TAYLOR                           (A) ROCKIN' IN THE SAME OLD WAY 1979 CHARLY    UK    CRL 5016
```

DREW TAYLOR

DREW TAYLOR	(A	(A) WINDOW	1981 ROXON	UK	ROX 004		

EDDIE TAYLOR

EDDIE TAYLOR	G V	(ALL	(A) MASTER OF THE MODERN BLUES	1966 TESTAMENT	US	2214
BIG WALTER HORTON	HCA	(A	(B) READY FOR EDDIE	1975 BIG BEAR		BEAR 6
OTIS SPANN	PNO	(A	(C) FEEL SO BAD	1976 DJM	UK	DJM 22065
FRED BELOW	D	(A	(D) BAD BOY A LONG WAY FROM CHICAGO	1978 P/VINE	JAP	PLP 3501
BOB HALL	PNO	(B	(E) BIG TOWN PLAYBOY	1980 CHARLY	UK	CRB 1015
STEVE BEAL	G	(F	(F) MY HEART IS BLEEDING	1980 L&R	GER	42009
ROGER HILL	G	(B				
BOB BRUNNING	B	(B	GRAHAM GALLERY	B	(B	PETE YORK	D	(B	PHILIP WALKER	G(C
GEORGE SMITH	HCA	(C	JIMMY JONES	PNO	(C	CHUCK JONES	B	(C	JOHNNY TUCKER	D(C
LITTLE H WILLIAMS	TAMB	(C	GEORGE KITTA	B	(F	ODIE PAYNE	D	(F	CAREY BELL	HCA	(F
SUNNYLAND SLIM	PNO	(F	FLOYD JONES		(A					

HOUND DOG TAYLOR

HOUND DOG TAYLOR	G V	(ALL	(A) & THE HOUSE ROCKERS	1974 SONET UK SNTF676 ALLIGATOR US 4701
BREWER PHILLIPS	G	(ABC*	(B) NATURAL BOOGIE	197 SONET UK SNTF678 ALLIGATOR US 4704
TED HARVEY	D	(ABC*	(C) BEWARE OF THE DOG	197 SONET UK SNTF701 ALLIGATOR US 4707
			(D) LIVE AT FLORENCES(1969)	1980 JSP	1020
			(*) 1972 ANN ARBOR FESTIVAL	

JAMES TAYLOR

JAMES TAYLOR	G V	(ALL	(A) JAMES TAYLOR	1968 APPLE UK SAPCOR 3	US	3352
DANNY KORTCHMAR	G	(BDEJKLN	(B) SWEET BABY JAMES	1970 WB	UK K46043	US	1843
RUSS KUNKEL	D	(DEKLHJN	(C) & THE ORIGINAL FLYING MACHINE	1971 EUPHORIA		EUPH 2
PETER ASHER	V	(ADEJLN	(C) & THE ORIGINAL FLYING MACHINE	197 SPRINGBOARD	US	4023
ALEX TAYLOR	V	(EJ	(D) MUD SLIDE SLIM	1971 WB	UK K46085	US	2561
KATE TAYLOR	V	(ED	(E) ONE MAN DOG	1972 WB	UK K46185	US	2660
HUGH TAYLOR	V	(E	(F) WALKING MAN	1974 WB	UK K56042	US	2794
CAROLE KING	PNO V	(BEKD	(G) RAINY DAY MAN	1975 DJM	UK DJSLM2007 TRIP US 9513
ABIGALE HANESS	V	(ED	(H) GORILLA	1975 WB	UK K56137	US	2866
CARLY SIMON	V	(EFHJKLN	(J) IN THE POCKET	1976 WB	UK K56197	US	2912
LELAND SKLAR	B	(DEHJKLN	(K) THE BEST OF	1976 WB	UK K56309	US	2979
BOBBYE HALL	PERC	(EJ	(L) J.T.	1977 CBS	UK 86029	US	34811
GEORGE BOHANON	TROM	(EHJ	(M) GREATEST HITS	1977 WB	US 3113	US	2979
CHRIS DARROW	FDL	(B	(N) FLAG	1979 CBS	UK 86091	US	36058
MICHAEL BRECKER	SAX	(EFJK	(O) DAD LOVES HIS WORK	1980 CBS		US	37009
LINDA RONSTADT	V	(EL	(BD) TWO ORIGINALS	1975 WB	UK K66029	
JOHN McLAUGHLIN	G	(E				

BARRY ROGERS	TROM	(EF	ART BARON	TROM	(E	LOUIS CENAMO	G V	(A	DON SCHINN	K	(A
RANDY BRECKER	TPT	(EF	DAN DUGMORE	G STEEL(KL	DAVID SPINOZZA	G	(KFN	DASH CROFTS	MAND(E
JOHN LONDON	B	(BK	RANDY MEISNER	B	(BK	JOHN HARTFORD	FDL	(ED	ANDY MUSON	B	(KF
CLARENCE MACDONALD	PNO(KHJL	RED RHODES	STEEL(BEK	RALPH MACDONALD	PERC	(KF	MILT HOLLAND	PERC	(KHJ
BYRON BERLINE	FDL	(K	KENNY ASCHER	K	(KF	ANDREW GOLD	V HCA(K	RICK MAROTTA	D	(KF
JIM KELTNER	D	(KHJ	BOBBY WEST	B	(BK	GAYLE LEVANT	HARP	(KHJ	DAVID SANBORN	SAX	(KLHLN
NICK DE CARO	ORG	(KHJ	VICTOR FELDMAN	PERC	(KHJ	HERB PEDERSEN	V	(K	JONI MITCHELL	V	(KD
GRAHAM NASH	V	(KHJL	DAVID CROSBY	V	(KHJ	CRAIG DOERGE	K	(EKJ	KEVIN KELLY	K	(D
BISHOP O'BRIEN	D	(A	SKAILA KANGA HARP		(A	PAUL McCARTNEY	B	(AF	GENE ORLOFF	STR	(F
HUGH McCRACKEN	G	(F	RALPH SHUCKETT	K	(FN	KENNY BERGER	SAX	(F	RICHARD HEWSON	STR	(A
MICK WAYNE	G	(A	FREDDIE REDD	K	(A	LINDA McCARTNEY	V	(F	DON GROLNICK	K	(FN
HOWARD JOHNSON	TUBA	(F	GEORGE YOUNG	SAX	(F	ALAN RUBIN	TPT	(F	GEORGE MARGE	OBOE(F
PETER GORDON	HRNS	(F	ANDY NEWMARK	D	(H	AL PERKINS	STEEL(H	WILLIE WEEKS	B	(HJ
DAVID GRISMAN	MAND	(HJ	JULES JACOB	CLAR	(H	ARTHUR ADAMS	G	(H	CHUCK FINDLEY	HRNS(H
RANDY NEWMAN	K	(H	LOWELL GEORGE	V	(H	VALERIE CARTER	V	(HJ	ART GARFUNKEL	V	(J
KENNY WATSON	PERC	(H	RED CALLENDER B TUBA	(JL	OSCAR BRASHEAR	HRNS	(J	ERNIE WATTS	SAX	(J
WADDY WACHTEL	G	(JN	STEVIE WONDER	HCA	(J	RUSS TITELMAN	PERC	(J	DAVID LINDLEY	G	(J
HERB PEDERSEN	BANJ	(J	BONNIE RAITT	V	(J	STEVE MADAIO	HRNS	(J	DAVID CAMPBELL	STR	(L
LEAH KUNKEL	V	(L	STEVE FORMAN	PERC	(N	DAVID LASLEY	V	(N	ARNOLD McCULLER	V	(N
LOUISE SCHULMANN	VLA	(N	JESSE LEVY CELLO	(N	ARIF MARDIN	STR	(N	RICHARD GREEN	FDL	(D

JOHNNIE TAYLOR

JOHNNIE TAYLOR	V	(ALL	WANTED ONE SOUL SINGER	19 ATLANTIC	US	7715
EDDIE WILLIS	G	(S	WHP'S MAKIN' LOVE	1968 STAX	US	2005
GEORGE ROUNDTREE	K	(S	RAW BLUES	196 STAX	US	2008
GREG COLES	B	(S	RARE STAMPS	196 STAX	US	2012
LEE NATHAN	D	(S	J T PHILOSOPHY CONTINUES	1969 STAX UK 1024	US	2023
JERRY JONES	D	(S	ONE STEP BEYOND	19 STAX	US	2030
CARL SMITH	PERC	(S	GREATEST HITS	197 STAX	US	2032
BRANDYE	V	(S	TAYLORED IN SILK	1973 STAX UK STX1012	US	3014
			SUPER TAYLOR	1974 STAX UK STX5022	US	5509
			BEST OF	1976 STAX UK STX1049	US	5522
			EARGASM	1976 CBS UK 81201	US	33951
			RATED EXTRAORDINAIRE	1977 CBS	US	34401
			EVER READY	197 CBS	US	35340
			REFLECTIONS	19 RCA	APL1 2527
			CHRONICLE VOL 1	1978 STAX UK 7001	US	88001
			CHRONICLE VOL 2	1978 STAX UK 7002	US	88009
			DISCO 9000	197 CBS	38004
			SHE'S KILLING ME	1979 CBS	US	36061
		(S) A NEW DAY	1980 CBS	US	36548
			BEST OF	1981 CBS	US	37127

KATE TAYLOR

KATE TAYLOR	V	(AB	(A) SISTER KATE	1971 COTILLION	US	SD9045
DANNY KORTCHMAR	G PERC(A	(B) KATE TAYLOR	1978 CBS	US	35089
J D SOUTHER	V	(A	(C) ITS IN THERE	1979 CBS	US	36034
CHARLES LARKEY	B	(A				
JOEL O'BRIEN	D	(A	SANDRA CROUCH	PERC	(A	DONNA PRATER	V	(A	LEE SKLAR	B	(A
JOHN HARTFORD	BAN	(A	LINDA RONSTADT	V	(A	JAMES TAYLOR	G	(A	CAROLE KING	V	(A
MERRY CLAYTON	V	(A	RUSS KUNKEL	D	(A	ANDREW LOVE	HRNS	(A	JOHN BIELAND	G	(A
ABIGAIL HANESS	V	(A	WAYNE JACKSON	HRNS	(A	RALPH SCHUCKETT	K	(A	OMA DRAKE	V	(A
PETER ASHER	V	(A	MEMPHIS HORNS		(A					

KING SIZE TAYLOR

```
        KING SIZE TAYLOR     V  (AB      (A) LIVE IM STAR CLUB HAMBURG      19   ARIOLA    GER   200 868 241
                                         (B) LIVE IM STAR CLUB VOL 2        19   ARIOLA    GER   200 869 241
```
T28   KOKO TAYLOR   T28

```
        KOKO TAYLOR          V  (ABC      (A) I GOT WHAT IT TAKES          1975 SONET UK SNTF687 US ALLIGATOR 4706
        MIGHTY JOE YOUNG     G  (A        (B) SOUTHSIDE BABY               1975 BLACK & BLUE                  33505
        SAMMY LAWHORN        G  (AC       (C) EARTHSHAKER                  1978 SONET UK SNTF775 US ALLIGATOR 4711
        ABE LOCKE            SAX (AC      ( ) KOKO TAYLOR                  19   CHESS US 1532
        VINCE CHAPPELLE      D  (AC       ( ) BASIC SOUL        19         CHESS   US 50018
        BILL HEID            K  (A        ( ) HEART OF A WOMAN             1982 SONET UK SNTF 868
        CORNELIUS BOYSON     B  (AC
        JOHNNY B MOORE       G  (C  PINETOP PERKINS  K  (C  MERVYN HINDS        HCA(C
```
T29   LITTLE JOHNNY TAYLOR   T29

```
        LITTLE JOHNNY TAYLOR    (ALL      (A) EVERYBODY KNOWS ABOUT MY GOODTHING 197 POLYDOR UK 2916 015 US RONN 7530
                                         (B) OPEN HOUSE                    1973 CONTEMPO   1003     US RONN 7532
                                         (C) SUPER TAYLORS                 1974 CONTEMPO           CLP 502
                                         (D) PART TIME LOVE                1980 CHARLY        UK   CRB 1012
                                         (D) PART TIME LOVE                197  GALAXY        US   0207
                                         (E) I SHOULDA BEEN A PREACHER     1981 RED LIGHTNING UK   RL 0030
                                         ( ) GREATEST HITS                 19   GALAXY        US   8207
                                         ( ) LITTLE JOHNNY TAYLOR          1979 RONN          US   7535
                                         (EP AS LONG AS I DONT SEE YOU     1980 CHARLY        UK   CTD 118
```
T30   LIVINGSTON TAYLOR   T30

```
        LIVINGSTON TAYLOR G K V(ABCDE     (A) LIVINGSTON TAYLOR            1970 WB US WS 3006     + ATCO 33334
        PAUL HORNSBY       K  (AB         (B) LIV                          1971 WB UK K46131 US CAPRICORN 863
        ROBERT POPWELL     B  (AB         (C) OVER THE RAINBOW             1973 CAPRICORN      US  CP 0114
        DAVE WOODFORD      WIND (B         (D) THREE WAY MIRROR            1979 EPIC           US     35540
        BILL STEWART       D  (BC         (E) ECHOES                       1979 CAPRICORN     US     0220
        TOMMY TALTON       G  (BC         (F) MANS BEST FRIEND             1980 EPIC          US     36155
        WALTER ROBINSON    B  (BC
        JOHNNY SANDLIN     B  (AB  GREG PRESTOPINO   V  (B  PETE CARR       G  (A  BUZZ FEITON    G  (C
        NEIL LARSEN        K  (C   JIN NAILS         B  (C  RICK MAROTTA    D  (C  TONY LEVIN B   (C
        VICTOR BRADY       STEEL(C  MIKE MAINIERI    PERC (C  GEORGE MARGE  CLAR (C  GLORIA AGOSTINI HARP(C
        ED FREEMAN         STR (C   JAMES TAYLOR     V  (C  CARLY SIMON     V  (C  MERETHA STEWART V  (C
```
T31   MICK TAYLOR   T31

```
        MICK TAYLOR        G V (A1         (A) MICK TAYLOR                  1979 CBS   35076        UK       82600
        LOWELL GEORGE      G  (A           (1) 1977 LIVE BAND
        PIERRE MOERLEN     D  (A
        JEAN ROUSSEL       PNO (A  NORMAN MITCHELL   TAMB (A  MIKE DRISCOLL  D  (A  KUMA HARADA    B  (A
        RICHARD BAILEY     D  (A   ALAN SPENNER      B  (A  RONNIE LEAHY    K  (1  STEVE THOMPSON B  (1
        COLIN ALLEN        D  (1
```
T32   R DEAN TAYLOR   T32

```
        R DEAN TAYLOR      V  (ALL         (A) I THINK THEREFORE I AM       1970 RARE EARTH              RS 522
        SCOTT ROGERS       V  (C           (A) INDIANA WANTS ME            197  TAMLA US STML11185  90007
                                          (B) L A SUNSET                   1975 POLYDOR        UK   2383 399
```
T32A   TED TAYLOR   T32A

```
        TED TAYLOR         V  (ALL         (A) & LITTLE JOHNNY              1974 RONN     US        0011
        DINO ZIMMERMAN     G  (C           (B) SHADES OF BLUE              19   RONN     US        7528
        DON BARRETT        B  (C           (C) TED TAYLOR                  1976 CONTEMPO UK        538
        JAMES STROUD       D  (C           (D) KEEPING MY HEAD ABOVE WATER 1978 MCA      US        3059
        WARDELL QUEZERQUE  K  (C           (E) KEEP ON WALKING             1980 CHARLY            CRB 1011
        MUSCLE SHOALS      HRNS (C          (F) IT'S TOO LATE(EP)          1980 CHARLY            CTD 111
        DOROTHY MOORE      V  (C
        JEWEL BASS         V  (C   DENNIS BELFIELD   B  (D  BOBBY RUFFINO   D  (D  JOEY BRASLER   D  (D
        RAY BRAVERMAN      K  (D   MICHAEL GIRARD   PERC (D  PAT ZICARI     SAX (D  TONY COLEMAN  TROM(D
```
T32B   ROD TAYLOR   T32B

```
        ROD TAYLOR         G V (A           (A) ROD TAYLOR                  1973 ASYLUM    SYLA 8755
        BONNIE BRAMLETT    V  (A
        DON CAVERHILL      D  (A   RY COODER         G  (A  JESSE ED DAVIS   G  (A  KENNY EDWARDS   B  (A
        STEVE FERGUSON     PNO (A   CRAIG SAFAN      PNO (A  STEVE VAN GELDER G FDL(A  ERNIE WATTS   SAX (A
        CHUCK FINDLEY      TPT (A   ANDREW GOLD      G ACC(A  JIM HORN       SAX (A  JIM KELTNER    D  (A
        LARRY KNECHTEL     PNO (A   DAVID LA FLAMME  FDL (A  LEE SKLAR       B  (A  GARY MALLABER   D  (A
        LEW McCREARY       HRN (A   JONI MITCHELL    V  (A  BUELL NEIDLINGER B  (A  BILL PAYNE K   (A
        CHUCK PLOTKIN      K  (A   RED RHODES    STEEL (A  JOEL TEPP        HCA CLAR(A
```
T32C   RODERICK TAYLOR   T32C

```
        RODERICK TAYLOR    V  (A           (A) STRAIGHT                     1980 METRONOME       GER 60379
        EARL SLICK         G  (A
        JEAN MILLINGTON    B V (A   CURLEY SMITH     D V  (A  DUANE HITCHING  K  (A  PETER IVERS   HCA (A
        JIMMY GREENSPOON   K  (A   MARK OLSON        K  (A  JEFFY RICH       B  (A
```
T32D   ROGER TAYLOR   T32D

```
        ROGER TAYLOR          (A           (A) FUN IN SPACE                 1981 ELEKTRA US 522 UK EMC 3369
```
T32E   TUT TAYLOR   T32E

```
        TUT TAYLOR         G  (ALL         (A) DORBROLIC PLECTORAL SOCIETY  19   TAKOMA   US      1050
        CLARENCE TAYLOR    G  (D           (B) FRIAR TUT                    19   ROUNDER  US      0011
        ROLAND WHITE         (D           (C) THE OLD POST OFFICE          19   FLYING FISH US   008
        CHRIS HILLMAN        (D           (D) DOBRO COUNTRY                19   UA       UK      29711
        BILLY RAY LATHAM     (D
        BILL KEITH           (D
```
T33   VINCE TAYLOR   T33

```
        VINCE TAYLOR       V  (ALL         (A) VINCE TAYLOR                 19   BARCLAY          280 149
                                          (B) 100% ROCK                    1977 BARCLAY 80984/5 RI 81088/9
                                          (C) VINCE TAYLOR (EP)            1979 SPADE             PFE 1
```
T33A   TAZMANIAN DEVILS   T33A

```
        BARRY LOWENTHAL    D  (A           (A) TAZMANIAN DEVILS             1980 WB US 3400    EURO 56812
        DUANE VAN DEMAN    B  (A
        DENNIS HEGAN       G V (A  PAT CRAIG         K  (A  DAVID CARLSON    G  (A
```

BRAM TCHAIKOVSKY

BRAM TCHAIKOVSKY	G V	(ABCD123	(A) STRANGE MAN CHANGED MAN	1979 RADAR UK 17 POLYDOR US 6211	
KEITH BOYCE	D	(A123	(B) RUSSIANS ARE COMING	1980 RADAR UK 26	
MICKY BROADBENT	V B G K	(AB123	(C) PRESSURE	1980 POLYDOR US 6273	
DENIS FORBES	G	(BCD123	(D) FUNLAND	1981 ARISTA UK 1164 GER 203 654	
KEITH LINE	D	(BC3	(1) SARAH SMILES	1978 CRIMINAL UK BRAM1	
ALBIE DONNELLY	SAX	(C	(2) LULLABY OF BROADWAY	1979 CRIMINAL UK BRAM5	
ANDY PARKER	SAX	(C	(3) PRESSURE (EP)	1980 RADAR UK RDR 3	
MIKE KEARNS	SAX	(C			
BOB ANDREWS	K	(C	NICK GARVEY B V (ACD23 RICHARD ITCHINGTON B (D BERNIE CLARKE K (D		
ANDY McMASTER	V	(D	LEW SOLOFF TPT (D JIMMY MAELEN PERC (D MIKE OLDFIELD PERC(A		

TEA

MARK STORACE	V	(AB	(A) TEA	1975 PHILIPS	6305 238
TURO PASCHAYAN	B V	(AB	(B) THE SHIP	1975 PHILIPS	9118 001
ARMAND VOLKER	G V	(AB			
PHILIPPE KIENHOLZ	K V	(AB	ROLI EGGLI D (A DIETER DIERKS D (B		

TEA COMPANY

(A) COME & HAVE SOME TEA WITH TEA COMPANY	196 SMASH US	67105

TEA & SYMPHONY

JEFF DAW	FLT G V	(A	(A) AN ASYLUM FOR THE MUSICALLY INSANE	1969 HARVEST UK	SHVL 761
JAMES LANGSTON	G V WIND	(A	(B) JO SAGA	1970 HARVEST UK	SHVL 785
NIGEL PHILLIPS	K V PERC	(A			
BOB LAMB	D	(A	RON CHESTERMAN B (A MICK HINCKS B (A GUS DUDGEON PERC (A		
CLEM CLEMPSON	G	(A			

TEA SET

NICK HAEFFNER	G	(	(A) CUPS & SAUCERS (EP)	1979 WALDOS RECORDS	BS 003
RON WEST	B	(			
DUNCAN STRINGER	G	(	CALLY D (NICK EGAN V (		

TEAR GAS

ZAL CLEMINSON	G	(AB	(A) PIGGY GO GETTER	PARAMOUNT US 5029 UK FAMOUS SFMA5751	
CHRIS GLEN	B V	(AB	(B) TEAR GAS	REGAL ZONOPHONE UK SLRZ1021	
HUGH McKENNA	K	(B			
TED McKENNA	D	(B	DAVEY BATCHELOR V (A EDDIE CAMPBELL K V (A WILLIE MONRO D V (A		

TEARDROP EXPLODES

JULIAN COPE	B V	(AB	(A) KILIMANJARO	1980 MERCURY US 4016 UK 6359 035	
DAVID BALFE	K SYN	(AB	(B) WILDER	1981 MERCURY UK 6359 056	
GARY DWYER	D	(AB			
ALAN GILL	G	(A	MICHAEL FINKLER G (A RAY MARTINEZ TPT (A HURRICANE SMITH TPT (A		
CLIVE LANGER	PROD	(AB	JAMES ELLER (B TROY TATE (B LUKE TUNNEY (B		
TED EMMETT		(B	JEFF HAMMER (B ALFIE AGIUS (B		

TEARDROPS

BOK BOK	(A	(A) FINAL VINYL	1980 ILLUMINATED	JAMS 2
TONY FRIEL	(A			
STEVE GARVEY	(A	TREV WAYNE (A HELEN BARBROOK (A		

TEAZE

BRIAN DANTER	B V	(A	(A) ON THE LOOSE	1978 AQUARIUS	AQR 516
MIKE KOZAK	D	(A	(B) LIVE	1978 AQUARIUS	520
CHUCK PRICE	G	(A	(C) ONE NIGHT STANDS	1979 CAPITOL US	11919
MARK BIADAC	G	(A	(D) BODY SHOTS	1980 AQUARIUS	AQR 528

TEDDY BEARS

PHIL SPECTOR	V	(A	(A) TEDDY BEARS SING	19 IMPERIAL US LP 12010
ANNETTE KLEINBARD	V	(A		
MARSHALL LIEB	V	(A		

RICHARD TEE

RICHARD TEE	K	(AB	(A) STROKIN'	1979 CBS US 35695 UK	83339
STEVE GADD	D	(B	(B) NATURAL INGREDIENTS	1980 CBS US 36380 UK	84194
ERIC GALE	G	(B			
MATTHEW BRAGG	B	(B	RALPH MACDONALD PERC (B HUGH McCRACKEN HCA (B TOM SCOTT SAX (B		
JON FADDIS	HRNS	(B	RANDY BRECKER HRNS (B BARRY ROGERS HRNS (B SELDON POWELL HRNS(B		
VALERIE SIMPSON	V	(B	ULLANDA McCULLOUGH V (B LANI GROVES V (B STRING SECTION (B		

WILLIE TEE

WILLIE TEE	(A) ANTICIPATION	19 UA US	UALA 655

TEE SET

FRANKLIN MADJA	B	(A	(A) MY BELLE AMI	19 QUALITY BM 597
DILL BENWICK	G	(A		
JOOP BLOM	D	(A	HANS VAN EIJCK K (A	

TED

TED GARDESTAD	V	(A	(A) BLUE VIRGIN ISLE	1978 EPIC UK 83653 POLS 300 IMP	
JEFF PORCARO	D	(A			
JIM KELTNER	D	(A	DAVID HUNGATE B (A RAY BROWN B (A BOB GLAUB B (A		
JAI WINDING	B K SYN V	(A	JAY GRAYDON G (A LEE RITENOUR G (A STEVE LUKATHER G(A		
FRED TACKETT	G	(A	JOHN COLLINS G (A LARRY MUHOBERAC K (A MIKE MELVOIN K (A		
JAMES NEWTON HOWARD	K	(A	DR JOHN K (A VICTOR FELDMAN PERC (A JERRY WILLIAMS PERC(A		
HAL BLAINE	PERC	(A	GARY COLEMAN PERC (A AL HENDRICKSON BAN (A STEVE PORCARO SYN (A		
EMIL RICHARDS	PERC	(A	JOHN MAYALL HCA V (A STEVE MADAIO TPT (A BOB FOWLER TPT (A		
GENE COE	TPT	(A	JERRY HEY TPT (A CAPPY LEWIS TPT (A DICK HYDE TROM(A		
TOM SHEPARD	TROM	(A	ABE MOST WIND (A JOHN LOWE WIND (A JIM HORN WIND(A		
BUDDY COLETTE	HRNS	(A	DAVID LUELL WIND (A TED NASH WIND (A WILLIE SCHWARTZ WIND(A		
GARY HERBIG	WIND	(A	STEPHEN NILSSON (A JANNE SCHAFFER G (A MIKE WATSON (A		
ROGER PALM		(A	DAVIS CASSIDY V (A VANETTA FIELDS V (A SHIRLEY MATTHEWS V (A		
STRINGS		(A			

TEEGARDEN & VANWINKLE

SKIP'VANWINKLE'KNAPE	V K B	(ABC	(A) AN EVENING AT HOME	19 ATCO US 33272
DAVE TEEGARDEN	D V	(ABC	(B) BUT, ANYHOW	19 WESTBOUND US 2003
MIKE BRUCE	G V	(C	(C) ON OUR WAY	19 WESTBOUND US 2010
BOB SEGER	V G	(C		
ERNIE FIELDS	HRNS	(C	BRENDA KNIGHT V (C MARLENE DRISCOLL V (C JO ANN HILL V (A	
JERRY SMITH	PNO	(C	TRACY NELSON V (C	

```
         NICK STIPANITZ      D V  (AB                              1979 EPIC       CAN    90534
         STEVE MAHON         B    (AB      (B) FRANTIC CITY        1980 ATTIC      GER 6 24407
         GORDON LEWIS        G    (AB
         FRANKIE KERR/VENOM V (AB DAVE RAVE     G    (A   GRANT SLATER  PNO (A  KELLY JAY  K   (A
         RICK MORRISON     SAX (B THE SHAKERS   V    (B   WALTER ZWOL   SYN (B
```

T37K   TELEPHONE   T37K

```
         JEAN LOUIS AUBERT G V (BC     (A) TELEPHONE           1977 MARCONI    FR    14506
         LOUIS BRTIGNAC    G V (BC     (B) CACHE TON VENIM     1979 EMI        FR    14737
         RICHARD KOLINKA   D   (BC     (C) AU COEUR DE LA NUIT 1980 EMI        FR 72279 VIRGIN UK 2195
         CORINE MARIENNEAU B V (BC
         COWBOY           SAX (C
```

T37L   JAHN TEIGEN   T37L

```
         JAHN TEIGEN        K V  (A    (A) THIS YEARS LOSER    1978 RCA  NOR    40028
         B HADAWAY          B    (A
         S COOLING          G    (A  H BORNHOLT   TIMB    (A  L NIELSEN   VLN (A  PETE KNUDSEN   STR (A
         T METALL           D    (A  JONAS FIELD     G   (A  A STAV     SAX (A  TORE SYVERTSEN V PERC(A
         WALTER QUINTUS    VLN   (A  BAARD SVENDSEN  K   (A
```

T38   TELEVISION   T38

```
         TOM VERLAINE      G V  (AB1   (A) MARQUEE MOON    1977 ELEKTRA US 7E1098   UK K52046
         RICHARD LLOYD     G V  (AB1   (B) ADVENTURE       1978 ELEKTRA US 6E 133   UK K52072
         BILLY FICCA       D    (AB1   (1) 1974/5
         FRED SMITH        B    (AB
         RICHARD HELL      B    (1   JOHN JANSEN  PROD (B
```

T38A   TELEVISION PERSONALITIES   T38A

```
                               (A) WHERE'S BILL GRUNDY          19   KINGS ROAD        001
                               (B) AND DONT THE KIDS JUST LOVE IT 198 ROUGH TRADE   UK ROUGH24
```

T38B   TELEX   T38B

```
         DAN LACKSMAN          (AB    (A) LOOKING FOR ST TROPEZ  1979 SIRE       UK   SRK  6072
         MICHAEL MOERS         (AB    (B) NEUROVISION            1980 SIRE NL58142 UK  SRK  6090
         MARC MOULIN           (AB
```

T39   JACK TEMPCHIN   T39

```
         JACK TEMCHIN          (A     (A) JACK TEMPCHIN     1978 ARISTA US 4193  UK SPART 1078
         PETE CARR         G   (A
         ROGER CLARK       D   (A   BOB WRAY      B   (A  BARRY BECKETT  K  (A  ANTHONY PARSONS FLT (A
         GLENN FREY        G V (A   HARVEY THOMPSON SAX (A  RANDY McCORMICK K (A  GAY BAKER      B   (A
         EDDIE STRUZICK    V   (A   THOM FLORA      V   (A  JENNIFER WARNES V  (A  JACKSON BROWNE  V  (A
```

T40   TEMPEST   T40

```
         JON HISEMAN       D    (AB    (A) TEMPEST        1973 BRONZE GER 86626   ILPS 9220
         MARK CLARKE     B K V (AB    (B) LIVING IN FEAR 1974 BRONZE             ILPS 9267
         PAUL WILLIAMS    V G K(A
         ALLAN HOLDSWORTH G V VLN(A OLLIE HALSALL   G K V(B
```

T41   TEMPLE CITY KAZOO BAND   T41

```
         DR JIM ZANE      KAZOO(A      (A) SOME KAZOOS     (EP)       1978 RHINO          RNEP 501
         RICHIE BALANCE   KAZOO(A      (B) PLATE FULL OF KAZOOS(KAZOO BROS) 1979 RHINO  EP  RNEP 504
         ZAZOOT SIMS      KAZOO(A
         TOM'CAT'KNAPP    KAZOO(A  DAVID ANDREWS   KAZOO(A  DON BUCHANAN   KAZOO(A GLEN COBAR KAZOO(A
         PAUL SANOIAN     KAZOO(A  JEFF GINSBERG   KAZOO(A  GREG GORDON    KAZOO(A TED KAZOOSKI   KAZOO(A
         ELIJAH GOLDSTEIN KAZOO(A  THE KAZOO BROTHERS BAND(B ELVIN KAZOOS  KAZOO(A JACKSON KAZOOS KAZOO(B
```

T42   TEMPTATIONS   T42

```
         OTIS MILES       V  (1234567  MEET THE TEMPTATIONS      1964 TAMLA UK STML11009 US GORDY 911
         MELVIN FRANKLIN  V  (1234567  SING SMOKEY               1965 TAMLA UK  TML11016 US GORDY 912
         EDDIE KENDRICKS  V  (1234     TEMPTIN' TEMPTATIONS      1966 TAMLA UK STML11023 US GORDY 914
         ELDRIDGE BRYANT  V  (2        GETTIN' READY             1966 TAMLA UK STML11035 US GORDY 918
         RICHARD STREET   V  (Z        GREATEST HITS             1967 TAMLA UK STML11042 US GORDY 919
         DAVID RUFFIN     V  (3        LIVE                      1967 TAMLA UK STML11053 US GORDY 921
         DENNIS EDWARDS   V  (4567Z    WITH A LOT OF SOUL        1967 TAMLA UK STML11057 US GORDY 922
         RICKY OWENS      V  (5        IN A MELLOW MOOD          1967 TAMLA UK STML11068 US GORDY 924
         DAMON HARRIS     V  (67       WISH IT WOULD RAIN        1968 TAMLA UK STML11079 US GORDY 927
         PAUL WILLIAMS    V  (123456   T V SHOW                  1967 TAMLA             US GORDY 933
                                       WITH THE SUPREMES         1969 TAMLA UK STML11096
         (1) 1959(DISTANTS)            LIVE AT THE COPA          1969              US GORDY 938
         (2) 1960                      CLOUD NINE                1969 TAMLA UK STML11109 US GORDY 939
         (3) 1962
         (4) 1968                      TCB      (SUPREMES)       1969 TAMLA UK STML11110 US TAMLA 682
         (5) 1971                      TOGETHER(SUPREMES)        1970 TAMLA UK STML11122
         (6) 1971                      PSYCHEDELIC SHACK         1970 TAMLA UK STML11147 US GORDY 947
         (7) 1971                      PUZZLE PEOPLE             1970 TAMLA UK STML11133 US GORDY 949
                                       LIVE AT THE TALK OF THE TOWN 1970 TAMLA UK STML11141 US GORDY 953
         ROBERT WARD      G   (ML      LIVE AT THE TALK OF THE TOWN RI 1979 MFP US  50419
         JOE MESSINA      G   (LM      CHRISTMAS CARD            1970              US GORDY 951
         ROBERT WHITE     G   (LM      GREATEST HITS   VOL 2     1970 TAMLA UK STML11170 US GORDY 954
         AARON SMITH      D   (LM      THE SKY'S THE LIMIT       1971 TAMLA UK STML11184 US GORDY 957
         URIEL JONES      K   (LM      SOLID ROCK                1972 TAMLA UK STML11202 US GORDY 961
         EARL VAN DYKE    K   (LM  (L) ALLDIRECTIONS             1972 TAMLA UK STML11218 US GORDY 962
         BOB BABBITT      B   (MLZ     (M)MASTERPIECE            1973 TAMLA UK STML11229 US GORDY 965
         WAH WAH RAGIN    G   (LMQ     GET READY                 1973 SOUNDS SUPERB UK 90004
         PAUL WARREN      G   (ML      1990                      1974 TAMLA UK STMA 8016
         LEDDIE WILLIS    G   (ML      ANTHOLOGY 1964/73         1974 TAMLA UK TMSP 6003 US GORDY 974
         RICHARD ALLEN    D   (ML      10TH ANNIVERSARY          1974 TAMLA                  M782
         ANDREW SMITH     D   (LM      HOUSE PARTY               1975 TAMLA UK STML12006 US GORDY 973
         LEROY TAYLOR     B   (LM  (Q)A SONG FOR YOU            1975 TAMLA UK STMA 8021 US GORDY 969
         EDDIE WATKINS    B   (ML      WINGS OF LOVE             1976 TAMLA UK STMA 8025 US GORDY 971
         EDDIE BROWN    PERC (LM       DO THE TEMPTATIONS        1976 TAMLA UK STML12040 US GORDY 975
         MAURICE DAVIS   TPT (ML       GREATEST HITS VOL 3       1977 TAMLA UK STML12061 US
         JACK BROCKENSHA PERC (LM      TEMPTATIONS               1977 TAMLA UK STMX 6002
         LJACK ASHFORD   PERC (ML      HEAR TO TEMPT YOU         1978 ATLANTIC UK K50413 US    19143
         TED LUCAS       HCA (ML       BARE BACK                 1978 ATLANTIC UK K50504 US    19188
         DON BALDWIN K WIND SYN(Q      SING SMOKEY               1979 MOTOWN    UK   STMR 9005
         OLLIE BROWN      D   (Q       20 GOLDEN GREATS          1980 MOTOWN UK STML12140
         ZACHARY FRAZIER  D   (Q       POWER                     1980 MOTOWN UK STML12136 US    994
         JAMES GADSON     D   (Q       TEMPTATIONS               1981 MOTOWN UK STML12159
```

                                           (CONTINUED)

T42 (CONTINUED)   TEMPTATIONS   T42

```
    EDDIE HAZEL        G   (Q
    WILLY NELSON       B   (Q    OTIS WILLIAMS      V   (Z    GLENN LEONARD      V   (Z    DAVID ENGLISH      V  (Z
    DON RENALDO        SRT (Z    BILL NEALE         STR G(Z   LARRY WASHINGTON   PERC (Z    JOHNNY GRIFFIN     ORG (LM
    PAUL RISER         STR (LM   NORMAN WHITFIELD  *PROD (LM  BILLY COOPER       G   (L     THOM BELL   PROD  K(Z
    BOBBY ELI          G   (Z    CHARLES COLLINS    D   (Z    ED W SHEA          PERC (Z
```

T43   TEN C C   T43

```
    ERIC STEWART       G V (ALL    (A) TEN CC                       1973 UK         UK UKAL 1005 US       53105
    GRAHAM GOULDMAN    G V (ALL    (B) SHEET MUSIC                  1974 UK         UK UKAL 1007 US       53107
    KEVIN GODLEY       D V (ABCDE  (C) 100CC                        1975 UK         UK UKAL 1012 US       53110
    LOL CREME          G V (ABCDE  (D) ORIGINAL SOUNDTRACK          1975 MERCURY UK 9102 500 US  SRM1 1029
    TERRY BOZZIO       D   (F      (D) ORIGINAL SOUNDTRACK ½ SPEED  1981 MERCURY UK 9102 500
    PAUL BURGESS       D   (FGHK   (E) HOW DARE YOU                 1976 MERCURY UK 9102 501 US  SRMI 1061
    RICK FENN          G   (GHK    (F) DECEPTIVE BENDS              1977 MERCURY UK 9102 502 US  SRMI 3702
    STUART TOSH        D   (GHK    (G) LIVE & LET LIVE              1977 MERCURY UK 6641 698 US  SRM2 8600
    TONY O'MALLEY      K   (G      (H) BLOODY TOURISTS              1978 MERCURY UK 9102 503 US  SRMI 6160
    TONY SPATH         PNO (FH     (I) GREATEST HITS                1979 MERCURY UK 9102 504 US POLYDOR6244
    JEAN ROUSSEL       K   (F      (J) THINGS WE DO FOR LOVE        1979 POLYDOR             US       6186
    DUNCAN MACKAY      K   (HK     (K) LOOK HEAR                    1980 MERCURY UK 9102 505 US WB   3442
    DEL NEWMAN         SRT (F      ( ) THE BEST OF                  1980 MERCURY NL 9279 567
                                   (L) 10 OUT OF 10                 1981 MERCURY UK 6359 048
```

T44   TEN WHEEL DRIVE   T44

```
    GENYA RAVAN        V HCA(ABC   (A) CONSTRUCTION No1             1969 POLYDOR    US 4008 UK   583 577
    ARAM SCHEFRIN      G V (ABCD   (B) BRIEF REPLIES                1970 POLYDOR    US 4024 UK  2425 022
    MIKE ZAGER         K CLAR (ABCD (C) PECULIAR FRIENDS            1971 POLYDOR    US 4062 UK  2425 065
    BILL TAXAS         B   (A      (D) TEN WHEEL DRIVE              1974 CAPITOL    US          ST 11199
    LEON RIX           D CELLO(A
    LOUIS HOFF         WIND (A    DENNIS PARISI    TROM (AB  JAY SILVA        WIND (A    RICHARD MEISTERMAN  TPT(A
    PETER HYDE         HRNS (A    BOB PIAZZA       B    (B   STEVE SATTEN     HRNS (A    JOHN GATCHELL       HRNS(BD
    DAVE LIEBMAN       WIND (B    JOHN ECKERT      HRNS (B   ALLEN HERMAN     D    (B    BLAKE HINES         B   (C
    DAVID WILLIAMS     D   (C     ALAN GAUVIN      WIND (C   DEAN PRATT       TPT  (CD   TOM MALONE    TROM  (C
    DANNY STILES       TPT (C     FRANK FRINT      TPT  (C   ANN SUTTON       V    (D    GERRY CHAMBERLAIN   TROM(D
    ED XIQUES          WIND (D    DON GROLNICK     K    (D   HARRY MAX        VLN  (D    BARRY LARAROWITZ D  (D
```

T45   TEN YEARS AFTER   T45

```
    ALVIN LEE          V   (ALL    (A) TEN YEARS AFTER              1967 DERAM     US 18009 UK SML1015
    LEO LYONS          B   (ALL    (B) UNDEAD                       1968 DERAM     US 18016 UK  SML1023
                                   (B) UNDEAD                       19   NOVA GER 6 21585
    CHICK CHURCHILL    D   (ALL    (C) STONEDHENGE                  1969 DERAM     US 18021 UK  SML1029
                                   (AC) T Y A/STONEDHENGE (DBL)     19   DERAM GER 3026/1 RI NOVA 628110
    RIC LEE            D(ABCDEFGHIJKLMN (D) SSSSSSSSH               1969 DERAM     US 18029 UK  SML1052
    DAVID POTTS        D   (1      (D) SSSSSSSSH                    1975 CHRYSALIS RI          UK CHR 1083
    GUS DUDGEON        PERC (A     (E) CRICKLEWOOD GREEN            1970 DERAM     US 18038 UK  SML1065
    MIKE VERNON        V   (C      (E) CRICKLEWOOD GREEN            1975 CHRYSALIS RI          UK CHR 1084
                                   (E) CRICKLEWOOD GREEN            19   DERAM GER 6 21589
    SIMON STABLE       PERC (C     (F) WATT                         1970 DERAM     US 18050 UK  SML1078
    HAROLD BURGON      V   (K      (F) WATT                         1975 CHRYSALIS RI          UK CHR 1085
                                   (G) ALVIN LEE & CO               1972 DERAM     US 18064 UK  SML1096
    (1) 1967                       (G) ALVIN LEE & CO               1979 LONDON US RI 50013
                                   (H) A SPACE IN TIME              1972 CHRYSALIS UK 1001  US CBS 30801
                                   (I) ROCK'N'ROLL TO THE WORLD     1972 CHRYSALIS UK 1009  US CBS 31779
                                   (J) RECORDED LIVE                1973 CHRYSALIS UK 1049  US CBS 32288
                                   (K) POSITIVE VIBRATIONS          1974 CHRYSALIS UK 1060  US CBS 32851
                                   (L) GOIN' HOME                   1975 CHRYSALIS UK 1077 US DERAM18072
                                   (M) ANTHOLOGY                    1976 CHRYSALIS UK 1107
                                   (N) CLASSIC PERFORMANCES         1977 CHRYSALIS UK 1134  US CBS 34366
                                   (O) PROFILE                      19   TELDEC          GERM   624011
                                   (P) LONDON COLLECTION            19   LONDON          US LC 50013
                                   (Q) HEAR ME CALLING              1981 DECCA      UKTAB24
                                   ( ) TEN  YEARS AFTER             1980 PICKWICK    UK SHM3038
```

T46   TEN YEARS LATER   T46

```
    ALVIN LEE          G V (AB     (A) ROCKET FUEL                  1978 POLYDOR 2310 605  +  2344 103
    TOM COMPTON        D   (AB     (B) RIDE ON                      1979 POLYDOR              2310 678
    MICK HAWKSWORTH    B   (AB
    BERNIE CLARKE      K   (A     MICK WEAVER      K    (A
```

T47   TENNENT MORRISON   T47

```
    DAVID MORRISON         (AB     (A) TENNENT MORRISON             1972 POLYDOR         UK   2383 152
    JOHN TENNENT       G V (AB     (B) KEEP IT CLEAN(AS JOE SOAP)   1973 POLYDOR         UK   2383 233
    RONNIE LEAHY       K   (A
    HERBIE FLOWERS     B   (A     JIMMY McCULLOCH      (AB  BRIAN ODGERS     (A    CLEM CATTINI       (A
    ROGER McKEW        G   (A     STEVE THOMPSON       (A   COLIN ALLEN      (A    DENNIS LOPEZ       (A
    MIK KAMINSKI       VLN (B     GERRY CONWAY     D   (B   JEFF PEARCE   B  (B
```

T47A   TENNESSEE FARM BAND   T47A

```
    LINDA HERSHFIELD   V   (A      (A) COMMUNION                    1977 FARM                    1013
    DAVID CHALMERS     D   (A
    THOMAS DOTZLER     V K SAX(A  MICHAEL SULLENS   B  (A   WALTER RABIDEAU  G V (A
```

T47B   TENNIS SHOES   T47B

```
                                   (A) MEDIUM WAVE   (EP)           19   BONAPARTE       UK    BONE 3
```

T47C   TERENCE   T47C

```
                                   (A) AN EYE FOR AN EAR           19   DECCA          IMP   DL75137
```

T47D   TENT   T47D

```
                                   (A) 6 EMPTY PLACES              1981 CHERRY RED BRED  17
```

T47E   TERESA   T47E

```
                                   (A) CLASS REUNION               1980 DREAM      US    3502
```

T47F   TERPSICHORE   T47F

```
                                   (A) TERPSICHORE (SILLY NOT TO)  1981 EMI        UK   EMS 1004
```

T48   TERRA COTTA   T48

```
    TOM ATKINSON       G   (1      (A) HARD TO KNOW    (EP)         197  TERRA COTTA          TC 001
    STEVE LUDLAM       G   (1      (1) 1978
    CHRIS WOODCOCK     D   (1
    TERRY COTTAM       V   (1     KELLY CANTLON    B   (1
```

TAMMI TERRELL	V	(ALL	(A) UNITED	1968	TAMLA	UK	STML11062
MARVIN GAYE	V	(A	(B) YOU'RE ALL I NEED	1968	TAMLA	UK	STML11084
			(C) IRRESISTIBLE	1969	TAMLA	US	652
			(D) EARLY SHOW	1969	MARBLE ARCH	UK	MAL 1110

DEWEY TERRY	V	(A	(A) CHIEF	1973	TUMBLEWEED		TW 3502
HARVEY MANDEL	G	(A					

KARL TERRY	(A	(A) CRUISIN'	1978	RAW		RWLP 105

SONNY TERRY	V HCA(	AT SUGARHILL	19	AMERICA			AM	6071
BROWNIE McGHEE	G V (	AT THE BUNKHOUSE	19	SMASH	US	27067		
DAVE LEE	PNO (	BACK COUNTRY BLUES	1978	MUSIDISC	FR	CV	956	
SVEND ERIK NORREGARD	(	BLUES IS MY COMPANION	19	VERVE	US			3008
PEPPERMINT HARRIS	(	BROWNIE & SONNY	19	ARC FOLK	US			242
		BLUES & SHOUTS	19	FANTASY	US			3317
		BROWNIE & SONNY	19	FANTASY	US			3340
		BROWNIE & SONNY	19	FANTASY	US			8091
		BROWNIE McGHEE BLUES	19	FOLKWAYS	US			2030
		BROWNIE McGHEE & SONNY TERRY	19	FOLKWAY	US			2327
		BROWNIE McGHEE SINGS THE BLUES	19	FOLKWAYS	US			3557
		BEST OF	19	PRESTIGE	US			7715
		BLUES FROM EVERYWHERE	19	TRANSATLANTIC			XTRA	1099
		BEST OF	19	STORYVILLE			SLP	217
		BROWNIE McGHEE SONNY TERRY	1971	STORYVILLE	FR			21020
		BROWNIE & SONNY'S BLUES	1960	ROULETTE	US			
		BROWNIE & SONNY'S BLUES	197	VOGUE	FR			12505
		BLUES & FOLK	19	BLUESVILLE	US			1005
		BLUES ALL ROUND	19	BLUEVILLE	US			1020
		BLUES IN MY SOUL	19	BLUESVILLE	US			1033
		BROWNIES BLUES	19	BLUESVILLE	US			1042
		COULDN'T BELIEVE MY EYES	197	BLUESWAY			BLS	6059
		DOWN HOME BLUES	19	SHARP	US			2003
		DOWN HOME BLUES	19	BLUESVILLE	US			1002
		GOING DOWN SLOW	1974	MAINSTREAM				L35784
		GOING DOWN SLOW	197	MAINSTREAM	US		MRL	407
		GUITAR HIGHWAY	19	VERVE	US			9019
		GET ON BOARD	19	FOLKWAYS	US			2028
		GET TOGETHER	19	VERVE	US			9010
		HOMETOWN BLUES	1974	MAINSTREAM	US		MRL	1019
		HOMETOWN BLUES	197	MAINSTREAM				56049
		HOMETOWN BLUES	19	MAINSTREAM				308
		HOMETOWN BLUES	1969	ACE OF HEARTS			ZAHT	182
		HOOTIN' & HOLLERIN'	1975	VOGUE	FR		LDE	894
		HOOTIN' & HOLLERIN'	19	CHOICE	US			503
		IN LONDON	1969	MARBLE ARCH	UK		MAL	843
		KEY TO THE HIGHWAY	1957	TRANSATLANTIC			XTRA	1004
		LONG WAY FROM HOME	1969	BLUESWAY			BLS	6028
		LIVE AT THE 2ND FRET	19	PRESTIGE	US			7803
		LIVIN' WITH THE BLUES	1960	FONTANA				688006
		LIGHTNIN' SONNY & BROWNIE	1965	SOCIETY			SOC	1009
		MIDNIGHT SPECIAL	1978	FANTASY	US		FAN	5973
		ON THE ROAD	19	TRANSATLANTIC			XTRA	1110
		PREACHIN' THE BLUES	1960	FOLKWAY	US			31024
		PREACHIN' THE BLUES	19	FOLKWAY	US			9019
		PENETENTIARY BLUES	1960	FONTANA				688 007
		SONNY TERRY & WOODY GUTHRIE	19	EMBER			CW	136
		SONNY TERRY	19	ARC FOLK				206
		SING & PLAY	19	SOCIETY	UK			1015
		SONNY TERRYS WASHBOARD BAND	19	FOLKWAYS				2006
		SONNY TERRY GUITAR & HARMONICA	19	FOLKWAYS				2035
		SONNY TERRY'S NEW SOUND	19	FOLKWAYS				3821
		SONNY IS KING	19	PRESTIGE				7802
		SONNY'S STORY	19	BLUESVILLE				1025
		SONNY'S STORY	1967	XTRA	UK			5025
		SONNY TERRY & LIGHTNIN' HOPKINS	19	BLUESVILLE				1059
		SONNY TERRY & HIS MOUTH HARP	19	STINSON				55
		SONNY TERRY	19	TRANSATLANTIC			XTRA	1064
		SHOUTS & BLUES	19	AMERICA			AM	6075
		SONNY & BROWNIE	1973	A&M	UK		AMLH64379	
		TRADITIONAL BLUES	1977	CHANT DUMONDE	FR		FL	52421
		TERRY & McGHEE	19	FANTASY	US			3254
		THE SOUND OF AMERICA	19	CHOICE				509
		TERRY McGHEE	19	FANTASY	US			3254
		WALK ON	1977	BULLDOG	UK		BDL	1018
		WHERE THE BLUES BEGAN	19	fontana				67599
		WORK SONGS PLAY SONGS	19	CHOICE				500
		YOU HEAR ME TALKING	1979	MUSE	FR		MR	5131

TERRY DOLAN	G V	(AB12	(A) THE DOUBTFUL HANDSHAKE	1980	LINE	GERM	LLP 5062
DAVID HAYES	B v	(A23B	(B) TOO CLOSE FOR COMFORT	1979	WILD BUNCH	ITALY	WB 5001
DAVE CARTER	B V	(B	(1) 1974 (2) 1975 (3) 1977				
ANDY KIRBY	D	(23					
JEFF MYER	D	(A3 MICHAEL WHITE	B	(3 STEVE DERR	G	(B LONNIE TURNER	B (B3
JOHN CIPOLLINA	G	(A123 GREG DOUGLASS	G	(A123 DAVID WEBER	D	(1 HUTCH HUTCHINSON	B (12
SID PAGE	VLN	(2 NICKY HOPKINS	K	(B2 JIM McPHERSON	K	(2 BONES JONES	D (B2
BILL BARON	D	(B					

JOE TEX

JOE TEX	V	(ALL	THE BEST OF	19	KING		US	935
HAYWARD BISHOP	D	(S	THE BEST OF	1965	PARROT		US	S71002
KARL HIMMEL	D	(S	HOLD ON TO WHAT YOU'VE GOT	1965	ATLANTIC		US	SD8106
BUDDY KILLEN		(R	HOLD ON	1965	CHECKER			2993
BOBBY WOOD	K	(SR	NEW BOSS	1965	ATLANTIC		US	SD8115
LOUIS JOHNSON		(R	GREATEST HITS	1967	ATLANTIC	UK 588089		
BOBBY EMMONS	K	(RS	LOVE YOU SAVE	1966	ATLANTIC		US	SD8124
JOHN CHRISTOPHER	G	(S	I'VE GOT TO DO A LITTLE BETTER	19	ATLANTIC		US	SD8133
REGGIE YOUNG	G	(SR	BEST OF	196	ATLANTIC		US	SD8144
TOMMY COGBILL	B	(S	LIVE & LOVELY	1968	ATLANTIC	UK 588104	US	SD8156
LARRIE LONDIN		(R	SOUL COUNTRY	1968	ATLANTIC	UK 588118	US	SD8187
CHARLES ROSE	HRNS	(R	HAPPY SOUL	1969	ATLANTIC		US	SD8211
JOSEPH THOMAS		(R	YOU BETTER GET IT	1969	ATLANTIC	UK 588130		
MIKE LEECH	B	(S	BUYING A BOOK	1969	ATLANTIC	UK 588193	US	SD8231
DALE QUILLEN	HRNS	(S	SINGS WITH STRINGS	19	ATLANTIC	UK 2465001	US	SD8254
LEROY HADLEY		(R	FROM THE ROOTS CAME THE RAPPER	196	ATLANTIC		US	SD8292
BEN CAULEY	HRNS	(S	SHOW ME	19	ATLANTIC	UK 2464004		
HARRISON CALLOWAY	HRNS	(SR	I GOTCHA	1972	DIAL		US	6002
HARVEY THOMPSON	HRNS	(SR	I GOTCHA	1972	MERCURY	UK 6338 093		
RON EADES	HRNS	(SR	(S) SPILL THE BEANS	197	DIAL		US	6004
JAMES BOOKER	PNO	(R	HE WHO IS WITHOUT FUNK	197	DIAL		US	6100
FARRELL MORRIS	PERC	(R	LONDON COLLECTOR SUPER SOUL	19	LONDON		US	50017
PAULA BEBEFIELD		(R	ANOTHER MANS WOMAN	1977	POWERPAK		US	305
BETH HAVIS	V	(R	HISTORY OF	19	PRIDE		US	0020
WAYNE BUTLER	HRNS	(R	BUMPS & BRUISES	1977	EPIC	UK 81931	US	34666
CHARLES CHALMERS	V	(R	(R) RUB DOWN	1978	EPIC	UK 82581	US	35079
SANDRA RHODES	V	(R	TURN BACK THE HANDS	19	PICKWICK			
DONNA RHODES	V	(R	SUPER SOUL	1979	LONDON	US	50017	
WAYNE JACKSON	HRNS	(R						
STRING SECTION		(R						

THE WAY WE LIVE

JIM MILNE	G K V	(A	(A) A CANDLE FOR JUDITH	1971	DANDELION	UK	DAN 8004
STEPHEN CLAYTON	D PERC	(A					
JOHN BRIERLEY	PROD	(A					

THEATRE OF HATE

		(A) WHO DARES WINS	1981	SSSSS	UK	SS1

THEE IMAGE

MIKE PINERA	G V	(AB	(A) THEE IMAGE	1975	MANTICORE	US	MA6 504
DUANE HITCHINGS	K V SYN	(AB	(B) INSIDE THE TRIANGLE	1975	MANTICORE	US	MA6 506
DANNY VOLBERG	D	(AB					

THEIVES

		(C) YUCATAN	1980	ARISTA	US	4232

THEM

VAN MORRISON	HVA V	(	ANGRY YOUNG THEM	1965	DECCA	UK LK4700	GER	17029
BILLY HARRISON	G	(1	THEM	1965	PARROT		US	PAS71005
ALAN HENDERSON	B	(1JK	THEM AGAIN	1966	DECCA LK 4751	US	PARROT	71008
RONNIE MILLINGS	D	(1	NOW & THEM	1968	TOWER		US	ST 5104
ERIC WIKSEN	PNO	(	TIME OUT,TIME IN FOR THEM	1968	TOWER		US	ST 5116
JACKIE McAULEY	ORG	(1	WORLD OF THEM (COMP)	1970	DECCA		UK	SPA 86
PAT McAULEY	D	(	(J)THEM	1970	HAPPY TIGER		US	HT 1004
PETER BARDENS	ORG	(	(K)THEM IN REALITY	197	HAPPY TIGER		US	HT 1012
JIMMY PAGE	G	(	BACKTRACKIN'	1974	LONDON		US	PS 639
RAY ELLIOT	K	(	THE BEGINNING	1972	DECCA		GERM	ND 772
DAVID HARVEY	D	(	BAD OR GOOD (COMP) (DBL)	1972	DECCA		GERM	3008 1/2
JIM ARMSTRONG	G	(	STORY OF THEM (COMP)	1977	LONDON		US	50001
KEN McDOWELL	V	(	THEM (COMP) (DBL)	1973	PARROT		US	71053
JOHN WILSON	D	(	THEM	1973	DERAM		UK	DPA 3001
KEN McLEOD		(	PROFILE (COMP)	197	DECCA		GER	624 005
MARK SCOTT		(	ITS ALL OVER NOW	1975	DECCA		GER	628 339
JERRY COLE	V	(J	HERE COMES GLORIA (COMP) (DBL)	1976	DECCA		GER	628 361
RAY RUFF		(J	ROCK ROOTS (COMP)	1976	DECCA		UK	ROOTS3
JOHN STARK	D	(K	BELFAST GYPSIES	1977	SONET		UK	SNTF 738
JIM PARKER	G	(K	BELFAST GYPSIES	19	GRAND PRIX		SWED	GP 9923
			(1) 1963					

THERAPY

		(A) BRINGING THE HOUSE DOWN	19		
		(B) ONE NIGHT STAND	19		
		(C) ALMANAC	1976	CBS 69017	+DJM DJF 20492

THIN LIZZY

PHIL LYNOTT	B V	(ALL	(A) THIN LIZZY	1971	DECCA	UK SKL 5082	US LONDON	594
BRIAN DOWNEY	D	(ALL	(B) SHADES OF A BLUE ORPHANAGE	1972	DECCA	UK TXS 108		
ERIC BELL	G	(ABC	(C) VAGABONDS OF WESTERN WORLD	1973	DECCA	UK SKL 5170	US LONDON	636
GARY MOORE	G	(DK	(D) NIGHT LIFE	1974	VERTIGO	UK 6360 116	US MERCURY	SRM11107
JOHN HELLIWELL	SAX	(H	(D) NIGHT LIFE	1975	VERTIGO	US 2002		
SCOTT GORHAM	G	(DEFGHJKLMNO	(E) FIGHTING	1975	VERTIGO	UK 6360 121	US MERCURY	SRM11108
SNOWY WHITE	G	(NL	(E) FIGHTING	1975	VERTIGO	US 2005		
BRIAN ROBERTSON	G	(DEFGHJN	(F) JAILBREAK	1976	VERTIGO	UK 9102 008	US MERCURY	SRM11081
PHIL COLLINS	PERC	(G	(G) JOHNNY THE FOX	1976	VERTIGO	UK 9102 012	US MERCURY	SRM11119
KIMBERLEY BEACON	V	(G	(H) BAD REPUTATION	1977	VERTIGO	UK 9102 016	US MERCURY	SRM11186
ROGER CHAPMAN	V	(E	(I) REMEMBERING	1976	DECCA	UK SKL 5249		
IAN MACLAGAN	PNO	(E	(J) LIVE & DANGEROUS	1978	VERTIGO	UK 6641 807	US WB	2 3213
DARREN WHARTON	K	(NLO	(K) BLACK ROSE	1979	VERTIGO	UK 9102 032	US WB	3338
JEAN ROUSSEL	K	(D	(L) CHINA TOWN	1980	VERTIGO	UK 6359 030	US UK	3496
FRANKIE MILLER	V	(D	( ) THE ROCKER	1977	LONDON		US	50004
MARY VISCONTI	V	(H	( ) PROFILE	19	TELDEC		GERM	624013
MIDGE URE	V	(LO	(M) ADVENTURES OF (COMP)	1981	VERTIGO	LIZ TV 1		
TIM HINKLEY	K	(LO	(N) KILLERS LIVE (EP)	1981	VERTIGO	LIZZY 812		
JON BOJIC	V	(H	(O) RENEGADE	1981	VERTIGO	UK 6359 083		
KEN MORRIS	V	(H						
TONY VISCONTI	REC	(H	JOHN EARLE	SAX	(J			

THIRD EAR BAND

COLIN SWEENEY	PERC (ABC	(A) ALCHEMY	1969 HARVEST	UK	SHVL 756
PAUL MINNS	OBOE (ABC	(B) THIRD EAR BAND	1970 HARVEST	UK	SHSP 773
RICHARD COFF	VLN (AB	(C) MACBETH	1972 HARVEST	UK	SHSP 4019
MEL DAVIS	CELLO(A	(D) EXPERIENCES (COMP)	1976 HARVEST HERITAGE	UK	SHSM 2007
JOHN PEEL	JEWS HARP (A				
DAVE TOMLIN	VLN (A	URSULA SMITH (B	SIMON HOUSE	VLN (C	DENIM BRIDGES G (C
PAUL BUCKMASTER	CELLO(C				

THIRD POWER

DREW ABBOTT	G V (A	(A) BELIEVE	1970 VANGUARD	US	VSD 6554
JEM TARGAL	B V (A				
JIM CRAIG	D V (A				

THIRD RAIL

ART RESNICK	K (A	(A) IN MUSIC	1967 EPIC	US	26327
K RESNICK	(A				
JOEY LEVINE	(A				

THIRD WORLD

PRILLY	V (A				
CAT COORE	G B (ABCDE	(A) THIRD WORLD	1976 ISLAND	UK	ILPS 9369
RICHIE	B G (ABCDE	(B) 96 DEGREES IN THE SHADE	1977 ISLAND	uk	ILPS 9443
IBO	K V (ABCDE	(C) JOURNEY TO ADDIS	1978 ISLAND	UK	ILPS 9554
CORNEL	D (A	(D) STORY'S BEEN TOLD	1979 ISLAND GER 200663 UK		ILPS 9569
CARROT	PERC (ABCDE	(E) PRISONER IN THE STREET	1980 ISLAND	UK	ILPS 9616
RUGS	G V (BCDE	(F) RISE IN HARMONY	1980 ISLAND	US	9574
WILLIE	D (BCDE	(G) ROCKS THE WORLD	1981 CBS	UK	85027
CHRIS WOOD	SAX (D				
REBOP	PERC (B				

THIRD WORLD

STEVE WINWOOD	K G V(A	(A) AIYE KETA	1973 ISLAND	UK	HELP 14
REMI KABAKA	V G D B(A				
ABDUL LOUGHTY AMAO	V WIND(A				

THIRD WORLD WAR

TERRY STAMP	G V (AB	(A) THIRD WORLD WAR	1971 FLY UK HIFLY4 GER POLYDOR 2310123
JIM AVERY	B (AB	(B) THIRD WORLD WAR II	1972 TRACK UK 2406 108 GERM 2310 123
MICK LIEBER	G (A	(B) THIRD WORLD WAR II	1972 POLYDOR GER 2310 200
JOHN KNIGHTSBRIDGE G	(B		
RAY FLACKE	G (B	JOHN HAWKEN PNO (B CRAIG COLLINGE D (B JIM PRICE HRNS (AB
WINGY	HCA (A	SPEEDY PERC (A FRED SMITH D (A BOBBY KEYS SAX (A
TONY ASHTON	K (A	PETE MARTIN G (A JOHN FENTON PROD (AB

THIRSTY MOON

NORBERT DROGIES	D (ABCD	(A) THIRSTY MOON	1973 BRAIN	GER1021
MICHAEL KOBS	K (AB	(B) YOU'LL NEVER COME BACK	1973 BRAIN	GER 1041
WILLI PAPE	WIND (AB	(C) YELLOW SUNSHINE	197 BRAIN	GERM 0040 124
JUNIOR WEERASINGHE	D(D	(D) STARCHASER	1981 SKY	GER 053
HARALD KONIETZKO	G B V(AB			
ERWIN NOACK	PERC (AB	JURGEN DROGIES G PERC(ABD HANS WENER RANWIG K V (AD SIEGFRIED PISALLA G V(A

THIRTEENTH FLOOR ELEVATORS

ROCKY ERICSON	V (ABC	(A) PSYCHEDELIC SOUNDS OF	1966 INTERNATIONAL ARTIST	US	LP1
DAN GALINDO	B (B	(A) PSYCHEDELIC SOUNDS OF	1978 RADAR RI	UK RAD13
JOHN IKE WALTON	D (A	(B) EASTER EVERYWHERE	1968INTERNATIONAL ARTIST	US	IA5
DANNY THOMAS	D (B	(B) EASTER EVERYWHERE	1979 RADAR RI	UK RAD15
STACY SUTHERLAND	G PROD(AB	(C) 13TH FLOOR ELEVATORS LIVE	1968 INTERNATIONAL ARTIST	US	IA8
BENNY THURMAN	B VLN(A	(D) BULL OF THE WOODS	1969 INTERNATIONAL ARTIST	US	IA9
TOMMY HALL	JUG (ABC	(E) AVALON 66	1977	FP 1001
RONNIE LEATHERMAN	D (A	(F) YOU REALLY GOT ME (EP)	1978 AUSTIN	UK	RE1
LELAN ROGERS	PROD (AB				
GORDON BYNUM	PROD (A				

THIRTY DAYS OUT

PHIL LOWE	D V (A	(A) THIRTY DAYS OUT	1971 REPRISE	US	6450
JACK MALKEN	G V (A				
MONTE MELNICK	B V K(A	JOHN MILCALLEF G V (A JIM DICKENSON K (A LARRY KNECHTEL K (A

THIRTY EIGHT SPECIAL

DONNIE VAN ZANT	V (ALL	(A) THIRTY EIGHT SPECIAL	1977 A&M	US 4638	UK	AMLH64638
STEVE BROOKINS	D (ALL	(B) SPECIAL DELIVERY	1978 A&M	US 4684	UK	AMLH64684
JACK GRONDIN	D (ALL	(C) ROCKIN' THE NIGHT	1980 A&M	US 4782		
KEN LYONS	B (ALL	(D) WILD EYED SOUTHERN BOYS	1981 A&M	US 4835	UK	AMLH64835
DON BARNES	G V (ALL	(E) SPECIAL FORCES	1982 A&M	US 4888		
JEFF CARLISI	G STEEL(ALL	(EP) HOLD ON LOOSELY	1981 A&M		UK	AMS 9160
TERRY EMERY	PNO (ABDE					
LARRY JUNSTROM	B (ALL	DAN HARTMAN V (A LANI GROVES V (A JOSLYN BROWN V (A
CARL HALL	V (A	BILLY POWELL K (C DALE KRANTZ V (C STEVE McRAY HCA (E
JIM BARNES	HCA (E	CAROL BRISTOW V (E LU MOSS V (E

THIS HEAT

GARETH WILLIAMS	K G B V(AB	(A) THIS HEAT	1979 PIANO	UK	THIS 1
CHARLES HAYWARD	PERC K V (AB	(B) DECEIT	1981 ROUGH TRADE	UK	ROUGH26
CHARLES BULLEN	G VLA V CLAR(AB				

JACQUES THOLLOT

JACQUES THOLLOT	D K (ABCD	(A) QUAND LE SON DEVIENT TROP AIGU	1971 FUTURA	GER 24
FRANCOIS JEANNEAU	SAX (BCD	(B) WATCH DEVIL GO	19 PALM	17
SIEGFRIED KESSLER	PNO (C	(C) RESURGENCE	1977 MUSICA	MUS 3021
BOB GUERIN	B (C	(D) CINQ HOPS	1978 FREE BIRD	FLY 03
NANA VASCONCELOS	PERC (C				
FREDERIQUE GEGENBACH	V (C	ELISE ROSS V (D FRANCOIS COUTURIER PNO (D JEAN PAUL CELEA B (D
CHRIS HOWARD	FLT (D	MICHEL GRAILLIER CLAR (D JEAN FRANCOIS CLARK B (B CHARLINE SCOTT V (B

B J THOMAS

Personnel			Album	Year	Label	Country	Cat.
B J THOMAS	V	(ALL	(A) I'M SO LONELY I COULD CRY	19	SCEPTER	US	535
PAUL WILLIAMS	V	(IM	(B) ON MY WAY	19	SCEPTER	US	570
MENTOR WILLIAMS	V	(I	(C) YOUNG & IN LOVE	19	SCEPTER	US	576
MARK JAMES	V	(IM	(D) GREATEST HITS	19	SCEPTER	US	518
JON STROLL	K V	(IL	(E) RAINDROPS KEEP FALLING	19	SCEPTER	US	580
AL GORGONI	G V	(IKL	(F) EVERYBODY'S OUT OF TOWN	19	SCEPTER	US	582
DOMINIC CORTESE	ACC	(I	(G) MOST OF ALL	1971	SCEPTER	US	586
TEDDY IRWIN	G	(I	(H) GREATETS HITS VOL 2	197	SCEPTER	US	597
KIRK HAMILTON	B	(IK	(I) ROCK'N'ROLL LULLABY	1972	SCEPTER	US	5101
ALLAN SCHWARTZBERG	D	(ILK	(J) B J THOMAS COUNTRY	1972	SCEPTER	US	5108
JIMMY MAELEN	PERC	(ILK	(K) SONGS	1973	PARAMOUNT	US	6052
GLEN SPREEN	STR	(IK	(L) LONGHORN & LONDON BRIDGES	1974	PARAMOUNT	US	1020
BARRY MANN	K V	(IK	(M) REUNION	197	ABC	US	858
DUANE EDDY	G	(I	(N) HELP ME MAKE IT	197	ABC	US	912
GEORGE DEVENS	VIBES	(I	(O) BEST OF	19	STARDAY	US	992
DAVE CARY	VIBES	(I	(P) ABC COLLECTION	19	ABC	US	30028
DARLENE LOVE	V	(I	(Q) 16 GREATEST HITS	197	TRIP	US	16/18
FANITA JAMES	B	(I	(R) HOME WHERE I BELONG	1977	MYRRH	UK	1060
JEAN KING	V	(I	(S) B J THOMAS	1977	MCA	US	2286
DAVE SOMERVILLE	V	(I	(T) EVERYBODY LOVES	1978	MCA	US	3035
RON HICKLIN	V	(I	(U) HAPPY MAN	1979	MYRRH	US	1072
TOM BAHLER	V	(I					

GENE MORFORD	V	(I	STEVIE WONDER	HCA	(I	JIMMY WEBB	K	(I	CAROLE KING	K	(I
CHARLIE LARKEY	B	(I	RON TUTT	D	(I	HUGH McCRACKEN	G	(IKL	DAVE BOONE	FDL	(I
STEVE TYRELL	PERC V	(IKL	WAYNE CARSON	G	(I	CHIP TAYLOR	V	(I	RODNEY JUSTO	V	(ILK
JOHN SEBASTIAN	G	(I	PETE DRAKE	STEEL	(IM	BOBBY EMMONS	K	(M	BOBBY WOODS		(M
GENE CHRISMAN	D	(M	MIKE LEECH	B	(M	CHIPS MOMAN	G	(M	JOHNNY CHRISTOPHER	G	(M
REGGIE YOUNG	G	(M	SHANE KEISTER	SYN	(M	STEVE GIBSON	G	(M	GEORG WADENIUS	G	(KL
BOB MANN	G	(LK	ERIC WEISSBERG	BAN	(K	PAUL GRIFFIN	K	(KL	ANDY MUSON	B	(KL
LINDA LAWLEY	V	(K	MARGRET DORN	V	(K	TOM MALONE	TPT	(K	LOU SOLOFF	TPT	(KL
LOU MARINI	SAX	(KL	DAVE BARGERON	TROM	(KL	GINI EASTWOOD	V	(K	DON GROLNICK	K	(KL
SHARON WALKER	V	(K	GENE CORNISH	V	(K	DINO DANELLI	V	(K	BILLY HOCHER	V	(K
ERIC THORNGREN	V	(K	JOHN TURI	V	(K	GERRY GOFFIN	V	(K	BARRY GOLDBERG	V	(K
MIKE BRECKER	SAX	(L	RANDY BRECKER	TPT	(L	RANDALL BRAMBLETT	K V	(L	PETER GORDON	HRNS	(L
ELLIOTT RANDALL	G	(L	RICHIE SUPA	G	(L	RICK MAROTTA	D	(L	BELL TREE	G	(L
PROF BRADFORD SINGERS	V	(L									

CARLA THOMAS

Personnel			Album	Year	Label	Country	Cat.			
CARLA THOMAS	V	(ALL	(A) GEE WHIZ	1961	ATLANTIC	US	SD8057			
			(B) COMFORT ME	1966	STAX/ATLANTIC	US	7706			
			(C) CARLA	1966	STAX/ATLANTIC	US	7709			
			(D) KING & QUEEN	1967	STAX/ATLANTIC	US	7716			
			(E) QUEEN ALONE	1967	STAX/ATLANTIC	US	7 718			
			(F) LOVE MEANS	1971	STAX	US	2044	UK	PLORDOR	2362023
			(G) MEMPHIS QUEEN	1975	STAX	Us	2019	UK STAX	STX 1038	
			(H) BEST OF	19	ATLANTIC	US	SD8232			
			(J) CHRONICLE	1979	STAX		STX 4124			

DAVID THOMAS

Personnel			Album	Year	Label	Cat.
DAVID THOMAS		(A	(A) SOUND OF SOUND	1981	ROUGH TRADE	ROUGH 30

IAN THOMAS

Personnel			Album	Year	Label	Country	Cat.
IAN THOMAS		(AB	(A) GOODNIGHT MRS CALABASH	1976	CHRYSALIS	UK	CHR 1126
			(B) IAN THOMAS	1976	DJM	UK	DJM 20440

IAN THOMAS BAND

Personnel			Album	Year	Label	Country	Cat.
DAVE COOPER	G	(AB	(A) STILL HERE	1978	ATLANTIC	US	19167
MICK OBERLE	D V	(AB	(B) SLIDER	1979	ATLANTIC		
DAVE SAWYER	B V	(AB					
HUGH SYME	K V	(AB	IAN THOMAS G K V(AB				

IRMA THOMAS

Personnel			Album	Year	Label	Country	Cat.			
IRMA THOMAS	V	(ALL	(A) IN BTWEEN TEARS	1973	FUNGUS	US	25150	UK RI	CHARLY1020	
JERRY WILLIAMS	PNO	(A	(B) WISH SOMEONE WOULD CARE	19	IMPERIAL	US				
JESSE CARR	G	(A	(C) TAKE A LOOK	196	MINIT	UK	40004			
POPS POPWELL	B	(A	(D) LIVE	1976	ISLAND	UK	HELP 29			
SQUIRM	D	(A	(E) SOUL QUEEN OF NEW ORLEANS	1978	MAISON SOUL	US	1005			
PAUL HORNSBY	K	(A	(F) SAFE WITH ME	1979	RCS	US	1004			
SWAMP DOGG BAND		(A	(G) HIP SHAKIN' MAMA	1981	CHARLY	UK	2019			
MIKE THOMAS	D	(E								
STAN KEMPER	D	(E	HAROLD COWART	B	(E	FREDDY WALL	G	(E	ROD ANTOON	K (E
PETE VERDOIS	SAX	(E	HAROLD COWART	STR	(E	CORA JEFFERSON	V	(E	ALICE JACKSON	V (E
RANDY JACKSON	B	(EF	CARSON WHITSITT	K	(E	JAMES STROUD	D	(F	ROGER HAWKINS	D (F

JOE THOMAS

Personnel			Album	Year	Label		Cat.
JOE THOMAS	FLT	(AB	(A) JOY OF COOKIN'	1974	PEOPLE		PLEO 15
MARVIN STAMM	HRNS	(B	(B) MAKE YOUR MOVE	1979	LRC 9327	+ TK	TKR 83374
GEORGE YOUNG	SAX	(B					
HIRAM BULLOCK	G	(B	RICHARD TRIFAN SYN (B				

MICKEY THOMAS

Personnel			Album	Year	Label	Country	Cat.			
MICKEY THOMAS	PERC V	(A	(A) ALIVE ALONE	1981	ELEKTRA	US	5E530			
JOE VITALE	D SYN V	(A								
DON FELDER	G	(A	GEORGE PERRY	B V	(A	PAUL HARRIS	PNO	(A	STEVE PORCARO	SYN (A
DON BALDWIN	SYN V	(A	MIAMI STRINGS		(A	MARTY GREBB	SAX	(A	MAXINE WILLARD	V (A
JULIA TILLMAN	V	(A	OREN WATERS	V	(A	CRAIG CHAQUICO	G	(A	NORTON BUFFALO	HCA (A
CORY LERIOS	K	(A	DON BONSANTI	SAX	(A	NEAL BONSANTI	SAX	(A	ROGER HOMEFIELD	TROM (A
KEN FAULK	TPT	(A								

NICKY THOMAS

Personnel			Album	Year	Label	Cat.
NICKY THOMAS		(ALL	(A) TELL IT LIKE IT IS	1971	TROJAN	TRLS 25
			(B) IMAGES OF YOU	19	HORSE	HRLP 701
			(C) LOVE OF THE COMMON PEOPLE	1976	TROJAN	TBL 143

```
RAY THOMAS        V FLT(AB       (A) FROM MIGHTY OAKS              1975 THRESHOLD        UK        THS 16
NICKY JAMES       V PERC(AB      (B) HOPES WISHES & DREAMS         1976 THRESHOLD        UK        THS 17
JOHN JONES        G V   (AB
MIKE MORAN        K     (AB  B J COLE   STEEL(A  DAVE POTTS      D   (A  MIKE SILVER    G V (A
TREVOR JONES      B V   (B   GRAHAM DEACON  D    (B  BARRY ST JOHN  V   (B  LIZA STRIKE V   (B
HELEN CHAPPELLE   V     (B
```

```
RUFUS THOMAS      V     (ALL     WALKING THE DOG                  1964 STAX             US        704
BILLY RED LOVE    PNO   ((E)     MAY I HAVE YOUR TICKET PLEASE    19   STAX             US        2022
JOE HILL LOUIS    G     (E       FUNKY CHICKEN                    1970 STAX             US        2028
HOUSTON STOKES    D     (E       LIVE AT PJs DOIN' THE PUSH & PULL 1970 STAX            US        2039
                                 DID YOU HEAR ME                  197  STAX US 3004 UK POLYDOR 2362028
                                 CROWN PRINCE OF DANCE            1974 STAX US 3008 UK STAX   STX1002
                                 (E)RUFUS THOMAS(EP)              1977 CHARLY           UK        CEP 101
                                 I AINT GETTIN' OLDER             19   AVID US 6046
                                 IF THERE WERE NO MUSIC           1977 PYE UK NSPL28241 US AVI   6015
                                 CHRONICLE(1 SIDE RUFUS /1 SIDE CARLA) 1979 STAX US   STX 4124
```

```
TIMMY THOMAS      (             (A) TOUCH TO TOUCH               1978 TK                         TKR 82510
                                ( ) WHY CANT WE LIVE TOGETHER     19   GLADES US 6501 POLYDOR 2956 002
                                ( ) YOU'RE THE SONG               1975 POLYDOR                   2310 377
                                ( ) MAGICIAN                      1977 TK               UK XL    14044
```

```
MALCOLM THOMLINSON V   (A      (A) ROCK'N'ROLL HERMIT            1980 CASABLANCA        US 7199
```

```
                               (A) A PRODUCT OF                  1981 T                UK        TELP1
                               (B) SET                           1982 T                UK        TELP2
```

```
BARBARA THOMPSON SAX PERC(ALL  (A) PARAPHERNALIA                 1978 MCA              UK   MCF  2852
JON HISEMAN      D    (DC       (B) JUBIABA                       1978 MCA              UK   MCF  2867
DILL KATZ        B    (DC       (C) WILDE TALES                   1979 MCA              UK   MCF  3047
COLIN DUDMAN     K SYN(DAC      (D) LIVE IN CONCERT               1980 MCA                   MCSP 309
ROY BABBINGTON   B    (AB
HAROLD FISHER    D    (A   DEREK WADSWORTH   HRN (B  HENRY LOWTHER    TPT (B  IAN HAMMER      TPT (B
GLYN THOMAS      PERC (B   PETER LEMER       K   (B  TREVOR TOMKINS   D   (B  BILL LESAGE PERC (B
```

```
ALI THOMPSON          (A       (A) TAKE A LITTLE RHYTHM           1980 A&M              UK  AMLH68512
DURBAN LAVERDE   B    (AB       (B) DECEPTION IS AN ART           1981 A&M              UK  AMLH64846
PHILIP WRIGHT    G V  (AB
JAMES LACELLES   PNO  (A   WILLIAM C LYALL   SYN (AB  TED McKENNA   D   (A  DAVE ROACH  SAX  (AB
JULIAM DIGGLE    PERC (A   DEBI DOSS         V   (AB  PETE FILLEUL  PNO (A  STUART ELLIOT   D (B
JEFF PHILLIPS    D    (A   ALAN MURPHY       G   (A   CHARLIE SPITERI  PERC (A  CAROL KENYON  V (AB
RICHARD BAILEY   D    (A   SONJA JONES       V   (A   JON KELLY     PROD (AB  RAY COOPER    PERC(B
JOHN HELLIWELL   SAX  (B   ED GOODMAN        HRNS (B  SYLVIA MASON  V   (B  ELLIE WARREN    V (B
```

```
MAYO THOMPSON    V    (A       (A) CORKY'S DEBT TO HIS FATHER     19   TEXAS REVOLUTION US  CFS  2270
```

```
RICHARD THOMPSON G V  (ALL     (A) HENRY THE HUMAN FLY            1972 ISLAND UK ILPS9197 US REPRISE2112
LINDA THOMPSON(PETERS)V(ALL    (B) I WANT TO SEE THE BRIGHT LIGHTS 1974 ISLAND         UK    ILPS 9266
TIMI DONALD      D    (ABCDEG   (C) HOKEY POKEY                    1974 ISLAND GER 88598 UK   ILPS 9305
PAT DONALDSON    B    (ABCDEG   (D) POUR DOWN LIKE SILVER          1975 ISLAND         UK    ILPS 9348
SANDY DENNY      K V  (AE       (E) GUITAR & VOCAL                 1976 ISLAND         UK    ICD8
DAVID SNELL      HARP (A        (E) R T LIVE!(MORE OR LESS)(DBL)   1977 ISLAND         UK    ISLA 9421
JEFF COLE        TROM (A        (F) FIRST LIGHT                    1978 CHRYSALIS GER 6307640 UK CHR1177
JOHN DEFERERI    SAX  (A        (G) SUNNY VISTA                    1979 CHRYSALIS NL 511247 UK  CHR1247
CLAY TOYANI      TPT  (A        (H) STRICT TEMPO                   1981 ELIXIR         UK    LP1
ABDU RAHIM       V    (G
SUE DRAHEIM      FDL  (A   BARRY DRANSFIELD  FDL (A   JOHN KIRKPATRICK ACC  (ALL ASHLEY HUTCHINGS  V B(ADE
SIMON NICOL G K V  (BCEFG  BRIAN GULLAND     KRUMM(B  RICHARD HARVEY   KRUMM(B  ROYSTON WOOD    V  (B
TREVOR LUCAS     V    (BF  C W S SILVER BAND     (BC  IAN WHITEMAN     K FLT(CDE ALY BAIN        FDL(CD
SIDONIE GOOSSENS HARP (C   DAVE MATTACKS     D (DEFGH NIC JONES        FDL (D  HENRY LOWTHER    TPT(D
JUDY DYBLE       V    (E   IAN MATTHEWS      V   (EF  MARTIN LAMBLE    D   (E  PETE ROSS       HCA(E
DAVE SWARBRICK   FDL  (E   DAVID PEGG            (EG  ANDY NEWMARK     D   (F  WILLIE WEEKS    B  (F
NEIL LARSEN      K    (F   CHRIS KARAN       PERC (F  DOLORES KEANE    WHISTLE (F DAVE BRADY    V  (F
HEATHER BRADY    V    (F   BILL CADDICK      V   (F   PHILIPPA CLARE   V   (F  JULIE COVINGTON V  (F
ANDY FAIRWEATHER LOW V (F  MADDY PRIOR       V   (F   PETA WEBB        V   (F  ANDY ROBERTS    DULC(A
DAVE BURLAND     V    (F   MICHAEL SPENCER ARSCOTT D(G SUE HARRIS      WIND (G  PETE WINGFIELD  K  (G
RABBIT BUNDRICK  K    (G   LUIS JARDIM       PERC (G  KATE McGARRIGLE  V   (G  ANNA McGARRIGLE V  (G
GLEN TILBROOK    V    (G   JULIAN LITTMAN    V   (G   MARC ELLINGTON   V   (G  OLIVE SIMPSON   V  (G
NICOLE TIBBELS   V    (G   LINDSAY BENTON    V   (G   DAVID BEAVAN     V   (G  BRUCE LYNCH     B  (G
GERRY RAFFERTY   V    (G   HAFSA ABDUL JABBAS V  (G
```

```
ROBBIN THOMPSON  G V  (AB      (A) ROBBIN THOMPSON               1976 NEMPEROR         US    440
VELPO ROBERTSON  G V  (A       (B) TWO B'S PLEASE                1980 NEMPEROR         US
ERIC HIEBERG     K V  (
BOB ANTONELLI    D V  (    MIKE LANNING      B V (
```

```
BIG MAMA THORNTON .V   (ALL    (A) STRONGER THAN DIRT            1969 MERCURY UK SMCL 20176 US  61225
CORNELL DUPREE   G    (H        (B) SHES BACK                     1968 BACKBEAT          US    68
RONNIE MILLER    G    (H        (C) IN EUROPE                     1966 ARHOOLIE          US F 1028
PAUL GRIFFIN     K    (H        (D) CHICAGO BLUES                 1967 ARHOOLIE          US F 1032
WILBUR BASCOMB   B    (H        (E) BALL & CHAIN                  1968 ARHOOLIE          US F 1039
JIMMY JOHNSON    D    (H        (F) JAIL                          1975 VANGUARD                79351
BUDDY LUCAS      SAX  (H        (G) SASSY MAMA                    1975 VANGUARD                79354
GEORGE SMITH     HCA  (H        (H) MAMA'S PRIDE                  1978 VANGUARD                VPC4000<
STEVE WACHSMAN   G    (H        (I) SAVED                         1973 PENTAGRAM         US 10005
WALTER HORTON    HCA  (H        ( ) THATS THE WAY IT IS           19   MERCURY   61249
BEE HOUSTON      G    (H
FRANCIS CLAY     D    (D   J D NICHOLSON     K   (H  BRUCE SIEVERSON  B   (H  TODD NELSON     D  (H
BILL POTTER      SAX  (H   EDDIE BOYD        K   (C  BUDDY GUY        G   (C  JIMMY LEE ROBINSON B(C
FRED BELOW       D    (C   FRED McDOWELL     G   (C  JAMES COTTON     HCA (D  OTIS SPANN  PNO    (D
MUDDY WATERS     G    (D
```

THOR

THOR	V	(A	(A) KEEP THE DOGS AWAY	1978 MIDSONG	US	2337
JOHN SHAN	G	(A				
TERRY McKEO						

PETER THORUP

PETER THORUP	G B V(A	(A) THIN SLICES	1978 METRONOME	EURO	15635
KEN GUDMAN	D	(A			
SANNE SALOMONSEN	V	(A	KENNETH KNUDSEN	K	(A	HANS FJELDSTED	K	(A

GEORGE THOROGOOD & THE DESTROYERS

GEORGE THOROGOOD	G V	(ALL	(A) GEORGE THOROGOOD & THE DESTROYERS	1977 ROUNDER 3013 US UK SONET SNTF760
MICHAEL LEVINE	B	(C	(A) GEORGE THOROGOOD & THE DESTROYERS	1978 SONET GER 69082
JEFF SIMON	D	(ALL	(B) MOVE IT ON OVER	1978 ROUNDER 3024 US UK SONET SNTF781
BILLY BLOUGH	B	(ABE	(C) BETTER THAN THE REST (1974)	1979 MCA US 3091 GER 62136 UKMCL1623
RON SMITH	G	(BA	(D) MORE GEORGE THOROGOOD	1980 ROUNDER US 3045 UK SONET SNTF850
UNCLE MEAT PENNINGTON	PERC(B	(E) BAD TO THE BONE	1982 EMI US 17076
HANK CARTER	SAX	(DE		

BILLY THORPE

BILLY THORPE	G V	(AB	(A) CHILDREN OF THE SUN	1979 POLYDOR UK 2391424
GIL MATTHEWS	D	(B	(A) CHILDREN OF THE SUN	1979 CAPRICORN US 0221
LEE SKLAR	B	(AB	(B) 21ST CENTURY MAN	1980 ELEKTRA US 6E 294
ALVIN TAYLOR	D	(A	(C) STIMULATION	1981 PASHA US 37499

THOSE NAUGHTY LUMPS

			(A) ICE CREAM	19 OPEN EYE UK OE 1002

THREE D

RICK ZWIC	V	(A	(A) 3D	1980 POLYDOR US 6254 UK 2391 445
KEW GINSBERG	G V	(A		
TED WENDER	K V	(A	NICK STEVENS B V (A MIKE FINK D (A	

THREE DOG NIGHT

DANNY HUTTON	V	(12K	(A) THREE DOG NIGHT	1969 UK STATESIDE 5006 US DUNHILL 50048
CHUCK NEGRON	V	(12K	(B) SUITABLE FOR FRAMING	1969 UK STATESIDE 5013 US DUNHILL 50058
CORY WELLS	V	(12K	(C) LIVE AT THE FORUM	1970 UK STATESIDE 5023 US DUNHILL 50068
MIKE ALLSUP	G	(12K	(D) IT AINT EASY	1970 UK PROBE SPBA6251 US DUNHILL 50078
JIM GREENSPOON	K	(12K	(E) NATURALLY	1971 UK PROBE SPBA6257 US DUNHILL 50088
JOE SCHERMIE	B	(1K	(F) GOLDEN BISCUITS	1971 UK PROBE SPB 1035 US DUNHILL 50098
FLOYD SNEED	D	(12K	(F) GOLDEN BISCUITS	1974 UK ABC ABCL5014
JACK RYLAND	B	(2K	(G) HARMONY	1971 UK PROBE SPB 1047 US DUNHILL 50108
SKIP KONTE	K	(2K	(H) SEVEN SEPARATE FOOLS	1972 UK PROBE SPTC 1 US DUNHILL 50118
(1) 1968/73 (2) 1973/			(I) AROUND THE WORLD	1973 UK PROBE PBSP 113 US DUNHILL 50138
			(J) CYAN	1974 UK ABC ABCL5039 US DUNHILL 50158
			(K) HARD LABOUR	1974 UK ABC ABCL5049 US DUNHILL 50168
			(L) GREATEST HITS	1974 UK ABC ABCL5064 US DUNHILL 50178
			(M) DOG STYLE	1974 US DUNHILL 50198
			(N) COMING DOWN YOUR WAY	1975 UK ABC ABCL5120 US ABC 888
			(O) AMERICAN PASTIME	1976 UK ABC ABCL5159 US ABC 928

THREE MAN ARMY

PAUL GURVITZ(CURTIS	(ALL	(A) A THIRD OF A LIFETIME	1971 PEGASUS UK PEG3
ADRIAN GURVITZ(CURTIS G(ALL		(A) A THIRD OF A LIFETIME (DIFF TRACKS)	KAMA SUTRA 2044
PETE ROBINSON	PNO (BC	(B) THREE MAN ARMY	1973 REPRISE UK K44254 US 2150
MIKE KELLIE	D	(A	(C) THREE MAN ARMY 2	1974 REPRISE UK K54015
BUDDY MILES	D	(A	(D) MAHESHA	1974 POLYDOR 2310 241
TONY NEWMAN	D	(BC		
BRIAN PARRISH	G	(A	RUBY JAMES V (C MADELINE BELL V (C DORIS TROY V (C

PERCY THRILLINGTON

PERCY THRILLINGTON	(A	(A) THRILLINGTON	1978 CAPITOL US 11642
(PAUL McCARTNEY)			

THRILLS

TONY MONACO	K V	(AB	(A) FIRST THRILLS	1980 CBS
DAVE FULLERTON	G V	(AB	(B) FRONY PAGE NEWS	1981 CBS
BILL GILBERT	B V	(AB		
ROB OWENS	D V	(AB		

THROBBING GRISTLE

GENESIS P ORRIDGE	B C	(ABCDE	(A) 1ST ANNUAL REPORT	197 INDUSTRIAL UK IR0001
COSEY FANNI TUTTI	G V(ABCDE	(B) 2ND ANNUAL REPORT	1977 INDUSTRIAL UK IR0002
CHRIS CARTER	K	(ABCDE	(B) 2ND ANNUAL REPORT(RECUT RI)	1979 FETISH UK FR2001
PETER CHRISTOPHERSON EFFECTS(ABCDE		(C) D O A	1978 INDUSTRIAL UK IR0004
			(D) 20 JAZZ FUNK GREATS	1979 INDUSTRIAL UK IR0008
			(E) HEATHEN EARTH	1980 INDUSTRIAL UK IR0009
			(F) GREATEST HITS	1981 ROUGH TRADE UK 23

THUMBS

STEVE WILSON	V	(A	(A) THUMBS	1979 RAMONA US RR1
MARTY OLSON	K	(A		
KEVIN SMITH	G V	(A	KARL HOFFMANN G B (A MARK MOOSE BRENNAN G B(A

THUNDER

JOHN PORTER McMEARS	G V(A	(A) THUNDER	1980 ATCO US 38129 EURO 50746
MO WERT	G V	(A	(B) HEADPHONES FOR COWS	1981 ATCO
DANNY HERSON	K V	(A		
CHOPPER ANDERSON	B V	(A	TRIS IMBODEN D (A

THUNDERCLAP NEWMAN

ANDY NEWMAN	K	(A	(A) HOLLYWOOD DREAM	1970 TRACK UK 2406 003
JIMMY McCULLOCH	G	(A		
SPEEDY KEEN	V G D(A	PETE TOWNSHEND (BIJOU DRAINS)B(A JIM AVERY B (JACK McCULLOCH D (
CHRIS MORPHET	HCA	(A		

THUNDERHEAD

MIKE DAGGER	V	(A	(A) THUNDERHEAD	1975 ABC US 919
PAT RUSH	G	(A		
RONNIE DOBBS	G	(A		

THUNDERMUG

BILL DURST	G	(A	(A) THUNDERMUG STRIKES	1972 AXE UK AXS502 US EPIC 32464	
JOE DE ANGELIS	V	(A	(B) TA DAA	1975 MERCURY	US	SRM1 1039
JIM CORBETT	B	(A			
ED PRANSKUS	D	(A			

JOHNNY THUNDERS

JOHNNY THUNDERS	G V	(A	(A) SO ALONE	1978 REAL UK RAL1 GER WB 56571	
STEVE MARRIOTT	K	(A			
PETER PERRETT	G V	(A	STEVE JONES	G	(A	BILLY RATH	B	(A	PAUL GRAY	D(A
PHIL LYNOTT	B	(A	MIKE KELLIE	D	(A	WALTER LURE	G	(A	PAT PALLADIN	V (A
PAUL COOK	D	(A	JOHN IRISH EARLE	SAX	(A	STEVE NICOL	D	(A	HENRI PAUL	G (A
STEVE LILLYWHITE	PROD K(A	CHRISSIE HYNDES	V	(A	KOULLA KAKOULLI	V	(A		

THUNDERTHIGHS (VOCAL BACKING)

CASEY SYNGE	V	(	KAREN FRIEDMAN	V	(	DARI LALOU	V	(	JUANITA FRANKLIN	V	(

THUNDERTRAIN

GENE PROVIST	G	(1	(A) TEENAGE SUICIDE	1977 JELLY	JPLP1
RICK PROVOST	B	(1	(1) 1976		
MACH BELL	V	(1	STEVEN SILVA	G	(1 BOB EDWARDS	D (1

TICKETS

STEVE RAPPO	D	(A	(A) 0001	1980 CBS	84423
KEVIN CARLSEN FLYNN	G V(A				
DOM TORCHE	K V	(A	HUBERT HERITIER	B V	(A	

TIERRA

		(A) TIERRA	1974 20TH CENTURY	US 412

ASMUS TIETCHENS

HANS IIM CESSTEU	SYN	(A	(A) BIOTOP	1981 SKY GER	057
TUSSI SCHEMANTE	SYN	(A			
STY SEEMI		(A	SAM SENS	SYN	(A ACHIM STUTESSEN	SYN	(A MISCHA SUTTENSE	SYN (A

TIGER

BIG JIM SULLIVAN	G	(AB	(A) TIGER	1976 RETREAT RTL6006 US WB 2940	
ALAN PARK	K	(B	(B) GOING DOWN LAUGHING	1976 EMI UK EMC 3153 US	11660
DAVID McCRAE	K	(A			
NICKY MOORE	HCA V G	(AB	ANDY BROWN	B V	(B	PHIL CURTIS	B	(A	LES WALKER	G V (AB
BILL McGILLIVRAY	G K V(B	RAY FLACKE	G	(A	BILLY RANKIN	D	(A		

TIGERS

TONY JACKS	G V	(A	(A) SAVAGE MUSIC	1980 A&M US AP4817 EURO WEA 58163	
NICK COLA	K V	(A			
ROSS McGEENEY	G V	(A	NIC POTTER	B	(A	PETE DOBSON	D	(A		

TIGHT LIKE THAT

DAVID H PEABODY	G V HCA(A	(A)HOKUM	1972 VILLAGE THING	VTS 12
DAVID GRIFFITHS	VLN G V(A			
BILL SHORTT	PERC (A	HUGH McNULTY	B V	(A ANDY LEGGETT	JUG (A

TILLER BOYS

		(A) BIG NOISE FROM THE JUNGLE(EP)	198 NEW HORMONE	ORG 3

ROGER TILLISON

ROGER TILLISON		(A	(A) ROGER TILLISON'S ALBUM	19 ATCO	US SD 33355
JESSE ED DAVIS	G	(A			
JIM KELTNER	D	(A	LARRY KNECHTEL	K	(A	

STEVE TILSTON

STEVE TILSTON	G V	(A	(A) ACOUSTIC CONFUSION	1971 VILLAGE THING	UK VTS 5
			( ) COLLECTION	1972 TRANSATLANTIC	UK TRA252
			( ) SONGS FOR THE DRESS REHEARSAL	1977 CORNUCOPIA	UK

TILT

JOHN PONDER	D V	(A	(A) MUSIC	1978 PARACHUTE US	9008
FRANK EWING	B	(A			
MIKE HARNER	G V	(A	DOUG KAHN	K	(A	

TIMBER

JUDY ELLIOTT	V	(AB	(A) PART OF WHAT YOU HEAR	19 KAPP	US KS3633
WAYNE BERRY	B G V(AB	(B) BRING AMERICA HOME	19 ELEKTRA US 74095	UK K42093
GEORGE CLINTON	K V HRNS(AB			
ROGER JOHNSON	G V TPT (AB	WARNER DAVIS	D	(AB	

TIMBERLINE

		(A) GREAT RUSH	1977 EPIC	US 34681

TIME

GARY MARGETZ	G V	(A	(A) TIME	1975 BUK	UK BULP 2005
TORRIS MARGETZ	B	(A			
ALEX JOHNSON	G V	(A	JOE DOLLY	D V	(A	

TIME BOX

MIKE PATTO	V	(	(A) ORIGINAL MOOSE ON THE LOOSE	1977 COSMOS COLLECTOR US	CCLPS9016
JOHN HALSEY	D	(			
OLLIE HALSALL	G	(	CHRIS HOLMES	K	(CLIVE GRIFFITHS	B	(

TIN HUEY

HARVEY GOLD	SYN K(A	(A) CONTENTS DISLODGED DURING SHIPMENT	1979 WB US BSK 3297	
RALPH CARNEY	K WIND V(A			
MICHAEL AYLWARD	G V	(A	CHRIS BUTLER	G V	(A JIM HAAS	V	(A MARK PRICE	B V	(A
STUART AUSTIN	D V	(A	STAN FARBER	V	(A	

TIN TIN

		(A) TIN TIN	1970 ATCO US	
		(B) ASTRAL TAXI	1971 ATCO US	33370

TINY TIM

TINY TIM	V UKE(ALL	(A) GOD BLESS TINY TIM	1968 REPRISE	US	6292
		(B) 2ND ALBUM	1968 REPRISE	US	6323
		(C) FOR ALL MY LITTLE FRIENDS	1969 REPRISE	US	6351
		(D) WITH LOVE & KISSES	19 BOUQUET		771

```
    KEITH TIPPETT      PNO  (ALL          (A) YOU ARE HERE I AM THERE        1970 POLYDOR GER 2383 050 UK 2384004
    ELTON DEAN         SAX  (ABG          (B) DEDICATED TO YOU               1971 VERTIGO                 6360 024
    MARK CHARIG        HRNS (ABG          (C) BLUE PRINT                     1972 RCA             UK    SF 8290
    NICK EVANS         TROM (ABG          (D) T'N'T                          1976 EMANEM          US      3307
    JEFF CLYNE         B    (A            (E) T'N'T                          1978 STEAM                 SJ104
    ALAN JACKSON       D    (A            (F) WARM SPIRITS COOL SPIRITS      1977 VINYL               VS 101
    GIORGIO GOMELSKY   BELLS(A            (G) FRAMES        (ARK)            1978 OGUN              OGD 003/4
    ROBERT WYATT       D    (B            (H) BOTH SIDES NOW                  19  POLYDOR            2359 007
    BRYAN SPRING       D    (B
    PHIL HOWARD        D    (B  TONY UTER       CONGA(B  ROY BABBINGTON    B   (BC NEVILLE WHITEHEAD  B  (B
    GARY BOYLE         G    (B  KEITH BAILEY    PERC (C  FRANK PERRY       PERC(C  JULIE TIPPETTS   G V (CFG
    TREVOR WATTS       SAX  (FG COLIN McKENZIE  B    (F  STAN TRACEY       PNO (DEG BRIAN SMITH     WIND (G
    LARRY STABBINS     WIND (G  HENRY LOWTHER   TPT  (G  PETER KOWALKE     HRNS (G  HARRY MILLER    B    (G
    LOUIS MOHOLO       D    (G  DAVE AMIS       TROM (G  MAGGIE NICHOLLS   V   (G
```

```
    SONNY CONDELL G V PERC(ABC            (A) TIR NA NOG                     1971 CHRYSALIS       UK    ILPS 9153
    LEO O'KELLY G V VLN   (ABC            (B) A TEAR & A SMILE               1972 CHRYSALIS       UK    CHR 1006
    BRIAN ODGERS      B   (C              (C) STRONG IN THE SUN              1973 CHRYSALIS       UK    CHR 1047
    DAVE MARKEE       B   (C
    JIM RYAN          B   (C  BARRY DE SOUZA  D    (BC ACE FOLLINGTON   D   (C  JEFF JONES      D   (C
    MATTHEW FISHER    K   (C  LARRY STEELE    B    (B
```

```
    KJELL'CHAPPY'ASPERUD D (ACD           (A) TITANIC                       1971 CBS                 64104
    JANNY LOSETH       G   (ACD           (B) SEA WOLF                       1972 CBS                 64791
    JOHN LORCK         D   (AC            (C) EAGLE ROCK                     1973 CBS                 65661
    ARICA SIGGS        B   (              (D) BALLAD OF A ROCK'N'ROLL LOSER  1975 CBS                 80786
    HELGE GROSLIE      K   (C             (E) RETURN OF DRAKKAR              1978 EGG               900542
    ROY ROBINSON       V   (ACD           (F) EYE OF THE HURRICANE           1980 SOUPLET      NL  201 856
    JOHN WILLIAMS      B G V(D
    KENNY AAS          ORG (A  ANDREW RAILSTON  D    (D
```

```
    RON RHOADES        K V (A             (A) THE FABULOUS TITANS (EP)       1980 EPIPHANY     US     003
    LLOYD ADAMS        D   (A
    DON FULTON         B V (A  SCOTT HILL      G V (A  CARROLL KNAPP    SAX (A
```

```
    LIBBY TITUS        V   (A             (A) LIBBY TITUS                    1977 CBS          US    PC 34152
    GRADY TATE         D   (A
    TONY LEVIN         B   (A  DON GROLNICK    K    (A  HUGH McCRACKEN   G   (A  ALAN RUBIN     HRNS(A
    DAVID NADIEN       VLN (A  KATHY KIENKE    VLN  (A  ALFRED BROWN     VLA (A  JANET HAMILTON CELLO(A
    PAUL SIMON         V   (A  RONNY ZITO      D    (A  CHUCK ISRAELS    B   (A  GEORGE YOUNG   SAX (A
    JOE BECK           G   (A  CHRIS PARKER    D    (A  RUSSELL GEORGE   D   (A  JOHN GUERIN    D   (A
    MAX BENNETT        B   (A  HIRTH MARTINEZ  G V  (A  MICHAEL MELVOIN  K   (A  GARTH HUDSON   K   (A
    RICK MAROTTA       D   (A  JOHN TROPEA     G    (A  PATTI AUSTIN     V   (A  LANI GROVES    V   (A
    WILL LEE           B   (A  GWEN GUTHRIE    V    (A  ROBBIE ROBERTSON G   (A  LARRY MUHOBERAC PNO (A
    MARVIN STAMM       TPT (A  DAVE TOFANI     FLT  (A  PHIL BODNER      FLT (A  DON BROOKS     HCA (A
    CRAIG DOERGE       K   (A  CARLY SIMON     V    (A  JAMES TAYLOR     V   (A
```

```
    JIM YOOMEY         D   (A             (A) TITUS GROAN                    1970 JANUS US 3024  UK DAWN DNLS3012
    STUART COWELL      K G (A
    TONY PRIESTLAND    WIND (A  JOHN LEE        B    (A
```

```
    LEMMIE LEMBRECHT   B V (A             (A) TO BE                          1977 BRAIN        GER    0060 053
    PETER FRANKEN      D   (A
    PETER WICHE        G   (A  ROLF KOHLER     B    (A  CLAUS ROBERT KRUSE K  (A
```

```
                                          (A) TOAD                          1972 RCA             UK    SF8241
```

```
    GARY RAZZANTE      B   (A             (A) TOAD HALL                      1968 LIBERTY      US    7580
    JOHN RICHARDSON    V PERC(A
    CHRIS SIGWALD      D   (A  THOMAS O MARCUS  G V (A  CLAPTON GUGLIAMO  G  (A
```

```
    BALDE SILVA G V HCA   (AB             (A) TOBY BEAU                      1978 RCA             UK    PL 12771
    STEVE ZIPPER     B V  (AB             (B) MORE THAN A LOVE SONG          1979 RCA             UK    PL 13119
    RON ROSE         G V BAN(AB           (C) IF YOU BELIEVE                 1980 RCA                    3575
    DANNY McKENNA    G V  (AB
    ROB YOUNG        D PERC(AB
```

```
    CLIFF BENNETT      V   (AB            (A) TOEFAT                         1970 PARLOPHONE   UK      7097
    KEN HENSLEY        G V (AB            (A) TOEFAT                         1970 RARE EARTH   US    RS 511
    LEE KERSLAKE       D V (A             (B) TOEFAT II                      1971 REGAL ZONOPHONE UK SLRZ 1015
    JOHN GLASCOCK      B   (              (B) TOEFAT II                      1971 RARE EARTH   US    RS 525
    JOE KONAS          B   (A
    MOX                HCA FLT (A
```

```
    IAN CUSSICK        V   (A             (A) TOLLHOUSE                      1978 NOVA         GER    623430
    DIRK STEFFENS      G   (A
    PETER WEIHE        G   (A  ROLF KOHLER     B V  (A  PETER FRANKEN    D PERC(A JEAN JACQUES KRAVETZ K(A
    HERB GELLER        SAX (A  BOB LANESE      TPT  (A  HANS UWE REIMERS SAX (A  RALE            V   (A
    JIM HOPKINS        V   (A  HEIKO EFFERTZ   V    (A
```

```
    KEN TAYLOR         B V (A             (A) TOKYO                           19  ARIOLA       GER  203 430
    FRITZ MATZKA       D   (A
    PETER WICHE        G   (A  ROLF KOHLER     B    (A  KLAUS LULEY      G V (A
```

JUKKA TOLONEN

```
JUKKA TOLONEN      G    (ALL    (A) TOLONEN                        1974 SONET UK SNTF652 SW LOVE LP 47
BILL OHRSTROM      PERC V(K     (A) TOLONEN                        1974 BRAIN GER 1059 US JANUS 3066
PEKKA POHJOLA      B    (A      (B) THE SUMMER GAMES               197            SW LOVE LP91
PEKKA POYRY        SAX  (AD     (C) THE HOOK                       197            SW LOVE LP113
REINO LAING        D    (A      (D) CROSSECTION                    1976 SONET UK SNTF699  US JANUS 7017
HEIKKI VIRTANEN    B    (AD     (E) HYSTERICA                      197            SW LOVE LP149
RONNE OSTERBERG    D    (A      (F) A PASSENGER TO PARAMARIBO      1978 SONET UK SNTF768 SW LOVE LP231
NORMAN FEARINGTON  D SYN(K      (F) A PASSENGER TO PARAMARIBO      1978 SONET NL 3028
JUKKA GUSTAVSON    K    (A      (G) MONTREUX BOOGIE                1979 SONET UK SNTF789 SW LOVE LP278
PARONI PAAKKUNAINEN SAX(D       (H) MOUNTAIN STREAM                1980 SONET UK SNTF818
ESA KOTILAINEN     K SYN(DF     (J) J T B                         1979 PICK UP PULP79302
ESKO ROSNELL       D    (D      (K) DUMS HAVE MORE FUN             1981 POLYDOR UK 2380 087
SAKARI KUKKO       WIND (D      (L) TOUCH WOOD                     1981 SONET    SNTF865
JOSSI AALTO        TROM (D
HARRY MERILAHTI    B    (JK   COSTE APETREA   G V(FJKL   CHRIS EKLUND    SAX (JF  BILL CARSON    D (FJ
JOACHIM KUHN       K    (J    MANS GRUNDSTROEM  B   (F   ILKA HANSKI     B   (F
```

TOM TOM CLUB

```
BEN ARMBRISTER        (A       (A) TOM TOM CLUB                    1981 ISLAND UK ILPS9686 GER 204 102
LORIC WEYMOUTH        (A
LAURA WEYMOUTH        (A     LANI WEYMOUTH      (A   TINA WEYMOUTH   (A   JAMES RIZZI       (A
ADRIAN BELEW          (A     STEVE STANLEY      (A   STICKY          (A   CHRIS FRANTZ      (A
MONTE BROWNE          (A     TYRONE DOWNIE      (A   KENDALL STUBBS  (A
```

TOMITA

```
ISAO TOMITA       K SYN(ALL     (A) SNOWFLAKES ARE DANCING         1975 RCA ARL1 0488  RI 81 LP3008
                                (B) PICTURES AT AN EXHIBITION      1975 RCA ARLI 0838  RI 81 LP 3010
                                (C) FIREBIRD SUITE                 1976 RCA              ARL1 1312
                                (D) THE PLANETS(WITHDRAWN)         1977 RCA              RL  11919
                                (E) BERMUDA TRIANGLE               1979 RCA              RL 12885
                                (F) KOSMOS                         1979 RCA              RL 42652
                                ( ) DAPHRIS ET CHLOE               19   RCA FR    PL13412
                                ( ) GREATEST HITS                  1981 RCA LP 3037
```

TOMORROW

```
KEITH WEST        V    (A       (A) TOMORROW                       1968 PARLOPHONE         PCS 7042
JOHN WOOD         B    (A       (A) TOMORROW                       1976 HARVEST   UK       SHSP 2010
STEVE HOWE        G    (A       (A) TOMORROW                       1968 SIRE      US   1003  97012
TWINK             D    (A       (A) TOMORROW                       1978 VISA                 1002
KEN LAWRENCE      D    (A
JOHN BURGESS      (        MARK P WIRTZ PROD K     (A
```

TOMORROW'S GIFT

```
ELLEN MEYER       V    (A       (A) TOMORROWS GIFT (DBL)           19   PLUS      GER  1+2
WOLFGANG TRESCHER FLT  (A       (B)GOODBYE FUTURE                  1973 AAMOK     GER  28515
CARLOS KARGES     G PERC(A
BERND KIEFER      B    (AB   GERD PAETZKE    D   (A   MANFRED RURUP    K  (AB  JOCHEN PETERSEN SAX (A
```

TONI & TERRY
BROWN GARTHWAITE

```
TONI BROWN        V G K(ABDG     (A) CROSS COUNTRY  (TONI & TERRY)  1973 CAPITOL             11137
TERRY GARTHWAITE  V G   (ABCDEF  (B) GOOD FOR YOU TOO (TONI)        1974 MCA               MCF 2558
BILL AIKENS       K    (A        (C) TERRY                          1975 ARISTA US 4055  UK  ARTY 124
DENNIS LINDE      V B  (A        (D) THE JOY     (TONI & TERRY)     1977 FANTASY             FT 537
KENNY MALONE      D    (A        (E) HAND IN GLOVE  (TERRY)         1978 FANTASYUS 9564  UK  FT 554
RUSS HICKS        G V  (A        (F) SAN FRANCISCO LTD(TERRY)       1976 CRYSTAL CLEAR   US     5004
JIM COLVARD       G    (A        (G) ANGEL OF LOVE  (TONI)          1980 FANTASY US 9585
VASSAR CLEMENTS   VLN  (A
CHARLIE McCOY     HCA V(A   BOBBY THOMPSON   G BAN(A   ROBERT EARL SCOTT  D  (F   DAVID AUSTIN   K  (D
DAVE DORAN        G    (A   JIM METHENY      V   (A   BILLY PUETT    HRNS (B   LLOYD GREEN    STEEL(B
CHUCK COCHRAN     ACC  (B   MARY HOEPFINGER  HARP (B   KURT McGETTRICK SAX (BC  TOMMY COGBILL  B  (B
JERRY CARRIGAN    D    (B   BOBBY WOOD       K   (B   BILLY SANFORD  G    (B   REGGIE YOUNG   G  (B
JOHN CHRISTOPHER  G    (B   CHIP YOUNG       G   (B   FARRELL MORRIS PERC (B   GEORGE TIDWELL HRNS (B
DENNIS GOODE      HRNS (B   BOBBY EMMONS     K   (B   BUDDY SPICHER  FDL  (B   WILLOW WRAY    V  (CDE
SONNY BURKE       K    (C   WILLIAM SMITH    K   (CD  PATRICE RUSHEN K    (C   ROGER KELLAWAY K  (C
PEGGY STERN       K    (CE  JAMES GADSON     D   (CD  HARVEY MASON   D    (C   JOHN GUERIN    D  (CE
VALENTINOS        V    (C   BOBBY WOMACK     V   (C   SCOTT MATTHEWS D    (C   BILL SUMMERS   PERC (C
WILLIE WEEKS      B    (C   RON CARTER       B   (C   CHUCK DOMANICO B    (C   DAVID GARTHWAITE B  (C
WAH WAH WATSON    G    (C   HOWARD ROBERTS   G   (C   JOE CRANE      G    (C   BOB FLURIE     G  (D
REGGIE McBRIDE    B    (C   STEVE MITCHELL   D   (D   JOHN BLAKELY   G    (D   ELVIN BISHOP   G  (D
BOBBYE HALL       PERC (D   TAJ MAHAL        G HCA(D   J D MANESS     STEEL(D   JIM HORN       HRNS (D
STEVE MADAIO      HRNS (D   JIMMY ROBERTS    WIND (D   BILL NAPIER    CLAR (D   JOHNNY ROTELLA CLAR (D
MICHELLE HARRIS DULC MAN(D  MARJIE ORTEN  DULC MAND(D  KENNETH NASH   PERC (E   JAY GRAYDON    G  (E
VICTOR FELDMAN    K    (E   CLARK GASSMAN    K   (E   MAC CRIDLIN    B    (E   GEORGE MRAZ    B  (E
SHEILAH GLOVER    V    (E   VICKI RANDLE     V   (E   DEE DEE DICKERSON V (E   DON SHEFFIELD  HRNS (B
KENT MIDDLETON PERC HCA(F   JOHN STAFFORD    HRNS (F   BRIAN ATKINSON TPT VIBES(F   CHUCK METCALF  B  (F
BILL SCHWARTZ     G    (F   PHILIP G SMITH   SAX (C
```

TONTON MACOUTE

```
CHRIS GAVIN       G B  (A       (A) TONTON MACOUTE                 1971 NEON       UK        NE 4
PAUL FRENCH       K V  (A
NIGEL REVELER     D    (A    DAVE KNOWLES WIND V(A
```

TONTOS EXPANDING HEADBAND

```
ROBERT MARGOULEFF SYN K(AB      (A) ZERO TIME                      1971 UK ATLANTIC K40251 US EMBRY0732
MALCOLM CECIL     SYN K(AB      (A) ZERO TIME                      1975 ATLANTIC US RI 18123
STEVE GADD        D    (B       (B) ITS ABOUT TIME                 1974 POLYDOR              2383 308
REG McBRIDE       B    (B
MARLO HENDERSON   G    (B    ARMAND HABDURIAN PERC (B   MICHAEL CEMBALO  G   (B
```

DAVID TOOP

DAVID TOOP	INSTR(A	(A) NEW & REDISCOVERED MUSICAL	1975 OBSCURE	UK	OBS 48	
BRIAN ENO	PROD (A					

TOOTS & THE MAYTALS

TOOTS HIBBERT	V (ALL	(A) FROM THE ROOTS	1973 TROJAN		TRLS 63
HUX BROWN	G (DFJ	(B) FUNKY KINGSTON	1973 DRAGON DRLS5002 ISLAND	ILPS9186
HAROLD BUTLER	K (HJ	(B) FUNKY KINGSTON	1973 ISLAND US 9330	
JACKIE JACKSON	B (DHJ	(C) IN THE DARK	1974 DRAGON DRLS5004 ISLAND	ILPS9231
PAUL DOUGLAS	B (DFHJ	(D) REGGAE GOT SOUL	1976 ISLAND		ILPS9374
RAD BRYAN	G (DF	(E) THE MAYTALS	1978 STATE		ETAT 16
RALEIGH GORDON	V (DFGHJ	(F) PASS THE PIPE	1979 ISLAND NL 200471 UK ILPS9534
JERRY MATHIAS	V (DFGHJ	(G) BEST OF	1979 TROJAN		TRLS 171
WINSTON WRIGHT	K (DFHJ	(H) JUST LIKE THAT	1980 ISLAND	UK ILPS9590
RANCHY McLEAN	B (F	(J) LIVE	1980 ISLAND		ILPS9647
JUNIOR KERR	G (D	(K) BEST OF TROJAN	1980 TROJAN UK 171	
CHINNA LINDO	G (D				

CARL HARVEY	G (J	GLADSTONE ANDERSON K (D	SONNY BINNS	K (D	STEVE WINWOOD	K (D
EMMANUEL RENTZOS	K (D	CHICAGO STEVE HCA (D	BOBBY ELLIS	TPT (D	EDDIE QUANSAH	TPT(D
JEROME FRANCISQUE	TROM (D	RICO RODRIGUES TROM (D	RAY ALLEN	SAX (D	DUDU PUKWANA	SAX(D
TOMMY McCOOK	SAX (D	GEORGE LEE SAX (D	DENSIL LANG	PERC (D	BROTHER JAMES	PERC(D
TONY UTER	PERC (D	BRUCE ROWLAND PERC (D	PABLO BLACK	K (D	WILLIE LINDO	G (H
MIKEY CHUNG	G (H					

TOPAZ

ROB STONER	(A	(A) TOPAZ	19 CBS US	34934	

TOP TOPHAM

TOP TOPHAM	G (A	(A) ASCENSION HEIGHTS	1970 BLUE HORIZON UK	763857
RICK HAYWARD	G (A				

JOHN MARSHALL	D (A	COLIN ALLEN D (A	HERBIE FLOWERS	B (A	EDDIE TRIPP	B (A
BRIAN ODGERS	B (A	STRING SECTION (A	PETE WINGFIELD	K (A	STEVE GREY	K (A
DUSTER BENNETT	HCA (A	MIKE VERNON PERC (A	TERRY NOONAN	TPT (A	BUTCH HUDSON	TPT(A
GREG BOWEN	TPT (A	NIGEL CARTER TPT (A	CHRIS PYNE	TROM (A	DANNY ELWOOD	TROM(A
JACK THIRLWELL	TROM (A	ALAN SKIDMORE SAX (A	DANNY MOSS	SAX (A	TONY COE	SAX (A
STEVE GREGORY	SAX (A	DON HONEYWELL SAX (A				

TORNADER

SANDY TORANO	G (A	(A) HIT IT AGAIN	1977 POLYDOR	US	PL 1 6098
LARRY ALEXANDER	V (A				

JOHNNY WINTER	G (A	JOE BECK G (A	STEVE FERRONE	D (A	RANDY BRECKER	HRNS(S
MICHAEL BRECKER	HRNS (A					

BERNIE TORME

BERNIE TORME	G V HCA FLT(A	(A) TURN OUT THE LIGHTS	1972 KAMAFLAGE UK	KAMLP2
PHIL SPALDING	B V (A				

NIGEL GLOCKLER	D (A	MARK HARRISON D (A	COLIN TOWNS	K FLT(A

TORNADOS

HEINZ BURT	V B G(	(A) SOUND OF (EP)	1962 DECCA	UK	DFE 8510
ROGER JACKSON	K (	(B) TELSTAR (EP)	1963 DECCA	UK	DFE 8511
GEORGE BELLAMY	G (	(C) MORE SOUNDS FROM (EP)	1963 DECCA	UK	DFE 8521
ALAN CADDY	VLN G(	(D) TORNADO ROCK	1963 DECCA	UK	DFE 8533
CLEM CATTINI	D (	(E) TELSTAR	196 LONDON	US	3279
		(F) AWAY FROM IT ALL	1963 DECCA	UK	LK 4552
		(G) WORLD OF	1972 DECCA	UK	SPA 253
		(H) REMEMBERING	1976 DECCA	UK	ROOTS 4

TORONTO

NICKI COSTELLO	B (AB	(A) LOOKING FOR TROUBLE	1980 SOLIDGOLD US 1000 A&M UK 64821
JIMMY FOX	D (AB	(B) HEAD ON	1981	A&M UK 64872
SHERON ALTON	G V (A	(C) GET IT ON CREDIT	1982 SOLIDGOLD US 1011
HOLLY WOODS	V (A		
SCOTT KREYER	K (A	BRIAN ALLEN G V (A	

RICHARD TORRANCE

RICHARD TORRANCE	V B G K(ALL	(A) EUREKA	1974 A&M UKAMLH68266 US SHELTER 2112
GARY ROWLES	G V PERC STEEL(ABC	(B) BELLE OF THE BALL	1975 A&M UKAMLH68312 US SHELTER 2134
MONTY STARK	B SYN(A	(B) BELLE OF THE BALL	1979 SHELTER RI 52019
KEN WEISSMAN	(A	(C) EUREKA III	1977 PHILIPS NL 6363133 US SHELTER?
DENNIS MANSFIELD	V D VIBES(ABCE	(D) BAREBACK	1977 CAPITOL SW 11610
JON LAMB	G B V PERC(BC	(E) DOUBLE TAKE	1978 CAPITOL SW 11699
RICHARD CANTU	PERC (BC	(F) ANYTHINGS POSSIBLE	1979 CAPITOL
DUANE SCOTT	V K PERC (AB		

TERRY LEE LICK	G V (E	DAVID WHITE B V (E	MELODY JEAN HORNEY K V (E	BILLY PAYNE	K (ED
VANDER LOCKETT	PERC (E	STEPHANIE BLACK V (A	BILL LINCOLN	G B (A	JOE McSWAYNE	B (A
BILL CUOMO	K (A	EDDIE TUDUR D (A	JAY SPELL	K V (A	JIM RICHARDSON	HRNS(C
FRED TACKETT	G (D	DAVID HUNGATE B (D	JEFF PORCARO	D (D	SAM CLAYTON	PERC(D
VANETTA FIELDS	V (D	MAXINE WILLARD V (D	JULIA TILLMAN	V (D	THOMAS SNOW	V (D
ERNIE WATTS	HRNS (D	HARVEY MASON D (D	WILTON FELDER	B (D	PETER CHRISTLIEB	HRNS(D
BUDDY COLLETTE	HRNS (D	JOHN HAENY PROD (D	BOB FINDLEY	HRNS (D		

PETER TOSH

PETER TOSH	G V K(ALL	(A) LEGALIZE IT	1976 VIRGIN UK V2061 US CBS 34253
CARLTON BARRETT	D (A	(B) EQUAL RIGHTS	1978 VIRGIN UK V2081 US CBS 34670
ASTON BARRETT	B (A	(C) BUSH DOCTOR	1978 ROLLING STONES CUN 39109
ROBBIE SHAKESPEARE	B (ABCD	(D) MYSTIC MAN	1979 ROLLING STONES CUN 39111
TYRONE DOWNEY	K (A	(E) WANTED DREAD OR ALIVE	.1981 ROLLING STONES CUN 39113
LARRY McDONALD	PERC (C		

RITA MARLEY	V (A	JUDY MOWATT V (A	BUNNY WAILER	V (AB	AL ANDERSON	G (AB
DONALD KINSEY	G (AC	ROBBIE LEE HCA (A	RAS LEE	HCA (A	EARL LINDO	(B
MIKEY CHUNG	K G (CD	SLY DUNBAR D (BCD	ROBBIE LYN	K (DC	YVONNE LEWIS	V (D
KEITH STERLING	PNO (DC	STICKY PERC (DC	ED ELIZALDE	G (D	SAMMY FIGUEROA	CONGA(D
SKULLY	D (D	ED WALSH SYN (D	GEORGE YOUNG	WIND (D	LOU MARINI	WIND (D
HOWARD JOHNSON	SAX (D	BARRY ROGERS TROM (D	MIKE LAWRENCE	TPT (D	TAMLINS	V (D
GWEN GUTHRIE	V (D	BRENDA WHITE V (D	LUTHOR FRANCOIS	SAX (C	KEITH RICHARDS	G (C
MICK JAGGER	V (C					

TOTALLY HOT
                    (A) TOTALLY HOT   1981 MOBILE   US   040
TOTO
    DAVID PAICH   K V (ABCD   (A) TOTO   1978 CBS   US 35317   UK 83148
    DAVID HUNGATE   B G (ABCD   (B) HYDRA   1979 CBS   US 36229   UK 83900
    JEFF PORCARO   D   (ABcD   (C) TURN BACK   1980 CBS   US 36813   UK 84609
    JOE PORCARO   PERC (ABCD   (D) IV   1982 CBS   UK 85529
    BOBBY KIMBALL   V   (ABCD
    GARY GRANT   TPT (D   STEVE PORCARO   K (ABCD STEVE LUKATHER G V(ABCD LENNY CASTRO   PERC(ABD
    JIM HORN   SAX (AD CHÉRYL LYNN   (A   MICHAEL BODDICKER K (AB RALPH DYCK   SYN(CD
    CHUCK FINDLEY   HRNS (A   ROGER LINN   (ABC MARTY PAICH   STR (ABD SID SHARP   STR (A
    REGGIE FISHER   (B   MIKE PORCARO CELLO (D   JAMES NEWTON HOWARD STR(D TOM SCOTT   SAX (D
    JERRY KEY   TPT (D   JIM PANKOW   TROM   (D   JON SMITH   SAX (D TOM KELLY   V (D
    TIMOTHY SCHMIDT   V   (D
TOUCH
    DON TULLUCCI   K V (A   (A) TOUCH   1969 DERAM   UK SML 1033
    JOHN BORDONARO   PERC V(A
    JOEY NEWMAN   G V (A   BRUCE HAUSER   B V (A JEFF HAWKES   V   (A
TOUCH
    CRAIG BROOKS   G V (AB   (A) ENERGIZER   1977 BRUNSWICK   US 754214
    GLENN KITHCART   D   (B   (B) TOUCH   1980 ATCO   US SD 38123
    MARK MANGOLD   K V (B   (B) TOUCH   1980 ARIOLA   UK 5036
    DOUG HOWARD   B V (B
TOUCHSTONE
    TOM CONSTANTEN   K   (A   (A) TAROT   1972 UA   US   5563
    PAUL DRESHER   G FLT(A
    GARY HIRSH   PERC (A   WES STEELE   B CELLO(A ART FAYER   VLN (A JIM BYERS   G   (A
    RUBBER DUCK   TAMB (A
TOURISTS
    ANNIE LENNOX   V K FLT(ABC   (A) TOURISTS   1979 LOGO UK 1018   GER 64019
    PETE COOMBES   G V (ABC   (B) REALITY EFFECT 1979 LOGO UK 1019   GER 64021
    DAVE STEWART   G   (ABC   (B) REALITY EFFECT 1979 EPIC US 36386
    JIM TOOMEY   D   (ABC   (C) LUMINOUS BASEMENT 1980 RCA RCALP5001 +   PL 25323
    EDDY CHIN   B   (ABC   (A) THE TOURIST   1981 RCA INT   UK INTS5096
ALLEN TOUSSAINT
    ALLEN TOUSSAINT   K G HCA(ALL   (A) WILD SOUNDS OF NEW ORLEANS 1958 RCA VICTOR   US   1767
    VINCENT TOUSSAINT G   (C   (B) TOUSSAINT   1971 TIFFANY US014   WAND WNS 14
    LEO NOCENTELLI   G   (C   (B) TOUSSAINT   1977 DJM   UK DJF 22070
    GEORGE PORTER   B   (C   (C) LIFE LOVE & FAITH 1972 REPRISE US 2062 UK K44202
    GEORGE PLUMMER   G   (C   (D) SOUTHERN NIGHTS 1975 REPRISE US 2186 UK K54021
    WALTER PAYTON   B   (C   (E) MOTION   1978 WB   US 3142 UK K56473
    JOSEPH MODELISTE   D   (C   (F) BOMP CITY   1973 WB   US   2616
    VANETTA FIELDS   V   (B
    JOE LAMBERT   D   (C   ALFRED ROBERTS   CONGA(C SQUIRREL   CONGA(C GARY BROWN   SAX (C
    ALVIN THOMAS   SAX (C   RED TYLER   SAX (C CLYDE KERR   TPT (BC FRANCIS ROUSSELLE TPT(C
    JEFF PORCARO   D   (E   POPS POPWELL   B   (E CHUCK RAINEY   B   (E LARRY CARLTON   G (E
    VICTOR FELDMAN   PERC (E   RICHARD TEE   K   (C PAULINHO DA COSTA PERC (E ETTA JAMES   V (E
    BONNIE RAITT   V   (E   DR JOHN   G K (B TERRY KELLMAN   G   (B FRED STAEHLE   D (B
    EDDIE HOHNER   B   (B   ED GREENE   D   (B EARL TURBINTON SAX (B FRED KEMP   SAX(B
    MERRY CLAYTON   V   (B
MEIKE TOUW
    MEIKE TOUW   V   (A   (A) TUTTI FRUTTI   1980 ARIOLA   NL   202 160
    HENK TORPEDO   (A
    HARRY DEWINTER   (A   DICK SCHULTE NORDHOLT B V(A ROBERT JAN STIPS K (A MARC BOON   (A
    PETE CALICKER   (A   MAX MOLLINGER   (A JAN CEES TANS   (A JOHN KRIEK   (A
    ERNST GLERUM   (A   HENK WIJTMAN   (A
TOWER OF POWER
    HUBERT TUBBS   V   (EG   (A) EAST BAY GREASE 1970 SAN FRANCISO   US SD204
    LENNY PICKETT   SAX (QBCDEGHJ   (B) BUMP CITY   1972 WB   UK K46167 US   2616
    GREG ADAMS   HRNS (ABCDEGHJ   (C) TOWER OF POWER 1974 WB   UK K46223 US   2681
    MIC GILLETTE   HRNS (ABCDEGHJ   (D) BACK IN OAKLAND 1974 WB   UK K46282 US   2749
    STEVE KUPKA   SAX (ACEGHJ   (E) IN THE SLOT   1975 WB   UK K56155 US   2880
    BRUCE CONTE   G V (CEGHJ   (F) URBAN RENEWAL   1975 WB   UK K56093 US   2834
    CHESTER THOMPSON   K   (CEGHJ   (G) LIVE & LIVING COLOUR 1976 WB UK K56221 US   2924
    FRANCIS PRESTIA   B   (ABCCFGH   (H) AINT NOTHIN' STOPPIN' US NOW 1976 CBS UK 81572 US 34302
    DAVID GARIBALDI   D   (CFGABD   (J) WE CAME TO PLAY 1978 CBS   UK 82239 US 34906
    LENNY WILLIAMS   V   (C   (K) BACK ON THE STREETS 1979 CBS   US 35784
    EMILIO CASTILLO   SAX V(AC
    BRENT BYARS   V   (CA RICK STEVENS   V   (A WILLIE FULTON   G V (A JAY SPELL   PNO (C
    BRUCE STEINBERG   HCA (C   BOOTCHE ANDERSON V   (E MARILYN SCOTT   V   (E PEPPER WATKINS V (E
    DAVID BARTLETT   V   (C   RON BECK   V D (EHJ FRANK BINER   V   (E ROGER RIFKIND V (D
    EDWARD McGEE   V   (H   MICHAEL JEFFRIES V   (J VICTOR CONTE   B   (J SKIP MESQUITE V WIND(A
RALPH TOWNER
    RALPH TOWNER   G K (ALL   (A) TIROS:SOLOS   1975 ECM   UK 1025
    JACK DEJONETTE   D   (G   (B) DIARY   1975 ECM   UK 1032
    EDDIE GOMEZ   B   (G   (C) MATCHBOX   1975 ECM   UK 1056
    GARY BURTON   VIBES(C   (D) SOLTICE   1975 ECM   UK 1060
    JOHN ABERCROMBIE   (E   (E) SARGASSO SEA   1976 ECM   UK 1080
                                       (F) SOUND OF SHADOWS 1977 ECM   UK 1095
                                       (G) BATIK   1978 ECM   UK 1127
COLIN TOWNLEY
    COLIN TOWNLEY   V   (AB   (A) TOWNLEY   1980 HARVEST   US   12007
                                       (B) MORE THAN A DREAM 1981 EMI UK 3371
COLIN TOWNS
    COLIN TOWNS   (A   (A) FULL CIRCLE   1978 VIRGIN   UK   V 2093

                                      [567]

PETE TOWNSHEND

```
PETE TOWNSHEND    G V K(AB        (A) WHO CAME FIRST            1972 TRACK UK 2408 201  US MCA  2026
TONY BUTLER       B    (B         (A) WHO CAME FIRST            197  DECCA US 79189
RONNIE LANE       G V  (A         (B) EMPTY GLASS               1980 ATCO  UK  K 50699  US 32100
BILLIE NICHOLLS   G V  (A
CALEB QUAYE       G    (A    RABBIT BUNDRICK  K    (B  KENNY JONES      D  (B   MARK BRZEZICKI   D  (B
RAPHAEL BUDD      HRNS (B    SIMON PHILLIPS   D    (B  JAMES ASHER      D  (B   PETE HOPE-EVANS  HCA (B
CHRIS THOMAS      PROD (B
```

TONWSHEND/LANE

```
PETE TOWNSHEND    G    (A         (A) ROUGH MIX                1977 POLYDOR UK 2442 147 US MCA 2295
RONNIE LANE       B G V(A         (A) ROUGH MIX                1080 POLYDOR RI 2482 488
CHRIS LAURENCE    B    (A
ERIC CLAPTON      G    (A    CHARLIE WATTS    D    (A  RABBIT BUNDRICK  K   (A  HENRY SPINETTI   D  (A
PETER HOPE EVANS  HCA  (A    GRAHAM LYLE      G    (A  BENNY GALLAGHER  ACC (A  CHARLIE HART     VLN (A
DAVE MARKEE       B    (A    MEL COLLINS      SAX  (A  IAN STEWART      PNO (A  JULIAN DIGGLE    PERC(A
TONY GILBERT           (A    CHARLES VORZANGER VLN (A  STEVE SHINGLES   VLA (A  CHRIS GREEN      CELLO(A
BOZ BURRELL       B    (A    JOHN ENTWISTLE   HRNS V(A BILLY NICHOLLS   V   (A
```

TOY

```
ALBERT HARRY WOODS K G V(AB       (A) BAD NIGHT               1970 PAYOLA NL 939/1  LOGO UK 4010
THEO VAN HEMELRYK  G V  (AB       (B) SPIT                    1981 PAYOLA NL 64389
RENATO MARCIANO    B    (A
PAUL ILLE          D    (A  MARK BOURNE  G PERC(B  PAOLO DAMANTS           K   (B  RENAAT BOEYKENS  B  (B
```

TOYAH

```
TOYAH WILCOX      V    (ABCDE      (A) SHEEP FARMING IN BARNET  1979 SAFARI UK SAP1  GER 63442
PETE BUSH         K    (AC         (B) TOYAH TOYAH             1980 SAFARI UK LIVE2  GER 63866
MARK HENRY        B    (AC         (C) BLUE MEANING            1980 SAFARI UK  IEYA666
JOEL BOGEB        G    (AC         (D) FOUR FROM TOYAH(EP)     1981 SAFARI UK  TOY1
STEVE BRAY        D    (AC         (E) ANTHEM                  1981 SAFARI UK VOOR1
CHARLES FRANCIS   B    (C
```

TOYAN

```
                                  (A) HOW THE WEST WAS WON     1981 GREENSLEEVES    UK GREL20
```

TRACE

```
RICK VAN DER LINDEN K (ABC        (A) TRACE                   1974 VERTIGO UK 6360852 US SIRE 7504
COR DEKKER        B    (C          (A) TRACE                   1974 PHILIPS GER 6423 075
JAAP VAN EIK      G    (AB         (B) BIRDS                   1975 VERTIGO UK 6413080 SIRE US 7514
PIERRE VANDER LINDEN D (A          (C) THE WHITE LADIES        1976 RCA GER 21815
IAN MOSLEY        D    (B
DARRYL WAY        VLN  (B    PETER DE LEEUWE  G D (C  DICK REMELINCK   WIND(C  HANS JACOBSE     K  (C
HETTI SMIT        V    (C    HARRY SCHAFER    V   (C
```

TRACKS

```
ANDREW ASHTON     G V  (A         (A) EVEN A BROKEN CLOCK IS RIGHT TWICE A DAY 1972 CAPITOL    1118
SCOTT KENNETH     B V  (A
ROY BITTAN        K B G V(A   STEV MEROLA      D HCA(A  EARL SLICK       G   (A
```

TRACTOR

```
JIM MILNE         G V B(A         (A) TRACTOR                 1972 DANDELION       UK      2310 217
STEVE CLAYTON B K D FLT(A
DAVE ADDISON      B    (
```

JEANIE TRACY

```
JEANIE TRACY      V    (A         (A) ME AND YOU              1982 FANTASY    US    6414
```

TRADER HORNE

```
JUDY DYBLE        K V  (A         (A) MORNING WAY             1970 DAWN UK DNLS3004 JANUS US 3012
JACKIE McAULEY    K G V(A1        (1) 1970 SUMMER
RAY ELLIOT        WIND (A
SAFFRON SUMMERFIELD G V(1    ANDY WHITE       D   (A  JOHN GODFREY     B   (A
```

TRADITION

```
                                  (A) SHOWCASE               1980 VENTURE     UK CUT 10
                                  (B) CAPTAIN GANGA & THE SPACE AGE 1981 VENTURE UK CUT 9
```

TRAFFIC

```
STEVE WINWOOD     G K V(ALL        (A) Mr FANTASY            1967 ISLAND UK ILPS 9061 US UA  6651
JIMMY JOHNSON     G    (G          (A) MR FANTASY            1967 ISLAND GER 85784
JIM CAPALDI       D V K(ALL        (B) TRAFFIC               1968 ISLANDUK ILPS 9081  US UA  6676
CHRIS WOOD        WIND (ALL        (C) LAST EXIT             1969 ISLAND UK ILPS 9097 US UA  6702
DAVE MASON        G V  (ABCE       (D) JOHN BARLEYCORN MUST DIE 1970 ISLAND UK ILPS 9116 US UA 5504
BARRY BECKETT     K    (GH         (D) JOHN BARLEYCORN MUST DIE 1970 ISLAND GER 6339 016
RICK GRECH        B    (EF         (E) WELCOME TO THE CANTEEN 1971 ISLAND UK ILPS 9166 US UA  5550
REBOP BAAH        CONGA(EGHF       (F) LOW SPARK OF HIGH HEELED BOY 1971 ISLAND UK ILPS 9180 US   9306
ROSKO GEE         B    (J          (F) LOW SPARK OF HIGH HEELED BOY 1971 ISLAND GER 85867
JIM GORDON        D    (EF         (G) SHOOT OUT AT THE FANTASY FACTORY 1973 ISLAND UK ILPS 9224 US 9323
DAVE HOOD         B    (GH         (H) ON THE ROAD    (LIVE DBL) 1973 ISLAND UK ILSD 2  US      9336
ROGER HAWKINS     D    (GH         (J) WHEN THE EAGLE FLIES   1974 ISLAND UK ILPS 9273  GER  88334
                                  (J) WHEN THE EAGLE FLIES   1974 ASYLUM            US   7E1020
                                  ( ) COLOURED RAIN         1967 ISLAND SWED  ILP800
                                  ( ) LIVE  (NOT RELEASED)  1970 ISLAND UK ILPS 9142
                                  ( ) BEST OF               1969 ISLAND UK ILPS 9112 US UA  5500
                                  ( ) BEST OF               19   ISLAND GER 88066
                                  ( ) HEAVY TRAFFIC         1975              US UA  4211
                                  ( ) MORE HEAVY TRAFFIC    1975              US UA LA526
                                  (EP) HOLE IN MY SHOE      1978 ISLAND UK  I EP 7
```

TRAMLINE

```
JOHN McCOY        V HCA(A          (A) SOMEWHERE DOWN THE LINE 1968 ISLAND       UK   ILPS9088
TERRY SIDGWICK    B V  (A          (B) MOVES OF VEGETABLE CENTURIES 1969 ISLAND  UK   ILPS9095
TERRY POPPLE      D    (A
MICK MOODY        G    (A    CHRIS BLACKWELL      PROD (
```

T129			BOBBY LEE TRAMMELL					T129

```
T129                              BOBBY LEE TRAMMELL                                    T129
     BOBBY LEE TRAMMELL    (AB         (A) ARKANSAS TWIST           19   ATLANTA    US   1503
                                       (B) I DARE AMERICA TO BE GREAT 19 SUNCOT    US   1102
T130                                   TRAMP                                             T130
     MICK FLEETWOOD       D  (BA        (A) TRAMP                  1969 MUSIC MAN 603 RI SPARK UK SRLM2001
     DANNY KIRWAN         G  (BA        (B) PUT A RECORD ON        1974 SPARK          UK   SRLP 112
     DAVE BROOKS          SAX (B
     DAVE KELLY           V  (BA  JO ANN KELLY    V   (BA BOB BRUNNING    B(BA BOB HALL        K  (BA
     IAN MORTON           PERC (B
T131                                   TRANQUILITY                                       T131
     TONY LUKYN           K V (A        (A) TRANQUILITY            1972 EPIC  UK 64729   US   31084
     KEVIN McCARTHY       G   (A        (B) SILVER                 197  EPIC            US   31989
     TERRY SHADDICK       G V (A
     BERNARD HAGLEY       G   (A  BERKELEY WRIGHT    G V (A   PAUL FRANCIS    D   (A
T131A                                  TRANSISTOR                                        T131A
     ROBERT JAN STIPS     K   (A        (A) ZIG ZAG               1980 ARIOLA    NL   201 163
     HENK WIJTMAN         D V (A
     HUBA DE GRAFF        K V (A  DICK SCHULTE NORDHOLT B V (A
T132                                   TRANSMITTERS                                      T132
     CHRIS GEORGE         LYRIC(A       (A) 24 HOURS              1978 EBONY       UK     EB1002
     MIKEL LEE            G   (A        (B) AND WE CALL THAT LEISURE TIME 1981 HEARTBEAT UK   HB4
     SAM DODSON           B G K(AB
     JIM CHASE            D   (AB VINCE CUTLIFFE    G   (A   JOHN QUINN      V  (A DAVE BABY   SAX (B
     SID WEELS            B   (B  JULIAN TREASURE   B (AB    ROB CHAPMAN     V K(B
T133                                   TRAPEZE                                           T133
     GLENN HUGHES         B  (ABCF       (A) TRAPEZE              1970 THRESHOLD    UK     THS 2
     MEL GALLEY           G  (ABCEFGH    (B) MEDUSA               1970 THRESHOLD    UK     THS 4
     DAVE HOLLAND         D  (BCEFGA     (C) YOU ARE THE MUSIC    1972 THRESHOLD    UK     THS 8
     PETE WRIGHT          B  (EFGH       (D) FINAL SWING          1974 THRESHOLD    UK     THS11
     ROB KENDRICK         G  (EF         (E) HOT WIRE             1974 WB    US 2828 UK     K56064
     PETE GALBY           G V (GH        (F) TRAPEZE              1975 WB    US 2887 UK     K56165
     B J COLE             STEEL(C        (G) HOLD ON/RUNNING      1978 AURA            AUL 708
     STEVE BRAY           D   (H         (H) LIVE IN TEXAS/DEAD ARMADILLOS 1980 AURA  UK  AUL 717
     ROD ARGENT           K   (C
     TERRY ROWLEY G K FLT (EGA JOHN JONES  V TPT  (A  KIRK DUNCAN   K   (C  JOHN OGDEN  PERC (CE
     FRANK RICOTTI        PERC (C  JIMMY HASTINGS  SAX  (C  KENNY COLE   V  (E   MISTY BROWNING  V(E
     CHRIS MERCER         SAX  (E
T133A                                  TRASHMEN                                          T133A
     BOB REEDS            B   (A         (A) SURFIN' BIRD         1964 SOMA      US    200
     DAL WINSLOW          G   (A
T134                               HAPPY & ARTIE TRAUM                                   T134
     HAPPY TRAUM          G  (ABCDEF     (A) HAPPY & ARTIE TRAUM  1969 CAPITOL           ST 586
     ARTIE TRAUM          G  (ABCFDG     (B) DOUBLEBACK           1971 CAPITOL           ST 799
     PATRICK ALGER        MAND (EF       (C) MUD ACRES            1972 ROUNDER US 3001 UK MATCHBOX 239
     RICK DANKO           B   (          (D) HARD TIMES IN THE COUNTRY 1975 ROUNDER US 3007
     ERIC KAZ                 (          (E) RELAX YOUR MIND(HAPPY) 1976 KICKING MULE US 110 UK SNKF 111
     TRACY NELSON             (          (F) AMERICAN STRANGER    1978 KICKING MULE US 301 UK SNKF 142
     AMOS GARRETT         G   (          (G) LIFE ON EARTH        1974 ROUNDER    US 3014
     MARIA MULDAUR        V   (          (H) BRIGHT MORNING STARS 1980 GREENHAYS  US 703
     BILL KEITH           STEEL(
     DOUG JAMES           PERC (F  BETTY McDONALD  V FDL(F   ANDY ROBINSON  VPERC(F  ROLY SALLEY  B (F
     JOHN SEBASTIAN       V HCA(F  HOWARD VOGEL    REC  (F   JODI VOGEL   CELLO(F  ERIC WEISSBERG  FDL(F
T134A                                  TRAVEL AGENCY                                     T134A
                                        (A) TRAVEL AGENCY        1968 VIVA      US   36017
T135                                   PAT TRAVERS                                       T135
     PAT TRAVERS          G V K(ALL      (A) PAT TRAVERS          1976 POLYDOR US 1 6079 UK 2383 395
     PETER MARS COWLING   B(ABCDEFGH     (B) MAKIN' MAGIC         1977 POLYDOR US 1 6103 UK 2383 436
     NICKO McBAIN         D   (CB        (C) PUTTIN' IT STRAIGHT  1977 POLYDOR US 1 6121 UK 2383 471
     TONY CAREY           K   (C         (D) HEAT IN THE STREET   1979 POLYDOR US 1 6170 UK POLD5005
     SUZIE McKINLEY       V   (C         (E) GO FOR WHAT YOU KNOW(LIVE) 1979 POLYDOR US 6202 UK POLS1011
     BERT HERMISTON       SAX (C         (F) CRASH & BURN         1980 POLYDOR US   6262 UK POLS1017
     SCOTT GORHAM         G   (C         (G) RADIO ACTIVE         1981 POLYDOR US 6313 UK 2391 499
     ROY DYKE             D   (A         (H) BLACK PEARL          1982 POLYDOR       UK 2391 553
     TOMMY ALDRIDGE       D   (DEFG
     PAT THRALL           G SYN(DEFG CLIVE EDWARDS  D  (B  GLENN HUGHES  V   (B  MICHAEL SCHRIEVE PERC(FG
     DAWN SHAHAN          V   (F  SANDY GENNARO    D  (GH DON HARRISS  K SYN(H
T135A                                  PAUL TRAVIS                                       T135A
     PAUL TRAVIS          G K V(A        (A) RETURN OF THE NATIVE 1975 A&M UK AMLS 68290
     TONY BRAUNAGEL       D   (A
     TERRY WILSON         B   (A  RABBIT BUNDRICK  K  (A  MARK WARNER   G   (A  SANDY DAVIS    V  (A
     HELEN CHAPPELLE      V   (A  BARRY LORD       V  (A  CHRIS MERCER  SAX (A  EDDIE QUANSAH  SAX (A
     PETER VANDERPIUSE    SAX (A  JACK EMBLOW ACC     (A  CHRIS LAURENCE B   (A
T135B                                  TRAX                                              T135B
                                        (A) HOME (EP)            19   LONELY    UK   LONSOME 1
T136                               JACK TRAYLOR & STEELWIND                              T136
     JACK TRAYLOR         G V (A         (A) CHILD OF NATURE      1973 GRUNT           FTR 0194
     CRAIG CHAQUICO       G   (A
     DANNY VIRDIER        B V (A  SKIP MORAIRTY    G V (A  DIANA HARRIS  K V (A  KENT MIDDLETON HCA PERC(A
     BILL LAUDNER         V   (A  RICK QUINTANAL   V  (A  DAVID FREIBERG K  (A
T137                                   TREES                                            T137
     CELIA HUMPHRIS       K V (AB1       (A) THE GARDEN OF JANE DELAWNEY 1970 CBS         63837
     BIAS BOSHELL         G V B(AB       (B) ON THE SHORE        1970 CBS              64168
     BARRY CLARKE         G   (AB1       (1) 1972
     DAVID COSTA          G   (AB1
     UNWIN BROWN          D V (AB  TONY COX        B   (B  MICHAEL JEFFERIES HARP (B  BARRY LYONS  B  (1
     ALUN EDEN            D   (1   CHUCK FLEMING   VLN (1
```

TREMBLERS
```
    PETER NOONE   V G K B  (A         (A) TWICE NIGHTLY                  1980 EPIC UK 84448 US JOHNSTON 36532
    GREGG INHOFER      K G V(A
    ROBERT WILLIAMS  D V (A   GEO CONNER      G V  (A   MARK BROWNE      B  (A   MIKE CAMPBELL        (A
    STAN LYNCH         (A   RON BLAIR        (A   JOHN FARRAR      (A   STEPHEN HAGUE        (A
    STEVE ALLEN        (A   NIGEL OLSSON     (A   BILL PITCOCK     (A   DARYL DRAGON         (A
```
T138   (BRIAN POOLE &) THE TREMELOES   T138
```
    BRIAN POOLE        V    (ABCHP   (A) BIG HITS OF 1962            1963 ACE OF CLUBS    UK   ACL 1146
    RICK WESTWOOD      G V  (        (B) TWIST & SHOUT               1963 DECCA          UK   LK  4550
    ALAN BLAKELY       G V  (        (C) IT'S ABOUT TIME             1965 DECCA          UK   LK  4685
    DAVE MUNDEN        D V  (        (D) HERE COME THE TREMELOES      1967 CBS           UK       63017
    LEN'CHIP'HAWKES    B V  (        (E) HERE COMES MY BABY           1967 CBS           US       26310
    AARON WOOLLEY         (         (F) EVEN THE BAD TIMES ARE GOOD   1967 CBS           US       26326
    BOB BENHAM            (         (G) SUDDENLY YOU LOVE ME          1967 CBS   US 26363      UK  63138
                                    (G) SILENCE IS GOLDEN             1975 EMBASSY    UK       31206
                                    (H) 58/68 WORLD EXPLOSION         1968 CBS  US 26388
                                    (J) LIVE IN CABARET               1969 CBS                 UK   63547
                                    (K) MASTER                        1970 CBS                 UK   64242
                                    (L) GREATEST HITS                 1970 CBS                 UK   64206
                                    (M) REACH OUT FOR THE TREMELOES   1973 EMBASSY             UK   31031
                                    (N) SHINER                        1974 DJM   UK DJLP 5441 +  DJF 20441
                                    (O) DON'T LET THE MUSIC DIE       1976 DJM           UK    DJF 20447
                                    (P) REMEMBERING                   1977 DECCA         UK       REM 5
```
T138A   TRETTIOARIGA KRIGET   T138A
```
    STEFAN FREDIN       (B          (A) KRIGSSANG                   1975 CBS            UK       80900
    DAG LUNDQUIST       (B          (B) HEJ PA ER!                  1978 MISTLUR    SWED MRL 4
    ROBERT ZIMA         (b          ( ) TRETTIOARIGA KRIGET         19   CBS            UK       80220
    CHRISTER AKERBERG   (B          ( ) MO ALLA ODDS                19   MISTLUR    SWED MLR 9
    MATS LINDBERG   SAX K(B
```
T138B   TRICKSTER   T138B
```
    PHIL BATES       G V  (AB       (A) FIND THE LADY               1977 JET UAS 30132   RI   JETLP 206
    JOHN FINCHAM     B V  (B        (A) FIND THE LADY               1977 JET  US 35478
    COLIN HEWINSON   K SYN(AB       (B) BACK TO ZERO                1979 JET UK JETLP221 US 35968
    MIKE SHEPPARD    G B V(A
    PAUL ELLIOTT     D PERC(AB MICHAEL GROTH    G V  (B
```
T138C   TRIANA   T138C
```
    JESUS DE LA ROSA  V    (ALL     (A) TRIANA                      1975 MOVIE PLAY      17 0678/7
    EDUARDO RODRIGUEZ G V  (ALL     (B) HYOS DEL AGOBIO             1977 GONG 170907/9
    JUAN JOSE PALACIOS D V(ALL      (C) SOMBRA Y LUZ                1979 MOVIE PLAY      17 1439/4
                                    (D) UN ENCUENTRO                1980 MOVIE PLAY      53 0678/5
                                    (E) TRIANA     CASSETTE         1981 MOVIE PLAY      53 2770/8
```
T138D   TRIBE   T138D
```
                                    (A) ETHNIC STEW                1974 ABC  US      807
                                    (B) TRIBAL BUMPIN'             1975 ABC  US      859
```
T139   TRIGGER   T139
```
    JIMMY DUGGAN        (A          (A) TRIGGER                    1978 CASABLANCA     UK  NBLP 7092
    RITCHIE HOUSE       (A
    TOM NIGRA           (A   DEREK REMINGTON       (A
```
T139A   TRILLION   T139A
```
    RON ANAMAN     B V  (AB         (A) TRILLION                   1978 EPIC          US       35460
    PAT LEONARD    K    (BA         (B) CLEAR APPROACH             1980 CBS           US       36206
    FRANK BARBALACE G V (BA
    THOM GRIFFIN   G V  (B    BILL WILKINS     D PERC(BA DENNIS FREDRICKSON V  (A
```
T139B   TRINITY   T139B
```
                                    (A) UPTOWN GIRL                1977 MAGNUM              DEAD 1003
                                    (B) ROCK IN THE GHETTO         1979 TROJAN             TRLS 170
```
T140   TRINITY RIVER BOYS   T140
```
    MICHAEL MURPHEY    G    (A      (A) TRINITY RIVER BOYS         1964 PROSPECTOR NOT RELEASED
    MICHAEL NESMITH    G V  (A
    JOHN RAINES        D    (A   JOHN LONDON      B  (A
```
T141   TRIO   T141
```
    JOHN SURMAN      SAX  (ABC      (A) THE TRIO                   1970 DAWN           UK   DNLS 3006
    BARRE PHILLIPS   B    (ABC      (B) CONFLAGRATION              1971 DAWN           UK   DNLS 3022
    STU MARTIN       D    (ABC      (C) LIVE AT WOODSTOCK TOWN HALL 1976 DAWN          UK   DNLS 3072
    HARRY BECKETT    TPT  (B
    MARC CHARIG      CORN(B   CHICK COREA      K  (B   NICK EVANS      TROM (B   MALCOLM GRIFFITHS   TROM(B
    DAVE HOLLAND     B    (B   JOHN TAYLOR      PNO (B   JOHN MARSHALL   D  (B   MIKE OSBORNE       CLAR(B
    ALAN SKIDMORE    WIND (B   STAN SULOMAN     WIND (B   KENNY WHEELER   HRNS(B
```
T141A   TRITONUS   T141A
```
    PETER K SEILER    K    (A       (A) TRITONUS                   1975 BASF          GERM     17 223841
    RONALD J D BRAND  B V G(A
    CHARLIE JOST      D PERC(A
```
T142   TRIUMPH   T142
```
    RIK EMMET      G    (ABCDE       (A) TRIUPH                    1976 ATTIC          LAT 1012
     G L MOORE     D    (ABCDE       (B) ROCK'N'ROLL MACHINE       1977 ATTIC          LAT 1036
    MIKE LEVINE    B    (ABCDE       (C) ROCK'N'ROLL MACHINE(COMP OF A B) 1979 RCA  12982
    LAURIE DELGRANDE K  (A           (D) JUST A GAME               1979 RCA  13224 RI INT5154
    BEAR DAVID     V    (B           (E) PROGRESSIONS OF POWER     1980 RCA  13524 RI INT LP3039
    GORD WASZEK    V    (B           (F) ALLIED FORCES             1981 RCA LP 6002
```

TRIUMVIRAT

HELMUT KOELLEN	B G V(B	(A) MEDITERRANEAN TALES	1972 HARVEST	EURO IC 062 29441
CURT CRESS	D (E	(B) ILLUSION ON A DOUBLE DIMPLE	1974 HARVEST US 11311 UK	SHSP 4030
BARRY PALMER	V (DE	(B) ILLUSION ON A DOUBLE DIMPLE	1977 EMI	EURO IC 062 29441
DIETER PETEREIT	B (E	(C) SPARTACUS	1975 HARVEST US 11392 UK	SHSP 4048
HANS JUERGEN FRITZ K V (ABCDEFG		(D) OLD LOVES DIE HARD	1976 CAPITOL US 11551 EURO	29622
HANS PAPE	B V (AB	(E) POMPEII	1977 CAPITOL US 11697 EURO	LC1305
HANS BATHELT	D (ABCD	(F) A LA CARTE	1978 CAPITOL US 11862	
DICK FRANGENBERG	B (D	(G) RUSSIAN ROULETTE	1980 HARVEST 45834	
ULLA WIESNER	V (B			

HANNA DOHTISCH	V (B	PETER CADERA	V (B	BRIGITTE THOMAS	V (B	ARNO STEFFEN	V (G
JEFF PORCARO	D (G	STEVE LUKATHER	G B (G	TIM MAY	G (G	ROBERT GREENRIDGE	D(G
NEAL STUBENHAUS	B (G	ALAN ESTES PERC	(G	PETER CHRISTLIEB	SAX (G	MIKE GONG	G V (G
DAVID HUNGATE	B (G	JIM HITE	(G	VANETTA FIELD	V (G	MAXINE WILLARD	V (G
JULIA TILLMAN	V (G	BRIGITTE WITT	V (G	HINNA DOLITZSCH	V (G	CATRIN PROPPER	V (G

TROGGS

REG PRESLEY	V (1	FROM NOWHERE	1966 FONTANA	UK ST 5355
CHRIS BRITTON	G (1	TROGGLODYNAMITE	1966 PAGE ONE	UK POL 001
PETE STAPLES	B (1	WILD THING	1966 ATCO	US SD 33193
RONNIE BOND	D (1	WILD THING	1966 FONTANA	27556
TONY MURRAY	B (	GIVE IT TO ME	1966 FONTANA	85001
COLIN FLETCHER	G (	CELLOPHANE	1967 PAGE ONE	POL 003
CALEB QUAYE	G (	BEST OF VOL 1	1967 PAGE ONE	FPR 001
IAN AMEY	G (	BEST OF VOL 2	1967 PAGE ONE	FOR 002
RICHARD MOORE	G (	LOVE IS ALL AROUND	1968 FONTANA	SRF 67576
PETER GREEN	G (	MIXED BAG	1968 PAGE ONE	POLS 012
		HIP HIP HOORAY	1968 HANSA	GERM 78595
		THE TOP OF THE TROGGS	1968 HANSA	GERM 77817
		TROGGLOMANIA	1969 PAGE ONE	POS 602
		CONTRAST	1970 SILVERLINE	DJSL 009
		THE TROGGS	1975 PENNYFARTHING	UK PEN 543
		THE TROGGS	1975 PYE	US 12112
		THE TROGG TAPES	1976 PENNYFARTHING	UK PELS 551
		A GIRL LIKE YOU	1975 DJM	DJML26047
		THE ORIGINAL TROGG TAPES	1976 DJM	DJM 44314
		THE ORIGINAL TROGG TAPES	1976 PRIVATE STOCK US	2008
		POP CHRONIK	19 HANSA	GERM 87574
		VINTAGE YEARS	1976 SIRE	3714 2
		WILD THING	1979 CHEVRON	CHV 155
		LIVE AT MAX'S KANSAS CITY	1980 BASEMENT 6006	
		LIVE AT MAX'S KANSAS CITY	1981 MKC US 214 UK	100
		BLACK BOTTOM	1981 NEW ROSE FR	4

DOMENIC TROIANO

DOMENIC TROIANO	G V (ALL	(A) DOMENIC TROIANO	1972 MERCURY US SRM1 639	UK 6338105
PENTI GLEN	D (A	(B) TRICKY	1973 MERCURY US SRM1 670	
HUGH SULLIVAN	K (A	(C) BURNING AT THE STAKE	1977 CAPITOL	11665
PRAKASH JOHN	B (A	(D) JOKES ON ME	197 CAPITOL	11772
WILLIAM SMITH	K V (AB	(E) FRET FEVER	1979 CAPITOL GERM 064 85893 US 11932	
ROY KENNER	PERC V (ABE			

TESSE CALDERONE	V (AB	SHAUN JACKSON	V (AB	BUNK GARDNER	SAX (A	BUZZ GARDNER	TPT (A
TJAY CANTRELLI	SAX (A	LONNIE SHETTER	CLAR (A	PAUL DELONG	D (E	DAVE TYSON	K V (E
BOB WILSON	B V (E	KEN RICE	D (B	WILLIE WEEKS	B (B	MONT STARK	SYN (B
GAYLE LEVANT	HARP (A	PAT HOLLOWAY	V (B	JOHN WEIDER	VLN (B	ERNIE WATTS	SAX (B
MARION CHILDERS	TPT (B	DOUG RICHARDSON	SAX (B	TOM SCOTT	TPT (B	WILLIAM GREEN	WIND(B
JOHN KELSO	SAX (B	RED RHODES STEEL	(A				

TRONICS

GABY DE VIVUENNE	(A	(A) LOVE BACKED BY FORCE	1981 ALIEN BEALIEN	UK 3

TROOPER

RAY McGUIRE	V HCA(ALL	(A) TROOPER	1976 EPIC UK 81618 US MCA	2149
BRIAN SMITH	G V (ALL	(B) TWO FOR THE SHOW	1977 US MCA	2214
HARRY KALENSKY	B V (A	(C) KNOCK 'EM DEAD KID	1977 EPIC UK 82296 US MCA	2275
TOMMY STEWART	D V (ALL	(D) FLYING COLOURS	1979 MCA UK MCF3039 US MCA	3173
RANDY BACHMAN	G (ABC	(E) THICK AS THIEVES	1978 MCA US	2377
FRANK LUDWIG	K V (BCDE	(F) TROOPER	1980 MCA US	5151
DONI UNDERHILL	B V (BCDEF	(G) HOT SHOT	1980 MCA US	3222
ROBERT DEANS	K (F			

JOHN TROPEA

JOHN TROPEA	G V SYN(ALL	(A) JOHN TROPEA	1976 JAYBOY JSL7 MARLIN	2200
WILL LEE	B V (ABC	(B) SHORT TRIP TO SPACE	1977 TK	14061
RICK MAROTTA	D (ABC	(C) TO TOUCH YOU AGAIN	1979 MARLIN US 2222 +TK UK	83355
EARL CHAPIN	HRNS (B			

DON GROLNICK	K (ABC	LEON PENDARVIS	ORG (BC	RUBENS BASSINI	PERC (ABC	DAVE TAYLOR TROM	(ABC
RALPH MACDONALD	PERC (B	JEFF KING	SAX (B	RON CARTALEMI	V (B	RANDY BRECKER	(ABC
JEFF KAWALEK	V (B	MICHAEL BRECKER	WIND (ABC	CHARLES BLACKWELL	V (B	DAVID SPINOZZA	G (B
DUNCAN CLEARY	V (B	MARGARET ROSS	HARP (B	BRIAN DRAKE	V (B	RICHARD DAVIS	B (B
BRUCE GOLDBERG	V (B	MIKE MAINIERI	VIBES (B	BILL GUERRA	V (B	ROMEO PENQUE	WIND(B
STEVE GADD	D (AB	RON JANNELLI	WIND (B	LANI GROVES	V (B	GEORGE YOUNG	HRNS(ABC
JIM BUFFINGTON	HRNS (B	LEW DEL GATTO	WIND (ABC	LOU MARINI	WIND (BC	EUMIR DEODATO	K (A
ELLEN SEELING	TPT (B	TONY PRICE	HRNS (B	JOHN GATCHELL	HRNS (A	ALAN RUBIN HRNS	(AC
ALLEN SCHWARZBERG	D (A	DON PAYNE	B (A	KENNY ASCHER	K (A	RON TROPEA	PERC(AC
NICK REMO	PERC (A	C CONRAD	(A	DAVE SANBORN	SAX (AC	BOB MINTZER	FLT (A
GEORGE OPALISKY	WIND (A	KEN BERGER	WIND (A	JEANNIE FINEBERG	SAX (B	SAM BURTIS	TROM(ABC
STEVE JORDAN	D (C	PAUL SCHAEFFER	K (C	RICHARD TEE	K (C	JON FADDIS	WIND(C
LUTHER VANDROSS	V (C	DIVA GRAY	V (C	JOCELYN SHAW	V (C	JIM MAELEN	PERC(C
BARRY ROGERS	HRNS (C	STRING SECTION	(ABC				

ROBIN TROWER

ROBIN TROWER	G	(ALL	(A) TWICE REMOVED FROM YESTERDAY	1973 CHRYSALIS CHR1039 GER 6307 513
JIMMY DEWAR	B V	(ABCDEFGH	(B) BRIDGE OF SIGHS	1974 CHRYSALIS CHR 1057
REG ISADORE	D	(AB	(C) FOR EARTH BELOW	1975 CHRYSALIS CHR1073
BILL LORDAN	D	(CDEFGHJ	(D) LIVE	1975 CHRYSALIS CHR1089
RUSTY ALLEN	B	(FG	(E) LONG MISTY DAYS	1976 CHRYSALIS CHR1107
PAULINHO DA COSTA PERC		(G	(F) CITY DREAMS	1977 CHRYSALIS CHR1148 GER 6307 610
JACK BRUCE	B	(J	(G) CARAVAN TO MIDNIGHT	1978 CHRYSALIS CHR1189 GER 6307 630
			(H) VICTIM OF FURY	1980 CHRYSALIS CHR1215
			(J) BRUCE,LORDAN, TROWER B L T	1981 CHRYSALIS CHR1324 GER 203 384

T149   T149

DORIS TROY

DORIS TROY   V   (ALL   (A) DORIS TROY   1970 APPLE US ST3371   UK SAPCOR 13
WINSTON DELANDRO G   (B   (B) STRETCHING OUT   1974 POLYDOR   PLEO 12
KEN ELLIOT   SYN (B   (C) RAINBOW TESTAMENT   19   POLYDOR   2956 001
HUX BROWN   G   (B   (D) JUST ONE LOOK   19   ATLANTIC UK 2464 001 US   8088
JACKIE JACKSON   B   (B
ROSETTA HIGHTOWER V   (B   PHIL CHEN   B   (B   ROY DAVIES   SYN (B   RAD BRYAN   G   (B
WINSTON WRIGHT   K   (B   JOANNE WILLIAMS V   (B   GLADSTONE ANDERSON V (B   WINSTON GRENNAN V (B
DORIS PAYNE   V   (B

T149A   T149A

ROGER TROY

ROGER TROY   V   (A   (A) ROGER TROY   1976 RCA   US   APLI 1910

T149B   T149B

TROYKA

MIKE RICHARDS   V D (A   (A) TROYKA   1970 COTILLION   US   SD9020
ROBERT EDWARDS   G MAND V(A
RUMOR LUKAWIETSKY B PERC V(A

T149C   T149C

TRUCK STOP

LUCIUS REICHLING V   (ABC   (A) TRUCK STOP   1973 TELEFUNKEN   GER 14742
RAINER BACH   G K V(ABC   (B) CANT STOP TRUCK STOP 1974 TELEFUNKEN   GER 14783
ERICH DOLL   G BAN(ABC   (C) KEEP ON TRUCKING   1975 TELEFUNKEN   GER 622142
CISCO BERND   B V (ABC
ECKART   (ABC HOFFMAN   WIND (ABC TEDDY IBING   D   (ABC MICHAEL REINECKE K G V(C

T150   T150

WILLIAM TRUCKAWAY

WILLIAM TRUCKAWAY V G K(A   (A) BREAKAWAY   1976 REPRISE US 6469 UK   K44165
ED BOGAS VLN MAND VIBES(A
BOBBY CASTRO   PERC (A   RUSSELL DASHIELL G   (A   TERRY DOLAN   G   (A   BILL DOUGLAS   B (A
JOHN NONZIATO   CONG V(A BUDDY EMMONS   STEEL(A   RICHARD GREENE VLN (A   LARRY HANKS JEWSHARP(A
DAVID HAYES   B   (A   DOUG KILMER   B   (A   WALT KOKEN BANJO FDL (A   FRANK MESTROPASQUA V (A
DOC STORCH   V   (A   JOHN WATSON   V   (A   CHARLES LLOYD FLT (A   NORM MAYELL   D V (A
DALLAS WILLIAMS V PERC(A STOVALL SISTERS V   (A   ARCELLO GARCIA V   (A   VICTOR QUINONES V (A
JOHN RODRIGUEZ V   (A

T150A   T150A

ANDREA TRUE CONNECTION

ANDREA TRUE   V   (A   (A) WHITE WITCH   1977 BUDDAH   5702
CHRISTOPHER CARROLL D (A
KEN WALLACE   K   (A   RALPH AGRESTA   G V (A TOM CAREY   B V (A   JOE BARBOSA G V (A

T150B   T150B

TRUE CONFESSIONS

JULIA BOURQUE   G V (A   (A) TRUE CONFESSIONS   1980 BOMB US 7033 LINE GER LLP5089
GLEN BINMORE   G V (A
BLANCHE BEUBE   K V (A   TERRY McCUBBEN D   (A MARK FOURNIER B   (A   JOHN HAMILTON   D (A

T151   T151

TRUK

MOBY ANDERSON   B   (A   (A) TRUK TRACKS   1971 CBS US 30005   UK   64367
BILL DAFFERN   D   (A
MIKE GRAHAM   V   (A   PAT GRAHAM   K   (A GLENN TOWNSEND G   (A

T151A   T151A

TRUST

BERNARD BONVOISIN V   (AB   (A) REPRESSION   1981 CBS UK   84958
NONO   G   (B   (B) SAVAGE   1982 EPIC UK   85546
VIVI   B   (B
MOHO   G   (B   NICKO D   (B

T151B   T151B

TRUTH

                                  (A) TRUTH   1975 ROULETTE   US   3014

T152   T152

TUBES

FEE WAYBILL   V   (ALL   (A) THE TUBES   1975 A&M US SP 4534 UK AMLH64534
BILL SPOONER   G   (ALL   (B) YOUNG & RICH   1976 A&M US SP 4580 UK AMLH64580
VINCE WELNICK   K   (ABCDEFG   (C) NOW   1977 A&M US SP 4632 UK AMLH64632
RICK ANDERSON   B   (ABCDEFG   (D) WHAT DO YOU WANT FROM LIVE 1978 A&M US SP 6003 UK AMLH68460
MICHAEL COTTEN   SYN (ABCDEFG   (E) REMOTE CONTROL   1979 A&M US SP 4751 UK AMLH64751
ROGER STEEN   G   (ABCDEFG   (F) COMPLETION BACKWARDS PRINCIPLE 1981 CAPITOL US 12151 UK 26285
PRAIRIE PRINCE   D   (ABCDEFG   (G) BEST OF   1981 A&M
RE STYLES   V DANCE(ACDE   (EP) WHITE PUNKS ON DOPE 1978 A&M AMS 7323
MINGO LEWIS   PERC (CDEF

T153   T153

TUBEWAY ARMY

GARY NUMAN   V K G(ABC   (A) TUBEWAY ARMY   1978 BEGGARS BANQUET UK BEGA 4
PAUL GARDINER   B   (AB   (A) TUBEWAY ARMY   1978 BEGGARS BANQUET GER 146510
JESS LIDYARD   D   (AB   (A) TUBEWAY ARMY   1978 BEGGARS BANQUET NL 660048
                                  (B) REPLICAS   1979 BEGGARS BANQUET UK   BEGA7
                                  (B) REPLICAS   1979 ATCO US 38117
                                  (B) REPLICAS   1979 BEGGARS BANQUET GER 146519
                                  (C) THAT'S TOO BAD(EP)   1979 BEGGARS BANQUET UK   BACK2

T153A   T153A

TANIA TUCKER

TANIA TUCKER   V   (ALL   (A) DELTA DAWN   1972 CBS US 31742
PIG ROBBINS   K   (F   (B) WHATS YOUR MAMA'S NAME 1973 CBS US 32272
JERRY CARRIGAN   D   (F   (C) WOULD YOU LAY WITH ME 1974 CBS US 32744
JACK WILLIAMS   B   (F   (D) GREATEST HITS   1975 CBS US 33355
BILLY SANFORD   G   (F   (E) GREATEST HITS   1975 EMBASSY 31180
GLENN KEENER   G   (F   (F) LOVIN' & LEARNIN'   1976 MCA US 2167   UK MCF2741
STEVE GIBSON   G   (F   (G) TANYA TUCKER   1976 MCA US 2141   UK MCF 2713
PETE DRAKE   STEEL(F   (H) HERES SOME LOVE   197 MCA US 2213   UK MCF 2722
CHARLIE McCOY   HCA (F   (J) RIDIN RAINBOWS   1976 MCA US 2253
BERGEN WHITE   V   (F   (K) YOU ARE SO BEAUTIFUL 1977 EMBASSY   UK   31568
CHARLIE DANIELS   FDL (F   (L) WOULD YOU LAY WITH ME 1978 EMBASSY   UK   31690

(CONTINUED)

       TANIA TUCKER   (CONTINUED)

```
    JANIE FRICKE         V   (F        (M) GREATEST HITS            1978 MCA    US 3032
    LARRY GATLIN         V   (F        (N) TEAR ME APART            1979 MCA              UK   MCF 3048
    JERRY CRUTCHFIELD    V   (F        (O) DREAM LOVERS             1981 MCA              UK   MCF 3109
    JERRY SWALLOW        G MAND(N
    BILL ANDERSON        G V (N   BEAU SEGAL      D    (N   STEVE GOLDSTEIN   K V  (N   JEFF EYRICH     B  (N
    LUTHER WATERS        V   (N   MAXINE WILLARD  V(N   JULIA TILLMAN     V    (N   RUSTY BUCHANAN  V  (N
    LYNDA LEE LAWLEY     V   (N   SUE RICHMAN  V  (N    SNDREA ROBINSON   V    (N   JERRY PETERSON  SAX (N
    OREN WATERS          V   (N
```

T154   TOMMY TUCKER   T154

```
    TOMMY TUCKER     V K D(A        (A) MOTHER TUCKER              1977 RED LIGHTNING  UK    RL 022
    LARRY HOLLOWAY   D     (A        ( ) HIGH HEELED SNEAKERS       19   CHECKER   US    2990
    WELDON DEAN YOUNG G   (A
    BRENDA JONES     B    (A   JOHNNY WILLIAMS  D    (A   EDDIE WILLIAMS   TPT (A   MICKEY BAKER    G  (A
    SCOTT ALLEN      B    (A   GENE ROBERTS     PNO  (A   DONNY HATHAWAY   K   (A   PAUL WILLIAMS   SAX (A
    BUDDY LEWIS      SAX  (A   DONNIE FITZ      V    (A   ROBERT BANKS     K   (A   GENE JOHNSON    K  (A
    GREG FITZ        K    (A   PAZANT BROTHERS  HRNS (A   LEO GATEWOOD     D   (A
```

T155   TUCKY BUZZARD   T155

```
    TERRY TAYLOR     G   (ABCD        (A) WARM SLASH               1969 CAPITOL    US    787
    DAVE BROWN       B   (ABCD        (B) COMING ON AGAIN          1971 CAPITOL    US    864
    TIM HENDERSON    V   (ABCD        (C) ALRIGHT ON THE NIGHT     1973 PURPLE UK TPSA 7510   BASF 291367
    NICK GRAHAM      K   (AB          (C) ALRIGHT ON THE NIGHT     1973 PASSPORT US 97001
    DON WELLER       HRNS (C          (D) BUZZARD                  1973 PURPLE UK TPSA 7512
    JOHN LEE         TROM (D          (D) BUZZARD                  1973 PASSPORT US 98001
    PAUL FRANCIS     D   (AB
    CHRIS JOHNSON    D   (CAD RON TAYLOR     G   (C   PHIL TALBOT   G   (D   PAUL KENDRICK   G V (CD
    TONY ASHTON      K   (D   RICKY DODD      SAX (D   JEFF WORKMAN  PNO (C   BILL WYMAN      PNO (D
    NOEL NORRIS      TPT (D   PHIL CORDELL    PNO (C
```

T155A   TONY TUFF   T155A

```
    SANTA           D   (A        (A) TONY TUFF               1980 GROVE MUSIC   UK    ILPS9619
    CLINTON FERRON  B   (A
    ALRICK FORBES   G V (A   ALBERT GRIFFITHS  G  (A   ANSEL COLLINS   K   (A   SKULLY        PERC(A
    MICHAEL PROPHET V   (A   YABBY U           V  (A
```

T155B   TENPOLE TUDOR   T155B

```
    TENPOLE TUDOR    (AB        (A) EDDIE, OLD BOB, DICK & GARY   1980 STIFF   UK   SEEZ 31
                                (B) LET THE FOUR WINDS BLOW       1981 STIFF   UK   SEEZ 42
```

T156   TUFF DARTS   T156

```
    JEFF SALEN      G   (A        (A) TUFF DARTS             1978 SIRE UK 6048
    JOHN DI SALVO   B   (A
    BOB BUTANI      G   (A   JAMES MORRISON  D   (   ROBERT GORDON   V   ( KEVIN COLNEY    V   (
    TOMMY FRENZY    V   (A   JOHN MORELLI    D   (A  JOHN CRISCIONE  V   (A RONALD ARDITO   V   (
    ART LAMONICA    V   (A   GEORGE YOUNG    SAX (A  LEW DELGATTO   SAX  (A RALPH SCHUCKETT PNO (A
    LANCE QUINN     G   (A   ERIC WEISSBERG  STEEL(A IAN HUNTER      K   (A BOB CLEARMOUNTAIN B(A
```

T157   TUNDRA   T157

```
    CHRIS STAINTON  K   (A        (A) TUNDRA               1976 DECCA   UK    SKLR5259
    GLEN TURNER     B   (A
    HENRY SPINETTI  D   (A   CHARLIE HARRISON  B V  (A
```

T157A   GORDON TURNER   T157A

```
    GORDON TURNER    (A        (A) MEDITATION          1969 CHARISMA   UK    CAS 1009
```

T157B   TUNES   T157B

```
                              (A) TRUTH JUSTICE & MANCUNIAN WAY(EP) 19 RHESUS   GO APE1
```

T157C   TURN UPS   T157C

```
    JOE GEAR         D   (A        (A) TURN UP             1980 CRACKED   US    CRLP2
    STEVINYL         G V (A
    R FINGERS DELLER B   (A
```

T157D   TURKEY   T157D

```
                              (A) TURKEY              197 CHRYSALIS UK/US 1010
```

T158   IKE & TINA TURNER   T158

```
    IKE TURNER         G V          ACID QUEEN    (TINA)       1975 UA       US LA495 UK UNS29875
    TINA TURNER        V            AIRWAVES                   1979 UA       US LA917
    P P ARNOLD         V            AND THE RAELETTES          19   TANGERINE US 15611
    VANETTA FIELDS     V   (R       BAD DREAMS                 1973 US                 UK UAS29549
    MERRY CLAYTON      V            BEST OF                    19   BLUE THUMB US 49
    BONNIE BRAMLETT    V            BLACK ANGEL                1976 MUSIDISC            CV1342
    EDWARD BURKS       TROM (NP      BLUES ROOTS   (IKE)        1972 UA       US 5576  UK UAG29326
    McKINLEY JOHNSON   TPT  (NP      BLACK MANS SOUL            19   POMPEII   US 6003
    MARY REED          SAX  (N       COME TOGETHER              1970 LIBERTY   US 7637  UK LBS83350
    JACKIE CLARK       G    (NP      CONFINED TO SOUL  (IKE)    19   UA    US 061
    SOKO RICHARDSON    D    (NP      THE COUNTRY OF TINA TURNER 19   UA       US 200
    WARREN DAWSON      B    (NP      CUSSIN' CRYIN' AND CARRYING ON 19 POMPEII US 6004
    J D REED           SAX  (N       DELILAHS POWER             1977 UA       US 707   UK UAS30040
    DAVID GARLAND      (P            DANCE WITH                 19   SUE      US 2003
    CLAUDE WILLIAMS    (P            DYNAMITE                   19   SUE      US 2004
    JIMMIE SMITH       (P            DONT PLAY ME CHEAP         19   SUE      US 2005
    ANDDRE CECCARELLI  D    (M       FANTASTIC                  1969 SUNSET   US 5265  UK SLS50205
    BERNIE ARCADIO     K    (M       FEEL GOOD                  1972 UA       US 5598  UK UAS29377
    JAYCEE CHANAVAT    G    (M       FUNKY MULE                 1975 DJM               DJSLM2010
    TONY BONFILS       B    (M       FESTIVAL OF LIVE PERFORMANCES  19 KENT    US 538
    MANU ROCHE         PERC (M       FESTIVAL OF LIVE PERFORMANCES  19 UNITED  US  7755
    GEORGES RODI       SYN  (M       GREATEST HITS              19   WB       US 1810  UK K36001
    GEORGE MARGE       OBOE (M       GREATEST HITS              197  UA       US LA592
    TOM MALONE         TROM (M       GREATEST HITS              197  SUNSET   US 5285
    WAYNE ANDRE        TROM (M       GREATEST HITS              196  SUE      US 1038
    BARRY ROGERS       TROM (M       GREATEST HITS              19   HALLMARK     563
    DAVE TAYLOR        TROM (M       GREATEST HITS              196  LONDON   UK HAC8248
    MICHAEL BRECKER    SAX  (M       GREAT ALBUM                1974 ALBUM             ALB  148
    LAWRENCE FELDMAN   SAX  (M       GOSPEL ACCORDING TO        19   UA
    GEORGE YOUNG       SAX  (M       GET IT GET IT              19   CENCO    US 104
    LEW DELGATTO       SAX  (M       HER MAN HIS WOMAN          1970 CAPITOL  US ST 571 VMP 1013
    RANDY BRECKER      TPT  (M       HUNTER                     1970 BLUE THUMB US BTS11
```

(CONTINUED)

[573]

JON FADDIS	TPT	(M
ALAN RUBIN	TPT	(M
PETER BUNETTA	D	(R
BILL HAYNES	B	(R
RONNY STOCKERT	K	(R
MICHAEL BODDICKER	SYN	(R
AIRTO MOREIRA	PERC	(R
MAXAYN LEWIS	V	(R
STEPHANIE SPRUILL	V	(R
DEBORAH LINDSEY	V	(R
JULIA TILLMAN	V	(R
DENISE ECHOLS	V	(R
AL CINER	G	(R
KEN MOORE	PNO V	(R
W D SMITH	ORG	(R
TONY WALTHERS	V	(R
MICHAEL STEPHENSON	V	(R
ED GREENE	D	(R
DENNIS BELFIELD	B	(R
MARY RUSSELL	V	(R
RICK KELLIS	SAX	(R
BILL OZ	HCA	(R

Title	Year	Label			
HUNTER	1970	HARVEST		UK SHSP4001	
IKE & TINA	1975	DJM		DJMD 8006	
IKE & TINA SHOW II	19	TOMATO	US		
IKE & TINA SHOW II	19	WB	US 1568		
IKE & TINA SHOW	19	LOMA	5112		
IKE & TINA SHOW	1966	WB	1579		
IKE TURNER ROCKS THE BLUES(IKE)	19	CROWN	US 367		
IKE TURNER & THE KINGS OF RHYTHM	1980	ACE		UK CH22	
IKE TURNER & THE KINGS OF RHYTHM	19	SUE	US 2004		
ITS GONNA WORK OUT FINE	19	SUE	2007		
IKE & TINA TURNER	19	CENCO	US 5031		
IN PERSON	1969	MINIT	US 24018	UK 40014	
I'M TORE UP	1978	RED LIGHTNIN'		UK RL0016	
LIVE IN PARIS	19	LIBERTY		LBS83468/9	
(L) LET ME TOUCH YOUR MIND(TINA)	1973	UA	US 5660	UK UAS29423	
(M) LOVE EXPLOSION	1978	UA		UK UAG30267	
(N) NUFF SAID	1971	UA	US 5530	UK UAG29256	
NUTBUSH CITY LIMITS	1973	UA	US 180	UK UAS29557	
OOH POO PAH DOO	19	HARMONY	US 30400		
OUTTA SEASON	19	SUNSET		UK SLS50314	
OUTTA SEASON	19	BLUE THUMB	US BT5		
ON STAGE	19	VALIANT		UK VS 118	
PEACHES	19	POLYDOR		UK 2916 020	
PLEASE PLEASE PLEASE	19	KENT	US 550		
QUEEN	1975	SPRINGBOARD	US 4033		
(R) ROUGH (TINA)	1979	UA		UK UAG30211	
REVUE	1975	NEW WORLD		MW 6006	
RIVER DEEP & MOUNTAIN HIGH	1975	A&M	US 4178	UK AMLP8013	
RIVER DEEP & MOUNTAIN HIGH	197	PHILLES	118	4011	
RIVER DEEP & MOUNTAIN HIGH	1966	LONDON		UK SHU 8298	
RIVER DEEP & MOUNTAIN HIGH	1970	MAYFAIR		UK AMLB1021	
RIVER DEEP & MOUNTAIN HIGH	197	MFP		UK 50443	
SO FAR	19	MUSIDISC		CV 1262	
SOUL OF	19	KENT	US 519		
SOUL OF	19	SUE	2001		
SOUL SELLERS(COMP)	1980	LIBERTY		UK LBR 1002	
SOMETHINGS GOT A HOLD OF ME	19	HARMONY	US 30567		
STRANGE FRUIT	1974	UA		UK UAG29316	
SWEET RHODE ISLAND RED	1974	UA		UK UAS29681	
SIXTEEN GREAT PERFORMANCES	1975	ABC	US 4014	UK ABCL5123	
SOULED FROM THE VAULTS	1975	DJM		DJLMD8006	
SUPER ORIGINAL SESSIONS	1975	MUSIDISC		ALB 169	
SO FINE	196	LONDON		UK SHU 8370	
SO FINE	196	POMPEII	US 6000		
TOO HOT TO HOLD	19	SPRINGBOARD	4011		
TOO HOT TO HOLD	19	PICKWICK	US 3284		
VERY BEST OF	1976	UA		UK UAS29948	
WORLD OF	1973	UA	US 064	UK UAD60043	
WORKING TOGETHER	1971	LIBERTY	US 7650	UK LBS83455	
WHAT YOU HEAR	1971	UA	US 995	UAD60005/6	

T159   NIK TURNER   T159

NIK TURNER	V WIND(AB	(A) XITINTODY	1978	CHARISMA	UK	CDS 4011
STEVE HILLAGE	G (A	(B) PASS OUT (INNER CITY)	19			
TIM BLAKE	SYN (A					
ALAN POWELL	PERC (A	MIQUETTE GIRAUDY SYN (A MORRIS PERT PERC (A MIKE HOWLETT B(A				

T160   TURNING POINT   T160

JEFF CLYNE	B (AB	(A) CREATURES OF THE NIGHT	1977	GULL	UK	GULP 1022
BRIAN MILLER	K (AB	(B) SILENT PROMISES	1978	GULL	UK	GULP 1027
DAVID T D BALL	SAX (AB					
PEPE LEMER	V (AB	PAUL ROBINSON D (AB				

T161   TURTLES   T161

HOWARD KAYLAN	K V (ALL	(A) IT AINT ME BABY	1965	WHITE WHALE US		WWS 7111
MARK VOLMAN	G V (ALL	(B) YOU BABY	1966	WHITE WHALE US		WWS 7112
JOHN SEITER	K V D(EGF	(C) HAPPY TOGETHER	1966	WHITE WHALE US		WWS 7114
AL NICHOL	K V B G(ALL	(C) HAPPY TOGETHER	1967	LONDON	UK	HAU 8330
DON MURRAY	D (1	(D) GOLDEN HITS	1967	WHITE WHALE US		WWS 7115
JIM PONS	G B V(3F	(E) BATTLE OF THE BANDS	1968	WHITE WHALE UK 8904 US WWS7118		
CHUCK PORTZ	B (12	(E) BATTLE OF THE BANDS	1968	LONDON	UK	SHU 8376
JIM TUCKER	G (123	(F) TURTLE SOUP	1969	WHITE WHALE US		WWS 7124
JOHN BARBATA	D (3E	(G) MORE GOLDEN HITS	1970	WHITE WHALE US		WWS 7127
(1) 1965		(H) WOODEN HEAD	1970	WHITE WHALE US		WWS 7133
(2) 1965		(J) HAPPY TOGETHER AGAIN	1975	PHILIPS		9299 425
(3) 1966		(K) HAPPY TOGETHER AGAIN(DBL)	1975	SIRE	US	3703
		(EP) 1968	1978	RHINO US RNPD 901		

T161A   TUXEDOMOON   T161A

STEVE BROWN	K V SAX (AB	(A) HALF MUTE	1980	RALPH	US	TX 8004
BLAINE REININGER	VLN V K G B(AB	(B) DESIRE	1981	RALPH US	UK PRE	PREX4
PETER PRINCIPLE	B G SYN(AB					
WINSTON TONG	V (B	VICKY ASPINALL VLN (B AL ROBINSON CELLO(B				

T161B   TUSH   T161B

DANNY LADEMACHER	(A	(A) WE'RE JUST THE BOYS	1980	EMI EURO 29679	

T161C   TOMMY TUTONE   T161C

TOMMY HEATH	G V (AB	(A) TOMMY TUTONE	1980	CBS US 36372	
JIM KELLER	G (A	(B) 2	1981	CBS	
MICKEY SHINE	D (AB				
TERRY NAILS	B (AB				

TWEEDS

```
    JEFF MEZZROW      G V B(A        (A) PERFECT FIT              1980 AUTOBAHN   TDS 1230
    GEORGE GODDING    V PERC(A
    MARK McHUGH       G V (A    GORDON WALLACE   D V (A   KENNY G      PNO (A
```

TWENTIETH CENTURY STEEL BAND

```
    MARTIN JAMES      PERC V(B        (A) WARM HEART, COLD STEEL   1975 UA        UK         UAK 29878
    MIKEY BRUMONT     PERC V(B        (B) YELLOW BIRD IS DEAD      1976 UA        UK         UAS 29980
    WINSTON FINDLEY   PERC V(B
    MICHAEL OLIVER    PERC(B    GODFRUN MOORE   PERC (B  GIDEON ROGERS   PERC (B  LUCIANO BRAVO   PERC(B
    TREVOR WILLIAMS   PERC V(B  COLLINS MOORE    D V (B  MIKE D'ALBERQUERQUE B (B TERRY TAYLOR    G (B
```

TWENTY SIXTY SIX

```
    VEIT MARVOS       K V (A          (A) AND THEN                1972 UA        UK         UAS 29314
    STEVE ROBINSON    SYN K(A
    GEFF HARRISON     V   (A    GAGEY MROZECK   G V (A   DIETER BAUER    B (A   KONSTANTIN BOMMARIUS D(A
```

20/20

```
    STEVE ALLEN       G V (A          (A) 20/20                   1980 PORTRAIT US 36205 UK PRT 83898
    RON FLYNT         B V (A          (B) LOOK OUT                1981 PORTRAIT US 37050
    MIKE GALLO        D   (A
    CHRIS SILAGYI G V SYN(A    PHIL SEYMOUR       V (A
```

TWICE AS MUCH

```
    DAVE SKINNER        (AB         (A) OWN UP                   1966 IMMEDIATE  UK         IMSP 007
    ANDREW ROSE         (AB         (B) THAT'S ALL               1968 IMMEDIATE  UK         IMSP 013
    NICKY HOPKINS     K   (
    JOHN McLAUGHLIN   G   (A    ANDY WHITE   D  (A   JIMMY PAGE    G   (A   JIM SULLIVAN    G (A
    ALAN WEIGHALL     G   (A    JOE MORETTI  G  (A   ERIC FORD         (A
```

DWIGHT TWILLEY

```
    DWIGHT TWILLEY G K V PERC(ALL    (A) SINCERELY              1976 SHELTER UK ISA5012  US  52001
    PHIL SEYMOUR      D B V(ABC      (B) TWILLEY DONT MIND      1977 SHELTER UK ISA5015 US ARISTA4140
    BILL PITCOCK IV   B G (ABCDE     (C) TWILLEY                1979 ARISTA        US      4214
    JOHNNY JOHNSON    B   (AB        (D) BLUE PRINT             1980 ARISTA        US      4251
    LEON RUSSELL      PNO B(A        (E) SCUBA DIVER            1982 EMI           US      17064
    ROGER LINN        G   (A
    JERRY NAIFEH      D   (ACD JIM LEWIS      B D (CD  JIMMY HASKELL  STR (A   NOAH SHARK    PERC(CE
    GREG BLOCH        VLN (C    BENMONT TENCH  K   (E  BRIAN QUALIS  B  (E
```

TWINK

```
    TWINK             D V (AB        (A) THINK PINK             1970 POLYDOR GER 2310057 UK 2343 032
    KID ROGERS        G V (B         (B) DO IT (EP) WITH THE FAIRIES) 1978 CHISWICK   UK   SW 26
    CHRIS CHESNEY     G   (B
    LITTLE JOHN       G   (B    DANGER SUN      B  (B  FINGERS FALCONER K  (B
```

TWINKEYZ

```
    DONNIE JUPITER    G B V(A        (A) ALPHA JERK            1979 PLUREX        1000
    HONEY             V G B(A
    KEITH McKEE       D V (A    TOM DARLING G V B  (A  DAVID L HOUSTON  B SYN(A
```

THE TWINKLE BROTHERS

```
    RALSTON GRANT     G V (CD         (A) DO YOUR OWN THING    1977 CARIB' GEMS
    ERIC BERNARD   B V PNO (CD         (B) LOVE (10")          1978 FRONT LINE    UK     FCL 5001
    NORMAN GRANT      D V (CD          (C) PRAISE JAH          1979 FRONT LINE    UK     FL 1041
    BONGO ASHER       PERC (CD         (D) COUNTRYMEN          1980 VIRGIN        UK     V 2169
    KARL HYATT        V PERC(CD        (E) ME NO YOU           1981 TWINKLE NG 632
    DERRICK BROWN     B   (C
    TERRY BARHAM      G   (D    ASHTON GRANT    G  (C   P HURLOCK    G  (C   MICHAEL DAN   PNO (C
    ARNOLD BRECKENRIDGE SYN(C   TOMMY McCOOK   HRNS (C  VIN GORDON  HRNS (C   RANCHIE       B (C
    DAVIDSON DUBOIS   G B (D    MICHAEL SMITH   D  (D
```

TWIST

```
    STEVE CORDUNER    D   (A          (A) THIS IS YOUR LIFE    1979 POLYDOR       UK     2383 552
    WIMS              G V (A
    PETE MARSH        G V (A    ANDY PASK       B  (A   STEVE NAIVE  K  (A   ELVIS COSTELLO  V (A
    JIMMY EDWARDS     V   (A
```

TWISTED SISTER

```
    DEE SNYDER        V   (A          (A) UNDER THE BLADE      1982 SECRET    UK SEC x9
    EDDIE OJEDA       G   (A
    JAY JAY FRENCH    G   (A    MARK MENDOZA    B  (A  A J PERO   D  (A   EDDIE CLARKE   G (A
```

CONWAY TWITTY

```
    CONWAY TWITTY   G V (ALL   SATURDAY NIGHT WITH CONWAY    1959 MGM        US  C801   3786
    LORETTA LYNN      V (GKPRT HITS                          1960 MGM        US         4799
    BOBBY WOOD        K (C     GREATEST HITS                 19   MGM        US         3849
    MIKE LEECH        B (C     TOUCH                         1961 MGM        US         3943
    HENRY STRZELECKI  B (C     HIT THE ROAD                  1964 MGM        US         4217
    JERRY CARRIGAN    D (C     CONWAY TWITTY                 1965 MGM METRO  US         110
    REGGIE YOUNG      G (C     ROCK 'N' ROLL STORY           19   CONTOUR        UK  2870 151
    JOHNNY CHRISTOPHER G (C    CONWAY TWITTY SINGS           19   DECCA US 74724
    TROY SEALS        G (C     LOOK INTO MY TEARDROPS        19   DECCA US 74828
    JOHN HUGHEY       STEEL(C  COUNTRY                       19   DECCA US 74913
    JACK HICKS        BAN (C   HERE'S CONWAY TWITTY          19   DECCA US 74990   UK MCA MUPS342
    DON SANDERS       SAX (C   HERE'S CONWAY TWITTY          1974 MCA            UK    MCF 2622
    TOM BRANNON       SAX V(C  NEVER ENDING SONG OF LOVE     1974 CORAL          UK    CDL 8006
    LISA SILVER       FDL (C   I'M SO USED TO LOVING YOU     197  CORAL US 20000
    FARRELL MORRIS      (C     SHAKE IT UP                   19   PICKWICK US 3360
    SHELLEY KURLAND   STR (C   STAR SPANGLED SONGS           19   M F P          UK   SPR90064
    LEA JANE BERINATI V (C     NEXT IN LINE                  1968 DECCA US 75062 MCA UK MUPS363
    GINGER HOLLADAY   V (C     YOU KNOW I WOULDN'T LIE       1969 DECCA US 75105 MCA UK MUPS386
    JANIE FRICKE      V (C     YOU CANT TAKE COUNTRY OUT OF CONWAY 1969 MGM     US          4650
    DWAYNE WEST       V (C     HELLO DARLIN'                 1970 DECCA US 75209 US MCA     19
                               I LOVE YOU MORE TODAY         1970 MCA            UK MUPS404
                               TO SEE MY ANGEL CRY           1970 MCA UK MUPS412 UK RI MCF2639
                               TO SEE MY ANGEL CRY           1970 DECCA US 75172
                               (G)WE ONLY MAKE BELIEVE       1971 DECCA US 75251  MCA UK MUPS423
                               CONWAY TWITTY                 1971 MGM            UK   2351 006
                               15 YEARS AGO                  1971 MCA   UK MUPS426 MCA RI MCF2647
```

(CONTINUED)

CONWAY TWITTY

15 YEARS AGO	1971	DECCA	US	75248		
I WONDER WHAT SHE'LL THINK	1972	MCA	UK	MUPS443	MCA RI	MCF2653
HOW MUCH MORE CAN SHE STAND	1971	DECCA	US	75276		
I CAN'T SEE ME WITHOUT YOU	1972	DECCA	US	75335		
(P) LEAD ME ON	1972	DECCA	US	75326		
GREATEST HITS VOL 1	1972	DECCA	US	75352		
I CANT STOP LOVING YOU	1972	DECCA	US	75361		
SINGS THE BLUES	1972	MGM	US	4837		
TWENTY GREAT HITS	1972	MGM	US	4884		
SHE NEEDS SOMEONE TO HOLD HER	1973	MCA	US	303		
(K) LOUISIANA WOMAN/MISSISSIPPI MAN	1974	MCA	US	335	UK	MCF2539
YOU'VE NEVER BEEN THIS FAR BEFORE	1974	MCA	US	359	UK	MCF2557
CLINGING TO A SAVING HAND	1973	MCA	US	376		
HONKY TONK ANGEL	1974	MCA	US	406		
COUNTRY PARTNERS	1974	MCA	US	427		
I'M NOT THROUGH LOVING YOU YET	1974	MCA	US	441		
LINDA ON MY MIND	1975	MCA	US	469	UK	MCF2706
(R) FEELIN'S	1975	MCA			UK	MCF2717
HIGH PRIEST OF COUNTRY MUSIC	197	MCA	US	2144		
TWITTY	197	MCA	US	2176		
BEST OF	1976	MCA			UK	MCF2737
NOW & THEN	1976	MCA	US	2206	UK	MCF2760
(T) UNITED TALENT	1976	MCA			UK	MCF2764
GREATEST HITS	1976	MCA	US	2235		
BEST OF VOL 2	1977	MCA			UK	MCF2788
PLAY GUITAR PLAY	1977	MCA	US	2262	UK	MCF2798
DYNAMIC DUO	1977	MCA	US	2278		
I'VE ALREADY LOVED YOU IN MY MIND	1977	MCA	US	2293		
GEORGIA KEEPS PULLING MY RING	1978	MCA	US	2328	UK	MCF 2845
GREATEST HITS	1977	MCA	US	2345		
HONKY TONK HEROES	1978	MCA	US	2372		
VERY BEST OF	1978	MCA	US	3043		
ROCK'N'ROLL (DBL)	1978	POLYDOR	FR	2624 031		
SINGS THE GREAT COUNTRY HITS	1978	TEE VEE	US	1010		
CONWAY	1978	MCA	US	3063	UK	MCF 2878
(C)CROSSWINDS	1979	MCA	US	3086	UK	MCF 3038
VERY BEST OF LOETTA & CONWAY	1979	MCA	US	3162		
COUNTRY ROCK	1979	MCA	FR	414039		
TWO'S A PARTY	1980	MCA	US	3190		
HEART & SOUL	1981	MCA	US	3210		
REST YOUR LOVE	1980	MCA	US	5138		

TWO GUNS

KENNY BARKER	G V	(A			(A) BALL OUT	1979	CAPRICORN	US	0224
BOBBY WILLIAMS	G V	(A							
MIKE SCONCE	B V	(A	PAT SPENCE	D	(A				

TYCOON

MARK KREIDER	B V K(AB				(A) TYCOON	1979	ARISTA US 4215	UK	ARTY 167
NORMAN MERSHON	V	(Ab			(B) TURN OUT THE LIGHTS	1981	ARISTA US 9555		
MICHAEL FONFARA	K SYN	(A							
MARK RIVERA	SAX V(AB	JON GORDON	G SYN(AB RICHARD STEINBERG	D(A BOB MESSANO			G V	(B
MIKE BROUN	D	(B	KEITH TAYLOR	K	(B				

TYGERS OF PAN TANG

ROBB WEIR	G V	(ABCD	(A) WILD CAT	1980	MCA US 3270	UK MCF3075	GER 202966	
JESS COX	V	(A	(B) SPELLBOUND	1981	MCA	UK MCF3104	GER 203621	
BRIAN'BIG' DICK	D	(ABCD	(C) CRAZY NIGHTS	1981	MCA	UK MCL3123	GER 204671	
ROCKY	B	(ABCD	(D) THE CAGE	1982	MCA	UK 3150		
JOHN SYKES	G	(BC	(EP) CRAZY NIGHT	1981	MCA		GER MCAT723	
CHRIS GARIDES	K	(B						
FRED PURSER	K G	(D	JON DEVERILL	V	(BCD			

SEAN TYLA & THE TYLA GANG

SEAN TYLA	G V	(ABCD	(A) YACHTLESS	1977	BESERKLEY UK BSERK 11 US	0057					
GERALD MOFFETT	G	(D	(A) YACHTLESS	1977	BESERKLEY GER 623 370						
BRIAN TURRINGTON	B	(AB	(B) MOONPROOF	1978	BESERKLEY UK BSERK 16 US	0059					
PAUL SIMMONS	D	(D	(B) MOONPROOF	1978	BESERKLEY GER 623 637						
KEN WHALEY	B	(BC	(C) JUST POPPED OUT	1980	LINE GER 5068 POLYDOR 2391 463						
REEBOP KWAKU BAAH PERC	(D		(C) JUST POPPED OUT	1980	POLYDOR US 6281						
BRUCE IRVINE	G	(ABC	(D) REDNECK IN BABYLON	1981	ZILCH GER 2324 184 UK RIEN 1						
STEVE JONES	V	(C									
PETER O'SULLIVAN	B	(A	MIKE DESMARAIS	D	(ABC DEKE LEONARD	G V K(A	BAM KING	G	(C
MARTYN WATSON	G V	(C	BUZZ CHANTER	G	(C	MALCOLM MORLEY	G	(C TEX COMER	B	(C
NICK GARVEY	B V	(C	MICK GROOM	B V	(CD BOB DAISLEY	B	(C ANDY BENNIE	B	(C
KEVIN KINSON	K	(C	KENNY LAGUNA	K V	(C FRAN BYRNE	D	(C TIM ROPER	D	(C
PETE THOMAS	D	(C	MIKE KELLIE	D	(C JOHN EARLE	SAX	(CD CARLENE CARTER	V	(CD
JOAN JETT	V	(C	MARK DODSON	V	(C					

ALVIN 'RED' TYLER

ALVIN'RED' TYLER		(AB	(A) ROCKIN & ROLL	19	ACE	US 1006
			(B) TWISTIN' WITH MR SAX	19	ACE	US 1021

BONNIE TYLER

BONNIE TYLER	V	(ABC	(A) THE WORLD STARTS TONIGHT	1977	CHRYSALIS US 1140 RCA UK PL25063			
KEVIN DUNN	B	(B	(B) NATURAL FORCE	1978	RCA		UK PL25152	
MICKY GIBBONS	D	(B	(B) ITS A HEARTACHE	1978	RCA US AFLI12821			
ROGER BARM	K	(B	(C) DIAMOND CUT	1979	RCA US AFLI3072		UK PL25194	
TAFF WILLIAMS	G V	(B						
STEVE WOLFE	G V	(B	PETER KING	V	(B			

TYNDALL

RUDOLF LANGER	K	(A	(A) SONNENLICHT	1980	SKY	GERM	SKY036
JURGEN KREHAN	K	(A	(B)				
			(C) REFLEXIONEN	1982	SKY	GER	SKY074

JUDIE TZUKE	V (ALL	(A) WELCOME TO THE CRUISE	1979 ROCKET	UK	TRAIN7
MO FOSTER	B (A	(B) SPORTSCAR	1980 ROCKET US 3249	UK	TRAIN9
PETER VAN HOOKE	D (A	(C) I AM PHOENIX	!)(! ROCKET	UK	TRAIN15
RAY RUSSELL	G (A	(D) STAY WITH ME TILL DAWN	1981 ROCKET US 27001
CHRIS PARREN	K (A	(E) ROAD NOISE	1982 CHRYSALIS UK CTY1405
JOHN PUNTER	PERC (A	(F) SHOOT THE MOON	1982 CHRYSALIS UK CDL 1382
ROY BABBINGTON	B (A
MIKE PAXMAN	PERC G(ABCDEF	SIMON PHILLIPS	D (A	PAUL HART	K SYN (A	PAUL MUGGLETON	V (BCDE
JOHN EDWARDS	B (BCEF	BOB NOBLE	K (BCEF	CHARLIE MORGAN	D (BCF	JEFF RICH	D (BCEF
ANDY CLARK	SYN CF	MARTIN DITCHAM	PERC (C	EUGENE ORGAN	G (C	MIKE ROGERS	G (C
DON SNOW	K (F	THE DRIBBLE BROS	V (F

ALISTAIR CAMPBELL	G V (ABC	(A) SIGNING OFF	1980 GRADUATE	GRADLP 2
ROBIN CAMPBELL	G (ABC	(B) PRESENT ARMS	1981 DEP	DEP 1
BRIAN TRAVERS	SAX (ABC	(C) PRESENT ARMS IN DUB	1981 DEP	DEP 2
MICHAEL VIRTUE	K (ABC	(D) THE SINGLES ALBUM	1982 DEP	DEP 5
EARL FALCONER	B (ABC
JIM BROWN	D (ABC	NORMAN HASSAN PERC (ABC

U BROWN	V (ALL	(A) SATTA DREAD	1977 KLIK	KLP 9018
SANTA	D (E	(B) LONDON ROCK	1977 THIRD WORLD	TWS 909
ROBERT SHAKESPEARE	B (E	(C) REVELATION TIME	1977 LIVE & LOVE	LALP 002
WINSTON WRIGHT	K (E	(D) STARSKY & HUTCH	1978 CANCER	CANSLP 001
WIRE LINDO	K (E	(E) MI BROWN SOMETHING	1978 FRONT LINE	UK	FL1003
BO PEE	G (E	(F) CAN'T KEEP A GOOD MAN DOWN	1979 FRONT LINE	FL1030
CHINNA	G (E
SCULLY	PERC (E

PETER WAY	B (ALL	(A) U F O	1971 BEACON UK BEAS12 US RARE EARTH 524
ANDY PARKER	D (ALL	(B) FLYING	1972 BEACON UK BES19 GERM NOVA21438
PHIL MOGG	V (ALL	(AB) U F O /FLYING	1973 DECCA	UK	SD30311/2
BERNIE MARSDEN	G (	(C) LIVE	1972 NOVA	GER	6 21454
MICK BOLTON	G (ABC	(D) PHENOMENON	1974 CHRYSALIS	CHR 1059
MICHAEL SCHENKER	G (DEFHJK	(E) FORCE IT	1975 CHRYSALIS	UK	CHR 1074
DANNY PEYRONEL	K (F	(F) NO HEAVY PETTING	1976 CHRYSALIS	UK	CHR 1103
PAUL RAYMOND	K (HJKL	(G) SPACE METAL	1976 NOVA	GERM	6 28363
PAUL CHAPMAN	G (MLO	(H) LIGHTS OUT	1977 CHRYSALIS	UK	CHR 1127
NEIL CARTER	G K V(OK	(J) STRANGERS IN THE NIGHT	1978 CHRYSALIS CJT5	CHR 1209
LARRY WALLIS	G (	(K) OBSESSIONS	1978 CHRYSALIS	CDL 1182
		(L) NO PLACE TO RUN	1979 CHRYSALIS	CDL 1239
		(M) THE WILD, THE WILLING & INNOCENT	1981 CHRYSALIS	CHR 1307
		(O) MECHANIX	1982 CHRYSALIS	CHR 1360
		( ) PROFILE	19 TELDEC	GERM	624007
		( ) C'MON EVERYBODY(1971)	1981 TELEFUNKEN	GER	624836

JOHN WETTON	B G V(ABC	(A) U K	1978 POLYDOR UK 2302 080	US 1 6146
TERRY BOZZIO	D (BC	(A) U K	1978 POLYDOR GER 2344 104
EDDIE JOBSON	VLN K(ABC	(B) DANGER MONEY	1979 POLYDOR UK 2302 089	US 1 6194
BILL BRUFORD	D (A	(C) NIGHT AFTER NIGHT	1979 POLYDOR UK 2302 096	US 1 6234
ALLAN HOLDSWORTH	G (A

CHARLIE HARPER	V HCA(ABCDE	(A) ANOTHER KIND OF BLUES	1979 GEM	UK	GEMLP 100
NICK GARRATT	G (ABCD	(B) BRAND NEW AGE	1980 GEM	UK	GEMLP 106
PAUL SLACK	B (ABC	(C) CRASH COURSE(WITH LTD EDITION EP) 1980 GEM UK GEMLP 111 GER 43423
PETE DAVIES	D (ABC	(D) DIMINISHED RESPONSIBILITY	1981 GEM	UK	GEMLP 112
STEVE ROBERTS	D (D	(E) LIVE KICKS	1980 UNIVERSE NL 23
ALVIN GIBBS	B (D
MEL WESSON	SYN (D	CAPTAIN SENSIBLE K (D

U ROY(EWART BECKFORD)	(ALL	(A) DREAD IN A BABYLON	1976 VIRGIN US 34234 UK	V 2048
ROBBIE SHAKESPEARE	B (C	(B) NATTY REBEL	1976 VIRGIN	UK	V 2059
SLY DUNBAR	D (C	(C) RASTA AMBASSADOR	1977 VIRGIN	UK	V 2092
CLINTON FEARON	B (C	(D) DREADLOCKS IN JAMAICA	1977 LIVE & LOVE	LALP 05
ALBERT GRIFFITHS	G V (C	(E) BEST OF	1977 LIVE & LOVE	LALP 08
RANCHIE	V G (C	(F) VERSION GALORE	1978 FRONT LINE	UK	FL1018
DUGGIE	G (C	(G) JAH SON OF AFRICA	1977 LIVE & LOVE	LALP 08
ANSEL COLLINS	K (C
EARL 'WIRE' LINDO	SYN(C	STICKY	PERC (C	WAYNE JARRETT	V (C	NAGGO MORRIS	V (C

BOB GREENFIELD	D (A	(A) DON'T HOLD BACK	1971 RCA	UK	SF 8168
DOUG FIEGER	B (A
JOHN COURY	K G (A	ROB STAWINSKI	D (A	PAT ARNOLD	V (A	BOBBY KEYS	SAX (A
GARY WRIGHT	K (A	JIMMY MILLER	PERC (A	JIM PRICE	SAX (A	DORIS TROY	V (A
ALAN WHITE	D (A	CHRIS WOOD	FLT (A	FLO BENDER	(A

LARRY MULLIN	D (AB	(A) BOY	1980 ISLAND UK ILPS9646 GER 202 913
ADAM CLAYTON	B (AB	(B) OCTOBER	1981 ISLAND UK ILPS9680 GER 204 185
THE EDGE	G (AB
BONO HEWSON	V (AB

	(A) STARBOOTY	19 ELEKTRA	UK	K52068

DAVE BINGHAM	V HCA(AB	(A) SOMEWHERE OUTSIDE	1966 YORKTOWN
JOHN READ	B (AB	(B) OFF THE WALL	1980 RAZOR CAN 003
GLYN BELL	G V (AB
ROGER MAYNE	G (AB	ROBIN BOERS	D (AB	SCOTT CUSHINE	K (B	ANDY GRAUTITUS	(B
BERT HERMISTON	SAX (B	SIMON WALLIS	SAX (B

U6   JAMES'BLOOD'ULMER   U6

```
    JAMES BLOOD ULMER  G    (ABC       (A) NO WAVE                          1980 MOERS MUSIC              MM01072
    AMIN ALI           B    (C         (B) MUSIC REVELATION ENSEMBLE        1980                    GERM
    SHANNON JACKSON    D    (C         (C) ARE YOU GLAD TO BE IN AMERICA    1980 ROUGH TRADE UK ROUGH 16
    DAVID MURRAY       SAX  (C
    G CALVIN WESTON    D    (C   OLIVER LAKE       SAX (C    OLU DARA       TPT (C    WILLIAM PATTERSON  G(C
```

U7   ULTIMATE SPINACH   U7

```
    BARBARA HUDSON     G V  (ABC       (A) ULTIMATE SPINACH                 1968 MGM   UK 8071      US      SE4518
    IAN BRUCE DOUGLAS  V K G HCA(AB     (B) BEHOLD & SEE                     1968 MGM   UK 8094      US      SE4570
    KEITH LAHTEINEN    D V  (AB         (C) ULTIMATE SPINACH                 1969 MGM                US      SE4600
    GEOFFREY WINTHROP  G V  SIT(AB
    RICHARD NESE       B    (AB  JEFF BAXTER      G V  (C    MIKE LEVINE     B   (C    RUSS LEVINE      D  (C
    TED MYERS          G V  (A   TONY SCHEUREN    K    (C    ALAN LORBER     PROD (A
```

U7A   ULTRA VIOLET   U7A

```
                                       (A) ULTRA VIOLET                    1974 CAPITOL            11244
```

U8   ULTRAVOX   U8

```
    JOHN FOXX          V    (ABCD      (A) ULTRAVOX                         1977 ISLAND UK ILPS9449 GER 28193
    STEVE SHEARS       K V  (ABD       (B) HA HA HA                         1977 ISLAND UK ILPS9505 GER 25499
    BILLY CURRIE       K VLN(ABCDE123   (C) SYSTEMS OF ROMANCE              1978 ANTILLES US 7069 UK ISLAND 9555
    ROBIN SINE         G    (D         (C) SYSTEMS OF ROMANCE               1978 ISLAND GER 26453
    WARREN CANN        D    (ABCDE123   (D) THREE INTO ONE (COMP)           1980 ISLAND UK ILPS 9614
    MIDGE URE          G V  (E23       (D) THREE INTO ONE (COMP)            1980 ANTILLES US 7079
    CHRIS CROSS        B    (ABCDE123   (E) VIENNA                          1981 CHRYSALIS UK CHR1296 GER 202701
                                       (F) RAGE IN EDEN                     1981 CHRYSALIS UK CHR1338 GER 203959
                                       (G) QUARTER                         1982 CHARISMA UK CHR1338
                                       (1) MAN WHO DIES    (EP)            1978 ISLAND UK IEP8
                                       (2) VIENNA          (EP)            1981 CHRYSALIS GER 600352
                                       (3) ALL STOOD STILL(EP)            1981 CHRYSALIS GER 12 2522
```

U8A   UMPS & DUMPS   U8A

```
    ALAN HARRIS        B V  (A         (A) THE MOON IS FIT                 1980 TOPIC        UK      12TS 416
    SUE HARRIS         DULC (A
    TUFTY SWIFT        FDL HCA(A  JOHN KIRKPATRICK CONC V(A  DEREK PEARCE  BANJO PERC V(A
```

U9   UNCLE DOG   U9

```
    CAROLE GRIMES      V    (A         (A) OLD HAT                         1972 SIGNPOST     UK      SG 4253
    DAVID SKINNER      K V  (A
    PHILLIP CROOKS     G    (A   TERRY STANNARD    D    (A   JOHN PORTER   G B  (A   SAMMY MITCHELL   G   (A
    JOHN PEARSON       D    (A   RABBIT BUNDRICK   K    (A
```

U9A   UNCLE JIM'S MUSIC   U9A

```
    GARY TOLBERT NICHOLSON G V  (A     (A) THERE'S A SONG IN THIS          19   / /  US
    THOMAS DUNSTAN     STEEL BAN V(A
    WESLEY PRITCHARD   B V  (A   JIM NORMAN   K G V   (A   MICHAEL MINDEL  VLN (A   ST PERRY         D  (A
    MARK HOFSTEIN      SAX  (A
```

U10   UNDERTAKERS   U10

```
    JACKIE LOMAX       G V  (A         (A) UNDERTAKERS                     1964 PYE NOT RELEASED
    BUGS PEMBERTON     D    (A
    CHRIS HUSTON       G    (A   GEORGE NUGENT    G    (A   BRIAN JONES    SAX(A
```

U11   UNDERTONES   U11

```
    FEARGAL SHARKEY    V    (ABC       (A) THE UNDERTONES                  1979 SIRE UK SRK6071 GER 200 681
    MICKEY BRADLEY     B    (ABC       (A) THE UNDERTONES (1 EXTRA TRACK)  1979 SIRE UK/US SRK 6081
    JOHN O'NEILL       G    (ABC       (B) HYPNOTISED                      1980 SIRE UK SRK6088 GER 202 203
    BILLY DOHERTY      D    (ABC       (EP) TEENAGE KICKS                  197  GOOD VIBRATION        GOT 4
    DAMIAN O'NEILL     G    (ABC       (C) POSITIVE TOUCH                  1981 ARDECK UK 103 EMI GER  64367
    NEILL KING         TPT  (C
    DICK BLEWETT       SAX  (C   PAUL CARRACK K   (C
```

U12   UNDISPUTED TRUTH   U12

```
                                       (A) UNDISPUTED TRUTH               1971 TAMLA UK STML11197 US GORDY 955
                                       (B) FACE TO FACE                   1972 TAMLA UK STMG 8004 US GORDY 959
                                       (C) LAW OF THE LAND                1973 TAMLA UK STML11240 US GORDY 963
                                       (D) HIGHER THAN HIGH               1975 TAMLA UK STML12009 US GORDY 972
                                       (E) DOWN TO EARTH                  1975 TAMLA UK STML11277 US GORDY 968
                                       (F) COSMIC TRUTH                   1975 TAMLA UK STMA 8023 US GORDY 970
                                       (G) BEST OF                        1977 TAMLA UK STMA 8029
                                       (H) METHOD TO THE MADNESS          197  WB    UK  K56289   US       2967
                                       (I) SMOKIN'                        1979 WB    UK  K56497   US       3202
```

U13   UNICORN   U13

```
    PETER PERRIER      D V  (ABCD      (A) UPHILL ALL THE WAY             1971 TRANSATLANTIC   UK       TRA238
    TREVOR MEE       G V FLT (A        (B) BLUE PINE TREES                1974 CHARISMA UK 1092 US CAPITOL 11334
    KEN BAKER          V K G(ABCD      (C) TOO MANY CROOKS                1976 HARVEST UK SHSP4054
    PAT MARTIN         B V  (ABCD      (C) UNICORN II                    1976 CAPITOL      US       ST 11453
    KEVIN SMITH        G    (BCD       (D) ONE MORE TOMORROW             1977 HARVEST      UK    SHSP 4067
    DAVID GILMOUR      STEEL(BC        (D) ONE MORE TOMORROW             1977 CAPITOL      US       ST 11692
    CHRIS PIDGEON      K    (CD
    HOWIE CASEY        SAX  (D   BILLY LIVSEY     K    (D
```

U13A   UNIQUES   U13A

```
                                       (A) YOU DONT MISS YOUR WATER      1980 CHARLY       UK    CTD 121
```

U13B   UNION   U13B

```
    RANDY BACHMAN      G V  (A         (A) ON STRIKE                     1981 POTRAIT UK 85121   US  37368
    FRED TURNER        B V  (A
    FRANK LUDWIG       K V  (A   CHRIS LEIGHTON    D PERC(A
```

U14   UNIT 4+ 2   U14

```
    BRIAN PARKER LYRICS     (          (A) FIRST ALBUM                   1965 DECCA        UK    LK 4697
    DAVE MEIKLE        G V  (1         (B) UNIT 4+2 FEATURING CONCRETE & CLAY196 LONDON  US    PS 427
    TOMMY MOELLER      K V  (1         (C) REMEMBERING                   1977 DECCA        UK    REM 6
    PETE MOULES        V    (1         (1) 1962
    HOWARD LUBIN       G V  (1
    BOB GARWOOD        B    (    HUGH LEM HALLIDAY D    (    RUSS BALLARD    G V  (    ROBERT HENRIT   D  (
```

```
U15A                    UNITED SONS OF AMERICA                                          U15A
   GERRY BLAKE      K V (A       (A) GREETINGS FROM THE U S OF A    19   MERCURY SR 61312 +    6338 036
   STEVE WOODS      V PERC(A
   RICHARD FREEMAN  G   (A    JERRY RITCHLEY   B   (A  MIKE HUESTIS     D PERC (
U15B                   UNITED JAZZ & ROCK ENSEMBLE                                       U15B
                              (A) LIVE IM SCHUTZENHAUS         19   MOOD GER   22666
                              (B) TEAMWORK                     19   MOOD GER   22999
                              (C) THE BREAK EVEN POINT       1979   MOOD GER   23600
U16                     UNITED STATES OF AMERICA                                         U16
   JOSEPH BYRD      K SYN(A       (A) UNITED STATES OF AMERICA   1968 CBS US  9619    UK   63340
   DOROTHY MOSKOWITZ V   (A
   GORDON MARRON  VLN SYN V(A RAND FORBES    B V  (A  CRAIG WOODSON   D PERC (A ED BOGAS     K (A
U16A                           UNITS                                                     U16A
   SCOTT RYSER     SYN V  (A     (A) DIGITAL STIMULATION       1980 '415'    US   003
   RACHEL WEBBER   SYN V  (A
   BRAD SAUNDERS   D   (A   JIM REYNOLDS   VIBES    (A
U17                        UNIVERS ZERO                                                  U17
   DANIEL DENIS    PERC (AB      (A) UNIVERS ZERO             1978 ATEM            7001
   MICHEL BERCKMANS WIND (AB     (B) HERESIE                  1979 ATEM 7005 UK RECOMMENDED   RR4
   MARCEL DUFRANE  VLN (A
   CHRISTIAN GENET B   (A   PATRICK HANAPPIER VLN (AB  EMMANUEL NICAISE    HCA (A    ROGER TRIGAUX G K(AB
   GUY SEGERS      B V (B
U17A                      UNIVERSAL ENERGY                                               U17A
                              (A) UNIVERSAL ENERGY           1977 HARVEST       UK   SHSP 4075
U17B                           UNIVERSE                                                  U17B
   GARY PAUL VAN   K V (A        (A) UNIVERSE                 1977 PBR INTERNATIONAL    PBR 7002
   DENNIS LEE ASKEW G V (A
   WALFREDO REYES  PERC (A
U17C                    UP WITH THE PEOPLE                                               U17C
                              (A) LIVE IT LIVE               1970 BUDDAH      US   ?
U18                         PHIL UPCHURCH                                                U18
   PHIL UPCHURCH   G B V(ALL     (A) YOU CANT SIT DOWN        1961 BOYD          US       398
   TENNYSON STEVENS    (J        (B) YOU CANT SIT DOWN II      196 UA            US      6162
   ERIC GALE       G   (J        (C) TWIST THE BIG HIT DANCES  196 UA            US      6175
   ARTHUR ADAMS    G   (H        (D) UPCHURCH                  196 CADET         US       826
   HARVEY MASON    D   (H        (E) THE WAY I FEEL           1969 CADET         US       840
   BOBBYE HALL     PERC (H       (F) FEELING BLUE             1968 MILESTONE     US      9010
   DOUG BASCOMB    B   (J        (G) PHIL UPCHURCH             19   MARLIN       US      2209
   BOB JAMES       K   (J        (H) DARKNESS DARKNESS        1972 BLUE THUMB US 6005 UK  ILPS9219
   STEVE GADD      D   (J        (J) UPCHURCH TENNYSON        1975 KUDU                 KU 22
   ANDREW SMITH    D   (J        (K) PHIL UPCHURCH            1978 TK                   TKR82542
   DAVID SANBORN   SAX (J
   CHUCK RAINEY    B   (H   JOE SAMPLE    K   (H  ELSA HARRIS     V   (E  CASH McCALL    V (E
   KITTY HAYWOOD   V   (E   DON SIMMONS   D   (H  BEN SIDREN      K   (H  DONNY HATHAWAY  K (H
U19                            UPP                                                       U19
   ANDY CLARK      K V (AB       (A) UPP                      1975 EPIC US   33439   UK  80625
   STEVEN AMAZING  B   (AB       (B) THIS WAY UPP             1976 EPIC US   34177   UK  81322
   JAMES COPLEY    D   (AB
   DAVID BUNCE     G   (B   JEFF BECK     G   (AB TOM SCOTT       SAX (B  JEANIE ARNOLD  V (B
   CHRISTY THOMPSON V   (B  GARY COLEMAN  PERC (B JIMMY GETZOFF   (B
U20                         UPSETTERS                                                    U20
   LEE PERRY           (        (A) RETURN OF DJANGO         1970 TROJAN            TRL  19
   JOHNNY MOORE        (        (B) THE GOOD THE BAD & THE UPSETTERS 1970 TROJAN    TBL 119
   VAL BENNETT         (        (C) EASTWOOD RIDES AGAIN     1970 TROJAN            TBL 125
   WINSTON WRIGHT      (        (D) PRISONER                 1970 TROJAN            TBL 127
   JIM JACKSON         (        (E) SUPER APE                1977 ISLAND      UK    ILPS9417
   HUX BROWN           (        (F) AFRICA'S BLOOD           1980 TROJAN            TBL 166
   EASY BECKFORD       (        (G) THE UPSETTERS COLLECTION 1981 TROJAN      UK    TRLS195
   BOB AITKENS         (
   GLEN ADAMS          (   ALVA LAVIS        (  CARLTON BARRETT     ( ASTON BARRETT        (
U20A                        URBAN VERBS                                                  U20A
   ROBIN ROSE          (AB       (A) URBAN VERBS     1      1980 WB   US BSK3418   UK K56810
   RODDY FRANTZ        (AB       (B) EARLY DAMAGE           1981 WB   US BSK3533   UK K56896
   LINDA FRANCE        (AB
   ROBERT GOLDSTEIN    (AB DANNY FRANKEL    D   (AB
U20B                        URBAN HEROES                                                 U20B
   EVERT NIEUWSTEDE V   (A       (A) WHO SAID...            1980 FLEET NL 202026 HANDSHAKE US 36962
   MARTIN ZONDEROP  B   (A
   JAAP DE JONCKHEERE G (A  JEROEN ERNST    K   (A  AD VAN DER REE   D   (A
U20C                        URBAN RENEWAL                                                U20C
                              (A) MURPHYS LAW            1975 DUNHILL       US   50194
U20D                          URBAN SAX                                                  U20D
   GILBERT ARTMAN      (AB       (A) UBRAN SAX              1978 COBRA       FR   37004
   SAX ORCHESTRA(16 SAX) (       (B) URBAN SAX 2            1979 COBRA       FR   37017
U21                       MICHAEL URBANIAK                                               U21
   MICHAEL URBANIAK VLN SAX(ALL  (A) FUSION                 1974 CBS   US 32852    UK 65744
   URSZULA DUDZIAK  PERC V(BCDF  (B) ATMA                   1974 CBS   US 33184
   CZESLAW BARTKOWSKI D  (BD     (C) FUSION III             1975 CBS   US 33542
   WOJCIECH KAROLAK K    (B      (D) INACTIN'               1975 SPIEGELEI      GERM 287847U
   RAY MANTILLA    PERC (B       (E) PARATYPHUS B           1975 SPIEGELEI      GERM   28771
   JOHN ABERCROMBIE G    (C      (F) BODY ENGLISH           1976 ARISTA US AL 4086
   ROMAN DYLAG     B    (D       (G) TRIBUTE TO KOMEDA      1976 BASF      US 21657
   WLODEK GULGOWSKI K    (C      (H) ECSTASY                1978 MARLIN             2221
   ANTHONY JACKSON B    (C       (I) SERENADE FOR THE CITY  1980 MOTOWN US      M 7944
   BRANISLAV KOVACEK D  (D       (J) HERITAGE               1980 PAUSA     US 7047
   GERRY BROWN     D    (C
   STEVE GADD      D    (C   LARRY CORYELL   G   (C  JOE CARO     G  (CF BERNARD KAFKA   V (CF
   HAROLD IVORY WILLIAMS K(F BASIL FEARRINGTON B  (F  STEVE JORDAN  D  (F ERROL CRUSHER BENNETT PERC(F
   ADAM MAKOWICZ   PNO  (D
```

MICK BOX	G(ABCDEFGHJKLMNOPS	(A)	VERY'UMBLE VERY 'EAVY	1970	VERTIGO	UK 6360 006	MERCURY	US SR61294
KEN HENSLEY	K V(ABCDEFGHJKLMNOP	(A)	VERY'UMBLE VERY 'EAVY	1971	BRONZE	RI ILPS9142	BRONZE 77RI	BRNA142
DAVID BYRON	V (ABCDEFGHJKL	(B)	SALISBURY	1971	VERTIGO	UK 6360 028	MERCURY	US SR61319
PAUL NEWTON	B (ABCK	(B)	SALISBURY	1971	BRONZE	RI ILPS9152	BRONZE 77RI	BRNA152
KEITH BAKER	D (BK	(C)	LOOK AT YOURSELF	1971	BRONZE	UK ILPS9169	MERCURY	US SRM1614
AL NAPIER	D (AK	(C)	LOOK AT YOURSELF	1977	BRONZE			RI BRNA169
NIGEL OLSSON	D (A	(D)	DEMONS & WIZARDS	1972	BRONZE	UK ILPS9193	MERCURY	US SRM1630
IAN CLARKE	D (CK	(D)	DEMONS & WIZARDS	1977	BRONZE			RI BRNA193
GARY THAIN	B (DEFGH	(E)	MAGICIANS BIRTHDAY	1971	BRONZE	UK ILPS9213	MERCURY	US SRM1652
LEE KERSLAKE	D (DEFGHJKLMNOS	(E)	MAGICIANS BIRTHDAY	1977	BRONZE			RI BRNA213
JOHN WETTON	B (JL	(F)	LIVE	1973	BRONZE	UK ILSD1	MERCURY	US SRM7503
TREVOR BOLDER	B V (MNOP	(F)	LIVE	1977	BRONZE			RI BRSP 1
COLIN WOOD	K (A	(G)	SWEET FREEDOM	1973	BRONZE	UK BRNA245	WB	US 2724
JOHN LAWTON	V (MNO	(G)	SWEET FREEDOM	1977	BRONZE			RI BRNA245
MEL COLLINS	SAX (J	(H)	WONDERWORLD	1974	BRONZE	UK ILPS9280	WB	US 2800
B J COLE	STEEL(J	(H)	WONDERWORLD	1975	BRONZE			RI BRNA280
CHRIS MERCER	SAX (O	(J)	RETURN TO FANTASY	1975	BRONZE	UK ILPS9335	WB	US 2869
JOHN SLOMAN	V (P	(J)	RETURN TO FANTASY	1977	BRONZE			RI BRNA335
MARK CLARKE	V (1	(K)	THE BEST OF	1975	BRONZE	UK ILPS9375	MERCURY	US SRM11070
CHRIS SLADE	D (P	(K)	THE BEST OF	1977	BRONZE			RI BRNA375
JOHN SINCLAIR	K (S	(L)	HIGH & MIGHTY	1976	BRONZE	UK ILPS9384	WB	US 2949
PETE GOALBY	V (S	(L)	HIGH & MIGHTY	1977	BRONZE			RI BRNA384
BOB DAISLEY	B (S	(M)	FIRE FLY	1977	BRONZE	UK ILPS9483	WB	US 3013
		(M)	FIRE FLY	1977	BRONZE			RI BRNA383
		(N)	INNOCENT VICTIM	1977	BRONZE	UK BRON504	WB	US 3145
		(O)	FALLEN ANGEL	1978	BRONZE	UK BRNA 512	CHRYSALIS	US S 1204
		(P)	CONQUEST	1980	BRONZE	UK BRNA 524		
		(Q)	URIAH HEEP	1980	MERCURY	US 8004		
		(R)	WONDERFUL	1980	CHRYSALIS	US 1227		
		(S)	ABOMINOG	1982	BRONZE	UK BRAN 538	GER 204 532	
		(T)	ABOMINOG JUNIOR (EP)	1982				

DICK WAGNER	G V (A	(A)	URSA MAJOR	1972	RCA	US LSP 4777	
GREG ARAMA	B (A						
RICKY MANGONE	D V (A						

DENNY FISCHELSCHER	D (A	(A) UTOPIA			1973 UA	UK UAG 29438					
JIMMY JACKSON	K (A										
LOTHAR MEID	B (A	ANDY MARX	G (A	JOE NAY	D (A	CHRIS KARRER	VLV (A				
ROLF ZACHER	V (A	JOHN WEINZIERL	G (A	GEO GREEN	D (A	JOE QUICK	G (A				
GEORGE BROWN	D (A	KRISTIAN SCHULZE	K (A	RENATE KNAUP	V (A	FALK ROGNER	K (A				
OLAF KUBLER	SYN PROD(A	SIEGFRID SCHWAB	G (A	PETER KRAMPER	SYN (A	EDGAR HOFFMAN	SAX (A				
KEITH FORSEY	D (A	RALF BASTEN	V (A								

RITCHIE TEETER	D (A	(A) 1979				
BRUCE BRODY	K (A	RITCHIE FLIEGLER	G (A	DONNIE NOSSOV	B(A	

	(A) PUNK ROCK	19	FESTIVAL	FR 680

JAY STORCH	K					
PETER SABATINO	V	LARRY WEST	B	LESLIE WEST	G ROGER MANSOUR	D

VALDY	V (AB	(A) VALDY			1975 A&M US 4538	UK AMLH64538			
JIM KELTNER	D (A	(B) VALDY & THE HOMETOWN BAND			197 A&M US 4592				
JERRY SCHEFF	B (A								
FRED TACKETT	G (G	DAVID PAICH	K (A	RICHARD GREENE	VLN (A	DALLAS TAYLOR	D(A		
JERRY McGEE	G (A	ELEANOR SEATKIN	CELLO(A	JOHN SEBASTIAN	HCA (A	JIM GORDON	D (A		
JIM HORN	FLT (A	ALAN MUNDE	BANJO(A	JESSE ED DAVIS	G (A	JAY DEE MANESS	G (A		
WILLIAM SMITH	K (A	KLAUS VOORMANN	B (A						

RITCHIE VALENS	V (A	RITCHIE VALENS	19	DELFI	US	1201
		RITCHIE	19	DELFI	US	1206
		RITCHIE	19	LONDON	US	HA 2390
		IN CONCERT	19	DELFI	US	1214
		GREATEST HITS	19	DELFI	US	1225
		GREATEST HITS II	19	DELFI	US	1247
		GREATEST HITS	19	LONDON	UK	HA 8196
		ORIGINAL	19	GUEST STAR	US	1484
		ORIGINAL LA BAMBA	19	GUEST STAR	US	1469
		RITCHIE VALENS	19	APEX	US	1201
		HIS GREATEST HITS	19	PRESIDENT		PTL 1001
		ROCK LI'L DARLIN'	19	JOY		JOYS 254
		RITCHIE VALENS	1979	LONDON	UK	HAR 8535

DINO VALENTI (CHESTER POWERS)	V (A	(A) DINO VALENTI	1968 CBS UK 63443	US EPIC 26335	

DAVE VALENTIN	FLT (ABC	(A) THE HAWK	1979 ARISTA	US 5006				
DAVE GRUSIN	K SYN(ABC	(B) LAND OF THE THIRD EYE	1980 ARISTA	US 5009				
MICHAEL VINAS	G (ABC	(C) PIED PIPER	1981 ARISTA	US 5505				
MARCUS MILLER	B (ABC							
BUDDY WILLIAMS	D (ABC	CRUSHER BENNETT	PERC (AC	OSCAR HERNANDEZ	K (ABC	LINCOLN GOINES	B (ABC
TITO MARRERO	D (ABC	ROGER SQUITERO	PERC (ABC	RAFAEL DE JESUS	PERC (ABC	LARRY ROSEN	PERC(A
ANGELA BOFILL	V (A	DENNIS BELL	K (B	JEFF MIRONOV	G (B	PATTI AUSTIN	V (B
LUTHER VANDROSS	V (B	BOBBY BROOM	G (C	VIVIAN CHERRY	V (C	YVONNE LEWIS	V (C
KACEY CYSIK	V (C	BILL O'CONNELL	K (C				

VAMPIRES

```
GARY GAREIS       V  (A        (A) WE'RE ON THE ROAD AGAIN      1978 NITTRIBITT GER        1006
UDO WALDER        G  (A
DIETER KLIER      K V (A   NORBERT ROSCH    B  (A  JURGEN FECHTER    D  (A
```

JOEL VANCE

```
JOEL VANCE        G V (A        (A) WHAT I DID ON MY VACATION     19   CADET      US    325
```

MARTHA & THE VANDELLAS

```
MARTHA REEVES     V  (ALL       (A) COME & GET YOU MEMORIES       1963                US GORDY 902
ROSALIND ASHFORD  V  (123       (B) HEAT WAVE                     1963 TAMLA UK STML11005 US GORDY 907
LOIS REEVES       V  (34        (C) DANCE PARTY                   1965 TAMLA UK STML11013 US GORDY 915
BETTY KELLY       V  (2         (D) WATCH OUT                     1966 TAMLA UK STML11051 US GORDY 920
ANNETTE BEARD     V  (1         (E) GREATEST HITS                 1966 TAMLA UK STML11040 US GORDY 917
SANDRA TILLEY     V  (4         (F) LIVE                          1968                US GORDY 925
                                (G) RIDIN HIGH                    1968                US GORDY 926
                                (H) SUGAR & SPICE                 196                 US GORDY 944
                                (J) NATURAL RESOURSES             196                 US GORDY 952
                                (K) BLACK MAGIC                   1974 TAMLA UK STML11204 US GORDY 958
                                (L) GREATEST HITS VOL 2           1974 TAMLA UK STML11223
                                (M) ANTHOLOGY                     1974 TAMLA UK STML12060 US TAMLA 778
                                (N) GREATEST HITS                 1981 TAMLA UK STMS5042
```

GINO VANELLI

```
GINO VANELLI      V PROD   (ALL  (A) CRAZY LIFE                   1973 A&M US 4395
JOE VANELLI       K PROD SYNBFGH (B) POWERFUL PEOPLE              1974 A&M US 3661      UK AMLS 63630
ROSS VANELLI      V PROD   (FGH  (C) STORM AT SUNUP               1975 A&M US 4533
JIMMY HASLIP      B  (F          (D) THE GIST OF THE GEMINI       1976 A&M            UK AMLH64596
MANUEL BADRENA    PERC (F        (E) A PAUPER IN PARADISE         1977 A&M            UK AMLH 64664
STEPHANIE SPRUILL V  (F          (F) BROTHER TO BROTHER           1978 A&M US 4722    UK AMLH 64722
JULIA TILLMAN     V  (F          (G) NIGHTWALKER                  1980 ARISTA        UK START 1148
MARK CRANEY       D  (F          (H) THE BEST OF GINO VANELLI     1980 A&M           UK AMLE 69043
CARLOS RIOS       G  (F
LEON GAER         B  (F  ERNIE WATTS      SAX (F   VICTOR FELDMAN  VIBES (F MAXINE WILLARD   V (F
RICHARD BAKER STR HRNS K(B  JOHN J MANDEL    PERC (B   LANI HALL    V  (B   GRAHAM LEAR      D (B
TONY GOLIA        PERC (B
```

VANDENBERG

```
ADJE VANDENBERG   G  (A         (A) VANDENBERG                    1982 ATCO       UK    50904
JOS ZOOMER        D  (A
DICK KEMPER       B  (A   BERT HEERINK     V  (A
```

CHRISTIAN VANDER

```
CHRISTIAN VANDER  K  (A         (A) TRISTAN ET ISEULT             1978 EGG        FR    90171
JANIK TOP         B  (A
STELLA VANDER     V  (A   KLAUS BLASQUIZ   V PERC  (A  LAURENT THIBAULT  PROD (A
```

VAN DER GRAAF GENERATOR

```
PETER HAMMILL     K V G(ALL      (A) AEROSOL GREY MACHINE         1968 FONTANA UK       6430 083
NIC POTTER        B  (BCJKMH     (A) AEROSOL GREY MACHINE         1968 MERCURY US       SR 61238
DAVE JACKSON      WIND K(BCDEFGJKMH (A) AEROSOL GREY MACHINE      1968 VERTIGO ITALY    6360 510
GUY EVANS         D  (ABCDEFGLKMHJ (B) THE LEAST WE CAN DO IS WAVE 1969 CHARISMA CAS1007 GER PHILIPS 6369901
HUGH BANTON       K G B(ABCDEFGKM (C) H TO HE WHO AM THE ONLY ONE 1970 CHARISMA CAS1027 GER PHILIPS 6369915
JOHN ANTHONY      PROD (ABC      (C) H TO HE WHO AM THE ONLY ONE  1970 DUNHILL US 50097
KEITH ELLIS       B  (AK         (D) PAWN HEARTS                  1971 CHARISMA CAS  1051
GRAHAM SMITH      K V VLN  (HJ    (E) GODBLUFF                    1975 CHARISMA CAS1109 US MERCURY 1069
CHARLES DICKIE K  CELLO(J        (F) STILL LIFE                   1976 CHARISMA CAS1116 US MERCURY 1096
CED CURTIS        G B  (M        (G) WORLD RECORD                 1976 CHARISMA CAS1120 US MERCURY 1116
PIERO MESSINA     K G  (M        (H) THE QUIET ZONE               1977 CHARISMA CAS1132
JERRY SALISBURY   HRNS (B         (J) VITAL LIVE       (DBL)      1978 CHARISMA CVLD101 US PVC 9901
MIKE HURWITZ      CELLO(B         (K) 1968//1971                  1973 CHARISMA          CS 2
JEFF?             FLT (A          (M) LONG HELLO                  1973 NO LABEL
ROBERT FRIPP      G  (CD          (N) REPEAT PERFORMANCE          1980 CHARISMABG8
                                 (O) REFLECTION                   19   FONTANA GER 9286 002
```

LON & DERREK VAN EATON

```
LON VAN EATON G V K D SAX(AB     (A) BROTHER                      1973 APPLE       UK    SAPCOR 25
DERREK VAN EATON V B G D (AB     (B) WHO DO YOU OUT DO            1975 A&M         US    SP 4507
RINGO STARR       D  (A
JIM GORDON        D  (AB KLAUS VOORMANN    B   (AB ANDY NEWMARK   D   (A   PAUL GLANZ    ORG (A
T J TINDALL       G  (A  MIKE HUGG         D   (A  ALEX GUEVARA   CONGA(A  RICHARD DAVIS B   (A
JIM KELTNER       D  (B  RICHARD PERRY     PERC (B  TOM HENSLEY   K   (B   VANETTA FIELDS V  (B
BOBBY HARTNAGLE   G  (B  CYNTHIA WEBB      V   (B  FRITZ POASKETT V   (B   RUSS TURNER   ORG (B
DAVID BEEBE       D  (B  TOM SEUFERT       G   (B  CHUCK FINDLEY  HRNS (B  LANI GROVES   V   (B
MARTHA REEVES     V  (B  TREVOR LAWRENCE   SAX (B  LYNDA LAURENCE V   (B   JAMES GADSON  D   (B
CLYDIE KING       V  (B  GARY WRIGHT       K   (B
```

VANGELIS

```
VANGELIS          K  (ALL        (A) DRAGON                       1971 CHARLY      UK    CRL 5013
MICHEL RIPOCHE    B  (AHK        (B) L'APOCALYPSE DES ANIMAUX     1973 POLYDOR           2489 113
BRIAN ODGERS      B  (AH         (C) EARTH                        1974 VERTIGO US 1019 UK 6499 693
TONY OXLEY        D  (AH         (D) HEAVEN & HELL                1975 RCA UK RS1025 RI 3012 US 5110
MICK WALLER       D  (A          (E) ALBEDO .39                   1976 RCA UK RS1080 RI 3017 US 5136
ARCHIRIS          G  (A          (F) SPIRAL                       1977 RCA UK PL25116 RI3022 US 2627
YEUNK HAK FUN     V  (K          (G) BEAUBOURG                    1978 RCA UK PL25155     US 3020
KOON FOOK MAN     V  (K          (H) HYPOTHESIS                   1978 AFFINITY           AFF 11
JON ANDERSON      V  (DL         (J) BEST OF                      1978 RCA UK PL25174 RI 3028
VANA VEROUTIS     V  (D          (K) CHINA                        1979 POLYDOR UK POLD5018 US  1 6199
ENGLISH CHAMBER CHOIR  (L        (L) SEE YOU LATER                1980 POLYDOR UK 2302 101
PETER MARSH       V  (L          (M) CHARIOTS OF FIRE             1981 POLYDOR UK POLS1026
CHERRY VANILLA    V  (L          (N) TO THE UNKNOWN MAN           1981 RCA               US 4397
CORI JOSIAS       V  (L
```

VAN HALEN

```
EDWARD VAN HALEN   G   (ABCDE        (A)  VAN HALEN                    1978 WB    US BSK3075        UK K56470
ALEX VAN HALEN     D   (ABCDE        (B)  VAN HALEN II                 1979 WB    US HS 3312        UK K56616
MIKE ANTHONY       B   (ABCDE        (C)  WOMEN & CHILDREN FIRST       1980 WB    US    3415        UK K56793
DAVE ROTH          V   (ABCDE        (EP) VAN HALEN  12"              197  WB                       PRO 705
JAN VAN HALEN      CLAR (E            (D)  FAIR WARNING                 1981 WB    US    3540        UK K56899
                                     (E)  DIVER DOWN                   1982 WB                      UK K57003
```

VANILLA FUDGE

```
MARK STEIN         K   (ABCDEFG      (A)  VANILLA FUDGE                1967 ATLANTIC UK 587 086   US 33224
VINCE MARTELL      G   (ABCDEFG      (B)  THE BEAT GOES ON             1968 ATLANTIC UK 587 100   US 33237
TIM BOGERT         B   (ABCDEFG      (C)  RENAISSANCE                  1968 ATLANTIC UK 587 110   US 33244
CARMINE APPICE     D   (ABCDEF       (C)  RENAISSANCE                  1973 MIDI GER 20045
                                     (D)  NEAR THE BEGINNING           1969 ATLANTIC UK 228 020   US 33278
                                     (D)  NEAR THE BEGINNING           1981 ATLANTIC RI UK K40075
                                     (E)  ROCK'N'ROLL                  1970 ATLANTIC UK 288 029   US 33303
                                     (F)  STAR COLLECTION              1974 MIDI                  MID 0033
         (AS THE PIGEONS)>>>(G) WHILE THE WORLD WAS EATING            1970 WAND US 687 METRONOME  GER 200108
                                     (BE) TWO ORIGINALS                1976 ATLANTIC    GERM        60116
```

CHERRY VANILLA

```
CHERRY VANILLA     V   (AB           (A)  BAD GIRL                     1978 RCA                UK  PL 25122
LOUIS LE PERE      G K V(AB          (B)  VENUS DE VINYL               1979 RCA                UK  PL 25217
ZECCA ESQUIBEL     K   (A
HOWIE FINKEL       B   (A    IAN STUART     V   (B  STUART ELLIOTT  D   (AB ALUN EDEN    D  (B
DAVE QUINN         B   (B    GEORGE FORD    B   (B  ROY BABBINGTON  B   (B  MORRIS PERT  PERC(B
MICHAEL MANUSCE    D   (
```

THIJS VAN LEER

```
THIJS VAN LEER FLT K SYN(ALL         (A)  INTROSPECTION                1972 CBS  US 32346    UK    65589
LETTY DE JONG      V   (A            (B)  INTROSPECTION II             1975 CBS                     65913
PAUL BUCKMASTER    K   (C            (C)  O MY LOVE                    1975 PHILIPS           6303 143
VICTOR FELDMAN     PERC (C            (D)  MUSICA PER LA NOTTE DI NATALE 1976 CBS                   69239
WILTON FELDER      B   (C            (E)  INTROSPECTION III            1978 CBS                     86034
JAMES GADSON       D   (C            (F)  NICE TO HAVE MET YOU         1978 CBS  US 35345    UK    86059
EUGENE CIPRIANO    OBOE (C
DAVID KEMPER       D   (C    ROSELIE VAN LEER  V  (C  NORMAN BENNO    OBOE(C  LOUIE SHELTON   G  (C
KING ERRISON       CONGA(C   RALPH MACDONALD PERC (C  RICHARD TEE     K   (F  ERIC GALE       G  (F
ANTHONY JACKSON    B   (F    HARVEY MASON    D   (F  EEF ALBERS      G   (F  STEVE KHAN      G  (F
JON FADDIS         HRNS (F   RANDY BRECKER   TPT (F  BARRY ROGERS    TROM(F  DAVE TAYLOR     TROM(F
JAMES BUFFINGTON   HRNS (F   JOHN CLARK      HRNS(F  FRED GRIFFIN    HRNS(F  ALEX FOSTER     SAX(F
MICHAEL BRECKER    SAX (F    RONNIE CUBER    SAX (F  TOM SCOTT       SAX (F  BROOKS TILLOTSON HRNS(F
DON CORRADO        HRNS (F   LOU MARINI      SAX (F  VIVIAN CHERRY   V   (F  BRENDA WHITE    V  (F
KEN WILLIAMS       V   (F    GWEN GUTHRIE    V   (F  RAYMOND SIMPSON V   (F  ZACH SANDERS    V  (F
BILL EATON         V   (F    LOUIS VAN DIJK  V   (D  ROGIER VAN OTTERLOO  (D STRINGS         (DF
```

TOWNES VAN ZANDT

```
TOWNES VAN ZANDT   G V (ALL          (A)  FOR THE SAKE OF A SONG       1968 POPPY PYS40001
PHILLIP DONNELLY   G V (H            (B)  OUR MOTHER THE MOUNTAIN      1969 POPPY PYS40004  TOMATO TOM 7015
BILLY EARL McLELLAND  G V(H          (C)  TOWNES VAN ZANDT             1970 POPPY PYS40007  TOMATO TOM 7014
CHIPS MOMAN        G V (H            (D)  DELTA MOMMA BLUES            1971 POPPY PYS40012  TOMATO TOM 7013
RANDY SCRUGGS      G MAND (H          (E)  HIGH,LOW & IN BETWEEN        1971 POPPY PYS5700   TOMATO TOM 7012
TOMMY COGBILL      B   (H            (F)  LATE GREAT                   1973 POPPY  LA 004    UA UK UAS29442
BOBBY EMMONS       K   (H            (F)  LATE GREAT                  197  TOMATO                 TOM 7011
EDDY ANDERSON      D   (H            (G)  LIVE AT THE OLD QUARTER      1977 TOMATO             TOM27001
TONI WINE          V   (H            (H)  FLYING SHOES                 1978 TOMATO                TOM 7017
JIMMY DAY          STEEL(H
GARY SCRUGGS       HCA (H    SPOONER OLDHAM   PNO (H  BILLY BURNETTE   V   (H
```

JOHNNY VAN ZANT

```
JOHNNY VAN ZANT    G V (AB           (A)  NO MORE DIRTY DEALS          1980 POLYDOR US 6289 NL 2391 472
ROBBIE GAY         G   (A            (B)  ROUND TWO                    1981 POLYDOR US 6322
ERIK LUNDGREN      G   (A
DANNY CLAUSMAN     B   (A    ROBBIE MORRIS   D   (A  PAUL BARRERE    G   (A  AL KOOPER   K    (A
ERNIE WATTS        WIND (A   JULIA TILLMAN   V   (A  RON HICKLIN     V   (A  JOHN BALHLER  V  (A
JERRY WHITMAN      V   (A    GENE MORFORD    V   (A  MARTI McCALL    V   (A  MYRNA MATTHEWS V (A
LORNA WILLARD      V   (A
```

VAPOUR TRAILS(VTs)

```
JOHN McBURNIE      G V (AB           (A)  VAPOUR TRAILS                1979 WB        US BSK3363 UK K56722
ANDY DALBY         G   (AB           (B)  V T s                        1980 CRIMINAL          UK STEAL1
PHIL CURTIS        B   (AB
JOHN FERRARO       D   (AB   STEVE HOLLY     D V (AB  BRIAN MANN      K   (AB  WILLIAM D SMITH K  (AB
MICHAEL OMARTIAN   K   (AB   DAVE ROSE       K   (AB  BRIAN CHATTON   K   (AB  DAVID BENOIT   K  (AB
BETSY COOKE        K V (AB   PAULINHO DA COSTA PERC (AB TOM SCOTT     SAX (AB  MEL COLLINS    SAX(AB
VIVIENNE McAULIFFE V   (AB   BILL CHAMPLIN   V   (AB
```

VARDIS

```
STEVE ZODIAC       G V (ABC          (A)  100MPH                       1980 LOGO              UK  MOGO 4012
ALAN SELWAY        B V (ABC          (B)  WORLD'S INSANE               1981 LOGO GER 64029    UK  LOGO 1026
GARY PEARSON       D   (ABC          (C)  QUO VARDIS                   1981 LOGO             UK  LOGO 1034
JUDD LANDER        HCA (B
ANDY BOWN          K   (B
```

VAPORS

```
DAVID FENTON       G V (A            (A)  NEW CLEAR DAYS               1980 UA   US 1049     UK  UAG 3030
HOWARD SMITH       D   (A            (B)  MAGNETS                      1981 LIBERTY US 1090  UK  LBG 30324
EDWARD BAZALGETTE  G   (A
STEVE SMITH        B V (A
```

```
BOBBY VEE        V  (ALL    DEVIL OR ANGEL                    196  LIBERTY US LST7165
SONNY CURTIS     G V  (C    BOBBY VEE                         196  LIBERTY US LST7181
BOB BOGLE        G    (D    WITH STRINGS & THINGS             196  LIBERTY US LST7186
NOKIE EDWARDS    B    (D    HITS OF THE 50s                   19   LIBERTY US LST7205
JERRY ALLISON        (C    TAKE GOOD CARE OF MY BABY          196  LIBERTY US LST7211  UK LBY 1004
JOE MAULDIN          (C    (C) MEETS THE CRICKETS             1962 LIBERTY US 7228     UK LBY 1086
DON WILSON       G   (D    (C) MEETS THE CRICKETS             1974 SUNSET    US SLS50357
MEL TAYLOR       D   (D    RECORDING SESSION                 196  LIBERTY US LST7232  UK LBY 1084
                           GOLDEN GREATS                     1962 LIBERTY US LST7245
                           MERRY CHRISTMAS                   196  LIBERTY US LST7267
                           NIGHT HAS A THOUSAND EYES         196  LIBERTY US LST7285  UK LBY 1139
                           (D) MEETS THE VENTURES            1963 LIBERTY US LST7289  UK LBY 1147
                           I REMEMBER BUDDY HOLLY            196  LIBERTY US LST7336  UK SBY 1188
                           SING NEW SOUND FROM ENGLAND       196  LIBERTY US LST7352
                           HITS OF THE SIXTIES               196  LIBETRY US LST7385
                           LIVE ON TOUR                      196  LIBERTY US LST7393
                           GOLDEN GREATS VOLII               196  LIBERTY US LST7464
                           LOOK AT ME GIRL                   196  LIBERTY US LST7482  UK SBY 1341
                           COME BACK WHEN YOU GROW UP         1967 LIBERTY US LST7534
                           JUST TODAY                        196  LIBERTY US LST7554  UK    83112
                           DO WHAT YOU GOTTA DO              196  LIBERTY US LST7592  UK    83130
                           GRITS GRILLS & RAILINGS           19   LIBERTY US LST7612
                           FOREVER KIND OF LOVE              1967 SUNSET          UK    5162
                           BOBBY VEE                         1966 SUNSET                5111
                           FAVOURITES                        19   SUNSET                1019
                           VERY BEST OF                      1971 SUNSET    UK SLS50271
                           NOTHING LIKE A SUNNY DAY          19   UA              UK 29457
                           LEGENDARY MASTERS                 1974 UA        US LA 025  UK UAD60055
                           VERY BEST OF                      1975 UA        US LA 332
                           TRIBUTE TO BUDDY HOLLY            1978 SUNSET      UK SLS50417
```

```
TATA VEGA        V  (AB     (A) FULL SPEED AHEAD              1976 TAMLA US 347   UK  STML12039
                            (B) TOTALLY TATA                 1977 TAMLA US 353   UK  STML12058
                            (C) TRY MY LOVE                  19   TAMLA US 360
```

```
MARTHA VELEZ     V  (ALL    (A) FIENDS & ANGELS              1969 LONDON UK SHK8395 SIRE US 97008
ERIC CLAPTON     G  (A      (A) FIENDS & ANGELS              1969 BLUE HORIZON    UK   763867
JACK BRUCE       B  (A      (B) HYPNOTIZED                   1972 POLYDOR US          PD5034
MITCH MITCHELL   D  (A      (C) MATINEE WEEPERS              1973 SIRE    US 7409  UK     0598
RICK HAYWARD     G  (A      (D) ESCAPE FROM BABYLON          1976 SIRE    US 7515  UK 9103 252
DUSTER BENNETT   HCA (A     (E) AMERICAN HEARTBEAT           1977 SIRE    US 6040  UK 9103 256
DAVE BIDWELL     D  (A
ANDY SYLVESTER   B  (A   STAN WEBB        G  (A   JEFF CONDON     HRNS (A   CHRIS WOOD       SAX (A
CHRISTINE PERFECT K (A   MICK WEAVER      K  (A   BRIAN AUGER     ORG  (A   PETER SHELLEY        (A
KEEF HARTLEY     D  (A   TERRY NOONAN     HRNS (A  PAUL KOSSOFF   G    (A   GARY THAIN       B   (A
SPIT JAMES       G  (A   JIM CAPALDI      D  (A   BUD PARKES      HRNS (A   DEREK WADSWORTH  HRNS(A
CHRIS MERCER     SAX (A  KEITH JOHNSON    HRNS (B  DAHAUD SHAAR   D    (B   JOHNNY ALMOND    SAX (A
JOHN PLATANIA    G  (B   NANCY WADE       K  (B   DON MOORE       B    (B   MIKE WINFIELD    B   (B
ALAN HAND        K  (B   JOHN KLINGBERG   B  (B   GERARDO VELEZ   CONGA(B   BILLY CURTIS    CONGA(B
COLLIN TILTON    WIND (B  GEORGE DEVENS   PERC (B  SPIDER BARBOUR  G   (B   CISSY HOUSTON    V   (B
JOSHIE ARMSTEAD  V  (B   JACKIE VERDELL   V  (B   RONNELLE STAFFORD V  (D   ASTON BARRETT    B   (D
CARLTON BARRETT  D  (D   AL ANDERSON      G  (D   EARL SMITH      G    (D   TYRONE DOWNIE    K   (D
WINSTON WRIGHT   K  (D   GLADSTONE ANDERSON K (D  BERNARD HARVEY  K   (D    LEE PERRY       PERC (D
BOB MARLEY       PERC (D  RITA MARLEY     V  (D   JUDY MOWATT     V    (D   MARCIA GRIFFITH  V   (D
DAVID SCANCE     V G K(E  BRIAN CUOMO     K  (E   JOHN SIEGLER    B    (E   PAUL MARCHETTI   D   (E
JOEL KRANTZ      V  (E   JOHN DI ROBERTIS V  (E   KEN NEMIROFF    V    (E   FRANK D'AGOSTINO V   (E
PAT ELLINGTON    V  (E   JOAN ELLINGTON   V  (E   JUDY ELLINGTON  V    (E   RON CARTALEMI    V   (E
JOHN ZANGRANDO   SAX (E  JOHN PAYNE       WIND (E  STEVE SAVAGE   PERC (E   BOB GERLAND     WIND (E
GEORGE CONSTANINOU STEEL(E  LARRY FAST    SYN (E  ERNEST ROYAL    HRNS (E   JOHN CLARK      HRNS(E
JAMES BUFFINGTON HRNS (E  WAYNE ANDRE     HRNS (E  JOHN GATCHELL  HRNS (E   JANICE ROBINSON HRNS(E
BUD MARTIN       SAX (E  MICHAEL CULLEN   SAX (E  PETER SOBEL     ZITHER(E
```

```
                            (A) VELVET FOGG                  1967 PYE            UK  NSPL18272
```

```
COLIN FOSTER     G  (A      (A) RIDE A HUSTLERS DREAM        1969 CBS       UK         63692
JOHN FORD        B  (A
RICHARD HUDSON   D  (A   JOHN JOYCE       V  (A
```

```
LOU REED         V G K(ABCDEFHJ  (A) VELVET UNDERGROUND WITH NICO 1967 VERVE   UK SVLP 9184    US 5008
JOHN CALE        B K  (ABE       (A) VELVET UNDERGROUND WITH NICO 196  VERVE      665114
STERLING MORRISON G   (ABCDEFJ   (A) VELVET UNDERGROUND WITH NICO 1971 MGM    UK 2315056 GER RI 2428 506
ANDY WARHOL      PROD (AE        (B) WHITE LIGHT WHITE HEAT   1967 VERVE   UK SVLP9201    US    5046
BILLY YULE       D  (DF          (B) WHITE LIGHT WHITE HEAT   1971 MGM     UK 2353 024 GER 710 015
MO TUCKER        B  (ABCDEJ      (C) VELVET UNDERGROUND       1969 MGM     UK  CS 8108      US4617
DOUG YULE G B D V K (CDFGJ       (C) VELVET UNDERGROUND       1971 MGM     UK 2353 022 GER 665 114
NICO             V  (AE          (D) LOADED                   1970 ATLANTIC 2400 111 COTILLION US 9034
TOM WILSON       PROD (B         (D) LOADED                   1972 ATLANTIC UK K40113  MIDI GER  20049
                                 (E) ANDY WARHOL'S V UNDERGROUND 1971 MGM  UK 2683 006
                                 (F) LIVE AT MAX'S KANSAS CITY 1972 ATLANTIC UK K30022 COTILLION 9500
                                 (G) SQUEEZE                  1972 POLYDOR  UK 2383 180
                                 (H) VELVET UNDERGROUND ,LOU REED 1973 VERVE UK 2315 258 PRIDE US 0022
                                 (J) VELVET UNDERGROUND LIVE  1974 MERCURY  UK 6643 900 US SRM27504
                                 (J) LIVE                     1976 MERCURY  GER 6643 017
                                 ( ) POP HISTORY No12         19   KAMA SUTRA UK 2612 021
                                 ( ) POP HISTORY No19         19   KAMA SUTRA UK 2625 019
                                 ( ) VELVET UNDERGROUND       1970 MGM       IMP GAS131
                                 ( ) VELVET UNDERGROUND       1976 MGM     UK 2354 033
                                 ( ) ARCHETYPES               1974 MGM     US 4950
                                 ( ) EVIL MOTHERS             19   SKYDOG        US  LP 003
```

BOB BOGLE	G	(12345R	WALK DONT RUN	196	LIBERTY UK LBY1002	US DOLTON	8003
DON WILSON	G	(12345R	THE VENTURES	196		US DOLTON	8004
MEL TAYLOR	D	(2345R	ANOTHER SMASH	196		US DOLTON	8006
NOKIE EDWARDS	B	(12	COLORFUL VENTURES	196		US DOLTON	8008
HOWIE JOHNSON	D	(1	TWIST PARTY	1962 LIBERTY UK LBY1072			
JERRY McGEE	G	(345R	TWIST WITH THE VENTURES	196		US DOLTON	8010
JOHNNY DURRILL	PNO	(45R	TWIST PARTY VOL 2	196		US DOLTON	8014
JOE BARILE	PERC	(SR	MASHED POTATOES & GRAVY	196		US DOLTON	8016
RED RHODES	STEEL	(S	DANCE PARTY	196		US DOLTON	8017
LARRY LINSTROT	PROD	(R	PLAY TELSTAR & LONELY BULL	1963		US DOLTON	8019
MIKE GUTIERREZ	PERC	(R	SURFING	1963 LIBERTY UK LBY1150		US DOLTON	8022
(1) 1960 (2) 1963 (3) 1967			COUNTRY CLASSICS	196		US DOLTON	8023
(4) 1967 (5) 1968			LETS GO	1963 LIBERTY UK LBY1169		US DOLTON	8024
			IN SPACE	1964 LIBERTY UK LBY1189		US DOLTON	8027
			FABULOUS	196		US DOLTON	8029
			WALK DONT RUN VOL 2	196	LIBERTY UK SLBY1228	US DOLTON	8031
			KNOCK ME OUT	1965 LIBERTY UK SLBY1252		US DOLTON	8033
			ON STAGE	1965 LIBERTY UK SLBY1270		US DOLTON	8035
			A GO GO	196	LIBERTY UK SLBY1274	US DOLTON	8037
			CHRISTMAS ALBUM	196	LIBERTY UK SLBY1285	US DOLTON	8038
			WHERE THE ACTION IS	196	LIBERTY UK SLBY1297	US DOLTON	8040
			BATMAN THEME	19		US DOLTON	8042
			GO WITH	196	LIBERTY UK SLBY1323	US DOLTON	8045
			WILD THING	196		US DOLTON	8047
			GUITAR FREAKOUT	196	LIBERTY UK SLBY1345	US DOLTON	8050
			SUPER PSYCHEDELICS	196	LIBERTY UK SLBY1372	US DOLTON	8052
			BEST OF	196	LIBERTY UK SLBY1375		
			GOLDEN GREATS	1965 LIBERTY UK 83046		US 8053	
			MILLION DOLLAR WEEKEND	1965 LIBERTY		US 8054	
			FLIGHTS OF FANCY	196	LIBERTY	US 8055	
			I LIKE IT LIKE THAT	1965 LIBERTY UK 83116			
			THE HORSE	196	LIBERTY	US 8057	
			GENIUS	1967 SUNSET		US 5160	
			UNDERGROUND FIRE	1969 LIBERTY UK 83193		US 8059	
			MORE GOLDEN GREATS	19	LIBERTY UK 83175	US 8060	
			HAWAII FIVE O	1969 LIBERTY UK		US 8061	
			SWAMP ROCK	1969 LIBERTY U K 83289		US 8062	
			DECADE	196	SUNSET	5137	
			10TH ANNIVERSARY ALBUM	1970 LIBERTY		US 35000	
			VENTURES	197	UA	US UAX 80	
			JIM CROCE SONGBOOK	197	UA	US 217	
			(R) NEW TESTAMENT	1971 UA		US 6769	
			(S) SHAFT	197	UA UK UAS29280	US 5547	
			SECRET AGENT MAN	19	LIBERTY		
			8 MILES HIGH	19	LIBERTY	US 8811	
			GUITAR POWER	19	SUNSET 1012		
			THE VENTURES DBL COMP	19	SUNSET NL 60022/3		
			SUPER GROUP	19	SUNSET 5271		
			LEGENDARY MASTERS	1974 UA UK UAD 60051			
			JOY	1974 UA UK UAS29340		US 5575	
			BEST OF THE POPS	1974 UA UK UAS29249			
			VERY BEST OF	1975 US EURO 050 96470		US UALA331	
			VERY BEST OF	1976 SUNSET UK SLS50386			
			RUNNING STRONG	197	SUNSET	US 5116	
			ROCKY ROAD	197	UA	US LA586	
			ROCK 'N' ROLL FOREVER	1973 UA		US 5649	
			IN SPACE	1978 PICKWICK		US 3604	

	(A) SONGS FROM SUNSHINE JUNGLE	1978 SPARK srlp125 NL ARIOLA 26121	

VIC VERGAT	(A) DOWN TO THE BONE	1981 HARVEST UK SHSP4117	

TOM VERLAINE	G V (AB	(A) TOM VERLAINE	1979 ELEKTRA US 216	UK 52156	
FRED SMITH	B PERC V(AC	(B) DREAMTIME	1981 WB	UK K56919	
JIMMY RIPP	G (C	(C) WORDS FROM THE FRONT	1982 VIRGIN	UK 2227	
TOMMY PRICE	D (C				
JOE VASTA	B (C	JAY DEE DAUGHERTY D (AC	ALLAN SCHWARTZBERG D (AC	LENE LOVICH SAX V(C	
DEERFRANCE	V (A	TOM THOMPSON D (A	MARK ABEL G (A	BRUCE BODY K (A	
RICKY WILSON	G (A				

JOHN VERITY	G V (A	(A) JOHN VERITY BAND	1974 PROBE UK SPB1087 US DUNHILL 50170		
GEOFF LYTH	K G (A				
GERRY SMITH	B (A	RON KELLY D (A	THUNDERTHIGHS V (A		

MIKE VERNON	V HCA PERC(AB	(A) BRING IT BACK HOME	1971 BLUE HORIZON	UK 2931 003					
COLIN ALLEN	D (B	(B) MOMENT OF MADNESS	1973 SIRE	US SAS 7410					
LAWRENCE GARMAN	HCA (B								
LEO LYONS	B (B	FUZZY SAMUELS	B (B	ANDY SYLVESTER	B (B	RIC LEE	D (B	
RICK HAYWARD	G (A	PETE WINGFIELD	K (AB	KENNY LAMB	D (A	DICK PARRY SAX	(A	
JOE JAMMER	G (B	MITCH MITCHELL	D (B	PAUL BUTLER	G (B	DEREK GRIFFITHS	G (B	
NICK SOUTH	B (B	BRUCE ROWLAND	D (B	CECIL MOSS	TPT(B	JOHN DONNELLY	TPT (B	
BILLY GRAHAM	TROM (B	HOWIE CASEY SAX	(B	RORY GALLAGHER	G (A	PAUL BUTLER	G (A	
LAURIE GARMON	HCA (A	PAUL KOSSOFF	G (A					

VERTO

```
    JEAN PIERRE GRASSET G SYN(AB      (A) KRIG / VOLUBILIS            1976 TAPIOCA FR 10007 POLE 0009
    GILLES GOUBIN      B    (A        (B) REEL 19/36                  1978 FLEAU                FL 7004
    CHARLES GOUBIN     G    (A
    CYRIL LEFEBVRE     G    (B    OCTAVE AGOBERT       (B    BENOIT WIDEMANN    SYN (B    DOMINIQUE GRASSET   G(B
    PHILIPPE PERRONET  D    (B    JEAN PIERRE FOUQUET B K(B   FRANCOIS ARTIGE    G   (B    PH GOUBIN   D    (A
    XAVIER VIDAL       VLN  (A    MICHAEL DEPALLE      D    (A   SERGE SOULIE      D   (A    DOMINIQUE DUBUISSON B(A
    OKAMOTO            V    (A    ALAIN THOMAS         B    (A   F ARTIGE          G   (A    MICHEL GOUBIN
```
EDWARD VESALA

```
    EDWARD VESALA      V D  (ALL      (A) NANA                       1970 BLUE MASTER          BLULP 125
    JUHANN AALTONEN    WIND (ABDEF     (B) HOT LOTTA                 1973 BLUE MASTER          SPEL  306
    ARILD ANDERSON     B    (A         (C) I'M HERE                  1973 BLUE MASTER          SPEL  311
    PETER KOWALD       B    (B         (D) NAN MADOL                 1974 JAPO 60007 +    ECM       1077
    PETER BROTZMANN    SAX  (B         (E) SATU                      1976 ECM                      1088
    KAJ BACKLUND       TPT  (D         (F) RODINA                    1976 LOVE                 LRLP  189
    SAKARI KUKKO       FLT  (D
    JOHANN POUTANEN    V    (D    TEPPO HAUTOANO     B    (D    ELISABETH LEISTOLA HARP (D   MIRCEA STANKO    HRNS (DF
    SEPPO PAAKKUNAINEN WIND(D    PENTTI LANTI      WIND (DF   CHARLIE MANANO     SAX  (D   TOMASZ STANKO    TPT  (EF
    PALLE MIKKELBERG   HRNS (E    TOMASZ SZUKALSKI  SAX   (EF   KNUT RIISNAES     FLT  (E   ROLF HALM        WIND(E
    TORBJØRN SUNDE     HRNS (E    TERJE RYPDAL       G     (E    PALLE DAUIELGSON   B   (E   PEKKA POYRY      SAX  (F
    ESA HELALSVUO      PNO  (F    PEKKA RECHARDIT           (F    PEKKA SARMANTO          (F   IRINA MILAN      V   (F
```
PATRICK VIAN

```
    PATRICK VIAN            (A         (A) BRUITS ET TEMPS ANALOGUES  1978 EGG          EURO       900 541
```
VIBRATORS

```
    IAN CARNOCHAN      G V  (1         (A) PURE MANIA                1977 EPIC US 35038 CAN 90433 UK 82097
    KNOX               G V K(ABC1      (B) V 2                       1978 EPIC              UK       82495
    JOHN ELLIS         G V SYN(ABC     (C) BATTERIES INCLUDED (COMP) 1980 CBS               UK       31840
    PAT COLLIER        G    (A         (1) 1978
    JOHN EDWARDS       D    (ABC1
    GARY TIBBS         B    (BC1  DON SNOW         K SAX(1    DAVE BIRCH       G    (1    CHRIS SPEDDING   G  (
    GREG VANCOOK       G    (C    BEN BRIERLEY  B     (C    SISTERS OF MERCY   V    (B
```
SID VICIOUS

```
    SID VICIOUS        V    (A         (A) SID VICIOUS               1979 VIRGIN            UK       V2144
```
MIKE VICKERS

```
    MIKE VICKERS            (AB        (A) I WISH I WERE A GROUP AGAIN 1968 COLUMBIA        UK       SCX  6180
    HUGH BURNS         G    (B         (B) A DAY AT THE RACES        1976 DJM               UK       DJSLM2034
    PAUL KEOGH         G    (B
    MIKE MORAN         K    (B    ALAN TARNEY        B    (B    TREVOR SPENCER    D    (B    CHRIS KARAN PERC (B
```
VICTIMS

```
    RICHARD            V HCA(A         (A) THE REAL WILD CHILD       1979 GOLDEN DISC       US        1001
    BARRY RYAN         G V  (A
    CHRIS DEY          B V  (A    M T HEART          D    (A    STEVE BERMAN       B    (A    JAMES ALEXANDER  D  (A
```
VIGRASS & OSBORNE

```
    PAUL VIGRASS       V    (AB        (A) QUEUES                    1972 UNI US 73129     UK        UDLS  501
    GARY OSBORNE       G V  (AB        (A) QUEUES                    1974 MCA              UK RI MCG 3521
    BARRY CLARKE       G MAND(B        (B) STEPPIN' OUT              1974 CBS US 33077     UK        80119
    MARK GRIFFITHS     G    (B
    PETER MORGAN       B    (B    TETSU YAMAUCHI     B    (B    PETER WATKINS      B    (B    HERBIE FLOWERS   B  (B
    BARRY DE SOUZA     D    (B    KENNEY JONES       D    (B    RAY COOPER        PERC (B    PETER WOOD       K  (B
    ALAN HAWKSHAW      K    (B    JEFF WAYNE         K    (B    DOREEN CHANTER     V   (B    IRENE CHANTER    V  (B
    JUANITA FRANKLIN   V    (B    JUDITH POWELL      V    (B    TIM RENWICK        G   (B
```
VICTORIAN PARENTS

```
    CLINTON BEALE      G V  (A         (A) SILENCE FOLLOWS           1981 POLYDOR      UK        POLS 1049
    DAVID PHIZACKLEA   B V  (A
    RAY THOMAS         D    (A    STEVE JOHNSON      G V  (A
```
GENE VINCENT

```
    GENE VINCENT       V    (ALL  BLUEJEAN BOP                        195 CAPITOL                    T764
    CLIFF GALLUP       G    (1    & THE BLUECAPS                      196 CAPITOL                    T811
    JACK NEAL          B    (1    VINCENT ROCKS,BLUECAPS ROLL         196 CAPITOL                    T970
    WILLIE WILLIAMS    G    (1    RECORD DATE                         196 CAPITOL                  T 1059
    DICKIE HARRELL     D    (12   SOUNDS LIKE                         196 CAPITOL                  T 1207
    PAUL PEEK          G    (2    CRAZY TIMES                        1960 CAPITOL                  T 1342
    TOMMY FACENDA      G    (2    CRAZY BEAT                          196 CAPITOL                    T20452
    BOBBY LEE JONES    G    (2    SHAKIN UP A STORM                   196 CAPITOL                    33SX 1646
    JOHN MEEKS         G    (*    GENE VINCENT                       1967 LONDON          UK        HAU 8333
    JIM GRANT          K    (*    BEST OF GENE VINCENT               1967 CAPITOL                    T20957
    RED RHODES         STEEL(*    BEST OF VOL 2                      1969 CAPITOL                    ST21144
                                  (*) I'M BACK & I'M PROUD           1969 DANDELION   US 102   UK  63754
    JIM GORDON         D    (*    GENE VINCENT                       1970 KAMA SUTRA    UK        2019
    MARS BONFIRE       G    (*    THE DAY THE WORLD TURNED BLUE      1971 KAMA SUTRA              2027
    SKIP BATTIN        B    (*    PIONEERS OF ROCK                   1972 STARLINE       UK   SRS  5117
                                  STORY VOL 1  1956/57               1973 PATHE          FR   064 81081
                                  STORY VOL 2     1958               1973 PATHE          FR   064 81082
    (1) 1956                      STORY VOL 3     1959               1973 PATHE          FR   064 81083
    (2) 1957                      STORY VOL 4     1960               1973 PATHE          FR   064 81084
                                  MEMORIAL ALBUM                       19 PATHE          FR   154 81001
                                  KING OF FOOLS                      1974 STARLINE       UK   SRS  5177
                                  GREATEST                             19 CAPITOL       IMP  052 80230
                                  SINGLE ALBUM                       1981 CAPITOL                 26233
                                  THE BOP THEY COULDN'T STOP         1982 MAGNUM FORCE   UK   007
                                  BOP THAT WONT STOP                 1974 CAPITOL             ST 11287
                                  GENE VINCENT STORY                 1975 CAPITOL       IMP  178 81798
                                  GREATEST                           1977 CAPITOL        UK  CAPS 1001
                                  ROCK'N'ROLL LEGEND(4LP BOXED SET)  1977 EMI           IMP  85071/4
                                  GREATEST                           1979 CAPITOL        UK  CAPS 1028
                                  BIRD DOGGIN                        1982 LINE GER  BULLDOG UK  3001
```

JAMES VINCENT

JAMES VINCENT	G	(A		(A) SPACE TRAVELLER	1977 CARIBOU	US	34237	
RONALD STOCKHERT	K	(A						
VERDINE WHITE	B	(A	HARVEY MASON D (A PATRICK M MURPHY		PERC (A			

MADS VINDING

MADS VINDING	B	(A		(A) DANISH DESIGN	1974 SONET	SLP	2560
JAN SCHAFFER	G	(A					
KJELL OHMAN	K SYN(A	OLA BRUNKERT D (A SABU MARTINEZ		CONGA (A			

V33 VINEGAR JOE

ELKIE BROOKS	V K (ABC		(A) VINEGAR JOE	1972 ISLAND UK ILPS9183 ATCO US 7007		
ROBERT PALMER	G V (ABC		(B) ROCK'N'ROLL GYPSIES	1972 ISLAND UK ILPS9214 ATCO US 7016		
PETE GAGE	K G V(ABC		(C) SIX STAR GENERAL	1973 ISLAND UK ILPS9262		
STEVE YORK	HCA B(ABC					
TIM HINKLEY	K (A	ROB TAIT D (A DAVE THOMPSON	K SAX(A DAVE BROOKS SAX (A			
CONRAD ISADORE	D (A	KEEF HARTLEY D (AB GASPAR LAWAL	PERC (A ROGER BALL HRNS(A			
MALCOLM DUNCAN	HRNS (A	JIM MULLEN G (B MIKE DEACON	K V (BC JOHN WOODS (BC			
PETE GAVIN	D (C					

V34 EDDIE 'CLEANHEAD' VINSON

EDDIE VINSON	V SAX(ALL	EDDIE CLEANHEAD VINSON	19	TRIP	US	5590
LARRY CORYELL	G (H	THE ORIGINAL CLEANHEAD	1972	PHILIPS	UK	6369 406
NEAL CREQUE	K (H	CHERRY RED BLUES	19	KING STARDAY	US	1087
CORNELL DUPREE	G (H	JAMMING THE BLUES	1975	BLACK LION		BLP 30168
CHUCK RAINEY	B (H	EDDIE VINSON	19	B&B		33021
BERNARD PURDIE	D (H	CLEANHEADS BACK IN TOWN	19	BETHLEHEM	US	BCP 5005
MIKE BLOOMFIELD	G (G	CLEAN MACHINE	1979	MUSE	FR	MR 5116
PATTI BROWN	K (G	(G)CHERRY RED	1967	BLUESWAY		6007
BUDDY LUCAS	SAX HCA(G	(H) YOU CANT MAKE LOVE ALONE	19	MEGA	US	1012
		( ) I WANT A LITTLE GIRL	1982	PABLO	UK	2310 866

V35 VIOLINSKI

MIK KAMINSKI	VLN (AB		(A) NO CAUSE FOR ALARM	1979 JET US 36133 UK JETLP 219		
JOHN MARCANGELO	K (AB		(B) STOP CLONING ABOUT	1980 JET UK JETLP 232		
JOHN HODSON	D (AB					
MIKE DE ALBUQUERQUE	G V(AB	BAZ DUNNERY G V (A PAUL MANN	V B (A ANDY BROWN B V(A			
IAIN WHITMORE	B V (B					

V35A VISAGE

STEVE STRANGE	(A		(A) VISAGE	1980 POLYDOR US 16304 UK 2490 157		
MIDGE URE	G (A		(A) VISAGE	1980 POLYDOR NL 2391 494		
BILLY CURRIE	VLN (A		(B) THE ANVIL	1982 POLYDOR UK 5060		
JOHN McGEOCH	G (A		(AB) VISAGE / THE ANVIL	1982 POLYDOR CASS UK DBMC1		
RUSTY EGAN	D (A					
DAVE FORMULA	K (A	BARRY ADAMSON B (A				

V35B FRANKIE VIRTUE & THE VIRTUES

(A) GUITAR BOOGIE SHUFFLE	1980 PRESIDENT UK PRX 16

V36 VISITOR 2035

CRAIG PRUESS	KTPT VIBES(		(A) VISITOR 2035	1978 ARIOLA	AHAL 8003
RAY DEEFHOLTS	G (		(B) CAIN (D)	19	
PETER STROUD	B (				
NIGEL ROBINSON	D PERC(				

V37 VITAL DUB

(A) WELL CHARGED	1977 VIRGIN UK V 2055

V38 JOE VITALE

JOE VITALE	D V (AB		(A) ROLLERCOASTER WEEKEND	1975 ATLANTIC US SD18114 UK K50121	
JOE WALSH	G (AB		(B) PLANTATION HABOR	1980 ASY US 529	
RICK DERRINGER	G (A				
NELSON'FLACO' PADRON PERC(A	PHIL KEAGY G (A GEORGE PERRY	B V (B RICKY WASHINGTON V (B			
WILLIE HALE	G (B	MARILYN MARTIN V (B JOEAN PERRY	V (B PAUL HARRIS K (B		
MICKEY THOMAS	V (B	JOE LALA PERC (B TIM SCHMIT	V (B DON FELDER G (B		
GREG DROMAN	V (B	BILL SZYMCZYK PROD (B BOBBY MAYO	K (B JIMMY PANKOW TROM(B		
LEE LOUGHNANE	TPT (B	WALT PARAZAIDER SAX (B MARTY GREBB	SAX (B GRAHAM NASH V (B		

V38A VITESSE

PETER VAN STRATEN	B V (E		(A) VITESSE	1975 REPRISE RI NL 54058	
HERMAN BROOD	K V (A		(B) VITESSE	1977 NEGRAM NL 25754	
PAUL BAGMEIER	B (A		(C) OUT IN THE COUNTRY	1978 EMI GER 26013	
HERMAN VAN BOEYEN	D V (ABCDEF		(D) ROCK INVADER	1979 NEGRAM NL 26378	
RON TEN BOKUM	G B V(A		(E) LIVE	1980 RCA UK 44024	
"BIG" JOHN	HCA (A		(F) GOOD NEWS	1981 RCA UK 30086	
ROB VAN DON SELAAR	K (A		(CD) VITESSE	1979 UA UK 30250	
FERRY WIENECKE	K (B				
MARGRIET	V (A	HILDE V (A RUDY DE QUELJOE	G (BCD MARK BOON G V (F		
ANDRE VERSLUYS	B V (BF	JAN VANDER MEY G V(BCDE HANRY VAN DIJK	G V (B NAPPA NOYA PERC(C		
PIM KOOPMAN	K VIBE(C	WILCO TORROE LEERDAM B V(CD JERNEY & JODY	V (C SANDER JANSSEN K (F		
FRED LEEFLANG	SAX (D	TONY DE BRUIN D (D PETER LANGERAK	G V (F JOCHEN FLUITSMA G V (F		

V39 MIROSLAV VITOUS

MIROSLAV VITOUS	B SYN G(ALL	(A) INFINITE SEARCH	1969 EMBRYO	US	SD 524
JOE ZAWINUL	PNO (B	(B) PURPLE	1970 CBS SONY	US	37181
JOE HENDERSON	SAX (AC	(C) MOUNTAIN IN THE CLOUDS	1972 ATLANTIC	UK K50406 US SD1622
BILLY COBHAM	D (D	(D) BASS =(C)	1972 ATLANTIC		30024
JOHN McLAUGHLIN	G (ABC	(E) MAGICAL SHEPHERD	1976 WB	UK K56219 US BS2925
HERBIE HANCOCK	K (ACE	(F) MIROSLAV	1978 FREEDOM	UK 41040 US 1040
JACK DE JOHNETTE	D (ACE	(G) FIRST MEETING	1980 ECM		1145
JON CHRISTENSEN	D (GH	(H) M V GROUP	1981 ECM		1185
JOE CHAMBERS	D (AC				
JAMES GADSON	D (E	AIRTO MOREIRA PERC (E CHERYL GRAINGER	V (E ONIKE V (E		
JOHN SURMAN	WIND (GH	KENNY KIRKLAND PNO (GH			

```
V39A                                 VIVA                                      V39A
    BANARA SCHENKER    K    (A        (A) WHAT THE HELL IS GOING ON    1982 CBS  GER        85372
    ANDY FACK          G    (A
    RALPH MURPHY       G    (A
V39B                               VIVABEAT                                    V39B
                                       (A) PARTY IN THE WAR ZONE    1981 CHARISMA    US    3102
V39C                                 VOG                                       V39C
    ONY KAYE           V    (A        (A) VOG                        1981 RCA        PL 28466
    RENNIE XOSA        B V  (A
    JIMI JOHALLIS      D    (A  ROBERT LEPICOLO  SYN K(A  BOBBY DIMONTE    G V  (A
V40                        VOICES OF EAST HARLEM                               V40
    BERNICE COLE       V    (         (A) RIGHT TO BE FREE      1970 ELEKTRA US 74080  UK  2469 007
    GERRI  GRIFFIN     V    (         (B) BROTHERS & SISTERS    197  ELEKTRA         UK  K42119
    CYNTHIA SESSIONS   V    (         (C) VOICES OF EAST HARLEM 1973 JUST           US  JUST 7
    JAMES MISSOURI     V    (         (D) CAN YOU FEEL IT       1974 JUST           US  JUST3504
V40A                               VOLKSMUSIC                                  V40A
    ALBRECHT METZGER   G V  (B        (A) SONGSAUS DER SCHAN    19
    WOLFGANG KALLERT   B V  (B        (B) MORGENS UM 7 ABENDS UM 8  1979 PLANE   GER
    STEFAN POPOVIC     D V  (B
    PETER SCHICK       K G V(B  HANS DIETER SUMPF G V  (B
V41                          ADELBERT VON DEYEN                                V41
    ADELBERT VON DEYEN ALL INST(AB    (A) STEMGAT               1978 SKY               SKY 019
                                      (B) MORDBORG              1979 SKY               SKY 029
                                      (C) ATMOSPHERE            1980 SKY               041
V41A                          ROGER VOUDOURIS                                  V41A
    ROGER VOUDOURIS            (ABC    (A) RADIO DREAM          1979 WB
                                       (B) A GUY LIKE ME        1980 WB
                                       (C) ON THE HEELS OF LOVE 1981 BOARDWALK   US
V42                                 VOYAGER                                    V42
    PAUL FRENCH        K V  (AB        (A) HALFWAY HOTEL        1979 MOUNTAIN UK TOPS124 US ELEKTRA 208
    PAUL HIRSH         K G V(AB        (B) ACT OF LOVE          1980 MOUNTAIN UK TOPS127 US RCA 3662
    CHRIS HOOK         B V  (AB        (C) THE WEB              1981 RCA  UK 5020
    JOHN MARTER        D    (AB
W1                               THE WACKERS                                   W1
    BOB SEGARINI       G V  (ABCD      (A) WACKERING HEIGHTS    1971 ELEKTRA    US        EKS 74098
    ANDY BISHOP V G B K    (ABCD      (B) HOT WACKS            1972 ELEKTRA    US        EKS 75025
    MICHAEL STULL      G V PNO(AB      (C) SHREDDER             1972 ELEKTRA    US        EKS 75046
    BILL KOOTCH TROCHIM V B G(ABCD     (D) WACK'N' ROLL    (NOT RELEASED)
    SPENCER T EARNSHAW     D (ABC
    BILL HENDERSON     D    (A  JACK SCHAEFFER    SAX   (AC  KATHIE KODAMA  KOTO (B   J P LAUZON    B G PNO(C
    DAN YEN MANTOR  CONGAS(C  FRANKIE HART V PERC    (C   JERRY MERCER     D  (C  RAY BLAKE        V    (C
    JANET ABRAMSON     V    (C  MARK ABRAMSON    PROD (C
W2                               WAGES OF SIN                                  W2
    TIM RENWICK        G    (A        (A) 1968
    COLIN FREEMAN           (A  PETER DINES K    (A  VIC FARRAR    (A  JERRY SHIRLEY    D(A
W3                               ADRIAN WAGNER                                 W3
    ADRIAN WAGNER      K    (ABC       (A) DISTANCES BETWEEN US 1974 ATLANTIC      UK    K50082
    JOHN CORNWALL      B    (C         (B) INSTINCTS            1977 CHARISMA      UK    CAS 1124
    MEL COLLINS        SAX  (B         (C) THE LAST INCA        1978 CHARISMA      UK    CAS 1135
    IVO HATFIELD       G    (C
    MORRIS PERT        D    (BC  BOB WESTON    G    (B  THUNDERTHIGHS    V   (B
W3A                                 WAH                                        W3A
                                      (A) NAH POO THE ART OF BLUFF  1981 ETERNAL CLASSIC1
W3B                               THE WAILERS                                  W3B
    KENT MORRILL       K    (          TALL COOL ONE           1964 IMPERIAL US 12262 UK LONDON
    MARK MARUSH        SAX  (          FABULOUS WAILERS AT THE CASTLE  19  ETIQUETTE US ALB1
    RICK DANGEL        G    (          WAILERS WAILERS EVERYWHERE   19  ETIQUETTE US ALB23
    BUCK ORMSBY        B    (          WAILERS & COMPANY        19  ETIQUETTE US ALB22
    MIKE BURK          D    (          OUT OF OUR TREE          19  ETIQUETTE US ALB26
    GAIL HARRIS        V    (          OUTBURST                 19  UA        US 6557
    ROBIN ROBERTS      V    (          WAILERS                  19  GOLDEN CREST US 3075
                                       WALK THRU' THE PEOPLE    1967 BELL       US 6016
W4                               BUNNY WAILER                                  W4
    BUNNY WAILER       V    (ABC       (A) BLACK HEART MAN      1976 ISLAND        uk    ILPS 9415
    CARLTON BARRETT    D    (A         (B) PROTEST              1977 ISLAND        UK    ILPS 9512
    ASTON BARRETT      G    (A         (C) SINGS THE WAILERS    1981 ISLAND        UK    ILPS 9629
    HEADLEY BENNETT    HRNS (C         (D) ROCK'N' GROOVE       1981 SOLOMONIC     IMP
    ROBBY SHAKESPEARE  B    (ABC
    TYRONE DOWNIE      K    (A  TOMMY McCOOK      FLT  (AB  PETER TOSH    G   (AB  WINSTON WRIGHT  K  (AC
    DIRTY HARRY      HRNS (AB  BOBBY ELLIS    HRNS (AB  HERMAN MARQUIS  HRNS (AB  WILLY PEP      PERC(A
    HAROLD BUTLER      K    (A  EARL CHINNA SMITH G  (AC  FRATTER       G   (A  HORSE MOUTH     D  (B
    MIKE RICHARDS      D    (A  EARL LINDO       K    (B  TOUTER        K   (B  KEITH STERLING  K  (BC
    SOLOMONIC ENCHANTERS V  (B  STICKY          PERC (C  DEAN FRASER    HRNS (C  NAMBO          HRNS(C
    SLY DUNBAR         D    (C
W4A                              WAILING SOULS                                 W4A
    WINSTON'PIPE'MATTHEWS V(AB     (A) WILD SUSPENSE        1979 ISLAND        UK    ILPS 9523
    LLOYD McDONALD     V    (AB        (B) FIREHOUSE ROCK      1981 GREENSLEEVES   UK    GREL 21
    HEADLEY BENNETT    SAX  (A
    RAD BRYAN          G    (AB  ANSELL COLLINS K   (A  GEORGE HAYE    V    (AB  TARZAN NELSON  PNO (A
    RUDOLPH DENNIS     V    (AB  NOEL SLY DUNBAR D   (A  RANCHIE McLEAN  B   (A  VIN GORDON     TROM(A
    STICKY THOMPSON  PERC (A  RICO             TROM (A  CEDRIC BROOKS  SAX  (A  NOEL SIMMS     PERC(A
    ROBBIE SHAKESPEARE G    (A  BOPEE BOWEN      G    (A  DICKAGE       HRNS (A
```

LOUDON WAINWRIGHT III

```
LOUDON WAINWRIGHT II  G V(ALL    (A) ALBUM 1                        1971 ATLANTIC  US SD8260 UK  2400 103
RICHARD CROOKS       D (CEFG      (A) ALBUM 1                        1971 ATLANTIC            UK  K40107
JOHN CROWDER         B    (FG     (B) ALBUM 2                        1972 ATLANTIC  US SD8291 UK  K40272
STEPHEN TUBIN        K    (FG     (C) ALBUM 3                        1972 CBS       US  31462 UK  65238
RON GETMAN   STEEL G  (FG         (D) ATTEMPTED MOUSTACHE            1974 CBS       US  32710 UK  65837
JIMMY MAELEN         CONGA(F      (E) UNREQUITED                     1975 CBS       US  33369 UK  80696
ELLIOTT RANDALL      G    (F      (F) T SHIRT                        1976 ARISTA    US  4063  UK  ARTY 127
JOANNE VENT          V    (F      (G) FINAL EXAM                     1978 ARISTA    US  4173  UK  SPART1042
GWYNNE MICHAELS      V    (F      (H) LIVE ONE                       1979 ROUNDER US 3050 RADAR UK RAD 24
ERIN ARNOLD DICKINS       (F
JEAN ARNOLD          V    (F  CHRISTIE THOMPSON V   (F  JON COBERT        V    (F  GEORGE MARGE       REC (F
MARVIN STAMM         HRNS (F  HANK JONES        K   (F  MARKIE MARKOWITZ  HRNS (F  RICHARD DAVIS      B   (F
JOE COCUZZO          D    (F  PETER LA BARBERA VIBES(F  MAGGIE ROCHE      V    (F  TERRE ROCHE        V   (F
ERIC WEISSBERG       BANJO(FG CHARLES BROWN III G  (CF  KENNETH KOSEK     FDL  (CFG GLEN MITCHELL     K V (FG
DAVID SANBORN        SAX  (CF PAUL PRESTOPINO      (F  DAVE TAYLOR        TROM (F  JOHN LISSAUER      CLAR(FG
DON HAMMOND          REF  (F  HARVEY ESTRIN     REC (F  JOHN HALL         G    (EG ARLEN ROTH         G   (G
HUGH McCRACKEN       G    (G  LARRY PACKER      FDL (G  ERROL BENNETT     PERC (G  TEDDY WENDER       PNO (C
GREG THOMAS          D    (E  RON COLBERTSON       (E  HARVEY BROOKS     B    (E  KLAUS VOORMANN     D   (E
LYLE RITZ            B    (E  RICHARD GREENE    VLN (E  MARTIN FIERRO     SAX  (E  ANNA McGARRIGLE    V   (E
THOMAS JEFFERSON KAYE G(C DON PAYNE          B   (E  CALVIN HARDY          (E  FRANK KLEIGER          (E
RANDY WALLACE            (E  MARTY GREBB       K   (E  CHRIS GUEST           (E  GEORGE GERDES          (E
JIM KELTNER          D    (E  JAY MIGLIORI     WIND (E  AUSTIN DELONE         (E  KATE McGARRIGLE    V (E
```

JOHN WAITE

```
JOHN WAITE           V    (A      (A) IGNITION                      1982 CHRYSALIS  UK  CHR 1376
IVAN KRAL            G K  (A
DONNIE NOSSOV        B V  (A  TIM PIERCE        G   (A  FRANKIE LA ROCKA  D    (A  CRISPIN CIOE       HRNS(A
ARNO HECHT           HRNS (A  PAUL LITTERAL    HRNS (A  PATTY SMYTH       V    (A  RAHNI KUGEL    V   (A
ILANA MORRILLO       V    (A  BRUCE BRODY  K       (A
```

THE WAITRESSES

```
PATTY DONAHUE        V    (A      (A) WASN'T TOMORROW WONDERFUL      1982 polydor    us  6346
ARIEL WARNER         V    (A
MARS WILLIAMS        WIND (A  DAVID HOFSTRA     B   (A  BILLY FICCA       D    (A  DAN KLAYMAN K      (A
CHRIS BUTLER         G    (A  TRACY WORMWORTH   B   (A  DON CHRISTENSEN   D    (A  RALPH CARNEY       SAX HCA(A
STUART AUSTIN        D    (A  RICK DAILEY       K   (A
```

TOM WAITS

```
TOM WAITS            G V  (ALL    (A) CLOSING TIME                  1973 ELEKTRA US SD5061 UK SYL 9007
MIKE MELVOIN         K    (C      (A) CLOSING TIME                  1976 ELEKTRA            UK  K53030
PETE CHRISTLIEB      SAX  (C      (B) HEART OF A SATURDAY NIGHT     1974 ASYLUM  US 7E1015 UK  K53035
JIM HUGHART          B    (CFGD   (C) NIGHTHAWKS AT THE DINER       1975 ASYLUM  US 7E2008 UK  SYSP 903
SHELLEY MANNE        D    (CD     (C) NIGHTHAWKS AT THE DINER       1976 ASYLUM            UK  K63002
LEW TABACKIN         SAX  (CD     (D) SMALL CHANGE                  1976 ASYLUM  US 7E1078 UK  K53050
DA WILLIE GONGA      K    (F      (E) FOREIGN AFFAIRS               1977 ELEKTRA US 7E1117 UK  K53068
RICK LAWSON          D    (F      (F) BLUE VALENTINE                1978 ASYLUM  US 6E 162 UK  K53088
ROLAND BAUTISTA      G    (FG     (G) HEART ATTACK & VINE           1980 ASYLUM  US 6E 295 UK  K52252
BYRON MILLER         B    (F      (1) TV SHOW ENGLAND 1979
FRANK VICARI         SAX  (F
RAY CRAWFORD         G    (F  CHARLES KYNARD    B   (F  CHIP WHITE        D    (F  BOBBYE HALL        PERC (F
HAROLD BATTISTE      PNO  (F  SHINE ROBINSON    G   (F  SCOTT EDWARDS     B    (F  EARL PALMER        D   (F
BIG JOHN THOMASSIE   D    (G  PLAS JOHNSON     SAX  (G  GREG COHEN        B    (G  RONNIE BARRON      K   (G
VICTOR FELDMAN       PERC (G  MICHAEL LANG     PNO  (G  MEL COLLINS       SAX  (1  TIM HINKLEY        K   (1
CLEM CLEMPSON        G    (G  HERBERT HARDESTY SAX  (F  BILL GOODWIN      D    (C  BONES HOWE         PROD   (BD
DELBERT BENNETT      TPT  (A  SHEP COOKE        G V (A  ARNI EGILSSON     B    (A  JESSE EHRLICH      CELLO(AD
```

JOHNNY WAKELIN

```
JOHNNY WAKELIN       V    (ALL    (A) REGGAE SOUL & ROCK'N'ROLL     1976 PYE  US 12131 UK  NSPL 18521
                                  (B) AFRICAN MAN                   1977 PYE            UK  NSPL 18487
                                  (C) DOUBLE TROUBLE                1978 PYE            UK  NSPL 18561
                                  (D) GOLDEN HOUR                   1979 PYE            UK  GH 680
```

RICK WAKEMAN

```
RICK WAKEMAN         K PROD(ALL   (1) PIANO VIBRATIONS              1971 POLYDOR     UK  2460 135
TIM RICE             V    (K      (A) 6 WIVES OF HENRY VIII         1973 A&M  US 4361   UK  AMLH64361
DAVE WINTOUR         B    (A      (B) JOURNEY TO THE CENTRE OF EARTH 1974 A&M US 3621   UK  AMLH63621
CHRIS SQUIRE         B    (AG     (C) KING ARTHUR                   1975 A&M  US 4515   UK  AMLH64515
CHAS CRONK           B    (A      (D) LISZTOMANIA                   1975 A&M  US 4546   UK  AMLK64546
LES HURDLE           B    (A      (E) NO EARTHLY CONNECTION         1976 A&M  US 4583   UK  AMLK64583
MIKE EGAN            G    (AGB    (F) WHITE ROCK                    1976 A&M  US 4614   UK  AMLH64614
DAVE LAMBERT         G    (A      (G) CRIMINAL RECORD               1977 A&M  US 4660   UK  AMLK64660
STEVE HOWE           G    (A      (H) BEST KNOWN WORKS              1978 A&M            UK  AMLH68447
ALAN WHITE           D    (AG     (J) RHAPSODIES                    1979 A&M  US 6501   UK  AMLX68508#
BILL BRUFORD         D    (A      (K) 1984                          1981 CHARISMA      UK  CDS 4022
TONY VISCONTI        G    (J      (L) THE BURNING                   19
BARRY DE SOUZA       D    (A
RAY COOPER           PERC (A  DAVID HEMMINGS    V   (B  FRANK RICOTTI    PERC (AGK DAVE COUSINS      BANJO (A
LISA STRIKE          V    (A  LAURA LEE         V   (A  BARRY ST JOHN     V   (A  SYLVIA McNEILL     V   (A
JUDY POWELL          V    (A  ASHLEY HOLT       V   (BCE GARY PICKFORD HOPKINS V (BC JEFF CRAMPTON    G   (C
ROGER NEWELL         B    (BCE BARNEY JAMES     D   (BC  JOHN HODGSON    PERC (C  JOHN DUNSTERVILLE  G V(E
TONY FERNANDEZ       D    (EFK MARTY SHIELD HRNS V  (E  REG BROOKS       HRNS V(E  BILL ODDIE        V   (B
ARS LAETA CHOIR      V    (B  ROGER DALTREY     V   (D  PAUL NICHOLAS     V   (D  LINDA LEWIS        V   (D
DAVID WILDE          PNO  (D  GEORGE MICHIE         (D  JOHN FORSYTHE         (D  ENG ROCK ENSEMBLE  V   (D
NAT PHILHARMONIC ORCH    (D  BRUCE LYNCH       B   (J  FRANK GIBSON      D    (J  NICO RAMSDEN       G   (J
STEVE BARNACLE       B    (K  TIM STONE         G   (K  VICKIE BROWN      V    (K  STEVIE LANGE       V (K
KEVIN KELLY          B    (L  MIKE GAREAU       D   (L  RONNIE LAWSON     K    (L  BRIAN MATHEWS     V  (L
CHAKA KHAN           V    (K  STEVE HARLEY      V   (K  JON ANDERSON      V    (K  KENNY LYNCH        V    (K
SONIA JONES          V    (K  GARRY BARNACLE   SAX  (K  ALAN BRAWER       G    (L  MIKE BRAUN         D  (L
ARLEN ROTH           G    (L  LIBERTY DEVITTO   D   (L  LONDON SYMP ORCHESTRA  (B  ENGLISH CHAMBER CHOIR(B
```

NARADA MICHAEL WALDEN

```
NARADA MICHAEL WALDEN D V(ALL     (A) GARDEN OF LOVE LIGHT        1977 ATLANTIC  US 18199  UK        K50329
JEFF BECK            G    (A                (B) I CRY, I SMILE            1978 ATLANTIC            UK        K50417
RAY GOMEZ            G    (AB               (C) AWAKENING                 1979 ATLANTIC  US SD19222 UK       K50570
T M STEVENS          B    (D                (D) THE DANCE OF LIFE         1979 ATLANTIC            UK        K50678
CARLOS SANTANA       G    (AC               (E) VICTORY                   1980 ATLANTIC  US SD19279 UK       K50473
HIRAM BULLOCK        G    (BC
NEIL JASON     B   (B    CLIFF CARTER     K   (BC   HERBIE MANN         SAX  (B    NORMA JEAN BELL    SAX  (AB
SAMMY FIGUEROA PERC (AB   RAFAEL CRUZ      PERC (B   CHRISTINE FAITH     V    (B    ELLEN DELESTON     V    (B
CHERYL ALEXANDER V (BC    WILL LEE         B   (A    DAVID SANCIOUS      K    (A    CISSY HOUSTON      B V  (A
PATTY SCALFA    V  (AC    BOB KNAPP        HRNS (A   ICARUS JOHNSON      G    (A    DON MERO           SYN  (A
LOIS COLIN      HARP (A   JAY GRAYDON      G   (C    PAT THRALL          G    (C    KENNY MAZUR        G    (C
KENI BURKE      B  (C     NATE PHILLIPS    B   (C    NORBERT SCOLEY      B    (C    GREG PHILLINGANES  K    (C
BOBBY LYLE      K  (C     MICHAEL BRECKER  HRNS (C   RANDY BRECKER       HRNS (C    AIRTO MOREIRA      PERC (C
POINTER SISTERS V  (C     JIM GILSTRAP     V   (CD   CARLA VAUGHN        V    (CD   ALEX BROWN         V    (C
ANGELA WINBUSH  V  (C     BILL LAMB        TPT (E    TAWATHA AGEE        V    (C    CORRADO RUSTICI    G V  (DE
RANDY JACKSON   B  (C     FRANK MARTIN     K   (DE   MARC RUSSO          SAX  (DE   DAVID GROVER       TPT  (D
WAYNE WALLACE   TROM (C   DANNY NOE        TROM       VICKI RANDLE       V    (D    NUHAD SABA MARTIN  V    (D
```

WENDY WALDMAN

```
WENDY WALDMAN V PNO G DULC(ALL    (A) LOVE HAS GOT ME            1973 WB              US BS 2735
DAVID KEMPER         D    (D                (B) GYPSY SYMPHONY             1974 WB              US BS 2792
KENNY EDWARDS        B G V(ABCD             (C) WENDY WALDMAN              1975 WB              US BS 2859
ANDREW GOLD   G V PNO (ABCD                 (D) THE MAIN REFRAIN           1976 WB              US BS 2974
WADDY WACHTEL        G    (BCD              (E) STRANGE COMPANY            1978 WB              US BS 3178
EMIL RICHARDS        PERC (C                (F) WHICH WAY TO MAIN STREET   1982 EPIC            US
LINDA RONSTADT       V    (D
MICHAEL BOTTS   D  (D     KARLA BONOFF     V   (ABCD NICK DE CARO       ACC  (D    PETER BERNSTEIN    B    (DE
DAVID FOSTER    K  (CD    STEVE CROPPER    G   (D    KING ERRISSON      PERC (D    TAJ MAHAL          V    (D
JIM HORN        WIND (ABD MILT HOLLAND     CONGA(D   VICTOR FELDMAN     PERC (AD   STEVE FERGUSON K G V(ACD
JAI WINDING     ORG (D    CHUCK FINDLEY    HRNS (ABD DON MENZA          HRNS (ABD  JAY MIGLIORI       HRNS(D
STEVE BEERS     D  (E     MARK GOLDENBERG G PNO G V(E CRAIG HULL        G V  (E    DEBBIE DOBKIN    V PERC(E
KAT HENDRIKSE   D  (E     PETER ROBINSON   PNO (A    PETER WHITE        K    (E    JENNIFER WARREN    V    (C
RON TUTT        D  (C     RUSS KUNKEL      D   (A    JOHN JOSEPH KELSON HRNS (A    JOE PORCARO        PERC(A
BOBBYE HALL     PERC (A   MARIA MULDAUR    V   (AB   KAREN ALEXANDER    V    (A    PETER IVERS        HCA (A
BARRY BECKETT   K SYN(B   ROGER HAWKINS    D   (A    JIMMY JOHNSON      G    (B    THOMAS ROADY       PERC(B
JOEL TEPP       HCA (A    GENE GARFIN      D   (A    LARRY BUNKER       VIBES(A    LEE SKLAR          B   (A
STEPEN PAIETLA  ACC (A    FRED STREINER    STR (A    CARMI SIMON    MAND G (AB     GREG PRESTOPINO    V   (AB
DAVID CAMPBELL  STR (A    PETE CARR        G   (B    DAVID HOOD         B    (B    JERRY MASTERS      B   (B
PAUL HUBINON    HRNS (B
```

WALDORF & TRAVERS

```
M WALDORF            V    (A                (A) NIGHT BLINDNESS            19   UA   UK     UAG30234
G TRAVERS            V    (A
HENRY SPINETTI  B   (A    DAVE MARKEE      B   (A    LAWRENCE JUBER     G    (A    PHIL PALMER G      (A
BILLY LIVSEY    K   (A    SIMON MORTON PERC    (A    PETER HOPE EVANS HCA    (A    STAN SULZMANN      HRNS(A
KENNY WHELLER   HRNS (A   RAY WARLIEGH HRNS    (A
```

WALES /O'REGAN

```
ERIC WALES     V G MAND K(A       (A) READY TO RUN             1977 MOUNTAIN        UK        TOPC5010
JERRY O'REGAN        G V  (A
JEFF ALLEN      V   (A    BARRY DE SOUZA   D   (A    ALLAN MAIR         D    (A    PETE ZORN          B   (A
ROGER SUTTON    B   (A    DAVE MARKEE      B   (A    RICHARD BRUNTON    G    (A    DAVE ROSE          K   (A
GEOFF WESTLEY   K   (A    B J COLE         STEEL(A   TONY COLE          WIND (A    STAN SULZMANN      HRNS(A
RON ASPERY      HRNS (A   JACK EMBLOW      ACC (A    VICKY BROWN        V    (A    LIZA STRIKE        V   (A
BARRY ST JOHN   V   (A    IRENE CHANTER    V   (A    ANNE CULLEN        V    (A
```

DAVID T WALKER

```
DAVID T WALKER       G    (AB               (A) DAVID T WALKER           1973 ODE             US    SP  77011
JOE SAMPLE           K    (A                (B) PRESS ON                 1974 ODE             US    SP  77020
JOHN LEHMAN          V    (A                (C) SIDEWALK                 19   REVUE           US    RS  7297
JERRY PETERS         K    (A                (D) PLUMM HAPPY              19   ZEA                   1000
BILLY PRESTON        K    (A                (E) ON LOVE                  1976 ODE             US    SP  77035
CLARENCE McDONALD    K    (A
PAUL HUMPHREY   D   (A    WILTON FELDER    B   (A    JIM GILSTRAP       V    (A    STEPHANIE SPRUILL  V    (A
BOBBYE HALL     PERC (A   CURTIS AMY       SAX (A    MERRY CLAYTON      V    (A    PATRICE HOLLOWAY V  (A
ANN ESTHER DAVIS V   (A
```

JERRY JEFF WALKER

```
JERRY JEFF WALKER G V (ALL        (A) MR BOJANGLES             1968 ATCO            US      33259
DAVID BROMBERG       G    (ABE              (B) DRIFTIN' WAY OF LIFE       1969 VANGUARD        US  VSD 6521
GARY ILLINGSWORTH K       (A                (C) FIVE YEARS GONE            1969 ATCO            US      33297
DONNY BROOKS         HARP (A                (D) BEIN' FREE                 1970 ATCO            US      33336
DANNY MILTON         DOBRO(A                (E) JERRY JEFF WALKER          1972 MCA  US  510    RI 1976  2358
JODY STECHER    FDL MAND(A                  (E) JERRY JEFF WLAKER          1973 MCA  UK MUPS 488 RI 1974 MCF 2518
BOBBY CRANSHAW       B    (A                (E) JERRY JEFF WALKER          1973 DECCA          US      75384
JERRY JEMMOTT        V    (A                (F) VIVA TERLINGUA             1973 MCA  US  382    RI 76  2350
RON CARTER           B    (A                (F) VIVA TERLINGUA             1973 MCA  UK MAPS7164
BILL LAVORGNA        D    (A                (G) WALKERS COLLECTIBLES       1974 MCA  US  450    RI 76  2355
KENNETH BUTTREY      D    (BIJ              (G) WALKERS COLLECTIBLES       1974 MCA  UK                MCF 2592
NORBERT PUTNAM       B    (BIJ              (H) RIDIN' HIGH                1975 MCA  US                2156
PETE WADE            DOBRO(B                (I) ITS A GOOD NIGHT FOR SINGING 1976 MCA US 2202   UK MCG 3522
HAROLD RUGG          STEEL(B                (J) A MAN MUST CARRY ON (DBL)  1977 MCA  US 2 8013  UK MCSP 281
WAYNE MOSS           G    (B                (K) CONTRARY TO ORDINARY       1978 MCA  US 3041    UK MCF 2851
DAVID BRIGGS         K    (BIJ              (L) JERRY JEFF                 1978 ELEKTRA US 6E163 UK    K52106
PATTERSON BARRETT    STEEL(EJ               (M) TOO OLD TO CHANGE          1979 ELEKTRA US 6E239
BEN CARUSO           B    (E                (N) BEST OF                   1980 MCA  US      5128
RAY WYLIE HUBBARD    V    (J                (O) REUNION                   1981 MCA  US      5199
WILLIE NELSON        G V  (J
DAVID COOK      STEEL(E   JEFF DUFINE      PNO (E    MARY EGAN           VLN  (EF   CRAIG HILLIS       G   (EF
ELLEN KEARNEY   V   (E    BOB LIVINGSTON K B V(EFHIJL RAUN MACKINNON    PNO  (E    MICHAEL McGARRY    D   (E
MICHAEL MURPHEY G   (E    ANDY NEWMARK     D   (E    GARY P NUNN       K V (EFHIJ   LARRY PACKER     G VLN(E
MICKEY RAPHAEL  HARP (EF  JIM RICHMOND     D   (E    JONATHAN SIMMONS   MAND (E    HERB STEINER       STEEL(EFJ
JOANNE VENT     V   (EF   KELLY DUNN       ORG (FHIJ JOHN INMON         G V  (HIJ  TOMAS RAMIREZ      WIND(HJLM
DONNY DOLAN     D   (HIJ  WELDON MYRICK    STEEL(IJ  JOHNNY GIMBLE      FDL  (IM   CHIP YOUNG         G V (I
```

(CONTINUED)

JERRY JEFF WALKER

BOBBY THOMPSON	BAN (I	SHANE KEISTER	K (I	DEBORAH ALLEN	V (I	REESE WYNANS	K (I
BOBBY RAMBO	G B V(JLM	RON COBB	SAX (JLM	LEO LEBLANC	STEEL(JLM	FRED KRC	D PERC V(JLM
DAVE PERKINS	G (JLM	KEITH SYKES	G (L	PENNY NEY	V (L	STEVE ZIRKEL	HRNS(L
MICHAEL MORDECAI	HRNS (LM	CAROLE KING	V (M	RICHARD PRICE	B (M	MARK HALLMAN	D (M
DAVID AMRAM	HRNS (M	FINGERS TAYLOR	HCA (M	GEORGE M JONES	PERC (M	STEVE KEITH	FDL (J
KAREN BROOKS	V (J	SHARI NEUWELL	V (J	VASSAR CLEMENTS	FDL (J	BEE SPEARS	B (J
DON McCLURE	K (J	SUSAN WALKER	V (J	HONDO CROUCH	V (J	CHARLES JOHN QUATRO	V(J
BILL JOOR	(J	JIMMY BAKER	TROM (J				

JOHNNY' BIG MOOSE' WALKER

JOHNNY WALKER	K (A	(A) RAMBLIN WOMAN	1969	ABC BLUESWAY	US	6036

JUNIOR WALKER & THE ALL STARS

JUNIOR WALKER	SAX V(	SHOTGUN	1965	TAMLA UK STML11017	US SOUL	701
WILLIE WOODS	G (	SOUL SESSION	1966	TAMLA UK STML11029	US SOUL	702
VIC THOMAS	K (	ROADRUNNER	1966	TAMLA UK STML11038	US SOUL	703
		LIVE	196	TAMLA UK STML11152	US SOUL	705
JAMES GRAVES	D (	HOME COOKIN'	196	TAMLA UK STML11097	US SOUL	710
		GREATEST HITS	196	TAMLA UK STML11120	US SOUL	718
		WHAT DOES IT TAKE TO WIN YOUR LOVE	196		US SOUL	721
		A GASSSS	1970	TAMLA UK STML11167	US SOUL	726
		LIVE	1970		US SOUL	725
		RAINBOW FUNK	1971	TAMLA UK STML11198	US SOUL	732
		MOODY JUNIOR	1972	TAMLA UK STML11211	US SOUL	733
		PEACE & UNDERSTANDING	1973	TAMLA UK STML11234	US SOUL	738
		GREATEST HITS VOL 2	1973	TAMLA UK STML11224		
		ANTHOLOGY	1974	TAMLA UK TMSP 1129	US	M2 786
		JR WALKER & THE ALL STARS	1974	TAMLA UK STML11274		
		HOT SHOT	1976	TAMLA UK STML12018	US SOUL	745
		SAX APPEAL	1976	TAMLA UK STML12033	US SOUL	747
		WHOPPER BOPPER SHOW STOPPER	1976	TAMLA UK STML12048	US SOUL	748
		MOTOWN SPECIAL	1977	TAMLA UK STMX 6005		
		20 SUPER HITS	1978	EMI EURO 062 60061		
		SMOOTH SOUL	1978	TAMLA UK STML12089	US SOUL	750
		BACK STREET BOOGIE	1979	WHITFIELD US 3331		

PHILLIP WALKER

PHILLIP WALKER	G V (AB	(A) SOMEDAY YOU'LL HAVE THESE BLUES	1980	SONET UK SNTF831	US ALIGATOR 4715
AL BRUNO	G (A	(B) BLUES SHOW LIVE AT PIT INN	1980	YUPITERU	JAP YR 23 4002
BILL MURRAY	K (A	( ) THE BOTTOM OF THE TOP	1975	PLAYBOY	US 118
JUNSHI YAMAGISHI	G (B				
DENNIS WALKER	B (AB	FREDDIE LEWIS	D (A	AL DEVILLE	TPT (A	ARCHIE FRANCIS D (A
VICTOR HILL	D (A	DAVID II	HRNS (A	JOHNNY BANKS	ORG (A	AARON TUCKER D (A
MILTON THOMAS	PERC (A	GEORGE SMITH	HCA (B	JOHNNY TUCKER	D (B	MITSUYOSHI AZUMA G (B

T BONE WALKER

T BONE WALKER	G V (ALL	T B WALKER	196	CAPITOL	T 1958
MIKE OMARTIAN	K (V	THE TRUTH	1968	BRUNSWICK US	754126
CHARLES BROWN	K (V	THE TRUTH	1968	MCA UK MUPS331	RIMCF2617
JAMES BOOKER	K (V	STORMY MONDAY BLUES	1968	STATESIDE UK	SSL 10223
MAX BENNETT	B (V	STORMY MONDAY	1973	BLUESWAY	BLS 6008
PAUL HUMPHREY	D (V	STORMY MONDAY	197	WET SOUL US	1002
BEN BENAY	G HCA(V	STORMY MONDAY BLUES	1978	CHARLY UK	CR 30144
RICHARD BENNETT	G (V	FUNKY TOWN	1969	STATESIDE UK	SSL 10265
JERRY LACROIX	HCA (V	FUNKY TOWN	1973	BLUESWAY	BLS 6014
DAVID FATHEAD NEWMAN	SAX(V	WELL DONE	19	HOME COOKING US	HCS103
MIKE STOLLER	K (V	DIRTY MISTREATER	1973	BLUESWAY	BLS 6058
JOE OSBORN	B V	(I) I WANT A LITTLE GIRL	1973	DELMARK US	DS 633
DEAN PARKS	G (V	FEELIN' THE BLUES	197	B & B	33019
SWEET INSPIRATIONS	V (V	(V) VERY RARE	1974	WB UK	K94001
DIZZY GILLESPIE	TPT (V	(T) T BONE BLUES	1975	ATLANTIC UK K40131	US SD8256
JON FADDIS	TPT (V	SINGING THE BLUES	197		
TONY STUDD	TROM (V	CLASSICS OF MODERN BLUES	1976	BLUENOTE	BLAD 533
ZOOT SIMS	SAX (V	JUMPS AGAIN	1980	CHARLY UK	CRB 1019
HERBIE MANN	FLT (V	FLY WALKER AIRWAYS	1974	POLYDOR US 5521	
WARREN BERNHARDT	K (V	EVERYDAY I HAVE THE BLUES	19	BLUESTIME US	9004
LOUIE SHELTON	G (V	GOOD FELLING	19	POLYDOR	24 4502
KING ERRISSON	CONGA(V				
JOHN TROPEA	SITAR(V	WILTON FELDER	B (V	LARRY CARLTON	G (V	AL COHN SAX(V
DAVID T WALKER	G (V	GERRY MULLIGAN	SAX (V	JERRY DODGION	WIND (V	JOE FARRELL WIND (V
FRANK VICARI	WIND (V	GARNETT BROWN	TROM (V	PAUL FAULISE	TROM (V	SELDON POWELL WIND(V
MARVIN STAMM	TPT (V	DANNY STILES	TPT (V	MIKE GIBSON	TROM (V	R S RANKIN G (T
BARNEY KESSEL	G (T	PLAS JOHNSON	SAX (V	JOE COMFORT	B (T	LLOYD GLENN PNO (T
OSCAR BRADLEY	D (T	GEORGES ARVANITAS	PNO (I	S P LEARY	D (I	RAY JOHNSON PNO (T
EARL PALMER	D (T	BILLY HADNOTT	B (T	HAL SINGER	SAX (I	JACKIE SAMSON B (I
JIM GORDON	D (V				

WALKER BROTHERS

JOHN MAUS WALKER	G VV (ALL	(A) THE WALKER BROTHERS	1965	STAR CLUB	158 026 STY
SCOTT ENGEL	V G K(ALL	(B) PORTRAIT	1966	STAR CLUB	158 028 STY
GARY LEEDS	V D (ALL	(B) PORTRAIT	1966	PHILIPS	BL 7732
STEVE GREY	K G (FJ	(C) IMAGES	1967	STAR CLUB GER 158 032	
CHRIS MERCER	SAX (K	(C) IMAGES	1967	PHILIPS	
DAVE McRAE	K (FJK	(D) STORY (COMP)	1967	PHILIPS 843476/7	6640 001
BARRY MORGAN	D (FJ	(E) MAKE IT EASY ON YOURSELF	1972	PHILIPS UK	6336 214
RONNIE ROSS	SAX (K	(E) MAKE IT EASY ON YOURSELF	19	CONTOUR RI	CN 2017
DOUG WRIGHT	D (F	(F) NO REGRETS	1975	GTO	GTLP 007
CHRIS KARAN	PERC (F	(G) GREATEST HITS	1975	PHILIPS	6640 009
ALAN PARKER	G (FJ	(H) IMMORTAL	1970	PHILIPS	6870 564
RITCHIE HITCHCOCK	G (F	(J) LINES	1976	GTO	6321 114
JUDD PROCTOR	G (F	(K) NITE FLIGHTS	1978	GTO	GTLP 033
LEN WALKER	G (F	( ) TAKE IT EASY ON YOURSELF	1965	PHILIPS UK	SBL 7691
B J COLE	STEEL(F	( ) SPOTLIGHT ON	1979	PHILIPS UK	6640 013
BRIAN ODGERS	B (F	( ) SUN AINT GONNA SHINE	1966	SMASH US	27082
BRIAN BENNETT	D (J				

(CONTINUED)

WALKER BROTHERS (CONTINUED) W13A

```
MORRIS PERT      PERC (K
SIMON PHILLIPS   D    (J   ALAN JONES    B   (J   JOHN MEALING       G   (J   PAUL KEOGH  G       (J
ALAN SKIDMORE    WIND (JK  JEFF DALY     WIND (J   DAVE WILUS         WIND (J   TRISTAN FRY         PERC (J
LES DAVIDSON     G    (K   JIM SULLIVAN  G   (K   PETER VAN HOOKE    D   (K   MO FOSTER   B       (K
FRANK GIBSON     D    (K   DILL KATZ     B   (K   ROGER CHURCHYARD   VLN (J
```

W13B WALL W13B

```
KELLY         V   (A        (A) BEACHEAD                          19   FRESH           UK      FLP 2
NICK WARD     G   (A        (B) PERSONAL TROUBLES & PUBLIC ISSUES 1980 FRESH                   LP 2
ANDY GRIFFITHS B  (A        (EP) GHETTO                           1980 FRESH                   FRESH 17
RAB RAE BEITH D   (A
PETE WILSON   K G (A
```

W13C ALWYN WALL BAND W13C

```
ALWYN WALL     G V (A       (A) THE PRIZE                         1977 MYRRH                   MYR  1057
NORMAN BARRETT G V (A
PHIL HOLMES    K V (A   TONY HUDSON    B    (A  NICK BROTHERWOOD   D   (A
```

W13D WALLENSTEIN W13D

```
BILL BARONE      G V (ABCD     (A) BLITZKRIEG              1971 BASF                    20 290646
HARALD GROSSKOPF D   (ABC      (B) MOTHER UNIVERSE         1972 BASF                    20 291138
JURGEN DOLLASE   K V (ALL      (C) COSMIC CENTURY          19   OHR                     KM 58 006
JERRY BERKERS    B V (AB       (D) STORIES SONGS & SYMPHONIES 19 OHR                    KM 58 014
JURGEN PLUTA     B PERC(DE     (E) NO MORE LOVE            1977 RCA                     PL  30010
JOACHIM REISER   VLN (CD       (F) CHARLINE               1978 RCA                     PL  30045
NICKY GEBHARD    D   (E        (G) BLUE EYED BOYS          1979 RCA                     PL  30061
GERD KLOCKER     G V (E        (H) FRAULEINS               1980 RCA       EURO          064 45932
DIETER MEIER     B   (C
ROLF DOLLASE     FLT (C   KIM MERZ     V    (FGH PETE BROUGH    G   (FGH MICHAEL DOMMERS    G(FGH
CHARLY TERSTAPPEN D  (FGH TERRY PARK   B    (FGH
```

W13E WALKIE TALKIES W13E

```
TONY BEARD    D    (A        (A) SURVEILLANCE                    1980 RIALTO UK 101 US 44059
ROB SPENSLEY  B V  (A
DAVE FULLER   G V  (A   ALAN MURPHY   G   (A   DAVE STEWART    K   (A   KEITH GEMMELL WIND (A
TONY MARONIE  BONGO(A   KIM BEACON    V   (A
```

W13F WALLACE COLLECTION W13F

```
RAYMOND VINCENT  VLN (AB       (A) FIRST COLLECTION        19   PARLOPHONE UK 7076
CHRISTIAN JANSEN B   (A        (B) WALLACE COLLECTION      1070 PARLOPHONE UK 7099 US CAPITOL 350
JACQUES NAMOTTE  CELLO(B
MARC HEROVETT    K   (B   SYLVAIN VAN HOLMAN G  (B  FREDDY NIEULAND    D V (B
```

W14 WALLY W14

```
PETE COSKER        G B V(AB      (A) WALLY                 1974 ATLANTIC US 18115 UK    K50051
PAUL GERRETT       K V  (A       (B) WALLY GARDENS         1975 ATLANTIC          UK    K50180
PAUL MIDDLETON STEEL B  (AB
ROGER NARRAWAY     D    (AB  NICK GLENNIE SMITH K V(B  JAN GLENNIE SMITH  V  (B  MADELINE BELL    V  (B
PETE SAGE VLN MAND B    (AB  ROY WEBBER     G V  (AB  RAY WEHRSTEIN      SAX(B
```

W15 WALRUS W15

```
DON RICHARDS   TPT (A        (A) WALRUS                    1971 DERAM UK SML1072 US JANUS 3051
ROY VOCE       SAX (A
BILL HOAD      WIND(A    STEVE HAWTHORN  B   (A   JOHN SCATES     G   (A   NICK GABB      D   (A
BARRY PARFITT  K   (A    NOEL GREENAWAY  V   (A
```

W15A SHEILA WALSH W15A

```
SHEILA WALSH   V   (A        (A) FUTURE EYES              1981 CHAPEL LANE     UK  CLS 8006
COLIN VALLANCE B   (A
CHRIS ROBINSON K   (A    RAY GOUDIE    D    (A   RALPH BOLLARD   B   (A   ROB MARSHALL   G   (A
NORMAN BARRETT G   (A    DAVE MORRIS   K    (A   PETE BROOKS     G   (A   DAVE BOLLARD   B   (A
DAVE KASAK     G   (A
```

W15B STEVE WALSH W15B

```
STEVE WALSH   V K D(A        (A) SCHEMER DREAMER          1980 KIRSHNER   US      36320
PHIL EHART    D    (A
TIM GEHRT     D    (A    STEVE MORSE    G   (A   ALAN SLOAN      VLN (A   JEFF LUX    G VIBES FLT(A
KERRY LIVGREN G    (A    TURNER GAUGH   B   (A   CECIL WELCH     TPT (A   SKIP LANE   SAX    (A
RICH WILLIAMS G    (A    DAVID BRYSON   B   (A   DUANE BUCKLER   B   (A   MERLE McLAIN   B (A
```

W16 JOE WALSH W16

```
JOE WALSH G V SYN B(ALL      (A) BARNSTORM                     1973 DUNHILL US 50130 PROBE UK  6268
KENNY PASSARELLI B V(ABC      (A) BARNSTORM                     1974 ANCHOR RI UK           ABCL 5022
JOE VITALE  FLT D K(ABCDF     (B) THE SMOKER YOU DRINK          1973 DUNHILL US 50140 PROBE UK  6275
AL PERKINS     STEEL(A        (B) THE SMOKER YOU DRINK          1974 ANCHOR RI UK           ABCL 5033
PAUL HARRIS    K   (A         (C) SO WHAT                       1974 DUNHILL US 50171
ROCKE GRACE    K V (B         (C) SO WHAT                       1974 ANCHOR                UK ABCL 5055
TOM STEPHENSON K   (C         (D) YOU CANT ARGUE WITH A SICK MIND 1975 ABC US ABCD 932 ANCHOR UK  5156
RANDY MEISNER  V   (C         (D) YOU CANT ARGUE WITH A SICK MIND 1981 MCA UK RI 1613
CLYDIE KING    V   (B         (E) SO FAR SO GOOD               1978 ANCHOR                UK ABCL 5240
VANETTA FIELDS V   (B         (F) BUT SERIOUSLY FOLKS          1978 ASYLUM US 6E 141 UK      K53081
JOE LALA       PERC (B        (G) BEST OF                      1979 ABC     US 1083
RICKY FATAAR   D   (          (EP) PLUS FOUR                   1977 ANCHOR                UK ABE  1202
JOHN STRONACH  V   (C         (H) THERE GOES THE NEIGHBORHOOD  1981 ELEKTRA US 5E523  UK      K52285
BRYAN GAROFALO B V (C
J D SOUTHER    G V (C    DAN FOGELBERG   G V (C   DAVID MASON     K   (D   WILLIE WEEKS    B  (DF
JAY FERGUSON   K V (DF   DON FELDER      G V (C   GLENN FREY      V   (CDF DON HENLEY      V  (CDF
ROCKY DZIDZORNU PERC (D  ANDY NEWMARK    D   (D   JOEY MURCIA     G   (F   TIM SCHMIT      V  (F
CHUCK RAINEY       (A    RON GRINEL      D   (C   GUILLE GARCIA   PERC(C   JODY BOYER      V  (C
```

W16A TRAVIS WAMMACK W16A

```
TRAVIS WAMMACK G V HCA (AB     (A) TRAVIS WAMMACK          1973 FAME      US 1801
RICK HALL       V    (B        (B) NOT FOR SALE            1975 CAPRICORN US 162 UK 2493 133
LEON SHERRILL   G    (B
PETE CARR       G    (B   DON CARTEE    D    (B   RANDY McCORMICK   K   (B   BARRY BECKETT   K (B
JOE HAMILTON    B    (B   LENNY LE BLANC B   (B   JIMMY EVANS       D   (B   RONNIE OLDHAM   K (B
STACY GOSS      HRNS (B   ROGER CLARK    D   (B
```

THE WANDERERS

```
      STIV BATORS       V    (A            (A) ONLY LOVERS LEFT ALIVE        1981 POLYDOR POLS 1028
      DAVID FREGANNA    B V  (A
      DAVE PARSONS      G V  (A   RICK ROCK        D  (A
```

WAR

```
      ERIC BURDON       V    (ABK           (A) BLACKMANS BURDON       1970 LIBERTY               LDS 8400   314
      DEACON JONES      V    (              (B) ERIC BURDON DECLARES WAR  1970 POLYDOR          UK  2310 041
      HAROLD BROWN      D  (ABCDEFGHJKLMNO  (C) WAR                    1971 UA  US LA5508        UK  LBG83478
      HOWARD SCOTT G  PERC(ABCDEFGHJKLMNO   (C) WAR                 RI 1979 MCA UK MCG4003 ISLAND 76  ILPS 9164
      B B DICKERSON B PERC(ABCDEFGHJKLMNO   (D) ALL DAY MUSIC           1972 UA  US LA5546        UK  UAS29269
      CHARLES MILLER  WIND(ABCDEFGHJKLMNO   (D) ALL DAY MUSIC        RI 1979 MCA UK MCF3020 ISLAND 76  ILPS 9177
                                            (D) ALL DAY MUSIC        RI 1981 LAX US 37111
      LONNIE JORDAN     K  (ABCDEFGHJKLMNO  (E) THE WORLD IS A GHETTO   1973 UA  US LA5652        UK  UAS29400
      PAPA DEE ALLEN  PERC(BCDEFGHJKLNO     (E) THE WORLD IS A GHETTO RI 1979 MCA UK MCF3021 ISLAND 76  ILPS 9171
                                            (E) THE WORLD IS A GHETTO RI 1981 LAX US 37112
      LEE OSKAR       HCA (ABCDEFGHJKLMNO   (F) DELIVER THE WORD        1973 UA  US LA 128        UK  UAG29521
                                            (F) DELIVER THE WORD     RI 1979 MCA UK MCF3022 ISLAND 76  ILPS 9194
                                            (G) LIVE                    1974 UA  US LA 193        UK  UAD60067/8
                                            (G) LIVE                 RI 1979 MCA UK MCF3040 ISLAND 76   ILSD 8
                                            (H) WHY CANT WE BE FRIENDS  1975 UA  US LA 441        UK  UAG29843
                                            (H) WHY CANT WE BE FRIENDS RI 1981 LAX US 37113
                                            (H) WHY CANT WE BE FRIENDS RI 1979 MCA UK MCF3023 ISLAND 76  ILPS 9378
                                            (I) GREATEST HITS          1976 UA  US LA 648  ISLAND     ILPS 9413
                                            (J) PLATINUM               1977 UA  US 690    ISLAND UK ILPS 9507
                                            (K) LOVE IS ALL AROUND     1976 ABC US ABCD 988      UK  ABCL 5207
                                            (K) LOVE IS ALL AROUND     1979 MCA UK MCF3025
                                            (L) YOUNGBLOOD(SOUNDTRACK) 1978 UA  US LA904   MCA  UK  MCF  2864
                                            (M) GALAXY                 1978 MCA US MCA 3030      UK  MCF  2822
                                            (N) MUSIC BAND             1979 MCA      3085 UK RI 79  MCF  4001
                                            (O) MUSIC BAND 2           1979 UA  UK 3050   US 3193
                                            (P) PLATINUM JAZZ  (DBL)   1979 MCA      305
```

CLIFFORD T WARD

```
      CLIFFORD T WARD  V K(ALL          (A) SINGER SONGWRITER       1972 DANDELION        UK   2310 216
      DEREK THOMAS      GABCDF          (B) HOME THOUGHTS FROM ABROAD 1973 CHARISMA US 6061 UK CAS 1066
      KEN WRIGHT        D  (ABCD        (C) MANTLEPIECES            1973 CHARISMA US 6065 UK CAS 1077
      BEV PEGG          B  (A           (D) NO MORE ROCK'N'ROLL     1975 PHILIPS          8109 500
      DAVID SKINNER     K  (A           (E) ESCALATOR              1975 CHARISMA        UK  CAS 1098
      JOHN SAWYER      VIBES(A          (F) WAVES                  1976 PHILIPS          9109 216
      WILL ROPER       FLT  (A          (G) NEW ENGLAND DAYS       1977 PHILIPS          9109 605
      JOHN MEALING      K   (F
      PAUL KEOGH        G   (F   PETE KING       SAX (F   TERRY EDWARDS  B(BCDF  CHRIS SPEDDING    G  (D
      ALAN PARKER       G   (D   MIKE MORAN      K   (D   BRIAN ODGERS   B (D    ANDREW STEELE     D  (D
      CHRIS KARAN      PERC (D   B J COLE       STEEL(D   PETE WINGFIELD PNO(D   MARTIE ECHITO     K D(G
      GENE HOLMES      G V  (G   MARC LEVINE     B   (G   MARC SINGER    D (G    SID SHARP     STRINGS (G
      KEITH SMART       D   (F   MICHAEL EASLEY  G   (G
```

HAYES WARE

```
      HAYES WARE        V    (A          (A) GHETTO WOMAN            1979  BASH   US   426
      BILLY BRANCH     HCA   (A
      SHORT GARY        D    (A   CRAIG 'SLOE GIN' WALTON B(A
```

LEON WARE

```
      LEON WARE         V    (A          (A) ROCKIN YOU ETERNALLY    1981  ELEKTRA  UK   K52282
```

WARHORSE

```
      NICK SIMPER          (AB           (A) WARHORSE               1970  VERTIGO          UK  6360 015
      MAC POOLE         D   (AB           (B) RED SEA                1972  VERTIGO          UK  6360 066
      ASHLEY HOLT       V   (AB
      FRANK WILSON    K PNO(AB  PETER PARKER     G   (B   GED PECK       G   (A
```

WARLOCK

```
                                         (A) WARLOCK               1972  BUDDAH  US  102
```

WARM DUST

```
      PAUL CARRACK      K    (ABC         (A) AND IT CAME TO PASS    1970  TREND            UK  TNLS 700
      DAVE PEPPER       D    (AC          (A) AND IT CAME TO PASS    1970  UNI              US  73109
      TEX COMER         B    (ABC         (B) PEACE FOR OUR TIME     1971  TREND            UK  6480 001
      LES WALKER        V    (ABC         (C) THIRD ALBUM            1972  BASF
      ALAN SOLOMON    SAX K V (ABC
      JOHN SURGUY     SAX G V (ABC KEITH BAILEY     D   (B
```

JOHNNY WARMAN

```
      JOHNNY WARMAN         (A            (A) WALKING INTO MIRRORS   1981  ROCKET   UK TRAIN 17
      JERRY MAROTTA     D   (A
      JOHN GIBLIN       B   (A   TONY LEVIN   B   (A   DAVE LAWSON   K   (A LARRY FAST    SYN(A
```

DAVE WARNERS

```
      DAVE WARNERS      V    (A           (A) MUG'S GAME             1978  MUSHROOM AUST        36759
      JOHN DENNISON    K V   (A
      JOHN RYAN         G    (A   PAUL NOONAN B V    (A   ALI JOHNSTONE  PERC  (A TONY DURANT STEEL V(A
      TREVOR LUCAS      V    (A   PETER SCHULTZ  BAN (A   BOB SPENCER    G    (A GAIL           V  (A
      DANNY             V    (A   DR PEPPER      V   (A   MARK MOFFAT    V    (A
```

JENNIFER WARNES

```
      JENNIFER WARNES  K V   (ALL         ( ) I CAN REMEMBER         1968  PARROT      US    71020
      KENNY EDWARDS    V G   (B           ( ) SEE ME                 1968  PARROT      US    71034
      MIKE FINNIGAN    V     (B           ( ) JENNIFER               1972  REPRISE     US     2065
      BRIAN RUSSELL    V     (B           (A) JENNIFER WARNES        1977  ARISTA US 4062  UK SPARTY 1006
      NICKY HOPKINS    K     (A           (B) SHOT THROUGH THE HEART 1979  ARISTA US 4217  UK SPART  1097
      PEGGY SANDVIG    K     (A
      JAY GRAYDON      G     (A   JIM HORN       WIND (A   DAVE McDANIELS  B  (A  RUSS KUNKEL     D  (A
      JOE CORRERO      D     (A   JIM PRICE    K V TROM (A  DANIEL MOORE    V  (A  MATTHEW MOORE   V  (A
      DAN SAWYER       D     (A   STEVE MADAIO   TPT  (A   SKIP MESQUITE   SAX (A  MAX HASKETT     TPT(A
      LAUDIR DE OLIVEIRA PERC(A   JIM MOORE      V    (A   ALAN LINDGREN   PNO (A  JOHN HUG        G  (A
      DOUG ROAHNE      G     (A   REINIE PRESS   B    (A   DENNIS ST JOHN  D   (A  BETH FICHET     V  (A
      HERB PEDERSEN    V     (A   DOUG G LIVINGSTON PNO (AB BRIAN WHITCOMB PNO (A  GAYLE LEVANT   HARP(A
      MICHAEL BOWDEN   B     (A   MATT BETTON    D    (A   DOUG HAYWOOD    V   (A  BEN BENAY       G  (A
```

(CONTINUED)

JENNIFER WARNES (CONTINUED)

DANNY KOOTCH	G	(A	ANDREW GOLD	D B K G	(B	BLONDIE CHAPLIN	G V	(B	JIM GORDON	D	(B
BOB GLAUB	D	(B	BROCK WALSH	K V	(B	DENNY SEIWELL	D	(B	BUZZY FEITEN	G	(B
ABRAHAM LABORIEL	B	(B	MARK OLSON	K	(B	MARTY GREBB	K	(B	BILL ELLIOTT	PNO	(B
WALT RICHMOND	K	(B	RICKY FATAAR	D	(B	CHICO GOLDSMITH	PERC	(B	ROB FRABONI	V	(B
PENNY NICHOLS	V	(B								

WARSAW PAKT

ANDY CALQUHOUN	B	(A	(A) WARSAW PAKT	1977 ISLAND	ILPS 9515
LUCAS FOX	D	(A			
JOHN WALKER		(A	CHRIS UNDERHILL	(A	JIMMY COULL	(A

DIONNE WARWICK

DIONNE WARWICK	V	(ALL	PRESENTING	1964 PYE UK NPL28037	SCEPTER US 508
ISAAC HAYES	V	(M	ANYONE WHO HAD A HEART	1964	SCEPTER US 517
KARL RICHARDSON	PROD	(Z	MAKE WAY FOR	1964 PYE UK NPL28046	SCEPTER US 523
BARRY GIBB V PROD G SRT		(Z	THE SENSITIVE SOUND OF	1965 PYE UK NPL28055	SCEPTER US 528
STEVE GADD	D	(Z	THE BEST OF	1966 PYE UK NPL28064	
GEORGE BITZER	K SYN	(Z	HERE I AM	1966 PYE UK NPL29071	SCEPTER US 531
GEORGE TERRY	G	(Z	IN PARIS	1966 PYE UK NPL28076	SCEPTER US 534
JOE LALA	PERC	(Z	HERE WHERE THERE IS LOVE	1967 PYE UK NPL28096	SCEPTER US 555
DANIEL BEN ZEBULON PERC		(Z	ON STAGE AND IN THE MOVIES	1967 PYE UK NPL28101	SCEPTER US 559
GARY BORION	SAX	(Z	WINDOWS OF THE WORLD	1967 PYE UK NPL28105	SCEPTER US 563
WHIT SIDENER	HRNS	(Z	MAGIC OF BELIEVING	1967	SCEPTER US 567
BRETT MURPHEY	HRNS	(Z	VALLEY OF THE DOLLS	1968 PYE UK NPL28114	SCEPTER US 568
DAN BONSANTI	HRNS	(Z	FREEWHEELIN'	1969 PYE UK NPL28120	
KEN FAULK	HRNS	(Z	SOULFUL	1969 PYE UK NPL28122	SCEPTER US 573
NEAL BONSANTI	HRNS	(Z	SOULFUL	1971 WAND UK WNS12	
ALBHY GALUTEN PROD SYN K		(Z	GREATEST MOTION PICTURE HITS	1969 WAND UK WNS 1	SCEPTER US 575
RICHARD TEE	PNO	(Z	GOLDEN HITS VOL 1	1969 WAND UK WNS 1	SCEPTER US 565
TIM RENWICK	G	(Z	GOLDEN HITS VOL 2	1970 WAND UK WNS 2	SCEPTER US 577
			I'LL NEVER FALL IN LOVE AGAIN	1970	SCEPTER US 581
GEORGE PERRY	B	(Z	VERY DIONNE	1971 WAND UK WNS 10	SCEPTER US 587
DENNIS BRYON	PERC	(Z	PROMISES PROMISES	1971 WAND UK WNS 11	SCEPTER US 571
ANITA LOPEZ	PERC	(Z	FROM WITHIN VOL 1	1972 WAND UK 1007	SCEPTER US 598
PETER GRAVES	HRNS	(Z	FROM WITHIN VOL2	1972 WAND UK 1008	
			GREATEST HITS VOL 1	1973 HALLMARK UK 789	
			GREATEST HITS VOL 2	1973 HALLMARK UK 803	
			DIONNE	1973 WB UK K46140 US 2585	
			THE DIONNE WARWICK STORY 1	1973 GOLDEN HOUR UK826	
			THE DIONNE WARWICK STORY 2	1973 GOLDEN HOUR UK 827	
			JUST BEING MYSELF	1973 WB UK K46186 US 2658	
			GREATEST HITS 3	1974 HALLMARK UK 829	
			THEN CAME YOU	1975 WB UK K56109 US 2846	
			GREATEST HITS 4	1975 HALLMARK UK 883	
			TRACK OF THE CAT	1975 WB UK K56178 US 2893	
			DIONNE WARWICK COLLECTION	1976 PICKWICK UK 001	
			FOREVER OLD	19	SCEPTER US 5110
			VERY BEST OF	19 UA	US UALA 388
			(M) A MAN & A WOMAN	1976 ABC UK ABCD613	
			LOVE AT FIRST SIGHT	1977 WB UK K56429 US 3119	
			DIONNE	1978 ARISTA UK SPART1096	
			NO NIGHT SO LONG	1980 ARISTA UK SPART1132	
			HOT LIVE & OTHERWISE	1981 ARISTA UK DARTY 10	
			GOLDEN COLLECTION	1981 K TEL UK NE1137	
			20 GREATEST HITS	1981 ORCHID UK 003 CASSETTE	
			FRIENDS IN LOVE	1982 ARISTA UK SPART1192	
			20 GOLDEN PIECES	1982 BULLDOG UK	
			HEARTBREAKER	1982 ARISTA UK 204974	

WAS(NOT WAS)

DAVID WAS	SAX K V	(A	(A) WAS(NOT WAS)	1981 ISLAND UK ILPS 7015
JACK TANN	PROD	(A		
DAN WAS	B SYN V	(A		

WASA EXPRESS

BO HALLGREN	K	(ABC	(A) WASA EXPRESS	1977 LOVE SWED 239
MALLA RONNANDER	HCA	(C	(B) ON WITH THE ACTION	1978 LOVE SWED 279 SONET UK SNTF771
CARY SHARRAF EL DIN	G	(ABC	(C) WASA EXPRESS	1979 SONET SNTF 810
BO HAGGSTROM	B	(ABC		
AKE ERIKSSON	D	(ABC		

WASHBOARD DOC, LUCKY & FLASH

JOSEPH 'WASHBOARD' DOCTOR		(A	(A) EARLY MORNING BLUES	1980 L&R 42010
CAB LUCKY	G V	(A		
JOHN 'FLASH' WHITNER	B V	(A	LOUISIANA RED	G V	(A

BABY WASHINGTON

BABY WASHINGTON		(ALL	THATS HOW HEARTACHES ARE MADE	1965 SUE US 1014 LONDON UK HAC8260
			ONLY THOSE IN LOVE	1966 SUE US 1042 LONDON UK HAC8292
			THE ONE & ONLY	196 TRIP US 8009
			SOUL OF BABBY WASHINGTON	196 UA US 21020
			WITH YOU IN MIND	19 DEEP US 16528 UK UA 1217

DELROY WASHINGTON

DELROY WASHINGTON	B V G PERC	(AB	(A) I SUS	1976 VIRGIN	UK	V2060
CANDY McKENZIE	V	(B	(B) RASTA	1977 VIRGIN	UK	V2088
BUNNY McKENZIE	B G	(AB				
JUNIOR MARVIN	G	(B	KARL PITTERSON	PERC	(B	ANGUS GAYE	D	(AB	AL ANDERSON	G	(AB
TREVOR STARR	G	(B	DICK CUTHELL PERC HRNS		(B	COURTNEY HEMMINGS	K	(AB	GEORGE OBAN	PERC	(AB
TONY ROBINSON	K	(AB	RICO	TROM	(AB	EDDIE THORNTON	HRNS	(AB	KEITH GEMMELL	WIND	(AB
JUNIOR KERR	G	(A	LADBROKE GROVE ST CHOIR		(A	DONALD GITS	G	(A	PAT THRALL	G	(A

GENO WASHINGTON(& THE RAM JAM BAND)

```
GENO WASHINGTON    V   (ALL    (A) HAND CLAPPIN' FOOT STOMPIN'          1966 PICCADILLY      UK    NPL38026
HERB PRESTIDGE         (        (A) HAND CLAPPIN' FOOT STOMPIN'          1980 PYE            UK    NSPL18618
STEVE GREGORY      WIND (        (B) SHAKE A TAIL FEATHER                1968 PICCADILLY      UK    NSPL38029
BUD BEADLE         SAX  (        (C) HIPSTERS FLIPSTERS                  1968 PICCADILLY      UK    NSPL38032
JEFF WRIGHT            (        (D) RUNNING WILD                        1968 PYE            UK    NSPL18219
JOHN ROBERTS          (        (E) SIFTERS,SHIFTERS,FINGER CLICK MAMA 1969 MARBLE ARCH     UK     MAL 816
CARL PALMER        D   (        (F) UP TIGHT                            1969 MARBLE ARCH     UK    MAL 1162
PETE GAGE          G   (        (G) GOLDEN HOUR                         1975 PYE            UK     GH 594
ROD BABY              (        (H) GENO'S BACK                          1976 DJM            UK    DJF 20486
BILLY DAVEY           (        (J) LIVE                                 1976 DJM            UK    DJF 20457
LIONEL KINGHAM     SAX (        (L) THAT'S WHY HOLLYWOOD LOVES ME       1979 DJM            UK    DJF 20561
BARRIE MARTIN      PERC (J       ( ) PUT OUT THE CAT                     197 TELDEC          GER      24665
DONNA FEIN         V   (L
PETE LAMONT        TROM (J   ROGER CHANTLER    G   (J    DAVID BALLENTINE  G V (J CHRIS STAINES    B V(J
MIKE MEROS         K   (L   JOE CHEMAY        B V (L    MIKE BAIRD        D   (L BRENT NELSON     D   (L
PAULINHO DA COSTA  PERC (L   GEORGE DOERING    G   (L    JOEL PESKIN       SAX (L CURT BOETCHER    V   (L
MUFFY HENDRIX      V   (L
```

GROVER WASHINGTON

```
GROVER WASHINGTON SAX  (ALL    (A) SOUL BOX   (DBL)                     1973 KUDU US 1213          KULD 501
BOB JAMES         K    (DE     (B) INNER CITY BLUES                     197 KUDU         KULD 11   KUL  3
LOUIS JOHNSON     B    (E      (C) ALL THE KINGS MEN                    197 KUDU                   KUL  7
GARY KING         B    (DE     (D) MISTER MAGIC                         1975 KUDU                  KUL  20
STEVE GADD        D    (E      (E) FEEL SO GOOD                         1975 KUDU                  KU   24
RALPH MACDONALD   PERC(DEFN    (F) SECRET PLACE                         1976 KUDU                  KU   32
RANDY BRECKER     TPT  (E      (G) SOUL BOX 1                           1976 KUDU                  KU   12
JON FADDIS        TPT  (DEN    (H) SOUL BOX 2                           1976 KUDU                  KU   13
JOHN FROSK        TPT  (E      (J) LIVE AT THE BIJOU                    1978 KUDU                  SOUL D02
BOB MILLIKAN      TPT  (E      (K) REED SEED                            1978 TAMLA                 STML12099
ALAN RAPH         TROM (E      (L) PARADISE                             1979 ELEKTRA US6E182   UK  K52130
BARRY ROGERS      TROM (E      (M) WINELIGHT                            1980 ELEKTRA US 6E305  UK  K52262
DAVE TAYLOR       TROM (E      (N) SKYLARKIN'                           1980 MOTOWN           UK  STML12131
PHIL UPCHURCH     B    (D      (O) BADDEST                              1981 MOTOWN           UK  TMSP 604
HARVEY MASON      D    (DF     (P) COME MORNING                         1981 ELEKTRA US 562   UK  K52337
ERIC GALE         G    (DFN
DAVID GRUSIN      PNO  (F   TONY JACKSON      B   (F    GEORGE MRAZ       B   (F  STEVE KHAN       G  (F
GERRY NIEWOOD     SAX  (F   JOHN BLAKE        VLN V K (K TYRONE BROWN     B   (K  LEONARD GIBBS V PERC(K
JAMES SIMMONS     K    (F   RICHARD L STEACKER G V (K  MILLARD VINSON    D   (K  ED WALSH         K  (N
JORGE DALTO       PNO  (N   ALEXANDER OTEY    TPT (N   MARCUS MILLER     B   (N  RICHARD TEE      K  (N
IDRIS MUHAMMAD    D    (N   PAUL GRIFFIN      K   (N   MARVIN STAMM      TPT (DKENNETH RICE      D  (E
JIMMY MADISON     D    (E
```

WASTED YOUTH

```
KEN SCOTT             (A      (A) WILD & WANDERING                     1981 BRIDGEHOUSE    UK BHLP 006
```

WASTELAND

```
                              (A) WANT NOT (EP)                        1979 DISASTER
```

SADAO WATANABE

```
SADAO WATANABE    SAX FLT(ABCD (A) ROUND TRIP                          1970 CBS SONY      50320
CHICK COREA       K    (A      (B) AUTUMN BLOW                         1977 INNERCITY      US    IC 6064
LEE RITENOUR      G    (BC     (C) CALIFORNIA SHOWER                   1979 MIRACLE              MLP3005
ERNIE WATTS       SAX  (BC     (D) HOW'S EVERTHING (DBL LIVE)          1980 CBS                    22081
PATRICE RUSHEN    K    (B      ( ) ORANGE EXPRESS                       19  ?
JACK DEJOHNETTE   D    (A
ANTHONY JACKSON   B    (BD  JON FADDIS       TPT (D   TOKYO PHILHARMONIC ORCH(D  HARVEY MASON    D  (BC
STEVE FORMAN      PERC (B   DAVE GRUSIN      K   (CD  CHUCK RAINEY      B   (C  PAULINHO DA COSTA PERC(C
OSCAR BRASHEAR    TPT  (C   GEORGE BOHANON   TROM (C   RICHARD TEE      K   (D  ERIC GALE        G  (D
JEFF MIRANOV      G    (D   STEVE GADD       D   (D   RALPH MACDONALD   PERC (D  MIROSLAV VITOUS B  (A
```

WATER

```
                              (A) DAMBURST             19  VERTIGO      UK  9286 575
```

WATER & POWER

```
RACHEL SANDERS    V    (A      (A) WATER & POWER                       1975 FANTASY        F9494
WARREN SAMS       V    (A
CHRISTINE ADAMS   V    (A   JAMES GADSON     D   (A   JAMES JAMERSON    B   (A  SONNY BURKE      K  (A
RAY PARKER JR     G    (A   BUD BRISBOIS     HRNS (A   GEORGE BOHANON   TROM (A  GARY COLEMAN     PERC(A
```

WATERFALL

```
                              (A) BENEATH THE STARS                   1981 GUNDOG    UK      LP003
```

MUDDY WATERS

```
MUDDY WATERS                   (A) AT NEWPORT                          1960 CHESS 1449       +   CRL  4513
(McKINLEY MORGANFIELD) G V(ALL (A) AT NEWPORT                          1967 MARBLE ARCH      UK MAL  661
JIMMIE ROGERS     G    (RSYa    (A) AT NEWPORT                          1973 CHECKER          UK 6467 306
WILLIE DIXON      B    (RSY     (B) MUDDY WATERS                        1964 PYE INT UK NPL28040 US CHESS203
PAUL BUTTERFIELD  HCA  (X       (B) MUDDY WATERS                        1967 MARBLE ARCH      UK MAL  723
FRED BELOW        D    (RSY     (C) FOLK SINGER                         1964 PYE INT NPL28048 US CHESS 1483
LEROY FOSTER      G    (S       (D) SINGS BIG BILL BROONZY              1964                  US CHESS 1444
BIG CRAWFORD      B    (RSY     (E) MUDDY BRASS & THE BLUES             1967 CHESS                   1507
ANDREW STEPHENS   B    (ARSY    (F) REAL FOLK BLUES                     1966 CHESS   UK CRL4515 US    1501
PAT HARE          G    (AS      (G) MORE REAL FOLK BLUES                196  CHESS               US   1511
FRANCIS CLAY      D    (ARSVY   (H) SUPER BLUES                         1966 CHESS   UK CRL4529
WILLIE SMITH      D    (SZabcde (I) SUPER SUPER BLUES BAND              1968 CHECKER LPS 3010 CHESS CRL 4537
ELGIN EVANS       D    (SL      (J) ELECTRIC MUD                        1968 CADET              LPS  314
LITTLE WALTER     HCA  (RSY     (K) SAIL ON                            19   CHESS                   1539
JERRY PORTNOY     HCA  (ade     (L) DOWN ON STOVALLS PLANTATION        19   TESTAMENT        US T2210
SAM LAWHORN       G    (STVXd   (M) AFTER THE RAIN                     1969 CADET LPS 320   CHESS  50017
OTIS SPANN        PNO  (PRSVYQ  (N) THEY CALL ME MUDDY WATERS          19   CHESS                   1553
LEVON HELM        D B  (X       (O) THE BEST OF MUDDY WATERS           19   CHESS          FR    9124 224
JAMES MADISON     G    (Sd      (M) AFTER THE RAIN                     1969 CHESS                CRL 4553
PAUL OSCHER       HCA  (PSc     (Q) FATHERS & SONS                     1969 CHESS     2 127    CRL 4556
SONNY WIMBERLEY   B    (S       (Q) FATHERS & SONS                     1969 CHESS                  50033
BO DIDDLEY        G V  (I       (R) McKINLEY MORGANFIELD AKA M WATERS  1972 CHESS                  60006
```

(CONTINUED)

MUDDY WATERS   (CONTINUED)

```
    JOE NEWMAN             TPT  (T    (S) VINTAGE MUD                     1970 SUNNYLAND                KS 100
    MARCUS JOHNSON         SAX  (S    (T) LONDON SESSIONS                 1972 CHESS 6310 121            60013
    CHARLES CALMESE        B    (Zd   (U) CANT GET NO GRINDING            1973 CHESS 6310 129            50023
    RORY GALLAGHER         G    (TW   (V) MUD IN YOUR EAR                 1973 MUSE                       5008
    CAREY BELL HARRINGTON  HCA (TW    (W) LONDON REVISTED                 1974 CHESS                     60026
    RICK GRECH             B    (TW   (X) WOODSTOCK ALBUM                 1975 CHESS                     60035
    STEVE WINWOOD          K    (TW   (Y) CHESS BLUES MASTERS             1977 CHESS NL 6641 639    2ACBM 203
    GEORGE FORTUNE         K    (TW   (Z) HARD AGAIN                      1977 BLUE SKY US 34449    UK  81853
    MITCH MITCHELL         D    (TW   (a) I'M READY                       1977 BLUE SKY US 34928    UK  82235
    JOHNNY WINTER          G    (UZade (b) 'UNK IN FUNK                   1974 CHESS                     60031
    BOB MARGOLIN           G    (XZabde (c)LIVE                           1972 CHESS                     50012
    HERBIE LOVELL          D    (T    (d) LIVE                            1977 BLUE SKY US 35712    UK  83422
    CHARLES'CHUCK' BERRY   G(L         (e) KING BEE                       1980 BLUE SKY US 37064    UK  84918
    GEORGE BUFORD          HCA  (V     ( ) CHICAGO 5 GOLDEN YEARS         1980 CHESS FR 427005
    LEONARD CHESS          PERC(RY     ( ) BACK IN THE GOOD OLD DAYS      19  SYNDICATE CHAPTER 001
    LUTHER TUCKER          G    (RY    ( ) GOOD NEWS                      19  SYNDICATE CHAPTER 002
    CHARLES STEPNEY        ORG  (P
    SELDON POWELL          SAX  (T  GARTH HUDSON  ACC K SAX(X   HOWLIN WOLF       V HCA(I   PHIL UPCHURCH      G  (PQ
    ROSETTA HIGHTOWER      V    (T  WALTER HORTON     HCA (RYa  FRED CARTER       B G  (U   ERNIE ROYAL        TPT(T
    PINETOP PERKINS        PNO(XZabcde HOWARD JOHNSON SAX (X    JOE DENIM         HCA (c   PETE COSEY         G  (P
    GARNETT BROWN          TROM (T  LUTHER JOHNSON    G (Vbde   MORRIS JENNINGS   D   (P   JAMES COTTON       HCA(ARSYZd
    CALVIN JONES           B(bcde  LOUIS SATTERFIELD B  (P     LITTLE WILLIE SMITH HCA ( TAT HARRIS          G  (ARY
    PERCY THOMAS           G V  (L  LOUIS FORD        V MAND(L  HENRY SIMS        G VLN(L   MIKE BLOOMFIELD    G  (Q
    DONALD DUNN            B    (Q  SAM LAY           D   (Q   BUDDY MILES        D   (Q   JEFFREY CARP       HCA(Q
    PAUL ASBELL           G    (Q
```

ROGER WATERS

```
    ROGER WATERS               (A    (A) THE BODY (SOUNDTRACK)           1970 HARVEST               UK  SHSP 4008
    RON GEESIN                 (A
```

GERAINT WATKINS

```
    GERAINT WATKINS     K V  (A    (A) GERAINT WATKINS & THE DOMINATORS 1979 VERTIGO                   9102 033
    ANDY FAIRWEATHER LOW G V(A
    MICKY GEE    G PERC V B(A  JOHN DAVID  B V PERC(A   DAVE CHARLES    D V  (A  HENRY SPINETTI      D V(A
    STEVE GREGORY       SAX  V(A  BUD BEADLE    SAX V  (A
```

JOHN L WATSON

```
    JOHN L WATSON          V   (A    (A) WHITE HOT BLUE BLACK            1970 DERAM                 UK  SMLR 1061
```

JOHNNY GUITAR WATSON

```
    JOHNNY GUITAR WATSON G V(ALL   (A) JOHNNY GUITAR WATSON             196  KING                  US       857
    EMRY THOMAS           D    (MNOPHQ (B) BLUES SOUL                    196  CHESS                 US      1490
    TOMMY ROBERTSON       TROM (MNO   (C) LARRY WILLIAMS SHOW WITH J G W 1965 DECCA                 UK  LK 4691
    KNUD JENSEN           SAX  (N     (D) BAD                            1966 OKEH                      OKS 14118
    WALT FOWLER           TPT  (NOQ   (E) TWO FOR THE PRICE OF ONE       1967 OKEH                      OKS 14122
    MAXWELL DAVIS         SAX  (J     (F) I CRIED FOR YOU                1967 CADET                     LPS 4056
    JIM WYNN              SAX  (J     (G) IN THE FATS BAG                1968 OKEH                      OKS 14124
    RENE HALL             G    (J     (H) LISTEN                         1973 FANTASY EURO 03861279 US     9437
    TED BRUNSON           G    (J     (I) GANSTER OF LOVE                19  POWERPAK                       306
    BARNEY KESSEL         G    (J     (J) THE GANGSTER IS BACK           1975 RED LIGHTNING         UK  RL 0013
    RUDY COPELAND         K V  (H     (K) I DONT WANT TO BE A LONE RANGER 1976 FANTASY              US      9484
    ANDRE LEWIS           K B  (H     (L) CAPTURED LIVE                  1976 DJM
    J D REED              SAX  (M     (M) AIN'T THAT A BITCH             1976 DJM  US DJM 3         UK  DJF 20485
    HENRY REED            G SAX(H     (N) A REAL MOTHER FOR YA           1977 DJM  US DJLPA7        UK  DJF 50505
    DARCUS                V    (P     (O) FUNK BEYOND THE CALL OF DUTY   1977 DJM  US       714     UK  DJF 20525
    BILL HALEY            SAX  (OQ    (P) GIANT                          1978 DJM  US        19     UK  DJF 20551
    MAXAYN LEWIS          V    (H     (Q) WHAT THE HELL IS THIS          1979 DJM  US        24     UK  DJF 20557
    PAUL DUNMALL          SAX  (M     (R) LOVE JONES                     1980 DJM                   UK  DJF 20568
    GREGORY DUVAS         TPT  (Q     (S) GETTIN DOWN                    1978 CADET    US 4056
    ALBERT WING           SAX  (Q     (T) VERY BEST OF                   1981 DJM                   UK  DJF 20576
    TONY COLEMAN          TROM (Q     (U) JOHNNY & THE FAMILY CLONE      1981 DJM                   UK  DJF 20574
    BOBBY HOWARD          B    (Q     (V) HOT LITTLE MAMA                19  BIG TOWN  BT1002
    MARCY THOMAS          V    (P
    PETER MARTIN          TPT  (M  WILMA WILSON    V  (Q  DEON ESTUS    B   (Q
```

ROBERT WATSON

```
    ROBERT WATSON         SAX K(A     (A) ESTIMATED TIME OF ARRIVAL      1978 PYE                   UK  NSPL28250
    WILBY FLETCHER        D    (A     (B) ALL BECAUSE OF YOU             1979 PYE                   UK  NSPL28276
    PAT PATRICK           SAX  (A
    CHARLES DAVIS         SAX  (A  SINCLAIR ACEY   TPT (A  FRANK WILLIAMS  TPT (A  DICK GRIFFIN    TROM(A
    MICHAEL TRENI         TROM (A  ARTHUR WHITE    SAX (A  VALERI PONOMAREN TPT (A  RICHARD CARUSO TROM(A
    BILL SAXTON           SAX  (A  CURTIS LUNDY    B   (A  TERUMASA HINO   TPT (A  DENNIS IRWIN   B  (A
    JOE CARO              G    (A  ROLAND PRINCE   G   (A  MONTI ELLISON   PERC(A  JABALI BILLY HART D(A
    WALTER DAVIS          K    (A  BILLY HIGGINS   D   (A  PAMELA WATSON   K V (A
```

WAH WAH WATSON

```
    WAH WAH WATSON        G V  (A     (A) ELEMENTARY                     1976 CBS  UK 81582         US   34328
    JULIA TILLMAN         V    (A
    MAXINE WILLARD        V    (A  ORRIN WATERS    V   (A  LUTHER WATERS   V   (A  RAY PARKER JR   G  (A
    OLLIE BROWN           D    (A  LOUIS JOHNSON   B   (A  SONNY BURKE     K   (A  JOHN BARNES     K  (A
    JOE SAMPLE            PNO  (A  CLARENCE McDONALD PNO (A MARK DAVIS     PNO (A  WILLIE WEEKS    B  (A
    HERBIE HANCOCK        K    (A  BENNIE MAUPIN   SAX (A  ERNIE WATTS     SAX (A  AARON SMITH     D  (A
    WILTON FELDER         B    (A  HENRY DAVIS     B   (A  JAMES JAMESON   B   (A  DAVID T WALKER  G  (A
    DAVID GRUSIN          K    (A
```

WATSONIAN INSTITUTE

```
    JOHNNY GUITAR WATSON  G V(A     (A) MASTER FUNK                     1978 DJM  US 13        UK DJF 20529
    BOBBY HOWARD          B V  (A     (B) EDP                            1981 DJM  US 27
    GIP NOBLE             K    (A
    EMRY THOMAS           D V  (A  TOMMY ROBERTSON TROM B V(A
```

ERNIE WATTS

```
ERNIE WATTS SAX FLT PERC V(AB      (A) LOOK IN YOUR HEART        1980 ELEKTRA       US      6E 285
PETE ROBINSON       K     (A        (B) CHARIOTS OF FIRE         1982 QWEST         US      3637
DAN DEAN            B     (A
ALEX ACUNA          D     (A   RON COOK        G     (A   PAULINHO DA COSTA  PERC(AB   RICHARD TEE    K   (B
CARLOS RIOS         G     (B   JOHN ROBINSON   D    ((B   IAN UNDERWOOD      SYN  (B   LARRY HALL TPT    (B
JAMES INGRAM        V K   (B   HOWARD HEWITT   V     (B   STEVE LUKATHER     G    (B   DON GRUSIN K SYN(B
QUINCY JONES        PROD  (B   MICHAEL OMARTIAN K STR(B   NEIL STUBENHAUS    B    (B   JERRY HEY  HRNS (B
BILL REICHENBACH    TPT   (B   PHILLIP INGRAM  V     (B   DAVID WILLIAMS     G    (B   GREG PHILLINGANES SYN(B
```

WATTS 103RD STREET BAND
W33   W33

```
CHARLES WRIGHT      V     (         (A) CORNBREAD & GRITS       1967 WB           US      1741
MELVIN DUNLOP       B     (         (B) IN THE JUNGLE BABE      1969 WB           US      1801
AL McKAY            G     (         (C) EXPRESS YOURSELF        1970 WB           US      1864
BERNARD BLACKMAN    G     (         (D) YOU'RE SO BEAUTIFUL     19   WB           US      1904
RAY JACKSON         TROM  (
JOHN RAYFORD        SAX   (   GABRIEL FLEMMING  TPT  (    BILL CANNON   SAX  (   JAMES GADSON    D  (
```

W34   WAVEMAKER   W34

WAVEMAKER

```
JOHN LEWIS          K     (AB        (A) WHERE ARE WE CAPTIAN    1975 POLYDOR    UK      2383 331
BRIAN HODGSON       K     (AB        (B) NEW ATLANTIS            1977 POLYDOR    UK      2383 434
TONY McVEY          PERC  (AB
JON KEHLIOR         PERC  (A
```

W34A   WAX   W34A

WAX

```
                                    (A) WAX ATTACK              1981 RCA        US      3608
```

W35   DARRYL WAY   W35

DARRYL WAY

```
DARRYL WAY          VLN K(ALL        (A) SATURATION POINT       1973 DERAM UK SML1104  LONDON JAP LAX1037
DEK MESSECAR        B V   (ABCE      (B) CANIS LUPUS            1973 DERAM UK SDL  14  LONDON JAP LAX1036
JOHN ETHERIDGE      G     (ABCE      (AB) SATURATION/CANIS      19   LONDON IMP 23113  NOVA GER 8005/1-2
IAN MOSLEY          D     (ABCDE     (C) NIGHT MUSIC            1974 DERAM UK SML1116  LONDON JAP LAX1116
JOHN HODKINSON      V     (C         (D) CONCERTO FOR ELEC VLN & SYN 1978 ISLAND        UK       ILPS 9550
FRANCIS MONKMAN     SYN   (D         (E) DARRYL WAY'S WOLF      1974 LONDON            US       PS    644
                                     ( ) ANTHOLOGY              1976 KING   JAP 1008
```

W35A   JEFF WAYNE   W35A

JEFF WAYNE

```
JEFF WAYNE                (A         (A) WAR OF THE WORLDS      1978 CBS    96000
```

W35B   WAZMO NARIZ   W35B

WAZMO NARIZ

```
JEFF BOYNTON        K     (A         (A) THINGS AREN'T RIGHT    1979 ILLEGAL         UK       ILP 003
JEFF HILL           G V   (A
BRUCE ZELESNIK      D     (A   JAMES E McGEEVY III B  (A
```

W35C   WEAPON OF PEACE   W35C

WEAPON OF PEACE

```
                                     (A) WEAPON OF PEACE        1981 SAFARI        UK SWOP 1
```

W36   WEATHER REPORT   W36

WEATHER REPORT

```
WAYNE SHORTER       SAX   (ALL       (A) WEATHER REPORT         1971 CBS UK 64521  US 30661  JAP 25AP 941
JOE ZAWINUL         K     (ALL       (B) I SING THE BODY ELECTRIC 1972 CBS UK 64943 US 31356 JAP 25AP 944
ALEJANDRO ACUNA     PERC  (FH        (C) SWEETNIGHTER           1973 CBS UK 65532  US 32210  JAP 25AP 945
CHESTER THOMPSON    D     (F         (D) MYSTERIOUS TRAVELLER   1974 CBS UK 80027  US 32494  JAP 25AP 946
JACO PASTORIUS      B     (FHJ       (E) TAIL SPINNIN'          1975 CBS UK 80734  US 33417  JAP 25AP 947
NARADA MICHAEL WALDEN D(F            (F) BLACK MARKET           1976 CBS UK 81325  US 34099  JAP 25AP 57
MIROSLAV VITOUS     B     (ABCDG     (G) LIVE IN TOKYO          1977 CBS SONY                SOPJ 12/13XR
DON ALIAS           PERC  (F         (H) HEAVY WEATHER          1977 CBS UK 81775  US 34418  JAP 25AP 357
MANOLO BADRENA      PERC  (HJ        (J) Mr GONE                1978 CBS UK 82775
ALPHONSO JOHNSON    B     (DEF       (K) 8.30                   1979 CBS UK 83670
DOM UM ROMAO        PERC  (BCDG      (L) NIGHT PASSAGE          1980 CBS UK 84597
ISHMAEL WILBURN     D     (D
AIRTO MOREIRA       D     (A   ALPHONZE MOUZON  D  (A   ERIC GRAVATT    D   (BCG ANDREW WHITE   HRNS B(BC
HUBERT LAWS         FLT   (B   WILMER WISE     HRNS (B   YOLANDE BAVAN   V   (B  JOSHIE ARMSTEAD    V  (B
ROBERT CHAPMAN      V     (B   RALPH TOWNER    G    (B   HERSCHEL DWELLINGHAM D (E  ALYRIO LIMA,   PERC (E
NGUDU CHANCLER      D     (E   TONTO           K    (E   MURUGA          PERC(C  STEVE GADD        D  (J
TONY WILLIAMS       D     (J   PETER ERSKINE   D    (J   DENIECE WILLIAMS V  (J  MAURICE WHITE     V  (J
JON LUCIEN          D     (J
```

W36A   JIM WEATHERLY   W36A

JIM WEATHERLY

```
JIM WEATHERLY       G V   (AB        (A) THE SONGS OF JIM WEATHERLY 1974 BUDDAH  US      5608
                                     (B) MAGNOLIAS & MISFITS    1975 BUDDAH     US      5637
```

W37   VIVIAN WEATHERS   W37

VIVIAN WEATHERS

```
VIVIAN WEATHERS     V PERC(A         (A) BAD WEATHER            1978 FRONT LINE          FL1025
WINSTON BENNETT     G     (A
KOJO OSEI           D     (A   WINSTON CURNIFFE D   (D   TONY OSEI       K   (A  EVER DEE          B  (A
FLOYD LAWSON        B PERC(A   JOHN VARNOM     PERC G(A   JANOS BAJTALA   K   (A
```

W38   THE WEB   W38

THE WEB

```
JOHN L WATSON       V     (AB        (A) FULLY INTERLOCKING     1968 DERAM US 18018  UK   SML 1025
TOM HARRIS          WIND  (ABC       (B) THERAPHOSA BLONDI      1970 DERAM           UK   SML 1058
JOHN EATON          G     (ABC       (C) I SPIDER               1970 POLYDOR         UK   2383 024
TONY EDWARDS        G     (ABC
DICK LEE SMITH      B     (AB  LENNIE WRIGHT D PERC   (ABC KENNY BEVERIDGE   PERC D(ABC   STRING SECTION (AB
DAVE LAWSON         K V   (C
```

W39   JIMMY WEBB   W39

JIMMY WEBB

```
JIMMY WEBB          V K   (ALL       (A) JIM WEBB SINGS JIM WEBB  1968 EPIC              US   26401
DAVID PAICH         K SYN(F          (B) WORDS & MUSIC          1970 REPRISE UK K44101   US   6421
GEORGE MARTIN       K SYN(F          (C) & SO ON                1971 REPRISE           US   6448
FRED TACKETT        G     (BDEF       (D) LETTERS                1972 REPRISE UK K44173   US   2055
DEAN PARKS          G     (FE         (E) LANDS END              1974 ASYLUM  UK SYL9014  US   5070
B J COLE            STEEL(E           (E) LANDS END              1974 ASYLUM  GER 43006
DEE MURRAY          B     (FE         (F) EL MIRAGE              1977 ATLANTIC UK K50370  US   18218
HARVEY MASON        PERC  (F
DAVID HUNGATE       B     (F   LARRY KNECHTEL   B   (F   NIGEL OLSSON    D   (FE JIM GORDON       D  (F
LOWELL GEORGE       G     (F   BARRY DE SOUZA   D   (E   PHILIP GOODHAND TAIT K (E DAVID HENTSCHEL SYN (E
BRIAN HODGES        B     (E   DAVEY JOHNSTONE  MAND(E   PAUL KEO        G   (E  JONI MITCHELL    V  (DE
JIM RYAN            G     (E   TOM SCOTT       SAX  (BE   RINGO STARR     D   (E  SUSAN WEBB       V  (DE
RAY RICH            D     (D   SKIP MOSHER      B SAX (D
```

EBERHARD WEBER

```
  EBERHARD WEBER    B CELLO(ALL    (A) COLOURS OF CHLOE            1974 ECM 1042
  RAINER BRUNINGHAUS   K(ABCD      (B) YELLOW FIELDS               1976 ECM 1066
  PETER GIGER      D   (A          (C) THE FOLLOWING MORNING        197 ECM 1084
  RALF HUBNER      D   (A          (D) SILENT FEET                  197 ECM 1107
  ACK VAN ROOYEN   HRNS (A         (E) FLUID RUSTLE                 197 ECM 1137
  GARY BURTON      VIBES(E
  CHARLIE MARIANO  SAX (BCD JOHN CHRISTENSEN D   (B    JOHN MARSHALL   D   (D   BILL FRISELL    G (E
  BONNIE HERMAN    V   (E   NORMA WINSTON    V   (E
```

VINCE WEBER

```
  VINCE WEBER      PNO (A          (A) BLUES 'N' BOOGIE            1977 RUSSEL      GER  32295
  INGA RUMPF       V   (A
```

THE WEDGE

```
  TOM BROWN        D   (A          (A) THE BIG BAD BOSS BEAT OF(EP)  1980 RHINO      RNEP 509
  FRED GRABERT     G   (A
  LOU MAXFIELD     G   (A   ACE THE BASS   B   (A   HAROLD BRONSON   PROD (A
```

WEEKEND MILLIONAIRE

```
  NICOLAS GORODETSKY V G K WIND(A  (A) WEEKEND MILLIONAIRE        1978 WB   UK   K56449
  JEAN MARESKA     PROD (A
  JEAN MICHEL NAVARRE V G (A  ALAIN THOMAS   B K V(A   NICOLAS DEGAULEJAC   D (A FRANCOIS SRTIGE    G(A
  PHILIPPE BENZEL  PERC (A  JEAN PHILIPPE DELRIEU K(A  CLAUDE ALVAREZ PEREYNE G K(A ROGER LOUBET    SYN (A
```

RANDY WEBSTER

```
  RANDY WEBSTER        (A          (A) BLUES TO AFRICA              19   FREEDOM     FLP 41014
```

RITCHIE WEEMS

```
  RITCHIE WEEMS        (A          (A) NATURAL BORN MAN           1965 DUNHILL      202
```

JOHN WEIDER

```
  JOHN WEIDER      G V (A          (A) JOHN WEIDER               1976 ANCHOR      UK ANCL 2018
  CHARLIE McCRACKEN B (A
  PIERCE KELLY     D   (A
```

WEIDORJE

```
  MICHEL ETTORI    G   (A          (A) WEIDORJE                  1978 COBRA        COB 37014
  JEAN PHILIPPE GOUDE K (A
  PATRICK GAUTHIER K   (A   KIRT RUST       D   (A   ALAIN GAILLARD   SAX (A  YVON GAILLARD    TPT V(A
  BERNARD PAGANOTTI B V (A
```

BOB WEIR

```
  BOB WEIR         G V (AB         (A) ACE                       1972 WB   US BS2627 UK   K 46165
  DAVID PAICH      K   (B          (B) HEAVEN HELP THE FOOL      1978 ARISTA US 4155   UK SPART1044
  DAVID FOSTER     K   (B          (B) HEAVEN HELP THE FOOL      1978 ARISTA GER 60467
  CARMEN TWILLIE   V   (B          (C) BOBBT & THE NIDNITES      1981 ARISTA
  DAVE TORBERT     B   (A
  MIKE BAIRD       D   (B   MIKE PORCARO    B   (B   TOM SCOTT        WIND (B  BILL CHAMPLIN   K V (B
  TOM KELLY        V   (B   NIGEL OLSSON    D   (B   DEE MURRAY       B   (B  WADDY WACHTEL    G   (B
  PEGGY SANDVIG    K   (B   LYNETTE GLOUD   V   (B   BILL KREUTZMANN  D   (A  PHIL LESH        B V (A
  JERRY GARCIA     G STEEL (A  KEITH GODCHAUX   PNO (A   DONNA GODCHAUX   V   (A  ED BOGAS        STRINGS(A
```

RUSTY WEIR

```
  RUSTY WEIR       G V (ALL        (A)STONED SLOW RUGGED         1975 ABC       US  AB 820
  LEONARD ARNOLD   G STEEL V(C     (B) DONT IT MAKE YOU WANNA DANCE 1975 20TH CENTURY US   T 469
  RUSTY YOUNG          (A          (C) RUSTY WEIR               1976 20TH CENTURY US   T 495
  CHRIS HILLMAN    B V (A          (D) BLACK HAT SALOON         1976 CBS       US   34319
  RICHIE FURAY         (A          (E) STACKED DECK             1977 CBS       US   34775
  HERB PEDERSEN        (A
  GIB GUILBEAU         (A   JIM MARRIOTT    V D (C   BOBBT SMITH      B V (C  TODD POTTER     G V (C
  KIM SNIDER       K V (C   BILL SMITH      K   (C   GLENN SPREEN     PNO (C  MIKE BALLEW     G   (C
  DON FRANCISCO    V   (C   SHANE KEISTER   K SYN(C
```

WEIRDO'S

```
  JOHN DENNY       V   (AB         (A) WHO? WHAT? WHEN? WHERE? WHY?  1979 BOMP EP US W3 LINE GER LSLP4001
  DIX DENNEU       G SYN(AB        (B) ACTION DESIGN            1980 RHINO EP   US RNEP 508
  WILLY WILLIAMS   B   (B
  CLIFF ROMAN G SAX SYN (AB DANNY BENAIR D   (A   ART FOX          D   (B  BILLY PERSONS   B (A
  KELLY QUINN      K   (A
```

TIM WEISBERG

```
  TIM WEISBERG     FLT V(ALL       (A) TIM WEISBERG             1971 A&M    US 3039
  TODD ROBINSON    G   (DEGH        (B) DREAMSPEAKER             1972 A&M    US 3045
  DOUG ANDERSON    B   (DEGBH       (C) HURTWOOD EDGE            1973 A&M    US 4352
  TY GRIMES        D   (EG          (D) TIM WEISBERG 4           1974 A&M    US 3658    UK   AMLH63658
  TOM DOUGHERTY    PERC (G          (E) LISTEN TO THE CITY       1975 A&M    US 4545    UK   AMLH64545
  BILL STEWART     D   (H           (F) LIVE AT LAST             197  A&M    US 4600
  RICK JAEGER      D   (BGH         (G) TIM WEISBERG BAND        1977 UA     US LA773   UK   UAG 30113
  JOHN HUG         G   (GKH         (H) ROTATIONS                1978 US     UA LA857   UK   UAG 30175
  TOWER OF POWER   HRNS (G          (I) TWIN SONS OF DIFFERENT MOTHERS 1978 EPIC  US 35339
  CHUCK LEAVELL    K   (GH          (J) NIGHT RIDER             1979 MCA    US 3084
  JIM KRUEGER      G   (B           (K) PARTY OF ONE            1980 MCA    US 5125
  MILT HOLLAND     PERC (B          (L) SMILE      (BEST OF)     1979 A&M    US 4749
  DAN FOGELBERG    G V (I
  MIKE MELVOIN     PNO (B   BOBBYE HALL     PERC (H   RONNIE EADES     SAX (H  NEIL LARSEN     K (GHK
  MICKEY RAPHAEL   HCA (H   HARRISON CALLOWAY TPT (H  HARVEY THOMPSON  SAX (B  BEN CAULEY      TPT (H
  FRED SELDON      SAX (H   ERNIE CARLSON   TROM (H   LYNN BLESSING K SYN(BDEK MARTY FOLTZ     D (D
  JUDEE SILL       G V K(D  TOM PELTIER     V   (D   ART JOHNSON      V   (D  LARRY KNECHTEL  B (B
  ED GREENE        D   (K   NEIL STUBENHAUS B   (K   ABRAHAM LABORIEL B   (K  GREG PHILLINGANES PNO(K
  JOHN JARVIS      PNO (K   RUSSEL FERRANTE PNO (K   BUZZ FEITEN      G   (K  MIKE SEMBELLO   G (K
  MICHAEL BODDICKER SYN (K  STEVE FORMAN    PERC (K   BILL CHAMPLIN    V   (K  CARMEN GRILLO   V (K
  LAURA CREAMER    V   (K   WILLIAM SMITH   K   (K
```

```
    LARRY WEISS        V  (A        (A) BLACK & BLUE SUITE          1974 20TH CENTURY          T428
    TOM HENSLEY        PNO (A
    LEE SKLAR          B  (A    RICK MAROTTA    D    (A  HUGH McCRACKEN    G K(A  JIMMIE HASKELL    K  (A
    JAMES HENDRIX      G  (A    JIM KELTNER     D    (A  DEAN PARKS        G (A  DAVID PARLATO      B  (A
    STRING SECTION        (A
```
W45   ERIC WEISSBERG   W45
```
    ERIC WEISSBERG  G V FDL (ALL    (A) FOLK BANJO STYLES          1966 POLYDOR        UK
    STEVE MANDELL   G V BANJ(CD      (B) NEW DIMENSIONS IN BANJO BLUEGRASS 19 ELEKTRA    US      EKS  7238
    CHARLIE BROWN   G V HCA (D       (C) DUELLING BANJO'S          1973 WB     US BS2683 UK      K46214
    MARSHALL BRICKMAN   (AB          (D) RURAL FREE DELIVERY(DELIVERANCE) 1973 WB  US 2720  UK   K46260
    TONY BROOKS     B V  (D
    RICHARD BROOKS  D    (D
```
W46   BOB WELCH   W46
```
    BOB WELCH          G V  (ALL    (1) BOB WELCH WITH HEAD EAST    1970 VOGUE      LDA 20344
    ROBERT HUNT        K V  (1       (A) FRENCH KISS                1977 CAPITOL UK/US EST11663 GER 85266
    CHRISTINE McVIE    K    (AB      (B) THREE HEARTS               1979 CAPITOL UK/US EST11907 GER 85807
    MICK FLEETWOOD     D    (AB      (C) I'M THE ONE                1979 CAPITOL UK/US EST12017 GER 86050
    STEVE NICKS        V    (B       (D) MAN OVERBOARD              1980 CAPITOL UK/US EST12107 GER 86231
    ALVIN TAYLOR       D    (ABDE    (E) BOB WELCH                  1981 RCA  UK 6019 US 4107
    LINDSAY BUCKINGHAM G V(A
    TODD SHARP         G    (BCD DAVID ADELSTEIN    SYN K(BCDE STEVE FOREMAN    PERC (B  DONNY FRANCESCO  D V (CD
    BRAD PALMER        B    (DE  ALAN BRAN      B   (D      RANDY MEISNER     V   (D  WENDY WALDMAN    V  (D
    MARTY JOWARD       SAX K(D   VENETTA FIELDS  V  (D      PAULETTE BROWN    V   (D  BUNNY HILL       V  (D
    NORTON BUFFALO     HCA  (D   DAVE RODRIGUEZ  B  (E      JOEY BRASLER      G   (E  AL BRAN          B  (D
    TOM KELLY          V    (E   ROBBIE PATTON   PERRC(E    ROGER VOUDOURIS   G   (C  HENRY MOORE D V  (1
```
W46A   BRANDI WELLS   W46A
```
    BRANDI WELLS       V    (A       (A) WATCH OUT                  1981 WMOT UK 2224    US 37668
```
W46B   CORY WELLS   W46B
```
    CORY WELLS              (A       (A) TOUCH ME                   197 A&M US    4673
```
W47   JUNIOR WELLS   W47
```
    JUNIOR WELLS     V HCA(ALL    (A) ON TAP                   1966 DELMARK        US    DS 635
    BUDDY GUY        G    (BCDKF  (B) IT'S MY LIFE BABY        1966 VANGUARD UKSRVL19028 US VSD79231
    FRED BELOW       D    (BEJ    (B) IT'S MY LIFE BABY        1966 FONTANA              TFL6084
    LEROY STEWART    B    (B      (C) SOUTH SIDE JAM           196 DELMARK         US    DS 612
    WALTER BEASLEY   B    (B      (D) HOODOO MAN BLUES         196 DELMARK         US    DS 628
    LITTLE AL        D    (B      (E) BLUES HIT BIG TOWN       196 DELMARK         US    DS 640
    WALTER WILLIAMS  G    (F      (F) COMING AT YOU            1968 VANGUARD UKSVRL19011 US VSD79262
    DOUGLAS FAGAN    SAX  (F      (G) YOU'RE TUFF ENOUGH       1968 MERCURY        UK    SMCL20130
    TOM CRAWFORD     B    (F      (G) YOU'RE TUFF ENOUGH       1968 BLUE ROCK      US      64002
    LEVI WARREN      D    (F      (H) SINGS AT THE GOLDEN BEAR 1968 BLUE ROCK      US      64003
    CLARK TERRY      TPT  (F      (J) IN MY YOUNGER DAYS       1971 RED LIGHTNING  UK    RL  007
    WALLACE DAVENPORT TPT (F      (K) PLAY THE BLUES           1972 ATLANTIC US 33364   UK K40240
    JIMMY OWEN       TPT  (F      (L) PLEADING THE BLUES       19 ISABEL           FR    900501
    TOM McINTOSH     TROM (F      (EP) BLUES WITH A BEAT       197 DELMARK               DJB  1
    HENRY GRAY       K    (J
    LOUIS MYERS      G    (EJ  DAVID MYERS     B    (EJ  SYL JOHNSON    G    (J   WILLIE DIXON    B  (EJ
    EUGENE LOUNGE    D    (J   EARL HOOKER     G    (J   LAFAYETTE LEAKE K    (J   DONALD HAWKINS  SAX(J
    JARRETT GIBSON   SAX  (J   JOHN WALKER     K    (JA  JACK MEYERS    B    (DJ  MUDDY WATERS    G  (E
    ELMORE JAMES     G    (E   ODIE PAYNE      D    (E   OTIS SPANN     G    (E   JOHNNIE JONES   PNO(E
    A C REED         SAX  (A   ROOSEVELT SHAW  D    (A   CHARLES MILES  SAX  (A   PHILIP GUY G      (A
    HERMAN APPLEWHITE B  (A   SAM LAWHORN  G   (A  (**) SEE BUDDY GUY ENTRY FOR K LINE UP
```
W48   MARY WELLS   W48
```
    MARY WELLS         V  (ALL    BYE BYE BABY              1961 TAMLA US 600 ORIOLE 63 UK 40051
    MARVIN GAYE        V  (*      ONE WHO REALLY LOVES YOU 1962 TAMLA             US       605
                                  TWO LOVERS               1962 TAMLA US 607 ORIOLE 63 UK 40045
                                  ON STAGE                 1962 TAMLA             US       611
                                  GREATEST HITS            1963 TAMLA US 616      UK    TML 11032
                                  TOGETHER *               1964 STATESIDE         UK      10097
                                  TOGETHER *               1964 TAMLA             US       613
                                  MY GUY                   1964 STATESIDE         UK      10095
                                  MY GUY                   1964 TAMLA             US       617
                                  MY GUY                   197 PICKWICK           CAN     3395
                                  MARY WELLS               1965 STATESIDE         UK      10133
                                  MARY WELLS               196 20TH CENTURY       US      4171
                                  MY BABY JUST CARES FOR ME 1966 TAMLA UK STML11006
                                  LOVE SONGS OF THE BEATLES 196 STATESIDE         UK      10171
                                  LOVE SONGS OF THE BEATLES 196 20TH CENTURY      US      4178
                                  GREATEST HITS            196 TAMLA US 616
                                  OOH!                     1966 MOVIETONE         US      71010
                                  VINTAGE STOCK            1967 TAMLA             US       653
                                  TWO SIDES OF             196 ATCO               US      33199
                                  SERVIN' UP SOME SOUL     1968 JUBILEE           US      8018
                                  SERVIN' UP SOME SOUL     1968 STATESIDE         UK      10266
                                  MY GUY                   1970 MOTOWN     UK SRS5040
                                  (EP) MARY WELLS          1966 TAMLA TME 2007
```
W48A   PHILLIP J WELLS   W48A
```
    PHILLIP J WELLS    ALL INST(A    (A) THE LAST SURVIVORS        1978 SOLID GOLD      SGRLP 101
```
W48B   MICHAEL WENDROFF   W48B
```
    MICHAEL WENDROFF   G HCA V(A      (A) SOUTHPAW                 1974 BUDDAH            BDS  5609
    BOB KULICK         G    (A        (B) LIVE                     1977 BUDDAH       US        5687
    STEVE MORGAN       V    (A
    MIKE MONTGOMERY    K    (A    JIM GREGORY     B    (A  GREGG DIAMOND PERC D V (A  JIMMY MAELEN    PERC V(A
    P J ROSS           V    (A    RALPH MOSS      V    (A  JOANNE VENT    V    (A   STRING SECTION     (A
```
W48C   WEREWOLVES   W48C
```
    BRIAN PAPGEORGE    V    (A       (A) THE WEREWOLVES           1978 RCA  AFLI2746    uk PL 12746
    BUCKNER BALLARD    V G B(A       (B) SHIP OF FOOLS            197 RCA   AFLI3079
    KIRK BREWSTER      G V  (A
    SEAB MEADOR        G    (A   BOBBY BARANOWSKI D   (A  MICHAEL KINDRED    K   (A  JOEY STANN HRNS (A
    PETER WOOD         ACC  (A
```

DAVID WERNER

```
    DAVID WERNER      G V K(ABC        (A) WIZZ KID                    1975 RCA  US 0350
    MAX KENDRICK      G    (A          (B) IMAGINATION                1976 RCA  UK 0922
    GARY LINK         B    (A          (C) DAVID WERNER               1979 EPIC US 36126    UK        83862
    MARK DOYLE      G K B V (C
    MOONEY            D    (C  ALBRITTON McLAIN  B   (C  KEN BISCHEL     SYN (C  RICHARD HUNTER   HCA (C
    TIM CAPELLO       SAX  (C  IAN HUNTER        V   (C  MAXINE DIXON    V   (C  TOM GLAISTER     D   (A
    JOE FARRELL       SAX  (A  LINDA NOVEMBER    V   (A  MAERETHA STEWART V   (A  TASHA THOMAS     V   (A
```
W48E   WENCHIN'   W48E
```
                                         (A) WENCHIN'                    1975 BUDDAH   US   5642
```
W48F   WEREWOLVES OF LONDON   W48F
```
    PAUL ROLAND       G V  (A          (A) MIDNIGHT RAGS               1980 ARMAGEDDON  UK   ARM9
    JOHN DANIELS      G    (A
    BRIAN GOULD       K    (A  PAUL NESBIT SAX      (A  SIMON BALESTRINI  B   (A  ROGER DIAMOND   D PERC(A
    MARTIN MEADS      D    (A  MAURICE MEMMOTT   VLN (A
```
W49   HOWARD WERTH & THE MOONBEAMS   W49
```
    HOWARD WERTH      G V  (A          (A) KING BRILLIANT      1975 CHARISMA UK CAS11-04 US ROCKET2180
    MIKE MORAN        K    (A
    FRED GANDY        B    (A  BOB WESTON        G   (A  ROGER POPE      D   (A  PHIL DUNNE       (A
    GUS DUDGEON       PERC (A
```
W50   FRANK WESS   W50
```
    FRANK WESS             (AB         (A) FLUTE OF THE LOOM            1973 ENTERPRISE       ENS5006
                                       (B) COMMODORE YEARS             1973 ATLANTIC         SD 2 306
                                       (C) WESS TO MEMPHIS             197  ENTERPRISE       ENS5001
```
W51   LESLIE WEST   W51
```
    LESLIE WEST       G V  (ALL        (A) MOUNTAIN                    1969 WINDFALL/BELL          4500
    N D SMART         D    (A          (B) LESLIE WEST BAND            1975 PHANTOM PHS 701 1976 1258
    FELIX PAPPALARDI  K B PROD(A       (C) THE GREAT FATSBY            1875 RCA US RS1009 PHANTOM US 0954
    NORMAN LANDSBERG  K    (A
    CORKY LAING       D    (BC MICK JONES   G       (B  DON KRETMAR    B   (BC SREDNI VOLLNER  HCA (BC
    KEN ASCHER        K    (B  BILL GELBER  B       (B  HILDA HARRIS   V   (B  TASHA THOMAS .  V   (B
    SHARON REDD       V    (B  CARL HALL    V       (B  MICK JAGGER    G   (C  JOEL TEPP       G   (C
    HOWIE WYETH       PNO  (C  GARY WRIGHT  PNO  (C  MARTY SIMON    PNO (C  NICK FERRANTELLA D  (C
    KEN HINKLE        B    (C  FRANK VICARI HRNS (BC  DANA VALERY    V   (C  JAY TRAYNOR     V   (C
```
W51A   TOMMY WEST   W51A
```
    TOMMY WEST        G V  (A          (A) HOMETOWN FROLICS            1976 LIFESONG US 6003     2794
    ROB STEVNS        K    (A
    CHARLIE BROWN     G    (A  WARREN NICHOLS  B   (A  DAVID SANBORN  SAX (A  GEORGE DEVENS  PERC(A
    PAUL PRESTOPINO   DOBRO(A  SUSAN MANCHESTER V  (A  ERIC WEISSBERG STEEL(A  TOM ROSSETLER  D  (A
    MARTY NELSON      V    (A  DAVID SPINOZZA  V   (A  DAVID MANSFIELD STEEL(A  TASHA THOMAS   V  (A
    RICK RICARDO      V    (A  GENI JACKSON    V   (A  MICHAEL KAMEN  HRNS(A  TERRY CASHMAN  V  (A
    KENNY KOSEK       FDL  (A  RICHARDS CROOKS D   (A  JOHN CROWDER   D   (A  MICHAEL RAGOGNE V  (A
```
W52   WEST BRUCE & LAING   W52
```
    LESLIE WEST       G V  (ABC        (A) WHY DONTCHA      1972 CBS  UK 65314   WINDFALL US 31929
    JACK BRUCE   B V K SYN HCA(ABC     (B) WHAT EVER TURNS YOU ON 1973 RSO  UK 2394 107 WINDFALL US 32216
    CORKY LAING       D    (ABC        (C) LIVE & KICKIN'   1974 RSO  UK 2394 128 WINDFALL US 32899
```
W53   WEST COAST POP ART EXPERIMENTAL BAND   W53
```
    BOB MARKLEY       PROD (ABCD       (A) PART ONE         1967 REPRISE US 6247 RI MIDI K24024
    DAN HARRIS        G V  (ALL        (B) VOL2             1967 REPRISE US 6270
    SHAUN HARRIS      G B V(ALL        (C) A CHILD'S GUIDE TO GOOD & EVIL 1968 REPRISE 5106      6298
    JIMMY BOWEN       PROD (           (D) WHERE'S MY DADDY?   19   AMOS            US   AAS 7004
    MICHAEL LLOYD   G K V(E            (E) LEGENDARY UNRELEASED ALBUM 1980 RASPBERRY SAWFLY  SAW 8001
```
W53A   WEST ROAD BLUES BAND   W53A
```
    TAKASHI NAGAI     V    (A          (A) WEST ROAD                   1975 BOURBON     JAP  BUC3001
    SHINJI SHIOTSUGU  G    (A
    JUNSHI YAMAGISHI  G    (A  TADASHI KOBORI   B   (A  TERUO MATSUMOTO D  (A  RYUICHIRO SENOH  HCA(A
    HIROSHI SATO      K    (A  RYUICHI IDE      K   (A  MARI KANEKO    V   (A
```
W53B   KEVIN WESTLAKE   W53B
```
    KEVIN WESTLAKE         (A          (A) STARS FADE                  1976 UTOPIA    US   1388
    JIMMY JEWELL      SAX  (A
```
W54   WET WILLIE   W54
```
    JIMMY HALL SAX    V HCA(ALL        (A) WET WILLIE        1971 CAPRICORN UK K40281 US SD 861
    JACK HALL         B V  (ALL        (A) WET WILLIE        1971 CAPRICORN RI        US    0138
    RICKY HIRSCH      G V  (ABCDEFGH   (B) WET WILLIE II     1972 CAPRICORN          US    0109
    JOHN ANTHONY      K V  (ABCDEFGH   (C) DRIPPIN' WET      1973 CAPRICORN UK K47512 US    0113
    LEWIS ROSS        D    (ABCDEFGH   (D) KEEP ON SMILIN'   1974 CAPRICORN UK 2429 115 US 0128
    WICK LARSEN       G    (B          (E) DIXIE ROCK        1975 CAPRICORN UK 2429 124 US 0149
    ELLA AVERY        V    (BDE        (F) WETTER THE BETTER 1976 CAPRICORN UK 2429 137 US 0166
    SUZI STORM        V    (B          (G) LEFT COAST LIVE   1977 CAPRICORN UK 2429 151 US 0182
    SCOTT BOYER       STEEL(B          (H) GREATEST HITS     1977 CAPRICORN          US    0200
    JAI JOHANNY JOHANSON  (BC          (J) MANORISMS         1978 EPIC      UK 82330  US 34983
    DONNA HALL        V    (DEF        (K) WHICH ONE'S WILLIE 1979 EPIC               US 35794
    JOYCE KNIGHT      V    (DE
    EARL FORD         TROM (DE  MIKE DUKE      K V(EFGJK TOM DOWD     PERC (E  MAMA HALL     K V (E
    SUSAN HALL        V    (E   PAUL HORNSBY   K   (F  LEO LABRANCHE  TPT (F  SKIP LANE     SAX (F
    DEZSO LAKATOS     SAX  (F   JEROME JOSEPH  CONGA(F  LESLIE PHILUS LIVELY D V(J  LESLIE HAWKINS V (F
    LARRY BERWALD     G    (JK  MARSHALL SMITH G V (JK  THEOPHILUS LIVELY D V (JK  PAULETTE BROWN B (K
    VANETTA FIELDS    V    (K   ANGELLE TROSCLAIR V (K  MIGHTY CLOUDS OF JOY V (K  STEVE MADAIO  TPT (K
    LENNY CASTRO      PERC (K   VICTOR FELDMAN PERC (K  CHUCK FINDLEY  HRNS (K  GARY HERBIG   SAX (K
    DAVID LUELL       SAX  (K   BOB PAYNE      TROM (K
```
W54A   JOHN WETTON   W54A
```
    JOHN WETTON     G V K B (A         (A) CAUGHT IN THE CROSSFIRE 1980 POLYDOR EG    UK   EGLP 107
    SIMON KIRKE       D PERC(A
    MALCOLM DUNCAN    SAX  (A  MARTIN BARRE     G   (A  PHIL MANZANERA  G   (A
```

(BIG) WHA KOO

```
DAVID PALMER        V   (ABC              (A) BIG WHA KOO                1977 ABC UK ABCL5208 US 971
RICK VAN MAARTH G V     (AC               (B) FRAGILE LINE               1977 EPIC US 36173
DANNY DOUMA       G V   (AC               (C) BERKSHIRE                  1978 ABC UK ABCL5238
DON FRANCISCO     PERC V(AC
CLAUDE PEPPER     D VIBES(AC PETER FREIBERGER   (C  RICHARD KOSINSKI  K V (ABC ANDREW SYLVESTER G B (A
REINIE PRESS      B SAX  (AC LEE RITENOUR     G  (A  EDDIE TUDURI      D   (B  ERIC GOTTHELF     B (B
CHUCK COCHRAN     G V  (B WILLIAM D SMITH    SAX (B  DAVID WOODFORD    K   (B  STEVE FORMAN      TROM(C
BRADFORD THOELKE  TROM (C DAN LEMELLE     SAX    (C  BUDDY McDANIEL    SAX (C  CLIFF ERVIN TPT   (C
```

WHALEFEATHER

```
MICHAL JONES      G V  (A    (A) WHALEFEATHER     1971 BLUE HORIZON UK2431 009 NASCO 9005
M E BLACKMON      K V  (A
LEONARD LE BLANC  B V  (A STEPHEN BACON    PERC (A
```

MIKE WHELLANS

```
MIK WHELLANS      G    (A    (A) DIRT WATER FOX    1976 DARA    MPA016
COLIN BAINE       G V  (A
BILLY JACKSON     B    (A CILLA FISHER  V   (A
```

WHIPPING POST

```
ASTRID COTTI      K V (A     (A) AFTER & REALLY LIVE  1978 MUSK PROJEKT   7777/2-3
GEORGE KLEE       WIND V PERC(A
FABI TONON        B    (A PUMI BRUNNER D PERC V(A    C B BUSSER    G V  (A   PIMI BENDEL G    (A
```

WHIRLWIND

```
NIGEL DIXON       V    (AB    (A) BLOWING UP A STORM  12"  1978 CHISWICK   WIK 7    CWK  3007
MICHAEL LEWIS     G    (AB    (A) BLOWING UP A STORM  10"  1978 CHISWICK CH4   GER 67058
CHRIS EMO         B    (AB    (B) MIDNIGHT BLUE        1980 CHISWICK CWK 3012 GER 67069
PHIL HARDY        D    (A
GARY HASSETT      (B
```

WHIRLY WORLD

```
IAN OLSON         V K SYN(A    (A) WIN OR LOSE (EP)   1980 MISSING LINK    MLEP 4
JOHN MURPHY       D PERC(A
GREG SUN          B PERC(A ARNIE HANNA      G   (A
```

ALAN WHITE

```
ALAN WHITE        D V  (A     (A) RAMSHACKLED        1976 ATLANTIC   US SD18167 UK K50217
PETER KIRTLEY     G V  (A
COLIN GIBSON      B PERC(A KEN CRADDOCK     K V  (A  ALAN MARSHALL     V  (A  BUD BEADLE     WIND(A
ANDY PHILLIPS     PERC (A STEVE GREGORY    WIND (A  HENRY LOWTHER     TPT (A
JON ANDERSON      V    (A STEVE HOWE    G    (A
```

BUKKA WHITE

```
BUKKA WHITE       G V  (ALL    (A) BUKKA WHITE(37/40   1964 CBS            52629
WASHBOARD SAM     PERC (A       (B) SIC 'EM DOGS       196  HERWIN     US     201
HARMONICA BOY     HCA  (C       (C) MEMPHIS HOT SHOTS  1968 BLUE HORIZON UK  7 63229
BILL BARTH        G    (C       (D) BLUES MASTERS VOL 4 196 BLUE HORIZON US     4604
TREVOR KEOHLER    PNO  (C       (E) MISSISSIPPI BLUES  1969 TAKOMA US 1001 GNP US  10011
ANCHOR            B    (C       (F) LEGACY OF THE BLUES 19 SONET       UK  SNTF 609
JIM CROSTHWAIT    PERC (C       (G) SKY SONGS VOL 1 63 1975 ARHOOLIE         F1019
BIG WILLIE        PERC (GH      (H) SKY SONGS VOL 2    1975 ARHOOLIE         F1020
JOE GRAY          D    (C       (J) PARCHMENT FARM     19 CBS      US 30036
LIGHTNIN' SLIM    (L            (K) BIG DADDY          1974 BIO  US 12049
WHISPERIN' SMITH  (L            (L) BATON ROUGE, MOSBY ST 1972 CAR  1932119
```

CHRIS WHITE

```
CHRIS WHITE       V PERC(A     (A) MOUTH MUSIC        1976 CHARISMA       CAS  1118
TOM PARKER        K    (A
CLEM CATTINI      D    (A Z JENKINS      G  (A  DAVE OLNEY       B  (A  SHEL TALMY      PERC (A
```

KIERAN WHITE

```
KIERAN WHITE V G B HCA (A     (A) OPEN DOOR          1975 GULL UK GULP1011 GER 622307
DAVE SHEEN        B D  (A
CHAS JANKEL       K G V(A ROGER BUNN     B   (A  DONAL LUNNEY    SYN G V(A GEOFF DRISCOLL  WIND(A
TIM STAFFEL       V    (A
```

LENNY WHITE

```
LENNY WHITE       D K B(ALL    (A) VENUSIAN SUMMER    1975 NEMPEROR   US 435   UK K50213
DOUG RAUCH        B    (A       (B) BIG CITY          1977 NEMPEROR   US 441   UK K50345
DOUG RODRIGUEZ    G    (A       (C) ADVENTURES OF ASTRAL PIRATES 1978 ELEKTRA US 6E121 UK K52065
RAY GOMEZ         G    (AB      (D) STREAMLINE        1978 ELEKTRA            UK K52108
JIMMY SMITH       ORG  (A       (E) BEST OF FRIENDS   1979 ELEKTRA   US 223
DON BLACKMAN      K SYN(A       (F) 29                1980 ELEKTRA            UK K52257
DAVID SANCIOUS    K    (A
JEFF SIGMAN       G    (C WELDON IRVINE    K   (A  ONAJE ALLAN GUMBS K  (AB PATRICK GLEASON   K (AB
PETER ROBINSON    K    (C HUBERT LAWS     FLT  (A  DENNIS MACKAY    PERC (A  LARRY YOUNG     ORG (A
TOM HARREL        G    (C LARRY CORYELL   G    (A  AL DIMEOLA       G   (A   BRIAN AUGER      K (B
HERBIE HANCOCK    K    (B VERDINE WHITE    B   (B  TOWER OF POWER   HRNS (B  JAN HAMMER       K (B
JERRY GOODMAN     VLN  (B NEAL SCHON      G    (B  LINDA TILLERY    V   (B   ALEX LIGERTWOOD  G (B
JACK MILLS        G    (B CLIVE CHAMAN    B    (B  BENNIE MAUPIN    SAX (B   LENNOX LAINGTON CONGA(B
PAUL JACKSON      B    (B MARCUS MILLER    B   (B  ALEX BLAKE       B  (BC   MIROSLAV VITOUS   B (B
MIKE GIBBS        PNO  (B LOIS COLIN      HARP (B  GARY KING        D  (B    DAVID JOHNSON   CONGA(B
NICK MOROCH       G    (C
```

MICHAEL WHITE

```
MICHAEL WHITE     (ALL    (A) THE SUN & MOON HAVE COME TOGETHER 1969 CAPITOL  US  SKOA 423
BABATUNDE         (J       (B) WEREWOLF           1970 CAPITOL   US
JOSEPH BARBOZA    (J       (C) 4TH WAY            1971 CAPITOL   US
NAPOLEON BROCK    (J       (D) SPIRIT DANCE       1972 IMPULSE   US  AS9215
DAVID DANIEL      (J.      (E) PNEUMA             1973 IMPULSE   US  AS9221
BRUCE FOWLER      (J       (F) THE LAND OF SPIRIT & LIGHT 1974 IMPULSE US AS9241
WALT FOWLER       (J       (G) FATHER MUSIC MOTHER DANCE 1974 IMPULSE US AS9268
DEWILLI GONGA     (J       (H) GO WITH THE FLOW   1975 IMPULSE   US  AS9281
MUFFY JAMES       (J       (J) THE X FACTOR       1978 ELEKTRA US 138 UK  K52095
HUBERT LAWS       (J       (K) WHITE NIGHT        1979 ELEKTRA US 183
KING ERRISON      PERC (J
BYRON MILLER      (J AIRTO MOREIRA     (J  EDWARD MYERS     (J  GREGORY PHILLINGANES (J
PETSYE POWELL     (J DUANE ROBERSON    (J  PATRICE RUSHEN   (J  MIKE SEMBELLO        (J
ALBERT WING       (J ROLAND BAUTISTA   (J  MARVIN BOXLEY    (J  PATTY BROOKS         (J
LEON CHANCLER     (J RAUL DE SOUZA     (J
```

TONY JOE WHITE

```
TONY JOE WHITE   G V HCA(ALL    (A) BLACK & WHITE              1968 MONUMENT US 18114  UK SMO  5027
TOMMY McCLURE    B      (BFE    (B) CONTINUED                  1969 MONUMENT US 18133  UK SMO  5035
SAMMY CREASON    D      (BFE    (C) TONY JOE                   1970 MONUMENT US 18142  UK SMO  5043
JAMES MILHART    D      (BF     (D) TONY JOE WHITE             1971 WB       US 1900   UK  K46068
MIKEE UTLEY      ORG    (BFE    (E) THE TRAIN I'M ON           1972 WB       US 2580   UK  K46147
DAVID BRIGGS     K      (AFE    (F) BEST OF                    1973 WB EURO 054 92274  UK  K56149
JERRY CARRIGAN   D      (AFE    (G) HOME MADE ICE CREAM        1973 WB       US 2708   UK  K46229
NORBERT PUTNAM   B      (AFE    (H) EYES                       197  20TH CENTURY           BT523
CHIP YOUNG       G      (A      (J) TONY JOE WHITE             1977 20th CENTURY           PS2030
JIMMY ISBELL     D      (A      (K) REAL THANG                 1980 CASABLANCA US 7233
TIPPY ARMSTRONG  G      (C      (DE) TWO ORIGINALS             1973 WEA GER 66028
JOHN HUGHEY      STEEL(C
ROGER HAWKINS    D      (C  DAVID HOOD      B  (C  BARRY BECKETT   K  (C  RONNIE BARON   K  (C
CHARLES CHALMERS SAX   (C  TOM DOWD        V  (C
```

WHITE HORSE

```
JON LIND         G V (A        (A) WHITE HORSE                1977 CAPITOL       US    ST 11687
BILLY NICHOLLS   PNO G V(A
KENNY ALTMAN     G B  (A  JEFF PORCARO     D  (A  PAUL BARRERE    G  (A  BILL PAYNE   SYN K(A
JOE PORCARO      PERC (A  GARY MALLABER    D  (A  BOB GLAUB       B  (A  CALEB QUAYE G   (A
RUSS KUNKEL      D    (A  FRED TACKETT     G  (A  CHUCK DOMANICO  B  (A  REGGIE KNIGHTON G(A
DAVY LIVINGSTONE STEEL(A  DAVID PAICH      PNO (A
```

WHITE CLOUD

```
THOMAS JEFFERSON KAYE G V (A   (A) WHITE CLOUD               1972 ?
JOANNE VENT      V    (A
RICHARD CROOKS   PERC (A  TEDDY WENDER     K V (A  KENNETH KOSEK   FDL V(A  DONALD PAYNE    B  (A
CHARLIE BROWN    G    (A  ERIC WEISSBERG BAN STEEL (A
```

WHITE HEAT

```
BOB SMEATON      V    (A        (A) IN THE ZERO HOUR         1981 VALIUM     UK    VALP 101
ALAN FISH        G    (A
BRYAN YOUNGER    G    (A  COLIN ROBERTS    B  (A  JOHN ROBERTS    D  (A  SIMON BOSWELL  K  (A
JOHN EARLE       SAX  (A  GEORGE WATERS    D  (
```

WHITE LIGHTNING

```
BUSTA CHERRY JONES B V (A       (A) WHITE LIGHTNIN'          1975 ISLAND     US    ILPS9325
DONALD KINSEY    G V  (A
WOODY KINSEY     D V  (A
```

WHITE MANSIONS (CONCEPT)

```
JESSI COLTER     V    (A        (A) WHITE MANSIONS           1978 A&M US 6004  UK  AMLX64691
WAYLON JENNINGS  G V  (A
JOHN DILLON V G K FDL (A  STEVE CASH      HCA V(A  ERIC CLAPTON    G  (A  BERNIE LEADON  G V (A
HENRY SPINETTI   D    (A  DAVE MARKEE     B   (A  TIM HINKLEY     K  (A  PAUL KENNERLEY V  (A
```

WHITE NOISE

```
DAVID VORHAUS    (ABC           (A) AN ELECTRIC STORM        1969 ISLAND US 9303  UK  ILPS 9099
JOHN WHITMAN     V    (A        (A) AN ELECTRIC STORM        1976 ANTILLES US 7011
DELIA DERBYSHIRE (A             (B) WHITE NOISE              1975 VIRGIN            v2032
BRIAN HODGSON    (A             (C) RE ENTRY                1980
PAUL LYTTON      PERC (A
ANNIE BIRD       V    (A  VAL SHAW         V  (A
```

WHITE WATER

```
JOHN VASTANO     G    (A        (A) OUT OF THE DARKNESS      1973 RCA        US    APLI 0091
RICHARD DOMANE   K TPT(A
PAUL PHILLIPS    HRNS (A  JOHN EMMA       SAX (A  BOB FIOCCO      B  (A  CONRAD CATALANO  D(A
```

WHITE RUSSIA

```
TREVOR WATKINS   V    (A        (A) EAST SIDE STORY         1981 ALADIN         85055
GERRIT MEYER     G    (A
UWE HOFFMAN      D    (A  T PIERS HEADLEY  B  (A
```

WHITE WITCH

```
RON GOEDART      V    (AB       (A) WHITE WITCH             1972 CAPRICORN   UK    K47505
BUDDY PENDERGRASS K   (AB       (A) WHITE WITCH             1972 CAPRICORN   US    0107
BUDDY RICHARDSON G    (AB       (B) A SPIRITUAL GREETING    1974 CAPRICORN   US    0129
BOBBY SHEA       PERC (AB
BILL PETERSON    PERC (B   CHARLIE SOUZA    B  (B  BEAU FISHER     D V (A
```

WHITEFACE

```
STEVE HARDWICK   G V  (A        (A) WHITEFACE              1979 MERCURY     US    SRM13765
KYLE HENDERSON   B V  (A        (B) CHANGE OF FACE         1981 MERCURY     US    SRM14017
DOUG BARE        K V  (A
BENNY RAPPA          D V (A
```

WHITESPIRIT

```
MALCOLM PEARSON  K    (A        (A) WHITESPIRIT            1980 MCA         UK    MCF 3079
PHIL BRADY       B    (A
BRUCE RUFF       V    (A  JANICK GERS      G  (A  GRAEME VRALLEN  D  (A
```

WHITEHEAT

```
                 WHITEHEAT                                 1975 RCA         US    0853
```

WHITEHOUSE

```
                                (A) ERECTOR                1980 COME        UK    881007
```

GEOFF WHITEHORN

```
GEOFF WHITEHORN  G V  (A        (A) WHITEHORN              1974 STATESIDE   JAP   ISS 80164
GERRY MORRIS     B    (A
JOHN RICHARDSON  D    (A  PETE ARNESON     K  (A  CLIFF DAVIS     D  (A  DICK MORRISSEY  SAX (A
TONY ATKINS      V    (A
```

WHITFORD- ST HOLMES

```
BRAD WHITFORD    G    (A        (A) WHITFORD- ST HOLMES    1981 CBS  US
DEREK ST HOLMES  V    (A
DAVE HEWITT      B    (A  STEVE PACE       D  (A
```

```
    BOBBY WHITLOCK    G V (ABCD     (A) BOBBY WHITLOCK        1972 DUNHILL US 50121 UK CBS   65109
    RICK VITO         G   (B        (B) RAW VELVET           1972 DUNHILL US 50131 UK CBS   65301
    DON PONCHER       D   (B        (C) ONE OF A KIND        1975 CAPRICORN US 0160
    KEITH ELLIS       B   (B        (D) ROCK YOUR SOX OFF    1976 CAPRICORN US 0168  UK 2429 139
    T J TINDALL       G BAN(C
    DICKIE BETTS      G   (C   CHUCK LEAVELL    PNO (C   KENNY TIBBETTS   B  (C   RICK ECKSTEIN   D (C
```

```
    JAKI WHITREN  G V BANJO(A        (A) RAW BUT TENDER      1973 EPIC             UK       65465
    PAT DONALDSON     B   (A
    GERRY CONWAY      D   (A   LINDSAY COOPER  BASSOON(A   ALBERT LEE       G  (A   MARIE GOOSENS   HARP (A
    ROB YOUNG       FLT   (A   HENRY VIII         JUG (A   JOHN VAN DERRICK VLN(A   GORDON HUNTLEY  STEEL(A
    FRANK RICOTTI   PERC  (A   IVAN CHANDLER        K (A   HARRY BECKETT    HRNS(A   STAN SULZMANN   SAX (A
    BRIAN BROCKLEHURST B  (A   STUART COWELL        G (A   MIKE LESLIE      G V(A
```

```
    PETE TOWNSHEND    G K V(ALL      (A) MY GENERATION       1965 BRUNSWICK     UK  LAT 8616
    ROGER DALTREY     V HCA(ALL      (A) "    "     "        1966 DECCA         US      74664
    JOHN ENTWISTLE    B K V(ALL      (A) "    "     "        1972 MCA           US      2044
    KEITH MOON        D V (ALL TO 1978 (A) "    "   "        1980 VIRGIN        UK      V2179
    KENNY JONES       D   (F        THE WHO                  1966 POLYDOR       FR  2383 137
    NICKY HOPKINS     PNO (KR       A QUICK ONE               1966 REACTION      UK      593002
    DAVE ARBUS        VLN (RK         "   "    "              1970 BACKTRACK     UK   2407 008
    ROD ARGENT        K   (T        WHO SELL OUT             1967 TRACK 612002   UK   613 002
    ANDY FAIRWEATHER LOW V (T         "   "    "              1970 BACKTRACK     UK   2407 009
    CHRIS STAINTON    K   (NL         "   "    "              1967 DECCA         US      74950
    ELTON JOHN        PNO V(G          "   "    "             1974 POLYDOR       GERM 2675 089
    ERIC CLAPTON      G   (G        A QUICK ONE/SELL OUT     19   TRACK         2683 038
    RON WOOD          G   (G          "   "    "              19   TRACK         GER 2644 002
    FUZZY SAMUELS     B   (G          "   "    "              197  MCA           US      2046
    CALEB QUAYE       G   (G        HAPPY JACK               1967 DECCA         US      74892
    MICK RALPHS       G   (G          "   "    "              197  MCA           US      2045
    GRAHAM DEACON     D   (G        MAGIC BUS                1968 DECCA         US      75064
    PHIL CHEN         B   (G.         "   "    "              1972 MCA           US      2047
    ALAN ROSS         G   (G        MAGIC BUS/MY GENERATION  1975 MCA           US   2 4068
    RICHARD BAILEY    D   (G        DIRECT HITS              1969 TRACK         UK   613 006
    DAVE WINTOUR      B   (G        TOMMY          DBL        1969 TRACK         UK   613 013/4
    TONY MURRAY       B   (G          "    "       DBL        1972 TRACK         2657 002
    NIGEL OLSSON      D   (G          "    "                  19   POLYDOR       GER 2612 006
    RAY COOPER        PERC (G          "    "                 196  DECCA         US      7205
    DAVEY JOHNSTONE   G   (G          "    "                  197  MCA           US      2-1005
    GERALD SHAW       ORG (G        TOMMY PART ONE           1972 TRACK         UK   2406 007
    TONY STEVENS      B   (G        TOMMY PART TWO           1972 TRACK         UK   2406 008
    ANN MARGARET      V   (G        (G) TOMMY SOUNDTRACK     1975 POLYDOR       PD 29502
    OLIVER REED       V   (G        THE BEST OF TOMMY        197  POLYDOR       NL  2383 130
    JACK NICHOLSON    V   (G        LIVE AT LEEDS            1970 TRACK         UK   24-6 001
    ROBERT POWELL     V   (G          "    "     "           1970 DECCA         US      79175
    PAUL NICHOLAS     V   (G          "    "     "           1972 MCA           US      2022
    TINA TURNER       V   (G          "    "     "           197  MCA           US      3023
    BARRY WINCH       V   (G          "    "     "           19   POLYDOR       NL   65 124
    ARTHUR BROWN      V   (G        MEATY BEATY BIG & BOUNCY 1971 TRACK         UK   2406 006
    VICTORIA RUSSELL  V   (G          "    "    "    "       1971 DECCA         US      79184
    BEN ARIS          V   (G          "    "    "    "       1972 MCA           US      2025
    MARY HOLLAND          (G          "    "    "    "       19   MCA           US      3025
    JENNIFER BAKER        (G        POP HISTORY VOL 4 (DBL)  1971 POLYDOR       GERM 2675 012
    SUSAN BAKER           (G        (K)WHO'S NEXT            1971 TRACK         UK   2408 102
    IMOGEN CLAIRE         (G        (K) "    "               1971 DECCA         US      79182
    JULIET KING           (G          "    "    "            1972 MCA           US      2023
    GILLIAN KING          (G        (L)QUADROPHENIA   (DBL)  1973 TRACK         UK   2657 013
    SIMON TOWNSHEND       (G          "    "    "            1973 MCA           US      10004
    LIZA STRIKE       V   (G        (N) "    "    "  SOUNDTRACK 1979 POLYDOR     GER 2644 001
    MYLON LEFEVRE     V   (G          "    "    "            1979 POLYDOR       UK   2625 037
    BILLY NICHOLLS        (G        INSTANT PARTY            19   BRUNSWICK     NL   173 269
    JESS RODEN        V   (G        POP HEROES               19   POLYDOR       GERM 2459 410
    MARGO NEWMAN          (G        THE WHO & JIMI HENDRIX(DBL) 19 KARUSSELL     GERM 2674 001
    SARAH McINTOSH        (G        WHO DID IT (WITHDRAWN)   19   TRACK         UK   2856 001
    VICKI BROWN       V   (G        GREATEST ROCK SENSATION  19   KARUSSELL     GERM 2345 104
    KIP TREVOR            (G        VERY BEST OF             19   POLYDOR       JAP  MFP 1163
    HELEN CHAPPELLE       (G        THE STORY OF THE WHO     19   POLYDOR       JAP  MPZ81012
    PAUL GURVITZ          (G        PERFECT COLLECTION       19   POLYDOR       JAP  MP 94478
    ALISON DOWLING        (G        I'M A BOY                19   POLYDOR       JAP  SLPM1354
                                    EXCITING                 19   POLYDOR       JAP  MP 1385
                                    GOLDEN DOUBLE ALBUM      19   POLYDOR       JAP  MP93556
                                    ODDS & SODS              1974 TRACK         UK   2406 116
                                      "    "   "             1974 MCA           US      2126
                                    BEST OF 1964 74          1975 POLYDOR       UK   2674 017
                                    BEST OF                  1975 POLYDOR       2482 172
                                    BEST OF                  19   POLYDOR       GERM 185  152
                                    BEST OF LAST TEN YEARS (DBL) 197 KARUSSEL GER 26740017 2662 323
                                    PORTRAIT OF              1975 POLYDOR       2482 100
                                    WHO (COMP)               197  IMPACT        6886 551
                                    WHO (COMP)               19   POLYDOR       FR   6371 450
                                    (R) WHO BY NUMBERS       1975 POLYDOR       UK   2490 129
                                    (R) "    "    "          1975 MCA           US      2161
                                    (R) "    "    "          19   MCA           US      3026
                                    (R) "    "    "          1975 POLYDOR       GER  2480 309
                                    STORY OF THE WHO         1976 POLYDOR       UK   2683 069
                                      "    "   "             19   POLYDOR       GERM 2668 015
                                    (T) WHO ARE YOU          1978 POLYDOR       UK   WHOD5004
                                    (T) "    "    "          1978 MCA           US      3050
                                    (T) "    "    "          1978 POLYDOR       EURO 2417 325
                                    WHO ARE YOU/LIVE AT LEEDS (DBL) 1980 POLYDOR CASS 3574 089
                                    KIDS ARE ALRIGHT         1979 POLYDOR       UK   2675 179
                                    (F) FACE DANCES          1981 POLYDOR       UK   WHOD 5037
                                    (F) FACE DANCES          1981 POLYDOR       EURO 2302 106
                                    HOOLIGANS                1981 MCA           US
                                    PHASES (BOXED SET)       1981 POLYDOR       UK   2675 216
                                    ITS HARD                 1982 POLYDOR       UK   WHODC5066
```

```
W73                              WICHITA FALL                                        W73
    LARRY WATSON     B    (A        (A) LIFE IS BUT A DREAM        1969 LIBERTY UK83208 IMPERIAL US12417
    DANNY ROUSH      G V  (A
    LEN FEIGIN       D    (A   PHILIP BLACK      G V (A
W73A                            BENOIT WIDEMANN                                       W73A
    BENOIT WIDEMANN  K    (A        (A) STRESS                     1980 BALLON NOW              BAL 13002
    CLEMENT BAILLY   D    (A
W74                              WIDOWMAKER                                          W74
    ARIEL BENDER     G    (AB       (A) WIDOWMAKER                 1976 JET UK 2310 432  UK RI JETLP 15
    STEVE ELLIS      V    (A        (A) WIDOWMAKER                 1976 UA               US     LA 642
    PAUL NICHOLS     D    (AB       (B) TOO LATE TO CRY            1977 UA  UK UAG30038  US     LA 723
    LLOYD LANGTON    G    (A
    BOB DAISLEY      B    (AB  JOHN BUTLER      V    (B   ZOOT MONEY      K   (A
W74A                             WIGGY BITS                                          W74A
                                 (A) WIGGY BITS                   1976 POLYDOR         US      1 6081
W75                              WIGWAM                                              W75
    JIM PEMBROKE     K V  (BCDHJKLM  (A) HARD & HORNEY             1969 LOVE            SWED LRLP 9
    RONNIE OSTERBERG D    (CHJKLMBD  (B) TOMBSTONE VALENTINE       1970 LOVE            SWED     LRLP19
    JUKKA GUSTAVSON  K    (BCDHL     (C) FAIRYPORT                 1971 LOVE            SWED LRLP44/55
    PEKKA POHJOLA    B VLN(BCDH      (D) WIGWAM                    1972 LOVE            SWED LRLP 511
    PEKKA RECHARDT   G    (HJKLM     (E) WICKED IVORY              1972 LOVE            SWED     LRLP52
    MANS GROUNDSTROEM B   (JKLM      (F) BEING                     1974 LOVE            SWED LRLP 92
    ESA KOTILAINEN   K    (JM        (G) PIGWORM                   1974 LOVE            SWED LRLP 103
    PAAVO MAIJANEN   B V  (JKLM      (H) LIVE FROM TWILIGHT ZONE   1975 LOVE            SWED LXLP517/8
    ILMARI VARILA    OBOE (C         (J) DEAD AT THE NUCLEAR NIGHTCLUB  1975 LOVE SWEDLRLP129 UK VIRGIN 2035
    TAPIO LOUHENSALO K    (C         (K) LUCKY GOLDEN STRIPES      1976 VIRGIN          UK       2051
    HANNU SAXELIN    WIND (C         (L) DARK ALBUM                1978 LOVE            IMP  LRLP 227
    RISTO RENSOLA    WIND (C         (M) RUMOURS ON THE REBOUND (DBL COMP) 1979 VIRGIN  UK   VGD 3503
    UNTO HAAPA AHO   WIND (C
    EERO KOIVISTOINEN SAX (CM  PEKKA POYRY      SAX   (C   HESSU HIETANEN  K   (KLM TIMO KOJO    V  (L
    COSTA APETREA    G    (M   MATS HULDEN  B   (D      JUKKA TOLONEN   G   (D   NIKKE NIKAMO    G  (D
W76                              DANNY WILD                                          W76
    DANNY WILD            (A        (A) WILD IN THE COUNTRY        1978  RAW                 RWLP 102
W77                              WILD ANGELS                                         W77
    JOHN HAWKINS     G    (C        (A) OUT AT LAST                1972 DECCA       UK    SKL 5134
    ROD COTTER       B    (C        (B) LETS GET BACK TO ROCK      1975 PYE         UK    GH  614
    ROB O'CONNOR     D    (c        (C) LIVE AT THE REVOLUTION     1970 B+C               BCM 101
    BILL KINGSTON    V    (C        (D) RED HOT'N'ROCKIN'          1970 B+C               BCM 102
    MAL GRAY              (C        (E) TOO LATE TO CRY            19   JET         UK    UAG 30038
    MITCH MITCHELL   G    (
    GEOFF BRITTON    D    (
W77A                             WILD BUTTER                                         W77A
    RICK GAREN       G V  (A        (A) WILD BUTTER                196
    JOHN SENNE       G V  (A
    STEVE PRICE      B V  (A   JERRY BUCKNER      K V  (A
W77B                             WILD BLUE YONDER                                    W77B
                                 (A) ENTHUSIASM                   1980 TOTALLYOUTOFCONTROLL  US 1
W77C                             WILD CHERRY                                         W77C
    TAMPA LANN       V    (A        (A) I LOVE MY MUSIC            1978 EPIC        US    35011
    BECK GOLDSTEIN   V    (A
    RANDY BRECKER    HRNS (A   MICHAEL BRECKER    HRNS (A
W78                              WILD HORSES                                         W78
    BRIAN ROBERTSON  G    (AB       (A) THE FIRST ALBUM            1980 EMI         UK    EMC 3326
    JIM BAIN         B    (AB1      (B) STAND YOUR GROUND          1981 EMI         UK    EMC 3368
    NEIL CARTER      G    (A
    CLIVE EDWARDS    D    (AB  JOHN LOCKTON      G    (B   REUBEN ARCHER   V   (1  LAURENCE ARCHER G (1
    FRANK NOON       D    (1
W78A                             WILD MAGNOLIAS                                      W78A
    BO DOLLIE        V TAMB(A       (A) WILD MAGNOLIAS             19   BARCLAY            80529
    MONK BREAUX      V CONGA(A
    'GATOR JUNE' JOHNSON  V TAMB(A
    'CRIP' ADAMS     V PERC(A  QUARTER MOON TOBIAS V PERC(A GALE JOHNSON  PERC V(A  BUBBA SCOTT PERC V(A
    JAMES SMOTHERS   PERC V(A  GITCHIE           D(A   EARL TURBINTON WIND(A   JULIUS FARMER   B  (A
    SNOOKS EAGLIN    G    (A   LARRY PANNA       D    (A   ALFRED ROBERTS CONGA(A
W78B                             WILD TCHOUPITOULAS                                  W78B
                                 (A) WILD TCHOUPITOULAS           1976 ISLAND      US    9360
W79                              WILD TURKEY                                         W79
    GLEN CORNICK     B G K(AB       (A) BATTLE HYMN                1971 CHRYSALIS   UK    CHR 1002
    TWEKE LEWIS      G    (AB       (B) TURKEY                     1972 CHYSALIS    UK    CHR 1010
    MICK DYCHE       G V  (B
    JEFF JONES       D    (AB  STEVE GURL       K   (B   GARY PICKFORD HOPKINS G V(AB  JON BLACKMORE   G V(A
W80                              WILD WALLY                                          W80
    WILD WALLY            (         (A) I GO APE                   1971 CONSTELLATION     CCS 5001
W81                              MARTY WILDE                                         W81
    MARTY WILDE      V    (ALL  DR DOOLITTLE                       1968 MARBLE ARCH UK    MAL 738
    BIG JIM SULLIVAN G    (AB   ROCK'N'ROLL                        1970 PHILIPS           6308 010
    BRIAN BENNETT    D    (AB   GOOD ROCKIN' THEN & NOW            1974 PHILIPS           6382 102
    LICORICE LOCKING B    (AB   BAD BOY                            19   EPIC       US    EPC 3686
    TONY BELCHER     G    (AB   (A)WILDE ABOUT MARTY (RI)          1969 EPIC US 3711 PHILIPS UK 13147
                               WILDCAT                             198  PHILIPS    SWED
                               (B) SHOWCASE                        1960 PHILIPS    UK
W82                              WILDERNESS ROAD                                     W82
    NATE HERMAN      G K V(ABC      (A) WILDERNESS ROAD            19   CBS         US    31118
    WARREN LEMING G V BANJ (ABC     (B) THREE GENUINE TRANSPLANT   19   REPRISE     US    PRO 556
    ANDY HABAN       B V  (ABC      (C) SOLD FOR PREVENTION OF DISEASE 1973 REPRISE US    2125
    RAY WARD              (A
    TOM HABAN       D V OBOE(ABC J A RICHARDSON   B    (A   RICK MANN    STEEL (C JIM HORN    SAX (C
    DON MENZA        SAX  (C   VENETTA FIELDS    V    (C   CLYDIE KING  V   (C  SHIRLEY MATTHEWS V (C
```

W82A   **WILDING BONUS**   W82A

```
    DANNY WILDING      FLT (A        (A) PLEASURE SIGNALS            1978 DJM  UK DJF 20553 US  VISA 7003
    PETE BONUS         G   (A
    PHIL COLLINS       D   (A   PHIL CHEN       B   (A  KIKI GYAN       K   (A  REBOP KWAKU BAAH PERC(A
    ASHTON TOOTLE      HRNS (A   PHIL TODD       HRNS (A  JOHN GOODSALL   G   (A  BAYETE           K  (A
    GREGG SHEEHAN      D   (A   JOHN GIBLIN     B G (A  PRESTON HEYMAN   D   (A  ROBIN LUMLEY     K  (A
    ANDY CLARK         K   (A   KATE ST JOHN    OBOE (A  MIKE SHRIEVE     D   (A  CHRIS PARREN     K  (A
```

W82B   **WILDLIFE**   W82B

```
    STEVE OVERLAND     G V (A        (A) BURNING                     1980 CHRYSALIS        UK  CHR 1288
    MARK BOOTY         K   (A
    CHRIS OVERLAND     G   (A   ROB SKEAT       K B (A  PETE JUPP       D   (A  RUPERT HINE K PERC V(A
    TREVOR MORAIS      D   (A   JOHN GIBLIN     B   (A  GEOFFREY RICHARDSON  (A
```

W83   **MIKE WILHELM**   W83

```
    MIKE WILHELM           (A        (A) WILHELM                     1976 ZIG ZAG  UK         UA ZZ1
    RICHARD OLSEN WIND PROD B K (A
    GINO RYMER         D   (A   KENNY STREIGHT  B   (A  DENNIS WILSON   V   (A  PETER MINTUM     K  (A
    J BETHARDS  TPT PERC B (A   CHRIS WILSON  G V   (A  RICK KUNSTER  G V   (A  SID PAGE         VLN (A
    DENNIS CORSO       V   (A   RICK PADEN  V       (A  CAPRICE REYNOLDS V   (A  JOHN ILLY        V  (A
```

W84   **BIG JOE WILLIAMS**   W84

```
    BIG JOE WILLIAMS   G V (ALL   BIG JOE WILLIAMS           1975 STORYVILLE              SLP224
    MARY WILLIAMS      V   (U     BIG JOE WILLIAMS(LEGACY No6) 197 SONET UK SNTF635 US GNP  10016
    SAM FOWLER         V HCA(M     BIG JOE WILLIAMS           19   EVEREST      US          218
    WILLIE EALEY       V PNO(M     BIG JOE WILLIAMS           19   WORLD PACIFIC US          21897
    LEE WILLIAMS       V   (M     BLUES FROM MISSISSIPPI DELTA 19  BLUES ON BLUE US          10003
    CHARLIE MUSSELWHITE HCA(T     BIG JOE & ROBERT PETE WILLIAMS 1975 STORYVILLE            SLP225
    ROGER ALLEN CLARK  D   (I     (B) BLUE ON HIGHWAY 49      196  DELMARK       US          DL 604
    JERRY BRIDGES      B   (I     BACK TO THE COUNTRY         19   TESTAMENT     US          2205
    RANSOM KNOWLING    B   (PB    (F)CLASSIC DELTA BLUES      1964 CBS           UK          63813
    J D SHORT          G V HCA(S   COUNTRY BLUES              19   SPECIALTY     UK          SNTF5014
                                  DONT LEAVE ME               19   POLYDOR                   616  011
                                  (I)DONT YOUR PLUMS LOOK MELLOW 19 BLUESWAY     UK          BLS 6080
                                  EARLY RECORDINGS            197  MAMLISH       US          1810
                                  HAND ME DOWN MY OLD WALKING STICK 1968 LIBERTY            LBS83207
                                  HELL BOUND & HEAVEN SENT    1964 FOLKWAYS      US          FTS31004
                                  (M)MALVINA MY SWEET WOMAN   1974 OLDIE BLUES   NL  OL      2814
                                  MISSIPPIPPI JOE WILLIAMS    19   FOLKWAYS      US          3820
                                  BLUES FOR NINE STRING       19   BLUESVILLE    US          1056
                                  LIVE AT FOLK CITY           1968 BLUESVILLE US 1067 XTRA UK 5059
                                  MISSIPPIPPI DELTA BLUES     19   SPIVEY        US          1005
                                  STUDIO BLUES                196  BLUESVILLE    US          1083
                                  BIG CRAWLIN' SNAKE          1970 RCA           US  INT     1087
                                  (P)NINE STRING GUITAR BLUES 196  DELMARK       US          627
                                  (P) "   "   "   "           196  FOLKWAYS      US          3820
                                  PINEY WOOD BLUES            196  DELMARK       US          602
                                  RAMBLIN' WANDERIN' BLUES    19   STORYVILLE                SLP 163
                                  (S) STAVIN' CHAIN BLUES     196  DELMARK       US          609
                                  (S) SUPER BLACK BLUES       196  GOODY         FR          10006
                                  (T)THINKING OF WHAT THEY DID 1969 ARHOOLIE     US          1053
                                  (U)TOUGH TIMES              1960 ARHOOLIE      US          1002
```

W84A   **CLAUDE WILLIAMS**   W84A

```
    CLAUDE WILLIAMS        (A        (A) KANSAS CITY GREATS         197 BIG BEAR  UK         BEAR 25
```

W84B   **JERRY WILLIAMS & ROADWORK**   W84B

```
    JERRY WILLIAMS     V   (A        (A) TOO FAST TO LIVE          1977 SONET SWED  SLP 2604 UK SNTF791
    PEDER SUNSAHL      D   (A
    INGEMAR RAGEFEDT   G   (A   CAJ HOGBERG B G PNO V  (A  DOUGIE LAWTON   G   (A  LARS AKE JOHANSSON PERC G(A
```

W84C   **DENIECE WILLIAMS**   W84C

```
    DENIECE WILLIAMS   V   (ALL   (A) THIS IS NIECY              1977 CBS  UK 81869
    AL McKAY           G   (AB    (B) SONGBIRD                   1977 CBS  UK 86946
    FREDDIE WHITE      D   (AB    (C) THATS WHAT FRIENDS ARE FOR 1978 CBS  UK 86068
    JOHNNY MATHIS      V   (C     (D) WHEN LOVE COMES CALLING    1979 CBS  UK 83202
    SYDNEY BARNES      V   (ABC   (E) MY MELODY                  1981 CBS  UK 84874
    STEVE MADAIO       TPT (AB
    RANDALL ALDCROFT   TROM (A   GALE ROBINSON    HRNS (A  RAY PIZZI       SAX (A  ERNIE WATTS      SAX (A
    CHARLES FEARING    G   (BC   JOHN ROWIN       G    (A  PAULINHO DACOSTA PERC(A  VICTOR FELDMAN   VIBES(B
    MICHAEL HARRIS     TPT (B    LOUIS SATTERDFIELD TROM(B  DON MYRICK      SAX (BC  ANDREW WOOLFOLK  SAX (B
    MARILYN ROBINSON   HRNS (B   JEFF PORCARO     D    (C  MAURICE WHITE D V PROD(AB  JERRY PETERS    K  (AB
    VERDINE WHITE      B   (AB   OSCAR BRASHEAR   TPT (AB  GEORGE BOHANON  TROM (AB  SIDNEY MULDROW   HRNS(A
    PLAS JOHNSON       SAX (A    TERRY HARRINGTON SAX (B   NATHAN WATTS    B   (B   MARLO HENDERSON  SAX(B
    DAVID GARIBALDI    D   (B    LARRY DUNN       SYN (B   CHUCK FINDLEY   TPT (B   CHARLES LOPER TROM (B
    AZAR LAWRENCE      SAX (B    GEORGE PATTERSON SAX (B   ALAN ROBINSON   HRNS (B  RAY PARKER  G PROD(B
    DAVID SHIELDS      B   (B    GREG PHILLINGANES K   (C  GARY COLEMAN    VIBES(C  MAXINE WILLARD   V  (C
    STEVE LUKATHER     G   (B    MIKE PORCARO     B   (C   GARY HERBIG     SAX (C   JULIA TILLMAN    V(C
    JERRY HEY          HRNS (C   WAH WAH WATSON   G   (C   EDDIE BROWN     PERC (C  LARRY JACOBS  V  (C
    LARRY FARROW       K   (C    OLLIE BROWN      PERC (C  DYANNE CHANDLER V   (C   GENE PAGE   STR HRN(C
    ED GREENE          D   (C    DAVID FOSTER     K PROD(C  BILL CHAMPLIN  V   (C   DAVID HUNGATE B  (C
    RICHARD FELDMAN    G   (C    SCOTT EDWARDS    B   (C   JACK ASHFORD    PERC (C  SYLVESTER RIVERS K (C
```

W84D   **DUKE WILLIAMS & THE EXTREMES**   W84D

```
    DUKE WILLIAMS      K V(ALL   (A) FANTASTIC FEDORA           1974 CAPRICORN US
    T J TINDALL        G V B(AB   (B) A MONKEY IN A SILK SUIT   1974 CAPRICORN US 0119
    BOBBY HARTNAGLE    G   (AB
    COTTON KENT        K   (AB   TOMMY HOUGH      B V (A  EARL SCOOTER    PERC V(A  DIMITRI CHIMES   G  (A
    EARL YOUNG         D   (AB   SKIP DRINKWATER  PERC (B  RON BAKER      B   (B   RALPH SCHUCKETT  K  (B
    LARRY WASHINGTON   PERC (B   BRUCE STEINBERG  HCA (B  CHRIS BOND      SYN (B
```

W85   **JODY WILLIAMS**   W85

```
    JODY WILLIAMS      G V (A        (A) LEADING BRAND(6 TRACKS)   1977 RED LIGHTNIN      RL0018
    BERNARD BARKSON    SAX (A
    HAROLD ASHBY       SAX (A   LAFAYETTE LEAKE  PNO (A  RED HOLLOWAY    SAX (A  WILLIE DIXON  B (A
    BOB GUTHRIE        D   (A
```

```
JOHN WILLIAMS       G   (ALL      (A) CHANGES                         1971 FLY UK HIFLY 5 US CBS 31091
HERBIE FLOWERS      G B (ABH      (B) HEIGHT BELOW                    1973 FLY              UK     HIFLY 16
FRANCIS MONKMAN     K   (H        (C) GREATEST HITS                   1974 CBS                     30051
BARRY MORGAN        D   (AH       (D) RHAPSODY                        1974 CBS                     73350
ADRIAN BRETT        WIND (H       (E) & FRIENDS                       1976 CBS                     73487
RICHARD HARVEY      REC (H        (F) SPANISH GUITAR                  1976 WESTMINSTER  UK    WG1001
VIC FLICK           G   (H        (G) BEST FRIENDS                    1976 RCA          UK    RS1094
LAWRENCE JUBER      G   (H        (AB) CHANGES /HEIGHT BELOW          1977 CUBE RI      UK    T00FA12
LES THATCHER        G   (H        (H) TRAVELLING                      1978 CUBE         UK    HIFLY27
HAROLD FISHER       D   (H        (J) BRIDGES                         1979 LOTUS        UK    WH 5015
STUART ELLIOTT      D   (H
PATRICK GOWERS      K   (H   DANNY THOMPSON    B   (A   JIM LAWLESS       PERC (A   CHRIS LAURENCE  B  (A
JOE MUDELE          B   (A   RAY COOPER      PERC (A   BARRY GUARD       PERC (A   ALAN PARKER     G  (A
CHRIS SPEDDING      G   (A   RICK WAKEMAN      K   (A   DAVID SNELL       HARP (A   CHRIS TAYLOR    WIND (A
ROY WILCOX          WIND (A   TONY COE         WIND (A   RONNIE CHAMBERLAIN WIND (A   KENNY WHEELER   TPT (A
STANLEY RODERICK    TPT (A   RALPH IZEN        TPT (A   DEREK WATKINS     TROM (A   NAT PECK        TROM (A
DON LUSHER          TROM (A   PAT HARLEY       TROM (A   RAY PREMRU        TROM (A   RONNIE VERRALL  PERC (A
TERRY COX           PERC (A   TRISTAN FRY      PERC (AB   BRIAN GASCOIGNE  PERC (B   CHARLOTTE NASSIM KOTO (B
VIRAM JASANI        TABLA(B   ROY BABBINGTON    B   (B   JOHN MARSHALL     D   (B   WILLIAM DE MONT CELLO (B
MORRIS LUBAN        VLA (B   BRIAN MOLLINSON    B   (B   CHRIS BOWERS-BROADBENT K(B   DARRYL RUNSWICK  B   (B
PETE MORGAN         B   (B   BARRY DE SOUZA    D   (B   KENNY CLAIRE      D   (B   TREVOR TOMKINS  D   (B
ALAN BRANSCOMBE     VIBES(B   DAVID CORKHILL   FLT (B   JACK ELLORY       FLT (B   GEORGE CROZIER  FLT (B
DUDLEY MOORE        ORG (B   ROLAND HARKER     G   (B   DICK ABEL         G   (B
```

```
LARRY WILLIAMS      V   (ALL      (A) LIVE                            1965 SUE          UK    ILP 922
JOHNNY GUITAR WATSON G  (ABD      (B) THE LARRY WILLIAMS SHOW         1965 DECCA        UK    LK  4691
PLAS JOHNSON        SAX (C        (C) HERE'S LARRY WILLIAMS           196  SPECIALITY US 2109 UK SNTF5008
ALVIN'RED'TAYLOR    SAX (C        (D) TWO FOR THE PRICE OF ONE        19   OKEH              OKS 14122
ERNIE FREEMAN       PNO (C        (E) MISSING & UNISSUED SIDES        19   SPECIALITY FR 2225
RENEE HALL          G   (C        (F) GREATEST HITS                   19   OKEH              OKS 12123
BARNEY KESSEL       G   (C
TED BRINSON         B   (C   RAY BROWN        B   (C   EARL PALMER       D   (C   GERALD WILSON   TPT (C
DAVE SHERIDAN       SAX (AB   TONY HURLEY      SAX (AB   PHILIP GOODHAND TAIT K (AB   IVOR SHAKLETON  G   (AB
KIRK RIDDLE         B   (AB   DICK FORCEY       D   (AB
```

```
MASON WILLIAMS      G V (ALL      (A) PHONOGRAM RECORD                1969 WB           US    WS1729
BILL CUNNINGHAM     G   (H        (B) MASON WILLIAMS EAR SHOW         1969 WB           US    WS1766
RICK CUNHA          G   (H        (C) MUSIC                           1969 WB           US    WS1788
AL CASEY            G   (H        (D) HAND MADE                       19   WB           US    WS1838
LARRY KNECHTEL      B   (H        (E) THEM POEMS & THINGS             196  JOY               JOY 118
HAL BLAINE          D   (H        (F) SHAREPICKERS                    10   WB           US    WS1941
TOMMY MORGAN        HCA (H        (G) FEUDIN BANJOS                   19   OLYMPIC      US    7105
STEVE LA FEVER      B   (H        (H) IMPROVED                        1971 WB           UK    K46120
MILT HOLLAND        PERC (H       (I) FRESH FISH                      197  FLYING FISH  US    FF059
PATTER SMITH        B   (H        (J) LISTENING MATTER                19   EVEREST      US    3265
DAVE DAWSON         V   (H
SUZETTE GRANT       G V (H   NANCY AMES        V   (H   ARTIE AZENZOR     PNO (H   JAN HYDE        D   (H
GARY CARLSON        G   (H   RONNIE TUTT       D   (H
```

```
PAUL WILLIAMS       V   (ALL      (A) DELTA BLUES SINGER              1973 SONET        UK    SNTF 654
ROGER SUTTON        B   (2        (A) IN MEMORY OF ROBERT JOHNSON     1973 INTERCORD    GER   28754
GLENN CAMPBELL      G   (A        (1) PAUL WILLIAMS SET 1967
BOB HALL            K   (A        (2) PAUL WILLIAMS SET 1968
KEITH ELLIS         B   (A
EDDIE YARLETT       G   (A   PAT DONALDSON     B   (A   ALUN DAVIES       G   (A   SPENCER DAVIS   G  (A
JON MARK            G   (A   ROY MILLS             (1   ROD SLADE         B   (1   TEDDY CHILDS       (1
JOHN ALMOND         WIND (12   JIMMY CRAWFORD       (12   JEFF CONDON      HRNS (12   ALAN WHITE      D  (2
JOHN WIGGINS            (2
```

```
TONY WILLIAMS       D   (A        (A) JOY OF FLYING                   1979 CBS US 35705 UK    83338
RONNIE MONTROSE     G   (A
HERBIE HANCOCK      K   (A   BRIAN AUGER   K    (A   JAN HAMMER         K   (A   STANLEY CLARKE  B  (A
GEORGE BENSON       G   (A
```

```
JAMES WILLIAMSON        (ALL      (A) CHICAGO                         19   B&B               FR 33034
DAVE MYERS          B   (B        (B) AIN'T SICK NO MORE              1973 BLUESWAY     BLS 6071
EDDIE TAYLOR        G   (B        (C) & SNOOKY PRYOR                  197  CAROLINE UK C1502 BIGBEAR  21
SNOOKY PRYOR        HCA (BCD       (D) HOME SWEET HOMESICK JAMES       1976 BIG BEAR     BEAR10
WILLIE SMITH        D   (B
BOB HALL            PNO (CD   BOB BRUNNING      B   (CD   JOHN HUNT        D   (CD   PETE YORK       D   (D
JIMMIE LEE ROBINSON B   (D
```

```
ROBIN WILLIAMSON        (ALL      (A) MYRRH                           1972 ISLAND            HELP 2
SYLVIA WOODS K HCA V B (C        (B) JOURNEY EDGE                     1977 FLYING FISH  US    033
CHRISTOPHER CASWELL WIND V(C     (C) AMERICAN STONEHENGE              1978 FLYING FISH  US    062
JERRY McMILLAN      VLN V(C       (C) AMERICAN STONEHENGE             1978 CRIMINAL     UK    STEAL 4
PETE GRANT          BAN G(C       (D) GLINT AT THE KINDLING           1979 CRIMINAL     UK    STEAL 6
LOUIS KILLEN        CONC (C       (D) GLINT AT THE KINDLING           1979 FLYING FISH  US    096
DIRK DALTON         B   (C        (E) SONGS OF LOVE & PARTING         1981 FLYING FISH  US    257
STU BROTMAN         B   (C
CAROL SHRIVE        VLN (F   MIKE GARSON       K   (E   DAVID CAMPBELL    VLA (E   JESSE ERLICH    CELLO(E
JUDY GAMERAL        DULC(E
```

SONNY BOY WILLIAMSON (1)

```
SONNY BOY WILLIAMSON  V HCA(A      (A) SONNY BOY WILLIAMSON         19   RCA                       FXM1 7215
(JOHN LEE WILLIAMSON)              (B) BLUEBIRD BLUES              1970 RCA INT                    INT  1088
JOE WILLIAMS       G    (B         (C) SONNY BOY VOL 1             1975 BLUES CLASSICS                  BC3
YANK RACHELL       MAND (B         (D) SONNY BOY VOL 2             1975 BLUES CLASSICS                  BC20
SPECKLED RED       PNO  (B         (E) SONNY BOY VOL 3             1975 BLUES CLASSICS                  BC24
WILLIE HATCHER     MAND (B
ROBERT LEE McCOY   G    (B   WALTER DAVIS    PNO (B   JOSH ALTHEIMER   PNO  (C   FRED WILLIAMS    D  (C
WASHBOARD SAM      PERC (C   ARMAND JACKSON  D   (C   BLIND JOHN DAVIS PNO  (C   ALFRED WLKINS    B  (C
BILL BROONZY       G    (C   MATT MURPHY     G   (D   TED SUMMIT       G    (C   RANSOM KNOWLING  B  (C
CHARLIE McCOY      G    (C   WALTER DAVIS    PNO (C
```

SONNY BOY WILLIAMSON (II)

```
SONNY BOY WILLIAMSON  V    (ALL    (A) SONNY BOY & MEMPHIS SLIM   1963 VOGUE                      LD  63930
(RICE MILLER)                      (B) DOWN & OUT BLUES           1964 CHESS US 1437 UK PYE       NPL 28036
BRIAN AUGER        K    (M         (B) DOWN & OUT BLUES           1967 MARBLE ARCH   UK RI         MAL   662
JOE HARRIOT        SAX  (M         (C) HELP ME                    1964 CHESS                       CRE  6001
ALAN SKIDMORE      SAX  (M         (D) & THE YARDBIRDS            1964 FONTANA       UK            TL5277
JIMMY PAGE         G    (M         (D) & THE YARDBIRDS            1964 MERCURY       US            21071
RICKY BROWN        B    (M         (D) & THE YARDBIRDS            196  FONTANA                     858 025
MICK WALLER        D    (M         (D) & THE YARDBIRDS            1968 FONTANA                     SFJL 960
ERIC CLAPTON       G    (D         (D) & THE YARDBIRDS            1975 PHILIPS                     6435 011
DUKE HUDDLESTON    SAX(P           (D) & THE YARDBIRDS            1980 MERCURY       US            8003
KEITH RELF         HCA  (D         (E) ONE WAY OUT               196  CHESS    US 1417 RI         CHV   417
JIM McCARTY        D    (D         (F) IN MEMORIUM               1965 CHESS                       CRL  4510
CHRIS DREJA        G B  (D         (G) REAL FOLK BLUES           196  CHESS         US            1503
PAUL SAMWELL SMITH B    (D         (H) MORE FOLK BLUES           196  CHESS         US            1509
ERIC BURDON        (Q              (I) SONNY BOY WILLIAMSON      19   STORYVILLE                  SLP   158
JOHN STEEL         D    (Q         (J) BLUES OF                  19   STORYVILLE                  671 170
HILTON VALENTINE   G    (Q         (K) PORTRAIT IN BLUES         19   STORYVILLE US 4016 UK       671 158
MATT MURPHY        G    (QJKPVW     (L) DONT SEND ME NO FLOWERS   1968 MARMALADE                  608 004
CHAS CHANDLER      B    (Q         (M) THE ORIGINAL              19   BLUES CLASSICS              BC    9
ALAN PRICE         K    (Q         (N) BUMMER ROAD               19   CHESS                       1536
MEMPHIS SLIM       PNO  (AJKX      (O) THIS IS MY STORY          19   CHESS                       50027
BILLY STEPNEY      D    (JKW       (P) DONT MAKE A MISTAKE       19   BLUES BALL    US            2004
MUDDY WATERS       G    (EV        (M) JAM SESSION               1975 CHARLY        UK            CR 30011
WILLIE DIXON       B    (EPVW      (Q) & THE ANIMALS             1975 CHARLY        UK            CR 30018
BUDDY GUY          G    (PVW       (U) KING BISCUIT TIME         1976 ARHOOLIE                    R 2020
LAFAYETTE LEAKE    PNO  (PVW       (V) BLUES MASTERS             19   CHESS                       2ACBM 206
OTIS SPAN          PNO (EPVW       (V) CHICAGO GOLDEN YEARS      1976 VOGUE         FR            427 804
WALTER DAVIS       PNO  (R         (W) BYE BYE BIRD              1979 BLUES NIGHT                 073 1668
BIG JOE WILLIAMS   G    (Y         (X) CHEST MASTERS             1981 CHESS    UK CXMD 4001
OLIVER HARRIS      B    (P         (Y) & BIG JOE WILLIAMS (1 SIDE) 1980 P VINE                    JAP PLP 9014
CLIFF BIVENS       V B  (PU
S P LEARY          D    (P   JOE WILLIE WILKINS G  (PU  FRED BELOW      D   (EPV ODIE PAYNE     D  (V
MILTON RECTOR      B    (V   JARRETT GIBSON    SAX (PV  CLIFTON JAMES   D   (PV  DAVE CAMPBELL  PNO (PU
FROCK              D    (U   CLARENCE LONNIE   PNO (U   JIMMY ROGERS    G   (EV  ROBERT LOCKWOOD G (EPNV
LUTHER TUCKER      G    (ENV AL DUNCAN         D   (V   JACK MYERS      B   (PV
```

WILLIE & THE RED RUBBER BAND

```
WILLIE REDDEN      G V  (AB        (A) WILLIE & THE RED RUBBER BAND 1968 RCA       US            LSP 4074
GLEN BALLARD       G B  (AB        (B) WE'RE COMING UP            1969 RCA         US            LSP 4193
CHARLES ADDINGTON  K    (AB
CONLAY BRADFORD    D    (AB  LARRY FIELD  G  (AB  JOHN BUCK WILKEN   G  (B   BEGIE CRUZER    K  (B
```

PETE WILLSHER

```
PETE WILLSHER      STEEL G(AB       (A) GUITAR MAGIC              19   JOY                       JOYS 158
STUART COWELL      G    (B          (B) STEEL SEASONS             1977 PYE                       NSPL18539
ROB HENDRY         G    (B
TONY KELLY         G V  (B   LUCE LANGRIDGE  D  (B   BOB LOVEDAY     FDL (B   GRAHAM WAYNE   B  (B
TRISTRAM FRY       PERC (B   RAPH RAVENSCROFT WIND (B  KEITH MILLER   K   (B   KEITH NELSON   BANJ(B
MANDI WILSON       V    (B
```

CHUCK WILLIS

```
CHUCK  WILLIS      V    (AB        (A) STOOP DOWN BABY.. LET YOUR DADDY SEE  1972 LAVAL   US   LVB 1327
                                   (B) THE KING OF THE STROLL     19   PIONEER       JAP P4587A
```

WILLOW

```
                                   (A) WILLOW                     1974 20TH CENTURY US 420
                                   (B) BRANCHING OUT              1974 20TH CENTURY US 450
```

VIOLA WILLS

```
VIOLA WILLS        V    (A         (A) WITHOUT YOU                1979 LINE GER     LLP 5023
```

DENNIS WILSON

```
DENNIS WILSON  V K D STR(A         (A) PACIFIC OCEAN BLUE         1977 CARIBOU US 34354   UK 81672
JAMIE JAMERSON     B    (A         (B) ONE OF THOSE PEOPLE        1980 ELEKTRA US 230
ED TULIJA          G V  (A
JOHN KANTON        G    (A   BOBBY FIGUEROA  D  (A   BILL LAMB       HRNS(A   LANCE BULLER   HRNS(A
CHARLIE McCARTHY   HRNS (A   ED CARTER     G B  (A   CHUCK DOMANICO  B   (A   EARLE MARKEY   G  (A
HAL BLAINE         D    (A   RICKY FATAAR    D  (A   MICHAEL ANDREAS HRNS(A   JANICE HUBBARD HRNS(A
KAREN LAMM-WILSON  V    (
```

CARL WILSON

```
CARL WILSON        V G K (A        (A) CARL WILSON                1981 CARIBOU UK 84840   US 37010
MYRNA SMITH        V    (A
GERALD JOHNSON     B    (A
JAMES STROUD       D    (A   JOEL PESKIN     SAX (A   JAMES GUERCIO   G B PERC (A
JOHN DALY          STEEL(A   ALAN KRIGGER    D   (A   RANDY McCORMICK CLAR K(A
```

JACKIE WILSON V (ALL

JACKIE WILSON

HES SO FINE	195	BRUNSWICK US	54042
LONELY TEARDROPS	1958	BRUNSWICK US	54045
DOGGIN' AROUND	1959	BRUNSWICK	
NIGHT	1960		
SO MUCH	1960	BRUNSWICK US	754050
SINGS THE BLUES	1960	BRUNSWICK US	754055
MY GOLDEN FAVOURITES	1960	BRUNSWICK US	754058
MY GOLDEN FAVOURITES	196	CORAL UK	LVA9135
A WOMAN A LOVER A FRIEND	1960	BRUNSWICK US	754059
TRY A LITTLE TENDERNESS	1961		
YOU AIN'T HEARD NOTHING YET	1961	BRUNSWICK US	754100
BY SPECIAL REQUEST	1961	BRUNSWICK US	754101
BY SPECIAL REQUEST	1961	CORAL UK	LVA9151
BY SPECIAL REQUEST	1961	CORAL UK	SVL3018
BODY & SOUL	1962	BRUNSWICK US	754105
BODY & SOUL	1962	CORAL UK	LVA9202
WORLDS GREATEST MELODIES	196	BRUNSWICK US	754106
WORLDS GREATEST MELODIES	196	CORAL UK	LVA9214
AT THE COPA	196	BRUNSWICK US	754108
AT THE COPA	196	CORAL UK	LVA9209
BABY WORK OUT	1962	BRUNSWICK US	754110
MERRY CHRISTMAS	196	BRUNSWICK US	754112
SHAKE A HAND	1962	BRUNSWICK US	754113
GOLDEN FAVOURITES	196	BRUNSWICK US	754115
SOMETHIN' ELSE	1964	BRUNSWICK US	754117
SOUL TIME	196	BRUNSWICK US	754118
SPOTLIGHT ON	1965	BRUNSWICK US	754119
SOUL GALORE	1966	BRUNSWICK US	754120
SOUL GALORE	196	CORAL UK	LVA9232
WHISPERS	1966	BRUNSWICK US	754122
HIGHER & HIGHER	1967	BRUNSWICK US	754130
HIGHER & HIGHER	1967	MCA UK	MUPS304
MANUFACTURES OF SOUL	196	BRUNSWICK US	754134
TOO MUCH	196	MCA UK	MUPS333
I GET THE SWEETEST FEELING	1968	BRUNSWICK US	754138
I GET THE SWEETEST FEELING	1968	MCA UK	MUPS361
GREATEST HITS	19	BRUNSWICK US	754140
DO YOUR THING	19	BRUNSWICK US	754154
DO YOUR THING	19	MCA UKMUPS 405	
ITS ALL A PART OF LOVE	1971	BRUNSWICK US	754158
YOU GOT ME WALKING	1973	BRUNSWICK US	754172
YOU GOT ME WALKING	1973	BRUNSWICK	BRLS3001
GREATEST HITS	197	BRUNSWICK US	754185
GREATEST HITS	1973	BRUNSWICK	BRLS3004
VERY BEST OF	1975	BRUNSWICK	BRLS3016
THIS LOVE IS REAL	1973	BRUNSWICK US	754167
BEAUTIFUL DAY	197	BRUNSWICK US	754189
NOWSTALGIA	19	BRUNSWICK US	754199
NOBODY BUT YOU	1977	BRUNSWICK US	754212
NOBODY BUT YOU	1977	BRUNSWICK	BRLA5002

LARRY JON WILSON (ALL

LARRY JON WILSON

(A) NEW BEGINNINGS	1975 MONUMENT US 33382 RI	MC 6635
(B) LET ME SING MY SONGS	1976 MONUMENT US 34041 RI	MC 6636
(C) LOOSE CHANGE	1977 MONUMENT US	MG 7615
(D) THE SOJOURNER	1979 MONUMENT US	MG 7631

LEROY WILSON (A

LEROY WILSON

(A) BEST OF	1978 UA US	LA 807

FRANK WILSON K V (A
MELVYN GALE K V (A
ALAN ROSS G V (A   STEVE STROUD   B   (A   ADRIAN SHEPARD   D   (A

WILSON /GALE

(A) GIFT WRAPPED SET	1980 JET UK	JETLP223

MARIO MILLO K V (A
TOWO PILT K V (A
DOUG BLIGH D (A   DUNCAN McGUIRE   B   (A

WIND CHASE

(A) SYMPHINITY	1976 FESTIVAL	36216

DEBORAH HARRY V PERC(A
GIL FIELDS D (A
WAYNE KIRBY B V K(A
IDA ANDREWS WIND (A   PETER BRITTAIN   G V (A   PAUL KLEIN   G V (A   ANTON CARYSFORTH   D(A
STEVE DE PHILLIPS B V (A   PETER C LEEDS   PERC (A   ARTIE KORNFELD PROD PERC(A   HARRIS WIENER   K V (A

WIND IN THE WILLOWS

(A) WIND IN THE WILLOWS	1968 CAPITOL	2956
(A) WIND IN THE WILLOWS	1979 CAPITOL RI	CAPS 1030

JESSE WINCHESTER

JESSE WINCHESTER G V K(ALL
AMOS GARRETT G (BC
MARTY HARRIS B V (DE
CHRIS CASTLE D (D
BOB COHEN G (DE
CHRISTIAN STROCH D (D
MAURICE BEAUCHAMP K (D
DONALD BROWN K (G
RON DAWN STEEL(DE
CARLISLE MILLER SAX (D   BRUCE MURCHISON   VLN (D   KEN PEARSON   K   (AD   DON HABIB   B (D
BOB LUCIER STEEL(D   DAVE LEWIS   D   (AE   LORRI ZIMMERMANN   V   (D   SHARON RYAN   V (D
MICKEY RAPHAEL HCA (E   PAUL BUTTERFIELD   HCA (D   RICKY SKAGGS   FDL (E   TOM SZCZESNIAK   ACC(E
JON CLARKE SAX (E   JAMES BURTON   G   (E   EMMYLOU HARRIS   V   (E   HERB PEDERSEN   V (E
ANNE MURRAY V (E   DIANNE BROOKS   V   (E   NICOLETTE LARSON   V   (E   ROBBIE ROBERTSON G (A
LEVON HELM D (A   BOB BOUCHER   B   (AB   DAVID REA   G V (A   GUY BLACK   D (A
AL CHERNEY VLN (A   ANDRE BENICHOU   G   (B   DOUG SCHMOLZE   G   (B   CHARLES VIBER   VLN(B
GORD FLEMING PNO (B   JIMMY OLIVER   B   (B   GENE COTTON   B   (B   NORMAN SMART   D (B

(A) JESSE WINCHESTER	1971 AMPEX	US A10104
(B) 3RD DOWN 110 TO GO	1972 BEARSVILLE US 2102	UK K45512
(AB) JESSE WINCHESTER/3RD DOWN	1976 BEARSVILLE	UK K85507
(C) LEARN TO LOVE IT	1974 BEARSVILLE US 6953	UK K55506
(D) LET THE ROUGH SIDE DRAG	1976 BEARSVILLE US 6964	UK K55512
(E) NOTHIN' BUT A BREEZE	1977 BEARSVILLE US 6968	UK K81853
(F) A TOUCH ON THE RAINY SIDE	1978 BEARSVILLE US 6984	
(G) TALK MEMPHIS	1981 BEARSVILLE US 6989	

JESSE WINCHESTER

RON FRANKEL	D	(B	SAM KELLY	CONGA(B	DON ABRAMS	PERC (B	CARL MARSH	SYN (G
EDDIE FISHER	D	(G	BLAIR CUNNINGHAM	D	(G	STEVE COBB	B	(G	WILLIE MITCHELL	K (G
WALTER PERSON	PERC (G	MICHALE TOLES	G	(G	ERMA SHAW	V	(G	CINDY FARR	V (G
ELIZABETH SMITH	V	(G	GARY BURKE	D	(G	BRAD STAHL	B	(G

W102   WINDS OF CHANGE   W102

BRIAN ADDISON	WIND (A		(A) ILLUSIONS		1979 EMI	UK	EMA 791
STAN SULZMANN	WIND (A
ANTON WEINBERG	WIND (A	DAVID WHITE	WIND	(A	TONY HYMAS	K SYN (A	JIM LAWLESS	PERC(A
STEVE GREY	K	(A	BARRY DE SOUZA	D	(A	RICHARD HARVEY	SIN (A	RICKY HITCHCOCK	G (A
PAUL WESTWOOD	B	(A	SIMON PHILLIPS	D	(A	HERBIE FLOWERS	B	(A	FRANK RICOTTI	PERC(A
LITTLECHAP STRINGS		(A

W103   PETE WINGFIELD   W103

PETE WINGFIELD	K V (AB		(A) BREAKFAST SPECIAL	1975 ISLAND	UK	ILPS9333
DELISLE HARPER	B	(A		(B) LOVE BUMPS & DIZZY SPELLS	1976 ISLAND NOT RELEASED
NEIL HUBBARD	V	(A
JOSEPH EDWARD WRIGHT	G (A	GLEN LE FLEUR	D	(A	CHRIS MERCER	SAX (A

W103A   WINGS (US)   W103A

	(A) WINGS	19 DUNHILL	US	DS50046

W104   THE WINKIES   W104

MICHAEL DESMARAIS	D	(A		(A) THE WINKIES	1975 CHRYSALIS	US	CHR 1066
PHILIP RAMBOW	G V	(A
GUY HUMPHREYS	G V	(A	BRIAN TURRINGTON	B V K(A

W104A   COLIN WINSKI   W104A

COLIN WINSKI		(A		(A) ROCK THERAPY	1980 CHRYSALIS	1318

W105   WINTER   W105

	(A) WINTER	197 EMI	UK	EMC 3266

W106   EDGAR WINTER   W106

EDGAR WINTER V SAX K	(ALL	(A) ENTRANCE	1970 EPIC	US 26503	UK 64083
JIMMY GILLEN	D	(A	(B) WHITE TRASH	1971 EPIC	US 30512	UK 64298
RANDAL DOLANON	G	(A	(AB) ENTRANCE WHITE TRASH	1976 EPIC	US 33770	UK 81191
GENE KURTZ	B	(A	(C) ROAD WORK	1972 EPIC	US 31249	UK 67244
JOHNNY WINTER G HCA V	(ABCF	(D) THEY ONLY COME OUT AT NIGHT	1973 EPIC	US 31584	UK 65074
RAY ALONGE	HRNS (A	(E) SHOCK TREATMENT	1974 EPIC	US 32461	UK 65640
EARL W CHAPIN	HRNS (A	(F) JASMINE NIGHTDREAMS	1975 BLUE SKY US 33483	UK 80772
BROOKS TILLOTSON	HRNS (A	(G) WITH RICK DERRINGER	1975 BLUE SKY US 33798	UK 69181
JERRY LA CROIX V SAX HCA(BCH	(H) RECYCLED	1977 BLUE SKY US 34858	UK 82228
JON SMITH	V SAX(BCH	(J) EDGAR WINTER ALBUM	1979 BLUE SKY US 35989	UK 83648
MIKE McCLELLAN	V TPT(BC	(K) STANDING ON ROCK	1981 BLUE SKY US 36494
KEITH BENSON	D	(J
BOBBY RAMIREZ	D	(BC	GEORGE SHECK	B	(BH	FLOYD RADFORD	G	(BH	RICK DERRINGER	G V(BCDEFG
TASHA THOMAS	V	(B	JANICE BELL	V	(B	CARL HULL	V	(B	MAERETHA STEWART	V (B
ALBERTINE ROBINSON V	(B	EILEEN GILBERT	V	(B	RAY BARRETTO	CONGA(B	RANDY HOBBS	B (CD
MARSHALL CYR	TPT (CH	TILLY LAWRENCE	TPT	(C	DAN HARTMAN B V G PERC(EDFGH	CHUCK RUFF	D V (EDFG
PAUL PRESTOPINO	G BAN(G	JOHN SIEGLER	B	(G	ROBERT ARNOLD	B	(H	BOZ SCAGGS	G (
JERRY WEEMS	G	(	RONNIE MONTROSE	G	(G	GEORGE RECILE	V	(H	DAN MINATRE	G (H
JOHNNY BADANAJEK	D	(D	RICK MAROTTA	D	(F	JAMES WILLIAMS	B	(J	CRAIG SNYDER	G (J
LARRY WASHINGTON	PERC(J	AL FERRANTE G MAND	(K	RONNIE LAWSON	K V	(K	SCOTT SPRAY	B (K
GREG CARTER	D PERC(K	MONIQUW WINTER	V	(K

W107   JOHNNY WINTER   W107

JOHNNY WINTER	G V HCA(ALL	(A) JOHNNY WINTER	1969 CBS	US 9826	UK 63619
EDGAR WINTER SAX K V	(ADMQSN	(B) PROGRESSIVE BLUES EXPERIMENT 1969 LIBERTY US LBR1001	UK 83240
JOHN TURNER	D	(ABDS	(B) PROGRESSIVE BLUES EXPERIMENT 1969 IMPERIAL US 12431
TOMMY SHANNON	B	(ABDS	(B) PROGRESSIVE BLUES EXPERIMENT 1973 SUNSET	UK 50264
DENNIS COLLINS	B	(D	(C) FIRST WINTER	1970 CBS	US 7513 BUDDAH UK 2359 011
MUDDY WATERS	V G	(PS	(D) SECOND WINTER (3 SIDES)	1970 CBS	US 9947	UK 66231
RICK DERRINGER	G	(FGLMSN	(E) STORY	1971 GRT	US 101 MARBLE ARCH UK 34
KENNY ASCHER	K	(N	(E) STORY	19 SONET	SWED 9972
RANDY JO HOBBS	B	(FLMOSGn	(F) JOHNNY WINTER AND...	1971 CBS	US 30221	UK 64117
RICHARD HUGHES	D	(LOMSN	(G) JOHNNY WINTER AND..LIVE	1971 CBS US 30475 RI 33651	UK 64289
JAMES COTTON	HCA	(PS	(H) ABOUT BLUES	1971 JANUS	US 3008
PINETOP PERKINS	PNO	(PS	(I) EARLY TIMES	1971 JANUS	US 3023
BOB MARGOLIN	G	(PS	(J) BEFORE THE STORM	197 JANUS	US 3056
CHARLES CALMESE	B	(PS	(K) AUSTIN TEXAS	1976 UA	US LA139
WILLIE SMITH	D	(PS	(L) STILL ALIVE & WELL	1973 CBS	US 32188	UK 65484
DAN HARTMAN	B	(MSR	(M) SAINTS & SINNERS	1974 CBS	US 32715	UK 65842
BOBBY CALDWELL	D	(GMS	(N) JOHN DAWSON WINTER III	1974 BLUE SKY US 33292	UK 80568
TASHA THOMAS	V	(M	(O) CAPTURED LIVE	1976 BLUE SKY US 33944	UK 69230
CARL HALL	V	(M	(P) NOTHIN' BUT THE BLUES	1977 BLUE SKY US 34813	UK 82141
LANI GROVES	V	(M	(Q) WHITE HOT & BLUE	1978 BLUE SKY US 35475	UK 82963
KANSAS	PERC (M	(R) RAISIN' CAIN	1980 BLUE SKY US 36343	UK 84103
BARBARA MASSEY	V	(M	(S) THE JOHNNY WINTER STORY(DBL) 1980 BLUE SKY	UK 22112
RANDY BRECKER	TPT (MN
ALAN RUBIN	TPT (M	LEW DELGATTO	SAX (MN	JO JO GUNNE	PERC (M	JON SMITH	SAX (M
I P SWEAT	B	(QS	BOBBY TORELLO	D	(QRS	PAT RAMSEY	HCA (QS	PAT RUSH	G (QS
RANDY ZEHRINGER	D	(FS	JEREMY STEIG	FLT (L	TODD RUNDGREN	K	(L	MARK KLINGMAN	PNO (LS
FLOYD RADFORD	G	(OS	CHUCK RUFF	D	(S	A WYNN BUTLER	SAX (AS	KARL GARIN	TPT (AS
JERRY PORTNOY	HRNS (S	PAUL PRESTOPINO	PERC (SN	JACKDAW	V	(S	DENNIS FERRANTE	V (S
WILLIE DIXON	B	(AS	WALTER HORTON	HCA (AS	NORMAN RAY	SAX (A	CARRIE HOSSELL	V (A
PEGGY BOWERS	V	(A	ELSIE SENTER	V	(A	JON PARIS B V HCA G (R	SUSAN WARFORD	V (R
KRISTY GRIGGS	V	(R	ALLAN MARTIN	V	(R	BERNADETTE MAZUR	V	(R	TOM STROHMAN	SAX (R
DAVE STILL	PERC (R	CINDY MURRAY	V	(R	MIKE BRECKER	SAX (N	DAVE TAYLOR	TROM(N

W108   JOHNNY & EDGAR WINTER   W108

```
W108                        JOHNNY & EDGAR WINTER                                    W108
   JOHNNY WINTER    G V  (A      (A) TOGETHER ,LIVE        1976 BLUE SKY  US 34033  UK  81338
   EDGAR WINTER     SAX V(A
   RICK DERRINGER   G    (A   FLOYD RADFORD    G   (A   RANDY JO HOBBS   B  (A   DAN HARTMAN   K  (A
   RICHARD HUGHES   D    (A   CHUCK RUFF       D   (A
W109                              RUBY WINTERS                                       W109
   RUBY WINTERS     V    (AB     (A) RUBY WINTERS         1978 CREOLE              CRLP 512
                                 (B) SONGBIRD             1979 K TEL               NE 1045
                                 (C) I WILL               1980 MILLENIUM    US     8006
W110                        WINTERS BROTHERS BAND                                    W110
   DONNIE WINTERS   G V  (AB     (A) COAST TO COAST       197  ATLANTIC        US 38106
   DENNIS WINTERS   G V  (AB     (B) WINTER BROTHERS BAND 1977 ATLANTIC UK K50343  US 36145
   GENE WATSON      B    (B
   KENT HARRIS      D    (B   DAVID DAVIS      K   (B   CHARLIE DANIELS  FDL (B   DON MURRAY  CONGAS(B
   DON WINTERS SNR  V    (B   TAZ DIGREGORIO   PNO (B
W110A                            WINTERGARDEN                                        W110A
                                 (A) WINTERGARDEN         1979 HARVEST    EURO 45265
W111                             STEVE WINWOOD                                       W111
   STEVE WINWOOD    K G V(ALL    (A) WINWOOD              197  UA            9964
   NICOLE WINWOOD   V    (CE     (B) WINWOOD & FRIENDS    197  SPRINGBOARD   US SPB4040
   BROTHER JAMES    PERC (A      (C) STEVE WINWOOD        1977 ISLAND     UK   ILPS 9494
   ALAN SPENNER     B    (C      (D) ARC OF A DIVER       1980 ISLAND     UK   ILPS 9576
   WILLIE WEEKS     B    (C      (E) TALKING BACK TO THE NIGHT 1982 ISLAND UK   ILPS 9777
   ANDY NEWMARK     D    (C
   JOHN SUSSWELL    D    (C   JUNIOR MARVIN    G   (D   JIM CAPALDI   D V (CA  REBOP        PERC(C
   ERIC CLAPTON     G    (BA  YARDBIRDS            (B   JEFF BECK     G   (B   GINGER BAKER  D  (BA
   LONG JOHN BALDRY V    (B   JACK BRUCE       B   (B   SONNY BOY WILLIAMSON (B  MUFF WINWOOD     (A
   SPENCER DAVIS    A    (A   PETER YORK       D   (A   DAVE MASON    G   (A   CHRIS WOOD    FLT(A
   RICK GRETCH      B    (A   NB (A&B) ARE COMPILATION ALBUMS OF STEVE'S PREVIOUS BANDS AND OTHER OUT TAKES
W112                                   WIRE                                          W112
   ROBERT GOTOBED   D    (ABCD    (A) PINK FLAG          1977 HARVEST US 11757 UK   SHSP 4076
   GRAHAM LEWIS     B V  (ABCD    (B) CHAIRS MISSING     1978 HARVEST           UK   SHSP 4093
   BRUCE CLIFFORD GILBERT G(AD    (C) 154                1979 HARVEST           UK   SHSP 4105
   COLIN NEWMAN     G V  (ABCD    (C) 154                1979 WB   US 3398
   MIKE THORNE      PROD K (BC    (D) DOCUMENT & EYEWITNESS 1981 ROUGH TRADE   UK   ROUGH 29
   KATE LUCAS       FLT  (BC
   TIM SOUSTER      VLA  (C   HILLY KRISTAL    V   (C   JOAN WHITING    WIND (C
W113                               WIRELESS                                          W113
   MIKE CRAWFORD    G    (AB    (A) POSITIVELY HUMAN ,RELATIVELY SANE 1979 MERCURY  US    3750
   STEVE McMURRAY   G    (AB    (B) NO STATIC           1980 ANTHEM          ANR 11025
   ALAN MARSHALL    B V  (AB
   MARTY MORIN      D    (AB
W114                             WISHBONE ASH                                        W114
   STEVE UPTON      D    (ALL    (A) WISHBONE ASH        1970 MCA UK MKPS2014 RI MCG3507
   MARTIN TURNER    B(A TO O     (A)  "    "            1970 DECCA US 75249 RI MCA 2343
   GLEN TURNER      G    (        (A)  "    "            197  BARCLAY FR 510002
   ANDY POWELL      G    (ALL    (B) PILGRIMAGE          1971 MCA UK MDKS8004 RI MCG3504
   TED TURNER       G    (ABCDE   (B)  "    "            197  DECCA US 75295 RI MCA 36
   LAURIE WISEFIELD G(FJKMNOPR   (B)  "    "            197  BARCLAY        FR 510007
   JOHN TOUT        K    (C        (C) ARGUS            1972 MCA UK MDKS8006 RI MCG3510
   GEORGE NASH      K    (D        (C)  "    "            197  DECCA US 75437 RI 2344
   GRAHAM MAITLAND  PNO  (D        (C)  "    "            197  BARCLAY        FR 410003
   PHIL KENZIE      HRNS (D        (D) WISHBONE FOUR      1973 MCA UK MDKS8011 RI MCG3503
   DAVE COXHILL     HRNS (D        (D)  "    "            197  MCA   US 327  RI 2348
   BUD PARKES       HRNS(D         (D)  "    "            197  MCA       MAPS6673
   FLACO PADRON     CONGAS(F       (D)  "    "            197  BARCLAY  FR410008
   ALBHY GALUTEN    SYN  (F        (E)LIVE DATES          197  MCA UK MCSP254 US 2 8006
   JOHN WETTON      B    (P        (E)"    "              197  BARCLAY FR 41012/13
   CLAIRE HAMMILL   V    (P        (F) THERES THE RUB     1974 MCA UK MCF2575 US 464
   TREVOR BOLDER    B    (R        (F)  "    "            197  BARCLAY FR 410029
   GASPAR LAWAL     PERC (P        (G) MILESTONES         1974 EMI   EURO 184 50373
   IAN KEW          K    (P        (H) MASTERS OF ROCK    1975 EMI   EURO 054 96269
   CISSY HOUSTON    V    (J        (J) LOCKED IN          1976 MCA UK MCF2750
   EUNICE PETERSON  V    (J        (J)  "    "            19   BARCLAY FR  410055
   SYLVIA SHEMWELL  V    (J        (K) NEW ENGLAND        1976 MCA UK MCG 3523
   PETE WOOD        K    (J        (K)  "    "            1976 ATLANTIC US        18200
                                   (K)  "    "            197  BARCLAY FR  414006
                                   (L) CLASSIC ASH        1977 MCA UK  MCF2795
                                   (L)  "    "            197  BARCLAY FR  414015
                                   (M) FRONT PAGE NEWS    1977 MCA UK MCG3524 US 2311
                                   (M)  "    "            197  BARCLAY FR  511001
                                   (N) NO SMOKE WITHOUT FIRE 1978 MCA UK MCG3528 US 3060
                                   (O) JUST TESTING       1979 MCA UK  MCF3052
                                   (P) NUMBER THE BRAVE   1981 MCA UK  MCF3103
                                   (Q) LIVE DATES II      1981 MCA UK MCG4012 NL 203050
                                   (R) TWIN BARRELS BURNING 1982 AVM UK ASH 1
                                   ( ) THE ORIGINAL WISHBONE ASH 1977 MCA   US 42006
W115                            WISHFUL THINKING                                     W115
   KEVIN SCOTT      V    (B      (A) LIVE               1967 DECCA          UK   SKL 4900
   BRIAN ALLEN      D V  (AB     (B) HIROSHIMA          1971 B&C                 CAS 1038
   TONY COLLIER     B V  (BC     (C) WISHFUL THINKING   19   ?
   JOHN FRANKLIN    G V  (ABC
   TERRY NEW        G V  (    RAY DANIEL     V   (A   ROGER CHARLES    B V (A
W116                              WITCHFYNDE                                         W116
   STEVE BRIDGES    V    (AB     (A) GIVE 'EM HELL      1980 RONDOLET     UK   ABOUT 1
   PETE SURGEY      B    (AB     (B) STAGEFRIGHT        1980 RONDELET     UK   ABOUT 2
   GRA SCORESBY     D    (AB
   MONTALO          G    (AB
```

BILL WITHERS

BILL WITHERS	V	(ALL	(A) JUST AS I AM	1971	SUSSEX	LPSX3		7006
BRYAN GAROFALO	G	(J	(B) STILL BILL	1972	SUSSEX	LPSX1		7014
JERRY KNIGHT	B	(GHJ	(C) LIVE AT CARNEGIE HALL	1973	SUSSEX	LPDX101		7025/2
KEN BURKE	B	(HJ	(D) 'JUSTMENTS	1974	SUSSEX	LPSX2		8032
RUSS KUNKEL	D	(HJ	(E) BEST OF	1975	SUSSEX	LPSX 10	US	8037
RALPH MACDONALD	PERC	(HJ	(F) MAKING MUSIC	1975	CBS	US 33704	UK	69183
PAUL SMITH	K	(J	(G) NAKED & WARM	1976	CBS	US 34327	UK	81580
MIKE JONES	SYN	(H	(H) MENAGERIE	1978	CBS	US 34903	UK	82265
RAY PARKER	G	(H	(J) 'BOUT LOVE	1978	CBS	US 35596	UK	83176
DEAN GANT	K	(H	(K) 20 BEST OF	1978	METRONOME		GERM	69 030
CLIFF COULTER	K	(GH	(L) BEST OF	1980	CBS		UK	84710
GROVER WASHINTON JR	SAX	(K	(M) GREATEST HITS	1981	CBS		UK	85049
ALVIN TAYLOR	D	(H
GEOFFREY LEIB		(G	DON FREEMAN		(G	LARRY NASH	K	(G	LARRY TOLBERT		(G
CLARENCE McDONALD	K	(H	MELVIN DUNLOP	B	(GB	DOROTHY ASHBY		(G	ERROL BENNETT	PERC(G
YOUSEFF RAHMAN		(G	BENORCE BLACKMON	G	(GB	ROCKY DZIDZORNU	PERC	(G	STEPHEN STILLS	V	(A
AL JACKSON	D	(A	DONALD DUNN	B	(A	BOOKER T JONES K G	PROD	(A	JIM KELTNER	D	(A
BOBBYE HALL	PERC	(A	CHRIS ETHRIDGE	B	(A	JAMES GADSON	D	(B	RAY JACKSON K WIND		(A

JIMMY WITHERSPOON

JIMMY WITHERSPOON	V G	(ALL	GROOVIN' & SPOONIN'	19	ORIGINAL SOUND			7107
GROOVE HOLMES	ORG	(B	(B) SINGS THE BLUES	1964	SOCIETY		UK	SOC968
TEDDY EDWARDS	SAX	(B	EVENING BLUES	1964	STATESIDE	10088	US PRESTIGE7300
FRANK BUTLER	D	(B	BLUES AROUND THE CLOCK	1965	STATESIDE	10105	US PRESTIGE7314
JIMMY BOND	B	(B	SOME OF MY BEST FRIENDS ARE THE BLUES	1965	STATESIDE	10114	US PRESTIGE7356
DANNY KALB	G	(J	BLUE SPOON	1965	STATESIDE	10139	US PRESTIGE7327
HARVEY MANDEL	G	(J	IN PERSON	1966	VOGUE	VRL3005 RI MODE 546
BARRY GOLDBERG	K	(J	LIVE	1968	STATESIDE	10232
CHARLIE MUSSELWHITE	HCA	(J	(J) BLUES SINGER	1969	STATESIDE	10289	US BLUESWAY6026
			SPOON IN LONDON	1966			US PRESTIGE7418
			BLUES FOR EASY LIVERS	1967			US PRESTIGE7475
ROBBEN FORD	G	(L	BEST OF	19			US PRESTIGE7713
			MEAN OLD FRISCO	19			US PRESTIGE7855
(*) LINE UP SEE ERIC BURDON ENTRY			GOING TO KANSAS CITY	19	RCA US LPM 1639 RI		ANLI1048
			(*) GUILTY	1971	UA UK	UAG29251 MGM US 4791
			SPOONFUL	19	BLUENOTE	US		LA534
			HEY MRS JONES	19	REPRISE	US		6012
			SPOON CONCERTS	19	FANTASY			24701
			AT MONTEREY FESTIVAL	19	HI FI JAZZ	US		421
			& BEN WEBSTER	19	VERVE	US		V68835
			BEST OF	1973	BLUESWAY			BLS 6051
			LOVE IS A 5 LETTER WORD	1975	CAPITOL	11360	US LAX RI 37115
			AINT NOBODYS BUSINESS	197	POLYDOR		UK	2460 206
			LIVE	1979	MCA		UK	MCF 3027
			BABY BABY BABY	19	PRESTIGE	US		7290
			HANDBAGS & GLADRAGS	19	ABC US	717
			HUHH	1973	BLUESWAY	US		6040
			TAKE THIS HAMMER	19	CONSTELLATION	US		1422
			JIMMY WITHERSPOON	19	CROWN	US		5156
			SINGS THE BLUES	19	CROWN	US		5192
			FEELIN THE SPIRIT	19	HIFI	US		422
			AT THE RENAISSANCE	19	HIFI	US		426

WIZARDS FROM KANSAS

ROBERT MENADIER	B V	(A	(A) THE WIZARDS FROM KANSAS	196	MERCURY	US	61309
MARC CAPLAN	PERC	(A
JOHN COFFIN	G	(A	ROBERT CRAIN	G	(A	HAROLD PIERCE	D	(A	MARK NAFTALIN	K	(A

WIZARDS CONVENTION

RAY FENWICK	G B V	(A	(A) WIZARDS CONVENTION	197	RCA		UK	RS 1085
MO FOSTER	B	(A
RICK VAN DER LINDEN	K	(A	EDDIE HARDIN	SYN V	(A	RIC LEE	D	(A	MARK NAUSEEF	D	(A
JOHN CROCKER	SAX	(A	JON LORD	PNO	(A	JOHN SLAUGHTER	G	(A	TONY ASHTON	V K	(A
PETE YORK	D	(A	LESLIE BINKS	D	(A	GLEN HUGHES	V	(A	HENRY SPINETTI	D	(A
ROGER GLOVER	B	(A	DAVID COVERDALE	V	(A	MIKE D'ABO	V	(A	MIKE SMITH		(A
JIMMY HELMS		(A	CHRIS BARBER BAND

JAH WOBBLE

JAH WOBBLE		(AB	(A) LEGEND LIVES ON	1980	VIRGIN UK V2159 GER 203 050
MARTIN ATKINS	D	(A	(B) V.I.E.P. (EP)	1980	VIRGIN	UK	V36112
SNOW WHITE	V	(A

WOOLY WOLSTENHOLME

WOOLY WOLSTENHOLME	V K B G	(A	(A) MAESTOSO	1980	POLYDOR	UK	2374 165
STEVE BROOMHEAD	V M AND G	(A
KIM TURNER	D V	(A	BILL NIXON	PERC	(A	BRIAN DAY	B	(A

BOBBY WOMACK

BOBBY WOMACK	G V	(ALL	(A) LIVE	19	LIBERTY			LST 7645
BARRY BECKETT	K	(BCDELMN	(B) COMMUNICATION	1972	UA	US 5539	UK UAS 29306
CLAYTON IVEY	K	(BCDELMN	(C) UNDERSTANDING	1972	UA	US 5577	UK UAS 29365
ROGER HAWKINS	D	(BCDELMN	(D) FACTS OF LIFE	1973	UA	US LA043	UK UAS 29456
JIMMY JOHNSON	G	(BCDELMN	(E) LOOKING FOR A LOVE AGAIN	1974	UA	US LA199	UK UAS 29574
DAVID HOOD	B	(DEC	(F) ICAN UNDERSTAND IT	1975	UA		UK UAS 29715
DAVE TURNER	G	(D	(G) GREATEST HITS	1975	UA	US LA346
TRUMAN THOMAS	K	(BCDE	(H) I DONT KNOW WHAT THE WORLDS COMING TO	1975	UA	US LA353	UK UAS 29762
TIPPY ARMSTRONG	G	(EC	(J) SAFETY ZONE	1976	UA	US LA544	UK UAS 29907
LARRY RHEINHARDT	G	(E	(K) B W GOES C W	1976	UA	US LA638	UK UAS 29979
GERRY MASTERS	B	(D	(L)HOME IS WHERE THE HEART IS	1976	CBS	US 34384	UK 81693
HARVEY THOMPSON	SAX	(BCLN	(M) PIECES	1978	CBS	US 35083
DALE QUILLEN	TROM	(BC	(N) ROADS OF LIFE	1979	ARISTA US 4222	UK ARTY 165
HARRISON CALLOWAY	TPT	(BCLN	(O) THE POET	1982	BG	US 10000
PAM GRIER	V	(BC
PATRICE HOLLOWAY	V	(BC	JANICE SINGLETON	V	(BC	PETE CARR	G	(DE	BRANDYE	V	(M
KERRY CAMPBELL	SAX	(M	WAH WAH WATSON	G	(J	SONNY BURKE	K SYN	(JL	JAMES GADSON	D	(JO
BILL SUMMER	PERC	(F	WILLIE WEEKS	B	(F	LOUIS JOHNSON	B	(F	HERBIE HANCOCK	K	(F

                        (CONTINUED)

POINTER SISTERS	V	(F	VALENTINOS	V	(FL	DETROIT HORNS	(M
LAWRENCE FRATENGELO	PERC	(M	GLEN GOINS	G	(M	MICHAEL HENDERSON B	(M
DWAYNE LOMAX	D	(M	RUDY ROBINSON	K	(M	DAVID RUFFIN V	(M
AARON WILLIS	G	(MN	ANTHONY WILLIS	G	(MN	EDDIE WILLIS G	(MN
EDDIE HINTON	G	(L	TOM ROADY	PERC	(L	MUSCLE SHOALS	(L
BROTHERHOOD	HRNS	(L	ALAN DEVILLE	TPT	(L	LESTER SMITH TPT	(L
ZAIMUS ROWAN	TROM	(L	FRIENDLY WOMACK JR	V	(LO	CECIL WOMACK V	(LO
REGGIE YOUNG	G	(CJ	RANDY McCORMICK	K	(N	JACK ASHFORD D	(N
HODGES/JAMES?SMITH	V	(N	ROBERT ROBERTIE	D	(H	CATHERINE GOTTHOFFER HARP	(H
PEACE	HRNS	(H	BILL WITHERS	V	(H	SOKO RICHARDSON D	(H
DAVID T WALKER	G	(O	PATRICK MOTEN	K	(O	DALE RAMSEY K	(O
PAULINHO DACOSTA	PERC	(O	THE WATERS	V	(O	SALLY WOMACK	(O
REGINA WOMACK		(O	BOBBY EMMONS	K	(C	MIKE LEECH B	(C

DETROIT SYMPHONY STRINGS	(M
BARBARA HUDY	HRNS(M
CANDI STATON	V (M
CHARLES FULLILVE	G (L
BEN CULLEY	TPT(L
DASHIELL HUMAY	SAX (L
CURTIS WOMACK	V(LO
WAYNE JACKSON	HRNS(N
BOBBY BABIES	V (H
DAVID SHIELDS	B (O
DOROTHY ASHBY	HARP(O
VINCENT WOMACK	(O
BOBBY WOOD	K (C

STEVIE WONDER	V HCA K	(ALL
SCOTT EDWARDS	B	(WV
DANIEL BEN ZEBULON	PERC	(V
GLORIA BARLEY	V	(V
LANI GROVES	V	(VWX
JIM GILSTRAP	V	(VWX
RAY PARKER	G	(V
SHIRLEY BREWER	V	(VXYfg
DENIECE WILLIAMS	V	(VXY
TREVOR LAWRENCE	SAX	(VYf
DAVID SANBORN	SAX	(VY
STEVE MADAIO	TPT	(VY
JEFF BECK	G	(V
BUZZY FEITEN	G	(VY
DEBRA WILSON	V	(V
LORIS HARVIN	V	(V
BEN BRIDGES	SITAR G	(Ydfg
MICHAEL SEMBELLO	V	(dXY
LARRY GITTENS	TPT	(dgf
JOSIE JAMES	V	(dgY
RON KERSEY	K	(d
JACQUELINE F ENGLISH	V	(Y
PHILLIP KIMBLE	V	(Y
EARL DEROUEN	V	(dfg
NATHAN WATTS	B	(Ydfg
HANK REDD	SAX	(Ydf
RICK ZUNIGAR	G	(dfg
ABDOULAYE SOUMARE	V	(d
JOE JOHNSON	V	(d
ALEXANDRA BROWN	V	(dfg
LAMINE KONTE	PERC V	(d
IBRAHIM CAMARA	PERC	(d
KATHY COLLIER	V	(d
SUSAYE GREENE BROWN	V	(dYf
DENNY DAVIS	D	(d
ANGELA ISAIAH WINBUSH	V	(df
MARVA HOLCOLM	V	(df
HANK DEVITO	STEEL	(f

				US			UK	
(A)TRIBUTE TO UNCLE RAY	1963	TAMLA	232		ORIOLE		40049
(B)LITTLE STEVIE WONDER	196	TAMLA					54191
(C)JAZZ SOUL OF LITTLE STEVE	1963	TAMLA	233		STATESIDE		10078
(D)12 YEAR OLD GENIUS	1963	TAMLA	240		ORIOLE		40053
(D)12 YEAR OLD GENIUS	1980	TAMLA			STMR		9003
(E)WITH A SONG IN MY HEART	196	TAMLA	250				
(F)AT THE BEACH(HEY MR HARMONICA MAN)	1965	TAMLA	255		STATESIDE		10108
(G)UPTIGHT	1966	TAMLA	268		STML11036		
(H)DOWN TO EARTH	1966	TAMLA	272		STML11045		
(J)I WAS MADE TO LOVE HER	1967	TAMLA	279		STML11059		
(K)GREATEST HITS	1968	TAMLA	282		STML11075		
(L)SOMEDAY AT CHRISTMAS	1969	TAMLA			STML11085		
(M)FOR ONCE IN MY LIFE	1969	TAMLA	291		STML11098		
(N)EIVETS REDNOW	1969	GORDY	932				
(O)MY CHERIE AMOUR	1970	TAMLA	296		STML11128		
(P)LIVE	1970	TAMLA	298		STML11150		
(Q)TALK OF THE TOWN	1970	TAMLA			STML11164		
(R)SIGNED SEALED DELIVERED	1970	TAMLA	304		STML11169		
(S)WHERE I'M COMING FROM	1971	TAMLA	308		STML11183		
(T)GREATEST HITS	1972	TAMLA	313		STML11196		
(U)MUSIC OF MY MIND	1972	TAMLA	314		STMA 8002		
(V)TALKING BOOK	1972	TAMLA	319		STMA 8007		
(W)INNERVISIONS	1973	TAMLA	326		STMA 8011		
(X)FULFILLINGNESS FIRST FINALE	1974	TAMLA	332		STMA 8019		
(X)FULFILLINGNESS FIRST FINALE	197	TAMLA	T633 251				
(Y)SONGS IN THE KEY OF LIFE	1976	TAMLA	340		TMSP 6002		
(a)PORTRAIT	1976	EMI	EURO		064 92636		
(b)ANTHOLOGY	1977	TAMLA	804		M 9 804		
(c)WONDERLAND	197	EMI	EURO 064 95182				
(d)THE SECRET LIFE OF PLANTS	1979	TAMLA			TMSP 6009		
(e)LIGHT MY FIRE	1979	M F P			50420		
(f)HOTTER THAN JULY	1980	TAMLA			STMA 8035		
(g)ORIGINAL MUSIQUARIUM (DBL)	1982	TAMLA			TMSD 6012		
( )GREATEST HITS 2	19	TAMLA EURO 91056					
(EP)A CALL IT PRETTY MUSIC	1964	STATESIDE					
(EP) STEVIE WONDER	1965	TAMLA			TME 2006		
(EP) FREE WITH SONGS IN THE KEY OF LIFE	76	TAMLA			TME 2020		

CHARLES K WILSON	V	(f	MELODY McCULLY	V	(fg
VICTOR PAZ	HRNS	(g	EARL McINTYRE	HRNS	(g
ALFRED WILSON	HRNS	(g	ROBERT ELDRIDGE	HRNS	(g
CLIFTON ANDERSON	HRNS	(g	ANTHONY TOOLEY	HRNS	(g
DELORES BARNES	V		RONNIE WILSON	V	
LARRY LATIMER	V PERC	(WXY	YUSUF ROAHMAN	PERC	(W
SYREETA WRIGHT	V	(XYf	JAMES JAMERSON	B	(X
ART BARON	TROM	(U	TASHA THOMAS		(W
RALPH HAMMER	G	(W	SHEILA WILKERSON	PERC	(W
SNEAKY PETE	STEEL	(X	MINNIE RIPPERTON	V	(XY
GREG PHILLINGANES	K	(Y	MICHAEL GRAY	V	(Y
RONNIE FOSTER	ORG	(Y	MARY LEE WHITNEY	V	(Yf
CHARITY McCRARY	V	(Y	LINDA McCRARY	V	(Y
GLEN FERRIS	TROM	(Y	DOROTHY ASHBY	HARP	(Y
BOBI HUMPHREY	FLT	(Y	GEORGE BENSON	G V	(Y
JIM HORN	SAX	(Y	SNUFFY WALDEN	G	(Y
EDDIE LEVERT	V	(f	MICHAEL JACKSON	V	(f
NOLAN SMITH	TPT	(f	WALTER WILLIAMS	V	(f
CHARLIE COLLINS	V	(f	RAY POUNDS	D	(Y
DENNIS MORRISON		(f	KIMBERLEY JACKSON	V	(Y
LONNIE MORGAN	V	(Y	ROSONA STARKS	V	(Y
JAYASACINANDANA DASA	V	(Y	VEDAVYASA DASA	V	(Y
RUKMINI	V	(Y	ETHEL ENOEX	V	(Y
DENNIS SWINDELL	V	(Y	SHERYL WALKER	V	(Y
JITAMRTYI DASA	V	(Y	CINMAYI DASA	V	(Y
BRENDA BARRETT	V	(Y	COLLEEN CARLETON		(Y
DAVE HENSON		(Y	EDNA ORSO		(Y
SUDANA BOBATOON	V	(Y	BERRY BRIGES	V	(Y
AL FANN	V	(Y	BARBARA FANN	V	(Y
MIMI GREEN	V	(Y	ADRIAN JAMES	V	(Y
LARRI NUCKENS		(Y	GARY VENEY		(Y
LINDA AMERICA	V	(Y	STARSHEMAH BOBATOON	V	(Y
RODNEY BROWN	V	(Y	DOE RANI EDWARDS	V	(Y
TRACY FANN	V	(Y	SUSIE FUZZELL	V	(Y
ANTHONY GIVENS	V	(Y	DERRICK GIVENS	V	(Y
CALVIN JOHNSON	V	(Y	IRMA LESLIE	V	(Y
KIM LEWIS	V	(Y	CAROLYN MASSENBURG	V	(Y
GWEN PERRY	V	(Y	GREGORY RUDD		(Y
MARIETTA WATERS	PERC	(Y	JOHN FISHBACH	PERC	(Y

JANICE ROBINSON	HRNS	(g	VIRGIL JONES		HRNS(g
ROBERT RATLEDGE	HRNS	(g	J D PARRAN		HRN(g
LORENZO WYCHE	HRNS	(g	FRANK WESS		HRN(g
BRITT WOODMAN	HRNS	(g	EUGENE GHEE		HRNS(g
DEAN PARKS	G	(WY	CLARENCE BELL		ORG (W
WILLIE WEEKS	B	(W	REGGIE McBRIDE		B (X
ROCKY	PERC	(X	JACKSON 5		V (X.
DAVID T WALKER	G	(W	MALCOLM CECIL		B (W
BOBBYE HALL	PERC	(XY	PAUL ANKA		V (X
EDDIE BROWN	PERC	(Yf	SURDRAY TUCKER		V (Y
ARTICE MAY	V	(Y	RAYMOND MALDONADO		TPT(Y
LINDA LAWRENCE	V	(Y	TERRY HENDRICKS		V (Y
MADELAINE JONES	V	(Y	GEORGE BOHANON		TROM(Y
HERBIE HANCOCK	K	(Y	GREG BROWN	D	(Y
NATHAN ALFRED	PERC	(Y	CARMELLO GARCIA		PERC(Y
DENNIS DAVIS	D	(fg	ISAIAH SANDERS		K (fg
BETTY WRIGHT	V	(f	ROBERT MALACK		SAX (f
JAMIL RAHEEM	V	(f	PAUL RISER		STR (fg
STEPHANIE ANDREWS		(f	BILL WOLFER		(f
RENEE HARDAWAY	V PERC	(Y	ADDIE COX		V (Y
MICHAEL WYCOFF	V	(Y	DURYODHANA GURU DASA		V(Y
YOGAMAYA DASI	V	(Y	BHAKTA GREGORY		V (Y
CAROLYN JOHNSON	V	(Y	JAMES LAMBERT		V (Y
BARADRAS	V	(Y	AGNIDEVA DASA		V (Y
BHAKTA EDDIE	V	(Y	BHAKTA KEVIN		V (Y
CAROLE COLE		(Y	NELSON HAYES		PERC(Y
JOSETTE VALENTINO		(Y	GLEN FERRIS		TROM(Y
CECILIA BROWN	V	(Y	GARY BYRD		V (Y
SHELLEY FANN	V	(Y	MILDRED GIVENS		V (Y
PAT JOHNSON	V	(Y	WILLIE MOORE		V (Y
TAN ADAMS	V	(Y	HENRY AMERICA		V (Y
KHALIF BOBATOON	V	(Y	JEAN BROWN		V (Y
AL JOCKO FANN	V	(Y	MELANI FANN		V (Y
AUDREY GIVENS	V	(Y	ANTONIO GIVENS		V (Y
JEANIA HARRIS	V	(Y	TROY HARRIS		V (Y
CARL LOCKHART	V	(Y	GAIL LOCKHART		V (Y
KIM NIXON	V	(Y	LISA NIXON		V (Y
KEITH SLAUGHTER	V	(Y	CHARLES BREWER		PERC(Y
AMALE MATHEWS	PERC	(Y	YOLANDA SIMMONS		(Y

BRENTON WOOD

```
BRENTON WOOD      V   (AB        (A) OOGUM BOOGUM           19   DOUBLE SHOT   US   1002
                                 (B) BABY YOU GOT IT        19   DOUBLE SHOT   US   1003
```

LAUREN WOOD

```
LAUREN WOOD       K V (ALL       (A) LAUREN WOOD            1979 WB    US BSK 3278
JIM KELTNER       D   (A         (B) CAT TRICK              1981 WB    US BSK 3517
MICHAEL BAIRD     D   (A
JEFF PORCARO      D   (A    ALVIN TAYLOR      D   (A   RICK SCHLOSSER   D   (A   ERNIE EREMUTA   B PERC(A
ABRAHAM LABORIEL  B   (A    DAVID HUNGATE     B   (A   BILL PAYNE   K SYN(A   JAI WINDING     K   (A
JAY GRAYDON       G   (A    STEVE LUKATHER    G   (A   RONNIE MONTROSE  G   (A   SUMNER MERING   G   (AB
FRED TACKETT      G   (A    NOVI NOVOG    VLA SYN (AB  JOHN KLEMMER    SAX  (A   ANDREW LOVE SAX     (A
PAUL LANI       PERC V(A    STEVE FORMAN    PERC (A   BOBBY LAKIND  PERC V    MICHAEL JACKSON PERC(A
SINCLAIR ROGERS LOTT PERC(A MICHAEL McDONALD  V   (A   JOHN TOWNSEND    V   (A   BILL CHAMPLIN   V   (A
ROSEMARY BUTLER   V   (A    PAT SIMMONS       V   (A   ARNO LUCAS       V   (A   BOBBY KIMBALL   V   (A
RICARDO LECAMPOS  V   (A    KIKI KOURY        V   (AB  DUNCAN MACKAY   SYN  (A   BEN CAULEY HRNS (A
BILL ELLIOTT  K SYN STR(B   BRIAN RAY         G   (A   RICK CHUDACOFF  B K  (B   PETER BUNETTA   D   (B
ALAN ESTES      PERC (B     ARNOLD McCULLER   V   (B   LESLIE SMITH     V   (B   TOMMY FUNDERBURK V  (B
CARRIE BARTON     B   (B    JOE KELLY         G   (B   LARRY TRENDWELL  G   (B   GEORGE SOPUCH   G   (B
AIRTO MOREIRA   PERC (B     JOHN BERGAMO    PERC (B   MICHAEL BODDICKER SYN (B   MARK PELSONE    K   (B
JERRY HEY        TPT (B     GARY GRANT    TPT    (B   BILL REICHENBACH TROM (B   GARY HERBIG  SAX (B
PHIL AYLING      SAX (B     DAVID WOODFORD   SAX (B   ROBBIE DUPREE    V   (B   TATA VEGA       V   (B
```

ROBERT WOOD

```
ROBERT WOOD     VIBES(ALL       (A) TAROT                  19   EDICI     FR    ED 6102
STEVE POTTS     WIND (A         (B) SONABULAR              19   EDICI     FR    ED 6103
KENT CARTNER      B   (A         (C) VIBRAROCK              19   POLYDOR         2393 137
RON PITTNER       D   (A         (D) TOMBAC VIBE            19   POLYDOR         2393 150
GILBERT ARTMAN    D   (B
OLIVER ZDRZALIK   G B (C    MARCEL BEL        D   (C   PATRICK FONTAINE  B   (C   OLIVER DIDIER        (C
PIERRE MOERLIN    D   (C    DIDDIER MALHERBE WIND (C   MIKE HOWLET       B   (C   PERRY YELDHAM    B   (D
PATRICE CRAMER    D   (D
```

RON WOOD

```
RON WOOD        G V (ABC        (A) I'VE GOT MY OWN ALBUM TO DO  1974 WB   US 2819    UK   K56065
WILLIE WEEKS      B  (AB        (B) NOW LOOK                1975 WB    US 2872    UK   K56145
IAN MacLAGAN      K  (ABCD      (C) GIMME SOME NECK         1979 CBS   US 35702   UK      83337
KEITH RICHARD   G   (ABC        (D) 1234                    1981 CBS   US 37473   UK      85227
MICK JAGGER     G V (AC
ALVIN TAYLOR      D   (D    MICK TAYLOR    G B (ABC  JEAN ROUSSEL     K   (AB   MICK WALLER    D   (A
PETE SEARS        B   (D    MARTIN QUITTENTON  D  (A   ROD STEWART      V   (A   IRENE CHANTER  V   (A
DOREEN CHANTER    V   (A    ANDY NEWMARK      D   (AB  BOBBY WOMACK     G   (BD  KENNY JONES    D   (B
BOBBY KEYS      SAX (CD     JIM KELTNER       D   (CD  DAVE MASON       G   (C   CHARLIE WATTS  D   (CD
MICK FLEETWOOD    D   (C    ROBERT POPWELL    B   (C   JIM HORN       HRNS  (D   IAN WALLACE    D   (D
CLYDIE KING       V   (D    SHIRLEY MATTHEWS  V   (D   NICKY HOPKINS    K   (D   ANITA POINTER  V   (D
ALAN MYERS        D   (D    CARMINE APPICE    D   (D   JAY DAVIS        B   (D   ROBIN LEMESURIER G (D
JIMMY HASLIP      B   (D    WADDY WACHTEL     G   (D
```

RON WOOD & RONNIE LANE

```
RON WOOD        G V  (A         (A) MAHONEYS LAST STAND     1976 ATLANTIC   US SD36126 UK K50308
RONNIE LANE B BAN G V (A
KENNEY JONES      D   (A    PETE TOWNSHEND G PERC (A   IAN McLAGAN      K   (A
BOBBY KEYS      HRNS (A     JIM PRICE      HRNS   (A   BRUCE ROWLAND  D V   (A   BENNY GALLAGHER  B  (A
MICK WALLER     PERC (A     RICK GRECH    B D VLN (A   IAN STEWART      K   (A   GLYN JOHNS       V  (A
BILLY NICHOLLS    V   (A
```

ROY WOOD

```
ROY WOOD G V B K HRNS WIND(ALL  (A) BOULDERS               1973 HARVEST   SHVL803 RI SHSM 2021
MOVE                      (F    (A) BOULDERS               1974 UA    US UALA168
PAUL ROBINS       K G  (GH      (B) WIZZARD BREW    (WIZARD)1973 HARVEST   SHSP4025 US UA LA042
PETER MACKIE      B V  (H       (C) SEE MY BABY JIVE (WIZARD)1974 HARVEST  SHSP4034
BILLY PAUL      SAX  (GH        (D) EDDIE & THE FALCONS (WIZARD)1974 WB  UK K56029    US UA LA219
JOHN KURLANDER    K   (H        (E) MUSTARD                1975 JET  UK JETLP12    US UA LA575
ANDY FAIRWEATHER LOW V (H       (F) THE ROY WOOD STORY     1976 HARVEST   SHDW408
JOHN BONHAM       D   (H        (G) SUPER ACTIVE WIZZO (WIZZO)1977 WB UK K56388    US     3065
CARL WAYNE        V   (H        (H) ON THE ROAD AGAIN      1979 WB         US BSK3247
ANNIE HASLAM      V   (HE
DAVE DONOVAN      V   (HE   DICK PLANT        V  (HE  RICK PRICE B V PERC(BCDEFG  BILL HUNT K HRNS V (BCDF
HUGH McDOWELL CELLO SYN(BCF NICK PENTELOW WIND V (BCDF MIKE BURNEY  WIND (BCDF   KEITH SMART    D   (BCDF
CHARLIE GRIMA    D(BCDFH    CARBAG CHOIR      V   (B   BOB BRADY      K V   (D   PHIL EVERLY    V   (E
ELECTRIC LIGHT ORCH  (F    BEACH BOYS            (F   NIGHTRIDERS          (F   GRAHAM GALLERY B   (G
BOB WILSON      TROM (G
```

ROYSTON & HEATHER WOOD

```
ROYSTON WOOD    V CONC(A        (A) NO RELATION            1977 TRANSATLANTIC   UK   TRA 342
HEATHER WOOD      V   (A
PETER BELLAMY     V   (A    SIMON NICOL       G   (A   PENNIE HARRIS  V DULC(A   PETE KIRTLEY  G MAND(A
TONY HALL MELODEON    (A    ASHLEY HUTCHINGS  B   (A
```

WOODY WOODMANSEYS U BOAT

```
WOODY WOODMANSEY  D   (A        (A) U BOAT                 1977 BRONZE     BRON    501
PHIL PLANT        B   (A
MARTIN SMITH      G   (A    FRANK MARSHALL  K SYN(A   PHIL MURRAY      V   (A
```

JEZZ WOODROFFE

```
JEZZ WOODROFFE    K   (A        (A) OPPOSITE DIRECTIONS     1980 GRADUATE    UK   GRADLP1
ERIC CAIRNS       D   (A
IRWEN SYLVESTER   D   (A    GIBSON JOHN  B    (A
```

STEVIE WOODS

```
STEVIE WOODS      V   (A        (A) TAKE ME TO YOUR HEAVEN  1982 COTILLION US   5229
```

TERRY & GAY WOODS

```
TERRY WOODS      V G B MANS(ALL   (A) WOODS BAND          1971 GREENWICH    UK   GSLP 1004
GAY WOODS      V CONC DULC(ALL    (A) WOODS BAND          1977 ROCKBURGH    UK   ROC  102
ED DEANE         B G K(AB         (A) WOODS BAND          197  MOONCREST    UK   CREST 29
PAT NASH         D V  (A          (B) BACKWOODS           197  POLYDOR      UK   2383 322
AUSTIN CORCORAN  B G  (A          (C) THE TIME IS RIGHT   1976 POLYDOR      UK   2383 375
JOHN RYAN        K    (A          (D) RENOWNED            1976 POLYDOR      UK   2383 406
TONY REEVES      B    (A          (E) TENDERHOOKS         1978 rockburgh    UK   ROC  104
MIKE GILES       D    (B
DAVE WINTOUR     B    (B   TONY CARR    CONGA    (B   DAVE MATTACKS   D     (C GEOFF WHITEHORN  G  (B
PETER ARNESEN    K    (B   JOE O'DONNELL  VLN  (B   DAVE PEGG       B     (C PAT DONALDSON    B  (CE
TIMI DONALD      D    (C   B J COLE     STEEL(C   BRIAN GOLBEY    FDL   (C JON GILLASPIE   K  (C
DAVID MORRISON   G    (C   TRISTIAN FRY VIBES   (C   PHIL PALMER    G     (E JIM RUSSELL D      (E
KATE McGARRIGLE  V PNO(E   KEITH DONALD  SAX    (E   MARTIN O'CONNOR ACC   (E NEIL TONER  MAND (E
FRAN BREEN       PERC (E   JOLYON JACKSON ORG   (E
```

.WOOL

```
ED WOOL          G V  (A         (A) WOOL              19   ABC         US   ABCS &'&
TOM HASKELL      G V  (A
PETER LULIS      D    (A  CLAUDIA WOOL      V   (A  ED BARRELLA    B    (A
```

HENRY WOOLF

```
HENRY WOOLF          (A         (A) TIBETAN BELLS      1972 ISLAND      UK   HELP3
NANCY HEMMING        (A
DREW GLADSTONE       (A
```

BRUCE WOOLLEY

```
BRUCE WOOLLEY    V    (AB        (A) ENGLISH GARDEN              1979 EPIC  UK   83893
DAVID BIRCH      G    (A         (B) BRUCE WOOLLEY & THE CAMERA CLUB 1981 CBS  US      36301
ROD JOHNSON      D    (A
MATTHEW SELIGMAN D    (A  TOM DOLBY     B    (A
```

WORLD OF OZ

```
CHRISTOPHER ROBIN    (A         (A) WORLD OF OZ        1969 DERAM       UK   SML1034
DAVID KUBINEC        (A
TONY CLARKSON        (A  DAVID REA      (A
```

WORLD SERVICE

```
ROLY KERRIDGE    D    (A         (A) DEFINITE UNCERTAINTIES  1979 COOPER       WARP001
KEVIN DUNFORD    B    (A
STEVEN LODDER    K VLN(A  GERRY HUNT   G SAX    (A  ALAN HAYMAN PERC FLT(A
```

SONNY WORTHING

```
SONNY WORTHING   K V  (A         (A) TEENAGE DREAM     1977 TRANSATLANTIC UK TRA 344
JIM CUOMO        WIND (A
ELLIOTT RANDALL  G    (A  PETE WINGFIELD  K V  (A  PETER VAN HOOKE D  (A PETE WILSHER   STEEL(A
ISAAC GUILLORY   G    (A  MO FOSTER     B    (A  RITCHIE         G  (A KEITH NELSON   BANJO(A
BARBARA SEXTON   V    (A  MARTIN DROVER TPT  (A  GEORGE CHISHOLM TPT (A TONY ROBERTS  SAX (A
JEFF DALY        SAX  (A  DAVID SNELL   HARP (A
```

WRABIT

```
LOU NADEAU       V    (A         (A) WRABIT            1982 MCA UK MCF3126
DAVID APLIN      D    (A
SCOTT JEFFERSON SLECK D(A  JOHN ALBANI G V    (A  CHRIS BROCKWAY  B V  (A LES PAULHUS K V  (A
DAVID KIRBY      K    (A  RON SMITH     B    (A  ROB LOUDEN      V    (A
```

BILL WRAY

```
BILL WRAY        V    (A         (A) FIRE & ICE        1981 LIBERTY      LT1098
JAMES BENTLEY WRAY  G V B(A
GEORGE ENETE     K    (A  GREG WORLEY   D    (A  JERRY HEY       HRNS (A GARY GRANT TPT   (A
BILL REICHENBACH TROM (A  LARRY WILLIAMS SAX (A  JIM HORN        SAX  (A JERRY PATERSON SAX (A
PAULINHO DACOSTA PERC (A  WENDY WALDMAN V    (A  DEBRA DABKIN    V    (A LISA DALBELLO  V  (A
RANDY BISHOP     V    (A
```

LINK WRAY

```
LINK WRAY        G V  (ALL       (A) LINK WRAY & THE WRAY MEN  1960 EPIC        US  LN3661
BILLY HODGES     K V  (CF        (B) JACK THE RIPPER    1963 SWAN        US  SLP  510
MORDICAI JONES K MAND (F ]SAME ? (C) LINK WRAY          1971 POLYDOR US 24 4064 UK 2489 029
BOBBY HOWARD   K MAND (C ]       (D) THERES GOOD ROCKIN TONIGHT 1973 UNION PACIFIC  UP 002
DOUG WRAY        D V G(CFQ        (E) BE WHAT YOU WANT   1973 POLYDOR US 5047  UK  2391 063
STEVE VERROCA    D V  (CF         (F) BEANS & FATBACK    1973 VIRGIN      UK  V 2006
COMMANDER CODY        (E         (G) ROCKIN' & HANDCLAPPIN'  1973 EPIC        UK  63267
JERRY GARCIA     G    (E         (H) RUMBLE             1974 POLYDOR US 6025 UK  2391 128
DAVID BROMBERG   D    (E         (J) INTERSTATE 10      1975 CAROLINE    UK  C 1511
BOBBY BLACK      STEEL(E         (K) STUCK IN GEAR      1976 VIRGIN      UK  V 2050
RUAN OLOCHLAINN  K SAX(K         (L) ROCK'N'ROLL RUMBLE 19   CHARLY      UK  CR 30171
GORDON SMITH     B    (K         (M) EARLY RECORDINGS(B)? 1978 CHISWICK /ACE    CH 6
ARCHIE LEGGET    B    (K         (N) GREAT GUITAR HITS  19   VERMILLION  US  1924
FREDDIE SMITH    D    (K         (O) SINGS & PLAYS      19   VERMILLION  US  1925
DAVE GREAVES          (J         (P) YESTERDAY & TODAY  19   RECORD FACTORY US 1929
CHARLEY CHARLES  D    (J         (Q) BULLSHOT           1979 CHARISMA UK CAS1143 US VISA 7009
JOHN DZERIGAN    B    (H         (R) LIVE AT THE PASADISO 1980 LINE GER LLP5019 US VISA 7010
BOZ SCAGGS       G V  (H         (R) LIVE AT THE PARADISO 1980 MAGNUMFORCE UK 008 RCA NL 44012
ROBIN WRAY       V    (Q
RHONDA WRAY      V    (Q  MARK JORDAN   K V  (H  RICK SCHLOSSER  D    (H TOM RUTLEY     B  (H
JOE CRANE      B V K(H  ANDY NARELL PERC K   (H  BERNIE KRAUSE   K    (H PETE ESCOVEDO CONGA(H
BRUCE STEINBERG  HCA  (H  LENNY PICKETT  SAX (H  EMILIO CASTILLO SAX  (H STEVE KUPKA    SAX(H
MIC GILLETTE     TPT  (H  GREG ADAMS    TPT  (H  GLENN WALTERS   V    (H SKIP DRINKWATER V (H
DOROTHY MORRISON V    (H  ZELLER HURD   V    (H  BILL COMBS      V    (H JOE SCOTT      V  (H
BILLY CROSS      G    (Q  ANTON FIG     D PERC(Q  RICHARD GOTTEHRER K PERC(Q CHRIS ROBINSON K (Q
ROB STONER       B    (Q  HOWIE WYETH   D    (Q  JOANNA MASSEY   V    (Q
```

WRECKLESS ERIC

WRECKLESS ERIC	G V (ABC	(A) WRECKLESS ERIC				1978 STIFF		UK	SEEZ 6	
DAVEY PAYNE	SAX (AC	(B) WONDERFUL WORLD OF W ERIC				1978 STIFF		UK	SEEZ 9	
DAVID WITTON	D (AC	(C) BIG SMASH (DBL)(COMP)				1980 STIFF UK SEEZ21 GER 6 28499				
CHARLIE HART	K (AC	(C) BIG SMASH (DBL)(COMP)				1980 STIFF US 36463				
MARTIN ACE	V (C									
BARRY PAYNE	B (AC	STEVE CURRIE	B (AC	JOHN GLYN	SAX (AC	STEVE GOULDING	D (AC			
NICK LOWE	G B (AC	GEIR WAADE	D (A	JOHN BROWN	B (BC	EUNON BRADY	G (B			
PETE SOLLEY	K (B	MALCOLM MORLEY	G (BC	JOHN EARLE	HRNS (BC	DICK HANSON HRNS	(BC			
JOE PARTRIDGE	G (B	GARY TAYLOR	V (B	PETE GOSLING	G (C	WALTER HACON	G (C			
DAVE OTWAY	D (AC	ROGER RETTIG	STEEL(C							

BIG JOHN WRENCHER

BIG JOHN WRENCHER	V HCA(AB	(A) BIG JOHNS BOOGIE		1975 BIG BEAR		BEAR 5
EDDIE TAYLOR	G (A	(B) MAXWELL STREET ALLEY BLUES		1978 BARRELHOUSE		BH 2
BOB HALL	PNO (A	(C) MEMPHIS TO MAXWELL		19 JAWES		9999
BOB BRUNNING	B (A					
PETE YORK	D (A					

BETTY WRIGHT
W132

BETTY WRIGHT	V (ALL	(A) MY FIRST TIME AROUND	1968 ATCO	US 33260				
GREGORY WILKERSON	D (G	(B) I LOVE THE WAY YOU LOVE ME	1971 ALSTON	US 33388	ATLANTIC	UK	K40364	
MICHAEL WILKERSON	B (G	(C) HARD TO STOP	1973 ALSTON	US 7026	ATLANTIC	UK	K40514	
WILL BRIDGEFORTH	G (G	(D) DANGER HIGH VOLTAGE	1975 ALSTON	US 4400	RCA	UK	SF8408	
ROBERT WEBB	V PERC(G	(E) EXPLOSION	1976 ALSTON	US 4402	RCA	UK	RS1063	
GARRY GREENE	SAX (G	(F) THIS TIME FOR REAL	1977 ALSTON	US 4406	TK	UK	XL14053	
MICHAEL SCOTT	TPT (G	(G) LIVE	1978 ALSTON	US 4408	TK		UK TKR82541	
KEVIN KENDRICKS	K (G	(H) TRAVELING IN THE CIRCLE	1979 ALSTON	US 4410	TK		UK TKR83352	
		(J) BETTY WRIGHT	1981 EPIC	US 36879		UK	84882	

GARY WRIGHT

GARY WRIGHT	K V (ALL	(A) EXTRACTION		1970 A&M	US 4277	UK	AMLS2004	
JIM KELTNER	D (DEC	(B) RING OF CHANGES (WONDERWHEEL)		1972 A&M			UKAMLH64362	
ANDY NEWMARK	D (DG	(C) FOOT PRINT		1971 A&M	US 4296	UK	AMLS64296	
DAVID FOSTER	K (DE	(D) DREAM WEAVER		1976 WB	US 2868	UK	K56141	
BOBBY LYLE	K (DFG	(E) LIGHT OF SMILES		1976 WB	US 2951	UK	K56278	
LORNA WRIGHT	V (DEGJ	(F) TOUCH & GONE		1977 WB	US 3137	UK	K56435	
BETTY SWEET	V (DE	(G) HEADIN' HOME		1979 WB	US 3244	UK	K56585	
DAVID POMERANZ	V (DE	(H) THAT WAS ONLY YESTERDAY		1976 A&M	US 3528			
SPOOKY TOOTH	(H	(J) THE RIGHT PLACE		1981 WB	US 3511	UK	K56877	
JIM GORDON	D (C							
HUGH McCRACKEN	G (ACG	ALAN WHITE	D (ACG	TREVOR BURTON	B (A	KLAUS VOORMAN	B (AC	
MIKE KELLIE	D (A	MICK ABRAHAMS	G (A	RONNIE MONTROSE	G (D	DORIS TROY	V (AC	
MADELINE BELL	V (A	NANETTE NEWMAN	V (AC	BRYSON GRAHAM	D (C	MIKE JONES	G (E	
TOM DUFFY	B (C	ART WOOD	D (EF	PETER REILICH	K (E	STEVE PORCARO	B (E	
JUSTIN WRIGHT	V (E	COLLIN ALLAN	D (C	JERRY DONAHUE	G (C	GEORGE P'HARA	G (C	
JIM PRICE	HRNS (C	BOBBY KEYS	SAX (C	KING CURTIS	SAX (C	LIZA STRIKE	V (C	
BARRY ST JOHN	V (C	PAT P ARNOLD	V (C	JIMMY THOMAS	V (C	RICHARD BAKER	K (F	
CLYDIE KING	V (F	VANETTA FIELDS	V (FG	SHIRLEY MATTHEWS	V (FG	PETER REILICH	SYN (F	
HIROSHI UPSHUR	SYN (F	GARY MIELKE	SYN (F	STEVE LUKATHER	G (G	LENNY CASTRO	PERC(GJ	
AUDIE WATKINS	PERC (G	MICHAEL BODDICKER	SYN (G	JAI WINDING	SYN (G	MICHAEL McDONALD	V (G	
PAULINHO DACOSTA	PERC (G	FRED TACKETT	G (G	JIM HORN	SAX (G	EMIL RICHARDS	PERC(G	
RALPH HUMPHREY	PERC (G	BUZZY FEITON	G (G	NEIL LARSEN	SYN (G	DAVID CROSBY	B (J	
GRAHAM NASH	V (G	JEFF PORCARO	D (G	ROLAND BAUTISTA	G (G	DEAN PARKS G SAX	B PROD(J	
MARTY WALSH	G (J	TRIS IMBODEN	D (J	BOB C BENBERG	D (J	DAVID KEMPER	D (J	
GEORGE HAWKINS	B (J	ROD PIAZZA	HARP (J	DAVID PACK	V (J	TIM SCHMIT	V (J	

LORNA WRIGHT

LORNA WRIGHT	V (A	(A) CIRCLE OF LOVE		19 ROCKET		2902		
LARRY CARLTON	G (A							
BILL CUOMO	K (A	JIM KELTNER	D (A	ANDRE FISHER	D (A	STEVE FORMAN	PERC(A	
MIKE PORCARO	B (A	ERNIE WATTS	SAX (A	JAY LEWIS	G B (A	KIM CARNES	V (A	
JAY GRAYDON	G (A	FRED TACKETT	G (A	RALPH HUMPHREY	D (A	CHET McCRACKEN	D (A	
DAVID FOSTER	SYN (A	KLAUS VOORMANN	B (A					

RICHARD WRIGHT

RICHARD WRIGHT	K V (A	(A) WET DREAM	1978 HARVEST UK SHVL818 US CBS 35559		
MEL COLLINS	SAX (A				
LARRY STEELE	B (A	REG ISADORE	D (A	SNOWY WHITE	G (A

WRITING ON THE WALL

WILLY FINLAYSON	G V (A	(A) POWER OF THE PICTS	1969 MIDDLE EARTH		MDLS 303
BILL SCOTT	K (A				
JAKE SCOTT	V B (A	LINNIE PATERSON	V (	JIMMY HUSH	D (A	ALBY GREENHALGH	WIND(A
SMIGGY	G (				

STEVE WRIGHT

STEVE WRIGHT		(A) HARD ROAD	1975 POLYDOR	UK 2480 249

WRITZ

STEVE ROWLES	G V (A	(A) WRITZ	1979 ELECTRIC UK TRIX 12 GER 146352	
STEVE FAIRNIE	V (A			
JULES HARDWICK	G SYN(A	BEV SAGE	V (A	NICK BATTLE	B (A	ARRY AXELL D (A

ROBERT WYATT

ROBERT WYATT	V K D(ALL	(A) THE END OF AN EAR	1970 CBS UK 64189 RI 80 EMBASSY 31846				
NEVILLE WHITEHEAD	B (A	(B) ROCK BOTTOM	1974 VIRGIN US 13112	UK	V2017		
MARK CHARIG	CORNET (A	(C) RUTH IS STRANGER THAN RICHARD	1975 VIRGIN	UK	V2034		
BRIAN ENO	K G (C	(BC) ROCK BOTTOM/RUTH IS STRANGER	1981 VIRGIN	UK	VGD 3505		
ELTON DEAN	SAX (A						
DAVE SINCLAIR	ORG (A	CYRIL AYERS	PERC (A	RICHARD SINCLAIR	B (B	LAURIE ALLEN	D (BC
HUGH HOPPER	B (A	IVOR CUTLER	K V (B	MONGESI FEZA	TPT (B	GARY WINDO	WIND(BC
ALFREDA BENGE	V (B	FRED FRITH	VLA PNO (BC	MIKE OLDFIELD	G (B	BILL McCORMICK	B (C
NISAR AHMAD KHAN	SAX (C	JOHN GREAVES B	(C				

BILL WYMAN V B G K	(AB	(A) MONKEY GRIP	1974 ROLLINGSTONE US COC79100 UK COC59102
DANNY KOOTCH	G	(AB	(B) STONE ALONE	1976 ROLLINGSTONE US COC79103 UK COC59105
JOE LALA	PERC	(A	(C) GREEN ICE(SOUNDTRACK)	1981 POLYDOR UK POLS1031
DAVE MATTACKS	D	(D	(D) BILL WYMAN	1981 A&M UK AMLH 68540
CHRIS REA		(D		

MAC REBENNACK	PNO	(AB	DALLAS TAYLOR	D	(AB	JOEY MURCIA	G	(A	DUANE SMITH	PNO (A
GEORGE TERRY	G	(A	BYRON BERLINE	FDL	(A	JACKIE GRAVES	TROM	(A	JOHN McEUEN	BANJ(A
ABIGALE HANESS	V	(A	LEON RUSSELL	PNO	(A	WILLIAM SMITH	PNO	(A	HUBIE HEARD	K (AB
BETTY WRIGHT	V	(A	GEORGE McCRAE	V	(A	GWEN McCRAE	V	(A	MARK COLBY	HRNS(AB
KEN FAULK	HRNS	(A	NEAL BONSANTI	HRNS	(A	DAVE LAWSON	SYN	(DGUILLE GARCIA PERC	(B
MARK NAFTALIN	K	(B	BONNIE POINTER	V	(B	CLYDIE KING	V	(B	ALBHY GALUTEN	SYN (B
PAUL HARRIS	K	(B	JOE VITALE	K D	(B	NICKY HOPKINS	K	(B	AL KOOPER	K (B
GREGG ERRICO	D	(B	BOB WELCH	G	(B	VAN MORRISON	SAX HCA G	(B	RUTH POINTER	V (B
WANETTA FIELDS	V	(B	TERRY TAYLOR G		(BD	JACKIE CLARK	G	(B	ROBERT GREENRIDGE D(B
JOE WALSH	G	(B	JIM KELTNER	D	(B	RON WOOD	G	(B	ROCKY DZIZDORNU	PERC(B
JOHN McFEE	FDL	(B	FLOYD COOLEY		TUBA (B				

MICHAEL WYCOFF	K V	(A	(A) COME TO MY WORLD	1981 RCA UK PL13823

MICHAEL WYNN	G V	(A	(A) READY TO FLY	1978 ARIOLA GER 26484
ROBERT MUSENBICHLER	G V	(A	(B) QUEEN OF THE NIGHT	1979 ARIOLA 50027
NORBERT SCHMITT	B V	(A		
TOMMY SCHMITT	K V	(A	FRITZ MATZKA D (A JOHAN DAANSEN G (A DAVE SPRUNG V (A
ACHIM FARR	SAX	(A		

JOHN DOE	B	(AB	(A) LOS ANGELES	1980 SLASH US 104
BILLY ZOOM	G	(AB	(B) WILD GIFT	1981 SLASH US 107
CHRISTINE CERVENKA	V	(A		
EXENE	V	(AB	DON BONEBRAKE D (AB RAY MANZAREK K PROD (A

POLY STYRENE	V	(A	(A) GERM FREE ADOLESCENTS	1978 EMI INS 3023
LARA LOGIC	SAX	(		
JACK AIRPORT STAFFORD G	(A	PAUL DEAN B (A CHRIS CHRYSLER D (RUDI THOMPSON SAX (A
GLYN JOHNS	SAX	(	B P HARDING D (A RICHARD BP TEES D (

COLIN MOULDING	B V	(ABCDE	(A) WHITE MUSIC	1978 VIRGIN UK V2095
ANDY PARTRIDGE	G V	(ABCDE	(B) GO TWO	1978 VIRGIN UK V2108
TERRY CHAMBERS	D	(ABCDE	(C) DRUMS & WIRES	1979 VIRGIN US 13134 UK V2129
BARRY ANDREWS	K	(AB	(D) BLACK SEA	1980 VIRGIN US 13147 UK V2173
DAVID GREGORY	K G	(CDE	(E) ENGLISH SETTLEMENT (DBL)	1982 VIRGIN UK V2223
JOHN LECKIE	PROD	(A	(EP) GO PLUS	1978 VIRGIN UK VS23312
STEVE LILLYWHITE	PROD	(A		
HUGH PADGHAM	PROD V	(E		

MICHAEL MARTIN	G V	(A	(A) PLIGHT OF REDMAN	1972 RARE EARTH US R5361 UK SREA4002
JOMAC SUAZO	B	(A	(A) PLIGHT OF REDMAN	1972 RARE EARTH NL 058 93622
R C GARISS	G PNO	(A	( ) XIT	19
LEEJA HERRERA	D PERC	(A	( ) SILENT WARRIOR	19

ROE BUTCHER	B	(A	(A) XDREAMISTS	1980 POLYDOR NL 2442 181
JOHN DOC DOCHERTY	G	(A		
BRIAN MOFFAT	D	(A	UEL WALLS G V (A

J J CAMPBELL	V	(	(A) YACHTS	1979 RADAR UK RAD19
GLYNN HAVARD	B V	(B	(A) S O S	1970 POLYDOR US 6220
MARTIN DEMPSEY	K	(B	(B) WITHOUT RADAR	1980 RADAR UK RAD27 US POLYDOR16270
MARTIN J WATSON	G V	(AB		
BOB BELLIS	D	(AB	HENRY PRIESTMAN K (AB MICK SKINNER B (GLYN HAVARD B V (B

STOMU YAMASHTA	K PERC	(ALL	(A) CONTEMPORARY	1972 L'OISEAU DSL01
STEVE WINWOOD	K V	(HI	(B) RED BUDDHA	1972 BARCLAY 920376 GER 16063
MICHAEL SHRIEVE	D	(HJI	(B) RED BUDDHA	1974 VANGUARD US 79343
ANDY POWELL	B	(C	(C) COME TO THE EDGE	1973 ISLAND HELP 12
PAT THRALL	G	(HI	(D) THE MAN FROM THE EAST	1973 ISLAND ILPS9228
PHIL MANZANERA	G	(	(E) FREEDOM IS FRIGHTENING	1973 ISLAND GER 87703 UK ILPS9242
AL DIMEOLA	G	(HJI	(F) ONE BY ONE	1974 ISLAND ILPS9269
ROSCO GEE	B	(H	(G) RAINDOG	1975 ISLAND ILPS9319
KLAUS SCHULZE	K	(HJI	(H) GO	1976 ISLAND GER 27448 UK ILPS9387
HUGH HOPPER	B	(EF	(I) GO LIVE FROM PARIS	1976 ISLAND UK ISLD 10
GARY BOYLE	G	(EFG	(J) GO TOO	1977 ARISTA US4138 UK SPARTY1011
DAVE WHITE	SAX	(C	(J) GO TOO	1977 ARISTA UK 99228
BRIAN GASGOIGNE		(EFG		

HISAKO YAMASHTA VLN	(DEFGH	DONI HARVEY		(J	PAUL JACKSON		(J	BROTHER JAMES	PERC(HIJ
JEROME RIMSON	B	(I	LINDA LEWIS	V	(J	KAREN FRIEDMAN	V	(K	PETER ROBINSON	(CDJ
JESS RODEN	V	(J	R HARRIS		TPT	(C	MORRIS PERT PERC		(CD	PHIL PLANT	B (CD
HIDEO FUNAMOTO	PERC	(D	ALYN ROSS	B	(D	GARY BOYLE	G	(DE	ROBIN THOMPSON	SAX (CD
JOJI HIROTA	C	(D	GORO KUII	V	(D	MIKAKO TAKESHITA	V	(D	SHIRO MURATA	FLT (D
YOSHIO TAIRA	K	(D	MAGGIE NEWLANDS	K	(D	SAMMI ABU		(EF	NIGEL MORRIS	D (EF
FRANK TANKOWSKI	G	(F	BERNIE HOLLAND	G	(FH	DAITO FUJITA	B	(G	HOZUMI TANAKA	D (G
TSUNEO MATSUMOTO	G	(G	MURRAY HEAD	V	(G	MAXINE NIGHTINGALE	V	(H	JULIAN MARVIN	G (H
LENNOX LAINGTON	PER	(H	KAREN FRIEDMAN	V	(H	CASEY SYNGE	V	(H	DARI LALOU V	(H
THUNDERTHIGHS	V	(H	HANS WERNER HENZE		(A	PETER MAXWELL DAVIES		(A	TORU TAKEMITSU	(A
DOREEN CHANTER	V	(J	RUBY JAMES	V	(J	LIZA STRIKE	V	(J	J GIFFE	TROM (C

YAMBU

RAMON RODRIGUEZ	B	(A	(A) YAMBU			1975 MONTUNO		MLP 506	
MILTON HAMILTON	K	(A							
REINALDO ALCANTARA	TIMB(A	MANNY RIVERA	BONGO(A	JOSE GONZALES	CONGA(A	JAY SIVA	TPT	(A	
JOSE MORRISON	TPT	(A	SAM BURTIS	TROM (A	FRANKIE MALABE	CONGA(A	EDDIE RODRIGUEZ	CONGA(A	
FREDDY HARRIS	G	(A	RODNEY JONES	G (A	MIGUEL SEVILLA	D	(A	LESETTE WILSON	V (A
CATY SEVITTA	V	(A	IZZY DAVILA	CORO (A	NESTOR SANCHEZ	CORO(A	WILLIE TORRES	CORO(A	

JIMMY YANCEY

JIMMY YANCEY	V PNO(ALL	(A) PURE BLUES	196	ATLANTIC US	SD1283		
MAMA YANCEY	V (AB	(B) CHICAGO PIANO VOL 1	1972	ATLANTIC US	SD7229	UK	K40406
MICHAEL CROSBY	B (B	(C) JIMMY YANCEY	VOL 1	19	OLDIE BLUES US		2802
		(D) JIMMY YANCEY VOL 2	19	OLDIE BLUES US		2813	

YANKEES

JON TIVEN	V SAX(A	(A) HIGH 'N' INSIDE			1978 LONDON UK SHY8531 US BIGSOUND 037				
SALLY YOUNG	G V (A								
PAUL OSSOLA	K B (A	MICKEY CURRY	D	(A	ROGER C REALE	B V (A	IVAN JULIAN	B V (A	
HILLY MICHAELS	D	(A	JIMMY McALLISTER	B (A	ROBERT ORSI	HCA V(A	VAN DUREN	V (A	
CHRISTINE OHLMAN	V	(A	DOC CAVALIER	V (A	ALEX CHILTON	V (A	TOMMY HOEHN	V (A	
JOHNNY PARADISE	V	(A	EDYTH	V (A	NELSON ADELARD	V (A	FREDERICK BOV	V (A	

ZAL YANOVSKY

ZAL YANOVSKY	(A	(A) ALIVE & WELL IN ARGENTINA	1971 KAMA SUTRA	UK	2316 003

YAQUI

RUDY REGALDO	D	(A	(A) YAQUI		1974 ?		
RONNIE REYES	G V	(A					
LARRY CRONIN	K SYN V(A	GEORGE OCHOA	HCA V K G(A	ART SANCHEZ	B G V(A	EDDIE SERRANO V CONGA(A	
ROY RODRIGUEZ	D PERC(A						

PETER YARROW

PETER YARROW	V (A	(A) THAT'S ENOUGH FOR ME	1973 WB		UK	K46263
GLADY ANDERSON	PNO (A					
CHRIS DEDRICK	V K G(A	JACKIE JACKSON	B (A	BARRY BECKETT	K (A	JESSE DIXON SINGERS V(A
JIMMY JOHNSON	G (A	DAVID BROMBERG	MAND (A	FONTZ	B (A	DENZIL LANG	PERC(A
HUKS BROWN	G (A	WINSTON GRENNAN	D (A	COLIN LOUGHAN	SAX (A	BRAD BRYAN	G (A
ROGER HAWKINS	G (A	ROY MARKOWITZ	D (A	TONY BUCHANAN	SAX (A	TOOTS HIBBERT	V (A
DAVID SPINOZZA	G (A	PAUL BUTTERFIELD	HCA (A	JOHN HUCKRIDGE	TPT (A	WINSTON WRIGHT	K (A
PETE CARR	G (A	DAVID HOOD	B (A				

YATHA SIDHRA

ROLF FICHTER K SYN G V (A	(A) MEDITATION MASS	1974 BRAIN	GER	1045
KLAUS FICHTER	D PERC(A			
MATTHIAS NICOLAR	G B (A	PETER ELBRACHT	FLT (A	

YARDBIRDS

TONY TOP TOPHAM	G (1	WITH SONNY BOY WILLIAMSON	1964 FONTANA TL5277	RI	SFJL 960		
KEITH RELF	V HCA(12345	" " " "	1967 FONTANA	UK	858 025		
JIM McCARTY	D (12345	" " " "	1966 MERCURY	US	SR 61071		
CHRIS DREJA	G (12345	" " " "	1975 PHILIPS		756435 011		
PAUL SAMWELL-SMITH B (123		FIVE LIVE YARDBIRDS	1964 COLUMBIA	UK	33SX 1677		
ERIC CLAPTON	G (2	FIVE LIVE YARDBIRDS RI	1979 CHARLY GER 3066	UK	CR 30173		
JEFF BECK	G (34	FOR YOUR LOVE	1965 EPIC	US	26167		
JIMMY PAGE	G (45	HAVING A RAVE UP	1965 EPIC US 26177 CBS GER GCXC 28				
		THE YARDBIRDS	1966 COLUMBIA	UK	SCX 6063		
(1) 1963 (2) 1964 (3) 1965		OVER UNDER SIDEWAYS DOWN	1966 EPIC US 26210 CAPITOL CAN 6202				
(4) 1966 (5) 1967		GREAT HITS	1967 EPIC US 26246	US RI	34491		
		LITTLE GAMES	1967 EPIC US 26313				
		PERFORMANCES BY CLAPTON BECK PAGE	1970 EPIC US 30135				
		ROCK GENERATION	19 BYG	FR	529701/2		
		LIVE YARDBIRDS WITH J PAGE	1971 EPIC US 30615				
		REMEMBER	1971 STARLINE	UK	SRS 5069		
		HITS OF THE YARDBIRDS	197 CAPITOL	US	DT 6229		
		MORE GOLDEN EGGS	19 BERKELEY	US	1003		
		ERIC CLAPTON & YARDBIRDS	19 SPRINGBOARD	US	4036		
		FAVOURITES	1977 EPIC US 34490				
		WITH ERIC CLAPTON	1975 CHARLY GER 3008	UK	CR 30012		
		WITH JEFF BECK	1975 CHARLY	UK	CR 30013		
		WITH JEFF BECK	1975 BYG	FR 200 139			
		YARDBIRDS (DBL)	1975 CHARLY GER 3088				
		SHAPES OF THINGS	19 BOMB	US	1045		
		SHAPES OF THINGS	19 SPRINGBOARD	US	4039		
		SHAPES OF THINGS	1977 CHARLY	UK	CDX 1		
		ATTENTION	19 FONTANA	GER	9294 902		
		YARDBIRDS (EP)	1977 CHARLY	UK	CEP 116		
		REFLECTIONS/EARLY YARDBIRDS	19 FONTANA	GER	9294 904		

YELLO

BORIS BLANK	ELECT V(AB	(A) SOLID PLEASURE	1980 RALPH	US	YL 80L	
DIETER MEIER	V (AB	(B) CLARO QUE SI	1981 RALPH US YL8159 UK DOIT 008			
CARLOS PERON	TAPES (AB	(B) CLARO QUE SI	1981 VERTIGO GER 6435 123			
CHICO HABLAS	G (AB					
BEAT ASH	D (B	ZINE EL ABADINE	V (B	WALT KAISER	D (A	FELIX HAUG	D (A

ATLEE YEAGER

ATLEE YEAGER	B V (AB	(A) PLANT ME NOW AND DIG ME LATER	1973 CHELSEA	US	0366		
MICHAEL STEVENS	G (AB	(B) FLYING AHEAD	197 DUNHILL	US	50084		
FRED STAEHLE	D (A						
MARK PAUL	D (A	ROBERT WACHTEL	D G(A	ROCKY HILTON	G (A	BILL COWSILL	G (A
RICH CLYBURN	G (A	KEITH JOHNSON	G (A	SAM McCUE	G (A	JIM GORDON K SAX (A	
BUD DEAL	SAX (A	BRUCE SHAFFER	K V (A	DON FRANCISCO	D V (A		

YELLOW DOG

HERBIE ARMSTRONG	G V	(AB			(A) YELLOW DOG			1977 VIRGIN UK V2083 GER 28936				
KENNY YOUNG	G V	(AB			(B) BEWARE OF THE DOG			1978 VIRGIN UK V2103 GER 26189				
PETE SOLLEY		(B			( )STRANGERS IN PARADISE			1981 ESCAPE		ES001		
ROD DEMICK	B	(B										
GARY TAYLOR	B	(A	GERRY CONWAY D	(A	ANDY ROBERTS	B	(A	PHIL PALMER	G	(B		
JIM GANNON	G	(A	MICK FEAT	B	(B	PETER VAN HOOKE	D	(B	PETER BARDENS	K	(B	
PAUL ATKINSON	D	(B	MO FOSTER	B	(B	JACK HALL	B	(B	NEVILLE ROBERTS		(B	
SIMON PHILLIPS	D	(B	JIMMY HALL	SAX	(B	THEOPHILUS K LIVELY D	(B	JACK SPENCE	PERC(B			

YELLOW MAGIC ORCHESTRA

RYUICHI SAKAMOTO	K PERC(A		(A) YELLOW MAGIC ORCHESTRA		1979 A&M UK AMLH68506 HORIZON US 736		
KENJI OHUMURA	G	(B	(B) X∞ MULTIPLES		1980 A&M UK AMLH68516	US 4813	
YUKIHIRO TAKAHASHI D V	(A		(C) B G M		1981 A&M UK AMLH64853	US 4853	
HARUOMI HOSONO	K B	(B	(D) SOLID STATE SURVIVOR		1982 ALFA UK 85664		
HIDEKI MATSUTAKE		(A					
BSHUNICHI HASHIMOTO V	(A	MASAYOSHI TAKANAKA	G(A	SANDI	V	(B	

YELLOW JACKETS

RUSSELL FERRANTE	K	(A		(A) YELLOWJACKETS		1981 WB	US 3573	UK K56920
JIMMY HASLIP	B	(A						
RICKY LAWSON	D	(A	ROBBEN FORD	G	(A	LENNY CASTRO	PERC (A	PAULINHO DACOSTA PERC(A
BOBBY LYLE	K	(A	LARRY WILLIAMS	WIND (A	JERRY HEY	TPT (A	ERNIE WATTS	SAX (A
BILL REICHENBACH	TROM (A		GARY HERBIG	WIND (A	KIM HUTCHCROFT	SAX (A		

YELLOW PAYGES

BILL HAM	G	(A		(A) VOLUME 1	1969 UNI	US 73045
BOB BARNES	B	(A				
DAN HORTTER	V HCA(A		DAN GORMAN D	(A		

YES

CHRIS SQUIRE	B V	(ALL	(A) YES		1969 ATLANTIC US 8243	UK	588 190
JON ANDERSON	V	(A>M	(A) YES		1971 ATLANTIC RI	UK	K40034
BILL BRUFORD	D	(ABCDEF	(B) TIME & A WORD		1970 ATLANTIC US 8273	UK 2400 006	
TONY KAYE	K	(ABC	(B) TIME & A WORD		1971 ATLANTIC RI	UK	K40085
PETER BANKS	G	(AB	(C) THE YES ALBUM		1971 ATLANTIC US 8283	UK 2400 101	
STEVE HOWE	G	(C>N	(C) THE YES ALBUM		1971 ATLANTIC RI	UK	K40106
RICK WAKEMAN	K	(DEFGJKLM	(C) THE YES ALBUM		1980 ATLANTIC US 19131		
ALAN WHITE	D	(FGHJKLM	(D) FRAGILE		1971 ATLANTIC US 7211	UK 2401 019	
PATRICK MORAZ	K	(HM	(D) FRAGILE		1971 ATLANTIC RI	UK	K50009
TREVOR HORN	V B	(N	(D) FRAGILE		1980 ATLANTIC US 19132		
GEOFF DOWNES	K	(N	(E) CLOSE TO THE EDGE		1972 ATLANTIC US 7244	UK	K50012
COLIN GOLDRING	REC	(C	(E) CLOSE TO THE EDGE		1980 ATLANTIC US 19133		
			(F) YESSONGS (TPL)		1973 ATLANTIC US 3 100	UK	K60045
			(G) TOPOGRAPHIC OCEANS (DBL)		1973 ATLANTIC US 2908	UK	K80001
			(H) RELAYER		1974 ATLANTIC US 18122	UK	K50096
			(H) RELAYER		1980 ATLANTIC US 19135		
			(J) YESTERDAYS		1975 ATLANTIC US 18103	UK	K50048
			(J) YESTERDAYS		1980 ATLANTIC US 19134		
			(K) GOING FOR THE ONE		1977 ATLANTIC US 19106	UK	K50379
			(L) TORMATO		1978 ATLANTIC US 19202	UK	K50518
			(M) YESSHOWS (DBL)		1980 ATLANTIC US 2/510	UK	K60142
			(N) DRAMA		1980 ATLANTIC US 16019	UK	K50736
			(O) CLASSIC YES		1981 ATLANTIC US 19320		

YESTERDAY & TODAY(Y&T)

DAVE MENIKETTI	G V(ABCD	(A) YESTERDAY & TODAY		1976 LONDON	US PS 677
JOEY ALVES	G V(ABCD	(B) STRUCK DOWN		1978 LONDON	US PS 711
PHIL KENNEMORE	B V(ABCD	(C) EARTHSHAKER		1981 A&M UK AMLH64872	
LEONARD HAZE	D V(ABCD	(D) BLACK TIGER		1982 A&M UK AMLH64910	

YOBS

NODDY OLDFIELD	(A	(A) CHRISTMAS ALBUM		1980 SAFARI	UK RUDE 1
EBENEZER POLAK	(A				
KID VICIOUS	(A	H J BEDWETTER (A			

YIPES

PETE STRAND	B	(AB	(A) YIPES	1979 MILLENIUM
PAT McCURDY	V K	(AB	(B) A BIT IRRATIONAL	1980 MILLENNIUM 7750
ANDY BARTEL	G V	(AB		
TEDDY FREESE	D	(AB	MICHAEL HOFFMAN G (AB	

PETE YORK

PETE YORK	D	(A	(A) PETE YORK PERCUSSION BAND	19 DECCA UK TXS 109

RUSTY YORK

RUSTY YORK	(A	(A) ROCK'N' MEMORIES	1981 JEWEL US 917

STEVE YORK'S CAMELO PARDALIS

STEVE YORK	B	(A			(A) MANOR LIVE		1973 VIRGIN	UK V 2003	
ELKIE BROOKS	V	(A							
OLLIE HALSALL	G V	(A	GRAHAM BOND K SAX	(A	TIM HINKLEY	K	(A	IAN WALLACE	D (A
MARC CHARIG	HRNS (A		JOHN LEE	TROM	(A	BOZ BURRELL	V	(A	DAVE THOMPSON	K (A
DAVE BROOKS	SAX	(A	MIKE PATTO	V	(A	ROB TAIT	D	(A	DIANE STEWART CONGA V(A
MICK MOODY	G	(A	PETE GAVIN	D	(A	LOL COXHILL	SAX	(A	BARRY DUGGAN	SAX (A
JIM MULLEN	G	(A	PETE GAGE		(A					

CHRIS YOULDEN

CHRIS YOULDEN	V	(AB			(A) NOWHERE CITY		1973 DERAM UK SML 1099 US LONDON 633		
DEREK GRIFFITHS	G	(B			(B) CITY CHILD		1974 DERAM UK SML 1112 US LONDON 642		
PETE WINGFIELD	K	(AB			(C) LEGEND		1979 US LONDON 50016		
CHRIS SPEDDING	G	(A							
ROSCO GEE	B	(B	JACK MILLS	G	(B	TERRY STANNARD	D	(B	NICK NEWELL SAX (B
MIKE COTTON	TPT	(B	DAVE CASWELL	TPT	(B	JOHN BEECHAM	TROM (B	JOY YATES	V (B
ANNA PEACOCK	V	(B	SUZANNA LYNCH	V	(B	DANNY KIRWAN	G	(A	RAY FENWICK G (A
FOGGY LYTTLE	G	(A	ROY BABBINGTON	B	(A	ANDY SYLVESTER	B	(A	BRUCE ROWLAND D (A
MIKE McNAUGHT	K	(A							

JESSE COLIN YOUNG

```
JESSE COLIN YOUNG  G V  (ALL        (A) SOUL OF A CITY BOY           1964 CAPITOL  US 2070  RI 74  11267
JEFF MYER          D    (CDEFGHJ     (A) SOUL OF A CITY BOY           1975 VINE     US 1009
SCOTT LAWRENCE     K    (CDEFGHJ     (B) YOUNGBLOOD                   1965 MERCURY  US              SR 61005
JIM ROTHERMEL      WIND (EFGHJ       (C) TOGETHER                     1972 WB       US 2588
KELLY BRYAN        B    (EF          (D) SONG FOR JULI                1973 WB       US 2734  UK K46262
OZZIE AHLERS       PNO  (E           (E) LIGHT SHINE                  1974 WB       US 2790  UK K56037
MARTY DAVID        B    (E           (F) SONGBIRD                     1975 WB       US 2845  UK K56110
JERRY CORBITT      V    (CEF         (G) ON THE ROAD                  1976 WB       US 2913  UK K56223
SUZI YOUNG         V    (CEFGHJ      (H) LOVE ON A WING               1977 WB       US 3033  UK K56358
RON STALLINGS      SAX  (CF          (J) AMERICAN DREAMS              1978 ELEKTRA  US 6E157 UK K52105
PETER WELKER       TPT  (FH
REX ALLEN          TROM (G  CHUCK PETERSON    SAX  (H  HANK DE VITO     STEEL(FH FELIX PAPPALARDI  V   (H
JEFF NEIGHBOR      B    (H  ZANE WOODWORTH    TPT  (JH CHUCK BENNETT    TROM (H  NICOLETTE LARSON  V   (H
JOHN BLAKELEY      G    (H  EVERETT FAREY     HRNS (H  GORDON MESSICK   TROM (H  DAVID HAYES       B V(GHJD
RICHARD ANDERSON   HCA  (DC PETER CHILDS      G    (BC EDDY OFFENSTEIN  G    (DC JOHN WILMETH      HRNS(C
JEFF LABES         K    (J  MICHAEL O'NEILL   G    (J  ALVIN TAYLOR     D    (J  DAVID LINDLEY     VLN (J
ANNA RIZZO         V    (J  PAMELA MOORE      V    (J  PAULETTE McWILLIAMS V (J  GREG WRIGHT       V   (J
STEPHANIE SPRUILL  V    (J  ROGER KENERLY SAINT V  (J  JIM GILSTRAP     V    (J  GWEN EVANS        V   (J
JOHN LEHMAN        V    (J  FRITZ HEIBRON     TROM (J  RAYMOND LOECKLIE SAX  (J  BENNETT FRIEDMAN  SAX (J
OSIE JOHNSON       D    (B  JOHN SEBASTIAN    HCA  (B  GEORGE DUVIVIER  B    (B
```

JOHNNY YOUNG

```
JOHNNY YOUNG   G V HCA (ALL        (A) CHICAGO BLUES BAND           1966 ARHOOLIE      US      1029
LOUIS MYERS        G    (E         (B) CHICAGO BLUES                1968 ARHOOLIE      US      1037
PAUL OSCHER        HCA  (D         (C) BLUES MASTER No9             197  BLUE HORIZON  US      4609
SAMMY LAWHORN      G    (D         (D) FAT MANDOLIN                 1970 BLUE HORIZON  UK      763852
S P LEARY          D    (AD        (E) I CANT KEEP MY FOOT FROM JUMPING 1973 BLUESWAY  BLS  6075
RICHARD EVANS      B    (D         (F) & HIS FRIENDS                197  TESTAMENT     US      2226
OTIS SPANN         PNO  (AD
BILL WARREN        D    (E
WALTER HORTON      HCA  (B  LAFAYETTE LEAKE   PNO  (B  JAMES COTTON     HCA  (A  JIMMY DAWKINS     G  (B
ERNEST GATEWOOD    B    (B  JIMMY LEE MORRIS  B    (A  LESTER DORSIE    D    (B
```

KENNY YOUNG

```
KENNY YOUNG            (AB        (A) CLEVER DOG CHASE THE SUN     1972 WB           US      2579
BOB FALLOON        G   (A         (B) LAST STAGE FOR SILVERWOOD    19   WB           US      2676
BRUCE EPSTIEN      G   (A
MARK WARNER        G   (AB  CHRIS SPEDDING   G    (A  DAVE EDMUNDS     G    (A  GERRY HOGAN      STEEL(A
FIACHRA TRENCH     K   (A   DAVE WINTOUR     B    (A  BARRY DESOUZA    PERC (A  DEAN PARKS       G   (B
LELAND SKLAR       B   (B   RUSS KUNKEL      D    (B  TOM CANNING      K    (B  JIM HORN   SAX   (B
RABBIT BUNDRICK    K   (B   CHRIS GUNNING    STR  (B  BOBBYE HALL      PERC (B  LOUIS SHELTON    G   (B
WILTON FELDER      B   (B   GARY COLEMAN     PERC (B  DAVE COHEN       G    (B  WAYNE PERKINS    G   (B
TRACY HARRILL      B   (B   MIKE KELLIE      D    (B  SUSAN TRAYNOR    V    (B  JOE SAMPLE  K    (B
```

LARRY YOUNG

```
LARRY YOUNG        K   (ALL       GROOVE STREET                   196  PRESTIGE     US      7237
                                  OF LOVE & PEACE                 19   BLUENOTE            BST 84242
                                  CONTRASTS                       19   BLUENOTE     US     BST 84266
                                  HEAVEN ON EARTH                 19   BLUENOTE     US     BST 84304
                                  LAWRENCE OF NEWARK              1973 PERCEPHON    US      34
                                  FUEL                            1976 ARISTA      US     AL 4051
                                  SPACEBALL                       197  ARISTA      US     AL 4072
```

MIGHTY JOE YOUNG

```
MIGHTY JOE YOUNG  G V (ALL        (A) CHICKEN HEADS               1974 OVATION      US      1437
BOB REIDY          PNO (E         (B) LOVE GONE                   19   OVATION      US      1443
SYLVESTER BOINES   B   (E         (C) MIGHTY JOE YOUNG            19   OVATION      US      1706
ALVINO BENNETT     D   (E         (D) BLUES WITH A TOUCH OF SOUL  19   DELMARK      US     DS 629
CHARLES BEECHAM    TPT (E         (E) LEGACY OF THE BLUES (VOL 4) 1972 SONET UK SNTF633 US GNP 10014
KEN SAJDAK         K   (F         (F) BLUESY JOSEPHINE            1976 BLACK & BLUE         33521
WILLIE MABON       PNO (F
CORNELIUS BOYSON   B   (F   WILLIE HAYES     D   (F  WALTER HAMBRICK  SAX (E
```

NEIL YOUNG

```
NEIL YOUNG       G V HCA(ALL      (A) NEIL YOUNG                  1969 REPRISE US RS6317 UK K44059
JOHN BARBATA       D   (F         (B) EVERYBODY KNOWS THIS IS NOWHERE 1969 REPRISE US RS6349 UK K44073
PATRICE HOLLOWAY   V   (A         (B) EVERYBODY KNOWS THIS IS NOWHERE 19 REPRISE US RI 2282
TIM DRUMMOND       B   (DFHLJNOG   (C) AFTER THE GOLDRUSH          1970 REPRISE US RS6383 UK K44088
SHIRLEY MATTHEWS   V   (A         (C) AFTER THE GOLDRUSH          19   REPRISE US RI 2283
JACK NITZSCHE      K G (ADFH       (D) HARVEST                     1972 REPRISE US RS2032 UK K54005
BOBBY NOTKOFF      VLN (B         (D) HARVEST                     1)   REPRISE US RI 2277
BEN KEITH  STEEL G V (DFHLNGO     (E) JOURNEY THROUGH THE PAST(COMP) 1972 REPRISE US RS2480 UK K54015
DAVID CROSBY     G V (DFJG        (F) TIME FADES AWAY             1973 REPRISE US RS2151 UK K54010
JOE YANKEE         B   (FG         (G) ON THE BEACH               1974 REPRISE US RS2180 UK K54014
NICOLETTE LARSON   V   (LNP        (H) TONIGHTS THE NIGHT         1975 REPRISE US RS2221 UK K54040
KENNY BUTTREY      D   (DH         (J) ZUMA                       1975 REPRISE US MS2242 UK K54057
BILLY TALBOT       B   (BCHJLNOGQR (K) LONG MAY YOU RUN           1976 REPRISE US 2253   UK K54081
GREG REEVES        B   (C          (L) AMERICAN STARS & BARS      1977 REPRISE US 2261   UK K54088
NILS LOFGREN       PNO V(CH        (M) DECADE    (TRIPLE)         1978 REPRISE US 3 2257 UK K64037
RALPH MOLINA       D V (BCHJLNOGQR (N) COMES A TIME               1978 REPRISE US 2266   UK K54099
DANNY WHITTEN    G V (BCH          (O) HAWKS & DOVES              1979 REPRISE US 2297   UK K54109
STEPHEN STILLS     V   (CDJK       (P) RUST NEVER SLEEPS          1979 REPRISE US 2295   UK K54105
JAMES TAYLOR       V   (D          (Q) LIVE RUST                  1980 REPRISE US 2 2296 UK K64041
GRAHAM NASH        V   (DFJG       (R) REACTOR                    1981 REPRISE US 2304   UK K54116
RICK DANKO         B   (G
JIM MESSINA        B   (A   LINDA RONSTADT    V   (DL  JOHN HARRIS      PNO (D  EMMYLOU HARRIS   V  (L
KARL HIMMEL        D   (LNP FRANK SAMPEDRO G STR(JLNOPQR CAROLE MAYEDO VLN (L  SPOONER OLDHAM   PNO (N
STRINGS                (N   RUFUS THIBODEAUX  FDL  (NO JOE OSBORN       B   (NP LARRIE LONDIN    D  (N
J J CALE           G   (N   FARRELL MORRIS    PERC (N  GRANT BOATRIGHT  G   (N  BUCKY BARRETT    G  (N
JOHN CHRISTOPHER   G   (N   JERRY SHOOK       G    (N  STEVE GIBSON     G   (N  RUSS KUNKEL   CONGA(N
DALE SELLERS       G   (N   RAY EDENTON       G    (N  RITA FEY    AUTOHARP   (N  TIM MULLIGAN   SAX(N
LONDON SYM ORCH        (D   RUSTY KERSHAW     G FDL(G  GLORIA R JONES   V   (A  GRACIA NITZSCHE  V  (A
ROBIN LANE         V   (A   LEVON HELM        D    (GO GEORGE WHITSELL G   (G  TOM SCRIBNER    SAW (O
DENNIS BELFIELD    B   (O   ANN HILARY O'BRIEN V(O  GONE WITH THE WIND ORCH (N
```

```
    ROY YOUNG        K V  (AB        (A) THE ROY YOUNG BAND        1971 RCA            UK        SF8161
    JON LEE          TROM (AB        (B) MR FUNKY                  1972 MCA    UK MKPS2022 RI  MCF2690
    ALAN DAVIES      D    (AB
    DAVE WENDELLS    G    (AB   HOWIE CASEY      SAX. (A   PAUL SIMMONS    B  (    EDDIE THORNTON   TPT (B
    RICKY DODD       SAX  (B    RONNIE MACDONALD SAX (B   ONNIE McINTYRE  G  (B   NICK SOUTH       B  (B
    ROD COOMBES      D    (B    ROBIN JONES      PERC (B  DORIS TROY      V  (A   BARRY ST JOHN    V  (A
    SUE GLOVER       V    (A    SUNNY LESLIE     V   (A   LIZA STRIKE     V  (A   KATHY KISSOON    V  (A
    ALAN TOWNSEND    HRNS (AB
```

```
    STEVE YOUNG      G V  (ALL       (A) ROCK,SALT & NAILS         1969 A&M             US   4177
    JOE ALLEN        B    (E         (B) SEVEN BRIDGES ROAD        1972 REPRISE         US   2081
    KENNY MALONE     D    (E         (B) SEVEN BRIDGES ROAD        1975 BLUE CANYON     US    505
    CHUCK COCHRAN    K    (E         (B) SEVEN BRIDGES ROAD        1976 SONET       UK  SNTF 705
    JIM COLVARD      G    (E         (C) HONKY TONK MAN            1976 MOUNTAIN RAILROAD US 52776
    DAVE KIRBY       G    (E         (D) RENEGADE PICKER           1976 RCA  US APLI1759 UK  PL11759
    LLOYD GREEN      STEEL(E         (E) NO PLACE TO FALL          1978 RCA  US AHLI2510 UK  PL12510
    KRISTIN WILKINSON VLA (E         (F) TO SATISFY YOU            1981 ROUNDER     US   3057
    KARL HIMMEL      D    (BDE
    BOBBY WOOD       K    (D    MIKE LEECH       B    (DE  JERRY SHOOK   G HCA(DE DALE SELLERS    G  (BDE
    MAC GAYDEN       G    (DE   BUDDY EMMONS     STEEL(DE  TRACY NELSON  V   (ED  KIM YOUNG       V  (DE
    CHARLIE McCOY    HCA  (BE   BUDDY SPICHER    VLN  (BE  LARRY BYROM   G   (E   TERRY McMILLAN  HCA(D
    JOHNNY GIMBLE FDL MAND(D    WELDON MYRICK    STEEL(B   JOSH GRAVES   DOBRO(B  PETER WADE      G  (B
    BOBBY THOMPSON   G    (B    HENRY STRZELECKI B    (B   JERRY SMITH   K   (B   PETE DRAKE      STEEL(B
    FRED CARTER      B    (B    DAVID BRIGGS     K    (B   RAY EDENTON   G   (B   JERRY CARRIGAN  D  (B
    D J FONTANA      D    (B    WILLIE ACKERMAN  D    (B   BOB MOORE     G   (B   J B BROWN          (B
    GEORGE BOURQUE   B    (B    SPOOK JAMES      B    (B   CHARLIE JOBES     (B   STEVE KEITH        (B
    NASHVILLE EDITION V  (B     PAUL TANNEN      V    (B   MARY HOLLADAY V   (B   GINGER HOLLADAY V  (B
    ANITA BALL       V    (D    KIM MORRISON     V    (D
```

```
    BOB YOUNG        V HCA(A        (A) YOUNG & MOODY              1977 MAGNET UK MAG5015 UA UA LA759
    MICK MOODY       G V  (A
    GRAHAM PRESKETT VLN B K(A   KAY GARNER   V    (A   TERRY STANNARD   D   (A   JEAN HAWKER     V  (A
    CLAIRE TORRY     V    (A
```

```
    PAUL YOUNG            (A        (A) THIS IS YOUNG AND RENSHAW  1972 BELL        UK    201
    FRANK RENSHAW        (A
```

```
    BARRY TAYLOR     D    (A        (A) THIS IS YOUR LIFE          1980 QUINTESSENCE EP     CAN 1205
    ART BERGMANN     G V  (A
    JIM BESCOTT      B V  (A    HOWARD OGILVIE     VLA (A
```

```
    TIM BENJAMIN     B G  (A        (A) NO NEWS                    1980 PLUREX        EP   NL 0013
    RONALD HEILOO    K V  (A
    HAROLD SCHELLINK G B  (A    PETER MERTENS   G B  (A   RON SCHOLTE   D V (A
```

```
    ALISON STRATTON  V    (AB       (A) COLOSSAL YOUTH            1980 ROUGH TRADE     UK    ROUGH  8
    PHILIP MOXHAM    B    (AB       (B) FINAL DAY(EP)             1980 ROUGH TRADE     UK
    STUART MOXHAM    G K  (AB
```

```
    HEATHER WOOD     V    (A        (A) GALLERIES                 1968 VANGUARD               VSD 79295
    DAVE SWARBRICK FDL MAND(A       (A) GALLERIES                 1968 TRANSATLANTIC   UK   TRA 172
    ROYSTON WOOD     V TAMB(A       (B) THE YOUNG TRADITION       19   TRANSATLANTIC   UK   TRA 142
    DOLLY COLLINS    V    (A        (C) SO CHEERFULLY ROUND       19   TRANSATLANTIC   UK   TRA 155
    CHRIS HOGWOOD    PERC (A        (D) YOUNG TRADITION SAMPLER   1977 TRANSATLANTIC        TRANSAM13
    PETE BELLAMY   V G CONC (A      (E) GALLERIES REVISITED       1979 TRANSATLANTIC        TRANSAM30
    DAVID MUNROW SHAWN    (A
    ROD SKEAPING     VLN  (A    ADAM SKEAPING      VLN (A
```

```
    JESSE COLIN YOUNG G V B(ALL     (A) YOUNGBLOODS               1967 RCA            US   LSP3724
    JERRY CORBITT    G B  (A        (B) EARTH MUSIC               1967 RCA            US   LSP3865
    JOE BAUER        D    (DHJKL     (C) ELEPHANT MOUNTAIN         1969 RCA            US   LSP4150
    LOWELL LEVINGER  K G  (DHKL      (D) ROCK FESTIVAL             1970 WB             US   WS 1878
    MICHAEL KANE     B    (LK        (E) CRABTUNES NOGGINS         197  WB             US   WS 1944
    RICHARD'EARTHQUAKE'ANDERSON HCA(DKL  (F) THE BEST OF           1970 RCA            US   LSP4399
                                    (F) THE BEST OF               19   RCA  RI             AYL13680
                                    (G) TWO TRIPS                 1970 MERCURY         US   SR 61273
                                    (H) RIDE THE WIND             1971 WB    UK K46100 US   WS 2563
                                    (J) SUNLIGHT                  1971 RCA   UK SF8218 US   LSP4561
                                    (K) GOOD & DUSTY              1971 WB             US   BS 2566
                                    (L) HIGH ON A RIDGETOP        1972 WB             US   BS 2653
                                    (M) GET TOGETHER              19   RCA INT             INTS1170
                                    (N) THIS IS       (DBL)       1972 RCA            US    6051
```

```
    RENE WERNEER    VLN V(A        (A) MADAME LA FRONTIERE        1976 PHILIPS         FR   9101 056
    PASCAL STIVE     K V  (A
    JACKY THOMAS     B V  (A    JACQUES HIGELIN   ACC (A   MICHEL SANTANGELI D V (A  GABRIEL YACOUB  G (A
    PIERRE CHEREEZ   G    (A    JACQUES WIEDERKER CELLO(A
```

```
    COLE YOUNGER     G K V(A        (A) COLE YOUNGER              1975 ANCHOR          UK   ANCL 2008
    LINTON NAIFF     K    (A
    ROD ALEXANDER    G    (A    JIM RYAN        G    (A   STEVE WALLER  G V (A   DELISLE HARPER  B  (A
    TOM CROMPTON     D    (A    LITTLE STEVIE SMITH HCA(A KEN FREEMAN   SYN   (A   DORIS TROY      V  (A
    ROSETTA HIGHTOWER V  (A     JIM EVANS       V    (A   BILL KIMBLE   V   (A
```

```
    BEN BENAY        G    (A        (A) THE DAILY TRIP            1964 MERCURY    US   21094
    MIKE DEASY       B    (A
    JERRY SCHEFF     B    (A    BUTCH PARKER     K    (A   JIM BELL      OBOE V(A  JIM TROXELL     D  (A
    CURT BOETTCHER   PERC (A    TOXIE FRENCH     VIBES(A  MIKE HENDERSON ORG  (A
```

```
    TIMI YURO        V    (A        HURT                            1961 LIBERTY    US LST7208
                                    HURT                            19   LIBERTY RI SLS 50201
                                    SOUL                            1962 LIBERTY LRP 3212  LBY 1042
                                    WHATS A MATTER BABY             1962 LIBERTY LRP 3263 LBY1154
                                    WHATS A MATTER BABY             19   LIBERTY RI 50399
                                    LET ME CALL YOU SWEETHEART      19   LIBERTY LST7234 LRP 3234 LBY1275
                                    MAKE THE WORLD GO AWAY          19   LIBERTY LST 7319
                                    THE AMAZING TIMI YURO           19   MERCURY  US 60963
                                    SOMETHINGS BAD IN MY MIND       1968 LIBERTY LST 7594 LBL 83198
                                    THE TIMI YURO ALBUM             1976 EMI NL 97969
                                    IN THE BEGINNING               1968 LIBERTY UK LBS 83128
                                    timi yuro                       19   LIBERTY 5107     RI 50032
                                    BEST OF                         19   LIBERTY LRP 3289 LBY 1290
                                    GREAT PERFORMANCES              19   LIBERTY UK 83115
```

```
    BILLY GIBBONS    G V  (ALL       (A) FIRST ALBUM               1970 LONDON         US PS 584
                                     (A) FIRST ALBUM    RI         1980 WB RI EURO 56601    US   3268
    DUSTY HILL       B V  (ALL       (B) RIO GRANDE MUD            1972 LONDON UK SHU8433   US PS 612
                                     (B) RIO GRANDE MUD            1980 WB RI EURO 56602    US   3269
    FRANK BEARD      D    (ALL       (C) TRES HOMBRES              1973 LONDON UK SHU8459   US PS 631
                                     (C) TRES HOMBRES              1980 WB RI EURO 56602    US   3270
                                     (D) FANDANGO                  1975 LONDON UK SHU8482   UK PS 656
                                     (D) FANDANGO                  1980 WB RI EURO 56603    US   3271
                                     (E) TEJAS                     1976 LONDON UK LDU 1     US PS 680
                                     (E) TEJAS                     1980 WB RI EURO 56604    US   3272
                                     (F) BEST OF                   197  LONDON             US PS 706
                                     (F) BEST OF                   197  TELEFUNKEN/NOVA GER  623361
                                     (F) BEST OF                   1980 WB RI              US   3273
                                     (G) DEGUELLO                  1979 WB  UK K56701       US   3361
                                     (H) EL LOCO                   1981 WB   UK K56929      US   3593
```

```
    JOSEPH RACAILLE  K SYN V(AB      (A) BARRICADE 3               1976 RECOMMENDE RR7 ISADORA FR 9002
    HECTOR ZAZOU     K SYN B(AB      (B) TRAITE DE MECANIQUE POPULAIRE  1970 SCOPA       1002
    ANDRE JAUME      SAX  (A
    HARVEY NENEUX    G    (A  PATRICK PORTELLA  CLAR (A   DAVID RUEFF      WIND (AB GILLY BELL    SYN (A
    FERNAND D'ARLES  D    (A  MANFRED LE LALO   SAX (B   CATHERINE ARMAND SAX  (B LOLA TALOT    SAX (B
    HUMPHREY NENEUX  V    (B  REMI DEMILLAC     VLN (B
```

```
    ANDRE HERVE      K G V(A         (A) Z.O.U.                    1975 POLYDOR        FR  2393 103
    MICHEL HERVE     B V  (A
    JOEL HERVE       G V  (A  STEPHAN HERVE    D    (A   MARIA POPKIEWICZ  V   (A
```

```
    DENNY ZAGER      G V(ALL         (A) 2525                      1969 RCA  US 4214
    RICK EVANS       G V  (ALL       (B) IN THE YEAR 2525          19   RCA  US    ANL1 1077
    MARK DALTON      B    (A         ( ) FOOD FOR THE MIND         19   VANGUARD  US 6568
    NORM CHRISTIAN   D    (A         ( ) ZAGER & EVANS             1970 RCA  US 4302
```

```
    MICHAEL ZAGER    K    (ABC       (A) LETS ALL CHANT            1978 PRIVATE STOCK UK 1042
    ROB MOUNSEY      SYN K    (A     (B) LIFE'S A PARTY            1979 PRIVATE STOCK UK 1045
    FRANCISCO CENTANO B  (A          (C) ZAGER                     1980 EMI   UL EMC 3328
    CLIFF MORRIS     G    (A
    RAY CRISARA      TPT  (A  ALAN SCHWARTZBERG D   (A   JEFF MIRANOV     G    (A  RUBENS BASSINI  PERC(A
    GEORGE MARGE     WIND (A  DAVE GAREY      PERC (A   GLORIA AGOSTINI  HARP (A  PHIL BODNER    WIND(A
    JOHN GATCHELL    HRNS (A  ALAN RUBIN   HRNS   (A   ROBERT MILLIKAN  HRNS (A  TOM MALONE TROM (A
    GERALD CHAMBERLAIN TRROM(A DAVE TAYLOR  TROM   (A   WALTER KANE      WIND (A  RONALD CUBER   WIND(A
    JAMES BUFFINGTON HRNS (A  BROOKS TILLOTSON HRNS (A  ALVIN FIELDS     V    (A  YOLANDA McCULLOGH  V(A
    DOLLETTE McDONALD V  (A   LONI CLARK    V     (A   MAERETHA STEWART V    (A  FRANK FLOYD     V  (A
    BILLY BAKER      V    (A
```

```
    LENNY ZAKATEK    V    (A         (A) LENNY ZAKATEK             1979 A&M  US 4777 UK  AMLH64777
    JOHN GIBLIN      B V  (A
    STUART ELLIOTT   D PERC(A  MAX MIDDLETON     K    (A   ROBERT AHWAI     G    (A  IAN BAIRNSON   G V (A
    MARILYN BAIRNSON V   (A    STEVE GREGORY    SAX  (A   GEORGE CHISHOLM  HRNS (A  STRINGS         (A
```

```
    ZAL CLEMINSON    G    (A
    LEROI JONES      G    (A  CHRIS GLEN    B   (A   BILLY RANKIN     (A  TED McKENNA    D   (A
```

```
    MAUNCIA PLATON   V    (A         (A) Z=7L                      1973 VERTIGO    UK 6499 738
    FRANCOIS CAHEN   K    (A
    JEFF SEFFER      SAX  (A  JOEL DUGREN      B    (A   JEAN YVES PIZAUD VLN  (A  JEAN MYTRUONG  D   (A
```

```
                                     (A) ZAP POW WOW               1976 VULCAN        VULP 004
                                     (B) REVOLUTION                1976 TROJAN        TRLS 130
                                     (C) ZAP POW                   1978 ISLAND    UK  ILPS 9547
                                     (D) REGGAE RULES              1981 RHINO     US 015
```

```
FRANK ZAPPA PROD  G V  (ALL        (A) FREAK OUT                        1966 VERVE UK            SVLP9154
DON SUGARCANE HARRIS VLN(HJKLS     (A)  "    "                          1966 VERVE US            5005
DON PRESTON    K B  (BCDEFGHLMOPQT (A)  "    "         (DBL)            197  VERVE UK            2683 004
IAN UNDERWOOD G K WIND(CEFHJKL     (A)  "    "         (DBL)            196  VERVE GERM          710007
              (MOQSRYNG            (B) ABSOLUTELY FREE                  1967 VERVE UK SVLP9174 RI 2317 035
RUTH UNDERWOOD K PERC (NRSTYZcGU   (B)  "       "                       1967 VERVE US            5013
DAVID ANDERLE         (A           (B)  "       "                       1967 VERVE GERM          710006
RONNIE AMBLER    WIND (             (C) WE'RE ONLY IN IT FOR THE MONEY   1967 VERVE UK SVLP9199 RI 2317 034
MIKE ALTSCHUL    WIND (PQ          (C)  "   "   "  "  "   "             1967 VERVE US            5045
HAROLD AYRES          (            (C)  "   "   "  "  "   "             1967 VERVE GERM          710012
JIMMY CARL BLACK D(ABCEFGHLNfDj    (D) LUMPY GRAVY                      1967 VERVE UK SVLP9223 RI 2317 046
TERRY BOZZIO     D  (XYZbK         (D)  "    "                          1967 VERVE US            8741
BIANCO           K  (              (E) CRUISIN WITH RUBEN & THE JETS    1968 VERVE UK SVLP9237 RI 2317 069
MAX BENNETT      B  (JK            (E)  "   "   "   "   "               1969 VERVE US            5055
TERRY BOLIN      D  (              (E)  "   "   "   "   "               1969 VERVE GERM          710020
NAPOLEON MURPHY BROCK SAX(STUYbcX  (F) MOTHER MANIA                     1969 VERVE UK SVLP9239 RI 2317 047
JACK BRUCE       B  (S             (F)  "    "                          19   VERVE               2351 017
RANDY BRECKER    HRNS (Z           (F)  "    "                          1969 VERVE US            5068
MICHAEL BRECKER  HRNS (Z           (F)  "    "                          1969 VERVE GERM          710021
CAPTAIN BEEFHEART V  (KYX          (G) UNCLE MEAT                       1969 BIZARRE UK 52024  US 2024
BILL BYERS       TROM (PQ          (G)  "    "                          1969 REPRISE GERM        64005
DALE BOZZIO          (ef           (G)  "    "                          196  TRANSATLANTIC  UK   TRA197
EDWIN BEACH          (A            (H) WEASELS RIPPED MY FLESH          1970 REPRISE UK K44019
BEN BARRETT          (A            (H)  "   "   "   "                   1970 BIZARRE        US   2028
JOHN BERGAMO     PERC (Z           (J) CHUNGAS REVENGE                  1970 REPRISE UK K44020
BLOODSHOT ROLLIN'RED HCA(U         (J)  "   "                           1970 BIZARRE        US   2030
ADRIAN BELEW     G  (Abl           (K) HOT RATS                         1970 REPRISE UK K44078 RI K59021
ARTHUR BARROW       (efhjkm        (K)  "   "                           1970 BIZARRE        US   6356
GARY BARONE      TPT (             (L) BURNT WEENY SANDWICH             1970 REPRISE UK K44083
JIMMY BOND       B  (D             (L)  "    "    "                     1970 BIZARRE        US   6370
DENNIS BUDIMIR   G  (D             (HL) WEASELS/BURNT WEENY(2 ORIGINALS) 19  REPRISE UK K64024
JOHN BALKIN      B  (D             (M) LIVE AT FILLMORE EAST            1971 REPRISE UK K44150
CHUCK BERGHOFFER B  (D             (M)  "   "   "   "                   1971 BIZARRE US        2042
DICK BARBER      V  (DC            (N) 200 MOTELS                       1971 UA UK 50003     US   LA9956
RAY COLLINS         (ABEGHS        (N)  "   "                           1971 UA             GERM 29218/9
DAVE CORONADO    SAX (             (O) JUST ANOTHER BAND FROM LA        1972 REPRISE UK K44179
ROBERT CAMARENA  V  (ST            (O)  "    "    "   "  "              1972 BIZARRE        US   2075
RONNIE CUBER     REEDS(Z           (P) THE GRAND WAZOO                  1972 REPRISE UK K44209
LEE CLEMENT      PERC (P           (P)  "   "    "                      1972 BIZARRE        US   2093
HERB COHEN           (B            (Q) WAKA JAWAKA                      1972 REPRISE UK K44203
LISA COHEN           (B            (Q)  "   "                           1972 BIZARRE        US   2094
VINCE COLAIUTA      (efhk          (R) OVERNIGHT SENSATION              1973 DICREET UK K41000 US 2149
GENE CIPRIANO    WIND (D           (S) APOSTROPHE                       1974 DISCREETUK K59201 US 2175
ERIC CLAPTON     G  (CD            (T) ROXY & ELSEWHERE                 1974 DISCREET UK K69201 US 2202
DON CHRISTLIEB   WIND (            (U) ONE SIZE FITS ALL                1974 DISCREET UK K59207 US 2216
MARGINAL CHAGRIN SAX (e            (V) MOTHERS DAY                      197  VERVE               2626 002
FRANKIE CAPP     D  (D             (W) ROCK FLASHBACKS                  1975 VERVE               2352 057
CHUNCKY             (P             (X) BONGO FURY                       1975 DISCREET UK K59209 US 2234
WARREN CUCURULLO    (efhk          (Y) ZOOT ALLURES                    1976 WB       UK K56298 US 2970
AYNSLEY DUNBAR   D  (GMNOPQJS      (Z) IN NEW YORK                      1978 DISCREET UK K69204 US 2/2290
TONY DURAN       G  (PQ            (a) STUDIO TAN                       1978 DISCREET UK K59210 US 2291
VINCENT DE ROSA  HRNS (D           (b) SHEIK YERBOUTI                   1979 CBS        UK 88339
EARL DUMLER      WIND (P           (b)  "   "                           1979 ZAPPA           US   2/1501
GEORGE DUKE      K V  (JNPQRSTUXac (c) SLEEP DIRT                       1979 DISCREET UK K59211 US 2292
EUGENE DINOVI       (A             (d) ORCHESTRAL FAVOURITES            1979 DISCREET UK K59212 US 2294
ALEX DMOCHOWSKI(ERRONEOUS B(PRSQ   (e) JOE'S GARAGE ACT 1               1980 CBS        UK 86101
DEBBIE              (ST            (e)  "   "   "   "                   1980 ZAPPA           US   1/1603
ROY ESTRADA      B V(ABCDEFGHLYkm  (f) JOE'S GARAGE ACTS 2&3            1980 CBS        UK 88475
VIRGIL EVANS        (A             (f)  "   "   "   "                   1980 ZAPPA           US   2/1502
ALAN ESTES       PERC (PD          (g) ZAPPA & THE MOTHERS              19   VERVE               2352 057
GENE ESTES          (AD            (h) TINSELTOWN REBELLION             1981 CBS        UK 88516 US 37336
DON ELLIS           (B             (j) YOU ARE WAHAT YOU IS             1981 CBS        UK 88560
JIM FIELDER      B  (A             (k) SHUT UP 'N PLAY YER GUITAR       1981 CBS        UK 66368
KIM FOWLEY          (A             (m) SHIP ARRIVING TOO LATE           1982 CBS        UK 85804
GABBY FURGGY     V  (L
LARRY FANOGA        (D
VICTOR FELDMAN   PERC (A  CAROL KAYE        (A    MARK PINSKE        (j    ERNIE TACK       HRNS (P
TOM FOWLER       B (RSTUXY MICHAEL LICKERT  (,,   JOEL PESKIN     SAX (PQ   VITO             (A
JANET FERGUSON   V (PQ    LYNN              (ST   LISA POPEIL      V  (m    AL VIOLA         G  (D
BRUCE FOWLER TROM (RSTXY  MIKE LANG         K  (D VAN DYKE PARKS      (     STEVE VAI        G(hjkm
CARL FRANZONI       (TA   DAVID LOGERMAN    (hj  DAVE PARLATO     B  (Y    KEN VASSEY       (R
WALT FOWLER      TPT (TY  ANDRE LEWIS       K  (bY GEORGE PRICE    B  (Y    NEIL VANG        (A
LOWELL GEORGE    G  (HKL  RICKY LANCELOTTI  (R    RICHARD PERISSI HRNS (D   HENRY VESTINE    (A
ROY GATON           (A    BILL MUNDI        (BCG  SPARKY PARKER    B  (Y    MARK VOLMAN      V (JMNO
BUZZ GARDNER     HRNS (HL DAVID MOIRE       V  (Yb JEAN LUC PONTY  K  (KRSk  RAY WHITE       G(Zhjkm
BUNK GARDNER  WIND (BCEFGHL SAL MARQUEZ   TPT  (PQRS DON PARDO     V  (Z    CHAD WACKERMANN  V  (jm
RUBEN DE GUEVARA B V (STY LOU MARINI    REED (Z    CHRIS PETERSON  V  (Q    DAVID WELLS      (A
JIM GORDON       D  (S    KERRY McNABB   V  (S    JOHN ROTELLA   PERC (ABDP TOM WILSON     PROD (A
SUSIE GLOVER     V  (S    ARTHUR MAEBE   HRNS (D  KURT RETAR          (AB   KEN WATSON       (A
JOHN GUERIN         (DJKS ED MANN    PERC(Zbelfkjm EMIL RICHARDS  PERC (D   ERNIE WATTS    SAX (P
JIM HAYNES       D  (D    TOM MALONE     HRNS (Z  TONY RIZZI      G  (D     BOB WEST         B  (D
RALPH HUMPHREY   D  (RST  MALCOLM McNABB  HRNS (P ALICE STUART       (      PETER WOLF     K(efhk
PAUL HUMPHREYS      (K    LINCOLN MAYORGA  K  (D  STUMUK          SAX (e    RON WILLIAMS     (A
BOB HARRIS       K V (M   SHELLEY MANNE   D  (D   CRAIG STEWART       (ej   JOHNNY GUITAR WATSON
GEORDIE HORMEL      (f    BOB MARTON  SAX V K (m  KEN SHROYER    TROM (DPQ              G V(U
ELLIOT INGBER   G  (A     JOANNE CALDWELL McNABB (D PAUL SMITH    K  (D     DENNIS WALLEY G(Xefhjk
JOHN JOHNSON        (A    TOM MARIANO     K  (1   JEFF SIMMONS B G V(JOTQ   NELLY WALKER     (G
DR JOHN          K  (     AL MANN        (efhm    JIM SHERWOOD WIND (BCEFGHLj IKE WILLIS    (efhjk
PETE JOLLY       K  (D    AL MALKIN      (e       EMMET SARGEANT     (A     JAMES YOUMAN     (Uc
JULES JACOB   WIND (D     TOMMY MARS  K V (behjkm JOE SAXON          (A     BOB ZIMMITTI  PERC (P
FRED JACKSON  WIND (P     LOU ANNE NEIL  HARP (ZY DAVID SAMUELS  PERC (Z    PAMELA ZARUBICA  (BC
PLAS JOHNSON        (P    TED NASH       WIND (D  RON SELICO      D  (K     GAIL ZAPPA     V  (Y
EDDIE JOBSON K VLN V (ZK  SHUGGIE OTIS    G  (K   ARTIE TRIPP        (EFGHL  AHMET ZAPPA      (j
SNEAKY PETE KLEINOW STEEL(Q TONY ORTEGA  WIND (P  TOMMY TEDESCO   G  (D     MOON ZAPPA       (jm
HOWARD KAYLAN    V  (JMNO PAT O'HEARN B WIND(DZkm RANDY THORNTON  V  (b     JIMMY ZITO    TPT (D
RAY KELLOFF         (A    DAVID OCKER    CLAR (bj SCOTT THUNES    B  (m
RUTH KOMANOFF       (     JIM PONS       V  (OMN  CHESTER THOMPSON D (TUXc
```

```
Z9                              JOE ZAWINUL                                          Z9

    JOE ZAWINUL        K  (ALL      (A) ZAWINUL                1971 ATCO  US 1579    UK    2400 151
    GEORGE DAVIS       FLT (A        (A) ZAWINUL                1972 ATLANTIC        UK RI K40349
    EARL TURBINTON     SAX (A        (B) RISE & FALL            19   VORTEX          US     2002
    WOODIE SHAW        TPT (A        (C) MONEY IN THE POCKET    19   ATCO            US     3003
    MIROSLAV VITOUS    B   (A        (D) CONCERTO RETITLED(COMP) 1976 ATLANTIC       US     1694
    JIMMY OWENS        TPT (A
    HUBERT LAWS        FLT (A  HERBIE HANCOCK   K  (A   WALTER BOOKER    B  (A   JOE CHAMBERS    PERC(A
    BILLY HART         PERC (A DAVID LEE        PERC (A  WAYNE SHORTER   SAX (A   JACK DE JOHNETTE WIND(A
Z9A                               ZAZU                                               Z9A
    JOHN MELNICK       K V (A        (A) ZAZU                   1975 WOODEN NICKEL   US 0791
    RANDY CURLEE       B V (A
    PAUL RIPUPERO      G V (A  MICKEY LEHOCKY    PERC (A
Z9B                               ZED                                                Z9B
    NIGEL JENKINS      G B (A        (A) ZED                    1981 ATLANTIC US 19299 DOUBLE 003
    GRAHAM JARVIS      D   (A
    PAUL WESTWOOD      B   (A  DAVE LAWSON      SYN (A  MIKE MORAN      K  (A
Z9C                               ZEN                                                Z9C
                                 (A) RUSSIAN ROULETTE          1981 LASER           UK    LPIP2
Z10                              ZEPHYR                                              Z10
    TOMMY BOLIN        G V (AB       (A) ZEPHYR                 1970 PROBE UK SPB 1006 US  CP4510
    CANDY GIVENS       K V (ABC      (B) GOING BACK TO COLORADO 1971 WB             US  WS1897
    JOHN FARIS         K SAX(AB      (C) SUNSET RIDE            1972 WB             US  WS2603
    ROBBIE CHAMBERLAIN     D(A
    BOBBY BERGE        D   (B  DAVID GIVENS B V (ABC   PAUL CONLEY    SYN (B  BUZZY LINHART   V (B
    P M WOOTEN         D   (C  JOHN ALFONSE CONGA(C  DAN SMYTH      K   (C  JOCK BARTLEY    G V (C
    BOBBY NOTKOFF      VLN (C
Z11                          WARREN ZEVON                                           Z11
    WARREN ZEVON G V K B HCA(ALL     (A) WANTED DEAD OR ALIVE            1969 IMPERIAL    US    LP 12456
    DAVID LINDLEY      FDL  (BD       (B) WARReN ZEVON                    1976 ASYLUM US 7E1060 UK  K53039
    WADDY WACHTEL PROD G V (BCDF      (C) EXCITABLE BOY                   1978 ASYLUM US 6E 118 UK  K53973
    BOB GLAUB          B   (BC        (D) BAD LUCK STREAK IN DANCING SCHOOL 1980 ASYLUM US 5E 509 UK  K52191
    LARRY ZACK         D   (B         (E) STAND IN THE FIRE              1980 ASYLUM US 5E 519 UK  K52265
    PHIL EVERLY        V   (B         (F) THE ENVOY                      198  ASYLUM           UK K52354
    GREG LADANY        PROD(DEF
    J D SOUTHER        V  (BDCF JACKSON BROWNE   G V (BDC LINDSEY BUCKINGHAM G V (B  MARTY DAVID   B  (B
    GARY MALLABER      D   (A  SID SHARP    STRINGS (B  BOBBY KEYS     SAX (B  JAI WINDING   K V(B
    GLENN FREY         G V (BD  DON HENLEY        V  (BDF ROY MARINELL  B  (BF JORGE CALDERON  V  (BCDF
    NED DOHENY         G   (B  BONNIE RAITT      V  (B  ROSEMARY BUTLER V  (B  CARL WILSON   V  (B
    JEFF PORCARO       D   (CF GREG LADANYI    PERC (C  KENNY EDWARDS  B  (CF RICK MAROTTA  D  (CDF
    ARTHUR GERST       HARP (C LUIS DAMIAN   JARANA (C  DANNY KORTCHMAR G  (CF MANUEL VASQUEZ    (C
    RUSS KUNKEL        D   (C  LEE SKLAR        B  (CDF JIM HORN       SAX (CF LINDA RONSTADT V  (CD
    LINDA WARNES       V   (C  JOHN McVIE       B  (C  MICK FLEETWOOD D  (C  KARLA BONOFF   V  (C
    SKIP BATTIN        B   (A  DRACHEN THEAKER  D  (A  ED CARAEFF     PERC (A SWEET TRIFLES  V  (A
    BRENT SEAWELL      B   (A  TOXEY FRENCH     D  (A  JON CORNEAL    D  (A  GENTLEMEN BOYS V  (BC
    DON FELDER         G   (D  JOE WALSH        G  (D  STEVIE NICKS   V  (B  JORDON ZEVON   V  (F
    DAVID LANDAU       G   (EF ZEKE ZIRNGIRBEL  G V (E  BOB HARRIS     K V (E  ROBERTO PIRON  B V (E
    MARTY STINGER      D   (E  STEVE LUKATHER   G  (F  MIKE POTTS     D  (F  STEVE FORMAN   PERC(F
    BOB GLAUB          B   (F  GRAHAM NASH      V  (F
Z11A               ZIGGYBYFIELD & THE BLACKHEART BAND                               Z11A
                                 (A) RUNNING                   1980 PVK        UK       PVK  1
Z12                               ZIOR                                               Z12
    KEITH BONSOR V K B FLT(A         (A) ZIOR                   1971 NEPENTHA       6437  005
    JOHN TRUBA         G V (A
    PETER BREWER D PNO HCA(A  BARRY SKEELS     B V (A
Z15                              ZOMBIES                                             Z15
    COLIN BLUNSTONE    V   (B        (A) BEGINS HERE            1965 DECCA          UK    LK 4679
    ROD ARGENT         K   (B        (B) ODESSEY & ORACLE       1968 CBS UK 63280   US DATE TES 4013
    HUGH GRUNDY        D   (B        (C) WORLD OF THE ZOMBIES   1970 DECCA          UK    SPA 85
    PAUL ATKINSON      G   (B        (D) TIME OF THE ZOMBIES    1973 EPIC  UK 65728 RI   68262
    CHRIS WHITE        B   (B        (D) TIME OF THE ZOMBIES    1973 EPIC           US    32861
    PAUL ARNOLD        B   (         (E) ROCK ROOTS     (COMP)  1976 DECCA          UK    ROOTS2
                                     (F) EARTHDAYS             19   LONDON         US    PS 557
                                     (G) ZOMBIES       (COMP)  19   PARROT         US    PAS71001
                                     (H) SHES NOT THERE (DBL)(COMP) 1976 NOVA       GERM  6/28378
Z16                               ZON                                                Z16
    DENTON YOUNG       V   (         (A) ASTRAL PROJECTOR       1978 EPIC           PEC 90442
    HOWARD HELM        K   (         (B) BACK DOWN TO EARTH     1979 EPIC              80026
    KIM HUNT           D   (         (C) I'M WORRIED ABOUT THE BOYS 1980 FALCON        80003
    JIM SAMSON         B   (
    BRIAN MILLER       G   (
Z17                              ZONES                                               Z17
    WILLY GARDNER      G V (A        (A) UNDER INFLUENCE(4 DIFF COVERS) 1979 ARISTA  UK    SPART 1095
    BILLY McISAAC      K V (A
    RUSSELL WEBB       B V (A  KENNY HYSLOP      D  (A
Z18                               ZOO                                                Z18
    PIERRE FANEN       G   (A        (A) ZOO                    19   BARCLAY 521172 RIVIERA521118
    JOEL DAYDE         V   (A        (A) ZOO                    19   MAJOR MINOR    UK    SMLP 74
    DANIEL CARLET  VLN SAX (AB       (B) I SHALL BE FREE        1971 RIVIERA             521147
    MICHEL RIPOCHE VLN SAX (AB
    TONY CANAL         TPT (A  ANDRE HERVE      K  (AB  MICHEL BONNECARRERE G(AB  MICHEL HERVE   B  (AB
    CHRISTIAN DEVAUX   D   (AB IAN BELLAMY       V  (B
Z19                               ZOO                                                Z19
    TROND NYRUD        WIND (B        (A) CAPTURED BY ZOO       1979
    KETIL STOKKAN      G V (B        (B) NOREGS HEITASTE        1980 SNOWFLAKE        CLP 3017
    SVERRI DAHL        K V (B        (C) Z PA MAKEN             1981 SNOWFLAKE            3022
    RUDI HOYNES        TROM (b        (D) GAYA                  1981 SNOWFLAKE            3029
    ROYER LARSEN       B   (B
```

Z20   **ZORRO**   Z20
                       (A) 'ARRODS DON'T SELL 'EM (EP)   19   BRIDGE HOUSE   BHEP 1

Z20A   **ZOUNDS**   Z20A
                       (A) CURSE OF THE ZOUNDS   1981 ROUGH TRADE   UK

Z21   **TAPPER ZUKIE**   Z21

TAPPER ZUKIE	(ALL	MAN AH WARRIOR	1977	MER	MER 101
		IN DUB	19	STARS	RI FRONT LINE FL1029
		M P L A	19	KLICK	RI FRONT LINE FL1006
		MAN FROM BOSRAH	19	STARS	
		PEACE IN THE GHETTO	1978	FRONT LINE	FL1009
		TAPPER ROOTS	1978	FRONT LINE	FL1032

Z22   **ZWOL**   Z22

WALTER ZWOL	K V (A	(A) ZWOL				1978	EMI		AMS 2003	
WOODY WEST	G (A	(B) EFFECTIVE IMMEDIATELY				1981	EMI		US 17014	
RALPH MURPHY	V (A									
DENNIS PINHAM	B V (A	DANNY SMITH	D (A	MARL GENDLE	G (A	JIM ISBELL		D (A		
GHIA	CONGA(A	DONNA RHODES	V (A	ROGER COOK	V (A	PHILIP DONNELLY		G (A		
RACHEL SIMPSON	V (A	KATHY JOHNSON	V (A	STACEY HAYDEN	G (A	TONY NEWMAN		B (A		
CHARLES CHALMERS	V SAX(A	SANDRA RHODES	V (A							

Z22A   **ZYANKALI**   Z22A

PETER JAKOBI	K V (A	(A) I COULD CRY A LOTTA BLUES			1972 PLANE	GER	1001
DIETER BECK	B G V(A						
SOL DE SULLY	PERC (A	BERNHARD TREUTWEIN	EFFECTS(	KLAUS WEISS	D (A WALTER BRANDT	G B (A	
WILLY MICHL	V G PERC(A						

Z23   **ZYGOAT**   Z23
                       (A) ZYGOAT   1975 POLYDOR   2383 270

Z24   **ZZEBRA**   Z24

TERRY SMITH	G (A	(A) ZZEBRA			1974 POLYDOR	2383 296		
GUS YEADON	PNO G V (A	(B) PANIC			1975 POLYDOR	2383 326		
LIAM GENOCKEY	D V (AB							
JOHN McCOY	B (AB	STEVE BYRD	G (B	ALAN MARSHALL	V (B	TOMMY EYRE	K (B	
LOUGHTY AMAO PERC	SAX V(AB	DAVE QUINCY	SAX (AB	JO NEWMAN	V (B	LESLEY DUNCAN	V (B	
KIM MOORE	V (B							

Index

The index lists the main headings of each entry and all the musicians included. The references are to entry codes not page numbers. Main entries are indicated by a line under the code, e.g. ACE A7.

Various cross references have been provided between maiden, former, stage, real names etc.; all elements of composite group names have been indexed.

An/Au

ANDRIDGE Rick S33 S71
ANDROID SISTERS F51
ANDROMEDA A63
ANDWELLA'S DREAM A63A
Andy (G) M109
ANDY Bob B163
ANDY Horace D82
ANDY Patrick P140C
ANGAROLA Joyce B268
ANGE A64
ANGEL A65
ANGEL Alexis T 048
ANGEL Claude R6A
ANGEL David B197
ANGEL CITY A65A
ANGELETTES F42
ANGELIC UPSTARTS A65B
ANGELO A65C
ANGELO Michael P53
ANGELOS John N63
ANGELWITCH A65D
ANGER Darol M136C
ANGER Merle C118
ANGERS Phil S72
ANGLETRAX A66
ANGULO Victor K90
ANGROVE Ray S261A
ANHOECK Hasso Jr S38
ANIMALS A67 W94
ANIMATED EGG A67F
ANKA Paul W119
ANITA GROUP SINGERS H26
ANNAN Tom R1
ANNAS John B183C
ANNEXUS QUAM A67A
ANNIS John Wesley H139
Annisette S30
ANNO DOMINI A67G
ANNUS John G26A
ANSELL Tony R118A S147
ANSELMO Walty K96C
ANSON Chris S76
ANSON David B254
ANSTATT Bill S3A
ANSTEE Clive B110 H151 J84
ANT Adam (GODDARD Stuart) A10
ANTHEM A67H
ANTHILL Danny S278
ANTHONE Robert B108B
ANTHONY John (K V) G22C W54
ANTHONY John (PROD) V11
ANTHONY Keith F41
ANTHONY Mark (G V) H135A
ANTHONY Mark (HRNS) A35D
ANTHONY Mike (B) V14
ANTHONY Mike (G) H63 M227
ANTHONY Michael (K) I12A
ANTI PASTI A67J
ANTON Greg S322
ANTONELLI Bob T79A
ANTONI Robert 'Starkey' N16
ANTONIUS Jerry H90
ANTOON Rod T70
ANTYMOS APOSTOLIS S1B
ANY TROUBLE A67C
ANYONES QUESTION A67K
ANYOVE Garfield A35A
AORTA A67D
AOUZI Serge C137
APACHE A67P
APE Ayus S243
APETREA Coste P109 S14B T104 W75
APHRODITES CHILD A67E
APLANALP Richard H34 K5 K6 N151 O39 P14 P155
APPALOOSA A67L
APLIN David W128A
APPEL Dave F27A M65A
APPEL Martin J S354
APPEL Mike S229
APPELL Dave P119
APPICE Carmine A27 A67N B64A C5 C129 D66 D124 F65 K2 N63 S242 S273 V15 W120
APPICE Vinny A131G B115 D53 G64C
APPLE & APPLEBERRY A68B
APPLEBY Acker S210
APPLEBY Geoff H185 S53B
APPLEBY Kathy I32
Applejack B109 B210 M159

APPLEJACKS A67M
APPLE PIE MOTHERHOOD BAND A68A
APPLETON Arthur E Jr R36
APPLETON Rob H124B S181
APPLETREE THEATRE A68
APPLEWHITE Herman W47
APPLING Kitty S269
APPLING Shane S269
APPS Roy H109
APREA Ron L51
APRETREA Coste P56A
APRIL WINE A69
APROSIO Daniel K10D
AQSAK MABOUL A71A
AQUABELLA Francisco D103
AQUARIAN DREAM A70
AQUATONES A71B
AQUILA A71
AQUILA Assunta Dell K80
ARAI Ichiro H35A
ARAMA Greg N63 U22A
ARANDA Mick S339A
AR BIZ Mik S280
AR BRAS Dan A72A F6 S280
ARBRE A72
ARBUS Dave D9 E8 P49A W72
ARC (US) A72B
ARC A73 B79
ARCADIO Bernie T158
ARCADIUM A73A
ARCHELETA Mike L82B
ARCHER Bruce H35
ARCHER Dee R102B
ARCHER James M214
ARCHER Laurence W78
ARCHER Maria
ARCHER Reuben W78
Archiris V13
ARCHULETA Dave D66 M136C
ARDITO Ronnie S100 T156
ARDLEY Neil A74 N62
ARDO DOMBEC A74B
ARDOLINI Tom N2
AREA A74A
AREA CODE 615 A75
AREAS Jose Chepito A76 B109 B210 C158 C208A C213 G26D H19 H78 I31 O35 S19 S36
ARELLANO Dave I6
ARELLANO Francisco A132
ARENDS Lawrence P4
ARENDT Peter A67P
ARES Tony A35
ARGENT A77
ARGENT Rod A77 A78 B160 B195 D9 F36 F56 I22 L43 L99 M38 N45A P77 R46 T153 W72 Z15
ARGY Steve Q5
Ari T8
ARIEL A79
ARIOLI Doug B52B
ARIS Ben W72
ARIZONA A80
ARKIN Rob G121 S216
ARKONA Hannes E50A
ARKUS Anatol B91A H13
ARKUS Fabian B91A
ARLIN Bobby H146a L34
ARLINE Calvin K30 L9
ARLISS John S216
ARMAGEDDON A81
ARMAND Catherine Z2
ARMAND Nick S329C
ARMAND Renee A132 C173 O13
ARMAND Rick N50A S329C
ARMANDO Ray B85 D50 F103D L67B M218 S111 S169
ARMATRADING Joan A82 J86
AR MERDY Yann-Fanch S280
ARMIGER Martin S224A
ARMIGER Michael S224A
ARMBRISTER Benjamin T104A
ARMENTROUT Jay B200
ARMIN Dick L74
ARMIN Famille C28A
ARMIN Paul L74
ARMISTEAD Brian D125A
ARMITT Ian B23 B156 D49
ARMOND Wayne D63
ARMOUR Jeff M4
ARMSTEAD Chandra R125

ARMSTEAD Joshie A96 B221 D39 K45 M53 P6 P72A R125 S128 S147A V21 W36
ARMSTRONG Bill (Fdl) J69
ARMSTRONG Bill (Hrns) D101 D133
ARMSTRONG Dan (Sit) D101
ARMSTRONG Dan (G) S65
ARMSTRONG Dan (B) B21 M5
ARMSTRONG Danny (Trom) S284
ARMSTRONG Dave C76
ARMSTRONG Frankie A82A
ARMSTRONG Herbie D46 F95 M203 Y6
ARMSTRONG Howard G72
ARMSTRONG Jim L71A T57
ARMSTRONG Kevin A82B L100A
ARMSTRONG Lil J79
ARMSTRONG Moe D5
ARMSTRONG Nick P142B
ARMSTRONG Paul M18
ARMSTRONG Ralph M40 P115
ARMSTRONG Robert C240
ARMSTRONG Tippy A28 C139 J52 K46 T15 N55 R137 W64 W118
ARNDT Udi A99 O36A
ARNELL Rene R5
ARNESEN Peter C208B C234E D5 G49 H132 H185 I8 K4 R153 T6A W69E W125
ARNEY Ian T144
ARNOLD A82C
ARNOLD Billy Boy A83 D66 J92A S323
ARNOLD Bruce O33C
ARNOLD David A23
ARNOLD Derek Q3
ARNOLD Harvey Dalton O43
ARNOLD Jerome A83 B282 D139 H70
ARNOLD Jimmy C9A
ARNOLD Jimmy G17
ARNOLD Joseph M211 P80 R168 S36
ARNOLD Kristine B154A P151
ARNOLD Leonard B154A W43
ARNOLD Mac S204
ARNOLD Malcolm D40
ARNOLD Micha E56B
ARNOLD Pat 'P.P.' A84 A101 B268 C83 D86 D111 F13 H179 J16B J75B K51 L107 M64 N4 N18 S162 S296 T158 U5 W133
ARNOLD Paul Z15
ARNOLD Robert (B) W106
ARNOLD Robert (TPT (Tpt V) S326
ARNONE Don C146 K36
ARNOTT Ray F65A
ARNOUX Jean M57B
ARNOW Leonard M232
ARONOWITZ Myles J18
ARRICH Cynthia S332B
ARRINGTON Steve S154
ARRIVAL A85
ARROGANCE A85A
ARROWS A85B
ARROYO Pascal B207B
ARS LAETA CHOIR W7
ARS NOVA A86
ART A87
ART & LANGUAGE A87A
ART BEARS A88
ART ENSEMBLE OF CHICAGO A89
ART OBJECTS A89A
ARTFUL DODGER A90
ARTHUR Bob M211 S36
ARTHUR Brooks M203
ARTHUR Dave M50
ARTHUR Theodore K45
ARTHUR Toni M50
ARTHURS Andy R16B
ARTHURS Leom N19
ARTHURWORREY Louise B19
ARTI & MESTIERI A91
ARTIE KORNFELD'S TREE K84A
ARTIGE Francois V26B W39D
ARTISTICS A91A
ARTISTS Ron S85A

ARTMAN Gilbert C137 H89A L17 U20D W119C
ARTS Arno P156B
Artski Q5
ARTWOODS A92
ART ZOYD A89B
ARVANITAS Georges D63 W13
ARZACHEL A92A
ASADA Takeshi S93A
ASANO Ryoji G55
ASANO Takami G55
ASBELL Paul H147 H150 W28
ASBURY JUKES S199
ASCARRUNZ Cesar C63C
ASCEND A93
ASCH Les J51
ASCHER Ken A135 C134 C164 C229 D86 E40 F103 F108A K69 L51 L80C M41 M46B M107 N6A O27 P137 R60C S50 S124 S125 S180 T25 T147 W51 W107
ASCOTT Brett C108A
ASGARD A94
Ash Beat Y5A
ASH Daniel B51A
ASH Jim C115A
ASH Jon B183D
ASH Lesley D99
ASH Robert O26
ASH Vic P131 R40B
ASHBOURNE Peter D63
ASHBY Beverley S250
ASHBY Dorothy C52A C180 E7 I28 M102 W116 W118 W119
ASHBY Harold R168 W85
ASHBY Jeanie M75
ASHBY Ken A80
ASHCROFT Mike D16
ASHDOWN Doug A95
ASHER Jane B59
ASHER James T121
ASHER Peter G60 P68D R22 R137 S196 S272 T25 T27
ASHETON Ron I10 N31
ASHETON Scott I10
ASHEY Gil R142A
ASHFORD Jack B135 C153 F92 G26A J91A P113 R45 R141 R142A S34 S73 S128 T42 W84C W118
ASHFORD Nickolas A96
ASHFORD Paul S263A
ASHFORD Rosalind V9
ASHFORD Ted B144 H78 M18 T158 U5 W133
ASHFORD & SIMPSON A96
ASHKAN A97
ASHLEE Bill M126
ASHLEY Joan A23
ASHLEY Mark P29A
ASHLEY Steve A30 A98 C152 C165 E41
ASHLEY Virginia S140
ASHMAN Aliki A25 A98A B171 C48 S264
ASHMAN Malcolm C88
ASHMAN Matthew A10
ASHMAN Micky D100
ASHMAN REYNOLDS A98A
ASHRA A99
ASHTON Andrew T135B
ASHTON Bob M26
ASHTON Hugh O47
ASHTON John P142C
ASHTON Mark A99A H73 R33
ASHTON Robert S168
ASHTON Tony A22 A100 A101 B220 C101 E60 F12 G95 H67 L64 L117 L120 M83 M121 P9 R64B S264 T63 T155 W117
ASHTON William see KRAMER Billy J.
ASHTON & LORD A100
ASHTON GARDNER AND DYKE A101
ASHWORTH Audie C14
ASHWORTH Don B85
ASHWORTH Jimmy D58
ASHWORTH Pete S295A
ASHWORTH Richard & WHITE DUB A101A
ASIA A99B
ASKELAND Nina L24C

ASKEW Adrian A113 L139
ASKEW Dennis Lee U17B
ASKEW Roger A72
ASKEY Deidra M227
ASKEY Gil M115
ASLAKSEN Duane E62B
ASLAM Annie R65
ASLEEP AT THE WHEEL A102
ASMUSSEN Claus S108C
ASMUSSEN Svend S108C
ASOH Remi F71A
ASPERUD Kjell'Chappy' T97
ASPERY Ron B11 C79 C204 D9 D132 G50 G71A H111 H132 H176 K63 L12A L53 M157 O18B P91 R46 R93A W10
ASPEY Gary A103
ASPEY Vera A103 A104
ASPINAL Neil B59
ASPINALL Vicki R17
ASQUITH Gary R63B
ASSAGAI A105
ASSASSIN OF SILENCE A104A
ASSELINE Jean-Pol M49
ASSEMBLED MULTITUDE A105B
ASSOCIATES A105A
ASSOCIATION A106
ASTLEY Jon M41A S93
ASTOR Astor H38A
ASTRONAUTS A106A
ASTROP Jon A5A
ASWAD A107
ASYLUM CHOIR R173
ATACAMA A108
ATAMANJUK Larry K53 S63
ATHAS Robert J48
ATHEY Dianne N24F
ATHLETICO SPIZZ 80 A108A
ATKIN Pete A109
ATKINS Alex L52
ATKINS Bill D139
ATKINS Bob L110B
ATKINS Boyd J21 M48
ATKINS Chet A110 E75 K32 N37 P38 P125 P151 R26
ATKINS Don M236A
ATKINS John C11A
ATKINS Martin 'Brian Brain' B197E W117A
ATKINS Steve D14C
ATKINS Tony W69E
ATKINSON Bill H54
ATKINSON Brian T107
ATKINSON Craig C199A
ATKINSON Hal B110
ATKINSON Iain D46A
ATKINSON James D97B
ATKINSON Jim B57F D13 F116
ATKINSON John D92
ATKINSON Paul (G) Z15
ATKINSON Paul (D) Y6
ATKINSON Tom T48
ATLANTA RHYTHM SECTION A111
ATLANTIC BRIDGE A112
ATLANTICS A112A
ATLANTIS A113
ATLAS A113A
ATOLL A114
ATOMIC ROOSTER A115
ATON Emperador G122A
ATON Randall G122A
ATOYALL Jay K38
ATTARD Caroline B189 S287
ATTAWAY Greg C160 K68C M27
ATTERSON Alex C78 D68
ATTILA A131A
ATTITUDES A116
ATTRACTIONS A116A C193
ATTSCHUL Barry L67B
ATWILL Rupert H119
ATTWOOD David A50
ATTWOOL Hugh E56
ATWOOD Bill C158 G84 I31 L10B M59 M151 M203 S7 S36
ATWOOD George H134
ATWOOD Sherrill P6 P126
AUBERT Jean Louis T37K
AUBERT Richard A114 K77A
AUBREY Martin E13
AUBREY SMALL A117
AUDAT Alain L17
AUDET Don S96
AUDIENCE A118

BRACKETT Alan M123 P46
BRADBURY .B. A32A
BRADBURY John S207
BRADEN Larry A32B
BRADFORD Bobby S267
BRADFORD Chris B40
BRADFORD Conlay W95
BRADFORD Dennis L119C
BRADFORD Frankie H150
BRADFORD James A83 R115
BRADFORD Jeff B23
BRADFORD Melba R115
BRADFORD, Prof,SINGERS T67A
BRADFORD Scott B197D
BRADLEY .C. S154
BRADLEY Harold Ray B17A C14 H26 H65 K32 M11 M18 N37 P63 P125 R173 S271
BRADLEY James H4
BRADLEY Kenny N48B
BRADLEY Michael (B) A31
BRADLEY Nick (D) S258
BRADLEY M.J. (D) M139B
BRADLEY Oscar W13
BRADLEY Pam T12B
BRADLEY Phillip M175C
BRADLEY Stephen R22
BRADLEY Tomi Lee C76
BRADLEY Wain L57C
BRADLEY-WILLIS Roger C29 K94
BRADSHAW Iain S332
BRADSHAW James H34 M151 O39
BRADSHAW Kim L142 S11
BRADSHAW Todd B56A
BRADSTREET Pete M95B
BRADY Bob F6 M180A N58B W122
BRADY Dana A132
BRADY Dave M12C S343 T79
BRADY Eunon S H135 H137B M106A W130
BRADY Heather M126 S343 T79
BRADY Michael G26A M136C
BRADY Paul P93
BRADY Phil W69B
BRADY Ron B1
BRADY Victor T30
BRAGA Paulinho R99
BRAGG Johnny P139A
BRAGG Matthew T37E
BRAHMAN B177C
BRAID Les S356
BRAILEY Jerome B183 F137 P29
BRAIN Alan I23A
BRAIN Brian see ATKINS Martin
BRAIN Brian B197E
BRAINBOX B197F
BRAINCHILD B197F
BRAINERD Dwight M227
BRAINS B197B
BRAINSTORM B198
BRAINSTORM B198A
BRAINTICKET B199
BRAITHWAITE Darryl H116 S93B
BRAITHWAITE Flame N39
BRAITHWAITE Junior M88
BRAKE Brian H51
BRAKE Crystal D66
BRAKES B199A
BRAMAH Martin F10
BRAMBLE Derek H81
BRAMBLETT Randall A37 B109 B199B B200 C207 H15 H195 K30 L9 S56 T67A
BRAMLETT Bonnie (Nee LYNN) A88 B84 B91 B109 B200 B202 C121 C133 C155 C207 H7D K30 L89 M10 M101 R54 R173 S124 T9A T32B T158
BRAMLETT Delaney B109
BRAMLETT B201 B202 C121 C173 E75 F109 L64 M101 R173
BRAMWELL Randy B81
BRAN Al W46
BRANCACCIO William J38B
BRANCH Billy B226A W18A
BRANCH Margaret B155 G61

BRAND Carolyn P3
BRAND Jack M118 S355
BRAND Rick L45
BRAND Ronald T141A
BRAND X B203
BRANDEIS Hans R127
BRANDES Joel M192D
BRANDES Mick T12A
BRANDI Lello O33D
BRANDIS Harry Brender G112A
BRANDON Kevin C62B
BRANDS Ger D37B
BRANDT Brie E7B
BRANDT Holger B91A
BRANDT Pamela D33D
BRANDT Walter Z22A
BRANDY WINE B203A
Brandye C153 J11 K46 S73 T26 W118
BRANERMANN Ray T32A
BRANKER Don R54
BRANNIGAN N24
BRANNON Tom N59 R127A T167
BRANSCOMBE Alan A74 B59 C191 F14 L111 M42 W86
BRANSTON Tim L59
BRANT Barry A65
BRANTLEY Jamie L60 N23
BRANTLEY Steve H7D L60 N23
BRANTNER Nipso P115
BRANYAN Dave S55
BRASHEAR Oscar C45 C147 C179 C241 D59B D86 E7 E55 F103C H35B H96 H150 H156 K48 L66A M82 M102 M146A M229 Q3A R22 S193A S250 S235 T25 W27 W84C
BRASLER Joey C217 J38A T32A W46
BRASS CONSTRUCTION B204
BRASSINGTON Mick M139
BRASWELL Gary N58C
BRATTON Creed G83
BRAUN Bill O15
BRAUN Chris B204A
BRAUN Klaus C241D
BRAUN Ludwig D143
BRAUN Michael K59 M233 P25 R144A T169 W7
BRAUN Richard C. A122
BRAUNAGEL Tony A99A B12 B145B B26B C118 C144 C214 G51 K20 K87 M94 M195 Q1 R3 S108 T135A
BRAUNE Rudiger R22A
BRAUER Andreas L104B
BRAUER Buzz C76
BRAUNN Eric I24
BRAUNSTEINER Paul N60A
BRAUTIGAN Richard B205
BRAVE BELT B10 B205A
BRAVERMAN Roy B42B K38A T32A
BRAVO David D50
BRAVO Luciano K24 S270
BRAVO Sonny B85
BRAWER Alan W7
BRAWN Bob C150
BRAWNE Doug C13
BRAXTON Anthony C186 G47
BRAXTON Marvin A116
BRAY Jim K84
BRAY Maria C185F
BRAY Steve T122B T133 M151
BRAY Tom C77 C216 E71A M151
BRAYFIELD Buddy O46
BRAYLEY Rex L129A
BRAYNE Steve F95A
BRAZIER George L128A
BRAZIL Jerry S101
BRAZIL Joe A28C
Bread see McDONALD Lloyd
BREAD B206
BREAD LOVE & DREAMS B207
BREAKAWAYS G29A
BREAKFAST SPECIAL B207A
BREAN Larry S124
BREANT Francois B207B
BREAU Lenny E54
BREATHLESS B207C
BREBNER Asa L15A R83
BRECHTLEIN Tom C186

BRECKENFELD Bruce G7A
BRECKENFELD Del G7A
BRECKENRIDGE Arnold T166
BRECKENRIDGE Simon S270
BRECKER Michael A27 A31 A35A A123 A131 B7 B57A B85 B154 B183 B208 B208A B225 C44 C62 C147 C189 C236 D39 D63 D115 F3A F4C F103D F122 G4 G10 G19 G64C H8 H137 J20 J48 J72 J88 K36 K37 L18 L41 L51 L98 L109 L119 M17 M75 M107 M111 M125 M138A M180 M223 N65 O27 O32 P6 P15 P29 P35 P40 P72A P99 P123 R60 R100 R164 R142A S17 S73C S111 S124 S125 S215 S229 S231 S247 S252 S262 T25 T67A T111A T147 T158 V17 W8 W77C Z8
BRECKER Randy A31 A35A A123 A131 B57A B85 B141 B154 B183 B208 B208A C44 C147 C164 C189 C213D C236 D39 D50 D63 D115 F3A F4C G4 G19 G64C H51 H136A H137 J20 J48 J72 J93C K36 K37 K81 L4A L41 L58B L119 M13 M17 M26 M46B M75 M79 M107 M111 M125 M218 N39 N65 P15 P29 P35 P71 P72A P123 P123C R60 R100 R142A R164 S17 S111 S124 S125 S215 S229 S231 S252 S262 T25 T37E T67A T111A T147 T158 V17 W8 W25 W77C W107 Z8
BRECKER BROTHERS B208
BREDICE Richard J105A
BREDOUW Jim A125
BREEN Fran W125
BREEN Joe B208B M89 R23
BREEZE Brian B77 B237 J71 L53
BREEZE B208C
BREGANTE Merel B245 H120 L110 N53 S330
BREGG Don C183A
BREIDENBACH Paul D68B
BREINENTHAL David F78
BREMNER Billy C42 E19 I20 J110 L53 L135 M10C N51 S268
BRENDA & THE TABULATIONS B208D
BRENDELL Steve L51
BRENER Neil D122
BRENNAN Ciaran C120
BRENNAN Eithne C120
BRENNAN John N4
BRENNAN John Bandini L31
BRENNAN Maire C120
BRENNAN Mark'Moose' T83A
BRENNAN Paul C120
BRENNAN Robbie C120 O2C S263A
BRENNEN John H120
BRENNER Roger C165 P54
BRENSTON Jackie R168
BRENT Billy S235
BRENT Charlie C150 S56
BRENT Rob D46A
BRERETON Jim G53
BRESSEN Gerner B36A
BRESSER Bob B182A
BRESSERS Toon N5B
BRETHREN B208E
BRETONE Ronnie C215A
Brett G1
BRETT Adrian I12 M9 P54 W86
BRETT Fiona O40
BRETT Paul B209 E50
BRETT MARVIN AND THE THUNDERBOLTS M44 M99
BRETTELL Bones C143
BREUER Harry C146
BREUKER Hermann E52 J10A
BREVAL Carol G116C
BREWER Charles W119
BREWER Don B209A F67B G80B
BREWER Mike B210
BREWER Neil D122
BREWER Peter Z12

BREWER Shirley E73 P6 S362 W119
BREWER & FARNER B209A
BREWER & SHIPLEY B210
BREWERS DROOP B211
BREWIS Pete M203
BREWSTER Dwight S73C
BREWSTER Jake M188A
BREWSTER John A65A
BREWSTER Kirk W48C
BREWSTER Rick A65A
BREZOVAR Jean Michel A64
BRIA Felix D30B
BRIAN David G114
BRIAN Richard G114
BRIAN Tony D68A
BRIANS Robin G40
BRICK B212
BRICKLES Jack M32
BRICKLEY Audrey O33
BRICKLEY Shirley O33
BRICKMAN Marshall W45
BRIDGEFORTH Will W132
BRIDGEMAN Duncan B230
BRIDGEMAN Noel C120 S139
BRIDGES Alicia B213
BRIDGES Ben P114 W119
BRIDGES Denim T60
BRIDGES Gil R32
BRIDGES Jerry B126 F83A W84
BRIDGES Steve W115A
BRIDGES Willie G72 K51 K55 S7 T20
BRIDGFORD Geoff B71
BRIDGWATER Cecil L58B
BRIDGWATER Dee Dee B214 C129
BRIDGMAN Dan F5A K5
BRIERLEY Ben V2B
BRIERLEY Frank B37
BRIERLEY John T56
BRIERLEY Marc B216 M71
BRIGADA Steve A90
BRIGATI David A131 B216A D38A G72 H54 L111 O15
BRIGATI Eddie A131 B216A G72 H54 J88 L111 O15 R34
BRIGATI B216A
BRIGGER Judith I11A
BRIGGS Ann B216B
BRIGGS Billy A102
BRIGGS Brian B216C
BRIGGS David (K) A59 A75 A95 B17A B61 B210 C14 C124 C182 C247 D99 D104 E75 F78 G72 G85A H35 H49 H62 H136 I3 J31 J53 K77 K95 L108 M32 M75 M108 N25 N37 P49 P63 P112 P137 R4 R31 R81 R127A R173 S10 S55A S73 S216 S257 S272 T21 W11 W64 Y18
BRIGGS David (G) L92
BRIGGS David (Clar) P125
BRIGGS Vic A67 A120 E26 S259
BRIGGS William Henry R64
BRIGHT Bette D34 L16C
BRIGHT Bobby G26A
BRIGHT Jeryl C20
BRIGHT Rob D48B
BRIGHT Ronald H58
BRIGHT WINTER B217
BRIGHTLY Anthony B116
BRIGHTMAN Jerry G121
BRIGHTON Shaun N24F
BRIGHTON Thomas F83C
BRILEY Martin D27B F81A G97 H185 M38
BRILL Wally B17B
BRILLEAUX Lee C204 D84 D123 E13
BRILLON Peter R124F
BRIM John J21
BRIMFIELD Bill R112
BRIMM Kathleen C50
BRIMSTONE Derek J57B
BRINCK John A136
BRINGAS Bernie R96A
BRINK Ruuel B85
BRINSFORD Martin K65
BRINSLEY SCHWARZ B218 E22

BRINSON Ted W87
BRION Jean Claude S280
BRIONES jesse K49A
BRIQUETTE Pete B181
BRISBOIS Bud A1 C76 C162 C235 F134 N25 Q12 P6 R22 W27B
BRISCOE Al C183A N26A P151
BRISCOE Andy A82C
BRISCOE Jewel E52B
BRISTOW Carol O43 T65
BRISTOW Dave A5 A30 S66
BRISTOW Mark M119
BRITISH DISASTERS B218A
BRITISH LIONS B219
BRIT EL Tony G64 S268
BR'TON Terry B81A
BRITT Eddie I24A
BRITT Melvin J7
BRITTAIN Mike P41
BRITTAIN Peter W100
BRITTEN Terry B89 C161C H175 M157 O18B R80 R110 R129
BRITTON Chris T144
BRITTON Geoff C70 E8 K66 M9 M80 R40B R146 W77
BRITTON Michael C72A
BRITTON-BROWN Beverly K38
BROAD Graham B31 C173 G81 K84 M7A O18 P110
BROADBENT Micky T34
BROADNAX Darrell M238
BROADSTREET David B219A
BROCK Al R38
BROCK Dave C18 H63 H147 V63 Z8
BROCK Napoleon Murphy D127 W63 Z8
BROCK Pierre P15
BROCK Tony B8 S223 S273 S303
BROCK Wolfgang K11
BROCKBANK Neil H124A
BROCKENSHAW Jack S128 T42
BROCKETT Mick N18
BROCKIE Hugh B57F
BROCKLAND Peter S358F
BROCKLEHURST Brian H70 J91 M45 S270 W71
BROCKS Gary B202
BROCKWAY Chris W128A
BROCKWAY Nick W102
BRODERICK Chris C230A
BRODIE Wallace O39
BRODOWICZ C.J. A32A
BRODY Bruce S170 V1 V25B W5A
BROEK Nicholas Ten M227
BROESELMASCHINE B278
BROKEN GLASS B220
BROKEN HOME B220A
BROLIN Johnny G92
BROLUND Stefan L79 S39
BROMBERG David A59 A121 B221 B278 C68A C173 D53 D74 D139 E2 E20 G72 H136A J48 K81 K96 L72 L80C M18 M238A O15 P41 R169 S7 S78 S112 S180 S252 W11 W129 Y4B
BROMHAM Del S24
BROMLEY Nigel D34B
BRONCO B222
BRON Gerry B178 M83
BRONDSTED Niels M147
BRONOWSKI Ken S137A
BRONSON Gary F137 P29
BRONSON Harold L134 W39C
BRONSON Mark S72
BRONSON Mervin C62 C189
BRONSTEIN Debra O18
BRONSTEIN Stan B87 B223 E37 J70 L51 S310A
BRONSTEIN Terri B223
BRONX CHEER B224
BRONZE Dave C110
BRONZE Herman B224A C243 V38A
BROOKE Ben A30A
BROOKE Chuck B109 H96 L71B R161 T12
BROOKE Gwyn H168
BROOKE-TAYLOR Tim G71A
BROOKER Gary B110 B224B C121 C127 D100 J110 L46 M157 P23 P140

BROOKES Oliver C165
BROOKINS Steve T65
BROOKLYN BRIDGE B224C
BROOKLYN DREAMS B225 F101C
BROOKMEAD MUMBLE CHOIR E18A
BROOKS Alan D68 P147A
BROOKS Basil H119
BROOKS Cedric 'Im' A6 C245 W4A
BROOKS Chris B272B L110
BROOKS Chuck B238
BROOKS Clive A92A E24 G112 L67
BROOKS Craig Evan A55 T116A
BROOKS Danny D106D
BROOKS Dave A82 D108 H177 J82 M80 T130 V33 Y10
BROOKS Denny A132 P129 S272
BROOKS Derek B112
BROOKS Dianne A85A B71 H35 H59 K53 M36 P151 S228 W101
BROOKS Don B71 C124 C164 C180 C247 E20A F128 J18 J31 J48 J53 M41 M232 O27 R142A S252 T98 W11
BROOKS Dudley P125
BROOKS Elkie B226 D4 F65 H50 Q2 S266 V33 Y10
BROOKS Ernie M233 R83
BROOKS Harvey A59 B149 B171 C13 C68A D27 D103 D139 E33 E42 F3A H59 K10 K81 K86A M94 R169 S58 S65 W5
BROOKS Jack K84
BROOKS Joanne H187 R146A
BROOKS Julius F92
BROOKS Karen W11
BROOKS Lala A42A C242
BROOKS Lanny O6C
BROOKS Lonnie B226A S323
BROOKS Michael (G) E59
BROOKS Mike (B) B109
BROOKS Micky (D) A51A
BROOKS Patty B9 B149 B238 N42 R142A S228 S325 W63
BROOKS Paul B227
BROOKS Pete W15A
BROOKS Ray G11B
BROOKS Reg B83 H132 P9 W7
BROOKS Richard W45
BROOKS Robin O7B
BROOKS Roger L75
BROOKS Stuart (B) B112 D133 P128 S285
BROOKS Stuart (Tpt) O18B S82A
BROOKS Terry R. B227A
BROOKS Tony W45
BROOKSHIRE Bob D81A
BROOKSHIRE Bruce D81A
BROOM Bobby V6
BROOM Phyllis B149
BROOME Tom B91
BROOMHEAD Steve H47 M67 W117B
BROONZY Big Bill S329 W93
BROSIUS Chris B272B B274A M96
BROTHER BUNG B228
BROTHER FOX & THE TAR BABY B228A
Brother James A60A C34 C83 D49 H17 H70 L37 P45 S108 T110 W111 Y2
Brother Jesus Retartdo see AUSTIN Philip
Brother Jomo R35B
Brother Nat S190
BROTHER TO BROTHER B228B
BROTHERHOOD B228C
BROTHERHOOD HORNS W118
BROTHERHOOD OF BREATH B229
BROTHERS JOHNSON J83
BROTHERWOOD Nick W13C
BROTMAN Stuart C179 K6 W92
BROTZMANN Peter G47 V26C
BROUDIE Ian L16C O30B T5B
BROUDY Saul G72
BROUGH Chris A118
BROUGH Pete W13D
BROUGHTON Alex B230
BROUGHTON Edgar B230
BROUGHTON Loz B230
BROUGHTON Sally B230
BROUGHTON Steve B230 C118 H29 O18

BROUM Milan O21
BROUSSARD Austin H31 L75 L115
BROUSSARD Jules D24 D85 G10 M203 S19 S284
BROUSSARD Sam H120 M232
BROUSSARD Tony H59 M111
BROUWER Bart S214B
BROVITZ Lee B149B
BROSKY Michael E51
BROWDER Bill F128 T134B
BROWDER Stony Jr D83 K38
BROWDER Tommy K38
BROWN Al M151
BROWN Alan D9
BROWN Alexandra C147 E31 F33 H96 K48 L28 L55 L63 L65 L143 W8 W119
BROWN Alfred V. C147 T98 W106
BROWN Andy (D) F87
BROWN Andy (K) L64 P10
BROWN Andy (B) B134A B188 F43A R175 T89 V35
BROWN Arthur B231 C18 I22 P31 P145A S43 W72
BROWN Barry M204
BROWN Bill (B) F105F S96
BROWN Bill (Hrns) K80 M143 O32
BROWN Billy (V) M1A
BROWN Buster B232
BROWN Cecilia W119
BROWN Charles (V) B232A
BROWN Charles (G) C42 C164 D139 E49 G97B K81 M78 P6 P72A R22 W5 W45 W51A W65A
BROWN Charles (K) W13
BROWN Charlie (Sax) A31 P149
BROWN Cheryl R45
BROWN Chris B93A R104
BROWN Clarence 'Gatemouth' B233 D30
BROWN Clyde D116
BROWN Dan I29
BROWN Danny Joe B233A M178A
BROWN Darryl C129 S73C
BROWN Dartanyan C90
BROWN Dave (Perc) L72
BROWN Dave (B G) T155
BROWN David (B) B199B C217 D12 K81 M167 S19 S36 S111
BROWN David (G) C217 J20 J69 K59 P25 S123
BROWN Dave (B V) E56
BROWN David (Sax) A37 B109 B200 C207 D4A
BROWN Dennis B234
BROWN Derrick T166
BROWN Desmond S74
BROWN Donald W101
BROWN Duncan A133
BROWN Earl F134
BROWN Ed (B) F39 M132D
BROWN Eddie (D) B238 C153 C213E F92 G17 H99 J91A K45 P44 S128 S250 S251 S333A T42 W84C W119
BROWN Ella C207 J52 M93
BROWN Elmer E7 R112
BROWN Errol H159A
BROWN Estelle N23
BROWN Fontaine S199B
BROWN Freeman D86 S85A
BROWN Friday M67
BROWN Garnett B53 C17 C129 C147 C164 C213E C241 D50 D66 D97A D132B E7 H19 J75A J93D K45 L66A M41 M75 P149 R21 R34 R60C S14C S250 W13 W28
BROWN Gary B71 C75 C155 D21B D86 G4 M157 P8D T118
BROWN Gaye A109
BROWN Geoff G7
BROWN George (D) U23
BROWN George (D)(K) K80 S111
BROWN Gerald M67
BROWN Gerry A35A C61 C129 C186 C189 K9B L41 M69 S73C U21

BROWN Greg F14 W119
BROWN Harold B268 O35 W17
BROWN Honey B268
BROWN Hux C139 J48 S125 T110 T149 U20 Y4B
BROWN J.B. Y18
BROWN J.T. F66 H170 J21 L52 L94 R128 S358
BROWN J.W. L64
BROWN James B235
BROWN James (K) B242A P137
BROWN Jean W119
BROWN Jeff F26
BROWN Jennifer F133
BROWN Jim(D) U1
BROWN Jimmy (WIND) B212 R40B
BROWN Jocelyn D63 H164C I2 T65
BROWN Joe (G V) B81A B236 C149 F140 S162
BROWN Joe (Banjo) P15
BROWN Joe (B) M17
BROWN John (B) F10 W130
BROWN John (V) P6
BROWN John (D) B199A
BROWN John(V G B)G11C
BROWN Joseph A Jr R115
BROWN Judy M111
BROWN Julian B231
BROWN Junior C30B
BROWN Keisa B236A
BROWN Kenji R141
BROWN Kim R65B
BROWN Kipps A60
BROWN Larry (D) A85B
BROWN Larry (G) J96
BROWN Laurie H11 K61
BROWN Leroy C229
BROWN Lester R124D
BROWN Lorenzo C153 H98
BROWN Louis L42
BROWN Marvin A1
BROWN Maxine T70
BROWN Mel B127 B236B
BROWN Michael (D) B245
B240 C198 H150 K45
BROWN Michael (K) B68 L45 M182 S286
BROWN Michael (D) P25
BROWN Mick (D V) D93H
BROWN Miquel O34
BROWN Morrie E. P49
BROWN Niles C60
BROWN Noel P25 S149
BROWN Norman B37
BROWN Ollie B139 C6B C17 C38 C155 C246 H98 H135A K44C L63 M203 O15 P26A P67 P113 P114 P126 R45 R133 R142A S34 S254B S362 T42 W31 W84C
BROWN Pat (D) L57A
BROWN Patti (K) R140 V34
BROWN Paulette B261 C213E O46 S36 S342 W46 W54
BROWN Pete (V) B171 B237 D58
BROWN Peter (B) F98 S169
BROWN Phil B114B N18 R52 S147A
BROWN Phyllis S160
BROWN Randy B238
BROWN Ray (B) B63 B84 B110 B139 B239 H102 M229 O8B P129 S14C S262 T37H W87
BROWN Ray (Tpt) G17 S325
BROWN Richard (K) B54
BROWN Richard (D) M175D N19
BROWN Richard (Sax) E55
BROWN Rick (B) A120 B23 F14 P8 S259 S338 W94
BROWN Rick (V) M168
BROWN Rick (D) A22B F126A
BROWN Robby L64
BROWN Robert see Washboard Sam
BROWN Rodney W119
BROWN Roger D128 N57 R11 S257

BROWN Rolly B91B
BROWN Ron F92 K45
BROWN Roy B240
BROWN Russell John K56
BROWN Ruth B241
BROWN Sam A86 B131 C44 M55A M78 S162
BROWN Sammy K. H31 S310A
BROWN Sarah M227
BROWN Selwyn S261
BROWN Sharon F103 O33A
BROWN Shirley B242
BROWN Sonny L67B P125
BROWN STANKY BAND B242A
BROWN Stanley G26A
BROWN Steve (D) T5B
BROWN Steven (K SAX) D14B S177A T161A
BROWN Stewart C148
BROWN Stu C86A
BROWN Stuart B159
BROWN Tom (D) G81E W39C
BROWN Tom (SAX) B23
BROWN Sue K61
BROWN Toni J100 T107
BROWN Tony A59 C237 D139 H35 M222D R144A W45
BROWN Tyrone W25
BROWN Unwin T137
BROWN Vicky B45A B208B B236 B268 C34 C79 E22 F42 H11 H52 H70 H111 K11 L63 M7A N14 N46A P15 R136 S124 S162 W7 W10 W72
BROWN Wilber L128
BROWN DUST B242B
BROWN William C. G92B K46 N55
BROWNE Colin W55A
BROWNE Dalton M221D
BROWNE Douglas I10
BROWNE Duncan B160 B243 H110 M140
BROWNE Ivan L49
BROWNE Jackson A59 B244 C45 C184A C233 K99A L79A N4 N53 P137 R22 R109 S124 S196 S213 T39 Z11
BROWNE Mark T137A
BROWNE Monte T104A
BROWNE Patrick S327B
BROWNE Phil S19
BROWNE Phineas C6B
BROWNE Severin B245
BROWNING Chuck C14
BROWNING Dave B37
BROWNING John K45
BROWNING Misty K51 P120 T133
BROWNING West D86
BROWNSTONE Kier S72
BROWNSTONE B246A
BROWNSVILLE STATION B246
BROX Annette B171 B247 D129 G112D K84 R92 S338 S349A
BROX Victor B39 B171 B247 D86 D129 F24 K84 R92 S338 S349A
BROZENA Fran B267
BRTIGNAC Louis T37K
BRU Reggie S51
BRUBECK Chris 'Cree' C189 S147A
BRUBECK Dan C189
BRUBECK Darius C189
BRUBECK Don B253
BRUCE Bobby B80 B109 C39 C156 C179 F5 G24 H60 P79 P118D P129 S270
BRUCE Bruce S14D
BRUCE Denny F3B H37 K88 B156 B171 B248 C121 C189
BRUCE Jack A60A A74 B131 L70 L103 M40 M79 M80 M84D M90A M111 M196 P119B P120 P122 R5 R60 R122A S182 T148 V21 W52 W119 Z8
BRUCE Martin S11
BRUCE Michael 'Monk' B103 C182 S73 T37I
BRUCE Neil H56A
BRUCE Steve B23 H111
BRUCE Tubby S262
BRUCE Wayne H195

BRUCE-DOUGLAS Ian U7
BRUCHHAUSER Uwe L121C
BRLCHMANN Michael H125B
BRUCK Thomas S26A
BRUFORD Bill A5A B249 F65 G21 G66 H29 H168 K54 N9 P40 P45 S233 U3 W7 Y7
BRUHN Hanno C247C
BRUINSMA Meine E3C
BRUIZER Clive L23
BRUMLEY Tom N21
BRUMONT T162
BRUNE Hans Joachim T11
BRUNEL Bunny A21 C186 S193
BRUNER Kirk F128 M65A
BRUNET Max F133A
BRUNETTI Daniel S230A
BRUNINGHAMS K94C
BRUNIUSSON Hans F123 S14B
BRUNKERT Ola A4 R3 S39 V32B
BRUNN Roger B217
BRUNNER Mark L16B
BRUNNER Pumi W55B
BRUNING Bob A50A B250 B277 D30 F66 K22A M90 P142 R128 T23 T130 W91 W131
BRUNNING HALL BLUES BAND B250
BRUNNING SUNFLOWER BLUES BAND B250
BRUNNINGHAUS Rainer W39A
BRUNO A1 W12A
BRUNO Bill O44A
BRUNO Bob C116
BRUNO Bobby P65B
BRUNO George A67
BRUNO Jack A68A B49 S84A
BRUNO Steve E39
BRUNSCHEN Gunther F124
BRUNSON Frankie B94A
BRUNSON Ted W30
BRUNTON Richard B138D H42 H110 H154 I20 J60 N57 R11 R40B S131 W10
BRUSH ARBOR B250A
BRUSHOR Skeet A51
BRUSON Frankie P59C
BRUTON Stephen B274B C123 C180 G24 G72 K95 K96 M227 S124 S342
Brutus E62A
BRUZZESE Jim B246
BRYAN Brad Y4B
BRYAN Kelly G107 Y12
BRYAN Rad 'Douggie' B117 C139 C245 D113A D130 H122 J17B J17D R30 R35B R84 T110 T149 U4A W4A
BRYAN Robert B54
BRYANS Richard A131A B16
BRYANT Andrew B280
BRYANT Brenda B141 B261 C156 G61
BRYANT Bobby B238 C213E
BRYANT Carmen H156
BRYANT David B261
BRYANT Eldridge T42
BRYANT Eugene P126
BRYANT Geoff P127
BRYANT Jimmy L65
BRYANT Joel M2
BRYANT Marilyn B221
BRYANR Kim A28B
BRYANR Phil S75A
BRYANT Robert 'Bobby' A131D B58A C153 E7 F103C K45 K48 L66A M102 M229 P93B R60C R142A S14C
BRYANT Warren M111
BRYDEN Bob C236
BRYER Paul F47
BRYLOWSKI Ron F137
BRYMEN Bruce D122C
BRYMER Jack M9
BRYNAN Lindsay Kay B57
BRYNE Robert C39D
BRYON Dennis A49 F7 W21B
BRYSON Bill C179 C200 D68B D71
BRYSON David W15B
BRYSON Everett Jnr A41 D87B R161

BRYSON Peabo B251 M65A R97
BRYSON Robert J16
BRYSON Wally F90 R35 T17
BRZEZICKI Mark T121
BUBBLE PUPPY B252
Bubbler see WAUL Franklin
BUCCO Sam B116A
BUCHAN Gillies H178
BUCHANAN Bob I23
BUCHANAN Buzzy C173 N43 S211
BUCHANAN Don F54 L134 T41
BUCHANAN Ian T134
BUCHANAN Jim D103 R173
BUCHANAN Kirk N58C
BUCHANAN Malcolm A15
BUCHANAN Neil M91
BUCHANAN Robbie C127 C213E D104 G101B L12 P114
BUCHANAN Roy B253
BUCHANAN Rusty C185E E77 O15 T153A
BUCHANAN Spoons R118A
BUCHANAN Steve F123
BUCHANAN Tony A95 G26A L92 Y4B
BUCHHOLZ Francis S47
BUCHTEL Forrest D85 M59
Buck B91
BUCK Dirty Dan B197
BUCK J. A120
BUCK Mike F3B
BUCK Nick G94 H161 K13 L115A M18 S3
BUCK Steve G77B
BUCKACRE B254
BUCKBY Pete C26A
BUCKEYE B254A
BUCKEYE POLITICIAN B254B
BUCKINGHAM Lindsey B254C B255 D106G E23 F66 G101B L12B R137 S34 S272 W46 Z11
BUCKINGHAM Steve B213 M65A
BUCKINGHAM NICKS B255
BUCKINGHAMS B255A
BUCKINS Mickey A123 B213 C43 D139 G85A J11 P80
BUCKLE Phil S261B
BUCKLER Duane S15B
BUCKLER Nick F114
BUCKLER Rick J19
BUCKLEY Bob C106
BUCKLEY David B43D
BUCKLEY Kieran D68A
BUCKLEY Neil C120
BUCKLEY Stuart D16
BUCKLEY Tim B256
BUCKMASTER Paul A74 B53 B141 B186 C34 C78 C171 F24 F21 H11 H121 J72 L142A M214 P76 R133 S82 S108 S124 S194B S331 T60 V17
BUCKNER Juanita D66
BUCKNER Jerry W77A
BUCKNER Lafe S261A
BUCKNER Milt B233
BUCKNER Susan J96
BUCKNER Teddy R142A
BUCKS Deborah E33C
BUCKWHEAT B257
BUCKWICH Ray A59
BUDA Max see EPP Fenrus
BUDAMEYER Dave G101A
BUDD Eric F49
BUDD Harold E59
BUDD Raphael T121
Buddy see HAYE George
BUDDY MILES EXPRESS B151
BUDDY ODOR B257A
BUDGIE B258
Budgie L16C S132 S159
BUDHOS Phil H137
BUDIHAS Randy E55A
BUDIMIR Dennis A31 B50 B240 C164 D59B F103C H8A H10 M65A M170 M229 N40 P129 R99 R111B S50 S228 Z8
BUDSON Richard F92
BUDZAK David H26C
BUELL Bruce B245
BUFF Ashley E64A
BUFFALO Mad Mississippi D127A
BUFFALO Norton B259 C164 C173 D101 M83 M159 T71A W46

BUFFALO SPRINGFIELD B260
BUFFETT Jimmy B261 E2
BUFFINGTON Bill D50
BUFFINGTON James C129 C213D D27 D50 J20 K36 L119 M12 M41 M107 N39 S168 T147 V17 V21 Z3B
BUFORD George 'Mojo' J79A S204 W28
BUGATTI Dominic B189 L142A
BUGGLES B261A
BUGLASS Glen K10C
BUHLER Craig J41 M108
BUIE Buddy A111
Bulgie see FARQUHARSON Charles
BULKIN Kelly E57 L56C
BULKIN Leslie E57 L56C
BULL B262 M216C
BULL John I18A
BULL Richie H128A K100 M166 P54 R129 S108
BULL Sandy B262D T22
BULL Steve C210 H125
BULL ANGUS B262E
BULLARD Cece N4
BULLARD Clyde D63
BULLARD Kim C107E P106
BULLDOG B262F
BULLDOG BREED B262A
BULLDOZER B262B
BULLEN Charles T66
BULLEN Hugh G67
BULLEN Jim C7
BULLEN Roger D11
BULLENS Cynthia 'Cindy' A41 B135 B263 C123 C185E E73 J72 M227 Q3A
BULLER Lance W97
BULLET B264
BULLFROG B262C
BULLING Erick A35C
BULLMEYER Wolfgang F81B
BULLOCK Annie Mae see TURNER Tina
BULLOCK Dan M1
BULLOCK David S202
BULLOCK Hiram A82 B125E B155 B208 F60 J20 J69 K36 L109 M107 M225 S17 S125 S231 S262 T71 W8
BULLOCK Pete A30 H194
BULLOCK Vernon N28
BULLOCK Wayne M32
BULLSEYE B264A
BULLY Ron G79B
BULTITUDE Paul A13
BUMBLE B William . B1
Bumble Bee Slim (EASTON Amos) B265
Bumper M150A
BUMPUS Cornelius D101 M174
BUNCE David U19
BUNCH B266
BUNCH Peter C107E
BUNDESEN Michael S108C
BUNDRICK John 'Rabbit' A82 A133 B4 B12 B25 B125B B138 B243 C13 C30 C214 D9 D49 D99 E59 F7 F108 G32 G51 G102 H11 H65 K20 K75 K87 M45 M58 M88 M94 M157 M195 N64 O26 R3 R5 R125 S108 S288A S339 T79 T121 T122 U9 Y14
BUNDT Michael N48C
BUNDY Charles C15A C124
BUNDY Rex G2A
BUNETTA A1 P137
BUNETTA Neil R125
BUNETTA Peter C213 D133 M229 P137 R125 T158 W119B
BUNKA Roman B266A E52
BUNKER Clive A131B B136 G35 H119 H168 J58
BUNKER Larry B256 F34 F103D J43 S269 W9
BUNKFELDT John E7C
BUNKIEWICZ Richard B242A
BUNN Alan C115
BUNN Allen see Tarheel Slim
BUNN Dick L126
BUNN Lyne S250B

BUNN Roger R149 W61
BUNNAGE Mick D39C
BUNNELL Dewey A50
BUNNELL George S294
BUNNELL Mike S216
Bunny see SIMPSON Fitzroy
BUNTING Ted C214 M195
BUNTING Ted C214 M195 S312A
BUONO Buddy R34
BUONO Bruce R34
BUOYS B267
BURBECK Charles L118
BURBRIDGE Graham KB4
BURCH Curtis H65 N29C R173
BURCH Daryl M132C
BURCH Vernon K46
BURCHARD Christian E52
BURCHETTE Wilburn B267A
BURCHILL Charlie S126
BURDEN Gary C232
BURDEN Ian H178A
BURDEN John C161C
BURDETT Steve M227
BURDETTE Marty E7C
BURDINE Lawrence K45
BURDON Eric A67 B268 H123 W17 W94
BURGEN David C76
BURGER Gary M181A
BURGESS Colin M103B
BURGESS Dave C71
BURGESS John T106
BURGESS Ken M202A
BURGESS Norman I13A
BURGESS Paul B247 C184 G76A R158 T43
BURGESS Pete B188
BURGESS Richard A74 E9 L16 N62 R140 T19
BURGESS Sonny B269
BURGESS Steve E62B
BURGH Steve A121 B207A B221 B226 C164 F83A G72 J69 P137 S180
BURGHARD Karen S249C
BURGI Chuck B22A B203 H9
BURGIN Dave M227 M229
BURGON Harold L37 T45
BURGOS Bob M105
BURI Andre B154E
BURIGAN Ken B269A
BURK Mike W3B
BURKE Clem B139 D56A
BURKE Dave S240
BURKE Gary D139 F116 R100 W101
BURKE Howard B154A
BURKE K.P. (HCA) C136B O33C
BURKE Ken (B) C17 L65
BURKE Kevin B185 B270 B280 G121
BURKE Mike C6B
BURKE Patrick F44 P23A
BURKE Pat (WIND) F90A
BURKE Reginald C17 G26A
BURKE Solomon B271
BURKE Sonny C17 E40 H8 J113 K45 K51 M65A M132D M177 P114 R115 S180 S254B S333A T107 W27B W31 W118
BURKE Val B223 S224
BURKEY Stix N48B
BURKS Clifford C146
BURKS Edward T158
BURLAND Dave H87 S343 T79
BURLESQUE B272
BURLING Tucker S249C
BURLISON Paul B274
BURLISON Stewart G36
BURMEISTER Bolle L47C
BURMEISTER Dietmas A19A
BURNEL Jean-Jacques B271A S292 T18A
BURNETT Bill B151B
BURNETT Chester see Howlin' Wolf
BURNETT J. Henry 'T-Bone' A41 B274B D139 F116
BURNETT Larry F50
BURNETT Rick G104
BURNETT Tony P47
BURNETTE Billy B272B B274A V18

BURNETTE Dorsey B272A B274
BURNETTE Hank C. B273
BURNETTE Johnny B274
BURNETTE Rocky B274A
BURNEVIK Tom C250C
BURNEY Mike W122
BURNHAM Hugo G7C
BURNHAM Jeremiah 'Jerry' F44C G72 J18 M37 Q15A
BURNIN' RED IVANHOE B275
BURNING SPEAR B276
BURNIP John M164
BURNS August S353
BURNS Beckie M111
BURNS Charles G17
BURNS Dennis A43 G67A P65A R60B
BURNS Dougie N56A
BURNS Eddie 'Guitar' B277 K24 L101 M19 P76 S266 S352 S270
BURNS Hugh A82 B77 B83 B208B B248 C75 H29 H132A M157 P124 R11 R12 R23 S257 V29
BURNS Jake S275
BURNS Jethro G72 P137
BURNS John G72 P137 R61
BURNS Karl C184 F10
BURNS Liza D48A
BURNS M. (SYN) S224A
BURNS Murray (K) A65A M141B
BURNS Phil M199
BURNS Randy B278
BURNS Ray see Captain Sensible
BURNS Rob (B) H111
BURNS Robert (D) L146
BURNS Ron F94
BURNS Russell F48E
BURNS Rusty P109A
BURNS Stephen S55
BURNSIDE TerrY M211
BURNZ Cha F47
BURR Clive I25
BURRAGE Harold M48
BURRANO Ron R102
BURREL Webb B166
BURRELL Auburn B149 C132 D27A L44 M157
BURRELL Boz B14 B83 B138 B191 C63 C79 H123 K54 K84 L37 N37 P72A P120 S131 S300 T122 Y10
BURRELL Debbie D24
BURRELL Kenny C146 M229 P125 S168
BURRID Jay C90
BURRIDGE Hollis C12
BURRISE A.D. N50D
BURRISE J.D. N50D
BURRIDGE Roger F6
BURROUGHS Clark J72
BURROUGHS William A35 H86A
BURROWIES Valerie B45C
BURROWS Brian 018A S214E
BURROWS Bryn F3
BURROWS Chris C115
BURROWS Clive M180 P131
BURROWS Frederick M163B S214
BURROWS Rob E. S214E
BURROWS Tony C185B C201A D39 D92 F53 F56 G71A J72 P131 S209
BURSCH Peter B278A H125B
BURSE Christoph 036A
BURSTIN Jeff J64A
BURT Dave M135
BURT David,C. C28A
BURT Eddie L58B
BURT Heinz see Heinz
BURT Jo R116
BURT Mick B82 C89
BURT Wayne J64A
BURTIS Sam B197 B282 D50 K69 M107 P72A S169 T147 Y2A
BURTON Aaron C162 M5
BURTON Barbara R164
BURTON Barry Byrd A45 G101A N37
BURTON Dave L67 R46

BURTON Fred B210 R168
BURTON Gary H23 R28B T119A W39A
BURTON James A132 B74 B202 B260 B279 C14 C38A C50 C77A C164 C237 E20 E42 E74 H5C H35 H61 H62 L19 L116 M36 M170 N21 N25 P33 P74 P125 R101 S160 S272 W101
BURTON Joe K45
BURTON John D106F
BURTON Kevin C26 H68
BURTON Lance B174
BURTON Larry C162
BURTON Lori J48 L51
BURTON Paul H93 L53 M63
BURTON Steve S249A
BURTON Trevor B26 C13 C30 G27 G111 H99 K87 M219 P84 W133
BUSBOYS B280A
BUSBY David C165
BUSCH Giny K16
BUSCH Rick C161C
BUSCH Siggi C201
BUSCHMANN Georg S289 S299B
BUSEY Gary K95
BUSFIELD Steve C63C G96 M151 O35
BUSH B279A
BUSH Chuckie M65
BUSH Kate B280 G2 H29
BUSH Paddy B280
BUSH Pete T122B
BUSH Richard A2D
BUSH Roger C200 F74 G121 K29 M64 N21 P32
BUSH Sam C200 D66B D70 H49 H65 N29C P137 R173 S120
BUSH Terry N26A
BUSHBAUM Ray C26
BUSHKIN Joe R34
BUSHLER Herb E5 P41 P53 S17
BUSHNELL Bob A59 A59B I2 I21 M75 M203 R169 S168
BUSHWELL Bob H23
BUSHY Ron I24 J104D
BUSKIN David P80A
BUSLOWE Steve L98 S199 S242
BUSSEY C.B. W55B
BUSSEY George H133
BUSTAMENTE Fernando S289A
BUSTER Bobby H159
BUSTOS Lewis D13 S7
BUTANI Bob T156
BUTCHER Damon C70 R146
BUTCHER George E40
BUTCHER Ken L59
BUTCHER Mike M210
BUTCHER Roe X4A
BUTERA Mike K12
BUTLER Aalon A2A B268
BUTLER Alan G75
BUTLER Albert Wynn D139 W107
BUTLER Artie B53 C146 C155 G97B I2 M203 R111B R140
BUTLER Bill (G) B281 C146 G61 H15 H78A M227
BUTLER Billy (V) B280B
BUTLER Chris (B) A23
BUTLER Chris (D) N41
BUTLER Chris (G) T94A W5B
BUTLER Doc A59
BUTLER Frank D27 W116A
BUTLER Geezer B115
BUTLER Gregg C165 S295A
BUTLER Harold B234 C245 M221D T110 W4
BUTLER Jerry B281 E71 I15 R60C
BUTLER Jesse D101
BUTLER Joe L133
BUTLER John (V) W74
BUTLER John (G) F67
BUTLER Kirk C196
BUTLER Lance B56
BUTLER Larry C50 F126 H26 M11 R127A T21
BUTLER Leslie C139
BUTLER Martin D48A
BUTLER Mattie B280D F103
BUTLER Paul C101 J50 K45 L75 V26A

CORTINAS Jaime A82C
CORTINAS John C80C
CORTINAS C187
CORUN Erroll K38
CORVETTES C188
CORWIN Tim 011
CORY John S9B
CORYELL Julie C189
CORYELL Larry B248 C61 C189 D27 F109A M78 M79 M218 P60A U21 V34 W62
COS C190
COSEY Pete H170 W28
COSGROVE Tom B208E C195 F109 K68D K81 P45 R164
COSH Paul G22 G71A
COSKER Pete G62B W14
COSMIC EYE C191
COSMIC JOKERS C192
COSMIC SOUNDS C192A
Cosmo H85 S303
COSSA Lou D5C
COSSACK Ken B183B
COSTA David C48 T137
COSTA Don B53
COSTA Ed C168A
COSTA Rudy M53
COSTANZO Sal P19A
COSTELL Dave L61B
COSTELLO Deirdre M1A
COSTELLO Elvis (McMANUS Declan) C193 L16C S232 T166A
COSTELLO Neil I26A K26A
COSTELLO Nicki C62D T112A
COSTER Tom B177 K13A M227 S19
Cota D68A
COTE Chris A5Q
COTELLA Thom B53
COTEZ Dean S289B
COTINOLA Frank F138
COTON Keith E13
COTRELL Arnie B93A
COTT Gerry B181
COTTAGE Michael S177B
COTTAM Terry B230 T48
COTTEN Michael P114 T152
COTTER Rod W77
COTTI Astrid W55B
COTTLER Ivy S124
COTTO Lourdes K38
COTTON Clayborne Brother B144 M144 M211 M23B
COTTON Ernest B193 L52 R128
COTTON Gene C194 W101
COTTON James C59 C195 H62 H170 M195 S204 T79B W28 W107 Y13
COTTON Jeff see SEMENS Jim
COTTON Mel G92D
COTTON Michael (B) J16A
COTTON Mike (TPT) B160 C34 F36 G27 K61 M18O S27 Y11
COTTON Paul G117C I12A P106
COTTON Roger L68A
COTTON Sandy C194
COTTON Stephen P110
COTTONSOUTH C195B
COTTONWOOD C195A
COTTRELL Skip M170
COUARD Jimmy C75
COUBIN Dennis B178
COUCH Peter N11A
COUCHARD Jean Pierre A64
COUCHIS Chris C195C R36B
COUCHIS Mike C195C
COUCHIS Pat C195C R36B T3
COUCHIS C195C
COUDRILLE Jonathan K83
COUGAR Jim S213
COUGAR Johnny (MELLENCHAMP John) C196
COUGHLAN John S255
COUGHLAN Richard A133 C34
COULAM Roger B152 C127 M108 P107
COULL Jimmy W21A
COULLET Rhonda M120 N10
COULON Jean J105B
COULON Pierre J105B
COULSON Diana 018
COULSON Dennis C197 M29
COULTER Alan F56 G65 M118 018B P89A

COULTER Cliff B236B C198 H150 K45 W116
COULTER Paddy A3
COULTER Pat C158 P137
COULTER Roy J79
COULTER Shanne C198
COULTER Tom R158
COUNT BISHOPS C199
COUNT FIVE C199A
COUNTRY COOKING C199C
COUNTRY GAZETTE C200
Country Joe see MACDONALD Country Joe
COUNTS C199B
COUNTY Jayne E32
COUNTY Wayne E32
COURBOIS Pierre C201 C209
COURSEY Faris H134
COURT John E33
COURTENAY Lloyd A85 C55
COURTIAL Bill A136
COURTLEY Bert F14
COURTNEY Aixa C201A
COURTNEY David C201A S34
COURTNEY Kenny H37
COURTNEY Lou P6 R22
COURTNEY Trevor S312
COURTS Randy C103C
COURY John U5
Cousin Joe seePLEASANT
Cousin Joe
COUSINS Dave C202 D49 H151 I22 S295 W7
COUSINS Pete S237
COUSINS Richard C214B
COUSINS Roy R150
COUSINS Tony C210
COUSSE Francois G66
COUTURIER Francois M40 T67
COVAY Don C203
COVE Glen L133
COVEN C203A
COVERDALE David C204 D40 G50 L120 W117
COVERLY Del C126
COVINGTON Charles L58B
COVINGTON Joey C205 C217 G84A H161 J46 K10 K13 S322
COVINGTON Julie A30
COWAN Andrew M21
COWAN Colin 040A
COWAN Dennis B178 S243
COWAN Greg 040A
COWAN John H65 N29C P137 R173
COWAN Martin 040A
COWAN Steve S96A
COWARD Danny J105C
COWARD Eddie B47B
COWART Donivan C237 L36A
COWART Harold B71 E36 F39 F105 L68B R34 T70
COWART Juanita M98
COWBELL Paul M166A
Cowboy T37K
COWBOY C207
COWBOYS INTERNATIONAL C207A
COWDEROY Alan G77A
COWE Simon J5 L80
COWE Terry R65
COWELL Dave F140B
COWELL Stanley C207B
COWELL Stuart F55 S270 S349A T99 W71 W96
COWGER Jim C111A
COWLING Peter Mars G52 P146 S267 S338 T135
COWSILL Bill Y5B
COWSILL Bob C76
COWSILL Jan T164
COWSILL John T164
COWSILL Susan T164
COWSILLS,The C76
COX. Addie W119
COX Andy B58B
COX Billy C14 C133 C208 D12 H99 M151
COX Chris T37H
COX DannyB210 C208A

COX Gary A90
COX Geoff A130A
COX Helen S35
COX Irv J46 J96
COX Jess T169A
COX Larry C140A N4
COX Mark R63B
COX Michael E26 M203 S313
COX Mick C208B
COX Peter C30 K87
COX Roy B252 D45A
COX Sam M53
COX Sylvia J7 L66A M131
COX Terry A62 B23 B47B B186 C165 D131 F55 G32 H121 H180 J36A J41 J72 K84 L63 M42 P60 P120 R48 S12 W86
COX Tony B266 C34 D92 E41 F6 G98 H110 S185 T137
COX Wally G17
COXHILL Dave A62 M80 R121 S141 W114
COXHILL Lol A133 C48 C165 C209 D10 G102 H101 H154 H194B K78 K84 M158A N41 040 Y10
COXON Gordon C175
COXTON Mike N25A
COYLE Joe K21A
COYNE Kevin C210 M79 S133
COZZI Cathe F51
CRABBY APPLETON C211
CRABTREE Francis N24
CRABTREE Lee A59 H139
CRABTREE Lu F133 P49
CRABTREE Roger J53
CRACK THE SKY C212
CRACKERS C212A
CRACKIN' C213
CRADDOCK Ken A25 B79 B174B G101 H116C H177 L80 M86 R7 R11 S103B W58
CRADDOCK Vincent Eugene see VINCENT Gene
CRAFT Paul A121 R137 S73B
CRAGGS Martin H20
CRAIG David B233
CRAIG Davie N57
CRAIG Desmond P108
CRAIG Gary S55B
CRAIG Jim T60A
CRAIG Judy C103
CRAIG Marvin L10A
CRAIG Patrick C205 T33A
CRAIG Ralph A51 H1
CRAIG Roger L94B
CRAIN Billy P37A
CRAIN Robert W116B
CRAIN Tom D12
CRAINE Don D109
CRALLAN Henry A133
CRAMER Floyd A110 K32 P125 S10
CRAMER Janis D97B
CRAMER Patrice W119C
CRAMER Ron C109A
CRAMER Sheri S269
CRAMPLE C212C
CRAMPS C212B
CRAMPTON Jeff W7
CRANE Billy K29
CRANE Bobby K29
CRANE Chuck M28
CRANE Joe H5 H146 P114 I107 W129
CRANE Kenny M227
CRANE Larry C196
CRANE Mitch S177B
CRANE Steve B6
CRANE Tony M136
CRANE Vincent A115 B231 B237 G5
CRANEY Mark P115 V9A
CRANFORD Brian S153
CRANHAM Phil B231
CRANITCH Matt N2B
CRANNER Dennis C58A
CRANSHAW Bobby B53 C164 C213D I25B M26 P132C S125 W11
CRANSTON ,Lamont BAND

CRANSTON ,Lamont BAND L14
CRANNY Mark M86
CRAPSTER Gary G40
CRARY Dan D68B
CRASH Darby G24A
CRASH James R8
CRASS C213A
CRASSELL Dave C235
CRASSELLI Dianne C103C
CRASWELL Dave P49A
CRASWELL Paul P49A
CRAVATS C213B
CRAVEN Bob S249C
CRAVER Mike R52A
CRAVIOTTO John C179 F45A L50 M174 S10
CRAWDADDYS C213C
CRAWEY Mark J58
CRAWFORD Andy S136
CRAWFORD Big Tom B95B W28 W47
CRAWFORD Bill C241B
CRAWFORD Chip F92
CRAWFORD Dave K45 S254B
CRAWFORD Diana C59
CRAWFORD Ernest 'Big' L94 M185 R128 S358 T9B
CRAWFORD Hank C155 C168A C213D M26
CRAWFORD Jimmy A40 W89
CRAWFORD Leslie G122
CRAWFORD Michael W113
CRAWFORD Randy C213E C241 H4 M102
CRAWFORD Ray W6
CRAWLER C214
CRAWLEY John F83D
CRAY,Robert BAND C214B
CRAYTON Pee Wee C214A S165
CRAZE C214C
CRAZY CAVAN AND THE RHYTHM ROCKERS C215
CRAZY ELEPHANT C215A
CRAZY HORSE C216
CREACH Papa John B169A C217 H161 J46 K10 M16
CREAM C218
CREAMER Laura D53C D70 J69 L20 M131A M203 N23 N42 P75 S73 S272 W44
CREAMER Mark D53C J69 L20 N23
CREASEY Clinton B118
CREASMAN George H162A
CREASON Sammy Lee A132 B180 B202 B261 C123 C180 F123A K95 K96 M227 S342 W64
CREATION C219
CREATION (Jap/U.S.) P20
CREATION REBEL C219A
CREATIVE ROCK C219B
CREATIVE SOURCE C220
CREATURES C220A
CREDIBILITY GAP C220B
Cree see BRUBECK,Chris
CREE Andy C106B
CREECH David P81
CREED C220C
CREED Helios C110
CREED Mary 018
CREEDENCE CLEARWATER REVIVAL C221
CREEK Cosmo (ANDREWS Walt) R139
CREEPY JOHN THOMAS C221A
CREESE Pete B160A
CREGAN Jim B47B B146 D118 F12 H26A H70 H123 L63 P76 R107 S273 S300 S309
CREIGAN Derek C47B
CREIGHTON James G. S84C
CRELLER Gary B259
CREME Lol B247 C222 H163 J110 M81 M67 R20 S35 T43
CRENSHAW Marshall C222B
CRENSHAW Robert C222B
CREQUE Neal V34
CRESCENDOS C222A
CRESPO Jimmy F60A L98
CRESS Curt E61B J4B J10A K10E K98 028D P34 T89 T143
CRESSIDA C223
CRESSWELL Brian A6A

CRESSWELL Tony M67 S4
CRESWELL-DAVIS Andy K83 S235
CRESTS C223A
CRETONES C223B
CRETU M. B174
CREWS Felton D27
CREWSON Roy F106
CRICHTON Ian S5A
CRICHTON John S5A
CRICKETS C224 H134
CRIDLIN Mac B110 D70 G10B M18 S322 T107
CRIEFF Tom B255
CRIGENO Nicky L25
CRIGER Peter K94C
CRIGGER Dave A120 P34
CRILL Chester H146 M113
CRILL Connie see EPP Fenrus
CRIMBLE Thomas S141
CRIMES Tory see CHIMES Terry
Cripple see NELSON Errol
CRISARA Ray K48
CRISCIONE John S100 T156
CRISIS C225
CRISP Roger R96
CRISPY AMBULANCE C226
CRISS Eddie P53
CRISS Pete C227 K67
CRISSINGER Roger 024B P49
CRISTINA C227A
CRISTLIEB Don G121
CRITCHLEY Bob D37
CRITCHLOW Les H184A
CRITICAL MASS C227B
CRITTERS C228
CROCE Ingrid C229
CROCE Jim C229
CROCKER Jean-Paul H26A
CROCKER John W117
CROCKETT David S77A
CROCKETT Greg R60C
CROCODILES C229A
CRODULA Brian S284
CROFTS Dash A31 C71 L56C S58 T25
CROLLY Peter C177A I21A
CROMAGNON ORGASM C229B
CROMAGNON C229B
CROMBIE Noel S221
CROME SYRCUS C229C
CROMPTON Andy M67
CROMPTON Jannie R10
CROMPTON Tom S28
CRONIN Dan P137
CRONIN Kevin R1A
CRONIN Larry Y4A
CRONK Chas B189 B231 H118 S295 W7
CRONKHITE Glenn B177
CRONLEY T.J. B246
CRONSHAW Andrew C230 M45
CROOK Reni B61B
CROOK Ted J71
CROOKES Allan P104A
CROOKS Phillip U9
CROOKS Richard B105 B207A B253 D139 F10BA F109 I2 L4A 015 R108A R125 R144A S114A W5 W51A W65A
CROOKS Sydney P87
CROOKS C230A
CROOM Mickey D123
CROPPER Clay C107A
CROPPER David P54
CROPPER Steve B97 B110 B155 B180 B202 B253 C6B C58 C69 C109 C158 C231 D5A D115 E15 E40 F100 F134 F139 G10 H59 H92 H120 I24A J22 J58 K46 L51 L65 M36 M75 M85 M132D N24E P114B R28B R56 R107 R173 R177 S20 S34 S252 S273 S284D W9
CROSBY Bill J15
CROSBY Bobby E7B S58
CROSBY David B244 B285 C232 C233 C234 E75 G10 H161 J46 J72 K10 K48 M27 M101 M170 N4 R109 S61 S70 S157 S196 S276 T25 W133 Y16
CROSBY Ethan C232
CROSBY Michael Y3

CROSBY AND NASH C233
CROSBY STILLS NASH AND YOUNG C234
CROSDALE Clarence 'Brooms' D47
CROSLOSE Glen N53
CROSS Billy D44B D139 G74 I24A M143A W129
CROSS Chris U8
CROSS Christopher A50 C234D K48 M16A
CROSS Ed H111B
CROSS David C137 K54
CROSS Keith C234E T5
CROSS Keith & Peter ROSS C234E
CROSS Robert A126
CROSS Tim O18 S140
CROSS D12A
CROSS COUNTRY C234A
CROSSAN George F75B
CROSSFIRE C234B
CROSSFIRES C234C
CROSSLEY Charlotte E49 S36
CROSSLEY Earl M5 R112
CROSSLEY Raymond G17
CROSSLEY Steve O2A
CROSSMAN Fred P131
CROSTHWAIT Jim W59
CROTTY P.J. H70
CROUCH Andre P126
CROUCH Dick P42A
CROUCH Hondo W11
CROUCH Sandra J95 M68 T27
CROUCHER Tom S19
CROUCIER Juan D93H
CROUDACE Gary F130
CROVELLA Beppe A91
CROW Alvin S7
CROW Jerry T134B
CROW C235
CROWBAR C236
CROWD C236A
CROWDER Gayle S137A
CROWDER John B105 I2 W5 W51A
CROWDER Robert D30 D66 H170
CROWE Ben K65
CROWE Dave P144
CROWE George S187A
CROWE J.D. C236B R78C
CROWE J.D. & The NEW SOUTH C236B
CROWE Simon B181
CROWE Terry R65
CROWELL Rodney C50 C124 C237 E20 H35 L36A
CROW'OOT C238
CROWLEY J.C. P98
CROWLEY Peter H76
CROWNS C39B
CROWTHER Emlyn S221
CROWTHER Pete B220A M164
CROWTHER Phil (B) I23A
CROWTHER Phillip (D) F40
CROY Dennis M96
CROY Rick B274A M96
CROYLE Joe C147
CROZIER George W86
CROZIER Larry B115A
CROZIER Sam see BROX Victor
CROZIER Trevor C165
CROZIER Van Q1A
CRUCIFICTION C238A
CRUDUP Arthur 'Big Boy' C239
CRUICKSHANK Gordon H69
CRIUCKSHANK Pete F40 G112
CRUISERS T53
CRUMB R. C240
CRUMLEY Pat S178
CRUMP Bruce M178A
CRUSADERS C241
CRUSE David M2 O14
CRUTCHFIELD Jerry L108 T153A
CRUTCHFIELD Paul K68A
CRUTCHFIELD Robin Lee D14B
CRUIZINGER Claudia R171
CRUZ Bobby F17
CRUZ Celia F17
CRUZ Javier S137A
CRUZ Mike C72A
CRUZ Rafael B85 B208 G64C G111 K36 M206 R13A S124 WB
CRUZER Beegie C14 C194 N37 S272 W95

CRY C241C
CRY FREEDOM C241D
CRYAN SHAMES C241A
CRYERS C241E
CRYPT KICKERS P78
CRYSLER Ken S245
CRYSTAL Lee S358B
CRYSTAL Ruby M106
CRYSTAL GRASS C241F
CRYSTAL MANSION C241B
CRYSTALS C242
CSAPO George B90
CSERNITS Billy R177
CUA Rick O43
CUBAN HEELS C242A
CUBER Ronnie A31 A123 A131 B57A B85 F4C G19 H164C K36 K69 L41 L80A L119 M17 M46B M107 M111 M225 O27 P72A P99 S157 S215 S262 T20 V17 Z3B Z8
CUBERT Joe R177
CUBY AND THE BLIZZARDS C243
CUCCIA Ron C243A
CUCURULLO Warren Z8
Cuddly Juddly S306
CUDDLY TOYS C243B
CUDWORTH Nick C210 S133
CUFF Mark H35 S73B
CUFFE Luurie C242A
CUFFLEY John C141 T14
CUISSET Jos D109A
CULLAM Alan B150A
CULLEN Angus C223
CULLEN Anne W10
CULLEN Michael V21
CULLEN Wayne D125
CULLERS Randy K95 L77
CULLEY Ben W118
CULLEY John B119 C223
CULLUM Bunky R65
CULP Phil A104A S177A
CULPAN David M80
CULPEPER C234C
CULPEPPER Tom F116
CULPO John G121
CULSHAW Gary B195
CULT C244
CULTRERI Cliff M105A
CULTURE C245
CUMBERBATCH Ken H17 H99
CUMBERBATCH Trevor K41
CUMMING Bryan B104B H8 M21 M229 O13 P114
CUMMING David T19A
CUMMINGS Benny, Singers L51
CUMMINGS Burton B9 C38 C246 G115 N26A P106
CUMMINGS Diana P41
CUMMINGS Donnie D106A
CUMMINGS Douglas P41
CUMMINGS George D85 P112
CUMMINGS George S120
CUMMINGS Julian P41
CUMMINGS Keith S198
CUMMINGS Kris C39B
CUMMINGS Mark B23A S322
CUMMINGS Pat L44
CUMMINGS Pete G81B
CUMMINGS Richard K68A
CUMMINGS Stephen S224A
CUMMINGS Vernon O47
CUMMINS Steve H37
CUMMINS Trevor H145
CUNDALL Steve D120
CUNDIEFF Larry M136C
CUNHA Rick C247 D68B H35 H77 S272 W88
CUNNINGHAM B.B. H139B
CUNNINGHAM Bill B190 C247 M102B N53 S272 W88
CUNNINGHAM Blair B242 J81 R23 W101
CUNNINGHAM Bob M79
CUNNINGHAM C. G79
CUNNINGHAM Carl B36 R56
CUNNINGHAM Casey B173
CUNNINGHAM Danny E32
CUNNINGHAM David E32 F74C
CUNNINGHAM Gayle D92 S108
CUNNINGHAM George E57 L42
CUNNINGHAM James M212
CUNNINGHAM Johnny S116A
CUNNINGHAM Mark D53

CUNNINGHAM Matthew L51
CUNNINGHAM Phil S116A
CUNNINGHAM Ronnie Lee L26 P77
CUNNINGHAM Steve M57A R53
CUNNINGHAM Tom K11
CUNNINGHAM Woody K68A
CUOMO Bill B170 C38A C123 E23 H116 L9A L92 M18 M123 N42 O15 R127A S58 S228A S272 T113 W133A
CUOMO Brian F48F G69 I22 V21
CUOMO Jim A33 B104A C119 F8 G46 H29 H65 I22 P5 S243 W128
CUOMO Richard R101
CUPP Pat & Flying Saucers C247D
CUPPLES Peter S312
CURE C247A
CURFEW C247B
CURIEL Juanita C129
CURLAN Bob D44B
CURLEE Randy Z9A
CURLY CURVE C247C
CURNIFFE Winston P108 W37
CURNOW Creeper T6B
CURNOW Ian P92D S54
CURNUTTE Jim A104A
CURRAN Tina F123
CURRENT Jim S249C
CURRIE Billy L144B N63A U8 V35A
CURRIE Cherie C248 C248A R163
CURRIE Cherie & Marie C248A
CURRIE George D18
CURRIE John P73
CURRIE Kevin B272 S333
CURRIE Laurie A15
CURRIE Marie C248 C248A
CURRIE Steve B168 S209 W130
CURRY Dave L57A
CURRY Mickey D63A H9 S53A Y3A
CURRY Peter S335A
CURRY Tim C249 S124
CURRY -Tom A35A
CURTIS Adrian see GURVITZ Adrian
CURTIS Andy R33
CURTIS Billy V21
CURTIS Ced V11
CURTIS Chris R147 S60
CURTIS Dave D165A
CURTIS Clem F90A
CURTIS Clifton S251
CURTIS Dave R147
CURTIS Eddie C67
CURTIS Ian J99A
CURTIS James S164B
CURTIS John M196 P119
CURTIS Linda P124
CURTIS Little Joe C250 R56
CURTIS Mac C250A
CURTIS Michael C216
CURTIS Nick D99 F70B
CURTIS Paul see GURVITZ Paul
CURTIS Peter D68
CURTIS Phil (formerly SHUTT Phil) B231 D39 D92 F101 R46 S217 T89 V18B
CURTIS Rick C216
CURTIS Sonny C121 C224 C250B D104 H34 V19
CURTIS Stan M47C
CURTISS A. C250C
CURTISS Jimmy B17C
CURULEWSKI John S314
CURVED AIR C251
CUSACK Julian S218
CUSACK Peter F123
CUSANO Vinnie H51 N65
CUSCUNA Michael D132B J48 H62 M222 U5C
CUSHNIE Scott A16 C217
CUSLAR Pere see MOERLEN Pierre
CUSSEAUX Zulema B57A F103 M12

CUSSICK Ian C251B L17A T103A
CUTHBERT Doug J15A
CUTHBERT Dick A82 D49 J16 M127 Q1 R53 R84 S74 S207 W23
CUTLER Chris (D) A35 A71A A88 B69 F123 O18 R67 S152
CUTLER Chris (G.B) B69 H101 L95A
CUTLER David A48
CUTLER Ian H194
CUTLER Ivor A74 C252 W135
CUTLER Phil O40
CUTLER Rick S106
CUTLIFFE Vince T132
CUTRARA Joel H194B
CUTTERI Cliff N34A
CXIGANY Laszlo G35A
CYANIDE C253
CYBER Ronnie T20
CYBORG John L. C110 C253A
Cyclops I17B
CYMANDE C254
CYMARRON C254A
CYMBELINES C254B
CYMONE Andre L82A
CYR Marshall N23 W106
CYR Ray C115A
CYRILLE Andrew B131 G90 M79
CYRKLE C255
CYRUS C255A
CYSIK Casey J20 V6
CZUKAY Holger C25 C145 C256 C257
CZUKAY, WOBBLE & LIEBEZEIT C257

D.A.F. D57D
D.B's D1C
D.C. NIGHTHAWKS D1
D.F.K.BAND D1A
D.M.Z. D1B
D.P.'s D51
D Rocky S276
D.V.C. D1D
DAANSEN Johan S42B W138
DABKIN Debra W128B
DABNEY Russell J113 P24B
D'ABO Michael D2 M80 S273 W117
DABON Robert G4 M149
DA CAMERA SINGERS P140
DA COSTA Glen A6 H105 R134
DA COSTA Paulinho A35C A123 A131 B53 B85 B110 B208 B226 C36 C38 C213E C241 D3 D83 D86 E7 E40 E55 F33 F88A F103C H150A H156 J10B J72 K36 L18 L56C L65 L109 L119C L143 M16A M75 M130 M131 M178A P8A P44 P114 Q3B R97 R99 R115 S14C S34 S64 S250 S273 T118 T148 V18B W24 W27 W32A W84C W118 W128B W133 DA CUICA Zeca A131
DACUS Donnie C100 H120 J69 M27 O10 P114B R123 S276 T6B
DADA D4
Daddy Bones R169
DADDY COOL D4A
DADDY LONGLEGS D5
DAFFERN Bill (D) T151
DAFFERN Willy (V) C31
DAGGER Mike T84A
DAGLAND Karen S333A
DAGLAND Karen S333A
DAGGER Mike T84A
DAGRADI Tony B131 L118 S56
DA GREASE Dewey see DEWEY Greg
DAHL Anders A4
DAHL Freddy S12A
DAHL Sverri Z19
DAHLBACK Erik B4

DAHLEN Bengt B4
DAHLSTROM Patti D5A
DAHME Jim E39
DAHMEN Udo K89
DAILEY Albert R159
DAILEY Don D5B P80
DAILEY Geoff G71
DAILEY Harry B261
DAILEY Rick W5B
DAILY Dwight B144
DAISLEY Bob C101 O33E R14 T170 U22 W74
DAKER Rhoda S207
DAKING Geoff B157
DAKOTA D5C
DAKOTAS D6 K93
Daku 'Potato' O34
DAKUS Wes D6A
DAL BELLO Lisa W128B
D'ALBUQUERQUE Mike D7 E34 R85 T162 V35
DALBY Andy B231 D39 G92D V18B
DALDIN Herman P60B
DALE Dick M191
DALE Glen F87
DALE Paul M91
DALE Peter K52
DALE Robin S2
DALE Rollice K17 O39
DALE Ted C96
DALEK 1 D6B
D'ALEO Angelo B80A D74
DALEY Dan F108A
DALEY Earl D6C
DALEY Joe B131
DALEY John A9
DALEY Joseph M53
DALEY Patt D26
DALEY Wayne S63
DALLAM James C162
DALLAWAY Rob C213B
DALL'SENSE Gilbert P9
DALLAS Karl D5B
DALLAS COUNTY D7A
DALLIO Patricia A89B
DALLON Lee S210A
DALLON Miki F20B
DALONZO Paul Jr G116C
DALTON Dirk W92
DALTON Eric F74
DALTON Erik S199B
DALTON Gary D53C J69
DALTON Jack C168
DALTON John K61
DALTON Kathy D8
DALTON Mark Z3A
DALTON Mitch E77A I20 M203
DALTON BROTHERS D8A
DALTREY Peter F5A K5
DALTREY Roger D9 W7 W72
DALWOOD Dexter C187
DALY Brian F55 F70B H151 S313
DALY Geoff A23 B19 C75 C159 F42 G11 G94 L11 Q2 S107 W13A W128
DALY George P112
DALY Jackie D38
DALY John W97A
DALY Peter Hugo D12A
DALY Steven O28C
DALZIEL Alan P36
DAMAGE Brian A6C A35
DAMAGE Donnie R151
DAMAIN Derek C251
DAMANTI Paolo T122A
D'AMATO Maria see MULDAUR Maria
DAMBRA Joey S132A
DAMBRA Louis S132A
DAMBRAU Jeff L8
D'AMBROSIA GIULIO C63B
DAMEN Jan B149C
DAMERON Tadd D27
DAMERY Norman G5
DAMIAN Luis F. B244 G24 Z11
DAMIANI Chip R64
D'AMICO Joey C212
D'AMICO Nick C140A
D'AMICO Tony H187

Dam/Dea

DAMMERS Jerry S207
DAMNATION D9A
DAMNED D10
D'MORE Jack R121A
DAMRICK Wally S238A
DAMRON Mark R68
Dan A66
DAN Gichy K38
DAN Michael M133 T166
DAN HICKS AND HIS HOT LICKS H112
DANAHER Thomas A129
DANCE D10B
DANCE BAND D10A
DANCIK Mitchell J112
DANDO SHAFT D11
D'ANDREA John H60 R54
DANDY Jim (MANGRUM J.D.) B114 F65
DANE Barbara C69 D11A H152
DANELLI Dino B262F C62 F90 N65 R34 T67A
DANGEL Rick F69 W3B
D'ANGELO Jean Yves K19
D'ANGELO Renato B28
D'ANGELY J.J. Bouchet E18B
DANGER Sun T165
DANGERFIELD Matt B196
DANGERFIELD Rodney D11B
DANGLER Jackie B261
DANIEL David W63
DANIEL Gregg K27A
DANIEL Jeffrey S85A
DANIEL Pebble N23 N25 T9
DANIEL Ray W115
DANIELAK Stefan'Wildschwein' E63 G106
DANIELS Bobby R127A
DANIELS Charlie A38 B109 C217 D12 D139 G104 K81 M93 M232 S55A S252 T153A W110
DANIELS Ed A96 B85 G4 J20 K36 L58B L119 M26 M227 R99 R142A S125
DANIELS Eric G79A
DANIELS Gideon B109
DANIELS Hall N5BC
DANIELS Jess K45
DANIELS John W48F
DANIELS Kenny K27A
DANIELS Larry 'Spider' C162
DANIELS Phil D12A
DANIELS Ritchie D42
DANIELS Sian S212
DANIELS Stephen D50 P96
DANIELS Willie C. M41 P67
DANJUMA Ras M133
DANKE Terry B57F
DANKO Rick B29 C155 D13 D139 F116 H15 L111 S252 T134 Y16
DANKO Terry D13 F116 H62
DANKOWITZ Edith I27
DANKWORTH Johnny A60A
DANN Earl D17
D'ANNA Elio N60 O33O P64
DANNA Jean-Luc S280
DANNEMAN Don C255
DANNY AND THE JUNIORS A42A D14
DANNY JOE BROWN BAND B233A
DANNY WILD AND THE WILDCATS W76
DANOFF Taffy F27A
DANOFF William F27A
DANSIE Jane F51
DANTER Brian T37C
DANYLS Bob F16B
DANZA Dave M179
DANZIG Glenn M163C
DAPPER Klaus B278A K76B
DARA Olu U6
DARBEY Gilly C185A
DARBY Alan C7 S140
DARC Daniel T18A
DARC Jana Lee R16A
Darcus W30
DARENSBOURG Joe B221 F5
DARIN Bobby D14A
DARK DAY D14B
DARK STAR D14C
DARKS Trevor A126 M211A
D'ARLES Fernand Z2
DARLING D15
DARLING David H62 S73C S231
DARLING Diane C194
DARLING Erik C164

DARLING Fred B181A
DARLING Larry M106B
DARLING Ronnie S173C
DARLING Tom T165A
DARLINGTON Wilf A103
DARLOW Eva P136
DARNALL John H52A
DARNELL August D83K83
DARNELL Bill M95B
DARNELL Dik I3A S238A
DARNSELL Joseph K3B
DAROU Alex K28 P35
DARREN Jenny D16
DARRINGTON Steve B211 J16B
D'ARROW Phillip D17A
DARROW Chris C18B D17
D60 F94 F109 K6 M10C M95D M113 N53 O10 P6C
R28A S272 T1 T25
DARROW Steven D17
DARSCH Bob C190
DARTS (U.K.) D18
DARTS (U.S.) D18A
DARTSCH Bob C190
DARVILLS Nigel M119
DARWAY Chris C22B
DASA Agnideva W119
DASA Cinmayi W119
DASA Duryodhana Guru W119
DASA Jayasacinandana W119
DASA Jitamrtyu W119
DASA Vedavyasa W119
DAS DRITTE OHR D18C
DASH Sarah J70 L4 M93
DASHIELL Russell A1 C238 D18B G96 H38 H52 M68 P118D S65 T150
DASI Yogamaya W119
DA SILVA Ana R17
DA SILVA Everton P2
DA SILVA Jose R99
DASKOFF Isabelle B15
DASTI Michel C28A
DATA Darrell B254
DATIMEN Udo K89
DAUGA Philippe B102
DAUGAARD Kim S108C
DAUGHERTY Bob F99A
DAUGHERTY Jay Dee N48A R118 S170 V25B
DAUGHERTY Pat B114
DAUGHTERS Kenny H193
DAUGHTERS OF ALBION D19
DAUGHTREY Dean A111 C25A C132 F102 K81 L44
DAUILELGSON Palle V26C
DAULTREY Dots C165
DAUNER Wolfgang D19A H34 P115 S73C
DAUVIN Pinky L74
DAVANI Dave P4
DAVE CLARK FIVE C122
DAVE DEE DOZY BEAKY MICK & TICH D20
DAVENPORT Barry G85
DAVENPORT Billy B85B B282 D139
DAVENPORT Bob T6
DAVENPORT Darius La Noue A129 B57D B194
DAVENPORT Paul B222
DAVENPORT Wallace W47
DAVERN Kenny C68A
DAVERSA Jay D127 S14C
DAVEY Billy W24
DAVEY AND THE BADMEN D20A
DAVICH Marty L62D
David II S96 W12A
DAVID Gary S272
DAVID Jay B41B S120
DAVID John (B) D85
DAVID John (B) A26 E19 F7 M128 W29A
DAVID John (HORNS) A96
DAVID Kal C68A D133A F3A I12A M135 R22
DAVID Martin (PERC) B67
DAVID Marty (B) H139A L111 M203 Y12 Z11
DAVID Randall M84
DAVID Richard B53
DAVID & JONATHAN D20B
DAVID CAMPBELL STRINGS K48

DAVID KATZ ORCHESTRA S34
DAVID PEEL AND THE LOWER EAST SIDE P53
DAVID SWAIN SECTION M192A
DAVIDOWSKI Steve D79
DAVIDS James C146
DAVIDSON Bill G11B
DAVIDSON Brent D21
DAVIDSON Colin H28A
DAVIDSON Dianne B200 C14 D21 F7 H52A R137 R173
DAVIDSON George B282
DAVIDSON Greg (Ella Guru) B72
DAVIDSON Howard N25A
DAVIDSON Jos S113 S204
DAVIDSON Lenny C122
DAVIDSON Les E8 S178 W13A
DAVIDSON Paul Mitchell C209
DAVIDSON Scott A85A
DAVIDSON Steve C56
DAVIE Hutch P49
DAVIE Jon G114 S66
DAVIES Alan (D) Y17
DAVIES Alun (G) D22 H70
L63 S181 S266 S352 W89
DAVIES B.G. P129
DAVIES Bassett S102A
DAVIES Brendetta D53C
DAVIES Brian P129
DAVIES Buddy G102
DAVIES Cam F18 M191
DAVIES Cyril B156 D23 K84
DAVIES Dave D54 K61
DAVIES Dennis B186
DAVIES Diana C209
DAVIES Digger P10
DAVIES Doug S63
DAVIES Ed O47
DAVIES Gail A132 D72A
DAVIES Iva I5A
DAVIES James A34 Q11
DAVIES Joe G102
DAVIES John (D) M121
DAVIES John (Tpt/K) H69
DAVIES Megan A67M M180A
DAVIES Noel S74
DAVIES Pete U4
DAVIES Peter Maxwell Y2
DAVIES Phil Q11
DAVIES R. E20
DAVIES Raymond Douglas (V/G/K) K61
DAVIES Rhell E59
DAVIES Rhett M81
DAVIES Richard S333
DAVIES Rick C112
DAVIES Rod S119
DAVIES Roger H125
DAVIES Ron D23A
DAVIES Roy B47C B77 B283 D27B D95A G47 J72 K51 R125 T149
DAVIES Russell A109
DAVIES Taffy G1
DAVIES Trevor (Dozy) D20
DAVIES Vicki D23A
DAVIES William P107
DAVILA Izzy Y2A
DAVILIO Anthony O27
DA VINCI Paul H42 R40B
CRESWELL-DAVIS Andy see CRESWELL-DAVIS Andy
DAVIS Ann Esther W10A
DAVIS Anthony R157
DAVIS Art S10 S168
DAVIS Betty D24
DAVIS Billy B24
DAVIS Bill D97A
DAVIS Biscuit B108B
DAVIS Blind John C135 J79 S329 T9B W93
DAVIS Bobby M68
DAVIS Bryan H19
DAVIS Bud T13A
DAVIS Buddy D12
DAVIS Butch R96
DAVIS Carlton 'Santa' A6 B95A B101 C139 I1A J17C L58A M149 P134 P140C R29 S45
S190 T155A U1
DAVIS Carolyn L119B
DAVIS Chalmers G85A
DAVIS Charles M79 S111 W30A
DAVIS Cliff (D) I8 N63 W69

DAVIS Cliff (SAX) B203A
C72 D66
DAVIS Costo B41
DAVIS Dai A109
DAVIS Danny (NOWLAN George) A110
DAVIS David W110
DAVIS Delford N50B
DAVIS Dennis F88 J7 W19
DAVIS Digger B230
DAVIS Don M105A N34A
DAVIS Donna B123 J11 K56A
DAVIS Doreen S213
DAVIS Douglas D99
DAVIS Douzell E55
DAVIS Eddie 'Lockjaw' D25
DAVIS Fannie M22
DAVIS Frank C124 D25A
DAVIS Frank J. C158 M144
DAVIS Gary C172B
DAVIS George (G) N39
DAVIS George (Flt) Z9
DAVIS George (K) J22
DAVIS Graham B137
DAVIS Harvey D63B
DAVIS Henry J113 K46 K51
L2 M218 P67 R6OC S333A W31
DAVIS Howard J84
DAVIS Huey C177C
DAVIS Ivory R115
DAVIS J.Michael B238
DAVIS Jack S340A
DAVIS James S85A
DAVIS Jay A67N A131G S117B
S273 W120
DAVIS Jeff (B) A45
DAVIS Jeff (D) L64
DAVIS Jeff (Tpt) N39
DAVIS Jesse Edwin A116 B23
B84 B144 B149 B210 B221
B244 C6B C123 C156 D26
D53C D99 D139 G121 H39 J41
K45 K46 L51 M53 M111 M132D
M159 M191 M227 N23 O16 P28
R98 R173 S10 S111 S252
S273 T32B T91 V3
DAVIS Jesse F42
DAVIS Jimmie L2
DAVIS Jimmy (B) D96
DAVIS Joe Lane B201 C179
C217 K51
DAVIS John (Horns) A96
H65A R142A
DAVIS John (K) J92
DAVIS Kim P109A
DAVIS Krystal B253 K47 M93
P25 S198A
DAVIS L.C. B87
DAVIS Larry R112
DAVIS Larry S115
DAVIS Larry(B) A28A
DAVIS Lincoln H35
DAVIS Link A102 E62B M211
57
DAVIS Lloyd P149
DAVIS 'Lockjaw' Eddie D25
DAVIS Louis John P15
DAVIS Lynn D127
DAVIS Marilyn C14
DAVIS Mark R141 S250 W31
DAVIS Marlena O33
DAVIS Martha M210A
DAVIS Maurice C153 T42
DAVIS Maxwell J21 W30
DAVIS Mel (Tpt) A131 H137
L65 L69 M12 P59B M75
DAVIS Mel (Cello) T60
DAVIS Mercedes B17
DAVIS Michael (B) M1
DAVIS Mike (Tpt) A23 B83
E24 F14 H50
DAVIS Mike (G) B19
DAVIS Miles D27 M40
DAVIS Mose C199B
DAVIS Nathan B197D
DAVIS Ned B253
DAVIS Orville H195 R73
DAVIS Paul (U.K.) G77A
DAVIS Paul (U.S.) A111
D27A M65A
DAVIS Paul 'Sandy' D27B
DAVIS Paul (G) C14
DAVIS Paul (Perc) M82
DAVIS Peter B94C
DAVIS Phil G81E
DAVIS Pluma B233 K45 P26
DAVIS Raheem Lee Michael

C155B E7 E55 L65 S250
DAVIS Ray S31 S235
DAVIS Ray M225
DAVIS Raymond F137 P29
DAVIS Richard (B) C40 C186
D66 F109 I2 J48 L69 M21 M78
M79 M125 M177 M203 M233 N65
O15 R22 R34 S78 S111 S124
S125 S168 S229 T147 V12 W5
DAVIS Richard (Horns) B139
DAVIS Rob M223
DAVIS Sandy see DAVIS Paul 'Sandy'
DAVIS Shelly B224C
DAVIS Spencer C35D D28 M18
M101 M191 W89
DAVIS Stanton B233
DAVIS Steve (K) B41
DAVIS Steve (Trom) G71C
DAVIS Sue S112A
DAVIS Terry S284
DAVIS Theresa C72 E55
DAVIS Thom J16C
DAVIS Tim M159 S111
DAVIS Wade 'Holmes' L69
DAVIS Walter W93 W94
DAVIS Walter D86 W30A
DAVIS Warner T93
DAVIS Willie D38A
DAVISON Brian 'Blinky' A84
D29 G66 H29 N44 R61
DAVISON Ray A30A
DAVISON Tony A72
DAVY Colin F21 L16A S355
DAVY Stephanie R144A
DAVY Steve S258
DAW Jef T36
DAWE Michael B57 P15 P119
DAWE Tim D29A
DAWES Biff B274A
DAWES Tom C255
DAWKINS Greg S85A
DAWKINS Jimmy 'Fastfingers'
D30 E67 R168 S323 Y13
DAWN Ron W101
DAWN Sandra P97
DAWN PATROL D29B
DAWSON Claire A98
DAWSON Colin F140B
DAWSON David C247 W88
DAWSON Jack S113
DAWSON Jinx C203A
DAWSON John G84 N32
DAWSON Larry F16B
DAWSON Mark A132 F128
DAWSON Mike D68B
DAWSON Steve S32A
DAWSON Warren T158
DAWTAS Negus S190
DAX Danielle L48A
DAY Billy H70
DAY Bobby (BYRD Robert) D30A
DAY Brian W117B
DAY Bruce P3
DAY Charles S120
DAY Chuck M18
DAY Doris M125A
DAY James C133 G100 K32
M211 V18
DAY Margot P53
DAY Mike (V) L59
DAY Mike (G) C35D C69B
DAY Mike (D) R12
DAY Rusty C5 N63
DAY Stephen P139H
DAY Stu C182
DAY Terry see MIALL Terry
DAY Wyatt A86
DAY BLINDNESS D30B
DAY OF THE PHOENIX D31
DAYAN Duytt H79
DAYDE Joel Z18
DAYE Cory D83
DAYE Stuart B31B L107 R39
DAYES Kenneth Lloyd C245
DAYEZ Michel J105B
DAYLIGHT D31A
DAYLIGHTERS B193
DAYS Guy N49
DAYSHIFT D31C
DAYTON Jeff L16B
DAYTON Peter N16B
DAYTON D31D
D'BOYLE Lance P114A
DEACON Graham B151 E60 F65
F76 J16 J27 K84 M157 S179
T73 W72

[644]

DOG WATCH D93D
DOGFEET D93A
DOGG Tyman C130 H185
DOGGER Bunk D34B D92
DOGGEREL BANK D93
DOGGETT Bill D93B
DOGGETTE Georg G35B
DOGS D93C
DOHENY Ned R101 S196 Z11
DOHERTY Billy U11
DOHERTY Dane D93E
DOHERTY Denny B99 D93F M61
M224
DOHERTY Mike S164
DOHONEY Michael J. C200
DOHTISCH Hanna T143
DOKKEN Don D93H
DOLAN Donny F128 L122 S269
W11
DOLAN Joe S346
DOLAN Mick H25
DOLAN Nick C185A
DOLAN Peter K49A
DOLAN Steve H25 S131
DOLAN Terry T54 T150
DOLANON Randel W106
DOLBY Tom A82 F84 G37A H124B
W126A
DOLDINGER Klaus D93G P34
DOLEMAN Ron M21
DOLENZ Micky M181
DOLIN Bob B103 C182
DOLITZSCH Hinna T143
DOLL Erich T149C
DOLL D94
DOLL BY DOLL D95
DOLLAR Beau M211
DOLLASE Jurgen C192 G3A
W13D
DOLLASE Rolf W13D
DOLLEZ Jean-Marc S280
DOLLINGER Tom M203
DOLLINS Adolph H170
DOLLIS Bo W78A
DOLLY Joe T93B
DOLPH Richard H65A
DOLPHIN Terry K68A
DOLPHIN D95A
DOLPHY Eric H10
DOMAGALSKI Victor H19
DOMAGISTRIS Manny B264A
DOMANE Richard W68A
DOMANICO Chuck B84 C179
C180 F34 H8A H60 K77 M68
M75 M125 M170 O15 P114 S50
S111 S180 S196 T107 W65 W97 N57
DOME D95B
DOMIN Monika Marie F8D
DOMINATORS W29A
DOMINIC John B161
DOMINIC Steve W26
DOMINICI Charlie F101C
DOMINIQUE Carl Axel S186
Domino L63
DOMINO Antoine 'Fats' D96
DOMINO Floyd (HABER Jim)
A102
DOMINOES H122
DOMLING Norbert M163E S38
DOMMERS Michael W13D
DON Jimmy B145B
DON AND DEWEY D97
DON ELLIOTT SINGERS N35
DON HARRISON BAND H38
DONABLE Ernest S329
DONAHUE Jerry A82 D49 E41
F6 F89 G27 G98 G110 H42 H74
K24 K75 M21 M45 M108 P75
P107 R11 S185 S313 W133
DONAHUE Patty W5B
DONALD Chris S78
DONALD Keith M221E W125
DONALD Peter H8A M74
DONALD Timi B148 C13 D37
D49 E41 F6 G103 H29 I20 K97
M25 M38 M108 P90 R106 T79
W125
DONALDSON Andy H46
DONALDSON Bobby C146 H15
S168
DONALDSON David C96B
DONALDSON George C96B
DONALDSON Lloyd 'Jah Bunny'
B120 M109 P80C P108 R61C
DONALDSON Lou D97A

DONALDSON Pat A30 A62 A82
B138 B266 C9 C13 C109 C165
D2 D37 D49 E41 F6 F21 F89
G27 G32 G98 G110 H11 H42
H48 H65 H110 J84 K28B K97
L30 L36A L63 M19 M21 M25
M38 M108 M121 M180 N63B
P107 P138 R15 R46 R106
R125 S108 S185 S339 T79
W71 W89 W125
DONALDSON Peter A4A
DONALDSON Robert C96B
DONALDSON Starr S31A
DONATO Chris C222B
DONATO Joao F103D
DONATO Michael C151
DONATO Peter D97B
DONDI Franz A5B
DONEGAN Anthony James
'Lonnie' D100
DONEGAN Patrick 'Chiki'
R61A
DONELLY John S270
DONEN David C35C R23
DONIGHT Will B27
DONLINGER Jim A67D L130A
DONNELLAN Jay L128 M204
DONNELLY Al (V) P53
DONNELLY Albie (SAX) A29
B181 C118 M127 P25 R162
S332 T34
DONNELLY Ben I18A
DONNELLY Jim H74
DONNELLY John B83 H70
V26A
DONNELLY Philip B272B
C124 C133 D99 K77 M196
V18 Z22
DONNER Ral D98
Donovan (LEITCH Donovan)
C182 D99
DONOVAN Bob M79
DONOVAN Dave H55 W122
DONOVAN Lizzie O6A
DONOVAN Nicholas O6A
DOOBIE BROTHERS D101 S124
DOODY Tom C241CA
DOOMED D102
DOONAN Michael H87
DOOR & THE WINDOW D102A
DOORS D103
Dopepea J17C
DORAN Dave B41 M125 S73
T107
DORE Charlie D104 G71A
DORFMAN Gary P53
DORFMAN Jay S350
DORMAN Lee C31 I24
DORMAN Randy R127A
DORN Gary L57
DORN Joel M41
DORN Jonathan M41
DORN Margaret B145B R142A
T67A
DORN Van M192B
DOROUGH Bob D27 F133 G10
P49 R31
DORSET Ray D105 M230
DORSETT Matt F135B
DORSEY George M75 M227
S168
DORSEY Georgia Tom T9B
DORSEY Glenn J93D
DORSEY Jack B177
DORSEY Lee D106
DORSEY Leslie C164 F133
DORSEY Tony M9
DORSIE Lester Y13
DOSPAPAS Mike C77A
DOSS Debi D54 S177D
DOSS Kenny D106E
DOS SANTOS Luis A131
DOTSON Rosa D30
DOTSON Ward G117B
DOTT Gerard I16
Dottie B91
DOTZLER Thomas T47A
DOUBLEDAY Marcus B144 E33
M151
DOUCET Michel S187C
DOUCETTE D106A
DOUCETTE Jerry B225 D106A
DOUCETTE Thom A38
DOUD David E8A

DOUD Earle D106B F109
DOUD Mike EBA
DOUG & THE SLUGS D106F
DOUG COOK BAND C179C
DOUGHERTY Jimmy A33B
DOUGHERTY Dean S331A
DOUGHERTY Tom W44
DOUGHTY Neal R1A
Dougie see BRYAN Rad
DOUGLAS Bill G96 T150
DOUGLAS Bonnie F134 P28
S63
DOUGLAS Bruce S327B
DOUGLAS Carl H73
DOUGLAS Chip M181
DOUGLAS Cleon M163
DOUGLAS Cynthia E123 J11
K56A
DOUGLAS David D96
DOUGLAS Don B261
DOUGLAS Ed S52
DOUGLAS Graeme E13 K100
DOUGLAS Greg A35D B259
F80 G84A M16 M18 M159
M167 M179 R40 T54
DOUGLAS Ian U7
DOUGLAS Jack C92 P25
R123
DOUGLAS Jerry C236B H35
DOUGLAS Jimmy S154
DOUGLAS Jonathan S272
DOUGLAS Kevin K47
DOUGLAS Leon M163
DOUGLAS Michael O29A
DOUGLAS Mike D62
DOUGLAS Nat B233
DOUGLAS Pam G94 O34 Q1
DOUGLAS Paul T110
DOUGLAS Robert P96
DOUGLAS Steve B56 C146
C156 D74 D106C D135A
D139 E14 H5 J36 M96 M163
M191 P75 R24 R173 T164
DOUGLAS Val D63 F86 I12
R35B
DOUGLASS Bill L10B
DOUGLASS Gregg S322
DOUIEB Gilles C113A
DOUKAS John E6 K40
DOUMA Danny D106G W54B
DOVE Glenn S201B
DOVE Michael M131
DOVE Myron B233
DOVE Nathaniel M238B S96
DOVELLS D106D
DOVER Dave B268 C165A
DOW Gary C20
DOWD Tom J31 S228 W54
W64
DOWE Brenton D107
DOWIE John D107A
DOWLE David A120 C204
L11 M146B R164A S300
DOWLER Steve L100
DOWLING Alison W72
DOWLING Basil see BROOKS
Clive
DOWLING Ed S56
DOWLING Pete B90 C18
DOWN John Headley see
HEADLEY-DOWN John
DOWN Sandra P97
DOWNER Andy D48B
DOWNES Bob D108 D118 E24
R122
DOWNES Geoff A99B B261A
Y7
DOWNEY Alan F70B P131
DOWNEY Brian L144B M196
T59
DOWNEY P. J33A
DOWNEY Rick B154
Downie C. P2
DOWNIE Tyrone B276 M88
M221D T104A T114 V21
W4
DOWNING Al C42 M26
DOWNING Bill P53
DOWNING K.K. J102
DOWNING Tom A5
DOWNING Walter R141
DOWNLINERS SECT D109
DOWNS Tim M82
DOWNTRIP D109A
DOYLE Bobby B141
DOYLE John L100B M47

DOYLE Mark B263 J105C P123
S34 W48D
DOYLE Peter D110
DOYLE Raphael C9 H11
DOYLE Tom P53
DOYLE Tony A6C
DOYLE-MURRAY Brian N10
DOZIER Gene S85A
DOZIER Lamont D109B
DOZIER Tiny S154
DOZIER Ugene P80 S228
Dozy see DAVIES Trevor
DOZY BEAKY MICK & TICH D20
DRAFFEN Willis B143
DRAGGOTA George M58
DRAGON D110A
DRAGON Darryl K14 M238 S336
T137A
DRAGON Dennis B56 E45 M10A
S333B
DRAGONAIRES L39A
DRAGONFLY D110B
DRAHEIM Sue A30 A98 E41 M94
R66 T79
DRAHER Dan R85A
DRAINS Bijou see TOWNSHEND
Pete
DRAKE Brian T147
DRAKE Jack M211
DRAKE John N63
DRAKE Nick D111
DRAKE Oma B282 C36 C156
C211 H150 J91A N23 P126 S10
S116 T27
DRAKE Pete B17A C77A D112
D139 F35A F126 H26 H62 J30
K32 K81 K95 L42 M13 M41 M68
M211 N23 P63 P125 R127A
R173 S187C S252 T22 T67A
Y18
DRAKE Richard A35A
DRAMATIS D112A
DRANES L.C. P26
DRANSFIELD Barry A98 C165
D49 D113 H180 H194 L84 T79
DRANSFIELD Robin D49 D113
L84 N45A
DRANSFIELDS D113
DRAPER Lauren I27
DRAPER Mick G11C
DRAPER Ray D86 R92
DRAZ Peter S104C
DREAD Mikey D113A
DREAM D114
DREAMS D115
DREARES Alfred C146
DREAS Mike C130
DRECHSLER Remigius O40B
DREHER Phil A39A
DREILICH Herbert K10A
DREITH Dennis B56 B274A M62
P75
DRIER Bobby H135A
DREJA Chris C121 W94 Y5
DRENNAN Ali S45
DRENNAN Jim M125
DRESDEN Martin F77
DRESSLAR Len P137
DREYFUSS Michael M37
Dribble Brothers T173
DRIFTERS A42A D116 M43
DRIFTWOOD D117
DRIGGINS Tony B246
DRIGGS Karl F98 K90
DRILL Dave R23
DRINKARD Cissy see HOUSTON
Emily
DRINKWATER Paul C238A
DRINKWATER Skip H97 M184
W84D W129
DRISCOE Chris S111
DRISCOL Mike B23
DRISCOLL Gary E38 R14
DRISCOLL Geoff M80 P131 R46
S141 W61
DRISCOLL Julie see TIPPETTS
Julie
DRISCOLL Ken L114
DRISCOLL Marion S270
DRISCOLL Marlene M1 T37H
DRISCOLL Mike H23 P124 T31
DRIVER Laurie A14
DRIVER D119
DROGAS Wally R148
DROGIES Jurgen T63A
DROGIES Norbert T63A

DROMAN Greg V38
DRONE M.J. (HOWELLS M.J.)
D120
DRONES D120
Droppy D82
DRORI Assa S116
DROS Bob B43A
DROUBAY Marc S336
DROUET Jean Pierre M40
DROUKAS Joe D120B
DROVER Martin A23 B47C C39A
C75 C109 F7 F8 F42 F86 G67
H50 H65 I20 J104C L12A L53
M157 P131 R174 S11 S141
S178 W128
DROY James P51
DRUG ADDIX D120A
DRUICK AND LORANGE D121
DRUID D122
DRUIDS OF STONEHENGE D122A
DRUMGOLE James K48
DRUMMOND Burleigh A48 P31
R46
DRUMMOND Celia (nee HUMPHRIS)
T137
DRUMMOND Don P134
DRUMMOND John D21
DRUMMOND Keith B116
DRUMMOND Pete T137
DRUMMOND Tim A132 B56 B75
B282 C14 C133 C179 C233
C234 D12 D13 D21 D139 H62
M32 M111 M211 N4 P75 S298
Y16
DRUSS Len A51 H1 M115
DRY CITY SCAT BAND D122B
DRYDEN Spencer B210 J46 K10
N32 S61
D'SILVA Amancio C191
DUANE Ed K10C
DUARTE Ernesto B43
DUBE Joe F108A L119B S254
DUBIN Michael J65
DUBOIS Davidson T166
DUBOIS John D72B
DUBUISSON Dominique V26B
DU CANN John see CANN John
Duchess (Bo Diddley's
sister) D66
DUCK Ian B23 C173A H148 J72
J110
DUCKLES Lawrence L10B
DUCKS D122C
DUCKS DELUXE D123
DUCLOS Herve F4B
DUCKWORTH Dell S120
DUCKWORTH Ian S295A
DUCKWORTH John S360
DUCKWORTH Jim F8C
DUCONGE Wendel D96
DUDANSKI Richard B45F O25 R17
DUDECK Gerd G47 G120 H57A K98
DUDEK Les A38 B57A B114B D1A
D124 M159 M229 S36
DUDES D125
DUDGEON Alec B51
DUDGEON Gus A118 B178 C78 J72
J86 K78 M50 R46 S130 T36 T45
W49
DUDGEON John S261A
DUDLEY Cordell D24
DUDLEY Lee P76B
DUDLEY Michael S193B
DUDLEY Ron K10
DUDLEY Tony A74
DUDMAN Colin T76
DU DOIT Brigette E66
DUDZIAK Viszula S73C U21
DUELKS Skip R83
DUESENBERG D125B
DUFALL Dick B209 F48B
DUFFELL Bee M188
Duffo D125A
Duffy D126
DUFFY John A121 S73B
DUFFY Ray C13 E41 F55 G6 J60
K24 M108 N45C S198
DUFFY Tom A73 B79 H87 L80
W133
DUFINE Jeff W11
DUFORT Dave A133 E8
DUFORT Denise G37
DUFRANE Marcel U17
DUFRESNE Didier B164A
DUGAN Irv D71

EDWARDS Jackie D82 E19C
EDWARDS Jang E19D
EDWARDS Jimmy T166A
EDWARDS John (B) G94 T173
EDWARDS John (D) S249C V28
EDWARDS John (Trom) H183 S31
EDWARDS Jonathan E20 H35 O33A
EDWARDS Joseph R124A
EDWARDS Juma H99
EDWARDS Keith S74A
EDWARDS Kenny B175 C63D C171 C180 D18 G60 K86 M108 R22 R137 S196 S269 S282 T32B W9 W21 Z11
EDWARDS Kevin S216B
EDWARDS Liz R174
EDWARDS Lyn P136
EDWARDS Lynnie E20
EDWARDS Max P2
EDWARDS Mike E34
EDWARDS Mike L95A
EDWARDS Nokie V19 V24
EDWARDS Pete 'Plug' L142 S302A
EDWARDS Rob C168 D10 T149B
EDWARDS Rod A98A C159 G35 M45 M58B P77B S177D
EDWARDS Ron T12
EDWARDS Roy E21 J8 R6
EDWARDS Scott A31 A52 A59 B47A B50 B127 B225 B226 C17 C38A C58 C173 C246 E40 E71 F92 H9 H92 J73A J91A J113 K45 M75 M160 M218 M229 R78 R101 R115 R142A S34 S36 S228 S254B S333A S362 W6 W84C W119
EDWARDS Si B41 M11
EDWARDS Skip B154A E23 F50
EDWARDS Steve (G) E38
EDWARDS Steve (G) M123
EDWARDS Stoney E20A
EDWARDS Teddy J97 W116A
EDWARDS Terry W18
EDWARDS Terry N41
EDWARDS Tony P59B S16 W38
EDWARDS HAND E21
EELA CRAIG E21A
Eelco see GELLING Eelco
EFENDI Curtis E21B
EFENDIS GARDEN E21B
EFETTE Steve F2
EFFERTZ Heiko T103A
EFFORD Bob C2 C161C F42 K84 S31
EFTHIMIAN Chris C95A
EGAN Joe C127 E22 F7 N57 R11 S257
EGAN Mark G110 M107 M138A S17
EGAN Mary G100 W11
EGAN Mike L63 W7
EGAN Nick H184A T36A
EGAN Rusty R79 S140 V35A
EGAN Walter E23 M57C
EGDEN Bill J8
EGG E24
EGGERMONT Joap G64
EGGLI Roli T35
EGGS OVER EASY E24A
EGILSSON Arni W6
EGO E24B
EGOSARIAN George J105C
EHART Phil H4 K9 L95C W15B
EHINGER Jim B104B B233 C184A S358 W93
EHRIG Joachim H. 'Eroc' E63 G106
EHRLICH Jesse A59 B15 B256 C161B G76C P28 R62 R111B S116 W6 W92
EHRMANN Gerd D143
EICHER Martin G84B
EICHER Stephan G84B
EICHLER Glenn F8A
EICHLER J. G79
EIDE Pjouken P117C 801 E24C
EIGHTEEN CARAT GOLD E25
EIJAS Andrew A4
EIK Alf Emil E25A
EILLEDGE Gareth N19
EIRE EMPIRE E26
EISBERNER Jeff C138C
EISEN Steve S314
EISENBARGER Tony B225
EISENBERG Fran S121
EISENBERG Naomi Ruth H112

EISERLING Ric S173C
EISLER Paul S100
EKHARDT Ernie C234
EKLUND Christer A4 B193 T104
EKLUND Peter A37
EKLUND Torbjorn H18
EKMAN Pelle H18
EKSEPTION E27
EL Edward C239
ELAM Lawrence M136B
ELASTIC BAND E28
ELBERT Donnie E29
ELBØL Jens M147
ELBRACHT Peter Y4C
EL CHICANO E30
EL COCO E31
ELDER Coon see COON
ELDER BAND
ELDER Lynn G96
ELDERS E31B
EL DIN Cary Sharraf W22
ELDERADO Frankie E33C
ELDRIDGE Ben A121 S73B
ELDRIDGE Bill P19
ELDRIDGE Robert W119
ELECTRA E31D
ELECTRA FIVE E31E
ELECTRIC BANANA E31F P128

ELECTRIC CHAIRS E32
ELECTRIC FLAG E33
ELECTRIC LIGHT ORCHESTRA E34
ELECTRIC PRUNES E35
ELECTRIC SANDWICH E34A
ELECTRIC STRING BAND E35A
ELECTRIC SUN E34B
ELECTRIC TOILET E35D
ELECTRICS E34C
ELECTRO Dan D55
ELECTROPHON E35B
ELEKLAD Mohamed M78
ELEKTRICS E34C
ELEM Robert 'Big Mojo' E35C H37 S329
Elephant (GLASS Dick) E36
ELEPHANTS MEMORY E37
ELEVATORS E37A
ELEVENTH HOUSE C189
ELEY Lewis S215
ELF E38
ELFENBEIN Jay K69
ELFMAN Danny O13A
ELFIELD Dennis W54B
ELGART Billy M229B
EL HABASHI Nagi L79
EL HABIB Absalm F121
EL HADI Suliaman L22
ELI Bobby B135 J92 L130 O14 P59C P80 T42
ELIAS Ivan K59 R144A S331A
ELIAS Manny I23A
ELIAS HULK E38A
ELIASSEN Dan B181B
ELIJAH HORN SECTION R54
ELIOT Earl R177
ELISCU Bob B91A P118
Elizabeth P49
ELIZABETH E39
ELIZALDE Ed T114
ELKINS Alfred B95B B193 C135 H170 J79 M129 P142 S358 W93
ELKINS Gilly C185A
Ella Guru see DAVIDSON Greg
ELLAR Colin D16
Ellen S334
ELLER James C42 L16C L135 T37A
ELLEY Jeannie H49
ELLI Joseph Jr C63C
ELLICOTT Rod B63 C158 P114
ELLIMAN Kevin R164
ELLIMAN Yvonne C35C C121 E40 L120 M101
ELLINGTON David C38A H52A R127C S269
ELLINGTON Eric E41
ELLINGTON Jay S213
ELLINGTON Joan D76 F48F V21
ELLINGTON Judy D76 F48F V21

ELLINGTON Karen E41
ELLINGTON Marc E41 F6 M108 T79
ELLINGTON Pat D76 F48F V21
ELLIOT Brian B49
ELLIOT Cass B99 E42 M61 M101 M224 S276
ELLIOT Colonel E43
ELLIOT Jack R169
ELLIOT Ken B21 H172 J94 M221A S67 S76 T149
ELLIOT Nigel B154B
ELLIOT Ramblin' Jack D139 O6 P137 S55A
ELLIOT Ray T57 T125
ELLIOT Rob C88 S67 S303
ELLIOT Tony S76
ELLIOTT Bill S220
ELLIOTT Bill (K) D133A E20 M96 M229B N45B O33A R148 W21 W119B
ELLIOTT Bobby H132
ELLIOTT David E44 K87
ELLIOTT Dennis F41 F84 H185 I8 L98
ELLIOTT Don (Vibes) A135 S125
ELLIOTT Don (B) M66
ELLIOTT Don (V) N35
ELLIOTT Graham M80
ELLIOTT Jeff M136C
ELLIOTT Joe D40B
ELLIOTT Judy A132 T93
ELLIOTT Ken (K) B21
ELLIOTT Kenneth (D) B127 P21
ELLIOTT Lindsay H26A
ELLIOTT Marion see STYRENE Poly
ELLIOTT Mary O18
ELLIOTT Mike F90A
ELLIOTT Oona F51
ELLIOTT Paul T138B
ELLIOTT Ron B61 C50 C220B E45 G26C L58 L89 M10A M203 N40 P16
ELLIOTT Stuart A22 B280 B286 D9 D36 D127C E77A H26A I20 O18B P31 R46 R51 S270 T77 V16 W86 Z4
ELLIOTT William S63
ELLIS E46
ELLIS Alan C101
ELLIS Art R31
ELLIS Bobby A6 B101 B234 B276 C139 C245 D71A G39 I12 L58A P140C R29 R35B R84 R134 T110 W4
ELLIS Brad A30B
ELLIS Chris D46B H184A
ELLIS Danny P25 R162
ELLIS Dave E47 M99 S270
ELLIS Denny S74C
ELLIS Don K81 Z8
ELLIS Glyn see FONTANA Wayne
ELLIS Herb H63 P129
ELLIS Ian C142 G92D S31
ELLIS Ivan G3B
ELLIS Jerry E37A
ELLIS Jimmy E22
ELLIS Jock K94A M86 M101
ELLIS Joe G84
ELLIS John (G) V28
ELLIS John (Oboe) C164 F78
ELLIS Joseph M203
ELLIS Keith B191 J105 K79 V11 W70 W89
ELLIS Ken C209
ELLIS Mark(G) R15B
ELLIS Mark (B) L12A
ELLIS Matthew E48
ELLIS Maurice C114 S93
ELLIS Mundy O18
ELLIS Nancy M203
ELLIS Pee Wee B157 C168A E49 F80 L67B M203 M238 P72A
ELLIS Robin M50
ELLIS Roger E19B
ELLIS Stephen S336
ELLIS Steve B39 E46 W74
ELLIS Terry J58

ELLISON Andy D28 J57 J75 R10
ELLISON James L4
ELLISON Lorraine E49A K81
ELLISON Mel B109
ELLISON Monti W30A
ELLISON Stan N45A
ELLNER Kenn C199A
ELLORY Jack B5 S157 W86
ELLSON Paul S304
ELLWOOD Alan A73A
ELLWOOD Robert A73A
ELMER GANTRY'S VELVET OPERA E50
ELMER James B261
ELMIGER Billy A28C
ELMORE Greg Q12
EL MOLINA BAND C39B
ELO Michael S108C
ELOY E50A
EL SADOUN Hadi H186
ELSON Derek D39C
ELSON Ken F140D
ELSON Richard B116A
ELSTAR John F94 H116A
ELSTON Charlie P75
ELSWIT Rik B63 D85 S120
ELTES Polly E59
ELUSION E50B
ELVIN Chris F40
ELVIN D.G. H128A
ELWOOD Danny T111
ELWORTHY Billy B169A F67B F101C
ELY Joe A35D E51
ELY Ken J4
ELY Vince H124B P142C
ELYBAM Rich Y5B
ELYE David Norris S72
ELZE Rudiger H125B R22A
Embamba D127
EMBLOW Jack C78 C251 D54 D99 F70B G50 H11 H67 J72 L142A M25 N57 S108 S209 S235 S295 T135A W10
EMBRYO E52
EMELIN John L122A
EMERGENCY E52A
EMERICK Geoff B59
EMERICK Randy C150
EMERINE Larry M75
EMERSON Bill A121 D85
EMERSON Billy 'The Kid' E52B L94 H5
EMERSON Howard A59 J69 S331A
EMERSON Keith A84 E52C – E53 F109 H29 N44 S273
EMERSON Vic H47 M67 S4
EMERSON LAKE AND PALMER E53
EMERY Pete K23
EMERY Steve J39B K63 K66 R142 S301
EMERY Terence (Perc) S157
EMERY Terry (Pno) T65
EMIGRE E53A
EMMA John C90 W68A
EMMANUEL Leroy C199B
EMMANUEL Mathew K41
EMMANUEL Tommy A22C
EMMERSON Les F59A S228A
EMMET Rick T142 T37A
EMMET Ted S136
EMMINES Bob B237
EMMONS Bobby B272 C14 C77A D53C E53B E57 G102 K30 K95 K96 L77 M78 N37 O15 P125 P137 S271 T55 T67A T107 V18
EMMONS Buddy B126 B210 C14 C39 C41 C77A C124 C164 D49 D53C D68B D70 D71 D93F E54 E73 E74 E75 G121 H49 H65 H102 L7 L36A L116 M27 M75 M95B N21 N23 N23A N37 O10 O46 P33 P74 R137 S58 S65 S116 S272 T150 Y18
EMO Chris W56
EMOTIONS E55
EMPENS Cam B57E
EMPERHOFF Wolfgang J10A
EMPEROR E55A
EMPHREY Caleb K45
ENCHANTERS M161

END E56
ENDRESSEN Sidsel L24C
ENDURO Charles M76A
ENETE George W128B
ENEVOLDSEN Robert K45
ENGBER Evan D88A
ENGEL Bertram B12A B268
ENGEL Brian L76B L124
ENGEL Burkhardt M45D
ENGEL Christian B59A
ENGEL Claud M49
ENGEL Mark N66
ENGEL Scott D8A W13A
ENGEL Soren D44B
ENGEL Tommi A99
ENGERLING BLUES BAND E56B
ENGH Anne E25A
ENGLAND E56A
ENGLAND DAN AND JOHN FORD COLEY E57
ENGLARD Don B81
ENGLE Tony C165
ENGLET Dan C28A
ENGLISCH Gerhard E21A
ENGLISH Billy N23A
ENGLISH Cherie P75
ENGLISH David see FRANKLIN Melvin
ENGLISH Jacqueline F. W119
ENGLISH Jimmy G85A
ENGLISH Joe B200 C173 K60 M9 S56 T9A
ENGLISH Paul N23A R173
ENGLISH CHAMBER CHOIR S177D V13 W7
ENGLISH CHORALE C201A
ENGLISH ROCK ENSEMBLE W7
ENGLISH TAPESTRY D68
ENID E58
ENKE Harmut A99
ENNES Willem A27 J2A S187
ENNIS Ralph S356
ENNIS Ray R6 S356
ENNIS Sue H75
ENO Brian A133 B186 C13 C145 D59 E24C E59 F121 L5A M81 M106 N45 Q13 R149 T8 T109A W135
ENODEX Ethel W119
ENRIGHT Tom S84A
ENRIQUE Mario J14
ENSINGER Matzi N46E
ENSOR Jeremy G97 P136
ENSSLIN Donald O24B
ENTESARI Fred A121B
ENTNER Warren G83
ENTWISTLE John D9 E60 F65 H110 L12 T122 W72
ENTWISTLE Keith S177D
EON E60A
EPHRON Mike H99
EPISODE SIX E61
EPITAPH E60B
EPP Fenrus (also BUDA Max; PARCELY Templeton; CRILL Connie) D17 K6 P14 R28A
EPPEL Dave C6
EPPING Rick S230
EPPOSLITTA Jim R16A
EPPS Joe O39
EPPS Preston E61A
EPPS Stuart S39 R46 S187
EPSILON E61B
EPSTEIN Bruce E40 Y14
EPSTEIN Howie P70 S98
EPSTEIN Jay A53A
EPSTEIN Michael S284C
EQUADORS B87
EQUALS E62
EQUATORS E62C
EQUINE Michael C56
ERAK Tom M123
ERBA Ermano Ghisia M211A
ERBE Micky-M238A
ERBEL Rainer C219B
ERBER Barb T12B
ERDMANN Dirk S38
ERELWINE Mike S73
EREMITA Ernie W199B
ERGO SUM E62A
ERICKSON Jimmy K44C
ERICKSON Pat B201
ERICKSON Roky E62B T64

GREEN Eddie (K) P37B
GREEN Eli M22
GREEN Emanuel 'Manny' D139
I2 J91A K81 O15
GREEN Eunice B19 M133
GREEN Gary G22 G41
GREEN Geo U23
GREEN George K84 N43A R122A
GREEN Graham O44 S193B
GREEN Guitar Slim see Guitar
Slim
GREEN Hurbie M75
GREEN Ian G92C Q1
GREEN Jack B168 G92D P128
GREEN Jack S329B
GREEN James B85B R168 S323
GREEN Jerome A83 B87 D66
GREEN Jesse R168
GREEN Jim S338
GREEN Joe J91A N23 P126
R133 S216
GREEN Joel C14
GREEN John D132
GREEN Karl H108
GREEN Kelly F120 S173C
GREEN Kim R53D
GREEN Larry C236
GREEN Lee L62
GREEN Lloyd B285 C14 C15
C155 L77 M33 N37 S10 S272
T107 Y18
GREEN Lyndon J27
GREEN Malcolm S221
GREEN Maxine D124 S36
GREEN Mi Mi W119
GREEN Mick K39 P89 S87
GREEN Peter B39 B83 B193
B250 D125A D129 F65F F66 G13
G94 M111 M129 S105 S166 S204
S211 S259 T144
GREEN Phil S339A
GREEN Rob G81
GREEN Steve M2
GREEN Stuart K42
GREEN Susaye S333A W119
GREEN Thurman P115
GREEN Urbie D50 M12 R100
S100 S168
GREEN William A11 D77 G121
K48 L66A R60C R97 S14C S325
T145
GREEN Willie Jnr. C179
GREEN BULLFROG G95
GREENAWAY Noel W15
GREENBAUM Norman D88A G96
GREENBAUM Peter See GREEN
Peter
GREENBERG Chick A121B S79
GREENBERG Dana L82A
GREENBERG Peter D1B
GREENBERG Phil F85C
GREENBERG Rick S350
GREENBERG Steven L82A
GREENBLATT Alan P61
GREENE Alan B207C
GREENE Aleta L58B
GREENE Dave S102B
GREENE Debbie A59 R22
GREENE Dennis S78
GREENE Ed A31 A35C B50 B53
B127 B194 B225 B256 B226 C12
C30 C38A C39 C58 C70A C153
C173 E57 E71 F4C F23A F92
F103D G17 G120A H8 H9 H122A
J73A J113 K45 K72 K94A L65
L107 M56 M65A M151 M160 M177
M227 M229 N23 P15 P76 P114
R54 R78 R87 R99 R101 R115
R142A S34 S58 S180 S180D
S228 S262 T118 T158 W44 W84C
GREENE Garry W132
GREENE Jack H49
GREENE Jeannie A28 D126E
G96A G96B H62 H169A K46 N55
P125 S36
GREENE Joe S252
GREENE Lorne O42
GREENE Marc T12
GREENE Marlin A28 G96A G96B
L50 N37 N55
GREENE Mike G96C
GREENE Mary C147
GREENE Peter Charles see
STIRLING Peter Lee
GREENE Richard B158 B210
C123 C200 C237 F27A F128 G9

H35 K81 K101 L110 M125
M229 M229A N32 O15 P49
Q15A R288 R148 S63 T25
T150 V3 W5
GREENE Ron M101
GREENE Schagzerig R127
GREENE Ted B284C
GREENE Two Button H14A
GREENFIELD Bob U5
GREENFIELD Dave S292
GREENFIELD Robert P81
GREENHALGH Alby W134A
GREENHALGH Tom M124
GREENHILL Mitch C179
GREENIDGE Robert C14 J41
L51 M17 M53 M191 M232
P15 P28 S124 S252 T143
GREENLEE Bob see RATTLES
Rattlesnake
GREENLEE Romell B43C
GREENMAN Chip F140A
GREENSLADE G97
GREENSLADE Arthur F14
F140
GREENSLADE Dave C166 F21
G97 G97A H66A H86 I8
GREENSPOON Jim B64A F8B
F94 F109 G24 M36 S265A
T32C T81
GREENWAY Brian A69 D125
GREENWAY Roland C236 K53
GREENWELL Jim L14
GREENWICH Ellie B139
B172A C229 G97B G109
S192B
GREENWOOD Al. F84 L98
S231A
GREENWOOD Chico E31F J27
J43A M114A M193
GREENWOOD Mick G98
GREENWOOD Nick G99 K35
GREENWOOD Paul A113A
GREER Hal C140
GREER Maretta F133
GREER Patty S238A
REER Rob C173
GREER Sonny M185
GREETHAM Charles D129
GREEZY WHEELS G100
GREFROH Nick A59
GREGER Max A59C
GREGG Bobby A59A C13 C51
C255 D139 G61 M37
GREGG Brian K39
GREGG Bruce S55B
GREGG Haden N53
GREGG Terry M95B
GREGOR Max J10A
GREGORIO Michael B244C
J88
GREGORY Bhakta W119
GREGORY Bill I31
GREGORY Byron C212B
GREGORY Byron L65
GREGORY David G2 X3
GREGORY D. Lloyd R60C
GREGORY George T. C195
GREGORY Glenn H82A
GREGORY James H16B L98
GREGORY Jim D108 F58
M154 W48B
GREGORY John B158 S63
GREGORY Michael A30 B95
C165 F132 H194
GREGORY Steve A25 B5 B25
B47C B79 B171 B209 C80
C101 F7 F14 F66 F88 G6
G49 G67 H65 H177 J5 K51
L63 L80 M145 M233 N18
N63B O20 Q6 P10 P124
P131 R46 R61A R86 R125
S176 S204 S211 S257 S285
T111 W24 W29A W58 Z4
GREGSON Clive A67C
GREGSON Milt P24B
GREIG Lanier F83E N50A
GREINER Gottfried L120
GREINER Manni S66A
GREMY Guy George L87
GRENJA Ed O32A
GRENNAN Winston C139 J48
K38 S125 T149 Y4B
GRESSETT Charlie B233
GRETTIE Anne D44B
GREVE Bob H96 R161
GREY Al B233

GREY Glenn C68
GREY Paul D10
GREY Robbie M175D
GREY Roger C55
GREY Steve T111 W13A W102
GREY Tom A121
GREZES Michael E69A
GRICE Brian D66 J9A
GRIDLEY TABERNACLE CHOIR
AND ORCHESTRA M166
GRIDLIN Maurice D135A
GRIEG Keith P88A
GRIEG Stan M129
GRIER Rosey J15
GRIERSON Ralph J93C N40
GRIFF Zaine G100A
GRIFFIN G101
GRIFFIN Bob C30
GRIFFIN Brian c15B
GRIFFIN Colin E56
GRIFFIN Dale 'Buffin' B219
M214
GRIFFIN Dick W30A
GRIFFIN Fred V17
GRIFFIN Gary B56 C62B L129
GRIFFIN Gerri V40
GRIFFIN James B206 F48
G101A
GRIFFIN Johnny D25 P34
GRIFFIN Martin H64 S290
GRIFFIN Paul A59 B262 C164
C185F D97A D132B D139 F60
F103 J48 J93D K55 K59 K81
L4A L69 L111 M26 M41 M75
M177 M203 N63D P149 R22
R25 R100 R159 R169 S124
S125 S262 T67A T79B W25
GRIFFIN Ray B242
GRIFFIN Reggie M65
GRIFFIN Stephen S327
GRIFFIN Thom T139A
GRIFFIN Timothy B168A
C136B
GRIFFIN Trevor P139D
GRIFFIN William A132 H11
GRIFFITH Bob J16B
GRIFFITH Johnny S128
GRIFFITH Marcia B163 M88
R134 V21
GRIFFITH Richard B183
GRIFFITHS Albert G39 P140C
T155A U4A
GRIFFITHS Andy W13B
GRIFFITHS Brian B98
GRIFFITHS Clive P37 T94
GRIFFITHS David (G/Vln)
H162 P42B T90
GRIFFITHS David (B) B209
GRIFFITHS Derek A77 B87
A92 B160 D91 S27 V26A Y11
GRIFFITHS Donald A107
B276
GRIFFITHS Geoff B119
GRIFFITHS Hugh P86
GRIFFITHS Jack H16 N59C
GRIFFITHS Jim C212
GRIFFITHS Malcolm A23
B229 C39A C109 C204 F7
F14 F42 F86 F88 G31 G67
H42 H154 K84 L23 M205
N63B R174 S186A T141 W71
GRIFFITHS Mark E41 H43
K24 M108 R80 S198 V30
GRIFFITHS Martin B74
GRIFFITHS Nick S140
GRIFFITHS Paul S237
GRIGG Roger S81A
GRIGGS Johnny B85
GRIGGS Kristy W107
GRIGGS Nigel S221
GRIGSBY Earl D12
GRILL Rob G83 G101B
GRILLO Carmen C70A W44
GRILLO M. J113
GRILLS Stuart S295A
GRIMA Charles D66 M180A
W122
GRIMALDI John A77
Grimes P53
GRIMES Carol C105 G102
K4 R106 R116 S348B U9
GRIMES Charlie H150 L50
M64
GRIMES Chris C96C
GRIMES Cloris J15
GRIMES Dougy C96C

GRIMES Howard G92 M172 P51
GRIMES Jed H87
GRIMES Jeffrey c53
GRIMES Tiny H63
GRIMES Ty B72 N21 W44
GRIMETHORPE COLLIERY BAND
H29
GRIMM David F51
GRIMM Joe P6 R169
GRIMM Steve B13A
GRIMMELL Chuck H150
GRIMMS G103
GRIN L107
GRINDELL Susan O13
GRINDERSWITCH G104
GRINEL Ron 'Crunchy' F82
K44C M191 S197 W16
GRINGO G105 S185
GRINNEDGE Robert B245 D72A
GRINSTEAD Dave C34
GRISHAM Doyle B261 C194
E57 P137 S32 T9
GRISMAN David C38A C211
E5 E20 G84 H86 M21 M136C
M229 M229A O15 O17 R22
R137 S27B S65 T22 T25
GRISWOLD Whit M227
GRITS Vanilla D8
GROB Jeff L119B
GROBSCHNITT G106
GROCHMAL Jack N23
Groco I12
GRODANIER Lisa B174
GRODY Dion O6C
GRODY Gordon B57A B105 F4C
I2 L119 M160 S121 S215
S262
Grock D59A
GROEBER Andreas see GEE
Andy
GROENING Jan C243 F132B
M237A
GROENKE Randy M113
GROETZINGER Alain R123B
GROFF Joe R15B
GROGAN Cavan C215
GROGAN Clare A45A
GROGER Fritz M136B
GROH Muck G112D I11A
GROLNICK Don A96 B65 B85
B110 B208 C44 C189 D115
F60 F103D F122 G60 H29 J48
J88 K17 M65A M75 M107 P72A
R22 R135A R137 R159 S17
S36 S124 S125 S180 S196
S215 S252 S262 T25 T44
T67A T98 T147
GROMBACHER Myron B80B D53
M11B
GROMBECH Niels S108C
GROMER Alois A57A B91A
N61C P118
GRONCKI Darlene N23
GRONCIN Jack T65
GRONDIN Paul L66B
GRONENTHAL Max B114B D1A
T12
GROOM Don O42
GROOM Lynn G40
GROOM Mick D123 T170
GROOM Roger N5
GROOME Andy L22B
GROOME Len N55
GROOMS Sherry N23 R4
GROOTNA G107
GROOVY Winston G108
GROPP Gerry J53
GROS Axel E59
GROSCHNER Rolf I14A
GROSHONG James R140A
GROSLIE Helge T97
GROSS David g11B
GROSS Henry C51B C229 -
G109 S78
GROSS Jeff C76
GROSS Jill H189
GROSS John B141 B171
GROSS Tim A14
GROSS Uli K44B
GROSS Zelda G109
GROSSART Andy R1
GROSSKOPF Harald A99 C192
G3A G109A S43 W13D
GROSSLERDER Gunther M153
GROSSMAN Hal M228

GROSSMAN Jerry S124
GROSSMAN Lloyd C173A
GROSSMAN Neal C173A
GROSSMAN Severin A32
GROSSMAN Stefan B18 C183
E70 G110 M238 R66 S125
GROSSMAN Steve D27
GROSSMITH Dave C191
GROSSMITH Derek D131 M50
GROSSO Monica S186
GROSVENOR Luther A87 D39B
G111 H40 J9 M214 S224 S257
W74
GROTH Michael T138B
GROUCUTT Kelly E34
GROUNDHOGS G112 H150 M44
GROUNDSTROEM Mans T15 W75
GROUP 87. G111A
GROUP THERAPY G111B
GROVE Ben F74C
GROVER Bob P88B
GROVER David B109 G121 H96
R161 W8
GROVER Pat B250 B277 M90
S166
GROVES Lani A123 B139 B41
B169A C155 D53 E49 E73 F60
G4 G64 G64C H137 H164C I2
J20 J69 K46 L109 L119 M46B
M157 O35 P6 P72A R28B R100
S17 S124 S262 S362 T37E T65
T98 T147 V12 W107 W119
GROVES Mick C25B
GROVES Moss B82
GROW UP G112B
GROWING CONCERN G112C
GROWL G112A
GRUBER Craig E38 O48 R14
GRUDE Wolfgang C96A
GRUDGE Michael B204
GRUE Thomas S249B
GRUEN Peter P109A
GRUMBKOW Joachim H125B
GRUN Uli B182A
GRUNBLATT Georges H89A
GRUND Alfred B92
GRUND Atli B92
GRUND Peter B92
GRUNDSTROEM Mans T104
GRUNDY Ed B142
GRUNDY Hugh Z15
GRUNDY Malcolm G64A
GRUNSKY Jack G112D S42E
GURPALLO Patrice G123
GRUPP Paul O46
GRUPPO SPORTIVO G113
GRUSHECKLY Joe I24A
GRUSIN Dave A123 B63 F119A
G4 G113A J43 L79 M102 M218
R99 R108 W25 W27 W31 V6
GRUSIN Don C213E R15 R99
W32A
GRUSKA Jay D106G G101B R81
GRUSKA Michele D106G R4
GRYPHON G114
G10'S F54
GUARD Barry B250 C161C D102
K22A M157 O18B W86
GUARD Catherine S272
GUARD Croxley S272
GUARD Dave B256
GUARDIAN ANGELS F74
GUARINO Jasper D126B S340
GUARINO Massimo C116A O33D
GUARNERI Mario C179
GUARRCINE Gianni C116A
GUASTELLA Joe F97
GUBER Barry P53
GUCCIO Mario M30A
GUOMAND Ken D49 S3G S249B
S295 T79D
GUENTHER I. C140 L74
GUERCIO James William B56
L10 M232 S197 W97A
GUERIN Bob T67
GUERIN Jean E62A
GUERIN John A31 A59 A132
B17A B47E B49 B110 B149
B194 B226 B245 B285 C15B
C36 C247 E15 E57 E62A E74
F34 F103D G10 G14 H5C H12A
H37A H39 H156 K99A L1 L108
M27 M125 M170 M229A N58C
O15 P33 P50 P115 P129 R22
R28B R76 R108 R164 S50 S58
S111 S196 S213 S327A T21
T98 T107 Z8

GUERINO Pete G112C
GUERRA Bill T147
GUERRERO Kiko I13B
GUESS Don H134
GUESS WHO G115
GUEST Christopher N10 W5
GUEST Elenor K72
GUEST Gus H158
GUEST Lynton L129A
GUEST Reg F55 H180
GUEST William K72
GUEVARA Alex V12
GUFFEY Bill S103A
GUGGER Max b154E
GUGLIAMO Clapton T102
GUICHARD Pierre A64
GUIDERA Tom A121 H35 R137
GUIDOTTI Bobby N46A P114
GUIDRY Robert see CHARLES
Bobby
GUILBEAU Floyd 'Gib' C96B
C160 C180 C216 D28 F74 G116
G121 N5A P32 R137 S114 S196
S269 S341 W43
GUILBEAU C155
GUILINO John D50
GUILLARD Alain F4B
GUILLARD Yves F4B
GUILLERY Adrian H59 J54
GUILLON Dominique L87
GUILLORY Isaac A33 B226 C241A
D99 G116A M38 P5 P124 S270
W128
GUILLOTINE G116C
GUIMUNGIE O'Neil E78
GUINN Marty N53
GUISHARD Jeffrey H111E
GUITAR Johnny C199
Guitar Buddy F66
Guitar Junior N46D
Guitar Slim (STEPHENSON James
also GREEN Guitar Slim) B17B
G116B
GUTTIERREZ Steven H96 L28
GULGOWSKI Wlodek D72 M45C
P109 U21
GULINO Danny S157
GULLAND Brian G14 M57D T79
GULLEY Dennis J14A
GULLEY Russell J14A
GULLICKSON Grant B164
GULLICKSON Lance B164
GULLIKSEN Eric O33C
GULLIVER G117
GULLIVER Randy E19B
Guly M212A
GUMBLEY Steve C209
GUMBO John D86
GUMBS F. E78
GUMBS Onaje Allan G110 W62
GUN G117A
GUN B.B. P53
GUN CLUB G117B
GUNDY Walter I16
GUNN John L22B
GUNN Peter I18A
GUNN Phil R42
GUNN Ray N31
GUNN Tommy A55
GUNN Tommy (G)P87A

GUNNARSON Rutger A4
GUNNELS Gene S294
GUNNING Chris Y14
GUNNING John Francis M18
GUNNIP Daniel M18
GUNNIP David M18
GUNTER Arthur G119
GUNTER Cornel C146
GUNTHER Michel A19A
GUNTHER Paul B233
GURL Steve B5 J93 K22A W79
GURLAND Bob B57A
GURLEY James B94 J95
GURTLER Bob P53
GURU GURU G120
GURU RAMDAS SINGERS R101
GURVITZ Adrian (CURTIS
Adrian) B20 E18 G117A G120A
M151 T82
GURVITZ Paul (CURTIS Paul)
B20 E18 G117A G120A M151 P29B
T82 W72
GUSS Beau M191
GUSTAFSON John A131E A133 B26A

B98 C127 C171 F24 F42 G31
G35 H4 H21 H185
M34 M136 O8 P76 Q4 R149
S39 S355A
GUSTAVSON Jukka T104 W75
GUSTAVSON Owe H18
GUSTIN Gerard C137
GUTCHEON Jeff B221 G72
G87 H182 M228 M229 S252
GUTE Joe R177
GUTHEIL Daryl S299A
GUTHRIE Arlo D101 G121
GUTHRIE Bob M185 W85
GUTHRIE Gwen A123 B141
C155 D63 F60 J20 J69 L109
M17 M107 M222A P126 S169
T98 T114 V17
GUTHRIE James A48
GUTHRIE Woody G121 T53A
GUTIERREZ Robert B244 G24
GUTIERREZ Steve B52A
GUTH John A35C
GUTMAN Jon C140A
GUY Art S173C
GUY Barry D108 S267
GUY Billy C146 P75
GUY Buddy G122 H159 H170
L94 M129 T79B W47 W94
GUY Denny G122A
GUY Eddie R46
GUY Philip G122 M129 W47
GUY Thomas G122A
GUYLER Nick B93A
GUZENSLAW Brothers N23A
GUZIE Andy P141A
GUZMAN Ed D101 R32
GWENDAL G123
GWINN Marty B47A R101
GWYNN Marty M111 N45C
GWYNNE Michael F51
GYAN Kiki O34 Q1 W82A
GYPSY G124
GYPSY A53A
Gypsy Dave D99
GYTHFELDT Paddy H5B

H. Annette I5B
H. Charlie D87A
H.P. LOVECRAFT H1
HAAN Jenny B5 B54 S303
HAAPALA Eino F123 S14B
HAAS Andy M95A S288A
HAAS Chris D57D L66C
HAAS Daniel A64
HAAS James E C180 C185A
D74 E15 E40 K59 M102 O2B
P85 Q3A R101 S36 S228A
T94A
HAAS Steve C189 P45
HAAS Wendy A136 C45 F8B
G26D M65A O35 S19
HAASE Roland S289
HAASTRUP Joni M53
HABAN Andy W82
HABAN Tom W82
HABDURIAN Armand T109
HABENICHT Martin A67A
HABER Jim see DOMINO
Floyd
HABERLAND Margit Maya
R63
HABERMAN Steve B42B C217
HABIB Don W101
HABIBYYA H2
HABLAS Chico Y5A
HACKAMORE BRICK H2A
HACKENSACK H3
HACKER Melvyn M47C
HACKETT John H4 P72
HACKETT Steve B34 G21
H4
HACKMAN Paul H89C
HACKSHAW Alan M125
HACON Walter W130
HADAWAY B. T37L
HADAWAY Henry R124
HADDEN Roger G25A H115
HADDRELL Bob H111
HADEN Charlie B131 M79
M138A

HADEN John P24A
HADJAJE Paul S280
HADJIATHANASSIOU George
HADLEY Gillian P51
HADLEY Leroy T55
HADLEY Tony S203A
HADNOTT Billy F134 W13
HAEDER Manfred F101D
HAEFFNER Nick T36A
HAEHL Steve S91
HAENY John D103 R148A
T113
HAESEVEETS J.L. C190
HAGA John H198
HAGAN Dennis T33A
HAGAN Donnell F103 O48
HAGANS Robert 'Buddy' D96
HAGAR Ernie C173
HAGAR Sammy H5 M187
HAGBERG Garry D112A
HAGEL John P53
HAGEN Dean P69
HAGEN Nina H5A
HAGEN Russell R22
HAGEN Tiny M136B
HAGER Jim H5C
HAGER John H5C
HAGERS H5C
HAGGERTY Terry H45 S189
HAGGSTROM Bo M45C
HAGLER Larry R137
HAGLER Sherry B108
HAGLER Stephen S246
HAGLEY Bernard J94 T131
HAGOOD Kenneth D27
HAGOPIAN Hovaness M192B
HAGSTROMM Bosse S186 W22
HAGUE Ian F21 J8
HAGUE Steve E23 J105A L20
T137A
HAHN Jerry H5D S125
HAHN Mark L102
HAHNFELD Jorg H18B
HAIDER Joe S73C
HAIG Al D27
HAIGHT Lenny M11
HAINES D. N63A
HAINES Chris F120A
HAINES Dennis D94 D112A
F8 N63A
HAINES James E38A
HAINES Jimmy D49
HAINES Norman C78 L104
HAIR H5B
HAKANSSON Kenny H18
HAKARNARSON Gunnar S358F
HAKIM Omar G3B
HAKIN Alan S157
HAKINSSON Kim P10
HAKKINEN Cisse H190
HALDANE Stan B188
HALE Bob G82
HALE Corky B226 C164 M65A
S257
HALE Gerry S181 T37H
HALE Jack B202 C50 C231
D86 D101 F50 G92 G101A
J85A M130 N57 P51 P137
S276
HALE Keith C175
HALE Malcolm S203
HALE Mike M106B
HALE Otis A1 S20
HALE Owen G85A
HALE Teddy Q5
HALE Willie see Little
Beaver
HALEE Roy B141 B149B N55
HALES Geoffrey A41 O33G
HALES Jeff C6B
HALEX Harry N4
HALEY Bill (V/G) H6
HALEY William John Clifton
'Bill' (Sax) W30
HALF JAPANESE H6A
HALFBREED H7
HALFORD Paul see MOPED
Johnny
HALFORD Rob J102
HALINKOVICH Anatole B197
HALKITIS Arris A67E
HALL Albert A109 A120 F14
F70B R48
HALL Anita h70
HALL Bart H156 S213

HALL Bob (Big Sunflower)
A50A B154B B250 B277 D128
F50B G112 K22A K81 M90
M238 P142 R122A R143 S31
T23 T130 W89 W91 W131
HALL Bobbye Porter A11 A37
A60 B8 B25 B80 B168 B169
B180 B282 B283 C9A C11B
C38A C52A C76 C111A C123
C158 C171 C180 C220 C235
D99 D101 D103 D139 E57 E71
F78 F134 G9 G17 H7B J46
J95 K48 K81 K95 L31 K96
L63 L107 L146 M16 M75 M101
M170 M227 M229 N40 N45B
N46 O15 O46 P3 P106 P126
R28B R101 R107 R113 R142A
S34 S36 S58 S65 S116 S160
S213 S269 T25 T107 U18 W6
W9 W10A W44 W16 W119 Y14
HALL Bruce R1A
HALL Carl A37 D53 K45 L4A
P6 P149 R22 S124 T65 W51
W107
HALL Carol H7C H98
HALL Cathy G116A
HALL Chris M157
HALL Christopher D33B
HALL Cliff D104 H111 M15A
O18B S34 S80
HALL Clinton R35B
HALL Coffi M60 M135
HALL Clarence D96
HALL Daniel Lee B27
HALL Daryl F121 H7A H9
G117
HALL Dave E34D
HALL Debbie J16 N41
HALL Derek S166
HALL Dolores A102 K48
M232A P6 R125
HALL Donna C207 H7D M93
W54
HALL Dwight 110B
HALL Earl P. N25
HALL George F19
HALL Ges P142B
HALL Harry F109
HALL Jack H7D W54 Y6
HALL James (K) D39 H116A
L117 M157
HALL Janine S11
HALL Jim (B) E9
HALL Jimmy (V/Hca/Sax) A38
D12 G104 H7D L146 S277 W54
Y6
HALL Joe B122 H7E
HALL John (D) E62
HALL John (V/G/K) B244 C45
H8 K8 K81 L89 L111 M53 O32
R22 R117A S124 W5
HALL John (K) P139
HALL Lani (Mrs Lani Alpert)
H8A V9A
HALL Larry A131 E7 J72
M225 R161 W32A
HALL Lon R1A
HALL Mama W54
HALL Pam M221D
HALL Patricia B168 S262
HALL Patti L55
HALL Randy D27
HALL Rene C96 C146 D97 W30
W87
HALL Richard 'Dirty Harry'
B276 H122 I12 P134 R84 W4
HALL Rick W16A
HALL SHARKEY C96
HALL Susan M96 S192B W54
HALL Terry S207
HALL TOAD T102
HALL Tom C15A M151
HALL Tommy T64
HALL Tony (Mel) C165 T6
W123
HALL Tony (Sax) G32
HALL Vivian 'Talent' A6
R84
HALL Wayne C196
HALL Willie B155 B180 B238
B242 C58 C231 E55 G102
H65A H92 K46 L90 M75 N23
S55A
HALL AND OATES H9
HALL-SMITH Vanessa F132
HALLAWELL Jame I. S290

Haller Val E32
HALLERAU Jean-Luc S280
HALLEY Dick B254
HALLGREN Bo W22
HALLIDAY Hugh 'Pigmy' U14
HALLIDAY Stuart A34 N27
HALLIFAX Kalvyn E31E
HALLIGAN Dick B141 K81 M13
S20
HALLIN Pete P125
HALLING Patrick H168
HALLING Peter D99 H168
HALLMAN Mark E51 K48 N12A
W11
HALLMARK Bill G62A
HALLS Mick B250
HALM Rolf V26C
HALMAN Terry P59B
HALPIN Mike S314
HALPRIN Diana S100
HALSALL Ollie A133 B191 C13
D7 E59 G103 F20 I20 K81 K97
O40 P37 R106 R175 S35 S238C
T40 T94 Y10
HALSEY John A82 C79 D37 H29
H123 I20 M15 P37 P45 P138 R60
HALSTEAD Layne B69
HALVERSEN Tom R178
HALYNISSON Haflidr E35A
HAM Bill F116 Y6B
HAM Greg M130A
HAM Lori S325
HAM Pete B16 H39 I33
HAM Phil S211
HAM Warren B142
HAMANE Michael A53
HAMANN Ken J31
HAMBERG Hilary B269A
HAMBERG Martin G35A
HAMBLETON Fergus H9A
HAMBLETON Greg H9A
HAMBLY Pat S249A
HAMBRICK Clayton S73B
HAMBRICK Warren Y15
HAMBURG Dan F133
HAMBY Mark S96A
HAMEL Peter Michael A19A B91A
H9B
HAMER Bert C184B
HAMER Ian B19 B59 S96 T76
HAMER Stu J8
HAMILL Claire H11 H168 J87B
W14
HAMILTON A. S251
HAMILTON Alexander J22
HAMILTON Andy M41A
HAMILTON Bob H46
HAMILTON Chico H10
HAMILTON Chuck J21
HAMILTON David P40
HAMILTON Dick B149
HAMILTON Dan H10A K38
HAMILTON Edwin F26
HAMILTON Glen A. B80B
HAMILTON Jackie M192
HAMILTON Janet T98
HAMILTON Joe W16A
HAMILTON John D73 R15 R150B
HAMILTON Kirk C234A N63D T67A
HAMILTON Mike F39 L109 P109A
HAMILTON Milton Y2A
HAMILTON Ralph C146 F134 R111
HAMILTON Scott R125
HAMILTON Tom A16
HAMILTON Tony P8BA
HAMILTON Wally B16A
HAMILTON FACE BAND H11A
HAMLETT Ian C3
HAMLISCH Marvin B53
HAMMEL Dave P54
HAMMER Chuck B186 R60
HAMMER Ian F14
HAMMER Jan A4A B64 B169 B253
C129 C147 D72 F17 H12 J76 M40
M84D M102 S19 S42C S73C W62
W90
HAMMER Jeff T37A
HAMMER Lonny N48A
HAMMER Ralph E. C155 S251
W119
HAMMER Robert C232
HAMMER H12A
HAMMERSMITH H12B
HAMMETT Rick M227

[659]

HAMMILL Peter F121 H13 S48 V11	HANSI BIEBL BAND B91D	HARE Pat B127 L94 P26 W28	HARRINGTON Jula A2E	HARRIS Peppermint T53A
HAMMON Randy S29	HANSKI Ilka T104	HARGIS Marlon E77	HARRINGTON Terry B256 K48 W84C	HARRIS Pete P47
HAMMOND Albert C78 F13 H14	HANSON Bob F133	HARGIS Regi B212	HARRIOT Joe A120 N44 P8 W94	HARRIS Peter P102D
HAMMOND Don W5	HANSON Bryan c57	HARGREAVES Trevor D92	HARRIOTT Derrick H33	HARRIS Phil A7 C131
HAMMOND Jeffrey J58	HANSON Chris B116	HARGRETT Charlie B123	HARRIS Addie S98	HARRIS Ray B5 Y2
HAMMOND John Paul B144 C203 D139 F19 H15 J46 J78	HANSON David G70	HARGROVE Linda A102 C151D H26 J30 N25 R173	HARRIS Alan K65 M45	HARRIS Richard F103
HAMMOND Kevin B30	HANSON Dick C42 D1C D10A E19 F47 G1 G49 G89 I18A L12A L59 M10C M41A P25 R162 S268 S283B S327B S332 S348 W130	HARINEN Leo I13A	HARRIS Alan UBA	HARRIS Roger F128
HAMMOND Laurence H14A		HARKER Malcolm I17A	HARRIS Andrew J79	HARRIS Ron L65
HAMMOND Laurie M46		HARKER Roland G10 J72 S266 W86	HARRIS Beaver M79	HARRIS Roy C35D
HAMMOND Paul A115 H21		HARKIN Brendan B27 F108A P19A S254	HARRIS Bill C144A	HARRIS Scottie R115
HAMMOND Peter S289A	HANSON Junior (MARVIN J.H.) B276 D49 H17 L11 L101 M88 R84 W23 W111	HARKIN Pattie Dandy F108A	HARRIS Bob L51 Z8 Z11	HARRIS Sean D61
HAMMOND Phil P19		HARKLEROAD Bill B72 M58	HARRIS Bunny H133	HARRIS Shakey Jake H37 M48 S329
HAMMOND Ronnie A111	HANSON Lars B13A R73	HARKNESS Col S214E	HARRIS Carol B254C	HARRIS Shane P53
HAMMOND Steve A40 A111 F21 F24 F29 H121 P76 S355	HANSON Rolf C86	HARLAND Kelly A125 L30	HARRIS Charles D. R101	HARRIS Shaun H37A M86A W53
HAMMOUDI Basil O30A	HANSON Ronnie S286B	HARLEQUINN H26C	HARRIS Clara O18	HARRIS Steve I25 K29A
HAMPSON Danny M175E	HANSON Silver L1A	HARLEY Andy A33	HARRIS Cliff (also FOX Cliff) M175	HARRIS Sue A30 H194 K65 T79 UBA
HAMPTON Dave T5B	HANSON Simon O40	HARLEY Mel A67C	HARRIS Damon T42	HARRIS Tat W28
HAMPTON Greg K49A	HANSON Steve O24C	HARLEY Pat W86	HARRIS Dan H37A M8GA W53	HARRIS Ted B282
HAMPTON Ian B43C S205	HANSON Tom P137	HARLEY Sam A22 A33 P19	HARRIS Davis B17A	HARRIS Tim F90A
HAMPTON John H125A	HANSSON Bo H18 H18A	HARLEY Steve (NICE Steven) H26A M35 P31 W7	HARRIS Dennis B135 C203 L69 M2 O14 P56B	HARRIS Tony E66 O18B
HAMPTON Lionel C186	HANSSON AND KARLSSON H18A		HARRIS Diana (K V) T136	HARRIS Troy W119
HAMPTON Michael B183 F137 P29	HANUMAN H18B	HARLEY Wayne P49	HARRIS Diane (V) A35D R31	HARRIS Tweed G26A H175
HAMS Dr John D21	HAPLIN Tom M203	HARLING Cyril L137	HARRIS Don S230	HARRIS Voyle R22
HAMSON George B47D	HAPPENER Paul O37	HARLINGTON Roy M166A	HARRIS Don 'Sugarcane' (Vln) D97 H34 H99 H150 L83A M68 M111 O38 P115 P150 Z8	HARRIS Walter L63
HAMTONES F43A	HAPPY THE MAN H19A	HARLIS H26B		HARRIS WYNONIE H37C
HANAPPIER Patrick U17	HAPSHASH Lanse T11	HARLOS Axel 'Felix' G106		HARRISON Al C129
HANCK Terry B109	HAPSHASH AND THE COLOURED COAT H19B	HARLOW Allen P19	HARRIS Eddie C17	HARRISON Bill (D) M176
HANCOCK Butch E51 F65D		HARLOW Larry A47 F17 I2	HARRIS Elsa U18	HARRISON Billy (G) H37B T57 P140 S176
HANCOCK David H167	HARADA Kuma B19 C39A G94 I23D J39 K24 M145 M194 M202C M206 P45 R40B S108 S312A T31	HARMAN Buddy (B) L64	HARRIS Emmylou B29 B221 C123 C124 C237 D139 E20 F74 H35 L36A L89 P33 P50 P151 R32 N37 P63 P125 S70 T137 S65 W101 Y16	HARRISON Bobby C23 F56 F110
HANCOCK Herbie B85 C186 D27 G26D H19 K36 L66A M102 M170 M218 P35 P114 R45 S19 S126 V39 W31 W62 W90 W118 W119 Z9		HARMAN Dave (DEE Dave) D20		HARRISON Brian (D) D113 L117
	HARADA Yujin F20A G55	HARMAN John M106B		HARRISON Brian (B) J15A
	HARALSON Bobby Neil R123	HARMAN Mark Henry K32 P106		HARRISON Bruce E78B
	HARBACH Stephen A30A	HARMON Buddy (D) C14 F126		HARRISON Charlie A22 C15A P151 R22 M27 M7 P106 S285 T157
HANCOCK Tommy F65D	HARBERS Elime P10B	HARMON H26 J30 J53 L72 M18 M197A N37 P63 P125 S10 S187C S252 S271 S272	HARRIS Eugene A35C	
HANCOX Paul C101 M162	HARBERT Richard F108A		HARRIS Frank K84A	HARRISON Clive A130A
HAND Cal K88	HARBRECHT Hans H19C	HARMON James G25	HARRIS Freddie K38 P15 P99 Y2A	HARRISON Dave D14C
HAND Roger E21 G35 N58B P77B R6 S177D	HARCK Ken B16 O10A	HARMON Joan B17 K53	HARRIS Gale W3B	HARRISON Don H38
	HARCOURT Charlie C56 H20 J14 J107 L80	HARMONIA H27	HARRIS Gene H35B	HARRISON Geff D48 H38A K44B T162A
HANDELSMAN Jonathan C222	HARCOURT'S HEROES H20	Harmonica Boy W59	HARRIS Geoff K65	HARRISON George B47D B59 B89A B202 C94 D139 F66 H9 H39 K34 L37 L51 L111 M100E P126 R173 S50 S115D S220 S252
HANDLEY Jerry B72	HARD ROAD H20A	Harmonica Fats C217	HARRIS Goodge B231	
HANDLEY Pete R177A	HARD STUFF H21	HARMONIUM H28	HARRIS Greg B49 M205A	
Handsome Dick see BLUM Richard	HARDAWAY Renee W119	HARMS Jesse C179 H111A	HARRIS Hi-Fi R70A R74	
	HARDAWAY Robert C61A L140 R22	HARNELL Joe M229	HARRIS Hi-Tide(BOYD or GITRY Willie) H35A M111	HARRISON Jerry (K/G) H39A R83 T8
HANDY Chip F123	HARDCAKE SPECIAL H19C	HARNER Mike T92A		HARRISON John B253 H64
HANESS Abigale B53 J65 K48 K86 M227 R39 S124 S272 T25 T27 W136	HARDE Cliff A120	HARNETT Eddi H83	HARRIS Hilda A35A A57 A96 B221 B262 C164 C213D D97A D139 E37 F109 H99 H137 K8l L4A L21 P72A P149 W51	HARRISON Lanny M180B
	HARDEN Bobby E73	HAROWITZ David S213		HARRISON Lee T22
HANEY Dave B261	HARDEN John I10	HAROWITZ Marc C108D M218		HARRISON Mark T111B
HANEY J.D. M181C	HARDERS Hanno S329A	HARP Andy S339A	HARRIS Ivory Joe H120	HARRISON Martin E52A F66A N61C
HANGMEN H15A	HARDESTY Herbert D96 K45 W6	HARP Gerald F50B	HARRIS Jack P31	HARRISON Mike (V/K) A87 H40 J109 S224
HANK THE KNIFE & The JETS H15B	HARDIE C. G29A	HARP Bill S29	HARRIS Jeania W119	
	HARDIN Andrew D72B	HARPER Carl D. G37A	HARRIS Jerry N53A	HARRISON Mike (B) M39
HANKIN Larry L133	HARDIN Ardis G92	HARPER Charlie U4	HARRIS Jet (B) B64 H36 R80 S80	HARRISON Neil D117 H40A
HANKINS Don G122 H170	HARDIN Eddie A131E D28 D66 F38 G50 H22 H24 W117	HARPER Delisle (or Lyle) A98 B4 B19 B77 B171 B209 B231 B268 C204 D27B E77A F117 G10 G13 G67 H17 K51 L47 M202A O2O S257 W103 Y24		HARRISON Nicky D117 M233
HANKS Larry T150			HARRIS Jett (D) S192B	HARRISON Nigel B139 D53A M82 N52 S119
HANLEY Junior K81	HARDIN Glen D. A132 C14 C38A C224 C237 D71 E20 F74 H35 L36A N25 P33 P125 R137 S272 S341		HARRIS Jo Ann B53 D139 P69	
HANLEY Mick M121E			HARRIS Jody C198	HARRISON Norman M108A
HANLEY Paul F10			HARRIS Joe A40 D96 N43A	HARRISON Olly P77A
HANLEY Steve F10	HARDIN Joseph K45	HARPER Don H132 H164C R66 S198	HARRIS Joey S272	HARRISON Patti H39
HANLON Alan C146	HARDIN Louis M192	HARPER Ginger R122	HARRIS Johanna H37A	HARRISON Phil H13 K83 S103C
HANLON Bob S86C	HARDIN Steve P109A	HARPER Joe E67 H159	HARRIS John (K) B41 D21 H52A K88 K95 L77 N57 S73 Y16	HARRISON Richard C177D
HANLON Chris B267	HARDIN Tim H23	HARPER Lee A57AD43A		HARRISON Robbie N57B
HANLON David D127B	HARDIN and YORK H24	HARPER Patrick R127A		HARRISON Rodney A94
HANLON John W97	HARDING B.P. X2	HARPER Rick R127A	HARRIS Johnny H36A	HARRISON Roger R20
HANLON Tom F103	HARDING Bob A29	HARPER Rod S69	HARRIS Jon F108A	HARRISON Spiderman J11
HANNA Arnie W56	HARDING Chris P62	HARPER Roy B280 H29 P85	HARRIS Keith J14	HARRISON Stan S199
HANNA Gillian G72A	HARDING Michael S177D	HARPER Teddy P59	HARRIS Kenneth N39	HARRISON Stuart H125
HANNA Jeff B91 M232 N53	HARDING Rob O10A	HARPERS BIZARRE H30	HARRIS Kent W110	HARRISON Terry M233
HANNA Mike H7D	HARDINGER Michael S108C	HARPHAM Buddy R57	HARRIS Lazy J79	HARRISON Timmy F109
HANNA Roland E49	HARDLE Dick B183B	HARPHAM James H70	HARRIS Major Handy R124A	HARRISON Wendall C213D
HANNAFORD Ross D4A	HARDLICKA Dan C38	HARPO Slim (MOORE James H31)	HARRIS Mark H194A	HARRISON Wilbert H41
HANNAFORD Tony M195	HARDMEAT H25	HARRASSMENT George H31A	HARRIS Marty W101	HARRISS Don T135
HANNAH John S299A	HARDWICK Jules W134C	HARREL Dale Jnr A53	HARRIS Michael (K) B231	HARRIT Niels G12
HANNAH Paul F101B	HARDWICK Steve W69A	HARREL Tom A136 P99 W62	HARRIS Michael (Tpt) C45 C164B E7 E55 W84C	HARROLD Melanie (also CARLIN Joanna) B183D H42 S235
HANNES Mick F103F	HARDY Calvin W5	HARRELL Cynthia L65		HARROP Graham P4
HANNETT Martin C184 J99A M233A	HARDY Cliff H183 P131	HARRELL Dickie V32	HARRIS Michelle T107	HARRY Deborah B139 D56A H42A W100
	HADRY Darryl G121	HARRELL James L121A P118A S8A	HARRIS Mickey (V) S192B	
HANNIBAL H16	HARDY Damon J. A6B	HARRELL Vern L90	HARRIS Mikie B172A	HARRY MUSKEE BAND M237A
HANNON Biff A122	HARDY Dave F127	HARRIER Tim P19	HARRIS Norman F92 H133 K45 L130 N65 O14 P59C P80 S124A S228	HARRYMAN Martyn D4
HANNS Liz P18	HARDY Eddie B87	HARRIGAN Mike H46		HARSH REALITY H43
HANS A PLAST H16B	HARDY Gerry L25	HARRILL Tracy Y14	HARRIS Oliver W94	HARSH Harwood O33C
HANSELMANN David E69E M136B	HARDY Hagood M238A	HARRELL Vivian D66	HARRIS Paul A4 A59 B149 B194 C58 D53 C196 D111 F78 K81 M27 M28 M64 M94 M101 M229 O12 P106 R109 R169 S65 S73 S157 S197 S276 T71A V38 W16	HART Adrian P104A
HANSEN Bert B224A	HARDY Helen B237 C79	HARRIMAN John Carr P73		HART Billy H19 H44 S73C W30A Z9
HANSEN Brian L45A	HARDY Joe G92B	HARRINGTON Bob K48		HART Bobby B194A M181
HANSEN Randy H16A H19 M31	HARDY Lyndon Lee C56	HARRINGTON Carey Bell B85B E67 H32 H159 J9A L126 N46C R85A S323 S329 T23 W28		HART Charlie B237 J104C L16A T122 W130
HANSEN Rudolf S30	HARDY Max P93B			HART Dick A74 A109
HANSEN V. D83A	HARDY Phil W56	HARRINGTON John C165	HARRIS Pennie K65 W123	HART Ernest G114
	HARDY Richard K48 N12A			
	HARE Colin H143			

HILL Mike G29A
HILL Noel P93
HILL Philip S157
HILL Raymond E52B P̲5̲6
HILL Rob A82C
HILL Robert C39A
HILL Roger A50A B277 F6
M180A P100 T23
HILL Ron H24
HILL Roy H118 S295
HILL Scott T97A
HILL Steve B142
HILL Tom G23
HILL Tony G25A W115 M168 P10
HILL Victor W12A
HILL Wayne G61 P79
HILLAGE Steve A92A A133 C137
E24 G66 H119 K35 T159
HILLARY Dale L74
HILLARY John D59D
HILLER George Miller H138A
HILLERY Art C217
HILLESTAD Per L24C
HILLFIELD BOYS CHOIR S74
HILLIARD Brenda B172A F103
M12
HILLIS Craig M232 W11
HILLMAN Chris B285 C96B C123
D69 E41 F74 F139 H120 M27
M28 M30 M64 M125A P33 P106
R109 S52 S197 T32E W43
HILLS Chris C189 F122 M69
P99
HILLS Cliff C96
HILTON Brian B57F
HILTON Rockie M30 Y5B
HILTON Roger S214
HILTON Thomas J62
HIMMEL Karl A132 B261 C14
D12 D21 D101 D104 D139 E54
G16 G102 H26 H65 K30 M211
M232 N57 R31 R173 T21 T55
Y16 Y18
HINCH John J102
HINCKS Mick L104 T36
HINDS Billy P151
HINDS David S261
HINDS Mervyn T28
HINDS Neville J48 S125
HINDS Peter L71B
HINE Eric D134
HINE Graham G1 M99
HINE Malcolm L59
HINE Rupert A133 C19 C34
D36 H121 M127 Q2 P64 P72
W82B
HINES Blake T44
HINES David B49
HINES Delroy B276
HINES Earl C179
HINES Gloria K48
HINES Justin H122
HINES Marcia H122A
HINES Roland John B135
HINES Stephen B224A
HING Hal C215A
HINKLE Ken W51
HINKLE Rick A22B
HINKLEY Tim A82 B66 B75 B161
B191 C79 C204 D84 H11 H110
H123 H179 J67 K81 K84 L37
M15 P72A R6 S131 S176 S270
S300 T59 V33 W6 W67 Y10
HINKLEY'S HEROES H123
HINO Motohiko P115
HINO Terumasa C189 L67B
W30A
HINSCHE Billy B56 D8 J72
HINSHAS Bill W180
HINSHAW Bill A131D N25
HINSLEY Harvey H159A Q42
HINTON Anthony B186
HINTON Eddie A59 B126 B200
C139 F123A F134 G61 G96B
H15 H62 J52 J53 N55 N65 O15
P112 S36 S172 W118
HINTON Michael (Tpt) J86
HINTON Mike (Perc) H45 R77B
HINTON Milt C86A C146 M26
R125 S168
HINTON Nancy H45
HINZE Chris S73C
HIPPS Johnathon S331A
Hippy Harry B234
HIPWELL Bob M37
HIRAYAMA Masako R173

HIROSHIMA H123A
HIROTA Jogi T2
HIROTA Michi B186
HIROTA Richi B186
HIRSCH Larry C38A J105A
HIRSCH Meyer C38A
HIRSCH Ricky A37 A82 B200
W54
HIRSCH Shelley G10
HIRSCHBERG Roscoe P112
HIRSCHEL Ira D106A
HIRSCHI Phillip M40
HIRSCHMAN Robert H42 M164
HIRSEN James L. F70
HIRSH Gary 'Chicken' M18
T116B
HIRSH Jay C185F M165A
HIRSH Paul V42
HIRST Rob B130 M146
HISCOCK Terry H188
HISEMAN Jon A74 B171 B248
C166 C167 C202 D19A H50
H86 L99 M111 T40 T76
HITCH Markly H124
HITCHCOCK David C34 G21
P84
HITCHCOCK Rick B208B C6
D9 D38B D132 M100 R12
W13A W102
HITCHCOCK Robyn H124B
S181
HITCHCOCK Russell A22C
HITCHINGS Duane A27 A67N
B16 B64A C5 C38A C182 M68
M151 N29 P83A R163 S77A
S273 T32C T56B
HITCHINS Paul S224A
HITE Bob C26
HITE Jim T143
HITE Richard C26
HITE Tyrone B113B
HIMEN H124A
HITSON Herman H99
HITZEK Lothar S38
HLAVSA Milan P94A
HLUBEK Dave M178A
HLUDZIK Gerry B267 D5C
HOAD Bill W15
HOARD Steve M168
HOBAN Bob P137
HOBART Ted O18
HOBBS Becky T1
HOBBS Elsberry D116
HOBBS Gary S112A
HOBBS John B274A B259
C203A D68B F74 F110C
H52A M96 M123 N25 N42 N43
O15
P126A
HOBBS Randy Jo H99 K16A
M13 M187 W106 W107 W108
HOBO H125
HOBSON Jim B201 L128 M18
M204
HOBSON Joyce B247
HOBSON Pwc R151A
HOBSON Tom K12
HOCH Gerd B264
HOCH Max T21
HOCHANADLE Jim M136C
HOCHENSMITH Hadley A50
G14
HOCHER Billy B262A F67A
HOCHSTETTER Christian
H99B
HOCHULI Rick M139A
HOCKEDY Johnny G81B
HOCKLEY Steve S85A
HODDEN Martin S116A
HODDER Jim H5 R148 S262
HODGDEN Gary B68
HODGE Alan C78 D92 R48
R129
HODGE Alex P92
HODGE Bob C58A C59
HODGE Dallas C59
HODGE Keith B243 L53 P77B
Q6
HODGE Pete D127D
HODGE Philip H119
HODGES Billy W129
HODGES Brian W39 H29
HODGES Charles (K) G92
M172 P51
HODGES Charlie (G) P125
HODGES Chas (B/G/Fid) A22
B82 B89 C89 H74 L36A O42
S321

HODGES Doug B42B
HODGES Frank M50
HODGES Gary B255 M132D
HODGES Hoppy C11B L12B
HODGES Kenny S203
HODGES Leroy B43C G92
M172 P51
HODGES Mabon M227 P25
HODGES Norval R112
HODGES Steve C87A
HODGES Teenie G92 P51
HODGES Yvonne L108 N23
R127A
HODGKINS Dave R53A S330
HODGKINSON Colin B11 H12
K84 S42C
HODGKINSON J.W. I8 R129
HODGKINSON Mick B43C
HODGKINSON Richard M141B
HODGKINSON Tim A88 E24
H57 H101 S152
HODGSON Brian I20 W34 W68
HODGSON Gavin C7
HODGSON John (Perc) W7
HODGSON Peter B27 B124B
R39 R75 R146A
HODGSON Roger C112 S333
HODINOTT Robby K60
HODJERA Michael C96A
HODKINSON John W35
HODSON John V35
HOEHN Tommy C106A H125A
Y3A
HOEKE Rob C243
HOELDERLIN H125B
HOENIG Michael A19A H126
T11
HOEPFINGER Mary T107
HOERNER Ed D86
HOEYMANS Henri S214B
HOFF Gerry J27
HOFF Heinz B182A
HOFF Janet Ferguson D127
HOFF Louis T44
HOFFERT Paul H59 K66A L74
Hoffman T149C
HOFFMAN Bill P37A
HOFFMAN Christian C177D
HOFFMAN David P. B246A
HOFFMAN Eugene R22
HOFFMAN Hajo S38
HOFFMAN Ingfried D93G
HOFFMAN Ken N58C
HOFFMAN Michael Y8B
HOFFMAN Peter F25 N48A
HOFFMAN Richard P53
HOFFMAN Uwe W68B
HOFFMAN Wolf A6D
HOFFMANN Doug E69B
HOFFMANN Edgar E52 U23
HOFFMANN Gregg S210B
HOFFMANN Karl T83A
HOFMANN Michael S6A
HOFSTEDE Henk N52A
HOFSTEIN Mark U9A
HOFSTRA David C107C
HOFSTRA David W5B
HOG HEAVEN H126A
HOGAN Danny B111
HOGAN Gerry B73 E19 H74
M214 Y14
HOGAN Silas H127
HOGARTH Nick N150A K70
HOGBERG Caj W84B
HOGG Andrew 'Smokey' H128
HOGG Dave A65D
HOGG Derek D108
HOGGARD Graham D33E
HOGGINS Robert M151
HOGGS Billy C177C
HOGINS Bob K60 M126 M126
M151 N43
HOGS HEAD H128A
HOGUE John Q1A
HOGWOOD Christopher C165
Y21
HOH Eddie B171 B256 F74
F94 G61 H63 K81 M68 M238
HOHL Jochen R66D
HOHNER Eddie T118
HOICHI Nobuo C110A
HOITSMA Derrick B108B
HOKENSON Eddie B225
HOKUS POKE H129
HOKUS POKUS H129A
HOLBROOK John B194 B216C
B282 H185

HOLBROOK Mike G96C P73
HOLCOLM Marva W119
HOLD Random H129B
HOLDEN Lorence R111
HOLDEN Martin G7D
HOLDEN Randy B150 O37A
HOLDER Herschel B116 F1
M15 M227 P25
HOLDER Ian A30 C165
HOLDER Jack B43C B114
H160
HOLDER Mitch K99A R99 S34
HOLDER Noddy A47A S151
HOLDER Ram Jam H130
HOLDERMAN Gary Norton D5
HOLDRIDGE Lee M111
HOLDSWORTH Allan B249 G66
H131 I9 L70 N62 P72A P115
S182 S267 T40 U3
HOLDT Eugene J. S249C
HOLEGUARD Roger N24C
HOLGARTH Richard G7D
HOLIDAI Peter R8
HOLIDAY John P92D
HOLLADAY Ginger B210 B261
C77A D12 D99 E51 E57 E73
F7 H26 H62 H65 G16 G102
L77 P63 P125 R137 T20
T167 Y18
HOLLADAY Marvin S168
HOLLADAY Mary B210 D12
D99 F7 H26 H62 H65 G102
F7 P125 R137 S36 T20 Y18
HOLLAND Amy M16A
HOLLAND Bernie A62 A82
B11 B159 F14 F41 G71A
G110 H123 H180 H181 J67
L63 S257 Y2
HOLLAND Dave (D) H66 J102
T133
HOLLAND David (B) B131
C186 D27 J102 K84 M229
R22 S19 S104 S267 T141
HOLLAND Dave (D) A4A H176
M40
HOLLAND Franc E56A
HOLLAND Geoff R68
HOLLAND Julian 'Jools'
C199 E32 H131C S232 S299
HOLLAND Maggie A6D H162
HOLLAND Mary W72
HOLLAND Milt A37 A132
B17A B47C B47E B63 B72
B29 B149 B170 B181A C201
C111A
C129 C155 C179 C180 C213
C220B D68B D72A D101 G10
G80 G121 H8 H8A K81 L50
L72 L89 L109 L110 M60C
M82 M86 M125 M136C M170
M229 N40 P28 P106 R22
R101 R161 S20 S58 S65
S124 S252 T25 W9 W44 W88
HOLLAND Nicky S140
HOLLAND Paul R33
HOLLAND Steve M178A
HOLLANDER Jan H224A
HOLLANDER Marc A71 C189
F123 H131A L26A
HOLLANDER Max C234A
HOLLANDER H131B
HOLLAR Keith B110
HOLLAWAY Brian D39 E66
HOLLERAN Ace R66C
HOLLESTELLE David B224A
HOLLESTELLE Hans R111C
S41B S214D
HOLLESTELLE Jan B208C
R111C S214D
HOLLESTELLE Martha P92B

HOLLEY Major J20
HOLLIDAY Doc D81A
HOLLIES H132
HOLLINGWORTH Roy S206
HOLLINGWORTH Steve C183A
HOLLINS Everett 'Blood'
I12B
HOLLIS Ken C184B
HOLLIS Mark G1
HOLLIS Peter C97
HOLLIS Plum M63
HOLLISTER Greg A67H R124F
HOLLMER Lars F123 S14B
HOLLOWAY Bob R56
HOLLOWAY Brenda C155 H131D
Y16

HOLLOWAY Brian G66 I20 R40B
HOLLOWAY Larry T154
HOLLOWAY Laurie H132A
HOLLOWAY Loleatta H51 H133
HOLLOWAY Patrice B63 C155
P126 S10 S148 T145 W10A Y16
W85
HOLLOWAY Ron R139
HOLLY & THE ITALIANS H133A
HOLLY Charles Hardin
'Buddy' C224 H134
HOLLY Steve B231 D39 J72
L7 M9 R23 V18B
HOLLYWOOD ARGYLES H134A
HOLLYWOOD BRATS H135
HOLLYWOOD FATS H135B
HOLLYWOOD STARS H135A
HOLM Frode E11A
HOLM Thomas G112D H18B
HOLMAN Fred M37
HOLMAN Laurence N50D
HOLMAN Mitchell I31 L8
HOLMAN Wild Bill S173C
HOLMER C. A32A
HOLMES Alan D54 F36 H11 K61
S194
HOLMES Bob M232
HOLMES Carol C77
HOLMES Chris B5 T94
HOLMES Christine F13
HOLMES Dan S60
HOLMES Dandy M84
HOLMES Dave O40
HOLMES Dennis S358G
HOLMES Derek St. N63 S9B
W69F
HOLMES Diane G72 P137
HOLMES Frank F70B
HOLMES Dick M167
HOLMES Gene W18
HOLMES Glen L86
HOLMES Groove M26 W116A
HOLMES Jake H136
HOLMES Jim B101
HOLMES Malcolm O29A
HOLMES Nick H52A
HOLMES Norma M41
HOLMES Phil W13C
HOLMES Rudy B116
HOLMES Rupert H137 S295
HOLMES Sherman H15
HOLOCAUST H137A
HOLROYD Les B37 M67
HOLST Rainer S38
HOLSTER Jack C118
HOLSTER David N53
HOLSTIEN Ed F137
HOLSTIEN Fred F137
HOLT Ashley W7 W19
HOLT Craig F110B
HOLT Derek C141 T14
HOLT Douglas M48B
HOLT Errol 'Flabba' D113A
L58A P134 R29 S45
HOLT Gary B57F
HOLT Harry S198B
HOLT Ian A6A
HOLT Isaac L65
HOLT Johnse L016A
HOLT Laroon A2
HOLT Lincoln 'Style' D113A
S44A
HOLT Molly R34
HOLT Morris see Magic Slim
HOLT Nick M48B
HOLT Ricky John S26
HOLT Steve H160
HOLT Tim F114
HOLTAN John Erik E52A
HOLTON Gary H85 H137B S288A
HOLTON Gary & Casino STEEL
H137B
HOLTS Roosevelt H138
HOLY MACKEREL H138A
HOLY MODAL ROUNDERS H139
HOLY MOSES H139A
HOLZ Uwe L104B
HOLZKAMP Dean F103C
HOLZWARTH Doug A80
HOM Wolfgang B107
HOMAN Jeff S112A
HOMBACH Volker T11
HOMBRES H139B
HOME H140
HOMEFIELD Roger I13A T71A

JASPER J43A
JASPER Chris I28
JASPER WRATH J43B
JAST Phil C129
JAUME Hector Z2
JAUNIAUX Catherine A71A F123 H131A
JAUREQUI David C21A
JAVAHER Darius C173
JAVORS Russell J69
Jay S55C
JAY David B51A
JAY Jon M169A
JAY Kelly C236 K53 T37J
JAY Laurie J14
JAY martin D93 H26A H42 K41 S178
JAY AND THE AMERICANS J44
JAYNE Mitch D71
JAYOURBA Kwasi M26
JAZZ ROCK EXPERIENCE J45
Jazzmo H65A
JEAME Lay L16E
JEAN Norma C99
JEAN Sandy B154
JEANNEAU Francois C62A C137 M40 T67
JEBADIAH J45A
JEFF dave A60
JEFF BECK GROUP B64 D99
JEFF LORBER FUSION L119C
JEFF STURGES AND UNIVERSE S311
JEFFERIES Michael T137
JEFFERS Jack M79
JEFFERS James G122A
JEFFERSON Cora T70
JEFFERSON Gene I25B
JEFFERSON Scott W128A
JEFFERSON AIRPLANE J46
JEFFERSON STARSHIP J46
JEFFES Simon H121 L15 P59 P64
JEFFREY Michael B261 F128
JEFFREYS Garland H8 J48 R6O
JEFFREYS Paul B54 C88 H26A
JEFFRIES Michael T119
JEFFRIES Norm C161E
JEFFRIES Nancy I21
JEFFS Bob C35D
JEFFS Ian C115
JEKANOWSKI Phil C195
JELL Joey L95C
JELLIMAN Paul K10C
JELLY Mike A23
JELLY J49
JELLY BEANS J49A
JELLYBREAD J50
JELLYMAN Laurie C161 R14
JELLYROLL J51
JELSCH Gerald A64
JEMMOTT Jerry B85 C203 G61
K45 K51 K81 M78 M227 P49 P60A
P149 R168 W11
JENKINS Alan D39E
JENKINS Arthur Jnr B77 B85
C44 C76 D86 G61 J20 K36 L51
M12 M17 M41 M75 M111 M143 O27
P72A R22
JENKINS Barry A67 B2 H84 K52
N5
JENKINS Billy B272
JENKINS Chris A23
JENKINS Crystal S73
JENKINS Cliff H43
JENKINS David P3
JENKINS Harold Lloyd see
TWITTY Conway
JENKINS John (Pno) M128
JENKINS Johnny (V) J52
JENKINS Karl A74 C63 D118 G98
H171 L95 N62 P91 R132 S182
S185
JENKINS Ken (B) B27
JENKINS Kenny (Flt) M177
JENKINS Lyle A101 A133 H50
S119 S264
JENKINS Martin D11 D68 H87
J41 M108 P90
JENKINS Marvin G17
JENKINS Martinette (or
Mortonette) E31 L55 L143
JENKINS Nigel B47B M106A R11
R40B Z9B
JENKINS Paul C6
JENKINS Sean E28
JENKINS Terry H111C J8

JENKINS Tomi C20
JENKINS Zed (or Z) R41A
W60
JENNER Bob A34
JENNER Martin B189 C47A
D39C N57 R15 R80
JENNER Peter A133 B230
JENNINGS Bill J52B
JENNINGS Chris B197F
JENNINGS Colin A131E G49
G89 T6A
JENNINGS Jack F108A H58
L63 N65
JENNINGS Jessi see CARTER
Jessi
JENNINGS Morris B251 C17
H58 H170 L65 M126 W28
JENNINGS Peter C223
JENNINGS Sherroil B223
JENNINGS Waylon C124 C169
C247 H35 H134 J53 W67
JENSEN Bjorn S12A
JENSEN Hans E27
JENSEN Knud W30
JENSEN Troels D44B
JENSON Doug J53A
JENSON Kennedy J53A
JENSON Steve S335A
JENSON INTERCEPTOR J53A
JERDEN Dave H39A
JEREMY AND THE SATYRS J54
JERICHO J55
JERIMIAH John A33E H170
Jerney V38A
JERNIGAN Tank O39
JEROME Tim F27A
JERONIMO J56
JERSEY Jack J56A
JERUSALEM J56B
JERVIS Derek P103A
JESSE DIXON SINGERS S125
S180
JESSIE Bob C95
JESTERS M136C
JET J57
JETER Rev Claude S125
JETHRO TULL J58
JETS J59
JETS J58A
JETS R152
JETT Harvey B114
JETT Joan J59A R163 T170
JETT Otis L64
JETTER Marleena M18
JEWEKS Nole B210
JEWEL Ian M9
JEWELL Jimmy A34 A82 B77
B277 D9 D92 D95A D132 F6
F7 G6 G62B H50 H132 J60
J110 L16A L46 L106 L136
M29 N56 R129 W53B
JEWKES Denise J46
JEWKIS Noel B144 G84A
JEWRY Bernard see FENTON
Shane
JEZOWSKI Andy N63
JIG SAW J61
JILLALA Sidi B4
JIM KWESKIN JUG BAND K101
JIMBP Akira C51C
JIMENEZ David K21A
JIMINEZ Flaco C179 S7
JIMINEZ Tony C62
JIMMERSON Herb M18 M225
P21
JIMMY JAMES AND THE
VAGABONDS J24
JIMMY JOYCE CHILDRENS
CHOIR M27
JINK Peter F45
JINKS Bernard T5
JIROUS Ivan P94A
JIVA J62
JIVE BUREAUX J63
JO 40 L80B
JO JO GUNNE J64 W107
JO JO ZEP AND THE FALCONS
J64A
JO MAMA J65
JOAN Danny H171B
JOANNOU Harris H56
JOB Detlef N61
JOBE Lequeint R141
JOBE Rivers S31
JOBES Charlie Y18
Jobriath J65A
JOBS Joby D63

JOBSKI B. B52
JOBSON Brian N11A
JOBSON Edwin 'Eddie' B138
C251 E60 F42 F65 G32 G50
H110 J58 K54 M34 M81 R149
U3 Z8
JOBSON Richard S140
JOBSON Wayne N11A
JO'BURG HAWK J66
JOCKO J. J66A
Jody V38A
JODY GRIND J67
JOE SOAP T47
JOE TEMAIRE AND FLOUZE
T38C
JOECKER Gundi B278A
Joel S19
JOEL Billy Joseph A115A
D66 H55A J69 M69 M233 S55A
JOEY DEE AND THE STARLIGH-
TERS D38A
JOFFE Ritch S78
JOHALLIS Jimi V39C
Johanna D88
JOHANNSON Ove S225
JOHANSEN David D53 J70 N34
JOHANSEN Jerl R178
JOHANSEN Joe F69
JOHANSON Jai Johnny
'Jaimoe' A37 A38 B200 C207
D12 G104 J52 M93 S56 T20
JOHANSON Lars Ake W84B
John The Greek L110B
JOHN Andrew J70A
JOHN Bobby G67
JOHN Clive (also SPACE
Clint) A34 B287 H140 J71
M63
JOHN Del F53
JOHN Elton Hercules
(formerly DWIGHT Reg)
A133 B23 B159 C107 D39
D100 D131 J72 J86 S252
S273 L51 W72
JOHN Gibson W124A
JOHN Johnny Little J73
JOHN Phillip 041
JOHN Prakash see Prakash
John
JOHN Richard B137
JOHN Robert J73A K81
JOHN Steven D47
JOHN Terry O18B
JOHN DUMMER BLUES BAND
D128
JOHN FRED AND HIS PLAYBOY
BAND F105
JOHN MAYALL'S BLUESBREAKERS
M111
JOHN PAYNE BAND P42
JOHN SPENCERS LOUTS S212
JOHN STEVENS AWAY S267
JOHN VERITY BAND V26
JOHNNY AND THE HURRICANES
J74
JOHNNY AND THE JAILBIRDS
J74A

JOHNNY KIDD AND THE
PIRATES K39
JOHNS Andrew D58
JOHNS Bobby R102A
JOHNS Eric E12 F6 H81
JOHNS Gary C4A
JOHNS Glyn F7 H79 M159
N48B O46 W21
JOHNS Glyn (Sax) X2
JOHNS Richard B45C
JOHNS Terry D54
JOHNS Tricia P75
JOHN'S CHILDREN J75
Johnson G2B
JOHNSON Alan N48
JOHNSON Alec N47A T3
JOHNSON Alphonso A78 B214
C147 C164B C241 D127 F88A
H131 H150A J20 J75A M40
R99 W36
JOHNSON Andy 'Snakehip'
A59 R137 S14
JOHNSON Angie R28B
JOHNSON Anthony M65
JOHNSON Art H156 W44
JOHNSON Aubrey H11
JOHNSON August 'Augie'

C147 F33 H96 L71B L79 L143
M18 M191 S36
JOHNSON Barry N60
JOHNSON Bill (V) C179
JOHNSON Billy (Pno) P26
JOHNSON Billy (D) H58 M2
JOHNSON Bobby H147
JOHNSON Brian (V) A2 G23
JOHNSON Brian (K) E31F
JOHNSON Bud I25B J97 S168
JOHNSON Calvin W119
JOHNSON Carl R121A S349
JOHNSON Carol E76A
JOHNSON Carolyn W119
JOHNSON Charles C129 D127
PBA
JOHNSON Chas (K) B224
JOHNSON Chris T155
JOHNSON Claude N39
JOHNSON Cliff O10A
JOHNSON Corinthian
'Kripp' D43
JOHNSON Courtney H65 N29C
R173
JOHNSON Cynthia L82A
JOHNSON Dana G90
JOHNSON Danny A67N A131G
C182 D53 S273
JOHNSON Darryl H59
JOHNSON Dave 'Baby'
(Wind) S340
JOHNSON David Earle
(Perc) H12 J76 P99 S56
W62
JOHNSON Dave (B) P126A
JOHNSON David Leonard
S345
JOHNSON David (K) O13
JOHNSON Dennis C90
JOHNSON Dennis Keith S336
JOHNSON Don (Tpt) R111
JOHNSON Don (V) B91 H35
T16A
JOHNSON Doug L130B
JOHNSON Drew R87
JOHNSON Earl M222
JOHNSON Eric C234 M132D
JOHNSON Ernest G122 M48
M129
JOHNSON Errisson see King
Errisson
JOHNSON 'Flim' S75
JOHNSON Flyn J. P83
JOHNSON Gale W78A
JOHNSON Gareth B137
JOHNSON Gary H78A
JOHNSON 'Gater June' W78A
JOHNSON Gene T154
JOHNSON General Norman
C67
JOHNSON George (G/Mand)
C178
JOHNSON George (G) D127
P126 R161
JOHNSON Gerald C234 D124
G45 M101 M159 P114 S111
S276 W97A
JOHNSON Howie (D) V24
JOHNSON Geri M53
JOHNSON Ginger G27 M23
JOHNSON Gordon B253 S75
S114A
JOHNSON Gordy L83A
JOHNSON Graham R65B
JOHNSON Grant F43
JOHNSON Greg 'Doc' S171
JOHNSON Greg L108
JOHNSON Gregory C20
JOHNSON Gus K84
JOHNSON Herman C179
JOHNSON Howard (Wind) A27
B29 B131 B282 C68A F133
H92 K45 L51 M17 M53 M79
M111 M227 M229 M233 O27
P35 R125 S17 S124 T25
T114 W28
JOHNSON Howard (G) K32
JOHNSON Hubert C177C
JOHNSON Icarus W8
JOHNSON J.J. (D) E32 F74C
S140
JOHNSON J.J. (Trom) D27
JOHNSON James R62
JOHNSON James C. A53A
JOHNSON James A. N46A
JOHNSON James M. (G) L42

JOHNSON Jamie J79
JOHNSON Janice T16A
JOHNSON Jerome G12A
JOHNSON Jerry B242
JOHNSON Jill F15
JOHNSON Jim (B) M132D S284D
B126 B272B C14 C30 C38A
C139 C155 D27A D66 E44 F23
F48 F123A G10 G61 G96A H40
H62 H92 J11 J14A J22 K87
L79 L80C L146 M10 M235 N55
O15 P79 R4 R101 R117A R168
R173 S36 S73 S125 S266 S273
S342 T127 W9 W118 Y4B
JOHNSON Jimmy (G) H31 J77
JOHNSON Jimmy (D) B194 J48
S124 T79B
JOHNSON Jimmy (Sax) P26
JOHNSON Jimmy (Tpt) G22B
JOHNSON Joe (B) F69
JOHNSON Joe (V) W119
JOHNSON Joel B183
JOHNSON John Z8
JOHNSON John (B) C106B
JOHNSON John (Sax) B81 S55B
JOHNSON John (Hrns) E7
JOHNSON Johnny (K) B87
JOHNSON Johnny M11 T164
JOHNSON Johnny Lee A37
JOHNSON Joseph D96
JOHNSON Kathy Z22
JOHNSON Keg H35B
JOHNSON Keith (Tpt) B282
E37 K68D M203 V21
JOHNSON Keith (Pno) J22
JOHNSON Keith (G) Y58
JOHNSON Kelly G37
JOHNSON Kenny C195 M159
JOHNSON Kirby P28 S124
JOHNSON Lamont B63
JOHNSON Larry (B) D24
JOHNSON Larry (G) J78
JOHNSON Leo M26
JOHNSON Leslie see Lazy
Lester
JOHNSON Linton Kwesi J48
J78A P108
JOHNSON Lonr.ie J79 M185
S204
JOHNSON Lorenza O28C
JOHNSON Louis A123 B85 C241
J10B M16A M102 P114 P126
R99 R161 T55 W25 W31 W118
JOHNSON Luther Jnr.'Guitar
Junior' J77 W28
JOHNSON Luther 'Georgia
Boy'(or Snake)J79A S204 W28
JOHNSON Mackinley C169 J53
R137 T58
JOHNSON Marcus R59 W28
JOHNSCN Mark N48A
JOHNSON Martha M95A
JOHNSON Marvin D44
JOHNSON Mike (V) M163
JOHNSON Mike (G) K88 M65A
JOHNSON Oliver P115
JOHNSON Osie Y12
JOHNSON Patricia M26 W119
C56
JOHNSON Paul (B) P114
JOHNSON Peter M75
JOHNSON Phil M68
JOHNSON Plas B56 C146 C162
C179 C180 C198 C206 C246
D36A D86 D97 J22 K45 K48
K72 L19 M21 M68 M229 O39
R62 R101 R126 R142A S36
S262 S273 W6 W13 W84C W87
Z8
JOHNSON Prudence L16B
JOHNSON Ralph (D) E7
JOHNSON Ralph (V) I15
JOHNSON Ray (K) N21 O39 W13
JOHNSON Ray (B) B233
JOHNSON Reggie M79
JOHNSON Richard H150
JOHNSON Robert (U.K.) F65
J75B S263
JOHNSON Robert (U.S.Blues)
J80
JOHNSON Robert (U.S.Rock)
H160 J81
JOHNSON Robert (U.S.Funk/V)
B183
JOHNSON Robert (D) H157 K1
JOHNSON Rod G37A W126A

JOHNSON Roger (A'Harp) A132
JOHNSON Roger (G/Tpt) T93
JOHNSON Roger (G) H156 S20
JOHNSON Ron (B) D86 H63 K6
L73 M151
JOHNSON Ron (G) G94
JOHNSON Ross C106A
JOHNSON Samuel B246A
JOHNSON Smokey D96
JOHNSON Stephen A122 B122
L68 V31
JOHNSON Syl M48 W47
JOHNSON Terry (D) M85
JOHNSON Terry (B) M204
JOHNSON Tex B202 C121
JOHNSON Thomas D96
JOHNSON Tommy D86 E75 F74
JOHNSON Victor B280A
JOHNSON Vinnie S213
JOHNSON W. F83E
JOHNSON Wayne M75 S276
JOHNSON Webster 'Scratch'
J48 M109 P80C R61C
JOHNSON Wilko D84 F24 J82
JOHNSON Willie H170 L125
JOHNSON BROTHERS see
BROTHERS JOHNSON
JOHNSTON Adrienne J84
JOHNSTON Andy M232
JOHNSTON Bob G16 S55A
JOHNSTON Brian C204 H70
M114A S300
JOHNSTON Bruce B56 C38 G10
H37A J72 J85 M27 M125A P85
Q3A R96A S6
JOHNSTON Craig M211B
JOHNSTON Howie V24
JOHNSTON Jack M114A
JOHNSTON Kimberley I21A
JOHNSTON Roger M181A
JOHNSTON Tom D101 J85A
JOHNSTONE Ali W20B
JOHNSTONE Bruce A35A N35
JOHNSTONE Davey A82 B23 C6B
C45 C107 C182 D39 E40 J72
J86 M50 M120 N45B P114 S34
S263B T18 W39 W72
JOHNSTONE Di J86
JOHNSTONE Jude B274B
JOLLIFFE Steve S258 T11
JOLLIMORE Keith A69 C183A
C236 L74
JOLLIVER ARKANSAW J86A
JOLLY Charlie R133
JOLLY Paul S349B
JOLLY Pete B141 B149 C39
C156 H5C H8A M68 R76 Z8
JOLLY Steve F110 S14
JOLT J87
JON & THE NIGHTRIDERS J87A
JON & VANGELIS J87B
JONAH J88
JONATHAN & DAVID D20B
JONES A1 A60 H162
JONES Alan (Sax) A49 J101A
JONES Alan (B) B124 B286
D100 L16C M35 R80 R110 S80
W13A
JONES Albert S198A
JONES Alfred E52
JONES Andrew K51
JONES Anthony H179
JONES B.J. M141
JONES Barry S74
JONES Bert M12
JONES Betty M65A
JONES Bill (Wind/K) B261
C194 F83A O46 R81
JONES Bill (B) M32
JONES Billy A67D
JONES Billy (G) A9D O43
JONES Bob (G) B152A D48A G61
M68 S345
JONES Bob (A) A62
JONES Bob (D) B144 B210 L130C
M22 R140 R168 S198
JONES Bobby (V) C155 D26
JONES Bobby (Sax) A57A B91A
JONES Bobby Lee V32
JONES Bones T54
JONES Booker T. A116 B78 B84
B84 B180 B202 C180 C237 D139
F72 H59 H92 J88A K17 K96 L79A
M75 M85 N23A R177 S71A S276
S342 W116
JONES Brenda (V) L55

JONES Brenda (B) T154
JONES Brian (Sax) B59
D16 M23 S35 U10
JONES Brian (also LEWIS
Elmo) (G) J89 R133
JONES Busta Cherry E59
F121 J16B J89A S92 S209
T8 W66
JONES Buster M238B
JONES Calvin R114 W28
JONES Carlberg M225 S325
JONES Casey B226A C162
J89B M5
JONES CASEY & THE
GOVERNORS J89B
JONES Charles 'Chuck'
S96 T23
JONES Cheryl R16A
JONES Chris C178B
JONES Christopher J90
JONES Clifford B95B
JONES Clive B119
JONES Creadel 'Red ' C98
JONES Curt S154
JONES Curtis J91
JONES Danny (D) B97 C203
JONES Danny (Steel) B80
JONES David P136
JONES David (Tpt) B59
JONES David see BOWIE
David
JONES David D17
JONES Davy (V) M181
JONES Davy (Wind) K61
JONES Deacon W17
JONES Dwain E49
JONES Edward H46 H178
JONES Elvin O30
JONES Elvin (D)C189 D27
I21
JONES Ernest M26
JONES Ernestine M93
JONES Euton 'Fergus'
M109 R61C
JONES Fred B259
JONES Gary G17 H65A
JONES George M. (Perc)
W11
JONES George (Tpt) J8
JONES Glennis S251
JONES Gloria B109 B168
B201 C155 C179 D26 F43
J91A K14 L89 M229 P126
S10 S116 Y16
JONES Glyn N63B
JONES Gordon S116A
JONES Grace J92
JONES Graham P120
JONES Gypsy J94
JONES Hank W5
JONES Harvey G92 S93B
JONES Hilary H162
JONES Hugh E11B
JONES Hugh D6B
JONES Jan E. K59B M65A
JONES Jeff B287 H108A
J90 M63 R53D S26 T96 W79
JONES Jerry T26
JONES Jimmy (Pno) T23
JONES Jimmy (D) L102
JONES Job G84A
JONES Joe O27
JONES John (Tpt) T133
JONES John (G) A67 F120A
T73
JONES John Evan J94
JONES John Paul B64 D99
D109 F13 H29 L36 P139G
J21 J92A M48 R59 R128
T9B W47
JONES Johnny (Pno) H170
JONES Jon K45
JONES Joss B93A P47
JONES Judith J7 L66A
JONES Kenny (or Kenney)
A82 B87 D9 D37C F4 F7
F65 L27 L64 L106 R133
S162 S273 T121 V30 W72
W120 W121
JONES Leroi Z5
JONES Lester B193 C225
JONES Linda G92 J92B
JONES Madeline W119
JONES Mai R177A
JONES Malcolm A133 B44

B155B
JONES Marshall O13
JONES Mary D24
JONES Mel B89
JONES Melvin K51
JONES Michael B280A S198A
JONES Michal W55
JONES Mike (Tpt) C160A
JONES Mick (G) C130
JONES Mick (G) F84 F100
H39 H40 H185 L98 R140
S224 W51 W133
JONES Mickey (D) R101
JONES Mickie (B) A65 B283
D139
JONES Micky (G) B287 J93
L53 M63
JONES Mike (Syn) W116
JONES Monroe J73
JONES Moody P142
JONES Mordicai W129
JONES Neil A49 F7
JONES Nic B32 C165 T6 T79
JONES Nick (Perc) F23 K52
JONES Nick (G) A93
JONES Nigel Mazlyn J93A
JONES Noah M82
JONES Paul (POND Paul)
B131 C121 B154B J93B K22A
K84 M80 P122 R10 R11
JONES Penny S273
JONES Percy B203 E59 H4
H29 H169 I22 L15 L95 N60
S182
JONES Peter (K) L92 S147
JONES Peter S312
JONES Pete (B) B197E
JONES Phalin B36 R56
JONES Phil B59 C211 N45B
P70 S98
JONES Philly Joe D27
JONES Priscilla (nee
COOLIDGE) B84 B180 C180
D139 S276
JONES Puma B117 R33A
JONES Quincy B85 S125 W32A
JONES Radio S290
JONES Randy K22A P59
JONES Ray (B) D6 K93
JONES Raymond (K) C99 F60
H42A M149 R132A S135
JONES Rena C96B
JONES Richard (B) P136
JONES Richard (K) C141
JONES Richard (V) C179
JONES Rickie Lee J93C L18
JONES Rob A82C
JONES Robert 'Congo' E19
S26
JONES Robin B67 D108 R122
Y17
JONES Rodney Y2A
JONES Ronnie B156 K81
JONES Ronny (G) L25
JONES Royce A48 O10 S262
JONES Rusty M68
JONES Sammy D41
JONES Sandie M141
JONES Scott L82A
JONES Shirley L55
JONES Shiva 'Shankar' K4
Q16
JONES Sonia T77 W7
JONES Steve (G) G20 P140D
S77 S132 T86 T170
JONES Steve (G) F74D
JONES Steve H109
JONES Steven B. M238
JONES Steve L. (D) C95
H111C
JONES Stuart S261B
JONES Terry D54 R12
JONES Thad H19 J20 S168
JONES Thunderclap K39
JONES Tim M195 S108
JONES Tina N41
JONES Trevor A133 T73
JONES Uriel F92 G17 S128
T42
JONES Valorie L55 R45
JONES Victor D50 P96
JONES Virgil M17 M111
P132C R125 S169 W119
JONES Will 'Dub' C146
JONES Will H62

JONES William L. H81
JONES Willie (B) B193
JONES Willie M45
JONES Wizz M45
JONES Wornell L107 M200
R173
JONES Yvonne R6A
JONES-DAVIS Sue B187 I20
R120
JONESES J93D
JONESY J94
JONGMANS Frans B149C
Joni I12
JONNET Ed Q1A
JONNIE Micki R139
JONS Irish D36A
JONSSON Wili G12
JONUSCHIES Jurgens A67A
JONUTZ Jerry C158
JONUTZ Larry C158
JONZ Joni D86
JOOK J94A
JOON Sister A59
JOOR Billy A102 W11
JOPLIN Janis B94 J95
JOPP Mike A17 D2
JORA Dirk S158A
JORDAN Colin B250
JORDAN Cyril F61 S206
JORDAN Danny M1
JORDAN Darrell P59C
JORDAN Earl C95
JORDAN Fred G92 K51
JORDAN Lonnie B168 B268
J96 O35 W17
JORDAN Louis B85 J97
JORDAN Mark B61 B175 B244
C6B E18A G122 H5 J75A J85A
K40 L19 L19 M101 M187 M203
M229 R22 W129
JORDAN Mike P137
JORDAN Perry Cordell H78
JORDAN Peter E32 N34 S310A
JORDAN Sheila K99
JORDAN Steve A96 A123 B155
B208 F4C G110 H164C M12
M43 M111 S215 S231 T147
U21
JORDAN Taft M227
JORDAN Vic S187C
JORDANAIRES A59 C50 D2 F126
G74 J98 K30 K95 M18 M41
M197A M211 P125 R101 R127A
S10 S342 T22
JORDIN Melanie E49
JORGE Renaldo F17
JORGENSEN Richard L82A
JORGENSEN Steen S180C
JORIO Luciano P41
JORIS Chris H131A
JOSCH Friedemann M163E
JOSEFUS J98A
JOSEFUS Peter F103F
JOSEFUS Stefan F103F
JOSEPH Hilton K45
JOSEPH Jerome B109 G104
H78A M93 W54
JOSEPH Ken H111E
JOSEPH Kim L63 M111
JOSEPH Quinton M2 O14
JOSEPH Richard C3
JOSEPH Sleepy Jack D47
JOSEPH Vivian S235
JOSEPH W.Raphael D47
JOSEPH Waldron D96
JOSEPHINE Geraldine S257
JOSIAS Cori V13
JOST Charlie T141A
JOUASSIN Patrick D51A
JOUBERT Joseph N2A
JOURNEY J99
JOWARD Jeff M210A
JOWARD Martin M210A S89
W46
JOWE HEAD see HEAD Jowe
J98B
JOY DIVISION J99A
JOY OF COOKING J100
JOY UNLIMITED J100A
JOYCE Chris D136 P85A
JOYCE Jan B263 G10 J72 M18
JOYCE Jimmy (Choir) M27
JOYCE Johnny B209
JOYCE Jon B263 C147 C185E
E15 E40 K59 O2B P85 Q3A
V22
JOYCE Mike C194

JOYCE Tim L23
JUANEZ Bud S64
JUBAL J101
JUBER Lawrence D38B E77A
K94B L7 M9 R12 R23 W9A W86
JUBILEE FOUR P125
JUDAS JUMP J101A
JUDAS PRIEST J102
JUDD J102A
JUDD Cuddley B77
JUDD Nick A118 C48 E59 F6
F104 S92
JUDD Phil S221
JUDE J103
Judge see FERGUSON Lloyd
JUDGE DREAD J104
JUDGE-SMITH Chris L131
JUDKINS Stephens see WONDER
Stevie
JUDSON Jean D8
JUDY NYLON J104A
JUGG Roman D10
JUICE J104B
JUICE NEWTON AND SILVER SPUR
N44
JUICE ON THE LOOSE J104C
JUICY GROOVE J104D
JUICY LUCY J105
Juke Joint Jimmy G19 G122
JUKIN' BONE J105C
JUKKA TOLONEN BAND J3A
JULES AND THE POLAR BEARS
J105A
JULIAN Ivan H90 J72 Y3A
JULIANO Tom G69
Julie B139
JULVERNE J105B
JULY J105D
JUMBO J106
JUMONVILLE Jerry B144 B201
B202 B225 C58 C179 C217 C237
D26 D53C D86 D101 G24 I24
J85A J105A K51 K96 L19 L36A
L89 M62 M101 M203 M232 P75
P96 R6 R22 R101 S34 S273
JUMP Phil H25 S131
JUNCALE Tony A136
JUNCO PARTNERS J107
JUNIOR Roger H171B
JUNIOR WALKER AND THE ALL
STARS W12
JUNIORS see DANNY & THE
JUNIORD
JUNIORS EYES J108
JUNKYARD ANGEL J109
JUNSTROM Larry T65
JUNTUNEN Don O2A
JUPITER Donnnie T165A
JUPP Mickey J110 L46
JUPP Pete W82B
JURIC Terry M222
JURKENS Tom M216A
JUSKIEWICZ Krzysztof Henryk
S141
JUSTICE Phil P13
JUSTICE Robert N66
Justin R60B
JUSTIN Craig O6C
JUSTIN Gary S132A
JUSTIN Mark L130A
JUSTIN Tom F99A
JUSTIN HINES AND THE
DOMINOES H122
JUSTINADO Angel B223
JUSTINE J112A
JUSTIS Bill J111
JUSTMAN Seth G19 G122
JUSTO Rodney A111 C25A T67A
JUSTWATER J112
JUUTI Timo H157C
JUVET Patrick J113
JYALL Debora R134A

K Joseph K1A
K.C. AND THE SUNSHINE BAND
K1
K.G.B. K2
KAAGMAN Jerney E4
KAATZ Al K30

KABAKA Remi A25 C30 J9 J105 M9 M94 P76 Q1 RB2 T62A
KABES Jiri P94A
KABAUERO Karlos D64
KABOODLESCHNITZER Freddie S147
KABOR Janos O24
KABUS Billy S3B
KAC Michael M70
KAE Fudgie M72
KAEGH Adriana K38
KAERNES The G110
KAFAMASZ Bob D9A
KAFFEL Phil M18
KAFFINETTI David B87 F112 H54 H73 R33
KAFI Carol R60C
KAFKA Bernard U21
KAFKA Krzystof F47
KAGALE Robbie R164
KAGAN David B7
KAGAN Harvey M95B M141 S7
KAGERMANN Thomas F8D
KAHN Dave S238A
KAHN Doug T92A
KAHN John B144 B210 C208A F7 F80 G9 G53 G84A H150 K81 M22 M28B M229 M229A O17 R168 S27B
KAHN Lewis A47 F17
KAHN Roger B161A
KAHN Spook J66
KAHRS Volker 'Mist' E63 G106
KAIHATSU Tim G122 M238
KAILING Reed G83 P98
KAISER Baron Adolf B92
KAISER Henry F123 L16E
KAISER Rodie P53
KAISER Ulrich A99
KAISER Walt Y5A
KAJANUS Georg see HULTGREEN Georg
KAJANUS/PICKETT K3
KAJDAN Jean Michel B207B
KAK K3B
KAKEN Serge R164
KAKOULLI Harry K3A S232
KAKOULLI Koulla O26 T86
KALA K4
KALB Danny B158 C164 G110 T134 W116A
KALB Jonathan M177
KALB Marty G58
KALE Jim G115
KALCKREUTH David V. O36A
KALDOR John L115A
KALEIDOSCOPE (U.K.) K5
KALEIDOSCOPE (U.S.) K6
KALEIDOSKOP BAND K6A
KALENBERG Miriam J58
KALENSKY Harry T146
KALFF Carl M237A
KALINOWSKY Jean lou S84
KALISH David B68A C6B J93C L19
KALISHES John S337
KALLERT Wolfgang V40A
KALLIO Ile H190
KALMA Ariel H89A N64A
KALMUSKY Ken 13
KALONOWSKI Jean Lou S84
KALPHAT Bobby J17B P134
KALSTAD Per L24C
KALTENECKER Harald B262C
KALYAN K6B
KALTER Steve G29
KAMEN Michael B186 C196 C229 C249 D56A F6D G109 N36 R66C S156 W51A
KAMEN Sasha D56A
KAMERON Jo'anna R6D
KAMIMURA Junko G55
KAMIN Ira B94 B144 B210 G84A R168
KAMINOWITZ Marvin S350
KAMINSKI James F27
KAMINSKI Mike E34 R106 T47 V35
KAMMINGA Arjean L95B
KAMOTA Reika N65
KAMOWSKI Paul M41A
KAMP Horst G25
KAMPEN Huib V. E27
KAMPER Hans A67A
KANDELBURGER Helmut D93G

KANDLER Rosalind B69
KANE Amory K7 P139G
KANE Arthur N34
KANE Brian B255
KANE Howie J44
KANE Irv M211 T9
KANE Jim L82C
KANE Michael Y22
KANE Walter D50 K69 M75 S262 Z3B
KANE Worthington L82C
KANEKAZI Junichi H35A
KANEKO Mari W53A
KANGA Skaila B189 C109 C161C C201A H29 H70 J16 J41 J72 L63 M38 P76 R46 T25
KANGAROO K8
KANNENBERG Ute M140A
KANNIS Johnny R9
KANSAS K9 W107
KANSTUL Zigmant A9
KANTER James A9
KANTER Amy C40A
KANTNER Paul C217 C232 H45 J46 K10 S157
KANTOR Gail A35A B49 B282 F122 H185 L4A M65A N46
KAPADIA Mahendra B278A
KAPEC John A52
KAPELL Dave E20A T22
KAPLAN Artie C51 D50 D76 I2 M37 M125 M203 P6 R21 R100 S157
KAPLAN Fred H135B
KAPLAN Jeff B240 C96 K6 K88 P14
KAPLAN Jordan L80C
KAPNER Mark M18
KAPOLLKE Milla G106
KAPONO Henry E40
KAPP Johnny F67
KAPROFF Armand P106
KAPTAIN KOPTER AND THE TWIRLY BIRDS C15A
KARAN Chris A62 A82 A98 B5 B25 B39 B47B B138 B187 C37 C47A C171 D135 F100 G50 H70 H167 J16 J86 M50 N62 P41 R15 T79 V29 W13A W18
KARANSKY Mike S349B
KARAS Paul L120 R33 S235 S283B
KARAT K10A
KARG Jorgen K10B
KARGES Carlo N61 R63 T106
KARL TERRY AND THE CRUISERS T53
KARLOFF Billy K10C
KARLSEN Tom R178
KARLSSON Bengt S39
KARLSSON Jan H18A
KARMAZYN Dennis K17 R137
KARMELK Ferdie B224A
KARN Mick J40 N63A
KAROLAK Wojciech U21
KAROLI Michael C25 C256
KAROLINE K10D
KARP Charlie D76 L38 M151
KARPA Uwe A47
KARPENKIEL Jogi G120 K76B
KARPENKEIL Waldo B278A K76B
KARPMAN Ron F70
KARR Pat C4A
KARRENBACH Thomas L24B
KARRER Chris A57A K10E P118 U23
KARSKI Les F65A S332
KARSON Gil L55
KARSTEIN Jimmy B84 B149 C14 C94 C121 C155
KART Ira M68 Q3A
KARTHAROO K11
KARUSH Larry H119
KARWATKY Reinhold D143
KASAK Dave W15A
KASEBERG H125B
KASPIER Jack L16E
KASHUR Pet S72
KASKE Stephan M243
KASLOW Andy L118
KASTEN Fritz J100
KASTNER Andrew K36 L19

KASTNER Matt B278
KASTRAN Dean O11
KASUALS K27A
KASZUBOWSKI Michael B91D
KATAHN Martin D139
KATAKUZINOS Demetris A131F
KATH Terry C100 L13
KATO Gary M134A R76
KATO Hiroshi J27
KATOH Kazuhiko S5
KATOH Mika S5
KATONA Gabriel B254A C141 D70 F139 H62 R32 R118 S228A
KATSAROS Doug B22A S242
KATTICA Tom S187B
KATZ David C37 D7 D131 G71A H23 J27 P76 S34 S93 S255
KATZ Dill B237 E8 F56 T76 W13A
KATZ Fred D139
KATZ Gary C51 F4C
KATZ Matthew J46
KATZ Marvin K92
KATZ Mike C150
KATZ Steve A52 B141 B158 D127B E70 H158 K81 L146 M233 R60
KATZIN Jim F11
KATZMAN Nick K11A
KAUFMAN Dave A21
KAUFMAN Eric P139F
KAUFMAN Kenny O6 R102
KAUFMAN Stefan A6D
KAUFFMAN Kirk H63A
KAUFFMAN Mark R86A
KAUFMANN Elizabeth S177D
KAUKONEN Jorma C217 C232 H161 J46 K10 K12
KAUKONEN Peter A35D J46 K10 K13 S157
KAUWSOLEA Koko G10A
KAVANA Ron J104C
KAVANAGH Annie F16 I20 R174
KAVANAUGH Kevin 'Close-out' S199
KAWALEK Jeffrey T147
KAWASAKI Ryo R13A
KAWASHIMA Kazu S93A
KAY Connie M203
KAY Janet R61C
KAY John K14 S265
KAY Richard see Doctor K
KAY Ted D11
KAYAK K16
KAYE Bob G82
KAYE Carol A131D B240 C11 C14 C155 F103D H5C H37A P15 P129 R87 R111B R135 Z8
KAYE Hereward C9 H11
KAYE Joel C164 D50
KAYE Kaplan R174
KAYE Lenny S170
KAYE Ony S97 V39C
KAYE Thomas Jefferson B144 C123 K16A W5 W65A
KAYE Tony (K) B16 B17 B178 D57 F63 H70 Y7
KAYE Tony (D) J74
KAYLAN Howard 'Eddie' A132 B139 B168 C182 C234C F68 G69 H120 L51 M27 M82 M91 M198 N13 Q5 S229 S270 S276 T161 Z8
KAZ Eric Justin A52 B57D B157 K17 M222D R22 S173 T134
KAZ Fred E60B
KAZANAN Thomas M78
KAZANOTT Kaz M227
KAZOO Alvin T41
KAZOO Jackson t41
KAZOO BROTHERS BAND T41
KAZOOSKI Ted T41
KEACH Jim C179
KEADY Dan F86A
KEAGGY Phil G43
KEAGLE Charlie B29
KEAGLE Lynn WIlson H75
KEAGY Phil V38
KEALEY David L. B154B
KEALEY Tom N43
KEAN Douglas K44A
KEANE Barry A69 B10 D97B

KELLIE Mike A87 B26 C30 C155 F8B F100 F101 F104 G27 G111 I20 J16B K87 L48 L64 L95 O26 P29B R106 S224 T82 T86 T170 W133 Y14
H117 L72 S274 T79C
KEANE Dolores C102 D38 T79
KEANE Kevin C35C
KEANE Sean C102 G10
KEARNES Kurt N57C
KEARNEY Ellen M37 M229 P114B S124 W11
KEARNEY Pete F133
KEARNS Brantley B221
KEARNS Mick T34
KEARNS Phil S180
KEARTON Tommy D11
KEATON Eddie G7E
KEAYS James M103B
KEBECK Chris D29A
KECK Mike B109
KEEBLE John S203A
KEEBLE Peter G16
KEEFER Lee M170
KEEL Linda K19
KEELEY David R3
KEELEY Dennis E59
KEELEY Ron R9
KEELS Bunky E54 J53
KEELY Andy R55
KEELY Ron S177C
KEELY Yvonne H26A I20 M35
KEEN John 'Speedy' C84A H76 K20 T84
KEENAN Brian C69 R39
KEENAN Paddy B185 M1A
KEENE Barry S216
KEENE Bob A51
KEENE Mickey A98A B77 H52 N58B R85
KEENE Tom P129 S272
KEENER Glenn L108 T153A
KEENLYSIDE Tom P139
KEES Bill M216A
KEESEE Carl B219A
KEETON Steve E51
KEEVIL Pam H70
KEFFORD Ace K21 M219
KEGLER Peter S289
KEHLIOR John A9 S122 W34
KEHN Jim M204
KEHUT Wasyl C28A
KEINZER Joachim B198A
KEISER Stan S164B
KEISLER Bill B57E
KEISING Bernie C76
KEISTER John Shane B272B B210 B261 C50 C124 C194 E51 E57 H7D H162A K96 L77 L108 L136A M108 M125 N25 N37 O15 R4 R81 R127A S32 S269 S272 T67A W11 W43
KEITH K21A
KEITH Barbara K8
KEITH Ben A59 B29 B148 B169 B183B B278 B282 C216 C233 D2 D12 D139 G72 H35 H182 K68D M32 M211 N4 N57 R62 R164 R173 S173 S252 S29B Y16
KEITH Bill E5 E20 K101 M125 M222D M227 M228 M229 M229A O33A Q15A S67 T32E T134
KEITH Brian B247 P95 S338
KEITH Bubba E57 J31 P109A
KEITH Gary F11A R127A
KEITH Randall S281
KEITH Steve C124 P139F W11 Y18
KEITH Venna H98
KEITHLINE J.F. S118
KEKANA Fana David B105
KELBE Hellmuth B199
KELFELD David A27
KELLER Peter Vernon G94
KELLAWAY Roger H39 M125 M229 O15 T107
KELLEHER Dan O25
KELLER Bobby F109
KELLER Conny F101D
KELLER Danny M86
KELLER Dennis F43
KELLER Jim C182
KELLER Ron F83A H7D
KELLER Stephen M53
KELLEY Bill D5C
KELLEY Jan F134
KELLEY Joe S81
KELLEY Kevin B285 F5 F43 H65 O6 R98
KELLEY Raymond F134
KELLICHEN Tom N19

KELLIS Rick B224A T158
KELLMAN Terry T118
KELLOFF Ray Z8
KELLOGG Burns B150 M162B
KELLOGG Ralph B150
KELLOGG Rick B109
KELLOUGH Manuel P126
KELLY Aubray R144A
KELLY Betty V9
KELLY Bill B267
KELLY Bobby O2C
KELLY Casey G96B K22 S269
K22A T130
KELLY Dennis S311
KELLY Frances S177D
KELLY Georgia K48
KELLY Jedd B73
KELLY Jim H143
KELLY Jim F75B
KELLY Jo Ann B250 C105 D128 G110 K22A K23 M44 T130
KELLY Joe P33 W119B
KELLY John (G) E52
KELLY John (B) G3
KELLY Jonathan (LEDINGHAM Jon) K24 T77
KELLY Kevin (Pno) A59 B8 B256
KELLY Kevin (V) R144A
KELLY Kevin (B) W7
KELLY Kim B23
KELLY Larry F111
KELLY Matthew B236B G76 G84 K60 N43
KELLY Mike S220
KELLY Pat L2B P125A S355
KELLY Pete E19 M1 P10
KELLY Pierce M196 W41
KELLY Ray B15 B245 S116
KELLY Richard C196
KELLY Roger S299
KELLY Sam (D) C25
KELLY Sam (Congas) W101
KELLY Sherman K58
KELLY Tom A50 B25 B194 C70A R1A W42 W46
KELLY Tony K25 W96
KELLY Wells B166B C62B H185 K58 K81 L129 M90 O32 O39 R22 R164
KELLY Winston 'Spots' R139
KELLY Wynton D27 L83
KELLY WIl3B
KELSEY Linda D93D
KELSO Beverley M88
KELSO John 'Jack' All B56 B127 B201 C59 C76 C180 C213 C234D C235 D5A D59B D86 E40 F92 F134 K17 K95 M75 M125A M163 N16A O39 P102B P137 Q3A R101 R164 S160 S262 T145 W9
KELSO-HERSTON D. T21
KELTNER Jim A116 A132 B23 B53 B71 B84 B180 B201 B202 B244 B248 B255 C11B C14 C38A C76 C94 C155 C156 C162 C164 C171 C179 C180 C182 C237 D5A D23A D26 D28 D36A D99 D100 D124 D139 E40 F50 F78 F128 G10 G24 G109 G121 H8A H39 H156 J85A K17 K45 K46 K51 K86 L50 L51 M39B M65B M75 M101 M125A M132D M159 M191 M227 M229 N40 O15 O27 P28 P114B P130 R22 R24B R60C R80A R101 R173 S55A S58 S111 S124 S196 S220 S252 S262 T25 T32B T37H T91 V3 V12 W5 W44A W116 W119B W120 W133 W133A
KELTON Robert M13A
KELTZ Peter C61A
KEMP Allen N21
KEMP Bill N57
KEMP Brian A62A
KEMP Craig N29B
KEMP Fred D96 T118
KEMP Gary S203A

KINICK John F51
KINKS K61
KINLERS Craig C233
KINNEY George G62A
KINNEY Howerd M170
KINNEY Norma H39 M144
KINORRA Phil A120
KINSEL Frank R101
KINSEY Donald M88 T114 W66
KINSEY Kim F44B
KINSEY Nic M57B
KINSEY Tony G78
KINSEY Woody W66
KINSLEY Billy L94B M136
KINSLEY Roots B276
KINSON Kevin T170
Kip B137
KIP John B225
KIPNER Steve C127 K61A
KIPPER Stan Quica M125
KIPPINGTON LODGE K62
KIPPS Charlie M12 R159
Kirby (G) B174B C251 G4B J39B
K63 K66 P119B S301
Kirby (Pno) C216
KIRBY Andy R40 T54
KIRBY Clive S192
KIRBY Dave C15 H26 H62 J30
J53 M11 N37 R127A S252 S272
Y18
KIRBY David W128A
KIRBY Joe G66
KIRBY Robert B231 C161 C202
S93 S295
KIRBY Wayne W100
KIRCHBERGER John M106B
KIRCHEN Bill C173
KIRCHER Pete H143 M106A O30B
S87
KIRCHIN Basil K64
KIRIAKIS George E20A T22
KIRK Benjamin R60C
KIRK James O28C
KIRK Jeff F90C
KIRK Richard H. C4B K64A
KIRK Robert N56A
KIRKBRIDE John K64C
KIRK Sidney H65A
KIRKE Peter P120
KIRKE Simon B14 B112 B138
C30 D133 F108 H11 K87 R3
R125 W54A
KIRKHAM Bill R53A
KIRKHAM Mildred 'Millie' A59
D139 K95 L72 P125
KIRKLAND Bill S9C
KIRKLAND Eddie H150
KIRKLAND Frank D66
KIRKLAND James N21
KIRKLAND Jesse J91A P126
R133
KIRKLAND Ken K47 S276 V39
KIRKLAND Leroy H63
KIRKLAND Robert A85A
KIRKMAN Terry A106
KIRKPATRICK Chuck A50 B71
B124A C76 D26 G7E
KIRKPATRICK Jesse M26
KIRKPATRICK John A30 B105
C206 H194 J5 K65 R11 R23
S108 S263 T79 U8A
KIRKPATRICK Katie P44
KIRKPATRICK Scott G7E M28
KIRKPATRICK Spencer H195
KIRKWOOD Brian S55D
KIRNBERGER Andy H19C
KIRSCH Barry R20
KIRSCH Danny G85A
KIRSCHNING Achim S47
KIRSHENBAUM Steven B52B
KIRTLEY Pete G46 G101 G102
H177 I23D R7 R86 S103B S348B
W58 W123
KIRWAN Danny F66 K66 P62
S204 S211 T130 Y11
KISH George F14
KISS K67
KISSELBACH Donnie D53
KISSMER Willi B278A
KISSOON Katie B160 E41 K28B
M19 M203 R46 R106 Y17
KISSOON Mac E41 K28B M19 R106
KISWINEY Dave N63 Q5
KITAJIMA Osamu A41 H150A O33G
KITCAT Martin G77A H169
KITCHEN Kevin K66
KITCHEN CINQ K67B

KITE K67A
KITHCART Glenn A55 T116A
KITRELL Christine B193
KITTA George T23
KITTERINGHAM Eric G5
KITTYHAWK K67C
KITZMILLER John N25
KIX K67D
KIX Lee E23 M57C
KIZER Brad C39B
KJAERSTAD Wenche P104
KJELDSEN Mark S130
KLAASSE Beer F45
KLAASSE Jakob L5A
KLAATU K68
KLAERS Hugo S315A
KLAIN Gary H23
KLAIN Manny N25
KLAMANN Detlef M216B
KLARWEINI Marti S175
KLASS Lou C146 F134
KLASSEN Kasi E63
KLATKA Tony B141
KLAUS LENZ BAND L52B
KLAVETT Dean L131
KLAWON Dan T17
KLAYMAN Dan W5B
KLEBE Gary S102
KLEC'H Mikael S280
KLEE George W55B
KLEE Ginny D54
KLEE Lucy D54
KLEER K68A
KLEENEX K68B
KLEIGER Frank W5
KLEIN Betsy F133
KLEIN Carole see KING
Carole
KLEIN Daniel G19 G122
KLEIN Harry B59 C34 F14
K75 S14
KLEIN Larry (B) M170
KLEIN Larry (D) N58C
KLEIN Paul W100
KLEIN Warren F94 F104A
KLEINBARD Annette T37D
KLEINE-TELBE Ralph H99B
KLEINOW Bernd B91D D66C
KLEINOW 'Sneaky' Pete
B49 B71 B130 B202 B210
B244 B245 B285 C6B C59
C96B C155 C156 C160 C180
C216 C236 D8 D28 D49
D68B D69 D72A E41 F19
F66 F74 H5C
K17 K22 K68C K81 L51 L89
M30 M125A M159 M160 M170
M211C N21 N42 O15 O27
P33 P76 R137 S8A S71A
S114 S213 S252 T6B W119
Z8
KLEIST Ken E72
KLEMM Dieter F70A
KLEMM Harald A67A
KLEMMER John B194 H150
M82 S262 W119B
KLETCHKOVSKY Nick B197D
KLEYN Bert F133A
KLIEMES Peter A135
KLIENT Bernd C124B
KLIER Dieter V7
KLIER Gottfried F68A
KLIMAK Ken D86
KLIMAS Larry P156A
KLIMES Peter M132E W6
KLINE Phil D14B
KLING Janne A4 L79
KLINGBERG John M203 V21
KLINGER Gunther M136B
KLINGMAN Mark 'Moogy'
C195 F109 K68D K81 L80C
O39 R164 W107
KLINKHAMMER Hans R20A
KLOATR Alan S280
KLOBER Chris C247C H48A
KLOCKER Gerd W13D
KLOET Rob N52A
KLOETZE Don B261
KLUCZYNSKI Marek B82
KLUGH Earl B85 J20 J43
K69
KLUSTER C145
KLVANA Mike H9
KLYMAXX K68E
KMCH Steve O6A
KNAAK Bernd E52A
KNACK K69A
KNADEN Martin C247C

KNAIL John S236
KNAPE Skip 'Van Winkle'
S73 T37I
KNAPP Bob M40 W8
KNAPP Bruce S355A
KNAPP Carroll 'Rico' T97A
KNAPP John G124
KNAPP Peter I1
KNAPP Robin E77C S192
KNAPP Skip M1
KNAPP Tom 'Cat' T41
KNAUB Don K48
KNAUP Renate A57A P118
U23
KNECHTEL Larry B17A B110
B206 B285 C6B C140A C161B
C171 C172A D5A D23A D26
D28 D36A D53C D72A E14
E57 F43 G9 G10 G14 G15
G83 G101A H10A H37A J36
J69 K14 K81 L111 L116 M30
M61 M84C M101 M125A M144
N25 O15 P74 P125 P129 R76
R87 R101 R126 R142A S123
S125 S160 S173C S198B S272
T32B T64A T91 W39 W44 W88
KNEDDY Carmen H156
KNEE Lew D34B
KNEIL Manfred M136C
KNEPPER Edmund L23A
KNEPPER Jimmy K81 M79
KNICKERBOCKERS K69B
KNIEMEYER Claus O7
KNIGHT Billy J66
KNIGHT Bob C162
KNIGHT Brenda T37I
KNIGHT Brendan K72 M1
KNIGHT Curtis H99 K70
KNIGHT Fred G102
KNIGHT Gladys K72
KNIGHT Gladys & the Pips
K72
KNIGHT Graham M89
KNIGHT Holly S214A
KNIGHT Jean K71
KNIGHT Jerry B226 D124
KNIGHT Jesse E52B L90
KNIGHT Joyce C207 W54
KNIGHT K.J. A35A N63
KNIGHT Larry B210 C15A
S216
KNIGHT Lonnie K77
KNIGHT Merald K72
KNIGHT Peter A30 H194 J75B
P84 S263
KNIGHT Robert G16
KNIGHT Stanley B114
KNIGHT Steve (K) M216
KNIGHT Tony B224 D46 S141
KNIGHT Warren 'Butch' F64
KNIGHTON Joan H50
KNIGHTON Reggie K73 S65
W65
KNIGHTS Dave P140 R156
KNIGHTSBRIDGE John G32
H90 H174 I13 L76B S295
T63
KNOPFLER Dave D75
KNOPFLER Mark D75 D139
L144B M41A M203 S262
KNOTT Ray B5
KNOW Bobby O36
KNOWLES David T108
KNOWLES Errol A136 E65
KNOWLES Geoff P110
KNOWLES Greg M220 P143
KNOWLES Keith M91
KNOWLES Tom C196 K32A
KNOWLES Willie A80
KNOWLING Ransom C135 C239
E67 S204 S329 T9B W84 W93
Knox H128B V28
KNOX Bruce B181B
KNOX Buddy B187A K74
KNOX Don S230
KNOX Nick C212B
KNOX Tom R41
KNUDSEN Hans R178
KNUDSEN J.D83A
KNUDSEN Keith B134A D101
J85A L19 M144 S124
KNUDSEN Kenneth B275 C185D
D31 L41 S69 T79D
KNUDSEN Pete B230 P117A
P117C T37L
KNUTSEN Pete R178
KOBAYSHI Katsuhiko F71A

KOBAYASHI Shigeyuki C253A
KOBE Greg Q5
KOBIALKA Daniel A48
KOBLUN Ken B260
KOBORI Tadashi H35A W53A
KOBS Michael T63A
KOCH Michael J56
KOCH Steve D46A
KOCHBECK Georg P20A
KOCJAN Krysia H110 K61 K75
N11 S270
KOCK Franz O47
KODA Cubby B246
KODAK Dave S263A
KODAMA Kathie W1
KODER Jay L119C
KODAMA Martin G15A
O6C
KOELLEN Helmut T143
KOEMAN Martin K16
KOENIG Art A86
KOERNER 'Spider' John K75A
K75B T134
KOERNER RAY AND GLOVER K75B
KOERTS Chris E4
KOERTS Gerard E4
KOFFMAN Moe D97B K53
KOFSTEIN Mark E7B
KOGEL Robbie K68D
KOGER Marijke F81C
KOHL Martin S338
KOHLER Rolf S329A T100
T103A
KOHLHASE Klaus A3A
KOHLIN Jan L79
KOHMSTEDT Martin G15A
KOHN Madelaine B53
KOHN Philip C251
KOHN Sigurd L24C
KOHON Harold S215
KOIVISTOINEN Eero P56A
P109 W75
KOJIMA Ian U5A
KOJO Timo W75
KOKEN Walt T150
KOKOMO A22 K76
KOKOMO Singers M15A
KOLB Dieter S332C
KOLBE Bernd E60B
KOLBE Martin & ILLENBERGER
Ralf K76A
KOLDENHOVEN Darlene L65
KOLINKA Richard T37K
KOLKOWSKI Aleksander B17B
KOLLARUS Gary G87
KOLLEKTIV K76B
KOLLENBERG Jerry N29B
KOLLER Hans D19A S73C
KOLLIS Ed A132
KOLOC Bonnie G72 K77 P137
KOLONOVITS Christian M153
S42B
KOMANOFF Ruth Z8
KOMINTERN K77A
KONAS Joe G56 T103
KONCALSKI Michael M238
KONCZEWSKI Christiane S93
KONDO Tatsuro H35A
KONDOR Robbie F83A H15
KONDOS John Alexander
C185H
KONDOS Nicholas Alexander
C185H
KONDZIELA David A135 M198
KONGO Roy Johnston P134
KONGOS John D2 K78 N45
KONIETZKO Harald L5 P33E
T63A
KONIKOFF Eli S231
KONIKOFF Sanford B27 B84
C14 C155 D26 K45 K46 M53
S111
KONITZ Lee D27 M75
KONOPIK Kono A67K
KONRAD Robert B15
KONTE Lamine W119
KONTE Skip B166 B225 C158
T81
KONZIELA Dave C76
KOOBAS K79
KOOL AND THE GANG K80
KOOLEN Jonah B207C
KOONTZ Randy P67
KOOPER Al A59 A67L B141
B144 B158 B194 B210 B282
C77A C172A C180 C182 D139
E13 E15 F102 H99 K81 L24
L37 L107 M27 M53 N53 O39

P39 R133 R169 S34 V18A
KOOPMAN Pim D66A K16 V38A
KOOTCH Danny see KORTCHMAR
Danny
KOOYMANS George B224A C243
G64
KOPELSON Danny F80
KOPLAN Michael C80B
KOPP Holger S329A
KOPPEL Anders S30
KOPPEL Ilse Maria S30
KOPPEL Thomas S30
KOPPENHAUER David C21A
KOPPES Peter C111B
KORAL Dawn A31
KORBA Tom J112
KORBER Gunter J38
KORBER Helmut C241D
KORBERG Tommy M45C S186
KORDA Paul D4 K82 M23 R33 S35
KORDULETSCH Jurgen A57
KORELL Lou F99A
KORENG Gisbert E31D
KOREVEC Loren C234A
KORGIS K83
KORMA Eddy P92B
KORN Barbara E7 E55 S36
KORNER Alexis B150A B156 B268
C2 C243 D23 G112D H179 J75B
J91 K45 K84 M129 M185 P34
P120 R122A
KORNER Neil G32 N5 R65
KORNER Sappho J34 K84
KORNFIELD Barry P41
KORNFELD Artie K84A W100
KORONA K84B
KORPS K85
KORTCHMAR Danny (KOOTCH
Danny) A116 B149 B175 B244
C38 C38A C54 C117 C123 C138
C158 C184A C233 D53C D139 E40
F68 F114A F133 G60 J65 K14
K48 K86 K99A M132D M191 M211C
N4 N23 P114 Q15A R22 R39 R81
R137 S17 S70 S196 S252 S272
S276 T25 T27 T164 W21 W136
Z11
KORULETSCH Jurgen A57A
KORUS Kate R17 S19
KOSAK Wayne J15A
KOSCHNIDDER Bernd B107
KOSEF Kenny B207A
KOSEK Kenneth B135 B221 C199C
F83A G72 I2 M21 O15 P41 S7
W5 W51A W65A
KOSH Paul C251 F42 G22
KOSHIDA Nisako N65
KOSINEC Tony K86A
KOSINS Kathy H98
KOSINSKI Richard 'Koz' S327A
W54B
KOSLEN Jonah S241
KOSOWSKI Eddie A72B
KOSS Ron S28A S59A S65
KOSSOFF Keith B47
KOSSOFF Paul 'Koss' B12 B112
B138 C30 D133 F108 G51 K87
V21 V26A
KOSSOFF KIRKE TETSU AND
RABBIT F108
KOSTER Koos D37B
KOSTER Pieter D37B
KOSTROSKI Wayne C115A
KOTCH John B227A
KOTHE Gerd J100A
KOTITAINEN Esa T104 W75
KOTKE Lenny G69
KOTKOV Ralph C111
KOTLER Cameron S284C
KOTTKE Leo K88
KOULOURIS Silver A67E
KOURY Ki Ki W119B
KOUVARIS L.A. R94
KOVACEK Branislav U21
KOVACEV Laca D19A
KOVARIK Dennis B226 C59 M89A
KOVATCH Tim M203
KOWALD Peter V26C
KOWALKE Pete C207 T20 T95
KOWALSKI Mike B56 C62B C216
D111 H110 L129 M94 O39
KOWALSKI Ted D62
KOZAK Mike T37C
KOZAK Wayne P119A
KOZUKI Jun F71A
KPIAYE John B120 J48 P80C
R61C
KRAAIJEVELD Frank B104A

Led/Lew

LEDGER Robert S281
LEDINGHAM Jon see KELLY Jonathan
LEDISSEZ Lionel E62A
LEDSTER Bill I13A
LEE Adrian B174B H111
LEE Alan M81
LEE Albert A82 B84 B244 C89 C121 C124 C155 C224 C237 D2 D66 D100 E19 E20 E44 E73 F21 G27 G95 G95 H35 H74 H177 L19 L36A L64 L120 M78 N43 P56 P107 W71
LEE Alvin D66 H29 H39 L37 L44 S55A T45 T46
LEE Arthur L38 L128
LEE Barbara C103
LEE Bernie P110
LEE Beverly S98
LEE Brenda (TARPLEY Brenda Mae) L39
LEE Byron L39A
LEE Charles 'Chuckle' L69
LEE Chris A29
LEE Christopher J75B
LEE Dave T53A
LEE David Z9
LEE Diana B8 R108
LEE Dixie L114
LEE Ed C3
LEE Edmond M111
LEE Freddy 'Fingers' L40
LEE Geddy R167
LEE George 'Sneaks'(Sax) A85 B4 B105 B276 K20 M94 R84 R125 S313 T110
LEE George (Wind) A71
LEE GINGER C177D
LEE Glenn 'Judge' P47
LEE Gregory P75
LEE Jack B221 G16 M211 N23
LEE Jackie 'Earl' B162
LEE Jackie H66A
LEE Jamie R100
LEE Jeannette P144
LEE John (D) A79 C59 D72B D78 O46 S45C
LEE Larry (G) H99
LEE Laura W7
LEE Leonard S99
LEE Marvin M120
LEE Michael S216
LEE Mikel T132
LEE Millard K45
LEE Paul S276
LEE Phil G30 P36 P42A P45
LEE Phyliss P53
LEE Rahm L65
LEE Randy L42
LEE Ras T114
LEE Ray L134
LEE Ric C101 C112 J70A T45 V26A W117
LEE Richard (B) B187
LEE Richard (Recorder) C165 T37H
LEE Richard (K) F133
LEE Richard (G) K68A
LEE Robbie T114
LEE Robert L42A
LEE Robert S216
LEE Rod M. S204
LEE Roderick C101
LEE Roger J113 P24B
LEE Sandra S63
LEE Sarah F121 L32A
LEE Sharon B238
LEE Stan I16
LEE Stan D64
LEE William F. IV (Will) A31 A82 A123 B199B B20B B253 C62 C164 C189 C213E D86 D115 D139 F4C F60 F108A F111 F122 G64C H29 H137 H164C I2 J20 K36 K37 S152 M17 M26 M53 M65A M86 M107 M125 M198 M225 N2A N65 P72A R25 R169 S17 S124 S180 S228 S231 T98 T147 W8

LEE RIDERS L42A
LEECH David H129B
LEECH Geordie R141A
LEECH Greg M205A
LEECH Mike B43C B210 C14 C75 C124 C133 D104 E54 E73 G85A K30 K77 K88 M78 M108 N37 O15 P63 P125 P137 R4 R31 R101 S271 T9 T21 T55 T67A T167 Y18
LEEDS Gary B59 H99 W13A
LEEDS Peter C. W100
LEEDS Steve B245 G120A
LEEFLANG Fred M237A O9A V38A
LEEGER Josje F81C
LEEJACK Ron C5
LEEKERS Edward K16
LEENDERS Gerrit Jan K16
LEEQUE Darryl P25
LEER Thomas L42B L42C
LEERDAM Wilco Torre V38A
LEES Carol F69B
LEES John B37 L43 M67
LEESE Eric D99 R62
LEESE Howard H75 H164A M123
LEEUFF Sam see STEWART David
LEEUW Lourens C243 M237A
LEFEBURE Cyril V26B
LE FEVER Steve B245 C208A H52 M95B
LEFEVRE Lorraine I36A
LEFEVRE Mylon A111 D12 L37 L44 L95C W72
LEFEVRE Pierce L44
LEFLEUR Glen A85 B189 C7 D95A D131 G66A G67 H17 H42 H70 J110 L16A L46 L47 M38 O20 R11 W103
LEFLOCH Michel A64
Left Hand Frank H159 R128
LEFT BANKE L24
LEFTENANT Arnett C20
LEFTENANT Nathan C20
LEFTWICH John M86
LEGAL WEAPON L45A
LE GATE Bob G76
LEGEND L46
LEGEND Bill B168
LEGEND Johnny & THE SKULLCAPS L45B
LEGG Adrian S313
LEGGAT Gordy P139B
LEGGAT Hughie F83 N62A P139B
LEGGET Archie A35 A133 C13 C209 C210 E59 G102 R140 W129
LEGGETT Andy P42B P81 S152 S326A T90
LEGION George C107E
LEGOVER L47
LEGRAND Christianne P140
LEGRAND Michel D27 R142A
LEGRAND Robert O14
LEGS DIAMOND L47A
LEGWORTHY Elizabeth S264
LEH George M227 S339A
LEHENAFF Claude F101C
LEHMAN John J72 J88A M18 R137 S36 W10A Y12
LEHMAN Kenny C95A C99
LEHMANN Edie R137
LEHMING Kyle E57 F50 J53
LEHNERT Bob S284D
LEHNING Vicki E57
LEHOCKY Mickey Z9A
LEHRNDORFER Franz B91A
LEIB Geoffrey M123 P80B W116
LEIBER Oliver B226
LEIBEZEIT Jaki R145
LEIGH Peter L47B
LEIGH Andy E35A E41 F23 L48 M108 P158 S198 S224
LEIGH Denis see FOXX Denis
LEIGH Geoff F57 H57 H101 S152
LEIGH Jode E56A L9A
LEIGHTON Chris A125 I25A
LEIM Paul G14 G40 N25 N53A

LEINBACH Bob F3A H8 O32 J41 J105A K51 R137
LEINEMANN L47C
LEINER Friedemann B157
LEISHMAN Larry B124B R75
LEISTOLA Elizabeth V26C
LEITCH Donovan see Donovan
LEITCH James R76
LEITH Jim M96
LEITH Richard A131D B240 M68
LE JEAN Karla D86
LE JEUNE Jonny L95B
LEKA Paul C76 C108B
LEKAS Jim Q4A
LEKHELA Sonia O34
LE LAN Dominique 'Black Beard' L87
LELAND Charles S337
LELAND John E57
LELAND Michael S337
LEMAIRE Jo & FLOUZE L48B
LEMAIRE Sonny E77
LE MAISTRE Malcolm H110 I16
LEMBEDE Maureen Koto J4
LEMBRECHT Lemmie C251B
LEMELLE Daniel W54B
LEMER Pepi A74 R12 S76 T160
LEMER Peter A93 B20 B67 C6 G66 O18 S76 S267 T76
LEMERCIER Patrick M57B
LE MESURIER Robin L76B
LEMING Kip R94
LEMING Jean Sebastien R78A
Lemmy see KILMISTER Ian
LEMOINE Patrice G66 P124 R78A
LEMON Brian I20
LEMON KITTENS L48A
LEMON PIPERS L49
LEMONNIER Francis K77A
LEMONS Overton Amos see LEWIS Smiley
LEMOS Elly B69
LEMUR Pete B237
LENART Paul F19A I32
LENGYELL Mikie D73
LENINGRAD Charlie L49A
LENINGRAD D. L49A
LENINGRAD Johnny L49A
LENINGRAD Mike L49A
LENINGRAD SANDWICH L49A
LENART Paul F20 M191
LENNEAR Claudia A132 C123 C155 C179 G96A H179 J16B K25 K51 K81 L50 L107 M53 M101 N55 R173 S276
LENNER Jimmy R35
LENNERS Rudy S47
Lenni B183D
LENNON Jeff N61B
LENNON John B59 B89A B186 E37 L51 M100E O27 S115D S252
LENNON Julian L51
LENNOX Annie T117
LENNOX Dave O9
LENNOX Rob K65
Lenny & Squiggy L51A
LENOIR J.B. L52
LE NOIR Jet T18A
LENOIR Phil B112
LENS L52A
LENSKA Rula R120
LENT Robin R111C
LENTIN Keith S86C S214A
LENTIN Mike D2 R156
LENTZ Rudy P92B
LENZ Gunter B197D D19A H34
LENZ Jack L110 S58
LENZ Klaus L52B S58
LEO Josh B192 B261 C38A C63D F114A E13A
LEON Craig C237 D48A M96 S319
LEON Mark B42B C217
LEONARD Brian H117 M23BA
LEONARD Darrell B201 B202 B221 C38A D26 D133A G24

LEONARD Deke see LEONARD Roger
LEONARD Glenn Carl T42
LEONARD James L24A
LEONARD Mark G101B
LEONARD Mickey S122A
LEONARD Pat T139A
LEONARD Nondi C199C
LEONARD Roger 'Deke' D114
E23 L53 M63 T170
LEONARD Ronald K99A
LEONARD Steve C223B
LEONARDI Michel E62A
LEONARDO Michael B116A
LEONARDS Bobby M163
LEONE Bob M125
LEONE John D66
LEDNETH Eddie S147
LEONHART Jay C40
LEOPARD L54
LEOPOLD Glenn G117C
LEOPOLD Jaime H112
LEOPOLD Pete A57A
LEOPOLD Reg S235
LEOPOLD Ullrich A57A
LE ORME L54A
LEPAK Al A59A
LE PAMPLEMOUSSE L55
LEPERE Louis V16
LE PEW Kinki M1
LE PIG Germun P118C
LEPICOLO Robert V39C
LEPING Lucille N26A
LEPINSKY Joyce L82A
LEPORE Richard E7
LEPPARD ,DEF A40B
LEPPARD Norman D129 O24A
LEPPIK Gene S156
LE QUE Darryl I23D P45
LERACE Dominic see IRIS Donny
LERCHEY David D43
LERIOS Cory P3 S284
LERNER Mike E13A
LEROIS Cay T71A
LE ROUX L56
LEROY Greg C172B C216 P69
LESH Phil B221 C232 G9 G84 H45 N4 N32 R77B S61 W42
LESKIW Greg G115
LESLEY Kim P19
LESLEY Mike L56A
LESLIE Irma W119
LESLIE Jack E31C
LESLIE Kyra J30 N24
LESLIE, KELLY & JOHN FOD COLEY L56C
LESLIE Mike W71
LESLIE Russo J30 N24
LESLIE Sunny B14 B25 B138 B189 C30 C155 D2 D39 D46 D49 D105 E18 E48 G51 G73 H66A H70 H110 J63 J72 J102 K78 K81 K87 L56B M80 M214 P4 R20 S31 S185 S209 S317 Y17
LESPRON Mickey E30
LESSAGE Didier C152A
LESSER Scott B139
LESTER Al G61 S36
LESTER Bobby M192C
LESTER Eddie F70B R20
LESTER Funky N53
LESTER Gerry M160A
LESTER Kelty E71
LESTER Ray M68
LESTER Robert 'Squirrel' C98
LESTER Tony B31
L'ESTRANG Christopher H189
L'ESTRANGE Liam S250A
LES VARIATIONS L57
LETANTE De Paris K6
LETECHEUR Albert M30A
LETONDRE Tom J96
LETOURNEUX Eric C113A
LETT Carl C213D
LEURION Jean Jacques R78A
LEUSCHNER Jochen D143 H19C
LEUZINGER Chris B210 N23
LEVAN Martin R12
LE VANG Neil E74 Z8
LEVANT Eddie O14
LEVANT Gayle B225 C17 C39 C169 C180 F78 G121 H8A H39

L12B L72 M84C P28 R97 S10 T25 T145 W21
LEVASSEUR Bill N60B
LEVASSEUR Gerard S280
LEVAY Sylvester F66A J10A N61C
LEVEL 42 L57B
LEVEN Jackie see ST. FIELD John
LEVENS Dick A109
LEVENSON Jon B183D
LEVENTON Annabel A109
LEVER Tim M175E
LEVERT Eddie W119
LEVERTON James E46 F8 F29 H94 J105 M15 S31
LEVI AND THE RIPCORDS L57A
LEVI Bongo A107
LEVI James H19
LEVI Tony H29
LEVIAS Greg J7 R60C
LEVIATHAN L57C
LEVIEV Milcho C147 M75
LEVIN Daniel A102
LEVIN Drake B228C M144 R70 R76
LEVIN Geoff C180 E36 S213
LEVIN Louis H8
LEVIN Pete N35
LEVIN Ray L87A
LEVIN Robb P59A
LEVIN Stewart J73A
LEVIN Tony A82 C108D C164 C182 D50 F115 F121 G2 G10 H8 H136A K29B K54 K84A L51 L58B M21 M41 M65A M78 M143 N62 N65 O27 P123 R25 R60 R118 S124 S125 S180 S252 T30 T98 W20A
LEVINE Burt T13
LEVINE Hank F48C
LEVINE Joey T61
LEVINE Keith C130 C207A F71 P144
LEVINE Marc F. R101 W18
LEVINE Mark C63C C220B P48
LEVINE Mike (B) T80 T142 U7
LEVINE Michael (Vln) G90
LEVINE Russ U7
LEVINE Stewart D104
LEVINGER Lowell 'Banana' Y22
LEVINrad Miriam F70B
LEVINSOHN Blake F101C
LEVIS Bob B226A R168
LEVITON Mark L134
LEVITT Dan B61 E45 L58 M10A
LEVITT Noel G2A
LEVITT AND McCLURE L58
LEVY Barrington L58A
LEVY Bob S19
LEVY Carl C114 S93
LEVY Howard P137
LEVY Jay M26
LEVY Jesse I2 K36 R25 S215 T25
LEVY Marcia B85 B169A B226 C121 C182 F114A G106A Q3B R173
LEVY O'Donel L58B M26
LEVY Ron K45
LEVY Stafford L58B
LEVY Yes P53
LEWARK David H5 M179
LEWIE Jona (LEWIS John) L59 M99
LEWINE Rob I21A
LEWINS Bob C50
LEWINS Steve C199 J82
LEWINSON Danny J34
LEWINSON Paul A132 S213
LEWINTHAL Paul P114C
LEWIS Andre E62B H17 M151 W30 Z8
LEWIS Becky J38A R142A S34
LEWIS Billy B23A B194A D116
LEWIS Bob A51 K76 K77
LEWIS Buddy T154
LEWIS Cappy T37H
LEWIS Cheryl F74C
LEWIS Dave (D) B43C W101
LEWIS Dave (G V) A63A L60
LEWIS Diana J72 T18
LEWIS Doug L119C
LEWIS Eddie O21
LEWIS Elmo see JONES Brian
LEWIS Elsie H34
LEWIS Ewan M221D

[674]

Lof/ Lyn

LOFGREN Nils C216 L107 M16
S276 Y16
LOFGREN Tom L107
LOGAN Bud E54
LOGAN Ed B202 C62 D86 G92
G101A M130 N57 P51 P125 S276
LOGAN John P106 S203
LOGAN Mal G26A
LOGAN T. R67
LOGAN Todd A37 H195
LOGEMAN David Z8
LOGGINS Dan S253
LOGGINS Dave B261 H7D L108
LOGGINS Ken C70A G15 G106A
L109 L110 M16A N53 S20 S55A
LOGGINS AND MESSINA L110
LOGIC Lora E66A R17 R53 S292
S354A X2
LOGIC SYSTEM L110A
LOHMANN Michael J4B
LOHR Tommy H125B
LOHR Werner H268 S38
LOHSE Wertehr L70A
LOILE Jim F139
LOIZZO Gary A51
LOJEWSKI Rainer E56B
LOKEY Tommy R173
LOLLIPOP SHOPPE L110B
LOMAS Roger D90
LOMAX Dwayne K46 W118
LOMAX Jackie B17 B149 B26 D26
H84 L111 L112 R22 U10
LOMAX ALLIANCE L112
LOMBAR Dru C207 G104 T9A
LOMBARD Carole P125
LOMBARDI Mike R39
LOMBARDO Sam E71A
LONDIN Larry A95 B57F C124
C194 C237 E57 E75 H35 H49
H117 J53 K30 K77 L108 M157
N25 N37 R4 S32 S269 T55 Y16
LONDON L113
LONDON Dobbie J93D
LONDON John C188 F109 M113
N25 N53 T25 T140
LONDON Lew G72
LONDON Mark B77
LONDON Mike K28B M19 R106
LONDON Richard (Svor Naan)
C213B
LONDON CHAMBER CHOIR M15A
LONDON PHILHARMONIC ORCHESTRA
E34
LONDON SYMPHONY ORCHESTRA G27
L120 N54 W7 Y16
LONDON WELSH CHOIR S177D
Lone Groover L113A
LONE STAR L114
Lonesome Sundown (GREEN
Cornelius) L115
LONEY Roy A. F61 L115A
LONG Danny K77
LONG Dino L81 M158B
LONG Gary C173A
LONG Joey F91
LONG Julie B42B
LONG Mike C156
LONG Shorty P125
LONG Steve N13
LONG HELLO L117A
LONG TALL ERNIE L115B
LONGBOTTOM Pete P104A
LONGBRANCH PENNYWHISTLE L116
LONGDANCER E41 L117
LONGHAIR Professor L118
LONGMIRE Wilbert L119 P115
LONGO John L4 M46B M149 M157
LONGORIA Carlos B242B
LONGSTAFF Gordon N44
LONIE Clive J94
LONIE Lonie P18D
LONNEN Steve S102A
LONNEUX Francis R51D
LONNIE Clarence W94
LONSDALE Shep C85
LOOK Richard C86A
LOOKING GLASS L119B
LOOKOFSKY Harry L45 M233 M233
LOONAM John P142B
LOONEY Phil P53
LOONEY Warren P114
LOOP Bill E19B
LOOS Charles C190 J105B L26A
LOOSIGIAN Billy A32
LOPAC Gary L16B

LOPER Charles C70A C156
C213E E7 F92 H8A H156
K48 Q12 R99 W84C
LOPEZ Amaury R13A
LOPEZ Anita W21B
LOPEZ Barbara B246A
LOPEZ Becky B9 C246 J10B
R142A
LOPEZ Chris N11A
LOPEZ Dennis A98 J72 M15A
P139G T47
LOPEZ Vini 'Mad Dog'
S229
LOPRESTI John 'Cooker'
B157 C107 C182 M65A S252
LOPREVITE Franco N60
LORANGE Kirk D121 H40
L101
LORBER Alan U7
LORBER Jeff L119C
LORCK John I97
LORD Barry T135A
LORD David K83
LORD Jon A92 A100 B174B
B208B C204 D40 H91 L120
M90A P9 R96 R147 S22
W117
LORD Tracy L85
LORDAN Bill A53A T148
LORDAN Erin J110
LORDAN Petrina J110
LORDS L121
LORENZ Dave M242A
LORENZ Ding B145A
LORENZ Gene G117C
LORENZ Wolfgang B92
LORENZINI Mimi E18B
LORENZO Randy C179
LORIX George O33B
LORMANN Klaus E34A
LORMOR Michael S295A
LOS BRAVOS L121B
LOSEKAMP Michael C255
LOSEKES BLUES GANG L121C
LOSETH Janny T97
LOSIER Gilles M21
LOS INCAS S125
LOST AND FOUND L121A
LOST GONZO BAND L122
LO TEMPIO Rick B17A
LOTHAR AND THE HAND
PEOPLE L122A
LOTT Carl B233
LOTT Sinclair Rogers
W119B
LOUBET Roger W39D
Loud Lance M226
LOUDEN Rob W128A
LOUDERMILK John D. L123
LOUDSPEAKERS L124
LOUENS Paul G47
LOUGHAN Colin S147 Y4B
LOUGHNANE Lee A65 B71
C100 R173 V38
LOUHENSALO Tapio W75
LOUIE Doug J15A
LOUIS Becky (or Becci)
R137 S34 S58
LOUIS Daniel B43
LOUIS Elmer D43A H57A P34
LOUIS Huey see LEWIS Huey
LOUIS Joe Hill L125 T74
LOUIS Rebecca D124 S252
S262
LOUIS Roger Hayward D96
LOUIS Roy P34
Louisiana Red (MINTER
Iverson) L126 W22A
LOUNDER MAN Gus B280A
LOUNGE Eugene W47
LOUNGE LIZARDS L126A
LOU'S L127
LOUSLEY Brian S283A
LOUSTAU Henri A64
LOUTS S212
LOVE L128
LOVE Airrion S31A
LOVE Andrew B43C B202
C133 C231 D86 D101 F50
G92 G101A H65 J85A K45
L19 M85 M130 M209 N23
N57 P51 P137 S124 S276
T27 W119B
LOVE Arthur L128
LOVE Billy 'Red' L125
T74
LOVE Brad A131A

LOVE Candy H19
LOVE Charles B143
LOVE Clayton L128A
LOVE Darlene B224A B226
C38A J73A P74 P125 S135B
S200 T67A
LOVE Jerry M32
LOVE Mike B56 C62B K58 L97
L129
LOVE Preston O39
LOVE Stephen H9 H164C I2
J65A L98 M27 N21 N32 S286
LOVE Steve JM46B
LOVE Stuart Q5
LOVE AFFAIR L129A
LOVE COMMITTEE L130
LOVE SCULPTURE L130C
LOVE TOGETHERNESS DEVOTION
L2
LOVECRAFT L130A
LOVEDAY Billy E31F
LOVEDAY Bob W96
LOVEDAY Martin O40
LOVEGROVE Kelly S249C
LOVELACE David C160 K68C
M27
LOVELACE Jimmy B85 D67
R77B
LOVELACE Ken L64
LOVELADY Billy M114A
LOVELADY Dave F93
LOVELESS Jim D67 R77B
LOVELL Herbie A59 A68 B149
B157 B160B B194 B262 D139
K45 M94 M203 P49 R169 S168
W28
LOVELL Mike J2
LOVERBOY L130B
LOVERING John F30
LOVETRO Gary S294
LOVGREN Bertil L79
LOVICH Lene D78E L131 S348
V25B
LOVIN' SPOONFUL L133
LOVINE Jimmy P70
LOVING Jim M141
LOVING Keith H58
LOVING AWARENESS L132
Low Andy Fairweather see
FAIRWEATHER LOW Andy
LOW Pit M136B
LOW NUMBERS L134
LOWARCH Dave B247
LOWE Albert J22
LOWE Colin M60
LOWE Dan F90B
LOWE Helen R161
LOWE Jeff A82A
LOWE Jim E35
LOWE John N25 T37H
lowe Mundell C213E
LOWE Nick (Bazza) B218 C42
C105 C193 C234E D10 D123
E19 F3B G79 J110 K62 L135
M10C M157 P25 W130
LOWE Phil T64A
LOWE Richard S23A
LOWE Sammy H63
LOWE Steven M188A
LOWE Thadeus James S205
LOWELL Jimmy S86C S214A
LOWENTHAL Barry T33A
LOWER EAST SIDE P53
LOWERY Jim H7
LOWERY Robert A51B
LOWNER Peter F8D
LOWREY Gene C50
LOWRY John S359
LOWTHER Clare D111 F6
LOWTHER Henry A60A A74 B9B
B237 B248 C2 C34 C109 C145A
C159 C204 C251 D7 D10B E24
E38 F6 F14 F42 F86 F125 G11
G32 G71A G102 H50 H64 H70
H116C H176 I20 K84 L104
L136 M6 M80 M83 M111 P76
P127 Q2 R85 S93 S152 T76
T79 T95 W58
Loy N64A
LOYA Bobby E30
LOYALE Dale H146A
LOYDE Lobby A137
LOZAGA Bon G66
LOZANO Pauline M203
Lu see EDMUNDS Robert

LUANDREW Albert see
Sunnyland Slim
LUBAHN Douglas C138
D103 D115 E75 P80A
R86A S232A
LUBAN Morris W86
LUBBOCK Jeremy L56C
R97
LUBIN Howard Lem H185
M180 S27 U14
LUCAFO Phil H78
LUCAS Alfred C146
S171
LUCAS Arno C213 D133A
J93C N40 R125 W119B
LUCAS Buddy B85 C146
D97A H99 R169 T79B
V34
LUCAS David B154
LUCAS Douglas J3
LUCAS Harold C144A
LUCAS Jon P6
LUCAS Kate W112
LUCAS Keith see CASH
Nick
LUCAS Paulina K54
LUCAS Pete D20
LUCAS Ray A27 C146
F60 H58 K17 K55 S128
LUCAS Reggie D27 F60
L41 M222A
LUCAS Rob B45C
LUCAS Roy B45C
LUCAS Sharalee L136A
LUCAS Soo I23C
LUCAS Stan s254B
LUCAS Ted T42
LUCAS Trevor B222 B266
C206 D49 E12 F6 F89 G110
G111 L137 S270 S295 T79
W20B
LUCCA Pape F17
LUCCI Mario P156B
LUCE John A104
LUCERO Geno G112A
LUCHESSI Joe B13A
LUCIA Peter H126A J30
LUCIANO Bravo T162
LUCIEN Jon J75A W36
LUCIER Bob W101
Lucifer see WALKER Pete
LUCIFER L138
LUCIFER'S FRIEND L139
LUCK Jerry S73
LUCKE Johannes T11
LUCKEY Lena R173
LUCKLEY Margi H87
LUCKLEY Stu H87
LUCKY Cab W22A
LUDDECKE Larry F19A
LUDEWIG Peter E31D
LUDLUM Steve T4B
LUDMAN Kim S339
LUDUS L139A
LUDWICK Rex F12B R173
LUDWIG Frank A69 I25A T146
U13B
LUDWIG Rex N23A
LUELL David A37 B225 C39
C158 F103C F128 K72 L1
M65A M93 M232 N45C S34
S281 T37H W54
LUENING Warren B53 D86 L50
LUER Karl Hermann L139
LUFT Lorna B139
LUGO Frank Q9
LUHRING Les G7e
LUHRMANN Joachim f8D
LUKATHER Steve A35C A50
A123 B53 B85 B194 C6B C45
C63D C70A C213E C227 D104
E7 E57 F100 H9 J10B J72
J93C K17 K99A L9A L56C
M10B M16A M75 M102 M111
M170 N4 N42 N53 R99 R142A
S34 S36 T1 T12 T37H T115
T143 W32A W84C W119B W133
Z11
LUKAWIETSKY Rumor T149B
LUKENS Malcolm B253 S173B
LUKER Mal S313
LUKISKI Terry B81
LUKYN Tony H73 S48 T131
LULEY Klaus T103B
LULIS Peter W125A

Lulu (LAWRIE Marie L27 L140
LUMAN Robert Glynn 'Bob'
L141
LUMIA Guy S215
LUMLEY Robin B195 B203 C251
E77A H169 L15 S23 S97 W82A
LUMLEY-SAULE John S295
LUMSDEN Allan C165 D17 H194
LUNCH Lydia C177D L141A
LUND Zeke S173B
LUNDGREN Erik V18A
LUNDGREN Ken B89
LUNDQUIST Dag T138A
LUNDY Curtis W30A
LUNETTA Rick D77
LUNGREN Zappo R38
LUNNY Andy M41A
LUNNY Donal B185 C120 K24
M221E O2C P93 S230 W61
LUNT Tony C41A
LUPICA Frank S91
LUPPER Kenneth P126
LURE Walter H76 T86
LURIE Elliot L119B
LURIG Heiner S38
LURKERS L142
LURO Dominique S280
LUSHER Don C2 K84 R40B S31
W86
LUSSENDEN Bill B158
LUSTGARTEN Edgar B17 F19
LUSTGARTEN Robert A59
LUSTREA Robert M115
Luther D139
LUTHER Donald D122C
LUTHJENS Gustav A19A
LUTTICK Johannes F133A
LUTTON Davey B168 E26 E46
H84 S209
LUTTRELL Terry R1A S246
LUTZ Michael B246
LUVVERS L140
LUX Casimierz B197A
Lux Interior C212B
LUX Jeff W15A
LUX Kaz A27
LUXURY Neville P148
LYALL Graham L92 S312
LYALL William L142A P81B
R164A
LYCETT Kevin M124
LYDON John see ROTTEN
Johnny
LYEFOOT Byron B160 K24
LYLE Bobby B52A B85 C1B
C147 H96 L2B L65 L71B L128
L143 M68 P72A W8 W133
Y6B
LYLE Graham A82 C121 D49
E22 F6 F7 G6 G10 L16A M29
T122
LYLE Joy G76C
LYLES Chipper I25B
LYMAN Mel K101
LYMAN Steve S2
LYMANNE Frankie L144
LYNAM John S327
LYNAS Stewart P25
LYNCH Bruce B224B B280
C201A H170 J20 J110 R46 S266
S334 T79 W7
LYNCH David P97
LYNCH Eddie C30B C97
LYNCH Frances S140
LYNCH George D93H
LYNCH Kenny W7
LYNCH Larry K40
LYNCH Sean N73A
LYNCH Stan N45B P70 S89
T137A
LYNCH Suzanne H70 I24A M80
N57 S266 Y11
LYNCH Tim F61
LYNDON Dewey see OLDHAM
Spooner
LYNDON Frank B80A
LYNES Roy S255
LYNG Karsten D31
LYNGSTAD-FREDRIKSSON Frida
A4
LYNN Barbara L144A

[676]

Mac

McVAY Kenny B233A
McVEA Jack B233
McVEIGH Ray P140D
McVEY Tony M203 W34
McVIE Christine (nee PERFECT)
B254C C101 F66 P62 V21 W46
McVIE John B83 B193 C121
D106G F66 G101B M111 P62 S166
S204 S211 Z11
MACVITTIE Bob S318
McWHIRTER George C59 D133A
McWILLIAMS Carl Frog C42
MACWILLIAMS Carlton D96
McWILLIAMS David M45A
McWILLIAMS John D12A
McWILLIAMS Paulette E52C H181
L1 M102 R142A Y12
MACY John I3A M232
MAD DOGS AND ENGLISHMEN C155
MAD MAGAZINE M45B
Mad Muffet S153
MAD RIVER M46
MADAIO Steve A7 A37 B127 B221
B225 B282 C11B C17 C38 C45
C52A C58 C76 C147 C151B C155
C195 C213 C246 D74 D139 E7
F139 G120A H96 I2 I24A K45
L19 L51 L71B L111L146 M18
M39B M65A M93 M101 M111 M227
M229 M232 P83 P96 P114 R22
R60C R39 R78 S14C S34 S36
S124 S228 S252 S273 S362 T25
T37H T107 W21 W54 W84C W119
W120
Madcat see Ruth Peter
MADDEN David B234 C245 H105
R134
MADDEN John B197E
MADDEN Paul A131A
MADDEN Steve R51B
MADDEN Tom J84
MADDISON George C39C
MADE IN SWEDEN M45C
MADEN Jim P6
MADER Medor L16E
MADERA Jose B85 K69 S17
MADEY Bryan S156 S286
MADGE Bill L104
MADIGAN Amy J49
MADISON Brenda S18
MADISON James 'Pee Wee' R114
W2B
MADISON Jimmy B256 C44 L58B
P41 W25
MADISON James C65
MADJA Franklin T37G
MADLIN Pete K6
MADNESS M46A
MADRID John S36
MADRID Richard M144
MADSEN Finn S108C
MADSEN Merdin 044A
MAdsius Rudi C241D
MADU Chyke M81
MADURA Godfrey S261
MADURA M46C
MAEBE Arthur A131D C153 C180
C233 E7 M180 P115 S311 Z8
MAEL Ron B102 S205
MAEL Russell B102 S205
MAELEN Frank M46B
MAELEN Jimmy A47 B135 B242B
B263 C182 C234A C249 D50 F22
F60 F101C G2 G64 H9 H29 H51
H99 H137 H187 I2 J20 J4B J113
K59 L4A L21 L57 L98 L119 M26
M46B M120 N65 032 032A P25
R25 R18 S263B T34 T67A T147
W5 W84B
MAELON Eddie G48
MAELON Jim G2
MAERCKLEIN Kip B109 M158B
MAESTRO Johnny (MASTRANGELO
John) B224C C223A
MAFFEI Frank D14
MAFFITT Clark P129
MAFFITT Floyd C. P129
MAFFITT Rocky C69B
MAGALEN Daniel M. R36
MAGANDINI Pete D127
MAGAZINE M47
MAGEE Craig D60
MAGGI Beau B161A
MAGGIE STREDDER SINGERS S206
MAGGINI Phil S79
MAGHETT Sam see Magic Sam
MAGIC M47A

MAGIC Blue R128
Magic Dick G19 G122
Magic Sam (MAGHETT Sam)
M48
MAGIC LANTERNS M47B
MAGIC MIXTURE M47C
MAGIC SAND M48A
Magic Slim (HOLT Morris)
M48B
MAGITS M48C
MAGMA M49
MAGNA CARTA M50
MAGNESS Brian E30
MAGNESS Kerry D103
MAGNETS M51
MAGNIFICENTS M51
MAGNO Gabriel I8 N63
MAGNUM M52
MAGNUM Jeff D32
MAGNUSSON Bob R22
MAGNUSSON Jacob A133
MAGRUDER Charles C164
MAGRUDER June C164
MAGRUDER Robbie B253
MAGUIRE Les G26
Maha Dev see CODLING Dave
MAHAL Inshirah M53
MAHAL Taj (FREDERICKS
Henry) B144 K45 M53 P112
R22 R98 T107 W9
Mahalakshmi M40
MAHAVISHNU ORCHESTRA M39
MAHER Clare M79
MAHER Fred F123 M102F
M105A N34A
MAHER George D76
MAHER Jimmy D76
MAHER John B284
MAHIEUX Jacques D133
MAHLER Stephan S158A
MAHOGANY RUSH M54
MAHOLO Louis C183
MAHON Steve T37J
MAHONES Gildo P98B
MAHONEY Dave M4
MAHONEY Desmond B116
MAHONEY James P15
MAIA Luizao R99
NAIDA Sal C18 M154 R149
S205
MAIDEN Tony B225 K36 P126
R161
MAIHACK James B210 S120
MAIJANEN Paavo P56A W75
MAILE Vic I18A M63
MAILER MACKENZIE BAND
M54A
MAILLOUX Pascal L66B
MAIMONE Tony P61 R53
MAIMOUN Maurice L57
MAIN Graham F48E
MAINEGRA Richard B272B
K30
MAINES Donnie A35D
MAINES Kenny A35D
MAINES Lloyd A35D E51
MAINHORSE M55
MAINIERI Mike B110 D75
H136A I2 J20 J48 J69 M12
M41 M55A M143 N65 R100
R137 S124 S125 S215 T30
T147
MAINION Michael H8
MAINLAND M55B
MAINTENANCE Paul S264
MAINWARING Richard 029A
MAIR Allan 026 W10
MAIR Onnie F85A
MAISANO Joel P76B
MAITLAND Adam 026
MAITLAND Graham G45 H65
H155 S220 W114
MAITLAND Lynn B186 D186
MAJOR Ray B219 M214
MAJOR, CANIS C25B
Major Lance M56
MAJOR SURGERY M57
MAKER Greg S169
MAKI Shimmy S124
MAKINELL Lyn B237
MAKINS Ted F14
MAKLER Gabriel R39
MAKOWICZ Adam U21
MALABE Frankie Y2A
MALACH Bobby C129 L41 M2
W119

Malachi M57A
MALAGRA Campo B183B
MALANALDO Ray F17
MALAROWITZ Alan S353
MALARSKY Leonard F134
S116
MALBERBE Braham J66
MALCOLM Calum H71A
MALCOLM Vic G23
MALDANALDO Ray B139 F17
H42A W119
MALE Kerrilee E12
MALEKANY Jerry D63
MALENKY Bob L126
MALFATI Radu B229 N50
S181A
MALHERBE Didier (also DE
GRASSE Bloomdido Bad) A35
A133 C137 C175 G66 H86A
H119H119 M211A S175 W119C
MALIBOOZ M57C
MALIBU Johnny S333B
MALICK Peter M184
MALICORNE M57B
MALIGNAGGI Joseph see
MALIN Joseph
MALIKIAN Zaven M203
MALIN Jim S157
MALIN Joseph (MALIGNAGGI
Joseph) I2
MALISAN Gino E66
MALISAN Tony E66
MALKEN Jack T64A
MALKIN Al Z8
MALKINE Sonja H119
MALLABER Gary A50 B56
B244 B259 C123 C172A D5A
D72A D124 E57 F100 K77
M21 M82 M159 M179 M203
M229 015 R22 R40A S111
S196 T12 T32B W65 Z11
MALLAH Linda C26B
MALLARD M58
MALLARD Oett S358 T9B
MALLARD Ollie G102 S348B
MALLEN Mike S213
MALLER John M151 M218
MALLETT Ian R65B
MALLIA Sauveur R6A
MALLINDER Stephen C4B
MALLOG David F4
MALLONY David B16
MALLORY Lee M156 S6
MALLOY Hugh H4
MALO M59
MALONE J.J. K33A
MALONE Kenny B41 B57F C14
C15 C50 C75 C133 C194 D21
D70 E54 E73 H85A H7D H26
H49 H52A J13 J53 K30 K77
L42 L77 L10B M11 N23 N37
P137 R4 R81 S32 T107 Y18
MALONE Marcus M84 S19
MALONE Mike B81 L74
MALONE Pat D77
MALONE Tommy A27 A131 B29
B57A B155 C62 C129 C147
F109 G19 H92 M12 M17 M107
M120 M233 R125 S10 S17
S124 S169 T44 T67A T158
Z3B Z8
MALONE Will D16 F101 I22
MALONEY Campbell M9
MALONEY Paddy 018
MALTESE Rodolfo B28
MALUCHNIK Doug S79
MAMA LION M60
MAMAS AND PAPAS M61
MAMAS PRIDE R124C
MAMMA JAMMERS R124C
MAN M63
MAN Koon Fook V13
MANANO Charlie V26C
MANASSAS M64
MANCE Junior G122
MANCERI John B57A
MANCHESTER David M65A
MANCHESTER Melissa B53 E15
M65A N10 S252
MANCHESTER Susan W51A
MANCHILD M65
MANCHOVITZ Henry see
MITCHELL Mitch
MANCINI Chris H19
MANCUSE Donald B115A
MANDALA M66

MANDALABAND M67
MANDEL Fred C182
MANDEL Harvey B171 C26 C44
F109 G61 H34 L128 M68 M111
M238 P150 R133 T52 W116A
MANDEL John J. V9A
MANDEL Johnny R99
MANDEL Mike B248 C136B C189
F122 H99 L41 M69 M218 P99
S73C
MANDEL Tom F81A H185 I24A
M143A
MANDELL Steve C164 M211 W45
MANDELLA John A115
MANDENGUE Dikoto Jean 034
MANDIN Francis C137
MANDL Derek 047
MANDLER Buddy 036A
MANDRAKE MEMORIAL M70
MANDRAKE PADDLESTEAMER M71
MANDRE Andre Lewis M73
MANDRILL M72
MANE Alan 026
MANESS Jaydee A59 B285 C6B
C39 D36A E74 F110C I23 M18
M125A S118 T107 V3
MANFRED Long D63
MANFRED MANN M8C
MANFRED MANN CHAPTER THREE
M80
MANFRED MANN'S EARTH BAND
M80
MANGELSDORF Albert G47 K94C
S73C
MANGIONE GAP M74
MANGOLD Mark A55 T116A
MANGONE Ricky U22A
MANGRUM J.D. see DANDY Jim
MANHATTAN Horns B71
MANHATTAN TRANSFER M75 M101
MANHATTANS M76
MANIAC Manny M76A
MANIACS M76A
MANIETTE Bo S225
MANION Eddie 'Clams' B172A
S199
MANISCALCO Mark K48
MANISCALCO Mike I12B
MANITOBA Handsome Dick D65
MANJER Kjell R178
MANKER Sid J111
MANKEY Earl E23 S205 W97
MANKEY Jim S205
MANKU Mark C58A R177
MANKOWITZ Roy M198
MANLEY Colin R64B
Mann D86
MANN Al Z8
MANN Barry L51 T67A
MANN Brian C36 L109 V18B
MANN Carl M77
MANN Charles K45
MANN Ed Z8
MANN Greg G64C
MANN Herbie B71 L80C M78
WB W13
MANN Jonny F115
MANN Manfred H111B H175 M80
R5
MANN Mono D1B R50 MANN Paul
V35
MANN Rick W82
MANN Robert (Or Bob) B199B
B208 B219A C234A C241 D115
H117 J88 K29B L4A M10B M65A
M216 M238A P6 R22 T67A
MANN Steve C96 L67 T12
MANN Sy M125
MANN Terry P53
MANN Woody F5 K23
Mannah R175A
MANNE Shelley W6 Z8
MANNING Carlton A6
MANNING Donald A6
MANNING Leo B250 S31
MANNING Phil C65
MANNING Rene N39
MANNING Terry H160
MANNING Tom M46
MANNING Unford A6
MANONE Jimmy S311
MANOR Wayne H135
MANRIQUEZ Bobby C86
MANSEAU Maurice B245 II N53
S330

MANSELINO Danny J18
MANSELL Tony F70B
MANSFIELD Alan P15
MANSFIELD Andy S289A
MANSFIELD David A41 A59 B263
D274B C196 D39 E20A F116
M27 T22 W15A
MANSFIELD Dennis E23 R173
T113
MANSFIELD Ken G29
MANSFIELD Tony D6 K93 N30A
MANSKA Rick S73
MANSOLINO Dan J18 Q15A
MANSON Art D36A
MANSOUR Roger V2
MANSUAK Chris R9
MANTERO Marcos I13B
MANTESE Mario H81
MANTILLA Raymond B125E C177D
C189 E49 M78 P41 P99 U21
MANTLEONE Ed F100
MANTLER Karen B131
MANTLER Mike B131 G90 M79
M102E
MANTON Robert P154
MANTOOTH Frank B21
MANTOR Dan W1
MANTRA M80A
MANUEL Bobby B78 B242 E55
G102 K46 L90 M3 N55 R173
MANUEL Richard B29 D13 D139
F116 L111 R22
MANUPUTI Richard G112A
MANUS Nick H4
MANUSCE Michael V16
MANX Andy A59C
MANZANERA Phil C13 C222 E24C
E59 F42 M34 M81 N45 Q13 R149
S221 V2
MANZAREK Ray D103 M82 N52
X1
MANZER Bobby S3A
Mao see CHUNG Mikey
MAPHIS Jody S55A
MAPHIS Joe M82A N21
MAR-KEYS B180 G61 M85
MARABUTO Ron M4
MARACLE Don D127B
MARANGOLA Agnostino G52A
MARATRAT Alain R123B
MARC TANNER BAND T12
MARCAL Armando M79
MARCANGELO John V35
MARCANGELO Richard B187 S178
MARCELLI John B13A
MARCELLINO Dennis B109 M144
R154
MARCELLINO Jocko S78
MARCELLINO Marc B72
MARCH Carl C58
MARCH Geoff D37
MARCH George (D) B63
MARCH George (Wind) M125
MARCHELLO Mickey G69
MARCHELLO Peppi G69
MARCHENA Guillerno P34
MARCHESI Lex F90
MARCHETTI Paul I22 V21
MARCHI Guy S239
MARCHI Randy S239
MARCIANO Renato T122A
MARCO Ken R39
MARCO Pirroni R63B
MARCONI Mike B103
MARCOTTE Jim A1
MARCOVECCHIO Felice C24B
MARCOVECCHIO Marco S74A
Marcus see MALONE Marcus
MARCUS Arnie R96A
MARCUS Rick M228
MARCUS Steve C63C C189 M79
MARCUS Thea H63
MARCUS Tony B131 M203
MARCUS Veit D48
MARCUS Wade C236 T16A
MARCUS HOOK ROLL BAND M83A
MARCY Bob B94C
MARDIN Arif A131 B71 B85 D53C
G72 H54 015 P123 S7 S228 S273
T25
MARDONES Benny M84A
MAREDI Selaelo Dan B105
MARESKA Michael A41A
MARETT Jim P73

[679]

MARGARET Ann W72
MARGE George B85 C164 D50
F108A G2 J20 J69 K36 L119 M41
M125 M143 N39 N42 R117A R125
S124 S215 S262 T25 T30 T158
W5
MARGEN David S19
MARGETTS Gary S223
MARGETTS Tristan L9A S223
MARGETZ Gary T93B
MARGO Mitch C234A R25
MARGO Phil C234A
MARGOLIN Bob B29 N46D W28
W107
MARGOLIS Kenny M163
MARGOSHES Steven H11A S263B
MARGOULEFF Robert H59 K90
P126 R15 R60C T109
MARIAH M84B
MARIANO Charlie C61 E52 G66
M84D O36 S73C S332D
MARIANO Tom Z8
MARIE ET LES GARCONS M84E
MARIENNEAU Corine T37K
MARIGNAN Lou P20A
Marijke S71A
MARIMBA Ed see TRIPP Art
MARIN Richard 'Cheech' C94
MARINE Michael B27B
MARINELL Roy Z11
MARINELLI George Jnr B104B
B164 O33G
MARINELLI Mike A27 F69 G9
MARINI Lou A27 A123 B155 B197
B263 D50 D63 G19 H92 L21 M69
M120 M233 P123 R125 S10 T67A
T114 T147 V17 Z8
MARINO Frank A69 M54 M84F
MARINO Vince M54 M84F
MARINOS Jimmy R133A
MARK Douglas 'Red' R53A S330
MARK Joe I2
MARK Jon M84C M86 M111 P10
S352 W89
MARK Lewis B161A
MARK ALMOND M86
MARKASKI Gary S241
MARKEE Dave A82 B25 B40 B174B
B189 B208B C63 C75 C78 C121
C185B D9 D54 D105 E22 G97 H65
H132A H173 L30 M50 M233 N63B
P131 R15 R46 S34 T96 T122 W9A
W10 W67
MARKELLIS Tony B221
MARKEN Tom L8
MARKER Gary R16A R98
Marker, Magic J104D
MARKEYS G61 M65
MARKGROF Dietrich O36A
MARKHAM Jimmy O16
MARKHAM Naffy see NAFTALIN
Mark
MARKLEY Bob M86A W53
MARKOWITZ Irwin 'Marky' B282
C40 D50 D66 F108A M75 O15
S125 S168 W5
MARKOWITZ Kate B268
MARKOWITZ Roy B53 F109 M41
M75 R164 S173 Y4B
MARKS Danny E19B
MARKS David M190A
MARKS Emeretta H92 H99
Markus M212A
MARKUSFELD Alain M87
MARLETTE Robert S270
MARLEY Bob M88 V21
MARLEY Rita B101 C139 M88
M88A T114 V21
MARLO Phil P65B
MARLOW Jerry C241B
Marlow The Magician L28
MARMALADE M89
MARNEL Theodore C76
MARNELL Brian E62B S3
MARNIE A1 D36
MAROCCO Frank F78 H150A O15
MARONIE Tony W13E
MAROONS B154C
MAROS Mike B56
MAROSHEK P. M96
MAROTTA Dave M86
MAROTTA Jerry A82 B219A B263
C42 C103C F108A G2 H9 O32
S124 W20A

MAROTTA Rick A96 B7 B199B
B208E B244 C51B C62 C94
C213E C22y D50 E15 E40
F42 F103D G10 G60 G97B
H9 H164C J20 J93D K36
K37 K81 K86 L4A L51 M17
M143 N40 N46A N64D N65
O27 O32 P45 P114 R22
E135A R137 R142A R144 S17
S36 S50 S124 S125 S196
S215 S262 T25 T30 T67A
T98 T147 W44A W106 Z11
MAROTTI Art S168
MAROUSE Denny M53
MARQUAM Robert E51
MARQUES Joe E55A
MARQUEZ Sal K94A M101 Z8
MARQUIS Herman A6 B101
B234 B276 C245 D130 H122
I12 M149 P135 R84 W4
MARRERO Nicholas A131 B85y9
E33 F17 M17 M75 M107 M225
P99 S252 S262
MARRERO Tito V6
MARRIOTT Beryl S344
MARRIOTT Jim W43
MARRIOTT Roger S344
MARRIOTT Steve B150A C148
H179 K45 K84 M89A S162
T86
MARRON Bobby A112A
MARRON Eddy D143
MARRON Gordon H. C61B P28
U16
MARS Freddy D63
MARS Hein A42
MARS Johnny M90
MARS Tommy Z8
MARSA Denise F115
MARSALA Jim B87
MARSALIS Ellis E3A
MARSDEN Andy G77B
MARSDEN Bernie B5 C112
C204 M90A P9 P24 P119B
U2
MARSDEN Beryl S105
MARSDEN Freddie G26
MARSDEN Gerry G26
MARSEILLE M91
MARSH Carl B97 B61B B242
P137 S274 W101
MARSH Chris R151A
MARSH Elizabeth R60
MARSH George B144 H5D
MARSH Henry G105 S8
MARSH Ian Craig H82A
H178A
MARSH Jack C164 H96
MARSH John Q3A
MARSH Pam A69
MARSH Peter E9 M80 N45C
T166A V13
MARSH Phil M18
MARSH Randall C151C
MARSH Ted H134A
MARSH Tex H66A
MARSH Tony A109 F94 M57
MARSHAL Ed P114
MARSHALL Alan (V) B39 G67
O24A W58 Z24
MARSHALL Alan (B) W113
MARSHALL Barry R66C
MARSHALL Benita S193B
MARSHALL Benny B186
MARSHALL Bill E31A
MARSHALL Bob C74 M152
M202C
MARSHALL Brian L52A
MARSHALL Ester S140
MARSHALL Frank W124
MARSHALL Fred S231
MARSHALL James C12 D12
MARSHALL Joe C146
MARSHALL John (D) A74
B231 B248 C50 C63 C189
D2 D35 F30A H154 H171 K84
K94C M84D M205 N62 P145A
S182 S209 T111 T141 W39A
W86
MARSHALL John (Sax) J8
P47
MARSHALL Johnny (Trom)
C2 F14 K84
MARSHALL Julian F74C
MARSHALL Keith M92A
MARSHALL Leslie L52A

MARSHALL Paul F112
MARSHALL Peter (B) D53C
K13 R28B
MARSHALL Pete (V) F103
MARSHALL Richard P80D
MARSHALL Rob W15A
MARSHALL Ron P6
MARSHALL Terry L. E55
MARSHALL Tom P6
MARSHALL Wendel C146
MARSHALL-HAIN M92
MARSHALL TUCKER BAND M93
MARSON John M83
MARSUPILAMI M95
MARTELL Arlene M41
MARTELL Vince V15
MARTENS Sido F136
MARTER John M164 V42
MARTHA AND THE MUFFINS
M95A
MARTHA AND THE VANDELLAS
M95A
MARTIN Allan W107
MARTIN Anne G13
MARTIN Barbara S333A
MARTIN Barrie W24
MARTIN Barry (G) K100 R52
MARTIN Barry (Wind) J27
MARTIN Benny D70 H49
MARTIN Bill M181
MARTIN Bob B268
MARTIN Brian M71
MARTIN Brian (D) M163B
MARTIN Bud V21
MARTIN Caleb P99
MARTIN Carl D72
MARTIN Carlos A131 L63
M107 P123
MARTIN Carol K92
MARTIN Charles Allen B42
S73
MARTIN Charlie P72 S73
MARTIN Chip M68
MARTIN Chris A6C S260
MARTIN Christine S124
MARTIN Chuck H42A
MARTIN Colin A91
MARTIN DannY L83A
MARTIN Dave (G) C95 E62
N56 P19 S177D
MARTIN Dave (B) S81A
MARTIN David (B) S14A
MARTIN Denny I24A
MARTIN Dewey B260 M95B
MARTIN Dick F19A
MARTIN Don M141B
MARTIN Everette B58B
MARTIN Figure D84
MARTIN Fonso S261
MARTIN Frank W8
MARTIN Gail R137
MARTIN George A9C A50 B59
M9 W39
MARTIN Grady A59 B17A C14
F19 G72 G121 H26 H62 H134
K95 M18 N23A P125 P137
R173 S10
MARTIN Guskin J112
MARTIN Harold C63C
MARTIN Isy R141
MARTIN Joe B172A
MARTIN John (Vln) C178
MARTIN John (K) G91A
MARTIN John 'Moon' M96 P75
R137 S199B
MARTIN Johnny (V) K45
MARTIN Keith S31
MARTIN Larry A121A D133
M238
MARTIN Lou G5 K43 L101
M202C
MARTIN Luci C99 R142A
MARTIN Mel A136 C158 F103C
H146 L10B S7 S19 S36 S180
S193A
MARTIN Michael X4
MARTIN Mike I3A
MARTIN Mick B207B
MARTIN Milo F112
MARTIN Mike M95C
MARTIN Moon see MARTIN
John
MARTIN Napoleon S171
MARTIN Nuhad Saba W8
MARTIN Pam I3A
MARTIN Pat U13

MARTIN Paul L128
MARTIN Peter G71C T63 W30
MARTIN Phil A82C
MARTIN Richard M68
MARTIN Rick T61
MARTIN Robert B200
MARTIN Roy I24A
MARTIN Schmitt D86B
MARTIN Sean S250A
MARTIN Steve L45 N53 O33C
MARTIN Stu B197D M40 T141
MARTIN Thomas E73 R33A
MARTIN Tony D8
MARTIN Tony Jnr. M125A
MARTIN Troy S249C
MARTIN Vince M95D M95E
MARTIN Vince & Fred NEIL
M95E
MARTINEZ Carlos G96C I8
MARTINEZ Frank M42A
MARTINEZ Hirth M96A T98
MARTINEZ Joel P116
MARTINEZ Johnny R152
MARTINEZ Luis A35D
MARTINEZ Mia K38
MARTINEZ Mickey C227A
MARTINEZ Miguel C234
MARTINEZ Nigel E77A G17
M97
MARTINEZ Paul C101 H3 L126
O40 P9 P92C P149 S266 S301
MARTINEZ Rafael L115A
MARTINEZ Ray A26 A34 C78
G124 M126 R140 T37A
MARTINEZ Robert Q9
MARTINEZ Rudy (Question
Mark) Q9
MARTINEZ Sabu V32B
MARTINI Jerry B144 C213
R154 S161
MARTINO Joe D63C
MARTINS J.P. M210
MARTNEY Jeff O39
MARTON Bob Z8
MARTT Mike F135B
MARTYN Beverley M94
MARTYN John A74 H11 K87
M45 M94 S9
MARTYN FORD ORCHESTRA B280
J72 S107
MARTYNEC Gene C151 E19B
K28 L72 M39C M160A R60
Maruga K81 P53
MARUSH Mark W3B
Marv A2E
MARVELLETTES M98
MARVIN BRETT & THE
THUNDERBOLTS M99
MARVIN Hank M100 R80 S80
MARVIN Junior see HANSON
Junior
MARVIN Julian Y2
MARVIN AND FARRAR S80
MARVIN WELCH AND FARRAR
S80
MARVOS Veit E52A T89 S169C
T162A
MARX Andy C96A C221A F66A
N61C U23
MARX Bill C96
MARX Richard H120
MARZ Rainer A113 E61B K96C
S42B S169C S332B T89
MARZ AND EPERJESSY M100A
MARZULLA Fred M178B
MAS Carolyne M100B
Mascara Snake B72
MASCARA M100B
MASCARO Debbie C113B
MASDEA Jim B184
MASDIN Arif L80A
MASEK Doug E15
MASKELA Hugh C213E
MASHBIR Mick C182
MASHMAKHAN M100D
MASION John F64
MASKED MARAUDERS M100E
Maskel I M221D
MASKIL Michael R33A
MASLIN Harry N24E
MASLON Jimmie Lee M100F
MASON Bob F133 N53
MASON Cheryl L51
MASON Colin H20
MASON Dave B149 B202 C30
C121 D39B D52 E42 F12 H39

H99 J9 K34 M9 M101 M102C M135
N4 P81B R60A S55 S147A S180
T127
MASON David (K) C77 E51 W16
MASON Gne P59A
MASON Gregory S192
MASON Harvey B85 B208 B214
B269A C44 C129 C220B D50 F88A
G4 G113A H19 H35B J20 K48
L56C L109 L111 L119 L143 M17
M102 M146C N39 R97 R99 R113
R161 S19 S51 S58 S64 S180
S193A S213 T107 T113 U18 V17
V32A W25 W27 W39 W133
MASON Hoppy M102
MASON Ian L92
MASON Jae M102A
MASON Jenny C234E
MASON Jim F139 K16A M233 R6
S284
MASON Jim (Hrns) M62
MASON John F131
MASON Kenneth C17 G17 M102
M146C
MASON Lol C118
MASON Madison c108D
MASON Martin C108A
MASON Marvin M102
MASON Nick H119 M102E P85
P136
MASON Robert C30 S247
MASON Roger B207A F114B N63A
MASON Ron K27A
MASON Ross B109
MASON Steve see NAIVE Steve
MASON Sylvia T77
MASON PROFFIT M102B
MASON WOOD CAPALDI & FROG
M102C
MASONHEIMER Willis B166
MASQUERADERS M102D
MASS PRODUCTION M103
MASSACRE M102F
MASSARO John M159
MASSATT Dee H171B
MASSE Laurel L4A M75
MASSENBURG Carolyn W119
MASSER Michael B85 R142A
MASSEY Andrew M166
MASSEY Barbara B169A D97A H99
L119B P6 P72A P149 R125 S266
W107
MASSEY Bobby O14
MASSEY Joanna W129
MASSI Nick (MACIOCI Nicholas)
F91
MASSON Bob P45
MASSON G. M206A
MASSON Michel P147
MASTELLOTTO Pat S86B
MASTERS M103A
MASTERS Barrie E13
MASTERS Gerry (or Jerry) B126
F23 F123A G96B H39B L80C R3
R117A W9 W118
MASTERS Greg I7 N48
MASTERS Michael C76
MASTERS Vance G115
MASTERS APPRENTICES M103B
MASTERSON Brian O2C S333D
MASTORY John S84A
MASTRANGELO Carlo B80A D74

MASTRANGELO John see MAESTRO
Johnny
MASTRIANNI Vic G16 N63
MASTRO Jim L98A
MASUO Yoshiaki P115
MATA Nydia 'Liberty' I27 N65
MATA Pat H38
MATARE Vitus L21A
MATAYA Clifford Q1
MATCHBOX M105
MATCHING MOLE M106
MATERIAL M105A
MATHE Patrick S11
MATHER Billy M84
MATHER Dann G22A
MATHERS Carl H62
MATHESON Andrew H135 M106A
MATHESON Brendon R151 S329C
MATHESON Greg A31 C36 C118
C155 C185E E7B J43 K94A L9A
L107 M74 M75 N42 R99
MATHESON Ron N62
MATHEW Darold J96
MATHEWS Amale W119

MATHEWS Brian W7
MATHIAS Jon P37A R118
MATHIAS Nathaniel 'Jerry' T110
MATHIEU Margot F123
MATHIJSSEN Lanny E72
MATHIS Claude D29A
MATHIS Johnny 'John John' L69
MATHISEN P132B
MATIC Don K. G81E
MATIVET Francois L17
MATLOCK Glen I10 R79 S77
MATOESIAN Tamara C70A J72
MATOS Bobby C229
MATOUSEK Jiri E52A
MATRAT Yves F4B
MATRIX M106B
MATRIX M106C
MATSUI Kazu C179 H150A
MATSUMOTO Shigeru P20
MATSUMOTO Teruo H35A W53A Y2
MATSUTAKE Hideki Y6A
MATTA Gregory L143 M191
MATTACKS Dave A30 A62 A82 A98 B25 B224B B266 C47A C77A C165 D9 D17 D39 D49 D88 D111 E41 E44 E59 F6 F7 F56 G51 G94 H42 H65 H110 H194 I16 J41 J110 K41 K75 L117 M9 M19 M21 M45 M50 M81 M83 M94 N20 N63D P90 P124 R12 R46 R80 S9 S179 S209 S215 S218 S263 S339 T21 T79 W125 W136
MATTHES Robby B59A
MATTHEW Dave S103
MATTHEWMAN Tim J63
MATTHEWS Al R33
MATTHEWS Anton L53
MATTHEWS Annie R92
MATTHEWS Bob G84
MATTHEWS Carl M108A
MATTHEWS Carolyn P129
MATTHEWS Dave (D) R66A
MATTHEWS Dave (Hms) S125
MATTHEWS David (K) M107
MATTHEWS Edgar C62 E18 H65A
MATTHEWS George C146
MATTHEWS Gil T80A
MATTHEWS Graham C159 S108
MATTHEWS Ian (MACDONALD Ian M.) C206 E41 F6 L111 M108 P90 P158 R106 T79
MATTHEWS Milt M108A
MATTHEWS Myrna B8 B256 C234D D74 D124 F139 H96 M179 N42 P75 P126 P129 S36 S58 S262 V18A
MATTHEWS Neal F83A J98 L72 N37 P63 P125 S342
MATTHEWS Pauline see DEE Kiki
MATTHEWS Rick P14
MATTHEWS Scott D70 D135A E62B G10B H5 P227 T107
MATTHEWS Shirley A11 A37 A132 B32A B91 B109 B134A B200 B201 B256 C123 C159 C173 C180 C217 C246 D101 D124 F43 F50 G26A H5 H52 I32 J72 K14 K16A K45 K95 L9 L44 L107 M18 M32 M191 N4 N13 O39 P6 P129 Q3A R137 R142A S34 S58 S73 S262 S276 T37H W82 W120 W133 Y16
MATTHEWS Wade E78B
MATTHEWS Winston 'Pipe' W4A
MATTHEWS SOUTHERN COMFORT M108
MATTHEWSON Ron A82 P42A R132 R174 S267
MATTICE Lionel J74
Mattle E77E
MATTIO Mike A28C
MATTOS Marcio S267
MATTOUS Edgar P51
MATTRESS S354A
MATTS David B56
MATTSON Victor C62
MATUMBI B110
MATUTE Raul C158
MATYCHAK Basil B166B
MATZ Peter G10
MATZIOL Klaus Peter E50A
MATZKA Fritz T103B W138
MAU Michael S284
MAUCERI Angelo M125
MAUCERN John B244
MAUCHER Charlie H26B J38 M109A
MAUDS M109B
MAUDSLEY F. F69C

MAUERER Renate H56 N60A
MAUGH Bugsy B282 R164
MAULDIN Joe C224 H134 V19
MAULIN Jimmy C103C
MAUNU Peter L1 P115 S281
MAUPIN Benny C186 D27 H19 H72 J75A M102 M110 S193A W31 W62
MAUPIN John C158
MAURI Joe E33C
MAURITZ Barbara L10B
MAURITZ Walla N60A
Maurizio C108C
MAURO Frank H90
MAURO Lou F22A
MAUS John see STEWART John
MAVETY Joe F8
Max A60 R63B
MAX M111A
MAX Harry A47 T44
MAX DEMIAN BAND D45C
MAX WEBSTER BAND M112
MAXFIELD Lou L134 W39C
MAXFIELD Mike D6 K93
MAXFIELD PARRISH M113
MAXWELL Billy A41
MAXWELL Colin J110
MAXWELL Dave N46D
MAXWELL Don C26A
MAXWELL Duris B32A B197C D106A H75 P119A
MAXWELL Jim S168 S170
MAXWELL Michael P18D
MAXWELL Rick A11
MAXWELL Thad S114 G121 S269 S341
MAY Artece W119
MAY Arthur S253
MAY Bo F51
MAY Brian D100 H185 Q8
MAY Phil E33F M114A P128
MAY Tim A35C A122 B53 B226 C213E H122A J91A P114 R4 R142A T143
MAY BLITZ M114B
MAYALL John C121 G112 H37 H50 M111 T37H
MAYBERRY Tony D51 K42
MAYBRAY Billy J16C
MAYEDO Carole Y16
MAYEL Pierre S280
MAYELL Norman B150 G96 S191 T150
MAYER John B186 C191 M75 R22
MAYER Markus C212C
MAYER Michael S158A
MAYER Silky J38A
MAYERS Max S193B
MAYES Frank B202 D26 S71A
MAYES Martin S261B
MAYES Sean B186 F135
MAYFIELD Curtis F103 I15 M115 R59
MAYFIELD Percy M116
MAYHAN Judy P129
MAYHEW John G21
MAYHEW Michael H19B
MAYHUGH J,Clifton B74A
MAYNE Roger U5C
MAYNELL Colin L46
MAYO Bob F84 F100 V38
MAYO David B61B S284D
MAYO Deborah H65B
MAYO Doug J17
MAYO Elaine F112
MAYO Joe G17
MAYO John D84
MAYO Mark H65B
MAYOR Simon H162
MAYORA Raul H121 P76
MAYORGA Lincoln O6 P82 P129 R111B S227A S228 S252 Z8
MAYS Bill C156 M75
MAYS Lyle M138A M170
MAYS Warren G7A
MAYTALS T110
Mayuto C11B R28B
MAZALON Larry S137A
MAZE M117
MAZER Elliot R137
MAZUR Bernadette W107
MAZUR Kenny P15 W8

MAZUR Marc K38
MAZZOCHI Dave M178B
MDENGE Martha A105 J16
MDUUU wtobi O34
MEACHAM Britt J14A
MEAD Frank J110
MEAD Lowther E52
MEAD Moggy S67
MEADE Basil K26A
MEADE Greg F8A
MEADE Richie F8A
MEADOR Seab W48C
MEADOR Steve C156 K48
MEADOWS Bill G7C
MEADOWS Bucky A102 L3
MEADOWS Edwin 'Punky' A65 B283 C96C
MEADOWS Patrick S175
MEADS Martin W48F
MEAGER Tat J102A S133
MEAGHER Ron B61
MEAKIN Roger E66
MEAL TICKET M118
MEALING John A33 B23 B189 D37 E60 G49 H23 I8 J16B M50 P34 S34 S255 S295 W13A W18
MEALY Steve C12
MEAN STREET DEALERS M119
MEASHAM David N54
Meatball G81E
Meatloaf I22 M120 N63
MECHAN Bruce B42
MECHELEN Clous S41B
MECK John H168
MECO M120
MEDBURY Ted M221
MEDDICK Haydn C132
MEDEIROS Elli S279
MEDEIROS Ronald T11B
MEDICA Leon B233 L56 N53
MEDICINE HEAD M121
MEDINA Jeff S198A
MEDINA Nito O35
MEDITATION M122
MEDIUM MEDIUM M121A
MEDLEY Bill M122A R87 R127A
MEDLIN Victoria M232A
MEDLOCKE Ricky B123 J14A L146
MEDLOCKE Shorty B123
MEDORA Eddie S326B
MEDORA Mike G46
MEDRESS Hank P119
MEDROSS Hank M65A
Medula H189
MEE Trevor U13
MEEHAN Tony H36 R80 S80
MEEK Anna C57
MEEK Jeremy L95A
MEEKER Bill B109 D1A G96 G106A S111
MEEKINS Buzzy B233A
MEEKS Charles K69 M218 R99
MEEKS Johnny N25 V32
MEERMAN Ani B224A
MEERMAN Cees E79 J2A
MEERMAN Reinhard N24B
MEGADAY Mark R8
MEGGIDO Mark T7
MEGGINSON John G103 I20 M23 M25 R106 S35
MEGNA Vince B174E
MEHLER John F139
MEI Lei Aloah B230
MEID Lothar A57A A59C N61C P34 U23
MEIER Dieter W13D Y5A
MEIER Ellen P20A
MEIER Frank E21B
MEIER Jurgen R22A
MEIFERT Armulf F30
MEIKLE Dave U14
MEINE Klaus S47
MEINEMA Jeune C243
MEINHARD Klaus S169C T89
MEISNER Randy E2 F78 F139 G16 M123 N21 O15 P106 R109 R137 T25 W16 W46
MEISTERMAN Richard A28C T44
MEKLER Gabriel J95 P16 R39 S265

MEKONS M124
MELAMED Vince E2 O15 N46A P69
Melanie (SAFKA Melanie) H110 M125
MELANSON Jon R51B
MELBOURNE Errol 'Ramah' J48
MELCHER Terry B285 F110C M125A N57 R96A
MELCHES Klaus B204A
MELENDEZ Carlos 'Kiko' R13A
MELENDEZ Juan R13A
MELFORD Michael B144 D70 G10B M227
MELHUISH Martin G53A
MELINA Ray L82C
MELKONIAN Philippe C137
MELLEMAMarcel P156B
MELLENCAMP John see COUGAR Johnny
MELLENTHIN Michael S38
MELLIN Peter A8A
MELNICK John Z9A
MELNICK Monte T64A
MELOTTI Joe A131
MELOUNEY Vince B71 F18A
MELSHENKER Steve S96A
MELTON Barry H45 H186 M18 M126 S204
MELTON Jim S181
MELTON Steve J11
MELTZ Wolfgang D103
MELTZER David S74C
MELTZER Tina S74C
MELVIN Mimi S111
MELVIN Roderick E59 K41
MELVOIN Michael A31 B50 B256 C11 C153 C164 D36A H8A H156 M68 M75 N43 O15 R101 S160 S321 T1 T37H T98 W6 W44
MELZ Wolfgang B130 M86
MEMBERS M127
MEMMOTT Maurice G38C W48F
MEMPHIS BEND M128
MEMPHIS HORNS B242 C158 C231 F7 G102 H38 H40 K45 K46 L26 L90 M75 M132D M130 M157 N32 P112 S10 S273 T27
Memphis Slim (CHATMAN Peter) C26 D66C D80A H150 M129 R59 S204 W94
MEMPHIS STRINGS G92
MEMPHIS SYMPHONY ORCHESTRA B242
MENADIER Robert W116B
MENAGE A TROIS M131
MENARDO Dominic M26
MEN AT WORK M130A
MENCARONI Mauro A20A
MENDELL Steve N23
MENDELSOHN Barbara M227
MENDELSOHN John C109B
MENDELSON Andy M131A P123
MENDELSON Benno M10C M47
MENDELSON Joe M39 M132
MENDELSON Richard M131A P123
MENDENHAL Dale L82A
MENDES Warren N11A
MENDOZA Mark D65 T166B
MENDYK Joe N60B
MENE James B105 P146
MENGARELLI Benno N24C
MENGARELLI Piero N24C
MENICCI Mike K84A
MENIKETTI Dave Y8
Mensi A65B
MENTAL M132A
MENTAL AS ANYTHING M132B
MENZA Don A31 C156 C158 C180 D36A D127 F134 G60 H150 K77 L50 M229 Q12 R87 W82
MENZEL Thomas M216B
MENZER Kim B275
MENZO Liza F50
MEPHISTOPHELES M132C
MERBACH Sabine G30A
MERBER Uli B47
MERCER Chris A62 B4 B25 B47C B209 C75 C80 C101

C145A C159 D27B D30 D36 D86 F21 F42 F86 F125 G64 G67 H50 H94 H170 J5 J34 J105 K51 L53 L63 L101 L104 L142A M7 M111 M157 M168 M195 M202A M233 N6 N18 P76 P127 Q1 R12 S134 S209 S257 S285 S301 S355A T133 T135A U22 V21 W13A W103
MERCER Dave A67G
MERCER Glenn F32A
MERCER Jerry A69 B253 M100D W1
MERCEREAU Bob B268
MERCHANT Jimmy L144
MERCIA Joey S276
MERCIER Peadar C102
MERCURIO Frank E65
MERCURIUS S.Flavius H29
MERCURY Eric F60 F109 M132D
Mercury Flyer J104D
MERCURY Freddy H185 Q8
MERENSTEIN Lewis C13
MERGER M133
MERGY Fred S120
MERILAHTI Harry T104
MERING Summer W119B
MERKLEIN Kip S111
MERKY Bobbie B174E
MERLIN G. C169
MERLINO Gene G121
MERLINO John D99
MERLINO Louis C62D
MERNIT Billy B263 M132E S124
MERNIT John C107C
MERO Don W8
MEROLA Steve T123A
MEROS Gene L19 P3
MEROS Mike R173 W24
MERRIAM Charlie D36A M96
Merrick see HUGHES Chris
MERRILL John P46
MERRITT Max M134
MERRITT Randy F103C
MERRY GO ROUND M134A
MERRIWEATHER Big Maceo B95B T9B
MERRYWEATHER Neil E79 G61 M60 M135
MERSEYBEATS M136
MERSHON Norman T169
MERTENS Peter Y19C
MERTON PARKAS M136A
MERWIN Andy B278
MERZ Kim W13D
MESA Omar M72
MESCAL Walt F43
MESONIER Martin L16E
MESPARREN Dave D43A
MESQUITE Skip C158 C208A D24 H146 P114 S27B T119 W21
MESSAGE M137
MESSANNO Bobby B242A S254 T169
MESSECAR Dek C34 W35
MESSENGER Bob C39
MESSENGER Doug M203
MESSENGER Tony J63
MESSER Howard C195C R36B
MESSER Tim P137
MESSICK Gordon Y12
MESSINA Jay A16 C236
MESSINA Jim A132 B210 B260 F139 K22 L110 M132E P106 S55A Y16
MESSINA Joe A67P S128 T42
MESSINA Nick M111
MESSINA Phil J48
MESSINA Pierro V11
MESSING Charlie G74
MESSING Paul N65
MESTROPASQUA Frank T150
MESUMECCI Max S193
METABOLIST M137
METAL URBAIN M136D
METALL T. T37C
METCALF Louie C68A
METCALFE Andy S181
METCALFE Byron R127A
METCALFE Chuck T107
METCALFE David F18C
METEORS M137A
METER Walter M210
METERS D86 M138
METHENY Jim T107
METHENY Pat M138A M170
METHEWS Scott S322

Met/Mit

METHI Terje P117A P117C
METHOD M139
METHOD ACTORS M138B
METHUSALEM M139A
METHUSELAH M139B
METKE Bob S338
METOYER Luke S251
METRO M140
METROPOLIS M14GA
METZ Albin J100A
METZGER Albrecht V40A
METZGER Bob M108
METZNER Doug M18
MEURER Rob C234D
MEURIs Peter T12A
MEUSSDORFFER Jack S18A
MEWBORN John C158
MEWRILL Allan R164A
MEWS Christian S158A
MEYDAM John H40A
MEYENDORF Paul S108C
MEYER Augie C39B M141 S7
MEYER Bobby K48
MEYER Carol M141
MEYER Eduard T11
MEYER Ellen T106
MEYER Freddi M141A
MEYER George G112D I11A R28 R38
MEYER George (K) H185
MEYER Gerrit W68B
MEYER Helmut D18C
MEYER Herman B197A
MEYER Jeffrey M18
MEYER Jonathan P115
MEYER Nicolle F105A
MEYER Skip S102
MEYERS Adam A68A
MEYERS Bill M102
MEYERS Craig F140A
MEYERS Jack W47
MEYERS Mike A35D J11
MEYERS Paul P140D
MEYERS Randy S73
MEYERS Ronnie E4
MEYERSON Mark D132B
MEYJES Ron B197A
MEYN Rob B208C
MEYNET Roland E62A
MEZO Gail A69
MEZZROW Jeff T161D
MHLONGO Vicky Busiswe C83 J4
MI SEX M141B
MIALL Terry Lee (also DAY Terry) A10 P59B M175
MIAMI HORNS L26
MIAMI Strings T71A
MICARA Mike B172A
MICARE Franklin R125
MICAS Stephan M142
MICCOLI David B255A
MICELY Joe F105
MICENHEIMER Mike N50D
Michael F43
MICHAEL David G96C
MICHAEL Gil B111
MICHAEL SCHENKER GROUP S41
MICHAELS Billy R50A
MICHAELS Carson M37
MICHAELS Dave H1
MICHAELS Elliot E32
MICHAELS Gordon M143
MICHAELS Gwynne W5
MICHAELS Hilly C196 F81A H51 M107 P72A
MICHAELS Jay B169A
MICHAELS John P53
MICHAELS Lee M144 M159 R123
MICHAELS Lloyd M79
MICHAELS Nick B90 C18
MICHAELS Ras R33A
MICHAELS Roy C56
MICHAL Ed R108
MICHALSKI John C199A
Michel C60
MICHEL Ted D139
MICHELS Lloyd B282
MICHIE Chris M203 P114
MICHIE George W7
Mick see WILSON Michael
MICKEL Mindy M111
MICKENS Robert K80
MICUS Stephen M142
MIDDAUGH Chris B56
MIDDEL Willy C243
MIDDLEBROOKS Ralph 013

MIDDLECLASS Gary P41A
MIDDLEMIST Kink C235
MIDDLETON Dick D125A
MIDDLETON Fraser P118E
MIDDLETON Graham P118E
MIDDLETON Greg H192 I17C
MIDDLETON Kent T107 T136
MIDDLETON L. S251
MIDDLETON Max B64 B70 B237 B280 H29 H181 L63 L111
MIDDLETON Max M145 M206 N14 P45 P119B R15 R46 S103B S300 Z4
MIDDLETON Orwin A59
MIDDLETON Paul G62B W14
MIDDLETON Ross P118E S290
MIDGLEY C.J.T. see Beau
MIDLER Bette B53 S252
MIDNIGHT FLYER M146B
MIDNIGHT HANDCLAP SECTION F81B
MIDNIGHT OIL M146
MIDNIGHT RAGS M146A
MIDNIGHT STAR M146C
MIDNIGHT SUN M147
MIDNIGHTERS B24
MIDNITE Steve C205
MIEKANTSCH Dieter M163E
MIELKE Gary P151 W133
MIER Harry B5
MIESSNER Brian A15
MIETTE Jean Jacques L17
MIGDEN Steve C165
MIGHTY BABY M148
MIGHTY CLOUDS OF JOY L107 W54
MIGHTY DIAMONDS M149
Mighty Flea see CONNERS Gene
MIGHTY SPARROW M149B
MIGIL 5 M150
MIGLIORE Tony E73
MIGLIORI Jay A131D B56 C76 C156 C162 D8 M75 P28 P75 R87 W5 W9
MIGLIORI Tony C14
MIHALY Tamas 024
MIHM Danny F61 L115A S206
MIJTS Frans M237A S348A
Mike R3
MIKE Billy S231A
MIKE HERON'S REPUTATION H110
MIKE SLOT AND BUMPER M150A
MIKEAL David M3A
MIKENAS Ed M60 R100
Mikey Boo see RICHARDS Mikey
MIKKELBORG Palle C61 L41 R178 S69 V26C
MIKSA Florian Pilkington see PILKINGTON-MIKSA Florian
MIKULS Richard R161
MIKUS Heinz F7A
MILAN Irina V26C
MILAN Pepe A35 P92 S175
MILANESE Luciano N60
MILANO Fred B80A D74
MILARKY John C242A
MILCALLEF John I64A
MILCHBERG Jorge G10
MILES Abe B240
MILES Barry D72 L119 M26
MILES Bob B7B
MILES Buddy D24 E33 H99 L107 M40 M151 T82 W28
MILES Charles W47
MILES Chip B203A
MILES Denise Pantos M151
MILES Helene W. A37 C164
MILES J930 K25 L111 M41 R100
MILES John (K/G) M152
MILES Johnnie (D) H129 K4
MILES Lee R62
MILES Louis R68
MILES Otis (later WILLIAMS Otis) T42
MILES Victoria J10A
MILESTONES M153
MILFORD Michael E54
MILFORD Stephen P92D
MILHART James W64
MILIO Peter L8 M18 M68
MILK ,CHRISTOPHER C109B
MILK'&'COOKIES M154

MILKWOOD M155
MILLAR Andrew Cameron D93A
MILLAR Greg S231
MILLAR Robin S134
MILLAR Ron F8C
MILLAR Todd A9 C169
MILLAS Larry I6
MILLENIUM M156
MILLER Abraham L2
MILLER Adam C13 J48 N45
MILLER Al L118
MILLER Albert B203A
MILLER Bill E62B
MILLER Bob (D) S333
MILLER Bob (G) M178B
MILLER Brian (K) B67 I29 R122 T160
MILLER Brian (G) Z16
MILLER Byron D127 F88A H19 L65 S19 W6 W63
MILLER Carlisle W101
MILLER Carol Lee B56
MILLER Charles B268 D86 H92 035 W17
MILLER Chip C207
MILLER Count J24
MILLER D.O. D95B
MILLER Dale C160A
MILLER Daniel F4A
MILLER Darcy C62
MILLER David L140
MILLER Denzil R142A
MILLER Eddie K45
MILLER Floyd S154
MILLER Frank R38
MILLER Frankie F65 F104 J75B J103 M15 M157 T58
MILLER Gene 'Bowlegs' J22 R168 P80 S36
MILLER George R35B
MILLER Geri F109
MILLER Glen John A47
MILLER Glenn C106 C161B
MILLER Harry B229 C63 C183 D108 D118 K54 N50 045 P146 T95
MILLER Jacob I19 M158
MILLER Jerry F45A M174
MILLER Jimmy B242A F12 G27 L103 M159 P93A R133 U5
MILLER Jimmie (G) L16D
MILLER Joe C107A H170
MILLER John C199C F5 K23
MILLER John (B) B256 C68A C156 K68D K81 R164
MILLER Keith S178 W96
MILLER Kim H133 014 S115
MILLER Leo S325
MILLER Leslie F4C R25 S262 C241 D27 F4C G110 G113A J20 J72 K47 K69 L24C R99 S169 V6 W25 W62
MILLER Merle F122 L4A M84A
MILLER Mike (Wind) E57 G16
MILLER Mike (G/B) P76
MILLER Nelson B276
MILLER Pete S209
MILLER Phil C209 G102 H57 M106 N9
MILLER Randy B204
MILLER Ric G71C
MILLER Rice see WILLIAMSON Sonny Boy II
MILLER Robert S316
MILLER Robin H4 K54 S131
MILLER Roger M163D
MILLER Ronald D. S169 S254B T79B
MILLER Steve S133 S115
MILLER Shorty 014
MILLER Smokey Joe E51
MILLER Stan E6
MILLER Steve (U.K.) C34 C209 D5 D128 F108 G102 H43 H57 K84 M158A
MILLER Steve (U.S.-K) B109 F80 G104 H147 H150 K81 L81 M68 M158B T9A T21
MILLER Steve (U.S.-G) B87 M135 M159 S111
MILLER Todd C169
MILLER Tommy C193 06C
MILLER Tracy A61
MILLER Vern R64 S339A
MILLER FRASER BAND F104
MILLETT Doug 032A

MILLIGAN Sean A133
MILLIKAN Bob C186 D50 L4A R142A W25 Z3B
MILLIKEN John D77 G122A
MILLINER Ras P134
MILLINER Steve A3 B112
MILLING Ronnie T57
MILLINGTON M160
MILLINGTON Jean B186 F18
MILLINGTON M160 M191 T32C
MILLINGTON June F18 I27 M160
MILLINS Paul K25
MILLIONS Bill F32A
MILLIUS Mike F58
MILLMAN David M80
MILLMAN Eva F101D
MILLO Mario M160A W99B
MILLS Aaron C20
MILLS Abe D53C 039
MILLS Albert L71A
MILLS Alison M53
MILLS Chas B23 F53 G71A P131 S209 S270
MILLS Eleanore F60
MILLS Fred D24
MILLS Jack A120 K25 W62 Y11
MILLS Jerry M232 046
MILLS John Stuart E79
MILLS John A79
MILLS Lorenzo A53
MILLS Michael C36
MILLS Paul M195
MILLS Richard F30A
MILLS Roy W89
MILLS Russell D95B
MILLS Stephanie P56B
MILLS Tony (B) B83
MILLS Tony S303
MILLS Wayne S72
MILLWARD Mike F93
MILLWARD Simon M137
MILNE Billy F8A
MILNE Ian K94B
MILNE Jim B60 T56 T124
MILNE Karen C99 S135
MILNER Bruce E72A
MILNER David L9A
MILNER Phil D6B
MILNER Simon S164
MILSAP Bobby S187C
MILSAP Mike F3C
MILSAP Ronnie P125
MILT MATTHEWS INC. M10BA
MILTON Danny W11
MILTON Eddie King B193
MILTON Jake B160A Q16
MILTON Larry R15B
MILTON Leslie C11
MILTON Ted B160A
Mim F7B
MIMMS Charles H97
MIMMS Garnet M161
MIMMS Ken H7D L126
Min S131
MINATRE Dan W106
MINCE Graham H69
MINCY Wayne R101
MINDBENDERS M162
MINDEL Michael U9A
MINELLI Sammy E32
MINER David A41 B274B R173
MINESON Dick D27
MINFIELD Rod J36A
Ming Leslie B3
MINGAY Roger 042
MINGE Jerry A66
MINGRAM James S120B
MINGUS Charles D27 M170
MINGUS Sharon J91A
MINHINNIT Ray H116A M157 P77
MINK Ben A52 H117 M40
MINK Peter K94C
MINK DEVILLE M163
MINNEAR Kerry G22
MINNELLI Liza C182
MINNS David H169
MINNS Paul T60
MINOGUE Terence C229
MINOR Bull C15
MINOR Carter H78A
MINOR David G14 G88
MINORS M202B
MINOTT Lincoln Sugar M162A
MINSHULL Lea M175A

MINSKY Ronald G61
MINSKY Susandra D83
MINT TATTOO M162B
MINTER Iverson see Louisiana Red
MINTER Lindsey N13
MINTER Paul N13
MINTER Vivian L126
MINTON Phil C209 N9 S186A
MINTRUM Peter S358E W83
MINTZER Bob F108A P19A T147
MIQUELON Joe S73
Mirabai S55A
MIRACLES R115
MIRAGE M163A
MIRAGE Michael A50
MIRAGE Rick M165A
MIRANDA Ismael F17
MIRANOV Jeffrey A. A96 B110 B155 B208 B263 C42 C103C F60 G164C H99 H164C I20 J20 J48 K37 K47 L63 M21 M26 M65A M111 N2A N65 R22 R25 R99 R125 R142A S124 S125 S252 V6 W27
MIRO Steve M163B N61A
MIRREN Agnes K65
MISCULIN Joey I24A
MISENER Bill C182
MISFITS M163C
MISHALI Thembi B105
MISHIRO Kenji C110A
MISLEJUK Friedhelm S289
MISHLEN Rick K81
Miss Christine G38
Miss Cinderella G38
Miss Mercy G38
Miss Ona R137
Miss Pamela G38
Miss Sandra G38
MISSION OF BURMA M163D
MISSOURI James V40
MISSUS BEASTLY M163E
Mr Jim M163C
Mr M . S228
Mr.Snips see Snips
Mr T. Being G66
Mr.Twister C109B
MR.BIG M164
MR.BLOE M165
MR.FLOODS PARTY M165A
MR.FOX M166
MISTERIOSO L'angelo C121
MISTERS M166A
MISTRESS M167
MISTY IN THE ROOTS M167A
MISUNDERSTOOD M16B
MITCH RYDER AND THE DETROIT WHEELS R177
MITCHELL Adam M39 M75 P39 R137
MITCHELL Bernardine B213 M65A
MITCHELL Billie H59
MITCHELL Billy (G) J5
MITCHELL Billy (V) C144A
MITCHELL Blue B144 C217 M102 M111 M169 032 R62 S111
MITCHELL Bob J96 039
MITCHELL Bruce A29 B247
MITCHELL Craig C76
MITCHELL Dan M221C
MITCHELL Danny M175B
MITCHELL Dave D30B J98A
MITCHELL Debbie S140
MITCHELL Glen W5
MITCHELL Grover R60C
MITCHELL Ian M169A
MITCHELL James C231 D57C D86 D101 F50 G92 G101A J22 M130 M172 N57 P51 P80 P137 S36 S276
MITCHELL Jeff D5C
MITCHELL John (D) C209 F14 N9
MITCHELL John (Hrns) B141 F51 M18
MITCHELL John (K) S209
MITCHELL Joanh B231 P145A
MITCHELL Joni (nee ANDERSON Roberta Joan) A59 B17A B29 B149 B244 C232 C233 H156 L1 M170 N4 S71A T25 T32B W39
MITCHELL Kim M112
MITCHELL Lindsay L98 P139
MITCHELL Liz B174

MITCHELL Mitch (also
MANCHOVITZ Henry) B248 C15A
C79 C189 E26 F109 H99 H123
R21 R96 V21 V26A W28
MITCHELL Mitch (G) W77
MITCHELL Norman B20 T31
MITOZA Rob S189
Mojo S31A
MOJO HANNAH M178
MOLAN Bill C165
Mole O25
MOLE John C167 L99 M196
MOLINA Ralph C216 L107
N57 R123A S10 Y16
MOLINAUX John R66
MOLINEAUX Othello P35
MOLKIE COLE M177A
MOLL Frank Endrick L70A
MOLL Jose Maria B43
MOLLAND Joey B16 B150A
L51 N12
MOLLARD Dominique S280
MOLLARD Padrig A72A S280
MOLLER Stig S249B
MOLLIN Fred C140 E15 H117
M10D
MOLLINGER Max G113 O9A
T118A
MOLLINSON Brian W86
MOLLOY Matt B185 C102 P93
MOLLOY Mick B73 O2C
MOLLY HATCHET M178A
MOLNAR Gyorgy O24
MOLO John E78B
Moloch M178D
MOLONEY Paddy C102 G10
M23 O18
MOMAN Chips B272B C124
K30 T67A V18
MOMBASSA Reg M132B
MOMENTS J11
MOMOLUVICH Laza P72
MOMS APPLE PIE M178B
MONACO Randy M70
MONACO Tony T82B
MONAGHAN Walt A5 I8 N63
S23
MONAHAN Jim S250B
MONAHAN Scott M57C
MONARCH Michael D57 H129A
S265
MONARDO Meco F109 R142A
MONARI Buck B17A P126
MONAY Iain H194B
MONCRIEFF Tom E23 N45B
Mond A65B
MONDAY Paul B233
MONDRAGON Joe S124
MONET Cristina C227A
MONET Kash B208 C68A
MONETTE Ray R32
MONEY M178C
MONEY Eddie M179
MONEY George 'Zoot' A40
M23 R78 C210 D100
E41 E46 F117 G94 G103 K84
M23 M25 M180 R106 S35 S243
W74
MONEY P.R. H110
MONGREL M180A
MONICKS Fred O30A
Monk see Bruce Mike
MONK Elaine L126
MONK Meredith M180B
MONK Thelonious D27
MONKEES M181
Monkey B45C
MONKMAN Francis A62 B280
C161 C201A C251 E24A E44
M180C R12 R65 S80 S144
S270 W35 W86
MONKS (1960's) M181A
MONKS (1970's) M181B
MONLEY Dave O33B
MONNAS Nick A12A
MONOCHROME SET M181C
MONOGHAN Walt N59
MONRO Willie T37
MONROE James E. D9A
MONROE M181D
MONSTERMAKER Mark M180B
MONTAGE M182
MONTAGU Jeremy H194
Montalo W115A
MONTALTO Bob H15
MONTANA Vincent J92 K45
N65 O14 P80 S124A S228

MOHOLO Louis A105 B153
D35 D118 N50 P146 T95
MONTANO Pete P53
MOIR Fenwick K32A
MOIR Les I26A K26A
MOIRE David L95C Z8

MONTANEZ Victor S125
MONTE CAZAZZA M182A
Montego Joe D66 D76 N63
O15
MONTEIRO Stan B177 C217
MONTE1TH Sandy C132
MONTEZ Chris M183
MONTEZUMA Johnny B261
MONTGOMERY Bob C224 H134
MONTGOMERY Bobby B17
MONTGOMERY Carol C224 D139
M11 S269
MONTGOMERY David A73 K58
P159
MONTGOMERY Gary B274B C38A
C168 S8A
MONTGOMERY James C59 M184
MONTGOMERY Joe L52
MONTGOMERY John M37
MONTGOMERY Lee A132
MONTGOMERY Little Brother
(Eurreal) M48 M185 R168
S358
MONTGOMERY Melba H26
MONTGOMERY Michael John
B145B
MONTGOMERY Mike B12 K87
L9 L57 W48B
MONTGOMERY Monk C241
MONTGOMERY Robbie B144 D86
F42 H52 K81 M203 R22
MONTGOMERY Sonja A59
MONTGOMERY Tammy see
TERRELL Tammi
MONTGOMERY Wes S168
MONTGOMERY Wynell P126
MONTGOMERY-CAMPBELL Hugh
A92A E24 H57 P126
MONTRELL Roy D96 D106
MONTROSE M187
MONTROSE Ronnie B63 G7B
H19 H51 M16 M187 M203 W90
W106 W119B
W133
MONTY PYTHON M188
MONUMENT M188A
MOODY James D27
MOODY Mick B174B C75 C79
C204 H42 M177 J105 J110
L46 M157 M180 R11 S176
T128 Y10 Y19
MOODY BLUES M189
MOON (RAY OWEN'S) R44
MOON (U.K.) M190
MOON (U.K.) S1 M190A
MOON Chuck P73
MOON Derek I26A
MOON Doug B72 K49A
MOON Eve M163 M189A
MOON James G16
MOON Jim P94 S203
MOON Keith B59 B64 C35D
D66 E60 F65 H29 H110 L51
M191 S338 W72
MOON Roger S287
MOONBEAMS W49
MOONDOG M192
MOONDOGS M191A
MOONEY Bill L87A
MOONEY Ed M216A
MOONEY John M192A
MOONEY Kevin A10
MOONEY Malcolm C25
MOONEY Ralph A132 B279
C169 J53
MOONEY Thom B263 H111A N16
N57C O15 P24 T17 W48D
MOONGLOWS M192C
MOONLIG Tommy H2A
MOONQUAKE M192B
MOONRAKERS M192D
MOONRIDER M193
MOONWEED Hi T see BLAKE
Tim
MOORCOCK Michael C18 H64
M194
MOORE Alan (D) J102 S327
MOORE Alan (Trom) S31
MOORE Alan (Pno) M173 N37
MOORE Albert B. S353
MOORE Anthony A29 A133
H101 M80 S152
MOORE Arnie F12B H59 S272
MOORE Benny E52B
MOORE Bob R31 R127A

MOORE Bobby L, C14 D139
H26 M41 M68 M174 M194A
M197A N37 P63 P125 R173
Y18
MOORE Brew D27
MOORE Brian 'Red' S101
MOORE Charles M1
MOORE Christy M221E P93
MOORE Colin O18
MOORE Collins T162
MOORE Daniel (V) B221 C38A
C77 C109 C123 C155 D66 H59
S269 S272 W21
MOORE Danny (Tpt) D97A
J93D M41 P149 T20
MOORE Darryl J91A
MOORE Dave N56
MOORE Debbie R57
MOORE Denny M53
MOORE Derek N18
MOORE Don V21
MOORE Dorothy T32A
MOORE Douglas S157
MOORE Dudley W86
MOORE Eddie H133 L130
M222A P132C S27B
MOORE Edward F92
MOORE Eric G57
MOORE Eric 'The Kid' C30A
MOORE Fred C68A
MOORE G.L. T142
MOORE Gary A78 B195 C167
D88 G1A G40 H169 L9A L99
L144B M196 P119B S139 T59
MOORE Gerald 'G.T.' H109
J90 M195 S108
MOORE Glen C189 O30 P45
S73C
MOORE Godfrun T162
MOORE Greg M131
MOORE Henry W46
MOORE J,Alan E73
MOORE James see HARPO Slim
MOORE Jim L4 L118 W21
MOORE Johnny (V) D116 F59B
MOORE Johnny (V) U20
MOORE Johnny (G) T28
MOORE Kenneth L. P126 T158
MOORE Kermit C147 C164 K36
MOORE Kevin C217
MOORE Kim E66 Z24
MOORE Larry M2
MOORE Laverna A59 L72 N37
MOORE Lorraine P99
MOORE Lyndsey K61
MOORE Lynn D66
MOORE Matthew B221 C38A
C77 C123 C155 D66 E40 H59
M190A S8A W21
MOORE Melanie K68A
MOORE Melba R57
MOORE Melvin B240 O39
MOORE Merrill M197
MOORE Michael (B) M21 M229
S215
MOORE Michael (Sax) R141
MOORE Nicky H3 T89
MOORE Nigel L142
MOORE Pamela M196A S73
S322 Y12
MOORE Pat G72A
MOORE Pete see MOORE
Warren
MOORE Phil M102
MOORE Richard S312A T144
P125A S13
MOORE Scotty L64 M197A
M211 P125 S342
MOORE Stephen C20
MOORE Steve S230
MOORE Stevie M197B
MOORE Susan M227
MOORE Tim C76 G117 K17
M198 R22
MOORE Tiny A1O2 R57
MOORE Tom M221C
MOORE Warren A132
MOORE Warren 'Pete' R115
MOORE Wayne N5A
MOORE Willie W119
MOORS Don M53
MOORSHEAD John B171 B247
D129 H84 L7 S105
Moose see BRENNAN Mark

MOBED Johnny (HALFORD Paul)
M199
MORAIRTY Skip T136
MORAIS Trevor B47B B226 C30
H70 H121 Q2 W82B
MORALES Carlos D24
MORALES Clancey P53
MORALES Enrique B43
MORALES Garcia J2
MORALES Janet B197D
MORALES Hernanos B43
MORALES Miguel B43
MORALES Pancho H9 H181
MORALES Richie B208 M200
S147A
MORALES Rocky C39D D13 S7
MORALES Urbano I13B
MORAN Gayle C189 M40 S18
MORAN Jerry A54
MORAN Mike A62 A109 A133
B160 B280 C6B C47A C75 C127
C201A D2 D36 F13 F65F F70B
F86 F120A G31 G32 G50 H111
K78 M83 M175B M233 R46 R124F
S238C S283B T10 T73 V29 W18
W49 Z9B
MORAN Paul B166A
MORAN Pete A60
MORANTE Massimo G52A
MORAZ Patrick D39 H168 J14
M55 M189 M200 R61 S233 Y7
MORAZ Rene M200
MORCOMBE Richard D93 P131
MORDECAI Michael W11
MORDUE Eddie B19 C109 H121
K81 S93
MORE M200B
MORE A. M200A
More Ears see FAGAN Glaister
MORECOMBE Dick S186A
MOREING Jody G26D
MOREIRA Airto A24 A131 B85
B208 B214 C100 C129 C151
C186 D27 D50 D127 H181 J20
J75A K36 M40 M170 O15 P45
P72A R77B S19 S104 S125 T158
V39 W8 W36 W63 W119B
MORELAND George I28
MORELL Gary J104D
MORELL John A131D M227 P129
MORELLI John B149B T156
MORENO Tony M136C
MORERO Lydia S284
MORETTI Joe D131 E74 H121
K39 T163
MOREVE Rushton S265
Morey E69A
MORFORD Gene B226 C235 J72
T67A K14 V18A
MORFORD Lewis B63 P33
MORGAN M201
MORGAN Barry A109 B152 C2
C6 C75 C78 C161C C201A O39
E48 E74 F13 F14 F101 G11 G97
H132A J63 J72 J84 K81 K84
L15 M50 M58 M125 P109 P131
P131 P141 R12 R129 R132 S95B
S209 S266 W13A W86
MORGAN Bret A60A
MORGAN Carol K81
MORGAN Charlie B280 O40 T173
MORGAN Chris C26 S135B
MORGAN Chuck B202
MORGAN Dave (Perc) M1
MORGAN Dave (B) B26
MORGAN Earl H105 R134
MORGAN Gary S274
MORGAN Glyn C238A
MORGAN Graham J4 J16 J86 N11
Q1
MORGAN Jack K27A
MORGAN James B231 H56
MORGAN John (K) S217
MORGAN John (V) C165
MORGAN John Russell S265
MORGAN Leslie B25
MORGAN Lanny H8A S262
MORGAN Lonnie W119
MORGAN Michael M221
MORGAN Michel C43
MORGAN Mike (G) F13
MORGAN Mike (G) M239 P41
MORGAN Peter (B) B21 H66
H121 S355 V30 W86
MORGAN Peter (D) C238A
MORGAN Ron E35

MORGAN Roy B47B G10 K22A S235 S283B
MORGAN Scott M1 R36A
MORGAN Steve W48B
MORGAN Tommy B141 C38 C51 C220B E57 M21 M65A N42 S124 W88
MORGAN Warren A137 F65A
MORGANFIELD Mckinley see WATERS Muddy
MORGANO Doug B233
MORGENHEIM Bruce R21
MORGENSEN Eric C153
MORGENSTEIN Rod D79
MORGENTHALER Mary Ann F3
MORI Maurizio A9B
MORILLO Barbara C11
MORIN Andre G116C
MORIN Bob K45
MORIN Ed P76
MORIN Frank G84 M211 Q12 S7
MORIN Jerry S162A
MORIN Jean G116C
MORIN Marty W113
MORIN Paul G116C
MORIN Ron-Paul M202
MORIZURE Rene K19
MORK Steve D17
MORLEY Malcolm B73 G65 G79 H93 L53 M10C M63 S14 T170 W130
MORLEY Rick C241B
MORLEY Tony D93D
MORMAN Ralph B283 P63A S31
MORMET Karl E19C
MORNING M204
MORNING GLORY M205
MORNING GLORY M205B
MORNING STAR M205A
MOROCH Nick W62
MORODER Giorgio M201A
MOROUSE Dennis B169A L51 M101 S362
MORPHET Chris T84
MORRANGELO Thomas B286 E31C
MORREL John H5C
MORRELTom C15 N23A
MORRETTI Joe C127
MORRILL Kent W3B
MORRILLO Ilana W5A
MORRIS Bobby C71 G121
MORRIS Clifford C164 F60 J92 M53 N2A R125
MORRIS Dave (K) B43E S260 W15A
MORRIS David (S) S210
MORRIS David (D) D87
MORRIS Denis B45F K29 C14 C124 C194 D104 E51 E57 F50 F78 G16 G96C H7D H62 H65 H162A J13 K77 K95 K96 L72 L77 L10B L136A M11 N37 046 R4 R31 R81 R127A S269 T55 T107 T167 Y16
MORRIS Gerbert B114A
MORRIS George M50
MORRIS Gerry D68 W69E
MORRIS Ian S164
MORRIS Jeff B36B
MORRIS Jimmy Lee S204 Y13
MORRIS John H125
MORRIS Joe S356A
MORRIS Kenny S132 T59
MORRIS Kerry M123
MORRIS Kevin E7D
MORRIS Leo B85
MORRIS Mark B. A38 C50 N37
MORRIS Naggo U4A
MORRIS Nigel B67 H154 I29 Y2
MORRIS Peter B118 S198
MORRIS Rex E48 S14 S31
MORRIS Robbie V18A
MORRIS Roger M202A
MORRIS Roger (G) P142C
MORRIS Roy K79
MORRIS Russell A37
MORRIS S. B101
MORRIS Scott F80
MORRIS Shelley D95
MORRIS Steve J99A
MORRIS Viv H93
MORRIS AND THE MINORS M202B
MORRISON David C140 T47 W125
MORRISON Dennis S362 W119

MORRISON Diane K16A
MORRISON Dorothy G10 K16A K81 N4 S36 W129
MORRISON George L120
MORRISON James T156
MORRISON Janet S322
MORRISON Jesse M26
MORRISON Jim (V) D103 H99
MORRISON Joe V29
MORRISON Kim B272B N23
MORRISON Les D77
MORRISON Monte J79
MORRISON Reggie S171
MORRISON Rex L43
MORRISON Rick A69 T37J
MORRISON Sterling V23
MORRISON Tommy M202C
MORRISON Van B29 H150 M203 T57
MORRISON Walter F137
MORRISON Wayne S227
MORRISSEY Dick A60A B84 B243 F14 G2 I8 J8 J87B K84 L80A M206 N63B R15 R132 S82A S178 S182 S264 W69E
MORRISSEY Joe C90
MORRISSEY Rex Rex H24
MORRISSEY Wendell P99
MORRONGIELLO Tommy D56A H185
MORROW Buddy F4B
MORROW Glenn D36
MORROW Jeff H38
MORSE Peter P129
MORSE Steve D79
MORTENSEN Allan M147
MORTER Doug A30 D68 H188 P138 T6
MORTIMER M206A
MORTIMER Gareth 'Morty' M206B R6
MORTIMER Terry C3
MORTIMER Malcolm B43C G22 L59 M195 S303
MORTON Benny M227
MORTON Bob M175A
MORTON Ian T130
MORTON Johnny S358
MORTON Mandy S227
MORTON Mike S227
MORTON Robin H71A
MORTON Rockette see BOSTON Mark
MORTON Shadow N34 S88
MORTON Simon B195 B226 C79 D38B H42 H65 M10B P5 P42A S82A W9A
MORTON Yogi H39A
Morty see MORTIMER Gareth
MOSCA Sal D27
MOSE Francis also BACON Francis G66
MOSE JONES M208
MOSES Bob C189 F109A K99 L67B M138A
MOSES David L84 M94
MOSES Kathy C151 G79B M39C
MOSES Larry N39
MOSES Lee H99
MOSES Pablo M207
MOSES Peter L24B
MOSES Smiley L84
MOSHER Skip M132C W39
MOSKALYK Myron L74
MOSKOWITZ Dorothy M18 U16
Mosley P86
MOSLEY Bob F45A M174 M209
MOSLEY Cliff L28
MOSLEY Ian G35 S177D T123 W35
MOSLEY Steve B221 G72 O15 P137 T103
MOSS Abe M229
MOSS Cecil B83 D30 L75 M23 V26A
MOSS Chris A83
MOSS Danny C2 K84 T111
MOSS Emanuel A59
MOSS Ian C158A I5A
MOSS John (D) A23 E17 L113
MOSS John (K) B41 N37
MOSS Larry S164A
MOSS Lu O43 T65
MOSS Michael P45
MOSS Peter F94 S243 S270
MOSS Ralph P20 W48B

MOSS Ron (B) P98
MOSS Ron (Trom) C2 C186
MOSS Tony B247 P153
MOSS Wayne A75 B41 D139 H52A K81 K88 L77 M11 M159 N37 S10 W11
MOSSEL Joap M54A
MOSSON Cordell F137 P29
MOST Abe K45 M170 N40 T37H
MOSTERT Alan Q16
MOSTERT Chris G72A M111 P114C S358E
MOTAUNG Audrey J66 P146
MOTELLO Elton M210
MOTELS M210A
MOTEN Patrick M130 W118
MOTHER EARTH M211
MOTHER GONG M211A
MOTHER GOOSE M211B
MOTHER HEN M211C
MOTHER McCREE'S UPTOWN JUG CHAMPIONS G84
MOTHER'S FINEST M212
MOTHERLODE M212B
MOTHERS OF INVENTION Z8
MOTHERS RUIN M212A
MOTHERSBAUGH Bob C185J D59
MOTHERSBAUGH Mark C185J D59
MOTHLE Mogotsi Ernest B105 J4 O18 P146
MOTIAN Paul B131 M78
MOTION M212C
MOTLEY Joan K80
Moto H133 J92
MOTORHEAD M213
MOTORS W15
MOTRON Daniel R78A
MOTT M214
MOTT THE HOOPLE H185 M214
MOTTAU Eddie B160B L51 M233 P53 S284C
MOTTOLA Tony C146 H9
MOUGHAN Dermot L86A
MOULDING Colin S244 X3
MOULE Eugene S358C
MOULES Pete U14
MOULIA Patrick C60
MOULIN Marc C109 T38B
MOULLET Patrice R78A
MOULTON Victor B36B
Moulty B114A
MOULU Jean Baptiste E69A
MOUNSEY Rob A96 B263 C42 F4C F60 G10 H164C J93C K37 M46B M53 M111 R125 R142A S123 S215 S231 S262
MOUNT Dave M223
MOUNT RUSHMORE M216C
MOUNT ZION SINGERS K46 W13
MOUNTAIN M216
MOUNTAIN ASH M216B
MOUNTAIN Kenny B66
MOUNTAIN FJORS ORCHESTRA S355A
MOUNTAIN BUS M216A
MOUSE M217
MOUZON Alphonse C189 D72 H19 J75A M200 M218 W36
MOVE M219 W122
MOVIES (U.K.) A82 M220
MOVIES (U.S.) M221
MOVING FINGER M221A
MOVING HEARTS M221E
MOVING GELATINE PLATES M221B
MOVING SIDEWALKS M221C
M221D T114 V21
MOWRAY Jack C106B
MOWREY Irvin B8A
Mox G116A H29 J14 J27 K75 S48 S108 T103
MOXHAM Philip Y20
Moxy A101
MOXHAM Stuart Y20
MOXY M222
MOYE Don A89
MOYNIHAN Johnny D38 D88 P93 S346 T6
MOYSE David A22C
MOYSE Nigel S267
MOZE Francis (also BACON Francis) A72A G66 M49
MRAZ George A4A T107 W25
MROZEK Gagey T162A
MROZECK Gerhard K44B

MTSHALI Thembi B105
MTUME James C189 D27 F60 F88A F122 H97 L41 M222A O14 P99 S73C
MU M222B
MU Myron L10B
MUCKLIN Bob S199
MUCKRAM WAKES M222C
MUD M223
MUD ACRES M222D
MUDELE Joe W86
MUDFLAPS Rhinestone D127A
MUDRY Gregg C236 K53
MUEHLEISEN Maury C229
MUELLER Bill S73
MUELLER Teddy A131C
MUELLER Veronique M200
MUFFINS M95A
MUFFINS M223A
MUGGLETON Paul O22 T173
MUGRAGE Mike O32
MUGWUMPS M224
MUHAMMED Aymin N11
MUHAMMAD Idris C134 C213D E49 F60 G4 J20 L119 M225 N39 W25
MUHAMMAD Jamillar K47
MUHAMMAD Meekaeel K80
MUHLBOCK Fred N61
MUHOBERAC Larry A132 C38A C39 C50 C61A C169 C247 D59B E57 N23 O15 P125 P137 S269 T37H T98
MUHREN Arnold C61A
MUIK Ben F1A
MUIR Dawn B199
MUIR Ian F75B
MUIR Jamie K54
MUIR Perrin M113
MUKAIYA Minoni C51C
MUKUNDA Vemu H110
MULDAUR Geoff B282 C13 E75 K101 M227 M228 T134
MULDAUR Jenny M227
MULDAUR Maria A59 B282 C68A D101 E70 F48 G9 G72 G84A K101 M222D M227 M228 M229 R137 R173 S173 T134 W9
MULDOON Clive B165A
MULDROW Gail G80
MULDROW Sidney E7 E55 G17 H35B W84C
MULE Gerry A121
MULELLAND Stan M53
MULESKINNER M229A
MULFORD Ashley H47 M67 S4
MULHERIN Joe G92B
MULHERN A.J. B278
MULHOLLAND Keith N64 R12A
MULHOLLAND Phil C55A
MULKEY John H110 M125
MULL Martin M227 M229B
MULLANEY Jan B124A B169A C35C
MULLEN Jim A120 A131 B47B B237 F14 H65 K76 M41A M206 P45 R46 V33 Y10
MULLEN Richard T134B
MULLEN Terry Q5
MULLENIX Lou G96B T20
MULLENTHIN Michael S38
MULLER Dave B197F
MULLER Horst D43A
MULLER Peter B91A
MULLER Randy B204
MULLER Wolfgang A99
MULLER-MENCKENS Matthias P33E
MULLEY Jo K83
Mulligan F24A
MULLIGAN Declan B61
MULLIGAN Gerry B63 D27 H10 W13
MULLIGAN Kevin P34
MULLIGAN Tim Y16
MULLIN Larry U5A
MULLINS Gene A. D139 G72
MULLINS Sam C50
MULLINS Steve D10A
MULLRICH Uwe E52
MUMFORD Gene C179
MUMFORD John A74 A101 B248 E60 G6 I20 J60 L95 M29 P131 S119
MUMPS M226
MUNCE Gary F69B
MUNCH Bryant H65A

MUNDAY Mark Muller F8
MUNDAY Michael K4B
MUNDE Alan C200 F74 H65 K29 P33 V3
MUNDEN Dave T138
MUNDI Billy B29 B49 B183B B210 B256 D139 E5 F80 M30 M94 M228 P49 R75 R164 S272 S282 ZB
MUNDY Mary C76
MUNGO JERRY M230
MINICH CHAMBER OPERA ORCHESTRA L120 P31
MUNKHOFT David T79C
MUNNINKSNA Bas C243
MUNNS Roger H24
MUNOZ Carlos B85 C77 G109
MUNOZ Eddie P102B
MUNRO Rab R156
MUNRO Rob H56A
MUNROE Tony B106
MUNROW-SHAW David Y21
MUNSEY Phil B111
MUNSON Art B94C C156 D5A D59B E15 J69 R87 S135B
MUNSTER Frankie N4BC
MUNT Fred S243
MURAKAMI Jon S311
MURAKAMO Minuro M78
MURATA Shiro Y2
MURCHISON Bruce W101
MURCIA Billy N04
MURCIA Joey B71 C155 F39 L24 L26 L68B W16 W136
MURCIANO Charlie F98
MURDOCH Allan M136B
MURDOCK Glenn M212
MURDOCK Roger D17A
MURE Billy S16B
MURE Gary F60 M21 P41 R125 S215
MURE Mary M53
MURIBUS George A136
MURIEL Carole B199
MURINO Laurent C152A
MURL Douny S96
MURPH Greg D101
MURPHEY Brett W21B
MURPHEY John A105A
MURPHEY Michael M232 S55A T140 W11
MURPHY Alan B23 B280 D131 R46 T77 W13E
MURPHY Dave B159
MURPHY Elliott M233
MURPHY Floyd P26
MURPHY Gerry C140B M67
MURPHY Hugh H110 R11 R162B
MURPHY J.F. & SALT M232A
MURPHY Jae M232
MURPHY Jeff S102
MURPHY John S102 W57
MURPHY Kevin A137 R161
MURPHY Matt (G) B87 B155 C195 P26 W93 W94
MURPHY Matthew (B) M233
MURPHY Mike M106C R1A
MURPHY Patrick A80 A116 D124 L111 M132D V32A
MURPHY Paul D1B
MURPHY Peter B51A
MURPHY Ralph Z22
MURPHY Shaun S73
MURPHY Turk B210
MURPHY William (B) B97 L90
MURPHY Willie K75A
MURPHY Willy (K) R22
MURRAY Anne B69 W101
MURRAY Barry S31
MURRAY Bill A50 N10
MURRAY Bill (K) W12A
MURRAY Bob S303
MURRAY Bonnie M108
MURRAY Cindy W107
MURRAY Dave I25
MURRAY David (Sax) U6
MURRAY Dee C6B C127 C234B D58 D39 D72A E15 E24 E44 E57 F38 H22 H62 J72 J86 S228A W39 W42
MURRAY Don C234C D12 T161 W110
MURRAY George B186 H39A I25B
MURRAY Ian B66
MURRAY Jim Q12
MURRAY Ken R93B
MURRAY Larry C169 H77 K95 S52 S269
MURRAY Martin H143A

O 01
O BAND 01
O LEVEL 01A
OAK 02
OAKES Geoff I5A
OAKEY Lyn L184
OAKLAHOMA 02A
OAKLEY 03
OAKLEY Berry A38 J52
OAKLEY Leon B210 S120
OAKLEY Philip H178A
OAKLEY Ritchie 03
OAKLEY Vic B287
OAKMAN Pete B236
OAKRIDGE BOYS C50 R117A S125
W13A W18
OATES Jerry C15
OATES John H9
OATES Ron C194 E54 H65 N37
R101 S269
OATES Warren K95
OATON Bill P72A
OATTS Jim C90 S238A
OBAN George A107 B276 N27D
R358 W23
O'BANNION John 02B
OBERASHER Marianne M211A
OBERG Bebben S14B
OBERG Ted L95B
OBERLE David G114 H168
OBERLE Mick T67A
OBERMEIIER Uschi A57
OBIEDO Ray D127 H19 S193A
S325
OBOMSAWIN Thomas B161A
O'BRECK Jim B181D
O'BRIEN Ann Hillary C42 Y16
O'BRIEN Bishop T25
O'BRIEN Bob C55
O'BRIEN Butch M1
O'BRIEN Chas C185B I26A
O'BRIEN Cubby C39
O'BRIEN Deke B73 02C
O'BRIEN Dennis R40B
O'BRIEN Gloria A122
O'BRIEN Jack H12A
O'BRIEN Jimmie P18D
O'BRIEN Joel Bishop C195 J65
K48 K68D L111 M198 S272 T27
O'BRIEN Larry B45B
O'BRIEN Stacey A121
OBRY Trombone S171
OBRYANTST Robert C241
OBSERVER ALL STARS 04
Obeidiktion Blackbyrd see
McKNIGHT Dwayne
OBYTON John N41
O'CANAIN Tomas N2B
O'CARROLL Rory H20A
OCASEK Richard C41 L98 M155
S319
OCCASIONAL WORD ENSEMBLE 05
OCEAN John L62 027
OCEANS Lucky see GOSFIELD
Reuben
OCHOA George Y4A
OCHOA Mario S19
OCHS Phil 06
OCKER David Z8
O'CONNELL Bill V6
O'CONNELL Chris A102
O'CONNELL Dan B42
O'CONNOR Billy B139
O'CONNOR Charles H158
O'CONNOR Derek H46
O'CONNOR Donald B242
O'CONNOR Dermot S22
O'CONNOR Gary A15 C55A
O'CONNOR Hazel 06A
O'CONNOR John D68 P138
O'CONNOR Kieran B21 M221A S670
S76
O'CONNOR Mark D79
O'CONNOR Martin W125
O'CONNOR Michael L42A P151
O'CONNOR Neil F76 06A
O'CONNOR Patrick A21A
O'CONNOR Rob W77
OCTOBER Gene C95
OCTOBER CHERRIES 06B
OCTOPUS 06C
OCTOPUS 07
O'CUTHBERT Martin 07A
ODA Randy R157
O'DANIEL John P109A
ODAY Alan K14
ODDIE Bill G71A W7
ODDSOCKS 07B
ODEGUARD Ken D139

O'DELL Ann B152 C10B E18
F42 G50 H70 08 P76 S355
O'DELL Dick R17
O'DELL Rick L14
ODELL Larraine C3
ODELL Roger C3 S82A
ODEN Bianca M53
ODEN Henry B144
Odetta I2
ODGERS Brian A109 C79
C201A D9 D36 F14 G32 G71A
J36A J72 M40 P41 P76 P141
R12 R60 S48 S194B S270
S352 T47 T96 T111 V13
WDIN 08B
O'DOHERTY Dec H158
O'DOHERTY M132B
ODOM Andrew 'Big Voice'
D30 08A
O'DOMHNAILL Padraig see
O'DOMNAILL Padraig
O'DOMHAILL Michail see
O'DOMNAILL Michael
O'DOMHNAILL Triona see
O'DONNELL Triona
O'DONAGHUE Michael G81A
O'DONNELL Al S346
O'DONNEL Ed D66
O'DONNELL Joe E8 H73 J16
M15 N41 09 R86 W125
O'DONNELL Michael
(O'DOMNHAILL Michail)
B185 C120
O'DONNELL Padraig
(O'DOMNHAILL Padraig)
C120
O'DONNELL Steve G49
O'DONNELL Triona
(O'DOMNHAILL Triona)
B185 C120
O'DONOGHUE Kathi C79
ODOR Buddy 09A
O'DOWD Mike A102
ODUMUSU Mike 034
ODYSSEY 010
OEHLER Dale S17
OEHLER Peter H38A
O'FARREL Pat C120
OFF BROADWAY 010A
OFFEN Arthur A22B
OFFENBACH 010B
OFFENSTEIN Eddy Y12
OFFITT Lillian H147
O'FLAHERTY Joseph N10
O'FLAHERTY Peter D134
O'FLYNN Dennis S273
O'FLYNN Liam P93
OGAN Gary P118D R173
OGDEN Jim A27
OGDEN John T133
OGDIN Bobby C194 F93A G16
H7D H117 K88 L77 S32 S269
OGE Joe G12A
OGILVIE Howard Y19B
OGILVY-FORBES Jamie E41
OGLETREE Mike C8 S126
O'GORMAN Bernie C35D
O'HARA Art S36
O'HARA Barrett N25
O'HARA Brian F93
O'HARA George L71A W133
O'HARA Jack E24A
O'HARA Patrick A116 C158
G84 L100 M151 M203 Q12
S27B S36
OHARA Rey S5
O'HEARN Patrick Z8
OHIO EXPRESS 011
OHIO KNOX 012
OHIO PLAYERS 013
OHLERT Jorg E34A
OHLMAN Christine S53A Y3A
OHLSEN Mark S314
OHMAN Kjell V32B
OHRSTROM Bill H18 T104
OHMURA Kenji Y6A
OILY RAGS C89
OINGO BOINGO 013A
O'JAYS 014
OJEDA Henry 'Big Red' C179
T166B
OJIVAS Patrick Erard A74A
Okamoto V26B
OKAN Humphrey G13
O'KEEFE Billy 043
O'KEEFE Danny 015
O'KEEFE Leo T96

OKLAHOMA BAPTIST
UNIVERSITY CHORALE G10
OKLAHOMA MAFIA 016
OLAFSSON Finn A8A
OLAFSSON Torsten A8A
OLANDER Ivan L24
OLATUNJI Babatunde D17
E49 J113 M78 W63
OLBREI Fred C6B
OLBINSON Les S303
OLCH Dean P83
OLD AND IN THE WAY 017
OLDAKER Jamie C121 F100
K51 L68B R173
OLDEMEIER Lutz M163E
OLDFIELD Mike A133 B69
B230 C13 C209 E59 G66
H101 N41 N45A 018 P109
S12 T34 W135
OLDFIELD Nobby Y8A
OLDFIELD Rachel C217
OLDFIELD Sally H4 018
018A P109 S12
OLDFIELD Terry G66 018
OLDHAM Andrew H147
OLDHAM Ronnie W16A
OLDHAM Spooner (LYNDON
Dewey) B244 C180 D139 E75
F74 F123A G109 G121 H15
J22 L50 M10A M27 M125A
M229 M235 R137 S116 V18
Y16
O'LEARY Goncy D86
O'LEARY John (D) B278
O'LEARY John (Harm) B250
D128 S349A
O'LEARY John (B) R68
O'LIST Davy A84 F42 J57
J58 M168 N44 R149
O'LIST Susie B230 D95
L100B
OLITZKY Steven S58
OLIVA Nick R39
OLIVE Alfonso A41B
OLIVE Palm F71 R17 S159
OLIVE Pat H159A
OLIVELLA Phil 015
OLIVER David R54
OLIVER Dennis S111
OLIVER Graham S32A
OLIVER Kristine M27
OLIVER Janis M27
OLIVER Jimmy (B) W101
OLIVER Jimmy (D) D116
OLIVER Joey H59
OLIVER Michael K24 S270
T162
OLIVER Mick S209
OLIVER Oli J14
OLIVER Peter S329B
OLIVER Thomas D133E
OLIVER Tommy J46
OLIVER Tony I18A
OLIVERA Joe C146
OLIVERA Raul J10
OLLIS Terry H64
OLLIVER George M66
OLLSON Kent S107
OLMOS Claude C152A J4A
M49
OLMOS Edward R164
OLNEY Dave B209 D93 K94B
M25 P138 S93 W60
O'LOCHLAINN Ruan B73 C199
C210 F42 L16A 02C R8
S288A W129
OLOFSSON Lars L79
OLOGHLIN Shirley R17
OLSEN Fred B144 B210 S198
OLSEN Keith B25 B174F F82
G81E M156 M237 S6
OLSEN Richard C81 I31 W83
OLSON Dave C214B
OLSON Ian W57
OLSON Keith G25
OLSON Mark B225 D106A R32
T32C W21
OLSON Marty T83A
OLSON Richie A125 S65
OLSON Skip B177 M167 Q12
R40
OLSSON Kai L117 018B
OLSSON Nigel B23 B98 C6B
C3B C5B C14B D28 D39 D72A
E15 E44 F38 G77 J72 J86
019 P95 P113 P114B R137
R173 S228A T137A U22 W39
W42 W72

OLSSON Pontus H18
OLSSON Wayne 018B
OLYMPIC 019A
OLYMPIC RUNNERS 020
OLYMPICS 021
OMA DRAKE SINGERS N23
O'MALLEY Tony A85 C208B
H65 K76 K81 R69 T43
O'MARA Cathleen F51
OMARCUS Thomas T102
OMARTIAN Mike A132 B85
B127 B194 B210 C36 C51
C61B C213 C234D C235 D74
E40 F92 F139 G9 G10 G15
H14 H37A J16B J43 J69 K16A
K45 L72 L110 L140 M16A M75
N16A 023 P98 R28B R78 R99
R101 R142A S34 S55A S58
S65 S160 S180D S198B S262
T21 V18B W13 W32A
OMARTIAN Stormie C234D D74
F139 023
O'MEARA Barbara P147A
OMEGA 024
OMEGA PLAYERS B69
OMERNIK Fred C115A
OMEZIAN Freddy K19
OMOSHETI Tunji F7
ONE (U.K.) 024A
ONE (U.S.) 024B
ONE HUNDRED PER CENT PROOF
024C
101'ERS 025
ONE TRUTH BAND M39
O'NEAL Brian B280A
O'NEAL Gene S187C
O'NEAL Kevin R121
O'NEAL Mick R121
O'NEAL Vinni B213
O'NEIL Danny S238A
O'NEIL Jim M162
O'NEIL Jimme F47M80
O'NEIL Noth S349B
O'NEIL Mike D99 H74 P107
O'NEILL Bob C133 S177
O'NEILL Brendon G5
O'NEILL Damian U11
O'NEILL Eoghan M221E
O'NEILL Jennifer M27
O'NEILL Jim M80
O'NEILL Jimmy (B) M208
O'NEILL John U11
O'NEILL Mike G106A K51 K60
N43 Y12
O'NEILL Nancy C62
O'NEILL TWINS K51
ONG Lance P114
Onike V39
ONLY Jerry M163C
ONLY ONES 026
ONO Yoko B59 E37 L51 027
P53
ONO GAGAKU SOCIETY M78
ONONOGBO Charles A105
ONSON Duru B91A
ONWARD BRASS BAND S125
OOBLEE DOOBLEE BAND D128
OOGAH BUNCH H51
OOZE Warren C164
OP Trevor S264
OPA 027A
OPALACH Paul R39
OPALISKY George L51 027
T147
OPATIK Dave R177
OPEN MIND 027B
OPEN ROAD 028
OPERATION BASEBALL 028A
OPPENHEIM Sarah 024B
OPPENHEIM Steve T13
OPTNER Jimmy C58A
OPTON Jim N60B
O'QUINN Keith D50
ORAN UTAN 028B
ORANGE Joe M78
ORANGE Walter C174
ORANGE JUICE 028C
ORANGE PEEL 028D
ORBACH Dan S213
ORBISON Roy 029
ORCHESTRA DE L'OPERA DE
PARIS E53
ORCHIDS 029B
ORD John H59
ORDINAIRES F105A

ORE Bobby N61B
O'REGAN Jerry W10
OREGON 030
ORENA Charles C178A
ORFORD Martin L52A
ORFORD Owen C178B
ORGAN Eugene C85 T173
Organ D. see DOWNIE Tyrone
ORGANISATION 030A
ORGIL Peter A94
ORHAM Jamie West H118
O'RIADA Sean C102
ORIENTAL WIND 029C
ORIGINAL MIRRORS 030B
ORIGINALS 031
ORIOLO Dan S118
ORION 031A
ORIZ Pedro K10C
ORLANDO Tony B53
ORLEANS 032
ORLOFF Gene C147 C164 I2 M41
015 P123 T25 W106
ORLONS 033
ORLOVE Harry R31
ORMOND Brian S40
ORMSBY Buck W3B
ORNELAS Willie H122A L110 N43
T1
ORNELLAS Dave J66
ORNITZ Kim S340A
OROSCO Ernie G26B
OROSCO Ray G26B
OROSCO Ruben G26B
O'ROURKE Jimmy F105
O'ROURKE John D33E
O'ROURKE Sean J3
ORPHAN 033A
ORPHAN EGG 033B
ORPHEUS 033C
ORR Benjamin C41 L98 M155
ORRALL Robert Ellis 032A
ORRIDGE Genesis P. T83
ORSI Robert S53A Y3A
ORSON Ann J72
ORSZACZKY Jackie M160A
ORTEGA Tony 'Batman' P115 Z8
ORTEL Walter E61B
ORTEN Marjie T107
ORTHOFER Will E21A
ORTIZ Joe I19
ORTIZ Jose I1
ORTIZ Luis B139 F17
ORZABAL Roland C77B
ORZECHOWSKI Benjamin see ORR
Benjamin
Osamu see KITAJIMA Osamu
OSANNA 033D
OSAPANIN Kofi B19
OSAPANIN Kojo B19
OSBORN Joe A50 B261 C14 C36
C39 C140A C172A C194 C235
C247 D59B D68B D71 E57 E73
F43 G10 G22A G83 H14 H37A H65
K16A K81 L111 L116 L136A L140
M61 M125A M157 N21 N25 N37
P74 P129 R4 R80A R101 R126
R127A S58 S123 S125 S160 S269
S272 W33 Y16
OSBORN Mike (G) M238
OSBORN Mike (Perc) C222B
OSBORNE Billy I32 L2
OSBORNE Charlie R15B
OSBORNE Chris J48 027 P53
OSBORNE Gary B45A C48 C107B
D39 F117 J72 L27 L106 V30
OSBORNE Jeffrey L2 033J
OSBORNE Michael (G/V) A131C
M47B
OSBORNE Mike (Wind) B67 B229
C183 T141
OSBORNE Ray H74
OSBORNE Riley G100 S269
OSBORNE Sonny S10
OSBOURNE Bobby G11B
OSBOURNE Johnny 033K
OSBOURNE Ozzie B115 C203A
033E
OSCAR 033F
OSCAR BENTON BLUES BAND B85A
OSCHER Paul W28 Y13
OSEI Kojo W37
OSEI Mike M133
OSEI Teddy 034
OSEI Tony M133 W37
OSELAND Mark D14C
O'SHAVE Wavis 033H

PENNY Bob B199A
PENNY Charra C173
PENNYCOCK Bruce B57F D97B
PENQUE Romeo C164 C213D D27 D50 I2 J20 L69 M227 R125 T147
PENRHOS Kids O18
PENROD Jerry A9 I24 R75
PENSE Lydia C158
PENTANGLE P60
PENTECOSTAL Comm Choir S273 S177D W122
PENTELOW Nick G27 J104C S177D W122
PENTHOUSE Peter P18C
PENTIFALLO Kenny 'Popeye' S199
PEOPLE P59A
PEOPLE BAND P59B
PEOPLES Rocky P126
PEOPLES Tommy B185
PEOPLES CHOICE P59C
PEP Willy W4
PEP BOYS C86
PEPE John C25B
PEPPER Alice D46
PEPPER Art M125
PEPPER Claude (also MACK John) B13A D87B D106G S117B S156 W54B
PEPPER Dave K60 W20
PEPPER Gib P60A
PEPPER Jim C189 F109A F133 M177 P60A
PEPPER Ravie P60A
PERAINO Victor A35 B231 P60B
PERALTA Denise E57
PERATHONER Serje R139B
PERAZA Armando B253 D127 M40 M68 M78 S19 S284
PERCY Steve S268
Pere Cushion De G66
PEREIRA Ralph A85
PERELES Jon F83E
PEREYNE Claude Alvarez W39D
PEREZ Angelito B5
PEREZ Felipe C156
PEREZ Jerry C198
PEREZ John M141 S7
PEREZ Jose C156
PEREZ Juan F39
PEREZ Mark 'Chico' C235
PERFECT Christine see McVIE Christine
Perico K94A
PERILLAT Nat D106
PERISSI Richard E7 N25 R97 S116 S311 Z8
PERKIN Dave (B) C161C
PERKINS A1 C62B C123 C180 C200 E2 F74 F78 F139 H52A H120 J31 M27 M64 M204 M232A N25 N40 P33 P50 P126 R62 R109 R133 S95 S197 S270 T25 W16
PERKINS Albert C156
PERKINS Bill B210 C52A C162 C198 K45 M68 S111 S262
PERKINS Carl C50 L64 M9 P63
PERKINS Clayton P63
PERKINS Dave K48 W11
PERKINS Donny R82
PERKINS Greg P63
PERKINS Jay P63
PERKINS Jim S356A
PERKINS Joe 'Pinetop' B29 G122 H32 N62 N40 R114 T28 W28 W107
PERKINS Jonathan (K) O30B S237 S244
PERKINS Luther C50
PERKINS Polly A6B
PERKINS Stan P63
PERKINS Terry C14
PERKINS Trudy D24
PERKINS Wayne A28 B169A B272B E75 G96A G96B H11 H4O K46 L146 M10 M27 M88 M170 N55 R133 S160 S172 S196 T20 Y14
PERKOFF King B144
PERLA Gene L67B
PERLEE G. K16
PERO A.J. T166B
PERO Leroy S171
PERON Carlos Y5A

PERON Jean-Herve F30
PEROSA Bruno B262C
PERPER Ed P53
PERRACRA Dennis A59
PERRARA Lloyd G102
PERREAULT Benoit I13A
PERREN Fred E40 P44
PERRETT Peter O26 T86
PERRIER Dominique D51A R6A
PERRIER Peter U13
PERRIERA Joe E30
PERRIN Brian C2 K84 S31
PERRIN Nigel R80
PERRIN Steve D78D
PERRINE Pep S73
PERRODIN Fats H31
PERRONET Philippe V26B
PERROT Nick O7B
PERRU Marc S280
PERRY Bill C38A G117C
PERRY Chris B150A K70
PERRY Crawford J93D
PERRY D.J. H101
PERRY David F19 M216
PERRY Derek D93A
PERRY Doane R101A
PERRY Edwin Damus B52B
PERRY Frank O45 T95
PERRY George 'Chocolate' B71 C12 C107A C234 F39 L86 N4 S276 S276A T71A V38 W21B
PERRY Gwen W119
PERRY Joan V38
PERRY Joe A16 J70 P63A S121
PERRY John G. A131B A133 B81A B208B B268 C8 C34 C251 D9 D131 E44 G35 G82 G97A G105 H26A H65 H70 K63 K66 L63 M7 M45 N57 P31 P64 P72 Q2 R60 S177D S182 S270 T14
PERRY John (G) O26
PERRY John (G) G97
PERRY Kevin S169
PERRY Lee P65 U20 V21
PERRY Lori N45B
PERRY Mark A43 G67A P65A R60B
PERRY Neil J107
PERRY Richard P114 R60C R142A S124 S252 V12
PERRY Ron M151
PERRY Steve (V) H5 J99
PERRY Stu B154D B201 J51 M157 S216
PERRYMAN Rufus G. see Speckled Red
PERRYMAN William Lee see Doctor Feelgood
PERSELL Richard S206
PERSH John R32
PERSHING D'Arnel B224A
PERSKIN Joel B56
PERSKIN Spencer M211 S101
PERSON Walter W101
PERSONNE Paul P65B
PERSONS Billy W43A
PERSSON Peps B193
PERSUADERS P66
PERSUASIONS J48 M18 M41 M170 P67 R144A S180
PERT Maggie B195
PERT Morris A60A A78 B83 B160 B195 B203 B231 B280 C201A D127C F8 F42 G2 G35 G94 H13 H70 I29 J94 K81 L15 M38 M94 M233 N46A O18 P5 P64 P72 Q2 R11 R12 R174B S283B S331 S355A T159 V16 W3 W13A
PERTH COUNTY CONSPIRACY P67A
PESKIN Joel C38A C58 D101 G24 H38 K94A M203 R22 R101 S251 W24 W97A Z8
PESKY GEE P68
PETARDS P68C
Pete the Hat J110
PETEAU Michel N64A
PETER BARDEN'S LOONERS S105

PETER & GORDON P68D
PETER JAY AND THE JAYWALKERS R62
PETER PAUL & MARY P68E
PETER Peter S180C
PETEREIT Dieter P34 T143
PETERIK Jim C90 I6 P68A S336
PETERKIN Keith R35B
PETERMAN Jim M159 S111
PETERS Bill P80E
PETERS Dale J31
PETERS David (D) A32D B183D B233 L56 N53
PETERS Ferdi D18C
PETERS Frans S41B
PETERS James C80C
PETERS Jeff B236 R131
PETERS Jerry C45 E7 E55 F88A G26A H35B K46 L28 M102 M151 M218 R99 W10A W84C
PETERS Jim R56A
PETERS Linda see THOMPSON Linda
PETERS Michael N52A
PETERSEN Bill M65A
PETERSEN Bob S268
PETERSEN Colin B71
PETERSEN Detlef L10
PETERSEN Jochen R28
PETERSON Bill (Perc) W69
PETERSON Bill (B) K88
PETERSON Bobby M13
PETERSON Brett C115A
PETERSON Bruce D42
PETERSON Carl S268
PETERSON Charles I31 L10B S120 Y12
PETERSON Chris Z8
PETERSON Chuck G96
PETERSON Colleen P68B
PETERSON Dick B150
PETERSON Eunice C164
PETERSON Garry G115
PETERSON Gary F85C N26A C38A D133A H62 J105A L107 R137 S251 S284 T153A W128B T106
PETERSON Jochen B139A R63
PETERSON Jon B61
PETERSON John H30
PETERSON Ken R45 R142A
PETERSON Lou O36
PETERSON Sylvia C103
PETERSON Tom B141 P83
PETERSON William B256 P75 P115 R60C
PETERSSON Tom C92 F140A
PETIT Dodie B194
PETRARI Francois G116C
PETRI Tony P93A
PETRICCA Frank P6
PETRONE Rick N35
PETRUCCELLI Paul A28C
PETRY Oliver G15A
PETS P69
PETTEWAY Jim M229
PETTICAN Steve F65
PETTICOATO Toto B47
PETTIFORD Oscar D27
PETTIS Junior M48B
PETTIT Austin G104
PETTIT Bob B93A
PETTO Frank F48F
PETTY Joe Dan G104
PETTY Norman H134
PETTY Philip P109A
PETTY Skeet C151D
PETTY Tom N45B P70 S89 O18 T164
PETTY Vi H134
PETZOLD Dietrich D66C
PEVERETT Lonesome Dave F81 S31
PEW Tracy B108A B196A
PEYRONEL Danny H85 U2
PEYTON Craig H51
PEYTON Randy C213D
PEZBAND P71
PEZIN Slim C1A D63
PFANNMULLER Hartmut E61B S42B S302D
PFAU Ruth D21
PFAYLER Jim O11

PFISTERER Alban 'Snoopy' L128
Phantom F117
PHANTOM Slim Jim S296A
PHANTOM BAND P71A
PHANTOM MOVERS L115A
PHARAOUS S14A
PHARES Scott H108A
PHEASANT N.H.K. A113A
PHEE Dave H111B
PHELPS Rodney K47
PHEW P71B
PHIFER Stan M63
PHIL & BOOGIE BRASS A101
PHILADELPHIA STRINGS K45
Philippe T18A
PHILIPPET Gary C185 M16
PHILIPPOT Ferdinand L48B
PHILIPS Dave H111E L53
PHILIPS Leonard Graves D64
Phill H105
PHILLINGANES Gregory A31 A123 B41B B85 B110 E57 F4C J10B K36 K69 M16A M65A M179 P71C P114 R97 R99 S34 S51 S325 W8 W32A W44 W63 W84C W119
PHILLIP Jim A74 A112 C166
PHILLIPS Andy W58
PHILLIPS Anthony G21 I22 P72 R174B
PHILLIPS Art R97
PHILLIPS Barre G66 R178 T141
PHILLIPS Bill C35B
PHILLIPS Bob (V) C14 L42 S58
PHILLIPS Bob (B) R104
PHILLIPS Bobby (G) H37A
PHILLIPS Brewer H194A T24
PHILLIPS Buster H92
PHILLIPS Colleena B169A C182 D36 M222
PHILLIPS Doug C195A
PHILLIPS Earl A83 H150 H170 P142 R59
PHILLIPS Eddie C219
PHILLIPS Esther O38 P72A
PHILLIPS Gary E6 K40
PHILLIPS George R32A
PHILLIPS Glenn P73
PHILLIPS Greg C87
PHILLIPS Harry C58A R177
PHILLIPS J.C. S349
PHILLIPS Jeff D36 T77
PHILLIPS Jerry P137
PHILLIPS Jimmy C246 P114 S162A
PHILLIPS John (V G) M61 P74 P147A
PHILLIPS John (Sax) C58 G24 R101 S311
PHILLIPS Larry M178C
PHILLIPS Linn F64
PHILLIPS Little Esther O38
PHILLIPS Lydia S284
PHILLIPS Marc H162A
PHILLIPS Marg E65
PHILLIPS Michelle (nee GILLIAM) O10 M61 P75
PHILLIPS Nathaniel C147 H96 L28 L143 M225 W8
PHILLIPS Nigel T36
PHILLIPS Paul H11E T19
PHILLIPS Paul (Hrns) W68A
PHILLIPS Joe B219A H19
PHILLIPS Phil S270
PHILLIPS Popeye F74
PHILLIPS Ray (D) B258
PHILLIPS Ray (B) N5
PHILLIPS Ricky B8 N57C
PHILLIPS Rob P72
PHILLIPS Robert (G) P76A
PHILLIPS Ronald G12A
PHILLIPS Rudiger D66C
PHILLIPS Sean B146
PHILLIPS Shawn D99 F125 L63 P76 T18
PHILLIPS Sid B82 S338
PHILLIPS Simon A60A A98 B64 B160 B195 B248 C75 C108 C129 C204 D110 E24C G32 G35 G50 G97A H70 J102 M35 M90A M140 M196 N14 O20 R5 R15

R149 R174 R174B S41 S177D S211 T121 T173 W13A W102 Y6
PHILLIPS Stacey B207A
PHILLIPS Tim S226
PHILLIPS Tom F80 R57
PHILLIPS Wesley J15
PHILLIPS MACLEOD P76A
PHILLIPSON Mike A74
PHIPPS Peter H129B R174B
PHIPPS Sam O13A P45
PHIZACKLEA David V31
PHLORESCENT LEECH AND EDDIE see FLO AND EDDIE
PHLUPH P76B
Phoebe P73
PHOENIX P77
PHOENIX Bobo D33
PHOENIX Katherine D9A
PHONEY & HARDCORE P76C
PHOTOGLO P76D
PHOTOS P77A
Phrazer C225
Piano Red see Doctor Feelgood
PIAZZA Bob (B) R25 T44
PIAZZA Bob (V) L87
PIAZZA Giorgio P1
PIAZZA Rod 'Gingerman' B13 D77 W133
PIAZZA Sammy C217 H161 J46 S284
PIAZZA Tom S111
PIBLIKO P77C
PIC & BILL P77D
PICARDO Rick W51A
PICARIELLO Fredrick see CANNON Freddy
PICARO Joe M68
PICCADILLY LINE P77B
PICCIRILLO Mike C38A J73A
PICCOLO Greg F3B M192A R138A
PICCOLO John S100
PICCOLO Ron B262E
PICHINS Charles P77D
PICKARD Sorrells S252
PICKEN John P47
PICKENS J.P. S74C
PICKENS Lee B142
PICKERING Bill H134
PICKERING John H134
PICKERING Nigel S203
PICKERING Stuart N61A
PICKETT Bobby D57 S318
PICKETT Bobby 'Boris' P78
PICKETT Courtland P79 S7A
PICKETT Kenny C219
PICKETT Lenny B134A B226 B259 B253 D72A E6 F83A H5 H75 J72 J85A L8 L63 L89 M102 S147A T119 W129
PICKETT Michael D66
PICKETT Nick C183 D128 E41 H194 K3 S8
PICKETT Wilson Fr P80
PICKFORD Loren A9
PICKFORD-HOPKINS Gary A58 B96 C112 E80 W7 W79
PICKHARDT Carl D139
PICKLE Peregrine M18
PICKUP Howard A14
PIDGEON Chris U13
PIDGEON P80D
PIEBES Ellen B224A
PIECES P80B
PIEK Fred F136
PIEKARSK Tom M137
PIERCE Andy P53
PIERCE Billy O10
PIERCE Dave J16B M118
PIERCE Harold C150 W116B
PIERCE Jeffrey Lee G117B
PIERCE Jim J53
PIERCE John A22D C70D I25A P114 R99 S213
PIERCE Larry D26
PIERCE Mervin O13
PIERCE Michael M149 N23
PIERCE Rick T4
PIERCE Tim S86B W6
PIERCE ARROW P80A
PIERCEFIELD Ted C90

POTTER Roger 'Butch' B48A B237 S186A S209
POTTER Steve C213C
POTTER Terry A30 C165 H194
POTTER Todd B252 W43
POTTER ST. CLOUD P118A
POTTERTON Gary F80 S7
POTTINGER Martin H13
POTTS David C85 P123A T45 T73
POTTS Mike Z11
POTTS Moe L24A
POTTS Sean C102
POTTS Steve W119C
POTTS Sylvester C177C
POTTS Wardell S85A
POULAS Vince J38A
POULET Madeline A101
POULOS Jon Jon B255A
POUNCHER Don M141
POUNDS Ray B110 G26A K36 P114 W119
POUSETTE-DART John P119
POUSETTE-DART BAND P119
POUSSEZ P118H
POUTANEN Johann V26C
POVEY Bill B59 G27 S108
POVEY Gavin A23 E17 I18A L62 M10C S268
POVEY John E31F M114A P128
POVEY Trevor D93A
POWALLA Franz L104B
POWDER BLUES P119A
POWDRILL Pat E31 F33 M232 N23
POWELL Alan C101 F24 H64 K38 K83 M194 T159
POWELL Andrew (K) B280 C201A D36
POWELL Andy (G) R65 W114
POWELL Andy (B) R46 Y2
POWELL Benny C179 D86 E7 F60 L66A M111 M229 R60C S325
POWELL Billy A33B L146 R143A T65
POWELL Bobby R129B S171
POWELL Chris (Sax) N66
POWELL Christian (B) M174
POWELL Clive see FAME Georgie
POWELL Cozy A62 B64 B70 B174B C112 D99 H70 K21 M90A P119B R14 S23 S216
POWELL Diane S227A
POWELL Dick (G/K) C229C S227
POWELL Dick (D) B5
POWELL Dick (Vln) S273
POWELL Don A47A S151
POWELL George P151
POWELL Gordon P149
POWELL James C146 P149
POWELL Jane C201A
POWELL Joe M203
POWELL Judith B39 H175 S276 V30 W7
POWELL Marilyn see WILSON Marilyn
POWELL Megan B69
POWELL Nick P101
POWELL Petseye B9 C180 D86 P80 R142A S325 W63
POWELL Rande G96C
POWELL Reg E41
POWELL Rick B161B J53 L35 R111A
POWELL Ricky A33B
POWELL Rigby C158
POWELL Robert B69 E77A W72
POWELL Roger (D) A9C C109 C165 D49 F23 H2 K28B K52 L117 M19 M94 M148 R106
POWELL Roger (K) B186 D53 H119 M120 P119C R164 S263B
POWELL Roger (V) H185
POWELL Scott S78
POWELL Seldon A96 B282 C146 C164 D74 D97B F60 J93D K81 L51 L111 M17 M41 M53 M75 M203 M227 N46 P6 P149 R21 R34 S16B T37E W13 W28
POWELL William O14
POWER Duffy J50B J41 K81 M108 P120 S270
POWER John J64A
POWER Kirk A55
POWER Larry K84
POWER Will P117B
POWERHOUSE FOUR P122

POWERS Charlie T22
POWERS Chester see VALENTI Dino
POWERS Congo C212B
POWERS Dale B139 M141C O11
POWERS Jimmy C59
POWERS Kevin S270
POWLES Gery C195A
POYRY Pekka P109 T15 T104 V26C W75
POZO Francisco C146
POZZO Sara H29
PRAEKER Manfred H5A L104B
PRAGUE Mick F114B N63A
PRAGVEC P122A
PRAHLACH Werni B199
Prakash John A52 B57F B279A C182 H187 P29 R60 T145
PRANSKUS Ed T85
PRAT Jean Paul R6A
PRATCHER Miles M22
PRATER Alan J15
PRATER David (V) P35 S13
PRATER David Darth (D) B7 S19
PRATER Donna T27
PRATON Mark S120B
PRATT Alan H56A
PRATT Andy M131A P123
PRATT Bill F112
PRATT Dean T44
PRATT Deborah J96
PRATT Richard J93D R6A
PRATT Stan S341
PRATTLE Steve R10
PRAY Sue S215
PRAYING MANTIS P123A
PRECLES Greg L71B
PREECE Red F14
PREHN Ole D31
PRELI Thom F74B
PRELL Michelin S104
PRELUDE C78 P124
PREMOLI Flavio P1
PREMRU Raymond A74 B5 S157 W86
PRENDERGAST Fiona D95
PRENDERGAST Jack C205
PRENDERGAST Michael see PENDER Mike
PRESBY Matt L42A
PRESCOD Frank I22
PRESCOTT Peter M163D
PRESCOTT Roger P116
PRESKETT Graham A62 A133 B174B C47A C48 C161 C204 D95 D132 F55 F86 G35 G50 G71A H40A H70 H110 H111B H168 H173 H175 K22A M7 M38 M45 M80 M14C M214 M239 S58B P88B R11 R12 S152 S206 Y19
PRESLEY Elvis P125
PRESLEY Reg T144
PRESLEY Steffen S3D
PRESMANES Jimmy P73
PRESS Reinhold B17A B53 B80 B110 B149 B256 C36 C38A C50 C61A C140A E15 E57 E74 F134 G10 G117C K72 P114B P129 W21 W54B
PRESSER Gabor L103
PRESSURE P125A
PRESTBURY Duncan M163B S214
PRESTI Paul H189
PRESTIA Francis Rocco T119
PRESTIGE Herb W24
PRESTON Billy B59 B201 B202 C94 C155 C241 D139 H39 L51 P126 R60C R133 K51 M101 N55 P126A R173 Z8
PRESTON Don (Syn) B131 F68 G25 G38 G81E L51 R67 S164B
PRESTON Don (V) H39
PRESTON H. S251
PRESTON James S189
PRESTON Leroy A102
PRESTON Raphael J87B
PRESTOPINO Greg C171 C179

C206 D17 G121 M21 M227 M229 R22 T30 W9
PRESTOPINO Paul A16 C108D C182 C236 D53 J48 N48A P25 P40 P41 R100 R108A S63 W5 W51A W106 W107
PRESTORA Don S275B
PRESTWICH Steve C158A
PRESTWICK Marvin S270
PRETENDERS P127
PRETTY THINGS P128
PREVIN Dory P129
PREVITE Franke B262E F101C
PREVO Lionel L115
PREVOST Gerard H89A
PREVOTAT Jean Pierre K19
PREZMAN Michel S280
PRICE Alan (K) A67 P131 W94
PRICE Alan (D) J16
PRICE Alan (G) L23
PRICE Billy B253
PRICE Brian H78
PRICE Chuck T37C
PRICE Dave (V/G/K) C159
PRICE David (G) B152A M141
PRICE George C233 E7 Z8
PRICE Graham C215
PRICE Jean O18A
PRICE Jim A7 A101 A118 B221 B202 C121 C155 D13 D86 F18 F100 G24 H22 H39 H116C K16 K34 K45 L16B L61B L111 M18 M111 M214 M227 P76 P130 R133 R173 T63 U5 W21 W121 W133
PRICE Joe H59
PRICE Judy E51
PRICE Lloyd P132
PRICE Lon A35C A82 B104B G120A J43 L4 M111 M232 N23 N25 R1
PRICE Mark T94A
PRICE Maryann H112 M229
PRICE Michael B127 R78 S180D
PRICE Morris B204
PRICE Peter D95B
PRICE Ray N23A
PRICE Richard W11
PRICE Rick B197B E34 M180A M219 P132A S93C W122
PRICE Rod B112 F81
PRICE Rodney B80
PRICE Ron A133
PRICE Ronn B254A R1A
PRICE Stephen P3 S157 S284 W77A
PRICE Thommy B286 V25B
PRICE Tony B57A D50 D66 S215 T147
PRICE Topper B91 C207
PRICE Vincent J10B
PRIDE Freddy A35B
PRIDE Norman E18A O15 P119 P149
PRIEST Steve S347
PRIESTER Julian C168A H19 H97 M78
PRIESTLAND Tony L48 T99
PRIESTMAN Henry Y1
Prilly T62
PRIMA Vera P132B
PRIMROSE Jackson R162B
PRINCE Andy S358C
PRINCE Falumi B105
PRINCE Mike D61 L47A
PRINCE Prairie B169 B210 E59 T152
PRINCE Ric P102D
PRINCE Roland P132C W30A
PRINCE Viv B64 E46 E35A P128
PRINCE Wez S192A
Prince Buster P123
Prince Candy S96
Prince Far I P134
Prince Hammer P135
Prince Jammy P135A S45
Prince Mohammed P135B
PRINCIPAL EDWARDS MAGIC THEATRE P136
PRINCIPATO Tom M227
PRINCIPLE Peter T161A
PRINDELL Robert E52B

PRINE David P137
PRINE John P137
PRINGLE Jim O39
PRINS Marlene A132
PRIOR Maddy A30 A98 C47 C78 C165 F65 H47 H48 J5 J58 M45 M67 O18 P138 S263 S295 T6 T79
PRIOR Steve S268
PRISM P139
PRISONAIRES P139A
PRITCHARD Barry F87
PRITCHARD Charlie C56
PRITCHARD Dave C178A I7 N48
PRITCHARD Holly R53
PRITCHARD Mel B37 M67
PRITCHARD Pete F75A
PRITCHETT Wesley R137 U9A
PRITIKIN Kitty S276
PRITSCHET Hans C212C
PRIVATE EYE P139B
PRIVATE LIGHTNING P139F
PRIVATE LINES P139E
PRIVATE SECTOR P139C
PROBST John M11
PROBY P.J. F77 P139G
PROCESSION P139D
PROCK Bernie F66A N61C
PROCOL HARUM P140
PROCOPE Russell M227
PROCTOR Judd L117 W13A
PROCTOR Phil F51
PRODUCT P140A
PRODY Samuel P139H
PROFESSIONALS P140D
PROFESSOR BRADFORD SINGERS T67A
PROKOP Skip B144 C236 H59 K81 K86A L74 P39
PROLES P140B
PROOF P140E
PROOPS Jim F16A
PROOTY Fred A28
PROPHET Michael P140C T155A
PROPPER Catrin T143
PROSKY Michelle C185F
PROTHEROE Brian A30 P141
PROTO Larry L90
PROTZMANN Henning K10A
PROUDFOOT Mike C35A
PROUDLY Fred L75
PROUDY Fred P118D
PROULX Andre M57B
PROUTY Fred G96B H160
PROVENCAL Richard C84B
PROVIDENCE P141A
PROVISOR Dennis G83 G101B H146A
PROVOST David T164
PROVOST Eddie A56A
PROVOST Gene T88
PROVOST Joe C198
PROVOST Rick T88
PRUDEN Phillip A1
PRUDENCE Ron G89
PRUDENCE Steve J16A
PRUDENCE P141B
PRUESS Craig E77A F117 R80 V36
PRUITT Cathy R24B
PRUITT David P21 R60C
PRUITT Jay J105A S269
PRUT Richard S338
PRYKA Steve N53
PRYOR James Edward 'Snooky' P142 W91
PRYOR Jill C34
PRYOR Les A29
PRYSOCK Arthur P142A
PRYSOCK Red H63
PSEUDO EXISTERS P142B
PSYCHEDELIC FURS P142C
PSYCHEDELIC PSOUL P142E
PSYCHOTIC PINEAPPLE P142D
PSYKA Rodney B207C I24A
PUBLIC FOOT THE ROMAN P143
PUBLIC IMAGE P144
PUCKETT Gary P145
PUCKETT Jerry L73 S125
PUDERS Peter T4A
PUDDLETOWN EXPRESS P145A
PUDIM Alafia L22

PUENTE Richie F98
PUENTE Tito F3A
PUERTA Joe A48 C171 P31 R46 S270
PUFITT Billy B261 C14 C50 C77A C213E E57 G72 H62 H65 M211 N23 N37 T9 T107
PUGGARD-MULLER Thomas C243C
PUGH Jan R154
PUGH Jim (Trom) A123 C186 J20M
PUGH John B26A J110
PUGH Martin A81 S258 S273
PUGH Michael G100
PUGH Steve A85B
PUGLESE G. (J. Sebastian) D103
PUGLIANO Jim J16C
PUGSLEY Steve S148
PUKWANA Dudu A105 B153 B229 C63 D37 G98 H110 J4 M94 P146 S185 T110
PULLEN John P76
PULLIAG Steve C132
PULLIAM Robert J73
PULMAN Barry H172A
PULSAR P147
PULSFORD Jan H11
PULST Bernd J38
PULTE Jim S199B
Puma B117
PUMA Tommy Li B85
PUMER Eddy F5A K5
PUNCH Mark A95 G26A R118A
PUNCHIN' JUDY P147A
PUNDANT Wasunt G16
PUNISHMENT OF LUXURY P148
PUNKSON Tommy K45
PUNSHON Dave B5
PUNTER John F42 M164 R16B R174 S4 T173
PUPILS P148A
PUPLETT Bill S36A
PUPPEL Fritz C117A
PURAS Roberto R13A
PURBROOK Colin H171
PURCELL John D40D
PURDIE Bernard B169A B208A B282 C155 C189 C213D D27 D97A D132A E49 F27A F108A G53 H9 H58 H181 I21 J48 K17 K45 K81 L111 M21 M26 M78 M177 M198 M227 O15 O33C P20 P72A P149 R100 R140 R164 R169 S262 S266
PURDIE Edward M39
PURDIE Pretty I21 V34
PURE FOOD AND DRUG ACT P150
PURE PRAIRIE LEAGUE P151
PURIFY Bobby P152
PURIFY James P152
PURIFY BROTHERS P152
PURIM Flora A24 C151B C186 D127 J75A S14C S19
PURNELL Donnie K67D
PURPLE Dave C241A
PURPLE GANG P153
PURPLE HEARTS P154
PURRFECT Pete (HOWELLS Pete) D120
PURRO Chuck C172 M184
PURSE Bill B71
PURSELL Bill A59 B17A C14 C50 D139 M197A
PURSER David P54
PURSER Fred P58 T169A
PURSEY Jimmy D125A P155 S86
PURTON Micky M67
PURVIS Bobby S220
PUSSY CAT P156
PUSTELNIK Ken F40 G112
PUTMAN Woodie B6
PUTMON Edward P15
PUTNAM Norbert A59 A75 B17A B61 B210 B261 C14 F78 G72 G85A H7D H40 J53 K77 K95 L108 M18 M75 M108 N32 N37 P49 P112 P125 R4 R137 S10 S22 W11 W64
PUTT William A79
PUZZLE P156A
PUZZLES P156B
PYE Chris K10C
PYE Frances R173
PYLE Andy B136 J105 K61 L37 L101 S31 S273 S339
PYLE Artimus A33B A111 L146
PYLE Pip A35 C209 G66 G102 H57 H86A L5A N9 S9 S175 S181A

RHODES Randy 033E
RHODES Ray D47
RHODES Robert B57 E1
RHODES Ron S83A T97A
RHODES Sandra see CHALMERS
Sandra
RHONE Doug B53 B80 G40
RHYNE Chris P115 S19 RHYTHM
John S203
RHYTHM Rocky R70A
RHYTHM CATS R77A
RHYTHM DEVILS R77B
RHYTHM HAWKS R77C
RHYTHM HERITAGE R78
RHYTHM ROCKERS C215
RHYTHM ROCKERS K33A
RIALE Carmen F94
RIBA Xaver A35
RIBAUDO Joey R39
RIBB Paul M71
RIBBERSON Michael E51
RIBEIRO Catherine R78A
RIBISI Albert P59A
RICARD John K81 R122A
RICARDO Bob S44
RICCI George B85 C164 I2 J31
M41 M125
RICCIARDELLA Mike B41C I12B
N25A
RICCIO Ric A21
RICE Boyd R78B
RICE Denzil M32
RICE Kenneth C220 K51 R39 T145
W25
RICE Larry R78C
RICE Mack F9
RICE Michael R76
RICE Randy B268
RICE Ronnie N29B
RICE Sam N25
RICE Spider P60A
RICE Sylvester A35D F65D
RICE Tim C176C C210 S35 W7
RICE Tony C236B H35 M21 R78C
Rich B166B
RICH Billy B282 D26 L111 M40
M53 M151 M227
RICH Charlie L64
RICH Chuck 013
RICH Don G121
RICH Gerry S48
RICH Herbie E33 M151
RICH Jeff (D) C70 J39B K66
M238 S301 T173
RICH Jeff (B) B38 T32C
RICH Johnny W26
RICH Lewis H106 K61
RICH Ray W39
RICH Tommy A54
RICH KIDS R79
RICH MOUNTAIN TOWER R79A
Rich Tea E66A
RICHARD Cliff (WEBB Harry
Rodger) BB1A H65 H111 R80
RICHARD Ferdinand E69A F123
RICHARD Fred B1
RICHARD Keith (RICHARDS Keith)
B59 K81 M39B N27C R133 T114
W120
RICHARD Michael C245
RICHARD Paul C24B
RICHARD Roland P147
RICHARD Rudolph H31
RICHARD Thadeus M9
RICHARD Tommy C35B
RICHARDS Andy C78 D46B L7 S295
RICHARDS Angelo P126
RICHARDS Arthur P16
RICHARDS Billy R111
RICHARDS Dave B178 E41 E76
G103 I20 K28B L95 M19 M23 P36
P90 R106 S35
RICHARDS David (K) K36
RICHARDS Debe R142A
RICHARDS Digby 018B R80A
RICHARDS Don W15
RICHARDS Dwight M149
RICHARDS Eddie F53
RICHARDS Emil A31 A116 B139
B194 D99 D103 D127 F19 G17
G81E H8A H39 H60 H156 L107 M68
M101 M170 M211C M218 M229 S116
T1 T37M W9 W133 Z8
RICHARDS Jimmy M5
RICHARDS Judy A69
RICHARDS Keith see RICHARD
Keith

RHODES Randy 033E
RICHARDS Mike T149B
RICHARDS Mikey "Boo" (or
"Booth") D63 F86 H105 I12
R35B R134 R150 S313 W4
RICHARDS Peter J89B
RICHARDS Rod R32 R102
RICHARDS Roy R111
RICHARDS Star P114B
RICHARDS Sue H169A
RICHARDS Terry C90
RICHARDS Thadius L7 M9
RICHARDS Tui R118A
RICHARDS Turley R81
RICHARDSON Alex C251
RICHARDSON Barry B73
RICHARDSON Buddy W69
RICHARDSON Cindy A123
B272B C43 F83A M10 P80
R81
RICHARDSON Del (Wendell)
C83 F86 F108 I12 034 R82
RICHARDSON Dennis H133
014 S115
RICHARDSON Devon A4
RICHARDSON Doug E31 F99A
K86 L55 M132D P102B T145
RICHARDSON Edna M111
RICHARDSON Geoffrey C8
C34 G49 H70 H121 P64 Q2
RICHARDSON Jessie R115
RICHARDSON Jim I8 T113
RICHARDSON Joe 'Groundhog'
C146 C203
RICHARDSON John L106
RICHARDSON John (D) R153
T102 W69E
RICHARDSON John (G) G61
H40A M135 N62A
RICHARDSON Karl B71 W21B
RICHARDSON Larry L130
RICHARDSON Peter L57C
RICHARDSON Phil (Vin)
B259
RICHARDSON Phillip (V)
S325
RICHARDSON Ralph B48 C30
F66
RICHARDSON Scott S2
RICHARDSON Soko M111 R62
T158 W118
RICHARDSON Steve H24
RICHARDSON Tim C183
RICHARDSON Tracy B57A
C217 M222 Q5
RICHARDSON Verna C58 M101
S276
RICHERT Ralf P156A
RICHEY Dennis M12
RICHEY George J30 S252
RICHEY Slim C200
Richie T62
RICHIE Chris D135A
RICHIE Lionel C174 M170
RICHMAN Alex B283
RICHMAN Jonathan R83
RICHMAN Sue E77 015 S31
T153A
RICHMOND Albert C164 J20
RICHMOND Dannie (or
Danny) J41 M86
RICHMOND Dave B207 J72
M80 M100 S80
RICHMOND Fritz B244 C179
F19 K101 M227 R169 T134
RICHMOND Ham B83
RICHMOND Jim W11
RICHMOND Mike D40D
RICHMOND Rodney S124
RICHMOND Sanford F99A
RICHMOND Walt B169A D13
R124E W21
RICHRATH Gary R1A
RICHWINE Gary C9A
Rick I Rick F2
RICKARD Frank H35
RICKERT Ralf C241

RICKET Noony L128
RICKFORS Michael H132
RICKS Jerry H9
Rico see RODRIGUES Rico

Rico the Knife D51
RICOTTI Frank A74 A109 B5
B40 B67 B47B B141 B174B
B189 B288 C34 C118 C201A
C251 D2 D9 D37 D38B D49
D92 D132 F14 F70B F100 G11
G32 H52 H67 H70 H110 J63
L80 M83 M100 M239 018A P10
P72 R11 R40B R46 R80 R84A
R85 R129 S31 S35 S108
S177D S185 S209 S253 S255
S270 S283B S334 T133 W7
W71 W102
RICOTTI AND ALBUQUERQUE
R85
RICUPERO Paul Z9A
RIDARICK David R86B
RIDDLE Kirk C115 L145 W87
RIDDLE Paul D12 M93
RIDDLE Ron H19A
RIDDLES Kevin A65D
RIDERS IN THE SKY R85B
RIDGEWAY Tom B200
RIDGUARD Nicky B116
RIDLEY Greg A87 G27 H179
K45 M89A S111 S162 S224
RIECHMANN Wolfgang R85C
RIEDEL Wolfgang E31D
RIEDELBANCH Mandy M95
RIEDY John D56A
RIEDY Bob R85A
RIEL Alex S30
RIETENBACK Joachim L139
RIFF Jane M34
RIFF RAFF R86
RIFF RAFF R86A
RIFKIN Joshua E70
RIFKIND Roger T119
RIGBY Will S177C
RIGDEN Roger C165
RIGEN Ule E34B
RIGGINS Nat L128A
RIGGS Bob F129A
RIGGS Jerry R86B
RIGGS R86B
RIGHAM Phil C140B
RIGHTEOUS BROTHERS R87
RIGHTMER Jerry S20
RIGOR MORTIS E60
RIISNAES Knut V26C
RIISNAES Unur R178
RIIS-OLSEN Jacob G51B
Rik S45B
RIKKI AND THE LAST DAYS
OF EARTH R88
RILEY Ben C44
RILEY Billy F31 L64
RILEY Billy Lee A111 C50
P137 R89 T21
RILEY Bob A31 M189A
RILEY Doug B219A K53 L72
L107 M10B M238A S73
RILEY Edgar Jnr. A131C B7B
RILEY Herman B240 D86 E7
F92
RILEY Howard S267
RILEY Jake L2
RILEY Jimmy D27 R89A R134
RILEY John C155 S57
RILEY Judge S329
RILEY Lawrence 'Judge'
C239 T9B
RILEY Marc F10
RILEY Michael S261
RILEY Paul C105 E19 L16C
M10C
RILEY Pete C141
RILEY Terry C13 R90
RILEY Tommy J71 L53 M128
RILEY Vinnie D136
RILEY Winston M88
RILLERA Butch J38A
RILLING Mikro 036A
RIMBAUD Penny C213A
RIMSON Jerome A127 C79 H73
H169 L144B P30 Q1 Y2
RINALDI Dan L82C
RINDER Laurin B84A E31 L55
R91
RING Little Bobby P151
RING OF TRUTH R92

RINGE Bernie L121C
RINGO Bob P151
RINGS R92A
RINGS R93
RINKER Julia N42
RINKY DINK AND THE CRYSTAL
SET R93A
RINSE Hubert P72
RINZLER Ralph B17A
RIO Chuck C71
RIO GRANDE R93B
RIOPELLE Tom L82
RIORDAN Vince C151A
RIOS Carlos M86 V9A W2A
RIOT R94
RIOT ROCKERS R95
RIOT SQUAD R96
RIP CHORDS R96A
RIP RIG & PANIC R96B
RIPARETTI Tony S3A
RIPCORDS L57A
RIPERTON Minnie C17 033G
R97 R144 S362 W119
Ripke B155A
RIPLEY Steve D139
RIPP Jimmy M189A V25B
RIPPETOE Jimmy A31
RIPOCHE Michel A67E V13
Z18
RIPPETOE Jimmy S114A
RIPPLE Max D34
RISBERG Jan A4
RISCH Tony P115
RISER David S128
RISER Paul A96 R142A S362
T42 W119
RISER Temple A59 P125 T20
RISERS R97A
RISING SONS R98
RISIKO Rob S333E
RISNER Angela C54
RISTON Jean M55
RISTORI Jean M200
Ritchie C117A
RITCHIE Billy C142
RITCHIE Ian D34
RITCHIE June K61
RITCHIE Roy A95
RITCHLEY Jerry U15A
RITENOUR Lee A31 A65C A122
B53 B85 B110 B127 B225 C39
C52A C111A C129 C164 C171
D127 E15 E40 E57 F92 F119A
G10 H8A H97 H122A J75A
J113 K45 L79 L109 M65A
M102 M111 M160 M218 N39
P114 P114B R78 R97 R99
R142A S34 S58 S124 S180D
S262 T1 T37H W27 W54B
RITTER Ike C39B
RITTER Krene B45E
RITTER Mark F101B
RITTER Preston E35
RITTER Rob C117B
RITTLER Burkhard M45D
RITZ Lyle B56 C96 E15 E45
E74 H5C H112 K81 M180 N40
P129 R76 R87 R137 W5
RITZ Richie R169
RIVERA Al 038
RIVERA Eddie C62
RIVERA Fred B201
RIVERA Manny Y2A
RIVERA Mark B154 F84 F115
T169
RIVERA Miguel D133A K48
N12A
RIVERA Pete R32
RIVERA Rubin A35C
RIVERA Scarlet B214 D139
J70 R100
RIVERS Johnny (RAMISTELLA
Johnny) P50 R101
RIVERS Sam C155
RIVERS Sylvester H98 J92
R45 R60C R115 WB4C
RIVERS Tony BB1A D9 H26A
H65 H175 K63 K66 L63 M7
M45 M90A P31 R51 R80 S182
S270 T14
RIVETS Rick N34
RIVITS R101A
RIVIERAS R101B
RIVKIN David L82
RIX Harry G27
RIX Jerry J10A

RIX Leon T44
RIX Luther D139 L80C
RIZZI James T104A
RIZZI Tony Z8
RIZZO Anna B144 G107 M18 Y12
RIZZO Pat A37 C11B C179 S161
RIZZO Tom B144
ROACH Dave T77
ROACH Max D27
ROACH Paul K27A
ROACH Rod H157A S28
ROAD R102
ROAD HOME R102B
ROADMASTER R102A
ROADS Curt S111
ROADWORK W84B
ROADY Tom C38A C39D F48 G10
H146 J11 J22 L79 M235 S20
W9 W118
ROAHMANI Yusuf W119
ROAHNE Doug W21
ROBB Bruce C231 R103A
ROBB Craig R103A
ROBB Dee R103A
ROBB Joe C231 J96 RJ03A
ROBB Steve C231
ROBB Tom B213 D27A L44 M65A
M157
ROBBI Paul P97
ROBBIE Sandie C143
ROBBINS Dennis K46 R123
ROBBINS Hargus 'Pig' B17A
ROBBINS Jerry P29A
ROBBINS Nick K3A
ROBBINS Paul F2B
ROBBINS Robyn S73
ROBBINS Rockie L82A
ROBBINS Ron 039
ROBBINS Steve P15
ROBBINS Vernie S125
ROBBINS Wacky J. A59
ROBBS Fabulous L107
ROBBS R103A
ROBERG Tex R104
ROBERSON Bryce H170
ROBERSON Duane W63
ROBERSON G10B
ROBERT RENTAL AND THE NORMAL
R66B
Robert The Rook J7
ROBERTIE Robert W118
ROBERTON Sandy E41 J110
ROBERTS Al Jnr R105
ROBERTS Alan D67
ROBERTS Alfred G100 K53 L118
T118 W78A
ROBERTS Alun S306
ROBERTS Andy A133 B178 C18
C78 D37 D78 D92 E41 E76 F117
G97 G103 H29 I20 K28B K83
L95 L117 M19 M23 M25 M108
T56 P90 P138 R106 S9 S35 T79
Y6
ROBERTS Bambi A132 F128
ROBERTS Bergert B278
ROBERTS Bill R80
ROBERTS Bruce (G) I11 R104
R125
ROBERTS Bruce (K) B53 R107
ROBERTS Caugley R142A
ROBERTS Chapman W36
ROBERTS Colin W65B
ROBERTS Dave (Trom) A1 F99A
M75
ROBERTS Don C15B C234D L110
ROBERTS Donna A132
ROBERTS Elliot C232
ROBERTS Frank H154 I29 J4
P34 P145
ROBERTS Gene T154
ROBERTS George S321
ROBERTS Gerry B181
ROBERTS Gil R51B
ROBERTS Howard A131D B63 M68
M135 R108 T107
ROBERTS J. S251
ROBERTS Jerry D104
ROBERTS Jim S63
ROBERTS Jimmy C68 L111 M111
T107
ROBERTS John W24 W69C
ROBERTS John R60C

ROPER Will W18
ROSA Enrico C24B
ROSA Mike J18 Q15A
ROSA Valerie M37
ROSALES Joey S249C
ROSALES Leo M59
ROSALES Melanie L82A R22
ROSALES Terry S249C
ROSALIA Pat M75
ROSAND Aaron IZ
ROSARIO Giovanni G58
ROSARIO Pablo B186
ROSBOTHAM Joseph G64A
ROSBURG Scott H16A S305
ROSCETTI Ed F51
ROSCH Art P112
ROSCH Norbert V7
ROSCOE Martin N48C
ROSE R139B
ROSE R139C
ROSE Andrew T163
ROSE Barry S233
ROSE Biff R139A
ROSE Bob C40 L4A M60 R164
ROSE Brian B42B
ROSE Charles A45 A133 B200 B210 C26 C155 D99 F23 F48 G61 G85A H7D H40 H169A J11 K30 K96 L9 L75 L80C M10 M235 N23 P79 S73 S340 T55
ROSE Dave D95A E8 L47 P131 R139B S34 V18B W10
ROSE Diana 'Di' R140A
ROSE Erie P13
ROSE Harvey B247
ROSE Kathy S173
ROSE Michael A107 B117
ROSE Mike C254 J4
ROSE Norman N10
ROSE Pam A35 C77A F50
ROSE Robin U20A
ROSE Ron T102A
ROSE Tim B99 R140
ROSE Tony B32 K65
ROSE Wally A1
ROSE William 'Skip' M238
ROSE GARDEN R140A
ROSE ROYCE R141
ROSE TATTOO R141A
ROSEBROUGH Richard A28A B97 C106A H160
ROSELINO Frank R99
ROSEN Abe C164
ROSEN Larry B223 V6
ROSEN Mike B266 E12 G112D H50 L134 M23 M176 S35 V33
ROSEN Steve L134
ROSENBAUM Enrico A53A
ROSENBERG Al E72
ROSENBERG Marshall A35C
ROSENBERG Martin S350
ROSENBERG Roger F83A L51
ROSENBERG Richie 'La Bamba' S199
ROSENBLOOM David C107C
ROSENBURG John B141 C186
ROSENFELD Eric P13 S110A
ROSENGARDEN Neal H54
ROSENGARTEN Bob C146
ROSENHAGEN Mark A22A
ROSENJARTEN Mark K68D
ROSENKIND Harry S6A
ROSENTHAL Ann E24 H57
ROSENTHAL Arnold D26 L61B
ROSENTHAL David R14
ROSENTHAL Jurgen E50A
ROSENTHAL Phil S73B
ROSENTHAL Steve I8 P53
Roshi S301
Rosi G3A
ROSICA Jimmy B224C
ROSKAMS Alan G13
ROSLIE Gerry S187B
ROSMAN Ronnie H126A J30
ROSMINI Dick A132 R171
ROSNELL Esko T154
ROSOLINO Frank M102
ROSOU Geno A67L
ROSS Alan B242A E60 E61 R142 S339 W72 W99A
ROSS Alyn S331 Y2
ROSS Andy E61
ROSS Annie F14
ROSS Cameo J96
ROSS Christopher H63 H194B
ROSS Colin C165
ROSS Dan S18A

ROSS Davy H71A
ROSS Debi B194
ROSS Diana G17 R142A S333A
ROSS 'Doctor' Charles Isiah A50A R143
Ross Elise T67
ROSS Jack M173
ROSS Jimmy J16C
ROSS Jimbo E31 R91
ROSS Lewis W54
ROSS Margaret F27A S124 S180 T147
ROSS Mark M86
ROSS Marv Q3B
ROSS Merria E31
ROSS Nathan A131D
ROSS P.J. W48B
ROSS Peter C234E H148 S264 T79
ROSS Rindy Q3B
ROSS Ronnie (Sax) A109 F42 K84 R60 W13A
ROSS Steve C203A S272
ROSS Valerie H194B
ROSS Willie O14
Ross The Boss S84
ROSSELSON Leon C47
ROSSET Renato N60
ROSSETTER Tom W51A
ROSSI Angelo C151B P3
ROSSI Bobby G72
ROSSI Francis (formerly Mike) B!'$B E77A I22 S255
ROSSI Mike S153
ROSSI Neil B221
ROSSI Philibert H89A
ROSSI Walter P80
ROSSINGTON Gary L146 R143A
ROSSINGTON COLLINS BAND R143A
ROSSINI Stephane N64A
ROSSMINI Dick D53C D68B F62A
ROSSO Michael C162
ROSSUNOLO Wally M151
ROSSY Jesse E59
ROSSY Jose A35C C20 C99 T8
ROSTEIN Jack S266
ROSTILL John F101 R80 S80
ROTA San C241B
ROTARY CONNECTION R144
ROTCHELLE Dave P101
ROTELLA Johnny A132 B256 C61B F5 M18 M65A M229 015 P151 S262 T107 Z8
ROTELLA Thom B225 M229 N43 S228
ROTH Arlen B59 A105 R144A W5 W7
ROTH Dave V14
ROTH Don N37
ROTH Edward M135 P14
ROTH Jerry N50C
ROTH Mark H59
ROTH Ulrich E7A E34B S47
ROTHCHILD Paul D103 L128 S65
ROTHENBERG Ned F11
ROTHER Michael C145 H27 N26 R145
ROTHERMEL Jim B221 G72 M203 P114 P137 Y12
ROTHERT Karl B47
ROTHFIELD Ron see Raja Ram
ROTHFIELD Susie F82A
ROTHSTEIN Bob M41
ROTHSTEIN Jack D131 H70 M9
ROBSTEIN Rob J18 M41
ROTHWELL Linda G64A
ROTHWELL Ric H106 M162
ROTTEN Johnny (LYDON John) P144 S77
ROUCHER B. A120
ROUGE C103C
ROUGH DIAMOND R146
ROUGH TRADE R146A
ROUJON Loeiz S280
ROULETTE Fred B177 M68 M238
ROUNDABOUT R147
ROUNDTREE George T26
ROUSEETE Jerry L21B

ROUSH Danny W73
ROUSKO Lyn Q5
ROUSSEAU Gilles P35A
ROUSSEAU John J16B
ROUSSEL Coco H89A
ROUSSEL Jean A82 A113 B226 B141 B155 B197 C44 C62 C129 C30 C83 C155 C201A C210 D22 D49 E73 F21 H11 H17 H50 H177 J4 J34 J105 K87 L63 L101 034 P15 P80 P111 W107 R82 S266 S334 T31 T43 T58 W120
ROUSSEL Pierrot H89A
ROUSSELET Richard J105B
ROUSSELLE Francis T118
ROUSSOS Demis A67E
ROUTEN Irma Jean M191 M211 N23 S36
ROUTH Jack C50
ROUTH Marcia N23 N25 T9
ROWAN Chris B177 R148
ROWAN Lorin B177 R148
ROWAN Paul A60 G110 P56
ROWAN Peter E5 017 M229A R148 S63
ROWAN Roger I20
ROWAN Zaimos W118
ROWANS P112 P123 R148
ROWBOTHAM Dave D136
ROWE Benny H150
ROWE Bob A60 F40
ROWE Dennis B3
ROWE Edward K45
ROWE Hansford G66 M94 018
ROWE Keith A56A F123
ROWE Kenny C29 S306
ROWEBERRY Dave A67 H11
ROWELL Ernie C77A
ROWIN John W. H35B L28 W84C
ROWINSON Freddy B127
ROWELL Tony M80
ROWLAND Bruce C48 C155 D26 E40 F6 F7 F42 F125 G6 G86 H65 H84 H116C L16A L101 M15 M34 M94 M202A 08 P76 S344 T110 V26A W121 Y11
ROWLAND Danny C124 H52A
ROWLAND Kevin D59A
ROWLAND Phil S153
ROWLAND Steve F13
ROWLANDS Jonathan R140
ROWLANDS (Gary) D72A E23 F68 L128 M111 R173 T113
ROWLES Steve W134C
ROWLEY Gordon S304
ROWLEY Mick S173B
ROWLEY Nick A133 H110 L80
ROWLEY Terry H66 H176 T133
ROWLINSON Steve P64
ROXAL Dallas R141A
ROXBURGH Edwin G10
ROXFORD Steve D119
ROXY R148A
ROXY MUSIC R149
ROY Badal D27 L67B M40
ROY Brigitte C137
ROY Claude I13A
ROY Davy C7
ROY Michael D63C
ROY LONEY AND THE PHANTOM MOVERS L115A
ROY YOUNG BAND D9 Y17
ROYAL Ernie D77A D132B J930 J97 K45 K51 K81 P149 R34 S168 V21 W28
ROYAL Marshal C198 M229 R142A
ROYAL Rico M227
ROYAL Sonny L75 P79 S340
ROYAL Theodore L4 M149
ROYAL GUARDSMEN R149A
ROYAL PHILHARMONIC ORCHESTRA D40 018 S177D
ROYAL SPADES see MAR-KEYS
ROYALS R150
ROYER Ray P140
ROYER Rob B206
ROYSTER Phillip B261 G16
ROYSTON Bruce M203
ROZELLE Robert L128
ROZZELLE Roland M160
RUBBER CITY REBELS R151
RUBBER DOLLS R151A
RUBBER DUCK T116B
RUBBO Andy H71C
RUBEN AND THE JETS R152

RUBENHOLD Leon O41
RUBETTES R153
RUBICON R154
RUBIN Abbie O13
RUBIN Alan A27 A31 A123 B67 B69 C109 D108 F30A L136 M15A P31 R122 R174 W86
RUBIN Alton R124A
RUBIN Danny J112
RUBIN John R155
RUBIN Lynn A37
RUBIN Marc M2
RUBIN Michael L110
RUBIN Nathan M18 M203
RUBIN Rockin' Dopsie B154B R124A
RUBIN Ron B237
RUBINHOLD Leon R16A
RUBINI Mike B53 C96 L110
RUBINOS R155
RUBINS Tom S250B
RUBINSTEIN David M174
RUBINSTEIN Jamie B288
RUBIO Steven N50D
RUBY (U.K.) R156
RUBY (U.S.) R157
RUBY Frank F60A F102
RUBY Ron G61
RUBY Roy B144
RUBY & THE ROMANTICS R157A
RUCKER Big Daddy O3B
RUCKER Washington K56A
ruckner Karl B283 G26C
RUDD Clifford M2
RUDD Gregory W199
RUDD Joe T20
RUDD Michael A79
RUDD Phil A2
RUDD Roswell B131 M79
RUDE Tum M57C
RUDELBERGER Fritz E21A
RUDES Jordan S210B
RUDI Steve J19
RUDNYTSKY Dorian N4 N36
RUDOLPH Paul C18 D58 E59 H64 K38 P84 R93
RUEBSAM Peter F105A
RUE MORGUE R50A
RUEDA Sue C21A
RUEFF David Z2
RUEFREX R158
RUFF Bruce V69B
RUFF Chuck H5 S31A W106 W107 W108
RUFF Hope R164
RUFF Ray T57
RUFF Willie C198 D103 039 W118
RUFFIN David R159 R160 T42 W18
RUFFIN Jimmy R160
RUFFIN Bobby J38A T32A
RUFFY Dave C210 R175A
RUFUS R161
RUGBYS R161A
RUGER Tommy T139
RUGG Harold 'Hal' B17A C124 E75 M11 R4 R173 S10 S271 W11
RUGINSTEIN Rugy R38
Rugs T62
RUGSTED Jens S30
RUHL Gary.G1B
RUITER Bert A27 E4 F77 M180 N53 R87
RUITER Ria B224A
RUIZ Dominique S193
RUIZ George B172A
RUIZ Hilton N39
RUIZ Mike C164A M154
Rukmini W119
RUMMANS Michael H135A K59B
RUMOUR L16C P25 R162
RUMPELSTILTSKIN R162B
RUMPF Inga A13 F130A K93B R162A W39B
RUMPH Steve T3
RUMPLESTILTSKIN R162B
RUMSEY Dave S36A
RUNAWAYS R163
RUNCIMAN Chris P136
RUNDGREN Todd B43C C195 D53 F81 F109 G80B H9 H185 K68D M120 N16 N29A N34 R164 S170 S205 S263B W107
RUNDQUIST Christy G81E

RUNNELS Rochelle S250
RUNNER R164A
RUNNING MAN R165
RUNSWICK Darryl A98 A109 A112 B67 B69 C109 D108 F30A L136 M15A P31 R122 R174 W86
RUNYAN Jerry G22C
RUPHUS R166
RUPPERT Uli I14A
RURUP Manfred R63 T106A
RUSE Humbert P72
RUSH R167
RUSH Allan K95 L77
RUSH Billy S199
RUSH Bobby R167A
RUSH Joe D105 K56 M230
RUSH Little Willie S199
RUSH Otis D30 G122 K46 R168
RUSH Pat T84A W107
RUSH Ray H134
RUSH Tom R169
RUSHEN Patrice H97 J75A L28 M40 P115 R97 R99 T107 W27 W63
RUSHENT Martin G22 G65 H178A L53 P86 S292
RUSHING Jimmy R170
RUSHTON Alan B171 D108 F30A R122 R165 R174
RUSHTON Nick S258
RUSKIN Richard 'Rick' D68B R171
Russ Li'l P117B
RUSSEL George L58B
RUSSEL Robert B238
RUSSELL Bill S102B
RUSSELL Brenda A13J B53 B238 C38 D86 H69 M16A P15 S228
RUSSELL Brian C38 C171 H59 H117 K53 M10B M238A P15 S274 W21
RUSSELL Emile B233 C146
RUSSELL Erik S169D
RUSSELL Gary M65A
RUSSELL Graham A22C
RUSSELL Frank C177A
RUSSELL Jeff B250
RUSSELL Jim C251 I18A K66 M108 S301 W125
RUSSELL John (D) D17 P6C
RUSSELL John (G) A19
RUSSELL Johnny R172
RUSSELL Joseph H8 P67
RUSSELL Karl C179
RUSSELL Kathe 'Special K' R139
RUSSELL Kevin S75A
RUSSELL LaRRY M144
RUSSELL Leland G73A
RUSSELL Leon B202 C14 C39 C121 C123 C155 C180 D23A D26 D139 F74 H39 J36 K45 K51 L51 M101 016 R24B R133 R135 R173 S200 T164 W136
RUSSELL Martin E58
RUSSELL Mary (nee McCREARY) B169A M14 R173 T158
RUSSELL Ray B45A B47B B67 B171 B247 C75 C108 D108 E77A F30A H173 K83 L142A M34 M157 R120 R122 R165 R174 S54 S235 S334 T173
RUSSELL Rick P54
RUSSELL Robin N28
RUSSELL Sweet Joe M41
RUSSELL Tom G40 R93B
RUSSELL Tony A74
RUSSELL Victoria W72
RUSSIA R174A
RUSSIAN A.N. C185J
RUSSO Cos M160A
RUSSO Marc F80 W8
RUSSO Mike M22
RUSSO Sonny B282
RUSSO Tony M49
RUSSOTTO Irv M32
RUST Kirt W41A
RUSTICI Corrado C63B N60 P64 W8
RUSTICI Danielo N60 033D
RUSTON Richard C208A
RUTH Emily A23
RUTH Peter 'Madcat' B123 S147A
RUTHER Edward Brumund S1
RUTHER Wyatt H10
RUTHERFORD Arthur S216B
RUTHERFORD Mike G21 H4 P72 P174B R174

SIMPSON Olive T79
SIMPSON Pete C236
SIMPSON Rachel Z22
SIMPSON Raymond A96 G4 J69
M17 M225 R142A S169 V17
SIMPSON Richie M132D S284D
SIMPSON Rose H110 I16
SIMPSON Steve C79 H123 L16A
L106 M118 M157 O18B P54
SIMPSON Tammy C43
SIMPSON Valerie A96 B141 F4C
F109 K81 P56B R142A S125 S128
S262 T37E
SIMPSON William L47C S140
SIMRIL Doug S36
SIMS Dick A82 B84 C121 K51
SIMS Earl T20
SIMS Frank A135
SIMS Frankie Lee S129
SIMS Gary C39 S58
SIMS George A135 C76
SIMS Gerald D66 J9A M126
SIMS Henry W28
SIMS Jamie S177C
SIMS Jimmy R102B
SIMS Kazoot T41
SIMS Larry H120 L110 S330
SIMS Lee M216A
SIMS Robert F134
SIMS Sid G72 P137 S269
SIMS Terry A97
SIMS Von Eva S125
SIMS Willie E52B
SIMS Zazoot T41
SIMS Zoot C139 M75 S180 W13
SIN Marco D77D
SINCEROS S130
SINCLAIR Charles K41
SINCLAIR Dave A133 C19 C34
H57 M106 W135
SINCLAIR David L98
SINCLAIR John B8 H85 L81A S31
U22
SINCLAIR Laurent T18A
SINCLAIR Perry K4
SINCLAIR Richard A133 C19 C34
C209 H57 N11A W135
SINCLAIRD David S169D
SINDLER John L16E
SINE Robin U8
SINFIELD Pete K54 P1 R149
S131
SINFONIA OF LONDON N44
SINGER Doyle G121
SINGER Hal D133 K81 W13
SINGER Jeff A34
SINGER M. S251
SINGER Marc F70B S152 W18
SINGER Ray J40 N51 S285
SINGH Guruvir see FIELDS
Jerry
SINGLETON Albert C58
SINGLETON Geoff C165
SINGLETON J. J91A
SINGLETON Shelby L28A
SINGLETON Willie S171
SINN Sunbie O29B
SINNAEVE Spider S299A
SINNOTT Declan H158 M221E
SINS Sam T88C
SINS OF SATAN S131A
SINSEL Brad T4
SINZHEIMER Hugo M137A
SIOMOS John B83 C187B D53
F100 J65A K68D R62 R164
SIORNOS John L8OC
Siouxsie S132
SIOUXSIE AND THE BANSHEES
S132
SIPL George A54 C38
SIQUENZA Rubin M163
SIR DOUGLAS QUINTET S7
SIR LORD BALTIMORE S132A
SIRACUSE Carl B267
SIREN S133
SIRENS R149 S132
SIRKEL Eric S134
SIRKEL AND CO. S134
SIROTKIN Steve N12A
Sister B. R130
Sister Joan A59
SISTER SLEDGE S135
Sivuca A24 E33 S125
6680 LEXINGTON S135B
SIXTEEN EARL S135A
SIXTY FOUR SPOONS S136

SIXTY NINE S137
SJÖBERG Finn F44
SKAFISH Jim S137A
SKAFISH S137A
SKAGGS Gino H147 H150
SKAGGS Ricky A121 B80 B221
C236B C237 H35 L36A W101
SKATALITES S138
SKATES Geoff B25
SKEAPING Adam B138 B280
C165 H194 S212 S280 Y21
SKEAPING Alexander K94B
SKEAPING Joseph B280 C118B
D17
SKEAPING Lucy F74C
SKEAPING Roderick C118B
C165 D17 H194 Y21
SKEAT Bill H42 I20 L47
R40B
SKEAT Rob W82B
SKEEFE Joe A53
SKEELS Barry Z12
SKEEN Robb N24E
SKELLERN Peter D27B
SKELLY Mick I9
SKELTON Ric D81A
Sketch L81B
SKEVIK Kare P141B
SKEWES Geoff L92
SKID ROW S139
SKIDMORE Alan A120 B19 B23
B67 B229 B280 B288 C63
C183 C208B C251 D2 D35 D49
D133 F14 F42 K84 K94C M83
M111 N44 N50 P8 S306 T111
T141 W13A W94
SKIDS S140
SKILL Mike R133A
SKILLIN David A3 H140
SKIN ALLEY S141
SKIN FLESH AND BONES BAND
B101
SKINNER Bunky Rochelle J18
SKINNER Clive B165A
SKINNER David B138 C119
F'42 G32 K4 M81 R46 T163
U9 W18
SKINNER Jack A132 K95
SKINNER Mick Y1
SKINNER Mike A56
SKINNER Ron B174A
SKINNER Sandford R87
SKIP BIFFERTY H84 S142
SKIPPER Buddy B41 C194 E57
L136A M11
SKIPPER Stan F39
SKLAR Buddy H146A
SKLAR Leland A52 A132 B25
B53 B110 B175 B194 B244
C38 C38A C58 C70A C123
C147 C180 C200 C233 C234
D27 D36A D53C D74 D99 D103
E15 E40 E57 F19 F68 F139
G10 G60 G121 H9 H120 K14
K17 K22 K48 K59 K86 K95
K96 K99A L12 L108 M10B M27
M198 M211C N42 N45C P50
P76 P114B R24B R81 R109
R142A S34 S70 S213 S124
S180D S272 S273 S276 T1
T6B T25 T27 T32B T80A W9
W44A Y14 Z11
SKOGLUND Bo H18
SKOLER Ron P53
SKOLNIK Steve F54A
SKORNIA Chris F3
SKORSKY John H46
SKREWDRIVER S143
SKRIABOW Alyx M95A
SKUDDER Skip S268
Skully see SIMMS Noel
SKY S144
SKY Patrick S10 S145
SKY KING S147A
SKY SAXON BLUES BAND S33
SKYBAND S146
SKYBOAT G16
SKYDOG BAND B278
SKYER Mark M68
SKYHOOKS S147
Skyjuice see BLAKE
Christopher
SKYLARK S148
SKYROCKETS S149
SKYWHALE S149A
SKYY S149B
SLACK Chris A2E
SLACK Paul U4

SLACK ALICE S150
SLADE S151
SLADE Chris H66A M80 M157
N63A O18B P41 T49 U22
SLADE Kenny C155
SLADE Murray F48E
SLADE Rod 'Boots' P131
W89
SLADE Terry C210 H56 R65
S329B
SLADEN Moray H46
SLAGER Johan K16
SLAGLE Steve K37
SLAIS Bill B109
SLAIS Reni B109
SLAMER Mike C118
SLAPIN Billy C164 M41
R125
SLAPP HAPPY S152
SLATER Bill P137
SLATER Grant T37J
SLATER Michael 'Mutter'
S235
SLATER Nelson S152A
SLATER Rodney B178
SLATOR Janice E66
SLATTERY Jeff H186
SLAUGHTER Henry P125
SLAUGHTER John W117
SLAUGHTER Keith W119
SLAUGHTER Rick (WERNHAM
Richard) M215
SLAUGHTER AND THE DOGS
S153
SLAVE S154
SLAVEN Ken L16A
SLAVEN Neil L136 P84
SLAVIN Sandy R94
SLEATH Wil P72
SLEDGE Debbie S135
SLEDGE James R115
SLEDGE Joni S135
SLEDGE Kathie S135
SLEDGE Kim S135
SLEDGE Percy S155
SLEEPLESS NIGHTS S155A
SLETTEN Curt M229 O39
S251
SLEXIA Dick P88B
SLICK Darby G88
SLICK Earl B13A B186 D56A
H185 L51 M160 O27 S117B
S156 T32C T123A
SLICK Grace C217 C232 G88
H45 J46 K10 S61 S157
SLICK Jerry G88
SLIDER Albie S86
SLIGTING Jan Willem B43A
SLIK S158
SLIM CHANCE L16A
SLIME S158A
SLITS S159
SLIVIN Alexandra K14
SLIVIN Joan K14
SLIWIN Joan B47C
SLOAN Allen D79 W15B
SLOAN Claudio R97
SLOAN Eleanor C165
SLOAN Jennifer B53
SLOAN P.F. G83 M30 S160
SLOAN Phil F18B
SLOAN Ron G121
SLOANE Milton C155
SLOANE Tommy J14
SLOIS Bill G10B
SLOMAN Jon L114 U22
SLONE Bobby C236B K29
R78C
SLOSSEN Rick K16A
Slot M150A
SLOW CHILDREN S160A
SLUGS, Doug & the D106F
SLUTSKY Martin M37
SLY AND THE FAMILY STONE
S161
SLYTHE Joe J63
SMALE Ian 'Ishmael' I26A
P53
SMALE Tim I26A
SMALL Blues Charlie see
KRBAVAC Karl
SMALL Charles F19 H59
SMALL Dag M220 P143
SMALL Drink S161A
SMALL George L51 O27 P25
SMALL Henry P139 S162A
SMALL Janet S83A
SMALL Jonathan A115A H55A

SMALL Linda C58 J105A
SMALL Michael M21
SMALL Mick G112A
SMALL Phil C158A
SMALL FACES S162
SMALL WONDER S162A
SMALLCOMBE Derek P139H
SMALLEY Dave R35
SMALLMAN Gary B197E P58
SMALLS Charles R140
SMARR Rod D85
SMART Keith B26 C13 D66
M180A N58B W18 W122
SMART Leroy S163
SMART Norman Dow II B160B
C195 H91B H182 I3 K8 K68D
M216 P33 R164 W51 W101
SMART Terry R80 S80
SMASH Chas M46A
SMEATON Bob W69C
SMEDEGARD Gert A8A
SMEDGAARD Carsten J70A
M147
SMEDLEY Julian B187 I20
O40 S243
SMEENK Paul S348A
SMELKO Dave R36
SMIDT Birgit D83A
Smiggy B148 D72B N43 W134A
SMIRKS S164
SMIT Frans A27 B197A
SMIT Hetti T123
SMITH, A GROUP CALLED
S164A
SMITH Aaron T42 W31
SMITH Adrian I25
SMITH Al P26
SMITH Alexander B180
SMITH Allan B230
SMITH Allen J79
SMITH Ammer D51
SMITH Andrew (D) A35A A96
C153 F92 G4 J20 M41 O27
S128 T42 U18
SMITH Andy (Banjo) G98
SMITH Angela D66
SMITH Anthony I5A
SMITH Anthony Allen M40
SMITH Art P15
SMITH Barry O33B
SMITH Bas K43
SMITH Bat F13B
SMITH Bill (K) J41 S339
W43
SMITH Bill (B) A115 B23
J16 O9 P131 S34
SMITH Bill (V) P77D
SMITH Bill Strong P80D
SMITH Bob (K) C56 C76 F109
J18
SMITH Bob (G) S164B
SMITH Bobby (B) W43
SMITH Brian (Wind) A74 C63
F14 K84 N62 P42A S108 S267
T95
SMITH Brian (B) P5
SMITH Brian (G) M123 S210
T146
SMITH Brian B84
SMITH Broderick C41A D72B
S266
SMITH Bruce L28 L119C N27D
P117
SMITH Carl T26
SMITH Catherine A132 H117
L72
SMITH Charlie (D) B148
D113 L117
SMITH Charles (Tpt) E52B
SMITH Chris (G) C200 P50
SMITH Chris (Trom) F14
SMITH Chris (Hca) B224B
SMITH Chris 'Judge' (Perc)
H13
SMITH Chuck C162 R168
SMITH Claydes K80
SMITH Colin A50A K81 M5
P100 R122A
SMITH Curly C15A F39 H185
J64 M191 T32C
SMITH Curt G77B
SMITH Dalton C61A C180
F99A F134 Q12
SMITH Danny S230
SMITH Danny (D) D17 L89 Z22
SMITH Darnell H65A
SMITH Dave (B) K94B

SMITH Dave (D) F67
SMITH David (D/V) S308A
SMITH David E. L58B
SMITH David C164
SMITH David K96
SMITH Dean B72 B257
SMITH Dennis (B) A13 S68
SMITH Dennis (D) D108
SMITH Dennis P28
SMITH Derek L63
SMITH Des M1A
SMITH Dick (D) D36 H91A M238A
S55B S274
SMITH Dick Lee W38
SMITH Don (B) M11
SMITH Donald (V) L41 S169
SMITH Donald (D) T11B
SMITH Doug I25
SMITH Duane W136
SMITH Earl 'Chinna' A6 B95A
B101 B276 D71A D113A H122
H172 I1A I12 J17C J17E L58A
M88 M149 M221D P2 P134 P140C
R33A R134 S190 U1 V21 W4
SMITH Elizabeth B43C W101
SMITH Emma O18
SMITH Feddie B259
SMITH Frank (Sax) C203A
SMITH Frank C. D139 M209
SMITH Fred (B) B139 L98A R118
T38
SMITH Fred (Reeds) H99 R115
SMITH Fred (D) A133 C13 E59
T63 V25B W129
SMITH Fred 'Sonic' (G) I10
M1
SMITH G. B87 C103C
SMITH G.E. H9 H51 J48 M143A
R50A S53A
SMITH Garth B284
SMITH Gary S336
SMITH George A74 B13 B127
P93B S165 S204 S329 T23 T79B
W12A
SMITH George Ohara A101
SMITH Gerald C185H
SMITH Gerry V26
SMITH Gordon C83 C210 D46 F62
S166 W129
SMITH Graham (Perc) B2
SMITH Graham (V) V11
SMITH Graham (Harm) B105 M50
N45C P131 S270
SMITH Grahame (Vln) A93 D54
G97 H4 H13 H42 S93 S306
SMITH Greedy M132B
SMITH Greg (K) J10B R142A
SMITH Greg (Sax) F114A
SMITH Greg (G) S243A
SMITH Harry A133
SMITH Henri F92
SMITH Herb H58
SMITH Herman J79
SMITH Hoges James W118
SMITH Howard V18D
SMITH Huey 'Piano' D86 S167
SMITH Hurricane I37A
SMITH J. B166A S273
SMITH Jack (Pno) K88
SMITH Jack (D) F31
SMITH James (D) A71
SMITH James (G) J69 M27 M111
SMITH James (V) A94 S284A
S311A
SMITH James (K) S254B
SMITH James Allen (K) D24 P15
SMITH James Herb M2
SMITH James (quali) M111 P114C
S358E
SMITH James 'Smitty' (G) D86
SMITH Jeff C77A L131
SMITH Jeffrey Ray D78E
SMITH Jerome (G) H157 K1
SMITH Jerome (D) M185
SMITH Jerry (B) B13 S165
SMITH Jerry (B) F70
SMITH Jerry (B V) A121B
SMITH Jerry (G) K27A
SMITH Jerry S23
SMITH Jerry (K) C14 H26 J13
L77 S272 T37I Y18
SMITH Jerry (Wind) C164
SMITH Jerry Lee (K) M85
SMITH Jessica May A50 A120
B17 B144 C211 D86 D101 D127
G121 J72 K81 L128 M229 R32
SMITH Jimmie T158
SMITH Jimmy (K) K94A S168 W62

[702]

[703]

D131 E48 E59 F13 F42 F70B G10
G74 H29 H66A H86 H171 J72
J110 K82
K97 L63 L106 M79 M102E M129
M157 N62 P45 R84A S44 S92
S179 S186A S194B S209 S220
V28 W18 W86 Y11 Y14
SPEED LIMIT S210
SPEEDOMETERS S210A
SPEEDWAY BLVD S210B
Speego S190
SPEER Billy G79B
SPEER Marc C194
SPEER Stewart M134
SPEIGHT Edward C209 D137
SPEISER Jerry M130A
SPELEOS Teddy H139A K8
SPELL J.A. B61B N55 S284D
SPELL Jay B261 G102 M111
M132D T113 T119
SPELLER Abe F16B L18B
SPELMANS W. D57D
SPENCE Alexander 'Skip' J46
M174 S210C
SPENCE Barry H20
SPENCE Dave I20
SPENCE Eddie D54 G35 S177D
S291
SPENCE Ken E79
SPENCE Jack Y6
SPENCER Bob W20B
SPENCER C.P. O31
SPENCER Dick C164 C213E F51
SPENCER George R60C
SPENCER Jeremy F66 S211
SPENCER John (G/K) G1 H20A
S212
SPENCER John (B) K39 P89
SPENCER Kevin S85A
SPENCER Larry D50
SPENCER Mike C199
SPENCER Nina D95
SPENCER Paul S210A
SPENCER Pauline C30B
SPENCER Peter S174
SPENCER Rarry F17
SPENCER Robert S147
SPENCER Roger I7 N48
SPENCER Sandy M45
SPENCER Trevor D104 D110 M38
M100 O18A P81B R129 S34 I14
V29
SPENCER-ARSCOTT Michael O22
T79
SPENCER DAVIS GROUP D28
SPENGLER Michael B172A
SPENNER Alan B138 C30 C39A
C80 C109 C155 C204 F42 F125
G86 H65 H70 K76 K87 L37 L76B
M15 M94 N63 R69 R82 R149
R162A R173 S224 I31 W111
SPENNER Diane F8 J16B K81
S238C
SPENSLEY Rob W13E
SPERANZA Guy R94
SPERLING Dee Dee D63A
SPERRY Danny G16
SPEVOCK Ed B5 B171 B237 C101
R142 S103B
SPHEERIS Jimmy P112 S213
SPHERICAL OBJECTS S214
SPHYNX T159
SPICHER Norman Keith 'Buddy'
A75 A102 B17A B41 C14 C15 D21
E54 F7 F78 G85A H26 H52A J30
J53 K96 L77 M11 M75 M159 M232
N37 P49 R4 R31 R111A R137 S32 T95
T21 T22 T107 Y18
SPICKARD Bob C74
SPICOLLA Sal P53
SPIDER S214A
Spider see DANIELS Larry
SPIDERS S214E
SPIDERS FROM MARS S214C
SPIDERZ S214B
SPIEGEL Cliff A130
SPIEKERMAN Erik O36A
SPIEGEL Ray D67
Spike S251
SPILLANE Dany M221E
SPILLER Norman G122
SPILLNER Wolfgang A74B
SPIN S214D
SPIN Charlie F105
SPINAZOLA Joseph P156A
SPINDT Donn R155

SPINELLA Bob C228
SPINELLI Phil L105A
SPINETTI Henry A22 A82
B208B C75 C79 C121 D9 D46
D100 E22 F7 F14 F36 F56
H11 H22 H42 H65 H106 H175
H193 J101A J110 K81 L30
L46 M239 N63B P81B R11
R12 R15 S34 S287 S313
T122 T157 W9A W29A W67
W117
SPINNER David S122A
SPINNEY Brad I2
SPINOZZA David A31 A123
B47C B161 B208 C134 C164
C229 D86 D97A E40 F60
F103D H54 H58 H136A J48
J69 K45 K69 L4A L51 L110
M9 M21 M41 M65A M89A M102
N63D
U27 P114 R22 S17 S124
S125 S215 S252 I25 T147
W51A Y8B
SPIRES Jakson B123
SPIRIT S216
SPIRIT OF JOHN MORGAN
S217
SPIRKA Gerhard A59C
SPIROGYRA S218
SPITBALLS S219
SPITERI Charlie T77
SPITTERI Charles E22
SPITZ Barbara G32
SPIVEY Red C14
SPIVEY Victoria J79
SPIZZ S219A
SPLIFF S219B
SPLINTER S220
SPLIT ENZ S221
SPLODGE Max S221A
SPLODGENESSABOUNDS S221A
SPOELSTRA Mark S222 T134
SPONTANEOUS COMBUSTION
S223
SPONTANEOUS MUSIC
ENSEMBLE S267
SPOOKY TOOTH N51 S224
SPOONER Bill T152
SPOONER Mal D46B
SPOONER Steve D59A
SPOONS Sam B178 S206
SPORER Mark A59
SPORER Mark A59
SPORI Klaus O40B
SPORTS S224A
SPORTSMAN Phones B. S354A
SPOTNICKS S225
SPOUSE Willy Jnr. R102B
SPRADLIN Paul G72A
SPRAGUE Billy H34 L128
M15i
SPRAUGE Bob S229C
SPRAUGE Kent B181A S198B
SPRAY Scott C76 W106
SPREADEAGLE S226
SPREAFICO Robin D95
SPREEN Glen A59 B17A F78
M108 P125 S339 T12 T67A
W43
SPREMICH Richard M59
SPREY Jeff N31
SPRIGG Ed C236
SPRIGGS Michael R4
SPRIGUNS S227
SPRING Alice see BARRY
Sandra
SPRING Bryan N62 P34 R84A
SPRING Frankie P126
SPRING Keith N2
SPRING S227A
SPRINGER Bob C76
SPRINGER Dennis L119C
SPRINGER John B155
SPRINGER Mark F80 K16A
L10B M203
SPRINGFIELD Allan C95A
SPRINGFIELD Dusty J72
K16A S228
SPRINGFIELD John B116
SPRINGFIELD Rick H122A
S228A
SPRINGS Alice D15
SPRINGS Helena D139M131
SPRINGSTEEN Bruce B172A
P25 S229
SPROAT Dave J107

SPROXTON Steve Li17
SPRUILL James H15 T13B
SPRUILL Stephanie C153
C156 C171 C241 E73 H181
I2 J72 K48 L26B L65 L89
L143 M18 M102 P126 R28B
R97 T158 V9A W10A Y12
SPRUNG Dave W138
SPUD S230
SPURGEON Douglas R22
SPURLING Spud K26A
SPURLOCK Tommy C200 M174
SPY S230A
SPYS S231A
SPYRO GYRA S231
SPYROPOULOS Alex N51
SQUARE Lester M181C
SQUARE Russell P117B
SQUEEZE S232
SQUIRE Barry L134
SQUIER Billy B57A P87A
S232A
SQUIRE Chris S233 S358F
W7 Y7
SQUIRE Paul P80E
Squirm T70
Squirrel Y118
SQUIRREL Johnny L62
SQUITERO Roger B139 H42A
V6
SSERC Truc H57A
STABBINS Larry C63 T95
STABENOW Horst F7A
STABLE Simon (DE LA
BEDOYERE Count) T45
STABLINI Ronald L28A
STACEY Kevin B171
STACEY Marti C95
STACEY Mike H40
STACHELHAUS Horst B107
M136B
STACK Kathy L26B
STACKHOUSE Houston N46C
STACKRIDGE S235
STACKWADDY S236
STACZEK Don J74
STADIUM DOGS S237
STADTLER Dick F70A
STAEBELL Bill A122
STAEHELY Al C217 D5A L111
M191 S216
STAEHELY John Christopher
J64 A73 M191 S216
STAEHLE Fred B144 O86 E40
M229 S124 T118 Y5B
STAEHR Jess B275 S69
STAERK Henning G51B
STAFFEL Tim M201 W61
STAFFELD, brian N63
STAFFORD Jack X2
STAFFORD John T107
STAFFORD Ronnelle C195
D53C K47 M41 S125 V21
STAG Danny I17B
STAGG Ross S279
STAHL Brad A59 W101
STAHL Butch M236A
STAINED GLASS S237A
STAINES Chris W24
STAINES Rik D14C
STAINLESS STEEL S238
STAINTON Chris B110 B191
C3U C80 C121 C155 F8 S330
H65 H185 J16B L37 N55 P138
R173 S224 T157 W72
STAIRSTEP S238B
STALEY G.T. N2
STALEY Tom A59A P63
STALLIBRASS Will C105 F24
Li6C S149
STALLING Bill L50B
STALLING Wayne B238
STALLINGS Carol C155
STALLINGS Jim R77 S7
STALLINGS Mark E31A
STALLINGS Rev. Ron B109
B144 F80 M211 R168 S7
S198 Y12
STALLION S238A
STALLWORTH Paul A116 B135
B141 B169 C11B E40 G24 H39
J43 J85A K86 L107 M39B
M132D M191 R28B S196 S252
STALTZMAN Lucy Chapman
S215
STAMM Marvin A123 A131 B85

B141 C40 C213D D50 D66 H9
H137 I2 J20 K68A K81 L58B
L80A L119 M26 M75 R21 R159
S125 T71 T98 W5 W13 W25
STAMP Paul 'Boomer' P139B
STAMP Terry S238C T63
STAMPEDERS S239
STAMPFEL Peter F133 H139
H189
STAMPS P125
STAMPS QUARTET F48
STAN Per S108C
STAND K21
STANDEFER Russ A35D
STANDELLS S240
STANDRING Colin H157A
STANFORD Tina Renee P96
STANGER Nigel K84 M111
STANKY BROWN BAND B242A
STANKO Mircea V26C
STANKO Tomasz V26C
STANLEY Brian D17A
STANLEY David G40 R93B
STANLEY George B242B
STANLEY James Lee K99A
STANLEY John B25
STANLEY Michael S241
STANLEY Pamela K99A
STANLEY Paul K67 S242
STANLEY Pete B23
STANLEY Ralph P32
STANLEY Richard H190
STANLEY Steven T104A

STANLEY-CLARKE Jessica M95
STANN Joey B172A M84A W48C
STANNARD Terry B23 B63 B188
B189 C48 E44 F8 G86 H65 J16B
K25 K76 K81 L101 M202A U9
Y11 Y19
STANSHALL Viv B178 B237 C18
E60 H46 O18 S243
STANTON Holly S243A
STANTON Kevin M141B
STANTON Tom C234C
STANTON Tony A60A
STANWICK Al S274
STAPINOPOULOS Christos C137
STAPLES Kevan R146A
STAPLES Neville S207
STAPLES Pete T144
STAPLES Pop C231
STAPLES SINGERS B29 K81
STAPLETON Bill F99A
STAR Jeremiah O6B
STAR Sable M226
STAR PARK S244
STARBUCK Gary E40
STARBUCK S245
STARCASTLE S246
STARDRIVE S247
STARDUST S248
STARDUST Alvin see FENTON
Shane
STARFIGHTERS S249A
STARF*CKERS S249B
STARFYRE S249C
STARGARD S250
STARJETS S250A
STARK John T57
STARK Monty B255 O35 T113
T145
STARK Paul J94
STARK NAKED S250B
STARKEY Barbara C179
STARKEY Richard see STARR
Ringo
STARKIE Robert S147
STARKS John K45
STARKS Rosona W119
STARLETS R10
STARLIGHTERS B23
STARLING Faysooux A121 H35
STARLING John A121 H35 R137
S73B
STARN Mike B141
STARNEY Chris S177C
STARR Edwin S251
STARR Mike C167
STARR Ringo (STARKEY Ringo)
STARR Richard see STARR
Ringo
STARR Ron D68D
STARR Terry B25 S34
STARR Trevor W23

STARRS Jeff I23A
STARRS Mike L139
STARRY EYED and LAUGHING
S253
STARS AND STIPS S253A
STARSES Jim J18
STARZ S254
STASHUK Gene R22
STASIC John P53
STASIUM Ea B203A S60
STASSINOPOULOS Chris A131F
STASZKO Ed F126A
STATES S254A
STATLER BROTHERS C50
STATMAN Andy B207A B221
C199C O15 S7
STATON Candi S254B W118
STATON Jeffrey B110 G10
STATON Michael B110 C127 G10
STATOS Demetrio A74A
STATUS QUO S255
STAV A. T37L
STAVRO Art B109 M68 S198
STAVROU Alexandra G10
STAWINSKI Rob U5
STAX John P128
STAXX Jet M210
STEACKER Richard L. W25
STEAD Arthur F100
STEAD Tom K33
STEADMAN Gary C131
STEADMAN Ivor M133
STEADY Freddy K96A
STEAKS Chuck Q12
STEALERS WHEEL S257
STEAMHAMMER S258
STEAMPACKET S259
STEBBING Simon P154
STEC Joe M156 S6
STECHER Jody B221 W11
STECKEL Brad F90B
STEDING Walter S259A
STEEL Bill M18
STEEL Casino B196 H135 H137B
STEEL Jan C63
STEEL John A67 W94
STEEL Larry H26A
STEEL Lynton B118
STEEL Paul P142B
STEEL Trevor P92D
STEEL Willie H170
STEEL MILL S260
STEEL-PERKINS Crispian C161
C251
STEEL PULSE S261
STEEL RIVER S261A
STEELE Andrew C208B D93 F13
F23 H106 P76A R11 R15 S93
S257 S313 W18
STEELE Bobby M163C
STEELE Carole S322
STEELE David B58B
STEELE Drew S333B
STEELE Jan S263B
STEELE Jan/CAGE John S261B
STEELE Larry A82 B268 D22
D131 G67 J8 J72 K24 L63 M219
S266 S270 S276 T96 Wi34
STEELE Ray S358F
STEELE Ronald S269
STEELE Terry J72
STEELER Wes T116B
STEELER Bob H161
STEELEYE SPAN S263
Steelfinger G81E
STEELMAN Larry R24B
Steelie see NELSON Anthony
STEELWIND T136
STEELY DAN S262
STEEN Bob C164
STEEN Chip B52A
STEEN Roger 1152
STEER Dave H63A
STEER Martin B231
STEERS Tony R12A
STEFAN Steffi C78
STEFANELLI David O32A
STEFANSKI Jacnusz S73C
STEFANSKI Jarus D19A
STEFFEN Arno T14J
STEFFENS Dirk B107 T103A
STEFKO Joe S263B
STEGGLES Tim N63A
STEGMEYER Doug J20 J69 P25
STEHR Falk L121C

SYLVESTER Robert P41

SYLVESTER Terry H132 S358A
SYLVESTER D24 S358E
Sylvia E22 M212A
SYLVIAN David J40
SYME Hugh R167 T69A
SYMMONDS Glenn A127 E65 K73
SYMONDS David F5A
SYMONETTE Neil E52C
SYMONS Redmond S147
SYMPHONIC SLAM S359
SYN S358F
SYNATHESIA S358G
SYNDICATE OF SOUND S360
SYNERGY S361
SYNGE Casey T87 Y2
SYNGE Cathy G105
SYNIAR Bill T12B
SYNIGAL Edgar K45
Syreeta see WRIGHT Syreeta
Syrinx M200
SYVERTSEN Tore T37L
SYXX Niki J87A
SZABO Gabor E65 H10
SZAWLOWSKI Billy A69
SZCZESNIAK Steve A72B
SZCZESNIAK Tom H117 L72 M10B W101
SZELESTE Stan C233 D26 H62 M32
SZITTAI Michael N65
SZPIRA Catherine M49
SZRZEK Josef S1B
SZUKALSKI Tomasz V26C
SZYMCZYK Bill C162 D93F F39 G19 V38

T.Albert E19C
T. Bobby S157
T. Kathy O34
T. Steve P116 T1
T.FORD AND THE BONESHAKERS T2
T.I.M.E. T3
T.K.O. T4
T.REX B168
T.T. REUTER T4A
T.2. T5
T.V. B181
T.V. KIDS T5A
T.V. PERSONALITIES T38A
T.V. 21 T5B
T-Zap see EDMUNDS Hughes
TABACKIN Lew C213E M75 M79 W6
TABAK Ron P139
TABBERT Billy M136B
Tabby see SHAW Donald
TABERT Wayne F94
TABET Phil B261
TABINO Frank L80C
TABOR June T6
TABY Niels H37B
TACHIANA Hajame P95A
TACK Ernie C147 C180 D127 Z8
TACKETT Fred A37 B23 B25 B53 B135 B226 B244 C38 C45 C164 C180 D5A D139 G24 G120A H122A J93C K95 L19 L89 L109 M132C M198 N43 P28 P114 P114B R22 R101 R107 S20 S34 S36 S124 S196 S273 T37H T113 V3 W39 W65 W119B W133
TACKTIKES George C72A
TAERMINA Ron Q12
TAFINI Serge K10D
TAFOYA Mike B197
TAG Chris R7A
TAGFORD Jimmy H180
TAGG Eric L41 R99
TAGGETT T6A
TAGLIAPIETRA Aldo L54A
TAGLIAVORE Sam N58C
TAIEB Laurent Q24
TAILLET Michel A114
TAILOR Delbert S51
TAIRA Yoshio Y2
TAIT Rob B48A A133 B79 B237

G66 H86 K83 V33 Y10
TAK Bobby C113B
TAKAHASHI Yukihoro S5 Y6A
TAKANAKA Masayoshi S5 Y6A
TAKAS Bill C164 L80C T44
TAKEDA Kazuo P20
TAKEDA Osamu C110A
TAKEHARA Craig M216A
TAKEKAWA Yukihide G55
TAKEMITSU Toru Y2
TAKERS U10
TAKESHITA Mikako Y94A
TALAMANTES Eddie K94A
TALBERT Pat R115
TALBERT Sonny B183 S326
TALBERT Wayne C195 S7 T6C
TALBOT Billy C216 L107 R123A S10 Y16
TALBOT Danny M136A
TALBOT John M102B T6B
TALBOT Mick C108A' J19 M136A S302A
TALBOT Phil T155
TALBOT Richard H161
TALBOT Terry M102B T6B
TALBOT BROTHERS T6B
TALIOFERRO Tally H79
TALISKER T7
TALISMAN Dave G71C
TALKAMO Ari H157C
TALKING HEADS T8
TALLARICO Carl F111
TALLENT Garry W. B172A H185 S229
TALLENT Glen E58
TALLENTS Martin S175
TALLEY Gary B190
TALLEY James P137 T9
TALLEY Mary Jo T9
TALLEY Nedra R135
TALLMAN Barry C236
TALLMAN Slide K53
TALMY Shel K61 N57 S192B W60
TALOT Lola Z2
TALTON Tommy A37 A38 B91 B199B B200 C207 L9 S56 T9A T20 T30
TALTON STEWART SANDLIN T9A
TAMBLYN Larry S240
TAMBOER Ad E4
TAMLINS B234 D130 T114
Tampa Red (WHITTAKER Hudson) B95B T9B
TAMPLIN Marv R115
TAMS John A30 H194
Tamsin G66
Tan Tan S190
TANAKA Hozumi Y2
TANAKA Jimmy C28A P80
TANAS Andy B114
TANDY Richard B26 D39 E34 M219
TANEGA Norma T10
TANGEL Doris F101D
TANGEN Johan P141B
TANGERINE DREAM T11
TANGERINE PEEL T11A
TANGERINE ZOO T11B
TANIMaurice L115A
TANK T11C
TANKOWSKI Frank Y2
TANNEN Holly C230
TANNEN Paul Y18
TANNENBAUM Chaim M21
TANNER John (Pno) D18B H38
TANNER Johnny (V) F59B
TANNER Marc T12
TANNER Tony C21A
TANNERS L16A
TANNET Steve R60B
TANNO Vinnie H157 K1
TANNUM Rich R124F
TANS Jan Cees G113 D9A T118A
TANSIN Joe B16
TANTRUM T12B
Tanyette N59
TANZ DER YOUTH T13
TAORMINA Ron M211
TAOS T13
TAPES T12A
TAPIA Adrian S36
TAPIA Covarruras J14

TAPLIN Rosanna A41
TAPP Charles H16A
TARACK Gerald S215
Taragon S48
TARBUTTON Jimmy B61B
TARENSKEEN Job A42 M137A
TARGEL Tem T60A
TARGET T13A
Tarheel Slim (BUNN Allen) T13B
TARKESTY Eli K45
TARNEY Alan B81A C161C D104 D110 D132 H175 M15A M100 R80 R129 S34 S80 T14 V29
TARNEY SPENCER BAND T14
TARPIN Marv R115
TARPLEY Brenda Mae see LEE Brenda
TARRACH Dicky R28 R38 S329A
TARRANT Robert 'Tarp' A28 B97 C14 C208
TARRANT Morris L64
TARSHIS Steve B223
TARTACHNY Paul B57
TARTILLO Curt S249C
TARWATER Craig D53C L38 S122
Tarzan see NELSON Errol
TASAVALLAN PRESIDENTTI T15
TASHIAN Barry H35 P33 R64
TASSE Laurence H91B
TASSI Carl L8
TASSLER Stephen S246
TASTE T16
TASTE OF HONEY T16A
Tata P114C
TATANE Eddie O18
TATE Bruce P59
TATE C.W. L90
TATE Dick L142A
TATE Fran L89 P15
TATE Grady M21 M26 P49 R107 S123 S124 S125 S168 S180 T98
TATE Joe S12B
TATE Judy M238A
TATE Ray S269
TATE Tommy L73
TATE Troy S83 T37A
TATE COUNTY DRUM CORPS F8C
TATLER Brian D61
TATTOO T17
TATUM James M151
TATUM John C182
TATUM Neil E38A
TAUPIN Bernie T18
TAVOLAZZI Ares A74A
TAX Mel B282
TAXAS Bill T44
TAXI GIRL T18A
TAXLOSS T19
TAXXI T19A
TAYLOR Alan C55
TAYLOR Alex (V) B261 S124 T20 T25
TAYLOR Allan C10 T21
TAYLOR Alvin A50 A52 B268 C6B H39 J72 O15 P126 S51 T80A W46 W116 W119B Y12
TAYLOR Alvin 'Red' D86 W87
TAYLOR Andy D134B
TAYLOR Art D27
TAYLOR Barry Y19B
TAYLOR Beloyd E7
TAYLOR Bob (D) E14
TAYLOR Bob (V) C139
TAYLOR Bob (Horns) L136A P125
TAYLOR C. C191
TAYLOR C.D. F51
TAYLOR Cecil M79
TAYLOR Charise D66
TAYLOR Chip E20A T22 T67A
TAYLOR Christopher A98 P54 S157 W86
TAYLOR Clive A49 F7
TAYLOR Conrad R39
TAYLOR Dallas C138 C234 G122 H5 M64 N4 O12 R109 S65 S276 V3 W136
TAYLOR Danny F83 N62A S117A
TAYLOR Dave (B) C57

TAYLOR Dave (Trom) A27 B141 C129 F115 G4 J20 L119 M26 M69 M75 M107 R125 S73C S215 T147 T158 V17 W5 W25 W107 Z3B
TAYLOR Dave (V) T22A
TAYLOR David L67
TAYLOR David (K) P61
TAYLOR Dennis B231 P145A
TAYLOR Derek H39 S235
TAYLOR Dick E31F P128 R133
TAYLOR Dolphin K10C R116
TAYLOR Drew T22B
TAYLOR Eddie 'Playboy' A8 A50A H32 H150 H159 J21 J73 M5 P142 R59 T23 W91 W131
TAYLOR Fingers W11
TAYLOR Gary C47A D2 D104 F13 F95 H42 H106 R11 R12 R40B S93 S257 S313 W130 Y6
TAYLOR Gávin S8
TAYLOR Gene C26 M96
TAYLOR Glenton C139
TAYLOR Graeme A30 G114 H168 H194 S227
TAYLOR Greg (K/Harm) B261 H7D N25 N53
TAYLOR Gregory (V) D66
TAYLOR Hal M55A
TAYLOR Harold J93D
TAYLOR Hounddog T24
TAYLOR Howard S249C
TAYLOR Hugh B261 S124 T25
TAYLOR Ian S210A
TAYLOR Jack H9A
TAYLOR James (V) B261 C233 G10 H8 J48 K48 M170 R137 S17 S70 S124 S272 T20 T25 T27 T30 T98 Y16
TAYLOR James J.T. (V) K80
TAYLOR James (Hrns) R60C
TAYLOR Jan M181D
TAYLOR Jeff F30C
TAYLOR Jeremy B105 D22
TAYLOR Jesse A35D E51
TAYLOR Jim (Pno) M68 M135
TAYLOR John (K) A74 B67 C183 D2 K94C M205 P36 R85 S182 S220 T141
TAYLOR Johnnie (V) F72 T26
TAYLOR Jon (B) J43A
TAYLOR Karen G92B
TAYLOR Kate S272 T25 T27
TAYLOR Keith T169
TAYLOR Ken T103B
TAYLOR KING SIZE T27A
TAYLOR Koko T28
TAYLOR Larry B194A C26 F109 H34 H37 H135B K88 M68 M111 S198B S329
TAYLOR Laura F50
TAYLOR Lawrence L90
TAYLOR Lem J96
TAYLOR Leroy N28 T42
TAYLOR Les E77
TAYLOR Linda G67 M145 M157 O18B R15 R46 S327B
TAYLOR Little Johnny (YOUNG Johnny) T29
TAYLOR Livingston T30
TAYLOR Lonnie G122 S204
TAYLOR Luther E52B
TAYLOR M. B252
TAYLOR Marcia Ann B144
TAYLOR Martin M208
TAYLOR Mel V19 V24
TAYLOR Michael H118
TAYLOR Michael C212
TAYLOR Mick B2 B248 D133 G66 G112D H50 K52 L89 M78 M111 M233 N41 R133 S134 S329 T31 W120
TAYLOR Mike L104 S178
TAYLOR Mike 'Taffy' Q3
TAYLOR Nick B142
TAYLOR Ollie W. H121
TAYLOR Pat J17 S284D
TAYLOR Paul Allan B61B
TAYLOR Phil M213
TAYLOR R.Dean T32
TAYLOR Rich (also O'SHEA Rich) L62
TAYLOR Richard A98 O8
TAYLOR Rick S305
TAYLOR Robert D110A

TAYLOR Rod A117 T32B
TAYLOR Roderick (also FALCONER Roderick) T32C
TAYLOR Roger D134B N63A T32D
TAYLOR Roger Meddows H185 Q8 S70
TAYLOR Ron (G) T155
TAYLOR Ronnie (Sax) B93A H145 I11 R125
TAYLOR Russell P49B
TAYLOR Sam H134 J97
TAYLOR Sarah Maria A50 R4 S124
TAYLOR Spider B201
TAYLOR Stephanie H117
TAYLOR Ted A62 C47A T32A
TAYLOR Terry E56 G122 T155 T162
TAYLOR Thumbs T22
TAYLOR Tiger A67G
TAYLOR Tommy C234D
TAYLOR Tony E26 G77C
TAYLOR Tot A13
TAYLOR Trevor F30A
TAYLOR Tut B221 R173 T32E
TAYLOR Vince T33
TAYLOR Vinnie S78
TAYLOR Virginia S8
TAYLOR Wesley C151D
TAYLOR William H65A
TAYLOR Zola P97
TAYLOR Zoot B19
TAZMANIAN DEVILS T33A
Tazz see JOHNSON Webster
TCHICAT John B275
TCHAIKOVSKY Bram M215 T34
TEA T35
TEA AND SYMPHONY T36
TEA COMPANY T35A
TEA SET T36A
TEAR GAS T37
TEARDROP Calvin I17B
TEARDROP EXPLODES T37A
TEARDROPS T37B
TEAZE T37C
TEBB John C55
TEBOW Robert G121
TED T37D
Ted The Loaf R65A
TEDDY BEARS T37D
TEDESCO Rosemarie G53A
TEDESCO Tom B17A B56 B110 C14 G10 H103 J36 K81 L109 M30 M86 M229 N25 P125 P129
TEE Richard A31 A35A A96 A123 B71 B77 B85 B131 B141 C44 C77 C108B C155 C213D D86 D132B E33 F103 F133 G4 G10 H9 H39 H103 H164C J22 J69 J93D K36 L109 L119 M12 M17 M41 M65A M75 M78 M102 M125 M143 M233 N2A N23 N39 P20 P72A P149 R99 S50 S111 S123 S124 S130 S188 S228 S252 S310 T37E T118 T147 V17 W21B W25 W27 W32A Z8
TEE Willie T37F W78A
TEE SET T37G
TEEGARDEN David S73 T37I
TEEGARDEN & VAN WINKLE T37I
TEEL Kurtis K73
TEEL Mark B144
TEENAGE HEAD T37J
TEENAGERS L144
TEES Richard X2
TEETER Ritchie D65 V1
TEGZA Michael B33 H1 L130A
TEIFFER Jerry M41
TEIGEN John P117A P117C P132B T37L
TEIPEL Theodore O24B
TEJADA Jose Luis B43
TEK Deniz R9
TELEMACQUE Ron A22 H174 J110
TELEPHONE T37K
TELEPHONE BILL AND THE SMOOTH OPERATORS T37H
TELEVISION T38
TELEVISION PERSONALITIES T38A

Tel/Tho

TELEX T38B
TELFORD Jim S290
TELFORD Mel B130
TELL Greg G26A M160A
TELLEZ Rob M59 S19
TELLONE Albany S229
TEMIZ Okay L79
TEMPCHIN Jack F138 T39
TEMMER Marsha K14
TEMPERLEY Joe D50 L51
TEMPERTON Rod A123 H81 J10B
TEMPEST T40
TEMPLAR Simon R74 S83
TEMPLE Michael S216
TEMPLE CITY KAZOO BAND T41
TEMPLEMAN Ted D101 H30 J85A
L19 L89 M16A M187 M203
TEMPO Nino B53 B127 B226 D74
L51 R137 S200
TEMPTATIONS S337 T42
TENBOKUM Rob B224A
10cc T43
TEN WHEEL DRIVE I44
TEN YEARS AFTER T45
TEN YEARS LATER T46
TENCH Benimont D139 L62D N45B
P70 S89 T164
TENCH Bob B64 B191 B268 G13
H17 H123 H179 H181 K51 L63
M203 S300
Tenda I of Zabandis S190
TENNENT John T47
TENNENT Norrie F51A
TENNENT-MORRISON T47
TENNESSEE FARM BAND T47A
TENNEY John B259 M203
TENNILLE Toni B56 G10 J72 P85
TENNIS SHOES T47B
TENORT Vance C147 H96 L65 L71B
L143
TENPOLE TUDOR T155B
TENSON Harlan B226A
TENT T47D
TENYRE Augustus 'T' J48
TENYUE Henry 'Button' M109
P80C R61C
TENYUE Patrick 'Zebullon' B71
B120 F108A H59 J18 J48 M75
M109 P80C Q15A R61C
W21B W119
TEPP Joel C216 H8 M21 M108 O15
S196 T32B W9 W51
TEPP Richard T3
TEPPER Jeff Moris B72
TERENCE T47C
TERESA T47E
TERESA Laura M47
TERHEGGEN Hubert F77
TERLAAK Bart O9A
TERLEP John S216
TERMAN Pope R28A
TERPSICHORE T47F
TERRA COTTA T48
TERRAN Anthony A131D B127 B240
B256 H8A N25 P28 R22 R78 S160
W6
TERRANOVA Joe D14
TERRELL Dorothy B223
TERRELL Jean S333A
TERRELL Sanders see TERRY
Sonny
TERRELL Tammi (nee MONTGOMERY)
G17 T51
TERRELL Ty R111
TERRI Salli M84C
TERRICIANO Lou R22
TERROADE Ken D86
Terry B77
TERRY Buddy L69
TERRY Clark W47
TERRY Dewey D97 H34 H99 T52
TERRY George A4 B71 C58 C121
C155 E33 F23 G61 H120 K51 L68B
M28 S276 W21B W136
TERRY Gordon L3 P74
TERRY Karl T53
TERRY Richard 113A
TERRY Sonny (TERRELL Sanders)
T53A
TERRY AND THE PIRATES E37 T54
TERRY BERRY PUBLIC LIBRARY
GLEE CLUB CHOIR C236
TERRY-SHORT Greg L145
TERSTALL Rob O8B
TERSTAPPEN Charly W13D

TERVELT Paul H1
TESCO Nicky M127
TESINSKY Frank K76
TESLUK Paul J74
Tessie B166
TESTA James M. M177A
TETER Marlena J88A
TETLON Ted F57
TEWFIK Samira E59
TEWIS Martin K92
TEWKES Denise J46
TEX Emil Den L4B
TEX Joe T55
TEX ROBERG BAND R104
TEXTOR Thomas C164
THACKER Alan B254
THACKER Clive A120 M121
N62 P131
THACKER Marsha E31
THACKERY Jim C59 H15 N46D
THAIN Gary A61 D133 H50
H104 U22 V21
THAKE Will L75
THALER Fred A35C
THALER Wayne F98
THAN Peter F20
THARPE Harriet B79A G19
THARPE Sister Rosetta L91
THATCHER Donna S36
THATCHER Keith S48
THATCHER Les A62 B47B B98
J72 K41 M100 W86
THAU Marty F66C N34 S319
THAUT Bill S314
THE WAY WE LIVE T56
THEAKER Drachen B231 F94
L128 P145A Z11
THEATRE OF HATE T56A
THEDFORD Bill C156 R137
S36
THEE IMAGE T56A
THEELAN Jan K66C
THIEVES T56C
THELIN Bjorn S225
THEM T57
THEMEN Art B248 K84
THEODOSIUS Rev Atrocius
N63
THERAPY T58
THERIAULT Stan H9A
THERIOT Charles K32
THEURZIET Edwin G113
THEUS Fats M26
THEWLIS Stan S149A
THIBAULT Laurent M87
THIBAUT Didier M221B
THIBODEAUX Merton H31
L115
THIBODEAUX Rufus B151B
H31 L3 L75 L115 Y16
THIELE Bob B108B
THIELE Christian 'Strat'
A57A
THIELEMANS Jean 'Toots'
D53 F3A J10A M17 M125
S125
THIELEPAPPE Brigitte S38
THIELEPAPPE Michael S38
THIELHEIM Emil 'Peppy'
B157
THIELMANN Ringo A24 O27A
THIERFELD W. B52 R63
THIERS Manfred R28
THIGPEN Ed B193
THILLOT Jean-Luc A114
THILO Jesper S108C
THINGUAES Frode R178
THIN LIZZY T59
THIRAUT Jean Pierre L17
THIRD EAR BAND T60
THIRD POWER T60A
THIRD RAIL T61
THIRD WORLD T62
THIRD WORLD (1973) T62A
THIRD WORLD WAR I63
THIRION Jo F123
THIRLWELL Jack T111
THIRSTY MOON T63A
THIRTEENTH FLOOR
ELEVATORS T64
THIRTY DAYS OUT T64A
THIRTY EIGHT SPECIAL I65
THIS HEAT T66
THITTICAT Suchard K42
THOBOURNE Clinton M17
THOELKE Brad M111 W54B

THOLLOT Jacques I67
Thomas P127
THOMAS Alain V26B W39D
THOMAS Alfred K45
THOMAS Alvin B17 K53 M149
M157 T118
THOMAS Angus M111
THOMAS B.J T67A
THOMAS Banner M178A
THOMAS Barry B37
THOMAS Bernard C201A
THOMAS Bill Q1A
THOMAS Bob (D) M78
THOMAS Bob (G) S116A
THOMAS Bobbi (V) B245
THOMAS Brigitte T143
THOMAS Broadway O38
THOMAS Bruce B39 C193 E41
K24 L27 M108 M193 Q17 S9
S270 S339
THOMAS Carla R56 T68
THOMAS Cassandra R171
THOMAS Charlie D116
THOMAS Chris (K) B59 C13
E59 G22 P127 R149
THOMAS Chris (G) L124
THOMAS Chris (Prod) T121
THOMAS Craig M136C
THOMAS Danny T64
THOMAS Dave B137
THOMAS David P61 R53
THOMAS David (G) T17
THOMAS David T6BA
THOMAS Deborah R45
THOMAS Dennis K80
THOMAS Derek W18
THOMAS Dick K52
THOMAS Dink E51
THOMAS Don A59 C108D M203
R169
THOMAS Doug I1
THOMAS Earl E55 K46
THOMAS Emry W30 W32
THOMAS Errol H65A S274
THOMAS Gary B161
THOMAS Gerry C53
THOMAS Glen B25A
THOMAS Glyn B161 P138 T76
THOMAS Grady F137 P29
THOMAS Greg F3A M27 M28
M53 M162B R173 W5
THOMAS Henry B19
THOMAS Ian T69
THOMAS IAN BAND T69A
THOMAS Ingrid H50
THOMAS Irma T70
THOMAS Jackie (Trom) H65A
THOMAS Jacky (B) S280 Y23
THOMAS James M53
THOMAS Jasper B87
THOMAS Jay A28C
THOMAS Jimmy H17 J4 M47C
M133 S185W133
THOMAS Joe M26 T71
THOMAS John (G) B258 B230
H56
THOMAS John (Tpt) C186
K51
THOMAS John (K) M58
THOMAS Creepy John see
CREEPY John Thomas
THOMAS Joseph T55
THOMAS K.O. A41 B274B K51
THOMAS Lafayette M13A
M185
THOMAS Leon E49 G92 L67B
S19
THOMAS Maggie B230 H101
THOMAS Marcy W30
THOMAS Mark O13
THOMAS Marvell B242 E55
F134 J22 K46
THOMAS Mary C242
THOMAS Max C118
THOMAS Michael (Sax) A89B
B109 J46 N53 S93 T71A V38
THOMAS Mike (D) T70
THOMAS Milton P115 W12A
THOMAS Nadra B49
THOMAS Nicky T72
THOMAS Paula R171
THOMAS Percy W28
THOMAS Pete C105 C193
H118 J10 L16 T170
THOMAS Phil (D) G122

THOMAS Phil (Cong) K77
THOMAS Phil (B) S177C
THOMAS Philippa W130
THOMAS Plug J94
THOMAS Priscilla F48
THOMAS Ray E18 J27 M189 T73
THOMAS Rob G72 S112A
THOMAS Ronnie H85
THOMAS Roy V31
THOMAS Rufus T74
THOMAS Steve (B) B264
THOMAS Steve (D) S103A
THOMAS Tasha A35A B208E
B221 B262 C229 D53 G109 K45
K81 L4A L119B M233 P6 P72A
R22 S124 S266 W48D W51 W51A
W106 W107 W119
THOMAS Terry C85
THOMAS Timmy L86 T75
THOMAS Trev C18
THOMAS Truman I28 P113 P126
R161 R173 W118
THOMAS Tyrone A43 P65A
THOMAS Vic W12
THOMAS Vincent A35D O13
THOMAS Whitney N53A
THOMAS-BAKER Ray C41
THOMASSIE Big John E. K51
W6
THOMASSON Hughie O43
THOMLINSON Malcolm T75A
THOMPKINS Russell S311A
THOMPSON Ali I77
THOMPSON Barbara A74 C166
H50 L99 M80 M83 T76
THOMPSON Bill K10
THOMPSON Bobby (Ban/K) A75
B41 B261 C15 C194 D2 D21
E57 E75 F7 H26 H52A J53 L77
L136A M11 M157 M159 N37 R4
R31 R127A R173 S272 T107
W11 Y18
THOMPSON Bobby (B) B41 B82
S159
THOMPSON Bobby (D) M36A
THOMPSON Bobby R124
THOMPSON Chester (D) B34B
G21 H4 J75A L58B W36 Z8
THOMPSON Chester (K) J7 J72
T119
THOMPSON Chris C8 D101 L11
M7A M80 N46A R5
THOMPSON Christie C185F
M145 R15 R53 U19 W5
THOMPSON Clinton O46
THOMPSON Danny A62 A98 B168
B237 C21 C78 C161 D11 D49
D99 D111 F35 G110 H95 H151
H188 I16 J41 K84 L63 M19
M42 M45 M50 M94 P41 P60
P120 R66 S273 S355A T6 W86
THOMPSON Darryl L41 M69
THOMPSON Dave (K/Sax) B237
G60A V33 Y10
THOMPSON Dave (B) C253
THOMPSON David (Perc) P59C
THOMPSON Dennis M1 N31
THOMPSON Dicky M159 S159
THOMPSON Dougie S333
THOMPSON Frank B36
THOMPSON Gary F103 F120
THOMPSON George Jnr. G12A
THOMPSON Gerald S85A
THOMPSON Graeme P88A
THOMPSON Hakim Emanuel S73C
THOMPSON Harvey A37 A45
A33B B200 B210 B261 B272B
C26 C390 C75 C155 C213E
D99 E57 F23 F114A G61 G85A
H7D H40 H169A J11 K30 L9
L34A L80C M10 M235 N23 P79
S56 S73 S340 T39 T55 W44
THOMPSON Iain D12B
THOMPSON Ivan D10A
THOMPSON James Winston see
DOCTOR ALIMANTADO
THOMPSON Jean L2B
THOMPSON Jerry B91 B200
THOMPSON Jimmy H65A
THOMPSON John (D) L95C
THOMPSON John (G) L136A
THOMPSON Kathy L136A
THOMPSON Keith C118B F74C
N9
THOMPSON Kix S207
THOMPSON Larry I3A S238A
THOMPSON Lee M46A

THOMPSON Leonore D132A
THOMPSON Les H9 J43 N53
THOMPSON Lincoln R35B
THOMPSON Linda (nee PETERS)
A30 A62 B266 D49 E41 F6 F89
G110 H74 H110 P36 R11 S195
T79
THOMPSON Lucky D27
THOMPSON Mack A83 D30 M48
THOMPSON Marcel M165A
THOMPSON Marshall C98
THOMPSON Mayo A87 R53 T78
THOMPSON Mike (K) C38A J73A
THOMPSON Mike (B) P120
THOMPSON Neil C39C
THOMPSON Pam R173
THOMPSON Paul E7D E59 E77A
F42 M34 M81 R149
THOMPSON Peter (B) S127
THOMPSON Peter (D/K) B286 H70
S119
THOMPSON Richard (G V) A30
A62 B266 C13 C165 C206 D49
D111 E41 F6 F23 G110 H110
H194 M19 M94 M108 P36 R11
R106 S185 S195 T79
THOMPSON Richard (Pno) S203
THOMPSON Richard (U.S.)
A106 B3 M227
THOMPSON Robin (Sax) G50
S331 Y2
THOMPSON Robbin (V G) T79A
THOMPSON Ron H94A
THOMPSON Rudi X2
THOMPSON Scott G60A
THOMPSON Sonny D30 K51 H170
THOMPSON Steve C210 D26 F117
H84 L7 L27 L37 M111 S211
S283 T31 T47
THOMPSON Steve 'Rud' M127
THOMPSON Sticky see THOMPSON
Uzziah
THOMPSON Sylvester A83
THOMPSON Thump D18
THOMPSON Tom (D) V35B
THOMPSON Tommy (G) D66 R52A
THOMPSON Tommy Lee (C) M238C
THOMPSON Tony C99 H42A R142A
S135
THOMPSON Trey B114B D1A
G106A
THOMPSON Uzziah (or Uriah)
'Sticky' B101 B117 B24 B276
C139 C245 D63 D71A D130 G39
H122 J17B J17D J17E J92 M49
P135 R29 R30 R35B R150 T104A
T114 U4A W4 W4A
THOMPSON TWINS T75B
THOMS Peter C85 E9 J104B
L12A L16 L37
THOMS Trev I19A
THOMSON Dave B154D
THOMSON Marla E7C
THOMSON Mike D99 O28
THOMSON Kenny I34
THONER Erik J10A
THOR T79C
THORN Kirk S237
THORN Mike N38A
THORNBERG Lee D101 D133A
F114A J105A K116 L19 L89 R46
THORNBURG Mike S216
THORNE Dave S212
THORNE Elliot A104A
THORNE John A2E
THORNE Mike W112
THORNGREN Doug M75
THORNGREN Eric B262F T67A
THORNHILL Alan A132 M136C
THORNTON 'Big Mama' Willie
Mae S329 T79B
THORNTON Blair B10
THORNTON Buddy M93
THORNTON Eddie B59 F7 F14
R84 W23 Y17
THORNTON Fonzi G19 H42A
R142A
THORNTON Les B166
THORNTON Morreen S71A
THORNTON Pattie G58
THORNTON Paul G58 P53
THORNTON Randy Z8
THORNTON Steve C40 R99 S169
THORNTON-ODEN Bianca G26D
M203
THORNYCROFT Bill K43

THOROGOOD George T80
THORP Bill (Str) S177D
THORPE Billy A137 T80A
THORPE John Q5
THORPE Mel H24
THORPE Paul L68A
THORPE Peter E38A
THORPE Richard L68A
THORPE Tony R153
THORUP Peter B11 C2 K84 T79D
THOSE NAUGHTY LUMPS T80B
THOURY Jean William B102
THRALL Pat A127 T135 W8 W23 Y2
THRASHER Andrew D116
THRASHER Gerhard D116
THRASHER Norman B24
THREE D. T80C
THREE DOG NIGHT T81
THREE MAN ARMY T82
THIELKELD Carter C59
THRILLINGTON Percy T82A
THRILLS T82B
THROBBING GRISTLE T83
THRONE Bob J51
THUMBS T83A
THUNDER Margo A27
THUNDER Theodore B31 E8 L47 O9 P131 S34
THUNDER T83B
THUNDERBIRDS F21
THUNDERBOLTS M44 M99
THUNDERBYRD M27
THUNDERCLAP NEWMAN T84
Thundercloud J104D
THUNDERHEAD T84A
THUNDERMUG T85
THUNDERS Johnny H76 N34 T86
Thundersticks S14D
THUNDERTHIGHS A42 B231 E37 F65 K24 M214 R60 S108 T87 V26 W3 Y2
THUNDERTRAIN T88
THUNES Scott Z8
THURBER Matt R92A
THURMAN Benny T64
THURMAN Ed P139A
THUROW Mathies D19A
THURSTON Colin H178A R20
THURSTON Scott H129A I10 N31
THYNE Robin M50 N11
TIANA Mayo C15B C155 J65
TIBBELS Nicole T79
TIBBETTS Ken A37 B91 B200 B253
TIBBLE Howard S268
TIBBS Gary C151C J110 O6A R149 V28
TICE Dave C199
TICHY John C173
TICKETS T88A
TICKLER Nigel S84B
TICKNER George J99
TIDBALL Dave T160
TIDWELL Diane E57 H49 L108 N37 S32 S269
TIDWELL George C14 E57 G72 H7D H65 N37 T107
TIEFENSEE Martin H37B L10
TIEKEN Dennis I13D
TIEPOLD Wolfgang S43
TIERNAN Mark B256
TIERNEY Ricky C182
TIERNEY Tony L140
TIERRA T88B
TIETCHENS Asmus C145 I88C
TIGARD Holly C15B
TIGER T89
TIGERS T89A
TIGHT LIKE THAT I90
TIKI Lord F65F
TILBROOK Adrian B11
TILBROOK Glenn C42 C193 S232 T79
TILFORD Brian B42B C217
TILL John J95
TILLER Paul B112
TILLER BOYS T90A
TILLERY Calvin S325
TILLERY Linda G26D L100 S19 W62
TILLEY Chuck B253
TILLEY Sandra V9

TILLEY Simon B93A
TILLI Dennis C61A
TILLISON Roger T91
TILLMAN Abe D57C
TILLMAN Bill B141
TILLMAN Curtis S329
TILLMAN Georgeanna M98
TILLMAN Ivory D57C
TILLMAN Jimmy M159 R59
TILLMAN Julia A59 A120 B43 B47A B47C B127 B226 C36 C38A C39 C58 C129 C141 C156 C180 C182 C213E C235 C241 D99 D127 E40 F114A F134 H19 H35B H59 H181 H193B I24 J7 J10B J72 K45 K46 K48 K81 L89 M36 M68 M101 M102 M179 M191 M225 N23 O35 P44 P83 P126 Q3A R15 R28B R32 R87 R97 R101 R126 R137 R142A S19 S36 S51 S73 S124 S180 S180D S251 S269 S325 T71A T113 T143 T153A T158 V9A V18A W31 W84C
TILLMAN Keith D128 D129 K22A M111 R121 S349
TILLOTSON Brooks C213D D50 J20 K36 M12 M41 V17 W106 Z3B
TILMAN Gerry C234
TILSTON Steve T92
TILT T92A
TILTON Collin C172 M203 V21
TILTON June S73
TIM Larry M21B
TIMBER T93
TIMBERLINE T93A
TIMBRELL H.J. P125
TIME T93B
TIMEBOX T94
TIMMS Daniel C38A C180 M174 P76
TIMONEY Mike G76A H163
TIMPERLEY Clive C32 O25 P33B
TIN HUEY T94A
TIN TIN T94B
TINAYJRE Gilles S280
TINDALL T.J. B135 E18A F92 H133 L130 P15 R22 S124A V12 W84D
TINFANO Denny B255A
TINI Ray Jnr. K46
TINNER Rene C25
TINSLEY James C129
TINY TIM T94C
TIPPELSKIRCH Mathias P118
TIPPENS Stan M214
TIPPET John K44A
TIPPETT Keith B231 C63 C80A C84A C109 D35 D118 H154 K54 M19 M42 M108 N50 O45 P146 S131 T95
TIPPETTS Julie (nee DRISCOLL) A120 B2 B131 C63 D118 E46 J9 O45 S259 S267 T95
TIPTON Glen J102
TIR NA NOG T96
TISBY Dexter P59
TISCHER Nando A57A
Tish B139
TISON Patrick S108
TITANIC T97
TITANS T97A
TITCOMB Brent C151
TITCOMB Gordon B135
TITELMAN Russ A37 B72 C11B C50 C179 C206 D53C L89 N40 S10 T125
TITLER Paul D109
TITLEY Jeff D55
TITIMUS Jeff D39
Tito B157
TITUS Libby S124 T98
TITUS GROAN T99
TIVEN John C40A C106A V11A Y3A
TJEN AKWOEI Monika B224A
TKAZYAK Jeff A122
TO BE T100
TOAD T101
TOAD Slimey M199
TOAD HALL T102

TOAN Canny C189
TOBALY Marc K59 L57
TOBIAS Oliver J16B
TOBIAS Quarter Moon W78A
TOBIAS Tim M115
TOBIN George J73A
TOBIN Karen H161
Toby C184
TOBY BEAU I102A
TODARO Tony F66
TODD Alan B209
TODD Gary L. B91A C251B
TODD Graham B81A B89 M202
TODD N46A R60 S80
TODD Jeff F31
TODD Pam S73
TODD Paul S149A W82A
TODD Phillip C85 O18 P138 W82A
TODD Richard D127D
TODD Tony C6
TODERS Dominick B58A
TODMAN Mike B150A
TOEFAT T103
TOESCA Louis M49
TOFANI David A96 B85 F4C K69 L51 M107 R125 S100 S123 S157 S215 S262 T98
TOFANI Giampaolo A74A
TOI Ted F18A
TOKENS R25
TOKYO T103B
TOKYO PHILHARMONIC ORCHESTRA W27
TOLBERT Larry C70A H8A H192 M131 P26A R45 S250 W116
TOLE Perry N11A
TOLEGIAN David F39
TOLER Dan A38 B91
TOLER David A38 B91
TOLES Michael E55 F134 H65A K46 L90 M172 S274 W101
TOLF Jan S39
TOLFREE Larry A62A J10 L81B
TOLHURST Kerryn D72B F81A
TOLHURST Laurence C247A
TOLLES Jim B207A G72A
TOLLETT Gary H134
TOLLETT Glenn C58
TOLLETT Ramona H134
TOLLHOUSE T103A
TOLLMAN Godfrey F105A
TOLLS Michael B242
TOLMAN Gerry S276
TOLMIE David G87
TOLONEN Jukka T15 T104 W75
TOLSON Pete B230 E26 E31F G92D P128
TOM PETTY AND THE HEARTBREAKERS P70
TOM ROBINSON BAND R116
TOM TOM CLUB T104A
TOMASULO Mike E31E

TOMBOEL Al A27
TOMICH Mike H110 I16
TOMITA Isao T105
TOMKINS Trevor A74 D118 G30 N62 R85 S95B T76 W86
TOMLIN Dave T60
TOMLINSON Dave A29 C103B
TOMLINSON Lee C143
TOMLINSON Malcolm B57F
TOMLINSON-CLARKE Marie A123 F83A R81
TOMMELEIN Frank M166A
TOMMY Glen R66
TOMMY AND THE BIJOUX H110
TOMMY JAMES AND THE SHONDELLS J30
TOMORROW Karl K27A
TOMORROW T106
TOMORROW'S GIFT T106A
TOMPKINS Deborah S272
TOMPKINS Pam E31
TOMPKINS Tom P141A
TOMPKINS Tom B151 P141A
THRONE Bob J51
THUMBS T83A
THUNDER Margo A27
THUNDER Theodore B31 E8 L47 O9 P131 S34
THUNDER T83B

THUNDERBIRDS F21
THUNDERBOLTS M44 M99
THUNDERBYRD M27
THUNDERCLAP NEWMAN T84
Thundercloud J104D
THUNDERHEAD T84A
THUNDERMUG T85
THUNDERS Johnny H76 N34 T86
Thundersticks S14D
THUNDERTHIGHS A42 B231 E37 F65 K24 M214 R60 S108 T87 V26 W3 Y2
THUNDERTRAIN T88
THUNES Scott Z8
THURBER Matt R92A
THURMAN Benny T64
THURMAN Ed P139A
THUROW Mathies D19A
THURSTON Colin H178A R20
THURSTON Scott H129A I10 N31
THYNE Robin M50 N11
!TONTO Kathy O47
TONTO EXPANDING HEADBAND I109
TONTOH Mac D110 O34 Q1
TONTON MACOUTE I108
Tony Brother H172
Tony Zap see EDMUNDS Hughes
TOOBAD Johnny F121 L32A
TOOGOOD Johnny J14
TOOK Steve Peregrine B168 M24 P84 S82
TOOKER John P49
TOOKES Darryl B139 S241
TOOLEY Anthony W119
TOOLEY Ron J20 L51 P35
TOOMEY Glenn K83
TOOMEY Jim A62 B160 K24 P10 T99 T117
TOON Cedric K80
TOON Earl K80
TOOP David I109A
TOOTLE Ashton H52 W82A
TOOTS AND THE MAYTALS T110
TOP Jannik C62A H89A M49 N64A
Top Ten D65
TOPAZ T110A
TOPHAM Anthony 'Top' B83 P62 T111 Y5
TORAIN Reg I15
TORANO Joe J93C
TORANO Sandy T111A
TORBALY Marc K59
TORBERT David G84 H186 K60 N32 W42
TORBERT Wayne F94
TORCH Dom T88
TORELLO Bobby T84A W107
TORFF Brian F83A
TORFS Peter B35A
TORK Peter M181
TORME Bernie G31 O33E T111B
TORNADER T111A
TORNADOS T112
TORNQUIST Greg B173
TORO Renaldo C250C
TORO Yomo F17
TORONTO T112A
TORPEDO Henk N27B T118A
TORPS Gary E57
TORPY Frank S347
TORRANCE Dean A9 E23 J36
TORRANCE Michael G17
TORRANCE Richard R173 S20 T113

TORRANCE Tim S177B
TORRENCE Toni D115
TORRES Bobby A135 B245 C155 D86 S148
TORRES Harrold C223A
TORRES Joe F94
TORRES Willie Y2A
TORREY Mary S272
TORROLL Mark S354
TORRY Claire B224B D49 D89 D93 F13 K41 L76B P31 P85 S313 Y19
TOSCANO Freddy M165A
TOSETTO Adi B154E
TOSH Peter M88 T114 W4
TOSH Stuart D9 G76A P31 P81B T43
TOSTI Blaise S272
TOTALLY HOT T114A
TOTH T. M39
TOTO T115
TCTSANT Fred F66
TOUAT Max E62A
TOUCH (U.K.) T116
TOUCH (U.S.) T116A
TOUCHSTONE T116B
TOUCHTON Tim J10A
TOUMAZIS Andreas S266
TOUNTAS Nick M68
TOURIST T117
TOURSEL Ralf E52A
TOUSSAINT Allen B17 B29 C155 D86 D106 G4 K53 L4 L44 L50 L63 L65 M9 M111 M157 R125 T118
TOUSSAINT Joe B233
TOUSSAINT Vincent T118
TOUT John L51 R65 W114
Touter see HARVEY Bernard
TOUW Meikle G113 O9A T118A
TOVEL Clyde L63
TOVEN Clay M225
TOWARD Frank S343
TOWB Suki P36
TOWE John A14 A43 C95 G20 S103
TOWER Rasmussen R54
TOWER OF POWER A116 B94 B109 B226 C237 F100 H45 H75 J85A L61A L63 L66A M16 M102 M123 M178A P126 R161 S19 S203 S273 T119 W44 W62
TOWERS Michael C182A
TOWNER Phil N30A O6B R61C S104C S289A
TOWNER Ralph A4A C189 O30 T119A W36
TOWNLEY Colin T119B
TOWNS Colin G31 K94B T111B T120
TOWNSEND Alan Y17
TOWNSEND Billy S20
TOWNSEND Dave P31
TOWNSEND Glen R101 T151
TOWNSEND John (V) B114B L110 S20 W119B
TOWNSEND John (Perc) D33B
TOWNSEND Rob A131E A133 D10A F12 M121 S35
TOWNSHEND Paul B209
TOWNSHEND Pete B186 C121 D9 G6 H10J J72 O40 T84 T121 T122 W72 W121
TOWNSHEND Simon W72
TOWNSHEND LANE T122
TOWNSON Chris J57 J75
TOY T122A
Toyah (WILCOX Toyah) T122B
TOYAN T122C
TOYANI Clay T79
TRABANDT Terry M1 R36A
TRACE T123
TRACEY John C212
TRACEY Stan A74 S95B T95
TRACEY Steve R83
TRACHSEL Kirk Q5
TRACIE Stan F14
TRACKS T123A
TRACTOR T124
TRACY Jeanie F80 T124A
TRACY Jerry C138C
TRACY Steve C138C E69B
TRADEL John C220
TRADER HORNE T125
TRADITION T126
TRAFFIC D28 T127

[709]

VERA Billy B104B
VERBEKE Patrick H196 K19
VERBRUGGE Foort M54A
VERCAMBE Laurent M57B
VERDEAUX Bruno C137
VERDEAUX Cyrille C137
VERDELL Jackie M203 V21
VERDICK Michael P106
VERDOIS Pete T70
VERDUSCO Darrell C179 M179
VERES Mariska P92B S101A
VERGAT Vic V25A
VERGOS Nick H65A
VERHAGEN Anton O37
VERHEES Evert B35
VERHOEVEN Nico K66C
VERITY John A77 B160 F56 P77
R140 V26
VERLAINE Tom S170 T38 V25B
VERLIN Ron S103A
VERNACCHIO Michael E57
VERNAZZA John B109
VERNIERI Larry D38A
VERNO Buz J70 S358B
VERNON Edward D115 R161A
VERNON Mike D30 D133 F77 K51
L75 L95B O20 S31 T45 T111
V26A
VERNON Terry G74
VEROUTIS Vana V13
VER PLANCK Marlene M41
VERRALL Ronnie E74 F70B S295
W86
VERRETT Harrison D96
VERROCA Steve C210 W129
VERSLUYS Andre V38A
VERTO V26B
VERUCCHIO Dick B254
VERWEY Robert B197A
VESALA Edward V26C
VESOVO Al M78 R113
VESTINE Henry C26 H150 S329
Z8
VETTESE Peter John J58
VEVEY E. C108C
Vi Ann P21
VIAN Patrick R53C V27
VIAUD Andre P35A
VIBER Charles W101
VIBRATORS V28
Vicar P72
VICARAGE Mo M211A
VICARI Frank A28C B85 G19 L9
L51 L80A M75 W6 W13 W51
VICIOUS Kid Y8A
VICIOUS Sid (BEVERLEY John)
F71 S77 S132 V28A
VICK Harold C213E G4 M17 M227
P149 R125
VICKERS Carle L2
VICKERS Harold D86A
VICKERS Howie (V) C161B
VICKERS Mike G22 M80 S35 S185
V29
VICKERY Chris B57F
VICKERY Graham J72 S84B
VICTIM Steve P53
VICTIMS V29A
VICTOR PERAINOS KINGDOM COME
P60B
Victoria B208 C76
VICTORIAN PARENTS V31
VIDACOVICH John L118
VIDAL Carlos C174D C241
VIDAL Joao A. B43
VIDAL Maria C103C J48 S242
VIDAL Xavier V26B
VIDICAN John K6
Vie K51
VIEL George F101D
VIERRA John L10B M18
VIERTEL Jack R22
VIEVERMANNS Mariette K66C
VIEWIG Tommy A39A
VIG Tommy B41B B110 C39 D86
E15 G10 M75 R107 S228 S273
T12
VIGEANT Victor M238
VIGIL Tom B268
VIGLIAR Giovanni A91
VIGRASS Paul C48 D39 F117 L27
V30
VIGRASS AND OSBORNE C48 V30
VILATO Orestes F17 P45 S19
VILLA Trond R166
VILLAIN Andreas O36A

VILLALOBOS Bobby P156A
VILLAREAL Frank C179
Vinagre S197D
VINAS Michael V6
VINCENT Gene (CRADDOCK
Vincent Eugene) C149 V32
VINCENT James L13 V32A
VINCENT Jim (G) C21B C63C
K56A
VINCENT Pamela B123 J11
K56A
VINCENT Pat D87A
VINCENTPaul A59C F66A
N43A N61C
VINCENT Raymond E66 W13F
VINCENT Reggie C182
VINCENT Steve C215
VINCENT Veronique F123
VINCHON Brigit M1A
VINCI Frankie F90
VINCI Gerry R97
VINCI John N25A
VINDING Mads B275 S69
V32B
VINEGAR JOE V33
VINNEDGE Char C208
VINNEGAR Leroy C241 D103
VINSEY Tony K27A
VINSON Eddie 'Cleanhead'
O38 U34
VINSON Millard W25
VINYAKRAM T.H. S85
VIOLA Al M75 R62 Z8
VIOLA Ron B104B
VIOLETTI Gary E69B
VIOLIN Vera A35
VIOLINSKI V35
VIR Guru G69C
VIRDIER Danny T136
VIRGIN Dingo see ALLEN
Daevid
VIRLA Novi Novog W119B
VIRTANEN Heikki T15 T104
VIRTUE Frank V35B
VIRTUE Michael U1
VIRTUES V35B
VISAGE V35A
VISAGGIO Michael F8A
VISCIGLIA Mike M21 S230A
VISCELLI Johnny F50A
VISCONTI Delaney O6A
VISCONTI Jessica O6A
VISCONTI Mary see HOPKIN
Mary
VISCONTI Tony B168 B186
C36 C37 C155 G22 G27
G100A H29 H151 J41 J110
M50 O6A O22 P41 R7 R8
S295 T59 W7
VISION Terry D56A
VISITOR 2035 V36
VISLOCKY John S230A
VISSEN Jan A42
VISSER Biem P76C
VISSER Johan K32C
VISTER Tor L24C
VISVIKIS Dennis A131F
VITAL DUB V37
VITALE Arturo A91
VITALE Joe C234 D53 E2
E60 F39 F100 F78 N4 N63
O43 P37A R109 S36 S276
S276A T71A V38 W16
VITALE Steve S97
VITESSE V38A
Vito Z8
VITO Greg N58C
VITO Rick C184A M27 M111
M229 P137 R22 R164 S203
W70
VITOUS Miroslav C189 D40D
M78 R178 S104 V39 W27 W36
W62 Z9
VITT Bill B210 C208A F80
VITTEK David H139A
VIVA V39A
VIVABEAT V39B
Vivi T151A
VIYATE Ryan B224A
VIZARD Ed A102
VIZZUTTI Al C186
VOAG L. H31A
VOCE Roy W15
VOELKER H.L. G40
VOG Vivienne T18A
VOG V39C
VOGEL Allan S63
VOGEL Bill Q1A

VOGEL Howard T134
VOGEL Jodi T134
VOGEL Karsten B275 S69
VOICE Bob B209 F48B
VOICE Steve L113
VOICE OF AFRICA B4
VOICES OF EAST HARLEM V40
VOICES OF HOPE H164C
VOIDOIDS H90
VOIGHT Jim P46
VOLASCO Tony M39
VOLBERG Danny T56B
VOLK Philip B228C R70
VOLKER Armand T35
VOLKS MUSIC V40A
VOLLMER Brian H89C
VOLLNER Sredni C203 R100
W51
VOLMAN Mark A132 B139 B168
C182 C234C F68 G69 H120
L51 M27 M82 M91 M198 N13
Q5 S229 S270 S276 T161 Z8
VOLPE Lou C76 C164
VOLQUARTZ Ove A67A
VON ARB Fernando K96A
VON BOHR Manfred B107
M136B
VON BUR Alan H171B
VON BUTTLAR Manfred F7A
VON COVAY Tony C203
VON DEYEN Adalbert V41
VON DIJK Michael B197A
VON GRUMBKOW Jochen B107
T11
VON HAMMER Michael R151
VON NASH Larry M132D
VON NEIENHOFF Liz A57
VON OSTEN Sigune L120
VON OVERHEICTT Eddy B198A
VON ROHR Chris K96A
VON SCHLIPPENBACH
Alexander G47
VON SCHMIDT Eric T134
VON SCHREIBER Steve L119B
VON SENGER Dominik P71A
VON SINNEN Karla G120
VON STRAUCH Sven N46E
VON STREETER James R111
VOOGT Peter E27
VOORMAN Klaus B23 B59 C58
C94 C171 D56A D90 D100 D139
F100 G10 H39 H170 J41 K34
K45 L19 L51 L64 L111 M80
M132D M191 M227 M229 N40
N55 O27 P28 P130 R60 R60C
R173 S124 S220 S252 S338
V3 V12 W5 W133A
VOORSLUIJS Giezel S337A
VORHAUS David C105 L5A M1A
P36 W68
VORZANGER Charles T122
VOS Tony E27
VOSBURGH Denny C182
VOSBURGH (D) F86B P83A
T56A
VOSS Holger S329A
VOSTER Ernst A59C
VOUDOURIS Roger V41A W46
VOX H.J. B169C
VOYAGER V42
VOZNIAK Jaroslav P94A
VRALLEN Graeme W69B
VRE Midge L144B
VRENEGOOR J.J. S328A
VROLIJK Marco S332D
Vshailendra H110
VUNDERLINK Rob D66A

WAADE Geir H137B W130
WAADELAND Carl H. H137B
WAALKEN Otto L10
WACHSMAN Steve T79B
WACHTEL Robert 'Waddy' A116
B38 B175 B244 B255 C11B
C38A C94 C180 D53C D72A E75
F42 F66 F82 F139 G60 G121
H62 K48 K86 L12B M132D M229
N40 N45B P114 P129 R22 R28B
R135A R137 S17 S34 S196
S220 S272 T21 T25 W9 W42
W120 Y5B Z11
WACHTEL Sidney A27

WACKERMAN Chad Z8
WACKERS W1
WACKFORD Michael S253
WADA George F71A
WADA Masani C253A
WADDELL Bruce F21
WADDINGTON Geoff S335A
WADDINGTON John N27D P117
WADDY Frank Kash B183
WADE Ann F139
WADE Bill C241C F101B M222
T79C
WADE Brett E35 J15A L26B
WADE Cliff B62 D16
WADE Joel J15A
WADE Jonathan B187
WADE Larry C17
WADE Nancy V21
WADE Pete B17A C194 E75
G72 H26 K77 M75 N37 P63
R4 R137 R173 T21 W11 Y18
WADE Roger H50
WADENIUS George B141 M45C
P109 S157 S186 T67A
WADHAM John C120
WADINGTON Pete D26
WADSWORTH Derek A74 B19
B288 C166 D118 F7 F14 G98
H50 H52 M80 P131 R61A R122
S31 S178 T76 V21
WAGENET Hal I31
WAGER Betsy C76
WAGES OF SIN W2
WAGNER Adrian C18 W3
WAGNER Alfred D86B
WAGNER Bo S245
WAGNER Dave C235
WAGNER Dick C182 C246 C249
F22 F129A H9 M233 R60 U22A
WAGNER Gary P24A
WAGNER Josef G2
WAGNER Klaus M166A
WAGNER Lawrence F104A
WAGNER Norm L83A M68
WAGNER Richie I13C
WAGNER Ron A122
WAGNER Willie K44B
WAGON Chuck D64
WAH W3A
WAHL Tommy M136B
WAHLMANN Eckhard M216B
WAILE Denny L82C
WAILER Bunny (LIVINGSTONE
Neville) T114 W4
WAILERS M88 W3B
WAILING SOULS W4A
WAINMAN Phil A99A B83 B95
R122
WAINWRIGHT Bob L86A
WAINWRIGHT Loudon III S55A
W5
WAIS Mir T18A
WAITE Chris C76
WAITE John B8 W5A
WAITE Tony D95
WAITES Craig D33E
WAITRESSES W5B
WAITS Tom R22 W6
WAITZMAN Daniel A27
WAKEFIELD Frank C199C G68
WAKEFIELD Kathy C52B
WAKEFIELD Tony C225
WAKELIN Bob M175E
WAKELIN Johnny W6A
WAKELING Dave B58B
WAKEMAN Alan A109 G37A
S182
WAKEMAN Dusty G81E
WAKEMAN Rick A62 B115 B168
B186 C202 G32 J72 M50 R60
S48 S270 S295 W7 W86 Y7
WALCOTT Collin A4A C189
H59 L67B M180B O30
WALD Allen K95
WALDEN Dana C69B
WALDEN Don O32A
WALDEN Doug C109A
WALDEN Narada Michael B64
B169 B253 C186 F121 G64C
H131 J75A M40 N60 P35 S19
S135 W8 W36
WALDEN Snuffy B225 B268
C109 F108 L9A R3 S131 S297
W119

WALDER Udo V7
WALDMAN Jack M96 P15
WALDMAN Randy C156 M102 P114
R97
WALDMAN Wendy B175 C109
F103D K38A M123 M229 R137
S272 W9 W46 W128B
WALDNER Bill A121B
WALDO Jimmy N29A
WALDORF M. (G) W9A
WALDORF Marcia D. B256
WALDORF & TRAVERS W9A
WALDRON Dan B123A
WALDRON Mal E52
WALDROP Donald Al I31
WALES Eric W10
WALES Howard A1 G9 G84 M68
WALES O'REGAN W10
WALK Fred B281 L81 M158B
WALK Joe T9A
WALKELEY Brian F23
WALKER Aaron 'T-Bone' W13
WALKER Ade M55B
WALKER Alan B159
WALKER Albert 'Ralph' C245
WALKER Billy B274A N43
WALKER Bob B211
WALKER Brooker K45
WALKER Cato K45
WALKER Chris C48
WALKER Cleveland R130
WALKER Colin E34 S253
WALKER Dave F66 I7 M167 R40
S31
WALKER David T. B180 B214
B281 C17 C213E C241 E71 F92
G17 H35B K17 K48 K56A K72
L61B L143 M65A M102 M218 O10
P44 P114 P126 R101 R175 S14C
S198B S228 S251 W10A W13 W31
W118 W119
WALKER David K94B
WALKER Dennis M238B W12A
WALKER Derrick B144
WALKER Dick A32B
WALKER Don C158A
WALKER Doug (G/B) C76
WALKER Doug (G) P47
WALKER Earl 'Baga' C139
D113A
WALKER Ebo N29C
WALKER Fred C17
WALKER George D127
WALKER Greg (B) B123 C234A
D127B J14A L144
WALKER Greg (V) H19 S19
WALKER Hugh L58B
WALKER James O14
WALKER Jay B43A B85A
WALKER Jeanine E73
WALKER Jerry L90
WALKER Jerry Jeff C116 C124
F128 W11
WALKER Jim P144
WALKER Jimmy (Perc) H133 J92
K69B R21
WALKER Jimmy (V) R87
WALKER John 'Big Moose' (K
V) A83 H147 H150 O8A R168
S57 S358 W11A W47
WALKER John (V/G) P102D S245
WALKER John W21A
WALKER Junior (DE WALT
Autry) F84 M229 W12
WALKER Kathy M16A
WALKER Larry M238
WALKER Len W13A
WALKER Les T89 W20
WALKER Lilian E76A
WALKER Martha F42
WALKER Mel B171 O38
WALKER Morgan M143A
WALKER Mick S217
WALKER Nelly Z8
WALKER Percy B193
WALKER Pete 'Lucifer' P153
WALKER Peter M151
WALKER Phillip S96 T23 W12A
WALKER Raymond L. F83A K30
K95 L72 N37 P63
WALKER Richie M123
WALKER Ritchie I7
WALKER Rob S277
WALKER Sharon T67A
WALKER Sheryl W119

WATTS Arthur H70
WATTS Barry Q1C
WATTS Charlie B156 E56 H170
J35 K84 P59B R122A R133 R173
S111 T122 W120
WATTS Dave J14
WATTS Ernie A11 A48 A52 A59
A74 A123 A131 A131D B127 B141
B221 C17 C45 C76 C151B C153
C162 C173 C182 C213E D28 D74
D86 D127 D142A C57 F92 F103C
F114A F119A G17 G26A G60 G121
H35B H156 J75A J93C J113 K45
K48 L41 L79 M68 M82 M89A M101
M102 M108 M111 M123 M131A
M151 M229 P114 P115 Q3A R4
R22 R24B R78 R87 R99 S14C S36
S180D S189 S216 S262 S325 T25
T32B T113 T145 V9A V18A W27
W31 W32A W84C W113A Y6B Z8
WATTS Jeff S260
WATTS John F54A
WATTS Lennie C185B
WATTS Nathaniel B110 G26A
L66A M102 P114 R142A W84C
W119
WATTS Noble C146
WATTS Peter 'Overend' B219
M214
WATTS Robin P1B
WATTS Ron B211
WATTS Steve E55A
WATTS Trevor S267 T95
WATTS 103RD STREET W33
WAUGH Pete B247
WAUL Franklin 'Blubber' A6
B234 C245 D113A P135 R35B
R150
WAWUIRE Phil F4A
WAVEMAKER W34
WAX W34A
WAY Andy D28
WAY Darryl C251 E32 F8 G66
J58 K94B T123 W35
WAY Helen, Singers H134
WAY Peter C151A U2
WAY WE LIVE see THE WAY WE
LIVE
WAYBILL Fee T152
WAYNE Carl M129 W122
WAYNE Graham W96
WAYNE Hayden M84A
WAYNE Jeff V30 W35A
WAYNE Mick B186 J108 O47 T25
WAYNE Trev T37B
WAYNE COCHRAN AND THE C.C.
RIDERS C150
WAYNE FONTANA AND THE MIND-
BENDERS M162
WAYS A1 D63B
WAZMO Nariz W35B
WAZNOR Pete I3A
WEAPON OF PEACE W35C
WEARD Roy D93D
WEATHER REPORT W36
WEATHERILL Winston F95A
WEATHERLY James Dexter G73A
W36A
WEATHERS John A58 B96 B171
B237 E80 G22 G86 L80C N27
WEATHERS Lila P108
WEATHERS Vivian P108 W37
WEATHERSBY Eltesa H164C
WEATHERSPOON David L90
WEATHERSTONE Jimmy D46A
WEAVER Archer L24B
WEAVER Blue A49 A60A B71 C100
C196 E18 F7 M214 R60 S295
S334
WEAVER Deany H134A
WEAVER George S56
WEAVER Ken C133 H99
WEAVER Mark S57
WEAVER Mick (also FROG Wynder
K.) A22 A61 B268 B283 C145A
C208A D54 E46 F7 F29 F125 G34
G86 H50 H65 H66A H94 J105 K81
L106 M15 M102C M108 M128 M157
P76 R125 S60 S285 S339 T46
V21
WEB W38
WEBB Bob F39 J31
WEBB Cassell F128 S269
WEBB Champ D103
WEBB Cynthia R34 S252 V12
WEBB Dean B245 C127 D68B D71
R137

WEBB Fred 131 M179 S284
WEBB Gary H134A
WEBB George L64
WEBB Harry Rodger see
RICHARD Cliff
WEBB Jimmy C155 G10 R101
WEBB John (Syn) N63A
WEBB John (D) B67
WEBB Keith D99 P11 R62
WEBB Marvin B143
WEBB Melvin S251
WEBB Norman P54
WEBB Peta T79
WEBB Ralston C139
WEBB Reg F140D
WEBB Robert (Perc) W132
WEBB Robert (K/V) E56A
WEBB Roy Dean P50
WEBB Russell S140 Z17
WEBB Spider P15
WEBB Stan A101 B71 B220
C26 C101 D133 P62 S31 V21
WEBB Steve R125
WEBB Steve L121A
WEBB Steve L81A
WEBB Susan M170 W39
WEBB Tom F70
WEBB Wendy M232
WEBBER Aj H66
WEBBER Andrew Lloyd see
LLOYD-WEBBER Andrew
WEBBER Bob C185A M192D
S318
WEBBER Charlie (Tpt)
S356A
WEBBER Julian Lloyd see
LLOYD-WEBBER Julian
WEBBER Rachel U16A
WEBBER Roy G62B W14
WEBER Charly (D) K44B
WEBER Chris D139
WEBER Clark A51
WEBER David C185 R40 T54
WEBER Eberhard D19A K94C
M138A W39A
WEBER George D13
WEBER Herbert L121C
WEBER Jack E31 M84
WEBER Jon H112
WEBER Kalle K44B L121C
WEBER Klaus C219B
WEBER Steve F133 H139
WEBER Vince R162A W39B
WEBER Virgil G83
WEBSTER Alan I21A
WEBSTER Ben S30
WEBSTER Danny S154
WEBSTER Dave T7
WEBSTER Guy B228C
WEBSTER John S283A
WEBSTER Jon F18C
WEBSTER Katie L75 L115
WEBSTER Randy W40
WEBSTER Terry R124
WECHSLER Larry C164
WECHSTER Julius B56 C96
WECK David B246
WEDGE W39C
WEDGWOOD Mike C34 C251
E60 J27
WEEK Henry B123 B246
WEEKEND MILLIONAIRE W39D
WEEKS David P136
WEEKS Willie A37 A53A
B47C B100 B186 B253 C11B
C171 C206 D101 F78 H39
H58 H59 J43 J93C L12B L18
L18A L63 M16A M41 M229
N40 P114 P114B R28B R133
R173 S124 S220 S273 T25
T79 T107 T145 W16 W31
W111 W118 W119 W120
Wee Marie S283
WEEMS Jerry B170 W106
WEEMS Ritchie W40A
WEENER Jeffrey L121B
WELKOM Steve F69B
WEERASINGHE Junior T63A
WEGENER Jeffrey L121A
WEHLER Mathias A99
WEHLAND M205B M209
WEHRMEYER Eric G113
WEHRSTEIN Ray P19 R106
W14
WEIDEL Bugs P70

WEIDELI Mojo K96C
WEILDER John 'Willi' A67 B218
E60 F12 F65 H140 J27 K39
M193 M202A S309 T145 W41
WEIDORJE W41A
WEIGEL Hans Ulrich T11
WEIGHELL Alan E40 J72 S295
T163
WEIHE Peter C251B T103A
WEIL Terry H151
WEILLER Jean Pierre H154
WEINBERG Anton W102
WEINBERG Max B124C B172A
H185 M120 S199 S229 S263B
WEINBERG P. M109B
WEINBERG Sid B141 C164 J20
WEINBERG Warren L65
WEINER Mark B141
WEINER Matthew D133A
WEINER Stephane S208
WEINGARDEN Bill H14A
WEINGARTEN Steve E39
WEINSTEIN Leslie see WEST
Leslie
WEINSTOCK Murray F44C M75
S65
WEINZIERL John A57 U23
WEIR Bob G9 G84 H45 K60
W42
WEIR John K70
WEIR Kenny P49B
WEIR Robb T169A
WEIR Rusty W43
WEIRDOS W43A
WEIRNEKEN A1 C59
WEIS Danny A9 B124B C246
E75 I24 M108 O12 R60 R75
WEIS Jerry B141
WEISBERG Gary S272
WEISBERG Larry K13 S216
WEISBERG Steve M232
WEISBERG Tim C38A C39 F78
M101 R62 W44
WEISBURG Richard B57
WEISGARD E. D83A
WEISS Betty S88
WEISS Cathy P36
WEISS Dawn A9
WEISS Donna A132 C155 C179
C180 C247 D139 K81
WEISS Doudon A33A S193
WEISS Herb H1
WEISS Ingrid R17
WEISS Jerry A47 B141 K81
M13
WEISS Klaus N43A Z22A
WEISS Larry W44A
WEISS Mary S88
WEISS Paul S. P53
WEISS Terry P83A
WEISSBERG Eric A85A B141
B199B C108D C164 C185F
C229 C234A D139 F22A F27A
F108A F128 G97B G109 H59
J20 J67A J69 J164 M18 M78
M125 P41 R140 S10 S78 T134
T156 W5 W45 W51A W65A
WEISSE Harald M243
WEISSER Skip C150
WEISSMAN Dick F27A
WEISSMAN Ken C72A T113
WEISSMAN Mitch S121
WEITZ John R40A
WEITZ Mark S294
WELBAUM Douglas B246A
WELBORN Larry C224 H134
WELBORN Bob C74 F66 P24 R81
W46
WELCH Bruce M100 R80 S80
WELCH Cecil W15B
WELCH Chris S206
WELCH Sandy S75A
WELDON Liam S280
WELDON Nick J10
WELDON Paul E19B
WELDON Peter M21
WELEVRED Hank H101
WELFARE STATE C209
WELHAM Hadrian F85
WELHAM Martin F85
WELKER Larry M238
WELKER Peter C158 Y12
WELLANDER Lasse A4
WELLBELOVED Dave G112
WELLER Dave E8
WELLER Don H52 H110 K81

L23 M57 M118 P131 R122A
T155
WELLER Freddy K81 R70
WELLER Paul G2 J19
WELLINGTON Canute L71B
S203A
WELLINGTON Ever M133
WELLS Brandi W46A
WELLS Brookside K38
WELLS Cory C180 T81 W46B
WELLS David Z8
WELLS Fred C177D
WELLS John L47
WELLS Junior (BLACKMORE
Amos) G122 M129 R22 W47
WELLS Kevin C42 K44A
WELLS Mary G17 W48
WELLS Peter R141A
WELLS Phillip W48A
WELLS Tommy C194
WELLS Tony K59 P24B
WELLSTOOD Dick D139
WELMAN Garry W26
WELNICK Vince T152
WELSH Alex H11
WELSH Chauncey D86
WELSH Keith I5A
WELTER Edmond A9
WELTON Mick S270
WENCHIN W48E
WENDELS Kim O47
WENDELLS Dave B82 Y17
WENDER Ted T80C W5 W65A
WENDROFF Michael L57 R60
W48B
WENEIMEYER Michael E52
WENNEMUTH Gerd S38
WENNER Mark N46D
WENNERMARK Eunice O39
WENNERSRTOM Vern T12B
WENZEL Jurgen N61
WERBROUCK Christian H196
WERD John D127
WEREWOLVES W48C
WEREWOLVES OF LONDON W48F
WERITZ Jurgen F7A
WERLEROFZOIETS Max (WERNER
Max) K16 S41B
WERMAN Tom C92 M178A N63
WERNEER Mireille S280
WERNEER Rene S280 Y23
Werner M136B
WERNER David W48D
WERNER Hans T63A Y2
WERNER Max see WERLEROFZOI-
eTS Max
WERNER Wendelin F8D
WERNHAM Richard see SLAUGH-
TER Rick
WERNICK Peter C199C
WERT Mo T83B
WERTH Howard A118 W49
WERTZ Bob M102
WERTZ Kenny C200 F74 S52
WESCH Norbert K6A
WES DAKUS AND THE REBELS
D6A
WESLEY Fred B85 B183 C17
E7 K46 M107 P29 R62
WESS Frank C164 F60 K51 M79
M227 T20 W50 W119
WESSBERG Bob K76
WESSON Mel S169D U4
WESSON Steve F65D
WEST Andy D79
WEST Bobby B72 B236B B240
B260 K81 M68 M95 P115 S10
T25 Z8
WEST Chris Y2
WEST Dottie R127A
WEST Dwayne F83A K30 T167
WEST Frank B282
WEST Gary S103A
WEST J.P. H137B
WEST Jack G22C
WEST James A48
WEST James Robert S270
WEST Jamie R23
WEST Jeff B272B
WEST Jerry H31
WEST Jim F86B
WEST John R. L61B
WEST Keith (V/G) M193 M202A
T106
WEST Larry H65B V2
WEST Leslie (WEINSTEIN
Leslie) C62 D66 J86A K34
L44 M216 V2 W51 W52

WEST 'Major' Griff S194
WEST Peter F51
WEST Rick F55
WEST Riff G22C
WEST Ron B58 T36A
WEST Roscoe A41 F116
WEST Sandy R163
WEST Tommy C51 C51B C229
G109 J88 M75 W51A
WEST Woody F101B Z22
WEST BRUCE and LAING W52
WEST COAST POP ART
EXPERIMENTAL BAND W53
WEST-MULLEN M178C
WEST-ORAM James D94
WEST ROAD BLUES BAND W53A
West Virginia Creeper C173
WESTBROOK Frank R32
WESTBROOK Marsha M40
WESTBROOK Mike S186A
WESTBROOK Pete H25
WESTBY Olvind R178
WESTERN Hilary P31
WESTFIELD Ricky K8D
WESTLAKE Kevin B2 B146 E12
J16B K52 L16A L48 S264 W53B
WESTLAKE Martin P72
WESTLEY Geoff B71 B189 D92
D95 J16 N41 W10
WESTLEY Ira F5
WESTLEY Jim B71
WESTMORELAND Kathy P125
WESTON Azzedin O13
WESTON Bob A97 A98A A99A B23
B112 B171 D49 F66 G32 H70 K66
W3 W49
WESTON Danny C61A
WESTON David B155
WESTON G. Calvin Y6
WESTON Gil G37
WESTON Harvey I20
WESTON Kim G17
WESTON Paul S55D
WESTON Ray R128
WESTON Tim C62B D87B
WESTON Veryan C209
WESTONE Harry F134
WESTOVER Charles see SHANNON
Del
WESTOVER Kym S89
WESTPHAL Gert B91A
WESTPHAL Lonzo L78
WESTPHAL Michael M140A
WESTPHAL Wolfgang S299B
WESTRUPP Walter H125B
WESTSTRATE Paul A42
WESTWOOD John A20
WESTWOOD Paul B45A C6 D38B
F56 G49 G94 H11 H175 J39 R80
S209 W102 Z9B
WESTWOOD Richard G112B
WESTWOOD Rick T138
WESTWOOD Steven G112B
WET WILLIE W54
WETHERALL Vince F23
WETLOR Alan C132
WETTON John A99B B34 C79 E21
E59 F12 F42 H54 J4B K54 M35
M81 M176 N58B R23 R33 R149
S131 S300 U3 U22 W54A W114
WEX Tex F48 S20
WEXLER Jerry G61 S228
WEYER David C195A
WEYER Francis J2
WEYMOUTH Lani T104A
WEYMOUTH Laura T104A
WEYMOUTH Loric T104A
WEYMOUTH Martina T8
WEYMOUTH Tina T104A
WHA-KOO W54B
WHALE Peter B218 K62
WHALEFEATHER W55
WHALEN Chris S272
WHALEY Don C237 J41 L20 L111
M108 N25
WHALEY Ken D123 G79 H93 L53
M63 M126 S206 T170
WHALEY Paul B150
WHALLEY Steve B183D
WHARTON Darron T58
WHEAT Mike K29A
WHEATBREAD Paul P145
WHEATER Tim M34 O18A
WHEATLEY David F74
WHEATLEY Glenn M103B
WHEATLEY Tim D125A G77A T6A
WHEELER Archie S311

WHEELER Buddy E14
WHEELER Harold S229
WHEELER James P26
WHEELER Ken (B) P47
WHEELER Kenny (Tpt) B4 B249
C2 D35 D108 F14 G47 K22A K84
M83 N44 N62 P131 S31 S267
T141 W9A W86
WHEELER Park S339A
WHEELER Paul A137 M94
WHEELER Steve B233A
WHEELOCK Morris B268
WHEELOCK Moses J96 O35
WHELAN Bill P93
WHELAN Dave R52
WHELEN Katheleen J18
WHELLANS Mike W55A
WHELLOCK John B84A
WHELPLEY Randy D60
WHETSTONE Richard E35
WHIGHAM Jiggs B204A
WHIPLASH Bobby R173
WHIPPING POST W55B
WHIRLWIND W56
WHIRLWIND M107
WHIRLY WORLD W57
Whispering Mick M45
WHITAKER Dave G36 K32A
WHITAKER Don S217
WHITAKER Harry M218
WHITAKER Stanley H19A
WHITBREAD Dennis E27
WHITCOMB Brian A31 B164 O33G
P76A S58 W21
WHITE A.G. B178 'Bubbles' D30
S243
WHITE Alan A40 B26 B79 C155
O26 D99 G27 G101 G110 H11 H39
H168 K87 L51 S103B U5 W7 W5B
W89 W133 Y7
WHITE Andrew (Horns) W36
WHITE Andy (D) B59 F70B T125
T163
WHITE Ann D74 K48 O13
WHITE Anthony B178 S35
WHITE Arthur W30A
WHITE Barry D53C
WHITE Bergen L108 R127A T153A
WHITE Betty S276
WHITE Beverley P137
WHITE Bill N63
WHITE Billy Joe P53
WHITE Bob (D) H145
WHITE Bob (Fd1) S187C
WHITE Brenda C155 D63 F60
M222A S169 T114 V17
WHITE Bubs B178 C30 S243
WHITE Buck C124 H55
WHITE Bukka W59
WHITE Cheryl C124
WHITE Chip W6
WHITE Chris W60 Z15
WHITE Clarence B49 B84 B202
B244 B285 C123 C155 C180 C200
E75 G121 K29 M125A M211C M229
M229A N5A N40 P32 T32E
WHITE Cynthia C17
WHITE D.Bergen B261 H62 J13
K95 L77 M11 N37 S269 S272 T21
WHITE Dave D14
WHITE Dave (Wind) B5 C63
C177D W102 Y2
WHITE Dave C241B
WHITE David (B) F39 J105A S89
T113
WHITE David (G/V) S310A
WHITE Eric K29
WHITE Fred C45 E7 E55 H58
H193B L65 W84C
WHITE Gary C116 C124 S112
WHITE Grahame C29 K94 L145
S306
WHITE J.De Witt N21
WHITE Jack M240A P98
WHITE Jay M191
WHITE Jerry M11
WHITE Joanne S329B
WHITE John M81
WHITE Ken C136A
WHITE Kieran N62 S258 W61
WHITE Kitty P125
WHITE Larry G40 N54
WHITE Lenny A120 A136 B81
C129 C186 D27 D72 G110 I25B
P35 S19 W62
WHITE Leonard H122
WHITE Mark M124

WHITE Martin B93A
WHITE Maurice E7 E55 L65
W36 W84C
WHITE Michael (Vln) H150
W63
WHITE Michael (B) T54
WHITE Mike (V/G) R177A
WHITE Nathaniel J113
WHITE Paul A35A
WHITE Peter (G) S104B
S270
WHITE Peter (K) W9
WHITE Philip S202
WHITE Ralph C178B R118A
WHITE Ray Z8
WHITE Richard F83C
WHITE Robert (G) C17 F92
G17 J91A S128 T42
WHITE Roland C200 K29
T32E
WHITE Ronald A132 R115
WHITE Rueben R142
WHITE S. H58
WHITE Sam J93D
WHITE Sharon H35
WHITE Simon A29
WHITE Snowy G94 K24 L63
L144B M194 P85 T59 W134
WHITE Stan P88A
WHITE Sue C76
WHITE Tony Joe C169 F123A
J53 R127A W64
WHITE Trevor (G) S205
WHITE Trevor (B) D17
WHITE Verdine C45 D50 E7
E55 M102 S250 V32A W62
W84C
WHITE CLOUD W65A
White Dub see ASHWORTH
Richard
WHITE HEAT W65B
WHITE HORSE W65A
WHITE LIGHTNIN' W66
WHITE MANSIONS W67
WHITE NOISE W68
WHITE RUSSIA W68B
WHITE SNAKE C204
WHITE WATER W68A
WHITE WITCH W69
WHITECAGE Mark P45
WHITEFACE W69A
WHITEHEAD Alan M89
WHITEHEAD Benny K95 L77
WHITEHEAD John M71 P59C
WHITEHEAD Neville D35 H34
I29 P81C P115 S331 T95
W135
WHITEHEAD Paul H13 M71
WHITEHEAD Robert N46C S204
WHITEHEAD Tim R174
WHITEHEAD Tom H150
WHITEHEAD Trevor J113
WHITEHEAT W69C
WHITEHORN Geoff B12 B89
B268 C79 C214 D110 H111B
I8 M80 W69E W125
WHITEHORSE Tom J69
WHITEHOUSE W69D
WHITEHURST Jerry C14
WHITEMAN Ian B266 C109
C165 D49 E41 F6 F23 G27
H2 H25 K52 M19 M94 M108
M148 N45A R106 S9 I79
WHITEMAN Joe O41
WHITEMAN Steve K67D
WHITESIDE Millie R142A
WHITESPIRIT W69B
WHITEWHISTLE Rob C76
WHITFIELD Gayle L108 P63
WHITFIELD Kenneth N53A
WHITFIELD Norman T42
WHITFORD Brad A16 N50A
W69F
WHITFORD Hal F69
WHITFORD/St.HOLMES W69F
WHITHEAD Paul H13
WHITING George S157
WHITING Jere F19
WHITING Joan W112
WHITING Joe J105C
WHITING Keith H40A
WHITING June O18
WHITING Steve M168
WHITLEY Trantham B263
WHITLOCK Betty K48
WHITLOCK Bobby B201 B202

C121 D52 D86 M64 W70
WHILLOCK Jeff B123A
WHITMAN Ian D37 L95
WHITMAN Jerry B226 M102
V18A
WHITMAN John W68
WHITMAN Larry C164A K12
WHITMORE Iain D54 S253 V35
WHITMORE Larry J53
WHITNER John 'Flash' W22A
WHITNEY Charlie A131E F12
H123 S300
WHITNEY John M179
WHITNEY Mary Lee W119
WHITREN Jaki P31 R125 W71
WHITSELL George C216 R123A
Y16
WHITSELL Leon C216 R123A
WHITSETT Carson B78 G92B
L73 M3 S125 T70
WHITT Sheila E7
WHITTAKER Harry F60
WHITTAKER Hudson see Tampa
Red
WHITTAKER Jeff J8 S276
WHITTAKER Keith D46A
WHITTAKER Mark D115
WHITTAKER Michael N53
WHITTAKER Mike H7
WHITTAKER Tim D34
WHITTED Danny G61
WHITTED Dennis B194 B282
F3A M227 N36 R22
WHITTEN Danny C216 R123A
S10 Y16
WHITTING Ed D99
WHITTINGTON Melvan L128
WHITTLE Tommy C34 F14 H70
I20
WHITTON Don L74
WHITTY Brian C241C
WHITWAM Barry H108
WHITWORTH Nat B37
WHIZZ G C109B
WHO Dan A66
WHO W72
WHOLEFLAFFER Art 'Tricky'
see OSSMAN David
WHYTE Joanna Q1
WHYTE Tom M195 S108
WIBERG Peter S225
WICHE Peter T100
WICHITA FALL W73
WICHTL Martin B21
WICK Stephen N18
WICKENS Paul C210
WICKERSHAM Peter R102B
WICKETT Alan G27
WICKLAND Bobby Dean S45C
WICKLE Nathaniel J113
WICKS Johnny R52
WICKS Stuart H50
WICZLING Bogdan F47
WIDEMANN Benoit A72A M49
V26B W73A
WIDGER Paul C140C
WIDIEZ Dominique A72A S280
WIDOWMAKER W74
WIEBE Charlotte J53A
WIECLURKE Manfred E50A
WIECZORKE Manfred J38
WIEDEKE Detlef F132B
WIEDERKEHR Walter G30A
WIEDERKER Jacques Y23
WIEDLIN Jane G52B
WIEGAND Dick C235
WIEGAND Larry C235
WIEGEL Dick C138C
WIEGRATZ Warren 'Vito' S354
WIELERT Achim E60B
WIENECKE Ferry V38A
WIENER Elizabeth F4B N64A
WIENER Harris W100
WIENER Matthew J93C
WIER Derek B82
WIESE Klaus P118
WIESNER Skip J105A
WIESNER Ulla T143
WIESS Randy H198
WIEZ Richard Ihnaton A109
WIGAN Camilla S93
WIGGIN Betty S81B
WIGGIN Dorothy S81B
WIGGIN Helen S'1B
WIGGINS Gerald R142A

WIGGINS Jerry G121
WIGGINS Johnny A40 W89
WIGGINS Leroy H26A
WIGGINS Londie N28
WIGGINTON Hurshal A102
G85A J13 L77
WIGGY BITS W74A
WIGHT Dave K65 L113
WIGLEY Danny D55
WIGWAM W75
WIJTMAN Henk T118A T131A
WIKSEN Eric T57
WILBRAHAM John R40B
WILBRINK Herman B149C
WILBUR Bob F4B M227
WILBURN Ishmael W36
WILBURN Major G12A
WILBURN Vincent D27
WILCOX Bugsy G17
WILCOX Colin K68D
WILCOX David M229
WILCOX Jimmy D53
WILCOX John G. H9 H51 H119
M120 M198 R164
WILCOX Roy F14 H121 W86
WILCOX Toyah see Toyah
WILCOX Willy B216C
WILCZEWSKI Dave C77A F101B
WILD Bill R152
WILD Danny W76
WILD David P60B
WILD Ken K94A L79 S64
WILD Oscar O6A
WILD ANGELS W77
WILD BLUE YONDER W77B
WILD BUTTER W77A
WILD CHERRY W77C
WILD HORSES W78
WILD MAGNOLIAS W78A
WILD MAN see KRANTZ
Wolfgang
WILD ROMANCE B224A
WILD TCHOUPITOULAS W78B
WILD TURKEY W79
Wild Wally W80
Wild Willy A57A
WILDCATS W76
WILDE Danny G86B P15 Q10
WILDE David W7
WILDE Marty W81
WILDE Wilbur J64A S147
S224A
WILDER Danny R53E
WILDER Gene T8
WILDER Joe M41 S168
WILDER Johnny H81
WILDER Keith H81
WILDER Tim C39C
WILDERNESS ROAD W82
Wildflower F9B
WILDFLOWER Riley M30
WILDING Danny W82A
WILDING Robert James R6
WILDING BONUS W82A
WILDLIFE W82B
WILDY Tom A22 D92
WILES David F11
WILFS David F11
WILHELM Don H75
WILHELM Eberhard C96A
WILHELM Mike C81 F61 W83
WILHOITE O. S154
WILKENSON Bonnie F1
WILKENSON Ed E67
WILKERSON Gregory W132
WILKERSON Jimmy M11
WILKERSON Michael W132
WILKERSON Morris R59
WILKES Daniel A113A
WILKES Ira F116
WILKESON Leon A113A L146
R143A
WILKEY Dave G94
WILKIE Franklin M93
WILKIE Nathaniel P24B
WILKIN John 'Bucky' B17A
C169 G72 J53 K95 P129 S272
T21 W95
WILKIN Mari John S272
WILKIN Ronnie A39
WILKIN Steve S358C
WILKING Ernie R34
WILKINS Bill T139A
WILKINS Don C118A
WILKINS Gene M178D

WILKINS Harry B143
WILKINS Jack F109
WILKINS Jim C168A S254A
WILKINS Joe Willie W94
WILKINS Lucy C198
WILKINS Marlene C198
WILKINS Terry L74
WILKINSON Bonnie A112A D54
WILKINSON Colin H118
WILKINSON Collette M41A
WILKINSON Dave C101
WILKINSON Harry C189 M232
WILKINSON Jeff N24E P13
WILKINSON John P125
WILKINSON Keith N6
WILKINSON Kevin F121 S237
WILKINSON Kristin C124 Y18
WILKINSON Miles G79B M36
WILKINSON Paul F74D
WILKINSON Robert F61A
WILKINSON Shield W119
WILLARD Lorna B256 B282 C156
C182 K81 M191 P6 V18A
WILLARD Maxine (WATERS Maxine
Willard) A59 A120 B43 B47A
B47C B127 C36 C38A C39 C58
C129 C141 C155 C156 C180 C217
C235 C241 D26 D99 D127 E40
F114A F134 G24 H19 H35B H60
H181 H193B I24 J7 J10B J72
K45 K46 K81 L89 M89A M101
M102 M225 N23 O35 P64 P75 P83
R15 R28B R32 R87 R97 R101
R126 R137 R142A S19 S51 S73
S124 S180 S180D S251 S325
T71A T113 T143 T153A V9A W31
W84C
WILLARS Michael L28
WILLEMSE Guus S187
WILLEMSTEIN Bea P92B
WILLENS Mike R85A
WILLETT Paul M62
WILLEY Larry M222B
WILLIAM R. H105
WILLIAMS Aaron M136
WILLIAMS Adam S74
WILLIAMS Adrienne E31 J101A
WILLIAMS Alan L106 R153
WILLIAMS Albert H170
WILLIAMS Alfie C129
WILLIAMS Arthur P24B
WILLIAMS Barnett S51
WILLIAMS Bernard R39
WILLIAMS Big Al M75
WILLIAMS Big Joe W84 W93 W94
WILLIAMS Blinky H150
WILLIAMS Bob (Tpt) J65 P156A
WILLIAMS Bob (B) P47 R104
WILLIAMS Bob (Hca) S73B
WILLIAMS Bobby (G/V) T168A
WILLIAMS Brian M192A S268
WILLIAMS Bryan E60
WILLIAMS Buddy J20 K13A L119
R99 R125 S128 U7
WILLIAMS Buster see WILLIAMS
Charles
WILLIAMS Carey M53
WILLIAMS Carl Jnr. D97A
WILLIAMS Carlena B253 C39
C123 H179 L128 M18 M89A M132D
M203 P85 R22 R87
WILLIAMS Carol B172A
WILLIAMS Cathy H101 P57
WILLIAMS Charles (Sax) M41
M227
WILLIAMS Charles (Cong) O14
WILLIAMS Charles (D) D96 D106
WILLIAMS Charles (G/V) M167
WILLIAMS Charles 'Buster' (B)
C241 D27 H19 P132C
WILLIAMS Chris A3A S67
WILLIAMS Cliff A2 B31 H140
WILLIAMS Colin C174
WILLIAMS Curtis P59
WILLIAMS Dallas T150
WILLIAMS Danny E77
WILLIAMS Dave (B) B84A B209
F99A L55
WILLIAMS Davey F123
WILLIAMS David (D) M102 U14
S304 T44
WILLIAMS David (G) A35C H192
J10B J15 K36 P114 R142A W32A
WILLIAMS Deniece B47C C155
F60 I24 K46 R28B S36 W36 W84C
W119

WINKLEMAN Bobby B170 M159
WINKIES W104
WINKLER Angelika J38
WINLEY Harold C144A
WINN Terrell C40A
WINSBERG Jean Louis S320A
WINSKI Colin W104A
WINSLOWE Dal T133A
WINSTANLEY Alan L16C S292 T58
Winston R150
WINSTON Bill C146
WINSTON Jimmy S162
WINSTON Teddy R114
WINSTON Warren R54
WINSTON Winnie B221 G72
WINSTONE Norma A74 H74 H132A
N62 P36 W39A
WINTER W105
WINTER Ann C80A
WINTER Dave K81
WINTER Edgar D53 H51 L4A M16A
M120 M187 R164 W106 W107 W108
WINTER Ian C41A
WINTER Johnny C195 D53 F71
H99 L4A T111A W28 W106 W107
W108
WINTER Keith N62 S82A
WINTER Kurt G115
WINTER Manny R40B
WINTER Mike S84
WINTER Monique W106
WINTER Tom B181
WINTER BROTHERS BAND W110
WINTERGARDEN W110A
WINTERS Dennis W110
WINTERS Donnie W110
WINTERS Drew S72
WINTERS Ian D4A
WINTERS Ruby W109
WINTERS Ted H134A
WINTHROP Dave C101 S68 S108
S290 S333
WINTHROP Geoffrey U7
WINTOUR Dave B25 C6B C38 D9
D100 F7B F36 G32 H70 H111 I8
M108 M157 O18B P89A R15 S34
S152 S257 S355A W7 W72 W125
Y14
WINTZ Doug F99A M65A O39
WINWOOD Muff D28 M154 S205
WINWOOD Nicole W111
WINWOOD Steve A25 B134 B4
B138 C30 C121 C155 C206 D28
D49 F8 F17 G66 H39 H99 H170
I12 J9 J16 K52 L37 M20 M94
P76 P122 R60 R173 S243 S339
T62A T110 T127 W28 W111 Y2
WINZKOWSKI Michael E61B
WIPPERMAN Tim S55A
WIPPICH Bernd R28
Wire see LINDO Earl
WIRE W112
WIRELESS W113
WIRRICK Tip M18 M225
WIRTH Emil M136B
WIRTZ Mark P. J102A T106
WISCH Ben O32
WISCONSIN Eddie H71C
WISDON Howard Lloyd R130
WISE Chubby G68
WISE Fred M93
WISE Gary C25B
WISE R. E78
WISE Richie D138
WISE Steve G38C
WISE Wilmer C129 W36
WISEFIELD Laurie H140 W114
WISEMAN Mac H49
WISER Glenn B46
WISHART Paul S140
WISHBONE ASH W114
WISHEU Stefan O40B
WISHFUL THINKING W115
WISLEY Max C35B
WISNER Jimmy S124
WISNIEWSKI Bill G2A
WISSERT Joel L133
WISSNET Stefan S6A
WITCHER Dennis A135
WITCHER Philip S192A
WITCHFYNDE W115A
WITHAM Mo E7D J110 L46 R80
S177D

WITHERINGTON Steve A7
WITHERS Bill C241 W116
WITHERS Pick A6O C78 D75
D139 E19 J16B J41 J90 M45
M50 N27 P124 R11 R12 S103C
WITHERSPOON Jimmy B268
W116A
WITKOP Ernst Jan P10B
WITKOWSKI Rick C212
WITT Brigitte T143
WITT Joachim L17A
WITTE Heiner E56B
WITTENBERG John D127
WITTENBERG Mark L109
WITTICH Roland D19A
WITTON David W130
WITTS Dick P13A
WIUM Per A8A
Wizard Stan H5
WIZARDS CONVENTION W117
WIZARDS FROM KANSAS W116B
Wizzard M212
WIZZARD W122
WOBBLE Jah P144 W117A
WODOK Peter S158A
WOEHRLE Kathy D127
WOEST Craig E7C
WOFFERN David S218
WOFFORD David L23C
WOFFORD Mike F92 R108
WOJCIECHOWSKI Kajtek A4
WOLBRANDT Peter G21B G120
H57A K89 P20A
WOLEN H. Lee J73A
WOLF W35
WOLF Bill B177 F133 G53
M228 P46
WOLF Bruno K101
WOLF E.E.III F43
WOLF Kai F105A
WOLF Peter G19 G35B H52
Z8
WOLF Udo D18C
WOLFE Jay M125
WOLFE Randy K45
WOLFE Steve T171
WOLFE Sydney R33A
WOLFER Bill J10B J15 R142A
W119
WOLFERT David C127 C164
M65A M227 S228
WOLFF Charles B197B
WOLINSKI David 'Hawk' B33
B71 B175 B192 C63D C100
E13A F114A M46C R161
WOLK Tom H9 M189A
WOLLAERT Roger L4B
WOLLSCHON Gerd F70A
WOLNER Lori P49B
WOLSTENHOLME Stewart
'Wooly' B37 M67 W117B
WOLTERS John D85
WOLTZ Paul O15
WOMACK Bobby B84 B202 C180
F33 J95 R173 T107 W118
W120
WOMACK Cecil P56B W118
WOMACK Curtis W118
WOMACK Friendly W118
WOMACK Regina W118
WOMACK Sally W118
WOMACK Vincent W118
WOMMACK Bobby A102
WONDER Stevie (JUDKINS
Stephen) F74 F88A F100 H51
K45 M9 M101 M151 M229 P114
P126 R97 R115 S362 T25
T67A W119
WONG Jimmy F60
WONG Joseph Arthur B204
WOO Phillip A96
WOOD Annagh N45
WOOD Art A92 P76A W133
WOOD Arthur C141
WOOD Bill B17A
WOOD Billatt S7
WOOD Bobby C14 C15 C75
C133 D53C D104 E73 H26 H64
K30 K95 K96 M41 M78 N23
N37 O15 P112 P125 P137 R31
R127A S203 S269 S271 T55
T67A T107 T167 Y18
WOOD Brenton W119A
WOOD Carolyn B224C
WOOD Chris A25 B4 C30 C214

F29 F109 H17 H84 H99 J9
L104 M94 M102C P76 T62
T127 V5 V21
WOOD Colin C209 S133 S267
U22
WOOD Danny C78
WOOD Davy C78
WOOD Deborah S93
WOOD Derek G27
WOOD Guthrie T53A
WOOD Heather D88 F82A H110
W123 Y21
WOOD Jerry F48A
WOOD John C13 T106
WOOD Lauren W119B
WOOD Margaret M8O
WOOD Mark L10A
WOOD Orville M221D
WOOD Paul H150
WOOD Peter A82 C78 C165
C251 K24 L16A L27 M10B N12
P25 P41 P85 R101A S253
S270 S306 S339 V30 W48C
WOOD Phil M151
WOOD Robert W119C
WOOD Ron B23 B29 B64 B106
C13 C121 D13 D100 D139 F4
F116 H39 I33 L37 M39B N27C
R133 R161 S22 S273 W72
W120 W121
WOOD Roy D66 E34 H55 H99
M219 N4B W122
WOOD Royston A30 A98 C165
D49 T79 W123 Y21
WOOD Steve C237 J41 L109
M108
WOOD Vicki N45
WOODARD Nathan B233
WOODCOCK Chris S227 T48
WOODCOCK Ian E11
WOODE Jimmy G112D
WOODFORD David A132 D87B
D106G D133A M21 M229 R22
S111 S339A T30 W54B W119B
WOODFORD Peter O15
WOODFORD Terry H169A
WOODFORK Bob R128
WOODGATE Dan M46A
WOODHAMS Danny 'Woody' C39
K32
WOODHEAD George R46
WOODHEAD John A7 R173 S272
WOODLAND Nicholas B77A S6A
WOODLEY Ken A28A C106A
WOODMAN Britt C213E F5 M75
M229 S168 W119
WOODMAN Scott P139F
WOODMANSEY Mick 'Woody'
B186 S53B S214C W124
WOODROFFE Jezz P92B W124A
W133A
WOODROW John L118
WOODRUFFE Gerald B115
WOODS Albert T122A
WOODS Danny C67
WOODS David (G) M37
WOODS David (Tpt) B57A
WOODS Edna K81
WOODS Elvin H189
WOODS Gay S263 W125
WOODS Holly T112A
WOODS John B79 J107 S23
V33
WOODS Leslie Penny E11B
WOODS Mick E12
WOODS Mike A50 C80 J70A
S270 S285
WOODS Nicky (Perc) M30
WOODS Peter R134A
WOODS Phil C44 J69 S111
S124 S125 S168 S189 S262
WOODS Ron (D) G61 M151
S122
WOODS Ron (Sax) P6
WOODS Sonny B24
WOODS Steve U15A W124B
WOODS Stu B105 B208E C195
C229 C234A D139 E40 F108A
F109 G109 I2 K59 K68D K81
L4A M75 N63D O39 P45 R164
W92
WOODS Sylvia M136C S270
WOODS Terry S263 S346 W125
WOODS Thomas C144A
WOODS Wayne C40A
WOODS Willie W12

WOODS-PEARSON Charles C86
WOODSON Craig U16
WOODSON Elbert R56
WOODSON Kitty L68B
WOODWARD Dave P119A
WOODWARD Martin A71
WOODWARD Rob L68
WOODWORTH Romulus A101
WOODWORTH Zane M53 Y12
WOODY Scott F5B
WOODY WOODMANSEY'S U-BOAT
W124
WOOL Claudia W125A
WOOL Ed W125A
WOOL Tony D68A
WOOL W125A
WOOLAM Steve E34
WOOLEY Cliff A48
WOOLEY David B39
WOOLF Clive C152
WOOLF Henry W126
WOOLF Peter C210
WOOLF Stephanie C124 M11
WOOLFOLK Andy C45 E7 W84C
WOOLFSON Eric P31
WOOLIE Joe S56
WOOLLAMS John D92
WOOLLEY Aaron T138
WOOLLEY Bruce W126A
WOOLLEY BRUCE & CAMERA CLUB
W126A
WOOLLEY Sue B171
WOOLLOFF John M200
WOOTEN Cassandra L51
WOOTEN Denise M26
WOOTEN Michael K48 N12A
WOOTEN P.M. Z10
WOOTON Bob C50
WOOTON Doug C118B
WOOTTON Roger C175 S152
WORDSWORTH Ian N33
WORDSWORTH Linda N33
WORDSWORTH Tom D56A
WORKMAN Flap M39B
WORKMAN Geoff H5 K73 M39B
T164
WORKMAN Jeff T155
WORKMAN Michael B91
WORKMAN Nanette M54
WORKMAN Reggie M78 M79
WORKSHOP GROUP S267
WORLD I20
WORLD OF OZ W127
WORLD SERVICE W127A
WORLEY Greg W128B
WORLEY Paul R81
WORMALD Alan F51A
WORMAN Ray C165
WORMAN Tim P110A
WORMWORTH Tracy W5B
WORRELL Bernie B183 F137
H39A P29 T8
WORSNOP Rick L114
WORTERS Nick S152
WORTH-POTTS Leo M65A
WORTH Michael P103A
WORTHING Sonny W128
WORTHY Reginald B268
WORTHY Ricky A22 C87 D92
WORTLEY Jim A109
WORTMAN Kurt M203
WOTTON Al F22
WOTTON Doug C118B
WRABIT W128A
WRAFTERS Tony G51A
WRATH Jasper J43B
WRATHER Steve F27
WRAY Bill W128A
WRAY Bob A28 B87 C39D C43
C213E F83A H7D H146 L35
M235 P80 P118D T39
WRAY Doug W129
WRAY James Bentley W128B
WRAY Link G74 W129
WRAY Malcolm S230
WRAY Rhonda W129
WRAY Robin W129
WRAY Willow T107
WRECKLESS Eric W130
WREN Steve H56
WRENCHER Big John A50A
W131
WRICE Larry C21B
WRIEDEN Hardy K6A
WRIGHT Adrian D78D
WRIGHT Art C153
WRIGHT Arthur B240

WRIGHT Berkeley T131
WRIGHT Betty L24 L86 W119
W132 W136
WRIGHT Bill C57A
WRIGHT Bobby N46A
WRIGHT Charles (V) W33
WRIGHT Charles (G) B240
WRIGHT D. C191
WRIGHT Dave E66A
WRIGHT David (D) F61
WRIGHT David (K) B58B
WRIGHT Debbie F137
WRIGHT Denny D100
WRIGHT Doug J91 N45C W13A
WRIGHT Edna B63 B224A B226
C38A E71 J73A K81 O35
WRIGHT Elmon C146
WRIGHT Eric D51
WRIGHT Ernest L85
WRIGHT Gary A35 G27 H39 K45
L48 L64 R140 S220 S224 U5 V12
W51 W133
WRIGHT Gavin M34 P40 P64 Q2
R174
WRIGHT Geoff G71A
WRIGHT Greg Y12
WRIGHT Gregg E51
WRIGHT Gregory M203
WRIGHT Gus S329
WRIGHT Helen R174
WRIGHT Henry P47
WRIGHT Hoshal E33 M53
WRIGHT Ian S54
WRIGHT Janet D127B S169
WRIGHT Jeff W24
WRIGHT John (D) B57 D46B
WRIGHT John Lincoln E1
WRIGHT Joseph Edward 11 see
JAMMER Joe
WRIGHT Joy H176
WRIGHT Justin W133
WRIGHT Ken W18
WRIGHT Kyle G10B
WRIGHT Lamar C146
WRIGHT Lawrie J14
WRIGHT Lennie S16 W38
WRIGHT Lorna W133 W133A
WRIGHT Mel B174A
WRIGHT Michael C147
WRIGHT Monroe S251
WRIGHT Nigel S82A
WRIGHT Norman D43
WRIGHT P.J. G27
WRIGHT Pat C242
WRIGHT Pete (B) T133
WRIGHT Pete (B) C213A
WRIGHT Philip Adrian H178A
O24C
WRIGHT Richard (K) B44 P85
W134
WRIGHT Richard (G) C209
WRIGHT Rick K45
WRIGHT Robert H40A S250
WRIGHT Robert (V) M96
WRIGHT Ronald K46
WRIGHT Shaun S278
WRIGHT Steve K40 O24C
WRIGHT Stevie E10 W134B
WRIGHT Syreeta H96 P126 S362
W119
WRIGHT Tim E59 P61
WRIGHT William E73
WRIGHT Winston B117 C139 G39
H105 J48 R150 S45 T110 T149
U1 U20 V21 W4 Y4B
WRIGHTSON Jimmy J5
WRIGLEY Bernard A103
WRIGLEY George P33
WRIGLEY Mitch P33
WRITING ON THE WALL W134A
WRITZ W134C
WROE Alan H38A K44B
WRONSKI Dave J87A
WU Wendy P77A
WUEAT Craig E7C
WURGLER Roby M139A
WUSTHOFF Gunther F30
WUYTS Frank A71A F123
WYANT Pete A131D
WYATT Frank H19A
WYATT Hank P53
WYATT Robert A35 A133 B44
C13 C63 C209 C210 E26 E59
H34 H57 H101 M81 M102E M106
P115 R17 S182 S261B T95 W135
WYATT Rodney S313

An interesting spin off from the production of
the index has been to see how often musicians
have appeared in different entries

We have prepared a list of these musicians in
the form of a small chart. If you would like a
copy   send a stamped addressed envelope or
outside U.K. send an international reply coupon
(from post offices)

Write to :
    'Chart'
    13,Stanton Road
    Regents Park,
    Southampton
    England,
    SO1 4HF.

'Thats all folks'